MOON HANDBOOKS

HAWAII

MOON HANDBOOKS

HAWAII

THE ALL-ISLAND GUIDE

SIXTH EDITION

ROBERT NILSEN

AVALON
TRAVEL

MOON HANDBOOKS: HAWAII
SIXTH EDITION

Robert Nilsen

Published by
Avalon Travel Publishing
5855 Beaudry St.
Emeryville, CA 94608, USA

ISBN: 1-56691-326-8
ISSN: 1534-052X

Editor: Grace Fujimoto
Series Manager: Erin Van Rheenen
Copy Editor: Deana Shields
Graphics Coordinators: Erika Howsare, Susan Snyder
Production: Alvaro Villanueva, Jacob Goolkasian, Marcie McKinley
Map Editor: Naomi Dancis
Cartography: Mike Morgenfeld, Kat Kalamaras, Heather Carlisle, Chris Folks, Allen Leech, Mark Stroud
Index: Asha Jonnson

Front cover photo: map of Hawaii © 1988 Raven Maps & Images

Distributed by Publishers Group West

Printed in China through Colorcraft Ltd., Hong Kong

Please send all comments,
corrections, additions,
amendments, and critiques to:

**MOON HANDBOOKS:
HAWAII
AVALON TRAVEL PUBLISHING
5855 BEAUDRY ST.
EMERYVILLE, CA 94608, USA**
email: atpfeedback@avalonpub.com
website: www.travelmatters.com

Printing History
1st edition—1987
6th edition—October 2001
5 4 3 2 1

To Sandy B.,
who from first glance
filled her dad with aloha.

CONTENTS

INTRODUCTION

INTRODUCTION **3–94**
The Land **4**
  Climate
Flora and Fauna **10**
  The Mystery of Migration; Plants, Flowers, and Trees; Bird Life; Other
  Hawaiian Animals; Whales
History **24**
  The Road from Tahiti; The World Discovers Hawaii; The Unification of
  Old Hawaii; Missionaries and Whalers; King Sugar; A Kingdom Passes;
  Modern Times
Government **44**
  Office of Hawaiian Affairs
Economy **47**
  Tourism; The Military; Sugar; Pineapples; Other Agriculture; Economic
  Power
People **54**
  The Issue of Race; The Hawaiians; The Chinese; The Japanese;
  Caucasians; Filipinos and Others
Language **66**
  Pidgin; Hawaiian
Religion **73**
  Hawaiian Beliefs; Great Gods; The Caste and *Kapu* System;
  Missionaries One and All
Arts and Music **83**
  Arts of Old Hawaii; Arts to Buy; Language of the Lei; Hula; That Good
  Old Island Music
Festivals, Holidays, and Events **94**

SPECIAL TOPICS

Land Statistics 6
Green Flash 8
Hurricane Facts 9
Kukui *(Candlenut)* 13
Hawaii National Wildlife Refuges . 18–19
Environmental Resource Groups 23
Ecotourism in Hawaii 49
Land Ownership 54
Hawaii Population by Island 55
State of Hawaii Ethnic Populations . . . 56
Capsule Pidgin 67
Capsule Hawaiian Glossary 69–73
Giclée 86

ON THE ROAD **95–158**
Sports and Recreation **95**
  Scuba and Snorkeling; Catching Waves; Fishing; Camping and Hiking;
  National Parks; State Parks; County Parks; Horseback Riding; Bicycling;
  Golf and Tennis; Hunting; Sightseeing Tours

Accommodations 112
 Hotels; Condominiums; Vacation Rentals; Bed-and-Breakfasts; Hostels
 and YM/WCA; Home Exchanges
Food and Drink 117
 Hawaiian Foods; International Dishes; Money-Savers; Fish and Seafood;
 Munchies and Island Treats; Tropical Fruits and Vegetables; Island Drinks
Getting There 126
 Wings to Hawaii; Domestic Carriers; Foreign Carriers; Tour Companies;
 By Ship
Getting Around 136
 By Air; Interisland Carriers; By Ship; Rental Cars; Rental Agencies;
 Motorcycles and Mopeds; By Boat; Public Transportation; Hitchhiking
Health and Safety 144
 Water Safety; Hawaiian Folk Medicine and Cures; Medical Services;
 Services for Travelers with Disabilities; Prostitution; Illegal Drugs; Theft
 and Hassles
What to Take 152
Information and Services 154
 Hawaii Visitors Bureau; Local Resources; Other Information; Money and
 Finances; Newspapers and Tourist Publications; Tidbits: Official and
 Unofficial

SPECIAL TOPICS

Water Safety Tips 97   Largest Cities and Towns 157
Seasickness 102

BIG ISLAND

INTRODUCTION **161–218**
 Overview
The Land 164
 Climate
Flora and Fauna 167
 Common Flora; Birds; Mammals; Marine Life; The Hakalau Forest
 National Wildlife Refuge
History 172
Government 173
Economy 174
People 176
Festivals, Holidays, and Events 176
Sports and Recreation 180
 Beaches; Scuba and Snorkeling; Catching Waves; Parasailing; Ocean
 Tours; Fishing; Camping and Hiking; Horseback Riding; Bicycling;
 Skiing; Golf; Tennis; Hunting; Land Tours; Air Tours
Shopping 204
 Shopping Centers; Food Stores; Specialty Shops

Accommodations. 207
Food 209
Getting There 210
Getting Around. 212
  Car Rentals; Alternative Transportation; Medical Services
Information and Services 217

SPECIAL TOPICS

Big Island Temperature
  and Rainfall *166*
Big Island Botanical Gardens *168*
Big Island Ethnicity *176*
Big Island Arts and Culture
  Information. *177*
Big Island Museums *179*
Big Island Golf Courses *197–198*
Big Island Tennis Courts *200*

KONA. 219–267
Kailua-Kona 222
  Sights; Beaches and Parks; Accommodations; Food; Entertainment;
  Recreation; Shopping; Services and Information; Transportation
Holualoa 250
South Kona. 255
  Honalo and Kainaliu; Kealakekua; Captain Cook and Vicinity; Farther
  South

SPECIAL TOPICS

Ancient Sport of Holua *227*
Kona Coffee *254*
Konane *263*

SOUTH KOHALA 268–288
The Coast 270
  Sights and Nearby Communities; Beaches and Parks
Practicalities. 275
  Luxury Resorts; Other Accommodations; Food; Shopping; Recreation

WAIMEA 289–300
  History
Sights 292
  Sights in Town
Practicalities. 294
  Accommodations; Food; Recreation; Shopping; Services and Information

NORTH KOHALA 301–311
Kawaihae Coast 303
North Coast Towns 305
  Hawi; Kapa'au; Pololu Valley

THE SADDLE ROAD 312–318
Mauna Kea; Mauna Kea Observatory Complex; Sights Along Route 200; Mauna Loa

SPECIAL TOPIC
Mauna Kea Observatories' Website. 317

HILO 319–348
Sights 321
Downtown; Gardens; Beaches
Accommodations. 331
Along Banyan Drive; Near Waiakea Pond; Near Downtown; Farther out from Town; Bed-and-Breakfasts
Food 337
Inexpensive; Moderately Priced; Fine Dining; Brewery
Other Practicalities 342
Entertainment; Recreation; Shopping; Services and Information

SPECIAL TOPIC
Macadamia Nut 326

HAMAKUA COAST...349–368
Honomu to Honoka'a. 350
Honomu and Vicinity; Laupahoehoe
Honoka'a to Kukuihaele 355
Honoka'a and Vicinity; Kukuihaele
Walpi'o Valley. 361
History; Recreation; Staying in the Valley; Waimanu Valley

SPECIAL TOPIC
Hamakua Macadamia Nut 356

PUNA 369–389
Southeast Coast. 371
Pahoa and Vicinity; Along the Coast; Kaimu
Along the Hawai'i Belt Road. 379
Kea'au; Mountain Towns
Volcano Village 381
Accommodations; Food; Recreation; Shopping

SPECIAL TOPIC
History of the Anthurium. 380

HAWAII VOLCANOES NATIONAL PARK 390–407
Introduction 390
Kilauea Caldera 396
Visitors Center Area; Crater Rim Drive

Chain of Craters Road. **401**
Other Park Areas **403**
   Ka'u Desert; Small Detours
Practicalities. **406**
   Accommodations; Food and Shopping

SPECIAL TOPIC
....
Volcano Activity *394*

KA'U **408–417**
Towns and Sights **409**
   Pahala; Punalu'u and Ninole; Na'alehu and Vicinity; Wai'ohinu; South
   Point; Ocean View

MAUI

INTRODUCTION. **421–476**
   Overview
The Land. **424**
   Climate
Flora and Fauna. **426**
History. **428**
Government **430**
Economy. **431**
People **433**
Festivals, Holidays, and Events. **433**
Sports and Recreation **436**
   Beaches; Scuba and Snorkeling; Catching Waves; Thrill Craft; Ocean
   Tours; Fishing; Camping and Hiking; Horseback Riding; Bicycling; Golf;
   Tennis; Hunting; Sporting Clays; Land Tours; Air Tours; Booking
   Agencies
Shopping **463**
   Shopping Centers; Food Markets; Specialty Shops
Accommodations. **466**
Food **468**
Getting There **469**
   By Air; By Interisland Ferry
Getting Around. **472**
   Rental Cars; Alternative Transportation; Medical Services
Information and Services **475**

SPECIAL TOPICS

Maui Temperature and Rainfall..... 425
Maui Botanical Gardens 427
Maui Ethnicity 433
Maui Museums
  and Historical Society 434
Maui Arts and Culture Information .. 435
Maui Outrigger Canoes............ 441
Maui Tennis Courts.............. 455
Maui Golf Courses............... 456

CENTRAL MAUI: THE ISTHMUS........................ 477–500

Kahului 477
  Sights; Accommodations; Food; Entertainment; Recreation; Shopping;
  Services
Wailuku... 487
  Sights; Accommodations; Food; Entertainment; Recreation; Shopping;
  Services
Kahakuloa—West Maui's Back Side 498

SPECIAL TOPIC

Maui Sand Dunes... 485

WEST MAUI 501–564

Lahaina 501
  Sights; Beaches; Accommodations; Food; Entertainment; Recreation;
  Shopping; Services and Information
Ka'anapali.. 533
  Beaches; Luxury Hotels; Condos; Food; Entertainment; Recreation;
  Shopping; Services and Information
Honokowai, Kahana, and Napili.................................. 546
  Accommodations; Food and Entertainment; Shopping and Services
Kapalua... 557
  Beaches and Bays; Accommodations; Food; Shopping; Recreation

SOUTH MAUI 565–599

Ma'alaea 565
  Sights; Practicalities
Kihei 569
  Beaches; Accommodations; Food; Entertainment; Shopping; Recreation;
  Services and Information
Wailea 584
  Beaches; Luxury Resorts; Food; Entertainment; Recreation; Shopping;
  Services and Information
Makena 595
  Accommodations and Food; Recreation

UPCOUNTRY 600–622

Makawao.. 601
  Sights; Practicalities
Pukalani 609

Kula **610**
Sights; Continuing South
Haleakala National Park **616**
Sights; Hiking and Camping

EAST MAUI **623–657**
The Road to Hana **623**
Pa'ia; Ha'iku; The Road Begins; Sights; Accommodations
Hana **639**
Sights; Beaches; Accommodations; Food; Shopping; Activities; Services
Beyond Hana **652**
Kipahulu: The Coastal Boundary of Haleakala National Park; Beyond
'Ohe'o Gulch

KAHO'OLAWE **658–662**
Overview; History

LANA'I **663–698**
Introduction **663**
Overview; The Land; Flora and Fauna; History; The People; Sports and
Recreation; Getting There; Getting Around; Services and Information
Lana'i City **680**
Accommodations; Restaurants; Shopping
Exploring Lana'i **689**
Munro Trail; Heading South; Kaunolu: Kamehameha's Getaway; The
East Coast: Keomuku and Naha; Shipwreck Beach; The Garden of the
Gods and Polihua

SPECIAL TOPICS

Lana'i City Temperature   *Lana'i Golf*
   and Rainfall . . . . *666*   *and Tennis* *675*
Lana'i Ethnicity *671*

MOLOKA'I **699–746**
Introduction **699**
Overview; The Land; Flora and Fauna; History; Economy; The People;
Festivals and Events; Sports and Recreation; Shopping; Accommodation
and Food; Getting There; Getting Around; Information and Services
Kaunakakai **720**
Sights; Accommodations; Food; Shopping
East to Halawa Valley **726**
Sights; Accommodations and Food
Middle Moloka'i and Kalaupapa **732**
Main Forest Road; Kualapu'u and Kala'e; The Kalaupapa Experience
Moloka'i's West End **740**
The Northwest; Maunaloa and the Southwest Coast

SPECIAL TOPICS

Moloka'i Temperature and Rainfall . . 703   Moloka'i Golf and Tennis 715
Moloka'i Ethnicity. 709

O'AHU

INTRODUCTION **749–796**
   Overview
The Land 754
   The Climate
Flora and Fauna 755
Government 757
Economy 757
People 759
Festivals, Holidays, and Events 760
Sports and Recreation 765
   Scuba and Snorkeling; Catching Waves; Thrill Craft; Ocean Tours;
   Fishing; Camping and Hiking; Horseback Riding; Bicycling; Golf; Tennis;
   Hunting; Land Tours; Air Tours; Spectator Sports
Shopping 783
   Shopping Centers; Food Markets; Bookstores; Flea Markets and Swap
   Meets
Accommodations and Food 785
Getting There 788
Getting Around 791
   Rental Cars; Alternate Transportation; Medical Services
Information and Services 795

SPECIAL TOPICS

O'ahu Temperature and Rainfall 755   O'ahu Museums and Galleries . 762–763
O'ahu Botanical Gardens 756   O'ahu Archives and Libraries 764
O'ahu Ethnicity 759   O'ahu Golf Courses 776–778
O'ahu Arts and Culture Information. . 761   O'ahu Tennis Courts 779

HONOLULU **797–844**
Sights 799
   'Iolani Palace Area; Mission Houses Museum; Kawaiaha'o Church;
   Honolulu Harbor Area; Pali Highway; Punchbowl, National Cemetery of
   the Pacific; University of Hawai'i; Manoa Valley; Bishop Museum; Other
   Museums and Galleries; Gardens; Honolulu Beaches and Parks;
   Honolulu Hiking
Accommodations 823
   Downtown and Toward Waikiki; Near the University; Near the Airport;
   Bed-and-Breakfasts
Food 826

Shopping Center Dining; Inexpensive Dining Around Town; Moderate
Dining Around Town; Hawaiian Regional Cuisine

Entertainment. 834
Shopping 836
Chinatown. 840
Sights; Shopping; Food

SPECIAL TOPIC
The Legends of Manoa Valley *815*

WAIKIKI 845–889
Sights 850
Diamond Head; Honolulu Zoo; Waikiki Aquarium; U.S. Army Museum of
Hawaii; Free Sights and Curiosities; Waikiki Beaches and Parks
Accommodations. 858
Military Personnel Only; Under $50; $50–100; $100–150; $150–200;
$200–250; $250 and up; Condominiums
Food 874
Inexpensive; Moderate; Upper End; Classy Dining; Along Kapahulu
Avenue
Entertainment. 882
Shopping 886

CENTRAL OʻAHU 890–901
ʻAiea, Pearl City, and Vicinity 890
Pearl Harbor Historical Sites; Beaches and Sights; Practicalities
Wahiawa and Vicinity 898
Sights; Practicalities

SPECIAL TOPIC
Pineapple *900*

THE LEEWARD COAST 902–910
ʻEwa End
Beaches and Sights up the Coast 905
Practicalities. 908
Accommodations; Shopping, Food, and Services

SOUTHEAST OʻAHU 911–919
Maunalua Bay to Makapuʻu. 911
Sights, Beaches, and Parks; Services
Waimanalo 918
Beaches and Parks; Food and Shopping

WINDWARD OʻAHU 920–943
Kailua and Vicinity. 922
Sights; Beaches; Accommodations; Food; Shopping; Services

Kaneʻohe and Vicinity 928
 Sights; Accommodations; Food; Shopping
North Kaneʻohe Bay 933
 Kahaluʻu; Waiahole and Waikane
Kaʻaʻawa Town and Vicinity 935
 Sights and Beaches; Practicalities
Punaluʻu and Hauʻula 937
 Punaluʻu; Hauʻula; Beaches; Practicalities
Laʻie to Kahuku 939
 Laʻie; Beaches; Practicalities; Kahuku

THE NORTH SHORE **944–960**
Along the Farrington Highway 945
 Waialua
Haleʻiwa and Vicinity 948
 Parks; Accommodations; Food; Shopping
Waimea Bay and Vicinity 954
 Accommodations; Food

KAUAʻI

INTRODUCTION **963–1012**
 Overview
The Land 966
 Climate
Flora and Fauna 969
History 972
Government 973
Economy 973
People 975
Festivals, Holidays, and Events 975
Sports and Recreation 978
 Beaches; Scuba and Snorkeling; Catching Waves; Water-Skiing; Ocean
 Tours; River Cruise; Fishing; Camping and Hiking; Horseback Riding;
 Bicycling; Golf; Tennis; Hunting; Land Tours; Air Tours
Shopping 999
 Shopping Centers; Specialty Shops, Arts, and Boutiques; Food Stores
Accommodations 1003
 Food
Getting There 1007
Getting Around 1009
 Alternative Transportation; Medical Services
Information and Services 1012

SPECIAL TOPICS

Kaua'i Temperature and Rainfall. . . . 968
Rooster Alert 970
Kaua'i Botanical Gardens 971
Mu and Menehune 972
Kaua'i Ethnicity 975
Kaua'i Arts and Culture Information . 976
Kaua'i Museums and
   Historical Society. 977

Outrigger Canoe Racing 979
Kaua'i Golf Courses 992
Kaua'i Tennis Courts. 994
Movies Made on Kaua'i. 996
Personalized Novel 1001
Time-Shares 1005

LIHU'E 1013–1034
Sights 1014
   Kaua'i Museum; Grove Farm Homestead; Other Sights; Beaches and
   Parks
Practicalities. 1021
   Accommodations; Food; Entertainment; Recreation; Shopping
The Environs 1033
   Puhi; Hanama'ulu

EAST SHORE 1035–1066
Wailua 1035
   Sights; Accommodations; Food; Entertainment; Recreation; Shopping
Kapa'a 1051
   Accommodations; Food; Entertainment; Recreation; Shopping;
   Information and Services
Heading North 1064
   Anahola and Vicinity

SPECIAL TOPIC
Coco Palms 1042

NORTH SHORE 1067–1101
Kilauea 1068
   Sights; Practicalities
Princeville. 1074
   Beaches; Accommodations; Food; Entertainment; Shopping; Recreation; Services
Hanalei 1084
   Sights; Beaches; Accommodations; Food; Entertainment; Shopping;
   Recreation; Services and Information
Road's End 1094
   Sights; Accommodations; Food
Na Pali Coast 1098

SPECIAL TOPICS
Road Etiquette. 1095   Fire Shower. 1096

SOUTH SHORE..1102–1129
Koloa..1102
   Sights; Accommodations; Food; Shopping; Recreation; Services
Po'ipu..1108
   Sights; Accommodations; Food; Entertainment; Shopping; Recreation;
   Information
Inland Towns...1126
   Lawa'i; Kalaheo

WEST END...1130–1153
Hanapepe Vicinity...1132
   'Ele'ele and Port Allen; Hanapepe; Sugar Towns
Waimea..1139
   Sights; Accommodations; Food; Recreation
To the End of the Road...1144
   Kekaha; Pacific Missile Range Facility; Polihale State Park
Mountain Parks..1147
   Waimea Canyon State Park; Koke'e State Park

SPECIAL TOPICS
Kaua'i Red Dirt 1132   Mana Plain...................1145
Coffee Processing..............1133

NI'IHAU AND THE NORTHWESTERN ISLANDS.....1154–1160
Ni'ihau: The Forbidden Island..................................1154
   History; Life Today
The Northwestern Islands.....................................1157
   Midway Islands

SPECIAL TOPICS
Ni'ihau Shellwork 1156

BOOKLIST...1161–1169
ACCOMMODATIONS INDEX.........................1170–1174
RESTAURANT INDEX................................1175–1182
INDEX..1183–1199

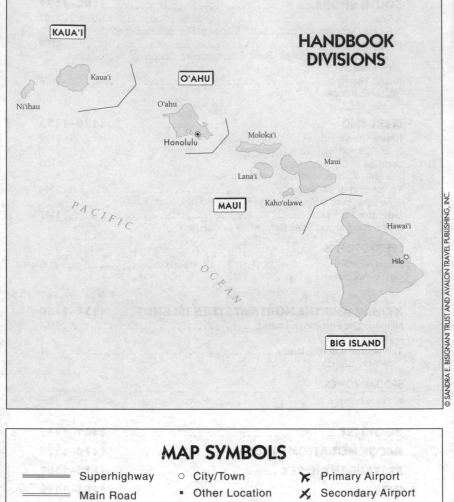

HANDBOOK DIVISIONS

KAUA'I

Ni'ihau

Kaua'i

O'AHU

O'ahu

Honolulu

Moloka'i

Lana'i

MAUI

Kaho'olawe

Maui

PACIFIC

OCEAN

BIG ISLAND

Hawai'i

Hilo

MAP SYMBOLS

═══ Superhighway	○	City/Town	✈	Primary Airport
── Main Road	▪	Other Location	✗	Secondary Airport
─ Other Road	•	Accommodation	✦	Snorkeling
------ Trail	▾	Restaurant/Bar	▲	Mountain
┼─┼ Railroad	★	Point of Interest	▲	State/County Park
⬡ US Interstate	⚑	Golf Course	✳	Volcanic Cone
◯ State Highway	△	Campground	≈	Waterfall
	▣	Gas Station	≈	Swamp/Marsh

MAPS

INTRODUCTION

INTRODUCTION
Hawaiian Archipelago 5
Polynesian Triangle 25

ON THE ROAD
Pacific Crossroads 127
Interisland Air Routes 137

BIG ISLAND OF HAWAI'I

INTRODUCTION
Hawai'i (The Big Island) 162
Mountains of Hawai'i 165
Big Island Land Ownership 175
Big Island Snorkeling 183
Big Island Campgrounds 190
Big Island Golf Courses 196
Kona International Airport 210
Hilo International Airport 211

KONA
Kona 220–221
Kailua-Kona 223
Kailua Kоauhou 224

SOUTH KOHALA
South Kohala 269

WAIMEA
Waimea .290

NORTH KOHALA
North Kohala 302

THE SADDLE ROAD
The Saddle Road 313

HILO
Hilo 320
Downtown Hilo 322
Hilo Vicinity 327

HAMAKUA COAST
Hamakua Coast 351

PUNA
Puna 370

Volcano Village 382

HAWAII VOLCANOES NATIONAL PARK
Hawaii Volcanoes National Park .391

KA'U
Ka'u .410–411

MAUI

INTRODUCTION
Maui 422
Maui Land Ownership 431
Maui Snorkeling 438
Maui Campgrounds 448
Maui Golf Courses 457
Kahului Airport 470

CENTRAL MAUI: THE ISTHMUS
Central Maui 478
Kahului 481
Wailuku .488
Road to 'Iao 491
West Maui's Back Side 499

WEST MAUI
West Maui 502
Downtown Lahaina 504
Ka'anapali 534
Honokowai to Kapalua 547

SOUTH MAUI
South Maui 566
Kihei 570
Wailea 585
Makena .595

UPCOUNTRY
Upcountry 602–603
Makawao 604
Haleakala National Park 617

EAST MAUI
East Maui 624–625
Pa'ia and Environs 626
Road to Hana 634
Hana 640

MAPS
(continued)

Beyond Hana 653

KAHO'OLAWE
Kaho'olawe 659

LANA'I
Lana'i 664
Lana'i City 681

MOLOKA'I
Moloka'i 700–701
Moloka'i Land Ownership 707
Kaunakakai 721

O'AHU

INTRODUCTION
O'ahu 750–751
O'ahu Land Ownership 758
O'ahu Snorkeling 766
O'ahu Campgrounds 771
O'ahu Golf Courses 775
Honolulu International Airport 788

HONOLULU
Greater Honolulu 798
Downtown Honolulu 800
Chinatown 841

WAIKIKI
Waikiki 846–847

CENTRAL O'AHU
Central O'ahu 891

THE LEEWARD COAST
The Leeward Coast 903

SOUTHEAST O'AHU
Southeast O'ahu 912

WINDWARD O'AHU
Windward O'ahu 921
Kailua 923
Kane'ohe .929

THE NORTH SHORE
The North Shore 945

Hale'iwa .949

KAUA'I

INTRODUCTION
Kaua'i 964
Kaua'i Land Ownership 974
Kaua'i Snorkeling 980
Kaua'i Campgrounds 987
Kaua'i Golf Courses 993
Lihu'e Airport 1008

LIHU'E
Lihu'e 1015
Lihu'e Vicinity 1018

EAST SHORE
East Shore 1036
Wailua .1038
Kapa'a .1052

NORTH SHORE
North Shore 1069
Princeville 1075
Hanalei .1085
Road's End 1094
Na Pali Coast 1099

SOUTH SHORE
South Shore 1103
Koloa 1104
Po'ipu 1110–1111

WEST END
West End 1131
Hanapepe 1135
Waimea 1140
Waimea Canyon 1148
Koke'e State Park 1150

**NI'IHAU AND
THE NORTHWESTERN ISLANDS**
Ni'ihau .1155
The Northwestern Islands 1158

ABBREVIATIONS

a/c—air-conditioning
AFB—air force base
B&B—bed-and-breakfast
BYO—bring your own
4WD—four-wheel drive
HVB—Hawaii Visitors Bureau

Hwy.—highway
mph—miles per hour
NWR—national wildlife refuge
OHA—Office of Hawaiian Affairs
PADI—Professional Association
   of Dive Instructors

P.O.—post office
Rt.—route
SASE—self-addressed stamped
   envelope
SRA—state recreation area
YH—youth hostel

PRICE RATINGS KEY

Accommodation listings in this book use the following price ranges for room rates per room, based on double occupancy high-season rates:

Under $50
$50–100
$100–150
$150–200
$200–250
$250 and up

ACKNOWLEDGMENTS

Since the passing of J. D. Bisignani, the original author of *Moon Handbooks: Hawaii,* I have taken on the great task of revising this book and others in his series of guides to Hawaii. Joe, you have been an inspiration to me and have laid a solid foundation for the present revision. I pray that I'm able to shoulder the responsibility. Even though you are gone, you've been with me with each word. To you, my good friend, a big thank you.

As always, the staff at Avalon Travel Publishing has been professional in every way. A sincere thank you to every one.

The following individuals require special thanks for their assistance in the revision of this book: Linda Nako, John Alexander, Barbara-Ann Anderson, Ouida Trahan, Sharon Miller, Jackie Horne, Linda Beech, Sue Pargett, Julie Applebaum, Donna Kimura, Nancy Daniels, Sally Proctor, Cameron Hewines, David Sayre, Mare Grace, Steve Glass, Margo Hobbs, Lorna Jeyte, Joan Early, Kathryn Grout, Howie Geib, Jane Chao, Hugh Montgomery, Rob Pacheco, Laura Aquino, Pat Wright, Jim Heine, Vincent Paiwa, Tom and Janice Fairbanks, Todd Castor, Kimberly Svetin, Melinda Mower, Robert Patey, Mel Akamine, Ellen Unterman, Gail Pickholz, Fusae Nakamura, Duke Walls, Mike Gerry, Ana Lee Apple, Henry Clay Richardson, Gigi Valley, Susan and Michael Hunter, Kimo Keawe, Glenn and Akiko Foster, Ruth Ann Becker, Bonnie Friedman, Marty Herald, Richard Marks, Charlene Kauhane, Eric Dixson, Phil Sammer, Pat Tom, Karen Tsui, Sophie and Lee, Craig Huish, Sharlynn, Candy Aluli, B. J. Whitman, Sonja Swenson, Connie Wright, Donna Jung, Sheila Donnelly, Shae Page, Linda and Bob Keane, E. J. and Diane Olsson, Robin Jumper, Shari Chang, Marjorie Ketcher, James and LeeAnn Hargraves, Bob Ingraham, Gabriela Taylor, Lizann Vidinha, Stephanie Reid, Carolyn Barnes, Jeff and Belle Shepard, Casey Reimer, Lauren Frye, Mike Hopkins, Margy Parker, Keoni Wagner, Haunani Vieira, Kathy Lane, and my wife, Linda Nilsen. A sincere "mahalo" to you all.

HELP MAKE THIS A BETTER BOOK

In today's world, things change so rapidly that it's impossible for one person to keep up with everything happening in any one place. This is particularly true in Hawaii, where situations are always in flux. Travel books are like automobiles: they require fine tuning and frequent overhauls to keep in shape. Help us keep this book in shape! We require input from our readers so that we can continue to provide the best, most current information available. Please write to let us know about any inaccuracies, new information, or misleading suggestions. Although we try to make our maps as accurate as possible, errors do occur. If you have any suggestions for improvement or places that should be included, please let us know about them.

We especially appreciate letters from female travelers, visiting expatriates, local residents, and hikers and outdoor enthusiasts. We also like hearing from experts in the field as well as from local hotel owners and individuals wishing to accommodate visitors from abroad.

If you take a photograph during your trip that you feel might be included in future editions, please send it to us. Send only good slide duplicates or glossy black-and-white prints. Drawings and other artwork are also appreciated. If we use your photo or drawing, you'll be mentioned in the credits and receive a free copy of the book. Keep in mind, however, that the publisher cannot return any materials unless you include a self-addressed, stamped envelope. Avalon Travel Publishing will own the rights on all material submitted. Address your letter to:

Robert Nilsen
Moon Handbooks: Hawaii
Avalon Travel Publishing
5855 Beaudry St.
Emeryville, CA 94608 USA
email: info@travelmatters.com
(please put book title in the subject line)
www.travelmatters.com

NOTE ON HAWAIIAN DIACRITICS

Aside from the five vowels and seven consonants, written Hawaiian uses two diacritical marks to distinguish spoken sounds. These are the *'okina,* or glottal stop, written as a reverse apostrophe (') before a vowel; and the macron *kahakō,* a short line written over a vowel indicating that the vowel is stressed. The *kahakō* is not used in this book. The *'okina* is used in Hawaiian place names, names of historical persons, and ordinary Hawaiian words, where appropriate. It is not used in business names if the business itself does not use this symbol. The name Hawai'i, written with an *'okina* refers to the island of Hawai'i, the Big Island; without the *'okina,* it refers to the state. The word Hawaiian, written without the glottal stop, refers to both the Polynesian inhabitants of the islands before Western contact and to those people of all races who currently reside in the state.

INTRODUCTION

ILES SANDWICH, UN OFFICIER DU ROI EN GRAND COSTUME.

No alien land in all the world
has any deep, strong charm for me,
but that one;
no other land could
so longingly and beseechingly
haunt my sleeping and waking,
through half a lifetime,
as that one has done.
Other things leave me,
but it abides.
      —Mark Twain, circa 1889

HAWAII STATE ARCHIVES

INTRODUCTION

The modern geological theory concerning the formation of the Hawaiian Islands is no less fanciful than the Polynesian legends sung about their origins. Science maintains that about 30 million years ago, while the great continents were being geologically tortured into their rudimentary shapes, the Hawaiian Islands were a mere ooze of bubbling magma 20,000 feet below the surface of the primordial sea. For millions of years this molten rock flowed up through fissures in the sea floor. Slowly, layer upon layer of lava was deposited until an island rose above the surface of the sea. The great weight then sealed the fissures, whose own colossal forces progressively crept in a southwesterly direction, to burst out again and again building the chain of what we now call the Hawaiian Islands. At the same time, the entire Pacific plate, afloat on the giant sea of molten magma, was slowly gliding to the northwest, carrying the newly formed islands with it.

In the beginning the spewing crack formed Kure and Midway islands in the extreme northwestern sector of the Hawaiian chain. This process continued for eons, and today 132 islands, islets, and shoals make up the Hawaiian Islands, stretching nearly 1,600 miles across an expanse of the North Pacific. Some geologists maintain that the "hot spot" now primarily under the Big Island remains relatively stationary, and that the 1,600-mile spread of the Hawaiian archipelago is due to a northwest drifting effect of about 3–5 inches per year. Still, with the center of activity under the Big Island, which itself is a relative youngster at about one million years old, Mauna Loa and Kilauea volcanoes regularly add more land to the only state in the country that is literally still growing. About 20 miles southeast of the Big Island is Lo'ihi Seamount, waiting 3,000 feet below the waves. Frequent eruptions bring it closer and closer to the surface; one day it will emerge as the newest Hawaiian Island and later, perhaps, merge with the Big Island itself.

THE LAND

The Hawaiian Islands sit right in the middle of the North Pacific straddling the tropic of Cancer. They take up about as much room as a flower petal floating in a swimming pool. The sea makes life possible on the islands, and the Hawaiian sea is a mostly benign benefactor providing all the basics. It is also responsible for an endless assortment of pleasure, romance, and excitement, and it forms a cultural link between Hawaii and its Polynesian counterparts. The slopes of the Hawaiian Islands rise dramatically from the sea floor, not gradually, but abruptly, like temple pillars rising straight up from Neptune's kingdom.

Physical Features

Hawaii is the southernmost state in the Union and the most westerly except for a few far-flung islands in the Alaskan Aleutians. The main islands lie just south of the tropic of Cancer at about the same latitude as Mexico City, Havana, Calcutta, and Hong Kong. Hawaii is the fourth smallest state, larger only than Connecticut, Rhode Island, and Delaware. Together, its 132 shoals, reefs, islets, and islands constitute 6,423 square miles of land. The eight *major* islands of Hawaii account for more than 99.9 percent of the total land area and are home to 100 percent of the population. They stretch over 400 miles across the Pacific from southeast to northwest: Hawai'i (the Big Island), Maui, Kaho'olawe (uninhabited), Lana'i, Moloka'i, O'ahu, Kaua'i, and Ni'ihau. The little-known Northwestern Islands, less than one-tenth of 1 percent of the state's total landmass, dot the North Pacific for more than 1,100 miles running from Nihoa, about 150 miles off Kaua'i's north shore, to Kure in the far northwest. The state has 822 miles of coastline and just over 1,000 miles of tidal shoreline. It ranges in elevation from Mauna Kea's 13,796-foot summit to Maro Reef, which is often awash by the sea.

Volcanoes

The Hawaiians worshipped Madame Pele, the fire goddess whose name translates equally well as "Volcano," "Fire Pit," or "Eruption of Lava."

When she was angry, Madame Pele complained by spitting fire and spewing lava that cooled and formed land. The Hawaiian Islands are perfect examples of **shield volcanoes.** These are formed by a succession of gentle submarine eruptions, which build an elongated dome much like a turtle shell. As the dome nears the surface of the sea, the eruptions combine with air and become extremely explosive due to the rapid temperature change and increased oxygen. Once above the surface they mellow again and steadily build upon themselves. As the island-mountain mushrooms, its weight seals off the spewing fissure below. Instead of forcing itself upward, the lava now finds less resistance in moving laterally. Eventually, the giant tube that carried lava to the top of the volcano sinks in upon itself and becomes a caldera. More eruptions occur periodically, but the lava is less dense and could be thought of as icing on a titanic cake. Then the relentless forces of wind and water take over to sculpt the raw lava into deep crevasses and cuts that eventually become valleys. The smooth, once-single mountain is transformed into a miniature mountain range, while generations of coral polyps build reefs around the islands, and the rising and falling of the surrounding seas during episodic ice ages combine with eroded soil to add or destroy coastal plains.

Lava

The Hawaiian Islands are huge mounds of cooled **basaltic lava.** The main components of Hawaiian lava are silica, iron oxide, magnesium, and lime. Lava flows in two distinct types, for which the Hawaiian names have become universal geological terms: **'a'a** and **pahoehoe.** They are easily distinguished by appearance, but chemically they're the same. Their appearance differs due to the amount of gases contained in the flow when the lava hardens. 'A'a is extremely rough and spiny, and will quickly tear up your shoes if you do much hiking over it. Also, if you have the misfortune to fall down on it, you'll immediately know why it's called 'a'a. Pahoehoe is billowy, ropy lava that looks like burned

HAWAIIAN ARCHIPELAGO

PACIFIC OCEAN

160° W

170° W

TROPIC OF CANCER

23.5° N

Kure
Midway
Pearl and Hermes Reef

Lisianski

Laysan

Gardner Pinnacles

French Frigate Shoals

Necker

Nihoa

Ka'ula

Ni'ihau
Kaua'i
O'ahu
Moloka'i
Lana'i
Kaho'olawe
Maui
Hawai'i

0   200 mi
0   200 km

MAIN ISLANDS

Kaua'i
Lihu'e
Ni'ihau

O'ahu
Honolulu

Moloka'i
Lana'i
Lahaina
Kaho'olawe
Maui

Hawai'i
Waimea
Hilo
Kailua

0   100 mi
0   100 km

pancake batter. Not nearly as dense as 'a'a, it can form fantastic shapes and designs.

Lava actually forms molten rivers as it barrels down the steep slopes of the volcanoes. Sometimes a lava river crusts over while the molten material on the inside continues to drain, until a **lava tube** is formed. Such a tube characteristically has a domed roof and a flat floor and would make a very passable subway tunnel. Some tubes measure more than 20 feet in diameter. One of the best examples is the Thurston Lava Tube at Volcanoes National Park on Hawai'i. Other lava oddities are **peridots** (green, gemlike stones called Pele's diamonds) and clear **feldspar.** Gray lichens that cover older volcanic flows are known as **Hawaiian snow,** and volcanic glass that has been spun into hairlike strands is known as **Pele's hair,** while congealed lava droplets are known as **Pele's tears.**

Lakes and Rivers
Hawaii has very few natural lakes because of the porousness of the lava: water tends to seep into the ground rather than form ponds or lakes. However, *underground* deposits where water has been trapped between porous lava on top and dense subterranean layers below account for many freshwater springs throughout the islands; these are tapped as a primary source for

irrigation and drinking water. Hawaii's only large natural lakes happen to be on the private island of Ni'ihau and are therefore seldom seen by the outside world. **Lake Waiau,** at 13,020 feet on the Big Island's Mauna Kea, ranks among the highest lakes in the United States. Honolulu's Salt Lake, once O'ahu's only natural inland body of water, was bulldozed for land reclamation. No extensive rivers are found in Hawaii except the **Waimea River** on Kaua'i; none are navigable except for a few miles of the Waimea. The countless "streams" and "rivulets" on the main islands turn from trickles to torrents depending upon rainfall. This is of greatest concern to hikers, who can find themselves threatened by a flash flood in a valley that was the height of hospitality only a few minutes before.

Tsunamis
Tsunami, a word of Japanese origin, is the more correct term for what is often popularly referred to as a "tidal wave." Tsunamis rank up there with the worst of them in sparking horror in human beings. But if you were to count up all the people in Hawaii who have been swept away by tsunamis in the last 50 years, the toll wouldn't come close to those killed on bicycles in only a few Mainland cities in just five years. A Hawaiian tsunami is actually a seismic sea wave generated by an

LAND STATISTICS

Area is expressed in square miles, coastline in miles, and highest point in feet.

Figures are approximate.

ISLAND	AREA	PERCENT OF STATE TOTAL	COASTLINE	HIGHEST POINT
Big Island	4,028	62.9	266	13,796
Mau'i	727	11.3	120	10,023
Kaho'olawe	45	0.7	29	1,477
Lana'i	140	2.2	47	3,370
Moloka'i	260	4	88	4,961
O'ahu	597	9.3	112	4,020
Kaua'i	552	8.6	90	5,243
Ni'ihau	70	1	45	1,281
Northwestern Islands	3	--	25	903
Total	6,423		822	

ROBERT NILSEN

Na Pali coast

tected by the gods. A giant tsunami inundated Waipi'o in the 1940s, catching hundreds of people in its watery grasp. Unbelievably, not one person was hurt. After the wave departed, many people rushed to the valley floor to gather thousands of fish that were washed ashore. Without warning, a second towering wave struck and grabbed the people again. Although giant trees and boulders were washed out to sea, not one person was harmed even the second time around. The safest place, besides high ground well away from beach areas, is out on the open ocean where an enormous wave is perceived only as a large swell. A tsunami is only dangerous when it is opposed by land.

Earthquakes

Earthquakes are also a concern in Hawaii and offer a double threat because they can generate tsunamis. If you ever feel a tremor and are close to a beach, evacuate as soon as possible. The Big Island, because of its active volcanoes, experiences hundreds of technical earthquakes every year, although 99 percent can only be felt on very delicate equipment. The last major quake occurred on the Big Island in late June 1989, reaching 6.2 on the Richter scale and causing about a million dollars' worth of damage. Fortunately, since 1868 (when an earthquake and tsunami killed 81 people) only two lives have been lost.

Hawaii has an elaborate warning system against natural disasters. Loudspeakers high atop poles along many beaches and coastal areas warn of tsunamis, hurricanes, and earthquakes. They are tested at 11 A.M. on the first working day of each month. All island telephone books contain a civil defense warning and procedures section with which you should acquaint yourself. Note the maps showing which areas traditionally have been inundated by tsunamis and what procedures to follow in case an emergency occurs.

earthquake that could easily have originated thousands of miles away in South America or Alaska. Some waves have been clocked at speeds up to 500 mph. The U.S. Geological Survey has uncovered data that indicates a 1,000-foot-high wall of water crashed into the Hawaiian Islands about 100,000 years ago. They believe a giant undersea landslide about 25 miles south of Lana'i was the cause. The wave was about 15 miles wide, and when it hit Lana'i it stripped land more than 1,200 feet above sea level. It struck the other islands less severely, stripping land up to 800 feet above sea level. The worst tsunamis in modern times have both struck Hilo on the Big Island: the one in May 1960 claimed 61 lives. Maui also experienced a catastrophic wave that inundated the Hana Coast on April 1, 1946, taking lives and destroying much property. Other waves have inexplicably claimed no lives. The Big Island's Waipi'o Valley, for example, was a place of royalty that, according to ancient Hawaiian beliefs, was pro-

CLIMATE

Of the wide variety of reasons for visiting Hawaii, most people have at least one in common: the weather! Nowhere on the face of the earth do human beings feel more physically comfortable

GREEN FLASH

Nearly everyone who has visited a tropical island has heard of the "green flash"—but few have seen it. Some consider the green flash a fable, a made-up story by those more intent on fantasy than reality, but the green flash is real. This phenomenon doesn't just happen on tropical islands—it can happen anywhere around the midriff of the earth wherever an unobstructed view of the horizon is present, but the clear atmosphere of a tropical island environment does seem to add to its frequency. The green flash is a momentary burst of luminescent green color that happens on the horizon the instant the sun sets into the sea. If you've seen the green flash you definitely know; there is no mistaking it. If you think you saw something that might have been green but just weren't sure, you probably didn't see it. Try again another day. The green flash requires a day when the atmosphere is very clear and unobstructed by clouds, haze, or air pollutants. Follow the sun as it sinks into the sea. Be careful not to look directly at the sun until it's just about out of sight. If the conditions are right, a green color lingers at the spot that the sun sets for a fraction of a second before it too is gone. This "flash" is not like the flash of a camera, but more a change of color from yellow to green—but an intense green—that is instantaneous, momentary, and gone. However romantic and magical, this phenomenon does have a scientific explanation. It seems that the green color is produced as a refraction of the sun's rays by the thick atmosphere at the extreme low angle of the horizon. This bending of the sun's light results in the green spectrum of light being the last seen before the light disappears. Seeing the green flash is an experience. Keep looking, for no matter how many times you've seen it, each time is still full of wonder and joy.

than in Hawaii, and a happy body almost always means a happy mind and spirit too. Cooling trade winds, low humidity, high pressure, clear sunny days, negative ionization from the sea, and an almost total lack of industrial pollution combine to make Hawaii *the* most healthful spot in America.

"So Good" Weather

The ancient Hawaiians had words to describe climatic specifics such as rain, wind, fog, and even snow, but they didn't have a general word for "weather." The reason is that the weather is just about the same throughout the year and depends more on where you are on any given island than on what season it is. The Hawaiians did distinguish between *kau* (summer, May–October) and *ho'oilo* (winter, November–April), but this distinction included social, religious, and even navigational factors, far beyond a mere distinction of weather variations. The average daytime temperature throughout Hawaii is about 80° F (26° C), with the average winter day registering 78° and the average summer day raising the thermometer only seven degrees to 85°. Nighttime temperatures drop less than 10°. Elevation, however, does drop temperatures about three degrees for every 1,000 feet; if you intend to visit the mountain peaks of Haleakala, Mauna Loa, or Mauna Kea (all more than 10,000 feet), expect the temperature to be at least 30° cooler than at sea level. The lowest temperatures ever recorded in Hawaii were atop Haleakala in January 1961 when the mercury dropped well below freezing to a mere 11°; the hottest day occurred in 1931 in the Puna District of the Big Island with a scorching (for Hawaii) 100°.

Precipitation

Hardly a day goes by when it isn't raining somewhere on *all* the main islands. If this amazes you, just consider each island to be a mini-continent: it would be the same as expecting no rain anywhere in North America on any given day. All islands have a windward (northeast, wet) and leeward (southwest, dry) side. It rains much more on the windward side, and much more often during winter than summer. (However, kona storms, because they come from the south, hit the islands' leeward sides most often.) Another important rain factor is the mountains, which act like water magnets. Moist winds gather around them and eventually build rain clouds. The ancient Hawaiians used these clouds—and the reflected green light on their underbellies—to spot land from great distances. Precipitation mostly occurs at or below the 3,000-foot level; thus, the upper slopes of taller mountains such as Haleakala are quite dry. The average annual rainfall on the seas surrounding Hawaii is only 25 inches, while a few miles inland around the windward slopes of mountains it can be 250 inches! Compare Lahaina and Mt. Pu'u Kukui, only seven miles distant from each other on West Maui, for a dramatic example of this phenomenon. Hot, arid Lahaina has an annual rainfall of only 15 inches; Pu'u Kukui can receive close to 40 *feet* of rainfall a year, rivaling Mt. Wai'ale'ale on Kaua'i as the "wettest spot on earth." Another point to remember: where there's rain there's also an incredible explosion of colorful flowers like an overgrown natural hothouse. You'll find this effect mostly on the windward sides of the islands. Conversely, the best beach weather is on the leeward sides: Ka'anapali, Waikiki, Kailua Kona, Po'ipu. They all sit in the "rain shadows" of interior mountains, and if it happens to be raining at one leeward beach, just move down the road to the next. One more thing about Hawaiian rains—they aren't very nasty. Much of the time just a light drizzle, they hardly ever last all day.

Because they are mostly localized, you can often spot them by looking for rainbows. Rain should never spoil your outings in Hawaii. Just "hang loose, brah," and go to the sunshine.

The Trade Winds

One reason Hawaiian temperatures are both constant and moderate is the trade winds, moderate breezes from the northeast blowing at about 5–15 miles per hour. These breezes are so prevailing that the northeast sides of the islands are always referred to as windward, regardless of where the wind happens to be blowing on any given day. You can count on the "trades" to be blowing an average of 300 days per year, hardly missing a day during summer and occurring half the time in winter. Usually calm in the morning, they pick up during the heat of the afternoon, then weaken at night. Just when you need a cooling breeze, there they are, and when the temperature drops at night, it's as if someone turned down a giant fan.

The trade winds are also a factor in keeping down the humidity. They will suddenly disappear, however, usually in winter, and might not resume

HURRICANE FACTS

Tropical Depression: low-pressure system or cyclone with winds below 39 mph.
Tropical Storm: cyclone with winds 39–73 mph.
Hurricane: cyclone with winds over 74 mph. These winds are often accompanied by torrential rains, destructive waves, and storm surges.

The National Weather Service issues a Hurricane Watch if hurricane conditions are expected in the area within 36 hours. A Hurricane Warning is issued when a hurricane is expected to strike within 24 hours. The state of Hawaii has an elaborate warning system against natural disasters. You will notice loudspeakers high atop poles along many beaches and coastal areas; these warn of tsunamis, hurricanes, and earthquakes. As the figures below attest, property damage has been great but the loss of life has, thankfully, been minimal.

MAJOR HURRICANES SINCE 1950

NAME	DATE	ISLANDS AFFECTED	DAMAGES
Hiki	Aug. 1950	Kaua'i	1 death
Nina	Dec. 1957	Kaua'i	—
Dot	Aug. 1959	Kaua'i	$5.5 million
Fico	July 1978	Hawai'i	—
'Iwa	Nov. 1982	Kaua'i, O'ahu	1 death; $234 million
Estelle	July 1986	Maui, Hawai'i	$2 million
'Iniki	Sept. 1992	Kaua'i, O'ahu	8 deaths; $1.9 billion

for a few weeks. The tropic of Cancer runs through the center of Hawaii, yet the latitude's famed oppressively hot and muggy weather is joyfully absent in the islands. Honolulu, on the same latitude as sweaty Hong Kong and Havana, has only a 50–60 percent daily humidity factor.

Kona Winds

"Kona" means "leeward" in Hawaiian, and when the trades stop blowing these southerly winds often take over. To anyone from Hawaii, "kona wind" is a euphemism for bad weather because it brings in hot, sticky air. Luckily, kona winds are most common October–April when they appear roughly half the time. The temperatures drop slightly during the winter, so these hot winds are tolerable, even useful for moderating the thermometer. In the summer they are awful, but luckily—again—they hardly ever blow during this season.

A "kona storm" is another matter. These subtropical low-pressure storms develop west of the Hawaiian Islands, and as they move easterly they draw winds up from the south. Usual only in winter, they can cause considerable damage to crops and real estate. There is no real pattern to kona storms—some years they come every few weeks, while other years they don't appear at all.

Severe Weather

With all this talk of ideal weather it might seem like there isn't any bad. Read on. When a storm does hit an island, conditions can be bleak and miserable. The worst storms occur in the fall and winter and often have the warped sense of humor to drop their heaviest rainfalls on areas that are normally quite dry. It's not infrequent for a storm to dump more than three inches of rain an hour; this can go as high as 10, making Hawaiian rainfalls some of the heaviest on earth.

Hawaii has also been hit with some walloping **hurricanes** in the last few decades. There haven't been many but they've been destructive. The vast majority of hurricanes originate far to the southeast off the Pacific coasts of Mexico and Latin America; some, particularly later in the season, start in the midst of the Pacific Ocean near the equator south of Hawaii. Hurricane season is generally considered June–November. Most hurricanes pass harmlessly south of Hawaii, but some, swept along by kona winds, strike the islands. The most recent and destructive was Hurricane 'Iniki, which battered the islands in 1992, killing eight people and causing an estimated $2 billion in damage. It had its greatest effect on Ni'ihau, the Po'ipu Beach area of Kaua'i, and on the leeward coast of O'ahu.

FLORA AND FAUNA

THE MYSTERY OF MIGRATION

Anyone who loves a mystery will be intrigued by the speculation about how plants and animals first came to Hawaii. Most people's idea of an island paradise includes swaying palms, dense mysterious jungles ablaze with wildflowers, and luscious fruits just waiting to be plucked. In fact, for millions of years the Hawaiian chain consisted of raw and barren islands where no plants grew and no birds sang. Why? Because they are geological orphans that spontaneously popped up in the middle of the Pacific Ocean. The islands, more than 2,000 miles from any continental landfall, were therefore isolated from the normal ecological spread of plants and animals. Even the most tenacious travelers of the flora and fauna kingdoms would be sorely tried in

crossing the mighty Pacific. Those that made it by pure chance found a totally foreign ecosystem. They had to adapt or perish. The survivors evolved quickly, and many plants and birds became so specialized that they were limited not only to specific islands in the chain but to habitats that frequently encompassed a single isolated valley. It was as if after traveling so far and finding a niche, they never budged again. Luckily, the soil of Hawaii was virgin and rich, the competition from other plants or animals nonexistent, and the climate sufficiently varied and nearly perfect for most growing things.

The evolution of plants and animals on the isolated islands was astonishingly rapid. A tremendous change in environment, coupled with a limited gene pool, accelerated natural selection. For example, many plants lost their protective thorns and spines because there were no grazing animals or birds to destroy them. Before settlement, Hawaii had no fruits, vegetables, coconut palms, edible land animals, conifers, mangroves, or banyans. The early Polynesians brought 27 varieties of plants that they needed for food and other purposes. About 90 percent of plants on the Hawaiian Islands today were introduced after Captain Cook first set foot here. Tropical flowers, wild and vibrant as we know them today, were relatively few. In a land where thousands of orchids now brighten every corner, there were only four native varieties, the least in any of the 50 states. Today, the indigenous plants and animals have the highest rate of extinction anywhere on earth. By the beginning of the 20th century, native plants growing below 1,500 feet in elevation were almost completely extinct or totally replaced by introduced species. The land and its living things have been greatly transformed by humans and their agriculture. This inexorable process began when Hawaii was the domain of its original Polynesian settlers, then greatly accelerated when the land was inundated by Western peoples.

The Greening of Hawaii

The first *deliberate* migrants to Hawaii were Polynesians from the Marquesas Islands. Many of their voyages were undertaken when life on their native islands became intolerable. They were prompted mostly by defeat in war, or by growing island populations that overtaxed the available food supply. Whatever the reasons, the migrations were deliberate and permanent. The first colonizers were known as "the land seekers" in the old Marquesan language—probably advance scouting parties who proved true the ancient chants, which sang of a land to the north. Once they discovered Hawaii, their return voyage to the southern homeland was relatively easy. They had the favorable trade winds at their backs, plus the certainty of sailing into familiar waters. Later, both men and women would set out for the new land in canoes laden with seeds and plant cuttings necessary for survival, as well as animals for both consumption and sacrifice.

Not all the domesticated plants and animals came at once, but the colonizers brought enough to get started. The basic food plants included taro, banana, coconut, sugarcane, breadfruit, and yams. The Polynesians also brought the paper mulberry from which tapa was made and the *ti* plant necessary for cooking and making offerings at *heiau*. Various gourds were grown to be used as bowls, containers, and even helmets for Hawaiian-style defensive armor. Arrowroot and turmeric were used in cooking and by the healing *kahuna* as medicines. 'Awa was brought by the high priests to be used in rituals; after chewing, the resulting juice was spat into a bowl where it fermented and became a mild intoxicant. Bamboo, the natural wonder material, was planted and used for countless purposes. The only domesticated animals taken to the new land were pigs, dogs, and chickens. Rats also made the journey as stowaways.

In the new land the Polynesians soon found native plants that they incorporated and put to good use. Some included: *olona,* which made the best-known fiber cord anywhere in the world and later was eagerly accepted by sailing ships as new rigging and as a trade item; koa, an excellent hardwood used for the manufacture of highly prized calabashes and the hulls of magnificent seagoing canoes; *kukui* (candlenut), eaten as a tasty nut, strung to make lei, or burned as a source of light like a natural candle. For a thousand years a distinct Hawaiian culture formed in relative isolation. When the first whites came they found a people who had become intimately entwined with their environment. The relationship between Hawaiians and the *'aina* (land) was spiritual, physical, and emotional: they were one.

PLANTS, FLOWERS, AND TREES

Much like the Polynesian settlers who followed, it was the drifters, castaways, and shanghaied of the plant and animal kingdom that were the first to reach Hawaii. Botanists say spores and seeds were carried aloft into the upper atmosphere by powerful winds, then made lucky landings on the islands. Some hardy seeds came with the tides and managed to sprout and grow once they hit land. Others were carried on the feathers and feet of migratory birds, while some made the trip in birds' digestive tracts and were ignominiously deposited with their droppings. This chance seeding of Hawaii obviously took a very long time: scientists estimate one plant arrival and establishment every 30,000–50,000 years. By latest count more than 1,700 distinct species of endemic (only Hawaiian) and indigenous (other islands of Polynesia) plants have been cataloged throughout the island chain. It is reasonably certain all of these plants were introduced by only 250 original immigrants; the 168 different Hawaiian ferns, for example, are the result of approximately 13 colonists. Most of the seeds and spores are believed to have come from Asia and Indonesia, and evidence of this spread can be seen in related plant species common to many Polynesian islands. Other endemic species such as the koa tree, which the Hawaiians put to great use in canoe building, have close relatives only in Australia. No other group of islands between Hawaii and Australia has such trees; the reason remains a mystery. Many plants and grasses came from North and South America and can be identified with common ancestors still there. Some species have become so totally Hawaiian that relatives are found nowhere else on earth. This last category has either evolved so dramatically they can no longer be recognized, or their common ancestors have long been extinct from the original environment. An outstanding example in this category is the silversword *('ahinahina),* found in numbers only atop Haleakala on Maui, with a few specimens extant on the volcanoes of the Big Island.

Hawaii's Flora

Hawaii's indigenous and endemic plants, flowers, and trees are both fascinating and beautiful, but unfortunately, like everything else that was native, they are quickly disappearing. The majority of flora considered exotic by visitors were introduced either by the original Polynesians or by later white settlers. The Polynesians who colonized Hawaii brought foodstuffs, gourds, *'awa,* and the *ti* plant. Non-Hawaiian settlers over the years have brought mangos, papayas, passion fruit, pineapples, and many other tropical fruits and vegetables associated with the islands. Also, most of the flowers, including protea, plumeria, anthuriums, orchids, heliconia, ginger, and most hibiscus, have come from every continent on earth. Tropical America, Asia, Java, India, and China have contributed

their most beautiful and delicate blooms. Hawaii is blessed with national and state parks, gardens, undisturbed rainforests, private reserves, and commercial nurseries that offer an exhaustive botanical survey of the island. The following is a sampling of the common native and introduced flora that add dazzling color and exotic tastes to the landscape.

Native Trees

Koa and 'ohi'a are two indigenous trees still seen on the main islands. Both have been greatly reduced by the foraging of introduced cattle and goats, and through logging and forest fires.

The koa, a form of acacia, is Hawaii's finest native tree. It can grow to more than 70 feet high and has a strong, straight trunk that can measure more than 10 feet in circumference. Koa is a quickly growing legume that fixes nitrogen in the soil. It is believed that the tree originated in Africa, where it was damp. It then migrated to Australia, where dry conditions caused the elimination of leaves, leaving only bare stems that could survive in the desert climate. When koa came to the Pacific Islands, instead of reverting to the true leaf, it just broadened its leaf stem into sick-

'ohi'a lehua tree

koa tree

LOUISE FOOTE

was also preferred for paddles, spears, even surfboards. Today it is still, unfortunately, considered an excellent furniture wood, and although fine specimens can be found in the reserve of Hawaii Volcanoes National Park on the Big Island, loggers elsewhere are harvesting the last of the big trees.

The 'ohi'a is a survivor and therefore the most abundant of all the native Hawaiian trees. Coming in a variety of shapes and sizes, it grows as miniature trees in wet bogs or as 100-foot giants on cool, dark slopes at higher elevations. This tree is often the first life in new lava flows. The 'ohi'a produces a tuftlike flower—usually red, but occasionally orange, yellow, or white, the latter being very rare and elusive—that resembles a natural pompon. The flower was considered sacred to Pele; it was said she would cause a rainstorm if you picked 'ohi'a blossoms without the proper prayers. The flowers were fashioned into lei that resembled feather boas. The strong, hard wood was used to make canoes, poi bowls, and especially temple images. 'Ohi'a logs were also used as railroad ties and shipped to the Mainland from Pahoa. It's believed that the "golden spike" linking rail lines between the U.S. East and West Coasts was driven into a Puna 'ohi'a log when the two railroads came together in Ogden, Utah.

le-shaped, leaflike foliage that produces an inconspicuous, pale yellow flower. When the tree is young or damaged it will revert to the original feathery, fernlike leaf that evolved in Africa millions of years ago. Koa does best in well-drained soil in deep forest areas, but scruffy specimens will grow in poorer soil. The Hawaiians used koa as the main log for their dugout canoes; elaborate ceremonies were performed when a log was cut and dragged to a canoe shed. Koa wood

KUKUI (CANDLENUT)

Reaching heights of 80 feet, the *kukui* (candlenut) was a veritable department store to the Hawaiians, who made use of almost every part of this utilitarian giant. As cure-alls, its nuts, bark, or flowers were ground into potions and salves and taken as a general tonic, applied to ulcers and cuts as an effective antibiotic, or administered internally as a cure for constipation or asthma attacks. The bark was mixed with water, and the resulting juice was used as a dye in tattooing, tapa cloth making, and canoe painting, and as a preservative for fishnets. The oily nuts were burned as a light source in stone holders, as well as ground and eaten as a condiment (mixed with salt) called 'inamona. Polished nuts took on a beautiful sheen and were strung as lei. Lastly, the wood itself was hollowed into canoes and seeds as fishnet floats.

LOUISE FOOTE

Lobelia

More species of lobelia grow in Hawaii than anywhere else in the world. A common garden flower elsewhere, in Hawaii it grows to tree height. You'll see some unique species covered with hair or spikes. The lobelia flower is tiny and resembles a miniature orchid with curved and pointed ends, like the beak of the native 'i'iwi. This bird feeds on the flower's nectar; it's obvious that both evolved in Hawaii together and exhibit the strange phenomenon of nature mimicking nature.

Tropical Rainforests

When it comes to pure and diverse natural beauty, the United States is one of the finest pieces of real estate on earth. As if purple mountains' majesty and fruited plains weren't enough, the country even contains tiny, living emeralds of tropical rainforest. A tropical rainforest is where the earth takes a breath and exhales pure sweet oxygen through its vibrant green canopy. Located in the territories of Puerto Rico and the Virgin Islands, and in the state of Hawaii, these forests comprise only one-half of 1 percent of the world's total, and they must be preserved. The U.S. Congress passed two bills in 1986 designed to protect the unique biological diversity of its tropical areas, but their destruction has continued unabated. The lowland rainforests of Hawaii, populated mostly by native 'ohi'a, are being razed. Landowners slash, burn, and bulldoze them to create more land for cattle and agriculture and, most distressingly, for wood chips to generate electricity! Introduced wild boar gouge the forest floor, exposing sensitive roots and leaving tiny fetid ponds where mosquito larvae thrive. Feral goats roam the forests like hoofed locusts and strip all vegetation within reach. Rainforests on the higher and steeper slopes of mountains have a better chance because they are harder for humans to reach. One unusual feature of Hawaii's rainforests is that they are "upside down." Most plant and animal species live on the forest floor, rather than in the canopy as in other forests.

Almost half the birds classified in the United States as endangered live in Hawaii, and almost all of these make their homes in the rainforests. For example, Maui's rainforests have yielded the po'ouli, a new species of bird discovered only in 1974. Another forest survey in 1981 re-discovered the Bishop's 'o'o, a bird thought to be extinct in the early 1900s. We can only lament the passing of the rainforests that have already fallen to ignorance, but if this ill-fated destruction continues on a global level, we will be lamenting our own passing. We must nurture the rainforests that remain and, with simple enlightenment, let them be.

BIRD LIFE

One of the great tragedies of natural history is the continuing demise of Hawaiian bird life. Perhaps only 15 original species of birds remain of the more than 100 native families that thrived before the coming of humans, these from only 20 or so original ancestors. Experts believe that the ancient Hawaiians annihilated about 40 species, including seven species of geese, a rare one-legged owl, ibis, lovebirds, sea eagles, and hunting creepers. Since the arrival of Captain Cook in 1778, 23 species have become extinct, with 31 more in danger. Hawaii's endangered birds account for more than 40 percent of the birds officially listed by the U.S. Fish and Wildlife Service as endangered or threatened. In the last 200 years, more than four times as many birds have become extinct in Hawaii as in all of North America. These figures unfortunately suggest that a full 40 percent of Hawaii's endemic birds no longer exist. Almost all of O'ahu's native birds are gone, and few indigenous Hawaiian birds can be found on any island below the 3,000-foot level.

Native birds have been reduced in number because of multiple factors. The original Polynesians helped wipe out many species. They altered large areas for farming and used fire to destroy patches of pristine forests. Also, bird feathers were highly prized for the making of lei, for featherwork in capes and helmets, and for the large kahili fans that indicated rank among the ali'i. Introduced exotic birds and the new diseases they carried are another major reason for reduction of native bird numbers, along with predation by the mongoose and rat—especially upon ground-nesting birds. Bird malaria and bird pox were also devastating to the native species. Mosquitoes, unknown in Hawaii until they were accidentally introduced at Lahaina in 1826, infected most native birds, causing a rapid reduction in bird life. However, the most damaging factor by far is the assault upon native forests by agriculture and land developers. The vast majority of Hawaiian birds evolved into specialists. They lived in only one small area and ate a very limited number of plants or insects—if these were removed or altered, the birds died.

Preservation

Theodore Roosevelt established the Northwest Islands as a National Wildlife Reserve in the early 20th century, and efforts have continued since then to preserve Hawaii's unique avifauna. Many fine organizations are fighting the battle to preserve Hawaii's natural heritage, including: Hawaii Audubon Society, University of Hawai'i, U.S. Fish and Wildlife Service, World Wildlife Fund, and Hawaii Department of Natural Resources. While visiting Hawaii make sure to obey all rules regarding the natural environment. Never disturb nesting birds or their habitat while hiking. Be careful with fire and never cut living trees. If you spot an injured or dead bird do not pick it up, but report it to the local office of the U.S. Fish and Wildlife Service. Only through the conscientious effort of all concerned does Hawaii's wildlife stand a chance of surviving.

Hawaiian Honeycreepers

One of the most amazing families of all the birds on the face of earth is known as Drepanidinae, or Hawaiian honeycreepers. More than 40 distinct types of honeycreepers currently exist, although many more are suspected to have become extinct even before the arrival of Captain Cook, when a record was started. All are believed to have evolved from *a single* ancestral species. The honeycreepers have differing body types. Some look like finches, while others resemble warblers, thrushes, blackbirds, parrots, and even woodpeckers. Their bills range from long, pointed honeysuckers to tough, hooked nutcrackers. They are the most divergently evolved birds in the world. If Darwin, who studied the birds of the Galapagos Islands, had come to Hawaii, he would have found bird evolution that would make the Galapagos seem like child's play.

More Endangered Endemic Birds

Maui is the last home of the **crested honeycreeper** *('akohekohe)*, which lives only on the windward slope of Haleakala from 4,500 to 6,500 feet. It once lived on Moloka'i but no longer. A rather large bird, it averages seven inches long and is predominantly black. Its throat and breast are tipped with gray feathers; bright orange decks its neck and underbelly. A distinctive fluff of feathers forms a crown. It primarily eats 'ohi'a flowers, and it's believed the crown feathers gather pollen and help propagate the 'ohi'a. The **Maui parrotbill** is another endangered bird found only on the slopes of Haleakala above 5,000 feet. It has an olive green back and yellow body. Its most distinctive feature is the parrot-like bill, which it uses to crack branches and pry out larvae.

The *po'ouli* is a dark brown, five-inch bird with a black mask and dark brown feet. It has a short tail and sports a conical bill. It was saved from extinction through efforts of the Sierra Club and Audubon Society, who successfully had it listed on the Federal List of Endangered Species. The bird has one remaining stronghold deep in the forests of Maui.

Two endangered waterbirds are the **Hawaiian stilt** *(ae'o)* and the **Hawaiian coot** *('alae ke'oke'o)*. The stilt is a 16-inch, very thin wading bird. It is primarily black with a white belly and long, pink sticklike legs. The adults will pretend to be hurt, pulling on an excellent "broken-wing" performance to lure predators away from their nests. The Hawaiian coot is a web-footed waterbird that resembles a duck. Found on all the main islands but mostly on Maui and Kaua'i, it has dull gray feathers, a white bill, and white tail feathers. It builds a large floating nest and vigorously defends its young. The **dark-rumped petrel** is slightly different from other petrels that are primarily marine birds. This petrel can usually be seen around the visitors center at Haleakala Crater about an hour after dusk May–October.

Survivors

The *'amakihi* and the *'i'iwi* are endemic birds not endangered at the moment. The *'amakihi* is one of the most common native birds. Yellowish-green, it frequents the high branches of 'ohi'a, koa, and sandalwood looking for insects, nectar, or fruit. It's less specialized than most other Hawaiian birds, the main reason for its continued existence. The *'i'iwi* is a bright red bird with a salmon-colored hooked bill. It's found mainly on Maui, Hawai'i, and Kaua'i in forests above 2,000 feet. It, too, feeds on insects and flowers. The 'i'iwi is known for its harsh voice, which sounds like a squeaking hinge but is also capable of a melodious song. The feathers of the 'i'iwi were highly prized by the ali'i for clothing decoration.

The **'elepaio** is found on several of the islands and is fairly common in the rainforest. This long-tailed, five-inch brown bird can be coaxed to come within touching distance of the observer. This bird was the special 'aumakua (personal spirit) of canoe builders in ancient lore. The **'apapane,** the most common native bird, is the easiest to see. It's a chubby, red-bodied bird about five inches long with a black bill, legs, wing tips, and tail feathers. It's quick and flitty and has a wide variety of calls and songs, from beautiful warbles to mechanical buzzes. Its feathers, like those of the 'i'iwi, were sought by Hawaiians to produce distinctive capes and helmets for the ali'i.

Pueo

This Hawaiian owl is found on all of the main islands, but mostly on Maui, especially in Haleakala Crater. The *pueo* is one of the oldest examples of an *'aumakua* in Hawaiian mythology. It was an especially benign and helpful guardian. Old Hawaiian stories abound in which a *pueo* came to the aid of a warrior in distress or a defeated army. Arriving at a tree in which a *pueo* had alighted, the soldiers are safe from their pursuers and are under the protection of "the wings of an owl." The many introduced barn owls in Hawaii are easily distinguished from a *pueo* by their heart-shaped faces. The *pueo* is about 15 inches tall with a mixture of brown and white feathers. The eyes are large, round, and yellow, and the legs are heavily feathered, unlike those of a barn owl. *Pueo* chicks are a distinct yellow color.

The Nene

The *nene,* or Hawaiian goose, deserves special mention because it is Hawaii's state bird

pueo

BOB RACE

and is making a comeback from the edge of extinction. The *nene* is found only on the slopes of Mauna Loa, Hualalai, and Mauna Kea on the Big Island, and in Haleakala Crater on Maui. It was extinct on Maui until a few birds were returned there in 1957, but some experts maintain the *nene* lived naturally only on the Big Island. *Nene* are raised at the Wildfowl Trust in Slimbridge, England, which placed the first birds at Haleakala, and at the Hawaiian Fish and Game Station at Pohakuloa, along the Saddle Road on Hawai'i. By the 1940s, fewer than 50 birds lived in the wild. Now approximately 125 birds live on Haleakala and 500 on the Big Island. Although the birds can be raised successfully in captivity, their life in the wild is still in question.

The *nene* is believed to be a descendant of the Canada goose, which it resembles. Geese are migratory birds that form strong kinship ties, mating for life. It's speculated that a migrating goose became disabled and remained in Hawaii along with its loyal mate. The *nene* is smaller than its Canadian cousin, has lost a great deal of webbing in its feet, and is perfectly at home away from water, foraging and nesting on rugged and bleak lava flows. The *nene* is a perfect symbol of Hawaii: let it be, and it will live.

OTHER HAWAIIAN ANIMALS

Insects

No one knows for sure, but it's highly probable the first animal arrivals in Hawaii were insects. Again, the theory is that most were blown here by ancient hurricanes or drifted here imbedded in floating logs and other pieces of wood. Like the plants that preceded them, their success and rapid evolution were phenomenal. A gravid female had to make the impossible journey, then happen upon a suitable medium in which to deposit her eggs. Here, at least, they would be free from predators and parasites with a good chance of developing to maturity. Again, the gene pool was highly restricted and the environment so foreign that an amazing ty of evolutionary changes occurred. Biologists believe only 350–400 original insect species are responsible for the more than 10,000 species that occur in Hawaii today. Of these 10,000, nearly 98 percent are found nowhere else on earth. Many are restricted to only one island, and most are dependent on a single species of plant or fruit. For this reason, when Hawaiian plants become extinct, many insects disappear as well.

It's very probable there were no pests before humans arrived. The first Polynesians introduced flies, lice, and fleas. Westerners brought the indestructible cockroach, mosquito larvae in their ships' stores of water, termites, ants, and all the plant pests that could hitch a ride in the cuttings and fruits intended for planting. Today visitors will note the stringent agricultural controls at airports. Some complain about the inconvenience, but they should know that in the past 50 years more than 700 new insect species have become established in Hawaii. Many are innocent enough, while others cause great problems for Hawaii's agriculture.

Land Snails

People have the tendency to ignore snails until they step on one, and then they find them repulsive. But Hawaiian snails are some of the most remarkable and beautiful in the world. It's one thing to accept the possibility that a few insects or plant spores could have been driven to Hawaii by high winds or on birds' feet, given the fact of their uncountable billions. But how did the snails get here? Snails, after all, aren't known for their nimbleness or speed. Most Hawaiian snails never make it beyond the tree on which they're hatched. Yet more than 1,000 snail varieties, from an original 22, are found in Hawaii, and most are inexplicably found nowhere else. The Polynesians didn't bring them, seawater kills them, and it would have to be a mighty big bird that didn't notice one clinging to its foot. Biologists have puzzled over Hawaiian snails for years. One, J. T. Gulick, wrote in 1858, "These Achatinellinae [tree snails] never came from Noah's ark." Tree snails are found on O'ahu, Maui, Moloka'i, and Lana'i, but not on Kaua'i. Kaua'i has its own land dwellers, and the Big Island has land snails that have moved into the trees. Like all the other endemic species, Hawaiian land snails now face extinction. Of the estimated 1,000 species existing when the Europeans came, 600 are now gone forever, and many others are threatened. Agriculture, the demise of native flora, and the introduction of new species add up to a bleak future for the snails.

Drosophila, The Hawaiian Fly

Most people hardly pay attention to flies, unless one lands on their plate lunch. But geneticists from throughout the world, and especially from the University of Hawai'i, make special pilgrimages to the volcano area of the Big Island and to Maui just to study the native Hawaiian drosophila. This critter is related to the fruit fly and housefly, but there are hundreds of native species that are singularly unique—more than one-third of the world's estimated total. The Hawaiian ecosystem is very simple and straightforward, so geneticists can trace the evolutionary changes from species to subspecies through mating behavior. The scientists compare the drosophila species between the two islands and chart the differences. Major discoveries in evolutionary genetics have been made through these studies.

Indigenous Land Animals

Before humans arrived, Hawaii had a paucity of higher forms of land animals. There were no amphibians and no reptiles, and except for a profusion of bird life, insects, and snails, only two other animals were present: the **monk seal** and the **hoary bat,** both highly specialized mammals.

The monk seal has close relatives in the Caribbean and Mediterranean, although the Caribbean relatives are now believed to be extinct, making the monk seal one of the two tropical seals left on earth. It's believed that the monk seal's ancestors entered the Pacific about 200,000 years ago when the Isthmus of Panama was submerged. When the land rose, no more seals arrived, and the monk seal became indigenous to Hawaii. The main habitat for the Hawaiian monk seal is the outer islands, from the French Frigate Atolls north to Kure Island, but infrequently a seal is spotted on the shores of one of the main islands. Though the seals' existence was known to the native Hawaiians,

HAWAII NATIONAL WILDLIFE REFUGES

BIG ISLAND

Hakalau Forest NWR
154 Waianuenue Ave., Room 219
Hilo, HI 96720
808/933-6915

Located between the 3,900–7,200 foot elevation on the windward slope of Mauna Kea, the Hakalau Forest refuge is instrumental in sustaining the naturally evolving middle elevation rainforest. It protects 'akiapola'au, Hawaiian 'akepa, Hawaiian creeper, Hawaiian hawk, 'o'u, Hawaiian hoary bat, 'amakihi, Hawaiian thrush, 'elepaio, 'i'iwi, and 'apapane in 11,000 acres of koa-'ohi'a habitat. Entry is authorized for hiking on the last weekend of the month only, by special use permit. Contact the manager.

MOLOKA'I

Kakahai'a NWR
U.S. Fish and Wildlife Service
300 Ala Moana Blvd.
P.O. Box 50167
Honolulu, HI 96850
808/541-1201

Five miles east of Kaunakakai along Highway 450, Kakahai'a NWR protects Hawaiian coot and Hawaiian stilt in 40 acres of freshwater ponds and marsh with dense thickets of bulrush. Established 1976. A beach park on refuge land is open to the public.

O'AHU

James C. Campbell NWR
O'ahu National Wildlife Refuge Complex
66-590 Kamehameha Hwy., Room 2C
Hale'iwa, HI 96712
808/637-6330

Near Kahuku on the northeastern shore of the island of O'ahu, this NWR protects Hawaiian gallinule ('alae'ula), Hawaiian coot ('alae ke'oke'o), Hawaiian stilt (ae'o), Hawaiian duck (koloa), black-crowned night herons, introduced birds, migratory shorebirds, and waterfowl. It covers 142 acres in two units: Punamano Pond is a natural spring-fed marsh, while the Ki'i Unit is a series of manmade ponds once used as sugarcane waste settling basins. Established in 1977. Open on specified weekends; contact manager for tours.

Pearl Harbor NWR
O'ahu National Wildlife Refuge Complex
66-590 Kamehameha Hwy., Room 2C
Hale'iwa, HI 96712
808/637-6330

Within Pearl Harbor Naval Base, this refuge protects Hawaiian gallinule, Hawaiian coot, Hawaiian stilt, Hawaiian duck, and black-crowned night herons on 40 acres of manmade wetlands. Established in 1977.

KAUA'I

Kilauea Point NWR
P.O. Box 87
Kilauea, HI 96754
808/828-1413

Kilauea Point NWR lies one mile north of Kilauea on a paved road; the headquarters and parking area are on Kilauea Point. Kilauea protects red-footed boobies, shearwaters, great frigate birds, brown boobies, red-tailed and white-tailed tropic birds, and Laysan albatross, as well as green sea turtles, humpback whales, and dolphins. It covers 31 acres of cliffs and headlands with native coastal plants. Open Mon.–Fri. 10 A.M.–4 P.M. The entrance fee is $2 adults, free for children under 16.

---

who called them 'ilio-holo-i-ka-uaua (dog running in the toughness), they didn't seem to play much of a role in their folklore or ecosystem. Whalers and traders certainly knew of their existence, hunting them for food and sometimes for skins. This kind of pressure almost wiped out the small seal population in the 19th century. Scientists were largely unaware of the monk seal until early in the 1900s. Finally, the seals were recognized as an endangered species and put under the protection of the Hawaiian Islands National Wildlife Refuge, where they remain in a touch-and-go battle against extinction. Today it's estimated that only 1,000 individuals are left.

The hoary bat (pe'ape'a) is a remarkable migratory animal that reached Hawaii from North and South America under its own power. The Hawaiian hoary bat no longer migrates, but its continental relatives still range far and wide.

Hule'ia NWR
P.O. Box 87
Kilauea, HI 96754
808/828-1413

At Hule'ia, viewing is best from the Menehune Fish Pond overlook along Halemalu Road west of Puhi Road. This refuge protects *koloa* (Hawaiian duck), Hawaiian coot, Hawaiian gallinule, and Hawaiian stilt. It covers 238 acres of seasonally flooded river bottomland and wooded slopes of the Hule'ia River Valley. Established in 1973. No general admittance.

Hanalei NWR
P.O. Box 87
Kilauea, HI 96754
808/828-1413

Hanalei NWR is on the north coast of Kaua'i, 1.5 miles east of Hanalei on Highway 56. Observe wildlife from Ohiki Road, which begins at the west end of Hanalei River bridge, or from the highway overlook in Princeville. This refuge protects *koloa* (Hawaiian duck), Hawaiian coot, Hawaiian gallinule, and Hawaiian stilt. It covers 917 acres of river bottomland, taro farms, and wooded slopes in the Hanalei River Valley. Established in 1972.

ATOLLS

Hawaiian Islands NWR
Hawaiian and Pacific Islands NWRs
300 Ala Moana Blvd.
P.O. Box 50167
Honolulu, HI 96850
808/541-1202

Hawaiian Islands NWR comprises far-flung islands and atolls strung 1,000 miles from Nihoa Island to Pearl and Hermes Reef—rugged volcanic remnants and sparsely vegetated low sandy islands. The refuge protects Laysan and black-footed albatross, sooty terns, white terns, brown and black noddies, shearwaters, petrels, red-tailed tropic birds, frigate birds, and boobies. Also protected are several land birds and ducks, the Hawaiian monk seal, and the green sea turtle. The refuge covers 1,800 acres of land and a quarter million acres of submerged reef and lagoons. Established in 1909. No general access.

Remote Pacific Refuges
Hawaiian and Pacific Islands NWRs
300 Ala Moana Blvd.
P.O. Box 50167
Honolulu, HI 96850
808/541-1202

Johnston Atoll NWR is about 825 miles southwest of Honolulu. It protects seabird nesting rookeries, sooty terns, gray-backed terns, shearwaters, red-footed boobies, brown boobies, masked boobies, lesser and great frigate birds, red-tailed tropic birds, and brown noddies. It's been a refuge since 1926. Managed with the Defense Nuclear Agency.

Baker Island NWR, 340 acres, and **Howland Island NWR,** 400 acres, are about 1,600 miles southwest of Hawaii, just north of the equator. Each encompasses emerged and submerged land. Low islands covered in grasses, vines, and bush sustain various seabirds and migratory birds.

Jarvis Island NWR is about 1,300 miles south of Honolulu and includes 1,100 acres of nesting area for at least eight species of migratory birds.

Rose Atoll NWR is the easternmost point of the Samoan archipelago and the southernmost U.S. national wildlife refuge. It covers 20 acres of islets, lagoon, and reef that support a dozen species of migratory birds. Administered jointly with the American Samoa government. Baker, Howland, Jarvis, and Rose NWRs were established in 1974.

The Hawaiian bat has become somewhat smaller and reddish in color over the years, distinguishing it from its larger, darker brown cousins. Its tail has a whitish coloration, hence the name. The hoary bat has a 13-inch wingspan, gives birth to twins in early summer, and unlike other bats, is a solitary creature, roosting in trees. It doesn't live in caves like others of its species. The bats normally live at altitudes below 4,000 feet, but some have been observed on Mauna Loa and Mauna Kea above 6,000 feet. The main population is on the Big Island, with smaller breeding grounds on Maui and Kaua'i. Sometimes bats are spotted on the other main islands, but it remains uncertain whether they inhabit the islands or simply fly there from their established colonies. Recently, a second species of bat (now extinct) has been identified from bone fragments taken from caves on four of the Hawaiian Islands.

Coral

Whether you're an avid scuba diver or novice snorkeler, you'll become aware of underwater coral gardens and grottoes whenever you peer at the fantastic seascapes below the waves. Although there is plenty of it, the coral in Hawaii doesn't do as well as in other more equatorial areas because the water is too wild and it's not quite as warm. Coral looks like a plant fashioned from colorful stone, but it's really the skeleton of tiny animals, zoophytes, that eat algae to live. Coral grows best on the west side of the islands where the water is quite still, the days are more sunny, and the algae can thrive. Many of Hawaii's reefs have been dying in the last 20 years, and no one seems to know why. Pesticides, used in agriculture, have been pointed to as a possible cause.

WHALES

Perhaps it's their tremendous size and graceful power, coupled with a dancer's delicacy of movement, that render whales so esthetically and emotionally captivating. In fact, many people claim that they feel a spirit-bond to these obviously intelligent mammals, which at one time shared dry land with us and then re-evolved into creatures of the great seas. Experts often remark that whales exhibit behavior akin to the highest social virtues. For example, whales rely much more on learned behavior than on instinct, the sign of a highly evolved intelligence. Gentle mothers and protective "escort" males join to teach the young to survive. They display loyalty and bravery in times of distress, and innate gentleness and curiosity. Their "songs," especially those of the humpbacks, fascinate scientists and are considered a unique form of communication in the animal kingdom. Humpback whales migrate to Hawaii every year November–May. Here, they winter, mate, give birth, and nurture their young until returning to food-rich northern waters in the spring. It's hoped that humankind can peacefully share the oceans with these magnificent giants forever. Then, perhaps, we will have taken the first steps toward saving ourselves.

Evolution and Socialization

Many millions of years ago, for an unknown reason, animals similar to cows—their closest land relative is the hippo—were genetically triggered to leave the land and readapt to the sea. Known as cetaceans, this order contains about 80 species of whales, porpoises, and dolphins. Being mammals, cetaceans are warm-blooded and maintain a body temperature of 96°, only 2.6 degrees less than humans. After a gestation period of about one year, whales give birth to fully formed young, which usually enter the world tail first. The mother whale spins quickly to snap the umbilical cord, then places herself under the newborn and lifts it to the surface to take its first breath. A whale must be taught to swim or it will drown like any other air-breathing mammal. The baby whale, nourished by its mother's rich milk, becomes a member of an extended family, or pod, through which it's cared for, socialized, and protected by many "nannies."

Physiology

The best way to spot a whale is to look for its "spout," a misty spray forced from a blowhole—really the whale's nostrils, which have moved from its snout to just behind its head. The spray from the spout is not water, but highly compressed air heated by the whale's body and expelled with such force that it condenses into a fine mist. A whale's tail is called a fluke; unlike the vertical tail of fish, a whale's tail is horizontal. The fluke, a marvelous appendage for propelling the whale through the water, is a vestige of the pelvis. It's so powerful that a 40-ton humpback can lift itself completely out of the water with only three strokes of its fluke. A whale's flippers guide it through the water. The bones in the flippers closely resemble those of the human arm and hand; small, delicate bones at the ends of the flippers look like fingers. On a humpback the flippers can be one-third as long as the body and supple enough to bend over its back, like a human reaching over the shoulder to scratch an itch.

A whale's eyes are functional but very small and not the primary sensors. Instead, the whale has developed keen hearing; the ears are small holes about as big around as the lead of a pencil. They have protective wax plugs that build up over the years. Like the growth rings in a tree, the ear plugs can be counted to determine the age of a whale; its life span is about the same as that of a human being. Because of strong ocean currents and the myriad dangers inherent in being at sea, whales enjoy a very light sleep, more like a rest similar to humans just awakening, a state that is not fully conscious but aware.

Types of Whales

Although all whales, dolphins, and porpoises are cetaceans, they are arbitrarily divided according to length. Whales are all those animals longer than 30 feet; dolphins range 6–30 feet; and porpoises are less than six feet long. There are basically two types of whales: toothed, which includes the sperm, killer, and pilot whales, as well as porpoises and dolphins; and baleen, including the blue, minke, right, fin, and humpback.

Toothed whales feed by capturing and tearing their prey with their teeth. The killer whale or orca is the best known of the toothed whales. With its distinctive black-and-white markings and propensity for aquabatics, it's a favorite at marine parks around the world. The orca hunts other cetaceans, oftentimes attacking in packs to overcome larger whales. A killer whale in the wild lives about four times as long as one in captivity, even if it is well cared for.

A baleen whale eats by gliding through the water with its mouth open, sucking in marine plankton and tiny shrimplike creatures called krill. The whale then expels the water and captures the food in row after row of a prickly, fingernail-like substance called baleen.

Hawaiian Whales and Dolphins

The role of whales and dolphins in Hawaiian culture seems quite limited. Unlike fish, which were intimately known and individually named, only two generic names described whales: *kohola* (whale) and *palaoa* (sperm whale). Dolphins were lumped together under one name, *nai'a;* Hawaiians were known to harvest dolphins on occasion by herding them onto a beach. Whale jewelry was worn by the *ali'i.* The most coveted ornament came from a sperm whale's tooth, called a *lei niho palaoa,* which was carved into one large curved pendant. Sperm whales have upward of 50 teeth, ranging in size 4–12 inches and weighing up to two pounds. One whale could provide numerous pendants. The most famous whale in Hawaiian waters is the humpback, but others often sighted include the sperm, killer, false killer, pilot, Curvier, Blainsville, and pygmy killer. There are technically no porpoises, but dolphins include the common, bottlenose, spinner, white-sided, broad- and slender-beaked, and rough-toothed. The mahimahi, a favorite eating fish found on many menus, is commonly referred to as a dolphin but is unrelated and is a true fish, not a cetacean.

The Humpbacks

The humpback gets its name from its style of exposing its dorsal fin when diving, which gives it a humped appearance. This dorsal fin also puts it into the rorqual family. There are about 10,000 humpback whales alive today, down from an estimated 100,000 at the beginning of the 20th century. The remaining whales are divided into three separate global populations: North Atlantic, North Pacific, and South Pacific groups. About 2,000 North Pacific humpbacks migrate from coastal Alaska beginning in November. Migration peaks in February, when humpbacks congregate mostly in the waters off Maui, with smaller groups heading for the waters off the other islands. In 1992, the **Hawaiian Islands Humpback Whale National Marine Sanctuary** was designated, encompassing waters off all six major islands. One hopes this will ensure a perpetual safe haven for the whales.

Adult humpbacks average 45 feet long and weigh in at a svelte 40 tons (80,000 pounds) or more. They come to Hawaii mainly to give birth to 2,000-pound, relatively blubberless calves (one per female), most of which are born by the end of January. The mother nurses her calf for about one year and becomes impregnated again the

humpback whale

BOB RACE

next year. While in Hawaiian waters the hump-backs generally don't eat. They wait until re-turning to Alaska, where they gorge themselves on krill. It's estimated they can live off their blub-ber without peril for six months. They have enor-mous mouths stretching one-third the length of their bodies and filled with more than 600 rows of baleen. Humpbacks have been known to blow air underwater to create giant bubble-nets that help corral krill. They rush in with mouths agape and dine on their catch.

Like other baleen whales, humpbacks feed in relatively shallow waters and sound (dive) for periods lasting a maximum of about 25 minutes. In comparison, the sperm whale, a toothed bot-tom-feeder, can stay down for more than an hour. On the surface a humpback will breathe about once every two minutes. They also sleep on the surface or just below it.

A distinctive feature of the humpback is the 15-foot flipper that it can bend over its back. The flippers and tail flukes have white markings that differ between individuals, much as do human fingerprints. These markings are used to identi-fy individual migrating humpbacks. Scientists photograph the distinctive tails and send prints to Seattle, Washington, a center of whale research. There a computer analysis identifies the indi-vidual or records it as a new specimen. There-after, any sightings become part of its life histo-ry. The humpback is the most aquabatic of all whales, and it is a thrilling sight to see one of these agile giants leap from the water and create a monumental splash.

The Humpback's Song
Unlike other whales, humpbacks have the spe-cial ability to sing. They create their melodies by grunting, shrieking, and moaning. No one knows exactly what the songs represent, but it's clear they're a definite form of communication. The singers appear to be "escort males" who tag along with and seem to guard a mother and her calf. Some scientists believe these are lone males and perhaps the song is territorial, or a mating call. The songs are exact renditions that last 20 minutes or longer and are repeated for hours. Amazingly, all the whales know and sing the same song, and the song changes from year to year. The notes are so forceful they can be heard above and below the water for miles.

Some of the deep bass notes carry underwater for 100 miles. Good recordings of the hump-backs' songs can be heard aboard the *Carthaginian II,* a restored 19th-century square-rigged ship just to the right of the loading dock in Lahaina Harbor on Maui. It serves as a floating museum dedicated to whales and whaling.

Whaling History
Humans have known about whales for many thousands of years. A Minoan palace on the is-land of Crete depicts whales on a 5,000-year-old mural. The first whalers were probably Scandi-navians who used stone harpoon heads to cap-ture their prey more than 4,000 years ago. Inuit have long engaged in whaling as a means of survival, and for centuries many peoples living along coastal waters have harpooned migrat-ing whales that ventured close to shore. The Basques had a thriving medieval whaling in-dustry in the 12th century centered in the Bay of Biscay, until they wiped out all the Biscayan right whales. The height of the classic whaling in-dustry that inspired Melville's *Moby Dick* oc-curred 1820–1860. The international whaling capital perfectly situated in the center of the win-ter whaling grounds was Lahaina, Maui. At that time 900 sailing ships roamed the globe in search of whales. Of these, 700 were Ameri-can, and they started the trend away from coastal to pelagic whaling by bringing their try-pots (blub-ber pots) aboard ship.

Although the killing was great during these years, every part of the whale was needed and used: blubber, meat, bone, teeth. Whale oil, the main product, was a superior lighting fuel and lu-bricant unmatched until petroleum came into general use in the mid-19th century. Today, every single whale by-product can be manufac-tured synthetically and there's absolutely no pri-mary need to justify slaughtering whales.

During the great whaling days, the whales ac-tually had a fighting chance. After all, they were hunted by men in wooden sailing ships that de-pended upon favorable winds. Once a whale was sighted by a sailor perched high in the rigging using a low-powered telescope, a small boat heaved off; after desperate rowing and dangerous maneuvering, the master harpooner threw his shaft by hand. When the whale was dead, it took every able-bodied man to haul it in.

Today, however, modern methods have wiped out every trace of daring and turned the hunt into technologically assisted slaughter. Low-flying aircraft radio the whales' locations to huge factory-ships that track them with radar and sonar. Once the pod is spotted, super-swift launches tear into them, firing cannon-propelled harpoons with lethal exploding tips. The killer launches keep firing until every whale in the pod is dead, and the huge factory-ship follows behind, merely scooping up the lifeless carcasses and hauling them aboard with diesel winches.

Many pirate whalers still roam the seas. The worst example perpetrated by these racketeers occurred in the Bahamas in 1971. A ship ironically carrying the name of *the* classic conservation group, *Sierra,* succeeded in wiping out every single humpback whale that wintered in Bahamian waters. Since 1971 not one whale has been sighted in the Bahamas, and whale-watchers lament that they will never return.

The Last Whalers
Thanks to world opinion and the efforts of benign but aggressive organizations such as Greenpeace and Earth Trust, the **International Whaling Commission** (IWC), a voluntary group of 17 nations, now sets standards and passes quotas on the number and species of whales that can be killed. Since the mid-1960s, blue, right, gray, bowhead, and humpback have become totally protected. However, many great whales such as the sperm, minke, sei, and fin are still hunted. Also, the IWC has no power of enforcement except public opinion and possible voluntary economic sanction.

The Japanese and Norwegians still hunt for whales, their operations often thinly disguised as "research." Native American Inuit and a few other indigenous peoples of the world, like the villagers of Lamalera on Lembata in Indonesia, hunt whales, but the number of whales taken by these groups is minuscule. The Japanese technically stay within their quotas, but they hire and outfit these and other nationals to hunt whales for them. Their main argument is that whaling is a traditional industry upon which they rely for food and jobs. This is patently false. Hardly more than 100 years old, pelagic whaling is a new industry to the Japanese. Much of the Japanese whale meat becomes pet food anyway, which is mainly exported.

Amazingly, a poll taken in Japan by the Whale and Dolphin Society of London found that 69 percent of the people opposed whaling. Finally, through the efforts of *ICEARCH* (International Cetacean Education And Research Conference), the first pillars of a bridge were laid between Japanese and Western scientists who are dedicated to finding a way for mankind and the great

ENVIRONMENTAL RESOURCE GROUPS

Anyone interested in Hawaii's environmental issues can contact the following for more information:

Earthjustice Legal Defense Fund (formerly Sierra Club Legal Defense Fund), 223 S. King St., 4th Fl., Honolulu, HI 96813, 808/599-2436, website: www.earthjustice.org

Greenpeace, 808/595-0057, website: www.greenpeace.org

The Nature Conservancy, 923 Nu'uanu Ave., Honolulu, HI 96817, 808/537-4508, website: www.tnc-hawaii.org

Rainforest Action Network, 221 Pine St., Suite 500, San Francisco, CA 94104, 415/398-4404, website: www.ran.org

Sierra Club Hawaii Chapter, P.O. Box 2577, Honolulu, HI 96803, 808/538-6616, website: www.hi.sierraclub.org

Earth Trust, 25 Kane'ohe Bay Dr., Suite 205, Kailua, HI 96734, 808/254-2866, website: www.earthtrust.org

A savvy monthly newsletter that focuses on environmental and political issues facing Hawaii today is *Environment Hawai'i,* 282 Ululani St, 1st Fl., Hilo, HI 96720, 808/934-0115, website: www.environment-hawaii.org; individual subscription rate is $35 per year. The well-researched and concisely written newsletter attempts to be fair to all parties concerned. Short on preaching and long on common sense, *Environment Hawai'i* is an excellent resource for anyone interested in the sociopolitical and environmental issues of the 50th state.

whales to live in harmony. In April 1993 these scientists came together on Maui for the first time to discuss the issue.

Whale-watching

If you're in Hawaii from late November to early May, you have an excellent chance of spotting a humpback. March is perhaps the best month. You can often see a whale from a vantage point on land, but this is nowhere near as thrilling as seeing them close up from a boat. Either way, binoculars are a must. Telephoto and zoom lenses are also useful, and you might even get a nifty photo in the bargain. But don't waste your film unless you have a fairly high-powered zoom: fixed-lens cameras give pictures with a lot of ocean and a tiny black speck. If you're lucky enough to see a whale breach (jump clear of the water), keep watching—they often repeat this a number of times. If a whale dives and lifts its fluke high in the air, expect it to be down for at least 15 minutes and not come up in the same spot. Other times they'll dive shallowly, then bob up and down quite often. If you time your arrival near sunset, even if you don't see a whale you'll enjoy a mind-boggling light show.

To learn more about whales and the Hawaiian Islands Humpback Whale National Marine Sanctuary, contact its office at 726 S. Kihei Rd., Kihei, HI 96753, 800/831-4888, website: www.t-link.net/~whale. Another good source of information is the **Pacific Whale Foundation,** 101 N. Kihei Road, Kihei, HI 96753, 808/879-8860, website: www.pacificwhale.org. Both these organizations have plenty of printed information about whales and other marine animals, and the Pacific Whale Foundation prints the free *Whalewatch News* tabloid, which details other information about these mammals and doings of the foundation. Additional research on whales and dolphins is being undertaken by the **Island Marine Institute,** 113 Prison St., Lahaina, HI 96761, 808/667-6165, website: www.whalewatchmaui.com.

HISTORY

THE ROAD FROM TAHITI

Until the 1820s, when New England missionaries began a phonetic rendering of the Hawaiian language, the past was kept vividly alive only by the sonorous voices of special *kahuna* who chanted the sacred *mele*. The chants were beautiful, flowing word pictures that captured the essence of every aspect of life. These *mele* praised the land *(mele 'aina),* royalty *(mele ali'i),* and life's tender aspects *(mele aloha).* Chants were dedicated to friendship, hardship, and favorite children. Entire villages sometimes joined together to compose a *mele*—every word was chosen carefully, and the wise old *kupuna* would decide if the words were lucky or unlucky. Some *mele* were bawdy or funny on the surface but contained secret meanings, often with biting sarcasm, that ridiculed an inept or cruel leader. The most important chants took listeners back into the dim past, even before people lived in Hawaii. From these genealogies *(ko'ihonua),* the *ali'i* derived the right to rule, since these chants went back to the gods Wakea and Papa from whom the *ali'i* were directly descended.

The Kumulipo

The great genealogies, finally compiled in the late 1800s by order of King Kalakaua, were collectively known as *The Kumulipo, A Hawaiian Creation Chant,* basically a Polynesian account of Genesis. Other chants related to the beginning of this world, but *The Kumulipo* sums it all up and is generally considered the best. The chant relates that after the beginning of time, there is a period of darkness. The darkness, however, mysteriously brims with spontaneous life; during this period plants and animals are born, as well as Kumulipo, the man, and Po'ele, the woman. In the eighth chant darkness gives way to light and the gods descend to earth. Wakea is "the sky father" and Papa is "the earth mother," whose union gives birth to the islands of Hawaii. First born is Hawai'i, followed by Maui, then Kaho'olawe. Apparently, Papa becomes bushed after three consecutive births and decides to vacation in Tahiti. While Papa is away recovering from postpartum depression and working on her tan, Wakea gets lonely and takes Ka'ula as his second wife; she bears him the island-child of

Lana'i. Not fully cheered up, but getting the hang of it, Wakea takes a third wife, Hina, who promptly bears the island of Moloka'i. Meanwhile, Papa gets wind of these shenanigans, returns from Polynesia, and retaliates by taking up with Lua, a young and virile god. She soon gives birth to the island of O'ahu. Papa and Wakea finally decide that they really are meant for each other and reconcile to conceive Kaua'i, Ni'ihau, Ka'ula, and Nihoa. These two progenitors are the source from which the *ali'i* ultimately traced their lineage, and from which they derived their god-ordained power to rule.

Basically, there are two major genealogical families: the **Nanaulu,** who became the royal *ali'i* of O'ahu and Kaua'i, and the **Ulu,** who provided the royalty of Maui and Hawai'i. The best sources of information on Hawaiian myth and legend are Martha Beckwith's *Hawaiian Mythology* and the monumental three-volume opus *An Account of the Polynesian Race,* compiled by Abraham Fornander 1878–85. Fornander, after settling in Hawaii, married an *ali'i* from Moloka'i and had an illustrious career as a journalist, Maui circuit judge, and finally Supreme Court justice. For years Fornander sent scribes to every corner of the kingdom to listen to the elder *kupuna*. They returned with firsthand accounts, which he dutifully recorded.

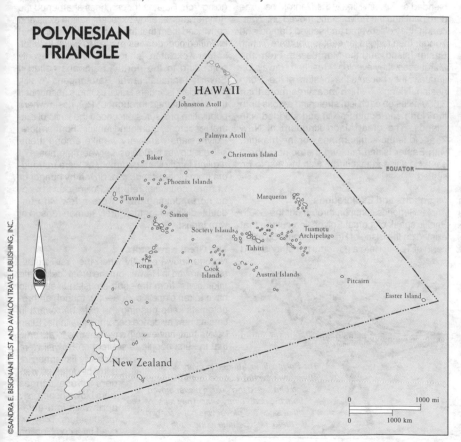

POLYNESIAN TRIANGLE

HAWAII

Johnston Atoll

Palmyra Atoll

Baker · Christmas Island

EQUATOR

Phoenix Islands

Tuvalu

Samoa

Marquesas

Society Islands

Tuamotu Archipelago

Tahiti

Tonga

Cook Islands

Austral Islands

Pitcairn

Easter Island

New Zealand

0   1000 mi

0   1000 km

Polynesians

Since prehistory, Polynesians have been seafaring people whose origins cannot be completely traced. They seem to have come from Southeast Asia mostly through the gateway of Indonesia, and their racial strain pulls features from all three dominant races: Caucasian, Negro, and Asian. They learned to navigate on tame narrow waterways along Indonesia and New Guinea, then fanned out eastward into the great Pacific. They sailed northeast to the low islands of Micronesia and southwest to Fiji, Vanuatu, and New Caledonia. Fiji is regarded as the "cradle of Polynesian culture"; carbon dating places humans there as early as 3,500 B.C. Many races blended on Fiji, until finally the Negroid became dominant and the Polynesians moved on. Wandering, they discovered and settled Samoa and Tonga, then ranged far east to populate Tahiti, Easter Island, and the Marquesas. From the Marquesas, they eventually reached Hawaii. Ultimately, they became the masters of the "Polynesian Triangle," which measures more than 5,000 miles on each leg, stretching across both the North and South Pacific and studded with islands. The great Maori kingdom of New Zealand is the southern apex of the triangle, with Easter Island marking the point farthest east; Hawaii, farthest north, was the last to be settled.

Migrations and Explorations

Ancient legends common throughout the South Pacific speak of a great Polynesian culture that existed on the island of Raiatea, about 150 miles north of Tahiti. Here a powerful priesthood held sway in an enormous *heiau* in the Opoa district called Toputapuatea. Kings from throughout Polynesia came here to worship. Human sacrifice was common, as it was believed that the essence of the spirit could be utilized and controlled in this life; therefore the mana of Toputapuatea was great. Defeated warriors and commoners were used as living rollers to drag canoes up onto the beach, while corpses were dismembered and hung in trees. The power of the priests of Opoa lasted for many generations, evoking trembling fear in even the bravest warrior just by the mention of their names. Finally, their power waned and Polynesians lost their centralized culture, but the constant coming and going from Raiatea for centuries sharpened the Polynesians' already excellent sailing skills and convinced them that the world was vast and that unlimited opportunities existed to better their lot.

Many explorers left to look for the "heavenly homeland to the north." Samoans called it Savai'i, Tongans Hawai, Rarotongans Avaiki, and Society Islanders Havai'i. Others abandoned the small islands throughout Polynesia where population pressures exceeded the limits of natural resources, prompting famine. Furthermore, Polynesians were very warlike among themselves; power struggles between members of a ruling family were common, as were marauders from other islands. So, driven by hunger or warfare, countless refugee Polynesians headed north. Joining them were a few who undoubtedly went for the purely human reason of wanderlust.

The Great Navigators

No one knows exactly when the first Polynesians arrived in Hawaii, but the great "deliberate migrations" from the southern islands seem to have taken place A.D. 500–800, though anthropologists keep pushing the date backward in time as new evidence becomes available. Even before that, however, it's reasonable to assume that the first people to set foot on Hawaii were probably fishermen, or perhaps defeated warriors whose canoes were blown hopelessly northward into unfamiliar waters. They arrived by a combination

The Polynesians, attuned to every nuance in their environment, noticed that a migratory land bird called the golden plover arrived from the north every year. They reasoned that since the plover was not a seabird, there must be land to the north.

LOUISE FOOTE

of extraordinary good luck and an uncanny ability to sail and navigate without instruments, using the sun by day and the moon and rising stars by night. They could feel the water and determine direction by swells, tides, and currents. The movements of fish and cloud formations were also utilized to give direction. Since their arrival was probably an accident, they were unprepared to settle on the fertile but barren lands, having no stock animals, plant cuttings, or women. Forced to return southward, many undoubtedly lost their lives at sea, but a few wild-eyed stragglers must have made it home to tell tales of a paradise to the north where land was plentiful and the sea bounteous. This is affirmed by ancient navigational chants from Tahiti, Moorea, and Bora Bora, which were passed from father to son and revealed how to follow the stars to the "heavenly homeland in the north." Possibly a few migrations followed, but it's known that for centuries there was no real reason for a mass exodus, so the chants alone remained and eventually became shadowy legend.

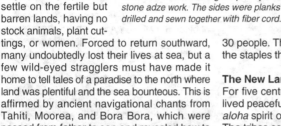

The canoe hull was a log shaped by masterly stone adze work. The sides were planks drilled and sewn together with fiber cord.

From Where They Came

It's generally agreed that the first planned migrations were from the violent cannibal islands that Spanish explorers called the Marquesas, 11 islands in extreme eastern Polynesia. The islands themselves are harsh and inhospitable, breeding a toughness into these people that enabled them to withstand the hardships of long, unsure ocean voyages and years of resettlement. Marquesans were a fiercely independent people whose chiefs could rise from the ranks because of bravery or intelligence. They must have also been a fierce-looking lot. Both men and women tattooed themselves in complex blue patterns from head to foot. The warriors carried massive, intricately designed ironwood war clubs and wore carved whale teeth in slits in their earlobes that eventually stretched to the shoulders. They shaved the sides of their heads with sharks' teeth, tied their hair in two topknots that looked like horns, and rubbed their heavily

muscled and tattooed bodies with scented coconut oils. Their cults worshipped mummified ancestors; the bodies of warriors of defeated neighboring tribes were consumed. They were masters at building great double-hulled canoes launched from huge canoe sheds. Two hulls were fastened together to form a catamaran, and a hut in the center provided shelter in bad weather. The average voyaging canoe was 60–80 feet long and could comfortably hold an extended family of about 30 people. These small family bands carried all the staples they would need in the new lands.

The New Lands

For five centuries the Marquesans settled and lived peacefully on the new land, as if Hawaii's *aloha* spirit overcame most of their fierceness. The tribes coexisted in relative harmony, especially since there was no competition for land. Cannibalism died out. There was much coming and going between Hawaii and Polynesia as new people came to settle for hundreds of years. Then, it appears that in the 12th century a deliberate exodus of warlike Tahitians arrived and subjugated the settled islanders. They came to conquer. This incursion had a terrific significance on the Hawaiian religious and social system. Oral tradition relates that a Tahitian priest, Pa'ao, found the mana of the Hawaiian chiefs to be low, signifying that their gods were weak. Pa'ao built a *heiau* at Waha'ula on the Big Island, then introduced the warlike god Ku and the rigid *kapu* system through which the new rulers became dominant. Voyages between Tahiti and Hawaii continued for about 100 years, and Tahitian customs, legends, and language became the Hawaiian way of life. Then suddenly, for no recorded or apparent reason, the voyages discontinued and Hawaii returned to total isolation.

The islands remained forgotten for almost 500 years until the indomitable English sailor, Captain James Cook, sighted O'ahu on January 18, 1778, and stepped ashore at Waimea on Kaua'i two days later. At that time Hawaii's isolation was so complete that even the Polynesians had forgotten about it. On an earlier voyage, Tupaia, a high priest from Raiatea, had accompanied Captain Cook as he sailed throughout Polynesia. Tupaia demonstrated his vast knowledge of existing archipelagos throughout the South Pacific by naming more than 130 islands and drawing a map that included the Tonga group, the Cook Islands, the Marquesas, even tiny Pitcairn, a rock in far eastern Polynesia where the mutinous crew of the *Bounty* found solace. In mentioning the Marquesas, Tupaia said, *"He ma'a te ka'ata,"* which means "Food is man" or simply "Cannibals." But remarkably absent from Tupaia's vast knowledge was the existence of Easter Island, New Zealand, and Hawaii.

The next waves of people to Hawaii would be white, and the Hawaiian world would be changed quickly and forever.

THE WORLD DISCOVERS HAWAII

The late 18th century was an extraordinary time in Hawaiian history. Monumental changes seemed to happen all at once. First, Captain James Cook, a Yorkshire farm boy fulfilling his destiny as the all-time greatest Pacific explorer, found Hawaii for the rest of the world. For better or worse, it could no longer be an isolated Polynesian homeland. For the first time in Hawaiian history, a charismatic leader—Kamehameha—emerged, and after a long civil war he united the islands into one centralized kingdom. The death of Captain Cook in Hawaii marked the beginning of a long series of tragic misunderstandings between whites and natives. When Kamehameha died, the old religious system of *kapu* came to an end, leaving the Hawaiians in a spiritual vortex. Many takers arrived to fill the void: missionaries after souls, whalers after their prey and a good time, traders and planters after profits and a home. The islands were opened and devoured like ripe fruit. Powerful nations, including Russia, Great Britain, France, and the United States, yearned to bring this strategic Pacific jewel under their own influence. The 19th century brought the demise of the Hawaiian people as a dominant political force in their own land and with it the end of Hawaii as a sovereign monarchy. An almost bloodless yet bitter military coup followed by a brief Hawaiian Republic

ended in annexation by the United States. As the United States became completely entrenched politically and militarily, a new social and economic order was founded on the plantation system. Amazingly rapid population growth occurred with the importation of plantation workers from Asia and Europe, which yielded a unique cosmopolitan blend of races like nowhere else on earth. By the dawning of the 20th century, the face of old Hawaii had been altered forever; the "sacred homeland in the north" was hurled into the modern age. The attack on Pearl Harbor saw a tremendous loss of life and brought Hawaii closer to the United States by a baptism of blood. Finally, on August 21, 1959, after 59 years as a "territory," Hawaii officially became the 50th state of the Union.

Captain Cook Sights Hawaii

In 1776 Captain James Cook set sail for the Pacific from Plymouth, England, on his third and final expedition into this still vastly unexplored region of the world. On a fruitless quest for the fabled Northwest Passage across the North American continent, he sailed down the coast of Africa, rounded the Cape of Good Hope, crossed the Indian Ocean, and traveled past New Zealand, Tasmania, and the Friendly Islands (where an unsuccessful plot was hatched by the "friendly" natives to murder him). On January 18, 1778, Captain Cook's 100-foot flagship HMS *Resolution* and its 90-foot companion HMS *Discovery* sighted O'ahu. Two days later, they sighted Kaua'i and went ashore at the village of Waimea. Though anxious to get on with his mission, Cook decided to make a quick sortie to investigate this new land and reprovision his ships. He did, however, take time to remark in his diary about the close resemblance of these newfound people to others he had encountered as far south as New Zealand, and he marveled at their widespread habitation across the Pacific.

The first trade was some brass medals for a mackerel. Cook also stated that he had never before met natives so astonished by a ship, and that they had an amazing fascination for iron, which they called *toe,* Hawaiian for "adze." There is even some conjecture that a Spanish ship under one Captain Gaetano had landed in Hawaii as early as the 16th century, trading a few scraps of iron that the Hawaiians valued even more than the Europeans valued gold. It was also noted that the Hawaiian women gave themselves freely to the sailors with the apparent good wishes of the island men. This was actually a ploy by the *kahuna* to test if the newcomers were gods or men—gods didn't need women. These sailors proved immediately mortal. Cook, who was also a physician, tried valiantly to keep the 66 men (out of 112) who had measurable cases of venereal disease away from the women. The task proved impossible as women literally swarmed the ships; when Cook returned less than a year later, it was logged that signs of VD were already apparent on some natives' faces.

Cook was impressed with the Hawaiians' swimming ability and with their well-bred manners. They had happy dispositions and sticky fingers, stealing any object made of metal, especially nails. The first item stolen was a butcher's cleaver. An unidentified native grabbed it, plunged overboard, swam to shore, and waved his booty in triumph. The Hawaiians didn't seem to care for beads and were not at all impressed with a mirror. Cook provisioned his ships by trading chisels for hogs, while common sailors gleefully traded nails for sex. Landing parties were sent inland to fill casks with fresh water. On one such excursion a Mr. Williamson, who was eventually drummed out of the Royal Navy for cowardice, unnecessarily shot and killed a native. After a brief stop on Ni'ihau, the ships sailed away, but both groups were indelibly impressed with the memory of each other.

Cook Returns

Almost a year later, when winter weather forced Cook to return from the coast of Alaska, his discovery began to take on far-reaching significance. Cook had named Hawaii the Sandwich Islands, in honor of one of his patrons, John Montague, the Earl of Sandwich. On this return voyage, he spotted Maui on November 26, 1778. After eight weeks of seeking a suitable harbor, the ships bypassed it, but not before the coastline was duly drawn by Lieutenant William Bligh, one of Cook's finest and most trusted officers. (Bligh would find his own drama almost 10 years later as commander of the infamous HMS *Bounty*.) The *Discovery* and *Resolution* finally found safe anchorage at Kealakekua Bay on the Kona Coast of the Big Island. It is very lucky for history that on board was Mr. Anderson, ship's chronicler, who left a handwritten record of the strange and tragic events that followed. Even more important were the drawings of John Webber, ship's artist, who rendered invaluable impressions in superb drawings and etchings. Other noteworthy men aboard were George Vancouver, who would lead the first British return to Hawaii after Cook's death and introduce many fruits, vegetables, cattle, sheep, and goats; and James Burney, who would become a long-standing leading authority on the Pacific.

By all accounts Cook was a humane and just captain, greatly admired by his men. Unlike many other supremacists of that time, he was known to have a respectful attitude toward any people he encountered, treating them as equals and recognizing the significance of their cultures. Not known as a violent man, he would use his superior weapons against natives only in an absolute case of self-defense. His hardened crew had been at sea facing untold hardship for almost three years; returning to Hawaii was truly like reentering paradise.

A strange series of coincidences sailed with Cook into Kealakekua Bay on January 16, 1779. It was *makahiki* time, a period of rejoicing and

Captain James Cook

festivity dedicated to the fertility god of the earth, Lono. Normal *kapu* days were suspended and willing partners freely enjoyed each other sexually. Dancing, feasting, and the islands' version of the Olympic games also took place. It was long held in Hawaiian legend that the great god Lono would return to earth. Lono's image was a small wooden figure perched on a tall, mastlike crossbeam; hanging from the crossbeam were long, white sheets of tapa. Who else could Cook be but Lono, and what else could his ships with their masts and white sails be but his sacred floating *heiau*? This explained the Hawaiians' previous fascination with his ships, but to add to the remarkable coincidence, Kealakekua Harbor happened to be considered Lono's private sacred harbor. Natives from throughout the land prostrated themselves and paid homage to the returning god. Cook was taken ashore and brought to Lono's sacred temple, where he was afforded the highest respect. The ships badly needed fresh supplies so the Hawaiians readily gave all they had, stretching their own provisions to the limit. To the sailors' delight, this included full measures of the *aloha* spirit.

The Fatal Misunderstandings

After an uproarious welcome and generous hospitality for over a month, it became obvious that the newcomers were beginning to overstay their welcome. During the interim a seaman named

William Watman died, convincing the Hawaiians that the *haole* were indeed mortals, not gods. Watman was buried at Hikiau Heiau, where a plaque commemorates the event to this day. Incidents of petty theft began to increase dramatically. The lesser chiefs indicated it was time to leave by "rubbing the Englishmen's bellies." Inadvertently, many *kapu* were broken by the English, and once-friendly relations became strained. Finally, the ships sailed away on February 4, 1779.

After plying terrible seas for only a week, *Resolution*'s foremast was badly damaged. Cook sailed back into Kealakekua Bay, dragging the mast ashore on February 13. The natives, now totally hostile, hurled rocks at the sailors. Orders were given to load muskets with ball; firearms had previously only been loaded with shot and a light charge. Confrontations increased when some Hawaiians stole a small boat and Cook's men set after them, capturing the fleeing canoe that held an *ali'i* named Palea. The Englishmen treated him roughly; to the Hawaiians' horror, they even smacked him on the head with a paddle. The Hawaiians then furiously attacked the marines, who abandoned the small boat.

Cook Goes Down

Next the Hawaiians stole a small cutter from the *Discovery* that had been moored to a buoy and partially sunk to protect it from the sun. For the

The Death of Captain Cook by John Webber, ship's artist on Cook's third Pacific exploration, circa 1779

first time, Captain Cook became furious. He ordered Captain Clerk of the *Discovery* to sail to the southeast end of the bay and stop any canoe trying to leave Kealakekua. Cook then made a fatal error in judgment. He decided to take nine armed marines ashore in an attempt to convince the venerable King Kalani'opu'u to accompany him back aboard ship, where he would hold him for ransom in exchange for the cutter. The old king agreed, but his wife prevailed upon him not to trust the *haole*. Kalani'opu'u sat down on the beach to think while the tension steadily grew.

Meanwhile, a group of marines fired upon a canoe trying to leave the bay; a lesser chief, No'okemai, was killed. The crowd around Cook and his men reached an estimated 20,000, and warriors outraged by the killing of the chief armed themselves with clubs and protective straw-mat armor. One bold warrior advanced on Cook and struck him with his *pahoa* (dagger). In retaliation, Cook drew a tiny pistol lightly loaded with shot and fired at the warrior. His bullets spent themselves on the straw armor and fell harmlessly to the ground. The Hawaiians went wild. Lieutenant Molesworth Phillips, in charge of the nine marines, began a withering fire; Cook himself slew two natives.

Overpowered by sheer numbers, the marines headed for boats standing offshore, while Lieutenant Phillips lay wounded. It is believed that Captain Cook, the greatest Western sailor ever to enter the Pacific, stood helplessly in knee-deep water instead of making for the boats because he could not swim! Hopelessly surrounded, he was knocked on the head; then countless warriors passed a knife around and hacked and mutilated his lifeless body. A sad Lieutenant King lamented in his diary, "Thus fell our great and excellent commander."

The Final Chapter

Captain Clerk, now in charge, settled his men and prevailed upon the Hawaiians to return Cook's body. On the morning of February 16 a grisly piece of charred meat was brought aboard: the Hawaiians, according to their custom, had afforded Cook the highest honor by baking his body in an underground oven to remove the flesh from the bones. On February 17, a group of Hawaiians in a canoe taunted the marines by brandishing Cook's hat. The English, strained to the limit and thinking that Cook was being desecrated, finally broke. Foaming with bloodlust, they leveled their cannons and muskets on shore and shot anything that moved. It is believed that Kamehameha the Great was wounded in this flurry, along with four *ali'i*; 25 *maka'ainana* (commoners) were killed. Finally, on February 21, 1779, the bones of Captain James Cook's hands, skull, arms, and legs were returned and tearfully buried at sea. A common seaman, one Mr. Zimmerman, summed up the feelings of all who sailed under Cook when he wrote, ". . . he was our leading star." The English sailed next morning after dropping off their Hawaiian girlfriends who were still aboard.

Captain Clerk, in bad health, carried on with the fruitless search for the Northwest Passage. He died and was buried at the Siberian village of Petropavlovsk. England was at war with upstart colonists in America, so the return of the expedition warranted little fanfare. The *Resolution* was converted into an army transport to fight the pesky Americans; the once-proud *Discovery* was reduced to a convict ship ferrying inmates to Botany Bay, Australia. Mrs. Cook, the great captain's steadfast and chaste wife, lived to the age of 93, surviving all her children. She was given a stipend of 200 pounds per year and finished her days surrounded by Cook's mementos, observing the anniversary of his death to the very end by fasting and reading from the Bible.

THE UNIFICATION OF OLD HAWAII

Hawaii was already in a state of political turmoil and civil war when Cook arrived. In the 1780s the islands were roughly divided into three kingdoms: venerable Kalani'opu'u ruled Hawai'i and the Hana district of Maui; wily and ruthless warrior-king Kahekili ruled Maui, Kaho'olawe, Lana'i, and later O'ahu; and Kaeo, Kahekili's brother, ruled Kaua'i. War ravaged the land until a remarkable chief, Kamehameha, rose and subjugated all the islands under one rule. Kamehameha initiated a dynasty that would last for about 100 years, until the independent monarchy of Hawaii forever ceased to be. To add a zing to this brewing political stew, Westerners and their technology were beginning to come in ever-increasing numbers. In 1786, Captain Jean de

François La Pérouse and his French exploration party landed in what's now La Pérouse Bay near Makena, foreshadowing European attention to the islands. In 1786 two American captains, Portlock and Dixon, made landfall in Hawaii. Also, it was known that a fortune could be made on the fur trade between the Pacific Northwest and Canton, China; stopping in Hawaii could make it feasible. After this was reported, the fate of Hawaii was sealed.

Hawaii under Kamehameha was ready to enter its "golden age." The social order was medieval, with the *ali'i* as knights owing their military allegiance to the king, and the serf-like *maka'ainana* paying tribute and working the lands. The priesthood of *kahuna* filled the posts of advisors, sorcerers, navigators, doctors, and historians. This was Polynesian Hawaii at its apex. But like the uniquely Hawaiian silversword, the old culture blossomed, and as soon as it did, began to wither. Ever since, all that was purely Hawaiian has been supplanted by the relentless foreign influences that began bearing down upon it.

Young Kamehameha

The greatest native son of Hawaii, Kamehameha, was born under mysterious circumstances in the Kohala District of the Big Island, probably in 1753. He was royal born to Keoua Kupuapaikalaninui, the chief of Kohala, and Kekuiapoiwa, a chieftess from Kona. Accounts vary, but one claims that before his birth, a *kahuna* prophesied that this child would grow to be a "killer of chiefs." Because of this, the local chiefs conspired to murder the infant. When Kekuiapoiwa's time came, she secretly went to the royal birthing stones near Mo'okini Heiau and delivered Kamehameha. She entrusted her baby

Kamehameha I as drawn by Louis Choris, ship's artist for the Von Kotzebue expedition, circa 1816. Supposedly it was the only time Kamehameha sat to have his portrait rendered.

to a manservant and instructed him to hide the child. He headed for the rugged and remote coast around Kapa'au. Here Kamehameha was raised in the mountains, mostly by men. Always alone, he earned the nickname "The Lonely One."

Kamehameha was a man noticed by everyone; there was no doubt he was a force to be reckoned with. He had met Captain Cook when the *Discovery* unsuccessfully tried to land at Hana on Maui. While aboard, he made a lasting impression, distinguishing himself from the multitude of natives swarming the ships by his royal bearing. Lieutenant James King, in a diary entry, remarked that Kamehameha was a fierce-looking man, almost ugly, but that he was obviously intelligent, observant, and very good-natured. Kamehameha received his early military training from his uncle Kalani'opu'u, the great king of Hawai'i and Hana who fought fierce battles against Alapa'i, the usurper who stole his hereditary lands. After regaining Hawai'i, Kalani'opu'u returned to his Hana district and turned his attention to conquering all of Maui. During this period young Kamehameha distinguished himself as a ferocious warrior and earned the nickname of "The Hard-shelled Crab," even though old Kahekili, Maui's king, almost annihilated Kalani'opu'u's army at the sand hills of Wailuku.

When the old king neared death, he passed on the kingdom to his son Kiwalao. He also, however, empowered Kamehameha as the keeper of the family war god Kuka'ilimoku: Ku of the Bloody Red Mouth, Ku the Destroyer. Oddly enough, Kamehameha had been born not 500 yards from Ku's great *heiau* at Kohala, and had heard the chanting and observed the ceremonies dedicated to this fierce god from his first breath. Soon after Kalani'opu'u died, Kamehameha found himself in a bitter war that he did not seek against his two cousins, Kiwalao and his brother Keoua, with the island of Hawai'i at stake. The skirmish lasted nine years, until Kamehameha's armies met the two brothers at Moku'ohai in an indecisive battle in which Kiwalao was killed. The result was a shaky truce with Keoua, a much-embittered enemy. During this fighting, Kahekili of Maui conquered O'ahu, where he built a house of the skulls and bones of his adversaries as a reminder of his omnipotence. He also extended his will to Kaua'i by marrying his half-brother to a high-ranking chieftess of that island. A new factor would resolve this stalemate of power—the coming of the *haole.*

The Olowalu Massacre
In 1790 the American merchant ship *Eleanora,* commanded by Yankee captain Simon Metcalfe, was looking for a harbor after its long voyage from the Pacific Northwest. Following a day behind was the *Fair American,* a tiny ship sailed by Metcalfe's son Thomas and a crew of five. Simon Metcalfe, perhaps by necessity, was a stern and humorless man who would tolerate no interference. While his ship was anchored at Olowalu, some natives slipped close in their canoes and stole a small boat, killing a sailor in the process. Metcalfe decided to trick the Hawaiians by first negotiating a truce and then unleashing full fury upon them. Signaling he was willing to trade, he invited canoes of innocent natives to visit his ship. In the meantime, he ordered that all cannons and muskets be readied with scatter shot. When the canoes were within hailing distance, he ordered his crew to fire at will. Over 100 people were slain; the Hawaiians remembered this killing as "the day of spilled brains." Metcalfe then sailed away to Kealakekua Bay and in an unrelated incident succeeded in insulting Kameiamoku, a ruling chief, who vowed to annihilate the next *haole* ship he saw.

Fate sent him the *Fair American* and young Thomas Metcalfe. The little ship was entirely overrun by superior forces. In the ensuing battle, the mate, Isaac Davis, so distinguished himself by open acts of bravery that his life alone was spared. Kameiamoku later turned over both Davis and the ship to Kamehameha. Meanwhile, while harbored at Kealakekua, the senior Metcalfe sent John Young to reconnoiter. Kamehameha, having learned of the capture of the *Fair American,* detained Young so he could not report, and Metcalfe, losing patience, marooned his own man and sailed off to Canton. (Metcalfe never learned of the fate of his son Thomas, and was later killed with another son while trading in the South Pacific.) Kamehameha quickly realized the significance of his two captives and the *Fair American* with its brace of small cannons. He appropriated the ship and made Davis and Young trusted advisors, eventually raising them to the rank of chief. They would all play a significant role in the unification of Hawaii.

Kamehameha the Great
Later in 1790, supported by the savvy of Davis and Young and the cannons from the *Fair American* (which he mounted on carts), Kamehameha invaded Maui, using Hana as his power base. The island's defenders under Kalanikupule, son of Kahekili who was lingering on O'ahu, were totally demoralized, then driven back into the death trap of 'Iao Valley. There, Kamehameha's forces annihilated them. No mercy was expected and none given, although mostly commoners were slain with no significant *ali'i* falling to the victors. So many were killed in this sheer-walled, inescapable valley that the battle was called *ka pani wai,* which means "the damming of the waters"—literally with dead bodies.

While Kamehameha was fighting on Maui, his old nemesis Keoua was busy running amok back on Hawai'i, again pillaging Kamehameha's lands. The great warrior returned home flushed with victory, but in two battles could not subdue Keoua. Finally, Kamehameha had a prophetic dream in which he was told that Ku would lead him to victory over all the lands of Hawaii if he would build a *heiau* to the war god at Kawaihae. Even before the temple was finished, old Kahekili attempted to invade Waipi'o, Kamehameha's stronghold. But Kamehameha summoned Davis and Young, and with the *Fair American* and an enormous fleet of war canoes defeated Kahekili at Waimanu. Kahekili had no choice but to accept the indomitable Kamehameha as the king of Maui, although he himself remained the administrative head until his death in 1794.

Now only Keoua remained in the way, and he would be defeated not by war, but by the great mana of Ku. While Keoua's armies were crossing the desert on the southern slopes of Kilauea, the fire goddess Pele trumpeted her disapproval and sent a huge cloud of poisonous gas and mud-ash into the air. It descended upon and instantly killed the middle legions of Keoua's armies and their families. The footprints of this ill-fated army remain to this day outlined in the mud-ash as clearly as if they were deliberately encased in wet cement. Keoua's intuition told him that the victorious mana of the gods had swung to Kamehameha and that his own fate was sealed. Kamehameha sent word that he wanted Keoua to meet with him at Ku's newly dedicated temple in Kawaihae. Both knew that Keoua must die. Riding proudly in his canoe, the old nemesis came gloriously outfitted in the red-and-gold feathered cape and helmet signifying his exalted rank, accompanied by a small band of warriors. When he stepped ashore he was killed by Ke'eaumoku, a friend and ally of Kamehameha, and his warriors were slain by Kamehameha's men. His body was ceremoniously laid upon the altar along with the others who were slaughtered and dedicated to Ku, of the Maggot-dripping Mouth.

Increasing Contact

By the time Kamehameha had won the Big Island, Hawaii was becoming a regular stopover for numerous ships seeking the lucrative sandalwood trade with China. In February 1791, Captain George Vancouver, still seeking the Northwest Passage, returned to Kealakekua, where he was greeted by a throng of 30,000. The captain at once recognized Kamehameha, who was wearing a Chinese dressing gown that he had received in tribute from another chief who in turn had received it directly from the hands of Cook himself. The diary of a crew member, Thomas Manby, relates that Kamehameha, missing his front teeth, was more fierce-looking than ever as he approached the ship in an elegant double-hulled canoe sporting 46 rowers. The king invited all to a great feast prepared for them on the beach. Kamehameha's appetite matched his tremendous size. It was noted that he ate two sizable fish, a king-size bowl of poi, a small pig, and an entire baked

dog. Kamehameha personally entertained the English by putting on a mock battle in which he deftly avoided spears by rolling, tumbling, and catching them in midair, all the while hurling his own spear a great distance. The English reciprocated by firing cannon bursts into the air, creating an impromptu fireworks display. Kamehameha requested from Vancouver a full table setting, with which he was provided, but his request for firearms was prudently denied. Captain Vancouver became a trusted advisor of Kamehameha and told him about the white people's form of worship. He even interceded for Kamehameha with his headstrong queen, Ka'ahumanu, and coaxed her from her hiding place under a rock when she sought refuge at Pu'uhonua O Honaunau. The captain gave gifts of beef cattle, fowl, and breeding stock of sheep and goats. The ship's naturalist, Archibald Menzies, was the first *haole* to climb Mauna Kea; he also introduced a large assortment of fruits and vegetables. The Hawaiians were cheerful and outgoing, and showed remorse when they indicated that the remainder of Cook's bones had been buried at a temple close to Kealakekua. John Young, by this time firmly entrenched into Hawaiian society, made no request to sail away with Vancouver. During the next two decades of Kamehameha's rule, the French, Russians, English, and Americans discovered the great whaling waters off Hawaii. Their increasing visits shook and finally tumbled the ancient religion and social order of *kapu*.

Finishing Touches

After Keoua was laid to rest, it was only a matter of time until Kamehameha consolidated his power over all of Hawaii. In 1794 the old warrior Kahekili of Maui died and gave O'ahu to his son, Kalanikupule, while Kaua'i and Ni'ihau went to his brother Kaeo. In wars between the two, Kalanikupule was victorious, though he did not possess the grit of his father nor the great mana of Kamehameha. He had previously murdered a Captain Brown, who had anchored at Honolulu, and seized his ship, the *Jackall*. With the aid of this ship, Kalanikupule now determined to attack Kamehameha. However, while en route, the sailors regained control of their ship and cruised to the Big Island to inform and join with Kamehameha. An army of 16,000 was raised and sailed for Maui, where they met only token resistance, destroyed Lahaina, pillaged the countryside, and subjugated Moloka'i in one bloody battle.

The war canoes sailed next for O'ahu and the final showdown. The great army landed at Waikiki, and though defenders fought bravely, giving up O'ahu by the inch, they were steadily driven into the surrounding mountains. The beleaguered army made its last stand at Nu'uanu Pali, a great precipice in the mountains behind present-day Honolulu. Kamehameha's warriors mercilessly drove the enemy into the great abyss. Kalanikupule, who hid in the mountains, was captured after a few months and sacrificed to Ku, the Snatcher of Lands, thereby ending the struggle for power.

Kamehameha put down a revolt on Hawai'i in 1796. The king of Kaua'i, Kaumuali'i, accepting the inevitable, recognized Kamehameha as supreme ruler without suffering the ravages of a needless war. Kamehameha, for the first time in Hawaiian history, was the undisputed ruler of all the islands of "the heavenly homeland in the north."

Kamehameha's Rule

Kamehameha was as gentle in victory as he was ferocious in battle. Under his rule, which lasted until his death on May 8, 1819, Hawaii enjoyed a peace unlike any the warring islands had ever known. The king moved his royal court to Lahaina, where in 1803 he built the "Brick Palace," Hawaii's first permanent building. The benevolent tyrant also enacted the "Law of the Splintered Paddle." This law, which protected the weak from the exploitation of the strong, had its origins in an incident of many years before. A brave defender of a small overwhelmed village had broken a paddle over Kamehameha's head and taught the chief—literally in one stroke—about the nobility of the commoner.

However, just as Old Hawaii reached its golden age, its demise was at hand. The relentless waves of *haole* both innocently and determinedly battered the old ways into the ground. With the foreign ships came prosperity and fanciful new goods after which the *ali'i* lusted. The *maka'ainana* were worked mercilessly to provide sandalwood for the China trade. This was the first "boom" economy to hit the islands, but it set the standard of exploitation that would follow. Kamehameha built an observation tower in La-

haina to watch for ships, many of which were his own returning laden with riches from the world at large. In the last years of his life Kamehameha returned to his beloved Kona Coast, where he enjoyed the excellent fishing renowned to this day. He had taken Hawaii from the darkness of warfare into the light of peace. He died true to the religious and moral *kapu* of his youth, the only ones he had ever known, and with him died a unique way of life. Two loyal retainers buried his bones after the baked flesh had been ceremoniously stripped away. A secret burial cave was chosen so that no one could desecrate the remains of the great chief, thereby absorbing his mana. The tomb's location remains unknown, and disturbing the dead is still one of the strictest *kapu* to this day. The Lonely One's kingdom would pass to his son, Liholiho, but true power would be in the hands of his beloved and feisty wife Ka'ahumanu. As Kamehameha's spirit drifted from this earth, two forces sailing around Cape Horn would forever change Hawaii: the missionaries and the whalers.

MISSIONARIES AND WHALERS

The year 1819 was of the utmost significance in Hawaiian history. It marked the death of Kamehameha, the overthrow of the ancient *kapu* system, the arrival of the first "whaler" in Lahaina, and the departure from New England of Calvinist missionaries determined to convert the heathen islands. Great changes began to rattle the old order to its foundations. With the *kapu* system and all of the ancient gods abandoned (except for the fire goddess Pele of Kilauea), a great void permeated the souls of the Hawaiians. In the coming decades Hawaii, also coveted by Russia, France, and England, was finally consumed by America. The islands had the first American school, printing press, and newspaper (the *Polynesian*) west of the Mississippi. Lahaina, in its heyday, became the world's greatest whaling port, accommodating more than 500 ships during its peak years.

The Royal Family

Maui's Hana District provided Hawaii with one of its greatest queens, Ka'ahumanu, born in 1768 in a cave within walking distance of Hana Harbor.

At the age of 17 she became the third of Kamehameha's 21 wives and eventually the love of his life. At first she proved to be totally independent and unmanageable and was known to openly defy her king by taking numerous lovers. Kamehameha placed a *kapu* on her body and even had her attended by horribly deformed hunchbacks in an effort to curb her carnal appetites, but she continued to flaunt his authority. Young Ka'ahumanu had no love for her great, lumbering, unattractive husband, but in time (even Captain Vancouver was pressed into service as a marriage counselor) she learned to love him dearly. She in turn became his favorite wife, although she remained childless throughout her life. Kamehameha's first wife was the supremely royal Keopuolani, who so outranked even him that the king himself had to approach her naked and crawling on his belly. Keopuolani produced the royal children Liholiho and Kauikeaouli, who became King Kamehameha II and III, respectively. Just before Kamehameha I died in 1819 he appointed Liholiho his successor, but he also had the wisdom to make Ka'ahumanu the *kuhina nui* or queen regent. Initially, Liholiho was weak and became a drunkard. Later he became a good ruler, but he was always supported by his royal mother, Keopuolani, and by the ever-formidable Ka'ahumanu.

Kapu Is Pau

Ka'ahumanu was greatly loved and respected by the people. On public occasions, she donned Kamehameha's royal cloak and spear: so attired and infused with the king's mana, she demonstrated that she was the real leader of Hawaii. For six months after Kamehameha's death, Ka'ahumanu counseled Liholiho on what he must do. The wise *kuhina nui* knew that the old ways were *pau* (finished) and that Hawaii could not hope to function in a rapidly changing world under the *kapu* system. In November 1819, Ka'ahumanu and Keopuolani prevailed upon Liholiho to break two of the oldest and most sacred *kapu* by eating with women and by allowing women to eat previously forbidden foods such as bananas and certain fish. Heavily fortified with strong drink and attended by other high-ranking chiefs and a handful of foreigners, Ka'ahumanu and Liholiho ate together in public. This feast became known as *'Ai Noa* (Free Eating). As the first morsels passed Ka'ahumanu's lips, the ancient gods of Hawaii tumbled. Throughout the land, revered *heiau* were burned and abandoned and the idols knocked to the ground. Now the people had nothing to rely on but their weakened inner selves. Nothing and no one could answer their prayers; their spiritual lives were empty and in shambles.

Missionaries

Into this spiritual vortex sailed the brig *Thaddeus* on April 4, 1820. It had set sail from Boston on October 23, 1819, lured to the Big Island by Henry 'Opukaha'ia, a local boy born at Napo'opo'o in 1792, who had earlier been taken to New England. Coming ashore at Kailua-Kona, where Liholiho had moved the royal court, the Reverends Bingham and Thurston were granted a one-year trial missionary period by King Liholiho. They established themselves on the Big Island and O'ahu and from there began the transformation of Hawaii. The missionaries were people of God, but also practical-minded Yankees. They brought education, enterprise, and most important a commitment to stay and build (unlike the transient seafarers). By 1824 the new faith had such a foothold that Chieftess Keopuolani climbed to the fire pit atop Kilauea and defied Pele. This was even more striking than the previous breaking of the food *kapu* because the strength of Pele could actually be seen. Keopuolani ate forbidden *'ohelo* berries and cried out, "Jehovah is my God." Over the next decades the governing of Hawaii slipped away from the Big Island and moved to the new port cities of Lahaina and, later, Honolulu.

Rapid Conversions

The year 1824 also marked the death of Keopuolani, who was given a Christian burial. She had set the standard by accepting Christianity, and a number of the *ali'i* had followed the queen's lead. Liholiho had sailed off to England, where he and his wife contracted measles and died. Their bodies were returned by the British in 1825, on the HMS *Blonde* captained by Lord Byron, cousin of *the* Lord Byron. During these years, Ka'ahumanu allied herself with Reverend Richards, pastor of the first mission in the islands, and together they wrote Hawaii's first code of laws based upon the Ten Commandments. Foremost was the condemnation of murder, theft, brawling, and the desecration of the Sabbath by work or play. The early missionaries had the best of intentions, but like all zealots they were blinded by the single-mindedness that was also their greatest ally. They weren't surgically selective in their destruction of native beliefs. *Anything* native was felt to be inferior, and they set about wiping out all traces of the old ways. In their rampage they reduced the Hawaiian culture to ashes, plucking self-will and determination from the hearts of a once-proud people. More so than the whalers, they terminated the Hawaiian way of life.

The Early Seamen

A good portion of the common seamen of the early 19th century came from the dregs of the Western world. Many a whoremongering drunkard had awoken from a stupor and found himself on the pitching deck of a ship, discovering to his dismay that he had been "pressed into naval service." For the most part these sailors were a filthy, uneducated, lawless rabble. Their present situation was dim, their future hopeless, and they would live to be 30 if they were lucky and didn't die from scurvy or a thousand other miserable fates. They snatched brief pleasure in every port and jumped ship at every opportunity, especially in an easy berth like Lahaina. They displayed the worst elements of Western culture—which the Hawaiians naively mimicked. In exchange for *aloha* they gave drunkenness, sloth, and insidious death by disease. By the 1850s the population of native Hawaiians tumbled from the estimated 300,000 reported by Captain Cook in 1778 to barely 60,000. Common conditions such as colds, flu, venereal disease, and sometimes smallpox and cholera decimated the Hawaiians, who had no natural immunities to these foreign ailments. By the time the missionaries arrived,

Kamehameha III

hapa haole children were common in Lahaina streets.

The earliest merchant ships to the islands were owned or skippered by lawless opportunists who had come seeking sandalwood after first filling their holds with furs from the Pacific Northwest. Aided by *ali'i* hungry for manufactured goods and Western finery, they raped Hawaiian forests of this fragrant wood so coveted in China. Next, droves of sailors came in search of whales. The whalers, decent men at home, left their morals back in the Atlantic and lived by the slogan "no conscience east of the Cape." The delights of Hawaii were just too tempting for most.

Two Worlds Tragically Collide

The 1820s were a time of confusion and soul-searching for the Hawaiians. When Kamehameha II died the kingdom passed to Kauikeaouli (Kamehameha III), who made his lifelong residence in Lahaina. The young king was only nine years old when the title passed to him, but his power was secure because Ka'ahumanu was still a vibrant *kuhina nui*. The young prince, more so than any other, was raised in the cultural confusion of the times. His childhood was spent during the very cusp of the change from old ways to new, and he was often pulled in two directions by vastly differing beliefs. Since he was royal born, he was bound by age-old Hawaiian tradition to mate and produce an heir with the highest-ranking *ali'i* in the kingdom. This mate happened to be his younger sister, the Princess Nahi'ena'ena. To the old Hawaiian advisors, this arrangement was perfectly acceptable and encouraged. To the increasingly influential missionaries, incest was an unimaginable abomination in the eyes of God. The problem was compounded by the fact that Kamehameha III and Nahi'ena'ena were drawn to each other and were deeply in love. The young king could not stand the mental pressure imposed by conflicting worlds. He became a teenage alcoholic too royal to be restrained by anyone in the kingdom, and his bouts of drunkenness and womanizing were both legendary and scandalous.

Meanwhile, Nahi'ena'ena was even more pressured because she was a favorite of the missionaries, baptized into the church at age 12. She too vacillated between the old and the new. At times a pious Christian, at others she drank all night and took numerous lovers. As the prince and princess grew into their late teens, they became even more attached to each other and hardly made an attempt to keep their relationship from the missionaries. Whenever possible, they lived together in a grass house built for the princess by her father.

In 1832, the great Ka'ahumanu died, leaving the king on his own. In 1833, at the age of 18, Kamehameha III announced that the "regency" was over and that all the lands in Hawaii were his personally, and that he alone was the ultimate law. Almost immediately, however, he decreed that his half-sister Kina'u would be "premier," signifying that he would leave the actual running of the kingdom in her hands. Kamehameha III fell into total drunken confusion, until one night he attempted suicide. After this episode he seemed to straighten up a bit and mostly kept a low profile. In 1836, Princess Nahi'ena'ena was convinced by the missionaries to take a husband. She married Leleiohoku, a chief from the Big Island, but continued to sleep with her brother. It is uncertain who fathered the child, but Nahi'ena'ena gave birth to a baby boy in September 1836. The young prince survived for only a few hours, and Nahi'ena'ena never recovered from her convalescence. She died in December 1836 and was laid to rest in the mausoleum next to her mother, Keopuolani, on the royal island in Mokuhina Pond. After the death of his sister, Kamehameha III became a sober and righteous ruler. Often seen paying his respects at the royal mausoleum, he ruled longer than any other king until his death in 1854.

The Missionaries Prevail
In 1823, the first mission was established in Lahaina, Maui, under the pastorate of Reverend Richards and his wife. Within a few years, many

of the notable *ali'i* had been, at least in appearance, converted to Christianity. By 1828 the cornerstones for Waine'e Church, the first stone church on the island, were laid just behind the palace of Kamehameha III. The struggle between missionaries and whalers centered around public drunkenness and the servicing of sailors by native women. The normally God-fearing whalers had signed on for perilous duty that lasted up to three years, and when they anchored in Lahaina they demanded their pleasure. The missionaries were instrumental in placing a curfew on sailors and prohibiting native women from boarding ships, which had become customary. These measures certainly did not stop the liaisons between sailor and *wahine,* but they did impose a modicum of social sanction and tolled the end of the wide-open days. The sailors were outraged; in 1825 the crew from the *Daniel* attacked the home of the meddler, Reverend Richards. A year later a similar incident occurred. In 1827, confined and lonely sailors from the whaler *John Palmer* fired their cannons at Reverend Richards' newly built home.

Slowly the tensions eased, and by 1836 many sailors were regulars at the Seamen's Chapel adjacent to the Baldwin home. Unfortunately, even the missionaries couldn't stop the pesky mosquito from entering the islands through the port of Lahaina. The mosquitoes arrived from Mexico in 1826 aboard the merchant ship *Wellington.* They were inadvertently carried as larvae in the water barrels and democratically pestered everyone in the islands from that day forward, regardless of race, religion, or creed.

Lahaina Becomes a Cultural Center
By 1831, Lahaina was firmly established as a seat of Western influence in Hawaii. That year marked the founding of Lahainaluna School, the first *real* American school west of the Rockies. Virtually a copy of a New England normal school, it attracted the best students, both native and white, from throughout the kingdom. By 1834, Lahainaluna had an operating printing press publishing the islands' first newspaper, *The Torch of Hawaii,* starting a lucrative printing industry centered in Lahaina that dominated not only the islands but also California for many years.

An early native student was David Malo. He was brilliant and well educated, but more importantly, he remembered the "old ways." One of the first Hawaiians to realize his native land was being swallowed up by the newcomers, Malo compiled the first history of precontact Hawaii, and the resulting book, *Mo'olelo Hawai'i* (Hawaiian Antiquities), became a reference masterpiece that has yet to be eclipsed. David Malo insisted that the printing be done in Hawaiian, not English. Malo is buried in the mountains above Lahainaluna where, by his own request, he is "high above the tide of foreign invasion." By the 1840s, Lahaina was firmly established as the "whaling capital of the world"; the peak year 1846 saw 395 whaling ships anchored here. A census in 1846 reported that Lahaina was home to 3,445 natives, 112 permanent *haole*, 600 sailors, and more than 500 dogs. The populace was housed in 882 grass houses, 155 adobe houses, and 59 relatively permanent stone and wood-framed structures. Lahaina would probably have remained the islands' capital, had Kamehameha III not moved the royal capital to the burgeoning port of Honolulu on the island of O'ahu.

Foreign Influence

By the 1840s Honolulu was becoming the center of commerce in the islands; when Kamehameha III moved the royal court there from Lahaina, the ascendant fate of the new capital was guaranteed. In 1843, Lord Paulet, commander of the warship *Carysfort*, forced Kamehameha III to sign a treaty ceding Hawaii to the British. London, however, repudiated this act, and Hawaii's independence was restored within a few months when Queen Victoria sent Admiral Thomas as her personal agent of good intentions. The king memorialized the turn of events by a speech in which he uttered the phrase, *Ua mau ke e'a o ka 'aina i ka pono* ("The life of the land is preserved in righteousness"), now Hawaii's motto. The French used similar bullying tactics to force an unfavorable treaty on the Hawaiians in 1839; as part of these heavy-handed negotiations they exacted a payment of $20,000 and the right of Catholics to enjoy religious freedom in the islands. In 1842 the United States recognized and guaranteed Hawaii's in-

dependence without a formal treaty, and by 1860 more than 80 percent of the islands' trade was with the United States.

The Great *Mahele*

In 1840 Kamehameha III ended his autocratic rule and instituted a constitutional monarchy. This brought about the Hawaiian Bill of Rights, but the most far-reaching change was the transition to private ownership of land. Formerly, all land belonged to the ruling chief, who gave wedge-shaped parcels called *ahupua'a* to lesser chiefs to be worked for him. The commoners did all the real labor, their produce heavily taxed by the *ali'i*. The fortunes of war, the death of a chief, or the mere whim of a superior could force a commoner off the land. The Hawaiians, however, could not think in terms of "owning" land. No one could *possess* land; one could only *use* land, and its *ownership* was a strange and foreign concept. As a result, naive Hawaiians gave up their lands for a song to unscrupulous traders, which remains an integral, unrectified problem to this day.

In 1847 Kamehameha III and his advisors separated the lands of Hawaii into three groupings: crown land (belonging to the king), government land (belonging to the chiefs), and the people's land (the largest parcels). In 1848, 245 *ali'i* entered their land claims in the *Mahele Book*, assuring them ownership. In 1850 the commoners were given title in fee simple to the lands they cultivated and lived on as tenants, not including house lots in towns. Commoners without land could buy small *kuleana* (farms) from the government at 50 cents per acre. In 1850, foreigners were also allowed to purchase land in fee simple, and the ownership of

> *Some were rapacious exploiters, seeking to deceive, loot, and leave. Hawaii has known them by the thousands through the years.*
> —Edward Joesting

Hawaii from that day forward slipped steadily from the hands of its indigenous people.

KING SUGAR

It's hard to say just where the sugar industry began in Hawaii. One story holds that a lone entrepreneur from China refined sugar on Lana'i just after 1800, but there seems to be no factual recording of his endeavor. The Koloa Sugar Plantation on the southern coast of Kaua'i successfully refined sugar in 1835. Following this, sugar refining was tried at numerous locations throughout the islands with varying degrees of success, but the industry burgeoned at Hana, Maui, in 1849. A whaler named George Wilfong hauled four blubber pots ashore and set them up on a rocky hill in the middle of 60 acres he had planted in sugar. A team of oxen turned "crushing rollers" and the cane juice flowed down an open trough into the pots, under which an attending native kept a roaring fire burning. Wilfong's methods of refining were crude, but the resulting high-quality sugar turned a neat profit in Lahaina. The main problem was labor. The Hawaiians, who made excellent whalers, were basically indentured workers. They became extremely disillusioned with their contracts, which could last up to 10 years. Most of their wages were eaten up by manufactured commodities sold at the company store, and it didn't take long for them to realize that they were little more than slaves. At every opportunity they either left the area or just refused to work.

Imported Labor

The **Masters and Servants Act of 1850,** which allowed importation of laborers under the contract system, ostensibly guaranteed an endless supply of cheap labor for the plantations. Chinese laborers were imported, but were too enterprising to remain in the fields for a meager $3 per month. They left as soon as opportunity permitted and went into business as small merchants and retailers. In the meantime, Wilfong had sold out, releasing most of the Hawaiians previously held under contract, and his plantation fell into disuse. In 1860 two Danish brothers, August and Oscar Unna, bought land at Hana to raise sugar. They solved the labor problem by importing Japanese laborers who were extremely hard-working and easily managed. The workday lasted 10 hours, six days a week, for a salary of $20 per month with housing and medical care thrown in. Plantation life was very structured, with stringent rules governing even bedtimes and lights out. A worker could be fined for being late or for smoking on the job. Even the Japanese couldn't function under these circumstances, and improvements in benefits and housing were slowly gained.

Sugar Grows

The demand for "Sandwich Island Sugar" grew as California was populated during the gold rush and increased dramatically when the American Civil War demanded a constant supply. The only sugar plantations on the Mainland were small plots confined to the Confederate states, whose products would hardly be bought by the Union and whose fields, later in the war, were destroyed. By the 1870s it was clear to the planters, still mainly New Englanders, that the United States were their market; they tried often to gain closer ties and favorable tariffs. The Americans also planted rumors that the British were interested in annexing Hawaii; this put pressure on the U.S. Congress to pass the long-desired **Reciprocity Act,** which would exempt sugar from import duty. It finally passed in 1875, in exchange for U.S. long-term rights to use the strategic naval port of Pearl Harbor, among other concessions. These agreements gave increased political power to a small group of American planters, whose outlooks were similar to those of the post–Civil War South, where a few powerful whites were the virtual masters of a multitude of dark-skinned laborers. Sugar was now big business and the Hana District alone exported almost 3,000 tons per year. All of Hawaii would have to reckon with the "sugar barons."

Changing Society

The sugar plantation system changed life in Hawaii physically, spiritually, politically, and economically. Now boatloads of workers came not only from Japan but from Portugal, Germany, and even Russia. The white-skinned workers were most often the field foremen *(luna).* With the immigrants came new religions, new animals and plants, unique cuisines, and a plantation language known as pidgin, or *da' kine.* Many Asians, and to a lesser extent the other groups, including the white plantation owners, intermarried with Hawaiians. A new class of people properly termed "cosmopolitan" but more familiarly and aptly known as "locals" was emerging. These were the people of multiple racial backgrounds who couldn't exactly say *what* they were, but it was clear to all just *who* they were. The plantation owners became the new "chiefs" of Hawaii who could carve up the land and dispense favors. The Hawaiian monarchy was soon eliminated.

A KINGDOM PASSES

The Beginning of the End

Like the Hawaiian people themselves, the Kamehameha dynasty in the mid-1800s was dying from within. King Kamehameha IV (Alexander Liholiho) ruled 1854–63; his only child died in 1862. He was succeeded by his older brother Kamehameha V (Lot Kamehameha), who ruled until 1872. With his passing the Kamehameha line ended. William Lunalilo, elected king in 1873 by popular vote, was of royal, but not Kamehameha, lineage. He died after only a year in office, and being a bachelor left no heirs. He was succeeded by David Kalakaua, known far and wide as the "Merrie Monarch," who made a world tour and was well received wherever he went. He built 'Iolani Palace in Honolulu and was personally in favor of closer ties with the United States, helping push through the Reciprocity Act. Kalakaua died in 1891 and was replaced by his sister, Lydia Lili'uokalani, last of the Hawaiian monarchs.

HAWAII STATE ARCHIVES

Queen Lili'uokalani

The Revolution

When Lili'uokalani took office in 1891, the native population was at a low of 40,000, and she felt that the United States had too much influence over her homeland. She was known to personally favor the English over the Americans. She attempted to replace the liberal constitution of 1887 (adopted by her pro-American brother) with an autocratic mandate in which she would have had much more political and economic control of the islands. When the McKinley Tariff of 1890 brought a decline in sugar profits, she made no attempt to improve the situation. Thus, the planters saw her as a political obstacle to their economic growth; most of Hawaii's American planters and merchants were in favor of a rebellion. She would have to go! A central spokesperson and firebrand was Lorrin Thurston, a Honolulu publisher who, with a central core of about 30 men, challenged the Hawaiian monarchy. Although Lili'uokalani rallied some support and had a small military potential in her personal guard, the coup was ridiculously easy—it took only one casualty. Captain John Good shot a Hawaiian policeman in the arm and that did it. Naturally, the conspirators could not have succeeded without some solid assurances from a secret contingent in the U.S. Congress as well as outgoing president Benjamin Harrison, who favored Hawaii's annexation. Marines from the *Boston* went ashore to "protect American lives," and on January 17, 1893, the Hawaiian monarchy came to an end.

The provisional government was headed by Sanford B. Dole, who became president of the Hawaiian Republic. Lili'uokalani surrendered not to the conspirators but to U.S. Ambassador John Stevens. She believed that the U.S. government, which had assured her of Hawaiian independence, would be outraged by the overthrow and would come to her aid. Incoming president Grover Cleveland *was* outraged, and Hawaii wasn't immediately annexed as expected. When queried about what she would do with the conspirators if she were reinstated, Lili'uokalani said that they would be hung as traitors. The racist press of the times, which portrayed the Hawaiians as half-civilized, bloodthirsty heathens, publicized this widely. Since the conspirators were the leading citizens of the land, the queen's words proved untimely. In January 1895 a small, ill-fated counterrevolution headed by Lili'uokalani failed, and she was placed under house arrest in 'Iolani Palace. Officials of the republic insisted that she use her married name (Mrs. John Dominis) to sign the documents forcing her to abdicate her throne. She was also forced to swear allegiance to the new republic. Lili'uokalani went on to write *Hawaii's Story* and the lyric ballad "Aloha O'e." She never forgave the conspirators and remained "queen" to the Hawaiians until her death in 1917.

Annexation

The overwhelming majority of Hawaiians opposed annexation and desired to restore the monarchy. But they were prevented from voting by the new republic because they couldn't meet the imposed property and income qualifications—a transparent ruse by the planters to control the majority. Most *haole* were racist and believed that the "common people" could not be entrusted with the vote because they were childish and incapable of ruling themselves. The fact that the Hawaiians had existed quite well for a thousand years before white people even reached Hawaii was never considered. The Philippine theater of the Spanish-American War also prompted annexation. One of the strongest proponents was Alfred Mahon, a brilliant naval strategist who, with support from Theodore Roosevelt, argued that the U.S. military must have Hawaii in order to be a viable force in the Pacific. In addition, Japan, victorious in its recent war with China, protested the American intention to annex, and in so doing prompted even moderates to support annexation for fear that the Japanese themselves coveted the prize. On July 7, 1898, President McKinley signed the annexation agreement, and this "tropical fruit" was finally put into America's basket.

MODERN TIMES

Hawaii entered the 20th century totally transformed. The old Hawaiian language, religion, culture, and leadership were all gone; Western dress, values, education, and recreation were the norm. Native Hawaiians were now unseen citizens who lived in dwindling numbers in remote areas. The plantations, new centers of social order, had a strong Asian flavor; more than

75 percent of the workforce was Asian. There was a small white middle class, an all-powerful white elite, and a single political party ruled by that elite. Education, however, was always highly prized, and by the late 19th century all racial groups were encouraged to attend school. By 1900, almost 90 percent of Hawaiians were literate (far above the national norm), and schooling was mandatory for all children ages 6–15. Intermarriage was accepted, and there was a mixing of the races like nowhere else on earth. The military became increasingly important to Hawaii. It brought in money and jobs, dominating the island economy. The Japanese attack on Pearl Harbor, which began U.S. involvement in World War II, bound Hawaii to America forever. Once the islands had been baptized by blood, the average Mainlander felt that Hawaii was American soil. A movement among Hawaiians to become part of the United States began to grow. They wanted a real voice in Washington, not merely a voteless delegate as provided under their territory status. Hawaii became the 50th state in 1959, and the jumbo-jet revolution of the 1960s made it easily accessible to growing numbers of tourists from all over the world.

Military History

A few military strategists realized the importance of Hawaii early in the 19th century, but most didn't recognize the advantages until the Spanish-American War. It was clearly an unsinkable ship in the middle of the Pacific from which the United States could launch military operations. Troops were stationed at Camp McKinley, at the foot of Diamond Head, the main military compound until it became obsolete in 1907. Pearl Harbor was first surveyed in 1872 by General Schofield. Later, a military base named in his honor, Schofield Barracks, was a main military post in central O'ahu. It first housed the U.S. 5th Cavalry in 1909 and was heavily bombed by the Japanese at the outset of World War II. Pearl Harbor, first dredged in 1908, was officially opened on December 11, 1911. The first warship to enter was the cruiser *California*. Ever since, the military has been a mainstay of the Hawaiian economy. Unfortunately, there has been long-standing bad blood between locals and military personnel. Each group has tended to look down upon the other.

Honolulu Star-Bulletin 1st EXTRA

SAN FRANCISCO, Dec. 7.—President Roosevelt announced this morning that Japanese planes had attacked Manila and Pearl Harbor.

WAR!
OAHU BOMBED BY JAPANESE PLANES

SIX KNOWN DEAD, 21 INJURED, AT EMERGENCY HOSPITAL

Headlines from the Honolulu Star Bulletin *announce two major events in recent Hawaiian history: Pearl Harbor attack (above) and statehood (below).*

Pearl Harbor Attack

On the morning of December 7, 1941, the Japanese carrier *Akagi,* flying the battle flag of the famed Admiral Togo of the Russo-Japanese War, received and broadcast over its public address system island music from Honolulu station KGMB. Deep in the bowels of the ship a radio man listened for a much different message, coming thousands of miles from the Japanese mainland. When the ironically poetic message "east wind rain" was received, the attack was launched. At the end of the day, 2,325 U.S. servicemen and 57 civilians were dead; 188 planes were destroyed; 18 major warships were sunk or heavily damaged; and the United States was in the war. Japanese casualties were extremely light. The ignited conflict would rage for four years until Japan, through the atomic bombing of Nagasaki and Hiroshima, was vaporized into submission. At the end of hostilities, Hawaii would never again be considered separate from America.

Statehood

A number of economic and political reasons explain why the ruling elite of Hawaii desired statehood, but put simply, the vast majority of people who lived there, especially after World War II, considered themselves Americans. The first serious mention of making "The Sandwich Islands" a state was in the 1850s under President Franklin Pierce, but it wasn't taken seriously until the monarchy was overthrown in the 1890s. For the next 50 years statehood proposals were made repeatedly to Congress, but there was stiff opposition, especially from the southern states. With Hawaii a territory, an import quota system beneficial to Mainland producers could be enacted on produce, especially sugar. Also, there was prejudice against creating a state in a place where the majority of the populace was not white.

During World War II, Hawaii was placed under martial law, but no serious attempt was made to intern the Japanese population as it was in California. There were simply too many Japanese, who went on to gain the respect of the American people by their outstanding fighting record during the war. Hawaii's own 100th Battalion became the famous 442nd Regimental Combat Team, which gained notoriety by saving the Lost Texas Battalion during the Battle of the Bulge and went on to be *the* most decorated battalion of the war. When these GIs returned home, *no one* was going to tell them that they were not loyal Americans. Many of these AJAs (Americans of Japanese Ancestry) took advantage of the GI Bill and received higher education. They were from the common people, not the elite, and they rallied grassroots support for statehood. When the vote finally occurred, approximately 132,900 voted in favor of statehood with only 7,800 votes against. Congress passed the Hawaii State Bill on March 12, 1959, and on August 21, 1959, President Eisenhower announced that Hawaii was officially the 50th state.

GOVERNMENT

Being the newest state in the nation, Hawaii has had the chance to scrutinize the others, pick their best attributes, and learn from their past mistakes. The government of the state of Hawaii is in essence no different from that of any other state except that it is streamlined and, in theory, more efficient. With only two levels—state and county—the added bureaucracy of town or city governments is theoretically eliminated. Unfortunately, some of the state-run agencies, such as the centralized Board of Education, have become "red-tape" monsters. Hawaii, in anticipation of becoming a state, drafted a constitution in 1950 and was ready to go when statehood was ratified. Politics and government are taken seriously in the Aloha State. For example, in the election to ratify statehood, hardly a ballot went uncast, with 95 percent of the voters opting for statehood. The bill carried every island of Hawaii except for Ni'ihau, where, coincidentally, the majority of people (total population 250 or so) are of relatively pure Hawaiian blood. In the first state elections that followed, 173,000 of 180,000 registered voters voted. In recent years, the number of votes cast in primary and general elections has slipped to unprecedented lows, as in the rest of the country.

State Government

Honolulu is the state capital of Hawaii and its seat of government. All major state-level executive, legislative, and judicial offices are located there. Hawaii's State Legislature has 76 members, with 51 elected seats in the House of Representatives and 25 in the State Senate. Members serve two- and four-year terms respectively. All officials come from 76 separate electorates based on population, which sometimes makes for strange political bedfellows. For example, Maui's split 7th Representative District encompasses much of West Maui and the islands of Lana'i and Moloka'i. This district combines one of Maui's richest tourist communities with Lana'i, where many people are Filipino former field workers (now hotel staff), and with economically depressed Moloka'i, where the vast majority of the native Hawaiians live on welfare. Perhaps even

stranger are the 12th Representative District, which takes in the eastern third of the island of Maui, and the 6th Senatorial District, which encompasses Kihei, Wailea, Makena, half of Upcountry, and Hana. Both are paired with the north coast of Kaua'i, an area that has no traditional political or cultural bond with Maui. The last redrawing of district lines was done in 1991.

O'ahu, which has the largest number of voters, elects 18 of 25 senators and 38 of 51 representatives, giving this island a majority in both houses. Kaua'i County, in comparison, elects 1.5 state senators and 2.5 representatives—the halves are shared with Maui County.

The state of Hawaii has an overwhelming Democratic Party orientation. Of the 76 members of the legislature, 54 are Democrats. Although not exclusive, Republican strongholds are portions of the metropolitan areas of Honolulu, Kane'ohe, and Kailua, on O'ahu.

The state is divided into four administrative counties: the **County of Kaua'i,** covering Kaua'i and Ni'ihau, with Lihu'e as the county seat; the **City and County of Honolulu,** which encompasses O'ahu and includes all of the Northwestern Hawaiian Islands, with Honolulu as its county seat; the **County of Hawai'i,** covering the Big Island, with Hilo as its county seat; and the **County of Maui,** administering the islands of Maui, Lana'i, Moloka'i, and uninhabited Kaho'olawe, with the county seat at Wailuku on Maui. Each county has an elected mayor. County councils are also elected to help administer each county. Honolulu, Hawai'i, and Maui Counties each have nine council members, while Kaua'i has seven.

Branches of Government

The **State Legislature** is the collective body of the House of Representatives and the Senate. They meet during a once-yearly legislative session that begins on the third Wednesday of January and lasts for 60 working days. (These sessions are oftentimes extended, and special sessions of up to 30 days are frequently called.) The Legislature primarily focuses on taxes, new laws, and appropriations. The **Executive Branch** is headed by the governor and lieutenant governor, both elected on a statewide basis for four years with a two-term maximum. The governor has the right to appoint the heads of 18 state departments outlined in the constitution. The department appointees must be approved by the Senate, and they usually hold office as long as the appointing administration. The present governor is Benjamin J. Cayetano, the second Hawaiian governor of the state and the first with any Filipino heritage. Mr. Cayetano has held this office since 1994. The **Judiciary** is headed by a state Supreme Court of five justices, an appeals court, and four circuit courts. All jurists are appointed by the governor and serve for 10 years with Senate approval. Twenty-seven district courts have local jurisdiction; the judges are appointed for six-year terms by the chief justice of the Supreme Court.

Special Departments

The Department of Education is headed by a board of 13 nonpartisan representatives elected for four-year terms, 10 from O'ahu and three from the other islands. The board has the right to appoint the Superintendent of Schools. Many praise the centralized board as a democratic body offering equal educational opportunity to all districts of Hawaii regardless of sociofinancial status. Detractors say that the centralized board provides "equal educational mediocrity" to all. The University of Hawai'i is governed by a Board of Regents appointed by the governor. They choose the president of the university.

Federal Government Representatives

The state of Hawaii elects two senators and two representatives to the U.S. Congress. Currently, all four are Democrats. The senators are Daniel Inouye and Daniel Akaka. Neil Abercrombie and Patsy Mink are the representatives.

Political History

Before World War II Hawaii was run by a self-serving yet mostly benevolent oligarchy. The one real political party was Republican, controlled by the Hawaiian Sugar Planters Association. The planters felt that, having made Hawaii a paradise, they should rule because they had "right on their side." The Baldwin family of Maui *was* the government, with such sup-

porters as the Rice family, which controlled Kaua'i, and William (Doc) Hill of Hawai'i. These were the preeminent families of the islands; all were represented on the boards of the Big Five corporations that ruled Hawaii economically by controlling sugar, transportation, and utilities. An early native politician was Prince Jonah Kuhio Kalaniana'ole, Queen Kapi'olani's adopted son and heir to the throne following Lili'uokalani, who joined with the Republicans to gain perks for himself and for his own people. Nepotism and political hoopla were the order of those days. The Republicans, in coalition with the native Hawaiians, maintained a majority over the large racial groups such as the Japanese and Filipinos who, left to their own devices, would have been Democrats. The Republicans also used unfair literacy laws, land ownership qualifications, and proof of birth in Hawaii to control the large numbers of immigrant workers who could threaten their ruling position. It was even alleged that during elections a pencil was hung on a string over the Republican ballot: if Hawaiians wanted to vote Democratic, they would have to pull the string to the other side of the voting booth. The telltale angle would be a giveaway. They would be unemployed the next day.

The Democrats Rise to Power

The Democrats were plagued with poor leadership and internal factionalism in the early years. Their first real rise to power began in 1935 when the International Longshoremen's and Warehousemen's Union (ILWU) formed a branch in Hilo on the Big Island. In 1937, an incident known as the "Hilo Massacre" occurred when policemen fired on and wounded 25 striking stevedores, which was the catalyst needed to bind labor together. Thereafter, the ILWU, under the leadership of Jack Hall, became a major factor in the Democratic party. Their relationship was strained in later years when the ILWU was linked to Communism, but during the early days, whomever the ILWU supported in the Democratic Party won.

The Democrats began to take over after World War II when returning Japanese servicemen became active in politics. The Japanese by this time were the largest ethnic group in Hawaii. A central character during the late 1940s and '50s was Jack Burns. Although a *haole,* this simple man was known to be for "the people" regardless of their ethnic background. During the war, as a police captain he made clear his view that he considered the Japanese exemplary Americans. The Japanese community never forgot this and were instrumental in Burns's election as governor, both in 1962 and 1966. The majority of people in the Asian ethnic groups in Hawaii tended to remain Democrat even after they climbed the socioeconomic ladder. The first special election after statehood saw the governorship go to the previously appointed Republican territorial governor William Quinn, and the lieutenant governorship to another Republican, James Kealoha, of Hawaiian-Chinese ancestry. The first congressperson elected was Japanese-American—Democrat Daniel Inouye. Since then, every governor has been a Democrat and one out of every two political offices is held by a person of Japanese extraction. Former governor George Ariyoshi was the first governor of Japanese ancestry in the United States.

OFFICE OF HAWAIIAN AFFAIRS

In 1979, a constitutional mandate created the Office of Hawaiian Affairs (OHA). This remarkable piece of legislature recognized, for the first time since the fall of the monarchy in 1893, the special plight of native Hawaiians. For 75 years, no one in government was eager to face the "native question," but since 1979, OHA has opened a Pandora's box of litigation and accusation. For example, in 1983, a presidential commission investigated U.S. involvement in the overthrow of Hawaii's last queen, Lili'uokalani, to decide if the federal government owed reparations to her Hawaiian people. After listening to testimony from thousands attesting to personal family loss of land and freedom, complete with old deeds documenting their claims, the commission concluded the United States was guiltless and native Hawaiians had nothing coming from Uncle Sam. Jaws dropped, and even those opposed to native Hawaiian rights couldn't believe this *white*wash. Then-governor George Ariyoshi said in a newspaper interview, "A recent congressional study did not accurately portray what went on here at the turn of the centu-

ry. . . . To say that the monarchy was not overthrown . . . is something that I cannot accept. It is not historically true."

Trouble in Paradise

Since then, OHA, as the vanguard of native political activism, has focused on gaining moneys guaranteed in the state constitution as recently as 1959 for "ceded lands." It has also been instrumental in regaining disputed Hawaiian lands and has helped in the fight to save the sacred and uninhabited island of Kaho'olawe, which was used as a bombing target from World War II until 1990. To simply state a complex issue, native Hawaiians have been eligible for benefits from revenues accrued from ceded lands and haven't been receiving them. These lands (1.8 million acres) were crown and government lands belonging to the Hawaiian monarchy and, therefore, to its subjects. When the kingdom was overthrown, the lands passed on to the short-lived Republic, followed by the U.S. Protectorate, and then finally to the state in 1959. No one disputed these lands belonged to *the people,* who were entitled to money collected from rents and leases. Since statehood, however, these tens of millions of dollars have gone into a "general fund" used by various state agencies, such as the Department of Transportation and the Department of Land and Natural Resources; the state is extremely reluctant to turn these funds over to what they derisively call an "unconstitutional special interest group." A Constitutional Convention in 1988 supposedly addressed this issue, but many problems still exist.

Native Hawaiian Rights

The question has always been, "Just what is a native Hawaiian?" The answer has always been ambiguous. The government has used the "blood quantum" as a measuring stick. This is simply the percentage of Hawaiian blood in a person's ancestry—customarily 50 percent qualifies a person as Hawaiian. The issue is compounded by the fact that no other group of people has been so racially intermarried for so many years. Even though many people have direct ancestry to pre-Republic Hawaiians, they don't have enough "Hawaiian-ness" to qualify. An overwhelming number of these people fall into the category of "locals": they "feel" Hawaiian, but blood-wise they're not. They suffer all of the negativity of second-class citizens and reap none of the benefits accorded Hawaiians. Those who do qualify according to blood quantum don't have the numbers or the political clout necessary to get results. In fact, many people involved with OHA would not qualify themselves, at least not according to the blood quantum! Strong factionalism within the native Hawaiian movement itself threatens its credibility. Many people who do qualify by the blood quantum view the others as impinging on their rightful claims. The most vocal activists point out that only a coalition of people who have Hawaiian blood, combined with those who "identify" with the movement, will get results. Political firebrands maintain "anti-Hawaiian rights" lobbyists such as the tourist industry, airlines, and large corporations are now stronger than the Hawaiians. They advise that the only way the Hawaiian rights movement can win is to become active "political warriors" and vote for legislators who will support their cause. The rhetoric of OHA is reminiscent of that of the equal rights movement of the 1960s.

Obviously compromise is necessary. Perhaps certain social entitlements (such as tuition grants) could be equal for all, whereas money and land entitlements could be granted by percentages equal to the claiming person's "blood quantum." OHA members appeal directly to the Hawaiian people and can build political constituencies at a grassroots level. Since they are elected by the people and not appointed by the government (the case with the Hawaiian Home Lands Department and the trustees of the Bishop Estate, two other *supposedly* Hawaiian institutions), the status quo political parties of Hawaii are wary of them. (Recently, a court finding has called into question the legitimacy of the voting system for OHA trustees, resulting in the appointment of several members by the governor.) What makes the issue even more ludicrous is that some of the state's most powerful corporate families opposed to Hawaiian rights have direct lineage not only to pre-Republic Hawaiian ancestors but to Hawaiian royalty. They themselves would receive "entitlements" from the ceded land according to blood quantum, but socioeconomically they are the natural enemies of OHA. The problem is difficult, and it is improbable that all concerned will get satisfaction. OHA maintains offices at 711 Kapi'olani Blvd., Honolulu, HI 96813, 808/594-1980, website: www.oha.org. It publishes a newspaper entitled *Ka Wai Ola o OHA* (The Living Water of OHA), which is available upon request.

ECONOMY

Hawaii's mid-Pacific location makes it perfect for two primary sources of income: tourism and the military. Tourists come in anticipation of endless golden days on soothing beaches, while the military is provided with the strategic position of an unsinkable battleship. The tourism sector nets Hawaii about $11 billion annually, about one-third the state's revenue of $33.5 billion, while military spending comes in at just over $3 billion, money that should keep flowing smoothly and even increase in the foreseeable future. These revenues mostly remain aloof from the normal ups and downs of the Mainland economy, and both attract either gung-ho enthusiasts or rabidly negative detractors. The remaining 60 percent comes in descending proportions from construction, manufacturing, and agriculture (mainly sugar and pineapples). As long as the sun shines and the balance of global power requires a military presence, the economic stability of Hawaii is guaranteed.

TOURISM

"The earthly paradise! Don't you want to go to it? Why, of course!" This was the opening line of *The Hawaiian Guide Book* by Henry Whitney, which appeared in 1875. In print for 25 years, it sold for 60 cents during a time when a round-trip sea voyage between San Francisco and Honolulu cost $125. The technique is a bit dated, but the human desires remain the same: some of us seek paradise, all seek escape, some are drawn to play out a drama in a beautiful setting. Tourists have been coming to Hawaii ever since steamship service began in the 1860s. Until World War II, luxury liners carried the financial elite on exclusive voyages to the islands. By the 1920s 10,000 visitors a year were spending almost $5 million—cementing the bond between Hawaii and tourism.

A $25,000 prize offered by James Dole of pineapple fame sparked a transpacific air race in 1927. The success of the aerial daredevils who answered the challenge proved that commercial air travel to Hawaii was feasible. Two years later, Hawaiian Air was offering regularly scheduled flights between the major islands. By 1950 airplanes had captured more than 50 percent of the transportation market, and ocean voyages were relegated to "specialty travel," catering to the elite. By 1960 the large airbuses made their debut; 300,000 tourists arrived on eight designated airlines. The Boeing 747 began operating in 1969. These enormous planes could carry hundreds of passengers at reasonable rates, so travel to Hawaii became possible for the average-income person. In 1970, two million arrived, and by 1990 close to six million passengers arrived on 22 international air carriers. In 2000, nearly seven million visitors chose Hawaii as their destination. The first hotel in Honolulu was the Hawaiian, built in 1872. It was pre-dated by the humble Volcano House, which overlooks Kilauea Crater on the Big Island and was built in 1866. The coral-pink Royal Hawaiian, built in 1927, is Waikiki's graciously aging grande dame, a symbol of days gone by. As late as the 1950s it had Waikiki Beach almost to itself. Only 10,000 hotel units were available in 1960; today there are more than 50,000 statewide and about 20,000 condo units as well.

Tourists: Who, When, and Where

Tourism-based income outstripped pineapples and sugar by the mid-1960s and the boom was on. Longtime residents could even feel a physical change in air temperature: many trees were removed from Honolulu to build parking lots, and reflected sunlight made Honolulu much hotter and at times unbearable. Even the trade winds, known to moderate temperatures, were not up to that task. So many people from the outlying farming communities were attracted to work in the hotels that there was a poi famine in 1967. But for the most part, islanders knew their economic future was tied to the "nonpolluting" industry of tourism. Most visitors are Americans,

and by far the largest numbers come from the West Coast. Sun-seeking refugees from frigid Alaska, however, make up the greatest proportional number, according to population figures. The remaining arrivals are, in descending numbers, from Japan, Canada, Korea, Australia, Germany, England, and Taiwan. Europe, as a whole, sends proportionately fewer visitors than North America or Asia, while the fewest come from South America, the Middle East, and Africa.

The Japanese market grew constantly until 1995, when it reached more than two million visitors per year. Since then, and due largely to the Asian economic crisis, numbers have fallen off, yet Japanese tourists still make up roughly 27 percent of the Hawaiian market. This is particularly beneficial to the tourist market because the average Western tourist spends about $150 per day, while a Japanese counterpart spends $230 per day. The average Japanese tourist, however, stays only about six days as opposed to 10 days for westbound travelers. Up until very recently the Japanese traveled only in groups and primarily stayed on O'ahu. Now the trend is shifting to independent travel, or to coming with a group and then peeling off, with a hefty percentage heading for the "Neighbor Islands" (all islands other than O'ahu).

The typical visitor is slightly affluent, and female visitors outnumber males three to two. The average age, at 35, is a touch higher than in most vacation areas because it reflects an inflated proportion of retirees heading for Hawaii, especially Honolulu, to fulfill lifelong "dream" vacations. A typical stay lasts about 10 days, down from a month in the 1950s; a full 56 percent are repeat visitors. On any given day there are about 80,000 travelers on O'ahu, 42,000 on Maui, 22,000 on Hawai'i, and about 18,000 on Kaua'i. Moloka'i and Lana'i get so few visitors, 1,000 and 1,100, respectively, that the figures are hardly counted.

In 1964 only 10 percent of the islands' hotel rooms were on the Neighbor Islands, but by 1966 the figure jumped to 25 percent, with more than 70 percent of tourists opting to visit the Neighbor Islands. Today four out of 10 hotel rooms are on the Neighbor Islands, with the figure steadily rising. The overwhelming number of tourists are on package tours, and the largest number of people congregate on O'ahu in Waikiki, which has nearly 80 percent average hotel occupancy and attracts twice as many visitors as do the Neighbor Islands together. Obviously, Waikiki is still most people's idea of paradise. Those seeking a more intimate experience can have it with a 20-minute flight from O'ahu to a Neighbor Island.

Joaquin Miller, the 19th-century poet of the Sierras, said, "I tell you my boy, the man who has not seen the Sandwich Islands, in this one great ocean's warm heart, has not seen the world." The times have certainly changed, but the sentiments of most visitors to Hawaii remain consistently the same.

Tourism-Related Problems

Tourism is both boon and blight to Hawaii. It is the root cause of two problems: one environmental, the other socioeconomic. The environmental impact is obvious, and is best described in the lament of singer Joni Mitchell's "Big Yellow Taxi": "They paved paradise and put up a parking lot." Put simply, tourism can draw too many people to an area and overburden it. In the process, it stresses the very land and destroys the natural beauty that attracted people in the first place. Tourists come to Hawaii for what has been called its "ambient resource": a balanced collage of indulgent climate, invigorating waters, intoxicating scenery, and exotic people all wrapped up neatly in one area that can both soothe and excite. It is in Hawaii's best interest to preserve this resource.

Most point to Waikiki as a prime example of development gone mad. It is super-saturated, and amazingly enough, hotel owners themselves are trying to keep development in check. Two prime examples of the best and the worst development can be found on Maui's south shore at Kihei and Wailea, less than five miles apart. Kihei is shoulder to shoulder high-rise condo, with hardly room for a peek at the ocean. You can bet those who made a killing building there don't live there. Just down the road, Wailea is a model of what development could and should be. The architecture is tasteful, low-rise, unobtrusive, and done with people and the preservation of the scenery in mind. It's obviously more exclusive, but access points to the beaches are open to everyone and the view is still there for all to enjoy. It points the way for development standards of the future.

Changing Lifestyle

Like the land, humans are stressed by tourism. Local people, who once took the "Hawaiian lifestyle" for granted, became displaced and estranged in their own land. Some areas, predominantly along gorgeous beaches that were once average- to low-income communities, are now overdeveloped, with prices going through the roof. The locals are not only forced to move out, but often must come back as service personnel in the tourist industry and cater to the very people who displaced them. At one time the psychological blow was softened because, after all, the newcomers were merely benign tourists who would stay a short time, spend a wad of money, and leave.

Today, condos are being built and a different sort of visitor is arriving. Many condo owners are well-educated businesspeople and professionals in the above-average income brackets. The average condo owner is a Mainlander who purchases one as a second or retirement home. These people are not islanders and have a tough time relating to the locals, who naturally feel resentment. Moreover, since they don't *leave* like normal tourists, they use community facilities, find those special nooks and crannies

---

ECOTOURISM IN HAWAII

Ecotourism is economically, culturally, socially, and environmentally sensitive and sustainable tourism that helps promote local communities and organizations and works in harmony with nature. Although small potatoes yet in the Hawaiian (and worldwide) tourism economy, ecotourism and its goals are growing in importance and will become a major factor in the economic vitality of tourism in the state. For more information on ecotourism in Hawaii, contact the Hawaii Ecotourism Association, P.O. Box 61435, Honolulu, HI 96822, 808/956-2866, website: www.planet-hawaii.com/hea, email: hea@aloha.net.

The following organization can also provide related information and contacts: The International Ecotourism Society, P.O. Box 668, Burlington, VT 05420, tel./fax 802/651-9819, website: www.ecotourism.org.

for shopping or sunbathing that were once exclusively the domain of locals, and have a say as voters in community governments. The islanders become more and more disenfranchised. Many believe that the new order instigated by tourism is similar to what has always existed in Hawaii: a few from the privileged class being catered to by many from the working class. In a way it's an extension of the plantation system, but instead of carrying pineapples, most islanders find themselves carrying luggage, cocktails, or broiled fish. One argument, however, remains undeniable: whether it's people or pineapples, one has to make a living. The days of a little grass shack on a sunny beach aren't gone, but you need a steady job or a wallet full of credit cards to afford one.

THE MILITARY

Hawaii is the most militarized state in the United States: all five services are represented. Camp H.M. Smith, overlooking Pearl Harbor, is the headquarters of CINCPAC (Commander in Chief Pacific), which is responsible for 70 percent of the earth's surface, from California to the east coast of Africa and to both poles. The U.S. military presence dates back to 1887, when Pearl Harbor was given to the Navy as part of the Sugar Reciprocity Treaty. The sugar planters were given favorable duty-free treatment on their sugar, while the U.S. Navy was allowed exclusive rights to one of the best harbors in the Pacific. In 1894, when the monarchy was being overthrown by the sugar planters, the USS *Boston* sent a contingency of marines ashore to "keep order," which really amounted to a show of force, backing the revolution. The Spanish-American War saw U.S. troops billeted at Camp McKinley at the foot of Diamond Head, and Schofield Barracks opened to receive the 5th Cavalry in 1909. Pearl Harbor's flames ignited World War II, and there has been no looking back since then.

About 44,000 military personnel are stationed in Hawaii (99 percent on O'ahu), with more than 54,000 dependents. This number has slowly but steadily been decreasing since 1988, when the military was at its greatest strength in the state, and is now lower than at any time since the mid-

1950s. The Army has the largest contingent with nearly 20,000, followed by the Navy at 11,000, Marine Corps at 7,000, Air Force at more than 5,000, and 1,500 or so with the Coast Guard. Besides this, 17,000 civilian support personnel account for 65 percent of all federal jobs in Hawaii. The combined services are one of the largest landholders, with more than 210,000 acres, accounting for five percent of Hawaiian land. The two major holdings are the 100,000-acre Pohakuloa Training Area on Hawai'i and 81,000 acres on O'ahu, which is a full 21 percent of the entire island. The Army controls 58 percent of the military lands, followed by the Navy at 25 percent, and the remainder goes to the Air Force, Marines, and a few small installations to the Coast Guard.

The Military Has No *Aloha*
Not everyone is thrilled by the strong military presence in Hawaii. Two factions, native Hawaiians and antinuclear groups, are downright angry. Radical contingencies of native Hawaiian-rights groups consider Hawaii an independent country, besieged and "occupied" by the U.S. government. They date their loss of independence to Lili'uokalani's overthrow in 1894. The vast majority of ethnic Hawaiians, though they consider themselves Americans, are concerned with loss of their rightful homelands—with no financial reparation—and about continuing destruction and disregard for their traditional religious and historical sites. A long list of grievances is cited by native Hawaiian action groups, but the best and clearest example was the controversy over the sacred island Kaho'olawe, which until 1990 was used as a bombing target by the U.S. Navy.

A major controversy raised by the military presence focuses on Hawaii as a nuclear target. The ultimate goal of the antinuclear protesters is to see the Pacific, and the entire world, free from nuclear arms. They see Hawaii as a big target used by the international power merchants on the Mainland as both pawn and watchdog—if war breaks out, they say, the Hawaiian Islands will be reduced to cinders. The military naturally counters that a strong Hawaii is a deterrent to nuclear war and that Hawaii is not only a powerful offensive weapon, but one of the best-defended regions of the world. Unfortunately, when you are on an island there is no place to go: like a boxer in a ring, you can run, but you can't hide.

Also, the military has been cited for disposing of stockpiles of chemical weapons by incineration on Johnston Island, a military installation southwest of the Big Island. Because there was no environmental impact study, scientists fear that wind and currents could carry the pollutants to the main Hawaiian Islands, destroying delicate coral reefs along the way.

SUGAR

Sugarcane *(ko)* was brought to Hawaii by its original settlers and was known throughout Polynesia. Its cultivation was well established and duly noted by Captain Cook when he first sighted the islands. The native Hawaiians used various strains of sugarcane for food, rituals, and medicine. It was never refined, but the stalk was chewed and juice was pressed from it. It was used as food during famine, as an ingredient in many otherwise unpalatable medicines, and especially as a love potion. Commercial growing started with a failure on O'ahu in 1825, followed by a successful venture a decade later on Kaua'i. Until the mid-1990s, this original plantation was still productive. The industry received a technological boost in 1850 when a centrifuge, engineered by David Weston of the Honolulu Iron Works, was installed at a plantation on East Maui. It was used to spin the molasses out of the cooked syrup, leaving a crude crystal.

Hawaii's biggest market has always been the Mainland. Demand rose dramatically during the California gold rush of 1849–50 and again a decade later for the Union Army during the American Civil War. At first Hawaiian sugar had a poor reputation that almost killed its export market, but with technological advances it became the best-quality sugar available.

Irrigation and Profit Politics
In 1876 the **Reciprocity Treaty** freed Hawaiian sugar from import duty. Now a real fortune could be made. One entrepreneur, Claus Spreckels, a sugar-beet magnate from California, became the reigning Sugar King in Hawaii. His state-of-the-art refineries on Maui employed every modern convenience, including electric

young sugarcane

LEAF JOINT (COLLARS)

STALK

LEAF

INTERNODE

NODE

ROOTS — SEED PIECE

LOUISE FOOTE

lighting; he was also instrumental in building marvelous irrigation ditches necessary to grow sugar on once-barren land. The biggest hurdle to commercial sugarcane growing has always been water. One pound of sugar requires one ton of water, or about 250 gallons. A real breakthrough came when the growers reasoned that fresh water in the form of rain must seep through the lava and be stored underground. Fresh water will furthermore float atop heavier salt water and therefore be recoverable by a series of vertical wells and tunnels. By 1898, planters were tapping this underground supply of water, and sugar could be produced in earnest as an export crop.

The Plantation System

Sugarcane also produced the plantation system, which was in many ways socially comparable to that of the pre–Civil War South. It was the main cause of the cosmopolitan mixture of races found in Hawaii today. Workers were in great demand, and the sugar growers scoured the globe looking for likely sources. Importing plantation workers started with the liberalizing of the **The Masters and Servants Act,** which basically allowed the importation of conscripted workers. Even during its heyday, people with consciences felt that this system was no different from slavery. The first conscripts were Chinese, followed by Japanese, and then myriad people including other Polynesians, Germans, Norwegians, Spanish, Portuguese, Puerto Ricans, Koreans, Filipinos, and even a few freed slaves from the southern United States.

Today, with production down on Kaua'i and Maui (commercial production has ceased on O'ahu and the Big Island), yearly sugar sales have fallen from those of a few decades ago, when they were a hefty $500 million, to less than $100 million currently, 50,000–60,000 acres. Nonetheless, the state's sugarcane-producing farms and their attendant refineries still employ a large number of workers. Newcomers, startled by what appear to be brush fires, are actually witnessing the burning of sugarcane prior to harvesting. While much reduced from its heyday, Hawaii's sugarcane industry is still solvent, producing more than two million tons of raw sugar annually.

PINEAPPLES

Next to cane, the majority of Hawaii's cultivated lands yield pineapples. The main farms are on O'ahu, on the northwest tip of Maui, and on the lower slopes of Haleakala on Maui, with Lana'i, once the world's largest pineapple plantation, now out of business. Pineapples were brought to the islands by Don Francisco Marin, an early Spanish agronomist, in the 1820s. Fresh pineapples were exported as early as 1850 to San Fran-

cisco, and a few cases of canned fruit appeared in 1876 at Hawaii's pavilion at the U.S. Centennial Exposition in Philadelphia. Old varieties of pineapples were pithier and pricklier than the modern variety. Today's large, luscious, golden fruits are the "smooth cayenne" variety from Jamaica, introduced by Captain Kidwell in 1886.

Dole

But Hawaiian pineapple, as we know it, is synonymous with one man, James Dole, who actually *made* the industry at the turn of the 20th century. Jim Dole started growing pineapples on a 60-acre homestead in Wahiawa, O'ahu. He felt that America was ready to add this fruit to its diet and that "canning" would be the conveyance. By 1903, he was shipping canned fruit from his Iwilei plant, and by 1920 pineapples were a familiar item in most American homes. Hawaii was at that time the largest producer in the world. In 1922, Jim Dole bought the entire island of Lana'i, whose permanent residents numbered only about 100, and started the world's largest pineapple plantation. By all accounts, Jim Dole was an exemplary human being, but he could never learn to "play ball" with the economic powers that ruled Hawaii, namely the Big Five. They ruined him by 1932 and took control of his **Hawaiian Pineapple Company.** Today, the Hawaiian pineapple industry is beleaguered by competition from Asia, Central America, and the Philippines, resulting in the abandonment of many corporate farms. Hit especially hard was Moloka'i, where Del Monte shut down its operations in the mid-1980s, and Lana'i, which stopped farming the prickly fruits in 1993. The other plantations are still reasonably strong, bringing in about $90 million dollars annually, twice as much on O'ahu as on Maui, but employment in the pineapple industry has dropped drastically in the last decade, and there are strong doubts these jobs will ever return.

OTHER AGRICULTURE

Every major food crop known can be grown in Hawaii because of its amazingly varied climates and rich soil. Farming ventures through the years have produced cotton, sisal, rice, and even rubber trees. Until the year 2000 (now surpassed by

Australia), Hawaii was the world's largest producer of the macadamia nut, considered by some the world's most useful and delicious nut. The islands' fresh exotic fruits are unsurpassed; juices and nectars made from papaya, passion fruit, and guava are becoming well known worldwide. Dazzling flowers such as protea, carnations, orchids, and anthuriums are also commercially grown. Hawaii has a very healthy livestock industry, headed by the Big Island's quarter-million-acre Parker Ranch, the largest singly owned cattle ranch in the United States. Poultry, dairy, and pork are also produced on many farms. The only coffee grown in the United States is grown in Hawaii on four islands. "Kona coffee" is of gourmet quality, well regarded for its aroma and rich flavor. Recently, chocolate manufacture was introduced to the Big Island, and production of this fine sweet is in full operation. *Pakalolo* (marijuana) is still a lucrative cash crop, but no official economic records exist. It's grown by enterprising gardeners on all the islands.

> *The land and industries of Hawaii are owned by old families and large corporations, and Hawaii is only so large.*
>
> —Jack London, circa 1916

Hawaiian waters are alive with fish, but its commercial fleet is woefully small and obsolete. Fishing revenues amount to only $53 million per year, which is ludicrous in a land where fish is the obvious natural bounty. Half of the 25 million pounds come from tuna, and 85 percent is fished by the commercial ventures on O'ahu. Native Hawaiians were masters of aquaculture, routinely building fishponds and living from their harvest. Where once there were hundreds of fishponds, only a handful are in use today. The main aquaculture is growing freshwater prawns, which produces some $5 million annually. With all of these foodstuffs, unbelievable as it may sound, Hawaii must import much of its food. Hawaii can feed *itself*, but it cannot support the six million hungry tourists who come to sample its superb and diverse cuisine every year.

ECONOMIC POWER

The Big Five Corporations

Until statehood, Hawaii was ruled economically by a consortium of corporations known as the Big

Five: **C. Brewer and Co.,** sugar, ranching, and chemicals, founded in 1826; **Theo. H. Davies & Co.,** sugar, investments, insurance, and transportation, founded in 1845; **Amfac Inc.** (originally H. Hackfield Inc.—a German firm that changed its name and ownership during the anti-German sentiment of World War I to American Factors), sugar, insurance, and land development, founded in 1849; **Castle and Cooke Inc.** (Dole), pineapple, food packing, and land development, founded in 1851; and **Alexander and Baldwin Inc.,** shipping, sugar, and pineapple, founded in 1895. This economic oligarchy ruled Hawaii with a steel grip in a velvet glove.

With members on every important corporate board, they controlled all major commerce, including banking, shipping, insurance, hotel development, agriculture, utilities, and wholesale and retail merchandising. Anyone trying to buck the system was ground to dust, finding it suddenly impossible to do business in the islands. The Big Five were made up of the islands' oldest and most well-established *haole* families; all included bloodlines from Hawaii's own nobility. They looked among themselves for suitable husbands and wives, so that breaking in from the outside even through marriage was hardly possible. The only time they were successfully challenged prior to statehood was when Sears, Roebuck and Co. opened a store on O'ahu. Closing ranks, the Big Five decreed that their steamships would not carry Sears's freight. When Sears threatened to buy its own steamship line, the Big Five relented.

Actually, statehood, and more to the point, tourism, broke their oligarchy. After 1960 too much money was at stake for Mainland-based corporations to ignore. Eventually the grip of the Big Five was loosened, but they are still enormously powerful and richer than ever. These days, however, they don't control everything; now their power is land. With only five other major landholders, they control 50 percent of the privately held land in Hawaii.

Land Ownership

Hawaii, landwise, is a small pie, and its slices are not at all well divided. Of the state's 6,423 square miles of land, the six main inhabited islands make up 98 percent. This figure does not include Niʻihau, which is privately owned by the Robinson family and inhabited by some of the last remaining pure-blooded Hawaiians; nor does it include uninhabited Kahoʻolawe. Of the 4,110,976 acres that make up the inhabited islands, 34 percent is owned by the state and 8 percent by the federal government; the remaining 68 percent is in private hands. While only 40 owners, with 5,000 or more acres each, own 65 percent of all private lands, the top 10 control 75 percent of that. To be more specific, Castle and Cooke Inc. owns 99 percent of Lanaʻi, while 40–60 percent of Maui, Oʻahu, Molokaʻi, Kauaʻi, and Hawaiʻi is owned by fewer than a dozen private parties.

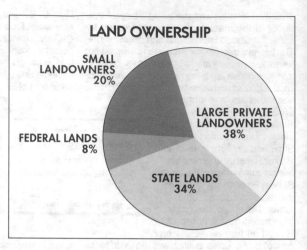

LAND OWNERSHIP

- SMALL LANDOWNERS 20%
- LARGE PRIVATE LANDOWNERS 38%
- FEDERAL LANDS 8%
- STATE LANDS 34%

The largest private landowner, with more than 367,000 acres (nearly 9 percent of the total land area of the state), is the Kamehameha Schools/Bishop Estate, which some years ago lost a Supreme Court battle allowing the state of Hawaii to acquire privately owned land for "the public good." More than in any other state, Hawaiian landowners tend to lease land rather than sell it, and many private homes are on rented ground. This was the case with many homes rented from the Bishop Estate. The state acquired the land and resold it to long-term lease holders. These lands had previously earned a slow but steady profit for native Hawaiians. As land prices continue to rise, only the very rich land developers are able to purchase long-term leases, and the people of Hawaii continue to become even more land poor.

PEOPLE

Nowhere else on earth can you find such a kaleidoscopic mixture of people as in Hawaii. Every major race is accounted for, with more than 50 ethnic groups adding not only their genes, but their customs, traditions, and outlooks. The modern Hawaiian is the future's "everyman": a blending of all races. Interracial marriage has been long accepted in Hawaii, and people are so mixed it's already difficult to place them in a specific racial category. Besides the original Hawaiians, themselves a mixed race of Polynesians, people in the islands have multiple ancestor combinations. Hawaii is the most racially integrated state in the United States, and although the newest, it epitomizes the time-honored American ideal of the melting-pot society.

THE ISSUE OF RACE

This polyracial society should be a model of understanding and tolerance, and in most ways it is, but there are still racial tensions. People tend to identify with one group, and though not openly hostile, they do look disparagingly on others. Some racial barbs maintain the Chinese are grasping, the Japanese too cold and calculating, the *haole* materialistic, Hawaiians lackadaisical, and Filipinos emotional. In Hawaii this labeling tendency is a bit modified because *people,* as individuals, are not usually discriminated against, but their *group* may be. Another factor is that individuals identify with a group not along strict blood lines, but more by a "feeling of identity." If a white/Japanese man married a Hawaiian/Chinese woman, they would be accepted by all groups concerned. Their children, moreover, would be what they chose to be and, more to the point, what they "felt" like.

There are no ghettos as such, but there are traditional areas where people of similar racial strains live, and where outsiders are made to feel unwelcome. For example, the Wai'anae District of O'ahu is considered a strong "Hawaiian" area where other people may meet with hostility, and the Kahala area of O'ahu mostly attracts upwardly mobile whites. Some clubs make it difficult for nonwhites to become members; certain Japanese, Chinese, and Filipino organizations attract only members from these ethnic groups; and Hawaiian 'ohana would question any person seeking to join unless he or she had some Hawaiian blood. Generally, however, the vast majority of people get along with each other and mix with no discernible problems.

The real catalyst responsible for most racial acceptance is the Hawaiian public school system. Education has always been highly regarded in Hawaii; the classroom has long been integrated. Thanks to a standing tradition of progressive education, democracy and individualism have always been basic maxims taught in the classroom. The racial situation in Hawaii is far from perfect, but it does point the way to the future in which all people can live side by side with respect and dignity.

Who and Where

Hawaii has an approximate population of 1.2 million, which includes about 100,000 permanently stationed military personnel and their dependents. It has the highest ratio of population to immigration in the United States and is the only state where whites are not the majority. White people are, however, the fastest growing group, due primarily to immigration from the U.S. West Coast. About 56 percent of Hawaiian residents were born in Hawaii; 26 percent were born on the Mainland U.S.; and 18 percent are foreign-born. The average age is 29, and men slightly outnumber women. This is due to the large concentration of predominantly male military personnel and to the substantial number of older bachelor plantation workers who came during the first part of the 20th century and never found wives. The population has grown steadily in recent times but has fluctuated wildly in the past. Most European sources gave estimates of between 300,000 and 400,000 for the population of the Hawaiian Islands before the arrival of Captain Cook. Some now estimate that number as low as 200,000 or as high as 800,000. In any case, following the arrival of Europeans, the native Hawaiian population declined steadily for a century. In 1876, it reached its lowest ebb, with only 55,000 permanent residents in the islands. This was the era of large sugar plantations; their constant demand for labor was the primary cause of

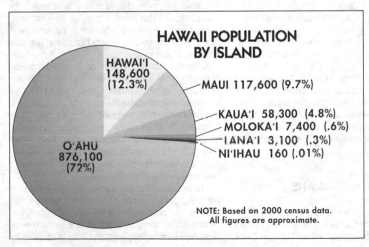

HAWAII POPULATION BY ISLAND

HAWAI'I 148,600 (12.3%)

MAUI 117,600 (9.7%)

KAUA'I 58,300 (4.8%)
MOLOKA'I 7,400 (.6%)
lANA'I 3,100 (.3%)
NI'IHAU 160 (.01%)

O'AHU 876,100 (72%)

NOTE: Based on 2000 census data. All figures are approximate.

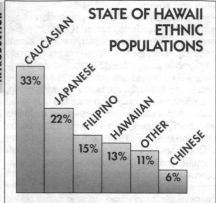

STATE OF HAWAII ETHNIC POPULATIONS

CAUCASIAN 33%

JAPANESE 22%

FILIPINO 15%

HAWAIIAN 13%

OTHER 11%

CHINESE 6%

importing various peoples from around the world, leading to Hawaii's racially integrated society. During World War II, Hawaii's population swelled from 400,000 just prior to the war to 900,000. These 500,000 were military personnel who left at war's end, but many returned to settle after getting a taste of island living.

Of the 1.2 million people in the islands today, 876,100 live on O'ahu, with slightly less than half of these living in the Honolulu metropolitan area. The rest of the population is distributed as follows: 148,600 on Hawai'i, with 47,000 living in Hilo; 117,600 on Maui, with the largest concentration, 53,000, in Wailuku-Kahului; 58,300 on Kaua'i, including 160 pure-blooded Hawaiians on Ni'ihau; 7,400 on Moloka'i; and just over 3,000 on Lana'i. The population density, statewide, is 188 people per square mile, approximately the same as California's. The population is not at all evenly distributed, with O'ahu claiming about 1,467 people per square mile, while the Big Island has barely 37 residents per square mile. Statewide, city dwellers outnumber those living in the country by nine to one. The average household size in Hawaii is 3.1 persons, down from 4.5 in 1940.

THE HAWAIIANS

The study of the native Hawaiians is ultimately a study in tragedy because it nearly ends in their demise as a viable people. When Captain Cook first sighted Hawaii in 1778, an estimated 300,000 natives were living in harmony with their ecological surroundings; within a little more than 100 years a scant 48,000 demoralized and dejected Hawaiians existed almost as wards of the state. Today, although more than 210,000 people claim varying degrees of Hawaiian blood (some official surveys record 140,000), experts say fewer than 1,000 are pure Hawaiian, and this is stretching it. A resurgence of Hawaiian ethnic pride is sweeping the islands as many people trace their roots and attempt to absorb the finer aspects of their ancestral lifestyle. It's easy to see why they could be bitter over what they've lost, since they're now strangers in their own land, much like Native Americans. The overwhelming majority of "Hawaiians" are of mixed heritage, and the wisest take the best from all worlds. From the Hawaiian side comes simplicity, love of the land, and acceptance of people. It is the Hawaiian legacy of *aloha* that remains immortal and adds the special elusive quality that *is* Hawaii.

Polynesian Roots

The Polynesians' original stock is muddled and remains an anthropological mystery, but it's believed that they were nomads who migrated from both the Indian subcontinent and Southeast Asia through Indonesia, where they learned to sail and navigate on protected waterways. As they migrated, they honed their sailing skills until they could take on the Pacific, and as they moved, they absorbed people from other cultures and races until they had coalesced into what we now know as Polynesians.

Abraham Fornander, still considered a major authority on the subject, wrote in his 1885 *An Account of the Polynesian Race* that he believed the Polynesians started as a white (Aryan) race that was heavily influenced by contact with the Cushite, Chaldeo-Arabian civilization. He estimated their arrival in Hawaii at A.D. 600 based on Hawaiian genealogical chants. Modern science seems to bear this date out, although it remains skeptical on his other surmises.

Thousands of years before Europeans even imagined the existence of a Pacific Ocean, Polynesians had populated the far-flung islands of the "Polynesian Triangle," which stretches from New Zealand in the south, east thousands of miles to

Easter Island, and finally to Hawaii, the northern apex. Similar language, gods, foods, and crafts add credibility to this theory. Other more fanciful versions are all long on conjecture and short on evidence. For example, Atlantis, the most "found" lost continent in history, pops up again, with the Hawaiians the supposed remnants of this advanced civilization. The slim proof is the Hawaiian *kahuna,* so well versed in the curative arts they had to be Atlanteans. In fact, they not only made it to Hawaii, but also to the Philippines, where their secret powers have been passed on to the faith healers of today. That the Hawaiians are the "lost tribe of Israel" is another theory, but this too is wild conjecture.

The "Land Seekers"

The intrepid Polynesians who actually settled Hawaii are believed to have come from the Marquesas Islands, 1,000 miles southeast of Hawaii. The Marquesans were cannibals known for their tenacity and strength, attributes that would serve them well. They left their own islands because of war and famine; these migrations went on for centuries. Ships' logs mention Marquesan seagoing canoes setting sail in search of new land as late as the mid-19th century. The first navigator-explorers, advance scouting parties, were referred to as "land seekers." They were led northward by a few terse words sung in a chant that gave a general direction and promised some guiding stars (probably recounting the wild adventures of canoes blown far off course that somehow managed to return to the southern islands of Polynesia). The land seekers were familiar with the stars, currents, habits of land birds, and countless other subtle clues that are overlooked by "civilized" people.

After finding Hawaii, they were aided in their voyage home by favorable trade winds and familiar waters. They set sail again in canoes laden with hopeful families and all the foodstuffs necessary to colonize a new land, anticipating a one-way ride with no return. Over the centuries, the fierce Marquesans mellowed into Hawaiians and formed a new benevolent culture based on the fertility god Lono. Then, in the 12th century, a ferocious army of Tahitians invaded Hawaii and supplanted not only the ruling chiefs but also the gentler gods with their war god Ku, who demanded human sacrifice. Abruptly, contact with Polynesia stopped. Some say the voyages, always fraught with danger, were no longer necessary. Hawaii was forgotten by the Polynesians, and the Hawaiians became the most rarefied race in the world. It was to these people that Captain Cook in 1778 brought the outside world. Finding Polynesians stretched so far and wide across the Pacific, he declared them "the most extensive nation upon earth."

The "Little People" of Hawaii

The Mu, Wa, and ʻEʻepa are all "little people" of Hawaii, but the most famous are the Menehune. As a group they resemble the trolls and leprechauns of Europe, but so many stories concern them that they appear to have actually existed in Hawaii at one time. Even in the late 18th century, an official census noted King Kaumualiʻi of Kauaʻi had 65 Menehune, who were said to live in Wainiha Valley. It's held that the Menehune drove out the Mu and the Wa. They also differed slightly in appearance. The Menehune are about two to three feet tall with hairy, well-muscled bodies. Their red faces have thick noses, protruding foreheads, and long eyebrows, and their hair is stringy. They love to frolic, especially by rolling down hills into the sea, and their favorite foods are shrimp and poi. They seldom speak, but their chatter sounds like the low growling of a dog. Nocturnal creatures, Menehune are frightened of owls and dogs.

The Mu are mute, while the Wa are noted for their loud blustering shouts. The Mu were thought to be black-skinned and to live deep in the forest on a diet of bananas. All had their specialties, but the Menehune were stonemasons par excellence. Many feats involving stonework are attributed to the Menehune. The most famous is the "Menehune Ditch" on Kauaʻi. They finished their monumental tasks in one night, disappearing by daybreak. Even in the 1950s, masons building with stone near Diamond Head insisted their work was disturbed at night, and a *kahuna* had to be called in to appease the Menehune. After that, all went well.

In a more scientific vein, the Tahitian word for Menehune means "commoner." Many feel they were non-Polynesian aboriginals who somehow made it to the islands and co-mingled with Hawaiians until their chiefs became alarmed that their little race would vanish. (Mohikia and

Analike are the respective names of a Menehune prince and princess who married Hawaiians and whose names have been preserved in legend.) The Menehune assembled en masse and supposedly floated away on an island descended from the heavens called "Kuaihelani." Some say they headed for the far-flung outer islands of Necker and Nihoa, where, oddly enough, stone gods found there are unlike any on the other Hawaiian Islands. But there the trail grows faint. Today, island mothers warn their misbehaving toddlers that the Menehune will come and take them away, but in most stories they are actually pixie-like and benign.

Causes of Decline

When Captain Cook stepped ashore on Waimea, Kaua'i, on the morning of January 20, 1778, he discovered a population of natives living in perfect harmony with their surroundings. Their agrarian society had flourished in the last thousand years. However, the ecological system of Hawaii has always been exceptionally fragile, its people included. White arrivals found a great people who were large, strong, and virile, but when it came to fighting even minor diseases they proved as delicate as hothouse flowers. To exacerbate the situation, the Hawaiians were totally uninhibited about sex between willing partners. Unfortunately, white sailors were laden with syphilis, gonorrhea, and all manner of other germs and common European diseases. Captain Cook tried desperately to keep sexually diseased members of his crew away from Hawaiian women, but it was impossible. The *hospitality* of Hawaiian women was legendary, and promises of "paradise" were actually used as a lure to get sailors for perilous cruises into the Pacific that could last for years. When Cook returned from the north in less than one year, there were already natives with telltale signs of venereal disease.

Hawaiian women brought venereal disease home, and it spread like wildfire. By the time the missionaries came in 1820 and halted the widespread fornication, the native population was only 140,000, less than half of what it had been only 40 years before. In 1804 alone, perhaps 100,000 died from 'oku'u (either typhoid or cholera). In the next 50 years measles, mumps, influenza, and tuberculosis ravaged the people. In 1853 a smallpox epidemic ate further into the doomed and weakened Hawaiian race, and leprosy ranged far and wide in the land. In addition, during the whaling years, at least 25 percent of all able-bodied Hawaiian men sailed away, never to return. By 1880 King Kalakaua had only 48,000 Hawaiian subjects, a cataclysmic decrease of the original population. Wherever the king went, he would beseech his people, *"Ho'oulu lahui"* ("Increase the race"), but it was already too late. Nature itself had turned its back on these once-proud people. Many of their marriages were barren, and in 1874 when only 1,400 children were born, a full 75 percent died in infancy. The final coup de grâce was intermarriage. With so many interracial marriages, the Hawaiians nearly bred themselves out of existence.

Painful Adjustments

In the 19th century, the old paternalism inherent in the Hawaiian caste system was carried on by the ruling *haole* families. The remaining Hawaiians looked to the ruling class of whites as they had to their own *ali'i*, and for many years this attitude discouraged self help. Many Hawaiians fervently accepted the Christianity that had supplanted their own religion because it was a haven against a rapidly changing world in which they felt more and more alienated. Though Hawaiians were not favored as good plantation workers and were branded as lazy, they were actually hard and dedicated workers. Like all people attuned to their environment, they chose to work in the cool of the mornings and late afternoons, and could make no sense of laboring in the intense heat of the day. As fishermen they were unparalleled, and they also made excellent cowboys on the ranches, preferring the open ranges to the constricting plantation fields.

Hawaiians readily engaged in politics and were impressed with all the hoopla and fanfare. They attended rallies, performed hula and songs, and in most instances sided with the whites against the Asians. They were known to accept money for their votes and almost considered it the obligation of the leader, whom they regarded as a sort of chief, to grease their palms. Educated Hawaiians tended to become lawyers, judges, policeman, and teachers, and there is still a disproportionate number of Hawaiians, population-wise, in these fields. Hawaiians were somewhat racist toward the Japanese and Chinese. However, they would readily intermarry because, true to *aloha*, they accepted individual "people" even though they might be prejudiced against their group. In 1910, although the native population was greatly reduced, there are still twice as many full-blooded Hawaiians as mixed bloods. By 1940 mixed-blood Hawaiians were the fastest-growing group, and full bloods the fastest declining.

Hawaiians Today

Many of the Hawaiians who moved to the cities became more and more disenfranchised. Their folk society stressed openness and a giving nature but downplayed the individual and the ownership of private property. These cultural traits made them easy targets for users and schemers until they finally became either apathetic or angry. About 140,000 people living in Hawaii have *some* Hawaiian blood. Most surveys reveal that although they number only 13 percent of the population, they account for almost 50 percent of the financially destitute families, arrests, and illegitimate births. Ni'ihau, a privately owned island, is home to about 160 pure-blooded Hawaiians, the largest concentration per capita in the islands. The Robinson family, which owns the island, restricts visitors to invited guests only. The second largest concentration of people with Hawaiian blood is on Moloka'i, where 4,600 Hawaiians, living mostly on Hawaiian Homes lands, make up 62 percent of the population. The majority of part- or full-blooded Hawaiians, 189,000 or so, live on O'ahu, where they are particularly strong in the hotel and entertainment fields. People of Hawaiian extraction are a delight to meet, and visitors so lucky as to be befriended by one long regard this friendship as the highlight of their travels. The Hawaiians have always given their *aloha* freely, and it is we who must accept it as a precious gift.

THE CHINESE

Next to Yankees from New England, the Chinese are the oldest migrant group in Hawaii, and their influence has far outshone their meager numbers. They have long been the backbone of the small, privately owned retail trade. They brought to Hawaii, along with their individuality, Confucianism, Taoism, and Buddhism, although many have long since become Christians. The Chinese population of about 68,000 makes up only 6 percent of the state's total, and the vast majority reside on O'ahu. Their key to success has been indefatigable hard work, the shrewdness to seize a good opportunity, and above all, an almost fanatical desire to educate their children. As an ethnic group they account for the least amount of crime, the highest per capita income, and a disproportionate number of professionals. They are some of Hawaii's most prominent citizens.

The First Chinese

No one knows his name, but an unknown Chinese immigrant is credited with being the first person in Hawaii to refine sugar. This Asian wanderer tried his hand at crude refining on Lana'i in 1802. He failed, but other Chinese were operating sugar mills by 1830. Within 20 years, the plantations desperately needed workers, and the first Chinese laborers brought to Hawaii were 195 coolies from Amoy who arrived in 1852 under the newly passed Masters and Servants Act. These conscripts were contracted for 3–5 years and given $3 per month plus room and board. This was for 12 hours a day, six days a week, and even in 1852 these wages were absolutely miserable. The Chinese almost always left the plantations the minute their contracts expired. They went into business for themselves and promptly monopolized the restaurant and small shop trades.

Bad Feelings

When they left the plantations, the Chinese were universally resented, due to prejudice, xenophobia, and their success in business. The first Chinese peddler in Honolulu was mentioned as early as 1823. The Chinese Consul in Hawaii was very conservative and sided with the plantation owners, giving his own people no support. When leprosy became epidemic in the islands, it was blamed on the Chinese. The Hawaiians called it *pake* disease, their derisive name for Chinese men, which, oddly enough, was an endearment in China meaning "uncle." Although leprosy cannot be blamed solely on the Chinese, a boatload of Chinese immigrants did bring smallpox in 1880. At the turn of the 20th century, a smallpox epidemic broke out again in Honolulu's Chinatown (where half the residents were really Japanese), and the area was promptly burnt to the ground by the authorities.

Amidst all this negativity, some intrepid souls prospered. The most successful entrepreneur was Chun Afong, who, with little more than determination, became a millionaire by 1857, raised 16 children, and almost single-handedly created the Chinese bourgeoisie in Hawaii. The Chinese were also responsible for making rice Hawaii's second most important crop (1867–1872). It was another Chinese person, Ah In, who brought the first water buffalo used to cultivate rice during this period.

The Chinese Exclusion Act

Although reforms on the plantations were forthcoming, the Chinese preferred the retail trade. In 1880 half of all plantation workers were Chinese, by 1900 10 percent were, and by 1959, only 300 Chinese worked on plantations. When the "powers that were" decided Hawaii needed compliant laborers, not competitive businesspeople, the monarchy passed the Chinese Exclusion Act in 1886, forbidding any more Chinese contract laborers from entering Hawaii. Still, 15,000 more Chinese were contracted in the next few years. In 1900 there were about 25,000 Chinese in Hawaii, but because of the Exclusion Act and other prejudices, many sold out and moved away. By 1910 their numbers were reduced to 21,000.

The Chinese Niche

Although many people in Hawaii considered all Chinese ethnically the same, they were actually quite different. The majority came from Guangdong Province in southern China. They were two distinct ethnic groups: the Punti made up 75 percent of the immigrants, and the Hakka made up the remainder. The Hakka had invaded Punti lands over a thousand years ago and lived in the hills overlooking Punti villages. In China, they remained separate from each other, never mixing; in Hawaii, they mixed out of necessity. Few Chinese women came at first, and the ones who followed were at a premium and gladly accepted as wives, regardless of ethnic background. The Chinese were also one of the first groups to willingly intermarry with the Hawaiians, from whom they gained a reputation for being exceptionally caring spouses.

By the 1930s, there was still resentment, but the Chinese were firmly entrenched in the merchant class. Their thriftiness, hard work, and family solidarity had paid off. The Chinese accepted the social order and kept a low profile. During Hawaii's turbulent labor movements of the 1930s and '40s, the Chinese community produced not one labor leader, radical intellectual, or left-wing politician. When Hawaii became a state, one of the two first senators was Hiram Fong, a racially mixed Chinese. Since statehood, the Chinese community has carried on business as usual as they continue to rise both economically and socially.

THE JAPANESE

Most scholars believe that (inevitably) a few Japanese castaways floated to Hawaii long before Captain Cook arrived and might have introduced the iron with which the islanders seemed to be familiar before the white explorers arrived. Other scholars refute this claim and say Portuguese or Spanish ships lost in the Pacific introduced iron. Nevertheless, shipwrecked Japanese did make it to the islands. The most famous episode involved a man named Jirokichi, who, lost at sea for 10 months, was rescued by Captain Cathcart of Nantucket in 1839. Cathcart brought him to Hawaii, where Jirokichi boarded with prominent families. This adventure-filled episode is recounted in the Japanese classic *Ban Tan (Stories of the Outside World)*, written by the scribe Yuten-sei. The first official arrivals from Japan were ambassadors sent by the Japanese shogun to negotiate with the United States in Washington. They stopped en route to Honolulu in March 1860, only seven years after Commodore Perry and his famous "Black Ships" had roused Japan from its self-imposed 200-year slumber.

A small group of Japanese plantation workers arrived in 1868, but mass migration was blocked for almost 20 years. King Kalakaua, among others, proposed that Japanese be brought in as contract laborers in 1881; it was thought that

Japanese subsistence farmers held promise as an inexhaustible supply of hardworking, uncomplaining, inexpensive, resolute workers. In 1886, because of famine, the Japanese government allowed farmers (mainly from southern Honshu, Kyushu, and Okinawa) to emigrate. Among these were members of Japan's little-talked-about untouchable caste, called *eta* or *burakumin* in Japan and *chorinbo* in Hawaii. They gratefully seized this opportunity to better their lot, an impossibility in their homeland.

The Japanese Arrive

The first Japanese migrants were almost all men. Under Robert Irwin, the American agent for recruiting the Japanese, almost 27,000 Japanese came, for which he received a fee of $5 per head. The contract workers received $9 plus room and board, and an additional $6 for a working wife. This pay was for a 26-workday month at 10 hours per day in the fields or 12 hours in a factory. Between 1897 and 1908, migration was steady, with about 70 percent men and 30 percent women. Afterwards, immigration was nearly halted because of a "gentlemen's agreement," a euphemism for racism against the "yellow peril." By 1900, more than 60,000 Japanese had arrived in the islands, constituting the largest ethnic group.

Until 1907 most Japanese longed to return home and faithfully sent back part of their pay to help support their families. Eventually, a full 50 percent did return to Japan, but the others began to consider Hawaii their home and resolved to settle . . . if they could get wives! Between 1908 and 1924, "picture brides" arrived whose marriages had been arranged *(omiai)* by family members back home. These women clung to the old ways and reinforced the Japanese ethnic identity. Excellent plantation workers, they set about making their rude camps into model villages. They felt an obligation that extended from individual to family, village, and their new country. As peasants, they were imbued with a feeling of a natural social order that they readily accepted . . . if treated fairly.

Changing Attitudes

Unfortunately, some plantation *luna* were brutal, and Japanese laborers were mistreated, exploited, and made to live in indecent conditions on the plantations. In unusual protest, they formed their first trade union under Yasutaro Soga in 1908 and gained better treatment and higher wages. In 1919 an unsuccessful statewide plantation strike headed by the Federation of Japanese Labor lasted seven bitter months, earning the lasting mistrust of the establishment. By the 1930s, the Japanese, frustrated at being passed over for advancement because they were nonwhite, began to move from the plantations, opening retail stores and small businesses. By World War II they owned 50 percent of retail stores and accounted for 56 percent of household domestics. Many became small farmers, especially in Kona, where they began to grow coffee. They also accounted for Hawaii's fledgling fishing fleet and would brave the deep waters in their small, seaworthy sampans. Like the Chinese, they were committed to bettering themselves and placed education above all else. Unlike the Chinese, they did not marry outside their ethnic group and remained relatively racially intact.

Americans of Japanese Ancestry (AJAs)

Parents of most Japanese children born in Hawaii before World War II were *issei* (first generation), who considered themselves apart from other Americans and clung to the notion of "we Japanese." They held traditional beliefs of unwavering family loyalty, and to propagate their values and customs they supported Japanese-language schools, which 80 percent of their children attended before the war. This group, who were never "disloyal," were, however, proud of being Japanese. Some diehards even refused to believe Japan lost World War II and were shamed by their former homeland's unconditional surrender.

Their children, the *nissei* or second generation, were a different breed altogether. In one generation they had become Americans, and they put into practice the high Japanese virtues of obligation, duty, and loyalty to the homeland; that homeland was now unquestionably America. After Pearl Harbor was bombed, many people were terrified that the Hawaiian Japanese would be disloyal to America and would serve as spies and even as advance combatants for imperial Japan. The FBI kept close tabs on the Japanese community, and the menace of the "enemy within" prompted the decision to place Hawaii under martial law for the duration of the war. Because of their sheer numbers it was impossible to place the Hawaiian Japanese into concentration camps as was done in California, but prejudice and suspicion toward them, especially from Mainland military personnel, was fierce. It has since been noted that not a single charge of espionage or sabotage was ever reported against the Japanese community in Hawaii during the war.

AJAs as GIs

Although Japanese had formed a battalion during World War I, they were insulted by being considered unacceptable as American soldiers in World War II. Those already in the armed services were relieved of any duty involving weapons. People who knew better supported the AJAs. One was Jack Burns, a Honolulu policeman, who stated unequivocally that the AJAs were trustworthy. They never forgot his support,

and thanks to a huge Japanese vote he was later elected governor. Some Japanese-Americans volunteered to serve in labor battalions, and because of their flawless work and loyalty, it was decided to put out a call for a few hundred volunteers to form a combat unit. More than 10,000 signed up!

AJAs formed two distinguished units in World War II: the 100th Infantry Battalion and, later, the 442nd Regimental Combat Team. They landed in Italy at Salerno and even fought from Guadalcanal to Okinawa. The 442nd distinguished themselves as *the* most decorated unit in American military history. They made excellent newspaper copy; their exploits hit front pages around the nation. They were immortalized as the rescuers of a Texas company pinned down during the Battle of the Bulge. These Texans became known as "The Lost Battalion" and have periodic reunions with the AJA GIs who risked and lost so much to bring them to safety.

The AJAs Return

The AJAs returned home to a grateful country. In Hawaii, at first, they were accused of being cocky. Actually, they were refusing to revert to the pre-war status of second-class citizens and began to assert their rights as citizens who had defended their country. Many took advantage of the GI Bill and received college educations. The Big Five corporations for the first time accepted former AJA officers as executives, and the old order began to wobble. Many Japanese became involved in Hawaiian politics, and the first elected member to Congress was Daniel Inouye, who had lost an arm fighting in the war. Hawaii's former governor, George Ariyoshi, elected in 1974, was the country's first Japanese-American to reach such high office. Most Japanese, even as they climb the economic ladder, tend to remain Democrats.

Today, one out of every two political offices in Hawaii is held by a Japanese American. In one of those weird quirks of fate, it is now the Hawaiian Japanese who are accused by other ethnic groups of engaging in unfair political practices—nepotism and discrimination. It's often heard that "if you're not Japanese, forget about getting a government job." Many of these accusations against AJAs are undoubtedly motivated by jealousy, but their record of social fairness is

The Japanese-American GIs returned as "our boys."

not without blemish, and true to their custom of family loyalty, they do stick together. Heavily into the "professions," they're committed to climbing the social ladder. The AJAs of Hawaii, now indistinguishable from "the establishment," enjoy a higher standard of living than most and are motivated to get the best education possible for their children. They are the least likely of any ethnic group to marry outside of their group—especially the men. There are now 250,000 people of Japanese ancestry in Hawaii, nearly one-quarter of the state's population.

CAUCASIANS

White people have a distinction separating them from all other ethnic groups in Hawaii: they are all lumped together as one. You can be anything from a Protestant Norwegian dockworker to a Greek Orthodox shipping tycoon, but if your skin is white, in Hawaii, you're a *haole*. What's more, you could have arrived at Waikiki from Missoula, Montana, in the last 24 hours, or your *kama'aina* family can go back five generations, but again, if you're white, you're a *haole*.

The word *haole* has a floating connotation that depends upon the spirit in which it's used. It can mean anything from a derisive "honky" or "cracker" to nothing more than "white person." The exact Hawaiian meaning is clouded, but some say it meant "a man of no background," because white people couldn't chant a genealogical *ha'i kupuna* telling the Hawaiians who they were. The word eventually evolved to mean "foreign white man" and today simply "white person."

White History
Next to Hawaiians themselves, white people have the oldest stake in Hawaii. They've been there as settlers in earnest since the missionaries of the 1820s, and were established long before any other migrant group. From the 1800s until statehood, old *haole* families owned and controlled almost everything, and although they were generally benevolent, philanthropic, and paternalistic, they were also racist. They felt (not without certain justification) they had "made" Hawaii, and, consequently, that they had the right to rule. These established *kama'aina* families, many of whom made up the boards of the

Big Five corporations or owned huge plantations, formed an inner social circle closed to the outside except through marriage.

Their paternalism, which they accepted with grave responsibility, at first only extended to the Hawaiians, who saw them as replacing their own *ali'i*. Asians were primarily considered instruments of production. These supremacist attitudes tended to drag on in Hawaii until quite recent times. Today, they're responsible for the sometimes sour relations between white and nonwhite people in the islands. Since the *haole* had the power over other ethnic groups for so long, they have offended each group at one time or another. Today, all individual white people are resented to a certain degree because of these past acts, even though they personally were in no way involved.

White Plantation Workers
In the 1880s, the white landowners looked around and felt surrounded and outnumbered by Asians. Many figured these people would one day be a political force to be reckoned with, so they tried to import white people for plantation work. Some of the imported workers included: 600 Scandinavians in 1881; 1,400 Germans 1881–85; 400 Poles 1897–98; and 2,400 Russians 1909–12. None worked out. Europeans were accustomed to much higher wages and better living conditions than provided on the plantations. Although they were workers, not considered the equals of the ruling elite, they were expected to act like a special class and were treated preferentially, receiving higher wages for the same jobs performed by Asians. Even so, many proved troublesome to the landowners, unwilling to work under the prevailing conditions; they were especially resentful of Hawaiian *luna*. Most moved quickly to the Mainland, and the Poles and Russians even staged strikes after only months on the job. A contingency of Scots, who first came as mule skinners and gained a reputation for hard work and frugality, became successful plantation managers and supervisors. There were so many on the Hamakua Coast of the Big Island that it was dubbed the "Scotch Coast." The Germans and Scandinavians were well received and climbed the social ladder rapidly, becoming professionals and skilled workers.

The Depression years, not as economically disastrous in Hawaii as in the continental United States, brought many Mainland whites seeking opportunity, mostly from the South and the West. These new people tended to be even more racist toward brown-skinned people and Asians than the *kama'aina haole*. They made matters worse and competed intensely for jobs. The racial tension generated during this period came to a head in 1932 with the infamous "Massie Rape Case."

The Massie Rape Case

Thomas Massie, a naval officer, and his young wife Thalia attended a party at the Officers Club. After drinking and dancing all evening, they got into a row and Thalia rushed out in a huff. A few hours later, Thalia was at home, confused and hysterical, claiming to have been raped by some local men. On the most circumstantial evidence, Joseph Kahahawai and four friends of mixed ethnic background were accused. In a highly controversial trial rife with racial tensions, the verdict ended in a hung jury.

While a new trial was being set, Kahahawai and his friends were out on bail. Seeking revenge, Thomas Massie and Grace Fortescue, Thalia's mother, kidnapped Joseph Kahahawai with a plan of extracting a confession from him. They were aided by two enlisted men assigned to guard Thalia. While questioning Kahahawai, they killed him and attempted to dump his body in the sea but were apprehended. Another controversial trial—this time for Mrs. Fortescue, Massie, and the accomplices—followed. Clarence Darrow, the famous lawyer, sailed to Hawaii to defend them. For killing Kahahawai, these people served *one hour* of imprisonment in the judge's private chambers. The other four, acquitted with Joseph Kahahawai, maintain innocence of the rape to this day. Later, the Massies divorced, and Thalia went on to become a depressed alcoholic who took her own life.

The Portuguese

The last time anyone looked, Portugal was still attached to the European continent, but for some anomalous reason the Portuguese weren't considered *haole* in Hawaii for the longest time. This was because they weren't part of the ruling elite, but merely workers, showing that at one time the word *haole* implied social standing and not just skin color. About 12,000 arrived 1878–87 and another 6,000 came 1906–13. They were accompanied during the latter period by 8,000 Spanish, who were considered one and the same. Most of the Portuguese were illiterate peasants from Madeira and the Azores, while the Spanish hailed from Andalusia. The majority of Spanish and some Portuguese tended to leave for California as soon as they made passage money. Those who remained were well received because they were white, but not *haole,* making a perfect "buffer" ethnic group. Unlike other Europeans, they would take any job, worked hard, and accepted authority. Committed to staying in Hawaii, they rose to be skilled workers and the *luna* class on the plantations. However, the Portuguese did not invest as much in education and became very racist toward the upwardly mobile Asians, regarding them as a threat to their job security.

By 1920, the 27,000 Portuguese made up 11 percent of the population. After that they tended to blend with the other ethnic groups and weren't counted separately. Portuguese men tended to marry within their ethnic group, but a good portion of Portuguese women married other white men and became closer to the *haole* group, while another large portion chose Hawaiian mates and grew farther away.

Although they didn't originate pidgin English, the unique melodious quality of their native tongue did give pidgin a certain lilt it has today. Also, the ukulele (which translates as "jumping flea") was closely patterned after the *cavaquinho,* a Portuguese stringed folk instrument.

The White Population

Today Caucasians make up the largest racial group in the islands at 33 percent of the population, or about 370,000 individuals. They are spread evenly throughout Kaua'i, O'ahu, Maui, and the Big Island, with much smaller percentages on Moloka'i and Lana'i. Numerically, the vast majority (265,000) live on O'ahu, in the more fashionable central valley and southeastern sections. Heavy white concentrations are also found on the Kihei and Ka'anapali coasts of Maui and the north Kona Coast of Hawaii. The white population is also the fastest growing in the islands because most people resettling in Hawaii are white Americans predominantly from the West Coast.

FILIPINOS AND OTHERS

The Filipinos who came to Hawaii brought high hopes of making personal fortunes and returning home as rich heroes; for most it was a dream that never came true. Filipinos had been American nationals ever since the Spanish-American War of 1898, and as such weren't subject to immigration laws that curtailed the importation of other Asian workers in the early 1900s. The first to arrive were 15 families in 1906, but a large number came in 1924 as strikebreakers. The majority were illiterate Ilocano peasants from the northern Philippines with about 10 percent Visayans from the central cities. The Visayans were not as hardworking or thrifty, but were much more sophisticated. From the first, Filipinos were looked down upon by all the other immigrant groups and were considered particularly uncouth by the Japanese. The value they placed on education was the least of any group, and even by 1930 only half could speak rudimentary English, while the majority remained illiterate. They were billeted in the worst housing, performed the most menial jobs, and were the last hired and first fired.

One big difference between Filipinos and other groups was that the men brought no Filipino women to marry, so they clung to the idea of returning home. In 1930 there were 30,000 men and only 360 women. This hopeless situation led to a great deal of prostitution and homosexuality. Many of these terribly lonely bachelors would feast and drink on weekends and engage in their gruesome but exciting pastime of cockfighting on Sunday. When some did manage to find wives, their mates were inevitably part Hawaiian. Today, there are still plenty of old Filipino bachelors who never managed to get home, and the Sunday cockfight remains a way of life.

Filipinos constitute 15 percent of Hawaii's population, with nearly three-quarters living on O'ahu. The largest concentration, however, is on Lana'i, where they make up 60 percent of that island's population. Some of these men are new arrivals with the same dream held by their countrymen for more than 70 years. Many visitors to Hawaii mistake Filipinos for Hawaiians because of their dark skin, and this is a minor irritant to both groups. Some streetwise Filipinos even claim to be Hawaiians, because being Hawaiian is "in" and goes over well with tourists, especially young women. For the most part, these people are hardworking, dependable laborers who do tough work for little recognition. They remain low on the social totem pole and have not yet organized politically to stand up for their rights.

Other Groups

About 11 percent of Hawaii's population is a conglomerate of other ethnic groups. Of these, one of the largest and fastest growing is Korean, with 25,000 people. About 8,000 Koreans came to Hawaii from 1903 to 1905, when their government halted emigration. During the same period about 6,000 Puerto Ricans arrived, but they have become so assimilated that only 4,000 people in Hawaii today consider themselves Puerto Rican. There were also two attempts made in the 19th century to import other Polynesians to strengthen the dying Hawaiian race, but they were failures. In 1869 only 126 central Polynesian natives could be lured to Hawaii, and from 1878 to 1885, 2,500 Gilbert Islanders arrived. Both groups became immediately disenchanted with Hawaii. They pined for their own islands and departed for home as soon as possible.

Today, however, 15,000 Samoans have settled in Hawaii, and with more on the way they are the fastest growing minority in the state. For inexplicable reasons, Samoans and native Hawaiians get along extremely poorly and have the worst racial tensions and animosity of any groups. The Samoans ostensibly should represent the archetypal Polynesians that the Hawaiians are seeking, but it doesn't work that way. Samoans are criticized by Hawaiians for their hot tempers, lingering feuds, and petty jealousies. They're clannish and are often the butt of "dumb" jokes. This racism seems especially ridiculous, but that's the way it is.

Just to add a bit more exotic spice to the stew, there are about 27,000 blacks, 5,000 Native Americans, and 6,000 Vietnamese refugees living on the islands.

LANGUAGE

Hawaii is part of the United States, and people speak English there, but that's not the whole story. If you turn on the TV to catch the evening news, you'll hear "Walter Cronkite" English, unless of course you happen to tune in to a Japanese-language broadcast designed for tourists from that country. You can easily pick up a Chinese-language newspaper or groove to the music on a Filipino radio station, but let's not confuse the issue. All your needs and requests at airports, car rental agencies, restaurants, hotels, or wherever you happen to travel will be completely understood, as well as answered, in English. However, when you happen to overhear islanders speaking, what they're saying will sound somewhat familiar but you won't be able to pick up all the words, and the beat and melody of the language will be noticeably different.

Hawaii—like New England, the Deep South, and the Midwest—has its own unmistakable linguistic regionalism. All the ethnic peoples who make up Hawaii have enriched the English spoken there with words, expressions, and subtle shades of meaning that are commonly used and understood throughout the islands. The greatest influence on English has come from the Hawaiian language itself, and words such as "aloha," "hula," and "lu'au" are familiarly used and understood by most Americans.

Other migrant peoples, especially the Chinese, Japanese, and Portuguese, influenced the local dialect to such an extent that the simplified plantation lingo they spoke has become known as "pidgin." A fun and enriching part of the "island experience" is picking up a few words of Hawaiian and pidgin. English is the official language of the state, business, education, and perhaps even the mind; but pidgin is the language of the people, the emotions, and life, while Hawaiian remains the language of the heart and the soul.

Note: Many Hawaiian words are commonly used in English, appear in English dictionaries, and therefore would ordinarily be subject to the rules of English grammar. The Hawaiian language, however, does not pluralize nouns by adding an "s"; the singular and plural are differentiated in context. For purposes of this book, and to highlight the Hawaiian culture, the Hawaiian style of pluralization will be followed for common Hawaiian words. The following are some examples of plural Hawaiian nouns treated this way in this book: *haole* (not haoles), hula, *kahuna,* lei, lu'au, and *nene.*

PIDGIN

The dictionary definition of pidgin is: a simplified language with a rudimentary grammar used as a means of communication between people speaking different languages. Hawaiian pidgin is a little more complicated than that. It had its roots during the plantation days of the 1800s when white owners and *luna* (foremen) had to communicate with recently arrived Chinese, Japanese, and Portuguese laborers. It was designed as a simple language of the here and now, and was primarily concerned with the necessary functions of working, eating, and sleeping. It has an economical noun-verb-object structure (although not necessarily in that order).

Hawaiian words make up most of pidgin's non-English vocabulary. It includes a good smattering of Chinese, Japanese, and Samoan; the distinctive rising inflection is provided by the melodious Mediterranean lilt of the Portuguese. Pidgin is not a stagnant language. It's kept alive by hip new words introduced by people who are "so radical," or especially by slang words introduced by teenagers. It's a colorful English, like "jive" or "ghettoese" spoken by American blacks, and it's as regionally unique as the speech of Cajuns from Louisiana's bayous. *Maka'ainana* of all socioethnic backgrounds can at least understand pidgin. Most islanders are proud of it, while some consider it low-class jargon. The Hawaiian House of Representatives has given pidgin an official sanction, and most people feel that it adds a real local style and should be preserved.

CAPSULE PIDGIN

The following are a few commonly used words and expressions that should give you an idea of pidgin. It really can't be written properly, merely approximated, but for now, *"Study da' kine an' bimbye it be mo' betta, brah! OK? Lesgo."*

an' den—and then? big deal; so what's next?

auntie—respected elderly woman

bad ass—very good

bimbye—after a while; bye and bye. "Bimbye, you learn pidgin."

blalah—brother, but actually only refers to a large, heavy-set, good-natured Hawaiian man

brah—all the bros in Hawaii are brahs; brother; pal. Used to call someone's attention. One of the most common words even among people who are not acquainted. After a fill-up at a gas station, a person would say "Tanks, brah."

chicken skin—goose bumps.

cockaroach—steal; rip off. If you really want to find out what *cockaroach* means, just leave your camera on your beach blanket when you take a little dip.

da' kine—a catchall word of many meanings that epitomizes the essence of pidgin. *Da' kine* is a euphemism for pidgin and is substituted whenever the speaker is at a loss for a word or just wants to generalize. It can mean: you know? watchamacallit; of that type.

geev um—give it to them; give them hell; go for it. Can be used as an encouragement. If a surfer is riding a great wave, the people on the beach might yell, "Geev um, brah!"

grinds—food

hana ho—again. Especially after a concert the audience shouts "hana ho" (one more!).

hele on—let's get going.

howzit?—as in "howzit, brah?" what's happening? how's it going? The most common greeting, used in place of the more formal "How do you do?"

huhu—angry! "You put the make on the wrong da' kine wahine, brah, and you in da' kine trouble if you get one big Hawaiian blalah plenty huhu."

lesgo—Let's go! Do it!

li'dis an' li'dat—like this or that; a catch-all grouping especially if you want to avoid details; like, ya' know?

lolo buggah—stupid or crazy guy (person). Words to a tropical island song go, "I want to find the lolo who stole my pakalolo."

mo' bettah—better, real good! great idea. An island sentiment used to be, "mo' bettah you *come* Hawaii." Now it has subtly changed to, "mo' bettah you *visit* Hawaii."

ono—number one! delicious; great; groovy. "Hawaii is ono, brah!"

pakalolo—literally "crazy smoke"; marijuana; grass; reefer.

pakiki head—stubborn; bull-headed

pau—a Hawaiian word meaning finished; done; over and done with. *Pau hana* means end of work or quitting time. Once used by plantation workers, now used by everyone.

seestah—sister, female

shaka—hand wave where only the thumb and baby finger stick out, meaning thank you, all right!

sleepah—slippers, flip-flops, zori

stink face—(or stink eye) basically frowning at someone; using facial expression to show displeasure. Hard looks. What you'll get if you give local people a hard time.

swell head—burned up; angry

talk story—spinning yarns; shooting the breeze; throwing the bull; a rap session. If you're lucky enough to be around to hear *kupuna* (elders) "talk story," you can hear some fantastic tales in the tradition of old Hawaii.

tanks, brah—thanks, thank you.

to da max—all the way.

waddascoops—what's the scoop? what's up? what's happening?

Pidgin Lives

Pidgin is first learned at school, where all students, regardless of background, are exposed to it. The pidgin spoken by young people today is "fo' real" different from that of their parents. It's no longer only plantation talk but has moved to the streets and picked up some sophistication. At one time there was an academic movement to exterminate it, but that idea died away with the same thinking that insisted on making left-handed people write with their right hand. It is strange, however, that pidgin has become the unofficial language of Hawaii's grassroots movement, when it actually began as a white owners' language that was used to supplant Hawaiian and all other languages brought to the islands.

Although hip young *haole* use pidgin all the time, it has gained the connotation of being the language of the nonwhite locals, and is part of the "us against them" way of thinking. All local people, *haole* or not, consider pidgin their own island language, and don't really like it when it's used by *malihini* (newcomers). If you're in the islands long enough, you don't have to bother learning pidgin; it'll learn you. There's a book sold all over the islands called *Pidgin to da Max*, written by (you guessed it) a *haole* from Nebraska named Doug Simonson. You might not be able to understand what's being said by locals speaking pidgin (that's usually the idea), but you should be able to *feel* what's meant.

HAWAIIAN

The Hawaiian language sways like a palm tree in a gentle wind. Its words are as melodious as a love song. Linguists say that you can learn a lot about people through their language; when you hear Hawaiian you think of gentleness and love, and it's hard to imagine the ferocious side so evident in Hawaii's past. With its many Polynesian root words easily traced to Indonesian and Malay, Hawaiian is obviously from this same stock. The Hawaiian spoken today is very different from old Hawaiian. Its greatest metamorphosis occurred when the missionaries began to write it down in the 1820s. There is a movement to reestablish the Hawaiian language, and courses in it are offered at the University of Hawai'i. Many scholars have put forth translations of Hawaiian, but there are endless, volatile disagreements in the academic sector about the real meanings of Hawaiian words. Hawaiian is, by and large, no longer spoken as a language except on Ni'ihau and in Hawaiian-language immersion classes, and the closest tourists will come to it is in place-names, street names, and words that have become part of common usage, such as "aloha" and "mahalo." A few old Hawaiians still speak it at home and there are sermons in Hawaiian at some local churches. Kawaiaha'o Church in downtown Honolulu is the most famous of these.

Wiki Wiki Hawaiian

Thanks to the missionaries, the Hawaiian language is rendered phonetically using only 12 letters. They are the five vowels, a-e-i-o-u, sounded as they are in Italian, and seven consonants, h-k-l-m-n-p-w, sounded exactly as they are in English. Sometimes "w" is pronounced as "v," but this only occurs in the middle of a word and always follows a vowel. A consonant is always followed by a vowel, forming two-letter syllables, but vowels are often found in pairs or even triplets. A slight oddity about Hawaiian is the glottal stop, called *'okina* in Hawaiian. This is an abrupt break in sound in the middle of a word, such as "oh-oh" in English, and is denoted in this book by a reverse apostrophe ('). A good example is *ali'i* or, even better, the O'ahu town of Ha'iku, which actually means "Abrupt Break."

Pronunciation Key

For those unfamiliar with the sounds of Italian or other Romance languages, the vowels are sounded as follows:

A—in stressed syllables, pronounced as in "ah" (that feels good!). For example, Haleakala is pronounced "hah-lay-AH-kah-lah." Unstressed syllables are pronounced "uh" as in "again" or "above." For example, Kamehameha would be "kuh-MAY-huh-MAY-huh."

E—short "e" is "eh," as in "pen" or "dent" (thus *hale* is "HAH-leh"). Long "e" sounds like "ay" as in "sway" or "day." For example, the Hawaiian goose *(nene)* is a "nay-nay," not a "nee-nee."

I—pronounced "ee" as in "see" or "we" (thus *pali* is pronounced "PAH-lee").

O—pronounced as in "no" or "oh," such as "KOH-uh" (koa) or "OH-noh" (ono).

U—pronounced "oo" as in "do" or "stew"; for example, "KAH-poo" *(kapu)* or "POO-nuh" (Puna).

Diphthongs

Eight vowel pairs are known as "diphthongs" (ae-ai-ao-au-ei-eu-oi-ou). These are the sounds made by gliding from one vowel to another within a syllable. The stress is placed on the first vowel. In English, examples would be s**oi**l and b**ai**l. Common examples in Hawaiian are lei (lay) and *heiau* (hayee-aoo).

CAPSULE HAWAIIAN GLOSSARY

The list on the following pages gives you a "taste" of Hawaiian and provides a basic vocabulary of words in common usage that you are likely to hear. Becoming familiar with them is not a strict necessity, but they will definitely enhance your experience and make talking with local people more congenial. Many islanders spice their speech with certain words, especially when they're speaking "pidgin," and you too can use them just as soon as you feel comfortable. You might even discover some Hawaiian words that are so perfectly expressive they'll become regular parts of your vocabulary. Many Hawaiian words have been absorbed into the English dictionary. The definitions given are not exhaustive, but are generally considered the most common.

Words marked with an asterisk (*) are used commonly throughout the islands.

'a'a rough clinker lava. 'A'a has become the correct geological term to describe this type of lava found anywhere in the world.

'ae—yes

ahupua'a—pie-shaped land divisions running from mountain to sea that were governed by *konohiki,* local *ali'i* who owed their allegiance to a reigning chief

aikane—friend; pal; buddy

'aina—land; the binding spirit to all Hawaiians. Love of the land is paramount in traditional Hawaiian beliefs.

akamai—smart; clever; wise

akua—a god, or simply "divine." You'll hear people speak of their family or personal

ali'i—a Hawaiian chief or noble

aloha*—the most common greeting in the islands; can mean both hello and good-bye, welcome and farewell. It can also mean romantic love, affection, or best wishes.

'a'ole—no

'aumakua—a personal or family god, often an ancestral spirit

auwe—alas; ouch! When a great chief or loved one died, it was a traditional wail of mourning.

'awa,—also known as *kava,* a mildly intoxicating traditional drink made from the juice of chewed 'awa root, spat into a bowl, and used in religious ceremonies

halakahiki—pineapple

hale*—house or building; often combined with other words to name a specific place, such as Haleakala (House of the Sun), or Hale Pa'i at Lahainaluna, meaning Printing House

hana*—work; combined with *pau* means end of work or quitting time

hanai—literally "to feed." Part of the true aloha spirit. A *hanai* is a permanent guest, or an adopted family member, usually an old person or a child. This is an enduring cultural phenomenon in Hawaii, in which a child from one family (perhaps that of a brother or sister, and quite often one's grandchild) is raised as one's own without formal adoption.

haole*—a word that at one time meant foreigner, but which now means a white person or Caucasian. Many etymological definitions have been put forth, but none satisfies everyone. Some feel that it signified a person without a background, because the first white men could not chant their genealogies as was common to Hawaiians.

hapa*—half, as in a mixed-blooded person being referred to as *hapa haole*

hapai*—pregnant; used by all ethnic groups when a *keiki* is on the way

haupia*—a coconut custard dessert often served at a lu'au

heiau*—A platform made of skillfully fitted rocks, upon which temporary structures were built as temples and offerings made to the gods.

holomu*—an ankle-length dress that is much more fitted than a mu'umu'u, and which is often worn on formal occasions

hono—bay, as in Honolulu (Sheltered Bay)

honu—green sea turtle; endangered

ho'oilo—traditional Hawaiian winter that began in November

ho'olaulea—any happy event, but especially a family outing or picnic

ho'omalimali*—sweet talk; flattery

huhu*—angry; irritated

hui*—a group; meeting; society. Often used to refer to Chinese businesspeople or family members who pool their money to get businesses started.

hukilau—traditional shoreline fish-gathering in which everyone lends a hand to *huki* (pull) the huge net. Anyone taking part shares in the *lau* (food). It is much more like a party than hard work, and if you're lucky you'll be able to take part in one.

(continued on next page)

CAPSULE HAWAIIAN GLOSSARY
(continued)

hula*—a native Hawaiian dance in which the rhythm of the islands is captured by swaying hips and stories told by lyrically moving hands. A *halau* is a group or school of hula.

huli huli—barbecue, as in *huli huli* chicken

i'a—fish in general. *I'a maka* is raw fish.

imu*—underground oven filled with hot rocks and used for baking. The main cooking method featured at a lu'au, used to steam-bake pork and other succulent dishes. The tending of the *imu* was traditionally for men only.

ipo—sweetheart; lover; girl- or boyfriend

kahili—a tall pole topped with feathers, resembling a huge feather duster. It was used by an *ali'i* to announce his or her presence.

kahuna*—priest; sorcerer; doctor; skillful person. In old Hawaii *kahuna* had tremendous power, which they used for both good and evil. The *kahuna ana'ana* was a feared individual because he practiced "black magic" and could pray a person to death, while the *kahuna lapa'au* was a medical practitioner bringing aid and comfort to the people.

kai—the sea. Many businesses and hotels employ *kai* as part of their name.

kalua—means roasted underground in an *imu*. A favorite island food is *kalua* pork.

kama'aina*—a child of the land; an old-timer; a longtime island resident of any ethnic background; a resident of Hawaii or native son or daughter. Hotels and airlines often offer discounts called *"kama'aina* rates" to anyone who can prove island residency.

kanaka—man or commoner; later used to distinguish a Hawaiian from other races. Tone of voice can make it a derisive expression.

kane*—means man, but actually used to signify a relationship such as husband or boyfriend. Written on a lavatory door it means "men's room."

kapu*—forbidden; taboo; keep out; do not touch

kupuna—a grandparent or old-timer; usually means someone who has gained wisdom. The statewide school system now invites *kupuna* to talk to the children about the old ways and methods.

kaukau*—slang word meaning food or chow; grub. Some of the best food in Hawaii comes from the *kaukau* wagons, trucks that sell plate lunches and other morsels.

kauwa—a landless, untouchable caste once confined to living on reservations. Members of this caste were often used as human sacrifices at *heiau*. Calling someone *kauwa* is still a grave insult.

kava—(see *'awa*)

keiki*—child or children; used by all ethnic groups. "Have you hugged your *keiki* today?"

kiawe—an algaroba tree from South America commonly found in Hawaii along the shore. It grows a nasty long thorn that can easily puncture a tire. Legend has it that the trees were introduced to the islands by a misguided missionary who hoped the thorns would coerce natives into wearing shoes. Actually, they are good for fuel, as fodder for hogs and cattle, and for reforestation, none of which you'll appreciate if you step on one of the thorns or flatten a tire on your rental car!

ko'ala*—any food that has been broiled or barbecued

kokua—help. As in "Your *kokua* is needed to keep Hawaii free from litter."

kona wind*—a muggy subtropical wind that blows from the south and hits the leeward side of the islands. It usually brings sticky hot weather and one of the few times when air-conditioning will be appreciated.

konane—a traditional Hawaiian game, similar to checkers, played with pebbles on a large flat stone used as a board

ko'olau—windward side of the island

kukui—a candlenut tree whose pods are polished and then strung together to make a beautiful lei. Traditionally the oil-rich nuts were strung on the rib of a coconut leaf and used as a candle.

kuleana—homesite; the old homestead; small farms. Especially used to describe the small spreads on Hawaiian Homes Lands on Moloka'i.

Kumulipo*—ancient Hawaiian genealogical chant that records the pantheon of gods, creation, and the beginning of humankind

la—the sun. Often combined with other words to be more descriptive, such as *La*haina (Merciless Sun) or Haleaka*la* (House of the Sun).

lanai*—veranda or porch. You'll pay more for a hotel room if it has a lanai with an ocean view.

lani—sky or the heavens

lau hala*—traditional Hawaiian weaving of mats,

hats, etc., from the prepared fronds of the pandanus (screw pine)

lei*—a traditional garland of flowers or vines. One of Hawaii's most beautiful customs. Given at any auspicious occasion, but especially when arriving or leaving Hawaii.

lele—the stone altar at a *heiau*

limu—edible seaweed of various types. Gathered from the shoreline, it makes an excellent salad. It's used to garnish many island dishes and is a favorite at lu'au.

lomi lomi—traditional Hawaiian massage; also, raw salmon made into a vinegared salad with chopped onion and spices

lua*—the toilet; the head; the bathroom

luakini—a human-sacrifice temple. Introduced to Hawaii in the 13th century at Waha'ula Heiau on the Big Island.

lu'au*—a Hawaiian feast featuring poi, *imu*-baked pork, and other traditional foods. Good ones provide some of the best gastronomic delights in the world.

luna—foreman or overseer in the plantation fields. They were often mounted on horseback and were renowned for either their fairness or their cruelty. Representing the middle class, they served as a buffer between plantation workers and white plantation owners.

mahalo*—thank you. *Mahalo nui* means "big thanks" or "thank you very much."

mahele—division. The "Great Mahele" of 1848 changed Hawaii forever when the traditional common lands were broken up into privately owned plots.

mahimahi*—a favorite eating fish. Often called a dolphin, but a mahimahi is a true fish, not a cetacean.

mahu—a homosexual; often used derisively like "fag" or "queer"

maile—a fragrant vine used in traditional lei. It looks ordinary but smells delightful.

maka'ainana—a commoner; a person "belonging" to the '*aina* (land), who supported the *ali'i* by fishing and farming and as a warrior

makai*—toward the sea; used by most islanders when giving directions

make—dead; deceased

malihini*—what you are if you have just arrived: a newcomer; a tenderfoot; a recent arrival

malo—the native Hawaiian loincloth. Never worn anymore except at festivals or pageants.

mana*—power from the spirit world; innate energy of all things animate or inanimate; the grace of god. Mana could be passed on from one person to another, or even stolen. Great care had to be taken to protect the *ali'i* from having their *mana* defiled. Commoners were required to lie flat on the ground and cover their faces whenever a great *ali'i* approached. *Kahuna* were often employed in the regaining or transference of *mana*.

manini—stingy; tight; a Hawaiianized word taken from the name of Don Francisco *Marin,* who was instrumental in bringing many fruits and plants to Hawaii. He was known for never sharing any of the bounty from his substantial gardens on Vineyard Street in Honolulu; therefore, his name came to mean "stingy."

manuahi—free; gratis; extra

mauka*—toward the mountains; used by most islanders when giving directions

mauna—mountain. Often combined with other words to be more descriptive, such as Mauna Kea (White Mountain)

mele—a song or chant in the Hawaiian oral tradition that records the history and genealogies of the *ali'i*

menehune—the legendary "little people" of Hawaii. Like leprechauns, they are said to shun humans and possess magical powers. Stone walls said to have been completed in one night are often attributed to them. Some historians argue that they actually existed and were the aboriginals of Hawaii, inhabiting the islands before the coming of the Polynesians.

moa—chicken; fowl

moana*—the ocean; the sea. Many businesses and hotels as well as places have *moana* as part of their name.

moe—sleep

mo'olelo—ancient tales kept alive by the oral tradition and recited only by day

mu'umu'u*—a "Mother Hubbard," an ankle-length dress with a high neckline introduced by the missionaries to cover the nakedness of the Hawaiians. It has become fashionable attire for almost any occasion in Hawaii.

nani—beautiful

nui—big; great; large; as in *mahalo nui* (thank you very much)

'ohana—a family; the fundamental social division; extended family. Now often used to denote a social organization with grassroots overtones.

(continued on next page)

CAPSULE HAWAIIAN GLOSSARY
(continued)

'okolehau—literally "iron bottom"; a traditional booze made from *ti* root. *'Okole* means "rear end" and *hau* means "iron," which was descriptive of the huge blubber pots in which *'okolehau* was made. Also, if you drink too much it'll surely knock you on your *'okole*.

oli—chant not done to a musical accompaniment.

ono*—delicious; delightful; the best. *Ono ono* means "extra or absolutely delicious."

'opihi—a shellfish or limpet that clings to rocks and is gathered as one of the islands' favorite *pu pu*. Custom dictates that you never remove all of the *'opihi* from a rock; some are always left to grow for future generations.

'opu—belly; stomach

pahoehoe*—smooth, ropey lava that looks like burnt pancake batter. It is now the correct geological term used to describe this type of lava found anywhere in the world.

pakalolo—"crazy smoke"; grass; smoke; dope; marijuana

pake—a Chinese person. Can be derisive, depending on tone in which it is used. It is a bastardization of the Chinese word meaning "uncle."

pali*—a cliff; precipice. Hawaii's geology makes them quite common. The most famous are the *pali* of Oahu where a major battle was fought.

paniolo*—a Hawaiian cowboy. Derived from the Spanish *español*. The first cowboys brought to Hawaii during the early 19th century were Mexicans from California.

papale—hat. Except for the feathered helmets of the *ali'i* warriors of old Hawaii, hats were generally not worn. However, once the islanders saw their practical uses and how fashionable they were, they began weaving them from various materials and quickly became experts at manufacture and design.

pa'u—long split skirt often worn by women when horseback riding. In the 1800s, an island treat was *pa'u* riders in their beautiful dresses at Kapi'olani Park in Honolulu. The tradition is carried on today at many of Hawaii's rodeos.

pau*—finished; done; completed. Often combined into *pau hana,* which means end of work or quitting time.

pilau—stink; bad smell; stench

pilikia—trouble of any kind, big or small; bad times

poi*—a glutinous paste made from the pounded corm of taro, which ferments slightly and has a light sour taste. Purplish in color, it's a staple at lu'au, where it is called "one-, two-, or three-finger" poi, depending upon its thickness.

pono—righteous or excellent

pua—flower

puka*—a hole of any size. *Puka* is used by all island residents, whether talking about a pinhole in a rubber boat or a tunnel through a mountain.

punalua—a traditional practice, before the missionaries arrived, of sharing mates. Western seamen took advantage of it, leading to the spread of contagious diseases and eventual rapid decline of the Hawaiian people.

pune'e*—bed; narrow couch. Used by all ethnic groups. To recline on a *pune'e* on a breezy lanai is a true island treat.

pu pu*—an appetizer; a snack; hors d'oeuvres; can be anything from cheese and crackers to sushi. Oftentimes, bars or nightclubs offer them free.

pupule—crazy; nuts; out of your mind

pu'u—hill, as in Pu'u 'Ula'ula (Red Hill)

tapa*—a traditional paper cloth made from beaten bark. Intricate designs were stamped in using beaters, and natural dyes added color. The tradition was lost for many years but is now making a comeback, and provides some of the most beautiful folk art in the islands. Also called Kapa.

taro*—the staple of old Hawaii. A plant with a distinctive broad leaf that produces a starchy root. It was brought by the first Polynesians and was grown on magnificently irrigated plantations. According to the oral tradition, the life-giving properties of taro hold mystical significance for Hawaiians, since it was created by the gods at about the same time as humans.

ti—a broad-leafed plant that was used for many purposes, from plates to hula skirts (never grass). Especially used to wrap religious offerings presented at the *heiau*.

tutu*—grandmother; granny; older woman. Used by all as a term of respect and endearment.

ukulele*—*uku* means "flea" and *lele* means "jumping," so literally "jumping flea"—the way the Hawaiians perceived the quick finger movements used on the banjo-like Portuguese folk instrument called a *cavaquinho*. The ukulele quickly became synonymous with the islands.

wahine*—young woman; female; girl; wife. Used by all ethnic groups. When written on a lavatory door it means "women's room."

wai—fresh water; drinking water

wela—hot. *Wela kahao* is a "hot time" or "making whoopee."

wiki*—quickly; fast; in a hurry. Often seen as *wiki wiki* (very fast), as in "Wiki Wiki Messenger Service."

USEFUL PHRASES

Aloha ahiahi—Good evening.
Aloha au ia 'oe—I love you!
Aloha kakahiaka—Good morning.
Aloha nui loa—much love; fondest regards
Hau'oli la hanau—Happy birthday
Hau'oli makahiki hou—Happy New Year
Komo mai—please come in; enter; welcome
Mele kalikimaka—Merry Christmas
'Okole maluna—bottoms up; salute; cheers; kampai

Stress

The best way to learn which syllables are stressed in Hawaiian is by listening closely. It becomes obvious after a while. Also, some vowel sounds are held longer than others; these can occur at the beginning of a word, such as the first "a" in *'aina* (land), or in the middle of a word, like the first "a" in *lanai* (veranda). Again, it's a matter of tuning your ear and paying attention. No one is going to give you a hard time if you mispronounce a word. It's good, however, to pay close attention to the pronunciation of street and place-names, because many Hawaiian words sound alike and a misplaced vowel here or there could be the difference between getting where you want to go and getting lost.

RELIGION

The Lord saw fit to keep His island paradise secret from humans for a few million years, but once we finally arrived we were awfully thankful. Hawaii sometimes seems like a floating tabernacle; everywhere you look there's a church, temple, shrine, or *heiau*. The islands are either a very holy place, or there's a powerful lot of sinning going on that would require so many houses of prayer. Actually, it's just America's "right to worship" concept fully employed in microcosm. All the peoples who came to Hawaii brought their own forms of devotion. The Polynesian Hawaiians praised the primordial creators, Wakea and Papa, from whom their pantheon of animistically inspired gods sprang. Obviously, to a modern world these old gods would never do. There were simply too many, and belief in them was looked down upon as mere superstition, the folly of semicivilized pagans. So, the famous missionaries of the 1820s brought Congregational Christianity and the "true path" to heaven.

Inconveniently, the Catholics, Mormons, Reformed Mormons, Adventists, Episcopalians, Unitarians, Christian Scientists, Lutherans, Baptists, Jehovah's Witnesses, Salvation Army, and every other major and minor denomination of Christianity that followed in their wake brought their own brands of enlightenment and never quite agreed with each other. The Chinese and Japanese immigrants established all the major sects of Buddhism, Confucianism, Taoism, and Shintoism. Allah is praised, the Torah is chanted in Jewish synagogues, and nirvana is available at a variety of Hindu temples. If the spirit moves you, a Hare Krishna devotee will be glad to point you in the right direction and give you a free flower for only a dollar or two. If the world is still too much with you, you might find peace at a Church of Scientology, or meditate at a Kundalini yoga institute, or perhaps find relief at a local assembly of Baha'i. Anyway, rejoice, because in Hawaii you'll find not only paradise but perhaps salvation.

HAWAIIAN BELIEFS

The Polynesian Hawaiians worshipped nature. They saw its forces manifested in a multiplicity of forms to which they ascribed godlike powers.

Daily life was based on this animistic philosophy. Hand-picked and specially trained storytellers chanted the exploits of the gods. These ancient tales, kept alive in a special oral tradition called *mo'olelo,* were recited only by day. Entranced listeners encircled the chanter and, in respect for the gods and in fear of their wrath, were forbidden to move once the tale was begun. This was serious business during which a person's life could be at stake. It was not like the telling of *ka'ao,* which were simple fictions, tall tales, and yarns of ancient heroes, related for amusement and to pass the long nights. Any object, animate or inanimate, could be a god. All could be infused with mana, especially a dead body or a respected ancestor.

'Ohana had personal family gods called *'aumakua* on whom they called in times of danger or strife. There were children of gods, called *kupua,* who were thought to live among humans and were distinguished either for their beauty and strength or for their ugliness and terror. It was told that processions of dead *ali'i* called "Marchers of the Night" wandered through the land of the living, and unless you were properly protected it could mean death if they looked upon you. Simple ghosts known as *akua lapu* merely frightened people. Forests, waterfalls, trees, springs, and a thousand forms of nature were the manifestations of *akua li'i,* "little spirits" who could be invoked at any time for help or protection. It made no difference who or what you were in old Hawaii; the gods were ever-present and they took a direct and active role in your life.

Behind all of these beliefs was an innate sense of natural balance and order, and the idea that everything had its opposite—similar to the Asian idea of yin-yang. The time of darkness when only the gods lived was *po.* When the great gods descended to earth and created light, this was *ao,* and humanity was born. All of these *mo'olelo* are part of *The Kumulipo,* the great chant that records the Hawaiian version of creation. From the time the gods descended and touched earth at Ku Moku on Lana'i, the genealogies were kept. Unlike in the Bible, these included the noble families of female as well as male *ali'i.*

Heiau

A *heiau* is a Hawaiian temple. The basic *heiau* was a masterfully built and fitted rectangular stone wall that varied in size from about as big as a basketball court to as broad as a football field. Once the restraining outer walls were built, the interior was backfilled with smaller stones, and the top dressing was expertly laid and then rolled, perhaps with a log, to form a pavement-like surface. All that remains of Hawaii's many *heiau* are the stone platforms. The buildings upon them, made from perishable wood, leaves, and grass, have long since disappeared.

Some *heiau* were dreaded temples where human sacrifices were made. Tradition says that this barbaric custom began at Waha'ula Heiau on the Big Island in the 12th century and was introduced by a ferocious Tahitian priest named Pa'ao. Other *heiau,* such as Pu'uhonua O Honaunau, also on the Big Island, were temples of refuge where the weak, widowed, orphaned, and vanquished could find safety and sanctuary.

Within *heiau,* ceremonies were conducted by the priestly *kahuna.* Offerings of chickens, dogs, fish, fruit, and tapa were laid on the *lele,* a huge stone altar, in hopes the gods would act favorably toward the people. Some buildings held the bones of dead *ali'i,* infused with their mana. Other structures were god houses in which idols resided, while still others were oracle towers from which prophecies were made. The gods were honored by *ali'i* and *maka'ainana* alike, but the *kahuna* prayed for the *ali'i,* while the commoners represented themselves. There was a patron god for every aspect of life, especially farming and fishing, but gods could be invoked for everything from weaving to help for thieves! Men and women had their own gods, with rituals governing birth, cutting the umbilical cord, sickness, and death. Ceremonies, often lasting for many days, were conducted by *kahuna,* many of whom had highly specialized functions. Two of the most interesting were: *kahuna kilikilo,* who could see a person die in a dream and save his or her life through offerings of white dogs, chickens, tapa, and *'awa;* and *kahuna kaula,* semi-hermits who could foretell the future.

Idols

The Hawaiian people worshipped gods who took the form of idols fashioned from wood, feathers, or stone. Some figures were more than six feet tall and crowned with elaborate head pieces.

Figures were often pointed at the end so they could be stuck into the ground. The eyes were made from shells, and until these were inlaid, the idol was dormant. The hair used was often human hair, and the arms and legs were usually flexed. The mouth was either gaping or formed a wide figure-eight lying on its side, and more likely than not was lined with glistening dog teeth. Small figures were made of woven basketry, expertly covered with feathers. Red and yellow feathers were favorites taken from specific birds by men whose only work was to roam the forests in search of them.

GREAT GODS

Ku

The progenitors of the gods were Wakea, the "sky father," and Papa, the "earth mother," but the actual gods worshipped in Hawaii were Ku, Kane and Kanaloa, and Lono. Ku was a universal god who represented the male aspect of nature, and Hina, the moon goddess, was his female counterpart. Ku was prayed to at sunrise and Hina at sunset. Ku's maleness was represented with pointed stones, while flat ones symbolized Hina's womanhood. Ku ruled the forest, land, mountains, farming, and fishing—his benevolent side. But Ku was better known as the god of war. It was Ku who demanded human sacrifice, especially in times of calamity or in preparation for battle. At times, Ku was represented by an 'ohi'a log, and a human sacrifice was made in the forest where it was cut and also at the post hole that held it upright at the heiau. When Ku was invoked, the strict and serious ceremonies could go on for more than a week. The entire 'aha (assembly) kept complete silence and sat ramrod straight

Ku

with the left leg and hand crossed over the right leg and hand in an attitude called *ne'epu*. At a precise command everyone simultaneously pointed their right hands heavenward. Anyone caught dozing or daydreaming, or who for some reason missed the command, instantly became the main course for Ku's lunch.

Kamehameha the Great carried a portable Ku into battle with him at all times, and this statue was known as Kuka'ilimoku (the Snatcher of Lands). It was held that during battle this effigy, whose gaping mouth gleamed with canine incisors, would cry out in a loud voice and stir Kamehameha's warriors on to victory. After a battle, the slain enemies were taken to the *heiau* and placed upon Ku's altar with their arms encircling two pigs. Now Ku became Kuwahailo (of the Dripping Maggot Mouth). With Ku's killing nature appeased, the people would pray for good crops, good fishing, and fertile wives. The scales were balanced and life went on.

Kane and Kanaloa

Kane is the Hawaiian word for "man" or "husband," and he was the leading god worshipped when the missionaries arrived. God of life, ancestor of all Hawaiians, Kane is the center of the Hawaiian creation myth, whose events are amazingly similar to those of Genesis. Kane comes forward from *po* (darkness) into *ao* (light) and, with the help of Ku and Lono, fashions a man from clay gathered from the four cardinal points of the compass. Once the body is formed, the gods breathe (some say spit) into the mouth and nostrils and give it life. The man is placed upon a paradise island, *Kalani i hauola,* and a wife is fashioned for him out of his right side. Like Adam and Eve, these two break the law by eating from the forbidden tree and are driven from paradise by the sacred white albatross of Kane. Kane is a forgiving god who demands no human sacrifice, because all life is sacred to him. He is a god of a higher order, not usually rendered as an idol. Instead he was symbolized by a single upright male stone splashed with oil and wrapped in white tapa. Kanaloa, the antithesis of Kane, was represented as a great squid, and often likened to the Christian devil. He warred with Kane and was driven out of heaven along with his minions. Kanaloa became the ruler of the dead and was responsible for "black" sorcery and for poisonous things. However, these two gods were often linked together. For example, prayers would be offered to Kane when a canoe was built and to Kanaloa to provide favorable winds. Farmers and diviners often prayed simultaneously to Kane and Kanaloa. Both gods were intimately connected to water and the intoxicating beverage 'awa.

Pele

The Hawaiian gods were toppled literally and figuratively in 1819 and began to fade from the minds of people. Two that remained prominent were Madame Pele, the fire goddess, who resides at Kilauea Volcano on Hawaii, and the demigod Maui, who is like Paul Bunyan and Ulysses rolled into one. Many versions account for how Pele wound up living in the Kilauea fire pit, but they all follow a general outline. It seems the beautiful young goddess, from a large family of gods, was struck by wanderlust. Tucking her young sister, in the convenient form of an egg, under her armpit, she set out to see the world. Fortune had its ups and downs in store for young Pele. For one, she was ravished by a real swine, Kamapua'a the pig god. Moreover, she fought desperately with her sister, Namaka o Kahai, over the love of a handsome young chief; Pele's sister stalked her and smashed her bones on the Hana Coast of Maui at a spot called Kaiwi o Pele (the Bones of Pele).

Pulling herself back together, Pele set out to make a love nest for her lover and herself. She chose the fire pit at Kilauea Volcano and has long been held responsible for its lava flows, along with anything else that deals with heat or fire. Pele can change her form from a withered old woman to a ravishing beauty; her moods can change from gentle to fiery hot. She is traditionally appeased with 'ohelo berries cast into her fire pit, but lately she prefers juniper berries

in the form of gin. Pele's myth was shattered by the Hawaiian queen Keopuolani, one of the earliest and most fervent converts to Christianity. In the 1820s this brave queen made her way to Kilauea fire pit and defiantly ate the 'ohelo berries sacred to Pele. She then cast stones into the pit and cried in a loud voice, "Jehovah is my god . . . it is my God, not Pele, that kindled these fires."

Still, stories abound of Pele's continuing powers. Modern-day kahuna are always consulted and prayers offered over construction of an imu, which falls under Pele's fire domain. It's said by traditional Hawaiians and educated haole alike that when Kilauea erupts, the lava miraculously stops before or circles around a homestead over which proper prayers were made to the fire goddess. In addition, the rangers at Volcanoes National Park receive hundreds of stones every year that were taken as souvenirs and then returned by shaken tourists, who claim bad luck stalked them from the day they removed Pele's sacred stones from her volcano. And, no one who has lived in the islands for any length of time will carry pork over the volcano at night, lest they offend the goddess. She's perhaps still angry with that swine, Kamapua'a.

The Strifes of Maui

Of all the heroes and mythological figures of Polynesia, Maui is the best known. His "strifes" are like the great Greek epics, and they make excellent tales of daring that elders loved to relate to youngsters around the evening fire. Maui was abandoned by his mother, Hina of Fire, when he was an infant. She wrapped him in her hair and cast him upon the sea, where she expected him to die, but he lived and returned home to become her favorite. She knew then that he was a born hero and had strength far beyond that of ordinary mortals. His first exploit was to lift the sky. In those days the sky hung so low that humans had to crawl around on all fours. A seductive young woman approached Maui and asked him to use his great strength to lift the sky. In fine heroic fashion, this big boy agreed, if the beautiful woman would, euphemistically, "give him a drink from her gourd." He then obliged her by lifting the sky.

The territory of humankind was small at the time. Maui decided that more land was needed, so he conspired to "fish up islands." He descended into the land of the dead and petitioned an ancestress to fashion him a hook out of her jawbone. She obliged, creating the mythical hook *Manai ikalani*. Maui then secured a sacred *'alae* bird that he intended to use for bait and bid his brothers to paddle him far out to sea. When he arrived at the deepest spot, he lowered *Manai ikalani* baited with the sacred bird, and his sister, Hina of the Sea, placed it into the mouth of "Old One Tooth," who held land fast to the bottom of the waters. Maui then exhorted his brothers to row but warned them not to look back. They strained at the oars with all their might and slowly a great landmass rose. One brother, overcome by curiosity, looked back, and when he did so, the land shattered into all of the islands of Polynesia.

Maui desired to serve humankind further. People were without fire, the secret of which was held by the sacred *'alae* birds, who had learned it from Maui's beneficent mother. Hina of Fire gave Maui her burning fingernails, but he oafishly kept dropping them into streams until all had fizzled out and he had totally irritated his generous progenitor. She pursued Maui, trying to burn him to a cinder, and Maui desperately chanted for rain to put out her scorching fires. When she saw her fires being quenched, Hina hid her fire in the barks of special trees and informed common mudhens where they could be found, but first made them promise never to tell humans. Maui learned of this and captured a mudhen, threatening to wring its scrawny, traitorous neck unless it gave up the secret. The bird tried trickery and told Maui first to rub together the stems of sugarcane, then of banana and even of taro. None worked, and Maui's determined rubbing is why these plants have hollow roots today. Finally, with Maui's hands tightening around the mudhen's neck, the bird confessed fire could be found in the *hau* tree and also the sandalwood, which Maui named *'ili ahi* (fire bark) in its honor. Maui then rubbed all the feathers of the mudhen's head for being so deceitful, which is why their crowns are featherless today.

Maui's greatest deed, however, was in snaring the sun and exacting a promise that it would go slower across the heavens. The people complained that there were not enough daylight hours to fish or farm. Maui's mother could not dry her tapa cloth because the sun rose and set so quickly. When she asked her son to help, Maui went to his blind grandmother for assistance. She lived on the slopes of Haleakala and was responsible for cooking the sun's bananas, which he ate every day in passing. Maui kept stealing his granny's bananas until she agreed to help. She told him to personally weave 16 strong ropes with nooses from his sister's hair. Some say these came from her head, but other versions insist that it was no doubt Hina's pubic hair that had the power to hold the sun god. Maui positioned himself, and as each of the 16 rays of the sun came across Haleakala, he snared them until the sun was defenseless and had to bargain for his life. Maui agreed to free him if he promised to go more slowly. The sun agreed, and from that time forward Haleakala (The House of the Sun) became Maui's home.

Lono and the Makahiki Festival

Lono was a benevolent god of clouds, harvest, and rain. In a fit of temper he killed his wife, whom he thought unfaithful. When he discovered his grave error, he roamed the countryside challenging everyone he met to a boxing match. Boxing later became an event of the Makahiki, the Harvest Festival, which was held in his honor. Lono decided to leave his island home, but he promised one day to return on a floating island. Every year at the beginning of *ho'oilo* (winter), starting in October, the Makahiki was held. It was a jubilant time of harvest when taxes were collected and most *kapu* were lifted. It ended sometime in February, and then the new year began. During this time great sporting events included surfing, boxing, sledding, and a form of bowling. At night, people feasted at lu'au to the rhythm of drums and hula. Fertility was honored, and willing partners from throughout the land coupled and husbands and wives shared their mates in the tradition of *punalua*.

Lono's idol was an *akua loa,* a slender 15-foot pole with his small image perched atop. Another pole fastened at the top formed a cross. Hanging from the cross pole were long banners of white tapa cloth, and the pole was festooned with the feathers and skins of seabirds. To this image the *kahuna* offered red and white fish, black coconut, and immature *awa*. This image, called "Long God," traveled in a procession clockwise around

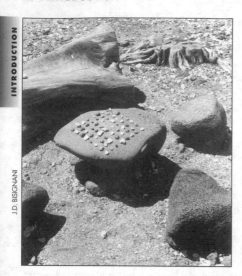

J.D. BISIGNANI

Konane *(Hawaiian checkers)* is often played during the Makahiki Festival

the island. It was met at every *ahupua'a* (land division) by the chief of that region, and new tapa was offered by the chieftess, along with roasted taro. The *maka'ainana* came and offered their produce from sea and land, and so the taxes were collected. At the end of the festival a naked man representing the god Kohoali'i ate the eyeball of a fish and one of a human victim and proclaimed the new year.

It was during the Makahiki that Captain Cook sailed into Kealakekua Bay. *Kahuna* saw his great "floating islands" and proclaimed the return of Lono. Uncannily, the masts of the sailing ships draped in canvas looked remarkably like Lono's idol. Cook himself was particularly tall and white-skinned, and at the sight of him, many natives fell to their knees and worshipped him as "Lono returned."

THE CASTE AND *KAPU* SYSTEM

All was not heavenly in paradise due to horrible wars, but the people mainly lived quiet, ordered lives based on a strict caste society and the *kapu* system. Famine was contained to a

regional level. The population was kept in check by herbal birth-control potions, crude abortions, and infanticide, especially of baby girls. The strict caste system was determined by birth, and there was no chance of changing one's status. The highest rank was the *ali'i,* the chiefs and royalty. The impeccable genealogies of the *ali'i* were traced back to the gods themselves and recorded in chants *(mo'o ali'i)* memorized and sung by professionals called *ku'auhau,* who were themselves *ali'i.* Ranking passed from both father and mother, and custom dictated that the first mating of an *ali'i* be with a person of equal status. After a child was produced, the *ali'i* was free to mate with lesser *ali'i* or even with a commoner. The custom of *punalua,* the sharing of mates, was practiced throughout Hawaiian society. Moreover, incest was not only condoned but sanctioned among *ali'i.* To conceive an offspring of the highest rank, *ni'au pi'o* (coconut leaf looped back on itself), the parents were required to be full brothers and sisters. These offspring were so sacred they were considered *akua* (living gods), and people of all ranks had to literally crawl on their stomachs in their presence. *Ali'i* who ran society's affairs were of lesser rank, and they were the real functionaries. The two most important were the land supervisors *(konohiki)* and caste priests *(kahuna).* The *konohiki* were in charge of the *ahupua'a,* pie-shaped land divisions running from mountain to sea. The common people came in contact with these *ali'i* because they also collected taxes and ruled as judges among the people.

Kahuna were highly skilled people whose advice was sought before any major undertaking, such as building a house, hollowing a canoe log, or even offering a prayer. The *mo'o kahuna* were the priests of Ku and Lono, in charge of praying and following rituals. These powerful *ali'i* kept strict secrets and laws concerning their various functions. The *kahuna* dedicated to Ku were severe: it was they who sought human sacrifice. The *kahuna* of Lono were more comforting to the people but were of lesser rank than the Ku *kahuna.* Other *kahuna* were not *ali'i* but commoners. The two most important were the healers *(kahuna lapa'au)* and the black magicians *(kahuna 'ana'ana),* who could pray a person to death. The *kahuna lapa'au* had a pharmacopoeia of herbs and spices that could cure more than 230 diseases. They employed baths and massage and used various colored stones to outline the human body and accurately pinpoint not only the organs but the internal origins of illness. The *kahuna 'ana'ana* were given a wide berth by the people, who did everything possible to stay on their good side! The *kahuna 'ana'ana* could be hired to cast a love spell over a person or cause untimely death; they seldom had to send a reminder of payment.

The common people were called the **maka'ainana,** "people of the land." They were the farmers, craftspeople, and fishermen. Their land was owned by the *ali'i,* but they were not bound to it. If the local *ali'i* was cruel or unfair, the *maka'ainana* had the right to leave. Very unjust *ali'i* were even put to death by their own people, with no retribution if their accusations proved true. The *maka'ainana* mostly loved their local *ali'i,* and vice versa. *Maka'ainana* who lived close to the *ali'i* and could be counted on as warriors in times of trouble were called *kanaka no lua kaua,* "a man for the heat of battle." They were treated with greater favor than those who lived in the backcountry, *kanaka no hi'i kua,* whose lesser standing opened them up to discrimination and cruelty. All *maka'ainana* formed extended families *('ohana)* and usually lived on the same section of land *(ahupua'a).* Inland farmers would barter their produce with fishermen; thus all shared equally in the bounty of the land and sea.

A special group called **kauwa** were a landless, untouchable caste confined to living on reservations. Their origins were obviously Polynesian, but they appeared to be descendants of castaways who had survived and become perhaps the aboriginals of Hawaii before the main migrations. It was *kapu* for anyone to go onto *kauwa* lands; doing so meant instant death. A *kauwa* driven by necessity to leave his lands was required to cover his head with tapa cloth, his eyes focused on the ground in a humble manner. If a human sacrifice was needed, the *kahuna* simply summoned a *kauwa,* who had no recourse but to mutely comply. Through the years after discovery by Cook, the *kauwa* became obscured as a class and mingled with the remainder of the population. But even to this day, calling someone *kauwa,* which now supposedly only means servant, is still considered a fight-provoking insult.

Kapu and Daily Life

Occasionally there were horrible wars, but mostly the people lived quiet and ordered lives based on a strict caste society and the *kapu* system. Famine was known but only on a regional level, and the population was kept in check by birth control, crude abortions, and the distasteful practice of infanticide, especially of baby girls. The Hawaiians were absolutely loving and nurturing parents under most circumstances, and would even take in *hanai* (adopted child or oldster), a lovely practice that lingers to this day.

A strict division of labor existed between men and women. Only men were permitted to have anything to do with taro, a foodstuff so sacred it

Punishment of a kapu-breaker was harsh and swift.

had a greater *kapu* than humans themselves. Men pounded poi and served it to women. Men were also the fishermen and builders of houses, canoes, irrigation ditches, and walls. Women tended gardens and were responsible for making tapa and tending to shoreline fishing. The entire family lived in the common house *(hale noa)*. But certain things were *kapu* between the sexes. The primary *kapu* were entrance by a woman into the *mua* (men's house), nor could they eat with men. Certain foods such as pork, coconut, red fish, and bananas were forbidden to women. It was *kapu* for a man to have intercourse before going fishing, engaging in battle, or attending a religious ceremony. Young boys lived with the women until they underwent circumcision *(pule ipu),* after which they were required to keep the *kapu* of men. A true Hawaiian settlement required a minimum of five huts: the men's eating hut, women's menstruation hut, women's eating hut, communal sleeping hut, and prayer hut. Without these five separate structures, Hawaiian "society" could not happen, since the *ia kapu* (forbidden eating between men and women) could not be observed.

Ali'i could also declare a *kapu,* and often did so. Certain lands or fishing areas were temporarily made *kapu* so they could revitalize. Even today, it is *kapu* for anyone to remove all the *'opihi* (a type of limpet) from a rock. The great King Kamehameha I even placed a *kapu* on the body of his notoriously unfaithful child bride, Ka'ahumanu. It didn't work! The greatest *kapu (kapu moe)* was afforded to the highest ranking *ali'i:* anyone coming into their presence had to prostrate themselves. Lesser ranking *ali'i* were afforded the *kapu noho:* lessers had to sit or kneel in their presence. Commoners could not let their shadows fall upon an *ali'i* or enter their houses except through a special door. Breaking a *kapu* meant immediate death.

Fun and Games
The native Hawaiians loved sports. A type of "Olympiad" was held each year during the Makahiki Festival. Events included boxing, swimming, diving, surfing, and running. A form of bowling used polished, wheel-shaped stones that tested for distance and accuracy. Hawaiians also enjoyed a more cerebral, chesslike game called *konane.* Intricately carved *konane* boards survive to this day. Hawaiians built special downhill courses for a runnered bobsled called *holua.* Strangely enough, the Hawaiians developed a bow and arrow but never employed it in warfare. It was merely a toy for shooting at targets or rats.

The greatest sport of all was surfing. **Surfing** originated with the Hawaiians, and many old records recount this singularly exhilarating activity. The boards, made of various woods, were greatly cared for, measuring up to 15 feet long and six inches thick. James King, a lieutenant with Cook, was "altogether astonished" by surfing, and Reverend Ellis wrote in 1826, ". . . to see fifty or a hundred persons riding on an immense billow . . . for a distance of several hundred yards together is one of the most novel and interesting sports a foreigner can witness in the islands."

Ghosts
The Hawaiians had countless superstitions and ghost legends, but two of the more interesting involve astral travel of the soul and the "Marchers of the Night." The soul, *'uhane,* was considered by Hawaiians to be totally free and independent of its body, *kino.* The soul could separate, leaving the body asleep or very drowsy. This disincorporated soul *(hihi'o)* could visit people and was considered quite different from a *lapu,* an ordinary spirit of a dead person. A *kahuna* could immediately recognize if a person's *'uhane* had left the body, and a special wreath was placed upon the head for protection and to facilitate reentry. A person confronted by an apparition could test to see if it was indeed dead or still alive by placing leaves of an *'ape* plant upon the ground. If the leaves tore when they were

In a sennit casket rested the bones of the dead.

LOUISE FOOTE

walked upon, the spirit was human, but if they remained intact it was a ghost. Also, you could sneak up and startle the vision, and if it disappeared it was a ghost. Also, if no reflection of the face appeared when it drank water from an offered calabash, it was a ghost. Unfortunately, there were no instructions to follow once you had determined you indeed had a ghost on your hands. Maybe it was better not to know! Some people would sprinkle salt and water around their houses, but this kept away evil spirits, not ghosts.

There are also many stories of *kahuna* restoring souls to dead bodies. First they had to catch one and keep it in a gourd. He then placed beautiful tapa and fragrant flowers and herbs about the body to make it more enticing. Slowly, the *kahuna* would coax the soul out of the gourd and get it to reenter the body through the big toe.

Death Marchers

One inexplicable phenomenon that many people attest to is Ka Huaka'i o Ka Po, "Marchers of the Night." This march of the dead is fatal if you gaze upon it, unless one of the marchers happens to be a friendly ancestor who will protect you. The peak time for "the march" is 7:30 P.M.–2 A.M. The marchers can be dead *ali'i* and warriors, the gods themselves, or the lesser *'aumakua*. When the *'aumakua* march there is usually chanting and music. *Ali'i* marches are more somber. The entire procession, lit by torches, often stops at the house of a relative and might even carry him or her away. When the gods themselves march, there is often thunder, lightning, and heavy seas. The sky is lit with torches, and they walk six abreast, three gods and three goddesses. If you get in the way of a march, remove your clothing and prostrate yourself. If the marching gods or *'aumakua* happen to be ones to which you pray, you might be spared. If it's a march of the *ali'i*, you might make it if you lie face upward and feign death. If you *do* see a death march, the last thing you'll worry about is lying naked on the ground and looking ridiculous.

MISSIONARIES ONE AND ALL

In Hawaii, when you say "missionaries," it's taken for granted you're referring to the small and determined band of Congregationalists who arrived aboard the brig *Thaddeus* in 1820, and the "companies" or "packets" that reinforced them over the next 40 years. They were sent from Boston by the American Board of Commissioners for Foreign Missions (ABCFM), which learned of the supposed sad and godless plight of the Hawaiian people from returning sailors and especially through the few Hawaiians who had come to America to study.

The person most instrumental in bringing the missionaries to Hawaii was a young man named Henry 'Opukaha'ia. An orphan befriended by a captain and taken to New England, he studied theology and was obsessed with the desire to return home to save his people from sure damnation. His widely read accounts of life in Hawaii were the direct cause of the formation of the Pioneer Company to the Sandwich Islands Missions. Unfortunately, 'Opukaha'ia died in New England from typhus in 1819, the year before the missionaries sailed.

"Civilizing" Hawaii

The first missionaries had the straightforward task of bringing the Hawaiians out of paganism and into Christianity and civilization. They met with extreme hostility—not from the natives, but from sea captains, sailors, and traders who were content with the open debauchery and wanton whoremongering that was the status quo in the Hawaii of 1820. The many direct confrontations between these two factions even included the cannonading of a missionary home by American sea captains who were denied the customary visits of island women, thanks to the meddlesome "do-gooders." The most memorable of these incidents involved "Mad Jack" Percival, the captain of the USS *Dolphin,* who bombed a church in Lahaina to show his rancor. In actuality, the truth of the situation was much closer to the sentiments of James Jarves, who wrote, "The missionary was a far more useful and agreeable man than his Catholicism would indicate; and the trader was not so bad a man as the missionary would make him out to be." The missionaries' primary aim might have been conversion, but the most fortuitous by-product was education, which raised the consciousness of every Hawaiian regardless of religious affiliation. In 40 short years Hawaii was considered a civilized nation well on its way into the modern world, and the American Board of Missions officially ended its support in 1863.

Some of Hawaii's finest museums and grandest architecture are part of the missionary legacy. Some of the most notable are: Moku'aikaua Church in Kona, Hawai'i, the first Christian church, founded in 1820; the Lyman House Museum of Hilo; Kawaiaha'o Church in Honolulu, founded 1821, and next door the superb Mission Houses Museum; Waine'e Church, the first stone church in Hawaii, founded in Lahaina in 1828, and the Baldwin Home just down Front Street; and Lahainaluna High School and Printing House, the first American school and publishing house west of the Rockies. The churches, but especially the homes and museums, not only offer a glimpse of religious life, but are some of the finest "windows" into 19th-century America. Their collections of artifacts, utensils, and general memorabilia put the life and times of 19th-century Yankees in a setting that could hardly be more different from New England.

Bonanza for Missionaries

Although the missionaries were the first, they by no means had the field to themselves. Hot on the same religious trail came the Catholics— French Sacred Hearts led by Father Bachelot, who arrived in Honolulu in July 1827 aboard *La Comete*. Immediately, Queen Ka'ahumanu, who had been converted by the Congregationalists, ordered them to leave. They refused. For the next 10 years the Catholic priests and their converts met with open hostility and persecution, which, in true missionary fashion, only strengthened their resolve. The humiliation of a young convert, Juliana Keawahine, who was tied to a tree and scourged, became a religious rallying point. After this incident the persecutions stopped. Honolulu's Our Lady of Peace Cathedral was completed in 1843, and 'Ahuimanu Catholic School, O'ahu's counterpart to Lahainaluna, opened for instruction in 1846. Today, Roman Catholicism, with 230,000 adherents, is the single largest religious group in Hawaii.

The Saints Come Marching In

A strange episode in Hawaii's history involved the Mormons. In 1850, the Latter-day Saints arrived direct from missionary work in California gold fields. By 1852, George Cannon had already translated the *Book of Mormon* into Hawaiian. The five original Mormon missionaries spent every moment traveling and converting the Hawaiians. They had a grand plan of constructing a "City of Joseph" on Lana'i, where they managed to gain a large tract of land. In 1858 the Mormon Wars broke out in Utah, and the missionaries were called home. One of their band, Walter Murray Gibson, who stayed to manage the fledgling Mormon church, became one of the most controversial and singularly strange fixtures in Hawaiian politics. When the Mormons returned in 1864, they found Gibson had indeed carried on the "City of Joseph," but he had manipulated all of the deeds and land grants into his personal possession. Furthermore, he had set himself up as an omnipotent grand patriarch and openly denounced the polygamous beliefs of the Mormons of the day. Immediately excommunicated, Gibson was abandoned to his fate, and the Mormons moved to O'ahu, where they founded a sugar plantation and temple in La'ie.

The Church of Jesus Christ of the Latter-day Saints now has approximately 40,000 members, the largest Protestant denomination in Hawaii. Their settlement on O'ahu at La'ie is now home to an impressive Mormon Temple and an island branch of Brigham Young University. Close by, the Mormons also operate the Polynesian Cultural Center, which is one of the top tourist attractions in all of Hawaii.

As for Gibson, he was elected to the legislature in 1876 and became a private counselor to King Kalakaua. In 1882, he worked himself into the office of "Premier," which he ran like a petty dictator. One of his more visionary suggestions was to import Japanese labor. Two of his most ridiculous were to drive non-Hawaiians from the islands (excluding himself) and to gather Oceania into one Pacific nation with Hawaii at the forefront. By 1887 he and Kalakaua had so infuriated the sugar planters that Gibson was railroaded out of the islands and Kalakaua was forced to sign a constitution that greatly limited his power. Gibson died in 1888, and his daughter Talulah and her husband sold the lands on Lana'i for a song after they tried but failed to grow sugarcane.

Non-Christian

By the turn of the 20th century, Shintoism and Buddhism, brought by the Japanese and Chinese, were firmly established in Hawaii. The first official Buddhist temple was Hongpa Hongwanji, established on O'ahu in 1889. All denominations of Buddhism account for 17 percent of the island's religious total, and there are about 50,000 Shintoists. The Hindu religion has perhaps 2,000 adherents, and roughly 10,000 Jewish people live throughout Hawaii. About 10,000 island residents are in new religious movements and lesser-known faiths such as Baha'i and Unitarianism. A large number of people in Hawaii remain unaffiliated.

INTRODUCTION

ARTS AND MUSIC

Referring to Hawaii as "paradise" is about as hackneyed as you can get, but when you combine it into "artists' paradise" it's the absolute truth. Something about the place evokes art (or at least personal expression) from most people. The islands are like a magnet: they not only draw artists to them, but they draw art *from* the artists. The list of literary figures who visited Hawaii and had something inspirational to say reads like a freshman survey in literature: William Henry Dana, Herman Melville, Mark Twain, Robert Louis Stevenson, Jack London, Somerset Maugham, Joaquin Miller, and of course James Michener.

The inspiration comes from the astounding natural surroundings. The land is so beautiful yet so raw; the ocean's power and rhythm are primal and ever-present; the riotous colors of flowers and fruit leap from the deep-green jungle background. Crystal water beads and pale mists turn the mountains into mystic temples, while rainbows ride the crests of waves. The stunning variety of faces begging to be rendered suggests that all the world sent delegations to the islands. And in most cases it did! Inspiration is everywhere, as is art, good or bad.

Sometimes the artwork is overpowering in itself and in its sheer volume. Though geared to the tourist's market of cheap souvenirs, there is hardly a shop in Hawaii that doesn't sell some item that falls into the general category of "art." You can find everything from carved monkey-face coconut shells to true masterpieces. The Polynesian Hawaiians were master craftspeople, and their legacy still lives in a wide variety of wood carvings, basketry, and weavings. The hula is art in swaying motion, and the true form is rigorously studied and taken very seriously. There is hardly a resort area that doesn't offer the "bump and grind" tourist's hula, but even these revues are accompanied by proficient local musicians. Nightclubs offer "slack key" balladeers; island music performed on ukuleles and on Hawaii's own steel guitars spills from many lounges.

Vibrant fabrics that catch the spirit of the islands are rendered into mu'umu'u and aloha shirts at countless local factories. They're almost a mandatory purchase! Pottery, heavily influenced by the Japanese, is a well-developed craft at numerous kilns. Local artisans fashion delicate jewelry from coral and olivine, while some ply the whaler's craft of etching on ivory, called scrimshaw. There are fine traditions of quilting, flower art in lei, and street artists working in everything from airbrush to glass.

ARTS OF OLD HAWAII

Since everything in old Hawaii had to be fashioned by hand, almost every object was either a genuine work of art or the product of a highly refined craft. With the "civilizing" of the natives, most of the "old ways" disappeared, including the old arts and crafts. Most authentic Hawaiian art exists only in museums, but with the resurgence of Hawaiian roots, many old arts are being revitalized, and a few artists are becoming proficient in them.

Magnificent Canoes

The most respected artisans in old Hawaii were the canoe makers. With little more than a stone adze and a pump drill, they built canoes that could carry 200 people and last for generations—sleek, well proportioned, and infinitely seaworthy. The main hull was usually a gigantic koa log, and the gunwale planks were minutely drilled and sewn to the sides with sennit rope.

INTRODUCTION

LOUISE FOOTE

Bone or shell was used as the cutting edge of the pump drill used to carve out canoes.

(mats) were made from *lau hala* (pandanus) leaves. Once split, the spine was removed and the leaves stored in large rolls. When needed they were soaked, pounded, and then fashioned into various floor coverings and sleeping mats. Intricate geometrical patterns were woven in, and the edges were rolled and well fashioned. Coconut palms were not used to make mats in old Hawaii, but a wide variety of basketry was made from the aerial root *'ie'ie*. The shapes varied according to use. Some baskets were tall and narrow, some were cones, others were flat like trays, while many were woven around gourds and calabashes.

A strong tradition of weaving and carving has survived in Hawaii, and the time-tested material of *lau hala* is still the best, although much is now made from coconut fronds. You can purchase anything from beach mats to a woven hat, and all share the desirable qualities of strength, lightness, and ventilation.

Apprenticeships lasted for years, and a young man knew that he had graduated when one day he was nonchalantly asked to sit down and eat with the master builders. Small family-size canoes with outriggers were used for fishing and perhaps carried a spear rack; large oceangoing double-hulled canoes were used for migration and warfare. On these, the giant logs had been adzed to about two inches thick. A mainsail woven from pandanus was mounted on a central platform, and the boat was steered by two long paddles. The hull was dyed with plant juices and charcoal, and the entire village helped launch the canoe in a ceremony called "drinking the sea."

Carving and Weaving
Wood was a primary material used by Hawaiian craftsmen. They almost exclusively used koa because of its density, strength, and natural luster. It was turned into canoes, woodware, calabashes, and furniture used by the *ali'i*. Temple idols were another major product of wood carving. A variety of stone artifacts were turned out, including poi pounders, mirrors, fish sinkers, and small idols.

Hawaiians became the best basket makers and mat weavers in all of Polynesia. *Ulana*

Featherwork
This highly refined art was found only on the islands of Tahiti, New Zealand, and Hawaii, while the fashioning of feather helmets and idols was unique to Hawaii. Favorite colors were red and yellow, which came only in a very limited supply from a small number of birds such as the *'o'o, 'i'iwi, mamo,* and *'apapane*. Professional bird hunters in old Hawaii paid their taxes to *ali'i* in prized feathers. The feathers were fastened to a woven net of *olona* cord and made into helmets, idols, and beautiful flowing capes and cloaks. These resplendent garments were made and worn only by men, especially during battle when a fine cloak became a great trophy of war. Featherwork was also employed in the making of *kahili* and lei, which were highly prized by the noble *ali'i* women.

Tapa Cloth
Tapa, cloth made from tree bark, was common throughout Polynesia and was a woman's art. A few trees such as the *wauke* and *mamaki* produced the best cloth, but other types could be utilized. First the raw bark was pounded into a feltlike pulp and beaten together to form strips (the beaters had distinctive patterns that also helped make the cloth supple). They were then decorated by stamping (using a form of block

printing) and then were dyed with natural colors from plants and sea animals in shades of gray, purple, pink, and red. They were even painted with natural brushes made from pandanus fruit, with an overall gray color made from charcoal. The tapa cloth was sewn together to make bed coverings, and fragrant flowers and herbs were either sewn or pounded in to produce a permanent fragrance. Tapa cloth is still available today, but the Hawaiian methods have been lost, and most comes from other areas of Polynesia.

BOB RACE

The ali'i wore magnificent feathered capes that signified their rank.

First Western Artists

When Captain Cook made first contact in 1778, the ship's artists immediately began recording things Hawaiian. John Webber and James Clevely made etchings and pen-and-ink drawings of Hawaiian people, structures, *heiau,* and everyday occurrences that struck them as noteworthy or peculiar. William Ellis, ship's surgeon, also a fair hand at etching, was attracted to portraying native architecture. These three left a priceless and faithful record of what Hawaii was like at the moment of contact. Louis Choris, ship's artist with Otto Von Kotzebue in 1816, painted early portraits of King Kamehameha and Queen Ka'ahumanu, the two grandest figures in Hawaii's history. Jacques Arago, aboard the *Uranie* with the French Captain de Freycinet in 1819, recorded some gruesome customs of punishment of *kapu* breakers and made many drawings of island people. Robert Dampier, who sailed on the *Blonde,* the ship that returned King Liholiho's body from England, recorded one of the earliest landscapes of Honolulu, a site that has continued to be depicted more on film by tourists than almost any other city on earth. These early artists set a trend that continues unabated to this day; artists endeavor to "capture" Hawaii, and they do so with every medium available.

Modern Masters

Countless artists working at all levels of accomplishment try to match their skills to the vigor and beauty of the islands. Some have set the standards, and their names have become synonymous with Hawaiian art. Heading this list of luminaries are Huc Luquiens, Madge Tennent, Tadashi Sato, Jean Charlot, and John Kelly.

Madge Tennent (1889–1972) was an Englishwoman who came to Hawaii via Samoa after spending years in South Africa and New Zealand. She worked in oils that she applied liberally and in bold strokes. Enamored with the people of Hawaii, her portraits are of a race striking in appearance and noble in character. Her works, along with those of other island artists, are displayed at the Tennent Art Foundation, on the slopes of Punchbowl on O'ahu.

Huc Luquiens, former chair of the art department at the University of Hawai'i, was a master at etching, especially in drypoint. His works, mainly island landscapes, are displayed in the Hawaiiana Collection of the Honolulu Academy of Arts.

Maui-born Tadashi Sato, a superbly accomplished muralist, has produced such famous mosaics as the 30-foot *Aquarius* (at the state capitol in Honolulu) and the 60-foot *Portals of Immortality* (at the Maui Memorial Gymnasium in Lahaina).

Frenchman Jean Charlot perfected his mural art in Mexico before coming to Hawaii in 1949. He is renowned for his frescoes and became a well-known art critic and the grand old man of Hawaiian art. He died in 1979 at 90.

John M. Kelly was in love with Hawaiian women; his etchings of them are both inspired and technically flawless. Kelly was infinitely patient, rendering his subjects in the minutest detail.

These artists are the "Big Five of Hawaiian Art"; their accomplishments are a gauge of what Hawaii can inspire in an artist. By observing their works you can get an instant art course and a comparative view of the state of the arts in Hawaii.

Contemporary Artists

The crop of new artists making their marks always seems bounteous, and their works, heavily influenced by the "feeling of Hawaii," continue to be superb. Every island has art galleries, co-ops, or unofficial art centers. One of the finest groups of island artists can be found along the "fence" of the Honolulu Zoo fronting Kapi'olani Park. The following list of artists, with a short description of their work, is by no means exhaustive. It merely shows the wide range of artwork available.

Roy Tabora specializes in dramatic sea-scapes of windwhipped palm trees and crashing surf illuminated by glorious sunsets. His work is a dramatic crescendo of sea, surf, and spirit, entwined to capture the awesome power that is Hawaii.

James Hoyle, a longtime Kaua'i resident, captures the spirit of Hawaii through color and movement. His media are oil, pastel, and polymer that he applies on canvas in a distinctive style of macro-pointillism. The sense that permeates all of Hoyle's work is that humankind cannot conquer nature but must learn to live in harmony with the *'aina,* which is very much alive.

Robert Nelson is a Maui artist who superbly transmits the integrated mystical life of land and

---

GICLÉE

Many galleries now offer unbelievable prints produced by a rather expensive computer-based method called *giclée*. A picture of the original is made into a transparency that is scanned to match subtle strokes and color variations perfectly, and then airbrushed at four million droplets per second (each one-fourth the diameter of a human hair) onto paper or canvas, creating a cyberspace copy of near-perfect similarity to the original.

---

sea. His watercolors are often diffused with the strange filtered light found beneath the waves. A conservationist, he has often depicted the gentle frolicking life of the whales that visit Hawaiian waters.

Bill Christian is a master of scrimshaw, which he renders on slate. He also produces fine oil paintings of the sea and old salts. A world-class artist, he has had his works displayed at art galleries on Maui as well as at the Smithsonian and at the New Bedford Massachusetts Whaling Museum.

Pegge Hopper is often compared to Madge Tennent. She works in bold colors and strokes. Her subject matter is islanders, especially the delicacy and inner strength of women. Her works are displayed at various galleries and are often available in limited-edition serigraphs.

Alapai Hanapi is a traditionalist sculptor who re-creates the motifs of his Hawaiian ancestors. He works in wood and stone with tools that he fashions himself. His driving force is cultural awareness, and through his art he tells of the old ways. His work is known for its simplicity.

Al Furtado is a freelance artist working in Honolulu. He specializes in capturing the movement of Hawaiian dance. His depictions are often larger than life, with a strong sense of vitality and motion.

Daniel Wang was born in Shanghai, where he learned the art of Chinese watercolors. Although born deaf and mute, he speaks loudly, clearly, and beautifully through his art. Daniel has a special technique in which the palm of his hand becomes his artistic tool. He can transmit intense inner emotions directly from his body to the canvas.

The following is a potpourri of distinguished artists displayed at various galleries around the islands. Any work bearing one of their names is authentic island art considered superior by fellow artists: William Waterfall, photographer; Satoru Abe, sculptor; Ruthadell Anderson, weaver; Betty Tseng Yu-ho Ecke, *dsui* painter; Claude Horan, sculptor, ceramics; Erica Karawina, stained glass; Ron Kowalke, painter; Ben Norris, painter; Louis Pohl, printmaker; Mamoru Sato, sculptor; Reuben Tam, painter; Jean Williams, weaver; John Wisnosky, painter; and John Young, painter.

ARTS TO BUY

Wild Hawaiian shirts or bright mu'umu'u, especially when worn on the Mainland, have the magical effect of making wearers "feel" like they're in Hawaii, while at the same time eliciting spontaneous smiles from passersby. Maybe it's the colors, or perhaps it's just the "vibe" that signifies "party time" or "hang loose," but nothing says Hawaii like alohawear. More than a dozen fabric houses in Hawaii turn out distinctive patterns, and many dozens of factories create their own personalized designs. These factories often have attached retail outlets, but in any case you can find hundreds of shops selling alohawear. Aloha shirts were the brilliant idea of a Chinese merchant in Honolulu, who used to hand-tailor them and then sell them to the tourists who arrived by ship in the glory days before World War II. They were an instant success. Mu'umu'u or "Mother Hubbards" were the idea of missionaries, who were appalled by Hawaiian women running about au naturel and insisted on covering their new Christian converts from head to foot. Now the roles are reversed, and it's Mainlanders who come to Hawaii and immediately strip down to as little clothing as possible.

Alohawear

At one time alohawear was exclusively made of cotton or from manmade, natural fiber based rayon, and these materials are still the best for any tropical clothing. Beware, however: polyester has slowly crept into the market. No material could possibly be worse for the island climate, so when buying your alohawear make sure to check the label for material content. Mu'umu'u now come in various styles and can be worn for the entire spectrum of social occasions in Hawaii. Aloha shirts are basically cut the same as always, but the patterns have undergone changes, and besides the original flowers and ferns, modern shirts might depict an island scene in the manner of a silk-screen painting. A basic good-quality mu'umu'u or aloha shirt is guaranteed to be worth its price in good times and happy smiles. The connoisseur might want to purchase *The Hawaiian Shirt, Its Art and History,* by R. Thomas Steele. It's illustrated with more than 150 shirts that are now considered works of art by collectors the world over.

Scrimshaw

This art of etching and carving on bone and ivory has become an island tradition handed down from the times of the old whaling ships. Although scrimshaw can be found throughout Hawaii, the center remains in the old whaling capital of Lahaina. There along Front Street a few shops specialize in scrimshaw. Today, pieces are carved on fossilized walrus ivory that is gathered by Inuit and shipped to Hawaii. It comes in a variety of shades from pure white to mocha, depending upon the mineral content of the earth in which it was buried. Elephant ivory or whale bone is no longer used because of ecological considerations, but there is a "gray market" in Pacific walrus tusks. Inuit can legally hunt the walrus. They then make a few minimal scratches on the tusks, which technically qualifies them to be "Native American art" and free of most governmental restrictions. The tusks are then sent to Hawaii as art objects, but the superficial scratches are immediately removed and the ivory is reworked by artisans.

scrimshaw

Scrimshaw is made into everything from belt buckles to delicate earrings and even into coffee-table centerpieces. The prices can go from a few dollars up into the thousands.

Wood Carvings

One surviving Hawaiian art is wood carving. Old Hawaiians used koa almost exclusively because of its density, strength, and natural luster, but koa is becoming increasingly scarce. Many items are still available, but they are costly. Milo and monkeypod are also excellent woods for carving and have largely replaced koa. You can buy tikis, bowls, and furniture at numerous shops. Countless inexpensive carved items, such as hula dancers or salad servers, are sold at variety stores, but most of these are imported from Asia or the Philippines and can be bought at any variety store.

Weaving

The minute you arrive in Hawaii you should shell out a few dollars for a woven beach mat. This is a necessity, not a frivolous purchase, but it definitely won't have been made in Hawaii. What is made in Hawaii is *lau hala*. This is traditional Hawaiian weaving from the leaves *(lau)* of the pandanus *(hala)* tree. These leaves vary greatly in length, with the largest more than six feet, and they have a thorny spine that must be removed before they can be worked. The color ranges from light tan to dark brown. The leaves are cut into strips from one-eighth to one inch wide and are then employed in weaving. Any variety of items can be made or at least covered in *lau hala*. It makes great purses, mats, baskets, and table mats.

Woven into a hat, it's absolutely superb but should not be confused with a palm-frond hat. A *lau hala* hat is amazingly supple and even when squashed will pop back into shape. A good one is expensive and with proper care will last for years. All *lau hala* should be given a light application of mineral oil on a monthly basis, especially if it's exposed to the sun. For flat items, iron over a damp cloth and keep purses and baskets stuffed with paper when not in use. Palm fronds also are widely used in weaving. They, too, are a great natural raw material, but not as good as *lau hala*. Almost any woven item, such as a beach bag, makes a good authentic yet inexpensive gift or souvenir.

Gift Items

Jewelry is always an appreciated gift, especially if it's distinctive, and Hawaii has some of the most original. The sea provides the basic raw materials of pink, gold, and black corals, which are as beautiful and fascinating as gemstones. Harvesting coral is very dangerous work. The Lahaina beds off Maui have one of the best black coral lodes in the islands, but unlike reef coral these trees grow at depths bordering the outer limits of a scuba diver's capabilities. Only the best can dive 180 feet after the black coral, and about one diver per year dies in pursuit of it. Conservationists have placed great pressure on the harvesters of these deep corals, and the state of Hawaii has created strict limits and guidelines on the firms and divers involved.

Pink coral has long been treasured by humans. The Greeks considered it a talisman for good health, and there's even evidence that it has been coveted since the Stone Age. Coral jewelry is on sale at many shops throughout Hawaii, its value determined by the color of the coral and the workmanship.

Puka shells (with small, naturally occurring holes) and *'opihi* shells are also made into jewelry. Many times these items are very inexpensive, yet they are authentic and great purchases for the price. Hanging macramé planters festooned with seashells are usually quite affordable and sold at roadside stands along with shells.

Hawaii produces some unique food items that are appreciated by many people. Various-size jars of macadamia nuts and butters are great gifts, as are tins of rich, gourmet-quality Kona coffee. Guava, pineapple, passion fruit, and mango are often gift-boxed into assortments of jams, jellies, and spicy chutneys. And for that special person in your life, you can bring home island fragrances in bottles of perfumes and colognes in the exotic smells of gardenia, plumeria, and even ginger. All of the above items are reasonably priced, lightweight, and easy to carry.

LANGUAGE OF THE LEI

The goddess Hi'iaka is Pele's youngest sister, and although many gods are depicted wearing flower garlands, the lei is most associated with her. Perhaps this is because Hi'iaka is the

BOB RACE

goddess of mercy and protection, qualities that the lei is deemed to symbolize. Hi'iaka traveled throughout the islands destroying evil spirits wherever she found them. In the traditional translation of "The Song of the Islands" by Reverend Samuel Kapu, the last verses read, "We all call to you, answer us o Hi'iaka, the woman who travels the seas. This is the conclusion of our song, o wreaths of Hawaii, respond to our call." A special day, May 1, is Lei Day in Hawaii. It started in 1928 as a project of Don Blanding, an island poet.

Hardly a more beautiful tradition exists anywhere in the world than placing a flower garland around the neck of someone special. The traditional time to give a lei is when someone is arriving or departing the islands, so every airport has lei sellers, mostly older women who have a little booth at the entrance to the airport. But lei are worn on every occasion, from marriages to funerals, and are equally apt to appear around the lovely neck of a hula dancer or as a floral hatband on the grizzled head of an old *paniolo*, or even draped around his horse's neck. In old Hawaii lei were given to the local *ali'i* as a sign of affection. When two warring chiefs sat together and wove a lei, it meant the end of hostilities and symbolized the circle of peace.

Lei Making

Any flower or blossom can be strung into a lei, but the most common are carnations or the lovely smelling plumeria. Lei, like babies, are all beautiful, but special lei are highly prized by those who know what to look for. Of the different stringing styles, the most common is *kui*—stringing the flower through the middle or side. Most "airport-quality" lei are of this type. The *humuhumu* style, reserved for making flat lei, is made by sewing flowers and ferns to a *ti*, banana, or sometimes *hala* leaf. A *humuhumu* lei makes an excellent hatband. *Wili* is the winding together of greenery, ferns, and flowers into short, bouquet-type lengths. The most traditional form is *hili*, which requires no stringing at all but involves braiding fragrant ferns and leaves such as *maile*. If flowers are interwoven, the *hili* becomes the *haku* style, the most difficult and most beautiful type of lei.

The Lei of the Land

Every major island is symbolized by its own lei made from a distinctive flower, shell, or fern. Each island has its own official color as well, though it doesn't necessarily correspond to the color of the island's lei.

The island of Hawai'i's lei is made from the red (or rare creamy white or orange) *lehua* blossom. The *lehua* tree grows from sea level to 9,000 feet and produces an abundance of tufted flowers. The official color of Hawai'i Island, like the lava from its active volcanoes, is red.

Kaua'i, oldest of the main islands, is represented by the *mokihana* lei and the regal color purple. The *mokihana* tree produces a small, cubelike fruit that smells like anise. Green when strung into Kaua'i's lei, the fruit turn a dark brown and keep their scent for months.

Maui is the pink island, and its lei is the corresponding small pink rose called the *lokelani*. These flowers are not native but were imported and widely cultivated at one time. In recent years they've fallen prey to a rose beetle, and sometimes when they're scarce *roselani* is substituted for Maui's lei.

Moloka'i is the silvery green island, and its lei is fashioned from the green leaves and small white flowers of the *kukui* tree. After it's shaped and polished, the *kukui* nut makes some of the most permanent and beautiful lei for sale in Hawaii. *Kukui* nut lei are quite common and make excellent gifts. Although not the official lei of any island, they could easily be the official lei representing all the islands.

Lana'i has one of the most traditional forms of lei in Hawaii. Both its color and its lei are represented by the orange *kaunaoa*. This plant commonly grows along beaches and roadsides. Its orange, leafless stems are twisted into strands to form a lei.

O'ahu, the color of the sun, is garlanded by the yellow *'ilima*. This flower is reminiscent of the *'o'o* bird, whose yellow feathers made the finest capes in Hawaii. The *'ilima* often bears double yellow flowers and will infrequently produce a light red flower too rare to be used in lei.

Kaho'olawe, the sacred island, is given the color gray and is represented by the silvery leaves and small, white, sweet-scented flowers of the *hinahina*. This heliotrope grows on sandy beaches just above the high-water mark; it's a very common plant throughout the Pacific.

Ni'ihau, the Forbidden Island, is home to some of the last remaining pure-blooded Hawaiians, and takes the color white. The island's lei is the rare *pupu* shell. This white shell sometimes has brown spots and is less than one-half inch long. The shell was once the home of a mollusk that died on the offshore reef. These *pupu* lei, considered fine jewelry, fetch a handsome price. Very cheap facsimiles made of *pikake* shells are sold everywhere; most have been imported from the Cook and Society Islands of the South Pacific.

The last island is the semi-submerged volcano of Molokini, just off Maui's south shore. Molokini is represented by the very traditional lei made from *limu kala*, a brown, coarse seaweed with feathery spiny leaves that makes a boa-type lei.

Besides these island lei, two others must be mentioned. A lei made from *maile* is perhaps the most traditional of all. *Maile* is a green, leafy vine. Its stiff, bonelike inner stem is removed, leaving the leaves and pliable bark intact, which are then twisted into lei. They might be ordinary to look at, but they have a delicious smell that is Hawaii. *Maile* is often used in conjunction with flowers to make top-notch lei. *Laua'e* is a common fern with large, coarse, shiny leaves. It is used to fluff out many lei; when bruised, the leaves have a mild scent of *maile*. Lei have one quality that is unsurpassed: they feel just as good to give as they do to receive.

HULA

The hula is more than an ethnic dance; it is the soul of Hawaii expressed in motion. It began as a form of worship during religious ceremonies and was danced only by highly trained men. It gradually evolved into a form of entertainment, but in no regard was it sexual. The hula was the opera, theater, and lecture hall of the islands all rolled into one. It was history portrayed in the performing arts. In the beginning an androgynous deity named Laka descended to earth and taught men how to dance the hula. In time the male aspect of Laka departed for the heavens, but the female aspect remained. The female Laka set up her own special hula *heiau* at Ha'ena Point on the Na Pali Coast of Kaua'i, where it still exists. As time went on women were allowed to learn the hula. Scholars surmise that men became too busy wresting a living from the land to maintain the art form.

Men did retain a type of hula for themselves called *lua*. This was a form of martial art employed in hand-to-hand combat that included paralyzing holds, bone-crunching punches, and thrusting with spears and clubs, which evolved into a ritualized warfare dance called *hula kui*. During the 19th century, the hula almost vanished because the missionaries considered it vile and heathen. King Kalakaua is generally regarded as saving it during the 1800s, when he formed his own troupe and encouraged the dancers to learn the old hula. Many of the original dances were forgotten, but some were retained and are performed to this day. Although professional dancers were highly trained, everyone took part in the hula. *Ali'i*, commoners, young, and old all danced. Early drawings by ships' artists like Arago, Choris, and Webber recorded hula scenes. Old folks even did it sitting down if their legs were too weak to perform some of the gyrations.

Hula Training

Only the most beautiful, graceful, and elegant girls were chosen to enter the hula *halau* (school). At one time, the *halau* was a temple in its own right, and the girls who entered at the ages of four or five would emerge as accomplished dancers in their early teens to begin lifelong careers of the highest honor. In the *halau,* the *haumana* (pupils) were under the strict and total guidance of the *kumu* (teacher), and many *kapu* were placed upon them. The hula was a subordination of gross strength into a sublime coupling of grace and elegance. Once a woman became a proficient and accomplished dancer, her hula showed a personal, semi-spontaneous interpretation based upon past experiences. Today, *hula halau* are active on every island, teaching hula and keeping the old ways and culture alive. Performers still spend years perfecting their techniques. They show off their accomplishments during the fierce competition of the Merrie Monarch Festival in Hilo every April. The winning *halau* is praised and recognized throughout the islands.

The Special World of Hula

Hawaiian hula was never performed in grass skirts; tapa or *ti*-leaf skirts were worn. Grass skirts came to Hawaii from the Gilbert Islands, so if you see grass or cellophane skirts in a "hula revue," it's not traditional. Almost every major resort offering entertainment or a lu'au also offers a revue. Most times, young island beauties accompanied by local musicians put on a floor show for the tourists. It'll be fun, but it won't be traditional. A hula dancer has to learn how to control every part of her or his body, including facial expressions, which help set the mood. The hands are extremely important and provide instant background scenery. For example, if the hands are thrust outward in an aggressive manner, this can mean a battle; if they sway gently overhead, they refer to the gods or to creation; they can easily become rain, clouds, sun, sea, or moon. Watch the hands to get the gist of the story, though in the words of one wise guy, "You watch the parts you like, and I'll watch the parts I like!" The motion of swaying hips can denote a long walk, a canoe ride, or sexual intercourse. Foot motion can portray a battle, a walk, or any kind of conveyance. The overall effect is multidirectional synchronized movement. The correct chanting of the *mele* is an integral part of the performance. These story chants, accompanied by musical instruments, make the hula very much like opera; it is especially similar in the way the tale unfolds.

Hula Music

Accompaniment is provided by chants called *mele* or *oli* and by a wide variety of instruments. The *ipu* is a primary hula instrument made of two gourds fastened together. It's thumped on a mat and slapped with the hand. In the background is the steady rhythm of the *pahu*, a large bass drum made from a hollowed coconut or breadfruit tree log and covered with a sharkskin membrane. Hawaii's largest drum, it was sometimes placed on a pedestal and used in ceremonies at the *heiau*. The *'uli 'uli* is a gourd or coconut filled with shells or pebbles and used like rattles, while *'ili 'ili* are stones clicked together like castanets. The *punui* is a small drum made from a coconut shell half and beaten in counterpoint to the *ipu*. Oftentimes it was played by the hula dancer, who had it fastened to her body as a knee drum. The *pu'ili* is a length of bamboo split at one end to look like a whisk, and when struck against the body it makes a rattling noise, while the *ka'eke'eke* and *kalau* are bamboo cut to various lengths and struck to make a rudimentary xylophonic sound. Two unique instruments are the *kupe'e niho 'ilio*, a dog's tooth rattle worn as an ankle bracelet by men only, now replaced by sea shells; and an *'ohe hano ihu*, a nose flute of bamboo that accompanied chants. None of these instruments are actually necessary to perform a hula. All that's needed are a dancer and a chant.

THAT GOOD OLD ISLAND MUSIC

The missionaries usually take a beating when it's recounted how much Hawaiian culture they destroyed while "civilizing" the natives. However, they seem to have done one thing right. They introduced the Hawaiians to the diatonic musical scale and immediately opened a door to latent and superbly harmonious talent. Before the missionaries, the Hawaiians knew little about melody. Though sonorous, their *mele* were repetitive chants in which the emphasis was placed on historical accuracy and not on "making music." The Hawaiians, in short, didn't *sing*. But within a few years of the missionaries' arrival, they were belting out good old Christian hymns, and one of their favorite pastimes became group and individual singing.

Early in the 1800s, Spanish *vaqueros* from California were imported to teach the Hawaiians how to be cowboys. With them came guitars and moody ballads. The Hawaiian *paniolo* (cowboys) quickly learned how to punch cows and croon away the long lonely nights on the range. Immigrants who came along a little later in the

19th century, especially from Portugal, helped create a Hawaiian-style music. Their biggest influence was a small, four-stringed instrument called a *braga* or *cavaquinho*. One owned by Augusto Dias was the prototype of a homegrown Hawaiian instrument that became known as the ukulele. "Jumping flea," the translation of ukulele, is an appropriate name devised by the Hawaiians when they saw how nimble the fingers were as they "jumped" over the strings.

King Kalakaua (the Merrie Monarch) and Queen Lili'uokalani were both patrons of the arts who furthered the Hawaiian musical identity at the turn of the 20th century. Kalakaua revived the hula and was also a gifted lyricist and balladeer. He wrote the words to "Hawaii Pono," which became the national anthem of Hawaii and later the state anthem. Lili'uokalani wrote the hauntingly beautiful "Aloha O'e," which is often pointed to as the "spirit of Hawaii" in music. Detractors say that its melody is extremely close to the old Christian hymn, "Rock Beside the Sea," but the lyrics are so beautiful and perfectly fitted that this doesn't matter.

Just prior to Kalakaua's reign a Prussian bandmaster, Captain Henry Berger, was invited to head the fledgling Royal Hawaiian Band, which he turned into a very respectable orchestra lauded by many visitors to the islands. Berger was open-minded and learned to love Hawaiian music. He collaborated with Kalakaua and other island musicians to incorporate their music into a Western format. He headed the band for 43 years until 1915, and was instrumental in making music a serious pursuit of talented Hawaiians.

Popular Hawaiian Music

Hawaiian music has a unique twang, a special feeling that says the same thing to everyone who hears it: "Relax, sit back in the moonlight, watch the swaying palms as the surf sings a lullaby." This special sound is epitomized by the bouncy ukulele, the falsettos of Hawaiian crooners, and by the smooth ring of the "steel" or "Hawaiian" guitar. The steel guitar is a variation originated by Joseph Kekuku in the 1890s. Stories abound of how Joseph Kekuku devised this instrument; the most popular versions say that Joe dropped his comb or pocketknife on his guitar strings and liked what he heard. Driven by the faint rhythm of an inner sound, he went to the machine shop at the Kamehameha Schools and turned out a steel bar for sliding over the strings. To complete the sound he changed the cat-gut strings to steel and raised them so they wouldn't hit the frets. Voila!—Hawaiian music as the world knows it today.

The first melodious strains of **slack-key guitar** *(ki ho'alu)* can be traced back to the time of Kamehameha III and the *vaqueros* from California. The Spanish had their way of tuning the guitar, and played difficult and aggressive music that did not sit well with Hawaiians, who were much more gentle and casual in their manners.

Hawaiians soon became adept at making their own music. At first, one person played the melody, but it lacked fullness. There was no body to the sound. So, as one *paniolo* fooled with the melody, another soon learned to play bass, which added depth. But, a player was often alone, and by experimenting he or she learned to get the right hand going with the melody and play the bass note with the thumb to improve the sound. Singers also learned that they could "open tune" the guitar to match their rich voices.

Hawaiians believed knowledge was sacred, and what is sacred should be treated with utmost respect—which meant keeping it secret, except from sincere apprentices. Guitar playing became a personal art form whose secrets were closely guarded, handed down only to family members, and only to those who showed ability and determination. When old-time slack-key guitar players were done strumming, they loosened all the strings so no one could figure out how they had them tuned. If they were playing, and some folks came by who were interested and weren't part of the family, the Hawaiians stopped what they were doing, put their guitars down, and put their feet across the strings to wait for the folks to go away. As time went on, more and more Hawaiians began to play slack key, and a common repertoire emerged.

An accomplished musician could easily figure out the simple songs, once they had figured out how the family had tuned the guitar. One of the most popular tunings was the "open G." Old Hawaiian folks called it the "taro patch tune." Different songs came out, and if you were in their family and were interested in the guitar, they took the time to sit down and teach you. The way they taught was straightforward—and a test of your sincerity at the same time. The old master would start to play. He just wanted you to listen and get a feel for the music—nothing more than that. You brought your guitar and *listened*. When you felt it, you played it, and the knowledge was transferred. Today, only a handful of slack-key guitar players know how to play the classic tunes classically. The best-known and perhaps greatest slack-key player was Gabby Pahinui, with The Sons of Hawaii. When he passed away he left many recordings behind. A slack-key master still singing and playing is Raymond Kane. Kane now teaches a handful of students his wonderful and haunting music. Not one of his students is from his own family, and most are *haole* musicians trying to preserve the classical method of playing.

Hawaiian music received its biggest boost from a remarkable radio program known as *Hawaii Calls*. This program sent out its music from the Banyan Court of the Moana Hotel from 1935 until 1975. At its peak in the mid-1950s, it was syndicated on more than 700 radio stations throughout the world. Ironically, Japanese pilots heading for Pearl Harbor tuned in island music as a signal beam. Some internationally famous classic tunes came out of the 1940s and '50s. Jack Pitman composed "Beyond the Reef" in 1948; more than 300 artists have recorded it and it has sold well over 12 million records. Other million-sellers include: "Sweet Leilani," "Lovely Hula Hands," "The Crosseyed Mayor of Kaunakakai," and "The Hawaiian Wedding Song."

By the 1960s, Hawaiian music began to die. Just too corny and light for those turbulent years, it belonged to the older generation and the good times that followed World War II. One man was instrumental in keeping Hawaiian music alive during this period. Don Ho, with his "Tiny Bubbles," became the token Hawaiian musician of the 1960s and early '70s. He's persevered long enough to become a legend in his own time, and his Polynesian Extravaganza at the Hilton Hawaiian Village packed visitors in until the early 1990s. He now plays at the Waikiki Beachcomber Hotel five nights a week. Al Harrington, "The South Pacific Man," until his recent retirement had another Honolulu "big revue" that drew large crowds. Of this type of entertainment, perhaps the most Hawaiian was Danny Kaleikini, who entertained his audience with dances, Hawaiian anecdotes, and tunes on the traditional Hawaiian nose flute.

The Beat Goes On

Beginning in the mid-1970s islanders began to assert their cultural identity. One of the unifying factors was the coming of age of "Hawaiian" music. It graduated from the "little grass shack" novelty tune and began to include sophisticated jazz, rock, and contemporary rhythms. Accomplished musicians whose roots were in traditional island music began to highlight their tunes with this distinctive sound. The best embellish their arrangements with ukuleles, steel guitars, and traditional percussion and melodic instruments. Some excellent modern recording artists have become island institutions. The local people say that you know if the Hawaiian harmonies are good if they give you "chicken skin."

Each year special music awards, **Na Hoku Hanohano**, or Hoku for short, are given to distinguished island musicians. The following are some Hoku winners considered by their contemporaries to be among the best in Hawaii. If they're playing on one of the islands while you're in Hawaii, don't miss them (some, unfortunately, are no longer among the living, but their recorded music can still be appreciated). **Barney Isaacs and George Kuo, Na Leo Pilimihana, Robi Kahakalau, Keali'i Reichel, Darren Benitez, Sonny Kamahele, Ledward Kaapana, Hapa, Israel Kamakawiwio'ole**, and **Pure Heart**.

Past Hoku winners who have become renowned performers include: **Brothers Cazimero**, who are blessed with beautiful harmonic voices; **Krush**, who are highly regarded for their contemporary sounds; **The Peter Moon Band**, fantastic performers with a strong traditional sound; **Henry Kapono**, formerly of Cecilio and Kapono; and **The Beamer Brothers**. Others include **Loyal Garner, Del Beazley, Bryan Kessler & Me No Hoa Aloha**, and **Susi Hussong**.

Those with Internet access can check out the Hawaiian music scene at one of the following websites: Hawaiian Music Island, www.mele.

com; Nahenahenet, www.nahenahe.net; and Hawaiian Music Guide, www.hawaii-music.com. While not the only sites, they are a good place to start. For listening to Hawaiian music on the Web, try: http://kkcr.org, www.kccn.com, and www.hotspots.hawaii.com/IRH.

FESTIVALS, HOLIDAYS, AND EVENTS

In addition to all the American national holidays, Hawaii celebrates its own festivals, pageants, ethnic fairs, and a multitude of specialized exhibits. They occur throughout the year, some particular to only one island or locality, while others such as Aloha Week and Lei Day are celebrated on all the islands. Some of the smaller local happenings are semi-spontaneous, so there's no *exact* date when they're held. These are some of the most rewarding, because they provide the best times to have fun with the local people. At festival time, everyone is welcome. Check local newspapers and the free island magazines for exact dates of events. For additional events of all sorts throughout the state, visit the calendar of events listing on the HVB website at http://calendar.gohawaii.com, the Hawaii vacation planner website at www.hshawaii.com/vacplanner/calendar, or visit the State Foundation of Culture and the Arts calendar, which features arts and cultural events, activities, and programs at www.state.hi.us/sfca/culturecalendar.html.

Note: Island-specific festivals and events are listed in the individual island chapters below.

Statewide Events

Wesak or Buddha Day is on the closest Sunday to April 8, and celebrates the birthday of Gautama Buddha. Ornate offerings of tropical flowers are placed at temple altars throughout Hawaii. Enjoy the sunrise ceremonies at Kapi'olani Park, Honolulu, with Japanese in their best *kimonos* along with flower festivals, pageants, and dance programs in many island temples.

May 1 is May Day to the communist world, but in Hawaii red is only one of the colors when everyone dons a lei for **Lei Day.** Festivities abound throughout Hawaii, but there are special goings-on at Kapi'olani Park, Honolulu.

Agricultural exhibits, down-home cooking, entertainment, and fresh produce are presented for four weekends starting in late May at the **50th State Fair,** at Aloha Stadium, Honolulu.

King Kamehameha Day, June 11, is a state holiday honoring Kamehameha the Great, with festivities on all islands. Check local papers for times and particulars. The following are the main events: O'ahu holds a lei-draping ceremony at the King Kamehameha statue in downtown Honolulu, along with parades complete with floats and pageantry featuring a *ho'olaule'a* (street party) in Waikiki; Kailua-Kona on the Big Island is hospitable with a *ho'olaule'a,* parades, art demonstrations, entertainment, and contests; on Kaua'i enjoy parades, *ho'olaule'a,* arts, and crafts centered around the Kaua'i County Building; Maui's Lahaina and Kahului are decked out for parades and pageants.

The **Aloha Festival** is a two-month-long celebration (Sept.–October) with more than 300 events on all of the islands, where everyone celebrates Hawaii's own "intangible quality," *aloha.* There are parades, lu'au, historical pageants, balls, and various entertainment. The spirit of *aloha* is infectious and all are welcomed to join in. Check local papers and tourist literature for happenings near you. For information, call 800/852-7690.

To promote cultural understanding and awareness among people of the different ethnic groups in the state, the **Hawaii International Film Festival** screens some of the best films from the East, West, and Oceania at various theaters around the island during November. Seminars and workshops are also held. For information, call 800/876-0567 or 800/752-8193 or visit the website at www.hiff.org

On **New Year's Eve** hold onto your hat, because they do it up big in Hawaii. Merriment and alcohol flow all over the islands. Firecrackers are illegal, but they go off everywhere. Beware of hangovers and drunken drivers.

ON THE ROAD

ON THE ROAD
SPORTS AND RECREATION

Hawaii is a playground for young and old with sports, games, and activities galore. Everyone can find something they enjoy, and most activities are free, relatively cheap, or once-in-a-lifetime thrills that are worth the money. The sea is the ideal playground. You can swim, snorkel, scuba, surf, bodysurf, windsurf, fish, sail, canoe, kayak, parasail, cruise, or stroll along the shore picking up shells or exploring tidepools. Every island offers tennis and golf, along with plenty of horseback riding, hiking, biking, and hunting, with more limited freshwater fishing. Spectator sports such as baseball, basketball, polo, and especially football are popular, and the Kona Coast of the Big Island is a mecca for world-class triathletes. Whatever your desire or physical abilities may be, there'll be some activity that strikes your fancy in Hawaii.

One of the best tonics for relaxation is to play hard at something you thoroughly enjoy, so you're deliciously tired and fulfilled at day's end. For you this might be hooking onto an 800-pound marlin that'll test you to the limit, or perhaps just giving yourself to the sea and floating on gentle waves. Hawaii is guaranteed to thrill the young, invigorate the once young, put a twinkle in your eye, and add a bounce to your step.

The following sports and recreation overview is designed to give you an idea of what's available. More in-depth information can be found in the travel chapters below. There you'll also find specific entries for localized sports like jet skiing, water-skiing, snow skiing, parasailing, and much more. Whatever else you may do in Hawaii, you owe it to yourself to do one thing: enjoy it!

SCUBA AND SNORKELING

If you think Hawaii is beautiful above the sea, wait until you explore below. The warm tropical waters and coral growth make it a fascinating haven for reef fish and aquatic plant life. Snorkel and dive sites, varying in difficulty and challenge,

ON THE ROAD

HAWAIIAN SHELLS

helmut

miter

cone

auger

cowrie

opohi

spindle

NOT DRAWN TO SCALE

DIANA LASICH HARPER

are accessible from all islands. Sites can be totally hospitable ones where families snorkeling for the first time can have an exciting but safe frolic, or they can be accessible only to the experienced diver. Every island has dive shops where you can rent or buy equipment, and where dive boats and instruction on all levels can be arranged. You'll soon discover that Hawaiian waters are remarkably clear, with excellent visibility. Below, fish in every fathomable color parade by. Lavender clusters of coral, red and gold coral trees, and more than 1,500 different types of shells carpet the ocean floor. In some spots (like O'ahu's Hanauma Bay) the fish are so accustomed to humans that they'll come looking for you. In other spots, lurking moray eels add the zest of danger. Sharks and barracuda pose less danger than scraping your knee on the coral or being driven against the rocks by a heavy swell. There are enormous but harmless sea bass and a profusion of sea turtles. All this awaits below Hawaii's waters.

Scuba

Scuba divers must show certification cards to rent gear from local shops, fill tanks, or take a charter dive. Plenty of outstanding scuba instructors will give you lessons toward certification, and they're especially reasonable because of the stiff competition. Prices vary, but you can take a three- to five-day semiprivate certification course, including all equipment, for $300–425. Divers unaccustomed to Hawaiian waters should not dive alone regardless of their experience. Most opt for dive tours to special dive grounds guaranteed to please. These vary also, but an *accompanied* single-tank dive where no boat is involved goes for about $85. For a double-tank boat dive, expect to spend $100. There are charter dives, night dives, and photography dives. Most companies pick you up at your hotel, take you to the site, and return you home. Basic equipment rental costs $30–50 for the day, and most times the water is so mild you'll need only the top of a wet suit.

Snorkeling

Scuba diving takes expensive special equipment, skills, and athletic ability. Snorkeling in comparison is much simpler and enjoyable to anyone who can swim. In about 15 minutes you

can be taught the fundamentals of snorkeling— you really don't need formal instructions. Other snorkelers or dive shop attendants can tell you enough to get you started. Because you can breathe without lifting your head, you get great propulsion from the fins and hardly ever need to use your arms. You can go for much greater distances and spend longer in the water than if you were swimming. Experienced snorkelers make an art of this sport and you too can see and do amazing things with a mask, snorkel, and flippers. Don't, however, get a false sense of invincibility and exceed your limitations.

You can buy or rent snorkel equipment in dive shops and in department stores. Sometimes condos and hotels offer free snorkeling equipment for their guests, but if you have to rent it, don't do it at a hotel or condo; go to a dive shop where it's much cheaper. Expect to spend $3.50–8 a day for mask, fins, and snorkel. A special option is an underwater camera. Rental of camera, film included, runs about $10–15. Many boats will take you out snorkeling. Prices

ON THE ROAD

WATER SAFETY TIPS

Observe the water before you enter. Note where others are swimming or snorkeling and go there. Don't turn your back on the water. Dive under incoming waves before they reach you. Come in *before* you get too tired.

When the wind comes up, get out. Stay out of water during periods of high surf. High surf often creates rip tides that can pull you out to sea. If caught in a rip tide, don't panic. Swim parallel to the shore until you are out of the strong pull. Be aware of ocean currents, especially those within reefs that can cause rip tides when the water washes out a channel.

If you are using water equipment, make sure that it all works properly. Wear a T-shirt when snorkeling; it could save you from a major sunburn.

Stay off of coral. Coral is damaged easily by standing on it or breaking it with your hands.

Leave the fish and turtles alone. Green sea turtles are an endangered species and a fine of up to $10,000 can be levied on those who knowingly disturb them. Have a great time looking, but give them space.

ON THE ROAD

REEF FISH

blue-spotted cowfish

Hawaiian lionfish

saddleback wrasse

manta ray

Potter's angelfish

bluestrip butterflyfish

mottled moray

NOT DRAWN TO SCALE

trumpetfish

manini

lagoon
humu

moorish idol

threadfin
butterflyfish

red-lipped
parrotfish

uhu

Achilles
tang

range from about $40 (half day, four hours) to $70 (full day, eight hours). Activities centers can also arrange these excursions for no extra charge.

Snuba

No, that's not a typo. Snuba offers a hybrid sport that is half snorkeling and half scuba diving. You have a regulator, a weight belt, mask, and flippers, and you're tethered to scuba tanks that float 20 feet above you on a sea-sled. The unofficial motto of snuba is "secure but free." The idea is that many people become anxious diving under the waves encumbered by tanks and all the scuba apparatus. Snuba frees you. You would think that being tethered to the sled would slow you down, but actually you're sleeker and can make better time than a normal scuba diver. The sled is made from industrial-strength polyethylene and is 2.5 feet wide by 7.5 feet long, consisting of a view window and a belly in the sled for the scuba tank. If you get tired, just surface and use it as a raft.

CATCHING WAVES

Surfing

Surfing is a sport indigenous to Hawaii. When the white man first arrived, he was astonished to see natives paddling out to meet the ships on long carved boards, then gracefully riding them in to shore on crests of waves. The Hawaiians called surfing *he'enalu* (to "slide on a wave"). The newcomers were fascinated by this sport, recording it on engravings and woodcuts marveled at around the world. Meanwhile, the Polynesians left records of surfing in petroglyphs and in *mele* of past exploits. A Waikiki beach boy named Duke Kahanamoku won a treasure box full of gold medals for swimming at the 1912 Olympic Games. Thereafter, he became a celebrity, introducing surfing to California, Australia, and the rest of the world. Surfing later became a lifestyle, popularized far and

... but a diversion, the most common is upon the water ... the men lay themselves flat upon an oval piece of plank ... they wait the time for the greatest swell that sets on shore, and altogether push forward with their arms to keep on its top, it sends them in with a most astonishing velocity ...."
—James King, circa 1779

wide by the songs of the Beach Boys in the 1960s. Now surfing is a sport enjoyed around the world, complete with championships, movies, magazines, and advanced board technology.

It takes years of practice to become good, but with determination, good swimming ability, and a sense of balance you can learn the fundamentals in a short time. At surf shops on all islands you can rent a board for very reasonable prices. The boards of the ancient *ali'i* were up to 20 feet long and weighed more than 150 pounds, but today's board is made from ultralight foam plastic covered in fiberglass. They're about six feet long and weigh 12 pounds or so. Innovations occur every day in surfing, but one is the changeable "skeg" or rudder allowing you to surf in variable conditions.

The sport of surfing is still male-dominated, but women champions have been around for years. The most famous surfing beach in the world is Sunset Beach and the Banzai Pipeline on North Shore O'ahu. Every year the nationally televised pro-tour Triple Crown of Surfing is held there, usually from late October to December. It's only a matter of time before surfing becomes an Olympic sport. One of the most brilliant books ever written on surfing is *Surfing, the Ultimate Pleasure,* by Leonard Lueras. It can be found at almost every surf shop.

Sailboarding

Technically called sailboarding, this sport is called windsurfing by most people, after the name of one of the most famous manufacturers of sailboards. A combination of surfing and sailing, the equipment is a rather large and stable surfboard mounted with a highly maneuverable sail. It may sound difficult, but most people find it slightly easier than surfing because you're mobilized by the wind and not at the mercy of the waves. You don't have to "read" the waves as well as a surfer, and like riding a bicycle, as long as you keep moving you can hold your balance. Boards and lessons are available on all the major islands. Sailboards are slightly more expensive than surfboards to rent, but you should be in business for about $35–50.

Kitesurfing

A cross between wakeboarding and flying a kite, kitesurfing (also known as kiteboarding) is one of the newest water sports to hit the island. With kitesurfing, a large foil-sail kite is attached by long ropes to a grab bar that is clipped to a harness that's worn around the waist. Steering is done by pulling one end of the bar or the other to raise or lower the kite, catching more or less wind. A wide ski is used, similar to a wakeboard ski, except that this one has a short rudder. Booties, a neoprene version of snowboard boots, keep you attached to the board. The proficient skim the water as fast and as freely as windsurfers. Those who really know how to use the wind to their advantage can get 20–30 feet of loft. Those who know the sport say that it's not for the timid, nor as easy as it might appear. Take lessons first. Both Maui and O'ahu have shops that give lessons and rent gear.

Boogie Boards

If surfing or sailboarding is a bit too much for you, try a boogie board—a foam or hard-shell board about three feet long that you lie on from the waist up. With the help of flippers for maneuverability, you can get tremendous rides on boogie boards. You can learn to ride in minutes and it's much faster, easier, and more thrilling than bodysurfing. Boogie boards are for sale all over the islands and are relatively cheap. You can rent one from a dive or surf shop for $5–7, or buy your own for $80–350.

FISHING

Hawaii has some of the most exciting and productive "blue waters" in all the world. A statewide "sport fishing fleet" comprises skippers and crews who are experienced professional anglers. You can also fish from jetties, piers, rocks, and the shore. If rod and reel don't strike your fancy, try the old-fashioned throw net, or take along a spear when you go snorkeling or scuba diving. There's nighttime torch fishing that requires special skills and equipment, and freshwater fishing in public areas. Streams and irrigation ditches yield introduced trout, bass, and catfish. While you're at it, you might want to try crabbing for Kona and Samoan crabs, or working low-tide areas after sundown hunting octopus, a tantalizing island delicacy.

Deep-Sea Fishing

Most game-fishing boats work the waters on the calmer leeward sides of the islands. Some skippers, carrying anglers who are accustomed to the sea, will also work the much rougher windward coasts and island channels where the fish bite just as well. Trolling is the preferred method of deep-sea fishing; this is usually done in depths of 1,000–2,000 fathoms (a fathom is six feet). The skipper will either "area fish," which means running in a crisscross pattern over a known productive area, or "ledge fish," which involves trolling over submerged ledges where game fish are known to feed. The most advanced marine technology, available on many boats, sends sonar bleeps searching for fish. On deck, the crew and anglers scan the horizon in the age-old Hawaiian tradition—searching for clusters of seabirds feeding on bait fish pursued to the surface by the huge and aggressive game fish. "Still fishing," or "bottom fishing" with hand lines, can yield some tremendous fish.

The Game Fish

The most thrilling game fish in Hawaiian waters is marlin, generically known as "billfish" or a'u to the locals. The king of them is the blue marlin, with record catches well over 1,000 pounds. There are also striped marlin and sailfish, which often go more than 200 pounds. The best times for marlin are during spring, summer, and fall. The fishing tapers off in January and picks up again by late February. "Blues" can be caught year-round, but, oddly enough, when they stop biting it seems as though the striped marlin pick up. Second to the marlin is tuna. 'Ahi (yellowfin tuna) is caught in Hawaiian waters at depths of 100–1,000 fathoms. It can weigh 300 pounds, but 25–100 pounds is common. There's also aku (skipjack) and the delicious ono, which average 20–40 pounds.

Mahimahi is another strong-fighting, deepwater game fish abundant in Hawaii. These delicious fish can weigh up to 70 pounds. Shore fishing and bait-casting yield papio, a jack tuna.

ON THE ROAD

SEASICKNESS

Many people are affected by motion sickness, particularly on sailing vessels. If you tend to get queasy, try one of the following to prevent symptoms. Oral medications widely available through pharmacies are **Dramamine, Bonine,** and **Triptone.** Running about $4 a pop, Dramamine and Bonine may cause drowsiness in some people; Triptone seems not to. Although these medications are usually taken just before boarding a ship, they might work better if a half dose is taken the night before and the second half is taken the morning of your ride. In all cases, however, take medication as prescribed by the manufacturer.

Those who don't want to take medication might try **Seabands,** elastic bands worn around the wrists that put gentle pressure on the insides of the wrists by way of a small plastic button. Seabands are available at pharmacies and at most scuba shops for about $8.50 and can be reused until the elastic wears out. Follow directions for best results.

Without medication or pressure bands, you can still work to counter the effects of motion sickness. The night before, try not to eat too much, particularly greasy food, and don't drink an excess of alcohol. During the ride, if your stomach begins to be upset, eat a few soda crackers. If you begin to feel dizzy, focus on the horizon or a mountaintop—something stationary—and try to direct your thoughts to something other than your dizziness or queasiness. With children (and perhaps adults as well), talking about what animal figures they can see in the clouds or how many houses they can spot along the shoreline may be enough to distract them until they begin feeling better.

Akule, a scad (locally called *halalu*), is a smallish schooling fish that comes close to shore and is great to catch on light tackle. *Ulua* is a shore fish that can be found in tidepools. They're excellent eating, averaging 2–3 pounds, and are taken at night or with spears. *'O'io* are bonefish that come close to shore to spawn. They're caught by bait-casting and bottom fishing with cut bait. Although bony, they're a favorite for fish cakes and *poki. Awa* is a schooling fish that loves brackish water. It can get up to three feet long and is a good fighter. A favorite for throw netters, it's even raised commercially in fishponds. Besides these there are plenty of goatfish, mullet, mackerel, snapper, sharks, and even salmon.

"Blue Water" Areas

One of the most famous fishing spots in Hawaii is **Penguin Banks** off the west coast of Moloka'i and the south coast of O'ahu. The "Chicken Farm" at the southern tip of Penguin Banks has great trolling waters for marlin and mahimahi. The calm waters off the Wai'anae Coast of O'ahu yield marlin and *'ahi.* The Kona Coast of the Big Island, with its crystal waters, shelters the most famous marlin grounds in Hawaii. Every year the **Hawaiian International Billfish Tournament** draws anglers from around the world to Kona. The marlin are found in 1,000 fathoms of water, but close in on the Kona Coast you can hook *ono* and hand line for *onaga* and *kahala.* Maui fishers usually head for the waters formed by the triangle of Maui, Lana'i, and Kaho'olawe, where they troll for marlin, *mahi,* and *ono,* or bottom fish for snapper. Kaua'i has excellent fishing waters year-round, with *ono, 'ahi,* and marlin along the ledges. Large schools of *'ahi* come to Kaua'i in the spring, and the fishing is fabulous with possible 200-pound catches.

Charter Boats

The charter boats of Hawaii come in all shapes and sizes, but all are staffed by professional, competent crews and captains with intimate knowledge of Hawaiian waters. You can hire a boat for a private or share charter, staying out for four, six, or eight hours. Some captains like to go for longer runs as there is a better chance of a catch and they can get farther into the water; some now do only private charters. Boat size varies, but four anglers per midsize boat is about average. No matter the size, most boats will take no more than six anglers. Although some provide it, be sure to bring food and drink for the day; no bananas, please—they're bad luck. Deep-sea fishing on a share basis costs approximately $120 per half day (four hours) or $150 full day, per person. On a private basis, expect $500 per half day or up to $800 for a full day. No fishing licenses are required. Tackle weighing 30–130 pounds is carried on the boats and is part of the service. It is customary for the crew to be given any fish that are caught, but naturally this doesn't apply to trophy fish; the crew is also glad to cut off steaks and fillets for your personal use. Honolulu's Kewalo Basin, only a few minutes from Waikiki, has the largest fleet of charter boats. Poka'i Bay also has a fleet, and others sail out of Kane'ohe Bay. On the Big Island, Kailua-Kona has the largest concentration of charter boats, with some boats out of Kawaihae. Maui boats run out of Lahaina or Ma'alaea Bay. Moloka'i has a few boats berthed at Kaunakakai, Lana'i has one, and on Kaua'i most boats sail out of Nawiliwili Harbor.

Freshwater Fishing

Due to Hawaii's unique geology, only a handful of natural lakes and rivers and a few reservoirs are good for fishing. The state maintains four "Public Fishing Areas" spread over Kaua'i, O'ahu, and Hawai'i. None are found on Maui, Lana'i, or Moloka'i. The two public fishing areas on O'ahu are **Wahiawa Public Fishing Area, a** 300-acre irrigation reservoir primarily for sugarcane near Wahiawa in central O'ahu, and **Nu'uanu Freshwater Fish Refuge: Reservoir no. 4,** in the Ko'olau Mountains above Honolulu. On Kaua'i, **Koke'e Public Fishing Area** is north of Kekaha, with 13 miles of stream, two miles of irrigation ditches, and a 15-acre reservoir offering only rainbow trout. On Hawai'i, the **Waiakea Public Fishing Area** encompasses a 26-acre estuarine pond within the city of Hilo.

Freshwater Fish

Hawaii has only one native freshwater game fish, the 'o'opu. This goby is an oddball with fused ventral fins. It grows to 12 inches and is found on all islands, especially Kaua'i. Introduced species include largemouth and smallmouth bass, bluegill, catfish, *tucunare,* oscar, carp, *pongee* (snakehead), and tilapia. The only trout to survive is the rainbow, found only in the streams of Kaua'i and the Big Island. The *tucunare* is a tough-fighting, good-tasting game fish introduced from South America, similar to the oscar from the same region. Both have been

compared to bass, but are of a different family. The tilapia is from Africa and has become common in Hawaii's irrigation ditches. It's a "mouth breeder," and the young will take refuge in their parents' protective jaws even a few weeks after hatching. The snakehead is an eel-like fish that inhabits reservoirs and is a great fighter. The channel catfish can grow to more than 20 pounds and bites best after sundown. There's also the carp, and with its broad tail and tremendous strength, it's the poor person's game fish. All of these species are best caught with light spinning tackle or with a bamboo pole and a trusty old worm. The catch limit of eight species of freshwater fish is regulated.

Fishing Licenses

A license is needed for freshwater fishing only. A **Freshwater Game Fishing License** is good for one year, from July 1 to June 30. Licenses cost $25 for non-island nonresidents, $10 for 7-day tourist use, $20 for 30-day tourist use; $5 for residents over age 15 and active duty military personnel, their spouses, and dependents over age 15, $3 for children ages 9–15; they are free to senior citizens and children under age nine when accompanied by an adult with a license. You can pick up a license at sporting goods stores or at the Division of Aquatic Resources on each of the main islands. Be sure to ask for its *Hawaii Fishing Regulations* and *Freshwater Fishing in Hawaii* booklets. All game fish except trout may be taken year-round. Trout, on Kaua'i only, may be taken for 16 days commencing on the first Saturday of August. Thereafter, for the remainder of August and September, trout can be taken only on Saturday, Sunday, and state holidays. Fishing is usually allowed in most State Forest Reserve Areas. Owners' permission must be obtained to fish on private property.

CAMPING AND HIKING

A major aspect of the "Hawaii experience" is the simple beauty of nature and the outdoors. Some visitors come to Hawaii to luxuriate at resorts and dine in fine restaurants, but everyone heads for the sand and surf, and most are captivated by the lush mountainous interior. What better way to savor this natural beauty than by hiking slowly through it or pitching a tent in the middle of it? Hawaii offers a full range of hiking and camping, and what's more, most of it is easily accessible. Camping facilities are located near many choice beaches and amid some of the most scenic mountain areas in the islands. They range in amenities from full housekeeping cabins to primitive hike-in sites. Camping permits can be obtained by walk-in application to the appropriate office, or by writing or phoning. Although there is usually no problem obtaining sites, when writing, request reservations well in advance, allowing a minimum of one month for letters to go back and forth.

Some restrictions to hiking apply because much of the land is privately owned, so advance permission to hike may be required. But plenty of public access trails along the coast and deep into the interior would fill the itineraries of even the most intrepid hikers. If you enjoy the great outdoors on the Mainland, you'll be thrilled by these "mini-continents," where in one day you can go from the frosty summits of alpine wonderlands down into baking cactus-covered deserts and emerge through jungle foliage onto a sun-soaked subtropical shore.

Equipment

Like everything else you take to Hawaii, your camping and hiking equipment should be lightweight and durable. Camping equipment size and weight should not cause a problem with baggage requirements on airlines: if it does, it's a tip-off that you're hauling too much. One odd luggage consideration you might make is to bring along a small Styrofoam cooler packed with equipment. Exchange the equipment for food items when you get to Hawaii. If you intend to car camp successfully and keep food prices down, you'll definitely need a cooler. You can also buy one on arrival for only a few dollars.

Consider a frame backpack or a convertible pack that turns into a soft-side suitcase, and a day pack. You'll need a lightweight **tent,** preferably with a rainfly and a sewn-in waterproof floor. This will save you from getting wet and miserable, and will keep out mosquitoes, cockroaches, ants, and the islands' few stinging insects. **Sleeping bags** are a good idea, although you can get along at sea level with only a blanket. Downfilled bags are necessary for Haleakala, Mauna

Kea, Mauna Loa, or any high-elevation camping—you'll freeze without one.

Campstoves are needed because there's very little available wood, it's often wet in the deep forest, and open fires are often prohibited. If you'll be car-camping, take along a multiburner stove; for hiking, a backpacker's stove will be necessary. The grills found at some campgrounds are popular with many families who often go to the beach parks for open-air dinners. You can buy a very inexpensive charcoal grill at many variety stores throughout Hawaii. It's a great idea to take along a **lantern.** This will add safety for car-campers. Definitely take a **flashlight,** replacement batteries, and a few small **candles.** A complete **first-aid kit** can be the difference between life and death, and it's worth the extra bulk. Hikers, especially those leaving the coastal areas, should take rain gear, a plastic ground cloth, a utility knife, a compass, a safety whistle, a mess kit, water purification tablets, biodegradable "Camp Suds" or similar soap, a canteen, nylon twine, a sewing kit (dental floss works as thread), and waterproof matches. In a film container pack a few nails, safety pins, fishhooks, line, and bendable wire. Nothing else does what these do and they're all handy for a million and one uses. If you find a staff or hiking stick at the beginning of a trail, consider using it—others obviously found it useful—but leave it at the trailhead for others to use when you return. Only a limited number of stores sell or rent camping and hiking equipment.

Hiking Tips

Keep your eye on two things to remain safe while hiking in Hawaii: humans and nature. The general rule is: the farther you get away from towns, the safer you'll be from human-induced hassles. Hike with someone—share the experience. If possible, don't hike or camp alone, especially if you're a woman. Don't leave your valuables in your tent, and always carry your money, papers, and camera with you. At the least, let someone know where you are going and when you plan to be back; supply an itinerary and your expected route, then stick to it. Stay on designated trails—this not only preserves the fragile environment, it also keeps you out of dangerous areas. While hiking, remember that many trails are well maintained, but trailhead markers are often missing. The trails themselves can be muddy, which can make them treacherously slippery and often knee-deep. Occasionally, trails will be closed for maintenance, so stay off these routes. Buy and use a trail map.

Wear comfortable clothing. Shorts and a T-shirt will suffice on many trails, but long pants and long-sleeve shirts are better where it's rainy and overgrown. Bring a windbreaker or raingear—it can rain and blow at any time. Wear sturdy walking or hiking shoes that you don't mind getting wet and muddy—it's almost guaranteed on some trails. Some very wet spots and stream crossings may be better done in tabi or other water shoes. Your clothes may become permanently stained with mud—a wonderful memento of your trip. Officials and others often ask hikers to pick clinging seeds off their clothes when coming out at the trailhead and to wash off boots so as not to unintentionally transport seeds to nonnative areas.

Always bring food because you cannot, in most cases, forage from the land. Carry plenty of drinking water, at least two quarts per day. Heat can cause your body to lose water and salt. If you become woozy or weak, rest, take salt, and drink water as you need it. Remember, it takes much more water to restore a dehydrated person than to stay hydrated as you go; take small, frequent sips. No matter how clean it looks, water in most streams is biologically polluted and will give you bad stomach problems if you drink it without purifying it first by boiling, filtering, or adding purification tablets. For your part, please don't use the streams as a toilet.

Use sunscreen. The sun can be intense and UV rays go through clouds. Bring and use mosquito lotion—even in paradise pesky bugs abound. Do not litter. Carry a dedicated trash bag and take out all that you bring in.

Some trails are used by hunters of wild boar, deer, or game birds. If you hike in hunting areas during hunting season, wear brightly colored or reflective clothing. Often, forest reserve trails have check-in stations at trailheads. Hikers and hunters must sign a logbook, especially if they intend to camp. The comments by previous hikers are worth reading for up-to-the-minute information on trail conditions.

Twilight is short in the islands, and night sets in rapidly. In June, sunrise is around 6 A.M. and sunset 7 P.M.; in December, these occur at 7 A.M. and 6 P.M. If you become lost, find an open spot and stay put; at night, stay as dry as you can. If you must continue, walk on ridges and avoid the gulches, which have more obstacles and make it harder for rescuers to spot you. Do not light a fire, but keep as dry as you can. Hawaii is made of brittle and crumbly volcanic rock. Never attempt to climb steep *pali* (cliffs). Every year people are stranded, and fatalities have occurred. Be careful of elevation sickness, especially on Haleakala, Mauna Loa, and Mauna Kea. The best cure is to head down as soon as possible. Be mindful of flash floods. Small creeks can turn into raging torrents with upland rains. Never camp in a dry creekbed. Fog is encountered only at elevations of 1,500–5,000 feet, but be careful of disorientation.

Heat can cause you to lose water and salt. If you become woozy or weak, rest, take salt, and drink water as you need it. Remember, it takes much more water to restore a dehydrated person than to keep hydrated; take small frequent sips. Generally, stay within your limits, be careful, and enjoy yourself.

Hiking Groups and Information

The **Department of Land and Natural Resources,** Division of Forestry and Wildlife, 1151 Punchbowl St., Room 325, Honolulu, HI 96813, 808/587-0058, is helpful in providing trail maps, accessibility information, hunting and fishing regulations, and general forest rules. This office offers an excellent, free *Recreation Map* for each of the four main islands.

The following organizations can provide information on organized hiking trips. **The Hawaiian Trail and Mountain Club,** P.O. Box 2238, Honolulu, HI 96804, 808/262-2845 or 808/488-1161, meets behind 'Iolani Palace on Saturday at 9 A.M. and Sunday at 8 A.M.; free for members and $2 for nonmembers. The hikes are announced in the *Honolulu Star Bulletin*'s "Pulse of Paradise" column. For the group's *Hiker's Guide*, send $1.50 and an SASE to the above address or check its website: www.geocities.com/yosemite/trails/3660. **Sierra Club, Hawaii Chapter** P.O. Box 2577, Honolulu, HI 96803, 808/538-6616, organizes weekly hikes, $1 for members and $3 for nonmembers. Information about the organization and its hikes is listed in its newsletter and on its website: www.hi.sierraclub.org.

ON THE ROAD

Sierra Club also sells the useful booklet *Hiking Softly in Hawai'i* ($5), which gives general information about hiking in Hawaii; preparation, etiquette, and precautions; a brief chart of major trails on each island, along with their physical characteristics; and other sources of information. Additional information about hiking in Hawaii can be found on the website www2.hawaii. edu/~turner/hikes.html, and about camping at www.visit.hawaii.org/hokeo/activity/camping.html. **Hawaii Audubon Society** can be reached at P.O. Box 22832, Honolulu, HI 96822 for information about bird-watching hikes, or call the **Hawaii Nature Center**, 808/955-0100, for information about hikes.

Hiking and Camping Books

For well-written and detailed hiking guides, complete with maps, check out *Maui Trails, Kauai Trails, Oahu Trails* and *Hawaii Trails* by Kathy Morey. See also Robert Smith's *Hawaii's Best Hiking Trails,* and his *Hiking Maui, Hiking Oahu, Hiking Hawaii* and *Hiking Kauai,* as well as *Hawaiian Hiking Trails* by Craig Chisholm.

Two helpful camping books are *Hawaii: A Camping Guide,* by George Cagala, and Richard McMahon's *Camping Hawai'i.*

Topographical Maps and Nautical Charts

For detailed topographical maps, contact **U.S. Geological Survey, Information Services,** P.O. Box 25286, Denver, CO 80225, 800/USA-MAPS or 703/648-4888, website: www.usgs.gov. Many types of maps are available at Borders Books throughout the islands. A wide range of topographical maps, nautical charts, and local maps can be purchased at independent shops like **Pacific Map Center,** 560 N. Nimitz Hwy., Suite 206A, Honolulu, HI 96817, 808/545-3600, and **Basically Books,** 46 Waianuenue St., 808/961-0144, in downtown Hilo on the Big Island. USGS, Defense Mapping Agency, University of Hawai'i, and Hawaii Geographical Society maps, as well as a limited selection of geographical-related books, can be purchased at **Hawaii Geographic Maps and Books,** 49 S. Hotel St., Honolulu, 808/538-3952 or 800/538-3950, open Monday, Wednesday, and Friday 10 A.M.–2 P.M. Also useful, but not for hiking, are the University of Hawai'i Press reference maps of each island.

For nautical charts, write **National Ocean Service,** Riverdale, MD 20737-1199, 301/436-6990 or 800/638-8972.

NATIONAL PARKS

Hawaii's two national parks sit atop volcanoes: **Haleakala National Park** on Maui and **Hawaii Volcanoes National Park** centered around Kilauea Crater on the Big Island. Camping is free at both, and permits are not required except for the cabins and campgrounds inside Haleakala crater. See the travel chapters for detailed information. Get free information by contacting the individual park headquarters: Hawaii Volcanoes National Park, P.O. Box 52, Hawaii National Park, HI 96718, 808/985-6000, website: www.nps.gov/havo; Haleakala National Park, P.O. Box 369, Makawao, HI 96768, 808/572-9306, website: www.nps.gov/hale. Or try the Hawaii office of the **National Park Service,** 300 Ala Moana Blvd., Honolulu, HI 96850, 808/541-2693.

STATE PARKS

Hawaii's 54 state parks, which include historical parks, recreation areas, recreation piers, waysides, monuments, and underwater parks, are managed by the Department of Land and Natural Resources, through its Division of State Parks branch offices on each island. Some are for looking at, some are restricted to day use, and at 14 (which may change periodically without notice) there is overnight camping. At seven of these parks, A-frames, self-contained cabins, or group accommodations are available on a fee basis with reservations necessary. At the others, camping is $5 per campsite for every night of use, $10 per person per night at the Na Pali Coast State Park campsites, and permits are required. RVs are technically not allowed.

Permits and Rules

Camping permits are good for a maximum stay of five consecutive nights at any one park, except for the Na Pali Coast State Park, which has one- and three-night limits at certain campsites. A permit to the same person for the same park is again available only after 30 days from the last day of previous use. Campgrounds are open every day on the Neighbor Islands but closed Wednesday and Thursday on O'ahu. Arrive after 2 P.M. and check out by 11 A.M., except again on O'ahu, where Wednesday checkout is 8 A.M. You must be 18 for park permits; anyone under that age must be accompanied by an adult. Alcoholic beverages are prohibited, along with nude sunbathing and swimming. Plants and wildlife are protected, but reasonable amounts of fruits and seeds may be gathered for personal consumption. Fires are allowed on cookstoves or in designated pits only. Dogs and other pets must be under control at all times (if allowed) and are not permitted to run around unleashed. Hunting and freshwater fishing are allowed in season with a license, and ocean fishing is permitted except when disallowed by posting. Permits are required for certain trails, pavilions, and remote camps, so check.

Cabins and Shelters

With one exception, housekeeping cabins, A-frames, and group lodges are available daily at seven state parks throughout the state; at Polipoli Spring on Maui, cabins are not available on Tuesday. See specific travel chapters for details. As with camping, permits are required and have the same five-day maximum-stay limitations. Reservations are necessary because of popularity, and a 50 percent deposit within two weeks of reservation is required. There is a 15-day cancellation requirement for refunds, with payment made in cash, money order, cashier's check, or certified check. If you pay by personal or business check, it must be received 30 days before arrival. The exact balance is due on arrival in cash; check-in is 2 P.M., checkout 11 A.M.

State Park Permit-Issuing Offices

Permit applications can be made by mail, by phone, or in person at one of the issuing offices, not more than one year in advance (30 days in advance for O'ahu). Reservations by letter must include your name, address, phone number, names and identification numbers of those over 18 years old in your party, type of permit requested, and duration of stay. Permits can be picked up from the issuing office on arrival with proof of identification. Office hours are Mon.–Fri.

8 A.M.–4 P.M. Usually, camping permits are no problem (O'ahu excepted) to secure on the day you arrive, but reserving ensures you a space and alleviates anxiety. The permits are available from the following offices: **O'ahu,** Division of State Parks, 1151 Punchbowl St., Honolulu, HI 96813, 808/587-0300; **Hawai'i,** Division of State Parks, 75 Aupuni St., Hilo, HI 96720, 808/974-6200; **Maui and Moloka'i,** Division of State Parks, 54 S. High St., Wailuku, HI 96793, 808/984-8109; **Kaua'i,** Division of State Parks, 3060 Eiwa St., Lihu'e, HI 96766, 808/274-3444. For lodging at **Koke'e State Park,** Kaua'i, write Koke'e Lodge, P.O. Box 819, Waimea, HI 96796, 808/335-6061 (9 A.M.–3:45 P.M.); and for **Malaekahana SRA,** O'ahu, write Friends of Malaekahana, P.O. Box 305, La'ie, HI, 96762, 808/293-1736 (10 A.M.–3 P.M.).

COUNTY PARKS

The state of Hawaii is broken up into counties, and the counties control their own parks. Of the more than 600 county parks, more than 100 are scattered primarily along the coastlines and are generally referred to as **beach parks.** Most are for day use only, where visitors fish, swim, snorkel, surf, picnic, and sunbathe, but more than 35 have overnight camping. The rules governing their use vary slightly from county to county, so check the individual travel chapters below, but most have about the same requirements as state parks. Again, the differences between individual parks are too numerous to mention, but the majority have a central pavilion for cooking, restrooms, and cold-water showers (solar heated at a few). Some have individual fire pits, picnic tables, and electricity (usually only at the central pavilion). RVs are allowed to park in appropriate spaces.

Fees and Permits

The fees are quite reasonable at $3–5 per night, per adult, with children about $1 each. One safety point to consider is that beach parks are open to the general public, and most are used with regularity. Quite a few people pass through, and your chances of encountering a hassle or rip-off are slightly higher than average. To get a permit and pay your fees for use of a county park, either write in advance or visit one of the following issuing offices. Most will accept reservations months in advance, with offices generally open during normal working hours. Write or visit the Department of Parks and Recreation, County Parks: **O'ahu,** 650 S. King St., Honolulu, HI 96813, 808/523-4525; **Maui,** War Memorial Gym, 1580-C Ka'ahumanu Ave., Wailuku, HI 96793, 808/270-7389; **Hawai'i,** 25 Aupuni St., Hilo, HI 96720, 808/961-8311; **Kaua'i,** 4444 Rice St., Moikeha Bldg., Suite 150, Lihu'e, HI 96766, 808/241-6660, or during off hours Lihu'e Police Station, 3060 Umi St., 808/245-6711; **Moloka'i,** Mitchell Pauole Center, Kaunakakai, HI 96748, 808/553-3204.

HORSEBACK RIDING

Horseback riding tours are available on each island, ranging from an easy walk along a shoreline bridle path to hard rides into mountainous interiors. But remember, all these tours are guided. On most you can canter, some let you gallop, but none will just let you take off on your own. Some stop at waterfalls, a few include a picnic lunch, and all offer fine island scenery. Important points to consider when thinking about a horseback ride are your level of expertise (or lack thereof) on a horse, the length of ride, and the terrain that the ride traverses—near the ocean, through thick valley forests, with broad vistas, or onto a working cattle ranch. Most operations have age and weight restrictions, often taking those only above age eight or 10 and below 225 pounds, so ask. While most rides run about 60–90 minutes for $60–100, you can find easy $30 45-minute rides as well as $250 five-hour adventures. The options are truly many.

BICYCLING

Bicycling in Hawaii can be both fascinating and frustrating. The countryside is great, and the weather is perfect, but for the most part, Hawaii is not as bicycle-conscious as many places in the country. Few bicycle trails and bicycle lanes exist. Most roads are well paved, and some have adequately wide shoulders.

Others have no shoulders at all. While coastal roads are generally flat and offer suburb views, they are often heavily trafficked. Because of steep climbs, many mountain roads can challenge the most dedicated riders, but these offer grand vistas to those who persevere. Many roads are full of twists and turns and, while fun to bike, do not offer much sight distance for a vehicle coming up behind. Traffic in and around the Honolulu metropolitan area is heavy, and riding a bicycle can be dicey. Traffic in small towns and out in the country is much less severe. Fortunately, there are many roads with little traffic, particularly on the Big Island, so bicycling can be a very enjoyable and rewarding experience. Off-road riders have some choice of trails, but the number is still small, with more found on the Big Island than anywhere else.

If you're planning on spending any length of time on a bicycle in Hawaii, you're probably better off bringing your own bike than renting. If you do rent a bicycle, consider getting a **mountain bike** instead of a delicate road bike, which will allow for the sometimes-poor road conditions and open up the possibilities of off-road biking. Even experienced mountain bikers should be careful on off-road trails, which are often extremely muddy and rutted. While the roads are sometimes congested, pedaling around is usually safe—a fun way of seeing the sights. Always use a helmet, always lock your bike, and always take your bike bag.

You can take your bike with you interisland by plane, but it will cost about $20 one-way—just check it in as baggage. Bikes must be packed in a box or hard case, supplied by the owner. Handlebars must be turned sideways and the pedals removed or turned in. Bikes go space available only—usually not a problem, except, perhaps, during bicycle competitions. In addition, a release of liability for damage must be signed before the airline will accept the bike. If you plan ahead, you can send your bike the previous day by air freight. You can also take your bike on the interisland ferry between Maui and Lana'i. It will cost you $20 each way, but you don't need to pack it.

Getting your bike to Hawaii from the Mainland or another country will depend upon which airline you take. Some will accept bicycles as baggage traveling with you (approximate additional charge of $50 from the Mainland U.S.) if the bikes are properly broken down and boxed in a bicycle box, while others will only take them as air freight, in which case the rates are exorbitant. Check with the airlines well before you plan to go or explore the possibility of shipping it by sea through a freight company.

For general information on biking in Hawaii, contact **Hawaii Bicycling League,** P.O. Box 4403, Honolulu, HI 96812-4403. This nonprofit organization promotes biking as recreation, sport, and transportation, encourages safe biking practices, conducts biking education, and advocates for biking issues. It publishes a monthly newsletter, *Spoke-n-Words,* filled with news of the organization's business, its bicycle safety program for kids, and rides that are open to the public, as well as current bicycle issues and sponsored bicycle competitions throughout the state. Group rides for all levels of abilities are sponsored almost every weekend, and nonmembers are welcome. If you are a bicycle rider living in the islands or simply want a subscription to the newsletter, write for membership information. For mountain biking and trail information on all the major islands, pick up a copy of *Mountain Biking the Hawaiian Islands,* by John Alford.

For additional information, have a look at the *Bicycle Regulations and Illustrated Safety Tips* booklet, put out by the Department of Transportation Services, City and County of Honolulu. Although written for the island of Oʻahu, the information is applicable to all the islands, except for a few minor details. On Oʻahu, pick up a copy at city hall or any satellite city hall or most bike shops. From the Neighbor Islands or if coming from outside the state, write or call for a copy: Bicycle Coordinator, City and County of Honolulu, 711 Kapiʻolani Blvd., Suite 1200, Honolulu, HI 96813, 808/527-5044. Also very informative for rules of the road and common sense biking tips is the *Rights and Responsibilities for Hawaiʻi's Bicyclists* booklet. This booklet and the *Bike Oahu* bicycle route map are available free from the State Bicycle/Pedestrian Coordinator, State Department of Transportation, 869 Punchbowl St., Honolulu, HI 96813, 808/587-2321, and may be available at city halls and tourist offices.

GOLF AND TENNIS

Golf

People addicted to chasing that little white ball around the links are going to be delighted with Hawaii. You can golf every day of the year on more than 80 golf courses scattered around the state. Many are open to the public and are built along some of the most spectacular scenery in the world, where pounding surf or flower-dappled mountains form the backdrop. You'll find everything from Lanaʻi's nine-hole Cavendish Golf Course, where you put your donation in an envelope on the honor system, to some of the most highly praised, exclusive, and exciting golf courses in the world. Master builders such as Robert Trent Jones and Jack Nicklaus have laid out links in the islands where major tournaments are yearly events. Fees range from as little as $7 for some little nine-holers up to $200 at the most exclusive resorts.

Municipal and public courses are open to everyone. Resort courses cater to the public as well as to resort guests. Private courses are for members only and their guests, although some set aside a day or two a week for nonmembers. Military personnel and dependents, Department of Defense personnel, and those who have access to military bases are welcome to golf at the military courses (only on Oʻahu). If you wish to golf at other than municipal or public courses, be sure to call ahead to verify accessibility. Many courses have pros and pro shops; most offer lessons. Many have driving ranges, some lighted. Virtually all have clubhouses with restaurants and lounges. Greens fees listed in the charts in the following island chapters are for non-Hawaii residents and for civilians at military courses. Many courses offer reduced *kama'aina* rates, special time rates, twilight hour rates, and summer specials. Be sure to ask about these rates as they often afford substantial savings. Some courses charge higher fees for non-U.S. residents. Military courses charge different greens fees for civilians than for military personnel, and the military fees differ depending upon rank.

Tennis

Tennis courts are found on every island of Hawaii and enjoyed by locals and visitors on a year-round basis. County courts, under the control and maintenance of the Department of Parks and Recreation, are open to the public for free. Play is on a first-come, first-served basis and is limited to 45 minutes if there are people waiting. Weekends are often fairly busy, but it's relatively easy to get a court on weekdays. Court rules apply and only soft-sole shoes are allowed. Some hotel and private courts are also open to the public, where fees range from complimentary to about $15 for nonguests. Most courts are of Laykold or plexi-pave asphalt. Many courts are lighted.

HUNTING

Most people don't think of Hawaii as a place to hunt, but actually it's quite good. Seven species of introduced game animals and 15 species of game birds are regularly hunted. Not all species of game animals are open on all islands, but every island offers hunting. Please refer to the travel chapters for full details on hunting on particular islands.

General Hunting Rules

Hunting licenses are mandatory to hunt on public, private, or military land anywhere in Hawaii. They're good for one year beginning July 1 and cost $15 residents and military, $95 nonresidents; free to senior citizens. Licenses are available from sporting goods stores and from the various offices of the Division of Forestry and Wildlife. This government organization also sets and enforces the rules, so contact it with any questions. Generally, hunting hours are from a half hour before sunrise to a half hour after sunset. Checking stations are maintained, where the hunter must check in before and after hunting.

Rifles must have a muzzle velocity greater than 1,200 foot-pounds. Shotguns larger than .20 gauge are allowed, and muzzleloaders must have a .45 caliber bore or larger. Bows must have a minimum draw of 40 pounds for straight bows, 35 pounds for a recurve bow, and 30 pounds for compounds. Arrows must be broadheads. The use of hunting dogs is permitted only for certain species of birds and game, and when dogs are permitted, only smaller caliber

rifles and shotguns, along with spears and knives, may be used—no big bore guns/shotguns. Hunters must wear orange safety cloth on front and back no smaller than a 12-inch square. Certain big game species are hunted only by lottery selection; contact the Division of Forestry and Wildlife two months in advance. Guide service is not mandatory, but is advised if you're unfamiliar with hunting in Hawaii. You can hunt on private land only with permission, and you must possess a valid hunting license. Guns and ammunition brought into Hawaii must be registered with the chief of police of the corresponding county within 48 hours of arrival. Also, firearms must be unloaded and in an appropriately locked case as checked luggage to be transported by plane to the state.

Information

Hunting rules and regulations are always subject to change. Also, environmental considerations often change bag limits and seasons. Make sure to check with the State Division of Forestry and Wildlife for the most current information. Request *Rules Regulating Game Bird Hunting, Rules Regulating Game Mammal Hunting,* and *Hunting in Hawaii.* Direct inquiries to: Department of Land and Natural Resources, Division of Forestry and Wildlife, 1151 Punchbowl St., Honolulu, HI 96813, 808/587-0166; on Maui, 54 S. High St., Wailuku, HI 96793, 808/984-8100; on Hawai'i, 19 East Kawili, Hilo, HI 96720, 808/974-4221; on Lana'i, P.O. Box 732, 911 Fraser Ave., Lana'i City, HI 96763, 808/565-6688; on Kaua'i, 3060 Eiwa St., P.O. Box 1671, Lihu'e, HI 96766, 808/274-3433; on Moloka'i, P.O. Box 347, Kaunakakai, HI 96748, 808/533-5019.

Game Animals

All game animals on Hawaii have been introduced. Some have adapted admirably and are becoming well entrenched, while the existence of others is still precarious. **Axis deer** originated in India and were brought to Lana'i and Moloka'i, where they're doing well. The small herd on Maui is holding its own. Their unique flavor makes them one of the best wild meats. They're hunted on Lana'i from mid-February to mid-May, by public lottery. **Feral pigs** are escaped domestic pigs that have gone wild and are found on all islands except Lana'i. The stock is a mixture of original Polynesian pigs and subsequently introduced species. The pigs are hunted with dogs and usually killed with a spear or long knife—not recommended for the timid or tender-hearted. These beasts' four-inch tusks and fighting spirit make them tough and dangerous. **Feral goats** come in a variety of colors. Found on all islands except Lana'i, they have been known to cause erosion and are considered a pest in some areas, especially on Haleakala. They're openly hunted on all islands, and when properly cooked, their meat is considered delicious. **Black-tailed deer** come from Oregon. Forty were released on Kaua'i in 1961; the herd is now stabilized at around 400 and they're hunted in October by public lottery. **Mouflon sheep** are native to Corsica and Sardinia. They do well on Lana'i and on the windswept slopes of Mauna Loa and Mauna Kea, where they're hunted at various times, also by public lottery. **Feral sheep** haunt the slopes of Mauna Kea and Mauna Loa at 7,000–12,000 feet. They travel in flocks and destroy vegetation. It takes determination and a good set of lungs to bag one, especially with a bow and arrow. **Feral cattle** on the Big Island and **rock wallabies** from Australia, which now make their home on O'ahu, are not hunted.

Game Birds

A number of game birds are found on most of the islands. Bag limits and hunting seasons vary, so check with the Division of Forestry and Wildlife for details. The **ring-necked pheasant** is one of the best game birds, found on all the islands. The **kalij pheasant** from Nepal lives only on the Big Island, where the **green pheasant** is also prevalent, with some found on O'ahu, Maui, and Lana'i. **Francolins,** gray and black birds from India and the Sudan, are similar to partridges. They are hunted with dogs on all islands and are great roasted. There are also **chukar** from Tibet, on the slopes of all islands; a number of **quail,** including the

Japanese and California varieties; **doves;** and the wild **Rio Grande turkey** found on all islands except Kaua'i and O'ahu.

SIGHTSEEING TOURS

Tours offered on all the major islands will literally let you cover an individual island from top to bottom; you can walk it, drive it, sail around it, fly over it, or see it from below the water. Water tours include half-day or full-day snorkel trips, kayak expeditions up rugged lava coastlines, submarine rides, and comfortable sunset cocktail/dinner cruises. Land tours are generally very gentle bus or van trips that show you the highlights of the islands, but some now offer adventure 4WD outings to the tops of mountains or into deep forest areas. Hiking tours are also a great option to get to places that you can't get to otherwise and to open up the natural beauty of the interior and natural life of the islands. Helicopter rides and fixed-wing air tours are the most usual and ubiquitous available, but several enterprising companies offer glider rides, hang gliding, paragliding, and even parachuting for the more adventurous traveler into the experience of excitement.

gray francolin

BOB RACE

ON THE ROAD

ACCOMMODATIONS

Hawaii's accommodations won't disappoint anyone. The state has an exceptionally wide range of places to stay with varieties both in style and in price. You can camp on a totally secluded beach two days down a hiking trail, have a dream vacation at one of the undisputed top resorts in the world, or get a package deal including a week's lodging in one of many island hotels for less than you would spend for a hotel at home. If you want to experience the islands as if you lived here, bed-and-breakfasts have become popular and easy to arrange. Condominiums are plentiful, and great for extended stays for families who want to set up home away from home or for a group of friends who want to save money by sharing costs. There is a smattering of youth hostels, YM/WCAs, and home exchanges. If you're a student, a summer session at the University of Hawai'i can mix education and fun.

Hawaii makes the greater part of its living from visitors, and all concerned desire to keep Hawaiian standards up and vacationers coming back. This means accommodations in Hawaii are operated by professionals who know the business of pleasing people. This adds up to benefits for you. Rooms in even the more moderate hotels are clean; the standard of services ranges from adequate to luxurious pampering. With the tips and advice given below, you should be able to find a place to stay that will match your taste and your pocketbook. For specifics, please refer to **Accommodations** in each of the travel chapters.

HOTELS

Even with the wide variety of other accommodations available, most visitors, at least first-timers, tend to stay in hotels. At one time, hotels were the only places to stay. Characters like Mark Twain were berthed at Kilauea's rude Volcano House, while millionaires and nobility sailed for Waikiki, where they stayed in luxury at the Moana Hotel or Royal Hawaiian, which both still stand as vintage reminders of days past. Maui's Pioneer Inn dates from the turn of the 20th century, and if you were Hawaii-bound, these and a handful that haven't survived were about all that was offered. Today, there are approximately 50,000 hotel rooms statewide, and every year more hotels are built and older ones renovated. They come in all shapes and sizes, from 10-room family-run affairs to high-rise giants. A trend turned some into condominiums, while the Neighbor Islands have learned an aesthetic lesson from Waikiki and built low-rise resorts that don't obstruct the view and that blend more readily with the surroundings. Whatever accommodation you want, you'll find it in Hawaii.

Types of Hotel Rooms

Most readily available and least expensive is a bedroom with bath, the latter sometimes shared in the more inexpensive hotels. Some hotels can also offer you a studio (a large sitting room that converts to a bedroom), a suite (a bedroom with sitting room), or an apartment with full kitchen plus at least one bedroom. Kitchenettes are often available, and each contains a refrigerator, sink, and stove usually in a small corner nook or fitted together as one space-saving unit. Kitchenettes cost a bit more but save you a bundle by allowing you to prepare some of your own meals. To get that vacation feeling while keeping costs down, eat breakfast in, pack a lunch for the day, and go out to dinner. If you rent a kitchenette, make sure all the appliances work as soon as you arrive. If they don't, notify the front desk immediately, and if the hotel will not rectify the situation ask to be moved or given a reduced rate. Hawaii has cockroaches, so put all food away.

Check-in is usually 3 P.M. or 4 P.M., although if your room is ready, they can get you in early. Call. Checkout is most often 11 A.M. or noon. Some of the more expensive hotels and resorts have express checkout, and a TV video checkout system is offered by others.

Amenities

All hotels have some of them, and some hotels have all of them. Air-conditioning is available in most, but under normal circumstances you won't need it. Balmy trade winds provide plenty of breezes, which flow through louvered windows and doors in many hotels. Ceiling fans are better. TVs are often included, but not always, as are entertainment centers with stereos and CD players; pay-per-view movies are almost always an option. In-room phones are usually provided, but a service charge of up to 85 cents per call is often tacked on, even for local calls. A few hotels have purposefully created an environment without phone, TV, or entertainment centers so that you can get plugged into your surroundings and stay disconnected form other distractions. Swimming pools are very common, even though the hotel may sit right on the beach. There is always a restaurant of some sort, a coffee shop or two, a bar, a cocktail lounge, and sometimes a sundries shop, clothing store, or art gallery. While most stock complimentary coffee and tea, goodies from the honor bar will be charged to your bill. Some hotels also offer tennis courts or golf courses either as part of the premises or affiliated with the hotel; usually an "activities desk" can book you into a variety of daily outings. Plenty of hotels offer laundromats on the premises, and the better places also have pickup and delivery laundry services. Hotel towels can be used at the beach and pool. Many hotels have installed lines that pull out over the bathtub and are to be used for drying wet clothes. Dry your swimsuits there because hotels don't want you to drape your wet suit over the balcony outside. Bellhops generally get about $1 tip per bag or $5 a load on a rolling cart, and maid service is free, though maids are customarily tipped $1–2 per time—a bit more if kitchenettes are involved, or if you've been a piggy. Parking is usually free unless you opt for valet service, which is provided at a nominal fee or by tip. Most have in-room safes for securing your valuable, but many charge $1.50–3.75 for the privilege. Most hotels offer a children's program with supervised activities, excursions, and food during weekday daytime hours—sometimes seasonally—most often for children 5–12. Cost ranges from free to $50 a kid. Hotels can often arrange special services like baby-sitters (in house or with a local licensed caregiver), all kinds of lessons, and special entertainment activities. A few even have bicycles and snorkeling equipment to lend. They'll receive and send mail for you, cash your traveler's checks, and take messages. For your convenience, each room should be equipped with a directory of hotel services and information, and some hotels also include information about area sights, restaurants, and activities.

Hotel Rates: Add 11.4 Percent Tax

Every year Hawaiian hotels welcome in the New Year by hiking their rates by about 10 percent. Hawaii, because of its gigantic tourist flow and tough competition, offers hotel rooms at universally lower rates than those at most developed resort areas around the world; so, even with the 11.4 percent tax (7.25 percent transient accommodations tax, plus 4.16 percent state excise tax), there are still many reasonable rates to be had. Package deals, especially to Waikiki, almost throw in a week's lodging for the price of an air ticket. The basic **daily rate** is geared toward double occupancy; singles are hit in the pocketbook. Single rates, when available, are cheaper than doubles, but not usually by much. Many hotels will charge for a double and then add an additional charge (often $10–75) for each extra person up to a certain number. Plenty of hotels offer the **family plan**, which allows children, usually 17 or 18 and under, to stay in their parents' room free if they use the existing bedding. If another bed or crib is required, there is an additional charge. Some hotels—not always the budget ones—let you cram in as many as can sleep on the floor for no additional charge. Only a limited number of hotels offer the **American plan**, in which breakfast and dinner are included with the night's lodging. In many hotels, you're provided with a mini-refrigerator and a coffee machine to make coffee and tea at no extra charge. **Discounts** of various sorts are offered, but these vary by hotel. Some of the typical discounts are AAA, AARP, car and room, room and breakfast, fifth-night free, and *kama'aina* (state resident) rates. **Business/corporate rates** are usually offered to anyone who can at least produce a business card. **Weekly and monthly** rates will save you approximately 10 percent off the daily rate. In all cases, make sure to ask about other-than-published rates because this information won't usually be volunteered. In addition to regular hotel charges and taxes, some luxury hotels and resorts now charge a "resort fee," generally $7.50–10, that is used to offset a variety of activities, services, and parking costs that would otherwise be charged for individually.

While some hotels have a single basic rate throughout the year, most have a tiered pricing policy based on times of the year. This often translates as regular- and value-season rates (which may be referred to differently at different hotels), while some also include holiday rates. Some hotels have a policy of **minimum stay,** usually three to seven days, during Christmas and New Year. While the difference between "high season" and "low season" is less distinct than it used to be, Hawaii's **peak season** still runs from just before Christmas until after Easter, and then again throughout the summer, when rooms are at a premium. Value-season rates, when rooms are easier to come by, are often about 10 percent below the regular rate.

In Hawaiian hotels you always pay more for a good view. Terms vary slightly, but usually "oceanfront" means your room faces the ocean and mostly your view is unimpeded. "Ocean view" is slightly more vague. It could be a decent view, or it could require standing on the dresser and craning your neck to catch a tiny slice of the sea sandwiched between two skyscrapers. "Garden view" means just that, and "mountain view" may mean that you have a view of a mountain or simply that you have a view away from the ocean. Rooms are designated and priced upward with garden view or mountain view being the least expensive, then ocean view and ocean front rooms. Suites are invariably larger and more expensive, and these usually get the best locations and views.

Note: Prices listed are based on a standard published rate, double occupancy, without taxes or other charges added, unless otherwise noted.

Paying, Deposits, and Reservations

The vast majority of Hawaiian hotels accept foreign and domestic traveler's checks, personal checks preapproved by the management, foreign cash, and most major credit cards. Reservations are always the best policy, and they're easily made through travel agents or by contacting the hotel directly. In all cases, bring documentation of your confirmed reservations with you in case of a mix-up.

Deposits are not always required to make reservations, but they do secure them. Some hotels require the first (or several) night's payment in advance. Reservations without a deposit can be legally released if the room is not claimed by 6 P.M. Whether by phone call, email, fax, or letter, include your dates of stay and type of room in your request for a reservation, and make sure that the hotel sends you a copy of the confirmation. All hotels and resorts have **cancellation requirements** for refunding deposits. The time limit on these can be as little as 24 hours before arrival, or as much as a full 30 days. Some hotels require full **advance payment** for your length of stay, especially during peak season or during times of crowded special events. Be aware of the time required for a cancellation notice *before* making your reservation deposit, especially when dealing with advance payment. If you have confirmed reservations, especially with a deposit, and there is no room for you, or one that doesn't meet prearranged requirements, you should be given the option of accepting alternate accommodations. You are owed the difference in room rates if there is any. If there is no room whatsoever, the hotel is required to find you one at a comparable hotel and to refund your deposit in full.

CONDOMINIUMS

Hawaii was one of the first states struck by the condominium phenomenon; it began in the 1950s and has increased ever since. Now condos are almost as common as hotels, and renting one is just about as easy. Condos, unlike hotel rooms, are privately owned apartments normally part of a complex or high-rise. The condo is usually an absentee owner's second or vacation home. An on-premises condo manager (or rental agency) rents out vacant units and is responsible for maintenance and security.

Things to Know

Staying in a condo has advantages and disadvantages over staying in a hotel. The main qualitative difference between a condo and a hotel is amenities. At a condo, you're more on your own. You're temporarily renting an apartment, so there won't be any bellhops, and rarely a bar, restaurant, or lounge on the premises, though many times you'll find a sundries store. The main lobby, instead of having that grand entrance feel of many hotels, is more like an apartment house entrance, although there might be a front desk. Condos can be studios (one big room), but mostly they are one- or multiple-bedroom affairs with a complete kitchen. Reasonable housekeeping items should be provided: linens, furniture, and a fully equipped kitchen. Most have TVs and phones, but remember that the furnishings are provided by the owner. You can find brand-new furnishings that are top of the line, right down to "garage sale" bargains. Inquire about the furnishings when you make your reservations. Maid service might be included on a limited basis (for example, once weekly), or you might have to pay extra for it.

Condos usually require a minimum stay, although some will rent on a daily basis, like hotels. Minimum stays when applicable are often three days, but seven is also commonplace, and during peak season two weeks isn't unheard of. Swimming pools are common, and depending on the "theme" of the condo, you can find saunas, weight rooms, hot tubs, or tennis courts. A nominal extra fee, often $15–20, is charged for more than two people. Generally speaking, studios can sleep two, a one-bedroom will sleep four, two-bedrooms will sleep six, and three-bedrooms will sleep eight. Most have a sleeper couch in the sitting room that folds out into a bed. You can find clean, decent condos for as little as $200 per week, all the way up to exclusive apartments for well over $2,000. Most fall into the $700–1,000 range per week. The method of paying for and reserving a condo is just about the same as for a hotel. However, requirements for deposits, final payments, and cancellation charges are much stiffer than in hotels. Make absolutely sure you fully understand all of these requirements when you make your reservations.

Their real advantage is for families, friends who want to share, and especially long-term stays, for which you will always get a special rate. The kitchen facilities save a great deal on dining costs, and it's common to find units with their own washers and dryers. To sweeten the deal, many condo companies offer coupons that can save you money on food, gifts, and activities at local establishments. Parking space is ample for guests, and like hotels, plenty of stay/drive deals are offered. Like hotels, condos usually charge $.60–1 for local calls, credit card calls, and collect calls. Some have in-room safes, but there will be a daily charge of $1.50–1.75 for their use. Pay-per-view, in-room movie service is usually available for $8.95–16.95 per movie. Many now also have a lost key fee, which may be as steep as $75, so don't lose it! If you can't produce it, you pay for it.

Hotel and Condominium Information

The best source of hotel/condo information for the vacationer is the Hawaii Visitors Bureau. While planning your trip, either visit one nearby or write to the bureau in Hawaii. (Addresses are listed in the **Information and Services** section later in this chapter.) Request a copy of the free *Connections Hawai'i*. This handy booklet lists all the hotel/condo members of the HVB, with addresses, phone numbers, facilities, rates, and general tips. Understand that these are not all of the hotels/condos in Hawaii, just members of HVB. Entertainment, dining, transportation, and general tips are also given.

For condo booking agencies on the different islands, see the individual travel chapter introductions below.

VACATION RENTALS

Vacation rentals are homes or cottages that are rented to visitors, usually on a basis of a week or longer. Some shorter rentals can be arranged. These rentals come with all the amenities of condo units, but they are usually free-standing homes. Meals are not part of the option, so that is your responsibility. There are numerous vacation rentals throughout the islands, and many of these advertise by word of mouth, ads in magazines, and websites. Perhaps the best way to locate a vacation rental, at least for the first time that you visit the island, is through a rental/real estate agent—a number are listed in the travel chapters of this book. This can be handled in Hawaii or by phone, fax, email, or mail. Everything from simple beach homes to luxurious hideaways is put into the hands of rental agents. The agents have descriptions of the properties and terms of the rental contracts, and many will furnish photographs. Be aware that some places, although not all, have out-cleaning fees in addition to the rental rate. When contacting an agency, be as specific as possible about your needs, length of stay, desired location, and how much you're willing to spend. If handled through the mail, the process may take some time; write several months in advance. Be aware that during high season, rentals are at a premium; if you're slow to inquire there may be slim pickin's.

BED-AND-BREAKFASTS

Bed-and-breakfast (B&B) inns are hardly a new idea. The Bible talks of the hospitable hosts who opened the gates of their homes and invited the wayfarer in to spend the night. B&Bs have a long tradition in Europe and were commonplace in Revolutionary America. Nowadays, lodging in private homes called bed-and-breakfasts is becoming increasingly fashionable throughout America, and Hawaii is no exception, with about 100,000 B&B guests yearly.

Points to Consider
The primary feature of bed-and-breakfasts is that every one is privately owned and therefore uniquely different from every other. The range of B&Bs is as wide as the living standards in America. You'll find everything from a semi-mansion in the most fashionable residential area to a little grass shack offered by a down-home fisherman and his family. This means that it's particularly important for the guest to choose a host family with whom his or her lifestyle is compatible.

Unlike at a hotel or a condo, you'll be staying *with* a host (usually a family), although your room will be private, with private baths and separate entrances quite common. You can make arrangements directly or you might want to go through agencies (listed below), which act as go-betweens, matching host and guest. It is best to call these agencies, but you can also write. Agencies have a description of each B&B they rent for, its general location, the fees charged, and a good idea of the lifestyle of your host family. What the agency will want to know from you is where you want to stay, what type of place you're looking for, the price range you're willing to pay, arrival and departure dates, and other items that will help them match you with a place. (Are you single? Do you have children? Smoker? etc.) You, of course, can do all the legwork yourself, but these people know their territory and

guarantee their work. If you find that a situation is incompatible, they will find another that works. They also inspect each B&B, and make sure that each has a license and insurance to operate. Most can also arrange discount rental car and interisland air fares for you.

Since B&Bs are run by individual families, the times that they will accept guests can vary according to what's happening in their lives. This makes it imperative to write well in advance: three months is good; earlier is too long and too many things can change. Four weeks is about the minimum time required to make all necessary arrangements. Expect a minimum stay (three days is common). B&Bs are not long-term housing, although it's hoped that guest and host will develop a friendship and that future stays can be as long as both desire. As with condos, B&Bs have different requirements for making and holding reservations and for payment. Most will hold a room with a credit card deposit or check covering a certain percentage of the total bill. Be aware, however, that some B&Bs do not accept credit cards or personal checks, so you must pay in cash, traveler's checks, or money orders. Always inquire about the method of payment when making your initial inquiries.

B&B Agencies
A top-notch B&B agency with over 200 homes is **Bed and Breakfast Hawaii,** operated by Evelyn Warner and Al Davis. They've been running this service since 1978, and their reputation is excellent. Write Bed and Breakfast Hawaii, P.O. Box 449, Kapa'a, HI 96746, 808/822-7771 or 800/733-1632, website: www.bandb-hawaii.com, email: reservations@bandb-hawaii.com.

One of the most experienced agencies, **Bed and Breakfast Honolulu** (statewide), at 3242 Kaohinanai Dr., Honolulu, HI 96817, 808/595-7533 or 800/288-4666, fax 808/595-2030, website: www.hawaiibnb.com, email: rainbow@hawaiibnb.com, owned and operated by Marylee and Gene Bridges, began in 1982. Since then, they've become masters at finding visitors the perfect accommodations to match their desires, needs, and pocketbooks. Their repertoire of guest homes offers more than 400 rooms, with half on O'ahu and the other half scattered around the state.

All Island Bed and Breakfast, 823 Kainui Dr., Kailua, HI 96734, 808/263-2342 or 800/542-0344, fax 808/263-0308, email: cac@aloha.net, can match your needs up with about 700 homes throughout the state.

Run by Susan Campbell, **Hawaii's Best Bed and Breakfast,** P.O. Box 563, Kamuela, HI 96743, 808/885-4550 or 800/262-9912, fax 808/885-0559, website: www.bestbnb.com, email: bestbnb@aloha.net, is a smaller business, but it has listings all over the state.

Since 1982, **Go Native Hawaii** has helped people find the right place to stay on the five major islands. Contact Go Native at 808/935-4178 or 800/662-8483, website: www.gonative-hi.com, email: reservations@gonativehi.com.

Hawaiian Islands Bed and Breakfast Vacation Rentals, 1277 Mokulua Dr., Kailua, HI 96734, 808/261-7895 or 800/258-7895, fax 808/262-2181, website: www.lanikaibb.com, is owned and operated by Rick Maxey, who can arrange stays on all islands and help with inter-island flights and car rental.

HOSTELS AND YM/WCA

While there are very few hostels in Hawaii, each of the four major islands has at least one, although only three are official American Youth Hostel members. All are located in major towns, and several are just a few blocks from the beach in Waikiki. These are basic accommodations that offer a common room, several bathrooms, bunk rooms, and a limited number of private rooms. Kitchens are usually available, as is long-term storage. Each offers other amenities, which may include transportation to and/or from the airport, local excursions, low car rental rates, and free use of water equipment. European travelers, surfers, and backpackers make up the bulk of visitors. Generally, a bunk bed runs about $15–18 and private rooms are $35–45.

YM/WCAs are also quite limited in Hawaii. All those with rooms are in Honolulu. They vary as far as private rooms and baths are concerned, so each should be contacted individually. Prices vary too, but expect to pay $25 single. Men or women are accepted at respective Ys unless otherwise stated.

HOME EXCHANGES

One other method of staying in Hawaii, open to homeowners, is to offer the use of your home for use of a home in Hawaii. This is done by listing your home with an agency that facilitates the exchange and publishes a descriptive directory. To list your home and to find out what is available, contact one of the following agencies: **Vacation Exchange Club** (Affiliate of Homelink, Int'l), P.O. Box 650, Key West, FL 33041, tel./fax 305/294-1448 or 800/638-3841; **Intervac U.S.,** P.O. Box 590504, San Francisco, CA 94159, 415/535-3497, fax 415/435-7440; **Worldwide Home Exchange Club,** 806 Brantford Ave., Silver Spring, MD 20904, 301/680-8950.

FOOD AND DRINK

Hawaii is a gastronome's Shangri-La, a sumptuous smorgasbord in every sense of the word. The varied ethnic groups that have come to Hawaii in the last 200 years have each brought their own special enthusiasms and cultures—and lucky for all, they didn't forget their cookpots, hearty appetites, and taste buds.

The Polynesians who first arrived found a fertile but barren land. Immediately they set about growing taro, coconuts, and bananas, and raising chickens, pigs, fish, and dogs, though the latter were reserved for nobility. Harvests were bountiful and the islanders thanked the gods with the traditional feast called the lu'au. Most food was baked in the underground oven, the *imu*. Participants were encouraged to feast while relaxing on straw mats and enjoying the hula and various entertainment. The lu'au is as popular as ever, a treat that's guaranteed to delight anyone with a sense of eating adventure.

The missionaries and sailors came next and their ships' holds carried barrels of ingredients for puddings, pies, dumplings, gravies, and roasts—the sustaining "American foods" of New England farms. The mid-1800s saw the arrival of boatloads of Chinese and Japanese peasants, who wasted no time making rice instead of bread the staple of the islands. The Chinese added their exotic spices, creating complex Sichuan dishes as well as workers' basics like chop suey. The Japanese introduced *shoyu* (soy sauce), sashimi, boxed lunches *(bento),* delicate tempura, and rich, filling noodle soups. The Portuguese brought their luscious Mediterranean dishes of tomatoes and peppers and plump spicy sausages, nutritious bean soups, and mouthwatering sweet treats like *malasadas* (holeless donuts) and *pao dolce* (sweet bread). Koreans carried crocks of zesty kimchi and quickly fired up grills for *pulgogi,* a marinated beef cooked over a fire. Filipinos served up their delicious *adobo* stews—fish, meat, or chicken in a rich sauce of vinegar and garlic.

Recently, Thai and Vietnamese restaurants have been offering their irresistible dishes next door to restaurants offering fiery burritos from Mexico and elegant marsala cream sauces from France. The ocean breezes of Hawaii not only cool the skin but waft with them some of the most delectable aromas on earth, to make the taste buds thrill and the spirit soar.

Special Note

Nothing is sweeter to the appetite than reclining on a beach and deciding just what dish will make your taste buds laugh that night. Kick back, close your eyes, and let the smells and tastes of past meals drift into your consciousness. The following should help you decide exactly what you're in the mood for and give you an idea of Hawaii's dishes and their ingredients. Particular restaurants and eateries will be covered in the travel chapters.

HAWAIIAN FOODS

Hawaiian cuisine, the oldest of the islands, consists of wholesome, well prepared, and delicious foods. All you have to do on arrival is notice the size of some of the local boys (and women) to know immediately that food to them is indeed a happy and serious business. An oft-heard island joke is that "local men don't eat until they're full; they eat until they're tired." Many Hawaiian dishes have become standard fare at a variety of restaurants, eaten at one time or another by

taro

BOB RACE

anyone who spends time in the islands. Hawaiian food in general is called *kaukau,* cooked food is *kapahaki,* and something broiled is called *ka'ola.* Any of these prefixes on a menu indicates that Hawaiian food is served. Usually inexpensive, these dishes will definitely fill you and keep you going.

Traditional Favorites

In old Hawaii, although the sea meant life, many more people were involved in cultivating beautifully tended garden plots of taro, sugarcane, breadfruit, and various sweet potatoes *('uala)* than with fishing. They husbanded pigs and barkless dogs *('ilio),* and prized *moa* (chicken) for their feathers and meat, but found eating the eggs repulsive. Their only farming implement was the *'o'o,* a sharpened hardwood digging stick. The Hawaiians were the best farmers of Polynesia, and the first thing they planted was taro, a tuberous root created by the gods at the same time as humans. This main staple of the old Hawaiians was pounded into poi. Every lu'au will have poi, a glutinous purple paste. It comes in liquid consistencies referred to as one-, two-, or three-finger poi. The fewer fingers you need to eat it, the thicker it is. Poi is one of the most nutritious carbohydrates known, but people unaccustomed to it find it bland and tasteless. Some of the best, fermented for a day or so, has an acidic bite. Poi is made to be eaten *with* something, but locals who love it pop it in their mouths and smack their lips. Those unaccustomed to it will suffer constipation if they eat too much.

While poi fell out of favor during the middle of the 20th century, it is once again becoming more popular, and several sizable factories now produce poi for sale. You can find plastic containers of this food refrigerated in many supermarkets and local food stores. In addition, deep-fried slices of taro root, plain or spiced, are now packaged and sold like potato chips.

A favorite popular dessert is *haupia,* a custard made from coconut. *Limu* is a generic term for edible seaweed, which many people still gather from the shoreline and eat as a salad, or mix with ground *kukui* nuts and salt as a relish. A favorite Hawaiian snack is *'opihi,* small shellfish (limpets) that cling to rocks. Those who gather them always leave some on the rocks for the future. Cut from the shell and eaten raw by all peoples of Hawaii, *'opihi* sell for $150 per gallon in Honolulu—a testament to their popularity. A general term that has come to mean hors d'oeuvres in Hawaii is *pu pu.* Originally the name of a small shellfish, it is now used for any finger food. A traditional liquor made from *ti* root is *'okolehao.* It literally means "iron bottom," reminiscent of the iron blubber pots used to ferment it.

Pacific Rim (a.k.a. Hawaiian Regional) Cuisine

At one time the "tourist food" in Hawaii was woeful. Of course, there has always been a handful of fine restaurants, but for the most part the food lacked soul, with even the fine hotels opting to offer second-rate renditions of food more appropriate to large Mainland cities. Surrounded by some of the most fertile and pristine waters in the Pacific, you could hardly find a restaurant offering fresh fish, and it was an ill-conceived boast that even the fruits and vegetables lying limply on your table were "imported." Beginning with a handful of extremely creative and visionary chefs in the early 1980s, who took the chance of perhaps offending the perceived simple palates of visitors, a delightfully delicious new cuisine was born. Based upon the finest traditions of Conti-

nental cuisine—including, to a high degree, its sauces, pastas, and presentations—the culinary magic of Pacific Rim boldly adds the pungent spices of Asia, the fantastic fresh vegetables, fruits, and fish of Hawaii, and, at times, the earthy cooking methods of the American Southwest. The result is a cuisine of fantastic tastes, subtle yet robust, and satiating but health-conscious—the perfect marriage of fresh foods prepared in a fresh way. Now restaurants on every island proudly display menus labeled "Hawaiian Regional" or some version of this. As always, some are better than others, but the general result is that the "tourist food" has been vastly improved and everyone benefits. Many of these exemplary chefs left lucrative and prestigious positions at Hawaii's five-diamond hotels and opened signature restaurants of their own, making this fine food much more available and affordable.

In 1998, a new and younger group called Hawaiian Island Chefs came together to further enhance the variety and offering of innovative foods made with island-grown produce and the bounty of the sea. In addition, this group strives to influence culinary programs in the state to help carry on this fine tradition. With the incredible mix of peoples and cultures in Hawaii, the possibilities are endless, and this new group of chefs intends to shepherd the experience along.

Lu'au

Thick cookbooks are filled with common Hawaiian dishes, but you can get a good sampling at a well-done lu'au. The central feature is the *imu,* an underground oven. Basically, a shallow hole is dug and lined with stones upon which a roaring fire is kindled. Once the fire dies down and the stones are super-heated, the ashes are swept away and the *imu* is ready for cooking. At one time only men could cook in this fashion; it was *kapu* for women. These restrictions have long been lifted, but men still seem to do most of the pit cooking, while women primarily serve. The main dish at a lu'au is *kalua* pork. *Kalua* refers to any dish baked underground. A whole pig *(pua'a)* is wrapped in *ti* and banana leaves and placed in the pit's hot center. The pig's stomach cavity is filled with more hot stones; surrounding it are bundles of food wrapped in *ti* leaves. These savory bundles, *lau lau,* contain the side dishes: fish, chicken, poi, sweet potatoes, breadfruit, and bananas. The entire contents are then covered with multiple layers of banana, *ti,* or sometimes ginger leaves, and a final coating of earth. A long tube of bamboo may stick up from the *imu* so that water (for steam) can be added. In about four hours the coverings are removed and the lu'au begins. You are encouraged to recline on *lau hala* mats placed around the central dining area, although tables and chairs are usually provided. There are forks and plates, but traditionally it is proper to use your fingers as utensils and a sturdy banana leaf as a plate. Professional lu'au cooks pride themselves on their cooking methods and their food, and for a fixed price you can gorge yourself like an ancient *ali'i.* All lu'au supply entertainment, and exotic drinks flow like the tides. Your biggest problem after one of these extravaganzas will be finding the strength to rise from your *lau hala* mat.

Lu'au range in price but are generally about $55–78 per adult and half that for children. This price includes entertainment. Most commercial lu'au are still put on by hotels, but many others are also very successful and well-regarded. Generally, lu'au run from about 5:30 to 8:30 P.M. On your lu'au day, eat a light breakfast, skip lunch, and do belly-stretching exercises! Lu'au food is usually served buffet-style, although some do it family-style. All lu'au have pretty much the same format, although the types of food and entertainment differ. The least expensive, most authentic, and best lu'au are often put on by local churches or community groups. They are not held on a regular basis, so peruse the free tourist literature where they advertise.

INTERNATIONAL DISHES

Chinese and Japanese cuisines have a strong influence on island cooking, and their well-known spices and ingredients are creatively used in many recipes. Other cuisines, such as Filipino, Korean, and Portuguese, are not as well known but are now becoming standard island fare.

Chinese

Tens of thousands of fortune cookies yield their little sprigs of wisdom every day to hungry diners throughout Hawaii. The Chinese, who came to Hawaii as plantation workers, soon discovered a brighter economic future by striking out on their own. Almost from the beginning, these immigrants opened restaurants. The tradition is still strong, and if the smallest town in Hawaii has a restaurant at all, it's probably Chinese. These restaurants are some of the least expensive, especially at lunchtime when prices are lower. In them, you'll find the familiar chop suey, chow mein, Peking duck, and fried rice. Take-out is common and makes a good, inexpensive picnic lunch.

Japanese

For the uninitiated, Japanese food is simple, aesthetically pleasing, and delicious. Sushi bars are plentiful, especially in Honolulu, using the freshest fish from local waters. Some common dishes include: teriyaki chicken, fish, or steak, which is grilled in a marinated *shoyu* (soy) sauce base; tempura, or mouth-size bites of fish and vegetables dipped in a flour and egg batter and deep fried; sukiyaki, or vegetables, meat, mushrooms, tofu, and vermicelli you cook at your table (in a prepared stock kept boiling with a little burner) then dip into a mixture of egg and *shoyu; shabu shabu,* similar to sukiyaki though without noodles and with the emphasis on beef; *donburi* (various ingredients on rice in a bowl), such as *ten donburi,* battered shrimp on rice; and various tofu dishes and miso soup, which provide some of the highest sources of nonmeat protein. Japanese restaurants span the entire economic range, from elegant and expensive to hole-in-the-wall eateries where the surroundings are basic but the food is fit for a samurai. Above all, cleanliness is guaranteed.

Filipino

Most people have never sampled Filipino food. This cuisine is spicy with plenty of exotic sauces. The following is a sampling found in most Filipino restaurants: *singang,* sour soup made from fish, shrimp, or vegetables, which has an acidic base from fruits like tamarind; *adobo,* a generic term for anything (chicken and pork are standards) stewed in vinegar and garlic; *lumpia,* a Filipino spring roll; *pancit,* many variations of noodles made into ravioli-like bundles stuffed with pork or other meats; *lechon,* a whole suckling pig stuffed and roasted; *siopao,* a steam-heated dough ball filled with chicken or other tasty ingredients; and *halo halo,* a confection of shaved ice smothered in preserved fruits and canned milk.

Korean

Those who have never dined on Korean dishes are in for a sumptuous treat. Specialties include: *kalbitang,* a beef rib soup in a thin but tasty broth; *pulgogi,* marinated beef and vegetables grilled over an open flame; *pulkalbi,* beef ribs grilled over an open flame; *pibimbap,* a large bowl of rice smothered with beef, chicken, and vegetables that you mix together before eating; kimchi, fermented cabbage and hot spices made into a zesty "slaw"; *kimchi chigyae,* a stew of kimchi, pork, vegetables, and spices in a thick soup base.

MONEY-SAVERS

Only one thing is better than a great meal: a great meal at a reasonable price. The following are island institutions and favorites that will help you eat well and keep prices down.

Kaukau Wagons

These are lunch wagons, but instead of slick, stainless-steel jobs, most are old delivery trucks converted into portable kitchens. Some say they're a remnant of World War II, when workers had to be fed on the job; others say that the meals they serve were inspired by the Japanese *bento,* a boxed lunch. You'll see these wagons parked along beaches, in city parking lots, or on busy streets. Usually a line of local people will be placing their orders, especially at lunchtime—a tip-off that the wagon serves delicious, nutritious island dishes for reasonable prices. They might have a few tables, but basically they serve food to go. Most of their filling meals are about $3.50, and "plate lunches" are the specialty.

Plate Lunch

One of the best island standards, these lunches give you a sampling of authentic island food that can include teriyaki chicken, mahimahi, *lau lau,* and *lomi* salmon among others. They're served on paper or Styrofoam plates, are packed to go, and usually cost less than $3.50. Standard with

a plate lunch is "two-scoop rice," a generous dollop of macaroni or other salad. Full meals, they're great for keeping down food costs and for instant picnics. Available everywhere from *kaukau* wagons to restaurants.

An innovation on the regular plate lunch is starting to pop up here and there in finer restaurants and even at a few *kaukau* wagons. This is a better quality plate lunch with the freshest ingredients, more health-conscious preparation, and a greater inventiveness in the foods chosen, and they're often served in a classier manner. As would be expected, these meals are not available everywhere yet and cost up to twice as much as the ordinary plate lunch, but they're still a good deal for this variation on a standard Hawaiian tradition.

Bento

Bento are the Japanese rendition of the box lunch. Aesthetically arranged, they are full meals. They are often sold in supermarkets and in some local eateries with take-out counters.

Saimin

Special "saimin shops," as well as restaurants, serve this hearty, Japanese-inspired noodle soup. Saimin is a word unique to Hawaii. In Japan, these soups would be called *ramen* or *soba,* and it's as if the two were combined to saimin. A large bowl of noodles in broth, stirred with meat, chicken, fish, shrimp, or vegetables, costs only a few dollars and is big enough for an evening meal. The best place to eat saimin is in a local hole-in-the-wall shop run by a family.

Okazu-ya

A Hawaiian adaptation of the Japanese restaurant that sells side dishes and inexpensive food, *okazu-ya* usually have a full menu of savory entrées as well as side dishes that take their inspiration, like much in the islands, from all the peoples who have made Hawaii their home. Sometimes, they specialize in one type of dish or another. Usually small family-run shops that cater to the local community, they have loyal clients who demand top quality and cheap prices. While not usually on the list of dieters' delights, the food you find at these fine places is filling and will sustain you through the day, yet some places are adapting to a "leaner" menu selection. Some but not all have *okazu-ya* as part of the restaurant name.

Early-Bird Specials

Even some of the island's best restaurants in the fanciest hotels offer "early-bird specials"—the regular-menu dinners offered to diners who come in before the usual dinner hour, which is approximately 6 P.M. You pay as little as half the normal price, and can dine in luxury on some of the best foods. The specials are often advertised in the "free" tourist books, which might also include coupons for two-for-one meals or limited dinners at much lower prices. Just clip them out.

Buffets

Buffets are also quite common in Hawaii, and like lu'au are all-you-can-eat affairs. Offered at a variety of restaurants and hotels, they usually cost $12 and up. The food, however, ranges considerably from passable to quite good. At lunchtime, they're lower priced than dinner, and breakfast buffets are cheaper yet. Buffets are always advertised in free tourist literature, which often includes discount coupons.

Tip

Many lounges and bars have a "happy hour," usually around sundown, when the price of drinks is reduced. Some also offer free *pu pu* during happy hour, and at the best, these *pu pu* could make a meal.

FISH AND SEAFOOD

Anyone who loves fresh fish and seafood has come to the right place. Island restaurants specialize in seafood, and it's available everywhere. Pound for pound, seafood is one of the best dining bargains in Hawaii. You'll find it served in every kind of restaurant, and often the fresh catch of the day is proudly displayed on ice in a glass case. The following is a sampling of the best.

Mahimahi

This excellent eating fish is one of the most common and least expensive in Hawaii. It's referred to as a "dolphin" but is definitely a fish, not a mammal. Mahimahi can weigh 10–65 pounds; the flesh is light and moist. This fish is broadest at the head. When caught it's a dark olive color, but after a while the skin turns iridescent shades of blue, green, and yellow. It can be served as a main course or as a patty in a fish sandwich.

A'u

This true island delicacy is a broad-bill swordfish or marlin. It's expensive even in Hawaii because the damn thing's so hard to catch. The meat is moist and white and truly superb. If it's offered on the menu, order it. It'll cost a bit more, but you won't be disappointed.

Ono

Ono means "delicious" in Hawaiian, so that should tip you off to the taste of this wahoo, or king mackerel. *Ono* is regarded as one of the finest eating fishes in the ocean, and its white, flaky meat lives up to its name.

Manini

These five-inch fish are some of the most abundant in Hawaii; they live in about 10 feet of water. They school and won't bite a hook but are easily taken with spear or net. Not often on a menu, but they're favorites with local people who know best.

Ulua

This member of the crevalle jack family ranges 15–100 pounds. Its flesh is white and has a steak-like texture. Delicious and often found on the menu.

Uku

This gray snapper is a favorite with local people. The meat is light and firm and grills well.

'Ahi

A yellowfin tuna with distinctive pinkish meat. 'Ahi is a great favorite cooked or served raw in sushi bars.

Moi

This is the Hawaiian word for "king." This fish has large eyes and a sharklike head. Considered one of the finest eating fishes in Hawaii, it's best during the autumn months.

Seafood Potpourri

Other island seafood includes *'opihi*, a small shellfish (limpet) that clings to rocks and is considered one of the best island delicacies, eaten raw; *'alo'alo*, similar to tiny lobsters; crawfish, plentiful in taro fields and irrigation ditches; *'ahipalaka*, albacore tuna; various octopuses and squid (calamari); and shark of various types.

'A'ama are the ubiquitous little black crabs that you'll spot on rocks and around pier areas. They're everywhere. For fun, local fishermen try to catch them with poles, but the more efficient way is to throw a fish head into a plastic bucket and wait for the crabs to crawl in and trap themselves. The *'a'ama* are about as big as two fingers and make delicious eating.

Limu is edible seaweed that has been gathered as a garnish since precontact times and is frequently found on traditional island menus. There's no other seaweed except *limu* in Hawaii. Because of this, the heavy, fishy-ocean smell that people associate with the sea but which is actually that of seaweed is absent in Hawaii.

Poke is raw, cubed fish, usually made into a seafood salad with salt, vinegar, seaweed, onions, or other such ingredients, that is often found in deli sections of supermarkets.

Sushi

A finger-size block of sticky rice, topped with a pickled vegetable and a slice of raw fish. A delicacy in Japan and appreciated in Hawaii as a fine food.

MUNCHIES AND ISLAND TREATS

Certain finger foods, fast foods, and island treats are unique to Hawaii. Some are meals in themselves, others are snacks. Here are some of the best and most popular.

Pu Pu

Pronounced as in "Winnie the Pooh Pooh," these are finger foods and hors d'oeuvres. They can be anything from crackers to cracked crab. Often, they're given free at lounges and bars and can even include chicken drumettes, fish kabobs, and tempura. At a good display you can have a free meal.

Crackseed

A sweet of Chinese origin, crackseed is preserved and seasoned fruits and seeds. Favorites include coconut, watermelon, pumpkin seeds, mango, plum, and papaya. Distinctive in taste, they take some getting used to but make great trail snacks. They are available in all island markets. Also look for dried fish (cuttlefish) on racks, usually near the crackseed. Nutritious and delicious, it makes a great snack.

Shave Ice

This real island institution makes the Mainland "snow cone" melt into insignificance. Special machines literally shave ice to a fluffy consistency. It's mounded into a paper cone and then an exotic island syrup is generously poured over it (you choose from dozens of flavors). Given a straw and a spoon, you just slurp away.

Taro Chips

Like potato ships, but made from the taro root. If you can find them fresh, buy a bunch as they are mostly available packaged.

Malasadas and Pao Dolce

Two sweets from the Portuguese, *malasadas* are holeless donuts and *pao dolce* is sweet bread. Sold in island bakeries, they're great for breakfast or as treats.

Lomi Lomi Salmon

This salad of salmon, tomatoes, and onions with garnish and seasonings often accompanies "plate lunches" and is featured at buffets and lu'au.

TROPICAL FRUITS AND VEGETABLES

Some of the most memorable taste treats from the islands require no cooking at all: the luscious tropical and exotic fruits and vegetables sold in markets and roadside stands or just found hanging on trees, waiting to be picked. Experience as many as possible. The general rule in Hawaii is that you are allowed to pick fruit on public lands, but the amount should be limited to personal consumption. The following is a sampling of some of Hawaii's best produce.

ON THE ROAD

Bananas
No tropical island is complete without them. There are more than 70 species in Hawaii, with hundreds of variations. Some are for peeling and eating while others are cooked. A "hand" of bananas is great for munching, backpacking, or picnicking. Available everywhere—and cheap.

Avocados
Brought from South America, avocados were originally cultivated by the Aztecs. They have a buttery consistency and nutty flavor. Hundreds of varieties in all shapes and colors are available fresh year-round. They have the highest fat content of any fruit except the olive.

Coconuts
What tropical paradise would be complete without coconuts? Indeed, these were some of the first plants brought by the Polynesians. When a child was born, a coconut tree was planted to provide fruit for the child throughout his or her lifetime. Truly tropical fruits, coconuts know no season. Drinking nuts are large and green, and when shaken you can hear the milk inside. You get about a quart of fluid from each. It takes skill to open one, but a machete can handle anything. Cut the stem end flat so that it will stand, then bore a hole into the pointed end and put in a straw or hollow bamboo. Coconut water is slightly acidic and helps balance alkaline foods. Spoon meat is a custard-like gel on the inside of drinking nuts. Sprouted coconut meat is also an excellent food. Split open a sprouted nut, and inside is the yellow fruit, like a moist sponge cake. "Millionaire's salad" is made from the heart of a coconut palm. At one time an entire tree was cut down to get to the heart, which is just inside the trunk below the fronds and is like an artichoke heart except that it's about the size of a watermelon. In a downed tree, the heart stays good for about two weeks.

Breadfruit
This island staple provides a great deal of carbohydrate, but many people find the baked, boiled, or fried fruit bland. It grows all over the islands and is really thousands of little fruits growing together to form a ball.

breadfruit

DIANA LASICH HARPER

Mangos
These are some of the most delicious fruits known to humans. They grow wild all over the islands; the ones on the leeward sides of the islands ripen April–June, while the ones on the windward sides can last until October. They're found in the wild on trees up to 60 feet tall. The problem is to stop eating them once you start!

Papayas
This truly tropical fruit has no real season but is mostly available in the summer. Papayas grow on branchless trees and are ready to pick as soon as any yellow appears. Of the many varieties, the "solo papaya," meant to be eaten by one person, is the best. Split one in half, scrape out the seeds, and have at it with a spoon.

Passion Fruit
Known by their island name of liliko'i, passion fruit make excellent juice and pies. The small yellow fruit (similar to lemons but smooth-skinned) is mostly available in summer and fall. Many grow wild on vines, waiting to be picked. Slice off the stem end, scoop the seedy pulp out with your tongue, and you'll know why they're called "passion fruit."

Guavas
These small, round, yellow fruits are abundant in the wild, where they ripen from early summer to late fall. They're often considered a pest—so pick all you want. A good source of vitamin C, they're great for juice, jellies, and desserts.

Macadamia Nuts
The king of nuts was brought from Australia in 1882. Now it's the state's fourth largest agricul-

tural product. Available plain, roasted, candied, or buttered. Until the year 2000, Hawaii produced more of these nuts than anywhere else in the world. Now it follows Australia in total production.

Litchis
Called nuts but really small fruits with thin red shells, litchis have a sweet, juicy white flesh when fresh and appear nutlike when dried.

Other Fruit
Along with the above, you'll find pineapples, oranges, limes, kumquats, thimbleberries, and blackberries in Hawaii, as well as carambolas (star fruit), wild cherry tomatoes, and tamarinds.

ISLAND DRINKS

To complement the fine dining in the islands, bartenders have been busy creating their own tasty concoctions. The full range of beers, wines,

The coconut was very important to the Hawaiians and every part was used. A tree was planted when a child was born as a prayer for a good food supply throughout life. The trunks were used for building homes and heiau and carved into drums to accompany hula. The husks became bowls, utensils, and even jewelry. 'Aha, sennit rope braided from the husk fiber, was renowned as the most saltwater-resistant natural rope ever made.

DIANA LASICH HARPER

and standard drinks is served in Hawaii, but for a real treat you should try mixed drinks inspired by the islands. Most look very innocent because they come in pineapples, coconut shells, or tall frosted glasses. They're often garnished with little umbrellas or sparklers, and most have enough fruit in them to give you your vitamins for the day. Rum is the basis of many of them; it's been an island favorite since it was introduced by the whalers of the 19th century. At fancy hotels expect to pay $6–7 for a drink; at other locations, about $5–6. Here are some of the most famous: mai tai, a mixture of light and dark rum, orange curaçao, orange and almond flavoring, and lemon juice; chi-chi, a simple concoction of vodka, pineapple juice, and coconut syrup—a real sleeper because it tastes like a milk shake; Blue Hawaii, made with vodka and blue curaçao; Planter's Punch, composed of light rum, grenadine, bitters, and lemon juice—a great thirst quencher; and Singapore Sling, a sparkling mixture of gin and cherry brandy with lemon juice and/or pineapple, lime, and orange juices.

Drinking Laws
There are no state-run liquor stores; all kinds of spirits, wines, and beers are available in markets and shops, generally open during normal business hours, seven days a week. The drinking age is 21, and no towns are "dry." Legal hours for serving drinks depend on the type of establishment. Hours generally are: hotels, 6 A.M.–4 A.M.; discos, and nightclubs where there is dancing, 10 A.M.–4 A.M.; bars and lounges where there is no dancing, 6 A.M.–2 A.M. Most restaurants serve alcohol, and in many that don't, you can bring your own.

Coffee
Kona coffee at one time held the distinction of being the only coffee grown in the United States. It's been grown for about 150 years in the upland district of Kona on the Big Island and is a rich, aromatic, truly fine coffee. If it's offered on the menu, have a cup. More recently, coffee from Maui, Moloka'i, O'ahu, and Kaua'i has entered the market. About 4,000 acres of former cane land has been turned into one huge coffee production on Kaua'i, making it by far the largest in the state.

GETTING THERE

With the number of visitors each year more than seven million, the state of Hawaii is one of the easiest places in the world to get to . . . by plane. About 10 large North American airlines (plus additional charter airlines) fly to and from the islands. About the same number of foreign carriers, mostly from Asia and Oceania, also touch down on a daily basis. Hawaii is one of the most hotly contested air markets in the world. The competition between carriers is fierce, and this makes for "sweet deals" and a wide choice of fares for the money-wise traveler. It also makes for pricing chaos. It's impossible to quote airline prices that will hold true for more than a month—if that long. But it's comforting to know that flights to Hawaii remain relatively cheap, and mile for mile they are one of the best travel bargains in the industry. Familiarize yourself with the alternatives at your disposal so you can make an informed travel selection. Now more than ever, you should work with a sharp travel agent who's on your side or do some research on the Web.

Airlines routinely adjust their flight schedules about every three months to account for seasonal differences in travel and route changes. Before planning a trip to and around the islands, be sure to contact the airlines directly or go through your travel agent for the most current information on routes and flying times.

When to Go

The prime tourist season starts two weeks before Christmas and lasts until Easter. It picks up again with summer vacation in early June and ends once more in late August. Everything is usually much more heavily booked and prices are inflated. Hotel, airline, and car reservations are a must at this time of year. You can generally save 10–50 percent and a lot of hassling if you go in the artificially created "off-season," September to early December and mid-April (after Easter) until early June. Recently, the drop in numbers of tourists during the off-season has not been nearly as substantial as in years past, indicating the increasing popularity of the islands at this time of year, but you'll still find the prices better and the beaches, trails, campgrounds, and even restaurants less crowded. The people will be happier to see you, too.

Airflight: The Early Years

On May 20–21, 1927, the people of the world were mesmerized by the heroic act of Charles Lindbergh, The Lone Eagle, as he safely piloted his sturdy craft, *The Spirit of St. Louis,* across the Atlantic. With the Atlantic barrier broken, it took only four days for Jim Dole, of pineapple fame, to announce an air race from the West Coast to Hawaii. He offered the same first prize of $25,000 that Lindbergh had claimed, and to sweeten the pot he offered $10,500 for second place. The **Dole Air Derby** applied only to civilian flights, though the military had already been at work attempting the Pacific crossing.

In August 1925, a Navy flying boat took off from near San Francisco, piloted by Commander John Rodgers. The seaplane flew without difficulty across the wide Pacific's expanse but ran out of gas just north of the Hawaiian Islands and had to put down in a stormy sea. Communication devices went dead, and the mission was given up as lost. Heroically, Rodgers and his crew made crude sails from the wings' fabric and sailed the plane to within 12 miles of Kaua'i, where they were spotted by an incredulous submarine crew. On June 28, 1927, Army lieutenants Lester Maitland and Alfred Hegenberger successfully flew a Fokker tri-motor land plane, *The Bird of Paradise,* from Oakland to O'ahu in just under 26 hours.

On July 14, 1927, independent of the air derby, two indomitable pilots, Ernest Smith and Emory Bronte, flew their *City of Oakland* from its namesake to a forced landing on the shoreline of Moloka'i. On August 16, 1927, eight planes lined up in Oakland to start the derby. The first to take off was the *Woolaroc,* piloted by Art Goebel and Bill Davis. It went on to win the race and claim the prize in just over 26 hours. Second place went to the appropriately named *Aloha,* crewed by Martin Jensen and Paul Schluter, coming in two hours behind the *Woolaroc.* Unfortunately, two planes were lost in the crossing

PACIFIC CROSSROADS

HAWAII

North America:
- Anchorage — 2780 mi.
- Seattle — 2678 mi.
- San Francisco — 2397 mi.
- Los Angeles — 2557 mi.

Asia/Pacific:
- Tokyo — 3647 mi.
- Hong Kong — 5543 mi.
- Manila — 5293 mi.
- Auckland — 4393 mi.
- Sydney — 5070 mi.
- Tahiti — 2741 mi.

TROPIC OF CANCER
EQUATOR
TROPIC OF CAPRICORN

NORTH AMERICA
SOUTH AMERICA
ASIA
JAPAN
PHILIPPINES
AUSTRALIA
NEW ZEALAND

2500 mi
2500 km

and two more in the rescue attempt, which accounted for a total of 12 dead. However, the race proved that flying to Hawaii was indeed feasible.

WINGS TO HAWAII

There are two categories of airlines you can take to Hawaii: **domestic,** meaning American-owned, and **foreign**-owned. An American law, penned in the early 1900s to protect American shipping, says that "only" an American carrier can transport you to and from two American cities. In the airline industry, this law is still very much in effect. It means, for example, that if you want a round-trip between San Francisco and Honolulu, you *must* fly on a domestic carrier. If, however, you are flying San Francisco to Tokyo, you are at liberty to fly a "foreign" airline, and you may even have a stopover in Hawaii, but you must continue to Tokyo or some other foreign city and cannot fly back to San Francisco on the foreign airline. Canadians have no problem flying a Canadian airline round-trip from Vancouver or Toronto to Honolulu because this route does not connect two U.S. cities, and so it is with all foreign travel to and from Hawaii. Travel agents know this, but if you're planning your own trip be aware of this fact.

Kinds of Flights

Depending on where you are coming from, you may have to fly from your home to a "gateway city," from where flights go to Hawaii, either direct or nonstop. On direct flights you fly from point A to point B without changing planes; it doesn't mean that you don't land in between. Direct flights do land, usually once to board and deplane passengers, but you sit cozily on the plane along with your luggage and off you go again. Nonstop is just that; you board and when the doors open again you're at your destination. All flights from the West Coast gateway cities are nonstop, "God willing"—because there is only the Pacific in between!

Stopover Flights

All airlines that fly to Hawaii land at Honolulu, and a few fly nonstop to Maui, Kaua'i, and the Big Island. Major carriers have interline agreements with the island carriers Hawaiian Airlines and Aloha Airlines for getting you to the Neighbor Islands from Honolulu, if one of those is your destination. This sometimes involves a plane change, but your baggage can be booked straight through.

Travel Agents

At one time people went to a travel agent the same way they went to a barber or beautician, loyally sticking with one. Most agents are reputable professionals who know what they're doing. They should be members of the American Society of Travel Agents (ASTA) and licensed by the Air Traffic Conference (ATC). Most have the inside track on the best deals, and they'll save you countless hours calling 800 numbers and listening to elevator music while on hold. Unless you require them to make very special arrangements, their services are free—they are paid a commission by the airlines and hotels that they book for you. In recent years these commissions have been greatly reduced, causing some to start charging a small fee for their services.

If you've done business with a travel agent in the past and were satisfied with the services and prices, by all means stick with him or her. If no such positive rapport exists, then shop around. Ask friends or relatives for recommendations; if you can't get any endorsements go to the Yellow Pages. Call two or three travel agents to compare prices. Make sure to give all of them the same information and to be as precise as possible. Tell them where and when you want to go, how long you want to stay, what class you want to travel, and any special requirements. Write down their information. It's amazing how confusing travel plans can be when you have to keep track of flight numbers, times, prices, and all the preparation information. When you compare, don't look only for the cheapest price. Check for convenience in flights, amenities of hotels, and any other fringe benefits that might be included. Then make your choice of agents and, if he or she is willing to give you individualized service, stick with that agent from then on.

Agents become accustomed to offering the same deals to many clients because they're familiar with the arrangements and because the deals have worked well in the past. Sometimes these are indeed the best, but if they don't suit you, don't be railroaded into accepting them. Any good agent will work with you. After all, it's your trip and your money.

Consolidators are companies that buy blocks of seats on certain flights and then turn around and sell them. Their buying price must be very cheap because their prices are some of the best that you can find. They often list their toll-free phone numbers in local phone directories and just as often run ads in large city newspapers—often in a Sunday Travel section. With the proliferation of the Internet, the number of online travel companies has also mushroomed, and these companies offer great deals. Again, the range in prices in substantial, so check around with many before you send your money.

Package Tours

For the independent traveler, practical package deals that include only flight, car, and lodging are okay. Agents put these together all the time and they just might be the best, but if they don't suit you, make arrangements separately. A package *tour* is totally different. On these you get your hand held by an escort, eat where they want you to eat, go where they want you to go, and watch Hawaii slide by your bus window. For some people, especially groups, this might be the way to do it, but everyone else should avoid the package tour. You'll see Hawaii best on your own, and if you want a tour you can arrange one there, often cheaper. Once arrangements have been made with your travel agent, make sure to take all receipts and letters of confirmation (hotel, car) with you to Hawaii. They probably won't be needed, but if they are, nothing will work better in getting results.

Mainland and International Fares

There are many categories of airline fares, but only three apply to the average traveler: first class, coach, and excursion. Traveling **first class** seats you in the front of the plane, gives you free drinks and movie headsets, a wider choice of meals, more leg room, and access to VIP lounges, if they exist. There are no restrictions, no penalties for advance-booking cancellations or rebooking of return flights, and no minimum-stay requirements.

Coach, the way that most people fly, is totally adequate. You sit in the plane's main compartment behind first class. Your seats are comfortable, but you don't have as much leg room or as wide a choice of meals. Movie headsets and drinks cost you a few dollars, but that's about it. Coach offers many of the same benefits of first class and costs about 30 percent less. You can buy tickets up until takeoff; you have no restrictions on minimum or maximum stays; you receive liberal stopover privileges; and you can cash in your return ticket or change your return date with no penalties.

Excursion or advance-payment excursion (APEX) fares are the cheapest. You are accommodated on the plane exactly the same as if you were flying coach. There are, however, some restrictions. You must book and pay for your ticket in advance (usually 7–14 days; sometimes up to 30 days). At the same time, you must book your return flight, and under most circumstances you can't change either without paying a stiff penalty. Also, your stopovers are severely limited and you will have a minimum/maximum stay period. Only a limited number of seats on any one plane are set aside for APEX fares, so book as early as you can. Also, if you must change travel plans, you can go to the airport and get on as a standby passenger using a discounted ticket, even if the airline doesn't have an official standby policy. There's always the risk that you won't get on, but you do have a chance, as well as priority over an actual standby customer.

Standby is exactly what its name implies: you go to the airport and wait around to see if any flights going to Hawaii have an empty seat. You can save some money, but you cannot have a firm itinerary or limited time. Since Hawaii is such a popular destination, standbys can wait days before catching a plane.

Charters

Charter flights were at one time only for groups or organizations that had memberships in travel clubs. Now they're open to the general public. A charter flight is an entire plane or a block of seats purchased at a quantity discount by a charter company and then sold to customers. Because they are bought at wholesale prices, charter fares can be the cheapest available. As in package deals, only take a charter flight if it is a "fly only," or perhaps includes a car. You don't need one that includes a guide and a bus. Most important, make sure that the charter company is reputable. It should belong to the same organizations (ASTA and ATC) as most travel agents. If not, check into the company at the local chamber of commerce.

More restrictions apply to charters than to any other flights. You must pay in advance. If you cancel after a designated time, you can be penalized severely or lose your money entirely. You cannot change departure or return dates and times. However, up to 10 days before departure the charter company is legally able to cancel, raise the price by 10 percent, or change time and dates. It must return your money if cancellation occurs, or if changed arrangements are unacceptable to you. Most charter companies are on the up-and-up and flights go smoothly, but there are horror stories. Be careful. Be wise. Investigate!

Tips

Flights from California take about five hours, a bit longer from the Northwest or Pacific Canada; you gain two hours over Pacific standard time when you land in Hawaii (three hours during daylight savings time). From the East Coast it takes about 11 hours and you gain five hours over eastern standard time. Flights from Japan take about seven hours and there is a five-hour difference between the time zones. Travel time between Sydney, Australia, or Auckland, New Zealand, and Hawaii is about nine hours. They are ahead of Hawaii time by 20 and 22 hours, respectively. Try to fly Mon.–Thurs., when flights are cheaper and easier to book. Pay for your ticket as soon as your plans are firm. If prices go up no charge is added, but merely booking doesn't guarantee the lowest price. Make sure the airlines, hotels, and car agencies get your phone number too—not only your travel agent's—in case any problems with availability arise (travel agents are often closed on weekends). It's not necessary, but it's a good idea to call and reconfirm flights 24–72 hours in advance.

First-row (bulkhead) seats are good for people who need more leg room, but bad for watching the movie. Airlines will give you special meals (vegetarian, kosher, low cal, low salt) often at no extra charge, but you must notify them in advance. If you're "bumped" from an overbooked flight, you're entitled to a comparable flight to your destination within one hour. If more than an hour elapses, you get denied-boarding compensation, which goes up proportionately with the amount of time you're held up. Sometimes this is cash or a voucher for another flight to be used in the future. You don't have to accept what an airline offers on the spot, if you feel it isn't being fair.

Traveling with Children

Fares for children ages 2–12 are often 30–50 percent of the adult fare, although the exact amount will depend on the season and flight; children under two not occupying a seat travel free. If you're traveling with an infant or active toddler, book your flight well in advance and request the bulkhead seat or first row in any section and a bassinet if available. Many carriers have fold-down cribs with restraints for baby's safety and comfort. Toddlers appreciate the extra space provided by the front-row seats. Be sure to reconfirm, and arrive early to ensure this special seating. On long flights you'll be glad you took these extra pains.

Although most airlines have coloring books, puppets, etc., to keep your child busy, it's always a good idea to bring your own. These can make the difference between a pleasant flight and a harried ordeal. Also, remember to bring baby food, diapers, and other necessities, as many airlines may not be equipped with exactly what you need. Make all inquiries ahead of time so you're not caught unprepared.

Baggage

You are allowed two free pieces of checked luggage—one large, the other small—and a carry-on bag. The two checked pieces can weigh up to 70 pounds each; an extra charge is levied for extra weight. The larger bag can have an overall added dimension (height plus width plus length) of 62 inches; the smaller, 55 inches. Your carry-on must fit under your seat or in the overhead storage compartment. Purses and camera bags are not counted as carry-ons and may be taken aboard. Surfboards and bicycles are about $50 extra. Although they make great mementos, remove all previous baggage tags from your luggage; they can confuse handlers. Attach a sturdy holder with your name and address on the handle, or use a stick-on label on the bag itself. Put your name and address inside the bag, and the address where you'll be staying in Hawaii if possible. Carry your cosmetics, identification, money, prescriptions, tickets, reservations, change of underwear, camera equipment, and perhaps a change of shirt or blouse in your carry-on.

Visas

Entering Hawaii is like entering anywhere else in the United States. Foreign nationals must have a current passport and most must have a proper visa, an ongoing or return air ticket, and sufficient funds for the proposed stay in Hawaii. A visa application can be made at any U.S. embassy or consular office outside the United States and must include a properly filled out application form, two photos 1.5 inches square, and a nonrefundable fee of $45. Canadians do not need a visa or passport but must have proper identification such as passport, driver's license, or birth certificate. Visitors from 29 countries do not need a visa to enter the United States for 90 days or less. As this list is amended periodically, be sure to check in your country of origin to determine if you need a visa for U.S. entry.

Agricultural Inspection

Everyone visiting Hawaii must fill out a "Plant and Animals Declaration Form" and present it to the appropriate official upon arrival in the state (or to the airline personnel). Anyone carrying any of the listed items must have these items inspected by an agricultural inspection agent at the airport. For Information on just what is prohibited, contact any U.S. Customs Office or check with an embassy or consulate in foreign countries.

Remember that before you leave Hawaii for the Mainland, all of your bags are again subject to an agricultural inspection, a usually painless procedure taking only a minute or two. To facilitate your departure, leave all bags unlocked until after inspection. There are no restrictions on beach sand from below the high-water line, coconuts, pre-packaged sugarcane, dried flower arrangements, fresh flower lei, pineapples, certified pest-free plants, seashells, seed lei, and wood roses. However, avocado, litchi, and papaya must be treated before departure. Some other restricted items are berries, fresh gardenias, roses, jade plants, live insects, snails, cotton, plants in soil,

soil itself, and raw sugarcane. Raw sugarcane is okay, however, if it is cut between the nodes, has the outer covering peeled off, and is split into fourths. For any questions pertaining to plants that you want to take to the Mainland, call the Agricultural Quarantine Inspection office on any island before your planned departure.

Foreign countries may have different agricultural inspection requirements for flights from Hawaii (or other points in the United States) to those countries. Be sure to check with the proper foreign authorities for specifics.

Pets and Quarantine

Hawaii has a very rigid pet quarantine policy designed to keep rabies and other Mainland diseases from reaching the state. All domestic pets are subject to **120 days' quarantine** (a 30-day quarantine is allowed by meeting certain pre-arrival and post-arrival requirements—inquire). Unless you are contemplating a move to Hawaii, it is not feasible to take pets. For complete information, contact the Department of Agriculture, Animal Quarantine Division, 99-951 Halawa Valley St., 'Aiea, HI 96701, 808/483-7151.

DOMESTIC CARRIERS

The following are the major domestic carriers to and from Hawaii. The planes used are primarily wide-body D10s, L10s, and 747s, with a smaller 737, 767, or the like flown now and again. A list of the "gateway cities" from which they fly direct and nonstop flights is given, but "connecting cities" are not. All flights, by all carriers, land at Honolulu International Airport except the limited direct flights to Maui, Hawai'i, and Kaua'i. Only the established companies are listed. Entrepreneurial small airlines such as the defunct Mahalo Air pop up now and again and specialize in dirt-cheap fares. There is a hectic frenzy to buy their tickets, and business is great for a while, but then the established companies lower their fares and the gamblers fold.

Hawaiian Airlines

Currently, Hawaiian Airlines operates direct flights between Honolulu and Seattle, Portland, San Francisco, Los Angeles, Las Vegas, and San Diego. It also has direct flights between

The Honolulu Advertiser **EXTRA**

CLIPPER LANDS AT 8:00

Thousands See Flight's Start At Golden Gate

An Early Morning Caller

Reaches Honolulu At 7:04; Cruises Over Island Until Crowds Arrive At Air Base

Pan American Airlines, now out of business, opened Hawaii to mass air travel with this historic 19 hour and 48 minute flight on Wednesday, April 17, 1935

Maui and Los Angeles. Scheduled flights to the South Pacific run twice a week from Honolulu to Pago Pago (Samoa) and Papeete (Tahiti). Hawaiian Airlines offers special discount deals with Dollar rental cars and select major-island hotels, and has a partnership agreement with American, Continental, and Northwest airlines. Contact Hawaiian Airlines at 800/367-5320 Mainland and Canada, 800/882-8811 in Hawaii, website: www.hawaiianair.com.

Aloha Airlines

Currently, Aloha Airlines flies daily flights from Honolulu to Oakland and Orange County that carry on to Las Vegas. Daily flights from Maui go to Oakland and Orange County, and these also carry on to Las Vegas. A flight from Kona to Oakland currently runs four days a week and does not carry on to Las Vegas.

In addition, Aloha now operates a weekly flight on Saturday to Midway Island and twice-weekly flights to Johnston Atoll in the South Pacific, which carry on to Majuro Atoll and Kwajalein. Aloha Airlines partners with United Airlines for easy flights to Mainland and Asian cities. For information, call 800/367-5250 Mainland and Canada or check online at www.alohaairlines.org.

United Airlines

Since its first island flight in 1947, United has become top dog in flights to Hawaii. The Mainland routes connect more than 100 cities to Hon-

olulu. The main gateway cities of San Francisco, Los Angeles, Chicago, and Vancouver have direct flights to Honolulu; flights from all other cities connect through these. United also offers direct flights to Maui from San Francisco and Los Angeles, from San Francisco and Los Angeles to Kona on the Big Island, and from Los Angeles to Lihu'e, Kaua'i. United also runs a seasonal (summer) flight once a week from San Francisco to Lihu'e. Continuing through Honolulu, United flights go to Tokyo (Narita), where connections can be made for other Asian cities. United offers a number of packages, including flight and hotel on O'ahu, and flight, hotel, and car on the Neighbor Islands. United interlines with Aloha Airlines and deals with Hertz Rent A Car. United is the "big guy" and intends to stay that way. Its packages are hard to beat; contact United at 800/241-6522, website: www.ual.com.

American Airlines

American offers direct flights to Honolulu from Los Angeles, San Francisco, Dallas-Fort Worth, and Chicago. It also flies daily from Los Angeles direct to Maui. American interlines with Hawaiian Airlines. Contact American at 800/433-7300, website: www.aa.com.

Continental Airlines

Flights from all Mainland cities to Honolulu connect via Los Angeles, Newark, and Houston. Also available are direct flights from Guam to

Honolulu. Continental interlines with Hawaiian Airlines. Call 800/525-0280 or 800/231-0856 for international information, or go online to www.fly-continental.com.

Northwest Airlines

Northwest flies into Honolulu from Los Angeles, San Francisco, Seattle, Minneapolis, and Detroit. Onward flights continue to numerous Asian cities. Call 800/225-2525 or check www.nwa.com.

Delta Air Lines

In 1985, Delta entered the Hawaiian market; when it bought out Western Airlines its share became even bigger. It has nonstop flights to Honolulu from Dallas-Fort Worth, Los Angeles, San Francisco, and Atlanta, and a direct flight to Kahului, Maui, from Los Angeles. Contact Delta at 800/221-1212, website: www.delta-air.com.

Trans World Airlines

TWA has daily nonstop flights from St. Louis to Honolulu, and since spring 2000 has started daily flights also to Kahului (Maui) and Kona (Big Island) from St. Louis. Call 800/221-2000 or check www.twa.com.

Note: As of this writing, Trans World Airlines has filed for bankruptcy, and it's not certain who will take over the airline's routes and planes.

FOREIGN CARRIERS

The following carriers operate throughout Asia and Oceania but have no U.S. flying rights. This means that for you to vacation in Hawaii using one of these carriers, your flight must originate or terminate in a foreign city. You can have a stopover in Honolulu with a connecting flight to a Neighbor Island. For example, if you've purchased a flight on Japan Air Lines from San Francisco to Tokyo, you can stop in Hawaii, but you must then carry on to Tokyo. Failure to do so will result in a stiff fine, and the balance of your ticket will not be refunded.

Canadian Airlines International

Nonstop flights from Canada to Honolulu originate in Vancouver and Toronto. Canadian has an interisland agreement with Aloha Airlines for travel to the neighboring islands. Contact Cana-

dian at 800/426-7000 in the U.S. or 800/665-7530 in Canada, website: www.cdnair.com.

Air New Zealand

Flights link New Zealand, Australia, and numerous South Pacific islands to Honolulu, with continuing flights to Mainland cities. All flights run via Auckland, New Zealand. Call 800/926-7255 or 800/262-1234 in the United States and 800/663-5494 in Canada for current information, or go online to website www.airnz.com.

Japan Air Lines

The Japanese are the second-largest group, next to Americans, to visit Hawaii. JAL flights to Honolulu originate in Tokyo (Narita), Nagoya, Osaka (Kansai), and Fukuoka. In addition, there are flights between Tokyo (Narita) and Kona on the Big Island. Call JAL at 800/525-3663, or go online to www.jal.co.jp.

Qantas

Daily flights connect Sydney with Honolulu; all other flights feed through this hub. Contact Qantas at 800/227-4500, website: www.qantas.com.au.

China Airlines

Routes to Honolulu with China Airlines are only from Taipei. Connections are available in Taipei to most Asian capitals. Call 800/227-5118 or surf to www.china-airlines.com.

Korean Air

Korean Air offers some of the least expensive flights to Asia. All flights are direct between Honolulu and Seoul, with connections there to many Asian cities. Call 800/438-5000 or try the website www.koreanair.com.

Other Airlines

Aside from the above airlines, large volume charter operators book flights to the various island with such carriers as **Canada 3000** and **American Trans Air.**

TOUR COMPANIES

Many tour companies advertise packages to Hawaii in large city newspapers every week.

They offer very reasonable airfares, car rentals, and accommodations. Without trying, you can get round-trip airfare from the West Coast and a week in Hawaii for $400–500 using one of these companies. The following companies offer great deals and have excellent reputations. This list is by no means exhaustive.

SunTrips

This California-based tour and charter company sells vacations all over the world. It's primarily a wholesale company but will work with the general public. SunTrips often works with Rich International Air. When you receive your SunTrips tickets, you are given discount vouchers for places to stay that are convenient to the airport of departure. Many of these hotels have complimentary airport pickup service and will allow you to park your car, free of charge, for up to 14 days, which saves a considerable amount on airport parking fees. SunTrips does not offer assigned seating until you get to the airport. They recommend you get there two hours in advance, and they ain't kidding! This is the price you pay for getting such inexpensive air travel. SunTrips usually has a deal with a car rental company. Remember that everyone on your incoming flight is offered the same deal, and all make a beeline for the rental car's shuttle van after landing and securing their baggage. If you have a traveling companion, work together to beat the rush by leaving your companion to fetch the baggage while you head directly for the van as soon as you arrive. Pick your car up, then return for your partner and the bags. Even if you're alone, you could zip over to the car rental center and then return for your bags without having them sit very long on the carousel. Contact SunTrips, 2350 Paragon Dr., P.O. Box 18505, San Jose, CA 95131, 800/786-8747 in California, 808/941-2697 in Honolulu, website: www.suntrips.com.

Pleasant Hawaiian Holidays

A California-based company specializing in Hawaii, Pleasant Hawaiian Holidays makes arrangements for flights, accommodations, and transportation only. For flights, they primarily use American Trans Air. Contact Pleasant Hawaiian Holiday, 2404 Townsgate Rd., Westlake Village, CA 91361, 800/242-9244, website: www.2hawaii.com.

Council Travel Services

These full-service budget-travel specialists are a subsidiary of the nonprofit Council on International Educational Exchange, and the official U.S. representative to the International Student Travel Conference. They'll custom-design trips and programs for everyone from senior citizens to college students. Bona fide students have extra advantages, however, including eligibility for the International Student Identity Card (ISIC), which often gets you discount fares and waived entrance fees. Groups and business travelers are also welcome. For full information, call 800/226-8624, or write to Council Travel Services at one of these offices: 530 Bush St., San Francisco, CA 94108, 415/421-3473, or 205 E. 42nd St., New York, NY 10017, 212/661-1450. Other offices are in Austin, Berkeley, Boston, Davis, Long Beach, Los Angeles, Miami, Portland, San Diego, and Seattle.

Student Travel Network

STA Travel is a full-service travel agency specializing in student travel, regardless of age. Those under 26 do not have to be full-time students to get special fares. Older independent travelers can avail themselves of services, although they are ineligible for student fares. STA works hard to get you discounted or budget rates. STA's central office is at 7202 Melrose Ave., Los Angeles, CA 90046, 213/934-8722 or 800/777-0112. STA maintains 39 offices throughout the United States, Australasia, and Europe, along with **Travel Cuts,** a sister organization operating in Canada. Many tickets issued by STA are flexible, allowing changes with no penalty, and are open-ended for travel up to one year. STA also maintains **Travel Help,** a service available at all offices designed to solve all types of problems that may arise while traveling. STA is a well-established travel agency with an excellent and well-deserved reputation.

Signature Vacations

Formerly Fiesta West, this company is Canada's largest complete-package tour operator, flying mainly from Toronto and Vancouver, but with flights also from Victoria, Calgary, and Edmonton. Prepackaged, all-inclusive one- to two-week tours are offered to all the major islands, but to the outer islands only seasonally. Signature Vacations uses Canada 3000 as its main air carrier. All Signature Vacations' bookings are done through travel agents; however, if you need assistance with a purchased tour package, you can call the company's 24-hour worldwide help line, 800/830-8111, or log on to its website, www.signature.ca.

EcoTours to Hawaii

Sierra Club Trips offers Hawaii trips for nature lovers who are interested in an outdoor experience. Various trips include hikes over Maui's Haleakala and, on Kaua'i, a kayak trip along the Na Pali Coast and a family camping spree in Kaua'i's Koke'e region. All trips are led by experienced guides and are open to Sierra Club members only ($35 per year to join). For information contact the Sierra Club Outing Department, 85 2nd St., 2nd Fl., San Francisco, CA 94105, 415/775-5500.

Earthwatch allows you to become part of an expeditionary team dedicated to conservation and the study of the natural environment. An expedition might include studying dolphins in Kewalo Basin Marine Mammal Laboratory or diving Maui's threatened reefs. If you become an assistant field researcher, your lodgings may be a dorm room at the University of Hawai'i, and your meals may come from a remote camp kitchen. Fees vary and are tax deductible. If you are interested in this learning experience, contact Earthwatch, 680 Mt. Auburn St., P.O. Box 403-P, Watertown, MA 02272, 617/926-8200.

Backroads, 801 Cedar St., Berkeley, CA 94710, 510/527-1555 or 800/462-2848, fax 510/527-1444, website: www.backroads.com, arranges easy-on-the-environment bicycle and hiking trips to the Big Island. Basic tours include a six-day hiking/camping tour ($698), a six-day hiking/inn tour ($1,295), and a five-day bicycle/camping tour ($649). Prices include hotel/inn accommodations or tent when applicable, most meals, and professional guide service. Airfare is not included, and bicycles and sleeping bags can be rented (BYO okay) for reasonable rates.

Educational Trips

Not a tour per se, but an educational opportunity, **Elderhostel Hawaii** offers short-term programs on five of the Hawaiian Islands. Different programs focus on history, culture, cuisine, and the environment in association with one of the colleges or universities in the islands. Most programs use hotels for accommodations. For information, write Elderhostel, 75 Federal St., Boston, MA 02110-1941, or call 617/426-7788.

BY SHIP

Cruise Ships

Cruise lines offering ships that touch in Hawaii for day trips only on their varied routes include the following. Most travel agents can provide information on these cruise lines:

Norwegian Cruise Lines, 800/327-7030, website: www.ncl.com

Holland America Lines, 800/426-0327, website: www.hollandamerica.com

Cunard, 800/528-6273, website: www.cunard-line.com

Carnival Cruise Line, 800/327-9501, website: www.carnival.com

Princess Cruises, 800/421-0522, website: www.princesscruises.com

Royal Caribbean International, 800/327-6700, website: www.royalcaribbean.com

Crystal Cruises, 800/446-6620, website: www.cruisecrystal.com

Freighter Travel

Travel by freighter is on a working cargo ship. While the routes are usually longer than cruise ship itineraries and the ships themselves do not contain all the luxuries and amenities of the cruise liners, fares are often 30–40 percent less per day than travel on a cruise ship. If you're especially interested in traveling by freighter, contact: **Freighter World Cruises,** 180 S. Lake Ave., Suite 335, Pasadena, CA 91101-2655, 626/449-3106 or 800/531-7774, website: www.freighterworld.com, email: freighter@freighterworld.com. This company is an agent that arranges passage for travelers on over 100 ships around the world. It publishes the *Freighter Space Advisory* newsletter. Also arranging travel is **Maris Freighter Cruises, USA,** 215 Main St., Westport, CT 06880, 203/222-1500 or 800/996-2747, fax 203/222-9191, website: www.cruisemaris.com/frieghters.html, email:

maris@freightercruises.com. Maris publishes the monthly *Freighter Travel Newsletter*. For additional information, check *Ford's Freighter* *Travel Guide & Waterways of the World* quarterly, which can be contacted at 19448 Londelius St., Northridge, CA 91324, 818/701-7414.

GETTING AROUND

BY AIR

Interisland air travel is highly developed, economical, and completely convenient. You can go almost anywhere at any time on everything from wide-bodied jets to single-engine air taxis. Hawaiians take flying for granted, using planes the way most people use buses. A shopping excursion to Honolulu from a Neighbor Island is commonplace, as is a trip from the city for a picnic at a quiet beach. Most interisland flights are 20–40 minutes long, with some shorter and a few longer. The moody sea can be uncooperative to mass transit, but the skies above Hawaii are generally clear and perfect for flying. Their infrequent gloomier moments can delay flights, but the major airlines of Hawaii have been flying nonstop ever since Hawaiian Air's maiden flight in 1929. The fares are competitive, the schedules convenient, and the service friendly.

Brief History

Little more than a motorized kite, the *Hawaiian Skylark* was the first plane to fly in Hawaii. On New Year's Day, 1911, it circled a Honolulu polo field, where 3,000 spectators, including Queen Lili'uokalani, witnessed history. Hawaiians have been soaring above their lovely islands ever since. The first paying customer, Mrs. Newmann, took off on a $15 joyride in 1913 with a Chinese aviator named Tom Gunn. In February 1920, Charles Fern piloted the first interisland customer round-trip from Honolulu to Maui for $150. He worked for Charles Stoffer, who started the first commercial airline the year before with one Curtiss biplane, affectionately known as "Charlie's Crate." For about 10 years sporadic attempts at interisland service amounted to little more than extended joyrides to deliver the day's newspaper from Honolulu. The James Dole Air Race in 1927 proved transpacific flight was possible, but interisland passenger service didn't really begin until Stanley C. Kennedy, a World War I flier and heir to Inter-Island Steam Navigation Co., began Inter-Island Airways in January 1929. For a dozen years he ran Sikorsky Amphibians, considered the epitome of safety. By 1941 he converted to the venerable workhorse, the DC-3, and changed the company name to **Hawaiian Air.**

By 1948, Hawaiian Air was unopposed in the interisland travel market, because regularly scheduled boats had already become obsolete. However, in 1946 a fledgling airline named Trans-Pacific opened for business. A nonscheduled airline with only one war surplus DC-3, it carried a hunting party of businessmen to Moloka'i on its maiden flight. By June 1952, it was a regularly scheduled airline in stiff competition with Hawaiian Air and had changed its name to **Aloha Airlines.** Both airlines had their financial glory days and woes over the next decade; by the end of the '60s both were flying interisland jets.

A healthy crop of small scheduled and unscheduled airlines always darted about the wings of the large airlines, flying to minor airfields and performing flying services uneconomical for the bigger airlines. Most of these tiny, often one-plane companies are swatted from the air like gnats whenever the economy goes sour or tourism becomes sluggish. In the past, they had names like Peacock and Rainbow, and after a brief flash of wings they were gone.

INTERISLAND CARRIERS

The only effective way for most visitors to travel between the Hawaiian Islands is by air. Luckily, Hawaii has excellent air transportation that boasts one of the industry's safest flight records. All interisland flights have a no smoking regulation. Items restricted on flights from the Mainland and from overseas are also restricted on flights within the state. Baggage allowances are the same as anywhere, except that due to space

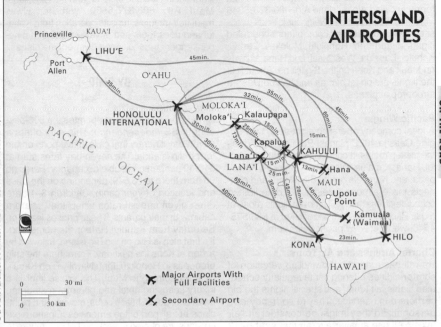

INTERISLAND AIR ROUTES

Princeville KAUA'I
LIHU'E
Port Allen
O'AHU
HONOLULU INTERNATIONAL
MOLOKA'I
Moloka'i Kalaupapa
Kapalua
Lana'i KAHULUI
LANA'I Hana
MAUI
Upolu Point
Kamuala (Waimea)
KONA HILO
HAWAI'I
PACIFIC OCEAN

45min.
35min.
32min.
35min.
30min.
30min.
30min.
25min.
13min.
15min.
15min.
15min.
15min.
13min.
25min.
38min.
35min.
28min.
40min.
65min.
40min.
45min.
23min.
60min.

0   30 mi
0   30 km

✈ Major Airports With Full Facilities

✈ Secondary Airport

ON THE ROAD

constraints, carry-on luggage on the smaller prop planes may be limited in number and size.

The following airlines have competitive prices, with interisland flights about $90 each way, with substantial savings for state residents. With both Hawaiian and Aloha, you can save $8–10 per ticket by purchasing a booklet of six **flight coupons.** These are available only in state at any ticket office or airport counter, and they are *transferable.* Just book a flight as normal and present the filled-in voucher to board the plane. Perfect for families or groups of friends. Hawaiian Airlines coupons are good for six months, Aloha Airlines coupons for one year.

Additionally, each airline offers passes good for unlimited travel anywhere that the airlines flies, but they are nontransferable and may only be used on consecutive days. You may purchase these passes in state or before you arrive in Hawaii. Hawaiian Airlines has the Hawaiian Island Pass: five days at $324, seven days at $345, 10 days at $409, and 14 days at $469. Fares for children ages 2–11 and seniors are about 10

percent less. Aloha Airlines offers one 7-day Island Pass for $321 with the same conditions.

Note: Although every effort has been made for up-to-date accuracy, remember that schedules are constantly changing. The following should be used only as a point of reference. Please call the airlines listed below for their latest schedules.

Hawaiian Air, 800/367-5320 Mainland and Canada, 800/882-8811 statewide, website: www.hawaiianair.com, is not only the oldest airline in Hawaii, it is also the biggest. It flies more aircraft, to more airports, more times per day than any other airline in Hawaii. It services all islands, including Moloka'i and Lana'i, and flies all jets.

Aloha Airlines, 800/367-5250 Mainland and Canada, website: www.alohaairlines.com, with its all-jet fleet of 737s, is also an old and venerable Hawaiian company with plenty of flights connecting O'ahu to Kaua'i, Maui, and both Kona and Hilo on Hawai'i. It offers more flights to Maui than any other island carrier.

Island Air (a subsidiary of Aloha Airlines and formerly called Aloha Island Air), 800/323-3345 Mainland, 800/652-6541 Neighbor Islands, website: www.alohaairlines.com, offers scheduled flights to and from Honolulu, Moloka'i, Lana'i; Kahului, Kapalua–West Maui, and Hana airports on Maui; and Kona on the Big Island. About half the flights are on jet aircraft and half on Dash-8 turboprop airplanes.

Pacific Wings

A local company operating eight-seat, twin-engine Cessna 402C planes, Pacific Wings does the pickup routes. It connects Honolulu to Kahului, Hana, Kapalua–West Maui, Moloka'i, Kalaupapa, and Kamuela on the Big Island, and connects these airports together, but on a limited schedule of less than half a dozen flights a day at most. Pacific Wings can be reached at 888/575-4546, website: www.pacificwings.com.

Charter Airlines and Air Tours

Hawaii has a good but dwindling selection of charter airlines offering some regularly scheduled flights, air tours, and special flights the big carriers don't service. They're so handy and personalized they might be considered "air taxis." All use smaller aircraft that seat 6–12 people and fly low enough that their normal interisland flights are like air tours. Stories abound of passengers being invited to ride copilot, or of a pilot going out of his way to show off a glimmering coastline or a beautiful waterfall. Many times you get the sense that it's "your" flight and the airline is doing everything possible to make it memorable. The commuter airlines are limited in plane size and routes serviced. Among themselves, prices are very competitive, but, except on their specialty runs, they tend to be more expensive than the three major interisland carriers. They're also not as generous on baggage allowance. You'll be charged more for the extra bulk, or some of it may not be allowed to accompany you on the plane.

Companies include **Big Island Air,** 808/329-4868 or 800/303-8868, operating out of Kailua-Kona, with charter service and flight-seeing tours around the Big Island on eight-passenger Cessna 402s. **Paragon Air,** 808/244-3356 or 800/428-1231, website: www.maui.net/~wings/index.htm, has charter flights to all of Hawaii's airports and

flight-seeing tours to Moloka'i and the Big Island. **Maui Air,** 808/877-5500, website: www. maui.net/~mauisle, runs its operation from Kahului and does tours and private charters in nine-passenger air-conditioned, twin-engine planes.

BY SHIP

Cruise Ships

American Hawaii Cruises operates the 800-passenger SS *Independence.* This ship offers a seven-day itinerary that calls at five ports on the four main islands. The seven-day fares start at $1,349 per person double occupancy. Fares go up from there to $3,549, depending on the class and location of your cabin. Children 3–17 are often given special rates when they share a cabin with their parents. These cruises leave on Saturday from Kahului Harbor, its home port. It's first stop is Hilo on the Big Island, followed by a stop at Kona the next day. From there the ship proceeds to Honolulu, then Nawiliwili on Kaua'i, before returning to Maui. This cruise liner is a luxury seagoing hotel and gourmet restaurant; swimming pools, health clubs, movies, and nightclubs are all part of the amenities. Onshore excursions are offered at each port of call. Airfare to Hawaii, interisland air flights, rental cars, and accommodation on any island after your cruise can be arranged for you by American Hawaii Cruises. For details contact: American Hawaii Cruises, Robin St. Wharf, 1380 Port of New Orleans Pl., New Orleans, LA 70130-1890, 800/513-5022, fax 504/599-5579, website: www.cruisehawaii.com.

Since December 2000, the MS *Patriot,* sister ship to the SS *Independence,* has also sailed these waters. Much newer and larger, it was totally renovated before being put back into service. This ship also leaves Saturday but starts her journey at the Aloha Tower in Honolulu, her home port, from where she follows the same clockwise route around the islands, stopping at all the same ports. Rates for this ship start at $1,599 and go up to $4,249 depending upon room location and time of year. For reservations, contact United States Lines at 877/330-6871, website: www.unitedstateslines.com.

Starting in December 2001, Norwegian Cruise Lines will run a weekly seven-day cruise with its luxury liner *Norwegian Leo*. This ship will leave Honolulu harbor Sunday evening and cruise to Kona for its first stop. Leaving there, it spends a day at sea before arriving at Fanning Island in the Republic of Kiribati. One day of sailing back returns the ship to Lahaina, from where it goes to Nawiliwili Harbor on Kaua'i and then back to port in Honolulu. For information and pricing, contact Norwegian Cruise Lines, 7665 Corporate Center Dr., Miami, FL 33126, 800/327-7030, website: www.ncl.com.

RENTAL CARS

Does Hawaii really have more rental cars than pineapples? O'ahu's Yellow Pages have six pages of listings for car rental agencies. There are more than 25 firms on Maui and a dozen or so on the Big Island and Kaua'i. Moloka'i has three, and Lana'i has one. You can rent anything from a 60-passenger Scenic-cruiser to a 60cc moped, but sedans and other passenger cars are the most common. Gaining in popularity, however, especially for the more adventurous travelers on the Neighbor Islands, are Jeeps and other 4WD vehicles. Still, it's best to reserve your car well before your arrival in Hawaii. If you visit the islands during the peak tourist frenzy without reserving your wheels in advance, you may be marooned at the airport.

There is a tremendous field of cars and agencies from which to choose, and vehicles are cheaper than anywhere else in America. Special deals come and go like tropical rain showers; swashbuckling price-slashings and come-ons are all over the rental car market. A little knowledge combined with some shrewd shopping around can save you a bundle. And renting a car is the best way to see the islands if you're going to be here for a limited time. Outside of O'ahu, it simply isn't worthwhile to hassle with the poor public transportation system or rely on your thumb.

Requirements

Car agencies impose various requirements on the renter, but the most important clauses are common. Before renting, check that you fulfill the requirements. Generally, you must be 21, although some agencies rent to 18-year-olds, while others still require you to be 25. You must possess a valid driver's license—licenses from most countries accepted, but if you are not American, get an International Driver's License to be safe. You should also have a major credit card in your name. This is the easiest way to rent a car. Some companies will take a deposit, but it will be very stiff. It could easily be $50 per day on top of your rental fees and sometimes much more. In addition, they may require a credit check on the spot, complete with phone calls to your employer and bank. If you damage the car, charges will be deducted from your deposit, and the car company itself determines the extent of the damages. Some companies *will not* rent you a car without a major credit card in your name, no matter how much of a deposit you are willing to leave, and this is often true for Hawaiian residents who want to rent a car on an island that they are not a resident of.

When to Rent

On this one, you'll have to make up your own mind, because it's a bet that you can either win or lose. But it's always good to know the odds before you plop down your money. You can reserve your car in advance when you book your air ticket, or play the field when you get there. If you book in advance, you'll obviously have a car waiting for you, but the deal that you made is the deal that you'll get—it may or may not be the best around, but it may be quite good. On the other hand, if you wait, you can often take advantage of on-the-spot deals. However, you're betting that cars are available. You might be totally disappointed and not be able to rent a car at all, or you might make a honey of a deal.

If you're arriving during the peak seasons of Christmas, Easter, or late summer vacation, absolutely *book your car in advance*. Rental companies have their numbers down pretty well and seem to have plenty of cars, but all may be accounted for during this period. Even if you can find a junker from a fly-by-night, it'll price-gouge you mercilessly. If you're going off-peak, you stand a good chance of getting the car you want at the price you want. It's generally best to book ahead; most car companies have toll-free numbers. At least call them for an opinion of your chances of getting a car upon your intended arrival.

Rates

The super-cheap rates on eye-catcher brochures refer to subcompacts. The price goes up with the size of the car. As with options on a new car, the more luxury you get, the more you pay. All major car rental companies in Hawaii use a flat rate option. The flat rate is best, providing a fixed daily rate and unlimited mileage. Some of the smaller local companies may have a mileage rate option. Mileage rate costs less per day, but you are charged for every mile driven. Mileage rates are best if you drive less than 30 miles per day—but even on an island that isn't much! With either rate, you buy the gas.

Rental rates vary by company, as do the names they use to refer to their types of vehicles. The following rates are fairly representative for most categories: subcompact, $45 a day, $225 a week; compact, $55/260; midsize, $65/300; full size, $75/350; luxury, $110/575; convertible and jeep, $100/500; van, $110/$575. Substantial discounts are offered for weekday, weekly, and monthly rentals. It's sometimes cheaper to rent a car for the week even if you're only going to use it for five days. If you'll be on more than one island, check to see if weekly and monthly rates can be split between Neighbor Islands. Most of the car companies, local and national, offer special rates and deals, like AAA rates. These deals fluctuate too rapidly to give any hard-and-fast information. They are common, however, so make sure to inquire. Don't expect that rental companies will let you know about any deal that they have. Also, peak periods have "blackouts," during which normally good deals no longer apply.

These rates aren't your only charges, however. On top of the actual rental fee, you must pay an airport access fee, airport concession fee, state tax, and a road tax surcharge—in total, an additional 25–30 percent. For cars not rented at the airports, you'll realize a savings of about 7.5 percent because some of the taxes can not be charged.

You may be asked about refueling options. Ordinarily, you fill the tank when you return the car or the company will fill the tank itself at an inflated rate. Some now offer you the option of prepaying for a half or full tank of gas at a reduced rate and they fill the car when it comes back. To get your money's worth this way, bring the car back exactly half empty or all the way empty, otherwise you may lose a little bit over pumping the gas yourself. Gas prices are generally higher in Hawaii than anywhere on the Mainland, and may be higher yet in "distant" locations like Hana, Moloka'i, and Lana'i.

Warning: If you keep your car beyond your contract, you'll be charged the highest daily rate unless you notify the rental agency beforehand. *Don't keep your car longer than the contract without notifying the company.* Companies are *quick* to send out their repossession specialists. You might find yourself in a situation with your car gone, a warrant out for your arrest, and an extra charge on your bill. A simple courtesy call notifying them of your intentions saves a lot of headaches and hassle.

Insurance

Before signing your car rental agreement, you'll be offered various "insurance" coverages. Although these too vary somewhat by company, they fall into general categories: loss/damage option runs about $15 a day; uninsured motorist protection, $7 a day; and liability protection, $13 a day. In addition, some also offer a personal effects protection for $5 a day in case your property gets stolen. Since insurance is already built into the contract (don't expect the rental agency to point this out), what you're really buying is a waiver on the deductible ($500–1,000), in case you crack up the car. If you have insurance at home, you will almost always have coverage on a rental car—including your normal deductible—although not all policies are the same, so check with your agent. Also, if you haven't bought the waiver and you have a mishap, the rental agency will put a claim against your credit card on the spot for the amount of deductible, even if you can prove that your insurance will cover. The company will tell *you* to collect from your insurance company because it doesn't want to be left holding the bag on an across-the-waters claim. If you have a good policy with a small deductible, it's hardly worth paying the extra money for the waiver, but if your own policy is inadequate, buy the insurance. Also, most major credit cards offer complimentary car-rental insurance as an incentive for using their cards to rent the car. Simply call your credit card company to see if this service is included.

In most cases, you'll get only one key for your rental car. Don't lose it or lock it inside. If you do lock it inside the vehicle, call AAA (or other auto emergency service that you have) and ask for assistance. Failing that, a local locksmith can open your car for a fee or the rental car agency can send out a second key by taxi, but both of these options can get quite pricey.

Driving Tips

Wear your seat belt—it's the law! Police keep an eye out for miscreants and often ticket those who do not use their restraints. Protect your small children as you would at home with car seats. Either bring one from home or rent one from a car rental company. Rental prices and availability vary, but all the agencies can make arrangements if you give them enough notice.

Mile markers on roads are great for pinpointing sites and beaches. The lower number on these signs is the highway number, so you can always make sure that you're on the right road.

There are few differences between driving in Hawaii and on the Mainland. Just remember that many people on the roads are tourists and can be confused about where they're going. Since many drivers are from somewhere else, there's hardly a "regular style" of driving in the islands. A farmer from Iowa accustomed to poking along on back roads can be sandwiched between a frenetic New Yorker who's trying to drive over his roof and a super-polite but horribly confused Japanese tourist who normally drives on the left.

In Hawaii, drivers don't honk their horns except to say hello, or in an emergency. It's considered rude, and honking to hurry someone might earn you a knuckle sandwich. Hawaiian drivers reflect the climate: they're relaxed and polite. Often, they'll brake to let you turn left when they're coming at you. They may assume you'll do the same, so be ready, after a perfunctory turn signal from another driver, for him or her to turn across your lane. The more rural the area, the more apt this is to happen.

It may seem like common sense, but remember to slow down when you enter the little towns strung along the circle-island route. It's easy to bomb along on the highway and flash through these towns, missing some of Hawaii's best scenery. Also, rural children expect *you* to be watchful and will assume that you are going to stop for them when they dart onto the crosswalks.

O'ahu's **H-1, H-2, and H-3 freeways** throw many Mainlanders a Polynesian "screwball." Accustomed to driving on superhighways, Mainlanders assume these are the same. They're not. O'ahu's superhighways are generally much more convoluted than most Mainland counterparts. Subliminally they look like normal freeways, except they've been tied into Hawaiian knots. There are split-offs, crossroads, and exits in the middle of exits. Stay alert and don't be lulled into complacency.

Respect Do Not Enter and Private Property signs—*Kapu* means the same thing.

Most insurance companies warn you that their cars are not supposed to be driven off paved roads—read your policy. This seems absolutely ridiculous for 4WD vehicles, but true nonetheless. When a road is signed for 4WD only, assume that that's the case for a good reason.

Speed limits change periodically along the highways of Hawai'i, particularly when they pass through small towns. Police routinely check the speed of traffic by use of radar equipment. Be aware of this so you don't go home with more than a suntan.

The State Department of Transportation has installed solar-powered emergency call boxes on highways that are linked directly to the 911 emergency telephone number. These boxes dot major roadways. Look for a yellow box on a tall pole topped by a small solar panel and blue light.

BYO Car

If you want to bring your own car, write for information to: Director of Finance, Division of Licenses, 1455 S. Beretania St., Honolulu, HI 96814. However, unless you'll be in Hawaii for a bare minimum of six months and will spend all your time on one island, don't even think about it. It's an expensive proposition and takes time and plenty of arrangements. From the West Coast U.S., the cost is at least $800 to Honolulu, and an additional $100 to any other island. To save on rental costs, it would be better to buy and sell a car there, or to lease for an extended period.

Four-Wheel Drives

For normal touring, it is unnecessary to rent 4WDs in Hawaii except on Lana'i, where they're

ON THE ROAD

a must, or if you really want to get off the beaten track on the other islands. They are expensive ($70–120 per day), and you simply don't need them. If you still want one, most car rental agencies have them, and some specialize in them. Because their numbers are limited, reservations are highly recommended.

RENTAL AGENCIES

When you arrive at any of Hawaii's airports, you'll walk the gauntlet of car rental booths and courtesy phones shoulder to shoulder along the main hallways. Of the two categories of car rental agencies in Hawaii, each has its advantage. In the first category are the big national firms. These big guys are familiar and easy to work with, sometimes offer special fly/drive deals with airlines, and live up to their promises. If you want your rental experience to be hassle-free, they're the ones. Also, don't be prejudiced against them just because they're so well known; sometimes they offer the best deals. Although these companies carry mostly sedans, some now also rent Jeeps, sport-utility vehicles, other 4WD vehicles, trucks, and vans.

Hawaii has spawned a good crop of local entrepreneurial rental agencies. Their deals and cars can range, like rummage-sale treasures, from great finds to pure junk. Local companies have the advantage of being able to cut deals on the spot. If nothing is moving from their lot on the day you arrive, you might get a real bargain. Unfortunately, mixed in this category is a hodgepodge of fly-by-nights. Some of these are small but adequate, while others are a rip-off.

The four major islands also have rental companies that deal in vanity vehicles like the Dodge Viper, Corvette, Ferrari, Porsche, Jaguar, and Lamborghine Diablo. These cars are purely for show, but if you don't mind dropping a couple of hundred dollars for a few hours in a sports car, give it a try.

National Agencies
All of the following national companies are represented in Hawaii. Only the 800 numbers are given below. For local numbers and for other agencies, see the individual travel chapters.

One of the best firms with an excellent reputation for service and prices is **Dollar Rent A Car,** 800/800-4000 worldwide, website: www.dollarcar.com. With an excellent reputation and very competitive prices, Dollar rents mostly Chrysler vehicles: sedans, jeeps, convertibles, and 4WDs. Great weekly rates, and all major credit cards accepted.

Alamo, 800/327-9633, website: www.goalamo.com, has good weekly rates. Mostly GM cars.

National Car Rental, 800/227-7368 worldwide, website: www.nationalcar.com, features GM and Nissan cars and accepts all major credit cards. Sometimes you can rent without a credit card if you leave a $100 per day deposit—less if you take full insurance coverage.

Avis, 800/321-3712 nationwide, website: www.avis.com, features late-model GM cars as well as most imports and convertibles.

Budget, 800/527-7000 worldwide, website: www.drivebudget.com, offers competitive rates on late-model Ford and Lincoln-Mercury cars and specialty vehicles. Budget manages the Sears auto rental network.

Hertz, 800/654-3011 worldwide, website: www.hertz.com, is competitively priced with many fly/drive deals. Hertz features Ford vehicles.

Thrifty, 800/367-2277 worldwide, website: www.thrifty.com, uses Chrysler vehicles.

Enterprise, 800/736-8222, website: www.pickenterprise.com, rents all types of vehicles at decent rates.

Car Pickup
The majority of agencies listed above have booths at all of the airport terminal buildings throughout Hawaii. If they don't, they have clearly marked courtesy phones in the lobbies. Just pick one up to get directions on where to wait for the agency's shuttle. Some of the larger local agencies also have courtesy phones and booths at airport terminals, but many only work out of their lots.

Travelers with Disabilities
Accessible Vans of Hawaii 296 Alamaha St., Suite C, Kahului, HI 96732, 808/871-7785 or 800/303-3750, fax 808/871-7536, website: www.accessiblevanshawaii.com, email: avavans@maui.net, is a private company owned and operated by Dave McKown, who has traveled the world with his paraplegic brother. Dave

knows firsthand the obstacles faced by people with disabilities, and his disabled associate does as well. Accessible Vans of Hawaii provides a full-service travel agency, booking rooms, flights, and activities for the physically disabled. Wheelchair-lift-equipped vans are rented on O'ahu, Maui, and the Big Island for $115 a day, $599 a week, or $2,250 a month, plus tax. Dave and his associate are good sources of information for any traveler with disabilities.

MOTORCYCLES AND MOPEDS

Driving a motorcycle can be liberating and exhilarating, yet motorcycle drivers are more vulnerable than drivers of cars and trucks. Enjoy your ride, but be very aware of traffic conditions. Drive safely and defensively, and always wear a helmet. Mopeds fall into the same vehicle category as bicycles, so become aware of all appropriate rules and regulations before you rent and ride.

Most motorcycles for rent in Hawaii are the big Harley-Davidsons, while some Japanese models are also available. Rates vary but run around $100 for half a day and $140–160 for 24 hours; longer rentals can be arranged. All drivers must be at least 21 years old, have a valid motorcycle license, and be in possession of a major credit card. Insurance is available. Companies want you to stay on good paved roads. Although wearing helmets is not required by state law, they are available.

BY BOAT

Ironically, in the country's only island state, which boasts a long sailing history, modern shipping, and port towns, ferry service between the islands, except for that between Maui and Lana'i and Maui and Moloka'i, is nonexistent. Periodically, there is a cry to reinstate some sort of coastal and interisland boat or ferry service. Some say visitors and islanders alike would enjoy the experience and be able to travel more economically. Others argue that Hawaiian waters are as dangerous and unpredictable as ever, and no evidence of need or enough passengers exists. For now, interisland travelers have to be content with seeing the islands from the air.

PUBLIC TRANSPORTATION

Public transportation is very limited in Hawaii, except for O'ahu's exemplary **TheBus.** TheBus, 808/848-4500, can take you just about anywhere you want to go on O'ahu for only $1 adult or 50 cents for students. Carrying more than a quarter million passengers per day, it's a model of what a bus system should be.

The MTS Line, popularly called the **Hele-On Bus,** 808/961-8744, is a very local bus system that services the Big Island. It's cheap and okay for short hops, but infrequent and slow for long distances. Travelers say they consistently make better time hitchhiking between Hilo and Kona than waiting for Hele-On to waddle by.

The **Kaua'i Bus,** 808/241-6410, runs limited routes with no service on Sundays or holidays. Still, for making shopping runs to Lihu'e or Kapa'a, it's an option if you have plenty of time on your hands.

Bus service is not available on Maui, Moloka'i, or Lana'i, but private, short-distance shuttle services seem to take up the slack in many tourist areas. There are a few remaining novelty pedicabs in Waikiki, and many hotels shuttle to and from airports. Check the travel chapter introductions below for details on what is available on each island.

HITCHHIKING

Hitchhiking varies from island to island, both in legality and method of thumbing a ride. On O'ahu, hitchhiking is legal, and you use the tried-and-true style of facing traffic and waving your thumb—but you can only hitchhike from bus stops. Not many people hitchhike and the pickings are reasonably easy, but TheBus is only $1 for anywhere you want to go, and the paltry sum you save by hitchhiking is lost in "seeing time." It's legal to hitch on Kaua'i and the police don't bother you on Hawai'i. Remember that Hawai'i is indeed a "big" island; be prepared to take some time getting from one end to the other. In Maui County (Maui, Moloka'i, Lana'i), thumbing a ride is now legal again. As one of her last duties, former mayor Linda Lingle signed a bill in early 1999 to give the right to hitch a ride back to the people. Where once you had to play the game with no thumb, now you can solicit rides with that old reliable method. You can get around quite well by thumb on Maui if you're not on a schedule, but traffic is very light on both Moloka'i and Lana'i, so you should expect to wait.

In general, you will get a ride, eventually, but in comparison to the amount of traffic going by, it isn't easy. Two things work against you: many of the drivers are tourists who don't want to bother with hitchhikers, and many locals don't want to bother with nonlocal hitchhikers. When you do get a ride, most of the time it will be from a *haole* who is either a tourist on his or her own or a new island resident. If you are hitchhiking along a well-known beach area, perhaps in your bathing suit and obviously not going far, you can get a ride more easily. Women should exercise caution and avoid hitchhiking alone.

HEALTH AND SAFETY

In a survey published some years ago by *Science Digest,* Hawaii was cited as the healthiest state in the United States in which to live. Indeed, Hawaiian citizens live longer than anywhere else in America: men to 76 years and women to 82. Lifestyle, heredity, and diet help with these figures, but Hawaii is still an oasis in the middle of the ocean, and germs just have a tougher time getting here. There are no cases of malaria, cholera, or yellow fever. Because of a strict quarantine law, rabies is also nonexistent. On the other hand, tooth decay, perhaps because of a wide use of sugar and the enzymes present in certain tropical fruits, is 30 percent above the national average. With the perfect weather, a multitude of fresh-air activities, soothing negative ionization from the sea, and a generally relaxed and carefree lifestyle, everyone seems to feel better in the islands. Hawaii is just what the doctor ordered: a beautiful, natural health spa. That's one of its main drawing cards. The food and water are perfectly safe, and the air quality is the best in the country.

Handling the Sun
Don't become a victim of your own exuberance. People can't wait to strip down and lie on the sand like beached whales, but the tropical sun will burn you to a cinder if you're silly. The burning rays come through more easily in Hawaii because of the sun's angle, and you don't feel them as much because there's always a cool breeze. The worst part of the day is 11 A.M.–3 P.M. Hawaii lies roughly between 19 and 22 degrees north latitude, not even close to the equator, but it's still more than 1,000 miles south of sunny southern California beaches. You'll just

have to force yourself to go slowly. Don't worry; you'll be able to flaunt your best souvenir, your golden Hawaiian tan, to your green-with-envy friends when you get home. It's better than showing them a boiled lobster body with peeling skin! If your skin is snowflake white, 15 minutes per side on the first day is plenty. Increase by 15-minute intervals every day, which will allow you a full hour per side by the fourth day. Have faith; this is enough to give you a deep golden, uniform tan. If you lie out on the beach or are simply out in the sun during the day, use sunblock lotion that has greater strength than you use at home—most people recommend SPF 25 or higher. If you do burn, try taking aspirin as quickly as you can. No one knows exactly what it does, but it seems to provide some relief.

Whether out on the beach, hiking in the mountains, or just strolling around town, be very aware of dehydration. The sun (and wind) tend to sap your energy and your store of liquid. Bottled water in various sizes is readily available in all parts of Hawaii. Be sure to carry some with you or stop at a store or restaurant for a filler-up.

Don't forget about your head and eyes. Use your sunglasses and wear a brimmed hat. Some people lay a towel over their neck and shoulders when hiking; others will stick a scarf under their hat and let it drape down over their shoulders to provide some protection.

Haole Rot
A peculiar condition caused by the sun is referred to locally as *haole* rot. It's called this because it supposedly affects only white people, but you'll notice some dark-skinned people with the same condition. Basically, the skin becomes

mottled with white spots that refuse to tan. You get a blotchy effect, mostly on the shoulders and back. Dermatologists have a fancy name for it, and they'll give you a fancy prescription with a not-so-fancy price tag to cure it. It's common knowledge throughout the islands that Selsun Blue shampoo has some ingredient that stops the white mottling effect. Wash your hair with it and then make sure to rub the lather over the affected areas, and it should clear up.

Bugs

Everyone, in varying degrees, has an aversion to vermin and creepy crawlers. Hawaii isn't infested with a wide variety, but it does have its share. Mosquitoes were unknown in the islands until their larvae stowed away in the water barrels of the *Wellington* in 1826 and were introduced at Lahaina. They bred in the tropical climate and rapidly spread to all the islands. They are a particular nuisance in the rainforests. Be prepared, and bring a natural repellent like citronella oil, available in most health stores on the islands, or a commercial product available in all groceries or drugstores. Campers will be happy to have mosquito coils to burn at night as well.

Cockroaches are very democratic insects. They hassle all strata of society equally. They breed well in Hawaii, and most hotels are at war with them, trying desperately to keep them from being spotted by guests. One comforting thought is that in Hawaii they aren't a sign of filth or dirty housekeeping. They love the climate like everyone else, and it's a real problem keeping them under control. Of a number of different roaches in Hawaii, the ones that give most people the jitters are big bombers over two inches long. Roaches are after food crumbs and the like, and very infrequently bother with a human. Be aware of this if you rent a room with a kitchenette or condo. If you are in a modest hotel and see a roach, it might make you feel better to know that the millionaire in the $600-a-night suite probably has them too. Bring your own spray if you wish, call the desk if you see them, or just let them be.

Poisonous Plants

A number of plants in Hawaii, mostly imported, contain toxins. In almost every case you have to eat a lot of them before they'll do you any real harm. The following is a partial list of the most common poisonous plants you'll encounter and the parts to avoid: poinsettia—leaves, stems, and sap; oleander—all parts; azalea—all parts; crown flower—juice; lantana—berries; castor bean—all parts; bird of paradise—seeds; coral plant—seeds.

Pollution in Paradise

Calling Hawaii the healthiest state in America doesn't mean that it has totally escaped pollution. It is the only state, however, in which all of the natural beauty is protected by state law, with a statewide zoning and a general development plan. For example, the absence of billboard advertising is due to the pioneering work of a women's club, The Outdoor Circle, which was responsible for an anti-billboard law passed in 1927. It's strictly enforced, but unfortunately high-rises and other ill-advised developments have obscured some of the lovely views that these far-sighted women were trying to preserve. Numerous environmental controversies, including nuclear proliferation and the ill effects of rampant development, rage on the islands.

The most obvious infringements occur on O'ahu, with 73 percent of the state's population, which places the greatest stress on the environment. An EPA study found that almost 20 percent of O'ahu's wells have unacceptably high concentrations of DBCP and TCP. Because of Hawaii's unique water lenses (fresh water trapped by layers of lava), this fact is particularly onerous. The "Great O'ahu Milk Crisis" of 1982 saw dairies shut down when their milk was found to have abnormally high concentrations of heptachlor, a chemical used in the pineapple industry. This was traced to the tops of pineapple plants sold as fodder, which tainted the milk.

Widespread concern existed over a 1,500-unit development on the Wai'anae Coast known as West Beach. According to environmentalists, the development will not only put a major strain on diminishing water resources, but impinge on one of the last fruitful fishing areas near long-established homes of native Hawaiians. O'ahu's H-3 Freeway was cut across an ecologically sensitive mountain range, and an alternative biomass energy plant is denuding the islands of its remaining indigenous *'ohi'a* trees. On the Big Island, plans are always lurking for resort development on South Point and even in the magnificent Waipi'o Valley. Also on the Big Island, a thermal energy plant was bitterly challenged because its builders insisted on locating it in the middle of sensitive rainforest when other, more ecologically acceptable sites were readily available. And just to be pesky, the Mediterranean fruit fly made its appearance and Malathion had to be sprayed. Compared to those in many states, these conditions are small potatoes, but they lucidly point out the holistic global concept that no place on earth is immune to the ravages of pollution.

WATER SAFETY

Hawaii has one very sad claim to fame: more people drown here than anywhere else in the world. Moreover, there are dozens of yearly swimming victims with broken necks and backs or with injuries from scuba and snorkeling accidents. These statistics shouldn't keep you out of the sea, because it is indeed beautiful—benevolent in most cases—and a major reason to go to Hawaii. But if you're foolish, the sea will bounce you like a basketball and suck you away for good. The best remedy is to avoid situations you can't handle. Don't let anyone dare you into a situation that makes you uncomfortable. "Macho men" who know nothing about the power of the sea will be tumbled into Cabbage Patch dolls in short order. Ask lifeguards or beach attendants about conditions, and follow their advice. If local people refuse to go in, there's a good reason. Even experts get in trouble in Hawaiian waters. Some beaches are as gentle as lambs; others, especially on the north coasts during the winter months, are frothing giants.

While beachcombing, or especially when walking out on rocks, never turn your back on the sea. Be aware of undertows (the waves drawing back into the sea). They can knock you off your feet. Before entering the water, study it for rocks, breakers, reefs, and riptides. Riptides are powerful currents, like rivers in the sea, that can drag you out. Mostly they peter out not too far from shore, and you can often see their choppy waters on the surface. If caught in a "rip," don't fight to swim directly against it; you'll lose and only ex-

haust yourself. Swim diagonally across it, while going along with it, and try to stay parallel to the shore. Don't waste all your lung power yelling, and rest by floating.

When bodysurfing, never ride straight in; come to shore at a 45-degree angle. Remember, waves come in sets. Little ones can be followed by giants, so watch the action awhile instead of plunging right in. Standard procedure is to duck under a breaking wave. You can survive even thunderous oceans using this technique. Don't try to swim through a heavy froth and never turn your back and let it smash you. Don't swim alone if possible, and obey all warning signs. Hawaiians want to entertain you and they don't put up signs just to waste money. The last rule is, "If in doubt, stay out."

Yikes!

Sharks live in all the oceans of the world. Most mind their own business and stay away from shore. Hawaiian sharks are well fed—on fish—and don't usually bother with unsavory humans. If you encounter a shark, don't panic. Never thrash around because this will trigger their attack instinct. If they come close, scream loudly.

Portuguese man-of-wars put out long, floating tentacles that sting if they touch you. It seems that many floating jellyfish are blown into shore by winds on the eighth, ninth, and 10th days after the full moon. Don't wash the sting off with fresh water, as this will only aggravate it. Hot salt water will take away the sting, as will alcohol (the drinking or rubbing kind), after-shave lotion, or meat tenderizer (MSG), which can be found in any supermarket and some Chinese restaurants.

Coral can give you a nasty cut, and it's known for causing infections because it's a living organism. Wash the cut immediately and apply an antiseptic. Keep the cut clean and covered, and watch for infection.

Poisonous sea urchins, such as the lacquer-black *wana,* can be beautiful creatures. They are found in shallow tidepools and will hurt you if you step on them. Their spines will break off, enter your foot, and burn like blazes. There are cures. Vinegar and wine poured on the wound will stop the burning. If those aren't available, the Hawaiian solution is urine. It might seem ignominious to have someone pee on your foot,

This "denizen of the deep" is much more afraid of you than you are of it.

but it'll put the fire out. The spines will disintegrate in a few days, and there are generally no long-term effects.

Hawaiian reefs also have their share of moray eels. These creatures are ferocious in appearance but will never initiate an attack. You'll have to poke around in their holes while snorkeling or scuba diving to get them to attack. Sometimes this is inadvertent on the diver's part, so be careful where you stick your hand while underwater.

Freshwater-borne bacteria deposited by the urine of infected animals into streams, ponds, and muddy soil cause **leptospirosis.** Two to 20 days after the bacteria enter the body, there is a *sudden* onset of fever accompanied by chills, sweats, headache, and sometimes vomiting and diarrhea. Preventive measures include: staying out of freshwater sources where cattle and other animals wade and drink; not swimming in freshwater if you have an open cut; and not drinking stream water.

HAWAIIAN FOLK MEDICINE AND CURES

Hawaiian folk medicine is well developed, and its cures for common ailments have been used effectively for centuries. Hawaiian *kahuna* were highly regarded for their medicinal skills, and Hawaiians were by far some of the healthiest people in the world until the coming of the Eu-

ropeans. Many folk remedies and cures are used to this day and, what's more, they work. Many of the common plants and fruits that you'll encounter provide some of the best remedies. When roots and seeds and special exotic plants are used, the preparation of the medicine is as painstaking as in a modern pharmacy. These prescriptions are exact and take an expert to prepare. They should never be prepared or administered by an amateur.

Common Curative Plants

Arrowroot, for diarrhea, is a powerful narcotic used in rituals and medicines. Kava *(Piper methysticum),* also called *'awa,* is chewed and the juice is spat into a container for fermenting into a medicine for urinary tract infections, rheumatism, and asthma. It also induces sleep and cures headaches. A poultice for wounds is made from the skins of ripe bananas. Peelings have a powerful antibiotic quality and contain vitamins A, B, and C, phosphorous, calcium, and iron. The nectar from the plant was fed to babies as a vitamin juice. Breadfruit sap heals cuts and makes a moisturizing lotion. Coconut is used to make moisturizing oil, and the juice can be chewed, spat into the hand, and used as a shampoo. Guava is a source of vitamins A, B, and C. Hibiscus has been used as a laxative. *Kukui* nut oil makes a gargle for sore throats and a laxative, plus the flowers cure diarrhea. *Noni,* an unappetizing hand-grenade-shaped fruit that you wouldn't want to eat unless you had to, reduces tumors, diabetes, and high blood pressure, and the juice is good for diarrhea. Sugarcane sweetens many concoctions, and the juice of toasted cane was a tonic for sick babies. Sweet potato is used as a tonic during pregnancy and juiced as a gargle for phlegm. Tamarind is a natural laxative and contains the most acid and sugar of any fruit on earth. Taro has been used for lung infections and thrush, and as a suppository. Yams are good for coughs, vomiting, constipation, and appendicitis.

Commonly Treated Ailments

For arthritis make a poultice of *koali* (morning glory) and Hawaiian salt; cover the area and keep warm. A bad-breath gargle is made from the *hapu'u* fern. The latex from inside the leaves of aloe is great for soothing burns and sunburn, as well as for innumerable skin problems. If you get chapped lips or windburned skin, use oil from the *hinu honu*. A headache is lessened with *'awa* or *'ape*. Calm nervousness with *'awa* and *lomi lomi*, Hawaiian-style massage. To get rid of a raspy sore throat, chew the bark of the root of the *'uhaloa*. A toothache is eased by the sticky narcotic juice from the *pua kala* seed, a prickly poppy.

Lomi Lomi

This traditional Hawaiian massage is of exceptional therapeutic value. It has been practiced since very early times and is especially useful in cases of fatigue, general body aches, preventive medicine, and sports injuries. When Otto Von Kotzebue arrived in 1824, he noted, ". . . Queen Nomahana, after feasting heartily, turned on her back, whereupon a tall fellow sprang upon her body and kneaded it unmercifully with his knees and fists as if it had been the dough of bread. Digestion was so assisted that the queen resumed her feasting." *Lomi lomi* practitioners must be accredited by the state.

MEDICAL SERVICES

Each major island has several hospitals that provide emergency room, long-term, and acute care facilities; clinics, for immediate care and first-aid treatment; and pharmacies, for drug pre-

scriptions and other medical necessities. Island by island lists of these facilities are in the specific travel chapters below.

Alternative Medicine

Most ethnic groups who migrated to Hawaii brought along their own cures. The Chinese and Japanese are especially known for their unique and effective treatments, such as herbal medicine, acupuncture, and shiatsu. The time-honored Chinese therapy of acupuncture is available throughout the islands. On O'ahu, contact the Hawaii Acupuncture Association, P.O. Box 11202, Honolulu, HI 96828, 808/538-6692, for referrals to state-licensed acupuncturists throughout the islands. Hawaii also has a huge selection of chiropractors. All types of massage are available throughout the islands, everything from shiatsu to Hawaii's own *lomi lomi* massage. The Yellow Pages on all islands list holistic practitioners, herbalists, naturopaths, chiropractors, as well as "massage."

SERVICES FOR TRAVELERS WITH DISABILITIES

A person with disabilities can have a wonderful time in Hawaii; all that's needed is a little preplanning. The following general advice should help.

Commission on Persons with Disabilities

This state commission was designed with the express purpose of aiding handicapped people. It is a source of invaluable information and distributes self-help booklets, which are published jointly by the Disability and Communication Access Board and the Hawaii Centers for Independent Living. Any person with disabilities heading to Hawaii should write first or visit their offices on arrival. For the *Aloha Guide to Accessibility* (Part I is free; $3–5 charge for Parts II and III), write or visit the head office at: Commission on Persons with Disabilities, 919 Ala Moana Blvd., Room 101, Honolulu, HI 96814, 808/586-8121; on Maui, 54 High St., Wailuku, HI 96793, 808/984-8219; on Kaua'i, 3060 Eiwa St. #207, Lihu'e, HI 96766, 808/274-3308. On Hawai'i, contact the Centers for Independent Living at 400 Haulani St., #16D, Hilo, HI 96820, 808/935-

3777, or 81-6627 Mamalahoa Hwy., Suite B-5, Kealakekua, HI 96750, 808/323-2221.

General Information

The key for a smooth trip is to make as many arrangements ahead of time as possible. Tell the transportation companies and hotels that you'll be dealing with the nature of your handicap in advance so that they can make arrangements to accommodate you. Bring your medical records and notify medical establishments of your arrival if you'll be needing their services. Travel with a friend or make arrangements for an aide on arrival. Bring your own wheelchair if possible and let airlines know if it is battery-powered; boarding interisland carriers requires steps. They'll board you early on special lifts, but they must know that you're coming. Many hotels and restaurants accommodate people with disabilities, but always call ahead just to make sure.

For specific services on each island, see the travel chapter introductions below.

PROSTITUTION

Though the small towns and villages are as safe as you can find anywhere in America, Hawaii isn't all good clean fun. Wherever there's constant tourist flow, a huge military presence, and high cost of living, there will be those people your mama warned you about. Most of the heavy night action occurs in Honolulu's Waikiki and Chinatown. Something about the *vibe* exudes sexuality. The land is raw and wild, and the settings are intoxicating. All those glistening bodies under the tropical sun and the carefree lifestyle are super-conducive to most anything you can imagine. It's long been known as a great place for boy meets girl, or whomever, but there also exists "play for pay."

Prostitution—The Way It Was

Ever since the first ship arrived in 1778, Hawaii has known prostitution. At that time, a sailor paid for a night with a woman with one iron nail. Funny, today they'll take a plastic card. Prostitution, rampant until the missionaries arrived in 1819, was a major cause of the tragic population decline of the Hawaiian race. The tradition has carried on into the 20th and 21st centuries. Iwilei

was a notorious red-light district in Honolulu in the early 1900s. The authorities, many of whom were clientele, not only turned a blind eye to this scene, but semi-legalized it. A policeman was stationed inside the "stockade" and police rules were listed on the five entrances. The women were required to have a weekly VD checkup from the Board of Health, and without a current disease-free certificate they couldn't work. Iwilei was even considered by some to be an attraction: when Somerset Maugham passed through the islands in 1916 on his way to Russia as a spy for England, he was taken there as if on a sightseeing tour. The long-established military presence in Hawaii has also helped keep prostitution a flourishing business. During World War II, troops were entertained by streetwalkers, in houses of prostitution, and at dance halls. The consensus of the military commanders was that prostitution was a necessary evil, needed to keep up the morale of the troops.

The Scene Today

You can go two ways on the "sleaze" scene in Hawaii: ignore it by remaining aloof and never seeing any, or look for and find it with no trouble. The following is neither a condemnation nor an endorsement of how you should act and what you should do. It's merely an interpretation and the choice is up to you.

The two areas notorious for prostitution today are in Honolulu: Kuhio and Kalakaua Avenues in Waikiki, which are geared toward the tourist, and Hotel Street in Chinatown, for servicemen and a much rougher trade. All sorts of women solicit—whites, blacks, and Asians—but the majority are young white women from the Mainland. They cruise along in the old-fashioned style, meeting eyes and giving the nod. As long as they keep walking, the police won't roust them.

Most hookers prefer Japanese clientele, followed by the general tourist and, lastly, the always-broke serviceman. In the terse words of one streetwalker queried about the preference for Japanese, she said, "They're small, clean, fast, and they pay a lot." If anyone in Waikiki can speak Japanese, a hooker can. They are not "equal opportunity employees." Western guys, whether white or black, don't stand much of a chance. The prostitutes are after the Japanese in a sort of crazy payback. The Japanese fish American waters, and the "pros" of Waikiki hook big Japanese fish.

A Honolulu policeman on his Kuhio Avenue beat said, "I can't do anything if they keep walking. It's a free country. Besides, I'm not here to teach anyone morals. . . . Last week a john "fell" out of an eight-story window and a prostitute was found with her throat slit. . . . I'm just on the front lines fighting herpes and AIDS. Just fighting herpes and AIDS, man." Unlike the days of Iwilei, there is absolutely no official control or testing for VD.

Then there is Chinatown; it's as rough as guts. The girls are shabby, the bars and strip joints are shabbier, and the vibe is heavy.

Women can find male prostitutes on most of the beaches of Honolulu and Waikiki. Mostly these transactions take place during the day. Although many men make a legitimate living as "beach boys" instructing in surfing and the like, some are really prostitutes. It's always up to the woman to decide how far the "lessons" proceed.

Massage Parlors, Etc.
Besides streetwalkers, Honolulu and some of the Neighbor Islands have their share of massage parlors, escort services, and exotic dance joints. For massage parlors and escort services you can let your fingers do the walking—through the Yellow Pages. Unfortunately, legitimate massage practitioners share the same listings with the other kind of massage parlors. If the listing reads something like "Fifi's Playthings—We'll rub it day or night, wherever it is," this should tip you off. Such parlors usually offer escort services too, for both men and women.

Exotic dance clubs are basically strip joints with a twist. The dancers are attractive women brought over from the Mainland. They can easily make good money every night dancing, and the majority are not prostitutes. An act lasts for three songs and gets raunchier as it goes. If you invite a dancer to have a drink, it'll cost you, but it will be a real drink. This gets you nothing but conversation. Working the sexually agitated male crowd are women who can best be described as "lap sitters." They're almost always older Korean women who've been through the mill. They'll charge you double for a fake drink, and then try to entice you over to a dark corner table, where they'll chisel more money from you for all you

can manage, or are brave enough to do, in a dark corner of a nightclub. Their chief allies are dim lights and booze.

ILLEGAL DRUGS

The use and availability of illegal, controlled, and recreational drugs are about the same in Hawaii as throughout the rest of America. Cocaine is available on the streets of the main cities, especially Honolulu. Although most dealers are small-time, the drug is brought in by organized crime. Cocaine trafficking fans out from Honolulu.

Another drug menace on the streets is "ice." Ice is smokable methamphetamine that will wire a user for up to 24 hours. The high lasts longer and is cheaper than cocaine or its derivative, "crack." Users become quickly dependent, despondent, and violent because ice robs them of their sleep as well as their dignity. Its use is particularly prevalent among late-night workers. Many of the violent deaths in Honolulu have been linked to the growing use of ice.

However, the main drug available and commonly used in Hawaii is marijuana, which is locally called *pakalolo*. Three varieties of psychoactive mushrooms contain the hallucinogen psilocybin; they grow wild but are considered illegal controlled substances.

Pakalolo Growing
In the 1960s, mostly *haole* hippies from the Mainland began growing pot in the more remote sections of the islands, such as Puna on Hawaii and around Hana on Maui. They discovered what legitimate planters had known for 200 years: plant a broomstick in Hawaii, treat it right, and it'll grow. *Pakalolo*, after all, is a weed, and it grows in Hawaii like wildfire. The locals quickly got into the act when they realized that they, too, could grow a "money tree." As a matter of fact, they began resenting the *haole* usurpers, and a quiet and sometimes dangerous feud has been going on ever since. Much is made of the viciousness of the backcountry "growers" of Hawaii. There are tales of booby traps and armed patrols guarding their plants in the hills, but mostly it's a cat-and-mouse game between the authorities and the growers. If you, as a tourist, are tramping about in the forest and hap-

pen upon someone's "patch," don't touch anything. Just back off and you'll be okay. Pot has the largest monetary turnover of any crop in the islands and, as such, is now considered a major source of agricultural revenue. There are all kinds of local names and varieties of pot in Hawaii. Dealers will sometimes approach you. Their normal technique is to stroll by and in a barely audible whisper say, "Buds?" The glory days are over, and many deals, especially on the streets, are rip-offs. All passengers leaving Hawaii are subject to a thorough "agricultural inspection," and you can bet they're not looking only for illegal papayas.

THEFT AND HASSLES

Theft and minor assaults can be a problem, but they're usually not violent or vicious as in some Mainland cities. Mostly, it's a local with a chip on his shoulder and few prospects, who will ransack your car or make off with your camera. A big Hawaiian or local guy will be obliged to flatten your nose if you look for trouble, but mostly it will be sneak thieves out to make a fast buck.

From the minute you sit behind the wheel of your rental car you'll be warned not to leave valuables unattended and to lock your car up tighter than a drum. Signs warning about theft at most major tourist attractions help fuel your paranoia. Many hotel rooms offer safes so you can lock your valuables away and relax while getting sunburned. Stories abound about purse snatchings and surly locals just itching to give you a hard time. Well, they're all true to a degree, but Hawaii's reputation is much worse than the

WARNING
DO NOT LEAVE
PURSE, WALLET OR
CAMERA IN LOCKED
OR UNLOCKED CARS

J.D. BISIGNANI

reality. In Hawaii you'll have to observe two golden laws: if you look for trouble, you'll find it, and a fool and his camera are soon parted.

Theft

The majority of theft in Hawaii is of the "sneak thief" variety. If you leave your hotel door unlocked, a camera sitting on the seat of your rental car, or valuables on your beach towel, you'll be inviting a very obliging thief to pad away with your stuff. You have to learn to take precautions, but they won't be anything like those employed in rougher areas of the world—just normal American precautions.

If you must walk alone at night, stay on the main streets in well-lit areas. Always lock your hotel door and windows and place valuable jewelry in the hotel safe. When you leave your hotel for the beach, there is absolutely no reason to carry all your traveler's checks and credit cards or a big wad of money. Just take what you'll need for drinks and lunch. If you're uptight about leaving money in your beach bag, stick it in your bathing suit or bikini. American money is just as negotiable if it is damp. Don't leave your camera or portable stereo on the beach unattended. Ask a person nearby to watch it for you while you go for a dip. Most people won't mind at all, and you can repay the favor.

While sightseeing in your shiny new rental car, which immediately brands you as a tourist, again, don't take more than what you'll need for the day. Why people leave a camera sitting on the seat of their car is a mystery! Many people lock valuables in the trunk, but remember that most good car thieves can jimmy it open as quickly as you can open it with your key. If you must, for some reason, leave your camera or valuables in your car, lock them in the trunk, stash them under a seat back that's been reclined, or consider putting them under the hood. Thieves usually don't look there, and on most modern cars you can only pop the hood with a lever inside the car. It's not fail-safe, but it's worth a try.

Campers face special problems because their entire camp is open to thievery. Most campgrounds don't have any real security, but who, after all, wants to fence an old tent or a used sleeping bag? Many tents have zippers that can be secured with a small padlock. If you want to

ON THE ROAD

go hiking and are afraid to leave your gear in the campgrounds, take a large green garbage bag with you. Transport your gear down the trail and then walk off through some thick brush. Put your gear in the garbage bag and bury it under leaves and other light camouflage. That's about as safe as you can be. You can also use a variation on this technique instead of leaving your valuables in your rental car.

Hassles

Another self-perpetuating myth about Hawaii is that "the natives are restless." An undeniable animosity exists between locals (especially those with some Hawaiian blood) and *haole*. Fortunately, this prejudice is directed mostly at the group and not at the individual. The locals are resentful of those *haole* who came, took their land, and relegated them to second-class citizenship. They realize that this is not the average tourist and they can tell what you are at a glance. Tourists usually are treated with understanding and are given a type of immunity. Besides, Hawaiians are still among the most friendly, giving, and understanding people on earth.

Haole who live in Hawaii might tell you stories of their children having trouble at school. They could even mention an unhappy situation at some schools called "beat-up-a-*haole*" day, and you might hear that if you're a *haole* it's not a matter of "if" you'll be beaten up, but "when." Truthfully, most of this depends upon your attitude and your sensitivity. The locals feel infringed upon, so don't fuel these feelings. If you're at a beach park and there is a group of local people in one area, don't crowd them. If you go into a local bar and you're the only one of your ethnic group in sight, you shouldn't have to be told to leave. Much of the hassle involves drinking. Booze brings out the worst prejudice on all sides. If you're invited to a beach party, and the local guys start getting drunk, make this your exit call. Don't wait until it's too late.

Most trouble seems to be directed toward white men. White women are mostly immune from being beaten up, but they have to beware of the violence of sexual abuse and rape. Although plenty of local women marry white men, it's not a good idea to try to pick up a local woman. If you're known in the area and have been properly introduced, that's another story. Also, women out for the night in bars or discos can be approached if they're not in the company of local guys. Maintain your own dignity and self-respect by treating others with dignity and respect. Most times you'll reap what you sow.

WHAT TO TAKE

It's a snap to pack for a visit to Hawaii. Everything is on your side. The weather is moderate and uniform on the whole, and the style of dress is delightfully casual. The rule of thumb is to pack lightly: few items, and light clothing both in color and weight. What you'll need will depend largely on your itinerary and your desires. Are you drawn to the nightlife, the outdoors, or both? If you forget something at home, it won't be a disaster. You can buy everything you'll need in Hawaii. As a matter of fact, Hawaiian clothing, such as mu'umu'u and aloha shirts, is one of the best purchases you can make, both in comfort and style. It's quite feasible to bring only one or two changes of clothing with the express purpose of outfitting yourself while here. Prices on bathing suits, bikinis, and summer wear in general are quite reasonable.

Matters of Taste

A grand conspiracy in Hawaii adhered to by everyone—tourist, traveler, and resident—is to "hang loose" and dress casually. Best of all, alohawear is just about all you'll need for comfort and virtually every occasion. The classic mu'umu'u is large and billowy, and aloha shirts are made to be worn outside the pants. The best of both are made of cool cotton. Rayon is a natural fiber that isn't too bad, but polyester is hot, sticky, and not authentic. Not all mu'umu'u are of the "tent persuasion." Some are very fashionable and form-fitted with peek-a-boo slits up the side, down the front, or around the back. A *holomu* is a mu'umu'u fitted at the waist with a flowing skirt to the ankles. They are not only elegant, but perfect for "stepping out."

Basic Necessities

As previously mentioned, you really have to consider only two "modes" of dressing in Hawaii: beachwear and casual clothing. The following list is designed for the midrange traveler carrying one suitcase or a backpack. Remember that there are laundromats and that you'll be spending a considerable amount of time in your bathing suit. Consider the following: one or two pairs of light cotton slacks for going out and about, and one pair of jeans for hiking and riding horses; two or three casual sundresses; three or four pairs of shorts for beachwear and for sightseeing; four to five short-sleeved shirts or blouses and one long-sleeved; three or four colored and printed T-shirts that can be worn anytime from hiking to strolling; a beach coverup; a brimmed hat for rain and sun; the crushable floppy type is great for purse or day pack, or pick up a straw or woven hat in the islands for about $10; two or three pairs of socks are sufficient, nylons you won't generally need; two bathing suits (nylon ones dry quickest); plastic bags to hold wet bathing suits and laundry; five to six pairs of underwear; towels (optional, because hotels provide them, even for the beach); a first-aid kit, pocket-size is sufficient; suntan lotion and insect repellent; a day pack or large beach bag. And don't forget your windbreaker, perhaps a shawl for the evening, and an all-purpose jogging suit. A few classy restaurants in the finest hotels require men to wear a sport coat for dinner. If you don't have one, most hotels can supply you with one for the evening.

In the Cold and Rain

Two occasions for which you'll have to consider dressing warmly are visits to mountaintops and boat rides when wind and ocean sprays are a factor. You can conquer both with a jogging suit (sweat suit) and a featherweight, water-resistant windbreaker. If you intend to visit Mauna Kea, Mauna Loa, or Haleakala it'll be downright chilly. Your jogging suit with a hooded windbreaker/raincoat will do the trick for all occasions. If you're going to camp or hike, you should add another layer, a woolen sweater being one of the best. Wool is the only natural fiber that retains most of its warmth-giving properties even if it gets wet. Several varieties of "fleece" synthetics currently on the market also have this

ability. If your hands get cold, put a pair of socks over them. Tropical rain showers can happen at any time so you might consider a fold-up umbrella, but the sun quickly breaks through and the warming winds blow. Nighttime winter temps may drop into the lower 60s or upper 50s, so be sure to have a sweater and long pants along.

Shoes

Dressing your feet is hardly a problem. You'll most often wear zori (rubber thongs) for going to and from the beach, leather sandals for strolling and dining, and jogging shoes for hiking and sightseeing. Teva and other types of outdoor strap sandals are good for general sightseeing and beach and water wear. A few discos require dress shoes, but it's hardly worth bringing them just for that. If you plan on heavy-duty hiking, you'll definitely want your hiking boots. Lava, especially 'a'a, is murderous on shoes. Most backcountry trails are rugged and muddy, and you'll need those good old lug soles for traction. If you plan moderate hikes, jogging shoes should do.

Specialty Items

Following is a list of specialty items that you might consider bringing along. They're not necessities but most will definitely come in handy. A pair of binoculars really enhances sightseeing—great for viewing birds and sweeping panoramas, and almost a necessity if you're going whale-watching. A folding, Teflon-bottomed travel iron makes up for cotton's one major shortcoming, wrinkles. Most accommodations have them, but you can't always count on it. Nylon twine and miniature clothespins are handy for drying garments, especially bathing suits. Commercial and hotel laundromats abound, but many times you'll get by with hand-washing a few items in the sink. A transistor radio/tape recorder provides news, weather, and entertainment, and can be used to record impressions, island music, and a running commentary for your slide show. Hair dryer: although the wind can be relied upon to dry wet hair, it leaves a bit to be desired in the styling department. As with the iron, most accommodations have these, but not all. Flippers, mask, and snorkel can easily be bought in Hawaii but don't weigh much or take up much space in your luggage.

INFORMATION AND SERVICES

The state operates **visitor information booths** at Honolulu International Airport, 808/836-6413; some are open 24 hours a day. These offer plenty of practical brochures and helpful information.

HAWAII VISITORS BUREAU

In 1903 the Hawaiian Promotion Committee thought tourism could be the economic wave of the future. They began the Hawaii Tourist Bureau, which became the Hawaii Visitors Bureau. The HVB is now a top-notch organization providing help and information to Hawaii's visitors. Anyone contemplating a trip to Hawaii should visit or write the HVB and inquire about any specific information that may be required. Their advice and excellent brochures on virtually every facet of living, visiting, or simply enjoying Hawaii are free. The materials offered are too voluminous to list, but for basics, request individual island brochures, maps, and vacation planners (also on the Web at www.hshawaii.com), and ask for *Connections Hawai'i,* an all-island members' directory of accommodations, restaurants, entertainment, and transportation. Allow two to three weeks for requests to be answered.

HVB Offices Statewide

Statewide offices include: **HVB Administrative Office,** Waikiki Business Plaza, 2270 Kalakaua Ave., Suite 801, Honolulu, HI 96815, 808/923-1811, website: www.gohawaii.com; **Visitor Information Office,** 808/924-0266, Royal Hawaiian Shopping Center, 4th Fl., 2201 Kalakaua Ave., Honolulu, HI 96815; **O'ahu Visitors Bureau,** 733 Bishop St., Suite 1872, Honolulu, HI 96813, 808/524-0722, website: www.visitoahu.com; **Big Island HVB, Hilo Branch,** 250 Keawe St., Hilo, HI 96720, 808/961-5797, website: www.bigisland.org; **Big Island, Kona Branch,** 75-5719 W. Ali'i Dr., Kailua-Kona, HI 96740, 808/329-7787; **Kaua'i HVB,** 4334 Rice St., Suite 101, Lihu'e, HI 96766, 808/245-3971, website: www.kauaivisitorsbureau.org; and **Maui HVB,** 1727 Wili Pa Loop, Wailuku, HI 96793, 808/244-3530, website: www.visitmaui.com.

North American Offices

West Coast: 180 Montgomery St., Suite 2360, San Francisco, CA 94104, 415/248-3800; 5355 Mira Sorrento Place #100, San Diego, CA 92121, 619/597-7586

Midwest: 625 N. Michigan Ave. #600, Chicago, IL 60611, 312/867-8886

East Coast: 1100 N. Glebe Road #760, Arlington, VA 22201, 703/525-7770

Canada: c/o Comprehensive Travel, 1260 Hornby St. #104, Vancouver, BC V6Z 1W2, 604/669-6691

European Offices

United Kingdom: P.O. Box 208, Sunbury on Thames, Middlesex TW16 5RJ, tel. 181/941-4009

Germany: c/o American Venture Marketing, Siemenstrasse 9, 63263 Neu-Isenburg, tel. 6102/722-411

South American Office

Uruguay: 1676 Of. 308, 11200 Montevideo, tel. 2/402-4171

Asia/Pacific Offices

Japan: Kokusai Bldg., 2F, 3-1-1, Marunouchi, Chiyoda-ku, Tokyo 100, tel. 3/3201-0430; Sumitomo Nakanoshima Bldg., 2F, 3-2-18, Nakano-shima, Kita-gu, Osaka 530, tel. 6/443-8015

Korea: c/o Travel Press, Seoul Center Bldg., 12th Fl., 91-1, Sokong-dong, Chung-gu, Seoul 100-070, tel. 2/773-6719

China: East-West Marketing Corp., 38 Da Pu Road, Hai Hua Garden, No. 4 Bldg., 27C, Shanghai 200023, tel. 21/6466-1077

Taiwan: c/o Federal Transportation Co., 8F, 61 Nanking East Road, Section 3, Taipei, tel. 2/2506-7043

New Zealand: c/o Walshes World, Dingwall Bldg., 87 Queen St., 2nd Fl., Auckland, tel. 9/379-3708

Australia: c/o The Sales Team, Suite 2, Level 2, 34 Burton St., Milsons Point, NSW 2061, tel. 2/9955-2619

LOCAL RESOURCES

Police, fire, ambulance: Dial **911** on all islands.
   Coast Guard Search and Rescue: Dial 800/552-6458 on all islands.

   For other numbers, such as crisis lines, consumer protection, weather and marine reports, see the individual travel chapters below.

Foreign Consulates
All of the foreign consulates and diplomatic offices are in Honolulu. Most major European, Asian, and Oceanic nations, along with many South American countries, have delegates in Honolulu. They are listed under "Consulates and Other Foreign Government Representatives" in the O'ahu Yellow Pages.

Post Offices
Post offices are located in all major towns and cities. Most larger hotels also offer limited postal services. Normal business hours are Mon.–Fri. 8 or 8:30 A.M. to 4 or 4:30 P.M.; some offices are open Saturday 8 A.M.–noon. The first three zip code digits, 967, are the same for all of Hawaii, except Honolulu, where it's 968. The last two digits designate the particular post office.

   The simplest way to receive mail is to have it sent to your lodgings if you'll be there long enough to receive it. Have it addressed to you in care of your hotel or condo, and include the room number if you know it. It'll be in your box at the front desk. If you plan frequent moves or a multiple-island itinerary with short stays on each island, have mail sent General Delivery to a post office in a town you plan to visit. The post office will hold your mail in general delivery for 30 days. It takes about five days for a first-class letter to arrive in Hawaii from the Mainland. It's a good idea to notify the postmaster of the post office where you will be receiving mail of the dates you expect to pick it up.

OTHER INFORMATION

Telephone
The telephone system in Hawaii is modern and comparable to any system on the Mainland. You can "direct dial" from Hawaii to the Mainland

> **The area code for all Hawaii is 808.**

and more than 160 foreign countries. Undersea cables and satellite communications ensure top-quality phone service. Any phone call to a number on that island is a local call; it's long distance when dialing to another island or beyond the state. As they do everywhere else in the United States, long-distance rates go down at 5 P.M. and again at 11 P.M. until 8 A.M. the next morning. Rates are cheapest from Friday at 5 P.M. until Monday at 8 A.M. Local calls from public telephones cost 30 or 35 cents. Emergency calls are always free. Public telephones are found at hotels, street booths, restaurants, most public buildings, and some beach parks. It is common to have a phone in most hotel rooms and condominiums, though a service charge is usually collected, even on local calls. Toll-free calls are preceded by 800, 888, or 877; there is no charge to the calling party. Many are listed in the text. For directory assistance call: local, 1-411; interisland, 1-555-1212; Mainland, 1-area code-555-1212; toll-free 1-800-555-1212.

Time Zones
There is no daylight savings time in Hawaii. When daylight savings time is not in effect on the Mainland, Hawaii is two hours behind the West Coast, four hours behind the Midwest, five hours behind the East Coast, and 11 hours behind Ger-many. Hawaii, being just east of the international date line, is almost a full day behind most Asian and

Oceanic cities. Hours behind these countries and cities are: Japan, 19 hours; Singapore, 18 hours; Sydney, 20 hours; New Zealand, 22 hours; Fiji, 22 hours.

Electricity

The same electrical current is in use in Hawaii as on the U.S. Mainland and is uniform throughout the islands. The system functions on 110 volts, 60 cycles of alternating current (AC). Appliances from Japan will work, but there is some danger of burnout, while those requiring the normal European current of 220 will not work.

Distance, Weights, and Measures

Hawaii, like all of the United States, employs the "English method" of measuring weights and distances. Basically, dry weights are in ounces and pounds; liquid measures are in ounces, quarts, and gallons; and distances are measured in inches, feet, yards, and miles. The metric system is known but is not in general use.

MONEY AND FINANCES

Currency

U.S. currency is among the drabbest in the world. It's all the same size and color; those unfamiliar with it should spend some time getting acquainted so that they don't make costly mistakes. U.S. coins include one cent (penny), five cents (nickel), 10 cents (dime), 25 cents (quarter), 50 cents (half dollar), and $1 (uncommon); paper currency is $1, $2 (uncommon), $5, $10, $20, $50, $100. Bills larger than $100 are not in common usage. Since 1996, new designs have been issued for the $100, $50, $20, $10, and $5 bills. Both the old and new bills are accepted as valid currency.

Banks

Full-service bank hours are generally 8:30 A.M.–4 P.M. Mon.–Thurs. and Friday until 6 P.M. There are no weekend hours, and weekday hours will be a bit longer at counters in grocery stores and other outlets. All main towns have one or more banks. Virtually all branch banks have ATM machines for 24-hour service, and these can be found at some shopping centers and other venues around the is-

land. ATMs work only when the Hawaiian bank you choose to use is on an affiliate network with your home bank. Of most value to travelers, banks sell and cash traveler's checks, give cash advances on credit cards, and exchange and sell foreign currency (sometimes with a fee). Major banks are American Savings Bank, Bank of Hawaii, Central Pacific Bank, and First Hawaiian bank.

Traveler's Checks

Traveler's checks are accepted throughout Hawaii at hotels, restaurants, and car rental agencies, and in most stores and shops. However, to be readily acceptable they should be in U.S. currency. Some larger hotels that frequently have Japanese and Canadian guests will accept their currency. Banks accept foreign-currency traveler's checks, but it'll mean an extra trip and inconvenience. It's best to get most of your traveler's checks in $20–50 denominations; anything larger will be hard to cash in smaller shops and boutiques, though not in hotels.

Credit Cards

More and more business is transacted in Hawaii using credit cards. Almost every form of accommodation, shop, restaurant, and amusement accepts them. For renting a car they're almost a must. With "credit card insurance" readily available, they're as safe as traveler's checks and sometimes even more convenient. Be sure to write down your credit card numbers in case they're lost or stolen. Don't rely on them completely because some establishments won't accept them, or perhaps won't accept the kind you carry.

NEWSPAPERS AND TOURIST PUBLICATIONS

Hawaii's two main English-language dailies are the *Honolulu Star Bulletin* and the *Honolulu Advertiser,* both with circulations around 100,000. The Japanese-English *Hawaii Hochi* has a circulation of 10,000, and the Chinese *United Chinese Press* sells 1,000 copies per day. All are published on O'ahu and are available on the other islands.

ON THE ROAD

Weeklies and Magazines

There's a stampede of weeklies in Hawaii; all major islands have at least one and O'ahu has at least six. On Kaua'i look for the *Kaua'i Times* and the slightly smaller *Garden Island*. Maui has the *Maui News*. The Big Island offers the *Hawaii Tribune Herald* out of Hilo and *West Hawaii Today*, published in Kailua. All of these papers are great for what's happening and for money-saving coupons for restaurants, rentals, and amusements. A few military newspapers are printed on O'ahu, as are a handful of foreign-language newspapers like the *Ashai Shinbun* from Japan and the *Korea Times*.

Aside from these newspapers, several dozen magazines are published in Hawaii, many on business, travel, and sports.

Free Tourist Publications

On every island, at airports, in hotel lobbies, at shopping malls, and on main streets are racks filled with free magazines, pamphlets, and brochures. Sometimes the sheer volume is overwhelming, but most have up-to-the-minute information on what's happening and many money-saving coupons. They're also loaded with maps and directions to points of interest. The best, published in a convenient narrow format, are *This Week . . . Oahu, Maui, Kauai, Big Island*, published weekly. *Guide to . . .* all major islands is in normal magazine format, with good maps. Regional magazines such as *Maui Gold* and *Kona Coast* are also well worth checking out, as is the weekly *Drive Guide* available from major car rental agencies.

TIDBITS: OFFICIAL AND UNOFFICIAL

Official Hawaii

The state flower is the yellow hibiscus. More than 5,000 species grow in Hawaii. The state tree is the *kukui*. The candlenut was one of the most useful trees of old Hawaii, providing food, medicine, and light. The state bird is the *nene*, a goose that came to Hawaii eons ago and adapted to the rugged terrain, becoming a permanent resident and losing its instinct for migration. The state fish, with a name bigger than itself, is the *humuhumunukunukuapua'a* (*humu*, for short). Found in a few scattered beds at depths of up to

---

LARGEST CITIES/TOWNS

ISLAND	CITY/TOWN	POP.
Big Island	Hilo	47,000
	Kailua-Kona	10,000
	Captain Cook	2,500
Maui	Kahului/Wailuku	53,000
	Kihei	11,000
	Lahaina	11,000
Lana'i	Lana'i City	2,800
Moloka'i	Kaunakakai	2,500
O'ahu	Honolulu	400,000
	Kailua Kaneohe	100,000
	Pearl City	40,000
	Waipahu	30,000
	Wahiawa	17,000
Kaua'i	Kapa'a	8,200
	Lihu'e	5,500

Note: All population figures are approximate.

---

100 meters is black coral, the state gem. The humpback whale that visits Hawaii every year was made the official mammal in 1979.

Hawaii's nickname is "The Aloha State." The motto, *Ua mau ke e'a o ka 'aina i ka pono* ("The life of the land is perpetuated in righteousness"), came from King Kamehameha III, when in 1843 Hawaii was restored to self-sovereignty after briefly being seized by the British. The anthem, "Hawai'i Pono," was written by the "Merrie Monarch," King Kalakaua, and put to music by the royal bandmaster, Henry Berger, in 1876. "Hawai'i Pono" at one time was the anthem of the Kingdom of Hawai'i and later of the territory before becoming the official state anthem.

Little-Known Facts

The Hawaiian Islands, from Kure Atoll in the north to the Big Island in the south, stretch 1,600 miles. South Point (Ka Lae) on the Big Island is the southernmost point of the United States. The islands are some 30 million years old and were entirely created by volcanic activity. Haleakala on Maui is the world's largest inactive volcano, while Hawaii's Mauna Loa is the world's largest active volcano, and Kilauea is the most active volcano in the world. Kaua'i's Mt. Wai'ale'ale is the wettest spot on earth, receiving about 450 inches of rain per year on average. Honolulu's 'Iolani Palace is the only royal palace in the United States. Hawaii had the first company (C. Brewer), American school (Lahainaluna), newspaper *(Sandwich Island Gazette),* bank (First Hawaiian), and church (Moku'aikaua, Kailua-Kona) west of the Rocky Mountains.

Tidbits

American captains Shaler and Cleveland brought the first horses aboard the *Lydia Byrd* and introduced them at Lahaina in 1803. Two were given to Kamehameha the Great, who was not impressed. Tattooing was common in old Hawaii; many people had the date of the death of a loved one tattooed on their body, and gouged their eyes and knocked out their own teeth as signs of mourning. The greatest insult was to inlay a spittoon with the teeth of a defeated enemy. The name of the channel between Lana'i and Kaho'olawe, Kealaikahiki, means "The Way to Tahiti." Voyagers got their bearings here for the long voyage south. "It will happen when Boki comes back" means something is impossible. Boki was a chief who sailed away in 1829 looking for sandalwood. He never returned. Only 20 of the 500 who sailed with him made it back to Hawaii.

DIANA LASICH HARPER

BIG ISLAND

In what other land save this one is the commonest form of greeting not "Good Day,"... but "Love?"... Aloha... It is the positive affirmation of one's own heart giving.

—*Jack London, 1916*

SHIP'S ARTIST, JOHN WEBBER

BIG ISLAND

INTRODUCTION

The island of Hawai'i is grand in so many ways. Its two nicknames, "The Orchid Island" and "The Volcano Island," are both excellent choices: the island produces more of the delicate blooms than anywhere else on earth, and Pele, the fire goddess who makes her mythological home here, regularly sends rivers of lava from the world's largest and most active volcanoes. However, to the people who live here, Hawai'i has only one real nickname, "The Big Island." Big isn't necessarily better, but when you combine it with beautiful, uncrowded, traditional, and inexpensive, it's hard to beat.

The Big Island was the first to be inhabited by the Polynesian settlers, yet it's geologically the youngest of the Hawaiian Islands at barely a million years old. Like all the islands in the Hawaiian chain, it's a mini-continent whose geographical demarcations are much more apparent because of its size. There are parched deserts, steaming fissures, jet-black sand beaches, raw semi-cooled lava flows, snow-covered mountains, upland pastures, littoral ponds, forests encased in stone, and lush valleys where countless waterfalls break through the rock faces of thousand-foot-high chasms. There are small working villages that time has passed by, the state's most tropical city, and an arid coast stretching more than 90 miles where the sun is guaranteed to shine. You'll find some of the islands' least expensive accommodations as well as some of the world's most exclusive resorts.

Historically, the Big Island is loaded with religious upheavals, the births and deaths of great people, vintage missionary homes and churches, reconstructed *heiau*, and even a royal summer palace. Here is the country's largest privately owned ranch, where cowboy life is the norm; America's oldest and once the only coffee plantations; artist communities; and enclaves of the counterculture, where people with alternative lifestyles are still trying to keep the faith of the 1960s.

Sportspeople love it here, too. The Big Island is a mecca for triathletes and offers snow skiing in season, plenty of camping and hiking, the best marlin waters in all the oceans of the world, great horseback riding, and as much water sports activity as anyone would care for.

Direct flights land on the Big Island, where the fascination of perhaps not "old" Hawaii, but definitely "simple" Hawaii, still lingers.

OVERVIEW

Kailua-Kona on the west coast and Hilo on the east side are the two ports of entry to the Big Island. At opposite ends of the island as well as of the cultural spectrum, the two have a friendly rivalry. It doesn't matter at which one you ar-

rive, because a trip to the Big Island without visiting both is unthinkable. Better yet, split your stay and use each as a base while you tour. The Big Island is the only Hawaiian Island big enough that you can't drive around it comfortably in one day, nor should you try. Each of the six districts is interesting enough to spend at least one day exploring.

Kona

Kona is dry, sunny, and brilliant, with large expanses of old barren lava flows. When watered, the rich soil blossoms, as in Holualoa and South Kona, renowned for its diminutive **coffee plantations.** The town of Captain Cook, named after the intrepid Pacific explorer, lies just above the very beach where he was slain because of a terrible miscommunication two centuries ago. Ironically, nearby is the restored **Pu'uhonua o Honaunau Heiau,** where mercy and forgiveness were rendered to any *kapu*-breaker or vanquished warrior who made it into the confines of this safe refuge.

Kailua-Kona is the center of Kona. The airport is just north of town near a major concentration of condos and hotels. The town itself boasts an array of art and designer shops; world-class triathletes come here to train, and charter boats depart in search of billfish and other denizens of the deep. Within Kailua is **Moku'aikaua Church,** a legacy of the very first packet of missionaries to arrive in the islands, and **Hulihe'e Palace,** vacation home of the Kamehameha line of kings. Dominating this entire coastline, **Mt. Hualalai** rises to the east, and northward the Kona District offers a string of fine beaches.

Kohala

Up the coast in South Kohala is **Hapuna Beach,** one of the best on the island. In 1965, Laurence Rockefeller opened the Mauna Kea Resort near there. Since then, this resort, along with its sculptured, coast-hugging golf course, has been considered one of the finest in the world. Just south is the Kona Village Resort, whose guests can spend the night in a "simple" grass shack on the beach. Its serenity is broken only by the soothing music of the surf and by the not-so-melodious singing of "Kona nightingales," a pampered herd of wild donkeys that frequents this area. Over the years, other expansive resorts and golf courses have been added, making this the island's luxury resort area, on a par with any in the state. Upcountry, at the base of the Kohala Mountains, is **Waimea** (Kamuela), center of the enormous **Parker Ranch.** Here in the cool mountains, cattle graze in chest-high grass, and *paniolo,* astride their sturdy mounts, ride herd in time-honored tradition. Hunters range the slopes of Mauna Kea in search of wild goats and boars, and the Fourth of July is boisterously acknowledged by the wild whoops of cowboys at the world-class Parker Ranch Rodeo.

North Kohala is primarily the hilly peninsular thumb on the northern extremity of the island. Along the coast are beach parks, empty except for an occasional local family picnic. *Heiau* dot the coast, and on the northernmost tip a broad plain overlooking a sweeping panorama marks the birthplace of Kamehameha the Great. The main town up here is **Hawi,** holding on after the sugar companies pulled out a few years ago. Down the road is Kapa'au, where **Kamehameha's statue** resides in fulfillment of a *kahuna* prophecy. Along this little-traveled road, a handful of artists offer their crafts in small shops. At road's end is the overlook of **Pololu Valley,** where a steep descent takes you to a secluded beach in an area once frequented by some of the most powerful sorcerers in the land.

BIG ISLAND

The Saddle Road

This cross-island road begins just outside of Hilo. It slices across the island through a most astonishing high valley or "saddle" separating the mountains of **Mauna Loa** and **Mauna Kea.** Passable, but the bane of car rental companies, the Saddle Road slides down the western slope of Mauna Kea to meet the Belt Road, from where it's an easy drive to either Waimea or Kona. From the Saddle Road, a spur road heads up to the top of Mauna Kea at 13,796 feet, where **astronomical observatories** peer into the heavens through the clearest air on earth.

Hilo

Hilo is the oldest port of entry, the most tropical town in Hawai'i, and the only major city built on the island's windward coast. The city is one tremendous greenhouse where exotic flowers and tropical plants are a normal part of the landscape, and entire blocks canopied by adjoining banyans are taken for granted. The town, which hosts the yearly Merrie Monarch Festival, boasts an early morning fish market, Japanese gardens, the **Lyman House Museum,** and a profusion of natural phenomena, including **Rainbow Falls** and **Boiling Pots.** Plenty of rooms in Hilo are generally easily available, and its variety of restaurants will titillate anyone's taste buds. Both go easy on the pocketbook while maintaining high standards.

Hamakua Coast

Hamakua refers to the entire northeast coast, where streams, wind, and pounding surf have chiseled the lava into towering cliffs and precipitous valleys known locally by the unromantic name of "gulches." Until recently, all the flatlands here were awash in a green sea of sugarcane; no commercial and few private fields remain. A spur road from the forgotten town of Honomu leads to **'Akaka Falls,** whose waters tumble over a 442-foot cliff—the highest sheer drop of water in Hawaii. North along the coastal road is **Honoka'a,** a one-street town of stores, restaurants, and crafts shops. The main road bears left here to the cowboy town of Waimea, but a smaller road inches farther north. It dead-ends at the top of **Waipi'o Valley,** cradled by cliffs on three sides with its mouth wide open to the sea. The valley is reachable only by foot, 4WD vehicle, or horseback. On its verdant floor a handful of families live simply by raising taro, a few head of cattle, and horses. Waipi'o was a burial ground of Hawaiian *ali'i,* where *kahuna* traditionally came to commune with spirits. The enchantment of this "power spot" remains.

Puna

Puna lies south of Hilo and makes up the majority of the southeast coast. Here are the greatest lava fields that have spewed from Kilauea, the heart of **Hawaii Volcanoes National Park.** An ancient flow embraced a forest in its fiery grasp, entombing trees that stand like sentinels today in **Lava Tree State Monument. Cape Kumukahi,** a pointed lava flow that reached the ocean in 1868, is officially the easternmost point

in Hawaii. Just below it a string of beaches feature ebony-black sand. Past the small village of Kalapana, the road skirts the coast before it dead-ends where it has been covered over by lava. Chain of Craters Road is now passable only from Hawaii Volcanoes National Park. This road spills off the mountain through a forbidding, yet vibrant, wasteland of old lava flows until it comes to the sea, where this living volcano fumes and throbs. Atop the volcano, miles of hiking trails crisscross the park and lead to the very summit of Mauna Loa. You can view the natural phenomena of steaming fissures, flowing lava, Devastation Trail, and Thurston Lava Tube, large enough to accommodate a subway train. Here, too, you can lodge or dine at Volcano House, a venerable inn carved into the rim of the crater.

Ka'u

Ka'u, the southern tip of the island, is primarily a desert-like arid region with pockets of green. On well-marked trails leading from the main road you'll discover ancient petroglyphs and an eerie set of footprints, the remnants of an ill-fated band of warriors who were smothered under the moist ash of a volcanic eruption and whose demise marked the ascendancy of Kamehameha the Great. Like Hamakua, Ka'u was a sugar-growing region. Sugar is no more and its loss created a tough economic environment, but macadamia nuts and other agricultural crops are being raised. Here are some lovely beaches and parks you'll have virtually to yourself. A tiny road leads to **Ka Lae** (South Point), the most southerly piece of ground in the United States.

THE LAND

Science and *The Kumulipo* oral history differ sharply on the age of the Big Island. Scientists say that Hawai'i is the youngest of the islands, being a little more than one million years old; the chanters claim that it was the first "island-child" of Wakea and Papa. It is, irrefutably, closest to the "hot spot" on the Pacific floor, evidenced by Kilauea's frequent eruptions and by Lo'ihi Seamount. The geology, geography, and location of the Hawaiian Islands, and their ongoing drifting and building in the middle of the Pacific, make them among the most fascinating pieces of real estate on earth. The Big Island is the *most* fascinating of them all—it is truly unique.

Size

The Big Island dwarfs all the others in the Hawaiian chain at 4,028 square miles and growing. It accounts for about 63 percent of the state's total landmass; the other islands could fit within it two times over. With 266 miles of coastline, the island stretches about 95 miles from north to south

MOUNTAINS OF HAWAI'I

Mauna Kea (13,796 ft.)
Mauna Loa (13,679 ft.)
Hualalai (8,271 ft.)
Kohala (5,480 ft.)
Kilauea (4,078 ft.)
Waimea (2,670 ft.)
Volcano (4,000 ft.)
Kona
Hilo

AVALON TRAVEL PUBLISHING, INC.

BIG ISLAND

and 80 miles from east to west. Cape Kumukahi is the easternmost point in the state, and Ka Lae is the southernmost point in the country.

The Mountains

The tremendous volcanic peak of **Mauna Kea** (White Mountain), in north-central Hawai'i, has been extinct for more than 3,500 years. Its seasonal snowcap earns Mauna Kea its name and reputation as a good skiing area in winter. More than 18,000 feet of mountain below the surface rises straight up from the ocean floor—making Mauna Kea actually 31,796 feet tall, a substantial 2,768 feet taller than Mt. Everest; some consider it the tallest mountain in the world. At 13,796 feet above sea level, it is without doubt the tallest peak in the Pacific. Near its top, at 13,020 feet, is **Lake Waiau,** the highest lake in the state and third highest in the country. Mauna Kea was obviously a sacred mountain to the Hawaiians, and its white dome was a welcome beacon to seafarers. On its slope is the largest adze quarry in Polynesia, from which high-quality basalt was taken to be fashioned into prized tools. The atmosphere atop the mountain, which sits mid-Pacific far from pollutants, is the most rarefied and cleanest on earth. The clarity makes Mauna Kea a natural for astronomical observatories. The complex of telescopes on its summit is internationally staffed and provides data to scientists around the world.

The **Kohala Mountains** to the northwest are the oldest and rise only to 5,480 feet at Kaunu o Kaleiho'ohel peak. This section looks more like the other Hawaiian Islands, with deep gorges and valleys along the coast and a forested interior. As you head east toward Waimea from Kawaihae on Route 19, for every mile you travel you pick up about 10 inches of rainfall per year. This becomes obvious as you begin to pass little streams and rivulets running from the mountains.

Mount Hualalai at 8,271 feet is the backdrop to Kailua-Kona. It's home to many of the Big Island's endangered birds and supports many of the region's newest housing developments. Just a few years ago, Mt. Hualalai was thought to be extinct, since the last time it erupted was in 1801. It is now known that within the last thousand years, the mountain has erupted about every two or three centuries. In 1929 it suffered an earthquake swarm, which means that there was a large movement of lava inside the mountain that caused tremors. Now USGS scientists consider Mt. Hualalai only dormant and very likely to erupt at some point in the future. When it does, it's expected to produce a tremendous amount of lava that will pour rapidly down its steep sides. From the side of this mountain has grown the cone Pu'u Wa'awa'a. At 3,967 feet, it's only slightly shorter than the very active Kilauea on the far side of Mauna Loa. Obsidian is found here and is one of the few place in Hawaii where this substance has been quarried in such quantities.

Even though **Mauna Loa** (Long Mountain) measures a respectable 13,679 feet, its height isn't its claim to fame. This active volcano, 60 miles long by 30 wide, comprises 10,000 cubic miles of iron-hard lava, making it the densest and most massive mountain on earth. In 1950, a tremendous lava flow belched from Mauna Loa's summit, reaching an astonishing rate of 6,750,000 cubic yards per hour. Seven lava rivers flowed for 23 days, emitting more than 600 million cubic yards of lava that covered 35 square miles. There were no injuries, but the villages of Ka'apuna and Honokua were partially destroyed along with the Magoo Ranch. Its last eruption in 1984 was small by comparison yet created fountaining inside the summit crater and a "curtain of fire" along its eastern rift.

The lowest of the island's major peaks, **Kilauea** rises only to 4,078 feet. Its pragmatic name means "The Spewing," and it is the world's most active volcano. In the last hundred years, it has erupted on the average once every 11 months. The Hawaiians believed that the goddess Pele inhabited every volcano in the Hawaiian chain, and that her home is now Halema'uma'u Crater in Kilauea Caldera. Kilauea is the most scientifically watched volcano in the world, with a permanent observatory built right into the crater rim. When it erupts, the flows are so predictable that observers run toward the mountain, not away from it! The flows, however, can burst from fissures far from the center of the crater in areas that don't seem "active." This occurs mainly in the Puna District. In 1959, Kilauea Iki Crater came to life after 91 years, and although the flow wasn't as massive as others, it did send blazing fountains of lava 1,900 feet into the air. Kilauea has been very active within the last few years, with eruptions occurring at least once a month and expected to continue. Most activity has been from a vent below Pu'u O'o crater. You might be lucky enough to see this phenomenon while visiting.

Tsunamis

Hilo has been struck with the two worst tsunamis in modern history. A giant wave smashed the islands on April 1, 1946, sweeping away 159 people and more than 1,300 homes; Hilo sustained most of these losses. Again, on May 23, 1960, Hilo took the brunt of a wave that rumbled through the business district killing 61 people. There is an elaborate warning system throughout the island; warning procedures and inundation maps are found in the front of the telephone directory.

Beaches and Ponds

The Big Island takes the rap for having poor beaches—this isn't true! They are certainly few and far between, but they are spectacular. Hawai'i is big and young, so distances are greater than on other islands, and the wave action hasn't had enough time to grind new lava and coral into sand. The Kona and Kohala Coast beaches, along with a few nooks and crannies around Hilo, are gorgeous. Puna's beaches are incredible black sand, and the southern part of the island has a string of hidden beaches enjoyed only by those intrepid enough to get to them.

Just north of the Kona airport is Makalawena, a beautiful white-sand beach. Inland is its associated wetland pond, probably the most important one on the Big Island. Other coastal ponds are in Kaloko-Honokohau National Historical Park (between the Kona airport and Kailua-Kona) and at Waikoloa Beach Resort.

CLIMATE

The average temperature around the island varies between 72 and 78° F. Summers raise the temperature to the mid-80s, and winters cool off to the low 70s. Both Kona and Hilo seem to maintain a year-round average of about 74 degrees, and the South Kohala Coast is a few degrees warmer. As usual, it's cooler in the higher

BIG ISLAND TEMPERATURE AND RAINFALL

TOWN		JAN.	MARCH	MAY	JUNE	SEPT.	NOV.
Hilo	high	79	79	80	82	82	80
	low	62	62	61	70	70	65
	rain	11	15	7	10	10	15
Kona	high	80	81	81	82	82	81
	low	62	64	65	68	68	63
	rain	4	3	2	0	2	1

Note: Temperature is expressed in degrees Fahrenheit; rainfall in inches.

elevations, and Waimea sees most days in the mid-60s to low 70s, while Volcano maintains a relatively steady 60 degrees. Atop Mauna Kea, the temperature rarely climbs above 50° or dips below 30, while the summit of Mauna Loa is about 10 degrees warmer. The lowest recorded temperature on the Big Island was 1° F inside the Mauna Kea summit crater in January 1970, while the highest ever recorded was in April 1931 at Pahala in Ka'u—a scorching (for Hawaii) 100°.

Precipitation

Weatherwise, the Big Island's climate varies not so much in temperature but precipitation. Hawai'i has some of the wettest and driest coastal areas in the islands. The line separating wet from dry can be dramatic. Waimea, for example, has an actual dry and wet side of town, as if a boundary line split the town in two! Houses on the dry side are at a premium. Kona and Hilo are opposites. The Kona Coast is almost guaranteed to be sunny and bright, receiving as little as 15 inches of rainfall per year but with an average of 28 inches. Both Kona and the Ka'u Desert to the south are in the rain shadow of Mauna Loa, and most rain clouds coming from east to west are pierced by its summit before they ever reach Kona. Hilo is wet, with predictable afternoon and evening showers—they make the entire town blossom. Though this reputation keeps many tourists away, the rain's predictability makes it easy to avoid a drenching while exploring the town. Hilo does get as much as 128 inches of rainfall per year, with a record of 153.93 inches set in 1971. It also holds the dubious honor of being the town with the most rainfall recorded by the National Weather Service in a 24-hour period—a drenching 22.3 inches in February 1979.

FLORA AND FAUNA

The indigenous plants and birds of the Big Island have suffered the same fate as those of the other Hawaiian Islands: they're among the most endangered species on earth and disappearing at an alarming rate. There are some sanctuaries on the Big Island where native species still live, but they must be vigorously protected. Do your bit to save them; enjoy but do not disturb.

COMMON FLORA

The Hawaiians called the **prickly pear cactus** *panini*, which translates as "very unfriendly," undoubtedly because of the sharp spines covering the flat, thick leaves. The cactus is typical of those found in Mexico and the southwestern United States. It was introduced to Hawaii before 1810 and established itself coincidentally with the cattle brought in at the time; *panini* is very common in North Kohala, especially on the Parker Ranch lands. It is assumed that Don Marin, a Spanish advisor to Kamehameha I, was responsible for importing the plant. Perhaps the early *paniolo* (cowboys) felt lonely without it. The *panini* can grow to heights of 15 feet and is now considered a pest, but nonetheless it looks as if it belongs. It develops small, delicious, pear-shaped fruits. Hikers who decide to pick the fruit should be careful of small, yellowish bristles that can burrow under the skin and irritate. The beautiful yellow and orange flowers measure three inches across. An attempt is being made to control the cactus in *paniolo* country. *El cosano rojo,* the red worm found in the bottom of Mexican tequila, has been introduced to destroy the plant. It burrows into the cactus and eats the hardwood center, causing the plant to wither and die.

More species of **lobelia** grow in Hawaii than anywhere else in the world. The lobelia flower is tiny and resembles a miniature orchid with curved and pointed ends, like the beak of the native *'i'iwi.*

The Big Island has more species of **gesneriad,** the African violet family, than anywhere else on earth. Many don't have the showy flowers that you normally associate with African violets but have evolved into strange species with huge, fuzzy leaves.

The *pu'ahanui,* whose name means "many flowers," is Hawaii's native hydrangea; it is common in the upland forests of the Big Island.

Ferns

If you travel to Volcanoes National Park you will find yourself deep in an amazing, high-altitude

J.D. BISIGNANI

Fiddlehead ferns are prevalent along trails where the lava has weathered.

tropical rainforest. This unique forest exists because of the 120 inches of annual rainfall, which turns the raw lava into a lush forest. Besides stands of 'ohi'a and koa, you'll be treated to a primordial display of ferns. All new fronds on ferns are called "fiddleheads" because of the way they unfurl and resemble the scrolls of violin heads. Fiddleheads were eaten by Hawaiians during times of famine. The most common ferns are *hapu'u,* a rather large tree fern, and *'ama'uama'u,* a smaller type with a more simple frond. A soft, furry growth around the base of the stalks is called *pulu.* At one time *pulu* was collected for stuffing mattresses, and a factory was located atop Volcanoes. But *pulu* breaks down and forms a very fine dust after a few years, so it never really became generally accepted for mattresses.

At high altitudes, young ferns and other plants often produce new growth that turns bright red as protection against the sun's ultraviolet rays. You'll see it on new foliage before it hardens. Hawai-

BIG ISLAND BOTANICAL GARDENS

The **Hilo Arboretum,** along Kilauea Ave. between Lanikaula and Kawili St., is maintained by the Department of Natural Resources, Division of Forestry. Open Mon.–Fri. 8 A.M.–3 P.M.; free for self-guided tour. The site is used for the propagation of rare and endangered plant species, for research, and for experimental pursuits. This arboretum contains examples of most of the trees present in Hawaii, including indigenous and imported specimens.

Nani Mau Gardens, 421 Makalika St., Hilo, 808/959-3541, is open daily 8 A.M.–5 P.M. Admission is $10, $5 per person for an optional tram tour. The 20-acre gardens feature separate areas: fruit orchards, heliconia garden, ginger garden, anthurium garden, orchid garden, orchid pavilion, gardenia garden, and bromeliad garden. This is the showiest garden on the island—a large, tame, and beautiful display. Plants are labeled.

Hawaii Tropical Botanical Gardens, 808/964-5233, open daily 8:30 A.M.–5 P.M., is a few miles north of Hilo. Admission is $15, children 6–16 $5. Here you are in the middle of a tamed tropical rainforest jungle, walking along one mile of manicured paths among more than 2,000 different species of trees and plants.

The **World Tropical Botanical Gardens,** 808/963-5427, near Laupahoehoe on the Hamakua Coast, is a garden in the making. While the plan is to cultivate some 30,000 species, arranged in evolutionary groupings, only about half is set up and open to the public. Open Mon.–Sat. 9 A.M.–5:30 P.M.; $5 adults and $2 teens.

Amy B. H. Greenwell Ethnobotanical Garden, 808/323-3318, along Rt. 11, between the communities of Kealakekua and Captain Cook. The garden is open Mon.–Fri. 8:30 A.M.–5 P.M. Guided tours are offered on the second Saturday of every month at 10 A.M., but visitors are welcome any time during daylight hours; $4 donation. This 12-acre interpretive ethnobotanical garden has indigenous Hawaiian plants, Polynesian introduced plants, and Hawaiian medicinal plants. The garden has remnants of the Kona field system, which dates from precontact times.

ians called this new growth *liko*. Today, people still make lei from *liko* because it has so many subtle and beautiful colors. 'Ohi'a *liko* is a favorite for lei because it is so striking.

BIRDS

You'll spot birds all over the Big Island, from the coastal areas to the high mountain slopes. Some are found on other islands as well, but the ones listed below are found only or mainly on the Big Island. Every bird listed is either threatened or endangered.

Hawaii's Own

The ***nene,*** or Hawaiian goose, is making a comeback from the edge of extinction. The *nene,* Hawaii's state bird, is found only on the slopes of Mauna Loa, Hualalai, and Mauna Kea on the Big Island, and in Haleakala Crater on Maui. Approximately 500 live on the Big Island.

Good places to view *nene* are in Volcanoes National Park at Kipuka Nene Campground, Summit Caldera, Devastation Trail, and at Volcanoes Golf Course, at dawn and dusk. They gather at the golf course because they love to feed on grasses. The places to view them on the Kona side are at Pu'ulani, a housing development north of Kailua Kona, and at Kaloko Mauka, another housing development on the slopes of Mt. Hualalai. At the top of the road up Mt. Hualalai is a trail, a good place to see the *nene*. Unfortunately, as the housing developments proliferate and the residents invariably acquire dogs and cats, the *nene* will disappear.

The **Hawaiian crow,** or *alala,* is reduced to fewer than 12 birds living on the slopes of Hualalai and Mauna Loa above the 3,000-foot level. It looks like the common raven but has a more melodious voice and sometimes dull brown feathers. The *alala* breeds in early spring, and the greenish-blue, black-flecked eggs hatch from April to June. It is extremely nervous while nesting, and any disturbance causes it to abandon its young.

The **Hawaiian hawk** (*'io*) primarily lives on the slopes of Mauna Loa and Mauna Kea below 9,000 feet. This noble bird, the royalty of the skies, symbolized the *ali'i*. The hawk exists only on the Big Island, for reasons that are not entirely clear. The *'io* population was once dwindling,

and many scientists feared that the bird was headed for extinction. The good news is that the *'io* is making a dramatic comeback.

The **'akiapola'au,** a honeycreeper, is a five-inch yellow bird hardly bigger than its name. It lives mainly on the eastern slopes in 'ohi'a and koa forests above 3,500 feet. It has a long, curved upper beak for probing and a smaller lower beak that it uses woodpecker-fashion. The *'akiapola'au* opens its mouth wide, strikes the wood with its lower beak, and then uses the upper beak to scrape out any larvae or insects. Listen for the distinctive rapping sound to spot this melodious singer. The *'akiapola'au* can be seen at the Hakalau Forest National Wildlife Refuge and along the Pu'u O'o Volcano Trail from Volcanoes National Park. It's estimated that only about 1,000 of these rare birds are left.

In addition, two other endangered birds of the Big Island are the *koloa maoli,* a duck that resembles a mallard, and the slate gray or white *'alae ke'oke'o* coot.

Marine Birds

Two coastal birds that breed on the high slopes of Hawaii's volcanoes and feed on the coast are the **Hawaiian dark-rumped petrel** (*'ua'u*) and the **Newell's shearwater** (*'a'o*). The *'ua'u* lives on the barren high slopes and craters, where it nests in burrows or under stones. Breeding season lasts from mid-March to mid-October. Only one chick is born per mother; it is nurtured on

The nene, the state bird, lives only on the slopes of Mauna Loa and Mauna Kea on the Big Island and in the crater of Haleakala, Maui.

BOB RACE

regurgitated squid and fish. The 'ua'u suffers heavily from predation. The 'a'o prefers the forested slopes of the interior. It breeds April–November and spends its days at sea and nights inland. Feral cats and dogs reduce its numbers considerably. In addition, the ae'o, Hawaiian black-necked stilt, has become endangered.

Forest Birds

The following birds are found in the upland forests of the Big Island. The 'elepaio is found on other islands but is also spotted in Volcanoes National Park. The 'amakihi and 'i'iwi are endemic birds not endangered at the moment. The yellowish green 'amakihi is one of the most common native birds. It is less specialized than most other Hawaiian birds, the main reason for its continued existence. The 'i'iwi is a bright red bird with a salmon-colored, hooked bill; it feeds on insects and flowers.

The 'apapane is abundant on Hawaii, especially atop Volcanoes, and since it is the most common native bird, is the easiest to see. It's a chubby, red-bodied bird about five inches long with a black bill, legs, wing tips, and tail feathers.

The **Hawaiian thrush** ('oma'o) is a fairly common bird found above 3,000 feet in the windward forests of Hawai'i. This eight-inch gray bird is a good singer, often seen perching with distinctive drooping wings and a shivering body. The best place to look for it is at the Thurston Lava Tube, where you can see it doing its baby-bird shivering-and-shaking act. A great mimic, it can sound like a cat or even like an old-fashioned radio with stations changing as you turn the dial.

The 'akepa is a four- to five-inch bird. The male is a brilliant orange to red, the female a drab green and yellow. It is found mainly on Hualalai and in windward forests.

The six-inch, bright yellow **palila** is found only on Hawai'i in the forests of Mauna Kea above 6,000 feet. It depends exclusively upon mamane trees for survival, eating its pods, buds, and flowers.

MAMMALS

Hawaii had only two indigenous mammals: the monk seal or 'ilio holu I ka uaua (found throughout the islands) and the hoary bat (found mainly on the Big Island), both of which are threatened or endangered. The remainder of the Big Island's mammals are transplants. But like anything else, including people, that has been in the islands long enough, they have taken on characteristics that make them "local."

The following animals are found primarily on the Big Island. The **Hawaiian hoary bat** ('ope'ape'a) is a cousin of the Mainland bat. Its tail has a whitish coloration, hence its name. The hoary bat has a 13-inch wingspan. Unlike other bats, it is a solitary creature, roosting in trees. It gives birth to twins in early summer and can often be spotted over Hilo and Kealakekua Bays just around sundown.

The **feral dog** ('ilio) is found on all the islands but especially on the slopes of Mauna Kea, where packs chase feral sheep. Poisoned and shot by local ranchers, their numbers are diminishing. Black dogs, thought to be more tender, are still eaten in some Hawaiian and Filipino communities.

The **feral sheep** are escaped descendants of animals brought to the islands by Captain Vancouver in the 1790s and of merinos brought to the island later and raised for their exceptional woolly fleece. These sheep exist only on the Big Island, on the upper slopes of Mauna Loa, Mauna Kea, and Hualalai. The fleece is a buff brown, and the sheep's two-foot-wide curved horns are often sought as hunting trophies. Feral sheep are responsible for the overgrazing of young mamane trees, which are essential to the endangered palila bird. In 1979, a law was passed to exterminate or remove the sheep from Mauna Kea so that the native palila could survive.

The **mouflon sheep** was introduced to Lana'i and Hawai'i to cut down on overgrazing and serve as a trophy animal. This Mediterranean sheep can interbreed with feral sheep to produce a hybrid. It lives on the upper slopes of Mauna Loa and Mauna Kea. Unfortunately, its introduction has not been a success. No evidence concludes that the smaller family groups of mouflon cause less damage than the herding feral sheep, and hunters reportedly don't like the meat as much as feral mutton.

The **feral donkey,** better known as the "Kona nightingale," came to Hawaii as a beast of burden. Domesticated donkeys are found on all islands, but a few wild herds still roam the Big Island along the Kona Coast, especially near the exclusive Kona Village Resort at Kaupulehu.

Feral cattle were introduced by Captain Vancouver, who gave a few domesticated head to Kamehameha; immediately a *kapu* against killing them went into effect for 10 years. The lush grasses of Hawaii were perfect and the cattle flourished; by the early 1800s they were out of control and were hunted and exterminated. Finally, Mexican cowboys were brought to Hawaii to teach the locals how to be range hands. From this legacy sprang the Hawaiian *paniolo*.

MARINE LIFE

Humpback Whales

Humpback whales, known in Hawaii as *kohola,* migrate to Hawaiian waters yearly, arriving in late December and departing by mid-March. The best places to view them are along the southern Kona Coast, especially at Kealakekua Bay and Ka Lae (South Point), with many sightings off the Puna coast around Isaac Hale Beach Park.

Hawksbill Turtle

Hawaii Volcanoes National Park stretches from the top of Mauna Kea all the way down to the sea. It is here, around Apua Point, that three of the last-known nesting sites of the very endangered hawksbill turtle *(honu 'ea)* are found. This creature has been ravished in the Pacific, where it is ruthlessly hunted for its shell, which is made into women's jewelry, especially combs. It is illegal to bring items made from turtle shell into the United States, but the hunt goes on.

Billfish

Although these magnificent game fish occur in various South Sea and Hawaiian waters, catching them is easiest in the clear, calm waters off the Kona Coast. The billfish—swordfish, sailfish, marlin, and *a'u*—share two distinctive common features: a long, spearlike or swordlike snout and a prominent dorsal fin. The three main species of billfish caught are the blue, striped, and black marlin. Of these three, the **blue marlin** is the leading game fish in Kona waters. The blue has tipped the scales at well over 1,000 pounds, but the average fish weighs in at 300–400 pounds. When alive, this fish is a striking cobalt blue, but when dead, its color changes to slate blue. It feeds on skipjack tuna; throughout the summer, fishing boats look for schools of tuna as a tip-off to blues in the area. The **black marlin** is the largest and most coveted catch for blue-water anglers. This solitary fish is infrequently found off the banks of Kona. Granddaddies can weigh 1,800 pounds, but the average is a mere 200. The **striped marlin** is the most common commercial billfish, a highly prized food served in finer restaurants and often sliced into sashimi. Its coloration is a remarkable royal blue. Its spectacular leaps when caught give it a great reputation as a fighter. The striped marlin is smaller than the other marlins, so a 100-pounder is a very good catch.

THE HAKALAU FOREST NATIONAL WILDLIFE REFUGE

The Hakalau Forest National Wildlife Refuge, acquired with the help of the Nature Conservancy but administered solely by the U.S. Fish and Wildlife Service, is a large tract of land north of the Saddle Road that borders Parker Ranch lands. It's upland forest and scrub that drifts down into solid rainforest harboring such birds as the *'akiapola'au, 'akepa, 'io,* Hawaiian creeper, *'oma'o, 'apapane, 'amakihi, 'elepaio, nene,* and *pueo.* The U.S. Fish and Wildlife Service is working hard to reconvert this refuge into natural habitat, and efforts include fencing, snaring, and hunting, ridding the area of feral pigs and cattle, and replanting with koa, 'ohi'a, opeka, pilo, and other native species while removing introduced and exotic foliage. It's a tremendous task that's mainly being shouldered by Dick Wass and Jack Jeffrey, rangers with the U.S. Fish and Wildlife Service. The refuge is not adequately staffed to accept visits by the general public at all times, but the Maulau Tract, the northernmost section of the refuge, is open for hiking and birding on the last weekend of every month. This area is a two-hour drive from Hilo, one-half of which is over a rugged dirt road traversable only by a 4WD vehicle. Additionally, the refuge is open the first three weekends of the month for public hunting of feral pigs. Numerous volunteer opportunities are available for various ongoing projects, either in the field or at the greenhouse, for a weekend or weeklong stint. If you *truly* have a dedication to help and aren't afraid to get your hands dirty, contact Dick or Jack for a very rewarding experience. To enter the refuge for any reason, first contact the office at least three weeks in advance to make arrangements; call 808/933-6915, fax 800/933-6917, or write to the Refuge Manager, Hakalau Forest NWR, 154 Waianuenue Ave., Room 219, Hilo, HI 96720. The refuge is very beautiful diamond in the rough, encompassing an incredible rainforest.

HISTORY

The Big Island plays a significant role in Hawaii's history. A long list of "firsts" have occurred here. Historians generally believe (backed up by oral tradition) that the Big Island was the first in the Hawaiian chain to be settled by the Polynesians. The dates now used are A.D. 600–700. Hawaii is geographically the closest island to Polynesia; Mauna Loa and especially Mauna Kea, with its white summit, present easily spotted landmarks. Psychologically, the Polynesian wayfarers would have been very attracted to Hawaii as a lost homeland. Compared to Tahiti and most other South Sea Islands (except Fiji's main islands), it's huge. It *looked* like the promised land. Some may wonder why the Polynesians chose to live atop an obviously active volcano and not bypass it for a more congenial island. The volcanism of the Big Island is comparatively gentle; the lava flows follow predictable routes and rarely turn killer. The animistic Hawaiians would have been drawn to live where the godly forces of nature were so apparent. The mana (power) would be exceptionally strong, and therefore the *ali'i* would be great. Human sacrifice was introduced to Hawaii at Waha'ula Heiau in the Puna District in the 13th century, and from there *luakini* (human-sacrifice temples) spread throughout the islands.

The Great One

The greatest native son of Hawaii, Kamehameha, was born under mysterious circumstances in the Kohala District, probably in 1753. Kamehameha became a renowned warrior and a loyal retainer to his uncle, Kalaniopu'u, the *moi* (ruler) of Hawai'i. Before Kalaniopu'u died, he made Kamehameha the keeper of the feathered family war god, Kuka'ilimoku, or Ku the Land Snatcher, while Kamehameha's cousins Kiwalao and Keoua engaged in a civil war over land rights.

Kamehameha, aided by disgruntled chiefs from Kona, waged war on both, and at Moku'ohai, Kiwalao was killed. Kamehameha went on to fight on Maui. By this time he had acquired a small ship, the *Fair American,* and using cannon manned by two white sailors, Isaac Davis and John Young, he defeated the Maui warriors at 'Iao Valley. If he could defeat Keoua at home, he would be king of all Hawaii.

The Gods Speak

A great oracle from Kaua'i announced war would end on Hawaii only after a great *heiau* was built at Pu'ukohola (Kawaihae), dedicated to the corpse of a great chief. Kamehameha instantly set about building this *heiau,* and through cunning, wisdom, and true belief placed the conquest of Hawaii in the hands of the gods. Meanwhile, a fleet of war canoes belonging to Kahekili of Maui attacked Kamehameha's forces at Waimanu, near Waipi'o. Aided again by the *Fair American* and Davis and Young, Kamehameha won a decisive battle and subdued Kahekili once and for all. Keoua seized this opportunity to ravage Kamehameha's lands all the way from Waipi'o to Hilo. He sent his armies south through Ka'u, but when the middle legions were passing the foot of Kilauea, it erupted and suffocated them with poisonous gas and a heavy deposit of ash. Footprints, encased in the cement-like ash, still mark their last steps.

Kamehameha and Keoua both took this as a direct sign from the gods. Kamehameha returned to Pu'ukohala and finished the *heiau.* Upon completion he summoned Keoua, who came by canoe with a small band of warriors resplendent in feather helmet and cape. He knew the fate that awaited him, and when he stepped ashore he was slaughtered. Keoua's body was laid on the altar, and at that moment the islands of

Hawaii were united under one supreme ruler, Kamehameha, The Lonely One. He ruled until his death in 1819, and his passing marked the beginning of the end for old Hawaii.

Great Changes

The great navigator and explorer, Captain Cook, was killed at Kealakekua Bay on February 14, 1779. Kalaniopu'u was still alive at the time and Kamehameha was only a minor chief. During Kamehameha's reign ships from the United States, England, and various European countries came to trade. Americans monopolized the lucrative sandalwood business with China, and New England whalers discovered the rich whaling waters. The Englishman, Captain Vancouver, became a trusted advisor of Kamehameha and told him about the white people's form of worship, while introducing plants and animals such as oranges, grapes, cows, goats, and sheep.

When Kamehameha died in 1819, Hawaii was ripe for change. His two great queens, Ka'ahumanu and Keopuolani, realized the old ways were coming to an end. They encouraged Liholiho (Kamehameha II) to end the *kapu* system. Men and women were forbidden to eat together, and those who violated this principal *kapu* were immediately killed to placate the gods before they retaliated with grave destruction. Keopuolani defied this belief when she sat down with Kauikeaouli, the seven-year-old brother of Liholiho. The gods remained quiet. Encouraged, Liholiho called for a great lu'au at Kailua, and he openly sat down to eat with his chiefs and chieftesses. Symbolically, the impotent gods were toppled with every bite, and *heiau* and idols were razed throughout the land.

Into this spiritual vortex sailed the brig *Thaddeus* on April 4, 1820. Those on board had set sail from Boston on October 23, 1819, lured to the Big Island by Henry 'Opukaha'ia, a local boy born at Napo'opo'o in 1792. Coming ashore at Kailua-Kona, the Reverends Bingham and Thurston were granted a one-year trial period by King Liholiho. Hawaii changed forever in those brief months. By 1824 the new faith had such a foothold that Chieftess Keopuolani climbed to the fire pit atop Kilauea and defied Pele. This was even more striking than the previous breaking of the food *kapu* because the strength of Pele could actually be seen. Keopuolani ate forbidden 'ohelo berries and cried out, "Jehovah is my God." Over the next decades the governing of Hawaii slipped away from the Big Island and moved to the new port cities of Lahaina and, later, Honolulu. In 1847, the Parker Ranch began with a two-acre grant given to John Parker. He coupled this with 360 acres given to his ali'i wife Kipikane by the land division known as the Great Mahele.

BIG ISLAND

GOVERNMENT

The county of Hawai'i is almost entirely Democratic and currently has only two Republican elected state legislative members. The current mayor is Harry Kim, a Democrat. The mayor is assisted by an elected county council consisting of nine members, one from each council district around the island.

Of the 25 state senatorial districts, Hawai'i County comprises three, all represented by Democrats. The 1st District takes in the whole northern section of the island: the Hamakua Coast, Mauna Kea, North and South Kohala, and part of North Kona. The 2nd District is mainly Hilo and its outlying area. The third comprises Puna, Ka'u, South Kona, and most of North Kona. Hawai'i County has six of 51 seats in the state House of Representatives. At this time, four representatives are Democrats, and the two Republicans represent the Kona and South Kohala strip.

ECONOMY

The Big Island's economy is the state's most agriculturally based. More than 6,000 farmhands, horticultural workers, and *paniolo* work the land to produce about one-third of the state's vegetables and melons and more than three-quarters of the fruit, especially papaya. Most of the state's taro is also produced on the Big Island, principally in the Waipi'o Valley and along the Hamakua Coast, and ginger production has become a major economic factor with more than six million pounds grown annually. The Big Island also produces 60 million pounds of macadamia nuts, the state's entire crop except for what's produced by small farms here and there on other islands. Hawaii has the oldest commercial coffee plantations in the state. Each year, due to the increased interest in gourmet Kona coffee, its share in the economy of the island increases, and it now grows more than 2.5 million pounds of coffee on about 2,500 acres. The Big Island is the only place in the country where cocoa beans for making chocolate are grown commercially. About 300 or more horticultural farms produce the largest number of orchids and anthuriums in the state, leaving the Big Island awash in color and fragrance. Other exotic flowers and foliage are also a growing concern. In the hills, entrepreneurs raise *pakalolo* (marijuana), which has become the state's most productive although illicit cash crop. More than $400 million worth is confiscated every year by law enforcement agencies (two-thirds of the total taken in the state), so you can imagine how much remains to hit the street.

Sugar

Hawai'i used to be the state's largest sugar grower, with more than 150,000 acres in cane. These commercial fields produced four million tons of refined sugar, 40 percent of the state's output. The majority of sugar land was along the Hamakua Coast, long known for its abundant water supply. At one time, the cane was even transported to the mills by water flumes. Another large pocket of cane fields was on the southern part of the island, mostly in Ka'u. With the closing of the last mill in 1996, sugar is no longer grown commercially on the island. Still, small entrepreneurial farms grow it on greatly reduced acreage. The big cane trucks have ceased to roll and the smokestacks stand in silent testimony to an era gone by.

Coffee

Coffee has been grown on the Big Island since 1828. The Kona District is a splendid area for raising coffee; it gives the beans a beautiful tan. Lying in Mauna Loa's rain shadow, it gets dewy mornings followed by sunshine and an afternoon cloud shadow. This coffee has long been accepted as gourmet quality; it is sold in the better restaurants throughout Hawaii and in fine coffee shops around the world. It's a dark, full-bodied coffee with a rich aroma. Approximately 600 small farms produce nearly $7 million a year in coffee revenue. Few, however, make it a full-time business. The production of Kona coffee makes up only about one-tenth of 1 percent of the coffee grown around the world. As such a rare bean, it's often blended with other varieties. When sold unblended it is quite expensive.

Cattle and Other Livestock

Hawai'i's cattle ranches produce more than five million pounds of beef per year, 50 percent of the state's total. More than 450 independent ranches dot the island, with total area over 650,000 acres, but they are dwarfed both in size and production by the massive Parker Ranch (now held as a public trust), which alone is three-quarters the size of O'ahu. While beef is the largest player in the livestock market, pork, dairy products, eggs, poultry, sheep, goats, and bees also are components, constituting perhaps half of the island's livestock revenues.

The Military

On average, about 60 military personnel are stationed on the Big Island at any one time, with about the same number of dependents. Most of these people are attached to the enormous Pohakuloa Military Reserve in the center of the island; a lesser number are at a few minor installations around Hilo and at Kilauea Volcano.

BIG ISLAND LAND OWNERSHIP

Hawai'i
2,578,073 Acres

- STATE
- FEDERAL
- HAWAIIAN HOMELANDS
- SMALL PRIVATE
- LARGE PRIVATE

Tourism

More than 4,000 island residents are directly employed by the hotel industry, and many more indirectly serve the tourists. There are slightly more than 9,500 hotel rooms, with the greatest concentration in Kona. Big Island hotels have the lowest occupancy rate in the state, rarely rising above 60 percent. The Big Island receives about 1.3 million tourists annually, about 22,700 on any given day, with 2.5 times as many people going to the Kona side as the Hilo side. Of the major islands, it ranks third in annual visitors, following O'ahu and Maui.

Land Ownership

Hawai'i County comprises more than 4.1 million acres. Of this total, the state owns about 1.2 million, mostly forest preserves and undeveloped land, and the federal government has nearly 340,000 acres in the Hawaii Volcanoes National Park, Pohakuloa Military Training Area, and Hakalau Forest National Wildlife Refuge. Large landowners control just over 1.5 million acres, and of these, the major players are the Bishop Estate, Parker Ranch, the Samuel Damon Estate, and the James Campbell Estate. Small landowners have more than 800,000 acres, and roughly 190,000 acres make up Hawaiian Home Lands.

PEOPLE

With 148,600 people, the Big Island has the second-largest island population in Hawaii, just over 12 percent of the state's total. However, it has the smallest population density of the main islands, with barely 37 people per square mile. Of these, 61 percent are urban dwellers while 39 percent live rurally. The Hilo area has the largest population with 47,000 residents, followed by North and South Kona with about 33,000, Puna at 28,000, South Kohala at 12,000, and the Hamakua Coast, North Kohala, and Ka'u each about 5,000–6,000. Within the last five years, the areas of Puna and South Kohala have experienced the greatest increases in population. The ethnic breakdown of the population is as follows: 34 percent Caucasian, 27 percent Japanese, 19 percent Hawaiian, 14 percent Filipino, 2 percent Chinese, 4 percent other.

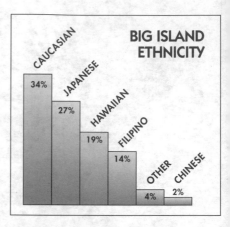

FESTIVALS, HOLIDAYS, AND EVENTS

The following events and celebrations are either particular to the Big Island, or they're celebrated here in a special way. Everyone is welcome to join in the fun, and most times the events are either free or nominally priced. There's no better way to enjoy yourself while vacationing than by joining in a local party or happening. Island-specific information is also available on the Web; check the calendar listing at www.bigisland.org for events on Hawai'i.

January

Thump in the New Year with a traditional Japanese **Mochi Pounding Festival** at Volcano Art Center, Volcanoes National Park.

During **The Volcano Wilderness Marathon and Rim Runs** the truly energetic run 26 miles through the desolate Ka'u Desert, while a 10-mile race around the Caldera Crater Rim features more than 1,000 participants.

February

February offers everything from the links to skiing at the **Mauna Kea Ski Meet** atop the Big Island's 13,000-foot volcano—weather and snow conditions dictate the exact time, which can vary from early January to March. Skiers from around the world compete in cup and cross-country skiing.

The **Annual Keauhou-Kona Triathlon** at Keauhou Bay is open to athletes unable to enter the Ironman and to anyone in good health. Each of its three events is half as long as in the Ironman, and it allows relay-team racing for each grueling segment.

The **Waimea Cherry Blossom Heritage Festival** showcases ethnic presentations, cultural events, parades, and plenty of food from around the world.

March

Mid-March rumbles in with the **Kona Stampede** at Honaunau Arena, Honaunau, Kona. *Paniolo* provide plenty of action during the full range of rodeo events.

Midmonth features beauty, grace, and athletic ability at the **Miss Aloha Hawai'i Pageant** at Hilo Civic Auditorium, Hilo.

The end of March is dedicated to Prince Kuhio, a member of the royal family and Hawaii's first delegate to the U.S. Congress. **Prince Kuhio Day** is a state holiday honoring the prince. It is held on March 26, his birthday.

April

Wesak, or **Buddha Day,** on the closest Sunday to April 8, celebrates the birthday of Gautama Buddha. Ornate offerings of tropical flowers are placed at temple altars throughout Hawaii.

The **Merrie Monarch Festival** in Hilo sways with the best hula dancers that the islands' *hula halau* have to offer. Gentle but stiff competition features hula in both its ancient *(kahiko)* and modern *(auana)* forms. The festival runs for a long weekend on a variable schedule from year to year. It's immensely popular with islanders, so hotels, cars, and flights are booked solid. Tickets usually go on sale at the first of the year and sell out in a month. This is the state's most prestigious hula competition. For information call the Hawaii Naniloa Hotel at 808/935-9168, or the HVB at 808/961-5797.

May

On May 1 everyone dons a lei for **Lei Day.** Festivities abound throughout Hawaii.

The **Captain Cook Festival** at Kailua-Kona offers Hawaiian games, music, and fishing.

Honoka'a Annual Western Week End at Honoka'a is a fun-filled weekend with a Western theme. It includes a cookout, parade, rodeo, and dance.

The annual **Spring Arts Festival** held at the Wailoa Center in Hilo is a juried art show featuring mixed media artwork by Big Island artists.

June

King Kamehameha Day, June 11, is a state holiday honoring Kamehameha the Great, a Big Island native son, with festivities on all islands. Check local papers for times and particulars. Kailua-Kona is hospitable with a *ho'olaule'a* (large festive party), parades, art demonstrations, entertainment, and contests.

Hilo flashes its brilliant colors with the **Annual Hilo Orchid Society Show,** at the Hilo Civic Auditorium, and the **Annual Big Island Bonsai Show,** Wailoa Center, Hilo (both sometimes scheduled for early July).

Bon Odori, also called O Bon Festival, the Japanese festival of departed souls, features dances and candlelighting ceremonies held at numerous Buddhist temples throughout the island. These festivities change yearly and can be held anytime from late June to early August.

July

Every year on the weekend closest to July 1, the weeklong **Pu'uhonua O Honaunau National Historical Park Annual Cultural Festival** is held at the national park south of Kealakekua Bay. This free event features traditional Hawaiian arts and crafts, music, dance, and food, and everyone is welcome.

The week of the **Fourth of July** offers the all-American sport of rodeo along with parades. Don't miss the **July 4 Parker Ranch Rodeo,** Paniolo Park, Waimea. The epitome of rodeo by Hawaii's top cowboys is set at the Parker Ranch.

Annual Na'alehu Rodeo, in Na'alehu, includes rodeo events, motorcycle and dune buggy races, lu'au, food booths, and Hawaiian entertainment.

The **Big Island Marathon** in Hilo consists of a full and half marathon starting and ending at the Hilo Hawaiian Hotel.

The **International Festival of the Pacific** features a "Pageant of Nations" in Hilo. Folk dances, complete with authentic costumes from throughout Asia and the Pacific, add excitement

---

BIG ISLAND ARTS AND CULTURE INFORMATION

East Hawai'i Cultural Council, Box 1312, Hilo, HI 96721, 808/961-5711, publishes *Art Centering,* a monthly newsletter of what's happening artistically and culturally on the Big Island. The publication includes a good monthly calendar of events with listings from exhibit openings to movies. Associated groups are the East Hawai'i Cultural Center, Big Island Art Guild, Big Island Dance Council, Hawai'i Concert Society, and Hilo Community Players.

Volcano Art Center, 808/967-8222, promotes visual and performing arts at Volcano and offers community art classes and workshops. The Art Center publishes the *Volcano Gazette,* a monthly newsletter detailing events it sponsors.

to the festivities. Other events include a parade, hula, and food from the Pacific.

The **Kilauea Volcano Wilderness Run** is held over rough lava, in and out of volcanic craters, and through 'ohi'a and fern forests within the Hawaii Volcanoes National Park.

With well-known headliners and newcomers alike, the annual **Big Island Slack Key Guitar Festival** is held in Hilo, sponsored by the East Hawai'i Cultural Center.

August

The first August weekend is **Establishment Day.** Traditional hula and lei workshops are presented at the Pu'ukohala Heiau in Kawaihae, where traditional artifacts are also on display.

The **Pro-Am Billfish Tournament,** held in the waters off Kona, precedes and is a qualifying meet for the more famous annual **Hawaiian International Billfish Tournament,** held about one week later. A world-renowned tournament and the Big Daddy of them all, the HIBT has been held every year since 1959. Since the beginning, the tournament organizer has been Peter Fithian. More than 90 percent of the fish caught are tagged and released. A percentage of the event's proceeds goes to the Pacific Ocean Research Foundation.

August 17 is **Admission Day,** a state holiday recognizing the day that Hawaii became a state.

Kailua-Kona hosts the annual **Queen Lili'uokalani Long Distance Canoe Race** every Labor Day weekend. Single-hull, double-hull, and one-person events are held over a two-day period. This 18-mile race is the longest in the state, with more than 2,500 paddlers in competition. Head up the coast to Kawaihae for the **Moikeha Hawaiian Sailing Canoe Race.**

September

In early September don't miss the **Parker Ranch Round-Up Rodeo** at Paniolo Park in Waimea.

The **Hawaii County Fair** at Hilo is an old-time fair held on the grounds of Hilo Civic Auditorium.

Aloha Festivals celebrates Hawaii's own "intangible quality," *aloha.* This two-month-long series of several dozen individual festivals includes parades, lu'au, athletic competitions, historical pageants, balls, and various entertainment. The spirit of *aloha* is infectious and all are welcome.

Check local papers and tourist literature for happenings near you, or go online to www.alohafestivals.com.

October

When they really "wanna have fun," super-athletes come to the **Ironman World Triathlon Championship** at Kailua-Kona. A 2.4-mile open-ocean swim, followed by a 112-mile bike ride, topped off with a 26.2-mile full marathon, is their idea of a good day. For information contact the Ironman Office, 808/329-0063, website: www.ironmanlive.com.

Lasting two weekends, the **Hamakua Music Festival** features island musicians and those of national fame. Jazz, classical music, and Hawaiian music are performed. For information, call 808/775-3378, or check www.hamakuamusicfestival.com.

November

Taste the best coffee commercially grown in the United States at the annual **Kona Coffee Cultural Festival** in Kailua-Kona. Parades, arts and crafts, and ethnic foods and entertainment are part of the festivities. It's the oldest food festival in the state—the 30th was held in 2000. For information, call 808/326-7820; website: www.konacoffeefest.com.

November 11, **Veterans Day,** is a national holiday celebrated by parades.

Christmas in the Country, atop Hawai'i's volcano, is a delight. Merrymakers frolic in the crisp air or relax around a blazing fire, drinking hot toddies. Plenty of arts and crafts, food, and Santa for the *keiki* round out the event. Contact the Volcano Art Center, Hawaii Volcanoes National Park, 808/967-8222.

The **Hawaii International Film Festival** showcases new and engaging films, mainly from Asian and Pacific Rim countries. On the Big Island, these films show at the Aloha Theater in Kainaliu, King Kamehameha's Kona Beach Hotel and Keauhou Cinemas in Kona, the Palace Theater and Hawaii Naniloa Hotel in Hilo, Honoka'a Peoples Theater, and the Na'alehu Theater. Call 800/752-8193 for information; website: www.hiff.org.

December

The people of Hilo celebrate a New England

BIG ISLAND MUSEUMS

Pacific Tsunami Museum, 130 Kamehameha Ave., 808/935-0926, open Mon.–Sat. 10 A.M.–4 P.M., is housed in the art deco–style First Hawaiian Bank building near the bayfront in Hilo. It's dedicated to those who lost their lives in the destructive tidal waves that hit and virtually destroyed the city in 1946 and 1960. Visual displays, video film, and computer links add to the educational focus of this organization, but most moving are the photographs of the last two terribly destructive tsunamis to hit the city. Admission is $5 adults, $4 seniors, and $2 students.

Hulihe'e Palace, a Victorian-style building in downtown Kailua-Kona, 808/329-1877, open Mon.–Fri. 9 A.M.–4 P.M., Saturday and Sunday 10 A.M.–4 P.M., is one of three royal palaces in the state. Used by the Hawaiian monarchs until 1916, it now contains countless items owned and used by the royal families. It's a treasure house and well worth a look. Adult admission is $5, $4 senior, $1 student. Guided or self-guided tours.

Parker Ranch Historic Homes, a few miles outside Waimea, 808/885-5433, is open daily 10 A.M.–5 P.M.; $7.50 admission. Pu'opelu, the ranch home of the Parker family, is a structure to be appreciated in and of itself, but it also houses artwork of world-prominent European artists, Chinese glass art, and antique furniture collected by Richard Smart, the last of the Parker line. Reconstructed on the grounds is Mana House, the original Parker ranch home from 1847, also open for viewing.

Kamuela Museum, west of downtown Waimea, 808/885-4724, open daily 8 A.M.–5 P.M., is a wonderfully eclectic private collection of Hawaiiana, upcountry *paniolo* life, Asian artifacts, and photos of the Parker family. This museum has many items that you might expect to find in a much larger big-city museum. Admission is $5, $2 for children under 12.

Parker Ranch Museum in the visitor center at the Parker Ranch Shopping Center, 808/885-7655, is

open daily 9 A.M.–5 P.M. (tickets until 4 P.M.) for adults $5, children $3.75. This is an exhibit of Parker family history and a brief history of ranching and *paniolo* life on the Big Island. Many display items plus a video are offered.

Kona Historical Society Museum, just south of the town of Kealakekua, 808/323-3222, is open Mon.–Fri. 9 A.M.–3 P.M.; $2 admission. Housed in a native stone and lime mortar general store from 1875, this museum has a small collection of glassware and photographs. An archive of Kona-area historical items is housed in the basement and is open by appointment only.

Lyman Mission House and Museum, 276 Haili St. in Hilo, 808/935-5021, open Mon.–Sat. 9 A.M.–4:30 P.M., first opened in 1932. The main building is a New England–style frame structure from 1839, the oldest wood-frame house on the island. It contains furniture and household goods from Reverend and Mrs. Lyman and other missionary families on the island. In a modern annex is a collection of Hawaiian artifacts and items of daily use in the Island Heritage Gallery and a very fine collection of rocks and minerals in the Earth Heritage Gallery. Admission $7 adults, $3 children 6–18.

Onizuka Space Center, 808/329-3441, is at the Kona International Airport. Its hours are 8:30 A.M.–4:30 P.M. daily except Thanksgiving, Christmas, and New Year's Day; $3 admission. This center is a memorial to Hawaii's first astronaut and a space education facility for adults and children. It includes interactive and static exhibits, models, audiovisual displays, and lots of reading material.

The **Laupahoehoe Train Museum,** 36-2377 Mamalahoa Hwy., near the Laupahoehoe Lookout, 808/962-6300, is a small but wonderful view into the life and times of trains and life along the train line of the Hamakua Coast. The museum is open daily 9 A.M.–4:30 P.M.

Christmas in memory of the missionaries with **A Christmas Tradition,** held at the Lyman House Memorial Museum, Hilo, 808/935-5021. On **New Year's Eve** hold onto your hat, be-

cause they do it up big in Hawaii. The merriment and alcohol flow all over the islands. Firecrackers are illegal, but they go off everywhere. Beware of hangovers and drunken drivers.

SPORTS AND RECREATION

You'll have no problem having fun on the Big Island. Everybody goes outside to play. You can camp and hike, drive golf balls over lagoons, smack tennis balls at private and public courts, ski, snorkel, windsurf, gallop a horse, bag a wild turkey, spy a rare bird, or latch onto a marlin that'll tail-walk across a windowpane sea. Choose your sport and have a ball.

BEACHES

Being the youngest island, Hawai'i has far fewer beaches than any of the other major Hawaiian Islands, and except for a handful of these shoreline retreats, they are small affairs often with volcanic rock intrusions. All beaches are open to the public. Most are accessed through beach parks, but some access is over private property. All hotels and condominiums must by law offer pathway access to beaches they front, and each has some parking set aside for public use.

Generally speaking, beaches and shorelines on the north and west have high surf conditions and strong ocean currents during winter months—use extreme caution—and those on the south and east experience some high surf during the summer months. A few county beaches have lifeguards. For lifeguard hours and locations, call the Department of Parks and Recreation, 808/961-8694. At some beaches, flags warn of ocean conditions. A yellow flag means use caution. A half-yellow, half-red sign signifies caution because of strong winds. A red flag indicates hazardous water conditions—beach closed, no swimming. In addition, yellow and black signs are sometimes posted to indicate other warnings: dangerous shore break, high surf spot, strong currents, presence of jellyfish, or beach closed.

Before you head to the beach, take a drive to the local shop for a cheap woven beach mat. Whalers General Store, ABC markets, other sundries shops, Longs Drug, Wal-Mart, Kmart, and the like have them for $1–1.50. Hotel sundries shops sometimes also carry the exact same thing for about a dollar more. On occasion, condos have them to borrow, and often B&Bs and vacation rental homes have them available for guests—but don't count on it.

East Side

The east side has few accessible beaches. The best are in the Hilo area. Hilo Waterfront beach is a nice long crescent of gray-white sand, but few use this beach for swimming. Locals head east to **Onekahakaha Beach, Leleiwi Beach,** and **Richardson Beach,** which are all small pockets of white sand bound by rugged lava shoreline. The only other beaches of note along this coast are the long black-sand **Waipi'o Beach** in Waipi'o Valley and the smaller **Waimanu Beach** in a valley farther north. The use of either is discouraged unless the water is glassy smooth.

South Side

Black sand typifies the beaches along the south coast. The best, near Kalapana and Kaimu, have been overrun by lava flows in the past 15 years. Yet, beaches that still draw swimmers in Puna are **Isaac Hale Beach** (also called Pohoiki) and the half-hidden **Kehena Beach.** In Ka'u, the best in the region and easiest to get to is **Punalu'u Beach.** Near the windswept South Point is **Green Sand Beach,** an oddity for sure but more to look at than for swimming, unless it's totally calm.

West Side

Miloli'i and **Ho'kena** are two local, fairly isolated beaches in South Kona. Although they're fine for a day out, you have to make an effort to get to either. North Kona has more beaches and is much more easily accessible: **Kahalu'u Beach** is the first, and while the swimming is fine the snorkeling is better. **Disappearing Sands Beach** (also called White Sand Beach) is also good when the sand is there; it's a popular spot for boogie boarders. Perhaps the most gentle for kids and an all-around good place to have your first dip into the Kona waters is **Kailua Bay Beach** in front of the King Kamehameha's Kona Beach Hotel. While there are pockets of sand beach at the Old Kona Airport State Recreation Area, Kaloko-Honokohau National Historical Park, and Kona Coast State Park, better beaches lie farther north.

The best beaches on the island dot the Kohala Coast. An almost perfectly crescent-shaped white-sand beach fronts the Kona Village Resort. The sandy bottom, clear water, and palm fringed shore let you know you're floating in paradise. Longer and straighter is the ever-popular **'Anaeho'omalu Beach,** which fronts the Outrigger Waikoloa Beach Resort. Not only is the swimming good here, but you can indulge in a wide variety of water sports. Diminutive beaches hug the coast at the Mauna Lani Resort, but the island's best beaches are just a few miles away. **Hapuna Beach** and **Mauna Kea Beach** are the crown jewels of Big Island beaches: white sand, gentle slopes, and long and narrow sand strips. Swimming is great and snorkeling is also noteworthy. If you had to choose one beach as the premier swimming beach on the island, it would definitely be one of these two. Both are fronted by first-class luxury hotels, and Hapuna Beach also has public facilities.

SCUBA AND SNORKELING

Scuba
Those in the know consider the deep diving along the steep drop-offs of Hawaii's geologically young coastline some of the best in the state. The ocean surrounding the Big Island has not had a chance to turn the relatively new lava to sand, which makes the visibility absolutely perfect, even to depths of 150 feet or more. There's also 60–70 miles of coral belt around the Big Island, which adds up to a magnificent diving experience. Only advanced divers should attempt deep-water dives, but beginners and snorkelers will have many visual thrills inside the protected bays and coves.

Scuba Shops and Tour Companies
About two dozen companies on the Big Island, mostly in Kona, offer scuba instruction, escorted dives, and scuba equipment rental.

One of the best outfits to dive with on the Big Island is **Dive Makai** in Kona, 808/329-2025, website: www.divemakai.com, operated by Tom Shockley and Lisa Choquette. These very experienced divers have run this service for years and have many dedicated customers. Both Tom and Lisa are conservationists who help preserve the fragile reef. They've worked very hard with the Diver's Council to protect dive sites from fish collectors and to protect the reef from destruction by anchors. Their motto, "We care," is not a trite saying, as they continue to preserve the reef for you and your children.

Another excellent diving outfit is **Jack's Diving Locker,** 75-5819 Ali'i Dr. in the Coconut Grove Marketplace, 808/329-7585 or 800/345-4807, website: www.divejdl.com, a responsible outfit that does a good job of watching out for its customers and taking care of the reef. Owners Teri and Jeff Leicher, along with their crew, run diving and snorkeling excursions along the Kona Coast from Kealakekua Bay to Keahole Point, which takes in more than 50 dive sites (most of which have permanent moorings to protect the reef from damage by anchoring). Jack's also specializes in snorkel sales and rentals, scuba equipment rentals, and certification classes. You can do a five-hour snorkel/sail on the *Blue Dolphin* or a multi-tank day or night dive on the larger *Na Pali Kai II.*

Eco-Adventures at the King Kamehameha's Kona Beach Hotel in Kailua, 808/329-7116 or 800/949-3483, offers a daily morning, afternoon, and night boat charters as well as beach dives. Its three-day open-water certification with all gear, books, and two days of diving runs $425. Hawaiian Divers is conveniently located and offers good value for your money.

Big Island Divers, 75-5467 Kaiwi St., 808/329-6068 or 800/488-6068, website: www.bigislanddivers.com, departing from Honokohau Harbor on its custom-built 35-foot dive boat, offers a very inexpensive scuba certification course that's given on four consecutive Saturdays or Wednesdays, so you must intend to stay on the Big Island for that length of time. The normal four-day course costs about $450. Dives range from a two-tank two-location dive for $70 to a three-tank three-location dive for $110. Complete snorkel gear is for rent, and introductory and night dives are available.

Kohala Divers, along Rt. 270 in the Kawaihae Shopping Center, 808/882-7774, website: www.kohaladivers.com, open daily 8 A.M.–5 P.M.,

BIG ISLAND

offers scuba certification for $300, snorkel rentals for $10, and scuba rentals for $22. Kohala leads two-tank dives for $85 and will take snorkelers along if there's room on the boat ($40). It's a bit far to go from Kailua-Kona but great if you're staying at one of the Kohala resorts or in Waimea. A full-service dive shop, this company is the farthest north along the Kohala Coast.

Kona Coast Divers, 74-5614 Palani Rd., Kona, 808/329-8802 or 800/562-3483, website: www.konacoastdivers.com, is owned and operated by longtime Kona Coast diver Jim Robertson. This outfit is efficient and to the point. Rates are: two-tank boat dive $70, night dive $55, introductory dive $95, boat riders and snorkelers $30. Full underwater gear is sold and rented.

Sandwich Isle Divers, 808/329-9188, website: www.sandwichisledivers.com, is owned and operated by Steve and Larry, longtime Kona Coast divers who know all the spots. They have a custom, six-passenger dive boat, great for small personalized trips for avid divers. Rates for instruction are competitive; day and night dives are available. Their office is in the Kona Marketplace.

Aloha Dive Company, 808/325-5560 or 800/708-5662, website: www.alohadive.com, operates out of Kona. Introductory dives run $125, a manta night dive $60, "local" dives $85, and "remote" dives $115–125.

If you want only a shore dive, try **Ocean Eco Tours,** 808/323-9695, website: www.oceanecotours.com. This company says it specializes in beginners. Certification courses taught.

Torpedo Tours Hawaii, 808/938-0405, website: www.torpedotours.com, does shore and boat dives and certification. Small groups are important here. To provide a little extra power, this company provides "torpedo" scooters for some dives, $55–99 from shore or $129 for a two-tank torpedo dive from a boat.

Kona Aggressor II is a "live-aboard" dive boat, 808/329-8182 or 800/344-5662, website: www.aggessor.com or www.pac-aggressor.com, departing Kona every Saturday for six days of diving along the Kona Coast toward South Point. Passengers dive up to five times per day and night, as the *Aggressor* completely fulfills its motto to "Eat, Sleep, and Dive." This is the Cadillac of dive cruises, and everything on board is taken care of. Rates run $1,895 per person.

The **Nautilus Dive Center,** 382 Kamehameha Ave., Hilo, 808/935-6939, website: www.downtownhilo.com/nautilus, open Mon.–Sat. 9 A.M.–4 P.M., is one of the longest established dive companies on the Hilo side. This full-service dive center offers instruction, rentals, and guided dives at prices that are less expensive than on the more frequented Kona side. But don't be fooled—the Hilo side has some very good diving as well. Two popular spots are Leleiwi Beach and Richardson Beach.

Two other shops in Hilo that offer boat and shore dives as well as other water activities are **Aquatic Perceptions,** 111 Banyan Dr.,808/935-9997, and **Planet Ocean Watersports,** 808/935-7277, 200 Kanoelehua Ave., website: www.hawaiidive.com.

Snorkeling

Kona's most popular snorkel sites include Kona Coast State Park, Pawai Bay, Disappearing Sands Beach, Kahalu'u Beach Park, Kealakekua Bay by the Captain Cook monument (often said to be the best on the island), and Pu'uhonua O Honaunau (outside the park boundaries). In the Kohala area, seek out Waikoloa Beach Park, Hapuna Beach Park, Mauna Kea Beach Park, Spencer Beach Park, Mahukona Beach Park, and Kapa'a Beach Park. Leleiwi Beach Park Richardson's Beach in Hilo area are favorites. Puna best snorkeling spot is Isaac Hale Beach Park.

Snorkel Rental

Larger hotels and some condos often have snorkel equipment for guests, but if it isn't free, it always costs more than if you rent it from a dive shop. Many activities booths and virtually all dive shops rent snorkel gear at competitive rates. Depending upon the quality of gear, snorkel gear runs from about $3 an hour or $9 a day to $9 an hour or $30 a day. Many of the places that rent snorkel gear also rent boogie boards, usually at about $5–8 a day.

Good old **Snorkel Bob's,** 808/329-0770, website: www.snorkelbob.com, in the parking lot right in front of Huggo's Restaurant in Kailua, offers some of the best deals for snorkel rental in Hawaii (free snorkeling maps and advice), and this gear can be taken interisland and turned in at any Snorkel Bob's location. De-

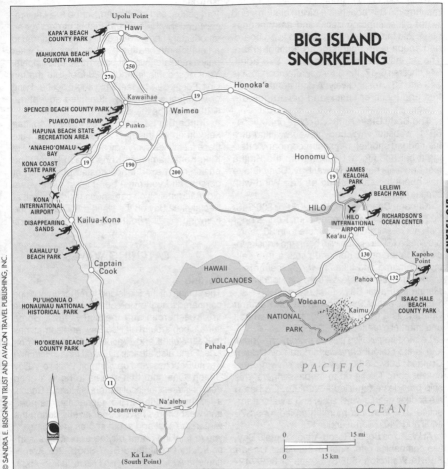

BIG ISLAND SNORKELING

Upolu Point
Hawi
KAPA'A BEACH COUNTY PARK
MAHUKONA BEACH COUNTY PARK
270
250
Kawaihae
Honoka'a
19
Waimea
SPENCER BEACH COUNTY PARK
PUAKO/BOAT RAMP
HAPUNA BEACH STATE RECREATION AREA
Puako
'ANAEHO'OMALU BAY
KONA COAST STATE PARK
19
190
200
Honomu
19
JAMES KEALOHA PARK
LELEIWI BEACH PARK
HILO
KONA INTERNATIONAL AIRPORT
Kailua-Kona
HILO INTERNATIONAL AIRPORT
RICHARDSON'S OCEAN CENTER
DISAPPEARING SANDS
Kea'au
KAHALU'U BEACH PARK
Captain Cook
HAWAII VOLCANOES
130
Kapoho Point
132
Pahoa
PU'UHONUA O HONAUNAU NATIONAL HISTORICAL PARK
Volcano
Kaimu
ISAAC HALE BEACH COUNTY PARK
NATIONAL
HO'OKENA BEACH COUNTY PARK
PARK
Pahala
PACIFIC
11
Na'alehu
OCEAN
Oceanview
0   15 mi
0   15 km
Ka Lae (South Point)

MooN

BIG ISLAND

pending on the type, snorkel gear will be $2.50–9 a day or $9–35 a week.

Jack's Diving Locker, 808/329-7585, along Ali'i Dr. in Kailua-Kona has snorkel, mask, and fins for $7.50 for 24 hours.

In Hilo, look for snorkel gear at **Nautilus Dive Center,** 382 Kamehameha Ave. at the edge of the downtown strip, 808/935-6939, where snorkel gear runs $5 a day. Also in Hilo, **Aquatic Perceptions,** near the Naniloa Hotel on Banyan Dr., 808/935-9997, rents a snorkel set for $6 a day.

Snorkel Boats

Snorkel cruises can be booked through the various activities centers along the Kona and Kohala coasts and at your hotel travel desk. Snorkeling, scuba, and snuba excursions are also provided by the following. The **Fair Wind,** 808/322-2788 or 800/677-9461 off-island, website: www.fair-wind.com, a well-established company with a 60-foot catamaran, has a great reputation and is sure to please. Its boat leaves daily from magnificent Keauhou Bay and stops at Kealakekua Bay in front of the Captain Cook monument. This boat has a diving platform and water slide, sunning deck, and easy access steps into the water. All equipment is on board, and snuba is an option for an additional fee. The 4.5-hour morning cruise runs $79 adult, $44 children 6–17; the 3.5-hour afternoon tour is $48 and $31, respectively. A continental breakfast and lunch or snack and beverages are served.

The Body Glove, 808/326-7122 or 800/551-8911, website: www.bodyglovehawaii.com, a full-fledged snorkel and scuba company offering a bar and lunch, departs from the Kailua pier and sails north to Pawai Bay. Body Glove has about the same setup as Fair Wind with similar rates.

Kamanu Charters, 808/329-2021 or 800/348-3091, website: www.kamanu.com, Kona's original snorkel sail, in business more than 30 years, provides a full day of fun with beer and snacks included in the price. Kamanu pilots a true sailing catamaran and takes fewer passengers—maximum of 24. Sails leave from the Honokohau Marina for Pawai Bay at 9 A.M. and 1:30 P.M., $48 adults and $29 for kids under 12. Kamanu Charters is a good choicesfor a fun-filled sail and snorkel experience.

Leaving from Kailua pier on a morning snorkel tour is the 60-foot *Lanakila* trimaran by **Dream Cruises,** 808/326-6000, website: www.dreamcruises.com. Taking up to 49 passengers, this ship provides a fun-filled adventure. On board are snorkel gear, a water slide, and a water trampoline. The four-hour morning cruise runs $70 adult and $40 children under 17.

At Waikoloa Beach Resort Anaeho'omalu Bay, two companies offer snorkel services. **Ocean Sports Waikoloa,** 808/886-9999 or 888/742-5234, website: www.hawaiioceansports.com, website: and **Red Sail Sports,** 808/886-2878 or 877/733-7245,www.redsail.com, both run morning snorkel tours from the beach on sleek catamarans for about $60. Red Sail also has sailings from Hapuna Beach.

A twist on the usual snorkel adventure is offered by **Torpedo Tours Hawaii,** 808/938-0405, which offers snorkel tours on the Kona Coast with battery-powered "torpedo" motors that pull you through the water at 2 mph. Shore- and boat-based excursions run $46–99.

Snuba

Part scuba, part snorkeling, snuba is a fairly recent underwater concept that is perfect for an introductory underwater adventure. Tethered to a flotation raft bearing a scuba tank, you wear only a regulator, weight belt, mask, and flippers. Your descent is limited to 20 feet, but the fun isn't. For those who feel timid about scuba diving or who just want a new, fun-filled adventure, snuba might be the answer.

Snuba Big Island, Inc., 808/326-7446, can set you up for this new adventure. Dives take place four times every day at the beach in front of King Kamehameha's Kona Beach Hotel. The basic snuba experience costs about $59 per person, and you must be at least eight years old. Alternately, you can snuba (and snorkel) at Kealakekua Bay on the twice-daily sail with the Fairwind's sailing boat for $137.50 per person.

CATCHING WAVES

Surfing

The surfing off the Big Island is rather uninspiring compared to that off the other islands. The reefs are treacherous and the surf is lazy. Some surfers bob around off Hilo Bay, and sometimes in Kealakekua and Wailua Bays on the Kona side. Puna also attracts a few off Isaac Hale and Kaimu Beaches, and up north off Waipi'o Valley Beach. One spot that seems to have a good deal of interest for local surfers is Honoli'i Beach, a few miles north of Hilo. Generally, the north and west shores have better swells during the winter, the east and south shores in summer. If you're thinking about buying or renting a surfboard, try **Orchidland Surf Shop,** 262 Kamehameha Ave., in downtown Hilo, 808/935-1533, or **Honolua Surf Co.,** 808/329-1001, at the Kona Inn Shopping Village in Kailua-Kona for starters. Be sure to ask there about what's happening with the water when you're on island. For surf lessons, try **Ocean Eco Tours,** 808/937-0494, in Hilo, or **Hawaii Lifeguard Surf Instructors,** 808/324-0442, on the Kona side.

Windsurfing

The Big Island seems nearly bereft of good windsurfing locations. By all accounts, 'Anaeho'omalu Bay at Waikoloa Beach Resort on the Kohala

Coast is the best place to sail. For instruction and rental equipment, check with **Ocean Sports Waikoloa,** 808/886-6666 or 888/742-5234, which rent boards at $20 an hour and gives 60 minutes of instruction for $45.

PARASAILING

UFO Parasailing, 808/325-5836 or 800/359-4836, website: www.ufoparasail.com, offers parasailing with a boat platform take-off and landing that's safe and easy for young and old alike. A "400 feet for seven minutes" atmospheric ride runs $45, and the "800 feet for 10 minutes" stratospheric ride is $55; there are reduced rates for early birds, and boat ride-alongs are $18. You, too, can dangle from a parachute and soar through the air. The boat leaves from the Kailua pier. Check in at the office across the street under Flashbacks Bar and Grill. Parasailing on the Big Island is done year-round.

OCEAN TOURS

Whether it's skimming across the ocean surface on a trim sloop, diving by submarine to view coral fields, or watching whales breach and play, many ocean tours excite visitors to the Big Island. Virtually all of these tours stay on the Kona side of the island. Some of the more popular options follow.

Zodiac
Captain Zodiac, 808/329-3199 or 800/422-7824, website: http://planet-hawaii.com/zodiac, will take you on a fantastic ocean odyssey beginning at Honokohau Small Boat Harbor just north of Kailua-Kona, from where you'll skirt the coast south all the way to Kealakekua Bay. A Zodiac is a very tough, motorized rubber raft. It looks like a big, horseshoe-shaped inner-tube that bends itself and undulates with the waves like a floating waterbed. These seaworthy craft, powered by twin Mercury 280s, have five separate air chambers for unsinkable safety. They'll take you for a thrilling ride down the Kona Coast, pausing along the way to whisk you into sea caves, grottoes, and caverns. The Kona Coast is also marked with ancient ruins and the re-

mains of villages, which the captains point out, and about which they relate historical anecdotes as you pass by. You stop at Kealakekua Bay, where you can swim and snorkel in this underwater conservation park. Round-trips depart at 8 A.M., and 1 P.M., take about four hours, and cost $67 adults, $54 children under 11. Captain Zodiac also provides a light tropical lunch of fresh exotic fruit, taro chips, fruit juice, iced tea, and sodas. All you need is a bathing suit, sun hat, towel, suntan lotion, camera, and sense of adventure.

Fair Wind, 808/332-2788, website: www.fair-wind.com, does similar tours on its 28-foot, rigid-bottom Zodiac raft, the *Orca,* but these tours leave from Kailua pier. Leaving at 8:30 A.M., morning tours run four hours with snorkel stops at Kealakekua Bay and one other location; $64 adult, $54 children. Three-hour afternoon tours start at 1 P.M. and make only the stop at Kealakekua Bay; $48 adult, $38 children.

Sea Quest, 808/325-5560, website: www.seaquesthawaii.com, runs a similar inflatable raft snorkel tour to Kealakekua Bay from Keauhou with numerous stops along the way to explore sea cave and other coastline features. Morning and afternoon departures cost $50–67.

Using a smaller inflatable raft for more intimate groups, **Dolphin Discoveries,** 808/322-8000, website: www.dolphindescoveries.com, also offers raft and snorkel trips to Kealakekua Bay from Keauhou Bay boat ramp. Morning and afternoon trips are given daily; $49–64 adult, $30–59 kids 5–15. These folks are very focused on the study of dolphins, whales, and other similar sea animals, so your trip will be educational. Part of your fee goes to support marine conservation programs.

Sailing
Sailing is a year-round adventure, and boats take advantage of the steady breezes and fine weather along the Kona Coast. In season (November–April), sailing companies offer fascinating whale-watching adventures as part of the bargain.

For a day of snorkeling, sailing, and whale-watching on a catamaran, contact **Kamanu Charters,** 808/329-2021, or **Dream Cruises,** 808/326-6000. From Waikoloa, **Ocean Sports**

BIG ISLAND

Waikoloa, 808/885-6666, and **Red Sail,** 808/886-2878, have snorkeling and whale-watching cruises several times per day. Mono-hulls are also used for true sailing experiences. Aside from Ocean Sports Waikoloa and Red Sail, **Honu Sail Charters,** 808/322-4668 runs half-day and sunset sail tours on its sleek sail-boat. Half-day tours including snorkeling and snacks run $80, while the sunset tour with *pu pu* is $60.

The *Maile,* berthed at Kawaihae Harbor, P.O. Box 44335, Kamuela, HI 96743, 808/326-5174 or 800/726-SAIL, is a 50-foot Gulfstar sloop available for luxury sailing charters and shorter-term whale-watching, snorkeling, and fishing expeditions. Skippered by Ralph Blancato, a U.S. Coast Guard–certified Master, the sloop offers competitive prices on half- or full-day charters, sunset sails, and long-term rental. Offering more than just a sailing trip, Blancato teaches his guests about marine life, reef ecology, and island environment. Aside from her commercial use, the *Maile* also functions as the research boat for both the Ocean Mammal Institute and the Oceanic Society.

Kayaking

Ocean kayaking has gained popularity in Hawaii in the last several years. Although the entire coastline would offer adventure for the expert kayaker, most try sections of the coast near Kealakekua Bay and east out of Hilo that offer excellent shoreline variation and great snorkeling.

While you can rent kayaks and go where you want, a few companies offer guided trips to exceptional places. Open-cockpit rental kayaks generally run about $25 for a single or $40 for a tandem, with all necessary gear and sometimes a car rack.

In Kailua, try **Ocean Safaris,** 808/326-4699, for half-day guided tours in the Keauhou area for $55 or an early-bird tour of Kailua Bay. Nearer to Kealakekua Bay are **Aloha Kayak Co.,** 808/322-2868 (in Honalo), and **Kona Boy's Kayaks,** 808/328-1234, and **Kealakekua Bay Kayak,** 808/323-3329 (in the town of Kealakekua).

For kayak rentals in Hilo, try **Aquatic Perceptions,** 808/933-1228, 111 Banyan Dr. near the Naniloa Hotel. Kayak rental starts at $15 for four hours single and goes up from there. The tours start at $25 per person. **Nautilus Dive Center** in Hilo, 382 Kamehameha Ave., 808/935-6939, rents quality kayaks at $25 a day.

A twist on the kayak business is offered by **Kohala Mountain Kayak Cruise,** P.O. Box 660, Kapa'au, HI 96755, 808/899-6922, website: www.kohalakayaks.com. On an outing with this company, you'll float several scenic miles of the Kohala irrigation flumes, over small ravines and through several tunnels in the remote, private lands of North Kohala. Completed in the early part of the 20th century and considered a feat of engineering, this 22-mile-long irrigation system (better known as the Kohala Ditch) supplied the Kohala Sugar mills with a steady supply of water until the plantation ceased business in 1975. Guided by experts using large, flat-bottom, double-hulled kayaks, you'll not only experience the beauty of the surrounding rainforest and rugged scenery but will also absorb a lesson in the history and culture of this area. No experience required. Bring an extra set of dry clothes. Floats are offered Mon.–Fri. at 9 A.M. and 1 P.M.; children 5–18 $65, adults $85. Meet at the office by the big banyan tree in Hawi.

Whale-Watching

Three-hour whale-watching tours on the 40-foot boat *Lady Ann* are offered by **Dan McSweeney's Whalewatching Adventures,** P.O. Box 139, Holualoa, HI 96725, 808/322-0028 or 888/WHALES6. While many are interested in looking only for the humpback whale, Dan, a marine biologist and whale researcher, takes visitors year-round so they can also learn about different kinds of whales and other ocean mammals that inhabit this coast. This is an educational trip, the best the island has to offer. If you want to see whales and learn about these beautiful mammals in the process, go with Dan. The *Lady Ann* leaves from the Honokohau Marina.

From December through May, most of the Zodiac, snorkel, scuba, catamaran, and sailing boats run whale-watching tours in addition to their other activities.

Glass-Bottom Boats

Captain Beans' Polynesian Cruise, 808/329-2955, is a Kona institution aboard its glass-bottom barge-like boat. Trips leave daily at 5:15 P.M. from Kailua Pier for $49 adults; age 21 and older only. During the very tame cruise you'll spot fish, listen to island music, and enjoy a sunset dinner. *Marian* of the **Kailua Bay Charter Company,** 808/324-1749, also does glass-bottom boat tours from the Kailua pier. With only 32 passengers, this cruise is much more personal. **Aloha Adventure Cruises,** 808/331-2992, runs a two-hour dolphin-watch/glass-bottom boat tour daily at 9 A.M. and noon from the Kailua pier for $44. Every weekday evening, the crew turns its attention above water and runs a sunset cruise departing at 5:30 P.M. This cruise features island music, *pu pu,* two cocktail drinks, and, of course, the fine sunset.

Submarines

Atlantis Submarine, 808/329-6626 or 800/548-6262, allows everyone to live out the fantasy of Captain Nemo on a silent cruise under the waves off Kailua-Kona. After checking in at the office at the King Square Shopping Center, a launch from Kailua Pier that takes you on a 10-minute cruise to the waiting submarine tethered offshore. You're given all of your safety tips on the way there. The underwater portion lasts about one-half hour. As you descend to 120 feet, notice that everything white, including teeth, turns pink because the ultraviolet rays are filtered out. The only colors that you can see clearly beneath the waves are blues and greens, because water is 800 times denser than air and filters out the reds and oranges. Everyone gets an excellent seat with a viewing port; there's not a bad seat in this 48-passenger submarine, so you don't have to rush to get on. Don't worry about being claustrophobic either—the sub is amazingly airy and bright, with aircraft-quality air blowers above the seats. Cruises run at 10 A.M., 11 A.M., 12:30 P.M., 1:30 P.M., and 2:30 P.M.; they cost $79 for adults and $39 for children.

The Atlantis sub is getting some competition from the *Nautilus II,* 808/326-2003, a semi-submersible very similar to the famous "ironsides" first used in the Civil War. This high-tech craft does not actually dive, but it offers a narrated one-hour tour in its spacious, air-conditioned lower deck, where you have great underwater scenes through its viewing windows. Departures leave daily from Kailua Pier. Cost is adults $29.95, children under 12 $19.95.

FISHING

Fishing Boats and Charters

The fishing around the Big Island's Kona Coast ranges from excellent to outstanding! It's legendary for marlin fishing, but there are other fish in the sea. Many charter boats with skilled captains and tested crews are ready, willing, and competent to take you out. The vast majority are berthed at Honokohau Small Boat Harbor just north of Kailua-Kona. The best times of year for marlin are July–September and January–March (when the generally larger females arrive). August is the optimum month. Rough seas can keep boats in for a few days during December and early January, but by February all are generally out.

To charter a boat, contact the individual captains directly, check at your hotel activities desk, or book through one of the following agencies. **Charter Services Hawaii,** operated by Ed Barry, 808/334-1881 or 800/567-5662, website: www.aloha.com/~hdc/charter, email: fishing@aloha.com, offers more than 50 boats in all sizes and price ranges. Ed also offers complete packages including room, car, and boat along with a cash prize of $1 million if you book through his agency and top the world record. If you're after a company that's knowledgeable about getting you onto a boat that will bring you to waters where you'll have the opportunity to catch one of the twirling and gigantic "big blues," this is the place to come. On the dock at Honokohau Harbor, the **The Charter Desk,** 808/329-5735 or 800/566-2487, and the **Charter Locker,** 808/326-2553, are two other reputable booking agencies that try to match you and your desire with the right boat and captain for best results. Other general booking agencies include: **Kona Activities Center** in Kailua-Kona, 808/329-3171, and **Kona Charter Skippers Assoc.,** P.O. Box 806, Kailua-Kona, HI 96740, 808/329-3600.

Most of the Island's 80 charter boats are berthed at Honokohau Harbor off Route 19, about midway between downtown Kailua and Kona Airport. Fish are weighed-in daily 11 A.M.–1 P.M. and again 3–5 P.M. Big fish are sometimes still weighed-in at Kailua Pier, in front of the King Kamehameha's Kona Beach Hotel for the benefit of the tourists. But Honokohau Harbor has

BIG ISLAND

eclipsed Kailua Pier, which is now tamed and primarily for swimmers, triathletes, and body-boarders. Congestion makes it difficult for charter boats to get in and out, so most the trade has moved up to Honokohau. A few boats also leave from Keauhou Bay and Kawaihae Harbor on the west side, and some use the river mouth in Hilo.

An excellent publication listing boats and general deep-sea fishing information is *Fins and Fairways, Hawaii,* P.O. Box 9014, Kailua-Kona, HI 96745, 808/325-6171 or 800/367-8014 from the Mainland, fax 808/325-6378, website: www.fishkona.com. This tabloid, published by Captain Tom Armstrong and available free at newsstands and in hotel/condo lobbies, is filled with descriptions of boats, phone numbers, captains' names, maps, and photos of recent catches. Write for subscription rates. For general fishing information and a listing of tournaments throughout the islands, pick up a copy of *Hawaii Fishing News* at a newsstand or supermarket.

Rainbow Falls

J.D. BISIGNANI

You can also contact **The Hawaiian International Billfish Assoc.,** 74-381 Kealakehe Pkwy, Kailua-Kona, HI 96740, 808/329-6155, for details on upcoming tournaments and on "what's biting and when."

Coastal and Freshwater Fishing

You don't have to hire a boat to catch fish! The coastline is productive too. *Ulua* are caught all along the coast south of Hilo, and at South Point and Kealakekua Point. Bays around the island produce *papio* and *halalu,* while *manini* and *'ama'ama* hit from Kawaihae to Puako. Hilo Bay is easily accessible to anyone, and the fishing is very exciting, especially at the mouth of the Wailuku River.

Licensed fishing is limited to the **Waiakea Public Fishing Area,** a state-operated facility in downtown Hilo. This 26-acre pond offers saltwater and brackish-water species. A license is required. You can pick one up at sporting goods stores or at the Division of Conservation and Resources Enforcement Office, 75 Aupuni St., Hilo, HI 96720, 808/974-6201.

CAMPING AND HIKING

The Big Island has the best camping in the state, with more facilities and less competition for campsites than on the other islands. More than three dozen parks fringe the coastline and sit deep in the interior; almost half offer camping. The others boast a combination of rugged hikes, easy strolls, self-guided nature walks, swimming, historical sites, and natural phenomena. The ones with campgrounds are state-, county-, and nationally operated, ranging from remote walk-in sites to housekeeping cabins. All require camping permits—inexpensive for the county and state parks, free for the national park. Camping permits can be obtained by walk-in application to the appropriate office or by writing. Although there is usually no problem obtaining sites, when writing, request reservations well in advance, allowing a minimum of one month for letters to go back and forth.

General Information

Most campgrounds have pavilions, fireplaces, toilets (sometimes pit), and running water, but usually no individual electrical hookups. Pavilions often have electric lights, but sometimes campers appropriate the bulbs, so it's wise to carry your own. Drinking water is available, but at times brackish water is used for flushing toilets and for showers, so read all signs regarding water. Back-country shelters have catchment water, but never hike without an adequate supply of your own. Cooking fires are allowed in established fire pits, but no wood is provided. Charcoal is a good idea. When camping in the mountains, be prepared for cold and rainy weather. Women, especially, should never hike or camp alone, and everyone should take precautions against theft, though it's not as prevalent as on the other islands.

County Parks

The county-maintained parks are open to the public for day-use, and permits are only required for overnight camping (tents or RVs). For information contact: Department of Parks and Recreation, County of Hawaii, 25 Aupuni St., Hilo, HI 96720, 808/961-8311. You can obtain a permit by mail or pick it up in person at Room 210, Mon.–Fri. 7:45 A.M.–4:30 P.M. (by 4 P.M. for permit application). If you'll be arriving after hours or on a weekend, have the permits mailed to you. Branch offices (most with reduced hours) are at Hale Halawai in Kailua-Kona, 808/327-3560; in Waimea Community Center in Waimea, 808/885-5454; in Yano Hall in Captain Cook, 808/323-3060; in Na'alehu, 808/929-9166, and in Pahala, 808/928-6206. Fees are $5 per day per adult; children 13–17, $2 per day; youngsters under 12, $1 per day. Pavilions for exclusive use are $25 per day with kitchen, $10 without. Camping is limited to one week for any one site June–August and for two weeks at any one site for the rest of the year. County parks that allow camping are as follows (counterclockwise around the island from Hilo): Kolekole, Laupahoehoe, Keokea, Kapa'a, Mahukona, Spencer, Ho'okena, Miloli'i, Whittington, Punalu'u, and Isaac Hale.

State Parks

Day-use of state parks is free, with no permit required, but you need one for tent camping and for cabins. Five consecutive nights is the limit for either camping or cabins at any one site. If you want a permit, at least one week's notice is

required regardless of availability. You can pick up your permit at the state parks office 8 A.M.–4 P.M. (applications accepted only 8 A.M.–noon), but again it saves time if you do it all by mail. Contact: Department of Land and Natural Resources, Division of State Parks, P.O. Box 936 (75 Aupuni St., Room 204), Hilo, HI 96721, 808/974-6200.

Tent camping is permitted only at Kalopa and MacKenzie State Recreation Areas. Kalopa SRA has cabins, and Hapuna Beach SRA has A-frame cabins. The four-person A-frames are a flat $20 per night. The group housekeeping cabins at Kalopa SRA are $55 for up to eight people. When writing for permits, specify exactly which facility you require, for how long, and for how many people. Mauna Kea State Park, along the Saddle Road near Pohakuloa Military Camp, is now closed to overnight use, but day use is still permitted.

Hawaii Volcanoes National Park

For overnight camping in Hawaii Volcanoes National Park, permits are required but available for free through the park visitors center. Your stay is limited to seven days per campground per year. A half dozen free walk-in primitive campsites and two trail cabins are in the park; you can't reserve them and you should expect to share them with other hikers. Applications for camping and hiking are taken only one day in advance before your first day. No open fires are permitted. At primitive campsites along the coast, there are three-sided, open shelters that offer only a partial covering against the elements. For information on camping and hiking in the park, write Hawaii Volcanoes National Park, P.O. Box 52, Hawaii National Park, HI 96718, or stop by the visitors center, 808/985-6000, open daily 7:45 A.M.–5 P.M.

A-frame cabins are provided at Namakani Paio Campground, and arrangements are made through Volcano House, Hawaii Volcanoes National Park, HI 96718, 808/967-7321 or 800/325-3535. This is the park's only drive-in campground, and tent camping is also possible. There is no charge for tent camping and no reservations are required. It's first-come, first-served. A cooking pavilion has fireplaces but no wood or drinking water, and there are no shower facilities for campers. The 10 small cabins available at

BIG ISLAND

BIG ISLAND

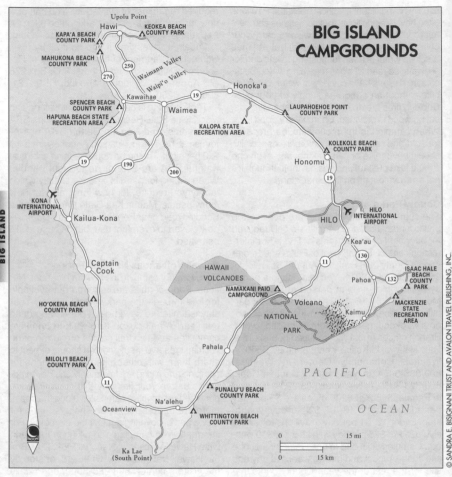

BIG ISLAND CAMPGROUNDS

© SANDRA E. BISIGNANI TRUST AND AVALON TRAVEL PUBLISHING, INC.

this campground can be reserved through Volcano House. Each sleeps up to four people and costs $40 single or double, $8 each for a third or fourth person. Linens, soap, towels, and a blanket are provided, but you would be wise to bring an extra sleeping bag as it can get cold. Each cabin contains one double bed, two single bunk beds, and an electric light, but no electrical outlets. There is a picnic table and barbecue grill for each cabin, but bring your own charcoal and cooking utensils. Check in at Volcano House after 3 P.M. and check out by noon.

Other Camping Areas

Camping is allowed by permit at three campsites on Bishop Estate land in Waipi'o Valley. For specific information and to obtain a free permit, contact the Kona office, 78-6831 Ali'i Dr., Suite 232, Kailua-Kona, HI 96740, 808/332-5300, at least two weeks in advance of your intended trip. They will send you an application, which you must sign and return. There are no toilets in the valley, so you must bring your own "Port-A-Potty" with you and take it out when you leave.

Camping is also permitted farther north along the coast in Waimanu Valley. Apply for a free camping permit from the Division of Forestry and Wildlife, P.O. Box 4849, Hilo, HI 96720, 808/974-4221, no more than one month in advance. Nine campsites are available, each with a fireplace, and three composting toilets are shared among the campers. Camping is limited to six nights.

Hiking the Big Island

Hiking on the Big Island is stupendous. There's something for everyone, from civilized walks to the breathtaking 'Akaka Falls to huff-puff treks to the summit of Mauna Loa. The largest number of trails, and the most outstanding according to many, lace Volcanoes National Park. After all, this is the world's most active volcano. You can hike across the crater floor, spurred on by the knowledge that it can shake to life at any moment. Or dip down off the mountain and amble the lonely trails in the Ka'u Desert or the remains of the King's Coastal Trail in Puna.

The most important thing to do before heading out in Volcanoes is to stop at park headquarters and inquire about trail conditions. Make absolutely sure to register, giving the rangers your hiking itinerary. In the event of an eruption, they will be able to locate you and send a helicopter if necessary. Follow this advice; your life may depend upon it! Everyone can enjoy vistas on Devastation Trail, Sulfur Bank, or at the Thurston Lava Tube without any danger whatsoever.

In the north sit Waipi'o, Waimanu, and Pololu Valleys. All offer secluded hiking and camping where you can play Robinson Crusoe on your own beach and gather island fruits from once-cultivated trees gone wild.

Bird-Watching and Hiking Tours

Hawaii has its fair share of birds. One type or other of the state's many species can be seen and heard wherever you are on the island, whether sunbathing along the shore, putting on a golf green, or hiking high on the mountainside. The most common will soon be obvious, but to see some of Hawaii's rare winged creatures you have to be adventurous, quiet, and willing to walk. Be sure to bring your binoculars. Anyone can appreciate birds where they are, but hardcore birders might want to go to spots where

the chance of getting a fleeting glimpse of that "rare one" will be greater.

If you're not familiar with good bird-watching spots on Hawaii, contact Rob or Cindy Pacheco at **Hawaii Forest & Trail**, 74-5035B Queen Ka'ahumanu Hwy., Kailua-Kona, HI 96740, 808/322-8505 or 800/464-1993, fax 808/331-8704, website: www.hawaii-forest.com, email: hitrail@aloha.net. This well-established naturalist company uses 4WD vehicles to get you to where the less common birds are. Its two exclusive bird-watching tours take you to the rainforests of the Pu'u O'o Ranch and Hakalau National Wildlife Refuge on the eastern slope of Mauna Kea. Other tours include the Valley Waterfall Adventure to the spectacular Pololu Valley of North Kohala, a Kahua cloud forest hike on the western slope of the Kohala Mountains, a tour to Hawaii Volcanoes National Park, a Ka'upulehu Cave adventure on Mt. Hualalai, a mule ride down into Pololu Valley, and the Mauna Kea Summit and Star Watching adventure. Other bird-watching and custom hiking tours can be arranged. All tours are limited to 10 people, are guided by knowledgeable naturalists, include food and beverage, provide all necessary equipment, and include pickup and drop-off at some accommodations in the Kona-Kohala area. The trips to Pololu Waterfall, Kahua Ranch cloud forest, and Ka'upulehu Cave run $89 adult or $79 children ages 8–12. These are half-day trips, as is the mule ride, which runs $95 and $85. Full-day bird-watching tours and the Mauna Kea summit trips are $139 adults and $99 children, while the volcano adventure runs $145 and $99. Any of these tours will certainly be a highlight of your vacation.

A well-established and reputable hiking company that will help you stretch your legs in the great outdoors yet have minimal impact on the land is **Hawaiian Walkways**, 808/775-0372 or 800/457-7759, website: www.hawaiianwalkways.com, email: hiwalk@aloha.net. This company also teaches you about the land you walk through and to appreciate its diversity and sanctity. Four basic hikes take you to Hawaii Volcanoes National Park to discover the secrets of the volcano, to the rim of Waipi'o Valley along a rediscovered mule trail for a peek into the Valley of Kings, up on the mist-shrouded slopes of Mt. Hualalai, and onto the broad expanse and into

BIG ISLAND

the hidden valleys of the Parker Ranch near Waimea. All except for the volcano hike go daily; the trip to the volcano runs on Thursday only or by request. Three of the hikes are easy to moderate, run 2–3 miles, and last 3–4 hours; the volcano discovery hike is longer at five hours and traverses about six miles. Custom hikes can also be arranged. The cloud forest botanical hike to Mt. Hualalai runs $75 per person, the Parker Ranch and Waipi'o Valley rim hikes $85. The rate varies ($85–135) for the volcano tour depending upon the length of hike requested. A small day pack, a walking stick, rain gear, lunch, and drinks are provided, as is expert commentary by knowledgeable guides. A hike with Hawaiian Walkways is not only good physical exercise, it's an introduction to the natural world of the Big Island. Two thumbs up.

For a more educational, "guided geologic adventure" on one of the earth's most changeable pieces of real estate, try **Hawaii Volcano GeoVentures,** P.O. Box 816, Volcano, HI 96785, tel./fax 808/985-9901, website: planet-hawaii. com/hea/volcano, email: geoventures@aloha.net.

Hawaii Earth Guides, 808/324-1717, focuses its hikes on Mt. Hualalai. Four different hikes from moderate to strenuous run 6–10 hours and offer you an up-close look at the terrain and wildlife on this often cloud-covered mountain.

The **Kona Hiking Club,** 808/328-8192, P.O. Box 569, Captain Cook, HI 96704, offers organized hikes on the island.

The Big Island **Audubon Society** group also runs periodic bird-watching excursions. For information, contact the group at P.O. Box 1371, Kailua-Kona, HI 96745, 808/329-9141.

Maps

On the Big Island, **Basically Books,** in downtown Hilo at 160 Kamehameha Ave., 808/961-0144, has an unbeatable selection of maps, including topographical maps for hikers, NOAA nautical and aeronautical charts, and Defense Mapping Agency charts of the Pacific. The collection covers most of the Pacific. On the Kona side, try **Big Island Marine, Inc.,** 73-4840 Kanalani St., #A-1, Kailua-Kona, HI 96740, 808/329-3719; or **Kona Marine,** 808/329-1012, in the Honokohau Small Boat Harbor, for nautical charts. The **Hawaii Forest and Trail** retail store, 808/331-8505, in Kailua

across from the entrance to Honokohau Marina, carries USGS maps.

HORSEBACK RIDING

Waipi'o Na'alapa Stables, 808/775-0419, offers one of the most unique rides on Hawai'i, with stables in the valley. The owner and her family have lived in Waipi'o Valley for over 25 years and know its history, geology, and legends intimately. There is pickup service from Kukuihaele "up top" for the 9:30 A.M. and 1 P.M. rides; $75 per person for 2.5 hours. If you have time, don't miss this wonderful adventure!

Waipi'o on Horseback, 808/775-7291, also offers horseback riding through fabulous Waipi'o Valley. These sightseeing rides ($75 for adult and $55 for kids) are good for all riding levels. Rides at 9:30 A.M. and 1:30 P.M. last 2.5 hours.

For a ride up on Waipi'o's rim, looking down into Hawai'i's largest and most spectacular valley, try **Waipi'o Ridge Stables,** 808/775-1007 or 808/492-4746, website: www.topofwaipio.com/horse.htm. This outfit offers a 2.5-hour rim ride to valley vistas, through former sugarcane land and past taro fields. The five-hour ride goes beyond this ride with a side trip to a waterfall where you stop for a swim and lunch. Rides leave at 8:45 A.M. and 12:45 P.M. from Waipi'o Valley Artworks in Kukuihaele.

Enjoyable rides are also offered by the **Mauna Kea Resort Stables** (for nonguests also), 808/882-4288, in Waimea—turn between K.M. Seeds and Ace Hardware and follow the signs. The resort has an arrangement with the Parker Ranch, which supplies a *paniolo* to guide you over the quarter-million acres of open range on the slopes of Mauna Kea, morning or afternoon. The stable is open Mon.–Sat. 9 A.M.–3 P.M. Rates are $40 per person for a one-hour ride and $70 for the two-hour ride; special trail rides available on request. Eight years old is the minimum age for riders; 210 pounds is the maximum weight.

Paniolo Riding Adventures, 808/889-5354, offers horseback riding on a working ranch in the Kohala Mountains north of Waimea. With your comfort in mind, Paniolo offers chaps, rain slickers, cowboy hats, and fleece saddle covers to keep you happy where the sun don't shine. Prices vary according to ride chosen, from novice

Sheri Hannum of Waipo Na'alapa Trail Rides

tain Cook. The wranglers lead you (4–6 people maximum) on a custom trail ride down to Captain Cook's Monument on the shores of Kealakekua Bay. This four-hour trip, departing at 9 A.M. (two hours of actual riding), includes snorkeling in the bay, along with a delicious picnic lunch. The price is $95.

Rain Forest Trailrides, 808/322-7126, takes you on horseback across the face of the Hualalai Mountains. Open daily, 9 A.M.–5 P.M., rides last 1–2.5 hours (the latter with lunch included) for $45–80.

Kapapala Ranch offers excursions onto its working ranch in Ka'u between the town of Pahala and the upper slopes of Mauna Loa. Rides run $65 for the two-hour experience. The ranch will also arrange overnight camping trips on the property that can be done by horse, hiking, pack mule, or vehicle. For reservations, call 808/968-6585.

Volcano Ranch offers several horseback adventures in Volcano Village. Options are the Village Ride, Ranch Ride, Roundup, and a trip to South Point. Rides range from two hours for $50 to four hours for $160. Contact the Volcano Inn in Volcano Village, 808/967-7293 or 800/997-2292.

Horse-Drawn Wagon Rides

Waipio Valley Wagon Tours, 808/775-9518, owned and operated by Peter Tolin, is a mule-drawn tour of the magnificent Waipi'o Valley. The 90-minute tours leave four times daily at 9:30 and 11:30 A.M., 1:30 and 3:30 P.M. The cost is $40 adults or $20 children under 12, including transportation down into the valley.

Wagon rides of a different sort are now offered at the Parker Ranch in Waimea. A wonderful family outing, these tame, 45-minute rides leave weekdays from the Parker Ranch Visitors Center every hour 10 A.M.–2 P.M. Tues.–Sat. and show you a portion of the working ranch up close. Children ages 3–12 ride for $12, while adults pay $15. No reservations are needed, but you can call the visitors center at 808/885-7655 for information.

Mule Rides

The only commercial mule ride on the Big Island is offered by **Hawaii Forest & Trail,** 808/322-8881. This company, which also offers various hiking and birding tours, takes riders on these sure-footed beasts into Pololu Valley and the

to cowpoke; daily rides are 2.5 and four hours long. After your guide matches you with an appropriate steed you head out onto the 11,000 acre range.

Kohala Na'alapa Stables, 808/889-0022, offers open range rides onto the historic Kahua and Kohala Ranch, high in the Kohala Mountains. Rides are offered daily at 9 A.M. and 1:30 P.M.; 2.5-hour rides are priced $75, 1.5-hour rides $55.

Using horses from its own working ranch in Waimea, **Dahana Ranch,** 808/885-0057, gives riders free-range trail rides on its own property. Rides go five times a day; 1.5-hour rides are $55, 2.5-hour rides are $100 but include a barbecue lunch. Experienced or not, no problem; riders from age three and up and those weighing up to 300 pounds are okay. Good upcountry range landscape.

Kings' Trail Rides O'Kona, 808/323-2388, website: www.konacowboy.com, has an office along Route 11, at mile marker 111, high above the Kona Coast between Kealakekua and Cap-north end of the island, starting from the old Kohala Ditch Company mule station. The ride takes you about 500 feet down the valley side to the black-sand beach of the valley mouth. These three-hour tours run twice daily; $95 adults, $85 kids 8–12.

BICYCLING

Pedaling around the Big Island can be both fascinating and frustrating. If you circle the island, it's nearly 300 miles around on its shortest route. Most pick an area and bike there. Generally, roads are well paved, but the shoulders are often torn up. With all the triathletes coming to Hawaii, and all the fabulous, little-trafficked roads, you'd think the island would be great for biking! It is, but you are better off bringing your own bike than renting. If you do rent, instead of a delicate road bike, get a cruiser for pedaling around town or along the beach or a mountain bike that can handle the sometimes poor road conditions as well as open up the possibilities of off-road biking. Even experienced mountain bikers should be careful on the often extremely muddy and rutted trails.

For off-street trails, pick up a copy of the Big Island Mountain Bike Association's comprehensive off-road, public-access trail guide at either HVB office or at most bike shops on the island. This guide is also available online at www.interpac.net/~mtbike. Aside from an introduction to the organization and safety tips, each trail is briefly described and accompanied by a rudimentary map, directions to the start of the trail, and any additional information that's necessary to complete the ride. The type of ride, length in distance, ride time, elevation change, and level of expertise needed are also listed. Trails vary from flat shoreline jaunts to rugged mountain workouts, for beginners to the advanced rider. Check it out before you ride; this information comes from experienced island riders. For additional information contact BIMBA at P.O. Box 6819 Hilo, HI 96720-8934, 808/961-4452.

Bicycle Shops and Rentals

Hawaiian Pedals Ltd., 808/329-2294, in the Kona Inn Shopping Plaza, rents mountain bikes at $15 for five hours, $20 for 24 hours, with discounted rates for longer needs. Performance bikes are slightly more expensive; tandems cost $35 all day. Bike racks and baby seats are also for rent.

Dave's Bike and Triathlon Shop, owned and pedaled by triathlete Dave Bending, is just a long stride or two from the beginning of the Ironman Triathlon in the Kona Square Shopping Center, 75-5669 Ali'i Dr., 808/329-4522. Dave's rents road, mountain, hybrid, and suspension bikes from $15 a day to $60 a week, and this includes a helmet, water bottles, a map, bicycle lock, and, most importantly, road advice. Dave is a font of information, one of the best bicycle men on the island.

The **Bike Works,** 74-5599 Lehua St., Suite F-3, next to Gold's Gym in the Old Kona Industrial Area, 808/326-2453, sells, services, and rents mountain and road bikes and bike gear. This Kailua-Kona full-service shop is perhaps the best on the island. Daily rates run $20–30 an hour. Five-hour and multi-day rates can also be arranged.

When in Hilo, check out **Hilo Bike Hub,** 808/961-4452, at 318 E. Kawila, for sales and service of all kinds of high-quality bikes and accessories. This shop and its owner are heavy into the mountain biking scene, including the Big Island Mountain Biking Association, and have information about all the island races. Crossbreed mountain bikes rent for $30 a day or $120 a week. Also in Hilo is **Mid Pacific Wheels,** 1133C Manono St., 808/935-6211, where you can get a more standard bike for $15 a day. At **Aquatic Perceptions,** 808/935-9990, you can rent a cruiser to pedal around Hilo for $3 an hour.

In Waimea, try either **C&S Outfitters,** 808/885-5005, or **Mauna Kea Mountain Bikes,** 808/883-0130, for wheels that will get you up to the high country. Rental rates are $25 for five hours, $30 for 24 hours, or $130 for a week; helmet and pump included.

Bicycle Tours

Mauna Kea Mountain Bikes runs four different group tours, for beginners to advanced riders. The beginner tour runs for 21 miles down Highway 250 over the shoulder of the Kohala Mountains to Hawi. This is a morning tour for a minimum of four riders; transportation back from Hawi is included. An intermediate ride travels back roads around Waimea and lets you get a feel for upcountry range country and farmland. The technical rainforest ride is a challenge, not long but lots of ups and downs through muddy single-track trails. The real crowning ride, however, is the one down Mauna Kea from the summit to the Saddle Road. On this one you have to be in very good shape and be focused. Rides last 2–4 hours and rates range $45–115. For details, call 808/883-0130 or 800/628-8687, or write P.O. Box 44672, Kamuela, HI 96743.

Aquatic Perceptions, 111 Banyan Dr. in Hilo, 808/933-1228, a multisport activity company, offers a bicycle Jungle Coastal Tour of Puna. Starting in Pahoa, the group mounts their mountain bikes and heads down the leisurely country roads to the south coast. From there, it travels along the sometimes-canopied, sometimes-steamy coastal road as far as the new black-sand beach and lava fields of Kaimu. The return to Hilo is by van. Cost is $69 per person. Half a dozen other bike tours are also offered, ranging from a ride around Kilauea Caldera to one along the North Kohala Coast. These rides are designed for an average rider, run 4–6 hours, and cost $125–135.

One of the newer biking opportunities on the island is a mountain biking tour to the rim of Waipi'o Valley, where you look over 1,000 feet into one of the island's most fascinating valleys. The Mauka Rim Ride takes you over back roads and through former sugarcane land to the very edge of the valley rim, where you get wonderful views into this huge valley. This ride also includes a trail ride to a waterfall and pool for a dip in the refreshing mountain water before your return and lunch. Meet at Waipi'o Valley Artworks in Kukuihaele at 8:45 A.M. to get fitted with a suspension bike. This ride is 3–4 hours long and runs $85 per person. Custom rides can also be arranged. For information, call **Top of Waipio** at 808/775-9393 or 800/492-4746 or go online to www.topofwaipio.com/bike.htm.

Kohala Eco-Adventures, 808/329-7116, website: www.cyclekona.com, also does a mountain bike tour on the north slope of the Kohala Mountains, traversing former sugarcane lands, traveling rural roads, and ending along the rugged coast near Keokea Park. All equipment, drinks, and snacks provided for $95. A half dozen other full- and part-day rides are offered, including a trip along the Hamakua Coast and through the coffee country.

For long-distance bicycle touring, contact one of the following island-based companies for specialized bike trips. The owners and tour leaders of **Island Bicycle Adventures,** 569 Kapahulu Ave., Honolulu, HI 96815, 808/734-0700 or 800/233-2226, are intimately familiar with bicycle touring and are members of the Hawaii Bicycling League. They offer tours to Maui, the Big Island, and Kaua'i. **Hawaiian Eyes Big Island Bicycle Tours,** P.O. Box 1500, Honoka'a, HI 96727, 808/775-7335, offers guided rides along the Hamakua Coast, down the Saddle Road, and around the island, among others.

Two Mainland-based companies also do multiday bicycle touring. **Backroads,** 801 Cedar St., Berkeley, CA 94710, 510/527-1555, fax 510/527-1444, 800/462-2848, website: www.backroads.com, email: goactive@backroads.com, goes easy on the environment with its bicycle and hiking trips to the Big Island. The eight-day circle-island bike tour offered October–April costs $1,895. Backroads also does a six-day Big Island hiking trip November–March that takes you into major scenic area of the island; $1,795. All on-island arrangements are included.

Bicycle Adventures, P.O. Box 11219, Olympia, WA 98508, 800/443-6060, website: www.bicycleadventures.com, email: office@bicycleadventrues.com, also organizes two road trips around the Big Island, mostly on less-used roads, which take in many of the best sights. The six-day trip connects Hilo to Kona around the south end, while the eight-day trip circles the island. Departures monthly. Rides average 45 miles a day with overnights planned mostly at Inns and small hotels. These all-inclusive tours cover everything you'll need. Rates are $1,598 and $1,890.

SKIING

Bored with sun and surf? Strap the "boards" to your feet and hit the slopes of Mauna Kea for one of the most unique ski adventures in the world. There are no lifts, so you need a 4WD to get to the top and someone willing to pick you up again at the bottom. You can rent 4WDs from car rental agencies, but if that seems like too much hassle just contact **Ski Guides Hawaii,** P.O. Box 1954, Kamuela, HI 96743, 808/885-4188, website: www.skihawaii.com. You can rent skis and this

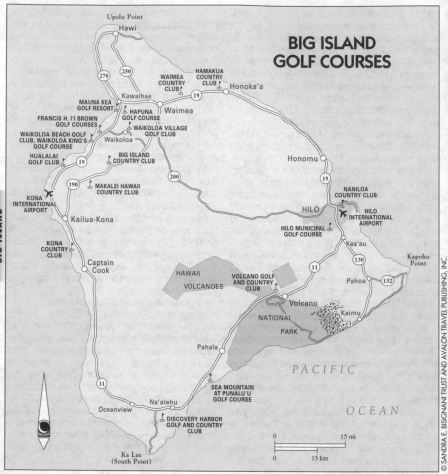

BIG ISLAND
GOLF COURSES

© SANDRA E. BISIGNANI TRUST AND AVALON TRAVEL PUBLISHING, INC.

company provides the "lifts" to the top. Skis, boots, and poles (or snowboards and boots) rent for $50 a day; the popular full-day ski tour with equipment, ride and driver, ski guide, and lunch costs $150 per person (minimum three). Other ski packages and cross-country ski tours are available and priced on request. For additional information, check out the Ski Association of Hawaii website at www.hawaiisnowskiclub.com.

You can expect snow December–May, but you can't always count on it. It's most probable during February and March, and very occasion-ally it stays until June or July. Generally speaking, your chances for skiable snow are better the few days after a moisture-laden front has moved across the island, blanketing the top with a white covering. It seems that more snow comes in La Niña years and less during El Niño.

GOLF

The Big Island has some of the most beautiful golf links in Hawaii. The Kohala-area courses

BIG ISLAND GOLF COURSES

COURSE	PAR	YARDS	FEES	CART	CLUBS
Big Island Country Club 71-1420 Mamalahoa Hwy. Kailua-Kona, HI 96740 808/325-5044	72	6,510	$120	incl.	$30
Discovery Harbor **Golf and Country Club** P.O. Box 621 Na'alehu, HI 96772 808/929-7353	72	6,343	$28	incl.	$12
Frances H. I'i Brown Golf Courses South Course North Course: 68-1310 Mauna Lani Dr. Kohala Coast, HI 96743 808/885-6655	72 72	6,025 6,086	$185 $185	incl. incl.	$35 $35
Hamakua Country Club P.O. Box 344 Honoka'a, HI 96727 808/775-7244	33	2,496 (9 holes)	$10	none	none
Hapuna Golf Course 62-100 Kauna'oa Dr. Kohala Coast, HI 96743 808/880-3000	72	6,029	$135	incl.	$35
Hilo Municipal Golf Course 340 Haihai St. Hilo, HI 96720 808/959-7711	71	6,325	$25 (weekday) $20 (weekend)	$14.50	$10
Hualalai Golf Club (resort guests only) P.O. Box 1119 Kailua-Kona, HI 96745 808/325-8480	72	6,032	$125	incl.	$50
Kona Country Club Mountain Course: Ocean Course: 78-7000 Ali'i Dr. Kailua-Kona, HI 96740 808/322-2595	72 72	6,470 6,579	$95 $110	incl. incl.	$30 $30

BIG ISLAND

(continued on next page)

BIG ISLAND GOLF COURSES
(continued)

COURSE	PAR	YARDS	FEES	CART	CLUBS
Makalei Hawaii Country Club 72-3890 Hawaii Belt Rd. Kailua-Kona, HI 96740 808/325-6625	72	6,698	$110	incl.	$25
Mauna Kea Golf Course 62-100 Mauna Kea Beach Dr. Kohala Coast, HI 96743 808/882-5400	72	6,737	$150	incl.	$35
Naniloa Country Club 120 Banyan Dr. Hilo, HI 96720 808/935-3000	35	2,740 (9 holes)	$37	incl.	$3
Sea Mountain at **Punalu'u Golf Course** P.O. Box 190 Pahala, HI 96777 808/928-6222	72	6,416	$42	incl.	$25
Volcano Golf **and Country Club** Box 46 Hawaii Volcanoes National Park, HI 96718 808/967-7331	72	6,547	$60	incl.	$16
Waikoloa Beach Golf Club 1020 Keana Place Waikoloa, HI 96738 808/885-6060	70	5,958	$125	incl.	$35
Waikoloa King's Golf Course 600 Waikoloa Beach Dr. Waikoloa, HI 96738 808/886-7888	72	6,010	$125	incl.	$35
Waikoloa Village Golf Club P.O. Box 383910 Waikoloa, HI 96738 808/883-9621	72	6,230	$80	incl.	$30
Waimea Country Club P.O. Box 2155 Kamuela, HI 96743 808/885-805	72	6,210	$45	incl.	$22.50

are considered by some to be the crown jewel of the state's golf options. Robert Trent Jones Sr. and Jr. have both built exceptional courses here. Dad built the Mauna Kea Beach Hotel course, while the kid built his at the Waikoloa Beach Resort. The Mauna Kea course bedevils many as the ultimate challenge. If the Kohala courses are too rich for your blood, a few in the Kailua area are less expensive, or you can hit nine holes in Hilo for about $25. How about golfing at Volcano Golf Course, where if you miss a short putt, you can blame it on an earthquake?

TENNIS

Many tennis courts dot the Big Island, and plenty of them are free. County courts are under the control of the Department of Parks and Recreation, which maintains a combination of lighted and unlit courts around the island. Usually of cement, these county courts can be reserved by calling the number listed. No fees are charged for these public courts, but play is on a first-come, first-served basis. Court rules apply and only soft-sole shoes are allowed. Please care for equipment and stick to time limits, especially if there are guests waiting. Some private and hotel courts are open to the public for a fee, while others restrict play to guests only. Most private courts have a plexi-pave or similar surface. Although each facility differs, private clubs usually have pro shops, offer equipment rental, and arrange clinics and lessons. Court play is regulated according to accepted rules, and proper attire is required, including proper shoes.

HUNTING

Huge unpopulated expanses of grassland, forest, and scrubby mountainside are very good for hunting. The Big Island's game includes feral pig, sheep, and goats, plus pheasant, quail, dove, and wild turkey. Public game lands are spread throughout the island; a license is required to take birds and game. For full information, contact the Department of Land and Natural Resources, Division of Forestry and Wildlife Office, 19 E. Kawili, Hilo, HI 96720, 808/974-4221.

LAND TOURS

Tours cover the Big Island from top to bottom. You can drive it, fly it, sail around it, hike it, or bike it.

Bus and Shuttle Tours

Most tour companies run vans, but some larger companies also use buses. Though cheaper, tours on full-sized coaches are generally less personalized. Wherever a bus can go, so can your rental car—but on a tour you can relax and enjoy the scenery without worrying about driving. Also, tour drivers are very experienced with the area and know many stories and legends with which they annotate and enrich your trip. Tours generally run $40–60 per person and either circle the island or have Kilauea Volcano as their main feature. Narrated and fairly tame bus tours are operated by **Roberts Hawaii,** 808/329-1688 or 808/966-5483, and by **Polynesian Adventure Tours,** 808/329-8008. **Jack's Tours,** 808/961-6666 or 808/329-2555, also runs various group bus tours to major sites on the island. **Dieter's Creative Tours,** 888/290-1000, website: www.dieters-hawaii.com, does guided minibus tours of Hilo and the volcano areas in German (other languages on request). German-language tours area also offered on Maui and O'ahu.

Four-wheel-drive van tour companies include: **Waipio Valley Shuttle,** 808/775-7121, offering a 90-minute tour down to Waipi'o Valley ($35 adult, $15 children) and a six-hour Mauna Kea summit tour ($80 per person), minimum four people. The Waipi'o Valley shuttle leaves from Kukuihaele, and the summit tour starts at the Parker Ranch Shopping Center in Waimea.

Adventure Van Tours

For a trip to the rim of the valley for a look down into Waipi'o, contact **Waipi'o Rim Backroad Adventures,** 808/775-1122 or 800/492-4746, website: www.topofwaipio.com/4x4.htm. This company's three-hour tour, for $85 per person, takes in former sugarcane land, backcountry roads, and unparalleled vistas overlooking the valley. A short hike brings you to a small waterfall and pool. On this adventure, you ride in comfort and lunch is provided.

BIG ISLAND

BIG ISLAND TENNIS COURTS

COUNTY COURTS

Under jurisdiction of the County Department of Parks and Recreation, 25 Aupuni St., Hilo, HI 96720, 808/961-8740. No fee for use, but reservations are recommended.

TOWN	LOCATION	NO. OF COURTS	LIGHTED
Hilo	Ainaole Park	1	No
Hilo	Hakalau Park	2	No
Hilo	Ho'olulu Park	8	Yes
Hilo	Lincoln Park	4	Yes
Hilo	Lokahi Park	2	Yes
Hilo	Malama Park	2	Yes
Hilo	Mohouli Park	2	No
Hilo	Pana'ewa Park	2	Yes
Hilo	Papa'aloa Park	2	Yes
Honoka'a	Honoka'a Park	2	Yes
Puna	Kurtistown Park	1	No
Kea'au	Kea'au Park	2	No
Ka'u	Ka'u High School	2	Yes
Ka'u	Na'alehu Park	2	Yes
Captain Cook	Greenwell Park	1	Yes
Keauhou	Keauhou Park	1	No
Kona	Old Kona Airport	4	Yes
Kona	Kailua Playground	1	Yes
Waimea	Waimea Park	2	Yes
Kapa'au	Kamehameha Park	2	Yes

HOTEL AND PRIVATE COURTS OPEN TO THE PUBLIC

TOWN	LOCATION	TEL. (808)	FEE	NUMBER OF COURTS	LIGHTED
Pahala	Sea Mountain Resort	928-6200	None	4	No
Keauhou	Keauhou Beach Resort	322-6112	$10/day	6	Yes
Kailua-Kona	Royal Kona Resort	334-1093	$6/day	6	Yes
Kailua-Kona	King Kamehameha's Kona Beach Hotel	334-9889	$5/hr	4	Yes
Waikoloa	Waikoloa Village	883-9704	$10	2	Yes
Waimea	Hawaii Prep Academy	881-4037	$20	4	Yes
Kohala	Outrigger Waikoloa Beach Resort	886-6666	$10/day	6	No
Kohala	Hilton Waikoloa Village Resort	881-2222	$25/hr	8	No
Kohala	Mauna Lani Tennis Garden	885-1485	$8/hr	10	No
Kohala	Mauna Kea Beach Resort	882-5420	$10/day	13	No

Mauna Kea Summit Adventures, 808/322-2366 or 888/322-2366, website: www.maunakea.com, owned and operated by Pat Wright, has been taking visitors on high-adventure trips around the Big Island for the last 15 years. Your comfort and safety, as you roam the Big Island, are ensured as you ride in sturdy GMC High Sierra vans with 4WD and a/c. The premier tour is an eight-hour journey to the top of Mauna Kea. Pat and his drivers not only fill your trip with stories, anecdotes, and fascinating facts during the ride, they top off the safari by setting up an eight-inch telescope so you can get a personal view of the heavens through the rarefied atmosphere atop the great mountain. Mauna Kea Summit Adventures picks you up at your hotel in Kailua-Kona at about 4 P.M. If you're staying on the Hilo side, you'll be met at a predetermined spot along the Saddle Road. The price is $135, with hot savory drinks and good warm parkas included. Special trips for photography, hiking, astronomy, and shore fishing can also be tailored to your needs.

Hawaii Forest and Trail, 808/331-8505 or 800/464-1993, offers much the same summit and stargazing tour from the Kona side at $135 per person.

Ascending to the summit of the mountain during the day is **Hawaiian Eyes Land Tours,** 808/937-2530. This tour leaves at 8 A.M. for a nine-hour trip, so there is no telescope use involved. However, on the way, you are taught about the mountain and the telescope so your trip is an educational experience. The tour is limited to six passengers and costs $99 per person. Hawaiian Eyes also does a Mauna Loa trip for the same price at same departure time.

Arnott's Lodge and Hiking Adventures, 98 Apapane Rd., Hilo, HI 96720, 808/967-7097, website: www.arnottslodge.com, offers hiking adventures to guests and nonguests who are looking for more than an ordinary group tour. While the tours do change periodically, several have remained popular. They include a Puna Rift Zone hike and a trip to South Point and hike to Green Sand Beach. Perhaps the most adventurous, and physically most taxing, are the night hike to the current lava flow in Volcanoes National Park and the sunset watch and stargazing at the top of Mauna Kea. These are full eight-hour trips—some longer. Rates run $43–48 for those staying at Arnott's Lodge in Hilo but are more expensive for others. Each trip takes only as many as the van will carry and they go only when the weather is conducive. Some restrictions on age and physical condition apply, so be sure to check with the staff at Arnott's Lodge, or check the website for the current list of adventures.

ATV Tours

ATV Outfitters Hawaii, 808/889-6000, website: www.outfittershawaii.com, runs a breezy four-wheel motorcycle tour across former Kohala sugar plantation land to coastal sights at the northern tip of the island. You'll ride over back roads and fields, through lush gullies, to the edge of ocean cliffs, and down to pebble beach. These fully equipped machines get to places that you wouldn't be able to access otherwise. Safe and reliable, these four-wheelers are easy to operate even for those who have had no experience on a motorcycle. Helmets, gloves, and goggles are supplied and instruction is given. To ride, you must be at least 16 years old and weigh 90–220 pounds. Wear long pants and closed-toe shoes.

Tour Tapes and Brochures

For a unique concept, rent Tour Tapes, narrated by Russ Apple, Ph.D., a retired national-park ranger and 1987 winner of the Historic Hawaii Foundation Award. Russ dispenses his knowledge about the Big Island as you drive along prescribed routes, mostly in and around Hawaii Volcanoes National Park. Tapes and decks are available in Hilo from the Hilo Hawaiian Hotel, Hawaii Naniloa Resort, and Lyman House Museum. They are also available at the Volcano Art Center.

The Big Island chapter of the HVB puts out the free *Hawaii's Big Island Driving Tour* brochure. Maps, photos, and text detail one-day and multiple-day self-drive itineraries of major historical and cultural points of interest, scenic spots, and other highlights around the island. Cursory coverage, but it introduces all areas of the island. Pick one up at either the Hilo or Kona HVB office.

BIG ISLAND

AIR TOURS

Helicopter Tours

Air tours are a great way to see the Big Island, but they are expensive, especially when the volcano is putting on a mighty display. Expect to spend a minimum of $115 for a front-row seat to watch the amazing light show from the air. Some discounts may be offered seasonally or for booking over the Internet. Kilauea volcano erupting is like winning the lottery for these small companies, and many charge whatever the market will bear. To get the best view of the volcanic activity, schedule your flight for the morning, or no later than 2 P.M. Later, clouds and fog can set in to obstruct your view. While the volcano is the premier focus of these tour companies, most also offer tours up the Hamakua Coast for a view of the sea cliffs, deep valleys, waterfalls, and the North Kohala Mountains, and some do a modified round-island tour that takes in the volcano, east and west coastlines, and Hamakua valleys and waterfalls. Helicopter flights from the Hilo Commuter Terminal are very competitively priced, with savings on volcano tours over the companies operating out of the Kona Commuter Terminal. However, more flights leave out of Kona because there are more tourists on that side. Additionally, flights by Blue Hawaiian Helicopters also leave out of the Waikoloa Heliport, across the highway from the entrance to Waikoloa Resort at the intersection of Queen Ka'ahumanu Highway and Waikoloa Road, and Mauna Kea Helicopters uses a helipad at the Mauna Lani Resort.

Everyone has an opinion as to which company offers the best ride, the best narration, or the best service. All the helicopter companies on Hawai'i are safe and reputable—nearly all pilots have been trained by the military—and most fly five-seat A-Stars, with a few four-passenger Bell Jet Rangers and Hughes 500s still in use. Most have two-way microphones so you can communicate with the pilot. Each gives a pre-flight briefing to go over safety regulations and other details. Remember, however, that the seating arrangement in a helicopter is critical to safety. The pre-flight crew is expertly trained to arrange the chopper so that it is balanced, and with different people of various sizes flying every day, their job is very much like a chess game. This means that the seating goes strictly according to weight. If you are not assigned the seat of your choice, for safety's sake, please do not complain. Think instead that you are part of a team whose goal is not only enjoyment but also to come back safe and sound. It's very difficult not to have a fascinating flight—no matter where you sit.

Nearly everyone wants to take photographs of their helicopter tour. Who wouldn't? Here are a few things to consider. Most of the newer helicopters are air-conditioned, which means that the windows don't open, so you might experience glare or some distortion. If you need absolutely clear shots, choose a chopper where the windows open or go with the one that flies with its doors off. Also, if you are the only one taking pictures on a tour and you're seated in the middle of the rear seat, you won't be happy. Again, ask for a ride in a smaller rig where everyone gets a window seat.

Volcano Helicopters, 808/961-3355, owned and operated by David Okita, is intimately familiar with the volcano area. While its choppers used to fly out of the town of Volcano, they now fly only from the Hilo Airport. The helicopter is a four-passenger Hughes 500D, and it's fast and maneuverable. Volcano Helicopters does a lot of contract work so tours don't fly every day, but when they do the rates are competitive. A 45-minute volcano flight costs $115, and a 55-minute tour can be tailored to your desires for $145.

Also flying out of the Hilo Airport in four-passenger Bell Jet-Ranger III helicopters is **Tropical Helicopters,** 808/961-6910, website: www.tropicalhelicopters.com. Tropical is a small company that gives personal attention to passengers. Its popular 45-minute volcano flight runs $99. An expanded 50-minute flight runs the same basic route but gives you additional overflight of waterfalls in the Hilo area for $158. The ultimate Feel the Heat flight, $138, takes you for an up-close look at the volcano activity—with the doors off!

Mauna Kea Helicopters, 808/885-6400 or 800/400-4354 in Hawaii, website: www.mkheli.com, flies from the small Kamuela Airport in Waimea but conveniently picks up passengers at the Mauna Lani Resort helipad for guests staying at the Kohala resort hotels. The two flights are a

Hamakua valley and waterfall flight for $145 and a circle-island for $310. Mauna Kea Helicopters also flies from Hilo on two flights that view the volcano and nearby waterfalls. The 50-minute flight is $160 while the shorter 40-minute flight runs $140. Mauna Kea Helicopters uses mostly A-Star craft but operates one Hughes 500, the doors of which can be removed for a real open-air flight.

Safari Helicopters flies from both Hilo and Kona, 808/969-1259 (Hilo), 808/329-4655 (Kona), or 800/326-3356 interisland or Mainland, website: www.safariair.com, email info@safariair.com. Flights from Hilo are the shortest and cheapest, 45–60 minutes for $149–189, and concentrate on the volcano and nearby waterfalls. A 2.5-hour flight, $339, leaves from Kona and crosses the island for a run down the Hamakua Coast before heading down to investigate the volcano and returning up the west coast to Kona. Safari uses a/c A-Star craft. This is a reputable company, and pilots give you a memorable flight. Safari also flies on Kaua'i.

With its spotless safety record, **Blue Hawaiian Helicopters**, 808/961-5600 or 800/745-2583, website: www.bluehawaiian.com, operates four A-Star helicopters from the Waikoloa Heliport on the Kona side and another four A-Stars from the Hilo airport. Volcano flights go from Hilo for $140. From Waikoloa, they do a two-hour circle island for $305 and a shorter Kohala Mountain and valley tour for $145. Blue Hawaiian also offers flights on Maui.

Flying out of Kona, **Sunshine Helicopters**, 808/882-1233 or 800/622-3144, website: www.sunshinehelicopters.com, runs a 45-minute Kohala Mountain and Hamakua Valley tour at $140 and a circle-island for $315. Sunshine offers a package with Atlantis Submarine for reduced rates on both activities. Sunshine also operates helicopter flights on Maui.

Fixed-Wing Air Tours

Big Island Air, 808/329-4868 or 800/303-8868, offers small-plane flights from Kona Airport (two-person minimum). A volcano tour in an eight-passenger Cessna 402 costs $135 per person, and a round-island/volcano flight for $185. Every seat is a window seat, but the wing is below the windows. The plane can be chartered for $550 an hour from Kona or $660 an hour from Hilo.

For smaller planes with wings above the windows, try **Island Hopper,** 808/969-2000, which offers flights from both the Hilo and Kona airports. Volcano and waterfall tours, $69–79, go from Hilo, but the longer flights from Kona are $149 for a volcano tour and $189 for a circle-island tour. With similar flights and prices are **Mokulele Flight Service,** 808/326-7070, out of Kona, and **Safari Aviation,** 808/935-8812, with flights out of Hilo.

From either Kona or Hilo, **Classic Aviation,** 808/329-8687, 800/695-8100, website: planet-hawaii.com/biplane, email: biplane@ilhawaii.net, offers flying adventures at $65–250 per person in its open-cockpit 1934 WACO replica biplane. This plane takes two passengers only, one on some flights. Sightseeing tours are the main focus here, but some tours offer aerial acrobatics for the real thrill seeker. Come pretend to be the Red Baron.

SHOPPING

The following is an overview of the main shopping areas and their locations around the island. Hawai'i has plenty of stores from large malls to small boutique shops, art galleries, bookstores, and gift shops. Almost every town has at least a gas station and market, and the bigger towns have supermarkets, health food stores, and local markets. Greater detail is in the individual travel chapters.

SHOPPING CENTERS

General shopping centers are found in Hilo, Kailua-Kona, and Waimea. Like most shopping malls, these have a variety of stores whose offerings include apparel, jewelry, dry goods, sporting goods, food, photography supplies, or outdoor rentals.

Kona Malls

Two commodities that you're guaranteed in Kailua-Kona are plenty of sunshine and plenty of shopping. **Kona Inn Shopping Village** is in central Kailua and has more than 40 shops selling everything from fabrics to fruits. Between the **King Kamehameha's Kona Beach Hotel Mall** and the new **Coconut Grove Marketplace** along Ali'i Drive, there are at least half a dozen small shopping plazas strung like beads catering heavily to the tourists. Heading inland from the pier along Palani Road are generally newer and larger shopping centers, more local shops where the people buy. Going up the way, they are the **King Kamehameha Mall, North Kona Shopping Center, Kopiko Plaza, Lanihau Center,** and the **Kona Coast Shopping Center,** each with a fine diversity of shops. Along Queen Ka'ahumanu Highway is the large, new **Crossroads Center** and the **Makalapua Center.** At the south end, **Keauhou Shopping Center** is conveniently located at the corner of Ali'i Drive and Kamehameha III Road, with everything from a post office to a supermarket.

Hilo Malls

The main shopping center in Hilo is the **Prince Kuhio Plaza,** 111 E. Pua'inako. This is Hilo's newest and the island's largest full-service and diversified shopping mall. Across the street is **Waiakea Center** with a Borders Books and Music, a natural foods store, and Wal-Mart. **Pua'inako Town Center** is up the road at 2100 Kanoelehua Avenue and has lots of food outlets. **Waiakea Kai Shopping Plaza,** near the Banyan Drive area, has a small clutch of stores and a movie theater. An older and somewhat eclipsed shopping center is **Kaiko'o Mall,** 777 Kilauea Ave., near the center of town. The **Hilo Shopping Center** is about one-half mile down on Kilauea Avenue. As a smaller mall, it has only a handful of local shops.

Waimea Malls

After the diversity of shopping malls in Kailua and Hilo, it's like a breath of fresh air to have fewer choices. In Waimea try the **Parker Ranch Shopping Center,** which has over 30 shops, including a pharmacy, a grocery, and general merchandise. Almost across the street is the **Waimea Center,** Waimea's newest mall. **Parker Square Shopping Mall** has a clutch of fine boutiques and shops.

FOOD STORES

Supermarkets

Groceries and picnic supplies can be purchased in almost every town on the island. Many of the markets in the smaller towns also sell a limited selection of dry goods and gifts. The general rule is, the smaller the market the higher the prices. The largest and cheapest stores with the biggest selections are found in Hilo and Kailua-Kona.

The island's major supermarkets, **KTA Superstores, Sack 'n Save,** and **Safeway,** each have at least one branch store in both Hilo and Kailua-Kona. KTA Superstores also has a supermarket in Waimea, while **Sure Save** stores have locations in Hilo and Kea'au. Waikoloa Village is serviced by the large and modern **Waikoloa Village Market.**

These smaller markets should meet your needs as you travel around the Big Island. Along the eastern Hamakua Coast you'll find **T. Kaneshiro Store** and **K.K. Super-Mart** in Honoka'a. On the Kohala peninsula look for **M. Nakahara** and **K. Takata** stores for general supplies in Hawi. The only place along the South Kohala Coast for supplies is **M's Puako General Store** in the tiny village of Puako. South of Kailua-Kona is **Kimura's Market** in Kainaliu, **Kamigaki Market** in Kealakekua, and **Shimizu Market** in Honaunau. South of Hilo in Pahoa is **Pahoa Cash and Carry.** In Volcano Village try **Kilauea General Store** and **Volcano Store** just before entering Hawaii Volcanoes National Park. The Ka'u District has **Pick and Pay** in Na'alehu, which bills itself as the southernmost market in the United States; **Wong Yuen Store** in Wai'ohinu; and the well-stocked **Ocean View General Store** in Ocean View.

Health Food Stores
Abundant Life Natural Foods, 292 Kamehameha Ave., in downtown Hilo, has been doing business since 1977. Open daily, it stocks a full selection of fresh fruit and vegetables, bulk and packaged foods, vitamins, minerals, and supplements, and has a food counter for ready-made and made to order wholesome eats. In a newer, larger store in the Waiakea Center is **Island Naturals.** This market and deli offers about the same services and products. While heading south from Hilo to Volcanoes, stop along Route 11 at **Kea'au Natural Foods** or in Pahoa at **Pahoa Natural Groceries.**

On the Kona side, try the full-service **Kona Natural Foods** in the new Crossroads Center. Its sister store, **Healthways II,** is in Waimea. South of Kailua in Kainaliu, look for the small but well-stocked **Evie's Natural Foods.** Aside from bulk and packaged foods, fresh produce and supplements, each store does fresh food preparation on premises and has prepared foods in a cooler case.

Farmers' Markets
On Wednesdays and Saturdays / A.M.–3 P.M., check out the **Hilo Farmers' Market** at Kamehameha Avenue and Mamo Street, fronting the bay in the center of the downtown area. This is a lively affair with an incredible variety of goods for sale.

For a real treat, visit the early-morning **Suisan Fish Market,** 85 Lihiwai St. near the river mouth in Hilo. At the Cooper Center in Volcano, you'll find produce, flowers, and baked goods at the **Volcano Farmers' Market** every Sunday 8–10 A.M. In Pahoa, **Caretakers of Our Land Farmers' Market** pulls out its wares on Saturday 7:30 A.M.–noon at the Sacred Heart Catholic Church. On Sunday 9 A.M.–1 P.M., head down the road to find food, flowers, clothing, and other items at the **Akebono Farmers' Market** at the back of the parking lot at the Akebono Theater.

For locally grown produce on the west side of the island try the **Kona Farmers' Market** every Wednesday and Saturday 7 A.M.–3 P.M. at the parking lot along Ali'i Drive across from Hale Halawai. The **Waimea Farmers' Market,** held every Satur. 7 A.M.–1 P.M., is where local farmers come to sell their produce, much of which is organic, at the Hawaiian Homes Hall about two miles east of town. Also on Saturday at about the same time is the **Parker School Farmers' Market.** held at the school grounds.

In addition to these organized markets, individual roadside stands pop up here and there around the island and sell fruit, vegetables, flowers, and more.

SPECIALTY SHOPS

Fine Art Galleries
While Hilo is not the hotbed of art galleries, one shop to look at is **Dreams of Paradise,** in the S. Hata Building along Kamehameha Avenue. This shop displays a wide variety of art from painting to fabric, and many of the artists live on the island.

While heading up the Hamakua Coast, visit the **Woodshop Gallery** along Honomu's main street, where large wood furniture, small wood boxes, paintings, pottery, glass, and all sorts of arts and crafts deserve a look. In Honoka'a, the **Bamboo Gallery** is a spacious showroom containing an eclectic mix of wood, fiber, canvas, and glass art, all displayed in a sparse Oriental style. At the end of the road in Kukuihaele is **Waipio Valley Artworks,** showcasing exclusive artwork of distinguished island artists.

If you are after an exquisite piece of art, a unique memento, or an inexpensive but distinctive

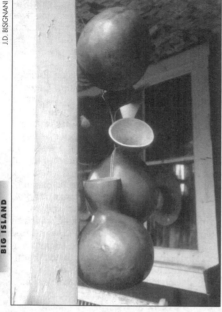

ipu, *a drum used to accompany hula*

souvenir, shop at the **Volcano Art Center** in Hawaii Volcanoes National Park. This is a real treasure and an exquisite showcase for island artists.

In the village of Kainaliu in South Kona, look for **The Blue Ginger Gallery,** displaying the owners' art as well as artists' works from all over the island.

Holualoa is an artists community. In town a converted and brightly painted coffee mill houses to the **Kona Art Center,** a community art co-operative since 1965. Also in town, half a dozen small but outstanding galleries include **Studio 7, Holualoa Gallery,** and **Ululani.**

Down in Kailua-Kona you'll find **Rift Zone Galleries** in the Coconut Grove Marketplace and **Kailua Village Artists,** which both carry a broad spectrum of art styles and media mostly by local artists. The ubiquitous **Wyland Galleries** has a shop at Waterfront Row. While featuring paintings by Wyland himself, it does showcase a handful of other big-name island artists.

Many of the luxury resorts along the Kohala Coast have an art gallery in their clutch of shops. One standout is the **Amaury St. Giles Modern Art Gallery** at the Hapuna Beach Resort. It's worth a look for eclectic modern pieces.

Along the north shore in Kapa'au across from the Kamehameha statue is **Ackerman Gallery,** showcasing the work of artist Gary Ackerman along with displays of local pottery, carvings, and one-of-a-kind jewelry.

Gift Shops

Sugawara Lauhala and Gift Shop is a virtually unknown Hilo institution making genuine *lau hala* weavings. Similarly, **Kimura's Lauhala Shop** in Holualoa has been selling and producing its famous *lau hala* hats ever since local weavers began bartering their creations for groceries in 1915.

For a genuine gift item, search the shelves of the **Hulihe'e Palace Gift Shop.** Not only will you find something to take home as a remembrance, you'll support this wonderful institution. **Alapaki's** at Keauhou Shopping Center sells traditional island arts and crafts, some of the tourist variety and some genuine. You can always find a good deal at **The Little Grass Shack** in Kealakekua, an institution in the area. It looks like a tourist trap, but don't let that stop you from going in and finding some authentic souvenirs.

Hilo has a few antique and collectible shops, but many more line the main drag in tiny Honoka'a up on the Hamakua Coast. Start at **Hawaiian Artifacts and Antiques** and just progress down the street.

Searchers of the New Age and metaphysicians of all stripes will find a book, a tape, an aroma, incense, or reading to fit their needs at **The Rainbow Path** in Kainaliu.

As on every island, **Hilo Hattie** is the place to stop for right-price, if not the most exceptional, gifts and clothing. Hilo Hattie has one shop in Hilo and a second in Kailua.

Bookstores

Two aspects of a quality vacation are knowing what you're doing and thoroughly relaxing while doing it. Nothing helps you do this better than a good book.

In Hilo, **Basically Books,** downtown at 160 Kamehameha Ave., has a good selection of

Hawaiiana, out-of-print books, and the island's best selection of maps and charts. It also features a very good selection of travel books. At the Prince Kuhio Plaza are the **Book Gallery** and **Waldenbooks,** both full-selection bookstores. Newest to town and the largest on the east side of the island is **Borders Books and Music** at the Waiakea Shopping Center.

Kailua-Kona also has a huge **Borders Books and Music** up above town on Henry Street. In town at the Kona Plaza Shopping Arcade is the **Middle Earth Bookshoppe,** smaller but more personal with a fine selection.

The **Kohala Book Shop** in Kapa'au purportedly is the largest used book store in the Pacific, and it does book searches.

Other shops with a wide selection of Hawaiiana are the gift shops at the **Lyman House Museum** and **Hulihe'e Palace.** Numerous gift shops throughout the island and hotel sundries shops also carry books on Hawaiian subjects. Books on health, cooking, natural foods, and nutrition can be found at **Abundant Life Natural Foods** and **Island Naturals** in Hilo, **Kona Natural Foods** in Kailua, and **Healthways** in Waimea. **The Rainbow Path** in Kainaliu carries books on metaphysics, spiritualism, and self-help.

For books on diving, snorkeling, reef fish, and marine topics, check dive shops and water sport activities shops. Some outdoor adventure shops carry books on camping, hiking, and natural history.

Film and Film Developing

Photographic film, print and slide, color and black and white, is available on Hawai'i, but color print film is most widely available. Camera shops carry the widest variety, but film can also be found at gift shops, sundries store, most activities outlets, and general merchandise stores throughout the island.

Longs Drugs, Wal-Mart, and **Kmart** all have film sales and developing at reasonable prices. For greater selection of film types and full-service options, try **Modern Camera Center** in Hilo, or **Zac's** or **Kona Photo Arts** in Kailua.

BIG ISLAND

ACCOMMODATIONS

Finding suitable accommodations on the Big Island is never a problem. The 9,500-plus rooms available at the island's 170 properties have the lowest annual occupancy rate of any in the islands at only 60 percent. Except for the height of the high seasons and during the Merrie Monarch Festival in Hilo, you can count on finding a room at a bargain. The highest concentration of rooms is strung along Ali'i Drive in Kailua-Kona—more than 5,000 in condos, apartment hotels, and standard hotels. Hilo has almost 2,000 rooms; many of its hotels have "gone condo," and you can get some great deals. The rest are scattered around the island in small villages from Na'alehu in the south to Hawi in the north, where you can almost count on being the only off-island guest. You can comfortably stay in the cowboy town of Waimea or perch above Kilauea Crater at one of the oldest hotel sites in the islands. Other options include vacation rentals, bed-and-breakfasts, and camping, which is superb, with a campsite almost guaranteed at any time.

The Big Island has a tremendous range of accommodations. Some of the state's greatest luxury resorts are within minutes of each other on the Kohala Coast. All are superb, with hideaway "grass shacks," exquisite art collections as an integral part of the grounds, picture-perfect gardens, world-ranked golf courses, and perfect crescent beaches. Kona has fine reasonably priced hotels like the King Kamehameha's Kona Beach Hotel and Royal Kona Resort in downtown Kailua, and the Keauhou Beach Hotel just south toward Keauhou. Interspersed among the big hotels are smaller hotels and condominiums with homey atmospheres and great rates. Hilo offers the best accommodations bargains. First-class hotels such as the Hilo Hawaiian and Naniloa are priced like midrange hotels on the other islands. Gems like the Dolphin Bay Hotel give you so much for your money it's embarrassing. And for a real treat, head to Hawaii Volcanoes National Park and stay at one of the bed-and-breakfasts tucked away there, or at Volcano House where raw nature has thrilled kings, queens, and luminaries like humorist Mark Twain for more than a century. If you want to get away from everybody else, it's no problem, and you don't have to be rich to do it. Pass-through towns like Captain Cook and Waimea have accommodations at very reasonable prices. You can try a self-growth retreat in Puna at Kalani Honua Oceanside Eco-resort or at the Wood Valley Buddhist Temple above Pahala.

Condo Booking and Reservations

The following is a partial list of companies with properties on the Big Island. Vacation rental agencies listed below can also offer this service for condominiums.

Aston Hotels and Resorts, 2250 Kuhio Ave., Honolulu, HI 96815, 808/931-1400 or 800/922-7886 Mainland, 800/445-6633 Canada, or 800/321-2558 in Hawaii, website: aston-hotels.com

Outrigger Hotels and Resorts, 2375 Kuhio Ave., Honolulu, HI 96815, 800/688-7444, website: www.outrigger.com

Marc Resorts Hawaii, 2155 Kalakaua Ave., Honolulu, HI 96815, 808/926-5900 or 800/535-0085, website: marcresorts.com, email: marc@aloha.net

Go Condo Hawaii, 800/452-3463, website: www.gocondohawaii.com

Hawaii Condo Exchange, 800/442-0404, website: http://hawaiicondoexchange.com

Hawaii Resort Management, 75-5776 Kuakini Hwy., Suite 105C, Kailua-Kona, HI 96740, 808/329-9393, fax 808/326-4136

Keahou Property Management, 76-6225 Kuakini Hwy., Suite C105, Kailua-Kona, HI 96740, 808/326-9075 or 800/745-5662, fax 808/326-2055

Sunquest Vacations, 77-6435 Kuakini Hwy., Kailua-Kona, HI 96740, 808/329-6488, 800/800-5662, or 800/367-5168 Mainland, fax 808/329-5480, website: www.sunquest-hawaii.com

Vacation Rentals

The following are major vacation rental agencies on the west side of Hawai'i, where the vast majority of vacation rentals are.

Hawaii Vacation Rentals, 808/882-7000 or fax 808/882-7607, 7 Puako Beach Dr., Kamuela, HI 96743, website: www.bigisland-vacation.com, email: seaside@aloha.net, handles properties almost exclusively in Puako.

South Kohala Management, 808/883-8500 or 800/822-4252, fax 808/883-9818, P.O. Box 384900 Waikoloa, HI 96738, website: www.southkohala.com, email: skm@kona.net, handles premium properties only at the luxury resorts in Kohala.

MacArthur & Company, 65-1148 Mamalahoa Highway, Kamuela, HI 96743, 808/885-8885 or 808/881-1550, website: www.letsgohawaii.com, email: mary@letsgohawaii.com, manages numerous rental homes mostly in the Kohala resort area, Puako, and Waimea.

Aldridge Associates, 808/883-8300, has vacation rentals in Waikoloa.

Century 21, 808/326-2121 or 800/546-5662, fax 808/329-6768, website: www.konaweb.com/vacations, handles mostly economy to midrange condo units in Kailua and Keauhou.

Property Network, 75-5799 Ali'i Dr., Kailua-Kona, HI 96740, 808/329-7977 or 800/358-7977, fax 808/329-1200, website: www.hawaii-kona.com, email: vacation@hawaii-kona.com, handles the full range of condos along the Kona Coast.

West Hawaii Property Services, 78-6831 Ali'i Dr., Suite 237, Kailua-Kona, HI 96740, 808/322-6696 or 800/799-5662, fax 808/324-0609, website: www.konarentals.com, email: whps@ilhawaii.com, has a good range of places from economy to deluxe.

Bed-and-Breakfasts

Aside from the major statewide agencies that arrange bed-and-breakfast accommodations (see the main **Accommodations** section in the On the Road chapter), the island of Hawai'i has it's own. Operating strictly for establishments on the Big Island is **Hawaii Island Bed and Breakfast Association.** This local organization monitors its members for quality standards. For information about HIBBA, contact P.O. Box 1890, Honoka'a, HI 96727, website: www.stayhawaii.com, email: hibba@aloha.net. The association's brochure lists member accommodations with addresses, telephone and fax numbers, email and website addresses, rates, and descriptions.

Hostels

The Big Island has some very reasonably priced hostels. Perhaps the truest hostel experience on the Big Island is in Volcano at **Holo Holo In,** 19-4036 Kalani Honua Rd., P.O. Box 784, Volcano Village, HI 96785, 808/967-7950, fax 808/9678025, website: www.enable.org/holo-holo, email: holoholo@interpac.net. The Holo Holo In is set up with a kitchen, dorms, private rooms, baths, a sauna, and a laundry, and is closed during the daytime. Rates are $17 per person for the dorm ($15 for AYH members), or $40 per couple for a private room. Please bring your own sheets or there will be a nominal extra charge.

Arnott's Lodge, 98 Apapane Rd., Hilo, HI 96720, 808/969-7097, fax 808/961-9638, website: www.arnottslodge.com, email: info@arnottslodge. com, offers a dormitory bunk for $17 and semi-private rooms with a shared bath, kitchen, and living room for $33–57. Arnott's also offers inexpensive hiking excursions.

Patey's Place, 75-195 Ala Ona Ona St., Kailua-Kona, HI 96740, 808/326-7018, fax 808/326-7640, will set you up in a bunk for $17.50 or a private room for $31.50–41.50. Patey's also runs van tours for guests.

The **Hotel Honoka'a Club,** P.O. Box 247, Honoka'a, HI 96727, 808/775-0678 or 800/808-0678, website: http://home1.gte.net/honokaac, email: honokaac@gte.net, has three private rooms for $35 and two communal rooms for $15 in its basement level. All rooms share a bath and kitchen facilities, and upstairs is a dining room.

In Mt. View is **Pineapple Park B&B Hostel,** P.O. Box 5844, Hilo, HI 96720, 808/968-8170 or 877/965-2266, website: www.pineapple-park. com, email: park@aloha.net. A bed in the bunk room runs $17, a double room runs $39, and a private room is $65.

Down on the south end of the Kona Coast is the quiet **Kaimana Guest House and Hostel,** P.O. Box 946, Captain Cook, HI 96704, 808/328-2207, website: www.kaimanavacations.com. Hostel beds run $20, a private single room is $30, and a private double room costs $40.

BIG ISLAND

FOOD

Lu'au
Tihati's Drums of Polynesia Lu'au at the Royal Kona Resort, 808/329-3111, occurs Monday, Friday, and Saturday. It's lots of fun but less traditional.

Royal Lu'au at the Outrigger Waikoloa Beach, 808/886-6789, on Sunday and Wednesday, gets good mention by locals.

Island Breeze Lu'au at King Kamehameha's Kona Beach Hotel, 808/326-4969, is held Sunday, Tuesday, Wednesday, and Thursday on the grounds of King Kamehameha's last residence.

Hale Ho'okipa—Friday Night Lu'au at Kona Village Resort, 808/325-5555, is the longest-running lu'au on the island. Highly recommended.

Old Hawaii Aha'aina Lu'au at the Mauna Kea Beach Hotel, 808/822-7222, is held on Tuesday. Perhaps the most traditional of the bunch, it gets high marks for the food and a fine seaside setting.

Legends of the Pacific at Hilton Waikoloa Village, 808/885-1234, takes place very Friday.

Paniolo Night at the Hapuna Beach Hotel, 808/880-3192, is a departure from the norm with its cowboy theme. Every Friday.

GETTING THERE

Almost all travelers to the Big Island arrive by air. A few lucky ones come by private yacht, or by the cruise ships that dock at Hilo and Kona. For the rest, the island's two major airports are at Hilo and Kona. Most flights to the Big Island have stopovers in Honolulu, but a few fly nonstop to the island.

Flights to the Big Island

Most island flights in the past landed at Hilo International Airport. With the Kona Coast gaining popularity, domestic flights from the Mainland have shifted to that side of the island, and the only direct international connection to the

Big Island lands there as well. United Airlines operates nonstop flights to the Big Island from the Mainland—daily flights from San Francisco and Los Angeles to Kona International Airport. Hawaiian Airlines also flies from Los Angeles to Kona, and Trans World Airlines has started a nonstop flight from St. Louis to Kona. In past peak seasons, United has run a flight to Hilo International Airport, but it's an on-and-off affair depending on the number of travelers. Japan Air Lines offers daily flights from Tokyo to Kona.

All other major domestic and foreign carriers fly you to Honolulu and have arrangements with either Hawaiian Airlines or Aloha Airlines for getting you to the Big Island. This sometimes involves a plane change, but your baggage can be booked straight through. If you fly from the Mainland with Hawaiian or Aloha, you have the added convenience of dealing with just one airline. Several charter airlines also fly to the Big Island nonstop from the Mainland.

Big Island Airports

The largest airport on the Big Island is **Hilo International Airport,** which services Hilo and the eastern half of the island. Formerly known as Gen. Lyman Field, it was named after Gen. Albert Kualii Brickwood Lyman, the first ethnic Hawaiian to become a brigadier general (1942) in the U.S. Army. This airport is remarkably close to downtown Hilo. It's a modern facility with full amenities, and its runways can handle jumbo jets. Interisland flights from here connect directly to Kona, Kahului, and Honolulu, from where you can get to any other airport in the state. The two-story terminal

KONA INTERNATIONAL AIRPORT

RUNWAY

TERMINALS

PARKING

To Kohala Resorts

ONIZUKA SPACE CENTER

RENTAL CAR BOOTHS

TERMINALS

PARKING

19

SCALE NOT AVAILABLE

COMMUTER TERMINAL

To Kailua-Kona, 7 miles

has an information center, a restaurant, vendors, restrooms, telephones, and lockers. Coin lockers large enough for a big backpack rent for 50 cents for 24 hours. Items left longer will be removed and assessed a storage fee. There is no bank, money exchange, or post office. As you face the terminal building, the departure lounge is in the center beyond the check-in counters and agricultural inspection station. Domestic arrivals are on the right and international arrivals are on the left. Each arrival area has baggage claim, restrooms, public telephones, and a small tourist information booth that's usually open 6 A.M.–8 P.M. To the left of the departure area are some helicopter tour company counters. Major car rental agencies have booths to the front of the terminal across the traffic lanes. There is no public transportation to or from the airport; a taxi for the three-mile ride to town costs about $8–12. Public parking is in a large lot behind the car rental booths. Parking fees run from 50 cents for the first half hour up to a maximum of $7 per day. Along the airport road, a short way in toward town, is the commuter terminal building, where several more helicopter companies have their offices and where you check in for their tours.

Kona International Airport is nine miles north of Kailua-Kona and handles the air traffic for Kona. The Kona airport is surrounded by fields of black lava. It handles a growing amount of air traffic from other island cities and all the Mainland and international flights, eclipsing Hilo as the island's major air transportation hub. Interisland flights arrive from Hilo, Honolulu, Kahului, and Lihu'e; Mainland and international flights arrive from San Francisco, Los Angeles, St. Louis, and Tokyo. During winter, charter flights also fly in from Vancouver. The terminal is a series of open-sided, nonconnected Polynesian-style buildings. Departures leave near the center of this cluster, where you also find the agricultural inspection; arrivals come to either end. Here too are lockers, telephones, restrooms, visitor information booths near both baggage claim areas, various food vendors, and other shops. Car rental agencies have booths across the circle road. Access to the public parking lot is 5:30 A.M.–9 P.M.; $1 first half hour, $1 each hour after that, and $7 maximum for 24 hours. There is no public transportation to the airport. A private cab to your hotel in Kailua-Kona will be $12 or more. The commuter terminal just down the road is for helicopter and fixed-wing tourist flight check-in.

Waimea-Kohala Airport is just outside Waimea (Kamuela). There are few amenities and no public transportation to town. Only commuter flights are scheduled between here and Honolulu. **Upolu Airport** is a lonely strip on the extreme northern tip of the island, with no facilities whatsoever and no scheduled flights. Both airports are serviced on request by small charter airlines.

BIG ISLAND

Interisland Carriers

Hawaiian Airlines can be contacted at 800/367-5320 Mainland and Canada, 800/882-8811 statewide, or on the Big Island at 808/935-0858 in Hilo or 808/326-1214 in Kona, website: www.hawaiianair.com. Between Honolulu and Kona, 14 flights (about 40 minutes) are spread throughout the day from approximately 5:15 A.M. to 8 P.M. Two of these flights stop in either Hilo or Kahului (Maui). A similar schedule applies to Hilo, with a few flights stopping in either Kahului or Kona on the way. All other Hawaiian Airlines flights originating in Hilo or Kona go through Kahului or Honolulu. Hawaiian Airlines partners with American Airlines, Continental Airlines, and Northwest Airlines.

Aloha Airlines, 800/367-5250 Mainland and Canada, 808/935-5771 on the Big Island, website: www.alohaair.com, also services the Big Island with flights from the neighboring islands. The 19 daily Honolulu to Kona runs start at 5:20 A.M., with the last at 8:45 P.M.; 15 Honolulu to Hilo flights depart throughout the day, 5:20 A.M.–8 P.M. Connecting through Honolulu, there are 11 daily flights to Lihu'e (Kaua'i). Aloha also flies from Kona and Hilo to Kahului (Maui) with three flights each spread throughout the day. Aloha also has one flight daily from Hilo to Kona. Aloha Airlines partners with United Airlines.

A subsidiary of Aloha Airlines, **Island Air,** 800/323-3345 nationwide, 800/652-6541 statewide, website: www.alohaairlines.com, flies direct from Kona to both Lana'i and Kapalua (Maui) once a day, carrying on to Honolulu. All Island Air flights to the Big Island are on Dash-8 turboprop airplanes.

Pacific Wings, P.O. Box 19, Pa'ia, HI 96779, 808/873-0877, website: www.pacificwings.com, is a local but reputable commercial airline that seems to fill the gaps that the bigger airlines often miss. On the Big Island, it services only the Waimea Airport. Daily flights depart Honolulu and arrive in Waimea at 5:55 P.M. These flights deplane and depart at 6:15 P.M. for Kahului (Maui), where they arrive at 6:50 P.M. Every day except Sunday, a plane leaves Waimea at 8 A.M. for Honolulu, arrival at 9:10 A.M. On Sunday, the flight leaves at 3:10 P.M. and arrives in Honolulu at 4:20 P.M. Pacific Wings also does flight-see tours from its base on Maui and is available for charters. For other information and flight schedules, contact the airline.

GETTING AROUND

The first thing to remember when traveling on the Big Island is that it *is* big, more than four times larger than Rhode Island. A complete range of vehicles is available for getting around, everything from rental cars to mopeds. Hawai'i, like O'ahu and Kaua'i, has some public transportation. Hitchhiking, while illegal, is still used by some to get around. Choose the conveyance that fits your style, and you should have no trouble touring the Big Island.

Highway Overview

Getting around the Big Island is fairly easy. There is one main highway called the Hawai'i Belt Road (also called Mamalahoa Highway) that circles the island, one cross-island highway called the Saddle Road, and a limited number of other highways and secondary roadways. The Hawai'i Belt Road has different numbers in various sections around the island, and this may lead to some confusion. Connecting Kailua-Kona and Hilo around the south end, the number is Highway 11. Major roads that lead off of it are

Napo'opo'o Road (which runs down to Kealakekua Bay), Ke Ala O Keawe Road (to Pu'uhonua O Honaunau National Historical Park), South Point Road (which drops down to the southernmost tip of the island), Chain of Craters Road (through Hawaii Volcanoes National Park to the lava-covered littoral Puna Coast), and Kea'au-Pahoa Road (Highway 130) from Kea'au to the hinterland of Puna. In Puna, Kapoho-Pahoa Road (Highway 132) and Kapoho-Kalapana Beach Road (Highway 137) make a circle with Highway 130 from Pahoa, down along the shore, and back again.

Going north from Kailua-Kona, the Hawai'i Belt Road (Highway 190), which starts off for the first few miles as Palani Road, cuts across the upper slopes of the volcanoes to Waimea. Slicing through coffee country as part of the Belt Road is Highway 180. From Honalo, Route 11 heads down toward Kailua, first as Kuakini Highway, which itself makes a tangent into town, and then as Queen Ka'ahumanu Highway. Heading north from Kailua, Queen Ka'ahumanu Highway becomes Route 19. In Kawaihae, it turns uphill to Waimea, becoming Kawaihae Road. In Waimea, Highways 19 and 190 merge, and Highway 19 becomes the designation as the Hawai'i Belt Road continues along and down the Hamakua Coast back to Hilo. Connecting Highway 19 and Highway 190 through the town of Waikoloa is Waikoloa Road. In Honoka'a, Highway 240 leaves the Belt Road and runs north to the edge of Waipi'o Valley. North Kohala is cut by two roads. Akoni Pule Highway (Highway 270) runs along the coast up and around the tip as far as the Pololu Valley. Connecting this road and the town of Waimea is the Kohala Mountain Road (Highway 250). Off limits to most rental cars, the Saddle Road (Highway 200) rises to about 6,500 feet between the tall peaks of Mauna Loa and Mauna Kea, making a shortcut between Hilo and Waimea or the Kohala Coast. From along the Saddle Road, rugged 4WD roads lead up to the observatories atop Mauna Kea and nearly to the top of Mauna Loa.

CAR RENTALS

The best way to tour the island is in a rented car, but keep these tips in mind. Most car companies charge you a fee if you rent the car in Hilo and drop it off in Kona, and vice versa. The agencies are prejudiced against the Saddle Road and the spur road leading to South Point, both of which offer some of *the* most spectacular scenery on the island. Their prejudice is unfounded because both roads are paved, generally well maintained, and no problem if you take your time. They'll claim the insurance will not cover you if you have a mishap on these roads. A good automobile policy at home will cover you in a rental car, but definitely check this before you take off. It's even possible, but not recommended, to drive to the top of Mauna Kea if there is no snow. Plenty of signs to the summit say "4WD only"; heed them, not so much for going up, but for needed braking power coming down. Don't even hint of these intentions to the car rental agencies, or they won't rent you a car.

No way whatsoever should you attempt to drive down to Waipi'o Valley in a car! The grade is unbelievably steep, and only a 4WD compound first gear can make it. Put simply, you have a good chance of being killed if you try it in a car.

Gas stations are farther apart than on the other islands, and sometimes they close very early. As a rule, fill up whenever the gauge reads half full.

Both Hilo International Airport and Kona International Airport have a gauntlet of car rental booths and courtesy phones outside the terminals.

Auto Rental Companies

The following are major firms that are represented at both the Hilo and Kona airports. Kona numbers begin with "329" and "327," Hilo with "961" or "935."

Dollar, 808/961-6059, 808/329-2744, or 800/800-4000, website: www.dollarcar.com

Alamo, 808/961-3343, 808/329-8896, or 800/327-9633, website: www.goalamo.com

National, 808/935-0891, 808/329-1674, or 800/227-7368, website: www.nationalcar.com

Avis, 808/935-1290, 808/327-3000, or 800/321-3712, website: www.avis.com

Budget, 808/935-6878, 808/329-8511, or 800/527-0700 nationwide, website: www.drivebudget.com

Hertz, 808/935-2896, 808/329-3566, 800/654-3011 worldwide, website: www.hertz.com

BIG ISLAND

Some years ago, local companies abounded, but today only one has survived with any significance. At **Harper,** in Hilo at 808/969-1478 and in Kona at 808/329-6688, or 800/852-9993 off-island, you can rent a car, truck, 7- to 15-passenger van, RV, or 4WD for driving up to Mauna Kea. Good competitive rates.

Motorcycles and Mopeds

D.J.'s Rentals, 808/329-1700, open daily 7:30 A.M.–6 P.M., is directly across from the King Kamehameha's Hotel in Kailua-Kona in an outdoor booth. D.J.'s rents mopeds, scooters, and motorcycles. Costs are: one-person mopeds $15 half day, $25 daily, and $125 a week; two-person scooters (capable of attaining highway speeds), $25 half day, $45 daily, and $225 a week. The top-of-the-line Harley costs $175 daily or $110 half day, a Big Twin Harley-Davidson costs $145 daily or $90 half day, and all other motorcycles rent at about 20 percent less. A half day is 7:30 A.M.–noon, and then again noon–6 P.M.

At Coconut Grove Marketplace in Kailua-Kona, **Safari Activities,** 808/334-0464, rents mopeds at $30 a day during daylight hours and $35 for 24 hours.

Motor Homes

If you don't want to stop at a hotel every night, why not take your hotel with you! **Island RV,** 75-5785 Kuakini Hwy., Kailua-Kona, HI 96740, 808/334-0464 or 800/406-4555, lets you do just that by renting an RV so you can go at your own pace and stop where you want. The RVs sleep up to six and come with all the necessary cooking and sleeping gear. The rental rate is $225 a day or $1,495 a week, but the weekly rate also includes airport pickup, itinerary planning, park registration fees, and the last night in a Kona hotel.

Harper car rental company also rents RVs, 808/969-1478 in Hilo, 808/329-6688 in Kona, or 800/852-9993.

ALTERNATIVE TRANSPORTATION

Hele-On Bus

The county of Hawai'i maintains the Mass Transportation System (MTS), known throughout the island as the Hele-On Bus. For information, schedules, and fares contact the Mass Transit Agency at 25 Aupuni St., Hilo, HI 96720, 808/961-8744. Hours are Mon.–Fri. 7:45 A.M.–4:30 P.M. The main bus terminal is in downtown Hilo at Mo'oheau Park, just at the corner of Kamehameha Avenue and Mamo Street. Recently, it's been completely rebuilt and modernized. Like bus terminals everywhere, it has a local franchise of derelicts and down-and-outers, but they leave you alone. The Hele-On Bus system now has a mostly modern fleet of large buses that are clean and comfortable. The Hele-On operates Mon.–Fri. approximately 6 A.M.–6 P.M., depending on the run, except for the route to Kona and Kohala, which also operate Saturdays, and the route to the North Kohala resorts, which operates daily. There are a number of intra-Hilo routes with additional intercity routes to points around the periphery of the island. If you're in a hurry then definitely forget about taking it, but if you want to meet the people of Hawai'i, there's no better way. The base fare is 75 cents, which increases whenever you go into another zone. Transfers are given free if you must change buses, but these must be used within an hour. Discount fares (monthly, one-way, round-trip, disabled, senior citizen, student) are available. Have change for exact fare when you board. You can also be charged an extra $1 for a large backpack or suitcase. Don't worry about that—the Hele-On is one of the best bargains in the country. Large-item surf boards, boogie boards, and bicycles are not allowed. There are five basic intercity routes connecting to Hilo. One goes from Kealia, south of Captain Cook, all the way to Hilo on the east coast via Kailua-Kona, Waikoloa, Waimea, Honoka'a, and Laupahoehoe. This journey (operating Mon.–Sat.) covers 110 miles in just over four hours and costs about $6, the most expensive fare in the system. From North Kohala, a daily bus from the Hilton Waikoloa Village Resort makes its way through Waimea to Hilo, making few stops. You can take the southern route from Ocean View Estates through Ka'u, passing through Na'alehu and Volcano, and continuing on to Hilo. This trip takes just 2.5 and costs $5.25. A fourth runs from Pahoa through Kea'au to Hilo, while the fifth goes down the coast from Honoka'a to Hilo. In the Kohala District, a bus runs every weekday morning from Kapa'au to Hilton Waikoloa Village and returns in the late afternoon.

Shuttle Services

Kona and Kohala are serviced by a three-part shuttle system that together is called the **Kona Coast Express**, 808/331-1582. The Kona Town Trolley runs from Keauhou pier at its southern end to King Kamehameha's Kona Beach Hotel, stopping at condos along this stretch as well as Huggo's and the Kona Inn Shopping Village. The Kohala Coast-Waikoloa Resort Express Bus makes stops at all the Kohala resorts and at the King's Shopping Center. The Kona Coast Express Bus connects passengers between these southern and northern sections of the system. Transfer stations are at the King's Shopping Center in Waikoloa and the King Kamehameha's Kona Beach Hotel in Kailua. An all-day pass on either the Kona Town Trolley or the Kohala Coast-Waikoloa Resort Express Bus is $5 per person. A $15 all-day pass lets you transfer from one section to the other and use the entire system. The Kona Town Trolley runs 7:40 A.M.–8:20 P.M., the Kohala Coast-Waikoloa Resort Express Bus runs 6 A.M.–10 P.M., and the connecting Kona Coast Express Bus runs 6 A.M.–10:20 P.M.; each runs at approximately 90-minute intervals.

Kailua-Kona also has the **Ali'i Shuttle**, 808/775-7121, which cruises Ali'i Drive but makes different stops than the Kona Town Trolley. This red, white, and blue bus runs every 90 minutes, 7:50 A.M.–9:10 P.M. At the north end it stops at the Lanihau Center, King Kamehameha's Hotel, Kona Inn Shopping Village, Hulihe'e Palace, and Royal Kona Resort. On the way south, pickups are at Magic Sands Beach and Kahalu'u Beach Park. On the south end it stops at Keauhou Shopping Center and Kona Country Club. Rides are $2 each way, $5 for a day pass, $20 for a weekly pass, or $40 for a monthly pass.

The tour bus company, Roberts Hawaii, also runs the **Kona Coast Shuttle** service connecting the Kohala Coast luxury resorts to Hilo Hattie and Kona Inn Shopping Village in Kailua-Kona. This service runs 7 A.M.–9 P.M., with seven round-trips a day. The charge is $10 for adults and $8 for children 2–12. Call to reserve a seat, 808/329-1688.

Taxis

Both the Hilo and Kona airports always have taxis waiting for fares. Fares are regulated at $4 for the first mile, $2 each mile after that, and 25 cents for an eighth of a mile. From Hilo's airport to downtown costs about $12, to the Banyan Drive hotels about $8. From the Kona Airport to hotels and condos along Ali'i Drive in Kailua fares run $19–32, north to Waikoloa Beach Resort they run about $40, and are approximately $60 as far north as the Mauna Kea Resort. Obviously, a taxi is no way to get around if you're trying to save money. Most taxi companies, both in Kona and Hilo, also run sightseeing services for fixed prices. In **Kona** try: Kona Taxi, 808/329-7779; Paradise Taxi, 808/329-1234; Laura's Taxi, 808/326-5466; or C&C Taxi, 808/329-6388. In **Hilo** try: Hilo Harry's Taxi, 808/935-7091; A-1 Bob's Taxi, 808/959-4800; and Percy's Taxi, 808/969-7060.

Inquire from the County Transit Agency, 800/961-8744, about money-saving coupons for "shared-ride taxi service." The coupons allow door-to-door taxi service within the urbanized areas of Hilo and Kona up to a nine-mile limit. Pre-purchased $2 coupons must be used for this service, and rides require one or two coupons. Service hours, participating taxi companies, and other restrictions apply.

An alternative in the Kona area is **Speedy Shuttle**, 808/329-5433. Speedy Shuttle runs multi-seat vans, so its prices are cheaper per person the more people you have riding. Sample rates from the Kona Airport are $15 to downtown Kailua-Kona, $23 to the south end of Kailua and the Keauhou area, and $26 for a ride up to Waikoloa Beach Resort. Speedy Shuttle has a courtesy phone at the airport for your convenience. Reservations a day ahead are not necessary but may be helpful to get a ride at the time that you want.

Hitchhiking

The old thumb works on the Big Island about as well as anywhere else. Although hitchhiking is technically illegal, the police seem to have much more important things to pay attention to than going after those just trying to get down the road. Stay off the roadway, be low-key, but make your intentions known. Some people hitchhike rather than take the Hele-On Bus not so much to save money but to save time! It's a good idea to check the bus schedule (and routes) and set out about 30 minutes before

BIG ISLAND

the scheduled departure. If you don't have good luck hitching a ride, just wait for the bus to come along and hail it. It'll stop.

MEDICAL SERVICES

Hospitals

On the east side, 24-hour medical help is available from Hilo Medical Center, 808/974-4700, and Honoka'a Hospital, 808/775-7211. While in Ka'u, seek help from the Ka'u Hospital in Pahala, 808/928-8331. On the west side, try Kona Community Hospital in Kealakekua, 808/322-9311, or **Straub Clinic and Hospital,** 808/329-9211. The new North Hawaii Community Hospital in Kamuela, 808/889-6211, services the northern part of the island.

Medical Clinics

For minor emergencies and urgent care in Kona, try **Kona-Kohala Medical Associates,** 808/329-1346 in Kailua. **Hualalai Urgent Care,** 808/327-4357, and **Kaiser Permanente,** 808/327-2900, are nearby. In Hilo, try **Kaiser Permanente,** 808/934-4000, or **Hilo Medical Associates,** 808/934-2000. In Waimea, use the **Lucy Henrigues Medical Center,** 808/885-7921.

Pharmacies

Longs Drugs, KTA Super Stores, and **Kmart** all have pharmacies. Others that should meet your needs are: **Village Pharmacy,** 808/885-4418, in Waimea; **Hilo Pharmacy,** 808/961-9267, along the bay front; **Kealakekua Pharmacy,** 808/322-1639, in Kealakekua; **Waikoloa Pharmacy,** 808/883-8484; and **Kamehameha Pharmacy,** 808/889-6161, in Kapa'au.

Alternative Health Care

The Big Island is blessed with some of the finest natural healers and practitioners in the state. For a holistic healing experience of body, mind, and soul, the following are highly recommended.

At the **School of Hawaiian Lomi Lomi,** P.O. Box 221, Captain Cook, HI 96704, 808/323-2416 or 808/328-2472, Margaret Machado, assisted by her husband Daniel, provides the finest *lomi lomi* and traditional Hawaiian herbal cures in the islands. Both are renowned *kupuna* who dispense a heavy dose of love and concern with every remedy prescribed.

Acupuncture and Herbs is the domain of Angela Longo. This remarkable woman is not only a superbly trained, licensed practitioner of traditional Chinese medicine and acupuncture, but she covers all bases by holding a Ph.D. in biochemistry from the University of California, Berkeley. For a totally holistic health experience, contact Angela at her Waimea office, 808/885-7886.

Angela's top student, **Karen MacIsaac,** has opened a Chinese herb and acupuncture clinic by appointment only, 808/329-4393, at 75-5995 Kuakini Hwy., Suite 126, Kailua-Kona, HI 96740.

The **Hawaiian Islands School of Body Therapy,** 808/322-0048, offers state-certified massage courses and mini-courses for the beginning or experienced therapist. Massage, anatomy, and physiology are part of the course work preparing the student for a Hawaii State License. Programs include a basic massage program taking 150 hours, an advanced massage program of 450 hours, and a third-level course designed for the professional that takes a minimum of one year's intensive study to complete.

A wonderful healing center is **Halemana** in Pahoa, 808/965-7783, where they'll soothe you with acupuncture and massage.

Academy of Massage Clinic, 211 Kino'ole St., Hilo, 808/935-2596, focuses on pre-licensing programs with an emphasis on sports massage, injury prevention and care, inner changes of body psychology, and *lomi lomi.* Semesters include a summer intensive and regular winter and fall classes. This is a great opportunity to receive a quality massage at a reasonable price while visiting Hilo.

INFORMATION AND SERVICES

For **police, fire, and ambulance** anywhere on the Big Island, dial **911**. For **nonemergency police** assistance and information call 808/935-3311 in Hilo or 808/323-2645 in Kona.

Civil Defense: In case of natural disaster such as hurricanes or tsunamis on the Big Island, call 808/935-0031. **Coast Guard Search and Rescue** can be reached at 800/552-6458.

Sexual Assault Crisis Line: Call 808/935-0677 for cases involving sexual assault or rape crisis.

For recorded information on **local island weather,** call 808/961-5582; for the **marine report,** call 808/935-9883; and for **volcano activity,** call 808/985-6000. For time of day, dial 808/961-0212.

Consumer Protection

If you encounter problems with accommodations, bad service, or downright rip-offs, try the following: the Chamber of Commerce in Hilo, 808/935-7178, or in Kailua-Kona, 808/329-1758; the Office of Consumer Protection, 808/974-6230; or the Better Business Bureau of Hawaii on Oʻahu, 808/536-6956.

Tourism Information

The best information on the Big Island is dispensed by the HVB Hilo Branch, 250 Keawe St., Hilo, HI 96720, 808/961-5797, and HVB Kona Branch, 75-5719 W. Aliʻi Dr., Kailua-Kona, HI 96740, 808/329-7787, website: www.bigisland.org.

The **visitor information booths** at the two island airports, 808/934-5838 in Hilo and 808/329-3423 in Kona, are good sources of information available on arrival. The Wailoa Center in downtown Hilo, 808/933-4360, open 8 A.M.–4:30 P.M. Mon.–Fri., also maintains visitor information and brochures about the island.

Post Office

Normal business hours are Mon.–Fri. 8 A.M.–4:30 P.M., Saturday 9 A.M.–1 P.M. The central post office on Hawaiʻi is in Hilo, and there are 25 branch post offices in towns around the island. For information, call 800/275-8777.

Reading Material

Libraries are located in towns and schools all over the island. The main branch is at 300 Waianuenue Ave., Hilo, 808/933-8888. It provides all information regarding libraries. In Kailua-Kona, the library is at 75-140 Hualalai Rd., 808/327-4327. Branch libraries are in Kapaʻau, Holualoa, Honokaʻa, Keaʻau, Kealakekua, Laupahoehoe, Mt. View, Naʻalehu, Pahala, Pahoa, and Waimea.

Free **tourist literature** and the narrow-format, magazine-style *This Week Big Island, Spotlight's Big Island Gold,* and *Big Island Beach and Activity Guide* are available at the airport, many hotels, and most restaurants and shopping centers around the island. They come out monthly or quarterly and contain money-saving coupons, information on local events and activities, shopping and restaurants, and island maps. The small-format magazine-style *Coffee Times* focuses on cultural and historical topics, while the newspaper-format *Hawaiʻi Island Journal* concentrates on issues of the day and has very good island calendars of events section. With a focus on activities and fun things to do, *101 Things to do on Hawaii The Big Island* is a great resource and also has money-saving coupons. Publications with local orientation are *Kohala Mountain News, Kona Times, Hamakua Times* and *The Waimea Gazette. Big Island Drive Guide* is available from the car rental agencies and contains tips, coupons, and good maps. The Hawaii AAA *Tourbook* is also very useful. Other publications of interest are the in-flight magazines of Aloha and Hawaiian Airlines.

Daily island newspapers include *Hawaii Tribune-Herald,* a Hilo publication, website: www.hilohawaiitribune.com, and *West Hawaii Today,* published in Kona, website: www.westhawaiitoday.com, both owned by the same parent company. Each costs 50 cents daily and $1 on Sunday. The *Kaʻu Landing* is a monthly out of Ocean View, website: www.kau-landing.com.

Island Radio

More than a dozen radio stations broadcast on the Big Island. Most broadcast only on either the Hilo or Kona side, while a few send signals to both sides. Popular stations: KIPA 620 AM, Rainbow Radio, plays easy listening contemporary music; KPUA 670 AM offers news and sports; KAOE 92.7 FM spins oldies and rock and roll; KWXX 94.7 FM combines island music and light contemporary rock; KNWB 97.1 FM broadcasts jazz and rock; and K-BIG 97.9 FM plays contemporary adult music.

Island Facts

Hawai'i has three fitting nicknames: the Big Island, the Volcano Island, and the Orchid Island. It's the youngest, most southerly, and largest (4,028 square miles) island in the Hawaiian chain. Its color is red, the island flower is the red lehua ('ohi'a), and the island lei is fashioned from the 'ohi'a-lehua blossom.

R.J. BAKER, 1908

BIG ISLAND

KONA

Kona is long and lean and takes its suntanned body for granted. This district *is* the west coast of the Big Island and lies in the rain shadows of Mauna Loa and Mauna Kea. You can come here expecting brilliant sunny days and glorious sunsets, and you won't be disappointed; this reliable sunshine has earned Kona the nickname "The Gold Coast." Offshore, the fishing grounds are legendary, especially for marlin that lure game-fishing enthusiasts from around the world. There are actually two Konas, north and south, and both enjoy an upland interior of forests, ranches, and homesteads while most of the coastline is low, broad, and flat. If you've been fantasizing about swaying palms and tropical jungles dripping with wild orchids, you might be in for "Kona shock," especially if you fly directly into the Kona Airport. Around the airport the land is raw black lava that can appear as forbidding as the tailings from an old mining operation. Don't despair. Once in town, trees form a cool canopy and flowers add color at every turn.

The entire Kona District is old and historic. This was the land of Lono, god of fertility and patron of the Makahiki Festival. It was also the spot where the first missionary packet landed and changed Hawaii forever, and it's been a resort since the 19th century. In and around **Kailua** are restored *heiau,* a landmark lava church, and a royal palace where the monarchs of Hawaii came to relax. The coastline is rife with historical sites: lesser *heiau,* petroglyph fields, fishponds, and a curious amusement ride dating from the days of the Makahiki. Below the town of Captain Cook is **Kealakekua Bay,** the first and main *haole* anchorage in the islands until the development of Honolulu Harbor. This bay's historical significance is overwhelming, alternately being a place of life, death, and hope from where the spirit of Hawaii was changed for all time. Here on the southern coast is a Hawaiian "temple of refuge," restored and made into a national historical park. The majority of Kona's sights are strung along Route 11. Except for Kailua-Kona, where a walking tour is perfect, you need a rental car to visit the sights; the Big Island's Hele-On Bus runs too infrequently to be feasible. If you're walking, pick up a copy of the pamphlet *Walking*

KONA

PACIFIC

BIG ISLAND

North Kona

K O N A

SEE "KAILUA-KONA" MAP

SEE "KAILUA-KEAUHOU" MAP

approximate range of Kona coffee production

To Waimea

To Kawaihae

190

BIG ISLAND COUNTRY CLUB

MAMALAHOA HWY

Pu'uanahulu

PU'U WA'AWA'A RANCH

Pu'u Wa'awa'a (3,967 ft)

Pu'u Papa (3,950 ft)

Hainoa (4,083 ft)

MAKALEI HAWAII COUNTRY CLUB

Pu'u Iki (3,417 ft)

Potato Hill

Hualalai (8,271 ft)

Hu'ehu'e Ranch

Hinaka Crater

KALOKO DR.

Honokohau (Palani Junction)

Pu'u La'la'au (6,526 ft)

Holualoa

Kahalu'u

DAI FUKUJI BUDDHIST TEMPLE

GREENWELL ETHNOBOTANICAL GARDEN

Honalo

Kainaliu

KONA HOSPITAL

Kealakekua

MARIA LANAKIA CHURCH

KONA HISTORICAL SOCIETY

Keikiwaha Point

BELT RD.

HAWAII BELT RD.

180

11

Kailua Kona

KALOKO INDUSTRIAL PARK

ONIZUKA SPACE CENTER

Kaloa

19

Kaloko Fishpond

KAMEHAMEHA PRESUMED BURIAL SITE

KALOKO-HONOKOHAU NATIONAL HISTORIC PARK

HONOKOHAU MARINA

OLD KONA AIRPORT STATE RECREATION AREA

KONA INDUSTRIAL AREA

WHITE SANDS BEACH COUNTY PARK

KONA COUNTRY CLUB

Keauhou Bay

Kahalu'u Bay

Keauhou Bay

Holualoa Bay

Kailua Bay

Pine Trees

NELHA FACILITY

Keahole Point

KONA INTERNATIONAL AIRPORT

KONA COAST STATE PARK

19

HUALALAI GOLF CLUB

FOUR SEASONS RESORT

KONA VILLAGE RESORT

Kaupulehu Pond

Kua Bay

Nawaikulua Point

Makalawena Beach

Kawili Point

Mahai'ula Bay

Makolea Point

Kiholo Bay

Waikoloa Beach

QUEEN KA'AHUMANU HWY

KA'AHUMANU HWY

OCEAN

COAST

ALEXANDER & BALDWIN SUGAR MILL
HIKIAU HEIAU STATE MONUMENT
NAPO'OPO'O BEACH COUNTY PARK

Na'po'opo'o
Ke'ei
Honaunau
ST. BENEDICT'S
PAINTED CHURCH

HONAUNAU RODEO

PU'U HONAUNAU
NATIONAL HISTORIC PARK
(CITY OF REFUGE)

Keokea
Kealia
Ho'okena

Loa Point
Kapulu Bay
Lepeamoa Rock
Ka'u Loa Point

HO'OKENA BEACH
COUNTY PARK

approximate range of
Kona coffee production

South
Kona

KIPAHOEHOE
NATURAL AREA
RESERVE

Ho'opuloa
Miloli'i

Kipahoehoe Bay

Arched Rock

MILOLI'I BEACH
COUNTY PARK

Moku O Kaha'ilani Rock
Miloli'i Bay
Pa'u Hinahina Bay

MACADAMIA
NUT FARM

HOLUA
(SLIDE)

Hawaiian
Ocean View
Estates

MANUKA STATE
WAYSIDE

MANUKA
NATURAL AREA
RESERVE

To Na'alehu and Volcanoes

0   10 mi

0   10 km

© SANDRA E. BISIGNANI TRUST AND AVALON TRAVEL PUBLISHING, INC.

Tour of Historic Kailua Village, put out by the Kona Historical Society.

Kailua-Kona is the heart of North Kona, by far the most developed area in the district. Its **Ali'i Drive** is lined with shops, hotels, and condos, but for the most part the shoreline vista remains intact because most of the buildings are low-rise. To show just how fertile lava can be when tended, miles of multi-hued bougainvillea and poinsettias line Ali'i Drive like a lei. Above Kailua to the east is the former coffee town and now artists' community of **Holualoa**. This upcountry village sits on the lower slope of **Mount Hualalai** (8,271 feet), and it's here that local people still earn a living growing vegetables and taro on small truck farms high in the mountain coolness. But it has been—and still is—coffee that is the most famous agricultural product of the upcountry region and its dominant economic force. Just a few miles north of Kailua, the land turns dry and huge swaths of black lava interspersed with arid scrubland become characteristic of the terrain from here through South Kohala to Kawaihae.

South Kona begins near the town of **Captain Cook.** Southward continues a region of diminutive coffee plantations where bushes grow to the shoulder of the road and the air is heady with the rich aroma of roasting coffee. South Kona is rural and far less populated. It's a rugged region, and the road stays high above the coastline. Farther south, rough but passable roads branch from the main highway and tumble toward hidden beaches and tiny fishing villages where time just slips away. From north to south, Kona is awash in brilliant sunshine, and the rumble of surf and the plaintive cry of seabirds create the music of peace.

KAILUA-KONA

SIGHTS

Ahu'ena Heiau

Directly seaward of King Kamehameha's Kona Beach Hotel, at the north end of "downtown" Kailua, is the restored Ahu'ena Heiau. Built on an artificial island in Kamakahonu (Eye of the Turtle) Beach, it's in a very important historical area. Kamehameha I, the great conqueror, came here to spend the last years of his life, settling down to a peaceful existence after many years of war and strife. The king, like all Hawaiians, reaffirmed his love of the *'aina* and tended his own royal taro patch on the slopes of Mt. Hualalai. After he died, his bones were prepared according to ancient ritual on a stone platform within the temple, then taken to a secret burial place just north of town which is believed to be somewhere near Wawahiwa'a Point. It was Kamehameha who initiated the first rebuilding of Ahu'ena Heiau, a temple of peace and prosperity dedicated to Lono, god of fertility. The rituals held here were a far cry from the bloody human sacrifices dedicated to the god of war, Kuka'ilimoku, that were held at Pu'ukohola Heiau, which Kamehameha had built a few leagues north and a few decades earlier. At Ahu'ena, Kamehameha gathered the sage *kahuna* of the land to discourse in the Hale Mana (main prayer house) on topics concerning wise government and statesmanship. It was here that Liholiho, Kamehameha's son and heir, was educated, and it was here that as a grown man he sat down with the great queens, Keopuolani and Ka'ahumanu, and broke the ancient *kapu* of eating with women, thereby destroying the old order.

The tallest structure on the temple grounds is the *'anu'u* (oracle tower), where the chief priest, in deep trance, received messages from the gods. Throughout the grounds are superbly carved *kia akua* (temple image posts) in the distinctive Kona style, considered some of the finest of all Polynesian art forms. The spiritual focus of the *heiau* was humanity's higher nature, and the tallest figure, crowned with an image of the golden plover, was that of Koleamoku, a god of healing. Another interesting structure is a small thatched hut of sugarcane leaves, Hale Nana Mahina, which means "house from which to watch the farmland." Kamehameha would come here to meditate while a guard kept watch from a nearby shelter. The commanding view from the doorway affords a sweeping panorama from the sea to the king's plantations on the slopes of Mt. Hualalai. Though the temple

KAILUA-KONA

BIG ISLAND

To Captain Cook and Volcano

To Waimea

To Airport and Kawaihae

To Captain Cook and Holualoa

To Captain Cook and Volcano

To Keauhou

HWY

182

HWY

HUALALAI

ALOHA KONA DR.

RD.

KUAKINI

Alii Dr

seawall

Kailua Bay

Kailua

KALANI ST.

ALA ONAONA

HENRY ST.

PALANI RD.

QUEEN

KA'AHUMANU

190

11

0   0.1 mi
0   0.1 km

CROSSROADS CENTER

WAL-MART

BORDERS BOOKS AND MUSIC

PATEY'S PLACE

MORMON CHURCH

HUALALAI URGENT CARE

KONA ISLANDER INN

KONA BILLFISHER

TRES HOMBRES

KONA REEF

HALE KONA KAI

ROYAL KONA RESORT

HUGGO'S RESTAURANT

COCONUT GROVE MARKETPLACE

ST. MICHAEL'S CATHOLIC CHURCH

LIBRARY

BANK OF HAWAII

PARKING

PARKING

KONA BAY HOTEL

WATERFRONT ROW

HALE HALAWAI O HOLUALOA CONGREGATIONAL CHURCH

KOBA INN SHOPPING VILLAGE

KONA MARKETPLACE

KAMEHAMEHA PLAZA

MOKU'AIKAUA CHURCH

HULIHE'E PALACE

KONA BANYAN COURT

KONA RANCH HOUSE

OCEAN VIEW INN

KONA SEASIDE

KONA SQUARE

FISH WEIGH SCALES

KAILUA PIER

AHU'ENA HEIAU

KOPIKO PLAZA

LANI'AU CENTER

HILO HATTE

BANK

POST OFFICE

FIRE STATION

KONA COAST SHOPPING CENTER

NORTH KONA SHOPPING CENTER

KONA BREWERY

KAMEHAMEHA MALL

KING KAMEHAMEHA'S KONA BEACH HOTEL

PARKING

KING

PARKING

KAILUA-KEAUHOU

ROYAL KONA RESORT

To Kailua-Kona

KONA REEF

KAILUA PLANTATION HOUSE BED & BREAKFAST

KONA TIKI

Kahului Bay

ASTON ROYAL SEA CLIFF RESORT

CASA DE EMDEKO SHOPPING CENTER

KONA BY THE SEA

ALI'I GARDEN MARKETPLACE

HALE MALUHIA COUNTRY INN BED AND BREAKFAST

To Holualoa

KONA BALI KAI

Holualoa Bay

Kamoa Point

LA BOURGOGNE

KONA MAGIC SANDS RESORT

WHITE SANDS BEACH COUNTY PARK (DISAPPEARING SANDS)

KAHALU'U

KU'EMANU HEIAU

Kahalu'u Bay

ST. PETER'S CATHOLIC CHURCH

KAHALU'U BEACH COUNTY PARK

HAPAI ALI'I HEIAU

KE'EKU HEIAU

KEAUHOU BEACH RESORT

KEAUHOU SHOPPING CENTER

KANALOA AT KONA

KEAUHOU RESORT

KONA COUNTRY CLUB

HOLUA SLIDE RUINS

BIRTHPLACE OF KAMEHAMEHA III

KEAUHOU

Keauhou Bay

KUAKINI HIGHWAY

HUALALAI RD.

HUALALAI RD.

HAWAI'I

BELT

ALI'I DRIVE

KAMEHAMEHA III RD.

MAMALAHOA

HIGHWAY

ROAD

Kuamo'o Bay

LEKE LEKE BURIAL GROUND

To Captain Cook

0   .5 mi
0   .5 km

grounds, reconstructed under the auspices of the Bishop Museum, are impressive, they are only one-third their original size. The *heiau* itself is closed to visitors but you can get a good look at it from the shore. Free tours offered by King Kamehameha's Kona Beach Hotel take you down to the *heiau* and include a tour of its own hotel grounds as well. The hotel portion of the tour includes a walk through the lobby, where various artifacts are displayed, and features an extremely informative botanical tour that highlights the medicinal herbs of old Hawaii. The hotel tours begin at 1:30 P.M. weekdays; call 808/329-2911. Don't miss this excellent educational opportunity, well worth the time and effort!

While in the area, make sure to visit the **Kailua Pier,** across the street from the *heiau*. Fishing boats are in and out all day, with most charters returning around 5 P.M. You'll have a chance to see some of the marlin for which Kona is noted, but if you have a sympathetic heart or weak stomach it might not be for you. This area is frantic with energy during the various "billfish tournaments" held throughout the year.

Moku'aikaua Church

Kailua is one of those towns that would love to contemplate its own navel if it could only find it. It doesn't really have a center, but if you had to pick one, it would be the 112-foot steeple of Moku'aikaua Church. This highest structure in town has been a landmark for travelers and seafarers ever since the church was completed in January 1837. Established in 1820, the church resolute beams are native 'ohi'a, pegged together and closely resembling the fine beamwork used in barns throughout 19th-century New England. The pews, railings, pulpit, and trim are all fashioned from koa, a rich brown, lustrous wood that begs to be stroked. Although the church is still used as a house of worship, it also has the air of a museum, housing paintings of historical personages instrumental in Hawaii's Christian past. The crowning touch is an excellent model of the brig *Thaddeus,* painstakingly built by the men of the Pacific Fleet Command in 1934 and presented to the church in 1975. The church is open daily from sunrise to sunset, and volunteer hostesses answer your questions 10 A.M.–noon and 1–3:30 P.M.

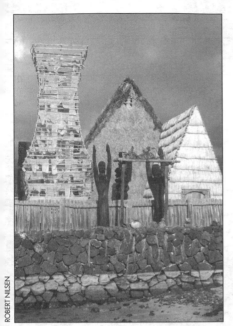

Ahu'ena Heiau

ROBERT NILSEN

Hulihe'e Palace

Go from the spiritual to the temporal by walking across the street from Moku'aikaua Church and entering Hulihe'e Palace. This two-story Victorian structure commissioned by Hawaii's second governor, John Kuakini, dates from 1838. A favorite summer getaway for all the Hawaiian monarchs who followed, especially King Kalakaua, it was used as such until 1914. At first glance, the outside is unimpressive, but the more you look the more you realize how simple and grand it is. The architectural lines are those of an English country manor, and indeed Great Britain was held in high esteem by the Hawaiian royalty. Inside, the palace is bright and airy. Most of the massive furniture is made from koa. Many pieces were constructed by foreigners, including the German Wilhelm Fisher. The most magnificent pieces include a huge formal dining table, 70 inches in diameter, fashioned from one solid koa log. Upstairs is a tremendous four-poster bed that belonged to Queen Kapi'olani, and two magnificent cabinets that were built by a Chinese convict serving a life sentence for smuggling opium. King Kalakaua heard of his talents and commissioned him to build the cabinets. They proved to be so wonderfully crafted that after they were completed the king pardoned the craftsman.

Prince Kuhio, who inherited the palace from his uncle, King Kalakaua, was the first Hawaiian delegate to Congress. He decided to auction off all the furniture and artifacts to raise money, supposedly for the benefit of the Hawaiian people.

claims to be the oldest house of Christian worship in Hawaii. The site was given by King Liholiho to the first Congregationalist missionaries, who arrived on the brig *Thaddeus* in the spring of that year. Taking the place of two previous grass structures, the construction of this building was undertaken in 1835 by the Hawaiian congregation under the direction of Reverend Asa Thurston. Much thought was given to the orientation of the structure, designed so the prevailing winds blow through the entire length of the church to keep it cool and comfortable. The walls of the church are fashioned from massive, roughhewn lava stone, mortared with plaster made from crushed and burned coral that was bound with *kukui* nut oil. The huge cornerstones are believed to have been salvaged from a *heiau* built in the 15th century by King Umi that had occupied this spot. The masonry is crude but effective—still sound after more than 150 years.

Inside, the church is extremely soothing, expressing a feeling of strength and simplicity. The

BIG ISLAND

ROBERT NILSEN

BIG ISLAND

Moku'aikaua Church

tion of spears reputedly belonging to the great Kamehameha himself.

Hulihe'e Palace, 808/329-1877, is on the *makai* side of Ali'i Drive, open Mon.–Fri. 9 A.M.–4 P.M., Saturday and Sunday 10 A.M.–4 P.M. You can look around on your own or ask the staff for a tour, which usually lasts 45 minutes. Admission is $5 adults, $4 seniors, $1 students. A hostess knowledgeable in Hawaiiana is usually on duty to answer questions.

The **Palace Gift Shop,** small but with quality items, is on the grounds next door to the palace. Open daily except Sunday. It offers a fine selection of koa sculptures of fish, sharks, and even a turtle, along with Hawaiiana books and postcards. Just outside is a saltwater pond with tropical fish.

Historical Walking Tour

The Kona Historical Society offers a leisurely one-hour to 90-minute guided walking tour of the Ahu'ena Heiau, Moku'aikaua Church, Hulihe'e Palace, and other nearby sights Tues.–Fri. at 9:30 A.M. and again on Friday at 1:30 P.M., for $10 per person. You can tour each of these sites on your own, but you can learn so much more from a knowledgeable guide. Make reservations at 808/323-2005, and wear comfortable shoes and a hat.

Along Ali'i Drive

Ali'i Drive heads south from Kailua, passing the majority of Kona's resorts on its way to Keauhou. On the mountain side of the road, a continuous flow of flowers drapes the shoulder like a femme fatale's seductive boa, while seaside the coastline slips along, rugged and bright, making Ali'i Drive a soothing sight.

At your first stop, near White Sands Beach, look for the historic **Hale Halawi O Holualoa Congregational Church** built in 1855 by Reverend John D. Paris. Services are still held every Sunday at 8 A.M. and 10 A.M. The base of the church is mostly original lava rock topped with a new roof. The cemetery area is peaceful and quiet and offers a perfect meditative perch from which to scan the coast below. Back on the road, look for signs to Kahalu'u Beach Park; pull in and park here. On the rocky northern shore of this bay is **St. Peter's Catholic Church.** Its diminutive size, capped by a blue tin roof that winks at you

Providentially, the night before the auction each piece was painstakingly numbered by the royal ladies of the palace, and the name of the person bidding for the piece was dutifully recorded. In the years that followed, the **Daughters of Hawai'i,** who now operate the palace as a museum, tracked down the owners and convinced many to return the items for display. Most of the pieces are privately owned, and because each is unique, the owners wish no duplicates to be made. It is for this reason, coupled with the fact that flashbulbs can fade the wood, that a strict *no photography* policy is enforced. The palace was opened as a museum in 1928!

Historical artifacts are displayed in a downstairs room. Delicate and priceless heirlooms on display include a tiger-claw necklace that belonged to Kapi'olani. You'll also see a portrait gallery of Hawaiian monarchs. Personal and mundane items are on exhibit as well—there's an old report card showing a 68 in philosophy for King Kalakaua—and lining the stairs is a collecfrom amidst the lava like a bright morning glory in an ebony vase, has earned it the nickname **Little Blue Church.** Built in 1889 on the site of an old, partially reclaimed *heiau,* the church is a favorite spot for snapshots. Inside, simplicity reigns with bare wood walls and a plain crucifix. The only splash of color is a bouquet of fresh flowers on the altar. To the right of the church as you face it are the remains of **Ku'emanu Heiau,** a temple where chiefs would pray for good surfing conditions. Their prayers must have worked, as surfers today still gracefully ride the

Liholiho, Kamehameha II

waves offshore within sight of this rock platform. On the grounds of the Keauhou Beach Resort, a 10-minute walk south from the church along the coast, are the remains of **Kapuanoni** and **Hapai Ali'i** *Heiau* and, just beyond that, the **Ke'eku**

Heiau. All are unrestored historical sites that still show signs of being used, and all offer vantage points from which to view the coast. Near the end of the road is **Keauhou Bay.** Here you'll find a cluster of historical sites, and the small boat harbor and boat ramp. Look for a monument marking the birthplace of Kamehameha III in 1814. Local people come to fish from the pier around 5 P.M. for *halalu,* a tough little fish to catch. Along the shoreline are a number of partially developed *heiau* sites. A small home stuck on a point of land on the edge of the bay is where John Wayne married his wife Pilar in 1954, and it marks the site of the first modern house built on the bay. Opposite the harbor, at the end of King Kamehameha III Road is Keauhou Park and beach access, an area of lawn, pavilion, and restrooms.

BIG ISLAND

ANCIENT SPORT OF *HOLUA*

In principle, *holua* was similar to snow sledding, and mostly a "chiefly" sport of the *ali'i.* Sleds were long two-runner affairs, perhaps six inches wide and eight feet long or longer, stabilized by cross bracing and grab bars on which the person would lie. These sleds were launched down a slope that was up to one mile in length and ended at or near the ocean. Only a few of these slopes remain, largely fallen into disrepair or taken apart to make way for modern constructions. The ruins are most prominent on the Big Island; the largest known sledding course was Kaneaka in Keauhou, the remains of which lie on the Kona Country Club *makai* golf course. These slopes were constructed of volcanic rock and filled in with small pebbles to make a flat top. It is believed that this flat top was then covered with layers of large leaves (maybe banana or *ti*) or thatching to provide a slippery surface for sledding. Once on the runway, there was no stopping until the sled got to the

bottom—or went over the side. The danger associated with this sport must have been an important component of its thrill. With no steering mechanism, the chance of disaster seems large. *Holua* seems to have slowly died out through the 1800s, perhaps, as some have suggested, after the Makahiki Festival—which may have been its principle forum—ceased to be a central component of the Hawaiian cultural tradition. No one in living memory is purported to have actually seen the sport in action. Only recently has there been much attention turned to its understanding. Few examples of a *holua* sled have survived—the best is displayed at the Bishop Museum in Honolulu—and few accounts relate anything about the sport. Aside from a few brave, modern souls who have tried short sections of slope for the thrill, this sport has not yet been brought back by the resurgence of ancient Hawaiian culture. Perhaps its time is still to come.

At the very end of the Ali'i Drive, past the Kona Country Club golf course, is the **Leke Leke Burial Grounds.** Laid to rest here are troops that fought under the leadership of Kekuaokalani, keeper of the war god Ku after the death of King Kamehameha I, in an attempt to sustain the traditional religious and social order of the Hawaiian people. More than 300 died here at Kuano'o Bay, using firepower obtained from the foreigners. This battle was the violent end to the old ways and symbolized the shaky introduction of the Western overlay on Hawaiian society.

North of Town

Honokohau Harbor, three miles north of Kailua-Kona, is a huge small-boat harbor and deep-sea fishing facility that has eclipsed the old Kailua Pier. This is the premier fishing harbor on the island and is used by other water-sport activities companies and sailboats. The harbor area is full of fishing-oriented shops, including Kona Marine for nautical charts, and is also home to the Harbor House Restaurant, where you can hear a yarn from Kona's old salts. Primarily, this is where you come to see huge marlin caught that day and talk to the skippers of the deep-sea fishing boats that go after them. When you pull into the marina, you'll see a road that goes off to the left. Head that way toward the tan building with a Texaco sign, to where the pier and the weigh-station are. The huge fish will be hoisted, measured, and photographed while the skippers and their crews clean and prepare the boats for the next day's outing. **Weigh in** is every day 11 A.M.–1 P.M. and 3–6 P.M.; call 808/334-1881 for information. If you are fascinated by deep-sea fishing, this is your chance to pick a likely boat and to get acquainted with the crew.

The future is now at the amazing Ocean Technology facilities just south of the airport between mile markers 95 and 94, where you'll find a turnoff heading toward the sea. This is the **Natural Energy Laboratory of Hawaii Authority (NELHA).** Incredible things are being done here. For example, cold water from several thousand feet below the surface of the ocean is placed in a turbine with warm surface water, a process that generates electricity and also provides desalinated water. In addition, the cold water is used for raising very un-Hawaiian things such as alpine strawberries, lobsters, abalone, sea cucumbers, commercial black pearls, and Japanese flounder, as well as for raising *limu,* a local edible seaweed. Others use its alternative energy source to make fish jerky, to grow shiitake mushrooms, and even to raise tropical fish that will become living bouquets of color in fish tanks around the world. Cyanotech, a leading manufacturer of marine products for worldwide nutrition and pharmaceutical markets, uses the facilities to make spirulina, available in health food stores. Tours are offered Thursday at 10 A.M.; call 808/329-7341 for reservations. If you choose to take a tour, don't be overwhelmed by the size of

St. Peter's Church

ROBERT NILSEN

the complex; the products are brought to a central area for your viewing. Afterward, you can request a tour of the facility. No tasting is offered, so bring your own snacks. For those who want to walk around on their own, maps are available. Behind this facility is the Ho'ona Historic Preserve, an area of home sites and graves from a late 19th-century Hawaiian community. Cutting across the NELHA area up near the highway is a section of the old King's Trail. The NELHA access road is open 6 A.M.–8 P.M.

Dedicated to Hawaii's own Col. Ellison S. Onizuka and to the men and women who tragically perished aboard the spacecraft *Challenger* on January 28, 1986, the **Onizuka Space Center** is at Kona International Airport, P.O. Box 833, Kailua-Kona, HI 96745, 808/329-3441, website: www.planet-hawaii.com/astronautonizuka. Hours are daily 8:30 A.M.–4:30 P.M. except Thanksgiving, Christmas, and New Year's Day; admission is $3 adults, $1 children. From this tragedy, a living memorial and space education facility was erected. Inside the modern, well-appointed building children and adults alike can marvel at human exploration of space by viewing exhibits like a "moon rock," a scale model of a space shuttle and space station, an interactive staffed maneuvering unit, a real space suit, and a theater showing educational videos throughout the day. There is a gift shop with plenty of fascinating reading material concerning the international effort to explore the heavens. Stop in before flying out.

BEACHES AND PARKS

It Kona is short on anything, it is beaches. The ones that it has are adequate and quite striking in their own way, but they tend to be small, few, and far between. People expecting a huge expanse of white sand will be disappointed. These beaches do exist on the Big Island's west coast, but they are north of Kailua-Kona in the Kohala District. Kona does, however, have beaches alive with marine life, providing excellent and safe snorkeling and top-notch tide pool exploration opportunities.

The following are the main beaches in and around Kailua-Kona. For descriptions of South Kona beaches see below.

Kamakahonu Beach

You couldn't be more centrally located than at "Eye of the Turtle" Beach. Find it in downtown Kailua-Kona next to Kailua Pier, in front of King Kamehameha's Kona Beach Hotel. Local people refer to it as "Kids' Beach" because it is so gentle and safe, perfect for a refreshing dip. Big kids come here to play too, when every year world-class athletes churn the gentle waters into a fury at the start of the Ironman Triathlon. Rent snorkel gear, kayaks, and other water gear for reasonable prices from the Beach Shack, in front of the hotel. Restrooms and telephones are on the pier.

Ali'i Drive Beaches

White Sands Beach County Park (a.k.a. **Magic Sands** or **Disappearing Sands**) is an excellent spot for a dip—if the sand is there. Every year, usually in winter, the sands are stripped away by heavy seas and currents, exposing rough coral and making the area too rugged for the average swimmer. People still come during those months because it's a good vantage point for observing migrating humpback whales. The sands always come back, and, when they do, the beach is terrific for all kinds of water sports, including body surfing and snorkeling. White Sands is known locally as a great boogie boarding and body surfing spot, and the annual Magic Sands Body Surfing Contest is held here in winter off the point. The best board surfing is just north of the beach in a break the locals call "Banyans." White Sands' amenities include drinking water, showers, and restrooms, making the beach a favorite spot with local people and tourists.

Kahalu'u Beach Park on Kahalu'u Bay has always been a productive fishing area. Even today, fishermen come to "throw net." You'll occasionally see large family parties surrounding their favorite fish with a huge *hukilau* net, then sharing their bounty among all participants. Because of this age-old tradition, the area has not been designated a marine conservation district. Kahalu'u became a beach park in 1966. This ensured that the people of Kona would always have access to this favorite spot, which quickly became surrounded by commercial development. Keauhou Beach Resort occupies the land just to the south. Amenities at the park include picnic

BIG ISLAND

tables, showers, restrooms, a lifeguard, and even a basketball court. The swimming is very good, but the real attraction is snorkeling. The waters are very gentle, and Kahalu'u is a perfect place for families or beginning snorkelers, as the water is generally only six to eight feet deep. However, stay *within* the bay because a powerful and dangerous rip current lurks outside. The shoreline waters are alive with tropical fish: angelfish, parrotfish, unicorn fish, the works. Unfortunately, Kahalu'u is often crowded, but it is still worth a visit.

Old Kona Airport State Recreation Area
In 1970 the old Kona Airport closed and the state of Hawaii turned it into a beach park. Take Kuakini Highway north from downtown until it ends. Facilities include showers, restrooms, and a picnic area near the water, plus athletic fields, a gymnasium and aquatic center, and a children's playground near the entrance. Parking is unlimited along the old runway, where you can also walk, bike, rollerblade, or jog. The park gate closes at 8 P.M. The white-sand beach is sandwiched between water's edge and the runway. You can enter the water at some shallow inlets, but the bottom is often rocky (be sure to wear water shoes) and the waters can be treacherous during high surf. The safest spot is a little sandy cove at the southern end of the beach. Swimming is generally not good here, but sunbathing is great. Snorkeling is fine at the northern end of the beach, and offshore a break at "Shark Rocks" makes Old Airport popular with Kona surfers. The waters in front of the park are a 217-acre marine life conservation district protected from motorized boat usage but open to scuba divers and snorklers.

Honokohau Beach
All types of people come to Honokohau Beach, including fishermen, surfers, and snorkelers, but it was primarily known as a **clothing-optional beach.** That status drastically changed when the area officially became part of **Kaloko-Honokohau National Historical Park.** At the Honokohau Small Boat Harbor, stay to the right and park almost at the end of the access road near the "boat graveyard" in a dirt parking lot. Clamber over the berm, follow the well-worn path into the vegetation, and keep walking for a few minutes to the beach.

This area, more toward Kaloko, was heavily populated during old Hawaiian days, and plenty of archaeological sites—mostly fishponds, ruins of houses, and a few petroglyphs—are found along the shoreline. Most of these sites are closed to protect them for posterity; if you come to an archaeological area, obey all posted signs and approach with great care and respect. Remember, it is imperative that you do not touch, disturb, or remove any historical artifacts. The coarse gray sand beach offers safe swimming in somewhat shallow water. There are no facilities.

Nudity is officially illegal within the park. Camping and open fires, also illegal, are citable offenses under federal regulations. Walk to the north end of the beach, where a trail leads inland through thick vegetation. Follow it to the "Queen's Bath" (called "Anchialine Bath" by the park service), a brackish pond surrounded by rock cairns. Because it is under consideration as a historical site, swimming in the pond is not recommended. There's sometimes a ranger back in here, and although the park is officially open, visitation is neither encouraged nor discouraged. **Kaloko Beach,** about a 10-minute hike north of Queen's Bath, has great snorkeling in only 10–20 feet of water. Here, you can explore a series of sea arches. The entire area is a favorite with green sea turtles, which make their presence known mainly in the evenings.

Dedicated in 1978, the 1,160-acre Kaloko-Honokohau National Historical Park can be entered either from Honokohau Small Boat Harbor or via Kaloko Gate and a mile-long rough road, just off Highway 19 across from the Kaloko Industrial Park. The gate is open daily 8 A.M.–3:30 P.M. For information, call the park office at 808/329-6881.

North Kona Beaches
The next beach you come to heading north is the famous **Pine Trees** surfing beach, near the NELHA facility just south of the airport. Where the long access road turns abruptly to the right, look for a well-worn dirt road leading to the left away from NELHA, and follow it to Pine Trees. Although famous with surfers and the site of many competitions, Pine Trees (none of which are in evidence) is not a good swimming beach. There are a few one towel coves along the rocky

shoreline where you can gain access to the water, but mostly it's a place from which to observe the action. You can also follow the road toward the NELHA facility a short way to **Wawaloli Beach,** a large, sandy, public beach, fronted by rock and coral. Here are a few volleyball nets, a restroom, and some picnic tables.

Kona Coast State Park
Recently opened and well marked, the Kona Coast State Park stretches north, encompassing several sandy secluded beaches in its 1,642-acre domain. The first is about two miles north of the airport between mile markers 91 and 90; open 9 A.M.–7 P.M. Follow the rugged but passable dirt road for about a mile and a half to one of the closest beaches to Kailua-Kona. The semi-improved area has a lavatory and picnic tables built around palm trees. The land rises before getting to the course-sand beach. The swimming here is safe in season, but always be careful.

Before you get to the official parking area, notice a walking path off to the right. It is a 10-minute walk to Mahaiula Bay and its magnificent **Mahaiula Beach.** This crescent of white sand stretches for about 200 yards, with shade trees coming down almost to the water's edge. Completely unimproved and secluded, it's a great beach to "get away from it all" for the day. Park access may be closed on Wednesdays.

Two miles farther north, between mile markers 89 and 88, look for the Pu'u Ku'ili cinder cone, whose vegetation has been given a crew cut by the trade winds. Turn here on a very rugged, 4WD-only dirt road that takes you down to **Makalawena Beach.** En route to this totally secluded area, you'll pass over rough lava and coral and eventually come to a gate, where you park. Proceed on foot, and you'll have your choice of three wonderful beaches ranging in size from 30 to 100 yards long; all are frequented by green sea turtles. Walk to the left past the biggest beach, and look for a path behind it that leads to a brackish but mostly freshwater pond where you can rinse off. Don't be alarmed by the harmless brine shrimp that nibble at your toes. They're much too small to do any real damage. If you do not have 4WD, you can still enjoy this area, but it means a hike of about 30 minutes. Be sure to bring water, es-pecially if you intend to spend the day. Alternately, you can walk north from Mahaiula Beach along a path, and in about five minutes you'll come to the remains of an abandoned estate that once belonged to the Magoon Family, longtime island residents and major stockholders in Hawaiian Airlines. After enjoying your short coastal hike, you will come to Makalawena. Remember not to take any chances during high surf, since there is no safety supervision whatsoever.

A few minutes farther north by car, just past the cinder cone, you'll find another road that starts off paved but almost immediately turns to lava and coral. If you have 4WD you can go to the end of the road and then walk to the beach, but you can also walk for about 15 minutes from the turnout near the highway. The well-worn path leads you to **Kua Bay,** a famous swimming and boogie-boarding beach.

ACCOMMODATIONS

Almost all of Kona's accommodations lie along the six miles of Ali'i Drive from Kailua-Kona to Keauhou. Most hotels/condos fall in the moderate to expensive range. A few inexpensive hotels are scattered here and there along Ali'i Drive, and back up in the hills is a "sleeper" or two, cheap but decent. The following list should provide you with a good cross section.

It's sad but true: except for the limited beach parks at Ho'okena and Miloli'i, south of Kailua-Kona, there is *no official camping* in all of the Kona District. Campers wishing to enjoy the coast must go north to the Kohala District to find a campground, or south to Ka'u. Some unofficial camping does exist in Kona, but as always, this generates certain insecurities. Bivouacking for a night or two in any of the unofficial camp spots should be hassle-free. Good luck!

Under $50
Patey's Place, 75-195 Ala Ona Ona St., Kailua-Kona, HI 96740, 808/326-7018, fax 808/326-7640, website: www.hawaiian-hostels.com, is a reasonably priced and friendly hostel. Upon arrival, it will appear as though a section of the living sea was taken from the coast and moved whole into a residential area of Kona. You will be

cohabiting with whales, mermaids, and dolphins, all rendered by airbrush *air*tist Paul Fullbrook, an Aussie artist who was undoubtedly a green sea turtle in his past life. Robert Patey, owner, is a long-time island resident who has plenty of *aloha* and will point you in the right direction. Rates are: bunk room $17.50; private room $31.50 single, $41.50 double. A $10 key and linen deposit is returned on departure. Patey's also provides free transportation *from* the airport if you stay two or more nights; airport drop-off for $5; various island tours for $40–55; body board, fishing gear, snorkel gear, and bike rentals at reasonable fees; lockers; safe deposit box; and free and invaluable information. The four-person bunkrooms are clean, lockable, and cooled by cross ventilation and ceiling fans. The hostel is also outfitted with four full bathrooms, three kitchens, a second-floor sunset deck, laundry facilities, gas barbecues, and an activities desk. You shouldn't expect, nor will you find, the standard of a five-star resort, but Patey's is an excellent choice for the adventurer, budget traveler, or anyone who enjoys a dynamic international crowd.

$50–100

For a reasonable and homey hotel, try the **Kona Tiki Hotel,** 75-5968 Ali'i Dr., Kailua-Kona, HI 96740, 808/329-1425, fax 808/327-9402, one of the first accommodations south of "downtown." At more than 50 years old, this is one of the oldest vacation hotels along the coast, and although of an old style, the place is kept up. Sandwiched between the ocean and the road, it's a bit noisy during the day but quiets down at night except for the lullaby of the rolling surf. The Kona Tiki features refrigerators in all rooms, some kitchenettes, a complimentary continental breakfast daily, and a small guest pool. The refurbished rooms are clean, with ceiling fans but no phones, and all units face the ocean so everyone gets a view. Prices are $54–58 for a standard room with queen or queen and twin bed, and $62–65 for a kitchenette; extra person $8, three-day minimum.

Kona Seaside Hotel is a basic but well-cared-for downtown hotel at 75-5646 Palani Rd., Kailua-Kona, HI 96740, 808/329-2455 or 800/560-5558, fax 808/329-6157. It's part of the island-owned Sand and Seaside Hotel chain.

Most rooms have a/c, cross ventilation, and lanai. There's a sun deck and central area with enclosed courtyard and swimming pool. Prices range from $80 standard to $115 deluxe, with AAA and AARP discounts and room and car packages available.

The **Kona Bay Hotel,** 75-5744 Ali'i Dr., Kailua-Kona, HI 96740, 808/329-1393 or 800/367-5102, website: www.unclebilly.com, email: resv@unclebilly.com, is a locally owned hotel in the center of town, run by Uncle Billy and his Kona family. Its best feature is the friendly and warm staff. The hotel is a remaining wing of the old Kona Inn, the rest of which was torn down to accommodate the shopping center across the road. The Kona Bay is built around a central courtyard and garden containing the Kimo's Family Buffet, pool, and bar. The rooms are a combination of moderate and superior with a/c, TV, and mini-fridge. Rates begin at $84–94, and $94–104 for a kitchenette; many discounts and package rates are available.

$150–200

King Kamehameha's Kona Beach Hotel in downtown Kailua-Kona at 75-5660 Palani Rd., Kailua-Kona, HI 96740, 808/329-2911 or 800/367-6060, website: www.konabeachhotel.com, email: reservations@hthcorp.com, is on a spot favored by Hawaiian royalty; Kamehameha the Great spent the last days of his life here. It's one of the only Kona hotels that has its own beach, adjacent to the restored Ahu'ena Heiau. The walls of the lobby are lined with historical artifacts; portraits of the Kamehameha royal family beginning with the great chief Kamehameha are displayed in the reception area; two *kahili* stand nearby as signs of royalty; and a feather cape and hat also adorn one wall. Other displays make up this mini-museum, and it's worth a look even if you are not staying here. Rooms each feature a lanai with a sweeping panorama of the bay or Mt. Hualalai. Prices for the 445 rooms range from $120 for a standard room up to $550 for a three-bedroom suite, additional person $25, and children under 18 stay free when sharing their parents' room. The hotel features two restaurants, the Billfish Bar, the Island Breeze Polynesian lu'au, tennis courts, a plethora of shops, a freshwater pool, and a beach.

The **Royal Kona Resort,** 75-5852 Ali'i Dr., Kailua-Kona, HI 96740, 808/329-3111 or 800/919-8333, website: www.royalkona.com, has figuratively and literally become a Kona landmark. The hotel, built like rising steps with the floor below larger than the one above, commands a magnificent view from its perch atop a beautiful promontory of black lava that anchors the south end of downtown Kailua. All 450 rooms are spacious, and each includes a lanai. Standard rates run from $140 for a garden view to $180 for an ocean view and $210 for an oceanfront room, with the oceanfront corner king rooms costing $250. Many packages are available. On the property, you can dine for breakfast, lunch, or dinner in the Tropics Cafe Restaurant, which has a lovely sun-soaked veranda with a sweeping view of the surrounding coastline. The Windjammer, an open-air lounge next door, features entertainment several evenings each week. The hotel also boasts a mini-shopping mall complete with a sundries store. The hotel pool, completely refurbished, has an upper kiddies' pool and a lower re-tiled main pool adjacent to the rolling surf, and an ocean-fed beach lagoon is sheltered from the force of the waves by huge black lava boulders. Between the main building and the beach tower is the coconut grove. Here, the *imu* is fired up every Monday, Friday, and Saturday evening, creating delectable morsels for the famous Kona sunset lu'au that comes complete with island entertainment that fills the grounds with music and laughter. The tennis courts, attended by a professional staff, are lit for nighttime play. Other full-service amenities include a self-serve laundry, free parking, beauty salon, exercise spa classes, baby-sitters, and no charge for children under 17 years of age sharing a room with their parents. The Royal Kona Resort keeps alive the tradition of quality service at a quality hotel.

The **Aston Keauhou Beach Resort,** 78-6740 Ali'i Dr., Kailua-Kona, HI 96740, 808/322-3441, 800/922 7866 from the Mainland, or 800/321-2558 in Hawaii, is built on a historic site that includes the remains of two *heiau,* a reconstruction of King Kamehameha III's summer cottage, two freshwater springs, and several fishponds. Kahalu'u Beach Park is adjacent with its white sand beach, and the entire area is known for fantastic tide pools. This famous Kona hotel has recently undergone an extensive $16 million renovation; it reopened in March 1999. The money was well spent and the result is a wonderful feeling of old-fashioned Hawaii. To set the mood, paintings by Hawaii's Herb Kane hang on the walls and reflect the heritage of the two dugout canoes in the lobby. Throughout the hotel, soothing greens and sand beige colors coordinate with the period-style furniture to make this a restful retreat. Rates range from $155 for a garden view up to $270 for deluxe oceanfront room, with suites to $420. Each of the 311 rooms has a/c, TV, phone, private lanai, and small refrigerator. The hotel has one restaurant and a lobby lounge where you'll hear free music nightly, as well as a swimming pool, sundries store, activities desk, and fitness center. In keeping with the new outlook, the hotel is offering daily activities and presentations in Hawaiian dance, music, arts and crafts, and a torch-lighting ceremony. A free cultural tour offered daily takes you around to the historical sites on the hotel grounds. For the tennis player, Island Slice Tennis is on the property. The hotel also offers a free shuttle service to local shopping, golfing, and dining. Although not the largest, the Keauhou Beach Hotel is the finest hotel property in the Kailua area.

Bed-and-Breakfast

While Kailua is chock-a-block with condos, B&Bs are few and far between. One excellent place set right on the ocean is the lovely **Kailua Plantation House B&B Inn,** 75-5948 Ali'i Dr., Kailua-Kona, HI 96740, 808/329-3727 or 888/357-4262, fax 808/326-7323, website: www.kphbnb.com, email: kphbnb@ilhawaii.net. This multistory honeymooners' retreat is truly a standout. It's like a beachside mansion and southern plantation house wrapped up in one. Each room is exquisitely decorated and has a private bath, color TV, and lanai. A pool/spa at oceanside is for all guests, and everyone is served an expanded continental breakfast each morning. Room rates run $160–235 a night, two nights minimum, and it's 20 percent extra for a third person. No children under age 12.

Condominiums

$50–100: Kona Magic Sands Resort couldn't get closer to the water. It sits on oceanside lava directly adjacent to White Sands Beach. Here, you can lounge at poolside and eat at Jameson's Restaurant without leaving the property. The studios have full kitchens, color TV, and phones. Rates run $85–95. For reservations, contact Hawaii Resort management at 800/622-5348.

Kitty-corner to the Keauhou Shopping Center and just a short walk from the Kona Country Club Golf Course is the **Keauhou Resort,** 78-7039 Kamehameha III Road, Kailua-Kona, HI 96740, 808/322-9122 or 800/367-5286, fax 808/322-9410, website: www.tropweb.com/keauhou.htm, email: keauhouresort@konanet.net, a townhouse complex of low-rise units in a garden of bougainvillea and other tropical plants. One- and two-bedroom units have electric kitchens, washers and dryers, telephones, and color TV, and there are two pools on the property. Rates run $70–97 a day for one-bedroom garden units to $102–145 for two-bedroom oceanview units; five-night minimum stay.

Kona Billfisher, 808/329-9277, offers full kitchens, pool, barbecues, limited maid service, and gazebo. One-bedroom units cost $70–85 daily for up to four persons, two-bedroom units $90–110 for up to six guests. Weekly and monthly rates and discounts are available.

$100–150: Kona Islander Inn condominium apartments, 75-5776 Kuakini Hwy., Kailua-Kona, HI 96740, 808/329-3181, are well appointed for a reasonable price. Conveniently located within walking distance of downtown Kailua-Kona, they're tucked into a tight but well-landscaped garden next door to St. Michaels' and Kealoaka-malamalama churches. The style is "early-20th-century plantation" shaded by tall palms. All rental units have phones, off-road parking, a/c, TV, and refrigerators. Rates are $99–109; five nights is the minimum stay. Reservations can also be made through Marc Resorts, 800/535-0085, or Hawaii Resorts Management, 800/622-5348.

Next to the Royal Kona Resort is the small and quiet **Hale Kona Kai,** 75-5870 Kahakai Road, Kailua-Kona, HI 96740, 808/329-2155 or 800/421-3996. These oceanfront apartments are fully equipped condo units with lanai, and a swimming pool and laundry facilities are on the premises. Room rates are $125–135 a night, three-night minimum.

Just outside the central Kailua area, at the start of "condo row," is **Kona Reef,** a Castle Resort property at 75-5999 Ali'i Dr., Kailua-Kona, HI 96740, 808/329-2959. Finely appointed units look out over the central garden and pool to the sea beyond. Each unit is set up with full kitchen and all you need for an easy stay. One-, two-, and three-bedroom suites run $135–330 and can sleep 4–8 people. For reservations, contact the condo or call Castle Resorts at 800/367-5004 Mainland or 800/272-5275 in Hawaii.

Outrigger's **Kanaloa at Kona,** 78-261 Manukai St., Kailua-Kona, HI 96740, 808/322-9625 or 800/688-7444, is in an upscale residential area at the southern end of Kailua-Kona in Keauhou. This is one of those special places where you feel you get more than you pay for. The one- and two-bedroom units are enormous. Bigger isn't always better, but in this case it is. Each unit comes equipped with a complete and modern kitchen, two baths, a lanai with comfortable outdoor furniture, and a wet bar for entertaining. Rates for the tastefully furnished units range from $125 for one bedroom to $310 for two bedrooms; the rooms can accommodate four and six people respectively at no extra charge. Many package rates and discounts are available. A security officer is on duty, and on the grounds you'll find three pools, a lighted tennis court, hot tubs, gas barbecues, an activities desk with free morning coffee, and even a restaurant and cocktail lounge overlooking the black-sand beach. The complex itself is made up of low-rise units and the grounds are finely landscaped. This is a place that feels like vacation. If you would like to escape the hustle and bustle but stay near the action, the Kanaloa at Kona is the place.

$150–200: A Marc Resort property, **Kona Bali Kai,** 76-6246 Ali'i Dr., Kailua-Kona, HI 96740, 808/329-9381 or 800/535-0085, fax 808/326-6056, is a very decent, comfortable place with a swimming pool, activities desk, concierge, and sundries shop on property. The studio, one-bedroom, and two-bedroom units each have a fully equipped kitchen, TV and VCR, and phone for local calls. All apartments are individually owned, so the decor differs, but most have muted colors and a tropical feel. Rates run $149–279. While some units are directly on the ocean, others are on the mountain side of Ali'i Drive, so they may or may not have an ocean view. This is a good choice for being close to town but not in the center of the hubbub.

The **Aston Royal Sea Cliff Resort,** 75-6040 Ali'i Dr., Kailua-Kona, HI 96740, 808/329-8021, 800/922-7866 Mainland and Canada, or 800/321-2558 in Hawaii, fax 808/326-1887, winner of the AAA three-diamond award, offers classy condo apartments. The alabaster contemporary building features rooms fronting a central garden courtyard. The unobstructed views of the coast from most rooms are glorious, and a perfect day-ending activity is a sunset enjoyed on your private lanai. Amenities include free tennis, daily maid service, cable color TV, freshwater and seawater swimming pools, jet spa and sauna, activities desk, and sundries shop. Units here are spacious and rates start with a studio at $170–190 and move to one bedroom $190–240, two bedrooms $220–280, with oceanfront villas at $550–600; the "family plan" allows children under 18 to stay at no charge when using existing beds.

$250 and up: Kona by the Sea, 75-6106 Ali'i Dr., Kailua-Kona, HI 96740, 808/327-2300, 800/922-7866 U.S. and Canada, or 800/321-2558 in Hawaii, is a rather new and beautifully situated condominium with extraordinary coastal views. Like many of Kona's properties, it has no beach, but there is a freshwater pool on the premises. From the balcony of your suite overlooking a central courtyard, you can watch the aqua-blue surf crash onto the black lava rocks below. Each spacious one- or two-bedroom unit has two bathrooms, tiled lanai, modern full kitchen, living room with fold-out couch, dining room, color cable TV, and central air. Like its near neighbor the Royal Sea Cliff Resort, this Aston property is also a AAA three-diamond award-winner. Prices are $235–290 for one-bedroom units and $290–345 for two-bedroom units.

Vacation Rental Agencies

With the multitude of condos and rental houses along this coast, there are plenty of agencies to do the looking for you. It's often better the first time around to let one of the agencies find one to fit your needs and then look for something else for next time while you're on the island. Try one of the following for condominium units or rental homes.

Sunquest Vacations 77-6435 Kuakini Hwy., Kailua-Kona, HI 96740, 808/329-6488, 800/800-5662, or 800/367-5168 Mainland, fax 808/329-5480, website: www.sunquest-hawaii.com, manages over 200 properties in the Kona area, mostly condos with over a dozen homes. By and large, these units are in the moderate range. They also arrange car rentals, tours, and activities.

Century 21 handles mostly economy to midrange condo units in Kailua and Keauhou. The office is on the waterfront in Kailua, 808/326-2121 or 800/546-5662, fax 808/329-6768, website: www.konaweb.com/vacations.

Property Network, 75-5799 Ali'i Dr., Kailua-Kona, HI 96740, 808/329-7977 or 800/358-7977, fax 808/329-1200, website: www.hawaii-kona.com, email: vacation@hawaii-kona.com, handles the full range of condos along the Kona Coast in about two dozen different properties, economy to luxury.

For mostly upper-end condo units in the Keauhou area, try **Keauhou Property Management Company,** 76-6225 Kuakini Hwy., Suite C-105, Kailua-Kona, HI 96740, 808/326-9075 or 800/745-5662, fax 808/326-2055.

Knutson and Associates, 75-6082 Ali'i Dr., Suite 8, Kailua-Kona, HI 96740, 808/329-6311 or 800/800-6202, fax 808/326-2178, website: http://planet-hawaii.com/knutson, manages midrange condo units and a few vacation homes mostly in the central Kona area.

With more than 70 properties, of which about two dozen are homes, **West Hawaii Property Services,** 78-6831 Ali'i Dr., Suite 237, Kailua-Kona, HI 96740, 808/322-6696 or 800/799-5662, fax 808/324-0609, website: www.konarentals.com, email: whps@ilhawaii.com, has a good range of places from economy to deluxe.

A smaller company with about half condo units and half homes is **C.J. Kimberly Realtors,** 75-5875 Kahakai Rd., Kailua-Kona, HI 96740, 808/329-4321 or 888/780-7000, fax 808/329-5533, website: www.cjkimberlyrealtors.com, email: cjkimberly@aloha.net.

Action Team Realty, 75-6082 Ali'i Dr., Suite A, Kailua-Kona, HI 96740, 808/329-8626 or 800/335-3347, website: www.konacondo.com, handles many condo units in more than a dozen properties in Kona.

FOOD

Inexpensive

"So, for the budget traveler," you've been asking yourself, "which is the best restaurant in town, with the most food at the lowest prices, with that down-home atmosphere?" **The Ocean View Inn,** 808/329-9998, is it! The gigantic menu of Chinese, American, Japanese, and Hawaiian food is like a mini-directory. Lunch and dinner range $8–12, and a huge breakfast goes for about $5. It's open daily except Monday, 6:30 A.M.–2:45 P.M. and 5:15–9 P.M., with the bar open daily 6:30 A.M.–9 P.M. Across from the seawall near King Kamehameha's Kona Beach Hotel, it's always crowded with local people, a sure sign that the food is good.

Stan's Restaurant, 808/329-4500, is an open-air establishment one notch up in both price and atmosphere from the Ocean View Inn next door. Here you have a cocktail lounge and a stab at atmosphere with some cozy lighting and rattan furniture. Breakfast is pleasing, with an assortment of island-inspired hotcakes and other specials. Dinners include salad, rice or whipped potatoes, fresh fruit, and dinner bread, and the best items are the many Hawaiian foods like *kalua* pig and *lala poi.* The food is good, but not great, and you generally get a square meal for a very reasonable price.

The **Royal Jade Garden,** in the Lanihau Center, 808/326-7288, open Sun.–Thurs. 10:30 A.M.–9:30 P.M., Fri.–Sat. until 10 P.M., is a Chinese restaurant where you get an amazing amount of well-prepared food for a moderate price. Run-of-the-mill chow mein, noodle soup, and meat dishes of chicken, duck, pork, or beef cost $6–8. More expensive items include lobster with black bean sauce and a variety of fresh fish and seafoods. But this place offers an unbeatable special every night: you choose three entrées plus fried rice or fried noodles for only $6.50 (fewer choices, less expensive). It's pre-prepared and placed on a hot table, but it's not cooked to death. You wind up with so much food that the most difficult part is keeping it on your plate. In the Royal Jade there's no decor, but if you are hungry and on a tight budget, this is one of the best values in town.

Although the Kona industrial area doesn't sound inviting, is a great place to find inexpensive food, along with stores where the *people* shop. To get to the industrial area, head for the airport, and about one minute north of the junction of Route 19 (the airport road) and Palani Road, make a left on Kaiwi Street. Or follow Kuakini Road, a major intersection off Palani Road just a minute from the seawall, to Kaiwi Street. The triangle formed by Kaiwi and Kuakini is primarily the old industrial area. The **French Bakery,** 808/326-2688, open weekdays 5:30 A.M.–3 P.M., Saturday 5:30 A.M.–2 P.M., is a budget gourmet deli/restaurant where the food is great and the prices are low. Not only does it have the full range of pastries you would expect, it has wonderful and inexpensive sandwiches and coffee.

Su's Thai Kitchen, 808/326-7808, also in the industrial area and open for lunch weekdays 11 A.M.–2:30 P.M. and for dinner nightly 5–9 P.M., is a semi-open-air restaurant with a distinctive touch of southeast Asia. You can sit inside, but choose a spot on the veranda, where there is absolutely no view but where the breezes blow and bamboo curtains are dropped for a feeling of privacy. The extensive menu offers a *pu pu* platter; lightly breaded and pan-fried shrimp combined with fresh mint, lime juice, garlic, and kafir; savory Thai soups mostly with a coconut base, with morsels of fish, scallops, or pork; salads; and a full selection of curries. Vegetarians will be happy with the numerous meatless items. The service is friendly, and the portions large for the money. Su's is a favorite with local people—the highest recommendation.

Harbor House, at the Honokohau Small Boat Harbor, 808/326-4166, open daily 10:30 A.M.–8:30 P.M., features Kona's longest bar. Harbor House is more or less an open-air pavilion, but it is actually quite picturesque as it overlooks the harbor. If you are interested in a charter fishing boat, this is the best place to come to spin a yarn with the local skippers who congregate here nightly at about 4:30 P.M. Over the bar hangs a gigantic 1,556-pound marlin, almost as big as the Budweiser sign. Strategically placed TVs make it a good sports bar, and the jukebox has a great selection of oldies and contemporary tunes. You can not only quaff a variety of draft beers here, but can order off the bill of fare for grilled bacon cheeseburgers with fries, shrimp and chips, crab-salad sandwiches, clam chowder, and the like. Harbor House is one of the truly *colorful* places in Kailua-Kona, and one of the best places to relax and have a hassle-free brew. It's also a place where the fish stories you tell might easily become exaggerated with the number of beers you drink.

Basil's Pizzeria and Restaurant in downtown Kailua-Kona, 808/326-7836, open daily 11 A.M.–10 P.M., is a place that makes its own pizza dough. Individual gourmet pizzas range $5.95–10.95, depending upon your choice of toppings; New York-style pizza, 14-inch and 16-inch, is $10.95–17.95. Besides pizza, Basil's offers soup of the day for $3.50, Italian antipasto at $7.95, angel hair primavera for $10.95, shrimp marinara for $14.95, eggplant parmigiana at $10.95, and an assortment of other fine Italian foods. A nightly "fresh catch special" is priced around $15, or you can order any number of sandwiches for under $7. Pizza by the slice is available 10 A.M.–5 P.M. only, and you can do take-out. If you don't care to come down, Basil's offers free delivery of any menu item in the Kailua area. So go ahead, recline on your condo lanai and call Basil's, and they'll be over *molto rapido.*

Aki's Cafe, 808/329-0090, is a moderately priced Japanese/American restaurant offering breakfast, lunch, and dinner. Breakfast can be three-egg omelets, an eggs Benedict scramble, pancakes, or a Japanese breakfast with eggs, miso soup, rice, and your choice of meat. Lunch can be California roll sushi, fried noodles to which you can add chicken or shrimp, or curry with rice. The dinner menu offers marinated New York steak, chicken teriyaki, garlic pasta, and fish and chips. Aki's is a centrally located, simple restaurant that adds a nice touch to ordinary food.

King Yee Lau, in the Ali'i Sunset Plaza across from the seawall at the south end of town, 808/329-7100, open Mon.–Sat. 11 A.M.–2 P.M., nightly 5–9 P.M., offers an all-you-can-eat lunch buffet and the usual Chinese dishes like pressed crispy duck, beef with ginger sauce, and shrimp with seasoned vegetables, most priced under $8. Many vegetarian selections are offered.

Kimo's Family Buffet, in the heart of Kailua in the courtyard of Uncle Billy's Kona Bay Hotel, 808/329-1393, serves very reasonably priced breakfast and dinner buffets, with a free hula show thrown in Tues.–Sun. evenings as part of the bargain. The breakfast buffet runs $5.95, dinner buffet $10.95, and a Sunday brunch $7.95. These prices can't be beat, but don't expect a lavish layout.

One of a small chain on the island, **Verna's Drive-In** on Kuakini Hwy. is where many local people go for inexpensive local fast food like plate lunches, sandwiches, omelets, burgers, and drinks.

In the Lanihau Center, **Chili by Max,** open Mon.–Sat. 10 A.M.–8 P.M., Sunday 11 A.M.–8 P.M., is famous for its award-winning oven-baked chili, made with beef or turkey. Also on the bill of fare are kosher hot dogs, chili dogs, chili nachos, baked potatoes, and ice cream.

The Lanihau Center's **Kona Grill,** open Mon.–Thurs. 6 A.M.–8 P.M., Friday to 10 P.M., Saturday 8 A.M.–10 P.M., and Sunday 8 A.M.–4 P.M., is a counter restaurant serving standard breakfasts and plates like teriyaki beef, *kalbi* ribs, and shrimp platters for about $6.50. The Kona Grill is not special, but the food is acceptable and inexpensive.

In the Kopiko Plaza, along Palani Road and just down from the Lanihau Center, you'll find several places to eat: **Yuni's,** 808/329-1018, is open daily 10:30 A.M.–8 P.M. This basic saimin stand offers charsiu saimin, seafood *udon,* and a variety of other noodle dishes for under $7.

Rocky's Pizza, 808/322-3223, open daily 11 A.M.–9 P.M. at the Keauhou Shopping Village, offers whole pizzas for $9.95–14.95 or slices for $1.75 each. Rocky's also features delicious sub sandwiches like hot pastrami on crusty bread; they are favorites with the locals, who like good food at a good price.

Delis and Coffee

You can't get "hotter" than **Lava Java,** 808/327-2161, one of Kona's popular coffeehouse/ restaurants, open daily 7 A.M.–10 P.M. in the Ali'i Sunset Plaza across from the seawall. Here, local people and tourists alike come to kick back, read the papers, and actually engage in the lost art of conversation. Sandwiches are served 9 A.M.–7 P.M. Try the turkey and cranberry sandwich for $6.25, a garden burger for $5.95, Polish dog for $3.75, or a pita pocket for $4.25. Lava Java has a counter offering muffins, cookies, root beer floats, Kona coolers made

BIG ISLAND

with tropical fruit sorbet, Italian sodas, and bulk coffee by the pound. Sharing the same space is a **Tropical Dreams** ice cream parlor.

A Piece of the Apple, also in the Ali'i Sunset Plaza, open Mon.–Sat. 8 A.M.–4 P.M., is a New York-style deli with a healthful twist. Offered are fresh carrot juice, fresh-squeezed orange juice, smoothies, and fresh-baked bagels. The deli section has two-fisted sandwiches like the Reuben, New Yorker (pastrami with Swiss cheese), vegetarian, and "Seinfeld" (smoked turkey, roasted red peppers, mozzarella, and red onions). Light appetites will enjoy a California salad with smoked turkey, avocado, and Swiss cheese, a chef salad, or a garden salad. You can sit inside, but the best spot is outside at a picnic table shaded by dwarf palms.

Down the road next to Huggo's is **Java on the Rock,** an early morning coffee bar serving freshly brewed Kona coffee, espresso, and a variety of pastries from Mamane Street Bakery in Honoka'a. Take-out is an option, but perhaps it would be better to sit along the waterfront and savor your drink while you enjoy the harbor scene. A friendly place with lots of "Aloha." Open daily 6–11 A.M. except major holidays.

A friendly gorilla greets you at the **Pot Belli Deli,** 808/329-9454, open weekdays 6 A.M.–4 P.M., not far from Su's. The refrigerated deli case holds such things as chicken, ham, or tuna salad sandwiches, spinach pie, and bagels with cream cheese. The shelves hold all the condiments

and extras you need for a terrific picnic lunch. You can get your order to go or eat at one of the few booths inside.

Moderate

Cafe Sibu, in the Kona Banyan Court, 808/329-1112, open daily 11:30 A.M.–2 P.M. for lunch and 5–9 P.M. for dinner, is an Indonesian restaurant serving savory marinated meats and vegetables spiced with zesty sauces and flame grilled. The restaurant, across from the seawall under the big banyan tree, has only a few outside tables and makes a light attempt at decor with a few antique Indonesian masks. If you're hungry, go for the *gado gado* for $9.95, an Indonesian salad layered with spices and peanut sauce that can be dinner for one or an appetizer salad for two or three. Saté, curry, and stir-fry dishes can be made with chicken, beef, pork, shrimp, or vegetables for $9.25–11.95, or try the truly authentic *ayam panggang pedis,* a grilled and marinated spicy chicken. Although slightly more expensive, the combination plates are good deals as they let you try a number of items. Lunch prices are a couple bucks cheaper. Cafe Sibu serves *the* best and *the* most interesting moderately priced food in Kailua-Kona.

Look for a bright *akachochin,* a red paper lantern, marking the entrance to **Restaurant Yokohama** in the Ali'i Sunset Plaza, 808/329-9661, open Tuesday, Friday, and Sunday for

Chef Sam Choy (left) and assistant

lunch 11 A.M.–2 P.M., and Tues.–Sun. 5:30–9 P.M. Inside is simplicity: Japanese kites, light wood furniture, and a few glowing lanterns. The classic lunches include *soba sukiyaki, teishoku, donburi,* or a fixed-plate lunch, such as *tonkatsu* pork cutlets, that includes an appetizer, salad, rice, and miso soup. Some traditional dinner entrées are cooked right at your table, like sukiyaki for $22, or *shabu shabu,* thin slices of beef and assorted vegetables boiled in stock for $24. Restaurant Yokohama also features sushi combination dinners costing $10–17. Although in a shopping plaza, both the atmosphere and cuisine are genuine.

The **Kona Ranch House,** 808/329-7061, at the corner of Kuakini Hwy. and Ololi Rd., is a delightful restaurant with something for everyone. It has two rooms: the family-oriented Paniolo Room, where hearty appetites are filled family style; and the elegant Plantation Lanai, where both palate and sense of beauty are satiated. This cheery restaurant is well regarded in town and epitomizes plantation dining. The Kona Ranch House is a classy establishment where you get more than you pay for. The menu is mostly standard American fare with a heavy dollop of fish and seafood. You may need reservations for breakfast on the weekends. Open daily 6:30 A.M.–2 P.M., and Sunday for brunch.

Cassandra's Greek Taverna, 808/334-1066, open Mon.–Sat. 11 A.M.–10 P.M., Sunday 4:30–9 P.M., tucked away along Ali'i Drive in the Kona Plaza Shopping Center, uses a predominant blue and white motif reminiscent of the Greek Isles. Lunch is served 11 A.M.–4 P.M., with most items under $9. Dinner expands the lunch menu and includes such offerings as traditional appetizers like *dolmades* (grape leaves stuffed with meat and rice) and *keftedes* (pan-fried Greek meatballs), and savory entrées like a *gyro* plate, Greek-style baby-back pork ribs, shrimp posidonian, or *souvlaki* made with chicken, beef, or lamb. Prices mostly range $13–24; a platter for two runs $44.95. A full bar is tucked in the corner. This is the place to come to for eastern Mediterranean food. Earthy, vibrant Greek music to stir the soul wafts through the air, and belly dancing is performed for guests on Friday and Saturday evenings.

On the second floor across from the pier, **Kona Galley,** 808/329-5550, open for lunch 11:30 A.M.–4 P.M. and for dinner 4–9 P.M., features bright paintings of sunsets, flowers, and ferns reflecting the island mood of the beach and bay below. Lunchtime has gourmet burgers and sandwiches. Dinner is more full-bodied, with dishes like chicken Jerusalem made with mushrooms, garlic, artichoke hearts, capers, and a Dijon dill sauce; scallops or shrimp Bombay; Pacific seafood medley; or a New York steak and lobster tail.

Quinn's, across from King Kamehameha's Kona Beach Hotel, 808/329-3822, is Kona's socially eclectic bar and grill where everyone from local bikers to pink-roasted tourists are welcomed. It's also a roost for night owls who come here to munch and have a beer when everything else in town is closed. The inside bar is cozy, friendly, and sports oriented. Quinn's is open daily for lunch 11 A.M.–5:30 P.M. and dinner 5:30 P.M.–1 A.M. (Sunday until 10 P.M.). Go for the fish. For lunch, a gigantic mound of shrimp and crab salad is wonderful. The fresh catch-of-the-day sandwiches with salad are a deal. Reasonably priced specialties include tenderloin tips sautéed in brandy with onions, shrimp and chips, and fish and chips. Fill up for under $10. Dinner entrées are savory: sautéed scallops, chicken stir-fry, and fresh catch sautéed or baked. Most entrées are $15–20 and all include soup or dinner salad, vegetable, rice, and Quinn's home-fried potatoes.

Cool down with a frosty margarita and watch life go by as you perch on a stool at the upstairs location of **Pancho and Lefty's,** 808/326-2171, open daily 11 A.M.–10 P.M. Happy hour, running 3–6 P.M., offers 12-ounce drafts for $1 and big, potent 16-ounce margaritas for $2.75. Menu selections begin with appetizers such as buffalo wings, skinny dippers (potatoes covered with bacon and cheese or guacamole), and nachos. Full dinners include taco salad, seafood salad with crisp greens, or fajitas—steak, chicken or seafood (fresh catch). Specials are enchilada rancheros, carne asada, tostadas, or Mexican burgers. Most everything is in the $12–18 range, with few items over $20. Pancho and Lefty's is a good-time place with satisfying food that's easy on the budget.

When you enter the Kaloko Industrial Park, just past mile marker 97 and about three miles north from Kailua-Kona, the setting makes you

BIG ISLAND

think you're after plumbing supplies. That's here too, but you'll also find terrific food prepared by one of Hawaii's greatest chefs at **Sam Choy's Kaloko Restaurant,** 808/326-1545, open weekdays 6 A.M.–2 P.M. and Tues.–Sat. 5–8 P.M. for dinner, reservations suggested. To get there, turn right onto Hinalani Street, go up one block and take a right onto Kanalani Street, and a left two blocks down onto Kauhola Street. Look for Sam's in a nondescript gray building halfway up the hill on the right, next to the lumberyard. The atmosphere is pleasant enough, but those who have dined on Sam's sumptuous creations come for the food! Breakfasts like the ultimate stew omelet (a three-egg omelet filled with Sam's beef stew) for $7.50, steak and eggs for $10.95, or any one of the various "loco moco" will keep you going most of the day. The lunch menu includes fresh island fish prepared *poke* style and then flash-fried for $7.50, saimin at $3, and Kaloko noodle mania for $7.50. For a gourmet dinner, choose Chinese-style honey duck with Ka'u orange sauce at $19.95, pork ribs and fried chicken for $13.95, or Sam's award winning seafood *lau lau* made with fresh fish, assorted veggies, and Waipi'o Valley taro leaves for $23.95. While not the cheapest in town, the portions are large and the flavors are perfect.

Up in the Crossroads Shopping Center on Henry Street is a wonderful gourmet restaurant that serves meals at moderate prices. This is Amy Ota's **Oodles of Noodles,** 808/329-9222. Don't be put off by the shopping center location—the food is great and the rich colorful decor, low light, and dark tile floor are conducive to a fine meal. Oodles serves a fusion of East and West, with such items as Japanese *udon,* Thai rice noodles, and Italian pasta, that leads to unique and surprising flavors. Almost everything has noodles of some sort in it, including the appetizers, soups, and salads, and with many items you can create your own combinations. Some menu selections include crisp Thai calamari in noodle nest, red miso ramen with shiitake mushrooms and tofu, Asian risotto Peking duck with herbs and spices, and aglio olio linguini with shellfish, and there are always featured specials. Most lunch and dinner entrées cost under $14, while the appetizers, soups, and salads run $6–10. Food here is a treat for the taste buds, and the variety of noodle dishes is outstanding. Amy's restaurant is an excellent choice.

With a menu that's at least twice as long as you might expect to find, **Bangkok House** Thai restaurant, 808/329-7764, serves plentiful food in a pleasing setting in the King Kamehameha Mall. Your choices include standard Thai fare plus many surprises. Most entrées run $8–10, with specials up to $15.

Bubba Gump's, next to Waterfront Row, is perhaps the newest of the midrange restaurants along Ali'i Drive. It's a fun family restaurant that, of course, does shrimp and seafood.

Overlooking the Royal Kona Resort tennis courts is **Tres Hombres,** 808/329-2173. This is a Mexican restaurant with a strong island influence. Taquitos, tostadas, burritos, chili rellenos, fajitas, and all the usual offerings are on the menu, as are fish and seafood items. Lunch and dinner have roughly the same menu, with few items more than $15. Before dinner, stop at the bar for a cool one and watch the sunset. Open Sun.–Thurs. 11:30 A.M.–9 P.M. and Friday and Saturday until 10 P.M. This is a good choice for Mexican.

If you thought you saw Elvis head up the stairway you might have been right. Follow him up to the second floor at **Flashbacks Bar and Grill,** 808/326-2840. Music of the '50s and '60s fills the air and the walls are hung with memorabilia of the era. If this doesn't put you in the mood for an old-fashioned burger or dog, what will? Try the Chubby Checker burger, a double patty with lettuce and tomato, for $8.95, or a chili cheese dog for $6.25. Appetizers, soups, salads, and sandwiches are also on the menu, as are more substantial meals like fried chicken, New York steak, and roast beef, which run mostly under $15. Across from the Kailua pier, Flashbacks opens at 11 A.M. and serves lunch and dinner; stop by 4–6 P.M. for happy hour. Hey, isn't that the Big Bopper over by the window?

Moving up a generation brings you to the **Hard Rock Cafe,** in the Coconut Grove Marketplace, 808/329-8866, where the '70s and '80s is the theme. Music accompanies your meal and memorabilia covers the walls. The Hard Rock has standard American fare with many burger and sandwich choices, plus items like hickory barbecued chicken, smoked pork chops, and fresh catch of the day, mostly under $12. Of course, there is a bar to serve drinks and a counter that sells Hard Rock merchandise. Open daily 11 A.M.–11 P.M. (11:30 P.M. on Friday and Saturday).

South of town in the Keauhou Shopping Center is the breezy, easy-going **Drysdale's Too** restaurant, 808/322-0070, where you can get burgers, sandwiches, hot dogs, gyros, and any number of meat and meatless dishes, plus soups, salads, tropical drinks, and beer. A friendly, comfortable place, it's somehow familiar, and you'll be happy that it won't cost an arm and a leg. Burgers and sandwiches run $5.50–7, while most entrées are less than $14.

Expensive

Oui oui, Monsieur, but of course we have zee restaurant *français.* It is **La Bourgogne,** 808/329-6711, open Mon.–Sat. 6–10 P.M., at the corner of Nalani Street, about three miles south of downtown Kailua-Kona along Route 11. For those who just can't live without escargot, real French onion soup, or scallop Provençale, you've been saved. How much will it set you back? Plenty, *mon petit!* Cold and hot appetizers include *pâté du chef* for $7.95, and escargots de Bourgogne for $7.95, while scrumptious French onion soup for $5 or homemade lobster bisque for $6.50 will follow. For salads, order greens with local goat cheese or greens with mango and lobster. Titillating seafood and poultry entrées, $21–30, feature fresh catch of the day; lobster braised with shallots, tomato, brandy, and cream; and roast duck breast with raspberries and pine nuts. Meat courses, $23–32, include delectable roast rack of lamb with creamy mustard sauce; tenderloin of venison with sherry and pomegranate sauce; and osso bucco veal shank in red wine. Top off your gourmet meal with fresh, made-in-house desserts like crème brûlée or a lemon tartlet. This restaurant, small and slightly out of the way, is definitely worth a visit for those who enjoy exceptional food—a memorable gastronomic experience. Definitely call for reservations, perhaps a couple of days in advance.

Jameson's-by-the-Sea, 77-6452 Ali'i Dr., 808/329-3195, is open for lunch weekdays 11 A.M.–2:30 P.M. and dinner every evening 5:30–10 P.M. Jameson's makes a good attempt at elegance with high-backed wicker chairs, crystal everywhere, white linen table settings, and a back-lit fish tank in the entry. The sea foams white and crashes on the shore just outside the restaurant's open windows. The quality of the food is very good, just shy of gourmet. People come here for fish, and they are never disappointed. The lunch menu lists appetizers like sashimi, salmon pâté, and fried calamari, and a variety of sandwiches. The dinner menu offers the same appetizers but adds a seafood platter with sashimi, shrimp, and fresh oysters. The dinner entrées range from fresh catches like *opakapaka, ono,* and mahimahi to fried shrimp and scallops with oyster sauce and Chinese pea pods. Other full meals include filet mignon with béarnaise sauce, baked stuffed shrimp, sesame chicken, and shrimp curry with mango chutney, mostly under $25. For dessert, save room for the assortment of homemade chiffon pies from $4.50.

At **Huggo's Restaurant,** on Ali'i Drive next door to the Royal Kona Resort, 808/329-1493, it's difficult to concentrate on the food because the setting is so spectacular. If you were any closer to the sea, you'd be in it, and of course the sunset is great. Because it is built on a pier, you can actually feel the floor rock. Huggo's is open Mon.–Fri. 11:30 A.M.–2:30 P.M. for full lunch service, 2:30–5 P.M. for late-lunch sandwiches only served at the bar, and 5:30–10 P.M. for dinner, with entertainment most nights. Lunch is reasonable, with tasties like Huggo's club, a pizza with your choice of toppings for around $8, or a classic Huggo's burger. The dinner menu is superb and starts with fresh *sashimi* and seafood chowder made from clams and fresh fish and seasoned with sherry, cream sauce, and butter. The best entrées come from the sea just outside the door and are priced daily at around $25. A fantastic selection is the stuffed fish, delicious with an exotic blend of tender bay shrimp and dijonnaise sauce. Also worth trying is shrimp scampi or Kona paella, made with fresh fish, Maine lobster claw, shrimp, and chicken all tossed with lemon and saffron and served with rice pilaf. Huggo's has been in business for more than 30 years and is consistently outstanding. Enjoy free *pu pu* Mon.–Fri. 4–6 P.M. while sipping a cocktail as the red Kona sun dips into the azure sea.

The Kona Inn Restaurant at the Kona Inn Shopping Village, 808/329-4455, open daily for lunch and dinner, is a lovely but lonely carry-over from the venerable old Kona Inn. On entering, notice the marlin over the doorway and a huge piece of hung glass through which the sunset sometimes forms prismatic rainbows. The bar and dining area are richly appointed in native koa and made more elegant with a mixture of turn-of-the-century wooden chairs, high-backed peacock thrones, polished hardwood floors, and sturdy open-beamed ceilings. If you want to enjoy the view, try a cocktail and some of the *pu pu* served until closing. Lunch is reasonable at the café grill. Open 11:30 A.M.–10:30 P.M., it serves mostly light foods, sandwiches, burgers, soups, and salads. Dinner is served 5:30–9:30 P.M., reservations recommended. The menu is heavy on fish and meat but offers a few Asian stir-fry dishes and pastas. Expect dinner entrées to run $15–22. The Kona Inn Restaurant epitomizes Kona beachside dining, and the view is simply superb.

Michaelangelo's, in Waterfront Row, 808/329-4436, is run by Mike Medeiros—a true *Mediterraneo* if there ever was one. It is open for lunch daily 11 A.M.–4:30 P.M. and for dinner until 10 P.M., with happy hour 11 A.M.–5 P.M. Savory selections include antipasto for $6.95–11.95, clam chowder for $5.95, and specialty salads that could make a meal. For lunch, try Kona Krust pizza or vegetarian pasta. The dinner menu, with most entrées in the $14–25 range, includes spaghetti boulinnaise, chicken Parmesan, Lava Fire Calamari, or Norwegian smoked salmon. A children's menu has items all priced at $4.95 to help keep costs down. The large oceanfront room is appointed with open-beamed ceilings joined by distinctive copper couplings, with Casablanca fans.

Also in Waterfront Row, the **Chart House,** 808/329-2451, open daily for dinner 5–10 P.M., is part of a small chain of restaurants that have built a good reputation for service, value, and well-prepared food. Primarily, it is a steak and seafood house with most meals costing $16–25. The location is very pleasant, away from the street noise and with a good view of the sea.

The **Kona Beach Restaurant,** at King Kamehameha's Kona Beach Hotel, 808/329-2911, is open daily for breakfast and dinner and is especially known for its Sunday champagne brunch served 9 A.M.–1 P.M., $21.95 adults, $9.95 children 6–12. The long tables are laden with fruit, vegetables, pasta salad, peel-and-eat shrimp, omelets, waffles, hot entrées from fresh catch to sashimi, and desserts so sinful you'll be glad that someone's on their knees praying at Sunday services. Friday and Saturday nights are very special because of the Prime Rib & Seafood Buffet at $21.95, which brings hungry people from around the island. A pasta bar buffet is hosted on Wednesday and Thursday for $12.95, while Monday and Tuesday sees a scrumptious Hawaiian dinner buffet for $13.95, both great deals. The Kona Beach Restaurant is an award-winning operation, sure to please. The restaurant itself is tasteful, but the best feature is an unobstructed view of the hotel's beach, especially fine at sunset.

Brewery

The **Kona Brewing Company** has been creating quality beer since the mid-1990s. It produces eight varieties from a light lager to a dark porter, perhaps the best known of which are Pacific Golden Ale, Fire Rock Pale Ale, and Longboard Lager. Bar beer is brewed on the premises at a rate of about 150 barrels a week, but the retail beer is brewed in California according to Kona Brewing Company's recipe. Free brewery tours and tastings are given daily at 10 A.M. and 3 P.M., but if you miss the tour, stop by the brewery and café anyway to try a beer or two. The café serves mostly pizza and sandwiches, nothing elegant, but a good complement to the brew. A seat at the bar gets you up close to all the action there, or you may choose a booth inside or a table out on the lanai where you can watch the sun go down as easily as the beer in your tall cool glass. Behind Zac's Business Center in the North Kona Shopping Center, Kona Brewing is open for lunch and dinner daily.

ENTERTAINMENT

Kona nights come alive mainly in the restaurants and dining rooms of the big hotels. The most memorable experience for most is free: watching the sunset from Kailua Pier and taking a leisurely stroll along Ali'i Drive. All of the lu'au have "Polynesian Revues" of one sort or another, which are generally good, clean, sexy fun, but of course these shows are limited only to the lu'au guests. For those who have "dancin' feet" or wish to spend the evening listening to live music, there's a small but varied selection from which to choose.

Around Town

Huggo's Restaurant, with its romantic waterfront setting along Ali'i Drive, features music 8:30 P.M.–12:30 A.M. The entertainment changes nightly: *karaoke,* smooth Jahwaiian, other mellow contemporary sounds, or a touch of rock now and again.

The **Aston Keauhou Beach Resort** soothes you with easy listening, Hawaiian style, at the veranda bar.

At the **Royal Kona Resort's Windjammer Lounge,** an open-air bar, sip a flavorful tropical concoction while watching the sun melt into the Pacific. Entertainment is offered several evenings a week, featuring jazz on Sunday afternoon. Call the resort at 808/329-3111 for a schedule of entertainment.

In downtown Kailua-Kona you can pick your fun at King Kamehameha's Kona Beach Hotel. Here, the **Billfish Bar** has live entertainment Tues.–Sun. 6–9:30 P.M., featuring mellow Hawaiian music. The bar is open until 10 P.M. daily with happy hour 5–7 P.M.

Kimo's Family Buffet at the Kona Bay Hotel offers a free hula show 6–8 P.M. Tues.–Sun. during dinner. As the entertainment is performed outdoors near the pool, passersby are also treated to lovely strains of Hawaiian music and swaying hips.

Around town, **Michaelangelo's** has dancing every night 10 P.M.–2 A.M. at its disco dance club at Waterfront Row. For a quiet beer, sports talk, or just hanging out with the local people try **Quinn's, Ocean View Inn,** or **Sam's Hideaway,** all in downtown Kailua-Kona.

For movies try the **Kona Marketplace Cinemas** in the Kona Marketplace or the **Hualalai Theater** at the corner of Hualalai Road and Kuakini Hwy. at the Hualalai Center.

Lu'au

Tihati's Drums of Polynesia Lu'au, at the Royal Kona Resort, 808/329-3111, held every Monday, Friday, and Saturday, offers an evening of entertainment and feasting, Hawaiian style. The lu'au begins at 5:30 P.M. and is followed by an open bar, lavish buffet, and thrilling entertainment for three fun-filled hours. Many supposedly authentic lu'au play-act with the *imu*-baked pig, but here it is carved and served to the guests. Prices are $53 adults, $25 children ages 6–12, free for children under age five. Reservations are strongly recommended.

King Kamehameha's Kona Beach Hotel, 808/326-4969, sways with Hawaiian chants during its famous **Island Breeze Lu'au** held every Sunday, Tuesday, Wednesday, and Thursday on the beach and grounds of King Kamehameha's last residence, Ahu'ena. The pig is placed into the *imu* every morning at 10 A.M. and the festivities begin in the evening with a lei greeting at 5:30 P.M. and a torch-lighting *imu* pageant at 6 P.M. Cocktails flow 6–8 P.M.; the 22-course lu'au dinner is served 6:30–8:30 P.M. Prices are $52 adults, $19.50 children 6–12, free for children five and under. Reservations are required. Call 808/326-4969 or stop by the lu'au desk in the lobby of the hotel.

RECREATION

Tennis

The Royal Kona Resort has four latexite courts, three of which are lighted for night play, that are open to resort guests and nonguests alike. Court fees are a reasonable $6 per hour. Avid tennis players should check the weekly rates. Instruction can be arranged and racquets rented for $3–8. Call the pro shop at 808/334-1093 to reserve court time, particularly for night play.

Island Slice Tennis, 808/322-6112, at the Keauhou Beach Hotel offers reserved tennis play for $10 a day on six lighted courts.

Snorkeling

For snorkeling equipment rental, try **Snorkel Bob's,** 808/329-0770, across from Huggo's; it has some of the best prices, equipment, and services on the island. Gear, which includes mask, snorkel tube, and fins, is rented for a 24-hour day or by the week. The snorkel set runs between $2.50 a day or $9 a week to $9 a day or $35 a week, depending on the quality. Rental boogie boards are also available.

Miller's Snorkeling, 808/326-1711, at the Kona Bali Kai condo rents complete snorkeling

Some of the island's best canoeists come to Kailua Bay to work out every evening.

BIG ISLAND

gear for $7 per day or $15 per week. It also rents boogie boards and beach accessories and is open daily 8 A.M.–5 P.M. Most dive shops also rent snorkel gear.

Bikes

Dave's Bike and Triathlon Shop, 808/329-4522, owned and pedaled by triathlete Dave Bending, is just a long stride or two from the beginning of the Ironman Triathlon across from King Kamehameha's Kona Beach Hotel in the Kona Square Shopping Center. Dave rents competition-quality road bikes, mountain bikes, hybrids, and full-suspension bikes, from $15 a day to $60 a week. Prices include helmet, water bottles, map, bicycle lock and, most importantly, road advice. Dave knows his stuff, so pay heed! If you want to do more than just pedal along the beach, come see Dave for the best gear and best advice in town.

Hawaiian Pedals, at the Kona Inn Shopping Village, 808/329-2294, rents basic mountain bikes and hybrids. A sister store, the **Bike Works,** 74-5599 Lehua St., Suite F-3, 808/326-2453, rents suspension mountain bikes and road bikes. Rates for 24 hours are $20 for mountain and hybrids, $25 for road and front-suspension bikes, and $30 for full-suspension mountain bikes. Five-hour and multi-day rates can also be arranged.

Safari Activities, 808/334-0464, at the Coconut Grove Marketplace, rents mountain bikes

for $15 for five hours and $20 for 24 hours, with reduced daily rates for longer periods. It also rents kayaks, snorkel gear, boogie boards, mopeds, and miscellaneous beach accessories.

Electric Car Rental

If you don't want to pedal around town, perhaps touring in a souped-up golf cart would be more your style. These electric vehicles look like bubbles on wheels. They run up to 25 mph and can go about 30 miles on a charge. They're fun and breezy, come in two- and four-seater models, and make a unique way to get to the beach. The vehicles rent for $39–50 for four hours, $69–75 for up to eight hours, and $80–99 for 24 hours. Ask about the multi-day rental bargains. Contact **Happy Haulers,** 808/334-1626 or 800/960-3651, at the Kona Square Shopping Center for rental information.

Submarine Tour

Two companies in Kailua offer a once-in-a-lifetime, below-the-surface-of-the-water experience to view undersea life at the fish eye level. **Atlantis Submarine,** 808/329-6626 or 800/548-6262, allows everyone to live out the fantasy of Captain Nemo on a silent cruise under the waves. This underwater dive lasts about a half hour and descends to 120 feet, where everything seems to turn to blues and greens. You cruise in air-conditioned comfort and have great viewing out the two-foot diameter windows.

Cruises run five times a day 10 A.M.–2:30 P.M.; the price is $79 adults and $39 children. Find the office near the pier at the Akona Kai Mall.

In contrast, the **Nautilus II,** 808/326-2003, is a semi-submersible that does not actually dive. This craft skims the water and the spacious below deck passenger compartment offers sights out the viewing window. Nautilus offers narrated one-hour tours from the Kailua Pier. Adults cost $29.95, children under 12 tour for $19.95. The Nautilus office is in the Kona Seaside Mall across from the pier.

Sunset Dinner Cruise
Captain Beans' Dinner Cruise departs Kailua Pier Sat.–Thurs. at 5 P.M. and returns at 8 P.M. On Friday, the boat leaves at 7 P.M., so if you are after a sunset cruise, don't go on a Friday. On board, you are entertained while the bar dispenses liberal drinks and the deck groans with an all-you-can-eat buffet. And you get a terrific panorama of the Kona Coast from the sea. You can't help having a good time on this cruise, and if the boat sinks with all that food and booze in your belly, you're a goner—but what a way to go! Minimum age is 21 years, $52 includes tax and tip. Reservations suggested; call 808/329-2955.

Miniature Golf
If the local golf courses are just too expensive or if you're just not sure enough about your game, spend some time first at the **Swing Zone** miniature golf course and practice at the Menehune Country Club 18-hole grass putting course that's shaped like the Big Island itself. One round runs $8 and includes a putter and balls, no players under age 12; golf rules apply. This course has no lights so it's daytime play only. Also at the Swing Zone is a full-size driving range that's lit at night; a pail of 60 balls costs $5. If these two aren't enough to wear you out, try the batting cage, also lit, where $1 buys 10 pitches. Open daily until 9 P.M., the Swing Zone is across the street from the Old Airport Beach Park; 808/329-6909.

SHOPPING

The Kailua-Kona area has an abundance of two commodities near and dear to a tourist's heart: sunshine and shopping malls. Below is a selection of Kona-area shopping centers and malls, including a general idea of what they contain.

Shopping Along Ali'i Drive
King Kamehameha's Kona Beach Hotel Mall, fully air-conditioned, features a cluster of specialty shops which include Resort Sundries, selling wine, liquor, and beer along with suntan lotions, gift items, magazines, novels, and T-shirts; Jewel Palace, sparkling with watches and fine jewelry fashioned from gold and silver; Silver Reef, featuring Hawaiian-motif jewelry, glassware, Japanese dolls, and porcelainware; Kailua Village Artists, hung with paintings and prints; several apparel and gift shops; and a coffee and ice cream shop.

Kitty-corner to King Kamehameha's Hotel is the **Kona Seaside Mall,** with most shops open daily 9 A.M.–6 P.M. Here you'll find Neptune's Garden, creating rainbows with its display of stained glass art fashioned into lamps, creative hangings, and vases, plus a few paintings. For clothing, try Tropical Tees, Sandal Stop, and Eel Skin Liquidators, and Bubi's Sportswear Center of Kona. Other shops are the Kona Coast Sunglass Company, and DJ's Rentals for motorcycles and scooters.

The **Kona Square Shopping Center,** next to the Seaside Mall, features Mermaid's By The Sea, a distinctive ladies' and children's clothing boutique bright with alohawear, pareu, sundresses and evening dresses, and a ceiling hung with cherubic angels if you're not sharing your Hawaii vacation with one of your own. Directly across from Mermaid's is Island Silversmiths, Kona's oldest modern-day shop, in business since 1973, so you know it's doing something right. This tiny mall also has Dave's Bike and Triathlon Shop, Happy Haulers electric cart rental, and the Nautilus II submersible office.

Just down the way, the **Kona Banyan Court** has a dozen shops with a medley of goods and services. Unison is a surfing shop with T-shirts, sandals, hats, and boogie boards. The most impressive shop in the complex is Big Island Jewelers, owned and operated by brothers Flint and Gale Carpenter, master goldsmiths. The shop motto, "Have your jewelry made by a Carpenter," applies to custom-made jewelry fashioned to their or your personal design. Big Island Jewelers, in business for more than 15 years, does repairs and also carries a full line of pearls and loose stones that you can have mounted into any setting you wish. Open daily.

Kitty-corner from Hulihe'e Palace is **Kona Marketplace,** which offers a variety of shops selling everything from books to bathing suits. Numerous restaurants are spread throughout the mall, as are the Middle Earth Bookshoppe, an antique shop, and the Kona Marketplace Cinemas. Here too is Kona Jewelers, specializing in fine jewelry and ceramics; the jam-packed Aloha From Kona specializes in baubles, bangles, postcards, handbags, and purses; and the Kona Flea Market stuck to the rear of the mall sells inexpensive travel bags, shells, beach mats, suntan lotion, and all the junk that you could want.

One of the largest malls in Kailua is the **Kona Inn Shopping Village.** It spreads south from Hulihe'e Palace in a long meandering series of buildings, taking the place of what was the old Kona Inn Hotel. This shopping village boasts more than 40 shops selling fabrics, fashions, art, fruits, gems and jewelry, photo and music needs, food, bicycles, souvenirs, and gifts. One shop in this mall is Hula Heaven, which specializes in vintage Hawaiian shirts and modern reproductions. Prices range from $50 for the "look-alikes" to $1,000 for the rarest of the classics. Because many of the items on display date from the '40s and '50s, the shop is like a trip back in time. Other stores include Kona Jewelry Factory, featuring island-inspired jewelry; Hawaiian Fruit and Flower Company for sweets and sweet-smelling flowers; Fare Tahiti Fabrics for incidental travel bags, pareu, and fabrics; Golden Orchid Originals, a women's resortwear and casual wear shop; Kona Inn Jewelry, for worldwide treasures—one of the oldest and best-known shops for a square deal in Kona; Flamingo's for contemporary island clothing and evening wear mainly for women; Alley Gecko's, showcasing colorful gifts from around the world; and Thomas Kinkade Gallery for paintings by this well-known artist.

Waterfront Row is a relatively new shopping and food complex in the center of downtown Kailua-Kona. Built of rough-cut lumber, it's done in period architecture reminiscent of an outdoor promenade in a Boston shipyard at the turn of the century. Here, Crazy Shirts sells unique island creations and Wyland Galleries of Hawaii displays island-inspired paintings and sculpture. Restaurants include the Chart House for steaks and seafood and Michaelangelo's for Italian cuisine.

Newest to the Kailua strip, just up from the Royal Kona Resort, is **Coconut Grove Marketplace.** This two-part shopping plaza, split by a sand volleyball court, has about a dozen shops and restaurants that include Rift Zone Gallery and Pia Mana Pearls. Island Salsa features one-of-a-kind designer T-shirts, creations by Roberta, the owner/artist, some of the best in Kona. It also features alohawear for the entire family, ladies' evening wear, swimwear, and dinner clothes. You can find other fine clothing and alohawear at Malia Kane and Tropics, and Jack's Diving Locker can set you up on a scuba tour. Hungry? You'll find Hard Rock Cafe and Lulu's Restaurant here.

Shopping Along Palani Road

There are several malls on both sides of Palani Road, which heads away from the water, starting at the King Kamehameha Hotel. They include the following.

Backing up against King Kamehameha's Kona Beach Hotel is the small **King Kamehameha Mall,** where you will find, among other shops, the Kona Wine Market, with the town's largest selection of wines, and Bangkok House Restaurant.

Kopiko Plaza is a small mall containing Tempo Music, where you can fulfill all of your music needs, including plenty of island sounds, and B&L Bike and Sports for the largest selection of sporting equipment in town. This is the official Ironman store. The mall also has a smattering of inexpensive restaurants, both for take-out and eating in. Across the road is the Kona location of **Hilo Hattie's,** 808/329-7200, open 8:30 A.M.–6 P.M., where you can find family fashions, gifts, souvenirs, music, and packaged island foods.

The **Lanihau Center,** along Palani Road between Kuakini Highway and Queen Ka'ahumanu Highway, offers Longs Drugs for sundries and photo supplies; an assortment of restaurants including Buns in the Sun, Kona Grill, and Royal Jade Garden; and other shops including Royal Hawaiian Heritage Jewelry. Here as well are a Sack 'n Save supermarket, three banks, and the Kailua-Kona post office.

Kona Coast Shopping Center features a KTA Super Store for groceries and sundries, and a Blockbuster Video where you can rent a movie for the evening, open daily 10 A.M.–midnight.

Along Queen Kaʻahumanu Highway

At the corner of Queen Kaʻahumanu Highway and Henry Street is the new **Crossroads Center.** The two big stores here are Wal-Mart and Safeway, but one other place of note is the fine restaurant Oodles of Noodles. Across Henry Street in its own building is a huge Borders Books and Music store for the town's largest selection of books, CDs, and maps.

The new **Makalapua Center** above the old Kona Industrial Area has a huge Kmart open 7 A.M.–10 P.M. daily for all general shopping needs, including clothing, household goods, and camping and athletic supplies. Liberty House also has a big store here for family fashions.

Keauhou Mall

If, god forbid, you haven't found what you need in Kailua, or if you suddenly need a "shopping fix," the **Keauhou Shopping Center** is at the corner of Aliʻi Drive and Kamehameha III Road in Keauhou. Look for flags waving in the breeze high on the hill marking the entrance. This mall houses over 40 shops and is one of the newest in the area. You can find all your food and prescription needs at KTA Super Store, the largest in the area. Head to Longs Drugs for everything from foot care products to photo developing, and Ace Hardware for nuts and bolts. For food, Drysdale's Too is an indoor/outdoor bar and grill where you can relax over a cold beer or choose from an extensive sandwich menu; you could also have a pizza at Rocky's Pizza, a morning pick-me-up at Daylight Donuts and Deli, or a jolt at Bad Ass Coffee. Other shops include the Showcase Gallery, for glassware, paintings, ceramics, and local crafts; Borderlines and Paradise Found Boutique for apparel; and Alapaki's Hawaiian Gifts for island gifts and souvenirs from black coral jewelry to koa bowls, and a replica of a Hawaiian double-hulled canoe made of coconut and cloth with traditional crab-claw sails to *tutu* dolls bedecked in colorful muʻumuʻu. For some practical purchases at wholesale prices, check Liberty House Penthouse. This outlet store sells items that have been cleared and reduced from the famous Liberty House stores. You can save on everything from alohawear to formal dresses.

Art and Specialty Shops

The **Palace Gift Shop** is on the grounds of Huliheʻe Palace. Open daily except Sunday, it has quality Hawaiian craft items nice enough for gifts or memorabilia and a good collection of postcards and books on Hawaiiana.

One of the few art galleries in Kailua is the **Rift Zone Gallery,** 808/331-1100, in the Coconut Grove Marketplace. This gallery displays

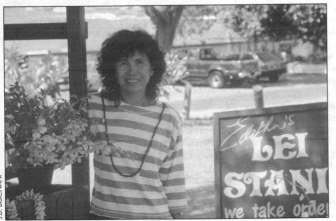

J.D. BISIGNANI

Editha's Lei Stand

the whole spectrum of artwork, almost exclusively from Big Island artists, including ceramics by Robert Joiner, bronze sculpture, paintings, wood art, and art glass. If you're looking to purchase art made in Hawaii, this is an excellent place to start.

Two other shops to look at for island art are **Kailua Village Artists,** 808/329-6653, a co-op gallery of Big island artists at the King Kamehameha's Kona Beach Hotel Mall, open daily 9:30 A.M.–5:30 P.M.; and **Wyland Galleries of Hawaii** at Waterfront Row, 808/334-0037.

Hawaii Forest and Trail is a tour company that leads wonderful birdwatching, hiking, and mule ride eco-adventures around the island. It now has a retail store across from the entrance to Honokohau Harbor that carries a small selection of hiking and outdoor supplies, adventure clothing, first-aid supplies, books, and USGS maps. While you're here, look into the company's tours. They are excellent.

Enjoy the beauty of Hawaii with flowers from **Editha's Lei Stand,** a.k.a. Oriental Flower Decor, in front of Huggo's Restaurant, open daily 10:30 A.M.–6 P.M. except Sunday with a slightly earlier closing. Editha creates lovely lei that run from $4 for a basic strand to $20 for a magnificent triple lei, along with a variety of fresh-cut flower arrangements. All of Editha's flowers are "certified" so if you want to take them home, you'll have no hassle with agricultural inspection. If you prefer direct shipping to the Mainland, that can be done as well.

Kailua Candy Company, 808/329-2522, is in the old Kona Industrial area on the corner of Kuakini Highway and Kiawi Streets. It was recognized as one of the "top 10 chocolate shops in the United States" in the February 1993 issue of *Bon Appetit* magazine. All the chocolates are made of the finest ingredients available, and all would try the willpower of Gandhi, but the specialty is the macadamia nut *honu,* Hawaiian for turtle. Shipping of all boxed candy is available at the cost of postage plus a handling fee. Every day 8 A.M.–6 P.M., have a free look into the kitchen and nibble samples of the products.

The **Banyan Tree Bazaar** (not really the name, but no one has bothered to give it one yet) is along Ali'i Drive across from the seawall. Look for blue and white umbrellas under which local merchants sell handcrafted and locally made necklaces, earrings, and bracelets. Others sell various artworks like stuffed animals, along with an array of inexpensive but neat tourist junk.

Food Markets

KTA Super Stores, open daily 6 A.M.–midnight, are generally the cheapest markets in town and are at the Kona Coast Shopping Center along Palani Rd. and at the Keauhou Shopping Center, at the extreme south end of Ali'i Drive at its junction with Kamehameha III Road. They're well stocked with sundries; an excellent selection of Asian foods, fresh veggies, fish, and fruit; and a smattering of health food. The market also contains a full-service pharmacy.

You'll also find a **Sack 'n Save** supermarket in the Lanihau Center, open 5 A.M.–midnight; and a **Safeway** in the newer Crossroads Center up on Henry Street.

Kona Wine Market, in the small King Kamehameha Mall, 75-5626 Kuakini Hwy., 808/329-9400, open daily 10 A.M.–8 P.M., Sunday noon–6 P.M., is the best wine shop on the Kona Coast. It features an impressive international selection of wine and varietals and a large cooler holds a fine selection of beer, both domestic and imported. Store shelves also hold wonderful gourmet munchies like Indian chutney, Sicilian olives, mustards, dressings, marinades, smoked salmon, hearty cheeses, and even pasta imported from Italy. Cigar smokers will also appreciate the humidor filled with fine cigars from around the world.

Kona Reef Liquor and Deli is south of town center at the Casa De Emdeko condominium. It's well stocked with liquor and groceries, but at convenience-store prices.

You'll find the **Kona Farmers' Market,** held every Wednesday and Saturday 7 A.M.–3 P.M. at the parking lot across from Hale Halawai, a great place for locally grown fruits and vegetables, flowers, coffee, and crafts.

About two miles south of the pier on the *mauka* side of Ali'i Drive is the outdoor **Alii Garden Marketplace,** open 8 A.M.–5 P.M. Wed.–Sun. Vendors sell local produce, flowers, and crafts.

Health Food Stores

Kona keeps you healthy with **Kona Natural Foods** in the Crossroads Shopping Center on Henry Street, 808/329-2296, open Mon.–Sat. 9

A.M.–8 P.M., Sunday to 7 P.M. Besides a good assortment of health foods, there are cosmetics, books, and dietary and athletic supplements. Vegetarians will like the ready-to-eat and inexpensive sandwiches, salads, soups, smoothies, and juices. Shelves are lined with teas, organic vitamins and herbs, and packaged foods. A cooler is filled with organic juices, cheeses, and soy milk. A refrigerator holds organic produce, while bins are filled with bulk grains.

A **General Nutrition Center,** in the Lanihau Center, open Mon.–Fri. 10 A.M.–8 P.M., Sat.–Sun. 10 A.M.–6 P.M., is stocked with vitamins, food supplements, and minerals.

Bookstores

In Kailua-Kona be sure to venture into **Middle Earth Bookshoppe,** 808/329-2123, tucked back in behind Kona Marketplace next to St. Michael's Church along Ali'i Drive. Open Mon.–Sat. 9 A.M.–9 P.M., Sunday to 6 P.M., this jam-packed bookstore has shelves laden with fiction, nonfiction, paperbacks, hardbacks, travel books, Hawaiiana, and lots of good maps. A great place to browse, much more intimate than the big chain stores.

The largest bookstore in town, however, is **Borders Books and Music,** 808/331-1668, at the corner of Queen Ka'ahumanu Highway and Henry Street. As at all Borders, you have a huge selection of paperbacks and hardcover books in all genre, a wide selection of maps, postcards, magazines, newspapers, and CDs. Special readings and musical events are held throughout the month, and Cafe Espresso is there for when you get thirsty.

Photo Needs

Zac's Business Center, 808/329-0006, in the North Kona Shopping Center, is open Mon.–Fri. 8 A.M.–7 P.M., Saturday 9 A.M.–6 P.M., and Sunday 10 A.M.–4 P.M. Although Zac's offers excellent photo lab services, this is much more than a photo store. Other services available are copies, fax, wrapping and shipping, printing, computer rental, and Internet connection ($8 an hour or $2.75 for 15 minutes).

Kona Photo Arts, 808/329-2566, in the North Kona Shopping Plaza, is open Mon.–Sat. 8 A.M.–6 P.M. It is a *real* photography store where you can get lenses, cameras, filters, and even

telescopes and binoculars. The processing prices are competitive, and custom developing is available. Kona Photo Arts has been in business for 25 years.

Longs Drugs' photo departments at both the Lanihau Center and Keauhou Shopping Center have excellent prices on film and camera supplies. Both **Kmart** and **Wal-Mart** have one-hour photo finishing departments.

SERVICES AND INFORMATION

Emergencies and Health

The **Kona Community Hospital,** 808/322-9311, is in Kealakekua, about 10 miles south of central Kailua-Kona with 24-hour emergency care. **Straub Clinic and Hospital,** 75-170 Hualalai Rd., at the corner of Kuakini Highway, 808/329-9211, is open 24 hours a day.

For minor emergencies and urgent care, try **Kona-Kohala Medical Associates,** 75-137 Hualalai Rd., across from the Kona Library, 808/329-1346; **Hualalai Urgent Care,** at the Crossroads Medical Center on Henry Street, 808/327-4357; and **Kaiser Permanente,** 75-184 Hualalai Rd. above the Straub Clinic and Hospital, 808/327-2900.

Longs Drugs, KTA Super Stores, and **Kmart** all have pharmacies.

Information

The **Big Island Visitors Bureau** maintains an office in the Kamehameha Plaza, at 75-5719 Ali'i Dr., 808/329-7787, open Mon.–Fri. 8 A.M.–noon, then again 1–4:30 P.M. The staff is friendly, helpful, and extremely knowledgeable about touring the Big Island, and there's a variety of free tourist literature.

Numerous information gazebos are at the various malls in town, usually open until early evening, that can handle your questions about everything from dining to diving.

The **Kailua-Kona Public Library,** 808/327-4327, is at 75-140 Hualalai Rd., up from Hale Halawai Park.

Services

The **First Hawaiian Bank, Bank of Hawaii,** and the **American Savings Bank** all have branches and ATM machines at or next to the Lanihau

Center on Palani Road. Bank of Hawaii also maintains ATM machines at KTA Super Stores and the Safeway supermarket.

The **Kailua-Kona post office** is at 74-5577 Palani Rd., just up from the Lanihau Center.

Mail Boxes and Business Center provides postal, shipping, and wrapping services at the Crossroads Shopping Center. You'll find another business and copy center at the North Kona Shopping Center. **Zac's Business Center** is a full-service business, computer, shipping, printing, and photo developing shop also at the North Kona Shopping Center.

For a self-serve laundromat, try either **Hele Mai Laundromat** at the North Kona Shopping Center or **Tyke's Laundromat,** 74-5483 Kiawe St., in the old Kona Industrial Area.

TRANSPORTATION

If you want to concentrate on the scenery and not the driving, take the **Ali'i Shuttle,** 808/775-7121. Painted red, white, and blue, the bus runs daily every 90 minutes (more or less) along Ali'i Drive 7:50 A.M.–9:10 P.M. and charges $2 each direction ($5 for a day pass, $20 weekly). The terminal points are Lanihau Shopping Center on the north end and Keauhou Shopping Center on the south end, with pickups at major hotels and beaches along the way. You can hail the bus and it will stop if possible.

The **Kona Town Trolley** also runs along Ali'i Drive, making stops at some of the same and some different points. The south terminus is the Keauhou pier and the north terminus is the King Kamehameha Hotel, where you can transfer to the Kona Coast Express Bus to take you up the coast to the Kohala resorts and shops. This bus runs daily 7:40 A.M.–8:20 P.M. at approximately 90-minute intervals; you can ride all day for $5 or $15 per day on the entire line. For information call 808/331-1582.

Taxis will also do the trick for getting around town but can be quite expensive when going long distances. An alternative that works particularly well with groups is **Speedy Shuttle,** 808/329-5433. Speedy Shuttle mainly services Kailua, Keauhou, and Kohala resort areas but will go farther for a price. It has a courtesy phone at the airport for your convenience in getting into town. Rates for single travelers from the airport to downtown Kailua run about $15 or $23 as far south as the Keauhou Beach Hotel. Going north, rates are about $26 to the Waikoloa Beach Resort or $32 to the Mauna Lani Resort area. Rates for groups are higher but the price per person drops dramatically.

HOLUALOA

Holualoa (The Sledding Course) is an undisturbed mountain community perched high above the Kailua-Kona Coast with many of the island's most famous artists creating art in galleries that line up paintbrush to easel along its vintage main street. Prior to its transformation to an art community, Holualoa had another history. In days past, general stores, hotels, restaurants, bars, and pool halls lined its streets. Before Hawaii found its potential for tourism and started to develop its coastal areas, rural Hawaii was primarily agricultural, and the farms, and consequently most of the people, were located on the mountainsides. Large agricultural areas sustained working communities, and Holualoa was one such population center. While agriculture is still a big part of the local economy, it has been bolstered by tourism and the arts.

Get there by taking the spur Route 182, known as **Hualalai Road,** off Route 11 (Queen Ka'ahumanu Highway) from Kailua-Kona, or by taking Route 180 (Mamalahoa Highway) from Honalo in the south or from Palani Junction in the north (where Route 190 and Route 180 meet). Route 180, a high mountain road that parallels Route 11, gives you an expansive view of the coastline below. Climbing Hualalai Road also affords glorious views of the coast. Notice the immediate contrast of the lush foliage against the scant vegetation of the lowland area. On the mountainside, bathed in tropical mists, are tall forest trees interspersed with banana, papaya, and mango trees. Flowering trees pulsating in the green canopy explode in vibrant reds, yellows, oranges, and purples. This is coffee country, so you'll see acres of coffee trees at numerous plantations along much of Route 180, with more along Route 11 farther to the south. If you want to get away from the Kona heat and dryness, head up to the well-watered coolness of Holualoa at 1,400 feet in elevation. When leaving Holualoa for points south, stay on Route 180, the Mamalahoa Highway, a gorgeous road with great views from the heights. Going north, take Route 180 until it meets Route 190, which leads uphill to Waimea. For the coast, Kaiminani Drive cuts down through the residential area of Kalaoa just north of Kailua-Kona, or, farther north, take Waikoloa Road to the South Kohala coastal region.

Galleries and Shops

After you wind your way up Hualalai Road through this verdant jungle area, you suddenly enter the village and are greeted by **Kimura's Lauhala Shop,** 808/324-0053, open weekdays 9 A.M.–5 P.M., Saturday until 4 P.M., closed Sunday. The shop, still tended by Mrs. Kimura and her daughters, Alfreida and Ella, has been in existence since 1915. In the beginning, Kimura's was a general store, but it always sold *lau hala* and became famous for its hats, which local people would make to barter for groceries. Famous on, and later off, the island, only *Konaside* hats have a distinctive pull-string that makes the hat larger or smaller. Mrs. Kimura, and most of her friends who helped manufacture the hats, are getting on in age and can no longer keep up with the demand. Many hatmakers have passed away, and few young people are interested in keeping the art alive. Kimura's still has hats, but the stock is dwindling. All *lau hala* weavings are done on the premises, while some of the other gift items are brought in. Choose from authentic baskets, floor mats, handbags, slippers, and of course an assortment of the classic sun hats that start at $40. Also for an authentic souvenir, look for a round basket with a strap, the original Kona coffee basket.

After Kimura's follow the road for a minute or so to enter the actual village, where the library, post office, and a cross atop a white steeple welcome you to town. The tiny village, complete with its own elementary school, is well kept, with an obvious double helping of pride put into this artists' community by its citizens. In the center of town is **Paul's Place,** a well-stocked country store, open weekdays 7 A.M.–8 P.M., weekends 8 A.M.–8 P.M.

Along the main road is a converted coffee mill, gaily painted and decorated, and currently the home of the nonprofit **Kona Arts Center,** open Tues.–Sat. 10 A.M.–4 P.M., which began as a labor of love by husband and wife artist team Robert and Carol Rogers. Uncle Bob, as he was affectionately known, passed away, but Aunt Carol is still creating art at the center. Both had an extensive background in art teaching. They moved from San Francisco to Holualoa in 1965 and began offering community workshop classes. Workshops and exhibitions continue, and there is always some class or other going on. Much of the work is displayed in the small gallery at the entrance, where you may find everything from hobby crafts to serious renderings, including paintings, basketry, sculptures, and even tie-dyed shirts. The center is very friendly and welcomes guests with a cup of Kona coffee. Stop by to view the art or observe a class in progress. For those who desire to put hand to piece, $25 gets you a month's membership, and you can attend workshops any or all days; a different project is done every day. The building is rickety and old, but it's obviously filled with good vibrations and love.

Across the road from the Kona Arts Center is **Dahlia's Flower Shop,** 808/322-3189, open daily except Sunday 9:30 A.M.–3 P.M., specializing in tropical flower arrangements, mums, and fresh *maile* lei. The prices are excellent, and Dahlia offers shipping to the Mainland and Canada. All of her flowers are "certified" so there is no hassle with agricultural inspection.

Opposite the Holualoa Library is the **Country Frame Shop and Gallery,** 808/324-1590, open Mon.–Sat. 9:30 A.M.–4:30 P.M. It specializes in framing artwork in koa but also displays works by local artists including Carla Sachi-Nifash, a watercolor artist who renders Hawaii in everything from still life to underwater scenes; furniture artist Mike Felig, who turns koa into contemporary and traditional pieces of furniture; Sue Swerdlow, who is a master at capturing color as it bursts from the jungle; and Jennifer Pontz, who etches glass with Hawaiian motifs. Functional pieces, such as cutting boards, are also sold. Much of the work here is modern in style and bold in stroke. The Country Frame Shop is well worth a visit, if only just to browse.

BIG ISLAND

"He's a potter, I'm a painter," is the understatement uttered by Mary Lovein, the female half of the artistic husband and wife team of Mary and Matthew Lovein. They produce and display their lovely and inspired artwork at **Holualoa Gallery,** 808/322-8484, website: www.aloha.net/~mlovein, open Tues.–Sat. 10 A.M.–5 P.M. Mary uses acrylics and airbrush to create large, bold, and bright seascapes and landscapes of Hawaii. Matthew specializes in *raku:* magnificent works of waist-high vases, classic Japanese-style ceramics glazed in deep rose, iridescent greens, crinkled gray, and deep periwinkle blue. Mary and Matthew collaborate on some of the larger pieces. Matt creates the vessel and, while it is still greenware, Mary paints its underglaze. Other artists featured in the shop are Herb Kane, world renowned for his dreamreality paintings of Hawaii and its people; Cecilia Faith Black, who does delicate jewelry; Patricia Van Asperen-Hume, who creates fused glassworks; and Frances Dennis, who handpaints romantic Hawaiian imagery on porcelain. Also displayed are works in ceramic, glass, wood, and carved plexiglass; most of the inspiring works are done in a contemporary or modernist style.

The flora and fauna of Hawaii, both above ground and beneath the waves, come alive in **Ululani,** 808/322-7733, website: www.ululani.com, open Tues.–Sat. 10 A.M.–4 P.M. The bright and airy studio, once the home of "grease monkeys," showcases the fantastic works of accomplished watercolorist Shelley Maudsley-White. Her original and state-of-the art *giclée* prints of hibiscus, exotic birds, plumeria-scented forests, and hilarious yet pointed marine works confirm her philosophy that "there is more happening on this earth than what meets the eye." With three partners, she has expanded to include other artists, including a few of the male persuasion. Aside from the paintings, you'll find T-shirts, prints, posters, and cards created from original works.

A premier shop in town, **Studio 7,** 808/324-1335, open Tues.–Sat. 10 A.M.–4 P.M., is owned and operated by Hiroki and Setsuko Morinoue, who both studied at the Kona Art Center. The shop showcases Setsuko and Hiroki's work, along with that of about other 20 Big Island artists. Hiroki works in many media but primarily does large watercolors or woodblock prints. Setsuko, Hiroki's wife, is a ceramicist and displays her work with about six other potters. Check out the "neoclassical" silk-screen prints, free-form bowls, and wooden bracelets. Strolling from room to room in Studio 7 is like following a magic walkway where the art is displayed simply but elegantly, a legacy of the owners' very Japanese sense of style.

A separate shop in the same building is **Koa T Gallery,** woodworking by Thomas A. Stoudt, 808/322-7755. Tom works small. His pieces are extremely functional, including salt and pepper shakers, stamp dispensers, ladies' vanity mirrors, bowls, koa walking sticks, koa-based lamps, lazy Susans, and little nightstand clocks.

Hale O Kula, in Holualoa's original post office toward the south end of the community, houses both **Hale O Kula Goldsmith Gallery,** 808/324-1688, and **Chesnut and Company Gallery,** 808/324-1446, both open Tues.–Sat. 10 A.M.–4 P.M. Sam, the goldsmith, doesn't need much room, so he has the back. He works mostly in gold, silver, and precious stones; he also creates bronze sculptures and ceramics . . . very, very small sculptures. Sam can also supply stones from his collection, which includes amazing specimens like malachite and polyhedroid, a quartz from Brazil. Chesnut and Company is small but jam-packed with treasures like *tansu,* Japanese furniture known for its joinery; bamboo and *lau hala* lamps by Gerald Ben; free-form prints in splendid colors of cobalt blue and rose by Nora Yamanoha; spirit masks and "garden goddesses" by Volcano artist Ira Ono; basketry from Bali and Holualoa; placemats fashioned from supple twigs and coconut fiber; and distinctive weavings, wall hangings, and original design tables by Peggy Chesnut.

Next to Kona Arts Center is **Cinderella's,** 808/322-2474, an antiques and collectibles shop open Tues.–Fri. 11 A.M.–5 P.M. Here you find furniture, art, knickknacks, jewelry, and much more.

A side road, easily spotted along Holualoa's main street, leads you to **Koyasan Daishiji Shingon,** a Japanese Buddhist mission with distinctive red-orange buildings and a stone-lantern lined entrance. The mission is basic, simple, and unpretentious, combining Japanese Buddhism with a Hawaiian air. The roof has the distinctive shape of a temple, but unlike those found in Japan, which are fashioned from wood, this is corrugated iron. Getting to the temple takes only a few minutes, and coming back down the road rewards you with an inspiring vista of Kona and the sea.

Note: Keep in mind that it is customary for most of the galleries to be *closed on Monday*.

Coffee Plantation

Holualoa and the mountainside south of here is prime coffee growing area. Literally hundreds of small farms produce beans to be turned into America's most favorite drink. The farms in this region produce about one third of the state's total coffee production, and there are several mills along the strip that process the beans. Everyone knows Kona coffee and those who drink this black brew hold it in high esteem for its fine character.

One mile south of Kimura's is the **Holualoa Kona Coffee Company** plantation and mill, 77-6261 Mamalahoa Hwy., Holualoa, HI 96725, 808/322-9937 or 800/334-0348, website: www.konalea.com, email: hkc@aloha.net. This mill is open to visitors weekdays 8 A.M.–4 P.M. for a free tour of the milling and roasting process and coffee tasting. If you haven't ever been introduced to how coffee gets from tree to cup, this would be a good opportunity to discover how it's done. Although a small operation, this mill handles coffee beans from dozens of area farmers. A retail shop on site sells estate coffee; it can also be ordered by mail.

Accommodations

The **Kona Hotel,** along Holualoa's main street, 808/324-1155, primarily rents its 11 units to local people who spend the work-week in Kailua-Kona's seaside resorts and then go home on weekends. They are more than happy, however, to rent to any visitor passing through and are a particular favorite with Europeans. The Inaba family opened the hotel in 1926, and it is still owned and operated by Goro Inaba and his wife Yayoko, who will greet you at the front desk upon arrival. A clean room with bare wooden floors, a bed and dresser, and shared baths down the hall goes for $20 single, $26 double, and $30 with twin beds. Call ahead for reservations. No meals are served, but Mrs. Inaba will make coffee in the morning if you wish. The hotel is simple, clean, and safe, and

the view from the back rooms is more than worth the price.

A wooden jewel box nestled in velvet greenery waits to be opened as it rests on the edge of Holualoa high above the wide, rippling, cerulean Pacific. **The Holualoa Inn Bed and Breakfast,** 76-5932 Mamalahoa Hwy., P.O. Box 222, Holualoa, HI 96725, 808/324-1121 or 800/392-1812, fax 808/322-2472, website: www.konaweb.com/HINN, email: inn@aloha.net, was the retirement home of Thurston Twigg-Smith, CEO of the *Honolulu Advertiser* and member of an old *kama'aina* family. Mr. Twigg-Smith built the original home in 1978, but tragically, it burned to the ground. Undaunted, he rebuilt, exactly duplicating the original. After living here a few years Mr. Twigg-Smith decided it was too quiet and peaceful and went back to live in Honolulu. In 1987 it was converted into a B&B. The home is a marvel of taste and charm—light, airy, and open. Follow the serpentine drive from Holualoa's main road into the midst of vibrant foliage daubed with red hibiscus, manicured thickets of ripening coffee, sun-yellow papaya, and wind-swirled palms. The home at the end of the drive pleasantly shocks the senses. Top to bottom, it is the natural burnished red of cedar and eucalyptus. Here the Hawaiian tradition of removing your shoes upon entering a home is made a pleasure. The floors, softly polished, cool, and smooth, massage your feet; the roof rides above the walls so the air circulates easily. The front lanai is pure relaxation, and stained glass puncturing the walls here and there creates swirls of rainbow light. Throughout the home are original artworks done by the Twigg-Smith family. A pool table holds king's court in the commodious games room, as doors open to a casual yet elegant sitting room where breakfast is served. A back staircase leads to a gazebo, floored with tile and brazenly open to the elements, while the back lanai is encircled by a roof made of copper. From here, Kailua-Kona glows with the imaginative mistiness of an impressionist painting, and, closer by, 40 acres are dotted with cattle raised by the family. Just below is the inn's pool, tiled in blue with a torch ginger motif. The six rooms run $150–195 and all differ in size and decor. A few years back, Mr. Twigg-Smith was offered $7 million for the home. Much to our benefit, he declined. This is a gem.

KONA COFFEE

A coffee belt runs like a band through Kona. Generally speaking, it's a swath of mountainside 800–1,400 feet in elevation, about two miles inland from the coast, from one to two miles wide, and perhaps 25 miles long. In this warm upland region, watered by cool morning mists and rains, warmed by the afternoon sun, and cooled by evening breezes, coffee trees have an ideal climate in which to grow. Within this band, about 2,500 acres are planted in coffee, producing about 2.5 million pounds of the beans annually, which amounts to about one-third of the state's production. Most coffee estates here are small, and there are about 600 individual growers. Kona has been known for decades as a region that produces exceptional coffee. Until a few short years ago, it was the only area in the state (and country) that grew coffee. Now, farms on each of the main Hawaiian Islands also produce the bean, and Kaua'i has become the biggest producer in terms of acreage and pounds harvested.

Arabica coffee trees are grown in Kona. Trees produce beans at a young age and will keep producing until at least 80 years old if properly tended. Newly formed, coffee "cherries," each containing two beans, are green. When they ripen they turn red. Kona coffee beans are picked by hand, a tough and tedious job, but one that produces quality fruits. Harvest takes place for about five months during winter. After picking, the beans are brought to the mill to be processed. The first step is wet milling, where the outer covering is removed and the slimy inner liquid released. The beans are then rinsed and dried to a specific moisture content, and the silver skin-like covering is taken off. Beans are then separated according to their shape and size by a shaker, graded by quality and substance, bagged, and weighed before they are certified for bulk shipping. Roasting is another matter. Most roasting is done either the traditional way in a drum roaster or by a newer hot air method. Various roasts include dark, medium, and Vienna, and the result is determined by the temperature and length of roasting time. After waiting a few hours for carbon dioxide to off-gas, roasted coffee is packaged.

About a dozen Kona coffee plantations are open for year-round visitation of their property and mills. A few are listed in the text; others have signs along the road you will see as you drive through this region.

At the south end of the village, up a steep lane is **Rosy's Rest** bed-and-breakfast, 808/322-7378, website: www.bnbweb.rosy.html. Surrounded by tropical flowers and fruit trees, Rosy's has a view of the coast and offers beautiful sunsets free of charge. The two units in a detached building run $80 a night. One is a studio with queen bed, kitchenette, and lanai, the other a one-bedroom with living room and kitchen. Clean and modern, there's a touch of old-world charm in the natural free-form wood furniture and railings made from branches.

Above Kailua on the road to Holualoa, surrounded by lush tropical foliage that permeates the air with a sweet perfume, perches **Hale Maluhia Country Inn Bed and Breakfast,** 76-770 Hualalai Rd., Kailua-Kona, HI 96740, 808/329-5773 or 800/559-6627, fax 808/326-5487, website: www.hawaii-bnb.com/halemal.html, email: hawaii-inns@aloha.net, a hideaway lovingly tended by hosts Ken and Ann Smith. Built and furnished in rustic Hawaiian style with a Victorian twist, the B&B offers accommodations in the main house or the separate Banyan Cottage. The interiors of the central house and cottage feature open-beamed ceilings, plenty of natural wood trim, koa cabinets, and full kitchens. On the property are an outdoor stone-and-tile Japanese *ofuro* (spa) with massage jets, and a massage table where your cares and aches will float away on the evening breeze. Two relaxing common areas are outfitted with board games, a pool table, a large library, and surround sound color TV/VCR (with a large video library), while five lanai present the natural drama of a Michelangelo sunset nightly; all are wheelchair friendly. Ken spoils you every morning with a sumptuous home-cooked breakfast buffet laden with tropical fruits and juices, fresh bread and pastries, savory breakfast meats, herbal teas, and robust Kona coffee. All rooms are decorated with Hawaiian and provincial antique furniture and feature private baths. Rates are $90–125 for a guest room in the main house, and $150 for the Banyan Cottage; discounts are offered for longer stays. Hale Maluhia (House of Peace) Is all that its name implies.

Food

The enticing aroma of rich coffee has been wafting on the breeze in this mountain community ever since the **Holualoa Cafe,** owned and operated by Meggi Worbach, opened its doors in 1992. Just up the hill from the Kona Hotel, the café, 808/322-2233, open Mon.–Sat. 6:30 A.M.–3 P.M., serves wonderful apple coffee cake, bagels, muffins, and coffee and espresso from mocha frapp's to double cappuccinos. Other offerings include smoothies, juices, and herbal teas. The café also serves as a revolving art gallery for local artists and displays a few boutique and souvenir items. You can sit inside at a table, perch at the counter, or enjoy your coffee and pastry alfresco on the veranda, from where the two-block metropolis of Holualoa sprawls at your feet.

SOUTH KONA

Kailua-Kona's Ali'i Drive eventually dead-ends in Keauhou. Before it does, King Kamehameha III Road turns up the mountainside and joins Route 11, which in its central section is called the Kuakini Highway. This road, heading south, quickly passes the towns of **Honalo, Kainaliu, Kealakekua, and Captain Cook,** and farther on whisks through the smaller communities of **Hanuanou, Keokea,** and **Kealia.** These mountainside communities lie along a 10-mile strip of Route 11, and if it weren't for the road signs, it would be difficult for the itinerant traveler to know where one village ends and the next begins. You'll have ample opportunity to stop along the way for gas, food, or sightseeing. These towns have some terrific restaurants, fine bed-and-breakfast accommodations, specialty shops, and unique boutiques. If you are up for some off-the-beaten-track sightseeing, you won't be disappointed. At Captain Cook, you can dip down to the coast and visit Kealakekua Bay, or continue south to **Pu'uhonua O Honaunau,** a reconstructed temple of refuge, the best in the state. Farther south still, little-traveled side roads take you to the sleepy seaside villages of **Ho'okena** and **Miloli'i,** where traditional lifestyles are still the norm.

HONALO AND KAINALIU

This dot on the map is at the junction of Routes 11 and 180. Not much changes here, and the town is primarily known for **Dai Fukuji Buddhist Temple** along the road. It's open daily 9 A.M.–4:30 P.M., free. Inside are two ornate altars; feel free to take photos but please remember to remove your shoes. A short distance down a side road is **St. Paul's Catholic Church.**

Kainaliu is larger and more of a town, with a choice of shopping, restaurants, and a theater. It's just a mile or two up the road from Honalo; it's as if these two communities mesh into one.

Accommodation

Teshima's Inn, 808/322-9140, is a small, clean, family-run affair in Honalo. Operated by Mr. and Mrs. Harry Teshima and family, it's somewhat like a Japanese *minshuku* with all rooms fronting a Japanese garden. To be sure of getting a room, call three days to a week in advance. If you just turn up, you have a slim chance of getting one of the five available rooms. Check in at the restaurant. The rooms, at $25 single, $35 double, and around $300 monthly, are spartan but very clean with a bed, bath, and shower.

Food

Teshima's Restaurant in Honalo, open daily 6:30 A.M.–1:45 P.M. and 5–9:30 P.M., is just like the homey inn that adjoins it. Here, in unpretentious surroundings, you can enjoy a full American, Hawaiian, or Japanese lunch for about $7 and dinner for $10–15. A specialty is the *bento* box lunch for $6 that includes rice balls, luncheon meat, fried fish, teriyaki beef, *kamaboku* (fish cake), and Japanese roll. Since 1940, Teshima's has been a mom-and-pop (and kids) family restaurant. If you're interested in a good square meal, you can't go wrong here.

Aloha Theater Cafe, 808/322-3383, open daily 8 A.M.–3 P.M. for breakfast and lunch, and dinner Thurs.–Sat. until 9 P.M., is part of the lobby of the Aloha Theater in Kainaliu. The enormous breakfasts ($5–8) feature locally grown eggs, homemade muffins, and potatoes. Lunchtime sandwiches, around $7.50, are super-stuffed with varied morsels, from tofu and avocado to turkey breast. There are also a variety of soups and salads and Mexican dishes like a quesadilla for $7.95. Full dinners, including taro-crusted fresh *ahi,* herbed chicken, and grilled steak, run $13–20. For a snack choose from an assortment of homemade baked goods that you can enjoy with an espresso or cappuccino. Order at the counter (table service for dinner), and then sit on the lanai that overlooks a bucolic scene with the coast below. This is an excellent place for food any time of the day.

Entertainment

The **Aloha Theater** in Kainaliu has a semi-professional local repertory company, the Aloha Community Theater, that puts on about six plays per year that run for about three weeks each. Check the local newspaper, HVB office, or look for posters here and there around town. The theater periodically hosts other types of stage performances, live music, dance, and art films and is a venue for the Hawaii International Film Festival in November. Show times and ticket prices differ for all performances in this completely refurbished and well-appointed theater (built 1929–32), so call the box office for details at 808/322-2323 or check out www.alohacafe.com.

Shopping

There is not much in the way of shopping in Honalu except for a kayak rental shop. You'll have much better luck in Kainaliu.

Next door to the Aloha Theater, the **Aloha Store,** 808/322-1717, open daily Mon.–Thurs. 9 A.M.–7 P.M., Fri.–Sat. until 8 P.M., and Sunday until 3 P.M., sells gifts and sundries. The store has a wonderful selection ranging from stuffed teddy bears to teapots, along with local clothing and jewelry. You can also find items like koa barrettes and bracelets, children's games and books, music tapes, necklaces, earrings, and sterling silver jewelry. There's a rack of aloha shirts, as well as candle holders, pottery, a smattering of honey and fruit gift items, and lotions and potions locally made. The bulletin board is great for finding out what's happening in the area, especially in the alternative scene.

The Blue Ginger Gallery, 808/322-3898, open Mon.–Sat. 9 A.M.–5 P.M., showcases the art of owners Jill and David Bever, as well as over 100 artists' works from all over the island. David creates art pieces in stained glass, fused glass, and wood. Jill paints on silk, creating fantasy works in strong primary colors. Using her creations as base art, she then designs one-of-a-kind clothing items that can be worn as living art pieces. The small but well-appointed shop brims with paintings, ceramics, sculptures, woodwork, fiber art, and jewelry. A section holds Asian artworks, including Polynesian masks, carved elephants, Buddha heads, and batiks from Indonesia. The Blue Ginger Gallery is a perfect place to find a memorable souvenir of Hawaii.

The Rainbow Path, in the Basque Bldg. downtown at number 79-7407, 808/322-0651,

The Aloha Theater in Kainaliu still caters to crowds as it has done for decades.

ROBERT NILSEN

is open Mon.–Sat. 9 A.M.–6 P.M. This intriguing shop specializes in books on Hawaii, metaphysics, self-help, personal discovery, and books for children. You can also find tapes and CDs that include Hawaiian chants, Native American Indian music, Celtic music, and music especially composed to induce relaxation and relieve stress. Your body is taken care of with ayurvedic medicine, incense, beeswax candles, bath and body products, and natural perfumes of island scents. The soul will stir with crystal pendants, pyramids, beaded necklaces, and dream catchers. Monday, Wednesday, and Saturday, metaphysical readings are given by appointment. Check the bulletin board for information about new-age practitioners. All who are on the path will find this bookstore an oasis.

Bad Ass Coffee Company, 808/322-9196, open daily 7 A.M.–9 P.M., is a coffee and espresso bar where they roast their own beans on the premises in a Royal No. 4 Roaster manufactured in 1910, probably the last operational roaster of its type left in the state. Pure Kona coffee of the best grade sells for $29.95 per pound. After watching the roasting, take your cup of coffee and a homemade pastry to the rear of the shop, where you'll find an indoor stone grotto area away from the noise of the street. This is the original Bad Ass coffee shop. From here, the revolution has spread.

Don't let the tourist junk piled outside **Hawaiian Crafts & Gifts,** 808/322-0642, stop you from going in. Owned by Jeffrey Matias and open Mon.–Sat. 9 A.M.–5 P.M., the shop has a very surprising interior, filled as it is with authentic jewelry, shells, and Jeff's own beadwork. Many of the items are purchased from local people and include hula instruments, *lau hala* weavings, Ni'ihau shellwork, Hawaiian fishhook pendants, *kukui* nut lei, and even an assortment of Hawaiian food products like mustard and salad dressings. Hanging on the walls are carvings of tikis, dolphins, turtles, and owls, the *'aumakua* of ancient Hawaii. For the children, there are Hawaiian dolls, and children of all ages will love a replica of a sea-going canoe with the distinctive crab claw sail. Jeff also imports unique jewelry from the Balkans! For those who can't live without another T-shirt, you'll find them, as well as artificial flower lei. Look for Hawaiian Crafts across from the Bad Ass Coffee Company.

At the south end of town, in the new Mango Court, is **Evie's Natural Foods,** 808/322-0739, open weekdays 8 A.M.–7 P.M., weekends 9 A.M.–5 P.M. This full-range health food store serves freshly made, organic and wholesome sandwiches, soups, and other delicious foods at its deli. It also has "grab 'n go" items in a cooler. Evie's stocks plenty of coffee, herbs, vitamins and minerals, some fresh produce, packaged natural foods, and an assortment of bulk grains.

This is one time that you'll enjoy an outbreak of **Pandamonium,** in downtown Kainaliu, open Mon.–Sat. 10 A.M.–6 P.M., 808/324-7799, a shop filled with locally handcrafted artwear and crafts. Racks also hold high quality hand-painted Indonesian clothing, a designer line of T-shirts by Dr. Bill, and, if you just happen to be feeling a bit peaked after a long day of shopping, Chinese herbs, vitamins, and minerals in a side concession room. Not only can you come here and dress your body, you can address what ails you as well.

As you are leaving the built-up area of Kainaliu, look for the **Island Books,** "Used Books Bought and Sold" sign. Open Mon.–Sat. 10 A.M.–6 P.M., this shop stocks a general mix of titles, but history, geography, Hawaiiana, and a good selection of used travel books are the specialty. Here's a great place to purchase some casual reading material and save money at the same time; 808/322-2006.

Oshima's General Store is well stocked with cameras and film, drugs, fishing supplies, magazines, and some wines and spirits. Also in town is **Kimura's Market,** a general grocery store with some sundries, and **H. Kimura Store** for bolts of fabric.

KEALAKEKUA

Kealakekua is one of the old established towns along the road, but it has a newer look with more modern buildings and small subdivisions. In town are a post office and library, a small shopping center, gas station, several eateries, a few gift shops, and an antiques store. Just south of town on the road up to the schools is **Christ Church Episcopal,** established in 1867 as the first Episcopal church in the islands.

BIG ISLAND

Kona Historical Society Museum

The main building of the Kona Historical Society Museum was originally a general store built around 1875 by local landowner and businessman H. N. Greenwell using native stone and lime mortar made from burnt coral. Now on both the Hawaii and National Registers of Historic Places, the building served many uses, including the warehousing and packaging of sweet oranges raised by Greenwell, purported to be the largest, sweetest, and juiciest in the world. The museum, 808/323-3222, open weekdays 9 A.M.–3 P.M. with a $2 donation for admission, is one-quarter mile south of Kealakekua. The main artifact is the building itself, but inside, you will find a few antiques like a surrey and glassware, and the usual photographic exhibits with themes like coffee growing—part of the legacy of Kona. The basement of the building houses archives filled with birth and death records of local people, photographs both personal and official, home movies, books, and maps, most of which were donated by the families of Kona. The archives are open to the public by appointment only.

The Kona Historical Society, P.O. Box 398, Captain Cook, HI 96704, is a nonprofit organization whose main purpose is the preservation of Kona's history and the dissemination of historical information. Sometimes the society sponsors lectures and films, which are listed in the local newspapers. They also offer 4WD tours of the Kona area ($55) three times per year, usually in March, July, and November, and a historical boat tour in late January ($20) that takes you from Kailua-Kona south along the coast. There is no fixed schedule, but if you are in the area during those times of year, it would be well worth the trouble to contact the museum to find out if these excellent tours are being offered. A Captain Cook lecture tour at Kealakekua Bay and an archaeological tour of Keauhou can also be arranged by appointment only, with a minimum of three people. However, walking tours of the historical district of Kailua ($10) are regularly scheduled Tues.–Fri. at 9:30 A.M. and again Friday at 1:30 P.M. The tours usually last about 90 minutes at a leisurely pace. Another excellent tour that gets to the heart of the area is the walking tour conducted at the historic **D. Uchida Coffee Farm,** listed on the National Register of Historic Places, begun by Japanese immigrants. This

Living History Farm tour ($15), offered Tuesday and Thursday at 9 A.M., takes you to a working farm with original authentic buildings, operating machinery, live animals, and costumed guides. It is a representation of what daily life was like when the farm operated 1925–1945 and how the farm and its workers fit into this multi-ethnic community. For any of these fine historical society tours, make reservations by calling 808/323-2005 or go to http://lehua.ilhawaii.net/~khs.

Amy B.H. Greenwell Ethnobotanical Garden

You can not only smell the flowers but feel the history of the region at the Amy B.H. Greenwell Ethnobotanical Garden, along Route 11 south of Kealakekua and marked by an HVB Warrior, 808/323-3318, website: www.bishop.hawaii.org/bishop/greenwell. The garden is open Mon.–Fri. 8:30 A.M.–5 P.M., with guided tours on the second Saturday of every month at 10 A.M.; suggested donation, $4. Greenwell died in 1974 and left her lands to the Bishop Museum, which then opened a 12-acre interpretive ethnobotanical garden, planting it with indigenous Hawaiian plants, Polynesian introduced plants, and Hawaiian medicinal plants. At the beginning of the walking path through the lower section of the garden, take a fact sheet that describes the garden, complete with self-guided tour map. Represented here are coastal zone plants, agricultural plants, lowland dry forest and upland wet forest plants. The garden has remnants of the Kona field system, dating from precontact times when a fantastic network of stone ridges linked 50 square miles of intensive agriculture.

Food

The **Korner Pocket Bar and Grill,** 808/322-2994, serving lunch and dinner weekdays 11 A.M.–10 P.M., until midnight Friday and Saturday, is a family-oriented/friendly biker bar where you can get excellent food at very reasonable prices. The Korner Pocket sits below the highway in the small shopping center on Haleki'i Street. Grill selections are a poolroom burger, fresh catch, or scrumptious bistro burger of grilled beef on crusty sourdough topped with fresh mushrooms saut'ed in wine garlic sauce. Dinners are tempting: garlic scampi; chicken aliko accented with zesty Japanese sauce of lemon, apple, laurel, and spices; and prime rib eight ball, its encore entrée. The complete bar is well stocked with wines and spirits, or you can wash down your sandwich with an assortment of draft beers. The Pocket rocks with live music Friday night, while Saturday usually brings jazz for quieter dining and dancing. The Korner Pocket looks as ordinary as a Ford station wagon, both inside and out, but the food is surprisingly good, and the owners, Paul and Judy, are very friendly.

Near the rise in Kealakekua, look for the **Canaan Deli,** 808/323-2577, open Mon.–Fri. 7 A.M.–4 P.M. and Sat.–Sun. 7 A.M.–1 P.M., a luncheonette with an Italian flair. You can't miss it, it's painted pink! The owners hail from Philadelphia and bring the "back East" deli tradition of a lot of food for little money along with them. You can't go wrong with a Philly cheesesteak sub for $5.50; or try a pizza smothered in cheese and delectables, ranging from a 15-inch cheese at $13 to an 18-inch Master with 10 toppings for $28. All sauces, breads, and the pizza dough are homemade. Breakfast specials include a three-egg omelet for $5.50, deli sandwiches $5–5.50, big fatso hoagies $6, burgers $5–6, and a loco moco for those a quart low on cholesterol

On your way out of town going south, stop by **Chris's Bakery** and pick up a snack for the road. A variety of pastries are available here, but Chris's is best known for *malasadas,* made fresh daily.

Shopping

The Grass Shack, a.k.a. The Little Grass Shack, 808/323-2877, open Mon.–Sat. 9 A.M.–5 P.M., sometimes Sunday noon–5 P.M., is an institution in Kealakekua, owned and operated by *kama'aina* Lish Jens. It looks like a tourist trap, but don't let that stop you from going in and finding some authentic souvenirs, most of which come from the area or from Ms. Jens's many years of traveling and collecting. The items *not* from Hawaii are clearly marked with a big orange sign that says, Sorry These Items Were Not Made In Hawaii. But the price is right. There are plenty of trinkets and souvenir items, as well as a fine assortment of artistic pieces, especially wooden bowls, hula items, exquisite Ni'ihau shellwork, and Hawaiian masks. A shop specialty is items made from curly koa. Each piece is signed with the craftsperson's name and the type of wood used. One of the artisans displayed here is master woodworker Jack Straka. Items are also made from Norfolk pine and *milo.* A showcase holds jewelry and tapa cloth imported from Fiji, and a rack holds tapes of classic Hawaiian musicians from the '40s and '50s. The shop is famous for its distinctive *lau hala* hats, the best hat for the tropics.

You can find Hawaiian crafts, T-shirts, locally made food items, and a whole assortment of other items at the **Kealakekua Flea Market,** held Tuesday, Thursday, and Saturday approximately 8 A.M.–3 P.M. along Haleki'i Street.

Tropical Temptations, 808/323-3131, open Mon.–Sat. 10 A.M.–5 P.M., is housed in a gaily painted yellow and green building. Climb the steps to the porch, where you'll find a service buzzer that will summon owner and chief tempter Lance Dassance, who will smile a welcome into his candy kitchen. Remember, however, that most of the business is wholesale and not really set up for drop-in visitors. Lance turns the best available grade of local fruits, nuts, and coffee beans into delicious candies. The fresh-fruit process uses no preservatives, additives, waxes, or extenders and no sugars except in the chocolate, which is also the best grade possible. A slow-drying process is used, so as few nutrients as possible are lost. A shop specialty is candy made from rare white pineapple, which grows for only eight weeks per year. Lance, if not too busy, will be happy to take you on a tour of the facility. He takes a personal pride in making the best candy possible and stresses that he uses only fruit ripened in the last 24 hours. Tropical Temptations must be the healthiest candy store in Hawaii.

The **Kamigaki Market** is also in Kealakekua.

Horseback Rides

Kings' Trail Rides O'Kona, 808/323-2388, is along the highway at mile marker 111. Rides from here go down a jeep and hiking trail to Kealakekua Bay and the Captain Cook monument. With morning departures, the four-hour trip includes two hours of riding followed by snorkeling in the bay and a picnic lunch. The price is $95 per person, limited to six riders. The ride office doubles as a retail shop and is open daily

7:30 A.M.–5 P.M. There you can purchase koa boxes and chocolate-covered coffee beans, along with cowboy items like spurs, western belts, and a full assortment of tack.

CAPTAIN COOK AND VICINITY

Captain Cook is the last of the big towns along this highway. You can get gas, food, and lodging here, and it is the gateway to the sights on the coast. Beyond this, the smaller towns are each but a few houses that create wide spots in the road. If you're in the area in March, have a look at the yearly Kona Stampede Rodeo at the Honaunau Rodeo Grounds, at the big bend in the road going down to Pu'uhonua O Honaunau, and watch the local cowboys rope steers.

Royal Kona Coffee Mill and Museum
South of Captain Cook, you can't help noticing the trim coffee bushes planted along the hillside. On the highway almost to Hanuanau, you find the Royal Kona Coffee Mill and Museum, 808/328-2511, website: www.royalkonacoffee.com, open daily for self-guided tours 8 A.M.–5 P.M. The tantalizing smell of roasting coffee and the lure of a "free cup" are more than enough stimulus to make you stop. Mark Twain did! The museum is small, of the no-touch variety with most exhibits behind glass. Mostly they're old black-and-white prints of the way Kona coffee

country used to be. Some heavy machinery is displayed out on the back porch. The most interesting item is a homemade husker built from an old automobile. While walking around, be careful not to step on a couple of lazy old cats so lethargic they might as well be stuffed. Perhaps a cup of the local java in their milk bowl would put spring in their feline steps! Inside, more or less integrated into the museum, is a small gift shop. You can pick up the usual souvenirs, but the real treats are gourmet honeys, jellies, jams, candies, and of course coffee. You can't beat the freshness of getting it right from the source. Refill anyone? Be sure to have a look at the mill while you are here. You can witness the entire process from harvest to roast.

Two other coffee farms in the area that also offer tours of their mills are: **Bayview Farm,** a half mile north of St. Benedict's Church along Painted Church Road, 808/328-9658, website: www.bayviewfarmcoffees.com; and **Ueshima Coffee Company,** on the way down to Napo'opo'o, 808/328-9851, website: www.ucc-hawaii.com.

Painted Church
Whether going to or coming from Pu'uhonua O Honaunau, make sure to take a short side trip off Route 160 to **St. Benedict's Painted Church.** This small house of worship is fronted by latticework, and with its gothic-style belfry looks like a little castle. Inside, a Belgian priest, John

Royal Kona Coffee Mill and Museum

Berchman Velghe, took house paint and, with a fair measure of talent and religious fervor, painted biblical scenes on the walls. His masterpiece is a painted illusion behind the altar that gives you the impression of being in the famous Spanish cathedral in Burgos. Father John was pastor here 1899–1904, during which time he did these paintings, similar to others that he did in small churches throughout Polynesia. Before leaving, visit the cemetery to see its petroglyphs and homemade pipe crosses.

Napo'opo'o

In the town of Captain Cook, Napo'opo'o Road branches off Route 11 and begins a roller-coaster ride down to the sea, where it ends at Kealakekua Bay. Many counterculture types once took up residence in semi-abandoned "coffee shacks" throughout this hard-pressed economic area, but the cheap, idyllic, and convenience-free life isn't as easy to arrange as it once was. The area is being "rediscovered" and getting more popular. On the way, you pass **Kahikolu Congregational Church** (1852), the burial site of Henry Opukaha'ia, a young native boy taken to New England, where he was educated and converted to Christianity. Through impassioned speeches begging for salvation for his pagan countrymen, he convinced the first Congregationalist missionaries to come to the islands in 1820.

Continue down Napo'opo'o Road to the once-thriving fishing village of Napo'opo'o (The Holes), now just a circle on the map with a few houses fronted by neat gardens. During much of the last century, Napo'opo'o was a thriving community and had an active port where commodities and animals were shipped. Now only remnants of the old pier remain. When Napo'opo'o Road nears the water, turn right for Kealakekua (Pathway of the God) Bay. At the end the end of the road is the rather ill-kept **Napo'opo'o Beach County Park,** with showers, picnic tables, and restrooms. The beach here is full of cobbles with a little sand strip along the water, but it draws locals and visitors alike who come to sunbathe. Nearby is Hikiau Heiau. Taking a side road around the south side of the bay will bring you to the more secluded white-sand **Manini Beach.**

Just south of Napo'opo'o, down a narrow and very rugged road is the sleepy seaside village of **Ke'ei.** This side trip ends at a canoe launch area and a cozy white-sand beach good in spots for swimming. The wide reef here is a fine snorkeling spot and a favorite of surfers. A channel to an underwater grotto has been sliced through the coral. On the shore are the remains of Kamaiko Heiau, where humans were once sacrificed. In 1782, on the flats beyond this village, the **Battle of Moku'ohai** was fought, the first battle in King Kamehameha I's struggle to consolidate power not only over the island of Hawai'i but eventually all the islands.

Kealakekua Bay

Kealakekua Bay has been known as a safe anchorage since long before the arrival of Captain Cook and still draws boats of all descriptions. The entire bay is a 315-acre **Marine Life Conservation District,** and it lives up to its title by being an excellent scuba and snorkeling site. Organized tours from Kailua-Kona often flood the area with boats and divers in the area just off the Captain Cook monument, but the bay is vast and you can generally find your own secluded spot to enjoy the underwater show. The area between Napo'opo'o and Manini Beach, an area at the southern tip of the bay, is also excellent for coral formations, lava ledges, and fish. If you've just come for a quick dip or to enjoy the sunset, look for beautiful, yellow-tailed tropicbirds that frequent the bay.

Relax a minute and tune in all your sensors because you're in for a treat. The bay is not only a Marine Life Conservation District with top-notch snorkeling, but it drips with history. *Mauka,* at the county park parking lot, is the well-preserved **Hikiau Heiau,** dedicated to the god Lono, who had long been prophesied to return from the heavens to this very bay to usher in a "new order." Perhaps the soothsaying *kahuna* were a bit vague on the points of the new order, but it is undeniable that at this spot of initial contact between Europeans and Hawaiians, great changes occurred that radically altered the course of Hawaiian history.

The *heiau* is carved into the steep *pali* that form a well-engineered wall. From these heights the temple priests had a panoramic view of the ocean to mark the approach of Lono's "floating island," heralded by tall white tapa banners. The *heiau* platform was meticulously backfilled with smooth, small stones; a series of stone footings, once the bases of grass and thatch houses used in the religious rites, is still very much intact. The *pali* above the bay is pocked with numerous burial caves that still hold the bones of the ancients.

Captain James Cook, leading his ships *Resolution* and *Discovery* under billowing white sails, entered the bay on the morning of January 17, 1778, during the height of the Makahiki Festival, and the awestruck natives were sure that Lono had returned. Immediately, traditional ways were challenged. An old crew member, William Watman, had just died, and Cook went ashore to perform a Christian burial atop the *heiau*. This was, of course, the first Christian ceremony in the islands, and a plaque at the *heiau* entrance commemorates the event. On February 4, 1778, a few weeks after open-armed welcome, the goodwill camaraderie that had developed between the English voyagers and their island hosts turned sour, due to terrible cultural misunderstandings. The sad result was the death of Captain Cook. During a final conflict, this magnificent man, who had resolutely sailed and explored the greatest sea on earth, stood helplessly in knee-deep water, unable to swim to rescue boats sent from his waiting ships. Hawaiians, provoked to a furious frenzy because of an unintentional insult, beat, stabbed, and clubbed the great captain and four of his marines to death. A 27-foot obelisk of white marble erected to Cook's memory in 1874 "by some of his fellow countrymen" is at the far northern end of the bay.

The land around the monument is actually under British rule, somewhat like the grounds of a foreign consulate. Once a year, an Australian ship comes to tend it, and sometimes local people are hired to clear the weeds. The monument fence is fashioned from old cannons topped with cannon balls. Here too is a bronze plaque, often awash by the waves, that marks the exact spot where Cook fell. You can see the marble obelisk from the *heiau,* but actually getting to it is tough. Expert snorkelers have braved the mile swim to the point, but be advised it's through open water, and Kealakekua Bay is known for sharks that come in during the evening to feed. A rugged jeep/foot trail leads down the *pali* to the monument, but it's poorly marked and starts way back near the town of Captain Cook,

almost immediately after Napo'opo'o Road branches off from Route 11. Behind the monument are the ruins of the Ka'awaloa village site, some of which can be seen in the trees.

Pu'uhonua O Honaunau National Historical Park

This historical park, the main attraction in the area, shouldn't be missed. Though it was once known as City of Refuge Park, the official name of Pu'uhonua O Honaunau is coming into more use in keeping with the emergence of Hawaiian heritage. One way to get there is to bounce along the narrow four miles of coastal road from Kealakekua Bay. The other more direct and much better road is Route 160, where it branches off Route 11 at Keokea around mile marker 104, a short distance south of Honaunau.

The setting of Pu'uhonua O Honaunau couldn't be more idyllic. It's a picture-perfect cove with

Re-created thatched structures at Pu'uhonua O Honaunau create a feeling of what this post was like centuries ago.

ROBERT NILSEN

BIG ISLAND

KONANE

*K*onane is a traditional board game played by Hawaiians that is similar to checkers. Old boards have been found at various locations around the islands, often close to the water. The "board" is a flat rock with small depressions ground into it. These depressions usually number around 100, but may be as many as 200. The depressions are filled with alternating white and black stones or shells. The game has many variations. In one, each of the two players removes one stone, creating two blank spots. One of the two players starts by jumping an opponent's stone, capturing it and taking it off the board. Play then moves to the other person, who in turn jumps the opposite color stone, removing it. The game continues like this, each person alternately jumping the opponent's stones, until one player is no longer able to make a jump, which ends the game.

many paths leading out onto the sea-washed lava flow. The tall royal palms surrounding this compound shimmer like neon against the black lava so prevalent in this part of Kona. Planted for this purpose, these beacons promised safety and salvation to the vanquished, weak, and war-tossed, as well as to the *kapu*-breakers of old Hawaii. If you made it to this "temple of refuge," scurrying frantically ahead of avenging warriors or leaping into the sea to swim the last desperate miles, the attendant *kahuna,* under pain of their own death, had to offer you sanctuary. *Kapu*-breakers were particularly pursued because their misdeeds could anger the always-moody gods, who might send a lava flow or tsunami to punish all. Only the *kahuna* could perform the rituals that would bathe you in the sacred mana and thus absolve you from all wrongdoing. This *pu'uhonua* (temple of refuge) was the largest in all Hawaii, and be it fact or fancy, you can feel its power to this day.

The temple complex sits on a 20-acre finger of lava bordered by the sea on all sides. A massive, 1,000 foot-long mortarless wall, measuring 10 feet high and 17 feet thick, borders the site on the landward side and marks it as a temple of refuge. Archaeological evidence dates use of the temple from the mid-16th century, and some scholars

argue that it was a well-known sacred spot as much as 200 years earlier. Actually, three separate *heiau* are within the enclosure. In the mid-16th century, Keawe, a great chief of Kona and the great-grandfather of Kamehameha, ruled here. After his death, he was entombed in *Hale O Keawe Heiau* at the end of the great wall, and his mana re-infused the temple with cleansing powers. For 250 years the *ali'i* of Kona continued to be buried here, making the spot more and more powerful. Even the great Queen Ka'ahumanu came here seeking sanctuary. As a 17-year-old bride, she refused to submit to the will of her husband, Kamehameha, and defied him openly, often wantonly giving herself to lesser chiefs. To escape Kamehameha's rampage, she made for the temple. Ka'ahumanu chose a large rock to hide under, and she couldn't be found until her pet dog barked and gave her away. Ka'ahumanu was coaxed out only after a lengthy intercession by Captain George Vancouver, who had become a friend of the king. The last royal personage buried here was a son of Kamehameha who died in 1818. Soon afterwards, the "old religion" of Hawaii died and the temple grounds were abandoned but not entirely destroyed. The foundations of this largest city of refuge in the Hawaiian Islands were left intact.

On the landward side of the refuge wall was the "palace grounds" where the *ali'i* of Kona lived. Set here and there around the sandy compound are numerous buildings that have been re-created to let you sense what it must have been like when *ali'i* walked here under the palms. The canoe shed, set directly back from the royal canoe landing site on the beach, was exceedingly important to the seagoing Hawaiians, and the temple helped sustain the mores and principles of the highly stratified and regimented society. Several fishponds lie in this compound that raised food for the chiefs, and a *konane* stone set next to the water *konane* is a game similar to chess—is a modern version of one of the games that the old Hawaiians played. It is easy to envision this spot as one of power and prestige. Feel free to look around, but be respectful and acknowledge that Hawaiians still consider this a sacred spot.

In 1961, the National Park Service opened Pu'uhonua O Honaunau after a complete and faithful restoration was carried out. Careful consultation of old records and vintage sketches from early ships' artists gave the restoration a true sense of authenticity. Local artists used traditional tools and techniques to carve giant 'ohi'a logs into faithful renditions of the temple gods. They now stand again, protecting the *heiau* from evil. All the buildings are painstakingly lashed together in the Hawaiian fashion, but with nylon rope instead of traditional cordage, which would have added the perfect touch.

Stop at the visitor center to pick up a map and brochure for a self-guided tour. Exhibits line a wall, complete with murals done in heroic style. Push a button and the recorded messages give you a brief history of Hawaiian beliefs and the system governing daily life—educate yourself. The visitor center, 808/328-2288, is open daily 7:30 A.M.–5:30 P.M. Entrance to the 180-acre park is $2 per person. The beach park section to the south of the compound is open 6 A.M.–midnight.

Every year on the weekend closest to July 1 (the first was held in 1971), a free weeklong cultural festival is held here, featuring traditional Hawaiian arts and crafts, music, dance, and food. Be sure to stop by for a peek into the past if you are in the area during this time.

Accommodations

Manago Hotel, P.O. Box 145, Captain Cook, Kona, HI 96704, 808/323-2642, fax 808/323-3451, has been in the Manago family for 85 years, and anyone who puts his name on a place and keeps it there that long is doing something right. The Manago Hotel is clean and unpretentious with an old-Hawaii charm. There is nothing fancy going on here, just a decent room for a decent price. The old section of the hotel along the road is clean but a little worse for wear. The rooms are small with wooden floors, double beds, and utilitarian dressers, no fans, and shared bathrooms. Walk through to find a bridgeway into a garden area that's open, bright, and secluded. The new section features rooms with wall-to-wall carpeting, new furniture, private baths, louvered windows, ceiling fans, and private lanai. The rates are $25 single or $28 double for a room with a shared bath, $38–43 single and $41–46 double in the new section, plus $3 for an extra person. There is also one Japanese room that goes for $57 single or $60 double.

Weekly and monthly discounts are available on all rooms. The views of the Kona Coast from the hotel grounds are terrific. Downstairs in the old building, the restaurant serves breakfast, lunch, and dinner every day except Monday.

Merryman's Bed and Breakfast, also now known as Areca Palms Estate, P.O. Box 489, Captain Cook, HI 96704, 808/323-2276 or 800/545-4390, website: www.konabedandbreakfast.com, email: arecapalms@konabedandbreakfast.com, is considered, even by other B&B owners, to be one of the best on the island. Innkeepers Janice and Steve Glass have taken over the fine tradition of the Merrymans and are willing to share their cedar home with you. The house itself is sprinkled with antiques and fine furniture. A smooth wood floor and area rugs cover the spacious living and dining rooms under a cathedral ceiling. The house is always perfumed by freshly cut flowers, and Hawaiian music plays in the background to set the mood. Bedspreads are thick, the quilts in floral designs, and carpets cover the bedroom floors. Set in a broad manicured lawn surrounded by tropical flowers and palms, the outdoor hot tub and deck is the premier spot on the property. Rates for the four rooms range $75–125, inclusive of the sumptuous breakfast feast, two nights minimum.

Just a few steps from the Royal Kona Coffee Mill is **Affordable Hawaii at Pomaika'i "Lucky" Farm B&B,** 83-5465 Mamalahoa Hwy., Captain Cook, HI 96704, 808/328-2112 or 800/325-6427, fax 808/328-2255, website: www.luckyfarm.com, email: nitab+b@ilhawaii.net. This B&B is part of a working coffee and macadamia nut farm that has views of the coast from the back lanai. Two rooms in the farmhouse run $50 a night, one shares a bath and both share the sitting room with its TV and library. These rooms are a little close to the road and so may be a bit noisy, but it all quiets down at night. The greenhouse, a newer addition down below, runs $60 a couple for each of its two rooms. Both have queen beds, private entrances, and private baths. Then there's the coffee barn. Converted to a bedroom, it's been left with its rough-sawn framing and bare walls, but a bathroom has been added. It rents for $50 single or $60 double. All guests are served a farm-healthy breakfast each morning and you can pick fruit from the trees on the property. For reservations, contact Nita Isherwood at Pomaikai Farm B&B.

Also on a working coffee and macadamia nut farm is **Rainbow Plantation B&B,** P.O. Box 122, Captain Cook, HI 96704, 808/323-2393 or 800/494-2829, fax 808/323-9445, website: www.aloha.net/~konabnb, email: sunshine@aloha.net, a peaceful country place where chickens, potbellied pigs, and peacocks rule the yard. Each of the rooms and cottages has a private entrance and bathroom. Rooms in the main house run $75–85, while the cottages, one a converted fishing boat, are $75–95, two nights minimum. Breakfast is served each morning on the lanai, and all may use the "gazebo" kitchen.

Lion's Gate, owned by Diane and Bill Shriner, P.O. Box 761, Honaunau, HI 96726, tel./fax 808/328-2335 or 800/955-2332, website: www.kona-coffee-country.com/lionsgate, email: liongte@aloha.net, offers three rooms on a working macadamia nut and Kona coffee farm. Minutes from the Pu'uhonua O Honaunau National Historical Park, Lion's Gate features a hot tub, refrigerator, and TV in all rooms, great views of the coast from the wraparound deck, a gazebo for relaxing, and, of course, complimentary Kona coffee and macadamia nuts. Rooms run $70–95.

The Dragonfly Ranch, P.O. Box 675, Honaunau, HI 96762, 808/328-9570, or 800/487-2159, website: www.dragonflyranch.com, email: dfly@aloha.net, owned and operated by Barbara Moore, offers "tropical fantasy lodging" at a country estate that's set amongst thick vegetation on the way down to Pu'unonua O Honaunau. Rooms are remarkable and range from the Honeymoon Suite featuring a king bed in a lattice room to the Lanai cubby, an open-air affair with only a roof. All rooms include a small refrigerator and basic cooking apparatus, indoor bathroom, private outdoor shower, cable TV, stereo, and small library. Rates run $85–200 with substantial discounts for longer stays. This is an open, airy place with lots of Buddhist symbols. In fact, rainbow streamers and a Buddha in a butterfly banner greet you as you turn in the drive. To some, the touted tropical fantasy may be a "tropical nightmare." The hosts are very friendly and inviting, indeed, but definitely have an alternative philosophy. Free-spirited adventurers will feel comfortable here; others may not. Dragonfly Ranch is one of those places people totally adore or else dash away from.

Food

Try the legendary pork chop dinner served at the **Manago Hotel Restaurant,** 808/323-2642, in downtown Captain Cook. This meal and other offerings on the menu are plain old American food with a strong Hawaiian overlay. It won't set your taste buds on fire but you won't be complaining about being hungry or not having a wholesome meal. The restaurant is open for breakfast 7–9 A.M., lunch 11 A.M.–2 P.M., and dinner 5–7:30 P.M.; closed Monday.

There are very few places in Captain Cook where you can get a meal. On the highway just below Merriman's B&B is **Billy Bob's Pork 'n Park** barbecue restaurant, 808/323-3371, where you can order up barbecued ribs, chicken, hot biscuits, coleslaw, and salad. Also available, partner, are prime rib, veggie enchiladas, a mean Caesar salad, hog fries, and chili. Everything on the menu is less than $10, and you can order anything for take-out. Lasso that little missus of yours and come on down.

You'll be dancing like Zorba, singing like Caruso, and leisurely digesting like a *lomi lomi*ed Kamehameha after entering **The Kona Theater Cafe,** in Captain Cook just across from the post office, 808/328-2244. Revitalized by Ted Georgakis, a half-Italian, half-Greek man with an island flair, the café has an ethnic atmosphere that allows you to casually yet passionately philosophize over a menu that offers breakfast all day, fresh baked sweets, hot lunches, deli sandwiches, full entr'es, and espresso.

Looking for authentic Hawaiian food served by delightful people? Try **Super Js** take-out in Honaunau for *lomi lomi* salmon, *laulau,* macaroni salad, *poi,* and a variety of plate lunches that run about $6. Don't go too late, however, as it usually closes around sundown.

People in the know give the **Ke'ei Cafe,** 808/328-8451, rave reviews. But, you'll ask yourself: What is a fine restaurant serving fusion foods doing way out here? Open for lunch and dinner, it's in the tiny community of Honaunau. Seemingly set on the edge of the world, this little eatery has a wonderful location as the mountainside drops off below it toward Kealakekua Bay and the National Historical Park. Small in size but big in stature, it's popular, so call for reservations. Start with a Greek salad or Brazilian seafood chowder, both $6.95.

BIG ISLAND

Entrées include pasta primavera with heady herbs and spices and roast half chicken in white wine peppercorn gravy, under $15, and fresh catch prepared with red Thai curry, pan seared in lemon caper butter, or sautéed, market price. Follow this with a coconut flan or tropical bread pudding dessert. Yum! While the menu is short, there is a good selection of beers and wines. This will be a memorable meal, and the drive will be worth it.

Shopping

The **Kealakekua Ranch Center,** in Captain Cook, is a two-story mall with fashions, general supplies, and a Sure Save Supermarket.

Along the highway at the north edge of town is **Wood Works,** a shop selling wood furniture and smaller collectible pieces made mostly from koa created by two of the island's respected furniture makers. A few steps away is **Antiques and Orchids** collectibles shop.

Bong Brothers, 84-5227 Mamalahoa Hwy., on the *makai* side of the road near mile marker 106, 808/328-9289, is open Mon.–Fri. 8:30 A.M.–6 P.M., Sunday 10 A.M.–6 P.M. It's housed in a coffee mill complex circa 1920, one of the oldest in Honaunau, and sells not only coffee but organic produce and health food deli items. The shelves hold dried mango, candied ginger, bulk coffee, chocolate-covered coffee beans, Puna honey, Sam's Organic Gourmet salad dressings, dried pineapple, apples, bananas, special sauces, and—no shop is complete without them—T-shirts. Also look for a stack of burlap coffee bags, some bearing the Bong Brothers logo, that make a nifty souvenir. Adjacent is **Gold Mountain Mill,** a functional roasting mill tended by Tom Bong and his dog Bear; if time permits they'll show you around the operation. Coffee from the surrounding area comes in about three times per week to be roasted in the still functional, vintage 1930s roaster.

Also in Honaunau is the **Shimizu Market.**

FARTHER SOUTH

Ho'okena

If you want to see how the people of Kona still live, visit Ho'okena. A mile or two south of the Pu'uhonua O Honaunau turnoff, or 20 miles south of Kailua-Kona, take a well-marked spur road *makai* off Route 11 and follow it to the sea. The village is in a state of disrepair, but a number of homey cottages and some semi-permanent tents are used mostly on weekends by local fishermen. Ho'okena also boasts the **Ho'okena Beach County Park** with pavilions, restrooms, and picnic tables, but no potable water. Camping is allowed with a county permit. For drinking water, a tap is attached to the telephone pole near the beginning of your descent down the spur road. The gray-sand beach is broad, long, and probably *the* best in South Kona for both swimming and body surfing. If the sun gets too hot, plenty of palms lining the beach provide not only shade but a picture-perfect setting. Until the road connecting Kona to Hilo was finally finished in the 1930s, Ho'okena shipped the produce of the surrounding area from its bustling wharf. At one time, Ho'okena was the main port in South Kona and even hosted Robert Louis Stevenson when he passed through the islands in 1889. Part of the wharf still remains, and nearby a fleet of outrigger fishing canoes is pulled up on shore. The surrounding cliffs are honeycombed with burial caves. If you walk a half mile north, you'll find the crumpled walls and steeple of **Maria Lanakila Church,** leveled in an earthquake in 1950. The church was another "painted church" done by Father John Velghe in the same style as St. Benedict's.

Miloli'i

This active fishing village is approximately 15 miles south of Pu'uhonua O Honaunau. Again, look for signs to a spur road off Route 11 heading *makai.* The road, leading through bleak lava flows, is extremely narrow but worth the detour. Miloli'i (Fine Twist) earned its name from times past when it was famous for producing *'aha,* a sennit made from coconut-husk fibers; and *olona,* a twine made from the *olona* plant and mostly used for fishnets. This is one of the last villages in Hawaii where traditional fishing is the major source of income and where old-timers are heard speaking Hawaiian. Fishermen still use small outrigger canoes, now powered by outboards, to catch *opelu,* a type of mackerel that schools in these waters. The method of catching the *opelu* has remained unchanged for centuries. Boats gather and drop packets of chum made primarily from poi, sweet potatoes, or rice. No meat is used so sharks won't be attracted. The **Miloli'i Beach County Park** is a favorite with local people on the weekends; camping is allowed by permit. Tents are pitched in and around the parking lot, just under the ironwoods at road's end. Notice that a number of the tents appear to be semi-permanent. There are flushing toilets, a basketball court, and a brackish pond in which to rinse off, but no drinking water, so bring some. Swimming is safe inside the reef and the tide pools in the area are some of the best on the south coast. A 15-minute trail leads south to Honomalino Bay, where there's a secluded white-sand beach great for swimming. But always check with the local people first about conditions! In the village, a small, understocked store is operated by Willie Kaupiko, though the whole family pitches in.

For those looking for peace and quiet, try **Kaimana Guest House and Hostel,** P.O. Box 946, Captain Cook, HI 96704, 808/328-2207, website: www.kaimanavacations.com, a two-story oceanside house in Miloli'i that has a kitchen, shared bath, and covered lanai. There's plenty of water equipment to borrow and great free stargazing. Hostel beds run $20, a private single room is $30, and a private double room is $40.

SOUTH KOHALA

The Kohala District is the peninsular thumb in the northwestern portion of the Big Island. At its tip is Upolu Point, only 40 miles from Maui across the 'Alenuihaha Channel. Kohala was the first section of the Big Island to rise from beneath the sea. The long-extinct volcanoes of the Kohala Mountains running down its spine have been reduced by time and the elements from lofty, ragged peaks to rounded domes of 5,000 feet or so. Kohala is divided into North and South Kohala. South Kohala boasts *the* most beautiful swimming beaches on the Big Island, along with world-class hotels and resorts. Inland is Waimea (Kamuela), the *paniolo* town and center of the massive Parker Ranch. Between the coast and Waimea lies the newer planned community of Waikoloa, with its clusters of condominiums, family homes, and a golf course. North Kohala, an area of dry coastal slopes, former sugar lands, a string of sleepy towns, and deeply incised lush valleys, forms the northernmost tip of the island.

South Kohala is a region of contrast. It's dry, hot, tortured by wind, and scored by countless old lava flows. The predominant land color here is black, and this is counterpointed by scrubby bushes and scraggly trees, a seemingly semi-arid wasteland. This was an area that the ancient Hawaiians seemed to have traveled through to get somewhere else, yet Hawaiians did live here—along the coast—and numerous archaeological sites dot the coastal plain. Still, South Kohala is stunning with its palm-fringed white-sand pockets of beach, luxury resorts, green landscaped golf courses, a proliferation of colorful planted flowers, and its deep blue inviting water. You don't generally travel here to appreciate the stunning landscape, although it too has its attraction, you come here to settle into a sedate resort community, to be pampered and pleased by the finer things that await at luxury resorts that are destinations in and of themselves.

BIG ISLAND

SOUTH KOHALA

To Hawi

To Hawi

Kawaihae

270

Kawaihae Bay

250

To Hawi

KAWAIHAE ROAD

Waiaka

Waimea

PU'OPELU

SADDLE ROAD

200

To Hilo

19

PUUKOHOLA HEIAU NATIONAL HISTORIC SITE

SAM'EL M. SPENCER BEACH COUNTY PARK

MAUNA KEA BEACH HOTEL AND GOLF COURSE

HAPUNA BEACH PRINCE HOTEL AND GOLF COURSE

HAPUNA BEACH STATE RECREATION AREA

Hapuna Bay

Waialea Bay

Puako Bay

Puako

PUAKO RD

PUAKO PETROGLYPH AREA

19

Kamakoa

Gulch

SADDLE ROAD JUNCTION

HAWAII BELT HIGHWAY

WAIKOLOA ROAD

Waikoloa Village

WAIKOLOA VILLAGE GOLF COURSE

Pu'u Hinai (1,439 ft)

190

MAMALAHOA

To Kailua-Kona

PACIFIC OCEAN

Kawaihae Bay

HOLOHOLOKAI BEACH PARK

"THE ORCHID AT MAUNA LANI MAUNA LANI BAY HOTEL
FRANCIS H. I'I BROWN GOLF COURSES

Honoka'ope Bay

OUTRIGGER WAIKOLOA BEACH RESORT
HILTON WAIKOLOA VILLAGE
THE SHORES AT WAIKOLOA
THE BAY CLUB

WAIKOLOA BEACH GOLF CLUB

'Anaeho'omalu Bay

THE KING'S SHOPS

WAIKOLOA KINGS GOLF COURSE

HELIPORT

WAIKOLOA KINGS GOLF COURSE

WAIKO OA PETROGLYPH AREA

Lava Flow

KA'AHUMANU HIGHWAY

Puco Bay

Kaweiki Bay

Ohiki Bay

Kiholo Bay

Nawaikulua Point

LOOKOUT

QUEEN KA'AHUMANU HIGHWAY

19

To Kailua-Kona

Pu'uanahulu

Kuhuwai Bay

KONA VILLAGE RESORT

PETROGLYPH AREA

FOUR SEASONS RESORT

0   2.5 mi
0   2.5 km

THE COAST

The shoreline of South Kohala, from 'Anaeho'omalu Bay north to Kawaihae Bay, is rich with some of the finest super-deluxe resorts in the state. This coast's fabulous beaches are known not only for swimming and surfing, but for tide-pooling and awe-inspiring sunsets as well. Also, two of the coast's main beaches offer camping and even rental cabins. There are little-disturbed and rarely visited archaeological sites, expressive petroglyph fields, the educational **Pu'ukohola Heiau,** and even a rodeo. No "towns" lie along the coast, in the sense of a laid-out community with a main street and attendant businesses and services. The closest facsimile is Kawaihae, with a small cluster of restaurants, shops, a gas station, boat landing, and commercial harbor, but it's just an oversized village. Waikoloa Village, a planned community up above the coast, is a reasonably large town that's been carved from the dry uplands.

As you begin heading north from Kailua-Kona on coastal Route 19 (Queen Ka'ahumanu Highway), you leave civilization behind. There won't be a house or any structures at all, and you'll understand why they call it the "Big Island." Perhaps to soften the shock of what's ahead, magnificent bushes loaded with pink and purple flowers line the roadway for a while. Notice too that friends and lovers have gathered and placed white coral rocks on the black lava along the road, forming pleasant graffiti messages.

Suddenly you're in the midst of enormous flows of old 'a'a and pahoehoe as you pass through a huge and desolate lava desert. At first it appears ugly and uninviting, but the subtle beauty begins to grow. On clear days you can see Maui floating on the horizon, and *mauka* looms the formidable presence of Mauna Kea streaked by sunlight filtering through its crown of clouds. Along the roadside, wisps of grass have broken through the lava. Their color, a shade of pinkish gold, is quite extraordinary and made more striking juxtaposed with the inky-black lava. Caught by your headlights at night, or especially in the magical light of dusk, the grass wisps come alive, giving the illusion of wild-haired gnomes rising from the earth. In actuality, it's

fountain grass imported from Africa. This is also where you might catch a glimpse of the infamous "Kona nightingales," wild jackasses that roam throughout this area and can be road hazards, particularly at dawn and twilight. Watch for "Donkey Crossing" road signs.

Around mile marker 70, the land softens and changes. The lava is older, carpeted in rich green grass appearing as rolling hills of pastureland. These long, flat stretches of road can give you "lead foot." Be careful! The police patrol this strip heavily, using unmarked cars, looking for unsuspecting tourists who have been "road hypnotized." From Kailua-Kona to the Waikoloa Beach Resort is about 25 miles, with another five miles to the Mauna Kea Beach Resort near Kawaihae. If you're day-tripping to the beaches, expect to spend an hour traveling each way.

If you're approaching Kohala from Hilo or the east side of the island, you can take one of two routes. The Saddle Road (Route 200) comes directly west from Hilo and passes between Mauna Kea and Mauna Loa. This very scenic road has the alluring distinction of being the least favorite route of the car rental agencies. The Saddle Road intersects Route 190, where you can turn north and drive for seven miles to Waimea, south for 33 miles to Kailua-Kona, or take the 13-mile shortcut Waikoloa Road to the coast. Route 19, the main artery connecting Hilo with the west coast, changes its "locally known" name quite often, but it's always posted as Route 19. Directly north from Hilo as it hugs the Hamakua Coast, it's called the Hawaii Belt Road. When it turns west in Honoka'a, heading for Waimea, it's called the Mamalahoa Highway. From Waimea directly west to Kawaihae on the coast Route 19 becomes Kawaihae Road, and when it turns due south along the coast heading for Kailua-Kona, its moniker changes again to Queen Ka'ahumanu Highway.

SIGHTS AND NEARBY COMMUNITIES

The following sights and beaches are listed from south to north. All except for Waikoloa Village lie along coastal Route 19.

ROBERT NILSEN

a modern petroglyph at Puako resembling an ancient carved figure

Ka'upulehu Petroglyphs

Just back from the ponds at the Kona Village Resort is a cluster of approximately 440 lava rock carvings, near where the ancient Kings Highway must have passed. This group of petroglyphs contains designs, many of them different from others along this coast. There are numerous human figures, some with paddles and fishing lines held in their hands, a turtle figure, and dozens that illustrate the lines of crab-claw sails of sailing canoes. While some of these carvings are speculated to be as much as 900 years old, others are obviously newer, as you can discern the date 1820 and some Western script—obviously done after contact with early white sailors. In 1998, the resort constructed a wooden boardwalk around the majority of these carved figures in order to protect the integrity of these fine works of art. Please stay on the wooden pathway during your self-guided tour. As this field lies on Kona Village property, you may need to contact the hotel in order to get permission to enter the property. Tours can be arranged through the concierge desk, 808/325-5555, where printed information and a map of the site are available.

Waikoloa Petroglyphs

Set along a reconstructed section of the King's Trail and surrounded by the Beach Course golf course is the Waikoloa Petroglyph field. Unlike others nearby, this grouping is done in an undulating area and also includes remains of temporary structures. While many and varied designs are seen here, a circular pattern is much in evidence. Cinder rock paths have been constructed throughout this petroglyph field. Stay on the paths; do not walk on the carvings. Approach this area from the King's Shops for a self-guided tour or take one of the free guided tours conducted by the shopping center, Tues.–Fri. at 10:30 A.M. or Saturday at 8:30 A.M. Wear sturdy shoes, a hat, and bring drinking water.

Puako Petroglyphs

These rock carvings, approximately 3,000 individual designs, are considered some of the finest and oldest in Hawaii, but carvings of horses and cattle signify ongoing art that happened long after Westerners appeared. Circles outlined by a series of small holes belonged to families who placed the umbilical cords of their infants into these indentations to tie them to the 'aina and give them strength for a long and good life. State archaeologists and anthropologists have reported a deterioration of the site due to vandalism, so please look but don't deface, and stay on established paths. Access is by a well-marked, self-guiding trail starting from Holoholokai Beach Park, on the north side of the Orchid at Mauna Lani Hotel.

Puako

This alluring area is *makai* on a side road off Route 19 about four miles south of Kawaihae.

Hawaiians lived here in times past, but a modern community has been building along the three-mile road past Puako Bay since the 1950s. This quiet, no-frills community is a mixture of working class homes, rental properties, and discreet vacation hideaways. Services amount to one reasonably well-stocked general store, a public telephone, and a vacation rental agency. A thin ribbon of white sand runs the length of the beach near the boat ramp that provides fair swimming. Sunsets here are magnificent, and you'll usually have the beach to yourself. The remainder of the shoreline through this community is mostly rock shelf with inlets and tide pools, for good fishing, snorkeling, and some surfing. Near-shore scuba diving is excellent, with huge caverns and caves to explore, and a colorful concentration of coral and marine life. There are half a dozen shoreline access routes along this strip road.

Along Puako Road is **Hokuloa Church,** built by Reverend Lorenzo Lyons in 1859. This musically talented reverend mastered the Hawaiian language and composed lovely ballads such as "Hawaii Aloha," which has become the unofficial anthem of the islands.

Between here and Hapuna Beach State Recreation Area just up the coast is **Waialea Bay Marine Life Conservation District,** a 35-acre preserve. Turn off Puako Road onto Old Puako Road and then turn down a rough road near pole number 69 to reach the shore. The white sand beach here is best in summer. The reef is wonderful for snorkeling, better at its southern end. Although a bit hard to get to, it's a favorite for the local community.

Pu'ukohola Heiau

Don't miss this restored Hawaiian temple, a National Historical Site one mile south of Kawaihae where coastal Route 19 turns into Route 270 heading into North Kohala. This site, covering 77 acres, includes **Mailekini Heiau** and the **John Young's Homestead** site. Below the *heiau,* in the trees near the sea, Kamehameha I kept a royal household, and below that, now sunk under sand in the bay, is another older *heiau* dedicated to the shark gods. Administered by the National Park Service, this sacred ground is open daily 7:30 A.M.–4 P.M.; free admission. As you enter, pick up a map highlighting the points of interest. It's worthwhile checking out the visi-

tor center, 808/882-7218, where the rangers provide excellent information. Trails throughout the park lead to its notable sites. It's hot and dry at this site, so bring water and wear a hat. Pu'ukohola (Whale Hill) received its name either because the hill itself resembles a whale, or because migrating whales pass very close offshore every year. It was fated to become a hill of destiny.

Kamehameha I built Pu'ukohola Heiau in 1790–01 on the advice of Kapoukahi, a prophet from Kaua'i who said that Kamehameha would unify all the islands only after he built a temple to his war-god Kuka'ilimoku. Kamehameha complied, building this last of the great Hawaiian *heiau* from mortarless stone that when finished measured 100 by 224 feet. The dedication ceremony of the *heiau* is fascinating history. Kamehameha's last rival was his cousin, Keoua Kuahu'ula. This warlike chief realized that his *mana* had deserted him and that it was Kamehameha who would rise to be sovereign of all the islands. Kamehameha invited him to the dedication ceremony, but en route Keoua, in preparation for the inevitable outcome, performed a death purification ceremony by circumcising his own penis. When the canoes reached the beach, they were met by a hail of spears and musket balls. Keoua was killed and his body laid on Kuka'ilimoku's altar as a noteworthy sacrifice. Kamehameha became the unopposed sovereign of the Big Island and, within a few years, of all Hawaii.

Every August on the weekend closest to Establishment Day, a free two-day cultural festival is held on the *heiau* grounds, including arts and crafts exhibitions, games, hula demonstrations, music and dance, and re-creation of ancient ceremonies in traditional dress.

Near the *heiau* is the house site of John Young, an English seaman who became a close advisor to Kamehameha, who dubbed him 'Olohana, "All Hands." Young taught the Hawaiians how to use cannons and muskets and fought alongside Kamehameha in many battles. He turned Mailekini Heiau into a fort, and over a century later the U.S. Army used it as an observation area during World War II. Young became a respected Hawaiian chief and grandfather of Queen Emma. Only he and one other white man have the honor of being buried at the Royal Mausoleum in Nu'uanu Valley on O'ahu.

Kawaihae Town

This port town marks the northern end of the South Kohala Coast. Here, Route 19 turns eastward toward Waimea, or turns into Route 270 heading up the coast into North Kohala. Not really more than a village, Kawaihae town is basically utilitarian, with wharves, fuel tanks, and a boat ramp. A service cluster has numerous shops, restaurants, and a gas station. Unless you're stopping to eat, you'll probably pass right through.

Waikoloa Village

If you're interested in visiting Waimea as well as seeing the South Kohala Coast, you might consider turning right off Route 19 near mile marker 75 onto Waikoloa Road. This route cuts inland for 13 miles, connecting coastal Route 19 with inland Route 190, which leads to Waimea. About halfway up, you pass the planned and quickly growing community of Waikoloa Village about six miles inland from Waikoloa Resort. Try to overlook the condo complexes along the road and head into the village itself, which is low-rise and quite tasteful. Waikoloa Village is a mixture of condominiums and single-family homes that is also home to Waikoloa Village Golf Club, whose course is open to the public, and Roussels restaurant at the clubhouse.

Waikoloa sits below the saddle that runs between Mauna Kea and the North Kohala Mountains. When the trade winds blow from the northeast, they funnel over this saddle and race down the slope, creating windy conditions that challenge golfers. For the dubious distinction of being a windy community, Waikoloa is sometimes jokingly called "Waiko-blow-a." The village is serviced by the **Waikoloa Highlands Shopping Center,** a small but adequate shopping mall with a gas station, full-service supermarket, First Hawaiian Bank, postal service store, small medical center, and a few restaurants and shops.

BEACHES AND PARKS

There are a number of excellent beaches along this coast, most with good to excellent facilities. In addition, all resorts offer access to their beaches with (limited) public parking.

Kahuwai Bay

This picturesque bay has a sandy bottom bounded by rocky shorelines on either side. It is a spot often chosen by green sea turtles to relax on the sand or to lay their eggs. Give them wide berth. Kona Village Resort fronts this bay and creates a fine Polynesian village background. Next door, the Four Seasons Resort sits on a narrow strip of sandy beach and one swimming lagoon. Down the coast a ways is Kuki'o Beach and farther on is Kua Bay.

Kiholo Bay

Near mile marker 81 on the highway is a pull-off and overlook that offers a good glimpse of this stark lava-covered coast. Down on the coast just north of the pull-off you'll see Kiholo Bay and Luahinewai Pond. The pond was a favorite stop for Hawaiian sailors going up the coast, who would have a swim in its cool waters before continuing on. Look for a stand of royal palms marking the spot, and follow the rough but passable 4WD road down to the beach, where you will find a large round wooden house that once belonged to Loretta Lynn. Close by, a path leads over the lava to a tiny cove made more dramatic by a black-sand beach.

'Anaeho'omalu Bay

After miles of the transfixing monochrome blackness of Kohala's lava flows, a green standout of palm trees beckons in the distance. Turn near mile marker 76 at the Waikoloa Beach Resort entrance, and follow the access road to historic 'Anaeho'omalu Bay, referred to locally as "A-Bay." Set back from the beach here is the Outrigger Waikoloa Beach Resort. The bay area, with its freshwater springs, coconut trees, blue lagoon, and white-sand beach, is a picture-perfect seaside oasis. Between the large coconut grove and the beach are two well-preserved fishponds where mullet was raised for consumption only by the royalty who lived nearby or were happening by in seagoing canoes. Throughout the area along well-marked trails are petroglyphs, a segment of the cobblestoned King's Highway, and numerous archaeological sites including house sites and some hard-to-find burial caves. The white-sand beach is open to the public, with access, parking, and beautiful lava stone showers/bathhouses. Although the sand is a bit grainy, the swimming, snorkeling, scuba diving, windsurfing, and just about any water sport are great. A walk north along the bay brings you to an area of excellent tide pools and waters heavily populated by marine life.

Holoholokai Beach Park

Adjacent to the Orchid at Mauna Lani Hotel on a well-marked access road, this picturesque beach park is open to the public daily 6:30 A.M.–7 P.M. and is improved with a bathroom, running water, picnic tables, and resort-quality landscaping. Unfortunately, the beach itself is mostly coral boulders with only tiny pockets offering very limited water access. However, the park is used very little and is perfect for relaxing under a palm tree or for a leisurely stroll to explore the many tide pools. A shoreline path leads past the Orchid at Mauna Lani to the Mauna Lani Bay Hotel, which fronts the wide sand beaches of Makaiwa Bay. From the back side of the parking lot is the trail to Puako Petroglyphs.

Hapuna Beach State Recreation Area

Approximately seven miles north of 'Anaeho'omalu is the *second*-best (some rate this the best), but most accessible, white-sand beach on the island. Hapuna Beach is wide and spacious, almost 700 yards long by 70 wide in summer, with a reduction by heavy surf in winter. A lava finger divides the beach into almost equal halves. During good weather the swimming is excellent and lifeguards are on duty. During heavy weather, usually in winter, the rips are fierce, and Hapuna has claimed more lives than any other beach park on all of Hawaii! At the north end is a small cove almost forming a pool that is always safe, a favorite for snorkeling with families and children. Many classes in beginning scuba and snorkeling are held in this area, and shore fishing is good throughout. At the south end, good breaks make for tremendous body surfing (no boards allowed), and those familiar with the area make spectacular leaps from the seacliffs. Picnic tables, pavilions, restrooms, and plenty of parking are available in this nicely landscaped park.

Camping is available in six A-frame screened shelters that rent for $20 per night and accommodate up to four. Provided are sleeping platforms (no bedding), electric outlets, cold-water showers, and toilets in separate comfort stations, plus a shared range and refrigerator in a central pavilion. Although the spot is a little rundown, the A-frames are very popular, so reservations and a deposit are required. You can receive full information from the Division of State Parks, P.O. Box 936, Hilo, HI 96721, 808/974-6200; or visit the office at 75 Aupini St., Room 204, in Hilo.

Kauna'oa Beach

Better known as Mauna Kea Beach because of the nearby luxury hotel of the same name, Kauna'oa is less than a mile north of Hapuna Beach and is considered the best beach on the Big Island by not only the local population, but also by those who judge such things from a broader perspective. In times past, it was a nesting and mating ground for green sea turtles, and although these activities no longer occur because of human pressure on the habitat, turtles still visit the south end of the beach. Mauna Kea Beach is long and wide, and the sandy bottom makes for excellent swimming. It is more sheltered than Hapuna but can still be dangerous. Hotel beach boys, always in attendance, are unofficial lifeguards who have saved many unsuspecting tourists. During high surf, the shoreline is a favorite with surfers. Like all beaches in Hawaii, this one is public, but to keep the number of nonguests down, only 10 parking passes are handed out each day on a first-come, first-served basis. Pick up a pass at the guardhouse as you enter the hotel grounds. These entitle you to spend the day on the beach, but on weekends they're gone early. Alternately, park at Hapuna Beach and return via an easy mile-long trail connecting Hapuna and Mauna Kea Beaches.

Spencer Beach County Park

Look for the entrance a minute or two past Pu'ukohola Heiau on Route 19 just before entering Kawaihae. The old beach road leads from the beach park up to the *heiau*, so you can combine a day at the beach with a cultural education. The park is named after Samuel Mahuka Spencer, a longtime island resident who was born in Waimea, served as county mayor for 20 years, and died in 1960 at Honoka'a. The park provides pavilions, restrooms, cold-water showers, electricity, picnic facilities, and even tennis courts. Day use is free, but tent and trailer camping are by county permit only. Spencer Beach is protected from wind and heavy wave action by an offshore reef and by breakwaters built around Kawaihae Bay. These make it the safest swimming beach along South Kohala's shore and a favorite with local families with small children. The wide, shallow reef is home to a wide spectrum of marine life, making the snorkeling entertaining. The shoreline fishing is also excellent.

PRACTICALITIES

LUXURY RESORTS

The South Kohala Coast has four resort areas, all providing luxury accommodations, fine dining, golf courses, full-service resort amenities, the best beaches on the island, and a smattering of historical and cultural sites. They are, in effect, self-sufficient mini-villages. The first north of Kailua-Kona is not referred to by one name but encompasses the adjacent properties of **Kona Village and the Four Seasons Resorts.** They are actually in the North Kona District but are discussed here as they are more similar to the South Kohala luxury resorts than to any hotel complex in Kailua or Keauhou to the south. Kona Village Resort, the oldest resort along this coast, is designed like a Polynesian village: low-slung, thatch roofs, palm trees, white-sand beach, and shoreline ponds. It's a welcome oasis in a land of stark black lava; it has kept up with the times and still offers one of the best destinations in the state. The Four Seasons Resort is the island's newest, a modern complex of tasteful buildings, a counterpoint to Kona Village, where you will find golf, tennis, and water sport opportunities. It's new and fresh, a delight for the senses.

Next up the way is **Waikoloa Resort,** the largest, busiest, and most commercial of the resort complexes. Here you have the Outrigger Waikoloa Beach Resort, a redesigned hotel that reflects the grandeur of Hawaii from the 1930s and '40s, the gargantuan Hilton Waikoloa Village, and three high-class condominiums. Here as well are the King's Shops, the only shopping center in the area, two superb golf courses, a multitude of tennis opportunities, a petroglyph field, remnants of the ancient King's Trail, anchialine ponds, and one of the best beaches on the coast. Just across the road is a commercial heliport.

Mauna Lani Resort comes next, also big but not as commercial. Here too you find two magnificent hotels, five (and counting) condominiums, two golf courses, tennis, beaches, fishponds, two petroglyph fields, and a long history. There is no shopping complex here, but each hotel has a bevy of retail shops. This is a quality high-end resort, without glitz or hype.

Farthest to the north is the **Mauna Kea Resort.** Smaller and more intimate, it contains the grande dame of Kohala hotels, the Mauna Kea, and its more recent addition, the Hapuna Beach Hotel. Like bride and groom, these two hotels with their golf courses are sufficient unto themselves, and they sit on the two finest beaches on the island. While there are no major historical sites on the property, they lie a mile or two south on one of the most significant and well-kept *heiau* on this island.

Kona Village Resort

So you want to go "native," and you're dreaming of a "little grass shack" along a secluded beach? No problem! The Kona Village Resort, P.O. Box 1299, Kailua-Kona, HI 96745, 808/325-5555, 800/432-5450 from anywhere in the state, or 800/367-5290 from the Mainland, website: www.konavillage.com, email: kvr@aloha.net, is a once-in-a-lifetime dream experience. On Kahuwai Bay, a picture-perfect cove of white sand dotted with coconut palms, the village lies seven miles north of the Kona Airport, surrounded by acres of seclusion. The accommodations are 125 distinctive "hales," individual renditions of thatch-roofed huts found throughout Polynesia and Hawaii. They are simple but luxurious and, in keeping with the idea of getting away from it all, have no TVs, radios, or telephones. All, however, do have ceiling fans and louvered windows to let the tropical breezes blow through. Beds are covered with distinctive quilts and pillows. Each hut features a wet bar,

BIG ISLAND

refrigerator, coffeemaker, and extra-large bathroom. At one time you had to fly into the hotel's private airstrip, but today you arrive by car. Almost exactly at mile marker 87, turn in, make a right within 100 yards, and follow the access road that leads through coal-black lava fields. Don't despair! Down by the sea you can see the shimmering green palm trees as they beckon you to the resort. Kona Village gives you your money's worth, with a lei greeting, free valet service, a private tennis center, water sports, numerous cultural activities, and a variety of cocktail parties and lu'au. Guided tours are also offered to the many historic sites in the area, shoreline tide pool exploring, and even a botanical tour of the grounds complete with legends and explanations of the ancient medicinal uses of the plants.

Meals are served in the Hale Moana, the main dining room, and at the Hale Moana Terrace, where a famous luncheon buffet is served daily. Hale Samoa is the fine dining restaurant, open

daily except Wednesday and Friday for dinner. Upon entering Hale Samoa, your spirits rise immediately with the sweep of cathedral ceiling. On the walls is an original painting by Herb Kane, Hawaii's foremost artist, that depicts *The Fair American,* a tiny ship commandeered by King Kamehameha that was instrumental in changing the history of old Hawaii. The walls also hold portraits of the hotel's original owner, Johnno Jackson, an oil driller from California, who in 1960 sailed in with his wife Helen, their Labrador dog, a monkey, and a parrot—all in a 42-foot schooner—landed on these shores and declared, "This is the spot!" Also on the grounds are Hale Ho'okipa, "House of Hospitality," where a lu'au is held on Friday nights, and a *paniolo* steak and seafood dinner every Wednesday. Drinks and tropical libations are offered at the Hale Samoa Terrace, Shipwreck Bar, and Bora Bora Bar at the pool.

Rates start at $450 per couple with full American plan (includes three meals) and go up to $795 for oceanfront huts. Deduct $110 for single occupancy and add $35 for children 3–5, $140 for children 6–12, and $190 for an extra adult. These rates also include transportation to and from the airport if you need it, all scheduled activities, use of the tennis and fitness centers, water-sports equipment, and all activities except scuba, snuba, massage, and the Friday night lu'au. The hotel's "Na Keiki in Paradise" is a children's program included in the room price that will entertain and educate children ages six and up throughout the day. There is a strict reservations and refund policy, so check. Hotel manager Fred Duerr has been at the facility since 1966, along with most of his highly professional and seasoned staff. They take pride in the hotel and do everything to help you have a rewarding, enjoyable, and relaxing stay at this premier resort. The Kona Village is a serene Hawaiian classic that deserves its well-earned reputation for excellence, and as a consequence gets 65 percent repeat visitors and 25 percent honeymooners.

Four Seasons Resort

The Four Seasons Resort, Hualalai, P.O. Box 1269, Kailua-Kona, HI 96745, 808/325-8000 or 888/340-5662, fax 808/325-8100, at historic Ka'upulehu, opened in late 1996. This 243-room resort is split into 36 low-rise bungalows in four

hale *at Kona Village Resort*

crescent groups that front a half-mile beach and several natural lagoons just down from Kona Village Resort. In among old lava flows from the Hualalai volcano, 32 of these units have ocean access and four are along the 18th green of the accompanying golf course. Contemporary Polynesian in style, the units are a mixture of dark mahogany wood, light wall colors and carpeting, pleasing medium brown rattan furniture, and gray slate flooring. Authentic Hawaiian art pieces from the late 1700s to the present are displayed throughout the hotel. There is no skimping on space, furnishings, or amenities in any of the rooms or suites. Large as well are the bathrooms, each of which looks out onto a private garden, lanai, or patio. The slate floors of the main rooms are covered with seagrass mats and the beds with material reminiscent of tapa cloth.

The resort's two restaurants will fill your every culinary need for all three meals of the day. Both the elegant **Puhu I'a Restaurant** and the casual **Beach Tree Bar and Grill** are oceanside. In addition, the **Hualalai Club Grille and Bar** at the golf clubhouse serves lunch, drinks, and fine-dining dinners in an informal setting. On the ocean side of the meeting room building and the outdoor Hoku stage theater is Kids for all Seasons, the hotel's service of supervised care for 5- to 12-year-olds, which provides fun-filled indoor and outdoor activities. Hualalai Tennis Club is open for hotel guests only. Adjacent to the tennis courts is the Sports Club and Spa, a full-service facility that offers instructional classes, a 25-meter lap pool, exercise machines, massage and spa therapies, and volleyball and half-court basketball courts. For the duffer, the Hualalai Golf Club offers 18 holes of challenging play along the ocean. Check out the interpretive center with its 1,200-gallon reef aquarium just downstairs from the lobby, where you can learn about the surrounding waters, this area of Hawaii, and the life and lifestyle of ancient Hawaiians. In addition to an ocean swimming lagoon, the resort has both freshwater and saltwater swimming pools set just back from the beach. For those interested, a water-sports kiosk on the beach can fix you up with needed gear or activities.

An exceptional place, this all-inclusive destination resort is not cheap. Rooms run $450–650 per night, suites $775–5,200, $90 for an extra adult.

Outrigger Waikoloa Beach Hotel

Following a $25 million renovation and facelift, the former Royal Waikoloan re-emerged as the artful Outrigger Waikoloa Beach Hotel, 69-275 Waikoloa Beach Dr., Waikoloa, HI 96738, 808/886-6789 or 800/688-7444, website: www.outrigger.com. On a perfect spot fronting the palm-fringed 'Anaeho'omalu Bay, the hotel looks out over ponds that once stocked fish for passing *ali'i*. The hotel lobby is a spacious open-air affair that lets the trade winds blow through across its cool sandstone floor. Six floors of rooms extend out in wings on both sides, flanking the landscaped courtyard and new swimming pool. Greeting you as you enter the lobby is a marvelous old koa outrigger canoe in front of a three-part mural by renowned Hawaiian artist Herb Kane of a royal canoe and Western frigate meeting off the Kona Coast. Walk farther and gaze down upon the landscaped courtyard, heavy with greenery and the pungent smell of tropical plants. The renovation has bequeathed a look and feel reminiscent of the 1930s and '40s with its decorative artistic touches, and it imparts a sense of less hectic times. The Outrigger Waikoloa Beach Hotel is a class act.

All 545 hotel rooms and suites have been completely refurbished and tastefully decorated in light soothing colors, with king-size beds, rattan furnishings, custom quilts, and island prints of a mid-20th century art deco style. Each room has a/c, color TV, *yakuta* robes, in-room safe, small refrigerator, marble vanities, and a private lanai. Rooms are reasonably priced at $210–350, while suites run $425–1,000 per night. Hotel services and amenities include an activities desk for all on-site and off-property excursions and several retail shops and boutiques. You can take part in daily Hawaiian cultural programs, use the business center, or have your kids properly cared for at the children's program. Enjoy the garden swimming pool, spa and fitness center, six tennis courts, and a grand beach with plenty of water activities. The hotel is just a few minutes' stroll past the royal fishponds to the beach or to the remains of a nearby ancient but now restored *heiau*.

The Outrigger Waikoloa Beach also has new dining facilities. Harking back to the days when Hawaiian music and news of the islands was transmitted to the world by radio, and when Pan Am Clipper Ships flew travelers to the islands, is **Hawaii Calls Restaurant,** the hotel's main dining room. Open for three meals a day, the decor says yesteryear but the menu is thoroughly modern with a mix of Continental and Asian cuisine. As part of this open-air restaurant, the **Clipper Lounge** serves tropical drinks as smooth as a Clipper's landing on a mirror lagoon. This lounge serves up a late bistro menu and nightly entertainment 5–11:30 P.M., while the more casual poolside **Nalu Bar and Grill** is open 10 A.M.–sunset for snacks, fill-'er-ups, and drinks. Fit for the royalty who once called this bay their home, the twice weekly Royal Lu'au draws appreciative guests for food and entertainment.

The Shores at Waikoloa

The Shores at Waikoloa, 69-1035 Keana Place, Waikoloa, HI 96738, 808/885-5001—or contact Aston Hotel and Resorts, 800/922-7866 Mainland and Canada or 800/321-2558 in Hawaii—comprises secluded luxury condominiums nestled away in the planned community of Waikoloa. Enter through a security gate to see the peaceful and beautifully manicured grounds of these white-stucco and red-tile-roof condominiums. A few minutes away are the best beaches on Hawaii and all of the activities offered by the large luxury hotels, if you wish to participate. The condominium offers an activities desk where your outings can be arranged, a swimming pool and hot tub, two complimentary tennis courts, and outdoor barbecues. The condos are decorated by the individual owners, so each room is unique, but there are guidelines and standards so every unit is tasteful and comfortable. All units are extremely spacious, with many boasting marble and terra cotta floors. All have huge bathrooms, full modern kitchens, laundry facilities, and light and airy sitting rooms complete with state-of-the-art entertainment centers. Rates range $275 for a one-bedroom to $580 for a three-bedroom golf villa. Low season brings a 10 percent reduction, and a number of packages are available. If you are after a luxury vacation within a vacation where you can get away from it all after you've gotten away from it all, The Shores at Waikoloa is a superb choice. The Shores is a AAA three-diamond award-winner.

The Bay Club

Surrounded by golf links, The Bay Club, 69-450 Waikoloa Beach Dr., Kamuela, HI 96743, 808/886-7979 or 800/305-7979, has an ideal location. Like all other accommodations in this planned community of Waikoloa Beach Resort, The Bay Club is luxury living in a secure environment. On the property are tennis courts, a swimming pool with poolside café, a sauna and spa, fitness center, and activities center. You can partake in as much as you like or just lounge to your heart's content. All individually owned, each spacious unit is decorated in a pleasing style that reflects the taste of the owner. The Bay Club wraps you in the warm arms of luxury and offers amenities that will fulfill your heart's desire. One- and two- bedroom units run $250–315, and the golf villas are $365–395.

Hilton Waikoloa Village

At the Hilton Waikoloa Village, 425 Waikoloa Beach Dr., Waikoloa, HI 96738, 808/886-1234 or 800/445-8667, fax 808/886-2900, website: www.waikoloavillage.hilton.com, the idea was to create a reality so beautiful and naturally harmonious that anyone who came here, sinner or saint, would be guaranteed a glimpse of paradise. The architecture is "fantasy grand," and the grounds are grandly fantastic. The three main towers, each enclosing a miniature fern-filled botanical garden, are spread over the grounds almost a mile apart and are linked by pink flagstone walkways, canals navigated by hotel launches, and a quiet, space-age tram. Attention to the smallest detail is immediately apparent, and everywhere sculptures, art treasures, and brilliant flowers soothe the eyes. The museum promenade displays choice artworks from Hawaii and Asia, and here and there around the property are brilliant artistic flourishes. Nearly everywhere you look you delight in beauty. Songs of rare tropical birds and the wind whispering through a bamboo forest create the natural melody that surrounds you. The beach fronting the property offers excellent snorkeling, while three gigantic pools and a series of lagoons are perfect for water activities and sunbathing. You can swim in a private lagoon accompanied by dolphins, dine in first-rate restaurants, relax to a message at the spa, pick up a memento at the retail shops, sweat over a game of tennis, or just let your cares slip away as you lounge in perfect tranquility.

Like the hotel in general, its seven restaurants are culinary powerhouses, and every taste is provided for. **Donatoni's** features classic Northern Italian cuisine; **Palm Terrace** presents breakfast and dinner buffets, with a different theme nightly; **Imari** serves traditional Japanese fare; The Chinese **Kirin** restaurant offers dim sum lunches and seafood dinners; **Kamuela Provision Co.** specializes in steak and seafood; **Orchid Cafe** provides light breakfasts and lunches; and **Hang Ten** has casual lunches and tropical drinks. The hotel's bars, lounges, and casual poolside dining are other options, while twice weekly the **Legends of the Pacific** lu'au delights guests with fine food and an extravagant dinner show.

With all this splendor, the most talked-about feature at the hotel is still **Dolphin Quest.** A specially constructed saltwater pond is home to Atlantic bottlenose dolphins from Florida's Gulf Coast. Daily, on a lottery basis for adults, but with two months in advance reservations available to children up to 19 years of age, guests are allowed to interact with the dolphins. Dolphin Quest is an educational experience. Here you don't ride the dolphins and they don't do tricks for you. In the half-hour session, guests wade in chest-deep water with the dolphins gliding by while a staff member imparts information concerning not only dolphins, but all marine life and human interdependence with it. The experience is voluntary on the dolphins' part—*they* choose to swim with *you* as a guest in their domain. Much of the proceeds from the program go toward marine research.

This resort is definitely a distinctive undertaking, a step apart from any other resort complex in the state. It has cut its own path and gone its own way. Yet with all the grandeur, it seems a bit like Disneyland on a lava flow; beautiful and expansive, yet incongruous and overblown. Forget intimacy. You don't come here to get away, you come here to participate. With 1,240 rooms on a 62-acre property, it's so big that entering the lobby can be like walking into Grand Central Station and navigating the walkways like pushing through throngs at a fair. For all that, the Hilton still offers plenty for everyone and gives you unlimited options for a great vacation. You be the judge: is this paradise or something else?

This futuristic hotel complex has set a new standard, but as you would expect, all this luxury comes at a price. Rates are $390–579 for standard rooms and $770–4,730 for suites.

The Orchid at Mauna Lani

In a tortured field of coal-black lava made more dramatic by pockets of jade-green lawn rises ivory-white Orchid at Mauna Lani, 1 N. Kaniku Dr., Kohala Coast, HI 96743, 808/885-2000 or 800/845-9905, website: www.orchid-maunalani.com. A rolling drive lined with *haku lei* of flowering shrubs entwined with stately palms leads to the open-air porte cochère. Enter to find koa and marble reflecting the diffused and soothing light of the interior. Straight ahead, off the thrust-proscenium Sunset Terrace, a living blue-on-blue still-life of sea and sky is perfectly framed. Nature, powerful yet soothing, surrounds the hotel. Stroll the grounds, where gentle breezes always blow and where the ever-present surf is the back beat of a melody created by trickling rivulets and falling waters as they meander past a magnificent free-form pool and trimmed tropical gardens of ferns and flowers. The hallways and lobbies open from the central area like the delicate ribs of a geisha's fan; walls are graced with Hawaiian quilts and excellent artwork on view everywhere; and every set of stairs boasts a velvety smooth koa banister carved with the pineapple motif, the Hawaiian symbol of hospitality. The Orchid is casually elegant, a place to relax in luxury and warm *aloha*.

In two six-story wings off the main reception hall, the 539 hotel rooms, each with private lanai and sensational view, are a mixture of kings, doubles, and suites. Done in neutral tones, the stylish and refined rooms feature handcrafted quilts, twice-daily room attendance, an entertainment center, fully stocked honor bar, in-room safe, and spacious marble bathrooms. Room rates begin at $385 for a garden view to $650 for a deluxe oceanfront room. Suites range from an executive one-bedroom to the magnificent Presidential Suite and cost $700–4,250.

Dining at the The Orchid can be everything from poolside casual to haute cuisine, prepared in various styles, using locally grown produce, herbs, meats, and seafood. The culinary results are not only mouth-watering but healthy and wonderfully nutritious. The Orchid's fine dining restaurant is **The Grill,** where crystal and dark koa wood set the scene and most dishes are either Hawaiian-style or northern Mediterranean-influenced. The Grill is open for dinner only; evening or alohawear requested. The **Orchid Court,** a casual restaurant featuring Pacific Rim and California cuisine, is the hotel's main dining room and is open for breakfast and dinner. Poolside, **Brown's Beach House** is the most casual restaurant, where you dine alfresco in a garden setting for lunch and dinner. Soft Hawaiian music accompanies a hula dancer in the evening. For a relaxing evening of drinks, a cigar, or billiards, and periodic live entertainment, lower yourself into an overstuffed leather chair at the **Paniolo Lounge and Polo Bar.**

The hotel offers first-rate guest services, amenities, and activities that include a small shopping mall with everything from sundries to designer boutiques, complimentary shuttle to and from Mauna Lani's famous championship golf courses, golf bag storage, 11 tennis courts (with seven lit for evening play), complimentary use of fitness center and snorkel equipment, an enormous swimming pool and sun deck, bicycles for short tours, safe-deposit boxes, on-property car rental, baby-sitting, **Keiki Aloha,** a special instructional day-camp program for children ages 5–12, and much, much more.

Mauna Lani Bay Hotel and Bungalows

As soon as you turn off Route 19, the entrance road, trimmed in purple bougainvillea, sets the mood for Mauna Lani Bay Hotel and Bungalows, 68-1400 Mauna Lani Dr., Kohala Coast, HI 96743, 808/885-6622 or 800/367-2323, website: www.maunalani.com, a 350-room hotel that opened in 1983. Enter through a grand portico, whose blue tile floor, a mimic of the ever-present sea and sky, immediately creates a sense of sedate but beautiful grandeur. Below is a central courtyard, where full-size palms sway amidst a lava-rock water garden; cascading sheets of clear water splash through a series of koi ponds, making naturally soothing music. A short stroll leads you through a virtual botanical garden to a white-sand beach perfect for island relaxation. Nearby are convoluted lagoons, and away from the shore you find the Tennis Garden, Racquet Club, a full-service health spa, exclusive shops,

and swimming pools. Surrounding the hotel is the marvelous Francis I'i Brown Golf Course, whose artistically laid-out fairways, greens, and sand traps make it a modern landscape sculpture.

The Mauna Lani offers superb dining options. The **Bay Terrace,** open daily for breakfast and dinner, offers the most casual dining, with a weekend seafood buffet that shouldn't be missed. The oceanfront **CanoeHouse,** open daily for dinner only, delights you with Pacific Rim cuisine. Up at the golf clubhouse overlooking the fairways, **The Gallery Restaurant** serves lunch and dinner, while **Knickers Bar and Lounge** serves libations. For lunch and cocktails, try the informal **Ocean Grill,** where you'll be comfortable in a bathing suit and cover-up, and for a perfect place to relax after a day of golf or tennis, seek out the **Honu Bar,** where you will find a pool table and an excellent selection of liqueurs, wine, and fine cigars.

Rooms at the AAA five-diamond award-winning Mauna Lani Bay Hotel run $300 garden view to $595 oceanfront, suites from $835, and one-, two-, and three-bedroom villas are $500–825. The exclusive two-bedroom bungalows rent for $4,000–4,500 a night but each comes complete with a personal chef, butler, and swimming pool. Weekly and monthly rates are available on the villas and bungalows; three-night minimum required. Rooms are oversized, the majority come with an ocean view, and each includes a private lanai, remote color TV and VCR, honor bar, in-room safe, and all the comforts of home. Guest privileges include complimentary use of the health spa (massage extra), snorkeling equipment, Hawaiian cultural classes, hula lessons, complimentary morning coffee, and resort and historic tours. For parents with young children who have come to the realization that "families who want to stay together don't always play together," the hotel offers a break from those little bundles of joy with the seasonal **Camp Mauna Lani Bay** for children ages 5–12. While you play, the kids are shepherded through games and activities. One of the favorite evening activities at the hotel takes place once a month at the Eva Parker Woods cottage. For this free event, Hawaiian musicians, dancers, and storytellers gather to share their cultural talents with community and resort guests. Ask the concierge for particulars.

Mauna Lani Condominiums

Sitting in the lap of luxury are two secure, private, modern, and very high-end condo properties. They are **Mauna Lani Point,** which is surrounded by golf fairways at oceanside, and **The Islands at Mauna Lani,** also surrounded by golf links but set away from the water. Each has superbly built, spacious units that leave nothing lacking. The Mauna Lani Point has one- and two-bedroom units that run $260–475 a night, while The Island rents one-bedroom units for $375–450, three-night minimum. All guests can make use of the activities and amenities within the Mauna Lani Resort complex. For reservations and information about either, contact Classic Resorts, 68-1050 Mauna Lani Point Dr., Kohala Coast, HI 96743, 808/885-5022 or fax 808/885-5015, website: www.classicresorts.com, email: info@classicresorts.com.

The Mauna Kea Beach Hotel

This hotel has set the standard of excellence along Kohala's coast ever since former Hawaii Governor William Quinn interested Laurance Rockefeller in the lucrative possibilities of building a luxury hideaway for the rich and famous. Beautiful coastal land was leased from the Parker Ranch, and the Mauna Kea Beach Hotel, 62-100 Kauna'oa Drive, Kohala Coast, HI 96743, 808/882-7222 or 800/882-6060, website: www.maunakeabeachhotel.com, opened in 1965. The Mauna Kea was the only one of its

kind for a few years, until others saw the possibilities, and more luxury hotels were built along this coast. Over the years, the Mauna Kea grew a bit aged and suffered stiff competition from newer resorts nearby. After an extensive restoration, the Mauna Kea reopened with youthful enthusiasm in December 1995 and shines again as the princess it always was. Class is always class, and the Mauna Kea again receives very high accolades as a fine resort hotel.

The Mauna Kea fronts the beautiful Kauna'oa Beach, the best on the island. Million-dollar condos also grace the resort grounds, and hotel guests tend to come back year after year. The hotel itself is an eight-story terraced complex of simple, clean-cut design. The grounds and lobbies showcase more than 1,000 museum-quality art pieces from throughout the Pacific, and more than a half million plants add greenery and beauty to the surroundings. The landings and lobbies, open and large enough to hold full-grown palm trees, also display beautiful tapestries, bird cages with their singing captives, and huge copper pots on polished brick floors. The award-winning Mauna Kea Golf Course surrounds the grounds, and a multi-court tennis park overlooks the ocean. Swimmers can use the beach or the round courtyard swimming pool, set just off the small fitness center, and horseback riding is available at the Parker Ranch up in Waimea. Perhaps the most unusual activity at the hotel is the evening manta ray viewing off Lookout Point.

The beach at the Mauna Kea, like others along this coast, will tempt swimmers and sunbathers alike.

One of the newest in Kohala, the Hapuna Beach Prince Hotel takes its rightful place among the luxury hotels along this coast.

ROBERT NILSEN

Exceptional food is served in this exceptional environment. Serving classic Euro-Asian cuisine for dinner only is the **The Batik,** the hotel's finest restaurant. For breakfast, lunch, or dinner in an open-air setting with grand views of the coast, try the **Pavilion** restaurant. **The Terrace** does lunch buffets, and the **19th Hole** is a more casual spot at the golf course clubhouse that serves food from the East and West through midday. Three lounges also grace the grounds, each with its own entertainment. At the Saturday-evening clam bake at the Hau Tree Cafe, you can feast on Maine lobster, garlic shrimp, and sumptuous steamed clams, and Tuesday evenings are extra special as a **luʻau** is performed at the Luʻau Gardens at North Pointe.

The beautifully appointed rooms, starting at $345, feature an extra-large lanai and specially made wicker furniture. From there, rates rise to $575 for better rooms, and suites run $570–1,150. They are, like the rest of the hotel, the epitome of understated elegance. A television-free resort at its inception, the hotel now has TVs in most of the rooms as part of the recent restoration.

Hapuna Beach Prince Hotel

Opened in 1994, the Hapuna Beach Prince Hotel, 62-100 Kaunaʻoa Dr., Kohala Coast, HI 96743, 808/880-1111 or 800/882-6060, website: www.hapunabeachprincehotel.com, fronts Hapuna Beach about one mile down the coast from the Mauna Kea Hotel. These two hotels, owned and operated by the Westin Hotel chain, are separate entities but function as one resort, joined as if in marriage. The princess, Mauna Kea, has finally found her prince. Long and lean, this hotel steps down the hillside toward the beach in eight levels. A formal portico fronts the main entryway, through which you have a splendid view of palm trees and the ocean. This entryway is simple in design yet welcoming in spirit. Chinese flagstone, stained reddish by iron oxide, paves the main entry floor. Walls are the color of sand, and the wood throughout is light brown or dark teak. Lines are simple and decoration subtle. An attempt has been made to simplify and let surrounding nature become part of the whole. As at the Mauna Kea, visitors are not overwhelmed with sensory overload. A shuttle connects the Hapuna Beach to the Mauna Kea and all services available at one are open to guests of the other.

Carpeted bedrooms are spacious, allowing for king-size beds, and the bathrooms have marble floors. Each well-appointed room has an entertainment center, comfy chairs, live plants, prints on the walls, and a lanai. Although rooms are air-conditioned, they all have louvered doors, allowing you to keep out the sun while letting breezes flow through. Rates for the 350 guest rooms start at $345 and go up to $520 a night; suites run $1,000–6,500.

Of the hotel's four restaurants, the **Coast Grill** is its signature establishment. It specializes in fresh seafood and meat dishes and is only open for dinner; reservations are recommended. The **Hakone** serves not only a Japanese buffet—an unusual treat and perfect opportunity to sample a variety of Japanese foods at one sitting—but offers individual entrées and items from its sushi bar. Resort evening attire is required. In the clubhouse, **Arnie's** serves standard American and health-conscious food and caters mainly to the golfers. In addition, you can get lunch items, afternoon snacks, and drinks at the **Beach Bar** down by the pool. Aside from the Beach Bar, the Reef Lounge serves up tropical drinks and nightly entertainment. Every Friday is Paniolo Night, and this Western buffet and dinner show, served at the Kohala Gardens, is always a hit.

The **Westin Kids Club** at the Hapuna offers a reprieve to parents who desire some time away from their energetic kids. Children 5–12 years old can fill their time with fun activities and educational projects. For Mom and Dad are the links-style Hapuna Golf Course and the hotel's physical fitness center. While the fitness center has weights, its main focus is on dance, yoga, stretching, and alignment techniques, with various massage therapies also available. Set in the garden below the lobby, the swimming pool is great recreation during the day and reflects the stars at night.

Information
To generate a forum for information, the luxury properties of South Kohala have come together as the **Kohala Coast Resort Association.** This organization produces as full-color brochure about its member properties and the Kohala Coast area. For this brochure, write 69-275 Waikoloa Beach Drive, Kohala Coast, HI 96743, or call 800/318-3637. Alternately, look for the information on the Web at www.kkra.org.

OTHER ACCOMMODATIONS

Condominiums
Up the hill in Waikoloa Village, fronting the 9th fairway of the golf course, you'll find **Waikoloa Villas,** 808/883-9144, or call Marc Resorts at 800/535-0085 for reservations. Rates for these condo units are one bedroom $159–179, two bedrooms $179–199, and three bedrooms $229–259, with a two-night minimum stay. Amenities include two swimming pools, spa, nearby golf, and weekly maid service. All units are fully furnished with complete kitchens, TV, and washers and dryers. The condo offers a money-saving condo/car package. Check in at the Marc Resorts office in the Waikoloa Highlands Shopping Center, Suite 213.

Vacation Rental Agencies
Along with a few high-end condos, luxury resorts are the mainstay of accommodations in coastal South Kohala. There are, however, a number of vacation rental homes and individual condo units available for those who want more privacy but still want the sun. Try the following agencies for options.

Hawaii Vacation Rentals, 7 Puako Beach Dr., Kamuela, HI 96743, 808/882-7000, fax 808/882-7607, website: www.bigisland-vacation.com, email: seaside@aloha.net, handles properties almost exclusively in Puako, with a few others up and down the coast, that range from a studio cottage at $125 a night to a three-bedroom oceanfront mansion for $1,000 a night. A five-night minimum stay applies. This company also represents one or two units in Puako Beach Condominium, the only condo in this residential neighborhood and the only reasonably priced accommodation in this diamond-studded neck of the woods. The three-bedroom units run $125 a night, three nights minimum, with a kitchen, laundry, TV, and swimming pool.

For exclusive condo units and mansion-style homes at various resort complexes along the South Kohala Coast, try **South Kohala Management,** P.O. Box 384900 Waikoloa, HI 96738, 808/883-8500 or 800/822-4252, fax 808/883-9818, website: www.southkohala.com, email: skm@kona.net. It handles premium properties only, with three nights minimum for condos and five nights minimum for homes.

MacArthur & Company has offices at both the Orchid at Mauna Lani Hotel and in Waimea at the Historic Spenser House, 65-1148 Mamalohoa Highway, Kamuela, HI 96743, 808/885-8885 or 808/881-1550, website: www.letsgohawaii.com, email: mary@letsgohawaii.com. MacArthur manages numerous rental homes

BIG ISLAND

mostly in the Kohala resort area, Puako, and Waimea with a few others in North Kohala and south in Kona, that range $60–1,000 a night.

Aldridge Associates, 808/883-8300, has vacation rentals in Waikoloa.

FOOD

Except for a few community-oriented restaurants in Waikoloa Village, a handful of reasonably priced roadside restaurants in Kawaihae, and a gaggle of eating establishments in the King's Shops, all of the food in South Kohala is served in the elegant but expensive restaurants of the luxury resorts. The resort hotels also provide the lion's share of the entertainment along the coast, mostly in the form of quiet musical combos and dinner shows. The following is a sampling of the very limited food options in South Kohala, independent of that offered at the luxury resorts, hotels, and condominiums.

Restaurants at the King's Shops

Hama Yu Japanese Restaurant is open daily 11:30 A.M.–3 P.M. and 5:30–9 P.M. With strikingly contemporary decor, Hama Yu serves authentic Japanese cuisine that's not cheap. Choose appetizers like soft-shell crab, yakitori, and a variety of sashimi and sushi. Dinners, mostly $20–26, include tempura, Japanese steak, and *tonkatsu*. Sit at western-style tables or choose the sushi bar.

The Grand Palace Chinese Restaurant, open daily 11 A.M.–9:30 P.M., serves appetizers ranging from deep fried won ton for $5 to a cold platter for $16. Soups run $9 for pork with mustard cabbage all the way up to $56 for shark's fin soup with shredded crabmeat. Chicken and duck dishes range from $9 for sweet and sour chicken to $48 for a whole Peking duck. Seafood includes sautéed shrimp with asparagus for $15 and squid with bean sprouts for $10. There are also your standard beef, pork, and vegetable dishes, as well as the unusual hot pot dishes and sizzling platters. With over 150 items on the menu and prices that are above average, this is not your ordinary Chinese restaurant but a dining experience.

The **Big Island Steakhouse,** featuring the Merry Wahine Bar, is open daily from 5 P.M.,

serving items like a *pu pu* platter with baby-back ribs, sashimi, and a variety of salads from simple onion and tomato to aloha salads with fish, chicken, or beef. Entrées, mostly $15–20, include Thai pasta with stir-fry vegetables and coconut prawns, but the menu is heavy on the red meats.

Newest to the King's Shops is **Roy's Waikoloa Bar and Grill,** 808/886-4321, well known throughout the islands for blending ingredients from East and West. Roy's produces imaginative cuisine that will titillate your taste buds. The menu changes daily and always features nightly specials, but some of what you might expect to find are cassoulet of escargot appetizers and ginger chicken and sesame shrimp salad. For main entrées, look for braised garlic parmesan lamb shank, lemongrass chicken breast, and blackened *'ahi.* Most dinner entr'es are in the $15–25 range, with lunches somewhat less. Open 11:30 A.M.–2 P.M. and again 5:30–9:30 P.M.; reservations recommended.

For a smaller and more moderately priced meal try **Hawaiian Chili by Max,** a window restaurant where you can have a variety of chilis and hot dogs, all well prepared and healthy. A separate area called **The Food Pavilion** will satisfy anyone on the run with everything from a Subway Sandwich to pizza and espresso coffee.

Beach Grill

More than just a clubhouse eatery, the Beach Grill restaurant at the Waikoloa Beach Course golf clubhouse, 808/886-6131, is a diverse dining establishment with a better than average wine list. Lunch items are mostly light sandwiches and burgers, *pu pu,* soup, and salads, with few surprises, but dinner is a different story. Here you can order fresh catch done any number of ways at market price, Hawaiian *huli huli* chicken, herb-crusted pork chops, scampi Alfredo, or saut'ed calamari, mostly in the $15–21 range. Each dinner comes with potatoes, rice, vegetables, and warm bread. The Beach Grill is conveniently located for all guests at Waikoloa Resort and is open for lunch 11 A.M.–4 P.M., dinner 5:30–9:30 P.M., and for appetizers and cocktails until midnight.

Blue Dolphin Restaurant

In Kawaihae Village along Route 270 is the Blue Dolphin, 808/882-7771, open for lunch

Mon.–Fri. 10:30 A.M.–2 P.M., for dinner Mon.–Sat. 5–9 P.M. The menu features the house shrimp salad, a variety of burgers, and sandwiches that mostly run under $9. It also serves plate lunches such as teriyaki beef or chicken and chicken lu'au. Dinner, $10–15, begins with the soup of the day and appetizers like sautéed mushrooms and fresh ceviche. Hawaiian entrées include *kalua* pork and mixed Hawaiian plate, with specialties like sautéed prawns and scallops, barbecued ribs, and a vegetarian mixed plate. If you're heading north and want to picnic along the way, the Blue Dolphin will be happy to pack things to go. While the food is okay, the Blue Dolphin is perhaps best known for its music. It keeps the beat cool with blues and jazz on Friday nights from 7 P.M. and rock and roll on Saturday.

Café Pesto

Who'd expect an upscale yuppie restaurant in the sleepy village of Kawaihae? Café Pesto, 808/882-1071, open Sun.–Thurs. 11 A.M.–9 P.M., Fri.–Sat. 11 A.M.–10 P.M., has a chic interior design with black-and-white checkerboard flooring and black tables trimmed with wood, similar to its sister café in Hilo. The bold gourmet menu tantalizes you with starters like *crostini* (French bread with a fresh, creamy herb garlic butter) and freshly made soups from $3.25. Daily specials might be wild green salad, bleu Caesar salad, or Greek pasta salad. Pasta dishes are scrumptious, including smoked-salmon pasta with mushrooms and sun-dried tomatoes, and fettuccine in saffron cream sauce. Lunch, served 11 A.M.–4 P.M., brings an assortment of hot sandwiches that includes everything from smoked ham to a chicken pita. Café Pesto also serves gourmet pizza with crust and sauces made fresh daily, all ranging in price up to about $20. Among its best pizzas are shiitake mushrooms and artichokes with rosemary Gorgonzola sauce. Dinner entrées are wild, with North Kohala fresh catch that can be grilled, seared, or sautéed for $19–22, and seafood risotto sumptuous with morsels of Keahole lobster, tiger prawns, jumbo scallops, and Pahoa corn all seared with sweet chili for $19. Café Pesto is a perfect place to stop for a civilized meal as you explore the Kohala Coast.

Kawaihae Harbor Grill

This restaurant in Kawaihae serves lunch 11:30 A.M.–2:30 P.M. and dinner daily 5:30–9:30 P.M.; 808/882-1368. Climb the steps to the large veranda from where you have a bird's-eye view of Kawaihae and unfortunately an unobstructed view of the petrochemical tanks across the road. Dinners include harbor grill *lau lau,* which is fresh catch, scallops, and crab steamed in *ti* leaves; steak and seafood combo; *huli*-style half chicken; and charbroiled rib eye steak, all $11–23. Lighter fare is also offered like a *pu pu* sampler, veggie platter, and crab cakes. Inside, the one-time village store is quite tasteful, with *lau hala* mats, lava lamps, and a glass partition that has been etched with an octopus and tropical fish. The Kawaihae Harbor Grill is tasteful and presented with pride.

Tres Hombres Beach Grill

Pancho Villa in aloha shirt and sombrero and riding a surfboard (!) would be instantly at home in Tres Hombres, 808/882-1031, in the Kawaihae Center, open 11:30 A.M.–midnight, dinners to 9 P.M. on weekdays and to 10 P.M. weekends. Besides being a south-of-the-border restaurant, Tres Hombres is an unofficial surfing museum filled with a fine collection of surfboards and surfing memorabilia donated by such legendary greats as Dewey Weber, Greg Knoll, and Jack Wise. The bamboo-appointed interior has a relaxed tropical effect. The extensive menu offers antojitos such as nachos, nachitos, calamari, and chimichangas for under $11. Substantial meals include all the Mexican favorites for $8–14, plus the grill also offers fish in tomato and pepper onion sauce, shrimp basted in lime butter, honey mustard chicken, and more unusual items like crab enchiladas and fish tacos, for up to $20. The full bar serves not only a range of beers and all the island favorites, but adds special concoctions like the Kawaihae Sunsets that will help you go down for the evening, and Mauna Kea Sunrises that, with a great deal of wishful thinking, will pop you back up. *Pu pu* are served 3–6 P.M. daily. Relax with an ice-cold margarita on the lanai of this casual restaurant, and experience an excellent change of pace from the luxury hotels just down the road.

BIG ISLAND

Roussels Waikoloa Village

For those wanting to stay along the coast, Roussels is a bit out of the way, but for those willing to venture inland, the restaurant lies like a pot of gold at the end of the rainbow. In Waikoloa Village, turn onto Paniolo Avenue, then onto Lua Kula Street, and finally onto Malia Street and follow it to the golf course clubhouse where the Roussels sign will direct you to the restaurant. Roussels, 808/883-9644, is open seven days a week, for lunch 11 A.M.–2:30 P.M., appetizers 2–9:30 P.M., and dinner Tues.–Sat. 5–10 P.M. Reservations recommended. Roussels' niche is spicy Cajun food. It's the only restaurant on the island whose main emphasis is food from the Creole South. The shrimp, oyster, and okra gumbo at $6 a cup is outstanding and a specialty, as is the shrimp Creole for $17. Whet your appetite with sautéed escargot in garlic butter or crabmeat crepe, $8–9. A salad selection is the next course before you move to the Cajun entrées, which include chicken Pontalba, duck in orange sauce, trout meunière amandine, and blackened fresh catch, $16–25. All entrées are served with salad, vegetables, and fresh-baked bread. Complement the meal with a choice wine, choose from an assortment of cakes, pies, and mousses baked daily, and end with a wonderful liqueur. Lunches are a bit faster and geared toward the local golf clientele. Salads, burgers, and sandwiches are main menu items, but a few dinner selections also appear on the lunch menu in smaller, less expensive portions. This is upscale Cajun cooking in an upcountry island setting.

Lu'au

A sumptuous old-style feast is held at the **Kona Village Resort.** It's worth attending this lu'au just to visit and be pampered at this private hotel beach. Adults pay around $73, children 6–12 $45, children 2–5 $22. Held every Friday, by reservation only, 808/325-5555. The *imu* ceremony is at 6:30 P.M., followed by cocktails; the lu'au stars at 7 P.M. and the entertainment gets going at 8 P.M. The Kona Village Resort lu'au has been happening every Friday night for over 30 years, making it the longest-running lu'au on the island.

The **Royal Lu'au** at the Outrigger Waikoloa Beach, 808/886-6789, is offered on Sunday and Wednesday from 5:30 P.M., with the *imu* cere-

mony beginning at 6 P.M. followed by an open bar, dinner, and Polynesian entertainment of song and dance. Prices are adults $55, children 6–12 $27, free for children five and under.

Legends of the Pacific at the Hilton Waikoloa Village is performed by Tihati Productions each Friday evening 6:30–8:30 P.M. A full buffet dinner, one cocktail, and a rousing show of Tahitian music and dance is performed at the Kamehameha Court on the resort grounds. Tickets are $58 adults, $25 kids 5–12. Call 808/886-1234 for reservations.

The Mauna Kea **Old Hawaii 'Aha'aina** Lu'au is presented every Tuesday at the North Pointe Lu'au Grounds. While dinner and entertainment start at 6 P.M., you may watch the *imu* preparation at 9 A.M. and the *imu* opening ceremony at 5:30 P.M. Dinner is a veritable feast, followed by entertainment by Nani Lim and her award-winning *hula halau.* Adults pay $68, children 5–11 are half price. For reservations, call 808/882-7222.

Put on your best cowboy duds and head on down to the **Paniolo Night** cookout and revue at the Hapuna Beach Hotel Kohala Garden. Not a typical Hawaiian lu'au, this is an old-fashioned Western cookout followed by music and entertainment with a country cowboy flair. Paniolo Night runs 6:30–9:30 P.M. every Friday; tickets are adults $68, children 5–12 $34. Don't dawdle like some pokey cow, call 808/880-3192 for reservations.

SHOPPING

The King's Shops

The Waikoloa Beach Resort community has its own small but very adequate shopping center. The King's Shops, open daily 9:30 A.M.–9:30 P.M., feature more than 40 different shops and restaurants, along with entertainment, special events, and a gas station. A number of Hawaiian artifacts and exhibits are displayed here and there around the center. Many shops carry clothing: **Crazy Shirts** has distinctive tops and tees; **Kunahs** has casual tropical wear, shorts, T-shirts, hats, and classic aloha shirts for men; **Noa Noa** has an excellent selection of imported fashions from throughout Southeast Asia; **Malia** carries fine women's wear; and **Kane By Malia** is for men. It's obvious what **Zac's Photo and**

Copy Center handles; **Whaler's General Store** carries light groceries and sundries; **Pacific Rim Collections** is where you will find Hawaiian quilts, masks from throughout the South Pacific, and carved whales and dolphins; and the **Endangered Species** shop stocks items from T-shirts to sculptures, many with an animal or floral motif, where a portion of the proceeds goes to the World Wildlife Foundation. For artwork, try either **Dolphin Galleries** or **Genesis Galleries; Under the Koa Tree** showcases Hawaiian artists who have turned their hands to koa woodwork and fine jewelry. The center wouldn't be complete without a place to eat, and you can find everything from fast food to a fine meal. There's something for everyone.

Although the schedule changes periodically, **free entertainment** is offered at the King's Shops every Tuesday 5:30–6:30 P.M. and Thursday 6–8 P.M. when a local *hula halau* comes to perform, and Sunday 4–6 P.M. when local musicians play traditional and contemporary Hawaiian music. These evenings are popular with both tourists and locals and are an excellent chance to have fun Hawaiian style.

Guided tours of native Hawaiian plants and the nearby petroglyph field start at 10:30 A.M. Tues.–Fri. from in front of the food pavilion. Additionally, a petroglyph tour also runs on Saturday from 8:30 A.M. These petroglyphs offer a link to the mythology and lore of ancient Hawaii. Wear comfortable clothing and bring water for this two-hour walk.

Kawaihae

The Kawaihae Shopping Center can take care of your rudimentary shopping needs. There's a **7-Eleven** convenience store, a gas station, a couple clothing shops, an ice cream parlor, and an art and gift shop, with restaurants on both levels. On your way through, you can also stop for fresh fish from local waters at **Laau's Fish Market,** open Mon.–Sat. 6 A.M.–6 P.M.

RECREATION

Golf

The resorts in South Kohala offer half a dozen of the best golf courses in the state, and they are all within a few miles of each other.

Surrounding the Mauna Lani Bay Hotel are the marvelous **Francis H. I'i Brown Golf Courses** (North and South courses), whose artistically laid-out fairways, greens, and sand traps make it a modern landscape sculpture. The courses are carved from lava, with striking ocean views in every direction. Call the Pro Shop at 808/885-6655 for information and tee times.

The Mauna Kea's classic, trend-setting **Mauna Kea Golf Course** was designed by the master, Robert Trent Jones, has been voted among America's 100 greatest courses and Hawaii's finest. It lies near the ocean and has recently been joined by the **Hapuna Golf Course,** designed by Arnold Palmer and Ed Seay, which has been cut into the lava up above the hotels. Both 18-hole courses give even the master players a challenge. For tee times at Mauna Kea, call 808/882-5400 and for Hapuna, call 808/880-3000.

Like rivers of green, the Waikoloa Beach **King's Golf Course** and **Beach Golf Course** wind their way around the hotels and condos of Waikoloa Beach Resort. Both have plenty of water and lava rock hazards. For the King's Course, call 808/886-7888 and for the Beach Course, call 808/886-6060.

Last to be constructed along the coast is the Four Seasons' **Hualalai Golf Club.** This Jack Niklaus course seems to be set in the starkest surroundings. Starting inland, you wind over the tortured lava, finally returning to the water. The Pro Shop handles reservations at 808/325-8480.

On the windy slope of Mauna Kea at Waikoloa Village is **Waikoloa Village Golf Club.** No slouch for difficulty, this Robert Trent Jones Jr. course is the most economical of the bunch. Call 808/883-9621 for a tee time.

If you are on vacation without your golf clubs and plan to play more than a round or two, consider renting clubs from **Island Discount Golf,** 75-5565 Luhia St., in Kailua-Kona, 808/334-1771, open daily. Rental rates start at $18 per day but go down for longer rental periods. These rental rates are cheaper than those at the golf courses.

Tennis

Virtually every hotel and condominium has at least a couple of tennis courts on its property. Most are for use by guests only, but a few tennis centers are open to the public, and these can always arrange lessons, round robins, and match play. All the following are non-lighted, day-use only courts. The Outrigger Waikoloa Beach Resort tennis center has six courts with a $10 daily court fee. Call 808/886-6666 for a court time. The most expensive in the area at $25 an hour are the eight courts at the Hilton Waikoloa Village Resort, 808/881-2222. Court time at the Mauna Lani Tennis Garden, 808/885-1485, is more reasonable at $8 an hour. With 13 courts, the largest court complex is at the Mauna Kea Beach Resort. Play for $10 a day; call 808/882-5420 to make arrangements.

Kohala Divers

In the Kawaihae Shopping Center, Kohala Divers, 808/882-7774, website: www.kohaladivers.com, email: theboss@kohaladivers.com, open daily 8 A.M.–5 P.M., is a full-service dive shop that offers scuba certification for $350, two-tank boat dives for $85, an introductory dive for $135, scuba rentals for $22, and snorkeling gear rentals for $10. If there's room on the boat, Kohala Divers will take snorkelers along for $40. Kohala Divers is also a retail shop where you can buy boogie boards, fins, masks, snorkels, and scuba equipment. If you are a scuba enthusiast, you can come here to get your tanks refilled or overhaul your diving gear. It's a bit far to go from Kailua-Kona—much closer from the Kohala resorts—but rates are competitive.

Outrigger Canoe Ride

A 35-foot replica double-hull outrigger sailing canoe takes guests for rides along the Kohala Coast. Be part of the crew for a voyage. Taking only up to six passengers, the *Hahalua Lele* leaves from the beach in front of the Orchid at Mauna Lani; rides cost $95 per person. At a quiet cove, the outrigger will stop for guests to snorkel and enjoy tropical island snacks. From January to April, the chance of seeing whales close up is good. Call 808/885-2000 for reservations and departure times.

Water Sports

For general water sports activities including scuba dives, snorkel gear rental and tours, catamaran or mono-hull sailing crusies, kayak rental, hydro bikes, boogie boards, windsurfing, and more, check with either **Ocean Sports Waikoloa**, 808/886-6666 or 888/724-5234, or **Red Sail Sports**, 808/886-2876 or 877/733-7245. These companies operate from 'Anaeho'omalu Beach, and Red Sail also has a few activities happening at Hapuna Beach.

BIG ISLAND

BOB RACE

WAIMEA

Waimea (also called Kamuela) is in the South Kohala District, but because of its inland topography of high mountain pasture on the broad slope of Mauna Kea, it can be considered a district in its own right. It also has a unique culture inspired by the range-riding *paniolo* of the expansive **Parker Ranch.** This spread, founded early in the 19th century by John Palmer Parker, dominates the heart and soul of the region. Waimea revolves around ranch life and livestock. Herds of rodeos and "Wild West shows" are scheduled throughout the year. But a visit here isn't one-dimensional. In town are homey accommodations and inspired country dining. For fun and relaxation there's a visitor and ranch center; Pu'opelu, the Parker mansion and art collection; a wonderful museum operated by John Parker's great-great-granddaughter and her husband; a litany of historic shrines and churches; and an abundance of fresh air and wide-open spaces, the latter not so easily found in the islands.

The town, at elevation 2,670 feet, is split almost directly down the center—the east side is the wet side, and the west is the dry side. Houses on the east side are easy to find and reasonable to rent; houses on the dry side are expensive and usually unavailable. You can literally walk from verdant green fields and tall trees to semi-arid landscape in a matter of minutes. This imaginary line also demarcates the local social order: upper-class ranch managers (dry), and working-class *paniolo* (wet). However, the air of Waimea, refreshed and cooled by *kipu'upu'u* (fine mists) and wind, combines with only 20 inches of rainfall a year into the best mountain weather in Hawaii. Waimea is also known as Kamuela, the Hawaiianized version of Samuel, after one of John Parker's grandsons. Kamuela is used as the post office address, so as not to confuse Waimea with towns of the same name on the islands of O'ahu and Kaua'i.

For decades, Waimea was a sleepy insular ranch community. World War II brought an end to its isolation as thousands of GIs descended on the town when Camp Tarawa was built for training. To cater to all these eager young men, the town had to gear up to provide services, which it did in a rousing way. After the war, the town settled back to its quieter times. Recently, Waimea has experienced a growth spurt. In 1980 it had no traffic lights and was home to about 2,000

BIG ISLAND

WAIMEA

To Hilo

BELT RD.

DON'S PAKE KITCHEN

19

DAN DE LUZ WOODS

KAMUELA LIQUOR

UILANI PLAZA

COOK'S DISCOVERIES

HAWAI'I

Kuhio Village

C&S OUTFITTERS

Police

'IMIOLA CHURCH

STATE OFFICES

FIRE STATION

PARKE RANCH STABLES

MEDICAL CENTER

SEE DETAIL

KAPIOLANI RD.

HOKUULA RD.

WAIALOA

WAIMEA PARK

PARKER SQUARE MALL

WAIMEA SCHOOL

KAWAIHAE

PANIOLO PARK

KAMUELA INN

LINDSEY RD.

MAMALAHOA HWY

RACE TRACK

MERRIMAN'S

OPELO PLAZA

OPELU RD.

EDELWEISS

WAIMEA VISITOR CENTER

WAIMEA COUNTRY STORE

LAE LAE RD.

PANIOLO PARK

JACARANDA INN

KAWAIHAE

Kohākōhau Stream

PARKER RANCH HISTORIC HOMES

190

To Kona

WAIMEA KOHALA AIRPORT

0   0.5 mi
0   0.5 km

MAMALAHOA

Halea'kā Gulch

Waikoloa Stream

POWER PLANT

KAMUELA MUSEUM

HAWAII PREP ACADEMY

250

AAAH, THE VIEWS

19

To Hawi

To Kawaihae

Kaʻauʻamano

DETAIL

KECK OBSERVATORY OFFICE

KOA GRILL

SPENSER HOUSE

WAIMEA CENTER

KAPIOLANI RD.

WAIMEA COUNTRY LODGE

PANIOLO COUNTRY INN

WAIMEA SCHOOL

LINDSEY RD.

WAIMEA PARK

PARKER RANCH SHOPPING CENTER

BANK

VISITOR CENTER

PARKER RANCH GRILL

NEW KAHILU THEATER

POST OFFICE

LIBRARY

TOWN HALL

MAMALAHOA HWY

people. Now the population has grown three-fold and there are traffic jams. Waimea is modernizing, and its cowboy backwoods character is rapidly changing.

Waimea is at the crossroads of the main east coast road (Route 19) from Hilo and Route 190 from Kailua-Kona. Route 19 continues west through town, reaching the coast at Kawaihae, where it turns south and cuts along the barren Kohala Coast to Kailua-Kona. The main artery connecting Waimea and Kailua-Kona is Route 190, also known as the Hawaii Belt Road. This stretch is locally called the Mamalahoa Highway. From Kailua-Kona, head out on Palani Road until it turns into Route 190. As you gain elevation heading into the interior, look left to see the broad and flat coastal lava flows. Seven miles before reaching Waimea, Saddle Road (Route 200) intersects this road from the right, and now the highlands, with grazing cattle amidst fields of cactus, look much more like Marlboro Country than the land of aloha.

The **Waimea-Kohala Airport,** 808/885-4520, is along Route 190 just a mile or so before you enter town. This airport is used by private planes and a few daily flights by a small commuter airline. Facilities amount to a waiting lounge and basic restrooms. Unless a flight is scheduled, even these may be closed.

HISTORY

John Palmer Parker was a seaman who left Newton, Massachusetts, on a trading vessel in 1809 and landed in Kealakekua, becoming a fast friend of Kamehameha the Great. Parker, then only 19, jumped ship and in 1816 married Kipikani, the granddaughter of King Kamehameha. Domesticated cattle, a present from Captain Vancouver to Kamehameha, had gone wild due to neglect and were becoming a dangerous nuisance all over the Big Island. Parker was hired to round up the best of them and to exterminate the rest. While doing so, he chose the finest head for his own herd. In 1847 King Kamehameha III divided the land by what was known as the Great Mahele, and John Parker was granted Royal Deed No. 7, for a two-acre parcel on the northeast slopes of Mauna Kea. His wife, being royal born, was

entitled to 640 acres, and with these lands and tough determination, the mighty Parker Ranch began.

Unfortunately, many members of the Parker family died young. The first-born, John Palmer Parker II, married Hanai. His brother, Ebenezer, married Kilea, an *ali'i* woman from Maui, who bore him four children. The oldest boy was Samuel Parker, known in Hawaiian as Kamuela, the co-name of Waimea town. Samuel married Napela, and together they had nine children. Samuel's father Ebenezer died at age 26. Kilea could never get over his death and visited his grave daily. Finally, she decided that she wanted to return to her family on Maui. She was advised by the people of the island not to go because of rough seas. Kilea did not heed the advice and along with her entourage was lost at sea.

John Palmer Parker II moved the family and ranch's central operation from the original homestead to Waimea in 1879. His wife, Hanai, gave birth to only one boy, who died within 12 months. Childless, they adopted one of their nephew Samuel's nine children as a *hanai* child, in a practice that continues to this day. He was the fifth child, John, who became John Palmer Parker III and who later married Elizabeth Dowsett, known as Aunt Tootsie. They had one girl, Thelma Parker, before John III died of pneumonia at age 19. Aunt Tootsie raised Thelma as a single parent and somehow managed to purchase Samuel Parker's and his eight children's half of the ranch. Thelma Parker married Gillian Smart. They had one boy, Richard Smart, before Thelma died at age 20 of tuberculosis. Aunt Tootsie literally took the bull by the horns to keep the ranch going, and when she passed away in 1943, she left everything to her grandson Richard. The ranch prospered under his ownership. After his death, the ranch became a charitable trust called the Parker Ranch Foundation Trust that benefits the people of Waimea and local communities long associated with its operation. Although the ranch at one time was a huge 500,000 acres, it is now down to 225,000 acres. When Richard Smart was alive, the Parker Ranch was the largest privately owned, single-owner ranch in the United States. Today, still at that size, it has 400 horses and 50,000 head of cattle that supply fully one-third of the beef in the Hawaiian Islands. The Parker Ranch Foundation Trust is the second largest landowner in the state, following the Bishop Estate. Find more information about the ranch and family at www.parkerranch.com.

SIGHTS

BIG ISLAND

Parker Ranch Historic Homes

Richard Smart, last heir to the gigantic Parker Ranch, opened **Pu'opelu,** a century-old family mansion, to the public just a few years before he passed away on November 12, 1992. On the grounds, the ranch's reconstructed original home is also open to visitors. Pu'opelu is off Route 190 a few minutes southeast of town and is open daily 10 A.M.–5 P.M., admission $7.50 adults, $5 children; 808/885-5433.

A formal drive lined with stately eucalyptus trees leads to the mansion. The home was begun in 1862 by an Englishman but bought by John Palmer Parker II in 1879. In 1910, Richard Smart's grandmother, Aunt Tootsie, added the living room, kitchen, and fireplace. In 1960, Richard Smart, who inherited the ranch lands and home from Aunt Tootsie, replaced the living room and raised its ceiling to 16 feet to accommodate his art collection, and he landscaped the grounds. He added elegant French doors and skylights, and the koa doorways were installed to match. Smart grew up in San Francisco and became enamored with the theater at a young age. He studied at the Pasadena Playhouse in the late '20s and later appeared on Broadway with such famous names as Carol Channing and Nanette Fabray. Smart performed in plays all over the United States, and recordings of his singing provide the background music as you tour the house.

Enter an elegant sitting room illuminated by a crystal chandelier to begin your tour. Inside this living museum, the works of prominent European artists are displayed, but since Smart's death, some artworks have been sold off and the collection diminished. The tour is self-guided, with all art pieces named. Besides paintings by famous artists, there are magnificent pieces of wooden furniture, tall cabinets holding yellow Chinese Peiping glass from the 19th century, silver tea sets, glassware, figurines, and magnificent chandeliers. Make sure to see the little side bedroom, called the Venetian Room, aptly decorated with paintings of gondolas and appointed with treasures from Venice. Lighting the room are two chandeliers, one pink and the other turquoise. Here, the filigreed art-deco mirrors are also fabulous. The feeling is of genteel elegance, but notice that the walls are rather rough board-and-batten covered with beautiful artwork. Recently opened is Richard Smart's bedroom, which is loaded with memorabilia from his stage performances and mementos given by the people he knew on Broadway. You get feeling of class, but it's obvious that you are on a ranch. In the emerald-green kingdom that is the Parker Ranch, Pu'opelu is the crown jewel.

Just outside Pu'opelu is the reconstructed New England "saltbox" **Mana Hale,** the original Parker Ranch homestead. The home was built in 1847 by family patriarch John Palmer Parker from the durable native koa found at high elevations on the ranch lands. The sons, who were by then married, built two homes, and as children came, added more rooms in the sprawling New England tradition. They also built one large community kitchen, at which the entire family cooked and dined. A replica shows how the home grew over the years, and it is a good indicator of how the Parker fortunes grew along with it. As the children's children got older, they needed a schoolhouse, so they built one at the corner of the original site. It still stands and is maintained by a *paniolo* and his family who live there. The exterior of the original home, covered by a heavy slate roof, was too brittle to move from its original site 12 miles away, but the interior was removed, numbered, and put back together again like a giant jigsaw puzzle in the reconstructed home. A model in the living room shows you what the original site looked like back in the 1800s. To preserve the rich wood interior of the home, all that's required is to wipe it down once a year with lemon oil. At first the home seems like a small cabin, just what you'd expect from the 1850s, but in actuality it's a two-story home with one bedroom downstairs and three upstairs.

SIGHTS IN TOWN

Parker Ranch Visitor Center and Museum

This is the first place to stop while in town. The visitor center, 808/885-7655, at the Parker Ranch Shopping Center, is open daily 9 A.M.–5 P.M. (last tickets sold at 4 P.M.); admission is adults $5, children $3.75. Tickets for joint admission to the museum and Pu'opelu are $10 for adults. After spending an hour at the center's museum and taking in the slide presentation, you'll have a good overview of the history of the Parker Ranch and, by extension, Waimea. Exhibits at the John Palmer Parker Museum depict the history and genealogy of the six generations of Parkers who have owned the ranch. In the museum, old family photos include one of Reverend Elias Bond, who presided over the Christian marriage of John Palmer Parker and his Hawaiian wife in 1820. Preserved also are old Bibles, clothing from the era, and an entire koa hut once occupied by woodcutters and range riders. There are fine examples of quilting, stuffed animals, an arsenal of old weapons, and even a vintage printing press. The 15-minute video in the comfortable Thelma Parker Theater begins whenever enough people have assembled after going through the museum. The video presents a thorough and professional rendition of the Parker Ranch history, along with sensitive glimpses of ranch life of the still very active *paniolo*. To the rear of the shopping center is an old wood-and-stone corral.

There isn't much happening around the old town entertainment-wise, but free hula lessons are given at the Parker Ranch Visitor Center on Monday afternoons.

'Imiola Church

Head east on Route 19 to "church row," a cluster of New England-style structures on the left, a few minutes past the Parker Ranch Visitor Center. Most famous among these old structures is 'Imiola (Seeking Life) Congregational Church. It was built in 1855 by the Reverend Lorenzo Lyons, who mastered the Hawaiian language and translated some of the great old Christian hymns into Hawaiian, as well as melodic Hawaiian chants into English. Restored in 1976, the yellow clapboard church with white trim would be

at home along any New England village green. When you enter, you'll notice an oddity: the pulpit is at the near side and you walk around it to face the rear of the church. The walls and ceilings are of rich brown koa, but the pews, supposedly of the same lustrous wood, have been painted pink! The hymnals contain many of the songs translated by Father Lyons. Outside is a simple monument to Reverend Lyons, along with a number of his children's gravesites. A tour of the church is free, and definitely worth the time.

Also in this row are the **Ka Ola Mau Loa** Hawaiian Church, and the Kamuela Hongwanji Mission.

Kamuela Museum

The Kamuela Museum, 808/885-4724, open every day of the year 8 A.M.–5 P.M., the largest privately owned museum in Hawaii, is a fantastic labor of love. For the octogenarian owners, founders, and curators, Albert and Harriet Solomon, it's a vocation that began in 1968 and fulfilled a prophecy of Albert's grandmother, who was pure Hawaiian and a renowned *kahuna* from Pololu Valley. When Albert was only eight years old, his grandmother foretold that he would build "a great longhouse near three mountains and that he would become famous, visited by people from all over the world." This prediction struck him so much that he wrote it down and kept it throughout his life. When grown, he married Harriet, the great-great granddaughter of John Palmer Parker, and the two lived in Honolulu for most of their adult lives, where Albert was a policeman. For 50 years the Solomons collected, collected, and collected! Harriet, being a Parker, was given heirlooms by family members, which are also on exhibit. The museum is west of town center on Route 19, 50 yards west of the junction with Route 250 heading toward Hawi. Admission to the museum, dedicated to Mary Ann Parker, John Parker's only daughter, is adults $5, children under 12, $2. Plan on spending at least an hour.

As you enter, the screen door bangs like a shot to signal Albert and Harriet that another visitor has arrived. Inside it's easy to become overwhelmed as you're confronted with everything from sombreros to a stuffed albatross, moose head, and South American lizard. An ex-

Tapa beaters and konane boards are all part of the amazingly diverse collection at the Kamuela Museum.

ROBERT NILSEN

tensive weapons collection includes Khyber rifles, Japanese machine guns, swords, and knives. If you enjoy Hawaiiana, check out the *kahili* and *konane* boards, poi pounders, stone sinkers and hooks, wooden surfboards, and a very unique "canoe buster." The museum has a few extremely rare stone idols and a good collection of furniture from Hawaiian nobility, including Prince Kuhio's council table. Antiques of every description include Japanese and Hawaiian feath-

ered fans, carved Chinese furniture, a brass diving helmet, some of the first Hawaiian Bibles, and even buffalo robes used by the pioneers. Everywhere are old photos commemorating the lives of the Parkers down through the years. Before you leave, go into the front room, where the view through a huge picture window perfectly frames a pond and three round-topped mountains in *paniolo* country.

PRACTICALITIES

ACCOMMODATIONS

Inns

As far as staying in Waimea is concerned, you won't be plagued with indecision. Of the three inns in town, two are basic and clean, with moderate rates; the third is a well-heeled renovated ranch home.

$50–100

The **Kamuela Inn,** P.O. Box 1994, Kamuela, HI 96743, 808/885-4243 or 800/555-8968, fax 808/885-8857, website: www.hawaii-bnb.com/kamuela.html, email: kaminn@aloha.net, a one-time basic cinder-block motel, has been transformed into a bright and airy 31-unit boutique hotel. It is down a short cul-de-sac off

Route 19 just before Opelu Road. Office hours are 7 A.M.–8 P.M. The owner takes personal pride in the hotel and offers each guest a complimentary continental breakfast. The pleasant grounds are appointed with flowers and manicured trees, and you'll find a swing to lull you into relaxation. The basic motel rooms are small, neat, and tidy with twin or double beds with wicker headboards, private bathrooms, and color TV, but no a/c (not needed) or phones. About one-third of the units have kitchens. The deluxe Penthouse is upstairs and breaks into two joinable units that can accommodate up to five guests. A new wing features the deluxe Executive Suites. This wing has tasteful larger rooms with hardwood floors, king-size or twin beds, a full kitchen in the executive suites, and a small anteroom that opens onto a private lanai, perfect for a quiet morning breakfast. Prices range from $59 for a basic room to $89–99 for suites with kitchenettes, and $185 for the deluxe suites. Reserve well in advance.

The Waimea Country Lodge, 65-1210 Lindsey Rd., Kamuela, HI 96743, 808/885-4100, fax 808/885-6711, is in downtown Waimea, but don't let "downtown" fool you because it's very quiet. Renovated in 1997, the rooms, many with kitchenettes and vaulted ceilings, have full baths and are well appointed with knotty pine furnishings, king- or queen-size beds with turned pine lamps at each end, wicker easy chairs, phones, and TVs. The barn-red board-and-batten inn sits off by itself and lives up to its place in *paniolo* country by giving the impression of a gentleman's bunkhouse. Rates are $84 standard, $90 superior, $98 with a kitchenette, $108 deluxe, and $10 for an additional person.

$150–200

Built in 1897 as the Parker Ranch manager's house, this plantation estate has gone through several metamorphoses and recently been extensively renovated and turned into **The Jacaranda Inn,** 65-1444 Kawaihae Rd., Kamuela, HI 96743, 808/885-8813, fax 808/885-6096, website: www.jacarandainn.com, email: tji@jacarandainn.com. This estate, with its racp berry-colored roof, dominates a broad lawn. A white ranch fence and bougainvillea hedge separate it from the road. Amidst towering trees, the main house retains the original Hawaii Victorian flavor, with rich koa wood and numerous antiques. Enter the huge living room with its imposing fireplace, and from there you can move to the dining rooms, library, billiard room, bar, or terrace. Separate oversized suites have also been constructed to the rear as guest rooms. They are all decorated according to different themes and colors, and while each shows individual character and style, they all have a similar romantic feel. These are not ordinary rooms; they are designed to pamper guests in luxury. The eight guest rooms, with pretty flower names like White Lily, Iris, Orchid, and Passion Flower, rent for $189–245 a night, three nights minimum, continental breakfast included. A separate guest cottage with three bedrooms and three baths, living room, full kitchen, and hot tub runs $400–650, five-night minimum.

Bed-and-Breakfasts

No place could be more appropriately named than **aaah, The Views,** P.O. Box 6593, Kamuela, HI 96743, tel./fax 808/885-3455, website: www.beingsintouch.com, email: tommare@aloha.net. This bed-and-breakfast, in a quiet residential neighborhood just downhill from central Waimea, has unimpeded views of Mauna Kea, Mauna Loa, and Mt. Hualalai to the south, and, of course, the ocean off the Kohala Coast to the west. Fine for the sunrise over the mountains, the sunsets on clear days are stupendous, and clear nights illuminate a star-studded sky. Aaah, The Views sits along a stream next to Parker Ranch land, so you may see cattle grazing nearby. Rooms in the two-bedroom suite of the detached house can be booked individually or together. Each has a sleeping room with a cozy loft and a small deck, and they share a good-sized bathroom with tub and shower. New and modern, these rooms are tastefully appointed and laid with berber carpet. While each room has a small refrigerator, microwave unit, and coffeemaker, a continental breakfast with plenty of fruits, pastries, cereals, and coffee is served each morning in the main house dining area or on a lanai that overlooks the stream. Room rates for two are $65–110, add $15 for an additional person.

For additional B&B options, try **Hawaii's Best Bed and Breakfast,** P.O. Box 563, Kamuela, HI 96743, 808/885-4550 or 800/262-9912, fax 808/885-0559, website: www.bestbnb.com, email: bestbnb@aloha.net. This Waimea business run by Susan Campbell has listings all over the state.

FOOD

Inexpensive

Daizen Okazuya is a simple restaurant known for its healthy Japanese food. Open Mon.–Fri. 5 A.M.–3 P.M., Saturday from 8 A.M. Take-out is available.

Also in the Waimea Center is **Young's Kalbi,** a Korean restaurant open daily except Monday, which serves dishes like *kalbi* chicken, shrimp tempura, oyster-sauce chicken, and spicy pork, all priced under $8. Young's is very basic but clean, and the food is good.

The cafeteria-style **Kamuela Deli,** offers sirloin steak, grilled ham steak, and boneless spicy chicken, all priced around $7. They also have breakfasts like corned beef hash or hamburger patties with eggs and hash browns. Deli sandwiches, priced under $5, include teriyaki beef, shrimp burgers, and ham sandwiches. Plate lunches are also available.

Don's Pake Kitchen, about two miles east of town on Route 19, open daily 10 A.M.–9 P.M., has a good reputation for food at reasonable prices even though most of its selections are of the steam-table variety. Chef's specials are ginger beef, oyster chicken, and shrimp-sauce pork, but many people come for the saimin. Don's also specializes in large pans of food that can feed entire families.

Waimea Coffee Company, in the Parker Square, is open Mon.–Fri. 7 A.M.–5 P.M., Saturday 8 A.M.–4 P.M. Order coffee beans in bulk and coffee by the cup. Lunch is served 11 A.M.–3 P.M., including turkey, ham, or tuna sandwiches, Caesar salad, quiches, and homemade soups.

The **Hawaiian Style Café,** in a modest building across from Parker Square, open Mon.–Fri. 6 A.M.–12:45 P.M., Sunday 7:30–11:30 A.M., and 4–8 P.M. Wed.–Sat., offers local and American standard food at very reasonable prices. Inside the blue-painted interior, short diner stools line a counter where the menu offers breakfasts of two eggs with Spam or bacon, a three-egg omelette with a side of pancakes, Hawaiian-style loco moco, and Belgian waffles with whipped butter, strawberries, and maple syrup, mostly under $6. Plate lunches, around $7, served with rice and potato or macaroni salad include broiled mahimahi, beef and tripe stew, or a steak plate. A little short on Martha Stewart panache but long on pride, the Hawaiian Style Café will fill you up while being easy on your wallet.

Perhaps slightly ignominiously located across from the Opelo Plaza along Route 19 at the Waimea Country Store and gas station is **Monroe's,** basically a pizza and espresso bar that also does hearty breakfasts, plate lunches, soups, salads, and sandwiches. Breakfast starts at 6:30 P.M.; dinner runs until about 9 P.M. Monroe's is a very local eatery that puts out tasty food in large portions. Anything on the menu can be ordered for take-out.

Moderate

Paniolo Country Inn, on Lindsey Street, 808/885-4377, open daily for breakfast, lunch, and dinner, specializes in full country-style breakfasts, burgers, lunch platters, and flame-broiled steaks. Breakfast selections include omelets, hot cakes, waffles, huevos rancheros, loco moco, and the *wikiwiki* breakfast of English muffin, banana bread or wheat toast, coffee, and small fruit juice. Breakfast selections generally run $3–7. Sandwiches and burgers cost around $7, with cowboy-size pizza for $6–27. More substantial Paniolo Platters like teriyaki short ribs, top sirloin, or porterhouse steak mostly go for $9–22. Prime rib dinners are served Fri.–Sun. evenings. The food is wholesome, the atmosphere American country, and the service prompt and friendly.

Maha's Cafe, in the vintage Spencer House at the Waimea Center, 808/885-0693, open daily except Tuesday 8 A.M.–4:30 P.M., offers island-style food made fresh daily. The owner, "Maha," learned to cook for her large Hawaiian family but has worked professionally as a pastry chef and a sous chef at a number of resorts including the Mauna Lani Bay Resort. Maha's has window service but also sit-down service inside. From her diminutive kitchen comes breakfasts of poi pancakes with coconut syrup for $3.50 and an assortment of too-tempting pastries including homestyle banana bread, papaya coffeecake, croissants, or pan biscuits $2.50, and always-fresh Kona coffee. Lunch can be Waipio Ways, a plate of broiled fresh fish with sliced and steamed Waipio taro and sweet potato on a bed of Kahua greens with ginger vinaigrette dressing for $9, smoked 'ahi with *lilikoi* salsa at $11, or Kohala Harvest, a vegetarian delight mounded with vine-ripened tomatoes, Waimea broccoli, mushrooms, cucumbers, bell peppers, sweet onions, spinach, and clover sprouts for $8. Aloha Ahiahi, a version of afternoon tea served 3–4:30 P.M., brings a sampler of Maha's pastries, including croissants, open-faced finger sandwiches, shortbreads, and cobblers. The classic and restored Spencer House was the first frame house ever built in Waimea, in 1852. Once the home of a Judge Bickerton, it was also put to use as a courthouse and as a hotel. The house was once surrounded by the lush green grasses of *pan-*

iolo country but is now in the middle of the black asphalt of the Waimea Center's parking lot!

Aioli's Restaurant, at Opelo Plaza, 808/885-6325, serves quick but tasty soups, salads, and sandwiches for lunch. The dinner menu changes every two weeks, and there is always a vegetarian entrée or two on the menu. Open daily except Monday, open just 8 A.M.–2 P.M. on Sunday.

Su's Thai Kitchen, 808/885-8688, long known in Kailua-Kona for its delicious and moderately priced Thai cuisine, has opened a branch restaurant in the Parker Ranch Center, open daily 9 A.M.–9 P.M. American and island-style breakfasts served until 11 A.M. run $2–6. For lunch, 10 A.M.–3 P.M., Su's offers Japanese specials like a mini-tempura platter and sukiyaki, along with Hunan beef and an assortment of Thai lunch specials priced $5–8. Dinner starts with an extra-large *pu pu* platter for $11 and other appetizers and steaming bowls of different Thai soups for under $10. Savory curries—red, yellow, or green—can be made with a combination of scallops, crab, fish, and shrimp for $17, with most priced around $10. A specialty is Volcano fish, flash-fried and then topped with Su's homemade sweet and sour sauce. Su's, although very basic in its decor, continues to enjoy a well-deserved reputation for excellent food.

Also in the Parker Ranch Center is **Morelli's Pizza,** 808/885-6100, open daily from 11 A.M. Besides whole pizzas, the oven yields pizza by the slice, garlic bread, and oven-baked sandwiches like turkey, pastrami, ham, or veggie, most for around $7. The pizzas range from a small cheese pizza for $6 to a three-topping monster tray at $18. To round out your meal, you can also order garden and chef salads and homemade soup. A small dining room with picnic tables is provided if you choose to eat there.

Adjacent to Waimea Center is **Koa House Grill,** 808/885-2088, a well-liked casual place for steak, ribs, and seafood. This is good standard American food at moderate prices. Nearby in the Parker Ranch Center is **Parker Ranch Grill,** 808/887-2624, perhaps the town's premier steakhouse, with beef and prime rib from the Parker Ranch. Some fish items also appear on the menu, as the Grill is now associated with Huggos, a seafood restaurant on the coast in Kailua. This is a good-time place, with country decor and two fireplaces.

A newer place establishing a fine reputation is **Bree Garden Restaurant,** on Kinohou Street, 808/885-8849, open Mon.–Sat. 11 A.M.–2 P.M. and 5–9 P.M. The menu is varied Continental and tries to use locally grown ingredients.

Fine Dining

The Edelweiss on Route 19 across from the Kamuela Inn, 808/885-6800, is Waimea's established gourmet restaurant, where chef Hans-Peter Hager, formerly of the super-exclusive Mauna Kea Beach Hotel, serves gourmet food in rustic but elegant surroundings. The Edelweiss is open Tues.–Sat. for lunch 11:30 A.M.–1:30 P.M. and for dinner 5–9 P.M. Inside, heavy posts and beams exude that "country feeling," but fine crystal and pure white tablecloths let you know you're in for some superb dining. The wine cellar is extensive, with selections of domestic, French, Italian, and German wines. Affordable lunches include offerings like soup, turkey sandwiches, and chicken salad in papaya for under $10. Dinner starts with appetizers such as melon with prosciutto, escargot, onion soup, and Caesar salad. Some Edelweiss specialties are saut'ed veal, lamb, beef, and bacon with pfefferling; roast duck braised with a light orange sauce; half spring chicken diablo; and of course German favorites like Wiener schnitzel and roast pork and sauerkraut, mostly $16–22. The cooking is rich and delicious, the proof a loyal clientele who return again and again.

Merriman's, in the Opelo Plaza, 808/885-6822, has received a great deal of well-deserved praise from travelers and residents alike for its excellent food. The restaurant, resembling a small house from the outside, is stylish with pink and gray tablecloths, multicolored table settings, and cushioned chairs of bent bamboo. Here, chefs create fusion cuisine from local organic ingredients when available. The menu changes every few months, but perennial appetizer favorites ($6–11) are sweet corn and shrimp fritters, vine-ripened Lokelani tomatoes with Maui onions, and spinach salad with balsamic vinaigrette dressing. Lunch fare ($6–10) includes coconut curry grilled chicken with peanut dipping sauce and rice; grilled eggplant sandwich with Puna goat cheese, basil, and hot sauce; and grilled shrimp on Asian linguine. Entrées ($15–32) are superb: Peking duck and stir-fry noodles with lop chong sausage, vegetables, and spicy Hoisin sauce; wok-charred *ahi;* and prime New York steak. Vegetarians can graze on pan-fried Asian cake noodles and Kabocha pumpkin stew. Some of the most delicious offerings, however, are the fresh catch at market price, prepared in various gourmet styles including sesame-crusted and sautéed with *lilikoi* sauce, grilled in mango chutney and coconut lime sauce, or saut'ed with pineapple vinaigrette. Owned and operated by Peter Merriman, one of Pacific Rim Cuisine's originators, Merriman's is a Big Island classic. Open for lunch weekdays 11:30 A.M.–1:30 P.M. and dinner daily 5:30–9 P.M.; call for reservations.

RECREATION

You can pretend that you're a *paniolo* riding the range at the **Dahana Ranch,** 808/885-0057 or 888/399-0057.Spend a few hours tending cattle on this working ranch and learn about the history and culture of ranching the Big Island. Dahana Ranch will take just about anyone "three years to 300 pounds."

Kohala Carriages offers a tame 45-minute **ranch wagon tour** on Parker Ranch land, Tues.–Sat. every hour on the hour 10 A.M.–2 P.M., leaving from the Parker Ranch Visitor Center. Rides cost $15 adult, $12 seniors over 60, and $10 ages 4–11. Reserve a seat by calling 808/885-7655. This tour includes entrance to the Parker Ranch Visitor Center, entrance to the Parker Ranch Historic Homes, and lunch at the Parker Ranch Grill for $39.

Every 4th of July, the Parker Ranch hosts a **rodeo** that is one of the best in the state.

The best place in town to shop for good quality bikes, water gear, and camping equipment is **C & S Outfitters,** 808/885-5005, behind Cook's Discovery near the police station. This is a full-service shop that rents, sells, and repairs bicycles and stocks surfboards, body boards, and kayaks. Stop here first in you're in need of such things.

A few miles east of town on the way to Honoka'a is the **Waimea Country Club** golf course, a pleasantly rolling course carved from rangeland at over 2,000 feet in elevation. Enter between mile markers 51 and 52.

SHOPPING

Waimea's accelerated growth can be measured by the shopping centers springing up around town. These mostly small malls house new boutiques that add to the shopping possibilities in Waimea's established centers.

Parker Ranch Shopping Center

This long-established mall has more than 30 specialty stores selling shoes, apparel, sporting goods, toys, food, and art. Focused on its country cowboy heritage, the **Parker Ranch Store** sells boots, cowboy hats, shirts, skirts, and buckles and bows. Many handcrafted items are made on the premises. Open daily. **Keep In Touch** offers distinctive T-shirts and resortwear, and **Malia Kamuela** has racks of resortwear for women. **Waimea Design Center and Art Gallery,** 808/885-6171, has Asian handicrafts and Hawaiian koa bowls and furniture. The center has a handful of restaurants and quick food places. Nearby, the **Big Island Coffee Company** offers samples of pure Kona coffee that you can then purchase off the rack. Bulk coffee comes in tiny burlap bags holding eight ounces of whole beans, or in a gift pack for $10. Other savories include pineapple cookies, macadamia nuts, and chocolate-covered whole coffee beans that'll keep you zipping right along. Displays hold souvenirs like carved tikis, hula dancers, straw hats for men and women, T-shirts, and sweatshirts, with about 90 percent from the Big Island, or at least the Hawaiian Islands.

Waimea Center

Well marked along the Mamalahoa Highway behind McDonald's is Waimea's newest mall, with most stores open weekdays 9 A.M.–5 P.M. and Saturday 10 A.M.–5 P.M. Among its shops you will find a **KTA Super Store** with everything from groceries to pharmaceuticals; **Zac's Photo and Copy Center,** for developing and photo needs, copies, shipping, Internet access, and other business needs; **Mail Boxes and Business Center,** for similar business needs; **Healthways II,** open Mon.–Sat. 9:30 A.M.–6 P.M., Sunday 10 A.M.–4 P.M., a well-stocked natural foods store; the **Men's Shop,** whose name says it all; **Kamuela Kids** for children's clothing; **Rhythm and Read-**

ing, selling tapes, CDs, records, videos, and gifts; and the **Kamuela Hat Company,** which will cover your dome with Stetson hats, straw hats, and planter's hats for both men and women (*paniolo* oriented, this store is excellent if you're after Western wear). The Waimea Center also has some fast-food eateries and inexpensive restaurants.

Across the street is **Waimea Craft Mall,** where local artists display wood, ceramic, canvas, and fiber art. Here too you will find an outlet for Hawaiian chocolate.

Parker Square

Along Route 19, heading west from town center, this small mall has a collection of fine boutiques and shops. Here, the **Gallery of Great Things,** 808/885-7706, really is loaded with great things. Inside you'll find novelty items like a carousel horse, silk dresses, straw hats, koa paddles for $700, Ni'ihau shellwork priced $100–25,000, vintage kimonos, an antique water jar from the Chiang Mai area of northern Thailand for $925, Japanese woodblock prints, and less expensive items like shell earrings for $8 and koa hair sticks for $4. The Gallery of Great Things represents about 200 local artists on a revolving basis, and the owner, Maria Brick, travels throughout the Pacific and Asia collecting art. With its museum-quality items, the Gallery of Great Things is definitely worth a browse. But remember, all items are one of a kind—"now you see them, now you don't."

Sweet Wind, 808/885-0562, open daily, is packed with books, beads, and unique gifts. This "alternative thought and resource center" also sells incense, aromatherapy tinctures, and crystals. The beads come from the world over, and a display case holds Native American rattles, drums, and silver and amber jewelry. Visiting Sweet Wind is soothing for body and soul.

The **Silk Road Gallery,** 808/885-7474, open daily except Sunday, is resplendent with Asian antiques, specializing in ancient creations from Japan, China, and Korea. In this tasteful shop you will discover such treasures as carved ivory *netsuke,* a favorite of the well-dressed samurai; ornate silk kimonos; Sung Dynasty vases; and Satsumayaki painted pottery from Japan. As you look around you may spot lacquer tables and bowls, ornate *tansu* (chests), straw san-

dals, an actual water wheel, sacred scrolls that hang in a place of honor in Japanese homes, a Chinese jade bowl with elaborate dragon handles, and an 18th-century Chinese moghul lotus bowl. The owners make frequent trips to Asia, where they personally pick all the items in their shop, at which the artistic wonders of the ancient Silk Road are still on display.

Other stores in the center include **Bentley's Home and Garden Center,** with crockery, glassware, books, *lau hala* bags, and ceramics; **Imagination Toys,** hung with kites, Hawaiian dolls, stuffed gorillas, parrots, and puzzles; and **Waimea Coffee and Company,** for small estate Kona coffee and light food and drink. The **Waimea General Store** sells mostly sundries with plenty of stationery, children's games, stuffed toys, books on Hawaiiana, and gadgets.

Other Shops

The word *kama'aina* was invented with Patti Cook in mind. The proprietor of **Cook's Discoveries,** 808/885-3633, open daily 10 A.M.–6 P.M., Patti has filled her shop with personally chosen items displaying her impeccable taste and knowledge about all things relating to Hawaii. Everything inside Cook's Discoveries, fashioned by craftspeople from throughout the state, says "Hawaii." Shelves hold lustrous koa boxes, bracelets, cribbage boards, and pen sets, all easily transportable. Look for traditional pieces, including a carved ivory pendant (fossilized walrus tusk) representing a human tongue, the "voice of authority," traditionally worn only by the highest *ali'i,* hung from a necklace of woven black silk (substituting for human hair). Other traditional pieces are *lei o mano* (lei of sharks' teeth), a clublike war weapon yielded in battle or when absolute and immediate persuasion was necessary, *kukui* nut lei, distinctive warrior helmets with mushroom-like protuberances atop, poi bowls, and decorated gourds once used for food storage. Contemporary "made in Hawaii" articles include handmade coconut lotion and soap, plenty of jewelry, carved tiki walking sticks, and brush and mirror sets. You'll also find *mu'umu'u* and pareu in tropical designs and colors, T-shirts emblazoned with Nenewe the shark god, exquisite Hawaiian quilts, books on Hawaiian subjects, and gourmet jars of jams, jellies, and sauces made from *lilikoi, ohelo* berries, and

BIG ISLAND

Waimea's famous strawberries. This is one-stop shopping for memorable Hawaiian gifts. Look for Cook's kitty-corner from the police station, just beyond Imiola Church.

Who would have thought that one of the best wine and liquor stores on the island would be in a country town like Waimea? Look for **Kamuela Liquor Store** east along the highway just past Cook's Discovery. It's been in business since 1946.

Across from the liquor store is **Dan De Luz's Woods,** a fine shop selling bowls and small boxes made from native woods.

Food Markets

For food shopping try the **KTA Super Store** at the Waimea Center, for everything from groceries to pharmaceuticals. Also at the Waimea Center is **Healthways II,** open Mon.–Sat. 9:30 A.M.–6 P.M., Sunday 10 A.M.–4 P.M., with canned and boxed items, bulk foods including grain, flour, and pasta, a good selection of organic vegetables and produce, a cold case holding drinks and cheeses, and an excellent supply of vitamins and minerals. At the Parker Ranch Shopping Center, **Kamuela Meat Market** features fine cuts of Parker Ranch beef.

The **Waimea Homestead Farmers' Market** is held every Saturday 7 A.M.–noon, when local farmers come to sell their produce, much of which is organic. Flowers, baked goods, and crafts are usually available. Look for a dozen or so stalls in the parking lot of the Hawaiian Home Lands Building along Route 19, about two miles east of town center heading toward Honoka'a.

Alternately, try the **Parker School Farmers' Market,** held Saturday 8 A.M.–12 P.M. at the Parker School.

SERVICES AND INFORMATION

The full-service **North Hawaii Community Hospital,** 808/885-4444, is across from the Keck Observatory Office along Route 19. Physicians are available at **Lucy Henriques Medical Center,** 808/885-7921, and at the **Kaiser Permanente Waimea Clinic,** 808/881-4500.

Angela Longo, in the Kamuela Office Center, 808/885-7886, is a practitioner of acupuncture and a Chinese herbalist. Angela combines principles from both East and West into a holistic approach to health and well-being.

The **post office** is in the Parker Ranch Shopping Center. The U.S. Postal Service designates Waimea as Kamuela, so as not to confuse it with the Waimeas on O'ahu and Kaua'i.

The **Waimea Community Visitor Center,** 808/885-6707, is west of town along Route 19, next to Parker Square. Operated by the nonprofit Waimea Main Street organization, this office provides free maps and brochures of the area and public restrooms. This is a good stop to learn about the rich cultural history of the area and what's happening in town today. Be sure to pick up a copy of their informative *A Guide to the Heart of Historic Waimea* brochure.

The **police** and **fire departments** are in a new civic center across the highway from Church Row.

NORTH KOHALA

In North Kohala, jungle trees with crocheted shawls of hanging vines stand in shadowed silence as tiny stores and humble homes abandoned by time melt slowly back into the muted earth. This secluded region changes very little, and very slowly. It also has an eastward list toward the wetter side of the island, so if you're suffering from "Kona shock" and want to see flowers, palms, banana trees, and Hawaiian jungle, head for the north coast. Here the island of Hawai'i lives up to its reputation of being not only big, but bold and beautiful as well.

North Kohala was the home of Kamehameha the Great. From this fiefdom he launched his conquest of all the islands. The shores and lands of North Kohala are rife with historical significance, and with beach parks where only a few local people ever go. Here cattle were introduced to the islands in the 1790s by Captain Vancouver, an early explorer and friend of Kamehameha. Among North Kohala's cultural treasures is **Lapakahi State Historical Park,** a must-stop offering "touchable" exhibits that allow

you to become actively involved in Hawaii's traditional past. Northward is **Kamehameha's birthplace**—the very spot—and within walking distance is **Moʻokini Heiau,** one of the oldest in Hawaii and still actively ministered by the current generation of a long line of *kahuna.*

Hawi was a sugar town whose economy turned sour when the sugar mill stopped operations. Hawi is making a comeback, along with this entire northern shore, which has seen an influx of small, boutique businesses and art shops. In **Kapaʻau,** a statue of Kamehameha I fulfills the chief's ancestral dominions fulfills an old *kahuna* prophecy. On a nearby side road stands historic **Kalahikiola Church,** established in 1855 by Reverend Elias Bond. On the same side road is the old **Bond Homestead,** one of the most authentic missionary homes in all of Hawaii. The main coastal road ends at **Pololu Valley Lookout,** where you can overlook one of the premier taro-growing valleys of old Hawaii. A walk down the steep *pali* into this valley is a walk into timelessness, with civilization disappearing like an ebbing tide.

NORTH KOHALA

In Kawaihae, at the base of the North Kohala peninsula, Route 19 turns east and coastal Route 270, known as the Akoni Pule Highway, heads north along the coast. It passes through both of North Kohala's two major towns, Hawi and Kapa'au, and ends at the *pali* overlooking Pololu Valley. All the historical sites, beach parks, and towns in the following sections are along this route.

Route 250, the back road to Hawi, is a delightful country lane that winds through gloriously green grazing lands for almost 20 miles along the leeward side of the Kohala Mountains. It begins in the western outskirts of

Waimea and ends in Hawi. One of the most picturesque roads on the island, it's dotted with mood-setting cactus and small "line shacks." Vistas open to the west and far below are expansive panoramas of rolling hills tumbling to the sea. At mile marker 8 is **Von Holt Memorial Park,** a scenic overlook perfect for a high mountain picnic. Just outside Hawi, Route 250 splits; going right takes you to Kapa'au, left to Hawi. If you're coming along coastal Route 270 from Kapa'au toward Hawi, look for the H. Naito Store, and make a left there to go back over Route 250 to Waimea; you don't have to go all the way to Hawi to catch Route 250.

Upolu airstrip is a lonely runway at Upolu Point, the closest spot to Maui. A sign points the way at mile marker 20 along coastal Route 270. Here, you'll find only a bench and a public telephone. The strip is serviced only on request by small propeller planes.

KAWAIHAE COAST

Lapakahi State Historical Park

This 600-year-old reconstructed Hawaiian fishing village, combined with adjacent **Koai'e Cove Marine Conservation District,** is a standout hunk of coastline 12 miles north of Kawaihae. Gates are open daily except holidays 8 A.M.–4 P.M. for a self-guided tour, but the ranger's knowledgeable anecdotes make a guided tour much more educational.

The small grass shack near some *lau hala* trees at the entrance stocks annotated brochures and yellow water jugs. As you walk counterclockwise around the numbered stations, you pass canoe sheds and a fish shrine dedicated to Ku'ula, to whom the fishermen always dedicated a portion of their catch. A salt-making area demonstrates how the Hawaiians evaporated seawater by moving it into progressively smaller "pans" carved in the rock. There are numerous homesites along the wood-chip trail. Particularly interesting to children are exhibits of games like *konane* (Hawaiian checkers) and *ulimika* (a form of bowling using stones) that the children are encouraged to try. Throughout the area, all trees, flowers, and shrubs are identified, and as an extra treat, migrating whales come close to shore December–April. Don't leave without finding a shady spot and taking the time to look out to sea. For information write Lapakahi State Historical Park, P.O. Box 100, Kapa'au, HI 96755, 808/889-5566.

Mahukona and Kapa'a Beach County Parks

Mahukona Beach County Park is a few minutes north of Lapakahi down a well-marked side road. As you approach, notice a number of abandoned buildings and warehouses; Mahukona was once an important port from which the Kohala Sugar Co. shipped its goods. Still there is a pier with a hoist used by local fishermen to launch their boats. The harbor is filled with industrial debris, which makes for some good underwater exploring, and snorkeling the offshore reef rewards

you with an abundance of sealife. Only 150 yards offshore (follow the anchor chain from the landing) in only 20 feet of water lie the remains of a wrecked steamboat, the only wreck in Hawaii that's accessible from shore. The wooden boat has almost completely deteriorated, but you will find a huge boiler, engine, shaft, and propeller. Swimming off the pier is also good, but all water activities are dangerous during winter months and high surf. Picnic facilities include a large pavilion and tables. There are also cold-water showers and restrooms, and electricity is available in the pavilion. Although numerous signs close to the pavilion say No Camping, both tent and trailer camping are allowed with a county permit near the parking lot.

Kapa'a Beach County Park is five minutes farther north. Turn *makai* on a side road and cross a cattle grate as you head toward the sea. This park is even less visited than Mahukona. The rocky beach makes water entry difficult. It's primarily for day use and fishing, but there are showers, a restroom, and a pavilion. Camping is allowed with a county permit. Neither of these two beaches is spectacular, but they are secluded and accessible. If you're interested in a very quiet spot to contemplate a lovely panorama of Maui in the distance, this is it.

Mo'okini Heiau and Kamehameha's Birthplace

At mile marker 20, turn down a one-lane road to Upolu airstrip. Follow it until it reaches the dead end at the runway. Turn left here on a *very* rough dirt road to Mo'okini Heiau—this road may not be passable. This entire area is one of the most rugged and isolated on the Big Island, with wide windswept fields, steep seacliffs, and pounding surf. Pull off at any likely spot along the road and keep your eyes peeled for signs of cavorting humpback whales, which frequent this coast November–May. After bumping down the road for about two miles, look for a tall transmission

BIG ISLAND

tower pointing its bony metal finger skyward, which marks the road to the *heiau*. Sometimes the road is closed with a locked gate and you'll have to walk five minutes uphill to gain access, but if the gate is open, you can drive in.

Only *ali'i* came to the *heiau* to purify themselves and worship, sometimes offering human sacrifices. In 1963, Mo'okini Heiau was the first Hawaiian site to be listed in the National Historical Sites Registry. Legend says that the very first temple at Mo'okini was built as early as A.D. 480. This incredible date implies that Mo'okini must have been built immediately upon the arrival of the first Polynesian explorers, who many scholars maintain arrived in large numbers a full two centuries later. More believable oral history relates that the still-standing foundation of the temple was built by the Tahitian high priest Pa'ao, who came with conquering warriors from the south in the 12th century, bringing the powerful *mana* of the fierce war-god Kuka'ilimoku. The oral tale relates that the stones for the temple were fitted in a single night, passed hand to hand by a human chain of 18,000 warriors for a distance of 14 miles from Pololu Valley. They created an irregular rectangle measuring 125 by 250 feet, with 30-foot-high and 15-foot-thick walls all around.

When you visit the *heiau,* pick up a brochure from a box at the entrance (often empty); if none are available, a signboard nearby gives general information. Notice that the leeward stones are covered in lichens, giving them a greenish cast and testifying to the age of the *heiau*. Notice a huge, flat stone near another embedded in the ground with the menacing atmosphere of a sacrificial altar. Nearby is a clone of the famous "Phallic Rock" on Molokai. Please be respectful as you walk around, as this temple is still in use, and stay on the designated paths that are cordoned off by woven rope. To the rear is an altar area where recent offerings are often seen; the floor of the temple is carpeted with well-placed stones and tiny green plants that give a natural mosaic effect. For at least eight and perhaps 15 centuries, members of the Mo'okini family have been the priests and priestesses of the temple. Today, the inherited title of *kahuna nui* rests with Leimomi Mo'okini Lum, a nearby resident. The entire *heiau* is surrounded by a wave-like hump, perhaps the remnant of an earlier structure, that resembles a castle moat. Be sure to visit the nearby "little grass shack," one of the best examples of this traditional Hawaiian architecture in the islands. Check how sturdy the walls are, and what excellent protection is provided by the grass-shingled roof. Also, be aware of the integration of its stone platform and how perfectly suited the shack is to provide comfort against the elements in Hawaii. Look through the door at a timeless panorama of the sea and surf.

A minute from the *heiau* along the dirt road, an HVB Warrior points to Kamehameha's birthplace,

Mo'okini Heiau

J.D. BISIGNANI

Kamehameha 'Akahi 'Aina Hanau. The entrance to the area is at the back side, away from the sea. Inside the low stone wall, which always seems to radiate heat, are some large boulders believed to be the actual "birthing stones" where the high chieftess Kekuiapoiwa, wife of the warrior *ali'i* Keoua Kupuapaikalananinui, gave birth to Kamehameha sometime around 1752. This male child, born as his father prepared a battle fleet to invade Maui, would grow to be the greatest of the Hawaiian chiefs—a brave, powerful, but lonely man, like the flat plateau upon which he drew his first breath. The temple's ritual drums and haunting chants dedicated to Ku were the infant's first lullabies. He would grow to accept Ku as his god, and together they would subjugate all of Hawaii. In this expansive North Kohala area, Kamehameha was confronted with unencumbered vistas and sweeping views of neighboring islands, unlike most Hawaiians, whose outlooks were held in check by the narrow, confining, but secure walls of steep-sided valleys. Only this man with this background could rise to become "The Lonely One," high chief of a unified kingdom.

Together, Mo'okini Heiau and King Kamehameha's birthplace make up the seven-acre **Kohala Historical Sites State Monument.**

NORTH COAST TOWNS

HAWI

As you come into Hawi along Route 270, you'll see a line of false-front buildings leaning shoulder-to-shoulder like patient old men knowing that something *will* happen, and it has! One of the buildings is an ancient movie theater that still shows films. Introducing you to the town are Sacred Heart Church and Hawi Jodo Buddhist Mission, two lovely temples of worship and symbols of Hawaii's diversified spirituality. In the middle of town, Route 250, crossing the Kohala Mountains from Waimea, intersects the main road.

Hawi was once a bustling sugar town that boasted four movie theaters in its heyday. In the early 1970s, the Kohala Sugar Co. pulled up stakes, leaving the one-industry town high and dry. Still standing is the monumental stack of the sugarworks, a dormant reminder of what once was. The people of Hawi have always had grit, and instead of moving away they toughed it out and have revitalized their town. Spirit, elbow grease, and paint were their chief allies. Hawi has risen from its slumber and is now making a comeback with new restaurants and shops opening their doors. Here, too, are a handful of local shops selling food and household goods, an information center, the only functioning hotel in North Kohala, and some remarkable crafts shops and boutiques.

The Kohala Visitor Center dispenses maps, information, and *aloha.* It's open daily just near the junction of Routes 270 and 250 in Hawi. Next door is the local laundromat, a semi-open-air affair that is open just about all the time. The area post office is a large new facility on Route 270 between Hawi and Kapa'au just near the H. Naito Store.

Accommodations

The 18-room **Kohala Village Inn,** 55-514 Hawi Rd., Hawi, HI 96755, 808/889-0419, was long known as Luke's Hotel. The hotel has always catered to local working people or island families visiting the area, as well as passing tourists. In central Hawi, it has a quiet little courtyard and in-room TVs. Rooms are a reasonable $47–77. Clean and adequate, the hotel has a friendly, quiet atmosphere.

Perhaps the most luxurious rental in this area is **Hale Puu Mamo,** a new architectural residence set above a horse pasture near Opolu Point, overlooking the channel toward Maui. This modern three-bedroom, two-bath house has all the comforts of home in an expansive setting. Rent is $250 a night, five night minimum. Contact MacArthur and Company, 808/885-8885.

Halfway between Hawi and Kapa'au, *mauka* of the highway in a residential neighborhood, is **Cook's Cottage,** a studio with a full kitchen and bath, TV, and laundry facilities, available for $60 a night or $315 a week. Contact Sue Cook at 808/889-0912.

Food

A glowing example of Hawi's modern restoration and revitalization is the **Bamboo Restaurant,** 808/889-5555, open Tues.–Sat. 11:30 A.M.–2:30 P.M. for lunch, 6–8:30 P.M. for dinner, and Sunday for brunch 11 A.M.–2 P.M., with live music on Friday and Saturday evenings. This venerable old building was built by the Harada Family 1911–1915, serving as a hotel that housed contract workers brought to North Kohala by buckboard and later relocated to work camps. As the sugar trade took root, merchants came to town, and the hotel began catering to this more upscale clientele. These traveling salesmen were the epitome of the stereotype, and they desired evening entertainment. "Ladies of the night" took up residence in a few back rooms, and, with the proximity to the cane fields, might aptly have been known as "sugar babies." The fortunes of the Harada family took a turn for the worse, and the building was bought in 1926 by the Takata family, who converted it to a grocery and dry goods store that served the community until 1991, when they moved, building a new store just down the road. The old building fell into disrepair but was reopened as a restaurant after 16 months of restoration. New touches were added, like the old wicker chairs that once rocked wealthy vacationers into a light slumber at Waikiki's Moana Hotel, but they left the best alone, preserving the original feel of the building. Upon entering, notice the floor, heavily trodden over the decades, every nick marking a memory. The original wavy window glass is intact and still bears the original painted signs reading, "Fruits, Groceries, Cigars, Candy, Meats, and Coca Cola." The restaurant section, to the left as you enter, is perfect for an evening of dining; to the right and upstairs are galleries selling artworks. Browse before or after dinner and appreciate that this little community is finding a way to restore itself.

Lunch at the Bamboo can be homemade soup or one of several salads. More substantial dishes are *kalua* pork and cabbage, stir-fried noodles, and Hawaiian tostada with vegetarian chili, and there is also an assortment of sandwiches and burgers. Dinner begins with *pu pu* such as margaritaville prawns and calamari strips or seared *poke.* From the ocean comes shrimp and fresh catch at market price, in different preparations like herb-grilled in Thai flavors, baked in a sesame and nori crust, or sautéed and covered with margarita sauce and mango relish, all in the $13–20 range. From the land comes flame-broiled rib-eye steak, leg of lamb, or pineapple barbecued chicken, $15–22; local-style stir-fry noodles run $8–11. Sunday brunch is a crowd-pleaser, with the regular lunch menu plus platters like eggs Bamboo—poached egg on a toasted English muffin with a slice of smoked ham, *kalua* pork, or vegetables and topped with *lilikoi* hollandaise sauce and served with fried potatoes or rice. While not too expensive, the food at the Bamboo Restaurant is the finest on the north coast.

Sun, surf, and the trek to Hawi made you a bit droopy? Salvation is at hand at the **Kohala Coffee Mill** in downtown Hawi, open daily. Inside the remodeled vintage building, order Kona coffee, espresso, cappuccino, pastries, and soft drinks. Shelves hold T-shirts, herbal teas, fruit jelly and jam, and honey.

For a south-of-the-border taste treat, stop at **Hula La's Burrito Bar,** 808/889-5668, across the street from the coffee shop. Hula La's is known for its gut-filling burritos, tasty concoctions with beans, pork, chicken, or fish, fresh greens, other tasty morsels, and homemade salsa, $5–7. The Mexican-style plate lunch is also filing. If a burrito or plate lunch sounds like too much, choose a quesadilla or an order of nachitos, nachos, or tacos. At this neat little eatery you can fill up for under $7 and be on your way in no time. Open daily for lunch and dinner, 11 A.M.–6 P.M.

Recreation

There is little in the way of organized recreation along the north coast, but what there is can be exciting. Perhaps the most unusual activity is a kayak ride down a section of the Kohala Ditch. Specially designed inflatable kayaks put in above Makapala and drift down the flume, into and out of tunnels and over gullies for about three miles. Prepare to get wet. Morning and afternoon rides are offered, $75 per person. Make reservations with **Kohala Mountain Kayak Cruise,** 808/889-6922, website: www.kohalakayaks.com, or stop into its office up from the banyan tree in the center of Hawi.

ATV Outfitters Hawaii will take you to out-of-the-way places on former Kohala sugar plantation land on its rugged four-wheel motorcycles. Contact ATV Outfitters at 808/889-6000, website: www.outfittershawaii.com.

Hawaii Forest and Trail offers a hiking experience along the Kohala Ditch trail to Kopoloa waterfall at the back of the Pololu Valley and a mule ride down the steep cliff face to the Pololu Valley floor and beach. Contact Hawaii Forest and Trail, 808/322-8881 or 800/464-1993.

Aside from these outdoor opportunities, the **Kahei Theater** on the west end of town in Hawi shows first-run movies Fri.–Sun. only; admission is $5 general, $4 seniors, $3 children 11 and under.

Shopping

The **Nakahara Store** has been serving people of Hawi for decades, near the main intersection in town. One part of the store has groceries, while the other is a basic dry goods shop. **K. Takata** store is the best-stocked grocery store in Hawi. It's along the highway in a new building east of the town center. **Kohala Health Food** in downtown Hawi, to the side of the Kohala Coffee Mill, is open daily until 6 P.M. A small but growing establishment, its shelves hold herbs, vitamins, minerals, some packaged natural foods, and local organic produce and fruit when available. The juice bar in the back will mix up a refreshing drink from fresh local fruit. **Pumehana Flowers,** 808/889-5541, is alive with flowers and plants. Inside are small gift items and a cooler holding lei, perfect for brightening the day of that "special person," and perhaps for brightening the evening prospects for you. **Kohala Trade Center,** a basic convenience store in downtown Hawi, is open Mon.–Fri. 10 A.M.–10 P.M., Saturday 11 A.M.–10 P.M., and Sunday noon–8 P.M.

Proof that two establishments can occupy the same place at the same time, the **Kohala Koa Gallery,** 808/889-0055, open Monday 10 A.M.–5 P.M., Tues.–Sat. 10 A.M.–9 P.M., Sunday 10 A.M.–4 P.M., shares the vintage N. Takata Building with the Bamboo Restaurant. Living up to its name, the gallery is lustrous with all types of koa artwork: furniture, covered photo albums, jewelry boxes, and sculptures, representing the work of more than 70 island artists. The furniture is mainly by Michael Felig, who creates rocking chairs that beg to be sat in and fine koa dining room ta-

bles. Works of other well-known artists on display include lovely boxes, creamy white hand-thrown crystalline-glazed ceramics with flower or fish motifs, tapa-covered notebooks, replicas of sailing canoes, a smattering of aloha shirts, hand-painted silkwares, jewelry with an ocean motif, and bright prints.

A brightly painted sign marks the entrance to **Hawaiian Moon,** 808/889-0880, open Mon.–Sat. 10 A.M.–5 P.M., Sunday 10 A.M.–4 P.M. Small, but packed with arts, crafts, and clothing, the shop displays the artistic woman's touch. Racks hold sundresses, pareu, shoulder bags, aloha shirts, and shorts. Look for a shelf of chubby women dolls, their hair done in silver and red foil, that are as cute as . . . chubby little women dolls! Artists include: Omodt, a husband and wife team that creates very distinctive low-fired pottery pieces, primarily in black and white or blue, including paperweights, earrings, and clocks, all with an island motif; Himani, who does hand-tinted, original black-and-white photos of Hawaiian dancers; Pacini, another husband and wife ceramic artist team making vases and sculptures with Hawaiian themes; and Steven Hatland (how did he pass the one-name requirement?), a ceramic artist who employs a distinctive blue and blue-green glaze on everything from fruit bowls to water pitchers. Smaller souvenir items include shell key chains, stuffed fish, leather bracelets, jewelry, and paperweights.

As Hawi Turns is a small but intriguing shop for women's fashions and distinctive crafts.

For handcrafted works of art in clay, have a look at **Sugar Moon.** This small gallery features the works of owners Tom and Julie Kostes.

KAPA'AU

Kapa'au is a sleepy community, the last town for any amenities on Route 270 before you reach the end of the line at Pololu Overlook. There's a gas station, grocery store, library, bank, and police station. Most young people have moved away seeking economic opportunity, but the old folks remain, and macadamia nuts are bringing some vitality back into the area. Here too, but on a smaller scale than in Hawi, local artists and some new folks are starting shops and businesses catering to tourists. The main attraction in town is **Kamehameha's statue,** in front of the Kapa'au Courthouse. The statue was commissioned by King Kalakaua in 1878, at which time an old *kahuna* said that the statue would feel at home only in the lands of Kamehameha's birth. Thomas Gould, an American sculptor living in Italy, was hired to do the statue, and he used John Baker, part Hawaiian and a close friend of Kalakaua, as the model. Gould was paid $10,000 to produce the remarkable and heroic sculpture, which was sent to Paris to be cast in bronze. It was freighted to Hawaii, but the ship carrying the original statue sank just off Port Stanley in the Falkland Islands, and the nine-ton statue was thought lost forever. With the insurance money, Gould was again commissioned and he produced another statue that arrived in Honolulu in 1883, where it still stands in front of the Judiciary Building. Within a few weeks, however, a British ship arrived in Honolulu, carrying the original statue, which had somehow been salvaged and unceremoniously dumped in a Port Stanley junkyard. The English captain bought it there and sold it to King Kalakaua for $850. There was only one place where the statue could be sent: to the then-thriving town of Kapa'au in the heart of Kamehameha's ancestral homelands. Every year, on the night before Kamehameha Day, the statue is painted with a fresh coat of house paint; the bronze underneath remains as strong as the great king's will.

Kamehameha County Park, down a marked side road, has a full recreation area, including an Olympic-size pool open to the public, basketball courts, and weight rooms in the main building along with outside tennis courts with night lighting and a driving range. There are a kiddie area, restrooms, and picnic tables, all free to use.

Kalahikiola Church

A few minutes east of town an HVB Warrior points to a county lane leading to Kalahikiola Congregational Church. The road is delightfully lined with palm trees,

pines, and macadamias like the formal driveway that it once was. Pass the weathering buildings of the Bond Estate and follow the road to the church on the hill. This church was built by Reverend Elias Bond and his wife Ellen, who arrived at Kohala in 1841 and dedicated the church in 1855. Reverend Bond and his parishioners were determined to overcome many formidable obstacles in building Kalahikiola (Life from the Sun) Church, so that they could "sit in a dry and decent house in Jehovah's presence." They hauled timber for miles, quarried and carried stone from distant gulches, raised lime from the sea floor, and brought sand by the jarful all the way from Kawaihae to mix their mortar. After two years of backbreaking work and $8,000, the church finally stood in God's praise, 85 feet long by 45 feet wide. The attached bell tower, oddly out of place, looks like a shoebox standing on end topped by four mean-looking spikes. Note that the doors don't swing, but slide—some visitors leave because they think it's locked. Inside, the church is dark and cool and, inexplicably, the same type of spikes as on the bell tower flank both sides of the altar. There is also a remarkable koa table. Pamphlets describe the history of the church.

The Bond Estate

The *most* remarkable and undisturbed missionary estate still extant in Hawaii (and one of two undisturbed mission districts in the world—the other is in Nepal) is the old Bond Homestead and its attendant buildings, including the now defunct but partially renovated Kohala Girls' School and the Kalahikiola Church. All three of these wonderful structures are on the National Historical Register. No tours are given, but you can have a look at the outside of the buildings on the homestead grounds and at the girls' school.

Keokea Beach County Park

Two miles past Kapa'au toward Pololu you pass a

Once the center of North Shore community life, the Bond Estate now waits patiently for a rebirth.

BIG ISLAND

small fruit stand and an access road heading *makai* to secluded Keokea Beach County Park. The park, on the side of the hill going down to the sea, is very picturesque and luxuriant. It is a favorite spot of North Kohala residents, especially on weekends, but it receives little use during the week. The rocky shoreline faces the open ocean, so swimming is not advised except during summer calm. There are a pavilion, restrooms, showers, and picnic tables. A county permit is required for tent and trailer camping.

Accommodations

In the village of Niuli'i, on the road down to Keokea Beach Park is **Kohala's Guest House,** P.O. Box 172 Hawi, HI 96719, 808/889-5606, fax 808/889-5572, website: http://home1.gte.net/ svendsen.index.htm, where you have a choice of studio or home. The studio comes with a queen-size bed and bath, kitchenette, color TV, and private entrance. The house has a full kitchen, living and dining areas, TV, and laundry facilities. The studio rents for $59 a night, and the house $45–125, depending on the number of bedrooms you need.

Above Kapa'au is the **Kohala Country Adventures Guest House,** an island-style home with three units that could be your base for exploring North Kohala. The largest unit has a living and dining area with TV, kitchenette, sun deck, and bedroom with king-size futon at $105

a night, multiple-night rentals preferred. The garden room, with its queen-size bed, also has a deck off the bedroom and rents for $85. Basically a room and a bathroom, the economy room rents for $60. Add $5 if you wish to have a light continental breakfast in the morning. Each unit has its own private entrance. For reservations, call Bobby Moreno at 808/889-5663 or go to www.kcadventures.com.

Food

Don's Family Deli, 808/889-5822, open daily for breakfast and lunch until 6 P.M., across the street from the Kamehameha Statue in Kapa'au, is a taste of New York in North Kohala. How can a visit to tropical paradise be complete without bagels and lox, lasagna, or a thick slice of quiche? Don's features Dreyer's ice cream, coffee and cappuccino, and homemade biscotti filled with nuts and that zesty anisette flavor. Don's will also fix you up with a tofu or mahimahi burger and offers a wide selection of meats and breads if you prefer to design your own picnic lunch.

Matthew's Place, 808/889-5500, open daily, offers local food, seafood, and pizza. You can't go wrong at this simple, clean, good, and inexpensive restaurant.

Shopping

For food shopping in Kapa'au try **Union Market,** along Route 270 coming into Kapa'au,

ROBERT NILSEN

Accessible by a trail over private land, Kapaloa Falls is the pearl of upper Pololu Valley.

808/889-6450, which sells not only general merchandise and meats, but also a hefty assortment of grains, nuts, fruits, and locally made pastries and breads. **H. Naito Store** is a general grocery, dry goods, and fishing supplies store in Kapa'au, 808/889-6851. The **Kamehameha Pharmacy** in downtown Kapa'au is a full-service pharmacy, 808/889-6161.

In Kapa'au, across from the Kamehameha statue, is **Ackerman Gallery**, 808/889-5971, open daily 9 A.M.–5:30 P.M., owned and operated by artist Gary Ackerman. Besides showcasing his own sensitive, island-inspired paintings, he displays local pottery, carvings, and one-of-a-kind jewelry. He also carries a smattering of artwork from throughout the Pacific. The artwork selections are tasteful and expensive. You can also choose a reasonably priced gift item, especially from the handmade jewelry section. Check out the display of beautiful hand-blown

glass by a local artist named Yamazawa. The distinctive, iridescent glaze is achieved by using volcanic cinders—you can bring home a true island memento that includes a bit of Madame Pele herself. Gary has expanded by opening another Ackerman Gallery just down the street. This lovely gallery, housed in an early-20th-century building, showcases the fine art of local island artists.

In the renovated Nanbu Hotel building in town is **Kohala Book Shop,** 54-3885 Akoni Pule Highway, Kapa'au, HI 96755, 808/889-6400, fax 808/889-6344, email: kohalabk@gte.net, reputedly the largest used bookstore on the state. It handles fiction and nonfiction, rare and unusual books, books on Hawaii and the Pacific, and even some cards and other gift items. Thousands of volumes line the shelves, and if you can't find what you're looking for, the owners will try to locate a copy by searching their sources for it. You can also search their listing of books by logging onto the www.abebooks.com website and finding the Kohala Book Shop link.

The **Rankin Fine Art Gallery,** 808/889-6840, occupies the historic Wo On (Harmony and Peace) General Store in Makapala, which served the Chinese community during plantation days. This gallery displays a wide range of island-inspired paintings and pottery and some cowboy art. Next door is lovely and historically significant **Tong Wo Temple** and cemetery, well worth a visit.

POLOLU VALLEY

Finally you come to Pololu Valley Overlook. It's about 12 miles from Pololu to Waipi'o Valley, with several deep-cut valleys in between, including the majestic Waimanu, the largest. From the lookout it takes about 15 minutes to walk down to the floor of Pololu. The trail is well maintained as you pass through a heavy growth of *lau hala,* but it can be slippery when wet. At the bottom is a gate that keeps grazing animals in; make sure to close it after you! **Kohala Ditch,** a monument to labor-intensive engineering, runs to the rear of these valleys. It carried precious water to the sugar plantations,

BIG ISLAND

and today carries adventurous kayakers for a very unusual thrill ride. Pololu and the other valleys were once inhabited and were among the richest wet taro plantations of old Hawaii. Today, abandoned and neglected, they have been taken over by introduced vegetation. The black-sand beach fronting Pololu is lined with sand dunes, with a small sandbar offshore. The rip current here can be very dangerous, so enter the water only in summer months. The rip fortunately weakens not too far from shore; if you're caught, go with it and ride the waves back in. Many people hike into Pololu for seclusion and back-to-nature camping. Make sure to boil the stream water before drinking. Plenty of wild fruits can augment your food supply, and the shoreline fishing is excellent.

BIG ISLAND

HAWAII STATE ARCHIVES

BIG ISLAND

THE SADDLE ROAD

Slicing across the midriff of the island in a gentle arch from Mamalahoa Highway near Waimea to Hilo is Route 200, the Saddle Road. Everyone with a sense of adventure loves this bold cut across the Big Island through a broad high valley separating the two great mountains, Mauna Loa and Mauna Kea. Along it you pass rolling pastureland, broad swaths of lava flows, arid desert-like fields that look a bit like Nevada, a *nene* sanctuary, trailheads for several hiking trails, mist-shrouded rain forests, an explorable cave, and spur roads leading to the tops of Mauna Kea and Mauna Loa. Here as well is the largest military training reserve in the state, with its live firing range, and the Bradshaw Army Airfield. What you won't see is much traffic or many people. It's a great adventure for anyone traveling between Kona and Hilo. Keep your eyes peeled for convoys of tanks and armored personnel carriers as they sometimes sally forth from Pohakuloa Military Camp, and also watch out for those who want to make this a high-speed shortcut from one side of the island to the other.

Road Conditions

The Saddle Road was constructed in 1942 and left as gravel until about 20 years ago. While the road up both sides is at a good incline, the saddle itself is reasonably flat and at about 6,000–6,500 feet. Car rental companies cringe when you mention the Saddle Road. Most still do not allow their cars on this road even though it is paved and well engineered. Check your rental agreement, as it'll be very specific on this point. They're terrified you'll rattle their cars to death. For the most part, these fears are groundless, as there are only short sections that may be rough, due mostly to military use. By and large, it's a good road, no worse than many others around the island—the Hilo side is wider and has better shoulders than the Kona side. However, it *is* isolated, and there are no facilities whatsoever along its length. If you do have trouble, you'll need to go a long way for assistance, but if you bypass it, you'll miss some of the best scenery on the Big Island. On the Kona side, the Saddle Road turnoff is about six miles south of Waimea along Route 190, about halfway between

© SANDRA E. BISIGNANI TRUST AND AVALON TRAVEL PUBLISHING, INC.

BIG ISLAND

Waimea and Waikoloa Road. From Hilo, follow Waianuenue Avenue inland. Saddle Road, Route 200, also signed as Kaumana Drive, splits left after about a mile and is clearly marked. Passing Kaumana Caves County Park, the road steadily gains elevation as you pass into and then out of a layer of clouds. Expect fog or rain.

MAUNA KEA

There is old lava along both sides of the road as you approach the broad tableland of the saddle. Much of the lava here is from the mid-1800s, but some is from a more-recent 1935 flow. About 25 miles up from the Kona side, and 28 miles out of Hilo, a clearly marked access road to the north leads to the summit of 13,796-foot Mauna Kea (White Mountain). A sign warns you that this

road is rough, unpaved, and narrow, with no water, food, fuel, restrooms, or shelters. Moreover, you can expect wind, rain, fog, hail, snow, and altitude sickness. Intrigued? Proceed—it's not as bad as it sounds. In fact, the road is paved for the first six miles to the Onizuka Center for International Astronomy and Visitor Information Center at 9,300 feet, where there are restrooms and drinking water. Beyond there, a 4WD vehicle is required, and if there's snow, the road may not be passable at all.

Just beyond the Onizuka Center is **Hale Pohaku** (House of Stone), which looks like a ski resort; many of the scientists from the observatory atop the mountain live here. From here, the road is graded, banked, and well maintained, with the upper four miles paved so that dust is kept to a minimum to protect the sensitive "eyes" of the telescopes. As you climb, you pass through the clouds to a barren world devoid of vegetation. The earth is a red, rolling series of volcanic cones. You get an incredible vista of Mauna Loa peeking through the clouds and what seems like the entire island lying at your feet. In the distance the lights of Maui flicker.

Off to your right is Pu'u Kahinahina, a small hill whose name means "hill of the silversword." It's one of the only places on the Big Island where you'll see this very rare plant. The mountaintop was at one time federal land, and funds were made available to eradicate feral goats, one of the worst destroyers of the silversword and many other native Hawaiian plants.

Lake Waiau, which translates as "Swirling Water," lies at 13,020 feet, making it the third-highest lake in the United States. For some reason, ladybugs love this area. This lake is less than two acres in size and quite shallow. Oddly, in an area that has very little precipitation and very dry air, this lake never dries up or drains away as it apparently is fed by a bed of melting permafrost four or more feet below the surface.

Here and there around the summit are small caves, remnants of ancient quarries where Hawaiians came to dig a special kind of fired rock that is the hardest in all Hawaii. They hauled roughed-out tools down to the lowlands, where they refined them into excellent implements that became coveted trade items. These adze quarries, Lake Waiau, and a large triangular section of the glaciated southern slope of the mountain have been designated **Mauna Kea Ice Age Natural Area Reserve.**

A natural phenomenon is the strange thermal properties manifested by the cinder cones that dot the top of the mountain. Only 10 feet or so under their surface is permafrost that dates back 10,000 years to the Pleistocene Epoch. If you drill into the cones for 10–20 feet and put a pipe in, during daylight hours, air will be sucked into the pipe. At night, warm air comes out of the pipe with sufficient force to keep a hat levitating.

Mauna Kea is the only spot in the tropical Pacific that was thought to be glaciated, until recent investigation provided evidence that suggests that Haleakala on Maui was also capped by a glacier when it was higher and much older. The entire summit of the Mauna Kea was covered in 500 feet of ice. Toward the summit, you may notice piles of rock—these are terminal

moraines of these ancient glaciers—or other flat surfaces that are grooved as if scratched by huge fingernails. The snows atop Mauna Kea are unpredictable. Some years it is merely a dusting, while in other years, such as 1982, there was enough snow to ski from late November to late July. Most skiers career down what's known as the "poi bowl," northwest of the observatories, but they will ski wherever there is enough snow to run.

Evening brings an incredibly clean and cool breeze that flows down the mountain. The Hawaiians called it the Kehau Wind, whose source, according to ancient legend, is the burning heart of the mountain. To the Hawaiians, this inspiring heavenly summit was the home of Poliahu, The Goddess of Snow and Ice, who vied with the fiery Pele across the way on Mauna Loa for the love of a man. He could throw himself into the never-ending embrace of a mythical ice queen or a red-hot mama. Tough choice, poor fellow!

Hiking on the Mountain

Hiking on Mauna Kea means high altitude hiking. Although the height of the mountain is not the problem, the elevation gain in a short hour or two of getting to the top is. It takes time for the body to acclimatize, and when you drive up from the ocean you rob yourself of the chance to acclimatize easily. What you may expect to experience normally are slight dizziness, a shortness of breath due to reduced oxygen levels, and reduced ability to think clearly and react quickly. Some people are more prone to elevation problems, so if you experience more severe symptoms, get to a lower elevation immediately. These symptoms include prolonged or severe headache, loss of appetite, cramped muscles, prolonged malaise or weakness, dizziness, reduced muscle control and balance, and heart palpitations. Use your head, know your limits, and don't push yourself. Carry plenty of water (more than you would at a lower elevation) and food. Wear a brimmed hat, sunglasses, sunscreen, and lip balm, a long-sleeved shirt and long pants, and sturdy hiking boots or shoes. Carry a windbreaker, sweater, and gloves, as it can be cold and windy at and near the top. Don't alter the natural environment. Take out all that you take in.

There are a few good day hike trails on the mountain. About six miles above the Visitor Center, a dirt track heads off the access road to the west and downhill to a parking lot. From the parking area, it's about one mile farther west, over the saddle between two small hills, to Lake Waiau and its placid waters. On the way, a trail from the top (about a 30-minute hike) crosses this path and heads down the mountain back to the Visitor Center. A couple of miles down this cross path is an adze quarry site. Perhaps the most convenient hike is that to the true summit of the mountain. Start from the roadway across from the University of Hawai'i 2.2-meter Telescope, cross over the guardrail, and follow the rough path down into the saddle and steeply up the hill, a distance of less than half a mile.

The Hawaiians were the finest adze makers in Polynesia. One of the best stone quarries was atop Mauna Kea.

MAUNA KEA OBSERVATORY COMPLEX

Atop the mountain is a mushroom grove of astronomical observatories, as incongruously striking as a futuristic earth colony on a remote planet of a distant galaxy. The crystal-clear air and lack of dust and light pollution make the Mauna Kea Observatory site *the* best in the world. At close to 14,000 feet, it is above 40 percent of the earth's atmosphere and 98 percent of its water vapor. Temperatures generally hover around 40–50 degrees during the day, and there's only 9–11 inches of precipitation annually, mostly in the form of snow. The astronomers have come to expect an average of 325 crystal-clear nights per year, perfect for observation. The state of Hawaii leases the tops of the cinder cones, upon which various institutions from all over the world construct telescopes. These institutions in turn give the University of Hawai'i up to 15 percent of their viewing time. The university sells the excess viewing time, which supports the entire astronomy program and makes a little money on the side. Those who work up here must come down every four days because the thin air makes them forgetful and susceptible to making minor calculation errors. Scientists from around the world book months in advance for a squint through one of these phenomenal telescopes, and institutions from several countries maintain permanent outposts here.

The first telescope that you see on your left is the U.K.'s **James Clerk Maxwell Telescope** (JCMT), a radio telescope with a primary reflecting surface more than 15 meters in diameter. This unit was operational in 1987. It was dedicated by Britain's Prince Philip, who rode all the way to the summit in a Rolls Royce. The 3.6-meter **Canada-France-Hawaii Telescope** (CFHT), finished in 1979 for $33 million, was the first to spot Halley's Comet in 1983.

A newer eye to the heavens atop Mauna Kea is the double **W.M. Keck Observatory.** Keck I was operational in 1992 and Keck II in 1996. The Keck Foundation, a philanthropic organization from Los Angeles, funded the telescopes to the tune of over $140 million, among the world's most high-tech, powerful, and expensive. Operated by the California Association for Research in Astronomy (CARA), a joint project of the University of California and Cal Tech, the telescopes have an aperture of 400 inches and employ entirely new and unique types of technology. The primary reflectors are fashioned from a mosaic of 36 hexagonal mirrors, each only three inches thick and six feet in diameter. These "small" mirrors have been very carefully joined together to form one incredibly huge, actively controlled light reflector surface. Each of the mirror segments is capable of being individually positioned to an accuracy of a millionth of an inch; each is computer-controlled to bring the heavenly objects into perfect focus. These titanic eyeballs have already spotted both the most distant known galaxy and the most distant known object in the universe, 12 and 13 billion light years from earth, respectively. The light received from these objects today was emitted not long after the "Big Bang" that created the universe theoretically occurred. In a very real sense, scientists are looking back toward the beginning of time! The Keck Observatory

A tour group awaits sunset at the Mauna Kea Observatory Complex.

ROBERT NILSEN

includes a gallery that's open to the public Mon.–Fri. 10 A.M.–4 P.M., a video presentation of the telescope, displays, a viewing area inside one of the domes, and restrooms. Alternately, one may visit the Keck Observatory office in Waimea for complete information about the telescope, without having to make the trek up to the top of the mountain.

In addition to these are the following: The **NASA Infrared Telescope Facility** (IRTF) does only infrared viewing with its three-meter mirror. Also with only infrared capabilities, the **United Kingdom Infrared Telescope** (UKIRT), in operation since 1979, searches the sky with its 3.8-meter lens. Directly below it is the **University of Hawai'i .6-meter Telescope.** Built in 1968, it was the first on the mountaintop and has the smallest reflective mirror. Completed in 1970, the **University of Hawai'i 2.2-meter Telescope** was a huge improvement over its predecessor but is now the second smallest telescope at the top. The **Caltech Submillimeter Observatory** (CSO) has been looking into the sky since 1987 with its 10.4-meter radio telescope. **Subaru** (Japan National Large Telescope) is a monolithic 8.3-meter mirror capable of both optical and infrared viewing. It is the most recently completed telescope on the mountain, fully operational since 2000. The **Gemini Northern 8.1-meter Telescope,** also with both optical and infrared viewing, is run by a consortium from the United States, United Kingdom, Canada, Chile, Ar-

gentina, and Brazil. Its southern twin is on a mountaintop in Chile, and together they have been viewing the heavens since 1999. Situated to the side and below the rest is the **Submillimeter Array,** a series of eight six-meter-wide antennae. About two miles distant from the top is the **Very Long Baseline Array,** a 25-meter-wide, centimeter wavelength radio dish that is one in a series of similar antennae that stretches about 5,000 miles from Hawaii to the Virgin Islands.

The entire mountaintop complex, plus almost all of the land area above 12,000 feet, is managed by the University of Hawai'i. Visitors are welcome to tour the complex and stop by the Visitor Center at the **Onizuka Center for International Astronomy,** website: www.ifa.hawaii.edu/info/vis, at the 9,300-foot level. This center is named in honor of astronaut Ellison Onizuka, born and raised on the Big Island, who died in the *Challenger* tragedy in 1986, is a must-stop for stargazers. Inside are displays of astronomical and cultural subjects, informational handouts, and computer links to the observatories on the hill above, as well as evening videos and slide shows. Often, small 11- to 13-inch telescopes are set up outside during the day to view the sun and sunspots and in the evening to view the stars and other celestial objects. The Visitor Center is about one hour from Hilo and Waimea and about two hours from Kailua-Kona. A stop here will allow visitors a chance to acclimatize to the thin, high-mountain air—another must. A stay of one hour here is recommended before you head up to the 13,796-foot summit. (Because of the high altitude and the remoteness of the mountaintop from emergency medical facilities, children under age 16 are prohibited from venturing to the summit. People with cardiopulmonary or respiratory problems or with physical infirmities or weakness, women who are pregnant, and those who are obese are also discouraged from attempting the trip.) The Visitor Center provides the last public restrooms before the summit and is a good place to stock up on water, also unavailable higher up. The Visitor Center is open Mon.–Fri. 9 A.M.–noon, 1–5 P.M., and 6–10 P.M., and Saturday and Sunday 9 A.M.–10 P.M. Free stargazing tours are offered daily 6–10 P.M. and a summit tour every Saturday and Sunday 1–5 P.M. (weather permitting). These programs are free of charge. For either activity, dress warmly. Evening temperatures will be 40–50 degrees in summer and might be below freezing in winter, and winds of 20 miles per hour are not atypical. For the summit tour, you must provide your own 4WD transportation from the Visitor Center to the summit. For more information or to check on the current hours of operation, as they do change periodically, call 808/961-2180. Call 808/969-3218 for the weather report and road conditions. For information on the Internet about the mountaintop observatories or the individual telescope installations, log onto the University of Hawai'i Institute for Astronomy website (www.ifa.hawaii.edu/) and follow the links from there.

If you plan on continuing up to the summit, you must provide your own transportation and it must be a 4WD vehicle. As the observatories are used primarily at night, it is requested that visitors to the top come during daylight hours and leave by one half hour after sunset to minimize the use of headlights and reduce the dust from the road, both factors that might disrupt optimum viewing. For rental vehicles, contact **Harper Car and Truck Rentals** in Hilo, 808/969-1478, which offers 4WD rentals certified for driving to the mountaintop. Alternately, make arrangements for a guided tour to the top. From the Kona side, try **Mauna Kea Summit Adventures,** 808/322-2366 or 888/322-2366, website: www.maunakea.com; or **Hawaii Forest and Trail,** 808/331-5805 or 800/464-1993, website: www.hawaii-forest.com. In Hilo, contact **Arnott's Hiking Adventures,** 808/969-7097, website: www.arnottslodge.com; or **Hawaiian Eyes Land Tours,** 808/937-2530. **Waipio Valley Shuttle,** 808/775-7121, picks up passengers in Waimea. Take extra layers of warm clothing and your camera. Photographers using fast film get some of the most dazzling shots *after* sunset. During the gloaming, the light show begins. Look down upon the clouds to see them filled with fire. This heavenly light is reflected off the mountain to the clouds and then back up like a celestial mirror in which you get a fleeting glimpse of the soul of the universe.

MAUNA KEA OBSERVATORIES' WEBSITES

University of Hawai'i 2.2-meter Telescope:
www.ifa.hawaii.edu/88inch
NASA Infrared Telescope Facility:
irtf.ifa.hawaii.edu
Canada-France-Hawaii Telescope:
www.cfht.hawaii.edu
United Kingdom Infrared Telescope:
www.jach.hawaii.edu/UKIRT/home.html
James Clerk Maxwell Telescope:
www.jach.hawaii.edu/JACpublic
/JCMT/home.html
Caltech Submillimeter Observatory:
www.submm.caltech.edu/cso
Very Long Baseline Array:
www.nrao.edu/vlba/html/VLBA.html
W.M. Keck Observatory:
www2.keck.hawaii.edu:3636
Subaru: www.naoj.org
Gemini Northern 8.1-meter Telescope:
www.gemini.edu
Submillimeter Array: sma2.harvard.edu

SIGHTS ALONG ROUTE 200

Pohakuloa

The broad, relatively flat saddle between Mauna Kea and Mauna Loa is an area known as Pohakuloa (Long Stone). At an elevation of roughly 6,500 feet, this plain alternates between lava flow, grassland, and semi-arid desert pock-

BIG ISLAND

marked with cinder cones. About seven miles west of the Mauna Kea Road, at a sharp bend in the road, you'll find a cluster of cabins that belong to the now-closed Mauna Kea State Recreation Area. No services are available here, but you can stop for a picnic. Nearby is a game management area, so expect hunting and shooting of wild pigs, sheep, and birds in season. A few minutes west is the **Pohakuloa Military Camp,** whose maneuvers can sometimes disturb the peace in this high mountain area.

Kipuka Pu'u Huluhulu

Birdwatchers or nature enthusiasts should turn into the Kipuka Pu'u Huluhulu parking lot across the road from the Mauna Kea Road turn-off. A *kipuka* is an area that has been surrounded by a lava flow, but never inundated, that preserves an older and established ecosystem. Here you will find a hunters' check-in station. From the parking lot, a hiking trail leads into this fenced, 38-acre nature preserve. Several loop trails run through the forest on the hill, and there are two exits on Mauna Loa Observatory Road, on its eastern edge. Pu'u Huluhulu means "Shaggy Hill," and this diminutive hill is covered in a wide variety of trees and bushes, which include *mamame, naio, 'iliahi* (sandalwood), koa, and 'ohi'a. Some of the birds most often seen are the greenish-yellow *'amakihi,* the red *'i'iwi* and *'apapane,* the dull brown and smoky-gray *'oma'o.* In addition, you may be lucky enough to spot a rare *'io,* Hawaiian hawk, or the more numerous *pueo,* short-eared owl. Even if you are not particularly drawn to the birds or the trees, this is a good place to get out of the car, stretch your legs, and get acclimatized to the elevation.

Pu'u O'o Trail

Just after mile marker 24 on the way up from Hilo in the trailhead for Pu'u O'o Trail. From the small parking lot along the road, this tail heads to the south about four miles where it meets Powerline Road, a rough 4WD track, and returns to the Saddle Road. This area is good for birdwatching, and you might have a chance to see the very rare *'akiapola'au* or *'apapane,* and even wild turkeys. This area is frequently shrouded in clouds or fog, and it could very well rain on you. You may want to walk only partway in and return on the same trail, rather than making the circle.

MAUNA LOA

The largest mass of mountain to make up the Big Island is Mauna Loa (Long Mountain). It lies to the south of Mauna Kea and dominates the southern half of the island. At 13,677 feet, it is about 100 feet shorter than Mauna Kea. The top of this mountain is the huge **Moku'aweoweo Caldera,** virtually as big as Kilauea Crater near Volcano. Connected to this caldera are the smaller but equally impressive North and South pits, each about as big as Halema'uma'u, which is within Kilauea Crater. Unlike Mauna Kea, Mauna Loa has had some recent volcanic activity, spilling lava in 1949, 1950, 1975, and 1980. The top of this mountain is within the Hawaii Volcanoes National Park boundary. One of the longest and perhaps the most difficult hiking trail in the park runs up from the Volcano area to Red Hill cabin and from there on up to the top of the mountain. A trail skirts the edge of the summit caldera partway around, and a hiking cabin perches on the eastern edge of the rim.

Mauna Loa Observatory Road, a rough gravel road, turns south off Route 200 and leads about 17 miles to the **Mauna Loa NOAA Observatory,** at 11,150 feet. This atmospheric observatory is not open to the public, but you can park near here. From the observatory, a 3.5-mile trail leads up to the caldera rim, and it's another two miles to the cabin. If you intend to hike this section, be aware that this is a very remote area. There are no services, restrooms, or water along the way. It can be cold and moist, and there is virtually no protection from the weather until you get to the cabin.

HAWAII STATE ARCHIVES

BIG ISLAND

HILO

Hilo is a blind date. Everyone tells you what a beautiful personality she has, but . . . But? . . . it rains—130 inches a year. Mostly the rains come in winter and spring and are limited to predictable afternoon showers, but they do scare some tourists away, keeping Hilo reasonably priced and low-key. In spite of, and because of, the rain, Hilo is gorgeous. It's one of the oldest permanently settled towns in Hawaii, and the largest on the windward coast of the island. Hilo's weather makes it a natural greenhouse. Botanical gardens and flower farms surround Hilo like a giant lei, and shoulder-to-shoulder banyans canopy entire city blocks. To counterpoint this tropical explosion, Mauna Kea's winter snows backdrop the town. The crescent of Hilo Bay blazes gold at sunrise, while a sculpted lagoon, Asian pagodas, rock gardens, and even a tiny island connected by a footbridge line its shores. Downtown's waterfront has the perfect false-front buildings that always need a paint job. They lean on each other like "old salts" who've had one too

many. Don't make the mistake of underestimating Hilo, or of counting it out because of its rainy reputation. For most, the blind date with this exotic beauty turns into a fun-filled love affair.

Hilo is a unique town in a unique state in America. You can walk down streets with names like Pu'u'eo and Keawe, and they could be streets in Anywhere, U.S.A., with neatly painted houses surrounded by white picket fences. Families live here. At nearly 40,000, Hilo has the second-largest population in the state after Honolulu. It is the county seat, has a bustling commercial harbor, has a long tradition in agriculture and industry, boasts a branch of the University of Hawai'i, and is home to the Hawai'i Community College. It was once the terminus of railway lines that stretched north along the Hamakua Coast, and south to Mt. View and Pahoa. There are roots and traditions, but the town is changing. Fishermen still come for the nightly ritual of soul-fishing and story-swapping from the bridge spanning the Wailuku River,

HILO

BIG ISLAND

To Hamakua Coast and Waimea

SEE DETAIL

Keokea Point

KEAUKAHA BEACH

Hilo Breakwater

Hilo Harbor

SILVA ST.

HILO INTERNATIONAL AIRPORT
(GENERAL LYMAN FIELD)

TERMINAL

CAR RENTALS

COMMUTER TERMINAL

POST OFFICE

AIRPORT RD.

KALANIANA'OLE AVE.

137

Reeds Bay

REEDS BAY BEACH PARK
HARRINGTON'S
HILO SEASIDE HOTEL

BANYAN DR.

HAWAII NANILOA RESORT

UNCLE BILLY'S HILO BAY HOTEL

HILO HAWAIIAN HOTEL

NANILOA COUNTRY CLUB

KEN'S HOUSE OF PANCAKES

WAIAKEA KAI SHOPPING CENTER

DON'S GRILL

BIG ISLAND CANDIES

KANOELEHUA AVE.

PARADISE PLANTS

WAIAKEA CENTER

PRINCE KUHIO PLAZA

11

To Puna and Volcano

HO'OLULU COUNTY PARK

FREDDIE'S

HUALANI ST.

KEKUANAO'A ST.

ST.

LEILANI

MID PACIFIC WHEELS

HILO BIKE HUB

HAWAII COMMUNITY COLLEGE

Hilo Bay

LILI'UOKALANI GARDENS

Coconut Island

SUISAN FISH MARKET

BOAT SLIPS

WAILOA AVE.

KAMEHAMEHA AVE.

WAIOLI CENTER
KING KAMEHAMEHA STATUE

Waiakea Pond

WAIAKEA VILLAS HOTEL

HILO SHOPPING CENTER

MEHANA BREWERY

HILO FORESTRY ARBORETUM

KILAUEA ST.

LANIKAULA ST.

KAPIULANI ST.

PU'AINAKO TOWN CENTER MALL

PU'AINAKO ST.

123

'Ale'ale'a Point

THE BAY HOUSE B&B

WILD GINGER INN

19

SEE "DOWNTOWN HILO" MAP

STATE BUILDING

COUNTY BUILDING

KAIKO'O MALL

CAFÉ 100

KINO'OLE ST.

ULULANI ST.

WAILOA RIVER STATE RECREATION AREA

PONAHAWAI ST.

POLICE STATION

KAPI'OLANI ST.

UNIVERSITY OF HAWAII AT HILO

KUKUAU ST.

MOHOULI ST.

KOMOHANA RD.

DOLPHIN BAY HOTEL

SHIPMAN HOUSE B&B INN

SCHOOL

Wailuku River

WAIANUENUE AVE.

WAILUKU RIVER STATE PARK

HILO MEDICAL CENTER

Rainbow Falls

20

KAUMANA DR.

To Saddle Road, Kona, and Waimea

2 mi

2 km

0

© SANDRA E. BISIGNANI TRUST AND AVALON TRAVEL PUBLISHING, INC.

DETAIL

ONEKAHAKAHA BEACH COUNTY PARK

JAMES KEALOHA BEACH COUNTY PARK

LEILEIWI BEACH COUNTY PARK

RICHARDSON OCEAN CENTER

RAINWOOD HOUSE B&B

FRIENDS OF FRIENDS

'UMA'U

KOLOA

'OEDE

MAUREEN'S BED & BREAKFAST

KOLEA

KIOEA

'IWENE

LOKAHA

KAMOKUNA

ONEKAHAKAHA

KEOKEA

KALANIANA'OLE AVE.

ARNOTT'S LODGE

SEASIDE RESTAURANT

ANDREWS AVE.

KEAUKAHA

while just down the street newly arrived chefs prepare Cajun blackened fish at a yuppie restaurant as midnight philosophers sip gourmet coffee and munch sweets next door. Hilo is a classic tropical town. Some preserved buildings, proud again after new facelifts, are a few stories tall and date from the early 1900s when Hilo was a major port of entry to Hawaii. Sidewalks in older sections are covered with awnings because of the rains, which adds an early-20th-century gentility. Because Hilo is a town, most Americans can relate to it: it's big enough to have one-way streets and malls, but not so big that it's a metropolis like Honolulu, or so small that it's a village like Hana. You can walk the central area comfortably in an afternoon, but the town does sprawl, and it's *happening*. Teenagers in "boom box" cars cruise the main strip, which is lined with fine restaurants, antiques and collectibles shops, professional businesses, and mom-and-pop shops. This once vibrant town looks half dead in sections, with stores and shops falling silent due to the modern phenomena of new and large shopping malls in the outlying areas. Yet, there is a movement toward revival, and some old buildings are being enlivened with new uses and bold new shops are taking the places of the old and gone. There's even a down-and-out section where guys hunker down in alleyways, smoking cigarettes and peering into the night. In the still night, there's the deep-throated sound of a ship's foghorn, a specter of times past when Hilo was a vibrant port. Hilo is the opposite of Kailua-Kona both spiritually and physically. There, everything runs super fast; it's a clone of Honolulu. In Hilo the old beat, the old music, that feeling of a tropical place where rhythms are slow and sensual, still exist. Hilo nights are alive with sounds of the tropics and the heady smell of fruits and flowering trees wafting on the breeze. Slow down and relax; you'll start to feel at home. Hilo remains what it always was—a town, a place where people live.

Hilo is the eastern hub of the island. Choose a direction, and an hour's driving puts you in a time-lost valley deep in *paniolo* country, or on the blackness of a recent lava flow, or above the steaming fumaroles of Hawaii Volcanoes National Park. In and around town are museums, riverbank fishing, cultural centers, plenty of gardens, waterfalls, a potholed riverbed, and lava caves. Hilo's beaches are small, rocky, and hard to find—perfect for keeping crowds away. Hilo is bite-size, but you'll need a rental car to visit most of the sights around town.

The main thoroughfares through the downtown area are Kamehameha Avenue, Kilauea Street, which merges into Keawe Street, and Kino'ole Street, all of which run parallel to the bay. The Bayfront Highway, Route 19, skirts the water and runs north up the Hamakua Coast and east past the Banyan Drive area to the beaches out in Keaukaha. Heading inland from the water from the river mouth to Rainbow Falls and Boiling Pots is Waianuenue Avenue, and off it branches Kaumana Drive, Route 200, which continues over the mountain as the Saddle Road. Kaneolehua Avenue starts at Banyan Drive and runs inland to Volcano. On both sides of this main thoroughfare are the town's newer commercial districts and the airport.

SIGHTS

DOWNTOWN

Lyman Mission House and Museum

The preserved New England-style homestead of David and Sarah Lyman, Congregational missionaries who built it in 1839, is the oldest frame building still standing on the Big Island. Lyman House was opened as a museum in 1932! In 1856, a second story was added, which provided more room and a perfect view of the harbor.

In 1926, Haili Street was extended past the home, and at that time the Wilcox and Lyman families had the house turned parallel to the street so that it would front the entrance.

The furniture is authentic "Sandwich Isles" circa 1850, the best pieces fashioned from koa. Much of it has come from other missionary homes, although many pieces belonged to the original occupants. The floors, mantels, and doors are deep, luxurious koa. The main door is a "Christian door," built by the Hilo Boys Boarding

BIG ISLAND

DOWNTOWN HILO

To Hamakua Coast and Waimea

To Airport

Hilo Bay

SINGING BRIDGE

MAUI'S CANOE

Wailuku River

19

PUBLIC PARKING

BAYFRONT

KAMEHAMEHA AVE.

HIGHWAY

WAILOA RIVER

STATE RECREATION AREA

WAILOA RECREATION AREA

CHAMBER OF COMMERCE

CRONIES BAR AND GRILL

PACIFIC TSUNAMI MUSEUM

BASICALLY BOOKS

MODERN CAMERA

KRESS THEATER

KRESS BUILDING

PALACE THEATER

PESCATORE

ORCHIDLAND SURFBOARDS

HONU'S NEST

FURNEAUX

BUS TERMINAL

S. HATA BUILDING

REUBEN'S MEXICAN FOOD

MO'OHEAU BANDSTAND

FARMERS MARKET

NAUTILUS DIVE CENTER

BEAR'S COFFEE SHOP

SATSUKI'S

BIG ISLAND VISITORS BUREAU

TSUNAMI GRILL

ABUNDANT LIFE NATURAL FOODS

KTA SUPER STORE

HILO SURPLUS

ROYAL SIAM THAI RESTAURANT

NAUNG MAI

BUDDHIST TEMPLE

LOW INTERNATIONAL FOOD

KEAWE

KALAKAUA

KEKAULIKE

KALAKAUA PARK

FEDERAL BUILDING/ POST OFFICE

DRIVE

WAILUKU

AVE.

EAST HAWAI'I CULTURAL CENTER

KILAUEA

MAMO

KINO'OLE

ULULANI

WAIANUENUE

HAILI

HAILI CHURCH

PONAHAWAI

FIRE DEPARTMENT

KAPI'OLANI

POLICE

LIBRARY

LYMAN MISSION HOUSE

LYMAN MUSEUM

100 yds

100 m

0

0

N

© SANDRA E. BISIGNANI TRUST AND AVALON TRAVEL PUBLISHING, INC.

School. The top panels form a cross and the bottom depicts an open Bible. Many of the artifacts on the deep windowsills are tacked down because of earthquakes. One room was used as a schoolroom/dayroom where Mrs. Lyman taught arithmetic, mapmaking, and proper manners. The dining room holds an original family table that was set with the "Blue Willow" china seen in a nearby hutch. Some of the most interesting exhibits are of small personal items like a music box that still plays and a collection of New England autumn leaves that Mrs. Lyman had sent over to show her children what that season was like. Upstairs are bedrooms that were occupied by the parents and the seven children. Their portraits hang in a row. Mrs. Lyman kept a diary and faithfully recorded eruptions, earthquakes, and tsunami. Scientists still refer to it for some of the earliest recorded data on these natural disturbances. The master bedroom has a large bed with pineapples carved into the bedposts, crafted by a ship's carpenter who lived with the family for about eight months. The bedroom mirror is an original, in which many Hawaiians received their first surprised look at themselves. A nursery holds a cradle used by all eight children. It's obvious that the Lymans did not live luxuriously, but they were comfortable in their Island home.

The Lyman House is at 276 Haili St., 808/935-5021, and is open Mon.–Sat. 9 A.M.–4:30 P.M., admission $7 adults, $3 children 6–18. Guided tours are given half a dozen times a day by experienced and knowledgeable docents who relate many intriguing stories about the building and its occupants. This building is on the National and State Registers of Historic Places.

Next door to the Lyman House, in a modern two-story building, is the museum. The first floor is designated the **Earth Heritage Gallery.** The mineral and rock collection here is rated one of the top 10 in the entire country, and by far the best in Polynesia. Marvel at thunder eggs, agates, jaspers, India blue mezolite, aquamarine lazurite from Afghanistan, and hunks of weirdly shaped lava. These displays are the lifelong collection of the great-grandson of the original Reverend Lyman. Anything coming from the earth can be exhibited here: shells named and categorized from around the world, petrified wood, glass paperweights, and crystals. Other exhibits explain the geology and vol-

canology of Kilauea and Mauna Kea, and an entire section is dedicated to the vanishing flora and fauna of Hawaii. The museum is educational and worth some time.

Upstairs is the **Island Heritage Gallery,** where a replica of a Hawaiian grass house, complete with thatched roof and floor mats, is proudly displayed. Nearby are Hawaiian tools: hammers of clinkstone, chisels of basalt, and state-of-the-art "stone age" polishing stones with varying textures used to rub bowls and canoes to a smooth finish. Hawaiian fiberwork, the best in Polynesia, is also displayed, as well as coconut, pandanus, and the pliable air root of the *ʻieʻie*. The material, dyed brown or black, was woven into intricate designs. You'll also see fishhooks, stone lamps, mortars and pestles, *lomi lomi* sticks, even a display on *kahuna*, with a fine text on the *kapu* system. Precontact displays give way to kimonos from Japan, a Chinese herbal medicine display, and displays dedicated to Filipino, Portuguese, and Korean heritage. Saying good-bye is a bust of Mark Twain, carved from a piece of the very monkeypod tree he planted in Waiʻohinu in 1866. In an adjoining room is the **China Art Collection,** a fine grouping of ceramic and jade pottery and statuary. While most pieces are from the last three centuries, a few are perhaps 2,000 years old. Periodic exhibitions are shown in a third gallery.

Walking Tour

Start your tour of Hilo by picking up a pamphlet/map entitled *Discover Downtown Hilo, A Walking Tour of Historic Sites,* free at the HVB office and many restaurants, hotels, and shops. This self-guiding pamphlet takes you down the main streets and back lanes where you discover the unique architecture of Hilo's glory days. The majority of the vintage buildings have been restored, and the architecture varies from the early-20th-century Kress and S. Hata Building to the continental style of the Hawaiian Telephone Building and the Zen Buddhist Taishoji Shoto Mission. Older is the Lyman House and nearby the New England-style Haili Congregational Church (1859; congregation founded in 1824) and St. Joseph's Catholic Church.

Hilo suffered a devastating tsunami in 1946 and again in 1960. Both times, most of the city was destroyed, but the 1930 Bishop National

Bank building survived, owing to its structural integrity. Appropriately, the **Pacific Tsunami Museum,** 130 Kamehameha Ave., 808/935-0926, website: www.tsunami.org, is now housed in this fine art-deco structure and dedicated to those who lost their lives in the devastating waves that raked the city. The museum has numerous permanent displays, an audio-visual room, computer linkups to scientific sites, and periodic temporary exhibitions. While there is general scientific information, what's perhaps the most moving feature of this museum are the photographs of the last two terrible tsunami that struck the city and the stories retold by the survivors of those events. Stop in Mon.–Sat. 10 A.M.–4 P.M. for a look, it's well worth the time. Admission is $5 adults, $4 seniors, and $2 students. Other permanent displays of photos relating to the tsunami are hung in the Kress Building farther down Kamehameha Avenue and on the lower level of Wailoa Center.

A little ways down and on the opposite side of the road is a bandstand and main city bus stop. The **Mo'oheau Bandstand** is all that's left of the dozens of structures that lined the ocean side of Kamehameha Avenue before the 1946 tsunami. Miraculously, this structure survived. The bandstand is sometimes used by the Hawai'i County Band for concerts and for other community events. An information booth at a kiosk near the bandstand and bus stop may have information to dispense about the city.

A remarkable building, the "Old Police Station" is at 141 Kalakaua St., opposite Kalakaua Park. Built in 1932 and placed on the National and State Registers of Historic Places and Buildings in 1979, this old colonial structure is now the home of the **East Hawai'i Cultural Center,** 808/961-5711, a nonprofit organization that supports local arts and hosts varying festivals, performances, and workshops throughout the year, here and at other locations on the island. It also hosts Shakespeare in the Park performances by a local repertory group that stages, directs, designs, and enacts Shakespearean plays under the large banyan tree in Kalakaua Park, across the street, during the month of July. If you're in Hilo at this time, it shouldn't be missed. Monthly juried and non-juried art exhibits are shown on the main floor gallery; a venue for various performing artists is upstairs. The bulletin board is always filled with announcements of happenings in the local art scene. Stop in as there is always something of interest on the walls, and because this organization is worthy of support. The Big Island Art Guild, Big Island Dance Council, Hawai'i Concert Society, and Hilo Community Players are all member groups. The center is open 10 A.M.–4 P.M. Mon.–Sat., donations accepted.

Set aside for public use by King Kalakaua himself, **Kalakaua Park** is a grassy area overseen by a huge banyan tree, a midtown oasis. A seated statue of King David Kalakaua, the Merrie Monarch, takes center stage. Across Waianuenue Avenue is the solid and stately **Federal Building** with its offices and downtown post office. This stone structure dates from 1917.

A short walk up the street brings you to the **Hilo Public Library,** 300 Waianuenue Avenue. Sitting at the entrance are two large stones. The larger is called the **Naha Stone,** known for its ability to detect any offspring of the ruling Naha clan. The test was simple: Place a baby on the stone, and if the infant remained silent, he or she was Naha; if the baby cried, he or she wasn't. It is believed that this 7,000-pound monolith was brought from Kaua'i by canoe and placed near Pinao Temple in the immediate vicinity of what is now Wailuku Drive and Keawe Street. Kamehameha the Great supposedly fulfilled a prophecy of "moving a mountain" by budging this stone. The smaller stone is thought to be an entrance pillar of the Pinao Temple. Just behind the library is the Wailuku River. Pick any of its bridges for a panoramic view down to the sea. Often, local fishermen try their luck from the Wailuku's grassy banks. The massive boulder sitting in the river's mouth is known as **Maui's Canoe.** During the tsunami of 1946, the railroad bridge that crossed the river at bay's edge was torn from its base like a weak Tinker Toy construction. The metal bridge that crosses the river today is known as the "singing bridge" because the mesh that creates the roadway hums or "sings" as rubber tires spin across it.

Around Banyan Drive

If your Hilo hotel isn't situated along Banyan Drive, go there. This bucolic road skirts the edge of the Waiakea Peninsula that sticks out into Hilo Bay. Lining the drive is an almost uninterrupted series of banyan trees forming a giant

Suisan Fish Auction is perfect for bargains and local color.

canopy, while the fairways and greens of the Naniloa Country Club Golf Course take up the center of the tiny peninsula. Skirting its edge are the Lili'uokalani Gardens and the town's best hotels. This peninsula was once a populated residential area, an offshoot of central Hilo. Like much of the city, it too was destroyed during the tsunami of 1960. Park your car at one end and take a stroll through this park-like atmosphere. A variety of shops and restaurants sit in the coolness under the trees. The four dozen banyans that line this boulevard (the first planted in 1933, the last in 1972) were planted by notable Americans and foreigners, including Babe Ruth, President Franklin D. Roosevelt, King George V, Hawaiian volcanologist Dr. Jaggar, Hawaiian Princess Kawananakoa, pilot Amelia Earhart, and then-senator Richard Nixon. A placard in front of each tree gives particulars. Time has taken its toll here, however, and as grand as this drive once was, it is now a bit overgrown and unkempt in spots, with much of the area needing a little looking after.

Lili'uokalani Gardens are formal Japanese-style gardens along the west end of Banyan Drive. Meditatively quiet, they offer a beautiful view of the bay. Along the footpaths are pagodas designed for relaxing, torii gates, stone lanterns, and half-moon bridges spanning a series of ponds and streams. Along one side sits a formal Japanese Tea House where women come to be instructed in the art of the tea ceremony. Few people visit the gardens, and if it weren't for the striking fingers of black lava and the coconut trees, you could easily be in Japan.

Coconut Island (Mokuola) is reached by footbridge from a spit of land just outside Lili'uokalani Gardens. It was at one time a *pu'uhonua* (place of refuge) opposite a human sacrificial *heiau* on the peninsula side. Coconut Island has restrooms, a pavilion, and picnic tables shaded by tall coconut trees and ironwoods. A favorite picnic spot for decades, kids often come to jump into the water from stone abutments here and older folks come for a leisurely dip in the cool water. The only decent place to swim in Hilo Bay, it also offers the best panorama of the city, bay, and Mauna Kea beyond.

Suisan Fish Auction is at the corner of Banyan Drive and Lihiwai Street, which crosses Kamehameha Avenue. This fish auction draws island fishermen of every nationality. The auctioneer's staccato is pure pidgin. Restaurateurs and housewives gather before 6 A.M. to eyeball the catch of the day. Boats tie up and fishermen talk quietly about the prices. Later tourists will amble by, and it usually winds up a bit past 8 A.M. Around the side, Rei's small snack shop sells sandwiches and piping-hot coffee. Often you'll see townsfolk shore-fishing behind the market.

Cross Kamehameha Avenue heading south and you'll see **Ho'olulu County Park,** with the Civic Center Auditorium, numerous athletic stadiums, and a city nursery brimming with orchids.

This seems to be the organized athletic center of town. To the west is **Waiakea Pond,** a brackish lagoon where people often fish. The **Wailoa River State Recreation Area,** which encompasses the lagoon, is a 132-acre preserve set along both sides of the spring-fed Wailoa River in the center of Hilo. City residents use this big broad area for picnics, pleasure walks, informal get-togethers, fishing, and launching boats. On the western side are picnic pavilions and barbecue grills. Arching footbridges cross the river connecting the halves. Stop at the **Wailoa Center** on the western side for tourist information and cultural displays (closed Sundays). The walls in the upstairs gallery of this 10-sided building are used to display works of local artists and cultural/historic exhibits, changed on a regular basis. On the lower level hang astonishing pictures of the 1946 and 1960 tsunami that washed through the city. The Wailoa Center sits in a broad swath of greenery, an open, idyllic parklike area that used to be a cramped bustling neighborhood known as Shinmachi. It, like much of the city, was almost totally destroyed during the tsunami of 1960. Nearby stands the **Tsunami Memorial** to the residents of this neighborhood who lost their lives in that natural disaster. Also close by is a **Vietnam War Memorial,** dedicated to those who died fighting that war, and a new **statue of King Kamehameha I,** a replica of that which graces the town of Kapa'au at the northern tip of the island. Park at the Wailoa Center on Piopio Street, off Pauahi Street. Additional parking for this landscaped area is on the western side of Park Street at the end of Pi'ilani Street.

Farther Afield

A few miles out of town, heading west on Waianuenue Avenue, are two natural spectacles definitely worth a look. Just past Hilo High School a sign directs you to Wailuku River State Park. Here is **Rainbow Falls,** a most spectacular yet easily visited natural wonder. You'll look down on a circular pool in the river below that's almost 100 feet in diameter; cascading into it is a lovely waterfall.

MACADAMIA NUT

Hawaii produces about two-thirds of the world's supply of macadamia nuts, and the majority of the state's crop is raised on the Big Island. About one million macadamia nut trees produce these tasty nuts at the Mauna Loa Macadamia Nut property outside Hilo, with an equally large property producing nuts in South Kona. Smaller growers raise this crop at different locations on the Big Island, as well as on Moloka'i, O'ahu, and Kaua'i.

A native of Australia, macadamia nut trees were first brought to Hawaii in the 1880s. A number of these trees were again introduced to Hawaii in 1921 for study but failed to produce an acceptably significant and even-quality product. After years of grafting and experimentation, more than half a dozen varieties of the tree proved to yield acceptable nuts, and this led to large-scale commercial ventures in the '50s. Macadamia nut trees grow to about 40 feet tall, branch out to about the same width, and have dark green leaves. Trees require at least five years before they begin to produce nuts, and perhaps 5–10 additional years before they are in full production. Once mature, they can produce for years, and some trees known to be over 70 years old are still yielding nuts. Trees flower at different times over many months and produce nuts most of the year. This requires harvesting on a periodic basis. While some nuts are shaken from the trees, most fall naturally and are picked up from the ground. The nuts have a leathery skin that breaks open to reveal a very hard brown shell. This shell is cracked open to give forth the fruit itself, a light-colored, crisp and creamy orb about the size of a marble. In larger commercial ventures, the nuts are collected, dried, cracked, and sorted mechanically, while small-time growers may do some of this work by hand. Many of the nuts are roasted and salted, but some are set aside to be put into a brittle, glazed with various concoctions, or dipped in chocolate. Additionally, the nuts are often added to sauces, desserts, pastries, and confections. Some now are pressing the nut for its oil. Macadamia nuts contain mostly monounsaturated fat and traces of several minerals. The nut's high burn and smoke temperature makes it great for cooking, and its smooth texture is appropriate for lighter foods.

The 80-foot falls deserve their name because as they hit the water below, their mists throw flocks of rainbows into the air. Underneath the falls is a huge cavern, held by legend to be the abode of Hina, mother of the god Maui. Most people are content to look from the vantage point near the parking lot, but if you walk to the left, you can take a stone stairway leading to a private viewing area directly over the falls. Here the river, strewn with volcanic boulders, pours over the edge. Follow the path for a minute or so along the bank to a gigantic banyan tree and a different vantage point. This falls may be best seen in the morning when the sunlight streams in from the front.

Follow Waianuenue Avenue for two more miles past Hilo Medical Center to the heights above town. A sign to turn right onto Pe'epe'e Falls Street points to the **Boiling Pots,** another section of Wailuku River State Park. Few people visit here. Follow the path from the parking lot past the toilets to an overlook. Indented into the riverbed below is a series of irregularly shaped depressions that look as though a peg-legged giant left his peg prints in the hot lava. Seven or eight resemble naturally bubbling hot tubs as

river water cascades from one into the next. This phenomenon is best after a heavy rain. Turn your head upriver to see **Pe'epe'e Falls,** a gorgeous, five-spouted waterfall. Although signs warn you not to descend to the river—risky during heavy rains—locals hike down to the river rocks below to sunbathe and swim in pools that do not have rushing water.

In 1881, Mauna Loa's tremendous eruption discharged a huge flow of lava. The river of lava crusted over, forming a tube through which molten lava continued to flow. Once the eruption ceased, the lava inside siphoned out, leaving the tube now called **Kaumana Caves.** The caves are only five miles out of downtown Hilo along Route 200, clearly marked next to the road. Oddly enough, they are posted as a fallout shelter. Follow a steep staircase down into a gray hole draped with green ferns and brightened by wildflowers. Smell the scent of the tropical vegetation. You can walk only a few yards into the cave before you'll need a strong flashlight. It's a thrill to turn around and look at the entrance, where blazing sunlight shoots through the ferns and wildflowers.

Not many travelers can visit a zoo in such a unique setting, where the animals virtually live in paradise. The 150 animals at this 12-acre zoo, where it rains about 130 inches a year, are endemic and introduced species that would naturally live in such an environment. While small and local, the zoo is a delight. The road to the **Pana'ewa Rainforest Zoo,** 808/959-7224, is a trip in itself, getting you back into the country. Follow Route 11 south past mile marker 4 until you see the sign pointing right down Stainback Highway to the zoo. Near the zoo is the **Pana'ewa Equestrian Center,** with a full-size horse racing track. On a typical weekday, you'll have the place much to yourself. The zoo, operated by the county Department of Parks and Recreation, is open daily 9 A.M.–4 P.M., closed Christmas and New Year's Day. Feedings are usually done around 9 A.M. and 3:15 P.M., so you may want to be around for them. Admission is free, although donations to the nonprofit Friends of the Pana'ewa Zoo are appreciated.

Here you have the feeling that the animals are not "fenced in" so much as you are "fenced out." The collection of about 50 species includes ordinary and exotic animals from around the world. You'll see a giant anteater from Costa Rica, pygmy hippos from Africa, a rare white Bengal tiger, and a wide assortment of birds like pheasants and peacocks. The zoo hosts many endangered animals indigenous to Hawaii like the Laysan duck, Hawaiian coot, *pueo,* Hawaiian gallinule, and even a feral pig in his own stone mini-condo. There are some great iguanas and mongooses, lemurs, and an aviary section with exotic birds like yellow-fronted parrots and blue and gold macaws. The central area is a tigers' playground; a tall fence marks this rather large area where tigers still rule their domain. It's got its own pond and tall grasses that make the tigers feel at home but also make them hard to spot. A touching spot is the **Astronaut Grove,** in memory of the astronauts who were killed in the regrettable explosion of the space shuttle *Columbia.* All are remembered, especially Ellison Onizuka, a native son of the Big Island. The zoo makes a perfect side trip for families and will certainly delight the little ones.

Mauna Loa Macadamia Nut Factory, 808/966-8612, is several miles south of Hilo off Route 11, nearly to Kea'au. Head down Macadamia Road for about three miles until you come to the Visitors Center. Inside is an informative free video explaining the development and processing of macadamia nuts in Hawaii. Walkways outside the windows of the processing center and chocolate shop let you view the process of turning these delicious nuts into tantalizing gift items. Then return to the snack shop for macadamia nut goodies like ice cream and cookies, and the gift shop for samples and an assortment of packaged macadamia nut items. While you're here, step out back and take a self-guided tour of the small garden where many introduced trees and plants are identified. The Visitors Center is open daily 8 A.M.–5 P.M.

GARDENS

Along Kilauea Avenue, between Lanikaula and Kawili Streets, the Department of Natural Resources, Division of Forestry maintains the **Hilo Forestry Arboretum,** open Mon.–Fri. 8 A.M.–3 P.M., closed Saturday, Sunday, and holidays; no charge. This arboretum and tree nursery contains many of the trees present in Hawaii, including indigenous and imported specimens. Have a look at the diagram map of the grounds in the office before you head out back for a self-guided tour of part of the property. The map attempts to name the trees by matching them with points on the map as you pass by, instead of referring to signs on each specimen. The trees are magnificent, and you will have this quiet area virtually to yourself. Originally the site was an animal quarantine station operated by the Territory of Hawaii; the 19.4 acres of the arboretum were established in 1920 by Brother Mathias Newell. Brother Newell was a nurseryman employed by the Catholic boys' school in Hilo. At that time the Division of Forestry was already actively introducing plant species from all over the world. For the 40 years between 1921 and 1961 the department was engaged in the development and maintenance of arboretums consisting primarily of plant species from Australia and Africa. Arboretum sites ranged from sea level to Mauna Kea. Plant materials were exchanged, and thousands of breadfruit cuttings were exported. Over 1,000 different tree species and 500 different fruit trees were field tested.

Here at the Hilo Arboretum over 1,000 trees were planted. A few trees such as the paper bark and some pines are more than 50 years old. Presently a small number of timber species are grown for reforestation purposes. Essentially the Hilo site is utilized for the propagation of rare and endangered plant species, for research, and for experimental pursuits.

Nani Mau Gardens is the largest in Hilo, and touring these spectacular displays is well worth an afternoon. At 421 Makalika St., Hilo, HI 96720, 808/959-3541, the gardens are open daily 8 A.M.–5 P.M. Admission is $10 adult, $6 children ages 6–18, and $5 per person for an optional tram tour. The gardens now consist of 20 sculpted acres, and 33 more are being developed. More than a botanical garden, Nani Mau is a "floral theme park" designed as a tourist attraction. Walks throughout the garden are very tame but very beautiful; umbrellas are provided during rainy weather, which adds its own dripping, crystalline charm to the experience. Plants are labeled in English, Latin, and Japanese. The gardens are a huge but ordered display of flowers, flowering trees, and shrubbery. The wildly colored plumage of tropical birds here and there competes with the colors of the exotic blooms. The gardens are broken off into separate areas: fruit orchards, hibiscus garden, anthurium garden, orchid garden, gardenia garden, and bromeliad garden, along with Polynesian and European gardens. The new 33 acres include an annual garden, white-sand beach, small waterfall, picture garden for photos, several pavilions, and a Japanese garden. It also features floral sculptures, a small reflective pond, and an assortment of flowers and shrubs laid out in geometric patterns, and even "aloha" and "Hilo Hawaii" spelled out. The Nani Mau Restaurant provides lunch only, 10:30 A.M.–1:30 P.M., and the tourist shop is exactly like a Japanese *omiyagi* (souvenir) shop. No wonder, since it's owned by ethnic Japanese, and the tour buses coming here are all filled with Japanese visitors. If you enjoy a clean outdoor experience surrounded by magnificent flowers, this is the place.

Just a few minutes north of town, on the Onomea scenic coastal route, is the **Hawaii Tropical Botanical Gardens,** 808/964-5233, website: www.htbg.com, open daily 9 A.M.–5 P.M. for self-guided tours. Admission is adults $15, children 6–16 $5, and kids five and under are free. Remember that the entrance fee not only allows you to walk through the best-tamed tropical rainforest on the Big Island but helps preserve this wonderful area in perpetuity. The gardens were established in 1978 when Dan and Pauline Lutkenhouse purchased the property in order to educate the public to the beauty of tropical plants in their natural setting. The gardens have been open for viewing since 1984. Mr. Lutkenhouse, a retired San Francisco businessman, purchased the 25-acre valley and personally performed the work that transformed it into one of the most exotic spots in all of Hawaii. The locality was amazingly beautiful but inaccessible because it was so rugged. Through a personal investment of nearly $1 million and six painstaking years of toil aided by only two helpers, he hand-cleared the land, built trails and bridges, developed an irrigation system, acquired more than 2,000 different species of trees and plants, and established one mile of scenic trails and a water lily lake stocked with *koi* and tropical fish. Onomea was a favorite spot with the Hawaiians, who came to fish and camp for the night. The valley was a fishing village called Kahali'i in the early 1800s. Later on it became a rough-water seaport used for shipping sugarcane and other tropical products. A remake of *Lord of the Flies* was filmed here some years ago, and it's easy to see why the area made the perfect movie set.

Start at the visitors center along the road, where you'll find a gift shop, the tiny Onomea Museum, self-guided tour maps, drinking water, restrooms, umbrellas for your convenience, and jungle perfume—better known as mosquito repellent! Cross the road to the garden entrance and descend into this lush valley. The steep trail into the valley is about 500 feet long; once into the heart of the garden, the trails are more level. Plants from the four corners of the globe, including Iran, Central China, Japan, tropical Africa, India, Borneo, Brazil, East Indies, South Pacific Islands, tropical America, and the Philippines, are named with a full botanical description. Native plants from Hawaii are included. As you walk, listen for the songs of the native birds that love this ancient spot. Choose one of the aptly named trails like Fern Circle, Heliconia Trail, or Waterfall Trail and lose yourself in the beauty of the surroundings. You are in the middle of a tamed jungle, walking along manicured paths. Stroll the Ocean Trail down to the sea, where the rugged coastline is dramatically pummeled by frothy waves, a sea arch provides dramatic sculpture, and turtles swim the bay. You can hear the waves entering submerged lava caves, where they blow in and out like a giant bellows. Away from the sea you'll encounter screened gazebos filled with exotic birds like cockatoos from Indonesia and blue-fronted Amazon parrots. Walk the inland trails past waterfalls, streams, ponds, a bamboo grove, palms, and innumerable flowers. For at least a brief time you get to feel the power and beauty of a living Garden of Eden.

BEACHES

If you define a beach as a long expanse of white sand covered by a thousand sunbathers and their beach umbrellas, then Hilo doesn't have any. If a beach, to you, can be a smaller, more intimate affair where a good number of tourists and families can spend the day on pockets of sand between fingers of black lava, then Hilo has plenty. Hilo's best beaches all lie to the east of the city along Kalaniana'ole Avenue, an area known as the Keaukaha Strip, which runs six miles from downtown Hilo to its dead end at Leleiwi Point. Not all beaches are clearly marked, but they are easily spotted by cars parked along the road or in makeshift parking lots.

Hilo Bayfront Park is a thousand yards of gray-black sand that narrows considerably as it runs west from the Wailoa River toward downtown. At one time it went all the way to the Wailuku River and was renowned throughout the islands for its beauty, but commercialism of the waterfront ruined it. By 1960, so much sewage and industrial waste had been pumped into the bay that it was considered a public menace, and then the great tsunami came. Reclamation projects created the Wailoa River State Recreation Area at the east end, and shorefront land became a buffer zone against future inundation. Few swimmers come to the beach because the water is cloudy and chilly, but the sharks don't seem to mind! The bay is terrific for fishing and picnicking, and the sails of small craft and sailboards can always be seen. It's a perfect spot for canoe races, and many local teams come here to train. Notice the judging towers and canoe sheds. In the early 1800s, King Kamehameha I reputedly had 800 canoes made and launched from this beach for an assault on Kaua'i to bring that distant island under his control. The armada never made it, but eventually Kaua'i came under the great king's influence by diplomatic means. Toward the west end, near the mouth of the Wailuku River, surfers catch long rides during the winter months, entertaining spectators. There is public parking along the eastern half near the canoe clubs or at the river mouth where the fishing boats dock.

Reeds Bay Beach Park is a largely undeveloped park area on the east side of the Waiakea Peninsula at the end of Banyan Drive. Technically part of Hilo Bay, the water is notoriously cold because of a constantly flowing freshwater spring, hence the name Ice Pond at its innermost end. Most people just picnic here, and fishermen frequent the area.

Keaukaha Beach at **Carlsmith Beach County Park,** on Puhi Bay, is the first in a series of beaches as you head east on Kalaniana'ole Avenue. Look for Baker Avenue and pull off to the left into a parking area near an old pavilion. This is a favorite spot with local people, who swim at "Cold Water Pond," a spring-fed inlet at the head of the bay. A sewage treatment plant fronts the western side of Puhi Bay. Much nicer areas await you just up Kalaniana'ole Avenue.

Onekahakaha Beach County Park has it all: safe swimming, white-sand beach, lifeguards, and all amenities. Turn left onto Onekahakaha Road and park in the lot of Hilo's favorite "family" beach. Swim in the large, sandy-bottomed pool protected by a manmade breakwater. Outside the breakwater the currents can be fierce, and drownings have been recorded. Walk east along the shore to find an undeveloped area of the park with many small tidal pools. Beware of sea urchins.

James Kealoha Beach County Park, also known locally as "Four Mile Beach," is next; people swim, snorkel, and fish here, and during winter months it's a favorite surfing spot. A large grassy area is shaded by trees and a picnic pavilion. Just offshore is an island known as Scout Island because local Boy Scouts often camp there. This entire area was known for its fishponds, and inland, just across Kalaniana'ole Avenue, is the 60-acre Loko'aka Pond. This site of ancient Hawaiian aquaculture is now a commercial operation that raises mullet, trout, catfish, perch, tilapia, and others. The Seaside Restaurant operates here.

Leleiwi Beach County Park lies along a lovely residential area carved into the rugged coastline. This park with its parking lot, three pavilions, trees, and rock wall is a favorite local spot for scuba divers. The shore here is open to the ocean, and currents may be strong. About one-quarter mile farther on is Richardson Ocean Park, known locally as **Richardson's Beach Park.** Richardson Ocean Center is here. Use a shower that's coming out of the retaining wall surrounding the house to wash off. A battered seawall skirts the shore. A tiny cove with a black-sand beach is the first in a series. This is a terrific area for snorkeling, with plenty of marine life, including *honu* (green sea turtles). Walk east to a natural lava breakwater. Behind it are pools filled and flushed by the surging tide. The water breaks over the top of the lava and rushes into the pools, making natural hot tubs. This is one of the most picturesque swimming areas on the island.

Lehia Park is the end of the road. When the pavement stops, follow the dirt track until you come to a large, grassy field shaded by a variety of trees. This unofficial camping area has no amenities whatsoever, and at times seems like a homeless settlement. A series of pools like those at Richardson's are small, sandy-bottomed, and safe. Outside of the natural lava breakwater, currents are treacherous. Winter often sends tides surging inland here, making Lehia unusable. This area is about as far away as you can get and still be within a few minutes of downtown Hilo.

Going north out of Hilo a few miles brings you to **Honoli'i Beach County Park.** Turn right onto Nahala Street, then left onto Kahoa, and follow it around until you see cars parked along the road. The water is down a steep series of steps, and while the black-sand beach is not much appreciated for swimming, it is known as one of the finest surfing spots on this side of the island.

ACCOMMODATIONS

Accommodations in Hilo are hardly ever booked up, and they're reasonably priced. Sounds great, but some hotels have "gone condo" to survive while others have simply shut their doors, so there aren't as many choices as there once were. During the Merrie Monarch Festival in April, the entire town is booked solid! The best hotels are clustered along Banyan Drive, with a few gems tucked away on the city streets.

ALONG BANYAN DRIVE

$50–100

The **Hilo Seaside Hotel,** 126 Banyan Way, 808/935-0821, 800/560-5557 statewide, or 800/367-7000 Mainland and Canada, website: www.sand-seaside.com, is owned by the Kimi family. Like the others in this small chain, it's clean and well kept and has Polynesian-inspired decor with a '60s or '70s feel. On the property is Luci's Grill, which serves basic Japanese and American breakfasts and dinners. Room prices are $80 standard, $110 deluxe, and $120 kitchenette; third person charge is $10. Add approximately $25 for a room/car package. Ask about off-season, AAA, and AARP rates, and a better rate is sometimes offered depending on the amount of business at the time. The grounds are laid out around a well-tended central courtyard garden, and the pool is secluded and away from the street. While flash and polish are not part of the routine, you will find two scoops of dignity and pride. At this family-style hotel with a motel atmosphere, the friendly staff goes out of its way to make you feel welcome. This is a good choice for a moderate price at a convenient location.

Uncle Billy's Hilo Bay Hotel is sandwiched between two larger hotels at 87 Banyan Dr., Hilo, HI 96720, 808/935-0861, 800/367-5102 Mainland, or 800/442-5841 in Hawaii, website: www.unclebilly.com, email: resv@unclebilly.com. The Hilo Bay's blue metal roof and white louvered shutters make it look a bit like "Long John Silver's Meets Polynesia." The lobby's rattan furniture and thatched longhouse theme are pure '50s-kitsch Hawaii. Definitely have a look. There is free parking and a guest pool. This is a no-frills establishment, but all rooms are clean and air-conditioned with a TV and phone. Rooms run $84–104 or studio kitchenettes $94–114, good value for the money, but don't expect anything too modern or too luxurious. Numerous discounts are available, so be sure to ask. The in-house restaurant serves reasonably priced food, and a free hula show is presented every evening at 6 P.M. Uncle Billy's General Store, where you can buy everything from beer to sundries and ice cream to resortwear, is part of the complex.

$100–150

The **Hilo Hawaiian Hotel,** 71 Banyan Dr., Hilo, HI 96720, 808/935-9361, 800/272-5275 in Hawaii, or 808/367-5004 Mainland and Canada, occupies the most beautiful grounds of any hotel in Hilo. From the vantage of the hotel's colonnaded veranda, you overlook formal gardens, Coconut Island, and Hilo Bay. Designed as a huge arc, the hotel's architecture blends well with its surroundings and expresses the theme set by the bay, that of a long, sweeping crescent. While neat, clean, well maintained, and with all necessary amenities, the hotel still has somewhat of a '70s feel. If you want flash and glamour, try one of the new resorts on the Kona side. For down-home quality with a touch of class, you can't do better than the Hilo Hawaiian. Prices at this property run $107–130 for a standard room, $141 for an ocean-view room, and $177–350 for suites; all rooms have a/c, phone, and cable color TV, plus there's a swimming pool on the property. Guest services include a gift shop, laundromat, free parking, and a front-desk safety deposit box. The Queen's Court restaurant, Wai'oli Lounge, a bakery and lunch shop, and the Banyan Bodyworks Clinic are all on the property for guests' convenience. This is one of the two best accommodations Hilo has to offer.

Hawaii Naniloa Resort, 93 Banyan Dr., Hilo, HI 96720, 808/969-3333, 800/442-5845 statewide, or 800/367-5360 Mainland and Canada, website: www.naniloa.com, email: hinani@aloha.net, is a massive, 325-room hotel offering first-class accommodations. Rates start at $100 for garden view, $120 for partial ocean view, and $140–160 for oceanfront rooms. Suites are available for $190–800. The third person charge is $15; children under 13 using existing beds are free. The Naniloa offers a/c and a TV in all rooms, hotel parking, a free airport shuttle, two restaurants and lounges, periodic entertainment at the Crown Room, a gift shop, laundromats, and a pool setting—just above the lava—that is the nicest in Hilo. For the active guest, the hotel offers an exercise room with sauna and whirlpool and the nine-hole Naniloa Country Club golf course just across the road. The original hotel dates back more than 60 years and has built a fine reputation for value and service. The Hawaii Naniloa has recently undergone extensive renovations and is now more beautiful than ever, and each year the Naniloa is the central venue for the much-appreciated Merrie Monarch Festival hula competition.

NEAR WAIAKEA POND

$50–100

Inland but along the edge of the lovely Waiakae Pond and right next to Wailoa River State Recreation Area is **Waiakea Villas Hotel,** 400 Hualani St., Hilo, HI 96720, 808/961-2841 or 877/961-2841, fax 808/961-6797, a condominium and business complex where some of the buildings have been turned into nightly rentals. The Waiakea Villas Hotel is not only surrounded by a lovely setting, but the grounds themselves are well tended and well landscaped. On the property but off to the side of the accommodations are three restaurants, a karaoke bar, and sports bar. You will also find free parking, a laundry room in every building, a swimming pool, a tennis court, koi ponds, and streams that run between the buildings. The buildings themselves are done in a type of pole construction with high-pitch roofs and lots of exterior wood. Room amenities include cooking facilities in nearly every unit, telephone, cable TV, ceiling fans, and private lanai. The standard hotel room runs $76, a room with efficiency kitchen $99, $119 with full kitchen, and suites range $169–299 a night; add $15 for extra persons. Weekly and monthly rates are available.

NEAR DOWNTOWN

Under $50

Near the Hilo Shopping Center is a funky, easy-going place called **Off The Wall Mini Hotel,** 10 Wilson St., 808/934-8000. Rooms have been partitioned on the upper floor of this older house to make the five rooms, each with single beds, double bed, or two double beds. One room has a bathroom, the others share, and the covered shower is in the garden out back. This is a non-smoking place, and everyone shares a common TV lounge. Rooms run $25–35 a night. There is no luxury here whatsoever and you get only the most basic of accommodations, but it is convenient and an easy place to hang out for someone on a tight budget.

$100–150

Dolphin Bay Hotel is a sparkling little gem—simply the best hotel bargain in Hilo, one of those places where you get more than you pay for. It sits on a side street in the Pu'u'eo section of town at the north end of Hilo Bay, at 333 'Iliahi St., Hilo, HI 96720, 808/935-1466, fax 808/935-1523, website: www.dolphinbayhilo.com, email: john-hilo@gte.net. John Alexander, the owner/manager, is at the front desk every day. He's a font of information about the Big Island and will happily dispense advice on how to make your day trips fulfilling. The hotel was built by his father, who spent years in Japan, and you'll be happy to discover this influence when you sink deep into the *ofuro*-type tubs in every room. All 18 units have small but sufficient modern kitchens. Rates are $59 single and $66 double for a standard room, $69 and $79 for a superior room, and $86 for a one-bedroom, $98 for a two-bedroom fully furnished unit; additional guests $10. Weekly rates are available upon request. Deluxe units upstairs have open-beamed ceilings and lanai and, with three spacious rooms, feel like apartments. No swimming pool or a/c here, but there are color TVs and fans with excellent cross ventilation. The grounds and housekeeping are immaculate. Hotel guests can partake of free bananas, papayas, and other exotic fruits found in hanging baskets in the lobby, as well as free coffee. Make reservations, because everyone who has found the Dolphin Bay comes back again and again.

The Wild Ginger Inn, 100 Pu'u'eo St., Hilo, HI 96720, 808/935-5556 or 800/882-1887 Mainland, fax 808/969-1225, website: www.wildgingerinn.com, email: info@wildgingerinn.com, is a refurbished plantation-style hotel from the '40s painted bubble-gum pink and vibrant green. It's a short two blocks from the north edge of downtown, a few steps from the Dolphin Bay Hotel. An open-air lobby leads to an encircling veranda overlooking the thick greenery of the central courtyard area, with a view of the bay in the distance. A double hammock and vintage rattan chairs in the lobby area are for your relaxation. Each of the more than 30 rooms, very basic but very clean, has a refrigerator, private shower and bath, and ceiling fan, but no telephones; some also have TVs and microwaves. A bunk in the six-person dorm room is $15 a night, while room rates run $39–69 single, $45–69 double, $50–75 triple, and $70–80 quad, depending upon the type of room: standard, garden, ocean view, or suite. Discounts are available for longer stays. A homestyle breakfast of fruit, juice, and pastries is included for all except those in the dorm. The inn is completely nonsmoking, with a special area provided for smokers in the garden. Internet access, laundry facilities, weekly barbecue, bike rental, front-desk security boxes, and daily activities and trips are all available to guests. The Wild Ginger Inn, with a friendly staff and good service, is an excellent choice for budget accommodations and is owned by the same people who have the InterClub Waikiki on O'ahu.

FARTHER OUT FROM TOWN

Under $50

Arnott's Lodge, 98 Apapane Rd., Hilo, HI 96720, 808/969-7097, fax 808/961-9638, website: www.arnottslodge.com, email: info@arnottslodge.com, is a very reasonably priced hostel, extremely well run, safe, clean, and friendly. Follow Kamehameha Avenue south until it turns into Kalaniana'ole Avenue; in about five minutes you'll see a white sign pointing to Arnott's. Those without private transportation can be picked up by a free shuttle service operating 8 A.M.–8 P.M., with outbound departures at 8 A.M., 12:30 P.M., and 5:30 P.M. A ride downtown or to the airport costs only $2, or $3 round-trip. Arnott's staff can also

BIG ISLAND

help with inexpensive interisland air tickets or expeditions, some offered by Arnott's. Other services are bicycle rental at $5–15 per day, snorkel gear rental at $5 per day, coin laundry, telephones, reasonable Internet access, and safe storage of valuables and backpacks at no cost. Dormitory bunks—male, female, and coed—at $17 are spotlessly clean and cooled by cross ventilation and ceiling fans. Single rooms with bath, kitchen, and living room shared with one other room are $33; a double room with the same setup is $44. With private baths, the singles and doubles run $47–57. A self-contained suite with two bedrooms, one with a double bed and the other with twins, includes a bathroom, kitchen, and living room for $110 for up to five people; each additional person is $10. Check-in is until 9 P.M. only. Camping on the lawn with your own tent is now an option for $7 per person. Leisure time can be spent in a central courtyard or in a separate gazebo, for those who want to burn the midnight oil or watch one of a huge selection of videos. A backyard covered lanai has pink, blue, and green picnic tables so enormous that you feel like you're back in kindergarten, along with barbecue grills for your convenience, and a meditation platform built in a tree. To help keep your costs down, Arnott's hosts an all-you-can-eat barbecue/mixer on Wednesdays and Saturdays from 7 P.M., where you can have teriyaki or veggie burgers, salsa and chips, fresh fruit salads, ice cream, and tossed salads for only $7. Arnott's is an excellent hostel offering a quality, hassle-free stay with an international clientele.

BED-AND-BREAKFASTS

B&Bs are located here and there around town. Several are strung out along the highway north of town, a number are out toward Richardson's Beach, and a handful are scattered above town in residential pockets.

A short way past the singing bridge, take the first right turn to get to **The Bay House B&B,** 42 Pukihae St., Hilo, HI 96720, 808/961-6311 or 888/235-8195, website: www.bayhouse-hawaii.com, email: bayhouse@interpac.net. This new house with its three guest rooms sits on the cliff over Hilo Bay, as close as you can get to downtown Hilo. Rooms run $100 a night and

each has a king bed, private bath, and oceanside lanai. Guests share a common room with TV, phone, and refrigerator and receive a breakfast of fruit, juice, pastries, and coffee. The Bay House is comfortable, plush, and quiet. No credit cards are accepted.

Accepting paying guests for 20 years and others for longer that that, Amy Gamble Lannan's **Lihi Kai** bed-and-breakfast, 30 Kahoa Road, Hilo, HI 96720, 808/935-7865, is a treasure and the longest running B&B in town. This sedate, contemporary-style house sits on the edge of a cliff just north of town and has a million-dollar view of Hilo Bay; it's less than two miles north of the singing bridge. Guests of the two rooms share a bathroom and partake with Amy of a filling breakfast of fruit, pastries, and coffee to start the day. A small swimming pool occupies part of the yard. While Lihi Kai is a treasure, Amy is the jewel. Full of life and love, with a witty sense of humor, she can offer you insight on where to eat, what to see, how to get around, and where to find adventure. Rooms are $55 a night plus $5 a night for less than three nights. Make reservations well in advance, as her guests keep coming back again and again.

On a bluff overlooking the ocean just over two miles north of town is **Hale Kai,** 111 Honoli'i Pali, Hilo, HI 96730, 808/935-6330, fax 808/935-8439, website: www.interpac.net/~halekai, email: bjornen@interpac.net. This modern house has a small pool and hot tub. A sitting room for guests is shared, but each room has its own bath. Room rates run $90–100 a night with the suite at $110—no credit cards. The house is very comfortable, and the breakfast of fruits, pancakes, and sausages gives you a good start on the day.

Just four miles north of town is **Our Place Papaikou's B&B,** P.O. Box 469, Papa'ikou, HI 96781, tel./fax 808/964-5250, website: www.our-placebandb.com, email: rplace@aloha.net. Set among thick vegetation in a little gulch, the three rooms of this cedar home open onto a large lanai that overlooks Kupua Stream, but if you can imagine it, the house would be just as much at home on a high Colorado mountainside. The Early American (double bed) and Oriental Room (Queen bed) run $60 a night and share a bathroom, while the Master Bedroom with its king bed and day bed is $80 a night, two-night minimum. The lofty Great Room, open to all guests, has a

ROBERT NILSEN

It's easy to feel that old-world charm at Maureen's B&B in Hilo.

cozy fireplace, TV, stereo, and a grand piano that loves to be tickled by someone who really knows how to play. When traveling up Highway 19, turn left at Pinky's convenience store, take the next two lefts, and turn down the driveway.

Holmes' Sweet Home B&B, 107 Ko'ula St., Hilo, HI 96720, 808/961-9089, fax 808/934-0711, website: www.stayhawaii.com/holmes.html, email: homswhom@gte.net, is the residence of John and Charlotte Holmes. On a quiet residential cul-de-sac high above town (more than 700 feet in elevation) with a view of Hilo Bay and the city lights, this B&B provides two comfy rooms priced $60–75 that feature a private entrance to a common room, guest refrigerator and microwave, and private bathrooms. A tropical continental breakfast is included.

On 22 acres of macadamia nut and tropical fruit orchards above the Boiling Pots, with views over Hilo and the ocean and the 120-foot Kulaniapia Waterfall on the property, is **The Inn at**

Kulaniapia, P.O. Box 11338, Hilo, HI 96721, 808/966-6373 or 888/838-6373, website: www. waterfall.net, email: waterfall@prodigy.net. This recently built B&B features large suites with private granite-tiled baths and covered balconies. The room rate is $99, with $20 for each additional guest.

The first place out along the Keaukaha strip is **Maureen's Bed and Breakfast,** 1895 Kalaniana'ole St., 808/935-9018 or 800/935-9018, fax 808/961-5596, email: maurbnb@ilhawaii.net. Surrounded by landscaped lawns and koi ponds, this B&B was built in 1932 from redwood and cedar brought from the Mainland. With its high-ceilinged living room, arched windows and doors, balconies, and a Japanese tea room, it has plenty of charm. Comfortable and pleasingly decorated, the rooms rent for $40 single or $65 double, and a filling breakfast is included. This is a bargain and an all around good place.

Friends of Friends, P.O. Box 5731 Hilo, HI 96720, 808/961-6556 or 800/672-7872, fax 808/961-6557, website: http://vrbo.com/vrbo/1335.htm, email: bbell@aloha.net, is a basement studio that's been converted into a homey living area. While it has a low ceiling, everything else is standard. Two entrances open into the sitting and sleeping areas, and the kitchen and bathroom are to the side. The unit comes with its own phone and cable TV. Rates are $70 per night for one to three nights, $60 for four to six nights, or $350 a week; without breakfast it's $10 less per night or $250 a week.

Out near the end of the road is **Ironwood House B&B,** P.O. Box 10922 Hilo, HI 96721, tel./fax 808/934-8855 or 888/334-8855, website: www.ironwoodhouse.com, email: ironwood@flex.com. The remodeled older home is bright and cheery, and the young couple who own the place make their guests feel at home. The three guest rooms are on the second floor; two have good views of the ocean, the other has views of the surrounding trees. The Bamboo Room and Hibiscus Room share a bath while the Blue Ginger Room has its own. Each has a ceiling fan, TV, and phone. Rates are $50–85 a night for a couple ($5–10 less for a single); the larger room can accommodate up to two extra people at $20 per person. A full continental breakfast, organic when possible, is served and can be packed to go if you'll be on the road.

BIG ISLAND

Extra Special

A house can have presence, and, if it's brushed by magic like the Tin Man in *The Wizard of Oz*, it can even attain a heart. The home we're referring to was a purchase motivated by love and occupied by a large, dynamic family. The Shipman House, known locally as "the Castle," perched on five verdant acres high above Hilo, has such a heart.

After a quarter century on the Mainland, Barbara Ann Andersen, great-granddaughter of William H. "Willie" Shipman, the original owner, returned with her children and her husband Gary to restore to its former grandeur the residence where she spent her childhood Easters and Christmases. The house was figuratively stripped to its petticoats and outfitted in grand style.

Shipman House B&B Inn, 131 Ka'iulani St., Hilo, HI 96720, tel./fax 808/934-8002 or 800/627-8447, website: www.hilo-hawaii.com, email: bighouse@bigisland.com, is the grandest B&B in all Hawaii, and to appreciate it fully, you must know its history, which goes back as far as the first tall ships that arrived from New England bearing the missionaries and their faith to the old kingdom. The first members of the family to reside in Hawaii were the Reverend William C. Shipman and his wife Jane, who arrived in the 1850s. The Reverend Shipman died young, leaving Jane alone and in need of a means to support herself and their three children; she accomplished this by opening a Hawaiian girls' boarding school in Hilo. Later she met and married Mr. Reed, a famous engineer responsible for most of Hilo's bridges and for whom, by strange coincidence, "Reed's Island," the section of Hilo where the mansion sits, was named.

One of the boys, William H. "Willie" Shipman, married Mary Melekahuia Johnson, one of the young Hawaiian ladies at his mother's school. Mary was descended from the ruling *ali'i,* and her grandfather was a high chief and advisor to King Kamehameha. Willie originally determined to study medicine, but one day his stepfather, Mr. Reed, made him an offer he couldn't refuse, saying, "Son, if you will give up medicine and take up the study of business, I'll give you a ranch to run." Willie knew a good opportunity when he saw it, and over the years he became one of the largest landholders on the Big Island, founding W.H. Shipman, Ltd., which is today

chaired by his grandson, Roy Blackshear—Barbara Ann's father.

In the early 1900s, Mary often implored Willie to take her for a drive, which would invariably pass by a lovely home being built on Ka'iulani Street. Holding his hand and looking into his eyes she would ask, "Willie, won't you buy me that house?" and he would reply, "I can't. The Wilsons own it." Finally, one day as they passed the house, Mary asked once again, but this time Willie smiled and said, "Yes, my dear. It's been ours for 30 days." They moved into the house in April 1903.

Mary was a dear friend of Hawaii's last queen, Lili'uokalani, who would stay at the Shipman house whenever she was in Hilo. While there the queen would preside over simple but elegant "poi luncheons," always seated at the place of honor at the huge round koa dining room table, where she could look out the bay windows at Hilo below. After lunch, Lili'uokalani would slip away to the "Library" to clandestinely savor a fine cigar.

To arrive at the Castle, ascend Waianuenue Avenue until you come to the fourth bridge from the sea, Ka'iulani Street; cross it, turn left, and you'll see the Castle. Climb the steps to the wraparound lanai, a necessity even for well-to-do families, who, like all Hawaii residents, spend a great deal of time outdoors. The broad landing provides a wonderful view of Hilo and the sea in the distance, with wild flowers and tangled greenery cascading into a tropical bowl at your feet. Two stained glass windows, encircled by a laurel wreath, the classic sign of a congenial home, greet you on entering. The Double Parlor, the first floor of the rounded three-story Tower that caps the home, is magnificent. Everywhere is glass—old-fashioned, handmade curved glass—its mottled and rippled texture giving a surrealistic twist to the panorama.

Pad along on the burnished fir flooring past koa-wainscoted walls to enter the Dining Room, where an enormous dining table and *pune'e* (movable couch) are still very functional. The back area of the home is called the Conservatory, really the center of the home for day-to-day life, where the family took their meals. Just off it is a Solarium and the Butler's Pantry, next to an "Otis in-home elevator," installed in the 1930s and probably Hilo's first. Here, too, is a bedroom, formerly reserved for guests like Jack London and his wife Charmagne. The peaceful Library, waiting to engulf an afternoon reader within its impressive 12-foot ceilings, is warmed by a brick fireplace with a koa mantel and is fringed by built-in floor-to-ceiling koa bookcases.

Ascend the central staircase to the second floor, where once upon a time a ballroom adorned in white wallpaper with twinkling stars swayed with dancing and music; nowadays part has been converted into a bedroom. At the back near the elevator, a window opening to a cat-walk leads to a small room built over the water tank. This served as great-grandfather Willie's "Office," his haven from the clamor of 10 children! In the back corner is a second bedroom. A spiral staircase ascends to the attic where a "canvas room" was the children's dormitory. A large, free-standing credenza holds hats and antique clothing. Also in the attic is the entrance to the Tower, a wine barrel of a room with wrap-around windows.

The main house offers three guest rooms with antique beds, mosquito netting, private bath, and stately views through enormous windows. Other guests will lodge in the Cottage, a separate building on the grounds, originally built for the ex-press purpose of accommodating visitors. The Cottage contains two spacious bedrooms, each with queen bed, window seats, and private bath. Both rooms have private entrances, ceiling fans, and a small refrigerator. This is strictly a no smoking establishment and a "no TV zone," and children are not encouraged as there are so many antiques in the house and a steep ravine outside. Room rates are $140–175 single or double; $25 per extra person, add $25 for a single-night stay.

In the early afternoon, drinks and hors d'oeuvres are served on the main house's lanai. The Library is open to guests, along with use of the 1903 Steinway piano whose keys were once tickled by Lili'uokalani. A complete historical tour is offered daily. Breakfast, served 7:30–9 A.M. (earlier upon request, and special diets are accommodated), is an expanded continental with homemade cereals, hot cereals on request, assorted local fruits (there are 20 varieties of fruit trees on the property), fruit juices, Kona coffee, yogurt, fruit bread, muffins, popovers, and cinnamon rolls. Check in is 3–6 P.M., and checkout is at 10 A.M. Shipman House is once again one of *the* finest homes in all Hawaii in which to spend a quiet and elegant visit.

BIG ISLAND

FOOD

INEXPENSIVE

Named after the famous all-Japanese fighting battalion that predated even the famous "442," the **Cafe 100,** 969 Kilauea Ave., 808/935-8683, open Mon.–Thurs. 6:45 A.M.–8:30 P.M., Fri.–Sat. until 9:30 P.M., is a Hilo institution. The Miyashiro family has been serving food at its indoor-outdoor restaurant here since the late '50s. Although the loco moco, a cholesterol atom bomb containing a hamburger and egg atop rice smothered in gravy, was invented at Hilo's Lincoln Grill, the Cafe 100, serving it since 1961, has actually patented this belly-buster and turned it into an art form. There are the regular loco moco, the teriyaki loco, the sukiyaki loco, the hot dog loco, the oyako loco, and for the health conscious, the mahi loco. With a few exceptions, they cost $5 or less. So, if your waistline, the surgeon general, and your arteries permit, this is *the* place to have one. Breakfast choices include everything from bacon and eggs to coffee and donuts, while lunches (mostly under $5) feature beef stew, mixed plate, and fried chicken, or an assortment of sandwiches from teriyaki beef to good old BLT. Make your selection and sit at one of the picnic tables under the veranda to watch the people of Hilo go by.

All trips to Hilo must include a brief stop at **Low International Food,** 808/969-6652, long occupying the corner of Kilauea and Ponahawai Streets and open daily except Wednesday 9 A.M.–8 P.M., where *everyone* comes for the unique bread. Some of the more fanciful loaves are made from taro, breadfruit, guava, mango, passion fruit, coconut, banana, pumpkin, and cinnamon. The so-you-want-to-taste-it-all rainbow bread is a combination of taro, guava, and sweet bread. Loaves cost around $6, and arrangements can be made to ship them anywhere in the country. Breakfast, lunch, and dinner plates, most under $5, range from the famous pot-roast pork tail with black bean sauce to turkey plate and Korean chicken. Choose a table under the pavilion and enjoy your picnic in downtown Hilo.

Open every day 7 A.M.–9 P.M., a place that's getting praise from local people is **Freddie's,** 454 Manono St., 808/935-1108. The decor might be called upscale Formica, but Freddie's serves down-home food, all for under $7. Lunch and all entrées are served with two scoops of rice, fries, or mashed potatoes. Among the items on the menu are saimin, teriyaki steak sandwich, chili dogs, and burgers.

If you want to eat anything but uninspired "American standard" in Hilo after 9 P.M., go to **Nori's Saimin and Snacks,** 688 Kino'ole St., 808/935-9133, stuck away and hard to spot (but worth it) in a little alley across from the bowling alley. Here you can have a totally "island experience" in a humble, honest restaurant that specializes in authentic "local grinds." Inside, where the service is slow but friendly, are Formica tables and chairs, counter stools, and the "that's what you really look like" glow of fluorescent lighting. Boiling pots hold saimin of all sorts, which is generously ladled into steaming bowls and topped with fresh vegetables. Or order a plate lunch such as yakitori chicken with a scoop of rice or a scoop of macaroni salad. Two people can eat until they waddle at Nori's for about $15. There's no atmosphere, but the food is authentic and good.

Mun Cheong Lau is a cheap Chinese joint in downtown Hilo at 172 Kilauea Ave., 808/935-3040 (take-out available), open daily except Tuesday 10 A.M.–9:30 P.M. If you want to eat with "the people," this is the spot. The servings are generous. For $8 you can fill up in this place. It's clean, the service is friendly, and the dining experience, while certainly not fancy, is definitely authentic.

Dotty's Family Restaurant, at the Prince Kuhio Plaza, 808/959-6477, is open for breakfast daily 7–11 A.M., for lunch Mon.–Sat. 10:30 A.M.–2 P.M., and for dinner Mon.–Thurs. 5–8 P.M., Friday 5–9 P.M. Dotty's is an institution where local people come for the hearty portions and the homestyle cooking. Breakfast favorites are corned beef hash and eggs or French toast made with thick slices of sweet bread from Punalu'u covered with real maple or coconut syrup. Lunch includes the grilled chicken supreme with mushrooms and Swiss cheese or Dotty's ultimate steak sandwich with slices of sirloin, sautéed mushrooms, onions, and Swiss cheese on a grilled potato roll. Those in the know come from around the island to dine on Dotty's famous oven-roasted turkey, fresh catch of the day, or barbecued pork ribs with house-made smoke-flavored sauce. Fresh vegetables, real mashed potatoes, and homemade soups (great chowder on Friday) come with all full meals, and order a piece of homemade pie for dessert. The decor is "American standard" with a Formica counter and leatherette booths.

Bear's Coffee Shop, 106 Keawe, 808/935-0708, is an upscale coffee shop renowned for its breakfasts, served daily 7–11:30 A.M. It features Belgian waffles (made from malted flour) and an assortment of egg dishes. Lunch is hearty sandwiches of turkey, pastrami, chicken fillet, tuna, or ham, along with a small but zesty selection of Mexican food as well as salads. You can get most anything for under $6. Beverages include Italian sodas, homemade lemonade, and a large selection of coffee, cappuccino, and caffè latte from the full espresso bar. All are perfect with desserts like carrot cake, Bear's brownies, cheesecake, and pies. A great place to relax, read the morning paper, and watch Hilo life go by.

Satsuki's, along the 200 block of Keawe St., 808/935-7880, receives the highest recommendation because when local people want a good meal at an inexpensive price they head here. It's open for lunch 10 A.M.–2 P.M., dinner 4:30–9 P.M., closed Tuesday. Specialties are oxtail soup and the Okinawa *soba* plate lunch. There are plenty of traditional favorites, and all meals come with miso soup, Japanese pickles and condiments, rice, and tea. Spotlessly clean and friendly. This is excellent food at excellent value.

Tsunami Grill, 250 Keawe St., 808/961-6789, open Monday 8 A.M.–2 P.M. only, Tues.–Sat. 8 A.M.–2 P.M. and dinner 5–9 P.M., Sunday dinner only 5–9 P.M., is the same type of restaurant as Satsuki's, with its own loyal local clientele. The food is excellent here, too, and the prices are unbeatable. You'll walk away stuffed on traditional Japanese food for about $10. For food of the raw variety, head across the street to **Ocean Sushi**, its sister shop, 808/961-6625, where most sushi on the menu is $2–4 apiece.

Miyo's, 808/935-2273, overlooks Waiakea Pond from its second story location at Waiakea Villas. Here you find "homestyle Japanese cooking" done the way you might find in Japan, in simple surroundings, at a very reasonable price. Fresh fish daily, and vegetarians options are available. You can't go wrong here. Open for lunch Mon.–Sat. 11 A.M.–2 P.M. and for dinner 5:30–8:30 P.M.

The **Happy Valley Seafood Restaurant,** 808/933-1083, at the Hilo Shopping Center, has a typically Chinese long list of menu items and reasonably priced live lobster.

Another favorite of locals is **Don's Grill,** 808/935-9099, open daily except Monday 10:30 A.M.–9 P.M., Friday to 10 P.M. This American/ Hawaiian family-style restaurant is known for good food at reasonable prices. Inside find wood-trimmed blue Formica tables in a very modern yet functionally tasteful setting. Here you find everything from *saimin* to fish to rotisserie chicken. Don's is a basic American standard restaurant where you can get a good square meal for a good price.

Ken's House of Pancakes is a place to get a good standard American meal for a good price. Open 24 hours every day of the year, it's conveniently located on the way to the airport at 1730 Kamehameha Ave., 808/935-8711.

Kitty-corner across the intersection is the local **Verna's**, 808/935-2776, for plate lunches, burgers, sandwiches, and a multitude of inexpensive fast local food with nothing much more than $5. Take out or sit at the picnic table to the side.

At the back of the renovated S. Hata Building, **Canoes Cafe**, 808/935-4070, has a large variety of inspired sandwiches, wraps, and salads available Mon.–Sat. 9 A.M.–2:45 P.M., 10 A.M.–2 P.M. on Sunday, or stop in at 8 A.M. for coffee and pastries.

Island Grinds serves plate lunches, burgers, a salad bar, and vegetarian entrées from its lunch wagon at the bayfront beach Mon.–Fri. 10 A.M.–2 P.M.

Lanky's Pastries and Deli, Hilo Shopping Center, 808/935-6381, open 6:30 A.M.–9 P.M., deli side from 6 A.M., is a perfect place to head if you have a sweet tooth that *must* be satisfied. The deli/bakery is especially known for its "long johns,"—long, thin sugar donuts filled with custard—but it also has all kinds of baked goods from bread to apple turnovers. The deli case holds sandwiches priced under $3, along with an assortment of *bento,* perfect for a picnic lunch.

Places for a refreshing scoop of ice cream are **Tropical Dreams Ice Cream** at the refurbished Kress Building downtown (you can get baked goods here too), **Hilo Homemade Ice Cream** at 1477 Kalaiana'ole along the road to the beaches, and the **Big Island Candies** shop on Hinano Street. Both Tropical Dreams and Hilo Homemade ice creams are local brands made here in town.

Hilo Seeds and Snacks at 15 Waianuenue Ave., **Kilauea Preserve Center** at the corner of Kilauea and Ponahawai Streets, and **Kaiko'o Seeds 'n Things** in the Kaiko'o Mall all sell authentic crackseed. If you've never tried this unique island snack, here's your opportunity.

MODERATELY PRICED

Restaurant Miwa, at Hilo Shopping Center, 808/961-4454, is open daily 10 A.M.–9 P.M., sometimes until 10 P.M. for meals and until 2 A.M. at the bar. Very beautifully appointed, Miwa is a surprise, especially since it's stuck back in the corner of the shopping center. Enter to find traditional shoji screens and wooden tables adorned with fine linens, along with a classic sushi bar. The menu is excellent, with appetizers like sake-flavored steamed clams and crab *sunomono* (seaweed, cucumber slices, and crab meat). A specialty is *nabemono,* a hearty and zesty soup/stew prepared at your table for a minimum of two people. Traditional favorites popular with Westerners include beef sukiyaki and *shabu shabu,* and there's also a variety of combination dinners that give you a wider sampling of the menu at good value. Restaurant Miwa is an excellent choice for a gourmet meal at a reasonable price in a congenial setting.

Very clean and down-home proud, the **Royal Siam Thai Restaurant,** 70 Mamo St., 808/961-6100, serves up tasty Thai treats Mon.–Sat. 11 A.M.–2 P.M. and 5–9 P.M. Appetizers include a crispy Thai noodle dish for $5 and two of the several soups are coconut chicken soup for $6 and a seafood soup for $9. Entrées range from simple fried rice dishes through curries and meat dishes to seafood selections, mostly in the $7–10 range. There are specials nightly. Vegetarian selections are numerous and portions are large. This little restaurant gets good reviews and has a local following.

Gaining an appreciative following is the tiny **Naung Mai** Thai restaurant at 86 Kilauea Ave., 808/934-7540.

Fiasco's, a good restaurant and nightspot, is at the Waiakea Kai Shopping Plaza, 200 Kanoelehua St., 808/935-7666, open Sun.–Thurs. 11 A.M.–10 P.M., weekends to 11 P.M., with dancing Thurs.–Sat. 9 P.M. until closing. Featuring a country inn flavor, Fiasco's has a cobblestoned entrance that leads you to the cozy, post-and-beam dining room appointed with stout wooden tables and captain's chairs, with semi-private booths lining the walls. The mahogany bar, a classic with polished lion's-head brass rails, offers comfortable stools and black leather booths. The menu begins with appetizers, mostly $4–7, like fried mozzarella, escargot, or a big plate of onion rings. Lighter appetites might enjoy the well-regarded soup and salad bar buffet at $9, or a grilled chicken Caesar salad for $8. Sandwiches and burgers also run about $8. Entrées include Mexican fare and American standards, with a few pasta dishes thrown in to round out the selection. Many are under $10, while the most expensive item on the menu is only $18. Fiasco's has a large selection of beers—island-made, domestic, and imports. Families can save money with a special children's menu.

Along Kamehameha Avenue is a hole-in-the-wall eatery with a handful of tables called **Honu's Nest,** 808/935-9321, that's gaining a good reputation and strong local clientele. Served are a variety of Japanese dishes like tempura, donburi, soba, curry, and full dinners with salad, miso, and rice. Nothing on the lunch menu is over $9; add about $2 for an evening meal—and reserve a table! This place closes early. The lunchtime *bento* is highly recommended.

Nihon Restaurant, 123 Lihiwai St., overlooking Lili'uokalani Gardens, 808/969-1133 (reservations recommended), presents authentic Japanese meals, an excellent sushi bar, and combination dinners along with cultural and artistic displays. What you get here is like what you'd expect in Japan, with most everything under $17. Open daily except Sunday for lunch 11 A.M.–1:30 P.M. and dinner 5–9 P.M., sushi bar until 10 P.M.

Reuben's Mexican Food, 336 Kamehameha Ave., 808/961-2552, open Mon.–Fri. 11 A.M.–9 P.M., Saturday noon–9 P.M., will enliven your palate with its zesty dishes. The interior has the feel of Old Mexico with its bright murals and collection of sombreros and piñatas. Mariachi music wafts through the room, and you better like it because Pancho Villa is keeping an eye on you from the wall! The lengthy menu is reasonable ($7–9), with selections like carne asada, steak tacos, chicken flautas, crab enchiladas, and a vegetarian bean chili verde burrito. All are served with beans and rice, and the portions are huge. The bar has a large selection of Mexican, American, and European *cerveza* for $2–3, but Reuben's is most famous for its margaritas—more than one will get you acting like a human *chimichanga.* ¡Olé!

FINE DINING

Queen's Court Restaurant at the Hilo Hawaiian Hotel on Banyan Drive, 808/935-9361, offers a nightly buffet that is *the* best in Hilo. Connoisseurs usually don't consider buffets to be gourmet quality, but the Queen's Court proves them wrong. Throughout the week, buffets include a prime rib and crab buffet Mon.–Wed., a legendary seafood buffet Thursday and Friday, and a Hawaiian seafood buffet on Sunday. All are extraordinary and would give the finest restaurants anywhere a run for their money. The buffets run $23–26, with a 25 percent discount for seniors. À la carte items for less than the price of the buffet are also available. The dining room is grand, with large archways and windows overlooking Hilo Bay. Sunday champagne brunch is more of the same quality at $23. Breakfast is served Mon.–Sat. 6:30 A.M.–9:30 A.M., $10 for the buffet or à la carte with such items as eggs any style, a short stack of griddle cakes, an "Omelet by the Bay," or a local scramble. Lunch is also reasonably priced and served 11:15 A.M.–1:15

P.M. except Sunday. Make reservations, especially on seafood night, because the Hilo Hawaiian attracts many Hilo residents who love great food.

Sandalwood Room is the main restaurant of the Hawaii Naniloa Hotel on Banyan Dr., 808/969-3333. Here, in an elegant ground-floor room overlooking the bay and lined with aromatic sandalwood, you can feast on Continental and Japanese cuisine. Open for breakfast 6:30–10:30 A.M., lunch 11 A.M.–2 P.M., and dinner 5–9 P.M. Order off the menu any night, most entrées run $12–22, or choose the crab leg and prime rib buffets on Friday and Saturday evenings for $23. The Sandalwood ranks up there as one of the few fine restaurants in Hilo. The adjoining cocktail lounge comes alive with karaoke music nightly except Friday and Saturday, when there's dancing to house music.

Modern and chic with a black and white checkerboard floor, linen on the tables, an open-air kitchen, a high ceiling with ceiling fans, and the calming effect of ferns and flowers, is **Café Pesto**, 308 Kamehameha Ave. in the historic S. Hata Bldg., 808/969-6640, open Sun.–Thurs. 11 A.M.–9 P.M., Fri.–Sat. until 10 P.M. One of Hilo's established restaurants, it offers affordable gourmet food in an open, airy, and unpretentious setting that looks out across the avenue to the bay. Pizzas from the 'ohi'a wood-fired oven can be anything from a simple cheese pie for $8 to a large Greek or chili-grilled shrimp pizza for $18; you can also create your own. Lunch calzones run about $10 but at dinner go for $15 with soup and salad. Lunchtime also features sandwiches and pasta. For dinner, try an appetizer like Asian Pacific crab cakes or sesame-crusted Hamakua goat cheese. Heartier appetites will be satisfied with the main dinner choices, which include mango-glazed chicken, island seafood risotto, and a combination of beef tenderloin, lobster tempura, and garlic prawns for $14–29. Follow this with a warm coconut tart, liliko'i cheesecake, or creme brûlée and you'll be set for the evening. Café Pesto also has a brass-railed espresso bar where you can order caffé latté or iced cappuccino to top off your meal in one of the best gourmet restaurants on the Big Island.

Sicilian fishermen would feel right at home at **Pescatore**, 235 Keawe St., 808/969-9090, open daily for lunch 11 A.M.–2 P.M., dinner 5:30–9 P.M., and breakfast Sat.–Sun. 7:30–11 A.M. The building has had multiple uses over the years and, as part of its colorful past, served as a house of ill repute. Completely redone, it has been transformed into a bright, cheery room with high-backed, red velvet armchairs and formally set tables with green linen tablecloths. Italian-style chandeliers, lace curtains, and koa trim add to the elegance. When the Italian in you desires antipasti, minestrone soup, cioppino classico alla pescatore, *gamberetti Alfredo,* or any number of other seafood dishes, head for Pescatore for some of the finest Italian food in Hilo. Many dinner entrées run $15–25.

Harrington's, 135 Kalaniana'ole St., 808/961-4966, is open nightly for dinner 5:30–9:30 P.M., Sunday until 9 P.M., and lunch Mon.–Fri. 11 A.M.–2 P.M.; the lounge opens at 5 P.M. The restaurant overlooks the ice pond at Reed's Bay in a convivial setting. A sunset cocktail or dinner is enhanced with the melodic strains of live jazz, contemporary, or Hawaiian music playing softly in the background on the weekends. The continental cuisine of mostly steak and seafood features appetizers ($4–9) like seafood chowder, mushroom tempura, and escargot in casserole. Although the eggplant parmigiana at $15 is vegetarian, other mostly meat entrées include prawns scampi, scallops chardonnay, calamari meunière, Slavic steak, prime rib au jus, and chicken marsala for $16–20. Much appreciated by locals, the menu hasn't changed much since the '70s. While not inspired, Harrington's turns out eminently pleasing food in a pleasant atmosphere.

The Seaside Restaurant, 808/935-8825, appropriately named, is out along the Keaukaha strip at 1790 Kalaniana'ole Ave. at an aqua farm operation. If you want, have a look at the ponds before you head in for your meal. About a dozen varieties of fresh water and salt water fish are available on the menu in a number of preparations, and for the those who would rather, a few steak, chicken, and pasta selections are also available. For fish, come to the Seaside. Most fish dinners range $16.95–24.95. All dinners come complete with salad, vegetables, rice, and apple pie. This is a popular place with locals, so make a reservation; open Tues.–Sun. 5–8:30 P.M.

BREWERY

Hilo has its own microbrewery, **Mehana Brewing Company,** 275 E. Kawili St., 808/934-8211, website: www.mehana.com. A small operation in business since 1996, this microbrewery crafts half a dozen varieties of light beer with no preservatives, brewed specially for the tropical climate. Stop at the small tasting room for a sample. If it's not too busy, someone may show you around. Open Mon.–Fri. 9 A.M.–5:30 P.M. and Saturday 10 A.M.–4 P.M.

OTHER PRACTICALITIES

ENTERTAINMENT

Hilo doesn't have a lot of nightlife, but neither is it a morgue.

One of the newest places for weekend music and dancing, and quick easy food every night of the week is **Cronies Bar and Grill,** 808/935-5158, at the corner of Waianuenue and Kamehameha Avenues. Mostly hamburgers, sandwiches, and *pu pu* in the $5–8 range, drinks, and live music Thursday and Friday. Belly up to the bar, toss some darts at the electronic dartboard, or use the billiard table in the back while the music plays up front.

Fiasco's at the Waiakea Kai Shopping Plaza, 200 Kanoelehua Ave., 808/935-7666, swings with live music Thursday, Friday, and Saturday. While the music always changes, disco, reggae, and rock are often heard. Doors open at 9 P.M., with a cover and relaxed dress code.

If you're looking for a night out in the Banyan Drive area, try the **Wai'oli Lounge** at the Hilo Hawaiian Hotel, where there is live music Wed.–Sat. nights, ranging from contemporary Hawaiian to soft rock, and complimentary *pu pu* daily 5–7 P.M. The hotel's lobby lounge also offers light live music on Fri.–Sat. 4–7 P.M. **Uncle Billy's Restaurant** at the Hilo Bay Hotel has a free hula show nightly 6–7:30 P.M. The **Sandalwood** restaurant at the Hawaii Naniloa Hotel also features a free hula show on Saturday night. In the cocktail lounge next door, DJ music and dancing are an option on Friday and Saturday evenings. For a quieter setting with live piano music, try the lobby lounge upstairs. **Harrington's** offers live jazz, contemporary, or Hawaiian music Thurs.–Sat.; good for dinner or just for relaxing.

Shooter's, 121 Banyan Dr., 808/969-7069, open 11 A.M.–2 A.M., is a bar and restaurant where you can dance seven nights a week. DJ music ranges from reggae to rock to rap depending upon the crowd and the night, with live music a couple times a month. The cavernous interior is like a giant rumpus room with cement floors, neon beer signs, a graffiti wall, and TVs at every angle; the decor is industrial chic. Don't be put off by the atmosphere, which can seem a bit stark and hard at first glance. Shooter's is friendly, has security, and boasts that "there hasn't been one confrontation since the day we opened." That's nice!

At Waiakea Villas, **Karaoke Box,** 808/935-6269, is a place to sing to your heart's content. Open Mon.–Thurs. 5–10 P.M., Fri.–Sat. until 2 A.M., closed Sunday. Right next door is the **Hale Inu Sports Bar.** Stop in for a cold one and a game on the big screen.

Movie Theaters

To catch a flick, try the **Waiakea Theaters,** at Waiakea Kai Shopping Plaza on Kanoelehua Ave., 808/935-9747, with three screens; or the **Prince Kuhio Theaters,** at the Prince Kuhio Plaza, 808/959-4595, with eight screens and tickets for $7 adults or $5 kids. Downtown in the refurbished Kress Building is the newer four-screen **Kress Cinemas,** 808/961-3456; tickets cost $7.50 adults, $4 children. The renovated **Palace Theater** 38 Haili St., 808/934-7777, shows art films and is the venue of the yearly Hawaii International Film Festival. Here you have stadium seating, a proscenium stage, and wonderful old murals. If you're into art-deco buildings and old cinemas, make this a stop. It's mostly open Friday evenings at 7 P.M.; tickets are $6.

RECREATION

Bicycling

The **Hilo Bike Hub,** 318 E. Kawila, 808/961-4452, is perhaps the best shop in town for quality mountain bikes and accessories; sales, repair, and rentals. Stop here for information about island races and ideas for where to bike on-road or off-road on the island. Crossbreed mountain bikes rent for $30 a day or $120 a week.

Mid Pacific Wheels, 1133-C Manono St., 808/935-6211, sells and rents midrange bikes. Bikes rent for $15 a day; helmets and bike rack are also available.

For cruiser rentals in the Banyan Drive area, try **Aquatic Perceptions,** 808/933-1228, near the Naniloa Hotel. This activity operator also arranges bicycle tours including one through the tropical district of Puna, from Pahoa down to and along the coast.

For recycled bicycles, sales, repair, or rentals, stop and talk with the owner of **Da Kine Bike Shop,** 12 Fureaux Lane, 808/934-9861, just a few steps from Kamehameha Avenue in downtown Hilo. Nothing is new here, but you might find a bike to cruise the beach or one maybe to buy and sell back at the end of your trip.

Scuba

The **Nautilus Dive Center,** 382 Kamehameha Ave., Hilo, 808/935-6939, website: www.downtownhilo.com/nautilus, email: dcrooy @gte.net, open Mon.–Sat. 9 A.M.–4 P.M., Sunday by appointment, owned and operated by certified instructor William DeRooy, is one of the longest established dive companies on the Hilo side. This full-service dive center offers three- to five-day PADI certification at a very reasonable $125 per person for a group of at least four or $300 for private lessons, and shore dives at $55 for one tank or $75 for two tanks for certified divers, including transportation. Boat dives can be arranged. New and used dive gear, scuba rental equipment, and snorkel gear rental at $5 for 24 hours are also available. DeRooy is willing to provide information over the phone for anyone coming to the Hilo side to dive or snorkel. He updates you on ocean conditions, suggests spots compatible with your ability, and even offers a free dive and snorkel map whether you're a customer or not. Bill is a font of information about the Big Island's water sports and shares it in the true *aloha* spirit. Definitely stop in!

PADI instruction, sales, and rental of scuba equipment, guided dives, snorkel gear, and kayaks are all available at **Aquatic Perceptions,** 111 Banyan Dr. near the Naniloa Hotel, 808/933-1228.

Golf

The only county-maintained golf course on the island is high above downtown Hilo. **Hilo Municipal Golf Course,** 340 Haihai St., 808/959-7711, is a 6,325-yard, par-71 undulating course where nonresidents can golf for $20 weekdays and $25 weekends. There are reduced rates for state and island residents. Cart rental is separate, and clubs may be rented. This is definitely a local course but does provide some challenge. Call ahead for tee times.

Occupying the center of the Waiakea Peninsula and surrounded by Banyan Drive is the **Naniloa Country Club** golf course. Maintained by the Naniloa Resort, this small nine-hole course is a par 35 over a flat 2,740 yards; $37 for two times around. It's an easygoing place where lots of people come to learn and practice.

Arnott's Expeditions

Arnott's Lodge, 808/969-7097, website: www.arnottslodge.com/activity.html, offers a variety of hiking adventures to its guests and to those who do not stay at the lodge but want more of an adventure than organized tours usually offer. Although the schedule of offerings changes periodically, some of Arnott's mainstays are the night hike to the lava flow in Volcanoes National Park, a Puna Rift Zone hike, a trip to South Point and hike to Green Sand Beach, and the sunset and stargazing trek from the top of Mauna Kea. These van tours each run a full eight hours and take only as many as the van will hold. Rates run $43–48, higher for those not staying at the lodge. All trips are made weather permitting and only if there are enough takers to make a go of them. Some restrictions apply, so be sure to check with the staff at Arnott's Lodge, or check out its website for the current list of adventures.

SHOPPING

Shopping Malls

Hilo has the best general-purpose shopping on the island. **Prince Kuhio Plaza,** 111 E. Pua'inako, open weekdays 9:30 A.M.–9 P.M., Saturday to 7 P.M., Sunday 10 A.M.–6 P.M., is the island's largest shopping mall with over 75 shops. It's basically an indoor covered mall with the addition of several large detached buildings. Jewelry shops, fashion and shoe stores, fast-food restaurants, and large department stores like Sears, JC Penney, and Liberty House make this a one-stop shopping experience. Here too you'll find Longs Drugs, Safeway, and a Hilo Hattie's store. Across Maka'ala is the newer **Waiakea Center** with a Border Books and Music, Island Naturals natural food store, Wal-Mart, and Office Max. These two malls together make the greatest concentration of Hilo Shopping. The strip mall **Pua'inako Town Center** is a little farther up Kanoelehua Avenue (Route 11), with lots of small shops, a Sack 'n Save Market, Rite-Aid, and plenty of fast-food outlets. Back down the highway and handy to the airport at 100 Kanoelehua Ave. is the older strip mall **Waiakea Kai Shopping Plaza,** with a small clutch of stores, restaurants, the Planet Ocean Watersports store, and a movie theater. The older shopping plazas are closer in toward the downtown area. Once full-service malls, many of their shop spaces are now vacant. **Kaiko'o Mall** is at 777 Kilauea Avenue near the state and county buildings, while **Hilo Shopping Center** sits along Kilauea Avenue at the corner of Kekuanao'a Street, with a handful of local shops, some excellent inexpensive restaurants, and a fine pastry shop. In this shopping center is a small **Japanese Immigrant Museum,** open Mon.–Fri. 9 A.M.–3:30 P.M.; $3 donation requested.

Shops

If you're looking for a simple yet authentic gift or souvenir try the **Lyman Museum gift shop,** which also has an excellent collection of books on Hawaiian subjects.

Sugawara Lauhala and Gift Shop, 59 Kalakaua St., is a virtually unknown Hilo institution operated by the Sugawara sisters, who have been in business for most of their 70-plus years. They make genuine *lau hala* weavings right on the premises of their character-laden shop. Their best hats sell for $75 and up, and they also have baskets from $15. If you are after the genuine article, made to last a lifetime, you'll find it here. One by one, the old-timers—the best weavers—are dying or losing their eyesight, so these unique woven products are becoming more and more scarce and will undoubtedly increase in value as time goes by.

Hanahou, 164 Kamehameha Ave., 808/935-4555, open Mon.–Sat. 10 A.M.–5 P.M., is a won-

one of Hilo's many vintage buildings

ROBERT NILSEN

derful little shop selling mostly vintage island treasures like *lau hala* weavings, baskets, pillows, hats, and sandals. Most items are made on the Big Island, but some are imported from Niue, east of Tonga.

Old Town Printer and Stationers, 160 Kamehameha Ave., open Mon.–Sat., has been in business for 35 years selling stationery, office supplies, postcards, note cards, and a terrific selection of calendars. It is in the same shop as Basically Books.

Ets'ko, 35 Waianuenue Ave., 808/961-3778, is Ginza and Paris in Hilo. This classy, eclectic little shop sells all sorts of arts and craft items, gifts, furniture, jewelry, and a small selection of silk and natural fiber clothing. Perhaps a hand-painted silk tie for him or a Japanese *tansu* chest for her is just the piece you're looking for. After you've shopped yourself into oblivion, head for the espresso bar at the back of the shop to rejuvenate yourself on coffee, Italian soda, or a wide variety of baked goods. Open Mon.–Fri. 9 A.M.–6 P.M., closing Saturday at 4 P.M.

Sig Zane Design, 122 Kamehameha Ave., 808/935-7077, open Mon.–Sat. 9 A.M.–5 P.M., is one of the most unique and distinctive shops on the island. Here, owner and designer Sig Zane creates distinctive island wearables in 100 percent cotton. All designs are not only Hawaiian/tropical but also chronicle useful and medicinal Hawaiian plants and flowers. Sig's wife, Nalani, who helps in the shop, is a *kumu hula* who learned the intricate dance steps from her mother, Edith Kanakaole, a legendary dancer who has been memorialized with a local tennis stadium that bears her name. You can get shirts, dresses, and pareu, as well as affordable house slippers, sweatshirts, T-shirts, *hapi* coats, and even futon covers. The shelves also hold *lau hala* hats, hand-bound koa notebooks, and basketry made from natural fibers.

If you're looking for surfboards, boogie boards, or surfwear, or just want to find out about surfing conditions in the area, stop by **Orchidland Surfboards,** 262 Kamehameha Ave., 808/935-1533, website: www.surfolhawaii.com. Established in 1972 and run by an avid surfer, this place will have what you need. Check its website for surf reports, conditions, and weather forecast.

Dreams of Paradise, 808/935-5670, is a gallery in the restored S. Hata Building, erected in 1912. Some artists showcased in Dreams of Paradise are Andrew Plack, a nature artist specializing in the flora and fauna of Hawaii; Gerard Beauvalet, a multitalented artist producing fine koa furniture as well as distinctive acrylic paintings—mostly depicting Polynesian women in natural poses of meditation and serenity—that are also reproduced as distinctive T-shirt designs; Beverly Jackson, who catches the sun in her stained glass renditions of breadfruit, lotus blossoms, and various Hawaiian flowers; and Terry Taube, a sculptor producing lava sculptures and renditions of animal life, especially *honu,* the green sea turtle. Shelves also hold gourmet food items, incidental bags, distinctive cooking aprons, and plenty of inexpensive but tasteful souvenirs.

Caravan Town, 194 Kamehameha Ave., is open daily except Sunday. It is one of the most interesting junk stores in Hilo. The shelves hold an internationally eclectic mix of merchandise that includes pendulum clocks, plaster Greek goddesses, luggage, and paper lanterns. Also, the shop specializes in over-the-counter Chinese herbs and medicines purportedly effective for everything from constipation to impotence.

Big Island Estate Jewelry, 300 Kamehameha Ave., open Mon.–Fri. 9 A.M.–6 P.M., Saturday 9 A.M.–4 P.M., is much more than its name implies, functioning as a pawn shop and discovery shop. Inside are antiques, collectibles, knickknacks, vases, musical instruments, and a good selection of used camera gear.

Off the main drag is **Mauna Kea Galleries,** 276 Keawe St., 808/969-1184, which has a broad collection of antiques, jewelry, paintings and prints, and other old Hawaiiana.

Also for antiques and collectibles is the venerable old **Oshima's,** 235 Waianuenue Ave., 808/969-1554.

The **Modern Camera Center,** 165 Keawe St., 808/935-3279, is one of the few full-service camera shops in Hilo.

Hilo Surplus Surplus, featuring raincoats, hats, military supplies, knives, backpacks, rubber rafts, and plenty of old and new military uniforms, can be found on Mamo Street.

On Kuhio Road, just outside the entrance to Hilo Harbor, is the **Mauna Loa Plantation Craft and Gift Center,** 808/933-2625, where you can pick up any number of locally made items—art,

BIG ISLAND

crafts, wearables, or edibles—from the Big Island.

If you're looking for that special island memento or souvenirs to bring home to family and friends, Uncle Billy covers all the bases and along with everything else offers the **Polynesian Market Place,** adjacent to the Hilo Bay Hotel on Banyan Drive. Open daily 8 A.M.–8 P.M., the marketplace sells a lot of good junk, liquor, and resortwear.

The **Hilo Hattie's** store at Prince Kuhio Plaza has all you need in island clothing, tourist style.

North of town several miles and just past the Hawaiian Tropical Botanical Gardens along the scenic coastal road is **Hawaiian Artifacts and Antiques,** 808/964-1729, open daily 9 A.M.–5 P.M., a shop owned and operated by Paul Gephart. Paul creates small wood boxes and ornaments, mainly from koa and 'ohi'a, and sculptures of whales, dolphins, birds, and poi bowls. He also has a small collection of tasteful jewelry and seashells, all at very decent prices.

Flowers

One of Hilo's greatest asset is its flowers. Its biggest cash crops are orchids and anthuriums. Flowers grow everywhere, but to see them in a more formalized way, visit one of the many nurseries in and around town. Most have excellent prices for floral arrangements sent back to the Mainland. The flowers arrive neatly packaged but unassembled, with a picture of the arrangement so you can put them together yourself. These hearty cut flowers will look fresh and vibrant for as long as two weeks, so a few days in the mail won't hurt them. For a start, try **Paradise Plants,** 40 Wiwo'ole St., 808/935-4043, a complete shop specializing in indoor-outdoor plants and tropical fruit trees. It sends orchids and other live flowers to the Mainland. Also featured is a large gift area with gifts from around the world. While browsing, check out the orchid garden, which ranks as Hilo's oldest.

Food Markets

For groceries and supplies try: **KTA Super Store,** downtown at 321 Keawe Ave. or in the Pu'ainako Town Center; **Safeway,** 111 E. Pu'ainako; **Sack 'n Save** at Pu'ainako Town Center; or **Sure Save,** 1990 Kino'ole. For a real treat visit the early morning **Suisan Fish Auc-**

A great place for organic farm-fresh fruits and vegetables is the weekly farmers' market in Hilo.

tion, 85 Lihiwai St., one of only a few open-air fish auctions in the state. A retail fresh-fish market is next door, open daily except Sunday 8 A.M.–5 P.M. Pick up a copy of the *Hawaii Fishing News* and *Fisherman's News* at the counter.

Since 1977, **Abundant Life Natural Foods** has been doing business in downtown Hilo at 292 Kamehameha Ave., 808/935-7411, open weekdays 8:30 A.M.–6 P.M., Saturday until 5 P.M., and Sunday 11 A.M.–3 P.M. The store's kitchen puts out daily specials of soup, salads, sandwiches, and *bento,* all for under $5, while the shelves are stocked with an excellent selection of fresh fruits and veggies, bulk foods, cosmetics, vitamins, and herbs. The bookshelves cosmically vibrate with a selection of tomes on metaphysics and new-age literature.

In the Waiakea Center next to Borders Books is **Island Naturals** market and deli, 808/935-5533. This full-service shop is open Mon.–Thurs. and Saturday 8:30 A.M.–8 P.M., Friday until 9

P.M., and Sunday 10 A.M.–6 P.M. Fresh fruit and produce line the shelves, as do packaged, refrigerated, and frozen natural foods, plus personal care items, supplements, vitamins, and minerals. The deli has ready to order foods and pre-made items. You'll get wholesome healthy foods here, with a good vibe from people who care about what they sell.

All you folks with that affinity for chocolate will certainly be pleased by the **Big Island Candies** factory and gifts shop in a new location at 585 Hinano St., 808/935-8890 or 800/935-5510, website: www.bigislandcandies.com, email: bic@interpac.net. Stop by to look through the glass at the delicacies being produced and choose your favorite off the many shelves of possibilities. Hawaiian macadamia nut cookies, chocolate-dipped shortbread, and macadamia nut biscotti only start the selections. This store also sells Hilo Homemade ice cream and is open every day 8:30 A.M.–5 P.M. You can even peruse the offerings and order off the net.

On Wednesday and Saturday mornings, stop by the corner of Kamehameha Avenue and Mamo Street for the **Hilo Farmers' Market.** This is a lively affair, great for local color, where you can get healthy locally grown produce and bouquets of colorful flowers at bargain prices. Across the street at The Market Place and also a few steps up the road under the big tent are more vendors selling flowers, arts and crafts, and other gift items.

Bookstores

Hilo has some excellent bookstores. **Basically Books,** downtown at 160 Kamehameha Ave., 808/961-0144, website: www.basically-books.com, open Mon.–Fri. 8 A.M.–5 P.M., Saturday from 9 A.M., has a good selection of Hawaiiana, out-of-print books, and an unbeatable selection of maps and charts. You can get anywhere you want to go with these nautical charts, road maps, and topographical maps, including sectionals for serious hikers. The store also features a very good selection of travel books, and flags from countries throughout the world. Owner and proprietress Christine Reed can help you with any of your literary needs.

The **Book Gallery,** at Prince Kuhio Plaza, 808/959-7744, is a full-selection bookstore featuring Hawaiiana, hardcovers, and paperbacks. Also at the Prince Kuhio Plaza is **Waldenbooks,** 808/959-6468, one of the city's largest and best-stocked bookstores.

The largest and newest bookstore in Hilo is **Borders Books and Music,** 808/933-1410, open daily at the Waiakea Center, across Maka'ala Street from the Prince Kuhio Plaza. Borders has tens of thousands of hardcover and paperback books, full Hawaiiana and travel sections, plenty of road maps, and over a dozen newspapers from around the world. Readings, music performances, book and CD signings, and other special events are scheduled throughout the month. If browsing makes you thirsty, stop for a snack at the shop's Cafe Espresso.

SERVICES AND INFORMATION

Medical

Hilo Medical Center, 1190 Waianuenue Ave., 808/974-4700, has both outpatient services and a 24-hour emergency room. Just up the street at 1292 Waianuenue Avenue is a **Kaiser Permanente** clinic, 808/934-4000.

The **Hilo Pharmacy,** 308 Kamehameha Ave. in the S. Hata Bldg., 808/961-9267, open Mon.–Fri. 8:30 A.M.–5:30 P.M., Saturday 8:30 A.M.–12:30 P.M., is a full-service pharmacy that also has a photo developing service. Others in town are **Shiigi Drug,** at the Kaiko'o Mall, 808/935-0001; **Longs Drugs,** 555 Kilauea Ave., 808/935-3357; and the pharmacies at the **KTA Super Store, Sure Save** grocery store, and **Wal-Mart.**

Information

Two good sources of maps and helpful brochures are **Big Island Visitors Bureau,** at the corner of Keawe and Haili Streets, 808/961-5797, open Mon.–Fri. 8 A.M.–noon and 1–4:30 P.M.; and the **Chamber of Commerce,** 106 Kamehameha Ave., 808/935-7178.

Schools and Libraries

The **Hilo Public Library** is at 300 Waianuenue St., 808/933-8888. The **University of Hawai'i at Hilo,** 200 W. Kawili, 808/974-7516, is a branch of the state university system that has a strong Hawaiian Language program. The

Hawaii Community College, in a separate campus a short distance away, is a more skills-focused facility.

Banks and Post Office

All the state's big banks have branches in Hilo. Try **City Bank** at Kaiko'o Mall, 808/935-6844; **Central Pacific Bank,** 525 Kilauea Ave., 808/935-5251; **Bank of Hawaii,** 120 Pauahi St., 808/935-9701; **First Hawaiian Bank,** 1205 Kilauea Ave., 808/969-2211; or **American Savings Bank,** 100 Pauahi St., 808/935-0084.

Hilo's main **post office,** open weekdays 9 A.M.–4:30 P.M., Saturday 9 A.M.–12:30 P.M., is an efficiently run, modern post office, clearly marked on the access road to the airport. It is extremely convenient for mailings prior to departure. A downtown postal station is in the Federal Building on Waianuenue Avenue.

Internet Connection

Bytes and Bites is open daily 10 A.M.–10 P.M. for your (Internet) connection to the world at $2.50 for 15 minutes or $8 an hour. Find it at 223-A Kilauea Ave., on the corner of Ponahawai across from Low International bakery and restaurant.

DIANA LASICH HARPER

HAMAKUA COAST

Along the shore, cobalt waves foam into razor-sharp valleys where cold mountain streams meet the sea at lonely pebbled beaches. Inland, the Hamakua Coast, once awash in a rolling green sea of sugarcane, is starting to be put to other uses. Along a 50-mile stretch of the Hawai'i Belt Road (Route 19) from Hilo to Waipi'o, the Big Island grew its cane for 100 years or more. Water was needed for sugar, a ton to produce a pound, and this coast has plenty. Huge flumes once carried the cut cane to the mills. In the 19th century so many Scots worked the plantations hereabouts that Hamakua was called the "Scotch Coast." Now most residents are a mixture of Scottish, Japanese, Filipino, and Portuguese ancestry. Side roads dip off Route 19 into one-family valleys where modest, weather-beaten homes of plantation workers sit surrounded by garden plots on tiny, hand-hewn terraces. These valleys, as they march up the coast, are unromantically referred to as "gulches." From the Belt Road's many bridges, you can trace silvery-ribboned streams that mark the valley floors as they open to the sea. Each valley is jungle, lush with wildflowers and fruit trees transforming the steep sides to emerald-green velvet. This is a spectacular drive, and the coast shouldn't be missed.

This stretch of the island has recently been named the "Hilo-Hamakua Heritage Coast" in an effort to draw attention to its historic and cultural significance. When in Hilo, pick up a copy of the *A Driver's Guide to the Hilo-Hamakua Heritage Coast* pamphlet and look for brown and white road signs indicating points of interest as you proceed along Route 19.

Onomea Scenic Drive

Route 19 heading north from Hilo toward Honoka'a is a must, with magnificent inland and coastal views one after another. Only five minutes from Hilo, you'll come to Papa'ikou town. Look for Pinky's convenience store on the right. Within a half mile, a road posted as a scenic drive dips down toward the coast. Take it. Almost immediately signs warn you to slow your speed because of the narrow winding road and one-lane bridges, letting you know what kind of area you're coming into. Start down this meandering lane past some very modest homes and into the jungle that covers the road like a living green tunnel. Prepare for tiny bridges crossing tiny valleys. Stop, and you can almost hear the jungle growing. This four-mile-long Onomea Scenic Drive is like a mini-version of Maui's Hana Road. Along this route are sections of an ancient coastal trail and the ruins of a former fishing village. Drive defensively, but take a look as you pass one fine view after another. This road runs past the Hawaii Tropical Botanical Gardens and rejoins Route 19 at Pepe'ekeo, a workers' village where you can get gas or supplies.

HONOMU TO HONOKA'A

The ride alone, as you head north on the Belt Road, is gorgeous enough to be considered a sight. But there's more! You can pull off the road into sleepy one-horse towns where dogs are safe snoozing in the middle of the road. You can visit plantation stores in Honomu on your way up to 'Akaka Falls, or take a cautious dip at one of the seaside beach parks. If you want solitude, you can go inland to a forest reserve and miles of trails. The largest town on the coast is Honoka'a, with supplies, handmade mementos, restaurants, accommodations, and even a golf course. You can veer west to Waimea from Honoka'a, but don't—yet. Take the spur road, Route 240, to Kukuihaele, and from there drop down into Waipi'o Valley, known as the "Valley of Kings," one of the most beautiful in all of Hawaii.

HONOMU AND VICINITY

During its heyday, Honomu (Silent Bay) was a bustling center of the sugar industry boasting saloons, a hotel/bordello, and a church or two for repentance, and was even known as "Little Chicago." Now Honomu mainly serves as a stop as you head elsewhere, but definitely take the time to linger and soak in the feel of classic village life that still permeates its streets. Honomu is 10 miles north of Hilo and about a half mile or so inland on Route 220, which leads to 'Akaka Falls. On entering, you'll find a string of falsefront buildings that are doing a great but unofficial rendition of a "living history museum." The town has recently awoken from a long nap and is now bustling—if that's possible in a two-block town—with wonderful art galleries, small gourmet café, a culinary school, and a B&B inn. At the south end of town, just at the turn to 'Akaka Falls, notice the **Odaishisan,** a beautifully preserved Buddhist Temple. Honomu is

definitely worth a stop. It takes only minutes to walk the main street, but those minutes can give you a glimpse of history that will take you back 100 years.

What you may not expect from this little town is a first-rate cooking school, run by Sonia Martinez, a native of Cuba, member of the International Association of Culinary Professionals, and gourmet cooking school owner since 1980. **The Cooking School at Akaka Falls Inn,** P.O. Box 190, Honomu, HI 96728, 808/963-5468, fax 808/963-6353, website: www.akakafallsinn .com, email: akakainn@gte.net, emphasizes organic ingredients, the use of foods produced on the island, and blending foods from the cultures that peopled the islands. Many ingredients come from the Inn's own gourmet garden in the back. Assisted by her son, Anthony Mathis, Sonia offers regular hands-on classes throughout the month for adults and children, and she tailors instruction to student's abilities, seasonally available foods, type of menu, and length of class. Many students opt for a package that includes a room at the attached B&B Inn. Classes usually run with a minimum of four and a maximum of six students, and they range from a full-menu afternoon class with a room for $185 a couple to $1,250 for a four-night package with field trips. Check several months in advance for openings.

Accommodations and Food

You'd feel comfortable in your bowler hat or calico dress ordering up a root beer float in the **Akaka Falls Inn and Gift Gallery,** 28-1676 Main St., Honomu, HI 96728, 808/963-5468, website: www.akakafallsinn.com, email: akakainn@gte.net, a semi-converted ice cream parlor that still retains the original ambience with bent iron stools, a foot rail, a marble countertop, and a mirrored breakfront. This is the

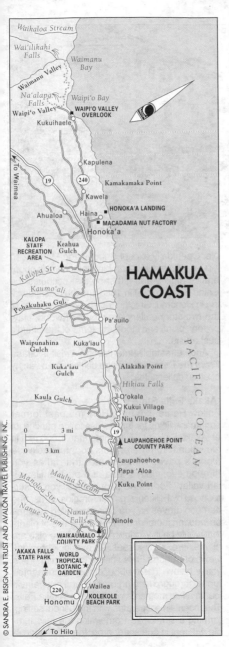

HAMAKUA COAST

Waikaloa Stream

Wai'ilikahi Falls

Waimanu Valley

Waimanu Bay

Na'alapa Falls

Waipi'o Bay

Waipi'o Valley

WAIPI'O VALLEY OVERLOOK

Kukuihaele

To Waimea

Kapulena

19 240

Kamakamaka Point

Kawela

Haina **HONOKA'A LANDING**

Ahualoa ■ **MACADAMIA NUT FACTORY**

Honoka'a

KALOPA STATE RECREATION AREA

Keahua Gulch

Kalopa Str.

Kaumo'ali

Pohakuhaku Gul.

Pa'auilo

Waipunahina Gulch Kuka'iau

Kuka'iau Gulch

Alakaha Point

Hikiau Falls

Kaula Gulch

O'okala

Kukui Village

Niu Village

19

▲ **LAUPAHOEHOE POINT COUNTY PARK**

Laupahoehoe

Papa 'Aloa

Kuku Point

Manolua Str.

Maulua Stream

Nanue Stream

Nanue Falls

Ninole

WAIKAUMALO COUNTY PARK

'AKAKA FALLS STATE PARK

WORLD TROPICAL BOTANIC GARDEN ★

220 Wailea

Honomu **KOLEKOLE BEACH PARK**

To Hilo

PACIFIC OCEAN

0   3 mi
0   3 km

© SANDRA E. BISIGN-ANI TRUST AND AVALON TRAVEL PUBLISHING, INC.

BIG ISLAND

Akita Building from 1923. Although the menu changes daily, the café section offers sandwiches for $4–7, quiche for $7, and green salads, fruit salads, and tamales for no more than $6. Shelves hold gourmet items like mango syrup, jams, chutneys, mustards, and oils, and a small freezer is packed with various flavors of ice cream, sold by the cone. Two additional rooms, serving as the gift gallery, are stuffed with quality souvenir items like koa bracelets and mirrors, artwork and beaded necklaces, calendars, cutting boards, cookbooks, and kitchen linens. As you meander through, look for potions and lotions, candles, pareu, T-shirts, and real Hawaiian quilts made by "a lady from Hilo." The café and gift shop are open 10 A.M.–5 P.M. Ascend a wainscoted stairway to the two-room bed-and-breakfast inn furnished in "plantation style" with hardwood floors, sash windows, and Casablanca fans. The two rooms, $55 single or $65 double and $25 for an extra person, are bright with Hawaiian quilts and rattan furniture. One features twin beds and a rollaway cot, while the other holds a queen bed and a day bed. A large tiled bathroom with tub and shower is shared by the two guest rooms, as is the comfortable parlor—perfect for relaxing. Peer through the windows into the backyards of Honomu, and in a few short few days you will be absorbed in the life of this simple village.

On the left as you drive along the main street is **Aloha Akaka Plate Lunch.** This little eatery is open daily except Wednesday 10 A.M.–5 P.M., where Nancy Tanemoto serves up charsiu (Chinese barbecued pork), miso with limpets, and saimin, all for easy-on-the-pocketbook prices. Sandwiches include a ham and cheese sub, hot tuna melt, and cheeseburger, and a variety of plate lunches can be had. The interior of the old building holds a few tables with chairs salvaged from Honomu's defunct theater and a counter with little red stools. The shelves are lined with pieces of remarkable driftwood, all natural sculptures made by Mother Nature. Aloha Akaka Plate Lunch is clean, friendly, and caught in a time warp harkening back to the days when a burger and a Nehi were the treat of the week!

Before entering town proper you'll spot **Jan's,** a convenience store selling cold beer and groceries.

Ishigo's General Store

Shopping

The **Woodshop Gallery/Café,** 808/963-6363 or 877/479-7995, website: www.woodshop-gallery.com, email: psm@ilhawaii.net, open daily 10:30 A.M.–6 P.M., along Honomu's main street, offers a wonderful opportunity for browsing among fine tropical wood furniture and artworks. This is one of the island's finest collections of arts and crafts. Shelves shine with the lustrous patina of bowls, mirrors, and furniture fashioned from koa, mango, *milo,* and macadamia wood, as well as from Norfolk pine, which can be turned to a translucent thinness. All pieces can be shipped, as can wood planks if you desire to create your own furniture or art piece. Jeanette and Peter McLaren, the shop owners, create stained glass works and furniture, respectively. Other artists produce additional furniture, art glass, ceramics, pottery, prints, paintings, and a great selection of turned bowls. Less expensive items include chopsticks, wooden spoons made of coconut and wood, combs, barrettes, and lovely vanity mirrors that come in a velvet bag. If you've worked up an appetite looking through the shop, head for the shop's espresso bar for a coffee, smoothie, sandwich, burger, or ice cream. Choose a table inside, or head for the lanai where you can watch the "action" in the two-block downtown of Honomu.

The **'Ohana Gallery,** 808/963-5467, operates with the philosophy that Hawaii's culture, history, and beauty are alive in the art of its peo-ple. Open daily except Sunday and Monday 10 A.M.–4 P.M., this is a combination fine arts cooperative gallery and gift shop that occupies the Ishigo Building, built in 1880 and the oldest building in Honomu. Gracing the shelves and walls of the two-story gallery are works of wood, clay, pottery, paint, and stone, by some of the island's best artists.

Another establishment worth a visit is **Glass From the Past,** with vintage bottles and a variety of other collectibles.

'Akaka Falls State Park

Follow Route 220 from Honomu past former sugarcane fields for three miles to the parking lot of 'Akaka Falls, at a little more than 1,000 feet in elevation. From here, walk counterclockwise along a paved "circle route" that takes you through everybody's idea of a pristine Hawaiian valley. For the 40-minute hike, you're surrounded by heliconia, ginger, orchids, ferns, and bamboo groves as you cross bubbling streams on wooden footbridges. Many varieties of plants that would be in window pots anywhere else are giants here, almost trees. An overlook provides views of Kahuna Falls spilling into a lush green valley below. The trail becomes an enchanted tunnel through hanging orchids and bougainvillea. In a few moments you arrive at 'Akaka Falls. The mountain cooperates with the perfect setting, forming a semicircle from which the falls tumble 442 feet in one sheer drop, the tallest single-tier waterfall in the state. After heavy rains, expect a mad torrent of power; during dry periods marvel at liquid-silver threads forming mist and rainbows. The area, maintained by the Division of State Parks, is one of the most easily accessible forays into Hawaii's beautiful interior.

Kolekole Beach Park

Look for the first tall bridge (100 feet high) a few minutes past Honomu, where a sign points to a small road that snakes its way down the valley to the beach park below. Slow down and keep a sharp eye out as the turnoff is right at the end of the bridge and easy to miss. Amenities include restrooms, grills, electricity, picnic tables, pavilions, and a camping area (county permit); no drinking water is available. Kolekole is very popular with local people, who use its pavilions for all manner of special occasions, usually on weekends. A black-sand beach fronts an extremely treacherous ocean. The entire valley was inundated with more than 30 feet of water during the great 1946 tsunami. The stream running through Kolekole comes from 'Akaka Falls, four miles inland. It forms a pool complete with waterfall that is safe for swimming but quite cold.

Wailea

Just a few miles beyond Kolekole Beach Park, above the highway on the old road, is the tiny community of Wailea. A former sugar town, it's now a sleepy village. Yet despite this sleepiness there is much energy and direction. Occupying one of the old storefronts, The WaiOla Community Wellness Center has set its sights on community involvement, health and wellness issues, and the preservation of cultural crafts. Also in town is the easygoing and casual **Akiko's Buddhist Bed and Breakfast,** P.O. Box 272, Hakalau, HI 96710, 808/963-6422, website: http://alternative-hawaii.com/akiko, email: msakiko@aloha.net. You need not be a Buddhist to stay, but you should come with an open mind and open heart. The bright yellow main house clues you in to the cheeriness and energy inside. Akiko's offers four Japanese-style rooms in the main building, a common kitchen, and bathroom with shower. An adjacent two-story plantation house also has four rooms, plus a living room, kitchen, and a basic bathroom with shower. A retreat studio is also available in a third building, with basic cooking appliances for longer stays. Breakfast is a group affair in the main house with fruits from the garden, fresh-baked bread, and other goodies created by the talented Akiko. While it is not required, you may want to attend one of the informal meditations held every morning at 5 A.M. in the main house meditation room, or tag along on one the morning walks. Yoga is done every Sunday morning. The rooms in the main house have futons on the floor; the plantation house has both beds and futons. Rates are $40 single or $55 double per night, and the plantation house can be rented for $155 a night. Weekly and monthly rates are $260 and $555 single or $355 and $750 double. The upstairs retreat studio has a two-week minimum and goes for $420 single or $585 double for that period. An easy place with good vibes and always plenty going on, you can rest and relax, participate or not, or head out to explore the countryside yourself.

'Akaka Falls

ROBERT NILSEN

BIG ISLAND

World Tropical Botanical Gardens

With an impressive name like this, this garden has to be good. But wait, the gardens are only in their infancy! Created on land that was sugarcane just a few short years ago, these gardens are destined to be a wonderful sight, and they already show signs of botanical prowess. What's more, the three-tier Umauma Waterfall is on the property and is sure to please. About half the acreage is open now to the public; walks take you past colorful exotic flowers and a selection of fruits and other tropical plants. The plan is to cultivate some 30,000 species—arranged in evolutionary grouping! This garden is open Mon.–Sat. 9 A.M.–5:30 P.M., and the entrance fee—which helps to further the cause—is a reasonable $5 adults and $2 teens; 808/963-5427, website: www.wbgi.com. Follow the signs up from the highway near mile marker 16.

LAUPAHOEHOE

This wave-lashed peninsula is a finger of smooth pahoehoe lava that juts into the bay. About halfway between Honomu and Honoka'a, the valley at one time supported farmers and fishermen who specialized in catching turtles. Laupahoehoe was the best boat landing along the coast, and for years canoes and, later, schooners would stop here. A plaque commemorates the tragic loss of 20 schoolchildren and their teacher who were taken by the great tsunami of 1946. Afterwards, the village was moved to the high ground overlooking the point. **Laupahoehoe Point County Park** now occupies the low peninsula; it has picnic tables, showers, electricity, and a county camping area. The sea is too rough to swim in but many fishermen come here, along with some daring surfers. Laupahoehoe makes a beautiful rest stop along the Belt Road. Turn near mile marker 27, after the highway comes back out of the valley. The road down to the park is narrow and winding and runs past several rebuilt homes and a restored Jodo Mission.

Near the Laupahoehoe scenic overlook is the **Laupahoehoe Train Museum,** 36-2377 Mamalahoa Hwy., P.O. Box 358, Laupahoehoe, HI 96764, 808/962-6300, email: ltmhawaii@aol.com. Open daily 9 A.M.–4:30 P.M., entrance by donation, this museum treats you to a taste of the olden days when trains hauled sugarcane, people, and goods up and down this rugged coast. The museum was once was the home of the Superintendent of Maintenance for this division, and it is now filled with train memorabilia, photographs, books, and furniture that were either from the house or typical of the era. The house itself has been lovingly restored and a track "wye" on the grounds is also being restored. You can see remnants of a loading platform out front. This museum is a worthy enterprise and a fine place to stop on your way up the road.

Ten miles inland from Laupahoehoe Point along a very rugged jeep trail is **David Douglas Historical Monument.** This marks the spot where the naturalist, after whom the Douglas fir is named, lost his life under mysterious circumstances. Douglas, on a fact-gathering expedition on the rugged slopes of Mauna Kea, never returned. His body was found at the bottom of a deep pit that was used at the time to catch feral cattle. Douglas had spent the previous night at a cabin occupied by an Australian who had been a convict. Many suspected that the Australian had murdered Douglas in a robbery attempt and thrown his body into the pit to hide the deed. No hard evidence of murder could be found, and the death was officially termed accidental.

Practicalities

As you drive up the highway, you dip into and out of the Maulua Gulch, the biggest and one of the most impressive so far up this coast. Just before Laupahoehoe, look for a sign to **Papa'aloa.** Although now silent, you can almost imagine the hubbub of activity when this town, and others like it on the coast, were alive with sugar production. Turn here, and head down the road to the **Papaaloa Neighborhood Store,** where local people go to buy the area's *best* smoked meats and fish, including marlin, beef, pork, and *laulau* made right at the store; plate lunches to go are also available.

In Laupahoehoe along Route 19, look for **M. Sakado Store,** open 7:30 A.M.–5:30 P.M., an old-fashioned Hawaiian-style convenience store. It sells basic items like milk, bread, and soft drinks, enough for a picnic. There's not too much else here but a post office, police station, and school. If you need gas, fill up at Sunny C's, the only place along the coast between Hilo and Honoka'a.

Keoki's Place, 808/962-0011, open Tues.–Sat. 10 A.M.–7 P.M., Sunday 10 A.M.–5 P.M., in a white and turquoise painted vintage building in Laupahoehoe Village, is a combination plate lunch restaurant and pizza parlor. Pizzas range $8–12 plus $1 for extra toppings, or cost $2 by the slice. Deli sandwiches like ham, turkey, chicken, tuna, avocado, veggie, or eggplant parmigiana are all under $5, with burgers a little higher. Plate lunches are the standard, from mahimahi to teriyaki beef. Desserts are homemade cheesecake and ice cream, and drinks include shakes and malts. The atmosphere is as local as you can get!

Pa'auilo

About 10 miles past Laupahoehoe is Pa'auilo, another ghost of a sugar town. Set close to the highway, the new town has a post office, Earl's snack shop, and a former plantation manager's house. In business for about 100 years, **Sandra's General Store** serves soda, sandwiches, and crackseed. Down toward the sea were plantation workers' camps, and on the coast are the old mill and docks where raw sugar was loaded for transport.

Kalopa State Recreation Area

This spacious natural area is 12 miles north of Laupahoehoe, five miles southeast of Honoka'a, three miles inland on a well-marked secondary road, and 2,000 feet in elevation. Little used by tourists, it's a great place to get away from the coast and up into the hills. Hiking is terrific throughout the park and adjoining forest reserve on a series of nature trails where some of the flora has been identified. Most of the forest here is endemic, with few alien species. Some of what you will see are 'ohi'a, koa, the *hapu'u* tree fern, and *kopiko* and *pilo,* both species of the coffee tree family. Near the entrance and camping area is a young arboretum. Beyond the arboretum is an easy three-quarter-mile nature loop trail through an 'ohi'a forest, and three-mile loop trail takes you along the gulch trail and back to camp via an old road. All trails are well marked and vary widely in difficulty. Bird life here may not be as varied as high up the mountainside, but still you can catch sight of 'elipaio, auku'u (a night heron), the white-eye, cardinal, and the Hawaiian hoary bat. The park provides an excellent opportunity to explore some of the lush gulches of the Hamakua Coast, as well as day-use picnicking, tent camping, and furnished cabins (state permit required) that can house up to eight people. Camping and cabin use is limited to five consecutive days per party. The bunk-style cabins, each with a bathroom and shower, rent for $55 for one to eight campers. Linens and blankets are provided, and you may cook in the recreation hall. For reservations, contact the State Park office, 75 Aupuni St. #204, Hilo, HI 96721, 808/974-6200.

BIG ISLAND

HONOKA'A TO KUKUIHAELE

HONOKA'A AND VICINITY

With a population of just over 2,000, Honoka'a (Rolling Bay) is the major town on the Hamakua Coast. In the past, it was a center for the both the cattle and sugar industries and a place where GIs stationed at Camp Tarawa in Waimea would come for R&R. Now it's mainly a tourist town, although the surrounding area is a center of the macadamia nut industry, and the town is a hotbed of controversy about land use issues now that sugar is no longer the economic behemoth of the region. From here, you can continue on Route 19 for 16 miles to Waimea or take Route 240 north for nine miles to the edge of Waipi'o Valley, which you should not miss. First, however, stroll the main street of Honoka'a, Mamane Street, where there are a number of shops specializing in locally produced handicrafts, a gallery or two, restaurants, and general merchandise stores next to antiques shops. Also in town are a small health center, a post office, two banks, a movie theater, public library, a nine-hole golf course, and a small visitor information center. It's also the best place to stock up on supplies or gasoline—there are stations on both Routes 19 and 240. If you are proceeding north along Route 240, the coastal route heading to Waipi'o Valley, just past mile marker 6 on the left, keep an eye peeled for a lava-tube cave right along the roadway. This is just a tease of the amazing natural sights that follow.

Festivals

The **Hamakua Music Festival**, 808/775-3378, website: www.hamakuamusicfestival.com, held yearly in early October and lasting two weekends, attracts not only island musicians but musicians of national and international fame. While there is always jazz, classical, and Hawaiian music on the schedule, other genre of music are sometimes also performed. Major concerts are performed on the weekends at the Honoka'a People's Theater, with related events and local musical groups performing during the week. Tickets usually run about $20 per concert, very reasonable for big name performers, and excess profits from the festival are used to fund local music scholarships and the salary for a local music teacher.

The annual **Taro Festival** is held in November and it celebrates the most cherished of traditional Hawaiian foods. Events include Hawaiian music, hula, chanting, taro exhibits, food made from taro, and crafts and games. The whole town gets into the swing of things and this day-long event is a hit.

Western Days Weekend is scheduled for the end of May. Genuine cowboys as well as city slickers from the Mainland pretending to be *paniolo* will throw their Stetsons in the air and yell "yippie yi yo kai yea!" when this event rolls around. It's a time for all cowboys to gather for

fun and games. Two rodeos are held during the weekend at the Honoka'a Arena for those who like that sort of rough and tumble affair—and for those who just like to watch. Aside from a lively parade that makes its way through town, there's horseshoe pitching, craft displays, a dinner and dance, and—everyone's favorite—the Saloon Girl contest. For information about either the Western Days Weekend or the Taro Festival, contact the Honoka'a Business Association, P.O. Box 474, Honoka'a, HI 96727, website: www.alternative-hawaii.com/hba.

Accommodations

Centrally located along Route 240 in downtown Honoka'a is the **Hotel Honoka'a Club**, P.O. Box 247, Honoka'a, HI 96727, 808/775-0678 or 800/808-0678, website: http://home1.gte.net/honokaac, email: honokaac@gte.net. Built in 1908 as the plantation manager's club, it's still infused with the grace and charm of the old days. Yet, what it lacks in elegance it makes up for in cleanliness and friendliness. The hotel, mostly used by local people, is old and well used but clean and comfortable, and the only accommodations right in town. From the back rooms, you get a view over the tin roofs of residential Honoka'a and the ocean. Follow a wainscoted hallway from the front office to your room. All rooms are upgraded with carpeting and fluffy quilts; each features a view and TV. There are more spartan but very clean rooms downstairs. These rooms run $80 for a two-room suite, $55–65 for an ocean view room with TV, private bath and, queen bed, and $45–50 for an economy room with a private bath. Rates include a simple continental breakfast. Hostel rooms, located in the basement, all with shared bath and kitchen facilities, are separated into three private rooms at $35 and two communal rooms (one sleeping three people and the other six people) that rent for $15, add $5 if you do not supply your own linens. The basement hostel rooms, although a bit dungeonesque, are clean, with windows to catch the breeze. The hotel's dining room, the Paniolo Plantation Inn, provides the continental breakfast for guests, and lunch, dinner, and cocktails for the general public.

About four miles up above town in the pasture and forest land of Ahualoa is **Mountain Meadow Ranch B&B**, P.O. Box 1697, Hono-

---

HAMAKUA MACADAMIA NUT INDUSTRY

The macadamia nut industry was started in Honoka'a when W.H. Purvis, a British agriculturist who had been working in Australia, brought the first trees to Honoka'a in 1882; one is still bearing! In 1924, W. Pierre Naquin, then manager of the Honoka'a Sugar Co., started the first commercial nut farm in the area. While the bulk of the macadamia nut industry has moved elsewhere on the island, nuts have continued to be grown and processed here almost continually since the early years.

ka'a, HI 96727, 808/775-9367, fax 808/775-8033, website: www.bnbweb/Mountain-Meadow.html, email: Wgeorge737@aol.com. The lower level of the ranch home has a living room with TV and VCR, sitting room with microwave and small refrigerator, two bedrooms, and its own entrance; a light continental breakfast is included in the room price. This unit runs $70 single or $80 double. A separate guest cottage with full kitchen, two bedrooms, and laundry room is also available, but no breakfast is included. There is a three-night minimum, and the rate is $125 a night or $700 a week. No smoking inside either unit.

The **Log Cabin** guesthouse in Ahualoa, P.O. Box 1994, Kamuela, HI 96743, 808/885-4243 or 800/555-8968, fax 808/885-8857, website: www.hawaii-bnb.com/kamuela.html, email: kaminn@aloha.net, is associated with Kamuela Inn in Waimea. It sits on a five-acre forested property in a cool mountain setting. The log-style walls and framing and barn roof give this large house a welcoming country feel. This house has a large living room with fireplace, upstairs library, full kitchen, five guest bedrooms, and a hot tub stuck in a garden gazebo. Room rates are $59 with shared bath, $99 with private bath, or $375 a night for the whole house, continental breakfast included.

Just east of town is the **Paauhau Plantation House**, P.O. Box 1375, Honoka'a, HI 96727, 808/775-7222 or 800/789-7614, fax 808/775-7223, website: www.bbhost.com/bbpaauhau-plantation, email: hawaii@pocketmail.com. This 1930s-style island house is a slice of what good living was like in years past. The drive leads up through the front metal gate, under stately palm trees to the plantation house. Surrounded by formal lawns and gardens, with a private tennis court on the property, this B&B has a billiard room, library, and TV den for guest use. In the main house is the master suite with its two bedrooms and connecting bath for $200 a night. The Yellow Room is also available for $100 a night. For something less formal, try one of the four cottages, each with its own bathroom and kitchen, for $100–140, two-night minimum.

Surrounded by pastureland just outside Kalopa State Recreation Area, **Mauka Bed and Breakfast**, P.O. Box 767, Honoka'a, HI 96727, 808/775-9983, website: www.stayhawaii.com/mauka.html, email: maukabb@gte.net, is a quiet and relaxing

spot. At 1,700 feet in elevation, it is also cool and refreshing. There is one studio here with a private entrance, queen bed, bathroom, TV, and VCR. The room rate of $60 a night includes a simple continental breakfast. No credit cards.

Food

Local people thought that Jolene was such a good cook, they talked her into opening **Jolene's Kau Kau Corner** in downtown Honoka'a, 808/775-9498, open Mon.–Fri. 10:30 A.M.–8 P.M., Saturday 10 A.M.–3 P.M.. Most tried-and-true recipes were handed down by her extended family, who lend a hand in running the restaurant. The restaurant, in a vintage storefront, is trim and neat, and the menu includes a variety of plate lunches like beef tips teriyaki, a shrimp plate, a steaming bowl of beef stew, saimin in two sizes, and burgers and fries, mostly under $6. The dinner menu, with many items $8–15, brings broiled mahimahi, shrimp tempura, shrimp and chicken baskets, a steak and seafood combination, and vegetarian stir-fry. Jolene's is as down-home and local as you can get, with friendly service, hearty dishes, and reasonable prices. This is one of the best places to eat along the northern Hamakua Coast!

Follow the comforting aroma of fresh-baked bread to **Mamane Street Bakery & Café**, 808/775-9478, open Mon.–Sat. 6 A.M.–5 P.M., owned and operated by Eliahu "Ely" Pessah, who is assisted by Emma, who has a smile sweeter than the cupcakes on the shelves. Ely bakes goodies including coconut turnovers, Danish pastries, and *ensemada,* a special type of cinnamon roll, but what the local people come in for are the honey-nut bran muffins, crunchy with chunks of macadamia nuts. Ely's oven also turns out ham and cheese croissants, mozzarella or marinara focaccia, or three-cheese focaccia. Eat in or take out while enjoying your purchase with a cup of steaming coffee or tea. Make sure to visit the "Gift Shop," constructed in free-form design with 52 different kinds of wood. Here, you'll discover painted fish, glass fish, wooden earrings, *lau hala* bracelets, carved elephants, a smattering of pottery, note cards, and Hawaiian dolls.

Almost across the street is the newer **Cafe Il Mondo,** 808/775-7711, an Italian pizzeria and coffee bar that's open Mon.–Sat. 11 A.M.–9 P.M.

BIG ISLAND

This is a cheery place with Italian music on the sound system and prints of Italian scenes on the walls. Here you feel the spirit of Italy. While pizzas, $12–18, are the main focus, you can also get tasty calzones, lasagna, sandwiches, salads, soup, ice cream, and gourmet coffee, of course!

The **Paniolo Plantation Inn,** at Hotel Honoka'a Club, is open daily for lunch 11 A.M.–2:30 P.M. and daily for dinner 5–8:45 P.M., with all meals prepared in a new and much upgraded kitchen. Cocktails are served in the bar until closing. Food is basically of the local American variety, with the infusion of plenty of fresh vegetables and locally grown produce, but the restaurant has that cowboy twist—it's associated with the Paniolo Country Inn restaurant in Waimea. The meals, although not gourmet, are wholesome, with plenty of well-prepared food. For something light, try a sandwich, burger, or salad—all under $7. Heartier menu items include steak, ribs, chicken, and lobster for $10–20. Paniolo pizza with your choice of toppings and a short Mexican section are also on the menu, and full bar service is available.

"On a Wing and a Prayer" is part of the logo welcoming you to **Simply Natural Ice Cream Parlor and Deli,** 808/775-0119, open Mon.–Sat. 9 A.M.–4 P.M., where the owner, Sharon, does the praying and Bernie the Cockatoo is the wing man and official greeter. Besides ice cream in tropical and standard flavors, a board offers a full sandwich and burger menu with plenty of soups, vegetarian items, and Mexican choices. Beverages include soft drinks, fresh-squeezed carrot juice, Kona coffee, espresso, and cappuccino.

Tex Drive In and Restaurant, 808/775-0598, open daily 5 A.M.–9 P.M., a little later on weekends, is an institution in town. Everyone knows it and everyone's been there—many times. The long-established Hamakua restaurant is known for its fresh *malasadas* (sugared, holeless Portuguese donuts), production of which is showcased behind plate glass windows inside. Get some! They're a treat. Every month, 15,000 of these tasty treats are sold. Tex has been remodeled with a fast-food look, a drive-up window, walk-up counter, and inside and outside tables, but the cavernous dining room in the back is still there and the food is

still as filling and reasonable as ever. It specializes in inexpensive local food like *kalua* pork, teriyaki chicken and beef, hamburgers, and fresh fish, and there are many ethnic items on the menu. Prices are very reasonable, with most dinners around $6 and sandwiches less. Local people and (an even better sign) the local police come here to chow down on good, easy-on-the-wallet food. Tex Drive In is along Route 19, at the corner of Pakalana Street.

Herb's Place, in downtown Honoka'a, is open for breakfast, lunch, and dinner daily from 5:30 A.M. You get basic meals and cocktails in this little roadside joint.

C.C. Jon's, a local ethnic eatery open for breakfast and lunch, is right on the road as you enter town. Most of the plate lunch dishes are under $5.

Keoki's Coffee Company, 808/775-1104, open 9 A.M.–5 P.M. daily, is on a side road that leads from the post office in town about a half mile down a steep hill toward the sea to the little community of Haina. It occupies part of what was the Hawaiian Holiday Macadamia Nut Factory. Currently coffee, a few snacks, and ice cream are served here. While here, have a look at the blown glass on display and at the glass-blowing operation.

Entertainment

The once run-down but classic "Last Picture Show" **Honoka'a People's Theater,** along the main drag, has been renovated to its old 1930s splendor. It's a big-screen theater, seating about 500, that has a new surround sound system. First-run movies generally show Fri.–Sun. evenings, with art movies shown on Tuesday and Wednesday. Showtime is 7 P.M. and tickets run $5 for adults, $3 for seniors and children. This theater is also used as a venue for the yearly Hawaii International Film Festival, for the autumn Hamakua Music Festival, and for other community events throughout the year. Call 808/775-0000 to hear what's showing.

Shopping

If you are at all interested in the history of Hawaii, make sure to stop by the **Hawaiian Artifacts and Antiques** shop along the main drag in downtown Honoka'a. This amazing curio and art shop is owned and operated by Lokikamakahiki "Loki" Rice, who ran it for many years with her husband James, who passed away in the spring of 1996. Loki, elderly and in failing health, keeps no set hours, opening when she feels like it, usually for a few hours in the afternoon, but never before 2 P.M. At first glance the shop may look inauthentic, but once you're inside, that impression quickly melts away. Loki, a full-blooded Hawaiian, was born and raised in Waipi'o Valley, and James traveled the Pacific for years. The stories from the old days are almost endless. Notice a tiki that serves as a main beam, and two giant shields against the back wall. They belonged to Loki's father, a giant of a man just under seven feet tall and more than 450 pounds—he had to have a special coffin made when he was buried on the island of Ni'ihau. Local people bring in their carvings and handicrafts to sell, many of which are hula implements and instruments like drums and rattles. Some of the bric-a-brac is from the Philippines or other South Sea islands, but Loki will identify them for you. Mingled in with what seems to be junk are some real artifacts like poi pounders, adzes, and really good drums. Many have come from Loki's family, while others have been collected by the Rices over the years. But the real treasure is Loki, who will share her aloha as long as time and the call from above permits.

At the east end of town, **Seconds To Go,** open daily except Sunday 9:30 A.M.–5 P.M., is owned and operated by Elaine Carlsmith. The collectibles and antiques shop specializes in Hawaiian artifacts; it brims with classic Hawaiian ties and shirts from the '50s, dancing hula-doll lamps, antique hardware and building materials, clawtoot bathtubs, old books, Japanese bowls, a good collection of plates and saucers, and a ukulele. Elaine also sells used fishing gear in case you want to try your luck.

The Honoka'a Trading Company, 808/775-0808, open daily 10 A.M.–5 P.M., is a discovery shop owned and operated by Denise Walker. Items come and go, but you can expect to find classic artwork from the Matson Steamship Lines, hula dolls, Japanese netsuke, poi bowls, costume jewelry, pots and pans, bottles, and old crockery. Denise has also filled this rambling building with a good selection of old books, Hawaiian instruments, Japanese fans, and vintage signs. Denise focuses not only on things *from* Hawaii, but on things brought *to* Hawaii. Much of the furniture and many of the antique items were brought to Hawaii by *kama'aina* and GI families.

If these shops haven't been enough for your antiques and collectibles needs, make your last stop at **Honoka'a Market Place,** 808/775-8255, where you can browse through furniture, clothing, and all sorts of old castoffs that now command a stiff price, and actually are, collectively, a window on the past.

Kama'aina Woods, 808/775-7722, in Honoka'a halfway down the hill leading to the Macadamia Nut Factory, is usually open daily except Sunday 9 A.M.–5 P.M., but this depends on the weather, the owner's inclination, and how the spirits are moving on any particular day. The shop is owned and operated by Bill Keb, a talented woodworker who specializes in fabulous bowls turned from native woods like koa, *milo,* extremely rare *kou,* and a few introduced woods like mango and Norfolk Island pine. All of the wooden art pieces, priced from affordable to not-so-affordable, are one-of-a-kind and utilitarian. Less expensive items are koa or *milo* bracelets, letter openers, and rice paddles.

The **Bamboo Gallery,** 808/775-0433, is a spacious showroom on the main drag where you will find an eclectic mix of wood, bamboo, fiber, canvas, multi-media, and glass art, all displayed in a sparse Oriental style. Nearby is **Hamakua Art Glass** with many more lovely examples of this art form. Toward the east end of town is **Starseed** for beads and gems.

S. Hasegawa has a few racks of local fashions and a few bolts of traditional Japanese cloth, as well as gifts and candies, cards, and cosmetics. This is an old-time general dry goods store. Next door is the very ethnic **Filipino Store** along the main drag; stop in to soak up a cultural experience and to find an array of exotic spices and food ingredients.

For groceries and even a few health food items, stop at **T. Kaneshiro Store** and **K.K. Super-Mart,** two well-stocked markets in town. A small selection of natural produce, fruits, packaged and canned items, supplements and vitamins is available at the **Honoka'a Natural Foods** store next to Hotel Honoka'a Club.

BIG ISLAND

KUKUIHAELE

For all of you looking for the "light at the end of the tunnel," Kukuihaele (Traveling Light) is it. A small plantation town, Kukuihaele now subsists on tourism. The new highway bypasses town. Take the old road down and in; it pops out again on the other side. At the far edge of town, on the cusp of the valley wall, is the **Waipi'o Valley Overlook,** an exceptional location for peering into this marvelous, mysterious, and legend-filled valley. For most tourists, this is as close as you'll get to the "Valley of Kings." But, oh, what a sight! Stand a while and soak in the surroundings: the valley and ocean, the black sand beach, the coastal cliffs, and the ever-changing clouds. During winter months you might be treated to a special sight when mama humpbacks bring their newborn babies to the bay below to teach them how to be whales.

On the old road just before town, the **Last Chance Store,** open daily except Wednesday and Sunday 9 A.M.–5 P.M., stocks basic grocery supplies plus a small assortment of handicrafts and gift items. The Last Chance has an excellent selection of domestic and imported beers, along with light snacks for a picnic lunch. The Last Chance Store is just that; there is no other shop beyond.

Waipi'o Valley Artworks, 808/775-0958 or 800/492-4746, open daily 9 A.M.–5:30 P.M., is an excellent shop in which to pick up an art object. There are plenty of offerings in wood by some of the island's best woodworkers that include carvings and bowls, but the shop also showcases various Hawaii-based artists working in different media. Definitely check out inspired prints, paintings, line drawings, pottery, and jewelry. You'll also find crafts, a smattering of souvenir items, a fairly extensive collection of books mostly on Hawaiiana, designer T-shirts, and other wearables. This is one of those wonderful finds, an out-of-the-way place that carries a good selection of excellent artwork at affordable prices—and they'll ship. The shop also features a counter serving ice cream, sandwiches, and soft drinks. Waipi'o Valley Artworks is the meeting place for **Waipio Valley Shuttle,** which will take you down to the valley, and for the hiking, biking, horseback, and van tours that explore the valley rim. All in all, Waipi'o Valley Artworks is the hub of activity in town.

Accommodations

A vintage home of a one-time plantation manager, **Waipio Wayside,** P.O. Box 840, Honoka'a, HI 96727, tel./fax 808/775-0275 or 800/833-8849, website: www.waipiowayside.com, email: wayside@ilhawaii.net, is now owned and operated by Jackie Horne as a congenial B&B Inn. Look for the Waipio Wayside sign hung on a white picket fence exactly two miles toward Waipi'o from the Honoka'a post office. You enter through double French doors onto a rich wooden floor shining with a well-waxed patina. The walls are hand-laid vertical paneling, the prototype that modern paneling tries to emulate. Here is a formal dining area and an informal seating area with books, a television, videos, and music. The home contains five bedrooms, each with private bathroom, ranging in price $95–135, $25 extra for an additional person beyond two. The Birds Eye Room has a three-night minimum and the Library Room a two-night minimum, with a $10 surcharge for single-night stays. Spacious and airy, all rooms are individually decorated by theme and hung with beautiful Battenburg lace curtains. The back deck, where you will find hammocks in which to rock away your cares, overlooks manicured grounds that gently slope to a panoramic view of the coast. Jackie, whose meticulous and tastefully appointed home is straight from the pages of a designer magazine, is also a gourmet cook. Breakfast is sometimes waffles with strawberries and whipped cream, sometimes omelets and biscuits, with fresh fruit from the property. Beverages are pure Hamakua coffee, juices, and gourmet teas from around the world, and there is always an assortment of snacks. A stay at Waipio Wayside is guaranteed to be civilized, relaxing, and totally enjoyable. As a benefit, Jackie will gladly arrange island activities for her guests.

Surrounded by green acres of pasture on the edge of the sea cliff next to the Waipi'o Valley Overlook is the **Cliff House,** 808/775-0005 or 800/492-4746. This two-story, two-bedroom house with full kitchen, laundry room, and lanai that looks over the ocean also has separate living and dining rooms. This house runs $150 a night for a couple, two nights minimum, with an extra person charge of $15. No credit cards. Check-in is at the Waipi'o Valley Artworks shop.

Right in the tiny community of Kukuihaele is **Moo's Log Cabin,** P.O. Box 5047, Kukuihaele, HI 96727, 808/775-8035. This true log cabin house, originally built on the Mainland, then dismantled and moved to its present site, is not your typical home in the islands. Yet, it is has a wonderful location a short distance from the edge of Waipi'o Valley and is set along a babbling stream. The house itself has two units, each with a private bathroom and kitchenette, both $85 a night for up to four people; the newer "teahouse" also has two rooms that together sleep three people for $110; 10 percent discount for three nights or more, add $10 for single-night stays. No breakfast is served, and no credit cards are accepted.

WAIPI'O VALLEY

Waipi'o is the way the Lord would have liked to fashion the Garden of Eden, if he hadn't been on such a tight schedule. You can read about this incredible valley, but you really can't believe it until you see it for yourself. Route 240 ends a minute outside of Kukuihaele at an overlook, and 900 feet below is Waipi'o (Curving Water), the island's largest and most southerly valley of the many that slice the harsh Kohala Mountains. The valley is a mile across where it fronts the sea at a series of high sand dunes, and six miles from the ocean to its back end. It's vibrantly green, always watered by Waipi'o Stream and lesser streams that spout as waterfalls from the *pali* at the rear of the valley. The green is offset by a wide band of black-sand beach. The far side of the valley ends abruptly at a steep *pali* that is higher than the one on which you're standing. A six-mile trail leads over it to Waimanu Valley, smaller, more remote, and more luxuriant.

Travelers have long extolled the amazing abundance of Waipi'o. From the overlook you can make out the overgrown outlines of garden terraces, taro patches, and fishponds in what was Hawai'i's largest cultivated valley. Every foodstuff known to the Hawaiians once flourished here; even Waipi'o pigs were said to be bigger than pigs anywhere else. In times of famine, the produce from Waipi'o could sustain the populace of the entire island (estimated at 100,000 people). On the valley floor and alongside the streams you'll still find avocados, bananas, coconuts, passion fruit, mountain apples, guavas, breadfruit, tapioca, lemons, limes, coffee, grapefruit, and pumpkins. The old fishponds and streams are alive with prawns, wild pigs roam the interior, as do wild horses, and there are abundant fish in the sea. Carrying on the traditions of farmers of old, some farmers in the valley still raise taro, and this has once again become one of the largest taro-producing regions on the island and one of the principal production centers in the state.

But the lovingly tended order, most homes, and the lifestyle were washed away in the tsunami of 1946. Now Waipi'o is largely unkempt, a wild jungle of mutated abundance. The valley is a neglected maiden with a dirty face and disheveled, windblown hair. Only love and nurturing can refresh her lingering beauty.

HISTORY

Legend and Oral History

Waipi'o is a mystical place. Inhabited for more than 1,000 years, it figures prominently in old Hawaiian lore. In the primordial past, Wakea, progenitor of all the islands, favored the valley, and oral tradition holds that the great gods Kane and Kanaloa dallied in Waipi'o, intoxicating themselves on 'awa. One oral chant relates that the demigod Maui, that wild prankster, met his untimely end here by trying to steal baked bananas from these two drunken heavyweights. One flung Maui against the rear valley wall, splattering blood everywhere, hence the distinctively red color of the earth at the far back reaches of the valley. Lono, god of the Makahiki, came to Waipi'o in search of a bride. He found Kaikilani, a beautiful maiden who lived in a breadfruit tree near **Hi'ilawe Waterfall,** which tumbles 1,000 feet in a cascade of three drops to the valley below and is the island's tallest waterfall.

Nenewe, a shark-man, lived near a pool at the bottom of another waterfall on the west side

BIG ISLAND

Waipi'o Valley

of Waipi'o. The pool was connected to the sea by an underwater tunnel. All went well for Nenewe until his grandfather disobeyed a warning never to feed his grandson meat. Once Nenewe tasted meat, he began eating Waipi'o residents after first warning them about sharks as they passed his sea-connected pool on their way to fish. His constant warnings aroused suspicions. Finally, the cape he always wore was ripped from his shoulders, and there on his back was a shark's mouth! He dove into his pool and left Waipi'o to hunt the waters of the other islands.

Pupualenalena, a *kupua* (nature spirit), takes the form of a yellow dog that can change its size from tiny to huge. He was sent by the chiefs of Waipi'o to steal a conch shell that mischievous water sprites were constantly blowing, just to irritate the people. The shell was inherited by Kamehameha and is now in the Bishop Museum. Another dog-spirit lives in a rock embedded in the hillside halfway down the road to Waipi'o. In times of danger, he comes out of his rock to stand in the middle of the road as a warning that bad things are about to happen.

Finally, a secret section of Waipi'o Beach is called **Lua o milu,** the legendary doorway to the land of the dead. At certain times, it is believed, ghosts of great *ali'i* come back to earth as "Marchers of the Night," and their strong chants and torch-lit processions fill the darkness in Waipi'o. Many great kings were buried in Waipi'o, and it's felt that because of their *mana,* no harm

will come to the people who live here. Oddly enough, the horrible tsunami of 1946 and a raging flood in 1979 filled the valley with wild torrents of water. In both cases, the devastation to homes and the land was tremendous, but not one life was lost. Everyone who still lives in Waipi'o will tell you they feel protected.

The remains of **Paka'alana Heiau** is in a grove of trees on the right-hand side of the beach as you face the sea. It dates from the 12th century and was a "temple of refuge" where *kapu* breakers, vanquished warriors, and the weak and infirm could find sanctuary. Paka'alana was a huge *heiau* with tremendous walls that were mostly intact until the tsunami of 1946. The tsunami sounded like an explosion when the waters hit the walls of Paka'alana, according to first-hand accounts. The rocks were scattered, and all was turned to ruins. Nearby, **Hanua'aloa** is another *heiau* in ruins. Archaeologists know even less about this *heiau,* but all agree that both were healing temples of body and spirit, and the local people feel that their positive *mana* is part of the protection in Waipi'o.

Recorded History

Great chiefs have dwelt in Waipi'o. King Umi planted taro just like a commoner and fished with his own hands. He went on to unite the island into one kingdom in the 15th century. Waipi'o was the traditional land of Kamehameha the Great and in many ways was the basis of his earthly and spiritual power. It was here that he was entrusted with the war god, Kuka'ilimoku, as King Kalani'opu'u was dying. Kamehameha came here to rest after heavy battles, and offshore was the scene of the first modern naval battle in Hawaii. Here, Kamehameha's war canoes faced those of his nemesis, Keoua. Both had recently acquired cannons bartered from passing sea captains. Kamehameha's artillery was manned by two white sailors, Davis and Young, who became trusted advisors. Kamehameha's forces won the engagement in what became known as the "Battle of the Red-Mouthed Gun."

When Captain Cook came to Hawaii, 4,000 natives lived in Waipi'o; a century later only 600 remained. At the turn of the 20th century many Chinese and Japanese moved to Waipi'o and began raising rice and taro. People moved in and out of the valley by horse and mule, and there were schools, stores, a post office, churches, and a strong community spirit. Waipi'o was painstakingly tended. The undergrowth was kept trimmed and you could see clearly from the back of the valley all the way to the sea. World War II arrived and many people were lured away from the remoteness of the valley by a changing lifestyle and a desire for modernity. The tsunami in 1946 swept away most of the homes, and the majority of the people pulled up stakes and moved away. For 25 years the valley lay virtually abandoned. The Peace Corps considered it a perfect place to build a compound in which to train volunteers headed for Southeast Asia. This too was later abandoned. Then in the late '60s and early '70s a few "back to nature" hippies started trickling in. Most only played "Tarzan and Jane" for a while and moved on, especially after Waipi'o served them a "reality sandwich" in the form of the flood of 1979.

Waipi'o is still very unpredictable. In a three-week period from late March to early April of 1989, 47 inches of rain drenched the valley. Roads were turned to quagmires, houses washed away, and more people left. Part of the problem is the imported trees in Waipi'o. Until the 1940s, the valley was a manicured garden, but now it's very heavily forested. All of the trees you will see are new; the oldest are mangroves and coconuts. The trees are both a boon and a blight. They give shade and fruit, but when there are floods, they fall into the river, creating logjams

that increase the flooding dramatically. Waipi'o takes care of itself best when humans do not interfere. Taro farmers too have had problems because the irrigation system for their crops was washed away in the last flood. But, with hope and a prayer to Waipi'o's spirits, they rebuild, knowing full well that there will be a next time. And so it goes.

Waipi'o Now

Waipi'o is at a crossroads. Many of the old people are dying or moving topside (above the valley) with relatives. Those who live here learned to accept life in Waipi'o and genuinely love the valley, while others come only to exploit its beauty. Fortunately, the latter underestimate the raw power of Waipi'o. Developers have eyed the area for years as a magnificent spot in which to build a luxury resort. But even they are wise enough to realize that nature rules Waipi'o, not humankind. For now the valley is secure. A few gutsy families with a real commitment have stayed on and continue to revitalize Waipi'o. The valley now supports perhaps 50 residents. More people live topside but come down to Waipi'o to tend their gardens. On entering the valley, you'll see a lotus-flower pond, and if you're lucky enough to be there in December, it will be in bloom. It's tended by an elderly Chinese gentleman, Nelson Chun, who wades into the chest-deep water to harvest the sausage-linked lotus roots by clipping them with his toes! Margaret Loo comes to harvest wild ferns. Seiko Kaneshiro is perhaps the most famous taro farmer because of his poi factory that produces Ono Ono Waipi'o Brand Taro. Another old-timer is Charlie Kawashima, who still grows taro the old-fashioned way, an art form passed from father to son. He harvests the taro with an *o'o* (digging stick) and after it's harvested cuts off the corm and sticks the *huli* (stalk) back into the ground, where it begins to sprout again in a week or so.

Aloha Distress

In the summer of 1992, the Bishop Museum requested an environmental impact survey on Waipi'o Valley because the frequency of visitors to the valley had increased tremendously. Old-time residents were complaining not only about the overuse of the valley, but about the loss of their quiet and secluded lifestyle. Some

BIG ISLAND

tour operators cooperated fully and did their best to help in the preservation and reasonable use of one of Hawaii's grandest valleys; others did not. Because of the impact study, commercial tours are not allowed to go to the beach area on the far side of the stream, which is now open to foot traffic only, and the valley is **closed on Sunday** to commercial tours.

There also seems to be some kind of socio-ethnic battle evolving in the valley. Long-term residents, mostly but not exclusively of Hawaiian decent, are staking out the valley as their own and have largely withdrawn the spirit of aloha from the melanin-challenged visitors to their wonderful valley. Their dissatisfaction is not wholly without basis, as some who have come to the valley have been quite disrespectful, trespassing on private property, threatening to sue landowners for injuries caused by themselves, or finding themselves stuck in a river that no one in their right mind would try to cross in a vehicle. Many wonderful, open, and loving people still live in the valley, but don't be too surprised to get the "stink face" treatment from others. Be respectful and stay on public property. If the sign says *Kapu* or Keep Out, believe it. It is everyone's right to walk along the beach, the switchback that goes to Waimanu, and generally waterways. These are traditional free lands in Hawaii open to all people, and they remain so. It's really up to you. With proper behavior from visitors, Waipi'o's mood can change, and *aloha* will return.

Driving

The road leading down to Waipi'o is outrageously steep and narrow, averaging a 25 percent gradient. If you attempt it in a regular car, it'll eat you up and spit out your bones. More than 20 fatalities have occurred since people started driving it, and it has only been paved since the early 1970s. You'll definitely need 4WD, low range, to make it; vehicles headed downhill yield to those coming up. There is very little traffic on the road except when surfing conditions are good. Sometimes Waipi'o Beach has the first good waves of the season, and this brings out the surfers en masse.

Waipio Valley Shuttle, 808/775-7121, has its office at Waipi'o Valley Artworks in Kukui-haele. It's best to make a reservation. Comfortable air-conditioned 4WD vans make the 90-minute descent and tour, Mon.–Sat. 8 A.M.–4 P.M. Along the way, you'll be regaled by legends and stories and shown the most prominent sights in the valley by drivers who live in the area. The tour costs $35 for adults, $15 for children under 11. Buy your ticket at the Artworks. This is the tamest, but safest, way to enjoy the valley. These guys know what they're doing—they've been in business since 1970. If you decide to hike down or stay overnight, you can make arrangements for the van to pick you up or drop you off for an added cost. The same company also offers a trip to the top of Mauna Kea.

RECREATION

Hiking

If you have the energy, the hike down the paved section of the road is just over one mile, but it's a tough mile coming back up! Once you're down in the valley, make a hard right and follow the dirt road to the beach or head straight ahead and plunge into the heart of the valley. You should remember before you go too far that you will have to cross one or more of the valley streams. There are no bridges; you'll have to wade through. None are deep or wide and are not usually a problem, but when steady rains swell the streams, stay out for your own sake, as you could easily be swept downstream.

Waipi'o Beach

Stretching over a mile, this is the longest black-sand beach on the island. A tall and somewhat tangled stand of trees and bushes fronts this beach. The surf here can be very dangerous, and there are many riptides. If there is strong wave action, swimming is not advised. It is, however, a good place for surfing and fishing. The road to the beach leads along the east wall of the valley and opens onto plenty of space to picnic under the trees. In order to get to the long expanse of beach across the mouth of the stream, you have to wade across it, stepping carefully over the boulders that lay on the bottom. To compound matters, waves sometimes wash water up the mouth of the stream. Be advised and be careful. Alternately, walk into the valley and find a public path that leads to the beach on the far side of the stream.

Waipi'o Beach

Horseback Riding in the Valley

For a fun-filled experience guaranteed to please, try horseback riding with **Waipi'o Na'alapa Stables,** 808/775-0419. Sherri Hannum, a mother of three who moved to Waipi'o from Missouri almost 30 years ago, and her husband Mark, own and operate the trail rides. The adventure begins at Waipi'o Valley Artworks in Kukuihaele, where you begin a 4WD ride down to the ranch, which gives you an excellent introduction to the valley since their spread is even deeper into the valley than the end of the line for the commercial valley tour! En route you cross three or four streams, as Mark tells you some of the history and lore of Waipi'o. When you arrive, Sherri has the horses ready to go. She puts you in the saddle of a sure-footed Waipi'o pony and spends two hours telling you legends and stories while leading you to waterfalls, swimming holes, gravesites, and finally a *heiau.* She knows the trails of Waipi'o intimately. The lineage of the horses of Waipi'o dates from the late 1700s. They were gifts to the *ali'i* from Captain George Vancouver. Waipi'o was especially chosen because the horses were easy to corral and could not escape. Today, more than 150 semi-wild progeny of the original stock roam the valley floor. If the fruits of Waipi'o are happening, Sherri will point them out and you can munch to your heart's delight. Tours lasting 2.5 hours cost $75 and start at 9:30 A.M. and 1 P.M. Full-day tours can be arranged, but a minimum of two and a

maximum of four riders is required. Sorry, no children under eight years old or riders weighing more than 230 pounds. Go prepared with long pants, shoes, and swimsuit.

Waipi'o On Horseback, 808/775-7291, also offers horseback riding through fabulous Waipi'o Valley. These sightseeing rides for all skill levels start at 9:30 A.M. and 1:30 P.M. and last about 2.5 hours. The cost of $75 for adult and $55 for kids under age 12 includes transportation from the Last Chance Store in Kukuihaele to the valley floor. Make reservations 24 hours in advance.

Wagon Tour

Waipio Valley Wagon Tours, P.O. Box 1340, Honoka'a, HI 96727, 808/775-9518, owned and operated by Peter Tolin, is one of the most fun-filled ways of exploring Waipi'o. This surrey-type wagon, which can hold about a dozen people, is drawn by two Tennessee mules. The fascinating 90-minute tours depart four times daily at 9:30 A.M., 11:30 A.M., 1:30 P.M., and 3:30 P.M. Cost is $40, children under 12 half price, children two and under free. To participate, make reservations 24 hours in advance, then check in 30 minutes before departure at the Last Chance Store, where a 4WD vehicle will come to fetch you. If you just drop by, you can ask at the store to see if there is space for you, but a last-minute opening is definitely not guaranteed. Lunch is not included, but if you bring your own, you can walk down to the beach and have a great picnic. The original wagon was built by Peter himself from parts ordered from the Mainland. Unfortunately, every part he ordered broke down over a nine-month trial period. Peter had all new parts made at a local machine shop, three times thicker than the originals! Now that the wagon has been "Waipi'onized," the problems have ceased. The only high-tech aspect of the wagon ride is a set of small loudspeakers through which Peter narrates the history, biology, and myths of Waipi'o as you roll along.

Upper Rim Adventures

The valley itself doesn't get all the attention. Recently, several other opportunities have opened for people to explore the east rim of the valley. You have your choice of hiking, horseback riding, mountain biking, and 4WD van exploration. Each adventure takes a different route, although some may overlap trails. All include a trip through former sugarcane land, and each brings you to wonderful vistas that overlook the broad expanse of the Waipi'o Valley from a height of over 1,000 feet. As you go, you'll be told stories and legends of the valley and vignettes of the culture and history of the area; some tours may even include a dip in a secluded pool under a tumbling waterfall.

Tours with **Hawaiian Walkways,** 808/775-0372 or 800/477-7759, website: www.hawaiianwalkways.com, email: hiwalk@aloha.net, led by Hugh Montgomery or one of his able staff, guide you through the rim-edge forest and over a long-abandoned former flume construction trail to the very edge of the valley. Here you can sneak up on and look down upon Hi'ilawe Waterfall and get to spots overlooking the valley that cannot be reached any other way. This is not just good physical exercise but also an education in the flora and fauna of the region, as Hugh is a proverbial font of knowledge about the area. The hike is moderate, takes about four hours, and goes daily for $85 per person. Lunch, drinks, and all necessary equipment are supplied. Meet at Waipi'o Valley Artworks.

The **mountain biking adventure** takes you over backroads and dirt trails to the edge of the valley. This ride includes a swim in a waterfall pool. Meet at 8 A.M. to be fitted with a suspension bike and taken to the trailhead. The ride is three to four hours long and includes lunch. Custom

and private rides can also be arranged from $150 and up depending upon the route and time involved. Reserve your spot by calling **Top of Waipio,** 808/775-9393.

Waipi'o Ridge Stables, 808/775-1007, offers a 2.5-hour rim ride for $75 and a five-hour valley rim and hidden waterfall ride for $145. Check-in is at 8:45 A.M. or 12:45 P.M. For more information and reservations, call 808/775-1007.

A three-hour 4WD tour is offered by **Waipi'o Rim Backroad Adventures,** 808/775-1122, that takes you in comfort to many of the same spots for exceptional vistas into the Waipi'o Valley. This catered ride runs $85 per person and is less physical but just as rewarding as the other adventures. The mountain biking, horseback riding, and 4WD tours meet at Waipi'o Valley Artworks in Kukuihaele. Additional information and reservations for all three are available at 800/492-4746 or get information on the Web at www.topofwaipio.com.

It is possible once again to hike a portion of the Hamakua Ditch Trail, constructed a century ago when water was needed to irrigate the Hamakua sugar plantations. Drive along Highway 19 to the outskirts of Waimea and turn right onto White Road. Proceed to the end of the road and park as much off the roadway as possible. Leave your $1 donation at the trailhead and cross through the gate. A gravel track leads around a water reservoir and on into the forest to the flume. Follow the flume and hiking trail about an hour upstream, where it eventually skirts the edge of the upper reaches of the Waipi'o Valley and from where there are superb vistas (on a clear day) into the valley and a long thin waterfall. About a half hour farther along the trail, you can look back down the valley to the ocean and beach. This area often clouds in by late morning, so hit the trail early.

STAYING IN THE VALLEY

Camping in Waipi'o

For camping in Waipi'o Valley you must get a permit from the Kamehameha Schools Bishop Estate, Kona Office, 78-6831 Ali'i Drive, Suite 232, Kailua-Kona, HI 96740, 808/332-5300. To get the permit, you must call at least two weeks in advance, giving the dates requested (four-day maximum) and number of people in your party. You will be mailed or faxed an application, and all adult members in your party must sign a "liability waiver" (parents or legal guardians must sign for any children) before the no-cost permit will be granted. Also, you must provide your own "Port-A-Potty" (yes, it's true) or "chemical toilet" and remove it when you leave. A small "camper style" potty, available in Hawaii, is sufficient. Camping is allowed in three designated areas only on the east side of Waipi'o Stream. A resident caretaker in the valley will check on campers. Many hikers and campers have stayed in Waipi'o overnight without a permit and usually have had no problem, but it is illegal! Remember, however, that most of the land, except for the beach, *is* privately owned.

The Waipi'o Overlook has a 24-hour parking limit. That's good for day use of the valley, but not sufficient for most campers or for those attempting the trek to Waimanu Valley beyond. Check with Waipi'o Valley Artworks for longer-stay parking arrangements.

Accommodations

Ever fantasized about running off to a tropical island and living a life of "high" adventure? *The* most secluded lodging in all of Hawaii is the **Waipi'o Treehouse**, P.O. Box 5086, Honoka'a, HI 96727, 808/775-7160, website: www.waipio.com, owned and operated by Linda Beech. The Treehouse is deep in Waipi'o Valley on three acres of land completely surrounded by holdings of the Bishop Estate. To get there, Linda or one of her caretakers will fetch you from topside in a sturdy 4WD, and ferry you across at least four streams until you come to her idyllic settlement at the foot of Papala Waterfall, which starts its cascade about 2,000 feet above the valley floor. This falls provides the water for a hydroelectric power plant (with solar backup) that runs everything from stereos to ceiling fans. Linda purchased the land years ago after returning to Hawaii, the place of her birth. She has had a most interesting life, living, working, and traveling throughout the Orient, and she returned to live in harmony with the land.

After much deliberation, Linda selected master boat builders Eric Johnson and Steven Oldfather to build The Treehouse in 1971, and she chose her 65-foot monkeypod tree as its perch.

Using an ingenious "three pin anchoring system," The Treehouse gently sways like a moored boat, allowing the tree to grow without causing structural damage. It has survived 120 mph winds and has proven a most "seaworthy" treehouse. Eric Johnson came back some years ago to reroof the structure and found it to be still square and level. Of this structure he says, "Here I pinnacled." Both men have given up professional boat building and have become very famous on the Big Island as custom home-builders.

Situated about 25 feet above the ground, The Treehouse is fascinating but quite basic. As you climb the steps past the hot shower, the first landing holds a flushing toilet; farther up is a barbecue grill. Inside, the 10- by 20-foot Treehouse is plain teak wood and screened windows all around, not much more. It's very comfortable with island-style furnishings and a full kitchen with all utensils, but it is not luxurious. The luxury is provided by Waipi'o itself, flooding the interior with golden light and the perfume of tropical flowers wafting on the breeze. All around, the melodious songs of indigenous birds and the ever-present wind and cascading waters serenades day and night. If you don't wish to perch high in a tree, Linda also offers The Hale, an earthbound but commodious two-story structure that's larger than the treehouse and where glass and screens open to the magnificent still-life surrounding you. All guests are invited to use a traditional Japanese *ofuro,* a hot tub. Remember, however, that The Treehouse is not a B&B—you should bring your own food and do your own light housekeeping. You'll be operating on a jungle efficiency level while here: no phones and no TV, but comfort and cleanliness. Because The Treehouse is so remote, it is necessary to make reservations well in advance. The Treehouse has one double bed and one single bed; rates are $200 per day for two or more nights or $250 for one night, and $25 per additional person over 12 years old. Rates for The Hale, which can sleep up to six, are the same. A 50 percent deposit is requested with the reservation, and a six-week cancellation notice prior to arrival is necessary for a refund. Nature still rules Waipi'o, and about 10 days per year the streams are flooded, making it impossible to get in or out. If you can't get in, a prompt refund will be made,

BIG ISLAND

and if you're lucky enough to be marooned, complimentary lodging and food will be cordially provided for the duration of your stay.

WAIMANU VALLEY

The hike down to Waipi'o and over the *pali* to Waimanu Valley is considered by many to be one of the top three treks in Hawaii. You must be fully prepared for camping and in excellent condition to attempt this hike. Also, water from the streams and falls is not good for drinking due to irrigation and cattle grazing topside; bring purification tablets or boil or filter it to be safe. To get to Waimanu Valley, a switchback trail, locally called the Z trail, but otherwise known as the **Muliwai Trail,** leads up the 1,200-foot *pali,* starting about 100 yards inland from the west end of Waipi'o Beach. The beginning of the switchback trail has a post with a painting that reads "Caution Menehune." Waimanu was bought by the state of Hawaii some years ago, and it is responsible for trail maintenance. The trail ahead is rough, as you go in and out of more than a dozen gulches before reaching Waimanu. After the ninth gulch is a trail shelter. Finally, below is Waimanu Valley, half the size of Waipi'o but more verdant, and even wilder because it has been uninhabited for a longer time. Cross Waimanu Stream in the shallows where it meets the sea. The trail then continues along the beach and back into the valley about a mile and a half, along the base of the far side, to Wai'ilikahi Falls, some 300 feet high. For drinking water (remember to treat it), walk along the west side of the *pali* until you find a likely waterfall. The Muliwai Trail to the Waimanu Valley floor is about 15 miles round-trip from the trailhead at the bottom of the *pali* in Waipi'o Valley, or 19 miles round-trip from Waipi'o Lookout. To stay overnight in Waimanu Valley you must have a (free) camping permit available through the Division of Forestry and Wildlife, P.O. Box 4849, Hilo, HI 96720, 808/974-4221, open Mon.–Fri. 8 A.M.–4 P.M. Apply not more than one month in advance. Your length of stay is limited to seven days and six nights. Each of the nine designated campsites along the beach has a fireplace, and there are three composting outhouses in the valley for use by campers. Carry out what you carry in!

Early in the 19th century, because of economic necessity brought on by the valley's remoteness, Waimanu was known for its *'okolehau* (moonshine). Solomon, one of the elders of the community at the time, decided that Waimanu had to diversify for the good of its people. He decided to raise domesticated pigs introduced by the Chinese, who roasted them with spices in rock ovens as a great delicacy. Solomon began to raise and sell the pigs commercially, but when he died, out of respect, no one wanted to handle his pigs, so they let them run loose. The pigs began to interbreed with feral pigs, and after a while there were so many pigs in Waimanu that they ate all the taro, bananas, and breadfruit. The porkers' voracious appetites caused a famine that forced the last remaining families of Waimanu to leave in the late 1940s. Most of the trails you will encounter are made by wild-pig hunters who still regularly go after Solomon's legacy.

According to oral tradition the first *kahuna lapa'au* (healing doctor) of Hawaii was from Waimanu Valley. His disciples crossed and recrossed Waipi'o Valley, greatly influencing the development of the area. Some of the *heiau* in Waipi'o are specifically dedicated to the healing of the human torso; their origins are traced to the healing *kahuna* of Waimanu.

PUNA

The Puna District, south of Hilo on the southeast coast, was formed from rivers of lava spilling from Mauna Loa and Kilauea again and again over the last million years or so. The molten rivers stopped only when they hit the sea, where they fizzled and cooled, forming a chunk of semi-raw land that bulges into the Pacific—marking the state's easternmost point at **Cape Kumukahi.** These titanic lava flows have left phenomenal reminders of their power. The earth here is raw, rugged, and jagged. It has not yet had sufficient time to age and smooth. Black lava flows streak the land and grudgingly give over to green vegetation. On the coast, cliffs stand guard against the relentless sea, and here and there lava tubes punctuate the coastline, leaving telltale signs of the mountains' might. Yet, the greatest of these features is the rift zone, where rupture lines dart out like streamers from a volcano's central crater. It is here along this zone that the unstable ground has slumped away and fallen into the ocean in great cataclysmic landslides and later settled to create benches of lowlands and the present coastline. It is along this rift zone that the mountain still shows its volatility, for the current active lava flow is disgorging from a vent along this line.

Pahoa is the major town in this region. It was at one time the terminus of a rail line that took commodities and people to Hilo. This was timber country and later sugarcane land, but since the mills have closed, it's waiting for other uses. Down the hill from town, **Lava Tree State Monument** was once a rainforest whose giant trees were covered with lava, like hot dogs dipped in batter. The encased wood burned, leaving a hollow stone skeleton. You can stroll through this lichen-green rock forest before you head farther east into the brilliant sunshine of the coast. Little-traveled side roads take you past a multitude of orchid, anthurium, and papaya farms, oases of color in a desert of solid black lava. A lighthouse sits atop Cape Kumukahi, and to the north an ancient paved trail passes beaches where no one ever goes.

Southward is a string of popular beaches—some white-sand, some black. You can camp, swim, surf, or just play in the water to your heart's delight, but realize that there are few places to stop for food, gas, or supplies. Also along the coast you can visit natural areas where the sea tortured the hot lava into caves, tubes, arches, and even a natural hot bath. There are historical sites where petroglyphs tell vague stories from

BIG ISLAND

PUNA

Cape Kumukahi

KUMUKAHI LIGHTHOUSE

KAPOHO TIDEPOOLS

PUALA'A PARK

ISAAC HALE BEACH COUNTY PARK

Pohoiki Bay

MACKENZIE STATE RECREATION AREA

137

HONOLULU LANDING

Opihi Rock

HAWAIIAN PARADISE COUNTY PARK

PUNA TRAIL

LAVA TREE STATE MONUMENT

Kau'eleau

'Opihikao

KALANI OCEANSIDE RESORT

KEHENA BEACH

PARADISE DR

132

Pahoa

STEAM VENTS

Kehena

130

Paki Bay

Haena

ANTHURIUM AND ORCHID FARMS

THE PAINTED CHURCH

Kaimu

Kalapana

AREA INUNDATED BY LAVA

Haena

130

To Hilo

Kea'au

Kurtistown

FUKU-BONSAI CULTURAL CENTER

BED & BREAKFAST MOUNTAIN VIEW

HAWAIIAN FLOWER GARDEN NURSERY

Mountain View

PINEAPPLE PARK B&B HOSTEL

PUNA FOREST RESERVE

WAO KELE O PUNA NATURAL AREA RESERVE

Pu'u O'o

SOME ROADS IN THIS AREA MAY BE CLOSED DUE TO VOLCANIC ACTIVITY. CHECK STATUS LOCALLY.

11

KAHAULE'A NATURAL AREA RESERVE

AKATSUKA ORCHID GARDENS

Glenwood

HAWAII VOLCANOES NATIONAL PARK

CHAIN OF CRATERS ROAD

OLA'A RAIN FOREST

SEE "VOLCANO VILLAGE" MAP

Volcano

Kilauea Iki Crater

Kilauea Caldera

CRATER RIM DRIVE

Tu Naalehu and Kona

5 mi

5 km

0

0

BELT ROAD

HAWAI'I

© SANDRA E. BISIGNANI TRUST AND AVALON TRAVEL PUBLISHING, INC.

the past, where ancient villages lay, and where generations of families placed the umbilical cords of their newborns into manmade holes in the rock. Hawaii Volcanoes National Park's eastern end covers the southwestern corner of the Puna District. The park's Visitors Center that used to stand just before the beginning of Chain of Craters Road burned down in the summer of 1989 when lava surged across the road, severing this eastern gateway to the park and causing an old Catholic church to be moved to a new location. This road is still closed and will undoubtedly remain so until the current volcanic activity ceases, so there is no park access from this side. Yet, raw lava flows and new black-sand beaches are there to be explored.

The **Hawaii Belt Road** (Route 11) is a corridor cutting through the center of Puna, running uphill straight toward the town of Volcano. Cutting through well-established villages, this road passes some of the largest and best-known flower farms in the state, and on both sides of this highway are scattered housing developments as new as the lava on which they precariously sit. Back in these hills, new-wave gardeners grow "Puna Butter" *pakalolo,* a significant, though illegal, economic force in the region.

On the border of Puna and the Ka'u District to the south are the village of **Volcano,** where you will find accommodations, restaurants, and shopping, and Hawaii Volcanoes National Park. Here the goddess Pele resides at Kilauea Caldera, center of one of the world's most active volcanoes. The Hawaii Belt Road continues southwest through the park and into Ka'u, the southernmost district of the Big Island, and, rounding the bottom of the island, travels up into Kona.

SOUTHEAST COAST

The most enjoyable area in the Puna District is the southeast coast, with its beaches and points of natural and historical interest. It is an easygoing, steamy, tropical region, one of the most typically old Hawaiian on the island. If you take Route 130 south from Kea'au, in about 12 miles you reach Pahoa. Like Kea'au, Pahoa is primarily a crossroads. You can continue due south on Route 130 to the seaside village of Kaimu, beyond where Route 130 used to join coastal Route 137 at Kalapana, feeding into Chain of Craters Road before much of this area was buried by lava flows. Along Route 130, about halfway between Pahoa and Kaimu, look for a small, unobtrusive sign that reads Scenic Overlook. Pull off and walk about 75 yards toward the sea until you find four steam vents. Many local people use them as natural saunas.

You might go directly east from Pahoa along Route 132. This lovely, tree-lined country road takes you past Lava Tree State Monument, which shouldn't be missed, and then continues to the coast, intersecting Route 137 and terminating at Cape Kumukahi. If this seems *too* far out of the way, head down Pohoiki Road where it branches just past the Lava Tree State Monument. Soon you bypass a controversial geothermal power station, then reach the coast at Isaac Hale Beach County Park. From there, Route 137 heads southwest down the coast to Kaimu, passing the best Puna beaches en route. Fortunately for you, this area of Puna is one of those places where no matter which way you decide to go, you really can't go wrong.

PAHOA AND VICINITY

You can breeze through this "one-street" town, but you won't regret stopping if even for a few minutes. A raised wooden sidewalk passing false-front shops is fun to walk along to get a feeling of the 1800s. Yet, a revitalized '60s counterculture element thrives in town along with the workaday local population. The shops here are an eclectic mix of food vendors, restaurants, antiques and crafts stores, and a new-age artist's gallery. The rest of town is a bit more utilitarian with a lumberyard, supermarkets, more restaurants, clothing stores, a church, schools, police and fire departments, post office, and the island's oldest movie theater. At one time Pahoa boasted *the* largest sawmill in America. Its buzz saw ripped 'ohi'a railway ties for the Santa Fe and other railroads. It was into one of these ties that the golden spike uniting the East and West coasts of the Mainland was driven. Many local people earned their livelihood from 'ohi'a charcoal that they made and sold all over the island until it was made obsolete by the widespread use of kerosene and gas introduced in the early 1950s. Pahoa's commercial heart went up in flames in 1955. Along the main street was a tofu factory that had a wood-fired furnace. The old fellow who owned the factory banked his fires as usual before he went home for the night. Somehow, they got out of control and burned all the way down to the main alley dividing the commercial district. The only reason the fire didn't jump the alley was because a papaya farmer happened to be around and had a load of water on the back of his truck, which he used to douse the buildings and save the town.

Pahoa is attempting to protect and revitalize its commercial center and bring new life to vintage buildings like the Akebono Theater, where classic movies are once again being shown. Pahoa has one of the highest concentrations of old buildings still standing in Hawaii that are easily accessible. Although the center of town has been bypassed by a new road, make sure to enter the town and stroll along the tiny backroads.

To replace timber and sugar, Pahoa is in the process of becoming the anthurium capital of the world. As you get close to Pahoa, coming from Kea'au, you'll see shade cloth draping acres of anthurium nurseries, sheltering magnificent specimens of the usually red flowers, plus plenty of white ones, a few green, and even black anthuriums. Papaya is also grown here in large quantities, and a number of farms are located below town toward the coast.

Lava Tree State Monument
In 1790, slick, fast-flowing pahoehoe lava surged through this 'ohi'a forest, covering the tree trunks from the ground to about a 12-foot level. The moisture inside the trees cooled the lava, forming a hardened shell. At the same time, tremors and huge fissures cracked the earth in the area. When the eruption ended, the still-hot lava drained away through the fissures, leaving the encased tree trunks standing like sentinels, only to burn away later. The floor of the forest is so smooth in some areas that the lava seems like asphalt. Each lava tree has its own personality; some resemble totem poles, and it doesn't take much imagination to see old, craggy faces staring back at you. Many still stand, while others have tumbled to the ground where you can look inside these pipe-like creations. The most spectacular part of the park is near the entrance. Immense trees loom over cavernous cracks (puka) in the earth and send their roots, like stilled waterfalls, tumbling down into them. To get to Lava Tree, take Route 132 east from Pahoa for about three miles and look for the well-marked entrance on the left. Drinking water is not available.

Road's end: lava flows create the most dramatic road obstructions.

ROBERT NILSEN

Accommodations

Right downtown, occupying the second floor of a building erected in 1910, is the **Village Inn**, 808/965-6444. A stairway with brass handrail leads to the second floor; as you ascend imagine how many others have grasped that very rail. You're greeted at the top by Koko—the resident parrot and king of his big cage—your musical entertainment during your stay here. This small hotel has five rooms, all with cable TV, lace curtains, and white wicker furniture like grandma used to have on her porch. Other furniture is reminiscent of the '30s and '40s, and ceiling fans help cool the rooms. While simple, everything is neat and clean. It's an establishment that has not been modernized. Rooms run $25–40 a night or $125–225 a week; some share a bathroom. Owner Bill Male runs the **Whimsies** antiques and collectibles shop on the first floor. His stock is always changing, but you can find such items as vintage jewelry, Hawaiian artifacts and stoneware, glassware, and aloha shirts. He'll buy, sell, and trade.

In the Leilani Estates subdivision south of town is the **Cliff House** vacation rental home. Set at the edge of the rift zone, you can see down across the lowlands to the ocean beyond. This modern, two-bedroom cedar house has a comfortable living area with TV and VCR, full kitchen and separate dining area, laundry room, and a lanai that stretches across the entire back of the house overlooking the back lawn. Private and secure, it's surrounded by thick vegetation, so your neighbors won't even know you're here. The house runs $95 a night, three-night minimum. Contact A Piece of Paradise, P.O. Box 1314, Pahoa, HI 96778, 808/965-1224, website: www.apoParadise.com, email: info@apoParadise.com.

For bed-and-breakfasts near Pahoa, contact **Pearl's Shell B&B**, 808/965-7015, website: www.stay-hawaii.com/pearls; or **Sunny Branch Acres**, 808/965-7516, website: www. stay-hawaii.com/sunnybranch, both in the Leilani Estates just a few miles southwest of Pahoa.

Food

Luquin's Place, 808/965-9990, open daily 11 A.M.–9 P.M., is a reasonably priced Mexican restaurant that offers enchiladas, burritos, tacos, and combination platters. It now serves drinks; margaritas are a house specialty.

A block away is **Mady's Cafe Makana**, 808/965-0608, open every day except Sunday 7:30 A.M.–3 P.M. Mady's is a full café and boutique. Pareu are one of the mainstays in the boutique, as are women's toiletries, candles, greeting cards, and carved wooden items. After shopping, stop in at the café for a bite to eat. Nearly everything is under $6. Fruit smoothies, hearty lentil soup, tamales, samosa, and veggie croissants are samplings from the menu. All choices are organic, healthy, and nutritious. Mady's also supplies baked goods and deli sandwiches to some of the health food stores in the area.

Let your mind and stomach be soothed with cosmic vibrations and libations at **Huna Ohana**, 808/965-9661, open daily 8 A.M.–6 P.M., Sunday 9 A.M.–1 P.M. The metaphysical bookstore and café is owned and operated by Dawn Horwitz. But it's more than that—you can also find videos and music, objects for meditation, jewelry, an assortment of gifts, and Internet access. Vegetarian foods are served in the back, so sit down for tofu scramble, multi-grain bagels and cream cheese, an assortment of croissants and blueberry muffins, or a tempeh burger. To get those cosmic vibes kicked into high gear, order a cup of espresso, choose a likely tome from the bookstore section, and kick back on an overstuffed couch or outside in the garden area.

Paolo's Italian restaurant, 808/965-7033, open Tues.–Sun. 5:30–9 P.M., is the place for fine dining in town. Dine inside at tables topped with blue-and-white-checkered tablecloths or have a seat in the patio outside. Start with an appetizer, like a bowl of minestrone soup or fresh mozzarella antipasto, and follow that with ravioli with spinach and ricotta or pasta with prawns. Special entrées, like chicken Marcella, cioppino, or pizza à la palios (gourmet pizza Italian style with capers, anchovies, tomato, oregano, and mozzarella), might be more to your taste. To round out the meal, have a cup of espresso or a caffé latté. Most meals are under $15.

Almost next door is **Sawasdee Thai Cuisine**, 808/965-8186. Open daily except Tuesday noon–8:30 P.M., this intimate eatery serves memorable Thai food with a fine blend of herbs and spices. Your mouth will not be disappointed. Using local organic ingredients, menu choices include appetizers like *po pia* spring rolls, soups such as *po tak* hot and sour seafood soup, and a variety of salads. Rice, noodle, and curry dishes make up the main entrée choices, most in the $7–12 range, and any can be made vegetarian if you wish.

Shopping and Services

When you pull into Pahoa you are greeted by the **Pahoa Village Center,** a small shopping center where you'll find a laundromat, a video store, and the Dairy Queen. A minute down the road is the full-service **Pahoa Cash and Carry** grocery store, 7-Eleven, and the Pahoa Casherette, which are enough for any supplies or incidentals that you may need.

Pahoa Natural Groceries, 808/965-8322, open weekdays 9 A.M.–9 P.M., Sunday 9 A.M.–6 P.M., specializing in organic food items, is one of the finest health food stores on the Big Island. It has an excellent selection of fresh veggies, organic grains, herbs and minerals, deli items, and a very good bakery selection. There's a kitchen on the premises, so the food is not only healthful but very fresh.

Adjacent is **Pahoa Natural Emporium,** 808/965-6634, open daily 10 A.M.–6 P.M., with a small but excellent selection of jewelry, Guatemalan clothing, Balinese batik, Yucatan hammocks, gifts, magazines, and cards. The Emporium also displays artwork, some by local artists, and a colorful selection of rugs. The shirts and dresses are all cotton and rayon. Some of the clothing is designed or handmade here in Puna. The back room displays a profusion of these vibrant rainbow-colored clothes.

You'll find two farmers' markets in town. On Saturday 7:30 A.M.–noon at the Sacred Heart Catholic Church is the more typical of these markets, with a variety of food and flowers. More a combination farmers' market and flea market is the interesting Akebono farmers' market, held Sunday 9 A.M.–1 P.M. in the parking lot of the theater.

Stop at **Happily** antiques shop for jewelry, wooden bowls, baskets, and hats. Open daily except Sunday 10 A.M.–5 P.M., this shop has been around a long time and is almost an institution in town. Alternately, check **Whimsies** antiques and collectibles shop below the Village Inn.

Along the elevated boardwalk are numerous shops for gifts and other diversions. **Lola, Tocaloma, and Jewelry Gallery** is where local artists display jewelry, canvas art, basketry, and ceramics.

There are many nurseries in the Pahoa area that ship mixed tropical flower bouquets and individual potted plants. For available arrangements, contact **Hawaiian Tropicals Direct,** P.O. Box 2069, Pahoa, HI 96778, 808/965-0704 or 800/840-3660, fax 800/840-2743; or **Hawaiian Greenhouse, Inc.,** P.O. Box 1, Pahoa, HI 96778, 808/95-8351 or 888/965-8351, website: www.hawaiian-greenhouse.com.

ALONG THE COAST

All of Puna's beaches, parks, and campgrounds lie along coastal Route 137 stretching for 20 miles from Pohoiki to Kaimu. Route 137 is also called Kapoho-Kalapana Beach Road or simply the "Red Road." Surfers, families, transients, even nude-sunbathing "buffs" have their favorite beaches along this southeast coast. For the most part, swimming is possible, but be cautious during high tide. There is plenty of sun, snorkeling sites, and good fishing, and the campgrounds are almost always available.

Cape Kumukahi

It's fitting that Kumukahi means "First Beginning" since it is the easternmost point of Hawaii and was recognized as such by the original Polynesian settlers. Follow Route 132 past Lava Tree for about 10 miles to the coast, where a lighthouse sits like an exclamation point on clinker lava. Along the way, get an instant course in volcanology: You can easily chart the destructive and regenerative forces at work on Hawaii. At the five-mile marker an HVB Warrior points out the lava flow of 1955. Tiny plants give the lava a greenish cast, and shrubs are already eating into it, turning it to soil. Papaya orchards grow in the raw lava of an extensive flat basin. The contrast between the black, lifeless earth and the vibrant green trees is startling. In the center of the flatland rises a cinder cone, a caldera of a much older mini-volcano unscathed by the modern flows; it is gorgeous with lush vegetation. An HVB Warrior points out the lava flow of 1960, and you can see at a glance how different it was from the flow of five years earlier. When Route 132 intersects Route 137, continue straight ahead down the unpaved road for about two miles to the Cape Kumukahi Lighthouse. People in these parts swear that on the fateful night in 1960 when the nearby village of Kapoho was consumed by the lava flow, an old woman (a favorite guise of Madame Pele) came to town begging for food and was turned away by everyone. She next went to the lighthouse asking for help and was cordially treated by the lighthouse keeper. When the flow was at its strongest, it came within yards of the lighthouse and then miraculously split, completely encircling the structure but leaving it unharmed as the flow continued out to sea for a considerable distance.

Route 137 continues north and in short order plunges into a forest of trees; the road turns into a rugged and rutted dirt lane that is often full of potholes and pools of water. Proceed with caution, this stretch is not kind to low-slung rental cars. If you continue, you will pass secluded private property and as-yet-undeveloped county park land and pop out on the other side at the bottom of the Hawaiian Shores Estates subdivision, which cascades down the hill from Pahoa. You're better off to turn south and enjoy other sites of the coast.

Kapoho

Although the old village of Kapoho was covered by lava a few short decades ago, a new community has been rebuilt to take its place. This new village has a mixture of retirees, working-class families, and vacation rentals. The section closest to the lighthouse is a gated community. You can snorkel in the tide pools along the coast in this village that can be used to snorkel. Those within the gated section are off-limits, but the rest can be enjoyed by anyone who takes the time to seek them out. Remember that this is a quiet rural community with pride in its natural resources, so be respectful when you visit. Turn onto Kapoho Kai Drive and head down into this small development. Park off the roadway along the road farthest down toward the water. It's a short way across the lava field toward the ocean before these pools become apparent. Wear shoes, as the lava is sharp. Best at high tide, the tide pools provide good snorkeling in a safe environment.

For vacation rental homes at Kapoho, contact **A Piece of Paradise,** P.O. Box 1314, Pahoa, HI 96778, 808/965-1224, website: www.apoParadise.com. The one-bedroom cottage rents for $95 a night, and the three two-bedroom homes run $120 or $150 a night, three nights minimum. Each is completely furnished with full kitchen and living areas and located a few short steps from the ocean and tide pools.

Puala'a Park and Thermal Spring

Back on Route 137, continue south under the dense tree cover. Between mile markers 10 and 11, just after the road narrows, you come upon **Puala'a Park,** also known as Ahalanui. Parking is across the road. Quietly opened by the County of Hawai'i on July 4, 1993, this lovely, 1.3-acre park was an ancient fishing village. Along the **Red Road** between Kapoho and 'Opihikao, the park features a pond that's been formed into a pool, thermally heated to a perfect temperature. It has a sandy bottom. Step in and relax in its soothing warmness. Some people use the pond to do watsu, a type of in-water massage. The swimming is safe except during periods of very high surf, when ocean water washes in over the outer cement wall. The park is perfect for families with young children. The pond is now watched over by a lifeguard, and toilets have been set up for your convenience.

Isaac Hale Beach County Park

You can't miss this beach park (often referred to as Pohoiki) on Pohoiki Bay at the junction of Route 137 and Pohoiki Road. Just look for a jumble of boats and trailers parked under the palms. At one time Pohoiki Bay served the Hawaiians as a canoe landing, then later became the site of a commercial wharf for the Puna Sugar Company. It remains the only boat launching area for the entire Puna Coast, used by pleasure boaters and commercial fishermen. Due to this dual role, it's often very crowded. Amenities include a pavilion, restrooms, and a picnic area; potable water is not available. Camping is permitted with a county permit. Experienced surfers dodge the rip-current in the center of the bay, and swimming is generally good when the sea is calm. Pohoiki Bay is also one of the best scuba and snorkel sites on the island. Within walking distance of the salt-and-pepper beach is another thermal spring in a lava sink surrounded by lush vegetation. It's popular with tourists and residents alike and provides a unique and relaxing way to wash away sand and salt. To find it, face away from the sea and go to the left along a small but well-worn path that leads between the water and a beach house. Be sure to ask permission if someone is around. The pools are warm, small, and tranquil. Harmless, tiny brine shrimp nibble at your toes while you soak.

MacKenzie State Recreation Area

This popular state park was named for forest ranger A. J. MacKenzie, highly regarded throughout the Puna District. He was killed in the area in 1938. The park's 13 acres sit among a cool grove of ironwoods originally planted by MacKenzie. A portion of the old King's Highway, scratched out by prisoners in the 19th century as a form of community service, bisects the area. Many people who first arrive on the Big Island hang out at MacKenzie until they can get their start. Consequently, the park receives its share of hard-core types, which has earned it a reputation for rip-offs. Mostly it's safe, but if you're camping, take precautions with your valuables. The entire coastline along MacKenzie is bordered by low but rugged black-lava seacliffs. Swimming is dangerous, but the fishing is excellent. Be extremely careful when walking along the water's edge, especially out on the fingers of lava; over the years, people have been swept away by freak waves. Within the park is a skylight of a collapsed lava tube, one end of which exits at the seacliff and the other a stone's throw inland. Take a flashlight and be careful if you venture inside. MacKenzie Park is along Route 137, two miles south of Pohoiki. Picnic facilities are available, but there is no drinking water. A state permit is required for overnight camping.

Kehena Beach

Pass the tiny village of 'Opihikao, where Kama'ili Road drops down from Route 130 to the Red Road. 'Opihikao was a major town along this coast in the 1800s but has faded away into quaint quietude. Just beyond this community the close canopy of trees opens, the road becomes wider, and the vistas broaden. Here are picture postcard coastal scenes as good as any

on the island. Cross over two sections of the 1955 lava flow and soon you come upon Kehena Beach. Kehena is actually two pockets of black-sand beach below a low seacliff. Entrance to the beach is marked only by a scenic pulloff, about four miles south of 'Opihikao; usually a half dozen cars are parked there. At one time Kehena was very popular, and a stone staircase led down to the beach. In 1975 a strong earthquake jolted the area, breaking up the stairway and lowering the beach by three feet. Now access is via a well-worn path, but make sure to wear sneakers because the lava is rough. The ocean here is dangerous, and often pebbles and rocks whisked along by the surf can injure your legs. Once down on the beach, head north for the smaller patch of sand, because the larger patch is open to the sea and can often be awash in waves. The black sand is hot, but a row of coconut palms provides shade. The inaccessibility of Kehena makes it a favorite "no-hassle" nude beach with many "full" sunbathers congregating here.

KAIMU

End of the Road

Just near the lava-inundated village of Kalapana, Routes 130 and 137 come to an abrupt halt where Madame Pele has repaved the road with lava. At the end of the line near the village of Kaimu you come to a barricaded area. Volcanic activity has continued virtually unabated beyond here since January 1983, when lava fountains soared 1,500 feet into the sky and produced a cone more than 800 feet tall. The initial lava flow was localized at Pu'u O'o vent, but after dozens of eruptive episodes it shifted eastward to Kupa'ianaha, which continuously produced about half a million cubic yards of lava per day. Today, it is mostly erupting once again from flank vents on Pu'u O'o. The lava flows eight miles to the sea, mostly through lava tubes. It has inundated almost 40 square miles, caused $61 million worth of property damage, and added more than 500 acres of new land to the Puna Coast—and it's still growing. Unfortunately, these lava flows have also completely covered the very popular **Kaimu Beach Park** (also known as Black Sand Beach), **Harry K. Brown Beach Park**, the national park's visitors center, and 13th-century Waha'ulu Heiau. For a full description of **Chain of Craters Road** and recent volcanic activity, see the following chapter on **Hawaii Volcanoes National Park.** Parts of the road are still open, but only *within* the park.

Volcanic activity has pretty much ceased in the Kaimu area and the lava solidified. You can walk out over this new lava but you can experience difficulty if you walk too far toward where the lava still flows. Some hazards you may encounter are brushfires, smoke, ash, and methane gas, which is extremely explosive. You can also fall through the thin-crusted lava into a tube, which will immediately reduce you to a burnt offering to Pele and unceremoniously deposit your ashes into the sea! New lava can cut like broken glass, and molten lava can be flung through the air by steam explosions, especially near the coastline. Seacliffs collapse frequently, and huge boulders can be tossed several hundred feet into the air. The steam clouds contain minerals that can cause burning eyes, throat and skin irritations, and difficulty breathing.

If you are still intrigued, realize that you are on the most unstable piece of real estate on the face of the earth. For those maniacs, fools, adventurers, and thrill-seekers who just can't stay away, give yourself up for dead, and proceed. Follow the old roadbed, up and down, over the lava. When you can no longer discern the road, pick your way across the undulating lava field, but don't get too close to the sea or the active flows. Observers say that every day, huge chunks fall off into the sea. As you look back at the mountain you can see heat waves rising from the land upon which you are standing. A camera with a zoom lens or a pair of binoculars accentuates this phenomenon. The whole mountain waves in front of you. As you walk closer to the sea, the lava cools and you can see every type there is: rope lava, lava toes, lava fingers. The tortured flow, which may crinkle as you walk over it, has created many imaginative shapes: gargoyles, medieval faces, dolphins, and mythical creatures. At the coast, when lava pours into the sea, it may create a white spume of steam lifting 200–300 feet into the air. No other place in the world gives you the opportunity to be the first person to tread upon the earth's newest land.

In Kaimu, you can safely walk the short distance over the lava to the ocean. At the end of the road, head straight toward the water and in 15 minutes you are there. This spot is near where Kaimu Beach Park used to be. Now, raw and rugged lava meets the sea and is slowly being turned into black sand once again.

The Painted Church

Star of the Sea Catholic Church is a small but famous structure better known as "The Painted Church." Originally located near Kalapana, this church was in grave danger of being overrun by a lava flow. An effort to save the historic church from the lava was mounted, and it has been moved to a location along Route 130, just above Kaimu. A brief history of the area asserts that the now-inundated Kalapana was a spiritual magnet for Roman Catholic priests. Old Spanish documents support evidence that a Spanish priest, crossing the Pacific from Mexico, actually landed very near here in 1555. Father Damien, famous priest of the Molokai Leper Colony, established a grass church about two miles north

inside the Painted Church

BIG ISLAND

J.D. BISIGNANI

and conducted a school when he first arrived in the islands in 1864. The present church dates from 1928, when Father Everest Gielen began its construction. Like an inspired but much less talented Michelangelo, this priest painted the ceiling of the church, working mostly at night by oil lamp. Father Everest was transferred to Lanai in 1941, and the work wasn't completed until 1964, when George Heidler, an artist from Atlanta, Georgia, came to Kalapana and decided to paint the unfinished lower panels in the altar section. The artwork itself can only be described as gaudy but sincere. The colors are wild blues, purples, and oranges. The ceiling is adorned with symbols, portraits of Christ, the angel Gabriel, and scenes from the Nativity. Behind the altar, a painted perspective gives the impression that you're looking down a long hallway at an altar that hangs suspended in air. The church is definitely worth at least a few minutes.

Accommodations

Kalani Oceanside Resort, RR 2 Box 4500, Kehena Beach, HI 96778, 808/965-7828 or 800/800-6886, website: www.kalani.com, email: kalani@kalani.com, is a nonprofit, international conference and holistic retreat center, a haven where people come when they truly want to step aside for a time. The entrance is a few miles east of Kaimu on Route 137 between mile markers 17 and 18, on the mountain side of the road. Look for a large Visitors Welcome sign and proceed uphill until you see the office and gift and sundries shop. Depending upon the yearly schedule, a variety of activities include massage, hula, meditation, yoga, lei-making, *lau hala*-weaving, and hikes, for men, women, couples, and families, gay and straight. The grounds have a botanical atmosphere, with a rain-fed swimming pool (clothing optional after 7:30 P.M.), hot tub, assembly studios, classrooms, cottages, and cedar lodges with kitchen facilities. It's the only place along the Puna Coast that offers lodging and homemade vegetarian fare. Kalani is not an oceanfront property and only some rooms have an ocean view over the trees. Rates are $50 single for a dorm room with shared bath, $75 single and $90 double for a private room with shared bath, $85 single and $105 double for a private room with private bath, and $100 single and $135 double for a guest cottage. Rates are about 30 percent higher than this from mid-December through the end of April. You can also camp for $20 a night, or less per person as a family. A blown conch shell calls you to breakfast at 8 A.M., lunch at noon, and dinner at 6 P.M. (nonguests welcome). The meals cost $8, $8, and $15 respectively, with a meal ticket pre-purchased at the office; or guests can purchase a "meal plan" for $27 that entitles you to all three. Food is served in the open-air dining hall, and fruits and vegetables from the property are used when possible. Entertainment by resident or local musicians is performed in a very casual setting at the Olelo Cafe next to the office Wed.–Sun. evenings until 11 P.M. The generator (and hence the lights) goes off at 11 P.M., but candles are provided for night owls. Kalani is not for everyone, but if you are looking for unpretentious peace and quiet, healthful food, and inner development, there's no better place on the island.

For a smaller and more secluded place to stay, try **Hale Kipa O Kiana** in Kaimu. This guesthouse offers one guest room with attached bath and private entrance for $60 a night. Contact the guesthouse at RR 2 Box 4874, Kalapana Shores, HI 96778, 808/965-8661, fax 808/965-0720, email: haleokiana@aol.com, website: www.halekipaokiana.com.

Food

Right where the roads ends you'll find **Verna's V Drive In** for quick and easy local eats. Have yourself a plate lunch, loco moco, or burger, fries, and a drink, before you head out for the short jaunt over the lava to the water.

ALONG THE HAWAI'I BELT ROAD

KEA'AU

Kea'au is the first town south of Hilo on Route 11, and although pleasant enough, it's little more than a Y in the road. Before the sugar mill closed in the mid-1990s, this was a bustling town with great swaths of the surrounding land in cane. Kea'au and the numerous subdivisions that have mushroomed on both sides of the highway running to Pahoa and up to Volcano have become bedroom communities to Hilo. At the junction of Route 11 (Hawai'i Belt Road) and Route 130 is **Kea'au Town Center,** a small shopping mall with a handful of variety stores, a laundromat, a post office, restaurants, a Bank of America, and gas station. Here, the Sure Save Supermarket has not only groceries but plenty of sundries and a decent camera department. Route 130 heads southeast from here to the steamy south coast, while Route 11 (Hawai'i Belt Road) heads southwest and passes through the mountain villages of Kurtistown, Mountain View, Glenwood, and Volcano at approximately 10-mile intervals, then enters Hawaii Volcanoes National Park. The Belt Road, although only two lanes, is straight, well surfaced, and scrupulously maintained. When heading to the Puna coast, it's easiest now to take the Kea'au Bypass Road around the east side of town, right past the old sugar mill, so you don't get bogged down in town traffic.

Food
The local **Dairy Queen,** in the Kea'au Town Center, not only makes malts and sundaes but serves breakfast, lunch, and dinner. Also in the shopping center is **Kea'au Natural Foods,** 808/966-8877, with a large stock of organic food items, herbs, and grains but no juice or snack bar. However, pre-made sandwiches from the deli case are always available. Have a look at the bulletin board for information on alternative happenings in the community. Open Mon.–Fri. 9 A.M.–8 P.M., Saturday 9 A.M.–9 P.M., and Sunday 10 A.M.–5 P.M. Have a beer while you wait for your laundry to wash at the **Suds 'n Duds** laundromat.

For a more congenial environment, try **Charley's Bar and Grill,** 808/966-7589, for a cool one or a light meal. This is perhaps the nicest place in town for a relaxing evening out.

Kea'au Cafe, 808/966-6758, is a simple unadorned restaurant that serves a mix of local, Japanese, and Korean foods. The ethnic foods are not traditionally prepared by any means, but everything is filling, portions are large, and hardly anything is more than $8. Open every day except Sunday 9 A.M.–8 P.M.

With only two little tables inside, the **Kea'au Chop Suey House,** 808/966-7573, is next door, with everything on the menu costing less than $7, including several vegetarian dishes.

On the far side of the shopping center you'll see **Verna's Drive-In,** which serves plate lunches.

MOUNTAIN TOWNS

Kurtistown
Near the highway in what might be considered the center of town are the post office, the J. Hara Store for sundries and groceries, and B.J.'s 76 Service Station. Just south of there, down 'Ola'a Road is the **Fuku-Bonsai Cultural Center.** This institution is a combination nursery, mail-order shop, bonsai display garden, and bonsai exhibition center. It is also the nonprofit Mid-Pacific Bonsai Foundation's Hawaii State Bonsai Repository. Have a walk through the garden and marvel at the miniature trees and plants demonstrating Japanese, Chinese, and Hawaiian styles, and note the similarities and differences. Inside are educational displays of tools, techniques, and more plants. Diminutive plants can be purchased in the shop to carry away, or they can be shipped anywhere in the country. Fuku-Bonsai is open Mon.–Sat. 8 A.M.–4 P.M. For anyone interested in raising bonsai or simply looking at these wonderfully sculpted plants, this is a worthy stop. For a mail-order catalog, contact P.O. Box 6000, Kurtistown, HI 96760, 808/982-9880, fax 808/982-9883, website: www.fukubonsai.com.

BIG ISLAND

Just over two miles up the road is the **Dan De Luz's Woods** showroom, 808/968-6607, which displays all sorts of turned wooden bowls, small wood boxes, and other small objects made of tropical island woods.

Look for a vintage plantation house painted blue a short ways beyond. This is **Tinny Fisher's Antique Shop,** owned and operated by Charles and Dorothy Wittig. What started as "yard sale treasures" about 10 years ago has turned into a unique curio, antiques, and collectibles shop. Open daily except Monday noon–6 P.M., the shop has all kinds of antiques and collectibles from Asia and Hawaii, including glass balls, Asian furniture, jewelry, and glassware galore. Tinny's also features a good Hawaiiana collection, with artifacts from the ancient days like *kukui* nut lamps, poi pounders, and stone knives.

Mountain View

Mountain View is a village of nurseries specializing in anthuriums. Many of them sport signs and some invite you to look around. **Hawaiian Flower Garden Nursery,** 808/968-8255 or 877/434-0555, open daily except Sunday, is one. There you can learn a little about the history of these fancy exotic flowers and see all sizes and colors. This is the home of the Toyama Red Anthurium, but they come in all shades from stark white to green and deep purple, and sizes from delicate tiny petals and those as big as a spade. Several other nurseries that not only grow but ship these lovely flowers are **Albert Isa Nursery,** P.O. Box 17, Mt. View, HI 96771, 808/968-6125; and **Hale Ohia Gardens,** P.O. Box 1042, Mt. View, HI 96771, 800/273-3848, fax 808/968-8047. For mail-order flowers, prices generally range $35–75 plus shipping costs, depending upon the mix.

Along the highway is a mini-mart, a post office, and **Verna's Too Drive In** serving plate lunches, burgers, and shakes. As you pass through, take a minute to explore the short side road into the village itself. It seems that every house has a garden of ferns, flowers, and native trees. On this old highway road through the village is **Mt. View Bakery,** home of the famous stone cookies—have them with milk! The **Mt. View Village Store,** fairly well supplied, is here as well.

Accommodations

Bed & Breakfast Mountain View, P.O. Box 963, Kurtistown, HI 96720, 808/968-6868 or 888/698-9896, fax 808/968-7017, website: www.bbmtview .com, email: info@bbmtniew.com, is owned and operated by Jane and Linus Chao, both internationally known artists. The couple's inspired artwork graces the home. A residence and artist studio, this B&B lies just outside the village of Mountain View along S. Kulani Road, on a landscaped four-acre parcel with a marvelous view north to Mauna Kea. Enter through an iron gate under a canopy of trees. The spacious guest rooms are modern in all amenities and equipped with king, queen, or twin beds; two have private bathrooms, two others share. Everyone has use of the common room for reading, TV, or simply appreciating the fine view. A full breakfast is served each morning in the dining room, and each day the offering is different. Room rates run $55–95 daily. For peace and serenity and inspiration of the artistic soul, there is no better place than Bed and Breakfast Mountain View.

HISTORY OF THE ANTHURIUM

Originally a native of Central America, the anthurium was introduced into Hawaii in 1889 by Samuel M. Damon, an English missionary. Damon discovered that Hawaii's climate and volcanic soil made an ideal environment for this exotic flower. Over the years, anthurium production has turned into a million-dollar export industry with all the major growers on the Big Island.

DIANA LASICH HARPER

Farther into this labyrinth of roads south of Mt. View, down along Pikake Street, is **Pineapple Park B&B Hostel,** P.O. Box 5844, Hilo, HI 96720, 808/968-8170 or 877/965-2266, website: www.pineapple-park.com, email: park@aloha.net. This is country living in modern style. A bed in the bunkroom runs $17 a night and a double room runs $39; these rooms share kitchen and bath facilities and have use of the common room. No breakfast is provided. A private room for $65 is available with breakfast, and a detached bungalow large enough for four people can be rented for $150 a night. Checkout is before 10 A.M., check-in until 9 P.M., and quiet time after 11 P.M. This is a smoke-free environment.

Glenwood

Between mile markers 19 and 20, this town offers a gas station and **Hirano's General Store** for a few basic provisions. A few minutes beyond town you pass **Akatsuka Orchid Gardens,** 808/967-8234, open daily 8:30 A.M.–5 P.M., except major holidays. If tour buses don't overflow the parking lot, stop in for a look at how orchids are grown. In the covered showroom, an incredible variety of orchids are on display and for sale, and neat little souvenirs are sold in the gift shop. Akatsuka ships cut flowers and potted orchids anywhere in the country. For a mail-order catalog, contact P.O. Box 220, Volcano, HI 96785, 808/967-6669, fax 808/967-7140.

VOLCANO VILLAGE

BIG ISLAND

You shouldn't miss taking a ride through the village of Volcano, a beautiful old settlement with truly charming houses and cottages outlined in ferns. Follow the signs off the main highway near mile marker 26 to the Old Volcano Highway, which is the main drag through the village. Tiny gravel roads lace this community, which sits virtually atop one of the world's undeniable "power spots." This is a heavily forested area with no sidewalks or street lights. Lighting is generally subdued, so it can be very dark at night. At about 4,000 feet, it gets surprisingly cool and, of course, it often rains—over 150 inches a year. Summer daytime temperatures average 75°, around 65° in winter. At night it drops to 55° in summer and into the 40s in winter. The fog rolls in most late afternoons, obscuring distant views but bestowing on the village an otherworldly charm. The area is so green and so vibrant that it appears surrealistic. With flowers, ferns, and trees everywhere, it is hard to imagine a more picturesque village in all of America. But even in this little parcel of paradise, things are changing, if slowly. The town of about 1,500 people now boasts two general stores, a hardware store, two small gift shops/galleries, a post office, a farmers' market, a winery, several restaurants, an abundance of accommodations, and several artists' studios.

Volcano Golf and Country Club

What's most amazing about this course is where it is. Imagine! You're teeing off atop an active volcano surrounded by one of the last pristine forests in the state. At the right time of year, the surrounding 'ohi'a turn scarlet when they are in bloom. The fairways are carved from lava, while in the distance Mauna Loa looms. Hit a poor shot and you can watch your ball disappear down a steam vent. The course began about 80 years ago when a group of local golfers hand-cleared three "greens," placing stakes that served as holes. Later this was improved to sand greens with tin cans for holes, and after an eruption in 1924 blanketed the area with volcanic ash that served as excellent fertilizer, the grass grew and the course became a lush green. After World War II the course was extended to 18 holes, and a clubhouse was added. Finally, Jack Snyder, a well-known course architect, redesigned the course to its present par-72 layout. Rates are $60 with shared cart; reduced rates for Big Island residents. To beat the heavy lunch crowd at Volcano House, try the restaurant at the course. The course is just north of the Belt Road, about two miles west of the park entrance. Turn on Pi'i Mauna Drive, sometimes called Golf Course Road. Phone 808/967-7331 for more information and tee times.

Volcano Winery

About one mile beyond the golf course at the end of Pi'i Mauna Road and off to your left are the buildings of the Volcano Winery, 808/967-7479, website: www.volcanowinery.com. This is

BIG ISLAND

To Hilo

WRIGHT RD.

HAUNINI RD.

KA HALE IKI KILAUEA
CHALET KILAUEA

VOLCANO INN

VOLCANO BED AND BREAKFAST

COOPER CENTER, FARMERS MARKET

LAUKAPU RD.

KEONELEHUA RD.

KILAUEA RD.

MY ISLAND BED AND BREAKFAST INN

OLD JAPANESE SCHOOLHOUSE
HALE KILAUEA

HOLO HOLO IN

KILAUEA LODGE AND RESTAURANT

KILAUEA GENERAL STORE, LAVA ROCK CAFE, KILAUEA KREATIONS, GAS STATION

THE COUNTRY GOOSE

VOLCANO COUNTRY COTTAGES

CARSON'S VOLCANO COTTAGES

POST OFFICE

OMA'S HAPU'U HIDEAWAY

HARDWARE STORE, GIFT SHOP, THAI THAI RESTAURANT, LAUNDROMAT

LOKAHI LODGE

HALE OHIA

OLD VOLCANO HWY.

THE VOLCANO STORE, SERT'S AT VOLCANO VILLAGE, GAS STATION

HAWAI'I BELT ROAD

FIRST
JADE AVE.
RUBY AVE.
PEARL AVE.

LIONA
SIXTH
EIGHTH
FOURTEENTH

NAHELENANI
ALAOHIA

THE GUESTHOUSE AT VOLCANO

0   0.5 mi
0   0.5 km

VOLCANO VILLAGE

To National Park, Kailua-Kona

the only winery on the Big Island and the southernmost in the United States. It's a hands-on operation where everything is done manually. Because the land is at an elevation of about 4,000 feet, the patented Symphony grape (a combination of grenache gris and muscat of Alexandria grapes) is grown to take best advantage of the climatic conditions, which are similar to those in Oregon and Washington. About 14 acres of this rough countryside are currently being cultivated with grapes, producing about three tons of grapes per acre, and another four acres have been planted in half a dozen other varieties to see if they too will produce acceptable wine. Bottled are dry and semi-dry wines, four wine and fruit blends including guava/chablis and jaboticaba/chablis, a lehua honey wine, and a macadamia honey wine. A local favorite, the jaboticaba blend is made with a Brazilian fruit of that name; the honey "wines" are made without any grapes. All bottles cost $13 apiece. Although no tours of

the winery are available, a tasting room is open daily 10 A.M.–5 P.M. Have a sip at the glass-covered koa bar and maybe you'll want to purchase a bottle for later in the evening or a six-bottle case to share with friends when you get home. There also is a small boutique on the premises selling T-shirts, jewelry, *kukui* nut leis, postcards, and other gift items.

ACCOMMODATIONS

There are a great number of accommodations in and around Volcano Village. While most are near the heart of the village, several are in the fern forests south of the highway and a few are around the golf course about two miles west of town. Most are bed-and-breakfasts, some are vacation homes where you take care of your own meals, and there is one hostel. These places run from budget and homey to luxurious and elegant, but most are moderate in price and amenities. Some of these establishments also act as agents for other rental homes in the area, so your choices are many. See also the Volcano House listing in the **Hawaii Volcanoes National Park** chapter below.

Under $50

Volcano has a hostel, and a fine one it is! Although a modern structure, this all-wood forest house is an old-style place with a comforting, traditional hostel feel. **Holo Holo In,** P.O. Box 784, Volcano Village, HI 96785, 808/967-7950, fax 808/967-8025, website: www.enable.org/holo-holo, email: holoholo@interpac.net, snuggles under the towering trees in a residential area of the village, next to an old Japanese schoolhouse at 19-4036 Kalani Honua Road. Owned, operated, and built by Satoshi Yabuki, a world traveler himself when he was younger, this is a one-man operation; his office hours are 6:30–9 A.M. and 4:30–9 P.M. Taking guests for nearly a dozen years, this hostel has been an AYH member since the late 1990s. On the downstairs level is a huge kitchen with all needed appliances and utensils and a library of books and information. You are more than welcome to cook, but please clean up after yourself. Here too are a laundry facility and a sauna ($4 per person per use). Upstairs are the men's and women's dorms and the TV room, and there are bathrooms up and down. Rates are $17 per person for the dorm ($15 for AYH members), or $40 per couple for a private room. Please bring your own sheets or there will be a nominal extra charge. This is a great little accommodation at a bargain price—a real find.

$50–100

At the end of Old Volcano Highway on the lower end of town, **Volcano Inn,** P.O. Box 490, Volcano Village, HI 96785, 808/967-7293 or 800/997-2292, fax 808/985-7349, website: www.volcanoinn.com, email: volcano@volcanoinn.com, has numerous rooms and several cottages at a separate location. The main three-story house is of modern design, with a common room and huge dining room where complimentary breakfasts are served to all guests. Single rooms run $45–55 a night and double rooms are $75–95. Each has a private entrance and bath, TV and VCR, refrigerator, and coffeemaker. The cottages on the south side of the highway in a

fern forest go for $65–135, and two are big enough for a small family. A 10 percent discount is given for AAA members. The inn also offers tours to various locations on the island, can book activities with other vendors, rents bicycles, and operates horseback riding tours.

On the downhill side of the highway, the **Country Goose Bed and Breakfast,** P.O. Box 597, Volcano, HI 96785, 808/967-7759 or 800/238-7101 from the Mainland, fax 808/985-8673, email: cgoose@interpac.net, is a very pleasant place with lots of knickknacks on the walls. The knotty pine on the walls, open-beamed ceiling, and decor all say easy country living. Comfortable and homey, rooms include private baths and entrances, and the common room is open to all guests. Everyone is served a hearty country-style breakfast each morning in the dining room. Nestled under 'ohi'a trees and ferns, half a mile from the highway, this little place is quiet. The gracious owner, Joan Early, has built herself a fine retreat here and loves to share it with others who love the area. Rooms rent for $70 a night for two, with an extra $10 for a third person. Joan also represents several one-, two-, and three-bedroom homes in the village and out near the golf course that are available for nightly, weekly, or longer stays.

A B&B with an excellent reputation is **My Island Bed and Breakfast Inn,** P.O. Box 100, Volcano, HI 96785, 808/967-7216, fax 808/967-7719, website: www.myislandinnhawaii.com, email: myisland@ilhawaii.net. The main house is a New England–style three-level house from the 1880s that was the Lyman summer home for many years. Rooms in this building rent for a reasonable $45 single to $70 double; some share a bathroom. A few steps away, the garden units go for $75–85. A private studio with bathroom and kitchenette, also in the garden, runs $85, and a fully furnished vacation house on the property goes for $120. No credit cards are accepted. All guests are served a "world-class" breakfast each morning in the main house. Spend some time in the exquisite flower garden here as it is a wonderful extra benefit to this property. In addition, My Island rents three other vacation homes in the village, two down below the highway and one up near the golf course.

Owned and operated by Bonnie Goodell, **The Guesthouse at Volcano,** P.O. Box 6, Volcano,

HI 96785, 808/967-7775, fax 808/967-8295, website: www.volcanoguesthouse.com, email: cmaplan@interpac.net, is a very friendly hideaway on the farthest back road of Volcano Village south of the highway. The fully furnished cottage is designed as a self-sufficient unit where guests are guaranteed peace and quiet on a lovely six-acre homesite. Bring your own food. Bonnie grew up in Hawaii and was for many years the education director for the Honolulu Botanical Gardens. She *knows* her plants and is willing to chat with her guests. The place is particularly good for families. Children have plenty of room to play, while their parents can roam the orchards on the property. The two-story guest home is bright and airy. Enter into a combo living room, kitchen, and dining area, with twin beds in a bedroom. Upstairs is a sleeping area with two twin beds and a queen bed. Futons can sleep even more. In the main house, a one-bedroom apartment called Claudia's Place has its own entrance and bathroom. It's completely wheelchair-accessible and will sleep up to three. The rate for either is $60, $10 for each additional person over two (off-season rates available). Two nights minimum, with the seventh night at no charge. Sometimes Bonnie will allow an emergency one-night stay if the house is not booked, but she charges $10 extra because the entire house has to be cleaned.

$100–150

Kilauea Lodge, P.O. Box 116, Volcano Village, HI 96785, 808/967-7366, fax 808/967-7367, website: www.kilauealodge.com, email: stay@kilauealodge.com, owned and operated by Lorna and Albert Jeyte, is the premier restaurant and lodge atop Volcano, as well as one of the very best on the island. The solid stone and timber structure was built in 1938 as a YMCA camp and functioned as such until 1962, when it became a "mom and pop operation," often failing and changing ownership. It faded into the ferns until Lorna and Albert revitalized it in 1987, opening in 1988. The lodge is a classic, with a vaulted, open-beamed ceiling. A warm and cozy "international fireplace" dating from the days of the YMCA camp is embedded with stones and plaques from all over the world. This building houses the restaurant and the office. An assortment of rooms, ranging $125–145 and including

a complete breakfast for all guests in the restaurant, are in three adjacent buildings on the property. The brooding rooms of the original guesthouse section were transformed into bright, cozy, romantic suites. The rooms, all differently appointed, range in decor from Hawaiian-European to Asian with a motif of Japanese fans. Each room has a bathroom with vaulted 18-foot ceilings and a skylight, a working fireplace, queen or twin beds, and swivel rocking chair. A separate one-bedroom cottage, in the ferns to the side, features a wood-burning stove (central heat too), wet bar, a queen-size bed, private bath, and small living room with queen-size pull-out sofa. In 1991, Kilauea Lodge opened seven new units centered around a commodious common room where you can read and snooze by a crackling fire. All rooms in the new section are very spacious, with vaulted ceilings (upstairs) and tastefully furnished with wicker furniture, white curtains, and fluffy quilts to keep off the evening chill. Many are hung with original artwork by Gwendolyn O'Connor. Check-in is 3–5 P.M. at the office; after that, check in at the restaurant. The Kilauea Lodge provides one of the most *civilized* atmospheres in Hawaii in one of its most powerful natural areas. The combination is hard to beat.

Conveniently located near stores and restaurants is **Oma's Hapu'u Hideaway,** a modern mountain house of cedar that's great for a family. Here you have all you need: a full kitchen, living room, bathroom, and two bedrooms downstairs, one with bunks that's great for kids, and a master bedroom loft upstairs. The house comes with TV and VCR and phone. It's a cozy place that goes for $95 a night for two with $15 extra for each additional person ($8 for kids 12 and under); the fifth night is free. The owners live across the street in a plantation house, and in the rear is **The Maid's Quarters,** a self-contained cottage with full kitchen, living room tiled with marble, fireplace, spacious bedroom, and completely updated bathroom. This is a lovely place, just right for a romantic couple. This cottage runs $85 a night, and both places are good value for the money. No breakfast is served. For information on either place, contact P.O. Box 611, Volcano, HI 96785, 808/985-8959, website: www.volcanovillage.net, email: todd@volcanovillage.net.

Hale Ohia

BIG ISLAND

Volcano Country Cottages, P.O. Box 159, Volcano, HI 96785, 808/967-7960 or 800/967-7960, website: www.volcanocottages.com, email: places@aloha.net, is conveniently located in the heart of the village at one of its oldest homes. Available are the Ohelo Berry Cottage for $95 for one night or $85 for two or more nights and the two-bedroom Artist's House for $125 or $105 for more than one night; $15 for each additional person beyond two. The studio cottage is a cozy one-room affair with kitchenette, bathroom, and room heater that snuggles into the back vegetation. It's perfect for a couple but can also sleep two kids on futons. A covered lanai outside the front door is a wonderful spot to sit during a light rain. Each morning, the fridge is stocked with a filling and tasty breakfast. Set closer to the front of the property under towering tsugi trees, the Artist's House contains a full kitchen, also stocked with morning goodies, a woodstove, and washer and dryer. It sleeps four comfortably and up to four more on pull-out futons. This is a gracious place, one of peace and tranquillity, with the added gift of artwork hung on the walls. Check-in is 3–5 P.M. Contact Kathryn Grout, manager, for information and reservations.

Follow a private mountain lane for a few minutes into an enchanted clearing where the artwork of a meticulous Japanese garden surrounds a gabled and turreted home and its attendant cottages of red-on-brown rough-cut shingles. Once the hideaway of the Dillinghams, an old and influential *kama'aina* family, **Hale Ohia,** P.O. Box 758, Volcano Village, HI 96785, 808/967-7986 or 800/455-3803, fax 808/967-8610, website: www.haleohia.com, email: haleohia@bigisland.com, is now owned and operated by Michael D. Tuttle, who purchased the property after falling hopelessly in love at first sight. The main house holds the Dillingham Suite, $110 per night, with its own sitting room, bath, and glass-covered lanai. Simple and clean, with hardwood floors and wainscoted walls, the home is the epitome of country elegance, Hawaiian style. Adjacent in the main house, occupying one bedroom, a big bath, and the main living room, is the Master Suite for $130. Hale Ohia Cottage, once the gardener's residence, has two stories, with the bottom floor front occupied by the Iiwi and Camellia suites, $75–95, which are wheelchair-accessible and can be combined for larger groups. Stained-glass windows with a calla lily-and-poppy motif add a special touch, while the low ceilings are reminiscent of the captain's quarters on a sailing ship. The first floor rear has a full kitchen and a covered lanai complete with barbecue grill that makes it perfect for evening relaxation. Narrow stairs lead to a full bath on the first landing, and the upstairs opens into a bright and airy parlor and adjacent bedrooms that can sleep five comfortably ($130). Hale Lehua, once a private study, is secluded down its own lava footpath and rents for $110.

The interior is cozy with its own fireplace, bamboo and wicker furniture, self-contained bathroom, covered lanai, partial kitchen, and leaded glass windows through which the surrounding fern forest will emit its emerald radiance. Similar but more luxurious is the Ihilani Cottage, at $125. To make your stay even more delightful, room rates include an "extended" continental breakfast, and guests are welcome to immerse themselves in the bubbling hot tub under a canopy of Japanese cedars and glimmering stars. No TV, no phones, and no smoking.

Ka Hale Iki Kilauea is a very romantic home away from home, canopied by the forest trees, screened from the road by tall ferns, and 50 feet through the jungle from the driveway. Much like a cabin with a porch all around, the inside opens to a high open-beamed ceiling, living room with a woodstove, and full kitchen. Sliding doors and picture windows all around frame the living green tapestry outside. In the bath is a huge tub fit for two; bathe by candlelight and open the full-length windows to let in the night air. Up the ladder-like narrow stairway is the bedroom and queen bed, where you can drift away with the moon and starlight gently filtering through the skylight windows. The rental rate is $135 a night for a couple and $15 more for an extra person, or $700 a week, breakfast included. For reservations, contact Joan Early at the Country Goose, 808/967-7759 or 800/238-7101, website: www.vbro.com/vrbo/1438.htm.

Green pines and native 'ohi'a shade **Hale Kilauea,** P.O. Box 28, Volcano, HI 96785, 808/967-7591, fax 808/985-7008. In the main lodge, a central common room is very comfortable with reading materials, fireplace, parlor games, and TV. The spacious and airy rooms in the main lodge, all with private baths, cost $85–125, $20 for an extra person, and are comfortable but not luxurious. Upstairs rooms are more deluxe with plush carpeting, knotty pine trim, refrigerator, small divan, and private lanai. Ask for a room in the rear so that you can overlook the quiet green forest. Two rooms across from the main building are warm and cozy, although quite small. They are private and the least expensive. The best deal, however, is a refurbished plantation cottage that sits across the road. The rate is $145, with special weekly and monthly rates. The wainscoted cottage provides a small but serviceable

kitchen, separate bedroom, and living room that can sleep a few more. Don't expect luxury, but a night in the cottage is a window into Hawaii's heritage of humble workers in humble homes. With all the rooms, including the cottage, a hearty continental breakfast is provided.

Deep in the fern forest, **Carson's Volcano Cottages,** P.O. Box 503, Volcano, HI 96785, 808/967-7683 or 800/845-LAVA, fax 808/967-8094, website: www.carsonscottage.com, email: carsons@aloha.net, owned and operated by Tom and Brenda Carson, offers two B&B rooms, one in its own studio cottage and the others in a three-room cottage. The richly decorated suites in the main house are upstairs and run $125–155 a night. The cottage accommodations all have private baths, entrances, and decks, and in the garden is a hot tub for everyone to use. The one-acre property is naturally landscaped with 'ohi'a and fern, and moss-covered sculptures of Balinese gods peek through the foliage. The studio cottage, $125 double, a miniature plantation house with corrugated roof and woodstove, has a mini-kitchen and a bath with a skylight—rustic country charm. The three-room cottage, $105–110 per room, has vaulted ceilings and queen beds, and rooms decorated in Hawaiian monarchy, Oriental, and tropical styles. Leaded glass windows open to a private porch. Tom and Brenda provide an extended continental breakfast for all guests in their dining room that might include banana bread, French toast, passion fruit juice, bagels and lox, or strawberry crepes. You'll be comfortable in front of the living room fireplace or enjoying the evening sky from the hot tub. The Carsons also rent several other one- and two-bedroom, fully furnished cottages in the village that start at $125 and a seaside retreat down in Kapoho if you are going that direction.

$150–200

Just up the road from the Kilauea Lodge is a cute little two-bedroom cottage, **Tutu's Place.** Built in 1929 by the Uncle Billy of hotel chain fame for "tutu" (grandma), it was bought several decades later by the Warner family. Mr. Warner was a minister and was involved in Hawaiian politics. His wife, Ruth Warner, lived in the cottage for 30 years until it was bought in 1995 by Lorna Larson-Jeyte, the owner of the Kilauea

Lodge, who used to visit as a child. Although it's been completely refurbished, people in the know say that the cottage is still imbued with the spirit of Ruth Warner. It's done in a theme of rattan and koa, with a fireplace in the living room, a full kitchen, and a wonderful little bathroom. For a small place, it has a surprisingly roomy feel. The rate is $155 for two people, including breakfast at the Kilauea Lodge, plus $15 for each additional person. To make reservations, call the Kilauea Lodge and ask for Tutu's Place.

Chalet Kilauea

Peeking from the *hapu'u* fern forest in a manicured glen is Chalet Kilauea, P.O. Box 998, Volcano Village, HI 96785, 808/967-7786 or 800/937-7786, fax 808/967-8660 or 800/577-1849, website: www.volcano-hawaii.com, email: reservations@volcano-hawaii.com, where you will be cordially accommodated by owners Lisha and Brian Crawford and their staff. Enter the second level of the main house to find a guest living room where you can while away the hours playing chess, listening to a large collection of CDs, or gazing from the wraparound windows at a treetop view of the surrounding forest, ferns, and impeccable grounds. Downstairs there's an outdoor lounge area and a black-and-white checkerboard dining room where wrought-iron tables sit before a huge picture window. A three-course candlelight breakfast is served here every morning. On the lawn, a free-standing gazebo houses an eight-person hot tub available 24 hours a day.

The main house, called The Inn at Volcano, is known for elegance and luxury. It holds four suites and two theme rooms, $135–395. The Oriental Jade Room is richly appointed with Chinese folding screens, samurai murals, Oriental carpet, and jade-green bedspread. The green marble bathroom adds to the green theme of the surrounding vegetation. The lanai outside is shared with the Out of Africa Room, which has a strong color theme of burgundy and brass. The Continental Lace Suite is fluff and lace, the bridal suite. Here the colors are white, gold, and pink; a wedding dress hangs in the corner to accentuate the theme. On the first floor, the Owners' Suite is designed for up to three people. Pink carpet covers the floor and a green floral spread tops the bed. With two shower heads in the shower stall, a couple can be happy showering together. Connected by a deck to the main house is the Treehouse Suite, a two-story unit with bath, sitting room, wet bar, and kitchenette downstairs, and a large bedroom on the upper floor. The surrounding glass makes the living forest part of the decor. A private lanai overlooks the garden, and a hand-crafted wooden circular staircase connects the two floors.

Chalet Kilauea also has many other accommodations in Volcano Village, including Castle Suites at Mauna Loa, a modern Victorian on the golf course, where rooms range $195–395. Both Lokahi Lodge, with rooms for $125–145, and The Lodge at Volcano, where rooms are a more reasonable $85–125, are done in modern style and big enough for groups. For those on a tighter budget, the Volcano Bed and Breakfast rents rooms for $45–65 and still has plenty of common space. In addition, six vacation homes dotted here and there about town in the secluded privacy of the forest are available for $125–225. Whatever your price range, Chalet Kilauea will have something for you, and breakfast is an option at most accommodations.

FOOD

The **Kilauea Lodge Restaurant,** open for dinner 5:30–9 P.M. nightly, reservations a must, is an extraordinary restaurant serving gourmet continental cuisine at reasonable prices. This is the premier restaurant in Volcano Village. A large fireplace dominates one side of the room with an inviting couch to its front. The hardwood floor reflects light from the two chandeliers that hang from the open-beamed wooden ceiling. Prints of Hawaiian scenes hang from the walls, and beer mugs line the stone mantle. A warm, welcoming, and homey place, the Kilauea Lodge Restaurant has fine dining in an unpretentious setting. A very friendly and professional staff serves the excellent food prepared by Albert, the owner. You'll start off with a fresh bread—studded like the fireplace, but with sunflower and sesame seeds. Appetizers such as mushroom caps stuffed with crab and cheese will titillate your palate, or try the baked brie cheese, a specialty. Entr'es, ranging $13–26, include soup, salad, and vegetables. The menu is strong on

BIG ISLAND

the meats, with its heavy German influence, but vegetarians will be delighted with their options too. Dinner features seafood Mauna Kea (succulent pieces of seafood served atop a bed of fettuccine) and paupiettes of beef (prime rib slices rolled around herbs and mushrooms in a special sauce). Always a great choice, the catch of the day is baked, broiled, or sautéed with a savory sauce. There is always a nightly special, and each dish is infused with herbs and pungent seasonings. Desserts are wonderful, and the meal is topped off with a cup of Irish or Italian coffee.

You can get away from the crowds and have a satisfying meal at **Volcano Country Club Restaurant,** 808/967-8228, at the golf course clubhouse. The green and white interior complements the fairways, which can be seen through the surrounding plate glass windows. A fireplace fills the center of this country kitchen style room. The food is quite good. Complete breakfast is served daily 8–10 A.M. (7 A.M. on weekends), a full lunch menu daily 10:30 A.M.–2:30 P.M. For breakfast choose omelets, hotcakes, or other standard American fare. Lunch selections include hearty sandwiches, salads, and burgers, as well as local favorites like teriyaki beef, saimin, or loco moco, with nothing on the menu over $9. Many stop by just for the Portuguese bean soup. The bar is well stocked, so enjoy an exotic drink, beer, or glass of wine after your round. This is a good choice for lunch.

Sharing the same building as the Volcano Store is the Asian-European fusion restaurant **Sert's at Volcano Village,** 808/967-8511. You know that times are a-changin' when a restaurant with a niche like this moves into town. No one seems to be complaining, however, and the addition to the food scene is positive. Lunch, from noon to 4 P.M., finds items like Caesar salad and spring rolls, vegetarian tofu curry and Dutch steak with potato on the menu. Reserve a seat for dinner, served 4–9:30 P.M., as this is a small place and popular. Choose calamari salad or stuffed escargot to start. Follow with an entrée like beef Penang or chicken puttanesca. There are always chef's specials and numerous fish selections. Most lunch items run less than $12 and dinner entrées up to $20. Make this a special night out.

Around the side is the **Steam Vent Cafe.** Associated with Sert's, this place is a self-serve café with pre-made sandwiches, salads, and tureens of soup, all $4–8, plus pastries and lots of coffee. If you start early, stop here. It's open 6:30 A.M.–8:30 P.M.

Situated behind the Kilauea General Store is **Lava Rock Restaurant,** 808/967-8526, the most local of the eateries in the village. The Lava Rock is open 7:30–10:30 A.M. for breakfast, until 5 P.M. for lunch, and dinner is served Tues.–Sat. until 9 P.M. Start your day with eggs, griddle items, or loco moco. For lunch you can get a plate lunch, burger, or sandwich, along with sides, fountain drinks, and coffee. Dinners are a bit heartier with the likes of teriyaki chicken and New York steak, and almost everything is under $12. A good choice. You can wear your jeans here and fit right in.

A fine addition to the restaurant scene in Volcano is **Thai Thai Restaurant,** 808/967-7969, open for dinner every day except Wednesday 5–9 P.M. This restaurant puts out food that will transport you to the Orient. It is establishing a good reputation in town for tasty food and large portions. Start with an appetizer (some as big as entrées), like deep-fried tofu or chicken satay. Traditional soups and salads come next, followed by curries or stir-fried selections, most of which came be made with your choice of shrimp, chicken, beef, or pork. Almost everything on the menu is in the $9–13 range, so it's not exorbitant.

Rainbow Moon Pizza, 808/967-8617, is a name without a place—there's no shop to walk into. What you do is call in your order, they bake the pizza at their commercial kitchen, and then deliver it to you. Finding you in the village is no problem for them as long as *you* know where you are. People in town say this is the best pizza that they've had—and they aren't kidding. This is gourmet pizza made from scratch—even the dough—so it may take an hour or so to reach you. It's worth the wait. It may be best to call ahead and ask for a specific delivery time later in the day. These pizzas are rectangular. The regular has eight pieces (equal to a 12-inch round), the double is two regulars of the same kind. Choices include vegetarian, meat, fish, and seasonal toppings, or you can create your own. Prices range $11–30. Call to find out what's available or look up the menu at www.volcanogallery.com/rainbow.htm. Rainbow Pizza takes orders Wed.–Sun. 4–9 P.M.

Wouldn't it be fun to have a full multi-course gourmet dinner prepared and delivered to your door by a trained chef and served on linen and fine china, with the dishes whisked away after you're finished so you can turn your attention to more romantic matters? Well, you can do just that here in the tiny village of Volcano for $25 per person plus gratuity and wine. Call the Culinary Crusaders, 808/985-7167, 24-hour advance notice requested. It is not inexpensive, and an experience to be remembered.

See also Kilauea House Restaurant in the **Hawaii Volcanoes National Park** chapter below.

RECREATION

The big attraction in the Volcano area is the great outdoors and the natural wonders of the national park. Seeing the "sights" around Kilauea Caldera is on everyone's list, as is driving the Chain of Craters Road, and some expend more energy by hiking the back country. Horseback riding at a local ranch and a guided overnight camping trip to the slopes of Mauna Loa are other options.

Volcano Ranch offers several horseback adventures starting with the very tame ride through the village, a two-hour saunter over the back roads for $50 per person. This is a great introduction to the village and good for the younger ones. For two to three hours and $100 you can have a ride at the working ranch; to get more involved ask for the daylong Roundup, $125, where you participate in some of the ranch activities. On special request, for $160 per person, the ranch will take a couple on a four-hour ride at South Point, where you have time to explore the wind-washed tip of the island.

Ever trekked with a llama? You can here in Volcano on an overnight hike to a camp partway up the slope of Mauna Loa. You walk; the llama carries the gear. This is a two-day affair and all transportation, food, and necessary equipment is provided. For either the llama trek or the horseback ride, contact Volcano Inn, 808/967-7293 or 800/997-2292.

SHOPPING

A **farmers' market** open every Sunday 8:15 A.M.–10 P.M. sells local produce, baked goods, used books, and other used items. It's along Wright Road at the Cooper Center. Come early for the food.

Volcano Store, 808/967-7210, also called the "upper store," is open daily 5:30 A.M.–7 P.M. and sells gasoline, film, a few camping supplies, and a good selection of basic foods, and general dry goods items. There are public telephone booths out front, and next door is the full-service post office.

Just down the road, **Kilauea General Store,** 808/967-7555, also called the "lower store," is open daily 7 A.M.–7:30 P.M. This store also sells gas, and although it is not as well stocked as a grocery, it does have a deli case, a good selection of beer and liquor, postcards, videos, and an excellent community bulletin board.

Set between these two is **True Value Hardware** for all your home and yard needs. Open daily 7 A.M.–5:30 P.M.

In a separate building next to the general store is **Kilauea Kreations,** a shop that specializes in quilts, quilting supplies, and art by local artists. For other art and crafts by local artists, as well as information about the area, have a look at the **Village Art Loft** above the hardware store.

Many artists have found a home at Volcano, and a few studios dot the backroads. Ask at stores for maps.

BIG ISLAND

HAWAII VOLCANOES NATIONAL PARK

INTRODUCTION

Hawaii Volcanoes National Park (HVNP) is an unparalleled experience in geological grandeur. The upper end of the park is the summit of stupendous Mauna Loa, the most massive mountain on earth. Mauna Loa Road branches off Highway 11 and ends at a foot trail for the hale and hearty who trek to the 13,679-foot summit. The park's heart is **Kilauea Caldera,** almost three miles across, 400 feet deep, and encircled by 11 miles of **Crater Rim Drive.** At the park **Visitors Center** you can give yourself a crash course in geology while picking up park maps, information, and back country camping permits. Nearby is **Volcano House,** Hawaii's oldest hotel, which has hosted a steady stream of adventurers, luminaries, royalty, and heads of state ever since it opened its doors in the 1860s. Just a short drive away is a pocket of indigenous forest,

providing the perfect setting for a bird sanctuary. In a separate detached section of the park is 'Ola'a Forest, a pristine wilderness area of unspoiled flora and fauna.

Crater Rim Drive circles Kilauea Caldera past steam vents, sulfur springs, and tortured fault lines that always seem on the verge of gaping wide and swallowing. On the way you can peer into the maw of **Halema'uma'u Crater,** home of the fire goddess, Pele, and you'll pass **Hawaiian Volcano Observatory** (not open to public), which has been monitoring geologic activity since the turn of the 20th century. Adjacent to the observatory is the **Thomas A. Jaggar Museum,** an excellent facility where you can educate yourself on the past and present volcanology of the park. A fantastic walk is **Devastation Trail,** a paved path across a desolate cinder field where gray, lifeless trunks of a

HAWAII VOLCANOES NATIONAL PARK

© SANDRA E. BISIGNANI IRLS) AND AVALON TRAVEL PUBLISHING, INC.

BIG ISLAND

suffocated forest lean like old gravestones. Within minutes is **Thurston Lava Tube,** a magnificent natural tunnel *"leid"* by amazingly vibrant fern grottoes at the entrance and exit.

The southwestern section of the park is dominated by the **Ka'u Desert,** not a plain of sand but a semi-arid slope of lava flow, cinder, scrub bush, and heat that's been defiled by the wind-blown debris and gasses of Kilauea Volcano and fractured by the sinking coastline. It is a desolate region, an area crossed by a few trails that are a challenge even to the sturdy and experienced hiker. Most visitors, however, head down the **Chain of Craters Road,** first through the 'ohi'a and fern forests, then past numerous secondary craters and down the *pali* to the coast where the road ends abruptly at a hardened flow of lava and from where visitors try to glimpse the current volcanic activity.

The indomitable power of Volcanoes National Park is apparent to all who come here. Mark Twain, enchanted by his sojourn through Volcanoes in the 1860s, quipped, "The smell of sulfur is strong, but not unpleasant to a sinner." Amen, brother! Wherever you stop to gaze, realize that you are standing on a thin skin of cooled lava in an unstable earthquake zone atop one of the world's most active volcanoes.

Established in 1916 as the 13th U.S. national park, HVNP now covers 377 square miles. Based on its scientific and scenic value, the park was named an International Biosphere Reserve by UNESCO in 1980 and given World Heritage Site status in 1982 by the same organization, giving it greater national and international prestige. With about 2.5 million visitors a year, this is one of the top visitor attractions in the state.

Admission to the park is $10 per vehicle (good for multiple entries over a seven-day period), $20 for an annual permit, $5 for bicycle traffic and hikers, and free to those 62 and over with a Golden Age, Golden Eagle, or Golden Access passport. These "passports" are available at the park headquarters and are good at any national park in the United States. For information about the park, write to Hawaii Volcanoes National Park, P.O. Box 52, Hawaii National Park, HI 96718-0052; call 808/985-6000 for a recorded message; or visit www.nps.gov/havo.

Geologic History:
Science Versus Madame Pele

The goddess Pele is an irascible old dame. Perhaps it's because she had such a bad childhood. All she wanted was a home of her own where she could house her family and entertain her lover, a handsome chief from Kaua'i. But her sea goddess sister, Namakaokaha'i, flooded her out wherever she went after Pele seduced her husband, and the pig god, Kamapua'a, ravished Pele for good measure. So Pele finally built her love nest at Halema'uma'u Crater at the south end of Kilauea Caldera. Being a goddess obviously isn't as heavenly as one would think, and whenever the pressures of life get too much for Pele, she blows her stack. These tempestuous outbursts made Pele one of the most revered gods in the Hawaiian pantheon because her presence and might were so easily felt.

For a thousand years Pele was appeased by offerings of pigs, dogs, sacred 'ohelo berries (her favorite), and now and again an outcast man or two (never women) who would hopefully turn her energy from destruction to more comfortable pursuits. Also, if Pele was your family's personal goddess, your remains were sometimes allowed to be thrown into the fire pit as a sign of great respect. In the early 1820s, the chieftess Kapi'olani, an ardent convert to Christianity, officially challenged Pele in an attempt to topple her like the other gods of old. Kapi'olani climbed down into Pele's crater and ate the sacred 'ohelo berries, flagrantly violating the ageless *kapu*. She then took large stones and defiantly hurled them into the fire pit below while bellowing, "Jehovah is my God. It is He, not Pele, that kindled these flames."

Yet today, most residents, regardless of background, have an inexplicable reverence for Pele. The Volcano post office receives an average of three packages a week containing lava rocks taken by tourists as souvenirs. Some hold that Pele looks upon these rocks as her children and taking them from her is kidnapping. The accompanying letters implore the officials to return the rocks because ever since the offender brought them home, luck has been bad. The officials take the requests very seriously, returning the rocks with the customary peace offering. Many follow-up "thank you" letters have been written to express relief that the bad luck has

ROBERT NILSEN

*on the edge of
Halema'uma'u Crater*

been lifted. There is no reference in Hawaiian folklore to this phenomenon, although Hawaiians did hold certain rocks sacred. Park rangers will tell you that the idea of "the bad-luck rocks" was initiated a few decades back by a tour bus driver who became sick and tired of tourists getting his bus dirty by piling aboard their souvenirs. *Voilà!* Another ancient Hawaiian myth! Know, however, that the rocks in Hawaii Volcanoes National Park are protected by federal law, much meaner and more vindictive than Pele.

Pele is believed to take human form. She customarily appears before an eruption as a ravishing beauty or a withered old hag, often accompanied by a little white dog. She expects to be treated cordially, and it's said that she will stand by the roadside at night hitching a ride. After a brief encounter, she departs and seems to mysteriously evaporate into the ether. Kindness on your part is the key; if you come across a strange woman at night, treat her well—it might not help, but it definitely won't hurt.

Eruptions

The first white man atop Kilauea was Reverend William Ellis, who scaled it in 1823. Until the 1920s, the floor of the caldera was exactly what people thought a volcano would be: a molten lake of lava. Then the forces of nature changed, and the fiery lava subsided and hardened over. Today, Kilauea is called the only "drive-in" volcano in the world, and in recent years it has

been one of the most active, erupting almost continuously since 1983 at vents along its eastern fault. When it begins gushing, the result is not a nightmare scene of people scrambling away for their lives, but just the opposite; people flock *to* the volcano. Most thrill-seekers are in much greater danger of being run over by a tour bus hustling to see the fireworks than of being entombed in lava. The volcanic action, while soul-shakingly powerful and not really predictable, is almost totally safe. The Hawaiian Volcano Observatory has been keeping watch since 1912, making Kilauea one of the best-understood volcanoes in the world. The vast volcanic field is creased by rift zones, or natural pressure valves. When the underground magma builds up, instead of *kaboom!* as in Mt. St. Helens, it bubbles to the surface like a spring and gushes out as a river of lava. Naturally, anyone or anything in its path would be burned to a cinder, but scientists routinely walk within a few feet of the still-flowing lava to take samples and readings. In much the way canaries detected mine gas, longtime lava observers pay attention to their ears. When the skin on top begins to blister, they know they are too close. The lava establishes a course that it follows much like an impromptu mountain stream caused by heavy rains.

This does not mean that the lava flows are entirely benign, or that anyone should visit the area during an eruption without prior approval by the park service. When anything is happening, the local radio stations give up-to-the-minute news, and the park service provides a recorded message at 808/985-6000. In 1790 a puff of noxious gases was emitted from Kilauea and descended on the Ka'u Desert, asphyxiating a rival army of Kamehameha's that just happened to be in the area. Eighty people died in their tracks. In 1881 a flow of lava spilled toward undeveloped Hilo and engulfed an area within today's city limits. In 1942, a heavy flow came within 12 miles of the city. Still, this was child's play in comparison with the unbelievable flow of 1950. Luckily, this went down the western rift zone where only scattered homes were in its path. It took no lives as it disgorged well over 600 million cubic yards of magma that covered 35 square miles! The flow continued for 23 days and produced seven huge torrents of lava that sliced across the Belt Road in three different areas. At its height, the lava front traveled six miles per hour and put out enough material to pave an eight-lane freeway twice around the world. In 1960, a flow swallowed the town of Kapoho on the east coast. In 1975, an earthquake caused a tsunami to hit the southeast coast, killing two campers and sinking a section of the coast by three feet.

The most recent—and very dramatic—series of eruptions that spectacularly began on January 3, 1983, has continued virtually unabated ever since, producing more than one cubic kilometer of lava. Magma bubbled to the surface about two miles away from Pu'u O'o. The gigantic fissure fountained lava and formed Pu'u O'o Cinder Cone, now 800 feet high and almost 1,000 feet across. Over a 3.5-year period, there were 47 episodic eruptions from this vent. On July 20, 1986, a new fissure broke upon the surface at Kupa'ianaha just outside the park in a nature reserve and formed a lava lake about one acre in surface size and 180 feet deep. At the end of April 1987 all activity suddenly stopped and the lava drained from the lake and tube system, allowing scientists to accurately gauge the depth. About three weeks later, it started up again when lava poured back into the lake, went through the tube system, and flowed back down to the ocean.

More episodic eruptions followed and from that point the flow turned destructive and started taking homes. It flowed about seven miles to the

coast through tubes and on the surface, wiping out Kapa'ahu, parts of Kalapana, and most of the Royal Gardens Subdivision, with more than 180 homes incinerated. In May 1989 it moved into the national park proper, and on June 22, it swallowed the park Visitors Center at Waha'ula. Since 1992, lava has been flowing into the ocean within the park. Unexpectedly, in January 1997 the dramatic activity shifted two miles westward to the Napau Crater, where lava erupted in spouts of fire and flows, and Pu'u O'o ceased spewing. Since February 1997, the majority of activity moved back to Pu'u O'o Cinder Cone, where there has been a continual shift of vent locations on the west and southwestern flanks and constant renewed activity inside the crater. Until 1997, remote Waha'ula Heiau was spared, but in August of that year lava inundated and buried the sacred spot. The destruction has caused more than $61 million worth of damage. Many of the homesteaders in the worst areas of the flow were rugged individualists and back-to-nature alternative types who lived in homes that generally had no electricity, running water, or telephones. The homes were wiped out. Some disreputable insurance companies with legitimate policyholders tried to wiggle out of paying premiums for lost homes, although the policies specifically stipulated loss by lava flow. The insurance companies whined that the 2,000° lava never really touched some of the homes, and therefore they were exonerated from covering the losses. Their claims were resoundingly repudiated in the courts, and people were paid for their losses.

VOLCANO ACTIVITY

For current information on volcano activity in the area, check the Hawaiian Volcano Observatory "Volcano Watch" website at hvo.wr.usgs.gov/volcanowatch. Related volcano and earthquake information for the Big Island is also available at hvo.wr.usgs.gov and from the Hawaii Center for Volcanology website at www.soest.hawaii.edu/GG/HCV/kilauea, or by calling 808/985-6000 for the Park Service's recorded message. Should there be any major increase in activity, local radio stations give up-to-the-minute news.

At its height, the output of lava was estimated at 650,000 cubic yards per day, which is equal to 55,000 truckloads of cement, enough to cover a football field 38 miles high. Since this activity started in 1983, it has averaged 300,000–600,000 cubic yards a day, added 560 acres of new land to the park and greater acreage to the areas outside the park, and buried about 13 miles of the Chain of Craters Road. For a history of the park's volcanic activity plus up-to-the-minute reports on current activity, see http://hvo.wr.usgs.gov. Related information is also available at www.soest.hawaii.edu/GG/HCV.

Mauna Loa

At 13,679 feet, this magnificent mountain is a mere 117 feet shorter than its neighbor Mauna Kea, which is the tallest peak in the Pacific, and by some accounts, tallest in the world. Measured from its base, 18,000 feet beneath the sea, it would top even Mt. Everest. Mauna Loa is the most massive mountain on earth, containing 10,000 cubic miles of solid, iron-hard lava, and it's estimated that this titan weighs more than California's entire Sierra Nevada mountain range! In fact, Mauna Loa (Long Mountain), at 60 miles long and 30 miles wide, occupies the entire southern half of the Big Island, with Hawaii Volcanoes National Park merely a section of its great expanse.

The summit of Mauna Loa with its mighty Maku'aweoweo Caldera and a broad swath of wilderness on the flank of the mountain rising up to it from Kilauea Caldera are all within park boundaries. This is the least visited part of the park, and in a sense the most separate. In order to visit here you have to hike.

The 17-mile hike to the summit of **Mauna Loa** is the most grueling in the park. The trailhead (6,662 feet) is at the lookout at the end of the pavement of Mauna Loa Road. Hikers in excellent condition can make the summit in three days round-trip, but four or five would be more comfortable. There is a considerable elevation gain, so expect freezing weather even in summer and snow in winter. Altitude sickness can also be a problem. En route you pass through *nene* country, with a good chance to spot these lava-adapted geese. Fences keep out feral goats, so remember to close gates after you. The first cabin is at Red Hill (10,035 feet) and the second is on the rim of Moku'aweoweo Caldera (13,250 feet) at the mountaintop. Water is from roof catchments and should be boiled. Mauna Loa's oval-shape Moku'aweoweo Caldera is more than three miles long and 1.5 miles wide and has vertical walls towering 600 feet. At each end is a smaller round pit crater. From November to May, if there is snow, steam rises from the caldera. The **Cabin Trail** runs along the south rim of the summit caldera, while the **Summit Trail** slips along the north rim to the highest point. The four-mile **Observatory Trail** will also get you to the summit from the Mauna Loa Weather Observatory on the north slope, but you must ascend via the Saddle Road. The summit treats you to a sweeping panorama that includes the great majority of the Big Island and Haleakala on Maui.

Special Notes

Everything in the park—flora and fauna, rocks, buildings, trails, etc.—is protected by federal law. Be respectful and do not carry anything away with you! Do not climb on any ancient rock structure and do not deface any petroglyph carvings. The *nene,* Hawaii's state bird, is endangered. By feeding these birds, visitors have taught them to stand in parking lots and by the roadside. What appears to be a humane and harmless practice actually helps kill these rare birds. Being run over by automobiles has become the leading cause of death of adult birds in the park. Please look, but do not try to approach, feed, or harass the *nene* in any way.

Bicycles are permitted in the park on paved roads only and paved sections of the Crater Rim Trail.

Hiking

There are over 150 miles of hiking trails within the park. One long trail heads up the flank of Mauna Loa to its top; a spiderweb of trails loops around and across Kilauea Caldera and into the adjoining craters; and from a point along the Chain of Craters Road, another trail heads east toward the source of the most recent volcanic activity. But by far the greatest number of trails, and those with the greatest total distance, are those that cut through the Ka'u Desert and along the barren and isolated coast. Many have shelters, and trails that require overnight stays provide cabins or primitive campsites.

Because of the possibility of an eruption or earthquake, it is *imperative* to check in at park headquarters, where you can also pick up current trail information and excellent maps. In fact, a hiking permit is required for most trails outside the Crater Rim Drive area and the stretch along the coast beyond the end of Chain of Craters Drive. Pick up your free permit no more than one day in advance. When hiking, wear long pants and closed-toe shoes or boots. Much of the park is hot and dry, so carry plenty of drinking water. Wear a hat, sunscreen, and sunglasses, but don't forget raingear because it

often rains in the green areas of the park. Stay on trails and stay away from steep edges, cracks, new lava flows and any area where lava is flowing into the sea.

If you will be hiking along the trails in the Kilauea Caldera, the free park maps are sufficient to navigate your way. To aid with hikes elsewhere, it's best to purchase and use larger and more detailed topographical maps. Two that are readily available and of high quality are the *Hawaii Volcanoes National Park* by Trails Illustrated and the Earthwalk Press's *Hawaii Volcanoes National Park Recreation Map.*

KILAUEA CALDERA

Many sights of Hawaii Volcanoes National Park are arranged one after another along **Crater Rim Drive.** Most of these sights are the "drive-up" variety, but plenty of major and minor trails lead off here and there.

Expect to spend a long full day atop Kilauea to take in all the sights, and never forget that you're on a rumbling volcano where a misstep or loss of concentration at the wrong moment can lead to severe injury or even death. Try to arrive by 9 A.M. with a picnic lunch to save time and hassles. Kilauea Caldera, at 4,000 feet, is about 10° cooler than the coast. It's often overcast, and there can be showers. Wear walking shoes and bring a sweater and/or windbreaker. Binoculars, sunglasses, and a hat will also come in handy.

Small children, pregnant women, and people with respiratory ailments should note that the fumes from the volcano can cause problems. Stay away from sulfur vents and don't overdo it, and you should be fine.

A very dramatic way to experience the awesome power of the volcano is to take a helicopter tour. The choppers are perfectly suited for the maneuverability necessary to get an intimate bird's-eye view. The pilots will fly you over the areas offering the most activity, often dipping low over lava pools, skimming still-glowing flows, and circling the towering steam clouds rising from where lava meets the sea. When activity is really happening, tours are jammed, and prices, like lava fountains, go sky-high. Remember, however, that these tours are increas-

ingly resented by hikers and anyone else trying to have a quiet experience, and that new regulations might limit flights over the lava area.

VISITORS CENTER AREA

The best place to start is at the Visitors Center and Park Headquarters. The turn-off is clearly marked along Highway 11 at mile marker 30. By midmorning it's jammed, so try to be an early bird. The center is well run by the National Park Service, which offers a free lecture and film about geology and volcanism, with tremendous highlights of past eruptions and plenty of detail on Hawaiian culture and natural history. It runs every hour on the hour starting at 9 A.M. Free ranger-led tours of the nearby area are also given on a regular basis. Also, a self-guided natural history museum gives more information about the geology of the area, with plenty of exhibits on flora and fauna. You will greatly enrich your visit if you take a half-hour tour of the museum, even though more volcano-specific information is available at the state-of-the-art Thomas A. Jaggar Museum a few minutes up the road.

For safety's sake, anyone trekking to the backcountry *must* register with the rangers at the Visitors Center, especially during times of eruption. Do not be foolhardy! There is no charge for camping, and rangers can give you up-to-the-minute information on trails, backcountry shelters, and cabins. Trails routinely close due to lava flows, tremors, and rock slides. The rangers cannot help you if they don't know where you are. Many day trails leading into the caldera from the rim road are easy walks that need no special preparation. The back-country trails can be very challenging, and detailed maps (highly recommended) are sold at the center along with special-interest geology and natural history publications prepared by the Hawaii Natural History Association. The Visitors Center is open daily 7:45 A.M.–5 P.M.; call 808/985-6000 for trail, camping, or volcanic activity information.

For those who are not traveling by rental car, the public Hele-On Bus stops in front of the Visitors Center Mon.–Fri., no scheduled stops on weekends. Pickup for the bus going to Hilo is at 8 A.M. and the cost is $2.25 for a ticket and $1 for a backpack. Coming from Hilo, the bus leaves at 2:40 P.M. from the Mo'oheau Bus Terminal downtown and arrives at Volcano about 3:45 P.M.

Volcano House

Have you ever dreamed of sleeping with a goddess? Well, you can cuddle up with Pele by staying at Volcano House. If your plans don't include an overnight stop, go in for a look. Sometimes this is impossible, because not only do tour buses from the Big Island disgorge here, but tour groups are flown in from Honolulu as well. A stop at the bar provides refreshments and a tremendous view of the crater. Volcano House still has the feel of a country inn. This particular building dates from the 1940s, but the site has remained the same since a grass hut was perched on the rim of the crater by a sugar planter in 1846. He charged $1 a night for lodging. A steady stream of notable visitors has come ever since: almost all of Hawaii's kings and queens dating from the middle of last century, as well as royalty from Europe. Mark Twain was a guest, followed by Franklin Roosevelt. Most recently, a contingent of astronauts lodged here and used the crater floor to prepare for walking on the moon. In 1866 a larger grass hut replaced the first, and in 1877 a wooden hotel was built. It is now the Volcano Art Center and has been moved just across the road. In 1885, an expansion added 14 rooms and the dining room, and 35 more rooms were constructed in the mid-1920s. An accident caused

the hotel to burn down in 1940, but it was rebuilt the next year.

The person who owned/operated Volcano House the longest was George Lycurgus, who took over management of the hotel in the 1890s. His son, Nick, followed him and managed the hotel until 1969. Since 1986, the hotel has once again been under local management.

Volcano Art Center

Art and history buffs should walk across the street to the Volcano Art Center, 808/967-7565, which is the original 1877 Volcano House, Hawaii's oldest hotel. You not only get to see some fine arts and crafts, but you can take a self-guided tour of this mini-museum, open daily 9 A.M.–5 P.M. except Christmas. A new show featuring one of the many superlative island artists on display is presented monthly, and there are always ongoing demonstrations and special events. Artworks on display are in a variety of media, including canvas, paper, wood, glass, metal, ceramic, fiber, and photograph. There is also a profusion of less expensive but distinctive items like posters, cards, and earthy basketry made from natural fibers collected locally. One of the functions of the art center is to provide interpretation for the national park. All of the 350 or 30 artists who exhibit here do works that in some way relate to Hawaii's environment and culture. Volcano Art Center is one of the finest art galleries in the entire state, boasting works from the best the islands have to offer. Definitely make this a stop.

As a community-oriented organization, the Volcano Art Center sponsors classes and workshops in arts, crafts, and language; an elderhostel program; and a season of performing arts, which includes musical concerts, dance performances, and stage plays. Some involve local performers, while others headline visiting artists. Performances, classes, and workshops take place at the Kilauea Theater at the military camp or in town at the Old Japanese Schoolhouse. Tickets for performances are sold individually at local outlets or you can buy a season ticket. For current information and pricing, call the center office at 808/967-8222 or check out the art center website at www.bishop.hawaii.org/vac for what's happening.

CRATER RIM DRIVE

There are so many intriguing nooks and crannies to stop at along Crater Rim Drive that you'll have to force yourself to be picky if you intend to cover the park in one day. Crater Rim Drive is a circular route; it matters little which way you proceed. Take your choice, but the following sights are listed counterclockwise beginning from Kilauea Visitors Center. Along this road you will travel from a tropical zone into desert, then through a volcanic zone before returning to lush rainforest. The change is often immediate and differences dramatic. Keep this in mind as you travel around the caldera. Your biggest problem on this route will be timing your arrival at the "drive-in" sights to avoid the steady stream of tour buses. Also remember that the Jaggar Museum closes at 5 P.M., so be sure to get around to that point with time enough to allow yourself to appreciate what it has to offer.

Sulfur Banks

You can easily walk to Sulfur Banks from the Visitors Center along a 10-minute trail. If you're driving, signs along Crater Rim Drive direct you, and your nose will tell you when you're close. As you approach these fumaroles, the earth surrounding them turns a deep reddish-brown, covered over in yellowish-green sulfur. The rising steam is caused by surface water leaking into the cracks where it becomes heated and rises as vapor. Kilauea releases hundreds of tons of sulfur gases every day, with Sulfur Banks being an example. This gaseous activity stunts the growth of vegetation. And when atmospheric conditions create a low ceiling, the gases sometimes cause the eyes and nose to water. The area is best avoided by those with heart and lung conditions.

Steam Vents

Within a half mile you'll come to Steam Vents, which are also fumaroles, but without sulfur. The entire field behind the partitioned area steams. The feeling is like being in a sauna. There are no strong fumes to contend with here, just the tour buses. A short hike from here leads to the Crater Rim Trail, where you can view the Steaming Bluff, which is more pronounced when it's cooler. **Kilauea Military Camp** is beyond the vents

and is not open to the public except for community events at the theater, the bowling alley, and the cafeteria. The camp serves as an R&R facility for active duty and retired military personnel.

Observatory and Museum

Some distance farther is **Kilauea Overlook**, as good a spot as any to get a look into the caldera, and there are picnic tables near the parking lot. Here too is Uwekahuna (Wailing Priest) Bluff, where the *kahuna* made offerings of appeasement to Pele. A Hawaiian prayer commemorates their religious rites. Unless you're stopping for lunch or making your own (appropriate) offering, it's perhaps better to continue on to the observatory and museum, where you not only have the view outside but get a scientific explanation of what's happening around you.

The **Hawaiian Volcano Observatory** has been keeping tabs on the volcanic activity in the area since the turn of last century. The actual observatory is filled with delicate seismic equipment and is closed to the public, but a lookout nearby gives you a dentist's view into the mouth of Halema'uma'u Crater (House of Ferns), Pele's home. Steam rises and you can feel the power, but until 1924 the view was even more phenomenally spectacular: a lake of molten lava. The lava has since crusted over and the floor is again black. Scientists do not predict a recurrence in the near future, but no one knows Pele's mind. This is a major stop for the tour buses. Information plaques in the immediate area tell of the history and volcanology of the park. One points out a spot from which to observe the perfect shield volcano form of Mauna Loa—most times too cloudy to see. Another reminds you that you're in the middle of the Pacific, an incredible detail you tend to forget when atop these mountains.

The newest addition to the national park is next door to the observatory, and offers a fantastic multi-media display of the amazing geology and volcanology of the area. The state-of-the-art **Thomas A. Jaggar Museum**, complete with a miniseries of spectacular photos on movable walls, topographical maps, inspired paintings, and TV videos, is open daily 8:30 A.M.–5 P.M., admission free. The expert staff constantly upgrades the displays to keep the public informed on the newest eruptions. The 30–45 minutes it takes to explore the teaching museum will enhance your understanding of the volcanic area immeasurably. Do yourself a favor and visit this museum before setting out on any explorations.

Halema'uma'u Crater

A string of interesting stops follows the observatory. One points out the Ka'u Desert, an inhospitable lava plain studded with a few scraggly plants. Next comes the **Southwest Rift**, a series of cracks running from Kilauea's summit to the sea. You can observe at a glance that you are standing directly over a major earthquake fault. Dated lava flows follow in rapid succession until you arrive at **Halema'uma'u Overlook** parking lot. A well-maintained cinder trail to the overlook is only one-quarter mile long and gives an up-close view of the crater. The area is rife with fumaroles leaking sulfur dioxide and should be avoided by those with respiratory problems. At the end you're treated to a full explanation of Halema'uma'u. Until this crater crusted over after an explosion in 1942, Halema'uma'u could be seen as a red glow and sometimes as a fabulous display of spouting lava from the Volcano House Hotel. From here, two trails make tracks across the caldera floor to the far side and back to park headquarters. Farther along the road is a spot that was once an observation point that caved in. You won't take the ground under your feet for granted!

Keanakako'i Crater

Keanakako'i Overlook is set on the rim of the diminutive crater of the same name. This was a prehistoric adze quarry from which superior stone was gathered to make tools. It was destroyed by a flow in 1877. If that seems in the remote past, realize that you just crossed a section of road that was naturally paved over with lava from a "quickie" eruption in 1982!

Devastation Trail

Most visitors hike along the half-mile Devastation Trail, which could aptly be renamed "Regeneration Trail." The half mile it covers is fascinating, one of the most-photographed areas in the park. It leads across a field devastated by a tremendous eruption from **Kilauea Iki** (Little Kilauea) in 1959, when fountains of lava shot 1,900 feet

into the air. The area was once an 'ohi'a forest that was denuded of limbs and leaves, then choked by black pumice and ash. The vegetation has regenerated since then, and the recuperative power of the flora is part of an ongoing study. Blackberries, not indigenous to Hawaii, are slowly taking over. The good news is that you'll be able to pick and eat blackberries as you hike along the paved trail, but the rangers are waging a mighty war against them. Notice that many of the trees have sprouted aerial roots trailing down from the branches: this is total adaptation to the situation, as these roots don't normally appear. As you move farther along the trail, tufts of grass and bushes peek out of the pumice. Then the surroundings become totally barren and look like the nightmare of a nuclear holocaust.

Thurston Lava Tube

If the Devastation Trail produced a sense of melancholy, the Thurston Lava Tube makes you feel like Alice walking through the looking glass. Inside is a fairy kingdom. As you approach, the expected signboard gives you the lowdown on the geology and flora and fauna of the area. Take the five minutes to educate yourself. The paved trail starts as a steep incline, which quickly enters a fern forest. All about you are fern trees, vibrantly green, with native birds flitting here and there. As you approach the lava tube, it seems almost manmade, like a perfectly formed tunnel leading into a mine. Ferns and moss hang from the entrance, and if you stand just inside the entrance looking out, it's as if the very air is tinged with green. If there were such things as elves and gnomes, they would surely live here. The walk through takes about 10 minutes, undulating through the narrow passage. At the other end, the fantasy world of ferns and moss reappears.

Hikes

The **Crater Rim Loop Trail** begins at Volcano House and parallels Crater Rim Drive. Hiking the entire 11.5 miles takes a full day, but you can take it in sections as time and energy permit. It's a well-marked and well-maintained trail; all you need are warm clothing, raingear, water, and determination. For your efforts, you'll get an up-close view of all of the sights outlined along Crater Rim Drive plus other views and vistas.

*Devastation Trail is
slowly returning to life.*

Halema'uma'u Trail provides some of the best scenery for the effort. It begins at park headquarters and descends into Kilauea Caldera, running about 2.5 miles to the Halema'uma'u Crater pit and crossing lava fields that are only 20–25 years old. Circle back via the Byron Ledge Trail, about three miles long, or arrange to be picked up at the Halema'uma'u parking area on the south side of the Crater Rim Drive.

Kilauea Iki Trail begins at the Thurston Lava Tube or at the Kilauea Iki Overlook. This four-mile trail generally takes two hours round-trip and passes over the floor of Kilauea Iki Crater, which was a sea of lava in 1959 when an exceedingly tall spume of lava spouted from the crater rim, creating this—and the most spectacular show the volcano has performed in memory. Start by taking the section of the Crater Rim Trail that follows the rim of the Kilauea Iki Crater, then branch west and descend the western edge of the crater wall. From there it's back across the crater floor and a zigzag up the eastern side. If conditions are right, the floor of the pit might steam as you walk across. It's easy to link up with the Byron Ledge Trail near the west end of this loop, from where you can walk into Halema'uma'u Caldera or back to park headquarters. On the south side of Kilauea Iki Crater, **Devastation Trail** links Pu'u Pua'i Overlook and the Devastation Trail parking area, from where there is a link trail to the Byron Ledge Trail on the Kilauea Caldera rim.

A shorter hike that takes you along the north edge of the rim and back via the Sulfur Banks is the **'Iliahi (Sandalwood) Trail,** a hike of just over one mile round-trip. Along this hike, you're not only treated to the sights and sounds of trees and birds, but also to the mysteries of steam vents, faults, and cracks.

Alternately, go left out of Volcano House and follow the **Earthquake Trail,** a section of the Crater Rim Loop Trail, along **Waldron Ledge.** The easy trail takes you along a paved section of the old Chain of Craters Road that was damaged by an 6.6 magnitude quake in 1983. Sections of the road are buckled, and part has slid down the edge of the rim.

CHAIN OF CRATERS ROAD

The Chain of Craters Road that once linked the park with Kalapana village on the coast was severed by an enormous lava flow in 1995 and can now only be driven to where the flow crosses the road beyond the Holei Sea Arch. Remember that the volcanic activity in this area is unpredictable, and that the road can be closed at a moment's notice. As you head down the road, every bend—and they are uncountable—offers a panoramic vista. There are dozens of pull-offs; plaques provide geological information about past eruptions and lava flows. The grandeur, power, and immensity of the forces that have been creating the earth from the beginning of time are right before your eyes. Although the road starts off in the 'ohi'a forest, it opens to broader views and soon cuts diagonally across the *pali* to reach the littoral plain. Much of this section of the road was buried under lava flows from 1969 to 1974. When the road almost reaches the coast, look for a roadside marker that indicates the Puna Coast Trail. Just across the road is the Pu'u Loa Petroglyph Field. The lower part of the road is spectacular. Here, blacker-than-black seacliffs, covered by a thin layer of green, abruptly stop at the sea. The surf rolls in, sending up spumes of sea water. In the distance, steam billows into the air where the lava flows into the sea. At road's end you will find a barricade staffed by park rangers and an information hut. Read the information and heed the warnings. The 20-mile drive from atop the volcano to the barricade takes about 30 minutes and drops 3,700 feet in elevation.

While hiking to the lava flow is not encouraged, park staff do not stop you from venturing out. They warn you of the dangers and the reality ahead. Many visitors do make the hike (more than three miles one-way), but there is no trail. The way is over new and rough lava that tears at the bottom of your shoes. If you go in the evening when the spectacle is more apparent, a flashlight with several extra batteries is absolutely necessary. To hike there and back could take three to four hours. If you decide to hike, bring plenty of water. There is no shade or water along the way, and the wind often blows along this coast. Do not hike to or near the edge of the water, as sections of lava could break off without warning. Depending upon how the lava is flowing, it may or not be worth the effort. When the lava is flowing, it is often possible to see the reddish glow at night from the end of the road, but you probably won't see much that's distinguishable unless you use high-power binoculars.

Craters

As you head down Chain of Craters Road you immediately pass a number of depressions for which the road is named. First on the right side is **Lua Manu Crater,** a deep depression now lined with green vegetation. Farther is **Puhimau Crater.** Walk the few steps to the viewing stand at the crater edge for a look. Many people come here to hear the echo of their voices as they talk or sing into this pit. Next comes **Ko'oko'olau Crater,** then **Pauahi Crater.** Just beyond is a turn-off to the east, which follows a short section of the old road. This road ends at the lava flow, and from here a trail runs to **Napau Crater.**

The first mile or more of this trail takes you over lava from 1974, through forest *kipuka,* past lava tree molds, and up the treed slopes of **Pu'u Huluhulu.** From this cone you have a view down on Mauna Ulu, from which the 1969–74 lava flow disgorged, and east toward Pu'u O'o and the currently active volcanic vents, some seven miles distant. Due to the current volcanic activity farther along the rift zone, you will need a permit to day hike beyond Pu'u Huluhulu; the trail itself may be closed depending upon where the volcanic activity is taking place. However, the trail does continue over the shoulder of Makaopuhi Crater to the primitive campsite at Napau Crater, passing more cones and pit craters, lava flows, and sections of rainforest.

Roadside Sights

For several miles, this road traverses lava that was laid down about 40 years ago; remnants of the old road can still be seen in spots. There are long stretches of smooth pahoehoe lava interspersed with flows of clinker 'a'a. Here and there, a bit of green pokes through a crack in

BIG ISLAND

the rock, bringing new life to this stark landscape. Everywhere you look, you can see the wild "action" of these lava flows, stopped in all their magnificent forms. At one vantage point on the way is **Kealakomo**, a picnic overlook where you have unobstructed views of the coast. Stop and enjoy the sight before proceeding. Several other lookouts and pull-offs have been created along the road to call attention to one sight or another.

The last section of road runs very close the edge of the sea, where cliffs rise up from the pounding surf. Near the end of the road is the **Holei Sea Arch,** a spot where the wave action has undercut the rock to leave a bridge of stone. This is small but a dramatic sight. Enjoy the scene, but don't lean too far out trying to get that perfect picture!

Pu'u Loa Petroglyphs

The walk out to Pu'u Loa Petroglyphs is delightful and highly educational and only takes one hour. The trail, although it traverses solid lava, is discernible. The tread of feet over the centuries has discolored the rock. As you walk along, note the *ahu,* traditional trail markers that are piles of stone shaped like little Christmas trees. Most of the lava field leading to the petroglyphs is undulating pahoehoe and looks like a frozen sea. You can climb bumps of lava, from eight to 10 feet high, to scout the immediate territory. Mountainside, the *pali* is quite visible and you can

pick out the most recent lava flows—the blackest and least vegetated. As you approach the site, the lava changes dramatically and looks like long strands of braided rope.

The petroglyphs are in an area about the size of a soccer field. A wooden walkway encircles them and ensures their protection. A common motif of the petroglyphs is a circle with a hole in the middle, like a donut; you'll also see designs of men with triangular-shaped heads. Some rocks are entirely covered with designs, while others have only a symbolic scratch or two. If you stand on the walkway and trek off at the two o'clock position, you'll see a small hill. Go over and down it, and you will discover even better petroglyphs that include a sailing canoe about two feet high. At the back end of the walkway a sign proclaims that Pu'u Loa meant "Long Hill," which the Hawaiians turned into the metaphor "Long Life." For countless generations, fathers would come here to place pieces of their infants' umbilical cords into small holes as offerings to the gods to grant long life to their children. Concentric circles were surrounded by the holes that held the umbilical cords. The entire area, an obvious power spot, screams in utter silence, and the still-strong *mana* is easily felt. The Big Island has the largest concentration of this ancient art form in the state, and this site holds its greatest number. One estimate puts the number at 28,000 petroglyphs!

petroglyphs

DAVID STANLEY

Waha'ula Heiau

Waha'ula Heiau (Temple of the Red Mouth) radically changed the rituals and practices of the relatively benign Hawaiian religion by introducing the idea of human sacrifice. The 13th century marked the end of the frequent comings and goings between Hawaii and the "Lands to the South" (Tahiti), and began the isolation that would last 500 years until Captain Cook arrived. Unfortunately, this last influx of Polynesians brought a rash of conquering warriors carrying ferocious gods who lusted for human blood before they would be appeased. Pa'ao, a powerful Tahitian priest, supervised the building of Waha'ula and brought in a new chief, Pili, to strengthen the diminished *mana* of the Hawaiian

chiefs due to their practice of intermarriage with commoners. Waha'ula became the foremost *luakini* (human sacrifice) temple in the island kingdom and held this position until the demise of the old ways in 1819. Not at all grandiose, the *heiau* was merely an elevated rock platform smoothed over with pebbles.

Waha'ula lay along the coast road near the eastern end of the park. This entire area is now completely inundated by recent lava flows. Until 1997, the *heiau* itself was a small island in a sea of black lava that miraculously escaped destruction, but in August of that year lava oozed over these 700-year-old walls and filled the compound. Madame Pele has taken back her own.

OTHER PARK AREAS

KA'U DESERT

Hilina Pali Road

About two miles down the Chain of Craters Road, the Hilina Pali Road shoots off to the southwest over a narrow roughly paved road all the way to the end at **Hilina Pali Lookout**—about nine miles. Soon after you leave the Chain of Craters Road the vegetation turns drier and you enter the semi-arid Ka'u Desert. The road picks its way around and over old volcanic flows, and you can see the vegetation struggling to maintain a foothold. On the way you pass one trailhead and Kipuka Nene Campground—closed at present to help the *nene* recover their threatened population. You should see geese here, but please leave them alone and definitely don't feed them. The road ends right on the edge of the rift, with expansive views over the benched coastline, from the area of current volcanic flow all the way to South Point. From here, one trail heads down the hill to the coast while another pushes on along the top of the cliff and farther into the dry landscape. At the pali lookout is a pavilion and restrooms, but no drinking water. This is not a pleasure ride as the road is rough, but it is passable. For most it probably isn't worth the time, but for those looking for isolation and a special vantage point, this could be it.

Ka'u Desert Trails

Ka'u Desert Trail starts along the Chain of Craters Road past the Jaggar Museum and heads southwest into the desolation. A second entry to this trail starts about eight miles south of the Visitors Center along Route 11, between mile markers 37 and 38. It's a short hike from this trailhead to the **Ka'u Desert Footprints.** The trek across the small section of desert is fascinating, and the history of the footprints makes the experience more evocative. The trail is only 1.6 miles round-trip and can be hustled along in less than 30 minutes, but allow at least an hour, mostly for observation. The predominant foliage is a red bottlebrush that contrasts with the bleak surroundings—the feeling throughout the area is one of foreboding. You pass a wasteland of *'a'a* and pahoehoe lava flows to arrive at the footprints. A metal fence in a sturdy pavilion surrounds the prints, which look as though they're cast in cement. Actually they're formed from pisolites: particles of ash stuck together with moisture, which formed mud that hardened like plaster.

In 1790 Kamehameha was waging war with Keoua over control of the Big Island. One of Keoua's warrior parties of approximately 80 people attempted to cross the desert while Kilauea was erupting. Toxic gases descended upon them, and the warriors and their families were enveloped and suffocated. They literally died in their tracks, but the preserved footprints, although romanticism would have it otherwise, were probably made by a party of people who came well after the eruption. This unfortunate occurrence was regarded by the Hawaiians as a direct message from the gods proclaiming their support for Kamehameha. Keoua, who could not deny the sacred signs, felt abandoned and shortly thereafter became a human sacrifice at Pu'ukohola Heiau, built by Kamehameha to honor his war god, Kuka'ilimoku.

From here **Mauna Iki Trail** heads east, crossing a 1974 flow, to connect with the Hilina Pali Road. The Ka'u Desert Trail continues south and swings around to the east, passing Pepeiao Cabin on the way to the Hilina Pali Overlook. From the cabin, **Ka'aha Trail** heads down to and along the coast to Ka'aha Shelter, where it meets a trail coming down from the overlook. From here, the **Puna Coast Trail** mostly parallels the coast, passing Halape and Keauhou shelters and 'Apua Point campsite before it meets the Chain of Craters Road near the petroglyph site. At the shelters, rain catchment tanks provide drinking water. In 1975, an earthquake rocked this area, generating a tsunami that killed two campers; more than 30 others had to be helicoptered to safety. All campers must register at the Kilauea Visitors Center. Registering will alert authorities to your whereabouts in case of a disaster. Hiking in the Ka'u Desert requires full hiking and camping gear. Bring plenty of water.

Lush 'ola'a fern forests stand in sharp contrast to the stark black lava fields only a short distance away.

SMALL DETOURS

Mauna Loa Road

About 2.5 miles west of the park entrance on the Belt Road, Mauna Loa Road turns off to the north. This road will lead you to the Tree Molds and a bird sanctuary, as well as to the trailhead for the Mauna Loa summit trail. As an added incentive, a minute down this road leaves 99 percent of the tourists behind.

Tree Molds is an ordinary name for an extraordinary place. Turn off Mauna Loa Road soon after leaving the Belt Road and follow the signs for five minutes to a cul-de-sac. At the entrance, a signboard tries hard to dramatically explain what occurred here. In a moment, you realize that you're standing atop a lava flow, and that the

scattered potholes were entombed tree trunks, most likely the remains of a once-giant koa forest. Unlike at Lava Tree State Monument, where the magma encased the tree and flowed away, the opposite action happened here. The lava stayed put while the tree trunk burned away, leaving the 15- to 18-foot-deep holes. While this site may not excite some visitors, realizing what happened here and how it happened is an eye-opener.

Kipuka Puaulu is a sanctuary for birds and nature lovers who want to leave the crowds behind, just under three miles from Route 11 up Mauna Loa Road. The sanctuary is an island atop an island. A *kipuka* is a piece of land that is surrounded by lava but has not been inundated by it, leaving the original vegetation and land contour intact. A few hundred yards away, small scrub vegetation struggles, but in the sanctuary the trees form a towering canopy a hundred feet tall. The first sign takes you to an ideal picnic area called Bird Park with cooking grills; the second, 100 yards beyond, takes you to Kipuka Puaulu Loop Trail. As you enter the trail, a bulletin board describes the birds and plants, some of the last remaining indigenous fauna and flora in Hawaii. Please follow all rules. The trail is self-guided, and pamphlets describing the stations along the way may be dispensed from a box near the start of the path. The loop is only one mile long, but to really assimilate the area, especially if you plan to do any birdwatching, expect to spend an hour minimum. It doesn't take long to realize that you are privileged to see some of the world's rarest plants, such as a small, non-descript bush called 'a'ali'i. In the branches of the towering 'ohi'a trees you might see an 'elepaio or an 'apapane, two birds native to Hawaii. Common finches and Japanese white eyes are imported birds that are here to stay. There's an example of a lava tube, a huge koa tree, and an explanation of how ash from eruptions provided soil and nutrients for the forest. Blue morning glories have taken over entire hillsides. Once considered a pest and aggressively eradicated, they have recently been given a reprieve and are now considered good ground cover—perhaps even indigenous. When you do come across a native Hawaiian plant, it seems somehow older, almost prehistoric. If a precontact Hawaiian could come back today, he or she would recognize only a few plants and trees even here in this preserve. As you leave, listen for the melodies coming from the treetops, and hope the day never comes when no birds sing. To hear the birds at their best, come in early morning or late afternoon.

Mauna Loa Road continues westward and gains elevation for approximately 10 miles. At the end of the pavement, at 6,662 feet, you find a parking area and lookout. A trail leads from here to the summit of Mauna Loa. It takes two long and difficult days to hike. Under no circumstances should it be attempted by novice hikers or those unprepared for cold alpine conditions. At times, this road may be closed due to extreme fire conditions.

'Ola'a Track

Off Route 11 close to Volcano village, turn on Wright Road (or County Rd. 148) heading toward Mauna Loa. On a clear morning you can see the mountain dead ahead. Continue for approximately three miles until you see a barbed-wire fence. The fence is distinctive because along it you'll see a profusion of *hapu'u* ferns that are in sharp contrast to the adjacent ranch property. Here is an *'ola'a* rainforest, part of the national park and open to the public, although park scientists like to keep it quiet. Be aware that the area is laced with lava tubes. Most are small ankle twisters, but others can open up under you like a glacial crevasse. Here is a true example of a quickly disappearing native forest. What's beautiful about an endemic forest is that virtually all species coexist wonderfully. The ground cover is a rich mulch of decomposing ferns and leaves, fragrant and amazingly soft. This walk is for the intrepid hiker or naturalist who is fascinated by Hawaii's unique foliage.

Remember, trails in this section of the park are poorly marked and quite confusing. You can get lost, and if no one knows you're in there, it could be life threatening. Also, be aware that you may be trampling native species or inadvertently introducing alien species. The park service is trying to bring the area back to its native Hawaiian rainforest condition through eradication of alien plants and elimination of feral pigs.

BIG ISLAND

PRACTICALITIES

ACCOMMODATIONS

If you intend to spend the night atop Kilauea, your choices of accommodations are few and simple. Volcano House provides the only hotel, but cabins are available at the campgrounds, and there are a handful of tent campsites along the hiking trails. For military personnel, lodging is offered at the Kilauea Military Camp.

Cabins and Camping

The main campground in Volcanoes, **Namakani Paio,** clearly marked off Route 11, is situated in a stately eucalyptus grove. There is no charge for tent camping and no reservations are required. It's first-come, first-served. A cooking pavilion has fireplaces, but no wood or drinking water is provided. Also, there are no shower facilities for those camping and hiking within the park, so make sure you're with people who like you a whole bunch. Ten small cabins are available through **Volcano House.** Each accommodates four people and costs $40 single or double, and $8 each for a third or fourth person. A $15 refundable key deposit gives access to the shower and toilet, and a $20 refundable deposit gets you linens, soap, towels, and a blanket (extra sleeping bag recommended). Each cabin contains one double bed and two single bunk beds and an electric light, but no electrical outlets. Outside are a picnic table and barbecue grill, but you must provide your own charcoal and cooking utensils. Check in at Volcano House after 3 P.M. and check out by noon.

For backcountry overnight camping, apply at the Kilauea Visitors Center (7:45 A.M.–4:45 P.M.) for a free permit no earlier than the day before you plan to hike. Camping is permitted only in established sites and at trail shelters. No open fires are permitted. Carry all the drinking water you will need, and carry out all that you take in.

Volcano House

If you decide to lodge at Volcano House, P.O. Box 53, Hawaii Volcanoes National Park, HI 96718, 808/967-7321 or 800/325-3535, don't be frightened away by the daytime crowds. They disappear with the sun. Since the mid-1980s, Volcano House has gone through a slow renovation and once again shines as what it always has been: a quiet country inn. The 42 rooms are comfy but old-fashioned. Who needs a pool or TV when you can look out your window into a volcano caldera? To the left of the reception area indoors, a crackling fireplace warms you from the chill in the mountain air, and this fire has burned virtually nonstop since the early days of the hotel. In front of the fireplace are stuffed leather chairs and a wonderful wooden rocker. Paintings and vintage photographs of the Hawaiian kings and queens of the Kamehameha line and magnificent photos of eruptions of the mountain hang on the walls. The hotel, now owned and operated by a *kama'aina* family, is an authorized concession of the park. Room rates are: main building with crater view $165–185, non-crater view $135; Ohia Wing nonstandard room $85, garden view $95; $15 extra for each additional person. No charge for children 12 and under occupying the same room as their parents. Rooms include koa wood furniture, Hawaiian quilted comforters, a telephone, and room heater, and each has a private bath or shower. Efficiently run, the hotel has a restaurant, lounge, two gift shops, 24-hour front desk service, maid service, and safe-deposit boxes. Besides that, you could hardly get closer to the crater if you tried.

Kilauea Military Camp

One mile west of the park entrance, within the park boundary, is the Kilauea Military Camp. Offering rooms and meals, this facility is open to active duty and retired military personnel, civilian employees of the Department of Defense, and their families. Dormitory rooms, one-, two-, and three-bedroom cottages, and apartments are open on a first-come, first-served basis. Services include a lounge bar, recreation facility, tennis courts, athletic fields, a general store, post office, laundromat, and gas station—all for guests only. Open to the public are the cafeteria, which serves three meals a day; the theater, which hosts community events; and the bowling alley, newly remodeled with state-of-the-art equipment, and its snack bar, open daily 3–10 P.M. Tours of the island can be arranged by the front office staff, and shuttle pickup from the Hilo airport can also be arranged with advance notice. For additional information, availability, and fees, write KMC Lodging, A Joint Recreation Service Center, Attn.: Reservations, Hawaii Volcanoes National Park, HI 96718, 808/967-7315, fax 808/967-8343, website: www.kmc-volcano.com, email: reservations@kmc-colcano.com.

FOOD AND SHOPPING

Food

Volcano House Restaurant offers a breakfast buffet daily 7–10:30 A.M. for $9.50 or $5.50 for children ages 2–11, that includes cereals, milk, and juices, an assortment of pastries, pancakes topped with fruit and macadamia nuts, sweet bread French toast, scrambled eggs, and Portuguese sausage. A lighter continental breakfast is $5.50. The lunch buffet, $12.50 adult or $7.50 per child is served daily 11 A.M.–2 P.M. Often terribly crowded because of the tour buses, the lunch buffet offers tossed greens and assorted vegetables, fresh fruit platters, stuffed mahimahi, pot roast, honey-dipped chicken, and drinks. If there are too many tour buses parked

outside during the lunch hour, give it a miss and try later. Dinner, nightly 5:30–9 P.M., starts with appetizers like sautéed mushrooms and a fruit platter. It moves on to entrées like seafood linguine, scampi, New York steak, catch of the day, and roast prime rib, the specialty. Most entr'es run $15–22. A child's menu is also available with dishes under $8. The quality is good and the prices reasonable; reservations are recommended.

For a nightcap, Uncle George's Lounge, just off the main entry, is a perfect spot to relax and watch the crater disappear into the dark. It closes when the restaurant stops serving.

Shopping and Services

If you are after an exquisite piece of art, a unique memento, or an inexpensive but distinctive souvenir, be sure to visit the **Volcano Art Center.** It's a treat.

When your little tummy starts grumbling, head for the snack shop at the hotel to appease it; it's open 9 A.M.–5 P.M. The hotel also has two gift shops that carry a wide assortment of tourist gifts, crafts, postcards, film, souvenirs, and a selection of logo wear. They are open 7 A.M.–7:15 P.M. Out along the road, the Jaggar Museum has a small gift shop that carries a fine selection of books and gifts relating to Hawaii's natural environment.

BIG ISLAND

KA'U

The Ka'u District is as simple and straightforward as the broad, open face of a country gentleman. It's not boring, and it does hold pleasant surprises for those willing to look. Formed entirely from the massive slopes of Mauna Loa, the district presents some of the most ecologically diverse land in the islands. The bulk of it stretches 50 miles from north to south and almost 30 miles from east to west, tumbling from the snowcapped mountains through the cool green canopy of highland forests. At lower elevations it becomes pastureland of belly-deep grass ending in blistering-hot black sands along the coast that are encircled by a necklace of foamy white sea. Much has been scored by recent lava flows and shaken by powerful earthquakes. At the bottom of Ka'u is **Ka Lae** (South Point), the southernmost tip of Hawaii and the southernmost point in the United States. It lies at a latitude 500 miles farther south than Miami and twice that below Los Angeles. Ka Lae was probably the first landfall made by the Polynesian explorers on the islands. A variety of archaeological remains support this belief.

Most people dash through Ka'u on the Hawaii Belt Road, heading to or from Volcanoes National Park. Its main towns, **Pahala** and **Na'alehu,** are little more than pit stops. The Belt Road follows the old Mamalahoa Trail where, for centuries, nothing moved faster than a contented man's stroll. Ka'u's beauties, mostly tucked away down secondary roads, are hardly given a look by most unknowing visitors. If you take the time and get off the beaten track, you'll discover black- and green-sand beaches, the world's largest macadamia nut farm, Wild West rodeos, and an electricity farm sprouting windmill generators. The upper slopes and broad pasturelands are the domain of hunters, hikers, and *paniolo,* who still ride the range on sure-footed horses. In Ka'u are sleepy plantation towns that don't even know how quaint they are, and beach parks where you can count on finding a secluded spot to pitch a tent. Time in Ka'u moves slowly, and *aloha* still forms the basis of day-to-day life.

The majority of Ka'u's pleasures are accessible by standard rental car, but many secluded coastal spots can be reached only by 4WD.

For example, **Ka'iliki'i,** just west of Ka Lae, was an important fishing village in times past. A few archaeological remains are found here, and the beach has a green cast due to the lava's high olivine content. Few tourists ever visit, although hardy souls come to angle the coastal waters. Spots of this type abound, especially in Ka'u's remote sections. But civilization has found Ka'u as well: When you pass mile marker 63, look down to the coast and notice a stand of royal palms and a large brackish pond. This is Luahinivai Beach, one of the finest on the island, where country and western star Loretta Lynn built a fabulous home. Those willing to abandon their cars and hike the sparsely populated coast or interior of Ka'u are rewarded with areas unchanged and untouched for generations.

TOWNS AND SIGHTS

PAHALA

Some 22 miles southwest of Volcano is Pahala, clearly marked off Route 11. The Hawaii Belt Road flashes past this town, but if you drive into it, heading for the tall stack of the Ka'u Sugar Co., you'll find one of the best-preserved examples of a classic sugar town in the islands. Not long ago, the hillsides around Pahala were blanketed by fields of cane and dotted with camps of plantation workers. It was once gospel that sugar would be "king" in these parts forever, but the huge stone stack of the sugar mill puffs no longer, while in the background the whir of a modern macadamia nut-processing plant breaks the stillness.

With 1,500 people, Pahala has the largest population in the district, even though some people left with the closing of the mill. In town you'll find the basics—a gas station, small shopping center, post office, Bank of Hawaii office, Mizuno's Superette, and a take-out plate lunch restaurant.

Wood Valley Temple
Also known as Nechung Dorje Drayang Ling, or Immutable Island of Melodious Sound, the Wood Valley Temple, P.O. Box 250, Pahala, HI 96777, 808/928-8539, fax 808/928-6271, website: www.planet-hawaii.com/nechung, email: nechung@aloha.net, is true to its name. This simple vermilion and yellow Tibetan Buddhist temple sits like a sparkling jewel surrounded by the emerald-green velvet of its manicured grounds, which are scented by an aromatic stand of majestic eucalyptus trees. The grounds, like a botanical garden, vibrate with life and energy.

The Buddha gave the world essentially 84,000 different teachings to pacify, purify, and develop the mind. In Tibetan Buddhism there are four major lineages, and this temple, founded by Tibetan master Nechung Rinpoche, is a classic synthesis of all four. Monks, lama, and scholars from different schools of Buddhism are periodically invited to come and lecture as resident teachers. The Dalai Lama came in 1980 to

BIG ISLAND

Wood Valley Buddhist Temple

ROBERT NILSEN

dedicate the temple and graced the temple once again in 1994 when he addressed an audience here of more than 3,500 people. Programs vary, but people genuinely interested in Buddhism come here for meditation and soul-searching as well as for peace, quiet, relaxation, and direction. Morning and evening services at 7 A.M. and 7 P.M. are led by the Tibetan monk in residence. Formal classes depend upon which guest teacher is in residence.

Buddhists strive to become wise and compassionate people. The focus of the temple is to bring together all meditation and church groups in the community. Plenty of local Christian and Buddhist groups use the nonsectarian facilities. Any group that is spiritually, socially, and community oriented and that has a positive outlook is welcome. Wood Valley Temple can't promise nirvana, but they can point you to the path.

The retreat facility is called the Tara Temple and at one time housed a Japanese Shingon Mission in Pahala. When the Shingon sect moved to a new facility in Kona, this building was abandoned and given to Wood Valley Temple. A local contractor moved it to its present location in 1978, cranked it up one story, and built the dormitories underneath. The grounds, hallowed and consecrated for decades, already held a Nichiren temple, the main temple here today, that was dismantled in 1919 at its original location and rebuilt on its present site to protect it from lowland flooding.

If you wish to visit, please do so on weekends and be respectful, as this is a retreat center. For those staying, either as guests or as part of a program, rates at the retreat facility are: private room single $30–40, double room $50; bunk in the dorm $25, with use of a large communal kitchen and shared bath. All require a two-night minimum stay or a $10 surcharge for only one night. Weekly discounts and group rates are available. Definitely call or write to make reservations and get directions.

Kapapala Ranch

Even though sugar is gone, ranching is not. Kapapala Ranch still manages a working enterprise between the town of Pahala and the upper slopes of Mauna Loa, and offers excursions onto the property. A two-hour trail ride runs $65, while a 4WD daylong work adventure is $100 per person, limit two. Also offered is an overnight camping experience on ranch land that can be done by horse, hiking, pack mules, or vehicle. Arrange cost with the ranch. For reservations, call 808/968-6585.

PUNALU'U AND NINOLE

Along the coast just south of Pahala are the small communities of Punalu'u and Ninole. Punalu'u was an important port during the sugar boom of the 1880s and even had a railroad. Notice the tall coconut palms in the vicinity, unusual for Ka'u. Punalu'u means "Diving Spring," so-named because freshwater springs can be found on the floor of the bay. Native divers once paddled out to sea, then dove with calabashes that

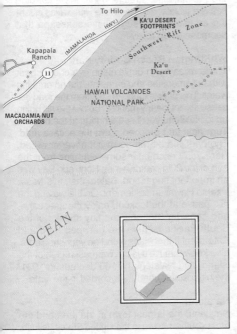

they filled with fresh water from the underwater springs. This was the main source of drinking water for the region.

Ninole is home to the **Sea Mountain Resort and Golf Course,** built in the early 1970s by a branch of the C. Brewer Company. The string of flat-topped hills in the background is the remains of volcanoes that became dormant about 100,000 years ago. In sharp contrast with them is **Lo'ihi Seamount,** 20 miles offshore and about 3,000 feet below the surface of the sea. This very active submarine volcano is steadily building and should reach the surface in just a few tens of thousands of years. Near Ninole is **Hoku-loa Church,** which houses a memorial to Henry Opukaha'ia, the Hawaiian most responsible for encouraging the first missionaries to go to Hawaii to save his people from damnation.

Punalu'u Beach County Park
Punalu'u Beach Park (near mile marker 56) is a county park with full amenities and famous for its black-sand beach. Here you'll find a pavilion, bathrooms, showers, drinking water, telephone, and open camping area (permit required). During the day there are plenty of tourists around, but at night the beach park empties, and you virtually have it to yourself. Punalu'u boasts some of the only safe swimming on the south coast, but that doesn't mean that it can't have its treacherous moments. Head for the northeast section of the black-sand beach near the boat ramp. Stay close to shore because a prevailing rip current lurks just outside the bay. Hawaiian green sea turtles use this beach for building their nests. When they're around, please give them plenty of room and don't harass them.

Ninole Cove Park, part of the Sea Mountain Resort, is within walking distance and open to the public. For day use, you might consider parking near the pro shop. As you walk to the beach from here you pass a freshwater pond, quite cold but good for swimming.

Practicalities
Sea Mountain Resort, P.O. Box 460, Pahala, HI 96777, 808/928-6200 or 800/344-7675, fax 808/928-8075, is a time-share condominium that also rents available units to the general public. Options include a studio at $80 garden view or $100 ocean view, one bedroom

BIG ISLAND

*Sea Mountain Resort
Golf Course*

ROBERT NILSEN

$100–125, and two bedrooms $125–155. Because of its rural location, Sea Mountain can offer secluded, first-class accommodations for reasonable prices. Your condo unit will be a low-rise, Polynesian-inspired bungalow with a shake roof. The standard units, all tastefully furnished, offer remote color TVs, full kitchens, full baths, ceiling fans, and a lanai. The resort itself has a swimming pool and spa pool, laundry facilities, four unlit tennis courts, and a golf course. Although the units vary, all are furnished in island theme, typically with rattan couches and easy chairs. The feeling throughout the resort is a friendly, home-away-from-home atmosphere. Outside your door are the resort's fairways and greens, backdropped by the spectacular coast. If you're after peace and quiet, Sea Mountain is hard to beat.

The **Sea Mountain at Punaluʻu Golf Course,** 808/928-6222, is a 6,400-yard, 18-hole, par-72 course. As it's set right on the coast, the winds can be strong and usually blow across the fairways, creating challenging play. Greens fees are $30 ($40 for visitors); clubs are available to rent. Range balls are $5 a bucket and golf lessons $25 an hour. The clubhouse, open daily 10 A.M.–2 P.M., serves a limited menu of sandwiches and *pu pu* and also offers a full bar and morning coffee available at 7 A.M.

A *kaukau* wagon often parks at Punaluʻu Beach, offering island sandwiches, cold drinks, and snacks.

NAʻALEHU AND VICINITY

Between Punaluʻu and Naʻalehu, the coastal area is majestic; stretching into the aqua-blue sea is a tableland of black lava with waves crashing against it in a surrealistic seascape that seems to go on forever.

Whittington Beach County Park

Three miles north of Naʻalehu is a county park with full amenities and camping, but no drinking water. This park is tough to spot from the road because it's not clearly marked. Before the hill going up to Naʻalehu you'll see a bridge at the bottom. Turn right and proceed down the access road. The park is a bit run-down but never crowded. Here you'll encounter some old ruins from the turn of the 20th century when Honuʻapo Bay was an important sugar port. Before that, this was a sizable Hawaiian settlement. On the way up the hill, pause at the lookout, enjoy the seascape, and consider that only the tiny specks of the South Pacific islands are between here and Antarctica! If that starts a chill on your shoulders, also know that Kaʻu is the warmest region of the island, and Naʻalehu hit 100 degrees in 1931, the highest temperature recorded in the state.

Naʻalehu

Naʻalehu, the largest town in the area and the most southern town in the United States, is lush.

Check out the overhanging monkeypod trees. They form a magnificent living tunnel as you go down Route 11 through the center of town. Every Fourth of July, a down-home rodeo is held in town for all the amateur riders of the district. Come and enjoy.

Accommodation

Becky's Paradise Bed & Breakfast, P.O. Box 673, Na'alehu, HI 96772, tel./fax 808/929-9690 or 800/235-1233, website: www.hi-inns.com/beckys, email: patti@bigisland-inns.com, is about 100 yards east of the theater, *mauka* of the road. Available in this modest but cheery 65-year-old plantation home are two spacious rooms with queen beds and one room with two double beds. Each has a private bath, and two have private entrances. They run $63 single or $75 double; a 25 percent discount is offered for stays of four nights or longer. To help you relax, the B&B features a backyard deck with a hot tub to unjangle the nerves. To get you started, a full breakfast of juice, fruit, and a griddle entrée is served every morning.

Food

On the west side of town, at the intersection with the Na'alehu Theater, grocery and hardware stores, a large, easily spotted sign marks the **Punalu'u Bake Shop and Visitor's Center,** 808/929-7343, open daily 9 A.M.–5 P.M. The bake shop, tempting with all kinds of pastries, is especially known for its *pao dolce,* sweet bread. Park and follow daily busloads of tourists down a cement pathway to the retail shop for baked goods, sandwiches, coffee, cold drinks, and a smattering of souvenirs. Punalu'u sweet bread is well known throughout the island. Have a look at the operation through the viewing windows. The cool and pleasing gardens here make a fine rest stop for the long stretches through this part of the island.

For a quick sandwich or full meal try the **Na'alehu Coffee Shop,** 808/929-7238, open daily. Many of the local people call this restaurant "Roy's," after the owner's first name. The menu is typical island cuisine with a Japanese flavor; the best item is the fresh fish from local waters. The restaurant is basic and clean, with most meals on the menu around $7. There's a wide assortment of souvenirs and tourist junk, and a

large koi pond outside. Look for the big yellow building near the shopping center as you enter town. The second local eatery in town is the **Shaka Restaurant,** just down from the theater.

Na'alehu Fruit Stand, 808/929-9009, open Mon.–Thurs. 9 A.M.–6:30 P.M., Friday and Saturday until 7 P.M., Sunday until 5 P.M., is a favorite with local people, always a tip-off that the food is great. Along with fresh fruit, it sells submarines, hot dogs, pizza, salads, soda, tea, coffee, fresh-baked goods, and a good selection of grains, minerals, vitamins, and health foods. The owners, John and Dorene Santangelo, are very friendly and willing to give advice about touring the Ka'u area; there's a good bulletin board for local events here. This is the best place on the south coast for a light meal or picnic lunch.

About 100 yards from the Na'alehu Fruit Stand, notice the baseball park. Here **Kalaiki Plate Lunch,** open daily 5:30 A.M.–4 P.M., run by the Hanoa family, serves hearty sandwiches and island favorites ready to go. This place is especially known for its full breakfasts, only $3–4.

Shopping and Supplies

In Na'alehu you can gas yourself or your car at the **Luzon Store,** open daily 7 A.M.–9 P.M. You can also find basic groceries and supplies in this jam-packed, friendly local establishment. There's a public telephone on the porch.

Na'alehu Shopping Center is along the road at the west end of town. In the small complex you'll find a small grocery store and Ed's Laundromat.

The **Na'alehu Theater,** 808/929-9133, is a large building also at the west end of town. It's a classic old-time theater usually open on weekends, and a venue of the Hawaii International Film Festival. Call for what's showing.

Turtle Union, open daily 10 A.M.–6 P.M., is a souvenir and neat tourist junk shop across from Whittington Beach. Inside, find hula skirts, wooden boxes, *kukui* nut lei, wooden platters, straw hats, and tiki carvings done by owner J. D.

WAI'OHINU

A tall church steeple welcomes you to the small town of Wai'ohinu. There's nothing remarkable about this village, except that as you pass through you'll be seeing an example of the real Hawaiian country lifestyle as it exists today. Wai'ohinu was an important agricultural region in centuries past, and King Kamehameha even had personal land here. Just before the well-marked Shirakawa Motel on the *mauka* side of the road is the **Mark Twain Monkeypod Tree.** Unfortunately, Wai'ohinu's only claim to fame except for its undisturbed peace and quiet blew down in a heavy windstorm in 1957. Part of the original trunk, carved into a bust of Twain, is on display at the Lyman House Museum in Hilo. A shoot from the original trunk has grown to become a sizable descendant of the town's original attraction.

Practicalities

The **Shirakawa Motel,** P.O. Box 467, Na'alehu, HI 96772, 808/929-7462, is a small, clean, comfortable, "hang loose bruddah" motel where your peace and quiet are guaranteed. The Shirakawa has been open since 1928. The original two-story hotel has now been converted to the home of the retired second-generation owners. Their son now runs the dozen-room motel, which consists of clean and utilitarian single-story detached buildings to the side. Prices are a reasonable $30 single, $35 double, $42 kitchenette. There's a 10 percent discount for a one-week stay, 15 percent for longer, plus fees of $8 for "rollaway children" and $10 for "rollaway adult" (if only it were that easy!).You may be greeted by Kai, a golden Lab, who has given up aggression for the "hang loose, no worries" island lifestyle.

A short hop west of town is **Macadamia Meadows B&B,** P.O. Box 756, Na'alehu, HI 96772, tel./fax 808/929-8097 or 888/929-8118, website: www.stayhawaii.com/macmed.html, email: kaleena@aloha.net, set as you might expect, in the middle of an eight-acre working macadamia nut farm. But this is more than just a B&B and farm; with the full-size tennis court, swimming pool, and basketball court, it seems like a mini-resort, and when you get restless, you can stroll through the orchard. The huge main house, with open kitchen, dining and living areas, and wraparound lanai, looks out on the back lawn and nut trees. In the main house are the spacious Mukupuni room for $75 and Honeymoon Suite for $99. In the newer detached building, the Pauli room runs $85, but when com-

bined with an adjacent room goes for $120 for up to four people. A hearty and palate-pleasing breakfast is served to all guests.

Margo Hobbs and Philip Shaw of **Margo's Corner,** P.O. Box 447, Na'alehu, HI 96772, 808/929-9614, email: margos@bigisland.com, can accommodate you in their strikingly original pentagonal guesthouse for $60 single or $75 double, which includes two vegetarian meals with the family. The guesthouse, with a private bath and shower, has a queen-size bed. Brightly painted outside, it's also a rainbow of cheery colors on the inside. Two nights minimum is preferred. Touring bicyclists and backpackers can camp for $25 per person in the yard among Norfolk pines; a shower is available. An organic vegetable garden is out back—food for your meals. No smoking and no excessive drinking, please. For your extra food needs, Margo's maintains a small but well-stocked health food store. Across from Discovery Harbor Golf Course, Margo's is about halfway between Na'alehu and the South Point Road, just south of Kama'oa Road. Call for exact directions and reservations.

In Wai'ohinu, about a mile west of Na'alehu, look for **Mark Twain's Square Café and Gift Shop,** open Mon.–Fri. 8 A.M.–5 P.M., Saturday 8 A.M.–4 P.M., owned and operated by the Fujikawa family. The luscious smells will lead you to fresh-baked bread, *manapua,* and an assortment of sandwiches all under $5, as well as plate lunches and daily specials like barbecued pork with rice and salad.

Ka'u Fishing Supply in Wai'ohinu offers fresh local fish that would make a perfect meal if you're cooking for yourself. Just down the road, you can pick up supplies at **Wong Yuen General Store and Gas Station,** 808/929-7223, open Mon.–Sat. 8:30 A.M.–5 P.M., Sunday to 3 P.M.

SOUTH POINT

The Hawaiians simply called this Ka Lae (The Point). Some scholars believe Polynesian sailors made landfall here as early as A.D. 150, and that their amazing exploits became navigating legend long before colonization began. A paved, narrow, but passable road branches off from Route 11 approximately six miles west of Na'alehu, and it drops directly south for 12 miles to land's end. Luckily the shoulders are firm, so you can pull over to let another car go by. Car rental agencies may warn against using this road, but their fears are unfounded. You proceed through a flat, treeless area trimmed by free-ranging herds of cattle and horses—more road obstacles to be aware of. Suddenly, incongruously, huge mechanical windmills appear, beating their arms against the sky. This is the **Kamoa Wind Farm.** Notice that this futuristic experiment at America's most southern point uses windmills made in Japan by Mitsubishi! The trees here are bent over by the prevailing wind, demonstrating the obviously excellent wind-power potential of the area. However strong the potential, the wind can also be a liability. You will notice that some of the windmills have been damaged by winds that were too strong. Farther along, a road sign informs you that the surrounding countryside is controlled by the **Hawaiian Home Lands Agency,** and that you are forbidden to enter. That means that you are not welcome on the land, but you do have the right to remain on the road.

Here the road splits left and right. Go right until road's end, where you'll find a parking area usually filled with the pickup trucks of local fishermen. Walk to the cliff and notice attached ladders that plummet straight down to where the fishing boats can anchor. Local skippers moor their boats here and bring supplies and their catch up and down the ladders. Nearby is a tall white structure with a big square sign on it turned sideways like a diamond. It marks the true *South Point,* the southernmost tip of the United States. At the very point you will notice holes curiously carved into rocks at the water's edge. These are reputed to be anchor points used by early Hawaiians to tie their canoes to the shore. Usually, a few people are line-fishing for crevalle or pompano. The rocks are covered with Hawaiian dental floss—monofilament fishing line that has been snapped. Survey the mighty Pacific and realize that the closest continental landfall is Antarctica, 7,500 miles to the south.

Back at the Hawaiian Homes sign, follow the road left and pass a series of World War II barracks being reclaimed by nature. This road, too, leads to a parking area and a boat ramp where a few seaworthy craft are bobbing away at their moorings. Walk toward the navigational marker

and you may notice more small holes drilled into the stone. These were used by Hawaiian fishermen to secure their canoes to shore by long ropes while the current carried them a short way offshore. In this manner, they could fish without being swept away. Today fishermen still use these holes, but instead of canoes they use floats or tiny boats to carry only their lines out to sea. The *ulua,* tuna, and *ahi* fishing is renowned throughout this area. The fishing grounds here have always been extremely fertile, and thousands of shell and bone fishhooks have been found throughout the area. Scuba divers say that the rocks off South Point are covered with broken fishing line that the currents have woven into wild macramé.

When the Kona winds blow out of the South Pacific, South Point takes it on the chin. The weather should always be a consideration when you visit. In times past, any canoe caught in the wicked currents was considered lost. Even today, only experienced boaters brave South Point, and only during fine weather.

There is no official camping or facilities of any kind at South Point, but plenty of boat owners bivouac for a night to get an early start in the morning. The lava flow in this area is quite old and grass-covered, and the constant winds act like a natural lawn mower.

Green Sand Beach

At the parking lot, check in with the Homelands office. They'll ask for a donation to park and walk along the coast to Green Sand Beach. Out front stands a short statue of a native Hawaiian wrapped in chains, symbolic of their situation as a disenfranchised people in their own land

The trail first leads to the boat ramp at Kaulana Bay; *kualana* means "boat landing." Head east from here past the gate. All along here are remnants of precontact habitation, including the remains of a *heiau* foundation. If you walk for three miles, you'll come to Papakolea, better known as Green Sand Beach, at Mahana Bay. The lava in this area contains olivine, a green semiprecious stone that weathered into sand-like particles distributed along the beach. The road heading down to Green Sand Beach is incredible. It begins as a very rugged jeep trail and disintegrates from there. Do not attempt this walk unless you have closed-toe shoes. Thongs will not make it. You're walking into the wind going down, but it's not a rough go—there's no elevation gain to speak of. The lava in the area is *'a'a,* weathered and overlaid by thick ground cover. An ancient eruption deposited 15–18 feet of ash right here, and the grasses grew.

About three miles on, you see what is obviously an eroded cinder cone at the edge of the sea. Peer over the edge to see the beach with its definite green tinge. This is the only beach along the way, so it's hard to mistake. Green Sand Beach definitely lives up to its name, but don't expect emerald green. It's more like a dull army olive green. Getting down to it can be treacherous. You'll be scrambling over tough lava rock, and you'll have to make drops of four to five feet in certain spots—or you could slide down the sand at the back end. Once you get over the lip of heavy-duty rock, the trail down is not so bad. When you begin your descent, notice overhangs, almost like caves, where rocks have been piled up to extend them. These rocked-in areas make great shelters, and you can see remnants of recent campfires in spots perfect for a night's bivouac. Down at the beach, be very aware of the wave action. The currents can be wicked here, and you should only enter the water on very calm days. No one is around to save you, and you don't want to wind up as flotsam in Antarctica.

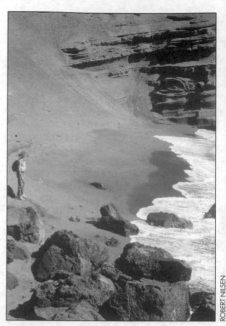

The wind is always strong at Green Sand Beach.

ROBERT NILSEN

OCEAN VIEW

Ocean View is often referred to as the largest subdivision in the state. In fact, it is a conglomeration of four subdivisions that is several miles wide and that pushes up the mountain about six miles and down toward the ocean another three. This unincorporated town of self-sufficient individuals who don't want to be bothered by anyone has been carved out of rough volcanic rubble with an overlay of scrub trees and bush. While not the most scenic, it is attractive in its own untamed way. Along the highway are a few services. You'll find a gas station, laundromat, sundries store, and not much else. This area has been hit hard by the downturn in the state economy, and often people have to drive long distances to get work—if they can find it at all.

Kula Kai Caverns

The newest and perhaps most curious offering of this region is the recently opened Kula Kai Caverns, P.O. Box 6313, Ocean View, HI 96737, 808/937-3083, one of the two lava tube caves in the state open to commercial tours (the other is the Ka'eleku Caverns in Hana, Maui). In contrast to the Ka'eleku Caverns on Maui, which are about 30,000 years old, the Kula Kai Cavern system is a mere baby at about 1,000 years old. A tour underground here gives you a look at the bowels of the largest mountain in the world, once used for shelter and as a place to collect water in this region of low rainfall. Like other lava tubes in the world, the Kula Kai Caverns shows fine examples of lava shelves, pillars, lava bombs, and other customary lava formations. As these interconnected tubes are so close to the surface in some spots, roots of *'ohi'a* trees have penetrated the ceiling of the cave and hang like hairy tendrils. An easy 20- to 30-minute interpretive walking tour ($12 for adults and $8 for kids) leads through the lighted section of the caverns. The more rigorous two-hour spelunking tour ($45) takes you deeper into the maze. Long pants and closed-toe shoes are required; gloves, knee pads, hard hats, and lights are provided.

Manuka State Wayside

The Manuka State Wayside is 12 miles west of South Point Road and just inside the Ka'u District. This civilized scene has restrooms, a pavilion, and a two-mile trail through a native and introduced forest, all of which lies within the Manuka Natural Area Reserve. The forested slopes above Manuka provide ample habitat for introduced, and now totally successful, colonies of wild pigs, pheasants, and turkeys. Shelter camping (no tents) is allowed on the grounds. This is an excellent rest or picnic stop, but bring your own drinking water. Within a couple of miles, you're in South Kona, heading up the coast toward Captain Cook and Kailua.

Accommodations

Bougainvillea Bed and Breakfast, P.O. Box 6045, Ocean View, HI 96737, tel./fax 808/929-7089 or 800/688-1763, website: www.hi-inns .com/bouga, email: peaceful@interpac.net, has views of the ocean and South Point. The inn is quiet and romantic, and each room has a private entrance and bath. Guests share the pool, hot tub, TV, and video library. There is nothing much out here, so at night there is great stargazing! A full breakfast is served each morning. Rooms are $59 single or $65 double; $15 for an extra person.

BIG ISLAND

MAUI

How shall we account for this nation spreading itself so far over this vast ocean? We find them from New Zealand to the south, to these islands to the north and from Easter Island to the Hebrides... how much farther is not known....

—Captain James Cook

HAWAII STATE ARCHIVES

INTRODUCTION

The Kumulipo, the ancient genealogical chant of the Hawaiians, sings of the demigod Maui, a half-human mythological sorcerer known and revered throughout Polynesia. Maui was a prankster on a grand scale who used guile and humor to create some of the most amazing feats of derring-do ever recorded. A Polynesian combination of Paul Bunyan and Hercules, Maui had adventures known as "strifes." He served humankind by fishing up the islands of Hawaii from the ocean floor, securing fire from a tricky mudhen, lifting the sky so humans could walk upright, and slowing down the sun god by lassoing his genitals with a braided rope of his sister's pubic hair. Maui accomplished this last feat on the summit of the great mountain Haleakala (House of the Sun), thus securing more time in the day to fish and to dry tapa. Maui met his just but untimely end between the legs of the great goddess, Hina. This final prank, in which he attempted to crawl into the sleeping goddess's vagina, left his feet and legs dangling out, causing uproarious laughter among his comrades, a band of warrior birds. The noise awakened Hina, who saw no humor in the situation. She unceremoniously squeezed Maui to death. The island of Maui is the only island in Hawaii and throughout Polynesia named after a god. With such a legacy the island couldn't help but become known by the slogan *"Maui no ka 'oi"* ("Maui is the best").

OVERVIEW

In a land of superlatives, it's quite a claim to call your island *the* best, but Maui has a lot to back it up. Maui has more miles of swimmable beach than any of the other islands. Haleakala, the massive mountain that *is* East Maui, is the largest dormant volcano in the world, and its hardened lava rising more than 30,000 feet from the sea floor makes it one of the heaviest concentrated masses on the face of the earth. There are legitimate claims that Maui grows the best onions and potatoes, but the boast of the best *pakalolo* may only be a pipe dream, since all the islands have great soil and weather and many enterprising gardeners.

West Maui

If you look at the silhouette of Maui on a map, it looks like the head and torso of the mythical

MAUI

MAUI

demigod bent at the waist and contemplating the uninhabited island of Kaho'olawe. The head is West Maui, and its profile is that of a wizened old man whose wrinkled brow and cheeks are the West Maui Mountains. The highest peak here is **Pu'u Kukui**, at 5,788 feet, located just about where the ear would be. If you go to the top of the head you'll be at **Kapalua**, a resort community that's been carved from pineapple fields. Fleming Beach begins a string of beaches that continues down over the face, stopping at the chin, and picking up again at the throat, covers the chest, which is South Maui. **Ka'anapali** is at the forehead; its massive beach continues almost uninterrupted for four miles, an area that in comparison would take in all of Waikiki, from Diamond Head to Ala Moana. The resorts here are cheek to jowl, but the best are tastefully done with uninterrupted panoramic views and easy and plentiful access to the beach. Between Ka'analapi and Kapalua, pineapple fields fringe the mountain side of the road, while condos are strung along the shore throughout the communities of **Honokowai, Kahana,** and **Napili.**

Lahaina is located at the Hindu "third eye." This town is where it's "happening" on Maui, with concentrations of craftspeople, artists, museums, historical sites, restaurants, and nightspots. Used in times past by royal Hawaiian ali'i and then by Yankee whalers, Lahaina has always been somewhat of a playground, and the good-times mystique still lingers. It's from Lahaina, across the waters of the 'Au'au Channel, better known as the "Lahaina Roads," that people can catch a glimpse of the island of Lana'i. At the tip of the nose is **Olowalu**, where a lunatic Yankee trader, Simon Metcalfe, decided to slaughter hundreds of curious Hawaiians paddling toward his ship just to show them he was boss. From Olowalu you can see four islands: Moloka'i, Lana'i, Kaho'olawe, and a faint hint of Hawai'i far to the south. The back of Maui's head is little known, but for the mildly adventurous it presents tremendous coastal views and Kahakuloa, a tiny fishing village reported to be a favorite stomping ground of great Maui himself.

Central Maui: The Isthmus

A low, flat isthmus planted primarily in sugarcane is the neck that connects the head of West Maui to the torso of East Maui, which is Haleakala. The Adam's apple is the little port of **Ma'alaea**, which has a good assortment of pleasure and fishing boats as well as the new **Maui Ocean Center.** Ma'alaea provides an up-close look at a working port not nearly as frenetic as Lahaina. The nape of the neck is made up of the twin cities of **Wailuku**, the county seat, and **Kahului**, where most visitors arrive at Maui's principal airport. These towns are where the "people" live. Some say the isthmus, dramatically separating east and west, is the reason Maui is called "The Valley Isle." Head into **'Iao Valley** from Wailuku, where the West Maui Mountains have been worn into incredible peaked monolithic spires. This stunning valley area played a key role in Kamehameha's unification of the Hawaiian Islands, and geologically it seems to be a more fitting reason for Maui's nickname.

East Maui and Haleakala

Once you cross the isthmus you're on the immensity of **Haleakala**, the one mountain that makes up the entire bulging, muscled torso of the island. A continent in microcosm, its geology encompasses alpine terrain, arid scrub desert, moonscape, blazing jungle, pastureland, and lava-encrusted wasteland. The temperature, determined by altitude, ranges from subfreezing to subtropical. If you head east along the spine, you'll find world-class sailboarding beaches, the artist and surfer village of **Pa'ia**, last-picture-show towns, and a few remaining family farms planted in taro. Route 360, the only coastal road, rocks and rolls you over more than 600 curves and shows you more waterfalls and pristine pools than you can count. After crossing more than 50 bridges, you come to **Hana**. Here, the dream Hawaii that people seek still lives. Farther along is **Kipahulu**, then **'Ohe'o Gulch**, known for its fantastic pools and waterfalls. Close by is where Charles Lindbergh is buried, and many celebrities have chosen the surrounding hillsides for their special retreats and hideaways.

On Haleakala's broad chest is the macho cowboy town of **Makawao**, complete with a Wild West rodeo contrasting with the gentle but riotous colors of carnation and protea farms down the road in **Kula. Polipoli Spring State Recreation Area** is here, a thick forest canopy with more varieties of imported trees than anywhere else in Oceania. A weird cosmic joke places **Kihei** just about where the armpit would be. Kihei is a mega-growth condo area ridiculed as an example of what developers shouldn't be allowed to do. Oddly enough, **Wailea,** just down the road, exemplifies a reasonable and aesthetic planned (although much more exclusive) community and is highly touted as a "model" development area. Just at the belly button, close to the kundalini, is **Makena,** long renowned as Maui's "alternative beach," but rapidly losing its status as the island's last "free" beach.

Finally, when you pilgrimage to the summit of Haleakala, it'll be as if you've left the planet. It's another world: beautiful, mystical, raw, inspired, and freezing cold. When you're alone on the crater rim with the world below garlanded by the brilliance of sunrise or sunset, you'll know that you have come at last to great Maui's heart.

THE LAND

After the Big Island of Hawai'i, Maui is the second largest and second youngest of the main Hawaiian Islands. The land was formed from two volcanoes: the West Maui Mountains and Haleakala. The **West Maui Mountains** are geologically much older than Haleakala, but the two were joined by subsequent lava flows that formed a connecting low, flat isthmus. **Pu'u Kukui,** at 5,788 feet, is the tallest peak of the West Maui Mountains. It's the lord of a mountain domain whose old weathered face has been scarred by a series of deep crags, verdant valleys, and inhospitable gorges. Rising more than 30,000 feet from the ocean floor, **Haleakala** is by comparison an adolescent with smooth, rounded features looming 10,023 feet above sea level, with a landmass four times larger than West Maui. The two parts of Maui combine to form 727 square miles of land with 120 miles of coastline. At its farthest points, Maui is 26 miles from north to south and 48 miles east to west. The coastline has the largest number of swimmable beaches in Hawaii, and the interior is a miniature continent with almost every conceivable geological feature evident.

Rivers and Lakes
Maui has no navigable rivers, but there are hundreds of streams. Two of the largest are **Palikea Stream,** which runs through Kipahulu Valley forming 'Ohe'o Gulch, and **'Iao Stream,** which has sculpted the amazing monoliths in 'Iao Valley. The longest, at 18 miles, is Kalialinui-Wai'ale Stream, which starts just below the summit of Haleakala, runs through Pukalani, and empties into the ocean near Kahului airport.

West Maui Mountains

ROBERT NILSEN

MAUI
TEMPERATURE AND RAINFALL

TOWN		JAN.	MARCH	MAY	JUNE	SEPT.	NOV.
Lahaina	high	80	81	82	83	84	82
	low	62	63	68	68	70	65
	rain	3	1	0	0	0	1
Hana	high	79	79	80	80	81	80
	low	60	60	62	63	65	61
	rain	9	7	2	3	5	7
Kahului	high	80	80	84	86	87	83
	low	64	64	67	69	70	68
	rain	4	3	1	0	0	2

Note: Temperature is expressed in degrees Fahrenheit; rainfall in inches.

A few reservoirs dot the island, but the two largest natural bodies of water are the 41-acre **Kanaha Pond,** on the outskirts of Kahului, and 500-acre **Kealia Pond,** on the southern shore of the isthmus; both are major bird and wildlife sanctuaries. Hikers should be aware of the countless streams and rivulets that can quickly turn from trickles to torrents, causing flash floods in valleys that were the height of hospitality only minutes before.

CLIMATE

Maui has similar weather to the rest of the Hawaiian Islands, though some aficionados claim that it gets the most sunshine of all. The weather on Maui depends more on where you are than on what season it is. The average daily temperature along the coast is about 78° F (25.5° C) in summer and during winter is about 72° F (22° C). On Haleakala summit, that average is 43–50° F (6–10° C). Nights are usually no more than 10 degrees cooler than days. Since Haleakala is a main feature on Maui, you should remember that altitude drastically affects the weather. Expect an average temperature drop of three degrees for every 1,000 feet of elevation, so at the top, Haleakala is about 30 degrees cooler than at sea level. The lowest temperature ever recorded on Maui was atop Haleakala in 1961, when the mercury dropped well below freezing to a low, low 11° F. In contrast, sunny Kihei has recorded a blistering 98° F.

Maui has wonderful weather, and because of near-constant breezes the air is usually clear and clean. Traffic and weather conditions never create smog, but because of burning cane fields Maui air will at times become smoky, a condition that usually rectifies itself in a day when the winds are blowing. On rarer occasions, a volcanic haze, known as "vog," filters over the island, being blown in from the Big Island. If it's hazy, doesn't smell of smoke, and nothing has been burning, it's probably vog.

Precipitation
Rain on Maui is as much a factor as it is elsewhere in Hawaii. On any day, somewhere on Maui it's raining, while other areas experience drought. A dramatic example of this phenomenon is a comparison of Lahaina with Pu'u Kukui, both on West Maui and separated by only seven miles. Lahaina, which translates as "Merciless Sun," is hot, arid, and gets only 15 inches of rainfall annually, while Pu'u Kukui can receive close to 500 inches (40 feet!) of precipitation. This rivals Mt. Wai'ale'ale on Kaua'i as the wettest spot on earth. Other leeward towns get a comparable amount of rain to Lahaina, but as you move Upcountry and around the north coast, the rains become greater. Finally, in Hana, rainfall is about five times as great as on the leeward side, averaging

more than 80 inches a year. The windward (wet) side of Maui, outlined by the Hana Road, is the perfect natural hothouse. Here, valleys sweetened with blossoms house idyllic waterfalls and pools that visitors treasure when they happen upon them. On the leeward (dry) side are Maui's best beaches: Kapalua, Ka'anapali, Kihei, Wailea, and Makena. They all sit in Haleakala's rain shadow. If it happens to be raining at one beach, just move a few miles down the road to the next. Anyway, the rains are mostly gentle, and the brooding sky, especially at sundown, is even more spectacular than usual.

FLORA AND FAUNA

Maui's indigenous and endemic plants, trees, and flowers are both fascinating and beautiful, but unfortunately, like everything else that was native, they are quickly disappearing. The majority of flora considered exotic by visitors was introduced either by the original Polynesians or by later white settlers. Maui is blessed with state parks, gardens, undisturbed rainforests, private reserves, and commercial nurseries, all of which offer brilliant and dazzling colors to the landscape.

Silversword
Maui's official flower is a tiny pink rose called a *lokelani.* The island's unofficial symbol, however, is the silversword. The Hawaiian name for silversword is *'ahinahina,* which translates as "gray gray," and the English name derives from a silverfish, whose color the plant is said to resemble. The silversword belongs to a remarkable plant family that claims 28 members, with five in the specific silversword species. It's kin to the common sunflower, and botanists say the entire family evolved from a single ancestral species. Hypothetically, the members of the silversword family can interbreed and produce remarkable hybrids. Some plants are shrubs, while others are climbing vines, and some even become trees. They grow anywhere from desert conditions to steamy jungles. On Maui, the silversword is found only on Haleakala, above the 6,000-foot level, and is especially prolific in the crater. Each plant lives 5–20 years and ends its life by sprouting a gorgeous stalk of hundreds of purplish-red flowers. It then withers from a majestic six-foot plant to a flat gray skeleton. An endangered species, silverswords are totally protected. They protect themselves, too, from radiation and lack of moisture by

growing fuzzy hairs all over their swordlike stalks. You can see them along the Haleakala Park Road at Kalahaku Overlook or by hiking along Silversword Loop on the floor of the crater.

Protea
These exotic flowers are from Australia and South Africa. Because they come in almost limitless shapes, sizes, and colors, they captivate everyone who sees them. They are primitive, almost otherworldly in appearance, and they exude a life force more like an animal than a flower. The slopes of leeward Haleakala between 2,000 and 4,000 feet are heaven to protea—the growing conditions could not be more perfect. Here live the hardiest, highest-quality protea in the world. The days are warm, the nights are cool, and the well-drained volcanic soil has the exact combination of minerals on which protea thrive. Haleakala's crater even helps by creating a natural air flow that produces cloud cover, filters the sun, and protects

silversword

MAUI BOTANICAL GARDENS

Kula Botanical Gardens, near the junction of Route 377 and Route 37 at the south end, 808/878-1715, has some 2,000 varieties of tropical and semitropical plants, including orchids, bromeliads, fuchsia, protea, *kukui* and sandalwood trees, and numerous ferns, on more than five acres at 3,300 feet of elevation. This privately owned garden is open daily 9 A.M.–4 P.M. for self-guided tours; $5 entrance fee.

Enchanting Floral Gardens, along Route 37 just south of Pukalani at mile marker 10, 808/878-2531, features about 1,500 species of native Hawaiian plants as well as exotic plants from around the world on eight acres. Open daily 9 A.M.–5 P.M. for self-guided tours; admission $5.

University of Hawai'i Agriculture Experimental Station, on Mauna Place just off Copp Road above Route 37 in Kula, offers 20 acres of constantly changing, quite beautiful plants, although the grounds are uninspired, scientific, rectangular plots. This garden is open Mon.–Thurs. 7:30 A.M.–3:30 P.M., closed for lunch. Although admission is free, visitors should check in with the station manager.

Garden of Eden, along the Hana Highway, is a 26-acre private garden of tropical plants and flowers, many labeled. Open 9 A.M.–2 P.M. every day; $5 admission.

Ke'anae Arboretum, above Ke'anae Peninsula on the Hana Hwy., is always open with no fee. In a natural setting with walkways, many identifying markers, and mosquitoes, this six-acre arboretum is split into two sections: ornamental tropical plants and Hawaiian domestic plants. The native forest swaths the surrounding hillsides.

Kahanu Gardens, a branch of the Pacific Tropical Botanical Gardens, is on the rugged lava coast west of Hana at the site of Pi'ilanihale Heiau. In this 123-acre garden, you'll find stands of breadfruit and coconut trees, a pandanus grove, and numerous other tropical plants from throughout Polynesia. Open Mon.–Fri. 10 A.M.–2 P.M.; two-hour guided tours $10, self-guided $5. Call 808/284-8912 for reservations.

Maunalei Arboretum is accessible to guided hikes only. Above Kapalua, this private botanical garden was started in the 1930s.

While not a botanical garden, **Polipoli Spring State Recreation Area** has some magnificent stands of redwoods, eucalyptus, conifers, ash, cypress, cedar, *sugi* and other pines. Various trails lead through the forest. Always open, but way off the beaten track. Similarly, **Hosmer Grove,** within Haleakala National Park at 6,800 feet in elevation, is an experimental forest project from the early 20th century that has fine examples of introduced trees like cedar, pine, fir, juniper, and *sugi* pine that were originally planted in hopes of finding a commercial, economically marketable wood for Hawaii. A short trail now winds through the no-longer-orderly stands of trees. Hike on your own or take a periodic ranger-guided tour. For more information, contact the Haleakala National Park Headquarters, 808/572-9306.

MAUI

the flowers. Protea make excellent gifts that can be shipped anywhere. As fresh-cut flowers they are gorgeous, but they have the extra benefit of drying superbly. Just hang them in a dark, dry, well-ventilated area and they do the rest. You can see protea, along with other botanical specialties, at the gardens, flower farms, and gift shops in Kula.

Carnations

If protea aren't enough to dazzle you, how about fields of carnations? Most Mainlanders think of carnations stuck in a groom's lapel, or perhaps have seen a table dedicated to them in a hothouse, but not fields full of carnations! The Kula area produces carnations that grow outside nonchalantly, in rows, like cabbages. They fill the air with their unmistakable perfume, and they are without doubt a joy to behold. You can see family and commercial plots throughout the upper Kula area.

Prickly Pear Cactus

Interspersed in countless fields and pastures on the windward slope of Haleakala, adding that final nuance to cattle country, are clusters of prickly pear cactus. The Hawaiians call them *panini,* which translates as "very unfriendly," undoubtedly because of the sharp spines covering the flat, thick leaves. These cactus are typical of those found in Mexico and the southwestern United States. They develop small pear-shaped fruits that are quite delicious. Hikers who decide to pick them should be careful of small yellowish bristles that can burrow under the skin and become very irritating. Prickly pears also have beautiful yellow and orange flowers.

Maui's Endangered Birds
Maui's native birds are disappearing. The island is the last home of the crested honeycreeper *('akohekohe),* which lives only on the windward slope of Haleakala from 4,500 to 6,500 feet. It once lived on Moloka'i, but no longer. The Maui parrotbill is another endangered bird, found only on the slopes of Haleakala above 5,000 feet. The *po'ouli* is a very rare dark brown bird that was saved from extinction through efforts of the Sierra Club and Audubon Society, who successfully had it listed to the Federal List of Endangered Species. The bird has one remaining stronghold deep in the forests of Maui.

Two endangered waterbirds found on Maui are the Hawaiian stilt *('ae'o)* and the Hawaiian coot *('alae ke'oke'o).*

Whale-watching
From shore you're likely to see whales anywhere along Maui's south coast. If you're staying at any of the hotels or condos along Ka'anapali or Kihei and have an ocean view, you can spot them from your lanai or window. Two good vantage spots are Papawai Point and McGregor Point along Route 30 just west of Ma'alaea. During whale-watching season, a Pacific Whale Foundation naturalist may be at one of these spots to help people locate whales and answer questions. In addition, a free talk on whales is sometimes conducted by a naturalist on the ocean observatory deck at the Kealia Beach Plaza weekdays around noon. Ma'alaea Bay is another favorite nursing ground for female whales and their calves. Another excellent viewpoint is Makena Beach, on the spit of land separating Little and Big Beaches. If you time your arrival near sunset, even if you don't see a whale you'll enjoy a mind-boggling light show.

HISTORY

The Kumulipo sings that Maui was the second island child of Wakea and Papa. Before the coming of white people and their written record, it's clear the island was a powerful kingdom. Wars raged throughout the land and kings ruled not only Maui, but the neighboring islands of Lana'i and Kaho'olawe. By the 16th century, a royal road called the Alaloa encircled the island and signified unity. Today, on West Maui, the road is entirely obliterated; only a few portions remain on East Maui. When white people began to arrive in the late 1700s, Maui became their focal point. Missionaries, whalers, and the new Hawaiian kings of the Kamehameha line all made Lahaina their seat of power. For about 50 years, until the mid-19th century, Maui blossomed. Missionaries built the first permanent stone structures in the islands. An exemplary New England–style school at Lahainaluna attracted students even from California cities. Here, too, a famous printing press brought not

only revenue but refinement, through the written word. The commercially viable sugar industry began in secluded Hana and fortunes were made; a new social order under the plantation system began. But by the turn of the 20th century, the glory years were over. The whaling industry faded away and O'ahu took over as the central power spot. Maui slipped into obscurity. It was revived in the 1960s when tourists rediscovered what others had known: Maui is a beauty among beauties.

Maui's Great Kings
Internal turmoil raged in Hawaii just before Captain Cook's arrival in 1778. Shortly after contact, the great Kamehameha would rise and consolidate all the islands under one rule, but in the 1770s a king named Kahekili ruled Maui. (Some contend Kahekili was Kamehameha's father.) The Hana district, however, was ruled by Kalaniopu'u of Hawai'i. He was the same king who

caused the turmoil on the day Captain Cook was killed at Kealakekua.

In 1776, Kalaniopu'u invaded Maui, but his forces were annihilated by Kahekili's warriors at Sand Hill near Wailuku, which means Bloody Waters. On November 26, 1778, Captain Cook spotted Maui but bypassed it because he could find no suitable anchorage. It wasn't until May 28, 1786, that a French expedition led by Captain Jean de François La Pérouse came ashore near Lahaina after finding safe anchorage at what became known as La Pérouse Bay. Maui soon became a regular port of call. In 1790 Kamehameha finally defeated Kahekili's forces at 'Iao Needle and brought Maui under his domain. The great warrior Kahekili was absent from the battle, during which Kamehameha used a cannon from the *Fair American*, a small ship seized a few years before. Davis and Young, two marooned seamen, provided the technical advice for these horrible but effective new weapons.

Maui's Rise

The beginning of the 19th century brought amazing changes to Hawaii, many of which came through Maui—especially the port of Lahaina. In 1793, Captain Vancouver visited Lahaina and confirmed La Pérouse's report that it was a fine anchorage. In 1802 Kamehameha stopped with his enormous Pelelu fleet of war canoes on his way to conquer O'ahu. He lingered for more than a year collecting taxes and building his Brick Palace at Lahaina. The bricks were poorly made, but the palace marked the first Western-style structure in the islands. He also built a fabulous straw house for his daughter, Princess Nahi'ena'ena, that was so well constructed it was later used as the residence of the U.S. Consul. In 1819 the first whaler, *The Bellina,* stopped at Lahaina and marked Hawaii's ascendancy as the capital of the whaling industry, a position that lasted until the majority of the whaling fleet was lost in the Arctic in 1871. During Lahaina's heyday, more than 500 ships visited the port in one year. Also in 1819, the year of his death, Kamehameha built an observation tower in Lahaina so he could watch for returning ships, many of which held his precious cargo. In that prophetic year the French reappeared, with a warship this time, and the drama began. The great Western powers of the period maneuvered to upstage each other in the quest for dominance of this Pacific jewel.

The Missionaries

In 1823 the first Christian mission was built in Lahaina under the pastorate of Reverend Richards, and the conversion of Hawaii began in earnest. In that year Queen Keopuolani, the first great convert to Christianity, died. She was buried in Lahaina not according to the ancient customs accorded an *ali'i,* but as a reborn child of Christ.

The Reverend Richards and Queen Ka'ahumanu worked together to produce Hawaii's first Civil Code based on the Ten Commandments. The whalers fought the interference of the missionaries to the point where attempts were made on Reverend Richards's life, including a naval bombardment of his home. Over the next decade, the missionaries, ever hard at work, became reconciled with the sailors, who donated funds to build a Seaman's Chapel. This house of worship was next to the Baldwin home, an early permanent New England–style house, which still stands on Front Street. The house originally belonged to the Spaulding family, but the Baldwins were such an influence that it was known by their name. Lahainaluna High School, in the cool of the mountains just north of Lahaina, became the paramount institution of secondary learning west of the Rocky Mountains. The newly wealthy of Hawaii and California sent their progeny here to be educated along with the nobility of the Kingdom of Hawaii.

Maui Fades

If the following 30 years of Maui's historical and sociological development were put on a graph, it would show a sharp rise followed by a crash. By midcentury, Maui boasted the first Constitution, Catholic Mass, Temperance Union, Royal Palace, and steamship service. A census was taken and a prison built to house reveling seamen. Kamehameha III moved the capital to Honolulu, and the 1850s brought a smallpox epidemic, the destruction of Waine'e Church by a "ghost wind," and the death of David Malo, a classic historian of precontact Hawaii. By the late 1860s, the whaling industry was dead, but sugar would rise to take its place. The first successful sugar plantation was started by George

MAUI

Wilfong in 1849 along the Hana Coast, and the first great sugar mill was started by James Campbell in 1861. The 1870s saw the planting of Lahaina's famous Banyan Tree by Sheriff W. O. Smith, and the first telephone and telegraph cable linked Pa'ia with Ha'iku.

The 20th Century

When the Pioneer Hotel was built in 1901, Lahaina was still important. Claus Spreckels, King Sugar himself, had large holdings on Maui and, along with his own sugar town, Spreckelsville, built the Ha'iku Ditch in 1878. This 30-mile ditch brought 50 million gallons of water a day from Ha'iku to Pu'unene so the "green gold" could flourish. The entrepreneur was able to buy the land for his sugar plantation cheaply. The highly superstitious Hawaiians of the time didn't value this particular plot of land, believing that the souls of those who had not made the leap to heaven were condemned to wander the wasteland. To them it was obviously cursed, supporting only grasses and scrub bushes, and they felt that they were getting the bargain, off-loading it onto the unsuspecting *haole*. Moreover, Spreckels was a gambler. In a series of late-night poker games with Kamehameha III he was able to win the water rights to a dozen or so streams in the area, thereby creating the possibility for his Ha'iku Ditch. Sugar and Maui became one.

Then, because of sugar, Lahaina lost its dominance and Pa'ia became *the* town on Maui during the 1930s, where it housed plantation workers in camps according to nationality. Maui slid more and more into obscurity. A few luminaries brought passing fame: Tandy MacKenzie, for example, born in Hana in 1892, was a gifted operatic star whose career lasted until 1954. In the 1960s, Maui, as well as all of Hawaii, became accessible to the average tourist. It was previously discovered by men like Sam Pryor, retired vice-president of Pan Am who made his home in Hana and invited Charles Lindbergh to visit, then to live and finally die in this idyllic spot. In the mid-1960s, the Lahaina Restoration Foundation was begun. It dedicated itself to the preservation of Old Lahaina and other historical sites on the island. It now attempts to preserve the flavor of what once was while looking to future growth. Today, Maui is once again in ascendancy, the second most visited island in Hawaii after O'ahu.

GOVERNMENT

The political boundaries of Maui County are a bit oddball. Maui County encompasses Maui Island, as well as Lana'i, Moloka'i, and the uninhabited island of Kaho'olawe. One historical geographical oddity consisted of an arc on East Maui, from Makawao past Hana and along the south coast almost to Kihei, which was a "shared" political area, aligned culturally with the Kohala District of the Big Island since Polynesian times. As a traditional carryover, these two districts were joined with each other until political lines were redrawn in 1991, severing that political connection. The real strangeness occurs in Maui's 6th Senatorial District and the 7th and 12th Representative Districts. The 7th Representative District includes much of West Maui and the islands of Lana'i and Moloka'i. The area of West Maui, with Ka'anapali and Lahaina, is one of the most developed and financially sound areas in all of Hawaii. It's a favorite area with tourists and one of the darlings of developers. On the other hand, Lana'i has a tiny population, a growing tourist industry, and, in comparison, a minuscule economy. Moloka'i has the largest per capita concentration of native Hawaiians, a "busted economy" with a tremendous share of its population on welfare, and a grassroots movement determined to preserve the historical integrity of the island and the dignity of the people. The 12th Representative District, which takes in the eastern third of the island of Maui, and 6th Senatorial District, which encompasses Kihei, Wailea, Makena, half of Upcountry, and Hana, are paired with the north coast of Kaua'i, from Kapa'a through Hanalei to the Na Pali Coast, an area that has no traditional political or cultural bond with Maui. You'd have to be a political magician to fairly represent all of the constituents in these widely differing districts.

The current mayor is James "Kimo" Apana. When elected in 1998, at age 36, he became the youngest mayor in Maui's history. Although

Maui, like the rest of the state, is overwhelmingly Democratic, Apana's win broke a 20-year Republican grip on the mayor's office. The mayor is assisted by an elected county council, with one council person from each district. Like the rest of the state, Maui County is over- whelmingly Democratic. Of the 25 state senators, Maui County is represented by three, all Democrats. Maui County has 5.5 of 51 seats in the State House of Representatives—the "half" represents a "shared" district with a portion of Kaua'i.

ECONOMY

Maui's economy is a mirror image of the state's economy: it's based on tourism, agriculture, and government expenditures. The primary growth is in tourism, with Maui being the second most frequently chosen Hawaiian destination after O'ahu. On average, Maui attracts more than two million tourists per year, and on any given day there are about 40,000 visitors enjoying the island. More than 17,000 rooms are available on Maui in all categories, and they're filled 75 percent of the time. The majority of the rooms are in Kihei

Wailea and the Ka'anapali to Kapalua strip. With tourists finding Maui more and more desirable every year, and with agriculture firmly entrenched, Maui's economic future is bright.

Agriculture and Ranching

Maui generates revenue through cattle, sugar, pineapples, and flowers, along with a substantial subculture economy in *pakalolo*. **Cattle grazing** occurs on the western and southern slopes of Haleakala, where 35,000 acres are owned

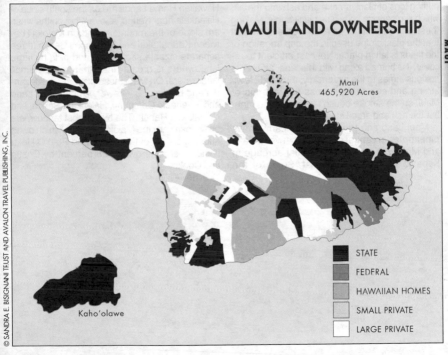

MAUI LAND OWNERSHIP

Maui
465,920 Acres

MAUI

STATE

FEDERAL

HAWAIIAN HOMES

SMALL PRIVATE

LARGE PRIVATE

Kaho'olawe

by the Haleakala Ranch, and more than 23,000 acres belong to the Ulupalakua Ranch. The upper slopes of Haleakala around Kula are a gardener's dream. Delicious onions, potatoes, and all sorts of garden vegetables are grown, but they are secondary to large plots of gorgeous flowers, mainly carnations and the amazing protea.

Sugar, actually a member of the grass family, is still very important to Maui's economy, but without federal subsidies it wouldn't be a viable cash crop. The largest acreage is in the central isthmus area, which is virtually all owned by the Alexander and Baldwin Company. Maui's two operating mills are at Pu'unene and Pa'ia. The Lahaina mill closed in 1996, and the cane fields on the Ka'anapali side have all been abandoned, the land given to pineapple production, developed into residential subdivisions, or simply left fallow. Those lodging in Ma'alaea and north Kihei will become vividly aware of the cane fields when they're burned off just prior to harvesting, putting tons of black smoke and ash into the air, which is otherwise known as black snow. Making these unsightly burnings even worse is the fact that the plastic pipe used in the drip irrigation of the fields is left in place. Not cost-efficient to recover, it is burned along with the cane, adding its noxious fumes to the air. Luckily, the wind blows strong and constantly across the isthmus of Maui, so the smoke doesn't hang around long, but the ash and smell stay longer.

Maui Land and Pineapple Company grows **pineapples** in central east Maui between Pa'ia and Makawao and on substantial acreage in Kapalua in the far northwest. Some of the pineapples shipped throughout the state and to the Mainland are whole fruits, while much is canned. Maui's first cannery (1914–1920) was in Honokohau, north of Kapalua. From 1920 to 1962, canning was done at the cannery in Lahaina. Today, Maui's only cannery is in Kahului, behind the Kaahumanu Shopping Center.

Military
The small military presence on Maui amounts to a tiny Army installation near Kahului and the Coast Guard facility at Ma'alaea.

Land Ownership
Maui County is about 750,000 acres in size, and of that 465,000 belongs to Maui, 165,000 to Moloka'i, 90,000 to Lana'i, and 28,800 to the uninhabited island of Kaho'olawe. Almost 30,000 acres is owned by the federal government—Haleakala National Park. The state controls about four times that acreage in its various forest and protected land holdings. Large chunks of Hawaiian Home Lands are on the south slope of Haleakala near Kaupo, above Kihei on the western slope of the mountain, and on Moloka'i between Kaunakakai and Mo'omomi Beach (three separate sizable sections). Land held by large landowners is greater than that held by small landowners. On Maui these players are Alexander and Baldwin, C. Brewer, Amfac, Maui Land and Pineapple Company, Haleakala Ranch, and Ulupalakua Ranch. The two largest landowners on Moloka'i are the Moloka'i Ranch, which owns about one-third of the island, and Pu'u O Hoku Ranch. Lana'i is owned 98 percent by Castle and Cooke.

PEOPLE

With 117,600 people, Maui has the third-largest island population in Hawaii, about 9.7 percent of the state's total, and the island's population density is 162 people per square mile. The Kahului-Wailuku area has the island's greatest density of population, with about 53,000 people. The Upcountry population is just over 33,000, while a little less than 20,000 live along the west coast. Hana District registers a handful over 2,000 people. For Maui County, 78 percent are urban while 22 percent live rurally. The ethnic breakdown of Maui Island is as follows: 42 percent Caucasian, 19 percent Filipino, 18 percent Japanese, 14 percent Hawaiian, 2 percent Chinese, and 5 percent other.

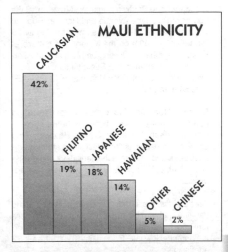

FESTIVALS, HOLIDAYS, AND EVENTS

January

Late January brings the college all-star **Hula Bowl** football game (televised) to the War Memorial Stadium in Kahului.

At the **Mercedes Championship,** the PGA tour plays golf at Kapalua, while the Senior PGA tour hosts the **Senior Skins Game** at Wailea.

February

Lunar New Year celebrations are held in the evening along Front Street in Lahaina and include a lion's dance, martial arts demonstrations, live music, food, and firecrackers, of course.

Marking the yearly return to Hawaiian waters of the humpback whale, February is whale month. The annual weeklong **Whalefest** happens in Lahaina with sailing and diving tours, demonstrations, and seminars; the **Great Whale Count** takes place islandwide; the **Annual Whale Day Celebration** is a Kihei event with lots of music, dance, and food; and **Whale Week on Maui** is a Wailea event with all sorts of events, including a regatta, fun run, and parade.

March

The Valley Island Road Runners sponsor the **Maui Marathon,** 808/871-6441, in mid-March from Kaahumanu Center in Kahului to Whalers Village in Ka'anapali.

The **East Maui Taro Festival,** 808/248-8972, website: www.hookele.com/tarofest, is celebrated in Hana with traditional ceremonies, music, food markets, symposiums, demonstrations, and exhibitions to honor one of the island's most basic food sources and the resurgence of Hawaiian cultural traditions.

April

The **Da Kine Hawaiian Pro Am** professional windsailing competition for men and women is held at Ho'okipa Beach, 808/827-7466. This is one stop on the world wavesailer's tour.

The "Ulupalakua Thing," previously known as the **Maui County Agricultural Trade Show,** is the largest event for displaying and promoting Hawaii-grown and -manufactured products. The show is held at the Tedeschi Winery at the

MAUI MUSEUMS AND HISTORICAL SOCIETY

Alexander and Baldwin Sugar Mill Museum, at the corner of Pu'unene Avenue and Hansen Road in Pu'unene, 808/871-8058, is a small but highly informative museum on the history and culture of sugar and sugar production on Maui and the corresponding plantation life. See a functioning sugar mill across the street. Open Mon.–Sat. 9:30 A.M.–4:30 P.M.; $4 admission.

Baldwin Home, on Front Street across from the harbor in Lahaina, is the two-story home of medical missionary Reverend Dwight Baldwin. This showcase museum is the oldest stone structure on the island, and it portrays the early days of the missions on Maui. Open daily 10 A.M.–4 P.M.; $3 admission.

Carthaginian II is a floating museum anchored at the Lahaina Harbor. This ship is a replica of a 19th-century brig, featuring whaling artifacts and exhibits on the humpback whale. Open daily 10 A.M.–4 P.M.; $3 admission.

Hale Pa'i is a printing house on the grounds of Lahainaluna School on the hillside above Lahaina. It has an operational replica printing press, original Lahainaluna press publications, and exhibits about the early days of Western contact in Lahaina. Open Mon.–Fri. 10 A.M.–4 P.M.

Lahaina Restoration Foundation, in the Bailey House, 808/661-3262, was begun in 1962. This privately funded organization seeks to preserve and maintain the flavor and authenticity of historical Lahaina and its old buildings.

Bailey House Museum, 2375-A Main St., Wailuku, 808/244-3326, is a repository of Hawaiian historical precontact objects, artifacts from the early days

of the missionaries on Maui, and the paintings of Edward Bailey. Once Bailey's home, it also served at one time as a dormitory for the Wailuku Female Seminary boarding school. Open by admission ($5) Mon.–Sat. 10 A.M.–4 P.M.

Maui Historical Society, 808/244-3326, is housed in the lower level of the Bailey House Museum. This society promotes interest in and knowledge of the history of Maui County and maintains an invaluable historical archive. It sponsors free lectures, classes, and events during the year.

Hana Cultural Center, 808/248-8622, is across from the entrance to Hana Bay. It preserves and restores historical artifacts, photos, and documents from the Hana area. On the grounds are a restored courthouse and jail. This cultural center also has four traditional-style buildings and maintains an ethnobotanical garden. Open daily 10 A.M.–4 P.M.; admission $2.

The private and nonprofit **Paper Airplane Museum** in Kahului, 808/887-8916, is a collection of model paper airplanes, photographs and artifacts from Maui's aviation history, and a collection of planes and other objects made from tin cans. An eclectic display, this museum will not fail to please and educate. Open daily at a storefront in the Maui Mall, donation suggested.

Whalers Village Museum, 808/661-4567, at the Whalers Village shopping mall in Ka'anapali, displays whaling artifacts and portrays the history and culture of whaling in Hawaii. This excellent display includes a reconstructed fo'c'sle and many photographs. In the courtyard is a 30-foot sperm whale skeleton. Self-guided learning experience while you shop. Open daily 9:30 A.M.–10 P.M.; free.

Ulupalakua Ranch; admission is charged. Call 808/874-0457 for information.

May

The annual **Lei Festival** takes place at the Outrigger Wailea Beach Hotel with a flower lei competition and Hawaiian music.

The annual **Barrio Fiesta** is held at the War Memorial Complex in Wailuku to celebrate Fil-

ipino culture. Food, music, dance, cultural competitions, and a Miss Barrio Fiesta contest are some of the events.

Da Kine Classic windsurfing event at Kanaha Beach in Kahului is part of the annual Maui Race Series for windsurfers.

Lahaina's signature cultural event is **In Celebration of Canoes.** This cultural gathering honors the voyaging canoe, which brought the ancestors of modern Hawaiians from the South Pacific. Cultural arts demonstrations, lu'au, musical performances, and the carving of canoes from logs are some of the activities. Representatives from Pacific island nations participate.

Held at the Ka'anapali Resort, the **Maui Music Festival,** 800/628-4767, website: www.mauimusicfestival.com, brings two days of contemporary jazz to the island.

June
The **Annual Upcountry Fair** at the Eddie Tam Center, Makawao, is an old-fashioned farm fair right in the heart of Maui's *paniolo* country. Crafts, food, and competitions are all part of the fair, as are the county 4-H championship and auctions.

June 10 is **King Kamehameha Day** in Lahaina. Festivities include a parade through town, crafts, and lots of food and entertainment.

Late June (or July) brings the annual **Kapalua Wine and Food Symposium,** where foods prepared by local master chefs get paired with international wines. Call 808/669-0244 for information.

The annual **Slack Key Guitar Festival** at the Maui Arts and Cultural Center in Kahului features some of Hawaii's best musicians.

The **Maui Film Festival,** 808/572-3456 or 808/579-9996, website: www.mauifilmfestival.com, shows a handful of art films at the Maui Arts and Cultural Center in Kahului and at a theater in Lahaina. Outdoor events also take place in Wailea. Other film showings take place throughout the year. Call for information on current showings.

July
Head for the coolness of Upcountry Makawao for the annual **Makawao Rodeo.** *Paniolo* are an old and very important tradition in Hawaiian life. Held at the Oskie Rice Arena, this old-time Upcountry rodeo can't be beat for fun and entertainment anywhere in the country. It's always accompanied by the Paniolo Parade through town.

The 4th of July brings the best fireworks display on Maui to the Ka'anapali Beach Resort. Thousands congregate for the show.

The **Vic-Maui** sailing race, website: www.vicmaui.org, runs every year from Victoria, British Columbia, Canada, to Ka'anapali. If you're a long-distance sail race fan, check out the progress of the boats at the race information office at the Lahaina harbor pier.

MAUI ARTS AND CULTURE INFORMATION

Lahaina Arts Society, 808/661-0111, is a nonprofit organization that has two galleries in the Old Lahaina Courthouse, open daily 9 A.M.–5 P.M. All artwork displayed is juried by the group's 175 members. Every other weekend, members also display their artwork under the banyan tree behind the courthouse. The Lahaina Arts Society also organized a year-round outreach program at a dozen sites throughout the island where classes are taught by society members.

The Lahaina Restoration Foundation, 808/661-3262, website: www.lahainarestoration.org, is a community organization in Lahaina created to preserve the flavor and authenticity of old Lahaina without the context of continued growth and development. It owns and maintains numerous historical buildings as museums and tries to educate the visiting public about the history of the area.

The **Lahaina Town Action Committee,** 808/667-9175, website: www.visitlahaina.com, organizes cultural events and other activities in Lahaina, including the ever-popular Friday evening Art Night. This group also sponsors the **Lahaina Visitor Center,** which has its office on the first floor of the Old Lahaina Courthouse.

The **Maui Historical Society,** 808/244-3326, website: www.mauimuseum.org, collects and preserves artifacts and disseminates information about the history and culture of Maui. It is in the basement of the Bailey House in Wailuku.

Friends of Moku'ula, 808/661-3659, website: www.mokuula.com, is a nonprofit organization striving to bring to public attention the importance of the old royal compound of Moku'ula in Lahaina and working toward its re-creation.

Late July or early August brings the **Hawaiian State Championship** windsurfing competitions to Kanaha Beach in Kahului.

August

The Japanese **Bon Odori** takes place in late July–August at Buddhist temples throughout the island, featuring dance, drumming, and lantern boats. Everyone is invited to participate.

Maui Onion Festival, at Whalers Village in Ka'anapali, 808/661-4567, celebrates the island's most famous commercial herb. All sorts of music, chef's demonstrations, and cooking-related events take place.

September

Labor Day weekend brings the well-respected **Maui Writers Conference,** 808/879-0061 or 888/974-8373, usually held at one of the fancy hotels on the island.

Late July or early August offers *the* most difficult marathon in the world. **The Run to the Sun** takes runners from sea level to the top of Haleakala (10,023 feet), more than 37 long grueling miles. For information, call 808/871-6441.

Head back up to Makawao for another excellent **Maui County Rodeo** as well as plenty of good happenings during the statewide **Aloha Week.**

Maui County Fair, at the Wailuku War Memorial Complex, brings out the kid in everyone. An old-fashioned fair with Western and homespun flavor, this event offers rides, booths, and games.

October

Wild costumes and outlandish behavior set the mood for **Halloween** in Lahaina, the largest celebration of Halloween in Hawaii, often called the "Mardi Gras of the Pacific," 808/667-9194.

The **Kaanapali Classic Senior PGA Golf Tournament** lures some of the game's living legends to the Ka'anapali links.

The **XTERRA World Championships** are held yearly in Wailea. This off-road triathlon combines a 1.5-mile ocean swim, 30K mountain bike ride, and an 11K run.

November

The **Hawaii International Film Festival** showcases new and engaging films, mainly from Asian and Pacific Rim countries, at the Maui Arts and Cultural Center in Kahului, 800/876-0567 or 800/752-8193, website: www.hiff.org.

The **Maui Invitational Basketball Tournament** holds a pre-season college team playoff at the Civic Center in Lahaina.

The **Aloha Classic Wave Sailing Championships** is held yearly at Ho'okipa Beach.

December

This month remembers Maui of old with the **Na Mele O Maui** festival in Lahaina and Ka'anapali. Hawaiian music, dance, arts, and crafts are featured.

The **Festival of Art and Flowers** in Lahaina incorporates displays of flowers grown on the island (including the beautiful protea), demonstrations, workshops, and music, plus hanging the Banyan Tree with lights and decorating the Old Courthouse for Christmas.

SPORTS AND RECREATION

Maui won't let you down when you want to go outside and play. More than just a giant sandbox for big kids, its beaches and surf are warm and inviting, and there are all sorts of water sports from scuba diving to parasailing. You can fish, hunt, camp, or indulge yourself in golf or tennis to your heart's content. The hiking is marvelous and the horseback riding on Haleakala is some of the most exciting in the world. The information offered in this chapter is merely an overview. Have fun!

BEACHES

Since the island is blessed with 150 miles of coastline, more than 32 of which are wonderful beaches, your biggest problem is to choose which one you'll grace with your presence. All beaches are open to the public. Most are accessed through beach parks, but some access is over private property. All hotels and condominiums must by law offer pathway access to beaches they front and each has some parking set aside for public use. The following should help you choose just where you'd like to romp about. But before you romp, pick up and read the brochures *Maui Beach Safety Tips,* by the American Red Cross, and *Beach and Ocean Safety Information,* found at most free information stands around the island.

West Maui

The most plentiful and best beaches for swimming and sunbathing are on West Maui, strung along 18 glorious miles from Kapalua to Olowalu. For an all-purpose beach you can't beat **D.T. Fleming Beach** or **Kapalua Bay Beach** on Maui's western tip. They have everything: safe surf (except in winter), great swimming, snorkeling, and bodysurfing in a first-class, family-oriented area. Then comes **Ka'anapali Beach,** bordered by the hotels and condos, the most well-known beach on the island. Black Rock, at the Sheraton, is the best for snorkeling. In Lahaina, **Lahaina Beach** is convenient but not private and just so-so. **Puamana** and **Launiupoko Beaches** have only fair swimming but great views and picnic areas. The beach at **Olowalu** has very good swimming and is one of the best and most accessible snorkeling spots on the island, while farther down, **Papalaua Wayside** offers seclusion on a narrow beach fringed by *kiawe* trees that surround tiny patches of white sand.

Kihei and Wailea

The 10 miles stretching from Ma'alaea to Wailea are dotted with beaches that range from poor to excellent. Ma'alaea Beach and **Kealia Beach** extend four miles from Ma'alaea to Kihei. These are excellent for walking, windsurfing, and enjoying the view, but little else. **Kama'ole Beach I, II,** and **III** are at the south end of Kihei. Top-notch beaches, they have it all—swimming, snorkeling, and safety. **Keawakapu Beach** is more of the same. Then come the great little crescent beaches of Wailea, which get more secluded as you head south: **Mokapu, Ulua, Wailea,** and **Polo.** All are surrounded by the picture-perfect hotels of Wailea, and all have public access. **Makena Beach,** down the road from Wailea, is very special. It's one of the island's best. At one time, alternative-lifestyle people made Makena a haven, and it still attracts free-spirited souls.

There's nude bathing in secluded coves, unofficial camping, and freedom.

Wailuku and Kahului

Poor ugly ducklings! The beaches in town are shallow, unattractive ones, and no one spends any time there. However, **Kanaha Beach** near the airport isn't bad at all, and it's a favorite of beginning windsurfers and kitesurfers. **H.P. Baldwin Beach** in Pa'ia has a reputation for hostile locals protecting their turf, but the beach is good, and you won't be hassled if you "live and let live." **Ho'okipa Beach** just east of Pa'ia isn't good for the average swimmer, but it is the "Sailboarding Capital" of Hawaii, and you should visit here just to see the exciting, colorful spectacle of people skipping over the ocean with bright sails.

Hana

Everything about Hana is heavenly, including its beaches. There's **Red Sand Beach,** small but almost too pretty to be real. Black-sand **Wai'anapanapa Beach,** surrounded by the state park and good for swimming and snorkeling, even provides a legendary cave whose waters turn blood red. **Hana Bay** is well protected and safe for swimming. Just south of town is the white-sand **Hamoa Beach,** described by James Michener as looking like the South Pacific.

Freshwater Swimming

There are several places for freshwater swimming in various stream pools on the road to Hana. One of the very best is **Twin Falls,** up a short trail from Ho'olawa Bridge. **Helio's Grave** is another good swimming spot between Hana and 'Ohe'o Gulch. Farther along at **Kipahulu** you'll find the paradise you've been searching for—gorgeous freshwater pools at the base of wispy waterfalls and fronted by a tremendous sea of pounding surf only a few yards away. Also, you can take a refreshing dip at **'Iao Stream** when you visit 'Iao Needle or in the next large valley north of there in **Waihe'e Stream.**

SCUBA AND SNORKELING

Maui is as beautiful from under the waves as it is above. There is world-class snorkeling and diving at many coral reefs and beds surrounding

MAUI SNORKELING

WAI'ANAPANAPA BEACH

Hana

360

Kipahulu

'Alenuihaha Channel

5 mi

5 km

0

0

Nahiku

360

Wailua

Ke'anae

HALEAKALA NATIONAL PARK

Kaupo

Ulumalu

360

Olinda

378

Pu'u 'Ula'ula (10,023 ft.)

31

Makawao

390

365

Ha'iku

398

390

Kula

377

36

Hali'imaile

Pukalani

Keokea

Pa'ia

37

370

Waiakoa

37

BALDWIN BEACH

Pu'unene

Ulupalakua Ranch

KAHULUI

311

31

Wailea

Waiehu

Wailuku

380

Kihei

Makena

Waikapu

30

KAMAOLE BEACHES

'AHIHI BAY

Kahakuloa

320

Ma'alaea

WAILEA BEACHES

"TURTLE TOWN"

340

30

Molokini Island

LA PEROUSE BAY

Waihe'e

'Alalakeiki Channel

Pu'u Kukui (5,788 ft.)

Lahaina

30

Olowalu

MILE MARKER 14

Kaho'olawe Island

'Au'au Channel

HONOLUA BAY

30

Kapalua

MOKULE'IA BAY

Kahana

KAPALUA BAY

NAPILI BAY

Honokowai

KA'ANAPALI BLACK ROCK

Ka'anapali

Pailolo Channel

MAUI

the island. You'll find some of the best, coincidentally, just where the best beaches are: mainly from Kihei to Makena, up around Napili and Kapalua bays, and especially around Olowalu. For a total thrill, try diving Molokini, the submerged volcano off Makena, just peeking above the waves and designated a Marine Life Conservation District. There are underwater caves at Nahuna (Five Graves) Point, just up from Makena landing; magnificent caves, arches, and lava tubes out at Lana'i; and a sunken Navy sub, the USS *Bluegill*, to explore. *Only* advanced divers should attempt the back side of West Maui, the coast at Kipahulu, and beyond Pu'uiki Island in Hana Bay. For these and other locations, with a brief description, check out the Maui Dive Shop's pamphlet, *Maui Dive Guide.*

Chuck Thorne is a diver who lives on Maui; he receives the highest accolades for *The Diver's Guide to Maui*, the definitive book on all the best dive/snorkel spots on the island. He's a no-nonsense kind of guy who's out to show you some great spots but never forgets about safety. While he's no longer available as a guide, his book is for sale at many scuba outlets, or you can write for it direct: Maui Dive Guide, P.O. Box 40, Hana, HI 96713. This book is an invaluable resource, well worth the money and the effort to check it out.

Scuba Shops and Tour Companies

Many boats will take you out diving. Some also do snorkel trips, deep-sea fishing, moonlight cruises, and other charters. All activities centers on the island can arrange these excursions for no extra charge. Although there is some crossover, typically boats leaving from Lahaina Harbor go to Lana'i or to spots along the west and north Maui coast to dive; those out of Ma'alaea or Makena go to Molokini or along the south coast of Maui.

Mike Severns Diving, 808/879-6596, website: www.mikesevransdiving.com, is one of the most experienced and respected diving companies on Maui. Mike is a marine scientist/explorer who's extremely knowledgeable about Maui both above and below the waves. He has his own boat and accepts both beginning and advanced divers, and he dives mostly along the south coast. Diving with Mike is an extraordinary educational experience. The two-tank dives run $120 and leave from the Kihei boat ramp; no

snorkel tours. Special three-tank and night dives can be accommodated.

Ed Robinson's Diving Adventures, 808/879-3584 or 800/635-1273, website: www.mauiscuba.com, offers a great deal for those staying in South Maui. The company operates a beach cabana at the Four Seasons Resort in Wailea and runs tours from two fully equipped boats to spots mostly in South Maui and to Molokini and Lana'i. Offered are free daily scuba clinics at the hotel, introductory and refresher dives, certification, and two- and three-tank boat dives.

Dive and Sea Maui, 1975 S. Kihei Rd., 808/874-1952, open Mon.–Sat. 7 A.M.–5 P.M., until noon on Sunday, is a full-service dive shop offering scuba dives, certification classes, air refills, equipment rentals, and dive/snorkel trips to Molokini Crater on a six-passenger Mako boat so that you are given individual attention and full value for the money.

The **Maui Dive Shop,** 1455 S. Kihei Rd., 808/879-3388 or 800/542-3483, website: www.mauidiveshop.com, with six other locations in Kihei and Lahaina, is Maui's largest scuba operation. The retail outlet is a full-service watersports store, and it and all locations offer shore and boat dives along with certification. Rates are moderate, and your experience will be memorable.

Lahaina Divers, 143 Dickenson St., Lahaina, 808/667-7496 or 800/998-3483, website: www.lahainadivers.com, next to Pacific Whale Foundation, offers a snorkeling experience; various scuba dives to Lana'i, Molokini, and the Maui coast; night dives; and certification courses. Lahaina Divers uses its own boats for all of the excursions and offers beverages and snacks on all trips. This company is well regarded and has an established reputation. Boats leave from Lahaina Harbor.

Pacific Dive, 150 Dickenson St., Lahaina, 808/667-5331 or 877/667-7331, website: www.pacificdive.com, offers open-water certification classes, beach dives, boat dives, night dives, and scooter dives. This full-service scuba/snorkel store does daily rentals on scuba and snorkel equipment, boogie boards, and other water gear, and also has a complete repair facility and air fill station for those already certified. Nitrox available.

MAUI

Dive Maui, 900 Front St, Lahaina, 808/667-2080, website: www.divemauiscuba.com, covers the whole range from shore and boat dives, night dives, certification, snorkel trips, and rentals. Boats leave from the most convenient boat ramp or pier.

Among the many other companies in South Maui, check out **Divers Locker,** 808/280-3483; **Provider,** 808/875-4004; or **Makena Coast Charters,** 808/874-1273 or 800/833-6483. In West Maui, try **Tropical Divers Maui,** 808/669-6284; **Extended Horizons,** 808/667-0611; or **Maui Diving,** 808/667-0633.

Snorkeling

Use the same caution when scuba diving or snorkeling as when swimming. Be mindful of currents. It's generally safer to enter the water in the center of a bay than at the sides where rips are more likely to occur. The following sites are suitable for beginners to intermediates: on Maui's western tip, Honolua Bay and nearby Mokule'ia Bay, both part of a Marine Life Conservation District; Kapalua and Napili Bays for usually good and safe conditions; in Ka'anapali, Black Rock at the Sheraton Hotel; and at Olowalu, where the ocean is very gentle with plenty to see. Also try the rocky headlands between the Kama'ole beaches in Kihei and farther down between the beaches in Wailea. 'Ahihi Bay and La Pérouse Bay in South Maui are great spots, and fairly isolated. On the windward side Baldwin Beach in Pa'ia and Wai'anapanapa State Park beach near Hana are both generally good. Under no circumstances should you miss taking a boat out to Molokini. It's worth every penny, even though it's getting rather crowded! Some boats also stop at Turtle Town off of Maui's last lava flow. Manele and Hulopo'e bays on Lana'i are like aquariums, both also marine life conservation districts. And there are plenty more.

Snorkel Equipment

Sometimes condos and hotels have snorkeling equipment free for their guests, but if you have to rent it, don't do it from a hotel or condo; go to a snorkel or dive shop where it's much cheaper. Expect to spend $5–10 a day for mask, fins, and snorkel, or $25–30 a week.

One of the best snorkel deals is through **Snorkel Bob's,** 808/879-7449 in Kihei, 808/667-2553 in Lahaina, and 808/669-9603 in Napili. Old Snorkel Bob will dispense info and full snorkel gear for only $9–29 a week. Add $7 a week if you add a dry snorkel tube. You can return it to any store on Maui or on a Neighbor Island if you'll be heading off Maui before the week is up. Daily rates are similarly reasonable. Slick-bottom boogie boards run $26 a week, and other water gear is also available for rent.

A & B Rentals and Sportswear, in Honokowai at the Da Rose Mall, 808/669-0027, open daily 9 A.M.–5 P.M., rents snorkel gear for $2.50 per day and $9 per week, as well as boogie boards.

In the Kahana Plaza, **Boss Frogs,** 808/669-6700, has snorkel gear for $2.50–9 per day or $9–30 per week. This shop also rents surfboards, boogie boards, and bikes.

West Maui Sports, behind Lahaina Cannery mall, 808/661-6252, rents ordinary snorkel gear for $2.50 a day or $10 a week, as well as body boards, kayaks, beach gear, and golf clubs.

In Lahaina, try **Duke's Surf and Rentals,** along Front St. at the south end of downtown, for snorkel gear at $3 a day or $18 a week, as well as surfboards, bikes, golf clubs, and an assortment of other items.

Numerous other shops on the island also rent snorkel gear at comparable but variable rates depending upon the quality of the equipment.

Snorkel Excursions

For a pure snorkeling adventure, unlike those offered by the tour boats, try **Snorkel Maui,** 808/572-8437, website: www.maui.net/~annf. Naturalist Ann Fielding is the author of *Hawaiian Reefs and Tide Pools* and *An Underwater Guide to Hawai'i,* which detail many of the invertebrates and reef fish you will encounter on one of her fantastic dives. Ms. Fielding instructs you in snorkeling and in the natural history and biology of what you'll be seeing below the waves. She tailors the dive to fit the participants. A basic half-day snorkel dive costs $75 adults or $65 kids.

Dozens of snorkel boat excursions take place in Maui's waters every week. Most boats leave either from Lahaina or Ma'alaea Harbor, while others leave from the beaches fronting the large hotels of Ka'anapali, Wailea, and Makena. Catamarans, mono-hulls, sailing ships, power boats, or rafts: snorkeling vessels come in all shapes and sizes. Prices range $50–80 for half-day adventures; full-day tours with lunch and sail could be $150.

For a magnificent day of sailing, exploring, and snorkeling, you can't beat **Trilogy Excursions,** 808/661-4743 or 888/628-4800, whose sleek catamarans leave Lahaina Harbor for a day trip to Lana'i, Ma'alaea Harbor for Molokini, or Ka'anapali Beach for trips up the coast.

Others to check out are: **Pride of Maui,** 808/242-0955; **Classic Charters'** *Four Winds II,* 808/879-8188; **Island Marine Activities'** *Lahaina Princess,* 808/661-8397; **Prince Kuhio,** 808/242-8777; **Blue Dolphin,** 808/661-3333; or **Boss Frogs'** *Frogman,* 808/874-6325.

Snuba

Snuba is half snorkeling and half scuba diving. You have a regulator, weight belt, mask, and flippers, and you're tethered to scuba tanks that float 20 feet above you on a sea-sled. The idea is that many people become anxious diving under the waves encumbered by tanks and all the scuba apparatus. Snuba frees you. If you would like to start diving, this is a wonderful and easy way to begin. Try **The Four Winds,** 808/879-8188, a snorkel-dive boat that goes to Molokini Crater, or **Island Scuba,** 808/661-3369. A few other outfits are now starting to offer snuba on Maui. A snuba experience runs $45–70.

CATCHING WAVES

Bodysurfing

All you need are the right wave conditions and a sandy beach to have a ball bodysurfing and boogie boarding. Always check conditions first—bodysurfing has led to some very serious neck and back injuries for the ill-prepared. The following are some decent beaches: Ulua, Wailea, Polo, or Makena, the north end of Kama'ole Beach Park I in Kihei, Napili Bay, D.T. Fleming, and Baldwin Park. Typical boogie board rental prices are $5 a day to $25 a week—similar to the rate for snorkel gear.

Surfing

While the north coast of O'ahu is known as the best surfing area in Hawaii—and arguably the best in the world—Maui has a few decent spots.

Try Honolua Bay, Napili Bay, Lahaina Harbor, Launiupoko Park, and Ho'okipa Beach. Many beginners stay at the more gentle beaches between Lahaina and Olowalu, Ma'alaea Beach, and the beaches in Kihei.

Maui does have one spot, however, that has gained worldwide notoriety over the last several years. This is "Jaws." On a good day, waves at Jaws rise 30–50 feet high! The conventional method of catching a wave—paddling belly down on your board until you gain enough speed and momentum to slip down the front of the wave—doesn't work here because of the height and speed of these waves. Ingenious (and maybe a bit crazy) surfers have come up with a solution—use a jet ski to gain speed and tow the surfer to the right spot before dashing out of harm's way. Some surfers use the tow rope as a big slingshot to propel themselves even faster from behind the jet ski. Surfboards used at Jaws have straps for the feet similar to a sailboard. So far, no one has died in this highly risky endeavor, but it seems likely that over time someone will bite it big. Jaws is about 10 minutes past Ho'okipa Beach on the road to Hana and then down a road toward the ocean. People are reluctant to give the exact location, although locals know the spot well. Some fear, and rightly so, that inexperienced surfers will give this monster a try, but homeowners in the area just don't like the traffic and congestion. On a high surf

---

MAUI OUTRIGGER CANOES

Historically, outrigger canoes have been made from the trunks of koa trees. Koa trees large enough to built a canoe are scarce these days, and most are legally protected. To have one made today from available logs would run $40,000–100,000. By far the majority of outrigger canoes in the islands these days are made from fiberglass. Much cheaper, they still must meet rigorous specifications. On Maui there are eight or nine canoe clubs, and most have 100-plus members. In all of Hawaii, outrigger canoeing is the team sport that has the greatest participation, with more than 10,000 active canoe club members in about 60 canoe clubs throughout the state.

day, there may be as many as 350 cars parked on the approach road.

Surfing Instruction

More than two dozen shops on Maui rent surfboards, and perhaps a dozen or more companies and individuals teach the basics of surfing. Some are listed below. You can get surfing lessons in groups or individually. Lessons generally run in the vicinity of $55–70 for a group lesson that lasts about two hours or about $80–90 for a private lesson. Many lessons are taught directly south of Lahaina Harbor, while some instruction is done at the beach parks between Lahaina and Olowalu or in Kihei. The surfing schools offer multiday packages.

Maui Surfing School, 808/875-0625, website: www.mauisurf.com, offers lessons at the beach just to the side of Lahaina Harbor. Ask for Andrea Thomas. Specializing in "beginners and cowards," the school guarantees results after one lesson. Another "learn in one day" guarantee is offered by **Nancy Emerson School of Surfing,** 808/244-7873, website: www.maui.net/~ncesurf/ncesurf.html. Also in Lahaina are **Goofy Foot,** 808/244-9283; **Surf Dog Maui,** 808/250-7873; and **Outrageous Adventures,** 808/669-1400. In Kihei, call **Maui Waveriders,** 808/875-4761, or **Maui Boardrides,** 808/870-7873.

Windsurfing

Ho'okipa Beach, just east of Pa'ia, is the "Sailboarding Capital of the World," and the big-money championship used to be held here every year in March and April. Today, the **Aloha Classic,** held in late October or early November, with prize money at $5,000–10,000, is as big as it gets. Smaller local and national competitions are held in spring and winter, usually at Kooks Beach, Kanaha Beach Park, in Kahului, but for details ask at any of the big windsurfing shops on the island.

Kanaha Beach Park has perfect gentle winds and waves for learning the sport, and the beach at Spreckelsville has virtually the same characteristics. Summer is best for windsurfing because of the winds, which blow steadily from the east. Mornings are good for the novice because winds are lighter. As winds pick up in the afternoon the more advanced board riders hit

the water. Any sailboard shop will point you in the right direction for location and gear according to your skill level. When the winds come from the south, most windsurfers head to the north end of Kihei and set in at Mai Poina 'Oe La'u Beach Park to sail on Ma'alaea Bay. Sometimes in the winter, you'll see boarders out on the water with the whales. Wherever you decide to try the water, pick up a copy of *Guidelines For Windsurfing on Maui* before you put together your gear. This helpful pamphlet is put out by the Maui Boardsailing Association, 808/871-4981.

Rental equipment with a board and one mast runs roughly $30 a day or $50 with two sails, to $350 and $500 for two weeks, depending upon the quality of gear. Group lessons for three or more usually run 2–3 hours, and private lessons that run 1–2 hours cost about $60–70. Remember—start with a big board and a small sail! Take lessons to save time and energy. To rent equipment or take lessons, try **Maui Windsurf Company,** 808/877-4816 or 800/872-0999, website: www.maui-windsurf.com; **Hi-Tech,** 808/877-2111, website: www.htmaui.com; **Second Wind,** 808/877-7467 or 800/936-7787, website: www.maui.net/~secwind; **Neilpryde Maui,** 808/877-7443 or 800/321-7443, website: www.neilprydemaui.com; **Extreme Sports Maui,** 808/871-7954, 877/376-6284, website: www.extremesportsmaui.com; **Maui Sails,** 808/877-7443; **Hawaiian Island Surf and Sports,** 808/871-4981 or 800/231-6958, website: www.hawaiianisland.com; **Hawaii Sail and Sport,** 808/879-0178, website: http://maui.net/~hisurf; **Sailboards Maui,** 808/871-7954; and **Windsurfing West Maui,** 808/871-8733.

For lessons only, inquire at one of the shops or directly with **Alan Cadiz's HST,** 808/871-5423 or 800/871-6943, website: www.hstwindsurfing.com; or **Action Sports Maui,** 808/871-5857, website: www.actionsportsmaui.com. **Al West's,** 808/871-8733 or 800/870-4084, website: www.mauivans.com, also does lessons and rents vans to transport your gear.

Kitesurfing

A cross between wakeboarding and flying a kite, kitesurfing (also known as kiteboarding) is one of the newest water sports to hit the island. If you want to see it, head for "kite beach," just west of Kanaha Beach park in Kahului.

Lessons by several shops in Kahului run from a two-hour kite control class to three-hour introductory lessons to a five-day advanced course. For most, the three-hour course works best; it runs about $185. Rental gear is also available at local shops. If you decide to really get into the sport, you can get set up for about $1,000. Perhaps the premier shop offering lessons and equipment is **Divinci Kites,** 22 Hana Hwy., 808/873-9463, website: www.davin-cikites.com. Others are: **Second Wind,** 808/877-7467 or 800/936-7787, website: www. secondwindmaui.com, and **Hawaiian Islands Surf and Sport,** 808/871-4981 or 800/231-6958, website: www.kitesails.com. Be sure to familiarize yourself with kitesurfing regulations. Pick up a copy of the *Safe Kiteboarding Guidelines,* printed by the Maui Kiteboarding Association. It's available at shops that rent or sell kiteboarding equipment, or check the website at www.maui.net/~hotwind/mka.html.

THRILL CRAFT

Usually the term "thrill craft" refers to jet skis, water-ski boats, speedboats, parasailing, and other such motorized watercraft. In years past, a controversy raged about their use. The feeling among conservationists was that these craft disturb humans, and during whale season they disturb the whales that come to winter over in the rather small Lahaina Roads and Ma'alaea Bay. This is definitely a case of "one person's pleasure is another person's poison." On March 31, 1991, a law was passed that bans these types of craft from operating in west and south Maui waters during whale season: December 15 through May 15. Although you might assume that this is due to the sound of the motors roaring through the waters—research has been done to determine if this too is a problem—the restriction was set in place because of the speed and unpredictable nature of these water craft.

Jet Skis
To try this exciting sport, contact **Pacific Jet Sport,** 808/667-2066, for use of jet skis and wave runners. From 9 A.M. to 4 P.M. daily, you can meet the shuttle boat on the beach in front of the Hyatt Hotel in Ka'anapali, and it will take you out to the pontoon boat and riding area where you'll get instruction on how to operate these water machines. Rates are $50 for a half hour or $70 an hour, and $10 extra for each additional person up to three for the wave runners. You must be 15 years old.

Banana Boat Rides and Water-skiing
A banana boat is an inflatable raft-like craft that is pulled through the water by a power boat. Riders don goggles and life vests, sit on two cushioned sections, hold on to strap grips, and thrill in the experience of pounding over the waves. All riders must be in good physical shape. Those with back problems or who are pregnant are advised not to ride. A 20-minute ride costs $20. Sign up with **The Banana Boat,** 808/667-1964, near the water at Ka'anapali Beach.

This company also does water-skiing for $50 a half hour for one or two people, or $90 an hour for up to four people.

Parasailing
If you've ever wanted to soar like an eagle, here's your chance with no prior experience necessary. Basically, a parasail is a parachute tethered to a speedboat. And away we go! The most dangerous part seems to be getting in and out of the shuttle boat that takes you to the powerboat from where you take off. On the powerboat a special harness attaches to a parachute. You're put in a life vest and strapped to the harness, which forms a cradle upon which you sit while aloft. Make sure, once you're up, to pull the cradle as far under your thighs as you can. It's much more comfortable. Don't be afraid to loosen your steel grip on the guide ropes, because that's not what's holding you anyway. In the air, you are as free as a bird and the unique view is phenomenal. The technology is simple, straightforward, and safe. Relax and have a ball. Cost is about $50 for a 10-minute joyride that lets out about 800 feet of line or $40 for a seven-minute ride where you are at the end of a 400-foot line. Some companies pull singles only; others take doubles. Boats leave from Mala Wharf and off Ka'anapali Beach. Try **Parasail in Paradise,** 808/661-4060; **UFO Parasail,** 808/661-7UFO; or **Parasail Kaanapali,** 808/669-6555.

MAUI

OCEAN TOURS

You haven't really seen Maui unless you've seen it from the sea. Tour boats take you fishing, sailing, whale-watching, dining, diving, and snorkeling. You can find powerboats, sailboats, catamarans, and Zodiac rafts that offer a combination of some or all of these options or just sail you around for pure pleasure—Maui presents one of the premier sailing venues in the Pacific. Many take day trips to Lana'i. Others visit Molokini, a submerged volcano with only half the crater rim above water; it has been designated a marine life conservation district. The majority of Maui's pleasure boats are berthed in Lahaina Harbor, and most have a booth right there on the wharf where you can sign up. Other boats come out of Ma'alaea Harbor, and a few companies are based in Kihei. The following are basically limited to sailing/dining/touring activities, with snorkeling often part of the experience. To add to the mix, there are even a few submarine tour possibilities, where you can see underwater sights without getting wet.

Excursions and Dinner Sails

Trilogy, 808/661-4743 or 888/628-4800, website: www.sailtrilogy.com, founded and operated by the Coon family, is a success in every way; its Lana'i Cruise is the best on Maui. Although the hand-picked crews have made the journey countless times, they never forget that it's your first time. They run catamarans that carry up to 50 passengers, and once aboard, you're served refreshments and Mama Coon's famous cinnamon rolls. Once at Lana'i, you can frolic at Hulopo'e Bay, which is great for swimming and renowned as an excellent snorkeling area. All gear is provided. While you play, the crew is busy at work preparing a delicious barbecue at the picnic facilities at Manele Harbor. You couldn't have a more memorable or enjoyable experience than sailing with Trilogy. But don't spoil your day; be sure to bring along (and use!) a wide-brim hat, sunglasses, sunscreen, a long-sleeve shirt, and a towel. For this full day's experience, adults pay $159, children (3–12) half price. Trilogy Excursions also runs a popular half-day trip to Molokini Crater, sailing daily from Ma'alaea Harbor—adults $79, children half price,

which includes breakfast, lunch, and all snorkeling gear; a five-hour midday picnic sail from Ka'anapali Beach for $89; and two-hour whale-watching sails during whale season, also from Ka'anapali Beach for $39.

If you've had enough of Front Street Lahaina, **Club Lanai,** 808/871-1144 or 800/531-5262, is a Maui-based company that runs day excursions and does whale-watches and cocktail cruises, too. You board your catamaran at Lahaina Harbor, leaving at 7 A.M. and returning at around 3:30 P.M. after a full day. En route you're served a breakfast. The club provides you with snorkel gear, and scuba diving can also be arranged at an extra charge. Family-oriented with plenty of activities for children of all ages, Club Lanai lets you set your own pace . . . do it all, or do nothing at all.

Navatek II, a state-of-the-art marvel built on O'ahu and engineered expressly for use in Hawaii, is actually a SWATH vessel (Small Water Plane Area Twin Hull) of revolutionary design that features two submerged hulls, remote-controlled submarines, connected by two half-moon arching struts that support the above-water superstructure. The design means that the ship handles the waves with amazing dexterity since no part of the above-water decks comes into actual contact with them. The result is the island's most steady, most nimble, and most comfortable craft. With the touch of a finger, ballast tanks in the submersibles can be either flooded or blown to balance the craft, while a joystick raises or lowers the bow, and a polished aluminum ship's wheel only the size of a hockey puck steers the agile SWATH. Fronting the pilothouse is stepped amphitheater seating, and behind is a comfortable tanning deck with lounge chairs, restrooms, and even hot showers, very welcome after a swim or snorkeling adventure. The glass-enclosed lower deck converts to a floating restaurant, with stage, dance floor, full table settings, kitchen, and complete bar. The *Navatek II* offers a Lana'i snorkel and whale-watch for $115 adults, $95 juniors 12–17, and $75 children ages 5–11, leaving daily except Sunday from Ma'alaea Harbor at 9 A.M. and returning at about 3 P.M. The cruise offers a delicious breakfast buffet, barbecue lunch, snorkeling, and sail. The Sunset Dinner Cruise, adults $87, children 2–11 $55, departs nightly around 5

P.M. and features *pu pu,* cocktail hour, and a complete three-course dinner and dessert served at your table by a professional waitstaff. For complete details contact Royal Hawaiian Cruises, 808/873-3475, website: www.royalhawaiiancruises.com.

Pacific Whale Foundation, 808/879-8811, runs *The Manute'a,* a 50-foot catamaran, offering a dolphin watch and snorkel adventure to Lana'i from Lahaina Harbor for $79. Pacific Whale Foundation has three other boats, one more leaving from Lahaina Harbor and two from Ma'alaea, which do whale, dolphin, and turtle sails in the $59–89 range.

The *Prince Kuhio,* 800/468-1287 or 808/242-8777 on Maui, offers a different kind of trip altogether. Comfort, luxury, and stability come with this 92-foot ship. Departing from Ma'alaea Harbor daily, the *Prince Kuhio* does a four-hour snorkel cruise to Molokini and turtle town ($75 adult, $40 children under 12), including a continental breakfast, buffet lunch, open bar, and champagne on the return voyage.

One of the least expensive cruises is a cocktail sail aboard the 44-foot catamaran *Frogman,* 808/874-6325. It departs from Ma'alaea Harbor and serves *pu pu,* mai tais, and beer on its trade wind sail. The quickest way to Molokini, which means more time in the water, is aboard the catamaran *Kai Kanani,* 808/879-7218, which departs from in front of the Maui Prince Hotel in Makena. Equipment and food are provided. Other resort catamarans leave from west side beaches, all doing a combination of snorkel sails, sunset cruises, and private charters. *Wind Warrior* sails from the beach in front of Whalers Village in Ka'anapali. *Teralani* leaves from the Sheraton, *Gemini* from the Westin Maui, and the *Kiele V* from the Hyatt Regency. Up the coast, the *Kapalua Kai* sails from the Kapalua Bay Hotel.

Scotch Mist, 808/661-0386, has one racing yacht, *The Scotch Mist II.* It is the oldest sailing charter on Maui (since 1970), and it claims to have the fastest mono-hull sailboat in Lahaina Harbor, boasting the lightest boat, the biggest sail, and the best crew. A sail/snorkel in the morning costs $55 per person; the afternoon sailing trip is best to catch the trade winds; or take the sunset sail (up to 25 passengers) complete with champagne for $45 per person. When

the time is right, a moonlight/starlight sail and a whale-watching sail are also offered.

The *Lavengro,* 808/879-8188, a 60-foot "Roaring 20s" pleasure craft that even saw coastal duty during World War II, offers a lovely sail on a tall, two-masted wooden ship. This ship and its glass-bottom catamaran companion, *Four Winds,* make morning snorkel runs to Molokini; $59 for the *Lavengro* and $69 for the *Four Winds.* The sloops **Flexible Flyer,** 808/244-6655, and *Cinderella,* 808/244-0009, also leave from Ma'alaea Harbor. With six passengers maximum, the *Cinderella* charges $135 per person for short tours. The entire ship can be chartered at the rate of $500 for four hours, $800 for a full day, or $360 for a two-hour sunset run. America's Cup contender *America II,* 808/667-2195, sailing out of Lahaina Harbor, can carry up to 28 passengers. It leaves twice daily at $30 a person and runs $32.95 for a sunset sail. **Paragon Sailing Charters,** 808/244-2087, runs its catamaran also on a twice daily schedule for $40–64 per person. The rate for *Island Star,* which runs private charters only, ranges $500–3,000.

Sunset cruises are very romantic and very popular. They last for about two hours and cost $40–70 for the basic cruise, but for a dinner sail expect to spend $70–90. Remember, too, that the larger established companies are usually on Maui to stay, but smaller companies come and go with the tide! The big 149-passenger *Maui Princess,* 808/667-6165, offers dinner cruises aboard its sleek 118-foot motor yacht for $75 ($35 children), which includes open bar, dinner, entertainment, and dancing. **Windjammer,** 808/661-8600, also does a salmon and prime rib dinner cruise for $71 on its 93-passenger three-masted schooner, with sailings daily at 5:30 P.M. and 7:30 P.M. Others to check out are the sunset cocktail cruise on the *Pride of Maui,* Island Marine's barefoot buffet sunset cruise, and the sunset cruise, dinner sail, and dance party hosted by Club Lanai.

Some companies offer cocktail sails and whale-watches for much cheaper prices, but many pack people in so tightly that they're known derisively as "cattle boats." Don't expect the personal attention you'd receive on smaller boats, and always check the number of passengers when booking.

Whale-watching

Anyone on Maui from November to April gets the added treat of watching humpback whales as they frolic just off Lahaina, one of the world's major wintering areas for the humpback. Almost every boat in the harbor runs a special whale-watch during this time of year. If you're susceptible to seasickness, take a ride in the morning, because the water usually gets a little choppier in the afternoon.

Whales Alive Maui, 808/874-6855, is a fantastic organization of dedicated scientists and naturalists who have made a career of studying the magnificent humpback whale and who operate whale-watches every day in season. Whales Alive Maui operates two-hour trips for a reasonable $30 through the **Ocean Activities Center,** 808/879-4485 or 800/798-0652. Part of the proceeds are donated to further the research of this fine organization. Whales Alive Maui leaves Ma'alaea Harbor twice daily in the afternoon on the *Makakai* and *Wailea Kai*. On each of these stable and seaworthy catamarans is a fully trained Whales Alive Maui naturalist who offers a very educational and entertaining interpretive narration. When one of these wonderful animals shows itself by breaching, spouting, or slapping a pectoral fin, the naturalist informs you of what's going on and especially how it relates to the social pattern of whale life. Simply by taking people out to see these magnificent creatures and teaching them about their lives, Whales Alive staff hope everyone will become aware of the whale's delicate place in nature and learn to appreciate its significance as something to be protected. There is no better way to have a truly Hawaiian experience of sea, surf, and natural beauty than enjoying a whale-watch sail with Whales Alive Maui.

Another highly educational whale-watch is sponsored by the **Pacific Whale Foundation,** Kealia Beach Plaza, Suite 25, 101 N. Kihei Rd., Kihei, HI 96753, 808/879-8811, website: www.pacificwhale.org, open daily 8 A.M.–5 P.M. A nonprofit organization founded in 1980, it is dedicated to research, education, and conservation, and is one of the only research organizations that has been able to survive by generating its own funds through membership, donations, and excellent whale-watch cruises. The foundation has one of the best whale-watches on

the island aboard its own ships, berthed for your convenience at Ma'alaea and Lahaina Harbors. The scientists and researchers who make up the crew rotate shifts and come out on the whale-watch when they're not out in the Lahaina Roads getting up close to identify and make scientific observations of the whales. Most of the information that the other whale-watches dispense to the tourists is generated by the Pacific Whale Foundation. Departures from Ma'alaea and Lahaina Harbors are several times daily. The foundation also offers an "Adopt-a-whale Program" and various reef and snorkel cruises that run throughout the year.

Rafting

For a totally different experience, try a rafting trip. Several rafting companies have sprung up in the last few years, so there's plenty of competition. These rafts are small rigid-bottom crafts with a sun shade; they seat 6–24 people. The vessels are highly maneuverable, totally seaworthy high-tech motorized rafts whose main features are their speed and ability to get intimate with the sea as the supple form bends with the undulations of the water. You're right on the water, so you'll get wet, and you often ride right on the inflatable rubber tubes. Like boat tours, these rafts do one or a combination of tours that involve whale-watching, snorkeling, sea caves, coastal cruises, or the circumnavigation of Lana'i. For half-day rides, expect a charge of $7–80; full-day adventures run $110–135. The first company in Maui waters was **Blue Water Rafting,** 808/879-7238, website: www.bluewaterrafting.com, which departs from the Kihei Boat Ramp for trips down along the rugged Makena Coast. **Royal Hawaiian Cruises** runs the *Maui Nui Explorer* out of Lahaina Harbor to Lana'i for half-day and full-day snorkel and whale-watch trips, $67–95, plus an alternate afternoon whale-watch trip in season for $29. Other options are **Ocean Rafting,** 808/661-7238 or 888/677-7238, website: www.hawaiioceanrafting.com; **Hawaiian Rafting Adventures,** 808/661-7333; and **Ultimate Rafting Ecotours,** 808/667-5678, website: www.maui.net/~ecoraft.

Kayaking

Kayaking has also become quite popular over the last decade. Much of the kayaking is done in the Makena area, but some companies take trips to the north coast and other locations. In the Rainbow Mall at 2439 S. Kihei Rd., **South Pacific Kayaks,** 808/875-4848 or 800/776-2326, website: www.mauikayak.com, offers a half-day introductory trip (with drinks and snacks) for $59, or an advanced explorer trip along the remote coastline of South Maui (including drinks and full lunch) for $89. Both tours include plenty of snorkeling opportunities as you glide in and out of tiny bays fashioned from jutting lava rock fingers. South Pacific Kayaks offers rentals of single and double kayaks and also does sales.

Kelli's Kayak Tours, 808/874-7652, has several tours to various sites around the island ranging $55–99. See also **Makena Kayak,** 808/879-8426, which has two- to four-hour trips at Makena for $55–85; **Big Kahuna Kayak,** 808/875-6395, website: www.maui.net/~paddle, which also does hiking and scuba tours; and **Kayak Eco-adventures,** 808/891-2223.

Perhaps the most unusual paddling activity on the island is the **Hawaiian Sailing Canoe Adventure.** This old-style double-hull canoe departs Ka'anapali Beach four times a day for two-hour rides for paddling and sailing; $44 per person for a real cultural experience.

Submarines
Undersea adventures have also come to Maui. With *Atlantis Submarine,* 808/667-2224 or 800/548-6262, website: www.atlantisadventures.com, you can dive to more than 130 feet to view the undersea world through glass windows. The basic tour in this 48-passenger true submarine starts at $79 adult and $49 for kids; you must be at least three feet tall to board. These trips leave from the Lahaina Harbor pier every hour from 9 A.M. and travel to the sub loading area about two miles east of town. The trip lasts about 50 minutes. Atlantis offers several combo packages with other island activities vendors.

Both the 34-passenger *Reefdancer,* 808/667-2133, and the 28-passenger *SeaView Adventures,* 808/661-5550, are submersibles that let you view underwater from the depth of no more than 10 feet—but it's a great view nonetheless. The **Reef Dancer** runs $33–45 for 60- and 90-minute tours, while the **Sea View** is $44 but includes snorkel time in its two-hour run. All tours leave from Lahaina Harbor.

FISHING

Fishing Charters
The fishing around Maui ranges from very good to excellent. A sizable fleet of charter boats with skilled captains and tested crews is ready, willing, and competent to take you out. Most are berthed at Lahaina Harbor while others are at Ma'alaea Harbor.

Some of the best boats at Ma'alaea Harbor include: *Carol Ann,* 808/877-2181; *No Ka Oi III* and *Maka Kai,* 808/879-4485, run by Ocean Activities Center; and *Makoa Kai,* 808/875-2251, captained by Dave Ventura, who does only private fishing charters. In Lahaina you can't go wrong with the *Judy Ann,* 808/667-6672; **Aerial Sportfishing Charters,** 808/667-9089; *The Finest Kind* and *Reel Hooker,* 808/661-0338; or *Lucky Strike II,* 808/661-4606.

CAMPING AND HIKING

Maui offers limited camping, and most of it is easily accessible. Camping facilities sit along the coast and amid the scenic forest areas of Haleakala. They range in amenities from housekeeping cabins to primitive hike-in sites. All require camping permits—inexpensive for the county and state parks, free for the national park. Camping permits can be obtained by walk-in application to the appropriate office or by writing. Although there is usually no problem obtaining sites, when writing, request reservations well in advance, allowing a minimum of one month for letters to go back and forth.

Haleakala National Park
Camping at Haleakala National Park is free, but there is an automobile entrance fee of $10, $5 for bikers and hikers. Permits are not needed to camp at Hosmer Grove, just a short drive from park headquarters, or at Kipahulu Campground along the coastal road 10 miles south of Hana. Camping is on a first-come, first-served basis, and there's an official three-day stay limit, but it's a loose count, especially at Kipahulu, which is almost always empty. The case is much different at the campsites inside Haleakala Crater proper. On the crater's floor are two primitive

MAUI

MAUI CAMPGROUNDS

WAI'ANAPANAPA

Hana

360

KIPAHULU

Wailua

Nahiku

Kipahulu

Ke'anae

YMCA CAMP
KE'ANAE

Kaupo

HALEAKALA PALIKU

HOSMER
GROVE HOUA NATIONAL

378 KAPALAOA PARK

Pu'u Ula'ula
(10,023 ft.)

31

Ulumalu

Makawao

Olinda

POLIPOLI
SPRING

360

365

398 390 Ha'iku Kula 377

36

Pa'ia Half'imaile Pukalani

Waiakoa

Keokea

Ulupalakua
Ranch

37

Pu'unene 370

KANAHANA

KAHULUI

311

Kihei

Wailea

Makena

Molokini Island

Waiehu 380

Waikapu

Wai'

Wailuku 30

Kahakuloa 340 320 Ma'alaea

Waihe'e

Pu'u Kukui
(5,788 ft.)

30

Kapalua Lahaina

WINDMILL BEACH

Kahana

Olowalu

Honokowai CAMP PECUSA

Ka'anapali

30

Kaho'olawe
Island

'Alenuihaha Channel

'Alalakeiki Channel

'Au'au Channel

Pailolo Channel

5 mi

5 km

0

tenting campsites, one at Paliku on the east side and the other at Holua on the northwest corner. For these you'll need a wilderness permit from park headquarters, picked up on the first morning of your trip. Because of ecological considerations, only 25 campers per night can stay at each site, and a three-night, four-day per month maximum stay is strictly enforced, with tenting allowed at any one site for only two consecutive nights. However, because of the strenuous hike involved, campsites are open most of the time. You must be totally self-sufficient and equipped for cold-weather camping to be comfortable at these two sites.

Also, Paliku, Holua, and another site at Kapalaoa on the south edge of the basin offer cabins. Fully self-contained with stoves, water, and nearby pit toilets, they can handle a maximum of 12 campers each. Bunks are provided, but you must have your own warm bedding. The same maximum-stay limits apply as in the campgrounds. Stays at these cabins are at a premium—they're popular with visitors and residents alike. Reservations must be made at least two months in advance by mail using only a special cabin reservation request form. A lottery of the applicants chosen for sites keeps it fair for all. These cabins are geared toward groups, with rates of $40 for 1–6 people or $80 for up to the limit of 12. To have a chance at getting a cabin, write well in advance for complete information to: Haleakala National Park, P.O. Box 369, Makawao, HI 96768, or call 808/572-4400 or 808/572-9306 for a recorded message.

State Parks

Of the eight state parks on Maui, two have overnight camping. Polipoli Spring State Recreation Area and Wai'anapanapa offer free tenting, and housekeeping cabins are available; reservations necessary. Permits are required at each, and RVs technically are not allowed. Day use is free and open to everyone.

The dozen housekeeping cabins at Wai'anapanapa have a maximum capacity of six and have all necessary amenities, while the one at Polipoli Spring (gas stove, no electricity) can handle up to 10 persons. As with camping, permits are required with the same five-day maximum stay (the cabin at Polipoli Spring is closed on Tuesday night). Reservations are

Haleakala crater

ROBERT NILSEN

absolutely necessary, especially at Wai'anapanapa, and a 50 percent deposit at time of confirmation is required. There's a three-day cancellation requirement for refunds, and payment is to be made in cash, by money order, certified check, or personal check, the latter only if it's received 30 days before arrival so that cashing procedures are possible. The balance is due on arrival. Cabins are $45 per night for up to four people, and $5 for each additional person up to the limit. These are completely furnished down to the utensils, with heaters for cold weather and private baths.

Usually, tent camping permits are no problem to secure on the day you arrive, but reserving ensures you a space and alleviates anxiety. Permits are available from the Maui Division of State Parks, 54 S. High St., Room 101, Wailuku, HI 96793, 808/984-8109. Office hours are Mon.–Fri. 8 A.M.–4 P.M. This office also issues permits for camping at Pala'au State Park on Moloka'i.

County Parks

Maui has 16 county parks. Only Kanaha Beach Park in Kahului has overnight camping, but it's closed every other Tuesday, Wednesday, and Thursday for maintenance. Camping fees are quite reasonable at $3 per night per adult, 50 cents for children, with no more than three consecutive nights at the park. To get a permit and pay your fees for use of a county beach park, either write in advance or visit the permit issuing offices Mon.–Fri. 8 A.M.–5 P.M.: Dept. of Parks and Recreation, Permit Office, 1580-C Ka'ahumanu Ave. (in the War Memorial Gym) Wailuku, HI 96793, 808/270-7389.

Private Campgrounds

YMCA Camp Keanae is perhaps the best known private campground on the island, and it's a beauty. It lies on the rugged north shore, halfway along the Hana Highway. This camp offers bunkhouses (you must provide your own bedding), tenting space, bathrooms with showers, and a gymnasium. Tents can be pitched on the broad grassy lawn. Bring your own cooking gear. The dining room and kitchen are open for large group use only. Check-in is 3–9 P.M. A fee of $15 per person or $30 per family is charged, with a three-day maximum stay. Y members get reduced rates. All accommodations are by reservation only. For information and reservations, call the camp at 808/248-8355, or contact the Maui Family YMCA office in Kahului at 808/242-9007, email: ymcacampKeanae@aol.com.

Camp Pecusa is about one-quarter mile east of Olowalu, along the coast east of Lahaina. Owned and operated by the Episcopalian Church of Hawaii, this camp often fills with groups staying in the cabins during the summer. Tent space is open any time of the year for public use. A fee of $5 is charged per person per night. No reservations are taken, but it's best to call to see if space is available, 808/661-4303.

Camping is also permitted at **Windmill Beach,** just north of Honolua Bay on the northwest coast, on land owned by Maui Land and Pineapple Company. This is primitive camping—there are *no* facilities. No reservations are necessary, but a permit is. Camping permits are issued by the company office at 4900 Honoapi'ilani Hwy. (across the highway from Napili Plaza), Mon.–Fri. 7 A.M.–3:30 P.M. Fees

are $5 per party with three nights maximum. For information, call 808/669-6201.

Hiking

The hiking on Maui is excellent. Most times you have the trails to yourself, and the hikes range from a family saunter to a strenuous trek. There is no access problem on the more-established routes, but for others you'll need special permission from the landowners. However, many public access trails skirt the coast and penetrate deep into the interior.

Perhaps the most adventurous hiking on Maui is along the 27 miles of trails within Haleakala National Park. This is all high-elevation hiking with virtually no shade cover or water available, so you must be well prepared. Two trails start at different locations along Haleakala Highway and drop into the crater basin, traversing it to its far end. Several secondary trails connect these two main trails, while a third heads out and over the Kaupo Gap to descend the mountain to the south.

Not all hiking on the island requires such preparation or endurance. The Polipoli Spring area offers many miles of trails much lower in elevation and through sheltered forests, yet they give you great views over the countryside. There are also short hikes at 'Iao Needle near Wailuku and longer hikes up the Waihe'e Stream and Waihe'e Ridge, both north of Wailuku. Longer, drier, and more exhausting is the Lahaina Pali Trail, which cuts across the mountain ridge from Ma'alaea to the coast road heading toward Lahaina.

Coastal trails are also an option, and the easiest to approach are sections of the old King's Highway at Wai'anapanapa State Park. Another section of this ancient paved trail can be accessed from the end of the road at La Pérouse Bay.

Tour Companies

Hike Maui, P.O. Box 330969, Kahului, HI 96733, 808/879-5270, fax 808/893-2515, website: www.hikemaui.com, email: hikemaui@hikemaui.com, as its name implies, offers walking tours to Maui's best scenic areas accompanied by Ken Schmitt, a professional nature guide, or one of his fine staff. Ken has dedicated years to hiking Maui and has accumulated an unbelievable amount of knowledge about this awesome island. He's proficient in Maui archaeology, botany, geology, anthropology, zoology, history, oceanography, and ancient Hawaiian cosmology, and the hikes are actually workshops in Maui's natural history. Ken has expanded his operation to include a small hand-picked staff of assistants, each trained in the sciences, with the soul of an adventurer and the heart of an environmentalist. The hikes require a minimum of four people and are limited to eight. All special equipment is provided, but you are requested to wear comfortable walking/hiking shoes. Gourmet lunches and fruits are included. These hikes take in sights from Hana to West Maui, the coast, forest, and crater summit of Haleakala, and range from the moderate to the hardy ability level. Good physical conditioning is essential. Half-day hikes last about five hours, and all-day hikes go for eight hours or more. The rates vary from $85 ($65 for children) to $135 ($110 for children). A day with Ken Schmitt or one of his dedicated guides is a classic outdoor experience. You'll be in the hands of experts. Don't miss it!

Mango Mitch Ecotours, P.O. Box 2511, Wailuku, HI 96793, 808/873-1848 or 800/552-6541, website: www.mauigateway.com/~mangos, email: mangos@mauigateway.com, is another well-established company that offers small groups customized half-day, full-day, and overnight hikes; kayak trips; 4WD adventures; and multiple-day expeditions to other islands. Half-day hikes and snorkel trips run $50–60; the full-day Hana-area hike and swim is $90. An overnight in Haleakala Crater runs $120. Call for info on other options and multiday trips. For Maui tours, refreshments and some gear are provided; all meals and equipment are provided on the overnight tours. Aside from the hiking experience itself, Mango Mitch imparts knowledge about Hawaii's natural history and culture to all his guests.

Maui Hiking Safaris, P.O. Box 11198, Lahaina, HI 96761, 808/573-0168 or 888/445-3963, fax 808/572-3037, website: www.maui.net/~mhs, email: mhs@maui.net, also offers organized group hikes for $49 a half day or $89 a full day, all gear, snacks, and beverages provided. Various hikes are offered through valleys and forests, to waterfalls and up along ridges, and each hike is narrated with special attention to history and

botany. Hikes generally are 4–8 miles in length, and groups go with no more than six people. Randy Weaver leads the tours.

Paths in Paradise, P.O. Box 667, Makawao, HI 96768, 808/573-0094, fax 808/573-1484, website: www.maui.net/~corvusco, email: corvusco@maui.net, offers various hikes, easy to strenuous, from half day to full day, most on Haleakala and its slope, with an emphasis on natural history and birds. Fees run $80–125 with discounts for children. All food and necessary gear are provided. Hikes are led by Renate Gassmann-Duvall, Ph.D.; tours in German are available.

Latitudes & Attitudes, 180 Dickenson St., Lahaina, HI 96761, 808/661-7720 or 877/661-7720, website: www.ecomaui.com, offers hikes on West Maui only. Usually 4–6 hours in length, covering 2–6 miles, these hikes take you to a private arboretum tucked up the mountainside, into a valley used by ancient Hawaiians, or through the thick jungle to a waterfall. Two of the hikes are moderate in endurance; the other is mildly strenuous. Not all hikes run every day. Rates are $70–110 for adults, with a minimum of four needed for a hike to go. All hiking equipment and breakfast and/or lunch are provided, and there is hotel pickup in the Kapalua and Ka'anapali area.

For hikes at the top end of Maui near Kahakuloa and to the bottom side along the old King's Trail below Makena, contact **Island Style Adventures,** 808/276-5976. You have several hike options with a local guide that run $95–110 per person.

HORSEBACK RIDING

Those who love sightseeing from the back of a horse are in for a big treat on Maui. Stables dot the island, so you have a choice of terrain for your trail ride: a breathtaking ride through Haleakala Crater, across rangeland, or into the rainforest. No riding is allowed on the beach. Choose the stable by area or type of ride offered. Unfortunately, none of this comes cheap, but you won't be disappointed by either the quality of trail hand or scenery. It's advisable to wear jeans (jogging suit bottoms will do) and a pair of closed-toe shoes. Sunscreen and a hat are also recommended on most rides. All stables have age and weight restrictions, so be sure to check with them directly for all details.

You'll have your choice of rides at **Ironwood Ranch:** sunset, mountain, pineapple field, or extended rides for experienced riders. The West Maui Journey, for all skill levels, costs $75 for 90 minutes and runs through the foothills of the mountains. Also for all riders are the two-hour sunset ride for $100 and a two-hour Picnic in Paradise ride that also takes you on a short hike through a bamboo forest for $135. For the advanced rider, the Ironwood Odyssey takes you up the mountain for $125. No one over 220 pounds please. Horses are matched to the rider's experience level and all rides are escorted. Ironwood Ranch, 808/669-4991, is at mile marker 29 along Route 30 above Napili. All rides are conducted on private ranch land, so meet at the pickup point across the highway from Napili Plaza.

Makena Stables, 808/879-0244, website: www.makenastables.com, is at the end of the highway at the edge of La Pérouse Bay; owners Helaine and Pat Borge will take you on a two-hour introductory ride through low-elevation rangeland, lava flows, and along the mountain trails of Ulupalakua Ranch; on three-hour morning or sunset rides; or on a five- to six-hour bay and lunch ride. Rides range $110–175, and only one ride goes a day. Riders must be at least 13 years old and weigh no more than 205 pounds.

Pony Express Tours offers trail rides into Haleakala Crater—full day $175, partial day $150, lunch provided. One- and two-hour rides ($45–85) are also offered across Haleakala Ranch land at the 4,000-foot elevation. Riders must be at least 10 years old, under 65, and not more than 235 pounds. Contact Pony Express Tours, P.O. Box 535, Kula, HI 96790, 808/667-2200, website: www.maui.net/~ponex.

Thompson Ranch Riding Stables, Thompson Rd., Kula, HI 96790, 808/878-1910, a family-operated stable that will even mount up children under 10, guides you over the lower slopes of Haleakala on one of Maui's oldest cattle ranches. At 3,700 feet, just outside of Keokea, rides go downhill from there. A 90-minute ride runs $50, while the two-hour ride is $60.

Adventures on Horseback, P.O. Box 1419, Makawao, HI 96768, 808/242-7445, website: www.mauihorses.com, offers waterfall rides

along the north coast over lands of a private estate in Ha'iku for $175. Rides go with a maximum of six riders, who must be at least 16 years old and five feet tall, and not over 225 pounds. Bring your own swimming suit and towel. A full-day "horse whisperer" program is also offered for $225.

Hotel guests are given priority for use of the horses at the **Hana Ranch Stables,** but you can call ahead to arrange a trail ride on this truly magnificent end of the island. The one-hour easy guided rides, two in the morning and one in the afternoon, go either along the coast or into the upper pastureland. Cost is $35 per person; riders must be seven years old. Private rides are given after 3 P.M. for $70 per person. For information, call 808/248-8811.

In Kipahulu you'll find **Oheo Stables,** 808/667-2222. Two rides (10:30 and 11:30 A.M.) are given every day, both three hours on the trail, and the destination is the highland above Makahiku and Waimoku Falls in Haleakala National Park. Only six riders maximum per ride; they must be 12 years old and not more than 225 pounds. Both rides include a continental breakfast, snacks, and drinks, while the later ride also includes lunch. The early ride is $119, the later ride $139.

Mendes Ranch and Trail Rides, 808/871-5222, website: www.maui.net/~mendes, offers two rides, twice daily over a small working ranch on the rugged north coast of Maui; $85 and $130 per person. Riders must be at least 11 years old and no more than 250 pounds. You'll have a look at the shoreline, pastureland, lush valleys, and waterfalls, and a real *paniolo* barbecue picnic is provided on the longer rides. This is a local experience led by real cowboys. Mendes Ranch is just past mile marker 6 on Route 330 north of Wailuku.

Charley's Trailride and Pack Trips takes you on overnight camping rides to Haleakala, supplying all meals—in on Wednesday out on Thursday, or in on Saturday and out on Sunday. Contact Charles Aki, c/o Kaupo Store, Hana, HI 96713, 808/248-8209 (call before 10 A.M. or in the evening); rates on rides of more than two people are $250 per person per night, which includes food and camping equipment; $225 per night without food included. For only two people, the rate is $300 per person per day. Meet at Charley's residence in Kaupo for a 9

A.M. departure; early reservations are required, along with a $75 deposit well in advance. A hat, warm clothing, rain ponchos, and boots are recommended for all rides.

Maui Mule Ride, 808/244-6853 or 808/878-1743, offers two-, five-, and six-hour rides into Haleakala Crater on these sure-footed beasts of burden, leaving from the visitors center parking lot near the top. Rates are $95, $155, and $190 per person, respectively. Long pants, shoes, and a jacket are a must, and it's best to bring sunglasses and a hat. A picnic lunch is provided on the longer rides, refreshments on all.

BICYCLING

Bicycle enthusiasts should be thrilled with Maui, but the few flaws might flatten your spirits as well as your tires. The countryside is great, the weather is perfect, but the roads are heavily trafficked and the most interesting ones are narrow and have bad shoulders. Pedaling to Hana will give you an up-close personal experience, but for bicycle safety this road is one of the worst. Haleakala is stupendous, but with a rise of more than 10,000 feet in less than 40 miles it is considered one of the most grueling rides in the world. And a paved bike path runs from Lahaina to Ka'anapali that's tame enough for everyone. Cycling on Maui as your primary means of transportation is not for the neophyte; because of safety considerations and the tough rides, only experienced riders should consider it.

Bicycle Rentals
Some bicycle rental shops will tell you that the Park Service does not allow you to take your bike up to Haleakala National Park—horse pucky! You *cannot* ride the bike on the hiking paths, but going up the road (40 miles uphill) is okay if you have the steam. You are given this misinformation because the bike rental shops don't want the wear and tear on their bikes, but for the prices they charge, they shouldn't squawk. For off-road riding, try the trails in Kula Forest Reserve near Polipoli Spring State Recreation Area.

South Maui Bicycles, 1993 S. Kihei Rd., 808/874-0068, open daily 10 A.M.–6 P.M., Sunday until 2 P.M., is a rental and bike repair shop that boasts the largest fleet on Maui from which to

choose. Rates are: street bikes $18 per day, $80 per week; mountain bikes $30 a day or $110 a week. Frank Hackett, the shop owner, will take time to give you tips including routes and the best times to travel.

West Maui Cycles, in Lahaina at 840 Waine'e St., 808/661-9005, is a full-service bike sale and rental store that also carries other sporting equipment. The store has mostly Cannondale, GT, and Schwinn bikes. Standard road bike rates run from $20 a day to $80 a week; 25 percent more for a high-end bike. Tandems run $35–50 a day, cruisers $10 a day or $50 a week, and electric bikes $25 a day. Mountain bikes vary from $20 a day to $200 a week, depending on suspension.

Cruisers can also be rented in Lahaina from **Duke's Surf and Rental,** across from Kamehameha School along Front Street, for $10 a day or $70 a week.

In Kahului, **The Island Biker,** 415 Dairy Rd., 808/877-7744, rents mostly mountain bikes along with its sales and repair services. They go for $25 a day, $85 a week, or $250 a month. Open Mon.–Sat. 9 A.M.–6 P.M. Also try **Extreme Sports Maui,** 808/871-7954, which has mountain bikes for $29 a day, $162 a week, or $405 a month.

For other bike rentals, try **A & B Rental and Sales,** in Honokowai at 3481 Lower Honoapi'ilani Rd., 808/669-0027, open daily 9 A.M.–5 P.M., which rents basic mountain bikes at $15 for 24 hours or $60 per week. Aside from running bike tours, **Haleakala Bike Company,** 808/572-2200, in Ha'iku also rents mountain bikes, all equipment, and a rack if you need one for $29 the first day, $20 after that, or $110 a week. Upgraded suspension increases the cost.

Haleakala Bicycle Tours
An adventure on Maui that's become famous is riding a specially equipped bike from the summit of Mt. Haleakala for 40 miles to the bottom at Pa'ia. These bikes are mountain bikes or modified cruisers with padded seats, wide tires, and heavy-duty drum brakes, front and back. Typically, these tours take about eight hours with about three hours on the bike. Most offer a shuttle pickup and drop-off at your hotel. For tours that go to the top of the mountain for sunrise, expect to get picked up about 3 A.M.—get to bed early! Every bike rider on tours that ride through the national park must wear a full motorcycle

helmet. Other tours that start outside the park will provide you with a regular bicycle helmet. Warm, layered clothing is a must, long pants and closed toe shoes recommended. Most bike companies have some guidelines—no pregnant women, minimum age of 12, must be at least five feet tall—but each company's requirements may be slightly different, so check. These safety requirements are not without reason. Although comparatively safe, a few deaths have occurred on these bike trips over the years.

A pioneer in this field is **Maui Downhill**, 199 Dairy Rd., Kahului, 808/871-2155 or 800/535-BIKE, website: www.mauidownhill.net. Included in the bike ride for $115 you get two meals (continental breakfast, brunch, or a gourmet picnic lunch), and a windbreaker, gloves, and helmet to use. To drench yourself in the beauty of a Haleakala sunrise, you have to pay your dues. You arrive at the base yard in Kahului at about 3:30 A.M. after being picked up at your condo by the courtesy van. Here, you'll muster with other bleary-eyed but hopeful adventurers and munch donuts and coffee, which at this time of the morning is more like a transfusion. Up the mountain, in the van, through the chilly night air takes about 90 minutes, with singing and storytelling along the way. Once atop, find your spot for the *best* natural light show in the world: the sun goes wild with colors as it paints the sky and drips into Haleakala Crater. This is your first reward. Next comes your bicycle environmental cruise down the mountain with vistas and thrills every inch of the way, with stops for sightseeing, food, and to let cars pass. For the not-so-early risers, other mountain descent tours are available for $60–125.

Maui Mountain Cruisers of Makawao, 808/871-6014 or 800/232-6284; **Mountain Riders,** 808/242-9739 or 800/706-7700; **Cruiser Phil's Volcano Rides,** 808/893-2332 or 877/764-2453; and **Emerald Island Bicycle Rides,** 808/573-1278 or 800/565-6615, are the other major touring companies, offering pretty much the same guided bike services at competitive rates.

A twist to this convoy guided bike tour is offered by **Haleakala Bike Company,** 808/572-2200, website: www.bikemaui.com, in Ha'iku. With this outfit, you meet at the bike store and get fitted with your bike and given all necessary equipment. For the sunrise tours, the van leaves at about 4:15 A.M. and brings you to the top of the mountain in the park for your sunrise experience. When the bike riders start down the mountain, the company van stays with them until they are comfortable with the bikes and route and then lets them go the rest of the way by themselves, taking their time or zipping down the hill as they like, stopping when they want and eating where they desire. The only requirement is to return by about 4 P.M. It's bike freedom. Later in the morning, another drop-off goes to the crater rim. These rides are $69 and $59. Later drop-offs at the park entrance go for $49.

Another company that does a go-at-your-own-pace tour is **Upcountry Cycles,** 808/573-2888 or 800/373-1678, website: www.maui.net/~wayner.

Aloha Bicycle Tours, 808/249-0911, website: www.maui.net/~bikemaui, does local style trips through Upcountry along the lower slopes of the mountain.

Chris's Bike Adventures, 808/871-2453, offers a variation on the theme, taking you on a mountain bike adventure down Haleakala, including a tour of the Tedeschi Winery and a walk along the lava fields around La Pérouse Bay. Or you can take an afternoon ride, winding up at the winery, where you can soothe your beaten bottom with a glass of *vino.* A tough off-road option takes you to the backside of the mountain.

Bicycle Touring

For long-distance bicycle touring, contact one of the following. The owners and tour leaders of **Island Bicycle Adventures,** 569 Kapahulu Ave., Honolulu, HI 96815, 808/734-0700 or 800/233-2226, are intimately familiar with bicycle touring and are members of the Hawaii Bicycling League. They offer tours to Maui, the Big Island, and Kaua'i. **Chris' Adventures,** P.O. Box 869, Kula, HI 96790, 808/871-2453, runs three-day "inn-to-inn" tours on Maui. Call for rates.

For those who like to strike out on their own, two routes are recommended. One takes you for a 50-mile loop from Wailuku (or Lahaina) up the Ka'anapali Coast and around the head of Maui back to Wailuku. The road starts out in good repair, but the traffic will be heavy until you pass Kapalua. Here the road begins to wind along the north coast. Since this road has been paved, traffic around the north end has picked up, so the road will not be just yours anymore. Around the north end there is no place to get service. Go prepared, and be on the lookout for cars.

The second route is from Kahului up to Kula or Pukalani via Pulehu Road and back down the mountainside via Pa'ia, Ha'iku, or Ulumalu, through irrigated cane fields, the cool Upcountry region, and the lush, sculpted north slope of Haleakala.

GOLF

Maui has 10 golf courses with 16 links; all but one have 18 holes. These range from modest municipal courses to world-class private clubs. Some are along the coast, while others back against the mountain with sweeping views of the lowlands. The high-class resort areas of Ka'anapali, Kapalua, and Wailea are built around golf courses.

TENNIS

There are many tennis courts on Maui, and plenty of them are free. County courts are under the control of the Department of Parks and Recreation, which maintains a combination of lighted and unlit courts around the island. No

MAUI TENNIS COURTS

COUNTY COURTS

Under jurisdiction of the Department of Parks and Recreation, 808/270-7230. Courts listed are in or near visitor areas and open to the public.

TOWN	LOCATION	NO. OF COURTS	LIGHTED
Hali'imaile	Hali'imaile Park	1	Yes
Hana	Hana Ball Park	2	Yes
Kahului	Kahului Community Center	2	Yes
Kihei	Kalami Park	4	Yes
	Waipu'ilani Park	6	Yes
Lahaina	Lahaina Civic Center	5	Yes
	Malu'ulu O Lele Park	4	Yes
Makawao	Eddie Tam Center	2	Yes
Pukalani	Pukalani Park	2	Yes
Wailuku	Wailuku War Memorial Complex	4	Yes
	Wells Park	7	Yes

HOTEL AND PRIVATE COURTS OPEN TO THE PUBLIC

TOWN	LOCATION	TEL. (808)	FEES	NO. OF COURTS	LIGHTED
Ka'anapali	Hyatt Tennis Center	661-1234	$20	6	Yes
	Maui Marriott Tennis Club	661-6200	10	5	No
	Royal Lahaina Tennis Ranch	661-3611	10	10	6
	Sheraton Maui Tennis Club	662-8208	10	3	Yes
Kapalua	Kapalua Tennis Center	665-0112	12	10	5
	Kapalua Tennis Garden	669-5677	10	10	4
Makena	Makena Tennis Club	879-8777	12	6	2
Napili Bay	Napili Kai Beach Resort	669-6271	10	2	No
Wailea	Wailea Tennis Club	879-1958	25	11	3

MAUI

MAUI GOLF COURSES

COURSE	PAR	YARDS	FEES	CART	CLUBS
The Dunes at Maui Lani Kahului, HI 96732 808/873-0422	$72	6,413	$75	incl.	$25
Elleair Maui Golf Club Kihei, HI 96753 808/874-0777	71	6,404	$59	Incl.	$30
Kaanapali Golf Courses Kaanapali, HI 96761 808/661-3691					
North Course	71	6,136	$140	Incl.	$30
South Course	71	6,067	$132	Incl.	$30
Kapalua Golf Club Kapalua, HI 96791 808/669-8044					
Bay Course	72	6,051	$175	Incl.	$35
Village Course	71	6,001	$175	Incl.	$35
Plantation Course	73	6,547	$200	Incl.	$35
Makena Golf Courses Makena, HI 96753 808/879-3344					
North Course	72	6,914	$140	Incl.	$35
South Course	72	7,017	$140	Incl.	$35
Maui Country Club Sprecklesville, HI 96779 808/877-7270 (Monday only for visitors)	72	6,339	$65 $38 (9 holes)	Incl.	$10
Pukalani Country Club Pukalani, HI 96768 808/572-1314	72	6,494	$50	Incl.	$20
Sandalwood Golf Course Wailuku, HI 96793 808/242-4653	72	6,469	$75	Incl.	$35
Waiehu Municipal Golf Course Wailuku, HI 96793 808/243-7400	72	6,330	$26 (weekdays) $30 (weekends)	$8	$15 (18 holes) $10 (9 holes)
Wailea Golf Club Wailea, HI 96753 808/875-5155, 875-5111					
Blue Course	72	6,758	$135	Incl.	$35
Gold Course	72	6,653	$145	Incl.	$35
Emerald Course	72	6,407	$145	Incl.	$35

MAUI

MAUI GOLF COURSES

© SANDRA E. BISIGNANI TRUST AND AVALON TRAVEL PUBLISHING, INC.

MAUI

fees are charged for these public courts, but play is on a first-come, first-served basis and limited to 45 minutes if there are people waiting. Weekends are often fairly busy, but it's relatively easy to get a court on weekdays. Court rules apply and only soft-sole shoes are allowed. Some resort and private courts are open to the public for a fee, while others restrict play to members and guests only. Most private courts have a plexi-pave or similar surface. Although each facility differs, private clubs usually have pro shops, offer equipment rental, and arrange clinics and lessons. Court play is regulated according to accepted rules, and proper attire is required, including proper shoes. The accompanying chart is a partial listing of what's available.

HUNTING

Maui's game includes wild pigs and feral goats; hunted birds are pheasant, partridge, francolin, quail, dove, and wild turkey. There are several public hunting sections around the island, and a license is required. For full information, write the Department of Land and Natural Resources, Division of Forestry and Wildlife Office, 54 S. High St., Wailuku, HI 96793, 808/984-8100.

SPORTING CLAYS

An outgrowth of hunting, sporting clays is a sport that helps develop and maintain your hand-eye coordination. Shooting is done from different stations around a course, and the object is to hit a small round clay disk. Different from trap or skeet shooting, sporting clays relies upon moving targets that mimic different animals and birds, hopping along the ground as if a rabbit, springing off the ground like a teal, or flying high like a pheasant. Hawaii has about half a dozen sporting clay grounds; two are on Maui and one is on Lana'i. Each is designed differently, but all provide the same basic service. Although options are available for the beginner to the advanced shooter, a typical round with a 20 gauge shotgun would take about an hour and cost around $100. Open daily 8:30 A.M.–dusk, **Papaka Sporting Clays,** 808/879-5649, is in Makena. Call for reservations and directions. **West-**

side Sporting Clays, 808/669-7468, is 3.3 miles beyond Office Rd. in Kapalua. Reservations recommended.

LAND TOURS

Bus and Van Tours

It's easy to book tours to Maui's famous areas, such as Lahaina, Hana, 'Iao Valley, and Haleakala. Normally they're run on either half- or full-day schedules (Hana is always a full day) and range anywhere from $40 to $70 with hotel pickup included. Big bus tours are run by **Roberts Hawaii,** 800/831-5541, website: www.robertshawaii.com, and they're quite antiseptic—you sit behind tinted glass in an air-conditioned bus. Other companies with smaller tour buses and vans also hit the high points but have specialty tours. Try **Ekahi Tours,** 808/877-9775 or 888/292-2422, website: www.ekahi.com; **Polynesian Adventure Tours,** 808/877-4242 or 800/622-3011, website: www.polyad.com; and **Akina Aloha Tours,** 808/879-2828. **Valley Isle Excursions,** 808/661-8687, offers a daily Hana trip with a picnic provided for $99 per adult, $89 seniors, $79 kids.

Temptation Tours, 808/887-8888 or 800/817-1234, website: www.temptationtours.net, operates the ultimate in luxury van tours for the discriminating traveler. The deluxe vans, more like limousines, seat each of the eight passengers in a comfortable captain's chair for trips to Hana and Haleakala. This outfit runs more than a half dozen tours, all out to Hana or up to Haleakala, many combined with other activities. One Hana tour combines with a great cave tour, while a second lets you fly by helicopter one-way. The Haleakala trips take you up for sunrise or let you experience a day on the mountain. Rates run $124–219.

Of course, if you really want to go in style on your own private tour to Hana or Haleakala, try stretch limousine tours by **Star Maui Limousine,** 808/875-6900, or **Town and Country Limousine,** 808/572-3400. These limo trips run around $170 per person, kids half that, and include hotel pickup, continental breakfast, lunch in Hana, full bar service, and stops and major sites on the way.

Motorcycle Tour

A twist on the tour business is offered by **Quality Motorcycle Tours**, P.O. Box 728, Wailuku, HI 96793, 808/242-1015, website: www.ride-maui .com, email: tours@ride-maui.com, also known as Ride Maui, which takes you down the highway on two wheels. This company offers various day-long tours or can customize one for you. One- and two-day overnight trips are also an option. The day starts about 8 A.M. and goes until about 6 P.M. Day rides are $200 single and $150 double, more for overnights. Food, drinks, helmets, and all equipment are provided. All bikes are Hondas. You must have a motorcycle validation on your license and be at least 25 years old. A major credit card is required for reservations; book two weeks in advance.

Jeep Tours

Maui Jeep Adventures, 808/876-1177, website: www.mauijeepadventures.com, has opened tours across the uplands and lowlands of the Ulupalakua Ranch. A *mauka* tour takes you up on the hillsides of this working cattle ranch, through pastures and past lava caves to panoramic scenes of the island. The *makai* tour takes you down to the water's edge to ancient Hawaiian settlements and tide pools. Tours are conducted in seven-passenger jeeps, and all are narrated by those who know the land. Morning and afternoon rides are offered, and each includes a picnic lunch. Rates are $79 adults, $49 kids, or private tours can be accommodated at $125 an hour with a minimum of three hours.

Personal Guided Tours

For a personalized tour where a guide drives your rental car and takes you to "local" places, try the following. **Guides of Maui**, 808/877-4060 or 800/231-8022, website: www.guides-ofmaui.com, offers a Hana tour, circle-island tour, or Hana and Haleakala combination tour. Trips start at 8 A.M. and return late afternoon; no tours on Saturday. Rates are per car, $235 with your rental car or $340, with hotel pickup, if the guide provides the car. A similar service is provided by **Hapa Papa's Tours**, 808/871-7608, where a trip to Hana, 'Iao Valley and Maui's backside, or other routes runs $39–99 per person depending on the tours.

Tape Tours

For those who desire a go-at-your-own pace alternative to van tours, yet want the convenience of an escort, **Best of Maui Cassette Tours** may be for you. Rent a quality tape or CD describing the Hana Highway and what to see and do along the way. This rental ($25) comes with a small pamphlet of sights, history, and legends; a route map; a video; and coupons. Pick up your cassettes 6 A.M.–1 P.M.; reservations are appreciated. Call Best of Maui at 808/871-1555 or stop by the office at 333 Dairy Rd., Kahului. You can also get one of these tapes at **Woo-wee Maui's Cafe** next door, where they will also provide you with a boxed lunch for the road for $6.95.

Offering roughly the same service at a similar price is **Hana Cassette Guide**, 808/572-0550. Pick up your tape and all the extras at the booth at the Shell gas station along Dairy Road in Kahului, or inside the station after the booth closes.

Some condos and other accommodations, as well as some other activities, have these tapes for use by their guests for free.

Astronomy Tour

Star Party, 808/281-0949 or 877/648-3759, website: www.starparty.net, offers a very unique tour of the heavens. A 15-passenger van takes small groups up the mountain for a sunset view and a night of gazing at the starts—weather permitting. The tour leaves at 2 P.M. and returns around 10 P.M.; $125 per person. Aside from the up-close look at stars, planets, and the galaxies through a portable computer-driven telescope, Star Party includes a picnic meal, hot drinks, and warm jackets to use. As you are above much of the earth's atmosphere, viewing can be tremendous. Those who have trouble with high altitude and lower levels of oxygen should not consider joining this tour. Hotel pickup is provided.

For a view of the heavens from closer to home, try **Maui Astronomy Tours**, 808/276-3407. This private observatory in Kihei offers a peek at the night sky, 8–10 P.M. every evening, through three different telescopes. Cost is $20.

The Sugar Cane Train Tour

The old steam engine puffs along from Lahaina to Pu'ukoli'i depot in Ka'anapali pulling old-style open-air passenger cars through cane fields and the Ka'anapali golf course. The six miles of narrow-gauge track are covered in 25 minutes (each way), and the cost round-trip is $15 adult and $8.50 for children 3–12; one-way fares are $11 and $6.50, respectively. The train runs throughout the day 8:55 A.M.–4:50 P.M. It's very popular so book in advance—more than 400,000 ride the train every year. All rides are narrated and the conductor even sings. It's not just great fun for children; everybody has a good time. All kinds of combination tours with other activities vendors are offered as well; they're tame, touristy, and fun. The price is right. Contact the Lahaina Kaanapali and Pacific Railroad at 808/667-6851 or 800/499-2307, website: www.sugarcanetrain.com.

AIR TOURS

Maui is a spectacular sight from the air. A few small charter airlines, a handful of helicopter companies, and a hang gliding outfit swoop you around the island. These joyrides are literally the highlight of many people's experiences on Maui, but they are expensive.

Helicopter Tours

All the helicopter companies in Hawaii are safe and reputable. Tours are narrated over specially designed earphones, and most have two-way microphones so you can communicate with the pilot. Some offer a video of your helicopter tour of Maui (or a generic tape of highlights) as a souvenir at the end of the flight for an extra $20 or so. Each gives a pre-flight briefing to go over safety regulations and other details. Remember that the seating arrangement in a helicopter is critical to safety. The pre-flight crew is expertly trained to arrange the chopper so that it is balanced. This means that the seating goes strictly according to weight.

Nearly everyone wants to take photographs of their helicopter tour, but most of the newer helicopters are air-conditioned, which means that the windows don't open, so you might experience glare or some distortion. For the best shots, choose a chopper where the windows open or go with the one that flies with its doors off.

On certain flights the craft will touch down for a short interlude, and on some flights a complimentary lunch will be served; most companies can make special arrangements to design a package especially for you. Helicopter rides are particularly attractive because you can sightsee from a perspective not possible from the ground and get close to areas not accessible by foot. There may be a tradeoff, however. Steep turns, quick descents, and unstable pockets of air can cause some riders to get airsick. Chopper companies are competitively priced, with tours of West or East Maui at around $100, with a Hana-Haleakala flight at about $150. Circle-island tours are approximately $200, but the best might be to

Alex Air helicopter

ROBERT NILSEN

include a trip to Moloka'i at approximately $200 to experience the world's tallest sea cliffs along the isolated windward coast. While the most spectacular rides take you over Haleakala Crater or perhaps to the remote West Maui Mountains, where inaccessible gorges lie at your feet, the 45-minute East Maui tour is the most popular. Know, however, that many hikers have a beef with the air tours: after they've spent hours hiking into remote valleys in search of peace and quiet, out of the sky comes the mechanical whir of a chopper to spoil the solitude.

Virtually all flights leave from the heliport at the back side of Kahului Airport—access off Haleakala Highway extension road. Only a handful leave from Kapalua-West Maui Airport. Each company has an office at the Kahului Airport where you check in, pay your money, and receive your pre-flight instructions. A parking lot here is free the first 15 minutes, $1 for 15–30 minutes, $1 each additional hour, maximum of $7 a day.

Alex Air, 808/871-0792 or 888/418-8458, website: www.helitour.com, a small personable company, runs a tight ship. It offers a wide variety of flights on two types of helicopters, ranging from the West Maui special at $69 to the circle-island tour for $195.

Sunshine Helicopter, 808/871-0722 or 800/469-3000, website: www.sunshinehelicopters.com, is another local, family-run outfit that flies the "Black Beauties." The seating is two-by-two, and pilots goes out of their way to give you a great ride over Maui. Aside from the usual tours, this company does charters and combinations with Atlantis Submarine tours.

Air Maui, 808/877-7005, website: www.air-maui.com, seems to be the "little guy," but it tries hard to please. An owner-operated company, Air Maui offers all the standards and can customize a tour for you. A good choice.

Hawaii Helicopter, 808/877-3900 or 800/994-9099 in Hawaii, 800/367-7095 Mainland and Canada, website: www.hawaii-helicopters.com, is a statewide company. Its helicopters have plush interiors for your comfort but may squeeze four people in the back, so the two middle ones don't always get a good view. Most of the helicopters flown by this company have two engines. Standard tours are offered as well as one that starts from Kapalua; one that takes in Maui, Lana'i, and

Moloka'i; and one that incorporates a flight to the Big Island for a look at volcanic activity.

Blue Hawaiian Helicopters, 808/871-8844 or 800/786-2583, website: www.bluehawaiian.com, operates on Maui and the Big Island. It's a company that does lots of advertising, gets a lot of passengers, and has done work for film companies. Offerings include standard flights plus a sunset tour and a combination fly/drive to/from Hana tour with Temptation van tours.

Fixed-Wing Tours

For a Maui joyride out of Kahului Airport, contact **Paragon Air**, 808/244-3356 or 800/248-1231, website: www.maui.net/~wings/index.htm. Paragon offers several different options, like a flight to Moloka'i with a tour of Kalaupapa for $199 or a flight to Moloka'i coupled with the mule ride down to Kalaupapa for $259. Others include a Big Island volcano tour for $499 and a five-island tour for $149. Paragon Air can also be hired for point-to-point charter travel.

An alternative for a Big Island volcano tour, a sunset tour, or private charter is **Maui Air**, 808/877-5500. Maui Air runs the two-hour volcano tour from either Kahului or Kapalua airport at $259 per person. Taking a slightly different route to the Big Island, the sunset tour leaves from Kahului Airport only and is $239 per passenger. Flights are conducted in nine-passenger, air-conditioned twin-engine planes and everyone gets a comfortable window seat with stereo headset for the tour narration.

Paragliding

For motorized hang gliding, contact **Hang Gliding Maui**, 808/572-6557, website: www.hanggglidingmaui.com. These powered flights run $95 for 30 minutes and $165 for an hour. Long tours and instruction can be arranged. Flights leave from the Hana Airport only.

Want to try paragliding off the side of Haleakala? Contact **Proflyght Hawaii Paragliding**, 808/874-5433 or 877/463-5944 website: www.paraglidehawaii.com, which will set you up on a tandem flight with a certified instructor. Depending upon launch site, flights can be 5–10 minutes or up to 40 minutes; rates are $75–275. All necessary equipment is provided, but you should wear warm comfortable clothing and sturdy shoes.

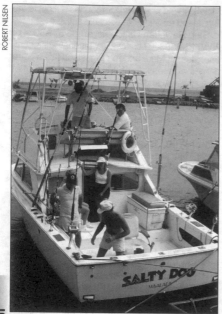

MAUI

the Salty Dog

BOOKING AGENCIES

Ocean Activities Center, 808/879-4370, is one of the biggest agencies for booking any and all activities on Maui. For much of the fun events like snorkeling, scuba diving, whale-watching, sunset cruises, and deep-sea fishing, the center has its own facilities and equipment, which means it not only provides you with an excellent outing but offers very competitive prices. Ocean Activities also books helicopter and land tours and rents and sells boogie boards, snorkel equipment, sailboards, and surfboards. It has sun and surf store/booking agencies in the Kihei-Wailea area at the Kea Lani Hotel, Mana Kai Maui Resort, and Maui Hill Resort, and at the Maui Marriott in Ka'anapali. Prices on all activities are very reasonable, and the service is excellent. If you had

to choose one agency for all your fun needs, this would be a good bet.

Another very reputable outfit with one booking office in Lahaina is **Barefoot's Cashback Tours,** 834 Front St., 808/661-8889 or 888/222-3601, website: www.tombarefoot.com, email: barefoot@maui.net. Barefoot's gives you up to a 10 percent discount on all your activities if you pay by cash or traveler's checks or a 7 percent discount with credit cards. It too can set you up with virtually any activity around the island or throughout the state. Stop in to see what adventure awaits at a reduced rate. Shop here; you'll be glad you did.

Activity Warehouse can provide the same service, often with last-minute reservations, and it also rents some ocean equipment. You can find Activity Warehouse in Lahaina, 578 and 602 Front St., 808/667-4000, and in Kihei, 1279 S. Kihei Rd., 808/875-4000. **Activity World,** 808/667-7777, has more than a dozen booths throughout the island, many at condos and resorts. They're convenient and offer good reductions in prices for all sorts of activities on the island. These are legitimate venders with solid reputations. You will, however, find a horde of other activities desks up and down Front Street and in other locations; you don't have to search for them—they'll find you, especially to make an exhausting high-pressured pitch for time shares! Avoid them—unless you want to listen to the rap in exchange for your reduced ticket price.

One of the easiest ways to book a fishing activity and sightsee at the same time is to walk along the Lahaina Wharf—an information booth here is operated by many of the companies who rent slips at the harbor. Check it out first, and then plan to be there when the tour boats return. Asking the passengers, right on the spot, if they've had a good time is about the best you can do. You can also check out the boats and do some comparative pricing of your own.

For boats and a full range of activities out of quiet Ma'alaea Harbor, contact the **Ma'alaea Activity Center,** 808/242-6982. The center does it all, from helicopters to horseback, but specializes in the boats berthed at Ma'alaea.

SHOPPING

This section provides general information about shopping on Maui; you'll find greater detail in the individual travel chapters. Happy bargain hunting!

SHOPPING CENTERS

Maui's various malls offer many one-stop shopping options. You'll find regularly known department stores as well as small shops featuring island-made goods.

Kahului and Wailuku

Along Ka'ahumanu Avenue, **Kaahumanu Center** is the largest shopping mall on the island, housing everything from Sears, JCPenney, and Liberty House to Sew Special, a tiny store featuring island fabrics. The mall is full-service with apparel and shoe stores, book and music shops, jewelry stores, health, beauty, and specialty shops. Local residents shop here. You can eat at numerous restaurants or enjoy a movie at Kaahumanu Theater.

Down the road is **Maui Mall,** featuring a photo center, Longs for everything from aspirin to film, and restaurants and food outlets. Sandwiched between these two modern facilities is **Kahului Shopping Center,** definitely "down-home" with old-timers sitting around outside. The shops here aren't fancy, but they are authentic, and you can make some offbeat purchases.

The newest and the second largest in town is the **Maui Marketplace Mall** on the south side of Dairy Road, where you can find Sports Authority, Eagle Hardware, OfficeMax, several banks, clothing shops, jewelry stores, and a Borders Books outlet.

The past few years have seen a rapid expansion of mercantile outlets in Kahului. In the triangle by Kahana Pond is **Triangle Square** center, and many of its shops are dedicated to sports. Several small malls line Dairy Road between Hana Highway and Hulilike Street.

Lahaina

You can't beat Lahaina's Front Street for the best, worst, most artistic, and tackiest shopping on Maui. This is where the tourists are, so this is where the shops are . . . shoulder to shoulder. The list is endless, but it includes art studios and galleries, T-shirts galore, scrimshaw, jewelry, silks, boutiques, leathers, souvenir junk, eelskins, and even a permanent tattoo memory of Maui. No wimps allowed! Lahaina also has the best special-interest shopping on Maui in various little shops along Front Street.

The following are the local malls: **The Wharf Cinema Center** on Front Street has a multitude of eating establishments, as well as stores and boutiques and a movie theater in its multilevel shopping facility. Nearly across the street are the **Pioneer Inn Shops,** again with clothing and gift shops, but all on street level. **Lahaina Market Place,** tucked down an alley off Front Street near Lahainaluna Road, features established shops along with open-air stalls. **Lahaina Square Shopping Center, Lahaina Shopping Center,** and **Anchor Square,** all between Route 30 and Front Street, have various shops; they are the most *local* of the Lahaina malls. The **505 Front Street Mall,** is at the south end of Front Street and offers distinctive and quiet shopping away from the frenetic activity.

The **Lahaina Cannery Mall,** on Lahaina's north end, features restaurants, boutiques, specialty shops, fast food, and plenty of bargains. It's the largest mall on West Maui and has some of the best shopping under one roof on the island. The newest mall in town is the open-air **Lahaina Center,** along Front St. at Papalaua Street. Stores include Hilo Hattie, Liberty House, Banana Republic, Wet Seal, Maui Dive Shop, Hard Rock Cafe, and the Front Street Theaters, plus plenty of fine eateries.

Ka'anapali to Kapalua

Whaler's Village, the only mall in Ka'anapali, is set right on the ocean and features a decent self-guided whaling museum. There are eateries, upscale boutiques, art galleries, a film processing center, and a sundries store. It's a great place to stroll, buy, and learn a few things about Maui's past. All the big resorts have shopping arcades. You'll need a suitcase stuffed with money to buy anything there, but it's a blast just walking around the grounds and checking out the big-ticket items.

Along Lower Honoapi'ilani Road, the villages of Honokowai, Kahana, and Napili all have small local shopping malls, mostly for everyday items. Two new and larger malls have opened on Honoapi'ilani Highway, however. At the junction where the old road splits from the newer highway is **Honokowai Marketplace,** with a first-rate restaurant, apparel stores, video shop, and sporting goods store. At **Kahana Gateway Mall** are three of Maui's finest restaurants, apparel shops, a laundromat, and even a sporting goods store. Farther along is **Napili Plaza,** with restaurants, shops, and a food market.

Aside from the swanky arcade at the Ritz-Carlton and **Honolua Store,** which has a mix of clothing, gifts, and deli foods, the only place to shop in Kapalua is **Kapalua Shops,** attached to the Kapalua Bay Hotel. The shops include high-end clothing retailers, an import store, art gallery, gift shop, and one restaurant.

Kihei and Wailea

Azeka Place, Azeka Place II, and **Longs Shopping Center** are all along South Kihei Road in what could be considered the center of Kihei. There's food shopping, clothing, gift, and specialty shops, with a few sporting goods stores, dive shops, and activities centers thrown in. Strung south along Kihei Road, one after another, are **Kukui Mall, Kihei Town Center, Kalama Village Marketplace, Dolphin Shopping Center, Kamaole Beach Center, Rainbow Mall, Kamaole Shopping Center,** and **Kai Nani Kai Village Plaza,** where restaurants, food outlets, boutiques, and all manner of gift shops can be found. Aside from these larger malls, numerous small arcades and individual shops dot the area.

The exclusive **Wailea Shopping Village** has an assortment of both chic and affordable boutiques and eateries within the fashionable resort area of Wailea. In addition, all the hotels within Wailea have ritzy shopping arcades of their own.

FOOD MARKETS

If you're shopping for general food supplies and are not interested in gourmet, specialty items, or organic foods, you'll save money by shopping at the big-name supermarkets in Lahaina, Kahului, and Kihei, often in malls. Smaller towns have general stores, which are adequate but a bit more expensive. You can also find convenience items at sundries shops in many condos and hotels, but these should be used only for snack foods or when absolutely necessary, because the prices are just too high.

Kahului and Wailuku

Most supermarkets are in Kahului. Three are conveniently located along Ka'ahumanu Avenue in or adjacent to the three malls, one right after the other. **Foodland,** open daily until 10 P.M., is in the Kaahumanu Center. Just down the road in the Kahului Shopping Center is the ethnic **Ah Fooks Super Market,** open Mon.–Fri. until 7 P.M., closing early Saturday and Sunday, specializing in Japanese, Chinese, and Hawaiian foods. Farther along in the Maui Mall is **Star Market,** open every day until 9 P.M., except on Sunday when it closes at 7 P.M. Just behind the Maui Mall on East Kamehameha Avenue is a **Safeway.** The biggest and most well-stocked in Wailuku is **Ooka Supermarket.** Along with the usual selection of items, it has a great ethnic food section. Open daily into the evening.

Kihei

In Kihei you've got your choice of **Foodland** in the Kihei Town Center or **Star Market** up the way on South Kihei Road.

West Maui

In Lahaina you can shop at **Foodland** and **Nagasako General Store** in the Lahaina Shopping Center. Nagasako's has all you need, plus a huge selection of Hawaiian and Asian items. Nagasako's is open daily 7 A.M.–10 P.M., Sunday until 7 P.M. If you're staying at a condo and doing your own cooking, the largest and generally least expensive supermarket on West Maui is the **Safeway,** open 24 hours daily, in the Lahaina Cannery Mall. North of Lahaina are the smaller but full-service **Star Market** in Honokowai and the **Napili Market** in Napili Plaza. All others are smaller convenience stores with more limited selection and higher prices.

Around and About

At **Pukalani Superette** in Pukalani, open seven days a week, you can pick up supplies and food to go, including sushi. Larger yet, with a greater selection, is **Foodland** in the Pukalani Terrace Center. In Hana, the **Hana Store** carries all the necessities and even has a selection of health foods and imported beers; open daily 7 A.M.–7:30 P.M.

Health Food

Those into organic foods, fresh vegetables, natural vitamins, and take-out snack bars have it made on Maui. The island's fine health food stores meet most of your needs. In Kahului, **Down to Earth Natural Foods,** 305 Dairy Rd., 808/877-2661. is an excellent full-service health food store complete with vitamins, minerals, and supplements, bulk foods, canned and boxed goods, and fresh vegetables and fruit. This store also has a deli counter, salad bar, and bakery. Open Mon.–Sat. 7 A.M.–9 P.M., Sunday 8 A.M.–8 P.M. A **Down To Earth Natural Foods** sister store is at 1169 Makawao Ave. in Makawao, 808/572-1488. Smaller, but with the same basic items and the same philosophy, it's open 8 A.M.–8 P.M. daily. **Westside Natural Food and Deli** in Lahaina is at the corner of Lahainaluna and Waine'e Streets, 808/667-2855. Open daily, it's a full-service health food store, featuring bulk items and a full selection of vitamins, minerals, and supplements. You can even get food to go from the salad bar and hot item counter. In Pa'ia is **Mana Natural Foods,** 49 Baldwin Ave., 808/579-8078, open daily 8 A.M.–8 P.M. This old establishment provides whatever you need for your trip to Hana. It has a full range of bulk and packaged items, supplements, drinks, a deli and hot food counter, and picnic foods.

Farmers' Markets

For the best and freshest fruits, veggies, baked goods, flowers, and sometimes crafts and clothing, search out the farmers' markets. Most of what is sold is local; some is organic. Gardeners bring their goods to the parking lot of Hawaiian Moon's in Honokowai on Monday, Wednesday, and Friday 7–11 A.M. and then move to the parking lot of Suda's Store in Kihei for the afternoons of the same days, 1:30–5:30 P.M. Be early for the best selection. The Longs Shopping Center in Kihei also hosts a farmers' market every Saturday 8 A.M.–noon, and another market is held at the Da Rose Mall in Honokowai every day but Saturday 7:30 A.M.–3:30 P.M. Kahului holds an organic farmers' market at the Kahului Shopping Center on Wednesday morning 8 A.M.–noon. If you're in Ha'iku on Saturday morning, stop by the Ha'iku Farmers' Market in front of the Ha'iku Town Center, 8 A.M.–noon for produce and crafts. All along the road to Hana are family fruit and flower stands. Many times no one is in attendance and the produce is paid on the honor system, at very reasonable prices.

SPECIALTY SHOPS

Some truly nifty and distinctive stores are wedged in among Maui's run-of-the-mill shopping centers; however, for real treasures you'll find the solitary little shop the best. Lahaina's Front Street has the greatest concentration of top-notch boutiques, but others are dotted here and there around the island. The following is only a sampling; many more are listed in the individual chapters.

Tattered sails on a rotted mast, tattooed seadogs in wide-striped jerseys, grim-faced Yankee captains squinting at the horizon, exotic (probably extinct) birds on the wing, flowers and weather-bent trees, and the beautiful, simple faces of Polynesians staring out from ancient days are faithfully preserved at **Lahaina Printsellers Ltd.,** one of the most unusual purveyors of art on Maui. The three shops, like minimuseums, are hung with original engravings, drawings, maps, charts, and naturalist sketches ranging in age 150–400 years. Each, marked with an authenticity label, can come from anywhere in the world, but the Hawaiiana collection is amazing in its depth. Many works feature a nautical theme, reminiscent of the daring explorers who opened the Pacific. The Lahaina Printsellers company has been collecting for years and is the largest collector of material relating to Captain Cook in the entire Pacific Basin. The shops keep Maui's art alive by representing modern artists as well. The three shops are at the Whaler's Village in Ka'anapali, the Lahaina Cannery Mall, and at the Grand Wailea Resort.

For a unique memento of Maui have your photo taken along Front Street in front of the

Pioneer Inn Shops. Here, you become the human perch for macaws and cockatoos. The birds are very tame, natural hams; they're the only thing on Maui guaranteed to be more colorful than your Hawaiian shirt. For about $25, vendors take your picture and deliver your developed photos the next day.

Pa'ia is quickly becoming an unofficial art center of Maui, along with being the windsurfing capital of Hawaii. Lahaina has slicker galleries, but you come much closer to the source in Pa'ia. The **Maui Crafts Guild** is an exemplary crafts shop that displays the best in local island art. All artists must be selected by active members before their works can be exhibited. All materials used must be natural, with an emphasis on those found only in Hawaii. Artists and craftspeople also work in Ha'iku and the vicinity, many with studios in the old Ha'iku or Pauwela canneries.

Upcountry's Makawao is a wonderful and crazy combination of old-time *paniolo,* matured hippies who now worry about drugs and their kids, those into alternative health, and up-and-coming artists. This hodgepodge makes for a town with general merchandise shops, exclusive boutiques, numerous art galleries, a health food store, and oriental health clinics, all strung along two Dodge City–like streets.

The **Maui Swap Meet** on Pu'unene Ave. in Kahului is open every Saturday 7 A.M.–noon and Wednesday 8 A.M.–1 P.M. Great junk! Wailuku is Maui's **antique attic** turned out on the street. About half a dozen odd little shops on Market Street display every kind of knickknack, curio, art treasure, white elephant, grotesque and sublime piece of furniture, jewelry, stuffed toy, game, or oddity that ever floated, sailed, flew, or washed up on Maui's beaches.

Whalers General Store and **ABC Discount Stores** are good places to look for sundries, but they can hardly be beat for prices on such things as snacks, bottles of liquor, beach towels, straw mats, straw hats, zori, gift items, Hawaiian-made products, and postcards. Anywhere on the island, you can pick up ordinary postcards, 3–5 for $1.

ACCOMMODATIONS

With about 18,000 rooms available, in some 225 properties, Maui is second only to O'ahu in the number of visitors it can accommodate. There's a tremendous concentration of condos, approximately 9,000 units, predominating in the Kihei, Ma'alaea, Honokowai, Kahana, and Napili areas; plenty of hotels, the majority in Ka'anapali and Wailea; and a growing number of bed-and-breakfasts. Camping is limited to a handful of parks, but what it lacks in number it easily makes up for in quality.

More than 90 hotels and condos have sprouted on West Maui, from Lahaina to Kapalua. The most expensive are along some of Maui's best beaches in Ka'anapali and Kapalua and include the Hyatt Regency, Westin Maui, Sheraton, Kapalua Bay, and Ritz-Carlton. The older condos in Honokowai are cheaper, with a mixture of expensive and moderate as you head north. Lahaina itself offers only a handful of places to stay: condos at both ends of town, three renovated old-style inns, and a handful of bed-and-breakfasts. Most people find the pace a little too hectic, but you couldn't get more in the middle of it if you tried. Ma'alaea Bay, between Lahaina and Kihei, has 11 quiet condos. Prices are reasonable, the beach is fair, and you're within striking distance of the action in either direction.

Kihei is "condo row," with close to 100 along the six miles of Kihei Road, plus a few hotels. This is where you'll find top-notch beaches and the best deals on Maui. Wailea, just down the road, is expensive, but the hotels here are world-class and the secluded beaches are gorgeous. Kahului often takes the rap for being an unattractive place to stay on Maui. It isn't all that bad. You're smack in the middle of striking out to the best of Maui's sights, and the airport is minutes away for people staying only a short time. Prices are cheaper and Kanaha Beach is a sleeper, with great sand, surf, and few visitors. Hana is an experience in itself. You can camp, rent a cabin, or stay at an exclusive hotel. Always reserve in advance and consider splitting your stay on Maui, spending your last few nights in Hana. You can really soak up this wonderful area, and you won't have to worry about rushing back along the Hana Highway.

Relax and enjoy la dolce vita.

To round things out, numerous B&Bs sit here and there around the island and on Moloka'i and Lana'i, and two hostels in Wailuku cater to the alternative traveler.

Condo Booking and Reservations

The following is a partial list of booking agents handling a number of properties on Maui. Aston, Outrigger, Marc, and Destination Resorts arrange only for their own properties. The rest offer a wider range of condos and vacation rentals.

Aston Hotels and Resorts, 2250 Kuhio Ave., Honolulu, HI 96815, 808/931-1400 or 800/922-7886 Mainland, 800/445-6633 Canada, or 800/321-2558 in Hawaii, website: aston-hotels.com

Outrigger Hotels and Resorts, 2375 Kuhio Ave., Honolulu, HI 96815, 800/688-7444, website: www.outrigger.com

Marc Resorts Hawaii, 2155 Kalakaua Ave., Honolulu, HI 96815, 808/926-5900 or 800/535-0085, website: www.marcresorts.com

Destination Resorts Hawaii, 3750 Wailea Alanui, Wailea, HI 96753, 808/879-1595 or 800/367-5246, fax 808/874-3554, website: www.destinationresortshi.com

Go Condo Hawaii, 800/452-3463, website: www.gocondohawaii.com

Maui Condominium and Home Realty, 2511 S. Kihei Rd., P.O. Box 1840 Kihei, HI 96753, 808/879-5445 or 800/822-4409 Mainland and Canada, fax 808/874-6144, website: www.mauicondo.com

Condominium Rentals Hawaii, 362 Huku Li'i Place, #204, Kihei, HI 96753, 808/879-2778, 800/367-5242 Mainland or 800/663-2101 Canada, website: www.crhmaui.com

Maui Beachfront Rentals, 256 Papalaua St., Lahaina, HI 96761, 808/661-3500 or 888/661-5200, fax 808/661-5200, website: www.mauibeachfront.com

AA Oceanfront Condo Rentals, 2439 S. Kihei Rd., Suite 102-A, Kihei, HI 96753, 808/879-7288 or 800/488-6004, fax 808/879-7500, website: www.makena.com

Kumulani Vacations and Realty, P.O. Box 1190, Kihei, HI 96753, 808/879-9272 or 800/367-2954, fax 808/874-0094, website: www.kumulani.com

Kihei Maui Vacations, P.O. Box 1055, Kihei, HI 96753, 808/879-7581 or 800/541-6284, fax 808/879-2000, website: www.kmvmaui.com

Klahani Resorts, P.O. Box 11108, Lahaina, HI 96761, 808/667-2712 or 800/669-6284, fax 808/661-5875, website: www.klahani.com

Maalaea Bay Rentals, 280 Hauoli St., Ma'alaea, HI 96793, 808/244-7012 or 800/367-6084, fax 808/242-7476, website: www.maalaeabay.com

Chase 'N Rainbows, 348 Lahainaluna Rd., Lahaina, HI 96761, 808/667-7088 or 800/367-6092, fax 808/661-8423, website: www.chasenrainbows.com

MAUI

Hostels

Maui has three reasonably priced hostels, two in Wailuku and one in Lahaina. **Banana Bungalow,** 310 N. Market St., Wailuku, HI 96793, 808/244-5090, 800/846-7835, or 800/746-7871, fax 808/846-3678, website: www.mauihostel.com, email: info@mauihostel.com, has office hours 8 A.M.–11 P.M. This laid-back hostel has bunks for $16 a night and rooms for $29 single, $40 double, and $50 triple. Extras include shuttle service, tours, on-site kitchen, and a hot tub in the garden. Just up the street and around the corner at 2080 Vineyard St. is the **Northshore Inn,** 808/242-8999 or 800/647-6284, fax 808/244-5004, web-

site: http://hostelhawaii.com, email: northshore @hostelhawaii.com. Look for the row of international flags on the streetfront balcony. Northshore offers most of the same amenities as Banana Bungalow. Bunks are $16, rooms $29 single and $38 double. **Patey's Place Maui Hostel,** 761 Waine'e St., 808/667-0999, website: www.hawaiian-hostels.com, email: maui@hawaiian-hostels.com, in Lahaina is a smaller, spartan, home-turned-hostel two blocks back from the water. It has a kitchen, TV room, and some storage. A bunk runs $20, a small single room $35, a private room with shared bath $40–45, and the private room with private bath $50–55.

FOOD

Lu'au

Old Lahaina Lu'au, 808/667-1998, on the beach at its location near the Lahaina Cannery Mall, has an excellent reputation because it is as close to authentic as you can get. Seating is Mon.–Sat. 5:30–8:30 P.M., but reserve at least 3–6 days in advance to avoid disappointment, perhaps two weeks in advance during peak season. The lu'au, featuring a "local's favorite," all-you-can-eat buffet and all-you-can-drink bar, costs $69 adults, children 2–12 $39. The traditional hula dancers use *ti*-leaf skirts, and the music is *fo' real.* The Old Lahaina Lu'au is one of the oldest, and it gets the nod from nearly everyone as being the best on the island.

Renaissance Wailea Beach Resort, 808/879-4900, recounts tales of old Hawaii with its professional hula show and lu'au every Tuesday, Thursday, and Saturday at 5:30 P.M. Hawaiian music, hula, drumming, and a fire dancer entertain as you dine through the evening on a wonderful assortment of foods expertly prepared by the chefs. Price includes open bar at $65 adults, $30 children 3–12. Reservations are required.

The Royal Lahaina Resort has been offering the nightly **Royal Lahaina Lu'au,** 808/661-3611, for years in its Lu'au Gardens. While definitely designed for the tourist, the show is entertaining and the food offered is authentic and tasty. Prices are $67 adults, children 12 and under $32; reservations suggested.

Wailea's Finest Lu'au, 808/879-1922, at the Outrigger Wailea Beach Resort, has garnered

awards for its lu'au fare and Polynesian show, and its fire/knife dancer has won international awards for his skill. Held Monday, Tuesday, Thursday, and Friday 5–8 P.M., $65 adults, children 6–12 $29.

Hyatt Regency Maui's **Drums of the Pacific,** 808/667-4720, is held every evening 5–8 P.M., for $68 adults, $44 teens, and $30 kids 6–12. This lu'au always gets high marks.

The **Maui Marriott** also presents its version of the lu'au and Polynesian show, starting the night with Polynesian games and activities. The Marriott's niche is its funny and entertaining twists. The evening starts at 5 P.M. and runs until 8 P.M. Cost is $72 adults, $30 children 6–12. Call 808/661-5828 for reservations.

While not the typical lu'au, per se, **The Feast at Lele,** 808/667-5353, website: www.feast-atlele.com, does a wonderful job of combining food with entertainment. Each of the five courses of this sit-down meal is accompanied by a Hawaiian, Tongan, Tahitian, or Samoan music and dance performance. Prepared under the direction of chef James McDonald, who also owns and operates the I'o and Pacific'O restaurants, the food is top-notch, and the show, designed by those who bring you the Old Lahaina Lu'au, is well-coordinated with the meal. This evening runs $89 adult and $59 for children, Tuesday, Wednesday, Thursday, Friday, and Saturday 6–9 P.M. (5:30–8:30 P.M. during winter) at the beachfront 505 Front Street Mall venue in Lahaina. Reservations a must.

GETTING THERE

BY AIR

Almost all travelers to Maui arrive by air. A few come by interisland ferry from Lana'i or Moloka'i, or one of the cruise ships that docks at Kahului. A limited number of direct air flights from the Mainland United States, Canada, and Japan are offered, but most airlines servicing Hawaii, both domestic and foreign, land in Honolulu and then carry on to Maui or offer connecting flights on "interisland carriers." More than 100 flights per day pass through Kahului Airport, while less than a dozen a day fly to Kapalua–West Maui airport.

Maui's Airports

There are three commercial airports on Maui, but the vast majority of travelers will be concerned with **Kahului Airport,** which accommodates 95 percent of the flights in and out of Maui. Kahului Airport is only minutes from Kahului city center, on the north-central coast of Maui. A full-service facility with all amenities, it has a few gift and snack shops, a restaurant, two tourist information booths, a newsstand, display cases of Hawaiian arts and crafts, a lost and found office, luggage storage office, bathrooms, public telephones, car rental agencies, and limited private transportation. Of the tourist information booths, one of which is in the arrival lounge and the other in the upstairs courtyard, at least one will be open 6:30 A.M.–10 P.M. daily. As you face the terminal building, the departure lounge is on your right, the arrival lounge is on your left, and splitting the two is an upper level courtyard with shops and a restaurant. For your entertainment, a hula and music show is performed here for two hours at midday. Between the baggage claim and car rental booths is a 10- by 20-foot, 1,200-gallon state-of-the-art aquarium with accompanying signboards, constructed and maintained by the Maui Ocean Center, which presents a sample of the lively and colorful world that surrounds the island. A few steps beyond the rental car booths at the front of the arrival building is the commuter terminal, and on the far side

of the runway is the heliport. Public parking at the airport costs $1 for the first half hour, $1 for each additional hour, or $7 maximum per day. There is metered parking at the commuter terminal. Major roads lead from Kahului Airport to all primary destinations on Maui.

Hawaiian Airlines opened the one-strip **Kapulua–West Maul Airport** in early 1987. You fly in over pineapple fields. This facility is conveniently located between the Ka'anapali and the Kapalua resort areas, on the *mauka* side of the Honoapi'ilani Highway at Akahele Street, just a few minutes from the major Ka'anapali hotels and condos of Honokowai and Kahana. As convenient as it is to this area of West Maui, it is not heavily used. Hawaiian Airlines no longer operates connecting flights to West Maui with the rest of Hawaii, and for now only Island Air and Pacific Wings schedule flights and have booths here. The small terminal is user-friendly with a snack bar, sundries shop, tourist brochures, and courtesy phones for car rental pickup in the baggage claim area. Parking is in the metered lot: $1 for the first one-half hour, $1 for each additional hour, or $7 maximum for the day.

The third airstrip is **Hana Airport,** an isolated runway with a tiny terminal on the northeast coast just west of Hana, serviced only by Pacific Wings. It has no amenities aside from a bathroom and telephone and transportation is available only to the Hotel Hana Maui via the hotel shuttle. People flying into Hana Airport generally plan to vacation in Hana for an extended period and have made prior arrangements for being picked up. The only rental cars in Hana are offered by Dollar, 808/248-8237—call before you come!

Flights to Maui

Until recently, United Airlines was the only carrier that offered nonstop flights from the Mainland to Maui. United flies daily nonstop to Maui from both San Francisco and Los Angeles. Now, Delta Air Lines and American Airlines also fly nonstop daily from Los Angeles to Kahului. Hawaiian Airlines offers daily flights connecting Kahului and

KAHULUI AIRPORT

To Kanaha Beach

COMMUTER TERMINAL

AIR CARGO BUILDING

CAR RENTAL BASE YARDS

PARKING

CAR RENTAL BOOTHS

ARRIVAL TERMINAL/ BAGGAGE CLAIM

CENTRAL BUILDING

T A R M A C

PARKING

DEPARTURE TERMINAL

To Kahului

SCALE NOT AVAILABLE

© SANDRA E. BISIGNANI TRUST AND AVALON TRAVEL PUBLISHING, INC.

MAUI

Los Angeles, with an onward connection to Las Vegas. Aloha Airlines flies daily between Kahului and Oakland, California, also connecting on to Las Vegas.

Interisland Carriers

Hawaiian Airlines can be reached at 800/367-5320 Mainland and Canada, 800/882-8811 statewide, or 808/872-4400 on Maui, website: www.hawaiianair.com. Flights to and from Honolulu (average flight time 35 minutes) run more than two dozen times per day in each direction. Hawaiian Airlines flights to Kahului, Maui, from Honolulu begin at 5:15 A.M., with flights thereafter about every 30 minutes until 10 P.M. Flights from Kahului to Honolulu begin at 6:15 A.M. and go all day until 9 P.M. There are two flights to/from Hilo daily, one at midmorning and one in the late afternoon. Kona, also on the Big Island, is ser-

viced with three flights from Kahului; one in the morning and two in the afternoon. For flights to Kaua'i, Lana'i, and Moloka'i, you must go through Honolulu. Moloka'i and Lana'i are connected by one daily direct flight.

Aloha Airlines, 800/367-5250 Mainland and Canada, 808/244-9071 Maui, website: www.alohaairlines.org, with its all-jet fleet of 737s, offers more flights to Maui than any other interisland carrier. It flies from Honolulu to Maui about 30 times per day beginning at 5:15 A.M. with the last flight at 8 P.M.; return flights to Honolulu start at 6:14 A.M., with the last at 9 P.M. Multiple flights throughout the day from Kaua'i—most go through Honolulu—begin at 6:30 A.M. and continue until 6:35 P.M.; to Kaua'i they start at 6:14 A.M. and continue throughout the day until 6:20 P.M. Four flights to Hilo are spread throughout the day, and the same number connect Kahului to Kona.

Island Air, 800/323-3345 nationwide, 800/652-6541 statewide, website: www.alohaairlines.org, connects Honolulu, Kahului, and Kona with the state's smaller airports, including Kapalua–West Maui, Lana'i, and Ho'olehua on Moloka'i. About half the flights are on jet aircraft and half on Dash-8 turboprop airplanes. Two flights a day connect Honolulu to Kahului, both making a stop on Moloka'i. Direct flights to and from Honolulu and Kapalua–West Maui Airport run six times daily 7:10 A.M.–5:08 P.M. Eight direct flights throughout the day connect Honolulu with both Lana'i and Moloka'i.

Operating eight-seat, twin-engine Cessna 402C planes, **Pacific Wings,** 888/575-4546 or 808/873-0877 on Maui, website: www.pacificwings.com, does the pickup routes, connecting Kahului nonstop with Hana, Kapalua–West Maui, Lana'i, Moloka'i, and Kamuela on the Big Island, and with Honolulu through one of these other airports. Pacific Wings also flies from Kapalua–West Maui, Moloka'i, and Kalaupapa to Honolulu.

Charter Airlines
If you've got the bucks or just need to go when there's no regularly scheduled flight, try one of the following for islandwide service. **Paragon Air,** 808/244-3356 or 800/428-1231 Mainland, website: www.maui.net/~wings/index.htm; **Pacific Wings,** 808/873-0877 on 888/575-4546 Mainland, website: www.pacificwings.com; or **Maui Air,** 808/871-8152, website: www.maui.net/~mauisle.

BY INTERISLAND FERRY

Lahaina-Lana'i Interisland Ferry
Expeditions runs a passenger ferry between Lahaina Harbor and Manele Bay on Lana'i. This shuttle service is not luxury travel but offers a speedy, efficient, and convenient transportation alternative to the plane when going to the Secluded Island. You are allowed to take luggage free of charge, but there's a $12 fee for a bicycle. The one-hour crossing leaves Lahaina's public pier daily at 6:45 A.M., 9:15 A.M., 12:45 P.M., 3:15 P.M., and 5:45 P.M.; it departs from Manele Bay at 8 A.M., 10:30 A.M., 2 P.M., 4:30 P.M., and 6:45 P.M. Adults pay $25 one-way, and children 2–11 pay $20; *kama'aina* rates are available. It's best to reserve your place. As only two bikes are permitted on each ferry, be sure to let the company know well ahead of time if you're planning to take one. Ground transportation on Lana'i from the pier at Manele Bay is provided by Lana'i City Service, which will take you up to Lana'i City for $20 round-trip or $10 round-trip to the Manele Bay Hotel. An added perk of this trip is that you will see dolphins from the boat most of the year and there's good whale-watching during the winter months. For information and reservations contact the ferry at 808/661-3756 on Maui or 800/695-2624 on Lana'i and elsewhere, 658 Front St., Suite 127, Lahaina, HI 96761, website: www.go-lanai.com.

Maui-Moloka'i Interisland Ferry
The *Maui Princess* used to sail daily between Kaunakakai and Lahaina, but for economic reasons the service was stopped in 1997, affecting many businesses on Moloka'i. Island Marine, the company that operates this ship, started ferry operation again in 2001 with the refurbished and faster *Molokai Princess,* which makes the crossing in about 75 minutes. Although the schedule is open to change, the yacht currently runs Mon.–Sat., leaving Kaunakakai at 6 A.M. and returning from Lahaina at 5 P.M. The fares are $40 one-way for adults and $20 for kids. For information and reservations call 808/667-6165 or 800/275-6969, or go online to www.mauiprincess.com/molokaiferry/index.html.

GETTING AROUND

If it's your intention to *see* Maui when you visit, and not just to lie on the beach in front of your hotel, the only efficient way is to rent a car. A few shuttles, taxis, and the good old thumb are available, but all these are flawed in one way or another. Other unique and fun-filled ways to tour the island include renting a bike or moped, but these conveyances are highly specialized and are more in the realm of sports than touring.

RENTAL CARS

Maui has about two dozen car rental agencies that can put you behind the wheel of anything from an exotic convertible to a used station wagon with chipped paint and torn upholstery. There are national companies, interisland firms, good local companies, and a few fly-by-nights that'll rent you a clunker. The national firms have booths at Kahului Airport. No rental agency has a booth at the Kapalua–West Maui Airport (there are courtesy phones), but one company has a booth at the Hana Airport. The rest are scattered around the island, with a heavy concentration in Kahului, on Halawai Dr. in Ka'anapali, and along S. Kihei Road. Those without an airport booth have either a courtesy phone or a number to call; some will pick you up and shuttle you to their lots. Stiff competition tends to keep the prices more or less reasonable. Good deals are offered off-season, with price wars flaring at any time and making for real savings. Even with all these companies, it's best to book ahead. You might not save money, but you can save yourself headaches.

Auto Rental Companies

The following major firms have booths at Kahului Airport—exit the arrival terminal and go to your right. Many pre-booked cars are waiting at these booths, but if you want to rent a car upon arrival, you must take a company shuttle to the base yard behind the airport parking lot to arrange for your car.

Dollar, 808/877-2731 in Kahului, 808/248-8237 in Hana, 800/342-7398 statewide, 800/800-4000 worldwide, website: www.dollar.com

Alamo, 808/871-6235 in Kahului and 808/661-7181 in Ka'anapali, or 800/327-9633, website: www.goalamo.com

National Car Rental, 808/871-8851, 808/667-9737 in Ka'anapali, or 800/227-7368 nationwide, website: www.nationalcar.com

Avis, 808/871-7575, 808/661-4588 Ka'anapali, 800/321-3712 nationwide, website: www.avis.com

Budget, 800/527-7000 on Maui, or nationwide 800/527-0700, website: www.drivebudget.com

Hertz, 808/877-5167 or 800/654-3011 nationwide, website: www.hertz.com

Enterprise, 808/871-1511 or 800/736-8222 nationwide, website: www.enterprise.com

Thrifty, 808/871-2860, 800/367-5238 statewide, or 808/367-2277 worldwide, website: www.thirfty.com

The following local companies are based in Maui. None have booths at the airport, but a few have pickup service through courtesy phones.

Word of Mouth Rent-A-Used Car, 150 Hana Hwy., 808/877-2436 or 800/533-5929, website: www.mauirentacar.com, pickup van provided, offers some fantastic deals on used, but not abused, cars. It's a reputable agency, having been around for 25 years. The office is open 8 A.M.–5 P.M., but a car can be left at the airport at earlier or later hours with prior arrangement.

Good Kar-ma, 536 Keolani Place, 808/871-2911, website: www.maui2000.com/carrental, close to the airport, has established a fine reputation. It rents compacts, jeeps, and station wagons mostly for a week or longer. These cars are a few years old, have seen use, and are not in pristine condition, but you won't stick out as a visitor. Cars run $99–189 a week, averaging about $129. Good Kar-ma rents to those under age 25 and will rent for cash. Airport pickup available. Others include: **Kihei Rent A Car,** 808/879-7257 or 800/251-5288; **Wheels R Us,** 808/871-6858 in Kahului, 808/667-7751 in Lahaina, and 808/875-1221 in Kihei; and **Maui Cruisers,** 808/249-2319 or 877/749-7889, which will put you in a car that will make you "look local."

Four-wheel Drive

Though 4WDs are much more expensive than cars, some people might feel safer in them when completely circling Maui or driving some roads in Upcountry. Also, unlike for cars, the rental companies offering 4WDs put no restrictions on driving past 'Ohe'o Gulch. Four-wheel drives can be obtained from **Dollar** and a few other of the "big boys," as well as the following. **Maui Rent A Jeep,** 808/877-6626 or 800/701-JEEP; **Wheels R Us,** 808/871-6858 in Kahului, 808/667-7751 in Lahaina, and 808/875-1221 in Kihei; **Kihei Rent A Car;** 808/879-7257 or 800/251-5288; or **Island Riders,** 808/661-9966 in Lahaina or 808/874-0311 in Kihei. Rates vary from company to company but are mostly around $75–100 per day, dependent on availability, model, and length of rental.

Vanity Vehicles

If you feel like stepping out in *style,* consider renting a flashy sports cars. **Island Riders,** 808/661-9966 in Lahaina or 808/874-0311 in Kihei, website: www.islandriders.com, rents a Dodge Viper, Ferrari 348TS, Prowler, Porsche, Corvette, and BMW convertible. These cars are classy, but they're not cheap, and you may have to be 25 years old to rent. However, for that one night of luxury, it may be worth it. Rates run from $200 for five hours to $425 for 24 hours. The **Aloha Toy Store,** 640 Front St., 808/661-1212, website: www.alohatoystore.com, also has a variety of these fancy cars, as does **Hawaiian Riders,** 808/662-4386 in Lahaina and 808/981-0889 in Kihei, website: www.hawaiianriders.com.

Motorcycles

A few companies also rent motorcycles for the intrepid traveler. Virtually all rental bikes are Harley-Davidson big hogs or sportsters. Rates vary but run around $100 for half a day and $140–160 for 24 hours; longer rentals can be arranged. All drivers must be at least 21 years old (25 for some companies), have a valid motorcycle endorsement on their license, and be in possession of a major credit card. Insurance is available. Companies want you to stay on good paved roads and don't usually allow trips to Hana. Although wearing helmets is not required by state law, they are available; some companies have you wear eye protection. For one of these big steeds, contact **Mavrik's,** 1215 S. Kihei Rd. in Kihei, 808/891-2299, or at Halawai Dr. in Ka'anapali, 808/661-3099. Also try **Island Riders,**

808/661-9966 in Lahaina or 808/874-0311 in Kihei; the **Aloha Toy Store,** 808/661-1212, in Lahaina; **Hawaiian Riders,** 808/662-4386, in Lahaina; **Hula Hogs,** 808/875-7433, in Kihei; or **Maui Bikers,** 808/871-6014, in Kahului.

Mopeds

For just running around town or to the beach mopeds are great. Expect to pay about $20 for two hours, $25 for four hours, and $40 for eight hours. Most companies ask for a cash deposit, and some will not let you have the mopeds overnight. Check with **Hawaiian Island Cruzers,** 2395 S. Kihei Rd., 808/879-0956; **Aloha Toy Store,** 640 Front Street, Lahaina, 808/661-1212; or **Hawaiian Riders,** 196 Lahainaluna Rd., Lahaina, 808/662-4386.

ALTERNATIVE TRANSPORTATION

Shuttle Service

There is no public bus service on Maui, but numerous shuttle services operate from the Kahului Airport to West Maui, between South Maui and West Maui, and within the resort developments of Lahaina, Ka'anapali and Wailea.

Speedi Shuttle, 808/875-8070, connects the Kahului Airport to virtually anywhere on the island. It operates daily during the hours that the planes fly. Pickup can be from either the airport or any hotel or condo if going to the airport. Use the telephone next to the information booth in the baggage claim area when at the airport. Rates vary according to distance and how many are in your party, but as an example, a party of two from the airport to Wailea would run about $28.

Airporter Shuttle, 808/875-7841, operated by Trans Hawaiian, runs a regular service to and from Lahaina and Ka'anapali, with pickup and drop-off in Honokowai and Kahana by reservation only. Shuttles run on the half hour, starting from the Kahului Airport at 9 A.M., with the last run from West Maui at 5 P.M. A courtesy phone and ticket booth are available at Kahului Airport next to the tourist information booth in the baggage area. The fare is $13 per person. Pickup is outside the baggage claim.

The free **Kaanapali Trolley** runs along the Ka'anapali strip about every half hour 9 A.M.–6

P.M., stopping at all major resorts, the golf course, and the Whaler's Village shopping complex. Look for the green jitneys. Pick up free printed tourist literature or ask at any hotel desk for the schedule.

The **Wailea Shuttle** is a complimentary van that stops at all major hotels and condos, The Shops at Wailea, and golf and tennis courts in Wailea every 20–30 minutes. It operates 6:30 A.M.–7 P.M. Be sure to check with the driver about the last pickup times if you are out in the evening. For information on the schedule and stops, call 808/879-2828.

Operated by Trans Hawaiian, the **West Maui Shopping Express** runs two routes: one from Lahaina to Ka'anapali, $1 per person each way, and the other from Ka'anapali to Kapalua, $2 per person each way. Stops include the hotels in Kapalua and Ka'anapali, condos along the west side, the Whalers Village shopping mall in Ka'anapali, and the Wharf Cinema Center, Hilo Hattie's, and the Lahaina Cannery Mall in Lahaina. Buses run about every hour from midmorning until midevening. Call 808/875-7841 for additional information on routes and times, or pick up a schedule at your hotel concierge desk.

The **South Maui Shopping Express** runs seven or eight times a day to/from Makena and the Maui Ocean Center, stopping at many of the hotels and condos on the way. Rides cost $2 per person for each point-to-point ride or $5 for an all-day pass. Connecting shuttles run from the Maui Ocean Center to Lahaina and Ka'anapali, stopping where the West Maui Shopping Express stops and at a few beaches along the highway between Ma'alaea and Lahaina. The fare is $10 for a systemwide pass. Call 808/875-7841 for exact pickup times and locations.

For those riding the Sugar Cane Train, shuttle transportation by the West Maui Shopping Express takes riders from the Wharf Cinema Center to Lahaina Station in time for each train departure (buy your train tickets beforehand). Another shuttle connects Whalers Village to the Pu'ukoli'i Station platform in Ka'anapali. The fare is $1.

Taxis

About two dozen taxi companies on Maui more or less operate in a fixed area. Most, besides providing normal taxi service, also run tours all over the island. While sedans predominate,

some minivans are being used as well. Taxis are expensive and metered by the distance traveled. For example, a ride from Kahului Airport to Ka'anapali is $50, to Kapalua $70, and about $35 to Wailea. Expect $5–10 in and around Kahului, and about $12 to the hostels in Wailuku. Any taxi may drop off at the airport, but only those with permits may pick up there. In the Kihei-Wailea area, try: **Yellow Cab of Maui,** 808/877-7000; **Wailea Taxi,** 808/874-5000; or **Kihei Taxi,** 808/879-3000. **Kahului Taxi Service,** 808/877-5681, operates in central Maui. In West Maui, options include **Alii Cab,** 808/661-3688; **AB Taxi,** 808/667-7575; and **Island Taxi,** 808/667-5656.

Classy Taxi, 808/665-0003, uses renovated old cars from the 1920s and '30s. A ride from Lahaina to Ka'anapali runs about $11, and from there to Kapalua it's about $18.

Several companies on the island offer limo service. These are expensive rides, however, and will run, for example, more than $120 one-way from the Kahului Airport to Ka'anapali. Private tours might run $60 for two persons for two hours or $90 for a full load for the same time frame. Ask your hotel concierge for assistance in arranging for this service, or contact one of the following: **Wailea Limousine,** 808/875-4114; **Kapalua Executive Transportation Service,** 808/669-2300; or **Bob and Sons Limousine Service,** 808/877-7800.

Hitchhiking

After three decades as a "criminal offense," hitchhiking is once again legal in Maui County. Use the old tried-and-true method of thumb out, facing traffic, with a smile on your interesting face. You can get around quite well by thumb, if you're not on a schedule. Hitching short hops along the resort beaches is easy. Catching longer rides to Hana or up to Haleakala can be done, but it'll be tougher because the driver will know that you'll be with him or her for the duration of the ride. Under no circumstances should women hitch alone.

MEDICAL SERVICES

Maui Memorial Medical Center, 221 Mahalani St., Wailuku, 808/244-9056, is the only full-service hospital on the island. Several clinics dot the island. Upstairs in the Dolphin Mall in Kihei is **Kihei Clinic and Wailea Medical Services,** 808/879-0114, open Mon.–Fri. 8 A.M.–7 P.M., Saturday until 6 P.M., and Sunday and holidays 9 A.M.–2 P.M. At **Urgent Care Maui/Kihei Physicians,** 808/879-7781, 1325 S. Kihei Rd., Suite 103, doctors, a clinical lab, and X-ray are available 6 A.M.–midnight daily. **Kihei-Wailea Medical Center,** 41 E. Lipoa St., 808/874-8100, has physicians, a pharmacy, physical therapy, and a clinical laboratory that's open Mon.–Fri. 8 A.M.–8 P.M., Saturday and Sunday until 5 P.M. **Kaiser Permanente** has a clinic in Lahaina, 910 Waine'e, 808/662-6900, and in Wailuku, 80 Ma-

halani St., 808/243-6000; open Mon.–Fri. 8 A.M.–5 P.M., closed noon–1 P.M., weekends, and holidays. In the center of Wailuku try **Maui Medical Group,** 2180 Main St., 808/242-6464; the group also has clinics in Lahaina and Pukalani. The **West Maui Healthcare Center** maintains an office at the Whalers Village shopping mall, 808/667-9721, open 8 A.M.–8 P.M. daily. The **International Healthcare Center,** 808/877-5844, at the Maui Marketplace, sees patients for walk-in urgent care issues 10 A.M.–10 P.M.

Numerous drugstores are spread throughout the island, including **Longs Drugs** in Kihei, 808/879-2033, Lahaina, 808/667-4390, and Kahului, 808/877-0068.

INFORMATION AND SERVICES

For **police, fire, and ambulance** anywhere on Maui, dial **911. Coast Guard Search and Rescue** can be reached at 800/552-6458. The **Sexual Assault Crisis Line** is 808/242-4357.

For recorded information on **local island weather,** call 808/877-5111; for the **marine report,** call 808/877-3477; and for conditions on Haleakala, call 808/571-5054. For time of day, dial 808/242-0212.

Consumer Protection and Tourism Complaints
If you encounter problems with accommodations, bad service, or downright rip-offs, try the following: Maui Chamber of Commerce, 250 Ala Maha, Kahului, 808/871-7711; the Office of Consumer Protection, 808/984-8244; or the Better Business Bureau (O'ahu), 877/222-6551.

Tourism Information
The best information on Maui is dispensed by the Maui HVB, 1727 Wili Pa Loop, Wailuku, HI 96793, 808/244-3530, website: www.visit-maui.com. For general information about Maui and specific accommodation and activities listings, ask for the official vacation planner, or check it on the Web at www.hshawaii.com/mvp.

The state operates two visitors information booths at Kahului Airport, one in the center building upper level and the other in the baggage claim area of the arrival terminal, 808/872-3892. Open daily 6:30 A.M.–10 P.M., they have plenty of

practical brochures and helpful information. Also, scattered around the arrival terminal lower level are numerous racks of free brochures, magazines, and other tourist literature.

Post Offices
There are 12 branch post offices on Maui, five on Moloka'i, and one on Lana'i. Window service is offered Mon.–Fri. 8:30 A.M.–5 P.M.; some offices are open Saturday 9 A.M.–1 P.M. For information, dial 800/275-8777.

Reading Material
The main branch of the **library** is at 251 High St., Wailuku, 808/243-5766; other branches are in Kahului, Lahaina, Makawao, Kihei, and Hana. The libraries hold a hodgepodge of hours through the week. Library cards are available free for Hawaii state residents and military personnel stationed in Hawaii, $25 for nonresidents for a card valid for five years, and $10 for three months for visitors.

Free tourist literature is well done and loaded with tips, discounts, maps, happenings, etc. Found in hotels, restaurants, and street stands, they include: *This Week Maui, Maui Gold, Maui Magazine, Maui Beach and Activity Guide, Maui Activities and Attractions,* and *The Best Guidebook.* The weekly *Drive Guide,* with excellent maps and tips, is given out free by all car rental agencies; similar is the *Driving Magazine of Maui. Maui Menus* is all about food; *101 Things to do*

Maui is a great resource and also has money-saving coupons; and *Maui Visitor* and *Maui No Ka Oi* contain more culture-oriented information.

The major local paper available on Maui is the *Maui News.* Published Mon.–Fri., it has good "Datebook" listings of local events. *Lahaina News* is a community paper of news, feature stories, and entertainment listings, available for 25 cents. It's a daily, as is the free *Maui Times.* The *South Maui Weekly* and *Haleakala Times* are weeklies, and *Gold Coast* and *MauiAina* are seasonal.

Island Radio
More than a dozen radio stations broadcast on Maui. Popular ones: KHPR 88.1 FM (also 90.7 FM) broadcasts from Honolulu and is the island's public radio station; KPOA 93.5 FM out of Lahaina does a mix of contemporary Hawaiian and standard rock; for easy listening tune to KUMU 94.7 FM; the format on KAOI 95.1 FM in Wailuku is mostly adult rock with a request line; KAPA 99.1 FM offers island sounds; KNUI 900 AM does traditional Hawaiian; and KAOI 1110 AM does news, talk, and sports.

Maui Facts
Maui is the second youngest and second largest Hawaiian Island after Hawai'i. Its nickname is the Valley Island. Its color is pink and its flower is the *lokelani,* a small rose.

SMILE
IT NO BROKE
YOUR FACE!

DIANA LASICH HARPER

M.G.L. DOMENY DE RIENZI

MAUI

CENTRAL MAUI: THE ISTHMUS

KAHULUI

It is generally believed that Kahului means "The Winning," but perhaps it should be "The Survivor." Kahului suffered attack by Kamehameha I in 1790, when he landed his war canoes here in preparation for battle at 'Iao Valley. In 1900 it was purposely burned to thwart the plague, then rebuilt. Combined with Wailuku, the county seat just up the road, this area is home to 28,000 Mauians, nearly one-quarter of the island's population. Here's where the people live. It's a practical, homey town, the only deep-water port from which Maui's sugar and pineapples are shipped out and other commodities shipped in, and it now has the island's only pineapple cannery. Although Kahului was an established sugar town by 1880, it's really only grown up in the last 40 years. In the 1960s, Hawaiian Commercial and Sugar Co. began building low-cost

housing for its workers, which became a model development for the whole of the United States. Most people land at the airport, blast through for Lahaina or Kihei, and never give Kahului a second look. It's in no way a resort community, but it has the best general-purpose shopping on the island, a few significant sites, the island's most noteworthy windsurfing site, and a convenient location to the airport.

SIGHTS

Kanaha Pond State Wildlife Sanctuary
This one-time royal fishpond is between downtown and the airport on the ocean side of the airport approach road. It's on the migratory route of various ducks and Canada geese, temporary

CENTRAL MAUI

Po'elua Bay

To Kapalua

340

KAHEKILI HWY

Kahakuloa

Moke'ehia Island

PACIFIC OCEAN

Kahului Bay

Spartan Reef

Waihe'e River

Waihe'e

WAIHE'E BEACH COUNTY PARK

WAIEHU MUNICIPAL GOLF COURSE

WAIEHU BEACH COUNTY PARK

Waiehu

N. Waiehu Stream

330

340

HALEKI'I-PIHANA HEIAUS STATE MONUMENT

Kahului Harbor

KANAHA POND STATE WILDLIFE SANCTUARY

KAHULUI AIRPORT

To Pa'ia and Hana

36

WAR MEMORIAL PARK

HELIPORT

HANSEN RD.

'Iao Needle

'IAO VALLEY STATE PARK

320

'IAO VALLEY RD.

'Iao Stream

Wailuku

32

KEOPUOLANI PARK

KAHULUI

KA'AHUMANU AVE.

36

37

To Haleakala

Wailuku Heights

30

THE DUNES AT MAUI LANI

380

Pu'unene

ALEXANDER AND BALDWIN SUGAR MILL MUSEUM

SUGAR MILL

PUUNENE RD.

Waikapu

HONOAPI'ILANI HWY

KUIHELANI HWY

305

MOKULELE HWY

370

MAUI TROPICAL PLANTATION

SANDALWOOD GOLF COURSE

380

311

To Ma'alaea and Lahaina

To Kihei

0   3 mi

0   3 km

MAUI

© SANDRA E. BISIGNANI TRUST AND AVALON TRAVEL PUBLISHING, INC.

home to dozens of vagrant bird species, but most importantly it's home to the endangered Hawaiian stilt (ae'o) and the Hawaiian coot ('alae ke'oke'o). The stilt is a slender, 16-inch bird with a black back, white belly, and stick-like pink legs. The coot is a gray-black duck-like bird that builds large floating nests. An observation pavilion is maintained on the south edge of the pond, accessed by a short walkway from a small parking area. This pavilion is always open and free of charge. Bring binoculars. Entry to the walking trails within the sanctuary is free to individuals or groups but by permit only from September to March. Apply Mon.–Fri. 8 A.M.–4:30 P.M. at the Department of Natural Resources, Division of Forestry and Wildlife office, 54 S. High St., Room 101, Wailuku, HI 96793. For more information call 808/984-8100. You must supply exact dates and times of your intended visit.

Kanaha Beach County Park

This is the only beach worth visiting in the area. Good for a swim (roped-off area) and a picnic, the broad beach here is flanked by plenty of trees so you can get out of the sun. In this strip of tall ironwood trees are broad lawns, picnic tables, barbecue pits, bathrooms, and a public phone. Permit camping is allowed at the western end of the park. This beach is used by one of the outrigger canoe clubs on the island, and you'll see their canoes drawn up on shore near their pavilion when they're not out on the water practicing their strokes. Kanaha is a favorite of windsurfers and it's also *the* best place to learn sailboarding. The wind is steady here but not too strong, and the wave action is gentle. Most use the section of beach farthest to the east, locally known as Kooks Beach. Many sailboard instructors bring their students here. From Ka'ahumanu Avenue or the Hana Highway, turn onto Hobron Avenue, and then immediately right onto Amala Street, and follow the signs to the park. Alternately, follow Keolani Place to the airport, swing back around and turn right on Ka'a Street. Pass the rental car agencies and carry on to Amala Street. There are two entrances to the park and plenty of parking. The only drawback might be the frequent and noisy arrivals and departures of aircraft at the airport, which is only a few hundred yards away.

A short way in toward the harbor from Kanaha beach park and across the road from the wildlife sanctuary is a stretch of beach known as "Kite Beach." Kitesurfers congregate here, as the kitesurfing and windsurfing areas have been segregated to reduce the risk of accidents. Having become popular in Hawaii over the last several years, this beach area is perhaps the best place in the state to see this new extreme sport. There is no official parking here; just pull off the road onto the edge of the sand dune.

Kahului Harbor

This is the island's principal commercial harbor, the conduit through which most goods flow in and out of the island, including pineapples and raw sugar. Several muscled piers along the water's edge are a hive of shipping activity. While there are no fishing boats or other tourist ventures operating at Kahului Harbor, it is home port for the SS *Independence*, which makes a one-week tour of the islands, starting and ending its journey here. Its sister ship, the SS *Patriot*, whose home port is Honolulu, docks here once a week, disembarking passengers for a day's sightseeing on the island before floating away to its next stop. Local anglers try their luck along both the breakwaters, and a canoe club launches its outriggers from Hoaloha Park for early morning practice on the smooth harbor waters.

Maui Community College

Just across the street from the Kaahumanu Center on Route 32, the college is a good place to check out bulletin boards for various activities, items for sale, and cheaper long-term housing. The Student Center is conspicuous as you drive in, and it's a good place to get most information about the school. Maui Community College, on the Web at mauicc.hawaii.edu, is a branch of the University of Hawai'i and the only college-level school in the county, although it maintains learning centers in Hana and on Moloka'i and Lana'i. Concentrating mostly on two-year-degree courses, the school's focus is on vocational and technical fields with some liberal arts added. Reasonably well known around the state is its culinary arts program.

Maui Arts and Cultural Center

This complex is surrounded by Maui Community College and Keopuolani Park. Opened in 1994,

MAUI

the $32 million Maui Arts and Cultural Center is a big draw for the island, attracting well-known local and national musicians, international dancers, visual arts exhibitions, and films. The Maui Film Festival uses this venue, as does the Hawaii International Film Festival. Educational programs are offered, and free art shows are held at the Shaffer Gallery Tues.–Sun. 10 A.M.–6 P.M. Call 808/242-7469 for information and tickets, which can also be picked up daily at the box office 10 A.M.–6 P.M. Check the Maui Arts and Cultural Center website for what's happening throughout the year: www.mauiarts.org.

War Memorial Park and Center

At the corner of Ka'ahumanu and Kanaloa Avenues is Wailuku War Memorial Park and Center, basically a large arena athletic venue. Here you'll find a football stadium, baseball field, gymnasium, Olympic-size swimming pool, tennis courts, and track. After years of being played at the Aloha Stadium in Honolulu, the college allstar Hula Bowl now takes place at the War Memorial Stadium and is scheduled to be played there at least until 2002. Around back behind the gym, in the recreation director's office, you can pick up county camping permits.

Keopuolani Park

Across Kanaloa Avenue from the War Memorial Park, and lying between the YMCA, the Maui Arts and Cultural Center, and Maui Community College, is the newly developed 110-acre Keopuolani Park, the largest county park on the island. Open 7 A.M.–10 P.M., this greenway has broad expanses of grass and sidewalks, jogging trails and exercise stations, as well as baseball and soccer fields, a sand volleyball court, children's play areas, horseshoe pits, picnic pavilions, and, in the corner near Ka'ahumanu Avenue, a skateboard park. Opened to the public in 1999, this is a welcome addition to the developed parklands of the island.

Paper Airplane Museum

For the curious, the unusual Paper Airplane Museum at the Maui Mall is an eclectic place displaying all sizes of model paper airplanes (not the folded-paper type) from those small enough to fit on the palm of a hand to those as large as a child, with plenty of photos, commentary, and artifacts on the island's aviation history. More than 2,500 model paper airplanes kits and other memorabilia are for sale in the gift shop. Known as "The Tin Can Man," the owner also displays airplanes and other objects that he's constructed with old soda cans. Open daily; admission is free to this nonprofit museum, yet donations are gladly accepted and will be used to support children's outreach programs. Contact the museum at 808/877-8916, or visit it on the Web at www.shaka.com/~edynray/pam/index.htm.

Alexander and Baldwin Sugar Mill Museum

The museum, 808/871-8058, is at the intersection of Pu'unene Avenue (Route 311) and Hansen Road, about a half mile from Dairy Road. Hours are Mon.–Sat. 9:30 A.M.–4:30 P.M.; admission is $4 adults, $2 children 6–17, ages five and under admitted free. (Avoid the area around 3 P.M. when the mill across the street changes shifts.) This small but highly informative museum could easily be your first stop after arriving at Kahului Airport only 15 minutes away, especially if you're heading to Kihei. When you get off the plane, you'll realize that you're in the midst of sugarcane fields. If you want to know the history of this crop and the people who worked and developed it, visit the museum. The vintage museum building (circa 1990) was the home of the sugar plantation superintendent, who lived surrounded by his work. Outside on the lawn are several old pieces of machinery from decades past, once used at the plantation. Inside is a small but well-stocked bookstore and gift shop featuring Hawaiiana and handmade clothing and artifacts, with goodies like guava and coconut syrups and raw sugar.

As you begin your tour, notice the ancient refrigerator in the corner that the

Hawaiian stilt

KAREN MCKINLEY

© SANDRA E. BISIGN-ANI TRUS' AND AVALON TRAVEL PUBLISHING, INC.

KAHULUI

Kahului Bay

Kahului Harbor

KANAHA BEACH PARK

To Kanaha Beach

To Kahului Airport

To Hana

KANAHA POND STATE WILDLIFE SANCTUARY

Kite Beach

To Waihe'e

To Lahaina

To Kihei

MAUI

MAUI ARTS AND CULTURAL CENTER

MAUI COMMUNITY COLLEGE

W&F WASHERETTE

KA'AHUMANU CENTER
FOODLAND

MAUI PINEAPPLE PLANT

MAUI BEACH HOTEL

MAUI SEASIDE HOTEL

HOALOHA PARK

LIBRARY

KAHULUI SHOPPING CENTER

AMERICAN SAVINGS BANK

FIRST BANK

BANK OF HAWAII

TWO FROGS HUGGING

HIDEAWAY RESTAURANT

OLD KAHULUI SHOPPING CENTER

MAUI MALL

WINDSURF SHOPS

MAUI MEDICAL CENTER

POST OFFICE

SAFEWAY

SWAP MEET

CATHOLIC CHURCH

TRIANGLE SQUARE

OBSERVATION PAVILION

MARCO'S GRILL

COSTCO
GAS STATION

WINDSURF SHOP

KMART

GAS STATION

DAIRY CENTER

MAUI MARKETPLACE

MAUI DOWNHILL

DOWN TO EARTH NATURAL FOODS

FIRE STATION

HONGWANJI

0.25 m
0.25 km

staff still uses. In the first room, you are given a brief description of the natural history of Maui, along with a rendition of the legends of the demigod Maui. Display cases explain Maui's rainfall and use of irrigation for a productive sugarcane yield. There is an old-fashioned copper rain gauge along with pragmatic artifacts from the building of the Hai'ku Ditch. A collection of vintage photos features the Baldwin and Alexander families, while a historical plaque recalls when workers lived in ethnic camps, each with its own euphemistic name (Chinese at Ah Fong, Japanese at Nashiwa, Portuguese at Cod Fish). This setup was designed to discourage competition (or cooperation) between the ethnic groups during labor disputes, and to ease the transition to the new land. These people are represented by everything from stuffed fighting cocks to baseball mitts from the 1930s. Included is an educational video on the various methods of sugarcane production. The museum is in the shadow of the state's largest sugar mill, and you can hear the wheels turning and the mill grinding. It's not an antiseptic remembrance, but a vital one where the history still continues. No tours are given at the mill across the street, but you can view a scale model to get an idea of what goes on inside its hulking exterior and just how selected machinery works.

ACCOMMODATIONS

Kahului features two economical motel/hotels, just right for the traveler looking for a good deal away from the island's tourist hubs, yet in a convenient location to many island sites, the airport, and business and government offices. These accommodations are west of Hoaloha Park on the harbor side of Ka'ahumanu Avenue (Route 32).

The **Maui Beach Hotel** is a low-rise affair with a Polynesian-style peaked roof over its lobby. On the lobby level are the front desk, a small gift shop, and the Red Dragon Chinese restaurant. Upstairs, daily buffets at the Rainbow Dining Room are good value, and cocktails and *pu pu* are served at the Rainbow Lounge near the dining room from 5 P.M. A small pool is also on the second floor, open 9 A.M.–9 P.M., but the main swimming pool is in the central courtyard off the main foyer hold, beyond which the lawn leads down to the narrow beach fronting Kahului Harbor. Rates for the Maui Beach are $98–125 for its standard to oceanfront rooms and $450 for an oceanfront suite. For reservations, contact the hotel directly at 808/877-0051 or 888/649-3222, fax 808/871-5797. For the convenience of its guests, a complimentary shuttle runs to the airport every half hour 6:30 A.M.–9 P.M.; reservations required. The Maui Beach Hotel has offered the same friendly hospitality to *kama'aina* and visitor alike since the 1960s.

About 100 yards to the east is the **Maui Seaside Hotel,** 808/877-3311 or 800/560-5552, part of the Sand and Seaside Hotels, a small island-owned chain. Friendly and economical, this too is a two-story facility with a swimming pool in the central courtyard, access to the beach, a lobby lounge, and Vi's Restaurant for breakfast and dinner. All rooms hold two double beds or a king bed, have color TV, a small refrigerator, ceiling fan, and air-conditioning. Some kitchenettes are available, and there is a self-service laundry on premises. More motel-like than the Maui Beach, the Maui Seaside is clean, neat, and well cared for, and shows obvious pride in the way it keeps up its property. AAA approved, rates are $98–135, or $127–164 with rental car; numerous discounts are offered. For reservations, call the hotel direct or central reservations at 800/367-7000, or fax 808/922-0052. Send email to sandsea@aloha.net, or visit the hotel's website at www.sand-seaside.com.

FOOD

The Kahului area has an assortment of inexpensive to moderate eating establishments and one that is a notch above the rest. Many are found in the shopping malls.

Inexpensive

Several basic restaurants and other food purveyors are along Dairy Road. **Maui Bakery Bagelry and Deli,** 201 Dairy Rd., 808/871-4825, is "home of the 50¢ bagel." Open Mon.–Sat. 6 A.M.–5:30 P.M. and 7 A.M.–3 P.M. on Sunday, the Bagelry makes fresh (preservative- and fat-free) rye, blueberry, whole-wheat, garlic, poppy seed, sesame, and onion bagels. Choose a buttered bagel or one smothered with a layer of cream cheese and have it wrapped to go, or eat it at one of the tables. Or try a tasty deli sandwich, served on a bagel, French bread, or rye. The bakery also makes mouthwatering cinnamon and walnut coffee-cake, fudge brownies, strudel, and loaves of French, rye, and whole-wheat bread.

If you're looking for a wholesome, natural deli item, fresh salad, hot entrée, or freshly baked pastry, there's not a better place to look than the deli counter at **Down to Earth Natural Foods,** 305 Dairy Rd. Open daily, it's also a full-service grocery store.

At the Dairy Center just up the road, you'll find the inexpensive eateries **Local Boys** for Hawaiian plate lunches and **Pi-ata's** Mexican restaurant. In the second half of this complex, near the corner of Dairy Road and Hana Highway, is **Maui Coffee Roasters,** 808/877-2877, for those who want a hot brew now or want take-home beans, available from all the islands. Other drinks, sandwiches, soups, salads, veggie burgers, and baked goods are also available in this good-time, upscale, yuppie-ish coffeehouse-type place.

Follow your nose in the Kaahumanu Center to **The Coffee Store,** 808/871-6860, open Mon.–Fri. 7 A.M.–9 P.M., Saturday 8 A.M.–7 P.M., and Sunday 8 A.M.–5 P.M. Light lunches include savories like a hot croissant or a spinach roll pastry puff. Coffee by the cup is $1.25 and up. The coffees, roasted on the premises, are from more than 20 gourmet varieties hand-picked in Africa, South America, Indonesia, and of course Hawaii, and include exotic beans like Jamaican Blue Mountain. Gifts and giftwear too!

The Maui Mall has a selection of inexpensive eateries. **Matsu Restaurant** is a fast-food Japanese restaurant with an assortment of daily specials for under $6, or a steaming bowl of various types of saimin for $5. Japanese standards include *katsu don buri,* tempura, or curry rice. Like a *soba-ya* in Japan. Adjacent are **Siu's Chinese Kitchen,** where most of the typical Chinese dishes are under $5, and **Maui Mixed Plate** for local hot entrées. All are good choices for a quick lunch during the day. Other international fast-food outlets can be found in the food courts at Maui Marketplace and Kaahumanu Center.

Finally, for those who need their weekly fix of something fried and wrapped in Styrofoam,

Kahului's streets behind Maui Mall are dotted with a slew of fast-food chain restaurants.

Moderate

The Maui Beach Hotel's **Rainbow Dining Room** serves food in the second-floor restaurant. You can fill up here at breakfast 7–9:30 A.M. Order à la carte Mon.–Fri. or try the Saturday and Sunday buffet for $7.50. A lunch buffet is served 11 A.M.–2 P.M. daily for $9.95. Order off the menu for dinner or choose the Japanese dinner buffet 5:30–8 P.M. for $17.95. On the lobby level, dine at the **Red Dragon Restaurant.** Open nightly, it features an all-you-can-eat Chinese buffet on Wednesday 5:30–8 P.M. for $21.95 per person.

Vi's Restaurant, 808/871-6494, at the Maui Seaside Hotel, serves a standard American fare breakfast 7–9 A.M. for $7 or less and dinner 6–8 P.M. for under $15. Vi's offers more than 20 dinners such as fresh fish and steak, and breakfasts include its well-known omelets and hotcakes, plus other island favorites.

In the Kahului Shopping Center is **Ichiban Restaurant,** 808/871-6977, an authentic and inexpensive Japanese eatery, open daily except Sunday 6:30 A.M.–2 P.M., dinner 5–9 P.M., featuring full and continental breakfast, along with Japanese, American, and local specialties. Much of the breakfast menu is typically American, like eggs and bacon, omelets, and pancakes, most around $6. The lunch menu includes teriyaki chicken or shrimp tempura, chicken cutlet, *don buri* dishes, a variety of *udon,* and basic noodles, most $5–8. Dinner features combination plates, with your choice of any two items like shrimp and vegetable tempura, sashimi, or teriyaki chicken for around $14, along with more expensive special combinations like steak and lobster, the most expensive item on the menu, for $20–26. In addition, the sushi bar is open for lunch and dinner, with individual pieces ranging $3.75–6.75.

Around back in the Kahului Shopping Center is the **Asian Cuisine Yakiniku and Sports Bar,** 808/877-7776. This oddly named place does in fact have a sports bar, and the food it serves is mostly Korean with select Japanese dishes thrown in as well. Try the marinated beef Bul Ko Ki for $14.95, tofu stew Sun Tubu Chi Ke for $9.95, or the simple mixed rice and vegetable Bi Bim Bap for $8.95.

MAUI

Koho Grill and Bar, at the Kaahumanu Center, 808/877-5588, is an easygoing, good-time place for lunch and dinner. Koho combines appetizers and salads with burgers, plate lunches, a few Mexican and Italian dishes, plus fish and standard American meat entrées. The food is nothing special, but you won't be disappointed either.

Also at the Kaahumanu Center, but upstairs, is **Moondoggy's,** 808/873-8550, a combination restaurant and brewpub. Much of the food is of the light and quick variety—salads, sandwiches, burgers, pizza—but prime rib, garlic chicken, fish tacos, and a Hawaiian plate are also on the menu, with most entrées under $10. This is one of only two brewpubs on Maui, and about 40–60 barrels of beer are brewed here every month—mostly light brews. Try the Bikini Light, Pu'uwai Gold, Dirty Lickin's, or other seasonal beers. Happy hour Mon.–Thurs. runs 4–6 P.M.

At the corner of Dairy Road and the Hana Highway is **Marco's Grill and Deli,** 808/877-4446, a casual place with black and white leather booths and cane chairs set around tiled tables. It's very Italian and you might hear Tony Bennett being played as background music. For breakfast try chocolate cinnamon French toast for $6.95, pancakes, omelets, or pastries. A quick lunch might be one of the many deli sandwiches or a hot sandwich from the grill, for under $11. Among the usual Italian fare are Italian sausage and linguine at $15.95 and veal parmesan for $18.95. Other specialties are vodka rigatoni or ravioli at $15.95 and seafood pasta at $20.95. Take-out is available for anything on the menu, or choose something from the deli case. Open 7:30 A.M.–10 P.M. daily.

The only on-the-water dining in Kahului is the **Hideaway** restaurant, next to Hoaloha Park, 808/873-6555. Hideaway does a breakfast and lunch buffet along with its à la carte menu, which is a combination of American standard and local dishes. The dinner menu is heavy on the meats and seafood, with the pork ribs a signature item. Entrées are all under $15.95, many less, and the *keiki* menu makes this a more affordable place for families. With dark wood overtones and low lighting, the Hideaway might also be a romantic spot for those who don't want to spend a bundle.

Fine Dining

Like many of his other establishments, Sam Choy's wonderful Maui restaurant has a very commercial location—it's at the Kaahumanu Center. **Sam Choy's Kahului,** 808/893-0366, serves breakfast 7–10:30 A.M., lunch 10:30 A.M.–3 P.M., and dinner 5–9 P.M. (Friday and Saturday to 9:30 P.M.). As usual, the atmosphere is casual and the food is artful. Choose a table in the back or a stool at the counter and watch the cooks prepare your food in the open kitchen. For breakfast try Sam's plantation-style breakfast, which is two eggs; your choice of meat; rice, hash browns or home fries; and toast and jelly for $6.50, or such things as steak and eggs for $10.95, or veggie moco at $6.95. Lunch offerings include plate lunches, and rice and noodle dishes, most below $9. Dinners are more expensive, $18–30, with such items as oven-roasted duck, Asian veal osso bucco, and Hoisin-glazed pork ribs, with the most pricey being the Hawaiian-style seafood bouillabaisse. Although Sam Choy's is decorated in a pleasing manner, people come for the food—the best in town. There are always large portions, and the presentation is as fine as the taste. It's always busy, so come early for lunch; dinner reservations recommended.

Groceries

For basic grocery items, try any of the following full-service stores in Kahului: **Star Market** at the Maui Mall, **Ah Fooks** at the Kahului Shopping Center, **Foodland** at the Kaahumanu Center, or **Safeway** at 170 E. Kamehameha Ave. behind the Maui Mall. **Down to Earth Natural Foods,** 305 Dairy Rd. across from Maui Marketplace, is open Mon.–Sat. 7 A.M.–9 P.M., and Sunday 8 A.M.–8 P.M. It's a full-service natural foods grocery with bulk items, canned and boxed goods, fresh vegetables and fruit, vitamins, minerals, and supplements, and health and beauty items. The store also has a deli counter, salad bar, hot entrée bar, and a bakery.

For a quick stop at a basic bottle shop try **Ah Fooks** at the Kahului Shopping Center or **Star Market** at the Maui Mall.

ENTERTAINMENT

The six-plex **Kaahumanu Theater,** on the second floor of the Kaahumanu Center, 808/873-3133, screens shows for $7 adults, $4 teens, and $2 children. At the Maui Mall, the **Maui Mall Cinema,** 808/661-3347, has eight screens, and tickets run $7.50 adults and $3.50 for those age 3–11.

If you like to see the pins fall, head for the **Aloha Bowling Center,** 808/243-9511, on Ka'ahumanu Avenue just up from Baldwin High School. More modern than its smaller cousin in Wailuku, its 20 lanes have computer score keeping. Open daily; adult evening play runs $2.75 a game.

Live bands perform Friday until 2 A.M. and Saturday afternoon at Moondoggy's at the Kaahumanu Center; a DJ spins plays hits on Saturday night. Expect a cover for the evening entertainment. Moondoggy's brews its own beer, so that's a draw, and since this restaurant has the same owner as the well-heeled Don Ho Grill on O'ahu, big-name bands are sometimes brought in to play.

You can hear free musical entertainment at both the Maui Mall and Kaahumanu Center, usually over the lunch hour or during early evening. These schedules vary throughout the month, but definitely stop and listen if the music is going when you are shopping.

The **Maui Arts and Cultural Center** has a varied program of music, dance, film, and visual arts showings at its complex near the harbor. This is one of the finest arts venues in the state, so check out what's on the program by calling 808/242-7469.

RECREATION

Kahului is by no means a recreational center, but it does offer options for sports and recreation. The War Memorial Center is the largest organized sports game venue on the island, a place to watch baseball, football, basketball, and track and field events. Of particular interest is the college all-star Hula Bowl, held here each fall. Nearby beaches are known throughout the world for excellent windsurfing and kitesurfing, the island's newest golf course is just outside of town, and while the mountain is a distance away, you can start your journey for a bike ride down the mountain here.

Kahului has the greatest concentration of windsurfing and water-sport shops on the is-

land, many of them at or near the corner of Hana Highway and Dairy Road. Shop here and comparison shop before going anywhere else.

Golf

Southwest of downtown Kahului in the rolling sand hills of the isthmus is the "Irish Linksland Design" course, **The Dunes at Maui Lani,** 808/873-0422. Undulating over the sand dunes, with plenty of elevation change, this course is a welcome addition to the range of courses offered on the island. Designed by Nelson and Haworth, the facility opened in 1999 with rudimentary facilities, but full-service pro shop, restaurant, and driving range were added in 2000. Greens fees run $75 regular, $37 twilight, reduced rates for residents.

SHOPPING

Because of its malls, Kahului has the best all-around shopping on the island. Combine this with the smaller shopping plazas, Kmart, Costco, and individual shops around town and you can find absolutely everything you might need. For something different, don't miss the **Maui Swap Meet,** 808/877-3100, on Pu'unene Avenue next to the post office every Saturday 7 A.M.–noon and Wednesday 8 A.M.–1 P.M.

MAUI SAND DUNES

The isthmus of Maui connects the island's two great mountains. This low broad plain was formed by lava that spewed over thousands of years, connecting the two mountains (and at one time also connecting Maui to Lana'i and Kaho'olawe) before the fire ceased and Maui drifted to the northwest. Over the eons, coral and sand formed along the periphery of the island and strong winds from the northeast lifted this mixture off the beaches along the isthmus's north shore and deposited it inland, forming sand dunes. The isthmus is fairly flat, but dunes have formed as low (mostly), rounded hills, principally on the western side of the isthmus. They rise to about 200 feet in height where they push against the mountainside at Wailuku.

You can also shop almost the minute you arrive or just before you leave at two touristy but good shops along Keolani Place. Less than a half mile from the airport are the **T-shirt Factory,** with original Maui designs and custom T-shirts for $5–25, as well as aloha shirts, sarongs, and pareu; and **Coral Factory,** for pink and black coral and jewelry set with semiprecious stones—the Coral Factory seems to be set up largely to cater to Japanese tour groups. When Keolani Place turns into Dairy Road you'll find **Airport Flower & Fruits, Inc.,** which can provide you with produce that's pre-inspected and admissible to the Mainland. It also has a large selection of lei, which can be packed to go. On Dairy Road between Haleakala and Hana highways are the two huge stores housing **Kmart** and **Costco.** Mainland American mercantilism has invaded.

The two-story **Kaahumanu Center** along Ka'ahumanu Avenue is Kahului's largest mall, has the widest selection of stores on the island with goods priced for the local market, and has plenty of free parking. The mall's central courtyard is covered with a big skylight and a huge sail-like expanse of canvas—a good way to let the light and breezes through. You'll find the big stores like **Liberty House, Sears,** and **JCPenney** anchoring this mall, with the smaller **Shirokiya** here as well. Numerous apparel, shoe, jewelry, and specialty stores and three restaurants and a brewpub fill this center, and a half dozen inexpensive international fast-food eateries are in the food court. Several of the specialty shops are a large **Waldenbooks** for one of the best selections of books on Maui, **Serendipity** for oriental furniture and home accessories, **GNC** for nutritional supplements, and **Wolf Camera** for all your camera needs. On the upper level, you can relax in the cool dark comfort of the **Kaahumanu Theater** and catch a movie. Entertainment is often offered at the center stage over the lunch hour and at about 7 P.M. in the evening, but not necessarily on a regular schedule.

The low-rise, open-air, and newly renovated **Maui Mall** is more pedestrian, yet it has a pleasant ambience as its buildings are set around courtyards. At the intersection of Hana Highway and Ka'ahumanu Avenue, Maui Mall has **Longs Drugs** for everything from aspirin to film, a **Star Market, GNC, Roy's Photo Center,** the unusual **Paper Airplane Museum,** a mega-plex theater, a handful of clothing and specialty stores, and a couple of places for quick foods. On Friday, there is free live entertainment at the mall's center stage.

While **Kahului Shopping Center,** 47 Ka'ahumanu Ave., has lost much of its vitality, you'll still find **Ah Fooks** supermarket, open daily from 6:30 A.M. and specializing in Asian foods; the smaller **Ji-Mi Asian Food Mart;** the moderate and pleasant **Ichiban Restaurant;** a **Salvation Army Thrift Store;** and **Central Pacific Bank.** Maui Organic Farmers' Market holds court here on Wednesday 8 A.M.–noon. This mall is less distinctive than the other two along Ka'ahumanu Avenue and seems to have suffered most because of the newer malls in town.

The Old Kahului Shopping Center, 55 Ka'ahumanu Ave., just across from the Maui Mall, is just that, an old building from 1916 that held a bank and a series of shops that was modernized and brought back to life in the late '80s. Once full of boutiques and specialty shops, it now only has two ordinary shops and a chiropractic office. **Lightning Bolt** specializes in surfboards and surf attire, modern fashions, women's apparel, hats, and sunglasses, while **Fabric Mart** has miles of cloth, and craft and sewing supplies.

The newest mall in Kahului, with a style from Anywhere U.S.A., occupies a huge area along Dairy Road. This is **Maui Marketplace,** and here you'll find such stores as **Borders Books and Music;** the **Sports Authority** for a large selection of athletic clothing and equipment, bicycles, and camping and fishing supplies; numerous clothing stores including **Hawaiian Island Creations;** a **Sunglass Hut,** the huge **Eagle Hardware and Garden** center for anything you might need for your house or yard; **OfficeMax** for your business needs; several jewelry stores; numerous other smaller shops; and a food court. For banking needs, try the **Bank of Hawaii** along Dairy Road.

Also new is the **Triangle Square** mall across from Kahana Pond, where you'll find **HST** and **Neilpryde Maui** for all water sports equipment and information. A boardsail away at the corner across from Kmart is **Hawaiian Island Surf and Sport,** which also carries a multitude of water sports equipment, new and used, for sale and rental. Next door is **Island Biker,** which sells and services road bikes and mountain bikes and rents mountain bikes. Numerous other water-sport shops are within a stone's throw of the Kanaha Pond.

At the **Dairy Center,** at the intersection of Dairy Road and Hana Highway, you'll find **Extreme Sports Maui** and **Kinko's** aside from several eateries, **Marco's Grill,** and **Maui Coffee Roasters.** Extreme Sports rents the usual water equipment, plus skateboards and bikes, and has a small climbing wall.

Of the freestanding shops in town, **Two Frogs Hugging,** 808/873-7860, at the corner of Ka'ahumanu and Pu'unene Avenues, is one of the most unusual with its collection of wooden furniture and wood and stone carvings imported mostly from Indonesia. Look for the two hugging frogs stone sculpture out front.

SERVICES

Kahului has numerous banks, most with ATM machines, and the majority are near the intersection of Ka'ahumanu and Pu'unene Avenues. There is a Bank of Hawaii, 27 S. Pu'unene Ave., 808/871-8250; First Hawaiian Bank, 20 W. Ka'ahumanu Ave., 808/877-2311; American Savings Bank branches at 275 Ka'ahumanu Ave., 808/871-5501, and 73 Pu'unene Ave., 808/871-8411; City Bank, at the Kaahumanu Center, 808/871-7761; and Central Pacific Bank, 85 W. Ka'ahumanu Ave., 808/877-3387.

The Kahului post office, 138 S. Pu'unene Ave. (Route 350), has hours Mon.–Fri. 8:30 A.M.–5 P.M. and Saturday 9 A.M.–noon. For information, call 800/275-8777.

The library, tucked quietly under the trees at 90 School St., 808/873-3097, is open Monday, Thursday, Friday, and Saturday 10 A.M.–5 P.M., Tuesday and Wednesday 10 A.M.–8 P.M.

The **W & F Washerette,** 125 S. Wakea, 808/877-0353, features video games to while away the time as well as a little snack bar. Soap and change machines, drop-off service, and dry cleaning available. Open daily 6 A.M.–9 P.M.

For medical emergencies, try **Maui Memorial Medical Center,** 221 Mahalani, 808/244-9056. Clinics include **Kaiser Permanente,** 20 Mahalani, 808/243-6000. Both these are between downtown Kahului and downtown Wailuku, with the medical center up behind the county police station, the clinic across the road from the police station. At the Maui Marketplace, **International Healthcare Center,** 808/877-5844, sees urgent care patients 10 A.M.–10 P.M.

If you need to check your email while on Maui, stop at **Kinko's,** 395 Dairy Rd., 808/871-2000, and use a computer for a reasonable 20 cents per minute, or avail yourself of any of the facility's other numerous copy and office services. For other copy, postal, and business services, try **Mail Boxes Etc.,** 415 Dairy Rd. across from Kmart, 808/877-0333; or **OfficeMax,** in the Maui Marketplace, 808/877-9448.

WAILUKU

Often, historical towns maintain a certain aura long after their time of importance has passed. Wailuku is one of these. Maui's county seat since 1905, the town has the feel of one that has been important for a long time. Wailuku earned its name, "Water of Destruction," from a ferocious battle fought by Kamehameha I against Maui warriors just up the road in 'Iao Valley. The slaughter was so intense that more than four miles of the local stream literally ran red with blood. In the 1800s, the missionaries settled in Wailuku, and their architectural influences, such as a white-steeple church and the courthouse at the top of the main street, give an impression of a New England town. Later in the century, sugar came to town and this vast industry grew with muscle and pumped great vitality into the community. After the turn of the 20th century, Wailuku strengthened its stance as the island's center of government, business, and industry, and the wealthy and influential built homes here. Wailuku maintained this strong position until the 1960s, when the sugar industry declined and the growth of tourism began to create other centers of population and industry on the island. Although still a vibrant government and population center, much of Wailuku's importance to the island's economy has been eclipsed.

To West Maui
Backside

WAILUKU

HAPPY VALLEY

'Iao Stream

WILI PA LOOP RD.

POST OFFICE

KALA ST.

330

'ULEI PL.

SAM SATO'S

MAUI TOURIST
BUREAU

MISSION ST.

MAKUA ST.

KAHAWAI ST.

KONAHEA ST.

MILL ST.

TASTY CRUST ST.

KANIELA ST.

BANANA
BUNGALOW

MARKET ST.

NORTH ST.

CENTRAL AVE.

MOLINA'S

WILD BANANA
GALLERY

FUJIYA ST.
SIAM THAI

MAUI BOWLING

JODO
MISSION

NANI ST.

A
SAIGON
CAFE

MAUI BAKE
SHOP

NORTHSHORE
INN

RAMON'S

SIMPLE
PLEASURES

'IAO
THEATER

330

To Kahului

SAENG'S

CHURCH ST.

SIG ZANE
DESIGN

ANTIQUE
SHOPS

OOKA
SUPERMARKET

VINYARD ST.

N HIGH ST.

E. MAIN ST.

FIRE STATION

CHURCH

GAS STATION

GAS STATION

S. MARKET ST.

PAPERBACKS
PLUS

MAUI MEDICAL
GROUP

WELLS ST.

WELLS
PARK

To 'Iao
Needle

PARK

STATE OFFICE
BUILDING

FEDERAL BUILDING

KANOA ST.

WAI'ALE RD.

KA'AHUMANU
CHURCH

BAILEY HOUSE
MUSEUM

LIBRARY

AUPUNI ST.

PAKAHI ST.

KOELI ST.

COUNTY OFFICE
BUILDING

PALUA ST.

'IAO SCHOOL

WAILUKU
PUBLIC SCHOOL

ICHIBAN
OKAZUYA

KAOHU ST.

KAIUA ST.

0   0.25 mi

0   0.25 km

MALAKO ST.

KAHO'OKELE ST.

OLD WAILUKU
INN

To Lahaina

MAKAHALA ST.

MAUI

MOON

While some of Wailuku is pretty, it's a mixed bag in other areas, including much of the downtown area. The town center, while once dignified, has lost its blush, yet there is some effort to revitalize it. Comely rows of plantation-era bungalows are scattered here and there around town, yet fading sections past their prime also exist, not always too far from the new and modern developments. Built on the rolling foothills of the West Maui Mountains, this adds some character—unlike the often-flat layout of many other Hawaiian towns. You can "do" Wailuku in only an hour, though most people don't even give it that much time. They just pass through on their way to 'Iao Needle, where everyone goes, or simply skirt the edge of town and head on to Kahakuloa, around the back side.

You *can* see Wailuku's sights from the window of your car, but don't shortchange yourself this way. Definitely visit the Bailey House Museum, and while you're out, walk the grounds of Ka'ahumanu Church. Clustered near these two are other historical buildings, several of which are listed on registers of historic places, both state and national. These include the Circuit Courthouse (1907), Old County Building (1927), Territorial Building (1931), Wailuku Public Library (1928), Wailuku Union Church (1911), and the Wailuku Public School (1904). One block away is the Church of the Good Shepherd (1911), and beyond that the 'Iao Theater (1928). This theater is the last remaining of the 19 theaters that dotted the island in the era between the world wars.

SIGHTS

Ka'ahumanu Church

It's fitting that Maui's oldest existing stone church is named after the resolute but loving Queen Ka'ahumanu. This rock-willed woman is the "Saint Peter" of Hawaii, upon whom Christianity in the islands was built. She was *the* most important early convert, often attending services in Kahului's humble grass-hut chapel. It is also worth noting that the church was erected on Maui king Kahekili's *heiau*—the squashing of one religion with the growing presence of another. In 1832, when the congregation was founded, an adobe church was built on the same spot and named in her honor. Rain and time washed it away, to be replaced by the island's first stone structure in 1837. In 1876 the church went through its fourth metamorphosis, the church tower and clock being delayed until 1884, and what remains is the white and green structure we know today. Its construction was supervised by the missionary Edward Bailey, whose home stands to the rear. A three-year renovation project ended in 1976, bringing the church back to form and allowing its placement on the National Register of Historic Places. Oddly enough, the steeple was repaired in 1984 by Skyline Engineers, who hail from Massachusetts, the same place from which the missionaries came 150 years earlier! You can see the church sitting there on High Street (Route 30), but it's sometimes closed during the week. Sunday services are at 9 A.M., when the Hawaiian congregation sings the Lord's praise in their native language. An excellent cultural and religious event to attend!

Bailey House Museum

This is the old Bailey House, built 1833–1850, with various rooms added throughout the years. From 1832 it housed the Wailuku Female Seminary, of which Edward Bailey was principal until the school closed in 1849. After that, the Baileys bought the property and lived here until the 1890s. Bailey then went on to manage the Wailuku Sugar Company. More important for posterity, he became a prolific landscape painter of various areas around the island. Most of his paintings, 26 in the museum's holdings, record the period 1866–1896 and are now displayed in the Bailey Gallery, once the sitting room of the house. The one-time seminary dining room, now housing the museum gift shop, was his studio. In July 1957 this old missionary homestead formally became the Maui Historical Society Museum, at which time it acquired the additional name of Hale Hoikeike, "House of Display." It closed in 1973 when it was placed on the National Register of Historic Places, then was refurbished and reopened in July 1975.

You'll be amazed at the two-foot-thick walls the missionaries taught the Hawaiians to build, using goat hair as the binding agent. Years of whitewashing make them resemble new-fallen snow. The rooms inside are given over to various themes. The Hawaiian Room houses excellent

the Bailey House

ROBERT NILSEN

examples of the often practical artifacts of pre-contact Hawaii, like stone tools, bone fishhooks, and wooden weapons; especially notice the fine displays of tapa cloth and calabashes. Hawaiian tapa, now nearly a lost art, was considered Polynesia's finest and most advanced. Upstairs is the bedroom. It's quite large and dominated by a four-poster bed. In this and an adjoining room, there's a dresser with a jewelry box, other pieces of furniture, toys for children, and clothes including hats and fine lace gloves. Downstairs you'll discover the sitting room and kitchen, heart of the house: the "feelings" are strongest here, and perhaps more so because original paintings by Edward Bailey adorn the walls. The solid 'ohi'a lintel over the doorway is as stout as the spirits of the people who once lived here. The stonework on the floor is well laid and the fireplace is totally homey.

Go outside! The lanai runs across the entire front and down the side. Around back is the canoe shed, housing a refurbished sennit-sewn outrigger canoe from the late 1800s, as well as Duke Kahanamoku's redwood surfboard from about 1910. On the grounds you'll also see exhibits of sugarcane, sugar pots, *konane* boards, and various Hawaiian artifacts around the lush and landscaped lawn. At 2375-A Main St., the Bailey House Museum is open Mon.–Sat. 10 A.M.–4 P.M. Admission is well worth the $5 for adults, $4 for seniors, and $1 for children 7–12. Upon arrival, a docent will introduce you to the

house and then let you make a self-guided tour at your leisure. Adjacent in the gift shop is a terrific selection of high-quality souvenirs, books, music, and Hawaiiana at better-than-average prices. All are done by Hawaiian artists and craftspeople, and many are created specifically for this shop.

The office of the **Maui Historical Society,** 808/244-3326, website: www.mauimuseum.org, email: office@mauimuseum.org, is in the basement of the Bailey House. It seems appropriate that this society, which collects and preserves artifacts and disseminates information about the history and culture of Maui, should be located on the grounds where Kahekili, Maui's last king, had his compound.

Kepaniwai Park

As you head up Route 320 to 'Iao Valley, you're in for a real treat. Two miles after leaving Wailuku, you come across Kepaniwai Park and Heritage Gardens. Here the architect, Richard C. Tongg, envisioned and created a park dedicated to all of Hawaii's people. See the Portuguese villa and garden complete with an outdoor oven, a thatch-roofed Hawaiian grass shack, a New England "salt box," a Chinese pagoda, a Japanese teahouse with authentic garden, and a bamboo house—the little "sugar shack" that songs and dreams are made of. Admission is free and there are pavilions with picnic tables often used by families for a Sunday picnic. This now-tranquil spot is where the Maui warriors fell to the invincible Kamehameha and his merciless patron war god, Ku. Kepaniwai means "Damming of the Waters"—literally with corpses. Kepaniwai is now a monument to humanity's higher nature: harmony and beauty.

Hawaii Nature Center, 'Iao Valley

At the upper end of Kepaniwai Park is the Hawaii Nature Center, 'Iao Valley, a private, nonprofit educational and interactive science center—good for kids and grown-ups alike and highly recommended. Open daily 10 A.M.–4 P.M., $6 adults, $4 children, this center boasts 30 exhibits that will beg you to participate, challenge your mind, and teach you about all aspects of Hawaiian nature at the same time. This seems an appropriate spot for a nature center as the West Maui Mountains harbor 12 distinct plant communities, about 300 species of plants, of which 10 are endemic to this locale, and literally thousands of varieties of animals and insects. On weekdays, one-mile 1.5-hour nature walks are guided through the valley to bring you face to face with some of the wonders that this valley has to offer. These hikes generally start at 11 A.M. and 2 P.M. and cost $25 adults and $23 children, which includes entrance to the exhibits. Reservations are required. Call 808/244-6500 for all activities and other nature-based programs. The center has a website at www.panworld.net/~hinature.

The Changing Profile

Up the road toward 'Iao Valley you come to a scenic area long known as Pali 'Ele'ele, or Black Gorge. This stream-eroded narrow slit canyon has attracted attention for centuries. It was one of the places in 'Iao Valley where *ali'i* were buried, so that no one would discover their final resting place. Amazingly, after President Kennedy was assassinated, people noticed his likeness portrayed there by a series of large boulders on one side of the valley wall; mention of a profile had never been noted or recorded there before. Bring your binoculars, as the pipe that once served as a rudimentary sighting instrument is gone. The likeness—with eyes closed in deep repose—is uncanny, and easily seen, unlike most of these formations, where you have to stretch your imagination to the breaking point. Recently, however, the powers that be (a committee of the State Department of Land and Natural Resources) have pronounced that this image is really that of the late-15th-century *kahuna* Kauaka'iwai. Legend has it that he was turned to stone to protect the *ali'i* buried in this valley. Go figure.

'Iao Valley State Park

This valley has been a sacred spot and a place of pilgrimage since ancient times. Before Westerners arrived, the people of Maui, who came here to pay homage to the "Eternal Creator," named this valley 'Iao, "Cloud Supreme" or "Supreme Light." Facing almost directly east, the valley catches the warming morning sunlight. According to legend, the gods Maui and Hina raised their daughter 'Iao in this valley. As

ROAD TO 'IAO

ROBERT NILSEN

'Iao Needle

'Iao grew, she became entranced with a half-man, half-fish god, and they became lovers. This arrangement did not please her father, who, in revenge, turned 'Iao's lover into a stone pinnacle, the peak we know as 'Iao Needle.

Historically, 'Iao Valley was a place set aside and did not belong to the traditional *ahupua'a* land-division system. No commoners were allowed into the valley except on special occasions, and royalty were buried here in secret graves. During the Battle of Kepaniwai in 1790, when King Kamehameha defeated Maui's King Kahekili, this valley was valiantly defended but overrun. Countless commoners perished while the *ali'i* escaped over the mountains to Olowalu.

In the center of this velvety green amphitheater-like valley is a pillar of stone rising more than 1,200 feet (actual height above sea level is 2,250 feet), its grassy plateau top at one time a natural altar and lookout for defense. Kuka'emoku, now commonly called "The Needle," is a tough basaltic ridge that remained after

water swirled away the weaker stone surrounding it, leaving only a saddle that connects it to the valley wall, unseen from below. 'Iao Valley is actually the remnant of the volcanic caldera of the West Maui Mountains, whose grooved walls have been smoothed and enlarged by the restlessness of mountain streams. Robert Louis Stevenson had to stretch poetic license to create a word for 'Iao when he called it "viridescent."

The road ends in a parking lot. Signs point you to paths, tame and well maintained, some even paved, with plenty of vantage points for photographers. If you take the lower path to the river below, you'll find a good-size, popular swimming hole; but remember, these are the West Maui Mountains, and it can rain at any time, causing water to rise rapidly. Pu'u Kukui, West Maui Mountains' tallest peak, lies on the western edge of this crater rim and gets about 400 inches of rain a year! On the east side of the stream below the bridge, a loop path leads though a garden of native plants. Beyond the bridge, steps lead up to an observation pavilion. You can escape the crowds, however, even in this heavily touristed area. As you head back, take the paved path that bears to the right. It soon becomes dirt, skirting the river, and the tourists magically disappear. Here are a number of pint-size pools where you can take a refreshing dip. A rudimentary path continues up this valley. About a mile up is a fork in the stream, beyond which it is not recommended to go.

'Iao is for day use only; hours are 7 A.M.–7 P.M. On your way back to Wailuku you might take a five-minute side excursion up to Wailuku Heights. Look for the road on your right. There's little here besides a mid- to upper-end residential area, but the view below over the isthmus is tops!

Maui Tropical Plantation and Country Store

This attraction is somewhat out of the ordinary. The 60-acre Maui Tropical Plantation, 808/244-7643, presents a model of a working plantation that you can tour by small tram. Most interesting is an up-close look at Maui's agricultural abundance. Displays of each of these products are situated around the taro patches at the plantation village. A 40-minute tram ride takes you through fields of cane, banana, guava, mango, papaya,

MAUI

pineapple, coffee, and macadamia nuts; flowers here and there add exotic color. Leaving every 45 minutes 10 A.M.–4 P.M., this tram runs $9.50 for adults and $3.50 for children 3–12. The plantation, with its restaurant, gift shop, and tropical flower nursery, is near Waikapu, a small village along Route 30 between Wailuku and Ma'alaea. If you visit over the noon hour, stop by the Plantation Cafe for lunch, open 10:30 A.M.–3 P.M. daily. The Country Store here sells Maui-produced goods and can mail gift packages of fruits, nuts, and coffee, while the nursery will ship flowers to anywhere in the country. Look for the windmill! Open daily 9 A.M.–5 P.M.

ACCOMMODATIONS

Visitors to Wailuku mostly stay elsewhere on Maui because there are only a few specialized and humble hostels and one historic bed-and-breakfast inn.

Under $50

The **Banana Bungalow**, 310 N. Market St., Wailuku, HI 96793, 808/244-5090 or 800/846-7835, fax 808/846-3678, website: www.maui-hostel.com, email: info@mauihostel.com, is on the edge of Happy Valley. Until a few years ago, this was a flophouse for locals who were down on their luck. Now it's a clean and spartan hostel, with a fresh coat of (yellow) paint, some artistic decorations, refurbished bathrooms up and down, and a renovated common room. Typically, you're liable to hear languages from a half dozen countries, and if you're into sailboarding or just after a cross-cultural experience, this is the spot. The Banana Bungalow offers basic accommodations, and if you care more about your experience than your sleeping arrangements, it's the place for you. Rates are $29 single, $40 double, $50 triple, or $16 for a bunk in a four- to six-person dorm (co-ed and female-only), and this includes the bed linens. Monthly rates can be arranged. Extra services include a free and convenient airport/beach shuttle; daily low-cost adventure tours with two new vans; laundry and storage facilities; a common room for conversation, TV, or music; free Internet access; inexpensive morning and evening meals at the communal kitchen, with free morning coffee; a hot

tub, barbecue grill, and hammocks in the garden under tropical fruit trees; discount rates on water equipment and lessons; and discount car rental deals. The daily tours, different every day, are sign-up tours open to anyone, guests or not, on a first-come, first-served basis. Office hours are 8 A.M.–11 P.M., but there is no curfew as there is a combination entry.

The **Northshore Inn,** 2080 Vineyard St., 808/242-8999 or 800/647-6284, fax 808/244-5004, website: hostelhawaii.com, email: northshore@hostelhawaii.com. is easily spotted with its row of international flags fluttering from the second-floor balcony. Enter via the alley sidewalk. With a capacity of about 45, this clean, light, and comfortable hostel caters mostly to young independent travelers and surfers. Skylights brighten the upstairs; potted plants add color to the walls; the homey sitting room offers a place for the international guests to talk, listen to music, or watch television; the balcony is a fine place to catch the evening air; and a bulletin board is filled with helpful information about Maui and the other islands. Bunk rooms go for $16 a bed, single rooms $29, and double rooms $38, exclusive of tax but including bed linens; all rooms share four bathrooms. There are laundry facilities; a safe for valuables; storage facilities for sailboards, backpacks, and large items; free use of boogie boards and snorkel equipment; cheap moped, bicycle, and surfboard rental; a full communal kitchen, free morning coffee; inexpensive dinners nightly; free evening movies; free Internet access; and a small garden in the back with an 80-year-old banyan tree and tropical fruit trees. Ask about low rental-car rates. The Northshore Inn won the respect of the community for transforming the former fleabag Wailuku Grand Hotel into a viable business and dealing equitably with the locals.

Molina's, 197 Market St., 808/244-4100, on the periphery of downtown Wailuku, offers utilitarian rooms at $35 a night, $125 a week, or $450 a month. Other rooms go for $45 a night, and a bunk in the dorm runs $18 per person. All rooms have bathrooms, TVs, and small refrigerators. The $25 key deposit is returned on exit. Although cleaned up in the last few years, Bogart playing a character with a five-day-old beard and a hangover might still be comfortable waking up at this basic, clean, and serviceable fleabag.

MAUI

Many renters are long-term, so be sure to call ahead to see if a room is available. Downstairs, Molina's Sports Bar is a neighborhood joint with satellite TV and live music on weekends.

$100–150

The first, best, and only fine place to stay in Wailuku is at the attentively renovated **Old Wailuku Inn at Ulupono,** now on the Hawaii Register of Historic Places. Built in 1924 for the son and daughter-in-law of Maui's first bank president, this was the queen of homes in one of Maui's most posh neighborhoods. Refurbished in 1997, this house was brought back to its early-20th-century charm, lovingly detailed, filled with period furniture that evokes the feeling of grandma's house, and decorated with Hawaiian and Asian antiques and artwork. It's a gem. Yet no modern amenity or comfort is left out. Each room has a TV, VCR, telephone, private bath, ceiling fan, and gorgeous Hawaiian quilt on its spacious bed. A fax machine, photocopier, and computer are also available for use. The house has central air-conditioning, but the cooling trade winds are generally enough to moderate the temperature. Catching the morning sun, the screened breakfast room looks out over the rear garden. The open-air front porch is a perfect spot for afternoon tea or reading a book from the extensive house library, and the living room is a fine place to relax in the evening. Each of the seven guest rooms is named for a Hawaiian flower, and their color and design motifs follow. The four upstairs rooms are spacious and grand, with native hardwood floors and 10-foot ceilings. The downstairs rooms are cozier, and two have their own courtyards. A gourmet breakfast accompanies each night's stay and, no matter what the offering, is tasty, filling, nutritious, and well presented. You'll be pampered. Born and raised on the island, the gracious and personable hosts, Tom and Janice Fairbanks, have intimate knowledge of what to do, what to see, and where to eat throughout the island and will gladly share their knowledge and recommendations with you. Rooms run $120–180 double occupancy, two nights minimum. Parking is on property. For information and reservations contact the Old Wailuku Inn at Ulupono, 2199 Kaho'okele St., Wailuku, HI 96793,

800/305-4899 or 808/244-5897, fax 808/242-9600, website: www.aitv.com/ulupono, email: Mauibandb@aol.com.

FOOD

Downtown

Wailuku has some of the best and the most inexpensive restaurants on Maui. The establishments listed below are all in the bargain or reasonable range. The decor in most is basic and homey, with the emphasis placed on the food. Even here in this nontouristy town, however, some of the restaurants are sprucing up and becoming a bit gentrified.

Saeng's, 2119 Vineyard, 808/244-1567, serves excellent Thai food at great prices. Dishes include appetizers like Thai crisp noodles for $4.95, green papaya salad for $6.50, and shrimp salad at $8.50. The savory soups, enough for two, include spicy coconut shrimp soup for $9.50 and po teak, a zesty seafood combination soup, for $10.95. Thai specialties such as pad thai vegetables, chicken Thai curry, and eggplant shrimp are all under $10, while vegetarian selections like stir-fry vegetables and Evil Prince tofu are under $7.50. Only the seafood plates are more expensive at $12.95. Although the interior is quite tasteful with linen tablecloths and paisley booths, the best seating is outside in the covered garden patio where a small waterfall gurgles pleasantly. Open Mon.–Fri. for lunch 11 A.M.–2:30 P.M. and dinner nightly 5–9:30 P.M.

Siam Thai is a small restaurant painted black and white at 123 N. Market, 808/244-3817, open Mon.–Sat. 11:30 A.M.–2:30 P.M., daily 5–9:30 P.M. It serves excellent Thai food with an emphasis on vegetarian cuisine, at prices that are comparable with Saeng's. Extensive menu; a perennial favorite.

Stop at **Fujiya,** 133 Market St., 808/244-0206, for a sit-down meal of fresh fish and sushi, or other Japanese favorites. Open Mon.–Fri. 11 A.M.–2 P.M. and Mon.–Sat. 5–9 P.M.

Ramon's, 2101 Vineyard, 808/244-7243, is back in business after expanding and remodeling—it now seats 200. You can now get 17 combination items on the Mexican side, along with the old favorites, and New York steak and other such dishes. Perhaps the most notable addition is that Ramon's has a sushi bar! Ramon's is open 11 A.M.–9 P.M. for lunch and dinner.

At 2092 Vineyard St. is **Maui Bake Shop and Deli,** 808/242-0064, open weekdays 6 A.M.–4 P.M., Saturday 7 A.M.–2 P.M.. This establishment has a full selection of home-baked goods and sandwiches for about $3.75, with soup du jour $5.95. Daily specials can be pizza, quiche, filled croissants, or even lox and bagels for under $5. Tantalizing baked goods include apple strudel, coconut macaroons, apricot twists, fruit tarts, and homemade pies. Enjoy your selection with an espresso, cappuccino, or hot tea. Maui Bake Shop is a common stop for morning nourishment.

Kitty-corner across the intersection and open Tues.–Fri. 11 A.M.–3 P.M. for vegetarian cuisine is **Simple Pleasures Cafe,** 808/249-0697. Short on hours, but heavy on quality, it offers soups and salads, pastries, samosa, crepes, lasagne, and quiche.

Next door and underneath the Northshore Inn is **Restaurant Mushroom,** 808/244-7117, a clean and reasonably priced place serving local, American, and Japanese foods. You can get mostly soups and sandwiches here as well as saimin and other Asian noodle dishes. It's perhaps best known for its pork and fish plates. Lunch 10:30 A.M.–2 P.M., dinner 5–8 P.M.; reasonably priced.

About a block down Vineyard is the small **Silk Road** restaurant, 808/249-2399, a mostly take-out place that serves Chinese and Westernized Korean dishes. Open Mon.–Sat. 10 A.M.–9 P.M.

If you're looking for a very local breakfast and lunch eatery, head for the **Happy Valley Cafe,** 808/249-0555. Directly across from the Banana Bungalow, it serves hot cakes, loco moco, omelets and the like for breakfast, mostly for under $5, and such items as plate lunches, sandwiches, noodles, and saimin for lunch at $6 and under.

The tiny **Ichiban Okazuya** take-out restaurant is just around the corner from the county office building on Kaohu Street. It's open 7 A.M.–2 P.M. and 4–7 P.M. for katsu, teriyaki, and other quick eats. It has a good reputation that's growing.

A little out of the way at 1792 Main St., but well worth the effort to find, is **A Saigon Cafe,** 808/243-9560. A great family place, clean but not fancy, this may be the best Vietnamese cuisine on the island. It gets a thumbs up from

everyone. Although there's no large sign yet advertising its location, it's a favorite local stop, and you'll know why once you try it. Start with spring rolls at $5.75 or shrimp pops for $7.25 and move on to one of the tasty soups like hot and sour fish soup for $9.20 or a green papaya salad for $5.50. Entrées, all under $10 except the Saigon fondue, which is cooked at your table, include a wide range of noodle, meat, fish, and vegetarian dishes, all with good portions. The menu is extensive. Open daily 10 A.M.–10 P.M., Sunday until 8:30 P.M., this restaurant is behind Ooka Super Market, below the bridge.

Not really in downtown, but on the edge of town toward Kahului near the underpass, is **Stillwell's Bakery and Cafe,** 1740 Ka'ahumanu Ave., 808/243-2243. Having established a fine reputation with locals, it's now becoming known to visitors. The surroundings are nothing special, but the food is worthy of the reputation, and the breads, baked goods, and cakes are delicious—and served at some fine restaurants on the island. Stop in for a pastry and coffee, a lunch sandwich and soup, or other hot entrée. Open Mon.–Sat. 6 A.M.–4 P.M.

Food off the Main Drag
If you get out of downtown and take Mill Street and Lower Main, you'll be rewarded with some of the *most* local and *least* expensive restaurants on West Maui. They are totally unpretentious, serving hefty portions of tasty, homemade local foods. If your aim is to *eat* like a local, search out one of them.

The **Tasty Crust Restaurant,** 1770 Mill St., 808/244-0845, opens daily 5:30 A.M.–11 P.M., Friday and Saturday until midnight. Similar to a diner, with bar stools at the counter, booths, and a few tables, the welcome sign says "This is where old friends meet." If you have to carbo-load for a full day of sailing, snorkeling, or windsurfing, order the famous giant homemade hotcakes.

Sam Sato's, 1750 Wili Pa Loop Rd., 808/244-7124, is in the Mill Yard. Sato's is famous for *manju,* a puff-like pastry from Japan usually filled with lima or *adzuki* beans. It's one of those places that, if you are a local resident, you *must* bring Sato's *manju* when visiting friends or relatives off-island. Aside from the *manju* there are noodles, saimin, sandwiches, and plate lunches for lunch, and omelets and banana hotcakes for breakfast. Many think that Sam serves the best dry mein noodles on the island. Most everything is under $5.50. Open Mon.–Sat. 7 A.M.–2 P.M., pickup until 4 P.M. A highly specialized place, but worth the effort.

Another well-established local place is **Nazo's Restaurant,** 808/244-0529, 1063 Lower Main St., second floor of the Puuone Plaza, an older yellowish two-story building. Park underneath and walk upstairs. Daily specials cost under $9, but Nazo's is renowned for its oxtail soup, a clear-consommé broth with peanuts and water chestnuts floating around, a delicious combination of East and West. Open Mon.–Sat. 10 A.M.–2 P.M. and again 5–9 P.M.

Tokyo Tei, 808/242-9630, in the same complex but downstairs, is another institution that has been around since 1937, serving Japanese dishes to a devoted clientele. Eating here is as consistent as eating at grandma's kitchen, with traditional Japanese dishes like tempura, various *don buri,* and seafood platters. If you want to sample real Japanese food at affordable prices, come here! Open daily 11 A.M.–1:30 P.M. for lunch, 5–8:30 P.M. dinner, open Sunday for dinner only.

Norm's Cafe, "Where food and people of good taste come together," is at 740 Lower Main St., 808/242-1667. A place of local atmosphere in a no-nonsense part of town, the inside is pink, white, and yellow, with booths and a few tables. Breakfast starts at 5 A.M. and includes items like pancakes, omelets, and loco moco. For lunch and dinner, try salads, sandwiches, or a more hearty dish like the bamboo-steamed *ono.* Nothing on the menu is more than $7. Norm's is an institution.

For authentic Korean food in Wailuku, try **Biwon Restaurant,** 808/244-7788, at 752 Lower Main near Norm's.

For a different taste treat, try the traditional-style *manju* and *mochi* made fresh daily at Wailuku's **Shishido Manju Shop,** 758 Lower Main St., 808/244-5222. If you're in the mood for hot *malasadas,* traditional or fancy, try either **Home Maid Bakery,** 1005 Lower Main, 808/244-7015, or **Simply Sweets,** 1816 Lower Main, 808/244-7709. Home Maid also does more contemporary *manju* with new flavors.

If you want to take home a taste of Maui, try the jelly, chutney, and mustard made with mango and other tropical fruits and onions at the **Maui Jelly Factory,** 1404 Lower Main, 808/242-6989.

Groceries

For general grocery shopping, go to **Ooka Super Market,** 1870 Main St., where you'll find not only the usual groceries but also a deli section and many ethnic foods. For decades, this has been Wailuku's major food supplier. A new addition, **Sack 'N Save** is in the Wailuku Town Center on the north edge of town along Waiehu Beach Road In Happy Valley, you can get a few basic necessities at **Takamiya Market** and **T.K. Supermarket,** both along Market Street.

ENTERTAINMENT

Wailuku is not a hotbed for entertainment by any stretch of the imagination, yet there a few items worthy of note. Live theater is offered by the **Maui Community Theater,** 68 N. Market St., in the remodeled 'Iao Theater building. Major productions occur four times a year, and the season starts in October. Plays are generally performed in the evening, with some matinee shows on the weekends. Tickets run $15 adult, $13 seniors and students. For information on what's currently showing or for ticket reservations, call the box office at 808/242-6969.

About the only place in town for live entertainment is the very local **Molina's Sports Bar** on Market Street, where you can catch live music Friday, Saturday, Sunday evenings, and an occasional Wednesday evening gig.

Maui Bowling Center, near the corner of Market and Vineyard, is an old-style 10-lane alley that hosts night leagues. The rate is $2.25 a game, shoes extra.

RECREATION

Golf

Just south of Waikapu, the fairways of **Sandalwood Golf Course,** 808/242-4653, lie on the lower slopes of the West Maui Mountains. A challenging course at 6,469 yards, greens fees run $75 general, $40 twilight, with reduced rates for Hawaii residents. You can avail yourself of the full pro shop and restaurant at the clubhouse.

Along the coast north of Wailuku in the village of Waiehu is the county-maintained **Waiehu Municipal Golf Course.** This is a family-friendly course used mostly by locals. Beautiful to play yet open to the bay, it can get strong winds. Greens fees are $26 during the week and $30 on weekends for nonresidents, and $8 and $9, respectively, for residents. Carts and clubs can be rented. Call 808/243-7400 for tee times.

Van Tours

There is little participatory sport or outdoor activity available to the visitor in Wailuku, yet the Banana Bungalow does offer daily van tours to various spots on the island in its new passenger vans. These tours are arranged by signing up at the hostel and are run on a first-come, first-served basis. While tours may change periodically due to interest, typical tours include a hike over swinging bridges into a lush nearby valley, a road trip to Hana, sightseeing and shopping to Lahaina and Ka'anapali, snorkeling in a protected marine sanctuary, a whale-watch (in season), hike in 'Iao Valley, drive to Haleakala for the sunset, and a leisurely day on a South Maui beach. Some tours last all day; others are shorter. For exact details and reservations, ask at the Banana Bungalow, 310 N. Market St., or call 808/244-5090.

SHOPPING

Most shopping in this area is done in Kahului at the big malls. But for an interesting diversion, some people shop closer to home. Wailuku's attic closets used to overflow with numerous discovery shops all in a row hung like promnight tuxedos, limp with old memories, and each with its own style. Today, most of these specialty shops are gone, but the few that hang on are all along Market Street. Here you'll find **Brown-Kobayashi,** 808/242-0804, for Asian art and furniture; **Bird of Paradise,** 808/242-7699, which handles blue willow china, vintage bottles, Depression and carnival glass, license plates from around the world, and even a smattering of antique furniture; **Gottling, Ltd.,** 808/244-7779, specializing in Oriental art and furnishings; **Good Fortune Trading Company,** 808/244-6033; and **Treasure Imports,** 808/244-7202.

Luckily for those who live or visit here, **Sig Zane Designs,** 808/249-8997, a well-known women's apparel shop from Hilo, has opened a shop here, and a coffee shop now serves drinks and treats almost across the street. A few steps up the road at 130 Market St., the wildly innovative **Wild Banana Gallery,** 808/242-4943, has opened its doors for those who appreciate alternative art. Stop in to see the *other* artwork being done on the island and, perhaps, meet one of the artists. At 1977 Main St., **Paperbacks Plus,** 808/242-7135, is the only book purveyor in town, dealing mostly used titles and some new Hawaiiana.

Limited shopping is also available in the small strip mall across the street from Ooka Super Market on Central Street and at the newer Wailuku Town Center mall that's on the north edge of town near the industrial area, just off Waiehu Beach Road (Route 340).

The best place in Wailuku to pick up a high-quality gift to take home is at the **Bailey House Museum gift shop.** Here you'll find books, CDs, clothing, and a wide assortment of crafts made by island artists with native materials at a decent price.

SERVICES

There's a Bank of Hawaii branch office at 2105 Main, 808/871-8200; an American Savings Bank, 69 N. Market St., 808/244-9148; and a First Hawaiian Bank, 27 N. Market St., 808/877-2377. The state office building, county office building, federal building, old courthouse, and library are all along High Street in the center of town, and the new post office, 808/244-4815, is out in the Mill Yard near the Maui Visitors Bureau office, 808/244-3530, on Wili Pa Loop Road.

For conventional health care, go to Maui Memorial Hospital, 221 Mahalani St. off Route 32, 808/244-9056, or Kaiser Permanente, 808/243-6000, near the hospital at the entrance to Mahalani Street. In the center of town at 2180 Main St. is Maui Medical Group, 808/242-6464.

Camping permits for county parks (currently only Kanaha Beach County Park) are available at the War Memorial Gym, 808/270-7389, Mon.–Fri. 8 A.M.–4 P.M. They cost $3 for adults, 50 cents for children, per person per night. State park permits can be obtained from the State Building, 54 S. High St., Rm. 101, Wailuku, HI 96793, 808/984-8109, weekdays 8 A.M.–4 P.M. only.

KAHAKULOA—WEST MAUI'S BACK SIDE

To get around to the back side of West Maui you can head north from Ka'anapali or north from Wailuku. A few short years ago, this road was in rugged shape, closed to all but local traffic and forbidden to rental cars by their companies. It's still narrow and very windy in part, but now it's paved all the way. What once took three hours might now take only an hour. Many people drive it these days, thus it has traffic, so it still has its hazards. Additionally, loose rock tumbles onto the roadway from embankments and *pali* (particularly after rainfalls), so be mindful and aware of debris. Drive slowly, drive carefully, and drive defensively. In large part, the road is the journey.

Sights
Before you start this 18-mile stretch, make sure you have adequate gas and water. From Wailuku, head north on Market Street through the area called Happy Valley. This road continues out of town as Route 330. Before it meets Route 340, or Kahekili Highway, which you'll follow toward Kahakuloa Bay and all the way around, you'll see an overgrown macadamia nut farm on the upland side of the road, a failed attempt at diversifying the agricultural base of this region. Just north of the bridge over 'Iao Stream, coming up Route 340 from Kahului, will be Kuhio Place on your left. Turn here and then again

onto Hea Place to **Haleki'i and Pihana Heiau State Monument,** which sits on a bluff overlooking lower 'Iao Stream. This was a place of great prominence during the centuries that Maui kings called Wailuku home and when a large population filled the surrounding land, cultivating it in taro. Although uninspiring, this 10-acre site is historical and totally unvisited. Originally constructed around 1240 for other reasons, Haleki'i became a house of images. Pihana was made a temple of war and rededicated to the war god Ku by Kahekili, Maui's last king. Legend says that the last human sacrifice on Maui was performed here for Kamehameha I as a demonstration of his control over the island. These *heiau* are on the National Register of Historic Places.

A short way north and down Lower Waiehu Road toward the water—a Shoreline Access sign will point the way—you'll reach **Waiehu Beach County Park.** This strip of sand meets the southern end of the Waiehu Golf Course and is a decent place for sunbathing, as well as swimming when the water is calm. On occasion surfers come for the waves, but mostly people come to use the athletic fields.

Back on Route 340 you come shortly to the small town of **Waihe'e** (Slippery Water), where you'll find the reconstructed **Waihe'e Protestant Church,** established in 1828 as one of the

Halek'i Heiau

ROBERT NILSEN

WEST MAUI'S BACK SIDE

Pailolo Channel

P A C I F I C   O C E A N

Oneloa Bay

HONOLUA BAY
(MARINE LIFE
CONSERVATION DISTRICT)

D.T. FLEMING
BEACH
COUNTY
PARK

Kapalua

Honolua

Honokohau
Bay

Honokohau

Po'elua Bay

340

Keahikano
(2,017 ft.)

Hononana Bay
Mokolea Point
★ Blowhole

POHAKU KANI
(BELLSTONE) ★

Honolua
(2,627 ft.)

Kahakuloa
Bay

Kahakuloa

Kahakuloa
Stream

Moke'ehia
Island

MOKE'EHIA
ISLAND
SEABIRD
SANCTUARY

KA-EKIII

AINA ANUHEA ★

Lanilili
(2,627 ft.)

Waihe'e
Ridge Trail

MALUHIA BOY
SCOUT CAMP ■

MENDES
RANCH

HULU ISLAND
SEABIRD
SANCTUARY

340

Waihe'e Valley Trail

Waihe'e Point

Waihe'e

▲ **WAIHE'E BEACH**
COUNTY PARK

'Iao Needle

WAIEHU MUNICIPAL
GOLF COURSE

▲ **WAIEHU BEACH**
COUNTY PARK

HAPPY VALLEY

Waiehu

330

★ **HALEKI'I-PIHANA HEIAUS**
STATE MONUMENT

Wailuku

340

To Lahaina ►

0   2 mi

0   2 km

first churches on the island, standing next to the Waihe'e School. Turn at the town park (softball on Saturday) and follow the sign pointing you to **Waiehu Municipal Golf Course;** call 808/243-7400 for tee times. Mostly local people golf here; it's full of kids and families on the weekend. The fairways, strung along the sea, are beautiful to play. Waiehu Inn Restaurant is an adequate little eatery at the golf course.

Like its sister on the south edge of the golf course, **Waihe'e Beach County Park** is tucked into its northern corner. It too is secluded and frequented mostly by local people. Some come here to snorkel or spear fish inside the reef. The reef is quite a ways out and the bottom is rocky, but the shore is sandy. Although both parks are for day use only, they'd probably be okay for an unofficial overnight stay. To reach this park, go left and follow the fence just before the golf course parking lot.

At mile marker 5, the pavement narrows and begins to climb the hillside. The road hugs the coastline and gains elevation quickly; the undisturbed valleys are resplendent. Here are several one-lane sections. Slow down and use the pull-offs if you want to take pictures of the wild coastline below or Haleakala in the distance. Soon you pass Maluhia Road, the access road to a Boy Scout camp and the Waihe'e Ridge Trail, which leads up into the West Maui Mountains. Across from the entrance to Maluhia Road is Mendes Ranch, and beyond that—oddly enough—is a new upper-end residential subdivision. With the paving of this coastal road, several commercial establishments have been opened along this back route. One of these is **Aina Anuhea,** a private garden between mile markers 8 and 9. While not spectacular, this garden is fine for a short stop. Walkways take you through the diminutive gardens, from where you're able to see not only the bay below but Haleakala off in the distance. Smitty will greet you as you come up the driveway, collect your $4 entrance fee, and set you on the right path. Following close at hand are **Seahorse Ranch,** 808/244-9862, and the homespun **Curley's Trailrides,** 808/244-7178, both of which offer trailrides down to the water through their own ranchland. Seahorse Ranch also offers lessons and other types of horse training.

In a few miles you skirt a tall headland—easily seen from Pa'ia and points along the north shore—and pass the **Kaukini Gallery,** 808/244-3371, probably the most remote gallery on the island. A place of arts, crafts, and gifts, the gallery displays works by more than four dozen island artists. From here the road rounds the shoulder and drops down to the fishing village of **Kahakuloa** (Tall Lord), with its dozen weatherworn houses and two tiny churches. St. Francis Xavier Mission, above the village on the east side of the stream, was founded in 1846. Being on the north coast, the turbulent waters constantly wash the beach of round black stones. Although a tiny community (you are greeted with Aloha, Welcome, and Farewell all on one sign), each house is well kept with pride, and a new house or two have popped up in the last decade or so. To cater to the increased through traffic, several roadside stands have popped up selling fruit, shave ice, banana bread, and other delicacies. Overlooking Kahakuloa on the western side is a pullout and promontory where you have good views over the rugged coast and back at the village. Here the road is at its absolute narrowest. The valley is very steep-sided and beautiful. Supposedly, great Maui himself loved this area.

A mile or so past Kahakuloa and near mile marker 15, you come to **Pohaku Kani,** the bell stone. It's about six feet tall and the same in diameter, and it sits directly on the inland edge of the road. The seascapes along this stretch are tremendous. The surf pounds along the coast below and sends spumes skyward, roaring through a natural blowhole. **Nakalele blowhole**

sits near the Nakalele Lighthouse coast guard beacon site. From the road, it's a short walk down to the water—good for the family. Enjoy the spume close-up and explore the tide pools, but be aware that it's a rough coastline with occasional heavy surf, churning seas, and lots of wind and spray. After the bell stone, the road becomes wider again but still curvy, the mileage markers start over and reduce in number, and you're soon at D. T. Fleming Beach Park. Civilization comes again too quickly.

Hiking Trails

The **Waihe'e Valley Trail** runs into this picturesque narrow valley. North of the town of Waihe'e turn left onto Waihe'e Valley Road. Proceed to the village and park in the pulloff near the middle of this community near where the pavement ends. Go right at the T-intersection and walk to a gate. Inside the gate, the trail first follows the maintenance road that skirts the stream, with the flume on the opposite bank. This level track then takes you over two suspension footbridges, through a bamboo forest, and under huge banyan trees until you reach the head dam, where you can leap off a rope swing into the pool. Count on at least two hours, more if you intend to swim in the pool.

Waihe'e Ridge Trail is a three-mile trek leading up the windward slopes of the West Maui Mountains. Follow Route 34 around the back side to Maluhia Road at the Mendes Ranch. Turn and follow the road up about one mile—almost to the Boy Scout camp—where there's a parking area and a trail sign. Go through the gate, cross the pasture, and head for the trees. The trail starts innocently enough but does become a switchback farther up and crosses some wet areas. The trail rises swiftly to over 2,560 feet. The views of Waihe'e Valley and Makamaka'ole Valley are spectacular. Maintained and marked by mileage markers, the trail continues on to Lanilili summit, where there are views of the northern slope of the mountain. This trail takes energy; count on three hours for the more than four miles there and back. If you think that you'll be on the trail after 5:30 P.M. or so, you'd better park your car down near the highway at the entrance to Makuhia Road, as the gate across this road closes at 6 P.M.; it opens at 7 A.M.

MAUI

M.G.L. DOMENY DE REINZI

WEST MAUI

LAHAINA

Lahaina (Merciless Sun) is and always has been the premier town on Maui. It's the most energized town on the island as well, and you can feel it from the first moment you walk down Front Street. Maui's famed warrior-king Kahekili lived here and ruled until Kamehameha, with the help of newfound cannon power, subdued Kahekili's son in 'Iao Valley at the turn of the 19th century. When Kamehameha I consolidated the island kingdom, he chose Lahaina as his seat of power. It served as such until Kamehameha III moved to Honolulu in the mid-1840s. Lahaina is where the modern world of the West and the old world of Hawaii collided, for better or worse. The *ali'i* of Hawaii loved to be entertained here; the royal surf spot, mentioned numerous times as an area of revelry in old missionary diaries, is just south of the Small Boat Harbor. In 1801 Kamehameha I built in Lahaina the islands' first Western structure, known as the Brick Palace; a small ruin still remains. Queens Keopuolani and Ka'ahu-

manu, the two most powerful wives of the great Kamehameha's harem of more than 20, were local Maui women who remained after their husband's death and helped to usher in the new order.

The whalers came preying for "sperms and humpbacks" in 1819 and set old Lahaina Town a-reelin'. Island girls, naked and willing, swarm out to meet the ships, trading their favors for baubles from the modern world. Grog shops flourished, and drunken sailors with their brown-skinned doxies owned the debauched town. The missionaries, invited by Queen Keopuolani, came praying for souls in 1823. Led by the Reverends Stuart and Richards, they tried to harpoon moral chaos. In short order, there was a curfew, a *kapu* placed on the ships by wise but ineffectual old Governor Hoapili, and a jail and a fort to discourage the strong-arm tactics of unruly captains. The Hawaiians adapted to the new order, but the Christian sailors damned the meddling

WEST MAUI

Oneloa Bay

Honolua Bay

Kapalua

D.T. FLEMING BEACH COUNTY PARK

Kapalua Bay

To Kahului

Napili Bay

Kahana

KAPALUA GOLF CLUB

Napili

KAPALUA WEST MAUI AIRPORT

HONOKOWAI BEACH COUNTY PARK

Honokowai

KAHEKILI BEACH PARK

Kahana Stream

Ka'anapali

SUGAR CANE TRAIN

KA'ANAPALI GOLF COURSES

Pailolo Channel

HANAKA'O'O BEACH COUNTY PARK

WAHIKULI CO. WAYSIDE

LAHAINA CIVIC CENTER

Pu'unoa Point

HALE PA'I

LAHAINALUNA HIGH SCHOOL

Lahaina

Kaua'ula Stream

PAUNAU BEACH COUNTY PARK

West Maui Mountains

Pu'u Kukui (5,788 ft.)

LAUNIUPOKO CO. WAYSIDE

Launiupoko Point

Kulanaokala'i Beach

Olowalu Stream

'Au'au Channel

Hekili Point

Olowalu

Mopua

Ka'ili'ili Beach

To Kihei and Kahului

Punahoa Beach

UKUMEHAME BEACH COUNTY PARK

Papalaua Gulch

Lahaina Pali Trail

PAPALAUA CO. WAYSIDE

TUNNEL

Ma'alaea

0   3 mi

0   3 km

Papawai Point

LOOKOUT

McGregor Point

MOON

MAUI

© SANDRA E. BISIGNANI TRUST AND AVALON TRAVEL PUBLISHING, INC.

missionaries. They even whistled a few cannonballs into the Lahaina homestead yard of the Reverend Richards, hoping to send him speedily to his eternal reward. Time, a new breed of sailor, and the slow death of the whaling industry eased the tension.

Meanwhile, the missionaries built the first school and printing press west of the Rockies at Lahainaluna, in the mountains just above the town, along with downtown's Waine'e Church, the first stone church on the island. Lahaina's glory days slipped by and it became a sleepy "sugar town" dominated by the Pioneer Sugar Mill, which operated from 1860 to 1996. In 1901, the Pioneer Inn was built to accommodate interisland ferry passengers, but few *came* to Lahaina. In the 1960s, Amfac Inc. had a brilliant idea. It turned Ka'anapali, a magnificent stretch of beach just west, into one of the most beautifully planned and executed resorts in the world. The Pioneer Sugar Mill had long used the area as a refuse heap, but now the ugly duckling became a swan, and Lahaina flushed with new life. With superb farsightedness, the Lahaina Restoration Foundation was begun in those years and almost the entire town was made a national historical landmark. Lahaina, subdued but never tamed, throbs with its special energy once again.

The Lahaina Restoration Foundation

Begun in 1961 by Jim Luckey, a historian who knows a great deal about Lahaina and the whaling era, the **Lahaina Restoration Foundation,** 808/661-3262, website: www.lahainarestoration.org, is now headed by Keoki Freeland, an old Maui resident and grandson of the builder of the Pioneer Inn. Its office is the upstairs of the Baldwin Home. The main purpose of the foundation is to preserve the flavor and authenticity of Lahaina without stifling progress—especially tourism. The foundation is privately funded and has managed to purchase or lease many of the important historical sites in Lahaina for their continued maintenance. It owns the Baldwin Home, Masters' Reading Room, the *Carthaginian II,* and the Seaman's Hospital, leases the Wo Hing Temple and the old Courthouse, and maintains Hale Pa'i, Hale Aloha, and the old prison. The people on the board of directors come from all socioeconomic backgrounds. You don't get on the board by how much money you give but by how much effort and time you are willing to invest in the foundation; the members are extremely dedicated. Merchants approach the foundation with new ideas for business and ask how they can best comply with the building codes. The townspeople know that their future is best served if they preserve the feeling of old Lahaina rather than rush headlong into frenzied growth. The historic village of Williamsburg, Virginia, is sometimes cited as Lahaina's model, except that Lahaina wishes to remain a "real" living, working town.

Parking

Traffic congestion is a problem that needs to be addressed. Be parked and settled 4:30–5:30 P.M., when traffic is heaviest. While there still are no traffic lights on Front Street, a spree of construction in the last several years has increased the number of lights on the highway from two to more than half a dozen. The other thing to know to make your visit carefree is where to stash your car. The two lots along Dickenson Street are centrally located and charge a reasonable daily rate, as are the lots along Lahainaluna Road and the small lots behind the Baldwin Home and the Lahaina Inn. A little more expensive but very central is the lot behind Burger King near the banyan tree. Also close is a smallish free public parking lot along Luakini Street, but it usually fills early in the day. These private lots charge $5–11 a day; exact fee is usually required as few lots have attendants on duty. Usually, you'll find a reduced overnight fee or an all-day special. Farther afield is an underground lot below the 505 Front Street Mall. The large lot at Prison and Front Streets is free but has a three-hour limit. The lots at Malu'ulu O Lele and Kamehameha Iki parks are also free and for use by park users only, but people do park and walk into town from there. Aside from these public parking lots, all shopping centers in town have parking; some are free, some charge, and some offer validated parking. Street parking has a three-hour limit. Watch your time as the "meter patrol" is very efficient, and your car may wind up in the pound if you're not careful! Parking fines are up to $35, and it will cost more than $100 if your car is towed. Those staying in Ka'anapali should leave cars behind and take

DOWNTOWN LAHAINA

To Ka'anapali
To Ka'anapali

KENUI ST.

HONOAPI'ILANI HWY.

PIZZA HUT

★ SEAMEN'S HOSPITAL

THE ▼ BAKERY

TRAIN DEPOT

KUHUA ST.

BAKER ST.

KAISER PERMANENTE CLINIC

PARKING

FIRST HAWAIIAN BANK

30

PAPALAUA ST.

GAS

To Lahainaluna →

LAHAINA CENTER

ANCHOR SQUARE

POST OFFICE

AM. SAVINGS BANK

LAHAINA SQUARE

PIONEER MILL

BANK OF HAWAII

GAS

LAHAINALUNA RD.

OLD LAHAINA CENTER

MAUI MYTH AND MAGIC THEATER

WESTSIDE NATURAL FOODS

WO HING TEMPLE

PARKING

TRILOGY

LAHAINA INN

PLANTATION INN

LAHAINA MARKETPLACE

SEAMEN'S CEMETERY

GAS

PATEY'S PLACE

WAINE'E ST.

MARIA LANAKILA CHURCH

PACIFIC WHALE FOUNDATION

PARKING

MASTER'S READING ROOM

PARKING

DICKENSON ST.

PARKING

SHINGON BUDDIST TEMPLE

HAUOLA STONE

★ BALDWIN HOME

MAUI ISLANDER

BRICK PALACE

LIBRARY

EPISCOPAL CEMETERY

CARTHAGINIAN II

PIONEER INN SHOPS

HALE ALOHA

PIONEER INN

BANYAN TREE

COURTHOUSE

WHARF CINEMA CENTER

FORT RUINS

PARKING

DAN'S GREENHOUSE

HALE PA'AHAO (THE PRISON)

KAMEHAMENA III SCHOOL

PRISON ST.

30

PARKING

MAUI MEDICAL GROUP

HONOAPI'ILANI

LUAKINI ST.

Lahaina Small Boat Harbor

EPISCOPAL CHURCH ★

LAHAINA HONGWANJII

PARKING

MAUI'ULU O LELE PARK

WAINE'E CHURCH

LAHAINA AQUATIC CENTER

KAMEHAMEHA IKI PARK

PARKING

SHAW ST.

LAHAINA RECREATION CENTER

505 FRONT ST. MALL

LAHAINA SHORES

BAMBULA INN

HWY.

ALOHA LANI INN

OLD LAHAINA HOUSE

KAUA'ULA ST.

To Maalaea, Kihei, and Kahului

0   0.25 mi
0   0.25 km

© SANDRA E. BISIGNANI TRUST AND AVALON TRAVEL PUBLISHING, INC.

MAUI

Area of Detail

30

WAHIKULI COUNTY WAYSIDE PARK

FIRE STATION

POST OFFICE

LAHAINA CIVIC CENTER

POLICE STATION

HONOAPI'ILANI HWY.

GARDEN GATE B&B

KANIAU RD.

THE GUEST HOUSE

HOUSE OF FOUNTAINS

WAI OLA

LOKIA ST.

AINAKEA ST.

LAHAINA

MAKAI INN

MALANAI ST.

FLEMING ST.

LAHAINA ROADS CONDO

ALOHA MIXED PLATE

MALA WHARF

GAS

OLD LAHAINA LUAU

LAHAINA CANNERY MALL

SNORKEL BOB'S

"JESUS COMING SOON"

LAHAINA JODO MISSION ★

Lahaina Roads

LAHAINALUNA RD.

To Hale Pa'i and Lahainaluna High School

Lahaina Harbor

30

FRONT ST.

SHAW ST.

AREA OF DETAIL

0   0.5 mi
0   0.5 km

HONOAPI'ILANI HWY.

PUAMANA

To Puamana Beach County Park

the West Maui Shopping Express shuttle for the day or hop on the Sugar Cane Train.

SIGHTS

In short, strolling around Lahaina offers the best of both worlds. It's busy, but it's bite-size. It's engrossing enough, but you can "see" it in half a day. The main attractions are mainly downtown within a few blocks of each other. Lahaina technically stretches, long and narrow, along the coast for about four miles, but you may only be interested in the central core, a mere mile or so. All along Front Street, the main drag, and the side streets running off it are innumerable shops, restaurants, and hideaways where you can browse, recoup your energy, or just wistfully watch the sun set. Go slowly and savor, and you'll feel the dynamism of Lahaina past and present all around you. Enjoy!

The Banyan Tree
The best place to start your tour of Lahaina is at this magnificent tree at the corner of Hotel and Front Streets. You can't miss it as it spreads its shading boughs over almost an entire acre. It is the largest banyan in the state. Use the benches to sit and reconnoiter while the sun, for which Lahaina is infamous, is kept at bay. Children love it, and it seems to bring out the Tarzan in everyone. Old-timers sit here chatting, and on

Saturday and Sunday, various artists gather here to display and sell their artwork under the tree's broad branches. Every Christmas, the tree is covered in lights, and numerous other festivities are held in its shade. This banyan was planted in April 1873 by Sheriff Bill Smith in commemoration of the Congregationalist Missions' golden anniversary. One hundred years later, a ceremony was held here and more than 500 people were accommodated under this natural canopy. Symbolic as it is, this banyan is truly the heart of Lahaina.

Courthouse
Behind the banyan tree on Wharf Street is the old county courthouse. Built in 1859 from coral blocks recycled from Kamehameha III's ill-fated palace, Hale Piula, it also served as governor's office, a post office, customs office, and the police station, complete with a jail in the basement. The jail is now home to the Lahaina Arts Society's **Old Jail Gallery,** where paintings and artifacts are kept behind bars, waiting for patrons to liberate them. The society has its main **Banyan Tree Gallery** on the first floor. Since its renovation in 1998, another project of the Lahaina Restoration Foundation, the **Lahaina Visitor Center,** 808/667-9193, has also occupied a room on the main floor, and here anyone can come for all sorts of tourist information and brochures about the town. Plans are for displays and demonstrations on cultural subjects to be

art under the banyan tree

J.D. BISIGNANI

MAUI

shown in the old courtroom on the second floor. Open daily 9 A.M.–5 P.M. Public bathrooms are upstairs; use either the stairway or the elevator.

Adjacent is the **fort,** built in the 1830s to show the sailors that they couldn't run amok in Lahaina. Even with its 20-foot-high walls, it was not much of a deterrent. When it was torn down, the blocks were hauled over to Prison Street to build the real jail, **Hale Pa'ahao.** A corner battlement of the fort was restored, but that's it, because restoring the entire structure would mean mutilating the banyan. The cannons, from a military vessel sunk in Honolulu Harbor a few years prior and now set along the wharf in front of the courthouse, are in approximately the location that they had been when they were fixtures on the fort wall.

Just south of the fort was one of the several canals that ran through Lahaina. At one point, this canal was widened to land small boats coming in from the ships anchored offshore. Just beyond it, in what is now part of the schoolyard, was the Government Market, a notorious place where all kinds of commodities, manufactured and human, were sold during the whaling days, and it was given the apt name of "Rotten Row."

Small Boat Harbor
Walking along the harbor stimulates the imagination and the senses. The boats waiting at anchor sway in confused syncopation. Hawser ropes groan and there's a feeling of anticipation and adventure in the air. Here you can board for all kinds of seagoing excursions. In the days of whaling there was no harbor; the boats tied up one to the other offshore in the "roads," at times forming an impromptu floating bridge. The whalers came ashore in their chase boats; with the winds always up, departure could be made at a moment's notice. The activity here is still dominated by the sea.

Although whaling has long since ceased to be and commercial fishing is not really a player either, the Lahaina Roads still play host to some big ships. More than four dozen modern cruise ships make a stop annually at Lahaina so their fun-seeking voyagers can taste a bit of what West Maui has to offer. Without a large pier, all ships park out in the deep water and, as in the days of old, passengers are tendered from ship to shore in smaller boats. These cruise ships tend to come in the winter, when the weather is warm and the waters of Alaska are just too cold.

Just as today, the old commercial and whaling boats used a light to guide their way to port. Beyond the *Carthaginian II* anchored at the harbor's mouth is the site of the Lahaina's first lighthouse. In 1840, before any were built along what would later be the West Coast of the United States, King Kamehameha III ordered a lighthouse to be constructed here. The original wooden nine-foot structure was rebuilt to 26 feet in 1869, and the present concrete structure installed in 1916. As might be expected, a whale oil lamp was first used for light, later to be supplanted by electricity.

The *Carthaginian II*
The masts and square rigging of this replica of the enterprising freighters that braved the Pacific tower over Lahaina Harbor. You'll be drawn to it . . .go! It's the only truly square-rigged ship left afloat on the seas. It replaced the *Carthaginian I* after that ship went aground in 1972 while being hauled to Honolulu for repairs. The Lahaina Restoration Foundation found this steel-hulled ship in Denmark; built in Germany in 1920 as a two-masted schooner, it tramped around the Baltic under converted diesel power. The foundation had it sailed 12,000 miles to Lahaina, where it underwent extensive conversion until it became the beautiful replica that you see today.

The *Carthaginian II* is a floating museum dedicated to whaling and to whales. It's open daily 10 A.M.–4 P.M., but arrive no later than 3:30 to see all the exhibits and videos. Admission is $3 adults, seniors $2, $5 for the whole family. On deck, check out the rigging, masts, and steering platform, and try to imagine sailing on a ship of this size for months around Cape Horn and then up and across the broad Pacific to Hawaii. Below decks is the museum containing artifacts and implements from the whaling days. There's even a whaling boat that was found intact in Alaska in 1972. The light in the hold is subdued, and while you sit in the little "captains' chairs" the humpbacks chant their peaceful hymns in the background, and whale researchers Debra and Mark Ferrari narrate a video documenting the life of humpbacks. Flip Nicklin's sensitive photos adorn the bulkheads.

The Brick Palace

A rude structure was commissioned by Kamehameha I in 1801 and slapped together by two forgotten Australian ex-convicts. It was the first Western structure in Hawaii, but unfortunately the substandard materials have all disintegrated or been moved and only the site remains, marked by a slab in front of the library. Kamehameha never lived in it, but it was occupied and used as a storehouse until the 1850s. Inland from this site was a taro field (now occupied by the library), said to have been tended by King Kamehameha I as an inspiration of labor to his subjects. Just to the right of the Brick Palace site, as you face the harbor, is **Hauola Stone.** Formed like a chair, it was believed by the Hawaiians to have curative powers if you sat on it and let the ocean bathe you. One legend says that it was a woman who was turned to stone and saved by the gods as she tried to escape those who were pursuing her. Best view at low tide.

Pioneer Inn

This vintage inn, at the corner of Hotel and Wharf Streets, is just exactly where it belongs. Stand on its veranda and gaze out at the banyan tree, harbor, and *Carthaginian II.* Presto . . . it's magic time! You'll see. It was even a favorite spot for actors like Errol Flynn and later Spencer Tracy, when he was in Lahaina filming *Devil at Four O'clock.* The green and white inn was built in 1901 to accommodate interisland ferry passengers, but its style seems much older. If ironwork had been used on the veranda, you'd think you were in New Orleans. A new and larger wing of rooms and shops was built behind it in 1965, and the two form a courtyard. Make sure to read the hilarious rules governing behavior that are posted in the main lobby, and give your regards to the old salt who's greeted guests at the front door for years. Although the second-floor rooms of the old section are no longer used (there are plans to renovate these as well), the inn still retains character and atmosphere despite its recent major renovation.

Baldwin Home

One of the best attractions in Lahaina is the Baldwin Home, on the corner of Front and Dickenson Streets. It was occupied by Doctor/Reverend Dwight Baldwin, his wife Charlotte, and their eight children, two of whom died in infancy. He was a trained teacher, as well as the first doctor/dentist in Hawaii. The building also served from the 1830s to 1868 as a dispensary, meeting room, and boarding home for anyone in need. The two-foot-thick walls are of cut lava, the mortar of crushed coral over which plaster was applied. Originally, the downstairs had four rooms; only later were the side rooms and upstairs added. The men slept downstairs in the boys room; upstairs were rooms for the girls. When needed, the upstairs was used by guests, boarders, or the sick, and could be occupied by several dozen at one time. As you enter, notice how low the doorway is, and that the doors inside are "Christian doors"—with a cross forming the upper panels and an open Bible at the bottom. The Steinway piano that dominates the entrance was built in 1859. In the bedroom to the right, along with all of the period furniture, is a wooden commode. Also notice the lack of closets; all items were kept in chests. Most of the period furniture and other items were not owned or used by the Baldwins but are representative of the era.

The doctor's fees are posted and are hilarious. Payment was by "size" of sickness: very big $50, diagnosis $3, refusal to pay $10! The Reverend Baldwin was 32 when he arrived in Hawaii from New England, and his wife was 25. She was supposedly sickly, and he had heart trouble, so they moved to Honolulu in 1868 to receive better health care. The home became a community center, housing the library and meeting rooms. Today, the Baldwin Home is a showcase museum of the Lahaina Restoration Foundation. It's open daily 10 A.M.–4 P.M., admission $3 adults (or $5 for the Baldwin House and the *Carthaginian II*), $2 seniors, and $5 for the family.

The oldest coral-block house in Hawaii was built in 1827 for Reverend William Richards and his family, who had come to serve in Lahaina three years earlier. Now gone, the house occupied the site of Campbell Park next door to the Baldwin Home.

Masters' Reading Room

Originally a missionaries' storeroom, the uniquely constructed coral-stone Masters' Reading Room was converted to an officers' club in 1834. It was restored to original condition in 1970. Next door to the Baldwin Home, these two venerable buildings constitute the oldest standing Western structures on Maui. Once the office of the Lahaina Restoration Foundation, it is now home to the Na Mea Hawai'i Store, a native Hawaiian arts and crafts shop.

Hale Pa'ahao

This is Lahaina's old prison, located midblock on Prison Street, and its name literally means "Stuck-in-Irons House." It was constructed by prisoners in 1852 from blocks of stone salvaged from the old defunct fort. It had a catwalk for an armed guard and cells complete with shackles for hardened criminals, but most were drunks who yahooed around town on the Sabbath, wildly spurring their horses. The cells were rebuilt in 1959, the gatehouse in 1988, and the structure is maintained by the Lahaina Restoration Foundation. The cells, curiously, are made of wood, which shows that the inmates weren't that interested in busting out. Have a look at the prison rules posted on the gatehouse wall on your way in. It's open daily; admission is free but donations are accepted.

Malu'ulu O Lele Park

"The Breadfruit Shelter of Lele" park—Lele was the former name of Lahaina—is a nondescript area at the corner of Shaw and Front, holding tennis and basketball courts, a baseball field, and a parking lot. It was at one time the most important spot in Lahaina. Here was a small pond with a diminutive island in the center. The 17-acre pond, Mokuhinia, was inhabited by a *mo'o*, a lizard spirit, said to be the deceased daughter of a proud Maui king, and protector of the tiny one-acre island, Moku'ula, home of Maui royalty and the Kamehamehas when they were in residence. King Kamehameha III and his sister Princess Nahi'ena'ena were raised together in Lahaina. They fell in love, but the new ways caused turmoil and tragedy. Instead of marrying and producing royal children, a favored practice only 20 years earlier, they were wrenched apart by the new religion. He, for a time, numbed himself with alcohol, while she died woefully from a broken heart. She was buried here, and for many years Kamehameha III could frequently be found at her grave, quietly sitting and meditating. Shortly afterward, the government of Hawaii moved to

Honolulu, and although part of this island remained a royal mausoleum, it slowly fell into disrepair. By the early years of the 20th century, water that fed this pond had been largely diverted for use in irrigating the surrounding sugarcane fields. All the remains of the island were taken away, the pond was filled, and the ground leveled for use as a park.

Friends of Moku'ula, website: www.mokuula.com., is a nonprofit organization based in Lahaina. It is trying to bring the historical and cultural significance of Malu'ulu O Lele to the public eye and to eventually re-create the pond and island.

Kamehameha Iki Park

Across the street from Malu'ulu O Lele Park was the site of Hale Piula (Iron-roof House), a two-story royal stone palace built in the late 1830s for King Kamehameha III. Never finished, its stones were later used to construct the old courthouse that now stands between the banyan tree and harbor. This mostly barren spot is now known as Kamehameha Iki Park. On this site the 62-foot double-hulled sailing canoe *Mo'o Kiha* (Sacred Lizard) has been built by the cultural group Hui O Wa'a Kaulua, and it's considered by them to be "Maui's flagship of Hawaiian culture and goodwill." Future plans for the park include additional canoes, canoe sheds, traditional-style buildings, landscaping, and educational and cultural training programs. Access to one of the two in-town beaches is here.

Waine'e Church and Cemetery

The church itself is not impressive, but its history is. This is the spot where the first Christian services were held in Hawaii, in 1823. A stone church was built here in 1832 that could hold 3,000 people, but it was razed by a freak hurricane in 1858. Rebuilt, it survived until 1894, when it was deliberately burned by an angry mob upset with the abolition of the monarchy in Hawaii and the islands' annexation by the United States. Another church was built, but it too was hit not only by a hurricane but by fire as well. The present structure was built in 1951 and renamed Waiola. In the cemetery is a large part of Maui's history: buried here are Hawaiian royalty. Lying near each other are Queen Keopuolani, her star-crossed daughter, Princess Nahi'ena'ena, and old Governor Hoapili, their

B. COWEN

The Wo Hing Temple was restored by the Lahaina Restoration Foundation.

royal tomb marked by two large headstones surrounded by a wrought-iron fence. Other graves hold missionaries, such as William Richards, and many infants and children.

Churches and Temples

You may wish to stop for a moment at Lahaina's churches and temples dotted around town. They are reminders of the mixture of faiths and peoples that populated this village and added their particular cultural styles. **Holy Innocents Episcopal Church,** built in 1927, is on Front Street, near Kamehameha III school. Known for its "Hawaiian Madonna," its altar and pulpit are resplendent with paintings of fruits, plants, and birds of the islands. Stop by on Sunday when the church is full and hear the sermon preached and hymns sung in Hawaiian. **The Episcopal Cemetery** on Waine'e Street, from 1863, shows the English influence in the islands. Many of the royal family, including King Kalakaua, became Anglicans. This cemetery holds the remains of many early Maui families, and of Walter Murray Gibson, the notorious settler, politician, and firebrand of the 1880s. Just behind is **Hale Aloha** (House of Love), a small structure built by Maui residents in thanksgiving for being saved from a terrible smallpox epidemic that ravaged O'ahu but bypassed Maui in 1853–54. The structure was restored in 1974. Also on Waine'e is **Maria Lanakila Church,** the site of the first Roman Catholic Mass in Lahaina, celebrated in 1841.

The present structure dates from 1928. Next to the church's cemetery is the **Seamen's Cemetery,** where many infirm from the ships that came to Lahaina were buried after failing to recover. Most stones have been obliterated by time, and only a few remain. Herman Melville came here to pay his last respects to a cousin buried in this yard. **Hongwanjii Temple** is also on Waine'e, between Prison and Shaw. It's a Buddhist temple with the largest congregation in Lahaina and dates from 1910, though the present structure was raised in 1927. Down Luakini Street is the tall clapboard plantation-era structure **Hokuji Mission Shingon Buddhist Temple.**

The **Wo Hing Temple** on Front Street is a Lahaina Restoration Foundation reconstruction. Constructed in 1912 as a social and religious hall for Chinese living and working in the area, it's perhaps the best example of such a structure in the state and has been placed on the National Register of Historic Places. Leased from a Chinese fraternal society, it was opened to the public in 1984 and shows the Chinese influence in Lahaina. Downstairs are displays, upstairs is the altar. In the cookhouse next door, you can see film clips of Hawaii taken by the Edison Company in 1899 and 1906. It's open daily 10 A.M.–4:15 P.M.; admission is by donation.

The **Lahaina Jodo Mission** is near Mala Wharf on Ala Moana Street. Heading west, leave the main section of town and keep going until you see a sign over a building that reads "Jesus

MAUI

Coming Soon." Turn left toward the beach and you'll immediately spot the three-tiered wooden pagoda. The temple bell welcomes you at the entrance gate, and a giant bronze Buddha sits exposed to the elements on a raised stone platform nearby. The largest outside of Asia, this seated Buddha image was dedicated in 1968 in commemoration of the centennial of the arrival of Japanese workers in Hawaii. The grounds are impeccable and serenely quiet. You may stroll around, and while the buildings are closed to the public, you can climb the steps of the main building to peek into the temple. The entire area is a perfect spot for solitary meditation if you've had enough of frenetic Lahaina. Buddha's birthday is celebrated here every April. The Pu'upiha Cemetery is across the street along the beach. It seems incongruous to see tombstones set in sand.

Mala Wharf
Built in 1922 and once an integral part of Lahaina commerce, the old Mala Wharf now stands decaying at the northern end of town. Next to it is a new boat launch ramp, which is used by local anglers and some ocean activities companies. There are restrooms here but no other amenities or services.

U.S. Seamen's Hospital
This notorious hospital from 1833 was reconstructed by the Lahaina Restoration Foundation in 1982. Here is where sick seamen were cared for under the auspices of the U.S. State Department. Allegations during the late 1850s claimed that the care here extended past the grave! Unscrupulous medicos supposedly charged the U.S. government for care of seamen who had long since died. The hospital is at Front and Baker, heading toward Ka'anapali, near the Jodo Mission. While the stony exterior of this building has been maintained, the building now houses Paradise TV, a company that produces the visitor channel for television. In the front yard is a 10,000-pound, swivel-end Porter anchor, found off Black Rock in Ka'anapali. This building was supposedly constructed for King Kamehameha III as a place where he could gamble, carouse, and meet his sister Nahi'ena'ena for love trysts away from the puritanical eyes of the missionaries.

Lahainaluna
Head up the mountain behind Lahaina on Lahainaluna Road for approximately two miles. On your left you'll pass the **Pioneer Sugar Mill,** in operation until 1996. At Lahainaluna (which means Above Lahaina) is the oldest school west of the Rockies, opened by the Congregationalist missionaries in 1831. Children from all over the islands, and many from California, came here if their parents could afford to send them away to boarding school. Today, the school is West Maui's public high school, but many children still come here to board. The first students were

Hale Pa'i, the oldest printing house west of the Rocky Mountains

ROBERT NILSEN

given not only a top-notch academic education but a practical one as well. They built the school buildings, and many were also apprentices in the famous **Hale Pa'i** (Printing House), which turned out Hawaii's first newspaper (1834) and made Lahaina famous as a printing center.

One look at Hale Pa'i and you think of New England. It's a white stucco building with blue trim and a wood-shake roof. It houses a replica printing press and copies of documents once printed there. Placed on the National Register of Historic Places in 1976 and restored in 1982, it's open Mon.–Fri. 10 A.M.–4 P.M. Owned by the state, Hale Pa'i is maintained by the Lahaina Restoration Foundation. If you visit the campus when school is in session, you may go to Hale Pa'i, but if you want to walk around, please sign in at the vice principal's office. Lahainaluna High School is still dedicated to the preservation of Hawaiian culture. Every year, in April, it celebrates the anniversary of the death of one of its most famous students, David Malo. Considered Hawaii's first native scholar, he authored the definitive *Hawaiian Antiquities,* an early history of the Hawaiian Islands. His final wish was to be buried "high above the tide of foreign invasion," and his grave is close to the giant "L" atop Mount Ball, behind Lahainaluna. At graduation, students from the school follow a decades-old tradition of surrounding the "L" with lighted tiki torches, making quite a sight from town. On the way back down to town, you have an impressive panorama of former cane fields, the port, Lahaina Roads, and Lana'i, and realize that Lahaina is not a big place, as you can see it all easily from end to end.

Heading East

Five miles east of Lahaina along the coastal road (Route 30) is the little village of **Olowalu.** Today, little more than the Olowalu General Store and Chez Paul French restaurant are here. This was the place of the Olowalu Massacre perpetrated by Captain Metcalfe, whose far-reaching results greatly influenced Hawaiian history. Two American seamen, Young and Davis, were connected with this incident, and with their help Kamehameha I subdued all of Hawaii. Only the remains of a pier and a few storage buildings mark the site of a once busy cane harbor and port facilities.

Behind the general store a half-mile dirt track leads to **petroglyphs;** make sure you pass a water tower within the first few hundred yards because there are three similar roads here. After about 20 minutes, you come to the remains of a wooden stairway going up to a rock face on an outcrop. Etched into the flat face of this deep red rock are a small group of human figures and one crab claw sailing canoe, which are believed to be about 300 years old. Some modern graffiti defaces this rock, so it's a little difficult to determine just what's what, still these petroglyphs are perhaps the most easily accessible of all such rock art on the island.

Near mile marker 14 is good snorkeling, some of the best on the island. Other good snorkeling is near the highway tunnel, where boats come to anchor just offshore. You will see them from the highway as you pass by. It's in this area that the old Lahaina Pali Trail heads up the rugged dry hillside to cross the ridge and drop down to the isthmus north of Ma'alaea.

If you continue east on Route 30, you'll pass **Papawai** and **McGregor Point,** both noted for their vistas (here you can see South Maui, Molokini, Kaho'olawe, and Lana'i) and as excellent locations to spot whales in season. The road sign merely indicates a scenic lookout.

BEACHES

The best beaches around Lahaina are just west of town in Ka'anapali or just east toward Olowalu. A couple of adequate places to spread your towel are right in Lahaina, but they're not quite on a par with the beaches just a few miles away.

In-Town Beaches

One beach stretches east of the harbor starting at Kamehameha Iki Park. It's crowded at times, on occasion used for beach volleyball, and there may be "wash up" at certain times of the year. It's cleaner and quieter at the east end down by Lahaina Shores Hotel. Close to the old royal compound, it was a favorite with the *ali'i.* There are restrooms, the swimming is fair, it's gentle for kids, and the snorkeling is acceptable past the reef. **Lahaina Beach** is at the west end of town near Mala Wharf. Follow Front to Pu'unoa Place and turn down to the beach. This is a good place for families with tots because the water is clear, safe, and shallow. There is beach access also at the turnaround on Kai Pali Place, the next two streets in toward town.

Puamana Beach County Park
About two miles before you enter Lahaina from the southeast along Route 30, you'll see signs for this beach park, a narrow strip between the road and the sea. The swimming and snorkeling are only fair. The setting, however, is quite nice with picnic tables shaded by ironwood trees. The views are terrific and this is a great spot to eat your plate lunch only minutes from town.

Launiupoko Wayside Park
A mile farther southeast, this park has restrooms and showers, but only a small enclosed kiddie beach that's best at high tide when it fills with water. This is more of a picnic area than anything else, although many come to sunbathe on the grass below the coconut trees. Beginning surfers like this spot and some beginning surf lessons are taught here because the waves are gentle.

South of here you'll see lots of shore fishers and others out for a quiet afternoon. Although not a designated park, the water is adequate for swimming. Find parking where you can under the trees.

East of Olowalu
Between Olowalu and the highway tunnel are **Ukumehame Beach County Park** and **Papalaua Wayside.** The first is a small park with picnic tables, barbecue pits, toilets, and a tiny lawn for sunbathing; swimming is okay. The second is an unimproved area with lots of ironwood trees for shade. This long narrow beach is a favorite of shore fishermen.

Wahikuli County Wayside
Along Route 30 between Lahaina and Ka'anapali, this park is a favorite with local people and excellent for a picnic. It has a rocky shore but is known as a good swimming spot. The drawback is that it's right on the busy highway. With three parking areas, it's as if the park was split into three units. Tennis courts are up across the street behind the main Lahaina post office.

Just up the highway, as if connected to this

wayside park, is **Hanaka'o'o Beach County Park.** This beach, which is actually the south end of Ka'anapali Beach, runs north past some of the most exclusive hotels on the island. Local canoe clubs put their canoes in the water here, and at certain times of the year paddling events are held at this beach.

ACCOMMODATIONS

Lodging in Lahaina is not of the usual tourist resort variety that people head to Ka'anapali for. Lahaina tends to be hot and hot to trot, especially at night. You can find good bargains here, and if you want to be in the thick of the "action," you're in the right spot.

Under $50
If you're looking for the least expensive place in town, try **Patey's Place Maui Hostel,** 761 Waine'e St., 808/667-0999, website: www.hawaiian-hostels.com, email: maui@hawaiian-hostels.com. This single-story house, with additional rooms added to the side for space, is spartan and reasonably clean. There's no luxury at this easy-going hostel, but it's serviceable. Guests can hang out on the cushions in the common TV room, a kitchen is available for simple food preparation and storage, and there are shared bathrooms with showers. A bunk in the dorm room runs $20 a night, the small single room $35, a private room with shared bath $40–45, and the private room with private bath $50–55. Used by those visiting the island on the cheap and by those who've come to find work, this could be a good place to garner information about what to see and do on Maui.

$50–100
The **Makai Inn,** 808/662-3200, fax 808/661-9027, is a former concrete block two-story apartment building turned into rental units. Compact and not landscaped like the big boys, it is right on the water where there's nothing blocking you from the sunset. Each of these 18 units is small, yet all have full kitchens and bathrooms, and most have queen beds. Furnished in tropical style, there are no TVs or phones in the units nor daily maid service, but there is a laundry room on premises and off-street parking. Units run $65–95 a night,

$10 extra for each person more than two, a low-end option for staying in this exciting town. Visit the inn on the Web at www.makaiinn.com, or send email to info@makaiinn.com.

$100–150

The **Pioneer Inn** is the oldest hotel on Maui still accommodating guests, and it was the only hotel on West Maui until 1963. The inn, 658 Wharf St., Lahaina, HI 96761, 808/661-3636 or 800/457-5457, fax 808/667-5708, website: www.pioneerinnmaui.com, email: info@pioneerinnmaui.com, has undergone more than a facelift since its early days. The semi-seedy old-timey essence has now been spiffed and polished. Now a Best Western hotel, the Pioneer Inn had half a million dollars poured into it in 1997–98, but all renovation was done in early-20th-century taste. For decades, the Pioneer Inn had absolutely no luxury whatsoever, only a double scoop of atmosphere. It was the place to come if you wanted to save money and be the star of your own movie with the inn as the stage set. Creaky stairways, threadbare carpets, low-light hallways, shared baths, and questionable merrymakers and occupants—the place had it all. Now the stairway doesn't creak anymore, new carpet has been laid, TVs installed, baths have shiny new tiles and some period fixtures, bedrooms have new furniture, trim and wall coverings renewed, and all rooms have air-conditioning. What does remain the same are the lanai, which, depending upon the room, look out over the banyan tree or the hotel courtyard and pool; the posted house rules; and the old salt who still stands at the front door. Rooms run $100–160; AAA and Best Western Gold Club discounts available. Downstairs food and drink are served daily at the grill and bar and on weekends in the courtyard, and local live music in always on the menu. Shops occupy the perimeter of the ground floor fronting the banyan tree and Front Street.

Another reborn classic is the **Lahaina Inn,** 127 Lahainaluna Rd., Lahaina, HI 96761, 808/661-0577 or 800/669-3444, fax 808/667-9480, website: http://lahainainn.com, email: inntown@lahainainn.com. Completely renovated and remodeled, this one-time dowdy orphan, the old, down-at-the-heels traveler's classic, Lahainaluna Hotel, emerged in 1989 as a lovely lady. Gone from this cockroach paradise are the weather-beaten linoleum floors, bare-bulb musty rooms, and rusted dripping faucets. In their place are antique-stuffed, neo-Victorian, tastefully appointed rooms that transport you back to the late 1800s. Each room is individually decorated, and period pieces include everything from wardrobes to nightstands, rugs, ceramic bowls, mirrors, pictures, lamps, and books. The only deference to modernity is the bathrooms with their new-but-old-style fixtures, the air-conditioning, telephones, and safes—no TV. You can still peer from the balcony of this vintage hotel—each room has a lanai with two hardwood rocking chairs and a table—or observe the masses below from behind heavy drapes and lace curtains. The 12 units include three spacious suites. Rates are $109–119 for the rooms and $169 for the parlor suites ($10 less during regular season) and include a complimentary continental breakfast, served every morning from about 7:30 A.M. at the sideboard at the end of the hall. There is a

The "old salt" greets all visitors to the Pioneer Inn.

ROBERT NILSEN

MAUI

two-night minimum stay only on Friday and Saturday; children over 15 are welcome. For dinner, you might try downstairs at the renowned David Paul's Lahaina Grill, which offers inn guests a discount. Free to guests, parking is in the public parking lot directly behind the inn.

A few blocks away from the hubbub, at 660 Waine'e St., Lahaina, HI 96761, 808/667-9766 or 800/922-7866, fax 808/667-2792, the **Maui Islander** is a very adequate hotel offering rooms with kitchenettes, studios, and one- and two-bedroom suites. Originally intended as a residential condo complex, these units are more spacious than most visitor accommodations. All have daily maid service, a/c, and TV, plus there's a swimming pool, lighted tennis court (hotel guests only), coin laundry facility, and a barbecue and picnic area on premises. Low-rise design in a garden setting lends a homey atmosphere; an activities desk at the front can help arrange outings. Basic hotel rooms start at $108, studios $132–144, and suites $162–276; 10 percent cheaper during value season. Studios and suites all have kitchens; one-bedroom, one-bath suites will hold four guests, the three-bedroom, three-bath suites up to eight. Take a botanical walk through the garden, where there are many varieties of exotic plants and flowers. This fine little hideaway is an Aston property.

The **Lahaina Roads** condo/apartment is at the far north end of town at 1403 Front Street. All units have fully equipped kitchens, TV, and maid service on request. One-bedroom units (for two) run $125, two-bedroom units (for four) are $200. There is a three-night minimum stay and a deposit required to hold your reservation. There is no beach here as it sits right along the seawall, but there is a freshwater pool, and you couldn't have a better view, as every unit faces the ocean. Parking is on ground level below the rooms. Rentals are handled through Klahani Resorts, P.O. Box 11108, Lahaina, HI 96761, 808/667-2712 or 800/669-6284, fax 808/661-5875.

$150–200

If Agatha Christie were seeking inspiration for *the* perfect setting for one of her mysteries, she would come to **The Plantation Inn**. The neo-Victorian building is appointed with posted verandas, hardwood floors, natural wood wainscoting and trim counterpointed by floral wall coverings, bedspreads, and deep-cushioned furniture. Rays of sunlight stray through stained-glass windows and wide double doors. Each uniquely decorated room is comfortable, with four-poster beds and private tiled baths with bold porcelain and brass fixtures; most have sofas. The complete illusion is early 1900s, but the modern amenities of a/c, remote TV and VCR, a fridge, daily maid service, and a soothing spa and pool are included. The back addition brings the total room count to 19. Most of the 12 new units have lanai overlooking the garden courtyard with its pool, spa, and guest pavilion. Prices are a reasonable $135 standard, $155 superior, $175 deluxe, $215 suite (some with kitchenette and hot tub), and all include a filling breakfast buffet at poolside prepared by Gerard's, the fine French restaurant on the first floor. The Plantation Inn also has money-saving options for dinner at Gerard's, rental cars, and package deals. While now associated with the Kaanapali Beach Hotel in Ka'anapali, it still maintains great autonomy. For full information contact the inn at 174 Lahainaluna Rd., Lahaina, HI 96761, 808/667-9225 or 800/433-6815, fax 808/667-9293, or visit www.theplantationinn.com, or send email to info@theplantationinn.com. On a side street away from the bustle, it's simply one of the best accommodations that Maui has to offer, and although a relatively new building, it fits well into the 19th-century whaling port ambience that Lahaina fosters.

Six-story **Lahaina Shores** was built before the Lahaina building code limited the height of new structures. At the south end of town, at 475 Front St., Lahaina, HI 96761, 808/661-4835 or 800/628-6699, the condo has become a landmark for incoming craft. The Shores offers a swimming pool and spa and is the only accommodation in Lahaina located on a beach. From a distance, the Southern-mansion facade is striking; up close, though, it becomes painted cement blocks and false colonnades. The fully air-conditioned rooms, however, are good value for the money. The basic room contains a full bathroom, large color TV, and modern kitchen. They're all light and airy, and the views of the harbor and mountains are the best in town. Studios run $150 mountain-view and $185 oceanfront; one-bedroom suites are $210 mountain-view and $240 oceanfront. The penthouse suites run $250 and $275 for mountain and ocean views, respectively. Reduced rates of 10–15 percent are given during low season. Other amenities include a front desk, daily maid service, laundry facilities, and an activities desk. This facility is associated with the interisland Classic Resorts group, which you can visit on the Web at www.classicresorts.com, or contact by email at info@classicresorts.com.

A 28-acre private community of condos on the south edge of town along the ocean, **Puamana** is a quiet hideaway away from the hustle and bustle of town, definitely a high-end property. The clubhouse here was the Pioneer Sugar Company's former plantation manager's residence (built 1923), and it's a beauty. Surrounding it are broad lawns and the townhouses. One-bedroom condo units run $125–175, two-bedroom units $150–275, and three-bedroom townhouses $300–500; three- to five-night minimum stay. Discounts are given for long stays. All units have fully equipped kitchens, all linens, TVs and VCRs, a/c, and outdoor barbecue grills. In addition, the former caretaker's cottage runs $150 a night for a couple or $175 for four. Puamana also features an oceanside swimming pool plus two others on property; a sauna, reading parlor, and lending library in the clubhouse; a guests-only tennis court; badminton and volleyball courts; and children's play areas. The only drawback is that it's wedged against the highway, but a thick hedge blocks out much of the noise. For the cottage, contact the Puamana Community Association, 808/661-3423, fax 808/667-0398, website: www.puamana-maui.com. For other rentals, contact Klahani Resorts, P.O. Box 11108, Lahaina, HI 96761, 808/667-2712 or 800/628-6731, fax 808/661-5875; or Whaler's Realty, 808/661-3484 or 800/676-4112, fax 808/661-8338.

B&Bs and Guesthouses

By and large, the B&Bs in Lahaina are clumped together in two areas of town: south of downtown near the water and halfway to Ka'anapali and up above the highway in the area known as Kapunakea.

Aloha Lani Inn, 13 Kaua'ula Rd., Lahaina, HI 96761, 808/661-8040 or 800/572-5642, fax 808/661-8045, website: www.maui.net/~tony, email: tony@maui.net, off Front Street, is a homey, cozy, and clean single-family home turned guesthouse. Across from the neighborhood beach, this guest home is a few minutes' walk south of downtown Lahaina. The two guest rooms, one with a queen bed and the other with two twins, rent for $69 and share a bathroom; two nights minimum. Guests have use of the kitchen; the living room with its books, television, and sound system; laundry facilities, and the backyard lanai under a mango tree. Strong complimentary coffee is available all day, but no breakfast is served. For information and reservations, talk with Melinda.

Next door is John and Sherry Barbier's **Old Lahaina House,** P.O. Box 10355, Lahaina, HI 96761, 808/667-4663 or 800/847-0761, fax 808/667-5615, website: www.oldlahainainn.com, email: info@oldlahainainn.com. This big salmon-colored house, surrounded by a wall of the same color, has four rooms, all with private baths, that range $60–95, breakfast included. All rooms include a/c, telephone, and TV, and everyone has access to the garden and the newly redone swimming pool and deck, which occupy the front yard. Reduced rental car rates can be arranged. Old Lahaina House is a relaxing, homey place, lived in by the family (so there are kids around).

In the streets behind, you'll find the **Bambula Inn Bed and Breakfast,** 518 'Ilikahi St., Lahaina, HI 96761, 808/667-6753 or 800/544-5524, fax 808/667-0979, website: www.bambula.com, email: bambula@maui.net. Here, two studios are separated at the back of the house so you're independent from the family. Each unit has a full kitchen, queen-size beds, private bath, TV, phone, and lanai. The detached cottage for $100 has a/c while the attached studio for $90 has ceiling fans; $20 for each additional person more than two, three nights minimum. Breakfast is brought to your room, and a complimentary sunset sail aboard the family sailboat *Bambula* is offered every evening, weather permitting. Contact Pierre for information and reservations. If these two rooms are full, ask about his other accommodation options.

The **GuestHouse,** 1620 Ainakea Rd., Lahaina, HI 96761, 808/661-8085 or 800/621-8942, fax 808/661-1896, website: www.mauiguesthouse.com, email: relax@mauiguesthouse.com, is a well-appointed contemporary B&B where the host provides free snorkel gear and even scuba lessons (for a fee). The GuestHouse caters largely to honeymooners and scuba enthusiasts. All rooms have queen beds, a/c, ceiling fans, TV, refrigerators, phones, and private lanai, and all have private baths. Full breakfast is provided. Everyone shares the living room, kitchen, barbecue, and laundry facility. Each of the four rooms runs $115 a couple or $95 single.

At 1565 Ku'uipo is **Wai Ola Vacation Paradise,** tel./fax 808/661-7901 or tel./fax 800/4WAIOLA, website: www.waiola.com, email: tai@maui.net. This private home has three units, all with private entrances. Just off the pool, the large one-bedroom apartment is more than 1,000 square feet, with full kitchen and amenities. It runs $135 a couple and $15 each extra person up to four. Newly remodeled, the studio apartment is about half as big but also has a full kitchen and all amenities. In the garden, it runs $115 a couple. The newest is the honeymoon Ku'uipo Room, with its own private lanai and larger king bed. It goes for $120 a night. Low season rates are $20 less. All well-appointed units have a/c, TV, VCR, and phones, and everyone has use of the free laundry facilities and the swimming pool. As a vacation rental, no food is served but all kitchens are stocked with basics. Very private; booked mostly by honeymooners. Contact Julie Frank at P.O. Box 12580, Lahaina, HI 96761, for information and reservations.

The **House of Fountains,** 808/667-2121 or 800/789-6865, fax 808/667-2120, website: www.alohahouse.com, email: hof@alohahouse.com, is farther up in this neighborhood at 1579 Lokia St., Lahaina, HI 96761. A modern house, with tile floor throughout, native wood furniture, and overall Hawaiian-style decor, this B&B is a restful and relaxing spot that also has a pool and hot tub on the back patio. Room rates for the five suites are $95–145 a night, with $20 for extra individuals, and this includes a filling breakfast of fruits and other goodies.

The peach color of the **Garden Gate Bed and Breakfast** beyond its private courtyard garden lets you know that this is an easy-going restful place. There are two bedrooms in the main house, one larger unit off an upstairs lanai to the side and an efficiency under that. Only the efficiency has a kitchen—the others have microwaves and refrigerators—but breakfast is served daily except Sunday. Everyone can use the barbecue and laundry facilities, and you can borrow bikes and beach gear. Rates run $79–95; three-night minimum stay. For information and reservations, call 808/661-8800 or 800/939-3217, fax 808/661-0209. Garden Gate is at 67 Kaniau Rd., Lahaina, HI 96761. Its website is www.gardengatebb.com. Send email to jaime@gardengatebb.com.

FOOD

Lahaina's menu of restaurants is gigantic; all palates and pocketbooks can easily be satisfied: there's fast food, sandwiches, sushi, happy hours, vegetarian, and elegant cosmopolitan restaurants. Because Lahaina is a dynamic tourist spot, restaurants and eateries come and go with regularity. The following is not an exhaustive list of Lahaina's food spots—it couldn't be. But there is plenty listed here to feed everyone at breakfast, lunch, and dinner. *Bon appétit!*

Quick Food and Snacks

Lappert's Ice Cream, next to the library, not only has rich ice cream, shave ice, and cookies, but also serves fat- and sugar-free ice cream—about the only thing on Maui that is fatfree! **Häagen Dazs** can also serve up your favorite flavor at both the Pioneer Inn shops and near Lahaina Market Place.

A good one for a quick snack is **Mr. Sub Sandwiches,** 129 Lahainaluna Rd. It features double-fisted sandwiches and packed picnic lunches.

Take Home Maui, 121 Dickenson St., 808/661-8067 or 800/545-MAUI from the Mainland for mail order, is a food store and delicatessen that specializes in packaging agriculturally inspected Maui produce such as pineapples, papayas, Maui onions, protea, potato chips, macadamia nut products, and even Kona coffee, which it will deliver to you at the airport before your departing flight. For an on-the-spot treat they prepare deli sandwiches for under $6, a variety of quiches, and sides of macaroni and potato salad. Take Home Maui is famous for its fresh-fruit smoothies, homemade soups, and picnic lunches. Choose a shaded spot on the veranda and enjoy your lunch while taking a break from the jostle of Front Street. Open 7:30 A.M.–6:30 P.M.

Your sweet tooth will begin to sing the moment you walk into **The Bakery,** 911 Limahana, near the Sugar Cane Train. You can't beat the stuffed croissants for under $3, or the sandwiches for under $5! The pastries, breads, and bagels are gooood! Opens daily at 5:30 A.M. and closes at 3 P.M. weekdays, 2 P.M. on Saturday, and noon Sunday, 808/667-9062.

Inexpensive

Across from the banyan tree is **Swiss Cafe,** 808/661-6776, a simple European-style eatery with seats outside under the trellis, where you can order hot and cold sandwiches, pizza, coffee, and juice for reasonable prices—nothing is over $8. Perhaps a bagel with cheese and tomato or fresh croissant will satisfy you for breakfast. All sorts of sandwiches and personal-size pizzas can be made for lunch, but the "melts" are the focus. Some stop by just for an espresso or iced mocha, while others come to cool off with a smoothie or ice cream. Open 9 A.M.–6 P.M., and while you're here, check your email for 15 cents a minute.

Tacos, burritos, and other south-of-the-border foods are served up with a Hawaiian attitude at **Maui Taco,** 808/661-8883, at Lahaina Square Shopping Center. This is excellent Mexiwaiian food with a punch, and everything on the menu is less than $7.

Smokehouse BBQ, 1307 Front St., 808/667-7005, serves baby back ribs, chicken, and fish smoked over a kiawe grill and smothered in special barbecue sauce. Also available for lunch are burgers and sandwiches, and always sides like rice, barbecued beans, and cole slaw. This is where local people and those in the know come for a very good but no-frills meal. If eating hearty without caring about the ambience (actually the sunset view couldn't be better) is your aim, come here. Open daily until 9 P.M. Take-out available.

The **Thai Chef,** 808/667-2814, will please any Thai food lover who wants a savory meal at a good price. Search for this restaurant stuck in a corner at the Old Lahaina Center, open Mon.–Fri. 11 A.M.–2 P.M. for lunch, dinner nightly 5–10 P.M. As in most Thai restaurants vegetarians are well taken care of with plenty of spicy

tofu and vegetable dishes. The extensive menu offers everything from scrumptious Thai soups with ginger and coconut for $8.95 (enough for two) to curries and seafood. Most entrées are under $14 with a good selection under $10. It's not fancy, but food-wise you won't be disappointed. Take-out is available. When in Kihei, visit Thai Chef's second restaurant in the Rainbow Mall.

Zushi's is a very reasonably priced Japanese restaurant selling sushi and various other Japanese dishes in Anchor Square on Waine'e Street. Zushi's serves lunch (take-out too) 11 A.M.–2 P.M., dinner 5–9:30 P.M. Authentic with most items under $6. Also in the plaza next to the Activities Information Center is a small take-out window with the imaginative name of **Local Food,** which sells local food in the form of plate lunches. Basic, cheap, filling, and good. In the Lahaina Square Shopping Center next door, **Denny's** serves up inexpensive standard American fare.

Sunrise Cafe, 693 Front St. next to the library, 808/661-8558, open 6 A.M.–6:30 P.M., is the kind of place that locals keep secret. It's a tiny restaurant where you can have excellent coffee and a sandwich or more substantial gourmet food at down-home prices. The nutritious and wholesome food includes breakfast specials like freshly baked quiche $6.95, and lunch salads from Caesar to fresh island fruit all priced under $9. Heartier appetites can choose various hot or cold sandwiches for under $7, pasta, plate lunches, and a more substantial fish or seafood dinner meal for under $12. A deli case holds scrumptious award-winning pastries, complemented by fine coffee selections always freshly brewed and a good selection of herbal teas. Eat inside or out on the back patio.

At the 505 Front Street Mall is **Bamboo Cafe,** 808/667-4051, which serves standard American breakfast 7–11 A.M., but inexpensive Thai and Vietnamese dishes for lunch and dinner until 9 P.M. with nothing on the menu over $11.

Next door to the new Old Lahaina Luau venue near Mala Wharf is **Aloha Mixed Plate,** 808/661-3322, a great spot for a simple, authentic, and award-winning meal and a cold drink. While noodle dishes, burgers, and sandwiches are on the menu, the specialties are the plate lunches. Available in three sizes, they run $2.95–8.95.

MAUI

Open 10:30 A.M.–10 P.M.; happy hour 3–7 P.M. You can't beat it.

If you're looking for Chinese food, try **Red Lantern,** 808/667-1884, next to the Lahaina Cannery Mall. Everyone will find something on this menu, which runs to over 100 items. Most dishes are in the $9–13 range, with special selections pricier.

Among the several eateries at the Wharf Cinema Center is the unpretentious **Yakiniku Lahaina,** which serves a fine rendition of Korean food.

Aside from the full range of produce, vitamins, health foods, and bulk foods, the **Westside Natural Foods** on Lahainaluna St., 808/667-2855, has some reasonably priced and healthy prepared hot and cold foods, fruit drinks, and smoothies. Items at the salad bar and hot-food counter are priced $6.50 a pound. Open Mon.–Sat. 7:30 A.M.–9 P.M., Sunday 8:30 A.M.–8 P.M.

The trendiest of the inexpensive eateries in town is the open-air **Cheeseburger in Paradise,** 811 Front St., 808/661-4855, open 10:30 A.M.–11 P.M., live music nightly. It's down by the sea overlooking the harbor out back. Served are a whole slew of burgers priced $6.75–8.50, Portuguese turkey burger for $8.50, the jumbo cheese dog covered with cheese and sautéed onions for $6.50, or the Maui classic BLT for $6.75. Other selections include the aloha fish and seasoned fries at $10.25, a huge Upcountry salad for $7.50, and calamari scallop gumbo for $6.95. Cheeseburger also has a full bar that sells imported and domestic beer, along with tropical concoctions. If you were going to pick one spot to have a beer, soak in the sights, and capture the flavor of old Lahaina, "the Burg" has all the trimmings.

Also a trendy place and up at the top end of the inexpensive spots is **The Hard Rock Café,** 808/667-7400, at the Lahaina Center on the corner of Front and Papalaua Streets. Open daily from 11:30 A.M., this is a large, breezy, screened restaurant keeping the rock-and-roll faith. Over the bar is a '59 Cadillac convertible woody, and on the walls are prints of rock stars and electric guitars, including a Gibson autographed by the Grateful Dead. The floors have a shiny patina, and the raised stools and round-top tables give you a view of the street and the sea beyond. Menu prices are moderate, with homemade onion rings at $4.29, Caesar salad

for $7.79, Cajun chicken sandwich at $8.79, barbecued ribs for $15.95, and the country char-broiled burger for $7.59. Sit inside at the bar or dining section or outside under the umbrellas. Food is served until 10 P.M. Sun.–Thurs., until 10:30 Friday and Saturday; the bar is open two hours longer every night, and there's live music on Saturdays.

Also reasonably cheap, and almost an institution in itself, is **Moose McGillycuddy's,** 808/667-7758. A wild and zany place, there is music nightly (live on Friday and Saturday), the sports channel on the many TVs hanging here and there, daily specials, early-bird specials (both breakfast and dinner), and a happy hour 3–6 P.M. The large portions are filling, and the menu reads like a book, with burgers, sandwiches, fajitas, *pu pu,* and much else, most under $9. Take a moment (or an hour) and have a look at all the stuff hanging on the walls.

Moderate

Kobe Japanese Steak House is at 136 Dickenson at the corner of Luakini, 808/667-5555, and open daily for dinner from 5:30 P.M. Service is *teppan yaki*-style, which means that the chef comes to you. His sharp blade flashes through the air and thumps the table, keeping the culinary beat as it slices, dices, and minces faster than any Veg-o-matic you've ever seen. The delectables of marinated meat, chicken, and vegetables are then expertly flash-fried at your own grill, oftentimes with aplomb in a ball of sake-induced flame. The experience is fun, the food very good, and the interior authentic Japanese. *Teppan* meals come complete with rice, soup, and tea. Expect to spend at least $18 for an entrée (less for the early-bird specials), $10 for an appetizer, and $11 for four pieces of sushi. Other style fish and meat entrées are also available for $17–29. Complement your meal with a glass of sake or Japanese beer. Aside from the food, karaoke entertainment on the weekend draws a lively crowd.

Set right at the harbor, the **Pioneer Inn Bar and Grill,** 808/661-3636, at the historic Pioneer Inn has a marine theme. It serves breakfast 6:30–11 A.M., offering buttermilk pancakes for $6.25, eggs benedict for $7.25, and a three-egg omelet for 8.25. Lunch and dinner, served 11 A.M.–10 P.M., start with such items as a hearty bowl of Portuguese soup for $5.50 or romaine Caesar salad for $8, and move on to a full selection of sandwiches for under $8.50, grilled steak for $21, spicy Thai chicken curry for $13.50, or fettuccine Alfredo for $19.95. In addition, the saloon is open for drinks 9 A.M.–10:30 P.M., with happy hour 3–6 P.M., and there is music some evenings. Friday, Saturday, and Sunday 6–9 P.M., food is also served at the inn's Courtyard Restaurant, and these meals are accompanied by soft live music. Since the Pioneer Inn is the oldest hotel in town, and a true landmark with a great lanai from which you can view the harbor, the experience is really one of history and atmosphere.

A casual open-air restaurant that overlooks the banyan tree from above the ABC Discount Store at the Wharf Cinema Center is **Zoolu Grille and Bar**, 808/667-6200. Open for lunch and dinner, there is a full bar and live entertainment nightly 6–10 P.M. Lunch brings salads, soups, and sandwiches in the $6–18 range, while dinner choices are more numerous and pricier. Appetizers like pot stickers, steamers, and blackened ahi sashimi run $12, while seafood, meat, and poultry entrées cost $16–28.

Kimo's, 845 Front St., 808/661-4811, is friendly and has great harbor and sunset views on the lower level. If you're in Lahaina around 6 P.M. and need a break, head here to relax with some "Kimo therapy." Popular, but no reservations taken. Kimo's offers seafood from $16.95, with most entrées $15–20, and is known for the catch of the day, usually the best offering on the menu; limited menu for children. Lunch prices are half the dinner prices, and you can get pu pu, burgers, and sandwiches. Dine upstairs or down. The downstairs bar has top-notch well drinks featuring brand-name liquors.

At 839 Front St., **Woody's Ocean Front Grill**, 808/661-8788, serves mostly salads and sandwiches under $10 for lunch, and more substantial fish and meat dishes that range $14–22 for dinner. Try ono onion rings or valley isle guacamole for starters. Sandwiches include the surfer's club, mahimahi, and Maui coconut shrimp, while dinner entrées might be blackened ahi, Woody's island ribs, and grilled New York steak. Tropical drinks and smoothies from the bar could round out your meal. In a casual setting, centrally located and right on the water,

Woody's is as dependable as the old woody station wagons that decades ago hauled surfers to the beach.

The Lahaina Fish Company, 831 Front St., 808/661-3472, open daily from 11 A.M. for lunch and 5–10 P.M. for dinner, buys from local fishermen so the fish is guaranteed fresh. Belly up to the Hammerhead Bar, fashioned from glass and brass, or choose a table that looks directly out onto Lahaina Harbor. Notice the vintage Coca Cola vending machine and a display of knots that were tied by the old salts who visited Lahaina. The limited lunch menu has sandwiches and other light foods, mostly for under $10. The evening dinner menu starts with dinner salads at $3.99, fried calamari at $9.99, or a bowl of fresh seafood chowder for $3.95. Entrées can be island fish and chips at $9.99, fisherman's pasta with fish and vegetables for $12.99, or sautéed sea scallops for $16.99. Meat and poultry dishes include Hawaiian teriyaki chicken for $12.99, lu'au-style pork ribs for $15.99, or top sirloin steak for $12.99. The fresh fish, depending on what's caught that day, is grilled, oven broiled, or blackened Cajun style and offered at market price, and every day brings a chef's special that ranges $18–22.

At 505 Front Street is **Hecock's**, 808/661-8810, open daily 7 A.M.–10 P.M. for food service, bar open until 2 A.M., owned and operated by Tom and Nancy, a husband and wife team who bring you good food at reasonable prices. Hecock's breakfast could be ranch eggs with a grilled New York steak for $9.25, or a three-egg scampi omelet for $6.75, along with the classics like French toast or buttermilk pancakes with the trimmings for under $7. The lunch menu offers a chef salad for $8.95, assorted burgers and sandwiches priced under $9.95. The dinner bill of fare includes fettuccine Alfredo $15.95, scampi for $22.95, and rack of lamb at $23.95. A children's menu, happy hour, daily specials, and an early-bird special offered 5–6 P.M. help to keep prices down.

Lahaina Coolers on Dickenson Street presents quick easy meals throughout the day in an open-air setting. Try pancakes, omelets, or eggs Benedict for breakfast; salads, sandwiches, and burgers for lunch; and pasta, tortillas, fresh fish, steak, and burgers for dinner. Nothing on the evening menu is over $16.95, with most in the

MAUI

$12–15 range. Coolers is a casual late-night place; you can get food until midnight and drinks until 2 A.M.

B.J.'s Chicago Pizzeria, 808/661-0700, on the second floor overlooking the seawall at 730 Front St., is known throughout the island for it deep-dish pizzas. Various choices, ranging from the ordinary cheese and tomato to shrimp thermador and "the works," run about $10–25. All made to order, they take some time but everyone agrees that they're worth the wait. Along with the pizza are various calzone and pasta dishes, and fine salads. Eat in or take out. B.J.'s has one of the largest beer selections on the island and live contemporary music every evening.

Compadres Mexican Bar and Grill, 808/661-7189, at the Lahaina Cannery Mall, has a full menu ranging from nacho appetizers through soups, salads, and sandwiches to a complete list of entrées, most in the $10–18 range. Sit down, relax, and enjoy your meal and the surroundings, or have a beer or margarita at the spacious long bar.

Fine Dining

When you feel like putting a major dent in your budget and satisfying your desire for gourmet food, you should be pleased with one of the following.

You won't be a pawn when you walk onto the black-and-white-checkered floor at **Longhi's,** 888 Front St., 808/667-2288, open daily 7:30 A.M.–10 P.M. Longhi owns the joint and he's a character. He feels that his place has "healing vibes" and that man's basic food is air. Longhi's has been around since 1976 and it's many people's favorite. Prices at Longhi's may seem expensive, but the portions are enormous and can easily fill two. If you don't want to stuff yourself, ask for a half order. Mornings you can order frittatas, like spinach, ham, and bacon. A good lunch choice is pasta Siciliana with calamari, spicy with marinara sauce; for dinner, the prawns amaretto and shrimp Longhi are signature dishes. Save room for the fabulous desserts or a cooling cocktail. Longhi's is a winner. It's hard not to have a fine meal here, and the wine list is outstanding. There's always a line, reservations accepted, never a dress code, and always complimentary valet parking! Live music is provided only on Friday and Saturday evenings.

The well-known Hawaiian chef Sam Choy has opened his **Sam Choy's Lahaina** at the Lahaina Center, 900 Front St, 808/661-3800. Like his other restaurants, this one has an open kitchen with stools around the periphery, but unlike the others you can sit at the tables here and see the ocean. Dinner only is served 5–9:30 P.M., and Sam's own beer (brewed on O'ahu) is on tap at the back. Sam always gives healthy portions and piles his food high. Start with the ahi pole, crab cakes, or popcorn shrimp appetizers, $6.95–10.95, then add a salad. Move on to an entrée like charsiu ribs, hibachi grilled chicken, seafood laulau, catch of the day, or a chow mein noodlemania, all $9.95–36.95. Everyone leaves filled and satisfied. A good choice for local-style fine food.

Next door to Sam's is **Ruth's Chris Steak House,** 808/661-8815. Relatively new to Lahaina, it has captured the attention of those Midwestern corn-fed-beef lovers. For a meal of meat and potatoes, this is your place. Entrées run $19–33 and include filet, rib eye, T-bone, and strip steaks, and pork, veal, and lamb chops. A few seafood items also appear on the menu. Ruth's, which has a full bar, is open for dinner only 5–10 P.M.; reservations are a necessity.

Pacific'O Cafe, 505 Front St., 808/667-4341, has garnered a solid reputation. Foods and flavors from the West, the East, and the Pacific are blended together, using only the freshest ingredients from the islands, to create a very delectable contemporary Pacific cuisine. Start with a fine Kula mixed green salad for $6.50 or roasted Maui onion and Puna goat cheese salad for $9.50. Lunch entrées, like the sesame-seared fish or smoked shrimp linguine pasta, are all reasonable at less than $15. Dinner entrées run $19–28 and might be fish tempura wrapped in wakame, grilled pork, tandoori spiced fish, or sesame-crusted lamb. The emphasis is on fish but meats are served as well. Comfortable seating, attentive servers, and the views out over the ocean might tempt you to linger over your meal and savor an excellent bottle of wine. Open daily for lunch 11 A.M.–3 P.M. and dinner 5:30–10:30 P.M.; there's live jazz Thurs.–Sat.

The **I'o** restaurant next door, 808/661-8422, is a newcomer to the restaurant scene in Lahaina. Open 5:30–10 P.M. for dinner only; reservations are a must. Like Pacific'O, I'o is owned by Chef

James McDonald, but unlike its neighbor, I'o is more experimental with its food and the ambience is more modern. Start your evening with tomato bread, served each night with a different dipping sauce. Appetizers include the "silken purse" steamed wonton, Pan Asian Rockefeller baked oysters, and the signature I'o crab cakes, $8–12. The main entrée might be a luscious crispy ahi, another signature dish, or foie gras–crusted and pan-fried fresh fish, or the wok stir-fried lobster Thai-hitian with mango curry sauce, $23–30. No matter what your choice, each dish is artfully inspired, and the symphony of flavors, particularly the sauces, complement one another. For dessert, order the goat cheese ice cream for a new experience, or have your meal with one of the many tropical-flavored martinis that the restaurant is known for. Sleek, open, and airy inside, there is also seating outside on the patio, where, if you time it right, you can watch the sunset paint the sky in bands of pink and red or the moon rise into the inky night sky.

David Paul's Lahaina Grill, 127 Lahainaluna Rd., 808/667-5117, open for dinner nightly 6–10 P.M., is one of Lahaina's finest gourmet restaurants. Here owner David Paul Johnson, famous for his sauces, presents "artwork on a plate." The dining room is quite lovely, with coved and pressed-metal ceilings from which hang punchbowl chandeliers illuminating the starched white table settings that surround the central bar. With low lighting and soft music, this well-appointed room is meant for a long romantic evening of salubrious relaxation. The waiters and waitresses, professional but friendly, definitely give you attentive service. The menu is diverse and can be served at the bar as well. Start with an Upcountry Kula corn chowder for $8, a Kona lobster-crab cake appetizer for $15, or baby romaine Caesar salad for $11. Entrées include David Paul's signature dishes, tequila shrimp and firecracker rice, made from tiger prawns marinated in chili oil, lemons, cilantro, cumin, and brown sugar in a blend of vanilla bean and chili rice for $28, and Kona coffee roasted rack of lamb for $38, plus others like Maui onion–crusted seared ahi for $30 and kalua duck with a reduced plum sauce for $29. Vegetarians will find at least one meatless entrée on each menu, and other dietary restrictions can be accommodated by the masterful chefs. No matter what is on the

changing menu, you can be assured that the ingredients are the freshest available. The very wicked dessert tray, with everything priced around $6, combined with a cup of rich roasted coffee, ends a wonderful meal.

Gerard's elegant restaurant is in the Plantation Inn, 174 Lahainaluna Rd., 808/661-8939, open daily for dinner only 6–9 P.M., with validated free parking nearby. The epitome of neo-Victorian charm, the room is comfortable with puff-pillow wicker chairs and always set with fine crystal atop starched linen. Fronting the building is a small dining garden, and inside the interior is rich with hardwood floors and an oak bar. Chef Gerard Reversade, trained in the finest French culinary tradition since age 14, creates masterpieces. He feels that eating is *the* experience of life, around which everything else that is enjoyable revolves. Gerard insists that the restaurant's waiters and waitresses share his philosophy, so along with the excellent food comes excellent service. The menu changes, but it's always gourmet. Gerard's is not cheap but it's worth every penny as nothing on the menu is less than excellent. Appetizers range $8.50–18.50, entrées $26.50–32.50, and desserts are $7.50. Some superb salad choices are the island greens with kiawe honey vinaigrette dressing, or spinach salad with grilled scallops, shaved parmesan cheese, and truffle sauce. Appetizers feature mouthwatering choices like shiitake and oyster mushrooms in a puff pastry. Full entrées like grilled rack of lamb with mint crust or savory stuffed breast of veal with spinach and herb sauce and glazed vegetables titillate the palate. Confit of duck with pommes frites served with mixed greens in a walnut-oil dressing is one of Gerard's superb signature dishes. Even if you possess great self control, you have less than an even chance of restraining yourself from choosing a luscious dessert like crème brûlée, chocolate mousse in cream puffs with raspberry sabayon, or even fresh strawberries glazed with suzette butter and macadamia nut cream. *C'est bon!*

Chez Paul, 808/661-3843, five miles east of Lahaina in Olowalu, is secluded, romantic, very popular, and French—what else! There are two seatings nightly at 6:30 and 8:30 P.M., by reservation only, credit cards accepted. Local folks into elegant dining give it two thumbs up. The wine list is tops, the desserts fantastic, and the

MAUI

food—*magnifique!* Start with luscious hors d'oeuvres like chilled artichoke soup with lobster salpicon, Bourgogne escargot, homemade duck pâté, or warm goat cheese bruschetta on greens, all priced $8–22. Entrées are delightful with fresh island fish poached in champagne, lobster in a saffron basil cream sauce, roasted venison with garlic and thyme flowers, or crispy duck with tropical fruits and pineapple sauce bigarade, all priced $28–38. Chez Paul is definitely worth the trip from Lahaina with a short stroll along the beach recommended as a perfect aperitif.

ENTERTAINMENT

Lahaina is one of those places where the real entertainment is the town itself. The best thing to do here is to stroll along Front Street and people-watch. As you walk along, it feels like a block party with the action going on all around you—as it does on Halloween. Some people duck into one of the many establishments along Front Street for a breather, a drink, or just to watch the sunset. It's all free, enjoyable, and safe.

Art Night
Friday night is Art Night in Lahaina. In keeping with its status as the cultural center of Maui, Lahaina opens the doors of its galleries, throws out the welcome mat, sets out food and drink, provides entertainment, and usually hosts a well-known artist or two for this weekly party. It's a fine social get-together where the emphasis is upon gathering people together to appreciate the arts and not necessarily on making sales. Take your time and stroll Front Street from one gallery to the next. Stop and chat with shopkeepers, munch the goodies, sip the wine, look at the pieces on display, corner the featured artist for comment on his/her work, soak in the music of the strolling musicians, and strike up a conversation with the person next to you who is eyeing that same piece of art with the same respect and admiration. It's a party. People dress up, but don't be afraid to come casually. Take your time and immerse yourself in the immense variety and high quality of art on display in Lahaina 6–10 P.M.

Halloween
This is one of the big events of the year. It seems that everyone dresses in costume, strolls Front Street, parties around town, and gets into the spirit of the evening. It is a party in the street with lots of people, dancing, music, color, and activities. In fact, it's becoming so popular with some that they fly in from Honolulu just for the night.

Nightspots and Dancing
All of the evening musical entertainment in Lahaina is in restaurants and lounges, except for the acclaimed Old Lahaina Lu'au and the Feast at Lele.

You, too, can be a disco king or queen on **Longhi's** black-and-white chessboard dance floor every weekend. Longhi's has live music on Friday and Saturday nights featuring island groups. **Moose McGillycuddy's** (just listen for the loud music on Front Street) is still a happening place with nightly music, though it's becoming more of a cruise joint for post-adolescents. Those who have been around Lahaina for a while usually give it a miss, but if you want to get your groove on with a younger crowd this place is for you.

The open-air **Cheeseburger in Paradise** rocks with live music nightly until 11 P.M. There's no cover charge, and you can sit upstairs or down listening to the tunes. Similarly, you can hear live soft rock music during dinner at **Zoolu** at the Wharf Cinema Center across from the banyan tree, 8–10:30 P.M., at **BJ's Chicago Pizzeria** overlooking the water, and at the **Pioneer Inn Grill and Bar** at the Pioneer Inn. Live jazz happens every Thurs.–Sat. evening at **Pacific'O** restaurant at 505 Front Street Mall.

Maui Brews not only has a long bar, a restaurant, and a game room, but the back room becomes a nightclub with loud music, colored lights, and plenty of people. There's music and dancing nightly until 2 A.M., and this seems to be the most happening place in town. Music ranges from rock to techno to reggae, and while a DJ sets the stage most evenings, there are live acts occasionally. Similarly, the **Mango Cafe Sports Bar and Game Room** turns the DJ loose Tues.–Sat. 9 P.M.–2 A.M. for music and dancing.

Theater Shows

Lahaina is lucky to have two theater shows, one large, the other more intimate. Performed at the 700-seat Maui Myth and Magic Theater with its thrust stage and amphitheater seating is 'Ulalena, a 1.5-hour historical review, cultural journey, and tale of legend and myth that is in essence the story of the Hawaiian people. While the content is thoroughly Hawaiian, it's told in a manner that's modern and Western—and that's part of its magic. Colorful, captivating, and imaginative, it is full of fun visuals, dramatic dance, and superbly moving music. This is a show not to be missed. Tickets run $40; showtimes are 6:30 P.M. and 9 P.M. Mon.–Sat. The Maui Myth and Magic Theater is at 878 Front Street, in the Old Lahaina Center; call 808/661-9913 for information and reservations.

Warren and Annabelle's is a slight-of-hand, up-close magic show that's performed in a 78-seat theater at 900 Front Street. Prior to the show itself, guests gather in the theater's cocktail lounge for appetizers and drinks ($6.75–22) to be serenaded on piano by Annabelle, a 19th-century resident "ghost." This show is open to those 21 years of age and older. Tickets run $36 per person and shows are performed twice an evening Mon.–Sat. Call 808/667-6244 for information and reservations.

Lu'au

Lahaina has two of the best dinner shows anywhere on the island. The Old Lahaina Lu'au is the most authentic lu'au on the island, and the all-you-can-eat buffet and all-you-can-drink bar has a well-deserved reputation. On the beach near the Lahaina Cannery Mall, it is the only lu'au on the island not associated with a hotel. Seating is Mon.–Sat. 5:30–8:30 P.M., but as it's so popular, be sure to reserve several days in advance, perhaps two weeks in advance during peak season; 808/667-1998. Tickets for adults are $69, $39 for children 2–12.

The Feast at Lele combines food and entertainment. While not the typical lu'au per se, the five-course meal is masterly coordinated with music and dance from the islands of Hawaii, Tonga, Tahiti, and Samoa. Reservations are a must; 808/667-5353. The dinner and show runs $89 adult and $59 for children, Tues.–Sat. 6–9 P.M. on the beach at the 505 Front Street Mall.

Cinemas

Lahaina Cinemas, once the only multiplex theater on West Maui, is on the third floor of the Wharf Cinema Center. First-run features only, movies start at about noon and run throughout the day. Adults $7, kids 2–11 $3.50, seniors $3.75; all seats $4 until 5 P.M. Lahaina's second cinema is Front Street Theaters. At the Lahaina Center, this four-screen theater charges $7 adult, $3.50 kids, and $4 matinee. Call 808/661-3347 for what's showing at either theater.

The Hawaii Experience Domed Theater, 824 Front St., 808/661-8314, has continuous showings on the hour daily 10 A.M.–10 P.M. (40-minute duration), for adults $6.95, children 4–12 $3.95. The idea is to give you a total sensory experience by means of the giant, specially designed concave screen. You sit surrounded by it. You will tour the islands as if you were sitting in a helicopter or diving below the waves. And you'll be amazed at how well the illusion works. If you can't afford to fly through Kaua'i's Waimea Canyon, dive with the humpback whales, watch the sunrise over Haleakala, or view the power of an oozing volcano, this is about as close as you can get. A second film on a different subject is also offered during the day. For both shows, tickets run $11.90 and $5.90, respectively. The lobby of the theater doubles as a gift shop where you can pick up souvenirs like carved whales, T-shirts, and inexpensive mementos.

Hula and Polynesian Shows

For a different type of entertainment, stop to see the free grown-up hula show, Wednesday and Friday at 2 P.M., or the keiki hula show, same days at 6 P.M., at Hale Kahiko in the parking lot of the Lahaina Center. Hale Kahiko is a reproduction Hawaiian village displaying implements and items of everyday use; open 9 A.M.–6 P.M.

Various weekly shows are also offered at center stage at the Lahaina Cannery Mall. Tuesday and Thursday at 7 P.M. there's a free Polynesian show, and a keiki hula show is presented Saturday and Sunday 1–2 P.M.

RECREATION

Lahaina is a center particularly for ocean-based activities on Maui. For further details on activity

off Lahaina

ROBERT NILSEN

providers, see **Sports and Recreation** in the Maui introduction, above.

Snorkel Bob's, 808/661-4421, at 1217 Front St. near the Mala Wharf, rents snorkel gear for $15 per week (daily rental also), which you can take to a neighboring island and return there for a small extra fee. Boogie boards are available at $13 per day or $26 per week, and Snorkel Bob's advice, whether you need it or not, is plentiful and free. Open 8 A.M.–5 P.M. daily, Snorkel Bob's can also fix you up with virtually any activity on the island through its activities desk.

Across from the banyan tree is **Duke's Surf and Rental,** where snorkel gears runs $2 a day or $18 a week. Ordinary surfboards and longboards go for anywhere from $10 for two hours to $20 a day or $120 a week. Water equipment is not the only stuff you can rent here; look also for cruiser bikes ($10 a day or $63 a week), golf clubs, and a whole assortment of other items.

West Maui Cycles, 808/661-9005, at the Lahaina Square Shopping Center, rents snorkel gear, surfboards, and boogie boards, but its big thing is the sale, service, and rental of road and mountain bicycles. Mountain bikes run $20–40 a day, depending upon the quality. Also available are cruisers at $10, road bikes $20–25, tandems at $35–50, and electric bikes at $25 a day, car racks extra. All bike rentals come with a helmet, pump, tool kit, and lock. Stop here for all your cycling needs on West Maui.

West Maui Sports, 808/661-6252, rents snorkel gear for $2.50 a day or $10 a week. Body boards are $2.50 a day or $15 a week, single kayaks $35 a day and $140 a week, tandem kayaks $50 a day or $150 a week. If you haven't brought it from home, beach chairs, coolers, umbrellas, and other beach gear can also be rented. Look for them behind Lahaina Cannery Mall next to Aloha Mixed Plate.

The Lahaina Recreation Center, along the highway as you enter town from the east, has baseball and soccer fields and a children's playground. The adjacent Aquatic Center, open daily until 4:30 P.M., has a kids' pool and an Olympic-size swimming pool.

Activity Companies

Companies that can set you up with most any activity offered on the island include the following. **Tom Barefoot's Cashback Tours,** 834 Front St., 808/661-8889 or 888/222-3601, website: www.tombarefoot.com, is a one-shop business that has a great handle on all types of tourist activities on Maui and throughout the state. It reduces the fee for activities by 10 percent for those who pay in cash or traveler's checks, and a 7 percent discount is given for payment by credit card. You can also explore information and book activities before you come to town. This company has been around for more than 25 years and is a leader in the business.

The purveyor with the largest number of activities booths around the island (over a dozen—mostly at condo resorts and shopping centers) is **Activity World,** 808/667-7777 or 800/624-7771, website: www.hawaiiactivity-world.com. In Lahaina, look for them at 910 Honoapi'ilani Hwy., the Wharf Cinema Center, Lahaina Shores, and Maui Islander. **Activity Mart,** 808/667-1989 or 800/450-7736, has an office at 624 Front St. and another at the Lahaina Cannery Mall, website: www.activity-mart.com. **Activity Warehouse,** 808/667-4000, across from Kamehameha III School along Front St., can also set up your activity schedule. The **Lahaina Ticket Company** can also arrange activities. Offices locations include the Old Lahaina Center, 808/661-0150, and at 764 Front St., 808/662-3430. For purely ocean activities, try the **Pier 1** booth at Lahaina Harbor, 808/667-0680.

A few of these companies, and others not mentioned, greatly discount their activities—but there is a tradeoff. Usually, to get this vastly reduced fare for an activity, you must attend a time-share presentation and sit through the hard sell that follows. If you are interested in buying into a time-share property anyway, getting cheap tickets in the process may not be a bad idea. However, most people just give it a miss, as they have better things to do on their vacations than be bombarded by high-pressure salesmen.

Hiking

The **Lahaina Pali Trail** is a Na Ala Hele (Hawaii Trail and Access System) trail. Five miles in length, it starts near mile marker 11, about one half mile west of the Lahaina Tunnel. Following an old established trail, it crosses the Kealaloloa Ridge at 1,600 feet, then descends to an access road that meets the highway near the junction of Highways 30 and 380. This trail is hot and dry, so bring plenty of water and wear a hat and sturdy hiking boots. It's a rigorous climb. Markers along the way indicate cultural and historical sites.

SHOPPING

Once learned, everybody loves to do the "Lahaina Stroll." It's easy. Just act cool, nonchalant, and give it your best strut as you walk the gauntlet of Front Street's exclusive shops and boutiques. The fun is just in being here. If you begin in the evening, go to the south end of town and park down by Prison Street; it's much easier to find a spot and you walk uptown, catching the sunset.

The Lahaina Stroll

On Prison Street, check out **Dan's Green House,** 808/661-8412, open daily 9 A.M.–5 P.M., specializing in *fuku-bonsai,* miniature plants originated by David Fukumoto. They're mailable (except to

Front Street, Lahaina

ROBERT NILSEN

MAUI

Australia and Japan), and when you get them home, just plop them in water and presto—a great little plant (from $26). Dan's also specializes in exotic birds like African gray parrots, macaws from Australia, common cockatoos, and various cheeky parrots, and has a few other miniature animals. Dan's is a great place to browse, especially for families.

As you head up Front Street, the first group of shops includes **Duke's Rentals,** where you can rent everything from snorkel gear and surf boards to cruiser bikes and golf clubs; **Sea Level Trading Company** with mostly women's alohawear and men's aloha shirts; and **Camellia** with a treasure chest laden with gifts and jewelry made from gold, silver, and ivory. Here as well is **Original Maui Divers,** which has some fancy jewelry including its specialty, black tree coral. Visit the "pin and ink" artist upstairs at **Skin Deep Tattooing,** 626 Front St., 808/661-8531, open daily 10 A.M.–10 P.M., until 5 P.M. Sunday, where you can get a permanent memento of your trip to Maui. Skin Deep features "new-age primal, tribal tattoos," Japanese-style intricate beauties, with women artists available for shy women clientele. The walls are hung with sample tattoos that you can choose from. A sobriety test is necessary to get tattooed. No wimps allowed! This is a legitimate place where the artists know what they're doing; they've been in business now for more than 20 years.

Moving down the Line

The following shops are all along Front Street. By no means exhaustive, this list just gives you an idea of some of the unique shops here.

In the old coral and stone Masters' Reading Room next to the Baldwin Home is **Na Mea Hawai'i Store,** 808/661-5707. This unique shop carries only native Hawaiian arts and crafts, block prints, clothing, printed fabric, tapa fabric, feather and shell lei, and food items, as well as a good selection of local music and books on Hawaiian subjects. This is the real thing. You won't find tourist junk or imported goods here. Open daily 10 A.M.–7 P.M.; stop in for an authentic gift from the island.

Between the Pioneer Inn and the seawall, walk onto the sandy floor of the Polynesian-style **Gecko Store,** where all the items, including shorts, T-shirts, bathing suits, and sweatshirts,

bear the bug-eyed sucker-footed logo of Hawai'i's famous clicking geckos. Next door is the **Lahaina Hat Co.,** where you can find the perfect chapeau to shield your head from the "merciless" Lahaina sun; and at **Maui Mercantile** you can find all sorts of clothing.

Golden Reef, 695 Front St., is open daily 10 A.M.–10 P.M. Inside is all manner of jewelry from heirloom quality to costume baubles made from black, gold, red, and pink coral, malachite, lapis, and mother of pearl. All designs are created on the premises. Everyone will be happy shopping here because prices range from $1 to $1,000 and more. Contrast these gems with **Bijoux Pour Vous** heirloom Hawaiian jewelry only a few steps away.

Noah himself would have been impressed with the **Endangered Species Store,** open daily 9 A.M.–10:30 P.M., where a life-size mountain gorilla, coiled python, flitting butterflies, and fluttering birds bid you welcome to this lovely jam-packed menagerie. The shelves hold world globes, maps, cuddly panda bears, posters of trumpeting elephants, sculptures of soaring eagles, parlor games, postcards, and memento flora- and fauna-inspired T-shirts of 100 percent cotton designed by local artists. A percentage of the profits from every purchase is set aside to advance environmental issues. Moreover, the store tries to deal with vendors who also contribute to the well-being of endangered species and the environment.

Back on the mountain side of the street, **Tropical Blues,** 754 Front, presents fine aloha shirts and women's alohawear. Next door at 752 Front, one of the four **Serendipity** shops on the island offers a unique collection of casual island wear, furniture, wood carvings, and accouterments of an Asian and Hawaiian nature. In this stretch you will also find **Tropical Addictions** for gifty items, candles, and knickknacks, **Sunspots** for distinctive T-shirts with outrageous sayings, and both an **ABC Discount Store** and **E-Z Discount** for sundries, gifts, snacks, and liquor.

The **Whaler's Locker,** 780 Front St., 808/661-3775, open 9 A.M.–10 P.M., is a sea chest filled with hand-engraved scrimshaw on fossilized walrus and mammoth ivory. Lahaina, historically a premier whaling port, has long been known for this sailor's art etched on everything from pocketknives to whale-tooth pendants. Display cases also hold gold and amber jewelry, Ni'ihau shellwork, Japanese netsuke, shark's teeth, and even some coral necklaces. If you are looking for a distinctive folk-art gift that truly says Maui, the Whaler's Locker is an excellent store from which to make your choice. The 780 Front St. building is the second oldest shop in modern Lahaina, dating back to 1871.

Sharing the same address is **The South Seas Trading Post,** 808/661-3168, open daily 8:30 A.M.–10 P.M. It indeed has artifacts from the South Pacific, like tapa cloth from Tonga, but also colorful rugs from India, primitive carvings from Papua New Guinea, and Burmese *kalaga* wall hangings with their beautiful and intricate stitching, jade from China, and bronze from Tibet. You can pick up a one-of-a-kind bead necklace for only a few dollars, or a real treasure that would adorn any home for a decent price. Sold are antiques and reproductions; the bona fide antiques have authenticating dates on the back or bottom sides.

In the courtyard just off Front Street and Lahainaluna Road is **The Lahaina Market Place,** a collection of semi-open-air stalls and a handful of storefronts, open daily 9 A.M.–9 P.M. Some vendors have roll-up stands and sell trinkets and baubles. Some is junk, but it's neat junk, and they all compete for your business. A mainstay of this alleyway market, **Maui Crystal** has fine examples of handmade glass sculpture and some crystals that are not made on premises. Pyrex and softer colored glass is used to form these creations, an activity you can watch through the glass windows of the small workshop. Two art galleries, facing Lahainaluna Road, back up against this courtyard.

The Far End
On both sides of Front Street beyond Lahainaluna Road the shops continue. The "sexually incorrect" will love **David's of Hawaii,** 815 Front St., where you can find all kinds of lewd postcards, T-shirts, and souvenirs. If T-shirts bearing sexually implicit puns offend you, keep strolling—it's nasty in there. Funky and audacious. Open daily 9 A.M.–10:30 P.M.

In the Old Poi Factory at 819 Front St. is **Pacific Visions,** selling hand-painted local garments done at Ha'iku, art-deco items from Los Angeles, San Francisco, and New York, and lots

of artifacts from Bali. Open daily. One of the oldest shops at the Poi Factory is **Valley Isle Promotions,** opened in 1974, which specializes in children's and women's clothing, along with 14-karat gold jewelry designed by the store's owner.

Scrimshaw is the art of carving and/or coloring ivory. Whaling and nautical scenes are perhaps the most common, but other designs are also found. **Lahaina Scrimshaw,** 845 Front St. (across from Wo Hing temple), 808/661-8820, open daily 9 A.M.–10 P.M., boasts its own master scrimshander, John Lee, who works in the window every day from about 7:30 A.M.–noon, and who is friendly and willing to answer questions about this sailor's art. Most of the scrimshaw is done on antique whale's teeth from the whaling era or on fossilized walrus and mastodon tusks. The scrimshaw offered is authentic, and made by about 40 artists, most of whom are from Hawaii.

At 844 Front St. is **Island Woodcarving** gallery, a prefect spot to choose a hand-carved art piece done in an island wood in a Hawaiian style.

Elephant Walk is a gift and clothing store that's fairly representative of others you'll find along Front Street, and the prices are good.

Crazy Shirts also has a great assortment of distinctive T-shirts and other clothes. Also in this store at 865 Front St. is the tiny but intriguing display of antiques, nautical instruments, scrimshaw, and whaling-related pictures.

Across the street is **The Whaler** for mostly new marine and nautical objects and some art glass.

At the **Sunglass Hut** shop, you can pick up shades for the strong tropical sun. Depending on the type, these sunglasses run $40–350. Also available is a wide range of watches—waterproof and not—some economical and others that will bust your budget.

Off the Main Drag
Wolf Camera, 139 Lahainaluna Rd., 808/667-6255, open daily, is a full-service, one-hour-developing camera store. It's good in West Maui for any specialized photo needs. A second one-hour lab is down the street and around the corner at 820 Front Street, while a third is found at the Pioneer Inn Shops.

Even if you haven't been out on a whale-watching tour, stop in at the Pacific Whale Foundation **Ocean Store,** 143 Dickenson St.,

808/667-7447, for a look at all the clothing, posters, jewelry, and gift items relating to the whale and other sea creatures. It's almost an education having a look here, and the proceeds help support this worthy organization.

Up the street at Dickenson Square is a **Whalers General Store,** for sundries.

The **Salvation Army Thrift Shop** on Shaw Street just up from Front Street has the usual collection of inexpensive used goods but occasionally some great buys on older aloha shirts. Open Mon.–Sat., regular business hours.

505 Front Street

With most shops open daily 9 A.M.–9 P.M., this mall offers a barrel full of shops and restaurants at the south end of Front Street, away from the heavy foot traffic. The complex looks like a New England harbor village, and the shopping is good and unhurried with validated underground parking for customers. Some shops include a **Whalers General Store** for sundries; **Ali'i Espresso Cafe; Foreign Intrigue Imports; Maui to Go** for arts and crafts; **Colors of Maui Clothing;** and the wonderful **Elizabeth Doyle Gallery,** which has lots of art glass, ceramics, and paintings—some island artists. The **Old Lahaina Book Emporium,** 808/661-1399, the best used-book store on this side on the island, is crammed full of hardcover and paperback books, right for a poolside read or serious study. This shop also has some new books and new and used CDs—trades are welcome; open Mon.–Sat. 10 A.M.–9 P.M. and Sunday until 6 P.M. Check your email at **505 Cafe** as you linger over a snack and coffee. Rates are 20 cents a minute, $6 a half hour, or $12 an hour; printouts are extra. Several other shops inhabit this mall, as do half a dozen restaurants.

The Wharf Cinema Center

The Wharf Cinema Center at 658 Front offers three floors of fast-food eateries, clothing and jewelry stores, souvenir shops, and a movie the-

ater. Most shops are open 9 A.M.–9 P.M. Playing first-run movies, the triplex **Lahaina Cinemas** occupies much of the third floor. Browse **Crazy Shirts** with its excellent selection of quality T-shirts. **Hawaiian Styles and Creations** offers tropical sportswear, and **Island Swimwear** carries bathing suits for men and women. There's a coffee bar where you can relax and read. **Island Coins and Stamps** on the second floor is a shop as frayed as an old photo album. It specializes in philatelic supplies. For postal needs and gifts, stop by the **Lahaina Mail Depot** on the lower level at the rear; open weekdays 10 A.M.–4:30 P.M., Saturday until 1 P.M. Across the walk is **Island Sandals,** 808/661-5110, a small shop run in the honest old-style way that produces fully adjustable tie sandals, styled from the days of Solomon. As the gregarious sandalmaker says, he creates the right sandal for $135 ($115 women's) and gives you the left as a gift. Stop in and have him trace your feet for an order. As he works, he'll readily talk about political, social, or local island issues, and definitely tell you why it's much better to have leather on the bottom of your feet than any manmade material. Out front is an **ABC Discount Store.** For those coming from Ka'anapali, the West Maui Shopping Express stops at the rear of this complex.

heleconia

Pioneer Inn Shops

Below Pioneer Inn is a clutch of shops that includes **Fundimentional,** mazemaster.com, for eye-catching 3-D art; **Products of Hawaii Too** for gift and craft items; **Watch-N-See** for timepieces and sunglasses; a **Lifestyle** alohawear clothing shop; and a **Whalers General Store.** Several other clothing stores are here as are **Waterfront Gallery** for jewelry, gifts, and artwork, **Häagen-Dazs** for ice cream treats, and an **Atlantis submarine** booth where you can arrange a memorable underwater Maui adventure. Most shops are open 9 A.M.–9 P.M.

On the sidewalk in front of these shops is a

stand where you can get your picture taken with a multicolored macaw on your shoulder (or with one on each shoulder and one sitting on your head!). Taken one day, the photos are ready the next day. The fee ranges upward from $20, depending upon the number and size of your photographs.

Old Lahaina Center
The Old Lahaina Center, in front of the midtown post office and between Front and Waine'e Streets, has an **Ace Hardware,** the **Lahaina Fishing Supplies** for fishing gear and marine hardware, **Lahaina One-Hour Photo,** the **Lahaina Pharmacy,** and **The Mail Room** for wrapping, shipping, and all postal supplies. In the midst of this complex is the **Maui Myth and Magic Center,** where the 'Ulalena theater show is performed, while along Papalaua Avenue are **Bank of Hawaii** and **American Savings Bank** branches. In the portion closest to Waine'e Street, you'll find **Nagasako General Store, Nagasako Variety,** a new **Foodland, Starbuck's Coffee,** and **Ji Mi's Asian Food Mart.**

Across Waine'e Street is the **Lahaina Square Shopping Center,** with its several inexpensive eateries, **West Maui Cycles** and **Gold's Gym.** You'll find an activities center, a water gear rental shop, and additional local eateries next door at **Anchor Square.**

The Lahaina Center
Lahaina's newest shopping center is at the corner of Front and Papalaua Streets at the north edge of downtown. The signature establishments of this mall are the **Hard Rock Café,** filled with memorabilia of rock-and-roll greats and serving American standards and cold beer; a **Banana Republic** for livable fashions; and **Hilo Hattie** for Hawaiian clothing and gifts. In the center you will also find **Local Motion Hawaii,** a hip clothing store selling tank tops, swimwear, and locally designed T-shirts; **Wet Seal** for young women's clothing, several other fashion shops; an **ABC Discount Store** for sundries and inexpensive beach gear; a **Dive Maui** outlet for water activities and equipment; and a **Made In Hawaii** shop for a good selection of local products. Cool yourself down at the **Paniolo Coffee Company** with a shave ice or milk shake, or give yourself a pick-me-up with a steaming espresso. You can

also cool down at the long bar at **Maui Brews**—a huge selection of bottle and draft beer—have a meal in the restaurant, spend some extra change in the game room, or come in the evening for music and dancing at the nightclub. For finer food, try either **Sam Choy's Lahaina** or **Ruth's Chris Steak House,** and follow that with an evening of magic at **Warren and Annabelle's.** Lahaina's second cinema complex, the **Front Street Theaters,** occupies one of the center buildings. Mon.–Fri. 2–8 P.M., arts and crafts displays and craft lessons cover the sidewalks of the center for everyone to enjoy. There is a pay parking lot here that's free with validation. The West Maui Shopping Express shuttle stops at the Hilo Hattie store more than 10 times a day on its route between Lahaina and Ka'anapali; $1 per person each way.

After shopping, stop by **Hale Kahiko** and have a look at the traditional-style Hawaiian buildings and items of everyday use displayed as a cultural showcase in a landscaped enclosure to the side of the parking lot. Open daily 9 A.M.–6 P.M. While here enjoy the hula show at 2 P.M. on Wednesday and Friday or the *keiki* hula show at 6 P.M. on Friday.

Lahaina Cannery Mall
As practical looking as its name on the outside—it is a converted pineapple cannery, after all—the center's bright, well-appointed, and air-conditioned interior features some of the best and most convenient shopping on West Maui; open daily 9:30 A.M.–9 P.M. The mall is at 1221 Honoapi'ilani Highway, near Mala Wharf. If you'll be staying at a condo and doing your own cooking, the largest and generally least expensive supermarket on West Maui is **Safeway,** open daily 24 hours. To book any activities, from a whale-watch to a dinner cruise, you'll find **Activity Mart** offering the right price. Sundries can be picked up at the **ABC Discount Store,** and you can beat the sun's glare by stopping into **Shades of Hawaii.** Clothing shops include **Crazy Shirts, Maui Water Wear, Escape to Maui, Panama Jacks** and **Bluse Ginger.** Food is available at **Compadres Mexican Bar and Grill** and **Mango Cafe,** as well as half a dozen smaller stalls in the food court. Although the mall is relatively new, don't let that fool you because some of Lahaina's oldest and best shops, like

MAUI

Lahaina Printsellers, are here. **Waldenbooks** has one of its excellent, well-stocked stores in the mall. One of the most unusual shops is **The Kite Fantasy,** featuring kites, windsocks, and toys for kids of all ages. You can buy kites like a six-foot flexifoil for more than $100 or a simple triangular plastic kite for only a few bucks. Cloth kites are made from nylon with nice designs for a reasonable $15.95. Another unique shop, well worth the effort of exploring, is **Totally Hawaiian Gift Gallery,** where you can find quilts, carved bowls, shellwork, and woodwork. If you're into designer coffees and cigars come to **Sir Wilfred's.** It's one of the few places on this side of the island for such delicacies. If you're hungry, try the deli case for pastries and the like, or order up a cup of soup, quiche, lasagna, or sandwich. A good assortment of gift items round out what's sold here. **Longs Drugs** is one of the cheapest places to buy and develop film. You can also find a selection of everything from aspirin to boogie boards. There's plenty of free parking at this mall, but the West Maui Shopping Express bus stops here a dozen times a day shuttling between Lahaina and Ka'anapali; $1 per person each way.

Booths are set up in the mall Mon.–Fri. 10 A.M.–4 P.M., displaying and selling Hawaiian art and crafts. Also, a free **Polynesian Show** is presented every Tuesday and Thursday evening 7–8 P.M., and there's a **Keiki Hula Show** every Saturday and Sunday 1–2 P.M.

Arts

Dubbed the "Art Capital of the Pacific." it's said that Lahaina is the world's third-largest art market. Who determined that to be so is a question unanswered, yet it is certain that you can view countless works of art here and spend a fortune acquiring it. Many artists on display at the galleries in Lahaina are local island artists and others are from throughout the state, although other Americans and numerous foreigners are also represented. Although not all, many of the galleries in town are open until 10 P.M.

Due to the renovation of the old Lahaina Courthouse in 1998, the Lahaina Arts Society had to vacate its digs in the basement of the old jail. Following the courthouse restoration, they've moved back. The **Old Jail Gallery** is once again in the basement, and the **Banyan Tree Gallery** has opened on the first floor; they are both open daily 9 A.M.–5 P.M. The Lahaina Arts Society is a nonprofit venture, and all artworks hung in its galleries are juried pieces of its 175 members, all island residents. You can get some good bargains here. Contact the Lahaina Arts Society at 808/661-0111 for information. Every other Saturday and Sunday 8 A.M.–5 P.M., society members display and sell their art at **Banyan Tree Craft Fair,** under the big banyan behind the courthouse. On alternate weekends, other artists and craftspeople display their wares at the same location at the **He U'i Cultural Arts Festival.** Sometimes you'll get demonstrations and music to boot. Many of the artists here are up and coming, and the prices for sometimes remarkable works are reasonable. They're trying to make a living by their skills, and most are not displayed at the well-known galleries in town.

The Village Galleries, with two locations at 120 Dickenson St., 808/661-4402 or 800/346-0585, open daily 9 A.M.–9 P.M., and at 180 Dickenson St., 808/661-5559, were founded by Lynn Shue in 1970 and are among the oldest continuous galleries featuring original works of Maui artists. At the original gallery at 120 Dickenson, enter to find everything from *raku* pottery to hand-blown glass and sculptures done in both wood and metal. Some of the accomplished painters on display are: George Allan, who works in oils; Joyce Clark, another oil painter noted for her seascapes; Betty Hay-Freeland, a landscape artist; Fred Kenknight, who uses watercolors to depict island scenes; Lowell Mapes, who also uses oil to render familiar landmarks and island scenes. The galleries also have inexpensive items like postcards, posters, and limited-edition prints, all perfect as mementos and souvenirs. The gallery at 180 Dickenson St. features more contemporary and abstract works.

The Wyland Gallery, 711 Front St., 808/667-2285, showcases the works of Wyland, renowned worldwide for his "whaling wall" murals of cavorting whales. Wyland's visionary oil and watercolor paintings of marvelous aquatic scenes adorn the walls, while his compassionate bronze renderings of whales and dolphins sing their soul songs from white pedestals. Other featured paintings are done by Al Hogue, William DeShazo, Neolito, and John Pitre. Also displayed are the organic sculptures of Dale Joseph Evers, a pioneer in functional furnishings, who has turned bronze and acrylic into dolphin-shaped tables. At 697 Front St., a second Wyland Gallery, 808/661-7099, vibrates with fantastic colors and images, and a third gallery is at 136 Dickenson, 808/661-0590. Galleries are open 9 A.M.–9 P.M. daily.

The two shops of **Galerie Lassen,** at 700 and 844 Front St., 808/661-1101 and 808/667-7707, showcase original and limited edition prints by Christian Riese Lassen, who boldly applies striking colors to bring to life his landscapes and two-worlds perspective of sea and earth. Complementing the exaggerated hues of Lassen's works is the subtle patina of Richard Steirs' cast-iron sculptures of supple whales and dolphins. Mr. Steirs, an Upcountry resident, is among the most admired sculptors on Maui with his limited edition castings.

The Lahaina Galleries, 728 Front St., 808/667-2152, is one of the oldest galleries on the island. Open until 9 P.M., the gallery, with a central room and two in the rear, is hung with the works of Dario Campanile, Andrea Smith, Guy Buffet, Aldo Luongo, and other widely acclaimed painters, and the mesmerizing acrylic sculptures of Frederick Hart. A branch gallery is at the Kapalua Shops in Kapalua.

Robert Lynn Nelson Studio, 802 Front St. on the corner of Lahainaluna Road, 808/667-2100, shows originals and prints only of Robert Lynn Nelson, the father of the modern marine art movement, which splits the canvas between land and undersea scenes. Although most well-known for his marine scenes, Nelson pursues other styles and themes that he is not known for, that you may only find displayed here in this gallery. A second gallery is at the West Maui Center on the mountain side of the highway.

Next door is the **Elan Vital Studio Galleries,** 808/661-0199. Elan Vital produces giant canvases of color, some bright and some somber, that seem like translucent plastic.

Displaying idyllic home scenes, waterfalls, snowscapes, and the like by Thomas Kinkade are the **Thomas Kinkade Galleries,** at 780 and 855 Front St., 808/667-7175. Open daily except Sunday 10 A.M.–10 P.M.

Flowers, birds, and Chinese fans make up the majority of works displayed at the **David Lee Galleries,** 712 Front St., 808/667-7740. David Lee uses natural powder pigments to create his vivid colors and even grinds lapis, pearl, turquoise, and gold for their colors, and paints on silk. Originals, lithographs, and posters.

Showing modern art with bright colors is **Sargents Fine Art** gallery right on the corner of Front Street and Lahainaluna Road. Some of what hangs on these walls are abstract sailing ships by Rick Lawrence, impressionist landscapes by Anne Good, surreal scenes by Vladimir Kush, and immense brightly painted fruit by Carmelo Sortino.

Nearly across Lahainaluna St. is the **Martin Lawrence Gallery,** 808/661-1788, which shows an eclectic collection of pop and contemporary art with such artists as Warhol, Chagall, Picasso, and Miro.

The **One World Gallery,** 808/661-3984, at 816 Front St., is a zany collection of modern art, jewelry, glass, ceramics, and multimedia art pieces, full of fun and with a sense of humor.

Lahaina Printsellers at the Lahaina Cannery Mall, open daily 9 A.M.–9:30 P.M., 808/667-7843 or 800/669-7843, website: www.printsellers.com, has walls festooned with beautiful prints of old Hawaii, including endangered birds, reef fish, and historical figures that featured prominently in Hawaii's past, and some nautical paintings. Printsellers specializes in antique maps and reproductions, especially those depicting the Pacific basin, and Captain Cook memorabilia. Original antique prints and maps, many from the beginning of the 19th century, can go all the way up to $100,000. The Hawaiian Nostalgia series, framed in bamboo, features less costly reproductions of advertising and commercial prints from the early and mid-1900s. Lahaina Printsellers also offers hand-rubbed koa frames and will be happy to send you a brochure of its selections if you would like to choose your artwork at home. With its heavy use of dark wood, many tables, and frames everywhere, this shop has the feel of an old library just waiting to be explored. Two other Lahaina Printsellers shops are at the Whalers Village in Ka'anapali and at the Grand Wailea Resort in Wailea.

Food and Liquor Stores

The following markets/supermarkets are in and around Lahaina. The larger ones also stock beer, wine, and liquor. **Safeway,** at the Lahaina Cannery Mall, open 24 hours, is a large supermarket complete with deli, fish market, floral shop, and bakery. **Foodland,** at the Old Lahaina Center, is a new and well-stocked supermarket. **Nagasako General Store,** also at the Old Lahaina Center, open daily 7 A.M.–10 P.M., Sunday until 7 P.M., has a smaller selection of ethnic Hawaiian, Japanese, Chinese, and Korean foods, along with liquor selections, fresh fish, and produce.

For bulk foods, health food items, vitamins, minerals, and supplements, and hot and cold prepared foods, try the full-service **Westside Natural Foods and Deli,** 808/667-2855, at the corner of Lahainaluna and Waine'e Street. Open daily, with shorter hours Sunday.

The Olowalu General Store, 808/661-3774, five miles east of Lahaina along Route 30, open Mon.–Fri. 6 A.M.–6:30 P.M., Saturday 7 A.M.–6:30 P.M., Sunday 7 A.M.–5 P.M., is fairly well stocked and the only place to pick up supplies in this area. It also has light snacks including sandwiches and hot dogs, a perfect stop if you are snorkeling or swimming on the nearby beaches.

Mr. Wine, 808/661-5551, on the corner of Lahainaluna and Waine'e Street, not only has a huge selection of wines and some beer, liquors, and liqueurs, but keeps the better wines and champagnes under cellar conditions in a climatically controlled room at 55° F and 70 percent humidity. Beat the hot Lahaina sun and stop in for a perfect bottle for the evening. Open Mon.–Sat. 11 A.M.–7 P.M.

SERVICES AND INFORMATION

For fire, police, or ambulance, dial 911 throughout the Lahaina area. The police station, fire station, and Lahaina civic center are above Wahikuli County Wayside Park between Lahaina and Ka'anapali.

Banking
In Lahaina during normal banking hours try the Bank of Hawaii, 808/661-8781, or the American Savings Bank, 808/667-9561, in the Old Lahaina Center; or First Hawaiian Bank, just a few steps away at 215 Papalaua St., 808/661-3655.

Post Office
The main post office is on the very northwest edge of town where Ka'anapali begins; the mid-

town postal branch is at the Old Lahaina Center. Both are open 8:30 A.M.–5 P.M. Mon.–Fri. and 9 A.M.–1 P.M. on Saturday; call 800/275-8777 for information.

Lahaina Mail Depot is a post office contract station at The Wharf Cinema Center, 808/667-2000. It's open weekdays 10 A.M.–4 P.M. (Saturday until 1 P.M.), and along with the normal stamps, etc., it specializes in sending packages home. Mailing boxes, tape, and packaging materials are all available, as are souvenir packs of coffee, nuts, candies, and teas, which might serve as a last-minute purchase, but they are expensive. In the Old Lahaina Center you'll find The Mail Room, 808/661-5788, for shipping and packaging services and supplies. Hours are Mon.–Fri. 9:30 A.M.–6 P.M., Saturday until 3:30 P.M.; closed for lunch.

Medical Treatment
A concentration of all types of specialists is found at the Maui Medical Group, 130 Prison St., 808/661-0051. Open Mon.–Fri. 8 A.M.–5 P.M. and Saturday 8 A.M.–noon; call for emergency hours. Professional medical care can also be found at the Kaiser Permanente clinic, 910 Waine'e St., 808/661-7400 during the same hours. Alternatively, the Lahaina Health Center, 180 Dickenson St. at Dickenson Square, Suite 205, 808/667-6268, offers acupuncture, chiropractic, therapeutic massage, and podiatry.

Pharmacies in Lahaina include: Lahaina Pharmacy at the Old Lahaina Center, 808/661-3119; Longs Drugs at the Lahaina Cannery Mall, 808/667-4384; and Valley Isle Pharmacy, 130 Prison St., 808/661-4747.

Information
The following groups and organizations should prove helpful: Lahaina Restoration Foundation, P.O. Box 338, Lahaina, HI 96761, 808/661-3262. The foundation is a storehouse of information about historical Lahaina; be sure to pick up its handy brochure, *Lahaina, A Walking Tour of Historic and Cultural Sites,* for an introduction to historically significant sites around town.

The Lahaina Town Action Committee, 648 Wharf St., Lahaina, HI 96761, 808/667-9175, sponsors cultural events and other activities throughout the year, including Art Night, and can provide information about what's happening in the area. It operates the Lahaina Visitor Center on the first floor of the Old Lahaina Courthouse. For popular events and activities happening in Lahaina, contact the events hotline at 808/667-9194, or visit the center's website at www.visitlahaina.com. Pick up its *Maui Historical Walking Guide* brochure. It has information mostly on Lahaina, but a bit on Ka'anapali and Kapalua as well.

The nonprofit Lahaina Arts Society, 808/661-0111, website: www.mauigateway.com/~las, has information about the art scene and art events in town. It maintains two galleries at the old courthouse and runs an art program for children.

The Lahaina Public Library is at 680 Wharf St., 808/662-3950, open Monday and Tuesday noon–8 P.M., Wednesday and Thursday 9 A.M.–5 P.M., and Friday 12:30–4:40 P.M.

KA'ANAPALI

Five lush valleys, nourished by streams from the West Maui Mountains, stretch luxuriously for 10 miles from Ka'anapali north to Kapalua. All along the connecting **Honoapi'ilani Highway** (Route 30), the dazzle and glimmer of beaches is offset by black volcanic rock. This is West Maui's resort coast. Two sensitively planned and beautifully executed resorts are at each end of this drive. Ka'anapali Resort is 500 acres of fun and relaxation at the south end. It houses six luxury hotels, a handful of beautifully appointed condos, a shopping mall and museum, 36 holes of world-class golf, tennis courts galore, and epicurean dining in a chef's salad of cuisines. Two of the hotels, the Hyatt Regency and Sheraton, are inspired architectural showcases that blend harmoniously with Maui's most beautiful seashore surroundings. At the northern end is another gem, the Kapalua Resort, 1,650 of Maui's most beautifully sculpted acres with its own showcases, prime golf, fine beaches, exclusive shopping, and endless activity.

Ka'anapali, with its four miles of glorious beach, is Maui's westernmost point. It begins where Lahaina ends and continues north along Route 30 until it runs into the village of Honokowai. Along this shore, Maui flashes its most captivating pearly white smile. The sights here are either natural or manmade, but not historical. This is where you come to gaze from mountain to sea and bathe yourself in natural beauty. Then, after a day of surf and sunshine, you repair to one of the gorgeous hotels or restaurants for a drink or dining, or just to promenade around the grounds.

History
Western Maui was a mixture of scrub and precious *lo'i*, irrigated terrace land reserved for taro,

the highest life-sustaining plant given by the gods. The farms stretched to Kapalua, skirting the numerous bays all along the way. The area was important enough for a "royal highway" to be built by Chief Pi'ilani, and it still bears his name. Westerners used the lands surrounding Ka'anapali to grow sugarcane, and **The Lahaina, Kaanapali, and Pacific Railroad,** known today as the "Sugar Cane Train," chugged to Ka'anapali Beach to unburden itself onto barges that carried the cane to waiting ships. Ka'anapali, until the 1960s, was a blemished beauty where the Pioneer Sugar Mill dumped its rubbish. Then Amfac, who owned the mill and this land, decided to put the land to better use. In creating Hawaii's first planned resort community, it outdid itself. Robert Trent Jones Sr. was hired to mold the golf course along this spectacular coast, while the Hyatt Regency and its grounds became an architectural marvel. The Sheraton-Maui was built atop, and integrated with, Pu'u Keka'a, "Black Rock," a wave-eroded cinder cone, and the architects used its sea cliffs as part of the walls of the resort. Here, on a deep underwater shelf, daring divers used to descend to harvest Maui's famous black coral trees. The Hawaiians believed that Pu'u Keka'a was a very holy place where the spirits of the dead left this earth and migrated into the spirit world. Kahekili, Maui's most famous 18th-century chief, often came here to leap into the sea below. This old-time daredevil was fond of the heart-stopping activity, and made famous "Kahekili's Leap," an even more treacherous sea cliff on nearby Lana'i. Today, the Sheraton puts on a sunset show where this "leap" is reenacted.

Unfortunately, developers picked up on Amfac's great idea and built condos up the road starting in Honokowai. Interested more in profit than beauty, they earned that area the dubious title of "condo ghetto." Fortunately, Maui Land and Pineapple Co. owned the land surrounding the idyllic Kapalua Bay. Colin Cameron, one of the heirs to this holding, had visions of developing 750 acres of the plantation, later expanded to 1,650 acres, and it opened in 1979 as the extraordinary Kapalua Resort.

Pu'u Keka'a

One of the most easily accessible and visually engaging snorkeling spots on Maui is at the Sheraton's Black Rock. Approach this either from the beach in front of the hotel where you can snorkel west around the rock, or from around back. Follow the main road past the Sheraton until it begins to climb the hill. Walk along the pathway that leads to the North Ka'anapali Beach and head for the remnants of an old pier. This pier was built as the end of a spur line of the sugarcane railroad and used to ship bags of sugar. After the Mala Wharf was constructed closer to Lahaina in the 1920s, the rail lines were taken up and cattle were shipped off island from here. The entire area offshore is like an underwater marine park. There are schools of reef fish, rays, and even lonely turtles. There is limited free public parking in Ka'anapali, so you may have to park in one of the few pay lots. Alternately, park at Kahekili Beach Park at the far north end of Ka'anapali near the Maui Kaanapali Villas, from where it's only a 15-minute walk.

Whaling Museum

The free **Whalers Village Museum,** 808/661-4567, at Whaler's Village shopping mall, has a few outside displays, but most items are inside on the upper level of the mall. The most dramatic outside display is the skeleton of a 30-foot sperm whale. This big boy greets you at the entrance to the mall as you come up the steps. There is also a whaling boat in a side courtyard. The compact display area upstairs on the mezzanine level is full of whaling history, photographs, drawings, artifacts from whaling ships, a reconstructed forecastle, a video on whaling, and many informative descriptions and stories about the whaling industry, whaling life, and the whalers themselves. After a walk through the museum, pick up a memento at the museum gift shop. Open 9:30 A.M.–10 P.M. daily. This is a must-see stop for anyone wishing a better understanding of whales, sailors, life on board, and this integral aspect of Hawaiian history.

Transportation

Ka'anapali is serviced by the free **Kaanapali Trolley** within the resort area. It runs throughout the day on a prescribed schedule and makes stops at each resort and the at Whalers Village shops. The **West Maui Shopping Express** runs south between Ka'anapali and the Wharf Cinema Center in Lahaina, and north to Kapalua. Rides are $1 each way between stops and operate 8 A.M.–10 P.M. daily, stopping at a dozen and a half resorts, condos, and shopping centers on the way. The **South Maui Express** connects Ka'anapali to the Maui Ocean Center in Ma'alaea, where there is a connecting shuttle that continues all the way to the Prince Resort in Makena. Fun for the entire family, the **Sugar Cane Train** takes the scenic route between Ka'anapali and Lahaina. For easy access to the airport in Kahului from Ka'anapali and Lahaina try the TransHawaiian **airporter shuttle.** The Kapalua-West Maui Airport is the most convenient for air travel to this end of the island, but there are only a limited number of daily flights in and out of this airstrip. Most air traffic to Maui still goes via Kahului.

BEACHES

Ka'anapali Beach

The two-mile stretch of pristine sand at Ka'anapali is what people come to experience in Maui, and they are never disappointed. Just as you leave Lahaina and enter Ka'anapali you'll find **Hanaka'o'o Beach Park.** It's a good swimming and sailboarding spot, with lifeguards, showers, and parking; and while so close, it's away from the hotel crowds. The Kahana Canoe Club is based here and you can often see rowers out on the water practicing their strokes. This beach, called Makaiwa, is also referred to as Canoe Beach. Between the beach and the road is an old cemetery with mostly Chinese characters written on the headstones.

Just north around the corner opens the expanse of Ka'anapali Beach, an uninterrupted stretch of sand running from the park to Black Rock. Ka'anapali Beach is sometimes referred to as Little Waikiki for all the resorts along its shore and the crowds of people who frequent it, and it has earned the moniker "Dig Me Beach" as it's known for people watching and those who come to be watched. Ka'anapali Beach is a center for water activities in West Maui. Aside from swimming and snorkeling, you can get surfing and windsurfing lessons, rent an ocean kayak, have a ride on a catamaran, outrigger canoe, or a motorized banana boat, or be lifted into the air by

MAUI

ROBERT NILSEN

North Ka'anapali Beach

parasail. Options abound. Although the hotels that line this beach are some of the most exclusive on the island, public access to the beach is guaranteed. There are numerous "right-of-way" walkways to the beach that run between the various properties, but parking your car here is definitely a hassle. Several of the hotels have set aside a few parking spaces in their area—usually less than a dozen spots—to accommodate the general public who come to enjoy the beach. Usually, these spaces are taken early in the day and remain full. A good idea is to park at either Hanaka'o'o or Wahikuli park and walk northward along the beach. You can park in the Hyatt's lower lot and enter along a right of way. There's access between the Hyatt and the Marriott (pay parking ramp), between the Marriott and the Kaanapali Alii, which also has limited parking, and between the Kaanapali Alii and the Westin Maui. There is also some parking near the Sheraton and at the Whalers Village parking ramp, but you must pass through the gauntlet of shops.

North Ka'anapali Beach

Past Black Rock the beach continues north. Quieter than the main Ka'anapali Beach, it's much less frequented, has no lifeguards, and only the Royal Lahaina Resort has frontage here. This North Ka'anapali Beach is also known as Keka'a Beach, and the section in front of Kahekili Park is locally called Airport Beach because a small airport was apparently located here at one time. Just north of the Royal Lahaina Resort, **Kahekili Park** is dedicated to Maui's King Kahekili. The newest beach park in the area, and open 6 A.M. to 30 minutes past sunset, is a commodious place with a broad lawn, palm trees, a pavilion for cooking, and tables for a picnic. The large shaded parking area can accommodate many cars, and you can count on always finding someone here. The beach, sometimes used for scuba lessons and not bad for snorkelers, runs uninterrupted to Black Rock.

Beach Walk

As in Wailea, a beach walkway has been created in Ka'anapali that runs along the sand from the Hyatt Regency in the south to the Sheraton in the north. This walkway is a convenient way to pass from one property to another: peruse your neighbor hotel, try one of the restaurants down the line, or walk to shop. During the cool hours of the day and at sunset, this walkway is also used by joggers out for exercise and those who want the perfect location to watch the sun go down. If you cut through the Sheraton property and duck out the other side, you can connect with a similar pathway that skirts the golf course and runs along the North Ka'anapali Beach to the Royal Lahaina Resort.

LUXURY HOTELS

The Ka'anapali Resort hotels are all in the $250 and up category—no budget accommodations here.

Hyatt Regency Maui

The moment you enter the main lobby of this luxury hotel the magic begins. An architectural extravaganza opens to the sky, birds fly freely, and magnificent potted plants and full-size courtyard palm trees create the atmosphere of a modern Polynesian palace at Ka'anapali's southern extremity, at 200 Nohea Kai Dr., Lahaina, HI 96761, 808/661-1234 or 800/233-1234, fax 808/667-4498, website: www.maui.hyatt.com. Nooks and crannies abound, and wildlife inhabits the impeccable landscaped gardens and ponds. The swimming pools are inspired by the islands: grottoes, caves, waterfalls, and a 150-foot slide are all built in. A swinging wooden bridge connects the sections, and you can have an island drink at a sunken poolside bar. There are four fine restaurants on property, half a dozen lounges, and the Drums of the Pacific lu'au. The covey of specialty shops and boutiques will please parents and the little kids will love it here too. Camp Hyatt for children ages 3–12 runs daily 9 A.M.–3 P.M. for $50 a child and includes activities and excursions that change daily, arts and crafts, lunch, and snacks. An evening camp 6–10 P.M. is also available, so put those little kiddies in the care of professionals and have a romantic night out. All beach activities, equipment rentals, and lessons, including a sail/snorkel ride on the *Kiele V* catamaran, can be arranged through the beach activities center at oceanside. Expend some energy at the health club and tennis center, or try the new Spa

Moana for the relaxing royal treatment. For less physical activity, check out the daily Hawaiian demonstrations in the lobby, the hotel wildlife tour, the art and garden tour, or the nightly astronomy show on the hotel roof. The lobby activities desk will help you make reservations for activities throughout the island, and if you're here on business, the business center can help take care of your office needs. Rates for the 815 rooms and suites are $285 for terrace rooms, $355 for golf/mountain rooms, $395 for ocean-view rooms, and $445 for oceanfront rooms. Rates are higher for the special Regency floors, and suites run $600–3,000. If you visit, valet parking is in front of the hotel, complimentary if you validate your ticket by dining at Spats or the Palm Court or spending $25 in one of the shops. Or you can self-park out front or around in the back. From here, both the north end of Lahaina, pretty at night with its colored lights reflecting on the water, and Lana'i, floating across the Lahaina Roads, are easily visible.

Sheraton Maui

The 510 rooms and suites of the Sheraton Maui, 2605 Ka'anapali Pkwy., Lahaina, HI 96761, 808/661-0031 or 800/782-9488, fax 808/661-0458, website: www.sheraton-maui.com, are built around Ka'anapali's most conspicuous natural phenomenon, Pu'u Keka'a, "Black Rock." Originally opened in 1963, the Sheraton reopened in 1997 after a two-year complete renovation. Open, bright, and breezy, the lobby looks out over the finely landscaped gardens and an enticing meandering pool with a water slide and spa. Three classy restaurants grace the hotel, as do two indoor lounges and a bar situated at poolside that features evening entertainment. The guest activities desk can arrange almost any activity that the island offers, and you can rent water equipment and have lessons from the beach activities booth. The snorkeling around Black Rock is the best in the area, and every evening there is a torch-lighting ceremony and cliff dives from the rock. As a guest, you can avail yourself of several daily catamaran rides aboard the *Teralani* or head for some sporting competition at the resort's tennis club. The fitness center, day spa, business center, and small clutch of shops are all for guest use. Kids can be taken care of as well through the daily Keiki

Aloha Club program. The north end of the Ka'anapali beach walk ends at the Sheraton, so you can walk all the way to the Hyatt at the south end without leaving the oceanside. Most rooms at the Sheraton face the ocean, and all are air-conditioned and have full amenities. Rates are $340–375 for garden and mountain views, $425–500 for ocean-view and oceanfront rooms, $625 for an Ohana family suite, and $800 for other suites.

The Westin Maui

At 2365 Ka'anapali Pkwy., Lahaina, HI 96761, 808/667-2525 or 888/625-4949, fax 808/661-5764, the Westin is actually a phoenix, risen from the old Maui Surf Hotel. True to the second life of that mythical bird, it is a beauty. Westin is known for its fabulous entranceways, lobbies, and quiet nooks. You won't be disappointed here. A series of strolling paths takes you through resplendent manicured grounds that surround an extensive multi-pool area, one of the largest on Maui. Waterfalls, water slides, and natural rock formations all blend to create civilized paradise. To the left of the main lobby is a collection of exclusive boutique shops and a business center. You'll find just what you want to eat or drink at any time of day at one of the hotel's six restaurants and lounges. The ocean activities center can set you up with all sorts of rentals on the beach or a ride on *Gemini,* the hotel's sailing catamaran. The kids are taken care of at the supervised daily Keiki Kamp. The daily kids' program runs 9 A.M.–3 P.M. at $45 a child, with an evening program 6:30–9:30 for $20. For the experience of all, each Friday 8 A.M.–4 P.M. brings Ho'olauna, a Hawaiian culture and arts program, and throughout the week are other activities set up especially for the guests. Perhaps a soothing massage or healing facial is what you're looking for. The Health Spa and Beauty Salon is open daily 6 A.M.–8 P.M. If you just want to soak in some beauty, have a tour of the hotel's $2 million art collection. The Westin Maui has more than 750 guest rooms. Standard terrace rooms run $280, a garden-view room $310, golf/mountain-view $365, ocean-view $395–445, oceanfront $470, and suites go upward from $850. A daily amenity and service fee of $8 will be added to your bill. Visit the hotel's website at www.westinmaui.com.

MAUI

Royal Lahaina Resort

Twenty-seven idyllic acres surround 542 rooms of the Royal Lahaina Resort, the largest complex in Ka'anapali, 2780 Keka'a Dr., Lahaina, HI 96761, 808/661-3611 or 800/222-5642, fax 808/661-3538, website: www.2maui.com. Here the tropical landscaping leads directly to the sun-soaked beach. The Royal Lahaina, one of the first properties to be developed, is divided into cottages and a tower. Rates range from a standard room at $270 to an oceanfront room at $440. Cottages rent for $350 and $460, suites $500–790; condo/car and other packages are available. The renovated rooms are decorated in a comfortable Hawaiian style with all amenities and private lanai; some of the cottages have kitchens. There are three restaurants at the resort, a nightly lu'au, music in the lounge and bar, and two swimming pools on the well-maintained grounds. A score of shops are at the hotel entrance for your convenience. The beach activities booth rents snorkel equipment, windsurfing boards, and kayaks, and arranges scuba lessons. The resort is also home to the **Royal Lahaina Tennis Ranch,** boasting 11 courts and a 3,500-seat stadium along with special tennis packages for those inclined.

Maui Marriott

The fifth of the big five hotels on Ka'anapali Beach is the Maui Marriott, 100 Nohea Kai Dr., Lahaina, HI 96761, 808/667-1200 or 800/763-1333, fax 808/667-8300. At the end of 2000, the Marriott finished a yearlong reconstruction process, which included, among other things, renovating the lobby and courtyard and turning some rooms into time-share units. With more than 600 rooms, a beach shack for water recreation activities, on-site tennis courts, two dozen shops, three restaurants and bars, an evening lu'au, and indoor and outdoor parking, the Marriott is one of the largest properties on West Maui, but not as elegant as some others in Ka'anapali. Open to the beach and facing the setting sun, the hotel is graced with cooling breezes that waft across its manicured court-yard and through the open atriums of both its buildings. Indoors, the many flowers and potted plants bring the outdoors inside. Outdoors, the grounds are more finely landscaped and tended than ever. The centerpiece of the new recon-

struction was the courtyard and swimming pool area. Totally reworked, it incorporated a huge pool with lagoons, waterfalls, a water slide, and a children's beach area, and is now one of the premier courtyard garden areas in Ka'anapali. The hospitable staff orchestrates the numerous daily handicraft and recreational activities, and there's plenty to keep every family busy. Snorkel sets, boogie boards, and kayaks can be rented at the beach activities center, and scuba lessons are given by Island Scuba. Room rates are $329 for a standard room, $369 for an oceanfront, and $414 for a deluxe oceanfront; suites run $489–1,499. Special honeymoon, tennis, golf, and family plans are available.

Ka'anapali Beach Hotel

Not as large or as luxurious as its famous neighbors, but an excellent hotel nonetheless, the Ka'anapali Beach Hotel is a bargain. At 2525 Ka'anapali Pkwy., 808/661-0011 or 800/262-8450, fax 808/667-5978, website: www.kbh-maui.com, this is undoubtedly the most "Hawaiian" of the hotels in Ka'anapali and perhaps in the state. As you arrive, you'll be greeted with *ho'okipa* (hospitality), and throughout your stay experience the *po'okela* (excellence) of the staff. There is no glitz here, just warm and friendly service, reasonably priced restaurants, a wonderful beachfront location, and nearly as many amenities as the big boys down the line. Guest service provides many free activities and demonstrations including lei-making, hula lessons, *lau hala* weaving, and a free torchlighting ceremony and sunset hula show nightly; the tour desk can always hook you up with any activity on the island. A delight is the 11 A.M. music and dance performance put on by the hotel staff on Monday, Wednesday, and Friday—they even have their own CD! If you're staying here, don't miss it; if you're not, drop on by anyway—everyone is welcome. Have a swim in the hotel's distinctive whale-shaped pool or check with the Trilogy Ocean Sports activities booth for water equipment to rent and water tours. Over the past few years, most of the rooms have been totally renovated and the rest of the property repainted and spiffed up. New wicker furniture, island-inspired wall coverings, unique sliding glass door arrangement for the lanai, and larger and updated bathrooms. The three restaurants provide a wide variety of food for everyone's taste, and the courtyard bar offers libations. The Aloha Passport for Kids program will keep the little ones busy as they go from spot to spot around the property collecting mementos from each "destination." Standard rooms range $170–265 for an ocean view, with suites priced $215–585; many special packages are available.

CONDOS

Generally less expensive than the hotels, most condos offer full kitchens, TVs, some maid service, swimming pools, tennis courts, and often convenience stores and laundry facilities. Combinations of the above are too numerous to mention, so it's best to ask all pertinent questions when booking. Off-season rates and discounts for longer stays are usually offered.

Right on the strip along the water are the fancy high-rise Kaanapali Alii and The Whaler condos. Set amidst the golf links and following the lay of the land are the low-rise Kaanapali Royal and Outrigger Maui Eldorado Resort. A short way north up the beach and off on a road by itself is Maui Kaanapali Villas.

Kaanapali Alii

The Kaanapali Alii lies in a finely landscaped yard right on the ocean. The four high-rise towers are aesthetically pleasing and are set off by flowers and greenery hanging from many of the balconies. If you need space, try here as each of the 200 or so large one- and two-bedroom units runs 1,500–1,900 square feet. All have full kitchens, dining and living rooms, two bathrooms, air conditioning, and washers and dryers. Services include free parking on premises, a beach activities center, complimentary tennis, daily maid service, room service, and many area activities, and restaurant bills can be put on your room charge as a service. On property are an exercise room, a swimming pool that overlooks the beach, whirlpool spa, and barbecues. Room rates are $300–700 a night, slightly lower during low season; three-night minimum. For information and reservations, contact Kaanapali Alii, 50 Nohea Kai Dr., Lahaina, HI 96761, 808/667-1400 or 800/642-6284, fax 808/661-5686, website: http://kaanapali-alii.com. Managed by Classic Resorts.

The Whaler on Kaanapali Beach

The Whaler comprises two high-rise buildings right on the beach next to Whalers Village shopping mall. Outwardly, it has less character than the Kaanapali Alii but offers numerous amenities. On property are a pool and spa, exercise room, tennis courts, sundries shop, and concierge desk. These units run from a 640-square-foot studio to a 1,950-square-foot two-bedroom two-bath suite. Rates are $195–540, slightly higher for some units during high season. There is a two-night minimum stay and several car/condo, honeymoon, and senior packages are available. Covered parking and signing privileges at some nearby restaurants. The Whaler is at 2481 Ka'anapali Pkwy., Lahaina, HI 96761, 808/661-4861 or 800/367-7052, fax 808/661-8315, website: www.the-whaler.com. Managed by Aston.

Maui Eldorado Resort

An Outrigger property, the Maui Eldorado Resort, 2661 Keka'a Dr., 808/661-0021, fax 808/667-7039, website: www.outrigger.com, slides down the hill alongside a fairway culminating in a beachfront cabana. There are also three swimming pools and a sundries store on property, and an activities desk will help you plan your day. These studios and one- and two-bedroom suites run $195–375 year-round. All have full kitchens, a/c, TV, in-unit safes, washers and dryers, and daily maid service. For toll-free reservations and information, call Outrigger at 800/688-7444. Some units here are also offered for rent directly by their owners or through independent agents such as Whaler's Realty, 800/367-5632.

Kaanapali Royal

A golfer's dream right on the course, the Kaanapali Royal at 2560 Keka'a Dr., 808/879-2205, fax 808/874-3497, has only two-bedroom, two-bath units that run $230 a night, slightly less during regular season and slightly more during peak season. Each suite has a full kitchen and a lanai that faces the fairway, a sunken living room, an entertainment center, and washer and dryer. Take advantage of the guest-only swimming pool, lighted tennis courts, and barbecue pit. Units are rented through agents only. Contact Whalers Realty, 808/661-3484 or 800/676-4112, website: www. whalersrealty.com; Maui Beachfront Rentals,

MAUI

808/661-3500 or 888/661-7200, website: www. mauibeachfront.com; or Chase'n Rainbows, 808/667-7088 or 800/367-6092.

Aston Maui Kaanapali Villas

Enjoy the surroundings of 11 sculpted acres at this affordable condo at 45 Kai Ala Dr., 808/667-7791 or 800/922-7866, fax 808/667-0366. The extensive grounds of cool swaying palms harbor three pools, a beach service booth, the Castaway Restaurant, activities desk, and a sundries shop. Rates begin at $145 for a hotel room with refrigerator. Studios with kitchens run $195–255, and it's $250–500 for one- and two-bedroom suites with a/c, cable TV, full kitchens, plus maid service daily. This property, at the far north end of the Ka'anapali development, has an added bonus of peace and quiet, although you remain just minutes from the action and a short stroll from Black Rock, a superb snorkeling area. These units are very large with spacious bedrooms; even the studios are capable of handling four people. A good choice.

FOOD

Every hotel in Ka'anapali has at least one restaurant, with several others scattered throughout the area. Some of the most expensive and exquisite restaurants on Maui are found in these hotels, but surprisingly, at others you can dine very reasonably. The only cheap eats in the area are the few fast-food restaurants at Whalers Village shopping mall

Reilley's Steak and Seafood House

This Irish restaurant and bar is in the clubhouse at Ka'anapali Golf Courses, 808/667-7477. Open for breakfast, lunch, and dinner, Reilley's is known for its daily all-you-can-eat prime rib dinner for $19.95. Other meat and seafood entrées are generally in the $20–28 range. Nightly dinner specials are offered, such as cottage pie on Monday. During the day, a simple pub menu is offered at the bar. Reilley's has a full bar—its single-malt Scotch selection is remarkable—so come and have a drink after a round of golf or just to watch the sun set over the fairway.

Luigi's

Luigi's is at the entrance to Ka'anapali Resort. The "All American" pizza prices start at $11.99 for a regular cheese-only item to $28.99 for a large House Special, super combination pizza smothered with toppings, or you can nibble a salad for only $3.99. Pasta ranges from $11.99 for a marinara sauce to $17.99 for meaty lasagna. Full-course meals include scallops Luigi for $17.99, eggplant parmesan for $15.99, and shrimp scampi for $19.99. Early-bird specials on pasta 5:30–6 P.M. run $10.95. This is a pleasant, family-oriented restaurant. Don't expect food like mama used to make, but it's not bad for adopted Italians. For reservations call 808/661-4500.

Downstairs is **Jonny's Burger Joint,** open 11:30 A.M.–1 A.M. for fist-size burgers and fries, cold drinks from the bar, and a game of pool or darts. Jonny's serves meat, veggie, fish, and chicken burgers with all the trimmings. It's a good-time place to relax after a day in the sun.

At Whalers Village

This shopping mall has three restaurants and a clutch of fast food joints. You can find everything from pizza and frozen yogurt to lobster tails. Prices range from bargain to pricey.

The well-established **Leilani's On The Beach,** 808/661-4495, has a downstairs Beachside Grill open 11 A.M.–11 P.M., and the upstairs fine-dining section is open for dinner 5–10 P.M. A daily dinner special is featured 5–6:30 P.M. The Beachside Grill offers plate lunches of barbecued ribs, paniolo steak, or stir-fry chicken all priced around $10, along with appetizers like sashimi at a daily quote, and creamy seafood chowder for $3.50. The burgers range $5.95–9.95. A more formal dinner from the upstairs broiler can be fresh fish of the day, filet mignon for $21.95 from the lava rock broiler, baby back pork ribs at $19.95 from the kiawe-wood smoker, or fettuccine pescatore for $16.95. A children's menu helps keep prices down, and cocktails are served until midnight. Entertainment daily 2:30–5:30 P.M.

Another favorite here is the partially indoors but mostly outdoors **Hula Grill and Barefoot Bar,** 808/667-6636. Open 11 A.M.–midnight, with dinner served 5–9:30 P.M. You can eat either in the casual Barefoot Bar under a thatch cabana or in the more formal dining area. Reservations are taken at the Hula Grill inside but not at the Barefoot Bar outside. No matter where you sit, however, the sunsets are always great. At the Barefoot Bar, try burgers, sandwiches, salads, and pizza. The dining room features seafood and steak. Expect entrées in the $20–25 range, with such choices as firecracker mahimahi, shrimp scampi, and Black Angus New York steak. Music runs 3–5 P.M. at the Barefoot Bar and 6–9 P.M. in the dining room.

The **Rusty Harpoon,** 808/661-3123, offers a pleasing atmosphere, a dozen satellite TVs showing sports events, and plenty of seafood items. It also has a bar that claims to serve the best daiquiris on Maui, along with happy hours 2–6 P.M. and 10 P.M.–2 A.M. Breakfast served 8–11 A.M. gets you started for the day with create-your-own three-egg omelets for $8.95, a homestyle breakfast with potatoes, eggs, and sausage links for $7.95, continental breakfast at $7.95, and a Belgian waffle bar with your choice of various fruit toppings and garnishes for $7.95. Lunch, 11 A.M.–5 P.M., is an extensive menu starting with appetizers like a house salad for $4.95 or crab-stuffed mushrooms for $9.95. Sandwiches are priced $8.95–9.95, burgers around the same. Dinner 5–10 P.M. offers entrées mostly in the $22–28 range, including linguine Mediterranean, pineapple teriyaki chicken, and rack of lamb, and lighter bistro fare is served from the bar until midnight. Don't forget about the sushi and seafood bar or the luscious desserts. To save money the Rusty Harpoon has a happy hour dinner special 5–6 P.M. and a children's menu.

Royal Lahaina Resort

You have three establishments from which to choose. The **Royal Ocean Terrace,** the resort's best dining, is open daily for breakfast buffet and dinner. The breakfast buffet runs $11.50 and is a very good deal. Most evening entrées are in the $16.50–21.50 range and include fresh catch, top sirloin, and island-style chicken that can be prepared in half a dozen ways. Sunday brunch 9 A.M.–2 P.M. is a winner. The attached lounge serves *pu pu* in the afternoon and provides entertainment every evening. It overlooks the ocean. **Beachcombers,** usually open Thurs.–Sat. evenings, is a bit more casual with nightly specials and the flavors of Hawaii and

the Pacific Rim countries. The poolside grille, **Made in the Shade** offers a casual fast food during the day, while you can get ice cream, sandwiches, and pastries from the **Royal Scope Ice Cream Parlor.**

At the entrance to the Royal Lahaina Resort, but an independent establishment, is **Basil Tomatoes,** 808/662-3210, an Italian grill that's open for dinner only 5:30–9 P.M.; reservations suggested. Basil's has garnered a fine reputation. Start with antipasto-like fried green tomatoes at $8 or cheese-stuffed artichokes at $12 and move on to the house salad for $8 or another fine bowl of greens. The entrées cover the whole range of pastas, meats, poultry, and fish, and are generally in the $21–30 range. To complement any dinner selection, choose from a variety of beers, wine, and aperitifs, and round out your meal with cup of coffee and a sweet dessert.

Castaway Cafe

The Maui Kaanapali Villas resort is the only Ka'anapali condo that has a restaurant. The casual Castaway Cafe is only steps from the beach and is open for breakfast, lunch, and dinner. Breakfast items include omelets, items from the griddle, and fruit, all for under $7. Burgers, sandwiches, and salads are served for lunch, and for dinner seafood, pasta, chicken, and steaks go for $13–19. Every day there are specials and the full bar can set you up with a drink any time until 9:30 P.M.

Ka'anapali Beach Hotel

The restaurants here are down-to-earth, reasonably priced, and provide food from the native Hawaiian diet that's unlike anything else in the area. The **Tiki Terrace** is the main food venue of the Ka'anapali Beach Hotel and offers casual dining in an open-air setting. Breakfast can be à la carte or buffet style and consists mostly of American standards. It runs 7–11 A.M. daily, except for Sunday when it gives way to a Champagne Sunday Brunch that runs 9 A.M.–1 P.M. More Hawaiian-inspired dishes are on the table for this brunch, $20.95, and the whole affair is accompanied by Hawaiian music. Dinner in the Tiki Terrace runs 5:30–9 P.M. and reservations are recommended, 808/667-0124. Expect your meal to run around $20. Many Hawaiian dishes are on the menu, and on Friday the Tiki Terrace does a *huli huli* barbecue of whole pig. Aside from the eats, a free hula show is given nightly at 6 P.M.

Open daily 6 A.M.–2 P.M. and 4–9 P.M., the **Ka'anapali Mixed Plate** restaurant serves all-you-can-eat buffet, $9 for early in the day and $12.50 for dinner. In the courtyard next to the whale-shaped pool, have a salad, sandwich, or burger from the **Tiki Bar and Grill,** 11:30 A.M.–6 P.M., or just stop for a drink when the *pu pu* are put out 3–6 P.M.

Westin Maui

The Westin's dining theme is the buffet. **'Ono Surf Bar and Grille,** on the pool level, is open all day for casual bistro dining. While the à la carte menu is an option, the 'Ono is known especially for its various buffets: island breakfast buffet at $18.95, barbecue lunch buffet for $13.95, and theme buffets every evening for $19.95–25.95. The 'Ono bar runs a happy hour daily 5–7 P.M., during which there is musical entertainment with the addition of a hula show on Friday and afternoon music on Friday and Saturday. Just a few steps away along the colonnade walk is **Sen Ju Sushi,** open nightly 5–9 P.M. for fresh sushi and other Japanese seafood dishes. At the far end of the hotel you'll find **Ko'Ala,** a seafood and barbecue buffet for $29.95 that's open nightly 5:30–9 P.M. Come 5:30–6 P.M. for the early-bird special at $25 and save a few bucks; live music 5:30–8:30 P.M. Perhaps the most well-known dining at the Westin is the champagne Sunday brunch, $29.95, served 9:30 A.M.–1 P.M. at the **Aloha Pavilion.** The Sunday brunch at this open-air venue is a tradition at the Westin, and it too is always accompanied by live music. Reservations a must; 808/667-2525.

Maui Marriott

Due to the reconstruction during 2000, all of the restaurants and bars at the Marriott have been completely changed. Serving breakfast and lunch is the poolside **Beachwalk Market and Pantry.** With mostly light fare on the menu, it's perfect for a midday snack. **Va Bene** also serves a bit more elegant breakfast, but in the evening it turns into the hotel's fine-dining Italian restaurant. Expanding the bar and its scope of appetizers, **Nalu Sunset Bar** (formerly the Makai Bar) is

still a great place for excellent *pu pu,* sushi, and evening entertainment as you watch the sun set into the distant ocean.

Hyatt Regency

The **Swan Court** is the Hyatt's signature restaurant, one of only a handful in Hawaii that have been awarded the AAA four-diamond rating. Save this one for a very special evening. You don't come here to eat; you come here to dine! Anyone who has been enraptured by those old movies where couples regally glide down a central staircase to make their grand entrance will have his or her fantasies come true. Although expensive, with entrées up to $38, you get your money's worth not only with the many wonderful tastes but also with the attention to detail. Dinner, 6–10 P.M., is grand and the style is Continental; reservations are recommended, and resort attire is required. The Swan Court offers a sumptuous breakfast buffet daily and a much-talked-about Sunday brunch. For reservations, call 808/667-4727. **Spats Trattoria,** open for dinner only, is downstairs near the entrance and decorated in heavy dark wood and carpets, premodern artwork, and low light. Spats specializes in "country homestyle" Italian food, with the average entrée around $24. Casual attire, reservations recommended. Music at Spats piano bar entertains 7:30–11:30 P.M. weekdays, but a disco takes over on weekends at 10 P.M. Set in the more casual setting of the garden, yet overlooking the grotto pool, is the open-air **Cascades Grille and Sushi Bar,** with a full complement of selections for lunch and dinner from about $20–30. After a full and pleasing meal, stop by the **Weeping Banyan Lounge** for a nightcap and soft music before heading off for a stroll along the beach.

Sheraton

A blend of Asia and America in theme, decor, and cuisine, the **Teppan Yaki Dan** is the hotel's signature restaurant. Appetizers like the spicy diablo shrimp or Eurasian pasta get you ready for the main meal of meat or fish, all cooked at your table *teppan yaki* style. It's a delight for the eyes and taste buds, but not cheap as most entrées run $21–32. Teppan Yaki Dan, 808/661-0031, serves Thurs.–Mon. 6–9 P.M., reservations recommended. Reservations are also recommended for the dinner-only **The Coral Reef** restaurant, elegant but with a bit of the old-world touch. It specializes in fish and seafood; you can start your meal with lobster tempura, oysters on the half shell, or a shrimp cocktail before moving on to the fresh catch, which can be done in 10 different preparations, like sautéed in wine and lime sauce, seared and crusted with macadamia nuts, marinated in a mixture of garlic, ginger, and soy sauce, or glazed with roasted peppers. Less expensive and less formal is the **Keka'a Terrace** restaurant where you can order all day long while surveying the gardens, pool, and Black Rock. Aside from the à la carte menu, a nightly buffet, different on each night of the week, can be selected. Most entrées run $18–25.

ENTERTAINMENT

Lu'au
The dinner show accompanying the lu'au at the Hyatt Regency features pure island entertainment. **Drums of the Pacific** is a musical extravaganza that you would expect from the Hyatt. There are torch-lit processions and excitingly choreographed production numbers, with all the hula-skirted *wahines* and *malo*-clad *kanes* that you could imagine. Flames add drama to the setting, and the grand finale is a fire dance. The Hyatt lu'au, 808/667-4720, is held

every evening 5–8 P.M., for $68 adults, $44 teens, and $30 kids 6–12.

Similarly, the lu'au at the Royal Lahaina Resort and Maui Marriott entertain you with music and dance while you stuff yourself on fine island cuisine. These two are fairly tourist-oriented but great fun nonetheless. Follow your nose nightly at 5 P.M. to the Luau Gardens for the **Royal Lahaina Lu'au** banquet and show, where the biggest problem after the Polynesian Revue is standing up after eating mountains of traditional food. Reservations needed, 808/661-3611; adults $67, children 12 and under $32. The **Maui Marriott Lu'au** presents its version, starting the night with an *imu* ceremony and Polynesian games. The Marriott's niche is its funny and entertaining twists. The evening starts at 5 P.M. and runs until 8 P.M. Cost is $72 adults, $30 children 6–12; 808/661-5828.

Musical Entertainment
The Ka'anapali Beach Hotel presents a free hula and music show in its courtyard at 6 P.M. for everyone's pleasure. In addition, Monday, Wednesday, and Friday around noon, the staff of this hotel put on a music and hula show for guests. It's good fun in a family atmosphere. Hawaiian music is also presented outdoors at 7 P.M. Monday, Wednesday, and Saturday on the center stage at Whalers Village.

Spats at the Hyatt has a quiet piano bar during evening dinner on weekdays, but turns to

MAUI

Staff provides noontime entertainment for guests at the Ka'anapali Beach Hotel.

ROBERT NILSEN

MAUI

disco after 10 P.M. on weekends. If you are into lively music try the **Hula Grill.** Across the way, Leilani's on the Beach has softer music in the afternoon. The 'Ono Grille at the Westin has music nightly 5–7 P.M. and during the afternoons on Friday and Saturday. Several other bars and lounges, like the Weeping Banyan Lounge at the Hyatt and the Lagoon Bar at the Sheraton, also offer soft evening background music.

Fourth of July

While there is some musical entertainment and other special activities throughout the resorts during the day, the biggest excitement is created by the fireworks celebration, with its multicolor puffballs, showers of streaming light, and blazing rocket trails. This is the best show on the island and can be seen for miles. Plenty of people crowd the beach, sit in hotel gardens, or stop along the resort roadways to have an upclose look at the color show. On this day it may be difficult to get to Ka'anapali if you're not staying there or haven't gone by midafternoon, and parking can be a struggle or simply unattainable.

RECREATION

Golf

Ka'anapali Resort, website: www.kaanapaligolf.com, is dominated by two gold courses. Designed by Robert Trent Jones Sr., the North Course is a challenge and requires masterful putting. While a bit shorter, the South Course by Arthur Synder calls for more overall accuracy. The clubhouse for both sits right at the resort entrance, and the pro shop rents clubs, arranges lessons, and can set you up on a putting green or the driving range. The Kaanapali Classic Senior PGA Tournament is played here. For nonresidents, greens fees run $140 for the North Course and $132 for the South Course, with twilight rates at half the regular fee. Call 808/661-3691 for tee times.

Tennis

The Royal Lahaina Tennis Ranch, Sheraton Maui Tennis Club, and the Maui Marriott Tennis Club are all operated by the same com-

pany. Rates are the same for all, and they rent racquets, shoes, balls, machines, and can arrange round robins, lessons, and clinics. The court fee runs $10 a person daily, racquets go for $2.50, and ball machines are $20 an hour. The Tennis Ranch at the Royal Lahaina has a 3,500-seat stadium that's rated for non-pro tournaments (it's occasionally used for concerts) and 10 other courts. Open 8 A.M. to noon and again 2–7 P.M. Call 808/667-5200 for court times. The Sheraton has three lighted courts open 8 A.M.–noon and 2–8 P.M.; 808/662-8208. Five courts are open at the Marriott 7 A.M.–8 P.M.; 808/661-6200 to arrange time on a court.

The Hyatt runs its own tennis center of five courts that's open from 7 A.M. All equipment is available, and lessons and clinics can be arranged. Court time runs $15 a day for guests or $20 for nonguests. To set a time for play, call 808/661-1234.

Water Activities

Water activities and gear are available at Ka'anapali, some from established activities booths, some from the hotels, and some from private vendors that operate right on the beach. Not all provide all services. The following is a sampling of what you might expect: Hobie Cats $45 an hour or $59 for a one hour lesson; single kayak $15 per hour, tandem kayak $25 per hour; sea cycle (pedal boat) $25 per hour; windsurf board $20 an hour or a 90-minute lesson for $59; boogie board $5 an hour; and snorkel gear $10 per day. Jet ski rental, a ride on a banana boat, and parasailing are other options. Scuba lessons and rentals can be arranged at the beach activities booths at each hotel. The *Gemini* at the Westin, the *Kiele V* from the Hyatt, the *Teralani* at the Sheraton, and others leaving from the beach in front of Whalers Village make sailings every day when weather permits. For a full listing, contact the information booth at Whalers Village, any of the activities desks at the hotels on this strip, or the Maui Ocean Activities booth at the Whalers Village, 808/667-1964. You can rent snorkel gear at Snorkel World and arrange water activities and all other activities islandwide at reduced rates at Activity World—both on Halawai Drive just off the highway north of the main Ka'anapali strip.

SHOPPING

Ka'anapali provides a varied shopping scene: the **Whalers Village** shopping complex, which is affordable; the **Maui Marriott** and **Royal Lahaina Resort** for some distinctive purchases; and the **Hyatt Regency, Westin Maui,** and **Sheraton,** where most people get financial jitters even window-shopping.

Whalers Village

This shopping complex is open daily 9:30 A.M.–10 P.M., and you can easily find anything you might need. Some of the shops are: **Reyn's,** for upscale tropical clothing; **Giorgiou** and others for expensive women's fashions; the exclusive **Louis Vuitton** for designer luggage; **Blue Ginger Designs,** for women's and children's resortwear and alohawear; **Dolphin Gallery,** with beautiful creations in glass, sculptures, paintings, and jewelry; **Lahaina Scrimshaw,** for fine scrimshaw pieces and other art objects ranging from affordable to expensive; **Endangered Species Store,** where you are greeted by a stuffed python (proceeds go to help endangered species); **Eyecatcher Sunglasses,** where you can take care of your eyes with shades from $150 Revos to $5 cheapies; **Jessica's Gems,** featuring the work of designer David Welty, along with coral jewelry and black Tahitian pearl rings; **Wolf Camera** for film developing; **Waldenbooks,** a full-service book shop; and an **ABC Discount Store** for sundries. There are many other shops tucked away here and there.

A fascinating shop is **Lahaina Printsellers,** 808/667-7617, featuring original and reproduction engravings, drawings, maps, charts, and naturalist sketches. The collection comes from all over the world, but the Hawaiiana collection is amazing in its depth, with many works featuring a nautical theme reminiscent of the amazing explorers who opened the Pacific or a naturalist theme showing the flora and fauna of the islands. This fine shop is open 8:30 A.M.–10:30 P.M.

The Whalers Village also has plenty of fast-food shops, three fine restaurants, West Maui Healthcare Center, a whaling museum, ATM machines, and a tourist information booth in the lower courtyard. The Kaanapali Trolley and West Maui Shopping Express make stops at the mall.

Be sure to catch the free **hula show** at 7 P.M. Monday, Wednesday, and Sunday, and the ever-changing sand sculpture in front of the stage on the lower level. Contemporary Hawaiian music is also performed at the center stage some evenings of the week. Every year in late July or early August, the Maui Onion Festival is held here at the mall, celebrating the most well known of Maui's agricultural crops with chef's demonstrations, food products, and music. Everyone is welcome.

There is free parking at the parking structure with validation from one of the mall shops. For others, the Whaler's Village parking lot charges $2 an hour or $20 maximum for the day, making parking an expensive proposition in Ka'anapali unless you have free parking as a guest of one of the hotels or condos here.

SERVICES AND INFORMATION

Banks

There are no banks in Ka'anapali; the closest are in Lahaina. Most larger hotels can help with some banking needs, especially with the cashing of traveler's checks. An ATM machine is on the lower level of the Whalers Village mall.

Medical

The West Maui Healthcare Center maintains an office on the upper level at the Whalers Village shopping mall, 808/667-9721; open 8 A.M.–8 P.M. daily. Doctors On Call, 808/667-7676, operates daily 8 A.M.–9 P.M. out of the Hyatt Regency and Westin Maui but makes house calls.

Information

Stop by the tourist information booth in the central courtyard at Whalers Village for specific information about the resort. For a source of general information on all aspects of the Ka'anapali area, contact Kaanapali Beach Resort Association, 2530 Keka'a Dr., Suite 1-B, Lahaina, HI 96761, 808/661-3271 or 800/245-9229. Visit the resort on the Web at www.kaanapaliresort.com, or send email to kbra@kaanapaliresort.com.

Rental Vehicles

Between Ka'anapali and Honokowai, along the edge of the highway on Halawai Drive, several rental companies service all of West Maui. Budget, Avis, Alamo, Dollar, and National car rental companies have offices and small lots here, as does Mavrik Motorcycles. While the availability is somewhat limited, the car rental companies do carry sedans and jeeps. Renting here eliminates one fee that is charged at the airport lots in Kahului. Mavrik only rents motorcycles.

HONOKOWAI, KAHANA, AND NAPILI

Between Ka'anapali and Kapalua are the villages of Honokowai, Kahana, and Napili, which service the string of condos tucked away here and there along the coast. All are practical stops where you can buy food, gas, and all necessary supplies to keep your vacation rolling. You head for this area if you want to enjoy Maui's west coast and not spend a bundle of money. They're not quite as pretty as Ka'anapali or Kapalua, but proportionate to the money you'll save, you come out ahead. These areas are not clearly distinct from one another so you may have some trouble determining where one ends and the next begins, but generally they are separated by some stretch of residential neighborhood. With the development of the new Ka'anapali Ocean Resort at the far northern end of Ka'anapali, the boundary between Ka'anapali and Honokowai will become less distinct. Napili, at the far north end of this strip, adjoins and in some ways is connected to Kapalua. Because of the distinct difference between the condo setting and the manicured resort, Napili is included in this section. To get to this area, travel north along Honoapi'ilani Highway past Ka'anapali and then take Lower Honoapi'ilani Road through Honokowai, and continue on it to Kahana and Napili. Three short connector roads link the new highway with the old road. For those who need to use it, the Kapalua–West Maui Airport sits above the highway in Kahana surrounded by acres of pineapple fields.

Beaches

The whole strip here is rather rocky and full of coral, so not particularly good for swimming except in a few isolated spots.

Honokowai Beach Park is right in Honokowai just across from Hawaiian Moons Market and Deli. Here you have a large lawn with palm trees and picnic tables, but a small beach. The water is shallow and tame—good for tots. The swimming is not as nice as at Ka'anapali, but take a dip after shopping. Snorkeling is fair, and you can get through a break in the reef at the north end.

Kahana Beach is near the Kahana Beach Resort; park across the street. Nothing spectacular, but the protected small beach is good for catching some rays and it's decent swimming between the bands of rock when the waves are

Napili Bay

J.D. BISIGNANI

MAUI

Map: HONOKOWAI TO KAPALUA

© SANDRA E. BISIGNANI TRUST AND AVALON TRAVEL PUBLISHING, INC.

MAUI

not to strong. There's a great view of Moloka'i and the beach is never crowded. Just south of there is **Pohaku Park.** It's a narrow strip with only a few parking stalls but is often used for picnics or by surfers—no restroom.

By far the best beach in this area, and one of the best on the island, is that at **Napili Bay.** This gentle crescent slopes easily into the water, and its sandy bottom gives way to coral so snorkeling is good here as well. There are rights of way to this perfect, but condo-lined, beach. Look for beach access signs along Napili Place and on Hui Drive. They're difficult to spot, but once on the beach there's better-than-average swimming, snorkeling, and a good place for beginning surfers and boogie boarders. No thrill craft are allowed on the waters of Napili Bay.

ACCOMMODATIONS

At last count there were well over three dozen condos and apartment complexes in the four miles encompassing Honokowai, Kahana, and Napili. There are plenty of private homes out there as well, which gives you a good cross-section of Hawaiian society. A multimillion-dollar spread may occupy a beach, while out in the bay is a local fisherman with his beat-up old boat trying to make a few bucks for the day. And his house may be up the street. Many of the condos built out here were controversial. Locals refused to work on some because they were on holy ground, and a few actually experienced bad luck jinxes as they were being built. The smarter owners called in *kahuna* to bless the ground and the disturbances ceased.

As usual, condos are more of a bargain the longer you stay, especially if you can share costs with a few people by renting a larger unit. And as always, you'll save money on food costs. The following should give you an idea of what's available in this area. Entries are arranged into their price categories by where their prices start, and within each category the hotels are in order from the south end moving north.

$50–100

At 3666 Lower Honoapi'ilani Rd., the **Honokowai Palms** condo is an old standby for budget travelers. A basic two-story cinder block affair, originally used as housing for workers constructing the Sheraton down the road, it's basically a long-term place now with a few rental units. The Palms is older, but not rundown; no tinsel and glitter, but neat, clean, and adequate. There is no view. Fully furnished with kitchens, TV, full baths, and queen- or king-size beds. A swimming pool and coin laundry are on the premises. A one-bedroom unit runs $75; three nights minimum. Contact the Klahani Resorts Corp. for details and reservations, 808/667-2712 or 800/669-6284, fax 808/661-5875.

Hale Maui is a very reasonably priced apartment hotel, P.O. Box 516 Lahaina, HI 96767, 808/669-6312, fax 808/669-1302, owned and operated by Hans Zimmerman. It offers one-bedroom apartments that can accommodate up to five people. All have a full kitchen, private lanai, color TV, and limited maid service, with washers and dryers and barbecue grills available to guests. Rates are $75–95, extra person $15, weekly and monthly discount rates available; three nights minimum. All units are bright, tasteful, and clean. The Hale Maui is an excellent choice for budget travelers who would rather spend money on having fun than on a luxurious hotel room.

Four floors high with a pool in the garden, **Hale Ono Loa** will give you a basic condo experience. Amenities include complete kitchens, separate living and dining areas, TV, lanai, partial maid service, and laundry facility. Hale Ono Loa, 3823 Lower Honoapi'ilani Rd., 808/669-0529 or 800/300-5399, fax 808/669-0631, has peak- and low-season rates with a $20 difference. High-season one-bedroom, ocean-view is $95, a two-bedroom ocean-view runs $185; three nights minimum, discounts for stays more than 28 days.

$100–150

On the *mauka* side of the road at 3626 Lower Honoapi'ilani Rd., 808/669-6622 or 800/367-5004, fax 808/669-9647, **Maui Park** is a regular kind of place that offers excellent value. Rooms start at $104 for a hotel room with a refrigerator. Studios run $114–121, suites $131–177. All studios and suites have full kitchens, and every room has a/c and a lanai. There is a large swimming pool on property, as well as a spa and barbecue area. This property is managed by Castle Resorts.

Noelani, a AAA-approved condo at 4095 Lower Honoapi'ilani Rd., 808/669-8374 or 800/367-6030, fax 808/669-7904, website: www.noelani-condo-resort.com, is last in the line before Kahana. All units are oceanfront, with fully equipped kitchens, ceiling fans, color TVs, VCRs (video rental available), washer/dryers in the nonstudio units, and midweek maid service. On the grounds are two heated pools, a hot tub, and a barbecue area. You're welcomed on the first morning with a complimentary continental breakfast served poolside, where you are given an island orientation by the concierge. You'll find peace and quiet here; you can't go wrong. Studios rent from $122, one bedrooms are $165, two and three bedrooms for $217 and $267; 10 percent discount offered after 28 days. Car/condo, senior, AAA, and honeymoon discounts are given.

At 4242 Lower Honoapi'ilani Rd., 808/669-5613 or 800/535-0085, **Kahana Villa Maui,** a modern, five-story condo, steps up the hillside and looks out over the channel to Lana'i and Moloka'i. Pleasantly and casually attractive with contemporary designs and Hawaiian artwork, each of the large units features a complete kitchen, color TV, video equipment in some rooms, washer/dryer, and daily maid service. This is a suite-only condo. On the property are a pool, hot tub, barbecue grills, tennis and volleyball courts, an activities desk, and a sundries store. An added special feature is highly acclaimed Erik's Seafood Grotto restaurant, privately operated but located on the property. High-season rates start at $120 for a one-bedroom garden-view unit that sleeps four to $178 for a deluxe ocean-view two-bedroom suite that sleeps six.

At 50 Napili Pl., 808/669-8002 or 800/541-0638, fax 808/669-8004, **Napili Surf Beach Resort** has reasonably priced full condo units at the south end of Napili Beach that attract mostly an older crowd with some younger families particularly during the summer months. Both the buildings and grounds have been upgraded recently. The grounds are not luxurious but nicely manicured, and have two pools and three shuffleboard lanes. Very clean rooms with full kitchens have ceiling fans, TVs, and their own lanai. Daily maid service is provided, and there's a laundry facility on premises. Garden-view studio units run $115, ocean-view studios and one-bedroom units run $159–255, respectively. Minimum stay is five nights, 10 during the Christmas holiday season; 10 percent discount for 30 days or longer. Car/condo packages and other special deals are offered. website: www.napilisurf.com.

At 46 Hui Dr., **Napili Sunset,** a AAA-approved condo, has two buildings on the beach and one away from the water. All units have fully equipped kitchens, ceiling fans, color TVs, and daily maid service, and share the pool, the beachfront barbecue grill, and a laundry area. Studio apartments in the building away from the beach go for $120, one-bedrooms $225, and two-bedrooms $315; all have reduced rates during the low season. For additional information and reservations contact Napili Sunset at 808/669-8083 or 800/447-9229, fax 808/669-2730, website: www.napilisunset.com.

$150–200
Smaller and older, yet offering great value is the **Maui Kai** condominium resort at 106 Ka'anapali Shores Place, 808/667-3500 or 800/367-5635, fax 808/667-3660, website: www.mauikai.com. These units each have a full kitchen, an entertainment center, a lanai that overlooks the water, and daily maid service. Relax at the swimming pool or inquire at the activities desk to arrange off-property tours. Studios run $145, one-bedrooms $175–185, and two-bedrooms $275, with rates reduced by about 10 percent during the value season. Two nights' minimum stay except for the last two weeks of December when there is a seven-night minimum.

The green tranquillity of the created oasis at **Aston Kaanapali Shores,** 3445 Lower Honoapi'ilani Rd., 808/667-2211 or 800/922-7866, fax 808/661-0836, offers an unsurpassed view of sun-baked Lana'i and Moloka'i just across the channel. You enter a spacious and airy open lobby, framing a living sculpture of palms and ferns. The grounds are a trimmed garden in large proportions dappled with sunlight and flowers. Soak away your cares in two whirlpools, one tucked away in a quiet corner of the central garden area for midnight romance, the other near the pool. Make use of the gift shop, fitness center, lighted tennis courts, and activities desk, or enroll the little ones in Camp Kaanapali, a program for children ages 3–8. Enjoy a romantic dinner at the Beach Club restaurant, which serves meals all day and offers entertainment in the evening. All studios and suites have been refurbished and include full kitchens, sweeping lanai, TV, a/c, and daily maid service. Prices range from an affordable studio at $185 to a two-bedroom oceanfront suite for $460. Several hotel rooms with refrigerators are also available at $160. The Aston Kaanapali Shores offers good value for the money.

At 3615 Lower Honoapi'ilani Rd., 808/669-8235 or 800/535-0085, the **Paki Maui Resort** is an excellent-value condo and presents airy and bright rooms with sweeping panoramas of the Lahaina Roads. Well-appointed studios for two begin at $175, to $330 for a two-bedroom oceanfront apartment for up to six people; additional guests $20. Amenities include maid service, a/c, cable TV, complete kitchens, pool with spa, and coin laundry facilities. Every unit has a private lanai overlooking a gem of a courtyard or the ocean. You can save money by getting a garden-view unit without sacrificing that delightful feeling that you are in the tropics. A complimentary mai tai party is held weekly for all guests. Although the Paki Maui is in town, it feels secluded the moment you walk onto this property, which forms a little oasis of tranquillity. There is no sand beach fronting the condo, but the snorkeling along the reef is excellent. An Aston-managed resort.

You know you're in Kahana when you pass Pohaku Park and spot the distinctive blue tile roofs of the **Sands of Kahana** complex, which forms a central courtyard area at 4299 Lower Honoapi'ilani Rd. (across the street from Kahana Villa Maui), 808/669-0400. The condo boasts the poolside Kahana Terrace Restaurant, which serves breakfast, lunch, and dinner. The sandy-bottomed beach fronting the property is very safe and perfect for swimming and sunbathing. The Sands of Kahana gives you extraordinarily large units for the money, with lots of glass for great views, and to sweeten the pot, they're beautiful and well appointed, mostly in earth tones and colors of the islands. Some studios in this complex are time-share units. Of the rental units, one-bedrooms at $150–225, two-bedroom units at $205–285, and three-bedroom units at $305–350 are massive with two lanai, two baths with a tub built for two, walk-in closets, and great ocean views. Each unit offers a gourmet kitchen, cable TV, daily maid service, and washer/dryer units. The property, with pool, three tennis courts, putting green, barbecue area, fitness center, and spa, exudes a sense of peace and quiet, and although there are plenty of guests, you never feel crowded. This is where you come when you want to get away from it all but still be within reach of the *action*. All arrangements are made through Sullivan Properties, P.O. Box 55, Lahaina, HI 96767, 808/669-1199 or 888/669-0400, fax 808/669-8409, website: www.sands-of-kahana.com.

The **Royal Kahana Resort's** flying V-wing shape gives all rooms a view of the ocean. Light in color and accented by floral patterns, all units have full kitchens, living areas, and washers and dryers, plus there are two tennis courts on the property for guest use only, a swimming pool by the beach, an activities desk, and a fitness center. Regular-season rates are $179–189 for a studio, $219–239 for a one-bedroom, and $269–389 for a two-bedroom unit; value season has rates reduced 10–15 percent with more drastic discounts at certain times of the year. The Royal Kahana is at 4365 Honoapi'ilani Road. Call 808/669-5911 or 800/447-7783, fax 808/669-5950. Alternatively, contact Outrigger Hotels and Resorts, which manages the property, at 800/688-7444.

Kahana Sunset has a superb spot on a wonderful little beach. Set alone on the small and protected Keoninue Bay, the finely sculpted gardens and trellised lanai set off the attractive and privately owned condo units that step down to the water. All units have full kitchens, private lanai, color TVs, washers and dryers, and daily maid service. Ceiling fans are used in each unit and louvered windows catch the cooling sea breezes. Rates are $165–190 for a one-bedroom unit, and two bedrooms run $180–285, with substantial off-season and monthly discounts. Some packages available. There is a two-night minimum, except during the year-end holidays. Some credit cards accepted. At 4909 Lower Honoapi'ilani Rd. For more information contact the complex at 808/669-8011 or 800/669-1488, fax 808/669-9170, website: www.kahanasunset.com.

Overlooking Napili Bay from the lava-rock shoreline is the two-story **Napili Shores** condominium, 5315 Lower Honoapi'ilani Rd., 808/669-8061 or 800/688-7444, fax 808/669-5407. All units surround a tropical garden, fishpond, manicured lawn, hot tub, and swimming pool. Although not large nor ostentatious, each unit is comfortable and contains a full kitchen, color TV, and large lanai. Rates run $160–200 for studios, $190–210 for one-bedroom units, with many packages available. There are two restaurants on the premises, the Orient Express Thai Restaurant and the Gazebo; da Store for food items, gifts, and sundries; an activities desk; and a guest laundry. The Napili Shores is an Outrigger property.

Opened in 1959, **The Mauian** is the oldest on the bay and it couldn't have a better location. Don't let the age fool you, however, as all 44 units have been recently and attentively renovated with new kitchens and bathrooms, pleasing period-style reproduction bamboo and hardwood furniture, and Hawaiian artwork that helps conjure up the feeling of a slower, more hospitable Hawaii. And you'll find hospitality here. Lots of it. This is a gem. The '50s-era buildings blend well with the garden, in which you'll find not only tropical flowers and bushes but also taro and medicinal plants. The open central lawn holds a pool and shuffleboard courts (join a tournament), and every unit has a lanai with a view of the beach and ocean. It's the kind of place where you might expect to hear slack-key guitar wafting across the garden, and you'll certainly hear the water lapping at the shore, lulling you to sleep at night. Ceiling fans and louvered windows create air flow; there is no air-conditioning. There also are no TVs or phones in the studios, but there is a TV and a phone as well as video and book libraries in the community Ohana Room, where a complimentary continental breakfast is served daily. Because of the hospitality and sense of 'ohana (family), many guests return year after year. Based on double occupancy, rates for low and high seasons are: $170/$195 for a beachfront unit, $160/$180 for beach-view units, and $140/$160 for garden units; $10/$15 each extra person. The Mauian is at 5441 Lower Honoapi'ilani Rd. For information and reservations call 808/669-6205 or 800/367-5034, fax 808/669-0129, website: www.mauian.com.

At 5900 Honoapi'ilani Rd., 808/669-6271 or 800/367-5030, fax 808/669-0086, website: www.napilikai.com, **Napili Kai Beach Resort** is the last in Napili before you enter the landscaped expanse of Kapalua. The Napili Kai Beach Resort, the dream-come-true of now deceased Jack Millar, was built before regulations forced properties back from the water. Jack Millar's ashes are buried near the restaurant under a flagpole bearing the United States and Canadian flags. The setting is idyllic, with the beach a crescent moon with gentle wave action. The bay itself is a swim-only area with no pleasure craft allowed. It's $185 for a garden-view hotel room to $575 for an oceanfront luxury two-bedroom suite, but amenities include a kitchenette (refrigerators in the hotel rooms), private lanai, air-conditioning in most units, complimentary snorkel gear, daily tea party, activities desk, and all the comforts of home. Several special packages are available. There are four pools, "Hawaii's largest whirlpool," an exercise room, a croquet lawn, putting greens, and tennis courts on property, and the Kapalua Bay Golf Course is just a nine-iron away. All rooms have Japanese touches complete with shoji screens. There's fine dining, dancing, and entertainment at the Sea House Restaurant overlooking the beach.

$200–250

At 4531 Lower Honoapi'ilani Rd., 808/669-5111 or 800/824-3065, fax 808/669-0974, website: www.kahanavillage.com, **Kahana Village** is a group of low beach houses surrounded by well-manicured lawns on three acres. Each of the pleasantly comfortable units is individually owned, so all have a slightly different character. All are light and breezy, appointed in earth tones, and each has a complete kitchen, color TV, VCR, and large lanai. Ground-level apartments are large at 1,700 square feet and feature three bedrooms and two baths. The upper-level units are a bit smaller but still spacious at 1,200 square feet and have two bedrooms (one as a loft), two baths, and high open-beam ceilings. There is a narrow pebble beach out front, and the property has a swimming pool, hot tub, and barbecue grills. Rates are $220–260 for second-floor units and $290–355 for ground-level units, 1–4 persons, and $20 per night for each extra person; five nights minimum. Low season rates

are about 20 percent less; 10 percent discount for stays longer than 14 days.

Napili Point Resort is one of the most beautifully situated complexes on Maui. This low-rise property sits on its own promontory of black lava separating Kahana and Napili, at 5295 Honoapi'ilani Rd. (next door to Napili Shores), 808/669-9222 or 800/669-6252, fax 808/669-7984, website: www.napilipointresort.com. The reef fronting the condo is home to a colorful display of reef fish and coral, providing some of the best snorkeling on the west end. It's not graced with a sand beach (it's 100 yards north along a path); however, nature was generous in another way. Each room commands an unimpeded panorama with a breathtaking sunset view of Lana'i and Moloka'i. You get a deluxe room for a standard price. Because of the unique setting, little development has occurred in the area, and the condo is very secluded though convenient to shops and stores. The two-story buildings offer fully furnished one- and two-bedroom units from a very affordable $219 to $329, less during regular season, with full kitchens, washers and dryers, walk-in closets, and large dressing and bath areas. Amenities include maid service, two pools, and barbecue grills. Two-bedroom units on the second floor include a loft with its own sitting area. Floor-to-ceiling windows frame the living still life of sea and surf so you can enjoy the view from every part of the apartment.

$250 and up

Aston's **Mahana at Kaanapali** is billed as an "all oceanfront resort," and in fact all apartments have an ocean view at no extra cost. The second that you walk into these reasonably priced condos and look through a large floor-to-ceiling window framing a swimming pool and the wide blue sea, your cares immediately begin to slip away. The condo sits on a point of beach at 110 Ka'anapali Shores Place, 808/661-8751 or 800/922-7866, fax 808/661-5510, and is one in the first group of condos north of Ka'anapali. Enjoy a complete kitchen plus pool, sauna, tennis, maid service, activities desk, and a money-saving family plan. Rates begin with studios at $235–265 to one-bedroom suites at $300–335 and huge two-bedroom suites (up to six people) for $455–515.

Open, airy, and with an atrium courtyard, **Embassy Vacation Resort,** a pink pyramid, occupies a sliver of beach. Each of the more than 400 air-conditioned suites has a kitchen, separate living area, large-screen TV, and lanai. Daily maid service is offered, as are a children's program, two restaurants, an activities desk, Trilogy Ocean Sports booth, and laundry facilities. Kids will love the water slide at the pool, while the adults may gravitate to the spa and fitness center. The resort's Ohana Grill is a casual restaurant that serves quick food like burgers, salads, and pizza for under $10. The North Beach Grille is the resort's better eatery, where you'll find a greater variety of entrées in the under $20 range and a nightly all-you-can-eat buffet. In a way, the Embassy is like a smaller version of the more exclusive resorts down the beach in Ka'anapali. Rates run $290–445 for a one-bedroom suite and $560 for a two-bedroom suite that sleeps six. A Marc Resort, the Embassy is at 104 Ka'anapali Shores Place, 808/661-2000 or 800/669-3155. There is shoreline access next to this resort.

Bed-and-Breakfast

True to its name, **Blue Horizons B&B** has good views of the blue Pacific looking to the west over Honokowai and Kahana. Set in a residential neighborhood below the Kapalua–West Maui Airport, this modern-style bed-and-breakfast offers three rooms. All have private bathrooms, one has a kitchenette, and two have refrigerators. The living room, kitchen, screened lanai, lap pool, barbecue grill, and washer/dryer are for everyone's use. Breakfast is included Mon.–Sat. Room rates run $79–99 for two, $15 an additional person; two nights minimum. The Blue Horizon is at 3894 Mahinahina St., perhaps the only B&B north of Lahaina on the west coast. Write or call: P.O. Box 10578, Lahaina, HI 96761, 808/669-1965 or 800/669-1948, fax 808/665-1615, website: www.maui.net/~chips, email: chips@maui.net.

Agencies

Aside from booking a room direct, you can work through a condo booking agency that will do all the arranging for you. For condos and homes throughout West Maui, try the following:

Kaanapali Vacation Properties, 808/667-7776 or 888/333-3066, fax 808/667-5544, website: www.mauivacation.com, has 18 units along this coast.

Whalers Realty, 808/661-3484 or 800/676-4112, fax 808/661-8338, website: www.whalersrealty.com, has more units in Ka'anapali properties than Honokowai, but does have a presence here.

With condos stretching from Lahaina to Napili is **Maui Beachfront Rentals,** 808/661-3500 or 888/661-7200, website: www.mauibeachfront.com.

With units in six properties, **Klahanai Resorts,** 808/667-2712 or 808/669-6284, fax 808/661-5875, website: www.klahani.com, deals mostly in the low- to midrange places.

FOOD AND ENTERTAINMENT

Inexpensive

At Da Rose Mall, just as you enter Honokowai proper, **Lourdes Kitchenette,** 808/669-5725, offers take-out or delivery service along with a few red picnic tables out front where you can eat. Open daily until 4 P.M., it prepares plate lunches and simple Filipino food such as adobo, with everything under $7. Lourdes is small, simple, clean, and adequate.

Pizza Hut, 808/669-6996, open Sun.–Thurs. 11 A.M.–11 P.M., weekends until midnight, offers carry-out and delivery pizza. For a quick bite, **Honokowai Okozuya Deli,** 808/665-0512, is available for an amazing selection of Chinese, Japanese, Italian, Mexican, and vegetarian foods. Both are in 5-A Rent a Space at 3600 Lower Honoapi'ilani Rd.

The following three restaurants are all at Napili Plaza. **Maui Taco** has reasonably priced, health-conscious fast food and a variety of drinks. Try a chimichanga for $5.95, a tostada for $5.25, tacos for about $3.25, or a two-fisted burrito that will keep you full all day for $6.95 or less. The salsa and guacamole are made fresh daily. No MSG or lard is used. For those who need a little pick-me-up during the day, stop at **The Coffee Shop,** open 6:30 A.M.–6 P.M. Down at the end of the line is **Mama's Ribs 'N Rotisserie,** a small take-out place that does all its cooking on the spot from fresh ingredients. Try a plate meal of ribs or chicken, done teriyaki- or traditional-style, with rice and barbecue beans, or choose a full rack of ribs or whole chicken. Side dishes are cole slaw, beans, macaroni salad, or rice. Aside from the full rack of ribs at $14.99, everything else is under $8.50. This is a local eatery of good repute. Mama knows best.

The **Gazebo**, 808/669-5621, open daily 7:30 A.M.–2 P.M., one of the best-kept secrets in the area, is a little brown gazebo with louvered windows next to the pool at the Napili Shores Resort. Be prepared for a line. Locals in the know come here for a breakfast of the Gazebo's famous banana, pineapple, and especially the macadamia nut pancakes for $5.75. There are also eggs and omelets of all sorts under $7.95. The lunch menu features a range of sandwiches for $5.25–7.50, along with burgers and lunch plates under $8.25. You can enjoy a world-class view sitting inside or outside the Gazebo for down-home prices.

Moderate

Whether you're a guest or not, a quiet and lovely restaurant in which to dine is **The Beach Club** at the Aston Kaanapali Shores. One of Honokowai's best-kept secrets, the restaurant is centered in the condo's garden area and opens directly onto the sea. The restaurant changes throughout the day from a casual café in the morning to a more formal candlelit room in the evening, but always the service is friendly. Breakfast, served 7–11:30 A.M., with early-bird specials until 9 A.M., is mostly standard American. Lunch, served 11:30 A.M.–3 P.M., offers sandwiches and lighter fare. The evening dinner menu, served 5:30–9:30 P.M., whets your appetite with scrumptious appetizers. Soup of the day and salad lead to main entrées like chicken marsala, grilled scallops, or clams pesto with linguine, with most in the $15–20 range. A children's menu is also offered, and entertainment is provided several nights a week.

Under the blue roof by the pool at the Sands of Kahana Resort, the open-air and moderately priced **Kahana Terrace Restaurant**, 808/669-5399, is just right for sunsets. Breakfast offerings feature omelets and items from the griddle; lunch is mostly sandwiches and burgers that go for less than $8. Appetizers like coconut shrimp and hot buffalo wings and various salads precede dinner entrées that can be fresh catch of the day at $17.95, New York steak for $18.95, or chicken-fried steak at $10.95. Every night brings a special dinner menu where you get even more for your money. This is not fine cuisine, but it is nutritious and satisfying. Live music nightly 5–7 P.M.

At the Kahana Manor Shops, 808/669-0266, **Dollie's** is open daily 11 A.M.–midnight, with happy hour 4–6 P.M. Dollie's features several TVs with satellite hookup for sporting events, cappuccino, and weekend entertainment. The good food and fair prices on Dollie's menu feature more than a dozen sandwiches, all priced $5.95–8.95; pu pu like nachos and potato skins; plates of various fettuccine for $9.95–11.95; and pizza by the tray for $15–20 or by the slice for $1.50 3–6 P.M. and 10 P.M. to closing. The sandwiches and other entrées are good, but the pizza is the best. The bar has a wide selection of domestic and imported beers, wines, and a daily exotic drink special. Dollie's, one of the few eateries in the area, is usually a laid back pub/pizzeria but can get hopping on the weekend and is perhaps the most happening place for late night get-togethers in Kahana.

The **China Boat** restaurant at 4474 Lower Honoapi'ilani Hwy. in Kahana, 808/669-5089, is open daily for lunch 11:30 A.M.–2 P.M. and dinner 5–10 P.M. It's almost elegant with its highly polished, black-lacquer furniture, pink tablecloths, scroll paintings, and island-inspired prints, but the food quality is variable. A typically large MSG-free Chinese menu offers seafood, beef, chicken, vegetables, pork, and noodle dishes at a reasonable price.

At the Kahana Gateway Mall, the **Outback Steakhouse**, 808/665-1822, is a meat house serving down under grilled and flame-broiled favorites. The Outback is open 4–10 P.M. for dinner, until midnight for drinks. Get your meal going with a Kookaburra wings appetizer or bonzer Brisbane Caesar salad. Sirloin, porterhouse, and tenderloins are favorites, as are smoked and grilled baby back ribs and seasoned and grilled chicken and shrimp. Most entrées run $16–20.

Koho's Grill and Bar at the Napili Plaza is an American standard, comfortably appointed with booths and tables, ceiling fans, wide-screen TVs with satellite feed, and a full-service bar. The menu offers chili cheese fries for $5.95, soups and dinner salads for $2.45, and fish and chips for $6.25. A sandwich board offers everything from BLTs to a club sandwich, all for under $6.25, while full-dress burgers are priced around $6. Plate lunches, all around $6.50, include teriyaki beef or chicken and mahimahi, and some standard fajitas run about $8.50 More substantial entrées include rib plate at $11.95 and a strip steak for $14.95. Open 11 A.M.–1 A.M. daily, with early-bird specials 4–7 P.M.

The **Orient Express**, 808/669-8077, at the Napili Shores Resort, is open daily for dinner only 5:30–10 P.M. The restaurant serves Thai and Chinese food with a flair for spices; duck salad and stuffed chicken wings are a specialty. The early-bird special, served before 6:30 P.M., is a five-course dinner for $11.95. The full menu of finely spiced foods includes Orient Express's well-known curry dishes; take-out available. Most entrées are in the $10–13 range. Overlooking the koi pond at the resort, this restaurant is a good choice. Sharing the same space is a sushi and *pu pu* bar, where everything is prepared before you at the counter. Nigiri sushi orders run $4.50–7, sashimi $9.50–15, with a few other items on the menu.

Expensive

Building on a well-deserved reputation, Jean-Marie Josselin has opened **A Pacific Cafe, Honokowai** in the Honokowai Marketplace; 808/667-2800, reservations requested. Open daily 5–10 P.M. You can expect most entrées in the $18–28 range. While some of the menu changes nightly, expect items like tiger-eye sushi or kalua pork and cabbage pot stickers for appetizers, and grilled Hawaiian *ono,* seared sea scallops in a crispy polenta crust, or Chinese-style roasted duck as main entrées.

At 4242 Lower Honoapi'ilani Rd., second floor of Kahana Villa, **Erik's Seafood Grotto** is open daily for lunch 11:30 A.M.–2 P.M. and dinner 5–10 P.M. Call 808/669-4806 for reservations. The bar menu is available all day, lunch comprises very reasonably priced plate lunches, and an early-bird special, which runs $12–14, is offered 5–6 P.M. Erik's is decorated in an appropriately nautical theme, with fish tanks, divers' helmets, and mounted trophy fish. Bouillabaisse, cioppino, and baked stuffed prawns are among the chef's specialties. Shellfish, lobster, steak, and poul-

try are on the menu, but the real focus is the wide variety of fish that can be prepared in numerous ways. Most dinners run $19–27, with a good selection of appetizers. Erik's is known to have the *best* selection of fresh fish on Maui—up to nine selections nightly. This is a quality restaurant with excellent service. The food is delicious but the prices are not cheap.

Finally McDonald's has a culinary purpose—to landmark **Roy's Kahana Bar and Grill,** 808/669-6999, at the Kahana Gateway Mall, open daily for dinner 5:30–10 P.M. At Roy's, the executive chef works kitchen magic preparing the best in Pacific Rim cuisine. Roy Yamaguchi, the inspirational founder, has a penchant for locating his Hawaii restaurants in pragmatic shopping malls. At Roy's Kahana, the surroundings are strictly casual, like a very upscale cafeteria. The enormous room, reverberating with the clatter of plates and the low hum of dinner conversations, has 40-foot vaulted ceilings, a huge copper-clad preparation area, heavy koa tables and booths, track lighting, and windows all around. Roy's philosophy is to serve truly superb dishes post haste, but impeccably, focusing on the *food* as the dining experience, not the surroundings. Although part of the menu changes every night, you could start your culinary extravaganza with island-style pot stickers with a spicy almond saté peanut sauce, grilled Sichuan spiced baby back pork ribs, crispy Upcountry green salad with a creamy spinach and tarragon dressing, or an individual *imu* pizza, all for less than $10. Move on to main dishes like lemon grass chicken, grilled filet mignon, or blackened yellowfin ahi. Expect entrées to be about $25. Desserts feature the chocolate macadamia tart or the signature fluffy dark-chocolate soufflé (allow 20 minutes to prepare). The full bar serves beer, mixed drinks, and personally selected wine by the bottle or glass. Roy's "elegant cafeteria" is no place to linger over a romantic cocktail. It's more like sipping the world's finest champagne from a beer mug. But the best by any other name is still the best!

Nicole Yamaguchi has a restaurant named in her honor, just next door to her dad's place at the Kahana Gateway, open daily from 5:30 P.M., 808/669-5000. **Roy's Nicolina Restaurant** features Euro-Asian cuisine heavily spiced with

California and Southwestern dishes. For example, try a gourmet pizza-like flatbread covered in red onions, tomatoes, and pesto; or Cajun shrimp and handmade sausage. Appetizers can be pan-fried calamari with anchovy mayonnaise, or seared goat cheese and eggplant with cilantro pesto and red pepper vinaigrette. Entrées are delicious and fascinating, offerings like roasted orange-ginger plum duck or Yankee pot roast with mashed potatoes and garlic spinach. While much of the menu at Nicolina's is the same across the hall at Roy's, about half is created only for this restaurant, and it too changes nightly. If dad's place is filled up, you'll love the quieter Nicolina's, a "Sichuan-spiced taco chip off the old block."

Since 1998 you've been able to get handcrafted beer on Maui's west side at the **Fish and Game Brewing Company and Rotisserie**, 808/669-3474, at the Kahana Gateway Mall. Of the half-dozen varieties always on tap, you could try the Plantation Pale Ale, Wild Hog Stout, or the lighter Honolua Lager. Beers run $3.75 a glass, or $5 for a sampler of five. The sports bar is in the back, and to the front is the deli counter and a sit-down space for lunch. Order your sandwiches and drink at the counter and have a look at the gourmet cheeses, seafood, and specialty meats that line the deli case. In the evening, the dark paneled dinner room is opened for full meals, and set behind glass in that room is the brewing apparatus. Start your dinner with spiced tomato steamed mussels, grilled brewers sausage, or oyster chowder. For the heart of the meal try fresh fish in one of four preparations, which include steamed Oriental and habanero cornmeal crusted, dungeness crab, or cioppino pasta. From the rotisserie and grill come such items as honey glazed duckling, marinated pork loin, and rack of lamb. Most entrées are under $23. The rich surroundings, fine food flavors, and quality beer will make for a satisfying evening.

At the Napili Kai Beach Resort, 808/669-1500, the **Sea House Restaurant** is open daily for breakfast 8–11 A.M., lunch noon–2 P.M., and dinner 6–9 P.M. (5:30 P.M. in winter); reservations suggested. Inside the semi-open-air restaurant, lunch appetizers like island noodle salad join with sandwiches and other entrées for inexpensive fare. Dinner choices, served with vegetables and rice pilaf or potato, include fresh catch for $24, jumbo shrimp for $20, seasoned and broiled rack of lamb for $25, and marinated chicken roulade at $17. Besides the normal menu, every night brings a special dinner menu, but the best is the lobster tail dinner on Thursday for $17.95. A full wine list includes selections from California and France. There are the sweet sounds of Hawaiian music nightly and a wonderful Friday night Napili Kai Foundation children's Polynesian show put on by local children who have studied their heritage under the guidance of the foundation. Dinner seating is at 6 P.M., the show at 7:30 P.M.; $35 adults, $20 children. If you just want to soak up the rays and gorgeous view of Napili Bay, you can wear your swimwear and have a cool drink or light fare at the Whale Watcher's Bar.

SHOPPING AND SERVICES

Honokowai Marketplace

This small mall right at the intersection where Lower Honoapi'ilani Rd. splits off the main highway is a new mall in the spirit of the Kahana Gateway Shopping Center and the Napili Village Shopping Center farther up the highway. Modern in design and convenient in location, it provides services for the tourist and resident alike. Here you'll find a **Star Market** for all basic food needs, **A Pacific Cafe Honokowai** restaurant, a **Maui Dive** shop, the **Golf in da Islands** golf rental shop, **Java Jazz** coffee shop, and a video rental shop.

Da Rose Mall

Look for this tiny mall at the south end of town at 3481 Lower Honoapi'ilani Rd., where you'll find **A & B Rental and Sales**, 808/669-0027, open daily 9 A.M.–5 P.M., specializing in bicycles, snorkel gear, boogie boards, and surfboards. Prices are: mountain bikes $15 for 24 hours, $60 per week; snorkeling gear $2.50 per day and $9 per week. Boogie boards, surfboards, and even fishing poles are rented by the day or week. The sportswear includes board shorts, sundresses, sarongs, aloha shorts, T-shirts, and sunglasses. In front is **Lourdes Kitchenette,** and around the side are **Treasures From the Sea** gift shop, and **Blooming Rose**

Boutique studio for women's fashions. Maui No Ka Oi farmers sell their produce at a **farmers' market** in the parking lot of Da Rose Mall Sun.–Fri. 7:30 A.M.–3:30 P.M. This is a good chance to pick up locally grown foods. Next door is an **ABC Store,** hours 6:30 A.M.–11 P.M., a minimarket selling everything from resortwear to wine.

5-A Rent a Space Mall
At 3600 Lower Honoapi'ilani Hwy., this mall is usually located by reference to the Pizza Hut here. Honokowai Okozuya Deli is the other eatery in this strip of shops. Here you'll find **Snorkels N' More,** 808/665-0804, open daily 8 A.M.–5 P.M., which has reasonable rates for sales and rental of snorkel gear, boogie boards, surfboards, other water equipment, and some golf clubs. There are usually a few bikes for rent as well, and same-day film processing.

Hawaiian Moons Natural Foods
Across from Honokowai Park, Hawaiian Moons stocks organic produce, natural foods, bulk foods, fish and meats, and supplements. Hawaiian Moons offers a good alternative to the area's standard grocery stores. If you're on the run, you can pick up a sandwich or juice drink at the deli counter. There is even an activities desk here if you want to schedule an activity for later. An offshoot of Hawaiian Moons in Kihei, this store is open Mon.–Fri. 7 A.M.–8 P.M. and weekends 8 A.M.–6 P.M.; 808/665-1339.

Monday, Wednesday, and Friday 7–11 A.M. you'll find the West Maui **farmers' market** in Moon's parking lot. Pick up fresh fruit, produce, flowers, and other food products for a day on the beach or dinner ingredients to cook at your condo.

Kahana Manor Shops
Aside from **Dollie's,** in the Kahana Manor Shops there is the **Kahana Manor Groceries,** a one-stop sundries and liquor store open Mon.–Sat. 7:30 A.M.–11 P.M.; the **Women Who Run With Wolves** boutique for beach and athletic wear and accessories for active women; the **Wiki Wiki One-Hour Photo** for all your camera needs; and **Boss Frogs** water activities shop, which rents snorkel gear and kayaks and does activity reservations.

Kahana Gateway Shopping Center
At this newest shopping addition to the Kahana area, easily spotted along Route 30 by McDonald's golden arches, you'll find a **gas station,** a **Whalers General Store, Bank of Hawaii,** and the **Koin-Op Laundromat.** However, the premier stop is **Roy's Kahana Bar and Grill,** one of the finest gourmet restaurants on Maui, and **Roy's Nicolina Restaurant** next door. But these aren't the only eateries here. Also try the **Fish and Game Brewing Company and Rotisserie,** one of only two on the island, and its accompanying restaurant, where you can get gourmet foods and specialty meats; and the more casual **Outback Steakhouse.** Also at the center is the **Maui Dive Shop,** 808/669-3800, a full-service water activities store where you can rent snorkel equipment, scuba gear, and beach accessories; **Gallerie Hawaii** for contemporary artwork; **Kafe Kahana,** 808/669-6699, which not only has the sweetest buns in town, but also sandwiches and salads; **Hutton's Jewelry; Ashley's Yogurt;** and **Leslie's Family Funwear** for contemporary fashions.

Napili Plaza
Napili's newest shopping center offers the full service **First Hawaiian Bank; Napili Supermarket,** open daily 6:30 A.M.–11 P.M., featuring fresh fish; **Mail Services Plus,** open daily 9 A.M.–6 P.M., Saturday until 1 P.M., closed Sunday, for all your postal and shipping needs. You may want to pick up a video for the night at **All Star Video,** or snorkel gear at **Boss Frog.** For food, the center has **Koho's Grill and Bar, Maui Taco,** and **Mama's Ribs and Rotisserie.**

Napili Village Shopping Center
At 5425 Lower Honoapi'ilani Rd., the **Napili Village General Store,** 808/669-6773, is a well-stocked little store and known landmark, good for last-minute items, with fairly good prices for where it is. You can pick up picnic items and sandwiches, groceries, sundries, and liquor. Open 7 A.M.–9 P.M. daily. Next door is **Snorkel Bob's,** 808/669-9603, where you can rent snorkel equipment (prescription masks available) for as little as $9 a week and boogie boards for only $26 per week. Bob lets you drop your gear at any of his shops for free.

MAUI

Next to this tiny shopping center at the Napili Shores Hotel is **da Store,** mainly a gift shop and convenience store that's open 8 A.M.–9 P.M. daily. Here as well is **Napili Tours & Activities** activities desk, 808/669-1350, where arrangements for all island activities and those on other islands can be taken care of. You need not be a guest of this condo to take advantage of its services. The staff here is very helpful and they have a rack of brochures for you to peruse.

KAPALUA

Kapalua sits like a crown atop Maui's head. One of the newest areas on Maui to be developed, the 1,650-acre Kapalua Resort, website: www.kapaluamaui.com, was begun in 1975. It's been nicely done. Within the resort are the Kapalua Bay and Ritz-Carlton luxury hotels, a half-dozen upscale condominium communities, exclusive shops, three championship golf courses, two tennis centers, sweeping vistas, and terrific beaches. Nearby are horseback riding stables, a sporting clays shooting range, and plenty of water activity options. All of this has been carved out of the former Honolua Ranch, an outgrowth of land granted to Reverend Baldwin (of Lahaina) in 1836, which eventually grew to be 24,500 acres by 1902. From the first, the Honolua Ranch grazed cattle and farmed fruits and coffee. This is pineapple country now, and these golden fruits have been raised here since 1912. Following the introduction of this crop, a cannery was built; camps, a store, and a church were set up for plantation workers; and a railroad was established for transporting the goods. Currently, Maui Land and Pineapple Company has about 9,000 acres of pineapple under cultivation, here and near Makawao, and is the largest producer of these sweet fruits in the United States.

High in the hills above Kapalua is the **Pu'u Kukui Preserve.** Donated by Maui Land and Pineapple company and managed by the Nature Conservancy, this 8,661-acre tract of rainforest real estate was dedicated in 1992 and is said to be the largest privately owned preserve in the state. It borders the remainder of the 13,000 acres that make up the whole of the West Maui Mountains rainforest, one of the most environmentally diverse areas in the state. Within its boundaries are several endangered species of birds, five endangered and brightly colored tree snails, and 15 distinct plant communities. Thickly wooded hillsides and deep ravines, a mist-shrouded mountaintop, boggy upland plateaus, and a swampy crater characterize this area. It is pristine wilderness that gets nearly as much rain (over 400 inches a year) as Mt. Wai'ale'ale on Kaua'i (said to have the highest rainfall in the world). It has, in miniature, characteristics similar to the Alaka'i Swamp on Kaua'i. There is no public access to this preserve, save for a once-a-year guided group hike arranged by lottery and sponsored by the Kapalua Nature Society. In response to this rich environment and the deep cultural and historical past of the region, the Kapalua Nature Society was formed to promote an awareness and appreciation for the diversity of the land and a respect for holding it in trust for future generations. Accessible to guided hikes and located on the lower slope of the mountain is the Maunalei Arboretum, a private botanical garden started in the 1930s. As a indication of the lengths that the landowners are willing to go in their stewardship of the natural environment, one need only look to a secluded and rather unusual sanctuary high above the West Maui Airport. There, land has been set aside and infrastructure begun on a gorilla preserve that will be the future home of Koko, the well-known great ape who talks in sign language.

Of the annual special events that take place at Kapalua, a few have broad interest. Held in late June, the Kapalua Wine and Food Symposium showcases culinary works of island chefs and couples these with select wines from around the world. The yearly Earth Maui Nature Summit conference is presented by the Kapalua Nature Society, which also sponsors an Earth Maui 5K Fun Run and Kapalua Fun Swim Challenge. These bring out plenty of enthusiastic local athletes, and part of the proceeds go to environmental organizations around the island. Both the Kapalua Open Tennis Tournament in September and the Senior Tennis Championship earlier in the year draw admiring crowds, but perhaps the most well-known event that takes place in Kapalua is the nationally broadcast Mercedes Championship golf tournament.

In 1993, the Bay Course was the first golf course in the nation to be certified by the Audubon Society as a cooperative sanctuary; by the next year, the Village and Plantation courses also had that designation. This certification means that, among other things, measures are taken to protect and promote wildlife habitat, to plant native species of vegetation, reduce water consumption, and restrict the use of chemicals for fertilizers and pest control.

Transportation

The complimentary **Kapalua Shuttle** runs throughout the resort for use by resort guests on an on-demand basis. While there is no regular schedule, it will make stops at the hotels and villas, tennis courts, golf courses, and the Kapalua-West Maui Airport. For information or pickup, call 808/669-3177.

BEACHES AND BAYS

Kapalua Beach

Just past Napili Bay is the equally as nice Kapalua Bay with its fine crescent beach—popular though usually not overcrowded. Look for access just past the Napili Kai Beach Resort. Park in the public lot and follow the path through the tunnel below the Bay Club restaurant to the beach. The well-formed reef has plenty of fish for snorkeling. Here are restrooms, showers, and a hotel beach concession.

Oneloa Beach

Around the point from Kapalua Beach, Oneloa is a small sandy beach down a steep path between condos, where swimming is good and locals come to surf. Seldom visited and private; parking available at the entrance to The Ironwoods.

D.T. Fleming Beach Park

One of Maui's best—a long, wide beach backed by wonderful shade trees. This beach park is on Honoapi'ilani Highway just past the Ritz-Carlton, where the road dips back down to the coast. Here you'll find parking, showers, barbecue grills,

and excellent swimming except in winter, when there's a pounding surf. There's fair snorkeling here and good surfing, but many younger kids come for body boarding. This is the beach for the Ritz-Carlton, so the south end closest to the hotel has become a bit exclusive while the rest maintains its very local flavor.

Mokule'ia Bay

Mokule'ia Bay is about 200–300 yards after mile marker 32. There is limited parking along the road, where cement stairs lead down to the water through a stand of trees. This beach has great bodysurfing but terribly dangerous currents in the winter when the surf is rough. Be careful. The surf here is known as "Slaughterhouse." Follow the trail to the left for the beach. The path straight ahead takes you to a rocky lava flow. This entire area, plus all of adjacent Honolua Bay, is a **Marine Life Conservation District** and the underwater life is fabulous—some of the best snorkeling in the area. Fish, crabs, eels, rays, octopus, and numerous other sea creatures use the bottom sand, multi-hued coral, and volcanic rock to play out their rhythm of life.

Honolua Bay

Just past Mokule'ia Bay heading north, look for a dirt road, then park, or park just after crossing the bridge. It's about a 10-minute walk to the beach from either spot. The bay is good for swimming, snorkeling, and especially surfing. Some people stay the night without much problem. For good views of the surfers, drive a little farther along the road and park along the cliff just as the road reaches the top, or drive down the dirt road at the edge of the pineapple field for a spot—there will be lots of cars on a good wave day.

Honokohau Bay

This rather sizable bay faces north and is the last bay before the "wilds" of the backside become predominant. Into the bay drains the water of the narrow but deep Honokohau Valley, from which water is taken by flume to irrigate the extensive fields of West Maui. A few houses constitute the community of Honokohau near mile marker 36. A rocky beach and thin strip of gray sand are located where the stream enters the bay, which generally has a sandy bottom close to shore. In the uplands above this valley are extensive pineapple fields, and from 1914 to 1920 the island's first pineapple cannery canned fruit here to be distributed to the world. Canning operations moved to Lahaina and continued there until 1962 when the business moved again to a new cannery in Kahului, which is still in operation.

ACCOMMODATIONS

Ritz-Carlton Kapalua

The green sweep of tended lawns fading into the distant sea foaming azure heralds your entrance into an enchanted realm as you wind your way down the roadway leading to the Ritz-Carlton Kapalua, a AAA five-diamond property at 1 Ritz-Carlton Dr., Kapalua, HI 96761, 808/669-6200 or 800/241-3333, fax 808/665-0026, website: www.ritzcarlton.com. At the porte cochere, a waiting bellman will park your car. Enter the main hall and relax in the formal parlor of overstuffed chairs, marble-topped tables, and enormous flower arrangements. Evenings in the hall bring mellow entertainment under soft illumination. Through a huge set of double doors is a terrace of Chinese slate. Below, in the floral heart of the hotel grounds, are the tri-level seashell-shaped swimming pools and fluttering palms. Reminiscent of the Orient, the roof line of this great hotel covers the two wings that descend the hill toward the sea, creating an enormous central area between. All this, coupled with the dark and rich woodwork, thick patterned carpets, floral drapery, pineapple-pattern wallpaper, and halls hung with the fine works by prominent island artists and 19th-century reproductions, defines the Ritz as the epitome of elegance and luxury.

On the beach, a sweeping crescent of white sand is embraced by two sinewy arms of jet-black lava. It becomes immediately obvious why the diminutive promontory was called Kapalua, "Arms Embracing the Sea," by the ancient Hawaiians who lived here. Notice on the rise above the sea a rounded shoulder of banked earth separated from the main hotel grounds by a low hedge of beach naupaka: the spirits of ancient *ali'i* linger here. This 13.5-acre burial ground harbors perhaps 2,000 graves dating from around 850 to the 1800s, and it also contains a section of the old paved King's

J.D. BISIGNANI

The outside moves inside at the Kapalua Bay Hotel.

MAUI

Trail that at one time circled the island. With the discovery of this site, the original construction plans were altered and the hotel was moved away from the area in an attempt to protect it. A *kahuna* was asked to perform the ancient *mele* to appease the spirits, and to reconsecrate the land, passing the *kahu* (caretaking) of it to the Ritz-Carlton. Although the small parcel was deeded to the state as the **Honokahua Preservation Site,** the hotel management and staff alike take their responsibility very seriously. Public access is restricted.

For those with physical fitness and pampering on their minds, the hotel has a fitness center complete with exercise machines, yoga classes, massage therapy, a beauty salon, sauna, and steam rooms. Other hotel offerings include the Ritz Kids children's program, the Aloha Fridays program of cultural activities, a croquet lawn, putting green, a business center, and a clutch of exclusive shops. At the corner of the property, the Kumulani Chapel or adjacent gazebo can be arranged for weddings.

In two wings off the main reception hall, the luxury rooms, all with their own private lanai and sensational view, are a mixture of kings, doubles, and suites. Done in muted neutral tones of coral or celadon, the rooms feature handcrafted quilts, twice-daily room attendance, turndown service, color TV, 24-hour room service, fully stocked honor bar, and an in-room safe. The spacious marble bathrooms offer wide, deep tubs, separate shower stalls and commodes, and double sinks. Rates begin at $295 for a garden view to $425 for a deluxe ocean view. The Ritz-Carlton Club, an exclusive floor with its own concierge, and featuring continental breakfast, light lunch, cocktails, cordials, and a full spread of evening hors d'oeuvres, is $495. Suites from an executive one-bedroom to the magnificent Ritz-Carlton Suite run $395–2,500. Many special packages are offered.

Kapalua Bay Hotel

This, like other grand hotels, is more than a place to stay; it's an experience, and the recent $25 million worth of renovation has ratcheted this experience up a notch or two. The hotel steps down the hillside from its 6th-level entrance. The main lobby is partially open and accented with an enormous skylight. Plants trail from the tall ceiling, and the walls are hung with paintings by Peggy Hopper. All colors are soothing and subdued. To one side is the Lehua Lounge. A tiny brook splits the Gardenia Court restaurant on the lower level, and the view over the garden lawns and out to sea is spectacular. The clean lines of the hotel, its sparse decoration, and contemporary elegance let the view speak for itself without distraction. The ocean view vies for your attention here, while the pool pulls you down to the garden and the beach lures you to the water. Not overly ornamented, guest rooms are done in muted colors—whites, tans, and tropical greens. Each spacious room is neatly laid out with an entertainment center, three telephones, electronic safe, a soft couch and easy chairs, and louvered doors to the lanai. The well-lit bathrooms have his and her sinks at each end of the room, separate dressing closets, and individual areas for the tub, shower, and commode. Marble, tile, and chrome are used throughout. Concierge service and twice-daily maid service are additional amenities. There are three restaurants and a lounge in the complex, a business center, fitness room, swimming pool and spa, beach activities center, a small arcade with plenty of shops, and a multitude of daily activities including Kamp Kapalua for kids. Every day 9 A.M.–3 P.M. in the lobby, craftspeople and artisans share their work with hotel guests. The least expensive room in the hotel is one with a garden view at $360. Ocean-view rooms run $410–480, $540–610 for oceanfront rooms, and suites from $1,000; $60 each additional person 18 and older. In addition, a dozen one- and two-bedroom oceanfront villa suites go for $400–550 a night. For reasonable sums, numerous packages are available. The Kapalua Bay Hotel, associated with the Halekulani and Waikiki Parc hotels in Honolulu, is part of the Luxury Collection. Contact the Kapalua Bay Hotel at One Bay Dr., Kapalua, HI 96761, 808/669-5656 or 800/367-8000, fax 808/669-4690, website: www.kapaluabayhotel.com.

Condominiums

Several groups of upscale vacation rentals dot this spacious resort, either fronting the water or overlooking the golf fairways. Condos in the Bay, Ridge, and Golf villas range from one-bedroom fairway units to two-bedroom oceanfront hideaways, and a handful of luxury homes are thrown into the mix. Each is individually owned so all are decorated differently, but all are equipped with full kitchens, a/c and fans, washers and dryers, telephones, and TVs, and all amenities that you'll need for your vacation. Daily maid service can be arranged. All groups of villas also have swimming pools, barbecue grills, and maintained gardens. One-bedroom villas with a fairway view start at $189 and climb rapidly to the two-bedroom oceanfront villas for $425. Daily rates for the luxury homes run $995 for three-bedroom to $4,000–5,000 for five-bedroom ones. Some golf and tennis packages and car/condo deals are also offered. Check-in is at the Kapalua Villas Reception Center, at 550 Office Rd. in a structure built in 1912 and used for decades as the plantation office. For information and reservations contact Kapalua Villas at 550 Office Rd., Kapalua, HI 96761, 808/669-8088 or 800/545-0018, fax 808/669-5234, website: www.kapaluavillas.com.

For rental options throughout the remainder of the resort, contact Kapalua Vacation Rentals, 808/669-4144, and Sullivan Properties, 808/669-0423.

FOOD

Ritz-Carlton Restaurants

Dining at the Ritz-Carlton is a wonderful gastronomic experience with three main restaurants from which to choose, plus two lobby lounges, a sushi bar, and a beachside café. **The Terrace Restaurant,** open daily for breakfast 6:30–11:30 A.M. (buffet to 10:30) and for dinner 5:30–10 P.M., informal and relaxed, overlooks the central courtyard with the dramatic sea vista beyond and features fish and seafood with undertones of Asian flavors. Although there is an extensive à la carte breakfast menu, the house specialty is a breakfast buffet for $17 or $13 for a lighter selection. For dinner, start with lobster shiitake spring rolls for $16 or island clam chowder at $8. Main courses include steamed *onaga* with ginger and mushrooms for $29, seared sesame-seed-crusted mahimahi with lemon grass butter $27, or Peking duck at $26. Monday evening brings an Asian buffet, Friday the buffet is seafood, Saturday's is Hawaiian, and Sunday it's Italian—all $42. Occasionally there's music.

The Anuenue Room, serving dinner Tues.–Sat. 6–9:30 P.M., is the hotel's most elegant restaurant, and it has continuously been awarded the AAA four-diamond rating. Reservations are recommended and resort attire is required. Formal yet intimate, the restaurant offers a nouveau Hawaiian cuisine. Appetizers, salads, and soups fit for the *ali'i* include baked Waianae snails and Puna goat cheese, crispy corn and sea urchin fritters, and *lomi lomi* salmon. An unusual soup is the roasted breadfruit soup, while limpets, seaweed, tomatoes, watercress, and other ingredients combine for a refreshing salad. The finest entrées include poached Kona lobster, *imu*-baked pheasant and taro risotto, and barbecued rack of lamb with mountain apple glaze and kukui nut crust. Desserts include passion fruit soufflé, flambéed island banana, and chocolate cake. Dinner for two could easily run $100. The food is wonderful but the view over the lawns, sea, and Moloka'i in the distance is an added pleasure.

The Banyan Tree, an informal outdoor restaurant, is open for lunch 11:30 A.M.–3:30 P.M., dinner 5:30–9 P.M., and Sunday brunch 10 A.M.–2:30 P.M. Food is a mix of the Orient and Hawaii. Fashioned like a Mediterranean court, the restaurant offers seating in high-backed chairs at teakwood tables, with mood lighting reminiscent of old oil lamps. Dine alfresco on the redwood deck and watch cavorting whales just offshore. Start with a warm tomato and feta tart, chilled island gazpacho, or arugula salad. Entrée selections are a barbecued kalua pork sandwich, seared mahimahi sandwich, and grilled chicken fettuccine, most $14–19, or gourmet pizza from a wood-burning oven.

At the **lobby lounge** you'll find appetizers, salads, sandwiches, fruit, coffee, and drinks to have while you sit and gaze out over the courtyard from the patio. Thurs.–Mon. 5–10 P.M. the freshest sushi is served. Down by the beach, on a patio surrounded by a manicured coconut grove, is the **Beachhouse**, serving tropical libations, healthy fruit smoothies, burgers, and sandwiches 11 A.M.–4 P.M.

Kapalua Bay Resort Restaurants

The resort has three dining spots. The elegant **Bay Club,** 808/669-8008, offers fine dining for dinner 6–9:30 P.M. on a promontory overlooking the beach and Moloka'i in the distance. Traditionally elegant, there is a dress code. With selections like the signature crab and rock shrimp cake, Kona lobster, and grilled duck breast, expect to spend at least $30 for a superbly prepared entrée with overtones of flavors from the Pacific and Asia. Piano music nightly. The open-air and contemporary **Gardenia Court** on the lower lobby level of the main building serves breakfast Mon.–Sat. 6–11 A.M. and Sunday brunch 9:30 A.M.–1:30 P.M. Dinners run Tues.–Sat. 6–9 P.M., while Friday seafood buffet starts at 5:30 P.M. Most entrées are in the $24–32 range. Resortwear required. In the entrance lobby, the **Lehua Lounge** serves *pu pu* and a light à la carte menu 6–10 P.M. and drinks 3–11 P.M. every evening, always with relaxing music to help let the cares of the day slip away.

Sansei

In the Kapalua Bay Shops is the exceptional Sansei seafood restaurant and sushi bar,

808/669-6286, which serves more than just Japanese sushi—a whole variety of Pacific Rim food and drinks from the bar. Open daily 5:30–10 P.M. for dinner, and Thursday and Friday for a late night dinner and laser karaoke from 10 P.M. until "closing." An early-bird special is offered 5:30–6 P.M. Sansei offers an extensive menu of sushi rolls and appetizers. While traditional sushi (and sashimi) can be ordered, the Sansei has made its reputation by taking these Japanese morsels to a higher level with eclectic combinations of ingredients and sauces, as in the mango crab salad handroll with its spicy Thai vinaigrette or the Kapalua Butterfly, which is snapper, smoked salmon, crab, and veggies in a crisp panko batter roll served with tangy ponzu sauce. An award-winning appetizer is the Asian rock shrimp cake, which is shrimp crusted with crispy noodles with ginger-lime-chili butter and cilantro pesto. While the sushi and appetizers could certainly fill you up, save room for an entrée. These delicacies include a special seafood pasta with tiger prawns, onion scallops, and Japanese noodles, a Sichuan crusted ahi tuna, Peking duck breast with mushroom and potato risotto and foie gras demi-glaze, and Colorado lamb T-bone chop. The menu items are imaginative and the blends of flavors exceptional.

Jameson's Grill and Bar

Don't underestimate this excellent restaurant just because it's between the golf clubhouse and tennis center. The Kapalua Bay Golf Course provides the backdrop and the restaurant provides the filling delicious food. The main room with its flagstone floor and open beam ceiling is richly appointed with koa wood, and large windows frame a sweeping view of the super-green fairways of the golf course. Sit inside or out on the patio. Breakfast and lunch are mostly light and easy meals; the real treat comes in the evening 5–10 P.M. when a more substantial dinner meal is served. Start with an appetizer like stuffed mushrooms for $8.95 or seared sashimi for $12.95, and move on to a soup or one of the many fine salads. Entrées include fish of the day at market price, lemon pepper chicken for $18.95, rack of lamb at $27.95, and New York strip steak. Follow your meal with dessert or sip wine selected from an extensive list. All items can be ordered take-out. An excellent restaurant with a lovely setting at 200 Kapalua Drive. Call 808/669-5653 for reservations.

The Plantation House

Above Kapalua at the Plantation Golf Course Clubhouse, you'll find the lovely Plantation House Restaurant, open daily 8–11 A.M. for breakfast, 11 A.M.–3 P.M. for lunch, and 6–10 P.M. for dinner, 808/669-6299. Inside, the split-level floor, gabled roof, natural wood, fireplace, and carpeted and marbled floor add elegance, but the real beauty is the natural still life that pours through the floor-to-ceiling French doors. Kapalua lies at your feet and the West Maui Mountains rise behind. For breakfast, the extensive menu offers fare like a hearty rancher's breakfast of two eggs, toast, two scoops of rice or breakfast potatoes, grilled ham, bacon, or Portuguese sausage all for $8; or smoked salmon Benedict at $10. For lunch, start with pan-fried crab cakes served with roasted pepper aioli for $8 or an oriental chicken salad for $8.50. A half-pound double-fisted Plantation House burger is available for $7.50 and a grilled chicken breast sandwich for $8.50. The dinner menu tempts your palate with the signature appetizers won ton Napoleon with tofu or ahi and curried spinach pot stickers. A favorite soup is the Tuscan-style bean soup with pesto oil. The chef prepares *pasta al giorno* for $16, or tops it with scallops or shrimp for $21, and sautéed jumbo prawns with garlic mashed potatoes run $21. The most popular of the many signature entrées is sautéed fish dusted with porcini mushroom powder and laid over a bed of spinach and garlic mashed potatoes. The food is a winner, and the views make it even more special.

Fleming's Restaurant

Fleming's "On the Greens at Kapalua" is the new restaurant at the Village Golf Course Clubhouse, 808/665-1000. As with the other clubhouse eateries at this resort, it has surprisingly good food, providing what can casually be referred to as golf gourmet. Breakfast, served 6:30–11 A.M. is eggs and griddle items. Lunch 11 A.M.–5 P.M. is mostly *pu pu*, soup, salad, and sandwiches. Dinner from 5 P.M. is definitely finer dining. Start with dungeness crab cakes, salmon ravioli, or salad, and move on to such entrées as fish of the day, veal chop, or rack of lamb adobo. Spiced with the flavors of the peo ple who have migrated to the islands, your meal will be satisfying no matter your choice.

Honolua Store

Set next to the entrance of the Ritz-Carlton, this small general store also serves reasonably priced light meals and sandwiches. The breakfast menu, served 6–10 A.M., offers "The Hobo"—eggs, sausage, and rice for $3.75—or two pancakes for $2.95. Plate lunches, sandwiches, grilled items, and salads all run under $7 and are served 10 A.M.–3 P.M., or pick something out of the deli case or take away a box lunch. Sit at a table on the front porch and overlook the broad lawns and tall pine trees of the exclusive planned community of Kapalua. This is by far the cheapest place in the area to eat.

SHOPPING

Kapalua Shops

A cluster of exclusive shops service the resort, including **McInerny** with fine women's apparel, **Kapalua Kids** for the younger set, and **Kapalua Logo Shop** if you want to show off that you've at least been to the Kapalua Resort, since all items of clothing sport the butterfly logo. Visit **La Perle** for pearls, diamonds, and other fashionable jewels; and **South Seas** for antiques, art, and more "ethnic" jewelry. For fine examples of Hawaiian quilts and other stitchery, try **Hawaiian Quilt Collection.** Lahaina Galleries has a wonderful collection of island artists on display, while the **Elizabeth Doyle Gallery** features art glass, and the **Island Woodcarving** gallery shows a variety of carved items in Hawaiian motifs. For a bit more of an intellectual stop, try **Kapalua Discovery Center** for a short historical, cultural, and natural history lesson about the area; open daily 10 A.M.–5 P.M., free. When you get hungry from all the shopping, stop into the **Sansei** restaurant and sushi bar for a taste of Japan and the Pacific with an eclectic twist. Adjacent to the Kapalua Bay hotel, these shops are open from 9 A.M. daily.

If you're here on Tuesday 10 A.M.–noon, come and listen to slack-key guitar and stories. On Thursday, be sure to see the free ancient hula show 10–11 A.M. On Friday 10:30–11:30 A.M. you can participate in a hula lesson, and 11:30 A.M.–12:30 P.M. there is contemporary Hawaiian music to enjoy. These shops are connected to those in Ka'anapali and Lahaina by the West Maui Shopping Express shuttle.

Honolua Store

This well-stocked, reasonably priced general store, open daily 6 A.M.–8 P.M., is a rare find in this expensive neck of the woods. The shelves hold beer, wine, and liquors, basic food items from bananas to sweets, books and gifts, and even a smattering of sunglasses, shorts, hats, aloha shirts, and logo wear. Breakfast and lunch are dispensed from the deli in the back, and boxes of pre-inspected pineapples can be purchased here to be taken back to the Mainland. Built in 1929 and metamorphosed over the years, this shop has served the needs of this community for nearly as long as there has been a community here, and it functioned in more than one way as the center of village life until the village was eclipsed by the Kapalua Resort in the mid-1970s.

RECREATION

Golf

Kapalua's three golf courses combine to make one of the finest golfing opportunities in the state. The Bay Course is an ocean course that extends up the hill into the trees. The signature hole 5 is a challenge with the fairway laid out around the curve of a bay. Pushing up against the surrounding pineapple fields, the Village Course is a mountain course that offers vistas over the distant ocean. At over 7,000 yards, the Plantation Course is the longest—it's used by the PGA for professional championships. For information and tee times, call 808/669-8044. In addition, the new Kapalua Golf Academy, 808/669-6500, is the largest such instructional facility in the state, offering clinics and lessons. Outdoors are target greens, putting greens, wedge areas, bunkers, a short game area, and an 18-hole putting course.

Tennis

The Kapalua Resort boasts 20 plexi-pave courts in two tennis centers, representing the largest private tennis facility in the state. Both offer pro shops, equipment rental, clinics, lessons, and tournaments. Some courts are lighted so evening play is possible. Court times run $10 per person for resort guests or $12 for others; call for reservations. The Tennis Garden, 808/669-5677, is near the Bay Course clubhouse, while the Village Tennis Center, 808/665-0112, is ensconced near the water below the Ritz-Carlton.

Other Activities

Kapalua Dive Company, 808/662-0872 or 877/669-3448, website: www.kapaluadive.com, services guests at both the Kapalua Bay Hotel and the Ritz-Carlton. Aside from the gear it rents, this company offers lessons and various dives, which include shore dives, scooter dives, and a kayak dive. Also of interest is its kayak/snorkel trip, which cruises the coast from Kapalua Bay to Honolua Bay.

Ironwood Stables has the only riding opportunities on this side of the island, from an easy jaunt through the lower foothills to a more advanced ride up the mountain. Rides range $75–125 for up to two hours. To reserve a spot and get information on where to meet, call the ranch at 808/669-4991.

Westside Sporting Clays, 808/669-7468, is 3.3 miles beyond Office Road in Kapalua. It's here that you can sharpen your shooting skills by firing at clays that mimic the movement of animals and birds. Options are available for beginning and advanced shooters. Open until dusk. Call for times and prices; reservations recommended.

Tours

Above the Kapalua Resort, the **Maunalei Arboretum** is open to tours. Within this private garden is a two-mile loop trail that takes you up to about 2,600 feet. This garden is the work of D. T. Fleming, a former Honolua Ranch manager, who collected a multitude of tropical plants from around the world. Hikes leave daily at 8 P.M. for the four-hour trip. Contact the villas reception center at 808/669-8088 or Maui Eco-adventures, 808/661-7720, to reserve your spot.

Kapalua is pineapple country—what could be better than to take a walk through pineapple fields and learn about this sweet golden fruit, its production, and the pineapple industry as a whole. Sponsored by the Kapalua Nature Society, plantation tours are held weekdays except holidays 9:30 A.M.–noon and again 1–3:30 P.M.; $26 per person. Wear a hat, closed-toe shoes, and clothes that you don't mind getting a little dusty. Tours leave from the Kapalua Villas reception center; call 808/669-8088 for additional information and reservations.

Kapalua Art School

In the former plantation blacksmith shop at 800 Office Road, the Kapalua Art School is a community center open to residents and resort guests alike. It offers classes on a rotating basis; subjects include watercolor, drawing, weaving, ceramics, dance, and yoga. In operation since 1995, this school functions on a drop-in basis and fees run about $30 for three-hour sessions. Call 808/665-0007 for information.

MAUI

M.G.L. DOMENY DE REINZI

SOUTH MAUI

MA'ALAEA

Ma'alaea is a small community in the southwestern corner of the Maui isthmus that is home to a small harbor, a handful of houses, a row of condominiums, several fine restaurants, the Maui Ocean Center aquarium, and a new and expanding shopping plaza. It sits on the edge of the huge and beautiful Ma'alaea Bay, often referred to as a whale's nursery because so many mother whales head here to birth and raise their young during their winter and spring stay in the islands. Until the advent of plane travel to and between the islands, Ma'alaea was a busy port for interisland steamer traffic, principally serving the Ma'alaea and Kihei areas. Constructed in its current configuration in 1952, **Ma'alaea Harbor** is a bite-size working port, one of two on the island where tour boats dock (the other being Lahaina Harbor). With the comings and goings of all types of craft, the harbor is colorful, picturesque, and always busy; it has the dubious distinction of being the second windiest harbor in the world,

with sustained winds averaging 25 knots. Upon entering the harbor, you are greeted by a small U.S. Coast Guard installation at the east end and Buzz's Wharf, a well-known restaurant, at the other. Between these two you'll find restrooms and the Ma'alaea Activities booth at harborside, which can book all sea, land, and air tours and activities for you. Across the street from the Coast Guard Station is Ma'alaea Store (est. 1946), and tucked in beside it is the Shinto fishermen's shrine Ebesu Kotohira Jinsha, which was constructed in 1914 and rebuilt in 1999. Up above the shrine and store are the aquarium and new gaggle of shops. The condominiums line Hauoli Street, which culminates in Haycraft Park, the western end of Ma'alaea Beach. Outside the breakwater is Ma'alaea's only well-known surf spot, called Freight Trains by locals and Ma'alaea Pipeline by others for its fast break.

For decades, Ma'alaea was little more than a sleepy village and harbor. It's still small, but the

MAUI

To Wailuku
To Kahului
MOKUELE HWY

KEALIA POND
WILDLIFE
REFUGE

Lahaina Pali
Trail

311

Kealia
Pond

31

BIRD SANCTUARY

SOUTH MAUI

To Lahaina

30

Ma'alaea
Ma'alaea
Beach

Ma'alaea Bay

McGregor
Point

KEALIA BEACH PLAZA

KIHEI
WHARF

MAI POINA 'OE IA'U
BEACH COUNTY PARK
CAPTAIN VANCOUVER MONUMENT

KALEPOLEPO BEACH
PARK

PI'ILANI

MAUI RESEARCH AND
TECHNOLOGY PARK

AZEKA PLACE
SHOPPING CENTER

31

ELLEAIR MAUI
GOLF COURSE

Kihei

To Kula

KALAMA BEACH PARK

37

KAMA'OLE BEACHES
COUNTY PARKS

Keokea

MOKAPU BEACH PARK
ULUA BEACH PARK
WAILEA SHOPPING VILLAGE
WAILEA BEACH PARK
POLO BEACH PARK

PALAUEA BEACH PARK

Maui
Meadows

Wailea

WAILEA
GOLF COURSE

WAILEA ALANUI RD

HWY

MARINE LIFE
CONSERVATION
DISTRICT

Molokini Island

Makena Bay

KEAWALA'I CHURCH (1832)

Onouli Beach
Pu'u Ola'i
Oneloa Beach

Makena

MAKENA
GOLF COURSE

SEABIRD
SANCTUARY

Ulupalakua Ranch
TEDESCHI WINERY

31

Kanahena
'Ahihi Bay

MAKENA ALANUI RD

'AHIHI-KINA'U
NATURAL
AREA RESERVE

MAUI'S LAST
VOLCANIC
ERUPTION SITE
(1790)

To Hana

'Alalakeiki Channel

Cape Kina'u
La
Perouse
Bay

Ancient Paved Road

0   3 mi
0   3 km

MAUI

influx of money and development is changing the face and character of the community. With greater traffic, Ma'alaea is busier and its visitors require more services. More than just a place to get on a snorkel boat or pass by on your way from Ka'anapali to Kihei, it's beginning to form an integrated identity all its own—a destination, not a byway. Luckily for those who live here, most changes are taking place up by the highway.

Maui's electric power generation plant sits outside of Ma'alaea. While it's not particularly conspicuous, you will spot the towers that rise above the surrounding sugarcane fields along Route 31 as it descends down to the ocean east of the village approaching the Kealia Pond Natural Wildlife Refuge. Two power generation units have been built, with only one currently in operation. Another unit is being planned, perhaps in anticipation of future island growth.

SIGHTS

Ma'alaea Beach

Consisting of three miles of windswept sand partially backed by Kealia Pond National Wildlife Refuge, Ma'alaea Beach has many points of access between Ma'alaea and Kihei along Route 31. The strong winds make this thin beach undesirable for sunning and bathing, but it's a windsurfer's dream. The hard-packed sand is a natural track for joggers, profuse in the morning and afternoon. The beachcombing and strolling are quiet and productive. From the Ma'alaea end, you can access the beach from Haycraft Park. If you're up by 6 A.M. you can see the Kihei canoe club practice at the Kihei end; they put their canoes in the water near the Kihei wharf just across the road from Suda's Store.

Maui Ocean Center

The most radical change for the community in years was the opening of the Maui Ocean Center. The Ocean Center is a large aquarium and marine park with several dozen indoor and outdoor displays and hands-on exhibits. Explore the realm of the reef in the Living Reef building, handle tide pool creatures at the Touch Pool, and learn about the fascinating turtles, stingrays, and whales in their separate exhibits. As an added benefit during winter months, whales can

be seen cavorting and breaching in the bay beyond the harbor. Perhaps the most unique feature at the center is the Underwater Journey, where you walk through a four-inch-thick, 54-foot-long transparent acrylic tunnel in the 750,000-gallon "open ocean" tank, Hawaii's largest aquarium, which offers a 240-degree view of the waterlife. There are no trained animal shows here, only periodic feedings and presentations by ocean naturalists at various locations throughout the center. This will be an enjoyable and educational experience as you learn about Hawaii's unique marine culture; all animals are indigenous or endemic. A stop here could easily be a half-day affair, so when you get hungry, have a quick bite at the Reef Cafe snack bar or try the Seascape Ma'alaea Restaurant for a more substantial lunch meal. Before leaving, pick up a memento of your day's visit at the gift shop. The Maui Ocean Center, 808/270-7000, is open daily 9 A.M.–5 P.M. (until 6 P.M. in summer); $18 adults, $12.50 children 3–12. Audio guides are available in English and Japanese for an additional $4. If you're without transportation, ride the South Maui Shopping Express from Kihei-Wailea-Makena to the Maui Ocean Center or the West Maui Shopping Express from the Lahaina-Ka'anapali area, $5 round-trip for either section or $10 for a one-day system-wide pass. When arriving or leaving Maui via the Kahului Airport, enjoy the new mini-aquarium that's between the baggage claim area and rental car booths. Maintained by MOC, this 1,200 gallon tank has the same beautiful marine life as the center in Ma'alaea. The center's website is www.mauioceancenter.com.

Kealia Pond National Wildlife Refuge

This refuge stretches between Ma'alaea and Kihei, mostly on the inland side of Route 31. Now set aside for stilts, coots, and other wildlife, this pond was once two productive fishponds used by Hawaiians living around the bay. Aside from the stilt and coot, other birds and fowl that inhabit the pond are Hawaiian duck, black-crowned night heron, golden plover, and ruddy turnstone. Migratory waterfowl such as the pintail and shoveller visit the refuge, and hawksbill turtles come to shore to lay eggs. There are no facilities. As with most such refuges, this shore environment lies in a delicate balance and changes according to the season. With the winter rains and runoff the pond may increase in size to over 400 acres; during periods of drought, parts of it may dry up all together, shrinking in size by more than half and leaving a salty residue on exposed ground. One of Maui's first air strips, the old Ma'alaea Airport, used to occupy the flats near here.

PRACTICALITIES

Accommodations

There are no hotels in Ma'alaea. Condominiums stand one after another along the water east of the harbor. For rooms, check with the Maalaea Bay Rentals agency, 808/244-7012 or 800/367-6084, fax 808/242-7476, website: www.maalaeabay.com. This agency has an office at the Hono Kai Resort, 280 Hauoli St., Ma'alaea, HI 96793, and handles more than 100 units in a majority of the condos along this road. All units are fully furnished with complete kitchens, TVs, telephones, and a lanai; and each property has a pool and laundry facility. Rates run $95–195 from mid-December to the end of April, with substantial discounts for summer and fall; five-night minimum, 10 nights during the Christmas holidays. Rates are reduced by 10 percent for monthly stays.

Food

The award-winning **Waterfront Restaurant** at the Milowai Condo, 808/244-9028, has a well-deserved reputation and a great view of the harbor and bay. It's owned and operated by the Smith brothers, who work both the front and the kitchen. The Waterfront is open for lunch 10 A.M.–1:30 P.M. daily except Saturday and from 5 P.M. for dinner. Choose a horseshoe-shaped booth tucked around the room's perimeter or a table out on the deck with sea breezes and the setting sun, and order a bottle of wine from the extensive international list. For starters, consider the Caesar salad for $8.95, Pacific oysters on the half shell at $9.95, or imported French escargot for $8.95. Definitely order the Maine lobster chowder, a famous specialty, for $7.95. The entrée scampi is $24.95, medallions of tenderloin is $25.95, while rack of lamb in a Sichuan peppercorn sauce is priced at $28.95.

However, the best choice is the fresh island fish, priced daily, which is prepared in a variety of ways: Sicilian; *à la meunière* in a white wine sauce with lemon; Bastille, which is imprisoned in angelhair potato and sautéed and topped with fresh scallions; Southwestern; Cajun; or sautéed, broiled, baked, or poached. Save room for one of the prize-winning desserts. The Waterfront provides an excellent dining experience, from the fine service to the wonderful food, and is well worth the price. Free parking in designated spots in the Milowai lot.

Buzz's Wharf restaurant, 808/244-5426, open daily 11 A.M.–11 P.M., specializes in seafood. The waterfront atmosphere and second-story views are first rate. It's a favorite spot and often busy. *Pu pu* selections include steamed clams for $12.95, escargot on the shell for $9.95, and coconut *panko* oysters on the half shell for $11.95. The lunch menu offers a Tuscan salad for $11.95, an assortment of burgers and fries for under $12, and a Cajun open-faced chicken sandwich for $8.95. For dinner, try prawns Tahitian, the captain's seafood platter, or a mouth-watering rib eye for $17–32. Enjoy a liter of house wine for $12 or cocktail for $6. End your meal with dessert followed by a stroll around the moonlit harbor.

Bamboo predominates in the tables, chairs, and room dividers of the new **Bamboo Bistro** at the Ma'alaea Harbor Village next to the Maui Ocean Center, 808/243-7374. Hardwood floors, jute carpeting, old-style lighting and ceiling fans, paintings by Avi Kiriaty, and large French doors that let in the ocean breezes and let you look out over the harbor add to the ambience. A full bar greets you as you enter this restaurant, and everyone walks by the glassed-in wall of wine bottles and can see into the kitchen through a plate-glass window on the way to their seats. Owned by the entrepreneurial and well-respected chef Peter Merriman, the Bamboo Bistro offers a nice twist to island eating. Along with the usual dinner appetizers and full meals you can order small portions to try various dishes without busting the budget—a tropical tapas, so to speak. While the furniture and furnishings bring you back a few decades, the food is as modern and experimental as you would expect. Served 11 A.M.–2 P.M., lunch might be Wainaku sweet corn and shrimp fritters with stir-fried beef, or a tomato and greens salad with grilled eggplant and Puna goat cheese sandwich. For dinner entrées, try the sesame crusted fish with spicy lilikoi sauce, prime top sirloin, adobo duck, or pan-fried Asian cake noodles with veggie stir-fry and black bean sauce. Food can also be served at the full bar. Reservations are recommended.

Cucina di Malia Un Trattoria, 808/242-7353, is an upscale eatery at the new Ma'alaea Harbor Village, open 5–11 P.M., Tues.–Sun. only. The focus is fine regional Italian cuisine in an elegant but "country" setting. Start your meal with antipasto, like clams, crustini, or herbed polenta, or a salad, $6.25–11.75, and move on to a gourmet pizza from the wood-burning oven for $11.50–14.75. One pizza option is smoked duck breast, carmelized onions and fennel, with fontina cheese. For something more substantial, choose from the pasta, rice, meat, and fish entr'es, $18–35, such as the salmon, ricotta, and mascorpone ravioli with lemon-basil cream sauce; grilled veal chop with gorgonzola cream sauce; or a roasted sea bass. The food here is authentic and the meal will be memorable. Reservations are best.

The **Tradewinds Deli and Mart,** at the Maalaea Mermaid, carries groceries, drinks, and alcohol, creates deli sandwiches, and also rents snorkel equipment and boogie boards.

Open daily except Monday 8 A.M.–5 P.M., the **Ma'alaea Store** is where you have a much better chance of buying fishing tackle than you do a loaf of bread, but it does have some very limited groceries, snacks, and sundries.

Shopping

Before a few years ago, the only shopping in Ma'alaea was at the **Ma'alaea Store** and the **Tradewinds Deli and Market.** Following the opening of the Maui Ocean Center, the **Ma'alaea Harbor Village** has opened next to the aquarium, with a **Whalers General Store** for sundries and food items, several clothing and jewelry shops, and an **Island Soap and Candle Works** store for scents and perfumes of the tropics. You can book your water tours with the ocean activities center, eat at two upscale restaurants, snack at several smaller eateries, and have a great time looking at the **surfing museum** at the **Shapers of Ma'alaea** water-sports store. The **Pacific Whale Foundation** also has a store here where you can pick up logo wear and books on whales and other marine subjects, or garner information about water tours run by the foundation.

KIHEI

Kihei (Shoulder Cloak) takes it on the chin whenever antidevelopment groups need an example at which to wag their fingers. For the last two decades, construction along both sides of Kihei Road, which runs the length of town, has continued unabated. Since there was no central planning for the development, mostly high-rise condos and a few hotels were built wherever they could be squeezed in: some are lovely, some are crass. There's hardly a spot left where you can get an unobstructed view of the beach as you drive along. That's the "slam" in a nutshell. The good news is that Kihei has so much to recommend it that if you refrain from fixating on this one regrettable feature, you'll thoroughly enjoy yourself, and save money, too.

The developers went "hyper" here because it's perfect as a tourist area. The weather can be counted on to be the best on all of Maui. Haleakala, looming just behind the town, catch-es rainclouds before they drench Kihei. Days of blue skies and sunshine are taken for granted. On the other side of the condos and hotels are gorgeous beaches, every one open to the public. Once on the beachside, the condos don't matter anymore. The views out to sea are unobstructed vistas of Lana'i, Kaho'olawe, Molokini, and West Maui, which gives the illusion of being a separate island. The buildings are even a buffer to the traffic noise! Many islanders make Kihei their home, so there is a feeling of real community here. It's quieter than Lahaina, with fewer restaurants and not as much action, but for sun and surf activities, this place has it all.

The six-mile stretch bordered by beach and mountain that makes up Kihei has always been an important landing spot on Maui. Hawaiian war canoes moored here many times during countless skirmishes over the years; later, Western navigators such as Captain George Vancouver

KIHEI

To Ma'alaea and Lahaina

Mokulele Hwy. to Kahului

SUGAR BEACH RESORT
NANI KAI HALE
KEALIA BEACH PLAZA
MAALAEA SURF RESORT
KIHEI WHARF
SUDA'S STORE

MAI POINA 'OE IA'U BEACH PARK
NONA LANI COTTAGES
WAILANA INN
MAUI LU RESORT
KIHEI GATEWAY PLAZA
KIHEI COMMERCIAL CENTER
BY THE SEA B&B

KALEPOLEPO BEACH PARK
MENEHUNE SHORES
KAUHALE MAKAI
LEINAALA
WAIPU'ILANI PARK
LONG'S CENTER
HALE KAI O KIHEI
AZEKA PLACE SHOPPING CENTER
STAR MARKET
POST OFFICE
AZEKA II
KIHEI PROFESSIONAL PLAZA
LIPOA CENTER

ELLEAIR MAUI GOLF COURSE

ST. TERESA'S CATHOLIC CHURCH
E. LIPOA ST.
KIHEI DIVE SHOP
WELAKAHAO RD.
KUKUI MALL
KIHEI TOWN CENTER
KALAMA PARK
KALAMA VILLAGE MARKET PLACE
KANANI RD.
LIHI KAI APT. HOTEL
MAUI VISTA
MAUI COAST HOTEL
KE ALI'I
KAMA'OLE BEACH PARK #1
DOLPHIN PLAZA
KAMAOLE BEACH CENTER
RAINBOW MALL
KAMA'OLE BEACH PARK #2
KAMAOLE SHOPPING CENTER
KAI NANI VILLAGE PLAZA
KAMA'OLE BEACH PARK #3
KEONEKAI RD.
KAMAOLE SANDS
MAUI HILL
KIHEI BOAT RAMP
MANA KAI MAUI RESORT
MAUI OCEANFRONT INN
To Wailea and Makena

KENOLIO RD.
OHUKAI ST.
KENOLIO RD.
ST.
KEONOULU ST.
KULANIHAKOI ST.
KIHEI RD.
S. KIHEI RD.
HALAMA ST.
P'ILANI HWY.

0   0.5 mi
0   0.5 km

found this stretch of beach a congenial anchorage. A totem pole across from the Maui Lu Resort marks the spot where Vancouver landed. During World War II, when a Japanese invasion was feared, Kihei was considered a likely spot for an amphibious attack. Overgrown pillboxes and rusting tank traps are still found along the beaches. Kihei is a natural site with mountain and ocean vistas. It's also great for beachcombing up toward Ma'alaea, but try to get there by morning because the afternoon wind is notorious for creating minor sandstorms.

Kihei's commercial sections are separated by residential areas. There is no one town center as such, although the highest concentration and greatest number of businesses are near the post office and the Azeka Place shopping centers. The new Maui Research and Technology Park has been built above the Elleair Golf Course in Kihei, sprucing up the image of the area a little and bringing in some high-tech white collar jobs at the same time, particularly of the dot.com variety. While only a handful of shiny new office buildings have been built so far, land has been set aside for many more.

BEACHES

Mai Poina 'Oe Ia'u Beach Park

On Kihei's northern fringe, fronting Maui Lu Resort, this beach offers only limited paved parking, otherwise just along the road. Showers, tables, and restrooms front the long and narrow white-sand beach, which has good safe swimming but is still plagued by strong winds by early afternoon. These trade winds are a windsurfer's delight, and here you can see upwards of 100 sporting enthusiasts out trying the wind when conditions are optimal.

Kalepolepo Beach Park

Next to the Whale Sanctuary office, this park has a small beach that's good for kiddies. Centuries ago, the thriving community of Kalepolepo occupied this area of Kihei and farmed the three-acre royal fishpond **Ko'ie'ie Loko I'a,** small but best preserved of the royal fishponds on Maui. Remnants of its rock wall can still be seen arcing through the water. Now much reduced in size, the walls once stood higher than high tide and wider than two men abreast. It's estimated that more than 2,000 pounds of fish a year were harvested from these waters when it was a functioning fishpond in the late 1500s.

Waipu'ilani Park
Just south of Kalepolepo is this park with its narrow beach, broad lawn, tennis courts, smattering of coconut trees, great sunsets, and windsurfers in season. Rather infrequented, it's like a big greenway to the sea for the condos that front it. The shoreline for over one-half of a mile south has been set aside as a State Beach Preserve. Access to it is at the end of West Lipoa Street. Off the coast here were three large fishponds that have now all but disappeared.

Kalama Park
This park is more suited to family outings, athletic games, and enjoying the vista than it is for beach activities. Kalama has a large lawn ending in a breakwater, a small beach in summer, and none in winter. However, there are 36 acres of pavil-

ROBERT NILSEN

Kamable Beach I

ions, tables, barbecue pits, volleyball, basketball, and tennis courts, a baseball diamond, a soccer field, and plenty of expanse to throw a Frisbee. With its great views of Molokini and Haleakala, it is considered the best family park in the area. At its extreme southern end, just across the highway bridge, is the diminutive Cove Park, where locals put small boats in the water and others come to surf.

Kama'ole I, II, and III
These beach parks, often referred to as Kam I, II, and III, are at the south end of town. All three have beautiful white sand, picnic tables, lifeguards, and all the amenities. The swimming and bodysurfing are good. At the North end of Kam I is an area called Charley Young Beach. Snorkeling is good here and for beginners on the reef between II and III, where much coral and many colorful reef fish abound. Kama'ole III has a kids' playground. Shopping and dining are nearby.

Kihei Boat Ramp
Just south of Kama'ole III Beach is the Kihei Boat Ramp, used by many ocean activities companies in the area to launch boats and rafts.

ACCOMMODATIONS

The emphasis in Kihei is on condos. With keen competition among them, you can save some money while having a more homey vacation. Close to 100 condos, plus a smattering of vacation apartments, cottages, and even a few small hotel resorts, are all strung along Kihei Road. As always, you pay more for ocean views. Don't shy away from accommodations on the *mauka* side of Kihei Road. You have total access to the beach and superior views of Haleakala, and you usually pay less money. The accommodations below are listed north to south. By and large, these places are north of the Azeka Place shopping centers and south of Kalama beach park, leaving the central section of town for businesses and homes.

$100–150
The Kihei area has one small hotel that's reasonably priced and well appointed. The **Maui**

MAUI

Coast Hotel, 2259 S. Kihei Rd., Kihei, HI 96753, 808/874-6284 or 800/895-6284, fax 808/875-4731; website: www.westcoasthotels.com/mauicoast, is Kihei's only true hotel. Completed in 1993 and renovated in 1999, the 265 rooms and suites here are bright and cheerful, blending Southwestern pastels and Hawaiian-style furniture. Adding to your comfort are standard amenities like remote-control color TV, a/c and ceiling fans, complimentary in-wall safes, coffeemakers, refrigerators, slippers to pad around in, full bathrooms that include a hot tub and a "who asked for one" bathroom scale. Wet bars are in all the larger suites. Guests are also treated to morning coffee, and washers and dryers are on every other floor. This seven-story hotel offers two spas with whirlpools, a swimming pool, lighted guests-only tennis courts, a restaurant, poolside bar with nightly entertainment, sundries shop, and free parking. Rates are $145–155 for a standard room, $165–349 for a suite, $20 each additional person, with discounted off-season and weekly rates. Rental-car packages are also available. The Maui Coast Hotel, set back from busy Kihei Road, offers a small oasis of peace and tranquillity with excellent rates for the amenities offered.

Maui Lu Resort, 575 S. Kihei Rd., Kihei, HI 96753, 808/879-5881, 800/922-7866, or 800/321-2558 in Hawaii, fax 808/879-4627, website: www.westcoasthotels.com/mauicoast, a 28-acre property at the north end of Kihei, attempts to preserve the feeling of old Hawaii with its emphasis on 'ohana. The Maui Lu is not designed as an ordinary hotel—it looks more like condo units—but none of the rooms have kitchens. Amenities here include an activities desk, tennis and volleyball courts, a Maui-shaped swimming pool, and a two tiny pocket beaches. While three buildings are next to the water, most rooms are in the newer wings up the hill near the entrance lobby. Rooms are priced $105–175 during value season and $125–205 during regular season. All hotel-style rooms include TV, a/c, refrigerators, and daily maid service. This is an Aston property.

$150–200

Maui Oceanfront Inn, 2980 S. Kihei Rd., is at the entrance to Wailea. In 2000, this intimate complex was given a complete makeover including buildings, furnishings, and grounds, and converted into a boutique hotel. While low-rise and looking much like a condominium, none of the studios and suites have cooking facilities. Each room has a TV and entertainment center, a/c and ceiling fans, in-room safe, and a small refrigerator. Rates are $159 for a mountain view, $179 for garden view, $189 for ocean view, and $259–379 for the suites. For reservations, call 808/879-7744 or 800/367-5004, fax 808/874-0145.

Condos and Cottages

One of the several condos at the far north end of Kihei, at the eastern end of Ma'alaea Beach, is **Sugar Beach Resort,** 145 N. Kihei Rd., 808/879-7765. All one- and two-bedroom units have full kitchens, ceiling fans and a/c, TV, and lanai, with guest-only tennis courts, swimming pool, spa, sauna, barbecue grills, sundries shop, sandwich shop, and activities desk on property. The activities desk can book you on virtually any land and sea excursion, while the sundries shop offers rental bikes, kayaks, snorkel gear, and beach equipment. All are individually owned and decorated. Rates run about $140–170 for one-bedroom and $185–250 for two-bedroom suites, but these rates vary a bit according to the rental agency. Contact the following agents for rooms here and at other nearby condos: Condominium Rentals Hawaii, 808/879-2778 or 800/367-5242 Mainland, 800/663-2101 in Canada; Rainbow Rentals, 808/244-1688 or 800/451-5366; or Maui Condominium and Home Realty, 808/289-5445 or 800/822-4409.

The cement high-rise **Nani Kai Hale,** 73 N. Kihei Rd., 808/875-0630, fax 808/875-8985, is very affordable at $109 per night for a one-bedroom standard for seven days or longer, $115 per night for fewer than seven days. One-bedroom ocean views run $125/$135, oceanfronts $145/$155; two-bedroom standards are $145/$155. The two-bedroom oceanfront units go for a $185 nightly rate only. Substantial savings are offered during off-season, a four-day minimum stay is required, and monthly rates are available. There's sheltered parking, a pool, laundry facilities, and barbecues on premises.

The Polynesian-style roofs and dark wooden siding might draw you to the two-story, luxury **Maalaea Surf Resort,** 12 S. Kihei Rd., 808/879-

1267 or 800/423-7953, fax 808/874-2884, but the fully furnished bright interiors, well-tended lawns, tennis courts, swimming pools, and white-sand beach will captivate you. Each unit has a/c and daily maid service. One-bedroom suites run $205–230, and two-bedroom units are $277–307. A fifth night is offered free during the value season. This and the two previously mentioned condos are at the far eastern end of Ma'alaea Beach, near the intersection of Highways 31 and 311.

The first place south of Suda's Store is **Nona Lani Cottages,** 455 S. Kihei Rd., 808/879-2497 or 800/733-2688, website: www.nanolanicottages.com, owned and operated by Dave and Nona Kong. These eight clean and neat units on the *mauka* side of the road have full kitchens and baths, queen beds, and daybeds. Laundry facilities, public phones, hammocks, chaise lounges, and barbecues are on the premises, and each unit has a raised lanai with tables. Rates are $78 a night during low season, $10 additional person and four-night minimum, and $88 a night during high season when there's a seven-night minimum stay. Weekly and monthly rates are available. These individual plantation-style units are about as down-home Hawaiian as you can get, a good place to come if you're looking for relaxation. The Nona Lani now also has a few rooms (no kitchens), which run $68 and $75, respectively, for low- and high-season.

A few steps away is **Wailana Inn,** an apartment turned condo rental. This two-story building has less than a dozen units, so it's quiet, and it's just a minute's walk to the beach. Each unit has a king or queen bed, kitchen or kitchenette, TV, a/c, and telephone. A sun deck with a hot tub is on the roof, and there is a washer and dryer on premises for your use. Spacious enough, these units have been totally remodeled and run $100 a night for a room with kitchen and $75 for the kitchenettes. Wailana Inn is at 14 Wailana Place near the Vancouver Monument, 808/874-3131 or 800/399-3885. The inn's website is www.wailanabeach.com.

Menehune Shores, 760 S. Kihei Rd., mailing address P.O. Box 1327, Kihei, HI 96753, 808/879-3428 or 800/558-9117, fax 808/879-5218, is a huge, family-oriented and moderately priced high-rise condo on the beach overlooking an ancient fishpond. The building itself is high-

lighted with replicas of Hawaiian petroglyphs. On the first floor is Jacques on the Beach restaurant, outside of which is a new swimming pool. The Menehune is used mostly by seniors, except during Christmas when families come. All units have an ocean view and rates are $110–185 for one- to three-bedroom condos in high season, three-day minimum. Low-season rates are about 10 percent less, discounts are given for monthlong stays, and special car/room packages can be arranged. Full kitchens include dishwashers, and washers and dryers are in each unit, which are individually owned, so furnishings vary. More than one-half of the units have recently been totally remodeled.

Kauhale Makai, 938 S. Kihei Rd., has fully furnished, individually decorated studios and suites that are a mixture of garden, mountain, and ocean view. All are clustered around a central courtyard garden. A swimming pool, kiddie pool, barbecues, putting green, and sauna are available, making it good for the family. Rates range $75–90 studio, $85–100 one-bedroom, and $115–160 two-bedroom, four-night minimum; weekly and monthly discounts given. All reservations are handled through Maui Condominium and Home Realty, P.O. Box 1840 Kihei, HI 96753, 808/879-5445 or 800/822-4409, fax 808/874-6144.

The boxy four-story **Leinaala** condos, 990 S. Kihei Rd., 808/879-2235 or 800/334-3305, may not attract everyone, but don't let the appearance fool you. Each of the 24 fully appointed units faces the beach across the lawns of the Waipu'ilani Park, and all are narrow units that run from the front of the building to the back. Set back from the road, this is a quiet spot where you can splash in the pool in peace. Winter rates are $115 and $150 for one- and two-bedroom units during high season. The best time for space is during the summer when rates are $25–30 less; four nights minimum. Weekly and monthly rates can be adjusted, and car rental packages arranged. Reduced rates for AARP and AAA.

Just down the back street at 1310 Uluniu Rd., Kihei, HI 96753, 808/879-2757 or 800/457-7014, fax 808/875-8242, is **Hale Kai O Kihei.** This apartment-like cinder block affair, simple and utilitarian, is clean, well-kept, and cute for what it is, and it's recently been spruced up. Each furnished unit has a direct ocean view with a lanai that looks over the pool, garden, and beach. There is also shuffleboard, barbecue grills, and coin laundry, with maid service on request. Reasonable rates are $110 for a one-bedroom unit ($75 for low season) and $145 for two bedrooms ($110 low season); three nights minimum—15 percent discount for stays of one month or greater. Cash payment only, no credit cards.

The following condos are all south of Kalama Park. First is **Lihi Kai Cottages,** 2121 Ili'ili Rd., Kihei, HI 96753, 808/879-2335 or 800/541-4524. These nine cottages are such a bargain they're often booked by returning guests, particularly during winter months. They're not plush, and there's no pool, but they're homey and clean, with little touches like banana trees growing on the property. Rates are $90 daily for three to six nights, $80 for seven or more nights; three nights minimum. Monthly rates are available on request, no credit cards accepted. For reservations, call or write the manager well in advance.

Maui Vista, 2191 S. Kihei Rd., 808/879-7966 or 800/535-0085, fax 808/633-5085, is a pleasing 10-acre condo complex that has 38 units managed by Marc Resorts. Three pools, six tennis courts, barbecue grills, and an activities desk are available to all guests. All studios and suites have kitchens, are modern in their appointments, spacious in layout, and have maid service. Studios run $149, one-bedroom suites $159–179, and two-bedroom suites $219–229, $20 less during "value" periods, $15 each extra person.

At **Kamaole Sands,** 2695 S. Kihei Rd., 808/874-8700 or 800/367-5004, fax 808/879-3273, all apartments come completely furnished with a full bath and kitchen, roomy living area, and lanai. Prices are: $135 studio, $155–190 one-bedroom, $230–280 two-bedroom, $335–345 three-bedroom, fifth night free; winter season rates slightly higher and rental car packages available. Stepping down the hillside, the Kamaole Sands is a full-service, family-oriented condo geared toward making the entire family comfortable. The Sandpiper Grill, situated poolside and for guests only, serves inexpensive breakfasts, lunches, and dinners on Friday featuring fresh island fish and pasta. One of the main features of the Kamaole Sands is its wonderful tennis courts, free to guests, with a tennis instructor to help you work on the fine points of your game. Here as well are a swimming pool, and

kids' pool, a jet spa, volleyball courts, and barbecue areas. The Kamaole Sands is bright and cheerful; it gives you a lot for your money.

Maui Hill is at 2881 S. Kihei Rd., 808/879-6321 or 800/922-7866, or 800/321-2558 Hawaii. If you want to rise above it all in Kihei come to this upbeat condo with a Spanish motif. This condo resort sits high on a hill and commands a sweeping view of the entire area. The one-, two-, and three-bedroom suites are spacious, bright, and airy; all have ceiling fans and a/c, cable TV, daily maid service, and full kitchens. A concierge service helps with your every need, and all sun and surf activities can be arranged at the activities desk. The grounds are secluded, beautifully maintained, and offer a pool with whale mosaic on the bottom, tennis courts, and spa. Regular-season rates are: one bedroom from $265 (up to four people), two bedrooms from $330 (up to six people), three bedrooms from $460 (up to eight people); substantial savings during low-season. A weekly complimentary mai tai party complete with games, singing, and door prizes is held for guests, along with a continental breakfast at 8 A.M. that offers an orientation on island activities. Guests can also enjoy a weekly afternoon lei-making class and a poolside scuba orientation several days per week. An Aston property.

At the south end of Kihei is **Mana Kai Maui** oceanfront resort, 2960 S. Kihei Rd., 808/879-2778 or 800/367-5242 Mainland or 800/663-2101 Canada, fax 808/879-7825. Features include front desk check-in, an activities desk, daily maid service, a sundries store, swimming pool, and an oceanside restaurant and bar on premises. Condo units have full kitchens, TV, private lanai, and ceiling fans. All hotel rooms, with outdoor access, a/c, and refrigerators, are on the garden level. Winter rates (January 6 to April 15) run $114–125 for the hotel rooms, $206–225 for a one-bedroom and $242–263 for a two-bedroom suite. Summer rates (until December 15) are about 10 percent cheaper, Christmas rates are 10 percent higher, and there is a 10 percent discount for stays of one month or more at any time of year.

Bed-and-Breakfasts

By The Sea B&B is tucked under tall palm trees down a side street near the windsurfing beach at the north end of Kihei. This private home has four units all with separate entrances that look over the back garden and pond. Rooms include a small kitchenette, large bathroom, ceiling fan, TV, and phone, plus daily breakfast; the second floor unit has a deck. Rates run $85–159, three nights minimum—no charge for the friendly advice on island activities and places to eat, or for the time you spend lounging in the hammock out back! Weekly discounts are offered and rental cars can be arranged. By The Sea B&B is at 20 Wailana Place, Kihei, HI 96753, 808/891-0348 or 888/879-2700, fax 808/879-5540.

Babson's Bed and Breakfast, 3371 Keha Dr., Kihei, HI 96753, 808/874-1166 or 800/824-6409, fax 808/879-7906, website: www.mauibnb.com, email: babson@mauibnb.com, offers a combination of B&B rooms and private cottage in the quiet residential area of Maui Meadows perched on the hillside above Kihei and Wailea. From this vantage point, you can watch the sun set over the Lahaina Roads with Kaho'olawe, Molikini, Lana'i, and even Moloka'i floating on the horizon, or pay closer attention to the finely landscaped gardens that surround the house. All rentals include cable, private bath, TV, telephone, and laundry facilities. Ann and Bob are happy to recommend their favorite scenic spots, activities, and restaurants, and will provide you with towels and a cooler for a day at the beach. Rates for the main home's B&B rooms, the Bougainvillea, Hibiscus Hideaway, and Molokini Master Suite, are $90–120 and include a continental breakfast Mon.–Sat.; 10 percent discount for stays longer than seven nights. The two-bedroom Sunset Cottage offers a sweeping ocean view, cathedral ceilings, two private baths, and full kitchen; it rents for $125 (no breakfast). All prices are for double occupancy; $15 for each extra person up to four in the cottage. There is a five-night minimum in the main house and seven-night minimum for the cottage. Ann and Bob go out of their way to make your stay enjoyable, having mastered the art of allowing you to enjoy it yourself.

Farther up in this neighborhood, at 815 Kumulani Dr., is **Eva Villa,** tel./fax 808/874-6407 or 800/884-1845, website: www.maui.net/~pounder, email: pounder@maui.net. Built with the clean lines of a contemporary design, Eva Villa is set in a finely landscaped yard sporting an attractive koi pond. Here you'll find a studio and two-room apartment that overlook the swimming pool. In a separate structure is a small cottage with its own kitchen. All units have phones and TV, a small refrigerator and eating area, and each has a private entrance. Rates run $95–140. The roof-top deck, pool, and hot tub are open to all guests, and everyone is provided a simple continental breakfast.

Rental Agencies
Numerous rental agencies handle condo units and rental homes in Kihei and South Maui.

Condominium Rentals Hawaii, 362 Huku Li'i Place, #204, Kihei, HI 96753, 808/879-2778 or 800/367-5242 Mainland or 800/663-2101 Canada, website: www.crhmaui.com, can arrange your stay in eight condos, all in Kihei.

Kihei Maui Vacations, P.O. Box 1055, Kihei, HI 96753, 808/879-7581 or 800/541-6284, fax 808/879-2000, website: www.kmvmaui.com, has units in over two dozen condos, mostly in Kihei, but a few in Ma'alaea and Wailea.

Maui Condominium and Home Realty, P.O. Box 1840, Kihei, HI 96753, 808/879-5445 or 800/822-4409, fax 808/874-6144, website: www.mauicondo.com, offers mostly economical to midrange units in Kihei.

AA Oceanfront Condo Rentals, 2439 S. Kihei Rd., Suite 102-A, Kihei, HI 96753, 808/879-7288 or 800/488-6004, fax 808/879-7500, website: www.makena.com, manages properties from north Kihei to Makena, economy to deluxe.

Kumulani Vacations and Realty, P.O. Box 1190, Kihei, HI 96753, 808/879-9272 or 800/367-2954, fax 808/874-0094, website: www.kumulani.com, email: info@kumulani.com, handles rentals in 10 condos in Kihei and Wailea.

FOOD

Inexpensive
At the north end, the first inexpensive eatery is **Suda's Snack Shop,** open Mon.–Sat. 6 A.M.–12:30 P.M. for burgers, plate lunches, and drinks. Adjacent to the Suda's Store, the snack shop is nothing special but is a good spot for a quick bite to eat.

Heat-flushed tourists hoping to chill out should head for **Stella Blue's Cafe,** at Longs Shopping

MAUI

Center, 808/874-3779, open daily 8 A.M.–9 P.M. This is an economical place, good for the family, where the kids will love the selections and adults can still order a beer or wine. Breakfast, served 8–11 A.M., features a continental breakfast for $7 or French toast for $6.25. Fresh hot bagels run $2.50, a tuna salad plate $7.25, and a tossed green salad is $3. Sandwiches, everything from roast beef to veggie, average about $7.50. From the grill you can have a tuna melt, veggie burger, or pastrami melt for under $7.75. Dinner includes spinach lasagna for $12.95 and chicken parmesan at $15.95.

Kalbi House, in a corner of Longs Shopping Center, open daily 9:30 A.M.–9:30 P.M. and Sunday 11 A.M.–9 P.M., offers a full range of Americanized Korean standards like barbecued short ribs, fried squid, noodles, stews, and small intestine soup, as well as plate lunches and combination plates, and a few Japanese dishes like chicken teriyaki. Most everything is under $12 except for the full-meal Bulgogi for $24.99; take-out available. The restaurant is basic but clean.

International House of Pancakes is toward the rear of Azeka Place. Open daily 6 A.M.–midnight, Friday and Saturday until 2 A.M. Same American standards as on the Mainland with most sandwiches and plate lunches under $8, dinners under $12, and breakfasts anytime around $6. Not exotic, but basic and filling with a good reputation in the area for inexpensive but passable fresh fish and daily specials.

Azeka's Ribs and Snack Shop at Azeka Place is an institution, very famous for its specially prepared (uncooked) ribs, perfect for a barbecue. Also available are plate lunches, burgers, and sushi.

Let the rich aroma of roasting coffee lure you to **The Coffee Store,** 808/875-4244, open daily 6 A.M.–10 P.M. at Azeka Place II. Breakfast fare features quiche for $3.75 or a breakfast quesadilla for $6.95. Lunch selections, always served with crusty homemade bread, include a Caesar salad at $4.95—or $6.95 for the large size that can easily feed two—and sandwiches like tuna, turkey, or vegetarian for $5.50 to $6.50. Daily homemade soup costs $3.95 including bread and coffee, stuffed quesadillas of all sorts go for $4–6, and wraps complete the menu. Enjoy coffee drinks that range in price $1–2.50, along with hot and iced herbal teas, hot chocolate,

and Italian cream sodas. A deli case is filled with luscious desserts sure to satisfy any sweet tooth, and, of course, you can purchase bulk coffee. You can dine inside or sit outside, especially in the evening to hobnob with local residents who come here to chat and enjoy a rich cup of coffee and snack or to check the Internet.

The fountain bar, jukebox, Formica tabletops, leatherette booths, distinctive color scheme, and period decorations and music peg **Peggy Sue** as a classic, theme hamburger joint—with a modern twist. You can order your Big Bopper burger for $8.25 or the Earth Angel garden burger for $7.25, or sample one of the salads, sandwiches, or burgers, most for under $10. No '50s joint worth its name would be without that cool summer favorite, so Peggy Sue serves up ice cream, shakes, sundaes, and fountain drinks. Stop in for the nostalgia rush. At Azeka Place II; 808/875-8944.

If you've been having too much fun and need a reviving cup of espresso, stop in at the **Kihei Caffe,** at Kalama Village Marketplace, 808/878-2230, open daily at 5 A.M., Sunday at 6 A.M., and enjoy your coffee along with an excellent assortment of sandwiches and baked goods. Order a complete breakfast of eggs, bacon, home fries, and biscuits with gravy for $6, or a giant raisin muffin for $2.75. Sandwiches, all under $6.50, are served on your choice of homemade bread—only cold sandwiches after 2 P.M. The café provides a few tables and stools inside and more outside, where you can watch the action on Kihei Road or across the road through Kama'ole Beach Park to the ocean.

A few steps away is **Alexander's,** 808/874-0788, open 11 A.M.–9 P.M. This local long-term establishment is definitely a cut above most fast-food restaurants, and it has taken a few steps along the upscale, yuppie, health-conscious road. The menu offers fresh fish, shrimp, and chicken sandwiches for $6.25–7.50. Plate lunches for $8 or under, sides, salads, and drinks, as well as larger baskets for $15.75–19.95, are also on the menu. Full meals are served with cole slaw and french fries or rice. All deep frying is done in canola oil but you can request broiling instead. You can't go wrong here. There's not much decor or atmosphere, but the food is delicious and makes a perfect take-out meal that can be enjoyed at the beach.

Sports Page Bar and Grill, at the Kamaole Beach Center, 808/879-0602, open 11 A.M.–midnight for cocktails and 11 A.M.–10 P.M. for food service, scores big with a full bar, a large-screen TV, and foosball and a pool table in the back. Order a mug of beer and a light snack like oyster shooters for $1 or teriyaki chicken breast strips for $6.95. The burger and sandwich menu goes all the way with a San Francisco '49er burger topped with bacon and cheese, a Chicago Cubs hot dog, or a Boston Celtics turkey sandwich, all for under $8.50. There's music some evenings and a cover may be charged. Mostly a working man's bar, although visitors are certainly welcome, its walls are covered with sports pictures, pennants, and posters. Families and even the athletically challenged will be comfortable here.

Also at Kamaole Beach Center is **Hawaiian Moon's Deli and Natural Foods,** open Mon.–Sat. 8 A.M.–9 P.M., Sunday until 6 P.M. Stop for a healthy deli sandwich and drink, or shop for groceries, vitamins, and bulk foods. Across the parking lot is **Maui Tacos** for tacos, burritos, and other standard Mexican food with a definite Hawaiian bump.

Kay's Cafe and Deli at Kai Nani Village Plaza serves smoothies, juices, coffees, and quick snack deli items.

Moderate

Margarita's Beach Cantina, 101 N. Kihei Rd in the Kealia Beach Plaza, 808/879-5275, open daily 11:30 A.M.–11:30 P.M., has a well-deserved reputation for good food at fair prices. Formerly vegetarian, it now serves meat and chicken dishes but still uses the finest ingredients, cold-pressed oils, and no lard or bacon in the bean dishes. The decor is classical Mexican with white stucco walls and tiled floors. There's an outdoor deck affording a great sunset view and sea breezes, or stop by for live music and dancing Friday 5–7 P.M. and Monday 5–8 P.M. The *carta* offers taco salads for $10.95, combination plates for $10.95–15.95, and money-saving daily lunch specials. Most entrées are in the $11–15 range, with nothing more than $20. Look for reduced price well drinks, beers, and margaritas during the 2:30–5:30 P.M. happy hour.

Restaurant Isana, 515 S. Kihei Rd., 808/874-5700, is open daily for the best Korean food in the area, and also has Japanese sushi 4–8 P.M.

You can either sit at the sushi bar or have dinner cooked at your table. Upstairs is the bar, which has a karaoke sing-along after 10 P.M. Most dinners are in the $10–18 range.

Jacques On the Beach is a relative newcomer to Kihei, and it follows the successful Jacques Bistro in Pa'ia. Both establishments have pretty much the same varied menu, and people know that they can come here for the conviviality. A few of the signature dishes are the giant New Zealand prawns appetizer at $10.95 and the entrées peanut chicken for $12.95 and island ribs at $18.95. Fresh fish and seafood and pastas are also prominent on the menu. Right of the beach at the Menehune Shores condominium, it's a wonderful spot for sunset.

Although you can get appetizers, salads, burgers, shrimp, and chicken at **Tony Roma's,** 808/875-1104, at the Kukui Mall, Tony's is a place for ribs, ribs, and more ribs. Prepared in several different ways, rib entrées run about $16, with most other entrées less. For those who want just a little extra, try the ribs combos for $13–25.

Chuck's Steak House at the Kihei Town Center, 808/879-4489, open Mon.–Sat. for lunch 11 A.M.–2:30 P.M., dinner nightly 5–10 P.M., is a family restaurant featuring American standards with an island twist. With a gray-on-gray interior, the restaurant provides a pleasant atmosphere, and although they do not take reservations, they will tell you how busy they are if you call ahead. The lunch menu is affordable with selections like a Reuben sandwich for $5.95 and plate lunches for under $7. The early-bird special, priced at a reasonable $11.95, is normally fresh fish or barbecued chicken, and includes the salad bar, homemade bread, and a choice of white rice or french fries. The dinner menu includes teriyaki steaks for $15.95 and a petite top sirloin priced at $14.95. Chuck's seafood selections include fresh fish or sautéed shrimp for about $20, and prime rib and lobster tail for $29.95.

In the Rainbow Plaza, **The Thai Chef Restaurant,** 808/874-5605, offers you a full menu of tasty Thai food at reasonable prices. Like at its sister restaurant in Lahaina, you can get appetizers like spring rolls for $7.50 or green papaya salad at $6.50, and various soups for around

$10. Entrées include red, green, or yellow curries for $9–11, with noodle, rice, and seafood dishes up to $14. There's a hefty selection for vegetarians, and desserts run $2–3. Well maintained, Thai Chef has a casual decor.

Tropical Mexican fare is offered *muy pronto* at **Cafe Navaca,** 808/879-0717, at 1945 S. Kihei Rd., open for breakfast, lunch, and dinner. Everything is made here every day, and no lard is used. All the usual favorites are on the menu in one form or another, plus such unusual items as grilled vegetable quesadillas, tequila-lime chicken, and chili-seared *ahi.*

In the Kamaole Center, **Canton Chef,** 808/879-1988, offers the usual long list of choices from appetizers to meat and seafood dishes. Spicy Sichuan items on the menu will fire up your day. Most entrées are in the $6–12 range.

KKO Kai Ku Ono, 808/875-1007, a semi-sports bar casual dining place, below the more upscale Kihei Prime Rib and Seafood House at Kai Nani Village Plaza, is open 7:30 A.M.–midnight with entertainment nightly. Grab a pizza and beer and cool off after a day at the beach with a game of pool or darts. Sandwiches, burritos, and pasta are available, with most items under $12. The full bar will set you up drinks, while you kick back and catch your favorite sporting event on one of the TVs.

Tucked into the rear of Kai Nani Village Plaza is the **Greek Bistro,** 808/879-9330, a wonderful addition to the restaurant scene, where the flavors and textures of the Greek and Mediterranean dishes will excite your palate. Dinner is served 5–10 P.M. and includes souvlakia, spanakopita, mousaka, and lamb kabob, all ranging $18–25. Other items are stuffed grape leaves for $8, Grecian village salad at $9, and several pasta dishes. If you're in doubt as to what would be tasty, try the A Taste of Greece platter, a sampling of several homemade entrées on the menu. Sit inside or out.

Expensive

Expanding from a very successful operation on Kaua'i, Chef Jean-Marie Josselin opened **A Pacific Cafe Maui,** 808/879-0069, at Azeka Place II. Open for dinner nightly 5:30–9:30, this restaurant presents the same kind of fine Hawaiian regional cuisine as at the original. Open, large,

and masculine, the simply elegant decor of the dining areas, set off by modernistic touches, surrounds the exhibition kitchen with its wood-fired pizza oven. Start with a tiger eye *ahi* sushi tempura with tomato and Chinese mustard sauce for $12 or a Caesar salad for $8.95. Soups might be a red Thai curry and coconut with fresh island fish and calamari for $6.75. Entrées average about $25, including grilled Pacific snapper with Indonesian sticky rice roll, Chinese-style roasted duck with garlic mashed potatoes, or penne pasta with shrimp, scallops, wild mushrooms, mussels, and purple asparagus. No matter what your choice, the ingredients will be the freshest, the service prompt, and the result memorable.

Jameson's Grill and Bar, 808/891-8860, is at the entrance to the Maui Coast Hotel. A well-appointed place, it's open for three meals a day. Lunch could be a simple Portuguese bean soup, fish and chips, or a barbecued chicken pizza. Dinners are a bit more formal, with such items as chilled tiger prawn appetizers, lemon pepper chicken, rack of lamb, or fresh catch of the day, with most entrées running $19–28. No matter what's on the menu, you always have well-prepared, nutritious food.

Upstairs at the Kai Nani Village Plaza at 2511 S. Kihei Rd. is **Kihei Prime Rib and Seafood House,** open from 5 P.M., 808/879-1954, offering most entrées for $20–32, including a well-stocked salad bar. Sashimi, lobster, and stuffed mushroom appetizers are under $10, and the early-bird specials, 5–6 P.M., include a salad bar. One of the best choices is medallions of lamb for $22. An island ambience is created with carvings by Bruce Turnbull and paintings by Sigrid, both well-known local artists.

Overlooking the beach, the casual **Five Palms** restaurant, 808/879-2607, at the Mana Kai Maui Resort at the south end of Kihei, is open for breakfast Mon.–Fri. 9–11:30 A.M. and a weekend champagne brunch 8 A.M.–2 P.M. Breakfast includes the usuals like eggs, sausages, pancakes, and the like, while the brunch also gives you the wider options of burgers, soups, salads, sandwiches, and some pastas. For lunch, try sandwiches, soup, pizza, or other entrées for $10–15. Dinner is served 5–9 P.M. (until 10 on Friday and Saturday), with flash-fry *ahi* for $10, Mediterranean green salad at $6, pulehu rack of lamb for $30, broiled lobster at market price, and many other delectable items on the menu, but the specialty is fish. So close to the water, the location and scenery are an integral part of the dining experience here.

Only steps from Wailea is the fine-dining Italian restaurant called **Carrelli's On the Beach,** 808/875-0001. Open for dinner only 6–10 P.M., bar until 11 P.M., all parking is complimentary valet only because of limited space. If you don't want to deal with parking, take a limo, $15 each way, from along this coast. The excellent reputation and proximity draw many guests from the resorts and condos of Wailea. The seating couldn't be better, with the restaurant set right on the beach, and it's the water and sparkling light off the waves rather than the interior decoration that draws your attention most. Start with an antipasti or calamari friette for $12 and move on to a green salad, Caesar, or soup for $8–18. Pastas include ravioli for $22 and risotto con pettini prosciutto for $28. A bit pricier are the scampi and veal dishes for up to $36. For a bit more casual treat, try a homemade pizza from the wood-fired oven. Although rich and expensive, one of the fine desserts, like tiramisu or tartufo (a gelato ball rolled in chocolate and served with mango puree), might make a fine finish to your meal.

ENTERTAINMENT

Kihei isn't exactly a hot spot when it comes to evening entertainment. You can dance at **Margarita's Beach Cantina** Friday and Monday. Try Jameson's poolside bar at the Maui Coast Hotel for nightly music in a relaxed setting. **Kahale Beach Club,** a local bar for people who work in the area, is a place that offers music and dancing on an occasional basis. To its front is the fun little bar **Life's a Beach,** which serves up evening entertainment along with burgers, sandwiches, salads, and *pu pu.* **Hapa's Brew Haus,** 41 E. Lipoa St., is a big place that once brewed its own beer. Now it serves other beers and offers a good-time atmosphere with games, entertainment, and dancing nightly on a big dance floor. Local live bands perform on Mondays and Fridays from about 9 P.M.; Hapa's occasionally gets a big name musician, and there will undoubtedly be a minimum cover. The

Pizazz café at Azeka Place II has established itself as the premier jazz venue in the area with live jazz Wed.–Sat.; $5 cover for the band. Up for karaoke? Try the Isana restaurant after 10 P.M. Many of the restaurants offer entertainment on a hit-and-miss basis, usually one artist with a guitar, a small dinner combo, or some Hawaiian music. These are usually listed in the free tourist brochures.

The **Kukui Mall Theater** at the Kihei Town Center is the only movie theater on this side of the island. It's a four-screen theater with shows starting at about noon. Admission is $7 for adults and $4 for seniors and kids.

SHOPPING

Shopping centers, both large and small, are strung along the entire coastal area of Kihei like shells on a dime-store lei. At many you can buy food, clothing, sporting goods, picnic supplies, sundries, photo equipment, cosmetics, resortwear, ice cream, pizza, dinner, and liquor. You can also book activities, order a custom bikini, or just relax with an ice-cold beer while your partner satisfies his or her shopping addiction. In Kihei, you have more than ample opportunity to spend your hard-earned vacation money that would be a sin to take back home. Aloha!

North End Shopping

At the very north end of Kihei, as you approach from Kahului or Lahaina, is the **Sugar Beach General Store,** with a small clutch of shops selling resortwear, snacks, and gifts. The activities company here can set you up for a fun afternoon or rent you a bicycle or water gear. Nearby at **Kealia Beach Plaza** is the **Felma General Store.** Upstairs in the front is the **Pacific Whale Foundation** office, open 9 A.M.–5 P.M. daily, and upstairs overlooking the water in the back is **Margarita's Beach Cantina.**

Suda's Store is a basic little market with limited food items, but with cold beer, fresh fish, and deli items. Open Mon.–Fri. 7:30 A.M.–5 P.M., Saturday closing at 4 P.M., Sunday 8 A.M.–3 P.M., it sits along the *mauka* side at 61 S. Kihei Road, across from the Kihei Canoe Club. Locally grown produce is sold in the parking lot here on Monday, Wednesday, and Friday 1:30–5:30 P.M. A

MAUI

few minutes down the road from Suda's heading for Kihei, look for the **Nona Lana Cottages,** where you can pick up a fresh-flower lei for a reasonable price.

Set along Pi'ilani Highway (Route 31), the main thoroughfare above Kihei that parallels Kihei Road, is **Kihei Gateway Plaza.** Even with the **South Shore Grinds** local food restaurant, **Aloha Gifts and Gallery** shop, and **Maui Clothing Outlet** store, it's perhaps most useful for its gas station and minimart. In the **Kihei Commercial Center** directly behind, you'll find **Casey's Bakehouse Cafe** for great breads, pastries and other treats, and **Kihei Wine and Spirits** for the widest selection of bottled wines, beers, liqueurs, hard liquor, gourmet foods, and cigars on this side of the island.

Longs Shopping Center

At 1215 S. Kihei Rd., almost opposite the post office, this shopping center is dominated by a huge **Longs Drugs,** stocked with electronics, photo equipment and film developing, sundries, cosmetics, stationery, a pharmacy, and even sporting goods. Around the center the **T-Shirt Factory** features all kinds of discounted wearable take-home gifts; **Mavrik Motorcycles,** rents the big hogs; and you can do everything from faxing to packing and shipping at **Mail Boxes Etc.** **American Savings Bank** is conveniently located here for all the shopping that you may be doing in this center and along the Kihei strip. A **farmers' market** is held in the parking lot every Saturday 8 A.M.–noon.

Azeka Place

Adjacent to the post office is the Azeka Place Shopping Center. In what might be considered the center of town, you'll find numerous small shops and fast-food eating establishments. There's also a great community bulletin board listing apartments, yard sales, and odds and ends. Most shops are open daily 9 A.M.–9 P.M. with shorter Sunday hours. **Rainbow Connection** features personalized and Polynesian gifts. **Island Memories** is stocked with carved koa boxes, shells, earrings, woven basketry, a good selection of pottery, and hula instruments, all made in Hawaii. **Tropical Tantrum** specializes in hand-painted clothing by local artists, mostly for women but with a few selections for men as well, and **Crazy Shirts** has its own distinctive line of clothing. In case you need a toggle bolt, try **Kihei Ace Hardware. Old Daze Antiques and Collectibles** is a stop for treasure hunters, and **B&B Scuba** rents underwater gear. **Wolf Camera** can develop your film, and while you're waiting, have a look at **Cinemagic Videos,** open nightly until 10 P.M., for your evening entertainment.

The Kihei **post office,** 1254 S. Kihei Rd., is open Mon.–Fri. 9 A.M.–4:30 P.M., Saturday until 1 P.M. Just down the street is a **Star Market** for all your grocery needs.

Azeka Place II

Just across the street from the original Azeka Place, this newer and larger shopping center features **Maui Dive Shop,** a full-service dive shop and activities center; **The Coffee Store,** a great place for a cup of coffee, a light lunch or late-night snack, or to check your email; **Bank of Hawaii,** a full-service bank with ATM machines; and **Roland's Shoes** for everything from slippers to hiking boots. For vitamins, minerals, and supplements try **General Nutrition Center;** head for **Sunglass Hut** for shades; and **Hula Hogs** rents motorcycles, which can be filled at the **gas station** at the corner. Toward the back of the center is **A Pacific Cafe Maui,** one of the finest restaurants in this strip. Started in 1950 as a one-store, mom-and-pop operation, the Azeka Place shopping centers comprise more than 50 shops and make the largest shopping complex in South Maui.

Lipoa Center

As the only major shopping center not on the main drag, Lipoa Center is a hop, skip, and a jump up Lipoa Street, just around the corner from Azeka II. Here you'll find a **First Hawaiian Bank, Kihei Professional Pharmacy, Ohana Physicians,** and **Gold's Gym.** Perhaps more of interest for the traveler are **Hapa's Brew Haus** for music and drink and the **Lipoa Laundry Center,** a clean and modern full-service laundry that's open Mon.–Sat. 8 A.M.–9 P.M., Sunday until 5 P.M.

Kukui Mall

At the Kukui Mall, across from Kalama Park are **Waldenbooks** and the apparel store **Local Mo-**

tion. Tired of the beach, or just need to beat the heat? Stop at the multiscreen **Kukui Mall Theater.** Hungry? Try **The Sweet Spot** ice cream shop or **Tony Roma's** for a full meal of ribs. Across the street at the corner is the **Aloha Marketplace** covered by awnings and trees, where you can shop for jewelry, clothing, carvings, and other touristy gifts.

Kihei Town Center

This small shopping center just south of the Kukui Mall offers a 24-hour **Foodland, Products of Hawaii Too** for gifts, the **Rainbow Attic** consignment shop, and several eateries, including the affordable **Chuck's Steak House** and **Aroma d'Italia.** Check the **Activity Outlet** for tours and activities.

Kihei Kalama Village Market Place

Look for this bargain-filled, semi-open-air warren of stalls under a tall roof superstructure at 1945 S. Kihei Rd., offering everything from tourist trinkets to fine art; clothes, crafts, and jewelry predominate. Around the periphery are other shops. Among them you will find **Serendipity,** a small, well-appointed boutique that displays imported items mainly from Malaysia and Brazil; **Clementines** for one-of-a-kind women's clothing; **Gallery and Gifts** with Hawaiian-made items; and the **Treasure Cove** next door with its arts, crafts, crystals, gifts, jewelry, and sculpture. Out front at the corner, **Maui Discount Activity World** will set you up with your day's activity. If you're hungry, you'll find all sorts of food options here as well: **Bubba Burgers, Bad Ass Coffee, Alexander's** for sandwiches, **Sala Thai Cuisine, Pita Paradies,** and **Cafe Navaca** for real Mexican eats.

The **Kalama Village Bakery** in the rear offers the best in baked goods. Stop in for a freshly baked loaf of homestyle bread to take home, or sit out back on the patio deck and eat your pastry there. Whole cakes and tortes are available, and birthday and wedding cakes can be ordered.

Dolphin Shopping Plaza

This small, two-story plaza at 2395 S. Kihei Rd. includes **Pro Photo lab** and **Tropical Disk** music store. **Boss Frogs** rents snorkel gear at reasonable prices, and **Hawaiian Island Cruis-**ers provides rental bikes and mopeds. Upstairs are **Kihei Medical Services** and **Kihei Chiropractic.**

Kamaole Beach Center

A small group of shops between Dolphin and Rainbow plazas, this center has **Honolulu Surf Company** clothing store for local fashions, **Aloha Books** for used books to read by the pool, and **Snorkel Bob's** to pick up snorkel gear for the week. You can get groceries and deli food at **Hawaiian Moon's Natural Foods,** or come by after a warm day on the beach for a cool beer at **The Sports Page Grill and Bar.**

Rainbow Mall

Yet another small mall just up the road at 2439 S. Kihei Rd. features **South Pacific Kayaks and Outfitters** and **Aloha Destination's Auntie Snorkel** for the sales and rental of snorkel gear, boogie boards, kayaks, and camping and hiking gear for very reasonable prices. Other shops in the mall are the **Maui Custom Beach Wear,** where you can buy off the rack or have a bikini made especially for you; **Premiere Video,** for evening entertainment if you're staying in a condo; and **Topaz,** a fine jewelry and watch store. **Rainbow Discount Liquor** is at the back of the mall. For food, **da Kitchen** serves up filling plate lunches and **The Thai Chef Restaurant** provides ethnic cuisine.

Kamaole Shopping Center

Last in this quick succession of small malls is the slightly larger Kamaole Shopping Center at 2463 S. Kihei Rd. This mall has several inexpensive eateries and various clothing, souvenir, and sundries stores. From its two floors of shops you can buy baubles, beads, and some nicer pieces at **Unique Jewels;** and groceries, liquor, and souvenirs at **Whalers General Store. Lappert's Aloha Ice Cream** sells island-made delights and fat-free yogurt. Also in the center is a **Maui Dive Shop,** a complete diving and water sports store offering rentals, swimwear, snorkels, cruises, and windsurfing lessons, and an **Ocean Activities Center** booth for booking water sports. **Postal Plus,** open Mon.–Sat. 9 A.M.–6 P.M., can take care of your stamp, box, and shipping needs, and offers computer connections.

MAUI

Kai Nani Village Plaza

This small cluster of shops sits at the south end of Kihei. Aside from the Greek Bistro, Kihei Prime Rib and Seafood House, KKO, and Annie's Deli eateries, you'll find the **Sunshine Mart** for sundries and food items.

Farmers' Markets

A small farmers' market is held in the parking lot in front of Suda's Store at 61 S. Kihei Rd., every Monday, Wednesday, and Friday 1:30–5:30 P.M. Besides fresh produce, stalls sell shells, T-shirts, and knickknacks of all kinds. There is also a farmers' market in the Longs Shopping Center every Saturday 8 A.M.–noon.

Food and Liquor Stores

Foodland, at Kihei Town Center (open 24 hours), and **Star Market,** 1310 S. Kihei Rd., are full-service supermarkets with a complete liquor, wine, and beer section.

Hawaiian Moon's Natural Foods at the Kamaole Beach Center is a small but full-service natural health food store. Stop in for bulk foods, groceries, herbs, organic fruits and vegetables, vitamins, minerals and supplements, juices, bottled water, soy drinks, and beer. There's even a freezer case for ice cream and a deli case for take-out sandwiches.

At the very south end of Kihei at Mana Kai Maui Resort, try **Keawakapu General Store** for groceries, sundries, snacks, and spirits. Open daily 7 A.M.–9 P.M.

Kihei Wine and Spirits, located in the Kihei Commercial Center at 300 Ohukai Rd., open weekdays 10 A.M.–6 P.M. and Saturday until 5 P.M., has a fantastic selection of wine and beer, a great little gourmet food section, and a variety of cigars. Even the most discriminating yuppie will find all necessary items for a first-class picnic at Kihei Wine and Spirits. Near the south end of town, **Rainbow Discount Liquor** at the Rainbow Mall has a good selection of liquor, imported beers, and wine.

RECREATION

Golf

The only golf course in Kihei is **Elleair Maui Golf Course,** 808/874-0777. Along Pi'ilani High-

way, it has gotten a shot in the arm and been tuned up significantly over the past few years with its new owners. Young and open, the course offers good views over town to the coast. Greens fees run a respectable $59.

Dive Shops and Marine Rentals

The **Maui Dive Shop**, 808/879-3388, has a main store and office at 1455 S. Kihei Rd. near the Star Market in Kihei, offering a full range of equipment, lessons, and rentals. Open daily 7:30 A.M.–9 P.M., it is one of the oldest and most respected companies in the business. Another location along this coast is at the Kamaole Shopping Center, 808/879-1533.

Dive and Sea Maui, 1975 S. Kihei Rd., 808/874-1952, is also a full-service dive shop offering dives, certification, air refills, equipment rentals, and dive/snorkel boat trips to Molokini Crater.

Snorkel Bob's, 808/879-7449, website: www.snorkelbob.com, is easy to spot at the Kamaole Beach Center. Bob has some of the best deals around for some very good gear. The weekly prices can't be beat at $9–29 for snorkel gear and about the same for boogie boards (day rentals available too). You also get snorkel tips and the semi-soggy underwater humor of Snorkel Bob.

Auntie Snorkel, 808/879-6263, at the Rainbow Mall and operated by Melissa and Mike McCoy, rents snorkel gear, along with boogie boards, beach chairs, and even ice chests. These are among the lowest prices in the area.

Also at the Rainbow Mall, **South Pacific Kayaks and Outfitters,** 808/875-4848 or 800/776-2326, website: www.mauikayak.com, open daily 8 A.M.–4 P.M., offers half a dozen kayak options from a half-day introductory trip for $59 to an advanced explorer tour along the remote South Maui coastline for $89. The longer tours include lunch, and all have plenty of snorkeling opportunities as you glide in and out of tiny bays fashioned from jutting lava rock fingers. South Pacific Kayaks offers rentals of single kayaks at $30 and double kayaks at $40, per day. For those who love the land more, several hiking trips can also be arranged.

Beach Sports Rentals, 808/249-7873, next to Suda's Store at the north end of Kihei, rents snorkel gear, boogie boards, surf boards, and all sorts of beach gear for competitive prices. They will deliver and pick up.

SERVICES AND INFORMATION

Medical

For minor medical emergencies try: Urgent Care Maui/Kihei Physicians, 1325 S. Kihei Rd., Suite 103, 808/879-7781, where doctors, a clinical lab, and X-rays are available 6 A.M.–midnight daily; Kihei-Wailea Medical Center, 41 E. Lipoa St., 808/874-8100, with physicians, a pharmacy, physical therapy, and a clinical laboratory, open Mon.–Fri. 8 A.M.–8 P.M., Saturday and Sunday until 5 P.M.; Kihei Clinic and Wailea Medical Service, 2349 S. Kihei Rd., 808/879-1440, open Mon.–Fri. 8 A.M.–7 P.M., Saturday until 6 P.M., and Sunday and holidays 9 A.M.–2 P.M. Chiropractic services are available at the Chiropractic Clinic of Kihei, 808/879-7246, 1847 S. Kihei Rd., which specializes in non-force techniques, and Kihei Chiropractic Center, 808/879-0638, at the Dolphin Plaza. There's also Kihei Acupuncture Clinic, 808/874-0544, run by Dr. Nancy Macauley, specializing in gentle needling techniques and offering a full selection of Chinese herbs.

Banks

There are several branch banks in Kihei: **Bank of Hawaii,** Azeka Place II, 808/879-5844; **First Hawaiian Bank,** Lipoa Center, 808/875-0055; **American Savings Bank,** Longs Center, 808/879-1977; and **Hawaii National Bank,** 1325 S. Kihei Rd., 808/879-8877.

Postal

The main **post office** in Kihei is at Azeka Place, 1254 S. Kihei Rd., 800/275-8777.

Mail Boxes Etc. at Longs Shopping Center, open weekdays 8 A.M.–6 P.M., Saturday 9 A.M.–5 P.M., Sunday 10 A.M.–3 P.M., offers fax services, copies, notary services, and packing and shipping. With basically the same services, **Postal Plus** is at the Kamaole Shopping Center.

Information

The member organization South Maui Destination Association has some information about South Maui: hotels, B&Bs, restaurants, activities, shopping, services, real estate, and more. Contact the association at: 101 N. Kihei Rd., Suite 4, Kihei, HI 96753, 808/874-9400, fax 808/879-1283, website: www.kihei.org, email: info@southmauivacations.com. Its *Maui Guide* can be seen online at www.mauiguide.com.

Laundry

Lipoa Laundry Center, 41 E. Lipoa, 808/875-9266, is also a full-service laundry and dry cleaning establishment. Open 8 A.M.–8 P.M. with shorter hours on Sunday.

Library

The **Kihei Public library,** 808/875-6833, is across the street from the Kihei Town Center. It has variable daily hours.

Transportation

The **South Maui Shopping Express** connects Kihei with Wailea and Makena to the south and west to the Maui Ocean Center in Ma'alaea, from where you can transfer to the West Maui Shopping Express if you want to continue on to Lahaina and Ka'anapali. The shopping express runs daily 6 A.M.–10:30 P.M. Fares are $2 point to point, $5 for a one-day pass for the section Makena to Ma'alaea, and $10 for a one-day pass for the whole system.

WAILEA

Wailea (Waters of Lea) isn't for the hoi polloi. It's a deluxe resort area custom-tailored to fit the egos of the upper class like a pair of silk pajamas. This section of South Maui was barren and bleak until Alexander and Baldwin Co. decided to landscape it into an emerald 1,450-acre oasis of world-class golf courses and destination resorts. Every street light, palm tree, and potted plant is a deliberate accessory to the decor so that the overall feeling is soothing, pleasant, and in good taste. To dispel any notions of snootiness, the five sparkling beaches that front the resorts were left open to the public and even improved with better access, parking areas, showers, and picnic tables—a gracious gesture even if state law does require open access! You'll know when you leave Kihei and enter Wailea. The green, quiet, and wide tree-lined avenues give the impression of an upper-class residential suburb. Wailea is where you come when quality is the most important aspect of your vacation. The brilliant five-star resorts are first-rate architecturally, and the grounds are exquisite botanical jewel boxes.

Aside from the beaches, the two main attractions in Wailea are the fantastic golf and tennis opportunities. Three magnificent golf courses have been laid out on Haleakala's lower slopes, all open to the public. Tennis is great at the Wailea Tennis Club and many of the hotels and condos have their own championship courts.

To keep up the quality, a few years ago Wailea Shopping Village was completely razed and built again in a fashion that would outdo even the fine upscale shops of Ka'anapali and Kapalua on the west end of the island.

Running along the water from one end of Wailea to the other is a 1.5-mile long beach walk. This walkway cuts across all properties from the Renaissance Wailea Beach Resort to the Kea Lani Hotel, and like the beaches, it's open to the public. Used often in the early morning or late afternoon for exercise by walkers and joggers, it's a convenient way to get to the next beach or to the next resort for lunch or dinner. Even if you're not staying in the area, take a stroll down the path and have a look at the wonderfully landscaped gardens and resort properties here.

You can get to Wailea by coming straight down South Kihei Road through the strip of condos and shopping centers. To miss this area and make better time, take Pi'ilani Highway, Route 31. This route takes you up on the hillside, where you have some nice views out over the water and can watch Kihei slip by in a blur below. Where this highway stops, Wailea Ike Drive snakes down the hill to Wailea Alanui Drive and deposits you in the "heart" of Wailea at the new shopping center.

Onward and Backward

If you turn your back to the sea and look toward Haleakala, you'll see its cool, green forests and peak wreathed in mysterious clouds. You'll want to run right over, but you can't get there from here! Outrageous as it may sound, you have to double back 18 miles to Kahului and then head up Route 37 for another 20 miles just to get to the exact same spot on Route 37 that you can easily see. On the map there's a neat little private 4WD road that connects the Wailea-Makena area with Upcountry in a mere three-mile stretch, but it's never open because it traverses private ranchland! If this situation is ever rectified, you'll be able to travel easily to the Tedeschi Winery and continue on the "wrong way" to Hana, or go left to Kula and Upcountry. For now, however, happy motoring!

BEACHES

If you're not fortunate enough to be staying in Wailea, the best reason for coming here is its beaches. These little beauties are crescent moons of white sand that usually end in lava outcroppings on both ends. This makes for sheltered swimmable waters and good snorkeling and scuba. Many of the hotel guests in Wailea seem to hang around the hotel pools, maybe peacocking or just trying to get their money's worth, so the beaches are surprisingly uncrowded. The following beaches are listed from north to south.

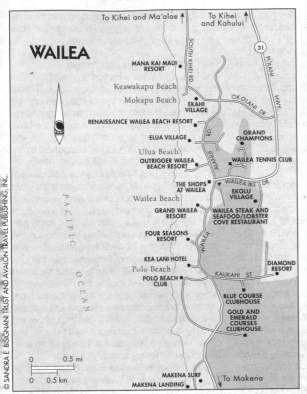

and protected waters are perfect for swimming. There's good snorkeling at the outcropping separating the beaches, or swim out to the first reef just in front of the rocks for excellent snorkeling.

Wailea Beach

The Outrigger, Grand Wailea, and Four Seasons resorts front this beach. One-half mile past The Shops at Wailea, turn right onto a clearly marked access road between the Grand Wailea and the Four Seasons; at the end of the drive there's good parking, as well as showers and toilets. A short but wide beach of white sand, Wailea offers good swimming and bodysurfing, but the snorkeling is only fair.

Polo Beach

Follow Wailea Alanui toward Makena. Turn right on Kaukahi Street just past the Kea Lani Hotel and right again at the clearly marked sign near the Polo Beach condo. Here also are paved parking, showers, and toilets. Polo Beach is good for swimming and sunbathing, with few tourists. There's excellent snorkeling in front of the rocks separating Polo from Wailea Beach—tremendous amounts of fish, and one of the easiest spots to get to.

Keawakapu

The first Wailea beach, almost a buffer between Kihei and Wailea, is just past the Mana Kai Resort. Turn left onto Kamala Place, or proceed straight on South Kihei Road until it dead-ends. Plenty of parking at both accesses, but no amenities. Keawakapu is a lovely white-sand beach with a sandy bottom. Good swimming and fair snorkeling. There's also a beginner's dive spot offshore.

Mokapu and Ulua

These two beaches are shoulder to shoulder, separated only by a rock outcropping. Turn right off Wailea Alanui at the first turn past the Renaissance Wailea Beach Resort. The beach is clearly marked, and there's a parking area, showers, and restrooms. Being resort beaches, they're both particularly well-kept. Beautiful white sand

LUXURY RESORTS

Renaissance Wailea Beach Resort

Always a beauty, the Renaissance Wailea, 3550 Wailea Alanui, Wailea, HI 96753, 808/879-4900 or 800/992-4532, fax 808/879-6128, is like a rich red cabernet that has aged superbly. The Renaissance is a superbly appointed resort with attention given to the most minute detail of comfort and luxury. When you enter the main lobby, you're actually on the fifth floor; the ones below terrace down the mountainside to the golden sands of Mokapu Beach. The lobby has original artworks on the walls and a sweeping marble staircase leading down to the Palm Court Restaurant. A bubbling spa fashioned from lava rock is surrounded by vines and flowering trees; another spa contains three little pools and a gurgling fountain, so that while the therapeutic water soothes your muscles, the music of the fountain soothes your nerves. The impeccable grounds have grown into an actual botanical garden. And everywhere there is water, cascading over tiny waterfalls, tumbling in brooks, and reflecting the amazing green canopy in tranquil lagoons.

The white-on-tan rooms are appointed with koa and rattan furniture. Beds are brightened with quilted pillows, and each room is accented with standing lamps, paintings of Hawaiian flora, an entertainment center with VCR and remote-control TV, wall safe, a glass-topped writing desk, even matching *happi* coats for an evening of lounging. Sliding doors lead to a lanai where you can relax or enjoy a quiet in-room meal. The bathrooms are small but adequate, with double marble-topped sinks and a queen-size tub. The hotel features the very private **Mokapu Beach Club,** a detached low-rise wing complete with its own pool and daily continental breakfast, where the hotel's impeccable service rises yet higher with valet service and 24-hour concierge. Room rates are $330 for a terrace view, $380 for a garden view, $430 for an ocean view, and $530 for a room in the Mokapu Beach Club; $40 each additional person over age 18. Suites run $1,000–3,300 for one-bedrooms and $1,450–3,800 for two-bedrooms. Varying rates include a family plan, where children under 18 stay free if they're in their parents' room, and also a variety of golf and tennis packages.

Renaissance Wailea Beach Resort has been acclaimed as a five-diamond resort by the AAA Motor Club for 10 consecutive years. You will enjoy the Palm Court, Hana Gion Japanese, and poolside Maui Onion restaurants, the lobby cocktail lounge, and the Wailea Sunset Luau is held three times weekly. The Renaissance offers valet parking, 24-hour room service, a fitness center, therapeutic massage and body care, a part-day children's program, free daily newspaper, a small shopping arcade, and a concierge desk to book you into every kind of outdoor Maui activity. The most amazing feature about the resort is its feeling of peace and tranquillity. Now part of the Marriott family of hotels.

Outrigger Wailea Beach Resort

The Outrigger Wailea Resort is a class act, and since its $25 million remodel in 2000, it's an even finer place. The entryway has been opened to let more light into the main building and reception area, and other public areas of the hotel have been reconfigured into new lounges and restaurants. The main lobby, supported by gigantic wooden beams, is still inviting with its informal setting, and it frames a wide panorama of the sea and Lana'i floating on the horizon. Walk out onto a stone-tiled portico and below, in a central courtyard ringed by palms, is a series of quiet lily ponds highlighted with red torch ginger and alive with serenading bullfrogs in the evening. Stroll the 22 meticulously landscaped acres and dip into one of the pools, take the kids to the new family pool with its water slide and play areas, or have a look at the Hawaiian fishermen's shrine near the shore. All rooms have been totally remodeled with simple and suitable furnishings and decorations, and throughout the property designs in the carpet, light fixtures, and other decorative features have been taken from Hawaiian mythology and symbolism.

The Outrigger Wailea Resort was the first large hotel property in Wailea. It has roots here. Not only that, but it makes the claim of being the "most Hawaiian hotel in Wailea." From the little touches to the large efforts, many would say that it is so. The hotel has established a position of Director of Hawaiian Culture and runs a Hawaiian cultural program called Ho'olokahi that not only educates the staff about its own Hawaiian heritage but also shares the Hawaiian culture with guests and brings the community to the hotel for cultural exchanges. The Hawaiian cultural program has a varied schedule of activities and workshops presented by knowledgeable Hawaiian elders and teachers. All you need to do to attend is sign up. Some activities are hula demonstrations and contests, lei-making, and ukulele instruction. On Aloha Friday, arts and crafts are displayed and sold and hula is performed in the hotel lobby. The resort also hosts a Hawaiian sailing canoe regatta, which is accompanied by numerous cultural activities and events. In addition, the restaurant Hula Moons is dedicated to Don Blanding, an early enthusiast of Hawaii and Hawaiian culture from the early 20th century, and it proudly displays some of Blanding's personal belongings and mementos of the times.

At least 70 percent of the resort's rooms have ocean views, which in most cases are actually oceanfront. Rooms are coordinated with light pastel tones of green-on-tan and beige. All have a large entertainment center with remote-control TV and small refrigerator. Granite bathrooms are well-proportioned with a full bath and shower, double sinks, and separate dressing area. Doors open to a terra cotta–floored lanai, flushed with sunshine and sea breezes, from where you have a private view of the Lahaina Roads. More amenities include room service, the Mandara Spa, a business center, a row of shops, self-service laundry, and complimentary valet parking in a covered parking lot. For children, the Cowabunga Kids Club fills the day with supervised activities for a nominal fee. For food and entertainment, head to the newly redesigned Hula Moons Restaurant or poolside Kumu Bar and Grill, pop into the new Mele Mele Lounge for a drink or *pu pu* while you chat or watch the sunset, or attend the award-winning lu'au and Polynesian show, "Wailea's Finest Luau." Outings and activities can be arranged at the concierge desk in the lobby. Room rates run $295 for a standard garden room to $495 for a deluxe oceanfront room, suites are available at $545, and the Voyagers Club rooms go for $525; $30 per extra person. Special family plans, room and car, honeymoon, golf, and other packages are available. The Outrigger Wailea Resort is at 3700 Wailea Alanui, Wailea, HI 96753, 808/879-1922 or 800/367-2960, fax 808/874-8331.

Grand Wailea Resort and Spa

A sublime interplay of cascading water, light diffused and brilliant, and the music of natural sound have been entwined with fine art, sculpted landscaping, and brilliant architecture to create the intangible quality of grandeur so apparent at the astounding Grand Wailea Resort and Spa, 3850 Wailea Alanui, Wailea, HI 96753, 808/875-1234 or 800/888-6100, fax 808/874-2411, www.grandwailea.com. On arrival the spume of a thunderous waterfall, misting a heroic sculpture

of the warrior king, Kamehameha, is the tangible spirit of the grand hotel. Inside the towering reception atrium, the water and sculpture interplay continues. Hula dancers both male and female, some with arms outstretched to the sun, others in repose or in a stance of power, are the visual *mele* singing of the ancient times. A mermaid, bronzed, bare-breasted, offers a triton shell of sweet water, and behind, sleek canoes float on a pond of blue. Ahead the glimmering sea, foaming surf, and wind-tossed palms dance to their immortal tune. Left and right, Fernando Botero's sculpted women—enormous, buxom, and seductive—lie in alluring repose.

In the garden, a formal fountain, surrounded by royal palms, is reflected in a rectangular pool inlaid with white and gold tile forming a giant hibiscus. The pool area surrounds a "volcano" and fronts Wailea beach. Here, a canyon river, complete with gentle current, glides you through a series of pools and past small grottoes where you can stop to enjoy a hot tub, swing like Tom Sawyer on a suspended rope, swim up to a bar for your favorite drink, or just slip along until you are deposited in the main pool. Waiting is the world's only water elevator, to lift you to the top again and again. Other meandering waterways and pools dot the property.

If Nero had the health and relaxation resources found at the hotel's Spa Grande, his fiddle playing would have vastly improved and Rome never would have burned. The magic begins as soon as you enter this marble-clad facility, the largest in the state and arguably the best equipped. Dip first into a Japanese *ofuro* that unjangles nerves and soothes muscles. From there, a cold dip to revitalize and then into the termé baths, followed by a cascading waterfall shower or jet rinse. Awaiting you are private massage rooms where you can choose a multitude of different massage, facial, and body treatments. Each room opens to the sea, whose eternal rhythm helps to create complete relaxation.

The Grand Wailea is a huge complex of five separate wings and a tower, with 780 guest rooms. These rooms feature private lanai that look out over the water and flower gardens below, while inside they are sanctuaries of pure luxury. All are appointed in soothing earth tones with complete entertainment centers, mini-fridge and bar, in-room safes, and twice daily maid service.

MAUI

Rates are $410–615 for standard rooms, and $750–1,900 for suites. Guests of the Napua Tower have concierge service and many special amenities. Rooms here run $710, suites $1,800–10,710. Numerous packages are offered.

For the dining and entertainment pleasure of its guests, the Grand Wailea has five restaurants, four bars and lounges, one nightclub, and a lu'au. To make a family visit perfect, **Camp Grande** holds court for children ages 5–12. Run by professionals, both day and night camps feature movies, a preschool playroom, arts and crafts, a computer learning center, video game room, and a kids' restaurant with their own dance floor and soda fountain. For those unfortunate enough to be in Hawaii on business, the hotel's business center is set up to take care of all equipment and service needs. Scuba diving lessons, a catamaran sail, and other water activities and rentals are arranged by an outside concession on hotel property near the beach. Periodic tours of the grounds and hotel art are offered—the Grand Wailea boasts a $30 million collection of art. The garden tour is free and given Thursday at 10 A.M. It starts at the concierge desk; sign up is required. Beginning from the Napua Gallery, the art tour is offered Tuesday and Friday at 10 A.M.; free to hotel guests, but $6.25 for nonguests. And finally, there is a nondenominational **chapel** that's used for weddings (the hotel does about 500 a year), a miniature cathedral with floor-to-ceiling stained-glass windows, as well as exclusive shops and boutiques for your shopping pleasure.

Four Seasons Resort Wailea

AAA five-diamond award winner the Four Seasons, on 15 acres at the south end of Wailea Beach, is oriented to the setting sun and opens itself up to the sweet sea breezes. Casually elegant, the open-air lobby is full of cushy chairs and couches, fountains, flowers, fans, and a grand staircase that glides down to the huge pool at beach level. On the way down, say "hello" to Ricky and Lucy, the hotel parakeets who make their home below the staircase. The pool and the colonnade of lobby pillars above it hint at a Romanesque architectural influence, yet the ambience and colors of the hotel say island natural. Original artwork and reproductions hang throughout the lobby and hallways, while huge fossilized

sea anemones are displayed on lobby tables, and birds and plants bring the outdoors inside. Countless little details make this resort pleasant and special.

The Four Seasons is a study of cream-on-cream, and this color scheme runs throughout the resort, offset by coral, almond, muted greens, and other pastels. Each large room has a bedroom and sitting area, an exceptionally large bath with separate shower and deep tub, a well-stocked wet bar, TV, room safe, and private lanai; 85 percent of the rooms have an ocean view and all have twice-daily room service. While air-conditioning is standard, rooms also have sliding screen doors or louvered French doors and overhead fans. Double rooms and suites are even more spacious, with the addition of a second bathroom and/or a dining area. Rates for the standard rooms run $305 for a mountain view to $595 for a prime ocean view, $80 per extra person. Depending upon the number of bedrooms and location, suites run $575–6,000. Rates on the Club Floor, which includes on-floor check-in, complimentary continental breakfast, afternoon tea, sunset cocktails and hors d'oeuvres, and a personal concierge, run $670–1,270, $150 extra person. The club lounge on this floor also provides books, newspapers, magazines, and board games. Golf, family, room and car, romance, and two-island packages are also available.

Other amenities include three top-notch restaurants, a lobby lounge that has entertainment nightly, five shops, a game room with a fine collection of surfing memorabilia, meeting rooms for conventions, complimentary valet parking, 24-hour room service, and an early-arrival/late-departure lounge where you can relax and enjoy the hotel services, store a small bag, or shower off the grit of travel. In addition, the supervised "Kids for all Seasons" program can keep your little ones ages 5–12 busy for all or part of the day, 9 A.M.–5 P.M., with games and activities. On site are two tennis courts and lawn croquet (for guests only); an expanded health club with exercise machines and a steam room that offers massage and personal training; and organized beach activities. Down by the beach, all beach chairs, cabanas, snorkel equipment (free rental for one hour), boogie boards, and the like are complimentary—added value for guests. These and most hotel amenities are in-

courtyard pool and gardens at the Kea Lani

J.D. BISIGNANI

cluded in the room charge. Although it's not cheap, you get a lot for your money and great service here at 3900 Wailea Alanui, Wailea, HI 96753. For information and reservations, contact the resort at 808/874-8000 or 800/334-6284, fax 808/874-6449, website: www.fourseasons.com.

Kea Lani Hotel

While Aladdin napped and dreamed of high adventure, his genie was at work building a pleasure dome more splendid than the great Khan's Xanadu. The Kea Lani Hotel, 4100 Wailea Alanui, Wailea, HI 96753, 808/875-4100 or 800/882-4100, fax 808/875-1200, website: www.kealani.com, is an alabaster fantasy bazaar where turrets and cupolas cover vaulted and coved ceilings suspended above towering pillars. Enter the central lobby, an open-air court with a bubbling fountain, completely sculpted and gilded; sultan's slippers would be appropriate here to pad around on the mosaic floors. A staircase leads to a tranquil pool area fronting a wide sweep of grass and perpetual blue sea. On the second level is a parlor, formal but comfortable, with giant shoji-like mirrors and sculpted harps and lyres embedded in the walls. Four restaurants and a lounge bar service the food needs of the guests.

Lodging at the Kea Lani is in one-bedroom luxury suites with separate living area priced $305–615, or in opulent two- and three-bedroom villas priced $1,400–1,800, with several room/car, room/meal, and romance packages as options. Enter the suites, very roomy at just under 900 square feet, to find a richly embossed carpet contrasting with white-on-white walls. These units sleep four. Double doors open to the master bedroom. The sitting room, formal but comfy, is appointed with puff-pillow chairs, a queen-size sleeper sofa, entertainment center, marble-topped tables, and a full bar with microwave and coffeemaker. All rooms are air-conditioned, but there are also ceiling fans. The bathroom, marble from floor to ceiling, features an oversize tub, two pedestal sinks, a huge stall shower, and cotton *yukata* for a day of lounging. The bi-level villas, sleeping 6–8, include more of the same but have greater floor space and more bedrooms. They are completely furnished with full and modern kitchens and laundry rooms. Outside each villa in its private courtyard is a plunge pool, slightly heated and perfect for two, and a gas barbecue.

The hotel's pool area is grand, just right for frolicking or for savoring an afternoon siesta. A free-form upper pool, boasting a swim-to bar, and serviced by the Polo Beach Grill, is connected to the lower pool by a 140-foot water slide. The lower area is family oriented with a football-shaped children's pool, but escape is at hand at the casbah pool, inlaid with multi-hued tiles forming an entwined moon and sun around it; adults can shelter in Camelot-like tents providing shade and privacy, or relax in one of two jet spas. Other amenities include a beach activities booth, an activities desk, in-house doctor's office, business center, complimentary fitness center, health and body spa, and a clutch of swank boutiques. The children have their own Keiki Lani children's program, open daily 9 A.M.–3 P.M., where children ages 5–12 are entertained with a mixture of fun and educational activities, and even given lunch.

Destination Resorts Hawaii

This complex is made up of six separate villages scattered along the coast or up around the golf course. Check-in is handled at the Destination Resorts office on the lower level of The Shops at Wailea. High- and low-season rates vary, with high season usually running from mid-December to the end of April. High season rates are quoted; low season rates will be 5–12 percent cheaper. **Ekolu Village,** near the Blue Course, has one- and two-bedroom condo units for $175–255. Also on the golf links, next to Wailea Tennis Club, is **Grand Champions,** with one-, two-, and three-bedroom units for $185–340. At the entrance to Wailea and the least expensive of the oceanfront properties, **Ekahi Village** has studio, one- and two-bedroom condos for $165–390. Tucked between the Renaissance and Outrigger, **Elua Village** fronts Ulua Beach and has one-, two-, and three-bedroom condos ranging $270–710. Right on Polo Beach is **Polo Beach Club,** the only high-rise condo building in the bunch. Rates here are $295–475 for one- or two-bedroom units. The newest and perhaps the most exclusive is **Makena Surf,** on a private section of coast a short way down the road toward Makena. Here one-, two-, and three-bedroom units run $360–700. All rates are based on double occupancy, with children 16 years and younger free; an additional $20 is assessed for each extra adult. Special golf, tennis, car, and romance packages are available. There is a three- to five-night minimum stay, 10–14 nights during the Christmas–New Year's season. The fifth or seventh night is free depending upon the village. An additional resort fee may be charged on check-in with each reservation. All units are plush and fully furnished, with kitchens, daily housekeeping service, a swimming pool or pools, barbecue grills, and some with tennis courts on the premises. All have gated entrances. The

beach, two golf courses, and additional tennis courts are nearby. Amenities include concierge services; reservations for dinners and all air, land, and sea activities; and arrangements for rental vehicles and water equipment. For information and reservations, contact the complex at 808/879-1595 or 800/367-5246, fax 808/874-3554, website: www.destinationresortshi.com.

Diamond Resort

Formerly a members-only resort, this condo property is now open to all but gets plenty of Japanese visitors. The Diamond Resort, 555 Kaukahi St., Wailea, HI 96753, 808/874-0500 or 800/800-0720, fax 808/874-8778, website: www.diamondresort.com, sits high above the Wailea Blue Golf Course and has a wonderful view over the ocean. The slate roof and stone exterior on the round portion of the main building make a wonderful first impression, and the pools and stream that cascade down between the buildings create a restful feeling. Let the resort's two restaurants fill your belly and the spa soothe your muscles. The spa features Japanese *ofuro,* Scandinavian saunas, and hot tubs. The 72 large, air-conditioned, one-bedroom guest suites have ocean, partial-ocean, or garden views and come with kitchenettes, TV and VCRs, and lanai. Rates run $200–340 a night, with numerous packages available, and this includes daily maid service and complimentary spa use.

FOOD

At the Renaissance

The **Palm Court** is the main dining room at the Renaissance, a first-rate restaurant. Walk though the lobby and look over the rail to the partially open-air restaurant below. The Palm Court is open for breakfast 6–11 A.M. and for dinner nightly from 5:30 P.M. Breakfast is Mediterranean à la carte or American buffet. The menu offers a different buffet every night featuring cuisines ranging from prime rib to seafood to Pacific Rim, all $32–35.

The **Sunset Terrace** in the lobby is a delightful perch on which to have a drink and survey the grounds and beach below. Every evening brings a dramatic torch-lighting ceremony. The drums reverberate and the liquid melancholy of the conch trumpet sends a call for meditation at day's end. Drinks include the full complement of island specialties, and you can order wonderful gourmet-quality *pu pu* while listening to the sweet sounds of island music.

Maui Onion is a convenient snack-type restaurant at poolside that's open 11 A.M.–6 P.M. for light lunches. Burgers, sandwiches, salads, smoothies, and Maui onion rings, the specialty, are on the limited menu. Prices are reasonable, especially if you don't want to budge from your lounge chair.

Last but not least, **Hana Gion** offers Kyoto-style Japanese food daily except Wednesday 6–9 P.M. in a small and intimate restaurant off the lobby. The focus here is on *teppan yaki* and sushi, but the à la carte menu is an option. Not cheap, but memorable.

Outrigger

Serving contemporary Hawaiian cuisine is **Hula Moons Restaurant,** the Outrigger's main dining establishment. Open daily for breakfast, lunch and dinner, this casual indoor/outdoor restaurant has been moved one floor up from the garden level. The name Hula Moons derives from the writings of Don Blanding, Hawaii's poet laureate, who arrived by steamship in 1924, dead broke, and remained for more than 40 years, all the while singing the island's praises. A few of the poet's personal belongings are still displayed—all whispering of the time when Hawaii was a distant land where only the rich and famous came to escape. Nice nostalgic touch. Open 10 A.M.–9 P.M., the **Kumu Bar and Grill** is a poolside eatery that serves light lunches and more substantial evening fare, accompanied by nightly music and hula. Newly created on the lobby level, **Mele Mele Lounge** serves tropical drinks and *pu pu* 11 A.M.–11 P.M., and serves as a place to relax, ponder your next outing, or just watch the sun set into the water beyond the garden. For the little ones, the **Wailele Snack Bar** is next to the kids' activity pool and serves a children's menu 10 A.M.–4 P.M., with lots of goodies that are easy and fun to eat.

Grand Wailea

The resort has an eclectic mix of restaurants, all landscaped around the central theme of water, art, and flowers, offering cuisine catering to all tastes and appetites. **The Grand Dining Room Maui** has perhaps the best seat in the house, overlooking the gardens and the sea. Open for breakfast only—both a daily buffet and à la carte menus are offered. A fun and informal restaurant more reasonably priced is the open-air **Bistro Molokini.** A mix of Italy and Hawaii, with a dash of the health conscious, menu items include wood-fired pizza, light sandwiches, and grilled seafood dinners. Open 11:30 A.M.–9:30 P.M.

Open daily 5:30 A.M.–9 P.M., **Cafe Kula** specializes in casual terrace dining. Here the freshest fruits, organic vegetables, and whole grains provide the foundation for most dishes. Enjoy salads and sandwiches, antipasto and pizza, fruits, pastries, and desserts. Some menu items are homemade granola at $5, grilled ahi filet for $13, and Maui Upcountry antipasto salad at $9.

Humuhumunukunukuapua'a is a thatched-roof Polynesian restaurant afloat on its own lagoon complete with 2,000 varieties of tropical fish in a huge aquarium. The specialties prepared at the Humuhumu come from throughout the Pacific. *Pu pu*— like prawn satay or crispy lobster shrimp cakes are great to nibble on while enjoying a special exotic drink. Entrées are delightful with offerings like pan-seared munchong or *paniolo* center-cut rib-eye steak. Delectable but not cheap; entrées in the $22–32 range. Open daily 5:30–10 P.M. for dinner only.

Perhaps the most elegant restaurant is **Kincha,** serving superb Japanese cuisine. Enter over stepping stones past a replica of a golden tea kettle used by Toyotomi Hideyoshi, revered as both a great warrior and a master of the *chanoyu,* the tea ceremony. Follow the stones past stone lanterns that light your way over a humpbacked bridge. Inside a raised *tatami* area awaits with sushi chefs ready to perform their magic, and private rooms are perfect for a very refined full meal. Sushi and sashimi are prominent on the menu. Entrées are Japanese favorites like *hotategai,* a broiled sea scallop, sake broiled salmon, and tempura, with prices from $26 on up. Open Thurs.–Mon., 5:30–9:30 P.M. only.

Four Seasons

At the Four Seasons Resort, the elegant **Seasons** restaurant is an experience in fine dining, consistently garnering the AAA four-diamond rating. With table linen, crystal, classical music,

MAUI

and jackets required for men, the Seasons is elegant, but not stuffy. The decor is teal and weathered bamboo, the windows open to let in sea breezes and moonlight, and the island cuisine is offered in a "homelike" presentation. Emphasis is on fresh island seafood. Selected appetizers are seared foie gras and ahi *poke,* while entrées might be sautéed *onaga,* wild pheasant with truffle, or Keahole lobster meunière. Expect entrées in the $35–42 range. Open for dinner only Tues.–Sat. 6–9:30 P.M.; live music and dancing until 10:30. Reservations are recommended and proper dress required.

The casual **Pacific Grill** restaurant combines a large selection of foods from the Orient and the West. The breakfast buffet is a long-established special, but an à la carte menu is also available. For dinner, some entrées are cooked in view of the guests. Pacific edge entrée specialties include steamed ehu Oriental style at $27 and mango-lime hulihuli chicken for $25. At the Pacific Grill, alohawear and activewear are the norm.

Ferraro's at Seaside serves as two distinct restaurants. For lunch, 11:30 A.M.–3 P.M., dine on healthy light fare, mostly seafood and grilled items. *Pu pu* and drinks are served 3–5 P.M. As Italian as Italian can be, Ferraro's opens at 6 P.M. and throws in Italian music for free. Start with an antipasti like deep-fried mozzarella and olives in tomato sauce for $9, and move on to tagliolini, a dish of clams, rock shrimp, and roasted bell peppers, for $25, grilled lamb chops with eggplant and zucchini gratin for $29, or parmesan and porcini crusted beef tenderloin for $30. Set almost on the water, Ferraro's is a great place to watch the sunset.

Kea Lani

An elegant breakfast at the Kea Lani happens at the **Kea Lani Restaurant**, 808/879-7224, where you can order à la carte or dive into the full-scale buffet 6:30–11 A.M. For a casual lunch or early dinner, with outdoor poolside seating 11 A.M.–6 P.M., try the **Polo Beach Grill and Bar** for a light salad, sandwich, or kiawe-grilled burger. If you're in the pool during these hours, you can swim up to the bar for a cool-down drink. For casual dining any time of the day, visit **Cafe Ciao,** rich with the smell of espresso, where the shelves hold homemade jellies, jams, chutney, pepper-

corn ketchup, and Italian olives. Choose fresh-baked bread, pastries, or a spicy focaccia from the bakery, pesto salad or a sandwich from the deli, or sit down for a meal at the trattoria where you'll find hot and cold appetizers, a selection of entrées, and pizza in the evening. The fine dining restaurant at the Kea Lani is **Nick's Fishmarket**, which produces Hawaiian regional cuisine with an emphasis on fish and seafood. A selection of entrées includes blackened salmon with Cajun spices, bouillabaisse with saffron, kiawe-broiled ahi with cracked pepper and bacon, and swordfish with sundried tomatoes, onions, garlic, and gorgonzola cheese. Expect entrées to cost $25–35, and quality to match. Open 5:30–10 P.M., dress code, reservations highly recommended.

Diamond Resort

The two resort restaurants are the **Taiko** and the **Le Gunji.** Taiko serves breakfast, lunch, and dinner and is open 7–10 A.M., 11 A.M.–1:45 P.M., and 5:30–9 P.M. The day starts with a Japanese- or Western-style breakfast for $13; lunch includes sandwiches and burgers, or Japanese soba, udon, or other traditional dishes for less than $12. Dinner entrées, like teriyaki chicken and lobster daiyaki, run $20–36; a whole range of sushi is also available. Le Gunji has limited seating at 6 P.M. and 8 P.M. only; reservations are a necessity and a dress code is enforced. Choose from five set menus, ranging $45–70. Food is a unique blend of French cuisine prepared in a Japanese *teppan yaki* style. Call 808/874-0500 for reservations.

An independent establishment, the **Bella Luna,** 808/879-8255, offers casual and light Italian food evenings only 5:30–8:30 P.M., except Sunday.

Golf Ball Soup

The following restaurants are along the golf links in the area, except for Joe's, which is at the Wailea Tennis Club. **Wailea Steak and Seafood,** 808/879-2875, on the 15th fairway of the Wailea Blue Course up from The Shops at Wailea, does dinner. Its name indicates the type of food the restaurant does best. For an appetizer, try coconut crusted shrimp or clam chowder. Fish might be basil herb salmon or King crab legs and meat a rack of lamb, prime rib, or filet mignon. Expect entrées in the $24–32 range. The sunset dinner special is served 5–6 P.M.; the portions are slightly smaller and run about $5 less.

Across the walk from the Wailea Steak and Seafood and open daily 5:30–10 P.M., the **Lobster Cove Restaurant,** 808/879-6677, is a seafood restaurant that shares space with **Harry's Sushi Bar.** Appetizers include garlic clams for $10.95, sweet and sour crispy shrimp at $11.95, and lobster cakes for $11.95. These would go well with the rock shrimp Caesar salad at $7.95. Entrées, limited but wonderful, might be seafood penne pasta for $21.95, spiny lobster and shrimp for $39.95, fresh island fish at market price, or a filet mignon at $29. Choose from an adequate wine list for a bottle to accompany your meal. You can order *pu pu* or make a meal from the offerings at Harry's. The choices of sushi are numerous and run $3.75–7 apiece, and are double that for a plate of sashimi. Also consider such items as California rolls or bowls of noodles.

A little up the hill and across the road at the Wailea Tennis Club is **Joe's Bar and Grill,** 808/875-7767. Open for dinner every evening 5:30–10 P.M., Joe's serves large and tasty portions of honest American, home-style comfort food in a relaxing atmosphere. Joe's is directly above the tennis courts in a wood-floored, open-beamed room, and cool breezes waft through the sliding glass partitions. Chief schmoozer Joe Gannon is the other half to Haliimaile General Store restaurant's chef Beverly Gannon. While the ambience and lighting set a welcome mood, the real treat is the food. Grilled quesadillas and Joe's gazpacho come first, with other appetizers and salads. Entrées include center-cut pork chop, herb-marinated New York steak, and Joe's famous meatloaf, one of the best sellers; all range $17–30. You know this is a family affair as Joe's daughter makes the mouthwatering desserts. The bar has a full range of beers and can make any mixed drink that you desire. Eat at Joe's, and have food the way you wish your mother used to make it.

The **SeaWatch** restaurant, 808/875-8080, at the Emerald Golf Course clubhouse, looks out over the fairway, but the most outstanding feature of its location is the view over Molokini and Kaho'olawe. The SeaWatch serves Hawaiian regional cuisine, and many selections are prepared over a kiawe-wood grill. Breakfast and lunch are served 8 A.M.–3 P.M. and are mostly egg and other grill items, or salads and sandwiches. A light grill menu is offered until 10 P.M. Dinner, served 5:30–10 P.M., is more refined, focusing on well-balanced flavors and ingredients. Start with crispy seared ahi with Tobiko caviar or a macadamia nut–crusted brie with pineapple relish. A sweet Kula organic green salad might complements your main entrée, which could be a crispy duckling confit, citrus ponzu pork chop, or miso-glazed tiger prawns. Fresh fish, prepared with a mango chutney macadamia crust or kiawe grilled, is always a fine choice. Entrées run $18–29. The wait people are attentive, the service is professional, and dinner is enhanced by classical piano accompaniment.

ENTERTAINMENT

Lu'au

Wailea has two lu'au that have been favorites for guests for years. At the Renaissance, the **Wailea Sunset Lu'au** shows Tuesday, Thursday, and Saturday from 5:30 P.M. An open bar accompanies the island-style foods that includes *poi, lomi lomi* salmon, and kalua pig. Entertainment is Polynesian review of hula and drumming that ends in a fiery knife dance. Adult tickets run $65, kids 5–12 are $30. If you don't go away full and with a smile on your face, it's your own fault. Call 808/879-4900 for reservations.

Wailea's Finest Luau is performed at oceanside by the Outrigger resort every Monday, Tuesday, Thursday, and Friday 5–8 P.M. An *imu* ceremony and torchlighting ceremony kick off the affairs. A sumptuous buffet dinner of Hawaiian favorites and hula show follow, and the night is finished by an enthralling fire knife dancer. Adults pay $65, children 6–12 are $29. To reserve, call 808/879-1922.

Music

If you haven't had enough fun on the Wailea beaches during the day, you can show off your best dance steps at the **Game at the Bar** nightclub at the Grand Wailea. This venue hops to the spin of a DJ every Wed.–Sat. 9 P.M.–1 A.M. Easy listening music is performed every evening at the **Sunset Terrace** lounge on the lobby level of the Renaissance Resort overlooking the gardens, and all hotels provide some venue for soft Hawaiian music, often with a little hula show included, like the **Kumu Bar** at the Outrigger Wailea, **Botero Lounge** at the Grand Wailea, or the lobby lounge at the Four Seasons.

RECREATION

Golf and Tennis

The 54 links to the Wailea golf course should not disappoint anyone. Studied and demanding, each offers its own challenges plus the beauty of the surrounding area. At more than 7,000 yards, the Gold Course demands attention to natural and man-made obstacles and design. It's consistently rated one of the top courses in the state. Sharing a clubhouse, the Emerald Course is the most compact but perhaps provides the most stunning scenery. Much tamer, the oldest of the three, and ranging the farthest, the Blue Course meanders like a lazy brook through the surrounding condominiums. Greens fees run between $90–145, club rentals $35, and the driving range $6; lessons also available. For tee times, call 808/875-7450.

Aside from its award-winning golf courses, Wailea Resort sports an 11-court tennis facility, with one championship court that can seat nearly 1,000 fans. Court fees run $25 an hour for resort guests and $30 for nonguests. Private lessons, clinics, and round robins can be arranged and equipment rented. For information or courts times, call 808/879-1958.

SHOPPING

The Shops at Wailea

Each major hotel in the resort has an arcade of shops for quick and easy purchases, but the real shopping opportunity in Wailea is at The Shops at Wailea, an upscale center with some 60 sophisticated stores. International retailers like **Loius Vuitton** and **Cartier** are here as are local and national firms like **Banana Republic, Bally, Reyns** and **Martin & MacArthur.** Clothing stores make up bulk of the shops, but five jewelry shops, eight art galleries, camera shops, and sundries stores have also found a place here. Head to **Island Camera** or **Wolf Camera** for all your photographic needs. **Activity Warehouse** can set you up with island excursions, and check at **ABC Stores** for that suntan lotion that you inadvertently left at home. Choose from the whole array of art displayed at **Lahaina Galleries, Dolphin Gallery,** and **Ki'i Glass Gallery** for a memento to take home. **Longhi's,** from Lahaina, has opened a fine-dining restaurant here, and **Lappert's** is the place to head for a sweet ice cream treat. Other restaurants include **Tommy Bahama's Tropical Cafe, Cafe Acropole, Wailea Bar and Grill,** and **Ruth's Chris Steak House. Destination Resorts,** the management company for a majority of the condo units in Wailea, has its reservations office on the lower level.

SERVICES AND INFORMATION

There are no banks or post offices in Wailea. Ask for help from your hotel front desk, or use facilities up the road in Kihei.

The **Wailea Shuttle** is a complimentary jitney that stops at all major hotels and condos, The Shops at Wailea, golf clubhouses, and tennis courts in Wailea about every 30 minutes. It operates 6:30 A.M.–8 P.M. Be sure to check with the driver about the last pickup times if you are out in the evening. With a little walking, this is a great way to hop from one beach to the next. For information on the schedule and stops, call 808/879-2828.

MAKENA

Just a skip south down the road is Makena Beach, but it's a world away from Wailea. This was a hippie enclave during the '60s and early '70s, and the freewheeling spirit of the times is still partially evident in the area even though Makena is becoming more refined, sophisticated, and available to visitors, but mostly it's mellow. For one thing, "Little Makena" is a famous (unofficial) clothing-optional beach, but so what. You can skinny-dip in Connecticut. The police come in and sweep the area now and again, and they've been known to arrest nude sunbathers on Little Makena to make the point that Makena "ain't free no more." Rip-offs can be a problem, so lock your car, hide your camera, and don't leave anything of value. Be careful of the *kiawe* thorns when you park; they'll puncture a tire like a nail. What's really important is that Makena is *the last* pristine coastal stretch in this part of Maui that hasn't succumbed to undue

development . . . yet. The Maui Prince Hotel and its adjacent golf course and tennis courts make up the 1,600-acre Makena Resort. Carved from land that was used for generations to graze cattle, this resort is as yet much less developed than Wailea up the road but has great potential for expansion.

Aside from the sundries shop at the Maui Prince Hotel, there's nothing in the way of amenities past Wailea, so stock up on all supplies. In fact, there's nowhere to get *anything* past the hotel except for the lunch wagons that are usually parked across from the state park entrance. The road south of the Maui Prince Hotel to La Pérouse Bay is by and large fairly good with a decent surface. It does, however, narrow down to almost a single lane in spots, particularly where it slides past small coves. Drive carefully and defensively.

Makena Beach is magnificent for bodysurf-

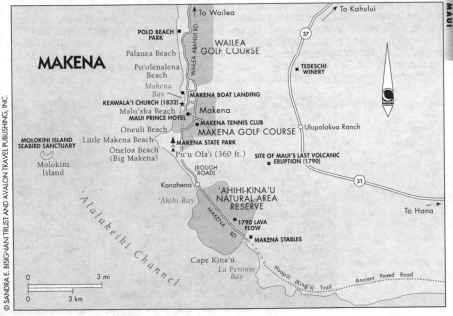

MAUI

© SANDRA E. BISIG-VAN TRUST AND AVALON TRAVEL PUBLISHING, INC.

ing if you have experience, and for swimming, but only when the sea is calm. Whales frequent the area and come quite close to shore during the season. Turtles waddled onto Makena to lay their eggs in the warm sand until early in the 1900s, but too many people gathered the eggs and the turtles scrambled away forever. The sunsets from **Red Hill** (Pu'u Ola'i), the cinder cone separating the big Makena beach from Oneuli Beach, are among the best on Maui; you can watch the sun sink down between Lana'i and West Maui. The silhouettes of pastel and gleaming colors are awe-inspiring. Oranges, russets, and every shade of purple reflect off the clouds that are caught here. Makena attracts all kinds: gawkers, burn-outs, adventurers, tourists, free spirits, and a lot of locals. It won't last long, so go and have a look now!

Keawala'i Church

In Makena, you'll pass this Congregational Church, established in 1832. The present stone structure was erected in 1855 and restored in 1952. Services are held every Sunday at 9:30 A.M. and 5 P.M., and many of the hymns and part of the sermon are still delivered in Hawaiian. Notice the three-foot-thick walls and the gravestones, many with a ceramic picture of the deceased. A parking lot, restrooms, and showers are across the road for the beach access, which is just down the road. Take Honoiki Road from the main highway, or come down the old coast road

from Polo Beach past Makena Boat Landing. The church is almost at the road's dead-end.

Small Beaches

You'll pass by the local **Palauea** and **Po'olenalena** beaches, via the coastal Old Makena Road, as you head toward Makena. There is no development here yet, no amenities, and usually few people, but good swimming and white sloping sands. **Nahuna (Five Graves) Point** is just more than a mile past Polo. An old graveyard marks the entrance. Not good for swimming but great for scuba because of deep underwater caves. Snorkelers can enjoy this area, too. A short distance farther on is the **Makena Boat Landing** (water, restrooms, showers), a launch site for kayakers and scuba divers. Makena Landing was a bustling port in the mid-1800s and a principal point for shipping goods and cattle from this end of the island to other majorisland seaports. **Oneuli,** on the north side of Red Hill, actually has a salt-and-pepper beach, with a tinge of red from the dirt of the hill. Turn down a rough dirt road for a third of a mile. Not good for swimming, but good diving, unofficial camping, and shore fishing. Open 9 A.M.–6 P.M.; no amenities and not many people. Signs warn you not to climb the hill—also from the Big Beach side—but obvious trails lead to the top and over its sides. The Maui Prince fronts **Malu'aka Beach.** There is public access from the end of the road near Keawala'i

Keawala'i Church, Makena

ROBERT NILSEN

Church and from the end of a dead-end road just past the resort, which swings back toward the Prince Resort.

Makena State Park
A few minutes past the Maui Prince Hotel, look for numerous *kaukau* wagons on the left where you might pick up a snack before turning right onto the park access road. Negotiate the excessive speed bumps for a few hundred yards to the parking lot and a few portable toilets; a second beach access is a few hundred yards farther on. This is **Oneloa Beach**, generally called **Big Beach** or **Makena Beach,** a nice long golden strand of fine sand that's open 5 A.M.–9 P.M. daily. Right leads you to **Pu'u Ola'i** (Earthquake Hill), a 360-foot cinder cone. When you cross over the point from Big Makena Beach you'll be on **Little Makena,** a favorite clothing-optional beach for locals and tourists alike. You'll know that you're on the right beach by the bare bums. Both beaches are excellent for swimming (beware of currents in winter), bodysurfing, and superb snorkeling in front of the hill (sometimes called Red Hill because of its color), yet there is not much shade at either. With families and clothed sunbathers moving in (especially on weekends), Little Makena is no longer so "remote" or isolated. The beginning of the end may be in sight, although there is a movement loosely organized to retain this small sanctuary as a place for those who still wish to swim in the buff.

'Ahihi-Kina'u Natural Reserve
Look for the sign four miles past Polo Beach. Even this far down toward the end of the road—or perhaps because of it—this stretch of the coast is becoming a bit more populated and fancy homes are popping up here and there. The jutting thumb of lava is **Cape Kina'u,** part of Maui's last lava flow, which occurred in 1790. Here you'll find a narrow beach, the small community of Kanahena, and a desolate, tortured lava flow. Within the reserve, several walking trails, one to a natural aquarium pool, start at pullouts along the road and lead to the water. Please stay on established paths and wear sturdy hiking shoes or boots. Dolphins often play off this point and whales can be seen near shore during winter months. Aside from the lava fields, 'Ahihi-Kina'u is also an underwater reserve, so

the scuba and snorkeling are first-rate. The best way to proceed is along the reef toward the left, or along the reef to the right if you enter at La Pérouse Bay. Beware not to step on the many spiny urchins in the shallow water. If you do, vinegar or urine will help with the stinging.

La Pérouse Bay
On the far side of Cape Kina'u is La Pérouse Bay, named after the French navigator Jean de François La Pérouse, first Westerner to land on Maui in May 1786. The bay is good for snorkelers and divers. The public road ends at the entrance to La Pérouse Bay, but with a 4WD you can get a distance down the rough track from here for good shore fishing and unofficial camping. If you walk farther around to the south you'll come across a string of pocket-size beaches, some with pebbles, others with sand. The currents can be tricky along here, so be careful.

Past the bay are remnants of the **Hoapili (King's) Trail,** still hikeable for perhaps five miles. This trail leads over smooth stepping stones that were at one time trudged by royal tax collectors. Many ancient house sites, *heiau,* canoe sheds, and other tangible remains are strewn throughout this archaeological district. Stay on the trail and leave everything as you find it! Spur trails lead down to the sea, including an overview of Cape Hanamanioa and its Coast Guard lighthouse. The trail eventually ends at private land. It could easily be a good day's hike exploring out this way, and remember that there is no help available. Bring a hat and plenty of water, water, and more water.

ACCOMMODATIONS AND FOOD

Maui Prince Hotel
A gleaming wing-shaped building, understated and almost stark on the outside, the Maui Prince Hotel, 5400 Makena Alanui, Makena, HI 96753, 808/874-1111 or 800/321-6248, fax 808/879-8763, is a fabulous destination resort that opens into an enormous central courtyard, one of the most beautiful in Hawaii. Japanese in its architecture and its sense of beauty, the courtyard is a protected haven of cascading waters, black lava rock, stone lanterns, breeze-tossed palms, and raked Zen-like gardens.

MAUI

Lean over the hardwood rails of the balconies on each floor and soak in the visual pleasure of the landscape below, where from these balconies cascade flowers and ferns in sympathetic mimicry of Maui's waterfalls.

All rooms have an alcove door so that you can open your front door yet still have privacy and allow the breeze to pass through. Oceanview and oceanfront rooms ranging $330–470 are beautifully accentuated in earth tones and light pastels. One-bedroom suites, priced $650–1,600, feature a giant living room, three lanai, a large-screen TV and VCR, and white terry cloth robes for lounging. The master bedroom has its own TV, listening center, and king-size bed. A nonsmoking wing is also available. The bathrooms have a separate commode and a separate shower and tub. The Prince also offers the very reasonable Prince Special that includes an ocean-view room, midsize rental car, and buffet breakfast for two priced only $275 per night per couple; other honeymoon, golf, tennis, and car packages are also available. For your food and entertainment needs, the Prince has three restaurants at the hotel and one at the golf clubhouse.

The Maui Prince faces fantastic, secluded Malu'aka Beach, almost like a little bay, with two points of lava marking it as a safe spot for swimming and snorkeling. Sea turtles live on the south point and come up on the beach to nest and lay their eggs. To the left you can see Pu'u Ola'i, a red cinder cone that marks Makena. The pool area is made up of two circular pools, one for adults, the other a wading pool for kids, two whirlpools, cabanas, and a poolside snack bar. There's volleyball, croquet, six plexi-pave tennis courts with a pro on the staff, and the 36 holes of the Makena Golf Course, which are the main athletic attraction of the Prince. The concierge desk offers complimentary activities, including a snorkel and scuba introduction. For the little ones, the Prince Kid's Club children's program can be arranged for healthy and supervised morning and/or afternoon activities. For the big people, see what the complimentary fitness center and spa can do for you. The boat *Kai Kanani* arrives each morning and will take you snorkeling to Molokini or arrange other activities throughout the island.

The Makena Resort **shuttle** runs on an "on demand" basis for resort guests only; it can take you to and fetch you from the Makena golf course and tennis courts, and all facilities in the Wailea resort. Arrange your ride through the hotel concierge.

The Prince has three restaurants. The fanciest restaurant is the **Prince Court,** featuring fine dining for dinner only 6–9 P.M., except for the truly exceptional Sunday champagne brunch, which is served 9 A.M.–1:30 P.M. The evening fare is Hawaiian regional cuisine and then some. Start with appetizers like kalua dusk lumpia and Kona lobster cake, or soups and salads that include five onion herb bisque and grilled portabello mushroom salad. From the grill, entrées include Hawaiian fresh catch *lau lau,* peppercorn-crusted loin of venison, and pan-roasted pork tenderloin, most for $22–30. In addition, Friday night brings a prime rib and seafood buffet for $38, and the Sunday brunch runs $36. The room is subdued and elegant, highlighted with snow-white tablecloths and sparkling crystal. The view is serene facing the courtyard or dramatic looking out to sea.

Hakone is a Japanese restaurant and sushi bar with all chefs from Japan. It serves complete dinners like *sukiyaki, isaribi,* and *shabu shabu* for under $35, and it also serves sushi and sashimi, plus a traditional *kaiseki* dinners for $58. A special Monday night dinner buffet is offered at $42 where you have your choice from a panoply of delightful dishes. In keeping with the tradition of Japan, the room is subdued and simple, with white shoji screens counterpointed by dark open beams. The floor is black slate atop packed sand, a style from old Japan.

The main dining room, serving breakfast and lunch, is the more casual and affordable **Cafe Kiowai.** On the ground level, it opens to the courtyard and fishponds. Breakfast brings griddle items and eggs, while you can get salads, sandwiches, wraps, and pizza for lunch. For now, food and accommodations in Makena mean the Maui Prince. The only exception is the **Makena Club House** restaurant at the golf course, which serves *pu pu* and grilled items for lunch for under $11.

For evening entertainment in Makena, the only option is the **Molokini Lounge.**

RECREATION

As the Maui Prince Hotel is a destination resort, on-site recreation possibilities include the beach, beach activities booth, a sailing catamaran, and the swimming pool. Golf at **Makena Golf Course** and tennis at **Makena Tennis Club** are just across the road and offer world-class courts and links. The golf course offers 36 holes; greens fees run $95–145, with twilight rounds cheaper. The six-court tennis club has two lighted courts for night play. Lessons, matches, and rentals are handled at the pro shop. Court fees run $18 an hour for resort guests and $22 for nonguests.

Makena Stables offers trail rides through this dry remote region at its location near the end of the road at La Pérouse Bay. Rides range $110–175, and you must be at least 13 years old and no more than 205 pounds. Call 808/879-0244 for the different rides available.

Loading from the beach in front of the hotel, the *Kai Kanani* sailing catamaran takes passengers to Molokini (the shortest route) for a half day of fun, food, and snorkeling. The ship runs 7–11:30 A.M. Tues.–Sat. for $69 per person.

HAWAII STATE ARCHIVES

UPCOUNTRY

Upcountry is much more than a geographical area to the people who live there: it's a way of life, a frame of mind. You can see Upcountry from anywhere on Maui by lifting your gaze to the slopes of Haleakala. There are no actual boundaries, but this area is usually considered as running from Makawao in the north all the way around to Kahikinui Ranch in the south, and from below the cloud cover down to about the 1,500-foot level. It swathes the western slope of Haleakala like a large, green floral bib patterned by pasturelands and festooned with wild and cultivated flowers. In this rich soil and cool-to-moderate temperatures, cattle ranching and truck farming thrive. Up here, *paniolo* ride herd on the range of the enormous 35,000-acre Haleakala Ranch, spread mostly around Makawao, and the smaller but still sizable 23,000 acres of the Ulupalakua Ranch, which *is* the hills above Wailea and Makena.

While Makawao retains some of its real cowboy town image, it has become more sophisti-cated, with some exclusive shops, fine dining restaurants, art galleries, and alternative healing practitioners. Pukalani, the largest town and expanding residential area, is a way station for gas and supplies, and is pineapple country. Kula is Maui's flower basket. This area is one enormous garden producing brilliant blooms and hearty vegetables. Polipoli Spring State Recreation Area is a forgotten wonderland of tall forests, a homogenized stand of trees from around the world. Tedeschi Winery in the south adds a classy touch to Upcountry—a place where you can taste wine and view the winemaking process. There are plenty of commercial greenhouses and flower farms to visit all over Upcountry, but the best activity is a free Sunday drive along the mountain roads and farm lanes, just soaking in the scenery. The purple mists of mountain jacaranda and the heady fragrance of eucalyptus encircling a mountain pasture manicured by herds of cattle portray the soul of Upcountry.

MAKAWAO

Makawao is proud of itself; it's not *like* a cowboy town, it *is* a cowboy town. Depending on the translation that you consult, Makawao means "Eye of the Dawn" or "Forest Beginning." Both are appropriate. Surrounding lowland fields of cane and pineapples give way to upland pastures rimmed with tall forests, as Haleakala's morning sun shoots lasers of light through the town. Makawao was settled late in the 1800s by Portuguese immigrants who started raising cattle on the upland slopes. It loped along as a *paniolo* town until World War II, when it received an infusion of life from a nearby military base below Kokomo. After the war it settled back down and became a sleepy village again, where as many horses were tethered on the main street as cars were parked. The majority of its false-front, one-story buildings are a half-century old, but their prototype is strictly "Dodge City, 1850." During the 1950s and '60s, Makawao started to decline into a bunch of worn-out old buildings. It earned a reputation for drinking, fighting, and cavorting cowboys, and for a period was derisively called "Macho-wao."

In the 1970s it began to revive. It had plenty to be proud of and a good history to fall back on. Makawao is *the* last real *paniolo* town on Maui and, with Kamuela on the Big Island, is one of the last two in the entire state.

The Oskie Rice Arena hosts the largest and most successful rodeo in Hawaii. Happening at the same time, the Paniolo Parade is a marvel of homespun humor, *aloha,* and an old-fashioned good time, when many people ride their horses to town, leaving them to graze in a public corral. They do business at stores operated by the same families for 50 years or more. Though many of the dry goods are country-oriented, a new breed of merchant has come to town. You can buy a wood stove, art glass, Oriental medicine, homemade baked goods, designer jeans, contemporary painting, and espresso coffee all on one street. At its eateries you can have fresh fish, a steamy bowl of saimin, Italian pasta, plate lunch, or a Mexican quesadilla. Artists of all mediums have found Makawao and the surrounding area fertile ground for their work, and the town has become a hotbed of alternative healing practitioners. Look on any bulletin board in town and you'll see a dozen fliers advertising formulas for better life, better health, reawakening of the spirit, Oriental health therapies, and new-age, new-health concepts.

Everyone, old-timers and newcomers alike, agrees that Makawao must be preserved, and they work together. They know that tourism is a financial lifeline, but shudder at the thought of

MAUI

upcountry rangeland

ROBERT NILSEN

UPCOUNTRY

Uaoa Bay

Honopou Point

Pa'ia Bay

HANA

Kui'aha

Waipi'o Bay

Huelo Point

36

Pa'ia

Ha'iku

HWY.

Ulumalu

Huelo

Kailua

'O'opuola Point

Nua'ailua Bay

Pauwal Point

To Kahului

UNION CHURCH

HOLY ROSARY CHURCH

390

398

365

Hali'imaile

BALDWIN AVE.

Kokomo

HUI NO'EAU

360

Ke'anae

37

Makawao

OSKIE RICE ARENA

Wailua

Pukalani

365

PUKALANI COUNTRY CLUB

POLO FIELD

PIIHOLO RD.

OLINDA RD.

370

37

377

OMA'OPIO RD.

HALEAKALA HWY.

Waihou Springs Trail

OLINDA COUNTRY COTTAGES

Honomanu Stream

Ke'anae Valley

W. Wailua Nui

ENCHANTING FLORAL GARDENS

KIMO RD.

Kula

Pelehu

KULA LODGE

SUNRISE PROTEA FARM

PULEHUIKI DR.

KAMEHAMEIKI DR.

HALEAKALA CRATER RD.

HOSMER GROVE

HOLY GHOST CHURCH

Waiakoa

UNIV. OF HA AGR. STA.

378

PARK HEADQUARTERS

Leleiwi Overlook

Ka'akaulua Gulch

COPP RD.

KEKAULIKE AVE.

RICE PARK

KULA BOTANICAL GARDENS

Kalahaku Overlook

HALEAKALA

Waiohuli Gulch

WAIPOLI RD.

Kaipoioi Gulch

Waiakoa Loop Trail

Pu'u 'Ula'ula (Red Hill) (10,023 ft.)

NATIONAL

Keokea

Boundary Trail

Upper Waiakoo Trail

Skyline Trail

PARK

DR. SUN YAT-SEN MEMORIAL PARK

KULA HWY.

THOMPSON RD.

POLIPOLI SPRING STATE RECREATION AREA

SILVERCLOUD UPCOUNTRY GUEST RANCH

37

Pu'u Keokea

MAKEE SUGAR MILL (1878)

Ulupalakua Ranch

Pu'u Makua (5,276 ft.)

Polipoli (6,472 ft.)

TEDESCHI WINERY

Pu'u Mahoe (2,660 ft.)

PI'ILANI

Manawainui Gulch

Kahululu Gulch

Kepuni Gulch

Kaupo

PI'ILANI HWY.

KAHIKINUI RANCH

31 HWY.

Huakini Bay

Mamalu Bay

Kamanawai Point

0   3 mi

0   3 km

Makawao becoming an Upcountry Lahaina. It shouldn't. It's far enough off the track to keep the average tourist away, but easy enough to reach and definitely interesting enough to make the side trip worthwhile.

The main artery to Makawao is through Pa'ia as you travel Route 36 (Hana Highway). In Pa'ia turn right onto Baldwin Avenue. From there it's about six miles to Makawao. You can also branch off Route 37 (Haleakala Highway) in Pukalani onto Route 365 (some maps show it as Route 40), which will also lead you to the town. The back way reaches Makawao by branching off Route 36 through Ulumalu and Kokomo. Just where Route 36 turns into Route 360, a road branches inland. This is Kaupakalua Road, Route 365. Take it through backcountry Maui, where horses graze around neat little houses and Haleakala looms above. At the first Y intersection there's a general store where you bear left. Pass a large junkyard and continue to Kokomo. Notice the mixture of old and new houses—Maui's past and future in microcosm. Here, the neat little banana plantation on the outskirts of the diminutive town says it all. Pass St. Joseph's Catholic Church and you've arrived through Makawao's back door. This is an excellent off-track route to take on your way to or from Hana. Alternately, you can also come up Kokomo Road, Route 398, through Ha'iku from the Hana Highway.

Upcountry Events

Makawao has put on a tremendous rodeo season every year since 1955. Most meets are sponsored by the Maui Roping Club. They start in the spring and culminate in the massive **Makawao Rodeo,** held over three days just before July 4. These events attract the best cowboys from around the state, with substantial prize money as reward. Both males and females try their luck in separate groupings. The numerous competitions include barrel racing; breakaway, team, and calf roping; and bull and bronco riding. The organization of the event is headed by longtime resident Brendan Balthazar, who welcomes everyone to participate with only one rule: "Have fun, but maintain safety." General admission is $10; call 808/572-2076 for information. Every year the rodeo is accompanied by the fun-loving Paniolo Parade.

MAKAWAO

To Ha'iku

365

ST. JOSEPH'S
CATHOLIC CHURCH

To Pa'ia

390

BREWSTER RD.

KAUPAKALUA RD.

KITADA'S
KAU KAU

DAVID WARREN
GALLERY

MASTER
TOUCH
GALLERY

MAKAWAO
STEAKHOUSE

BALDWIN AVE.

GOODIES

MAUI
HANDS

TROPO

RODEO
GENERAL
STORE

CAFE O
LEI

COLLECTIONS

HI HEARTH AND
LEISURE

S. REEVE GALLERY

UPCOUNTRY
LEGENDS

VIEWPOINTS
GALLERY

NAKUI ST.

DRAGON'S DEN

COURTYARD
CAFE

OLA'S MAKAWAO

KOMODA'S

POLLI'S MEXICAN
RESTAURANT

HOT ISLAND
GLASS

LITTLE TIBET ETHNIC
JEWELRY STORE

CASANOVA ITALIAN
RESTAURANT AND DELI

MIRACLES
BOOKERY

GALLERY MAUI

OLINDA RD.

DOWN TO EARTH
NATURAL FOODS

RANDY JAY BRAUN
GALLERY

POST OFFICE

PARKING

PIIANA ST.

ELAN VITAL'S ART
WORLD

STOPWATCH BAR
AND GRILL

GAS STATION

365

AI ST.

MAUI PL.

KEHAU PL.

390

MAKAWAO AVE.

MAUI SCHOOL OF
THERAPEUTIC MASSAGE

SCALE NOT AVAILABLE

EDDIE TAM
CENTER

To Pukalani

MAUI

MOON

The daylong **Upcountry Fair** happens at the Eddie Tam Center in mid-June. It's a real county event, where you'll find all sorts of craft displays, games, competitions, and food booths, as well as the 4-H judging and animal auction.

Polo

Upcountry plays polo. The Maui Polo Club sponsors matches in the spring and fall. From April to June, matches are held at the Haleakala Ranch polo arena, about one mile above Pukalani and just off Highway 377. The September through November matches take place above Makawao at the Olinda outdoor polo field. All matches are held on Sundays at about 1 P.M., and admission runs $3 per person. For further information and directions during the polo season, call 808/877-7744 or check the Maui Polo Club website at www.mauipolo.com.

SIGHTS

A few minutes south of town along Baldwin Avenue is the **Hui No'eau Visual Arts Center,** a local organization that features traditional and modern arts housed at Kaluanui, a mansion built in 1917 by the Baldwin family on their 10-acre estate. The member artisans and craftspeople produce everything from ceramics to *lau hala* weaving, drawings to sculpture. The old house is home to the center office, gift gallery, and periodic shows, while the former stable and carriage house have become studios. Throughout the year classes, lectures, and exhibits are offered, along with an annual Christmas Fair featuring their creations. One of the best features of visiting Hui No'eau (Club of Skills) is the resplendent mansion itself. Built in a neo-Spanish motif with red-tiled roof and light pink stucco exterior, Kaluanui sits among the manicured grounds that feature a reflection pond just in front of the portico. At 2841 Baldwin Ave., the gift shop and gallery are open Tues.–Sun. 10 A.M.–4 P.M. (a $2 donation is suggested), and you'll often find someone around working in the studios. For information, contact the center at 808/572-6560 or visit its website at www.maui.net/~hui.

Just south of there, at mile marker 5 along Baldwin Ave., Hali'imaile Road turns to the south and leads to the small pineapple town of **Hali'imaile.** This tiny community, a combination of old plantation town and new development, offers a wonderful restaurant, the Haliimaile General Store—well worth driving the distance for—and a well-shaded county park that features picnic tables, ball fields, and lighted tennis courts.

Take Olinda Road north out of town. All along it custom-designed houses have been built. Look for **Po'okela Church,** a coral-block structure built in 1843. **Seabury Hall,** a private boarding school for grades 6–12, sits among trees above Makawao. In May, it hosts a day-long arts and crafts fair, with entertainment, food, games, and auctions. An annual event for nearly 30 years, it has become the best-known and best-subscribed crafts fair on the island. In four miles you pass **Rainbow Acres,** 808/573-8313. Open Tues.–Thurs. 9 A.M.–4 P.M., this nursery specializes in cactus and succulents. Then shortly comes the Maui Bird Conservation Center—not open to the public. Near the top of Olinda turn left onto Pi'iholo Road, which loops back down. Along it is **Aloha O Ka Aina,** 808/572-9440, a nursery specializing in ferns. Open Wed.–Sat. 9 A.M.–4 P.M.

Hiking Trail

The **Waihou Spring Trail** is the easiest hiking access in the area, but in reality it's little more than a good walk. The trailhead is just below the intersection of Olinda Road and Pi'iholo Road. Running entirely through a forest canopy of pine and eucalyptus, this trail, flat and wide for most of its length, only narrows when it drops steeply down into a ravine as it gets close to the spring—now virtually always dry. The trail starts out by running through a experimental tree-growing area. Shortly you come to a T-intersection. Going right, you keep to the main trail; left brings you in a half-mile loop back to the main trail. From an overlook on the main path, the trail zigzags down to the boulder-strewn bottom of a narrow ravine, a cool and quiet sanctuary. Usually dry, a dripping curtain of water must cover the back wall during the rains. Neither strenuous or lengthy, this one-mile hike is nonetheless good exercise.

PRACTICALITIES

Accommodations

Built in 1924, the plantation house **Hale Ho'okipa Inn,** 32 Pakani Place, has been turned into a lovely B&B. Not a modern rendition, this well-loved place has real world, lived-in charm, and is filled with comfortable period-style and antique furniture and furnishings and artwork by Hawaiian artists. Three rooms have their own private baths, while the two-bedroom suite shares a bath and has use of the big country kitchen. A continental breakfast is served each morning in the rooms. Rates run $85–105 a night for the rooms and $140–155 for the suite. The inn is within walking distance of town, up above the Eddie Tam Center. For information and reservations, contact the inn at 808/572-6698, fax 808/573-2580, or visit its website at www.maui-bed-and-breakfast-inn.com. Send email to mauibnb@maui.net.

MAUI

Olinda Country Cottages and Inn, 808/572-1453 or 800/932-3435, website: www.mauibn-bcottages.com, email: olinda@mauibnbcottages.com, is up above Makawao past mile marker 11, at 2660 Olinda Road. On an old pro-tea farm at about 4,000 feet of elevation, and backed up against Haleakala Ranch, this B&B is secluded, spacious, and homey. The main house has two rooms upstairs and a suite below, with two separate cottages for plenty of privacy. The two bedrooms in the house have a private en-trance and share a sitting room, and each has a private bath. Breakfast is provided each morning for these rooms. The downstairs suite and indi-vidual cottages are more like small homes with all the amenities. As each has a kitchen, breakfast is served only the first morning. All have plenty of country-style furnishings and antiques, and the color and design work well. The bedrooms run $120 a night, the suite $130, and the cottages $195–220. The rooms and suite have a two-night minimum, the cottages three. No smoking inside, and no children under eight years old. Highly recommended for quiet and seclusion, yet close enough to get to a fine restaurant in town. With gregarious hosts and good value, the only drawback for some folks might be the windy road leading up to the B&B.

Down near Hali'imaile is **Peace of Mind** va-cation rentals, 1290 Hali'imaile Rd., Makawao, HI 96768, 808/572-5045 or 888/475-5045, web-site: www.maui.net/~pom, email: pom@maui.net. Peace of Mind overlooks the broad pineapple fields of this agricultural region, and from the property you have views of the north coast and the great mountainside sweep of Haleakala. Rooms in the main house are not extravagant but clean and serviceable at $40 single or $45 double. Guests share a bathroom, comfy living room and kitchen, and the outdoor patio. A sep-arate cottage sleeps 1–4, has a bright and effi-cient kitchen, small living room with TV, and a lanai. At $75 a night, it's a bargain. Breakfast is not included as you have full use of the kitchen.

Food

An excellent place to eat is **Polli's Mexican Restaurant,** 808/572-7808, open daily 7 A.M.–10 P.M. The sign, Come In and Eat or We'll Both Starve, greets you at the front. The meals are au-thentic Mexican, using the finest ingredients.

Formerly vegetarian—they'll still prepare any menu item in a vegetarian manner—they use no lard or animal fat in their bean dishes. You can have breakfast entrées for $6–8, a full lunch for under $9, or dinner for $10–16. Margaritas are large and tasty, the cervezas cool and refreshing. Monday night is barbecue night, Tuesday is kids' night. Still down home, still wholesome meals, still a happening place, this is one of Makawao's favorites.

A surprising and delicious dining experience, the best restaurant in town, is found at **Casano-va Italian Restaurant and Deli,** 808/572-0220, across from Polli's at the main intersection of town. The deli is open daily for breakfast and lunch. The interior is utilitarian—a refrigerated case loaded with cold cuts, shelves stocked with Italian delectables and cheeses, and a few tables for eating. Specials are offered, but the best dishes are the fresh-made lasagna, ravioli, and spaghetti, all smothered in different sauces. Many of the best restaurants on Maui order their pasta from Casanova's. Order your meal at the counter. The best place to sit is on the front porch where you can perch above the street and watch Makawao life go by. Upcountry-yup-pie-elegant, Casanova's restaurant occupies the adjoining section of the building, open daily except Sunday for lunch 11:30 A.M.–2 P.M., and nightly for dinner 5:30–11:30 P.M., featuring pizza, pasta, and other fine Italian cuisine. Of course, pasta is the staple, but meat, fish, and poultry en-trées are also popular. While you wait, you can watch the pizza maker toss the dough before putting it in the wood-burning oven. Expect en-trées in the $12–25 range. While the food is as good as the deli fare next door, many come for the music and dancing, which may go until 12:30–1 A.M., live on Friday and Saturday evenings, with a DJ on Wednesday and Sun-day. Having a nightclub atmosphere, a large dance floor, and a first-class sound system, it draws people not only from Upcountry but also from Central and South Maui. Casual attire is fine, but remember, Upcountry gets cool at night, so you might need something to cover your arms and shoulders.

Makawao Steak House, 808/572-8711, near the bottom end of town, is open daily for dinner from 5:30 P.M., with early-bird specials until 6:30. Casual, with wooden tables, salad bar, and good fish selections, dinners run upward to around $25. The steak dishes, and especially the Monday night special prime rib, are the best. The Makawao Steak House has been around a long time and maintains a good, solid reputation. The lounge is open from 5 P.M. until closing.

At 1127 Makawao Ave. you'll find the **Stopwatch Bar & Grill**, 808/572-1380. Open for lunch and dinner, the grill serves burgers and plate lunches along with more substantial steak, fried chicken, and fish entrées, with live entertainment and dancing on Friday and Saturday evenings. Full bar.

Sheltered down a short alley behind the Reeve Gallery is **Café O Lei**, 808/573-9065, which offers simple but filling soups, salads, and sandwiches daily for lunch. Courtyard seating.

Kitada's Kau Kau, 808/572-7241, makes the best saimin on Maui—according to all the locals. It's a town institution, across from the Makawao Steak House in a small plantation-style wood-frame building. Very local, nothing fancy, it's open Mon.–Sat. 6 A.M.–1:30 P.M. The sharp slap of the screen door announces your entry. Order at the counter, then pour yourself a glass of water and take a seat. The saimin is inexpensive, and there are also plate lunches, burgers, and sandwiches that mostly run less than $6.

Komoda's is a general store that has been in business for more than 80 years. It sells a little of everything, but the bakery is renowned far and wide. It's open 7 A.M.–5 P.M. except Wednesday and Sunday, Saturday until 2 P.M. People line up outside to buy their cream buns and homemade cookies—all gone by 9 A.M.

If you need a break from looking at all the art, head to the **Courtyard Cafe**, 808/572-4877, in the courtyard behind Viewpoints Gallery. This little eatery is open Mon.–Sat. 8 A.M.–6 P.M., Sunday 8 A.M.–2 P.M. People come just for the coffee, but you can also get an egg or waffle breakfast, fresh pastries, or hot or cold sandwiches that run mostly $6.50–8.50.

The **Haliimaile General Store**, 808/572-2666, open Mon.–Fri. 11 A.M.–2:30 P.M., and again 5:30–9:30 P.M., with a Sunday brunch 10 A.M.–2:30 P.M., serves elegant gourmet food to anyone lucky enough to find this Upcountry roadhouse. In Hali'imaile village along Hali'imaile Road between Baldwin Avenue and the Haleakala Highway, the restaurant is housed in what was this pineapple town's general store. Climb the steps to a wide veranda and enter to find the vintage utilitarian wood-floored interior transformed into an airy room with tropical fish hung from the ceiling, primitive ceramics and sculptures placed here and there, and original paintings of brilliant colors. It's as if the restaurant is part contemporary boutique and art gallery, and the old grocery shelves are filled with distinctive gift and gourmet food items. Choose a table in the casual front room, perch on a canvas chair at the copper-top bar in front of the open kitchen, or ask for a table in the back room, more formal with dark wood paneling, ceiling fans, track lighting, and floral displays. Master chef Beverly Gannon presents creative "Hawaiian regional cuisine with an American and international twist," while her Irish husband, master schmoozer Joe Gannon, presents an equally magnificent Blarney Stone atmosphere! While the menu changes seasonally, a sampling of what you might expect includes appetizers like the sashimi Napoleon, Asian pear and duck taco, or Bev's crab dip served on boboli bread, all under $14. These are an experience in themselves but serve to prepare you for the main course to come. Entrées include *paniolo* barbecue ribs, coconut seafood curry, aged Midwest beef rib eye, rack of lamb Hunan style, and chili verde enchiladas, ranging $16–24. Save room for a masterful dessert created by pastry chef and daughter Teresa Gannon. Piña colada cheesecake anyone? The food is always healthy and fresh, the portions are plentiful, and the meal won't bust your budget. Whatever your choice, you'll leave with a full belly and a smile on our face. The setting is casual and alohawear is okay, but because of the elevation long sleeves and pants might be in order. The Haliimaile General Store has been reborn, and its spirit lives on in this wonderful restaurant.

Food Markets

Down to Earth Natural Foods, 1169 Makawao Ave., 808/572-1488, open daily 8 A.M.–8 P.M., is a first-rate health food store that originated in Wailuku and later opened a branch here in Makawao. Inside you'll find shelves packed with minerals, vitamins, herbs, spices, and mostly organic fruits and vegetables. Bins hold bulk

MAUI

grains, pastas, honey, and nut butters, while a deli case holds sandwiches and drinks. You can even mix up a salad from the salad bar to take out, or choose a hot entrée from the food bar. At $5.99 a pound, the hot entrées are one of the best bargains in town for a meal. Down to Earth has a philosophy by which it operates, "to promote the living of a healthy lifestyle by eating a natural vegetarian diet; respect for all forms of life; and concern for the environment."

Rodeo General Store, 3661 Baldwin Ave., is a one-stop shop with a wide selection of natural foods, pastries, produce, fresh fish, wines, spirits, and cigars. Open 6:30 A.M.–10 P.M. daily.

Liquor Shack and Deli, 1143 Makawao Ave., 808/572-7775, can provide all the fixings for a lunch, and a full range of liquid refreshments.

In Hali'imaile, **Maui Fresh** is an outlet for Maui Pineapple Company. Available are fresh and canned pineapples and seasonal fruits and vegetables. A small plantation museum offers visitors a snapshot of the pineapple industry and the company operation. Open 10 A.M.–6 P.M. Mon.–Sat., this store is next to the plantation office along Hali'imaile Road.

Art Galleries

The Courtyard of Makawao is a consortium of shops at 3620 Baldwin Ave. near the bottom end of town where you can dine, peruse fine art, collect country crafts, or watch as glassblowers pursue alchemical art. In the reconstructed Makawao Theater building, **Maui Hands,** 808/572-5194, is open daily except Sunday 10 A.M.–6 P.M. This artists' "consignment shop" specializes in Maui-made art and crafts like semiprecious stone necklaces, sterling and gold jewelry, prints, bamboo work, *raku* pottery, primitive basketry, and even some T-shirts. **Viewpoints Gallery,** 808/572-5979, open daily 10 A.M.–6 P.M., is an artists' cooperative specializing in locally created paintings, sculptures, handicrafts, and jewelry. Some of the art displayed includes: oil paintings by Kathleen MacDonald; impressionistic oils by George Allen; the mixed-media art of Joelle Chichebortiche; and the combination pastel and oils by Diana Dorenzo. Most of the artists live in the area, and with enough notice will come to meet you if time permits. This shop is a perfect place to spend an afternoon eyeing the contempo-

rary art scene so vibrant in Upcountry. Every month brings a new exhibit. Outside is a pleasant courtyard, around which are several more shops. Here you will find Bill and Sally Worcester making magic at **Hot Island Glass,** 808/572-4527, open daily 10 A.M.–5 P.M., except Sunday when the shop is open noon–4 P.M. These very talented glassblowers, assisted by their son Michael, turn molten glass into everything from simple paperweights to gorgeous vases. Just line up at their window and watch the artists work. Between the three of them they have won almost every meaningful art award on Maui and in their former home state of Oregon. Incidental pieces run as cheap as $10, but the masterpieces go for several thousand. Don't worry about shipping or packing glass; they're also masters at packing so things don't break on the way home.

For more fine art, painting, pottery, wood sculpture, and more, check out **David Warren Gallery** across from the Courtyard, and visit the **Master Touch Gallery** for fine jewelry. Farther up Baldwin Avenue is the **Sherri Reeve Gallery,** where you'll find the inspiring watercolor florals of the artist. Across the street is **Ola's Makawao,** which displays contemporary American handmade crafts.

While Baldwin Avenue has been the scene of most studios and shops, new businesses have slowly begun to occupy buildings along Makawao Avenue. South of Casanova's is **Gallery Maui,** with a wide selection of art and wood furniture by island artists. Next door at 1156 Makawao Ave. is the **Randy Jay Braun Gallery,** which displays Braun's photo art plus art in other media. A few steps away is **Elan Vital's Art World,** one of the largest galleries in the state, where giant canvases of thick lustrous color swirl in shape and form.

Shopping

Makawao is changing quickly, and nowhere is this more noticeable than in its local shops. The population is now made up of old-guard *paniolo,* yuppies, and alternative people. What a combo! Some unique and fascinating shops here can provide you with distinctive purchases.

When Mimi Merrill opened **Miracles Bookery,** 3682 Baldwin Ave., 808/572-2317, hours Mon.–Sat. 9 A.M.–8 P.M., Sunday 9 A.M.–7 P.M., she put her heart, soul, and all of her resources into the place. Miracles Bookery specializes in books on new-age spiritualism, astrology, Tarot, children's classics, Hawaiiana, poetry, and "pre-loved" books. A different astrologer, palmist, or Tarot reader is "in residence" every day. Miracles also has unique gift items: angels, petroglyph reproductions, candles, puzzles, Native American jewelry, bumper stickers with an attitude, posters, and music of all kinds from spiritual to rock.

At the corner is the tiny **Little Tibet Ethnic Jewelry Store**, open 10 A.M.–5 P.M. Mon.–Sat. for brass and bronze jewelry and religious art and accouterments.

Upcountry Legends, 808/572-3523, open daily 10 A.M.–6 P.M., Sunday 11 A.M.–5 P.M., sells hand-painted silk shirts, ladies apparel, sterling silver jewelry, huggable teddy bears and other stuffed animals, greeting cards, candles, and baskets.

Collections Boutique, 808/572-0781, open daily till 6 P.M., Saturday until 4, imports items from throughout Asia: batik from Bali, clothes from India, silk Hawaiian shirts, jewelry, lotions, cosmetics, accessories, sunglasses, and handicrafts from various countries.

HI Hearth and Leisure, 808/572-4569, has the largest line of wood-burning and gas stoves in Hawaii. That's right, stoves! Nights in the high country can get chilly, and on top of Haleakala downright cold. Here as well are barbecue grills,

fireplaces, chimneys and accessories, a good selection of cutlery, and a few homemade food items.

Listen for tinkling wind chimes to locate **Goodies,** 808/572-0288, open 9:30 A.M.–5:30 P.M., Sunday 10 A.M.–5 P.M., a boutique that looks like a spilled treasure chest. Crystals, silk and cotton casual and elegant clothing, dolls, children's wear, stuffed animals, locally crafted trays, and magic wands fill this shop.

About the only shop in town for men's clothing is **Tropo,** 808/573-0356, where you can find shorts, polo shirts, aloha shirts, and even hats and ties. Owner Avi Kiriaty helps to design the clothing on sale here. Open Mon.–Sat. 10 A.M.–6 P.M., Sunday 11 A.M.–4 P.M.

Down a narrow alley a few steps from the intersection of Baldwin and Makawao Avenues is **The Dragon's Den Herb Store**, 808/572-2424, a shop stuffed full of Chinese herbs and medicines, minerals, crystals, teas, gifts, and books on Eastern healing arts. The **Dragon's Den Healing Center**, 808/572-5267, occupies the same building. Also in the alley is **Grace Health Clinic**, 808/572-6091, which specializes in chiropractic, massage, and traditional Oriental medicine, and half a dozen other health professionals. Check the bulletin board here for medical practices and community events. For other alternative practices, contact **Maui School of Therapeutic Massage,** 808/572-2277, at 1043 Makawao Ave., or **Maui School of Yoga Therapy,** 808/572-1414.

PUKALANI

This way-station town, at the intersection of Routes 37 and 365, is a good place to get gas and supplies for a driving trek through Kula or a trip up Haleakala. It's a rapidly growing community with many new housing developments around its periphery. There are no outstanding cultural or historical sights in Pukalani, but a fine golf course graces its southern edge. Across the street from the major shopping center is a large community park with ball fields, basketball courts, and a great swimming center with an Olympic-size swimming pool.

At the **Pukalani Terrace Center,** the largest shopping mall in Upcountry, are an **Ace Hardware, Foodland** grocery store, **Paradise Video,**

a **Bank of Hawaii** and **American Savings Bank,** both of which have teller machines, a **Maui Medical Group** clinic office, and a **post office.** In the corner of the mall, the full-service **Upcountry Laundry and Dry Cleaning** is open daily 8 A.M.–9 P.M. except Sunday, when it closes at 5 P.M. There is a wide variety of economical eateries here, including a **Subway** sandwich shop, **Royal King's Garden** Chinese restaurant (no MSG), **Mama Son's Barbecue** Korean restaurant, and **Ono Loco Food** mixed-plate shop.

One of the best restaurants in the area is the **Pukalani Country Club Restaurant,** 808/572-1325, open daily 7:30 A.M.–2 P.M. and 5–9 P.M. at the Pukalani Country Club. It has a salad bar and sandwiches but specializes in "local" and Hawaiian foods such as kalua pig and *lau lau* plates at reasonable prices. Most patrons are local people, so you know that they're doing something right.

The only Upcountry golf course on Maui, **Pukalani Country Club,** offers 18 holes of inexpensive golf. In the bargain come spectacular views over the isthmus and up toward Haleakala. Turn south at the Pukalani Terrace Center and follow the road for four or five blocks to reach the golf course.

Farther up the road at the corner of Aewa Place is the **Upcountry Cafe,** 808/572-2395, in a faded pink and gray building. Open daily except Tuesday 6:30 A.M.–3 P.M., Sunday until 1 P.M., and again for dinner Wednesday and Thursday 5:30–8:30 P.M., Friday and Saturday until 9 P.M., the café has brought wholesome and unpretentious dining to Upcountry. Inside, wooden tables, bent-back chairs, a tiled counter, and a black-on-white Holstein motif set the ambience in this American/island standard restaurant. The Upcountry Cafe is a perfect economical breakfast or lunch stop while touring Kula.

Behind the café is **The Grateful Bread,** 808/572-6084, open Mon.–Sat. 7:30 A.M.–4:30 P.M., where everything is baked fresh daily. Here you can choose from mouthwatering breads, pastries, and cakes, plus soups, salads, and sandwiches.

At the intersection of Makawao Avenue is the **Pukalani Superette,** a well-stocked grocery store, especially for this neck of the woods, that's open Mon.–Fri. 6 A.M.–9 P.M. with shorter hours on the weekends.

Down from the superette, going toward Makawao, is a second smaller shopping center, the **Pukalani Square,** where you'll find an **'Ohana Physicians** clinic, **Paradise Pharmacy,** the Maui **Nature Conservancy** office, and a **First Hawaiian Bank.**

At 112 Ho'opalua Dr., not far out of Pukalani on the way toward the lower Kula area, is the **Kula Hula Inn.** This Christian B&B has two rooms in the main house and two separate units. The rooms have their own bathrooms, and one has a separate entrance and lanai. They rent for $85–95. For $115 you can get the three-room Suite Plumeria. The larger and more private two-bedroom Hula Moon Cottage with full bath and kitchen goes for $130. An extra $15 per person is added to the bill when there are more than two people in a unit. Breakfast is included daily except Sunday for all except the cottage, where it's optional for an additional charge. This is a secure gated property surrounded by a large lawn, so it's good for kids. For information, contact the inn at 808/572-9351 or 888/485-2466, fax 808/572-1132. Visit the inn's website at www.kulahula.com and send email to kulahula@maui.net.

KULA

Kula (Open Country) could easily provide all of the ingredients for a full-course meal fit for a king. Its bounty is staggering: vegetables to make a splendid chef's salad, beef for the entrée, flowers to brighten the spirits, and wine to set the mood. Up here, soil, sun, and moisture create a garden symphony. Sweet Maui onions, cabbages, potatoes, tomatoes, apples, pineapples, lettuce, herbs, asparagus, and artichokes grow with abandon. Herefords and Black Angus graze in knee-deep fields of sweet green grass. Flowers are everywhere: beds of proteas, camellias, carnations, roses, hydrangeas, and blooming peach and tangerine trees dot the countryside like daubs from van Gogh's brush. As you gain the heights along Kula's lanes, you look

back on West Maui and a perfect view of the isthmus. You'll also enjoy wide-open spaces and rolling green hills fringed with trees like a lion's mane. Above, the sky changes from brooding gray to blazing blue, then back again. During light rainy afternoons, when the sun streams in from the west, you could easily spot a rainbow on the hillside, as if sprouting from the rich green pastureland. Kula is a different Maui—quiet and serene.

Getting There
The fastest way is the route to Haleakala. Take Route 37 through Pukalani, turn onto Route 377, and when you see Kimo Road on your left and right, you're in Kula country. Following Route

ROBERT NILSEN

protea

37 a few miles past Pukalani gets you to the same area, only lower on the mountain slope. If you have the time, take the following scenic route. Back in Kahului start on Route 36 (Hana Highway), but shortly after you cross Dairy Road look for a sign pointing to Pulehu-Oma'opio Road on your right. Take it! You'll wade through acres of sugarcane, and in six miles these two roads will split. You can take either because at the top they both deposit you in the middle of things to see. Once the roads fork, you'll pass some excellent examples of flower and truck farms. The cooperative vacuum cooling plant is in this neighborhood, a place where many farmers store their produce. Cross Route 37 (Kula Highway) and turn onto Lower Kula Road. Explore this road for a while before heading straight uphill via (Lower) Kimo Drive, Pulehuiki Drive, Kamehameiki Road, or Copp Road, which bring you through some absolutely beautiful countryside to Route 377.

SIGHTS

Botanical Gardens

Follow Route 377 south—it turns into Kekaulike Avenue after Haleakala Crater Road, Route 378, turns up the mountain. Look for the **Kula Botanical Gardens** on your left just before the road meets again with Route 37. These privately owned gardens, 808/878-1715, are open daily 9 A.M.–4 P.M.; be sure to start by 3 P.M. to give yourself enough time for a thorough walk-around. Admission is $5, children 6–12 are $1. Here are nearly six acres of identified tropical and semi-tropical plants on a self-guided tour. There is also a stream that runs through the property, a koi pond, and small aviary. Some of the 2,000 different varieties of plants include protea, orchid, bromiliad, fuchsia, and ferns, and the native koa, *kukui,* and sandalwood. First opened to the public in 1971, the gardens are educational and will give names to many flowers and plants that you've observed around the island. It makes for a relaxing afternoon. A wonderful spot. Enter through the gift shop.

Across from mile marker 10 on the Kula Highway, the privately owned **Enchanting Floral Gardens** is newer and more commercial than Kula Botanical Garden, yet worthy of a look. Its eight acres are neatly laid out, with many of the 1,500 varieties of flowers and plants identified. Stroll down the path and be captivated by the abundance. Plan on about an hour to see the entire lot. Open 9 A.M.–5 P.M. daily, entrance $5; 808/878-2531.

The **University of Hawai'i Agriculture Experimental Station** maintains 20 acres of flowers and other agricultural plants that change with the seasons. On Mauna Place above Route 37; open Mon.–Thurs. 7 A.M.–3:30 P.M. Check in with the station manager at the office—closed during the lunch hour. A self-guided tour map

MAUI

is available at the office. While there are experimental plots for other ornamental flowers, vegetables, and fruits, the main focus of this facility is hybridized protea for commercial production. Perhaps best from October through May, it's more a stop for scholarly interest as you can find more showy plants at the botanical gardens and flower shops nearby.

Flower Shops

Upcountry Harvest sits next door to the Kula Lodge and is open daily 8 A.M.–5:30 P.M., 808/878-2824 or 800/575-6470. Don't miss seeing the amazing fresh and dried flowers and arrangements. Here you can purchase a wide range of protea and other tropical flowers that can be shipped back home. Live or dried, these flowers are fantastic. Gift boxes starting at $38 are well worth the price. The salespeople are friendly and informative, and it's educational just to visit.

The **Sunrise Protea Farm** and gift shop is less than half a mile up Haleakala Crater Road. The shop sells gift items, local Maui produce, homemade sweets, sandwiches, and fruit juices. In the flower shop you'll find fresh and dried flowers and arrangements that can be sent anywhere in the country; fresh bouquets from $40, dried arrangements from $30. An easy stop on the way back from Haleakala. Open weekdays 8 A.M.–4 P.M., weekends 7 A.M.–5 P.M.; 808/876-0200 or 800/222-2797 for phone orders. The shop has a website at www.sunriseprotea.com.

The nursery and flower shop **Proteas of Hawaii,** 808/878-2533 or 800/367-7768, website: www.hawaii-exotics.com, is across the road from the University of Hawai'i Agricultural Experimental Station; hours are 8 A.M.–4:30 P.M. Fresh protea baskets, tropical bouquets, and individual flowers can be purchased and shipped anywhere. Prices start at about $40, or $20 for lei.

Polipoli Spring State Recreation Area

If you want quietude and mountain walks, come here, because few others do. Just past the Kula Botanical Gardens look for the park sign on your left leading up Waipoli Road. This 10-mile stretch is only partially paved; the first half zigzags steeply up the hill, and the second half, although fairly flat, is dirt and can be very rutted, rocky, or muddy. Hang gliders use this area, jumping off farther up and landing on the open grassy fields

along the lower portion of this road. Hunting is also done in the forests here, and trails lead off this road to prescribed hunting areas. As usual, the trip is worth it. Polipoli has an established forest of imported trees from around the world: eucalyptus, redwoods, cypress, ash, cedar, and *sugi* pines. Much of the area was planted in the 1920s by the state and in the '30s by the Civilian Conservation Corps. These trees do well here as the park lies right in that band where moisture-laden clouds seem to hang around the mountain. There is a great network of trails in the immediate area, and even one that leads up to the top of the mountain. One of the most popular is the **Redwood Trail,** which you can take to a shelter at the end. These trails are for hiking and mountain biking only—no motorcycles or horses. At 6,200 feet, the camping area can be brisk at night. Camping is free but permits are required and are available from the Division of State Parks, 54 S. High St., Room 101, Wailuku, HI 96793, 808/984-8109. Water, picnic tables, and outhouses are provided at the camping spot, which is a small grassy area surrounded by tall eucalyptus trees. The cabin here is a spacious three-bedroom affair with bunks for up to 10 people. It starts at $45 a night for 1–4 people and goes up $5 per additional person. It's rustic, but all camping and cooking essentials are provided, including a wood-burning stove. If you want to get away from it all, this is your spot.

Upcountry Hiking Trails

Most of these trails form a network through and around Polipoli Spring State Recreation Area, and are all accessible from the camping area at 6,200 feet. **Redwood Trail,** 1.7 miles, passes through a magnificent stand of redwoods, past the ranger station and down to an old Civilian Conservation Corps camp at 5,300 feet where there's a rough old shelter. **Tie Trail,** 0.5 mile, joins Redwood Trail with **Plum Trail,** so named because of its numerous plum trees, which bear during the summer. **Skyline Trail,** 6.5 miles, starts atop Haleakala at 9,750 feet, passing through the southwest rift and eventually joining the **Haleakala Ridge Trail,** 1.6 miles, at the 6,500-foot level, then descends through a series of switchbacks. You can join with the Plum Trail or continue to the shelter at the end. Both the Skyline and Ridge trails offer superb vistas of Maui.

Others throughout the area include: **Polipoli,** 0.6 miles, passing through the famous forests of the area; **Boundary Trail,** four miles, leading from the Kula Forest Reserve to the ranger's cabin, passing numerous gulches still supporting native trees and shrubs; and **Waiohuli Trail** descending the mountain to join Boundary Trail and overlooking Keokea and Kihei with a shelter at the end. **Waiakoa Trail,** seven miles, begins at the Kula Forest Reserve Access Road. It ascends Haleakala to the 7,800-foot level and then descends through a series of switchbacks, covering rugged territory and passing a natural cave shelter. It eventually meets up with the three-mile **Waiakoa Loop Trail.** All of these trails offer intimate forest views of native and introduced trees, and breathtaking views of the Maui coastline far below.

Other Sights

In the basement of the Kula Lodge, tucked away as if in a wine cellar, is the **Curtis Wilson Cost Gallery,** 808/878-6544 or 800/508-2278, website: www.costgallery.com. One of Maui's premier artists, Cost captures scenes reflecting the essence of Upcountry Maui; handles color, light, and shadow to perfection; and portrays the true pastoral nature of the area. This is traditional realism with a touch of imagination. Stop in and browse daily 8:30 A.M.–5 P.M., or visit his other shop on Front Street in Lahaina.

Holy Ghost Catholic Church, on Lower Kula Road in Waiakoa, is an octagonal house of worship (Hawaii's only), raised in 1897 by the many Portuguese who worked the farms and ranches of Upcountry. It was rededicated in 1992 after extensive renovation and has many fine hand-carved and hand-painted statues and an elaborate altar that was sent by the king and queen of Portugal when the church was built. This church is worth a look, not only for the museum-quality woodwork inside, but for the great view over the isthmus. In 1983, it was placed on the National Register of Historic Places.

Near the intersection of Highways 37 and 377 is **Rice Park,** a grassy wayside rest area that has a few picnic tables, bathrooms, and a public phone. From here, you get a good view over the lower mountain slope, the coast at Kihei and Wailea, and the isthmus.

In Waiakoa, there's a gas station; down on the main highway is the **post office.** Across the highway from the post office is a Montessori School that hosts a Christmas Faire every year just prior to the holiday season.

Accommodations and Food

The **Kula Lodge,** RR 1, Box 475, Kula, HI 96790, 808/878-1535 or 800/233-1535, fax 808/878-2518, website: www.kulalodge.com, email: info@kulalodge.com, is on Route 377 just past Kimo Road and just before Haleakala Crater Road. Lodging here is in five detached chalets ranging $100–175; check-in is at the lodge restaurant. Two of the chalets have fireplaces with wood provided, four have lofts for extra guests, and all have lanai and excellent views of lower Maui. With their dark wood, carpets, and cathedral ceilings, they are almost contemporary in appearance. The Kula Lodge is a fine establishment with a wonderful location. Elevation 3,200 feet. Perhaps the only drawback is the clamor created when riders on the Haleakala downhill bike trips arrive in a large group for breakfast. Be up early so as not to be disturbed.

The lobby and dining area of the **Kula Lodge Restaurant,** 808/878-1535, are impressively rustic, with open beamwork and framing, dark wood, and stone. This building started as a private residence when it was built more than 50 years ago. The walls are covered with high-quality photos of Maui: windsurfers, silverswords, sunsets, cowboys, and horses. The large main dining room has a giant bay window with a superlative view. Breakfast is served daily 6:30–11:15 A.M., lunch 11:45 A.M.–4:15 P.M., and dinner 5–9 P.M.; Sunday brunch runs 6:30 A.M.–1 P.M. The menus are surprisingly large. Try Hawaiian buttermilk griddle cakes or vegetarian Benedict for breakfast, or a fresh fish sandwich or grilled chicken breast for lunch. Start dinner with artichoke and mushroom gratinée or a Kula farm green salad, and move on to a salmon filet, filet mignon pepper steak, or farfalle pasta. The assortment of gourmet desserts includes a tasty mango pie, and one of these should round out your meal. There may be entertainment in the evenings. Before or after dinner, sit at the bar for a drink or warm yourself on the couches that front the stone fireplace.

MAUI

Kula View Bed and Breakfast, 808/878-6736, at 140 Holopuni Road below Highway 37, offers a room on the upper level of the home with private entrance, private lanai, and sweeping views of Upcountry and across the isthmus to the West Maui Mountains. Surrounded by two lush acres, peace is assured in your bright and cheery room appointed with queen-size bed, wicker furniture in a breakfast nook, and a shower; telephone and TV available upon request. The rate is $85 a night, single or double occupancy, and this includes a simple continental breakfast. Weekly discounts are available; cash and traveler's checks only. For reservations, contact host Susan Kauai at P.O. Box 322, Kula, HI 96790.

In the tiny community of Waiakoa on Lower Kula Road you'll find **Morihara Store,** open daily 8 A.M.–8 P.M. for basic necessities. Across the street is the spacious but spartan **Cafe 808,** open daily 6 A.M.–8 P.M., serving down-home local food, with nothing on the menu more than $8.95.

CONTINUING SOUTH

Keokea

Continue south on Route 37 through the town of Keokea, where you'll find gas, a small selection of items at Henry Fong's and Ching's general stores, two rural churches, including St. John's Episcopal Church, and an excellent park for a picnic. At the far end of the village is **Keokea Gallery,** open Tues.–Sat. 9 A.M.–5 P.M., which displays works by Maui artists. Next door is **Grandma's Maui Coffee,** open every day 7:30 A.M.–5 P.M. You can enjoy fresh pastries for breakfast until 10 A.M., and sandwiches, taro burgers, and pies for lunch. The real treat, however, is the coffee, grown on the slope below and roasted in an old-fashioned, hand-crank, 115-year-old coffee machine in the shop. Stop in for a sip or take a package to go. Partway down Thompson Road south of town are Thompson Ranch Riding Stables and Silvercloud Upcountry Guest Ranch.

For the diehard history buff, there is an old structure up above town that represents a link to the past, when Chinese workers inhabited the area in greater numbers than they do today.

This is the **Kwack Hing Society Building** on Middle Road, a two-story green structure with cream trim that has signboards on either side of the front door that are carved with Chinese characters. A smaller plantation-style building sits to the side. Both have been well maintained. Here, local Chinese would congregate for all sorts of social purposes.

Almost as evidence of that Chinese connection is **Dr. Sun Yat-sen Memorial Park,** farther along the highway. A small triangular county park, here you'll find a statue to this famous Chinese physician/politician, two carved stone lions, and picnic tables. Dr. Sun Yat-Sen spent some of his younger years studying in Honolulu and also had a brother who lived on Maui. It seems that Dr. Sun's movement to overthrow the Manchu dynasty, which ruled China until 1911, was precipitated here in Hawaii.

Tedeschi Winery

Past Keokea you'll know you're in ranch country. The road narrows and herds of cattle graze in pastures that seem like manicured gardens highlighting *panini* (prickly pear) cactus. You'll pass Ulupalakua Ranch office and then almost immediately come to the Tedeschi Winery tasting room on the left, 808/878-6058. Open for tasting daily 9 A.M.–5 P.M., the winery sells bottles of all its wines and cushioned boxes for transporting it. Here, Emil Tedeschi and his partner Pardee Erdman, who also owns the 23,000-acre Ulupalakua Ranch, offer samples of their wines. This is one of two wineries in Hawaii. When Erdman bought the ranch and moved here in 1963, he noticed climatic similarities to the Napa Valley and knew that this country could grow decent wine grapes. Tedeschi comes from California, where his family has a small vineyard near Calistoga. The partners have worked on making their dream of Maui wine a reality since 1974.

It takes time and patience to grow grapes and turn out a vintage wine. While they waited for their carnelian grapes (a cabernet hybrid) to mature and be made into a sparkling wine, they fermented pineapple juice, which they call Maui Blanc. If you're expecting this to be a sickeningly sweet syrup, forget it. Maui Blanc is surprisingly dry and palatable. In 1984 the first scheduled release of the winery's carnelian sparkling wine, Maui Brut, celebrated the patience and craftsmanship of the vintners. Maui Blush, a zinfandel-like light dinner wine, and Maui Nouveau, a young red wine that's no longer available, were then added to the list. Most recently, Plantation Red, a very dry, oaky, red wine; Maui Splash, a sweet dessert wine that is a combination of pineapple and passion fruit; the fruity Pineapple Sparkling Wine; the mellow Ulupalakua Red table wine; and the dry salmon-colored Rose Ranch Cuvée have made their debut. You can taste these wines at the white ranch house among the tall proud trees just off the highway, once visited by King Kalakaua in 1874. From here, free tours run at 10:30 A.M. and 1:30 P.M. to the working winery buildings just a few steps away. Hugging the ground closer to the road is a 100-year-old plaster and coral building that used to be the winery's tasting room. Formerly, it served as the jailhouse of the old Rose Ranch owned by James Makee, a Maui pioneer sugarcane planter. Look for the 25-acre vineyard one mile before the tasting room on the ocean side of the highway. Tedeschi wines are available in restaurants and stores around the island. The winery's website is www.maui.net/~winery.

Across the street are remains of the old **Makee Sugar Mill.** Down the road are the Ulupalakua Ranch office and the ranch store and deli, which is open regular business hours. Hanging around the store like old plantation workers after a hard day's work are several carved and painted lifelike figures, representing various groups of people who've contributed to Maui's past. Sit down and have a chat.

The ranch runs half-day jeep tours over its property, either down close to the water or up on the mountain side. These rides give guests an unprecedented view of a sizable section of Maui that is normally off limits. For information, contact **Maui Jeep Adventures,** 808/876-1177.

At the end of April, an agriculture trade show called **The Ulupalakua Thing** gives growers and producers an opportunity to show their goods and hand out samples. Products grown and manufactured throughout the state are on display, making this the largest such agricultural event in Hawaii. The Ulupalakua Thing is held at the Ulupalakua Ranch on the grounds of Tedeschi Winery.

Silvercloud Upcountry Guest Ranch
A good place for groups, this fine country accommodation has six rooms in the main house and five studios in an adjoining building. The cottage on the hillside up behind is very private and an excellent retreat for newlyweds. Appropriately ranch-style, all are surrounded by pastureland and, at nearly 3,000 feet in elevation, have unobstructed views down on the green lower slopes of the mountain. Rooms in the large well-appointed main house run $85–135, and everyone has access to the kitchen, living room, and dining room. Each bedroom has a private bath but no telephone, and the upstairs rooms have a balcony that overlooks the front lawn. The studios run $105 and $145 and come with a bath, kitchen, and private lanai. Renting for $150 a night, the cottage is a fully furnished unit with its own wood stove for heat. Breakfast is included for all guests and is served on the back lanai of the main house, surrounded by a flower garden. There will be a $15 surcharge for one-night stays and a 10 percent discount for those who stay longer than five nights. Rates increase about 10 percent from December 15 to the end of February. The guest ranch is along Thompson Road, just out of Keokea, and lies just up the slope from the Thompson Ranch horse corral. Contact the Silvercloud at RR 2, Box 201, Kula, HI 96790, 808/878-6101 or 800/532-1111, fax 808/878-2132. Visit the website at www.silvercloudranch .com and send email to slvrcld@maui.net.

MAUI

HALEAKALA NATIONAL PARK

Haleakala (House of the Sun) is spellbinding. Like seeing Niagara Falls or the Grand Canyon for the first time, it makes no difference how many people have come before you; it's still an undiminished, powerful, personal experience. The mountain is a power spot, a natural conductor of cosmic energy. *Kahuna* brought their novitiates here to perform final rites of initiation. During their heyday, intense power struggles took place atop the mountain between the healing practitioners, the *kahuna lapa'au,* and their rivals the *kahuna ana'ana,* the "black magic" sorcerers of old Hawaii. **Kawilinau,** the "Bottomless Pit," a natural feature on the basin floor, was the site of an ancient battle between Pele and one of her siblings, and thus held tremendous significance for both schools of *kahuna.* Average Hawaiians did not live on Haleakala, but came now and again to quarry tool-stones. Only *kahuna* and their apprentices lived here for any length of time, as a sort of spiritual preparation and testing ground. Today, students of higher consciousness from around the world are attracted to this natural cosmic empire because of the rarefied energy. They claim that it accelerates personal growth and compare it to remote mountain and desert areas in the Holy Lands. Even the U.S. Air Force has a facility here, and their research indicates Haleakala is *the* strongest natural power point in America. Not only is there an energy configuration coming from the earth itself, but there is also a high focus of radiation coming from outside the atmosphere. No one is guaranteed a spiritual experience on Haleakala, but if you're at all sensitive, this is fertile ground.

Natural Features

Haleakala is the world's largest dormant volcano, composed of amazingly dense volcanic rock, almost like poured cement. Counting the 20,000 feet or so of it lying under the sea makes it one of the tallest mountains on earth. Perhaps this mass accounts for the strange power of Haleakala as it sits like a mighty magnetic pyramid in the center of the North Pacific. The park's boundaries encompass 28,655 variable acres, which stretch from Hosmer Grove to Kipahulu and include dry forests, rainforests, alpine desert, and a subtropical coastline. The most impressive feature is the "crater" basin itself. It's 3,000 feet deep, 7.5 miles east to west, and 2.5 miles north to south, accounting for 19 square miles, with a circumference of 21 miles. A mini mountain range of nine cinder cones marches across the basin floor. They look deceptively tiny from the observation area, but the smallest is 600 feet, and the tallest, Pu'u O Maui, is 1,000 feet high. Haleakala was designated as a national park in 1961. Before that it was part of the Big Island's Volcanoes National Park. The entire park is a nature preserve dedicated to Hawaii's quickly vanishing indigenous plants and animals, and it was recognized as an International Biosphere Reserve by the United Nations in 1980. Only Volcanoes and Haleakala national parks are home to the **nene,** the Hawaiian wild goose, and the **silversword,** a fantastically adapted plant.

Note: A discussion of the Kipahulu section of the national park and its hiking and camping options is found in the "Beyond Hana" section below.

Weather

As high as it is, Haleakala helps to create its own weather. Sunshine warms air that rises up the mountainside. When this moisture-laden air pushes into a cooler strata, it creates a band of clouds that moisten the forest and create what is known as the cloud forest. Often, these clouds will push up into the basin itself, gushing up through the Ko'olau and Kaupo gaps, sometimes obscuring the basin from view. In the cool of the evening, these clouds retreat back down the mountainside, leaving the basin clear once again. As air temperature drops about three degrees for every 1,000 feet, the top may be more than 30° cooler than the sunny beaches along the Kihei Coast below. Haleakala also traps moisture from the trade winds, so the high mountain slopes above Hana get about 400 inches of rain a year, creating thick forest cover, while the

© SANDRA E. BISIGNANI TRUST AND AVALON TRAVEL PUBLISHING, INC.

HALEAKALA NATIONAL PARK

To Kahului

▲ (6,849 ft.)

HOSMER GROVE

PARK HEADQUARTERS

HALEAKALA CRATER RD.

Leleiwi Overlook

Kalahaku Overlook (9,324 ft.)

Pu'u 'Ula'ula (Red Hill) (10,023 ft.) ▲

White Hill ▲

VISITOR CENTER

HALEAKALA OBSERVATORIES

HOUA ▲

Halemau'u Trail

Silversword Loop

Bottomless Pit (Kawilinau)

Pu'u O Maui ❋

Kamaoali'i ❋

Ka Lu'u O Ka O'o ❋

Pu'u O Pele ❋

Pu'u Naue ❋

Halali'i ❋

Ka Moa O Pele ❋

Sliding Sands

Pu'u Maile ❋

HALEAKALA WILDERNESS

Pu'u Kumu ❋

Ko'olau Gap

Mauna Hina ❋ (8,907 ft.) ▲

Horokehua ❋

Namana O Ke Akua ❋

Oilipu'u ❋

Kaluaiki ❋

PALIKU ▲

(8,105 ft.) ▲

Kalapawili Ridge

Haupaakea Peak (9,157 ft.) ▲

KAPALAOA ▲

(8,20 ft.) ▲

Kaupo Gap

(6,300 ft.) ▲

Kaupo Trail

(4,772 ft.) ▲

To Kaupo and Hwy. 31 (4 miles)

SCIENTIFIC RESEARCH AREA (CLOSED)

Kipahulu Valley

Palikea Stream

Palikea (2,224 ft.)

Koukouai Gulch

Falls at Makahiku

Ohe'o Gulch

Waimoku Falls

KIPAHULU AREA

RANGER STATION

To Hana

KIPAHULU CAMPGROUND

31

To Kaupo

NOTE: BE AWARE OF FREE RANGE CATTLE ALONG THE HIGHWAY, ESPECIALLY AT NIGHT

MAUI

0   1 mi

0   1 km

slopes above Makena and farther around to Kaupo, mostly dry and scrubby, get only a dozen inches yearly. Average temperatures at the park headquarters run 52° in winter and 59° in summer, with minimum and maximums of 30° and 78°, respectively. Rainfall averages 1–2.5 inches from May to October and 4.5–10 from November to April.

The Experience

If you're after *the* experience, you must see the sunrise or sunset. Both are magnificent, but both perform their stupendous light show with astonishing speed. The sun, as it rises or sets, infuses the clouds with streaks, puffs, and bursts of dazzling pastels, at the same time backlighting and edging the basin in glorious golds and reds. If conditions are right, a rainbow may hang over the basin at sunset. Prepare for an emotional crescendo that will brim your eyes with tears at the majesty of it all. Engulfed by this magnificence, no one can remain unmoved. For this show of shows, the weather must be cooperative, and you may not be able to tell how it will be from down below. Misty, damp clouds can surround the basin, blocking out the sun, or pour into the basin, obscuring even it from view. Don't forget the wind. It's usually breezy at the top, which tends to drop the temperature even more, so wear appropriate clothing: jacket, hat, and gloves. The *Maui News* prints the hours of sunrise and sunset (on a daily basis) as they vary with the season, so make sure to check. The National Weather Service provides a daily weather recording at 808/871-5054. For more specific information, you can call the park headquarters at 808/572-4400 or 808/572-9306 for a recorded message. Plan on taking a minimum of 90 minutes to arrive from Kahului, and to be safe, arrive at least 30 minutes before dawn or dusk, because even one minute is critical. For sunrise, the view from the edge of the basin is best. For sunset, hike up to the enclosure on top of Red Hill or sit just over the edge of the hill so you're out of the wind, on the west side of the parking lot.

Note: If you want to avoid downhill bikers and tourists you can also get a great view from the Kalahaku Overlook. When you drive back down the mountain, shift into a low gear to control your speed to prevent riding the brakes.

"Crater" Facts

Haleakala was formed primarily from pa'hoehoe lava. This lava is the hottest natural substance on earth, and it flows like swift fiery rivers. Because of its high viscosity, it forms classic shield volcanoes. Plenty of 'a'a is also found in the mountain's composition. This rock comes out partially solidified and filled with gases, then breaks apart and forms clinkers. You'll be hiking over both, but be especially careful on 'a'a, because its jagged edges will cut you as quickly as coral. The basin is primarily formed from erosion, not from caving in on itself—hence not a crater, per se. The erosion on Hawaii is quite accelerated due to carbonic acid buildup, a byproduct of the quick decomposition of abundant plant life. The rocks break down into smaller particles of soil which are then washed off the mountain by rain, or blown off by wind. Natural drainage patterns form, and canyons begin to develop and slowly eat their way to the center. The two largest are

The adventurous gather at the crater rim to watch the sun rise on Maui.

J.D. BISIGNANI

MAUI

Ko'olau Gap at the upper end of the Ke'anae Valley in the north and **Kaupo Gap** in the south. These canyons, over time, moved their heads past each other to the center of the mountain, where they took several thousand feet off the summit and formed a huge amphitheater-like basin, most often referred to as Haleakala Crater.

Some stones that you encounter while hiking will be very light in weight. They once held water and gases that evaporated. If you knock two together, they'll sound like crystal. Also, be observant for **Maui diamonds.** They are garnet stones, a type of pyroxene or crystal.

The cinder cones in the basin are fascinating. They're volcanic vents with a high iron content and may form electromagnetic lines from the earth's center. On top, they are like funnels, transmitters and receivers of energy, natural pyramids. Climbing them violates park rules made to protect endangered plants and threatened insects that pollinate them. Notice the color of the compacted earth on the trails. It's obvious why you should remain on them. All the plants (silverswords, too) are shallow-rooted and live by condensing moisture on their leaves. Don't walk too close to them because you'll compact the earth around them and damage the roots. The ecosystem on Haleakala is very delicate, so please keep this in mind to better preserve its beauty for future generations.

SIGHTS

You'll start enjoying Haleakala long before you reach the top. Don't make the mistake of simply bolting up the mountain without taking time to enjoy what you're passing. Route 37 from Kahului takes you through Pukalani, the last big place to buy supplies. There it branches to clearly marked Route 377; in six miles it becomes the zigzag of Route 378 or **Haleakala Crater Road.** Along the way are forests of indigenous and introduced trees, including eucalyptus, beautifully flowering jacaranda, and stands of cactus. The vistas change rapidly from one vantage point to the next. Sometimes it's the green rolling hills of Ireland, and then instantly it's the tall, yellow grass of the plains. This is also cattle country, so don't be surprised to see herds grazing as you roll past.

Headquarters

After paying your entrance fee, the first stopping point in the park is **Hosmer Grove Campground** (see below), a short way down a secondary park road on your left. Proceed past this turnoff a few minutes and you'll arrive at **park headquarters,** elevation 7,000 feet, open daily 7:30 A.M.–4 P.M. Campers can get their permits here and others will be happy to stop for all manner of brochures and information concerning the park, for water, or to use the toilet or pay phone. There are some silverswords outside, and a few *nene* can occasionally be seen wandering the area. After you pass the park headquarters, zig and zag a couple more times, there's parking for Halemau'u Trail on your left (see below). Following are two overlooks, **Leleiwi** and **Kalahaku.** Both offer tremendous views and different perspectives on the basin. They shouldn't be missed—especially Kalahaku, where there are silverswords and the remnants of a travelers' lodge from the days when an expedition to Haleakala took two days.

Visitor Center

Near road's end is the visitor center, elevation 9,740 feet, approximately 10 miles up the mountain from headquarters, a half-hour drive. You get one of the best views into the basin from here. It's open from sunrise to 3 P.M. and contains a clear and concise display featuring the geology of Haleakala. Maps and books are available, and periodic ranger talks are particularly informative, delving into geology and the legends surrounding the great mountain. Various ranger-led hikes are also given, including the hike down Sliding Sands Trail, daily interpretive talks at the summit, and the Hosmer Grove forest walk. Additional interpretive talks and ranger-led hikes are conducted at the Kipahulu ranger station. Check with the park headquarters or the visitor center for times and days of programs. All mule and horse rides into the basin and bike trips down the mountainside through the park start from the parking lot to the front of the visitor center. By 10 A.M., there will be lots of people at the top, so enjoy the time between when the bikers leave and the buses arrive.

Bikes going down the mountain travel about 20–25 miles an hour, sometimes faster. If you're caught behind a string of bikes on your way

MAUI

down, just slow down and wait for them to pull over and let you pass.

HIKING AND CAMPING

Walks

One of the topside paths leads to **Pa Ka'oao** (White Hill). An easy quarter-mile hike will take you to the summit, and along the way you'll pass stone shelters and sleeping platforms from the days when Hawaiians came here to quarry the special tool-stone. It's a type of whitish slate that easily flakes but is so hard that when you strike two pieces together it rings almost like iron. Next comes **Pu'u 'Ula'ula** (Red Hill), the highest point on Maui, at 10,023 feet. Atop is a glass-encased observation area (open 24 hours). This is where many people come to view the sunset. From here, if the day is crystal clear, you can see all of the main Hawaiian Islands except Kaua'i. To add some perspective to size and distance, it's 100 miles from the top of Haleakala to the volcanic peak Mauna Kea on the Big Island to the southeast. Behind you on the slope below is **Maui Space Surveillance Complex,** a research facility with eight telescopes that's manned by the University of Hawai'i and the Department of Defense. Closed to the public; tours of the facility are no longer given.

The easy **Hosmer Grove Nature Trail** leads you through a stand of introduced temperate zone trees planted in 1910 to see if any would be good for commercial lumber use. There are perhaps a dozen different species of trees here, and the walk should take a half hour or so over mostly level ground. Originally planted in separate areas, these trees and others have intermingled now. Here you will see Jeffrey pine, ponderosa pine, lodgepole pine, incense cedar, eucalyptus, Norway spruce, eastern red cedar, Douglas fir, and Japanese *sugi.* Several signs are posted along the trail to explain what the trees are and how the forest developed.

Halfway up the hill and a completely different environment, a quarter-mile nature walk leads you from a parking lot to the Leleiwi Overlook. Along the way you find low shrubs and alpine plants rather than trees and thick vegetation.

Various **ranger-led walks** are given during the week, leaving either from the visitors center or from Hosmer Grove campground. On Monday and Thursday at 9 A.M., a naturalist leads a hike down into the Waikamoi cloud forest from Hosmer Grove, and on this hike you'll learn about trees, birds, and natural features of the area. Three hours, three miles, moderately strenuous. A ranger-led hike also goes down the Sliding Sands trail on a Cinder Desert Hike on Tuesday and Friday at 9 A.M. from the trailhead at the visitor center parking lot. The two-mile walk takes about two hours and is moderately strenuous.

Hikes

There are three major trails in Haleakala Wilderness Area (Halemau'u, Sliding Sands, and Kaupo) and several connecting trails—about 27 miles of trails in all. **Halemau'u Trail** starts at the 8,000-foot level along the road about three miles past the park headquarters. It descends quickly by way of switchbacks to the 6,600-foot level on the basin floor, offering expansive views of Ko'olau Gap along the way. En route you'll pass Holua Cabin, Silversword Loop and the Bottomless Pit (a mere 65 feet deep), and junctions with both the Sliding Sands and Kaupo trails before you reach Paliku Cabin. If you go out via the Sliding Sands Trail and visitors center, you shouldn't have any trouble hitching back to your car left at the Halemau'u trailhead.

Sliding Sands begins at the summit of Haleakala near the visitors center. This could be considered the main trail into the basin and gives you the best overall hike, with up-close views of cinder cones, lava flows, and unique vegetation. It joins the Halemau'u Trail more than a mile west of the Paliku Cabin. Near Kapalaoa Cabin, you can turn left to the Bottomless Pit and exit via Halemau'u Trail, or circle around by way of other connecting trails and exit the way you came. Exiting the Halemau'u Trail is a good choice, but you'll have to hitch back to your car at the visitors center.

The **Kaupo Trail** is long and tough. It descends rapidly through the Kaupo Gap to the park boundary at 3,880 feet. Below 4,000 feet the lava is rough and the vegetation thick. It then crosses private land, which is no problem, and after a steep and rocky downhill grade along well-marked trails deposits you in the semi-ghost town of Kaupo, on the dry rugged southern slope of the mountain. You'll have to hitch west just

The silversword is a severely endangered plant; please treat it with respect.

to get to the scant traffic of Route 31, or head nine miles east to Kipahulu and its campground, and from there back along the Hana Road.

For those inclined, **Maui Mule Ride** offers horse and mule tours into the basin. Hikers should also consider a day with the professional guide service **Hike Maui**. The guide's in-depth knowledge and commentary will make your trip not only more fulfilling but enjoyably informative as well.

Hikers

Serious hikers or campers must have sturdy shoes, good warm clothes, rain gear, plenty of water, down sleeping bags, and a serviceable tent (unless you've reserved one of the cabins). Hats and sunglasses are needed. Compasses are useless because of the high magnetism in the rock, but binoculars are particularly rewarding. No cook-fires are allowed in the basin, so you'll need a stove. Don't burn any dead wood—the soil needs all the decomposing nutrients it can get. Drinking water is available at all of the cabins within the basin, but the supply is limited and must be treated before use so bring what you will need. This environment is particularly delicate. Stay on the established trails so that you don't cause undue erosion. Leave rocks and especially plants alone. Don't walk too close to silverswords or any other plants because you'll compact the soil. Leave your pets at home; ground-nesting birds here are easily disturbed. If

nature "calls," dig a very shallow hole, off the trail, and pack out your used toilet paper since the very dry conditions are not conducive to it biodegrading.

Camping

Admission to the park is $10 per car, $5 for bikers, hikers, and motorcycles, and is good for seven days (national park discount passes are honored), but camping is free with a necessary camping permit from park headquarters. The Hosmer Grove campground is at the 6,800-foot level, just before park headquarters; the free camping here is limited to three nights and to 25 people, but there's generally room for all. There's water, pit toilets, picnic tables, grills, and a pavilion. It was named after Ralph Hosmer. While here take a stroll along the half-mile forest loop that threads its way through the grove of trees that Hosmer planted.

Kipahulu Campground is a primitive camping area on the coast near 'Ohe'o Stream. It's part of the park, but unless you're an intrepid hiker and descend all the way down the Kaupo Trail, you'll come to it via Hana.

There are campsites in the basin at **Holua**, **Kapalaoa**, and **Paliku**. All three offer cabins, and tent camping is allowed at the first and last. Camping at any of these is extremely popular, and reservations for the cabins must be made at least 60 days in advance by mail using only a special cabin reservation request form. Each

ROBERT NILSEN

MAUI

cabin is reserved for one group of up to 12 people only. A lottery of the applicants chosen for sites keeps it fair for all. Environmental impact studies limit the number of campers to 25 per area per day. Camping is limited to a total of three days per month, with no more than two consecutive days at each spot. Rates for cabin use are $40 for up to six persons and $80 to a maximum of 12 people. For complete details and reservation form contact: Haleakala National Park, P.O. Box 369, Makawao, HI 96768, 808/572-9306. Visit the park's website at www.nps.gov/hale.

Making Do

If you've come to Hawaii for sun and surf and you aren't prepared for alpine temperatures, you can still enjoy Haleakala. For a day-trip, wear a windbreaker or jacket and your jogging suit or a sweater, if you've brought one. Make sure to wear socks, and even bring an extra pair as makeshift mittens. Use your dry beach towel to wrap around inside your sweater as extra insulation, and even consider taking your hotel blanket, which you can use Indian fashion. Make rain gear from a large plastic garbage bag with holes cut for head and arms; this is also a good windbreaker. Take your beach hat, too. Don't worry about looking ridiculous in this get-up—you will! But you'll also keep warm! Remember that for every thousand feet you climb, the temperature drops three degrees Fahrenheit, so the summit is about 30° cooler than at sea level. As the sun reaches its zenith, if there are no rain clouds, the basin floor will go from about 50 to 80 degrees. It can flip-flop from hot to dismal and rainy a number of times in the same day. The nights may drop below freezing, with the coldest recorded temperature inside the basin a bone-chilling 14°. Dawn and dusk are notorious for being bitter. Because of the altitude, be aware that the oxygen level will drop, and those with any impairing conditions should take precautions. The sun is ultra-strong atop the mountain, and even those with deep tans are subject to burning. Noses are particularly susceptible.

MAUI

M.G.L. DOMENY DE REINZI

EAST MAUI
THE ROAD TO HANA

MAUI

On the long and winding road to Hana's door, most people's daydreams of "paradise" come true. A trip to Maui without a visit to Hana is like ordering a sundae without a cherry on top. The 50 miles from Kahului to Hana are some of the most remarkable in the world. The Hana Highway (Route 36) starts out innocently enough, passing Pa'ia. The inspiration for Pa'ia's gaily painted storefronts looks like it came from a jar of jelly beans. Next come some north-shore surfing beaches where windsurfers fly, doing amazing aquabatics. Soon there is a string of "rooster towns," so named because that's about all that seems to be stirring. Then Route 36 becomes Route 360 and at mile marker 3 the *real* Road to Hana begins.

The semi-official count tallies more than 600 rollicking turns and 57 one-lane bridges, inducing everyone to slow down and soak up the sights of this glorious road. It's like passing through a tunnel cut from trees. The ocean winks with azure blue through sudden openings on your left. To the right, streams, waterfalls, and pools sit wreathed with jungle and wildflowers. Coconuts, guavas, mangos, and bananas grow everywhere on the mountainside. Fruit stands pop up now and again as you creep along. Then comes Ke'anae with its arboretum and taro farms indicating that many ethnic Hawaiians still live along the road. There are places to camp, picnic, and swim, both in the ocean and in freshwater streams.

Along with you, every other car traveling the Hana Highway is on the road to take in the beauty that this coast has to offer. Nearly all visitors pass through, some stay a day or a week, while others take up residence. Islanders, mainlanders, and foreigners alike are enticed by the land, and under its spell they put down roots. George Harrison has a house a few miles down the coast in Nahiku, and Jim Nabors, Kris Kristofferson, and Carol Burnett also maintain homes here.

Then you reach Hana itself, a remarkable town. The great Queen Ka'ahumanu was born here, and many celebrities live in the surrounding hills seeking peace and solitude. Past Hana, the road becomes even more rugged and besieged by jungle. It opens up again around 'Ohe'o Gulch. Here waterfalls cascade over stupendous cataracts, forming a series of pools until they reach the sea. Beyond is a rental car's no-man's land, where the passable road toughens and Haleakala shows its barren volcanic face scarred by lava flows and covered by dry-land forest.

PA'IA

Pa'ia (Noisy) was a bustling sugar town that took a nap. When it awoke, it had a set of whiskers and its vitality had flown away. At the beginning of the 19th century, many groups of ethnic field workers lived here, segregated in housing clusters called "camps" that stretched up Baldwin Avenue. Pa'ia was the main gateway for sugar on East Maui, and even a plantation railroad functioned here until about 30 years ago. During the 1930s, its population, at more than 10,000, was the largest on the island. Then fortunes shifted toward Kahului, and Pa'ia lost its dynamism, until recently. Pa'ia was resuscitated in the 1970s by an influx of paradise-seeking hippies, and then again in the '80s came another shot in the arm from windsurfers. These two groups have metamorphosed into townsfolk and have pumped new life into Pa'ia's old muscles. The practical shops catering to the pragmatic needs of a "plantation town" were replaced. The storefronts were painted and spruced up. A new breed of merchants with their eyes on passing tourists has taken over. Now Pa'ia focuses on boutiques, crafts, artwork, and food. It also has a golf course in the neighborhood of Spreckelsville. Opened in 1925, this well-kept private course is the oldest functioning golf course on the island. Since you've got to pass through on your way to Hana, it serves as a great place not only to top off your gas tank but also to stop for a bite and a browse. The prices are good for just about everything, and the nearby village of Ku'au boasts one of the island's best fish restaurants. Pa'ia, under its heavy makeup, is still a vintage example of what it always was—a homey, serviceable, working town.

PACIFIC OCEAN

EAST MAUI

Honopou Point

Waipi'o Bay

Huelo Point

HWY.

Huelo

vin Falls

Kailua

'O'opuola Point

360

Nua'ailua Bay

Paohokamua Falls

Ko'anae

Pauwalu Point

Haipuaena Falls

Wailua

Ke'anae Falls

Waiohue Bay

Nahiku

HANA HWY

Honomanu Stream

Ke'anae Valley

Kano Stream

W. Wailua Nui

Kuhiwa Valley

Upper Nahiku

360

HANA AIRPORT

Natural Arch

Ka'eleku

378

Kawaipapa Gulch

Hana Bay

Hana

MAUI

HALEAKALA NATIONAL PARK

Palikea

Kipahulu Valley

Pu'u Kaukanu ▲

Kapi'a Stream

Pu'u 'Ula'ula (Red Hill) (10,023 ft.)

Waiho'i Valley

Kaki'o

Hamoa

Pu'uiki

Pohakuloa Bay

Ha'o'u

Koali

Mu'olea

Manawainui Gulch

Kahalulu Gulch

Wailua

Wailua Cove

Kepuni Gulch

Stream

Kipahulu

31

Puhilele Point

PI'ILANI HWY

Kaupo

Lelekea Bay

Natural Arch

Huakini Bay

Mamalu Bay

Kamanawai Point

Alenuihaha Channel

EAST MAUI COVERAGE

0   3 mi

0   3 km

© SANDRA E. BISIGNANI TRUST AND AVALON TRAVEL PUBLISHING, INC.

PA'IA AND ENVIRONS

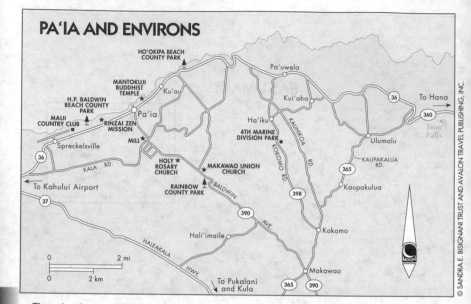

HO'OKIPA BEACH
COUNTY PARK

Pa'uwela

MANTOKUJI
BUDDHIST
TEMPLE

Ku'au

Kui'aha

36

To Hana

H.P. BALDWIN
BEACH COUNTY
PARK

Pa'ia

360

Twin
Falls

MAUI
COUNTRY CLUB

RINZAI ZEN
MISSION

Ha'iku

4TH MARINE
DIVISION PARK

Ulumalu

Spreckelsville

MILL

36

KALA RD.

HOLY
ROSARY
CHURCH

MAKAWAO UNION
CHURCH

KAUPAKALUA
RD.

365

Kaupakulua

To Kahului Airport

RAINBOW
COUNTY PARK

BALDWIN

398

37

390

AVE

Kokomo

Hali'imaile

HALEAKALA

0   2 mi

0   2 km

HWY.

To Pukalani
and Kula

Makawao

365   390

© SANDRA E. BISIGNANI TRUST AND AVALON TRAVEL PUBLISHING, INC.

There is a large public parking lot at the west end of Pa'ia, across the highway from the Maui Crafts Guild. As Pa'ia is so small, it's best to leave your car here and walk around town.

Sights

A mile or so before you enter Pa'ia on the left is **Rinzai Zen Mission**—reached by going through H. P. Baldwin Park. The grounds are pleasant and worth a look. **Mantokuji Buddhist Temple** on the eastern outskirts of Pa'ia heralds the sun's rising and setting by ringing its huge gong 18 times at dawn and dusk. Built in 1921, this temple is a fine example of a Zen mission structure and perhaps the best representative on Maui. The yearly *obon* festival is celebrated here with ceremony and dance.

H. P. Baldwin Beach County Park is on your left about seven miles past Kahului on Route 36, just past Maui Country Club and the well-to-do community of Spreckelsville. This spacious park is good for swimming, shell-collecting, and decent winter surfing. It has full amenities. Unfortunately, hassles and robberies have been known to occur—there are a lot of "park at your own risk" signs. Be nice, calm, and respectful. At the far western end of this beach, with access

through the community of Spreckelsville, is a protected spot just fine for kids.

Ho'okipa Beach Park is about 10 minutes past Pa'ia. There's a high grassy sand dune along the road and the park is down below, where you'll enjoy full amenities—unofficial camping occurs. Swimming is advisable only on calm days, as there are wicked currents. Primarily a surfing beach that is now regarded as one of the best sailboarding areas in Hawaii, this is home to the Aloha Classic, held yearly in October or November. The world's best sailboarders come here, trying to win the substantial prize money. Bring binoculars.

Going up on Baldwin Avenue (Route 390) you pass the Pa'ia **sugar mill,** a real-life Carl Sandburg poem. A smaller sister mill to the one at Pu'unene, it's a green monster trimmed in bare lightbulbs at night, dripping with sounds of turning gears, cranes, and linkbelts, all surrounded by packed, rutted, oil-stained soil. Farther along Baldwin Avenue sits **Holy Rosary Church** and its sculpture of Father Damien. The rendering of Damien is idealized, but the leper, who resembles a Calcutta beggar, has a face that conveys helplessness while at the same time faith and hope. It's worth a few minutes' stop. Coming next is **Makawao Union Church,** and it's a beauty. Like a Tudor mansion made completely of stone with lovely stained-glass windows, the entrance is framed by two tall and stately royal palms. Farther up is tiny **Rainbow County Park,** one of the few noncoastal parks on Maui. Set in the bend of the road, the grassy lawn here would be okay for a picnic.

Accommodations

One of the few place to lodge in Pa'ia is at the **Nalu Kai Lodge,** 808/579-8009, just behind the Wine Cooler where Baldwin Avenue meets the Hana Highway; ask for Myrna. This plain and simple two-story cement building offers clean, quiet, adequate rooms. Don't expect anything fancy, just the necessities. No TV and no telephones. Rates vary—Myrna bargains—but expect to spend about $40 for one night or $350 for a month. There are seven units, one double and six singles. Many people stay long-term.

Someone looking for very inexpensive accommodations can find space in a house at 151 Hana Hwy., only a few steps from the center of Pa'ia. Basically a house turned into a rental pad, beds go for $60 a week. Call 808/579-8015 for more information.

About a mile away in the tiny community of Ku'au next to Mama's Fish House is the **Kuau Plaza Condo,** 808/579-8080, fax 808/579-8533. Rooms have private baths and color televisions. Laundry facilities are on premises. Here again it's nothing special, but it gets you close to Maui's best surfing spots and it's just a skip down the road from Pa'ia. Rooms and suites generally run $40–70 a night.

Fronting the beach next to Mama's Fish House is **Mama's Beachfront Cottages.** Close to the action but not bothered by the hubbub of town, these cottages are much more the tropical hideaways than the two aforementioned properties. Hid by foliage from the restaurant and the neighbor houses, one-bedroom and two-bedroom units, each nicely furnished, come complete with a modern kitchen and entertainment center, a/c, telephone, and lanai with gas grill. The smaller units run $135–150 a night, while the larger units go for $300. Contact the cottages at 799 Poho Place, Paia, HI 96779, or call 808/579-9764 or 800/860-4852, fax 808/579-8594, website: www.mamasfishhouse.com.

For other options, try **Kuau Cottages,** 808/579-8700, which has rooms for $70 a night; or a Pa'ia home, 808/579-8728, where a room runs $175 week and the studio $250 week. Check the several bulletin boards around town for all varieties of accommodations that rent by the night, week, or month.

Food

Picnic's, 30 Baldwin Ave., 808/579-8021, is open daily 7 A.M.–5 P.M. Breakfast and lunch offer everything from eggs and pancakes to plate lunches and vegetarian sandwiches, like

Mantokuji
Buddhist Temple

ROBERT NILSEN

MAUI

the famous spinach nut burger, all under $8. The best options are boxed picnic lunches that add a special touch if you're heading to Hana. They start from the basic Upcountry Picnic, which includes sandwiches and sides at $8.50 per person, to the Holo Holo Pikiniki for four, with all the fixings for sandwiches, herb-roasted chicken, sides, condiments, dessert, and even a tablecloth all in a Styrofoam ice chest for $52. Picnic's is one of the best stops along the Hana Road even for a quick espresso, cappuccino, or frozen yogurt. Or treat yourself with the fresh-baked pastries like macadamia nut sticky buns and the apple and papaya turnovers: worth the guilt!

At the corner is **Paia Fish Market Restaurant,** 808/579-8030, a casual sit-down restaurant with picnic tables inside. Specializing in charbroiled fish, the menu also includes more than a dozen types of fish, all at market price, that can be prepared in one of four different manners. You can also have charbroiled chicken, blackened sashimi, seafood salad, or fresh fish to take home and prepare yourself. The lunch and dinner menus include burgers, pasta, and fajitas. This is a perennial favorite.

Across the street and also on the corner, a great place to people-watch or be watched is **Milagros Bar and Restaurant,** 808/579-8755. Milagros does burgers, sandwiches, and fish; eat inside or outside on the patio along the sidewalk. This is semi-Mexican fare with sandwich and burger lunches in the $6–8 range and dinners like seafood enchiladas and grilled ahi burritos mostly $12–16. Milagros has a full bar, so you can ease into the evening with a tropical margarita, south-of-the-border beer, glass of fine wine, or well drink.

Jacques Bistro, 808/579-6255, at 89 Hana Hwy., has seating inside at tables with white linen or on the patio out back under shade trees. The lunch menu includes mostly sandwiches, salads, and fish, and might be a mahi sandwich for $6.95 or tomato mozzarella salad for $7.95. For dinner, try spicy peanut chicken, *paniolo* cut steak, or seafood linguine. Most entrées are under $19. The bar has a fine selection of wines and a full line of well drinks. Jacques is a casual spot, an easy place to dine and drink.

The **Bangkok** Thai cuisine restaurant, 808/579-8979, an indoor/outdoor café with a courtyard area surrounded by palm trees, is open for lunch Mon.–Fri. 10 A.M.–1 P.M. and dinner daily 5–9:30 P.M. Appetizers ranging $5.50–7.95 include Thai crispy noodles and sateh chicken. Try a green papaya salad or a spicy seafood coconut soup before your entr'e, which might be the Evil Prince shrimp or fish for $9.95, or seafood combo with broccoli at $11.95. In addition, there are many curry, noodle, fish, and vegetarian dishes. Desserts include tapioca and warm coconut milk at $2.95. Food here is good value, decently presented, and authentic. Soft drinks and bar drinks available.

For a quick bite you have **Charley's,** 808/579-9453, a saloon with pool tables and restaurant specializing in pizza, pasta, and sandwiches, open 7 A.M. for breakfast, from 11:30 for lunch, and 5 P.M. for dinner. Charley's is a gathering place for breakfast, and has items like huevos rancheros for $7.75. For lunch, select a fish sandwich for $7.25 or burgers for around $8. Some dinner specials, like fettuccine Alfredo or chicken marsala, at about $15, are more pricey but still very reasonable. Soups, salads, and appetizers are priced equally well. This is a big rambling amiable place where tourists and locals alike come for a pleasant time, and the bar is a pleasant afternoon hangout for locals.

The **Vegan Restaurant,** 115 Baldwin Ave., 808/579-9144, open daily noon–9 P.M., is an extraordinary health-conscious restaurant, a "hippie" hangout that others into healthy food frequent. You won't come here for the decor—brightly colored wall hangings on no-nonsense walls—you'll come for the large portions of incredibly delicious food. The Vegan serves only vegetarian food made with organic products and uses no meat, dairy, eggs, or animal products of any kind; the food is mostly cholesterol-free. Standard menu items include hummus salad at $5.95, the Vegan burger for $4.95, and tofu soft tacos for $9.95; specials nightly. Luscious smoothies are priced at $2.95. Sit at one of the few tables inside, or call ahead for orders to go.

Moana Bakery and Cafe, 808/579-9999, is another good choice. Food is served 8 A.M.–9 P.M., and baked goods are always available from the deli case. Breakfast is mostly eggs, griddle items, and saimin, while lunch choices include salads and sandwiches. Dinner is more substantial, with dishes like island pesto pasta, chili seared ahi, and medallions of filet mignon,

$7.95–23.95. Live music Wednesday, Thursday, Friday, and Sunday evenings.

A short way up Baldwin Avenue, the **Paia Coffee Company,** 808/579-9296, offers more than coffee. Of course, you can get your morning jolt of espresso, caffe latte, or straight black cup of joe, but you might also like to try a crepe. On Friday, it's all-you-can-eat pasta night for $5. You can't beat it.

Offering an alternative for the java jock is the easygoing **Anthony's Coffee,** 808/579-8340, on Baldwin Avenue, where you can get coffee by the cup or a pound to go. Come for breakfast and pastries or try a lunch sandwich or ice cream as you hang out and read the paper.

Mama's Fish House, reservations highly recommended, 808/579-8488, is just past Pa'ia in Ku'au and on the left heading toward Hana. Look for the turnoffs near the blinking yellow light; you'll see a vintage car with a sign for Mama's, a ship's flagpole, and a fishing boat marking the entranceway. There's plenty of off-road complimentary valet parking. Mama's, serving lunch 11 A.M.–2:30 P.M., cocktails and *pu pu* until dinner at 5 P.M., has earned the best reputation possible— it gets thumbs up from local people even though it is expensive. It's perhaps the best upscale beach shack on the island, right on the water surrounded by coconut trees and tiki torches with outrigger canoes drawn on the lawn out front. The fish is fresh daily, with some broiled over *kiawe,* while the vegetables come from local gardens and the herbs are Mama's own. Fish entrées run $30–35, others $28–46. For a meal with the same special flavors but easier on the pocketbook, stop by for lunch. Special Hawaiian touches, wonderful food, friendly professional service, and a great view of Maui's north shore, add to the enjoyment of every meal. A terrific idea is to make reservations here for the evening's return trip from Hana.

Mana Natural Foods, 49 Baldwin Ave., 808/579-8078, open daily 8 A.M.–8 P.M., is a well-stocked health-food store, maybe the best on Maui, that's kind of funky and still not "modernized." Inside the old building you'll find local organic produce, vitamins, grains, juices, bulk foods, and more. For take-out, try the salad bar or hot entrée bar, or look for picnic items in the cooler. Outside, check out the great community bulletin board for what's selling and happening around Pa'ia and to find rental housing.

Just before Baldwin Avenue along the Hana Highway is **Nagata Store,** a general grocery store with a seafood department open Mon.–Fri. 6 A.M.–7 P.M., Saturday 6 A.M.–6 P.M., Sunday 6 A.M.–1 P.M.

The **Wine Cooler,** at the corner of Baldwin Ave. and the Hana Hwy., is a well-stocked bottle shop with a superb selection of wines, liquor, and ice-cold beer. Microbreweries are well represented. Open Monday noon–10 P.M., Tues.–Sun. 9 A.M.–10:30 P.M.

Shopping

Maui Crafts Guild is on the left just as you enter Pa'ia, at 43 Hana Hwy., P.O. Box 609, Pa'ia, HI 96779, 808/579-9697. The guild's website is www.mauicraftsguild.com. Open daily 9 A.M.–6 P.M., the Crafts Guild is one of the best art outlets in Hawaii. It's owned and operated by the artists themselves, now numbering more than two dozen, all of whom must pass a thorough jurying by present members. All artists must be islanders, and they must use natural materials found in Hawaii to create their work except for some specialized clay, fabrics, and printmaking paper. Items are tastefully displayed and you'll find a wide variety of artwork and crafts including pottery, prints, woodwork, stone art, bamboowork, fiber art, silk painting, and jewelry. Different artists staff the shop on different days, but business cards and phone numbers are available if you want to see more of something you like. Prices are reasonable and this is an excellent place to make that one "big" purchase.

Along the Hana Highway before you get to Baldwin Avenue is **Paia Trading Co.,** a discovery shop open Mon.–Fri. 9 A.M.–5 P.M. with collectibles like glass, telephones, aloha shirts, lanterns, jewelry, license plates, oil lamps, flotation balls, old bottles, and a smattering of pottery and antique furniture. Next door is **Boutique II,** open daily 10 A.M.–6 P.M., Sunday to 4 P.M., filled with ladies' apparel and alohawear. **Nuage Bleu,** a boutique open daily 10 A.M.–5 P.M., features distinctive fashions and gift items, mostly for women. **Jaggers,** open daily 9 A.M.–5 P.M., carries alohawear, fancy dresses, replicas of vintage aloha shirts for men, and some umbrellas. **Maui Hands** is near and has prints, turned wood, and some paper art pieces. Across the street is a shaved ice shop; **Sand and Sea,** primarily a

MAUI

sculpture gallery featuring dolphins; and **Paia Bay Gallery** for unique island art.

Around the corner and open daily until 6 P.M. is **Paia Mercantile,** displaying a collection of quilts, wooden boxes, hand-blown glass, jewelry, and many more intriguing craft items. Here too is **Moon Beam Tropics,** carrying women's sundresses, men's aloha shirts, shorts, T-shirts, and other island wear. Walk along the opposite side of Baldwin Avenue for a half block and you'll find a drawerful of boutiques and fashion shops, including **Old Plantation Store** for Hawaiian gifts, crafts, and clothing; and **Lotus Moon** for jewelry. **Jukebox** has a good selection of new and used CDs and tapes and some vinyl records, and **Mandala Ethnic Arts** carries furniture, clothing, gifts, statues, and alternative art from South and Southeast Asia. All are interesting shops and worth a peek. A bit farther along Baldwin Avenue is a branch **Bank of Hawaii** building and, quite a bit farther up, the new **post office** and a laundromat. Windsurfers can look for boards and gear at **Sailboards Maui.** At this and other surf shops in town, you can dress yourself for the beach and get a board to ride over those waves.

Pa'ia has two gas stations: **76,** which has made-to-order sandwiches at its minimart, and **Chevron.** These gas stations are the last places to fill your tank before reaching Hana. Next door is **Paia General Store** for groceries, supplies, and sundries, with a take-out snack window called the **Paia Drive Inn,** where most "local food" is under $7. Next to that, in what was at one time the Lower Pa'ia Theater, are a flower shop and **Simmer** sailboard shop. Simmer sells clothing, boards, components, and accessories, does sail repair, and rents boards. Lessons are given through HST in Kahului. Across the street is the Pa'ia Mercantile Shopping Complex, a collection of little shops selling items from surfing equipment to beads and gifts.

Heading down the road to Hana you'll see a **community center** on your right, the Mantoku-ji Buddhist temple on your left, and a little farther on the **Kuau Market,** a convenience store to get snacks for the road. Just around the bend is **Mama's Fish House,** and shortly after Ho'okipa Beach. Near mile marker 14 on the mountain side of the highway you'll come across **Maui Grown Market and Deli.** Housed in a vintage corrugated roof plantation-style building with a porch out front, it carries mostly sandwiches, salads, smoothies and packaged food items, with a limited supply of fresh produce. Lunch boxes are a specialty. Open daily 6:30 A.M.–7 P.M. (until 6 P.M. on Sunday), this is the last place before you really start to wind your way down the Hana Highway. A public phone is out front. Aside from side trips to Ha'iku, Kui'aha, and Ulumalu, you'll have clear sailing down the road to Hana.

HA'IKU

Around mile marker 11, Ha'iku Road heads up the hill to the little community of Ha'iku. From Upcountry, follow Kokomo Road down the hill after turning off of Route 365 below Makawao. Kokomo Road runs past the 4th Marine Division Park, a community park of athletic fields and a few picnic tables that was the site of the World War II 4th Marine Division camp. Ha'iku is an old cannery town, canning, boxing, and sending millions of pineapples and guavas to the world over the decades. After the cannery companies stopped production, their industrial buildings were renovated and turned into shops and studios, and have become, along with the Pa'uwela Cannery down the road, a center for artists and craftsmen. In the largest of the old cannery buildings, the pineapple cannery, now called **Ha'iku Marketplace,** you'll find among the many shops a **True Value Hardware** store, the **Haleakala Bike Company** shop for sales and rental, **Haiku Video, Ha'iku Pharmacy, Ha'iku Laundromat, Postal Plus,** and the **Ha'iku Grocery Store,** open seven days a week and a good place to pick up supplies. For what's happening in and around town, check out the community bulletin board. To the side of the huge parking lot in a separate building is **Trattoria Haiku,** 808/575-2820, a wonderful Italian eatery. Open daily except Monday and Tuesday for dinner only, this restaurant serves honest family food. Appetizers include grilled eggplant with tomatoes and mozzarella; entr'es might be seared ahi, angelhair pasta and spinach, spaghetti and meatballs like grandma used to make, or Italian sausage and penne pasta.

Also at the main intersection is **Fukushima Store,** a mini-mart open daily 6:30 A.M.–8 P.M., Sunday until 5 P.M. Here too you'll find a community bulletin board. For a quick bite to eat, stop around the corner at **Haiku Gourmet Takeout and Deli.** Across Ha'iku Road is the **post office,** and tucked behind it is **Ha'iku Town Center,** the second of the big remodeled cannery buildings that's slowly been turned into space for other use. This was the guava cannery. Among other shops is **Sativa,** a small shop dealing almost entirely with the numerous and various products made from the hemp plant. Next door is **Veg Out,** 808/575-5320, a vegetarian restaurant open Mon.–Sat. 8:30 A.M.–7:30 P.M. Every Saturday 8 A.M.–noon, you can find a **farmers' market** in front of this center for local produce and crafts.

Ha'iku Road runs east, wending its way along the mountain, in and out of gulches, over bridges, and through thickly vegetated forests to the community of Kui'aha. This is a great way to see the back roads of lower mountain Maui. There are lots of roads in this area, and many people have settled here, carving out their little bit of paradise. An alternate road to Kui'aha from the Hana Highway starts just past mile marker 12. Look for West Kui'aha Road and make a right heading for the old **Pa'uwela Cannery,** which is less than five minutes up the road. This huge tin can of a building has been divided into a honeycomb of studios and workshops housing fine artists, woodworkers, potters, T-shirt makers, and surfboard and sailboard makers. These artists and craftspeople come and go, so you're never sure just who will be occupying the studios. However, all welcome guests to come and browse, and buy. **Maui Art Works** is one of these place, and it also offers classes. Stop at the **Pauwela Cafe** for a cold drink, hot coffee, salad, sandwich, or pastry. Sit inside or out. Open Mon.–Sat. 7 A.M.–3 P.M., Sunday 8 A.M.–2 P.M. Have a peek at the **Hawaiian Fish Prints Gallery** next door. For other needs, try the small **Ohashi General Store** across the street; open 8 A.M. to about 7 P.M.

Not along the coast but in the rangeland above Ulumalu is **Lanikai Farm,** P.O. Box 797, Ha'iku, HI 96708, 808/572-1111, fax 808/572-3498. The farm's website is www.maui.net/~lanibb. Send email to lanibb@maui.net. This "Victorian-European style" newer home lies next to the Ko'olau Forest Reserve and is surrounded by tropical fruit trees. The guest rooms have private entrances, TV, small refrigerators, and lanai, and there is use of the washer/dryer and barbecue grill. A scrumptious breakfast of European-style breads and fresh fruit is served every morning. Rates are $65 single, $70 double, or $100 for two rooms; two nights minimum. A studio rental without breakfast runs $80, or two rooms for $105. The athletically inclined might want to have a turn on the squash court on property.

THE ROAD BEGINS

The Road to Hana holds many spectacles and surprises, but one of the best is the road itself . . . it's a marvel! The road was hacked out from the coastline and completed in 1927, every inch by hand using pick and shovel. Crushed volcanic rock was the first surface material. Rebuilt and partially paved in 1962, only in 1982 was the road fully paved. Nature and machines have taken their toll on the road, and in the early 1990s, the Hana Highway was widened and again resurfaced. Today it's smooth sailing, although stretches are periodically closed for repair. An ancient Hawaiian trail followed the same route for part of the way, but mostly people moved up and down this coastline by boat. What makes the scenery so special is that the road snakes along Maui's windward side. There's abundant vegetation and countless streams flowing from Haleakala, carving gorgeous valleys. There are a few scattered villages with a house or two that you hardly notice, and the beaches, although few, are empty. Mostly, however, it's the "feeling" that you get along this road. Nature is close and accessible, and it's so incredibly "South Sea island" that it almost seems artificial. But it isn't.

Road to Hana Tips

You've got 30 miles of turns ahead when Route 36 (mile marker 22) becomes Route 360 (mile marker 0) and the fun begins. The Hana Highway has the reputation of being a "bad road," but this isn't true. It's narrow, with plenty of hairpin turns, but it's well banked, has clearly marked bridges, and there's frequent maintenance going

MAUI

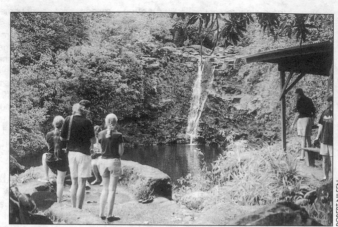

*waterfalls along the
Hana Highway*

ROBERT NILSEN

on (which can slow you up). Years back, it was a harrowing experience. When mudslides blocked the road, drivers were known to swap their cars with those on the opposite side and carry on to where they were going. The road's reputation sets people up to expect an ordeal, so they make it one, and, unfortunately, drive accordingly. Sometimes it seems as though tourists demand the road to be rugged, so that they can tell the folks back home that they, too, "survived the road to Hana." This popular slogan appears on T-shirts, copyrighted and sold by Hasegawa's famous store in Hana, and perpetuates this belief. You'll have no problem, and you'll see much more if you just take it easy.

Your speed will often drop below 10 miles per hour and will rarely exceed 25. Standard-shift cars are better for the turns. Cloudbursts occur at any time so be ready for slick roads. A heavy fall of fruit from roadside mango trees can also coat the road with slippery slime. Look as far up the road as possible and don't allow yourself to be mesmerized by the 10 feet in front of your hood. If your tire dips off a rough shoulder, don't risk losing control by jerking the wheels back on immediately. Ride it for a while and either stop or wait for an even shoulder to come back on. Local people trying to make time will often ride your rear bumper, but generally they won't honk. Pull over and let them by when possible. Pulloffs on this road are not overabundant, so be sure to choose your spot carefully. As a safety measure and courtesy to others, yield to all oncoming traffic at each bridge.

Driving from Kahului to Hana will take three hours, not counting some recommended stops. The greatest traffic flow is 10 A.M.–noon; returning "car trains" start by 3 P.M. and are heaviest around 5 P.M. Many white-knuckled drivers head for Hana as if it were a prized goal, without stopping along the way. This is ridiculous. The best sights are before and after Hana; the town itself is hardly worth the effort. Expect to spend a long day exploring the Hana Road. To go all the way to 'Ohe'o Stream and take in some sights, you'll have to leave your hotel at sunup and won't get back until sundown. If your budget can afford it, plan on staying the night in Hana (reservations definitely recommended) and return the next day. This is a particularly good plan if you have an afternoon departing flight from Kahului Airport. Also, most tourists seem terrified of driving the road at night. Actually it's easier. There is far less traffic, road reflectors mark the center and sides like a runway, and you're warned of oncoming cars by their headlights. Those in the know make much better time after dark! In case of **emergency,** roadside telephones are *makai* between mile markers 5 and 6, at the Halfway to Hana refreshment stand, and at Pua'a Ka'a State Wayside. Only 3,000 people live along the entire north coast of East Maui leading to and including Hana.

SIGHTS

Twin Falls

A favorite of locals, the trail to Twin Falls should take about 20–30 minutes. It's one of the first places to stop and enjoy along the road. Park near mile marker 2 just before the Ho'olawa Bridge. A new metal gate marks the jeep trail. This is private property and people live back here, but everyone seems to use it as if it were open to all. There's even a fruit stand at the entrance and a sign along the jeep trail pointing to the falls. On the way, a couple of side trails go off to the left and down to the steam. Guavas grow in this area and you might find ripe fruit at the right time of the year—there used to be a guava cannery in Ha'iku not far away. Before you get to an irrigation ditch, a small trail heads off to the left and leads to the stream and falls. The first pool is fed by two falls that give the area its name. A trail to the right goes up to the top of the falls and on to a second falls a short distance above. There you'll have more privacy. If you continue on to the irrigation ditch, cross it, and enter a secondary ravine, the trail will lead to another small falls.

Huelo

A few miles past the new bridge and pulloff for Twin Falls is Huelo. Huelo means "Famous Owl," a name given for the birds that used to inhabit trees in the area. In the 1840s, Huelo was bustling sugar town surrounded by cane fields; it even sustained a mill. Later, the area grew pineapple, but it's now just a quiet "rooster town" famous for **Kaulanapueo Church,** built in 1853. The structure is made from coral that was hauled up block by block from Waipi'o Bay below and is reminiscent of New England architecture. It's still used on the second and fourth Sundays of each month at 10 A.M., and a peek through the door reveals a stark interior with straight-backed benches and a front platform. The pit on the ocean side of the church building was used to make the lime and mortar mix. Few bother to stop, so it's quiet and offers good panoramas of the village and sea below. At the broad turnoff to Huelo, between mile markers 3 and 4, there's a public telephone and a row of mailboxes.

Kailua

The next tiny community is Kailua. Plenty of mountain apple trees flourish along this stretch. The multicolored trees are rainbow eucalyptus, introduced in the late 1800s from Australia and some of the most beautiful trees in Hawaii. Close by is a cousin, *Eucalyptus robusta,* which produces great timber, especially flooring, from its reddish-brown heartwood. This tree, due to its resins, gets extremely hard once it dries, so it must be milled immediately or you can do nothing with it. A few minutes beyond Kailua, notice a sudden difference in the humidity and in the phenomenal jungle growth that becomes even more pronounced.

Waikamoi Ridge

This nature walk (mosquitoes!) is a good place to stretch your legs and learn about native and introduced trees and vegetation (some are labeled). The turnout, good for about half a dozen vehicles, is not clearly marked along the highway past mile marker 9, but look for a metal gate at roadside and picnic tables in a clearing above the road. The well-defined, gradual trail leads through tall stands of trees. You know you're on the right path when you pass the signboard that says "Quiet, trees at work." This trail is about one mile long and takes less than an hour. On the way, you will get glimpses of the highway and stream below. The bamboo forest is most interesting when the wind rustles the trees so that they knock together like natural percussion instruments. Picnic tables are available at the start and end of the trail. Tall mango trees tower over the upper picnic area. Return via the same trail or walk down the jeep path.

Back on the road, and at the next bridge, is excellent drinking water. There's a stone barrel with a pipe coming out, and local people come to fill jugs with what they call "living water." It doesn't always run in summer but most times can be counted upon.

About one-half mile beyond Waikamoi Ridge the road crosses another stream where there's limited parking. Walk along the stream a short way to this waterfall. Although it may be slippery, you can go around the right side and up to another falls and cascade. Back on the road, you can see still other falls much farther up this valley.

ROAD TO HANA

PACIFIC OCEAN

KAULANAPUEO CHURCH

To Pa'ia and Kahului

Huelo

Pu'u Kuka'i (574 ft.)

360

Kailua

WAIKAMOI RIDGE TRAIL NATURE WALK

GARDEN OF EDEN

Puohokamoa Falls

Haipua'ena Falls

KEOPUKA ISLET SEABIRD SANCTUARY

KAUMAHINA STATE WAYSIDE

HONOMANU COUNTY PARK

CAMP KE'ANAE

Ke'anae

Keanae Valley

Nu'ailele Stream

KE'ANAE ARBORETUM

MAKU MANU ISLAND SEABIRD SANCTUARY

ST. GABRIEL'S CHURCH

Wailua

WAILUA WAYSIDE PARK

OVERLOOK

Waikani Falls

PUA'AKA'A STATE WAYSIDE

Kapa'ula Stream

Wailua Iki Stream

360 HANA HWY

Opuhanao Point

Nahiku

POOL AT ULAINO

Upper Nahiku

Kuhiwa Valley

Heleleike and Stream

Mokuhina Stream

Honomanu Stream

KEHANU GARDENS PI'ILANIHALE HEIAU

ULAINO RD.

KA'ELEKU CAVERNS

KA'ELEKU RD.

ALA'ELE RD.

HANA AIRPORT

WAI'ANAPANAPA STATE PARK

Natural Arch

HEIAU

Ancient Paved Trail

Nanu'alele Point

Hana Bay

HANA BEACH COUNTY PARK

Hana

KOKI BEACH PARK

Hamoa

Hamoa Beach

WAIOKA VILLAGE

Pu'uiki

31

To Kipahulu

Kapi'a Stream

Waiohonu Stream

3 mi

3 km

0

0

© SANDRA E. BISIGNANI TRUST AND AVALON TRAVEL PUBLISHING, INC.

Garden of Eden

This finely landscaped property is a private arboretum and botanical garden. Entrance $5; open daily 9 A.M.–2 P.M. Have a stroll here among the 26 acres of tropical trees and flowering bushes, over 500 of which are labeled for easy identification, or walk out to the Puohokamoa Falls overlook where you have a fine view down onto this graceful waterfall. There are restrooms here and a place to picnic, so make a stop on your way down the road.

Puohokamoa Falls

Following is Puohokamoa Falls, where you'll find a nice pool and picnic table. A short trail takes you to the pool and its 30-foot cliff, from which local kids jump off. You'll also find a trail near the falls, and if you go upstream about 100 yards you'll discover another invigorating pool with yet another waterfall. Swimming is great here, and the small crowd may be gone. If you hike downstream about one-half mile *through* the stream (no trail), you come to the top of a 200-foot falls from where you can peer over the edge. Be very conscious of water conditions and the dangers of being near the cliff edge.

Wayside Rest and Park

Less than two miles past Waikamoi Ridge are **Kaumahina State Wayside,** along the road, and the largely undeveloped **Honomanu County Park** down at Honomanu Bay. Some camp here unofficially with splendid views out to sea overlooking the rugged coastline and the black-sand beach of Honomanu Bay. Honomanu is not good for swimming because of strong currents, but is good for surfing. There are no amenities at Honomanu, but Kaumahina has picnic tables and restrooms. From Kaumahina, you're rewarded with splendid views down the coast to the Ke'anae Peninsula. Slicing deep into the heart of the mountain, Honomanu Valley has 3,000-foot cliffs and 1,000-foot waterfalls.

At **Nua'ailua Bay,** one bay farther on, two roads lead down to the water on either side of the stream. This spot is one where locals come to fish or surf and to spend a leisurely day by the ocean.

Ke'anae

Running back about five miles toward the center of the mountain, Ke'anae Valley is the largest on the north side of Haleakala. It and the Kaupo Valley on the mountain's southern slope were filled in by lava flows or landslides, greatly reducing their original size.

Usually clearly marked on the right side of the highway—the sign at times has gone missing—will be the six-acre **Ke'anae Arboretum,** established in 1971. A hike through this facility will exemplify Hawaiian plant life in microcosm. There are two sections, one of ornamental tropical plants (identified) and the other of Hawaiian domestic plants. Toward the upper end of the arboretum are taro fields, and the hillsides

ROBERT NILSEN

taro fields

MAUI

above are covered with the natural rainforest vegetation. You can picnic along Pi'ina'au Stream. Although the trail is hard to pick out, hardier hikers can continue for another mile or so through the rainforest; at the end of the trail is a pool and waterfall. As there is a gate across the entrance to the arboretum (at a sharp curve in the road), pull well off the road to park your car and walk in.

YMCA Camp Keanae is just before the arboretum. It looks exactly as its name implies, set on a gorgeous grassy slope. There are three bunkhouses (you must provide your own bedding), two bathrooms with showers, a gymnasium, and, for large groups only, a dining room and kitchen. Tent camping is allowed on the lawn; bring your own cooking gear. Arrival time is between 3 and 9 P.M., three-day maximum stay, $15 per person or $30 per family. Y members have reduced rates. All accommodations are by reservation only. For more information contact the camp at 808/248-8355, email: ymcacampKeanae@aol.com; for reservations contact the Maui Family YMCA office in Kahului at 808/242-9007.

Ke'anae Peninsula is a thumb-like appendage of land formed by a lava flow that came down the hollowed-out valley from Haleakala Crater. Its rocky shoreline is a favorite of local fishermen, perhaps appropriate as *ke'anae* means "mullet." A fantastic lookout is here—look for a telephone pole with a tsunami loudspeaker atop it at mile marker 17, and pull off just there. Below you'll see neat little farms, mostly growing taro. Shortly before this lookout, and about 200 yards past the arboretum, a public road heads down into the peninsula to a turnaround by the church. If you walk, park well off the roadway just as you get down the hill. The road makes an arc around to the parking lot beyond the church. About a mile, this stroll should take less than half an hour, but you may want to stop to chat. Most people living here are native Hawaiians. They still make poi the old-fashioned way: listen for the distinctive thud of poi-pounding in the background. Though *kapu* signs abound, the majority of people are friendly, and someone has even set up a fruit stand. If you visit, be aware that this is one of the last patches of ground owned by Hawaiians and tended in the old way. Be respectful, please. Notice the

lava-rock missionary church. Built in 1860, **Lanikili 'Ihi 'Ihi O Lehowa O na Kaua Church** was rebuilt in 1969. Neat and clean, it has straight-back, hardwood pews and a pleasant altar inside. Services are held twice a month. The cemetery to the side is groomed with tropical flowers while the grounds are rimmed by tall coconut trees. A ballpark and public telephone stand next to the church.

Fruit Stands

Past Ke'anae between mile markers 17 and 18 is the **Halfway to Hana** roadside refreshment stand, where you can buy banana bread, shave ice, ice cream, sandwiches, fruit, and something to drink. Notice the picture-perfect, idyllic watercress farm on your left.

Do yourself a favor and look for **Uncle Harry's Fruit Stand,** clearly marked on the left past the Ke'anae Peninsula just beyond the Ke'anae school. Unfortunately, this *kahuna,* who knew a great deal of the natural pharmacology of old Hawaii and was a living encyclopedia on herbs and all their healing properties, has passed away, but his spirit lives on. Past mile marker 18 on the right is a fruit stand operated by a fellow named Joseph. He not only has coconuts, pineapples, and papayas, but also little-tasted exotic fruits like mountain apples, star fruit, strawberry guavas, and Tahitian lemons. An authentic fruit stand worth a stop. Another one, operated by a Hawaiian woman, is only 50 yards farther on the left. If you have a hankering for fruit, this might be the spot. Other fruit stands pop up now and again on this road. It's just a down-home cottage industry. No definite times necessarily, just open whenever. Look for them as you pass, stop to refresh yourself, and leave a little for the local economy.

Wailua

At mile marker 18, you come to Wailua. Similar to Ke'anae, it too is covered in taro but not to as great an extent, and is a picturesque spot. Turn left here on Wailua Road and proceed to St. Gabriel's Church. Just beyond it you'll find the **Miracle of Fatima Shrine,** so named because a freak storm in the 1860s washed up enough coral onto Wailua Beach that the church could be constructed by the Hawaiian congregation. There is a lovely and relatively easy-access waterfall nearby. Pass the church, turn right, and park by the large field. Look for a worn path (may be private, but no signs or hassle) that leads down to the falls. Look inland up the valley and you'll see a long sliver of a falls just below the roadway that clings to the *pali*. You can look down on this village and valley from several pull-offs and the Wailua Wayside Park, all past the Wailua Road turnoff along the Hana Highway.

Wailua Wayside Park

Cut into the ridge directly along the roadway is the small parking lot of this tiny wayside park. Drive slowly and keep your eyes peeled as the sign comes up quickly and you have little time to signal your turn to get off the road. A short series of steps leads up under a canopy of overhanging *hao* tree branches to a flat grassy area about 20 feet above the road. From here you have an expansive view down onto Wailua and up along the face of the *pali*. From the rear of the parking area, you can peer into the adjoining *mauka* valley, and when it rains several waterfalls cascade down the valley walls inland. No facilities. From here, you can see the Ke'anae Valley and Ko'olau Gap. Look closely. From this vantage point it is obvious how lava and rubble from the Haleakala basin poured down the mountain filling this once deep-cut valley. A pulloff on the ocean side of the roadway about one-half mile farther provides you with perhaps a better view down into Wailua Valley.

Pua'a Ka'a State Wayside

This spot is about 14 miles before Hana. There's no camping, but there are a few picnic tables and restrooms. Across the road from the parking lot is a short path that leads to Kopili'ula and Waikani Falls. A very public place, it's not the best scenery along the road and these are not the best pools for swimming.

Nahiku

The village, named after the Hawaiian version of the Pleiades, is reached by a steep but now paved three-mile road and has the dubious distinction of being one of the wettest spots along the coast. The well-preserved and tiny village church near the bottom of the road was constructed in 1867 (renovated in 1993) and is just big enough for a handful of pews. You may see school kids playing ball in the yard next to the church, the only place in the community open and large enough. The turnaround at oceanside is where many locals come to shore-fish. Often during the summer months, beginning around 3 P.M., an extended family pod of dolphins enters Nahiku Bay to put on an impromptu performance of water acrobatics just for the joy of it. At one time Nahiku was a thriving Hawaiian village with thousands of inhabitants. Today it's home to only about 70 people, the best-known being former Beatle George Harrison. A few inhabitants are Hawaiian families, but mostly the people are wealthy Mainlanders seeking isolation. After a few large and attractive homes went up, the real estate agents changed the description from "desolate" to "secluded." What's the difference? About $1 million per house! At the turn of the 20th century this was the site of the Nahiku Rubber Co., the only commercial rubber plantation in the United States. Many rubber trees still line the road, although the venture collapsed in 1912 because the rubber was poor due to the overabundance of rainfall. Some people have augmented their incomes by growing *pakalolo* in the rainforest of this area. However, the alternative-lifestyle people who first came here and have settled in have discovered that there is just as much money to be made raising ornamental tropical flowers, and have become real "flower children." Many have roadside stands along the Hana Highway where payment for the flowers displayed is on the honor system. Leave what is requested—prices will be marked.

Near mile marker 29 in Upper Nahiku, you'll come upon **Nahiku Ti Gallery** for gifts and crafts, a pastry and refreshment shop, and a little stand selling baked breadfruit bread and smoked fish kabobs.

ACCOMMODATIONS

Bed-and-breakfast establishments and similar accommodations lie along the road to Hana, many in or near Huelo. Only a few are listed below.

$50–100

Surrounded by trees, bamboo, and wildflowers, **Halfway to Hana House** is a small and peaceful getaway with views over the lush north coast. As it's a one studio apartment on the lower level of the house, there are no distracting noises. Its private entrance leads into a comfortable room with double bed and mini kitchen. In a separate room is the bath, and a breakfast patio is out back. Breakfast of pastries and fruit from the property is waiting every morning if you desire. Room rates are $75 single and $85 double with breakfast, $70 and $75 without; three nights minimum, 10 percent discount for a week or more. A kayak and scuba enthusiast, the owner can tell you about good ocean spots to visit. Contact: P.O. Box 675, Ha'iku, HI 96708, 808/572-1176, fax 808/572-3609, or visit the website at www.maui.net/~gailp. Send email to gailp@maui.net.

Ali'i Hono Hu'ako Tropical Plantation, down behind Kaulanapueo Church on a 300-foot cliff above Waipi'o Bay, is a peaceful 38-acre retreat and alternative working plantation farm that retains a connection to the past in the guise of a *heiau* while it looks toward the peace and tranquillity of the future. The property is dotted with tropical permaculture orchards and gardens, and the stream was blocked to form a naturally heart-shaped pond. Amidst bamboo, a globe-like kiva meditation hall sits about the main house and office, below which is a heated swimming pool and spa. The two suites on the garden level of the house rent for $90 and $95 a night, or together for $135. The gazebo suite at poolside below the nine-sided office is often used by newlyweds; it runs $150. Overlooking much of the farm and surrounding forested hillsides, the bamboo hexa-hale goes for $125. The cliff house, set on the precipice of the 300-foot *pali* next to a waterfall, with a commanding view of the bay, is yours for $250. Any stay less than three nights requires an additional housekeeping fee. Breakfast of organic fruits from the property, home-baked muffins and croissants, juice, and tea will be placed in your refrigerator for your first morning. After the first day, there is a nominal charge for breakfast if you order it, but you can fix whatever you want as each unit is equipped with a kitchenette. Come, relax, refresh, and reinvigorate, or participate in one of the activities offered. For additional information and reservations contact: P.O. Box 600, Ha'iku, HI 96708, 808/573-1391, fax 808/573-0141. The planta-

tion's website is www.retreatmaui.com. Send email to bnb@retreatmaui.com.

The lush and verdant grounds of the **Kailua Maui Gardens** is in the tiny community of Kailua. Set amidst a landscape of tropical trees and flowering plants are four cottages, one garden apartment, and a three-bedroom house, yet surprisingly each unit maintains a great deal of privacy. The swimming pool, spa, and barbecue are for everyone's use. For 2–3 nights, the cottages run $90–115, the apartment $95, and the house $250; rates decrease for longer stays. Two nights minimum. The whole property can also be rented for up to 18 people. Gay friendly. For information and reservations, write Kailua Maui Gardens, S.R. 1, Box 9, Ha'iku, HI 96708, or call 808/572-9726 or 800/258-8588, fax 808/572-5934. Visit the website www.maui.net/~kmg or send email to kmg@maui.net.

$100–150

About one mile down a dirt road near Twin Falls is **Maluhia Hale B&B,** P.O. Box 687, Ha'iku, HI 96708, 808/572-2959, website: www.maui.net/~djg, email: djg@maui.net. Off the main route, this 2.5-acre quiet and relaxing spot is enveloped by greenery yet has the wide ocean vista spreading at your feet. A detached open-beam plantation-style cottage with screened porch and a sitting room has a king bed, a nearly full kitchen, and a detached bathing room that has a clawfoot tub and shower; very commodious. The cottage can accommodate three. Light, open, and airy, it rents for $110 a night with breakfast, $20 for an extra person; two nights minimum.

Down at the end of the Hana Road is the **Tea House Cottage.** This B&B is "off the grid," generating its own power by photovoltaic cells and collecting its own water. Quiet, with no distractions, the Tea House Cottage offers broad views of the ocean. The one cottage has a Japanese "feel," with a living room, kitchen, bedroom, and screened lanai; a few steps away is the redwood bathhouse. Art on the walls is by the owner/artist, and it complements the rattan furniture and oriental rugs. The room rate is $110 double or $95 single a night; three nights minimum, seventh night no charge. A daily breakfast is provided. A tunnel through the trees leads you to the house, and walkways run throughout the property, one to a small stupa built some

25 years ago by a Tibetan monk. For more information: P.O. Box 335, Ha'iku, HI 96708, 808/572-5610. Visit the cottage on the Web at www.maui.net/~teahouse. Send email to teahouse@maui.net.

$150–200

In the community of Huelo, with a spectacular view up the coast toward Hana, is **Huelo Point Lookout.** Here, the main house and three cottages are scattered around the acreage, which is finely landscaped with tropical trees and bushes. The rock-wall swimming pool is inviting, and a soak in the hot tub under a cloudless night sky befits a day on the island. Wake up to the sound of birds singing in the trees, have your breakfast on the lanai, and spend your day leisurely hanging out here or venture out to see the island sights. Once a fisherman's cottage, surrounded by banana trees and heliconia, the remodeled Star Cottage has an indoor/outdoor bathroom, a solarium, and a queen bed and double futon, $155–185. Although smaller,

Haleakala Cottage studio has a full kitchen and king bed in one room, $135–165. Outside is an enclosed shower and a covered lanai. The Rainbow Cottage is a newer building, renting for $235–325. Downstairs are the living room and kitchen; a 22-foot tall wall of glass offers the best views of the coast from either floor. Make your way up the handmade wooden spiral staircase to the upstairs bedroom where a king bed lies under a large skylight. Outside is your own private hot tub. The Sunrise Suite in the main house has a wall of sliding glass doors that faces east for perfect sunrise views, its own kitchen, and large bath. This suite rents for $325–350 a night, but the entire main house can also be rented for families or groups of up to eight people for $2,450–2,650 a week, one week minimum. Cash or traveler's checks only; no credit cards accepted. For additional information: P.O. Box 117, Paia, HI 96779, 808/573-0914 or 800/871-8645, fax 808/573-0227. Visit the website www.maui.net/~dreamers or send email to dreamers@maui.net.

HANA

Hana is about as pretty a town as you'll find anywhere in Hawaii, but if you're expecting anything stupendous you'll be sadly disappointed. For most it will only be a quick stopover at a store or beach en route to 'Ohe'o Stream: the townsfolk refer to these people as "rent-a-car tourists." The lucky who stay in Hana, or those not worried about time, will find plenty to explore throughout the area. The town is built on rolling hills that descend to Hana Bay; much of the surrounding land is given over to pasture, while trim cottages wearing flower corsages line the town's little lanes. Before the white people arrived, Hana was a stronghold conquered and reconquered by the kings of Maui and those of the north coast of the Big Island. The most strategic and historically laden spot is Ka'uiki Hill, the remnant of a cinder cone that dominates Hana Bay. This area is steeped in Hawaiian legend, and old stories relate that it was the demigod Maui's favorite spot. It's said that he transformed his daughter's lover into Ka'uiki Hill and turned her into the gentle rains that bathe it to this day.

Changing History

Hana was already a plantation town in the mid-1800s when a hard-boiled sea captain named George Wilfong started producing sugar on his 60 acres there. Over the years the laborers came from the standard mixture of Hawaiian, Japanese, Chinese, Portuguese, Filipino, and even Puerto Rican stock. The *luna* were Scottish, German, or American. All have combined to become the people of Hana. After having grown to half a dozen plantations and producing for decades, sugar production faded out by the 1940s and Hana began to die, its population dipping below 500. Just then, San Francisco industrialist Paul Fagan purchased 14,000 acres of what was to become the **Hana Ranch.** Realizing that sugar was *pau,* he replanted his lands in *pangola* range grass and imported 300 Hereford cattle from another holding on Moloka'i. Their white faces staring back at you as you drive past are now a standard part of Hana's scenery. Today, Hana Ranch has about 3,000 acres and raises more than 2,000 head of cattle. Hana's population, at 1,900, is about 48 percent Hawaiian.

MAUI

Fagan loved Hana and felt an obligation to and affection for its people. He also decided to retire here, and with enough money to materialize just about anything, he decided that Hana could best survive through limited tourism. He built the Hotel Hana-Maui, which catered to millionaires, mostly his friends, and began operation in 1946. Fagan owned a baseball team, the San Francisco Seals, and brought them to Hana in 1946 for spring training. The community baseball field behind the hotel was made for them. This

was a brilliant publicity move because sportswriters came along; becoming enchanted with Hana, they gave it a great deal of copy and were probably the first to publicize the phrase "Heavenly Hana." It wasn't long before tourists began arriving.

Unfortunately, the greatest heartbreak in modern Hana history occurred at just about the same time, on April 1, 1946. An earthquake in Alaska's Aleutian Islands sent huge tsunamis that raked the Hana Coast. These destroyed hundreds of homes, wiping out entire villages and tragically sweeping away many people. Hana recovered, but never forgot. Life went on, and the men began working as *paniolo* on Fagan's spread and during roundup would drive the cattle through town and down to Hana Bay where the animals were forced to swim to waiting barges. Other entire families went to work at the resort, and so Hana lived again. It's this legacy of quietude and old-fashioned *aloha* that attracted people to Hana over the years. Everyone knows that Hana's future lies in its uniqueness and remoteness, and no one wants it to change. The people as well as the tourists know what they have here. What really makes Hana "heavenly" is similar to what's preached in Sunday school: everyone wants to go there, but not everyone makes it.

Hana Festivals

As is the case in most Hawaiian towns, Hana has many local festivals and events. First in the year is the fireworks on New Year's Eve over Fagan's cross. In late March, the weekend **Taro Festival,** with its traditional ceremonies, games, music, authentic foods and a food market, arts and crafts exhibitions, and hula demonstrations, thrills everyone. People come from all over the state to watch and participate; make plans well in advance. Later in June or early July, the children of town get treated to the **Makeke,** a children's festival, when all sorts of games and celebrations are held. For decades, Hana has had a tie with the great American sport. To honor this connection, a softball tournament is held over the Labor Day weekend, pitting families and friends against one another in friendly but serious competition. As with all of the state, the **Aloha Festival** is celebrated with gusto. Parades, lu'au, a fishing tournament, and many other activities are organized.

SIGHTS

Hana Bay

Dominating the bay is the red-faced **Ka'uiki Hill.** Fierce battles raged here, especially between Maui chief Kahekili and Kalaniopu'u of Hawaii, just before the islands were united under Kamehameha. Kalaniopu'u held the natural fortress until Kahekili forced a capitulation by cutting off the water supply. It's believed that Kamehameha himself boarded Captain James Cook's ship after a lookout spotted it from this hill. More importantly, Queen Ka'ahumanu, Kamehameha's favorite and the Hawaiian *ali'i* most responsible for ending the old *kapu* system and leading Hawaii into the "new age," was born in a cave here in 1768. Until very recent times fish-spotters sat atop the hill looking for telltale signs of large schools of fish.

To get there, simply follow Uakea Road when it splits from the Hana Road at the police station, and follow the signs to the bay. Take it right down to the pier and **Hana Beach County Park,** open 6 A.M.–10 P.M. Hana Beach has full amenities, and the swimming is good. It's been a surfing spot for centuries, although the best breakers occur in the middle of the bay. Until the '40s, cane trains rode tracks from the fields above town out onto the pier, where the cut stalks were loaded onto boats to be taken to the mill for processing. To explore Ka'uiki look for a pathway to the right of the pier and follow it. Hana disappears immediately; few tourists walk out this way. Walk for a few minutes until the lighthouse comes clearly into view. The footing is slightly difficult but there are plenty of ironwoods to hang onto as the path hugs the mountainside. A few pockets of red-sand beach eroded from the cinder cone are below. A copper plaque erected in 1928 commemorates the spot of Ka'ahumanu's birth. Proceed straight ahead to the lighthouse sitting on a small island. To cross, leap from one jagged rock to another. If this doesn't suit you, take your bathing suit and wade across a narrow sandy-bottomed channel. Stop for a few moments and check the wave action to avoid being hurled against the rocks. When you've got it timed, go for it! The view from up top is great.

Fagan Memorial

Across from the Hotel Hana-Maui, atop Lyon's hill, is a lava-stone cross erected to the memory of Paul Fagan, who died in 1960. The land is privately owned, but it's okay to walk up there if there are no cattle in the pasture; inquire at the hotel first. The road to the top starts at the hotel guest parking lot, and although it starts out all right, it gets deceptively steep toward the top.

From atop the hill you get the most panoramic view of the entire Hana area. After a rain, magic mushrooms have been known to pop up in the "cow pies" in the pasture surrounding the cross.

Wananalua Church

Near the hotel is the Wananalua Congregational Church, built from coral blocks in 1838 and placed on the National Register of Historic Places in 1988. Sunday service is at 10 A.M. The missionaries deliberately and symbolically built it on top of an old *heiau,* where the pagan gods had been worshipped for centuries. It was the custom of chiefs to build *heiau* before entering battle, and this area is supposed by some to be a site of battle between forces of King Kamehameha I from the Big Island and Maui soldiers. Since Hana was always contested ground, dozens of minor *heiau* can be found throughout the region.

Across the street is the newer and lovely St. Mary's Catholic Church. Its wood construction and decorative detail contrast vividly with the plain, sturdy, rather unornamented Wananalua Church. Mass is celebrated Sunday 9 A.M., weekdays 7 A.M., and Friday 5 P.M. Visitors welcome.

Hana Cultural Center

Along Uakea Road on the right, kitty-corner from the Hana Bay entrance road, this center is open daily 10 A.M.–4 P.M. (but may open at noon on Sunday); $2 donation gladly accepted. Founded in 1971, the Hana Cultural Center, 808/248-8622, occupies an unpretentious building (notice the beautifully carved koa doors, however) on the grounds of the old courthouse and jail. The center houses fine examples of quiltwork: one, entitled "Aloha Kuuhae," was done by Rosaline Kelinoi, a Hana resident and the first woman voted into the State Legislature. There are pre-contact stone implements, tapa cloth, and an extensive shell collection. Your donation entitles you to visit the courthouse and jail next door. Simple but functional, with bench and witness stand, it makes Andy and Barney of Mayberry look like big time. This tiny courthouse was used regularly 1871–1978, and is still used monthly for the same purpose. It's been placed on the Hawaii Register of Historic Places. The jail, "Hana Lockup," was also built in 1871 and finally renovated in 1997. The townsfolk knew whenever it held an inmate because he or she became the groundskeeper and the grass would suddenly be mowed.

In the ancient Hawaiian style and using traditional materials, a sleeping house, cook house, meeting house, and canoe shed have been constructed to the side and below the center to give you an idea of what types of buildings were used in Hawaii in the past. On the terrace below these structures is a small **ethnobotanical garden** of medicinal and agricultural native plants. Pick up a brochure about the plants inside the museum. Be sure to stop at the cultural center while in Hana to

Wananalua Church

J.D. BISIGNANI

learn a bit about local history and culture. The center's website is www.planet-hawaii.com/hana.

Ka'eleku Caverns

One of Hana's newest adventures is spelunking. There are 50 known caves on Maui and 150 on the Big Island. Only a short section of the Thurston Lava Tube in Hawaii Volcanoes National Park and two to three others can be entered. Some 30,000 years old, Ka'eleku (Standing in the Dark) Cave near Kahanu Gardens in Hana is the only cave on Maui that's open to the public, and it's a beauty. This cave, like all others in Hawaii, is actually a lava tube 30–40 feet below the surface, so the cave follows the lay of the land up the mountainside. No matter what the temperature is outside, it's always a moderate 64–72 degrees inside. You enter through a skylight and make your way down the steps to the floor of the cave, which once flowed with molten lava. Let your eyes adjust to the darkness before proceeding downhill. As liquid lava surged through this tube it scored the walls, leaving striations. Here and there, you will also see benches and ledges along the sides where lava cooled faster on the periphery than the middle. Some rubble has fallen from the ceiling or off the walls creating small mounds, but the trail skirts or traverses these obstructions. You can walk upright all the way, no kneeling or crawling involved, and there's no problem with claustrophobia. Other natural features are lava stalactites and stalagmites, drip columns, a bowling alley-like channeling with gutters down both sides, ropy pahoehoe lava levees, clinkers of rough 'a'a, side loops, convergent channels, and over tubes. A very unusual feature, perhaps peculiar to this cave alone, is delicate, filigreed grape-like botryoid clusters. And the colors, who would have thought? There is gray, blue, brown, gold, and copper—quite astounding. One of the mysteries of this cave is that the air flows in two different directions. Through the lower portion, the flow is downward and out a series of skylights; in the upper section, the air flows uphill, exiting at a yet undiscovered spot. As this cave has only recently been open to visitors, it's still in very pristine condition. Care must be taken not to touch delicate formations or accidentally crush or break anything fragile. "Cave softly and carry a big light" is the owner's motto. Maui Cave Adventures is run by Chuck Thorne, and he can set you up with a tour. All tours are guided, very informative, and safe. Chuck is happy to share with you what he knows about this cave as well as other caves in the state. Check in is at the kiosk at the cave entrance, about one-half mile along Ulaino Road after turning off the Hana Highway. An informative schematic drawing of the cave, with explanation, is displayed at the parking lot. A hard hat, light, and drinks are provided. Wear long pants, closed-toe shoes, and a T-shirt—something that you don't mind getting a little dirty. If you have any interest in caving or have never even been underground before, you'll be glad you had a look at this one. A one-hour walking tour costs $29 per person, and adventurers must be at least eight years old. The two-hour "wild" tour is $69 per person, with an age requirement of 15 years old. For those who just want a taste of what's below, the 30-minute tour at $12.50 might be just right; minimum age of seven. Two-person minimum for tours to run. For information and advanced reservations, contact the company at Maui Cave Adventures, P.O. Box 40, Hana, HI 96713, 808/248-7308 (8 A.M.–8 P.M.), or visit the website www.mauicave.com. Send email to info@mauicave.com.

Kahanu Gardens

Turn off Hana Highway onto Ulaino Road and proceed toward the ocean. Here, the pavement soon gives way to a dirt track and leads about a mile and a half to Kahanu Gardens, just past a shallow stream. The gardens are open Mon.–Fri. 10 A.M.–2 P.M., but may be closed at any time if, because of heavy rains, the stream (no bridge) is too high or moving too swiftly to cross. This 123-acre tropical garden runs down to the tortured lava coastline. Part of the National Tropical Botanical Garden system, the Kahanu Gardens contain domestic and imported tropical plants, including a huge native pandanus forest and large and varied collections of breadfruit and coconut trees. While one of the purposes of the garden is to propagate and protect Hawaiian and Polynesian ethnobotanical plants, within its property is **Pi'ilanihale Heiau**, Hawaii's largest, with massive walls that rise more than 50 feet and a broad top that's twice as long as a football field and half that wide. A National Historical Landmark, this heiau is probably from the 14th century and

MAUI

possibly a royal compound associated with Pi'ilani, a Maui king from around 1500 who seems to have unified the island as one political unit. Two-hour guided walking tours are given for $10 per person (schedule open to change); meet at the gate. Alternatively, you may walk through on your own for $5. The walk is level, but leave yourself 1–1.5 hours for the tour. Contact the gardens at 808/248-8912, or visit the website at www.ntbg.org, for information and reservations.

Just before the NTBG is the private **Kaia Ranch Tropical Botanical Garden,** a 10-acre site open daily 9 A.M.–5 P.M. for self-guided tours; $3 entrance fee.

Pool at Ulaino

Past Kahanu Gardens, Ulaino Road continues to roughen, crosses two more streams, passes several homesites being carved out of the bush, and ends after more than a mile at a parking area near the ocean. This may not be drivable during heavy rains with a 2WD rental car but may be passable with a 4WD vehicle. Walk across the boulders that form the beach at the mouth of the stream and stay along the *pali* for 100 yards or so until you come upon what some people call Blue Pond or Blue Pool tucked behind some larger rocks. This hideaway is an old local favorite, a clothing-optional swimming spot where a waterfall drops freshwater into an oceanside pool. Not always blue, it's sometimes murky when water brings large amounts of sediment down from the hillside above. As always at pools, be aware of stones and branches that might come over the top and give you a knot on your noggin as a souvenir of your time in paradise.

Hana Airport

Less than a mile in toward town from Ulaino Road, on 'Alal'ele Road, a sign points left to Hana Airport, where **Pacific Wings,** 808/873-0877, schedules some flights. All flights to Hana go through Kahului, from where you can get connecting flights to other Hawaiian cities and the Mainland. Hotel Hana-Maui operates a shuttle ($5 per person) between the airport and the hotel for its guests, and will take others when not full. There is no public transportation in Hana, and only **Dollar Rent A Car,** 808/248-8237, can provide wheels for you—make reservations be-

fore arriving in Hana. The booth is open 8 A.M.–5 P.M. daily at the airport. Aside from the airline counters, there is only a public telephone and restrooms here at this tiny terminal.

Blue Hawaiian helicopters makes one run up the Hana Coast that stops at the Hana Airport. Here, it connects with ground transportation by **Temptation Tours,** so you can go one way by air and the other by land, a fly-drive offering. Neither company has an office at the Hana Airport.

The real adventurer may want to take note that power hang gliding flights are offered at the Hana Airport, but by appointment only. Contact **Hang Gliding Maui,** 808/572-6557, to arrange a 30- or 60-minute flight over the Hana Coast.

Wai'anapanapa State Park

Only three miles outside Hana, and down a road that's clearly marked along the highway at mile marker 32, this state park offers not only tent and RV camping but housekeeping cabins sleeping up to six. Set some distance from the beach and tenting area, the cabins offer hot water, electricity, a full kitchen, bathroom, bedrooms, and bedding, and rent for $45 a night for up to four people and $5 for each additional person. A deposit is required. They're very popular so book far in advance by writing Division of State Parks or visiting its office at 54 S. High St., Wailuku, HI 96793, 808/984-8109. The grassy camping area has picnic tables, water, showers, and restrooms. Even for those not camping, Wai'anapanapa is a "must-stop." Pass the office to get to the beach park and its black-sand beach. The swimming is dangerous during heavy surf because the bottom drops off quickly, but on calm days it's mellow. The snorkeling is excellent, and it should be, as Wai'anapanapa means "Glistening Waters." Just offshore is a clearly visible natural stone bridge. Some very brave local kids come and jump off the rocks here—for the thrill, no doubt.

A short, well-marked trail leads to **Wai'anapanapa Caves.** The tunnel-like trail passes through a thicket of vines and *hau,* a bush used by the Hawaiians to mark an area as *kapu.* The two small caves are formed from lava. The water trapped inside is clear. These caves mark the site of a Hawaiian legend, in which a lovely princess named Popu'alaea fled from her cruel husband Ka'akae. He found her hiding here and killed her. Bringing a sense of truth to this legend, hordes of tiny red shrimp occupy these caves at certain times of the year, turning the waters red, and this the Hawaiians take as a reminder of the poor slain princess.

Along the coastline here are remnants of an ancient paved Hawaiian trail known as the **King's Highway.** You can follow it for a short distance. To get to the section running north toward the airport, cross the black-sand beach and head up the far side. This trail is reasonably well maintained but fairly rugged due to lava and cinders and stays on or near the cliffs most of the way. This walk takes about two hours. A section of the trail also runs south past the cabins along the coast toward Hana. Along the way you'll pass small bays, lava cliffs, blow holes, and an old *heiau*. The vegetation is lush, and long fingers of black lava stretch out into cobalt-blue waters. Expect about a three hour hike.

Along this road to the state park and at various spots along the Hana Highway, small roadside stands offer flowers or fruit for sale by the honor system.

BEACHES

Red Sand Beach

Named Kaihalulu (Roaring Sea), this is a fascinating and secluded beach area, but unfortunately the steep walk down can be treacherous. The path skirts the side of a cliff, and the footing is made tough because of unstable and crumbly cinders. Grave accidents have occurred, and even locals often won't make the trip. Follow Uakea Road past the turnoff to Hana Bay. Proceed until you pass the public tennis courts on your right and the community center on your left. The road dead-ends shortly. Head through the open lot between the community center and hotel property, where you pick up a worn path. Ahead is a Japanese cemetery with its distinctive headstones, some now being lost to wave erosion and a degrading shoreline. Below are pockets of red sand amidst fingers of black lava washed by sky-blue water. There are many tide pools here. Keep walking around Ka'uiki Head until you are obviously in the hollowed-out amphitheater of the red cinder cone. Pat the walls to feel how crumbly they are—the red "sand" is

eroded cinder. The water in the cove is fantastically blue against the redness.

Across the mouth of the bay are little pillars of stone, like castle parapets from a fairy kingdom, that keep the water safe for swimming. This is a favorite fishing spot for local people and the snorkeling is good, too. The beach is best in the morning before 11 A.M.; afterward it can get hot if there's no wind and rough if the wind is from the north—remember the beach's name. The coarse red sand massages your feet, and there's a natural hot tub area in foamy pools of water along the shore.

Koki Beach

The beach is a mile or so out of town heading toward 'Ohe'o. Look for Haneo'o Road on your left with a sign directing you to Koki and Hamoa Beaches. Koki is only a few hundred yards on the left, at the first set of pullouts by the water. This beach is a mixture of white sand and red sand from the hill next to it. The riptides are fierce in here so don't swim unless it's absolutely calm, but locals surf here when conditions are right—usually in the summer. The winds can whip along here, too, even though at Hamoa Beach, less than a mile away, it can be dead calm. Koki is excellent for beachcombing and for a one-night unofficial bivouac.

A very special person named Smitty lived in a cave on the north side of the beach. A distinguished older man, he "dropped out" years back and came here to live a simple monk's existence. He kept the beach clean and saved a number of people from the riptide. He was a long-distance runner who would tack up a "thought for the day" on Hana's public bulletin board. People loved him and he loved them in return. In 1984 the roof of his cave collapsed and he was killed. When his body was recovered, he was in a kneeling position. At his funeral, all felt a loss, but there was no sadness because all were sure that Smitty had gone home.

Hamoa Beach

Follow this loop road a few minutes past Koki Beach to the other side of this small thumb of a peninsula to Hamoa Beach. Between Koki and Hamoa are the remnants of the extensive Haneo'o fishpond, part of which is still discernible. This entire area is an eroding cinder

MAUI

Hamoa Bay and Beach

J.D. BISIGNANI

cone known as **Kaiwi O Pele** (Bones of Pele). This is the spot where the swinish pig god, Kamapua'a, ravished her. Pele also fought a bitter battle with her sister here, who dashed Pele on the rocks, giving them their anatomical name. Out to sea is the diminutive 'Alau Island, a remnant left over by Maui after he finished fishing up the Hawaiian Islands.

You can tell that Hamoa Beach is no ordinary beach the minute you start walking down the paved, torch-lined walkway. This is the semiprivate beach of the Hotel Hana-Maui. But don't be intimidated, because no one can own the beach in Hawaii. Hamoa is terrific for swimming and snorkeling on calm days or bodysurfing or surfing on days when the wind is up a little. The hotel guests are shuttled here by buses throughout the day, so if you want this lovely beach to yourself arrive before midmorning and stay after late afternoon. There is a pavilion that the hotel uses for its lunch buffets, as well as restrooms and showers.

ACCOMMODATIONS

$50–100

Joe's Place, 808/248-7033, a very modest but clean self-serve guesthouse, is a home that's been split into eight guest rooms. A Maui-style sign reads, "The brown front door may be open. If so, you are welcome to go inside and look around. All available rooms are open and the rates are posted in each room." Rooms for singles or doubles cost $45, $55 with a private bath. Also available is a room for $65 that can sleep three. Cash or traveler's checks only. Checkout time is at 10 A.M. and check-in is at 3 P.M. "or as soon as room is available." Reservations are held until 6 P.M. There's kitchen access, a communal TV room, daily towel change, and maid service on request at an extra charge.

Hana Maui Vacation Rental is a small place with three new units. Neat and tidy, one has a kitchen while the other two have only microwaves. All have bedrooms separate from the cooking area, bathrooms with showers, and separate entrances. While not large, it's certainly adequate, and the price is right. The room with a kitchen runs $65 a night, with the microwave $55; maximum three per room. Monthly and *kama'aina* rates available. Call or write for reservations: P.O. Box 455, Hana HI, 96713, tel./fax 808/248-8087 or 800/991-2422.

Kulani's Hideaway, 808/248-8234, has two units that rent for $65 double occupancy. Nothing special, they are, however, comfortable and conveniently located on the road down to the state park.

Adjacent to the Hana Cultural Center, the **Aloha Cottages** are owned and operated by Zenzo and Fusae Nakamura and are the best bargain in town. The studio and cottages are meticulously clean, well built, and sparsely appointed. For $65–95, $10–25 per additional guest, you get two bedrooms and bath, a full kitchen, living room, linoleum floors throughout, a deck, and outdoor grills, but no television or phones. Mrs. Nakamura is very friendly and provides daily maid service. In season, fruit trees on the property provide free fruit to guests. For reservations, contact: P.O. Box 205, Hana, HI 96713, 808/248-8420.

At **Josie's Hana Hideaway,** Josie offers two spartan rooms in the rear of her house and one up at the front. Each large and comfy unit (the front unit is smaller than the ones behind) has a bedroom/sitting room with a kitchenette in the corner, color TV by the queen bed, a full bathroom, and a separate entrance. If you want, you can prepare your meal in the kitchenette on the upper lanai. The daily room rate is $55 single or $65 double, $10 for an extra person, and five- and seven-day rates available. Josie also rents the one-bedroom house next door for $75 a night, and a cabin behind it for $75 a night. Aside form these, Josie also rents three other houses of various sizes in town that range $80–200 a night. No credit cards or personal checks. To find Josie's turn off the Hana Highway onto Ka'uiki Street, near Pa'ani Mai Park, and go down to the bend in the road, where you will find Josie's Hana Hideaway. For information, call Josie Diego at 000/240-0410 or 808/248-7727, or write P.O. Box 265, Hana HI, 96713. The hideaway's website is www.hanahideaway.com.

Hana Accommodations offers a service whereby you can rent a private house or studio on the lush, tropical Hana Coast. You have seven units to choose from, ranging from a two-story plantation-style house sleeping four and complete with lanai, full kitchen, barbecue, and your own private mini-garden for $150, to the hideaway studio just right for a cozy couple at $70. Several other homes are available around town, like the Garden House ($110 downstairs and $140 upstairs), which has full amenities, and the smaller Lani Makaalae studio, for $80, which gives you a kitchenette, lanai, and an outdoor tub/shower under a plumeria tree. Contact Tom Nunn at 808/248-7868 or 800/228-4262, fax 808/248-8240, or email: info@hana-maui.com. The service's website is www.hana-maui.com.

A second and larger agency in Hana renting everything from a seaside cottage to large plantation homes scattered throughout the Hana area, **Hana Ali'i Holidays** offers a dozen and a half homes, cottages, and studios to choose from. One of the smallest is the Hauoli Lio Cottage, which is on a horse ranch and perfect for two at $85 a night. At the other end is Hale Kilohana, which is a two-story, three-bedroom island house with all amenities, only a short walk to the beach, for $250 a night. Weekly and monthly rentals are also available. Some units are nonsmoking, some have a minimum of two nights' stay. Contact Duke; he'll set you up with something that's just right for your needs. He runs a

a bed-and-breakfast
in Hana

MAUI

ROBERT NILSEN

quality business with quality homes: P.O. Box 536, Hana, HI 96713, 808/248-7742 or 800/548-0478, fax 808/248-8595. Visit Duke's website at www.hanaalii.com, or send email to info@hanaalii.com.

$100–150
On the road that leads to the airport, **Tradewinds Cottages** rents two detached houses set in the garden that have full kitchens and bathrooms, queen beds and sleeper sofas, color TV, and ceiling fans. The Tradewinds Cottage runs $135 a night, maximum of six, while the Hana Cabana is $110 a night, maximum of four; $10 each additional person after the first couple. Information: Hana's Tradewinds Cottages, P.O. Box 385, Hana, HI 96713, 808/248-8980 or 800/327-8097. Visit the cottages' website at www.hana-maui.net, or send email to twt@maui.net.

A magnificent place on the lower road into town, **Hana Hale Malamalama** sits on a steep hillside overlooking an ancient fishpond that's been rebuilt. This is a culturally significant site, and numerous artifacts have been found here. Great care has been taken to aesthetically landscape the property so that the buildings seem to fit in as if they have been here for years. Four units make up the compound. Next to the pond, the Royal Suite occupies a two-floor, 1,800-square-foot house made in the Philippines, transported here, and reconstructed. The Garden Suite is in a rock garden. Up on the bluff are the Tree House Cottage and Poolside Bungalow. The Royal Suite runs $195, the Garden Suite $110, Poolside Bungalow $150, and the Tree House Cottage $160. This is a perfect place for a honeymoon or for a couple who just want a little luxury and class without spending an arm and a leg. Two units next door are also rented, the Bamboo Inn Studio at $140 and the Bamboo Inn Villa for $180. Call John Romain for reservations, 808/248-7718, or try: Hana Hale Malamalama, P.O. Box 374, Hana, HI 96713. Visit the website at www.hanahale.com or send email to hanahale@maui.net.

Hana Kai Maui Resort, the only condo rentals in town at 1533 Uakea Rd., is well maintained and offers a lot for the money. Rates are: studios $125–145, deluxe one-bedrooms $145–195; fifth night free, and weekly and monthly rates available. All have private lanai (with exemplary views of the bay), maid service, laundry facilities, and barbecues, but no phone or television. The views couldn't be better as the grounds, laid out in a lovely garden highlighting the interplay of black lava rock and multihued blooms, step down the mountainside to Popolana Beach on Hana Bay. For additional information, contact: P.O. Box 38, Hana, HI 96713, 808/248-8426 or 800/346-2772, fax 808/248-7482. The resort has a website at www.hanakaimaui.com. Send email to hanakai@maui.net.

$150–200
Set high above the west end of town is **Ekena,** a luxurious vacation rental owned and operated by Robin and Gaylord Gaffney. The upper and lower floors are separate, but only one level is rented at a time—unless the entire building is desired—so you won't be disturbed by anyone. So spacious are these that each floor could be rented by two couples, one on each end, who want to share the cost and enjoy each others' company. Both floors have large living rooms, fully equipped kitchens, two master bedrooms and spacious bathrooms. Ekena is a wonderful pole building with a huge deck and spectacular views both down to the coast and up the mountainside. As it sits high up the hill, it almost always is graced with trade winds, so even if it's dead calm in town it may be breezy up there. At the upper end of the vacation rental bracket, it's not cheap but it's good value for the money. The Jasmine level with one bedroom goes for $185 a night, two bedrooms $250. The Sea Breeze level is $350. Both together run $600 a night. Three nights minimum, no kids younger than 14. For information and reservations, contact: T. Isetorp, P.O. Box 728, Hana HI 96713, 808/248-7047, or visit Ekena on the Web at www.maui.net/~ekena. Send email to ekena@maui.net.

Hamoa Bay House and Bungalow sits in a copse of trees and bamboo just off the Hana Highway above Hamoa Beach. Inspired by the architecture of Bali, at Hamoa Bay two stone lions holding umbrellas greet you at the driveway. The main house and a second-story studio in the back are both for rent. The main house has two bedrooms while the upstairs unit has a living room/bedroom. Both have full kitchens and baths, plus ceiling fans, TV, phones, and barbecues. The studio has a hot tub/shower on the screened porch, while the house has an outdoor shower. Laundry facilities are available. Either makes a fine romantic getaway. Rates for the house are $200 for two or $300 for four, with a three-night minimum. For the upstairs studio, it's $175 a night, with a two-night minimum. Cash, personal and traveler's checks only; no credit cards. No smoking, and no children under 14. Contact the property at P.O. Box 773, Hana, HI 96713, 808/248-7884 or 808/248-7047, or visit the website www.hamoabay.com. Send email to hamoabay@maui.net.

The second most famous Hana accommodation, the **Heavenly Hana Inn,** resembles a Japanese *ryokan*. It's within the bamboo fence, just past the school on the way into town. Walk through the formal garden and remove your shoes on entering the open-beamed main dining hall. Skylights brighten this central area around a hearth. The inn is homey and delightful, and tea and meditation rooms flank the front entrance, adding a sense of tranquillity. Having undergone renovations, the inn is more beautiful than ever in its simplicity. A variety of woods give warmth to the living areas, shoji screens hide what need not always be present, and the decoration is perfectly authentic. The three suites seem like little apartments broken up into sections by shoji screens. Each has a sleeping room, bathroom with soaking tub, a sitting room with television but no telephone, and its own private entrance. One suite has a second bedroom, and no smoking is allowed inside. Special gourmet breakfasts are served at $15 per person with at least one week's prior notice, and lunch or tea service can also be accommodated upon request with advance notice. These suites run $185–250 a night, with a two-night minimum. For more information, contact the inn at P.O. Box 790, Hana, HI 96713, 808/248-8442, website: www.heavenly-hanainn, email: hanainn@maui.net.

$250 and up

The legacy of Paul Fagan, who built it in the late 1940s, **Hotel Hana-Maui** is as close to a family-run hotel as you can get. Most personnel have either been there from the beginning, or their jobs have passed to their family members, and the hotel has had only eight managers in the last 50 years. Guests love it that way, proven by an astonishing 80 percent of repeat visitors, most of whom feel like they're staying with old friends. Unfortunately, the hotel suffered a downturn in the late '90s but seems to be on the upswing once again. The public areas in the hotel are done in muted tans and browns. It's open and airy with flagstone floors and easy furniture of hardwood and bamboo. The low-slung main buildings cluster around gardens, while the newer Sea Ranch Cottages line the ocean on land that slopes down to the water. Rooms, all with their own lanai, surround the beautifully appointed grounds where flowers add a splash of color to the green-on-green blanket of ferns and gently sloping lawn. All suites have a wet bar and large comfortable lounge area with rattan furniture covered in billowy pillows. The floors are a deep rich natural wood counterpointed by a light reed mat in the central area. The beds, all king-size or two twins, are covered with handmade Hawaiian quilts, while Casablanca fans provide all the cooling necessary. The guest-cottage rooms have large free-standing pine armoires; all rooms have two walk-ins. The bathrooms, as large as most sitting rooms, are tiled with earth-tone ceramic. You climb a step to immerse yourself in the huge tub, then open eye-level windows that frame a private mini-garden like an expressionist's still life.

The hotel staff adds an intangible quality of friendliness and *aloha*. There is a library for use by guests, and a few shops for clothes, necessities, and gifts, and a superb art gallery. The hotel restaurant is open for breakfast, lunch, and dinner, and the Paniolo Bar serves drinks from the late morning until 10:30 P.M. Thursday and Sunday bring a free hula show to the dining room at 7:30 P.M., and Thurs.–Sun. 6:30–9 P.M. the soft lilt of Hawaiian music and song wafts through the house from the bar. Other facilities and activities include a wellness center, two heated swimming pools, tennis courts, superb horseback riding, a three-hole practice golf course, free bicycle use by guests, hikes to archaeological sites, and a daily lunch barbecue at the hotel's facilities on Hamoa Beach. All activities are easily arranged by visiting the activities desk, which can be counted on to keep family and children happy with Hawaiian language lessons, lei-making, or swaying hula lessons. Free shuttle service is provided by the hotel throughout the area in its vintage vehicles.

MAUI

Rates start at $375 for a garden-view room and progress up to $695 for the sea ranch cottage suites. There is a $50 extra charge for each additional adult; kids 12 and below stay free. The entire scene isn't stiff or fancy, but it is a memorable first-class experience! Contact Hotel Hana-Maui at P.O. Box 9, Hana, HI 96713, 808/248-8211 or 800/321-4262, or visit the hotel on the Web at www.hotelhanamaui.com.

FOOD

Hotel Hana-Maui

As far as dining out goes, there's little to choose from in Hana. The Hotel Hana-Maui main dining room offers breakfast, lunch, and dinner. Prices vary according to your choice of options, but expect to spend $10–20 for breakfast and lunch and $22–32 for a dinner entr'e. Reservations are highly recommended. Hotel guests have first preference, but the hotel will try its hardest to seat you. Afternoon snacks are also served at the Paniolo Bar 2:30–6 P.M. The bar menu included such items as sandwiches, pizza, and dim sum. Served 7:30–10 A.M., breakfast is all manner of fresh fruits and juices, hot pastries, buttermilk waffles or pancakes, and eggs and omelets. Lunch, 11:30 A.M.–2 P.M., includes Cobb salad, turkey baguette, Hawaiian club sandwich, and a flame-broiled fish sandwich. Special dinner menus are prepared daily, but you can begin with a sashimi plate or lobster taro cake, and then move on to an assortment of grilled, seared, and broiled fowl and seafood, or locally grown beef and lamb, all basted in a variety of sauces. Desserts are too tempting to resist. Dinner is served 6–9 P.M.

The barbecue lunch cookout at Hamoa Beach, offered 11:30 A.M.–1:30 P.M. daily, is another alternative. Make reservations at the activities desk in the hotel lobby.

Entertainment at the hotel—and that, quite frankly, is it for the whole town—is an informal hula and Hawaiian music shows put on by local families during the Thursday and Sunday dinners. Aside from that, nightly music is performed at the bar, usually by one or two local musicians on ukulele and/or guitar, who fill the entire building with good cheer and melodious song. The Paniolo Bar is open daily 11:30 A.M.–10:30 P.M. For alternate entertainment, try the frequent evening baseball games at the ballpark behind the hotel.

Hana Ranch Restaurant

The Hana Ranch Restaurant, 808/248-8255, serves very tasty family-style meals, but it can be stampeded by ravenous tourists heading up or down the Hana Road. Reservations recommended. It's a sturdy place with wood floors, rattan furniture, and heavy slabs of wood as tables. Seating is inside or on the lanai under a timber framework. Breakfast, daily 8–10 A.M., is served inside and from an adjoining service window. Lunch, also served from the service window, is an assortment of sandwiches, saimin, and plate lunches that's available daily 11 A.M.–3 P.M. Shaded picnic tables are to the side. Dinner is served inside Friday and Saturday evenings 6–8 P.M., and Wednesday is pizza night. The dinner menu includes appetizers like garlic mushrooms or loco moco quesadilla for $5.95. Portuguese bean soup is on the menu, as are prime rib of beef, honey barbecue smoked ribs, fresh catch, and strip steak and shrimp, mostly for $22–27. The salad bar can stand on its own or complement any meal. A short wine list is available, or you can choose some other drink or beer from the bar. Not gourmet by any means, it is tasty, filling, and decently priced. The outside window is open 4–7 P.M. for plate lunches, burgers, and sandwiches on days that the restaurant is closed. Besides the Hotel Hana-Maui, this is the only place to have an evening meal in Hana.

Tu Tu's

Tu Tu's Snack Shop, open Mon.–Sat. 8 A.M.–4 P.M. at the community center building fronting the beach, offers window service plus a few tables on the porch. Eggs, loco moco, French toast, and other breakfast items all under $4.50, sandwiches to $4, and plate lunches under $6.50. Other items include salads, saimin, hamburgers, drinks, and ice cream. This building was donated to the community by Mrs. Fagan, the wife of Paul Fagan, the original owner of the Hotel Hana-Maui.

SHOPPING

Hasegawa's General Store

In the ranks of general stores, Hasegawa's would be commander-in-chief. This institution, run by Harry Hasegawa, had been in the family for 80 years before it burned to the ground in the fall of 1990. While your gas tank was being filled, you could buy anything from a cane knife to a computer disk. There were rows of food items, dry goods, and a hardware and parts store out back. Cold beer, film, blue jeans, and picnic supplies—somehow it was all crammed in there. Everybody went to Hasegawa's, and it was a treat just to browse and people-watch. Now revived and housed in the old movie theater building, this store still serves the community and visitors that for so long sustained it. It's just as packed as ever, has the only one-day film processing in town, as well as its only ATM machine. Open Mon.–Sat. 7 A.M.–7 P.M., Sunday 8 A.M.–6 P.M.; 808/248-8231.

On Thursday 9:30 A.M.–3:30 P.M. at the old Hasegawa Service Station you may find a **farmers' market and crafter market**.

Hana Ranch Store

From the Hana Road, make the first right past St. Mary's Catholic Church and go up to the top of the hill to find the Hana Ranch Store, open daily 7 A.M.–7:30 P.M., 808/248-8261, a general store with an emphasis on foodstuffs. It carries a supply of imported beers, a wide selection of food items, film, videos, and some gifts. The bulletin board here gives you a good idea of what's currently happening in town.

Hana Treasures

In the small complex next to the Hana Ranch Restaurant, look for Hana Treasures, open Mon.–Fri. 10 A.M.–4 P.M., Saturday and Sunday until 3 P.M., operated by Cheryl, a Hana resident who is friendly and willing to offer local information. The small shop features airbrushed T-shirts by Ilana artists, an assortment of Hawaiian gifts and souvenirs, particularly those made in the Hana area, and a display case of silver necklaces, bracelets, and rings.

Hana Coast Gallery

At Hotel Hana-Maui, this gallery displays an excellent collection of fine art by Hawaiian residents. Not only is the work of very high quality, the whole gallery is set up to show off each piece to its fullest. Works include: watercolors, turned wood bowls, Oriental brush paintings, bronze sculpture, woodblock prints, jewelry, basketry, and wood furniture. The gallery, 808/248-8636, is open daily 10:30 A.M.–6 P.M.

ACTIVITIES

Hana Bay Kayak

Arranged through the Hotel Hana-Maui activities desk, 808/248-8211, this adventure heads to Hana Bay for a two-hour session and can take as many as eight people. Kayak and snorkel tours are given at 9:30 A.M. and 2 P.M.; $59 per person, half price under age 12. They'll even videotape underwater for you as you snorkel.

Horseback Riding

Horseback rides are given at the Hana Ranch Stables. The one-hour trail rides, either along the coast or in the upper pastures, leave at 8:30 and 10 A.M. and again at 1:30 P.M. Rides cost $35 per person, and riders must be seven years old. Private rides can be arranged 3–5 P.M. for $70 per person.

Jogging Trail

A walking/jogging trail is maintained on Hana Ranch property, on what was the narrow-gauge sugarcane railroad bed. The trail runs for a bit more than two miles and starts partway up the path to the Fagan Memorial. Walk south.

Power Hang Gliding

The only commercial ultralight motorized paragliding on the island runs out of the Hana Airport, and only then by appointment. **Hang Gliding Maui** offers tandem flights that run 30- to 60-minutes for $95–165. This open-cockpit, slow speed tour gets you as close to a bird's-eye view of the area as is possible. For information and reservations, call 808/572-6557.

SERVICES

Hana Community Health Center
Along the Hana Road at the Y intersection, clearly marked on the right just as you enter town, is Hana Medical Center, 808/248-8294. Open weekdays 8 A.M.–6 P.M. (until 8 P.M. on Tuesday and Thursday) and Saturday 8 A.M.–noon; closed Sunday. Walk-in, nonemergency treatment. For emergencies, use the phone at the hospital entrance.

Police Station
The police station is at the Y intersection between Hana Highway and Uakea Road, just as you enter town. For emergencies call 911; otherwise, 808/248-8311.

Money, Mail, and Library
The Bank of Hawaii, 808/248-8015, is open Mon.–Thurs. 3–4:30 P.M., Friday 3–6 P.M.; cash advances on Visa and Mastercard can be made there. For an ATM bank machine go to Hasegawa's store. The **post office** is open weekdays 8 A.M.–4:30 P.M.; community bulletin board outside. Both are next door to the Hana Ranch Restaurant. The excellent Hana school/public library, 808/248-7714, is at the new Hana School on the western edge of town; open Monday, Tuesday, and Friday 8 A.M.–4 P.M. (from 9 A.M. on Tuesday), and Wednesday and Thursday 11 A.M.–7 P.M.

Gas
There is one gas station in town. The Chevron station next to the horse stables is open daily 7 A.M.–6:30 P.M. (from 7:30 A.M. on Sunday). It has a public bathroom and telephone. Gas in Hana is expensive, about 30–35 cents per gallon higher than elsewhere on the island. Fill up before leaving town—the nearest gas station west is in Pa'ia; going south around the bottom, the closest is in Keokea.

Rental Cars
At the airport, **Dollar Rent A Car,** 808/248-8237, is the only show in town. It's best to call in advance to ensure a reservation. Cars may be available on short notice during low season, but don't count on it.

BEYOND HANA

About a half mile south of Hana is mile marker 51. From there, the mile markers decrease in number as you continue around the south coast back to Kahului. Now you're getting into adventure. The first sign is that the road becomes narrower, then the twists and turns begin again. After 'Ohe'o Gulch, there are a few miles that are still unpaved, and this is followed by a long stretch that's nothing more than a patchwork quilt of filled potholes. You know you're in a rural area with not much traffic when you come across the sign "Caution: Baby Pigs Crossing." There is one phone, no gas, only a fruit or flower stand or two, one *kaukau* wagon, and one store until you reach Ulupalakua Ranch. Although the road is good for most of the year, during heavy rains sections do still wash out and become impassable. The fainthearted should turn back, but those with gumption are in for a treat. There are roadside waterfalls, thick luscious forests, cascading streams filling a series of pools, pocket-size ranches, a hero's grave, tiny plantation communities, some forgotten towns, isolated homesteads, million-dollar retirement retreats, and desolate scrubby ranchland. If you persevere all the way, you pop out at the Tedeschi Winery, where you can reward yourself with a glass of bubbly before returning to civilization.

Waioka Pool
Also referred to by some as Venus Pool, a legend says Waioka Pool was once used exclusively by Hawaiian royalty. At the Waiohonu bridge just past mile marker 48, cross over the fence and hike (public access trail) through the fields above the river to its mouth. There you'll find a series of waterfalls below the bridge and a freshwater pool scoured out of the solid rock walls of this water course. Used by Hawaiian royalty during centuries past, it's now a refreshing, usually solitary place for a swim or to sunbathe on the smooth rocks. Be safe and stay

out of the ocean—the surf, which can be just over the narrow sandbar, is strong. At certain times of the year you may see giant turtles just off the rocks a short way farther down the coast. In the fields above and to the north of Waioka Pool are the remains of an old sugar mill and part of the King's Highway, a paved pathway that once ran along the coast.

Wailua Falls

About six miles after leaving Hana, Wailua and Kanahuali'i Falls tumble over steep lava *pali,* filling the air with a watery mist and filling their pools below. They're just outside your car door, and a minute's effort will take you to the mossy grotto at the base. There's room to park. If not for 'Ohe'o up ahead, this would be a great picnic spot, but wait! Sometimes roadside artists park here, and basket-makers or fruit-sellers ply their trade. Check out the taro fields that have been created on the ocean side of the road. If you are going back toward Hana on this road, you will see another falls high above Wailua Falls on the mountain above. In a few minutes, about one-half mile before you enter the park, you pass a little shrine cut into the mountain. This is the **Virgin by the Roadside.** It's usually draped with a fresh lei.

KIPAHULU: THE COASTAL BOUNDARY OF HALEAKALA NATIONAL PARK

This is where the enormous **Kipahulu Valley** meets the sea. The majority of this valley, about a third of the national park area, is off limits to the public, set aside as a biological preserve. Palikea Stream starts way up on Haleakala and steps its way through the valley, leaving footprints of waterfalls and pools until it spends itself in the sea. The area was named the Seven Sacred Pools by some unknown publicity person in the late '40s. The area should have been held sacred, but it wasn't. Everything was right here. You can feel the tremendous power of nature: bubbling waters, Haleakala red and regal in the background, and the sea pounding away. Hawaiians lived here, but the numerous *heiau* that you might expect are missing. Besides that there aren't seven pools; there are a few dozen! The name "Seven Sacred Pools" is falling into disfavor because it is inaccurate, with local people and the National Park Service preferring the proper name Kipahulu, Pools of 'Ohe'o, or 'Ohe'o Gulch, instead. In the late 1990s, 52 acres were added to the park near the pools, including ad-

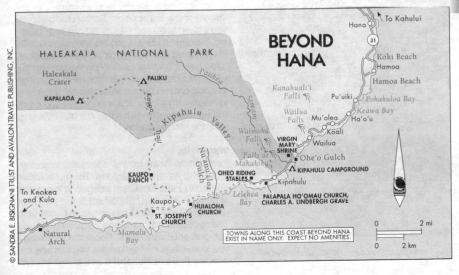

ditional shoreline and the Kanekauila Heiau. It's about 10 miles out of Hana.

Visitor Center

As you progress along the road, you'll come to a large cement arched bridge (excellent view) and then a parking area to your left with a ranger's station/visitors center, restrooms, and public telephone. The visitors center is relatively new, and from its lanai you can see the Big island looming on the horizon on a clear day. Information on the Kipahulu District of the national park, area trails and their conditions, the native Hawaiian people who lived in the area and their lifestyle, and the natural resource of the district are all well explained. Check out the koa canoe. It was cracked when the tsunami struck the area in the 1940s. The center also stocks a selection of books about the area. A small bulletin board outside displays other information. The center is open 9 A.M.–5 P.M. daily. The rangers are friendly and informative, so before doing any

exploring stop in and ask about trail conditions. They know a tremendous amount of natural history concerning the area and can inform you about the few dangers in the area, such as the flash flooding that occurs in the pools. Interpretive talks are given at the ranger station daily at 12:30, 1:30, 2:30, and 3:30 every afternoon, and occasional cultural programs are offered. Call the ranger station, 808/248-7375, for information. You can hike the trail by yourself but ranger-led hikes are also given. A short one-mile hike goes to the Bamboo Forest daily at 9:30 A.M. Those intending to hike or camp should bring their own water. The vast majority of the people go to the easily accessible lower pools, but a stiff hike up the mountain takes you to the upper pools, a bamboo forest, and a fantastic waterfall; 99 percent of park visitors are gone by sundown. From the parking lot, a short dirt track leads down to the large grassy camping area.

The Lower Pools

Head along the clearly marked path from the parking area to the flat, grass-covered peninsula. The winds are heavy here as they enter the mouth of the valley from the sea. A series of pools to choose from is off to your left. It's delightful to lie in the last one and look out to the sea crunching the shore just a few yards away. Move upstream for the best swimming in the largest of the lower pools. Be careful, because you'll have to do some fairly difficult rock climbing. The best route is along the right-hand side as you face up the valley. Once you're satiated, head back up to the road along the path on the left-hand side. This will take you up to the bridge that you crossed when arriving, one of the best vantage points from which to look up and down this amazing valley. This trail is a half-mile loop from the ranger station.

Waterfalls

Few people head for the waterfalls; however, those who do will be delighted. The trail is called **Waimoku Falls Trail,** and it begins at the ranger station. The falls at Makahiku are a half mile uphill and Waimoku Falls is two miles distant. The toughest part is at the beginning as you huff-puff your way uphill. Soon, the trail brings you to an overlook from where you can see the lace-like **Falls at Makahiku** as it plummets 181

relaxing at the Lower Pools, 'Ohe'o Gulch

feet to the rugged valley floor below. A short way beyond this is a shorter second falls, where the pool has undercut the opposite bank and the water then cascades down through a narrow gorge and series of stepped pools. During summer, guava and other fruit drops to the ground, creating a pungent or downright smelly fragrance along the trail. The path continues over two new metal bridges that cross more cascades and pools, and then zigzag up the opposite bank. After passing some enormous mango trees, you head through a high jungle area. Suddenly you're in an extremely dense bamboo forest—an incredible experience in itself. The trail is well cut as you pass through the green darkness of this stand. If the wind is blowing, the bamboo will sing a mournful song for you. Here you get the first glimpse of the waterfall—a tease of what's ahead. This trail gets somewhat sloppy and slippery in sections, and about a quarter mile of boardwalk had been built over small streams and the worst of the soggy ground. Emerge into more mangos and thimbleberries and there's the creek again. Turn left and follow the creek, without crossing yet, and the trail will become distinct again. There's a wooden walkway, and then, eureka! . . . Waimoku Falls. It cascades over the *pali* and is so high that you have to strain your neck back as far as it will go. It's more than a waterfall; it's silver filigree. You can stand in the shallow pool below surrounded by a sheer rock amphitheater. The sunlight dances in this area and tiny rainbows appear and disappear. If you are there during the rains, you may see more than one extra waterfall coming off the cliff above.

One word of warning. As at all such waterfalls on the islands, where the pool beckons to slake the heat and the surrounding scenery is so captivating, rocks and boulders periodically dislodge from the *pali* above and tumble into the pool below. How else have the boulders in the pool gotten to where they are? Usually, although not always, these falling rocks are accompanied by sounds of rock striking rock. Always keep an ear out for danger and an eye upward. At popular and oft-visited waterfalls, warning signs are posted to warn you of such dangers and to keep you out of harm's way. Know the dangers and heed the warnings.

Camping

Kipahulu is part of Haleakala National Park, and camping is free (obtain permit at the visitor center) in designated sites only for a three-day limit. No backcountry camping or camping along the streams. Groups of more than 12 should obtain permits from the park superintendent at Park Headquarters, P.O. Box 369, Makawao, HI 96768, 808/572-9306. The campgrounds are primitive and mostly empty, except for holiday weekends when they can be packed. From the parking lot follow the camping sign and continue down the hill on the rutted dirt track. Bear right to a large grassy area overlooking the sea, where signs warn not to disturb an archaeological area. Notice how spongy the grass is here. Move to the trees to escape the wind. Here are clean outhouses, picnic tables, and barbecue grills, but no potable water, so make sure to bring plenty of your own to drink.

BEYOND 'OHE'O GULCH

Some of Route 31 beyond 'Ohe'o is genuinely rugged and makes the car companies cry. But it can be driven, and even the tourist vans make it part of their regular route. Be aware, however, that rough weather can bring landslides; the road may be closed by a locked gate with access available only for official business and local residents. Check the bulletin board at the ranger station for road conditions! If the road is closed, a sign in Hana will warn you of this condition. In 1.5 miles you come to the well-kept clapboard **St. Paul's Church,** which sits right next to the highway. Services are conducted here twice a month. A little farther along and down a side road is **Palapala Ho'omau Church** (founded 1864) and its tiny cemetery, where Charles Lindbergh is buried. People, especially those who are old enough to remember the "Lone Eagle's" historic flight, are drawn here like pilgrims. The public is not really encouraged to visit, but the human tide cannot be stopped. If you go, please follow all of the directions posted. Right next to the church cemetery is the tiny **Kipahulu Lighthouse Point County Park,** which sits on the edge of the cliff overlooking the frothy ocean below. Several trees and picnic tables provide a quiet and shaded place for a bite to eat and a rest. Up the road is

Samuel F. Pryor's Kipahulu Ranch. Mr. Pryor was a vice president of Pan Am and a close chum of Lindbergh's. It was he who encouraged Lindbergh to spend his last years in Hana.

Kipahulu Ranch has seen other amazing men. In the 1800s a Japanese samurai named Sentaro Ishii lived here. He was enormous, especially for a Japanese of that day, more than six feet tall. He came in search of work, and at the age of 61 married Kehele, a local girl. He lived in Kipahulu until he died at the age of 102.

Past Sam Pryor's place is **Oheo Riding Stables,** up a long driveway from the road. From here two rides a day are taken through the lush vegetation to spots overlooking Makahiku and Waimoku Falls, both in the national park. About three hours are spent in the saddle; six guests maximum per ride.

Past here the road really begins to get rugged and narrow, but only about four miles remains unpaved.

Kaupo

Once you get to the Kaupo Gap, the tropical vegetation suddenly stops and the landscape is barren and dry for most of the year. Here Haleakala's rain shadow creates an environment of yellow grassland dotted with volcanic rock. Everywhere are *ahu,* usually three stacked stones, that people have left as personal prayers and wishes to the gods. Just after Kaupo, the dirt road becomes a beat-up patchwork that wheels along past rangeland and ranches with the ocean far below. When the road dips to the ocean, you are in Kaupo Ranch. Near the mouth of the deepest valley to slit this side of the island, you'll find a pebble beach that seems to stretch a mile. At mile marker 32, look down to the coast and see two rough volcanic peninsulas. On the westernmost sits a *heiau.* A short way beyond, before the road dips down the hillside, is a pulloff where you can walk out on a bluff and overlook these peninsulas. A good but distant view of these peninsulas is also possible from another pull-off between mile markers 28 and 29. Beyond that, the road gains elevation and the landscape becomes more arid except for the green carpet of trees high up on the mountainside. From there, you can look down on Maui's last lava flow and La Pérouse Bay. Near mile marker 23, the new road surface starts, and be-

fore the road tucks back into the trees you get great views of the coast. Be aware of free-range cattle, which can be in the middle of the road around any turn, all the way along this road through Kaupo. Enjoy the road, because in a few minutes you'll be back in the civilized world.

The vistas open up at the beginning of the Kaupo Gap just when you pass **Hui Aloha Church.** Built in 1859, this church sits on a level grassy spot below the road near the sea; the road down may be very rough and impassable except with a 4WD vehicle. Eight miles from 'Ohe'o, the village of **Kaupo** and the **Kaupo Store** follow Hui Aloha Church. After so many years of erratic hours and unpredictable closures, Kaupo Store now has regular hours, Mon.–Sat. 10:30 A.M.–5:30 P.M. A real anachronism, the store serves double duty as unofficial dusty museum and convenience store. Along with the antiques hanging on the walls and filling the shelves (not for sale), the store stocks cold juices and beer, ice cream and chips—mostly snacks and traveling food.

Only a few families live in Kaupo, old ones and new ones trying to live independently. During decades past, Kaupo Store, which was established in the mid-1920s, was the center of this community. If only the walls could talk, what stories they would tell. Kaupo is the last of a chain of stores that once stretched all the way from Ke'anae and were owned by the Soon Family. Nick Soon was kind of a modern-day wizard. He lived in Kaupo, and among his exploits he assembled a car and truck brought piecemeal on a barge, built the first electric generator in the area, and even made from scratch a model airplane that flew. He was the son of an indentured Chinese laborer.

A short distance past Kaupo is **St. Joseph's Church.** Built in 1862, it has recently been remodeled, and services are held here periodically.

Wonders never cease! About 100 yards west of the Kaupo Store is **Auntie Jane's** *kaukau* wagon, owned and operated by Auntie Jane Aki, who, along with her *paniolo* husband Charles, owns and operates a small cattle ranch. Their organic beef is made into the large juicy burgers offered on the limited menu. Definitely stop by if only just to "talk story" with Auntie Jane, a lifelong Hawaii resident, who came to the Kaupo area 40 years ago. Open from "about 11 A.M. to about when the sun goes down, everyday except Thursday" (when she goes for supplies), Auntie Jane offers big juicy regular burgers for $5, along with local ice cream, $5 large and $3 small, and $1 sodas. These huge burgers are loaded with all the trimmings and a meal in themselves. Auntie Jane says, "Everything is made my way, not McDonald's way." When she first opened, Auntie Jane had no sign to advertise her business. To remedy that, the island artist Piero Resta created one for her. What a blessing. Have a look. Also along with her husband, Jane owns and operates **Charley's Trailrides,** which offers guided overnighters from Kaupo to Haleakala Crater. Auntie Jane has "plenty aloha," which is as nourishing to the soul as her burgers are to the belly. Fill up!

BOB RACE

MAUI

M.G.L. DOMENY DE REINZI

KAHO'OLAWE

OVERVIEW

The island of Kaho'olawe (the Carrying Away—as if by currents) is clearly visible from many points along Maui's south shore. From Lahaina and Ma'alaea, the outline of Kaho'olawe on the horizon resembles the back and dorsal fin of a whale half out of the water, ready to dive. In fact, many whales and dolphins do congregate around the island in summer to calve their young and mate for the coming year. Until recently Kaho'olawe was a target island, uninhabited except for a band of wild goats that refused to be killed off.

Kaho'olawe was a sacred island born to Wakea and Papa, the two great mythical progenitors of Hawaii. The birth went badly and almost killed Papa, and it hasn't been any easier for her ill-omened child ever since. Kaho'olawe became synonymous with Kanaloa, the mangod. Kanaloa was especially revered by the *kahuna 'ana'ana,* the "black sorcerers" of old Hawaii. Kanaloa, much like Lucifer, was driven

from heaven by Kane, the god of light. Kanaloa held dominion over all poisonous things and ruled in the land of the dead from his power spot here on Kaho'olawe. Kanaloa was also revered as the god of voyaging by early Polynesians and as such held an important place in their cast of deities.

For years, a long, bitter feud raged between the U.S. Navy, which wanted to keep the island as a bombing range, and Protect Kaho'olawe Ohana, a Hawaiian native-rights organization, which wants the sacred island returned to the people. The Navy finally agreed to stop bombing and return the island to the state of Hawaii, bringing the Ohana one step closer to its goal.

The Land

Kaho'olawe is 11 miles long and six miles wide, with 29 miles of coastline. Its 45 square miles make it the seventh largest of the main Hawaiian Islands, larger only than Ni'ihau, and its mean elevation of about 600 feet is lower than all the other islands except for that small private enclave. The tallest hill, Moa'ulanui, is in the east-

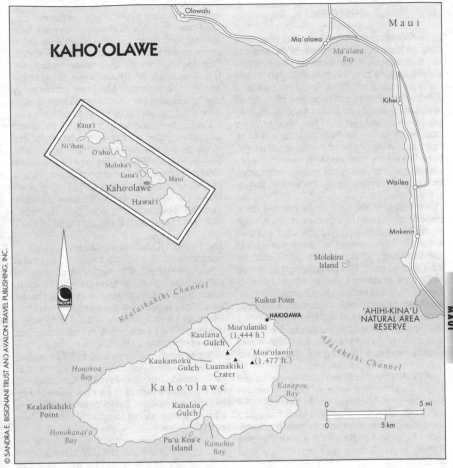

ern section at 1,477 feet. Across the shallow Luamakika Crater is the nearly-as-tall hill Moa'ulaniki, at 1,444 feet. There are no natural lakes or ponds on the island, and all streams except for one or two are seasonal. As Kaho'olawe lies in Maui's rain shadow (it's six miles across to South Maui), it receives only about 25 inches of rain a year.

The land is covered by sparse vegetation and is cut by ravines and gulches. Much of the island, particularly the south and east coasts, is ringed by steep *pali,* but the land slides off more gradually to the north and west. There are few beaches on the island, but the best are at the west end between Honokoa Bay and Honokanai'a Bay (some references say Hanakanaea Bay). Also known as Smuggler Cove, Honokanai'a Bay is said to be the site of a treasure buried on the beach in 1880 and as yet unclaimed. Kealaikahiki (the Way to Foreign Lands) Point is the island's western tip, and this rock was used as a beacon during centuries past for canoe travelers to and from the island to the south.

HISTORY

It's perfectly clear that small families of Hawaiians lived on Kaho'olawe for countless generations and that religious rites were carried out by many visiting *kahuna* over the centuries, but mostly Kaho'olawe was left alone. There are scores of archaeological sites and remnants of *heiau* all over the bomb-cratered face of Kaho'olawe, perhaps from as early as A.D. 1150. Most of these sites are close to water near the area known as Hakioawa in the northeast corner of the island, but a few others have been discovered inland. One site of archaeological interest is an adze quarry, up top and said to be the second largest in the state.

In the early 1800s, Kaho'olawe was used as a place of banishment for criminals. It was a harsh sentence, as the island had little food and less water. Yet, many survived and some managed to raid the nearby islands of Maui and Lana'i for food and women! The first attempt at sheep ranching was started in 1858 but was not successful. This was followed by a second venture, which also proved largely unproductive because of the great numbers of wild goats that had by that time established themselves on the island. By the turn of the 20th century, Kaho'olawe was already overgrazed and a great deal of its bare topsoil blown away into the sea.

In 1917 Angus MacPhee, a cattleman, leased Kaho'olawe from the territorial government for $200 per year. The lease would run until 1954 with a renewal option, if by 1921 MacPhee could show reasonable progress in taming the island. Harry Baldwin bought into the **Kaho'olawe Ranch** in 1922, and with his money and MacPhee's know-how, Kaho'olawe turned a neat profit. Within a few years Kaho'olawe Ranch cattle were being shipped regularly to markets on Maui. MacPhee did more than anyone to reclaim the land. He got rid of many of the goats and introduced horses and game birds. While the island supported indigenous vegetation such as 'ohi'a, mountain apples, and even Hawaiian cotton and tobacco, MacPhee planted eucalyptus and range grass from Australia, which caught on well and stopped much of the erosion. Gardens were planted around the homestead and the soil proved to be clean and fertile.

The Navy Arrives

In 1939, with the threat of war on the horizon, MacPhee and Baldwin, stimulated by patriotism, offered a small tip of Kaho'olawe's southern shore to the U.S. Army as an artillery range. One day after the attack on Pearl Harbor, the U.S. Navy seized all of Kaho'olawe "to further the war effort" and evicted MacPhee, immediately disenfranchising the Kaho'olawe Ranch. The island was supposed to be returned after the war, but when the lease ran out in 1954 the island was appropriated by presidential decree for use solely by the military. No compensation was ever given to MacPhee or his family. Kaho'olawe has since become the most bombarded piece of real estate on the face of the earth. During World War II the Navy praised Kaho'olawe as being *the* most important factor in winning the Pacific War, and it held Kaho'olawe until the fall of 1990.

The Protect Kaho'olawe Ohana

Founded in 1976, the Protect Kaho'olawe Ohana (PKO) is an extended group favoring traditional values based on *aloha 'aina* (love of the land), which is the primary binding force for all Hawaiians. They would like the island to return to Hawaiian Lands inventory with the *kahu* (stewardship) in the hands of native Hawaiians. The point driven home by the Ohana is that the military has totally ignored and belittled native Hawaiian values, which are now beginning to be asserted. They maintain that Kaho'olawe is not a barren wasteland, but a vibrant part of their history and religion. Indeed, Kaho'olawe was placed on the National Register of Historic Sites in 1981.

In a formal agreement with the PKO and the state of Hawaii in 1980, the U.S. Navy granted legal access to the island for four days per month. The PKO built a *halau* (longhouse), and members used the time on Kaho'olawe to dedicate themselves to religious, cultural, and social pursuits. The Ohana look to Kaho'olawe as their *pu'uhonua* (refuge), where they gain strength and knowledge from each other and the *'aina*. Hopefully Kaho'olawe's future as a sacred island is now secure.

Changing Hands

In 1990, then-president George Bush issued an order to immediately halt the bombing of

The Protect Kaho'olawe Ohana resolutely builds a longhouse.

J.D. BISIGNANI

Kaho'olawe, and at the same time established a congressional commission to create the terms and conditions for returning the island to the state. At that time, Ka Lahui Hawaii, the Native Nation of Hawaii, founded in Hilo in 1987, demanded that the island, as "totally ceded lands," be given to them as part of their sovereign nation. The Protect Kaho'olawe Ohana, in a more moderate stance, suggested "land banking" the island under the control of the state or federal government until the United States recognizes the sovereignty of the Ka Lahui Hawaii. In the meantime, the PKO continues to lobby for exclusive rights to the stewardship of Kaho'olawe. On May 7, 1994, Kaho'olawe was returned to the state of Hawaii.

Transition

With the transfer of the island back to state protection, Kaho'olawe has become an "island reserve." Congress dedicated $400 million over a 10-year period (the Navy will be gone in 2003) toward cleaning the island of scrap and unexploded ordnance, and for the rejuvenation of the environment. What appears to be a huge amount of money is already being used at a rapid pace and appears to be only enough to start the process of making the island safe and healthy. The Kaho'olawe Island Reserve Commission (KIRC) was established by state law to oversee and manage this effort until the Navy leaves. The reserve includes the island of Kaho'olawe plus the waters surrounding it to a distance of two miles. This total area is one of restricted access.

Now that the goats are gone and some of the ordnance cleaned up, the greatest problem seems to be erosion. While vegetation has a hold in some valleys and clings to spots where goats could not feed, much of the soil covering the island's plateau and gentle slopes has been blown off, exposing red, hardpan earth. Much work has been done; various approaches tried to establish grasses and other plants, and dams of grasses have been placed to prevent dirt from washing down gullies to the sea. Still, much more needs to be done. Introduced species are overtaking the dwindling native plants, and field mice are swiftly eating native seeds. Two other serious problems that must be overcome are the remaining unexploded ordnance, which is both expensive and risky to remove and dispose of, and the perpetual lack of water. While the ordnance cleanup effort continues by the military, Mother Nature must be coaxed to help out with water. With similar natural conditions to South Maui, the island gets only minimal rain each year. Freshwater comes from rain catching, and few streams ever run.

The only habitation sites on Kaho'olawe are the traditional structures put up by the PKO near Hakioawa and the military installation on the west end of the island. There is currently virtually no infrastructure on the island except for a few rutted dirt roads. Over the years, several thousand people have visited the island, mostly to help with the cleanup efforts or to participate in religious and cultural activities. Kaho'olawe might become a great cultural resource, a place where Hawaiians could go to practice age-old traditions in a sympathetic environment, but it probably will never be a place for any large-scale habitation.

MAUI

While exact plans for the future are still undecided, it seems most likely that the island will be kept out of the hands of developers and open to visitors for cultural purposes if the risk factor finally drops low enough. How the island will be managed and what status it will eventually attain is still to be determined.

The Book on Kaho'olawe

Inez MacPhee Ashdown lived on the island with her father and was a driving force in establishing the homestead. She has written a book, *Recollections of Kaho'olawe,* that chronicles the events from 1917 until the military takeover and is rife with myths, legends, and historical facts about Kaho'olawe.

Information

Unless you are one of the lucky few, you must be content to view Kaho'olawe from across the water. For information about current happenings relating to this tortured island, log on to the PKO's website: www.kahoolawe.org. Alternately, try that of the KIRC at www.state.hi.us/kirc (or www.hawaii.gov/kirc), or the Navy information site at www.efdpac.navfac.navy.mil/news/kaho/hp1.htm. To contact the PKO, write: P.O. Box 152, Honolulu, HI 96810. For the KIRC: 811 Kolu Street, Suite 201, Wailuku, HI 96793, 808/243-5020 or 800/468-4644, email: administrator@kirc.state.hi.us.

For other general information about the island, log onto the Bishop Museum's Kaho'olawe page at www.bishopmuseum.org/bmanthro/kaho.

HAWAII STATE ARCHIVES

LANA'I

INTRODUCTION

Lana'i (Day of Conquest), in the long dark past of Hawaiian legend-history, was a sad and desolate place inhabited by man-eating spirits and fiendish bloodcurdling ghouls. It was redeemed by spoiled but tough Prince Kaulula'au, exiled there by his kingly father, Kaka'alaneo of Maui. Kaulula'au proved to be not only brave, but wily too; he cleared Lana'i of its spirits through trickery and opened the way for human habitation. Lana'i was for many generations a burial ground for the *ali'i* and therefore filled with sacred *mana* and *kapu* to commoners. Later, reports of its inhospitable shores filled the logs of old sailing vessels. In foul weather, captains navigated desperately to avoid its infamously treacherous waters, whose melancholy whitecaps still outline Shipwreck Beach and give credence to its name.

The vast majority of people visiting the Hawaiian Islands view Lana'i from Lahaina on West Maui but never actually set foot upon this lovely quiet island. For two centuries, first hunters and then lovers of the humpback whale have come to peer across the waters of the 'Au'au Channel, better known as the "Lahaina Roads," in search of these magnificent giants. Lana'i is a victim of its own reputation. Most visitors were informed by even longtime residents that Lana'i, nicknamed "The Pineapple Island," was a dull place covered in one large pineapple plantation: endless rows of the porcupine plants, sliced and organized by a labyrinth of roads, contoured and planted by improbable-looking machines, and tended by mostly Filipino workers in wide-brimmed hats and goggles. Although changing somewhat, this image still persists. It's true that Lana'i had the largest pineapple plantation in the world, 15,000 cultivated acres, which accounted for about 90 percent of U.S. production. The remnants of these fields are still obvious in the swirls of feral fields as you approach the island by air. Now only about 100 acres remain in cultivation out by the airport—as a testimony to a bygone era—and these fruits are raised for local consumption only. All other pineapples on the island are raised by local gardeners. But the island has 74,000 acres that remain untouched and perfect for exceptional outdoor experiences, ranging from golf to mountain biking to snorkeling.

Because of its past reputation as a place where almost no one went and recent shift from pineapple production to tourism that caters to the well-to-do who want their peace and quiet, Lana'i is once again becoming known as the "Secluded Island."

OVERVIEW

The people of Lana'i live in one of the most fortuitously chosen spots for a working village in the world: Lana'i City. All but about two dozen of the island's 3,100 permanent residents make their homes here. Nestled near the ridge of mountains in the northeast corner of the Palawai Basin, **Lana'i City** (elevation 1,600 feet) is sheltered, cooled, and characterized by a mature and extensive grove of Cook pines planted in the

early 1900s by the practical New Zealand naturalist George Munro. This evergreen canopy creates a parklike atmosphere about town while reaching tall green fingers to the clouds. A mountainous spine tickles drizzle from the water-bloated bellies of passing clouds for the thirsty, red, sunburned plains of Lana'i below. The trees, like the bristled hair of an annoyed cat, line the **Munro Trail** as it climbs Lana'ihale, the highest spot on the island (3,370 feet). The Munro Trail's magnificent panoramas encompass sweeping views of no less than five of the eight major islands as it snakes along the mountain ridge, narrowing at times to the width of the road itself.

Maunalei Gulch, a vast precipitous valley, visible from "The Trail," was the site of a last-ditch effort of Lana'i warriors to repel an invasion by the warrior king of the Big Island at the turn of the 18th century. Now its craggy arms

ROBERT NILSEN

the south coast of Lana'i

LANA'I

provide refuge to mouflon sheep as they execute death-defying leaps from one rocky ripple to the next. On the valley floors roam axis deer, and, until recently, on the northwest grasslands were the remnants of an experimental herd of pronghorn antelope brought from Montana in 1959. After saturating yourself with the glories of Lana'i from the heights, descend and follow a well-paved road from Lana'i City to the southern tip of the island. Here, **Manele** and **Hulopo'e** bays sit side by side. Manele is a favorite spot of small sailing craft that have braved the channel from Lahaina. Hulopo'e Bay, just next door, is as salubrious a spot as you can hope to find. It offers camping and all that's expected of a warm, sandy, palm-lined beach. With its virtually untouched underwater marine park, Hulopo'e is regarded as one of the premier snorkeling spots in the entire island chain.

You can hike or 4WD to **Kaunolu Bay,** one of the best-preserved ancient Hawaiian village sites. Kamehameha the Great came to this ruggedly masculine shore to fish and frolic his summers away with his favorite cronies. Here, Kahekili leaped from a sea cliff to the ice-blue waters below, and challenged all other warriors to prove their loyalty to Kamehameha by following his example and hurtling themselves off what today is known as **Kahekili's Leap.**

You can quickly span a century by heading for the southeast corner of Lana'i and its three abandoned villages of **Lopa, Naha,** and **Keomuku.**

Here legends abound. *Kahuna* curses still guard a grove of coconut trees, which are purported to refuse to let you down if you climb for their nuts without offering the proper prayers. Here also are the remnants of a sugar train believed to have caused its cane enterprise to fail because the rocks of a nearby *heiau* were disturbed and used in its track bed. A decaying abandoned Hawaiian church in Keomuku insists on being photographed.

You can head north along the east shore to **Shipwreck Beach,** where the rusting hulk of a liberty ship, along with timbers and planks from the great wooden square-riggers of days gone by, lie along the beach, attesting to the authenticity of its name. Shipwreck Beach is a shore stroller's paradise, a real beachcomber's boutique. Also along here are some thought-provoking petroglyphs. Other petroglyphs are found on a hillside overlooking the former "pine" fields of the Palawai Basin.

If you hunger for a totally private beach, head to the northwest corner of the island. En route, you'll pass through a scarce remnant of Hawaiian dryland forest at **Kanepu'u Preserve** and a fantastic area of ancient cataclysm aptly called **The Garden of the Gods.** This raw, baked area of monolithic rocks and tortured earth turns incredible shades of purple, red, magenta, and yellow as the sun plays upon it from different angles. If you're hot and dusty and aching for a dip, continue north to trail's end where the desolation of the garden suddenly gives way to the gleaming brightness of virtually unvisited **Polihua Beach.**

After these daily excursions, return to the green serenity of Lana'i City. Even if you're only spending a few days, you'll be made to feel like you're staying with old friends. You won't have to worry about bringing your dancing shoes, but if you've had enough hustle and bustle and yearn to stroll in quietude, sit by a crackling fire, and look up at a crystal-clear sky, head for Lana'i. Your jangled nerves and ruffled spirit will be glad you did.

THE LAND

The sunburned face of Lana'i seems parched but relaxed as it rises in a gentle, steady arc from sea level. When viewed from the air it looks like an irregularly shaped kidney bean. The sixth largest of the eight main islands, Lana'i is roughly 140 square miles, measuring 18 miles north to south and 13 miles east to west at its longest points, with 47 miles of coastline. A classic single-shield volcano, at one time Lana'i was probably connected to Maui, Moloka'i, and Kaho'olawe as a single huge island. Marine fossils found at the 1,000-foot mark and even higher in the mountains indicate its slow rise from the sea. Its rounded features appear more benign than the violent creases of its closest island neighbors; this characteristic earned it the unflattering appellation of "Hump." More lyrical scholars, however, claim the real meaning has been lost to the ages or may in fact mean "Day of Conquest," but Lana'i does look like a hump when viewed from a distance at sea.

Its topography is simple. A rugged mountain ridge runs northwest to southeast through the eastern half of the island, and its entire length is traversed by the Munro Trail. The highest peak is Lana'ihale (3,370 feet). This area is creased by precipitous gulches: the two deepest are Maunalei and Hauola at more than 2,000 feet. The topography tapers off steadily as it reaches the sea to the east. Beaches stretch from the white sands of Polihua, past Shipwreck Beach in the north, terminating at the salt-and-pepper sands of Naha on the east. Beyond a short section of sea cliff lie the beautiful rainbow arches of Manele and Hulopo'e in the south. Until 1993, Palawai, Lana'i's central basin, was completely cultivated in manicured, whorled fields of pineapple. Early in the 1900s, Palawai was covered in cactus; now cattle graze across sections of the plain and some wheat is grown. The southwest and west coasts have phenomenal sea cliffs accessible only by boat. Some of the most majestic are the **Kaholo Pali,** which run south from Kaumalapau Harbor, reaching their most amazing ruggedness before Kaunolu Bay. At many spots along this stretch the sea lies more than 1,500 feet below. Starting at Lana'i City in the center, a half hour of driving in any direction presents a choice of this varied and fascinating geography.

Climate
The daily temperatures are quite balmy, especially at sea level, but it can get blisteringly hot in the basin and on the leeward side, so be sure to carry plenty of water when hiking or four-wheel-driving. At 1,600 feet, Lana'i City gets refreshingly cool in the evenings and early mornings, but a light jacket or sweater is adequate, al-

LANA'I CITY
TEMPERATURE AND RAINFALL

	JAN.	MARCH	MAY	JUNE	SEPT.	NOV.
High	70	71	75	80	80	72
Low	60	60	62	65	65	62
Rainfall	3	3	2	0	2	4

Note: Temperature is expressed in degrees Fahrenheit; rainfall in inches.

though thin-blooded residents bundle up. While it's sunny most days, fog rolls into town occasionally, evoking an ethereal, mysterious feel and sense of magic.

Water

Lying in the rain shadow of the West Maui Mountains, even Lana'i's windward side receives only 40 inches of rainfall a year. The central basins and leeward shores taper off to a scant 12 inches, not bad for pineapples and sun worshippers. Lana'i has always been short of water, but wells now help satisfy the needs of the residents. Its scruffy vegetation and red-baked earth are responsible for its inhospitable reputation. There are no real rivers, and the few streams, found mostly in the gulches of the windward mountains, carry water only when the rains come and are otherwise dry. Most ventures at colonizing Lana'i, both in ancient and modern times, were kept to a minimum because of this water shortage. The famous Cook pines of Lana'i City, along with other introduced greenery, greatly helped the barrenness of the landscape and provided a watershed. They tickle the underside of and drink water from the clouds that graze the highland ridge. But the rust-red earth remains unchanged, and if you get it onto your clothes, it'll remain there as a permanent souvenir.

FLORA AND FAUNA

Most of Lana'i's flora and fauna have been introduced. In fact, the Cook pine and the regal mouflon sheep were a manmade attempt to improve the natural, often barren habitat. These species have adapted so well that they now symbolize Lana'i, as the ubiquitous pineapple once did. Besides the mouflon, Lana'i boasts axis deer and a few feral goats. A wide variety of introduced game birds include the Rio Grande turkey, ring-necked pheasant, and an assortment of quail, francolins, and doves. Like the other Hawaiian Islands, Lana'i, unfortunately, is home to native birds that are headed for extinction. Along the Munro Trail and on the windward coast you pass through forests of Cook pines, tall eucalyptus stands, shaggy ironwoods, native koa, and silver oaks. Everywhere, dazzling colors and fragrances are provided by Lana'i's flowers.

Flowers

Although Lana'i's official flower is the *kauna'oa*, it's not really a flower, but an airplant that grows wild. It's easily found along the beach at Keomuku. It grows in conjunction with *pohuehue*, a pinkish-red, perennial seashore morning glory. Native to Hawaii, the *pohuehue* grows in large numbers along Lana'i's seashore. It's easy to spot, and when you see a yellow-orange vinelike airplant growing with it, you've found Lana'i's *kauna'oa*, which is traditionally fashioned into lei. The medicinal *'ilima*, used to help asthma sufferers, is found in large numbers in Lana'i's open fields. Its flat, open yellow flower is about one inch in diameter and grows on a waist-high shrub. Two other flowers considered by some to be pests are the purple *koali* morning glory and the miniature red and yellow flowering lantana, known for its unpleasant odor. Both are abundant on the trail to the Garden of the Gods.

Cook Pines

These pines were discovered by Captain Cook in the South Pacific, and some say that the first were brought here by Captain Vancouver as a future supply of ship masts. Imported in great numbers by George Munro, they adapted well to Lana'i and helped considerably to attract moisture and provide a firm watershed. Exquisitely ornamental, they can also be grown in containers. Their perfect cone shape makes them a natural Christmas tree, used as such in Hawaii; some are even shipped to the Mainland for this purpose.

Endemic Birds

The list of native birds still found on Lana'i gets smaller every year, and those still on the list are rarely seen. The *'amakihi* is about five inches long with yellowish-green plumage. The males deliver a high-sounding tweet and a trilling call. Vegetarians, these birds live mostly on grasses and lichen, building their nests in the uppermost branches of tall trees. Some people believe that the *'amakihi* is already extinct on Lana'i.

The *'ua'u* or Hawaiian petrel is a large bird with a 36-inch wingspan. Its head and back are shades of black with a white underbelly. As this "fisherbird" lives on squid and crustaceans that it regurgitates to its chicks. Unfortunately, the Hawaiian petrel nests on the ground, sometimes

LANA'I

laying its eggs under rocks or in burrows, which makes it an easy prey for predators. Its call is reported to sound like a small yapping dog.

The *'apapane* is abundant on the other main islands, but dwindling rapidly on Lana'i. It's a chubby red-bodied bird about five inches long with a black bill, legs, wingtips, and tail feathers. It's quick, flitty, and has a wide variety of calls and songs from beautiful warbles to mechanical buzzes. Its feathers were sought by Hawaiians to produce distinctive ornate featherwork.

Axis Deer

This shy and beautiful creature came to Lana'i via Moloka'i, where the first specimens arrived in 1868 as a gift from the Hawaiian consul in Hong Kong. Its native home is the parkland forests of India and Sri Lanka. The coats of most axis deer are golden tan with rows of round lifetime spots, along with a black stripe down the back and a white belly. They stand three to four feet at the shoulder, with bucks weighing an average of 160 pounds and does about 110. The bucks have an exquisite set of symmetrical antlers that always form a perfect three points. The antlers can stand 30 inches high and more than 20 inches across, making them coveted trophies. Does are antlerless and give birth to one fawn, usually between November and February, but Hawaii's congenial weather makes for good fawn survival anytime of year. Axis deer on Lana'i can be spotted anywhere from the lowland *kiawe* forests to the higher rainforests along the Munro Trail. Careful and proper hunting management should keep the population stable for many generations. The meat from axis deer is reported to have a unique flavor, different from Mainland venison—one of the finest tasting of all wild game.

Mouflon Sheep

Another name for these wild mountain sheep is Mediterranean or European bighorn. One of only six species of wild sheep in the world, mouflon are native to the islands of Sardinia and Corsica, whose climates are quite similar to Hawaii's. They have been introduced throughout Europe, Africa, and North America. Although genetically similar to domestic sheep, they are much more shy, lack a woolly coat, and only infrequently give birth to twins. Both rams and ewes are a similar tannish brown, with a snow-white rump, which is all that most people get to see of these always-alert creatures as they quickly and expertly head for cover. Rams weigh about 125 pounds (ewes a bit less) and produce a spectacular set of recurved horns. They need little water to survive, going for long periods on only the moisture in green plants. On Lana'i they are found along the northwest coast in the grasslands and in the dry *kiawe* forests.

HISTORY

Kaka'alaneo peered across the mist-shrouded channel between West Maui and Lana'i and couldn't believe his eyes. Night after night, the campfire of his son Kaulula'au burned, sending its faint but miraculous signal. Could it be that the boy was still alive? Kaulula'au had been given every advantage of his noble birth, but still the prince had proved to be unmanageable. King Kaka'alaneo had even ordered all children born on the same day as his son to be sent to Lahaina, where they would grow up as his son's friends and playmates. Spoiled rotten, young Kaulula'au had terrorized Lahaina with his pranks and one day went too far: he destroyed a new planting of breadfruit. Even the chief's son could not trample the social order and endanger the livelihood of the people. So finally the old *kahuna* had to step in. Justice was hard and swift: Kaulula'au must be banished

axis deer

BOB RACE

LANA'I

to the terrible island of Lana'i, where the man-eating spirits dwelled. There he would meet his fate, and no one expected him to live. But weeks had passed and Kaulula'au's nightly fires still burned. Could it be some ghoulish trick? Kaka'alaneo sent a canoe of men to investigate. They returned with incredible news. The boy was fine! All the spirits were banished! Kaulula'au had cleansed the island of its evil fiends and opened it up for the people to come and settle.

Oral History

In fact, it's recorded in the Hawaiian oral genealogical tradition that a young Kaulula'au did open Lana'i to significant numbers of inhabitants in approximately A.D. 1400. Lana'i passed through the next few hundred years as a satellite of Maui, accepting the larger island's social, religious, and political dictates. During this period, Lana'i supported about 3,000 people who lived by growing taro and fishing. Most inhabited the eastern shore facing Maui, but old home sites show that the population became established well enough to homestead the entire island. Lana'i was caught up in the Hawaiian wars that raged in the last two decades of the 1700s, and was ravaged and pillaged in 1778 by the warriors of Kalaniopu'u, aging king of the Big Island. These hard times marked a decline in Lana'i's population; accounts by Western sea captains who passed even a few years later noted that the island looked desolate, with no large villages evident. Lana'i began to recover and saw a small boost in population when Kamehameha the Great established his summer residence at Kaunolu on the southern shore. This kept Lana'i vibrant for a few years at the beginning of the 19th century, but it began to fade soon thereafter. The decline continued until only a handful of Hawaiians remained by the 20th century. The old order ended completely when one of the last traditional *kanaka,* a man named Ohua, hid the traditional fish god, Hunihi, and died shortly thereafter in his grass hut in the year 1900.

Early Foreign Influences

No one knows his name, but all historians agree that a Chinese man tried his luck at raising sugarcane on Lana'i in 1802. He brought boiling pots and rollers to Naha on the east coast, but after a few years of hard luck gave up and moved on. About 100 years later a large commercial sugar enterprise was attempted in the same area. This time the sugar company even built a narrow-gauge railroad to carry the cane. A story goes that after disrupting a local *heiau* to make ballast for the rail line, the water in the area, never in great abundance to begin with, went brackish. Again sugar was foiled.

In 1854 a small band of Mormon elders tried to colonize Lana'i by starting a "City of Joseph" at Palawai Basin. This began the career of one of Hawaii's strangest, most unfathomable yet charismatic early leaders. Walter Murray Gibson came to Palawai to start an idyllic settlement for the Latter-day Saints. He energetically set to work improving the land with funds from Utah and hard work of the other Mormon settlers. The only fly in Gibson's grand ointment occurred when the Mormon Church discovered that the acres of Palawai were not registered to the church at all but to Walter Murray Gibson himself! He was excommunicated and the bilked settlers relocated. Gibson went on to have one of the strangest political careers in Hawaiian history, including championing native rights and enjoying unbelievable influence at the royal Hawaiian court. His land at Palawai passed on to his daughter who became possessed by the one evil spirit Kaulula'au failed to eradicate: she tried to raise sugarcane, but was fated, like the rest, to fail.

A few other attempts proved uneconomical, and Lana'i languished. The last big attempt at cattle raising produced The Ranch, part of whose lands make up the Cavendish Golf Course in Lana'i City. This enterprise did have one bright note. A New Zealander named George Munro was hired as the manager. He imported all manner of seeds and cuttings in his attempt to foliate the island and create a watershed. The Ranch failed, but Munro's legacy of Cook pines stands as a proud testament to this amateur horticulturist.

The Coming of Pineapples

The purchase of Lana'i in 1922 was one of the niftiest real estate deals in modern history. James D. Dole, the most enterprising of the pineapple pioneers, bought the island—lock, stock, and barrel—from the Baldwins, an old missionary family, for $1.1 million. That comes to only $12 per acre, though many of those acres were fairly scruffy, not to mention Lana'i's bad economical track record. Dole had come from Boston at the turn of the 20th century to figure out how to can pineapple profitably. Dole did such a remarkable job of marketing the "golden fruit" on the Mainland that in a few short years, Midwestern Americans who'd never even heard of pineapples before were buying cans of it regularly from the shelves of country grocery stores. In 1922, Jim Dole needed more land for his expanding pineapple fields, and the arid basin of Palawai seemed perfect.

Lana'i Plantation was an oligarchy during the early years, with the plantation manager as king. One of the most famous of these characters was H. Broomfield Brown, who ran Lana'i Plantation in the '30s. He kept watch over the fields from his house through a telescope. If anyone loafed, he'd ride out into the fields to confront the offender. Mr. Brown personally "eyeballed" every new visitor to Lana'i: all prostitutes, gamblers, and deadbeats were turned back at the pier. An anti-litter fanatic, he'd even reprimand anyone who trashed the streets of Lana'i City. During the labor strikes of the 1960s, workers' grievances were voiced and Lana'i began to function as a more fair enterprise. With pineapple well established on the world market, Lana'i finally had a firm economic base. From a few thousand fruits in the early days, the flow at its peak reached a million fruits per day during the height of the season. They were shipped from the manmade port at Kaumalapau, which was specially built in 1926 to accommodate Lana'i's "pines."

Crushed Pineapples

At its height, Lana'i had 18,000 acres of pineapples under production (15,000 acres for most of its heyday). These acres made up the largest single pineapple plantation in the world. Virtually the entire island was operated by The Dole Co., whose name had become synonymous with pineapples. In one way or another, everyone on Lana'i owed their livelihood to pineapples, from the worker who twisted his ankle in a pine field to the technician at the community hospital who X-rayed it. Now, all has changed and only a few plots remain, mostly for use by the hotels.

Foreign production, especially in the Philippines, has greatly increased, and the Lana'i pineapple industry has folded. As acreage was taken out of pineapple production, and as the population of the island and number of visitors have increased, the company has experimented with raising various organic vegetables, grains, and cattle to diversify the island's economy. This seems to be a pet project of the owner, and the hope is to make the economy of Lana'i more locally sustainable and less dependent on imports from the other islands and the Mainland.

Changing Lana'i

Most are amazed that George Munro's pines still shelter a tight-knit community that has remained untouched for so long. But all that's changing, and changing quickly. Two new hideaway luxury hotels have risen, and they're beauties. The coming of these resorts has brought the most profound changes to Lana'i since James Dole arrived at the turn of the 20th century. Castle and Cooke, practically speaking, owns the island (98 percent). David Murdoch is the CEO and owner of Castle and Cooke, and the hotels are his babies. He developed them and the two golf courses, and continues to develop residential lots (up to 700 in the next 10 years) through a permutation of companies that is now called the Lana'i Company. This company employs a staff of about 1,200 or so, more than all the workers needed to tend the pineapple fields, which was just over 500 people. The hotels have brought an alternative job market, new life to the downtown area, and a housing spurt. One fact was undeniable concerning Lana'i: if you wanted to make a living you either had to work the pineapple fields or leave. Now that has changed. To stop the disenfranchisement of the local people, which was generally the case with rapid development, the Lana'i Company has built several new housing projects, which have come with a promise. Local people, according to seniority with the company and length of residence on Lana'i, have first choice. One group of houses is multiple-family, geared to the entry-level buyer, and the second is single-family homes. Million-dollar homes are also starting to pop up above town and now begin to line the fairways of the new golf courses. This isn't all *heart* on the part of the Lana'i Company. It wants to ensure that the hotels will have a steady and contented workforce to keep them running without a hitch and to make the whole venture economically viable.

Downtown Lana'i is inadequate. It couldn't possibly handle the hotel guests and all the new workers and their families who have moved to the island. Old buildings have been refurbished, some torn down and replaced, with more upscale businesses taking their place. The tired little shops in town are on Lana'i Company property, most with month-to-month leases. The Lana'i Company again promises to be fair, but like the rest of Lana'i, they'll have a choice: progress or perish. Most islanders are optimistic, keeping an open mind and adopting a "wait and see" attitude concerning the inevitable changes and the promises that have been made for a better life.

THE PEOPLE

Lana'i is characterized by the incredible mix of racial strains so common in Hawaii—Filipino, Japanese, Hawaiian, Chinese, and Caucasian. It is unique, however, in that 60 percent of its people are Filipino. The Filipinos, some recent immigrants, were solicited by Castle and Cooke to work as laborers on the pineapple plantation. Mostly single young men, the majority Ilocano, some may have come to join relatives already on Lana'i. Here they learned English and from Lana'i they spread out. As workers they were perfect: industrious and quiet. At night you wonder where they all are. Due to the tremendous shortage of eligible women, most workers stay home or fish or have a beer in the backyard with buddies. And on Sundays, there is the illegal (officially nonexistent) cockfight. For high living, everyone heads for Maui or Oahu.

The next largest racial groups are Japanese (14 percent), Hawaiian (12 percent), and Caucasians (11 percent). The Japanese started as the field workers before the Filipinos but now, along with the whites, are Lana'i's professionals and middle management. The races coexist, but there are still unseen social strata. There's even a small Chinese population (1 percent), who continue their traditional role as shopkeepers. Finally, about 2 percent fall into the "mixed" category, with many of these Filipino-Hawaiian.

Community
Lana'i has a strong sense of community and uniqueness that keeps the people close. For example, during a bitter three-month strike in 1964, the entire community rallied and all suffered equally: laborers, shopkeepers, and management. All who remember say that it brought out the best in the island tradition of *aloha*. If you really want to meet Lana'ians, just sit in the park in the center of Lana'i City for an hour or two. You'll notice a lot of old-timers, who seem to be very healthy. You could easily strike up a conversation with some of them.

Other Faces
It once might have struck you that most of the people you saw around Lana'i were men. That in itself was a social comment about Lana'i, where men worked the fields and women stayed at home in their traditional roles, nurturing and trying to add the pleasantries of life. Now you will see more and more women about, many who work at the hotels. You might notice that there are no famous crafts of Lana'i and few artists working commercially. This is not to say there is no art on Lana'i, but the visitor rarely sees it. One reason that Lana'i produces so little commercial art is that it's a workers' island with virtually no unemployment, so everyone is busy

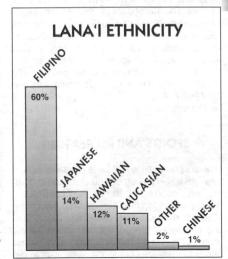

LANA'I

making a living. Old-timers are known to make superb fishing poles, nets, and even their own horseshoes. The island ladies are excellent seamstresses and, with the rising interest in hula, make lovely lei from the beautiful *kauna'oa*, Lana'i's flower. If you turn your attention to the young people of Lana'i, you'll see the statewide problem of babies having babies. Although the situation is getting better, teenage parents are still not uncommon. Young guys customize their 4WDs although there's no place to go. If as a young person you wish to remain on Lana'i, then in almost every case your future will be tied to the Lana'i Company. If you have other aspirations, it's "goodbai to Lana'i." These islanders are some of the most easygoing and relaxed people you'll encounter in Hawaii, but with the electronic age extending its long arms of communication, even here they're not nearly as "backwater" as you might think.

Events

All official holidays are honored and celebrated. As anywhere in the state, Lana'i celebrates special events in its own unique way, and each ethnic group has festivities that the whole island participates in. Some community events include **Community Kite Flying** day, held at Lana'i City in March. **May Day** is important throughout the state and events here take place at Lana'i High School. The **4th of July** (or another day in early July) brings the **Pineapple Festival** to Hulopo'e Beach on Lana'i, when all the town gathers to enjoy music, crafts, demonstrations, and, of course, lots of pineapple. A farmers' market is held for produce and home-baked goods, and a cooking contest is conducted for amateurs and professionals alike. To cap off the event, fireworks light the night sky.

SPORTS AND RECREATION

There's no question that Lana'i's forte is its natural unspoiled setting and great outdoors. Traffic jams, neon lights, blaring discos, shopping boutiques, and all that jazz just don't exist here. The action is swimming, hiking, snorkeling, fishing, horseback riding, and some hunting. Tennis and golf round off the activities. Lana'i is the place to revitalize your spirits—you want to get up with the birds, greet the sun, stretch, and soak up the good life.

Snorkel and Scuba

Lana'i, especially around Manele and Hulopo'e Bays, has some of the best snorkeling and scuba in Hawaii. If you don't have your own equipment, and you're not a guest at one of the hotels, you could buy gear from Pine Isle or Richards stores or rent from the Adventure Lana'i Company. If you're the adventurous sort, you can dive for spiny lobsters off Shipwreck or Polihua, but make absolutely sure to check the surf conditions as it can be super treacherous. It would be best to go with a local person.

Trilogy Ocean Sports, 888/628-4800, operates the new *Trilogy III* catamaran and a rigid-bottom inflatable raft from Manele Boat Harbor for a number of sailing options. The four-hour snorkel/sail ($95) leaves Monday, Wednesday, and Friday at 8:45 A.M., and Saturday at 10 A.M. Two scuba adventures, $130–140, leave around the same time, every day except Sunday. Rafting tours with dolphin watch (whale-watch, in season) are also offered ($75–95) throughout the week at various times. For those who don't care to start from a boat, beach dives are also offered twice a day weekdays at Hulopo'e Beach for $65–75. Book directly or through the concierge desk at the Manele Bay Hotel or at the Lodge at Ko'ele. Trilogy, in the business for years, has worked out all the kinks, and their boat, crew, and services are truly state-of-the-art. No matter how many times they make the trip, they never seem to forget that it's a new and exciting adventure for you, and they go out of their way to be helpful, upbeat, and caring without being intrusive. *Trilogy III's* aft is set up for easy entry and exit, with steps going down to the water level. Just make like a seal and slither in and out! If the winds are up, the captain will be happy to set sail as they head toward Kahekili's Leap and other famous Lana'i landmarks. The experience is not just underwater, but also in the magnificent views of this pristine island that hasn't changed since the days of the Polynesian explorers. On morning sails, you return in the early afternoon with plenty of time left for more sightseeing or just relaxing. For those on Trilogy boats coming from Lahaina, the company has a pavilion at Manele Harbor that's used to feed their guests, and from where they are taken to Hulopo'e Bay to snorkel and swim or tour the island by van. This pavilion is also used by Trilogy for theme parties, so if you have a group you may want to inquire what they can do for you. The company's website is www.sailtrilogy.com.

Spinning Dolphin Charters, owned and operated by Captain Jeff Menze, a long-time Lana'i resident, P.O. Box 491, Lanai City, 96763, 808/565-6613, will take you fishing (children welcome), snorkeling, and whale-watching in season; six person maximum. Captain Jeff is a commercial fisherman and master diver who knows all of the best spots in Lana'i's waters. Offered are whole-day and half-day adventures, special off-the-beaten-path dives, and private boat charters.

Kayaking

Trilogy Excursions has at least three kayak adventures that it offers on Lana'i along with its sailing excursions. Tours are lead by guides along the south and north shores and run $125 per person, and that includes lunch and transportation. Contact Trilogy at 888/628-4800.

Swimming

Lana'i City has a fine swimming pool. In town near the high school, it's open to the public during summer, usually 10:30 A.M.–5 P.M. daily except Wednesday, and on a limited schedule during other seasons. Each of the two resorts has its own swimming pool and spa—for use by registered guests only. By far the best swimming beach on Lana'i is at Hulopo'e Bay, but a few other spots for a dip can be found along the coast from Shipwreck Beach to Naha.

Fishing

Only the **Spinning Dolphin Charters,** 808/565-6613, operates a fishing boat out of Lana'i, for full- or half-day charters from one to six people, but that's not to say there are no fish. On the contrary, one of the island's greatest pastimes is this relaxing sport. Any day in Lana'i City Park, you'll find plenty of old timers to ask where the fish are biting. If you have the right approach and use the right smile, they just might tell you. Generally, the best fishing and easiest access on the island is at Shipwreck Beach running

west toward Polihua. Near the lighthouse ruins is good for *papio* and *ulua,* the latter running to 50 pounds. Many of the local fishermen use throw-nets to catch the smaller fish such as *manini,* preferred especially by Lana'i's elders. Throw-netting takes skill usually learned from childhood, but don't be afraid to try even if you throw what the locals call a "banana" or one that looks like Maui (a little head and a big body). They might snicker, but if you laugh too, you'll make a friend. Mostly you'll fish with rod and reel using frozen squid or crab, available at Lana'i's general stores. Bring a net bag or suitable container. This is the best beachcombing on the island and it's also excellent diving for spiny lobster. There is good shore fishing (especially for *awa*) and easy accessibility at Kaumalapau Harbor, from where the pineapples used to be shipped and where the supplies for the island now come. There is also superb offshore fishing at Kaunolu, Kamehameha's favorite angling spot on the south shore. You can catch *aku* and *kawakawa,* but to be really successful you'll need a boat. Finally, Manele Hulopo'e Marine Life Conservation Park has limited fishing, but as the name implies, it's a conservation district, so be sure to follow the rules prominently posted at Manele Bay.

Camping

The only official camping permitted to nonresidents is at Hulopo'e Bay, administered by the Lana'i Company. Reservations for one of the six official campsites on the grass up from the beach are a must, although unbelievably there's usually a good chance of getting a space. Lana'i Company officials state that they try to accommodate any "overflow" unreserved visitors, but don't count on it. Since Lana'i is by and large privately owned by Castle and Cooke Inc., the parent company of the Lana'i Company, you really have no recourse but to play by their rules. It seems they want to hold visitors to a minimum and keep strict tabs on the ones that do arrive.

Nonetheless, the campsites at Hulopo'e Bay are great. Lining the idyllic beach, they're far enough apart to afford some privacy. The showers are designed so that the pipes, just below the surface, are solar heated. This means a good hot shower during daylight and early evening. Campsite use is limited to six nights, and you must be 18 years of age or older to make an application. The fee includes a one-time $5 registration, plus $5 per person per night. For reservations write to the Lana'i Co., P.O. Box 310, Lanai City, HI 96763, attn. Camping, or call 808/565-3978. Permits, if not mailed in advance, are picked up at the Lana'i Company office. If visiting on the spur of the moment from a neighboring island, it's advisable to call ahead.

Note: While hiking or four-wheel driving the back roads of Lana'i, especially along Naha, Shipwreck, and Polihua beaches, a multitude of picture-perfect camping spots will present themselves, but they can be used only by Lana'i residents, although there's little supervision. A one-night bivouac would probably go undetected. No other island allows unofficial camping, and unless it can be statistically shown that potential visitors are being turned away, it seems unlikely that the Lana'i Company will change its policies. If you're one of the unlucky ones who have been turned down, contact parent company Castle and Cooke with your protest: 650 Iwilei Rd., Honolulu, HI 96817, 808/548-4811.

Hiking and Jogging

All the paved roads and many of the gravel roads in Lana'i City are decent for walking and jogging. Although the traffic is not heavy, be careful if you're on the roadway.

One trail on the island has been marked, the **Koloiki Ridge Trail.** Pick up a map at either of the resort front desks. Start at the rear of the Lodge at Ko'ele and head up through the golf course into a tall stand of pine trees. Cross under the power lines and into Hulopo'e Valley, where an abandoned road heads up to the Munro Trail. Once there, turn right and head south, walking into and out of Kukui Gulch, until you round a very eroded "moonscape" on your right. A short way farther, turn left down an old jeep trail for perhaps 5–10 minutes. Head through a tunnel in the trees to the flat open Koloiki lookout. From here, you can look down into Naio and Maunalei gulches and out toward Maui and Moloka'i.

Shorter and easier is **Fisherman's Trail,** a 1.5-mile shoreline trail that runs from Hulopo'e Bay to the west, below the Manele Bay Hotel. A project of the State Na Ala Hele trail system, this was once part of an ancient trail that circled the island.

Horseback Riding

The Stables at Ko'ele, 808/565-4424, open daily and just a few minutes from the Lodge at Ko'ele, offers a variety of mounted excursions. Trail rides run 1–2.5 hours for $40–80. Three- and four-hour trail rides with lunch are $110–140. Private rides can be arranged for $70–180, as can a full day ride to the top of the mountain for $400. Other rides are available, including a 15-minute children's pony ride and carriage rides. Lana'i enjoys a ranching heritage that goes back to the 1870s. Many of the trails that you'll be fol-

eighth hole at The Experience at Ko'ele

ROBERT NILSEN

LANA'I GOLF AND TENNIS

GOLF COURSE	PAR	YARDS	FEES	CART	CLUBS
Cavendish Golf Course no phone	36	3,058	Donation	None	None
The Challenge at Manele at the Manele Bay Hotel 808/565-2222	72	7,039	$185 nonguest $135 hotel guest	Incl.	$40
The Experience at Ko'ele at the Lodge at Ko'ele 808/565-4653	72	7,014	$200 nonguest $145 hotel guest	Incl.	$40

TENNIS COURTS LOCATION	TEL. (808)	FEES	NO. OF COURTS	LIGHTED
The Lodge at Ko'ele Tennis Courts	565-4555	no fees	3	Yes
Manele Bay Hotel Tennis Center	562-2387	$25	6	No
Lana'i School (Lana'i City)	(no phone)	no fees	2	Yes

lowing date from those early days. Riders must be in good health, weigh less than 250 pounds, and be at least nine years old and stand four foot, six inches in height—except for the pony rides. Everyone must wear long pants and closed-toe shoes. Safety helmets will be provided for all riders.

Golf and Tennis
Golfers will be delighted to follow their balls around **Cavendish Golf Course** on the outskirts of Lana'i City. This nine-hole, 3,058-yard, par-36 course (use the blue tees the first time around, the white tees if you want to go a second nine hotels) is set among Cook pines and challenging local residents since the 1930s. It's free to all, but visitors to the island are requested to leave a donation for maintenance at the first tee, which, unless you're familiar with the course, could be a bit hard to find. Ask—it's straight up from the clubhouse. Even this unassuming community course has a "signature" hole with some difficulty. It's the ninth hole, and its green is about 50 feet higher than the tee, plus you must golf through a narrow opening in the trees to reach the green. You'll find this course at the end of Nani Street.

The **Experience at Ko'ele,** a Greg Norman-designed course, won the *Fortune Magazine* Best New Golf Course of 1991 award. This magnificent course, set in the mountains above the Lodge, not only offers challenging links, but a fantastic series of views of Moloka'i and Maui on a shimmering canvas of sea. With four sets of tees ranging from forward to tournament, the course yardage varies accordingly from 5,425 yards to 7,014 yards. The course also boasts the only bent-grass greens in the state. Two of the finest holes are the number 8,444-yard parfour, which cascades 250 feet from ridgetop to glen below, and the short but maximum water-challenged number 9, a 180-yard par-three. For information and tee times, call 808/565-4653.

The **Challenge at Manele,** designed by the legendary Jack Nicklaus, officially opened on Christmas Day, 1993. Employing the five-tee concept, the par-72 course ranges in length 5,024–7,039 yards. This course is set above the cliff edge, along the sparkling ocean at the Manele Bay Hotel. Three of the main holes, including the signature number 12 par-three hole, demand a tee shot over the greatest water hazard in the world, the wide Pacific. Call 808/565-2222 for tee times.

You can play **tennis** at two lighted courts at the Lana'i School 7 A.M.–8:30 P.M. They have rubberized surfaces called royal duck and are fairly well maintained—definitely okay for a fun game. The Lodge at Ko'ele and the Manele Bay Hotel have plexi-pave courts and their use is complimentary for hotel guests but $25 per hour for nonguests. The six courts at Manele Bay are newer than the three at the Lodge and in better condition. Equipment rental (rackets and ball machines), court times, and fees can be arranged at the pro shops or through the concierge desks. Private lessons and clinics are available.

Hunting

The first cliché you hear about Lana'i is that it's one big pineapple plantation. The second is that it's a hunter's paradise. The first was true, the second still is. Both private and public hunting are allowed. As virtually all of Lana'i is privately owned, about two-thirds of the island is set aside as a private reserve, and one-third is leased to the state for public hunting and is cooperatively managed.

The big game action for public hunting is provided by mouflon sheep and axis deer. Various days are open for the hunting of game birds, which include ring-necked and green pheasant; Gambel's, Japanese, and California quail; wild turkey; and a variety of doves, francolins, and partridges. The public hunting area is restricted to the northwest corner of the island. Brochures detailing all necessary information can be obtained free of charge by writing to Department of Land and Natural Resources, 1151 Punchbowl St., Honolulu, HI 96813. Contact Derwin Kwon at the Lana'i regional office, P.O. Box 732, 911 Fraser Ave., Lanai City, HI 96763, 808/565-7916. Licenses are required ($15 resident, $100 nonresident) and can be purchased by mail from Department of Land and Natural Resources or picked up in person at the office on Lana'i.

Public archery hunting of mouflon sheep is restricted to the last Saturday in July and first Saturday in August. The muzzleloader rifle season occurs on the second and third Saturday in August, and for rifles, shotguns, and bows and arrows for the nine following Saturdays. Tags are required and hunters are restricted by public drawing. Axis deer regular season (rifle, shotgun, and bows) opens on the nine consecutive Saturdays starting from the last Saturday in March; it's also restricted by public drawing. Muzzleloader season is the two Saturdays before

that, and archery season for axis deer is the two Saturdays preceding the muzzleloader season. Bag limits are one mouflon ram and one buck.

On the private land, only axis deer are hunted. Hunting is done year-round, although the best trophy season is May–November. Hunting dates must be mutually agreed upon by the hunter and the rangers, as there are a limited number of rangers and this is a three-day process, although the hunt itself is only one long day affair. Write three to six months in advance for best results. The rate is $275 per day for a regular hunting permit, or $50 for an archery hunting permit that is good until the Hawaiian hunting license expires. Guide service is not officially mandatory, but you must prove that you have hunted Lana'i before and are intimately knowledgeable about its terrain, hunting areas, and procedures. If not, you *must* acquire the services of a guide. Guide service is $750 a day, and this includes a permit and all necessities, except lodging and meals, from airport pickup to shipping the trophy. For all hunters, a Hawaii state hunting license and a hunter safety card are required. For full details write to Gary Onuma, Chief Ranger, The Lana'i Co., Game Management, P.O. Box 310, Lanai City, HI 96763, 808/565-3981, fax 808/565-3984.

Sporting Clays

An outgrowth of hunting, sporting clays is a sport that helps develop and maintain your hand-eye coordination. Shooting is done from different stations around a course, and the object is to hit a small round clay disk. Different than trap or skeet shooting, sporting clays relies upon moving targets that mimic different animals and birds, hopping along the ground as a rabbit, springing off the ground like a quail, or flying high like a pheasant. Here you can have all the enjoyment of hitting a target without the guilt of killing a living animal. **Lana'i Pine Sporting Clays,** 808/559-4600 or 800/321-4666, is a high-tech operation that services both beginners and the advanced shooter. To satisfy everyone's needs, there are skeet and trap ranges here as well. A number of shooting competitions are held here every year, including the Hawaii Pacific Open Ducks Unlimited Shoot in October.

Register at the pro shop and pick up your needed supplies and accessories there. A paved path connects each of the 14 stations; take a golf cart or walk the course. The basic package, including 100 targets, gun rental, cartridges, eye and ear protection, and safety vest runs $135 per person; $75 for 50 targets. For experienced shooters, guns, cartridges, targets, and carts can be rented separately, and you may use your own gun. Instruction is also given for beginners at $65; private lessons are available. Pull!

Archery

Set up next to Lana'i Pine Sporting Clays is the newer **Lana'i Pine Archery** course. With 12 targets set 15 and 35 yards from the firing line, this is enough to give everyone a challenge. Open 9:15-2:30 daily, the pro shop will set you up with all the needed equipment for your ability. Instruction runs $45, and course use for those who already know how to shoot is $35 or $25 with your own gear. Call 808/563-4600 for information or to arrange course time.

Adventure Tours

An independent company that caters largely to hotel guests, **Adventure Lana'i Company** can take you along the north coast of Lana'i on a kayak/snorkel trip, on a 4WD expedition of the highlights around the island, biking down to Shipwreck Beach, or on several other outings on the island. Half-day outings cost $69 per person. Guided tours and introduction are provided, and private tours can be arranged. Rentals can be accommodated. Adventure Lana'i has camping gear, kayaks, mountain bikes, and snorkel gear at competitive prices. See your hotel concierge or arrange directly: P.O. Box 1394, Lanai City, HI 96763, 808/565-7373, website: www.adventurelanai.com.

Hotel Lana'i rents mountain bicycles for $24 on a day-by-day basis, 7 A.M.–7 P.M. If you are staying at the Lodge at Ko'ele, check with the concierge about rental bicycles and an accompanying picnic backpack.

GETTING THERE

By Air

Hawaiian Airlines, 800/367-5320 Mainland and Canada, on Lana'i 800/882-8811, flies to Lana'i. It currently has a direct daily early-morning flight from Honolulu that returns via Moloka'i. The daily afternoon flight from Honolulu comes through Moloka'i, returning directly to Honolulu. Morning and afternoon flights to Kahului go via Moloka'i and/or Honolulu.

Daily flights are available to and from Lana'i by **Island Air,** 808/565-6744 or 800/652-6541 Neighbor Islands, or 800/367-5250 Mainland and Canada. Using some jets and some turbo-props, Island Air flies to and from Honolulu 10 times daily, with once daily to Kona on the Big Island.

Based in Kahului, the small commuter and tour operator **Pacific Wings** also flies regularly scheduled flights to and from Lana'i twice daily on weekdays with an abbreviated schedule on weekends. Call 888/575-4546 for information and reservations.

Lana'i Airport is a practical little strip about four miles southwest of Lana'i City, out near the remaining pineapple fields. The pleasing new terminal offers a departure lounge, gift shop, bathrooms, and public phones. If you are staying at any of the three hotels, a shuttle will transport you into town and drop you at the appropriate place for a $10 use fee. Complimentary airport pickup can also be arranged with Dollar Rent A Car if you rent from them. Otherwise **Rabaca's Limousine Service,** 808/565-6670, can shuttle you into town for $5 per seat or $10 minimum for ride.

By Boat

Expeditions, a passenger ferry, plies daily between Lahaina and Manele Bay. This shuttle offers speedy and convenient alternative transportation to the island. The crossing takes less than one hour and the ferry leaves Manele Bay at 8 A.M., 10:30 A.M., 2 P.M., 4:30 P.M., and 6:45 P.M. From Lahaina's public loading pier, ferries leave at 6:45 A.M., 9:15 A.M., 12:45 P.M., 3:15 P.M., and 5:45 P.M. The adult fare is $25 one-way while children 2–11 pay $20; *kama'aina* rates available. It's best to reserve a place. Luggage is taken free of charge, except for a $20 fee for bicycles. As only two bikes are permitted on each ferry, be sure to let the company know well ahead of time so your bikes can go with you. Ground transportation on Lana'i from the pier at Manele Bay is provided by Lana'i City Service, which will take you up to Lana'i City for $20 round-trip or $10 round-trip to the Manele Bay Hotel. An added perk of this trip is that you will see dolphins from the boat most of the year and there's good whale-watching during the winter months. For information and reservations contact the shuttle at 808/661-3756 on Maui or 800/695-2624 on Lana'i and elsewhere, website: www.go-lanai.com, or write 658 Front St., Suite 127, Lahaina, HI 96761.

One other possibility for getting to Lana'i is going by pleasure boat from Maui. These tour boats specialize in snorkeling, whale-watching, and the like, but may be willing to drop you off and pick you up at a later date. As there are no fixed rates for this service, you'll have to make your own arrangements with the boat captains at Lahaina Harbor. Remember that, in effect, you're going standby, but there is generally room for one more. This alternative is particularly attractive to campers, as they anchor on Lana'i at Manele Bay, just a five-minute walk from the campsites at Hulopo'e. Try Trilogy, 808/661-4743 or 888/628-4800, the only boat tour company with permission to land on Lana'i.

GETTING AROUND

Shuttle and Limousine Service
No public bus service operates on Lana'i, but **Lana'i City Service,** 808/565-7227, operates a free airport shuttle service during their business hours (7 A.M.–7 P.M.) if you're renting a car/jeep from them. Lana'i City Service also meets all ferries at the pier at Manele Bay and shuttles passengers to Manele Bay Hotel for $10 round-trip or up to Lana'i City for $20 round-trip. Otherwise shuttle service is handled by **Rabaca's Limousine Service,** 808/565-6670. To/from the airport or anywhere in and around Lana'i City, the charge is $5 a seat, and from Lana'i City to Manele Bay Hotel or the pier at Manele Harbor it's $10 per seat; two seat minimum on all rides.

The only limousine service on Lana'i is offered by Rabaca's. Rabaca has three stretch limos that are available 24 hours a day. Itineraries are set by the guest. Contact for rates: 808/565-6670, fax 808/565-6670, email: rabaca@aloha.net.

Lana'i Resort Shuttle
A shuttle service is offered for guests of the two big resorts and Hotel Lana'i. This shuttle runs daily 7 A.M.–midnight every 30 minutes on the hour and half hour, and picks up passengers at the front of each hotel. A connecting shuttle runs to and from the airport, $10 per person round-trip, meeting all arriving and departing planes.

Rental Car
For a car, or better yet, a jeep, try **Lana'i City Service, Dollar Rent A Car,** 808/565-7227 or 800/533-7808, at 1036 Lana'i Ave. in Lana'i City. You'll be outfitted with wheels and given a drive guide with information about road conditions and where you're allowed and not allowed to drive with their vehicles. Pay heed! Make sure to tell them your plans, especially if you're heading for a remote area. Lana'i City Service is a subsidiary of Trilogy Excursions and has a franchise with Dollar Rent A Car. It rents compacts for $59 per day, midsize cars for $79, eight-passenger minivans for $129, 4WD Jeep Wranglers for $129 per day, and 4WD Jeep Cherokees of $145 a day. Ask about weekly, monthly, and *kama'aina* rates. No insurance is available for vehicles rented on Lana'i, except for no-fault insurance, which is required by law. Lana'i City Service offers free shuttle service to and from the airport if you rent with them. This service operates only during their regular business hours, 7 A.M.–7 P.M. If you need to be at the airport before they start in the morning or after they close in the evening, there will be a $10 pickup charge if you drop off the vehicle at the airport. A fee of $20 is charged for picking up a vehicle left at the ferry pier.

Lana'i City Service has the only gas station on the island and it's open 7 A.M.–7 P.M. daily. With the few roads on the island, you won't be using much gas, but you'll have to fill the tank up on a rental vehicle when you return it. The price of gas varies, but in usually 30–50 cents a gallon more expensive here than the average price on Maui.

Using a 4WD Rental
With only 30 miles of paved road on Lana'i and rental cars firmly restricted to these, there is no real reason to rent one unless you are here just to golf. The *real* adventure spots of Lana'i require a 4WD vehicle, which on Lana'i is actually useful and not just a yuppie showpiece, since mind-boggling spots on Lana'i are reachable only on foot or by 4WD. Unfortunately, even the inveterate hiker will have a tough time because

the best trailheads are quite a distance from town, and you'll spend as much time getting to them as hiking the actual trails.

Many people who have little or no experience driving 4WDs are under the slap-happy belief that they are unstoppable. Oh, that it were true! They do indeed get stuck, and it's usually miserable getting them unstuck. The rental agencies will give you up-to-the-minute info on the road conditions and a fairly accurate map for navigation. They tend to be a bit conservative on where they advise you to take their vehicles, but they also live on the island and are accustomed to driving off-road, which balances out their conservative estimates. Also, remember that road conditions change rapidly: a hard rain on the Munro Trail can change it from a flower-lined path to a nasty quagmire, or wind might lay a tree across a beach road. Keep your eye on the weather, and if in doubt don't push your luck. If you get stuck, you'll not only ruin your outing and have to hike back to town, but you'll also be charged for a service call, which can be astronomical, especially if it's deemed to be due to your negligence. Most of your dirt road driving will be in 2WD, but certain sections of some roads and other roads during inclement weather will require a *compound* 4WD gear, low range.

Jeep Tours

Personalized, escorted jeep tours on the island can be arranged through **Rabaca's Limousine Service,** 808/565-6670. Let them know your preferences and they'll tailor a tour for you. The rate is $50 an hour with a maximum of four passengers. There is a two-hour minimum, but it usually takes at least three hours to get to some place on the island, have a look around, and get back. If you are unsure about driving dirt roads or may not want to rent a jeep for the out-of-the-way places, leave the driving to the professionals. It can be a good deal. You can also inquire here about kayaking, mountain biking, hiking, photography, fishing, and hunting options. Rabaca can either arrange this for you or send you in the right direction to match your needs.

Hitchhiking

Hitching is legal in Maui County and that includes Lana'i. Islanders are friendly and quite good about giving you a lift. Lana'i, however, is a

workers' island, and the traffic is really skimpy during the day. You can only reasonably expect to get a ride from Lana'i City to the airport or to Manele Bay since both are on paved roads and frequented by normal island traffic, or to Shipwreck Beach on the weekends. There is only a very slim chance of picking up a ride farther afield, toward the Garden of the Gods or Keomuku, for example, so definitely don't count on it.

SERVICES AND INFORMATION

Information

For general information about Lana'i, and activities and services on the island, contact Destination Lana'i, P.O. Box 700, Lanai City, HI 96763, 808/565-7600 or 800/947-4774, fax 808/565-9316, website: www.visitlanai.net, email: dlanai@aloha.net.

Additionally, maps, brochures, and pamphlets on all aspects of staying on Lana'i are available free from the Lana'i Company, P.O. Box 310, Lanai City, HI 96763, 808/565-3000.

For an upclose look at local news and what's happening in the community, have a look at the monthly *Lana'i Times* newspaper.

Useful Phone Numbers

Emergency: 911; police, 808/565-6428; weather and surf conditions, 808/565-6033; Lana'i City Service gas station, 808/565-7227; Department of Land and Natural Resources, 808/565-7916; Lana'i Airport, 808/565-6757; Lana'i Community Hospital 24-hour emergency service, 808/565-6411; Lana'i Family Health Center, 808/565-6423.

Money

Try full-service First Hawaiian Bank, 808/565-6969, in Lana'i City for your banking needs. Bank of Hawaii, 888/643-3888, also has a branch here. Banks are open Mon.–Thurs. 8:30 A.M.–4 P.M., Friday until 6 P.M., but they may be closed for lunch. Both have ATM machines outside their offices for after-hours banking. All major businesses on the island accept traveler's checks and some now also accept credit cards.

Post Office

The Lana'i post office, 808/565-6517, at its new location on Jacaranda Street, just a few steps off

LANA'I

the city park, is open weekdays 9 A.M.–4:30 P.M., and Saturday 10 A.M.–noon. You can find boxes and padded mailers for your beachcombing treasures at the two general stores in town.

Lana'i Community Library

At 6th and Fraser Avenues, the public library is open Tuesday, Thursday, and Friday 8 A.M.–4 P.M., Wednesday 1–8 P.M., and Saturday 11 A.M.–4 P.M.

Lana'i Playhouse

On the corner of Lana'i Avenue and 7th, Lana'i Playhouse, 808/565-7500 is the only theater on the island; it runs current-release movies. Open Fri.–Tues.; tickets run $7 adults and $4.50 kids and seniors.

Laundromat

The laundromat is open every day from "morning until nighttime": 6:30 A.M.–8:30 P.M. Bring coins.

LANA'I CITY

Lana'i City (pop. 3,100) would be more aptly described and sound more appealing if it were called Lana'i Village. A utilitarian town, it was built in the 1920s by Dole Pineapple Company. The architecture, field-worker plain, has definitely gained "character" in the last 70 years. It's an excellent spot for a town, sitting at 1,600 feet in the shadow of Lana'ihale, the island's tallest peak. George Munro's Cook pines have matured and now give the entire town a green, shaded, park-like atmosphere. It's cool and breezy—a great place to launch from in the morning and a welcome spot to return to at night. Most visitors head out of town to the more spectacular sights and never take the chance to explore the back streets.

Houses

As you'd expect, most houses are square boxes with corrugated roofs, but each has its own personality. Painted every color of the rainbow, they'd be garish in any other place, but here they break the monotony and seem to work. The people of Lana'i used to make their living from the land and can still work wonders with it. Around many homes are colorful flowerbeds, green gardens bursting with vegetables, fruit trees, and flowering shrubs. When you look down the half-dirt, broken-pavement roads at a line of these houses, you can't help feeling that a certain nobility exists here. The houses are mud-spattered where the rain splashes red earth against them, but inside you know they're sparkling clean. Many of these narrow lanes are one-way streets—watch for signs!

The modern suburban homes that line the few blocks at the extreme south end of town are mostly from the late 1980s and early '90s. Most of these belong to Lana'i's miniature middle class and would fit unnoticed in any up-and-coming neighborhood on another island. On the north edge of town are few new apartments and multifamily buildings that were put up in the mid-1990s. On the slope above town, set along the golfcourse fairways, are the more recent townhouses and luxury homes that will, over the years, become more predominant if development goes as planned. A similar luxury home development is growing along the golf fairways to the side of Manele Bay Hotel.

Around Town

Lana'i City streets running east-west are numerical starting with 3rd Street and running to 13th Street; the streets running north-south have alphabetical first letters and include Fraser, Gay, Houston, Ilima, Jacaranda, Ko'ele, and Lana'i Avenues, with a few more streets beyond this central grid. If you manage to get lost in Lana'i City you should seriously consider never leaving home.

If you sit on the steps of Hotel Lana'i and peer across its huge front yard, you can scrutinize the heart of downtown Lana'i City. Off to your right are offices, the community hospital and health center sitting squat and solid. In front of them, forming a type of town square, is Dole Park where old-timers come to sit and young mothers bring their kids for some fresh air. No one in Lana'i City rushes to do anything. Look around and you'll discover a real fountain of youth: the many octogenarians walk with a spring in their step. Years of hard work without being hyper or anxious is why they say they're still

LANA'I CITY

To Garden of the Gods
and Polihua Beach

TENNIS COURTS

To Shipwreck Beach

STABLES

430

THE LODGE AT
KOELE

THE
EXPERIENCE AT
KOELE GOLF
COURSE

KEOMUKU RD.

CAVENDISH
GOLF COURSE

DOLE PARK (detail)

MARIA M'S
BOUTIQUE

BANK

THEATER

LANA'I FAMILY
STORE

TANIGAWA'S

DOLE
PARK

DESTINATION
LANA'I

AKAMAI
TRADING

RICHARD'S
SHOPPING
CENTER

BANK

PINE ISLE
MARKET

KOELE AVE.

LANA'I

3RD
ST.

MAHANA

NANI

AVE.

ST.

ST.

6TH
ST.

JACARANDA

KO'ELE

LANA'I

IIMA

HOUSTON

GAY

AVE.

AVE.

AVE.

AVE.

AVE.

ST.

FRASER
AVE.

4TH
AVE.

5TH
AVE.

COFFEE
WORKS

POST
OFFICE

CLINIC

HEART OF LANA'I

SCHOOL

LOCAL GENTRY

BLUE GINGER
CAFE

LAUNDROMAT

GIFTS WITH ALOHA

HOSPITAL

LANAI ART
PROGRAM

DOLE PARK

8TH
ST.

HOTEL LANA'I

GYM

ADVENTURE
LANA'I COMPANY

PELE'S OTHER
GARDEN

PUUANI PL.

KAUNA'OA

TENNIS
COURTS

SEE DETAIL

POOL

POLICE

PELE'S
GARDEN

INTERNATIONAL FOOD
AND CLOTHING

ST.

9TH
ST.

LANAI CITY
SERVICE

ST.

DLNR

10TH
ST.

11TH
ST.

QUEENS
ST.

PALAWA
ST.

12TH
ST.

AHA

MANA

OLOPA
ST.

13TH
ST.

AKAHI ST.

AKOLU

0   0.25 mi

0   0.25 km

FIRE
STATION

440

KAUMALAPAU HWY.

MANELE RD.

To Airport

To Manele Bay

LANA'I

MooN

Although mostly humble, homes on Lana'i show plenty of pride.

J.D. BISIGNANI

around. The park is surrounded by commercial Lana'i. There's nowhere to *go* except over to the school yard to play some tennis or to Cavendish Golf Course for a round of nine holes. Lana'i City has a movie theater, and its now showing pictures once again. You can plop yourself at the Blue Ginger Cafe or Tanigawa's for coffee, or stay in the park if you're in the mood to strike up a conversation—it won't take long.

Meander down Lana'i Avenue past a complex of former agricultural buildings and shops. Once full of heavy equipment, this is where Lana'i showed its raw plantation muscle. Part of it has now been tamed and is the site of a new senior citizen's housing complex. Beyond the commercial buildings on both sides of the downtown park are the rows of plantation houses, now with newer subdivisions farther to each end. Do yourself a favor—get out of your rental car and walk around town for at least 30 minutes. You'll experience one of the most unique villages in America.

ACCOMMODATIONS

$100–150

Being the only hotel on the island until 1990, you'd think the lack of competition would have made **Hotel Lana'i** arrogant, indifferent, and expensive. On the contrary: it is delightful. The hotel has gone through a few cosmetic changes since it was built in 1923 as a guest lodge, then called "The Clubhouse," primarily for visiting executives of Dole Pineapple Co., the progeny of which still owns it. Its architecture is simple plantation-style Hawaiiana, and its setting among the tall Cook pines fronted by a large lawn is refreshingly rustic. With a corrugated iron roof, board and batten walls inside and out, wooden floors, and two wings connected by a long enclosed veranda, it looks like the main building at a Boy Scout camp. But don't be fooled. The 10 remodeled rooms may not be plush, but they are cozy as can be, and four open onto the front lanai. All have been painted in lively colors, and are immaculate with refurbished private baths. All have pine dressers and tables, floor lamps, area rugs, and ceiling fans, and patchwork quilts like grandma used to make cover each comfortable bed. Original artwork, done specifically for the hotel by island artist Denise Henning, graces the rooms and public areas. A newly renovated cottage behind the main building, at one time the caretaker's house, has its own private yard and bath. Room rates are $95–140, which includes a complimentary continental breakfast 7–9:30 A.M. of pastries from the kitchen, juice, and coffee; checkout is 11 A.M. Contact Hotel Lana'i at P.O. Box 520, Lanai City, HI 96763, 808/565-7211 or 800/795-7211 (7 A.M.–8 P.M. local time), fax 808/565-6450, website: www.onlanai.com.

The hotel has the only in-town bar, where guests and islanders alike have a quiet beer and twilight chat. The dining room, which occupies the center of the hotel, is paneled in knotty pine boards and lined with hunting trophies. So if you're lured by the quiet simplicity of Lana'i and wish to avail yourself of one of the last family-style inns of Hawaii, stay at the lovely little Hotel Lana'i.

$250 and up

A stately row of Cook pines bids welcome as they line the red brick driveway leading to **The Lodge at Ko'ele,** a grand manor house perched in genteel quietude just a 15-minute walk from downtown Lana'i City. An upland country hotel befitting this area of trees and cool summers, it's gracefully done in neo-Victorian style. Here, a huge pineapple mural painted above the front entrance greets everyone upon arrival. The name for this section of the island, Ko'ele means dark sugarcane. The Lodge at Ko'ele, P.O. Box 310, Lanai City, HI 96763, 808/565-7300 or 800/321-4666, with its encircling veranda and sweep of broad lawn, exudes gracious relaxation. You enter into the Great Hall where the back ceiling is a translucent skylight through which the sun casts diffused beams onto the formal Victorian parlors below. Encircled by a rich koa balcony, the Great Hall holds two immense fireplaces, the largest in Hawaii. Parlor settings of velvet chairs, cushy couches, wicker lounges, credenzas covered in flowers and ferns,

and lustrous end tables are perfect for a lazy afternoon of perusing the newspapers and magazines of the world or listening to soft island music every evenings. At each corner of the spacious Great Hall is a hexagonal room of beveled windows: one for dining; one for music; one a library; and the last a game room with backgammon, chess, and dominoes. Complimentary afternoon tea is served 3–5 P.M. for hotel guests in the music room.

Out front is a croquet pitch, to the side a bowling green. Out back through glass French doors are the swimming pool and fitness center, gazebo and reservoir, Japanese strolling garden, orchid house, palm and fruit gardens, and an executive putting green—a professionally designed "miniature" but real golf course. Here, with putter and a glass of chilled champagne and chocolate-dipped strawberries, you can test your skill against tiny sand traps, puddle-size water traps, and challenging Chihuahua-inspired doglegs both left and right.

Walk along the wide covered veranda past a row of rocking chairs to the two wings off the Great Hall, where you will find the 102 guest rooms, which range in price from $375 for a garden view to $2,000 for the best suite. A "renewal" project of the entire property was completed in 2000. Once inside, you can take the brass-doored elevator but climb instead the sweeping wooden staircases bearing carved pineapples, the symbol of hospitality, and walk the broad

LANA'I

ROBERT NILSEN

the Lodge at Ko'ele

hardwood hall hung with the works of island artists (ask the concierge for an art list for the hotel), letting period wall lamps light your way. Rooms are furnished in a combination of wicker and heavy knotty pine, with a four-poster bed—each topped with a carved pineapple—covered by a downy quilt, while billowy printed curtains flutter past a window seat. Along with this early 1900s charm comes a full entertainment center, in-room safe, and wet bar. Each room has its own lanai with tile floor and wooden furniture. The bathroom, perhaps blue- or black-on-white marble, features a pedestal sink and deep soaking tub with old-fashioned brass knobs, and separate commode. Each room also has multiple phones, ceiling fans, even walking sticks for an afternoon foray into the surrounding hills.

An unexpected favorite for many guests is the hotel's Visiting Artist Program. Started in 1992, this ongoing cultural event brings writers, musicians, chefs, poets, filmmakers, and a whole host of other creative people to the hotel for free informal gatherings and presentations. Two in-house restaurants are here to serve the guests. You can find sundries (and film developing) at the hotel shop, open 8 A.M.–9 P.M., and all hotel and island activities, including croquet, tennis, golf, hunting, horseback riding, jeep tours, sporting clays, and beach and boating activities, can be arranged by the concierge. There is shuttle service to meet all arriving and departing planes, to and from Lana'i City, Hotel Lana'i, and to Manele Bay Hotel. For more information log on to www.lanai-resorts.com.

While overlooking Manele Bay, **The Manele Bay Hotel** property is dealt with here as it's the only other hotel accommodation on the island. Glass doors curved in a traditional Roman arch sympathize with the surging Pacific as you enter the seaside 250-room Manele Bay Hotel, fashioned in a fusion of Mediterranean, Oriental, and Hawaiian design and motif. The open reception area, all marble and glass, holds two massive murals of Lana'i and the wide Pacific dotted with islands. Heroic paintings depict pioneering Polynesians in a double-hulled canoe sighting the Hawaiian Islands and the rascal Prince Kaulula'au, redeemer of Lana'i, standing triumphantly on a windswept beach after banishing the vexatious specters of Lana'i. The lower lobby in contrast has a decidedly Oriental feel, with hints of Hawaii and the Southwest. High on the upper walls are painted huge murals depicting Chinese scenes. Below, salubrious chairs and cushions invite you to relax, Asian-style adornments please the eye, and a huge Hawaiian-theme chandelier provides light. Gold and filigree mirrors, lamps of Chinese flute players, carved elephant tusks, and billowy curtains add a touch of style. For an elegant evening, order a drink or come to hear the evening entertainment at the Hale Aheahe Lounge. The hotel library is a genial room filled with leather-bound tomes, globes, and models of sailing ships. Overhead, the recessed wooden ceiling has been painted with various emblems of Hawaii; the floor is the intricate paisley of tasseled Persian carpets. Sit in a highbacked chair just near the balcony and enjoy the vantage point overlooking Hulopo'e Court below.

From the main reception area, descend a grand staircase and pass a formidable lava rock wall draped with the purples and pinks of living bougainvillea. Here is the grand cloverleaf pool encircled by a marble apron. Nearby, the hotel spa and fitness center is complete with steam rooms, saunas, fitness machines, free weights, and professional staff. The formal gardens, two on the east and three on the west, and each with its own theme, are tranquil oases where rivulets drop into koi ponds surrounded by patches of broad-leafed taro and swaying stands of bamboo. It's a marvelous setting, but perhaps the best outdoor feature of all is the unobstructed natural beauty of Hulopo'e Bay.

The hotel rooms and suites are mainly in wings east and west. East rooms bear marine names derived from the sea; the west rooms are named after flowers. These oversize guest rooms ranging in price $350–650, designed with Mediterranean and Oriental themes, offer four-poster mahogany beds covered with thick quilts, wicker lounge chairs, wet bars, and user-friendly entertainment centers. Marble-tiled bathroom features extra-deep soaking tubs, double sinks and vanity, separate commodes, and glass-enclosed shower stalls big enough for two. Each room has its own private lanai that either overlooks one of the gorgeous gardens or offers an ocean panorama. The hotel also offers a number of suites that range in price $675–2,700. A typical midrange suite offers a formal parlor and separate master bedroom with a dressing room attached. On the Butler Floor, someone will pack and unpack clothing, draw a hot bath, pour cold champagne, make dinner reservations, and act as your personal liaison at the hotel.

The hotel also offers valet parking, tennis courts, a beach kiosk, a children's program, a gift shop, three restaurants, and a cocktail lounge where music is performed nightly 5:30–9:30 P.M. Saturdays and Sundays are special with *keiki* hula dancers who come to perform their special magic in the Hulopo'e Court. Another treat is to walk a few minutes to the hotel's **Lana'i Conference Center,** where the antechamber holds museum-quality artifacts. In glass cases, you will find stone implements ranging from *'ulu maika,* Hawaiian bowling stones similar to Italian boccie, to *poho kukui* (*kukui* nut oil lamps). Most of these implements, including a petroglyph stone, have been gathered from Lana'i. There is also a very impressive replica of a Hawaiian double-hulled canoe.

Contact the Manele Bay Hotel at P.O. Box 310, Lanai City, HI 96763, 808/565-7700 or 800/321-4666, website: www.lanai-resorts.com.

B&Bs and Vacation Rentals

For a more homey stay on the Pineapple Island, try one of the few bed-and-breakfast inns or vacation rentals on Lana'i, all of which are in Lana'i City. These places offer a substantially cheaper alternative to staying on Lana'i than the resorts and they get you into the community.

Dreams Come True, 808/565-6961 or 800/566-6961, fax 808/565-7056, website: www.go-native.com/inns/0117.html, email: hunter@aloha.net, a true B&B in the oldest part of town at 12th and Olapa Street, is surrounded by lots of trees and flowers. Three rooms in this comfortable plantation house are rented to guests, each with its own bathroom and use of the common room, which is full of Asian art. Decent size for the island, one room has a queen bed and a single while the others just have queen beds. An expanded continental breakfast, with fresh-squeezed lilikoi juice from their own trees, is served each morning. The rate is $98.50 single or double; $10 extra for a child in the same room as parents. In house massage can be arranged by appointment only, and the owners sell their handmade jewelry. The owners, Michael and Susan Hunter, also have three vacation rental houses in town, all newly renovated, fully furnished, and only few minutes from the main house. The two-bedroom, two-bath Pink House runs $198 a night; the three-bedroom, three-bath Jasmine House is $290 a night; and the four-bedroom, four-bath Lana'i Plantation House in $390 a night. Find out more about these properties at www.10kvacationrentals.com/dreamscometrue/index.pht.

Hale Moe, 808/565-9520, on the south side of town at 502 Akolu St., P.O. Box 196, Lanai City, HI 96763, website: www.lanaibandb.com, rents three rooms, each with a bathroom, or the entire house. Usually no breakfast is served, but guests can make use of the kitchen. Two rooms go for $80 and the third is $90. The whole house can be rented for $250.

Denise Henning of Heart Of Lana'i Art Gallery rents two master bedrooms, each with its own bath, private entrance, and covered lanai. Guests have use of the kitchen; no breakfast is served. Rates are $90 a night, three nights minimum preferred. Weekly and monthly arrangements can be accommodated. Contact: P.O. Box 98, 758 Queen St., Lanai City, HI 96763, 808/565-6678 or 888/565-7815, email: den@aloha.net.

Several fully equipped houses can be rented from Phylis McOmber, 808/565-6071. One is a two-story affair that can sleep up to eight; the others sleep 5–6 persons. Rates for all run $35 per person per night.

Hale O Lana'i, 808/247-3637, fax 808/235-2644, is a newer two-bedroom, two-bath house on 4th and Lana'i Avenue that has all the amenities for a fine vacation stay. It rents for $95–125 a night, two nights minimum; or $585–695 on a weekly basis. For more information about the house go to www.hotspots.hawaii.com/beachrent1.html, or email hibeach@lava.net.

Aside from these, try Dolores Fabrao, 808/565-6134, who rents rooms in the family house, 538 Akahi St., for $50 single, $60 double. She also has a larger room that's often used by hunting groups; $25 per person with four or more.

Rental Agents

Okamoto Realty was Lana'i's first house rental agency and it handles upscale property. Although the number of houses in its listing varies, you're likely to find three-bedroom affairs at

$150–175 a night for up to seven people, or a four-bedroom, three-bath cedar house for $395 a night that will sleep 10. All houses are completely furnished including linens and kitchen utensils, and most have washer/dryer and TV. Houses are rented by the day (with a two-night minimum), week, or month. Write Okamoto Realty, 730 Lana'i Ave., #112, P.O. Box 552, Lana'i City, HI 96763, 808/565-7519, fax 808/565-6106, for current information.

Handling some vacation rental properties on the island is **Lana'i Realty.** They have homes for $100–145 a night with a two-night minimum. Contact the agency at P.O. Box 676, Lanai City, HI 96763, 808/565-6597 or 800/943-0989.

RESTAURANTS

Aside from the resort hotels, Lana'i City is the only place on the island where you can dine, shop, and take care of business. The food situation on Lana'i used to be discouraging. Most everything had to be brought in by barge, and the fresh produce, fish, and meat was at a premium. People surely ate differently at home, but in the two tiny restaurants open to the traveler, the fare was restricted to the "two-scoop rice and teri beef" variety, with fried noodles and Spam as the pièce de résistance. But, "the times they are a-changin'!" Now, there are more options from which to choose, and more culinary variety.

By far the best restaurant in town is **Henry Clay's Rotisserie** at the Hotel Lana'i, 808/565-7211; open for dinner 5:30–9 P.M. daily. Set just off the entry porch, this barrel-vaulted room also has tables on the back patio. Evening appetizers run the gamut from oyster shooters at $1.45 apiece to Cajun shrimp for $10.95. A soup or salad prepares the way for an entrée, be it eggplant creole and angel hair pasta at $16.95, "plate style" barbecue ribs at $17.95, fresh catch, or roasted venison loin for $36.95. Gourmet pizzas are also served and don't forget the homemade desserts. This is down-home country cooking with a Cajun twist and island influence. Have a look through the glass window into the kitchen to see the large commercial rotisserie full of chicken and other meat. Order a variety of beers or a glass of wine with your meal or simply stop by the bar for a drink. It's the only bar in town, other than at the big hotels; open 5:30 P.M. until closing.

The banging screen doors announce your presence as you enter the plantation-era wainscoted **Blue Ginger Cafe,** 808/565-6363, open daily 6 A.M.–2 P.M. and 3–9 P.M., which could actually be called chic for Lana'i. Upon entering, baked goods let you know that not long ago it was Dahang's Bakery, a Lana'i institution whose motto, "Mo betta grind ova hea," has also survived. It offers a full breakfast menu with choices like two eggs with sausage for $4.75, along with plenty of side orders, and fresh pastries. Plate lunches are $6.50 or so, while a bowl of saimin goes for $2.95. Burgers, sandwiches, pizza, and ice cream are also on the menu at comparable prices. Varying nightly, dinner specials, served with rice "toss" salad or macaroni salad, run $8–16. Eat inside or on the front veranda, where you can see everything there is to see in Lana'i City. If you *really* like it here, take home one of their T-shirts. Look for the blue roof.

An authentic workers' restaurant, **Tanigawa's,** open daily except Wednesday for breakfast and lunch 6:30 A.M.–1 P.M., is one of those places that you must visit at least for morning coffee. Totally down-home, but a pure cultural experience, you can also get hot cakes, omelets, burgers, and plate lunches. Arrive before 7 A.M. when many of the older people come to "talk story." Just one look around at the crinkled faces will reveal the tough but sweet spirit of Lana'i.

For a healthy, quick, light meal, try **Pele's Other Garden,** 808/565-9628. This juice bar, pizzeria, and deli is open Mon.–Fri. 11 A.M.–7 P.M., Saturday until 2 P.M. Eat in or take out. Try a turkey, veggie, or other sandwich for $6.99 or less, or a hot entrée, like a cheese quesadilla or black bean and brown rice burrito, for $3.50–6.50. Pizzas run $13–26, or choose a salad or something else from the deli case. A picnic basket might be a good choice if you're going to be away from town all day. Be sure to check the special board, as you never know what scrumptious delicacy will be offered each day. Connected through the back door is **Pele's Garden,** a small health foods store that also stocks a limited selection of natural health supplies.

The newest shop in town is **Coffee Works,** 604 Ilima St., 808/565-6962. Stop in for an espresso, latte, or cappuccino, herb tea, or refreshing ice cream.

Hotel Restaurants

In harmony with the rest of the Lodge at Ko'ele, the dining rooms are impeccably furnished. Serving all day, **The Terrace,** set in a section off the Great Hall and the more casual of the two restaurants, looks out over the exotic gardens, while the separate dinner-only **Formal Dining Room** lends Itself to evening attire—jackets required. Breakfast selections include continental breakfast, eggs Benedict, and sweet rice waffles with *lilikoi*-coconut chutney. At midday satisfy your hunger with jumbo shrimp with papaya relish, grilled pastrami of striped marlin on a tomato fennel salad, spinach pasta with grilled scallops, or smoked salmon and herbed goat cheese. Dinner, like the other daily fare, is made from the freshest island ingredients. Choose standards like rack of lamb, prime rib, a superbly prepared catch of the day, or, for a special treat, the Lana'i mixed pheasant, quail, and axis deer sausage with Pinot Noir sauce.

In the Formal Dining Room you'll have a grand dining experience. It always gets rave reviews form diners who are into serious eating. Once again, the freshest island ingredients are used to prepare each meal that leaves the kitchen. Not only are they sumptuous but they are presented in a pleasing manner. All this elegance doesn't come cheap, however. Expect prices in the $40–50 range for an entrée.

The **Clubhouse** at the **Experience at Ko'ele** golf course is open 10:30 A.M.–3:30 P.M. daily, serving excellent soups, sandwiches, and salads at very reasonable prices. Everyone is welcome, and the standing room only lets you know that the food is very good. Try a Korean barbecued beef sandwich, Caesar salad, or one of the many pasta dishes for $7–13. Indoor or outdoor seating, with a great view of the 18th green.

The master chef at the Manele Bay Hotel's formal **Ihilani Dining Room** offers two fixed menus nightly, along with a complete menu of à la carte suggestions. Expect entrées in the $35–45 range. The Ihilani serves dinner only Tues.–Sat. 6–9:30 P.M.—jackets required. Begin with ravioli of Hawaiian goat cheese in a sauce of parsley and sun-dried tomatoes, or Maine lobster with Hayden mango and arugula salad. Second courses can be a delicately roasted squab breast in a marmalade of onions and a Moloka'i sweet potato puree. Entrées are roasted Chinese duck with Hawaiian seasoning, Oriental rice, and pickled ginger plum sauce, or an array of curries from Thai shrimp red curry and pan-fried *onaga* in a North Indian style. Grill selections include catch of the day, or Colorado lamb chops with polenta topped by a roasted garlic sauce. All of this, with a superb view of the bay and beach— magnifique!

The less formal but still extremely elegant **Hulopo'e Court** offers breakfast and dinner of contemporary Hawaiian regional cuisine, with prices similar to the Ihilani. This is perhaps the best breakfast spot on the island. Begin the day with a continental breakfast, choose all manner of traditional favorites from the breakfast buffet, or make an à la carte selection. Lunch and dinner begin with appetizers like Chinese spring rolls, seared *ahi* in a spicy crust, or a fresh dim sum basket. Soups and salads include Maui onion soup, Caesar salad with croutons, or Lana'i field greens in a *lilikoi* vinaigrette. Entrées are fresh pasta, Chinese noodles with duck covered in a chili oyster sauce, or penne pasta primavera. You can also have a gourmet pizza of Tandoori chicken or Peking duck. An excellent selection of domestic and imported beer and wine completes the meal.

The least formal dining setting is poolside at **The Pool Grille,** an alfresco restaurant serving lunch and afternoon snacks 11 A.M.–5 P.M. daily. Start with an appetizer like chicken quesadilla or cocktail of Pacific shrimp. Lighter appetites will enjoy main course salads including marinated grilled vegetables, Cobb salad, or seafood salad. The sandwich board features a good old-fashioned club, a grilled beef burger, or hot dog. Special offerings are Hawaiian favorites like grilled fresh catch, or a steamy bowl of savory saimin.

One must not forget the **Clubhouse Restaurant** at the Challenge at Manele golf course, which has superb underwater scene murals painted on its walls by John Wulbrandt. The view from here is perhaps the best on the property, overlooking both the hotel and bay, with Haleakala on Maui in the background, particularly on a night when the full moon is rising early. Food is served daily 11 A.M.–4 P.M., dinner

Thurs.–Sun. 5–9 P.M. Small plates are the theme here. Some selections on this hot and cold *"pu pu"* menu are shrimp satay, spiced lamb, and grilled *ahi* with white bean cassoulet, all for under $15 a plate.

SHOPPING

Except for the clutch of shops at the Lodge at Ko'ele and Manele Bay Hotel, and the gift shop at the airport, shopping on Lana'i means shopping in Lana'i City. Be aware that all but a few are closed on Sunday, and remember that some shops in town may close their doors for an hour or longer at midday for a siesta.

The two grocery stores in town are fairly well stocked with basics. The markets are almost next door to each other. **Pine Isle Market,** 808/565-6488, run by Kerry Honda and open 8 A.M.–7 P.M. every day except Sunday, is Lana'i's closest equivalent to a supermarket, although it also carries hardware and general merchandise. **Richards Shopping Center,** 808/565-6047, is open Mon.–Sat. 8:30 A.M.–6:30 P.M. A small grocery and sundries store, it supplies all your basic camping, fishing, and general merchandise needs, including clothing and medicines, some groceries, liquor, and odds and ends.

Lying between these two is **Akamai Trading Company,** 808/565-6587, which sells gifts, T-shirts and party supplies, espresso and other types of coffee, ice cream, and also does film processing. At the back of the store is "The Closet" for slightly used clothing. Open daily 9 A.M.–5:30 P.M. (until 5 P.M. on Sunday).

Around the corner is **International Food and Clothing Center,** 808/565-6433, where you can pick up not only things to eat, but also hardware and hunting supplies. They have their own butcher, but no clothing any more. This is an old-fashioned general store, definitely a local place; open weekdays 8 A.M.–6 P.M., until 1:30 on Sunday, closed Saturday. On the next street over a couple of small shops sell CDs and tapes and a few snacks.

Even tiny Lana'i has a health food store. Opened in 1995, it was the first new store in town in years. **Pele's Garden,** 808/565-9629, stocks a limited but generous range of packaged items, herbs, juices, vitamins and minerals, natural health and beauty supplies, and even a few books. It's a full-service health food store in miniature. Owned by Ms. Beverly Zigmond, this fine store is open Mon.–Fri. 9:30 A.M.–6:30 P.M. She'll have most of what you might desire, and you may get a whole nutrition lesson at no extra cost. Out front and connected to her store is **Pele's Other Garden,** opened in 1997 and run by her brother and his wife, a deli, juice bar, and pizzeria that offers cool refreshment and healthy quick food.

On the far side of the city park is the **Lana'i Family Store,** 808/565-6485, for video rentals and furniture. Next door at **Maria M's Boutique,** 808/565-9577, you can find clothing items, accessories, jewelry, and makeup; open Mon.–Fri. 9:30 A.M.–noon and 2–5 P.M.

Gifts With Aloha, 808/565-6589, a small shop that carries art and craft items from local and other Hawaii residents, is just down the road. Some items include cloth and clothing, jewelry, quilts, and candles. You should be able to find something for that special occasion here, Mon.–Sat. 9 A.M.–6 P.M.

Behind Gifts With Aloha is **The Local Gentry,** 808/565-9130, a clothing boutique for women that's open Mon.–Fri. 10 A.M.–6 P.M. and Saturday until 5 P.M.

Nearby is the **Lana'i Art Program** gallery, 808/565-7503, open daily at irregular hours as it's staffed by volunteers, which has taken the spirit of the Zimbabwe saying "If you can walk, you can dance," and changed it into "If you've got life, you've got art." This co-op of local Lana'i citizens has created a nonprofit organization dedicated to developing the artistic talents of its members and has a strong kids program. Classes, chaired by guest artists, are periodically offered in photography, woodworking, Japanese doll-making, fabric-making, drama and cultural arts, painting, glass, ceramics, and pen and ink drawing. The showroom offers purchases like hand-dyed silk scarves, stenciled T-shirts, naturally dyed incidental bags, notecards, lovely pareu for women. Pottery and silk painting seem to predominate. The work is always changing, but you are sure to find a distinctive island memento that couldn't be more genuine. All are welcome, resident or not, so you can drop in on a workshop, pay for your supplies, and create your own art.

Now in a bright yellow plantation-era house at 758 Queen St., behind Hotel Lana'i, **Heart of Lana'i Art Gallery,;** 808/565-6678, features watercolors of island scenes by Denise Henning, wooden bowls and ukuleles by Cyrus Keanini, and oil paintings by Macauio Pascual and Pam Andeliu. The works are casually displayed but of top quality. With no fixed hours, it's best to call ahead to be sure that the gallery is open.

Are you looking for fresh food to cook yourself? Try the farmers' market at Dole Park, Saturday morning 7–9 A.M.

For snacks and sundries, you can also try the shop at Lana'i City Service. For last-minute souvenirs, have a look at the **airport gift shop** in the terminal building.

EXPLORING LANA'I

MUNRO TRAIL

The highlight of visiting Lana'i is climbing the Munro Trail to its highest point, Lana'ihale (3,370 feet), locally called **The Hale.** As soon as you set foot on Lana'i the silhouette of this razorback ridge with its bristling coat of Cook pines demands your attention. Set off for The Hale and you're soon engulfed in its cool stands of pines, eucalyptus, and ironwoods, all colored with ferns and wildflowers. George Munro, a New Zealander hired as the manager of the Lana'i Ranch a short time before Jim Dole's arrival, is responsible. With a pouch full of seeds and clippings from his native New Zealand, he trudged all over Lana'i planting, in an attempt to foliate the island and create a permanent watershed. Driven by that basic and primordial human desire to see things grow, he climbed The Hale time and again to renew and nurture his leafy progeny. Now, all benefit from his labors.

The Trail
There are two basic ways to go to The Hale, by foot or 4WD. Some local people go on horseback. Head out of town on Keomuku Road toward Shipwreck Beach. It's preferable to start in the morning; cloud cover is common by early afternoon. At mile marker 1, still on the Lana'i City side of the mountains, take the first major gravel road to the right. The sign here should read Cemetery Road. In about one-quarter mile the road comes to a Y intersection—go left. You immediately start climbing and pass through a forested area. Continue and the road forks; again bear left. Always stay on the more obviously traveled road, and don't be fooled by the short cuts that have been constructed for water

drainage. The side roads may look muddy or be overgrown and it's obvious which is the main one. Robert Frost would be disappointed.

As you climb, you pass a profusion of gulches, great red wounds cut into Lana'i's windward side. First comes deep and brooding **Maunalei (Mountain Lei) Gulch,** from where Lana'i draws its water through a series of tunnels bored through the mountains. It's flanked by **Ko'olana'i Trail,** a rugged and dangerous footpath leading all the way to the coast. Past the communication towers is **Ho'okio Gulch,** a battleground where Lana'i's warriors were vanquished in 1778 by Kalaniopu'u and his ferocious fighters from the Big Island. All that remains are a few room-size notches cut into the walls where the warriors slept and piled stones to be hurled at the invaders. After Ho'okio Gulch, a trail bears left, bringing you to the gaping mouth of **Hauola Gulch,** more than 2,000 feet deep. Keep your eyes peeled for axis deer, which seem to defy gravity and manage to cling and forage along the most unlikely and precipitous cliffs. Be very careful of your footing—even skilled Lana'i hunters have fallen to their deaths in this area.

The jeep trail narrows on the ridge to little more than 10 feet across. On one side are the wild gulches, on the other the whorling fingerprints of the former pineapple fields. At one point on the way, there's even a picnic table with a view down the west side at one of the short pulloffs. Along the trail, in season, you can munch strawberries, common guavas, and as many thimbleberries as you can handle. At the crest of The Hale, let your eyes pan the horizon to see all the main islands of Hawaii (except for Kaua'i). Rising from the height-caused mirage of a still sea is the hazy specter of O'ahu to the north, with Moloka'i and Maui clearly visible just

10 miles distant. Haleakala, Maui's magical mountain, has a dominant presence viewed from The Hale. Sweep right to see Kaho'olawe, bleak and barren, its body shattered by years of bombs, a victim of controversial war games now ended, that with great volunteer help is slowly on the mend. Eighty miles southeast of Kaho'olawe is the Big Island, its mammoth peaks, Mauna Loa and Mauna Kea, looming like ethereal islands floating in the clouds.

Just past the final lookout is a sign for **Awehi Trail,** which leads left to Naha on the beach. It's extremely rough and a drive down would definitely require 4WD in compound low gear. Access to this road is not permitted by the rental car company, so you'll have to walk if you want to explore this route. Follow the main road down this dusty decline and take either Ho'ike Road, which flattens out and joins with Route 440 just south of Lana'i City, or head straight ahead and join the highway near where it heads down the hill to Manele Bay. If you have time for only one outing on Lana'i or funds budgeted for only one day of 4WD rental, make sure to treat yourself to the unforgettable Munro Trail.

HEADING SOUTH

Joseph Kali'ihananui was the last of the free Hawaiian farmers to work the land of Lana'i. His great-grandson, Lloyd Cockett, lived in Lana'i City until a few years ago. Joseph made his home in the arid but fertile Palawai Basin, which was later bought by Jim Dole and turned into the heart of the pineapple plantation. Just south of Lana'i City on Route 440 (Manele Road), the Palawai Basin is the crater of the extinct single volcano of which Lana'i is formed. Joseph farmed sweet potatoes, which he traded for fish. He gathered his water in barrels from the dew that formed on his roof and from a trickling spring. His lands supported a few cattle among its now-extinct heavy stands of cactus. Here, too, Walter Murray Gibson attempted to begin a Mormon colony, which he later aborted, supposedly because of his outrage over the idea of polygamy. Nothing noteworthy remains of this colony, but high on a hillside overlooking Palawai are the Luahiwa Petroglyphs.

Luahiwa Petroglyphs

Heading south on Manele Road, look to your left for six tall pine trees and the back side of a stop sign at Ho'ike Road. Ho'ike Road was once paved but has now disintegrated into gravel. Parenthetically, during the pineapple days, major roads that ran through the pineapple fields were paved in order to keep the big trucks running from field to warehouse even when rains made the fields slick with mud. These roads were lines with stone, quarried and set in place by Korean stone masons in the early 1900s. While the rows of pineapples are gone, whorls of grass still grow in the fields. A telltale sign that these fields were recently cultivated are the ever-present bits and pieces of black plastic irrigation pipe and weed cloth that can be seen here and throughout the Palawai basin, an ugly remnant of the plantation days that will be around for years.

After turning left onto Ho'ike, head straight down the road about one mile. When the road comes up a low rise, turn left and follow this secondary road, keeping the ditch on your right. Proceed about one-half mile until you come to a silver water pipe about 12 inches in diameter. Follow this pipe, heading back toward Lana'i City, jogging right up onto the dike, crossing the pipe, and continue on the upper road about three-tenths of a mile to rocks on your right at the base of the hill.

Walk up the hill to the boulders on which appear the petroglyphs. Once, brownish black and covered in lichen, their appearance has changed somewhat following an accidental grass fire, which, oddly enough, exposed additional petroglyphs in a ravine to the south that had not been remembered by island residents. Their natural arrangement resembles an oversize Japanese rock garden. Dotted on the hillside are sisal plants that look like bouquets of giant green swords. As you climb to the rocks be very careful of your footing—the ground is crumbly and the vegetation slippery. The boulders cover a three-acre area; most of the petroglyphs are found on the south faces of the rocks. Some are hieroglyphics of symbolic circles, others are picture stories complete with canoes gliding under unfurled sails. Dogs snarl with their jaws agape, while enigmatic triangular stickmen try to tell their stories from the past. Equestrians gallop, showing that these stone picture-books were done even after the coming of the white man. The Luahiwa Petroglyphs are a very special spot where the ancient Hawaiians still sing their tales across the gulf of time. Unfortunately, some modern graffiti now mares the stones.

Hulopo'e and Manele Bays

Proceed south on Route 440 to Lana'i's most salubrious spots, the twin bays of Manele and Hulopo'e. At the crest of the hill, just past the milepost, you can look down on the white, inviting sands of Hulopo'e to the right, and the rockier small boat harbor of Manele on the left. The island straight ahead is Kaho'olawe, and on very clear days you might be able to glimpse the peaks of Hawaii's Mauna Loa and Mauna Kea. Years and years ago, Manele was the site of an ancient Hawaiian village and it was the principal port for the island until the current commercial harbor was built at Kaumalapa'u. **Manele Bay** is a picture-perfect anchorage where a dozen or so small boats and yachts are tied up on any given day. Ferries from Maui drop off passengers here, and tour boats also tie up here. In the trees overlooking the harbor are a few picnic tables and a public bathroom. Manele and Hulopo'e are a Marine Life Conservation District with the rules for fishing and diving prominently displayed on a large bulletin board at the entrance to Manele. Because of this, the area is superb for snorkeling, and you can often see a pod of spinner dolphins playing in the water.

The tidepools here are also past of this marine reserve, and can provide great fun and exploration. No boats are allowed within Hulopo'e Bay except for Hawaiian outrigger canoes, and you may see the canoe club using the bay for practice.

Hulopo'e Bay offers very gentle waves and soothing, crystal-clear water. The beach is a beautiful expanse of white sand fringed by palms with a mingling of large boulders that really set it off. Aside from the day-use picnic areas with lawns and grills, this is Lana'i's official camping area, and six sites are available. All are well spaced, each with a picnic table and fire pit. A series of shower stalls made of brown plywood provides solar-heated water and just enough privacy, allowing your head and legs to protrude. After refreshing yourself you can fish from the rock promontories on both sides of the bay, or explore the tide pools on the left side of the bay out near the point. It's difficult to find a more wholesome and gentle spot anywhere in Hawaii For the more adventurous, walk the path the skirts the headland around to Manele Bay. Alternately, take the Na Ala Hele Fisherman's Trail from the beach and along the shore below the hotel and golf course to the farthest fairway.

Kaumalapa'u Harbor

A side trip to Kaumalapau Harbor might be in order. This manmade facility, which used to ship more than a million pineapples a day during

Hulopo'e Bay is a fine spot to watch dolphins frolic.

STAN BUTLER

LANA'I

peak harvest, was the only one of its kind in the world. Activity is now way down, with only one ferry a week on Thursday to deliver supplies, yet it is still Lana'i's lifeline for off-island goods. As you've probably already rented a vehicle, you might as well cover these few paved miles from Lana'i City on Route 440 just to have a quick look. En route you pass Lana'i's odoriferous garbage dump, which is a real eyesore. Hold your nose and try not to notice. The harbor facility itself is no-nonsense commercial, but the coastline is reasonably spectacular, with a glimpse of the island's dramatic sea cliffs. Also, this area has super-easy access to some decent fishing, right off the pier. An added bonus for making the trek to this lonely area is that it is one of the best places on Lana'i from which to view the sunset, and you usually have it all to yourself.

KAUNOLU: KAMEHAMEHA'S GETAWAY

At the southwestern tip of Lana'i is Kaunolu Bay, a point where currents from both sides of the island converge. At one time, this vibrant fishing village surrounded Halulu Heiau, Lana'i's most important religious spot, and a sacred refuge where the downtrodden were protected by the temple priests who could intercede with the benevolent gods. Halulu Heiau is perhaps named after the man-eating bird Halulu from Tahiti, one of the legendary birds that guided Polynesians from the south to the Hawaiian Islands. Kamehameha the Great would escape Lahaina's blistering summers and come to these very fertile fishing waters with his loyal warriors. Some proved their valor to their great chief by diving from Kahekili's Leap, a man-made opening in the rocks 60 feet above the sea. The remains of more than 80 house sites and a smattering of petroglyphs dot the area. The last inhabitant was Ohua, elder brother of Joseph Kali'ihananui, who lived in a grass hut just east of Kaunolu in Mamaki Bay. Ohua was entrusted by Kamehameha V to hide the *heiau* fish-god, Kuniki; old accounts by the area's natives say that he died because of mishandling this stone god. The natural power still emanating from Kaunolu is obvious, and you can't help feeling the energy that drew the Hawaiians to this sacred spot.

Getting There

Proceed south on Manele Road from Lana'i City through Palawai Basin until it makes a hard bend to the left. Here, a sign points you to Manele Bay. Do not go left to Manele, but proceed straight and stay on the once-paved pineapple road. The rental car company doesn't allow their vehicles on this and most other former plantation roads, but you can hike. Head straight through the old pineapple fields until you come upon two orange pipes (like fire hydrants) on the left and right. Turn left here onto a rather small road. Follow the road left to a sign that actually says "Kaunolu." This dirt track starts off innocently enough as it begins its plunge toward the sea, and you pass two abandoned dryland farms along the way that once experimented with herbs and vegetables that didn't require much water. Only two miles long, the local folks consider it the roughest road on the island. It *is* a bone-cruncher, so take it super slow if you Ôre in a vehicle. Plot your progress against the lighthouse on the coast. This road is not maintained. Because of natural erosion; it may be too rugged for any vehicle to pass. This area is excellent for spotting axis deer and wild turkeys. The deer are nourished by *haole koa,* a green bush with a brown seed pod that you see growing along the road. This natural feed also supports cattle, but is not good for horses, causing the hair on their tails to fall out.

Kaunolu

The village site lies at the end of a long dry gulch that terminates at a rocky beach, suitable in times past as a canoe anchorage. This entire area is a mecca for archaeologists and anthropologists. The most famous was the eminent Dr. Kenneth Emory of the Bishop Museum; he filed an extensive research report on the area in the 1920s. A more recent research team covered the are in the mid-1990s. In response to its importance, Kaunolu has been designated an Archaeological Interpretive Park and been given the status of a National Historical Landmark. At its terminus, the road splits left and right. Go right to reach a large *kiawe* tree with a picnic table under it. Just in front of you is a large pile of nondescript rocks purported to be the ruined foundation of Kamehameha's house. Numerous other stone remnants dot the slope on both sides of the gulch. Unbelievably, this sacred area is sometimes trashed out by disrespectful and ignorant picnickers. Hurricane 'Iwa also had a hand in changing the face of Kaunolu, as its tremendous force hit this area head on and even drove large boulders from the sea onto the land. As you look around, the ones that have a whitish appearance were washed up on the shore by the fury of 'Iwa.

The villagers of Kaunolu lived mostly on the east bank and had to keep an ever-watchful eye on nature because the bone-dry gulch could suddenly be engulfed by flash floods. In the center of the gulch, about 100 yards inland, was Pa'ao, the area's freshwater well. Pa'ao was *kapu* to menstruating women, and it was believed that if the *kapu* was broken, the well would dry up. It served the village for centuries. It's totally obliterated now; in 1895 a Mr. Hayselden tried to erect a windmill over it, destroying the native caulking and causing the well to turn brackish—an example of Lana'i's precious water being tampered with by outsiders, causing disastrous results.

The Sites
Climb down the east bank and cross the rocky beach. The first well-laid wall close to the beach on the west bank is the remains of a canoe shed. Proceed inland and climb the rocky bank to the remains of Halulu Heiau. Just below in the undergrowth is where the well was located. The *heiau* site has a commanding view of the area, best described by the words of Dr. Emory himself: "The point on which it is located is surrounded on three sides by cliffs and on the north rises the magnificent cliff of Palikaholo, terminating in Kahilikalani crag, a thousand feet above the sea. The ocean swell entering Kolokolo Cave causes a rumbling like thunder, as if under the *heiau*. From every point in the village the *heiau* dominates the landscape." As you climb the west bank, notice that the mortarless walls are laid up for more than 30 feet. If you have a keen eye you'll notice a perfectly square fire pit right in the center of the *heiau*.

This area still has treasures that have never been catalogued. For example, you might chance upon a Hawaiian lamp, as big and perfectly round as a basketball, with an orange-size hole in the middle where *kukui* nut oil was burned. Old records indicate that Kuniki, the

temple idol itself, is still lying here face down no more than a few hundred yards away. If you happen to discover an artifact, do not remove it under any circumstance. Follow the advice of the late Lloyd Cockett, a *kupuna* of Lana'i, who said, "I wouldn't take the rock because we Hawaiians don't steal from the land. Special rocks you don't touch."

Kahekili's Leap
Once you've explored the *heiau*, you'll be drawn toward the sea cliff. **Kane'apua Rock**, a giant tower-like chunk, sits just offshore at the end of the cliff. Below in the tide pool are basin-like depressions in the rock-salt evaporation pools, the bottoms still showing some white residue. Follow the cliff face along the natural wall obstructing your view to the west. You'll see a break in the wall about 15 feet wide with a very flat rock platform. From here, **Shark Island**, which closely resembles a shark fin, is perfectly framed. This opening is Kahekili's Leap, perhaps named after a Lana'i chief, not the famous chief of Maui. Here, Kamehameha's warriors proved their courage by executing death-defying leaps into only 12 feet of water, and clearing a 15-foot protruding rock shelf. Scholars also believe that Kamehameha punished his warriors for petty offenses by sentencing them to make the jump. Kahekili's Leap is a perfect background for a photo. Below, the sea surges in unreal aquamarine colors. Off to the right is Kolokolo Cave, above which is another, even more daring leap at 90 feet. Evidence suggests that Kolokolo is linked to Kaunolu Gulch by a lava tube that has been sealed and lost.

Petroglyphs
To find the petroglyphs, walk directly inland from Kane'apua Rock, using it as your point of reference. On a large pile of rocks are stick figures, mostly with a bird-head motif. Some heads even look like a mason's hammer. This entire area has a masculine feeling to it. There aren't the usual swaying palms and gentle sandy beaches. With the stones and rugged sea cliffs, you get the feeling that a warrior king would enjoy this spot. For their enjoyment, the vacationing chiefs often played *konane*, and a few stone boards can still be found from this game of Hawaiian checkers. Throughout the area is *pili* grass, used by the

Hawaiians to thatch their homes. Children would pick one blade and hold it in their fingers while reciting *"E pili e, e pili e, 'au hea ku'u hale."* The *pili* grass would then spin around in their fingers and point in the direction of home. Pick some *pili* and try it yourself before leaving this wondrous, powerful area.

THE EAST COAST: KEOMUKU AND NAHA

Until the turn of the 20th century, most of Lana'i's inhabitants lived in the villages of the now-deserted east coast. Before the coming of Westerners, 2,000 or so Hawaiians lived along these shores, fishing and raising taro. It was as if they wanted to keep Maui in sight so that they didn't feel so isolated. Numerous *heiau* from this period still mark the ancient sites. The first white men also tried to make a go of Lana'i along this stretch. The Maunalei Sugar Co. tried to raise sugarcane on the flat plains of Naha but failed and pulled up stakes in 1901—the last time that this entire coastline was populated to any extent. Today, the ancient *heiau* and a decaying church in Keomuku are the last vestiges of habitation, holding out against the ever-encroaching jungle. You can follow a jeep trail along this coast and get a fleeting glimpse of times past.

The shallow coastline that wraps around the north and east coast of Lana'i opposes the shallow south coast of Moloka'i. Although many fewer than on that coast of Moloka'i, the majority of ancient fishponds of Lana'i were here, and their remnants can still be seen. Because of the shallow nature of the water and its rocky bottom, swimming is not particularly good along most of this coast except for a few isolated sandy spots. In fact, the water cannot be seen well from the road most of the way to Naha because of the growth of trees and bushes along the beach. Numerous pullouts and shore access roads have been created, however, so you can get to the water. Unfortunately, inconsiderate visitors have left these pullouts a bit trashy with junk tossed to the ground rather than taken out.

Getting There

Approach Keomuku and Naha from one of two directions. The most straightforward is from north to south. Follow Keomuku Road from Lana'i City until it turns to dirt and branches right (south) at the coast, about a half hour. This road meanders for about 12 miles all the way to Naha, another one-half to one hour. Though the road is partial gravel and packed sand and not that rugged, you will need a 4WD in spots. Watch for washouts and fallen trees. It's paralleled by a much smoother route that runs along the beach partway down the coast, but it can only be used at low tide. Many small roads connect the two, so you can hop back and forth between them every 200–300 yards. Consider three tips: First, if you take the beach road, you can make good time and have a smooth ride, but could sail past most of the sights since you won't know when to hop back on the inland road; second, dry sand can easily bog down even a 4WD vehicle, making an expensive rescue mission for a tow truck, so be wise and only drive where sand is hard-packed; third, be careful of the *kiawe* trees—the tough, inch-long thorns can puncture tires as easily as nails.

The other alternative is to take Awehi Trail, a rugged jeep track, about halfway between Lopa and Naha. This route is not open to rental jeeps, but you can hike. This trail leads up the mountain to the Munro Trail, but because of its ruggedness it's best to take it down from The Hale instead of up. A good long day of rattling in a jeep would take you along the Munro Trail, down Awehi Trail, then north along the coast back to Keomuku Road. If you came south along the coast, it would be better to retrace your steps instead of heading up Awehi. When you think you've suffered enough and have been bounced into submission by your jeep, remember that many of these trails were carved out by Juan Torqueza. He trailblazed alone on his bulldozer, unsupervised, and without benefit of survey.

Keomuku Village

There isn't much to see in Keomuku Village other than an abandoned Hawaiian church. This was the site of the Maunalei Sugar Co. The town was pretty much abandoned after 1901 when the sugar company ceased operations, but a ranching operation did utilize this area until the mid-1900s. Most all the decaying buildings were razed in the early 1970s. A few hundred yards north and south of the town site are examples of some original fishponds. They're tough to see (overgrown with mangrove), but a close observation gives you an idea of how extensive they once were. The **Hawaiian church** is worth a stop—it almost pleads to be photographed. From outside, you can see how frail it is, so if you go in, tread lightly. The altar area, a podium with a little bench, remains. A banner on the fading blue-green walls reads *"Ualanaano Jehova Kalanakila Malamalama,* October 4, 1903." Only the soft wind sounds where once strong voices sang vibrant hymns of praise.

A few hundred yards south of the church is a walking trail. Follow it inland to **Kahe'a Heiau** and a smattering of petroglyphs. This is the *heiau* disturbed by the sugarcane train; its desecration was believed to have caused the sweet water of Keomuku to turn brackish. The people of Keomuku learned to survive on the brackish water and kept a special jug of freshwater for visitors.

Heading South

Farther south a Japanese cemetery and monument were erected for the deceased workers who built **Halepaloa Landing,** from where the cane was shipped. Today, only rotting timbers and stonework remain, but the pier offers an excellent vantage point for viewing Maui, and it's a good spot to fish.

The road continues past **Lopa,** ending at **Naha.** Both were sites of ancient fishponds; the one at Naha can still be discerned at low tide. On the way, you'll pass several roads heading inland that lead to hunting areas. You also pass a few coconut groves. Legend says that one of these was cursed by a *kahuna*—if you climb a tree to get a coconut you will not be able to come down. Luckily, most tourists have already been cursed by "midriff bulge" and can't climb the tree in the first place. When you get to Naha check out the remnants of the paved Hawaiian walking trail before slowly heading back from this decaying historical area.

SHIPWRECK BEACH

Heading over the mountains from Lana'i City to Shipwreck Beach offers you a rewarding scenario: an intriguing destination point with fantastic scenery and splendid panoramas on the way. Head north from Lana'i City on Keomuku Road. In less than 10 minutes you crest the mountains, and if you're lucky the sky will be clear and you'll be able to see the phenomenon that guided ancient navigators to land: the halo of dark brooding clouds over Maui and Moloka'i, a sure sign of landfall. Shorten your gaze and look at the terrain in the immediate vicinity. Here, in the gulches and gullies, wounded earth bleeds red while offering patches of swaying grass and wildflowers. It looks like the canyons of Arizona have been dragged to the rim of the sea. As you wiggle your way down Keomuku Road, look left to see the rusting hull of a World War II Liberty Ship sitting on the shallow reef almost completely out of the water. For most, this derelict is the destination point on Shipwreck Beach.

The Beach

As you continue down the road, little piles of stones, usually three, sit atop a boulder. Although most are from modern times, these are called *ahu,* a traditional Hawaiian offering to ensure good fortune while traveling. Under no circumstances disturb them. Farther down, the lush grasses of the mountain slope disappear, and the scrub bush takes over. The pavement ends and the dirt road forks left (west) to Shipwreck Beach, or straight ahead (south) toward the abandoned town of Naha. If you turn left you'll be on an adequate sandy road, flanked on both sides by thorny, tire-puncturing *kiawe* trees. In less than a mile is a large open area to your right. If you're into unofficial camping, this isn't a bad spot for a one-night bivouac—the trees here provide privacy and an excellent windbreak against the constant strong ocean breezes. About two miles down the road is Federation Camp, actually a tiny village of unpretentious beach shacks built by Lana'i's workers as "getaways" and fishing cabins. Charming in their humbleness and simplicity, they're made mostly from recycled timbers and boards that have washed ashore. Some have been worked on quite diligently and skillfully and are actual little homes, but somehow the rougher ones are more attractive. You can drive past the cabins for a few hundred yards, but to be on the safe side, park just past them and begin your walk.

Petroglyphs

At the very end of the road is a cabin that a local comedian has named the "Lana'i Hilton." Just off to your left *(mauka)* are the ruins of a lighthouse. Look for a cement slab where two graffiti artists of bygone days carved their names: "John Kupau and Kam Chee, Nov. 28, 1929." Behind the lighthouse ruins an arrow points you to "The Bird Man of Lana'i Petroglyphs." Of all the petroglyphs on Lana'i these are the easiest to find; trail-marking rocks have been painted white by Lana'i's Boy Scouts. Follow them to a large rock bearing the admonition "Do Not Deface." Climb down the path with a keen eye—the rock carvings are small, most only about 10 inches tall. Little childlike stick figures, they have intriguing bird heads whose symbolic meaning has been lost.

Hiking the Beach

The trail along the beach goes for eight long hot miles to Polihua Beach. That trip should be done separately, but at least walk as far as the Liberty Ship, about a mile from the cabins. The area has some of the best beachcombing in Hawaii; no telling what you might find. The most sought-after treasures are glass floats that have bobbed for thousands of miles across the Pacific, strays from Japanese fishnets. You might even see a modern ship washed onto the reef, like the Canadian yacht that went aground in the spring of 1984. Navigational equipment has improved, but Shipwreck Beach can *still* be a nightmare to any captain caught in its turbulent whitecaps and long ragged coral fingers. This area is particularly good for lobsters and shore fishing. And you can swim in shallow sandy-bottom pools to refresh yourself as you hike.

Try to time your return car trip over the mountain for sundown. The tortuous terrain, stark in black and white shadows, is awe-inspiring. The larger rocks are giant sentinels: it's easy to feel the power and attraction they held for the ancient Hawaiians. As you climb the road on the windward side with its barren and beaten terrain, the feelings of mystery and mystique attributed to spiritual Lana'i are obvious. You come over the top and suddenly see the plateau—manicured, rolling, soft, and verdant and the few lights of Lana'i City beckoning.

THE GARDEN OF THE GODS AND POLIHUA

The most ruggedly beautiful, barren, and inhospitable section of Lana'i is out at the north end. After passing through a broad stretch of former pineapple fields, you come to Kanepu'u Preserve, the island's only nature reserve and best example of dryland forest. Just as you pop out the far side of the preserve, you reach the appropriately named Garden of the Gods. Waiting is a fantasia of otherworldly landscapes—barren red earth, convulsed ancient lava flows, tortured pinnacles of stone, and psychedelic striations of vibrating colors, especially moving at sunrise and sunset. Little-traveled trails lead to Ka'ena (The Heat) Point, a wasteland dominated by sea cliffs where adulterous Hawaiian wives were sent into exile for a short time in 1837. Close by is Lana'i's largest *heiau,* dubbed Ka'enaiki, so isolated and forgotten that its real name and function were lost even to Hawaiian natives by the middle of the 19th century. After a blistering, sun-baked, 4WD drubbing, you emerge at the coast on Polihua, a totally secluded, white beach where sea turtles once came to bury their eggs in the natural incubator of its soft warm sands (Polihua means "Eggs in Bosom").

Getting There

Lana'i doesn't hand over its treasures easily, but they're worth pursuing. To get to the Garden of the Gods, head past the Lodge at Ko'ele, and turn left onto the road that runs between the tennis courts and the riding stable. After about one minute, there's an intersection where you should turn right. Follow this road through former pineapple fields, keeping the prominent ridge on your right. Proceed for about 20 minutes until you pass through the Kanepu'u dryland forest preserve. Disregard the roads to the right and the left. Once out the back side of the preserve, you soon begin to see large boulders sitting atop packed red earth, the signal that you're entering the Garden of the Gods. It's about another hot half hour drive down to Polihua Beach, and on the way you'll find a marker on the left for Ka'ena Road, which leads to magnificent sea cliffs and Ka'enaiki Heiau.

ROBERT NILSEN

Garden of the Gods

Basically, you're heading toward the western tip of Moloka'i, which you can keep in your sights in the distance across the channel. Have no illusions about this road. It's long and bumpy, but if you want a beach to yourself, preserver. Definitely do not attempt the lower reaches of this road without 4WD.

Kanepu'u Preserve
Straddling the road leading to the Garden of the Gods, this 590-acre preserve is the best remaining example of dryland forest on Lana'i and a sampling of what covered much of the lower leeward slopes of the Hawaiian Islands before the coming of man. In this forest you'll find *olopua,* a native olive tree, *lama,* a native ebony, *na'u,* Hawaiian gardenia, the *'iliahi* sandalwood tree, and numerous other plant varieties, 49 species of which are found only in Hawaii, as well as many species of birds. Over the centuries, these dryland forests were reduced in size by fire, introduced animals, and the spread of nonnative weeds and trees. Erosion control measures, such as the planting of native shrubs and seeds, have been implemented to cover bare spots and fill contour scars. Under the care of the Nature Conservancy and local conservation groups, this forest and others like it are being protected.

As you pass through this preserve, stop at the self-guided loop trail to get a close-up look at some of the trees in the forest. It's about a 15-minute walk over level ground, if you stop and read the posted signs. Overlooking this trail and set on a nearby rise is Kanepu'u (Kane's Hill) Heiau.

Guided hikes are occasionally offered through the preserve. Call the hikeline, 808/537-4508, for more information about these hikes or 808/565-7430 for general information about the preserve.

The Garden of the Gods
There, a shocking assault on your senses, is the bleak, red, burnt earth, devoid of vegetation, heralding the beginning of the garden—a Hawaiian Badlands. The flowers here are made of rock, the shrubs are the twisted crusts of lava, and trees are baked minarets of stone, all subtle shades of orange, purple, and sulfurous yellow. While most is obviously created by natural erosion, some piles of stone are just as obviously erected by man. The jeep trail has been sucked down by erosion and the garden surrounds you. While the beginning seems most dramatic, much more spreads out before you as you proceed down the hill. Stop many times to climb a likely outcropping and get a sweeping view. While you can't see Lana'i's coastline from here, you do have a nice view of Moloka'i across the channel. The wind rakes these badlands and the silence penetrates to your soul. Although eons have passed, you can feel the cataclysmic violence that created this haunting and delicate beauty.

LANA'I

The Garden of the Gods is perhaps best in the late afternoon when slanting sunlight enriches colors and casts shadows that create depth and mood.

Polihua Beach

After leaving the Garden of the Gods, you can bear left to lonely **Ka'ena Point,** where you'll find Lana'i's largest *heiau,* a brooding setting full of weird power vibrations. Straight ahead, the trail takes you done to the coast. Abruptly the road becomes smooth and flat. Like a mirage too bright for your eyes, an arch is cut into the green jungle, framing white sand and moving blue ocean. As you face the beach, to the right it's flat, expansive, and the sands are white, but the winds are heavy; if you hiked eight miles, you'd reach Shipwreck Beach. A few shade trees edge the sand so you can get out of the heat. More interesting is the view to the left, which has a series of lonely little coves. The sand is brown and coarse and large black lava boulders are marbled with purplish-gray rock embedded in long, faulted seams. Polihua is not just a destination point where you come for a quick look. It takes so much effort coming and going that you should plan on having a picnic and a relaxing afternoon before heading back through the Garden of the Gods and its perfectly scheduled sunset light show.

MOLOKA'I

INTRODUCTION

MOLOKA'I

Moloka'i is a sanctuary, a human time capsule where the pendulum swings inexorably forward, but more slowly than in the rest of Hawaii. It has always been so. In ancient times, Moloka'i was known as Pule O'o, "Powerful Prayer," where its supreme chiefs protected their small underpopulated refuge, not through legions of warriors but through the chants of their *kahuna*. This powerful, ancient mysticism, handed down directly from the goddess Pahulu, was known and respected throughout the archipelago. Its *mana* was the oldest and strongest in Hawaii, and its practitioners were venerated by nobility and commoners alike—they had the ability to "pray you to death." The entire island was a haven, a refuge for the vanquished and *kapu*-breakers of all the islands. It's still so today, beckoning to determined escapees from the rat race!

The blazing lights of supermodern Honolulu can easily be seen from the west end of Moloka'i, while Moloka'i as viewed from O'ahu is fleeting and ephemeral, appearing and disappearing on the horizon. The island is home to the largest number of Hawaiians. In effect it is a tribal homeland: more than 4,000 of the island's 7,400 inhabitants have more than 50 percent Hawaiian blood and, except for Ni'ihau, it's the only island where they are the majority. The 1920s Hawaiian Homes Act allowed *kuleana* of 40 acres to anyone with more than 50 percent Hawaiian ancestry. *Kuleana* owners form the grassroots organizations that fight for Hawaiian rights and battle the colossal forces of rabid developers who have threatened Moloka'i for decades.

OVERVIEW

Kaunakakai and West

Kaunakakai, the island's main town, once looked like a Hollywood sound stage where Jesse James or Wyatt Earp would feel right at home. The town is flat, with few trees, and three blocks long. Ala Malama, its main shopping street, is lined with false-front stores; pickup trucks are parked in front where horses and buggies ought to be. To the west are the prairie-like plains of Moloka'i, some sections irrigated and now planted in profitable crops. The northern section of the island contains **Pala'au State Park,** where a campsite is always easily found, and **Phallic Rock,** a natural shrine where island women came to pray for fertility. Most of the west end is owned by the mammoth 54,000-acre **Molokai Ranch.** Part of its lands supports several thousand head of cattle and herds of axis deer imported from India in 1867.

The 40-acre *kuleana* are here on the uplands, as well as abandoned Dole and Del Monte pineapple fields. The once-thriving pineapple company town of **Kualapu'u** is now a semi-ghost town since the Del Monte pulled up stakes in 1985. Dole shut down the pineapple fields around **Maunaloa** in 1975, after which the town took a swift nose dive into neglect. Having recently undergone a massive face-lift, Maunaloa is holding on as the Molokai Ranch is expanding its operations to include more tourism-related activities. The Kualapu'u area now produces coffee and attracts its scattered Filipino workers mostly on weekends, when they come to unofficially test their best cocks in the pit. Look for the small A-frame shelters in yards here that house these creatures.

On the western shore is the Kaluakoi Resort, perched above the island's best beaches. Here, 6,700 acres sold by the Molokai Ranch to the Louisiana Land and Exploration Company and later sold to another concern are slowly being developed as homesites. Already there are houses scattered here and there. This area, rich with the finest archaeological sites on the island, is a hotbed of contention between developers and preservationists. The Kaluakoi Resort with its hotel, condominiums, and golf course, however, is often pointed to as a well-planned development, a kind of model compromise between the factions. Its low Polynesian-style architecture blends well with the surroundings and is not a high-rise blight on the horizon.

The East Coastal Road

Highway 450 is a magnificent coastal road running east from Kaunakakai to Halawa Valley. A slow drive along this writhing country thoroughfare rewards you with easily accessible beach parks, glimpses of fishponds, *heiau,* wildlife sanctuaries, and small one-room churches strung along the road like rosary beads. Almost every mile has a historical site, like the **Smith and Bronte Landing Site** where two pioneers of trans-Pacific flight ignominiously alighted in a mangrove swamp, and **Paikalani Taro Patch,** the only one from which Kamehameha V would eat poi.

On Moloka'i's eastern tip is **Halawa Valley,** a real gem accessible by car. This pristine gorge has a series of waterfalls and their pools, and a beach park where the valley meets the sea. The majority of the population of Halawa moved out in 1946 after a 30-foot tsunami washed their homes away and mangled their taro fields, leaving a thick salty residue. Today only a handful of those from the old families and a few alternative lifestylers live in the valley among the overgrown stone walls that once marked the boundaries of manicured and prosperous family gardens. Just south on the grounds of Pu'u O Hoku Ranch is **Kalanikaula,** the sacred *kukui* grove of Lanikaula, Moloka'i's most powerful *kahuna* of the classic period. This grove was planted at his death and became the most sacred spot on Moloka'i. Today the trees are dying.

The Windward Coast
Kalaupapa (Flat Leaf) is a lonely peninsula formed by lava flow from the 400-foot-high Kauhako Crater, the highest spot on this relatively flat nub of land. Kalaupapa leper colony, completely separated from the world by a hostile pounding surf and a precipitous 1,600-foot *pali,* is a modern story of human dignity. Kalaupapa was a howling charnel house where the unfortunate victims of leprosy were banished to die. Here humanity reached its lowest ebb of hopelessness, violence, and depravity, until one tiny flicker of light arrived in 1873—Joseph de Veuster, a Belgian priest known throughout Hawaii as Father Damien. In the greatest example of pure *aloha* yet established on Hawaii, he became his brothers' keeper. Tours of Kalaupapa operated by well-informed former patients are enlightening and educational.

East of Kalaupapa along the windward (northeast) coast is a series of amazingly steep and isolated valleys. The inhabitants moved out at the beginning of the 20th century except for one pioneering family that returned some years ago to carve out a home. Well beyond the farthest reaches of the last road, this emerald-green primeval world awaits. The *pali* here mark the tallest sea cliffs in the world (although some dispute this designation), with an "average incline of more than 55 degrees." Many spots are far steeper. About halfway down the coast near Umilehi Point, the cliffs are at their highest at 3,300 feet. Farther to the east and diving headfirst out of a hanging valley is **Kahiwa (Sacred One) Falls,** the highest in Hawaii at 1,750 feet. You get here only by helicopter excursion or by boat in the calmer summer months. For now, Moloka'i remains a sanctuary, reminiscent of the Hawaii of simpler times. Around it the storm of modernity rages, but still the "Friendly Island" awaits those willing to venture off the beaten track.

THE LAND

With 260 square miles, Moloka'i is the fifth largest Hawaiian Island. Its northwestern tip, at 'Ilio Point, is a mere 22 miles from O'ahu's eastern tip, Makapu'u Point. Resembling a jogging shoe, Moloka'i is about 38 miles from heel to toe and 10 miles from laces to sole, totaling 166,425 acres, with just over 88 miles of coastline. Most of the arable land on the island is owned by the 54,000-acre Molokai Ranch, primarily on the western end, and the 14,000-acre Pu'u O Hoku Ranch on the eastern end. Moloka'i was formed by three distinct shield volcanoes. Two linked

together to form Moloka'i proper, and a later eruption formed the flat Kalaupapa Peninsula.

Physical Features

Although Moloka'i is rather small, it has a great deal of geographical diversity. Western Moloka'i is dry with rolling hills, natural pastures, and a maximum elevation of only 1,381 feet. The eastern sector of the island has heavy rainfall, the tallest sea cliffs in the world, and craggy narrow valleys perpetually covered in a velvet cloak of green mosses. Viewed from the sea it looks like a 2,000-foot vertical wall from surf to clouds, with tortuously deep chasms along the coastline. Mount Kamakou is the highest peak on Moloka'i, at 4,961 feet. The south-central area is relatively swampy, while the west and especially northwest coasts around Mo'omomi have rolling sand dunes. Papohaku Beach, just below the Kaluakoi Hotel on western Moloka'i, is one of the most massive white-sand beaches in Hawaii. A controversy was raised when it was discovered that huge amounts of sand were dredged from this area and hauled to O'ahu; the Molokai Ranch was pressured and the dredging ceased. A hefty section of land in the north-central area is a state forest where new species of trees are planted on an experimental basis. The 240-acre Pala'au State Park is in this cool upland forested area. Moloka'i's south shore is also worthy of note as it has about 28 miles of reef, the state's only continuous barrier reef.

East Moloka'i Mountains

ROBERT NILSEN

MOLOKA'I
TEMPERATURE AND RAINFALL

	JAN.	MARCH	MAY	JUNE	SEPT.	NOV.
High	79	79	81	82	82	80
Low	61	63	68	70	68	63
Rain	4	3	0	0	0	2

Note: Temperature is expressed in degrees Fahrenheit; rainfall in inches.

Manmade Marvels

Two manmade features on Moloka'i are engineering marvels. One is the series of 62 ancient fishponds strung along the south shore like pearls on a string—best seen from the air as you approach the island by plane. The outlines of dozens can still be seen, but the most amazing is the enormous **Keawanui Pond,** covering 54 acres and surrounded by a three-foot-tall, 2,000-foot-long wall. It's on the National Register of Historic Places. The other is the modern **Kualapu'u Reservoir** completed in 1969. The world's largest rubber-lined reservoir, it can hold 1.4 billion gallons of water. Part of its engineering dramatics is the Moloka'i Tunnel, which feeds it with water from the eastern valleys. The tunnel is eight feet tall, eight feet wide, and almost 27,000 feet (five miles) long.

Climate

The average island daytime maximum temperature runs 75–85° F (24–29° C), winter to summer. The yearly average rainfall is 27 inches; the east receives a much greater percentage than the west.

FLORA AND FAUNA

Land animals on Moloka'i were brought by man: pigs, goats, axis deer, and cattle. The earliest arrival still extant in the wild is the *pua'a* (pig). Moloka'i's pigs live in the upper wetland forests of the northeast, but they can actually thrive anywhere. Hunters say the meat from pigs that have lived in the lower dry forest is superior to those that acquire the muddy taste of ferns from the wetter upland areas. Pigs on Moloka'i are hunt-

ed mostly with the use of dogs who pin them by the ears and snout while the hunter approaches on foot and skewers them with a long knife.

Offspring from a pair of **goats** left by Captain Cook on the island of Ni'ihau spread to all the islands; they were very well adapted to life on Moloka'i. Originally from the arid Mediterranean, goats could live well without any surface water, a condition quite prevalent over most of Moloka'i. They're found primarily in the mountainous area of the northeast.

The last free-roaming arrivals to Moloka'i were **axis deer.** Moloka'i's deer came from the upper reaches of the Ganges River, sent to Kamehameha V by Dr. William Hillebrand while on a botanical trip to India in 1867. Kamehameha V sent some of the first specimens to Moloka'i, where they prospered. Today they are found mostly on western Moloka'i, though some travel the south coast to the east.

Bird Life

A few of Hawaii's endemic birds can be spotted by a determined observer at various locales around Moloka'i. They include: the Hawaiian petrel *('ua'u);* Hawaiian coot *('alae ke'oke'o),* prominent in Hawaiian mythology; Hawaiian stilt *(ae'o),* a wading bird with ridiculous stick legs that protects its young by feigning wing injury and luring predators away from the nest; and the Hawaiian owl *(pueo),* a bird that helps in its own demise by being easily approached. Moloka'i has a substantial number of introduced game birds that attract hunters throughout the year.

The nonprofit organization **Nene O Moloka'i** operates a facility that breeds, releases, and monitors the state bird, the *nene.* About four miles east of Kaunakakai, it offers free tours

MOLOKA'I

daily at 9 A.M., but you must make an appointment to visit. To learn more about these friendly geese, call 808/553-5992 or visit the organization's website at www.aloha.net/~nene.

Flora

The *kukui* or candlenut tree is common to all the Hawaiian Islands; along with being the official state tree, its tiny white blossom is Moloka'i's flower. The *kukui,* introduced centuries ago by the early Polynesians, grows on lower mountain slopes and can easily be distinguished by its pale green leaves. Low and dry, the western end of Moloka'i is typified by shrubby bushes and gnarled trees. Only in the windy desert-like Mo'omomi sand dune area does hearty native shore vegetation still survive. In the upper reaches of the north shore valleys, the vegetation as rich, diverse, and luxuriant as the wet areas of the other islands.

Conservation Controversy

It has long been established and regretted that introduced animals and plants have destroyed Hawaii's delicate natural balance leading to the extinction of many of its rare native species. A number of well-meaning groups and organizations are doing their best to preserve Hawaii habitat, but they don't always agree on the methods employed. Feral pigs, indiscriminate in their relentless hunt for food, are ecological nightmares that virtually bulldoze the rainforest floor into fetid pools and gouged earth where mosquitoes and other introduced species thrive while driving out the natives. Moloka'i's magnificent Kamakou Preserve, Upper Pelekunu Valley, and the central Moloka'i ridges are some of the last remaining pockets of natural habitat on the island. The Kamakou Preserve, 2,774 pristine acres, is covered, like the others, in 'ohi'a forest, prime habitat for the almost-extinct *oloma'o* (Moloka'i thrush), *kakawahie* (creeper), and the hearty but beleaguered '*apapane* and '*amakihi.* No one disagrees that the wild boar must be managed to protect these areas, but they do not agree on *how* they should be managed. The Nature Conservancy in its dedication to preserving the rainforest backed a policy to snare the wild boar, maintaining that this was the best possible way of eliminating these pests while placing

the forest under the least amount of stress. In opposition to the practice of snaring is Pono, a local organization of native Moloka'i hunters that maintains snaring pigs is inhumane, causing the animals to starve to death or to die slowly from strangulation. Pono also abhors the wasting of the meat, and the indiscriminate killing of sows.

Aside from the **Kamakou Preserve,** the Nature Conservancy also maintains 5,759 acres of the Pelekunu Valley on the remote north coast of the island, where there is no public access. There is periodic access, however, to the **Mo'omomi Preserve,** a 921-acre area of sand dunes west of Mo'omomi Beach that is safe harbor for several species of endangered plants, seabirds, and green sea turtles. The Nature Conservancy conducts hikes once a month into the Kamakou and Mo'omomi preserves. If you wish to attend, call well in advance for dates and to reserve your spot; 808/553-5236. For more information log onto the organization's website at www.tnc.org.

HISTORY

The oral chant *"Moloka'i nui a Hina. . ."* ("Great Moloka'i, child of Hina") refers to Moloka'i as the island-child of the goddess Hina and the god Wakea, male progenitor of all the islands; Papa, Wakea's first wife, left him in anger as a result of this unfaithfulness. Hina's cave, just above Kalua'aha on the southeast coast, can still be visited and has been revered as a sacred spot for countless centuries. Another ancient spot, Halawa Valley, on the eastern tip of Moloka'i, is considered one of the oldest settlements in Hawaii. As research continues, settlement dates are pushed farther back, but for now scholars agree that early wayfarers from the Marquesas Islands settled Halawa in the mid-seventh century.

Moloka'i, from earliest times, was revered and feared as a center for mysticism and sorcery. In fact, an ancient name for the island is Moloka'i Pule O'o (Moloka'i of the Potent Prayers). **'Ili'ili'opae Heiau** was renowned for its powerful priests whose incantations were mingled with the screams of human sacrifice. Commoners avoided 'Ili'ili'opae, and even powerful *kahuna* could not escape its terrible power. One, Kamalo, lost his sons as sacrifices at the *heiau* for their desecration of the temple drum. Kamalo sought revenge by invoking the help of his personal god, the terrible shark deity Kauhuhu. After the proper prayers and offerings, Kauhuhu sent a flash flood to wipe out Mapulehu Valley where 'Ili'ili'opae was located. All perished except for Kamalo and his family, who were protected by a sacred fence around their home.

This tradition of mysticism reached its apex with the famous Lanikaula, "Prophet of Moloka'i." During the 16th century, Lanikaula lived near Halawa Valley and practiced his arts, handed down by the goddess Pahulu, who predated even Pele. Pahulu was the goddess responsible for the "old ocean highway," which passed between Moloka'i and Lana'i and led to Kahiki, lost homeland of all the islanders. Lanikaula practiced his sorcery in the utmost secrecy and even buried his excrement on an offshore island so that a rival *kahuna* could not find and burn it, which would surely cause his death. Hawaiian oral history does not say why Palo, a sorcerer from Lana'i and a friend of Lanikaula, came to spy on Lanikaula and observed him hiding his excrement. Palo burned it in the sacred fires, and Lanikaula knew that his end was near. Lanikaula ordered his sons to bury him in a hidden grave so that his enemies could not find his bones and use their *mana* to control his spirit. To further hide his remains, he had a *kukui* grove planted over his body. **Kalanikaula** (Sacred Grove of Lanikaula) is still visible today, though most of the trees appear to be dying.

Incursions from Outside

Captain James Cook first spotted Moloka'i on November 26, 1778, but because it looked bleak and uninhabited he decided to bypass it. It wasn't until eight years later that Captain George Dixon sighted the island and decided to land. Very little was recorded in his ship's log about this first encounter, and Moloka'i slipped from the attention of the Western world until Protestant missionaries arrived at Kalua'aha in 1832 and reported the native population at approximately 6,000.

In 1790 Kamehameha the Great came from the Big Island as a suitor seeking the hand of Keopuolani, a chieftess of Moloka'i. Within five years he returned again, but this time there was no merrymaking: he came as a conquering chief on his thrust westward to capture O'ahu. His war canoes landed at Pakuhiwa Battleground, a bay just a few miles east of Kaunakakai between Kawela and Kamalo; it's said that warriors lined the shores for more than four miles. The grossly outnumbered warriors of Moloka'i fought desperately, but even the incantations of their *kahuna* were no match for Kamehameha and his warriors. Inflamed with recent victory and infused with the power of their horrible war-god Ku of the Maggot-dripping Mouth, they slaughtered the Moloka'i warriors and threw their broken bodies into a sea so filled with sharks that their feeding frenzy made the waters appear to boil. Thus subdued, Moloka'i slipped into obscurity once again as its people turned to a quiet life of farming and fishing.

Molokai Ranch

Moloka'i remained almost unchanged until the 1850s. The Great Mahele of 1848 provided for private ownership of land, and giant tracts were formed into the Molokai Ranch. About 1850, German immigrant Rudolph Meyer came to Moloka'i and married a high chieftess named Dorcas Kalama Waha. Together they had 11 children, with whose aid he turned the vast lands of the Molokai Ranch into productive pastureland. A man of indomitable spirit, Meyer held public office on Moloka'i and became the island's unofficial patriarch. He managed Molokai Ranch for the original owner, Kamehameha V, and remained manager until his death in 1897, by which time the ranch was owned by the Bishop Estate. In 1875, Charles Bishop had bought half of the 70,000 acres of Molokai Ranch, and his wife, Bernice, a Kamehameha descendant, inherited the remainder. In 1898, the Molokai Ranch was sold to businessmen in Honolulu for $251,000. This consortium formed the American Sugar Co., but after a few plantings the available water on Moloka'i turned brackish and once again Molokai Ranch was sold. Charles Cooke bought controlling interest from the other businessmen in 1908 and remained in control of the ranch until 1988 when it was sold to Brierly Investments, a business concern from New Zealand.

MOLOKA'I

MOLOKA'I

Changing Times

Very little happened for a decade after Charles Cooke bought the Molokai Ranch from his partners. Moloka'i did become famous for its honey production, supplying a huge amount to the world up until World War I. During the 1920s, political and economic forces greatly changed Moloka'i. In 1921, Congress passed the **Hawaiian Homes Act,** which set aside 43,000 acres on the island for people who had at least 50 percent Hawaiian blood. By this time, however, all agriculturally productive land in Hawaii had already been claimed. The land given to the Hawaiians was very poor and lacked adequate water. Many Hawaiians had long since left the land and were raised in towns and cities. Now out of touch with the simple life of the taro patch, they found it very difficult to readjust. To prevent the Hawaiians from selling their claims and losing the land forever, the Hawaiian Homes Act provided that the land be leased to them for 99 years. Making a go of these 40-acre parcels *(kuleana)* was so difficult that successful homesteaders were called "Moloka'i Miracles."

In 1923 Libby Corporation leased land from Molokai Ranch at Kaluako'i and went into pineapple production; Del Monte followed suit in 1927 at Kualapu'u. Both built company towns and imported Japanese and Filipino field laborers, swelling Moloka'i's population and stabilizing the economy. Many of the native Hawaiians subleased their tracts to the pineapple growers, and the Hawaiian Homes Act seemed to backfire. Instead of the homesteaders working their own farms, they were given monthly checks and lured into a life of complacency. Those who grew little more than family plots became, in effect, permanent tenants on their own property. Much more importantly, they lost the psychological advantage of controlling their own future and regaining their pride as envisioned in the Hawaiian Homes Act.

Modern Times

For the next 50 years life was quiet. The pineapples grew, providing security. Another large ranch, **Pu'u O Hoku** (Hill of Stars) was formed on the eastern tip of the island. It was originally owned by Paul Fagan, the amazing San Francisco entrepreneur who also developed the Hana Ranch on Maui. In 1955, Fagan sold Pu'u O Hoku to George Murphy, a Canadian industrialist, for a meager $300,000. The ranch, under Murphy, became famous for beautiful white Charolais cattle, a breed originating in France.

In the late 1960s "things" started quietly happening on Moloka'i. The Molokai Ranch sold 6,700 acres to the Kaluakoi Corp., which they controlled along with the Louisiana Land and Exploration Company. In 1969 the long-awaited Moloka'i reservoir was completed at Kualapu'u; finally west Moloka'i had plenty of water. Shortly after Moloka'i's water problem appeared to be finally under control, Dole Corp. bought out Libby in 1972, lost millions in the next few years, and shut down its pineapple production at Maunaloa in 1975. By 1977 the acreage sold to the Kaluakoi Corp. started to be developed, and the Molokai Sheraton (now the Kaluakoi Hotel) opened along with low-rise condominiums and 270 fee-simple home sites ranging 5–43 acres selling for a minimum of $150,000 ($350,000 for oceanfront sites). Future plans for this area included two more resorts, additional condominiums, shopping facilities, bridle paths, and an airstrip (it's only 20 minutes to Honolulu). Lo and behold, it seemed that sleepy old Moloka'i with the tiny Hawaiian Homes farms was now prime real estate and worth a fortune.

To complicate the picture even further, Del Monte shut down its operations in 1982, throwing more people out of work. In 1986 it did resume planting 250-acre tracts, but now all the pineapple is gone. Recently, coffee has been put into production near the old pineapple town of Kualapu'u, some experimental plots of fruits and vegetables have been planted, and the Molokai Ranch has brought in sheep and cattle. After Brierly Investments bought the Molokai Ranch, bigger changes have started to take place, including a total face-lift for the town of Maunaloa and greater emphasis on tourism for a slice of the ranch's income. These new avenues of diversification are still in their infant stages but might possibly lead to greater economic strength and stability. Today Moloka'i is in a period of flux in other ways. There is great tension between developers, who are viewed as "carpetbaggers" interested only in a fast buck, and those who consider themselves the last remnants of a lost race holding on desperately to what little they have left.

ECONOMY

If it weren't for a pitifully bad economy, Moloka'i would have no economy at all. At one time the workers on the pineapple plantations had good steady incomes and the high hopes of the working class. With all the pineapple jobs gone, Moloka'i was transformed from an island with virtually no unemployment to a hard-luck community with a high rate of the people on welfare. With the start of the coffee plantation and the slowly growing tourism industry, this bleak economic situation has lessened somewhat. Inexplicably, Moloka'i also has the highest utility rates in Hawaii. Some say this is due to the fact that the utility company built a modern biomass plant and didn't have enough biomass to keep it operating—the people were stuck with the fuel tab. The present situation is even more ludicrous when you consider that politically Moloka'i is part of Maui County. It is lumped together with Ka'anapali on Maui's western coast, one of Hawaii's poshest and wealthiest areas, where the vast majority of people are recent arrivals from the Mainland. This amounts to almost no political/economic voice for grassroots Moloka'i.

Agriculture

The word that is now bandied about is "diversified" agriculture. What this means is not pinning all hope to one crop like the ill-fated pineapple, but planting a potpourri of crops. Attempts at diversification are evident as you travel around Moloka'i. Fields of corn, wheat, fruits, nuts, and coffee are just west of Kaunakakai; many small farmers are trying truck farming by raising a variety of garden vegetables that they hope to sell to the massive hotel food industry in Honolulu. Watermelon, bell pepper, onions, and herbs are perhaps the most well known, and one farm, some say the largest in the state, grows sweet potatoes. The problem is not in production, but transportation. Moloka'i raises excellent crops, but not enough established transport exists for the perishable vegetables. A barge service, running on a loose twice-weekly schedule, is the only link to the market. The lack of storage facilities on Moloka'i makes it tough to compete in the hotel food business, which requires the freshest produce. Unfortunately, vegetables don't wait well for late barges.

Development

When development was new, a debate raged between those in favor of tourist development, which they said will save Moloka'i, and grassroots organizations which insist unchecked tourism development would despoil Moloka'i and give no real benefit to the people. A main character in the debate was the Kaluakoi Corp., which wanted to build condos and sell more

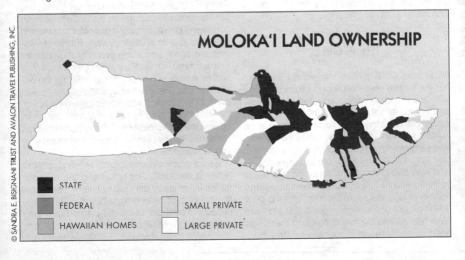

MOLOKA'I LAND OWNERSHIP

STATE
FEDERAL
HAWAIIAN HOMES
SMALL PRIVATE
LARGE PRIVATE

MOLOKA'I

home lots. It claimed that this, coupled with a few more resorts, would bring in jobs. The people know that they will be relegated to service jobs (maids and waiters), while all the management jobs go to outsiders. Most islanders felt that only rich people from the Mainland could afford million-dollar homes and condos, and that eventually they will become disenfranchised on their own island. Claims were that outsiders have no feeling for the 'aina (land) and would destroy important cultural sites whenever growth dictates. While quieted much over the years, this issue is only barely under the surface and erupts quickly when any talk of development it in the winds.

A few years back the Kaluakoi Corp. hired an "independent" research team to investigate the area around Kawakiu Iki Bay, known to be an ancient adze quarry. After weeks of study, this Maui-based research team reported that Kawakiu was of "minor importance." Hawaii's academic sector went wild. The Society of Hawaiian Archaeology dispatched its own team under Dr. Patrick Kirch, who stated that Kawakiu was one of the richest archaeological areas in Hawaii. In one day they discovered six sites missed by the "independent" research team, and stated that a rank amateur could find artifacts by merely scraping away some of the surface. Reasonable voices call for moderation. Both sides agree Moloka'i must grow, but the growth must be controlled, and the people of Moloka'i must be represented and included as beneficiaries.

THE PEOPLE

Aside from the tiny island of Ni'ihau, Moloka'i has the largest percentage of Hawaiian population, and this is perhaps due in part to relatively small commercial development on the island throughout its history, which did not bring in large numbers of ethnic workers. While sugar was tried early on with some success, it never grew to vast size, and the pineapple production on the island was also limited. Only ranching has really persevered and this doesn't require any large number of laborers. More recently, with the slow development of tourism, white collar workers have filtered into the workforce and there has been some increase in tourism-related jobs.

Local Hawaiians make up 48 percent of Moloka'i's population; 21 percent are Filipino, 18 percent Caucasian, 9 percent Japanese, 1 percent Chinese, and 3 percent various other groups.

Moloka'i is obviously experiencing a class struggle. The social problems hinge on the economy—the collapse of pineapple cultivation and the move toward tourism. The average income on Moloka'i is quite low and the people are not consumer-oriented. Tourism, especially "getaway condos," brings in the affluent. This creates friction; the "have-nots" don't know their situation until the "haves" come in and remind them. Today, most people hunt a little, fish, and have small gardens. Some are small-time pakalolo growers who get over the hard spots by making a few dollars from some backyard plants. There is no organized crime on Moloka'i. The worst you might run into is a group of local kids drinking on a weekend in one of their favorite spots. It's a territorial thing. If you come into their vicinity they might feel their turf is being invaded, and you could be in for some hassles. All this could add up to a bitter situation except that the true nature of most of the people is to be helpful and friendly. Just be sensitive to smiles and frowns and give people their space.

Ethnic Identity

An underground link exists between Moloka'i and other Hawaiian communities such as Waianae on O'ahu. Moloka'i is unusual in that it is still Hawaiian in population and influence, with continuing culturally based outlooks that remain unacceptable to Western views. Ethnic Hawaiians are again becoming proud of their culture and heritage, as well as politically aware and sophisticated, and are just now entering the political arena. Few are lawyers, doctors, politicians, or executives; with ethnic identity returning, there is beginning to be a majority backlash against these professions. Among non-Hawaiian residents, it's put down or unacknowledged as a real occurrence.

Social problems on Moloka'i relate directly to teenage boredom and hostility in the schools, fueled by a heavy drinking scene. A disproportionate rate of teen pregnancy is a direct by-product. Teachers unofficially admit that they prefer a student who has smoked pakalolo to one who's been drinking. It mellows them out.

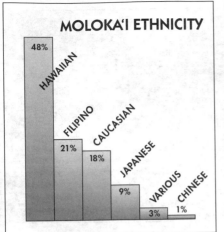

MOLOKA'I ETHNICITY

HAWAIIAN 48%
FILIPINO 21%
CAUCASIAN 18%
JAPANESE 9%
VARIOUS 3%
CHINESE 1%

The traditional educational approach is failing.

Ho'opono'opono is a fascinating family problem-solving technique still very much employed on Moloka'i. The process is like "peeling the onion," where a mediator, usually a respected *kupuna*, tries to get to the heart of a problem. Similar to group therapy, it's a closed family ordeal, never open to outsiders, and lasts until all emotions are out in the open and all concerned feel "clean."

FESTIVALS AND EVENTS

Like all the other islands, Moloka'i celebrates all federal and state holidays and major events. In addition to these, there are specific events which has a particular importance on this island. A few of these follow.

January
The **Makahiki Games** are a revived version of the ancient Hawaiian Olympics. Includes food, arts, and crafts and is held at Kaunakakai Park.

May
Music, song, and hula contests are the focus of the day at the **Moloka'i Ka Hula Piko,** held at Papohaku Beach Park on the west end of Moloka'i. This event, which includes craft and art demonstrations and Hawaiian foods, is held to honor the birth of hula, traditionally held to have been on top of Ka'ana Hill above Maunaloa.

September
The **Wahine O Ke Kai Outrigger Canoe Race** for women takes off at the end of September in Hawaiian-style canoes from the remote Hale O Lono Beach on Moloka'i's west end to Kahanamoku Beach in Waikiki. In crossing, the teams must navigate the always-rough Kaiwi Channel.

October
The **Moloka'i Hoe Outrigger Canoe Race** is the men's version of this canoe contest, which also starts from Hale O Lono Beach and races to Kahanamoku Beach on O'ahu.

SPORTS AND RECREATION

Since Moloka'i is a great place to get away from it all, you would expect an outdoor extravaganza. In fact, Moloka'i is a "good news, bad news" island when it comes to recreation, especially in the water. Moloka'i has few excellent beaches with the two best, Halawa and Papohaku, on opposite ends of the island; **Papohaku Beach** on the west end is treacherous during the winter months. Surfers and windsurfers will be disappointed with Moloka'i except at a few locales at the right time of year, while bathers, sun worshippers, and families will love the small secluded beaches with gentle waves located around the island.

Moloka'i has a small population and plenty of undeveloped "outback" land. This *should* add up to great trekking and camping, but the land is mostly privately owned and the tough trails are poorly maintained. However, permission is usually granted to trek across private land, and those bold enough to venture into the outback will virtually have it to themselves. Day-hiking trails and lightly used camping areas with good facilities are no problem. Moloka'i has tame, family-oriented beach parks along its southern shores, superb hunting and fishing, two excellent golf courses, and a handful of tennis courts. Couple this with clean air, no industrial pollution, no city noise, and a deliciously casual atmosphere, and you wind up with the epitome of relaxation.

MOLOKA'I

MOLOKA'I

No. 20 Beach, Moloka'i

J.D. BISIGNANI

East End Beaches

The beaches of Moloka'i have their own temperament, ranging from moody and rebellious to sweet and docile. Heading east from Kaunakakai along Route 450 takes you past a string of beaches that vary from poor to excellent. Much of this underbelly of Moloka'i is fringed by a protective coral reef that keeps the water flat, shallow, and at some spots murky. This area was ideal for fishponds but leaves a lot to be desired as far as beaches are concerned. The farther east you go, the better the beaches become. The first one you come to is at **One Ali'i Park,** about four miles east of Kaunakakai. Here you'll find a picnic area, campsites, good fishing, and family-class swimming where the kids can frolic with no danger from the sea. Next you pass **Kakahai'a Beach Park** and **Kumimi Beach,** one of a series of lovely sandy crescents where the swimming is fine. Just before you reach Puko'o, a small dirt road on your right goes to a hidden beach perfect for a secluded swim.

Halawa Bay, on Moloka'i's far east end, is the best all-around beach on the island. It's swimmable year-round, but be extra careful during the winter months. The bay protects the beach for a good distance; beyond its reach the breakers are excellent for surfing. The snorkeling and fishing are good to very good.

West End Beaches

The people of Moloka'i favor the beaches on the northwest section of the island. **Mo'omomi Beach** is one of the best and features good swimming, fair surfing, and pleasurable snorkeling along its sandy, rocky bottom. You have to drive over a very rutted dirt road to get there. Although car rental agencies are against it, you can make it, but only in dry weather. From Mo'omomi you can walk west along the beach and find your own secluded spot.

Very few visitors go south from Maunaloa town, but it is possible and rewarding for those seeking a secluded area. As you enter Maunaloa town a crushed coral track goes off to your right. Follow it through the Molokai ranchland and down the hill to **Hale O Lono Harbor,** start of an Outrigger Canoe Race. The swimming is only fair but the fantasy feeling of a deserted island is pervasive.

Papohaku and **Kepuhi** beaches just below the Kaluakoi Hotel are excellent, renowned for their vast expanses of sand. Unfortunately, they're treacherous in the winter with giant swells and heavy rips, which make them a favorite for surfers. Anyone not accustomed to strong sea conditions should limit themselves to sunning and wading only to the ankles. During the rest of the year this area is great for swimming, becoming like a lake in the summer months. About a mile north of Kepuhi Bay is an ideal beach named **Kawakiu.** This area is well established as an archaeological site, and access to the beach was a hard-fought controversy between the people of Moloka'i and the Molokai Ranch. Good swimming, depending upon tide conditions, and unofficial camping.

Snorkel and Scuba

Some charter fishing boats arrange scuba and snorkeling excursions, but scuba and snorkeling on Moloka'i are just offshore and you don't need a boat to get to it. Beginners will feel safe at **One Ali'i Park**, where the sea conditions are mild, though the snorkeling is mediocre. The best underwater area is the string of beaches heading east past mile marker 18 on Route 450, and especially at mile marker 20. You'll wind up at Halawa Bay, which is tops. Mo'omomi Beach on the northwest shore is very good, and Kawakiu Beach out on the west end is good around the rocks, but stay away during winter. For those staying at Molokai Ranch, Halena and Kolo beaches along the south coast also offer descent snorkeling.

Moloka'i Fish and Dive in Kaunakakai, 808/553-5926, is a full-service snorkel shop. It has very good rental rates ($9 a set), can give you directions to the best spots, and can arrange excursions.

Bill Kapuni's Snorkel and Dive Adventure, 808/553-9867 or 888/553-9867, P.O. Box 1962, Kaunakakai, HI 96748, website: www.molokai-aloha.com/kapuni, email: bk@molokai-aloha.com, is an excellent way to enjoy Moloka'i's underwater spectacle. Owner Bill Kapuni, a native Hawaiian, is intimately familiar with both the marine life that you will encounter and the Hawaiian myths and legends of his heritage. Bill's trips, 7:30 A.M., 10:30 A.M., and 1 P.M., including complimentary snacks, are $45 for snorkeling and $85 for a two-tank dive. Bill offers professional PADI instruction and has a compressor to fill tanks for certified divers. All trips operate on a Boston Whaler, six person maximum.

Kayaking

Whether its to the calm south shore with its reef and many fishponds, or the rugged north shore and its isolated valleys, **Lani's Kayak Tours and Rentals,** 808/558-8563, can get you there. Destinations may depend upon the season and water conditions. South shore trips are $45 and north shore trips $65, $10 extra for snorkeling gear.

The Molokai Ranch runs a rather tame but thoroughly fun kayak tour along the south shore inside the reef for $40.

If you want to take off on your own or be guided through the placid reef, try **Moloka'i Outdoor Activities,** 808/553-4477. Single and double kayaks are available at $10 per hour or $25 per day, or $15 per hour or $40 per day, respectively. See them at Hotel Moloka'i.

Sailing

Moloka'i is nearly devoid of charter sailboats. However, for those who like to feel the salty sea breeze in their hair, hear the snap of a full-furled sail, or enjoy the sunset from the deck of a sailing ship, try an excursion with **Moloka'i Charters,** 808/553-5852, P.O. Box 1207, Kaunakakai, HI 96748. The only charter sailing ship on the island is its 42-foot sloop *Satan's Doll,* berthed at the Kaunakakai wharf. Tours offered are a two-hour sunset sail for $40 and a full-day sail to Lana'i for swimming and snorkeling for $90. In season, whale-watching tours are also run for $50. Four-person minimum; priced per person.

Surfing

The best surfing is out on the east end past mile marker 20. Pohakuloa Point has excellent breaks, which continue eastward to Halawa Bay. Mo'omomi Beach has decent breaks as does Kepuhi Beach in front of Kaluakoi Resort (also good for windsurfing); Kawakiu's huge waves during the winter months are suitable only for experts. If you need to rent a surfboard, try **Moloka'i Outdoor Activities,** 808/553-4477.

Fishing

The Penguin Banks of Moloka'i are some of the most fertile waters in Hawaii. Private boats as well as the commercial fishing fleets out of O'ahu come here to try their luck. Trolling produces excellent game fish such as marlin, mahimahi, *ahi* (a favorite with sashimi lovers), and *ono*, with its reputation of being the best-tasting fish in Hawaii. Bottom fishing, usually with live bait, yields *onaga* and *uku*, a gray snapper favored by local people. Moloka'i's shoreline, especially along the south and west, offers great bait-casting for *ulua* and '*ama 'ama. Ulua* is an excellent eating fish, and with a variance in weight from 15 to 110 pounds, can be a real whopper to catch

MOLOKA'I

from shore. Squidding, *limu* gathering, and torch-fishing are all quite popular and productive along the south shore, especially around the old fishpond sites. These remnants of Hawaii's one-time vibrant aquaculture still produce mullet, the *ali'i's* favorite; an occasional Samoan crab; the less desirable, introduced tilapia; and the better-left-alone barracuda.

The **Alyce C.,** 808/558-8377, is a 31-foot, fully equipped diesel-powered fishing boat, owned and operated by Captain Joe Reich, who can take you for full- or half-day charters and offers whale-watching tours in season. Rates run $300 for a half-day and $400 for a full-day charter of the boat.

Fun Hogs Hawaii, 808/567-6789, also offers half- or full-day fishing excursions, as well as two-hour sunset cruises. This company will also take a group body boarding, give instruction, and provide gear. Charters for other purposes are welcome.

The **Moloka'i Fish and Dive Co.,** 808/553-5926, also arranges deep-sea charters as well as excursions and shoreline sailing.

If you want to stay inside the reef and try for something smaller but just as sporty, **Moloka'i Flat Bottom Boat** should be your choice. This company will take you out for reef fish on a half-day or full-day adventure. The 3.5-hour half-day runs $75 per person and the full-day $150; two-person minimum. Contact Junior Rawlins, 808/558-8380 for reservations. His family also runs the Moloka'i Horse and Wagon Ride.

Camping

The best camping on Moloka'i is at **Pala'au State Park** at the end of Route 470, in the cool mountains overlooking Kalaupapa Peninsula. It's also the site of Moloka'i's famous Phallic Rock. Here you'll find pavilions, grills, picnic tables, and freshwater. What you won't find are crowds; in fact, most likely you'll have the entire area to yourself. The camping here is free, but you need a permit, good for seven days, from the park headquarters office in Kalae, 808/567-6923, or from the Division of State Parks in Wailuku on Maui.

Camping is permitted for up to a week at **Waikolu Lookout** in the Moloka'i Forest Reserve, but you'll have to follow a tough dirt road (Main Forest Road) for 10 miles to get to it. A free permit must be obtained from the Division of Forestry and Wildlife in Ho'olehua next to the post office, in the building that says "Molokai Water System."

County park, seaside camping is allowed at **One Ali'i Park,** just east of Kaunakakai, and at **Papohaku Beach Park,** on the west end. These parks have full facilities. Papohaku is isolated and quiet, but due to its location and easy access just off the highway, One Ali'i is often crowded and noisy. Also, you are a target here for any rip-off artists. A county permit is required and available from County Parks and Recreation at the Mitchell Pauole Center in Kaunakakai, 808/553-3204, Mon.–Fri. 8 A.M.–4 P.M.; fees are $3 per day for adults, $.50 for children under age 17.

tentalow,
Moloka'i Ranch

Camping is limited to three consecutive days and a total of 15 days in a year.

Hawaiian Home Lands, P.O. Box 198, Ho'olehua, HI 96729, 808/567-6104 or 808/567-6296, fax 808/567-6665, offers camping at **Kioea Park,** one mile west of Kaunakakai. The permit to this historical coconut grove costs $5 a day. Be sure to reserve well ahead of time; graduation, summer, and December are usually booked. One of the most amazing royal coconut groves in Hawaii, it's a treat to visit, but camping here, though quiet, can be hazardous. Make sure to pitch your tent away from any coconut-laden trees if possible, and vacate if the winds come up.

Camping on private land is offered by **Moloka'i Horse and Wagon Ride,** 808/558-8380, at their beach property out on the east end next to the Mapulehu Mango Grove. Rates are $15 per day for two people if you have your own gear, or $25 if you use their equipment.

You may be able to camp free (unofficially) at Mo'omomi Beach on the island's northwest shore on a grassy plot near the pavilion, or at isolated Kawakiu Iki Bay farther to the west. You can't officially camp at Halawa Bay Beach Park either, but if you continue along the north side of the bay you'll come to a well-used but unofficial campground fringed by ironwoods and recognizable by old fire pits. This area does attract down-and-outers so don't leave your gear unattended.

Hiking

Moloka'i should be a hiker's paradise and there are exciting, well maintained, easily accessible trails, but others cross private land, skirt guarded *pakalolo* patches, are poorly maintained, and tough to follow. This section provides a general overview of some hiking possibilities available on Moloka'i. Full info is given in the respective sections.

One of the most exciting hassle-free trails descends the *pali* to the **Kalaupapa Peninsula.** You follow the well-maintained mule trail down, and except for some "road apples" left by the mules, it's a totally enjoyable experience suitable for an in-shape family. You *must* have a reservation with the guide company to tour the former leper colony, however.

Another excellent trail is at **Halawa Valley,** following Halawa Stream to cascading Moaula

Falls, where you can take a refreshing dip if the famous *mo'o,* a mythical lizard said to live in the pool, is in the right mood. This trail is strenuous enough to be worthwhile and thrilling enough to be memorable. In years past anyone could walk up into Halawa Valley; however, due to abuse, disrespect, degradation of the land, and a few law suits, it was closed to the public for two years. It has been opened again, but entrance is restricted to those who go in with **Halawa Falls Cultural Hike.** Tour leaders Pilipo Solitorio, born and bred in the valley, or his son, not only show you the way but give you a private historical and cultural lesson on the way. This valley is one of the most ancient populated sites in the islands and many remnants of the past still dot the floor of the valley. You meet at the Puko'o Neighborhood Store and caravan into the valley. The hike starts around 10 A.M. and a walk of 1.5–2 hours brings you to the falls where you can swim and rest. A return by 1:30–2 P.M. in the afternoon rounds out an enjoyable half day adventure. Hikes, $25 per adult, do not run every day, so for an exact schedule call 808/553-4355 in the early evening.

Moloka'i Forest Reserve, which you can reach by driving about 10 miles over the rugged Main Forest Road (passable by 4WD only in the dry season), has fine hiking. On the way you'll find the Sandalwood Measuring Pit and just at the reserve boundary the Waikolu Lookout. The hale and hearty who push on will find themselves overlooking Pelekunu and Wailau, two fabulous and enchanted valleys of the north coast.

The **Meyer Ranch** in Kala'e has opened part of its 1,800 acres to guided hiking tours along the *pali.* All hikes include a tours of the Moloka'i Museum and Cultural Center before heading up to the ranchland. These hikes run $30 per person with a minimum of three, and are usually finished around noon. Call the museum and cultural center at 808/567-6436 to make arrangements.

The Molokai Ranch also offers a number of unique cultural hiking tours across its land at the west end of the island. For schedules, times, and fees, call the ranch Outfitters Center at 808/552-2791.

Horseback Riding

For riding options on Moloka'i, there's more to choose from these days than a few years ago.

MOLOKA'I

The **Moloka'i Horse and Wagon Ride,** 808/558-8380, near Puko'o also does rides along with the wagon ride through the Mapulehu Mango Grove and up to the 'Ili'ili'opae Heiau, largest on the island. Both horse rides and wagon rides are $50 per person.

The **Molokai Ranch,** 808/552-2791, offers a variety of rides over its lands for ranch guests and nonguests. Included are a paniolo roundup for $75, a cattle drive ride for $85, and a trail ride for $75. Their tame wagon ride runs $25.

On the far eastern tip of the island, Pu'u O Hoku Ranch now offers several trail rides through its working ranch, that range from a one-hour ride at $55 to a four-hour ride for $105. Specialized rides are also offered, like one with lunch and a swim runs $120, a six-hour waterfall ride goes for $180, and the sunset/dinner ride is $125. These rides let you see scenery that is generally not open to others than those who work on the ranch. For information, call 800/558-8109.

Wagon Ride

One of the most fun-filled cultural experiences that you can have is to spend an afternoon on the **Moloka'i Horse and Wagon Ride,** 808/558-8380, email: wgnride@aloha.net. Rides are given Mon.–Sat. starting in late morning. Call at least a day in advance. Rates are $50 for the wagon ride (minimum of eight required), $50 if you would like to go along on horseback. The experience starts and ends from a hidden beach just past mile marker 15 on the east end of the island along Route 450. As you drive, look to the right for a sign to Mapulehu Mango Grove; you'll follow the road to a small white house on the beach. After loading, the wagon leaves the beach and rolls through the mango grove and proceeds down a tree-shrouded lane with anecdotes along the way. In about 20 minutes you arrive at 'Ili'ili'opae Heiau, among the largest Hawaiian places of worship in the islands. You are told about the history of the *heiau,* pointed out exotic fruits and plants in the area, and led atop the *heiau* for a photo session. You then return to the beach for a barbecue lunch and a demonstration of coconut husking, throw-netting, and maybe even a hula lesson. You can also count on the Hawaiian tradition of hospitality. These guys know how to treat you well. This is a totally local operation completely devoid of glitz, glamour, and hype. Run by Junior Rawlins, wagonmaster, and his wife, Nani, it's a *real* experience, so don't expect anything fancy or pretentious.

Mule Ride

Coupled with a tour of the Kalaupapa settlement, the **Molokai Mule Ride** runs tours from topside down to the peninsula. The well-trained mules will transport you round-trip down and up the 1,600-foot *pali* face, negotiating the switchbacks with ease. The ride each way is about 90 minutes. Conducted 8 A.M.–3:30 P.M. daily except Friday, this tour is $150 per person and includes the ground tour of the settlement and lunch; add $18 per person (minimum two) if you need transportation from the Moloka'i Airport if you're flying in for the day for the tour. No riders over 240 pounds please; all must be at least 16 years old and in good physical shape. Molokai Mule Ride can also arrange the ground tour for you ($40) if you desire to hike down the hill, or a fly-in from Ho'olehua Airport to the peninsula and ground tour for $109. Other options are the ground tour and a fly-in from either Maui or Honolulu for $189, or a hike-in and fly-out to the Moloka'i Airport for $80. For further information and reservations, contact the company at 808/567-6088 or 800/567-7550, or write P.O. Box 200, Kualapuu, HI 96757, website: www.muleride.com, email: muleman@aloha.net.

Bicycling

For the only sales and repair of bikes on Moloka'i, and for guided bike tours of Pu'u O Hoku ranchland way out on the eastern tip of the island, see **Moloka'i Bicycle,** 808/553-3931. Open Tuesday, Wednesday, Thursday 3–6 P.M. and Saturday 9 A.M.–2 P.M., this bike shop is in a warehouse type building at 80 Mohala Street, just up from the highway. It hardly looks like a bike shop so keep your eyes peeled. Moloka'i Bicycle has the largest rental pool on the island, aside from those at the ranch. Rental rates are: regular mountain bikes, $15 a day or $75 a week; mountain bikes with front suspension, $20 a day or $85 a week; road bikes, $25 a day or $110 a week. Guided ride rates run $65 per person (minimum two) for three to five hour rides and $45 per person for one- to three-hour rides. Call

808/553-5740 for reservations. The company's website is www.bikehawaiicom/molokaibicycle.

Molokai Ranch offers several levels of bike riding over numerous courses across their ranch land. Half- and full-day guided tours are run for $30 and $75, respectively, and traverse a great deal of the rugged ranch land. These course offer trails for the beginner to the advanced rider. A night ride is also an option. Renting bikes from the Outfitters Center is $20 a day or $30 for full suspension.

Moloka'i Outdoor Activities, 808/553-4477, at Hotel Moloka'i, rents beach cruisers for $15 a day or $65 a week; ATBs for $17.50 a day or $75 a week; and mountain bikes for $23 a day or $105 a week.

Golf

Moloka'i's two golf courses are as different as custom-made and rental clubs. The **Kaluakoi Golf Course,** 808/552-2739, is a picture-perfect beauty that would challenge any top pro. Laid out by master links designer Ted Robinson, it's out at the Kaluakoi Resort. The 6,564-yard, par-72 course winds through a beautiful setting including five holes strung right along the beach. There's a complete pro shop, driving range, and practice greens. Golf lessons by the hour are also available. Greens fees for 18 holes are $45 for resort guests and $80 for nonguests; twilight specials available.

Moloka'i's other golf course is the homey **Ironwood Hills Golf Club,** 808/567-6000. Open 7 A.M.–5 P.M. daily, this rarely used but well-maintained mountain course is nine holes, par 34, and 3,086 yards long. Pay the affordable greens fee to the office manager or to a groundskeeper who will come around as you play; $15 for nine holes or $20 if you want to loop the course twice. Twilight rates, club rental, riding and hand carts are also available. The course is up in the hills in Kala'e at 1,200 in elevation, just before the Meyer Sugar Mill—look for the sign. Ironwood Hills is turning from a frog to a prince. Recent work has concentrated on improving the grounds. Even today there is no pro shop or snack shop available—all these will come in time—and only a small mobile building as an office.

Tennis

Public courts are available at Moloka'i High School in Ho'olehua and at the Community Center in Kaunakakai, but you may have to reserve a spot with the office in the Mitchell Pauole Center next door for the courts in town. Two courts are available at the **Ke Nani Kai Condos,** at the Kaluakoi Resort, which are free to guests. Two courts at the **Wavecrest Condo** east of Kaunakakai on Route 450 are also free to guests.

MOLOKA'I GOLF AND TENNIS

GOLF COURSE	PAR	YARDS	FEES	CART	CLUBS
Ironwood Hills Golf Club Kala'e 808/567-6000	34	3,086	$15/9 holes $20/18 holes	$8 (9 holes) $3 (pullcart)	$12
Kaluakoi Golf Course at the Kaluakoi Resort 808/552-2739	72	6,564	$45 guest $80 nonguest	Incl.	$11

TENNIS COURTS					
TOWN	LOCATION	TEL. (808)	FEES	NO. OF COURTS	LIGHTED
Kaunakakai	Community Center	(no phone)	none	2	Yes
Ho'olehua	Moloka'i High School	(no phone)	none	2	Yes

Hunting

Some of the best hunting on Moloka'i is on the private lands of the 54,000-acre **Molokai Ranch,** 808/552-2741, open to hunting year-round. However, the enormous fees charged by the ranch have effectively stopped hunting on their lands to all but the very determined or very wealthy. Ecological conditions may also affect hunting at certain times of the year. A permit to hunt game animals including black buck, aoudad sheep, eland antelope, and axis deer costs $400 per day for a guided hunt with an additional fee of $250 per person (up to three). Game fees are $1,000 for each of the animals, except that the trophy fee (certain animals of a certain size) is $1,500! Game bird hunting is also offered during regular state hunting season, following state rules and regulations, at $150 per day.

Public hunting lands on Moloka'i are open to anyone with a valid state hunting license. Wild goats and pigs can be hunted in various hunting units year-round on weekends and state holidays except when bird hunting is in effect. Bag limits are two animals per day. Hunting game birds (ring-necked pheasants, various quails and doves, wild turkeys, partridges, and francolins) is open on public lands from the first Saturday in November to the third Sunday in January. A special dove season runs late January through March. For full information, license, and fees contact the Division of Forestry and Wildlife, P.O. Box 347, Kaunakakai, HI 96748, 808/533-5019.

Adventure Tours

Walter Naki knows Moloka'i—its mountains, seas, shores, trails, flowers, trees, and birds. His one-man action-adventure company, **Ma'a Hawaii,** P.O. Box 1269, Kaunakakai, HI 96748, 808/558-8184, loosely translates as "used to, accustomed to, or familiar with." A native Hawaiian raised on the island and versed in its myths and mysteries, Walter has won the Hawaiian decathlon five times and has won renown in statewide spearfishing and free diving contests. If it has to do with the outdoors Walter does it. Hunting for axis deer, wild boar, or goats on private land costs $200 per day for bow hunters and $300 per day for rifle hunts (two hunters per day only). Hiking and

"camera safaris" over many of the same hunting trails cost $50 for a half day (up to six people only), while snorkeling, skin diving, spear fishing, and reef fishing are $50 per half day. Kayak, whale-watching, and north shore trips are available on request. He's one of the few who takes guests to the "backside" (north shore) of the island. Walter is a great guide, but he is definitely "fo real," absolutely genuine with no glitz or glamour. He will do everything that he can to make your day safe and enjoyable, even stopping at his friend's taro patch to give you a glimpse of preserved island life. If you seek a unique experience where you can touch the spirit of Moloka'i, travel for a day with Walter Naki.

Land Tours

Only a few limited tours are offered on Moloka'i. Mostly, it's you and your rental car. **Moloka'i Off-road Tours and Taxi,** 808/553-3369, offers half- and full-day narrated tours by air-conditioned van; reservations required. A six-hour tour for $49 hits many of the highlights of the island. Also offered is a four-hour tour of the upcountry area around Kala'e for $36. Tours start at the Kaluakoi Hotel and pick up at the airport and in Kaunakakai.

Air Tours

An amazing way to see Moloka'i—particularly its north coast—is by helicopter. This method is admittedly expensive, but dollar for dollar it is *the* most exciting way of touring and can get you places that no other means can. A handful of companies operate mostly from Maui and include overflights of Moloka'i. Though a helicopter trip will put a big hole in your budget, most agree they are among the most memorable experiences of their trip. Try **Sunshine Helicopters,** 808/871-0722 or 800/469-3000; **Hawaii Helicopters,** 808/877-3900 or 800/367-7095; and **Blue Hawaiian Helicopters,** 808/871-8844 or 800/786-2583.

Paragon Air, 808/244-3356 or 800/428-1231, does a five-island scenic flight that includes the north coast of Moloka'i. If you are lucky, your regularly scheduled flight from Kahului to Ho'olehua will also fly along the north coast and give you a glimpse, although not real close, of this spectacular line of *pali* and valley.

Activities Desk

Aside from the desk at the Kaluakoi Resort, the private concessionaire activities desk at Hotel Moloka'i, **Moloka'i Outdoor Activities,** is the only activities desk on the island—and it handles everything. The staff members here are well versed on what recreational possibilities are available on the island, and go out of their way to make it happen for you. From them you can rent bikes and kayaks, snorkel gear, surfboards and windsurfing equipment, camping gear, and a host of accessories. They can guide you on a bike tour of the coffee plantation, kayak tour inside the fringe reef, or teach you how to surf or windsurf. They even teach Hawaiian crafts classes. This company can set you up with any of the other activity providers on the island, connect you with activities on other islands, and as a travel agency, can arrange transportation, lodging, and car rental. Contact them for all your island activity needs: HC 01 Box 28, Kaunakakai, HI 96748, 808/553-4477 or 877/553 4477, web site: www.molokai-outdoors.com, email: outdoors@aloha.net. They are open Mon.–Sat. 8 A.M.–6 P.M., Saturday until 5 P.M.

SHOPPING

Coming to Moloka'i to shop is like going to Waikiki and hoping to find a grass shack on a deserted beach. Moloka'i has only a handful of shops where you can buy locally produced crafts and Hawaiiana. Far and away, most of Moloka'i's shopping is centered along Ala Malama Street in downtown Kaunakakai. All three blocks of it! Here you'll find the island's only health food store, three very good food markets, a drugstore that sells just about everything, and a clutch of souvenir shops. Away from Kaunakakai the pickin's get mighty slim. Heading west you'll find the **Kualapu'u General Store** off Route 470 on the way to Kalaupapa, and a sundries store and gift shop Kaluakoi Hotel on the far west end. The Maunaloa Road (Route 460) basically ends in Maunaloa town. Go there! The best and most interesting shop, **The Big Wind Kite Factory,** is in town and is worth a visit in its own right. It's accompanied by the **Plantation Gallery,** an intriguing souvenir shop of Hawaiian and imported items. Heading east from Kaunakakai is another shoppers' wasteland with only the sundries store at the Molokai Shores condo and the Puko'o Neighborhood Store for anything to buy.

ACCOMMODATION AND FOOD

One quick overview can paint, in broad strokes, the picture of where accommodations are located and where food can be found on Moloka'i. While seemingly enough for visitor, places to stay are not numerous. The main town of Kaunakakai has one fine renovated and refurbished island-style hotel and one condominium. To the east is another condominium, and in this eastern section of the island are the bulk of its vacation rentals and B&Bs, not surprising since the greatest number of people live in Kaunakakai and along the southeast coastline. The west end has the upper end accommodations. Opened more than 20 years ago as a top notch hideaway resort, the Kaluakoi Hotel and Golf Club has many good years and then gradually began a slide into disrepair. Surrounding this resort are three upscale condominiums. Up the hill in Maunaloa are the newest and most unusual accommodation options on the island. The Molokai Ranch started a high-end camping/activity experience a number of years ago that, through its ups and downs, has been a great experience for those lucky enough to have made the trek. In 1999, the ranch opened The Lodge, and it is now the most luxuriant accommodation on the island. Built in retro island ranch style, this operation is a gem.

Food is another item all together. Kaunakakai has a handful of small eateries, mostly geared toward the local population, but the best is the bunch is the restaurant at Hotel Moloka'i. Another to watch will be the new brewpub restaurant in town. It started brewing beer and serving food in 2000. To the east of town, there is only one place to eat, and that is the Neighborhood Store in Puko'o. After years of successful operation, the Kualapu'u Cookhouse, headquarters of "The Slow Food Chain," closed. There are rumors that it will reopen under new management, but. . .who knows? It was a good place for a bite to eat when out on the road. Places to eat at the west end are few and far

MOLOKA'I

between. The Kaluakoi Hotel has one mediocre restaurant and snack bar, so those who are staying there must go into Kaunakakai or up the hill to Maunaloa if they want something different. Those who stay at the ranch camps are provided food on site. For others there are two options. The casual Village Grill has reopened and serves food in the stonegrill cooking style. Alternately, the lodge Dining Room serves wonderful pacific rim food, and is the best restaurant on the island.

GETTING THERE

Only Hawaiian Airline, Island Air, and Pacific Wings have regularly scheduled flights to Ho'olehua Airport. Molokai Air Shuttle and Paragon Air also fly to the island but on an on-call or charter basis. Pacific Wings also flies to Kalaupapa, to connect with tours of the peninsula.

Hawaiian Airlines, 808/567-6510 on Moloka'i, 800/882-8811 in Hawaii, or 800/367-5320 Mainland, has two regularly scheduled flights each way connecting Moloka'i and Honolulu. The morning flight from Honolulu and the afternoon flight to Honolulu go through Lana'i. Flights to all other cities in Hawaii go through Honolulu.

Island Air, 808/567-6115 or 800/652-6541 Hawaii, or 800/323-3345 Mainland, offers flights connecting Moloka'i with O'ahu and Maui. There are 12 daily flights to/from Honolulu 5:50 A.M.–6:30 P.M. The two daily flights from Hana to Moloka'i go through Kahului, from where there are an additional four daily flights.

Pacific Wings, 888/575-4546, connects Moloka'i with Kahului once a day and Honolulu three times a day, using eight-seat, twin-engine Cessna 402C aircraft. It also has six flights a week connecting Kalaupapa Peninsula with the Ho'olehua Airport "up top."

Molokai Air Shuttle, 808/567-6847 Moloka'i or 808/545-4988 O'ahu, flies a Piper Aztec to/from Honolulu and Moloka'i for $59.95 roundtrip or $34.95 one-way. This is not a scheduled route: you call and let them know when you want to fly and they will tell you what's available that day. This is a very good fare, however, arrival in Honolulu is along Lagoon Drive, which is on the opposite side of the runways from the main terminal building, so it's not convenient for con-

necting flights, but is fine if you're just being picked up in the city.

Paragon Air, 808/244-3356 or 800/428-1231 Mainland, does islandwide air charters in small aircraft, including from Moloka'i to Honolulu.

Moloka'i Airport
The **Ho'olehua Airport** has a small terminal with an open-air baggage claim area to the far right, check-in counters next to that, and the waiting lounge on the left side. In the baggage claim area, Dollar and Budget have rental car booths, and each has a base yard a few steps away across the public parking lot out front. Parking runs 25 cents for two hours. Ground transportation waits at the front but doesn't hang around long after a plane arrival. There is no public transportation on Moloka'i, but one company does offer taxi service. Also at the terminal you'll have a lounge and lunch counter (6 A.M.–6 P.M. daily) with not-too-bad prices, toilets, and public telephones in the baggage claim area and in the lobby. Pick up a loaf of excellent Moloka'i bread, the best souvenir available, or a lei from the small gift shop. Tourist brochures are available from a rack in the arrival area, or from the tourist information booth if someone is on duty. On your way out of the airport, you are greeted first thing with the sign "Aloha. Slow Down. This is Moloka'i."

By Sea
The *Maui Princess* used to sail daily between Kaunakakai and Lahaina, but for economic reasons the service was stopped in 1997, affecting many businesses on Moloka'i. Island Marine, the company which operates this ship started ed ferry operation again in 2001 with the refurbished and faster *Moloka'i Princess,* which is able to make the crossing in about one hour and 15 minutes. Although the schedule is open to change, the yacht currently runs Mon.–Sat., leaving Kaunakakai at 6 A.M. and returning from Lahaina at 5 P.M. The fares are $40 one-way for adults and $20 for kids.

The *Maui Princess* does, however, offer several day tour packages to Moloka'i from Maui. The cruise/car and cruise/van tour packages run $139 per person. For information and reservations contact the company at 808/667-6165 or 800/275-6969, website: www.mauiprincess.com.

GETTING AROUND

Rental Cars

Moloka'i offers a limited choice of car rental agencies—make reservations to avoid being disappointed. Rental car booths close after the last flight of the day has arrived. Rental car companies on Moloka'i dislike their cars being used on dirt roads (there are plenty) and strongly warn against it. No jeeps are available from the national chains but the island-based company does rent them. **Dollar Rent A Car,** 808/567-6156 or 800/800-4000, provides professional and friendly service; **Budget Rent A Car,** 808/567-6877 or 800/527-7000, is another option. These companies have booths and base yards only at the airport. Pick up a copy of the *Molokai Drive Guide* magazine for maps and useful information on sights and activities.

The new guy in the market is a local company called **Island Kine Auto Rental.** In Kaunakakai, its slant is to rent the kind of vehicle that the big companies don't and to be competitive in pricing with the kind that they do. It has a small fleet of four-door compact and midsize sedans, 4WDs, 10- and 15-passenger vans, and pickups, all used but well maintained. As with the other companies, these cars are not to be taken off paved roads. Let them know what kind of car you need and for how long and they'll let you know what the rate will be. They even do a courtesy pick up at the airport and give you a brief introduction to what's to see and do on the island. For further information and reservations, contact the company at P.O. Box 1018, Kaunakakai, HI 96748, 808/553-5242, fax 808/553-3880, website: http://molokai-car-rental.com, email: info@molokai-car-rental-com.

There are only four gas stations on the island: two in Kaunakakai, one in Maunaloa, and one at the Neighborhood Store in Puko'o, on the eastern end of the island. Fill your tank before turning in your rental car as there is not a station at or near the airport. Gas prices are generally 20–30 cents higher on Moloka'i than on Maui.

Public Transportation

No public bus transportation services Moloka'i. **Moloka'i Off-road Tours and Taxi,** 808/553-3369, does transfers to and from the airport 8 A.M.–6 P.M. for $7 per person ($8 after hours), minimum of three.

Hitchhiking

The old thumb gives fair to good results on Moloka'i. Most islanders say they prefer to pick up hitchhikers who are making an effort by walking along, instead of lounging by the side of the road. It shows that you don't have a car but do have some pride. Getting a ride to or from Kaunakakai and the airport is usually fairly easy. To other destinations, it's more problematic.

INFORMATION AND SERVICES

Telephone numbers for service agencies that you might find useful: emergency, 911; police, 808/553-5355; weather 808/552-2477; County Parks and Recreation, 808/553-3204; Division of Forestry, 808/553-1745; Hawaiian Home Lands, 808/567-6104 or 808/567 6296; Kaunakakai post office, 808/553-5845.

Moloka'i Visitors Association

The MVA, 808/553-3876 or 800/553-0404 statewide, or 800/800-6367 Mainland and Canada, can help with every aspect of your trip to Moloka'i. From their office at the intersection of the highway and the wharf road, they dispense up-to-the-minute information on hotels, car rentals, activities, and services, and some brochures and island maps. Moloka'i Visitors Association should be your first contact if you are contemplating a visit to Moloka'i. Open Mon.–Sat. regular business hours. For more information log on to www.molokai-hawaii.com, email: mva@molokai-hawaii.com.

For general information about the island, try the websites www.molokai-aloha.com and www.molokai.com.

Banks

There are two banks on the island, both in downtown Kaunakakai and each open Mon.–Thurs. 8:30 A.M.–4 P.M., Friday until 6 P.M. Each has an ATM. They are Bank of Hawaii, 808/553-3273, and American Savings Bank, 808/553-3263.

Library

The Moloka'i Public Library (1937), 808/553-5483,

is next to the government buildings at the west end of town. While its hours may vary by season, they generally are Monday, Tuesday, Thursday, and Friday 9 A.M.–5 P.M., Wednesday noon–8 P.M.

Newspapers
For a local look at what's happening on the island of Moloka'i, check out either of the island's two newspapers. The larger and more mainstream is *The Dispatch* (www.aloha.net/~mmkdisp), published in Maunaloa, while the more humble *Moloka'i Advertiser-News* (www.hotspots-hawaii .com/man.html), is published in Kaunakakai by solar power.

Medical
Moloka'i is a small place with a small population so there is not as much available here in the way of medical treatment as on Maui or the other larger islands. Yet Moloka'i has Moloka'i General Hospital, 808/553-5331, which is at the end of Home 'Olu Street just above Ala Malama Avenue in Kaunakakai. There are half a dozen doctors on the island and half as many dentists. Try Molikai Drugs, 808/553-5790, in the Kamo'i Professional Center, one block off the main drag, for prescription drugs, first aid items, potions, lotions, and sundries. It's open Mon.–Sat. 8:45 A.M.–5:45 P.M.

Laundry
Moloka'i Dry Cleaning, next to the Pizza Cafe, is open Mon.–Fri. 9 A.M.–5 P.M., Saturday 9 A.M.–1 P.M.. Across from the Moloka'i Drive Inn, the Ohana Laundromat is open 6 A.M.–9 P.M. daily. There is also a small laundromat behind Outpost Natural Foods.

KAUNAKAKAI

No matter where you're headed on the island you have to pass through Kaunakakai (Beach Landing), the tiny port town and economic and government center that is Moloka'i's hub. An hour spent walking the three blocks of Ala Malama Street, the main drag, and its side streets, gives you a good feeling for what's happening. If you need to do any banking, mailing, or shopping for staples, Kaunakakai's the place. Hikers, campers, and even day-trippers should get all they need here since shops, both east and west, are few and far between, and mostly understocked. Evenings are quiet here, with no neon or glamour, no traffic or stop lights, and that's just the way that people want to keep it.

SIGHTS

Head toward the water and you'll see **Kaunakakai wharf** stretching out into the shallow harbor for a half mile. Not a natural harbor, the approach to the wharf had to be cleared through coral. Townsfolk like to drive their cars onto the causeway, but it's much better to walk out. On the landing are the harbor office, public toilets, boat moorings, a boat launch, and the Moloka'i Ice House, an ice producer and place that sells the freshest fish on the island. The twice-weekly barge to the island stops here and commercial fishing and sailing boats leave from its moorings. The fishing from the wharf isn't great but it's handy and you never can tell. If you decide to stroll out, look for the remains of Lot Kamehameha's summer house, "Malama" (circa 1864), a raised platform surrounded by stone, near the canoe shed along the shore west of the road. This site and the adjacent land is now part of the as-yet undeveloped Malama Cultural Park, which only has restrooms, parking, and access to the water. To its side is the Moloka'i Voyaging Canoe Society building.

Kapuaiwa Coconut Grove
A three-minute drive or a 15-minute walk west brings you to this 11-acre royal coconut grove planted in the 1860s for Kamehameha V (Lot Kamehameha), or Kapuaiwa to his friends. Kapuaiwa Coconut Grove was originally built because there were seven pools here in which the *ali'i* would bathe, and the grove was planted to provide shade and seclusion. The grove also symbolically provided the king with food for the duration of his life. The grove has diminished from the 1,000 trees originally planted, but more than enough remain to give a sense of grandeur

KAUNAKAKAI

MOLOKAI GENERAL HOSPITAL

OILI

HOME OIU

KOLAPA

LAUNDROMAT
OUTPOST NATURAL FOODS
SEE DETAIL
ST. SOPHIA'S CHURCH
SUNDOWN DELI
PAASCUA STORE
OVIEDO'S
GYM
POOL

GAS
MOLOKA'I FISH AND DIVE
MOLOKA'I MANGO
ALA MALAMA ST.
FIRE DEPARTMENT
TENNIS COURTS

STATE OFFICE BUILDING
FRIENDLY MARKET
POST OFFICE
POLICE

LIBRARY
K. FINE ART GALLERY
KAMO'I
MITCHELL PAUOLE CENTER
COUNTY OFFICES

MOLOKA'I WINE N' SPIRITS
KANEMITSU BAKERY

To West End
BANK
ALOHI
BALLPARK
LOURDES
ROBANG'S
IMAMURA'S

460
GAS
MOLOKA'I BICYCLE
KAMO'I PROFESSIONAL CENTER
TAKES
MISAKI'S
IMPORTS GIFT SHOP

MAUNALOA HWY.
MVA
ACE HARDWARE
LAUNDROMAT
'AILOA

MOLOKA'I BREWING COMPANY
MOLOKA'I DRIVE-IN

HIO
MOLOKA'I PIZZA CAFE
MOLOKA'I DRY CLEANING
MOLOKA'I SURF
SCHOOL
OKI
450
"DUKE" MALIN REGIONAL PARK

KAUNAKAKAI
MOHALA
KAMEHAMEHA V HWY.
To East End

MALAMA CULTURAL PARK
To the Wharf
BEACH
SCALE NOT AVAILABLE

"MALAMA" HOUSE SITE ★

MOLOKA'I

to the spot. Royal coconut palms are some of the tallest of the species, and besides providing nuts, they served as natural beacons pinpointing the spot inhabited by royalty. These that remain are more than 80 feet tall. Now the grove has a parklike atmosphere and mostly you'll have it to yourself. Pay heed to the signs warning of falling coconuts. An aerial bombardment of hefty five-pounders will rudely customize the hood of your rental car. Definitely do not walk around under the palms if the wind is up. Just next to the grove is **Kioea Park,** where camping is permitted for $5 a day through the Hawaiian Home Lands Department.

Church Row

Sin has no chance against the formidable defensive line of churches standing altar-to-altar along the road across from Kapuaiwa Coconut Grove. A grant from Hawaiian Home Lands provides that a church can be built on this stretch of land to any congregation that includes a minimum number of Hawaiian-blooded parishioners. The churches are basically one-room affairs that wait quietly until Sunday morning when worshippers come from all over the island. Let there

be no doubt: old Satan would find no customers around here, as all spiritual loopholes are covered by one denomination or another. Visitors are always welcome, so come join in. Be wary of this stretch of road—all services seem to let out at the same time on Sunday morning, causing a minuscule traffic jam.

In-Town Parks

Right in the center of town is the Mitchell Pauole Center, which has the police, fire, county, and parks and recreation offices. Directly across the street is the Kaunakakai Ball Park; behind it are the community tennis courts and swimming pool, and more open spaces for athletic games. Adjoining this county land, but with access from the highway, is the new "Duke" Malin Regional park, which has additional ball fields, restrooms, and a pavilion with picnic tables.

Classic Fishponds

Moloka'i is known for its fishponds, which were a unique and highly advanced form of aquaculture prevalent from at least the early 13th century. Moloka'i, because of an abundance of shallow, flat waters along its southern shore, was

small Moloka'i church

J.D. BISIGNANI

able to support a network of these ponds numbering more than five dozen during their heyday. Built and tended by the commoners for the royal *ali'i*, they provided succulent fish that could easily be rounded up at any time for a meal or impromptu feast. The ponds were formed in a likely spot by erecting a wall of stone or coral. It was necessary to choose an area that had just the right tides to keep the water circulating, but not so strong as to destroy the encircling walls. Openings were left in the wall for this purpose. **Kaloko'eli Pond** is about two miles east of Kaunakakai along Route 450. Easily seen from the road, it's an excellent example of the classic fishpond. You can proceed a few more minutes east until you come to a coconut grove just a half mile before One Ali'i Beach Park. Stop here for a sweeping view of **Ali'i Fishpond,** another fine example.

ACCOMMODATIONS

Besides camping, Kaunakakai has only two places to stay. Head here for adequate accommodations if you want to save money.

Molokai Shores

This condo, only 1.5 miles east of downtown Kaunakakai, has full kitchens, large living rooms, and separate bedrooms. The white walls contrasting with the dark brown floors are hung with tasteful prints. Plenty of lounge furniture is provided along with a table for outside dining and barbecues. The upper floor of the three-story building offers an open-beam ceiling including a full loft. Some units have an extra bedroom built into the loft. All units look out over the ocean. The grounds are very well kept, quiet, and restful. The swimming pool fronts the gentle but unswimmable beach, and nearby is a classic fishpond still in good shape. The only drawback is the architecture: it's pragmatic and neat, but not beautiful. Rates are $144 one-bedroom oceanfront, $189 two-bedroom oceanfront; $15 for each additional person. For information, call 808/553-5954 direct or call central reservations, 800/535-0085, fax 800/633-5085. A Marc Resorts Hawaii management property.

Hotel Moloka'i

This 45-room hotel was built in 1966 by an architect (Mr. Roberts) enamored with the South Seas, who wanted to give his hotel a Polynesian village atmosphere. He succeeded. The buildings are two-story, semi–A-frames with sway-backed roofs covered with split-wood shingles that fit snugly in a coconut grove next to the water. The upstairs units are larger and more airy that the downstairs studios, but both feature lanai, phone, TV, a small refrigerator, and daily housekeeping service. This hotel had its heyday before the big resort and the big money came to the island. After a change of ownership

MOLOKA'I

in 1998, Hotel Moloka'i was closed for extensive room renovation and landscaping. By the beginning of 1999, the hotel was once again entertaining guests and has again become a happening place on the island. In a way, it's a throwback to the casual and slower '60s. Not only tourists come looking for this slice of Hawaii, but also Hawaiian residents come to visit. Hotel Moloka'i was always known for good dining, weekend live entertainment, a well-appointed gift shop, a swimming pool, and a poolside lounge, and it now continues that tradition. The restaurant and bar are open daily and rooms run $80–135. For the convenience of guests, there is an on-site laundry facility and the island's most comprehensive activities desk. Hotel Moloka'i is just before mile marker 2, east of town. The only drawback is that the hotel is next to the highway, but overall traffic noise is not much of a concern. Overall, this is a great choice. For current information on dining and room availability, contact Hotel Moloka'i directly at P.O. Box 1020, Kaunakakai, HI 96748, 808/553-5347, fax 808/553-5047; or Castle Resorts and Hotels, 800/367-5004 Mainland and Canada or 800/272-5275 in Hawaii, website: www.hotel-molokai.com.

FOOD

Like the hotel scene, Moloka'i has only a handful of places to eat, but among these are veritable institutions that if missed make your trip to Moloka'i incomplete. The following are all on Kaunakakai's main street, or just a minute away. Just ask anyone where they are.

The **Kanemitsu Bakery**, 808/553-5855, has been in business for more than 70 years and is still run by the same family. The bakery is renowned for its numerous varieties Moloka'i breads. Mrs. Kanemitsu's cookies are scrumptious, and anyone contemplating a picnic or a day hike should load up. The bakery is open Wed.–Mon. 5:30 A.M.–6:30 P.M. At the front counter you can order a sandwich made from bread that is baked in the back, and none are more than $4. There's a lunch counter too where you can get eggs, pancakes, omelets, and local Hawaiian foods, open Wed.–Mon. 5:30–11:30 A.M. Kanemitsu Bakery is known far and wide

for its "hot bread." In fact, traditionally this is one thing that you had to bring back for family and friends if you made a trip to Moloka'i. Fresh-baked hot bread is available from the bakery only 10 P.M.–3 A.M. Go down the alley next to Imamura's and duck through the chain link fence to reach the bakery's back door. If the door isn't open, you may have to bang on it. Tell the person how many loaves you want and they'll be brought to the door. It's perhaps best to check out the price of bread during the day.

Rabang's serves a variety of inexpensive Filipino food, in addition to the eggs and omelets for breakfast, local-style plate lunches for lunch, and ice cream. Next door is Rabang's Market for a limited selection of groceries, some prepared foods, and a few true Filipino delicacies like balut. Open 7:30 A.M.–10 P.M. daily.

Oviedo's Lunch Counter, 808/553-5014, in the last building on the left along Ala Malama, is a strictly Filipino restaurant where every item on the menu is only about $7.75. Choose from ethnic selections like pork adobo, chicken papaya, tripe stew, sweet and sour ribs, pig's feet, mongo beans, and eggplant pimakbet. Oviedo's is small, run-down, but clean. The decor is worn linoleum floors and Formica tables. Basically a take-out place, there are a few tables inside if you care to eat there.

Next door to Oviedo's is the newer **Sundown Deli**, 808/553-3713. Making reasonably priced sandwiches, salads, and soups in a shop that's hardly big enough to turn around, this place is establishing a fine reputation. Open Mon.–Fri. 10:30 A.M.–6 P.M., until 2 P.M. on Saturday; order at the counter or call your order in to pick up.

Kamo'i Snack 'N Go is in the new Kamo'i Professional Center. Stop here for Dave's ice cream, candies, cold drinks, and other snacks. Open daily until 9 P.M.

The **Moloka'i Drive-In,** open daily 6 A.M.–10 P.M., is along Kamehameha Highway in a bluish-gray, flat-roofed building that has the look of the '60s. You order from the window and then take your meal to eat under an awning, or step into the air-conditioned inside to find a few tables. Breakfast offers omelets, eggs, Spam, bacon, or ham along with sides of rice, hash browns, or toast for under $5. Lunch is chili dogs, nachos, subs, fish, shrimp, and chicken burgers, with a special featured every day. The

MOLOKA'I

drive-in is actually tasteful, bright, and clean. It's a local place with decent food and very affordable prices, but you won't find food for the health-conscious here. It would make a great stop for a picnic lunch to go, especially if you're heading to Halawa and points east.

Don't let the name **Moloka'i Pizza Cafe,** 808/553-3288, fool you! Although this bright and cheery restaurant makes designer pizza, the emphasis is on *café*. Wharfside of the junction of Routes 450 and 460, this eatery is open daily 10 A.M.–10 P.M. (until 11 P.M. on Friday and Saturday, from 11 A.M. on Sunday). The café has fast food with a flare. Pizzas come in three sizes and range in price from a Moloka'i small for $8.25 up to their giant Big Island with everything including green peppers, onions, sausage, beef, and bacon for $22.50. Sandwiches can be an Italian sub laden with turkey, ham, and roast beef, or a plump fresh-baked pocket sandwich. Hearty appetites will enjoy meals like pasta in marinara sauce, barbecued spareribs (great!), or the fresh catch. Order it! Caught in these waters, the fish comes in the back door, is filleted, cooked, and served to you as fresh as it can be. Wednesday, Thursday, and Sunday specials are Mexican, Hawaiian *laulau*, and prime rib. Desserts too! The Moloka'i Pizza Cafe delivers—perfect for anyone staying in a condo. Take-out available.

The **Hotel Moloka'i Restaurant,** 808/553-5347, is the fanciest place in town and the best restaurant on the island east of Maunaloa. Right on the water, it has the superb location. Breakfast, lunch, and dinner are served every day of the week, and there are always breakfast and dinner specials. Nightly entertainment for guests consists of an hour or so of music by a local group, and on the weekends, local and off-island bands play live dance music into the night. Breakfasts are a mixture of standard American and island treats, while lunch is mostly salads and sandwiches with a few other plate entrées. The kitchen shines best at dinner, when you can order such items as fresh catch of the day, coconut shrimp, paniolo-style pork ribs, or an herbed and charbroiled chicken breast, all for less than $18 an entré. This is tasty food at good value.

The newest eating establishment in town is also a brewery. **Moloka'i Brewing Company,** 808/553-3946, at 10 Mohala St., brews several types of beer on premises, from a sweet mild ale to a typical pale ale and rich dark brown porter. Hours of operation are Sun.–Thurs. 6:30 A.M.–9 P.M., Friday and Saturday until 11 P.M., serving breakfast, lunch, and dinner. Various *pu pu* run $6.95; sandwiches, mostly of the meat and fish variety, are less than $8.95, and fish plates like encrusted mahi mahi run $12.50. It's a good stop for a cold one and a quick bite, and you can be assured that they'll work out the kinks over the months.

Outpost Natural Foods, 808/553-3377, serves wholesome, healthy, nutritious quick foods from its inside window Sun.–Fri. 10 A.M.–3 P.M. Here you can find various sandwiches for less than $6, burritos for up to $4.25, salads, veggie and tempeh burger around $5, and the daily lunch specials for under $6. The best vegetarian food on the island. In addition, there is an assortment of fresh juices and smoothies. While there, pick up any groceries that you'll need for your time on the island.

If you're in the mood for a bite to eat before you leave the island, the lunch counter at the airport has burgers, sandwiches, and plate lunches. It's open whenever the terminal building is open. If you need to fortify yourself with a drink before you get on the plane, slip around the side to the adjacent lounge. It's open every day until around 8:30 P.M.

For fresh fish, try the **Ice House** on the Kaunakakai wharf. Open roughly 9 A.M.–6 P.M. daily, they carry the freshest fish on the island and have a good selection of *poki,* a marinated raw fish.

SHOPPING

Moloka'i Fish and Dive in downtown Kaunakakai, 808/553-5926, sounds very practical, and it is, but it has a good selection of souvenirs, T-shirts and fashions, books (including a couple written by shop owner James Brocker), maps of Moloka'i, island music, jewelry, and a good assortment of film along with its fishing equipment. Basically, a little bit of everything. They can give you detailed information about fishing and water sports on Moloka'i, and they rent some water gear like snorkel sets, boogie boards, or a rod and reel for $9 a day.

Moloka'i Island Creations, connected to Moloka'i Fish and Dive and also open daily 9:30 A.M.–4:30 P.M., features authentic Moloka'i designs on ladies' blouses, tank tops, and men's T-shirts. It also has original Moloka'i glassware, china, and porcelain, along with Hawaiian cards and notebooks. Fashions also include pareu, children's alohawear, shorts, hats, aloha shirts, mu'umu'u, swimwear, a good selection of jewelry, and a rack of cosmetics and perfumes in island scents.

Imamura's, open daily except Sunday 8:45 A.M.–5:45 P.M., is a very friendly down-home shop that sells everything from flip-flops to fishnets. It also specializes in lei-making needles and has a great selection of inexpensive luggage. The shelves hold beach mats and hats, T-shirts, pots and pans, and kitchen utensils. The sales staff are all friendly and slow-paced; when you return, they'll smile a welcome.

Across the street is the newer **Imports Gift Shop,** which has an assortment of clothing, gifts, souvenirs, post cards, and a few snacks. Open Mon.–Sat. until 9 P.M.

Lourdes Shoes Clothing and Jewelry is a basic local shop offering a smattering of alohawear, handbags, jogging shoes, baby clothes, towels, and women's clothing.

Moloka'i Mango, 808/553-3300, Mon.–Sat. 9 A.M. 7:30 P.M., is a place to find entertainment for the evening. There is no movie theater in Kaunakakai, but since 1998 there has been one in Maunaloa. People who want to watch a big screen show must now travel to the west end for it—and they do. If not, rent your movie here.

For those into wholesome health food, **Outpost Natural Foods,** 808/553-3377, is at 70 Makaena Place across from the government buildings. It's the only store of its kind on Moloka'i, but it's excellent. It's open Mon.–Thurs. 9 A.M.–6 P.M., Sunday until 5 P.M., and Friday until 4 P.M. The fruits and vegetables are locally and organically grown as much as possible. Along with the usual assortment of health foods you'll find bulk grains, granola, nuts, and dried fruits. The jam-packed shelves also hold rennetless cheese, fresh yogurt, nondairy ice cream, vitamins, minerals, supplements, and a good selection of herbs, oils, spices, and natural health care products. If you can't find what you need, ask Dennis, the owner, or the general manager on duty. The

juice bar, open Sun.–Fri. 10 A.M.–3 P.M., is a great place for a healthy lunch and cold drink.

For general shopping along Ala Malama Street, the **Friendly Market,** open Mon.–Fri. 8:30 A.M.–8:30 P.M., Saturday to 6:30 P.M., is by far the best-stocked grocery store on Moloka'i. There's a community bulletin board outside. It might list cars for sale, Hawaiian genealogies, or fund-raising sushi sales. Have a look!

Just down the street **Takes Variety Store,** which also carries hardware, is open daily except Saturday. **Misaki's Groceries and Dry Goods** a few steps farther along sell just about everything in food and general merchandise that you'll require. Open daily.

For that special evening, try **Moloka'i Wines 'n Spirits,** open daily until late evening, which has a very good selection of vintage wines, beer, and liquor, as well as gourmet treats. Although not the only place on Moloka'i that sells wine and beer, it is the only shop on the island with such selection.

On the second floor of the Moloka'i Center across from the library is **Kamakana Fine Arts Gallery,** 808/553-8520. This gallery is the only such art gallery on the island and is an important forum for Moloka'i island artists to display their work, which includes hand painted, "quilt design" paper, turned wooden bowls, exquisite pencil drawings, cloth quilts, and ukulele. The gallery is open Mon.–Fri. 9:30 A.M.–5:30 P.M. and Saturday until 2 P.M. Stop in and support Moloka'i artists or at just least peruse what's being shown. You'll certainly find something that pleases.

Moloka'i Drugs, 808/553-5790, open daily 8:45 A.M.–5:45 P.M., closed Sunday, is the only full-service pharmacy and drugstore on the island. Don't let the name fool you because it sells much more than potions and drugs. You can buy anything from sunglasses to film, watches, toys, baby food, small appliances, and garden supplies. It has the best selection of film on Moloka'i, with a very good selection of books, especially Hawaiiana. Film processing, including slides, takes 48 hours. It too has moved from its spot on the main street to the town's newest mall, the small Kamo'i Professional Center, one street back. Also in this center is **Kamo'i Snack 'N Go** for ice cream, candies, snacks, and cold drinks; open daily until 9 P.M.

MOLOKA'I

Moloka'i Surf, open daily except Sunday 9 A.M.–6 P.M. in its shop along the highway, has bathing suits, sandals, T-shirts, shorts, and alohawear.

If you're in town on Saturday morning, be sure to have a look at the **farmers' market,** held 7 A.M.–noon on the sidewalk in front of the bank buildings, for local produce and craft items.

The two full service gas station and mechanic shops on the island are **Rawlin's Chevron Service,** 808/553-3214, at the corner of the highway and the wharf road; and **Kalama'a Service,** 808/553-5586, one block up. These two shops generally have the same hours: Mon.–Thurs. 6:30 A.M.–8:30 P.M., Friday and Saturday until 9 P.M., and Sunday 7 A.M.–6 P.M.

EAST TO HALAWA VALLEY

The east end of Moloka'i, from Kaunakakai to Halawa Valley, was at one time the most densely populated area of the island. At almost every milepost is a historical site or point of interest, many dating from precontact times. A string of tiny churches attests to the coming of the missionaries in the mid-1800s, and a crash-landing site was an inauspicious harbinger of the deluge of Mainlanders bound for Hawaii in the 1900s. This entire stretch of Route 450 is almost entirely undeveloped, and the classical sites such as *heiau,* listening stones, and old battlegrounds are difficult to find, although just a stone's throw from the road. The local people like it this way, as most would rather see the south shore of Moloka'i remain unchanged. A determined traveler might locate the sites, but unless you have local help, it will mean hours tramping around in marshes or on hillsides with no guarantee of satisfaction. Some sites such as **'Ili'ili'opae Heiau** are on private land and require permission to visit. It's as if the spirits of the ancient *kahuna* protect this area.

SIGHTS

It's a toss-up whether the best part about heading out to the east end is the road itself or the reward of Halawa Valley at the end. Only 30 miles long, it takes 90 minutes to drive. The road slips and slides around corners, bends around huge boulders, and dips down here and there into coves and inlets. Out on the far end, the cliff face and protruding stones have been painted white so that you can avoid an accident, especially at night. Sometimes the ocean and road are so close that spray splatters your windshield. Suddenly you'll round a bend to see an idyllic house surrounded by palm trees with a gaily painted boat gently rocking in a protected miniature cove. Behind is a valley of verdant hills with colors so vibrant they shimmer. You negotiate a hairpin curve and there are Lana'i and Maui, black on the horizon, contrasted against the waves as they come crashing in foamy white and blue. Down the road chugs a pickup truck full of local people. They wave you a "hang loose" as their sincere smiles light up your already glorious day. Out in one of the innumerable bays are snorkelers, while beyond the reef, surfers glide in exhilarating solitude.

The local people think of the road as "their road." Why not? They use it as a sidewalk, playground, and extension of their backyards. Dogs snooze on it, while the rumps of grazing stock are only inches away from your fender. The speed limit is 35, but go slower and enjoy it more. The mile markers stop at mile 17, then four miles farther you come to the best part. Here, the well-tended two-lane highway with the yellow stripe plays out. The road gets old and bumpy, but the scenery gets much more spectacular. It's about nine miles from where the bumpy part begins until you reach the overlook at Halawa Valley. Come with a full tank of gas, plenty of drinking water, a picnic lunch, and your sense of wonder.

One Ali'i Beach Park

A few minutes east of Kaunakakai the road brings you to a stand of perhaps 80 coconut palms, a place where you can get an excellent view of one of the string of fishponds that are famous in this area. One Ali'i Beach Park, only a few minutes farther along, is actually split into two units. Although this park is open for camping, it's too close to the road, not well shaded, and a *a scenic coconut grove and fishpond typical of east Moloka'i*

MOLOKA'I

bit too overused to be comfortable. The swimming here is only fair for those who like a challenging surf, but excellent for families with little children who want calm waters. Restrooms and showers are available and the grounds are generally in good shape. Those not camping here would find it pleasant enough for a short stop, but it's nothing compared with what's farther east along the road.

A View from the Heights
About two minutes past One Ali'i, Makanui Road (the sign says Kawela Plantation I) leads up the hillside on the *mauka* side of the road. A two-minute ride up this road exposes the beginnings of a condo development. As you gain height (one of the only roads that allows you to do so) you'll have an excellent view of the coastline with a panorama of the fishponds below and Lana'i and Maui floating on the sea. Beyond this road are two others just like it, leading into a largely undeveloped subdivision with much the same overview.

Kawela
The Kawela area was a scene of tragedy and triumph in Moloka'i's history. Here was **Pakuhiwa,** the battleground where Kamehameha I totally vanquished the warriors of Moloka'i on his way to conquering O'ahu. In nearby Kawela Gulch are the remains of **Pu'ukaua,** the fortress that Kamehameha overran. The fortress oddly

doubled as a *pu'uhonua,* a temple of refuge, where the defeated could find sanctuary. Once the battle had been joined, and the outcome inevitable, the vanquished could find peace and solace in the very area that they had so recently defended.

Today the area offers refuge as **Kakahai'a Beach County Park** and across the highway, the **Kakahai'a National Wildlife Refuge. The** beach park is not used heavily: it, too, is close to the road. This is also an excellent area for coconut trees, with many nuts lying on the ground for the taking. The refuge is an area where birdwatchers can still be captivated by the sight of rare endemic birds.

Kamalo to Puko'o
This six-mile stretch is loaded with historical sites. Kamalo is one of Moloka'i's natural harbors and was used for centuries before most of the island commerce moved to Kaunakakai. In the late 1800s, **Kamalo Wharf** was the island's principal landing site—turn off the highway at mile marker 10, just at the bend on the road. There may be some fishing shacks here, and outrigger canoes from a local club. Tracks once ran out on the wood and stone "mall" to help unload ships. Only remnants of this pier remain. From here, turn around and have a look at the mountains. You'll be facing the highest point on the island.

Saint Joseph Church, next in line, was built in 1876 by Father Damien and restored in 1995.

It's small, no more than 16 by 30 feet, and very basic. Inside is a small wooden altar adorned with flowers. A picture of Father Damien and one of St. Joseph adorn the walls. Outside is a black metal sculpture of Damien and a small graveyard. It is said that Father Damien purposefully located the church here, to offer the Hawaiians an alternative to giving offerings at Pu'ili Heiau, which lies just inland.

One mile or so past St. Joseph's is the **Smith and Bronte Landing Site.** These two aviators safely crash-landed their plane here on July 14, 1927, completing the first trans-Pacific civilian flight in just over 25 hours. All you can see is a mangrove swamp, but it's not hard to imagine the relief of the men as they set foot even on soggy land after crossing the Pacific. They started a trend that would bring more than six million people a year to the islands. A mile or beyond that is **Keawanui Fishpond.** At 54 acres and with a 2000 foot long wall, it is the largest on the island. The Wavecrest Resort Condominium is nearby at mile marker 13.

Before Puko'o are three noteworthy sites. **Kalua'aha Church** looks like a fortress with its tiny slit windows and three-foot-thick plastered walls and buttresses. Built in 1844 by the Protestant missionaries Reverend and Mrs. Hitchcock, it was the first Christian church on Moloka'i and is considered by some to be the most significant building on the island. Used for worship until the 1940s, it has since fallen into disuse. In 1967, the bell and steeple came down, the roof is caving in, and the rest is mostly in ruins. While parishioners had repair plans, it is doubtful that the structure can be saved without major rehabilitation.

Our Lady of Sorrows Church, another built by Father Damien in 1874 and rebuilt in 1966, is next. Inside are beautiful pen-and-ink drawings of the Stations of the Cross imported from Holland. Mass on Sunday at 7:15 A.M. Across the street is a fine example of a fishpond.

Following on the ocean side is the deep shade of the **Mapulehu Mango Grove,** one of the largest in the world with more than 2,000 trees and 32 varieties. Planted by the Hawaiian Sugar Co. in the 1930s in an attempt to diversify, but now owned by the Bishop Estate, the trees came from all over the world, including Brazil, India, and Formosa. Unfortunately, most of the United States was not educated about eating exotic fruits, so the mangos rotted on the tree unpicked, and the grove became overgrown. While mangos are now well known and these trees still producing prodigiously, it seems that the cost would be too high to trim this grove back into shape to make it economical. So the grove still stands unused and uncared for. To compound matters, the Mediterranean fruit fly has become a problem.

Then comes **'Ili'ili'opae Heiau,** one of Hawai'i's most famous human-sacrifice temples, and a university of sorcery, as it were, where *kahuna* from other islands were tutored. All of the wooden structures on the 286 by 87 foot stone platform have long since disappeared. Legend holds that all of the stone was carried across the island from Wailau Valley and perfectly fitted in one night of amazing work. Legend also holds that the sorcerers of 'Ili'ili'opae once sacrificed two sons of a local *kahuna* for some childish misbehavior at the temple. Outraged, he appealed to a powerful shark-god for justice. The god sent a flash flood to wipe out the evil sorcerers, washing them into the sea where the shark-god and other sharks he had called for the feast waited to devour them. Since the temple is now on private land it is necessary to receive permission to visit it. This *heiau* is now on the National Register of Historic Places. Tours of the *heiau* and nearby Mapulehu Mango Grove are given by Moloka'i Horse and Wagon Ride.

At Puko'o, near mile marker 16, is the private **Mana'e Canoe Club** with its well-tended lawns and tiny inlets. There have been controversies about public access to the beach on the bay across from the canoe club, which has been the norm for generations. The situation culminated in public protests and walks to the beach. There is, however, public access to the old wharf area directly west of the canoe club, but is only fair for swimming. There is also beach access on the east side of this lagoon, where there is better swimming.

Just past Puko'o is the **octopus stone,** a large stone painted white next to the road. It is believed that this signifies a cave inhabited by a mythical octopus, and that the stone still retains magical powers. Across the road are the remains of **Paikalani Taro Patch,** reputedly to have been three acres in size. Said to have been constructed by Pi'ilani, king of Maui, both Kamehameha I and Kamehameha V got taro to make poi from it.

More East End Beaches

Waialua Beach, also called Peabody Beach, almost at mile marker 19, is one of the best beaches on the island for swimming, snorkeling, and beginner surfing. A freshwater stream entering the ocean is very convenient for rinsing off.

Two minutes past mile marker 19 is a sand and coral beach where you can walk knee-deep out to the reef. At high tide, it's chest high.

Just before mile marker 20, a stone fishpond perimeter wall has been restored near to its original form, with a six-foot-wide flat top, outlet gate, and shrine to the fish deity. A grassroots restoration project, this is perhaps the best example of what a functioning fishpond looked like in centuries past.

Mile Marker 20 Beach, known locally as Murphy's Beach, with its huge strand of white sand and protected lagoon, is the main beach on the east end. Pull off at a handy spot and enjoy the great snorkeling, although the swimming is only mediocre. It's very safe and perfect for a family outing. Just past the beach there is a pull off parking area on a rock point. At times, local youngsters come here to jump off the rocks into the water. In and out of another bay, you come to Pohakuloa, also called Rock Point, a well-known surfers spot.

Note: All of these beaches have sharp coral. Wear a pair of reef walkers or good old sneakers. You do not want to go out there barefoot!

On to Halawa Valley

Past Puko'o, the road gets very spectacular. Many blow-your-horn turns pop up as you wend around the cliff face following the natural roll of the coastline. Coming in rapid succession are incredibly beautiful bays and tiny one-blanket beaches, where solitude and sunbathing are perfect. Be careful of surf conditions! Some of the fruitful valleys behind them are still cultivated in taro, and traditional community life beckons young people from throughout the islands to come and learn the old ways. Offshore is the crescent of **Moku Ho'oniki Island,** now a seabird sanctuary but used at times during World War II for bombing practice. The road swerves inland, climbing the hills to the 14,000 acres of **Pu'u O Hoku (Hill of Stars) Ranch.** People often mistake one of the ranch buildings along the road for a store. It's the ranch office, but the people inside can direct you to an overlook where you can see the famous and sacred *kukui* grove where Lanikaula, one of the most powerful sorcerers of Moloka'i, is buried. The different-looking cattle grazing these hilly pastures are French Charolais, imported by Pu'u O Hoku Ranch and now flourishing on these choice pasturelands. The road comes to a hairpin turn where it feels like you'll be airborne. Before you is the magnificent chasm of Halawa Valley with its famous waterfalls sparkling against the green of the valley's jungle walls. Hundreds of feet below, frothy aquamarine breakers roll into the bay.

Halawa Valley and Bay

This choice valley, rich in soil and watered by Halawa Stream, is believed to be the first permanent settlement on Moloka'i, dating from around A.D. 650. Your first glimpse is from an overlook along the road from which you get a spectacular panorama across the half-mile valley to Lamaloa Head forming its north wall, and westward, deep into its two-mile cleft, where lies Moaula Falls. Many people are so overwhelmed when they gaze from the overlook into Halawa that they don't really look around. Turn to your right and walk only 15 yards directly away from Halawa. This view gives a totally different perspective of a deep-V valley and the pounding surf of its rugged beach—so different from the gently arcing haven of Halawa Bay. For centuries, Halawa's farmers carved geometric terraces for taro fields until a tsunami of gigantic proportions inundated the valley in 1946 and left a plant-killing deposit of salt. Most people pulled out and left their homes and gardens to be reclaimed by the jungle.

Follow the paved road into the valley until you see a house that was obviously a church at one time. Cross Halawa Stream and follow the road as far as you can. Here you have a choice of bathing in the cool freshwater stream or in the surf of the protected bay. Don't go out past the mouth of the bay because the currents can be treacherous. This area is great for snorkeling and fishing, and is one of the only good surfing beaches on Moloka'i.

MOLOKA'I

Halawa Bay is a beach park, but it's not well maintained. There are toilet facilities and a few dilapidated picnic tables, but no official overnight camping, and the water is not potable. You can bivouac for a night on Pu'u O Hoku Ranch land at the far north end of Halawa Bay under a canopy of ironwood trees, but be aware that this area attracts rip-offs and it's not safe to leave your gear unattended.

Moa'ula Falls

One of *the* best walks on Moloka'i, mosquitoes notwithstanding, is to the famous 250-foot Moa'ula (Red Chicken) Falls. Halawa Stream can be a trickle or torrent, depending upon recent rains. If Moa'ula Falls is gushing, the stream too will be roaring. The entire area up toward the falls harbors the remains of countless taro patches and home sites. Groves of *kemani* trees mark the sites where *ali'i* were buried; their tall trunks at one time were used by Hawaiian fishermen and later by sailors as a landmark. Legend recalls that a female lizard, a *mo'o*, lives in the gorgeous pool at the bottom of the falls. Sometimes she craves a body and will drag a swimmer down to her watery lair. The only way to determine her mood is to place a *ti* leaf (abundant in the area) in the pool. If it floats you're safe, but if it sinks the lady lizard wants company—permanently! Minor gods who live in the rocks above Moa'ula Falls pool want to get into the act too. They'll drop tiny rocks on your head unless you make an offering (a penny under a *ti* leaf will do). Above Moa'ula Falls you can see **Upper Moa'ula Falls,** and beyond that the cascading brilliance of 500-foot **Hipuapua Falls.** For some years the trail to this waterfall was closed; it goes across private property. You can once again gain access but only through a guided tour led by a man who was born and raised in the valley. (See **Hiking** for details.)

ACCOMMODATIONS AND FOOD

First down the line is **Ka Hale Mala,** just less than five miles east of Kaunakakai on Kamakana Place. This vacation rental is the ground floor of a family house, set amidst a tropical garden. Here you have a large living room, full kitchen and bath, and a laundry room,

Moa'ula Falls, Halawa Valley

ROBERT NILSEN

plus use of a bicycle or snorkel gear. Rates are $70 without breakfast or $80 with. For more information, contact Cheryl Corbiell, P.O. Box 1582, Kaunakakai, HI 96748, tel./fax 808/553-9009, website: www.molokai-bnb.com, email: cpgroup@aloha.net.

Depending on your point of view the **Wavecrest Resort** is either a secluded hideaway, or stuck out in the sticks away from all the action. It's east of Kaunakakai on Route 450 just at mile marker 13. You'll find *no* hustle, bustle, anxiety, nightlife, or restaurants, and only basic supplies at the Wavecrest General Store at the entrance. This condominium sits on five well-tended acres fronting a lovely-to-look-at lagoon that isn't good for swimming. It catches the morning sun and looks directly across the Pailolo Channel to Ka'anapali on Maui. Enjoy a putting green, shuffleboard court, newly refurbished swimming pool, and two lighted tennis courts free to guests. Be aware that there are no phones in any of the units. For those who need to call, there are two pay phones at the front office. In each unit is a fully furnished kitchen, spacious living room, ceiling fan, television, and lanai. A laundry room is located on each floor for guest use. Even if you feel that you're too far from town, remember nothing is going on there anyway. Another attraction is that local fishermen may put in just next to the Wavecrest and sell their fish for unbeatable prices. Guests can barbecue on gas grills provided. One-bedroom ocean or garden view $119, one-bedroom oceanfront $149; two-bedroom oceanfront $189; $15 per extra person. Car/condo packages are also available. Attractive monthly and low-season discounts available. Call the Wavecrest direct, 808/558-8103, or Friendly Isle Realty, 808/553-3666 or 800/600-4158, fax 808/553-3867. Friendly Isle Realty manages numerous other units in each of the condominiums on the island and also several homes on the west end and along the beaches on the east end. For more information log on to www.molokairealty.com.

Kamalo Plantation, HC 01, Box 300, Kaunakakai, HI 96748, tel./fax 808/558-8236, is a five-acre tropical garden, where Glenn and Akiko Foster welcome guests. About 10 miles east of Kaunakakai, and across from Father Damien's St. Joseph Church, Kamalo Plantation is surrounded by well-vegetated grounds and even has a *heiau* on the property. The Fosters can accommodate you in a fully contained private studio cottage with king bed, full kitchen, indoor and outdoor showers, and deck for $85, two night minimum. The cottage is secluded on the property and has a sitting area, necessary cooking appliances, an outside deck, and a barbecue grill in its own little gazebo. The tropical decor makes this comfy cottage a home away from home. A breakfast of fruit and baked breads and a tour of the grounds are part of the price. A fine place, perfect for a quite getaway. The Fosters also have the **Moanui Beach House** for rent across from the beach at mile marker 20. This newly renovated A-frame sits up on the hillside overlooking a horse pasture and the water. With two bedrooms, one and a half baths, and a full kitchen, this house is just right for a small family and goes for $140 double occupancy with $20 for each additional person, three night minimum. For more information try www.molokai.com/kamalo, email: kamaloplantation@aloha.net.

Almost next door is **Kumu'eli Farms B&B,** P.O. Box 1829, Kaunakakai, HI 96748, tel./fax 808/558-8284, or 808/558-8281, email: dcurtis@aloha.net. This lovely, contemporary-style wooden house has only one rental suite, which is set to the side of the main house. It has a private entrance off the connecting deck, and there is a lap pool off the back deck. The suite has a queen bed, ceiling fan, TV, and refrigerator, and runs $100 a night, two nights minimum. A homemade breakfast is served each morning. For more information, contact Dorothe or David Curtis, long-time Moloka'i residents.

Just past the Puko'o Neighborhood Store, going east, is a casual ocean front house with two bedrooms and two baths, a full kitchen, and only steps from the water. This cute little place runs $150 a night during the winter or $125 at other times, three night minimum. This and a half dozen other properties nearby on the east end (and three or four out at Kaluakoi Resort on the west end) are handled by Swenson Real Estate, P.O. Box 1979, Kaunakakai, HI 96748, 808/553-3648 or 800/558-3648, fax 808/553-3783, website: http://island-realestate.com/vacation.html, email: diane@island-realestate.com.

Some distance farther is the **Waialua Beach House,** a three-bedroom, two-bath, oceanfront home with all the conveniences. This island-style house sleeps up to six and runs $135 per night, three nights minimum, with an $85 cleaning fee. For information and reservations, call 808/599-3838 or 888/579-9400, fax 808/537-2322, or try website www.hawaiibeachhouse.org, email: hawaiibeachhouse@hotmail.com.

At the far eastern end of the island, overlooking the lands of Pu'u O Hoku Ranch is **Pu'u O Hoku Country Cottage,** a vacation rental that was once a guest cottage at the ranch manager's residence. Check in at the ranch office along the highway near mile marker 25. If you're looking for a place to really be away, this is it. This cottage is a large two-bedroom house that has been renovated but is still charming in its simplicity. It has a living room with a wall of glass, dining room, and full kitchen. Each of the two bedrooms has a private bath. With a couch in the living room, it can sleep six. No TV, radio, or telephone unless requested. Feel free to use the swimming pool up at the main lodge. The rental rate is $85 a night or $510 a week with the seventh night free. The lodge is also available for group rental and would make a great place for a conference or retreat. The lodge has 11 bedrooms, seven bathrooms, a huge main room, and an industrial kitchen. Originally built for Paul Fagan, who later built Hotel Hana-Maui, this lodge will house up to 23 individuals and is surrounded by acres of lawn and trees. The rate for the lodge is $900 a night, two nights minimum. Contact: Pu'u O Hoku Ranch, HC 01 Box 900, Kaunakakai, HI 96748, 808/558-8109, fax 808/558-8100, website: www.puuohoku.com, email: hoku@aloha.net.

The only place to find food on this end of the island is the **Neighborhood Store,** 808/558-8498, in Puko'o. This convenience store carries basic necessities. Connected is a lunch window that serves breakfasts and lunches, like sandwiches for $4 and plate lunches for $6–7. Open daily except Wednesday 8 A.M.–6 P.M. daily.

MIDDLE MOLOKA'I AND KALAUPAPA

As you head west from Kaunakakai on Route 460 toward Ho'olehua Airport you pass fields planted in various crops. These are Moloka'i's attempt at diversified agriculture since the demise of pineapple. The cultivated fields give way to hundreds of acres filled with what seems like skeletons of dead trees. It's as if some eerie specter stalked the land and devoured their spirits. Farther along and just before a bridge, the **Main Forest Road** intersects, posted for 4WD vehicles but navigable in a standard car during dry weather. This track leads to the Sandalwood Measuring Pit, a depression in the ground that is a permanent reminder of the furious and foolhardy trading of two centuries ago. Farther on is the Kamakou Preserve, a largely intact region of native trees and wildlife. Here too along little-used trails are spectacular views of the lost valleys of Moloka'i's inaccessible northeast shore.

West on Route 460 another branch road, Route 470, heads north through Kualapu'u, Del Monte's diminished pineapple town, to road's end at Pala'au State Park, Moloka'i's best camping area and home to the famous Phallic Rock. Near the state park entrance is the lookout for **Kalaupapa Peninsula** and the beginning of the mule trail, which switchbacks down more than 1,600 feet to the humbling and uplifting experience of Kalaupapa.

MAIN FOREST ROAD

Head west on Route 460 from Kaunakakai, and just before mile marker 4 turn right before the bridge (just past the Seventh-Day Adventist Church). After a few hundred yards you pass the Homelani Cemetery. Here, a red dirt road called Main Forest or Maunahui Road heads into the mountains. Your car rental agency will tell you that this road is impassable except in a 4WD, and they're right—if it's raining! But, even if it isn't, this road is rough. Follow the rutted road up into the hills and you'll soon be in a deep forest of 'ohi'a, pine, eucalyptus, and giant ferns thriving since their planting early in the 1900s. The cool, pleasant air mixes with rich earthy smells of the forest. At 5.5 miles you enter the Moloka'i Forest Preserve. At just under six miles there's a bend to the right. Proceed a few hundred yards and on your left is a wood shop with turned wood bowls for sale! Ignore many small roads branching off.

After nine miles is the **Sandalwood Measuring Pit** (Lua Moku 'Iliahi), or Pit of the Sandalwood Ship, a depression in the ground in the shape of a ship's hull. Now bordered by a white pipe fence, it's not very spectacular, and this is a long way to go over a rough road to see a shallow hole in the ground, but the Sandalwood Pit is a permanent reminder of the days of mindless exploitation in Hawaii when money and possessions were more important than the land or the people. Hawaiian chiefs had the pit dug to measure the amount of sandalwood necessary to fill the hold of a ship. They traded the aromatic wood to Yankee captains for baubles, whiskey, guns, manufactured goods, and tools. The traders carried the wood to China where they made huge profits. The trading was so lucrative that the men of entire villages were forced into the hills to collect it, even to the point where the taro fields were neglected and famine gnawed at the door. It only took a few years to denude the mountains of their copious stands of sandalwood, even more incredible when you consider that all the work was done by hand and all the wood was carried to the waiting ships on the coast using the *maka'ainana* as beasts of burden.

Travel past the Sandalwood Pit (beware the mud) for about one mile and you'll come to **Waikolu (Three Waters) Overlook.** From here you can peer down into the pristine valley 3,700 feet below. If rains have been recent, hundreds of waterfalls spread their lace as they fall to the green jungle. The water here seeps into the ground, which soaks it up like a huge dripping sponge. Father Damien tapped a spring at the bottom end of this valley to supply fresh water to his flock at Kalawao. A water tunnel, bored into the valley, collects the water and conducts it for more than five miles until it reaches the 1.4 billion-gallon Kualapu'u Reservoir. Drive to this area only on a clear day, because the rain will not only get you stuck in mud, but also obscure your view with heavy cloud cover. Camping is allowed at the overlook park. Get your free permit from the Department of Land and natural Resources office in Ho'olehua.

Past the Waikolu Overlook is the Kamakou Reserve. **Hanalilolilo Trail** begins not far from Waikolu Lookout and winds through high mountain forests of 'ohi'a followed by the Pepe'opae Bog until it comes to a breathtaking view of Pelekunu Valley. Hiking trails through this area are poorly marked, poorly maintained, and strenuous—great qualifications for those who crave solitude and adventure. Alternately, continue walking the 4WD road into the preserve. After about 4.5 miles, at a spot where the road makes a sharp right turn, the **Pepe'opae Trail** heads into the bog over a boardwalk, ending after 1.5 miles at the Pelekunu Lookout. Pelekunu means "smelly" (due to no sunshine). Don't let the name fool you. Hawaiians lived happily and well in this remote, north shore valley for centuries. Time, aided by wind and rain, has turned the 3,300-foot sea cliffs of Pelekunu into some of the tallest in the world. Today, Pelekunu is more remote and isolated than ever. There are no permanent residents, although islanders come sporadically to camp in the summer, when the waters are calm enough to land on the coast.

The 2,774-acre **Kamakou Preserve,** established by the Nature Conservancy of Hawaii in 1982, seeks to preserve this unique forest area,

home to five species of endangered Hawaiian birds, two of which are endemic only to Moloka'i. There are 250 species of Hawaiian plants and ferns, 219 of which grow nowhere else in the world. Even a few clusters of sandalwood trees tenaciously try to make a comeback. The land was donated by the Molokai Ranch, which keeps control of the water rights. Two officials of the ranch are on the conservancy board, which causes some people to look suspiciously at their motives. Most trails have been mapped, and hunting is encouraged throughout most of the area. Up-to-the-minute information and maps are available from the preserve manager: P.O. Box 220, Kualapuu, HI 96757, 808/553-5236.

KUALAPU'U AND KALA'E

Kualapu'u was a vibrant town when pineapple was king and Del Monte was headquartered here. Now, coffee is king and some of the town's former vibrancy has resurfaced. It is the only town where you can find basic services on the way to Kalaupapa.

Right at the turnoff onto Farrington Avenue is the restored Plantation Store and an adjacent espresso bar. Displayed in the store are many attractive gifts, arts, and crafts done by Moloka'i and other island residents. The lunch counter has pastries, sandwiches, and various coffee and juice drinks. This is now coffee country, so pick up a bag of Mululani Estate or Muleskinner coffee at the store or try a cup at the lunch counter. Both are open Mon.–Sat. 7 A.M.–4 P.M.

Walking tours are given at the 500-acre **Coffees of Hawaii** coffee plantation that take you through the fields for an up-close look at the coffee plants, then heads to the mill and roasting room to see what happens to the beans once they're picked. These tours are generally offered Mon.–Fri. 9 A.M.–1 P.M. and cost $7 per person; 24-hour advance reservations required. For more information, contact the plantation at 808/567-9270 or 800/709-2326, website: www.coffee-hawaii.com.

A minute down Farrington Avenue you'll come to the **Kualapu'u Market,** open daily except Sunday 8:30 A.M.–6 P.M. Here you'll find a selection of foodstuffs, fresh produce and beef, and general merchandise.

MOLOKA'I

Open 7:30–11:30 A.M. and 12:30–4:30 P.M., the Kualapu'u post office is to the side of the market.

Notice also the world's largest rubber-lined reservoir across the highway from town. Holding 1.4 billion gallons, its water comes via a five-mile-long, eight-foot-round tunnel from the water-filled valleys to the east.

Purdy's Macadamia Nut Farm

A few miles west of Kualapu'u, on Lihi Pali Ave, is **Purdy's Na Hua 'O Ka Aina Farm.** A former airline employee, Mr. Purdy grew up just down the road. When the airline pulled out of Moloka'i, he decided to stay home, become a farmer, and teach people about the exquisite macadamia nut. His farm has 50 trees that are about 70 years old. These trees still produce nuts prodigiously and continuously for 10 months of the year—September–June—with nuts at all different stages of maturity on the tree at one time. When mature, nuts fall to the ground. Harvested from the ground, they are taken to be cracked and either kept raw or roasted and lightly salted. This one-acre grove of trees is farmed naturally, but Mr. Purdy has put in about 250 trees at another location on the island that are fertilized and treated with pesticides. Purdy's is the only mac nut farm on Moloka'i, and his yield is about 250–300 pounds of unshelled nuts per tree, as opposed to the 150–200 pounds on the thousand-acre farms of the Big Island. Visit the shop at the farm where Mr. Purdy tells everyone about the trees. Have a go at cracking one of the nuts, and have a taste of its rich fruit. Bags of nuts are sold at his gift shop—a little treat to yourself for the road—and can be mailed anywhere in the country for you. Free admission; open Mon.–Fri. 9:30 A.M.–3:30 P.M. and Saturday 10 A.M.–2 P.M. The nut farm's website is www.molokai.com/eatnuts.

Moloka'i Museum and Cultural Center

Along Route 470, two miles past Kualapu'u in the village of Kala'e, you'll discover the old R. W. Meyer Sugar Mill, now part of the Moloka'i Museum and Cultural Center, 808/567-6436. Open Mon.–Sat. 10 A.M.–2 P.M., the self-guided mill tour is $2.50 adults, $1 students 5–18, and this includes the cultural center building with its displays, gift and book shop, and historical video is free. Proceeds go into a fund to construct a new museum building. Built in 1878, the restored mill (1988) is on the National Register of Historic Places. It is in functioning order and clearly shows the stages of creating sugar from cane. As the smallest commercial mill in the state, it was used only until 1889, and it ground cane from 30 nearby upland acres. The museum and cultural center focus on preserving and demonstrating Hawaiian arts and handicrafts like quilting, *lau hala* weaving, wood carving, plus demonstrations of lei-making and hula. The idea is to share and revive the arts of Hawaii, especially those of Moloka'i, in this interpretive center. As

Meyer Sugar Mill Museum

ROBERT NILSEN

an outgrowth, the center is used as the Elder-hostel campus for Moloka'i. In August, the annual Moloka'i music and dance festival takes place at the center. Hula is performed, local musicians play, and the whole community turns out.

Just beyond the center is the Meyer ceme-tery. You can enter, but be respectful. It is here that Rudolph Meyer, his wife, and children are buried. Up in among the trees above the mill is the Meyer home—not open to the public. Par-tially restored in 1973, it's now in disrepair. Per-haps one day it to will be restored again and preserved as another tangible link to the fami-ly that helped shape the history and economy of the island. The three acres that the cultural center sits on were graciously donated by the Meyer family. Aside from sugarcane, coffee, vegetables, fruits, and dairy cattle were raised on Meyer land, and the present Meyer Ranch still occupies a large tract of the surrounding upland area.

Kala'e Cocks

A minute or two past the sugar mill is a surreal-istic scene amidst the bucolic highland fields of knee-deep grass. Keep your eyes peeled for a tall cyclone fence topped with nasty looking barbed wire. Inside are row after row of tiny green A-frames, like the pup tents of a brigade of GIs on bivouac. Restrained by leashes just long enough to prevent mortal combat are hundreds of plumed, crowing roosters. Moloka'i's Filipino population has long been known for cockfighting, an illegal activity, but no law prevents the raising of the fighting birds. These glorious cocks, dis-playing their feathers while clawing the earth, challenge each other with quite a show of devil-may-care bravado. The spectacle is easily seen from the road.

Pala'au State Park

A few minutes past Kala'e are the stables for Molokai Mule Rides, which take you down to Kalaupapa. Even if you're not planning a mule ride, make sure to stop and check out the beau-ty of the countryside surrounding the mule sta-bles. Follow the road until it ends at the parking lot for Pala'au State Park.

In the lot, two signs direct you to the Phallic Rock and to the Kalaupapa Overlook (which is not the beginning of the trail down to the penin-sula). Pala'au State Park offers the best camping on Moloka'i although it's quite a distance from the beach. Follow the signs from the parking lot for about 200 yards to **Phallic Rock** (KauleoNana-hoa), one of the best examples of such a stone in the state. Nanahoa, the male fertility god inhab-iting the anatomical rock, has been performing like a champ and hasn't had a "headache" in centuries! Legend says that Nanahoa lived near-by and one day sat to admire a beautiful young girl who was looking at her reflection in a pool. Kawahua, Nanahoa's wife, became so jealous when she saw her husband leering that she at-tacked the young girl by yanking on her hair. Nanahoa became outraged in turn and struck his wife, who rolled over a nearby cliff and turned to stone. Nanahoa also turned to stone in the shape of an erect penis, and there he sits point-ing skyward to this day. Barren women have come here to spend the night and pray for fertil-ity. At the base of the rock is a tiny pool the size of a small bowl that collects rainwater. The women would sit here hoping to absorb the child-giving *mana* of the rock. You can still see offer-ings and of course graffiti.

Return to the parking lot and follow the signs to **Kalaupapa Overlook.** Jutting 1,600 feet below, almost like an afterthought, is the penin-sula of Kalaupapa, which was the home of the lost lepers of Hawaii, picked for its remoteness and inaccessibility. The almost-vertical *pali* served as a natural barrier to the outside world. If you look to your right you'll see the mule trail switchbacking down the cliff. Look to the south-east sector of the peninsula to see the almost perfectly round **Kauhako Crater,** remnant of the separate volcano that formed Kalaupapa.

THE KALAUPAPA EXPERIENCE

No one knew how the dreaded disease came to the Hawaiian Islands, but they did know that if you were contaminated by it your life would be misery. Leprosy has caused fear in the hearts of man since biblical times, and in the 1800s King Kamehameha V and his advisors were no ex-ception. All they knew was that lepers had to be isolated. Kalawao Cove, on the southeast shore of Kalaupapa Peninsula, was regarded as the most isolated spot in the entire kingdom. So, starting in 1866, it was to Kalawao that the lepers of Hawaii were sent to die. Through crude diagnostic testing, anyone who had a suspicious skin discoloration, ulcer, or even bad sunburn was rounded up and sent to Kalawao. The islanders soon learned that once sent, there was no return. So the afflicted hid. Bounty hunters roamed the countryside. Babies, toddlers, teenagers, wives, grandfathers—none were immune to the bounty hunters. They hounded, captured, and sometimes killed anyone who had any sort of skin ailment. The captives were ripped from their villages and loaded on a ship. No one would come near the suspected lepers on board and they sometimes sat open to the elements in a cage. They were allowed only one small tin box of possessions. As the ship anchored in the always choppy bay at Kalawao, the cage was opened and the victims were tossed overboard, followed by a few sealed barrels of food and clothing that had been collected by merciful Christians. Those too weak or sick or young drowned; the unlucky made it to shore. The crew waited nervously with loaded muskets in case any of those on shore attempted to board the ship.

Hell on Earth

Waiting for the newcomers were the forsaken. Abandoned by king, country, family, friends, and apparently the Lord himself, they became animals—beasts of prey. Young girls with hardly a blemish were raped by reeking deformed men in rags. Old men were bludgeoned, their tin boxes ripped from their hands. Children and babies cried and begged for food. The arrivals made rude dwellings of sticks and stones, while others lived in caves or on the beach open to the elements. Finally, the conscience of the kingdom was stirred, and while the old dumping ground of Kalawao was not

abandoned, new lepers were mostly exiled to the more hospitable Kalaupapa side of the peninsula, just a mile or so to the west.

The Move to Kalaupapa

These lepers sent to Kalaupapa were treated more mercifully. Missionary groups provided food and rudimentary clothing, and *kokua* (helpers) provided aid. An attempt was made to end the lawlessness and depravity, and provide some semblance of civilized society. Still, the lepers were kept separate, and for the most part lived outdoors or in very rude huts. They never could come in direct contact with the *kokua* or anyone else who came to the peninsula. If they met a healthy person walking along a path, they had to grovel at the side. Many *kokua*, horrified by Kalaupapa, left on the next available boat. With little medical attention, death was still the only release from Kalaupapa.

Light in Hell

It was by accident or miracle that **Joseph de Veuster, Father Damien,** a Catholic priest, came from Belgium to Hawaii. His brother, also a priest, was supposed to come, but he became ill and Father Damien came in his place. Damien spent several years on the Big Island of Hawaiʻi, building churches and learning the language and ways of the people, before he came to Kalaupapa in 1873. What he saw touched his heart. He was different from the rest, having come with a sense of mission to help the lepers and bring them hope and dignity. The other missionaries saw Kalaupapa not as a place to live, but to die. Damien saw the lepers as children of God who had the right to live and be comforted. When they hid under a bush at his approach, he picked them up and stood them on their feet. He carried water all day long to the sick and dying. He bathed their

Father Damien just weeks before his death from Hansen's disease

wounds and built them shelters with his own two hands. When clothes or food or materials ran short, he walked topside and begged for more. Other church groups were against him and the government gave him little aid, but he persevered. Damien scraped together some lumber and fashioned a flume pipe to carry water to his people, who were still dying mainly from pneumonia and tuberculosis brought on by neglect. Damien worked long days alone, until he dropped exhausted at night.

Father Damien modified **St. Philomena Church,** a structure that was originally built in Honolulu by Brother Bertrant in 1872, and shipped it to Moloka'i in segments. Father Damien invited his flock inside, but those grossly afflicted could not control their mouths, so spittle would drip to the floor. They were ashamed to soil the church, so Damien cut squares in the floor through which they could spit onto the ground. Slowly a light began to shine in the hearts of the lepers and the authorities began to take notice. Conditions began to improve, but there were those who resented Damien. Robert Louis Stevenson visited the settlement, and after meeting Damien wrote an open letter that ended ". . . he is my father." Damien contracted leprosy, but by the time he died in 1889 at age 49, he knew his people would be cared for. In 1936, Damien's native Belgium asked that his remains be returned. He was exhumed and his remains sent home, but a memorial still stands where he was interred at Kalaupapa. After lengthy squabbles with the Belgian government, Father Damien's right hand was returned to Kalaupapa in 1995 and has been reinterred as a religious relic. In 1995, he was beatified by Pope John Paul II. A number of books have been written about Damien's life, perhaps the best of the bunch is *Holy Man, Father Damien of Molokai,* by Gavan Daws.

The Light Grows Brighter

Brother Dutton, who arrived in 1886, and Mother Marianne Cope, a Franciscan nun from Syracuse, New York, who came in 1888 with two other Sisters of Saint Francis, carried on Damien's work. In addition, many missionary groups sent volunteers to help at the colony. Thereafter the people of Kalaupapa were treated with dignity and given a sense of hope. In

1873, the same year that Damien arrived at Kalaupapa, Norwegian physician Gerhard Hansen isolated the bacteria that causes leprosy, and shortly thereafter the official name of the malady became Hansen's disease. By the turn of the 20th century, adequate medical care and good living conditions were provided to the patients at Kalaupapa. Still, many died, mostly from complications. Families could not visit members confined to Kalaupapa unless they were near death, and any children born to the patients—who were now starting to marry—were whisked away at birth and adopted, or given to family members on the outside. Even until the 1940s people were still sent to Kalaupapa because of skin ailments that were never really diagnosed as leprosy. Many of these indeed did show signs of the disease, but there is always the haunting thought that they may have contracted it after arrival at the colony.

In the mid-1940s sulfa drugs were found to arrest most cases of Hansen's disease, and the prognosis for a normal life improved. By the 1960s further breakthroughs made Hansen's disease noncontagious, and in 1969 the quarantine on patients was eliminated. Patients at Kalaupapa were then free to leave and return to their homes. No new patients were admitted, but most, already living in the only home they'd ever known, opted to stay. In total over the years, there have been about 8,000 unfortunate individuals who have been exiled to this forgotten spit of land. Almost as if it were an accident of fate designed to expunge evidence of the damning past, the community hospital along with all its records burned to the ground in the early '90s. No help was afforded by the local fire truck, which was unable to be started. Nonetheless, medical treatment continues and all needed care is still provided. The community of resident patients numbers less than 45 today (down from a high of about 1,800 in 1917)—the average age is about 70—and state caretakers and federal employees in the community now outnumber patients. In all of Hawaii today, there are about 450 people registered with Hansen's disease; all but those at Kalaupapa live at home with their families. Each year on average, about 18 new cases are diagnosed in the state. Still the number of patients continues to drop as the old-timers die. In 1980, Kalaupapa and adjoining lands were designated Kalaupapa National Historical Park, jointly administered by the state Department of Health, but the residents are assured a lifetime occupancy and free care.

The Kalaupapa Peninsula and its three adjoining valleys are technically a separate county within the state structure called Kalawao. While there is a sheriff, there are no elected officials, but residents can and do vote in state and national elections. Of this area, 12 acres have been designated parkland, about 500 are Hawaiian Home Lands, and the rest is state property. In the past, much of the peninsula was fenced off as rangeland for cattle, but more recently the cattle and goats have pretty much destroyed the native vegetation, which is now overgrown by alien species.

Getting There

It shouldn't be a matter of *if* you go to Kalaupapa, but *how* you go. You have choices. You can fly, walk, or ride a mule. No matter how you go, you *cannot* walk around Kalaupapa unescorted. You *must* take an official tour, and children under 16 are not allowed. If you're going by mule, arrangements are made for you by the company, but if you're walking down or flying in you have to call ahead to Richard Marks at **Damien Tours,** 808/567-6171, the only tour company now operating, and he will give you an exact place and time to meet once down on the peninsula. Typically, this is a 9:45 A.M. pickup at the Kalaupapa Airport for those who fly in, followed by a 10 A.M. pickup at the bottom end corral for those who hike or ride the mules down. Damien Tours charges $32 for a fascinating, four-hour tour conducted by one of the residents. Definitely worth the money; the insight you get from the resident tour guide is priceless and unique. No food or beverages, except water, are available to visitors, so make sure to bring your own.

"I'd rather be riding a mule on Moloka'i" is an eye-catching bumper sticker sported by those lucky enough to have made the decent to Kalaupapa aboard sure-footed mules. After several years of closure for trail repair, the **Molokai Mule Ride** is now back in business. The well-trained mules will transport you down the 1,600-foot *pali* expertly negotiating 26 hairpin switchbacks on the trail to the bottom. After your tour of the settlement, these gutsy animals carry you right back up so you too can claim your bumper sticker and ride-completion certificate. You are on the mule about 90 minutes each way. This tour runs $150 and includes the ground tour of the settlement and lunch. No riders over 240 pounds please; you must be at least 16 years old and in good physical shape. For reservations, call 808/567-6088 or 800/567-7550.

If you're hiking to Kalaupapa, follow the mule trail cut by Manuel Farinha in 1886. Go about 200 yards past the stables and look for a road to the right. Follow this track down past pastureland to the trailhead, where there is a small metal building with an odd faded sign that reads "Advance Technology Center Hawaii USA," near an old overgrown observation point for the peninsula. The 3.8-mile, 90-minute trail going down the steep north face of the *pali* is well maintained and only mildly strenuous. You should be in good physical condition to hike it, however, as it can take a toll on your knees going down, and requires strength and endurance on the way up. It may be preferable to leave before the mules do in the morning (around 8:15 A.M.), but in any case give yourself enough time to make it to the bottom before the tour pickup at 10 A.M. The trail will be rutted and muddy in spots, and you'll have to step around the road apples, so wear hiking boots if possible, sneakers at a minimum. A zigzag of 26 turns (they're numbered) gets you down to the bottom and one long zag will bring you to the beach and the mule corral beyond. There is no swimming at this beach, which is pending status as a turtle sanctuary, and is an area where monk seals have been known to give birth to their young.

While you were once able to fly in and out directly from Ho'olehua, top side Moloka'i, or walk down and fly up, this service is currently not available. Now if you want to fly either one-way or round-trip between Ho'olehua and Kalaupapa, you must fly via Honolulu with **Pacific Wings,** the only airlines that services both destinations with regular service. One-way will cost $186, round-trip $372. Pacific Wings also offers a regularly scheduled round-trip flights from Honolulu for $186. Flights are limited so call for schedules, 808/873-0877 on Maui, or 888/575-4546 elsewhere. **Paragon Air,** 808/244-3356 or 800/428-1231, offers round-trip charter flights from both Kahului and Kapalua, Maui, for $199, and this in-

J.D. BISIGNANI

seeing the sights at Kalawao

MOLOKA'I

cludes your air fare, tour fee, and a simple lunch. All flights get you to Kalaupapa in time for the start of your tour and pick you up when your tours ends at about 3 P.M. for your return flight. If you want to fly in, you must still arrange for the ground tour through Damien Tours (or be sponsored by someone who lives in Kalaupapa) before you will be sold a ticket. If you decide to fly, notice the breakers at the end of the runway sending spray 90 feet into the air. The pilots time their take-offs to miss the spray!

The Tour

Damien Tours will pick you up by bus either at the airport or at the mule corral. From there, you start your tour by a drive into the main Kalaupapa settlement, where all residents live, and where the hospital, park service office, post office, several churches, and pier are located. Driving past the old visitor center, you arrive at the pier. While many supplies come by plane, a ferry comes once a year to bring bulkier goods. Across from the pier is the remodeled St. Francis Church and next to it, the unassuming Father Damien Memorial Hall, a mini-museum dedicated to Father Damien, Brother Dutton, and Sister Marianne Cope. Both can be visited if time permits. The tour then takes you past the remains of the old burnt hospital and the Bishop Home, a residence for female patients, to a stop at the new visitor center. This new center has displays of the settlement and a few books and other items for sale. From there, you head over the flank of Pu'u 'Uao (405 feet), the highest point on the peninsula, to the old Kalawao settlement site for a stop at St. Philomena Church. This is perhaps the most moving part of the tour as the church and its cemetery are about the only physical remains of the works of Father Damien. During. Father Damien's time, there were nearly 300 mostly small and humble buildings in Kalawao, many of which were constructed with the help of this holy man. Lunch is at Judd Park nearby, next to where the first leprosy hospital stood, and from this bluff you have a great view overlooking the precipitous north Moloka'i coast. Pu'u 'Uao was the volcanic caldera out of which lava flowed to create the Kalaupapa Peninsula. Its crater top contains a small lake about the size of a baseball infield that is said to be over 800 feet deep. On your return, you'll pass several graveyards that line the road to the airport, the last resting place to the thousands of victims who were cruelly treated by their disease and the society in which they lived.

MOLOKA'I'S WEST END

Long before contact with the Europeans, the west end of Moloka'i was famous throughout the Hawaiian Islands. The culture centered on Maunaloa, the ancient volcanic mountain that formed the land. On its slopes the goddess Laka learned the hula from her sister and spread its joyous undulations to all the other islands. Not far from the birthplace of the hula is Kaluako'i, one of the two most important adze quarries in old Hawaii. Without these stone tools, no canoes, bowls, or everyday items could have been fashioned. Voyagers came from every major island to trade for this dense, hard stone. With all this coming and going, the always-small population of Moloka'i needed godly protection. Not far away at Kalaipahoa, the "poison wood" sorcery gods of Moloka'i lived in a grove that supposedly sprouted to maturity in one night. With talismans made from this magical grove, Moloka'i kept invading warriors at bay for centuries.

Most of the island's flat useable land is out that way. The thrust west began with the founding of the Molokai Ranch, whose 54,000 acres make up about 50 percent of the good farm and range land on the island, and about one-third of the island. The ranch was owned last century by Kamehameha V, and after his death it was sold to private interests who began the successful raising of Santa Gertrudis cattle imported from the famous Texas King Ranch. The ranch still employs *paniolo,* with the life of riding the range and rodeo still strong. Today, anywhere between 6,000–10,000 head of Brahman and Brangus cattle roam ranch land with about 80 horses to do the work.

THE NORTHWEST

The northwest section of Moloka'i, centered at **Ho'olehua,** is where the Hawaiian Home Land parcels are located. The entire area has a feeling of heartland America, and if you ignore the coastline in the background you could easily imagine yourself in the rolling hills of Missouri. Don't expect a town at Ho'olehua. All that's there is a little post office and a government office.

Mo'omomi Beach

The real destination is Mo'omomi Beach. Follow Route 460 until it branches north at Route 480 a mile east of the airport. Follow Route 480 until it turns left onto Farrington Avenue in Ho'olehua, and continue for about four miles until it turns into a red dirt road. This road can be extremely rutted, even tipping your car at a very precarious angle. Be advised! Continue for 10–15 minutes until you come to a Hawaii Home Lands recreational pavilion. Below you is Mo'omomi Beach. This area is a favorite with local people who come here to swim, fish, and surf. The swells are good only in winter, but the beach becomes rocky at that time of year. The tides bring the sand in by April and the swimming until November is good. Unofficial camping is probably okay on this grassy area, and a toilet and water are available at the pavilion.

Mo'omomi Beach goes back in Hawaiian legend. Besides the mythical lizards that inhabited this area, a great shark-god was born here. The mother was a woman who became impregnated by the gods. Her husband was angry that her child would be from the spirit world, so he directed her to come and sit on a large rock down by the beach. She went into labor and began to cry. A tear, holding a tiny fish, rolled down her cheek and fell into the sea and became the powerful shark-god. The rock upon which his mother sat is the large black one just to the right of the beach.

If you feel adventurous you can head west along the beach. Every 10 minutes or so you come to a tiny beach that you have entirely to yourself. Since this area is so isolated, be extremely careful of surf conditions. About two miles west of Mo'omomi is **Keonelele,** a miniature desert strip of sand dunes. The wind whips through this region and pushes the sand into rows. Geologists haunt this area trying to piece together Moloka'i's geological history. The Hawaiians used Keonelele as a burial site, and strange footprints found in the soft sandstone supposedly foretold the coming of white men. Today, Keonelele is totally deserted; although small, it gives the impression of a vast wasteland. A 921-acre plot west of Kaiehu Point, including much of the Keonelele area is now overseen by the Nature Conservancy as the **Mo'omomi Preserve.** This coastal ecosysytem, mostly unaltered over the centuries, safeguards 22 native plant species—four of which are endangered—that do well in this very wind-blown and harsh environment. The Hawaiian green sea turtle also frequents these sands, making this preserve a sanctuary for this creature. While the Hawaiian owl, plover, and numerous sea birds visit this distant stretch of shore, numerous birds which used to live here have now gone extinct, leaving only their bones in the sand to tell of their presence here. Within the preserve, use only the beach or the marked trails and 4WD roads.

Papohaku Beach

The best attraction in the area doesn't have a price tag. Papohaku Beach is the giant expanse of white sand running south from the Kaluakoi Resort. The sands here are so expansive that they were dredged and taken to O'ahu in the 1950s. During the winter months a great deal of sand is stripped away and large lava boulders and outcroppings are exposed. Every spring and summer the tides carry the sand back and deposit it on the enormous beach. Camping is permitted at the **Papohaku County Beach Park** just past the resort. Pick up your permit at the Mitchell Pauole Center in Kaunakakai, 808/553-3204, before you come all the way out here. Here you'll find a large grassy play area, toilets, showers, picnic tables, grills for cooking, and a virtually empty beach. A sign on the road past the park tells you to watch out for deer. This road runs through a huge Papohaku Ranchlands home development area, with several beach access roads and parking areas that lead to other spots along this huge expanse of beach.

The last beach access at the end of the paved road leads to a secluded and protected small bay and fine sand beach that is even safe during winter months when other beach areas are not. Locals refer to this beach as Dixie Maru Beach as a fishing boat of that name once sunk in the bay. The Kaupoa Trail starts from the south end of this beach and runs into Molokai Ranch lands—about a 30–40 minute walk.

One of the attractions of Moloka'i is its re-

moteness. Here the sky is clear and at night the stars are brilliant. Yet, even here you know that you're not too far from the crush of humanity for directly across the Kaiwi Channel you can clearly see the glow of Honolulu, Wailua, and Kaneohe shimmering in the distance, and, closer at hand, the more muted lights of Maunaloa on the hill above.

Kawakiu Beach

This secluded and pristine beach on the far northwestern corner of Moloka'i was an item of controversy between the developers of the Kaluakoi Corp. and the grassroots activists of Moloka'i. For years access to the beach was restricted, and the Kaluakoi Corp. planned to develop the area. It was known that the area was very important during precontact times and rich in unexplored archaeological sites. The company hired a supposed team of "experts" who studied the site for months and finally claimed that the area had no significant archaeological importance. Their findings were hooted at by local people and by scholars from various institutions who knew better. This controversy resulted in Kawakiu Beach being opened to the public with plans of turning it into a beach park; the archaeological sites will be preserved.

The swimming at Kawakiu is excellent with the sandy bottom tapering off slowly. To get there go to the Paniolo Hale Condo at Kaluakoi Resort and park at the end of the dirt road that heads toward the sea, past the last paved parking lot of the condo. Walk across the golf course fairway to the beach. Follow it north for three-quarters of a mile, dodging the tide until you come to the very private Kawakiu Beach—definitely not recommended during periods of high surf, when swimming would be too dangerous anyway. No rules or prying eyes here, so if you would like to swim au naturel, this is the place. If you have lots of time and energy, walk on farther to the smaller and rocky but more private Kawakiu Iki Beach, or farther on to the ancient adze quarry and abandoned Coast Guard station on 'Ilio Point. You can also drive there by following the dirt road past the condos until it branches inland. It eventually swings back and takes you to Kawakiu. The road is rough, and the hike mildly strenuous, but Kawakiu is definitely worth it.

MOLOKA'I

Kaluakoi Hotel

Much of the west end of Moloka'i is the Kaluakoi Resort. This complex includes the Kaluakoi Hotel, three resort condominiums, the Kaluakoi Golf Course, private home sites, and Papohaku, Hawaii's largest white-sand beach.

The **Kaluakoi Hotel and Golf Club,** P.O. Box 1977, Maunaloa, HI 96770, 808/552-2555 or 800/435-7208 statewide, or 888/552-2550 Mainland, fax 808/552-2821, is the destination point for many who come to Moloka'i. The low-rise buildings, made primarily of wood, blend with the surrounding countryside. The well-kept grounds are covered in manicured trees and shrubbery. Rooms are done in light pastels and earth colors. Dynamic color is provided by the large windows that open onto the fairways and the sea beyond. All rooms have color TV, VCRs (video rental is at the front desk), and small refrigerators, and those on the second floor have open-beam construction. Some of the rooms have stovetops, while the cottages have kitchenettes. Many rooms sit along the fairways of the golf course and most have at least a partial ocean view. Because of the constant cool breezes, no air-conditioning is necessary, but there are ceiling fans. The least expensive hotel room is a standard garden view at $105, the most expensive a one bedroom oceanview suite at $275. Privately owned condo units go from $170 for a studio to $275 for a one-bedroom oceanfront cottage. The third-person charge is $15. A guest laundry is on premises. At more than 20 years old, this resort is beginning to show its age and is becoming a little frayed around the edges. While not luxury anymore, it is, nonetheless, quite adequate. Over the past few years, a number of organizations have looked into buying the hotel, but none have clinched the deal. It seems that everyone just waits for deep pockets to bring the shine back into the place and restore it to its former state of loveliness.

The hotel dining room serves breakfast and dinner, while a snack shop is open for lunch. The lounge serves drinks all day, and it's situated just off the pool deck, beyond which is the golf course. Consult the activities desk for what's doing around the island. It can help you make all arrangements. On property you'll find the small A Touch of Molokai clothing shop, along with the West End Sundries store, which sells snacks, magazines, and liquor. The Laughing Gecko shop stocks antiques, art, jewelry, Hawaiiana, and locally designed T-shirts made on Moloka'i. For more information try www.kaluakoi.com, email: kaluakoi@juno.com.

Kaluakoi Condos

Some of the units at the resort complex, collectively called the **Kaluakoi Villas,** are managed by the Castle Group. Each studio, suite, and cottage has been tastefully decorated and includes a color TV, lanai, kitchen or kitchenette, and guests can use the resort's restaurants and all its recreational facilities. Rates range $128–154 for a studio, $155–185 for a suite, and $206 for the cottage; fourth night free. Contact: 1131 Kaluako'i Rd., Maunaloa, HI 96770, 808/552-2721 or 800/367-5004 United States and Canada, 800/272-5275 statewide.

Built in 1981, the **Ke Nani Kai** condos are *mauka* of the road leading to the Kaluakoi Hotel, and they cost $149–159 for one of the fully furnished one-bedroom apartments; two bedrooms rent at $179–199. All apartments are large and in excellent condition. On property are a swimming pool and two tennis courts, and you're only a few steps away from the Kaluakoi golf course. Contact Ke Nani Kai, P.O. Box 289, Maunaloa, HI 96770, 808/552-2761 or 800/888-2791 or 800/535-0085, fax 808/633-5085. A Marc Resort Hawaii management property.

Newer yet, **Paniolo Hale** is another condo complex set in the trees surrounded by fairways. These buildings have more style than others on the area, and the whole complex a little classier. The swimming pool, paddle tennis, and barbecue grill are for the use of all guests. Maid service is provided for stays of one week or longer, and each unit has a washer and dryer. Garden and ocean studios run $95–115 and $185–205, $115–230 for one bedroom, and $145–265 for two bedrooms; three nights minimum except over the Christmas holiday season, when it's one week. Two-bedroom units have a hot tub and enclosed lanai. Contact Paniolo Hale, P.O. Box 190, Maunaloa, HI 96770, 808/552-2731 or 800/367-2984, fax 808/552-2288, website: www.paniolohaleresort.com, email: stay@paniolohaleresort.com.

Food

The Kaluakoi Resort's **Ohia Lodge**, 808/552-2555, is an uninspired restaurant serving breakfast 6:30–10:30 A.M. and dinner 6–8:45 P.M. daily. It is the only restaurant at the resort and, aside from the Village Grill and the lodge Dining Room at Molokai Ranch in Maunaloa, the only one on the west end of the island. Nice sunset views; reservations suggested. The garden-side snack bar is open daily 11 A.M.–4 P.M., selling sandwiches, burgers, and plate lunches, with most everything under $6. The **Ohia Lounge** is open all day and provides live local entertainment on Friday and Saturday.

MAUNALOA AND THE SOUTHWEST COAST

According to legend, the hilltop area Ka'ana above Maunaloa was the first place in the islands that the Hawaiians received hula instruction. Today, there are many *hula halau* on Moloka'i, and the yearly Moloka'i Hula Ka Piko festival is held down the hill at Papohaku State Park to honor this ancient music and dance form.

Most people heading east-west between Kaunakakai and the Kaluakoi Resort never used to make it into Maunaloa town. That's because Route 460 splits just east of Maunaloa, and Kaluako'i Road heads north toward the Kaluakoi Resort and away from the town. Until recently, with the pineapples gone and few visitors, the town barely hung on. Built in 1923, Maunaloa was a wonderful example of a plantation town. It was a little patch of humble workers' houses carved into a field. In front you were likely to see a tethered horse, a boat, or glass fishing floats hanging from the lanai. Overhead you could see a kite flying—a sign that you had arrived in Maunaloa. The townsfolk were friendly and if you were looking for conversation or a taste of Hawaiian history, the old-timers hanging around under the shaded lean-to near the post office were just the ticket.

But the winds of change have started to blow in Maunaloa and the force increases. The Molokai Ranch, which owns the town, has instituted a new grand development scheme to completely "rejuvenate" the town. Most of the old homes, many falling apart and maybe uninsurable, have been torn down and have been replaced by new, similar-style homes. Bunched together away from the downtown area, these homes are set closer together than the old houses were. Starting at about $139,000, they are affordable for many and well below the state average. Local people have been given first choice, and many have taken the deal. Additionally, streets have been paved and new ones laid out. A new sewer system and water reservoir have been installed, along with other segments of a modern infrastructure. While several of the old standby commercial establishments have remained, like the post office, general store, police substation, churches, and *The Dispatch* newspaper office, the town has gotten a new face. Already a movie theater, KFC franchise, gift shop, gas station, restaurant, ranch activities center, and the ranch lodge are up and running. An old-town museum features several renovated old buildings moved from other locations in town and the Maunaloa Cultural Park is a spot where community events are staged. Future plans include more business establishments and new residential areas for custom homes. With all these changes there is certain to be some disagreement about their effect. While many take a wait-and-see attitude, others who live and/or work in town seem to think that the changes are for the better.

The only public shore access on this corner of the island is **Hale O Lono** harbor and beach. Turn just after the ranch outfitter and follow Mokia Street past the ranch lodge south out of town and keep to the major track of crushed coral. This road runs for a couple of mile down to the harbor. Hale O Lono is an old harbor that services the ranch, a few commercial boats related to the ranch, and the occasional passing ship. From here, the sand of Papohaku Beach was shipped to O'ahu in the 1950s. With its small but fine white-sand beach, Hale O Lono is the launch point for the annual Bankoh Moloka'i outrigger canoe championship races to Waikiki.

If you are staying at the Molokai Ranch, other spots along the coast might be of interest. About a mile east of Hale O Lono is **Halena Beach**, where there is an old Boy Scout camp and pavilion. East of there down the coastal dirt track is **Kolo Beach,** a fine long strand that sports the dilapidated **Kolo Wharf** at its far end. Kolo Wharf

MOLOKA'I

was where Moloka'i once shipped its pineapples. Now only naked pilings stand to mark the spot. On the far western end of the island is **Kaupoa Beach,** an old-time favorite of island residents.

Molokai Ranch Accommodations

The only place to stay in Maunaloa in at the Molokai Ranch, but you don't just sleep there; you also find food and activities. Accommodations are either in the lodge or in three camps, placed in isolated yet picturesque spots. Paniolo Camp is set up near the rodeo arena, Kolo Camp overlooks the water near the old Kolo Wharf on the south shore, and Kaupoa Camp sits on a perfect white-sand double crescent beach at the extreme west end, a place that's good for swimming and tidepooling, with an occasional monk seal on the beach or dolphin in the bay. Paniolo and Kaupoa Camps have "tentalows," and Kolo has yurts. Wood-frame structures covered with heavy canvas, all are set up on wooden platforms that hold umbrella-covered patio tables, chairs, and benches. Inside are comfortable queen beds, a chest of drawers, and a chair. Set off to the side of the lanai is a composting toilet and half-roof shower that uses solar energy to heat the water. Electricity in each camp is powered by solar batteries; no televisions or phones. All this is done to impact the environment as little as possible. This is rustic simplicity—but luxurious camping. Rates are $145 for Paniolo Camp and $195 for the other two, children 4–12 are $75; *kama'aina* rates are reduced. These prices include a hearty morning breakfast served at an open-air pavilion on site, daily maid service, and transportation within the ranch; lunches run $12 and dinner $25.

In 2000, **The Lodge at Molokai Ranch** opened for the greater pleasure (and comfort) of those visiting the ranch. This two-story 22-room lodge reflects the days of the 1920s and '30s, with its early ranch decor and Hawaiiana tourist memorabilia. It's a Hawaiian ranch lodge in the true sense of the word, with a central hall flanked by wings of bedroom suites. In the main hall, you can easily make yourself comfortable as you sit back on a fine leather coach or wicker chair in front of the warming stone fireplace beneath the high ceiling that rises above you on the shoulders of rough-hewn timber posts and beams. Deep-patterned tropical foliage fabric covers the furniture and pillows, artwork reflecting earlier years of tropical Hawaii, the golden glow of table lamps, rustic accessories, and a chandelier made from deer horn fill the room. Relax to the live entertainment every evening or grab a book from the upstairs library and sit yourself down in one of the second floor nooks that overlook this hall. The bedrooms are as salubrious, also done in the decor of days past, but with all modern amenities. Room rates are $295–350, $75 for an additional guest, and this rate includes a children's program of outdoor

Molokai Ranch Lodge

ROBERT NILSEN

adventure and crafts. For anyone staying at the ranch needing transportation to and from the airport, there is an additional $20 fee. The lodge also has a restaurant, bar with billiard table, fitness center, massage service at the spa, an outdoor swimming pool, and the island's only elevator. A wide variety of activities on ranch property and along the coast are offered through the Outfitters Center. For information and reservations contact Molokai Ranch, P.O. Box 259, Maunaloa, HI 96770, 877/726-4656, website: www.molokai-ranch.com, email: info@molokai-ranch.com.

Food
The **Village Grill,** 808/552-0012, introduces "stonegrill cooking' to its guests. Well-known down under, this type of cooking is relatively new to the United States. With stonegrill cooking, the guest cooks his or her own main dish on a hot stone slab that's brought to the table from the kitchen at about 750°. Mostly ranch-style cuisine, prime rib, teri chicken, fish, and seafood are the main foods. Other offerings are pasta, salads, and dessert; entrées are in the $9–18 range. Drinks are also available from the bar. The bar, which once did duty at the Pearl City Tavern in O'ahu, has been retopped in bronze with cowboy designs added. The Village Grill is open Mon.–Fri. 11:30 A.M.–2 P.M. for lunch, and nightly 6–9 P.M. for dinner.

Maunaloa Dining Room is the lodge restaurant, serving the island's most upscale cuisine, with a superb vista over ranchland and a view of O'ahu and the lights of Honolulu at night (so near yet so far!). This is Moloka'i Rim Cuisine, gourmet ranch food. When the temperature is warm and balmy sit outside on the verandah, when it cools down in the evening, move to one of the tables inside. Breakfast, served 6:30–10 A.M., lunch, and Sunday brunch are 11 A.M.–1:30 P.M., while dinner is 6–9 P.M. Try an appetizer like crispy coconut shrimp and entr'es like honey and macadamia nut crusted rack of lamb. If you desire, the restaurant will even do a picnic lunch for two, with all you'll need for a day's outing. The lodge lounge offers an easy-going atmosphere, whether sitting on a rawhide bar stool or at a table along the lanai. Open 4–11 P.M., this is a full-service bar and you can also order food off the bar menu.

To some people's delight and others' chagrin, there is now a **KFC Express** in town in the theater building. Usual fare, but limited; usual prices. Open Tues.–Sun. 11 A.M.–7:30 P.M., until 8 P.M. Friday and Saturday.

Activities and Recreation
There was a theater is Maunaloa until the mid-1970s, after which the only one on the island was in Kaunakakai. When that one closed, the island was without until the new **Maunaloa Town Cinemas** was built in 1997. This triplex theater shows first-run movies and not only draws people from Maunaloa, but also from Kaluako'i and Kaunakakai as well. Ticket run $5.50 adults, $3.50 children; call 808/552-2616 for what's showing.

For outdoor adventure, you must go to the Molokai Ranch **Outfitters Center,** where all sorts of outdoor activities can be arranged. If you're staying at one of the camps, activities are arranged through the camp staff. These activities include horseback riding (corral roundup and trail rides), ocean kayaking and outrigger canoeing, full or half-day mountain-biking tours, cultural walks, a ropes course, raft and snorkeling trips, and whale-watching in season; all equipment is provided. A separate charge is made for each activity; most $35–75 apiece. Those staying at the ranch get priority for activities, but anyone may participate. For those not staying at the ranch, the rates are somewhat higher. While at the Outfitters Center, choose a souvenir at the logo shop or have a peek at the mini-museum for a survey of the island's history and culture and a small display of photos and artifacts. Open daily 7 A.M.–7 P.M.; 808/552-2791 or 888/729-0059.

Shopping
A good reason to make the trek to Maunaloa is to visit the **Big Wind Kite Factory,** 808/552-2364, open Mon.–Sat. 8:30 A.M.–5 P.M., Sunday 10 A.M.–2 P.M., owned and operated by Jonathan Sosher and his wife Daphane. The hand-crafted kites and windsocks from this down-home cottage industry are the same ones that sell at outlets around the state. All are made on the premises by Jonathan, Daphane, son Zachary, and a few workers, who come up with designs like butterflies, rainbow stars, and hula girls in *ti*-leaf

skirts—ask for a free factory tour. Jonathan will give you a lesson in the park next door on any of the kites, including the two-string-controllable ones. Prices range $35–65 for a rip-stop nylon kite; they make beautiful, easily transportable gifts that'll last for years. The shop itself is ablaze with beautiful colors, as if you've walked into the heart of a flower. This is a happy store. The Big Wind Kite Factory is *the* most interesting shop on Moloka'i. The company's website is www.molokai.com/kites.

In the second half of this building, the **The Plantation Gallery,** sells a variety of crafts by local artists—Hawaiian quilt pillowcases, Pacific isle shell jewelry, scrimshaw (on deerhorn), earrings, bracelets, boxes, bamboo xylophones, and other wood objects. Part of the boutique has batiks, Balinese masks, wood carvings, quilts, and sarongs; especially nice are carved mirror frames of storks, birds, and flowers. And if you just can't live without a blowgun from Irian Jaya, this is the place. Here too you'll find perhaps the island's best selections of books on Hawaii, post cards, and a selection of T-shirts, Hawaiian shirts, and sarongs. After you've run through a million tourist shops and are sick of the shell lei, come here to find something truly unique.

Maunaloa General Store, 808/552-2346, is open Mon.–Sat. 8:30 A.M.–6 P.M. It's a well-stocked store where you can pick up anything that you'll need if you'll be staying in one of the condos at Kaluako'i. You can buy liquor, wine, beer, canned goods, meats, and vegetables.

Across from KFC and theater, tucked into the side of the general store is the west end's only **gas station.** The price of gas here is virtually no different than anywhere else on the island. Open 9 A.M.–5 P.M. Mon.–Fri. and Saturday 10 A.M.–4 P.M., this station also carries drinks, sundries, and has an ATM machine. There is no bank in Maunaloa.

O'AHU

It is the meeting place of East and West. The very new rubs shoulders with the immeasurably old. And if you have not found the romance you expected you have come upon something singularly intriguing.

—W. Somerset Maugham

M.G.L. DUMONT DE RIENZI

INTRODUCTION

It is the destiny of certain places on earth to be imbued with an inexplicable magnetism, a power that draws people whose visions and desires combine at just the right moment to create a dynamism so strong that it becomes history. The result for these "certain places" is greatness . . . and O'ahu is one of these.

It is difficult to separate O'ahu from its vibrant metropolis, Honolulu, whose massive political, economic, and social muscle dominates both the entire state and its home island. But to look at Honolulu *as* O'ahu is to look upon only the face of a great sculpture, ignoring the beauty and subtleties of the whole. The words "Honolulu," "Waikiki," and "Pearl Harbor" conjure up visions common to people the world over. Immediately, imaginations flush with palm trees swaying, a healthy tan, bombs dropping, and a golden moon rising romantically over coiled lovers on a white-sand beach.

O'ahu is called the "Gathering Place," and to itself it has indeed gathered the noble memories of old Hawaii, the vibrancy of a bright-eyed fledgling state, and the brawny power so necessary for the future. On this amazing piece of

land adrift in the great ocean, 885,000 people live; nearly eight times that number visit yearly, and as time passes O'ahu remains strong as one of those "certain places."

OVERVIEW

O'ahu is partly a tropical garden, bathed by soft showers and sunshine, and swaying with a gentle but firm rhythm. You can experience this feeling all over the island, even in pockets of downtown Honolulu and Waikiki. However, its other side is brash—dominated by the confidence of a major American city perched upon the Pacific Basin whose music is a pounding staccato jackhammer, droning bulldozer, and mechanical screech of the ever-present building crane. The vast majority of first-time and return visitors land at Honolulu International and spend at least a few days on O'ahu, usually in Waikiki.

People are amazed at the diversity of experiences the island has to offer. Besides the obvious (and endless) beach activities, it offers museums, botanical gardens, a fantastic zoo and

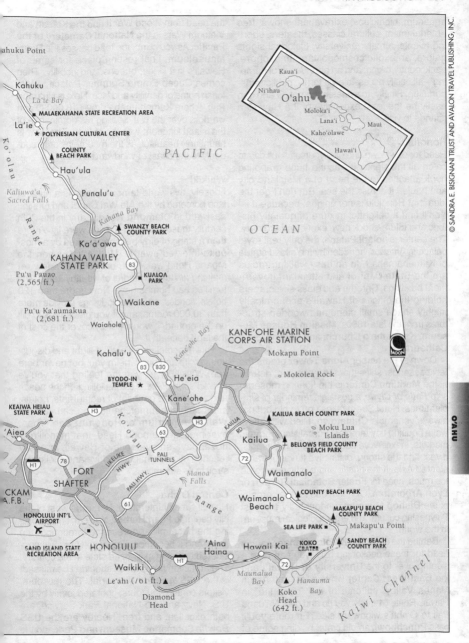

ahuku Point

Kahuku

La'ie Bay

■ MALAEKAHANA STATE RECREATION AREA

La'ie

★ POLYNESIAN CULTURAL CENTER

▲ COUNTY
BEACH PARK

Hau'ula

Punalu'u

*Kaliuwa'a
Sacred Falls*

Kahana Bay

PACIFIC

OCEAN

▲ SWANZY BEACH
COUNTY PARK

Ka'a'awa

KAHANA VALLEY
STATE PARK ▲

Pu'u Pauao
(2,565 ft.)

83

■ KUALOA
PARK

Waikane

Pu'u Ka'aumakua
(2,681 ft.)

Waiahole

Kane'ohe Bay

KANE'OHE MARINE
CORPS AIR STATION

Kahalu'u

Mokapu Point

○ Mokolea Rock

83 830

BYODO-IN
TEMPLE ★

He'eia

Kane'ohe

KEAIWA HEIAU
STATE PARK ▲

H3

'Aiea

H3

KAILUA RD.

▲ KAILUA BEACH COUNTY PARK

○ Moku Lua
Islands

78

Kailua

H1

63

■ BELLOWS FIELD COUNTY
BEACH PARK

FORT
SHAFTER

LIKELIKE HWY.

PALI
TUNNELS

*Manoa
Falls*

72

Waimanalo

CKAM
A.F.B.

PALI HWY.

61

Range

Waimanalo
Beach

● COUNTY BEACH PARK

HONOLULU INT'L
AIRPORT

MAKAPU'U BEACH
COUNTY PARK

SEA LIFE PARK ■

Makapu'u Point

SAND ISLAND STATE
RECREATION AREA

HONOLULU

H1

'Aina
Haina

Hawaii Kai

KOKO
CRATER

▲ SANDY BEACH
COUNTY PARK

Waikiki

Le'ahi (761 ft.) ▲

*Maunalua
Bay*

72

Diamond
Head

Koko
Head
(642 ft.) ▲

*Hanauma
Bay*

Kaiwi Channel

Kaua'i

Ni'ihau

O'ahu

Moloka'i

Lana'i

Maui

Kaho'olawe

Hawai'i

MOON

O'AHU

aquarium, nightclubs, extravagant shows, free entertainment, cultural classes, theaters, sporting events, a major university, historical sights galore, an exotic cosmopolitan atmosphere, backcountry hiking, and an abundance of camping—all easily accessible via terrific public transportation. Finally, to sweeten the pot, O'ahu can easily be the least expensive of the Hawaiian Islands to visit.

Honolulu

Head for downtown and give yourself a full day to catch all the sights. It's as if a huge grappling hook attached to the heart of a Mainland city and hauled it across the sea. But don't get the idea that Honolulu is not unique, because it is! You'll find a delightful mixture of quaintly historic and future-shock new, exotic and ordinary. The center is 'Iolani Palace, the only real royal palace in America, heralded by the gilded statue of Kamehameha I. In an easy walking radius are the State Capitol and attendant government buildings. Chrome and glass skyscrapers holding the offices of Hawaii's economically mighty shade small stone and wooden structures from the late 1800s: Mission Houses Museum, Kawaiaha'o Church, and St. Andrew's Cathedral.

Down at the harbor Aloha Tower greets the few passenger ships that still make port; nearby at the Maritime Center is the floating museum ship *Falls of Clyde,* a nostalgic reminder of simpler times. Hotel Street takes you to old but not always venerable Chinatown, filled with alleyways housing tiny temples, herbalists, aromatic markets, inexpensive eateries, rough nightspots, dives, and the strong, distinctive flavor of transplanted Asia. If the hustle and bustle gets to be too much, head for Foster Botanical Garden or Lyon Arboretum. Or hop a bus for the serenity of the Bishop Museum, undoubtedly *the* best Polynesian cultural and anthropological museum in the world.

Behind the city is the Ko'olau Range. As you head for these beckoning hills, you can take a sidetrip over to the University of Hawai'i and the East-West Center while passing through Manoa Valley, epitome of the "good life" in Hawaii. Route 61 takes you up and over Nu'uanu Pali to O'ahu's windward side. En route you'll pass Punchbowl, an old crater holding some of the dead from World War II and the Korean and Vietnam Wars in the National Cemetery of the Pacific. As you climb, the road passes the Royal Mausoleum, final resting place for some of Hawaii's last kings, queens, and nobility. Then comes Queen Emma Summer Palace, a Victorian home of gentility and lace. Next is Nu'uanu Pali, where Kamehameha drove 16,000 O'ahu warriors over the cliff, sealing his dominance of the island kingdom with their blood. The view is hauntingly beautiful, as the mountains drop suddenly to the coast of windward O'ahu.

Waikiki

Loosely, this world-famous beach is a hunk of land bordered by the Ala Wai Canal and running eastward to Diamond Head. Early in the 20th century these two golden miles were little more than a string of dirty beaches backed by a mosquito-infested swamp. Until 1901, when the Moana Hotel was built, only Hawaii's few remaining ali'i and a handful of wealthy *kama'aina* families had homes here. Now, more than 120 hotels, condos, and other lodgings provide more than 30,000 rooms, and if you placed a $20 bill on the ground, it would barely cover the cost of the land beneath it.

This hyperactive area will delight and disgust you, excite and overwhelm you, but never bore you. Waikiki gives you the feeling that you've arrived *someplace.* Besides lolling on the beach and walking the gauntlet of restaurants, hotels, malls, and street merchants, you can visit the Waikiki Aquarium or Honolulu Zoo. Then, ever-present Diamond Head, that monolith of frozen lava so symbolic of Hawaii, is easily reached by a few minutes' drive and a leisurely stroll to its summit.

Central O'ahu

Hawaii's major interstate, H-1, runs west of the city center to Pearl Harbor. You can't help noticing the huge military presence throughout the area, and it becomes clear why Hawaii is considered the most militarized state in the country. The attraction here, which shouldn't be missed, is the USS *Arizona* Memorial. The museum, visitors center, and tours, operated jointly by the U.S. Navy and the National Park Service, are both excellent and free. Nearby are the USS *Bowfin* Submarine Museum and Park and the

USS **Missouri,** both worthy stops.

Pearl Harbor is ringed by rather ordinary communities, suburbs of Honolulu. Because of its topography and climate it was a mainstay of the sugar industry until quite recently. In Waipahu, the museum village **Hawaii's Plantation Village** gives you a glimpse of what life was like for those living and working the ever-present sugar plantation. Farther up the plateau the land has been put to other uses. Early in the 19th century, huge pineapple plantations were started on the rich soil, and today vast tracts are still planted in this fruit. The demonstration gardens of Del Monte and Dole are good places to stop for an introduction to the history of pineapple production on the island. Also dominating huge areas of this central plain are the broad and beautiful **Schofield Barracks** Army base and **Wheeler Air Force Base,** two of the island's important military installations and significant players in America's armed conflicts in the Pacific and Asia.

Leeward Coast

The western edge of the island is the **Wai'anae Coast.** The towns of **Ma'ili, Wai'anae,** and **Makaha** are considered one of the last domains of the locals of O'ahu. This coastal area has escaped mass development so far, and it's one of the few places on the island where ordinary people can afford to live near the beach. Sometimes an attitude of resentment spills over against tourists; mostly, though, lovely people with good hearts live here, who will treat you as nicely as you're willing to treat them.

World-class surfing beaches along this coast are preferred by many of the best-known surfers from Hawaii. Many work as lifeguards in the beach parks, and they all congregate for the annual surfing championships held in Makaha. Here is a perfect chance to mingle with the people and soak up some of the last real *aloha* left on O'ahu.

Southeast O'ahu

Head eastward around the bulge of Diamond Head, passing exclusive residential areas; you quickly find a string of secluded beaches that are better for surfing than swimming. The next bulge in the shoreline is **Koko Head,** below which lies **Hanauma Bay,** an underwater conservation park renowned for magnificent family-class snorkeling. **Koko Crater** is a short dis-

tance away, and within its circling arms lies the little-visited **Koko Crater Botanical Garden,** which specializes in dry land plants. Below **Makapu'u Point,** the easternmost tip of the island, is **Sea Life Park,** an extravaganza of the deep, and just up the coast is the sleepy village of **Waimanalo.** The beach at Waimanalo is considered one of the best on the island, and it's hard to believe the city's just 10 miles back.

Windward O'ahu

On the windward side, **Kailua** and **Kane'ohe** have become suburban bedroom communities for Honolulu; this entire coast has few tourist accommodations, so it remains relatively uncrowded. The beaches are excellent, with beach parks and camping spots one after another, and the winds make this side of the island perfect for windsurfing. Inland of downtown Kane'ohe is **Valley of the Temples,** where a Christian cross sits high on a hill, and Buddha rests calmly in **Byodo-In Temple.**

Just up Route 83, the coastal highway, comes **Waiahole,** O'ahu's outback, where tiny farms and taro patches dot the valleys and local folks move with the slow beat of bygone days. Then a quick succession of beaches follows, many rarely visited by more than a passing fisherman. **Punalu'u** comes next, offering some of the only accommodations along this coast. In **La'ie** is the **Polynesian Cultural Center,** operated by the Mormon Church. **Brigham Young University** is here too, along with a solid **Mormon temple** that's open to visitors.

North Shore

The North Shore is famous for magnificent surf. From **Hale'iwa** to **Sunset Beach,** world-class surfers come to be challenged by the liquid thunder of the **Banzai Pipeline, Waimea Bay,** and other well-known surf breaks. Art shops, boutiques, and restaurants are concentrated in Hale'iwa, the main North Shore town, but secluded hideaways line these sun-drenched miles. Beyond the former sugar town of **Waialua** lies the long and nearly unvisited **Mokule'ia Beach** and **Dillingham Airfield,** where you can take a glider ride or air tour of the island. The road ends with a very rugged jeep trail leading to **Ka'ena Point,** renowned for the most monstrous surf on the North Shore.

O'AHU

THE LAND

When Papa, the Hawaiian earth mother, returned from vacationing in Tahiti, she was less than pleased. She had learned through a gossiping messenger that her husband, Wakea, had been playing around. Besides simply philandering, he'd been foolish enough to impregnate Hina, a lovely young goddess who bore him island children. Papa, scorned and furious, showed Wakea that two could play the same game by taking a handsome young lover, Lua. Their brief interlude yielded the man-child O'ahu, sixth of the great island children. Geologically, O'ahu is the second oldest main island after Kaua'i. It emerged from beneath the waves as hissing lava a few million years after Kaua'i and cooled a little quicker than Papa's temper to form Hawaii's third largest island.

Land Facts

O'ahu has a total land area of 597 square miles, and measured from its farthest points it is 44 miles long by 30 miles wide. The 112-mile coastline holds the two largest harbors in the state, **Honolulu** and **Pearl.** The **Ko'olau Range** runs north-south for almost the entire length of the island, dramatically creating windward and leeward O'ahu. The **Wai'anae Range** is smaller, confined to the western section of the island. It too runs north-south, dividing the **Wai'anae Coast** from the massive **Leilehua Plateau** of the interior. **Mount Ka'ala,** at 4,020 feet, in the northern portion of the Wai'anae Range, is O'ahu's highest peak. Even with these two mountain ranges, 45 percent of O'ahu is less than 500 feet in elevation, the lowest of the six major islands. Much of the huge Leilehua Plateau is covered in pineapple. Lying between the two mountain ranges, it runs all the way from Waialua on the North Shore to 'Ewa, just west of Pearl Harbor. At its widest point, around Schofield Barracks, it's more than six miles across.

O'ahu's most impressive natural features were formed after the heavy volcanic activity ceased and erosion began to sculpt the island. The most obvious are the wall-like *pali* cliffs—mountains eroded by winds from the east, valleys cut by streams from the west. Perfect examples of these *pali* are seen from Waimanalo to the north end of Kane'ohe Bay, and examples of eroded valleys are **Nu'uanu** and **Kalihi.** Other impressive examples are **Diamond Head, Koko Head,** and **Punchbowl,** three "tuff-cone" volcanoes created after the heavy volcanic activity of early O'ahu. A tuff cone is volcanic ash cemented together to form solid rock. Diamond Head is the most dramatic, formed after a minor eruption about 100,000 years ago and rising 761 feet from its base.

O'ahu has the state's longest stream, **Kaukonahua,** which begins atop Pu'u Ka'aumakua at 2,681 feet in the central Ko'olau Range and runs westward 33 miles through the Leilehua Plateau, emptying at the North Shore. En route, it runs through the **Wahiawa Reservoir,** which, at 302 acres, forms the second largest body of fresh water in Hawaii. O'ahu's tallest waterfalls are 80-foot **Kaliuwa'a** (Sacred Falls), just west of Punalu'u; and **Waihe'e Falls,** in famous Waimea Park on the North Shore, which have a sheer drop of more than 40 feet. O'ahu's main water concern is usage that outstrips supply.

THE CLIMATE

O'ahu, like all the Hawaiian Islands, has equitable weather year-round. The average daily temperature is 80° F. The mountainous interior of O'ahu experiences about the same temperatures as the coastal areas because of the small difference in elevation. However, the *pali* are known for strong, cooling winds that rise up the mountainside from the coast. The coldest temperature recorded on the island was 43° in Kane'ohe on the windward coast, while the hottest was 96° at Wai'anae on the leeward coast.

apapane

LOUISE FOOTE

O'AHU TEMPERATURE AND RAINFALL

TOWN		JAN.	MARCH	MAY	JUNE	SEPT.	NOV.
Honolulu	high	80	82	84	85	82	81
	low	60	52	68	70	71	68
	rain	4	2	0	0	0	4
Kane'ohe	high	80	80	80	80	82	80
	low	67	62	68	70	70	68
	rain	5	5	2	0	2	5
Waialua	high	79	79	81	82	82	80
	low	60	60	61	63	62	61
	rain	2	1	0	0	1	3

Note: Temperature is expressed in degrees Fahrenheit; rainfall in inches.

Precipitation is the biggest differentiating factor in the climate of O'ahu. Generally, the entire leeward coast, the "rain shadow," from Ka'ena to Koko Head, is dry. Wai'anae, Honolulu International Airport, and Waikiki average only 20–25 inches of rain a year. The Leilehua Plateau in the center of the island does a little better at about 40 inches a year. Rain falls much more frequently and heavily in the Ko'olau Mountains and along the windward coast. The bay town of Kane'ohe sees 75–90 inches a year, while the Nu'uanu Reservoir in the mountains above Honolulu gets a whopping 120–130 inches yearly, with some years substantially greater than that. The maxim throughout the islands is "don't let rain spoil your day." If it's raining, simply move on to the next beach, or around to the other side of the island where it'll probably be dry. You can most often depend on the beaches of Waikiki and Wai'anae to be sunny and bright. No matter where you go for that day on the beach, however, the temperature of the ocean water will run 75–80° year-round.

FLORA AND FAUNA

You would think that with O'ahu's dense human population, little room would be left for animals. In fact, they are environmentally stressed, but they do survive. The interior mountain slopes are home to **wild pigs,** and a small population of **feral goats** survives in the Wai'anae Range. Migrating **whales** pass by, especially along the leeward coast where they can be observed from lookouts ranging from Waikiki to Koko Head. Half a dozen introduced game birds are found around the island, but O'ahu's real animal wealth is its indigenous bird life.

Birds

The shores around O'ahu, including those off Koko Head and Sand Island, but especially on the tiny islets of Moku Manu and Manana on the windward side, are home to thriving colonies of marine birds. On these diminutive islands it's quite easy to spot a number of birds from the **tern** family, including the white, gray, and sooty tern. All have a distinctive screeching voice and approximate wingspan of 30 inches. Part of their problem is that they have little fear of humans. Along with the terns are **shearwaters.** These birds have a normal wingspan of about 36 inches and make a series of moans and wails, oftentimes while in flight. For some reason shearwaters are drawn to the bright lights of the city, where they fall prey to house cats and automobiles. Sometimes Moku Manu even attracts the enormous **Laysan albatross** with its seven-foot wingspan. **Tropic birds** with lovely, streamer-like tails are quite often seen along the windward coast.

To catch a glimpse of exotic birds on O'ahu you don't have to head for the sea or the hills.

O'AHU BOTANICAL GARDENS

Honolulu Botanical Gardens comprises five separate gardens supported and maintained by the county. All are open daily 9 A.M.–4 P.M. No admission fee, except for Foster Botanical Garden.

1) **Foster Botanical Garden,** 180 N. Vineyard Blvd., Honolulu, 808/522-7065, is a 13-acre oasis of exotic trees and rare plants. Guided tours are available Mon.–Fri. at 1 P.M. Admission is $5 for nonresidents, $3 for residents, $1 for children 6–12, and free for those younger.
2) At **Ho'omaluhia Botanical Garden,** 45-680 Luluku Rd., Kane'ohe, 808/233-7323, some guided hiking tours are offered
3) **Koko Crater Botanical Garden,** inside Koko Crater, 808/522-7060, specializes in succulents, cacti, and other dry land plants.
4) **Lili'uokalani Botanical Garden,** between Kuakini and School Streets, Honolulu, 808/522-7060. features mostly native Hawaiian plants.
5) **Wahiawa Botanical Garden,** 1396 California Ave., Wahiawa, 808/621-7321, contains 27 acres of cultivated trees, flowers, and ferns from around the world.

Ha'iku Gardens, 46-336 Hai'ku Rd., Kane'ohe, has many acres of flowers, ornamental trees, and ponds. A restaurant is on-site.

Lyon Arboretum, 3860 Manoa Rd., Honolulu, 808/988-0464, is a research facility of the University of Hawai'i. Dr. Lyon planted 194 acres of trees, flowers, and bushes in the late 1800s. Open Mon.–Sat. 9 A.M.–3 P.M. Some guided tours offered.

Moanalua Gardens, 1352 Pineapple Pl., 808/833-1944, is a former Damon Estate property. The gardens are open to public for self-guided walks weekdays 7 A.M.–6 P.M. and from 7:30 A.M. on weekends.

Senator Fong's Plantation and Gardens, 47-285 Pulama Rd., Kane'ohe, 808/239-6775, is open daily 10 A.M.–4 P.M., except Christmas and New Year's Day. The 725 acres encompass natural and cultivated flower, tree, palm, and fern gardens. Admission is $10 adults, $8 seniors, and $6 children 5–12.

Waimea Arboretum and Botanical Garden, at Waimea Falls Park, 808/638-8655, collects, grows, and preserves rare Hawaiian flora. Flowers and plants are labeled.

The city streets and beach parks are constantly aflutter with wings. Black **mynah birds** with their sassy yellow eyes are common mimics around town. **Sparrows,** introduced to Hawaii through O'ahu in the 1870s, are everywhere, while **munia,** first introduced as cage birds from Southeast Asia, have escaped and can be found almost anywhere around the island. Another escaped cage bird from Asia is the **bulbul,** a natural clown that perches on any likely city roost and draws attention to itself with loud calls and generally ridiculous behavior.

If you're lucky, you can also catch a glimpse of the *pueo* (Hawaiian owl) in the mountainous areas of Wai'anae and the Ko'olau Range. Also, along trails and deep in the forest from Tantalus to the Wai'anae Range you can sometimes see elusive native birds like the *'elepaio, 'amakihi,* and fiery red *'i'iwi.*

GOVERNMENT

Oʻahu has been the center of government for about 160 years, since King Kamehameha III permanently established the royal court here in the 1840s. In 1873–74, King David Kalakaua built ʻIolani Palace as the central showpiece of the island kingdom. Liliʻuokalani, the last Hawaiian monarch, lived after her dethronement in the nearby residence Washington Place. While Hawaii was a territory, and for a few years after it became a state, the palace was used as the capitol building, the governor residing in Washington Place. Modern Oʻahu, besides being the center of state government, governs itself as the **City and County of Honolulu.** The county covers the entire island of Oʻahu as well as the far-flung Northwestern Islands, except for Midway, which is under federal jurisdiction.

The island of Oʻahu has three times as many people as the other islands combined. Nowhere is this more evident than in the representation of Oʻahu in the state House and Senate. Oʻahu claims 18 of the 25 state senators and 37 of the 51 state representatives. These lopsided figures make it obvious that Oʻahu has plenty of clout, especially Honolulu urban districts, which elect more than 50 percent of Oʻahu's representatives. Frequent political battles ensue, since what's good for the city and county of Honolulu isn't always good for the rest of the state. More often than not, the political moguls of Oʻahu, backed by huge business interests, prevail.

Like the rest of the state, the voters on the island of Oʻahu are principally Democratic in orientation, but not in as great a percentage as on the other islands. The current mayor is Jeremy Harris, Democrat. He is assisted by an elected county council consisting of nine members, one from each council district around the island. The Oʻahu state senators are overwhelmingly Democratic, with only three Republicans. Democratic state representatives also outnumber Republicans, but not by quite as huge a margin. Most of the 13 Republican districts are in urban Honolulu and the suburban communities of Kailua and Kaneʻohe.

ECONOMY

Economically, Oʻahu dwarfs the rest of the islands combined. It generates income from government spending, tourism, and agriculture. A huge military presence, an international airport that receives the lion's share of visitors, and a sizable agricultural sector keep Oʻahu in the economic catbird seat. The famous "Big Five" maintain their corporate offices in downtown Honolulu, from where they oversee vast holdings throughout Hawaii and the Mainland. These offices are in about the same spots they were when their founders helped overthrow the monarchy. For the Big Five, things are about the same as then, except that they're going strong, while the old royalty of Hawaii has vanished.

Tourism

The flow of visitors to Oʻahu has remained unabated ever since tourism outstripped sugar and pineapples in the early 1960s, becoming Hawaii's top moneymaker. Of the more than six million people who visit the state yearly, more than one-half stay on Oʻahu. This means that on any given day, Oʻahu plays host to about 80,000 visitors. Waikiki is still many people's idea of paradise. Most all the rest, en route to the Neighbor Islands, at least pass through. Hotels directly employ more than 18,000 workers, half the state's total, not including all the shop assistants, waiters and waitresses, taxi drivers, and everyone else needed to ensure a carefree vacation. Of the state's 70,000 accommodation units, Oʻahu claims 36,000; of those, more than 31,000 are in Waikiki. The Oʻahu hotels consistently have the highest occupancy rates in the state, hovering around 80 percent. In contrast, the average daily room rate is the lowest in the state, making accommodations on Oʻahu slightly more of a bargain than on the other islands. The tourism industry generates

OʻAHU

about $11 billion of yearly revenue from direct visitor spending. With the flow of visitors seemingly endless, O'ahu has a bright economic future.

Military

Hawaii is the most militarized state in the United States, and O'ahu is the most militarized island in the state. The U.S. military has been on O'ahu since 1887, when Pearl Harbor was opened to the U.S. Navy as part of the "Sugar Reciprocity Treaty." The Spanish-American War saw U.S. troops billeted at Camp McKinley at the foot of Diamond Head, and Schofield Barracks opened to receive the 5th Cavalry in 1909. Pearl Harbor's flames ignited World War II, and there has been no looking back since then. On O'ahu today, the combined military services hold about 100,000 acres, a full 26 percent of the island. Much of this land, used for maneuvers, is off-limits to the public. Besides Pearl Harbor, so obviously dominated by battleship gray, the largest military lands are around Schofield Barracks and the Kahuku-Kawailoa Training Area. About 44,000 military personnel are stationed on O'ahu (99 percent of those in the state), with a slightly higher number of dependents.

Agriculture

You'd think that with all the people living on O'ahu, coupled with the constant land development, there'd be hardly any room left for things to grow. But that's not the case. The land is productive, though definitely stressed.

Changing times and attitudes led to a "poi famine" that hit O'ahu in 1967 because very few people were interested in the hard work of farming taro, the source of this staple. While O'ahu has, by far, the smallest acreage in farms and the smallest average size of farm in the state, it still manages to produce a considerable amount of sugarcane, pineapples, and the many products of diversified agriculture. Pineapples cover 11,500 acres, with the biggest holdings on the Leilehua Plateau belonging to Dole, a subsidiary of Castle and Cooke. In the hills, entrepreneurs raise *pakalolo,* which has become the state's most productive cash crop. O'ahu is also a huge agricultural consumer, demanding more than four times as much vegetables, fruits, meats, and poultry to feed its citizens and visitors than the remainder of the state combined.

O'AHU LAND OWNERSHIP

O'ahu
384,128 Acres

- ■ STATE
- ■ FEDERAL
- ■ HAWAIIAN HOMELANDS
- □ SMALL PRIVATE
- □ LARGE PRIVATE

O'AHU

Land Ownership

The island of Oʻahu is about 600 square miles in size. Although Honolulu County also includes the string of Northwest Islands, only Oʻahu is inhabited. This island, smaller than the Big Island and Maui, and only slight larger than Kauaʻi, has nearly three-quarters of the state's population. The federal government owns vast tracts on Oʻahu, mostly military bases and military-use areas. While smaller in area, the state also owns many acres, particularly rugged mountain sections of both the Koʻolau and Waiʻanae ranges. There are two Hawaiian Home Lands sections on Oʻahu, one in Waimanalo and the other in Nanakuli on the Waiʻanae Coast. These are just where you might expect them, as many native Hawaiians live in these areas. Of the large landowners, the Bishop Estate, Castle and Cooke, and the James Campbell Estate control the vast majority of land, but larger in size are the plots of land held by small landowners.

PEOPLE

For most visitors, regardless of where they've come from, Oʻahu (especially Honolulu) will be the first place they've ever encountered such an integrated multiracial society. Various countries may be cosmopolitan, but nowhere will you meet so many individuals from such a diversity of ethnic groups, and mixes of these groups. You could be driven to your hotel by a Chinese-Portuguese cab driver, checked in by a Japanese-Hawaiian clerk, served lunch by a Korean waiter, and serenaded by a Hawaiian-Italian-German musician, while an Irish-English-Filipino-French chambermaid tidies your room. This racial symphony is evident throughout Hawaii, but it's more apparent on Oʻahu, where the large population creates more opportunity for a racial hodgepodge. The warm feeling you get almost immediately upon arrival is that everyone belongs.

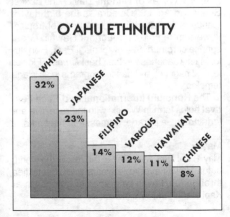

O'AHU ETHNICITY

WHITE 32%
JAPANESE 23%
FILIPINO 14%
VARIOUS 12%
HAWAIIAN 11%
CHINESE 8%

Oʻahu Population Figures

Oʻahu's 876,100 or so residents account for 72 percent of the state's population. All these people are on an island comprising only 9 percent of the state's land total. About 400,000 people live in greater Honolulu, the built-up area from 'Aiea to Koko Head. The next most populous urban centers after Honolulu are the Kailua-Kaneʻohe area with about 100,000 residents, followed by Pearl City and Waipahu with a combined total of about 70,000. On the Leilehua Plateau, 47,000 live in Mililani Town and Wahiawa. The strip of towns on the leeward coast, including Waiʻanae, totals about 33,400 inhabitants. In the last decade, the areas that have had the greatest increase in population are Wahiawa and 'Ewa. On Oʻahu, 96 percent of the population are urban dwellers while only 4 percent live rurally.

With all of these people, and such a finite land resource, real estate on the island is sky-high. The average single-family home on Oʻahu sells for $375,000 ($50,000 higher than the state average), while a condo averages about $180,000. And for plenty of prime real estate, these figures would barely cover the down payment!

So where is everybody? Of the major ethnic groups, you'll find the Hawaiians clustered around Walʻanae and on the windward coast near Waimanalo and Waiahole; the whites tend to be in Wahiawa, around Koko Head, in Waikiki, and in Kailua-Kaneʻohe; those of Japanese ancestry prefer the valleys heading toward the *pali,* including Kalihi, Nuʻuanu, and Tantalus; Filipinos live just east of the airport, in downtown Honolulu, and in Wahiawa; the Chinese are in Chinatown and around the Diamond Head area.

O'AHU

Of the minor ethnic groups, the highest concentration of blacks is in the Army towns around Schofield Barracks; Samoans live along with the Hawaiians in Wai'anae and the windward coastal towns, though they are most concentrated in downtown Honolulu not far from Aloha Tower; Koreans and Vietnamese are scattered here and there, but mostly in Honolulu. The ethnic breakdown of O'ahu's 876,100 residents is as follows: 32 percent Caucasian, 23 percent Japanese, 14 percent Filipino, 11 percent Hawaiian, 8 percent Chinese, and 12 percent other.

FESTIVALS, HOLIDAYS, AND EVENTS

O'ahu has more festivities and events than all the other islands, and these times provide great social opportunities for meeting people. Everyone is welcome to join in the fun, and most times the events are either free or nominally priced. There's no better way to enjoy yourself while vacationing than by joining in with a local party or happening.

January

January 2: **Queen Emma Museum Open House.** This is Queen Emma's birthday, and the public is invited to visit her summer home and view a well-preserved collection of her personal belongings; 808/595-3167.

The Narcissus Festival in Honolulu's Chinatown starts with the parade and festivities of Chinese New Year, with lion dances in the street, fireworks, a beauty pageant, and a coronation ball; call 808/533-3181 for locations.

The **Cherry Blossom Festival** in Honolulu can begin in late January and last through March. Events include a Japanese cultural and trade show, tea ceremony, flower arranging, queen pageant, and coronation ball. Check newspapers and free tourist magazines for dates and times of various Japanese cultural events.

February

NFL Pro Bowl. Aloha Stadium, Honolulu. Annual all-star football game offering the best from both conferences. Call 808/486-9300 for more information.

Punahou School Carnival. Honolulu. Arts, crafts, and a huge rummage sale at one of Hawaii's oldest and most prestigious high schools. Great ethnic foods. You'd be surprised at what Hawaii's oldest and most established families donate to the rummage sale. Call 808/944-5711 for details.

March

Enjoy the kites at the annual **O'ahu Kite Festival** at Kapi'olani Park or the **Honolulu Kite Festival** at Sandy Beach. For fun and competition.

Hawaiian Song Festival and Song Composing Contest. Kapi'olani Park Bandstand in Waikiki. Determines the year's best Hawaiian song. Presented by top-name entertainers.

Kamehameha School Annual Song Contest. Blaisdell Center Arena, Honolulu. Competition among secondary-grade students of Hawaiian ancestry.

April

Easter Sunday. Sunrise Service at the National Memorial Cemetery of the Pacific, Punchbowl Crater, Honolulu.

Annual Hawaiian Festival of Music. Waikiki Shell, Honolulu. A grand and lively music competition of groups from all over the islands and the Mainland. A music lover's smorgasbord offering everything from symphony to swing and all in between.

April 8: **Wesak or Buddha Day** on the closest Sunday to April 8. Celebrates the birthday of Gautama Buddha. Ornate offerings of tropical flowers at temples throughout Hawaii. Great sunrise ceremonies at Kapi'olani Park, Honolulu. Mainly Japanese in their best *kimono.* Flower festival pageant and dance programs in all island temples.

The **Honolulu International Bed Race Festival** holds forth in Waikiki with the race, live entertainment, a parade, games, and fireworks.

May

May 1: **Lei Day.** May Day to the rest of the world, but in Hawaii everyone wears a lei. Festivities throughout Hawaii with special goings-on at Kapi'olani Park, Waikiki.

O'AHU ARTS AND CULTURE INFORMATION

These organizations dispense information on Hawaiian arts and crafts.

Both Honolulu daily newspapers, the *Honolulu Advertiser* and the *Star Bulletin,* run calendars of current and upcoming cultural events around the island.

The Committee for Arts and Culture's *Art Resource Directory,* website: www.hcc.hawaii.edu/artweb/directory.html, is a thorough compilation of art and cultural organizations on the island of O'ahu.

Arts With Aloha, Honolulu Academy of Arts, 900 S. Beretania St., Honolulu, HI 96814, 808/538-8713, website: www.artswithaloha.com, is an association of major arts and cultural organizations in Honolulu that provides quick and easy information about its member organizations through a printed brochure and on a website.

Bishop Museum, 1525 Bernice St., Honolulu, HI 96817, 808/847-3511, website: www.bishop.hawaii.org, is the world's *best* museum covering Hawaii and Polynesia, with exhibits, galleries, archives, demonstrations of Hawaiian crafts, and a planetarium. On the premises, Shop Pacifica has a complete selection of books and publications on all aspects of Hawaiian art and culture.

Hawai'i Craftsmen, P.O. Box 22145, Honolulu, HI 96823, 808/596-8128, website: www.hawaiicraftsmen.org, increases awareness of Hawaiian crafts through programs, exhibitions, workshops, lectures, and demonstrations.

Honolulu Academy of Arts, 900 S. Beretania St., Honolulu, HI 96814, 808/532-8701, website: www.honoluluacademy.org, collects, preserves and exhibits works of fine art. The academy offers public art education programs related to its collections as well as tours, classes, lectures, films, and publications.

Mayor's Office of Culture and the Arts, 530 S. King St., Rm. 404, Honolulu, HI 96813, 808/523-4674, website: www.hcc.hawaii.edu/artweb, is the City and County of Honolulu's official organ for visual and performing arts information islandwide.

Pacific Handcrafters Guild, P.O. Box 29389, Honolulu, HI 96820-1789, 808/254-6788, website: www.alternative-hawaii.com/profiles/crafters/phg.htm, focuses on developing and preserving handicrafts and fine arts of all mediums. The guild sponsors four major crafts fairs annually.

The **State Foundation on Culture and the Arts,** 44 Merchant St., Honolulu, HI 96813, 808/586-0300, website: www.state.hi.us/sfca, was begun by the State Legislature in 1965 to preserve and promote Hawaii's diverse cultural, artistic, and historical heritage. It manages grants and maintains programs in folk arts and art in public places.

Brothers Cazimero Annual May Day Concert is one of the most anticipated musical events of the year. These musicians perform at the Waikiki Shell in the evening, as they have done for a quarter of a century.

Memorial Day. Special military services held at Honolulu, National Memorial Cemetery of the Pacific, on the last Monday in May.

50th State Fair, at Aloha Stadium, Honolulu. Agricultural exhibits, down-home cooking, entertainment, and produce. Lasts four weekends.

June

Mission Houses Museum Fancy Fair and **Festival of Hawaiian Quilts,** Honolulu. A top-notch collection of Hawaii's best artists and craftsmen for the fair, and Hawaii's best stitchery for the quilt show. A great chance to browse and buy. Also, food and entertainment; 808/531-0481.

June 11: **King Kamehameha Celebration** is a Hawaiian state holiday honoring Kamehameha the Great, Hawaii's first and greatest universal king. Lei-draping ceremony at King Kamehameha statue and parades complete with floats and pageantry featuring a *ho'olaule'a* (street party) in Waikiki. Civic Center, downtown Honolulu.

Annual King Kamehameha Hula Competition. Blaisdell Center, 808/536-6540.

The **Taste of Honolulu** brings together food from some 30 restaurant and wine vendors plus big name local entertainment for this weekend-long festivity at the Civic Center.

O'AHU MUSEUMS AND GALLERIES

Bishop Museum, 1525 Bernice St., Honolulu, 808/847-3511, open daily 9 A.M.–5 P.M., contains the best collection in the world on Polynesia in general and Hawaii specifically. A true cultural treat that should not be missed.

The Contemporary Museum, 2411 Makiki Heights Dr., Honolulu, 808/526-0232, open Tues.–Sat. 10 A.M.–4 P.M., Sunday noon–4 P.M., focuses on exhibitions, not collections, although there are permanent displays. Changing exhibits reflect different themes in contemporary art.

Damien Museum, at Saint Augustine Catholic Church, 130 Ohua Ave., Waikiki, 808/923-2690, displays photographs, papers, artifacts, and mementos of the legendary Father Damien. Open weekdays only 9 A.M.–3 P.M. Donations gratefully accepted.

Hawaii Maritime Center at Pier 7, Honolulu Harbor, 808/536-6373, open daily 8:30 A.M.–8 P.M., chronicles the exploration and exploitation of Hawaii by the seafarers who have come to its shores. Visit the famous double-hulled canoe *Hokule'a* and the tall-masted *Falls of Clyde.*

Hawaii's Plantation Village, 94-695 Waipahu St., Waipahu, 808/677-0110, is an open-air museum portraying sugar plantation life and the ethnic mix of plantation workers through restored buildings and memorabilia. Open for guided tours only Mon.–Fri. 9 A.M.–3 P.M., Saturday 10 A.M.–3 P.M.

Honolulu Academy of Arts, 900 S. Beretania St., Honolulu, 808/532-8701, open Tues.–Sat. 10 A.M.–4:30 P.M., Sunday 1–5 P.M., collects, preserves, and exhibits works of art, classic and modern, with a strong emphasis on Asian art. The academy offers permanent and special exhibitions, plus tours, classes, lectures, and films. Across from the Academy of Arts, the affiliated **Academy Art Center at Linekona** displays student artwork, mostly of a contemporary Hawaiian nature.

'Iolani Palace, 'Iolani Palace Grounds, Honolulu, 808/538-1471, is the only royal palace in the United States. Features include vintage artwork and antiques. Guided tours are offered Tues.–Sat. 9 A.M.–2:15 P.M.

The excellent **Mission Houses Museum,** 553 S. King St., Honolulu, 808/531-0481, open Tues.–Sat. 9 A.M.–4 P.M., comprises two homes, a printing house, and a library; an early mission compound. Guided tours.

Pacific Aerospace Museum, at the Honolulu International Airport, 808/839-0777, is open daily 9

Annual Pan-Pacific Festival—Matsuri. Dances and festivities, parades and performances, music, arts and crafts in Honolulu at Kapi'olani Park and other locations. It's a show of Japanese culture in Hawaii. Also, Bon Odori, the Japanese festival of departed souls, features dances and candle-lighting ceremonies at numerous Buddhist temples throughout the islands. These festivities change yearly and can be held anytime from late June to early August.

July

Trans Pacific Yacht Race, from Los Angeles to Honolulu during odd-numbered years. Yachties arrive throughout the month and converge on the Ala Wai Yacht Basin, where "party" is the password.

July 4: **Hawaiian Islands Tall Ships Parade.** Tall-masted ships from throughout the islands parade from Koko Head to Sand Island and back to Diamond Head. A rare treat and taste of days gone by. Other celebrations along Waikiki Beach.

The **Prince Lot Hula Festival** is a great chance for visitors to see authentic and noncompetitive hula from some of the finest hula *halau* in the islands. A free annual event held at the beautiful Moanalua Gardens in Honolulu; 808/839-5334. Also includes gift and craft sales, quilts, demonstrations, and food vendors.

Queen Lili'uokalani Keiki Hula Competition, Blaisdell Arena, Honolulu. Children ages 6–12 compete in a hula contest. Caution: Terminal Cuteness.

A.M.–10 P.M., Wednesday until 6 P.M. The focus is on aerospace travel and the aviation history of Hawaii, with interactive displays and an interpretive film.

Queen Emma Summer Palace, 2913 Pali Hwy., Honolulu, 808/595-3167, is open daily 9 A.M.–4 P.M., except major holidays. This restored historic home, built about 1848, contains the furniture and mementos of Queen Emma and her family. Some items belong to other members of the royal family.

Exhibits at the **Queen's Medical Center Historical Room,** 1301 Punchbowl St., Honolulu, 808/547-4397, display the history of the Queen's Medical Center (founded 1859) and the history of medicine in Hawaii. Open weekdays 8:30 A.M.–3:30 P.M.; no charge.

Tennent Art Foundation Gallery, 201-203 Prospect St., Honolulu, 808/531-1987, shows the work of Madge Tennent and other, mostly contemporary, works of art.

Tropic Lightning Museum, directly up from Macomb Gate on Schofield Barracks, 808/655-0438, is a military museum covering the history of Schofield Barracks Army Base and the 25th Infantry Division. Open Tues.–Sat. 10 A.M.–4 P.M.

University of Hawai'i Art Gallery, University of Hawai'i, Manoa, 808/956-6888, is on the third floor of the student center. It showcases faculty, student,

and traveling exhibitions. Open during the academic year Mon.–Fri. 10 A.M.–4 P.M. and Sunday noon–4 P.M. The gallery closes between exhibitions.

U.S. Army Museum of Hawaii, Fort DeRussy, Waikiki, 808/438-2821, open Tues.–Sun. 10 A.M.–4:30 P.M., covers the military history of Hawaii from the time of Kamehameha I to the activities of the U.S. Army in east Asia and the Pacific islands.

At the **USS *Arizona* Memorial,** Pearl Harbor, 808/422-2771, free Navy launches take you on the tour of "Battleship Row," including the sleek 184-foot white concrete structure that spans the sunken USS *Arizona*. Open daily 7:30 A.M.–5 P.M. No reservations: first-come, first-served. Launches leave every 15 minutes. The visitors center offers graphic materials and film, reflecting events of the Pearl Harbor attack.

USS *Bowfin* Submarine Museum, Pearl Harbor, 808/423-1341, is open daily 8 A.M.–5 P.M. Guided tours of this fully restored World War II submarine offer insight into the underwater war. Fascinating. It's next door to the *Arizona* Memorial.

It was on the **USS *Missouri*,** Pearl Harbor, 808/973-2494 that the documents ending World War II hostilities were signed. This refurbished World War II ship is a fitting counterpoint to the USS *Arizona*, the destruction of which pushed the United States into the war. Open 9 A.M.–5 P.M. daily.

Annual Ukulele Festival, held on the last Sunday of the month at Kapi'olani Park Bandstand, Waikiki. Hundreds of ukulele players from throughout the islands put on a very entertaining show.

The annual **Dragon Boat Festival** provides fun entertainment for all at the Ala Moana Beach Park.

For the music aficionado, the **Hawaii International Jazz Festival** offers great music from island and international musicians at the Hawaii Theatre and/or other venues around town, website: www.hawaiijazz.com.

August
The **Pacific Taro Festival** at Windward College celebrates this important staple crop with food, music, and cultural performances.

September
Aloha Festivals celebrate Hawaii's own "intangible quality," *aloha*. There are parades, lu'au, historical pageants, balls, and various other entertainment on all islands. The spirit of *aloha* is infectious and all are welcomed to join in. Check local papers and tourist literature for happenings near you. Downtown parades attract thousands, and even parking lots do their bit by charging a $1 flat fee during these festival times. The savory smells of ethnic foods fill the air from a multitude of stands, and the Honolulu Symphony performs at the Blaisdell Center, while free concerts are given at the Waikiki Shell. Over 300 planned activities at various locations on all islands. This is the state's largest multi-ethnic event; 800/852-7690.

Moloka'i to O'ahu Canoe Race. Women (men in October) in Hawaiian-style canoes race from a remote beach on Moloka'i to Fort DeRussy Beach in Honolulu. In transit they must navigate the rough Kaiwi Channel.

October

Moloka'i to O'ahu Canoe Race. Men (women in September) navigate Hawaiian-style canoes across the rough Kaiwi Channel from a remote beach on Moloka'i to Fort DeRussy Beach, Honolulu.

Annual Orchid Plant and Flower Show. Hawaii's copious and glorious flowers are displayed. Blaisdell Center Exhibition Hall, Honolulu. Blaisdell Center.

November

November 11: **Veterans Day Parade.** National holiday. A parade from Fort DeRussy to Queen Kapi'olani Park, Waikiki. American Legion, 808/949-1140.

Mission Houses Museum Holiday Craft Fair. Quality items offered by Hawaii's top craftsmen in an open-air bazaar; 808/531-0481.

Triple Crown of Surfing. Hawaiian Pro, World Cup of Surfing, Pipeline Masters. The best surfers in the world come to the best surfing beaches on O'ahu. Wave action determines sites except for the Masters, which is always held at Banzai Pipeline, North Shore, O'ahu. Big money and national TV coverage.

The annual **World International Hula Festi-**

O'AHU ARCHIVES AND LIBRARIES

Bishop Museum Library and Archives, 1525 Bernice St., Honolulu, HI 96817, 808/848-4148, features an extensive historical and cultural collection. Open Tues.–Fri. 10 A.M.–3 P.M. and Saturday 9 A.M.–noon.

Episcopal Church of Hawaii, 229 Queen Emma Square, Honolulu, HI 96813, 808/536-7776, displays records and photos of church history in Hawaii from 1862.

Hawaiian Historical Society, 560 Kawaiaha'o St., Honolulu, HI 96813, 808/537-6271, manages an extensive collection of 19th-century materials on Hawaiian Islands, including 3,000 photos, 10,000 books, maps, microfilm. Don't miss it. Open Mon.–Fri. 10 A.M.–4 P.M. The historical society is adjacent to Hawaiian Mission Children's Society—the two should be seen together.

Hawaiian State Archives, 'Iolani Palace Grounds, Honolulu, HI 96813, 808/586-0329, open Mon.–Fri. 7:45 A.M.–4:30 P.M., contains the archives of the government of Hawaii, including private papers of Hawaiian royalty and government officials, photos, illustrations, and etchings recording Hawaiian history. For anyone seriously interested in Hawaii. Shouldn't be missed.

Hawaii Chinese Historical Center, 111 N. King St., Rm. 410, Honolulu, HI 96813, 808/521-5948, features rare books, oral histories, and photos concerning the history of Chinese in Hawaii. Open 12 hours per week; call.

Hawaii State Library, 'Iolani Palace Grounds, Honolulu, HI 96813, 808/586-3500, is the main branch of statewide library system.

Mission Houses Research Library, 553 S. King St., Honolulu, HI 96813, 808/531-0481, is open Tues.–Fri. 10 A.M.–4 P.M. and Saturday by appointment. Holdings include records, personal journals, letters, microfilm, and photos of early 19th-century Congregational missionaries to the Hawaiian Islands; it's the archive of the Congregational Church in the Pacific. Shouldn't be missed.

Robert Allerton Library, 900 S. Beretania St., Honolulu, HI 96814, 808/532-8700, is an indispensable site for information about the arts, containing 35,000 books on art and Hawaiiana. Started in 1927, it's been recently remodeled and is now more user-friendly. It's at the Honolulu Academy of Arts; books can only be used on site.

University of Hawai'i Library at Manoa, 2550 McCarthy Mall, Honolulu, HI 96822, 808/956-7204, includes the Hamilton Library on the fourth floor, which holds the Hawaiian/Pacific Collection.

val is held at the Waikiki Shell for participants from several countries. Individual, female, male, and combined events are held.

Hawaii International Film Festival. Two-week event showing the best art films from the East, West, and Oceania. Over two dozen locations on all islands; 808/528-3456.

December

Pacific Handcrafters Guild Winter Fair, Thomas Square, Honolulu. A chance to see the "state of the arts" all in one locality. Perfect for early-bird and unique Christmas shopping. The best by the best, just in time for Christmas. Browse, buy, and eat ethnic foods at various stalls. This guild also holds spring, summer, and fall fairs. Call 808/254-6788 for information.

Annual Honolulu Marathon. An institution in marathon races. One of the best-attended and very prestigious races in the country, where top athletes from around the world turn out to compete. Call 808/734-7200.

The annual **Honolulu City Lights** festival starts off the Christmas season with the lighting of a Christmas tree at City Hall, followed by an electric light parade and other entertainment.

Annual Rainbow Classic. Invitational tournament of NCAA collegiate basketball teams. University of Hawai'i, Manoa.

Aloha Bowl and **O'ahu Bowl** are two post-season collegiate football games played at Aloha Stadium on Christmas Day.

On **New Year's Eve** hold onto your hat, because they do it up big in Hawaii. The merriment and alcohol flow all over the islands. Firecrackers are illegal, but they go off everywhere. Beware of hangovers and drunken drivers.

To counter the alcohol-inspired activities, the alcohol-free **First Night Honolulu,** a festival of music and other events, is sponsored at the Honolulu City Hall the last night of the year until midnight.

SPORTS AND RECREATION

SCUBA AND SNORKELING

O'ahu has particularly generous underwater vistas open to anyone donning a mask and fins. Snorkel and dive sites, varying in difficulty and challenge, are accessible from the island. Sites can be totally hospitable, good for families and first-time snorkelers who want an exciting but safe frolic; or they can be accessible only to the experienced diver. All over the island are dive shops from which you can rent or buy all equipment, and where dive boats and instruction on all levels can be arranged. There are dozens of well-known dive sites around the island, with many of these clustered along the Wai'anae Coast, the eastern half of the North Shore, and the southeastern corner of the island. Some features of note include drop-offs, walls, sea caves, arches, and sunken ships and planes.

Dive Shops and Rentals

In the Honolulu area, try the following. **Waikiki Diving,** 424 Nahua St., 808/922-2121, website: www.waikikidiving.com, does PADI certification, beach and boat dives. **South Seas Aquatics,** 2155 Kalakaua Ave., Suite 112, 808/922-0852, is a full-service dive shop with competitive pricing for certification, tours, and rentals. **Ocean Concepts,** 808/677-7975, website: www.oceanconcepts.com, has several shops around the island. **Reef Trekkers,** 808/943-0588, website: www.reeftrekkers.com, has established a good reputation for scuba tours.

Surf and Sea, 62-595 Kamehameha Hwy., 808/637-9887, website: www.surfnsea.com, is a complete dive shop on the North Shore in Hale'iwa offering certification, rentals, charters, and tours. Also offering educational dive options in Hale'iwa is **Deep Ecology,** 808/637-3992, website: www.deepecology.com.

Aloha Dive Shop at the Hawaii Kai Shopping Center (on the way to Hanauma Bay), 808/395-5922, website: www.alohadiveshop.com, does it all from snorkeling to boat dives. Excellent rates, good service. This shop is owned and run by Jackie James, the "First Lady of Diving" in Hawaii, with nearly 30 years of experience.

In Kailua, try the full service dive shops: **Aaron's Dive Shop,** 307 Hahani St., Kailua, 808/262-23233, website: www.hawaii-scuba.com;

O'AHU

or **Windward Dive Center,** 789 Kailua Road, 808/263-2311, website: www.divehawaii.com.

Snorkeling

While there are countless places to snorkel around the island, several spots are easily accessible to visitors. Perhaps the best spot right at Waikiki is Sans Souci Beach or the area right in front of the Natatorium. Going a little farther around the coast brings you to Hanauma Bay, perhaps the best, and certainly the most popular, spot on the island. Along the windward shore, Lanikai Beach with its offshore island and Goat Island at Malaekahana Park offer good options. Shark's Cove and Three Tables at Waimea are good but you have to be careful of the surf. On the leeward side, try Electric Beach at Kaha Point, which is just at the start of the road up the Wai'anae Coast.

Snorkel Rentals

Snorkel Bob's, 808/735-7944, at the corner of Kapahulu Ave. and Date St., has very inexpensive deals on snorkeling. Prices start at $3.50 a day or only $9 per week for full snorkel gear, which you can take to Maui, Kaua'i, and Big Island locations and return to his shops there for free. The better equipment (still a deal) runs to $29 a week. Snorkel Bob's also has underwater cameras, boogie boards for $6.50 a day or $26 a week, and wet suits at $15 a week. It's best to stop in and peruse the selection for just what you need. **Hanauma Bay Snorkeling,** 808/373-5060, rents full equipment for $6.25 a day and underwater cameras for $17. The company offers tours to Hanauma Bay from Waikiki for $18.75, including transportation, equipment, instruction, a fish I.D. chart, and a map of the reef. Also try **Paradise Snorkel Adventures,** 808/923-7766, which rents top-of-the-line equip-

J.D. BISIGNANI

exploring the reefs of O'ahu

ment for $6.95 a day and runs a shuttle to Hanauma Bay for $9.95 with equipment. Disposable underwater cameras go for $19.95, and the better ones are $20–25, for 24 or 36 exposures, respectively. Also running shuttle tours to Hanauma Bay from Waikiki is **Tommy's Tours,** 808/373-5060. They offer snorkel rental plus transportation for $17.50 adults. At Koko Marina, **Hanauma Bay Snorkel and Gifts,** 808/396-7083, also offers short shuttles and cheap rates.

Snuba
Snuba Tours of Oahu, 808/396-6163, offers snuba tours that include instruction and transportation. Free swim time runs about 30 minutes, and the total tour time is about 90 minutes. Three times a day, weekdays except Tuesday, tours are offered to Hanauma Bay for $65. For $60, Mon.–Sat., you can snuba the waters of Maunalua Bay on any of three tours. A four-hour tour for $99 is also run to the Wai'anae Coast Mon.–Sat., starting at 11 A.M.

CATCHING WAVES

Surfing
All the Hawaiian Islands have incredibly good surfing conditions, but O'ahu has the best. If there is such a thing as "the perfect wave," O'ahu's waters are a good place to look for it.

Conditions here are perfect for both rank beginners and the most acclaimed surfers in the world. Waikiki's surf is predictable, and just right to start on, while the **Banzai Pipeline** and **Waimea Bay** on the North Shore have some of the most formidable surfing conditions on earth. **Makaha Beach** in Wai'anae is perhaps the best all-around surfing beach, frequented by the living legends of this most graceful sport. Summertime brings rather flat wave action around the island, but the winter months are a totally different story, with monster waves on the North Shore and heavy surf at times even in the relative calm of Waikiki. *Never* surf without asking about local conditions, and remember that "a fool and his surfboard, and maybe his life, are soon parted." For **surfing conditions,** call 808/973-4383. Heed all warnings!

Surfing Lessons
Enterprises in Waikiki offer beach services. Often these concessions are affiliated with hotels, and almost all hotel activities desks can arrange surfing lessons for you. A lesson and board go for about $40, half that for the board alone. Most guarantee that they will get you standing, but as in skiing, a few good lessons to start you off are well worth the time and money. Some reputable surfing lessons along Waikiki are provided by Outrigger Waikiki Hotel and Hilton Hawaiian Village. Also check near the huge rack of surfboards along Kalakaua Avenue, just near

O'AHU

Kuhio Beach at the Waikiki Beach Center, where you'll find beach boy enterprises at competitive rates. Surfing schools usually charge a bit more for their services, but you get great instruction and a wide range of options. A one-hour group lesson will run $50, a private lesson $90; day and multiple-day lessons are also available. In Honolulu, try **Hans Hedemann Surf School,** 808/924-7778, for instructions and lessons; on the North Shore, contact **Eco-Surf Tours,** 808/638-9503, or **Surf and Sea,** 808/637-9887.

Windsurfing

Far and away the most famous windsurfing beach on O'ahu is Kailua Beach Park on the windward coast. Daily, a flotilla of windsurfers glide over its smooth waters, propelled by the always blowing breezes. Along the shore and in town enterprises build, rent, and sell sailboards. The North Shore also offers decent windsurfing.

Windsurfing Lessons and Rentals

Kailua Sailboard Company, with a perfect location only a minute from the beach in Kailua at 130 Kailua Rd., 808/262-2555, open 9 A.M.–5 P.M. daily, is a full-service sailboard and kayak store. Sailboard rentals are $39 per day, half day $29; weekly rates are also available. Beginning group lessons are $49 for a three-hour session. In addition, boogie boards cost $10 per day. Ocean kayaks run $25 a half day, $32 full day, and $125 a week. Double kayak rentals are $32, $42, and $195, respectively.

Naish Hawaii, 155 A Hamakua Dr., 808/262-6068 or 800/767-6068, open 9 A.M.–5:30 P.M. daily, is a very famous maker of custom boards, production boards, sails, hardware, accessories, and repairs. T-shirts, bathing suits, beach accessories, hats, and slippers are also for sale. Naish is the largest and oldest windsurfing company in Hawaii. The famous Naish Windsurfing School, at Kailua Beach, gives 90 minutes of personal instruction and an additional half-hour of board use for $55 including all equipment; $75 for two people, or $35 per person for a group.

In the North Shore, see **Surf and Sea,** 808/637-9887, in Hale'iwa, or **Eco-Surf Tours,** 808/638-9503, for lessons and rentals.

Boogie Boarding

The most highly acclaimed boogie-boarding beach on O'ahu is Sandy Beach. It also has the dubious distinction of being the most dangerous beach in Hawaii, with more drownings, broken backs, and broken necks than anywhere in the state. Waikiki is tame and excellent for boogie boarding, while Waimanalo Beach, on the southeast side, is more for the intermediate boogie-boarder.

THRILL CRAFT

Parasailing

For a once-in-a-lifetime treat try **Aloha Parasail,** 808/521-2446. Strapped into a harness complete with lifejacket, you're towed aloft to glide effortlessly over the waters off Waikiki. Aloha Parasail has free hotel pickup. Others are **Sea Breeze Water Sports,** 808/396-0100, at the Koko Marina Shopping Center, and **Hawaiian Parasail,** 808/591-1280. Rides go for around $50 and last about 10 minutes. Boats usually have up to six riders so you might be on the water for about an hour.

Jet Skiing

Jet skiing is not allowed in Waikiki. Head to the Koko Marina Shopping Center and check with **Hawaiian Ocean Thrills,** 808/539-9400; **Hawaii Sports,** 808/395-3773; or **Get Wet Hawaii,** 808/395-7255, which operate their machines in Maunalua Bay. Expect to pay about $50 for a half hour. Get Wet Hawaii and Hawaii Sports also provide water skiing and wakeboard equipment, rentals, and lessons. Rates run $39 for a 15-minute pull, $49 for 20 minutes, $59 for 30 minutes, and $69 for beginners with a lesson.

OCEAN TOURS

Sail and Dinner Cruises

If you're taking a tour at all, your best bet is a sail or dinner cruise. They're touristy, but a lot of fun, and actually good value. Many times money-saving coupons for them are found in the free tourist magazines, and plenty of street buskers in Waikiki give special deals. The latter are mostly on the up and up, but make sure that you know exactly what you're getting. Most of these cruises depart around 5:30 P.M. from the Kewalo Basin Marina, or from one of the piers near the Aloha Tower, and cruise Waikiki toward Diamond Head before returning about two hours later. On board is a buffet, an open bar, live entertainment, and dancing. Costs vary but run from about $50 on up, per person.

High-tech hits the high seas on the **Navatek I,** 808/973-1311 or 800/548-6262, website: www.atlantisadventures.com, a unique bi-hulled ship that guarantees the "most stable ride in the islands." Sailing from Pier 6, you have a choice of various cruises, including a midday lunch cruise, $45 adult and $26.50 children; a sunset dinner cruise, $120 and $72, featuring gourmet food and some of the best island entertainers; and a moonlight skyline dinner cruise, $69 and $49. Operated by Atlantis Adventures.

Dream Cruises, 808/592-5200 or 800/400-7300, website: www.dream-cruises.com, offers a seasonal (April–December) dolphin-watching tour along the leeward coast. Early and late morning 2.5-hour sails leave from Wai'anae's small boat harbor and include a small breakfast; $61.50 adults, $37.75 for children 17 and under, transportation from Honolulu included. December–April, several daily whale-watching tours leave from Honolulu's Kewalo Basin and cruise off Waikiki and Diamond Head; $23.95 adults and $16.95 for children. Other offerings include the twice-an-evening dinner/dance cruise off Waikiki ($48.95/$27.95). The newer midday Pacific Splash fun cruise ($62.95/$31.95) and the Morning Splash brunch cruise ($46.95/$25.95) take you to a mooring spot where you can play with the water toys, swim, and use the two-story water slide and trampoline. Snuba equipment and jet skis rent for an additional $40 and $30 (prepaid), respectively.

Paradise Cruises, 808/983-7827 or 800/334-6191, website: www.paradisecruises.com, also does dinner cruise and show combinations on the *Star of Honolulu, Starlet I,* and *Starlet II* ships. The *Starlet I* and *Starlet II* leave out of the Kewalo Basin 5:15–5:30 P.M. for two-hour cruises. Prices range $29–72 adult for the Sunset Grill or Dinner Cruise. The *Star of Honolulu* offers three options from $62 to the $164 five-star, seven-course French dinner cruise with all the extras; it departs from Pier 8 near Aloha Tower. During the day, *Starlet II* does a water adventure day off Waikiki for $46.95 adult. The daytime cruise of the *Star of Honolulu* includes a tour of the south O'ahu coast, Pearl Harbor, and a view of the USS *Arizona* Memorial and USS *Missouri* from the water. Continental breakfast and lunch are included for $39 adult and $20 children.

The *Ali'i Kai* catamaran packs them in for a sunset dinner cruise and live band dance. At $52 adult and $29 for kids 4–11, the ride includes dinner, a Polynesian show, three free cocktails, and dancing. For $70 adult, $50 child, you can have all that plus a seat at the Magic of Polynesia illusion show in town. Call 808/539-9400 for reservations. Another barge-like catamaran, although not as large as the *Ali'i Kai,* offering similar a dinner cruise with live entertainment, is the **Voyager** Catamaran Sail, which leaves at 5:30 P.M. from Kewalo Basin. Tickets run $40 adults and $26 for kids.

For the pure thrill of running under the wind, have a sail with **Maitai** Catamaran, 808/922-5665. Ninety-minute trips leave several times a day for $20 per person, while the sunset cocktail cruise goes for $30. These cruises leave from the pier in front of the Hilton Hawaiian Village and cruise the waters off Waikiki. On the North Shore, try the catamaran **Ho'o Nanea** out of Hale'iwa harbor, 808/638-8279, which does sailing, snorkeling, and whale-watching tours. Tours from **Wild Side Specialty Tours,** 808/255-5812, website: www.sailhawaii.com, include snorkeling and whale- and dolphin-watching on its sailing boat. The size of the boat limits the number of guests to six, and a sailing charter runs $95 per person for a half day.

Captain Bob's, 808/942-5077 or 800/262-8798, tours Kane'ohe Bay aboard the *Barefoot I* catamaran daily (except Sunday) and features a picnic lunch and all the water activities that you can handle on its four-hour sail 10:30 A.M.–2:30 P.M. Prices run $69 adults, $55 for ages 13–17, and $49 for kids 3–12. You can work off lunch snorkeling or playing volleyball on the beach. The food is passable, but the setting offshore with the *pali* in the background is world-class. Transportation from Waikiki is included. Boats depart from He'eia Kea Harbor north of Kane'ohe.

Also operating on Kane'ohe Bay and out of He'eia Kea Harbor is **Club Kona Ocean Sports,** 808/226-2267, which runs a pontoon boat out to the sandbar, where kayaks and banana boats can be rented and snorkel gear used. This company, which caters largely although not exclusively to Japanese, runs daily except Sunday. The **Coral Queen,** 808/235-2192, runs its glass-bottom boat from He'eia Kea Harbor as well for daily trips to the Kane'ohe Bay, $10 adults or $5 for children 3–11.

Underwater Cruises

As beautiful as O'ahu is topside, it can be more exquisite below the waves. **Atlantis Submarines,** 808/973-9800, 800/548-6262, website: www.atlantisadventures.com, costs $59 adult, $39 children 12 and under, and departs daily every hour on the hour 7 A.M.–4 P.M. from the Hilton Hawaiian Village, where you board the Hilton Rainbow Catamaran, which ferries you to the waiting sub. Once aboard, you're given a few instructions and then it's "run silent, run deep, run excited" for about 45 minutes. The sub is amazingly comfortable. Seats are arranged so that everyone gets a prime view through the large windows, and the air is amazingly fresh. The larger futuristic sub measures 96 feet and carries 64 passengers; the smaller is 65 feet long and carries 48 passengers. Outfitted with videocams, it allows the passengers to view the undersea world in every direction, while listening to explanations of the varied sea life through a multilanguage audio system. A thrill of a lifetime.

A similar tour is offered by **Voyager Submarines,** 808/539-9440. Although you can't live in this yellow submarine, it'll escort you to the sea of green. From the comfort of the sub, you can view the wonders of life below the waves. From Kewalo Basin, a catamaran takes you to the sub lying offshore, where you and 47 others will board the yellow sub. Running 8 A.M.–3 P.M., each tour lasts about 90 minutes and runs $81 for adults. Captain, captain, full speed ahead.

Kayaking

Go Banana Kayaks, 799 Kapahulu, 808/737-9514, is into kayaks. Single-person kayaks run $30 per day, $42 for two-person kayaks; lessons and guided tours are available. Aside from renting kayaks, the store sells kayak and canoe gear and equipment.

Near the beach in Kailua, **Kailua Sailboard Company,** 808/262-2555, website: www.kailu-asailboards.com, also rents kayaks. It's a good company with a great location and competitive prices. A guided tour of the coast and islands off Kailua Beach runs $79. Good service, good prices, free pickup in Waikiki. Its prices are about the same as **Twogood Kayaks Hawaii,** 808/262-5656, 345 Hahani St. in Kailua, website: www.aloha.com/~twogood, which also offers kayak rentals, sales, and lessons. Full-day rental $32, tandem $42, and the kayak will be dropped off for free at the Kailua Beach Park ($10 delivery fee for other locations in Kailua). Half-day and multiday rates are also an option. Open Mon.–Fri. 9 A.M.–5 P.M., Sat.–Sun. 8 A.M.–5 P.M.

FISHING

Deep-Sea Fishing

O'ahu's offshore waters are alive with game fish. Among these underwater fighters are marlin, *'ahi, ono,* mahimahi, and an occasional deep-water snapper. The deep-sea boats generally troll the Penguin Banks and the generally calm waters along the Wai'anae Coast, from Barbers Point to Ka'ena Point.

The vast majority of O'ahu's fleet moors in **Kewalo Basin,** in Honolulu Harbor along Ala Moana Boulevard next to Fishermen's Wharf. The boat harbor is a sight in itself, and if you're contemplating a fishing trip, it's best to head down there the day before and yarn with the captains and returning fishermen. This way you can get a feel for a charter to suit you best.

For a charter organization try **Hawaii Charter Skippers Association,** 808/591-9100. Many private boats operating out of Kewalo Basin include: *Sea Verse,* 808/591-8840; **Island Charters,** 808/593-9455; **Kamome Sport Fishing,** 808/593-8931; *Maggie Joe* and *Sea Hawk,* 808/591-8888; **Kuu Huapala Fishing Co.,** 808/596-0918; and **The Wild Bunch,** 808/596-4709.

A few boats operate out of **Pokai Bay,** in Wai'anae on the leeward coast, and a few berth in Hale'iwa on the North Shore, like *Chupu Charters,* 808/638-7655.

Freshwater Fishing

The state maintains two public freshwater fishing areas on O'ahu. The **Wahiawa Public Fishing**

Area is 300 acres of fishable waters in and around the town of Wahiawa. It's basically an irrigation reservoir used to hold water for cane fields. Species regularly caught here are large and smallmouth bass, sunfish, channel catfish, *tucunare,* oscar, carp, snakehead, and Chinese catfish. The other area is the **Nu'uanu Reservoir no. 4,** a 25-acre restricted watershed above Honolulu in the Ko'olau Mountains. It's open for fishing only three times per year in May, August, and November. Fish caught here are tilapia and Chinese catfish.

CAMPING AND HIKING

Few people equate visiting O'ahu with camping. The two seem mutually exclusive, especially when you focus on the mystique of Waikiki and the dominance of a major city like Honolulu. But among state, county, and private campgrounds, you have about 20 spots to choose from all over the island.

State Parks

O'ahu boasts 22 state parks, recreation areas, waysides, and monuments. A majority offer a beach for day use, walking paths, picnic areas, toilets, showers, and/or pavilions. The state parks close their gates and parking lots at night. Those *not* offering camping are open 7 A.M.–7:45 P.M. from April 1 to Labor Day, closing during the remainder of the year at 6:45 P.M.

Four state parks currently offer tent camping: **Sand Island State Recreation Area,** just a few minutes from downtown Honolulu; **Keaiwa Heiau State Recreation Area,** in the interior on the heights above 'Aiea; **Malaekahana Bay State Recreation Area,** a mile north of La'ie on the windward coast; and **Kahana Valley State**

O'AHU CAMPGROUNDS

MALAEKAHANA STATE RECREATION AREA
Kahuku
KOKOLOLIO BEACH COUNTY PARK
KAIAKA BEACH COUNTY PARK
HAU'ULA BEACH COUNTY PARK
MOKULE'IA BEACH COUNTY PARK
Hale'iwa
SWANZY BEACH COUNTY PARK
KAHANA VALLEY STATE PARK
KUALOA REGIONAL PARK
KEA'AU BEACH COUNTY PARK
Wahiawa
LUALUALEI BEACH COUNTY PARK
Wai'anae
KEAIWA HEIAU STATE RECREATION AREA
MA'ILI BEACH COUNTY PARK
Kane'ohe
Kailua
BELLOWS FIELD BEACH COUNTY PARK
NANAKULI BEACH COUNTY PARK
WAIMANALO BAY BEACH PARK
Waimanalo
HONOLULU
SAND ISLAND STATE RECREATION AREA
WAIMANALO BEACH COUNTY PARK

Kaua'i Channel
PACIFIC OCEAN
PACIFIC OCEAN

NOTE: PARKS ARE OPEN FOR CAMPING ON A ROTATING BASIS. CHECK FIRST.

0   5 mi
0   5 km

O'AHU

Park between Punalu'u and Ka'a'awa on the windward coast.

To camp at Sand Island, Keaiwa Heiau, or Kahana Valley park, you must acquire a permit from the Dept. of Land and Natural Resources, Division of State Parks, P.O. Box 621 (1151 Punchbowl St.), Honolulu, HI 96809, 808/587-0300, open weekdays 8 A.M.–3:30 P.M. Camping fees are $5 per campsite for every night of use. O'ahu campsite **permit reservations** can be made only 30 days prior to the first day of camping, but *must* be made at least one week in advance. Write for a permit application form. Information needed includes your name, address, phone number, names and identification numbers of all persons over 18 years of age in your party, type of permit requested, duration of your stay, and specific dates requested. The permits can be picked up on arrival with proof of identification.

On O'ahu campsites are at a premium and people line up at 8 A.M. on the first-floor breezeway on the Beretania Street side of the issuing office, just outside the double glass doors, where you are given a number on a first-come, first-served basis (usually no hassle except on three-day holiday weekends). After this, go to the third floor where the office is.

Camping is allowed *only* from Friday 8 A.M. to Wednesday 8 A.M. (closed all day Wednesday and Thursday for camping—other activities okay), with the shutdown for, supposedly, regrowth and maintenance. Camping on Sand Island SRA only is Friday through Monday. Camping is allowed for only five consecutive days in any one month, and don't forget a parking permit for your vehicle, which must remain within the locked park gates at night.

Camping at Malaekahana State Recreation Area is handled by the Friends of Malaekahana, P.O. Box 305, La'ie, HI 96762, 808/293-1736 or fax 808/293-2066. Reservations are taken up to 12 months in advance and at least 14 days before planned arrival. Check-in is handled 3–5 P.M.; checkout time is noon. The office is open Mon.–Fri. 10 A.M.–3 P.M. Write or call for information and reservation applications. Firearms, fireworks, pets, and drinking of alcoholic beverages are prohibited in the park, and a quiet time is enforced 10:30 P.M.–8 A.M. Half a dozen beach houses, which sleep up

to 10, run $66 a night during the week and $80 on weekends. Tent campers pay $5 a night. A few yurts on the property can be rented when not occupied by students during the school year. The yurts do not have bath or cooking facilities, but they have floors and electricity. Outside hot showers and bathroom facilities are shared. Bring mosquito repellent. The pavilion can be rented for day events or for the day and night ($250)—it sleeps 15. Parking is limited. Make sure to call and make arrangements with the staff if you will be arriving later than office hours. The park gate is locked—for your security—7 A.M.–7 P.M.

County Parks

There are nearly 300 county parks on the island of O'ahu. The city and county of Honolulu has opened 13 (these change periodically) of its 62 beach parks around the island to tent camping, and most allow trailers and RVs. A free permit is required, and camping is allowed only from Friday at 8 A.M. until the following Wednesday at 8 A.M., at which time your campsite must be vacated (no camping Wednesday and Thursday evenings). A few of these parks have camping only on the weekends and one allows it only during summer months, so be sure to ask for particulars. These campsites are also at a premium, but you can write for reservations and pick up your permits on arrival with proper identification. For information and reservations write or visit City and County of Honolulu, Dept. of Parks and Recreation, Permit Section, 650 S. King St., Honolulu, HI 96813, 808/523-4525. Permits are also available from the satellite city halls around the island.

Note: All of the beach parks are closed during designated months (they differ from park to park) throughout the year. This is supposedly for cleaning, but really it's to reduce the possibility of squatters moving in. Make sure, if you're reserving far in advance, that the park will be open when you arrive. Don't count on the Parks and Recreation Department to inform you!

Hiking

The best way to leave the crowds of tourists behind and become intimate with the beauty of O'ahu is to hike it. Although the Neighbor Islands receive fewer visitors, a higher percentage of people hike them than Oʻahu. Don't get the impression that you'll have the island to yourself, but you will be amazed at how open and lovely this crowded island can be. Some cultural and social hikes can be taken without leaving the city, like a stroll through Waikiki and a historical walking tour of downtown Honolulu and Chinatown. But others—some mere jaunts, others quite strenuous—are well worth the time and effort.

Remember that much of Oʻahu is privately owned, and you must have permission to cross this land, or you may be open to prosecution. Usually private property is marked by signs. Another source that might stomp your hiking plans with their jungle boots is the military. A full 25 percent of Oʻahu belongs to Uncle Sam, and he isn't always thrilled when you decide to play in his back yard. Some of the finest walks (like to the summit of Mt. Kaʻala) require crossing military lands, much of which has been altered by very unfriendly looking installations. Always check and obey any posted signs to avert trouble. Many of the most accessible trails on Oʻahu are in the hills behind Honolulu in the Makiki-Tantalus area. The far side of the Koʻolau Range above Kailua holds other hiking trails that are also easy to get to. Others farther to the north are more remote and less frequented. The most popular of these, the trail to Sacred Falls, was shut down a few years ago due to a landslide and deaths of several hikers. See the travel chapters below for specific trail references.

Hiking Groups and Information

Since 1997, the ecotour operator **Oʻahu Nature Tours,** P.O. Box 8059, Honolulu, HI 96830, tel. 808/924-2473 or 800/861-6018, website: www.oahunaturetours.com, email: natureguide@oahu-naturetours.com, has offered daily hiking tours that focus on native birds and plants. The Diamond Head Crater Sunrise tour, 6–8 A.M., runs $20, and this is followed by the Volcanic Coastal Excursion to the southeast corner of the island, which runs 9 A.M.–12:30 P.M. for $37. An afternoon Hawaiian Rainforest Waterfall tour into the Koʻolau Range lasts 2–5:30 P.M. and also runs $37. When combining the sunrise tour with either of the other tours, the fee is $52. Conducted by owner Michael Walther and with a limit of six participants, each tour is an environmental education experience as well as a fun outing. Transportation and all equipment is provided.

Mauka Makai Excursions, tel. 808/593-3525 or 877/326-6248, website: www.oahu-ecotourism.com, offers several eco-friendly drive and hiking tours around the island that focus on cultural history and places of archaeological importance. Full- and half-day trips take you to North Shore or windward Oʻahu sites. Trips run $35–60 for adults, $10 less for kids 6–17 years old.

Camping Gear and Rentals

If you've come without camping gear and wish to rent some try **The Bike Shop,** 1149 S. King St., Honolulu, 808/596-0588, renting two-person tents and backpacks at $35 for a weekend or $70 for the week. A $200 deposit, returned when you return their equipment, is required. **Omar the Tentman,** 94-158, Leoole St., Waipahu, 808/677-8785 rents a wider variety of equipment and offers prices for one- to three-day or four- to seven-day periods. A six-person dome tent runs $52/$57, sleeping bags $15/$20, stoves $14/18, and lanterns (you supply to fuel) $14/$18. They have no backpacking tents.

For sales, try **The Bike Shop.** Also, **The Sports Authority** has a great variety of outdoor sports and camping equipment at decent prices. Much of the camping gear is more useful for car and beach camping than backpacking but it does offer a selection. Most convenient is their store in the Ward Gateway Center. **Powder Edge** has two shops, at the Aloha Tower Marketplace and the Ward Village Shops, and a website for some outdoor equipment (www.powderedge.com).

Topographical Maps

On Oʻahu, a wide range of topographical maps can be purchased at the **Pacific Map Center,** 560 N. Nimitz Hwy., 206A, Honolulu, HI 96817, 808/545-3600, or at **Hawaii Geographic Maps and Books,** 49 S. Hotel St., Honolulu, 808/538-3952 or 800/538-3950, open 10 A.M.–2 P.M. Monday, Wednesday, and Friday.

HORSEBACK RIDING

A different and delightful way to see Oʻahu is from the back of a horse. The following outfits operate trail rides on different parts of the island. **Kualoa Ranch,** 808/237-8515, by reservation only, at the north end of Kane'ohe Bay, offers 45-minute rides along the base of the *pali* for $28 and 90-minute rides into Ka'a'awa Valley for $45. Rides also are given as part of the ranch's all-day adventure packages. Hotel pickup available. The stable at **Turtle Bay Hilton,** 808/293-8811, on the North Shore, welcomes both resort guests and nonguests. Gentle guided trail rides through the ironwood forest and along the beach are run several times daily; adults $35, children age nine and above $22 for the 35-minute saunter. Ride every day in the hills above Waimanalo with **Correa Trails Hawaii.** Correa offers easy one-hour rides along the lower windward side of the Ko'olau Range at 10 A.M., noon, 2 P.M., and 4 P.M. Rides run $49.95 per person, you must be at least age eight and weigh no more than 275 pounds. Call for reservations, 808/259-9005. The stable is at 41-050 Kalaniana'ole Hwy. just outside of Waimanalo. On the North Shore, **Happy Trails Hawaii,** 808/638-7433, gets you on horseback for easy rides along the edge of the canyon looking into Waimea Valley. The one-hour and 90-minute rides run $38 and $48, respectively. The age requirement is six years old and you cannot weigh more than 235 pounds to ride.

BICYCLING

Pedaling around O'ahu can be both fascinating and frustrating. The roads are well paved, but the shoulders are often torn up. Traffic in and around Honolulu is horrifying, and the only way to avoid it is to leave very early in the morning. Many, but not all, of the city buses have been equipped with bike racks, so it's easier than before to get your bike from one part of the city to another or out of town. Once you leave the city, traffic, especially on the secondary interior roads, isn't too bad. Unfortunately, all of the coastal roads are heavily trafficked. Pedaling around Waikiki, although congested, is usually safe, and a fun way of seeing the sights. Always use a helmet, always lock your bike, and always take your bike bag.

Bike Rental and Bike Shops

For bicycle rentals try: **The Bike Shop,** 808/596-0588, 1149 S. King St.; **Big Mountain Rentals,** 2426 Kuhio Ave., 808/926-1644; **Blue Sky Rentals,** 808/947-0101, at 1920 Ala Moana Ave.; or **Paradise Isle Rentals,** 1879 Kalakaua Ave., 808/946-7777. Most rental bikes are mountain bikes or hybrids. Expect to pay about $15–20 a day or $50–70 a week, depending upon the type. For 1–4 hours on a cruiser or mountain bike, you'll be charged up to $10.

For sales and repairs try: **The Bike Shop,** 1149 S. King St., 808/596-0588; **The Bike Factory,** 740 Ala Moana Blvd., 808/596-8844; **Island Triathlon and Bike,** 569 Kapahulu Ave., 808/732-7227; **McCully Bicycle,** 2124 S. King St., 808/955-6329; and **Raging Isle Surf and Cycle,** 66-250 Kamehameha Hwy. in Hale'iwa, 808/637-7707.

GOLF

With 38 public, private, municipal, and military golf courses scattered around such a relatively small island, it's a wonder that it doesn't rain golf balls. These courses range from modest nine-holers to world-class courses whose tournaments attract the biggest names in golf today. Prices range from $10 a round up to $145. An added attraction of playing O'ahu's courses is that you get to walk around on some of the most spectacular and manicured pieces of real estate on the island. Some afford sweeping views of the coast, such as the **Ko 'Olina Golf Club,** while others, like the **Pali Golf Course,** have a lovely mountain backdrop, or, like Waikiki's **Ala Wai Golf Course,** are surrounded by city spread. The Ala Wai Golf Course also must be one of the busiest courses in the country as some 500 rounds of golf are played there daily! In 1994, the PGA rated the **Ko'olau Golf Course** the toughest course in the United States. Tough or easy, flat or full of definition, O'ahu provides ample opportunity and variety for any golfer.

For ease of use for municipal golf courses, the City and County of Honolulu has set up an automated tee time reservation and information system. Call 808/296-2000 to make or check your reservation or to have your inquiry answered.

TENNIS

Grease up the old elbow, because Oʻahu boasts 181 county-maintained tennis courts, 124 of which are lighted. Most courts also have backboards. To get information on where they are located, call the Dept. of Parks and Recreation, Tennis Division, at 808/971-7150. Alternately, you can stop by the Diamond Head Tennis Center at 3908 Paki Ave., Honolulu, and pick up a copy of a complete list. The accompanying chart is a partial listing of what's available.

HUNTING

Game on Oʻahu includes wild pig and goat, plus a variety of pheasant, francolin, quail, partridge, and dove. For information on hunting on Oʻahu, contact the Department of Land and Natural Resources, Division of Forestry and Wildlife, 1151 Punchbowl St., Honolulu, HI 96813, 808/587-0166. For recorded hunting information, call 808/587-0171.

LAND TOURS

Guided land tours are much more of a luxury than a necessity on Oʻahu. Because of the excellent bus system and relatively cheap rental cars, you spend a lot of money for a narration and to be spared the hassle of driving. If you've come in a group and don't intend to rent a car, they may be worth it. Sea cruises and air tours are equally luxurious, but provide glimpses of this beautiful island you'd normally miss. The following partial list of tour companies should get you started.

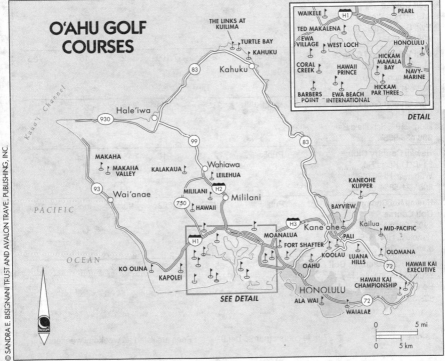

© SANDRA E. BISIGNANI TRUST AND AVALON TRAVEL PUBLISHING, INC.

O'AHU GOLF COURSES

COURSE	STATUS	PAR	YARDS	FEES†	CART	CLUBS
Ala Wai Golf Course 404 Kapahulu Ave. Honolulu, HI 96851 808/733-7387	Municipal	70	6,208	$42	$16	$25
Barbers Point Golf Course NAS, Barbers Point, HI 96862 808/682-1911	Military	72	6,394	22/28	10	5
BayView Golf Park 45-285 Kane'ohe Bay Dr. Kaneohe, HI 96744 808/247-0451	Public	60	3,399	62/73	incl.	21
Coral Creek Golf Course 91-1111 Geiger Rd. Ewa Beach, HI 96706 808/441-4653	Public	72	6,025	125	incl.	30
Ewa Beach International Golf Course 91-050 Fort Weaver Rd. Ewa Beach, HI 96706 808/689-8351	Semiprivate	72	5,998	90	incl.	35
Ewa Village Golf Course Mango Tree Road Ewa Beach, HI 96706 808/681-0220	Municipal	72	7,100	42	16	25
Fort Shaffer Golf Course USAG-HI Golf Bldg. 2104, Schofield Barracks, HI 96857 808/438-9587	Military	34*	2,900	18/22	8	8
Hawaii Country Club 94-1211 Kunia Rd. Wahiawa, HI 96786 808/621-5654	Public	72	5,916	45/65	incl.	20
Hawaii Kai Championship Golf Course 8902 Kalaniana'ole Hwy. Honolulu, HI 96825 808/395-2358	Public	72	6,222	90/100	incl.	30
Hawaii Kai Executive Golf Course 8902 Kalaniana'ole Hwy. Honolulu, HI 96825 808/395-2358	Public	55	2,386	28/33	8.50	15

* 9-hole course   ** 27-hole course (par 36 per 9)   † Fees are listed as weekday/weekend

COURSE	STATUS	PAR	YARDS	FEES†	CART	CLUBS
Hawaii Prince Golf Club 91-1200 Fort Weaver Rd. Ewa Beach, HI 96706 808/944-4567	Resort	36**	3,350	$135	incl.	$35
Kahuku Golf Course P.O. Box 417 Kahuku, HI 96731 808/293-5842	Municipal	35*	2,699	10	4	12
Kalakaua Golf Course USAG-HI Bldg. 2104- Schofield Barracks, HI 96857 808/655-9833	Military	72	6,186	27	8	8
Kapolei Golf Course 91-701 Farrington Hwy. Kapolei, HI 96707 808/674-2227	Semiprivate	72	6,136	70/90	incl.	30
Ko ʻOlina Golf Course 92-1220 Aliʻinui Dr. Kapolei, HI 96707 808/676-5300	Resort	72	6,867	145	incl.	50
Koʻolau Golf Course 45-550 Kionaole Rd. Kaneʻohe, HI 96744 808/236-4653	Public	72	6,797	110	incl.	35
Leilehua Golf Course USAG-HI Bldg. 2104- Schofield Barracks, HI 96857 808/655-4653	Military	72	6,521	33	8	8
Luana Hills Country Club 770 Auloa Rd. Kailua, HI 96734 808/262-2139	Semiprivate	72	6,164	50/80	incl.	30
Makaha Golf Club 84-627 Makaha Valley Rd. Waianae, HI 96792 808/695-9578	Public	72	6,369	55/65	incl.	30
Mid-Pacific Country Club 266 Kaelepulu Dr. Kailua, HI 96734 808/261-9765	Semiprivate	72	6,509	125	incl.	25
Mililani Golf Club 95-176 Kuahelani Ave. Mililani, HI 96789 808/623-2222	Semiprivate	72	6,455	89/95	incl.	25

OʻAHU

(continues on next page)

O'AHU GOLF COURSES
(continued)

COURSE	STATUS	PAR	YARDS	FEES†	CART	CLUBS
Moanalua Golf Club 1250 Ala Aolani St. Honolulu, HI 96819 808/839-2411	Semiprivate	36*	2,972	$20/25	$14	No
Olomana Golf Links 41-1801 Kalaniana'ole Hwy. Waimanalo, HI 96795 808/259-7926	Public	72	6,304	65	incl.	25
Pali Golf Course 45-050 Kamehameha Hwy. Kane'ohe, HI 96744 808/266-7612	Municipal	72	6,524	12/16	16	30
Pearl Country Club 98-535 Kaonohi St. Aiea, HI 96701 808/487-3802	Semiprivate	72	6,232	65/70	incl.	30
Ted Makalena Golf Course 93-059 Waipio Point Access Rd., Waipahu, HI 96797 808/675-6052	Municipal	71	5,946	42	10	15
The Links at Kuilima 57-049 Kamehameha Hwy. Kahuku, HI 96731 808/293-8574	Resort	72	6,795	125	incl.	30
Turtle Bay Country Club 57-049 Kamehameha Hwy. Kahaku, HI 96731 808/293-8574	Resort	36*	3,204	55	incl.	20
Waikele Golf Course 94-200 Paioa Place Waipahu, HI 96797 808/676-9000	Semiprivate	72	6,261	107/112	incl.	30
West Lock Golf Course 91-1126 Okupe St. Ewa Beach, HI 96706 808/675-6076	Municipal	72	5,849	42	16	15

* 9-hole course   ** 27-hole course (par 36 per 9)   † Fees are listed as weekday/weekend

O'AHU

O'AHU TENNIS COURTS

COUNTY COURTS

Under the jurisdiction of the Department of Parks and Recreation Tennis Division, 3908 Paki Ave., Honolulu, HI 96815, 808/971-7150. Courts listed are in Honolulu, Waikiki, and main towns only.

TOWN	LOCATION	NO. OF COURTS	LIGHTED
'Aiea	'Aiea District Park	2	Yes
'Ewa	'Ewa Beach Community Park	4	Yes
Kahala	Kahala Community Park	2	No
Kailua	Kailua District Park	8	Yes
Kaimuki	Kaimuki Community Park	2	Yes
Kane'ohe	Kane'ohe District Park	6	Yes
Ke'ehi	Ke'ehi Lagoon Courts	12	Yes
Koko Head	Koko Head District Park	6	Yes
Manoa	Manoa Valley District Park	4	Yes
Maunawili	Maunawili Valley Park	2	Yes
Mililani	Mililani District Park	4	No
Pearl City	Pearl City	2	Yes
Sunset Beach	Sunset Beach Neighborhood Park	2	Yes
Wahiawa	Wahiawa District Park	4	Yes
Wai'alua	Wai'alua District Park	4	Yes
Waianae	Waianae District Park	8	Yes
Waikiki	Ala Moana Park	10	Yes
Waikiki	Diamond Head Tennis Center	10	No
Waikiki	Kapi'olani Tennis Courts	4	Yes
Waimanalo	Waimanalo District Park	4	No
Waipahu	Waipahu District Park	4	Yes

HOTEL AND PRIVATE COURTS THAT ARE OPEN TO THE PUBLIC

TOWN	LOCATION	TEL. (808)	FEE	NO. OF COURTS	LIGHTED
'Aina Haina	Honolulu Tennis Academy	373-1282	$20/hr.	2	Yes
'Ewa Beach	Hawaii Prince Golf Club	944-4567	5/hr.	2	Yes
Kahuku	Hilton Turtle Bay Golf and Tennis Resort	293-8811	10/day	10	Yes
Kopolei	J.W. Marriott Ihilani Resort	679-0079	24/hr.	6	Yes

Bus and Shuttle Tours

If you're going to take a land tour, you must have the right attitude, or it'll be a disaster. Your tour leader, usually driving the van or bus, is part instructor, comedian, and cheerleader. There's enough "corn" in his or her jokes to impress an Iowa hog. On the tour, you're expected to become part of one big happy family, and most importantly, to be a good sport. Most guides are quite knowledgeable about O'ahu and its history, and they honestly try to do a good job. But they've done it a million times before, and their performance can be as stale as week-old bread. The larger the tour vehicle and the shorter the miles covered, the worse it is likely to be. If you still want a tour, take a full-day jaunt in a small van: you get to know the other people and the guide, who'll tend to give you a more in-depth presentation. Tips are cheerfully accepted. Also, be aware that some tours get kickbacks from stores and restaurants they take you to, where you don't always get the best bargains. Most companies offer free hotel pickup and delivery. Lunch or dinner is not included unless specified, but if the tour includes a major tourist spot like Waimea Falls Park or the Polynesian Cultural Center, admission is usually included.

About half a dozen different tours offered by most companies are variations on the same theme, and the cost is fairly uniform. One of the more popular is a **circle-island tour,** including numerous stops around Waikiki, the windward coast, North Shore, and the center of the island. These usually run about $50, half that for children. An afternoon and evening Polynesian Cultural Center tour, including admission and dinner show, costs close to $70. Tours to Pearl Harbor and the Arizona Memorial and to Diamond Head both run around $25.

Some reputable companies include: **Polynesian Adventure Tours,** 808/833-3000, website: www.polyad.com; **Roberts Hawaii,** 808/539-9400, website: www.robertshawaii.com; **E Noa Tours,** 808/591-2561, website: www.enoa.com; and **VIP Trans,** 808/922-5711. With tours mostly focused on the Pearl Harbor area is **Discovering Hidden Hawaii Tours,** 808/946-0432, website: www.discoverhawaiitours.com. Hotel activities desks and activities centers around Waikiki can also arrange tours for you or point you in the right direction.

Offering a different angle on the land tour is **Hawaii Film and Celebrity Tours.** This company runs a circle-island tour twice daily, but it focuses on locations where movies and TV shows have been filmed. Some of the movies filmed on O'ahu were *From Here to Eternity* and *Tora Tora Tora,* which portrayed different aspects of World War II; *Gidget Goes Hawaiian,* which eased us through the halcyon days after the war; and *Jurassic Park,* which brought us all to a

fanciful future. These films showed glimpses of Hawaii, but *Hawaii Five-O* and *Magnum P.I.* helped more than the movies to bring an understanding of the islands to TV viewers all over the world. Adults $55, children 4–12 $45. For information and reservations, call 808/926-3456.

Special Walking Tours
The following are special tours that you should seriously consider.

Walking Tour of Chinatown, 808/533-3181, by the Chinese Chamber of Commerce, leaves every Tuesday at 9:30 A.M. from in front of its offices at 42 N. King Street. The cost is $5 for the 2.5-hour tour. The **Hawaiian Heritage Center** offers a similar historical and cultural two-hour tour of Chinatown, leaving from the Ramsey Galleries at 1128 Smith St. every Friday at 9:30 A.M. The cost is $5 per person. Call 808/521-2749 for reservations.

The American Institute of Architects (AIA) offers a walking tour of downtown Honolulu and Chinatown, exploring the old edifices of the city. This walking tour starts from the institute's office at 1128 Nu'uanu Ave. at 9:30 A.M. on Tuesday and Saturday and returns about noon. The price is $15 per person or $25 per couple, and reservations and prepayment by credit card are necessary; 808/545-4242.

Walking Tour of Honolulu is a three-hour tour led by a very knowledgeable volunteer from the **Mission Houses Museum.** Starting with a walk through the houses of the museum, you're led on a wonderfully anecdoted walk through the historical buildings of central Honolulu for only $15 (reduced fees for seniors, *kama'aina,* military, and students). Tours are given on Thursday only and start at 9:45 A.M. from the Mission Houses Museum. Reservations are required; call 808/531-0481.

Honolulu Time Walks, 2634 S. King St., Suite 3, Honolulu, HI 96826, 808/943-0371, offers fascinating interpretive walking tours focusing on the city's colorful past. The tours, ranging in price $5–40 (most about $10), sometimes including dinner, are thematic and change regularly. Expect topics like A Journey to Old Waikiki, Mysteries of Mo'ili'ili, Scandalous Days of Old Honolulu, and the very popular Ghosts of Honolulu. Master storyteller Glen Grant, in costume, hosts many of the tours. Thematic bus and trolley tours are also offered, and several historical shows are performed at the Waikiki Heritage Theater in the International Marketplace. Extremely authentic and painstakingly researched, these tours and shows are immensely educational and entertaining. You can't find better. Reserve!

The **Hawaii Nature Center,** 2131 Makiki Heights Dr., Honolulu, HI, 808/955-0100, is a nonprofit organization dedicated to environmental education through a hands-on approach. Primarily geared toward school-age children, but welcoming the young at heart, the Hawaii Nature Center offers weekend community programs for families and the public to share in the wealth of Hawaii's magnificent natural environment through interpretive hikes, earth care projects, and nature crafts. This is a wonderful opportunity for visitors to explore Hawaii through direct interaction with the environment.

The volunteer organization **Clean Air Team,** 808/948-3299, hosts a hike up Diamond Head every Saturday 9 A.M.–noon, regardless of weather, leaving from the front entrance of the Honolulu Zoo. There is no cost for this hike, but a donation of $5 is accepted to further programs of this nonsmoker's rights advocacy group. Additionally, this group runs a hike to Jackass Ginger waterfall and natural swimming pool on Sunday, leaving at 9 A.M. from near the Mahatma Gandhi statue in front of the Honolulu Zoo. A $10 contribution is requested, and transportation is by public bus.

If you don't want to follow the leader, but still desire to get out and stretch your legs while soaking up a bit of the local color, try a **city walking tour.** To promote good health and exercise, the Hawaii Department of Health has put together a fun brochure/map briefly outlining 15 different walks in the downtown Honolulu, Waikiki, and Diamond Head areas. Pick up a copy in person or write to the Physical Activity Promotion Project, Hawaii Department of Health, Room 210, 1250 Punchbowl St., Honolulu, HI 96813, and ask for the *Honolulu Walking Map.* Be sure to include a business-size SASE.

AIR TOURS

When you soar above Oʻahu, you realize just how beautiful this island actually is, and considering that the better part of a million people live in this relatively small space, it's amazing just how much undeveloped land still exists in the interior and even along the coast. The following are some air tours worth considering. Remember that small one- or two-plane operations come and go as quickly as cloudbursts. They're all licensed and regulated for safety, but if business is bad, the propellers stop spinning.

Fixed Wing Tours

Novel air tours are offered from Dillingham Airfield, along the northwest coast, a few miles down the Farrington Highway west of Haleʻiwa. Once in the air, you can soar silently above the coast with **Glider Rides,** 808/677-3404, an outfit offering one- or two-passenger piloted rides infinitely more exciting than the company's name. A plane tows you aloft and you circle in a five-mile radius with a view that can encompass 40 miles on a clear day. The rides are available daily 10:30 A.M.–5 P.M. on a first-come, first-served basis. Cost is $60 each if there are two passengers and $100 for a single person; rides last about 20 minutes. Check in with "Mr. Bill."

Also at the Dillingham Airfield is **Soar Hawaii Sailplanes,** 808/637-3147. This company offers 10-, 20-, 30-, 40-, 50, and 60-minute rides for $39–99 for two persons; aerobatic rides for one passenger (with parachute!) are the same length as the standard rides but $10 less per ride. A reduction in rates is usually offered during the summer season. Open 10 A.M.–6 P.M.; reservations are recommended.

Skysurfing Glider Rides, 808/256-0438, is the third company to offer these engine-less flights. One- and two-person flights are similar in flight time and cost to the competitors.

Also operating out of the Dillingham Airfield is **Stearman Biplane Rides,** 808/637-4461. A ride in one of these old-style birds brings back the days of barnstormers and pioneer aviation. Stearman runs 20-minute flights for $125 and 40-minute flights for $175 in its open-cockpit biplane.

A throwback to the days when tourists arrived in the islands by clipper planes is a seaplane tour by **Island Seaplane Service,** 808/836-6273, on a floating dock at 85 Lagoon Dr., on the back side of the Honolulu International Airport. These planes take off and land in Keʻehi Lagoon, just like the Pan Am China Clippers did in the 1930s.

Two runs are offered: a half-hour circle of southeastern O'ahu to get a look at Honolulu, Waikiki, Diamond Head, and the lower windward *pali,* and a one-hour ride that gives you all of that plus takes you all the way up the windward coast, circling back over the Leilehua Plateau and Pearl Harbor before landing. Six flights a day fly from about 9 A.M.–4:45 P.M. and run $79 per person for the shorter flight, $129 for the longer. Reservations required. Van service from Waikiki is available.

Islands in the Sky is a one-day flying extravaganza offered by **Hawaiian Airlines.** Using regularly scheduled flights, this daily tour goes from Honolulu to Kona on the Big Island, on to Maui, and then back to O'ahu for $332 adults or $312 for kids ages 2–11. Stops in Kona and on Maui include dinner and sightseeing transportation, and transport to and from your hotel in Honolulu is also included. Call 808/838-1555 for reservations or arrange this trip at any Hawaiian Airlines ticket office.

Eco Air Tours Hawaii, 808/839-1499, flies out of Honolulu in a nine-passenger twin-engine Piper Chieftain. A six-island full-day scheduled excursion is offered Wednesday, Thursday, and Friday, at $249 per person; minimum six passengers to fly. Half-day tours and a two-hour flight over O'ahu, Kaua'i, and Ni'ihau are also available. All flights include a narration on ecology, culture, and history of the islands. Ground tours are an added option with the six-island flight, and private charters can be scheduled at $400 an hour for the plane. Reservations are necessary at least 24 hours in advance.

Helicopters

Helicopter companies rev up their choppers to flightsee you around the island, starting at about $75 per person for a short 15- to 20-minute trip over Honolulu-Waikiki. Prices rise up from there to about $190 for a one-hour full-island narrated tour. Several companies even offer a night flight over Waikiki for a spectacular light show for about $100. Usually, transport to and from the heliport is included in the cost. Sometimes discounts are offered, so ask.

Chopper companies are all at the backside of the Honolulu International Airport, except Cherry Helicopters, 808/293-2570, which operates out of the Hilton Turtle Bay Resort on the

North Shore. **Makani Kai Helicopters,** 808/834-5813, website: www.makanikai.com, offers standard options at a fair price using Astar six-passenger aircraft. This company is licensed to pick up and drop off at the Hilton Turtle Bay Resort, so you don't need to drive all the way to Honolulu for a ride if you're staying on the North Shore. **Magnum Helicopters,** 808/833-1133, uses Robinson helicopters and carries three guests maximum for the best viewing. Aside from the regular tours, they can customize island and interisland tours at about $475 an hour. **Sandstone Helicopters,** 808/833-5678, operates more like a "limo in the sky" as the entire aircraft is rented without sharing space; $425. The 30-minute runs highlight sites not easily seen from the ground. Flights usually operate Mon.–Fri. only.

Parachuting

Three companies offer parachuting at the Dillingham Airfield. These drops are tandem with an instructor, unless you have certification for solo flights. After gaining about 10,000 feet, you'll free fall for a minute and parachute for several more, landing lightly on the grass (God willing!) next to the airstrip. Rates vary somewhat, as do drop elevations, but expect a fee of about $150–200. For this thrill ride, contact **Drop Zone,** 808/637-7007; **Pacific International Skydiving,** 808/637-7472; or **Skydiving Hawaii,** 808/637-9700.

Hang Gliding

North Shore Hang Gliding, 808/637-3178, sells hang gliders and can hook you up with a tandem instructor for lessons toward certification. The staff can also give you tips on where to fly on O'ahu if you're already certified.

SPECTATOR SPORTS

O'ahu is home to a number of major sporting events throughout the year. Many are "invitationals" that bring the cream of the crop from both collegiate and professional levels.

Football is big in Hawaii. The University of Hawai'i's Rainbows play during the normal collegiate season at Aloha Stadium near Pearl Harbor. The December **Aloha Bowl** and the **Oahu**

Bowl are postseason collegiate games. You can hear the pads crack in February, when the NFL sends its best players to the **Pro Bowl.**

Basketball is also big on O'ahu. The University of Hawai'i's Rainbow Warriors play at the **Neal S. Blaisdell Center** in Honolulu at 777 Ward Street. The **Outrigger Hotels Rainbow Classic** tournament gathers eight heavy-hitting college teams from around the country for holiday sports entertainment. Mid-April sees some of the nation's best collegiate hoopballers make up four teams to compete in the **Aloha Basketball Classic.**

Water sport festivals include surfing events, usually from October through February. The best known are the **Triple Crown of Surfing, Hawaiian Pro Surfing Championships,** and the **Duke Kahanamoku Classic.** You can watch some of the Pacific's most magnificent yachts sail into the Ala Wai Yacht Basin in mid-July, completing their run from Los Angeles in the annual **Trans Pacific Yacht Race.**

SHOPPING

You can't come to O'ahu and *not* shop. Even if the idea of it doesn't thrill you, the lure of almost endless shops offering every imaginable kind of merchandise will sooner or later tempt even the most "big-waste-of-time" mumbler through their doors. So why fight it? And if you're the other type, who feels as though a day without shopping is like being marooned on a deserted island, have no fear of rescue, because everywhere on the horizon is "a sale, a sale!"

You can use "much much more" as either an aspersion or a tribute when describing O'ahu, and nowhere does this qualifier fit better than when describing its shopping. More than a dozen major and minor shopping centers and malls are in Honolulu and Waikiki alone! Population centers around the island all have shopping centers in varying degrees—at the very least, a parking lot rimmed with a half dozen shops that can provide immediate necessities.

On the Neighbor Islands, a major shopping mall is usually found only in the island's main city, with mom 'n' pop stores and small superettes taking up the slack. On O'ahu, you've got these too, but you're never very far from some serious shopping centers. The tourist trade fosters the sale of art and artifacts, jewelry and fashions, and numerous boutiques selling these are strung around the island like a shell necklace. Food costs in supermarkets tend to be reasonable because O'ahu is the main distribution center, and with all the competition, prices in general seem to be lower than on the other islands. If your trip to Hawaii includes a stop on O'ahu, do most of your shopping here, because of the cut-rate prices and much greater availability of goods. When most Hawaiians go on a shopping spree, they head for O'ahu. Don't underestimate a simple trip to the grocery store. Often, but not always, you can find uniquely Hawaiian gifts like coffee, macadamia nut liqueur, coconut syrup, and even an assortment of juices much cheaper than in the gift shops. Remember, even thrift and consignment shops may hold some treasures, like older T-shirts, many with distinctive local flavor.

SHOPPING CENTERS

Honolulu Shopping Centers

Since it serves as the main terminal for TheBus, you could make a strong case that **Ala Moana Shopping Center** is the heart of shopping on O'ahu. At one time billed as the largest shopping center in the country, today it settles for being the largest in the state, with its hundreds of stores covering 50 acres. It's on Ala Moana Boulevard, just across from the Ala Moana Beach Park. **The Ward Centre,** with its complex of half a dozen buildings, is just a few blocks west of the Ala Moana Center along Ala Moana Boulevard. It's a relatively new shopping center that's gaining a reputation for some exclusive shops. Adding to the multiplicity of shopping options in the big city is the **Kalaha Mall,** lying just east of Diamond Head and catering to the eastern suburbs of Honolulu.

Waikiki Shopping

Shopping in Waikiki is as easy as falling off a surfboard. In two or three blocks of Kuhio and Kalakaua Avenues are no less than seven shopping centers. If that's not enough, there are hundreds of independent shops, plus plenty of street vendors. Main shopping centers include **Royal Hawaiian Shopping Center,** the **Waikiki Shopping Plaza,** and the **International Market Place,** an open-air shopping bazaar across from the Sheraton Moana Hotel. The **Hyatt Regency Shopping Center** is on the first three floors of the Hyatt Regency Hotel, at 2424 Kalakaua Ave., and it has high end boutiques. The **King's Village** is at 131 Ka'iulani Ave., the **Waikiki Trade Center** is on the corner of Seaside and Kuhio Avenues, and the **Rainbow Bazaar** is a unique mall at the Hilton Hawaiian Hotel.

Around the Island

Heading east from Waikiki on Route 72, you'll come to the **'Aina Haina Shopping Center** and **Niu Valley Center** on your left, just a prelude to what's to come. Also on the left are the **Hawaii Kai Town Center** and **Hawaii Kai Shopping Center,** followed quickly by and set across from the pond from the **Koko Marina Center.** All have plenty of shops of all varieties. Kailua and Kane'ohe bedroom communities have their shopping malls. Try the **Kane'ohe Bay Shopping Center, Windward Mall,** or the **Windward City Shopping Center** in town, or the **Ko'olau Center** along Kahekili Highway, which cuts inland. While there are shops scattered here and there along the North Shore, by far the greatest concentration is in Hale'iwa, where surf gear, art, boutiques, and plenty of restaurants are found in the **North Shore Marketplace** and **Hale'iwa Shopping Center.** The **Pearlridge Shopping Center** in Pearl City is a full shopping complex with over 150 stores, and, although only half the size, the **Waikele Shopping Center** is the place to head for factory outlet stores and some great savings. The **Wai'anae Mall** along the Farrington Highway serves the Wai'anae Coast with a supermarket, drugstore, fast foods, and sporting goods, and the **Wahiawa Town Center** and the **Mililani Town Center** are good places to start when up in the center of the island.

FOOD MARKETS

Around the island plenty of mom 'n' pop grocery stores provide fertile ground for a cultural ex-change, but they're expensive. O'ahu's large supermarkets include **Times, Safeway, Foodland,** and **Star Markets.** Preference is highly individual, but Times has a good reputation for fresh vegetables and good prices. Japanese **Daiei** has several stores around the island. They've got some bargains in their general merchandise departments, but because they try to be everything, their food sections suffer, especially the fruits and vegetables.

Chinatown offers a market at the Cultural Plaza, at the corner of Mauna Kea and Beretania Streets. Besides produce, you'll find fresh fish, meats, and poultry; the **Oahu Fish Market** is in the heart of Chinatown along King Street. The shops are run-down but clean, and sell everything from octopus to kimchi.

Health Food Stores

Brown rice and tofu eaters can keep that special sparkle in their eyes with no problem on O'ahu—there are some excellent health food stores. Most have a snack bar where you can get a delicious and nutritious meal for bargain prices. **Down to Earth,** 2525 S. King St., 808/947-7678, is an old standby where you can't go wrong; great stuff at great prices. **Kokua Market Natural Foods Co-op,** 2643 S. King St., 808/941-1922, is a full-service store with organic and fresh produce, cheese, milk, juices, bulk foods, and breads. Around the island, **Celestial Natural Foods,** at the Hale'iwa Shopping Plaza on the North Shore, 808/637-6729, is also top-notch; and **The Source Natural Foods,** 808/262-5604, at 32 Kainehe in Kailua on the windward side, is open daily as it has been for years. For vitamins, minerals, and dietary supplements, try **Vim and Vigor Foods** at the Ala Moana Center, 808/955-3600, or the Pearl Kai Shopping Center, 808/488-5160. Other sources are the half dozen **General Nutrition Center** stores on the island.

People's Open Market

A highly organized venture overseen by the county, the People's Open Market has been going strong since 1973. This rotating farmers' market offers the best and freshest products from farm and sea at prices lower than at any store. A wonderful practice in and of itself, it also helps to vitalize the local economy while offering a place for people to gather in an age-old tradi-

O'AHU

tion. The market is held at 22 different locations and times throughout the week—every day except Sunday. On Monday, Wednesday, and Saturday, the market is in the greater Honolulu area. On Tuesday and Friday, it moves up to Central O'ahu and the leeward coast, while on Thursday it's on the windward side. Three market sites easy to locate are the City Hall parking lot deck, 11:45 A.M.–12:30 P.M. on Monday; Queen Kapiolani Park, 10–11 A.M. on Wednesday; and Waimanalo Beach Park, 7:15–8:15 A.M. on Thursday. Call 808/522-7088 for full information on locations and times. Come indulge in the sights and smells.

BOOKSTORES

O'ahu has plenty of excellent bookstores. In Honolulu, **Waldenbooks** has several locations, including at the Pearlridge Center, 808/488-9488; Kahala Mall, 808/737-9550; and Waikiki Shopping Plaza, 808/922-4154. **Barnes and Noble Booksellers**, 808/737-3323, has one store at 4211 Wai'alae Ave. **Borders Books and Music** also has two full-selection stores in Honolulu, one in the Waikele Center, 808/676-6699, and the other at the Ward Centre, 808/591-8995. On the windward side, **Bookends**, 808/261-1996, in Kailua has the best selection. For a fine selection of Hawaiiana try the **Bishop Museum Bookshop** at the Bishop Museum, 1525 Bernice St., 808/848-4158, the **Mission Houses Museum** in downtown Honolulu at 553 S. King St., 808/531-0481, and **Native Books and Beautiful Things**, 808/596-8885, at the Ala Moana Shopping Center. The **Palace Shop** at 'Iolani Palace has a selection of books on the monarchy era, and the **Queen Emma Summer Palace Gift Shop** has additional volumes on Hawaiian royalty. Both the **Honolulu Academy of Arts** and the **Contemporary Museum** have fine bookshops that focus on the arts, with many titles on various aspects of Hawaiian art. You can find a good selection of books on Hawaiian outdoors, hiking, camping, and recreation, as well as fine maps at the **Hawaii Geographic Maps and Books** shop, 808/538-3952, at 49 S. Hotel St. in Honolulu. The **East-West Center bookstore** also carries a substantial collection of Hawaiiana as well as books on Asia, many of them published by the center. For books on the natural environment and flora of Hawaii, try the gift shops at Lyon Arboretum and Foster Botanical Garden.

FLEA MARKETS AND SWAP MEETS

Amidst the junk, these are the cheapest places to find treasures. Two operate successfully on O'ahu and have a regular following. **Aloha Flea Market** is at Aloha Stadium every Wednesday and Saturday 6 A.M.–3 P.M. It's the biggest flea market on O'ahu, selling everything from bric-a-brac to real heirlooms and treasures. An independent operation for over 20 years, it has now been taken over by the state.

Kam Swap Meet, inside the Kam Drive-In Theater (look for the two big screens), 98-850 Moanalua Road, Pearl City, is open Wednesday, Saturday, and Sunday 5:30 A.M.–3 P.M. Regular stall holders to housewives cleaning out the garage offer great fun and bargains.

ACCOMMODATIONS AND FOOD

The innkeepers of O'ahu would be personally embarrassed if you couldn't find adequate lodging on the island. So long as O'ahu has to suffer the "slings and arrows" of development gone wild, at least you can find all kinds, qualities, and prices of places in which to spend your vacation. Of the more than 70,000 rooms available in Hawaii, 37,000 are on O'ahu, with 33,000 of them in Waikiki alone! Some accommodations are living landmarks, historical mementos of the days when only millionaires came by ship to O'ahu, dallying as if it were their own private hideaway. When the jumbo jets began arriving in the early 1960s, O'ahu, especially Waikiki, began to build frantically. The result was hotel skyscrapers that grew faster than bamboo in a rainforest. These monoliths, which offered the "average family" a place to stay, marked a tremendous change in social status of visitors to O'ahu. The runaway building continued unabated for two decades, until the city politicians, supported by the hotel keepers themselves, cried "Enough!" and the activity finally slowed down.

Now a great deal of money is put into refurbishing and remodeling what is already built. Visitors can find breathtakingly beautiful hotels that are the best in the land next door to more humble inns that can satisfy most anyone's taste and pocketbook. On O'ahu, you may not get your own private beach with swaying palms and hula girls, but it's easy and affordable to visit one of the world's most exotic and premier vacation resorts.

The Range

Rooms on O'ahu may be found in all sorts of hotels, condos, and private homes. Some venerable old inns along Waikiki Beach were the jewels of the city when only a few palms obscured the views of Diamond Head. However, most of Waikiki's hotels are now relatively new high-rises. In Waikiki's five-star hotels, prices for deluxe accommodations, with all the trimmings, can run $250 per night or more. But a huge inventory of rooms go for half that amount and less. If you don't mind being one or two blocks from the beach, you can easily find nice hotels for $75–125. Waikiki's side streets also hold many apartment-hotels that are, in effect, condos. In these you get the benefit of a full kitchen for under $150. Stays of a week or more bring further discounts.

Central Honolulu has one fine business hotel and a few no-frills hotels in and around Chinatown. Some upscale hotels around Ala Moana put you near the beach but away from the heavy activity of Waikiki. For those passing through, a few overnight-style hotels are near the airport. For those looking for less expensive accommodations, the city has a handful of YM/WCAs, youth hostels, and hostel hotels.

The remainder of the island, outside Waikiki, was mostly ignored as far as resort development was concerned, except for the venerable Turtle Bay Hilton on the North Shore and the new and luxurious J.W. Marriott Ihilani Resort on the Wai'anae Coast. In the interior towns, and along the south and leeward coasts, you'll be hard pressed to find a hotel room because there simply aren't any—only condo rentals. Even

today, only a handful of hotels, inns, and condos are found on the windward coast, at Kahalu'u, Punalu'u, and La'ie. This windward coast has more vacation rentals and bed-and-breakfasts, as does the north coast.

Hotel/Condo Booking and Reservations

The following is a partial list of booking agents handling properties on O'ahu:

Aston Hotels and Resorts, 2250 Kuhio Ave., Honolulu, HI 96815, 808/931-1400 or 800/922-7886 Mainland, 800/445-6633 Canada, or 800/321-2558 in Hawaii, website: www.aston-hotels.com

Outrigger Hotels and Resorts, 2375 Kuhio Ave., Honolulu, HI 96815, 800/688-7444, website: www.outrigger.com

Marc Resorts Hawaii, 2155 Kalakaua Ave., Honolulu, HI 96815, 808/926-5900 or 800/535-0085, website: www.marcresorts.com

Go Condo Hawaii, 800/452-3463, website: www.gocondohawaii.com

J.D. BISIGNANI

Hilton Hawaiian Village

Hostels

O'ahu has several very reasonably priced hostels operating currently, a half dozen within a Frisbee toss of the beach in Waikiki, and a couple more near the university and up along the North Shore.

An official American Youth Hostel member, the always-busy **Honolulu International Youth Hostel**, 2323-A Seaview Ave., Honolulu, HI 96822, 808/946-0591, fax 808/946-5904, is near the University of Hawai'i. Bunks, per night, run $12.50 for members and $15.50 for nonmembers. Call ahead for reservations. In Waikiki, you'll find the **Hale Aloha Youth Hostel**, 808/926-8313, fax 808/922-3798, at 2417 Prince Edward St., with bunks at $17 members and $20 nonmembers.

Also in Waikiki are several hostels not associated with youth hostel organizations but still providing basic inexpensive accommodations. They include **Inter-Club Waikiki**, 2463 Kuhio Ave., 808/924-2636, 800/322-3798, fax 808/922-3993; **Waikiki Beachside Hotel and Hostel**, 2556 Lemon Road, 808/923-9566, fax 808/923-7525; **Polynesian Hostel Beach Club**, 2584 Lemon Road, 808/922-1340, 877/504-2924, fax 808/923-4146; **Banana Bungalow Waikiki Beach**, 2463 Kuhio Ave., Honolulu, HI 96815, 808/924-5074, 888/246-7835, fax 808/924-4119; and **Island Hostel**, tel./fax 808/942-8748, at 1946 Ala Moana Blvd. Types of rooms, services, amenities, and restrictions differ somewhat among these establishments. Expect to pay $16–20 for a bunk and $35–75 for a room, per night.

The North Shore has two hostels. **Backpacker's Vacation Inn and Hostel**, 59-788 Kamehameha Hwy. in Waimea, 808/638-7838, 888/628-8882 in Hawaii, fax 808/638-7515, has bunks for $15–17 and rooms for $45–55. At 62-202 Lokoea Pl., Haleiwa, HI 96712, 808/637-7146, the **Surfhouse** offers bunks at $15 a night and a private room at $45 a night.

Lu'au

The following is a listing of the lu'au available on O'ahu at the present time. The **Royal Hawaiian Lu'au** on the Ocean Lawn of the Royal Hawaiian Hotel, every Monday 6–8:30 P.M., 808/931-7194, *is* the classic Hawaiian feast, complete with authentic foods, entertainment, and richly spiced with *aloha*. Authenticity is added by lawn seating on traditional *lau hala* mats (table seating too) while the sun sets on Waikiki Beach and the stars dance over Diamond Head. Entertainment is an hour-long Polynesian extravaganza featuring Tahitian and traditional hula, a Samoan fire dance, and bold rhythmic drumming, and the buffet is a lavish feast of traditional favorites. You are presented with a fresh flower lei and welcomed at the open bar for mai tais and other tropical drinks. Cost is $78 adults, $48 for children 5–12.

Germaine's Lu'au, 808/949-6626 or 800/367-5655, often claimed by local people to be *the* best, is held at a private beach at Barber's Point, Tues.–Sun. 5:45–8:45 P.M. Of all the lu'au on the island, Germaine's is the most down-home Hawaii of the bunch. The cost for dinner, cocktails, and the Polynesian show runs $49 for adults and $27 for kids 6–12. A free shuttle (reservations required) from Waikiki area hotels can be booked when calling for tickets.

Paradise Cove Lu'au at the Ko 'Olina Resort boasts a wonderful dinner with arts and crafts displays, games, and other activities on a private beach along the leeward coast. Held daily 5–8:30 P.M., tickets run $52.50 for adults, $42.50 youth 13–18, and $32.50 for kids 6–12, with enhanced packages at greater cost. Paradise Cove is in a well-run, well-landscaped 12-acre park-like setting, and the production is definitely tourist oriented. Transportation by shuttle bus from Waikiki is included in the price. The shuttle bus departs from various hotels starting at 3:45 P.M. and returns by about 9:30 P.M. Call 808/973-5828 or 800/775-2683 for reservations.

In La'ie on the windward coast, try the **Ali'i Lu'au** at the Polynesian Cultural Center. The dinner and show run daily except Sunday 5:30–9 P.M. The cost is $65 adult and $44 children and this includes entrance to the Polynesian Cultural Center. The Ali'i Lu'au introduces you to a well-rounded Hawaiian feast, the *imu* ceremony, and a reenactment of a royal court procession before the show begins. For reservations, call 808/293-3333 or 800/367-7060.

O'AHU

GETTING THERE

The old adage of "all roads leading to Rome" applies almost perfectly to O'ahu, though instead of being cobblestones, they're sea lanes and air routes. Except for a handful of passenger ships still docking at Honolulu Harbor, and some limited nonstop flights to the Neighbor Islands, all other passengers to and from Hawaii are routed through Honolulu International Airport.

Honolulu International Airport

This international airport is one of the busiest in the country, with hundreds of flights to and from cities around the world arriving and departing daily. In a routine year, more than 15 million passengers utilize this facility. The three terminals (directions given as you face the main entranceway) are: the main terminal, accommodating all international and Mainland flights; the interisland terminal, a separate building at the far right end of the main terminal, handling flights between the islands by Hawaiian and Aloha airlines; and the commuter terminal, farther to the right side, taking care of the commuter and smaller interisland air carriers.

The ground floor of the **main terminal** is mostly for arriving passengers and contains the baggage claim area, baggage lockers, car rental agencies, and international and domestic arrival doors, which are kept separate. The second floor is for departing passengers, with most activity centered here, including ticket counters, shops, lounges, currency exchange, baggage handlers, the Pacific Aerospace Museum, a business center, and the entrance to most of the gates. From both levels you can board taxis and TheBus to downtown Honolulu and Waikiki.

The **interisland terminal** services flights aboard Hawaii's two major interisland carriers. It has its own snack bars, car rental information, lounges, information booths, and restrooms. It's only a leisurely 10-minute stroll between the two terminals, which is fine if you don't have much baggage; if you do, there are plenty of shuttles every few minutes.

Shuttles also service the **commuter terminal,** which lies beyond the interisland terminal. This terminal is used by Island Air, Pacific Wings, and Phoenix Air (for flights to Midway Island), each of which has a ticket counter in the terminal lobby. Here too you'll find a baggage area, telephones, restrooms, and a restaurant and cocktail lounge.

HONOLULU INTERNATIONAL AIRPORT

Services, Information, Tips

For general airport information and arrival and departure information, call 808/836-6413.

The main **information booth** is on the ground level just near the central escalators. Besides general information, it has good maps of the airport, O'ahu, Honolulu, and Waikiki. Also, inquiry booths lined up along the ground level at the interisland terminal are friendly and helpful, but not always stocked with as many maps as the main information booth.

Lost and found booths are on the ground level of the main terminal and at the interisland terminal; call 808/836-6547. The **post office** is across the street from the main entranceway toward the interisland terminal.

Storage lockers are on both levels of the main terminal. Coin locker rental is for up to 48 hours at $3 for 24 hours. Baggage lockers and a long-term baggage storage facility are in the parking structure. These lockers run $6 for 24 hours, two days max. Prices at the baggage storage depend on the size of baggage and length of storage, but generally run $3–10 per day. You *must* have your claim ticket to retrieve your belongings. The service is well run and efficient.

Money can be a hassle at the airport, especially getting change, which is a downright rip-off, and very bad public relations for visitors. Unfortunately, no one will give you change, putting you at the mercy of $1 bill-change machines located throughout the airport. These machines happily dispense 85 cents for every $1 you put in, so if you want to make a phone call, or the like, you're out of luck. The snack bars will only change money for you with a purchase. For a state that prides itself on the *aloha* spirit and depends on good relations with its visitors, this is a ridiculously poor way of greeting people or giving them a last impression before they return home. There are several **foreign currency exchange** booths at the airport as well as ATM machines.

To refresh and relax, you might visit the **Airport Mini-Hotel**, 808/836-3044, fax 808/834-8985, in the main terminal, second level, central area, with 19 private, single-bed rooms. You can have a shower for $9, which includes soap, towel, shampoo, deodorant, and hair dryer. An eight-hour sleep and a shower runs $38, four hours is $33, three hours runs $28, and two hours goes for $23. If you need a room after 9

P.M. you should make reservations as it probably will be full. If this seems a bit pricey, just use the public bathrooms for a quick wash, then choose any one of three small gardens near the central concourse to take a little nap. If you're there just for a short snooze, airport security won't bother you.

Pacific Aerospace Museum

In the central lobby on the second floor of the overseas terminal building, this small museum has several interactive aerospace displays and a 27-minute film on the aviation history of Hawaii. Open daily 9 A.M.–10 P.M., Wednesday until 6 P.M. Entrance is free but donations are accepted; 808/839-0777. The museum gift shop has a wide variety of items, including hats, books, videos, models, and posters, all relating to aviation and aerospace—perhaps the best selection on the island. Set some time aside to drop by for a look before you get on the plane to leave.

Airport Transportation

The free **Wiki Wiki Shuttle** takes you between the terminals and arrival/departure gates. Staffed by courteous drivers, it is efficient—most of the time. When it's not, a nickname could be the "Tricky Tricky Shuttle." Transfer time between the two main and interisland terminals is only about 10 minutes, which does not include baggage transfer. If you'll be going on to a Neighbor Island make sure the carrier you are using has an interline agreement with the Hawaiian domestic carrier. If not, you must fetch your own bags, place them on the shuttle, and bring them with you to the interisland terminal.

Car rental agencies are lined up at booths on the ground floor of both terminals; their lot offices are in the parking area outside the main terminal. Many courtesy phones for car rental agencies not at the airport are in and around the baggage claim area; call for a free van to pick you up and take you to the nearby facility. This procedure even saves the hassle of maneuvering through heavy airport traffic—you usually wait at the island in the middle of the road just outside the baggage claim area. Make sure to specify the number of the area where you'll wait.

If you're driving to the airport to pick up or drop off someone, you should know about **parking.** If you want to park on the second level of the parking garage for departures, you must take the elevator either up to the fourth floor or down to ground level, and from there cross the pedestrian bridge. There's no way to get across on levels two and three. Parking is $1 for the first half hour, $1 for each additional hour, or $10 maximum for a 24-hour period.

Public transportation to downtown Honolulu, especially Waikiki, is abundant. Moreover, some hotels have courtesy phones near the baggage claim area; if you're staying there, they'll send a van to fetch you. Current charges for taxis, vans, TheBus, and limousine service are posted just outside the baggage claim area, so you won't have to worry about being overcharged.

Only **taxis** that contract with the airport can pick up at the terminal. All others can drop off there but are allowed to pick up only outside the terminal, at a car rental office, for example. From the terminal to Waikiki costs about $21–26, not counting bags. Splitting the fare with other passengers can save money. Some companies charge a flat fee of $15 from outside the terminal to Waikiki. Vans and motorcoaches leave from the central island in the roadway just outside the baggage claim. They charge about $8, but a wait of up to 45 minutes for one is not out of the ordinary. Moreover, they drop passengers at hotels all over Waikiki, so if you're not one of the first stops by chance, it could be an hour or so after reaching Waikiki before you're finally deposited at your hotel.

Airport Express charges $8 per person ($4 for children) between the airport and Waikiki. When going to the airport, you must reserve two days in advance.

You can take **TheBus** (no. 19 or no. 20) to Waikiki via the Ala Moana Terminal, from which you can get buses all over the island. If you're heading north, pick up bus no. 20, 51, or 52 just outside the airport. TheBus only costs $1, but you are allowed only baggage that you can hold on your lap without infringing on other riders. Drivers are sticklers on this point.

Interisland Carriers
Hawaiian Airlines, 800/367-5320 nationwide, 800/882-8811 statewide, 808/838-1555 on

O'ahu, website: www.hawaiianair.com, offers the most flights. From Honolulu to Kaua'i, nearly two dozen nonstop flights go 5:30 A.M.–P.M.; flights to Maui begin at 5:15 A.M. with one every 20–30 minutes until 10 P.M.; flights to Hilo and Kona on the Big Island leave about every hour or so 5:20 A.M.–7 P.M. Also, although fewer, daily flights are offered twice a day to Lana'i and Moloka'i, and between all the major island airports

Aloha Airlines, 800/367-5250 Mainland and Canada, 808/484-1111 on O'ahu, website: www.alohaairlines.com, connects Honolulu to Kaua'i, Maui, and both Kona and Hilo on the Big Island of Hawaii. Aloha's routes to Kaua'i are: from Honolulu, 26 nonstop flights 5:30 A.M.–8 P.M.; to Maui, about 28 flights daily, with one departing every 20 minutes or so 5:15 A.M.–8 P.M.; to Kona, 19 flights daily 5:15 A.M.–6:55 P.M.; and to Hilo, 15 flights 5:20 A.M.–6:45 P.M.

Island Air, 800/323-3345 nationwide, 800/652-6541 statewide, and 808/484-2222 on O'ahu, website: www.alohaairlines.com, connects Honolulu, Kahului, and Kona with the state's smaller airports, including Kapalua-West Maui, Lana'i, Ho'olehua on Moloka'i. About half the flights are on jet aircraft and half on Dash-8 turboprop airplanes. Eight flights each connect Honolulu with Lana'i and Moloka'i; six go to Kapalua, West Maui Airport; while one or two run to Kahului and Kona. Between the islands, flights connect Kahului to Moloka'i and Kona to Kapalua and Lana'i.

Pacific Wings does the pickup routes. It connects Honolulu to Kahului, Hana, Kapalua–West Maui, Moloka'i, Kalaupapa, and Kamuela on the Big Island, and connects these airports together, but on a limited schedule of less than half a dozen flights a day at most. Pacific Wings can be reached at 888/575-4546, website: www.pacificwings.com.

Charter Airlines
If you've got the bucks or just need to go when there's no regularly scheduled flight, try one of the following for islandwide service: **Paragon Air,** 808/244-3356 or 800/428-1231 Mainland, website: www.maui.net/~wings/index.htm; **Pacific Wings,** 808/873-0877 or 888/575-4546 Mainland, website: www.pacificwings.com; or **Maui Air,** 808/871-8152, website: www.maui.net/~mauisle.

GETTING AROUND

Touring Oʻahu is especially easy, since almost every normal (and not so normal) mode of conveyance is readily available. You can rent anything from a moped to a limo, and the competition is very stiff, which helps keep prices down. A few differences separate Oʻahu from the other islands. To begin with, Oʻahu has a model public transportation system called TheBus—not only efficient, but very inexpensive. Also, Oʻahu is the only island that has a true expressway system, though along with it came rush hour and traffic jams. A large part of Oʻahu's business is processing people, even if it's only to send them on to another island. The agencies operating these businesses on the island are masters at moving people down the road. With the huge volume of tourists who visit every year, it's amazing how smoothly it works.

RENTAL CARS

Every reputable nation-, state-, and islandwide car rental agency is here, along with some car rental hucksters that'll hook you and land you like mahimahi if you're not careful. The rule of thumb is, if the deal sounds too good to be true, it is. The competition is fierce among the reputable agencies, however, and their deals are all equally good. Always check with your travel agency for big savings on fly/drive or stay/drive packages. Six pages of car rental agencies grace the Honolulu *Yellow Pages*, from firms that rent Mercedes convertibles down to low-budget operations with a few dented and dated Datsuns. Don't get the impression that all the backyard firms are rip-offs. You can get some great deals, but you have to choose wisely and be willing to settle for a less-than-prestigious car.

Reserving a car on Oʻahu is doubly important because of the huge turnover that can occur at any time. Be aware of **drop-off charges;** for example, if you rent in Waikiki and leave the car at the airport, you'll be charged. It's convenient to rent a car at the airport. But it's also convenient to take an inexpensive shuttle to and from Waikiki and rent there. Many firms have offices in Waikiki, and you can even rent a car from your hotel desk and have it delivered to you. This saves you the hassle of dealing with traffic and unfamiliar roads during arrival and departure, and avoids drop-off fees—but you don't always get the cheapest rates.

National Agencies

All of the following national companies have locations in Waikiki. The local phone numbers given are for the main location at Honolulu International Airport and locations in Waikiki. Call for more details.

Dollar Rent A Car, 808/831-2330 or 808/944-1544, 800/800-4000 worldwide, website: www.dollarcar.com

Alamo, 808/833-4585 or 808/947-6112, 800/327-9633, website: www.goalamo.com

National Car Rental, 808/831-3800 or 808/973-7200, 800/227-7368 worldwide, website: www.nationalcar.com

Avis, 808/834-5536 or 808/973-2610, 800/321-3712 nationwide, website: www.avis.com

Budget, 800/527-7000 in Hawaii, 800/527-0700 worldwide, website: www.drivebudget.com

Enterprise, 808/836-7722 or 808/922-0090, 800/736-8222 nationwide, website: www.enterprise.com

Hertz, 808/831-3500 or 808/971-3535, 800/654-3011 worldwide, website: www.hertz.com

Thrifty, 808/831-2277 or 808/971-2660, 800/367-2277 worldwide, website: www.thrifty.com

Local Agencies

These firms are established rental companies. Some may rent without a major credit card, but they will undoubtedly require a stiff deposit. Sometimes they even rent to those under 21. You usually make out all right with **Paradise Isle Rental,** 808/946-7777 or 808/926-7777, at 151 Uluniu Ave. and 1879 Kalakaua Ave. in Waikiki, which carries Jeeps, SUVs, convertibles, motorcycles, and mopeds. **VIP (Very Inexpensive Prices) Car Rentals,** 808/488-6187 near the airport or 808/924-4605 in Waikiki, handles sedans, jeeps, and stationwagons. **JN Car and Truck Rental,** 808/831-2724, has all sorts of sedans, convertibles, trucks, and vans. Check **Harper,** 808/848-8999, for automobiles and trucks.

Vanity Rentals

The most distinctive and fun-filled cars on O'ahu are the sports cars and luxury imports available from **Ferrari Rentals,** 808/942-8725, in Waikiki at 2002 Kalakaua Ave. This company has a fleet of American and European classic cars, like Viper, Corvette, Ferrari, Porsche, Jaguar, Mercedes, and BMW. The magnificent Lamborghine Diablo goes for the equally magnificent price of $1,300 per day, while they let the lowly Corvette out for the mere pittance of only $260 per day.

Paradise Isle Rentals, 808/946-7777 or 808/926-7777, at 151 Uluniu Ave. and 1879 Kalakaua Ave. in Waikiki, also rents luxury cars like the Prowler, Viper, Mercedes, and Corvette convertible.

Motorcycles and Mopeds

For rentals, try **Paradise Isle Rentals,** 808/922-2224, at 151 Uluniu in Waikiki, where you can ride away with the wind in your face on a Nighthawk, Ninja, or Harley-Davidson for $79–99 a day, or scoot away on a 50cc moped for a daily rate of $20. Other options include **Adventure on 2 Wheels,** 1946 Ala Moana Ave., 808/944-3131, and 2002 Kalakaua Ave., 808/941-2222; and **Big Mountain Rentals,** 2426 Kuhio Ave., 808/926-1644. **Coconut Cruisers,** 2301 Kalakaua Ave., 808/924-1644, rents motorcycles that run $90–170 for three hours or $100–215 for up to 12 hours. **Cruzin Hawaii Motorcycles,** 1980 Kalakaua Ave., near the Ambassador Hotel, 808/942-9595, rents only Harleys. Open 9 A.M.–7 P.M., it rents the Big Twin at $79 for three hours, $149 all day, and $179 for 24 hours. Sportsters run $79 for three hours, $99 all day, and $129 for 24 hours.

ALTERNATE TRANSPORTATION

TheBus

If Dorothy and her mates had TheBus to get them down the Yellow Brick Road, she might have chosen to stay in Oz and forget about Kansas. TheBus, TheBus, ThewonderfulBus is the always-coming, slow-moving, go-everywhere friend of the budget traveler. Operated by O'ahu Transit Services, Inc. (OTS), it could serve as a model of efficiency and economy in any city of the world. What makes it more amazing is that it all came together by chance, beginning as an emergency service in 1971. It now services more than a quarter million passenger rides a day. Aside from crisscrossing the city, these brown, yellow, and orange coaches go up and down both the windward and leeward coasts, through the interior, while passing through all of the major and most of the minor towns in between, and most often stopping near the best sights.

Route signs and numbers are on the front of the bus and near the bus doors. The **fare** is only $1 adult, 50 cents for students between ages 6–19, while kids under six who can sit on a parent's lap aren't charged at all. The fare is paid in *exact change* upon entering. A four-day unlimited-use **visitors pass** is also available for $10. Adult **monthly bus passes,** good at any time and on all routes, are $25, but be aware that they are good only from the first to the last day of every month. If you buy a pass in midmonth, or even later, it's still full price. A student monthly pass is $12.50. Passes for senior citizens and disabled passengers are good for two years and cost $20. Seniors (65 or older) must furnish proof of age and will be given the pass within a few minutes of having an ID photo taken. Monthly passes are available at **TheBus Pass Office,** open Mon.–Fri. 7:30 A.M.–3:30 P.M., at 811 Middle St., 808/848-4500, website: www.thebus.org. Bus no. 1 Kalihi stops within a few feet of TheBus Pass Office.

Transfers are free and are issued upon request when entering TheBus, but you can only use them for ongoing travel in the same direction, on a different line. They are also timed and dated, good for approximately 30 minutes to one hour.

Only baggage that can be placed under the seat or on one's lap is permitted—no metal-frame backpacks; baby strollers that fold up are allowed. Seeing-eye dogs and other similar service animals can accompany a passenger, but all other animals must be in a carrier that fits under the seat or on the lap. No smoking is allowed, and eating or drinking is not permitted. Please use radios or similar devices with headphones only.

Some buses are now equipped with bike racks, which makes it easier to get around town or out of town without having to jostle with all the traffic. Bike racks carry two bikes only. First, let the bus driver know that you wish to load your bike. Then pull down to unfold the rack, if it isn't down already, and securely set the bike wheels into the slots. Pull up on the securing arm to lock your bike in, then board. When leaving the bus, be sure to let the driver know that you want to unload your bike, or it may go to the next stop without you. For additional instructions, consult the *How to Use the New Bike Rack for Buses* booklet, available from TheBus office.

There are about 80 routes in the system. Get full **route and schedule information** by calling TheBus at 808/848-5555, 5:30 A.M.–10 P.M., or by visiting the information booth at the Ala Moana Terminal and satellite city halls, where you can pick up fliers and maps. For other general information and attractions along the routes call 808/296-1818 with access code 8287. The-Bus lost and found office can be contacted at 808/848-4444. One inexpensive guide to major bus routes and attractions is the *TheBus Map and Guide Book*. Another excellent little guide is *Hawaii Bus and Travel Guide,* by Milly Single-tary. Both are available in most bookstores for around $5.

The following are some popular destinations and their bus numbers: **Aloha Tower,** no. 19, 20, or 47; **Airport,** no. 19 or 20; *Arizona* **Memorial, Pearl Harbor,** no. 20, 47, or 49; **Bishop Museum,** no. 2 School; **Chinatown,** no. 2 or 13; Hanauma Bay, no. 22; **Honolulu (downtown),** no. 2, 13, or 47 **Punchbowl,** no. 15; **Polynesian Cultural Center,** 52 Wahiawa-Circle Isle, 55 Kane'ohe–Circle Isle; **Queen Emma Summer Palace,** no. 4; **Sea Life Park,** no. 22 or 58; **University,** no. 4, 6, or 18; **Waikiki Beach,** no. 2, 4, 8, 20, or 58. The **Beach Bus,** no. 22, starts on Kuhio Ave. near Kalakaua Ave. and services all of the beach areas, including Hanauma Bay and Sandy Point; Sea Life Park is its terminus. Once a seasonal service, the Beach Bus now operates year-round.

Circling the island by bus is a terrific way to see the sights and meet people along the way. The circle route takes about four hours if you ride the entire loop, but you can use the transfer system to give yourself a reasonable tour of only the sights that strike your fancy. The **circle-island** bus no. 52 Wahiawa–Circle Isle goes inland to Wahiawa, north to Hale'iwa, along the North Shore, down the windward coast to Kane'ohe and back over the *pali* to Honolulu. Bus no. 55 Kane'ohe–Circle Isle follows the same route but in the opposite direction.

Trolley and Shuttles

The **Waikiki Trolley,** 808/593-2822, an open-air trolley-like bus, will take you on a tour of Waikiki and surrounding areas for $18 adults, $12 kids age 12–17, and $8 for children 4–12 years old. This all-day pass lets you board, exit, and re-board at any stop along a specific route. Multiday passes for four consecutive days on multiple routes are available for $42, $28, and $12, respectively. Starting from the Royal Hawaiian Shopping Center in Waikiki, the trolley runs three routes, with several overlapping stops, mostly at 20- to 30-minute intervals. The red line (Honolulu City route) operates 8:30 A.M.–6:45 P.M., leaving its last starting point at 4:30 P.M. This line basically connects Waikiki with historical and cultural sights in downtown Honolulu. The yellow line (Shopping and Dining route) runs from 9 A.M. to about 11 P.M. and brings visitors to the Ala Moana and Ward shopping centers. The blue line (Ocean Coast route) starts at 8:30 A.M. and runs until a little after 7 P.M. It heads east to the coastal sights of southeast O'ahu. The purple and orange lines are newer and operate differently, and tickets run $22 adult and $8 children 4–11. The purple line (First Adventures route) runs to Diamond Head, Punchbowl, and the Pali Lookout, while the orange line (Hidden Treasures route) takes you to the University of Hawai'i at Manoa and Moanalua Gardens. Trolleys on the orange and purple lines make two runs per day, one at midmorning and the other at midday. Pick up a map/brochure from any activities desk or call the number above. Tickets can be purchased from booths at the Royal Hawaiian Shopping Center and at Ward Warehouse.

The open-air **Rainbow Trolley** makes one circuitous route through Waikiki and downtown Honolulu. Get on and off as often as you like at any of over two dozen stops. The rides are narrated so you get a commentary on the various sites in town. Rates run $18 adult and $8 children ages 2–11 for a two-day pass, and $30 and $10,

O'AHU

respectively, for a four-day pass. Buy passes from the driver or the booth at the Waikiki Beachcomber Hotel; no reservations are taken. Trolleys run approximately 8:30 A.M.–11:30 P.M. daily. For information, call 808/539-9495 or 877/533-5334.

In addition to this trolley, several shuttles run only to specified sites. All leave from various hotels in Waikiki. The **Arizona Memorial Shuttle Bus** runs about every 90 minutes 7 A.M.–1 P.M. to the memorial, and until about 5 P.M. back from the memorial. Call 808/839-0911 for reservations (a must); $3 per person, one-way. The **Hilo Hattie/Dole Cannery Bus** runs daily to those two shopping sites, leaving every 20 minutes 7 A.M.–6 P.M. No charge. For exact schedule, call 808/537-2926. The **Waimea Valley Shuttle** runs daily from Waikiki to the North Shore's best known tourist attraction for $20 per person, with pickup between 8–8:30 A.M. and a return to Waikiki by about 4 P.M. For a schedule and boarding locations, call 808/638-8511.

Taxis

The law says that taxis are not allowed to cruise around looking for fares, so you can't hail them. But they do and you can, and most police officers have more important things to do than monitor cabs. Best is to summon one from your hotel or a restaurant. All are radio-dispatched, and they're usually there in a flash. The fares, posted on the taxi doors, are set by law and are fair, but still expensive for the budget traveler. The rates do change, but expect about $2 for the flag fall, and then 25 cents for each additional one-eighth mile. The airport to Waikiki is about $25, though luggage costs extra. Most cab drivers are quite good, but you may pause to consider if your cab sports the bumper sticker "Caution! I drive like you do!"

Of the many taxi companies, some with good reputations are: **Sida,** a cooperative of owner-drivers, at 808/836-0011; **Aloha State Cab,** 808/847-3566; **Charley's,** 808/531-1333; and **City Taxi,** 808/524-2121. If you need some special attention like a Rolls-Royce limo, try: **Cloud 9 Limousines,** 808/524-7999. It is one of at least three dozen limo services on the island.

Travelers with disabilities and people in wheelchairs can call **Handi-Cabs of the Pacific,** 808/524-3866.

Hitchhiking

Hitchhiking varies from island to island, both in legality and method. On O'ahu, hitchhiking is legal, and you use the tried-and-true style of facing traffic and waving your thumb. But city ordinance specifies that you can only hitchhike from a bus stop! Not many people try so the pickings are reasonably easy. TheBus, however, is only $1 for anywhere you want to go, and the paltry sum that you save in money is lost in "seeing time."

Two things against you: Many of the people are tourists and don't want to bother with hitchhikers, and many locals don't want to bother with nonlocal hitchhikers. When you do get a ride, most of the time it will be from a *haole* who is either a tourist on his own or a recent island resident. If you are just hitchhiking along a well-known beach area, perhaps in your bathing suit and obviously not going far, you can get a ride more easily. Women should exercise caution and avoid hitchhiking alone.

MEDICAL SERVICES

Full-service hospitals include: **The Queen's Medical Center,** 1301 Punchbowl St., Honolulu, 808/538-9011; **Castle Medical Center,** 640 Ulukahiki St., Kailua, 808/263-5500; **St. Francis Medical Center,** 2230 Liliha, Honolulu, 808/547-6011; **Straub Clinic and Hospital,** 888 S. King St., Honolulu, 808/522-4000; **Kuakini Medical Center,** 347 N. Kuakini St., Honolulu, 808/536-2236; and **Wahiawa General Hospital,** 128 Lehua St. in Wahiawa, 808/621-8411.

Medical services and clinics include: **Kaiser Permanente,** 3288 Moanalua Road, Honolulu, 808/432-0000; **Doctors on Call,** 808/971-6000 (for Japanese-speaking doctors call 808/923-9966), for emergencies and "house calls" to your hotel, 24 hours a day; **Kuhio Walk-in Medical Clinic,** 2310 Kuhio Ave., Suite 223, in Waikiki, 808/924-6688; **Urgent Care clinic,** 808/597-2860, 2155 Kalakaua Ave., Suite 308, with lab and x-ray capability; and **Waikiki Health Center,** 277 'Ohua Ave., 808/922-4787, for low-cost care including pregnancy and confidential VD testing, open Mon.–Thurs. 9 A.M.–8 P.M., Friday until 4:30 P.M., Saturday until 2 P.M.

For dental referral call the **Hawaii Dental Association** 24-hour information hotline, 808/536-2135.

Dozens of **pharmacies** dot the island, including: **Kuhio Pharmacy,** at the corner of Kuhio and Nahua, 808/923-4466; **Center Pharmacy,** 302 California Ave. in Wahiawa, 808/622-2773; **Longs Drugs,** in Honolulu at the Ala Moana Shopping Center, 808/941-4433, at the Kane'ohe Bay Shopping Center, 808/235-4511, and at over 20 other locations around the island; **Waianae Drugs,** 85-910 Farrington Hwy., Waianae, 808/696-6348; and **Waipahu Drug,** 94-748A

Hikimoe, 808/677-0794. In addition, Safeway and Times Super Markets also have pharmacies in their stores.

For **alternative health care** try: **Acupuncture Clinic,** 111 N. King St., 808/545-8080; **East-West Acupuncture and Herbs,** 1481 S. King St., 808/942-0244; **Honolulu School of Massage,** 1136 12th Ave., 808/733-0000. **Chiropractic Referral Service,** 808/478-4022, offers free information and referral to qualified chiropractors. For other chiropractors, acupuncturists, and alternative health care providers, please refer to the Yellow Pages.

INFORMATION AND SERVICES

Emergencies
For **police, fire, or ambulance** anywhere on O'ahu, dial **911.** For **nonemergency police** assistance and information, call 808/529-3111.

Civil Defense: In case of natural disaster such as hurricanes or tsunamis on O'ahu, call 808/523-4121 or 733-4300. The **Coast Guard Search and Rescue** can be reached at 800/552-6458.

Sex Abuse Treatment Center Hotline: Call 808/524-7273 for cases involving sexual assault or rape crisis.

Weather, Marine Report, and Time of Day
For recorded information on local island weather, call 808/973-4380; for marine conditions, phone 808/973-4382; and for the surf report, call 808/973-4383. For time of day, call 808/983-3211.

Consumer Protection and Tourist Complaints
If you encounter problems with accommodations, bad service, or downright rip-offs, try the following: **The Chamber of Commerce of Hawaii,** 808/545-4300; **Office of Consumer Protection,** 808/587-3222; or the **Better Business Bureau,** 808/536-6956. For general information, or if you have a hassle, try the City Hall's **Office of Information,** 808/523-4385, or the **Office of Complaint,** 808/523-4381.

Tourism Information
Perhaps the most convenient spot to garner tourist information is the **Visitor Information Office,** Royal Hawaiian Shopping Center, 4th

Fl., 2201 Kalakaua Ave., Honolulu, HI 96815, 808/924-0266.

The state operates **visitors information booths** at Honolulu International Airport, 808/836-6413; some are open 24 hours a day. These offer plenty of practical brochures and helpful information.

Post Offices
There are over a dozen post offices in Honolulu, and one in each of the major towns on the island. Window service is offered Mon.–Fri. 8:30 A.M.–4 P.M.; some offices are open Saturday 10 A.M.–noon. For all postal information on O'ahu, call 800/275-8777. The main post office in Honolulu is at 3600 Aolele St. near the airport, which has window hours weekdays 7:30 A.M.–8:30 P.M. The downtown station is at 335 Merchant Street. In Waikiki, the post office is at 330 Saratoga Road; in Kailua, at 335 Hahani St.; in Wai'anae, at 86-014 Farrington Hwy.; in Hale'iwa, at 66-437 Kamehameha Hwy.; and in Wahiawa, at 115 Lehua St.

Reading Material
Besides special-interest Chinese, Japanese, Korean, Filipino, and military newspapers, two major dailies are published on O'ahu. The *Honolulu Advertiser* is the morning paper, and the *Honolulu Star Bulletin* is the evening paper. They combine to make a Sunday paper. The alternative press *Honolulu Weekly* adds a different perspective to the mix. Aside from feature articles on pertinent local issues, it does a calendar of local

O'AHU

arts and events. This free weekly is available throughout O'ahu at over 600 locations. A money-saving paper is the *Pennysaver,* featuring classified ads on just about anything.

Don't miss out on the **free tourist literature** available at all major hotels, shopping malls, the airport, and stands along Waikiki's streets. They all contain up-to-the-minute information on what's happening, and a treasure trove of free or reduced-price coupons for various attractions and services. Always featured are events, shopping tips, dining and entertainment, and sightseeing. The main ones are: *This Week Oahu,* the best and most complete; *The Best of Oahu;* and *Spotlights Oahu Gold,* with good sections on dining and sightseeing. Free tabloids like the *Waikiki Beach Press* and *Waikiki News* offer entertainment calendars and feature stories of general interest to visitors. *Oahu Drive Guide,* handed out by all the major car rental agencies, has some excellent tips and orientation maps. Especially useful to get you started from the airport.

There are 23 public libraries on O'ahu, and these include: Hawaii State Library, in Honolulu at 478 S. King St., 808/586-3500; Kailua Library, 239 Ku'ulei Road, 808/266-9911; Waikiki-Kapahulu Library, at 400 Kapahulu, 808/733-8488. Library cards are available free for Hawaii state residents and military personnel stationed in Hawaii, $25 for nonresidents (valid for five years), and $10 for up to three months for visitors. The library system offers numerous services, including reference information during library hours at 808/586-3621, Internet access from library computers, and statewide access to the entire library collection. Business hours for each library differ, so check with the one you want to visit. Brochures listing hours and other general information are available at all libraries.

Island Facts

O'ahu's nickname is "The Gathering Place." Its color is yellow, the island flower is the *'ilima,* and the island lei is strung from its bold blossoms. At 597 square miles, O'ahu follows Hawai'i and Maui in size and has nearly the same area as Kaua'i.

HAWAII STATE ARCHIVES

HONOLULU

Honolulu is the most exotic city in the world. It's not any one attribute that makes this so; it's a combination of things. Honolulu's like an ancient Hawaiian goddess who can change her form at will. At one moment you see a black-eyed beauty, swaying provocatively to a deep and basic rhythm, and in the next a high-tech scion of the computer age sitting straight-backed behind a polished desk. The city is the terminus of "manifest destiny," the end of America's relentless westward drive, until no more horizons were left. Other Mainland cities are undoubtedly more historic, cultural, and perhaps, to some, more beautiful than Honolulu, but none come close to having all of these features in the same overwhelming combination. The city's face, though blemished by high-rises and pocked by heavy industry, is eternally lovely. The Ko'olau Mountains form the background tapestry from which the city emerges; the surf gently foams along Waikiki; the sun hisses fire-red as it drops into the sea, and Diamond Head beckons with a promise of tropical romance.

In the center of the city, skyscrapers rise as silent, unshakable witnesses to Honolulu's economic strength. In glass and steel offices, businesspeople wearing conservative three-piece uniforms are clones of any found on Wall Street. Below, a fantasia of people live and work. In nooks and crannies is an amazing array of arts, shops, and cuisines. In a flash of festival the streets become China, Japan, Portugal, New England, old Hawaii, or the Philippines.

New England churches, a royal palace, bandstands, tall-masted ships, and coronation platforms illustrate Honolulu's history. And what a history! You can visit places where in a mere twinkle of time past, red-plumed warriors were driven to their deaths over an impossibly steep *pali,* or where the skies were alive with screaming Zeros strafing and bombing the only American city threatened by a foreign power since the War of 1812. In hallowed grounds throughout the city lie the bodies of fallen warriors. Some are entombed in a mangled steel sepulcher below the waves, others from three wars rest in a natural bowl of bereavement and silence. And a

O'AHU

GREATER HONOLULU

O'AHU

To Waimanalo

KAHALA HILTON

Kahala

KEALA OLU

KAHALA AVE

KAHALA MALL

HUNAKAI AVE.

KILAUEA AVE.

KALANIANA'OLE HWY.

Maunalani Heights

10TH

DIAMOND HEAD STATE MONUMENT

AVE.

DIAMOND HEAD RD.

St. Louis Heights

MONSARRAT

Kaimuki

ST LOUIS DR

WAI'ALAE AVE.

LUNALILO

KAPAHULU AVE.

Mo'ili'ili

DATE ST.

ALA WAI BLVD

KALAKAUA AVE.

ALA WAI YACHT HARBOR

SEE "WAIKIKI" MAP

Ala Wai Canal

(EWERS)

Manoa

UNIVERSITY OF HAWAII

EAST-WEST CENTER

MANOA VALLEY INN AND Y.H.

O'AHU AVE.

DOLE AVE.

METCALF

BERETANIA ST.

KING ST.

MCCULLY ST.

KALIA

Mamala Bay

LYON ★ ARBORETUM

PU'U UALAKA'A STATE WAYSIDE

Makiki Heights

MANOA RD.

WAI'OLI TEA ROOM

PUNAHOU SCHOOL

NEHOA

YWCA

WILDER

PENSACOLA

PIIKOI

KEWALO BASIN COUNTY PARK

PAGODA HOTEL

ALA MOANA PARK

ROUND TOP DR.

MAKIKI HEIGHTS DR.

TANTALUS DR.

To Kailua and Nu'uanu Pali Lookout

QUEEN EMMA SUMMER PALACE

61

Pacific Heights

ROYAL MAUSOLEUM

THE CONTEMPORARY MUSEUM

PUNCHBOWL

PROSPECT

HONOLULU ACADEMY OF ARTS

BLAISDELL CENTER

KAPI'OLANI

QUEEN ST.

ALA MOANA BLVD

Kewalo Basin

VICTORIA WARD CENTRES

KAKA'AKO STATE PARK

TENNENT GALLERY

O'AHU CEMETERY

NU'UANU AVE.

ULIHA ST.

NU'UANU ST.

SEE "CHINATOWN" MAP

SCHOOL ST.

BISHOP

Chinatown

Honolulu Harbor

Sand Island

SEE "DOWNTOWN HONOLULU" MAP

To Kane'ohe

LIKELIKE HWY

63

KAMEHAMEHA SCHOOLS

BISHOP MUSEUM

Kalihi

KING ST.

DILLINGHAM BLVD.

IWILEI

HILO HATTIE

KALIHI ST.

NIMITZ HWY

92

Sand Island

SAND ISLAND STATE RECREATION AREA

To Pearl City

MIDDLE RD.

MAUNALOA

DOLE CANNERY SQUARE

LA MARIANNA YACHT CLUB

STATE BOAT HARBOR

KE'EHI LAGOON BEACH PARK

Ke'ehi Lagoon

SAND ISLAND ACCESS RD.

SEAPLANES

PU'ULOA DR.

LAGOON DR.

HONOLULU INTERNATIONAL AIRPORT

To Pearl Harbor

0 1 mi

0 1 km

nearby royal mausoleum holds the remains of those who were "old Hawaii."

Honolulu is the pumping heart of Hawaii. The state government and university are here. So are botanical parks, a fine aquarium and zoo, a floating maritime museum, and the world's foremost museum on Polynesia. Art flourishes like flowers, as do professional and amateur entertainment, extravaganzas, and local and world-class sporting events. But the city isn't all good clean fun. The seedier side includes "girlie" shows, raucous GI bars, street drugs, and street people. But somehow this blending and collision of East and West, this hodgepodge of emotionally charged history, this American city superimposed on a unique Pacific setting works well as Honolulu, the "Sheltered Bay" of humanity and its dreams.

SIGHTS

The best way to see Honolulu is to start from the middle and fan out on foot to visit the inner city. You can *do* downtown in one day, but the sights of greater Honolulu require a few days to see. It's a matter of opinion where the center of downtown Honolulu actually is, but the King Kamehameha statue in front of Ali'iolani Hale is about as central as you can get, and a perfect landmark from which to start. If you're staying in Waikiki, leave your rental car in the hotel garage and take TheBus no. 2 for downtown sightseeing.

Parking and Transportation, Downtown Honolulu

If you can't bear to leave your car behind, head for Aloha Tower. In front of Aloha Tower is Irwin Park and to the side is a parking lot. Enter to find plenty of parking. The traffic is not as congested here and the large lot is open 24 hours. The rate is $2 with validation for up to three hours 7:30 A.M.–4:30 P.M. and $1 for each 20 minutes beyond that. After 4:30 P.M. weekdays and all day on weekends, the rate is $2. Similar rates are charged at another lot just east of the Maritime Museum near Pier 4. You should have plenty of time for the local attractions that are well within walking distance, and you may also have time if you want to go as far as Chinatown. A handful of parking structures can be found in the business district of town a few blocks inland.

For various sights outside the downtown area, your rental car is fine. Some shuttles running out to the *Arizona* Memorial are more expensive than TheBus, but so convenient that they're worth the extra few coins. The **Waikiki Trolley,** 808/593-2822, conducts a Honolulu City Line circle route that runs between Waikiki and the downtown area, including the Bishop Museum. It looks like an old-style trolley but it's a bus that's been ingeniously converted. The trolley departs daily at 20-minute intervals 8:30 A.M.–6:45 P.M. from the Royal Hawaiian Shopping Center. You can get off and on at any of the 25 stops along the way or ride along for the entire two-hour trip.

'IOLANI PALACE AREA

The **Statue of King Kamehameha** is at the junction of King and Mililani Streets. Running off at an angle is **Merchant Street,** the oldest thoroughfare in Honolulu, and you might say it's "the beginning of the road to modernity." The statue is much more symbolic of Kamehameha's strength as a ruler and unifier of the Hawaiian Islands than as a replica of the man himself. Of the few drawings of Kamehameha that have been preserved, none is necessarily a good likeness. Kamehameha was a magnificent leader and statesman, but by all accounts not very good-looking. This statue is one of three. The original, lost at sea near the Falkland Islands en route from Paris where it was bronzed, was later recovered, but not before insurance money was used to cast this second one. The original is in the town of Kapa'au, in the Kohala District of the Big Island, not far from where Kamehameha was born, but although they supposedly came from the same mold, they somehow seem quite different. The third stands in Washington, D.C., dedicated when Hawaii became a state. The Honolulu statue was dedicated in 1883, as part of King David Kalakaua's coronation ceremony. Its black and gold colors are striking, but it is

OAHU

Map labels: KUKUI ST., FORT ST., PALI, ST. ANDREW'S CATHEDRAL, MILLER ST., QUEEN'S MEDICAL CENTER, LAUHALA ST., LISBON ST., WASHINGTON PLACE, PUBLIC PARKING, BERETANIA ST., WAR MEMORIAL, OUR LADY OF PEACE, BISHOP ST., MUNICIPAL BUILDING, PAUAHI ST., MALL, STATE CAPITOL, PUNCHBOWL ST., BETHEL ST., FORT ST. MALL, ALAKEA ST., RICHARDS ST., 'IOLANI BARRACKS, STATE ARCHIVES, HONOLULU HALE (CITY HALL), SOUTH KING ST., MISSION HOUSES MUSEUM, KING ST., ASTON EXECUTIVE CENTER, 'IOLANI PALACE, LIBRARY, KAWAIAHA'O ST., BANDSTAND, KAWAIAHA'O CHURCH, KAMEHAMEHA STATUE, FIRST HAWAIIAN CENTER, POST OFFICE, CEMETERY, MISSION LN., MERCHANT ST., JUDICIARY BUILDING, QUEEN ST., MILILANI ST., SOUTH ST., 92, NIMITZ HWY., HALEKUAWILA ST., DOWNTOWN HONOLULU, PARKING, ALOHA TOWER DR., FEDERAL BUILDING, 0 200 yds, ALOHA TOWER MARKETPLACE, FALLS OF CLYDE, PARKING, ALA MOANA, 0 200 m, ALOHA TOWER, HAWAII MARITIME CENTER, 92, RESTAURANT ROW, To Airport, O'AHU, Honolulu Harbor, To Waikiki

most magnificent on June 11, King Kamehameha Day, when 18-foot lei are draped around the neck and the outstretched arms.

Behind Kamehameha stands **Ali'iolani Hale,** now the State Judiciary Building. This handsome structure, designed by an Australian architect and begun in 1872, was originally commissioned by Kamehameha V as a palace, but was redesigned as a general court building. It looks much more grand than 'Iolani Palace across the way. Kamehameha V died before it

was finished, and it was officially dedicated by King Kalakaua in 1874. Less than 20 years later, on January 17, 1893, at this "hall of justice," the first proclamation by the Members of the Committee of Safety was read, stating that the sovereign nation of Hawaii was no more, and that the islands would be ruled by a provisional government. On the ground floor of this building, the **Judiciary History Center,** 808/539-4999, offers free exhibits weekdays from 9 A.M. to 3:30 or 4 P.M. Docents are available for individuals or small groups on Thursday and Friday; for larger groups, call to make an appointment.

Next door is the **Old Federal Building,** which is home to several state department offices and the downtown post office station. To their rear are the old Customs and Courts houses and, to the east, additional court buildings.

'Iolani Palace

As you enter the 11-acre parklike palace grounds, notice the emblem of Hawaii in the center of the large iron gates. They're often draped with simple lei of fragrant *maile*. The quiet grounds are a favorite strolling and relaxing place for many government workers, especially in the shade of a huge banyan, purportedly planted by Kalakaua's wife, Kapi'olani. The building, with its glass and ironwork imported from San Francisco and its Corinthian columns, is the only true royal palace in America. (Queen Emma Summer Palace in Nu'uanu Valley and Hulihe'e Palace on the Big Island, while royal residences, were never the seat of power.) 'Iolani (Royal Hawk) Palace, begun in late 1879 under orders of King Kalakaua, was completed in December 1882 at a cost of $350,000. It was the first electrified building in Honolulu, and it had a direct phone line to the Royal Boat House, located near where the Aloha Tower stands today.

Non–Hawaiian Island residents of the day thought it a frivolous waste of money, but here poignant scenes and profound changes rocked the Hawaiian Islands. After nine years as king, Kalakaua built a **Coronation Stand** that originally stood directly in front of the palace but was later moved to the left where you see it today. In a belated ceremony, Kalakaua raised a crown to his head and placed one on his queen, Kapi'olani. During the ceremony, 8,000 Hawaiians cheered, while Honolulu's foreign, tax-paying businessmen boycotted. On August 12, 1898, after only two Hawaiian monarchs, Kalakaua and Lili'uokalani (his sister), had resided in the palace, the American flag was raised up the flagpole following a successful coup that marked Hawaii's official recognition by the United States as a territory. During this ceremony, loyal Hawaiian subjects wept bitter tears, while the businessmen of Honolulu cheered wildly.

Kalakaua, later in his rule, was forced to sign a new constitution that greatly reduced his own power to little more than figurehead status. He traveled to San Francisco in 1891, where he died. His body was returned to Honolulu and lay in state in the palace. His sister, Lili'uokalani, succeeded him; she attempted to change this constitution and gain the old power of Hawaii's sovereigns, but the businessmen revolted and the monarchy fell. 'Iolani Palace then became the main executive building for the provisional government, with the House of Representatives meeting in the throne room and the Senate in the dining room. It served in this capacity until 1968. It has since been elevated to a state monument and National Historical Landmark.

'Iolani Palace is open to 45-minute guided tours only, starting every 15 minutes Tues.–Sat. 9 A.M.–2:15 P.M.; $15 adults, $10 *kama'aina,* $5 children 5–12, with no children under five admitted. The palace is open the same hours on the first Sunday of every month for free admission to *kama'aina;* other visitors are charged the regular fees. These tours are popular, so make reservations at least a day in advance. The **'Iolani Palace Gallery,** in the basement of the palace, is also open to visitors, but on a self-guided basis. This gallery contains the Hawaiian crown jewels and other royal accouterments. No reservations are needed to view this site, which is open 9 A.M.–4 P.M. on days that the palace is open. The cost of viewing the galleries is the same as that for the tours, except that children under five are admitted and there is no charge for them. To view the galleries and take a tour, fees are $20 adult, $15 *kama'aina,* $5 children 5–12. Tickets are sold at a window at the 'Iolani Barracks, behind the Royal Bandstand, open Tues.–Sat. 8 A.M.–3:30 P.M. Also in the barracks, the palace gift and book shop is open Tues.–Sat. 8:30 A.M.–3:30 P.M. For information and reservations call 808/522-0832 or go online at http://openstudio.hawaii.edu/iolani.

Palace Grounds

Kalakaua, known as the "Merrie Monarch," was credited with saving the hula. He also hired Henry Berger, first Royal Hawaiian Bandmaster, and together they wrote "Hawaii Pono," the state anthem. Many concerts were given from the Coronation Stand, which became known as

O'AHU

a royal insignia at the 'Iolani palace

ROBERT NILSEN

the **Royal Bandstand.** Behind it is **'Iolani Barracks** (Hale Koa), built in 1870 to house the Royal Household Guards. When the monarchy of Hawaii fell to provisional government forces in 1893, only one of these soldiers was wounded in the nearly bloodless confrontation. The barracks were moved to the present site in 1965 from nearby land on which the State Capitol was erected.

To the right behind the palace are the **State Archives,** 808/586-0329. This modern building, dating from 1953, holds records, documents, and vintage photos. A treasure trove to scholars and those tracing their genealogy, it is worth a visit by the general public to view the old photos on display. Open Mon.–Fri. 9 A.M.–4 P.M.; free. Next door is the **Hawaii State Library,** housing the main branch of this statewide system. As in all Hawaii state libraries, you are entitled to a card on your first visit and are then eligible to take out books. Library cards are available free for Hawaii state residents and military personnel stationed in Hawaii, $25 for nonresidents, and $10 for up to three months for visitors. The central courtyard is a favorite lunch spot for many of the government workers. Some of the original money to build the library was put up by Andrew Carnegie. This main library branch is open 9 A.M.–5 P.M. Monday, Friday, and Saturday, 10 A.M.–5 P.M. on Wednesday, and 9 A.M.–8 P.M. on Tuesday and Thursday; for information, call 808/586-3500.

Government Buildings

Lili'uokalani was deposed and placed under house arrest in the palace for nine months. Later, after much intrigue that included a visit to Washington, D.C., to plead her case and an aborted counterrevolution, she sadly accepted her fate and moved to nearby **Washington Place.** This solid-looking structure fronts Beretania Street and was originally the home of sea captain John Dominis. It was inherited by his son John Owen Dominis, who married a lovely young Hawaiian aristocrat, Lydia Kapa'akea, who became Queen Lili'uokalani. She lived in her husband's home, proud but powerless, until her death in 1917. Washington Place is now the official residence of the governor of Hawaii. To the right of Washington Place is the eternal flame **War Memorial.** Erected in 1974, this memorial replaced an older one and is dedicated to the people who perished in World War II. A courtyard and benches are provided for quiet meditation.

Directly behind 'Iolani Palace is the magnificent **Hawaii State Capitol,** built in 1969 for $25 million. The building itself is a metaphor for Hawaii: the pillars surrounding it are palms, the reflecting pool is the sea, and the cone-shaped rooms of the Legislature represent the volcanoes of Hawaii. It's lined with rich koa wood from the Big Island and is further graced with woven hangings and murals, with two gigantic, four-ton replicas of the State Seal hanging at both entrances. The inner courtyard has a 600,000-tile mosaic, *Aquarius,* rendered by island artist Tadashi Sato, and on one side is a poignant sculpture of *Father Damien of the Lepers.* The State Legislature is in session January to March, and opens with dancing, music, and festivities at 10 A.M. on the third Wednesday in January, public invited. Peek inside, then take the elevator to the fifth floor for outstanding views of the city.

A few steps away, on the corner of Punchbowl and King Streets, stands **Honolulu Hale,** Honolulu City Hall. Built in 1928, with additions in 1951, this office building is open 7:45 A.M.–4:30 P.M. weekdays and houses the office of the mayor, the city council, and a few city departments. It too has a courtyard where music, art, and other public events are held.

St. Andrew's Cathedral

To the left of Washington Place, the governor's residence, is St. Andrew's Cathedral. Construction started in 1867 as an Anglican church but wasn't really finished until the late 1950s. Many of its stones and ornaments were shipped from England, and its stained glass windows and bell tower are of particular interest. Hawaii's monarchs worshiped here, and the church is still very much in use. Open 6 A.M.–6 P.M. Mon.–Fri.; a free guided tour is offered following the 10 A.M. Sunday service.

MISSION HOUSES MUSEUM

The days when tall ships with tattered sails crewed by rough seamen bore God-fearing missionary families dedicated to Christianizing the savage islands are alive in the halls and buildings of the Mission Houses Museum, 553 S. King St., Honolulu, HI 96813, 808/531-0481, website: www.lava.net/~mhm, email: mhm@lava.net, now a registered National Historical Landmark. Across from Kawaiaha'o Church (oldest in Honolulu), the complex includes two main houses, a printing house annex, a research library, and a fine, inexpensive gift shop. It's operated by the nonprofit Hawaiian Mission Children's Society, whose members serve as guides and hosts. Many are direct descendants, or spouses of descendants, of the Congregationalist missionaries who built these structures. One-hour tours are conducted at various times throughout the day

Tues.–Sat. 9 A.M.–4 P.M. (closed Sunday and Monday). Guided tours of the Frame House are offered 9:30 A.M.–3 P.M. Admission is $8 adults, $7 *kama'aina* and military, $6 seniors, $4 students age 13 and above, and $3 children ages 4–12.

Construction

If you think that precut modular housing is a new concept, think again. The first structure that you enter is the **Frame House,** the oldest wooden structure in Hawaii. Precut in Boston, it came along with the first missionary packet in 1819. Since the interior frame was left behind and didn't arrive until Christmas Day, 1820, the missionary families lived in thatched huts until it was erected. Finally the Chamberlain family occupied it in 1821. Many missionary families used it over the years, with as many as four households occupying this small structure at the same time. This is where the Christianizing of Hawaii truly began. This structure was renovated in 1996, and most artifacts and furniture are from the 1820–1860 period, with some reproductions.

The missionaries, being New Englanders, first dug a cellar. The Hawaiians were very suspicious of the strange hole, convinced that the missionaries planned to store guns and arms in this "fort." Though assured to the contrary, King Liholiho, anxious to save face and prove his omnipotence, had a cellar dug near his home twice as deep and large. This satisfied everyone.

Notice the different styles, sizes, and colors of bricks used in the structures. Most of the ships of the day carried bricks as ballast. After unloading cargo, the captains either donated or sold the bricks to the missionaries, who incorporated them into the buildings. A common local material was coral stone: pulverized coral was burned with lime to make a rudimentary cement, which was then used to bind cut-coral blocks. The pit that was used for this purpose is still discernible on the grounds.

Kitchen

The natives were intrigued with the missionaries, whom they called "long necks" because of their high collars. The missionaries, on the other hand, were a little more wary of their "charges." The low fence around the complex was symbolic as well as utilitarian. The missionaries were obsessed

O'AHU

with keeping their children away from Hawaiian children, who at first ran around naked and played many games with overt sexual overtones. Almost every evening a small cadre of Hawaiians would assemble to peer into the kitchen to watch the women cook, which they found exceedingly strange because their *kapu* said that *men* did the cooking. In the kitchen, actually an attached cookhouse, the woodburning stove kept breaking down. More often than not, the women used the fireplace with its built-in oven. About once a week, they fired up the oven to make traditional New England staples like bread, pies, cakes, and puddings. The missionaries were dependent on the Hawaiians to bring them fresh water. Notice a large porous stone through which they would filter the water to remove dirt, mud, and sometimes brackishness.

The Hawaiians were even more amazed when the entire family sat down to dinner, a tremendous deviation from their beliefs that separated men and women when eating. When the missionaries assembled to dine or meet at the "long table," the Hawaiians silently stood at the open door to watch the evening soap opera. The unnerved missionaries eventually closed the door and cut two windows into the wall, which they could leave opened but draped. The long table took on further significance. The one you see is a replica. When different missionaries left the islands, they, like people today, wanted a souvenir. For some odd reason, they elected to saw a bit off the long table. As years went by, the table got shorter and shorter until it was useless.

Residents

Originally housing four families, the house was made a duplex in 1824 and into a home for one family in 1851. Although many families lived in it, two of the best known were the Binghams and the Judds. Much of the furniture here was theirs. Judd, a member of the third missionary company, assumed the duties of physician to all the missionaries and islanders. He often prescribed alcohol of different sorts to the missionary families for a wide variety of ailments; many records remain of these prescriptions, but not one record of complaints from his patients. The Binghams and Judds got along very well, and entertained each other and visitors, most often in the Judds' parlor because they were a little better off. The

women would often congregate here to do their sewing, which was in great demand, especially by members of the royal household. Until the missionary women taught island girls to sew, providing clothing for Hawaii's royalty was a tiresome and time-consuming obligation.

The missionaries were self-sufficient and had the unbounded energy of youth, as the average age was only 25. The husbands often built furniture for their families. Reverend Bingham, a good craftsman, was pressed by Queen Ka'ahumanu to build her a rocking chair after she became enamored of one made for Mrs. Bingham. The queen weighed almost 400 pounds, so building her a suitable chair was no slim feat! Still, the queen could only use it in her later years when she'd lost a considerable amount of weight. After she died, the Binghams asked for it to be returned, and it sits in their section of the house. Compare Bingham's chair to another in the Judds' bedroom, jury-rigged by a young missionary husband from a captain's chair. An understatement, found later in his diary, confirmed that the young man was not a carpenter.

When you enter the Judds' bedroom, note how small it is, and consider that two adults and five children slept here. As soon as the children were old enough, they were sent back to the Mainland for schooling, no doubt to relieve some of the congestion. Also notice that the windows were fixed, in the New England style, and imagine how close it must have been in these rooms. The Binghams' bedroom is also small, and not as well furnished. Bingham's shaving kit remains, and is inscribed with "The Sandwich Isles." In the bedroom of Mary Ward, a missionary woman who never married, the roof was raised to accommodate her canopy bed.

Another famous family that lived in the complex was the Cooke family. When the missionary board withdrew its support, the Cookes petitioned them to buy the duplex, which was granted. Shortly thereafter, Mr. Cooke, who had been a teacher, formed a partnership with one Mr. Castle, and from that time forward Castle and Cooke grew to become one of Hawaii's oldest and most powerful corporations.

Chamberlain House

The largest building in the compound is the coral-block Chamberlain House. This barnlike structure was completed in 1831 and used as a warehouse and living quarters for Levi Chamberlain's family. Chamberlain was the accountant and business agent for the mission, so goods for all mission stations in the islands were stored in most of the structure, while the family occupied three modest rooms. Exhibits are shown on the second floor.

Printing House

The missionaries decided almost immediately that the best way to convert the natives was to speak to them in their own language and to create a written Hawaiian language that they would teach in school. To this end, they created the **Hawaiian alphabet,** consisting of 12 letters, the five vowels and seven consonants. In addition, to disseminate the doctrines of Christianity, they needed books, and therefore a printing press. On the grounds still stands the Printing House, built in 1841 but first used as annex bedrooms of the Frame House by the Hall family. The original printing house, built in 1823, no longer exists. In the Printing House is a replica of the Ramage press brought from New England, first operated by Elisha Loomis. He returned to the Mainland when he was 28 and soon died of tuberculosis, but not before he had earned the distinction of being the first printer west of the Rockies. Here were printed biblical tracts, textbooks, and anything that the king or passing captains were willing to pay to have printed. Although it took eight hours of hard work to set up one page to be printed, it is estimated that in the 20 years the press operated under the missionaries, more than seven million pages were produced.

Gift Shop

While on the grounds be sure to visit the bookstore and gift shop. It's small but has an excellent collection of Hawaiiana, some very inexpensive but quality items (such as tapa bookmarks), and an outstanding collection of Ni'ihau shellwork, considered the finest in Hawaii. The shelves hold tasteful items like wood carvings, bread boards, hats, weavings, chimes, flags of old Hawaii, and stuffed pillows with classic Hawaiian quilt motifs, as well as a good collection of Hawaiian dolls, for kids and adults. Between the bookstore and the research library are restrooms.

Special Programs

Along with other programs, the museum hosts Hawaii's only **Living History Days** program, with actors who dress in fashions of the period and assume the roles of missionaries in 1830s Honolulu. Feel free to interact and ask questions, but remember that they stay in character, so the answers may surprise you. The living history program is usually offered every Wednesday and on the second Saturday of the month, 9 A.M.–4 P.M., regular admission except for *kama'aina* who get in free. Other special programs are also offered, like a candlelight Christmas affair, crafts and quilt fairs, quilt classes, and tea with the 19th-century Reverend Hiram and Mrs. Sybil Bingham in their parlor; call 808/924-1911 for details. Also, consider the historic walking tour offered by the museum, which guides you through the houses of the museum and then on to downtown Honolulu, hitting all the historic sights with an extremely knowledgeable narration by one of the museum's guides. The walking tour is conducted on Thursday only 9:45 A.M.–12:45 P.M.; reserve two days in advance. The cost, which includes entrance to the mission houses, is $15 for adults, $14 for military and *kama'aina,* $13 for seniors, $11 for college students and other students ages 13–18, $10 for children ages 4–12, and free for children under four. For anyone wanting to delve into the history of the mission, the reference library is open Tues.–Fri. 10 A.M.–4 P.M. and Saturday by appointment.

KAWAIAHA'O CHURCH

This church, so instrumental in Hawaii's history, is the most enduring symbol of the original missionary work in the islands. A sign welcomes you and bids the blessing, "Grace and peace to you from God our Father." Hawaiian-language services are given here every Sunday, along with English-language services. The church was constructed 1837–42 according to plans drawn up by Hiram Bingham, its minister. Before this, at least four grass shacks of increasing size stood here. One was destroyed by a sailor who was reprimanded by Reverend Bingham for attending services while drunk; the old sea dog returned the next day and burned the church to the ground. Kawaiaha'o (Water of Hao) Church is constructed from more than 14,000 coral blocks quarried from offshore reefs. In 1843, following Restoration Day, when the British returned the Hawaiian Islands to sovereignty after a brief period of imperialism by a renegade captain, King Kamehameha III uttered here the profound words in a thanksgiving ceremony that were destined to become Hawaii's motto, *"Ua mau ke e'a o ka 'aina i ka pono"* ("The life of the land is preserved in righteousness").

Other noteworthy ceremonies held at the church were the marriage of King Liholiho and his wife Queen Emma, who bore the last child born to a Hawaiian monarch. Unfortunately, little Prince Albert died at the age of four. On June 19, 1856, Lunalilo, the first king elected to the throne, took his oath of office in the church. A bachelor who died childless, he always felt scorned by living members of the Kamehameha clan and refused to be buried with them at the Royal Mausoleum in Nu'uanu Valley; he is buried in a tomb in the church's cemetery. Buried along with him is his father, Charles Kana'ina, and nearby lies

Kawaiaha'o Church

J.D. BISIGNANI

O'AHU

the grave of his mother, Miriam Kekauluohi. In the graveyard lies Henry Berger and many members of the Parker, Green, Brown, and Cooke families, early missionaries to the islands. Queen Lili'uokalani's body lay in state in the church before it was taken to the Royal Mausoleum. A jubilation service was held in the church when Hawaii became a state in 1959. Kawaiaha'o holds beautiful Christmas services with a strong Polynesian and Hawaiian flavor. Hidden away in a corner of the grounds is an unobtrusive adobe building, remains of a schoolhouse built in 1835 to educate Hawaiian children.

HONOLULU HARBOR AREA

Hawaii Maritime Center

The development of this center is a wonderful concept whose time has finally come. It's amazing that a state and former nation, whose discovery and very birth are so intimately tied to the exploration, navigation, and exploitation of the sea, had never had a center dedicated exclusively to these profoundly important aspects of its heritage. Now the Hawaii Maritime Center, at Pier 7, Honolulu Harbor, 808/536-6373, is exactly that. Open since 1989, the center consists of three attractions: the Maritime Center building with displays of Hawaii's past; the classic, fully rigged, four-masted *Falls of Clyde* floating museum; and the reproduction of a Hawaiian sailing canoe, the *Hokule'a,* which has sailed back in time using ancient navigational methods to retrace the steps of Hawaii's Polynesian explorers. Take TheBus no. 19 or 20, or the Waikiki Trolley from Waikiki. Admission for all attractions is $7.50 adults, $6 seniors and children 6–17, and free for the younger kids; open 8:30 A.M.–8 P.M. every day except Christmas. Admission includes a 48-minute tape tour that guides you through the museum. Don't just walk past or save this for the last, as it explains the exhibits and gives insight into what you're seeing. Also, stop in at the gift shop for a collectible of Hawaii's vintage past.

The main building of the center is the two-story museum. Upon entering you find a glass case filled with trophies and memorabilia from the days of King Kalakaua. His words have a sadly prophetic ring. "Remember who you are.

Be gracious, but never forget from whence you came for this is where your heart is. This is the cradle of your life." Notice the phones installed throughout the capital in 1887, a few years before California had electricity. Kalakaua had previously installed telephones between his boathouse and the palace in 1878, just two years after Bell's invention. The bottom floor of the center recalls ancient fishing methods and the traditional division of land and sea resources among the people. Another fascinating display traces the development of surfing through the ages, from original boards, more like seagoing canoes at 18 feet long, until the modern debut of the fiberglass board. You can spot a vintage album of *Surfin' Safari* by the Beach Boys. Here, too, is a land-surfing sled used for games during the Makahiki Festival. Trails to accommodate it were up to a mile long. Built on steep hills, they were paved in stone, layered with earth, and topped with slippery grass. Once launched there was no stopping until the bottom. Yippee! One corner of the museum is dedicated to tattooing, Polynesian and Western. It shows traditional tattoos worn by both men and women, and then how the Western style became more popular, as Hawaii was a main berth for sailors, who sported these living souvenirs from around the world. **Mail buoys** sound uninteresting, but these tidbits of old Hawaiiana are fascinating, and the tradition is still alive today. Passing ships, mainly from Peru and Equador, still radio Honolulu Harbor that they are dropping one of these gaily painted metal cans. Someone, anyone, who hears the message fetches it. Inside are little gifts for the finder, who takes the enclosed mail and sends it on its way.

The second floor is dedicated to the discovery of Hawaii, both by the Polynesians and Westerners. Through ledgers, histories, and artifacts, it traces original discovery, Western discovery, the death of Captain Cook, and the role of the sea otter pelt, which brought the first whalers and traders after sandalwood. The whaling section is dripping with blood and human drama. Look at the old harpoons and vintage film footage. Yes, film footage, and photos. A remarkable display is of scrimshaw from the whaling days. Sailors would be at sea 5–7 years and would have untold hours to cre-

ate beauty in what were dismal conditions. Suspended from the ceiling are replicas of double-hulled sailing canoes and one of only two fully restored skeletons of the humpback whale (this one is in diving position). One corner is a replica of H. Hackfeld and Co., a whaling supply store of the era. The rear of the second floor shows steamships that cruised between Hawaii, Japan, and the East Coast; a nature exhibit of weather, marine life, and volcanoes; and an auditorium with a video on the *Hokule'a*.

Behind the museum is the seafood Pier Seven Restaurant and an area called Kalakaua Park, a garden and observation area perfect for lunch. Eighty-one steps lead to the "crow's nest" and "widow's walk," with great views of the harbor and city.

Falls of Clyde

This is the last fully rigged, four-masted ship afloat on any of the world's oceans; it has been designated as a National Historic Landmark. She was saved from being scrapped in 1963 by a Seattle bank that was attempting to recoup some money on a bad debt. The people of Hawaii learned of her fate and spontaneously raised money to have the ship towed back to Honolulu Harbor. The *Falls of Clyde* was always a worker, never a pleasure craft. It served the Matson Navigation Company as a cargo and passenger liner 1898–1920. Built in Glasgow, Scotland, in 1878, she was converted in 1906 to a sail-driven tanker; a motor aboard was used mainly to move the rigging around. After 1920, she was dismantled and towed to Alaska, becoming little more than a floating oil depot for fishing boats. Since 1968, the *Falls of Clyde* has been a floating museum, sailing the imaginations of children and grownups to times past, and in this capacity has perhaps performed her greatest duty.

Hokule'a

The newest and perhaps most dynamic feature of the center is the *Hokule'a*. This authentic re-creation of a traditional double-hulled sailing canoe captured the attention of the world when in 1976 it made a 6,000-mile round-trip voyage to Tahiti. It was piloted by Mau Piailug, a Caroline Islander, who used only ancient navigational

OAHU

The Falls of Clyde *lies at the Hawaii Maritime Center.*

ROBERT NILSEN

techniques to guide it successfully on its voyage. This attempt to relive these ancient voyages as closely as possible included eating traditional provisions only—poi, coconuts, dried fish, and bananas. Toward the end of the voyage some canned food had to be broken out!

Modern materials such as plywood and fiberglass were used, but by consulting many petroglyphs and old drawings of these original craft, the design and lines were kept as authentic as possible. The sails, made from a heavy cotton, were the distinctive crab-claw type. In trial runs to work out the kinks and choose the crew, she almost sank in the treacherous channel between O'ahu and Kaua'i and had to be towed in by the Coast Guard. But the *Hokule'a* performed admirably during the actual voyage. The experiment was a resounding technical success, but it was marred by bad feelings between members of the crew. Both landlubber and sea dog found it impossible to work as a team on the first voyage, thereby mocking the canoe's name, "Star of Gladness." The tension was compounded by the close quarters of more than a dozen men living on an open deck only nine feet wide by 40 feet long. The remarkable navigator Piailug refused to return to Hawaii with the craft and instead sailed back to his native island. Since then, the *Hokule'a* has made six more voyages, including one to distant Papa Nui, logging more than 60,000 miles, with many ethnically mixed crews who have gotten along admirably.

The *Hokule'a,* owned by the Hawaii Maritime Center but sailed by the Polynesian Voyaging Society, makes Pier 7 its home berth when not at sea. This double-hulled canoe, a replica and much older brother of the significantly larger ones that Captain Cook found so remarkable, will fascinate you, too. This canoe has been joined by another, the *Hawai'iloa,* which also has made a long trip to Polynesia and back. While not on the water, it too is docked at the Hawaii Maritime Center. For more information about the Polynesian Voyaging Society, check its website at http://leahi.kcc.hawaii.edu/org/pvs.

Aloha Tower

Next door to the Hawaiian Maritime Center, at Pier 9, is the Aloha Tower, a beacon of hospitality welcoming people to Hawaii for eight decades. When this endearing and enduring tourist cliché was built in 1926 for $160,000, the 184-foot, 10-story tower was the tallest structure on O'ahu. As such, this landmark emblazoned with the greeting and departing word, "Aloha," with clocks embedded in all four walls, became the symbol of Hawaii. Before the days of air transport, ocean liners would pull up to the pier to disembark passengers, and on these "Boat Days," festive well-wishers from throughout the city would gather to greet and lei the arriving passengers. The Royal Hawaiian Band would even turn out to welcome the guests ashore. Almost as a re-creation of days past, similar "Boat Days" activities are held at the pier when interisland cruise ships depart for their weeklong sail around the islands.

Aloha Tower was originally connected to surrounding buildings. Visitors to the islands entered the huge ground floor U.S. Customs rooms, which at one time processed droves of passengers coming to find a new life. Today, crowds come to find bargains at the adjacent Aloha Tower Marketplace. When refurbished in 1994, the tower's attached buildings were removed, making the tower stand out with more prominence. Only a few harbormasters on the top floor oversee the comings and goings of cargo ships. The observation area on the top floor is reached by elevator, which has the dubious distinction of being one of the first elevators in Hawaii. The elevator is a bit like a wheezy old man, huffing and puffing, but it still gets you to the top. Once atop the tower, you get the most remarkable view of the harbor and the city. A high-rise project planned for next door would surely have ruined the view, but due to good sense and citizens with clout, this ill-considered idea has thankfully met a timely end. A remarkable feature of the vista is the reflections of the city and the harbor in many of the steel and reflective glass high-rises. It's as if a huge mural were painted on them. The tower is open free of charge daily 9 A.M.–7:30 P.M. April–September and until 7 P.M. October–March.

PALI HIGHWAY

Cutting across O'ahu from Honolulu to Kailua on the windward coast is Route 61, better known as the Pali Highway. Before getting to the famous Nu'uanu Pali Lookout at the very crest of the Ko'olau Mountains, you can spend a full and enjoyable day sightseeing. Stop en route at Punchbowl's National Memorial Cemetery, followed by an optional side trip to the summit of Tantalus for a breathtaking view of the city. Open 7 A.M.–7:45 P.M., Pu'u 'Ualaka'a State Wayside, also known as Round Top, is where Honolulu lies at your feet. Numerous hiking trails cross Tantalus Drive as it circles its way up and then down these mountain ridges. You can also visit the **O'ahu Cemetery** and **Royal Mausoleum State Monument** in the vicinity. Take the H-1 freeway to Vineyard Boulevard (exit

22), cross the Pali Highway to Nu'uanu Avenue, and follow it to the mausoleum. In a minute or two, if you continue up Nu'uanu Avenue, it intersects the Pali Highway. This small chapel, built in 1865 by Kamehameha IV, holds the bodies of most of the royal family who died after 1825. Their bodies were originally interred elsewhere but were later moved here. The mausoleum at one time held 18 royal bodies but became overcrowded, so they were moved again to little crypts scattered around the three-acre grounds. Of the eight Hawaiian monarchs, only King Kamehameha I and King William Lunalilo are buried elsewhere—King Kamehameha I somewhere on the Big Island and Lunalilo at Kawaiaha'o Church. Few tourists visit this serene place, which is open weekdays 8 A.M.–4 P.M. Across Nu'uanu Ave. and down just a bit is the O'ahu Cemetery. Founded in 1844, it hold the graves of some of the oldest and best-known island families.

Next comes Queen Emma Summer Palace and the Dai Jingu Temple, a Baptist college, and a Catholic church. It almost seems as though these sects were vying to get farther up the hill to be just a little closer to heaven. A sign, past Queen Emma Summer Palace, points you off to **Nu'uanu Pali Drive.** Take it! This few-minutes' jog off the Pali Highway (which it rejoins) takes you through some wonderful scenery. Immediately the road is canopied with trees, and in less than half a mile there's a bubbling little waterfall and a pool. The homes in here are grand, and the entire area has a parklike effect. One of the nicest little roads that you can take while looking around, this side trip wastes no time at all.

Queen Emma Summer Palace

Called Hanaiakamalama, this summer home is more the simple hideaway of a well-to-do family than a grand palace. The 3,000-square-foot interior has only two bedrooms and no facilities for guests. John George Lewis put the house on the property in 1848. He purchased the land for $800 from a previous owner by the name of Henry Pierce, and then resold it to John Young II. The exterior has a strong New England flavor, and indeed the house was prefabricated in Boston, but it definitely has a neoclassical flourish with its tall round Doric columns. The simple square home, with a front lanai, was purchased by John Young II, Queen Emma's uncle, in 1850. When he died, she inherited the property and spent many relaxing days here, away from the heat of Honolulu, with her husband King Kamehameha IV. The huge rear room was added in 1869 for a visit by the Duke of Edinburgh. Emma used the home little after 1872, and following her death in 1885 it fell into disrepair.

Rescued from demolition by the Daughters of Hawaii in 1913, it was refurbished and has operated as a museum since 1915. In the 1970s, the Summer Palace was added to the National Register of Historic Sites. The palace, at 2913 Pali Hwy., Honolulu, HI 96817, 808/595-3167, is open daily 9 A.M.–4 P.M., except for major holidays; admission $5, seniors $4, children 16 and under $1. Although it's just off the Pali Highway, the one and only sign comes up quickly, and many visitors pass it by. If you pass the entranceway to the O'ahu Country Club just across the road, you've gone too far.

As you enter, notice the tall *kahili,* symbols of noble rank in the entranceway, along with *lau hala* mats on the floor, which at one time were an unsurpassed specialty of Hawaii. Today they must be imported from Fiji or Samoa. The walls are hung with paintings of many of Hawaii's kings and queens, and in every room are distinctive Hawaiian artifacts, such as magnificent feather capes, fans, and tapa hangings. Many of the furnishings belonged to Queen Emma, while others were from other royal family members.

The furnishings have a very strong British influence. The Hawaiian nobility of the time were enamored with the British. King Kamehameha IV traveled to England when he was 15 years old; he met Queen Victoria, and the two became good friends. Emma and Kamehameha IV had the last child born to a Hawaiian king and queen on May 20, 1858. Named Prince Albert after Queen Victoria's consort, he was much loved but died when he was only four years old on August 27, 1862. His father followed him to the grave in little more than a year. The king's brother, Lot Kamehameha, a bachelor, took the throne but died very shortly thereafter, marking the end of the Kamehameha line; after that, Hawaii elected her kings. Prince Albert's canoe-shaped cradle is here,

made in Germany by Wilhelm Fisher from four different kinds of Hawaiian wood. His tiny shirts, pants, and boots are still laid out, and there's a lock of his hair, as well as one from Queen Emma. In every room there is royal memorabilia. The royal bedroom (originally the dining room) displays a queen-size bed, covered with an exquisite bedspread or quilt that changes periodically. In the Cloak Room, originally built as the bedroom but later used as the dining room, is a fine example of a royal feather cloak. Throughout the house, there's vintage Victorian furniture, a piano built in London by Collard and Collard, and even a stereopticon given as a gift from Napoleon III. A royal cabinet made in Berlin holds porcelains, plates, and cups. After Queen Emma died, it stood in Charles R. Bishop's drawing room but was later returned. In the cellar of the house are the servants' quarters, and the original cookhouse once stood to the side where the paved patio is today. Queen Emma once owned 65 acres of the surrounding land. The two acres that remain are beautifully manicured, and the house is surrounded by shrubbery and trees, many of which date from when the royal couple lived here. Restrooms are around back, attached to the gift shop, which is open the same hours as the palace. Managed by the Daughters of Hawaii, it's small but packed with excellent items like greeting cards, lei, books, beverage trays (reproductions of the early Matson Line menus), little Hawaiian quilt pillows, needlepoint, wraparounds from Tahiti, T-shirts with Queen Emma Summer Palace logo, and Ni'ihau shellwork, the finest in Hawaii.

Walk around back past the neighborhood park basketball court and keep to the right. Soon you'll see a modest little white building. Look for a rather thick and distinctive rope hanging across the entranceway. This is the Shinto temple **Dai Jingu.** It's not nearly as spectacular as the giant trees in this area, but it is authentic and worth a quick look. Shake the bell rope and clap your hands three times as you walk up to the entranceway. For fun, place 25 cents into the *oni kuji* wooden box and out comes a good luck fortune on the back of a small piece of paper. So, for a quarter, find out about love, marriage, business, health, and that sort of thing, and help out the temple at the same time.

Nu'uanu Pali Lookout

This is one of those extra-benefit places where you get a magnificent view without any effort at all. Merely drive up the Pali Highway to the well-marked turnout and park. The lookout closes at 8 P.M. Rip-offs happen, so take all valuables. Before you, if the weather is accommodating, an unimpeded view of windward O'ahu lies at your feet. Nu'uanu Pali (Cool Heights) lives up to its name; the winds here are chilly and extremely strong, and they funnel right through this notch in the mountain ridge. You may need a jacket or windbreaker. On a particularly windy day just after a good rainfall, various waterfalls tumbling off the *pali* will actually be blown uphill! A number of roads, punched over and through the *pali* over the years, are engineering marvels. Originally a foot path, later expanded to a horse trail, the famous "carriage road" built in 1898 was truly amazing. It was built by John Wilson, a Honolulu boy, for only $37,500, using 200 laborers and plenty of dynamite. Droves of people come here, many in huge buses, and they all go to the railing to have a peek. By walking down the old road built in 1932 that goes off to the right, you actually get private and better views. You'll find the tallest point in the area, a huge needle-like rock. The wind is quieter here.

Nu'uanu Pali figures prominently in Hawaii's legend history. It's said, not without academic skepticism, that Kamehameha the Great pursued the last remaining defenders of O'ahu to these cliffs in one of the final battles fought to consolidate his power over all of the islands in 1795. If you use your imagination, you can easily feel the utter despair and courage of these vanquished warriors as they were driven ever closer to the edge. Mercy was neither shown nor expected. Some jumped to their deaths rather than surrender, while others fought until they were pushed over. The estimated number of casualties varies considerably, from a few hundred to a few thousand, while some believe that the battle never happened at all. Compounding the controversy are stories of the warriors' families, who searched the cliffs below for years and supposedly found bones of their kinsmen, which they buried. The Pali Lookout is romantic at night, with the lights of Kailua and Kane'ohe in the distance, but the best nighttime view is from Tantalus Drive, where all of Honolulu lies at your feet.

PUNCHBOWL, NATIONAL CEMETERY OF THE PACIFIC

One sure sign that you have entered a place of honor is the hushed and quiet nature that everyone adopts without having to be told. This is the way it is the moment that you enter this shrine. The Hawaiian name, Puowaina (Hill of Sacrifice), couldn't have been more prophetic. Punchbowl is the almost perfectly round crater of an extinct volcano. It holds the bodies of more than

O'AHU

ROBERT NILSEN

the precipitous edge of the Windward pali as seen from the Nu'uanu Lookout

Punchbowl Cemetery

J.D. BISIGNANI

33,000 men and women who fell fighting for the United States, from World War II to Vietnam, and a few notable individuals who have served the country in other ways. At one time, Punchbowl was a bastion of heavy cannon and artillery trained on Honolulu Harbor to defend it from hostile naval forces. In 1943 Hawaii bequeathed it to the federal government as a memorial; it was dedicated in 1949, when the remains of an unknown serviceman killed during the attack on Pearl Harbor were first interred. One of the more recent to be buried here was astronaut Ellison Onizuka, who died in 1986 aboard the *Challenger* space shuttle. To attest to its sacredness and the importance of those who lie buried here, more than two million visitors stop here yearly to pay their respects, making this the most visited site in the state. In addition, the annual Easter sunrise service held here draws thousands.

As you enter the main gate, a flagpole with the Stars and Stripes unfurled is framed in the center of a long sweeping lawn. A roadway lined with monkeypod trees adds three-dimensional depth to the impressionistic scene, as it leads to the steps of a marble, altar-like monument in the distance. The eye has a continuous sweep of the field, as there are no elevated tombstones, just simple marble slabs lying flat on the ground. The field is dotted with trees, including eight banyans, a special tree and symbolic number for the many Buddhists buried

here. Brightening the scene are plumeria and rainbow shower trees, often planted in Hawaiian graveyards because they produce flowers year-round as perennial offerings from the living to the dead when they can't personally attend the grave. All are equal here: the famous, like Ernie Pyle, the stalwart who earned the Congressional Medal of Honor, and the unknown who died alone and unheralded on muddy battlefields in godforsaken jungles. To the right just after you enter is the office, 808/532-3720, with brochures and restrooms. The cemetery is open free of charge 8 A.M.–5:30 P.M. September 30–March 1 and until 6:30 P.M. March 2–September 29, except for Memorial Day when the grounds are open 7 A.M.–7 P.M. Guided walking tours are conducted by the American Legion Mon.–Fri. at 11 A.M. These two-hour tours cost $15 per person, and reservations must be made by calling 808/946-6383. Tour buses, taxis, and limousines line up at the front. Don't leave valuables in your car.

To get to Punchbowl take the H-1 freeway to Route 61, the Pali Highway, and exit at 21B. Immediately get to the right, where a sign points you to Punchbowl. You'll make some fancy zigzags through a residential area, but it's well marked and you'll come to Puowaina Street, which leads you to the main gate. Notice landmarks going in, because as odd as it sounds, no signs lead you back out and it's easy to get lost.

The Monument

Like a pilgrim, you climb the steps to the monument, where on both sides marble slabs seem to whisper the names of 28,778 servicemen, all MIAs whose bodies were never found or those who were buried at sea, but whose spirits are honored here. The first slabs on the right are for the victims of Vietnam, on the left are those from World War II, and you can see that time is already weathering the marble. Their names stand together, as they fought and died . . . men, boys, lieutenants, captains, private soldiers, infantrymen, sailors . . . from everywhere in America. "In proud memory . . . this memorial has been erected by the United States of America."

At the monument itself, built in 1966, is a chapel, and in the middle is a statue of a woman, a woman of peace, a heroic woman of liberty. Around her on the walls are etched maps and battles of the Pacific War whose names still evoke passion: Pearl Harbor, Wake, Coral Sea, Midway, Iwo Jima, the Gilbert Islands, Okinawa. Many of the visitors are Japanese. Many of Hawaii's war dead are also Japanese. Four decades ago we battled each other with hatred and malice. Today, on bright afternoons we come together with saddened hearts to pay reverence to the dead.

UNIVERSITY OF HAWAI'I

Established in 1907, the University of Hawai'i at Manoa is the main campus of a 10-branch university system (www.hawaii.edu). The Manoa campus teaches about 15,000 students in undergraduate and graduate programs and, like the rest of he state, is a multicultural and multiracial establishment. You don't have to be a student to head for the University of Hawai'i, Manoa Campus. For one, it houses the **East-West Center,** which was incorporated in 1975 and officially separated from the university; here nations from Asia and the Pacific present fascinating displays of their homelands. Also, Manoa Valley itself is one of the loveliest residential areas on O'ahu. To get to the main campus follow the H-1 freeway to exit 24B (University Avenue). Follow University Avenue to Dole Avenue, and make a right onto campus. Stop immediately at one of the parking lots and get a parking map! Parking restrictions are strictly enforced, and this map not only helps to get you around, but saves you from fines or having your car towed away. Parking is a flat $3 for visitors each time you use the lot, so think about taking TheBus no. 4, which services this area quite well from Waikiki.

Two six-week summer sessions beginning late May and in early July are offered to bona fide students of accredited universities at the University of Hawai'i at Manoa, including courses in Hawaiian language and history and Pacific Island studies. For information, catalog, and enrollment, write Summer Session Office, Outreach College, University of Hawai'i, Sakamaki C-400, 2530 Dole St., Honolulu, HI 96822, 808/956-7221 or 800/862-6628, website: www.outreach.hawaii.edu.

Campus Center

Make this your first stop. As you mount the steps, notice the idealized mural of old Hawaii: smiling faces of contented natives all doing interesting things. Inside is the **Information Center,** which dispenses info not only about the campus, but also about what's happening socially and culturally around town. Stop here for a campus map and self-guided tour brochure, and, if you're into it, pick up brochures on public artwork and significant plants on campus. The food in the cafeteria is institutional but cheap, and has a Hawaiian twist. The best place to eat is either the Manoa Gardens in the Hemenway Center next door to the Campus Center or at the Paradise Palms Cafe next to Hamilton Library.

The **University Bookstore** on the lower level is excellent, open Mon.–Fri. 8:15 A.M.–4:45 P.M., Saturday 8:15–11:45 A.M. The bookstore is worth coming to for its excellent range of specialty items, like language tapes and a whole range of Hawaiiana. The **University Art Gallery,** 808/956-6888, website: www.hawaii.edu/artgallery, is on the third floor—worth a look. Free! The exhibits change regularly but the gallery is only open during regular school sessions (August–May) Mon.–Fri. 10 A.M.–4 P.M. and Sunday noon–4 P.M. Call for what's on exhibition. Next to the gallery is a lounge filled with overstuffed chairs and big pillows, where you can kick back and even take a quick snooze. This is not a very social campus. By 4:30 or 5 P.M. the place is shut up and no one is around. Don't expect students gathered in a common reading room, or the activity of social and cultural events. When school lets out at the end of the day, people simply go home.

East-West Center

Follow Dole Avenue to East-West Road and make a left. Free tours, Wednesdays only at 1:30 P.M., originate from Imin Center-Jefferson Hall opposite Kennedy Theater. For more info contact the Friends of the East-West Center, 808/944-7691. The center's 21 acres were dedicated in 1960 by the U.S. Congress to promote better relations between the countries of Asia and the Pacific with the United States. Many nations, as well as private companies and individuals, fund this institution of cooperative study and research. The center's staff, with help from University of Hawai'i students and scholars and professionals from throughout the region, focus on four broad but interconnected issues: regional security, social and cultural changes, the changing domestic political scene in nations of the region, and regional economic growth and its resultant consequences. John Burns Hall's main lobby dispenses information on what's happening, along with self-guiding maps. Imin Center–Jefferson Hall, fronted by Chinese lions, has a serene and relaxing Japanese garden behind, complete with a little rivulet and a teahouse named Jakuan, "Cottage of Tranquillity." The murals inside are excellent, and it also contains a large reading room with relaxing couches. While here, check out the bookstore, which carries an impressive selection of Hawaiiana and books on Asia, or have a peek at the East-West Center Gallery, 808/944-7111.

The impressive 23-ton, solid teak Thai Pavilion was a gift from the king of Thailand, where it was built and sent to Hawaii to be reconstructed. These salas are common sights in Thailand. The Center for Korean Studies (not part of the East-West Center) is also outstanding. A joint venture of Korean and Hawaiian architects, its inspiration was taken from the classic lines of Kyongbok Palace in Seoul. Most of the buildings are adorned with fine artworks: tapa hangings, murals, calligraphy, paintings, and sculpture. The entire center is tranquil, and along with the John F. Kennedy Theater of Performing Arts

just across the road, is indeed fulfilling its dedication as a place of sharing and learning, culture and art.

MANOA VALLEY

Manoa Valley, a tropical palette of green ablaze with daubs of iridescent color, has a unique designation most aptly described as "urban rainforest." Although not technically true, the valley, receiving more than 100 inches of rainfall per year, is exceptionally verdant even by Hawaiian standards. However, it wasn't always so. In the late 1800s, the overpopulated valley was almost denuded of trees, only to be reforested by Dr. Lyon, the founder of Lyon Arboretum, who planted trees gathered from around the world. A literal backwater, the runoff from Manoa would flood the relatively dry Waikiki until the Ala Wai Canal was built in the 1920s as a catchment for its torrential flash floods. Only a short drive from arid Waikiki, Manoa was the first place in Hawaii where coffee was grown and where pineapple was cultivated. The great Queen Ka'ahumanu, who died here in 1832, favored the cool hills of the valley as a vacation spot to escape the summer heat. Manoa, favored by royalty ever since, has maintained itself as one of the most fashionable residential areas in Hawaii, even boasting its own country club at the turn of the 20th century, which is yet memorialized by the Manoa Cup held yearly at the O'ahu Country Club. In 1893, just before annexation, a bewildered and beaten group of royalists came to Manoa to hide out. They were subsequently captured by a contingency of pursuing U.S. Marines and imprisoned in an area called The Pen, on the grounds of the now defunct Paradise Park.

Taking Manoa Road you pass **Punahou School,** one of the oldest and most prestigious high schools in Hawaii. Built in 1841 from lava rock, children of the missionary families of wealthy San Franciscans attended, getting the best possible education west of the Rockies. Manoa Road eventually crosses O'ahu Avenue—an extension of University Avenue. Follow it to **Wai'oli Tea Room,** 3016 O'ahu Ave., owned and operated by the Salvation Army. Set within a small parklike property, the restaurant features fresh-baked pastries and serves break-

THE LEGENDS OF MANOA VALLEY

Kahala-o-puna, known for her exceptional beauty, was betrothed to Kauhi, a young chief who was driven mad by unfounded jealousy. He falsely accused his lovely wife of faithlessness and killed her five times, only to have her resurrected each time by her sympathetic guardian *amakua*. Finally, left for dead, Kahala-o-puna was found by a young prince who fell in love with her. Beseeching his animal spirits, he brought her to life one last time, and through them turned the jealous Kauhi into a shark. Kahala-o-puna, warned never to go into the ocean, disobeyed, and was seized in the massive jaws of Kauhi, who fatally crushed the life from her, never to be rekindled. The warm misty rains of Manoa are the tears of the mother of Kahala-o-puna, and the gentle winds are the soft sobs of her bereaved father, who together forever lament the loss of their beloved daughter.

Another legend sings of the spring, Wai-a-ke-akua, created spontaneously by the great gods Kane and Kaneloa, who came to visit this valley. While overindulging in 'awa they became intoxicated and decided that they would dawdle in the lovely valley. Lying down, the gods could hear water running underground, so Kane took his great staff and struck the earth, causing Wai-a-ke-akua to appear. Because of the spring's divine origin, it became known as "water of the gods," making it *kapu* to all but the highest *ali'i*. When Kamehameha conquered Oahu, only he could drink from the spring, which flows with cool sweet water to this day.

fast, lunch, and high tea. Also featured here is the **Little Grass Shack** supposedly lived in by Robert Louis Stevenson when he was a resident of Waikiki. Visit the chapel with its distinctive stained-glass windows. Wai'oli Tea Room is open daily 8 A.M.–4 P.M.

Paradise Park, 3737 Manoa Rd. (at the very end), closed in late 1993, is 13 acres of lush tropical plants founded by James Wong about 30 years ago. Magnificent blooms compete with the wild plumage of 50 species of exotic birds. However, the **Treetop Restaurant,** literally at treetop level and offering very good food and superlative views, is still operating. It serves lunch buffet only, and is a bargain at $9.95 weekdays and $12.95 on weekends.

The **Lyon Arboretum,** 3860 Manoa Rd., 808/988-0464, is situated on 194 acres at the upper end of Manoa Road. Open to the public, it's principally a research facility and academic institution of the University of Hawai'i, a quiet shaded retreat from the noise of the city. While well cared for and orderly, this is not a highly manicured garden, just a natural beauty and profusion of greens. It not only has sections set aside for research and horticultural plants, but there is an herb garden, ethnobotanical garden, and hundreds of tropical plants that include ginger, *ti,* heliconia, hibiscus, palms, and bromiliads. You can visit on your own Mon.–Sat. 9 A.M.–3 P.M., but guided tours are also offered Tuesday

10–11:30 A.M. and on Saturday 1–2:30 P.M. Call ahead and reserve. Walking tour maps are available after you sign in and leave your $1 donation. The arboretum book and gift shop is a great place to pick up a memento or select one of numerous books on the flora of Hawaii and other Hawaiian subjects. Do not park in the arboretum parking lot if you're planning to walk up the Manoa Valley Trail to Manoa Falls. Park just off the roadway about one-quarter of a mile back down the road or a bit farther down in the residential neighborhood.

BISHOP MUSEUM

Otherwise known as the Museum of Natural and Cultural History, this group of stalwart stone buildings holds the greatest collection of historical relics and scholarly works on Hawaii and the Pacific in the world. It refers to itself as a "museum to instruct and delight," and in one afternoon walking through its halls you can educate yourself about Hawaii's history and people and enrich your trip to the islands tenfold.

Officially named Bernice Pauahi Bishop Museum, its founding was directly connected to the last three royal women of the Kamehameha dynasty. Princess Bernice married Charles Reed Bishop, a New Englander who became a citizen of the then-independent monarchy in the

1840s. The princess was a wealthy woman in her own right, with lands and an extensive collection of "things Hawaiian." Her cousin, Princess Ruth Keʻelikolani, died in 1883 and bequeathed Princess Bernice all of her lands and Hawaiian artifacts. Together, this meant that Princess Bernice owned about 12 percent of all Hawaii! Princess Bernice died less than two years later and left all of her landholdings to the **Bernice Pauahi Bishop Estate,** which founded and supported the Kamehameha School, dedicated to the education of Hawaiian children. (Though this organization is often confused with the Bishop Museum, they are totally separate. The school shared the same grounds with the museum, but none of the funds from this organization were, or are, used for the museum.) Bernice left her personal property, with all of its priceless Hawaiian artifacts, to her husband, Charles. Then, when Queen Emma, her other cousin, died the following year, she too desired Charles Bishop to combine her Hawaiian artifacts with the already formidable collection and establish a Hawaiian museum.

True to the wishes of these women, he began construction of the museum's main building on December 18, 1889, and within a few years the museum was opened. In 1894, after 50 years in Hawaii, Bishop moved to San Francisco, where he died in 1915. He is still regarded as one of Hawaii's most generous philanthropists. In 1961, a science wing and planetarium were added, and two dormitory buildings are still used from when the Kamehameha School for Boys occupied the same site.

To get there, take exit 20A off the H-1 freeway, which puts you on Route 63, the Likelike Highway. Immediately get into the far right lane. In only a few hundred yards, turn onto Ber-

Princess Bernice

HAWAII STATE ARCHIVES

nice Street, where you'll find the entrance to the museum. Or, exit H-1 onto Houghtailing Street, exit 20B. Keep your eyes peeled for a clearly marked but small sign directing you to the museum. TheBus no. 2 (School-Middle Street) runs from Waikiki to Kapalama Street, from which you walk two blocks.

Admission and Information

The museum is at 1525 Bernice St., Honolulu, HI 96817, 808/847-3511, website: www.bishop.hawaii.org, and is open seven days a week 9 A.M.–5 P.M., except Christmas Day. Admission is $14.95 adults, $11.95 for those ages 4–12 and for seniors; kids under four and museum members are free, but some exhibits and the planetarium are closed to children under six. *Kamaʻaina,* military, and other discounts are available but you must ask. It's sometimes best to visit on weekends because many weekdays bring teachers and young students who have more enthusiasm for running around than checking out the exhibits. Food, beverages, smoking, and flash photography are all strictly prohibited in the museum. The natural light in the museum is dim, so if you're into photography you'll need super-fast film (400 ASA performs only marginally). Before leaving the grounds make sure to visit **Hawaiian Halau,** where a hula is performed Mon.–Fri. at 11 A.M. and 2 P.M. The **planetarium** opens up its skies daily at 11:30 A.M., 1:30 P.M., and 3:30 P.M., and Fri.–Sat. evenings at 7 P.M. by reservation; call 808/848-4136. Both the library and archives are open to the public, the library Tues.–Fri. 1–4 P.M. and the archives Tues.–Fri. 10 A.M.–3 P.M., while both open Saturday 9 A.M.–noon. Special exhibits are shown in the Castle Memorial Building—Sue, the most complete *Tyrannosaurus rex* fossil, had her

Bishop Museum

Hawaiian debut here in 2000. For library reference services, call 808/848-4148, for the archives, 808/848-4182. The snack shop has reasonable prices, and **Shop Pacifica,** the museum bookstore and boutique, has a fine selection of materials on Hawaii and the Pacific, plus some authentic and inexpensive souvenirs. Although it has a limited menu, try the museum café, **Woody's Restaurant** for a snack.

Exhibits

It's easy to become overwhelmed at the museum, so just take it slowly. The number of exhibits is staggering: more than 180,000 artifacts; about 20 million(!) specimens of insects, shells, fish, birds, and mammals; an extensive research library; a photograph collection; and a fine series of maps. The main gallery is highlighted by the rich tones of koa, the showpiece being a magnificent staircase. Get a map at the front desk that lists all of the halls, along with descriptions, and a suggested route to follow. Guided tours are given Mon.–Fri. at 10 A.M. and noon. Throughout the week, the hall offers demonstrations in various Hawaiian crafts like lei-making, featherwork, and quilting 9 A.M.–2 P.M. The following is just a small potpourri of the highlights.

To the right of the main entranceway is a fascinating exhibit of the old Hawaiian gods. Most are just called "wooden image" and date from the early 19th century. Among them are: Kamehameha's war-god, Ku; the tallest Hawaiian sculpture ever found, from Kaua'i; an image of a god from a temple of human sacrifice; and lesser gods, personal *'aumakua* that controlled the lives of Hawaiians from birth until death. You wouldn't want to meet any of them in a dark alley! Outside, in what's called the **Hawaiian Courtyard,** are implements used by the Hawaiians in everyday life, as well as a collection of plants that are all identified. The first floor of the main hall is perhaps the most interesting because it deals with old Hawaii. Here are magnificent examples of *kahili,* feathered capes, plumed helmets . . . all the insignia and regalia of the *ali'i.* A commoner sits in a grass shack, a replica of what Captain Cook might have seen.

Don't look up! Over your head a 55-foot sperm whale hangs from the ceiling. It weighed more than 44,000 pounds alive. You'll learn about the ukulele, and how vaudevillians spread its music around the world. Hula-skirted damsels from the 1870s peer provocatively from old photos, barebreasted and with plenty of "cheesecake." Tourists bought these photos even then, although the grass skirts they're wearing were never a part of old Hawaii but were brought by Gilbert islanders. See authentic hula instruments like a "lover's whistle," a flute played through the nose, and a musical bow, the only stringed pre-European Hawaiian instrument.

Don't miss the koa wood collection. This accomplished artform produced medicine bowls, handsome calabashes, some simple home

O'AHU

bowls, and others reputed to be the earthly home of the wind goddess, which had to be refitted for display in Christianized 'Iolani Palace. A model *heiau* tells of the old religion and the many strange *kapu* that governed every aspect of life. Clubs used to bash in the brains of *kapu*-breakers sit next to benevolent little stone gods, the size and shape of footballs, that protected humble fishermen from the sea. As you ascend to the upper floors, the time period represented becomes increasingly closer to the present. The missionaries, whalers, merchants, laborers, and Westernized monarchs have arrived. Yankee whalers from New Bedford, New London, Nantucket, and Sag Harbor appear determined and grim-faced as they scour the seas, harpoons at the ready. Great blubber pots, harpoons, and figureheads are preserved from this perilous and unglamorous life. Bibles, thrones, and the regalia of power and of the new god are all here.

OTHER MUSEUMS AND GALLERIES

Honolulu Academy of Arts

Enjoy the magnificent grounds of this perfectly designed building, a combination of East and West with a Hawaiian roof and thick white stucco walls reminiscent of the American Southwest, created by architect Bertram Goodhue and benefactor Anna Rice Cooke expressly as a museum. The museum, at 900 S. Beretania St. opposite Thomas Square, 808/532-8701, website: www.honoluluacademy.org, is open Tues.–Sat. 10 A.M.–4:30 P.M., Sunday 1–5 P.M. Admission fees are $7 general and $4 for seniors, students, and military personnel. Members and children under 12 get in free, as does everyone on the first Wednesday of the month. Guided docent tours are conducted daily at 11 A.M., Sunday at 1:15 P.M. The academy houses a brilliant collection of classic and modern art, strongly emphasizing Asian artwork.

James Michener's outstanding collection of Japanese *ukiyo-e* is here. The story goes that an unfriendly New York cop hassled him on his way to donate it to a New York City museum, while a Honolulu officer was the epitome of *aloha* when Michener was passing through, so he decided that his collection should reside here. This collection is rotated frequently and displayed in a specially designed gallery to highlight and protect the prints. Magnificent Korean ceramics, Chinese furniture, and Japanese prints, along with Western masterworks from the Greeks to Picasso, make the academy one of the most well-rounded art museums in America. Some collections are permanent while others change, so the museum remains dynamic no matter how many times you visit. Discover delights like Paul Gauguin's *Two Nudes on a Tahitian Beach,* James Whistler's *Arrangement in Black No. 5,* John Singer Sargent's *Portrait of Mrs. Thomas Lincoln Hansen Jr.* An entire wing is dedicated to religious art, while another holds furniture from medieval Europe. The courtyards are resplendent with statuary from the 6th century A.D. and a standing figure from Egypt, circa 2500 B.C. The Hawaiian climate is perfect for preserving artwork.

In addition to the art exhibitions, educational programs, films, and concerts are supported by the museum and held in the Academy Theater, and the Robert Allerton Library is a fine reference library open to the public for research. Stop at the Academy Shop, specializing in art books, museum repros, Hawaii out-of-prints, jewelry, notebooks, and postcards. The Garden Cafe is open Tues.–Sat. 11:30 A.M.–2 P.M. It has a light but terrific menu, and besides, a trip to the academy demands a luncheon in the café.

The Waikiki Trolley and TheBus nos. 2 and 13 stop out front, but if you are driving, parking is in a lot to the rear of the Academy Art Center; $1 with validation, $2 per hour during the day, or $4 flat rate in the evening. A second lot to the side of the main building is open to the public only in the evening at the same rate.

Academy Art Center at Linekona

Catty-corner from the Academy of Arts, and affiliated with it, is the Academy Art Center. Built in 1908 as McKinley High School, and later used as Lincoln (Linekona) Elementary School, it is now on both the national and state registers of historic places. The building was renovated and reopened in 1990 as a place where art students can do and display their artwork, and where annual and special exhibitions are held. As the displays change periodically, what you'll get is potluck. It's a functioning art center, so it's a good place to see what kinds of artwork young, contemporary Hawaiian artists are doing. Works

O'AHU

are displayed in a large, wooden-floored room with a high vaulted ceiling, perhaps the old school gymnasium, where banks of windows provide plenty of natural light.

The Contemporary Museum

Under the direction of Georgiana Lagoria, at 2411 Makiki Heights Dr., 808/526-0232, website: www.tcmhi.org, the museum welcomes you with two copper-green gates that are sculptures themselves. This open and elegant structure, the former Spalding House, yields seven galleries, a gift shop, art library, and an excellent ritzy gourmet restaurant, the Contemporary Cafe. Acquired through the generosity of the *Honolulu Advertiser*'s stockholders, the building was donated to the museum as a permanent home in 1988. The focus is on exhibitions, not collections, although works by David Hockney are on permanent display, and there are others by such well-known artists as Andy Warhol and Jasper Johns. Always-changing exhibits reflect different themes in contemporary art—the art from 1940 onward. Open Tues.–Sat. 10 A.M.–4 P.M., Sunday noon–4 P.M., closed Monday and major holidays; admission $5 general, $3 students and seniors, except on the third Thursday of the month when admission is free. Parking is also free.

Surrounding the building are three magnificent acres sculpted into gardens perfect for strolling and gazing at the sprawl of Honolulu far below. Led by museum volunteers, a 45-minute tour of the gardens is offered by appointment only. Guided tours of the exhibitions are also given Tues.–Sat.; call 808/536-1322 for details at least a week in advance.

Aside from the main galleries, works are displayed at the museum galleries at the First Hawaiian Center, 999 Bishop St., which is open Mon.–Thurs. 8:30 A.M.–4 P.M. and Friday until 6 P.M. Admission is free.

Tennent Art Foundation Gallery

At 201-203 Prospect St., on the *ewa* slope of Punchbowl, the foundation is open Tues.–Sat. 10 A.M.–noon, Sunday 2–4 P.M., 808/531-1987. Free. There is a library and the walls hold the paintings of Madge Tennent, one of Hawaii's foremost artists, as well as many other contemporary works. It's beautiful, quiet, and worth a visit. Head up Ward Avenue until it meets Prospect Street. Turn left and proceed until Prospect Street veers off to the right. From there it's not far. Look for the salmon-colored wall and gate. The gallery now sits behind a condo.

GARDENS

Foster Botanical Garden

Many of these exotic trees have been growing in this 13.5-acre manicured garden for more than 100 years. In the mid-1800s it was the private estate of Dr. Hillebrand, physician to the royal court; he brought many of the seedlings from Asia. Now that the garden is on the National Register of Historic Places, two dozen of these trees enjoy lifetime protection by the state, while others are examples of rare and endangered species. A few of the huge and exceptional trees are kapok, bo, banyan, and Mindanao gum, several from the 1850s, while other sections of the garden show orchids, palms, poisonous plants, herbs, and "primitive" plants. At 180 N. Vineyard Blvd., 808/522-7065, the gardens are open daily 9 A.M.–4 P.M. except Christmas and New Year's Day. Admission is $5 for nonresidents, $3 for residents, $1 for children 6–12, and free for those younger. Guided tours are given Mon.–Fri. at 1 P.M.; call 808/522-7066 for reservations. Free self-guided brochures are available. Give yourself at least an hour for a leisurely stroll; bring insect repellent. Along with four others on the island, these gardens are administered by the Honolulu Botanical Gardens. Before leaving, stop in for a look at the Foster Garden Gallery and Bookstore for books, postcards, tapa cloth, T-shirts, and other such gift items. The closest stop on TheBus is no. 4 from Waikiki.

A stone's throw to the north over the freeway and set along the Nu'uanu Stream are the 7.5 acres of the **Lili'uokalani Botanical Garden.** Once the private garden of the last Hawaiian monarch, it's now part of the Honolulu Botanical Garden system. Unlike the imported magnificence of the Foster Botanical Garden, this garden features mostly native Hawaiian plants.

Moanalua Gardens

The private gardens of the Damon Estate, at 1352 Pineapple Pl., 808/833-1944, were given to the original owner by Princess Bernice Bishop in

O'AHU

1884. Just off the Moanalua Freeway, and open to the public, these gardens are not heavily touristed, a welcome respite from the hustle and bustle of the city. Some magnificent old trees include a Buddha tree from Ceylon and a monkeypod called "the most beautifully shaped tree" in the world by *Ripley's Believe It or Not*. You can walk on your own through the garden, weekdays 7 A.M.–6 P.M. and from 7:30 A.M. on weekends; no charge.

The nonprofit cultural and educational **Moanalua Garden Foundation,** not affiliated with the Damon Estate, presents the noncompetitive Prince Lot Hula Festival in the Moanalua Gardens yearly on the third Saturday of July. In addition, this foundation sponsors guided hikes into Kawananui Valley (the valley that the H-3 freeway runs through) four times a year on Sundays. These hikes introduce people to the historical and cultural artifacts and the botanical diversity of the valley. This three-mile, four-hour round-trip hike is $5 per person. For information and arrangements, call the foundation at 808/839-5334.

HONOLULU BEACHES AND PARKS

The beaches and parks listed here are found in and around Honolulu's city limits. World-famous Waikiki has its own section (see "Waikiki," below). The good thing about having Waikiki so close is that it lures most bathers away from other city beaches, which makes them less congested. The following list contains most of Honolulu's beaches, ending at Fort DeRussy Beach Park, just a few hundred yards from where the string of Waikiki's beaches begins.

Ke'ehi Lagoon Beach Park
At the eastern end of Honolulu International Airport, this park is at the inner curve of Ke'ehi Lagoon, just off Route 92 (the Nimitz Highway). The water at this park is somewhat polluted, but people do swim here and a canoe club makes use of it. Mostly, local people use the area for pole fishing and crabbing, picnicking, and ball games. There are restrooms, pavilions, picnic facilities, a pay phone, and lots of parking. Entrance to the Disabled American Veterans Memorial is through the park.

Sand Island State Recreation Area
You enter this park by way of the Sand Island Access Road, clearly marked off the Nimitz Highway. On the way, you pass through some ugly real estate—scrapyards, petrochemical tanks, warehouses, and other such beauties. It's not bad once you get past this commercial/industrial strip. Don't get discouraged, keep going! Once you cross the metal mesh bridge and pass the entrance to the U.S. Coast Guard base, you enter the actual park, 14 acres landscaped with picnic and playground facilities. Follow the road into the park. From here, you get a view of downtown Honolulu, with Diamond Head making a remarkable counterpoint. The park is excellently maintained, with pavilions, cold-water showers, walkways, and restrooms; the park closes at 7:45 P.M. However, the camping area is usually empty (state permit required). The sites are out in the open, but a few trees provide some shade. Unfortunately, you're under one of the main glide paths for Honolulu International Airport. Many local people come to fish, and the surfing is good, but the beaches for snorkeling and swimming are fair at best. The currents and wave action aren't dangerous, but remember that this part of the harbor receives more than its share of pollutants. For delicious and inexpensive lunches, make sure to stop at Penny's Drive-In, next door to Dancers strip joint, on your way down the access road.

La Mariana Yacht Sailing Club
This small marina at 50 Sand Island Access Rd. is a love song in the middle of an industrialized area. The marina is Annette La Mariana Nahinua's labor of love that has remained true since 1955. You can read her fantastic story on the menu of the marina's Hideaway Restaurant, the only real restaurant on Sand Island. In 1955 this area was forgotten, forsaken, and unkempt. Ms. Nahinua, against the forces of nature and the even more unpredictable and devastating forces of bureaucracy, took this land and turned it into a yacht harbor. The main tools were indefatigable determination, God listening to her prayers, and a shovel and rake. It's one of the last enclaves of old Hawaii, a place to come for dinner, a drink, or just to look at the boats. The nighttime bartender is friendly but stoic after decades of seeing and hearing it all. Annette,

the founder, is now a little gray-haired woman, a motherly type in Birkenstocks, who lives right here above the Hideaway. In the daytime she wanders around spreading her magic while talking to old salts or new arrivals.

The marina is adjacent to an open waterway, which means that you don't have to pay for anchorage. It comes under the old "rights of sailors" to find a free port in which to berth. This unique setup has created an atmosphere in which a subculture of people have built subsistence shacks on the little islands that dot the bay. Some also live on old scows, shipshape yachts, or on very imaginative homemade crafts, afloat and semi-afloat on this tranquil bay. Many are disillusioned and disenfranchised Vietnam vets who have become misanthropes. You'll see the Stars and Stripes flying from their island hooches. Others are yachties who disdain being landlubbers, while others are poor souls who have fallen through the social net. La Mariana is a unique statement of personal freedom in a city where unique statements are generally not tolerated.

Kaka'ako (Point Panic) Waterfront Park
This small state facility was carved out of a piece of land donated by the University of Hawai'i's Biomedical Research Center, and at one time was used as a dump. Next to Kewalo Basin Harbor, follow Cooke or Ohe Street off Ala Moana Boulevard to the park. From the huge parking lot, walking paths lead over the rise (which blocks out the noise of the city) to a grand promenade and picnic tables set under stout trellises. This area is poor for swimming (known for sharks), but it's great for fishing and surfing. If you're lucky, you may even spot a manta ray, which are known to frequent these waters. Unfortunately, novices will quickly find out why it's called Point Panic. As at the Kewalo Basin Park across the opening to the adjacent harbor, a long seawall with a sharp dropoff runs the entire length of the area. The wave action is perfect for riding, but all wash against the wall. Beginners stay out! The best reason to come here is for the magnificent and unobstructed view of the Ala Moana Beach, the Waikiki skyline, and Diamond Head beyond. While rather underused at present, there are plans to add more facilities in the future and

hold musical concerts and cultural events here. To the side of the park is the Children's Discovery Center.

Kewalo Basin Park
Kewalo Basin Marina, developed in the '20s to hold Honolulu's tuna fleet, is home to many charter boats for water activities, including fishing, parasailing, sunset tours, and underwater excursions. Pay parking is to the side. On the ocean side of the marina, stretching along the breakwater, is this state park (free parking) with its promenade and covered picnic tables. Surfers congregate here for the good waves that develop due to the offshore reef, which continues all the way along the front of Ala Moana Beach Park. If you're here in the very early morning hours, check out the Honolulu Fish Auction at Kewalo Basin. Your dinner might be coming off one of these boats.

Ala Moana Beach Park
Ala Moana (Path to the Sea) Beach County Park is by far Honolulu's best. Most visitors congregate just around the bend at Waikiki, but residents head for Ala Moana, the place to soak up the local color. During the week, this beautifully curving white-sand beach has plenty of elbow room. Weekends bring families that come for every water sport O'ahu offers. The swimming is great, with manageable wave action, plenty of lifeguards, and even good snorkeling along the reef. Board riders have their favorite spots, and bodysurfing is excellent. The huge area has a number of restrooms, food concessions, tennis courts, softball fields, a bowling green, and parking for 500 cars. Many O'ahu outrigger canoe clubs practice in this area, especially in the evening; it's great to come and watch them glide along. A huge banyan grove provides shade and strolling if you don't fancy the beach, or you can bring a kite to fly aloft with the trade winds. Ala Moana Park stretches along Ala Moana Boulevard between the Ala Wai and Kewalo Basin boat harbors. It's across from the Ala Moana Shopping Center on the east end and Ward Centre on the west end, so you can rush right over if your credit cards start melting from the sun.

'Aina Moana (Land from the Sea) Recreation Area used to be called Magic Island because it was reclaimed land. It is actually the point of land stretching out from the eastern edge of Ala Moana Beach Park, contiguous with it. All the beach activities are great here, too.

HONOLULU HIKING

Judd Trail
This is an excellent trail to take to experience Oahu's "jungle" while visiting the historic and picturesque Nu'uanu Pali nearby. From the Pali Highway, Route 61, turn right onto the Old Pali Highway, then right again onto Nu'uanu Pali Drive. Follow it for just under a mile to Reservoir No. 2 spillway. The trail begins on the ocean side of the spillway and leads through fragrant eucalyptus and a dense stand of picture-perfect Norfolk pines. It continues through the forest reserve and makes a loop back to the starting point. En route you pass Jackass Ginger Pool. In the immediate area are "mud slides," where you can take a ride on a makeshift toboggan of *pili* grass, *ti* leaves, or a piece of plastic, if you've brought one. This activity is rough on your clothes, and even rougher on your body. The wet conditions after a rain are perfect. Afterward, a dip in Jackass Pool cleans the mud and refreshes at the same time. Continue down the trail to observe wild ginger, guava, and *kukui,* but don't take any confusing side trails. If you get lost head back to the stream and follow it until it intersects the main trail.

Tantalus and Makiki Valley Trails
Great sightseeing and hiking can be combined when you climb the road atop Tantalus. Trails in this area offer magnificent views, and, in fact, it has the greatest concentration of easy-access hiking trails on the island. To get there, head past Punchbowl along Puowaina Drive; just keep going until it turns into Tantalus Drive. The road switchbacks past some incredible homes and views until it reaches the 2,000-foot level, where it changes its name to Round Top Drive, then heads down the other side. To approach from the other side, take Ke'eaumoku Street across H-1.

Turn right on Nehoa, then left in one block to Makiki Street. Follow this a short distance to Round Top Drive and you're on your way. Trailhead signs are along the road.

One place to start is at the half-mile-long **Moleka Trail,** which offers some excellent views and an opportunity to experience the trails in this area without an all-day commitment. The trails are excellently maintained by the State Division of Forestry and Wildlife. Your greatest hazard here is mud, but in a moment you're in a handsome stand of bamboo, and in 10 minutes the foliage parts onto a lovely panorama of Makiki Valley and Honolulu in the background. These views are captivating, but remember to have "small eyes"—check out the variety of colored mosses and fungi, and don't forget the flowers and fruit growing around you. A branch trail to the left leads to Round Top Drive, and if you continue the trail splits into three: the right one is the **Makiki Valley Trail,** which cuts across the valley for about one mile, ending up at Tantalus Drive; **'Ualaka'a Trail** branches left and goes for another half mile, connecting the Makiki Valley Trail with Pu'u 'Ualaka'a State Park; straight ahead is the **Maunalaha Trail,** which descends for just over one-half mile to the bottom of the valley at the Hawaii Nature Center and Forestry Baseyard.

On the mountainside of the road across from the Moleka Trailhead, the **Manoa Cliff Trail** heads inland and swings in a 3.5-mile arch back around to meet Tantalus Drive. Intersecting this trail at approximately the halfway point is the **Pu'u 'Ohi'a Trail,** which leads to the highest point on Tantalus and the expected magnificent view. It continues inland via the **Pauoa Flats Trail,** which ends at a lookout over Nu'uanu Valley and its reservoir. Partway along this trail, the **Nu'uanu Trail** heads west down to connect with the Judd Trail. A short way farther, the **'Aihualama Trail** heads to the east to Manoa Falls and eventually down the Manoa Valley via the **Manoa Valley Trail** to the end of Manoa Valley Road, exiting near Lyon Arboretum.

ACCOMMODATIONS

The vast majority of O'ahu's hotels are strung along the boulevards of Waikiki. Most are neatly clustered, bound by the Ala Wai Canal, and run eastward to Diamond Head. These hotels will be discussed in the Waikiki section. The remainder of greater Honolulu has few accommodations, but those that do exist are some of O'ahu's cheapest. Most are clean, no-frills establishments, a handful just beyond the edge of Waikiki, one or two downtown, some near the university, with a few others at the airport.

DOWNTOWN AND TOWARD WAIKIKI

Under $50

O'ahu has a number of YM/WCAs from which to choose, and two of three official youth hostels in the state. The Ys vary as far as private rooms and baths are concerned, facilities offered, and prices.

The **YMCA Central Branch,** 401 Atkinson Dr., Honolulu, HI 96814, 808/941-3344, fax 808/941-8821, website: www.centralymca-honolulu.org, is the most centrally located and closest to Waikiki. Call ahead and make reservations. There is no curfew, no visitors allowed in the rooms, no loud noise permitted after 10 P.M., no smoking or drinking, no cooking in rooms, and a $10 key deposit, but the Y does have an outside swimming pool, sauna, weight room, gym, and racquetball court that are open to all guests. There are single and double rooms, shared and private baths. Rates for rooms with shared baths (men only) are $29 a night single or $40 double; weekly and monthly rates available. For rooms with a private bath (open to men and women), rates are $36.50 a day single and $51.50 double; rates go down after eight consecutive days. This Y is just up from the eastern end of Ala Moana Park across from the tall Ala Moana Hotel, only a 10-minute walk to Waikiki.

YMCA Nu'uanu (men only), 1441 Pali Hwy., Honolulu, HI 96813, 808/536-3556, at the intersection of S. Vineyard Blvd., is a few minutes' walk from downtown Honolulu. You'll find a mod-

ern, sterile facility with a pool and private rooms with a communal bathroom; $30 a night, $160 a week, with a $5 key deposit.

YWCA Fernhurst (women only), 1566 Wilder Ave., Honolulu, HI 96822, 808/941-2231, fax 808/949-0266, just off Manoa Rd., across from the historical Punahou School, offers single and double rooms with shared baths. Daily rates are $30 single or $25 shared, with long-term rates available. Breakfast and dinner are included weekdays. Security is 24 hours. Women from around the world add an international flavor. Reserve by phone, fax, or email: fernhurst@ywcaoahu.org.

The **Town Inn,** 250 N. Beretania St., Honolulu, HI 96817, 808/536-2377, is on the edge of Chinatown, and it's an old standby as an inexpensive but clean hotel. It's away from all the Waikiki action, and the spartan, linoleumed rooms rent for $38 or $42–49 for the air-conditioned ones. Plenty of travelers pass through here—there are long-term guests as well—and the hotel's restaurant serves authentic Japanese food at moderate prices. There are no TVs at the Town Inn, there's a charge for all phone calls, a key deposit is required, and there is no cooking in the rooms.

$100–150

The **Pagoda Hotel,** 1525 Rycroft St., Honolulu, HI 96814, 808/941-6611 or 800/367-6060, website: www.pagodahotel.com, email: reservations@hthcorp.com, is behind Ala Moana Park between Kapi'olani Blvd. and S. King Street. Because this hotel is away from the "action," you get very good value for your money. Rooms are in one low-rise and one high-rise tower. All rooms in the Terrace Tower come with kitchenettes and run $110–155 for studio, one-, and two-bedroom suites. The Hotel Tower has mostly standard rooms at $110, but a few deluxe rooms cost $120 and a couple of suites go for $195. Substantial discounts are given to residents. All rooms have TV, a/c, in-room safe, and small refrigerator. There's free parking, laundry facilities, a sundries shop, two swimming pools, as well as access to the well-known Pagoda Restaurant, a favorite of locals for its Asian ambience, koi pond, and manicured garden. The Pagoda Hotel is locally owned and operated.

$150–200

The only hotel right in downtown Honolulu is the **Aston at the Executive Center,** 1088 Bishop St., Honolulu, HI 96813, 808/539-3000 or 800/922-7866, fax 808/523-1088, website: www.astonhotels.com. This triangular glass and steel building is a perfect place for businesspeople and is as convenient for other visitors. Rooms look out over city streets and provide fine views of the night city lights. Each air-conditioned room is fitted with an entertainment center, telephones, data ports, and in-room safe. A continental breakfast and local newspaper are available for all guests, and an on-site restaurant, daily maid service, 24-hour business center, coin laundry, swimming pool, fitness center, and sauna are all amenities. Business suites with a refrigerator run $160–190, while the one-bedroom suites with kitchen are $220–250. If you need to be in the city for business or other reasons, the Aston at the Executive Center is a perfect location.

The 36-story, 1,200-room **Ala Moana Hotel,** 410 Atkinson Dr., Honolulu, HI 96814, 808/955-4811, 800/367-6025, fax 800/944-6839, website: www.alamoanahotel.com, is just off the Waikiki strip. It's between Ala Moana and Kapi'olani Boulevards, with a walking ramp connecting it directly with the Ala Moana Shopping Center. Rooms start at $125 for the Kona Tower, run $155–215 for the Waikiki Tower, and are $250–2,300 for a suite; corporate and government rates are available. Each room has a/c, TV, a mini-fridge, direct-dial telephones, data ports, and all the comforts that you would expect from a quality hotel. The hotel contains a third-level swimming pool, sundries shop, laundry facilities, the Rumours nightclub, a cocktail lounge, Japanese and Chinese restaurants, meeting and banquet space, and **Aaron's** restaurant on the top floor for elegant dining.

NEAR THE UNIVERSITY

Under $50
YMCA Atherton Branch, 1810 University Ave., Honolulu, HI 96822, 808/946-0253, fax 808/941-7802, website: www2.hawaii.edu/~ymca, email: ymca001@hawaii.rr.com, is across the street from the main entrance of the University of Hawai'i. Men and women students are given long-term residence here during the school year and also during summer sessions. Rooms are private singles and shared doubles, generally available for rent to nonstudents only during the summertime, and only then if there is room available. The room rate for short stays is $30 a night, but this must be accompanied by a one-time membership fee of $5. Inquire about room availability before you arrive. While a good option for students, it is not the best for those just visiting.

The **Honolulu International Hostel,** 2323-A Seaview Ave., Honolulu, HI 96822, 808/946-0591, fax 808/946-5904, is also near the university. It's an official Hostelling International hostel, so members with identity cards are given priority, but nonmembers are accepted on a space-available day-by-day basis. This hostel has 43 beds and two private rooms. A bed in a dormitory runs $12.50 a night for members and $15.50 for nonmembers. The office is open 8 A.M.–noon and again 4 P.M.–midnight. It has travel and sightseeing information, and hosts some weekly events. This YH is always busy, but it takes reservations by phone with a credit card. For information and non–credit card reservations write to the manager and include an SASE. There is no curfew and the expectation is that everyone keeps appropriate quiet hours. A full kitchen is open for use and there is a grill on the back patio for daytime barbecuing. A washer and dryer are available for guest use and there's limited off-street parking. Kick back in the communal room for TV, free movies, or to meet other travelers. For information about Hostelling International–American Youth Hostels and membership cards write HI-AYH National Office, P.O. Box 37613, Washington, DC 20013-7613.

NEAR THE AIRPORT

Under $50
At 3085 N. Nimitz Hwy. is **The Shower Tree,** 808/833-1411. A converted warehouse-type building, this place is a bit like a hostel, with double-bed rooms for $27.25–32.70 and bunks from $18. If all you need is a shower and a rest during a layover, it's $7.50. The bathroom and TV

lounge are down the hall. Only five minutes from the airport, the Shower Tree provides transportation to and from and luggage storage.

On the second level of the airport building, near the central courtyard, is the **Airport Mini-Hotel,** 808/836-3044. With 19 private, single-bed rooms, an eight-hour sleep and a shower runs $35, four hours is $32, three hours runs $26, and two hours goes for $20. For just a shower, including soap, towel, shampoo, deodorant, and hair dryer, it's $8.50. Reserve.

$100–150
One of the closest hotels to the airport is Best Western's **The Plaza Hotel,** 3253 N. Nimitz Hwy., 808/836-3636 or 800/800-4683, fax 808/834-7406, website: www.bestwestern-honolulu.com. This 12-story tower has 274 small but a/c rooms, each with king or queen bed, a full bath, entertainment center, and a small refrigerator. Amenities include a restaurant, coin laundry, sundries shop, small swimming pool, and courtesy van service to and from the airport. Rates run $110 for a standard, $122 for a superior, and $132 for a deluxe room, with discounts for AAA members, seniors, government employees, and military personnel. While not in the center of the city nor out along the sands of Waikiki, it is convenient for air travel, close to the military facilities that surround Pearl Harbor, and near the USS *Arizona,* USS *Missouri,* and USS *Bowfin* attractions.

With nearly the same amenities as the Best Western, the **Honolulu Airport Hotel,** 3401 N. Nimitz Hwy., 808/836-0661 or 800/800-3477 Mainland or Canada, fax 808/833-1738, website: www.honoluluairporthotel.com, is even a bit closer to the airport terminal. Here you have just over 300 rooms on four floors, your choice of a standard room at $112, superior at $125, a room on the executive floor at $136, or a suite for $295. Seniors and AAA members get 25 percent off, while other discounts are offered for airline, military, and government personnel. There is free hotel parking and complimentary shuttle service to and from the airport.

BED-AND-BREAKFASTS

The **Manoa Valley Inn,** 2001 Vancouver Dr., Honolulu, HI 96822, 808/947-6019 or 800/634-5115, fax 808/946-6168, website: www.aloha .net/~wery, email: manoain@aloha.net, offers a magnificent opportunity to lodge in early-20th-century elegance. Formerly the John Guild Inn, this "country inn" is listed on the national and state registers of historic places. Built in 1915 by Milton Moore, an Iowa lumberman, the original structure was a very modest, two-story, box-like home. It was situated on seven acres, but the demand for land by growing Honolulu has whittled it down to the present half acre or so. Moore sold the house to John Guild in 1919. A secretary

Manoa Valley Inn

O‘AHU

to Alexander and Baldwin, Guild added the third floor and back porch, basically creating the structure that you see today. The home went through several owners and even did a stint as a fraternity house. It ended up as low-priced apartment units until it was rescued and renovated in 1982 by Rick Ralston, the owner of Crazy Shirts and one of Hawaii's successful self-made men, a patron of arts and antiques. He outfitted the house from his warehouse of antiques with furnishings not original to the house but true to the period. Since then it has been sold several times and undergone additional refurbishing and landscaping.

Rooms with double beds and a shared bath run a reasonable $99–120, while the larger rooms with private baths and queen- or king-size beds are $140. One suite with a king bed goes for $190, and the detached cottage with its double bed runs $150. A continental breakfast and local phone calls are all included in the room charge. The exemplary continental breakfasts are prepared on the premises. In the morning, the aroma of fresh-brewed coffee wafts up the stairs. The daily and Sunday newspapers are available. Pick one and sink into the billowy cushions of a wicker chair on the lava-rock-colonnaded back porch. Free off-street parking is provided. Check-in is at 3 P.M., checkout at 11 A.M.

Run by Jubal Jones, **Adam and Eve B&B,** 4405 Kilauea Ave., Honolulu, HI 96816, 808/732-2979, website: www.adamandeveplanet.com, offers rooms and breakfast in this Kahala home. The smallest room, with a definite Japanese feel, is the Pikake Room, which runs $50 a night. The Ginger and Mango suites are $100–150 a night. The Ginger Suite is best for families as it has a king bed and two twin beds. All rooms have private baths, and weekly rates are available. In addition, the Ohana Cottage runs $150 a night.

FOOD

The restaurants mentioned below are outside of the Waikiki area, although many are close, even within walking distance. Others are near Ala Moana, Chinatown, downtown, Kaimuki, and the less touristed areas of greater Honolulu. Some are first-class restaurants; others, among the best, are just roadside stands where you can get a satisfying plate lunch. The restaurants are listed according to price range and location, with differing cuisines mixed in each range. Besides the sun and surf, it's the amazing array of food found on O'ahu that makes the island extraordinary.

SHOPPING CENTER DINING

Ala Moana Shopping Center
The following are all at the Ala Moana Shopping Center along Ala Moana Boulevard. Most are in the **Makai Food Court,** a huge central area where you can inexpensively dine on dishes from San Francisco to Tokyo—most for under $10. Counter-style restaurants serve island favorites, reflecting the multiethnic culinary traditions from around the Pacific. You take your dish to a nearby communal dining area, which is great for people-watching.

Patti's Chinese Kitchen, first floor facing the sea, has all the ambience you'd expect from a cafeteria-style Chinese fast-food joint, plus lines about a block long. But don't let either discourage you. The lines move incredibly quickly, and you won't get gourmet food, but it's tasty, plentiful, and cheap. The Princess-Queen Special is steamed rice, fried rice or noodles, plus chow mein, plus two entrées like sweet and sour pork or a chicken dish—for around $4. The Queen is the same, but add an entrée, and you can even have four entrées, which fills two large paper plates. The princesses who eat this much food aren't tiny-waisted damsels waiting for a rescuing prince—they can flatten anyone who hassles them on their own.

Plate lunches, noodle soups, pizza, and munchies can be ordered from the **Ala Moana Poi Bowl.** The **Island Burger** has, well, burgers, while **Lahaina Chicken** does chicken in a variety of ways. For noodles, stop at **Naniwa-ya Ramen** or **Tsuruya Noodle Shop,** or if you want the Italian variety, try **Mama'a Spaghetti.** Head for **Yummy Korean BBQ** for hot and spicy Korean plates.

On the top level near the Sears end, the

China House, 808/949-6622, is open daily for lunch and dinner. This enormous dining hall offers the usual selection of Chinese dishes but is famous for its dim sum (served 11 A.M.–2 P.M.); you pick and choose bite-sized morsels from carts. For more class and a finer environment, head for **Assaggio,** 808/942-3446, on the ground level next to Liberty House. This award-winning Italian restaurant serves tasty dishes that your mama would be proud to put on the table. You might not expect to find a fine restaurant in a department store, but Alan Wong has opened the Pineapple Room restaurant and Patisserie Bar on the third floor of the Liberty House department store. These two establishments plus his Regional Cuisine Marketplace on the fourth floor are swiftly establishing a great reputation.

Ward Warehouse

This shopping center, at 1050 Ala Moana Blvd., has a range of restaurants, from practical to semi-chic, all reasonably priced. **Benkei,** 808/591-8713, is a Japanese restaurant beautifully appointed with a rock garden at the entranceway that continues to the inside. It's bright and airy, neo-Japanese traditional. Prices are reasonable, with set menu dishes like *unagi kabayaki,* miso-fried fish, and plate lunches, as well as a wide selection of *don buri,* yakitori, and tempura. Open Mon.–Sat. 11 A.M.–2 P.M. for lunch, for dinner from 5 P.M. Nearby you'll find **Korean Barbecue Express** and **L&L Drive-In** for a quick bite to eat.

The Old Spaghetti Factory, 808/591-2513, is a huge place that feels a bit like you might imagine a San Francisco eatery at the turn of the 20th century—almost Victorian. It serves a wide variety of pasta not quite like Mama makes, but passable, and at a reasonable price. Try chicken parmigiana, spinach and cheese ravioli, or meatballs, Italian sausage, and spaghetti with meat sauce, all for under $9. Following your meal, linger over an Italian soda, coffee, tea, draft beer, or house wine. Open Mon.–Fri. for lunch 11:30 A.M.–2 P.M., daily for dinner 5–9 P.M., and Saturday right through.

More modern, upscale, and expensive is **Kincaid's Fish Chop & Steak House,** 808/591-2005, on the second floor with views out over Kewalo Basin Marina. Kincaid's dinner menu includes sirloin steak for $18, pasta and roast chicken Dijon for $13, and grilled mixed seafood at $20. The lunch menu includes many sandwiches in the under-$10 range, Korean *kalbi* ribs, Sonora pork chops with garlic plum sauce, and grilled northern Pacific salmon. Soups and salads are à la carte, and a few desserts round out the list.

For those into health foods, **Aloha Health Food,** primarily a vitamin and mineral store, has some prepared food and drinks in a cooler. Right across is **Coffee Works,** specializing in gourmet coffee and tea. It has a bakery with sandwiches and croissants. So take your vitamins on one side and get jazzed on the other. For fresh fruit juices and smoothies try the **Juice Stop.**

The **Chowder House,** 808/596-7944, on the ground floor has fresh-grilled *'ahi,* snow crab salad, Manhattan clam chowder, bay shrimp cocktail, deep-fried shrimp, daily specials, and an all-you-can-eat crab night on Thursday.

Ward Centre

This upscale shopping center is directly across the street from Ala Moana Park and next door to the Ward Warehouse. The following are some of its restaurants and eateries, where you can enjoy not only class, but quality as well.

Chocoholics would rather visit the **Honolulu Chocolate Company** than go to heaven. Mousse truffles, Grand Marnier truffles, chocolate eggs with pistachio or English walnut all will send you into eye-rolling rapture. If you enter, forget any resolve about watching your weight. You're a goner!

For a quick lunch try **Mocha Java Cafe,** a yuppie, upscale, counter-service-type place with a few tables. It has a selection of sandwiches with an emphasis on vegetarian. If you want a designer lunch, that's the place to go.

The best-known restaurant in the complex is **Keo's Thai Cuisine,** 808/596-0020, known for its mouthwatering Thai dishes and for its beautiful decor. The menu is extensive, with plenty of dishes for non-meat-eaters. Prices can be quite reasonable for Thai noodles, chicken, shrimp, or vegetarian, around $8; house salad, green papaya salad, and spring rolls for about $6; and tofu, shrimp, or chicken satay for under $10. Try the delicious soups like spicy lemongrass or Thai ginger. Entrées like the

Evil Jungle Prince have quite a spicy reputation, or tame down with Asian watercress stir-fried with garlic, yellow bean sauce, and beef, shrimp, or veggies. Spices can be tuned up or down to suit the customer, and vegetarians are also catered to. Keo's has another location at the Ambassador Hotel in Waikiki, and operates the **Mekong I and II,** simpler and less expensive restaurants, at 1295 S. Beretania and 1726 S. King St., respectively. Keo's is known for its beautiful flower displays of torch ginger, orchids, or plumeria on every table, and you may eat inside or outside.

The **Yum Yum Tree,** 808/592-3580, is an affordable American standard family restaurant that features pies and cakes from its bakery, along with homestyle fresh pasta. It has an extensive dining area, quite cheerful with dark wood floors, ferns, hanging greenery, and an open-beam ceiling. Breakfast, lunch, and dinner 7 A.M.–midnight; cocktails until closing.

Overlooking Ala Moana Park, **Compadres Mexican Bar and Grill,** 808/591-8307, open Mon.–Fri. 11 A.M.–1 A.M., Sat.–Sun. noon–1 A.M., serves from a smaller, late menu 10 P.M.–1 A.M. Although part of a small chain with restaurants in Maui, Palo Alto, and Napa Valley, Compadres offers made-to-order health-conscious Mexican cuisine that was voted the Best on O'ahu by the small but discerning local Mexican population. The decor is a mixture of South Seas and south of the border. The menu is huge and no lard is used in any of the dishes except carnitas, which are pork anyway. Try the big, double-handed burritos or the Quesadillas Internacionales, which join flavors from many countries. Besides these, the menu comprises standard burritos, tacos, and plenty of vegetarian selections, and no dish is more than $18. The bar complements the meal with a full selection of domestic and imported beer, a selection of microbrewery beers, 10 different kinds of tequila, margaritas by the glass or pitcher, and island exotic drinks. Compadres is an excellent choice for a "budget gourmet" meal in a hospitable atmosphere where the prices are right and the service excellent. There's even live music offered now and again. You can't go wrong!

Ryan's Grill, 808/591-9132, open 11:15 A.M.–2 A.M., is an ultramodern yet comfortable establishment appointed with black leather chairs, chrome railings, marble-topped tables, and a hardwood floor, which are all dominated by a huge bar and open kitchen. The menu offers standards along with nouveau cuisine and includes onion soup, sesame chicken salad, and tossed fettuccine with sliced breast of chicken and Cajun sauce. Sandwiches are everything from hot Dungeness crab to a grilled chicken club, all for about $10. More substantial meals from the grill include Cajun seafood jambalaya and pasta dishes. The bar prepares all of the usual exotic drinks and has plenty of draft beer selections from which to choose. Most menu items, along with plenty of munchies and *pu pu,* are served until 1 A.M., so Ryan's Grill makes a perfect late night stop.

Offering pizza, pasta, and (as they say) pizzazz, **Scoozees a Go Go Bakery and Deli,** 808/597-1777, is a modern and tasteful restaurant and deli. Imported pastas, prosciutto, cheese, stromboli, and fresh baked goods are available from the counter. Menu items include Italian sausage and pepper sandwich, marinated chicken breast grilled with orange macadamia nut pesto, and a multitude of pastas and pizzas for around $8–12. Italian desserts, soft drink, coffees, and smoothies round out what's available. Hours are Sun.–Thurs. 11 A.M.–10 P.M., Fri.–Sat. until 11 P.M., and Saturday from 9 A.M. for brunch.

Sushi Masa, 808/593-2007, serves reasonable Japanese food like tempura, shrimp, and vegetables, chicken teriyaki, and tanuki udon for under $9. You can get a sashimi combination plate for $22 or a sushi special for $16.50–18.50.

Upstairs is **Brew Moon Restaurant and Micro Brewery.** Food is casual American with a blend of the islands, but the real reason for stopping by should be the beer. Usually on tap are a half dozen beers brewed on site, with others offered seasonally, and a number of these fine concoctions have won awards at various beer festivals around the country. Open 11 A.M.–10 P.M., till midnight on the weekends, and the bar stays open until 2 A.M.

Aloha Tower Marketplace

Some years ago, a law was passed in Hawaii allowing beer to be sold at the place at which it was made. This allowed breweries to open pubs on premises. **Gordon-Biersch Brewery & Restau-**

rant, 808/599-4877, has taken advantage of this opportunity and opened a fine establishment at the Aloha Tower Marketplace. Four beers are brewed here, all lagers, with the addition of seasonal favorites: Export, a smooth, medium hop, full-bodied beer similar to a pilsner but less bitter; Marzen, an Oktoberfest beer with a little extra oomph from a combination of malts; Dunkles, a dark beer served unfiltered in the old Bavarian tradition; Blonde Bock, a sweet light golden drink. Aside from these beers, there is a selection of wines, coffees, soft drinks, milk, and juices, but no tropical mixed drinks. The lunch and dinner menus are similar, aside from the sandwiches offered at lunch and more hearty main dishes in the evening. Appetizers include fried calamari for $9.50 and crispy artichoke hearts for $6.50, and the small pizzas run $9.95. These and the various salads are just preparation for the main courses, like a roasted chicken with fontina cheese, pancetta, and honey mustard sandwich or fettuccine pasta at $7.95–12.95 for lunch, or barbecue salmon with cashew rice or double-cut pork chops with mashed potatoes ranging $14.95–22.95 for dinner. Dine inside or out. Inside, with its leather booths, is more elegant and quieter for conversation. In the more casual alfresco portico, sit at stout wooden tables under canvas umbrellas and watch the tugboats shuttle ships through the harbor as the lights of the city sparkle across the water. The inside bar is good for a quiet drink, while you can boogie at the outside bar, where different bands come to play Wednesday to Saturday.

Across the walkway, **Don Ho's Island Grill,** 808/528-0807, serves lunch and dinner daily and turns into a nightclub 11 P.M.–2 A.M. for dancing and live DJ music on Thursday, Friday, and Saturday. Cashing in on one of the best-known names in island music, this is a casual, easy-going place with good food to match. Try surfboard-shaped pizzas, fresh fish, and Hawaiian desserts.

At the entrance to the Marketplace is **Chai's Island Bistro,** 808/585-0011, a great stop for Hawaiian Regional cuisine but also the most happening place in town for the sweet sounds of island music, provided by famous island artists Tues.–Sat. 7–9 P.M. For lunch, try such delicacies as fresh spinach gnocchi, pan-seared marinated pork tenderloin with merlot demiglaze, or grilled Atlantic salmon with truffle Madeira sauce. The dinner menu is partially the same with additional intriguing entrée items. Chai's has established a great reputation and works hard at keeping the accolades coming. Lunch entrée prices run $11–20, dinner prices $29–40.

Restaurant Row

This new-age complex at 500 Ala Moana Blvd. (across from the Federal Building) points the way to "people-friendly" development in Honolulu's future. It houses shops and businesses, free public parking and a nine-plex movie theater, but mostly restaurants, all grouped together around a central courtyard and strolling area. Some restaurants are elegant and excellent, while others are passable and plain. But they are all in a congenial setting, and you can pick your palate and style preference as easily as you'd pick offerings at a buffet. Start at the central fountain area with its multicolored modernistic Lego-inspired tower.

A premier restaurant here is **Sansei Seafood Restaurant and Sushi Bar,** 808/536-6286. Following on the great success of the original Sansei in Kapalua, Maui, owner D. K. Kodama has opened this fine restaurant here in Honolulu. Employing the same concept, but in a much larger space, the Sansei offers a full range of traditional favorites and experimental sushi, main course entrées, and a large selection of domestic and imported wines and sake. Not only is the food eminently tasty, it's a joy to eat and is presented in a stylish manner. The sushi is adaptive, and many of the sauces, innovations in themselves, go way beyond soy sauce and wasabi. Sushi is the focus here and this is a great place to try several. While the meal menu includes mostly fish and seafood, some meat and poultry are also available. Sample items off the menu are an award-winning Asian rock shrimp cake appetizer, spider roll sushi that's crispy tempura soft shell crab with a sweet and hot Thai sauce and unagi glaze, and roast Peking duck breast over mushroom and potato risotto with a foie gras demi-glaze. When possible, locally grown greens picked daily are used, and, oddly enough but perhaps not surprising for this avant garde establishment, the desserts are as all-American as apple pie. But the Sansei is more than a restaurant. Sushi is priced from

OAHU

$3.95, entrées run $16–24. Open until 1 A.M. for karaoke and food with reduced prices on sushi and the bar menu after 10 P.M., it's become a favorite late-night spot. The Sansei is a winner and sure to please the discriminating palate.

The **Sunset Grill,** 808/521-4409, is on the corner. With wraparound windows, a long and open bar, and comfortable maple chairs, it lives up to its name. This is the place to come for a quiet evening drink in the downtown area. The food is prepared in full view on a *kiawe*-fired grill, wood-roasting oven, and Italian rotisserie. Choices include pasta, gourmet salads, calamari, fresh fish, oysters, chicken, veal, and lamb. Lunch is a wide variety of plump juicy sandwiches of turkey, sausage, beef, fish, or chicken. The chefs at the Sunset aren't afraid to blend East with West in a wide variety of creations. Open weekdays 11 A.M.–10 P.M., Saturday and Sunday 5:30–11 P.M.

Others in the Row include **Ruth's Chris Steakhouse, Josie's** for Mexican, the Italian **Boci** restaurant, and **Payao Thai Restaurant.** In the middle of the complex is **The Row,** an outdoor bar with finger food, and nearby is the **Ocean** nightclub, one of the happening night places in town.

INEXPENSIVE DINING AROUND TOWN

The following restaurants are in and around the greater Honolulu area.

In central Honolulu, mostly along Bishop Street's financial district, you'll find excellent and inexpensive restaurants that cater to the district's lunch crowd.

At the corner of Pali Highway and Vineyard is **People's Cafe,** 808/536-5789. It's run by Newton and Adelle Oshiro, and two going on three generations of the same Japanese family have been serving the full range of excellent and inexpensive Hawaiian food at this down-home restaurant. Plate lunches and other lunches run about $6. Combination lunches like the Laulau plate, which is lomi salmon, pipikaula, chicken lu'au or chicken long rice, poi or rice, are about $10 and served on sectioned trays. While there's no decor to speak of, the place is clean and the people are very friendly. If you want a real Hawaiian meal at a reasonable price, this is the place to come. The People's Cafe is open Mon.–Fri. 10 A.M.–7:30 P.M., Saturday until 2:30 P.M.

Down to Earth Natural Foods and Deli, 2525 S. King St., 808/947-7678, open daily 7:30 A.M.–10 P.M., is a kind of "museum of health food stores" serving filling, nutritious health food dishes for very reasonable prices. Get sandwiches (like a whopping avocado, tofu, and cheese) and other items such as veggie stroganoff, eggplant parmigiana, and lasagna at the deli counter, or try the salad and hot entrée bars to other prepared foods. Many items at the hot entrée bar go for $5.95 a pound. Healthwise, you can't go wrong!

Kokua Market Natural Foods Co-op, 2643 S. King St., 808/941-1922, is open to the public daily 8:30 A.M.–8:30 P.M. It's a full-service store with organic and fresh produce, cheese, milk, juices, bulk foods, breads, a small deli case full of sandwiches, and prepared entrées and hot soups.

Suehiro's, 1824 S. King, 808/949-4584, is open daily for lunch 11 A.M.–2 P.M. and dinner 5–9 P.M., with take-out service. It gets the nod from local Japanese people. The menu here is authentic, the decor strictly Americana, and the food well prepared and moderately priced.

Another of the same is the **Hungry Lion,** 808/536-1188, at 1613 Nu'uanu Avenue. Open 6 A.M.–11:30 P.M. daily and 24 hours on Friday and Saturday, it serves everything from Asian food to steaks. Many local people come here after a night out. Nothing special, but decent wholesome food on Formica tables.

At the Hawaii Maritime Center you'll find the seafood establishment **Pier Seven Restaurant,** 808/524-2233, tucked away in the rear overlooking Honolulu Harbor. It's open for lunch weekdays and dinner every day.

Getting two thumbs up from locals who appreciate fine homecooked food but care less about the surrounding decor is **Helena's Hawaiian Food,** 1364 N. King St., 808/845-8044.

Out in the same direction, but not as far, is the well-known **Tamashiro Market,** 808/841-8047, which sells fresh fish and carries a fine selection of poki.

Sekiya's Restaurant and Deli, 2746 Kaimuki Ave., 808/732-1656, looks like a set from a 1940s tough-guy movie. The food is well prepared and the strictly local clientele will be amazed that you even know about the place. Open 8:30 A.M.–10 P.M., Friday and Saturday until 11 P.M.

Hale Vietnam, 1140 12th Ave. in Kaimuki, 808/735-7581, is building an excellent reputation for authentic and savory dishes at very moderate prices. It gets the highest praise from local people, who choose it again and again for an inexpensive evening of delicious dining. Hours are daily 11 A.M.–10 P.M.

Another winner in Kaimuki is the **Big City Diner,** 3565 Wai'alae Ave., 808/738-8855. Open for breakfast, lunch, and dinner, it serves huge portions and is so much a local favorite that you'll have to wait in line to get a seat on Saturday morning. Your breakfast might be Our Favorite Big Breakfast of three eggs and choice of meat, Loco Moco, or Murphy's Famous Fresh Apple Pancakes. The lunch and dinner menu are pretty much the same, and from them you can order, among others, chow mein noodles, hamburger steak with grilled onions and mushrooms, baby back ribs with guava barbecue sauce, kimchi fried rice, burgers, or sandwiches. Most come for the food, but there's also satellite TV, live Monday night sports, and karaoke every evening starting at 10 P.M.

Penny's Lunch Wagon, 205 Sand Island Access Rd., 808/845-6503, is one of the least expensive and most authentic Hawaiian plate-lunch stands you can find. The most expensive lunch is the Hawaiian Plate, which is *kalua* pig, *lau lau, lomi* salmon, and the works for $6.95. Open Mon.–Fri. 5 A.M.–2:45 P.M., Saturday to 2:30 P.M. Penny's is out of the way, but definitely worth a stop, especially if you've been out at Sand State Recreation Area.

Art and the Sandwich

In Honolulu there are a few opportunities to feed your mind and soul along with satiating your appetite.

The **Garden Cafe,** at the Honolulu Academy of Arts, 900 S. Beretania, 808/532-8734, is a classy place for lunch. Open Tues.–Sat. 11:30 A.M.–2 P.M.; dine inside or out. Menu items include chilled tomato and avocado soup with coriander garnish, soup or salad and half sandwich, and warm sandwiches, mostly for under $9. An assortment of desserts and beverages can

also be ordered. The food is delicious, but be aware that the portions are not for the hungry, being designed primarily for patrons of the arts who seem to be wealthy matrons from the fashionable sections of Honolulu who are all watching their waistlines.

Don't let the Porsches, Mercedeses, and BMWs parked vanity plate to vanity plate in the parking lot discourage you from enjoying the **Contemporary Cafe,** at the Contemporary Museum, 2411 Makiki Heights Dr., 808/523-3362 (reservations recommended). The small but superb menu is as inspired as the art in the museum, and the prices are astonishingly inexpensive. Dine inside or out, or perch on the porch. Appetizers are sautéed mushrooms, fruit, or smoked salmon for under $10. Salads include home-smoked mahimahi and papaya vinaigrette salad, Malaysian shrimp salad, Greek salad, or chicken salad for under $11. Sandwiches include smoked breast of turkey or 'ahi Caesar for under $10. Desserts run from cheesecake to flourless chocolate roulade, and beverages include homemade lemonade and cappuccino. For a wonderful cultural outing combined with a memorable lunch, come to the Contemporary Cafe. Open Tues.–Sat. 11 A.M.–2 P.M. for the main menu, and 2–3 P.M. for drinks and desserts only. Sunday hours are noon–3 P.M. It's just so . . . contemporary!

MODERATE DINING AROUND TOWN

Fisherman's Wharf, 1009 Ala Moana Blvd. on the Kewalo Basin, 808/538-3808, is a Honolulu institution. This restaurant has been here since 1952, when it took over from Felix's Italian Garden Restaurant, which had been on this spot since the '40s. The restaurant's design gives you the feel of being aboard ship. Its theme is nautical, displaying a collection of ship's accessories, riggings, and figurines, and trophy catches from the sea. The place exudes the feel of a Honolulu of days past, and you can sit and watch through the windows as fishing boats and cruise ships arrive and depart as they have done for decades, or look out past Waikiki to Diamond Head. For lunch, start with oysters on the half shell or fresh steamed clams. Follow this with

Boston-style clam chowder and a Caesar salad. Lunch sandwiches range $5.95–11.95, or choose fresh fish done in a variety of ways at market price, broiled oysters and shiitake mushrooms for $11.95, or the seafood medley $29.95. The dinner menu is similar, but without the sandwiches and with the addition of pastas and other special entrées. Upstairs, the Captain's Bridge is like a cabaret club that serves light meals, soups, and salads, with a full range of drinks. Friday and Saturday nights there's karaoke, so come up and sing.

The Hideaway Restaurant, 808/848-2800, at La Mariana Sailing Club, 50 Sand Island Access Rd., is the only real restaurant in this neck of the woods. The Hideaway serves appetizers like sashimi, lumpia, and sautéed mushroom buttons. From the broiler come steaks, pork chops, and burgers with all the fixings. From the sea, seafood brochette, shrimp scampi served over linguini, or *ahi* Cajun-style will fill your plate. Chicken, lobster, and nightly specials round out the menu. The lunch menu is simpler, with soups, salads, hot and cold sandwiches, and a handful of fish and stir-fry selections. The chef is also known for his onion rings. They're not on the menu; you have to know about them. Now you know. While the decor has recently been upgraded, it's still very Polynesian and nautical in essence. Inside hang Japanese glass floats that at night are diffused with different colors, providing mood lighting for the cozy black booths and wooden tables with wicker chairs, tiki posts, and decorations scavenged from defunct former restaurants in town. The Hideaway is an out-of-the-way place, local, and real Hawaiiana. At a working marina, this is where all the yachties come. Half hidden behind a stand of trees, only one small sign at the entrance points the way. The restaurant serves food Mon.–Fri. 11:30 A.M.–2 P.M. and 5–9 P.M., Sat.–Sun. noon–5 P.M. On Friday and Saturday 9 P.M.–midnight, Ron Miyashiro and Singers croon the night away to piano music, so stop by for a drink at the bar and enjoy.

Auntie Pasto's, 1099 S. Beretania at the corner of Pensacola, 808/523-8855, is open Mon.–Thurs. 11 A.M.–4 P.M. for lunch and until 10:30 P.M. for dinner, and weekends 4–11 P.M. only for dinner. The quiet, comfortable vibe is upbeat pizza parlor; you can even bring your own wine. Most of the Italian menu entrées are $8.50–12, and these include eggplant parmesan, calamari steak, and veal marsala. Soups come by the cup or bowl, and salads range from a garden green salad to a chicken Caesar. Antipasto plates, sides, and desserts run $3–6. No reservations necessary.

Won Kee Seafood Restaurant, 100 N. Beretania in the Chinatown Cultural Plaza, 808/524-6877, is an eatery where you get delicious seafood, a place for Honolulu's in-the-know crowd. Tasteful surroundings. Free parking on Maunakea Street.

Right next door to the Won Kee is the **Forum Restaurant,** 808/599-5022. Open daily 11 A.M.–2:30 P.M. and 5–11 P.M., this too is a classy joint with everything from the usual rice dishes to braised imperial shark fin soup for $38 per person.

The **Legend Seafood Restaurant,** 808/532-1868, two doors down from the Won Kee, emphasizes fish and seafood but also serves inexpensive Hong Kong–style dim sum in small, medium, large, and super-size plate sizes.

The Chart House, 1765 Ala Moana Blvd. across from Ala Wai Yacht Harbor, 808/941-6660, is open daily 4 P.M. until 2 A.M., with food served 5:30–9:30 P.M. Seafood and beef are its specialties with most entrées in the $18–28 range. It offers a happy hour until 7 P.M., *pu pu* until midnight, and nightly entertainment.

India House, 2632 S. King St., 808/955-7552, is open daily for lunch and dinner. Extraordinary Indian dishes include a wide selection of curries, vegetarian dishes, special *naan* bread, kabobs, and fish *tikka*. Specialty desserts include homemade ice cream and toppings.

HAWAIIAN REGIONAL CUISINE

As large a city as Honolulu is, it's able to support many innovative restaurants where locally grown foods are combined with preparation techniques from around the world to produce new and intriguing flavors. The following are restaurants where something new is always on the menu and the combination of ingredients, textures, and tastes is sure to please. Reservations are recommended.

In the semi-industrial area of Iwilei at 580 N. Nimitz Hwy., **Sam Choy's Breakfast, Lunch,**

and Crab, 808/545-7979, is as popular as every other Sam Choy restaurant in the islands; reservations recommended. The Kona poke and beef stew omelets are much-requested breakfast items, while various crab and other seafood entrées appear for dinner depending on the season. Always generous portions at reasonable prices. Sam brews beer at this site and the brewpub is open until midnight. Here you get *pu pu* specials and there's live music on Wednesday evenings. Valet parking. Hours of operation are breakfast Mon.–Fri. 6:30–10:30 A.M. and until 11:30 A.M. on Sat. and Sun., lunch until 4 P.M., and dinner nightly from 5–10 P.M.

Indigo, 1121 Nu'uanu Ave. in Chinatown, 808/521-2900, serves what some classify as Eurasian cuisine. Chef Glenn Chu offers such savory items as Chinese steamed buns filled with eggplant and sun-dried tomatoes, crispy goat cheese wonton filled with fruit sauce, roasted tomato garlic crab soup, or grilled Mongolian rib-eye beef with chili black sauce. Some vegetarian items available. Open for lunch Tues.–Fri. 11:30 A.M.–2 P.M. and dinner Tues.–Sat. 6–9:30 P.M. There's live music and dancing at the adjacent Green Room Bar and Lounge on Saturday 6–8:30 P.M.

Alan Wong's is a Best Restaurant of the Year award winner. Try such delicacies as shredded *kalua* pig wrapped in taro pancake on poi vinaigrette with lomi tomato relish, grilled lamb chops with coconut macadamia nut crust, or a vegetarian entrée consisting of mashed potatoes, black bean salsa, grilled asparagus, and roasted shiitake mushrooms. Yum! Alan Wong's is just north of Waikiki at 1857 S. King St., 808/949-2526. Alan Wong has also opened the Pineapple Room restaurant for upscale dining and Patisserie Bar for coffee, drinks, and pastries on the third floor of the Liberty House department store at Ala Moana Center and the Regional Cuisine Marketplace for fine island foodstuffs on the fourth floor.

At 3660 Wai'alae Ave. near where the road crests the hill in Kaimuki is **3660 On the Rise,** 808/737-1177, a casually elegant place where you can watch the cooks create behind the glass wall of the kitchen. While the menu changes somewhat every night, Chef Russell Siu's "first flavors" include frizzled shrimp wrapped in shredded phyllo pastry or potato-crusted crab cakes, while "second flavors" are soups and salads. "Feature presentations" might be Asian pesto stuffed breast of chicken or Chinese steamed fillet of snapper lightly seared and simmered in a Chinese black bean broth. Round out your meal with one of the "sweet endings": harlequin crème brûlée or mile-high Wai'alae pie, perhaps, or indulge in a cup of coffee or glass of cognac or port. Delightful presentation and attentive service. Open Sunday and Tues.–Thurs. 5:30–9 P.M., Friday and Saturday until 10 P.M., closed Monday; reservations necessary.

On Jin's Cafe, 401 Kamake'e behind Pier 1 Imports at the Victoria Ward Centers, 808/589-1666, is a pleasant surprise. Chef On Jin Kim, who used to run the kitchen at the Hanatei Bistro before it closed, has opened a much smaller and more intimate restaurant here to everyone's delight. Open for lunch Mon.–Fri. 11 A.M.–2 P.M. and dinner Tues.–Sun. 5–9 P.M., Friday and Saturday until 10 P.M. The food is eclectic with definite Pacific and European overtones. The clean modern style, marble tables decorated with orchids, tile floor, and semi-open kitchen set the mood. Lunch is inexpensive with plate lunches and sandwiches that run $5.25–7.50, but even these show class. Dinners are the best, more sophisticated and more expensive but not outrageous. Appetizers like charred ahi and chicken satey run about $6–8, a French onion soup $4.50, while the entrées like seared salmon, bouillabaisse, duck, and chicken scaloppini are mostly $17.50–22. Savor the sauces.

One of the newest fine restaurants to enter the market is **Chef Mavro Restaurant,** 808/944-4714, 1969 S. King St., at the corner of McCully, open for dinner only, daily except Monday. Formerly the executive chef of the Four Seasons Resort on Maui and prior to that the executive chef at the Halekulani in Waikiki, chef Mavro is now king of his own domain, and he reigns with distinction. The restaurant is not large but comfortable and personal, tastefully elegant yet not extravagant. Booths line the perimeter of the room, tables are set in the middle, paintings of tropical flowers and raku pottery with flowers line the walls, and low lighting, linen, and crystal set the mood. Chef Mavro offers a mix of à la carte and prix fixe menus with three, four, or six options, with or without wine. While the food is exceptional in its own right, an important factor of dining here is the pairing of wine and food, a complementary union where neither overpowers the other. Each item is introduced and explained as it's set on the table, and wines are chosen for each individual dish. Nearly the entire menu changes every six weeks, but no matter what the choices, the freshest of Hawaiian produce

and seafood are always infused with subtle yet intense flavors and prepared with a French flare, resulting in a tropical cuisine with a French soul. This is an exceptional restaurant with masterful food. For a special night out, this is a great choice. Dining here can be expensive, but it's worth every penny.

ENTERTAINMENT

Music and Dancing

Anna Banana's, 2440 S. Beretania, 808/946-5190, is the "top banana" for letting your hair down and boogying the night away. It's out by the university just across from Star Market. This dance joint has a laid-back atmosphere, reasonable beer prices, usually a small cover that goes to the band, no dress code, and a friendly student crowd. Dancing is upstairs on Thursday, Friday, and Saturday, light dining downstairs, and a backyard to cool off in between sets. Great place, great fun! Open 11:30 A.M.–2 A.M.

Ocean Club at Restaurant Row, 500 Ala Moana, 808/526-9888, is Honolulu's newest hot spot. Open 4:30 P.M.–A.M., it has a DJ and dancing to contemporary hits. Large dance floor. The "cocktail hour," with reduced-price *pu pu* and light meals, runs 4:30–8 P.M., while happy hour on Friday starts at 8 P.M. The age limit for entrance is 23. Apparently the owners want a more sophisticated crowd, not just a bunch of rowdy first-timers.

Rumours Nightclub, in the Ala Moana Hotel, 410 Atkinson St., 808/955-4811, is an established DJ disco that cranks up around 9 P.M. and features the newest in dance and rock videos. Dress code; $5 cover.

TGI Fridays, 950 Ward Ave., 808/524-8443, is a lively night spot. Good food, large portions, reasonable prices, and music.

The **Pier Bar** at the Aloha Tower Marketplace has an elevated stage with live acts throughout the week, ranging from Hawaiian to contemporary rock to R&B. The music is potluck, but you're right on the harbor, so you can watch the sunset and always have a great time. Just a few steps away are **Don Ho's Island Grill** and **Gordon-Biersch Brewery & Restaurant,** both of which offer evening entertainment to accompany their fine menus.

Chai's Island Bistro, also at Aloha Tower Marketplace, has some of the best island musicians performing weekly. Hawaii's first lady of song, Melveen Leed, sings on Tuesday, the Brothers Cazimero take the stage on Wednesday, Thursday is the duo Hapa, and Azure McCall sings Friday and Saturday. Each is a class act and together they make the best lineup of local musicians on the island. Music runs 7–9 P.M. Reservations are suggested. Free valet parking.

For a complete listing of what's happening in town on the music and dance scene for the weekend and coming week, have a look at the Calendar of Events section of the Friday edition of the newspaper.

Note: Also see the **Waikiki** chapter.

Freebies

At **Centerstage,** Ala Moana Shopping Center, various shows are presented—mostly music (rock, gospel, jazz, Hawaiian) and hula. Performances usually start at noon. The **Keiki Hula Show,** every Sunday at 10 A.M., is fast becoming an institution. Here, hula is being kept alive, with many first-time performers interpreting the ancient movements that they study in their *halau.*

The **Royal Hawaiian Band,** founded more than 150 years ago, performs Friday at noon on the 'Iolani Palace Bandstand, and on Sunday at 2 P.M. at the Kapi'olani Bandstand. Call 808/527-5666 for other band performance locations, or visit the band website at www.royal-hawaiianband.com.

Everyone is invited to enjoy the free **Wednesday noontime music** at Tamarind Park, on the corner of King and Bishop Streets, where anything from rock and roll to jazz to traditional may be performed.

Honolulu Hale (City Hall) presents periodic free musical concerts in the central courtyard and art exhibitions in the central courtyard, Lane Gallery, or Third Floor Gallery. All are welcome Mon.–Fri. 8 A.M.–5 P.M.

Various hula, Hawaiian music, and other cultural programs are performed around dusk on Saturday and Sunday at the Kuhio Beach Banyan Tree Park.

Sometimes the university has free noontime shows by local bands at the student center and Friday evening jam sessions at the Manoa Gardens restaurant. Call the information center, 808/956-7235, for current happenings.

Hilo Hattie, 700 Nimitz Hwy., the largest manufacturer of alohawear in the state, conducts free tours of the factory, complete with complimentary shuttle ride from Waikiki (the shuttle also passes Dole Cannery Square). Up to 40,000 garments are on display in the showroom, plus countless gifts and souvenirs. It's hard to resist spending: prices and craftsmanship are good, and designs are the most contemporary. Open daily 7 A.M.–6 P.M., 808/537-2926 or 800/272-5282.

Performance Arts

Like any big city, Honolulu has a whole host of musical and performance art venues and high-quality productions. Some of the best-known are as follows:

The **Honolulu Symphony,** website: www.honolulusymphony.com, performs indoors at the Neil S. Blaisdell Center Concert Hall and outdoors at the Waikiki Shell. Various programs take place throughout the year, with most tickets ranging $15–50, with students and seniors half price. For information and tickets at the Blaisdell Center, contact 808/538-8863; for information about shows at the Waikiki Shell, call 808/591-2211.

Hawaii Opera Theater, website: www.hawaiiopera.org, also puts on shows at the Neil S. Blaisdell Center Concert Hall. The season runs January through March. For tickets, call 808/596-7858.

Diamond Head Theater performs at its own location, 520 Makapu'u Ave., just below Diamond Head. This company has been presenting theatrical shows since 1915 and never fails to impress. Performances are Thurs.–Sat. at 8 P.M., and tickets range $10–40. Call the box office at 808/734-0274 for information and tickets or check online at www.startech.com/diamondhead.

Built in 1922 and renovated inside in 1996, the **Hawaii Theatre** has thrilled crowds with its variety of shows over the years. This theater hosts local and off-island music and theater shows, and is a venue of the annual Hawaii International Film Festival. The Hawaii Theatre is at 1130 Bethel St. at the edge of Chinatown, and there is ample nearby pay parking. For what's happening, stop by the box office Tues.–Sat. 9 A.M.–5 P.M. and one-half hour before shows, call 808/528-0506, or surf to www.hawaiitheatre.com.

The **Academy Theater** at the Honolulu Academy of Arts hosts a full schedule of film, music, and theatrical performances throughout the year, along with lectures and other educational functions. Tickets for film showings runs $5, and those for other events vary in price. Call 808/532-8768 for information.

On the University of Hawai'i, Manoa campus, the **Kennedy Theatre** hosts university stage productions. The building, designed by the noted architect I. M. Pei, is of interest in itself but is of greater interest for theater buffs because it is made to easily stage both Western- and Asian-style productions. For information, call 808/956-7655.

For first-run commercial Hollywood movies, try **Restaurant Row 9 Theater,** 808/526-4171, at Restaurant Row, or the **Kahala 8 Theater,** 808/733-6243. About the only place in town to see art films at a commercial theater is the **Varsity Twins,** 808/973-5833, at 1106 University Ave. near the university. The University of Hawai'i Outreach College, website: www.outreach.hawaii.edu, also shows art films through its International Cinema Program. Films are shown at Krauss Hall room 012 on Thursdays at 7:30 P.M. These films are free to the public, but a donation of $3 is suggested. Call 808/956-3836 for the lineup.

Girlie Bars and Strip Joints

Many of these "lounges," as they're called, are strung along the 1600 and 1700 blocks of Kapi'olani Blvd. and in the little alleys running off it. They open and shut frequently. Inside are two types of women: the dancers and the lap sitters. Most patrons are local men or GI types, with only a smattering of tourists. Personal safety is usually not a problem, but a fool and his money are soon parted in these bars.

Chinatown's **Hotel Street** has hookers, both male and female, walking the heels off their shoes. They cruise during the day, but the area really comes alive at night. Mostly, these people are down-and-outers who can't make it against the stiff competition along the main areas of Waikiki. The clientele is usually servicemen and hard-core locals. A few clubs in this area offer strippers. Always be prepared for fights and bad vibes in any of these joints.

SHOPPING

If you don't watch the time, you'll spend half your vacation moving from one fascinating store to the next. Luckily, in greater Honolulu the majority of shopping is clustered in malls, with specialty shops scattered around the city, especially in the nooks and crannies of Chinatown.

Ala Moana Shopping Center

This is the largest shopping center in the state, and if you want to get all of your souvenir hunting and special shopping done in one shot, this is the place. It's on Ala Moana Blvd. just across from the Ala Moana Beach Park, open Mon.–Sat. 9:30 A.M.–9 P.M., Sunday 10 A.M.–7 P.M. The center has free parking lots for those who care to drive in, but the mall can also be reached by Waikiki Trolley, TheBus no. 8, and the Ala Moana Shuttle, which runs every 15 minutes daily throughout business hours from half a dozen locations in Waikiki for $1 each way. Recently, the Ala Moana Shopping Center has taken off its comfortable Hawaiian shirt and shorts and donned designer fashions by Christian Dior and Gianni Versace. Local people are irritated, and they have a point, to a point. The center has plenty of down-home shopping left, but it now caters as much to the penthouse as it does to the one-room efficiency. It used to be where the *people* shopped, but now portions are being aimed at the affluent tourist, especially the affluent Japanese tourists who flaunt designer labels like politicians flaunt pretty secretaries. If anything, the shopping has gotten better, but you'll have to look around a bit more for bargains.

Plenty of competition keeps prices down, with more than enough of an array to suit any taste and budget. There are about 200 stores, including all of Hawaii's major department stores like **Sears, JCPenney,** and **Liberty House,** with the recent inclusion of a **Neiman Marcus.** Utilitarian shops and boutiques feature everything from wedding rings to swim fins, while the food court and other restaurants feed hungry shoppers. It's also a great place to see a cross-section of Hawaiian society. Another pleasantry is the free Keiki Hula Show every Sunday at 10 A.M. on the Centerstage, but there are literally hundreds of other performances throughout the year. The center maintains an information kiosk near Centerstage to answer any questions and point you in the right direction.

The following is a mere sampling of what you'll find. The restaurants in the **Makai Food Court** are exceptional, if not for taste, at least for price, and are unbelievable for the variety of cuisines represented. In a huge open area you'll find dishes from Bangkok to Acapulco, from Tokyo to San Francisco. Most of these restaurants have only counters for ordering, with tables in a common dining area. Great for people-watching. In addition, free-standing restaurants and others in the department stores prepare a variety of excellent foods.

House of Music sells records and tapes. On the ground floor, this is a good store to shop in for those island sounds that'll immediately conjure up images of Hawaii whenever they're played. For books, try **Waldenbooks,** which has a large selection of books and a very inclusive Hawaiiana section. Books make inexpensive, easy-to-transport, and long-lasting mementos of your trip to Hawaii. For maps and more, shop the **Rand McNally Map and Travel** shop. **Longs Drugs** has good prices for film, but for cheap and fast developing try **Fromex One Hour Photo. The Crack Seed Center** offers the best array of crackseed (spiced nuts, seeds, and fruits), which has been a treat for island children for years. Prices are inflated here, but the selection can't be beat, and you can educate yourself about these same products in smaller stores around the island. Crackseed is not to everyone's liking, but it does make a unique souvenir.

OAHU

Spirolina hunters can get their organic fix at **Vim and Vigor,** featuring vitamins, supplements, and minerals, and those needing a chocolate fix should head for **Godiva. Shirokiya** is a Japanese-owned department store between JCPenney and Liberty House on the mountain side of the complex. It has a fascinating assortment of gadgetry, knickknacks, handy items, and nifty stuff that Nippon is so famous for. It's fun just to look around, and the prices are reasonable. Japanese products are also available at **S.M. Iida Limited,** a local store dating back to the early 1900s, featuring garden ornaments and flower-arrangement sets. Specialty shops in the center include **Products of Hawai'i, Too, Hawaiian Quilt Collection,** and **Irene's Hawaiian Gifts,** selling a wide assortment of island-made goods and souvenirs, from cheap to exquisite. **Tahiti Imports** sells bikinis, mu'mu', and a wide selection of handicrafts from throughout Polynesia. Aside from all these shops, Honolulu maintains a satellite city hall here, there is a post office, and both United and Continental have airlines offices at the mall.

Victoria Ward Centers

This cluster of over 120 shops and nearly two dozen eateries occupying five buildings is just a few blocks west of Ala Moana Shopping Center, across from Kewalo Basin and the west end of Ala Moana Beach Park. Shopping hours run Mon.–Sat. 10 A.M.–9 P.M. and Sunday 10 A.M.–5 P.M. The centers can be reached by Waikiki Trolley and TheBus nos. 8, 19, and 20. The modern two-story **Ward Warehouse** complex lives up to its name as a warehouse, with a motif from bygone days when stout wooden beams were used instead of steel. The wide array of shops includes inexpensive restaurants and clothing stores, but the emphasis is on arts and crafts. Give the tots their first lesson in impulse buying at **Child's Play,** an educational toy store, or at **Bambini,** for mother and child fashions, or show them how a pro does it by wandering into **Blue Ginger** for men's and women's fashionable alohawear. Repent past gluttony at **Aloha Health Foods,** primarily a vitamin and mineral store. Perhaps you can dress your feet at **Thongs 'n Things,** with everything in thongs from spiked golfing thongs to Teva sandals, the best all-around footwear for the island. Other shops include **Runners Route,** selling jogging shoes, shorts, and some backpacks; **Le Lotus Bleu** and **Villa Roma** for ladies' fashions; and **Beyond the Beach,** which stocks men's and women's alohawear, casual clothing, and sunglasses. Be sure to stop at **Native Books and Beautiful Things** for unique and authentic high-quality gifts, crafts, artwork, clothing, food items, and books made in Hawaii. Aside from the items it sells, this cooperative offers demonstrations, classes, and other activities on an ongoing basis. Perhaps the premier shop in the Warehouse is **Nohea Gallery** (*nohea* means beautiful or handsome in Hawaiian), which displays works by more than 500 local artists and craftspeople. Some of the finest works are created by more than 100 island woodworkers who make everything from rocking chairs and rolltop desks to traditional canoe paddles using rich grained woods like koa, mango, and rosewood. One of the most acclaimed woodworkers on display is Kelly Dunn, who turns bowls from Norfolk Island pine that are so thin you can actually see through them. Other artists displaying their talents include: Kurt McVay, who creates masterpieces in glass; Diana Lehr, who uses oils and pastels to capture the dramatic skyscapes and colors of Hawaii's sunsets and sunrises; Fabienne Blanc, who works in ultravibrant watercolors creating surrealistic close-up images of plants and foliage; Russell Lowrey, who works with watercolors and pastels, creating soft, feminine images of the islands; and Rick Mills, another glass artist who favors cobalt blue. Distinctive and affordable treasures include backgammon games, jewelry boxes, bowls, all kinds of jewelry, prints, and even distinctive postcards. Nohea Gallery is where you can see the "heart of Hawaii" through the eyes of its artists. Have a look!

The **Ward Farmers' Market** is just across Auahi Street, a great place to pick up fresh produce, fruits, nuts, fish, poultry, and flowers. To the side is **Ward Gateway Center,** where **Sports Authority** is the biggest shop, and behind is an **Office Depot** and **Nordstrom Rack.** Across Kamake'e St., **Ward Village Shops** include a **Pier 1 Imports,** several clothing outlets, a **Starbucks Coffee,** and a **Kua 'Aina Sandwich** shop.

Down Ala Moana Boulevard from Ward Warehouse and across the street from the Ward Village Shops is **Ward Centre,** a new string of stores that's gaining a reputation for some exclusive shops and upscale eateries. It also has one of the few microbreweries on the island. The Ward Centre is appointed in light wood and accentuated by brick floors that give the feeling of an intimate inside mall, although much is outside. Here you can find that just-right piece of jewelry at **Black Pearl Gallery;** fashions at **Allure, Kamehameha Garment Co.,** and **Rain Bow Tique;** and artworks at the **Gallery at Ward Centre.** Next to the gallery is the **Honolulu Chocolate Co.** Like a smug little devil, it tempts with chocolate truffles, mocha clusters, and fancy nut rolls. So sin! You're on vacation. Vibrating from a remote corner of the mall, where mystics feel more at home, is **Sedona,** a metaphysical new-age store. Inside, its shelves and cases are stocked with aromatherapy and massage oils, natural crystals, agates, books, jewelry, figurines, carvings, posters, postcards, and consciousness-lifting tapes. Recharge your spiritual batteries with a personal psychic reading done by various practitioners in a private upstairs area.

Borders Books and Music has a full-selection outlet here, with books, music, newspapers and magazines from around the world, a very good Hawaiiana section, ongoing events, and a gallery and coffee shop upstairs. Open Mon.–Thurs. 9 A.M.–11 P.M., Fri.–Sat. to midnight, and Sunday 9 A.M.–10 P.M. Call 808/591-8995 for book information, 808/591-8996 for music.

Aloha Tower Marketplace

Constructed in 1994, the Aloha Tower Marketplace is one of the newest mall/shopping plazas in Honolulu, one frequented not only by tourists but by locals. Set to the side of the Aloha Tower and fronting the working harbor of Honolulu, where ships from all over the world load and unload their goods, this marketplace is an old warehouse that's been tastefully converted into an upscale group of more than 100 shops offering food and beverages, apparel, art, gifts, jewelry, and specialty items. Shops are open Mon.–Sat. 9 A.M.–9 P.M. and Sunday until 6 P.M. An indoor-outdoor affair, where the sea breezes blow right through, the center atrium area lies in the shadow of the tower. This central courtyard atrium is also the spot for musical entertainment performed free throughout the day. The outside area in front of the tower is called the Boat Days

Bazaar, and it's filled with cabana-type booths selling mostly apparel, gifts, and souvenirs. Inside, find fashions at **Daniella** and **Beyond the Beach,** among others. **Magnet Five-O** has all sorts of magnets from floor to ceiling. If you can't find one here, you haven't looked hard enough. The **World of Time** carries everything from Swatch watches to pocket watches, **Powder Edge** has outdoor gear, you can find musical instruments at **Hawaiian Ukulele and Hula Supply,** and **Island Art Gallery** carries artwork to hang on your wall. Then there is **Perfumania,** and its name says it all. Browse through **Hula Prints** or peruse **Martin & MacArthur** for mostly koa wood furniture and furnishings. Also check out the **Endangered Species Store,** which stocks nature-inspired gift items. Part of the profits go to protect endangered species of the world. Most of the shops in this complex are locally owned, nonchain outfits. Have a walk through and support the local economy.

After having a look at the shops, sit down for a snack at one of the many food vendors. Try **Gordon-Biersch Brewery & Restaurant** for lunch and a chilled local brew, or **Baja Betty's** for other drinks; **Villa Pizza** for a quick bite; or **Belinda's Aloha Kitchen, Don Ho's Island Grill, Chai's Island Bistro,** or **Big Island Steakhouse** for a more substantial meal. Free noontime and early evening concerts are given at the main stage, but The Pier Bar, Gordon-Biersch, Don Ho's, the Big Island Steakhouse, and Chai's all have evening entertainment in their own establishments virtually every night of the week.

A vintage-looking, open-air trolley runs between the marketplace and Waikiki, charging $2 each direction for adults and $1 for children 3–11. The trolley starts around 9:15 A.M. and runs every 30 minutes until 9 P.M. Pickups are at 14 hotels and landmarks in Waikiki, and it drops you off right in front of the marketplace. Alternately, take TheBus no. 19, 20, or 47 from Waikiki and no. 55, 56, 57, or 8 on the return to Waikiki; or park in the pay parking lots in front of Aloha Tower or near Piers 5 and 6.

Dole Cannery Square

Look for the giant pineapple rising 200 feet into the air. A landmark of Honolulu, it was built in Chicago and erected here in 1928. It is still used as a reservoir and holds 100,000 gallons of water, which is piped throughout the Dole Cannery, whose outer buildings were transformed in 1988 to a minimall located at 650 Iwilei Road. Upon entering the atrium area, look high on the walls to see reproductions of Dole pineapple can labels. They're pop art, conveying a feeling of simpler times past. Downstairs you can watch a video about Dole and the cannery. Here also is a **Food Court,** providing snacks, salads, sandwiches, and soups for a quick lunch. On the two levels you'll find a cluster of shops laid out as traditional storefronts, but many seem to be empty—perhaps victims of the slow Hawaiian economy. Check **Blue Hawaii Surf Outlet** for many of your beach needs, **Famous Footwear** for shoes, and **Honolulu Jewelry Creation** for those small and expensive gifts. To satisfy your sweet tooth, head for that mountain of sin at the **Rocky Mountain Chocolate Factory.**

In the factory itself, workers stay busy processing the fruit with the newest generation of the marvelous Ginaca machine, first built in 1913 by Henry Ginaca, a draftsman hired by James Dole to modernize the industry. This whirring wonder can peel, core, cut, slice, and dice 100 fruits per minute. Within 20 minutes of reaching the machine, the canned fruit's ready for the grocer's shelf. Millions of Hawaii's fruits are canned, juiced, and sliced here for shipment around the world. In the summertime, at the height of the harvest, this factory can process more than three million cans of fruit per day!

Only a short walk away at 700 Nimitz Hwy. is the well-known **Hilo Hattie** shop. At this store you can find a incredible variety of island fashions, gifts, crafts, and food items at very reasonable prices. This is a good introduction to what the islands have to offer, and to make it a sweeter deal, the store offers free transportation to its store from Waikiki on its own shuttle buses.

Kahala Mall

The Kahala Mall is the major shopping mall on the eastern side of Honolulu in the upscale Kahala area. **Liberty House, Longs Drug, Star Market,** and the eight-plex **Kahala Theaters** anchor this mall, surrounded by dozens of apparel outlets, gift shops, and novelty stores, as well as electronics chains, jewelry stores, and specialty shops. As with most malls, there are about a dozen fast food outlets, from pizza to plate lunch and sushi, at which to refresh yourself for more shopping. Both **Barnes and Noble** and **Waldenbooks** have shops here. On the east end of the city, this is the shopping center of choice. Serviced by the Waikiki Trolley and TheBus nos. 22 and 58.

Bargains and Discounts

The Muumuu Factory, 1423 Kapi'olani Blvd., offers great sales—get there early and bring your helmet and shoulder pads to fight off the crowds. **Goodwill Thrift Shop,** 780 S. Beretania St., displays the same bargains as on the Mainland, but with a wide assortment of alohawear. **Pzazz,** 1419 Kalakaua Ave., has won accolades for being the best designer resale shop in town for moderately priced quality women's clothing. Also try the **Manufacturers Outlet,** a bevy of outlet shops under one roof at Dillingham and Kokau Streets in Iwilei. Every Saturday 8 A.M.–2 P.M. in a parking lot at Queen and South Streets, the **Honolulu Street Market** sets up for the sale of food, clothing, crafts, and other island-made items.

Miscellaneous

Hawaiian Islands Stamp and Coin, 1111 Bishop St., street level in the International Savings Building, displays rare coins, stamps, and paper money of Hawaii, the United States, and worldwide.

R. Field Wine Co., 1460 S. Beretania, is a purveyor of exquisite food, fine wines, crackers, cookies, cheeses, imported pastas, and caviar. Most of the wines are top-shelf Californian, with a nice variety of their reserve wines going back to 1968. Older French wines, as well as German wines, are also available, and while you're here peruse the humidor for a fine cigar. Most recent has been the addition of local organic produce and other Hawaiian food products. Look here for something for that special evening.

Everyone, sooner or later, needs a good hardware store. You can't beat the selection at **Kilgo's,** 180 Sand Island Rd.

O'AHU

CHINATOWN

Chinatown has seen ups and downs in the last 150 years, ever since Chinese laborers were lured from Guangdong Province to work as contract laborers on the pineapple and sugar plantations. They didn't need a fortune cookie to tell them that there was no future in plantation work, so within a decade of their arrival they had established themselves as merchants, mostly in small retail businesses and restaurants. Chinatown is roughly an area contained by Vinyard Boulevard and Nimitz Highway on the north and south and Bethel Avenue and River Street on the east and west. Twice this area has been flattened by fire, once in 1886 and again in 1900. The 1900 fire was deliberately set to burn out rats that had brought bubonic plague to the city. The fire got out of control and burned down virtually the whole district. Some contended that the fire was allowed to engulf the district in order to decimate the growing economic strength of the Chinese. Chinatown reached its heyday in the 1930s, when it thrived with tourists coming and going from the main port at the foot of Nu'uanu Avenue.

Today, Chinatown is a mixed bag of upbeat modernization and run-down sleazy storefronts. Although still strongly Chinese, there are Japanese, Laotians, Vietnamese, and even an Irish pub. This is Asia come to life: meat markets with hanging ducks and a host of ethnic Asian foods with their strange aromatic spices all in a few blocks. The entire district takes only minutes to walk and is a world apart from "tourist" O'ahu. Crates, live chickens, incredible shops, down-and-outers, tattoo parlors, and temples all can be found in this quarter. When Hotel Street meets River Street, with the harbor in the background, it all abruptly ends. This is a different Honolulu, a Pacific port, crusty and exciting.

Chinatown is relatively safe, especially during the daytime, but at night, particularly along infamous Hotel Street, you have to be careful. When the sun sinks, the neon lights and the area fires up. Transvestites and hookers slide down the street, shaking their wares and letting you know that they're open for business. Purchasing might leave you with a few souvenirs that you'd never care to *share* with the folks back home.

Not many tourists come this way. But walking down Hotel Street is really an adventure in and of itself. If you stay on the main drag, right down the middle, you'll be okay. At Hotel and Nu'uanu Streets you'll find the Honolulu Police Department downtown substation. A lot of nondescript places open to the street like a wound, oozing the odor of stale beer and urine. As you walk down Hotel Street toward the river it gets sleazier. But it's not all down and dirty here. On the periphery of Chinatown at the bottom end on Nu'uanu Ave. is **O'Toole's** pub, open for beer and hard drinks, and music Wed.–Sat. evenings.

Several parking lots and structures are conveniently located along or near Nu'uanu Avenue.

SIGHTS

Look for the pagoda roof of the former **Wo Fat Restaurant** on the corner of Hotel and Maunakea Streets. Until it closed shop in the late '90s, this was the oldest chop suey house in Honolulu, started in 1886 by Mr. Wo Fat, a baker. It's a good landmark for starting your tour. **Hawaii Theatre,** a Chinatown landmark (circa 1922), has been renovated inside and once again is open to the public. One-hour tours of this historic building are given every Tuesday at 11 A.M., and the $5 admission is partially raised to refurbish the building's exterior. Call 808/528-0506 for additional information. You can easily do Chinatown on your own, but for another view and some extremely knowledgeable guides try the **Chinese Chamber of Commerce** tour, 808/533-3181, which has been operating as a community service for almost 30 years. A guide will show you around Chinatown for only $5. This tour is offered only Tuesday mornings at 9:30 A.M. and starts from the chamber office at 42 N. King Street. Or try the **Hawaiian Heritage Center** Chinatown Historical and Cultural Walking Tour, which starts from the Ramsay Galleries at 1128 Smith St., every Friday at 9:30 A.M. The two-hour tours are $5 per person, minimum of three for tours to go; call 808/521-2749 for reservations, or write to P.O. Box 37520, Honolulu, HI 96837. An excellent source of general information is the **Hawaii Chinese Historical Center,** 111 N. King St., Honolulu, HI 96817. Another walking tour, but one that goes beyond the confines of Chinatown to take in historical structures in the rest of downtown Honolulu, is that given by the American Institute of Architects (AIA), 808/545-4242. This walking tour starts from their office at 1128 Nu'uanu Ave. at 9:30 A.M. on Tuesday and Saturday and returns about noon. The price is $15 per person or $25 per couple, and reservations and prepayment by credit card are necessary.

If you want to clear your head from the hustle and bustle, visit the **Kuan Yin Temple,** where Buddha is always praised with some sweet-smelling incense, or peek into the **Taoist Temple.** If that's not enough to awaken your spiritual inner self, visit the **Izumo Taisha Jinja,** a Japanese Shinto shrine. All the accouterments of a shrine are here—roof, thick coiled rope, bell, and prayer box. This one houses a male deity. You can tell by the cross on the top. There's a ferroconcrete example of a torii gate. If you've never visited a Japanese Shinto shrine, have a look here but be respectful and follow the rules. **Lum Sai Ho Tong,** across the street from the Shinto shrine on River Street, is a basic Chinese Buddhist temple, very small and usually closed after 2 P.M.

For peace and quiet, or to check out some old-timers playing checkers or dominoes, cross the river and enter **Aala Triangle Park,** or treat yourself by walking a few minutes north to **Foster**

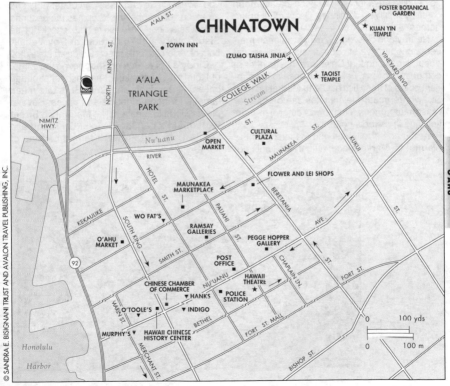

Botanical Garden, 180 N. Vineyard, for a glimpse of rare and exotic flora from around the world.

SHOPPING

For shopping head to the **Chinatown Cultural Plaza Shopping Center,** on the corner of Maunakea and Beretania Streets, but note that it has been struggling lately and shops come and go with regularity. It's more fun to look at than to shop in. You'll find such stores as Dragongate Bookstore, Phuc Hing Gift and Bookstore, Tak Wah Tong Chinese Herbalist, Excellent Gem and Diamonds, and Peninsula Jewelry. The Cultural Plaza Moongate Stage is the centerpiece. Here they perform Chinese dances and plays, and herald in the Chinese New Year. If there is a presentation happening, attend. Out back, in a little parklike area, local men spend the afternoon chatting or playing dominoes, Go, or other board games.

Nearby and close to the river is an open market, a cooperative of open-air stalls selling just about everything that Chinatown has to offer at competitive prices. Follow your nose to the pungent odors of fresh fish at **O'ahu Market** on King St., where ocean delectables can be had for reasonable prices. Numerous other fish markets line the streets nearby.

At the corner of Hotel and Maunakea is the **Maunakea Marketplace,** a tight little jumble of shops with souvenirs, gifts, and an indoor food court, with mostly Asian vendors. One block away at Hotel and Kekaulike Streets is the **Kekaulike Market** with more of the same diversity, and here **Paradise Produce Co.** handles an incredible variety of fresh edibles. Many other shops sell ethnic foods and ingredients.

The **Wingon Co.,** 131 Hotel, has porcelain ware, but the feature is the big crocks of crackseed. If you want it the way it *was* made, this is it.

Several antique and collectible shops line the lower end of Nu'uanu Avenue, many of which carry estate sale items.

Pegge Hopper Gallery, 1164 Nu'uanu St., 808/524-1160, is open Mon.–Fri. 11 A.M.–5 P.M. and Saturday 11 A.M.–3 P.M. Ms. Hopper is one of the three most famous working artists in all of Hawaii. Her original works grace the walls of the most elegant hotels and homes in the islands. If you would like to purchase one of her bold and amazing serigraphs, this shop has the best and widest selection. While you're here, check out the **Sisu Gallery** and **The Studio of Roy Venter,** both of which are only a few step down the street.

Cindy's Lei & Flower Shoppe, on the corner of Hotel and Maunakea, has fresh lei at cheap prices. At Beretania and Smith St. is **Lita's Lei,** famous for good products and prices. Several others along Maunakea, like **Maunakea Street Florist, Lin's Lei Shop, Violet Lei Stand** and **Lina's Leis and Flowers** form a garland of flower shops.

Chinese Medicine

Ted J. Kaptchuk, O.M.D., in his excellent book *The Web That Has No Weaver*, says, "Actually, Chinese medicine is a coherent and independent system of thought that has been developed over two millennia." Chinese practitioners, unlike most of their Western counterparts, look at the entire individual, not just the acute symptom, and try to pinpoint what they refer to as "internal disharmony." Their diagnosis might be "dampness in the liver" or "fire in the kidney," for which they may prescribe a combination of acupuncture, herbs, dietary supplements and even exercise. The practitioners listed below are all licensed to practice Chinese medicine. A visit, where they will check your overall appearance and a number of "pulses," costs about $10. The herbs that they prescribe, usually dispensed from a wall of drawers labeled with Chinese characters, will probably cost under $10 depending upon the malady. While there are a multitude in Chinatown, at 112 N. King St. is **Fook Sau Tong,** a Chinese herb specialist. Look in the window to see coiled snake skin, a few dried-out snakes, some flat-looking lizards, and who-knows-what. If you need the bounce put back in your step, maybe some tonics or a few needles in the ear are just what the doctor will order.

FOOD

You can eat delicious ethnic food throughout Chinatown. If not Honolulu's best, the entire district, food-wise, is definitely Honolulu's cheapest. On almost every corner you've got places like **Mini Garden Noodle House** and **Ting Yin Chop Suey** for breakfast, lunch, and dinner. They're basic and cheap eateries whose ambience is a mixture of Formica-topped tables and linoleum floors. In almost all, the food is authentic, with most featuring Asian food. You can easily get meals here for around $5. Some eateries appear greasier than the Alaska Pipeline, so you'll have to feel them out. The local people eat in them regularly, and most are clean enough.

One place that you shouldn't miss is **Shung Chong Yuein,** a Chinese cake shop at 1027 Maunakea. Look in to see yellow sugar cakes, black sugar cakes, shredded coconut with eggs, salted mincemeat, Chinese ham with egg, lotus seeds, and steamed buns. For noodle dishes of all kinds try **Yat Tug Chow,** and for a crackseed snack head to **Wah Da Trading** or **Sigma Industries.**

Rosarina Pizza, 1111 Maunakea St., 808/533-6634, is an alternative to the Asian cuisine. They will sell you a slice of pizza for only $1.50, or a whole pie ranging from a small cheese for $8 to a large combo at $16. You can also order a 12-inch pastrami and provolone for $5, or an à la carte dinner like spaghetti with meat sauce or sausage, cannelloni, or manicotti, all for under $8.

Also try **Zaffron,** 69 N. King St., for Indian cuisine, open Tues.–Sat. 6–9:30 P.M. for tandoori, curry, and other usual selections.

A local bar with an easy-going atmosphere and a *pu pu* and pita-deli sandwich menu is **Hanks Cafe Honolulu,** 1038 Nu'uanu Ave., 808/526-1410. Open noon–2 A.M. weekdays, 5 P.M.–midnight on Saturday, and 4–10 P.M. on Sunday; there's a weekday happy hour 4–6 P.M. Monday is open-mike comedy night, while musicians hold forth the rest of the week. While you're there, have a look at the paintings on the walls—all Hank's.

At the Chinatown Cultural Plaza

As with the shops in the plaza, the restaurants also come and go. One to check is **Buddhist Vegetarian Restaurant,** 808/532-8218. The Buddhist Vegetarian Restaurant is basic and about as antiseptic as a monk's cell, but the food is healthy. The varied menu includes inexpensive dim sum dishes, stir-fry vegetables, spicy hot and sour soup, and many braised or fried vegetable or tofu dishes. Most are in the under-$10 category, but the Buddhist supreme vegetarian plate goes for $23.95. Lunch is served 10:30 A.M.–2 P.M., dinner 5:30–9 P.M.

Doong Kong Lau Seafood Restaurant offers Hakka cuisine and sizzlers. It's on the river side of the Cultural Plaza, 808/531-8833. Inside it's utilitarian with leatherette seats and Formica tables. You come here for these foods. Savories include stir-fried squid with broccoli, stir-fried scallops with garlic sauce, stir-fried oysters with black beans, sizzle plates like seafood combo, or shark fin with shredded chicken, all for reasonable prices. The menu reads, "The chief recommends deep fried shrimp with toast." Who's to argue with the chief! Open 9 A.M.–9 P.M.

At another stall in this complex is the **Royal Kitchen,** 808/524-4461, a very popular place with local families and businesspeople. It's especially known for its take-out baked *manapua,* soft dough buns stuffed with pork, charsiu, or vegetables, and for its Chinese sausage, *lupcheung,* charsiu, roast pork, and roast duck. Open very early in the morning.

Chinatown's Vietnamese Restaurants

A recent phenomenon is a number of excellent Vietnamese restaurants that have sprung up like bamboo sprouts along Chinatown's streets. The majority are meticulously clean, and the moderately priced food is "family-pride-gourmet." The decor ranges from oilcloth tablecloths topped by a "bouquet" of plastic flowers and a lazy Susan filled with exotic spices and condiments, to "down-to-earth chic" with some mood lighting, candles, and even linen place settings. As a group, they represent the best culinary deals on O'ahu today. Many selections, like the grilled seasoned meatballs or marinated pork, come with noodles, fresh lettuce, mint, cucumber, bean sprouts, and ground peanut sauce that you wrap in layers of rice paper to make your own version of what can best be described as an "oriental taco." Simply moisten a few sheets of the rice paper in the bowl of water provided and wrap away. Great fun, and they'll show you how! There are plenty of savory vegetarian menu choices as well.

Maxime Vietnamese Restaurant, 1134 Maunakea St., 808/545-4188, open daily 9 A.M.–9 P.M., except Wednesday when they close at 4 P.M., is as authentic as its name is contrived. To get an idea, ask to use the bathroom. You'll pass through the cramped but meticulously clean kitchen filled with boiling pots that are tended by about three generations of the family. In the dining room, it's just Formica tables and red Naugahyde chairs, but the people couldn't be more friendly. Try Maxime's special noodles with pork, shrimp, crab, bean sprouts, lettuce, and pork soup on the side for only $6.50, or an order of shrimp rolls—light aromatic rolls with shrimp, pork, and garden vegetables and rice noodles rolled up in rice paper served with sauce for $4.50. The selections of *pho* soup, which can be beef or chicken *(pho ga),* come with rice noodles, onions, Chinese parsley, basil, bean sprouts, and wine. Beverages include lemonade, iced coffee with condensed milk, jasmine tea, fresh coconut juice, sweet and sour lemon juice, and soybean milk. Top off your meal with desserts like caramel custard or sweet beans with coconut milk for under $3.

A Little Bit of Saigon, 1160 Maunakea, 808/528-3663, open daily 10 A.M.–10 P.M., is the fanciest of the lot, although it is still quite basic. Specialties are "roll ups" that include savory beef, pork, or chicken, served with lettuce, fresh herbs, vegetables, sweet and sour fish sauce, and peanut or pineapple and anchovy sauce along with thin rice paper that you use to roll your own for $5.50–11.95. Good yet inexpensive selections are stir-fried vegetables that you can have either by themselves or with fresh fish, prawns, chicken, beef, tofu, or scallops. For the hearty appetite try the five-course dinner for two at $29.95 that gives a good sample of the menu. Finish with banana and tapioca dessert, $2.50.

To Chau Vietnamese Restaurant, 1007 River, 808/533-4549, and **Ha Bien,** 198 N. King St., serve basic Vietnamese fare for under $8 for most dishes. They're around the corner from the action of Hotel Street and are family-oriented.

HAWAII STATE ARCHIVES

WAIKIKI

Waikiki (Spouting Water) is like a fresh young starlet from the sticks who went to Hollywood to make it big, and did, though maybe too fast for her own good. Everyone always knew that she had a double-dip of talent and heart, but the fast lane has its heartaches, and she's been banged around a little by life. Even though her figure's fuller, her makeup's a little askew, and her high heels are worn down, she has plenty of chutzpah left, and when the curtain parts and the lights come up, she'll play her heart out for her audience.

Waikiki is a classic study of contradictions. Above all, it is an example of basic American entrepreneurialism taken to the nth degree. Along the main strip, high-powered business-people cut multimillion-dollar deals, but on the sidewalks it's a carnival midway with hucksters, handbillers, and street people selling everything decent and indecent under the tropical sun. To get a true feeling for Waikiki, you must put this amazing strip of land into perspective. The area covers only seven-tenths of a square mile, which at a good pace, you can walk the length of in 15 minutes. On any given day, about 110,000 people crowd its beaches and boulevards, making it one of the most densely populated areas on earth. Sixty thousand of these people are tourists; 30,000 are workers who commute from various towns of O'ahu and cater to the tourists, and the remaining 20,000 actually call Waikiki home. The turnover is about 80,000 new tourists per week, and the pace rarely slackens. To the head shakers, these facts condemn Waikiki as a mega-growth area gone wild. To others, these same figures make Waikiki an energized, fun-filled place to be, where "if you don't have a good time, it's your own fault."

For the naive or the out-of-touch looking for "grass-shack paradise," the closest they'll come to it in Waikiki is painted on a souvenir ashtray. Those drawn to a smorgasbord of activities, who are adept at choosing the best and ignoring the rest, can't go wrong! People and the action are as constant in Waikiki as the ever-rolling surf.

History

The written record of this swampy area began in the late 1790s. The white man, along with his historians, cartographers, artists, and gunpowder,

O'AHU

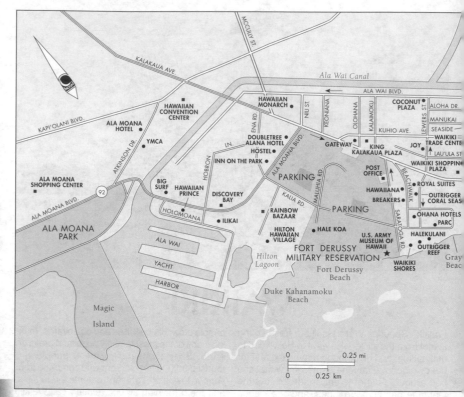

O'AHU

was already an undeniable presence in the islands. Kalanikupule, ranking chief of O'ahu, hijacked the *Jackall,* a small ship commanded by Captain Brown, with which he intended to spearhead an attack against Kamehameha I. The chief held the *Jackall* for a while, but the sailors regained control just off Diamond Head and sent the Hawaiians swimming for land. The ship then hastened to Kamehameha to report the treachery, and returned with his armada of double-hulled canoes, which beached along Waikiki. The great king then defeated Kalanikupule at the famous battle of Nu'uanu Pali and secured control of the island. Thereafter Waikiki, pinpointed by Diamond Head, became a well-known landmark.

Waikiki's interior was low-lying swampland, long known to be good for fishponds, taro, rice, and bananas, but hardly for living. The beach, however, was always blessed with sunshine and perfect waves, especially for surfing, a sport heartily loved by the Hawaiians. The royalty of Hawaii, following Kamehameha, made Honolulu their capital and kept beach houses at Waikiki. They invited many visiting luminaries to visit them at their private beach. All were impressed. In the 1880s, King Kalakaua was famous for his beach house hospitality. One of his favorite guests was Robert Louis Stevenson, who spent many months here writing one of his novels. By the turn of the 20th century, Waikiki, which had been little more than a handful of grass shack cottages, had become a highly exclusive vacation spot.

In 1901 the Moana Hotel was built, but immediately a protest was heard because it interfered with the view of Diamond Head. In 1906, Lucius Pinkham, then director of Hawaii's Board of Health, called the mosquito-infested area "dangerous and unsanitary," and pro-

WAIKIKI

ALA WAI
GOLF COURSE

ILIMA   ALOHA SURF   *Ala Wai Canal*

SAND VILLAS

NOHONANI
NAHUA
WALINA
KANEKAPOLE

ALA WAI BLVD.

WAIKIKI SUNSET

PAOAKALANI AVE.
KAPAHULU AVE.

RAMADA
PRINCE EDWARD

WAIKIKI
BUSINESS PLAZA
KOA AVE.
KALAKAUA AVE.

ULUNIU AVE.
LILI'UOKALANI AVE.
KEALOHILANI AVE.
OHUA AVE.

KUHIO AVE.

WAIKIKI
BEACHSIDE
HOSTEL

LEMON

MARRIOTT

HOSTEL

QUEEN KAPIOLANI

HONOLULU
ZOO

MONSARRAT AVE.

PAKI AVE.

ROYAL HAWAIIAN
SHOPPING CENTER

ROYAL HAWAIIAN   *SEE DETAIL*

SHERATON
WAIKIKI

*Waikiki
Beach*

THE FENCE (ART)

WAIKIKI SHELL

*Kuhio
Beach*

KAPI'OLANI PARK
BANDSTAND

KAPI'OLANI
PARK

KALAKAUA AVE.

TENNIS COURTS

DIAMOND
HEAD TENNIS

*Queens
Beach*

WAIKIKI AQUARIUM

NATATORIUM

NEW OTANI

To Kahala

M a m a l a   B a y

W HOTEL   DIAMOND
HEAD BEACH

*Sans Souci
Beach*

DETAIL

To Diamond Head

NAHUA
HONOLULU
PRINCE

KANEKAPOLE
MIRAMAR

LILI'UOKALANI
AVE.

CORAL
REEF

KUHIO AVE.

WAIKIKI TOWN
CENTER

PACIFIC
MONARCH

ULUNIU AVE.

ROYAL
GROVE

ST. AUGUSTINE
CATHOLIC
CHURCH

BEACHCOMBER

KING'S
VILLAGE

HOSTEL

INT'L MARKET
PLACE

KOA AVE.

WAIKIKI HANA

HYATT
REGENCY

WAIKIKI BEACH
TOWER

MOANA
SURFRIDER
OUTRIGGER
WAIKIKI

WAIKIKI
BEACHSIDE

PACIFIC
BEACH

PRINCESS
KAIULANI

CIRCLE

KUHIO BEACH PARK

NOT ALL HOTELS ARE SHOWN

posed to drain the swamp with a canal so that "the whole place can be transformed into a place of unique beauty." By the early 1920s, the Ala Wai Canal was built, its dredgings used to reclaim land, and Waikiki was demarcated. By the end of the 1920s, the Royal Hawaiian Hotel, built on the site previously occupied by the royal beach house, was receiving very wealthy guests who arrived by ocean liner, loaded down with steamer trunks. They ensconced themselves at Waikiki, often staying for the duration of the season.

For about 40 years, Waikiki remained the enchanted domain of Hollywood stars, dignitaries, and millionaires. But for the brief and extraordinary days of World War II, which saw Waikiki barricaded and barbed-wired, GIs—regular guys from the Mainland—were given a taste of this "reserved paradise" while on R&R. They brought home tantalizing tales of wonderful Waikiki, whetting the appetites of middle America.

Beginning just before statehood and continuing through the '60s to the mid-'70s, hotels and condos popped up like fertilized weeds, and tourism exploded with the advent of the jumbo jet. Discounted package tours began to haul in droves of economy-class tourists. Businesses catering to the tastes of penny-pinchers and first-timers elbowed their way into every nook and cranny. For the first time Waikiki began to be described as tacky and vulgar. For the old-timers, Waikiki was in decline. The upscale and repeat visitors started to snub Waikiki, heading for hidden resorts on the Neighbor Islands. But Waikiki had spirit and soul, and never gave in. Its declining hotels started a campaign to regain their illustrious images. Millions upon millions of dollars have been poured into renovations and remodeling. Luxury hotels renting exclusive and expensive rooms have reappeared and are doing a booming business. To give you some perspective, Waikiki has roughly 120 hotels with 33,000 guest rooms, 200 condominiums, 300 bars and lounges, and 250 restaurants, not to mention the hundreds of shops and entertainment spots.

Waikiki Today

The Neighbor Islands are pulling more and more tourists away, and depending on your point of view, this is either a boon or a bust for Waikiki. Direct flights to Maui, the Big Island, and Kaua'i allow more tourists than ever to bypass O'ahu, but still a whopping 80 percent of the people visiting the islands spend at least one night in Waikiki hotels, which offer, on average, the lowest room rates in Hawaii. The sublime and the gaudy are neighbors in Waikiki. Exclusive shops are often flanked by buskers selling plastic hula dolls. Burgers and beer mingle their pedestrian odors with those of Parisian cuisine. Though Waikiki in many ways is unique, it can also come off as "Anytown, U.S.A." But most importantly it somehow works, and works well. You may not find "paradise" on Waikiki's streets, but you will find a willing "dancing partner," and if you pay the fiddler, she'll keep the beat.

Non-Americans, especially Japanese, still flock for dream vacations, mostly staying at Waikiki hotels, many of which are owned by Japanese firms. Mainlanders and locals alike are disgruntled when they see the extent to which Waikiki has become a Japanese town. The visiting Japanese have been soundly warned by the tour operators before they arrive to never talk to strangers, especially someone on the street. Unfortunately for them, this means a vacation in which they never really leave their Japanese cocoon. They're herded into Japanese-owned shops and restaurants where prices are inflated, and from which the tour operators get kickbacks. Local shopkeepers, not on the list, are aggravated. They say that the once-timid Japanese visitors will now show irritation if the shopkeeper doesn't speak Japanese, and will indignantly head for the door if there is no one provided to deal with them in their native tongue. Also, these visitors have been taught to bargain with American shopkeepers, who they are told inflate prices. This makes for some rugged interaction when the price is already fair but the Japanese visitors won't believe it. While on average the Japanese tourist spends $340 per day, as opposed to a Mainlander who spends $130 per day, the Japanese really don't spread their money around as much as you would think. The money spent in Japanese shops primarily goes back to Japan. It's an incestuous system that operates in Waikiki.

Getting Around

By far and away the best way to get around Waikiki is on foot. For one, it's easily walked from one end to the other in less than 20 minutes, and walking saves you hassling with park-

overview of Waikiki from Diamond Head

ing and traffic jams. Also, TheBus and taxis are abundant. Those who have opted for a rental car should note that many of the agencies operate Waikiki lots, which for some can be more convenient than dropping your car at the airport on the day of departure. Check to see if this suits you. The following information is specific to Waikiki, and offers some limited alternatives.

In mid-1987, **pedicabs**, for all intents and purposes, were outlawed in Waikiki. There used to be 150–160 pedicabs that offered short taxi rides. They took people shopping, sightseeing, and between hotels, but basically they were a joyride. Mainstream businesspeople considered them a nuisance, and there were rumors that some drivers dealt drugs, so they were finally outlawed. Now only a handful of legal pedicabs operate in and around Waikiki. They're not allowed to go along Kalakaua Avenue, pick up or drop off at hotels, or use any of the main drags. They stay on the back streets or in the park, where they are constantly watched by the police. Charges are a hefty $3 per minute. The main customers are Japanese tourists who marvel at being peddled around town by a muscular *gaijin* (foreigner) in a rickshaw-type conveyance never seen in their own homeland any longer.

The **Waikiki Trolley,** 808/593-2822, offers tours throughout Waikiki and downtown Honolulu on five different routes, all starting at or running past the Royal Hawaiian Shopping Center. Day and multiday passes let you get on and off as much as you like. The trolley is really an open-air bus, but it's well done and plenty of fun. Pick up a route map at an activities desk or from a hotel concierge, or call the number above for times and stops.

Waikiki does an excellent job of conveying traffic, both auto and pedestrian, along Kalakaua Avenue, the main drag fronting Waikiki Beach. The city has installed very clear yet unattractive combinations of stoplights and street names. These are metal L-shaped beams, painted a dull brown, that straddle the roadways, clearly pinpointing your location. Unfortunately, they match the area about as well as work boots match a hula dancer. To give the feeling of an outdoor strolling mall, sidewalks along Kalakaua have been widened and surfaced with red brick, and the section right along the sand has been updated with stone walkways, old-fashioned

lamp posts, and water fountains. If you're driving, pay attention to one-way street signs. Kalakaua Avenue, for example, is one-way going south, Ala Wai Boulevard runs north, and Kuhio Avenue runs both ways—for most of its length. Many of the short cross streets also have one-way traffic only. What appears to be inconvenient at first actually helps the traffic flow and reduces congestion.

The **Kapi'olani Park Kiosk** is on the corner of Kapahulu and Kalakaua Avenues. The kiosk uses vintage photos to give a concise history of Kapi'olani Park. An overview map shows all the features of the park. Information is available here concerning events at the aquarium, zoo, Waikiki Shell, the Art Mart (a collection of island artists selling their creations along the Zoo), and the Kapi'olani Bandstand, where you're treated to free concerts by top-name bands and orchestras.

Public parking in Waikiki can be a hassle, although there are plenty of parking garages, most attached to hotels and shopping centers. A good place to park not far from the beach is the strip running parallel to Kapi'olani Park at one end and along Saratoga Street at the other. There are plenty of two-hour parking meters available, especially if you arrive before 9 A.M. Also, inexpensive (for Waikiki) parking is available at the ramp adjacent to the Waikiki Theatre along Seaside Road, but only after 5:30 P.M. Parking at the Fort DeRussy parking lot runs $2.50 for the first hour, $1.50 for additional hours, and $24 for a maximum of 24 hours. Parking at hotel or private parking lots can be very expensive. Hotels usually charge $8–10 for their daily rate; some have valet parking while at others you self-park. Parking lot fees often run $8–12 overnight.

Visitor Information

Numerous activities booths are strewn throughout the Waikiki area, most touting one or a number of particular attractions. They're set up to sell, so expect their pitch.

Your best source of general information for Waikiki, Honolulu, and the entire inland is the **HVB Visitor Information Service** office, which is on the fourth floor of the Royal Hawaiian Shopping Center, A401, 808/924-0266. Office hours are Mon.–Fri. 8 A.M.–4:30 P.M., closed weekends and holidays.

SIGHTS

To see Waikiki's attractions, you have to do little more than perch on a bench or loll on a beach towel. Its boulevards and beaches are world-class for people-watching. Some of its strollers and sunbathers are *visions,* while others are real *sights.* And if you keep your ears open, it's not hard to hear every American accent and a dozen foreign languages. Some actual sights are intermingled with the hotels, boutiques, bars, and restaurants. Sometimes, too, these very buildings are the sights. Unbelievably, you can even find plenty of quiet spots—in the gardens of Kapi'olani Park, and at churches, temples, tea-rooms, and ancient Hawaiian special places sitting unnoticed amidst the grandiose structures of the 20th century. Also, both the Honolulu Zoo and Waikiki Aquarium are well worth a visit.

DIAMOND HEAD

If you're not sandwiched in a manmade canyon of skyscrapers, you can look eastward from any-where in Waikiki and see Diamond Head. Dia-mond Head *says* Waikiki. Western sailors have used it as a landmark since the earliest days of contact, and the Hawaiians undoubtedly before that. Ships' artists etched and sketched its motif long before the names of the newfound lands of Hawaii, Waikiki, and O'ahu were standard-ized and appeared on charts as Owyhee, Whytete, and Woohoo. The Hawaiian name was Le'ahi (Brow of the Ahi); legend says it was named by Hi'iaka, Madame Pele's younger sis-ter, because she saw a resemblance in its sil-houette to the yellowfin tuna. The name "Dia-mond Head" comes from a band of wild-eyed English sailors who found calcite crystals on its slopes and thought they'd discovered diamonds. Hawaii had fulfilled so many other dreams, why not a mountain of diamonds? Kamehameha I immediately made the mountain *kapu* until his advisor, John Young, informed him that what the seamen had found, later known as "Pele's tears," were worthless, except as souvenirs. No fortune was made, but the name stuck. Diamond Head was considered a power spot by the

Hawaiians. Previously, Kamehameha had wor-shipped at a *heiau* on the western slopes, of-fering human sacrifice to his bloodthirsty war-god, Ku.

Geologically, the 761-foot monolith is about 350,000 years old, formed in one enormous ex-plosion when seawater came into contact with lava bubbling out of a fissure. No new volcanic activity has been suspected in the last 200,000 years. The huge rock is now Hawaii's state mon-ument and a national natural landmark. Its crater serves as a Hawaii National Guard depot; vari-ous hiking trails to the summit bypass installa-tions left over from World War II. The southeast *(makai)* face has some of the most exclusive and expensive real estate in the islands. The Kahala Mandarin Oriental Hotel is regarded by many to be one of the premier hotels in the world, and nearby is the super-snobbish Waialae Coun-try Club. Many private estates—homes of multi-millionaires, Hollywood stars, and high-powered multinational executives—cling to the cliffside, fronting ribbons of beach open to the public by narrow rights-of-way that oftentimes are hemmed in by the walls of the estates.

The Hike

The most recognized symbol of Hawaii, Dia-mond Head is the first place you should head for a strikingly beautiful panorama of Waikiki and greater Honolulu. Getting there takes only 15 minutes from Waikiki, either by TheBus no. 58 or by car following Kalakaua Avenue south from Waikiki and turning onto Monsarrat Avenue just beyond the Honolulu Zoo. Monsarrat turns into Diamond Head Road, then quickly a sign points you to Diamond Head Crater. Pass through a tunnel and into the militarized section in the cen-ter of the crater; the trail starts at the end of the parking lot. Although the hike is moderate, you should bring along water, a flashlight (a must), and binoculars if you have them. Run by the Di-vision of State Parks, the park is open daily 6 A.M.–6 P.M., and the entrance fee for hikers is $1 per person or $5 if you drive in. The trail is seven-tenths of a mile long and was built to the summit of Le'ahi Point in 1908 to serve as a

U.S. Coast Artillery Observation Station. It was heavily fortified during World War II, and part of the fun is exploring the old gun emplacements and tunnels built to link and service them.

Wildflowers and chirping birds create a peaceful setting. When you come to a series of cement and stone steps, walk to a flat area to the left to find an old winch that hauled the heavy building materials to the top. Here's a wide panorama of the sea and Koko Head to the east, and notice too that atop every little hillock is an old gun emplacement. Next comes a short but dark tunnel (flashlight!) and immediately a series of 99 steps. You can avoid the steps by taking the trail to the left, but the footing is slippery and there are no guard rails. Following the steps is a spiral staircase that leads down into a large gun emplacement, through which you walk and come to another tunnel. If you haven't brought a flashlight, give your eyes a few minutes to adjust and follow someone who has brought one. Once on top, another stairway and ladder take you to the very summit.

HONOLULU ZOO

The trumpeting of elephants and chatter of monkeys emanates from the jungle at the 42-acre Honolulu Zoo, 151 Kapahulu Ave., 808/971-7171, website: www.honoluluzoo.org, open daily except Christmas and New Year's Day, 9 A.M.–4:30 P.M., with special evening concerts featuring local artists every Wednesday 6–7 P.M. June–August. For the free evening show, the gates reopen at 4:35 P.M. and there is no admission. For the Sunday Music Series, there is free admission after 3:30 P.M. and the concert starts at 4:30 P.M. General admission is $6 for 13 years and older, $4 for locals, children 6–12 with an adult $1, and children under five free; the Honolulu Zoo family pass is $25. Other special programs include a tour with a zookeeper, a campout with breakfast and tour, and a moonlight stroll through the zoo.

The zoo holds the expected animals from around the world: monkeys, giraffes, lions, big cats, a hippo, even a sun bear (what else in Hawaii!). The Honolulu Zoo has the only large snake in Hawaii—a male Burmese python named Monty—housed in the Reptile House.

(Only the zoo can legally import snakes, geckos, iguanas, and similar reptiles.) Many islanders love this exhibit, because snakes in Hawaii are so exotic! Just as exotic is the new Komodo Dragon exhibit. From Indonesia, Komodo dragons are the world's largest lizards, often measuring three meters long. But the zoo is much more than just a collection of animals. It is an up-close escapade through the jungle of Hawaii, with plants, trees, flowers, and vines all named and described. Moreover, the zoo houses Hawaii's indigenous bird life, which is fast disappearing from the wild: Hawaiian gallinules, coots, hawks, owls, and the *nene,* the state bird, which is doing well in captivity, with breeding pairs being sent to other zoos around the world. The zoo is also famous for its Manchurian cranes, extremely rare birds from East Asia, and for successfully mating the Galapagos turtle. A **petting zoo** of barnyard animals, small reptiles, and amphibians is great for kids, and the tropical bird and African savanna sections are also sure to please. Before leaving, have a look at the Zootique shop where you can pick up T-shirts, postcards, posters, stuffed animals, books, and other gift items. The parking lot on the Kapahulu Ave. side costs a quarter an hour.

WAIKIKI AQUARIUM

The first Waikiki Aquarium (then called the Honolulu Aquarium) was built in 1904, its entranceway framed by a torii gate. Rebuilt and restocked in 1954, it was in the 1970s that it took on its current focus as an outreach and educational facility. The aquarium has recently undergone a facelift with a new entranceway, "touch tanks," and an opening directly to the sea. At 2777 Kalakaua Ave. in Kapi'olani Park, the aquarium, 808/923-9741, website: www.otted.hawaii.edu/aquarium, is open daily except Christmas Day, 9 A.M.–5 P.M., with entrance until 4:30 P.M. Admission is $7 adults, $5 seniors, students, *kama'aina,* and military, $3.50 youths 13–17, and free to children under 12. An audio wand tour in English and Japanese, included in the price of admission, explains the exhibits. Walk from points in Waikiki, take TheBus no. 2, or use the Waikiki Trolley red or blue line.

O'AHU

Although more than 400 species of Hawaiian and South Pacific fish, flora, and mammals live in its sparkling waters, the aquarium is much more than just a big fish tank. The floor plan contains four galleries of differing themes, all related to marine communities of the Pacific. One exhibit shows fish found in waters from Polynesia to Australia. Tanks hold sharks, turtles, eels, rays, clams, a seahorse, and colorful coral displays. Another exhibit, perhaps the most amazing of all, contains live coral that seem more like extraterrestrial flowers than specimens from our own seas. Some are long strands of spaghetti with bulbous ends like lima beans, others are mutated roses, or tortured camellias, all moving, floating, and waving their iridescent purples, golds, and greens in a watery bouquet. An Edge of the Reef exhibit shows how the low coastal waters and immediate shoreline relate to sustain the very busy reef environment.

Watch the antics of the monk seals, shameless hams, from the side of their 85,000 gallon tank, which now has a "variegated coastline" of natural nooks and crannies patterned after sections of O'ahu's coast. Hawaiian monk seals are one of only two species of tropical seals on earth. Endangered, only about 1,500 individuals still survive, and the "performances" are more of a detailed description of the seals' day-to-day life in their dwindling environment. The three seals inhabiting the tank are all males, since placing a breeding couple would almost certainly result in the birth of a pup. Marine biologists anguished over the decision. It was felt that seals raised in captivity and then released back into the natural environment might introduce a devastating disease to the native population. This was considered too great a danger to risk.

The aquarium contains a bookshop with a tremendous assortment of titles on sealife and the flora and fauna of Hawaii, plus great gifts and mementos. The University of Hawai'i, which has run the aquarium since 1919, offers seminars and field trips through the aquarium, everything from guided reef walks to minicourses in marine biology; information is available at the aquarium. The Waikiki Aquarium is a very special opportunity for fun and education that will be enjoyed by the entire family. Don't miss it!

U.S. ARMY MUSEUM OF HAWAII

This museum, with the hulks of tanks standing guard, is one long corridor where you feel the strength of the super-thick reinforced walls of this once-active gun emplacement. At Battery Randolph in Fort DeRussy, on the corner of Kalia and Saratoga Roads, the U.S. Army Museum of Hawaii, 808/438-2821, is open Tues.–Sun. 10 A.M.–4:30 P.M., except Christmas and New Year's Day, for self-guiding tours. Entrance is free, but an optional hour-long audiocassette can be rented for $3.50 that will guide you through the museum. Guided tours can be arranged for large groups by calling several weeks in advance. Battery Randolph once housed two 14-inch coast artillery rifles meant to defend Honolulu and Pearl Harbors. The architecture is typical of the Taft Period forts constructed between 1907 and 1920. The battery is listed in the National Register of Historic Places. As you enter there is a shop dedicated to "things military," flying jackets to wall posters. Walk the halls to learn the military history of Hawaii traced as far back as Kamehameha I. Here are rifles, swords, and vintage photos of Camp McKinley, an early-20th-century military station in the shadow of Diamond Head.

A side room holds models of artillery used to defend Waikiki from times when Battery Randolph was an active installation. One room shows how the guns worked in a method called "disappearing guns." The gun would raise up and fire. The recoil of the gun would swing it back down and lock in position. After it was reloaded a 50-ton counterweight would pop it up ready to fire. The explosive sound would rattle the entire neighborhood, so they were seldom test-fired.

Exhibits show the fledgling days of Army aviation in Hawaii, when on July 13, 1913, 14 officers began a military flying school. There are beautiful models of military equipment, especially one of an old truck unit. Then comes the ominous exhibit of "Rising Japan" with its headlong thrust into World War II. Hawaii, grossly overconfident, felt immune to attack because of the strong military presence. Photos from the 1930s and '40s depict the carefree lifestyle of visiting celebrities like Babe Ruth and Shirley

Temple, which ended abruptly on December 7, 1941, in the bombing of Pearl Harbor.

An entire room is dedicated to the Pearl Harbor attack and is filled with models of Japanese planes, aircraft carriers, and real helmets and goggles worn by the Zero pilots. Most interesting are the slice-of-life photos of Hawaii mobilized for war: defense workers, both men and women, sailors, soldiers, entertainers, and street scenes. Pamphlets from the time read, "Know Your Enemies," and there's a macabre photo of people gathered at a stadium to see a demonstration of the devastating effect of flame throwers that would be employed upon the Japanese enemy. Bob Hope is here entertaining the troops, while a 442nd Regimental Battle Flag bears testament to the most decorated unit in American history, comprised mostly of *nisei* Japanese from Hawaii. Then come photos and exhibits from the soul-wrenching conflicts in Korea and Vietnam.

A gallery on the upper level tells of the heroics of Hawaiian soldiers who have been awarded the Congressional Medal of Honor and Distinguished Service Cross for combat valor, almost all posthumously. Go outside to the upper level exhibit to see one of the old guns still pointing out to sea, which seems incongruous with sunbathers just below on the quiet and beautiful stretch of beach. On the upper deck are depth charges, torpedoes, and shells, along with a multimedia slide show. Your eyes will take a few minutes to refocus to the glorious sunshine of Waikiki after the cold gloom of the bunker. Perhaps our hearts and souls could refocus as well.

FREE SIGHTS AND CURIOSITIES

On the beach near the Sheraton Moana Surfrider Hotel are the **kahuna stones,** a lasting remnant of old Hawaii. The Hawaiians believed these stones were imbued with *mana* by four hermaphroditic priests from Tahiti: Kinohimahu, Kahaloamahu, Kapunlmahu, and Kapaemahu (*mahu* in Hawaiian signifies homosexuality). They came to visit this Polynesian outpost in ancient times and left these stones for the people, who have held them in reverence for more than 600 years. About 40 years ago, a group of local historians went looking for the stones but couldn't find them. Around that time, there was a bowling alley along the beach, and when it was finally torn down, it was discovered that the stones had been incorporated into the foundation. Today, the vast majority of visitors and islanders alike no longer revere the stones, often using them as a handy spot to scrape sand off their feet. *Kupuna* versed in the old ways say that the *mana,* once put in and strengthened by reverence, is now dissipating.

Even if you're not a guest at the following hotels, you should at least drop by their lobbies for a quick look. Dramatically different, they serve almost as a visual record of Waikiki's changing history. Those who have a fondness for the elegance of days gone by should take a tour of the **Sheraton Moana Surfrider** and steep in the history of the hotel, admiring its early 20th century artifacts and memorabilia. The Moana, Waikiki's oldest hotel, dating from 1901, is a permanent reminder of simpler times when its illustrious clientele would dance the night away at an open-air nightclub suspended over the sea. The Moana houses the Banyan Court, named for the enormous banyan tree just outside. From here, *Hawaii Calls* beamed Hawaiian music to the Mainland by shortwave for 40 years beginning in 1935. In its heyday, the show was carried by more than 700 stations. The hotel's architecture is a classic example of the now quaint "colonial style." Free one-hour tours are offered weekdays at 11 A.M. and 5 P.M. starting at the second floor lobby.

The **Royal Hawaiian Hotel,** built in 1927 on the site of the old royal beach house, once had fresh pineapple juice running in its fountains. Now surrounded by towering hotels, it's like a guppy in a sea of whales. However, it does stand out with its Spanish-Moorish style, painted in distinctive pink, and is surrounded by huge old tropical trees and huge coconut palms. In the old days, only celebrities and luminaries came to stay—who else could afford $3 per day? Although it's younger than the Moana, many consider it the grande dame of Hawaiian hotels. The entranceway is elegantly old-fashioned, with rounded archways, overstuffed couches, and lowboys. At the end of the main hallway, Diamond Head is framed in the arches.

Across the street from the Sheraton Moana are the giant, modernistic, twin towers of the

Hyatt Regency Waikiki. The lobby, like those of most Hyatts, is wonderful, with a huge waterfall and a jungle of plants, all stepped down the series of floors, making an effect like the Hanging Gardens of Babylon.

The **Pacific Beach Hotel,** farther down the street at 2490 Kalakaua Ave., is a first-rate hotel and a great place to stay in its own right. But if you don't, definitely visit the Oceanarium Restaurant just off the lobby, which has an immense three-floor-high aquarium dedicated to holding 280,000 gallons of sea water and scores of colorful tropical fish. The old mafia dons used to send their rivals to "sleep with the fishes"; here, you have an opportunity to dine with the fishes. Usually you go snorkeling to watch the fish eat, but in this particular instance the fish watch you eat.

As you walk along Kalakaua Avenue, directly across from the Kuhio Beach section is **St. Augustine Catholic Church.** This modernistic building squashed between high-rises is worth a quick look. The interior, serene with the diffused light of stained glass, looks like a series of A-frames. The **Damien Museum** is housed in a separate building to the rear, displaying photos and other artifacts of Father Damien, the Belgian priest who humanely cared for the lepers of Kalaupapa, Moloka'i, until his own death from complications of leprosy. The museum is open Mon.–Fri. 9 A.M.–3 P.M. and is free, although donations are gratefully accepted as they are the museum's only source of revenue.

The **Urusenke Teahouse,** 808/923-3059, is an authentic teahouse donated to Hawaii by the Urusenke Foundation of Kyoto. It is at 245 Saratoga Rd., which lies along the Waikiki side of Fort DeRussy. Every Wednesday and Friday 10 A.M.–noon, tea master Takashi Machita performs the ancient aesthetic art of *chanoyu* (tea ceremony). A minimum donation of $2 is asked of those who want to watch the ceremony and partake of the frothy *matcha,* a grass-green tea made from the delicate tips of 400-year-old bushes, and the accompanying sweets. Long pants are requested. To find delight and sanctuary in this centuries-old ritual among the clatter and noise of Waikiki offers a tiny glimpse into the often puzzling duality of the Japanese soul.

Delineating Waikiki from the rest of the city is the nearly two-mile-long **Ala Wai Canal.** Created in the '20s to drain the swamps that filled this flat oceanfront land, it now channels runoff from the mountains to the sea. The banks of the canal are used extensively by walkers, joggers, and runners, particularly shortly after sunrise and again before sunset; many come here to sit, relax, and watch the parade of paddlers practice for outrigger canoe races. It's cheap entertainment for one of Hawaii's favorite sports. Fishermen also make use of the canal, trying their luck near its mouth near the Ala Moana bridge.

Just across the canal from Waikiki proper is the new and impressive **Hawaii Convention Center.** Built to attract more convention business to the state, it's a combination of large and small meeting halls, exhibition rooms, and banquet facilities, with high-tech sound and light capabilities and instantaneous translation services. Appealing to the aesthetic side of anyone who takes the time to look inside are several waterfalls and pools, tall palm trees, numerous artworks, and a glass ceiling that brings the outside in.

WAIKIKI BEACHES AND PARKS

In the six miles of shoreline from Kahanamoku Beach fronting the Hilton Hawaiian Village at the west end of Waikiki to the section of Kahala Beach fronting the Kahala Mandarin Oriental Hotel, there are at least a dozen choice spots for enjoying swimming or surf activities. The central Waikiki beaches are so close to each other that you can hardly tell where one ends and another begins. They are basically just names for different sections of one long strand of sand. All are generally gentle, but as you head around Diamond the beaches get farther apart and have their own personalities. Sometimes they're rough customers, particularly during winter months. As always, never take *moana* for granted, especially during periods of high surf. There are at least six lifeguard stations in Waikiki, staffed daily year-round 9 A.M.–5:30 P.M. Now that you've finally arrived at a Waikiki beach, the one thing left to do is kick back and R-E-L-A-X.

Waikiki Beach stretches for two miles, broken into separate areas. A multitude of concession stands offer everything from shave ice to

Largest on the island, the Ala Wai Yacht Harbor anchors the west end of Waikiki Beach.

canoe rides. It's not news that this beach is crowded. Sometimes when looking at the rows of glistening bodies, it appears that if one person wants to tan his other side, everybody else has to roll over with him. Anyone looking for seclusion here is just being silly. Take heart—a big part of the fun is the other people.

Umbrella stands set up along Waikiki Beach fronting Kalakaua rent boogie boards, surf-boards, paddle boats, and snorkel gear. They're convenient, but their prices are much more than many shops offering the same. The guys by the big banyan tree are slightly cheaper than those set up by the breakwater just before Kapi'olani Park. However, all offer decent prices for surfing lessons and rides in outrigger canoes, which get you three waves and about 20 minutes of fun. Find other outrigger canoe rides—you help paddle—in front of the big hotels. Try the Outrigger Waikiki. They're great fun and a bargain at $7 per person.

Kahanamoku Beach

This stretch of sand fronting the lagoon at the Hilton Hawaiian Village is named after Hawaii's most famous waterman, Duke Kahanamoku. The manmade beach and lagoon were completed in 1956. A system of pumps pushes water into the lagoon to keep it fresh. The swimming is great, and a concession stand offers surfboards, beach equipment, and catamaran cruises.

Fort DeRussy Beach

You pass through the right-of-way of Fort DeRussy military area, where you'll find rest-rooms, picnic facilities, volleyball courts, and food and beverage concessions. Lifeguard service is provided by military personnel—no duty is too rough for our fighting men and women! A controversy raged for years between the military and developers who coveted this valuable piece of land. The government has owned it since the early 20th century, and has developed what once was wasteland into the last stretch of non-cement, non-high-rise piece of real estate left along Waikiki. And it's a beauty. Since the public has access to the beach and since Congress has voted that the lands cannot be sold, it'll remain under the jurisdiction of the military.

Gray's Beach

This section's name comes from Gray's-by-the-Sea, a small inn once located here. The narrow white-sand beach lies in front of the Halekulani Hotel, which replaced Gray's. Rights-of-way run on either side of the hotel, or get to the beach from around behind the military museum. The sea is generally mild here and the swimming is always good, with shallow waters and a sandy bottom. Offshore is a good break called Number Threes, a favorite with surfers.

The next section is referred to as **Royal Moana Beach**, because it lies between Waiki-ki's oldest manmade landmarks, the Royal Hawaiian and Moana Surfrider hotels. Access is unlimited off Kalakaua Avenue. The inshore waters here are also gentle and the bottom is sandy and generally free from coral. Offshore are three popular surfing areas: Paradise, Pop-ulars, and Canoes. Many novices have learned to surf here because of the predictability of the waves, but with so many rookies in the water

O'AHU

and beach activities going on all around, you have to remain alert for runaway boards and speeding outrigger canoes.

Prince Kuhio Beach and Beach Park
When people say "Waikiki Beach," this is the section to which they're usually referring. This county-maintained park fronts Kalakaua Avenue as far as Kapahulu Avenue. Here, you'll find surfing, canoeing, and generally safe year-round swimming along the gently sloping, sandy-bottomed shoreline. The Waikiki Beach Center is at the in-town end of this beach, where you'll find comfort stations, concession stands, and lifeguards. Be careful of the rough coral bottom at the Diamond Head end of Kuhio Beach. A long retaining wall called Slippery Wall fronts the beach, creating a semi-enclosed saltwater pool. Covered with a coating of slick seaweed, Slippery Wall definitely lives up to its name. Though local youngsters play on the wall, the footing is poor and many knees have been scraped and heads cracked after spills from this ill-advised play. The surf on the seaward side of the wall churns up the bottom and creates deep holes that come up unexpectedly, along with an occasional rip current. A statue of Duke Kahanamoku, Hawaii's most famous native son, stands in this park. Under the big banyan tree near here, a free presentation of torchlighting, hula, and music is presented on Saturday and Sunday evenings.

Kapi'olani Regional Park
In the shadow of Diamond Head is Kapi'olani Park, a quiet 140-acre oasis of greenery, just a coconut's roll away from the gray cement and flashing lights of central Waikiki. It has proved to be one of the best gifts ever received by the people of Honolulu. King Kalakaua donated this section of crown lands to them in 1877, requesting that it be named after his wife, Queen Kapi'olani. In times past, it was the site of horse and car races, polo matches, and Hawaii's unique *pa'u* riders, fashionable ladies in long flowing skirts riding horses decked out with lei. The park was even the site of Camp McKinley, the U.S. Army headquarters in the islands 1898–1907.

The park remains a wonderful place for people to relax and exercise away from the hustle of Waikiki. The park is a mecca for jogging and aerobics, with many groups and classes meeting here throughout the day. It also serves as the starting point for the yearly **Honolulu Marathon,** one of the most prestigious races in the world. Its **Waikiki Shell,** an open-air amphitheater, hosts many visiting musical groups, especially during Aloha Week. The Honolulu Symphony is a regular here, providing free concerts, especially on summer evenings. Nearby, the **Kapi'olani Bandstand** hosts the Royal Hawaiian Band on Sunday afternoons. Also, under the shade of the trees toward Waikiki Beach, plenty of street entertainers, including clowns, acrobats, and jug-

The waters of Waikiki Beach are gentle most any day of the year.

glers, congregate daily to work out their routines to the beat of conga drums and other improvised music supplied by wandering musicians. Families and large groups come here to picnic, barbecue, and play softball. The park grounds are also home to the free **Kodak Hula Show,** Waikiki Aquarium, Natatorium War Memorial, and Honolulu Zoo. Just in front of the zoo, by the big banyan, are hundreds and hundreds of pigeons, the "white phantoms of Waikiki." In the morning they are especially beautiful darting through the sunshine like white spirits.

Although Kapi'olani Beach Park is only a short stroll down the beach from Waikiki central, it gets much less use. This is where local families and those in the know come to get away from the crowds, just a few beach-blanket lengths away. In the park and along the beach are restrooms, volleyball courts, picnic tables, lifeguard towers, and a concession stand. At water's edge near the aquarium is the **Waikiki Natatorium,** a saltwater swimming pool built in 1927 as a World War I memorial. This pool was allowed to decay over the years until it was closed in 1980. The main gate and outer walls have recently been refurbished, and plans are in the works to do the same to the pool enclosure. Be careful of the rocky areas to the front of its stone enclosure. The section of the beach between Kuhio Beach Park and the Natatorium is called **Queens Beach.** The swimming is generally good here, with the best part at the Waikiki end, where it's at its widest and the bottom is gently sloping sand. Within this section, an area called The Wall has been designated as a special bodysurfing and boogie boarding area. Supposedly, board riders are restricted from this area, but if the surf is good they're guaranteed to break the rules. Experts can handle it, but novices, especially with runaway boards, are a hazard. Beyond the Natatorium is **Sans Souci Beach,** the quiet southern end. Many families with small children come to Sans Souci because it is so gentle.

The **Waikiki Marine Life Conservation District** occupies an area that stretches from the "groin" (a seawall at the end of Kapahulu Ave.) to the Natatorium, basically the Queens Beach area, and out 500 yards into the water. As it's a fish management area, fishing is not allowed, but other water sports can be enjoyed.

Around Diamond Head

Kaluahole Beach is on the Waikiki side of Diamond Head. The water conditions are safe all year-round, but the beach is small and lies along a seawall. Once a large beach, it was paved over for building purposes. It has one public right-of-way, poorly marked and sandwiched between private homes. It's almost at the end of Kalakaua Avenue. Park at Kapi'olani Park and walk. The surfing in this area is generally good, and the breaks are known as Tongg's, named after a local family that lived along this shore.

A short way farther are **Makalei Beach County Park,** with some picnic tables and shade trees, and **Le'ahi Beach County Park,** with less shade but lots of grass. Bus or walk—there is no parking.

Diamond Head Beach Park is an unlimited access area that covers almost two acres of undeveloped shoreline off Beach Road. Unfortunately, the beach is very narrow and surrounded by unfriendly rock and coral. The waters, however, are quite protected and generally safe, except in periods of high surf. This area is good for fishing and finding quiet moments. A Coast Guard lighthouse station is just above the park. Surfing breaks offshore are known as Diamond Head and Lighthouse.

Kuilei Cliffs Beach Park lies below Diamond Head Road, with access available from three lookout areas along the road. You must walk down the cliff trails to the beaches below. Here are plenty of secluded pockets of sand for sunbathing, but poor swimming. The surf is generally rough, and the area is always frequented by surfers. When the winds are right, windsurfers also come. Offshore is hazardous with submerged rocks, but this makes it excellent for diving and snorkeling—for experts only! Currents can be fierce, and you can be dashed against the rocks. Whales can sometimes be spotted passing this point, and to add to the mystique, the area is considered a breeding ground for sharks. Most visitors just peer down at the surfers from Diamond Head Road, or choose a spot of beach for peace and quiet. There are three parking areas along the road. At one of these is a memorial plaque dedicated to the famous American aviator Amelia Earhart. Lining these parking areas are "unofficial" gardens of grass and flowers, envisioned, planted,

O'AHU

and maintained by a couple of surfing oldsters who wanted to replace the hardpan dirt that flanked the top of the cliff with something more visually pleasing that would also cut down on the dust.

Farther east is a protrusion of land known as Black Point, the western end of ritzy residential Kahala. This section is the Beverly Hills of Honolulu, as many celebrities have homes here. The least expensive home in this section easily pushes $1 million asking price. On the Diamond Head side of Black Point is **Ka'alawai Beach.** The swimming is good here and generally safe because of a protecting reef. Many locals come to this area to fish, and it is good for bodysurfing and snorkeling. The waters outside the reef are excellent for surfing and produce some of the biggest waves on this side of the island. Access is by public right-of-way marked off Kulumanu Place, by small side roads that run off Kahala Avenue, or by walking along the shoreline from Kuilei Beach.

Kahala Beach parallels Kahala Avenue from Black Point to the Kahala Mandarin Oriental Hotel and can be reached by marked rights-of-way between the high fences of estates in the area. The swimming is not particularly good, but there are plenty of pockets of sand and protected areas where you can swim and snorkel. Local people come to fish, and the surfing is good beyond the reef. The Kahala Mandarin Oriental is at the eastern end of this beach. The swimming there is always safe and good because the hotel has dredged the area to make it deeper.

Where Kapakahi Stream enters the sea along Kahala Beach, the county has constructed **Waialae Beach County Park.** Waialae is a popular windsurfing and fishing spot, and it may be crowded on weekends. Split by the stream that's crossed by a footbridge, it's a small beach park with basic amenities in a beautiful location. Looking to the east, Koko Head gives the impression that there is an island off in the distance, but it's just the way O'ahu bends at this point.

ACCOMMODATIONS

Waikiki is loaded with places to stay: 120 properties holding 33,000 rooms jammed into one square mile. These come in all categories from deluxe to dingy, and there are many cross-over accommodations that have amenities and services typical to both hotels and condos. Your problem won't be finding a place to stay, but choosing from the enormous selection. During peak season (Christmas to Easter and again in summer) you'd better have reservations, or you could easily be left out in the *warm*. The good news is that, room for room, Waikiki is the cheapest place to stay in the state. Hotels along the beach tend to be slightly more expensive than their counterparts on a side street or back lane. The beachfront hotels have the surf at the doorstep, but those a block away have a little more peace and quiet. The following listings are not exhaustive. They couldn't be! Here are just some from all categories, which you can use as a barometer to measure what's available.

MILITARY PERSONNEL ONLY

Hale Koa, 808/955-0555 or 800/367-6027, fax 808/955-9670, website: www.halekoa.com, email: reservations@halekoa.com, is the Fort DeRussy Armed Forces Recreational Center. On the beach at Fort DeRussy, this hotel is solely operated for active-duty U.S. military personnel, Department of Defense civilians, and a few other categories of former military and defense-related personnel. But anyone can walk in and have a look around. This well-run and well-maintained hotel has all the dining facilities, entertainment options, activity programs, and amenities of other large hotels in Waikiki. Depending upon military rank or government status, there is a bewildering array of prices for the seven categories of rooms, all at rates well below the going rate for similar hotels in Waikiki—especially as it's right on the beach, and a wonderful section at that. Call for specifics.

UNDER $50

Hale Aloha Youth Hostel, the only member of Hostelling International–American Youth Hostel Association in Waikiki, is at 2417 Prince Edward St., Honolulu, HI 96815, 808/926-8313, fax 808/922-3798, two streets behind the Hyatt Regency. A dorm room bunk is $17 for members and $20 for those who are not International Youth Hostel Association members. Dorm rooms are not sexually integrated, and you must be at least age 18 to stay unaccompanied by an adult. Couples can rent a studio for $42 members and $48 nonmembers. It's recommended that reservations be made at least two weeks in advance, particularly during peak season. Credit cards can be used for reservations; the business office is open 7 A.M.–3 A.M. Open 24 hours. There is no curfew, but there is a seven-day maximum stay. Baggage may be stored for $5 for the day after checkout if you have a late flight. Key deposits will not be refunded if keys are not returned by 11 A.M., checkout time. Visitors are not allowed at any time, and neither alcohol nor smoking is permitted. Lockers—small, gym locker-types not big enough for a backpack but adequate for valuables—are available, but you must provide your own lock. The hostel gets visitors from around the world. It's clean and safe. The common area, kitchen, and bathrooms are shared by all.

The **Waikiki Beachside Hotel and Hostel** is at 2556 Lemon Rd., Honolulu, HI 96815, 808/923-9566, fax 808/923-7525, website: www.HoKondo.com, email: HoKondo@aol.com. Rates start at $16.50 per person for a bunk bed in the dorm and increase to $35 for a semiprivate room. A one-bedroom apartment with kitchen that sleeps four goes for $55 a night (up to $75 during the winter and summer months). All rooms have full baths and kitchens with refrigerator, a/c, and TV. On property there's a lounge, pool table, laundry facilities, and some parking. A clean, well-furnished, well-kept place—this is a good choice.

Just down the road is the **Polynesian Hostel Beach Club,** 2584 Lemon Rd., Honolulu, HI 96815, 808/922-1340 or 877/504-2924, fax 808/923-4146, website: http://hostelhawaii.com, email: polynesian@hostelhawaii.com. Only one block from the beach, the Polynesian is in a converted condo-apartment building. A space in a shared room with shared bath runs $17, single/double rooms with in-room baths are $33–46, and a private studio with kitchen goes for $55–77. The hostel has a common room for reading and TV watching, free movies, a communal kitchen, storage lockers for valuables, laundry facilities, free use of some water equipment, and some hostel-sponsored activities. Internet connection is available. When arriving, there is an airport shuttle; for adventure, inexpensive van excursions depart throughout the week to points around the island. Somewhat rough around the edges, this conveniently located hostel is a good place to meet people from other countries. The management here also runs the Northshore Inn in Wailiku on Maui.

The **Banana Bungalow Waikiki Beach,** 2463 Kuhio Ave., Honolulu, HI 96815, 808/924-5074, 888/246-7835, fax 808/924-4119, website: www.bananabungalow.com, email: hires@bananabungalow.com, is in a 12-story tower near the corner of Uluniu Avenue. With so much room, this place can hold over 300 guests at one time. Co-ed dorms run $20 a night and private rooms are $70. To stay you must have an I.D. and an air ticket out of Hawaii. Also, reservations are a must and will be secured by a valid credit card. All rooms have private baths, TV, and phones, and linens are supplied. Private rooms have safes, but for others there are only small safe deposit boxes for valuables at the front desk. A free continental breakfast is available for all guests each morning 8–10:30 A.M., and a kitchen is available. The hostel has a common area and game room with ping pong and pool tables, washers and dryers for laundry, about a dozen computers set up for Internet access, and organized in-house activities and daily tours of the island. When staying here, you don't have to go far to eat or drink. On property are a bar and a Mexican restaurant. Phone cards are sold, and boogie boards, snorkel gear, and other water equipment are rented at a very reasonable fee. When arriving or departing, use the free airport shuttle.

In the same complex at 2463 Kuhio Ave. is **InterClub Waikiki,** 808/924-2636 or 800/324-3798, fax 808/922-3993, website: www.interclubwaikiki.com, email: interclubwaikiki@aol.com. Co-ed and women's shared rooms run $18 per night, with four persons maximum per room, and private rooms are $55 and up. All rooms have a full bath and come with refrigerator, a/c, and television. The hostel provides a common area, laundry facilities, a barbecue grill, and inexpensive Internet access.

On the other end of Waikiki at 1946 Ala Moana Blvd., inside the Hawaiian Colony Building across from Fort DeRussy, is **Island Hostel**, tel./fax 808/942-8748. Each hostel room has a bathroom, small refrigerator, a/c, and linens. Bunks run $16.50 per person, and private rooms cost $40-50 a night. A communal kitchen is in the office, and the lounge is open for community activities. Laundry facilities, lockers, and telephones are available, and there is some water equipment to borrow.

For additional listings of inexpensive YM/WCAs and AYH hostels in other areas of the city, see the **Accommodations** section in the Honolulu chapter.

$50-100

When the hostels are full try the **Waikiki Prince Hotel** just next door to Hale Aloha YH, at 2431 Prince Edward St., Honolulu, HI 96815, 808/922-1544, fax 808/924-3712. This little hotel is about the cheapest in Waikiki at $40-55 per night during low season—April-November. Weekly rates get you a seventh night free. While the rooms are quite small, everything is as neat as a pin. All rooms have air-conditioning and cable television, and there's a coin laundry and limited parking on premises. At a very reasonable price, this is a good quiet alternative to the noisier and busier hostels in the area.

The **Royal Grove Hotel**, 151 Uluniu Ave., Honolulu, HI 96815, 808/923-7691, fax 808/922-7508, website: www.royalgrovehotel.com, email: rghawaii@gte.net, built in 1951 and run by the Fong family since 1970, gives you a lot for your money. You can't miss its "paint-sale pink" exterior, but inside it's much more tasteful. Rooms in the older and cheaper wing run $42.50-75 for two, $10 for an extra person; the newer upgraded wing with a/c is $57-75. Most are studios and one-bedroom apartments with full facilities. A tiny pool in the central courtyard offers some peace and quiet away from the street. The Royal Grove passes the basic tests of friendliness and

cleanliness. It's used but not abused. During low season, April-November 30, it offers reduced weekly and monthly rates.

At the far west end of Waikiki, across Ala Moana Blvd. from the Ala Wai Yacht Harbor is the **Big Surf Hotel**. An older high-rise, this hotel maintains small but clean rooms at a very affordable price. Rooms, with twin or double beds and each with its own small lanai, are studios and one- or two-bedroom suites with kitchens that range $30-75 low season to $35-102 during high season. Each unit has a/c, ceiling fans, and daily maid service. For reservations, write Big Surf Hotel at 1690 Ala Moana Blvd., Honolulu, HI 96815, or call 808/946-6525, fax 808/949-1142.

The **Waikiki Hana Hotel,** 2424 Koa Ave., Honolulu, HI 96815, 808/926-8841 or 800/367-5004, sits just behind the massive Hyatt Regency on a quiet side street. The hotel has just 73 rooms, so you won't get lost in the shuffle, and the friendly staff go out of their way to make you feel welcome. The Waikiki Hana is surrounded by high-rise hotels, so there's no view, but the peace and quiet just one block from the heavy action more than makes up for it. Rooms start at a very reasonable $81 and go to $121 for a deluxe with kitchenette. All rooms have telephones, a/c, color TV, and in-room safes, and are gaily appointed with bright bedspreads and drapes. The Super Chef Gourmet Restaurant, on the ground floor of the hotel, is one of the best in Waikiki for atmosphere, food, and very reasonable prices. On-site parking is another good feature in crowded Waikiki, but the charge is $10 a day. For a quiet, decent but basic hotel in the heart of Waikiki, the Waikiki Hana can't be beat. A Castle Resorts property.

The minute you walk into the **Aston Coconut Plaza Hotel,** 450 Lewers St., 808/923-8828 or 800/922-7866, fax 808/923-3473, with plantation decor in its lobby, you feel at home and comfortable. With the Ala Wai canal to its side, the hotel is not in the midst of the action, but it's only a few blocks to dining and entertainment. Rates are $80-105 for hotel rooms and up to $175 for suites; off-season is cheaper, with special day rates for bona fide business travelers on a space-available basis. All rooms are fully air-conditioned, and the suites have kitchenettes. There is a small pool off the lobby, where a complimentary continental breakfast is offered daily.

$100–150

Ohana Hotels is a branch of the Outrigger Hotels and Resorts family of accommodations. Ohana has 15 properties in Waikiki offering nearly 5,000 rooms. Some are near the beach, while others lie on quiet back streets. All fall into the moderate category. Although not luxurious, they do offer good accommodations, and all have full baths, air conditioning, TV, and entertainment centers. Rooms are basic, simple, and clean, and a number of the properties have recently been renovated. Several of the Ohana Hotels, like their more ritzy sisters, the Outrigger Hotels, have restaurants, lounges with entertainment, shops, and swimming pools on property, and similar services. Rates vary from hotel to hotel but five start with rooms at $109, an additional seven from $129, and three have rooms from $139. The majority of rooms are no more expensive than $169, but a handful of suites and studios, many with kitchenettes, go up to $199 or $209. Additional adults in a room are $20 per night. The best of the bunch are the **Ohana Reef Lanai, Ohana Waikiki Tower,** and **Ohana Waikiki Village,** all only steps away from the beach. Also in the palpitating heart of Waikiki are the old standbys **Ohana Edgewater** and **Ohana Coral Seas.** Most of the remainder are a few blocks back from the water. To help save money on these reasonably priced rooms, Ohana offers a $99 SimpleSaver rate, plus room and car, room and breakfast, and multiple-day package reductions. For information and reservations, contact Ohana Hotels at 303/369-7777 or 800/462-6262, fax 800/622-4852, website: www.ohanahotels.com, email: reservations @ohanahotels.com.

The Breakers, 250 Beachwalk, Honolulu, HI 96815, 808/923-3181 or 800/426-0494, fax 808/923-7174, website: www.breakers-hawaii.com, email: breakers@aloha.net, is a very friendly family-style two-story hotel, where if you're a repeat visitor, the staff remembers your name, and with only 65 units, they get plenty of repeat guests. Only minutes from the beach, this little gem of a hotel somehow keeps the hustle and bustle far away. Certainly, this is what staying at Waikiki was like before the high-rises blocked the sight of the beach from street level. While The Breakers is a cinderblock affair, it's been tastefully decorated and is eminently well kept. Every room has a complete kitchenette and overlooks the shaded courtyard of coconut and banana trees. In the garden is an ample swimming pool, and off to the side you can relax with a snack or light meal and tropical drink at the Cafe Terrace pool bar and lounge. The rates for studios are $91–98 single and $94–100 double; garden suites run $125–151. For additional persons in any room, there is an additional $10 per person fee. Studios hold up to three, suites five. All units have a/c, color TV, and a safe. There's limited parking. The Breakers claims to be "Waikiki's most distinctive resort hotel" and it's right. It's a winner.

Next door at 260 Beachwalk is the **Hawaiiana Hotel,** 808/923-3811 or 800/367-5122, fax 808/926-5728, another low-rise hotel with a distinctly local flavor. The Hawaiiana is a bit more boxy than the Breakers but is painted in pleasing whites and light blues. Two pools set off the nicely landscaped garden, onto which each of the fewer than 100 rooms in the six buildings has a view. All rooms have air-conditioning, a kitchenette, and electronic safe; most have showers, but a few have baths. Complimentary morning coffee and juice are served at poolside, barbecue grills are set up for guest use, and a free hula show is put on for guests every Sunday at 6:30 P.M. In addition, the hotel offers limited parking and laundry facilities. Rates for rooms, single or double, run $85–95, the one-bedrooms are $135, and suites go for $165–190. There's no glitz here, just good honest value and close proximity to the beach.

One notch up in quality is Castle Resorts' **Inn on the Park,** 1920 Ala Moana Blvd., 808/946-8355 or 800/367-5004, fax 808/946-4839, which looks out over the green at Fort DeRussy. Rooms here have all the same amenities plus there's a swimming pool. Standard city view rooms are $103, ocean view rooms are $125, and a studio with kitchenette is $135. Many special deals are offered, so ask. Castle Resorts always gives you your money's worth.

Another in the same category is the **Holiday Inn Waikiki,** 1830 Ala Moana Blvd., 808/955-1111 or 888/992-4545, fax 808/947-1799. Rooms here are clean, decent, away from the action, and reasonably priced at $120–130, with reduced rates at various times of the years according to availability.

Moving a few blocks back from the main drag takes you away from the congestion of town and puts you in a perfect spot to view the mountains that back this lovely city. The **Aston Aloha Surf Hotel,** 444 Kanakapolei, 808/923-0222 or 800/423-4515, fax 808/924-7160, is in such a location. Open, airy, bright, and modern, this hotel overlooks the Ala Wai Canal yet is near to what's happening in Waikiki. Room rates are $95 for a hotel room, $110–140 for a studio, and $160–180 for a suite.

Across the street but newer and more contemporary in design is the **Waikiki Sand Villa Hotel,** 2375 Ala Wai Blvd., Honolulu, HI 96815, 808/922-4744 or 800/247-1903, fax 808/923-2541, website: www.waikikisandvillahotel.com, email: reserve@waikiki-hotel.com. Reasonably small, with just over 200 rooms, it's still has all the amenities of a big hotel, including a large pool, sundries shop, and on-site restaurant. A complimentary breakfast is served daily. Housed in one tower and a three-story Mediterranean-style building to the rear, rooms run $82–111, while the larger and more spacious studios are $141. Prices run $10–15 more from about Christmas to Easter.

A sister hotel, the **Waikiki Gateway Hotel,** 2070 Kalakaua Ave., Honolulu, HI 96815, 808/955-3741 or 800/247-1903, fax 808/923-2541, website: www.waikiki-gateway-hotel.com, email: reserve@waikiki-hotel.com, is across from the King Kalakaua statue in Fort DeRussy. Slightly pyramidal in shape, this hotel is the home of Nick's Fishmarket (one of the town's best dinner choices), a sundries shop, and small pool, and it serves a daily complimentary breakfast. Rooms rates run $82–111, with about a 10 percent increase from about Christmas to Easter.

Ramada Vacation Suites, 431 Nohonani St., Honolulu, HI 96815, 808/923-7336, fax 808/923-1622, is a low-rise local place with 80 units, where each looks out over the garden courtyard with its swimming pool, spa, and coconut trees. Comfortably decorated with tropical decor, these rooms contain all the amenities to make your stay relaxing. Studio rooms are $110 and one-bedroom suites run $150. Shuttle service is provided to sites around the island and also to the airport for pickup and drop-off for a nominal fee.

On-site parking is limited. Dwarfed by the surrounding hotels and condos, Ramada Vacation Suites is like an old-time oasis amidst new-fangled Waikiki.

$150–200

The 21-floor **Miramar at Waikiki,** 2345 Kuhio Ave., Honolulu, HI 96815, 808/922-2077 or 800/367-2303, fax 808/926-3217, website: www.miramarwaikiki.com, is in the heart of Waikiki but off the main drag. This hotel offers generous rooms, with lanai, a/c, TV, a swimming pool, restaurants and lounges, and fee guest parking. Rates range $115–175 for rooms and $200–375 for suites, $20 extra per person, with numerous corporate, military, and special rates available.

The **Queen Kapiolani Hotel** is at 150 Kapahulu Ave., Honolulu, HI 96815, 808/922-1941 or 800/533-6970, fax 808/922-2694. With its off-the-strip location and magnificent views of Diamond Head, this is one of the best, and definitely the quietest, hotels for the money in Waikiki. You're only seconds from the beach, and the hotel provides a spacious lobby, parking, a restaurant, TV, a/c, shops, and a swimming pool. Rates begin at $120 standard to $170 for an ocean view and go up to $185 for studios with kitchenettes. Suites with kitchenettes run $270–400 a night. The hotel has been rejuvenated with a $2 million face-lift. The stately marble columns have been redone, new wallpaper applied, and the shopping area upgraded. The overall effect is open and airy with the living mural of Diamond Head in the background. Also featured, in the Peacock Dining Room, is one of the best buffets in Waikiki. An excellent choice for the money.

The **'Ilima Hotel,** 445 Nohonani St., Honolulu, HI 96815, 808/923-1877 or 800/367-5172, fax 808/924-8371, website: www.ilima.com, email: mail@ilima.com, overlooks the Ala Wai Canal and golf course. This high-rise condo-style hotel has the friendly *ahoha* spirit and maintains a quiet and safe environment. As soon as you enter you are greeted by paintings that depict in bold strokes scenes from Hawaiian mythology. Studio units begin at a reasonable $109, one-bedroom suites at $170, two-bedroom suites at

$210, with $10 each for extra persons. For families of up to six, the three-bedroom two-bath penthouse suite at $330 a night is an option. These rates are $10–20 less during low season, April through mid-December, and discounts are given for those over age 55 and for corporate travelers. All units are spacious, have full kitchens, a/c, TV, and maid service, and each has recently been remodeled with new floor and wall coverings, linens, and decorations. For amenities, you'll find a small pool, exercise room, and sauna, laundry facilities, a travel desk, and limited free parking. At the 'Ilima you get all the necessities at a very reasonable rate. A great choice.

Directly across from the beach, the **Aston Waikiki Circle Hotel**, 2464 Kalakaua Ave., 808/923-1571 or 800/922-7866, fax 808/926-8024, has one of the best locations in Waikiki at a very reasonable rate. An older landmark hotel that has been totally refurbished in a clean and cheery, whimsically modern mode, the building is in fact built in the round so that only some of the rooms have a view of the ocean. With 14 guest floors, this hotel is dwarfed by its neighbors, but it makes it all the more intimate for its guests. Guest rooms run $145 for a city view, $160 for a partial ocean view, and up to $185 for a view facing the ocean. Rooms and amenities include a/c, private lanai, cable TV, laundry facilities, on-premise restaurant, parking, and a tour desk. For its location, this is a bargain.

Upon arrival, step onto a path of white tile leading through a tiny but robust garden to a translucent dome sheltering the outdoor reception area of the **Aston Waikiki Joy Hotel**, a lotus flower that blooms in the heart of Waikiki, at 320 Lewers St., Honolulu, HI 96815, 808/923-2300 or 800/922-7866, fax 808/924-4010. Immediately, marble steps rise to a veranda, where every morning a complimentary continental breakfast is served accompanied by the soft background chanting of a tiny fountain. The hotel, with only 94 rooms, is divided into two towers, the Hibiscus and the Gardenia. It's intimate enough to make everyone feel like an honored guest. Typical hotel rooms, $125–170, and suites, $195–230, are amazingly spacious, and bigger yet are the executive one-bedroom suites with kitchen, $280. The hotel rooms each feature a refrigerator and writing desk. A king-size bed with a slanted headboard perfectly designed for propping pillows is the "nerve center" of the room with controls for everything within easy reach. The suites in the Gardenia Tower feature a bedroom and attendant sitting area complete with couch and a large private lanai. Here too, bathrooms feature a wonderful hot tub. The Waikiki Joy is also very special with a 15-room karaoke studio (reservations recommended). The hotel restaurant is Cappuccino's, a European-style bistro featuring live entertainment on the weekends. The Waikiki Joy, aptly named, is the epitome of the adage that "wonderful things come in small packages," but in this case, the wonderful thing *is* the package!

$200–250

Outrigger Hotels and Resorts manages the greatest number of hotel and condo rooms in the state for any single owner-operator. Outrigger is an island-owned chain that has five high-end properties in Waikiki, 15 economy Ohana Hotels properties also in Waikiki (see above), hotels and condos on the other three major islands, and additional properties throughout the South Pacific. Its flagship property, and fanciest Waikiki hotel, is the **Outrigger Waikiki**, which sits right on the beach next to the Royal Hawaiian Shopping Center, between the classic Royal Hawaiian Hotel and Sheraton Moana Surfrider. A few properties to the west and also on the beach is the **Outrigger Reef**, the company's number two property in Waikiki. Next door to that stands the **Waikiki Shores**, its premier resort condominium on O'ahu. On Lewers St., only a few steps away, is the **Outrigger Islander Waikiki**, and behind the International Market Place sits the **Outrigger East**. All these properties have multiple restaurants on property, and most have lounges and in-house entertainment on a daily basis. In addition, the Outrigger Waikiki presents the very popular entertainment show, Society of Seven, in its Main Showroom, and the equally thrilling show, Yes!, at the Polynesian Palace Showroom at the Ohana Reef Towers, a sister hotel. Each property has a pool, laundry facilities, shops, a travel desk, a/c rooms, in-room refrigerators and safes, and all amenities that you'd expect from a quality establishment. Three

O'AHU

have Voyager Club accommodations, which give you added perks and services for a little extra expense. Room rates for the Outrigger Waikiki and Outrigger Reef run $220–450 a room and suites cost $440–1,300. At the Outrigger East and Outrigger Islander Waikiki, rates start at $175, while studios and suites at the **Waikiki Shores** run $205–550. Outrigger can help you reduce your expenses by taking advantage of one of their many discount programs, like a free night with a minimum stay; room and car package; bed-and-breakfast package; and island-hopper, over 50, AAA, AARP, military, and corporate rates. Having been around for decades, the Outrigger gives good value and plenty of service, and knows how to treat its guests right. For additional information or reservations, contact Outrigger Hotels at 303/369-7777 or 800/688-7444, fax 800/622-4852, website: www.outrigger.com, email: reservations@outrigger.com.

At the far eastern end of the bay next to Kapi'olani Park and just below Diamond Head is a small group of hotels and condos, amidst a handful of apartments and single family homes. One landmark of this area is the refurbished **The New Otani Kaimana Beach Hotel,** 2863 Kalakaua Ave., Honolulu, HI 96815, 808/923-1555 or 800/356-8264, fax 808/922-1555, website: www.kaimana.com, email: kaimana@pixi .com. Built in 1964, it has the look of that era, but all has been updated. The New Otani has all the amenities and niceties that you'd expect from such a hotel, but a big plus is that it sits on the quiet Sans Souci Beach. On property are two fine restaurants and a lounge, a travel desk, laundry facilities, a fitness center, and off-street parking. Rooms run $155–320 and suites are $220–865; $25 per additional person.

A few steps away is the **Diamond Head Beach Hotel,** 2947 Kalakaua Ave., 808/922-1928 or 800/367-2317, fax 808/924-1982, website: www.diamondheadbeachhotel.com. Small and slender in stature, this hotel rises up at a slight angle, making the top floors narrower than the bottom floors. Tucked between tall apartments, most rooms offer little horizon view, except for those at the ocean end of the building. Rooms have full and modern conveniences and amenities, and the hotel provides daily complimentary breakfast and staffs an activities desk. Rates run $188–211 for rooms and $252–560 for suites.

Sometimes you just hit it lucky and find yourself in a situation where you get more for your money than you expected, and delightfully so. The **Waikiki Beachcomber Hotel,** 2300 Kalakaua Ave., Honolulu, HI 96815, 808/922-4646 or 800/622-4646, fax 808/923-4889, website: www.waikikibeachcomber.com, is definitely one of those *sometimes* things. The Beachcomber is right in the heart of town—you couldn't be more central. The Beachcomber, living up to its name, is just a minute from the beach, and the professional and amiable staff knows exactly what you want and how to deliver it. Recently renovated to the tune of $5 million, the 500 guest rooms, outfitted in new furniture and carpet, and painted in soothing tropical tones, all feature a private lanai, a/c, TV, phone, room safe, and convenient refrigerator. The Hibiscus Cafe, a casual restaurant on the second floor, serves meals all day, from a light breakfast starter to an international evening entrée. On the property are a swimming pool, boutique shops, covered parking, and laundry facilities. Offered through the summer months, the Beachcomber Kids program can entertain and feed children while their parents are off doing other activities. Enjoy the voice and humor of one of Hawaii's consummate entertainers, Don Ho, as he presents his musical extravaganza Sun.–Thurs. evenings as he has done in Waikiki for years. To add to its image as an entertainment center, the Beachcomber also presents the Magic of Polynesia Show, a nightly illusionist spectacular, in its 700-seat showroom. The rates for guest rooms range $180–215, while the sumptuous suites run $315 and $515. There is a $25 charge for an additional adult, and children under 17 stay free in their parents' room. A bargain special at only $140 puts you in a city view room with a rental car included or a breakfast buffet for two, while other special rates are also available. To stay within budget while having a quality experience, the Beachcomber is a sure bet!

Just off Lewers St. at 2233 Helumoa Rd. is the modern but casual **Waikiki Parc Hotel,** 808/921-7272 or 800/422-0450, fax 808/923-1336, website: www.waikikiparc.com, where the beach is just a stroll away. The entranceway is done in marble, carpet, and subdued lighting, and coolness seems to permeate the entire property.

Subdued elegance is the mode here—the building and surroundings speak for themselves. Rooms are not spacious, but efficient, yet eminently comfortable and pleasing, some with lanai and others with balconies. On the ocean-view side, you look down on the distinctive orchid pool at its sister, the Halekulani, across the street. Depending upon location in the building, rooms run $190–270 a night, and this includes a complimentary breakfast at the Parc Cafe, the hotel's main dining room, or the Japanese restaurant Kacho, both of which are also open for lunch and dinner. The Parc Cafe features reasonably priced buffets at all meals (à la carte available as well), but the specialty is the weekend evening prime rib and seafood buffet. The hotel pool is on the eighth floor, and there too you can get light meals and refreshments. Several special room packages are available to reduce your charges. Validated valet parking is standard.

Twinkling lights descending the residential valleys of the Koʻolau Range with Diamond Head framed in perfect symmetry are an integral part of the natural room decor of the **Aston Waikiki Sunset Hotel,** 229 Paoakalani St., Honolulu, HI 96815, 808/922-0511 or 800/922-7866, one of Waikiki's newest suite-hotels. Although *feeling* like a condominium, the Waikiki Sunset offers all of the comfort and convenience of a hotel, including 24-hour front desk service, daily maid service, and amenities like a swimming pool, sauna, tennis court, travel desk, minimart, and even a restaurant. The entrance, cooled by Casablanca fans whirring over marble floors, sets the mood for this charming hotel tucked away only one block from the Waikiki strip. One-bedroom units range $180–260, and two-bedroom units run $340–425, making this an appropriate size for families. All feature full kitchens for in-room cooking and dining. All suites feature a private lanai, an entertainment center with remote-control color TV, and a tiled bath with a Japanese-style *ofuro,* a soaking tub perfect for the start of a cozy evening.

Almost next door at 2452 Kalakaua Ave. is the smaller but just as sumptuous **Aston Waikiki Beachside Hotel,** 808/931-2100 or 808/922-7866, fax 808/931-2129. This boutique hotel is a place of style and class, from the pink floral carpet covered Italian Travertine marble floor to the hand-painted silk artwork hanging on the walls.

Every little touch says classical elegance. Outside, a tiny courtyard is serenaded by a bubbling Italian fountain, perfect for complimentary breakfast of coffee and croissants. In the 12 floors above, only 77 luxurious rooms await, ranging in price $190–395. Each tastefully decorated room comes with twice-daily maid service, a mini-fridge, entertainment center, room safe, and a free morning newspaper. To make your visit even more carefree, the concierge service will help with all your activities and travel plans. While not cheap, this is a gem.

Standing as one of the pillars of the eastern end of the strip is **Pacific Beach Hotel,** 2490 Kalakaua Ave., 808/922-1233 or 800/367-6060, fax 808/922-0129, website: www.pacificbeach-hotel.com, email: reservation@hth.com. This two-tower, 830-room hotel has a perfect spot along the shore and is only on the edge of most of the busy shopping bustle. Rooms have full baths, lanai, a/c, complete entertainment centers, refrigerators, and coffee makers. On property are a swimming pool, two tennis courts, a fitness center, a bevy of shops, laundry services, and valet or self parking. The concierge or tour desk will arrange activities for the family and the kids' program is set up to take care of the younger set. For the convenience of guests, the Pacific Beach has three restaurants, the unique Oceanarium, which has a three-story aquarium wall; Neptune's Garden, where the focus is on seafood; and Shogun, for Japanese dining fine enough to win local appeal. Room rates run $180–205 for standard and partial ocean-view rooms, $225–275 for ocean-view rooms, and $275–310 for oceanfront rooms. In addition, a handful of suites on the top floors of each tower run $650–1,500 a night and provide you the best of the best. For location, amenities, and ease of use, this fine hotel is hard to beat.

At 1956 Ala Moana Blvd., 808/941-7275 or 800/222-8733, fax 808/949-0996, website: www.alana-doubletree.com, the "intimate boutique hotel" **Doubletree Alana Waikiki Hotel** provides all needed amenities in a casual and relaxed atmosphere. All rooms are comfortably outfitted and have a/c, TV, computer hookups, lanai, and Italian marble entryways and baths. Rooms run $195–220, suites $250–550, and the Royal Amethyst Suite (a combined three-suite unit with board room) goes for $2,000.

OʻAHU

Artworks adorn the walls and works by local artists hang in the hotel's gallery. A full-service business center is available for those on working assignments, and everyone can enjoy the fitness center and swimming pool. Convenient for guests, one of Waikiki's best restaurants, Padovani's Bistro and Wine Bar, makes the Doubletree Alana its home.

$250 AND UP

Sheraton Princess Ka'iulani Hotel

Across the road from her sister hotel, the Sheraton Moana, is the Sheraton Princess Ka'iulani Hotel, 120 Ka'iulani Ave, Honolulu, HI 96815, 808/922-5811 or 800/782-9488, fax 808/931-4577, website: www.princess-kaiulani.com. With grace and grandeur, the Princess takes her place as one of the royalty of this strip, and this is immediately apparent as you enter the hotel lobby. Princess Ka'iulani was the last generation of Hawaiian royalty, but unfortunately she died at the young age of 24, some six years after the end of the monarchy. This hotel is built on what was her estate, 'Ainahau, and it's a big place with 1,150 rooms. Rooms run from $199 for a standard to $330 for a deluxe ocean view, with suites running upward of $500. Guest service helps with arranging activities and dining, kids can be taken care of through the hotel's *keiki* program, and you can safely deposit your car in the hotel parking lot. When looking for food, you need not look far. The Princess Ka'iulani has the Lotus Moon Chinese restaurant, Momoyama Japanese restaurant, and the open-air Pikake Terrace, known for its evening buffets and nightly Hawaiian entertainment—music wafts across the torchlight pool for the enjoyment of all. In addition, the Princess presents the theatrical performance Creation: A Polynesian Odyssey, nightly in its 'Ainahau showroom.

Waikiki Beach Marriott Resort

The Waikiki Beach Marriott (formerly the Hawaiian Regent Hotel), 2552 Kalakaua Ave., Honolulu, HI 96815, 808/922-6611 or 800/367-5370, fax 808/921-5255, has a long history of treating guests like royalty. The hotel now stands on what was the original site of Queen Lili'uokalani's summer cottage. The grand tradition of the hotel is reflected in the open sweeping style, and after more than two decades, it appears extremely modern because its design was so visionary when it was built. With over 1,300 units, the hotel ranks as the third-largest hotel in Hawaii after the Hilton Hawaiian Village and the Sheraton Waikiki. While there are many categories of rooms, most fall into the $210–360 range, with larger rooms and suites up from there. All rooms are oversize and include cable TV, a/c, nightly turndown service, and in-room safes. You can step across the street to mingle with the fun-seekers on Waikiki Beach or relax at one of the hotel's two pools. A championship Laykold tennis court is open from sunrise to sunset, with lessons and rackets available. The hotel offers exclusive shops in an off-lobby mall, and an on-site beauty shop and Japanese acupressure/massage service can revitalize you after a hard day of having fun in the sun. The hotel is renowned for its fine dining and entertainment; somewhere on property, there's entertainment every evening. Cafe Regent, an open-air restaurant just off the main lobby, is open for breakfast; the Ocean Terrace, designed for kicking back and watching life go by, is a poolside bar that serves lunch at very good prices; and The Summery specializes in Continental cuisine for breakfast, lunch, and dinner. A perfect spot to perch while listening to relaxing Hawaiian music is the Lobby Bar. If you're after peace and quiet, head for the Garden Courtyard in the center of the hotel, where you can sit among flowers and full-grown coconut and bamboo trees. Periodically throughout the week, you can attend activities here to learn lei-making, hula, or even Hawaiian checkers from *kupuna* who come just to share their *aloha*. The Marriott is a first-class hotel that really knows how to make you feel like a visiting monarch. Rule with joy!

Hilton Hawaiian Village

This mammoth first-rate resort, a 22-acre oasis of tranquillity, sits in its own quiet corner of Waikiki. The Hilton, at 2005 Kalia Rd., Honolulu, HI 96815, 808/949-4321 or 800/445-8667, fax 808/947-7898, website: www.hawaiianvillage.hilton.com, is at the far western end of Waikiki, lying between Fort DeRussy and Ala Wai Yacht Harbor. Enter along 200 yards of the private hotel driveway, passing the Rainbow Bazaar mall with its exclusive shopping and dining. Facing you are the Hilton's six "towers," the Tapa, Diamond Head, and Rainbow, the prestigious Ali'i Tower, and the newest, Lagoon and Kalia. With just shy of 3,000 rooms, this resort complex is by far the largest in the state, having nearly twice as many rooms as its nearest rival. The huge multistoried rainbow on the entire ocean side of the Rainbow Tower is, according to the *Guinness Book of World Records,* the tallest ceramic-tile mosaic in the world. All the rooms are deluxe with magnificent views. Amenities include color TV, a/c, self-service bar, refrigerator, 24-hour room service, voice mail, and a safe for personal belongings. The Ali'i Tower pampers you even more with a private pool, turndown service, and concierge service. The Lagoon Tower overlooks the huge hotel lagoon, while the others lie back from the water. The Kalia, newest of the bunch, has been set up with the business traveler in mind. It has its own set of shops and houses the new Mandara Spa. Rates are $220–430 throughout the Village, with suites up to $3,900.

The towers form a semicircle fronting the beach, not a private beach because none can be private, but about as private a public beach as you can get. Few come here unless they're staying at the Hilton. It's dotted with palms—tall royal palms for elegance, shorter palms for shade. The property has three pools. The main pool, surrounded by luxuriant tropical growth, is the largest in Waikiki. The lagoon area creates the music of water in bubbling rivulets, tiny waterfalls, and reflecting pools. Torches of fire, and ginger, banana trees, palms, ferns, and rock gardens are the grounds. The concierge can arrange a free guided tour of the grounds by a groundskeeper, who will explain the habitat, life cycle, and characteristics of each plant.

The *action* of Waikiki is out there, of course, just down the shore, but you don't feel it unless you want to. Relax and enjoy the sunset accompanied by contemporary Hawaiian music at any of the several bars and lounges. Exotic and gourmet dining from throughout the Pacific rim is available at the Village's 10 restaurants, especially the hotel's signature Bali by the Sea and Golden Dragon restaurants. Additional restaurants are just across the driveway at the Rainbow Bazaar shopping mall, while more boutique shops can be found in each of the towers. Reflecting the large-scale nature of this resort, a long list of free activities and entertainment is scheduled throughout the week. Of special note is the Friday sunset King's Jubilee entertainment of Polynesian music and dance, accompanied by fireworks over the water, as well as the Saturday Polynesian music and dance show. The hotel has everything to keep its "villagers" contented and happy. As a complete destination resort where you can play, relax, shop, dine, dance, and retreat, the Hilton Hawaiian Village knows what it's about and has found its center. After a $150 million renovation and expansion, the Hilton Hawaiian Village is in even better shape to cater to its guests.

Hyatt Regency Waikiki

The Hyatt is a hotel resort of grand proportions. Although it's easy to spot, you'll find it at 2424 Kalakaua Ave., 808/923-1234 or 800/233-1234, fax 808/923-7839, website: www.hyatt.com. Standing directly across from the beach, two geometrical towers rise up in symmetry to the warm tropical sun. Anchoring these modernistic pillars are three floors of shops and restaurants, a new spa, and meeting and convention space. As if in imitation of a jungle forest, the entrance atrium sports copious tropical greenery and a broad waterfall that spills into a refreshing pool. Up the stairs on the second level is the front desk. Over 1,200 rooms occupy this mini-city, and each is large and plush with the latest in adornments and amenities. Nothing is skimped on when it comes to guest comforts, but this luxury comes at a price. Hotel room rates run $250–465 a night, while suites are $750–3,500. Special deals and packages are always available, but these may change throughout the year. As with many other Hyatt hotels, this one provides professional spa service. At Na Ho'ola, you can maintain your workout regime at the fitness center or be pampered with massage, sauna, body work, or Hawaiian healing treatments of herbal preparations. Don't want to walk across the street to the beach? Then have a dip in the hotel pool or the hot tub. Five restaurants, serving everything from award-winning Chinese cuisine to Texas-size barbecue ribs, grace this hotel, and there is the customary lounge and bar for relaxation. Soft sounds of Hawaiian music

OʻAHU

waft through the hotel every evening from the lobby bar, while more energetic rock and roll is played at the Texas Rock 'n Roll Sushi Bar. With practiced efficiency, the Hyatt will provide a memorable stay.

Hawaii Prince Hotel

The dynamic seascape of the tall masted ships anchored in the Ala Wai Yacht Harbor reflects in the shimmering pink-tinted glass towers of the Hawaii Prince Hotel, at 100 Holomoana St., Honolulu, HI 96815, 808/956-1111 or 800/321-6248, fax 808/946-0811, the city's newest luxury hotel. The twin towers, Diamond Head and Ala Moana, are scaled by a glass elevator affording wide-angled vistas of the Honolulu skyline. Decorated in green and tan with light burnished maple, the rooms, all ocean view, feature a marble-topped desk with full mirror, a/c, functional windows, and a full entertainment center. Each room has its own refrigerator, walk-in closet with complimentary safe, and a king-size bed. The marble bathrooms have separate shower stalls, tubs, and commodes with a full set of toiletries. Room rates are from $300 for an Oceanfront Marina to $440 for an Oceanfront Top (floors 30–33), while suites range $550–2,500; $40 per extra person. Special business rates are offered (ask when booking), and golf and other packages are available. Ride the elevator to the fifth floor, where you will find a keyhole-shaped pool and canvas shade umbrellas overlooking the harbor below. Here as well is the Promenade Deck Snack Shop, serving coffee, jumbo hamburgers, and other munchies beginning at 11 A.M. The business center on the 29th floor gives you access to a secretary, computers, fax machines, modems for email, and a conference room. Fees vary according to services rendered. Other amenities include three excellent restaurants—the Prince Court, Hakone, and Marina Front Cafe—a lobby lounge, a full fitness center, valet parking, and a courtesy shuttle. The Hawaii Prince boasts its own golf course, an Arnold Palmer–designed 27-hole championship course, and two tennis courts, at the Hawaii Prince Golf Club, at 'Ewa Beach, 35 minutes away, the only one of its kind belonging to a Waikiki hotel. The Hawaii Prince, at the "gateway to Waikiki," is away from the action of the frenetic Waikiki strip, but close enough to make it easily accessible.

Sheraton Waikiki

Dominating the center of Waikiki are the 30 floors and 1,852 rooms of the Sheraton Waikiki Hotel, 2255 Kalakaua Ave., Honolulu, HI 96815, 808/922-4422 or 800/782-9488, fax 808/923-8785, website: www.sheraton-waikiki.com. Built in 1971 as one of the area's first convention centers, it has a perfect location on the beach—and a long stretch of the beach. Recent refurbishment brings the spirit of the sea into the hotel. In conjunction, the *honu* (green sea turtle), which has come back from the brink of extinction and feeds in the evening in the waters of Waikiki, has been incorporated into the hotel logo. Rooms are basically either ocean view or city view, and all have full amenities, including air-conditioning, TV and movies, mini-refrigerators, and in-room safes. Rooms with views away from the water run $260–335. With an ocean view or ocean front room, rates are $350–485. Suites start at $675. The hotel has a clutch of two dozen shops for apparel, jewelry, gifts, camera needs, and sundries; two freshwater swimming pools; a fitness center; new business center; and plenty of parking. On the dining and entertainment side, the Sheraton has the only nightclub in Waikiki on the beach, two cocktail lounges, nightly poolside Hawaiian music entertainment, and three fine restaurants, including the Hanohano Room (its signature restaurant on the 30th floor), the Ciao! Italian restaurant, and the more casual Ocean Terrace Restaurant, which is known for its buffets. Guests have signing privileges at the other Sheraton properties in Waikiki, all three of which are only minutes away. Free to guests are fun runs Mon.–Sat. at 7 A.M. with marathoner Max Telford, aerobic fitness training, tai chi, and a leisurely guided historical tour along the beach various days of the week. Water activities like sailing, surfing, snorkeling, outrigger canoe and catamaran rides can all be arranged at the hotel beach center. Outside activities can be arranged through the activities desk, while guests who have early arrivals or late-night departures can make use of the lockers, showers, restrooms, and lounge in the Hospitality Center 6:30 A.M.–9:30 P.M. The Keiki Aloha Club can keep your kids busy with age-appropriate, supervised activities, and baby-sitting services are also available. As the second largest resort complex in Hawaii, the Sheraton Waikiki offers something for everyone.

Sheraton Moana Surfrider

The Moana, 2365 Kalakaua Ave., Honolulu, HI 96815, 808/922-3111 or 800/325-3535, fax 808/923-0308, website: www.sheraton.com, is the oldest and most venerable hotel in Waikiki. More than just recapturing early 20th century grandeur, the Moana has surpassed itself by integrating all of the modern conveniences. The original Italian Renaissance style is the main architectural theme, but like a fine opera, it joins a variety of themes that blend into a soul-satisfying finale. Later construction and restoration has connected the three main buildings, the Banyan, Tower, and Diamond wings, to form an elegant complex of luxury accommodations, gourmet dining, and distinctive shopping. The renovated Moana, filled with memories of times past, is magical. It's as if you stood spellbound before the portrait of a beautiful princess of long ago, when suddenly her radiant granddaughter, an exact image, dazzling in jewels and grace, walked into the room.

You arrive under the grand columns of a porte cochere, where you are greeted by doormen in crisp white uniforms and hostesses bearing lei and chilled pineapple juice. The lobby is a series of genteel parlor arrangements conducive to very civilized relaxation. Art, urns, chandeliers, sofas, koa tables, flowers, vases, and pedestaled glass-topped tables wait in attendance. An elevator takes you to the second floor, where a room filled with 100 years of memorabilia whispers names and dates of the Moana's grand past.

Upstairs, the rooms are simple elegance. Queen-size beds, rattan chairs, and fat fluffy pillows and bedspreads extend their waiting arms. All rooms have a/c, and the Banyan Wing features a remote-control master keyboard for TV, lights, and music. But this is the Moana! Bathrooms are tile and marble appointed with huge towels and stocked with fine soaps, shampoos, creams, makeup mirrors, and a bathroom scale, which you can hide under the bed.

Being the first hotel built in Waikiki, it sits right on the beach with one of the best views of Diamond Head along the strip. A swimming pool with sundeck is staffed with attentive personnel, and the activities center can book you on a host of activities, including a classic outrigger canoe ride or a sunset sail on a catamaran. Four restaurants, a grand ballroom, a snack bar, and three lounges take care of all your dining needs. Many rooms overlook the central Banyan Court, scene of a nightly entertainment that can be chamber music or soft Hawaiian tunes. Open the windows, allowing the breezes to billow the curtains while the waves of Waikiki join with the music below in a heavenly serenade. Rooms are $265–530, with suites priced from $950. The Sheraton Moana Surfrider is a superb hotel offering exemplary old-fashioned service. Whether you're a guest here or not, feel free to join one of the guided tours of the hotel's restored and refurnished original section, offered twice weekdays at 11 A.M. and 5 P.M.

Royal Hawaiian Hotel

The Royal Hawaiian, second oldest hotel built along Waikiki, at 2259 Kalakaua Ave., Honolulu, HI 96815, 808/923-7311 or 800/325-3535, fax 808/924-7098, website: www.royal-hawaiian.com, provides an ongoing contemporary experience in early 20th century charm. Affectionately known as the Pink Palace, this Spanish-Moorish-style hotel has also recently completed a $25 million restoration, which has recaptured the grand elegance of the historic boat days. Doors first opened in 1927, at a cost of $4 million, an unprecedented amount of money in those days for a hotel. The Depression brought a crushing reduction to Hawaiian tourism, bringing the yearly total down from a whopping 22,000 to under 10,000 (today more visitors arrive in one day), and the Royal Hawaiian became a financial loss. During World War II, with Waikiki barbed-wired, the hotel was leased to the Navy as an R&R hotel for sailors from the Pacific Fleet. After the war, the hotel reverted to Matson Lines, the original owner, and reopened in 1947 after a $2 million renovation. Sheraton Hotels purchased the Royal in 1959, built the Royal Tower Wing in 1969, sold the hotel in 1975, but continued to remain as operating manager.

When you visit the Royal Hawaiian, the most elegant lobby is not where you check in. Rather, follow the long hallway toward the sea. This becomes an open breezeway, with arches and columns in grand style. Here is the heart, with Diamond Head framed in the distance.

Original double doors featured one solid door backed by a louvered door so you could catch the ocean breezes and still have privacy. Today, the hotel is fully air-conditioned, so the old doors have been removed and new solid rosewood doors carved in the Philippines have replaced them. Rooms might have four-poster beds, canopies, twins, or kings, depending upon your preference. All rooms have remote-control TV, refrigerators, electronic safes, and computer hookups on telephones for lap-top computers. Furniture is French provincial, with bathrooms fully tiled. Completely renovated rooms in the original section have kept the famous pink motif but are slightly more pastel. They have a marble tile bathroom, a brass butler, and louvered drawers. The tall ceilings are even more elegant with molded plaster cornices. Guests are treated to banana bread on arrival, a daily newspaper upon request, and turndown service. A Hospitality Suite is provided for early morning check-ins or late checkouts and offers complimentary shower facilities. The Royal Tower, an addition dating from 1969, is preferred by many guests because every room has an ocean view and the bathrooms generally larger. From the balcony of most, you look down onto the swimming pool, the beach, palm trees, and Diamond Head in the distance. Not as large as its neighbors, the Royal Hawaiian has 527 rooms, 34 of which are suites. A basic guest room is $335–625, with suites ranging upward from $800.

The main dining room at the Royal is the Surf Room, open all day every day, and perhaps best known for its Friday evening seafood buffet. Lighter food is also available at the Beach Club.

If you stay at the Royal Hawaiian, you can dine and sign at the Moana Surfrider, Sheraton Waikiki, or Princess Ka'iulani, all operated by Sheraton Hotels. One of the best features of the Royal, open to guest and nonguest, is the remarkable lu'au every Monday night. Drinks and entertainment are provided daily at the hotel's famous Mai Tai bar.

Halekulani

The Halekulani Hotel at 2199 Kalia Rd., Honolulu, HI 96815, 808/923-2311 or 800/367-2343, fax 808/926-8004, website: www.halekulani.com, was an experiment of impeccable taste that paid off. Some years ago the hotel was completely rebuilt and refurnished with the belief that Waikiki could attract the luxury-class visitor, and that belief has proven accurate. Since opening, the hotel has gained international recognition and has been named as a member of the prestigious Leading Hotels of the World and Preferred Hotels and Resorts Worldwide. It is one of few AAA five-diamond award hotels in Hawaii and the only one on O'ahu. In addition, its signature restaurant, La Mer, has also been given a five-diamond award rating, and the Orchids Dining Room has received a four-diamond award, making the Halekulani one of the best.

The soothing serenade of the Halekulani begins from the moment you enter the porte cochere, where an impressive floral display welcomes you. The property was first developed in

pool and courtyard at the Halekulani

1907 by Robert Lewers as a residential grouping of bungalows, none of which survive. However, still preserved is the Main Building, dating from the 1930s when the hotel became a fashionable resort owned by Juliet and Clifford Kimball. The Main Building, a plantation-style mansion, houses the hotel's La Mer restaurant, along with Orchids Dining Room, serving breakfast, lunch, and dinner; Lewer's Lounge for an intimate cocktail and nightly entertainment; the very genteel Living Room, where you can enjoy refreshments; and the veranda where the afternoon tea is held. Notice the Main Building's distinctive "Dickey Roof," patterned after a Polynesian longhouse, perfectly sloped in such as way as to catch island breezes while repelling a sudden rain squall.

Wander the grounds to be pleasantly surprised that so much is given to open space, accented with trimmed lawn, reflecting pools, and bubbling fountains. The heated Orchid Pool, with its signature mosaic orchid, is always inviting and within earshot of the foaming surf. Close by is House Without a Key, an indoor/outdoor buffet restaurant also serving light snacks and perhaps one of the best locales in all of Waikiki for a sunset cocktail. Enter the guest room through a solid teak door into an antechamber that opens into the room, done in seven shades of white. Awaiting is a platter of fine china bearing a display of fresh fruit and complimentary "Bakeshop" chocolates. King-size beds require only a small portion of the rich Berber carpet–covered floors. For ultimate relaxation and added convenience, all rooms feature a writing desk, small couch, reclining chair, and Oriental-style lamps. Additional amenities include a remote-controlled entertainment center, mini-fridge, three telephones, and in-room safe. Sliding louvered doors lead to a private tiled lanai. Prices are $325–520 for guest rooms, $700–1,400 for suites, with the Presidential and Royal suites $4,000–4,500. A third-person charge for over 18 years of age is $125 or $40 for a child if a roll-away bed is needed. Additional amenities include swimming pool, beach service, daily newspapers, free local telephone calls, a full-service fitness center, and free admission to numerous historical and cultural attractions around town. The Halekulani awaits to show you its version of classic island charm. You won't be disappointed.

Kahala Mandarin Oriental

Long considered a standard-setter for Hawaiian deluxe hotels, the Kahala Mandarin Oriental, 5000 Kahala Ave., Honolulu, HI 96816, 808/739-8888 or 800/367-2525, fax 808/739-8800, website: www.mandarinoriental.com, is not actually in Waikiki, but in Kahala, an exclusive residential area just east of Diamond Head. The hotel, built over 30 years ago and refurbished in 1996–97 to the tune of $80 million, is proud that many of its key employees have been there from the first days and that they have formed lasting friendships with guests who happily return year after year. Surrounded by the exclusive Wai'alae Country Club (not even hotel guests are welcome unless they are members), the hotel gives a true sense of peace and seclusion and rightly boasts a "Neighbor Island Experience" only minutes from bustling Waikiki. Adjacent to the lobby is the Verandah lounge. An indoor-outdoor affair, tea and light foods are served here in the afternoon 2–5 P.M., and entertainment is scheduled every afternoon and evening. Beyond the lounge and overlooking the garden and bay is the hotel's signature restaurant, Hoku's. One of many imaginative restaurants in town, Hoku's serves a grand combination of ethnic dishes encompassing the Pacific, East, and West from its open kitchen, and is open for lunch weekdays, dinner daily, and for Sunday brunch. Down a grand staircase and directly below Hoku's is the more informal and open-air Plumeria Beach Cafe, which offers à la carte and buffet choices every day from morning until evening. If that is not enough, the poolside Honu Bar is a perfect spot for a quiet afternoon or evening drink, serving *pu pu* 4–8 P.M.

The Kahala Mandarin has 371 rooms. Average rooms are extra large and have full entertainment centers with 27-inch televisions, bathrooms with his and her sections, a wet bar, small refrigerators, and in-room safes. Rates are $310 for a garden-view room, $340–380 for a mountain-view room, up to $490 for a lagoon or ocean-view room, and $630–690 for a room on the water; add $100 for a third adult in any room. Suites run $590–4,070. Numerous promotions and packages are available.

The hotel, fronting the sheltered Maunalua Bay, features a perfect crescent beach, the most secluded of hotel beaches in the city. Also on property are a swimming pool and beach cabana

O'AHU

with all water-sports gear available, including kayaks, rafts, boogie boards, and snorkel gear. Behind, a waterfall cascading from a free-form stone wall forms a rivulet that leads to a dolphin lagoon and a series of saltwater ponds teeming with reef fish. A daily 30-minute in-water dolphin experience is offered by an independent company, Dolphin Quest, and runs $95 per adult and $75 for kids 5–12 years old. A Hawaiian Cultural program offers classes free to guests that might be lei-making, hula dance, or ukulele instruction. Other offerings are its arcade shops, scheduled shuttle service to Waikiki and major shopping malls, fitness and executive business centers, and the Keiki Club for kids 5–12 years old. The Kahala Mandarin is a AAA five-diamond award winner and pays excellent attention to detail and service. While not for everyone, there's no doubt you get all that you pay for.

W Hotel Honolulu

The W Honolulu Hotel is at 2885 Kalakaua Ave., Honolulu, HI 96815, 808/922-1700, 877/946-8357, fax 808/923-2249, website: www.whotels.com. Small and intimate, at the quiet end of Waikiki on Sans Souci Beach, this is a chic modern affair at the forefront of contemporary design and features, with a touch of Asian, yet the elegance is understated. Each spacious room has a superb view of Diamond Head or the ocean, and only the best of amenities and finest of service are allowed. While not aimed exclusively to this group, the W Honolulu Hotel caters to business travelers. To satisfy your most discriminating tastes, the Diamond Head Grill, one of the city's chicest food purveyors, is in the building. This hotel comprises only four dozen rooms, so each guest is treated with a familiarity that is not possible at a larger resort. Rooms are $325–375, suites run $500–550, with the two-bedroom penthouse at $3,000; $45 extra guest charge, no charge for kids under 18 using existing bedding. Business discounts are offered.

CONDOMINIUMS

The following condominiums are arranged by their starting prices. The rates may range out of their respective categories depending on size and amenities.

$100–150

An island company that has numerous properties around the state, and five in Waikiki, is **Marc Resorts,** 808/922-9700 or 800/535-0085, fax 808/922-2421, website: www.marcresorts.com, email: marc@aloha.net. Marc Resorts basically has condominium units in various configurations, with the addition of hotel rooms in some buildings. The studios and suites come with kitchenettes or full kitchens, and the hotel rooms have small refrigerators. While some amenities differ according to property, all are air-conditioned. Most have swimming pools, lanai, laundry facilities, sundries shops, and a restaurant. A few have daily complimentary continental breakfast, while others have weekly managers mai tai parties. In Waikiki, the best of the Marc properties is **Waikiki Royal Suites,** 255 Beachwalk, where rates run $199–329. Prices at **Marc Suites Waikiki, Island Colony,** and **Waikiki Marc** start a bit lower at $139, and the most economical is the **Hawaiian Monarch,** a hotel-like property with rooms for $119–149.

You can capitalize on the off-beach location of the **Aston Honolulu Prince,** 415 Nahua St., Honolulu, HI 96815, 808/922-1616 or 800/922-7866, where you'll find a hotel/condo offering remarkably good value for your money. The hotel/condo invites you into its fully furnished one- and two-bedroom suites. All offer a/c, color cable TV, fully equipped kitchens, and daily maid service. Prices begin at $95 for a standard room, $145 one bedroom, and $175 two bedroom, with discounts during low season. The apartments are oversize, with a huge sitting area that includes a sofa bed for extra guests. The Honolulu Prince is not fancy, but it is clean, decent, and family-oriented, and has recently gone through a major renovation. A fine choice for a memorable vacation at affordable prices.

$150–200

You can't beat the value at the **Aston Pacific Monarch** condo resort directly behind the Hyatt Regency at 2427 Kuhio Ave., Honolulu, HI 96815, 808/923-9805 or 800/922-7886, fax 808/924-3220. It offers some great features for a moderately priced hotel. Fully furnished studios begin at $130 and go up to $150; one-bedroom condo apartments cost $160–190, all a/c, with

J.D. BISIGNANI

Waikiki offers ample opportunity to enjoy the sunset on the beach.

on-site pay parking. The rooms are bright and cheery with full baths, living/dining areas, kitchens or kitchenettes, and cable TV. End units of each floor are larger, so request one for a large or shared party. The swimming pool, with a relaxing hot tub, perches high over Waikiki on the 34th floor of the hotel, offering one of the best cityscapes in Honolulu. The lobby is sufficient but small. Save money and have a great family experience by setting up temporary house-keeping at the Pacific Monarch.

All you have to do is literally roll out of bed, walk out your door, and pick a spot on Waikiki Beach when you stay at the **Aston Waikiki Shores Condominium**, 2161 Kalia Rd., Honolulu, HI 96815, 808/926-4733 or 800/367-2353. Individually owned, each unit has different decor, but most are tasteful with island-style furnishings, and all are immense. Typical is a one-bedroom laid out with a sitting area, living room, dining area, two baths with dressing rooms, and a kitchen complete with microwave, dishwasher, coffeemaker, and garbage disposal. To make your stay more pleasant, there's daily maid service, private lanai, cable TV, in-room washers and dryers, beach towels, and limited parking, and children stay free with their parents. Rates, especially for what you get, are very reasonable, starting at $180 for a studio with deluxe ocean view, $260 for a one-bedroom unit, and up to $495 for a two-bedroom deluxe ocean front.

$250 and up
A tunnel of white thunbergia tumbling from a welcoming arbor leads to the entrance of the **Aston Waikiki Beach Tower Hotel**, 2470 Kalakaua Ave., Honolulu, HI 96815, 808/926-6400 or 800/922-7866, fax 808/926-7380, one of Waikiki's newest mini-luxury condo hotels. A lustrous patina shines from brown on tan marble floors while glass-topped tables of black and gold lacquer hold magnificent displays of exotic blooms, and fancy French mirrors and cut glass chandeliers brighten the small but intimate reception area. Enter your suite through a vestibule onto a white carpet leading to a combination dining/living room, accented with contemporary paintings and koa trim. The ultramodern kitchen is complete with standard-size refrigerator, a rice cooker, four-burner stove and oven, and dishwasher. The master bedroom has its own entertainment center and huge private lanai from which you can overlook Waikiki. The full bathroom has a huge walk-in closet holding a safe, steam iron and board, and a washer and dryer. Rates range $500–540 for one-bedroom suites, $595–725 for two-bedroom suites, with the addition of more opulent units up to $1000. Special amenities include twice daily maid service, concierge desk, valet parking, a swimming pool, spa and sauna. For a condo, this one is right up there at the top and you get all the extra amenities that make your stay a pleasure, plus you have the beach at your doorstep.

OAHU

FOOD

The streets of Waikiki are an international banquet, with more than a dozen cuisines spreading their tables for your enjoyment. Because of the culinary competition, you can choose restaurants in the same way that you peruse a smorgasbord, for both quantity and quality. Within a few hundred yards are all-you-can-gorge buffets, lu'au, dinner shows, fast food, ice cream, and jacket-and-tie restaurants. The free tourist literature runs coupons, and placards advertise specials for breakfast, lunch, and dinner. Bars and lounges often give free *pu pu* and finger foods that can easily make a light supper. As with everything in Waikiki, its restaurants are a close-quartered combination of the best and the worst, but with only a little effort it's easy to find great food, great atmosphere, and mouthwatering satisfaction.

Note: At many of the moderately priced restaurants listed below and at all of the expensive restaurants *reservations are highly recommended.* It's much easier to make a two-minute phone call than it is to have your evening spoiled, so please call ahead. Also, many of the restaurants along the congested Waikiki strip provide valet parking (usually at no charge) or will offer validated parking at a nearby lot. So check when you call to reserve. Attire at most Hawaiian restaurants is casual, but at the better restaurants it is dressy casual, which means closed-toe shoes, trousers, and a collared shirt for men, and a simple but stylish dress for women. At some of the very best restaurants you won't feel out of place with a jacket, but ties are not usually worn.

INEXPENSIVE

Eggs and Things, 1911 Kalakaua Ave., just where it meets McCully, 808/949-0820, is a late-night institution open 11 P.M.–2 P.M. the following afternoon. The clientele in the wee hours is a mix of revelers, hotel workers, boat captains, and even a hooker or two. The decor is wooden floors and Formica tables, but the waitresses are top-notch and friendly. The food is absolutely excellent and it's hard to spend more than $10. Daily specials are offered 1–2 A.M., while the morning special runs 5–8 A.M. Waffles and pancakes are scrumptious with fresh fruit or homemade coconut syrup. Besides the eggs and omelets the most popular item is fresh fish, which is usually caught by the owner himself, Mr. Jerry Fukunaga, who goes out almost every day on his own boat. Casual attire is acceptable, and BYO wine or beer is okay.

Around the corner is **The Dynasty Restaurant,** 808/947-3771, at 1778 Ala Moana Blvd., in Discovery Bay. It has an enormous menu of various Hong Kong Chinese cuisines that is acceptable but not memorable. The servers are friendly and courteous, and it's open daily 11 A.M.–3 A.M. For a very late night repast after "doing the town," the food definitely hits the spot!

Almost across the street and tucked into a nook close to the Hilton Hawaiian Village is the **Saigon Cafe,** 1831 Ala Moana Blvd., 808/955-4009, open daily 6:30 A.M.–10 P.M. The Saigon Cafe is a friendly, meticulously clean, unpretentious, family-run affair that definitely offers "budget gourmet" food. Order tureens of soup for two, spiced with lemongrass and hot garlic sauce, and with floating dollops of seafood, chicken, beef, tofu, or pork for under $7. Roll your own spring rolls, which come with slices of meat, fresh vegetables, mint, dipping sauces, and transparently thin rice paper that you dip in water to soften before rolling away. Noodle dishes are large and hearty, while breakfast brings an assortment of eggs, pancakes, and waffles. It's hard to spend more than $10 on a meal that is not only delicious, but fresh, made to order, and healthy as well. Great choice!

Da Smokehouse, 444 Hobron Ln., 808/946-0233, open daily 11 A.M.–midnight, is one of those places where the food is excellent and you can even get take-out and delivery. Your choices are smoked beef, pork, chicken, and ham all served picnic style, with two choices of sides including homemade potato salad, baked beans, rice, coleslaw, or french fries. Prices are reasonable, and desserts like *lilikoi* pie, cheesecake, mud pie, and sorbet are only a couple of bucks. A small delivery charge makes Da Smokehouse a perfect alternative to inflated room service prices at surrounding hotels, or for a home-cooked dinner in your condo. You'll love it!

Ruffage Natural Foods, 2443 Kuhio, 808/922-2042, is one of a very few natural food restaurants in Waikiki. It serves a wide assortment of tofu sandwiches, burritos, natural salads, tofu burgers, fresh island fruits, and smoothies for lunch and dinner, 9 A.M.–7 P.M. Everything is homemade, and the restaurant tries to avoid, as much as possible, processed foods. Just about everything on the menu is less than $7. Aside from the menu items, food supplements, minerals, vitamins, and things of that nature are also available. It's a small hole-in-the-wall type eatery that's easy to miss. A few wooden tables outside under a portico are the ambience.

Ezogiku is a chain of Japanese restaurants. Open till the wee hours, these no-atmosphere restaurants serve inexpensive hearty bowls of Sapporo *ramen* (renowned as the best), curry rice, and *gyoza*. It has three locations in Waikiki at 2143 Kalakaua Ave., 2420 Koa Ave., and 2546 Lemon Road. Ezogiku is a no-frills kind of place. Small, smoky, counter seating, and totally authentic. It's so authentic that on the dishes they spell *ramen* as *larmen*. You not only eat inexpensively, but you get a very authentic example of what it's like to eat in Japan . . . cheaply. Eat heartily for around $7.

Man Lee's Chinese Restaurant, 124 Kapahulu, 808/922-6005, is a basic Chinese restaurant that offers daily lunch and dinner specials. The atmosphere is quiet since it's around the corner from most of the action, and the food is acceptable but not memorable. A belly-filler only, it's open 11 A.M.–9:30 P.M.

Perry's Smorgy, with locations at 2380 Kuhio Ave. and at the Ohana Coral Seas Hotel, 250 Lewers St., is the epitome of the budget traveler's "line 'em up, fill 'em up, and head 'em out" kind of restaurant. What you'll find is good old American food. There is no question that you'll waddle away stuffed, but forget about any kind of memorable dining experience. When you arrive, don't be put off by the long lines. They move! First, you run a gauntlet of salads, breads, and potatoes, in the hopes that you'll fill your plate. Try to restrain yourself. Next comes the meat, fish, and chicken. The guys serving up the roast beef are masters of a whole lot of movement and very little action. A paper-thin slice is finally cut off and put on your plate with aplomb. Pressure comes from the long line of tourists behind, who act as if they have just escaped from a Nazi labor camp. The breakfast buffet, 7–11 A.M., at $5.25 is actually very good, with all the standard eggs, meats, juices, and rolls, and the food in general, considering the price, is more than acceptable. You can't complain. The lunch buffet, 11:30 A.M.–2:30 P.M., is priced equally well, and the all-you-can-eat dinner, 5–9 P.M., is a bargain at $9.25.

Building on its success in Lahaina, Maui, as a fun-loving place with good eats and affordable prices, all in a location that gives great sunsets, with the added benefit of lively music in the evening, **Cheeseburger in Paradise** opened shop in Waikiki right across from the beach at 2500 Kalakaua Ave. Try an omelet, pancakes, or French toast to get you going in the morning. For the rest of the day, burgers, meat or meatless, sandwiches, salads, and fries will do. Lots of options, lots of logo items too. You won't have to try too hard to get out the door for under $15.

There are enough Formica-tabled, orange-colored, golden-arched, belly-up-to-the-window places selling perfected, injected, and inspected ground cow, chicken, and fish to feed an army . . . and a navy, and marine corps too. Those needing a pre-fab meal can choose from the royal Burger King and Dairy Queen, Jack-in-his-Box, Ronnie McDonald, Pizza Hut-2-3-4, and dippy Zippy's Drive-In. **Zippy's** is a local chain and has much more than the usual hamburger and fries. Fast food addicts easily find pushers throughout Waikiki!

MODERATE

Caffelatte, 339 Saratoga Rd. (across from the post office), 808/924-1414, is open daily except Tuesday for dinner, on the second floor of a clapboard "New England-Hawaiian style" house encircled by a veranda. The cosmopolitan interior, simple and basic, is adorned with wrought-iron tables set with starched white linens. Hardwood floors, framed paintings both traditional and modern, a horseshoe bar, and subdued globed lighting complete the casual but stylish effect. The prix fixe menu features a few selections for each of its three courses, and every night brings new items to the menu, so you never know what wonderful food the chef will create. Whatever your choice, leave a little room for the rich desserts. The bar serves Italian wine by the bottle or glass, along with bubbling spumante and various champagnes. Italy in Hawaii? . . . *Perche no?*

At the Ohana Edgewater Hotel you'll find **Chuck's Steak House,** 808/923-6111, open 4:30–10 P.M. daily. While there are others on the outer islands, this one is *the original.* Opened in 1959 and still going strong, they're doing something right! Chuck's has a simple menu—steak, with the addition of a few pork, chicken, and seafood items. All meals come with rice or fries, salad bar, baked beans, and bread. The early-bird special is $8.95, while most entrées run $14–19. There is nothing extraordinary here, just plain good food prepared in a straightforward manner.

The **Super Chef Gourmet Restaurant,** at the Waikiki Hana Hotel, 2424 Koa Ave., 808/926-7199, is a sleeper. It is definitely one of *the* best moderately inexpensive restaurants in Waikiki, where you can get an *almost* gourmet meal for a terrific price. Being in a small hotel on a side street keeps the crowds away, so the quality of the food and service never suffers. The restaurant decor is not spectacular, but it is classy with small linen-covered tables and drum-seat chairs in a open and cheery room. The staff is very friendly, and the chefs prepare each meal individually behind a tile counter. Breakfast is served from 8 A.M. and dinner from 5 P.M. The portions are moderate but definitely not minuscule, and on top of it the cooking is just a half step below excellent. Definitely worth a try.

The **Peacock Dining Room,** at the Queen Kapiolani Hotel, 150 Kapahulu, 808/922-1941, open 5:30–9 P.M., offers one of the most outstanding buffets in Waikiki for both price and quality. These Thurs.–Sun. buffets are a combination of Hawaiian and Japanese foods, $16.95 on Thursday, $19.95 the other days. The room itself is tasteful with white tablecloths and full service. Every time you return to the buffet just leave your empty plate and it will be taken away for you. Help yourself from an amazing array of entrées that are expertly prepared. The salad bar is

extremely varied, and the desserts will make you wish that you saved room. Excellent value.

Carlos Castaneda wouldn't even notice as he walked past two psychedelic green cactuses into **Pepper's,** 150 Ka'iulani Ave., 808/926-4374, open daily for dinner only 4 P.M.–1:30 A.M. The interior is Yuppie-Mex with a wraparound rectangular bar with a fat wooden rail and low ceilings done in a Mexican-style stucco. The specialties of the house are prepared in a wood-fired oven for that hearty outdoor flavor in the heart of "Rancho Waikiki." Head "south of the border" for burrito madness, complete flautas dinner, or selections from the lava-rock grill like marinated chicken breast or baby-back ribs. You can also pick Mexican favorites like tacos, enchiladas, and fajitas, all served with rice, beans, and Mexican salad. Nothing on the Mexican side is more than $15, with most around $10. Eat, *hombre!*

The **Shore Bird Beach Broiler,** open for breakfast buffet and dinner, is on the beach at the Outrigger Reef Hotel at 2169 Kalia Rd., 808/922-2887, giving this restaurant the best gourmet location in all of Waikiki. Here you'll find a limited but adequate menu of cook-your-own selections for under $18. Walk through the lobby to the beach for a remarkable sunset while dining. Included is a good, fresh salad bar of vegetables and fruits. Beverages are included, the setting is wonderful, and the value excellent. Across the lobby, the Shore Bird Oceanside Bar and Grill offers a grill menu until 1 A.M. Following evening live entertainment, karaoke is offered nightly at the bar for all those Don Ho wannabes.

The **House of Hong,** 260 Lewers St., 808/923-0202, open daily 11 A.M.–10:30 P.M., Sunday from 4 P.M., is a standard, no surprises Chinese restaurant with a flair. The decor borders on tasteful with some tables outfitted in starchy white tablecloths accented by inlaid wall murals and painted ceilings of China scenes. Daily lunch specials run $6.25, but nothing except seafood items is over $10. Early-bird dinner specials are as much a bargain and you'd be hard pressed to find dinner entrées for over $15. Not great, but no complaints either.

The **Oceanarium** at the Pacific Beach Hotel, 2490 Kalakaua Ave., 808/922-1233, offers a full breakfast, lunch, and dinner menu. For lunch, try the tropical fruit plate or an entrée such as

Cajun five-spice chicken. Dinner appetizers such as Cajun calamari begin at $5.25, while entrées such as shrimp scampi and New York steak run are $17.50–23.50, and specials such as live Maine lobster and set dinners are $25.95 and up. The Oceanarium is done in elegant muted colors as if you were under water.

The **Shogun Restaurant,** also at the Pacific Beach Hotel, is an award winner and a favorite spot for residents to take their visiting guests. Shogun offers breakfast and lunch buffets, à la carte menus, dinner specials, and a *teppan* and sushi bar. Definitely make reservations; 808/921-6113.

Trattoria, in the Edgewater Hotel, 2168 Kalia Rd., 808/923-8415, serves savory dishes from northern Italy. Particularly good are the veal plates with an appropriate bottle of Italian wine. The interior is upscale with bent-wood chairs and white linen tablecloths set with crystal. Antipasti selections include escargot at $8.75 and calamari salad for $7.50. Combine these with pasta dishes like spaghetti puttanesca, a savory dish of fillet of anchovy and melted butter cooked in a hot sauce with tomatoes and black olives for $12. Complete dinners range in price $17–26; early-bird specials before 6:30 P.M. run $9.95. Trattoria is a good choice for a moderate restaurant with a pleasant atmosphere and better-than-average cooking. Dinner only.

Duke's Canoe Club, Waikiki 808/922-2268, at the Outrigger Waikiki Hotel, has an unbeatable location fronting Waikiki beach. Basically a steak and seafood restaurant, it's a happening place, with plenty of Duke Kahanamoku and surfing memorabilia on the wall, with cocktails and lively local music every evening. The day starts with a filling breakfast buffet for $9.95. Lunch runs 11 A.M.–5 P.M. with dinner going until 10 P.M. Aside from the steak and fish items there are such selections as huli huli chicken, Big Island pork ribs, and shrimp scampi, all $13.95–23.95. While the food is tasty, you generally come here as much for the atmosphere, music, and chance to see the sun sink into the sea. Just another part of the restaurant, the Barefoot Bar has pastry and coffee in the morning and lighter sandwiches, burgers, pizza, and plate lunches throughout the day. Full bar.

Whether you've tried Thai food or not, **Keo's in Waikiki,** 808/943-1444, at the Ambassador Hotel near where Kalakaua and Kuhio Avenues merge, is a good choice. Keo's has the full range of Thai entrées, from meat selections through noodles, seafood, and vegetarian dishes, and all can be adjusted from mild to fiery hot to suit your taste. Try a spicy lemongrass soup or green papaya salad to start your meal. These and appetizers are priced mostly under $8, while entrées, like Thai garlic beef with mushrooms, Thai crispy fish with red chili, Pad Thai noodles with vegetables, or yellow curry with chicken, generally run $9–13. With basically the same menu, Keo's is open daily for lunch 11 A.M.–2 P.M. and from 5 P.M. for dinner. Reservations would be a good idea as this is a popular place.

If you've ever eaten at or even peered into a Planet Hollywood restaurant, the **Planet Hollywood Honolulu,** 2155 Kalakaua Ave., 808/924-7877, will be no surprise. The place is filled with movie memorabilia and celebrity costumes, a monument to television and film. It's a happy place with enjoyable background music. Have a look around while you wait for your food. Mostly, salads, sandwiches, and burgers, a fair selection of pasta, and more hearty meat dishes are on the menu. And then, of course, there are the tropical drinks and rich desserts. While the food won't win any Oscars, it'll fill you up, get you on your way, and not set you back too much. Expect items in the $12 and under range. Open until midnight.

Along the same lines, but with a decor focus on music, is the **Hard Rock Café,** 808/955-7383, at the corner of Kalakaua Ave. and Kapi'olani Blvd. across from the Hawaii Convention Center. All-American burgers, sandwiches, and grill items fill the menu, with lots of drink options. An easy-going, convivial eatery with heady music; a real rock 'n' roll experience. Open 11:30 A.M.–11 P.M. daily, Friday and Saturday until 11:30.

UPPER END

Ciao! is the fine Italian restaurant at the Sheraton Waikiki. It offers a pizza and pasta buffet every night for $10.95 along with its menu selections. Items from the menu include appetizers for under $9, pizza for $11.50–16, pasta marinara for $11.50, and open face lasagna with shrimp and scallops for $17.95. Filet mignon, rib-eye, and New York steaks come from the

OAHU

broiler for $21–37.50, a grilled and marinated boneless chicken breast with mixed greens and roasted potatoes is $15.50, and the live Maine lobster, steamed or broiled, runs $32.50. Of course, there is a good selection of Italian and California wines to accompany any meal. No reservations.

Benihana, at the Hilton Rainbow Bazaar, 2005 Kalia Rd., 808/955-5955, is open daily for lunch and for dinner. Meals are designed to fit *gaijin* taste, and cooks flash their knives and spatulas at your table—as much a floor show as a dining experience. Good, basic Japanese food, *teppan*-style, but not cheap with many meals in the $40 range.

The word "genius" is oftentimes overused and misapplied, causing it to lose its oomph, but when it comes to creativity with food, Roy Yamaguchi is a genius, par excellence! **Roy's Restaurant,** 6600 Kalaniana'ole Hwy. in Hawaii Kai Corporate Plaza, 808/396-7697, open Sun.–Thurs. 5:30–9:30 P.M., until 10:30 P.M. Fri.–Sat., from 5 P.M. Saturday and Sunday, presents Pacific Rim Cuisine at its very best. Though technically not in Waikiki but in Hawaii Kai about 20 minutes away, it is definitely worth the trip. Through experimentation and an unfailing sense of taste, Roy's has created dishes using the diverse and distinctive flavors of French, Italian, Chinese, Japanese, Thai, and Hawaiian cuisine and blended them into a heady array of culinary delights that destroy the adage that "East is East and West is West." The twain have definitely met, and with a resounding success. Roy's dining room is "elegant casual" much like the food, featuring an open kitchen, and although pleasant enough, it is not designed for a lengthy romantic evening. Roy's dining philosophy seems to be the serving of truly superb dishes posthaste with the focus on the "food as the dining experience," not the surroundings. While the menu changes somewhat every evening, you might find charred *'ahi* and *opakapaka* pot stickers and wild mushroom and escargot cassoulet for appetizers, various salads, or an individual *imu*-oven pizza, most under $8. Entrées like grilled loin of lamb with rosemary, crabmeat, and risotto sauce, a teriyaki grilled chicken, or rosemary-seared yellowtail hamachi tuna are mostly in the $20–27 range. Desserts are also superb and include individually prepared (order at beginning of din-

ner) fresh fruit cobbler in sauce anglaise, or a richer than rich chocolate souffle. Roy's is a dining experience that is universally appreciated.

Another fine establishment is **Padovani's Bistro,** at the Alana Doubletree Hotel, 1956 Ala Moana Blvd., 808/946-3456. With rich dark wood, a low ceiling, a semi-Art Deco styling, the casually elegant restaurant is downstairs and the wine bar is upstairs. The wine bar has about 50 wines by the glass, appetizers, gourmet cheeses, and rich desserts. In the restaurant, expect breakfasts for up to $12, lunches in the $12–18 range, and dinner of meat and seafood for $18–39. Formerly head chef of the Manele Bay Hotel on Lana'i, Padovani combines haute cuisine with the ingredients and flavors of Hawaii and Asia. Valet parking.

House Without a Key, open for breakfast, lunch, and dinner, is a casual outdoor-indoor restaurant in a magnificent oceanside setting at the Halekulani Hotel. Named after the first novel written about Charlie Chan, Honolulu's famous fictional detective, the restaurant offers unsurpassed views in every direction, and is perhaps the best spot on the island to enjoy a sunset cocktail. Although casual, the seating is very comfortable with padded chairs at simple wood-trimmed tables. Like the environment, the menu too is more casual with prices much easier on the budget. Entertainment, nightly 5–8 P.M., performed by The Islanders or the Hiram Olsen Trio, is great for dancing under the stars. In addition, you'll be entranced by the graceful beauty of the hula dances done by former Miss Hawaii, Kanoe Miller, and Debbie Nakanelua. Remember, the door is never locked at House Without a Key.

White, purple, and yellow orchids tumble from trellises, cascade from clay planters, and always grace your table at **Orchids Dining Room,** open for three meals a day, another seaside, indoor-outdoor restaurant at the Halekulani. Specializing in contemporary American cuisine, Orchids is also famous for its fabulous Sunday brunch. Beautifully appointed with teak wood and Hawaiian eucalyptus flooring, the setting is casual-elegant with white starched linen tablecloths, captain-style chairs with blue and white pillows, and of course heavy silver and crystal. Arranged with a tri-level central dining area that spreads out to a covered veranda, all tables enjoy a panoramic view of the sea with Diamond Head in the distance. Start the day with a continental or American breakfast, or try it Japanese style with grilled fish, steamed rice, pickles, miso soup, seaweed, and green tea. Lunch is also casual, with the Sunday brunch drawing visitors and residents alike. The dinner specialty is seafood, although meat and poultry are available. Entrées are luscious *onaga* done in an Oriental style, broadbill swordfish, baked prawns, and roasted rack of lamb. Most entrées run $28–36.

The **Golden Dragon**, 808/946-5336, open nightly except Monday for dinner 6–10 P.M., would tempt any knight errant to drop his sword and pick up chopsticks. One of the two fine restaurants at Hilton Hawaiian Village, the Golden Dragon's walls are decorated with portraits of emperors, and the plates carry the Golden Dragon motif. The interior color scheme is a striking vermilion and black, with the chairs and tables shining with a lacquerware patina. The Golden Dragon isn't your average chop suey house, but the menu has all of the standard Cantonese fare from lemon chicken to . . . well, chop suey noodles, but it doesn't end there. The food is expertly prepared, and two fine choices are the exotic Imperial Beggar's Chicken, feeding two for $39.50, which is a chicken wrapped in lotus leaves, encased in clay, and baked (requires 24 hours notice to prepare); and Chef Chang's Signature Selection (for two), which includes seafood and vegetable egg rolls, crispy wontons, island pork charsiu, hot and sour soup, stir-fry chicken, wok-seared scallops, beef with snow peas, lobster and shrimp, and duck fried rice, with green tea ice cream for $32 per person. For a first-class restaurant with impeccable food and service, the prices at the Golden Dragon are very reasonable.

Hakone, the Hawaii Prince Hotel's fine Japanese restaurant, is appointed with shoji screens and wooden tables with high-backed chairs in front of a glass wall that frames the still life of the Ala Wai Yacht Harbor. Dishes are typical, with set menus *(teishoku)* like chicken teriyaki and katsura steak, mostly in the under $30 range, and the Kaiseki Hakone, a full seven course meal for $65. A Japanese lunch buffet is also served.

Michel's, at the Colony Surf Hotel, 2895 Kalakaua Ave., 808/923-6552, open daily for dinner only, is literally on the beach, so your appetite is piqued not only by sumptuous morsels, but by magnificent views of the Waikiki skyline boldly facing the Pacific. The interior is "neo-French elegant," with the dining rooms painted in soft pastels, white tablecloths, crystal chandeliers, heavy silver service, and tasteful paintings. The bar is serpentine and of polished koa. Food is French Continental and dinner is *magnifique* with such entrées as fresh Maine lobster, potato-crusted *onaga*, lamb loin with foie gras, and filet Wellington of beef tenderloin; $26–39. The dining experience at Michel's is completely satisfying with outstanding food and outstanding service, all in an outstanding setting.

Almost next door is the **Diamond Head Grill,** 808/922-3734, at the W Honolulu Hotel. This chic eatery serves three meals a day, and the menu items are as light and modern as the decor. The breakfast menu has everything from a vegetable frittata to Belgian waffles. Lunch could be a cool Cobb salad or seafood linguine. While not overly complex, dinner entrées are well seasoned and freshly creative. Fire-roasted opakapaka with Kahuku corn ragout and creamy potato, and lemongrass and Asian pesto scented rotisserie chicken are two options.

Matteo's, in the Marine Surf Hotel, 364 Seaside, 808/922-5551, open 6 P.M.–2 A.M., is a wonderfully dark and romantic Italian restaurant that sets the mood even outside by welcoming you with a red canopy and brass rail that leads to a carved door of koa and crystal. Inside is stylish, with high-backed booths, white tablecloths, and marble-top tables. On each is a rose, Matteo's signature. Dinners begin with hot or cold antipasti priced $7–13, such as portobello crustini, artichokes alla Matteo's, or seafood medley vinaigrette. Light tare of *insalada e zuppe* (salad and soup) matched with garlic bread or pizza bread make an inexpensive but tasty meal. Entrée suggestions are chicken or veal *rollatini* (rolled meat stuffed with bell peppers, mushrooms, onions, spinach, and mozzarella), or *bragiola* (rolled beef with mozzarella cheese, garlic, and fresh basil, baked with marinara sauce), all under $20. Complete dinners come with Matteo's special salad, pasta, vegetables, and coffee or tea and include mahimahi Veronica (sautéed fish in lemon sauce and seedless grapes) or veal parmigiana and are priced under $29. Pastas are very reasonable and besides the usual linguine dishes include gnocchi and manicotti. An extensive wine list complements the food. Full bar. This restaurant gets the thumbs up from local critics and has garnered awards of excellence. If you are out for a special evening of fine dining and romance, Matteo's will set the mood, and the rest is up to you.

Hy's Steak House, 2440 Kuhio Ave., 808/922-5555, is one of those rare restaurants that not only is absolutely beautiful (decorated like a Victorian sitting room) but serves great food as well. Its menu offers things other than steaks and chops, but these are the specialties and worth the stiff-upper-lip price.

Restaurant Suntory, Royal Hawaiian Shopping Center, 808/922-5511, is a very handsome restaurant with different rooms specializing in particular styles like *shabu shabu, teppan yaki,* and sushi. The prices used to be worse, but they're still expensive. However, the food preparation and presentation are excellent, and the staff is very attentive. Open for lunch and dinner.

Furusato Sushi at the Hyatt Regency at 2424 Kalakaua Ave., 808/922-4991, is expensive but a top-notch Japanese restaurant. The food and service are authentic, but they are geared toward the Japanese tourist who expects, and almost demands, to pay high prices. Free valet parking is great for this congested part of Waikiki. Three other exceptional restaurants worth visiting for authentic Japanese food are **Miyako** at the New Otani Beach Hotel, 808/923-4739; **Kacho** at the Waikiki Parc Hotel, 808/931-6645; and the **Kyo-ya,** 2057 Kalakaua Ave., 808/947-3911. All have excellent reputations.

One of the most unusual of restaurants in Waikiki is the **Top of Waikiki** at the Waikiki Business Plaza. The food and drink are good here, but you get a great view over the town as the round restaurant makes a slow revolution. Seating is tiered so that everyone has a good view. Come before sunset and watch the lights of the city come on and (hopefully) the sun sink into the sea. Start with an appetizer like sautéed escargot in parsley butter for $8.95 before moving on to shrimp scampi at $21.95. Other entrées include a New York steak at $24.50, salmon supreme at $19.95, and baked chicken breast for $17.95. Sunset special entrées are offered 5–7 P.M. for $12–18.

CLASSY DINING

Softly the soprano sea sings, while the baritone breeze whispers in melodious melancholy, as you float ephemerally above the waves at **La Mer,** the open-air signature dinner restaurant at the Halekulani Hotel. Splendid in their appointment, the walls, filigreed panels of teak covered in Chinese silkscreen, are predominantly browns and whites, the traditional colors of Hawaiian tapa. The superb Continental French menu, with its numerous selections of seafood, is bolstered by a huge wine list and a platter of select cheeses to end the meal. Entrées like medallions of fresh Scottish salmon, bouillabaisse, breast of Barbary duck, and round of lamb are generally in the $35–45 range with two set dinner menus at $85 and $105. La Mer sets the standard, and if you were to choose one restaurant for a night of culinary bliss, this is a perfect choice.

The Hilton Hawaiian Village, at 2005 Kalia Rd., is one of the finest destination resorts in Hawaii. Its signature restaurant complements the resort perfectly. **Bali by the Sea,** 808/941-2254, open Mon.–Sat. for dinner 6–10 P.M., may sound like Indonesian cuisine, but it's more Continental than anything else, and it's a consistent AAA four-diamond award winner. The setting couldn't be more brilliant. Sit by the open windows so that the sea breezes fan you as you overlook the gorgeous beach with Diamond Head off in the distance. Choose appetizers like escargot in phyllo with warm ratatouille or charsiu and shiitake potstickers. Ranging mostly $28–32, entrées include a magnificent selection of fish from Hawaiian waters, each prepared in a manner to bring out its essential flavor, and many covered with a special sauce. Meat entrées are marinated breast of chicken, casserole of lobster, or rack of lamb. Bali by the Sea is a superb choice for an elegant evening of fine dining. Reservations recommended.

The signature restaurant at the Sheraton Waikiki is the **Hanohano Room,** atop the building on its 30th floor. From here, the vista before you sweeps from Pearl Harbor to Diamond Head, and behind you, the city of Honolulu runs up into the hills. While noteworthy during the day, the view at night is stunning with the twinkle of city lights below. Aside from the usual breakfast fare, the Hanohano Room serves a breakfast buffet that, while not cheap, seems to have endless options. Along with breakfast Saturday morning, the room hosts the ever-popular Parry and Price live radio show on KSSK. The 8 A.M.–1 P.M. Sunday champagne brunch buffet is an outstanding feed, but pricey. In the evening, the restaurant features Pacific Island cuisine. Choose your selection of entrées from such items as chicken stuffed with lobster meat to filet mignon and lobster tail, ranging $26.95–48.95. If all the choices are too difficult, try one of the four select menu combinations, $53–75. A wonderful meal may be even more romantic here to the sounds of light piano music or later in the evening when a local trio called Stardust plays contemporary jazz and top 40 tunes. The dance floor is always open. Dress code.

One of the most laudable achievements in the restaurant business is to create an excellent reputation and then to keep it. **Nick's Fishmarket** at the Waikiki Gateway Hotel, 2070 Kalakaua, 808/955-6333, open nightly for dinner 5–10 P.M., until 11 P.M. on Friday and Saturday, has done just that—and keeps doing it. Many gourmets consider Nick's *the* best dining in Waikiki, and it's great fun to find out if they know what they're talking about. Adventurous and highly skilled, the chefs here, like the master of an old sailing ship, will take you to culinary ports of call rarely, if ever, visited. Highly professional waiters, knowledgeable about every dish, are friendly and efficient, and always at hand to suggest just the right wine from the extensive list to perfectly complement your choice of dish. Start with fresh-baked oyster Rockefeller, blackened sashimi, or, if you're in the mood, how about Russian beluga caviar (don't ask how much). The New England clam chowder is unbeatable, while the Caesar salad prepared at your table has long won honors as the best available west of California! Although Nick's is primarily renowned for its fish and lobster, don't overlook the veal, steaks, and chicken with sides of pasta. An excellent choice is one of Nick's complete dinners or lobster combinations. Most entrées run $29–36 while the lobster dishes run upwards of $42. The sinless along with those expecting salvation "tomorrow" will enjoy the dessert menu. A Cafe Menu has been added, from which you can order while listening to live entertainment in the lounge area 5:30–10 P.M. and until midnight on Friday and Saturday. Items on the Cafe Menu are all very reasonably priced under $12. Dancing to live music is featured nightly 5:30 P.M.–1:30 A.M. along with special events, such as wine-tasting evenings, scheduled throughout the year. If you had only one evening in Waikiki and you wanted to make it memorable, you'd have a hard time doing better than Nick's Fishmarket.

ALONG KAPAHULU AVENUE

Once Kapahulu Avenue crosses Ala Wai Boulevard, it passes excellent inexpensive to moderately priced restaurants, strung one after the other. Kapahulu was the area in which the displaced Chinese community resettled after the great Chinatown fire at the turn of the 20th century. Kapahulu basically means "poor soil," and unlike most areas of Hawaii could barely support vegetables and plants. Undaunted, the Chinese brought in soil with wagons and wheelbarrows, turning the area productive and verdant. While not actually in Waikiki, the restaurants along Kapahulu Ave. are only a short drive away for those staying in Waikiki.

Sam Choy's Diamond Head Restaurant, 449 Kapahulu Ave., 808/732-8645, is open for dinner Mon.–Thurs. 5:30–9:30 P.M. and Fri.–Sun. 5–10 P.M. Reservations are accepted, and there is complimentary validated parking. Island chef Sam Choy and his staff prepare food using mostly local produce, meat, and fish, mixing and embellishing the varied ethnic cuisine traditions of the islands. There are set and daily special menus. One of the nice things here is that you always have many *pu pu* appetizers to choose from, making it easier to sample small portions of food that you wouldn't otherwise have tried. Some signature entrées include Sam's seafood *lau lau,* veal osso bucco with Oriental noodles, honey macadamia nut-crusted pork chops, and oven-roasted duck. Expect most entrées in the $20–28 range. The restaurant also has a full bar and wine selection, and the decor is as soothing as the food is delicious.

The **Rainbow Drive-In** at the corner of Kana'aina Avenue is strictly local, with a kids' hangout feel, but the plate lunches are hearty and well-done for under $5. Another of the same, **K C Drive-In,** just up the road a few blocks at 1029 Kapahulu, specializes in waffle dogs and shakes and even has carhops. Both are excellent stops for picking up plate lunches on your way out of Waikiki heading for the H-1 freeway.

The sit-down **Irifune Japanese Restaurant,** 563 Kapahulu, 808/737-1141, is open for lunch Tues.–Fri. 11:30 A.M.–1:30 P.M., for dinner Tues.–Sun. 5–9 P.M., directly across from Zippy's, a fast-food joint. Irifune serves authentic, well-prepared Japanese standards in its small dining room. Most meals begin at $8, with a nightly special for around $10. One item that Irifune has become especially known for is its garlic *'ahi,* which goes for $11. Irifune is a great deal for Japanese food, much cheaper and easily as good as most other Japanese restaurants on the Waikiki strip. Known more for its food than its decor, it's a winner! Get there early; it's a popular place.

The next restaurant in line is **Ono Hawaiian Foods,** 726 Kapahulu, 808/737-2275, open Mon.–Sat. 11 A.M.–7:45 P.M., an institution in down-home Hawaiian cooking. This is the kind of place that a taxi driver takes you when you ask for "the real thing." It's clean and basic, with the decor being photos of local performers—all satisfied customers—hung on the wall. If you want to try *lomi lomi* salmon, poi, or *kalua* pig, this is *da' kine place, brah!* Prices are cheap.

If you have a sweet tooth, try **Leonard's Bakery,** 933 Kapahulu. Specializing in hot *malasadas* and *pao dolce,* Leonard's has garnered an islandwide reputation since 1952.

The Pyramids, 758-B Kapahulu Ave., 808/737-2900, is the place to head for Greek and Mediterranean cuisine. Open Mon.–Sat. for lunch buffet 11 A.M.–2 P.M. and daily for dinner 5:30–10 P.M., it's a small place so reservations are recommended. Being here, you might imagine yourself to be inside King Tut's tomb with hieroglyphics and painted stone blocks on the walls. Live music and belly dancing accompany the meal every evening. All the usual favorites are on the menu: tabouleh and shawarma salads; hommos, baba ghanouj, falafel, and stuffed grape leaves appetizers; and entrées like shish kabob, mousaka, and kebbeh. Dinner prices, $13.95–18.95 for entrées, are a few dollars more than those at lunch. The lunch menu also has a few sandwiches, while the dinner menu has some vegetarian options. This is about the only Middle Eastern restaurant on the island, and it's very convenient to Waikiki.

ENTERTAINMENT

Waikiki swings, beats, bumps, grinds, sways, laughs, and gets down. If Waikiki has to bear being called a carnival town, it might as well strut its stuff. Dancing (disco and ballroom), happy hours, cocktail shows, cruises, lounge acts, Polynesian extravaganzas, and the street scene provide an endless choice of entertainment. Small-name Hawaiian trios, soloists, pianists, and sultry singers featured in innumerable bars and restaurants woo you in and keep you coming back. Big-name island entertainers and visiting international stars play the big rooms. Free entertainment includes hula shows, ukulele music, street musicians, jugglers, artists, and streetwalkers. For a good time, nowhere in Hawaii matches Waikiki. The Friday edition of the newspaper contains a Calendar of Events section that lists events and activities throughout the area for the weekend and coming week. Also see the **Honolulu** chapter for other listings.

Bars and Lounge Acts
The **Irish Rose Saloon,** 227 Lewers, presents live entertainment nightly with dancing till 4 A.M. and features sporting events on its big-screen TV. Happy hour is 3–8 P.M. It's right across the street from the Ohana Coral Seas Hotel.

In the International Market Place, **Coconut Willy's Bar and Grill** offers free entertainment, with no minimum or cover.

Many hotel cocktail bars and restaurants will offer evening entertainment. One is the Oceanside Bar and Grill at the Outrigger Reef Hotel, where you can catch live local music 4–8 P.M. Following this, you can sing as karaoke takes over 9 P.M.–2 A.M.

Duke's Canoe Club in the Outrigger Waikiki Hotel has a great lineup of well-known local talent playing every night of the week 4–6 P.M. and then later from 10 P.M. to midnight.

For modern jazz in a hip and happening place,

visit the lounge of the **Diamond Head Grill** at the exclusive W Hotel Honolulu, at the far end of Kapi'olani Park below Diamond Head. This has become one of the city's hot spots.

The **Paradise Lounge** at the Hilton Hawaiian Village presents the harmonies of Olomana, a well-appreciated old-time trio, Wednesday, Friday, and Saturday evenings. Also at the Hilton, the **Tapa Bar** offers entertainment nightly; no cover.

A tradition at the **Lobby Bar** at the Waikiki Marriott (formerly the Hawaiian Regent Hotel) is its no-cover evening entertainment by well-respected Waikiki musicians. Be sure to stop in Thursday at 5:30 P.M. to catch the music of the lovely Genoa Keawe, who's been singing since the 1930s.

The **Banyan Court** at the Sheraton Moana Surfrider Hotel was the home of the famous Hawaii Calls radio show of years gone by. Now you don't have to dial in. Just walk down and sit under the banyan tree for the sweet sounds of contemporary Hawaiian music and hula every evening 5:30–8:30 P.M.

The Halekulani offers superb nightly entertainment. There is no lovelier location for a sunset cocktail than **House Without a Key,** where The Islanders or The Hiram Olsen Trio perform contemporary tunes nightly 5–8:30 P.M. Gracing the stage are two former Miss Hawaii beauty queens, Kanoe Miller and Debbie Nakanelua, who perform their inspired hula. Sunday brunch at the hotel's **Orchids Dining Room** is made even more genteel with the musical strains of harpist Susanne Hussong, accompanied by flutist Susan Gillespie, who perform the hit songs of Broadway musicals. Nightly 8:30–10 in the Orchids Dining Room and 10:15–midnight from the wood-paneled **Lewers Lounge** flows contemporary jazz selections with either Noly Paa on piano or the duo of Jim Howard on keyboard and Bruce Hamada on bass and vocals.

Poolside at the Sheraton Waikiki you can find several Hawaiian music and dance groups performing on a rotating schedule. These include Moe Keale, Ku'uipo Kumukahi, and Kanilau. Visit the **Hanohano Room** on the 30th floor of the Sheraton for the jazz and contemporary music of Stardust Mon.–Sat. and Night Grove on Sunday.

For jazz, head for the gentle ambience of the veranda lounge at the Kahala Mandarin, where vocalist Loretta Ables holds court Tues.–Sat. 7:30–11 P.M. Other evenings it's the sound of classical guitar, while every afternoon 2:30–4:30 P.M. there is the heavenly sound of a harpist.

Professional funster **Frank De Lima** holds court at the Captain's Table Lounge in the Hawaiian Waikiki Beach Hotel, Friday and Saturday 8:30–9:30 P.M. De Lima, supported by a two other loonies, is guaranteed to tickle your funny bone, "island style." Tickets are $7; two drink minimum; no reservations.

Discos, Dancing, and Nightclubs

Nick's Fishmarket restaurant at the Gateway Hotel, 2070 Kalakaua Ave., swings with contemporary dance music every Friday and Saturday 9 P.M.–1:30 A.M. Expect a mixed but mostly mature crowd who have stayed on to dance after a magnificent meal, which Nick's is known for.

The Wave, 1877 Kalakaua Ave., is a rock and roll and new wave hotspot with live music nightly. The Wave has become an institution of late-night fun and dancing. The crowd is mixed, and you can choose to dance, perch upstairs in the balcony behind glass where you can check out the dancers below, or have a few drinks and some conversation. The Wave is a sure bet for a night of fun.

The **Waikiki Hard Rock Café,** the fast-food joint of nightspots, has jazzed up its act by putting on live music for dancing Friday and Saturday evenings. It's at Kalakaua Ave. and Kapi'olani Blvd., directly across from the State Convention Center.

The following are disco nightclubs in and around Waikiki. Most have videos, a theme, a dress code of alohawear and shoes (no sandals), and start hopping around 9 P.M. with the energy cutoff around 4 A.M.

The **Cellar,** 205 Lewers St., features mostly rock and roll spun by the DJ. The place jumps till 4 A.M. and has plenty of special nights like Thirsty Tuesdays and Ladies' Night. Put on your dancin' shoes and casual attire.

Everyone trumpets the mating call at **Moose McGillycuddy's Pub and Cafe,** 310 Lewers in Waikiki, 808/923-0751, especially every Wednesday, which is Ladies' Night, and Sunday, when there's a bikini contest. Moose serves breakfast, lunch, and dinner in the downstairs restaurant; head upstairs for the music and dancing.

The nightclub rocks 9 P.M.–4 A.M. every night with live music until about 1 A.M. To help get the evening started, happy hour runs 4–8 P.M. and various specials on *pu pu* in the pub are always posted. This is a wild and zany place: good food, good fun, cheap drinks, and a young energetic crowd. Try here to answer the call of the wild.

The Esprit, at the Sheraton Waikiki, presents dance music from the '70s to the present Sun.–Thurs. 8:30 P.M.–12:30 A.M. and Friday and Saturday 9 P.M.–1:30 A.M. by the local bands The Krush and Honolulu. Come casual or dressed to the hilt. Good dance floor, $3 cover with a one-drink minimum, and it's the only nightclub right on the beach.

Eurasia, 2552 Kalakaua Ave., is a disco that's attracting dancers who once filled other discos in the area that have since closed their doors. Also try **Scruples Beach Club,** 2310 Kuhio Ave., for international DJ disco music.

The **Zanzibar Nightclub,** 2255 Kuhio Ave., is supposedly the largest nightclub in Waikiki. Dance to live music or DJ tunes; $5 cover.

Red Lion Dance Palace, 240 Lewers St., 808/922-1027, offers live rock and roll Wed.–Sat. and high-tech video and disco the remaining nights. Nice dance floor. Beachwear is okay. Open 11 A.M.–4 A.M.

In business for nearly 30 years, the gay-friendly nightclub **Hula's Bar and Lei Stand** now operates at 134 Kapahulu Ave. There's music and dance that everyone can get down to.

Exotic live dancers, like exotic live plants, need a unique atmosphere in which to bloom. Both seem to crave light, one sunlight, the other a spotlight. Most of the flashy fleshy nightspots of Waikiki used to be a few blocks away along Kapi'olani Boulevard, but they have been moving ever closer to the heart of Waikiki. Now they are strung along Kuhio Avenue, where they're easily recognizable by garish neon lights advertising their wares. The Kuhio Avenue exotic dance spots are supposedly a step up in class from their Kapi'olani Boulevard counterparts, but when their dancers strip to the buff, the difference is hardly noticeable . . . or very noticeable, depending upon point of view. The names of the strip joints really don't matter—just look for the signs of "exotic dancers." Usually a $10 cover and $5 for a drink.

Dinner Shows and Polynesian Extravaganzas

While hotel concierge staff and various ticket agents around town can sell or arrange tickets to the following shows, each show has its own dedicated ticket booth at the establishment where it performs. It's best to check in the morning for ticket availability or several days in advance during summer and winter peak seasons.

The **Don Ho Show,** an institution that played at the Hilton Hawaiian Village for years, is no longer. Mr. Ho has moved to the Waikiki Beachcomber Hotel at 2300 Kalakaua Ave., where he plays

the distinctive mural
at The Wave

J.D. BISIGNANI

one show nightly, Sun.–Thurs. at 7 P.M. For dinner (5:30 P.M.) and the show, tickets run $52; for cocktails (6:30 P.M.) and the show, it will be $32; reduced *kama'aina* rates. Gone is the glitz and glamour, leaving just Ho, his organ, his back-up band, and guest performers, much in the same way as he performed at Duke Kahanamoku's Club in the 1960s. Don Ho is still a great performer, and "the godfather of modern Hawaiian music." For information, call 808/923-3981.

The new multimillion dollar 700-seat showroom at the Waikiki Beachcomber Hotel fills with magical vibrations when headliner John Hirokawa suddenly appears out of nowhere. The **Magic of Polynesia** is a journey into the realm of enchantment and beauty that the entire family can enjoy. Sleight of hand, disappearing maidens, swaying hula dancers, fantastic costumes, and audience participation are all part of the magical extravaganza. Two shows nightly at 5:30 P.M. and 8 P.M. Dinner seating at the first show runs $67 for adults and $47 for kids ages 4–12; cocktail seating for the second show runs $39 for adults and $29 for children. Call 808/971-4321 for information and reservations.

Society of Seven, a well-established local ensemble, appears nightly at the Outrigger Main Showroom performing musical tunes from the last 50 years, with plenty of humor and antics thrown in for good measure. In various permutations, this band has been performing locally since the late '60s. Show times are 6:30 P.M. and 8:30 P.M. (8:30 P.M. only on Mon.), and tickets run $34.50 if you only want cocktails with your show or $52.50–59 for dinner with the show. Call 808/922-6408 for reservations or information.

Performing two shows nightly except Monday in the Ohana Reef Tower Hotel's Polynesian Palace Showroom is the **Yes! International Revue,** an absorbing collaboration of magic, dance, illusion, mime, and acrobatics. Ticket prices run $34.50 for the cocktail shows, $52.50–99 for the dinner show. Performance times are 6:30 P.M. and 8 P.M. For tickets and reservations, call 808/923-7469.

The 'Ainahau Showroom at the Sheraton Princess Ka'iulani Hotel presents **Creation: A Polynesian Odyssey,** a story of the origins of man and the movement of the Polynesian peoples across the Pacific islands to Hawaii, ending with scenes of luxury liners, statehood, and the hope for a prosperous future. Overall, this is a quick glimpse of the people who have made Hawaii home. Dramatically produced, with plenty of flash and flair, this show is an eyeful. Two shows nightly at 6 P.M. and 8:30 P.M. with dinner or cocktails. Cocktail show prices are $21–32 and the dinner show fare runs $55–105, depending upon your choice of food. Contact 808/931-4660 for information and tickets.

Free or Small Fee Entertainment

The **Royal Hawaiian Band** plays free concerts on Sunday afternoons at 12:45 P.M. and 2 P.M. at the bandstand in Kapi'olani Park, oftentimes with singers and hula dancers, and again on Friday at 12:15 P.M. at the 'Iolani Palace in downtown Honolulu. Formed in 1836, the band plays mostly classical music and Hawaiian traditional tunes. Also in the park, free concerts are periodically given by local and visiting musicians at the Waikiki Shell.

Every evening at King's Village behind the Hyatt Regency, a changing-of-the-guard show is performed by the King's Guards in uniforms from the period of the monarchy to give you a peek into one of the rituals of royal ceremony. This 6:15 P.M. ceremony is followed by a short hula demonstration on Wednesday, Friday, and Sunday.

The **Kodak Hula Show** is very popular. The show is held Tues.–Thurs. at 10 A.M. at the Waikiki Shell in Kapi'olani Park, but people start lining up at 8 A.M.; be there by 9 if you want a seat. You sit on bleachers with 3,000 people, while Hawaiian *tutu* bedecked in mu'umu'u, lei, and smiles play ukuleles and sing for the *ti*-leaf-skirted dancers. You can buy film and even rent a camera, as befits the show's sponsor, the Eastman Kodak Company—snap away with abandon. The performance dates back to 1937, and some of the original dancers, now in their eighties, still participate. At the finale, the dancers line up on stage with red-lettered placards that spell out H-A-W-A-I-I, so you can take your own photo of the most famous Hawaiian postcard. Then the audience is invited down for a free hula lesson. People who are too hip hate it, and *kama'aina* shy away from it, but if you're a good sport, you'll walk away like everyone else with a big smile on your face.

O'AHU

A potpourri of contemporary entertainment is also found in Kapiʻolani Park on weekends. Just across from the zoo, musicians, jugglers, clowns, unicyclists, and acrobats put on a free, impromptu circus.

The **Royal Hawaiian Shopping Center** provides free crafts demonstrations and lessons at various times throughout the week: quilting, coconut frond weaving, hula, lei-making, ukulele instruction, and *haku* (floral wristband) weaving. The Polynesian Cultural Center performs a short show of song and dance Monday, Wednesday, and Friday at 6 P.M. and Tuesday, Thursday, and Saturday at 10 A.M., at the fountain courtyard, where a mini-torch-lighting ceremony is also presented daily at 6 P.M. Free musical entertainment is also scheduled throughout the day at the same courtyard. For specific times for the crafts, call 808/922-0588.

A free hula show and fireworks are performed every Friday 6:30–7:30 P.M. at the super pool next to the main lobby at the Hilton Hawaiian Village. Anyone can come and stand for the show, but if you occupy one of the seats you must purchase at least one drink.

Also staging a free hula show, albeit in a more mundane setting, is the Waikiki Town Center. Come to the second floor of the shopping mall Monday, Wednesday, Friday, and Saturday at 7 P.M. for the fun.

A slice of old Hawaii comes to life on Saturday and Sunday evenings at 6:45 P.M. under the banyan tree at Kuhio Beach Park. **Molehu I Waikiki,** a torchlighting ceremony complete with Hawaiian music and authentic hula performed by various *halau,* is offered free to the public. Head for the Duke Kahanamoku statue and you'll be in

the right spot. You might want to bring your beach mats for this casual show.

Every Friday evening 8–10 P.M., Kalakaua Avenue comes alive with the music and dance of hula as the **Waikiki Strolling Hula** makes seven stops between the Royal Hawaiian Shopping Center and King Kalakaua Plaza.

Sometimes, "free" tickets to some of Waikiki's most popular Polynesian Extravaganzas are handed out by condo time-share outfits stationed in booths along the main drags. For attending their sales presentations, usually 90 minutes, you can get tickets, but they might be the toughest freebies you've ever earned. The presentation is a pressure cooker where hardened sales pros try every imaginable technique to get you to sign "right now, because this is the only time that this deal can be offered." If you're really interested in time-sharing, the deals aren't too bad, but if you're there only for the tickets, what a waste of time!

The **IMAX Waikiki** theater, half a block up Seaside Ave. from Kalakaua Ave., 808/971-5033, screens several shows everyday from about noon to 9:30 P.M. These exciting documentary films on Hawaiian subjects (there are usually three different offerings) run about 40 minutes in length and are scheduled on a rotating basis. Adults $9.50, children 2–11 $8, seniors and military $8.75. Call for current showings and ticket prices. Two other theaters in the same complex show regular first-run movies.

Just for the thrill of it, ride the outside glass elevators of either the Sheraton Waikiki or Ilikai Hotel. Great sights.

From 6:30 to 11:30 P.M. (weather permitting), you can hire a horse carriage to pull you for a 15-block ride around Waikiki for $10 adults and $5 children.

SHOPPING

The biggest problem concerning shopping in Waikiki is to keep yourself from burning out over the endless array of shops and boutiques. Everywhere you look someone has something for sale, and with the preponderance of street stalls lining the boulevards, much of the merchandise comes out to greet you. The same rule applies to shopping as it does to everything in Waikiki—class next door to junk. Those traveling to the

Neighbor Islands should seriously consider a shopping spree in Waikiki, which has the largest selection and most competitive prices in the islands. A great feature about shopping in Waikiki is that most shops are only a minute or two from the beach. This enables your sale-hound companion to hunt while you relax. There's no telling how much money your partner can save you! "Ingrate! This bathing suit could have cost

$50, but I got it for $25. See, you saved $25 while you were lying here like a beached whale." Everyone concerned should easily be mollified. Charge!

The Fence

The best place to find an authentic island-made souvenir at a reasonable price is at The Fence, along the fence of the Honolulu Zoo fronting Kapi'olani Park. Also referred to as Artists of O'ahu/Sunday Exhibit and Art Mart, The Fence gathers some of the island's best artists to display and sell their works on Tuesdays and weekends 10 A.M.–4 P.M. Individual artists are allowed to display only one day a week. The Fence was the good idea of Honolulu's former mayor, Frank Fasi, who decided that O'ahu's rich resource of artists shouldn't go untapped. There are plenty of excellent artists whose works are sure to catch your fancy. Also, about once a month on a Saturday or Sunday, booths are set up on the grassy area closer to the zoo, and an arts and crafts fair is held.

Gifts, Souvenirs, Sundries

ABC Stores scattered throughout Waikiki were founded by a local man, Sid Kosasa, who learned the retail business from his father. This "everything store" sells groceries, sundries, and souvenirs. Prices are good, especially on specials like lotions and beach mats. Very convenient.

Those who just can't return home without a deep Hawaiian tan should visit **Waikiki Aloe,** 2168 Kalakaua Ave. It specializes in skin-care products, lotions, and tanning supplies.

The **Waikiki Business Plaza,** 2270 Kalakaua Ave., houses jewelry stores. In one stop you can get a pretty good idea of prices and availability. Look for jewelry boxes laden with jade, gold, turquoise, pearls, coral, and *puka* shells, and eel, snake, and leather goods.

Most people just can't leave the island without buying an aloha shirt or a mu'umu'u. Any why not? They say Hawaii. Dozens of shops in Waikiki handle these trademark items, but to get an idea of what's out there at a decent price try **Touch of Aloha** at 205 Lewers St. Alternately, search the numerous shops at the International Market Place. For something more classy (and more expensive), look to the upscale shops in the larger shopping malls or the boutiques at the luxury hotels along this strip.

For classic Hawaiian shirts head for **Bailey's Antique and Aloha Shirts,** 517 Kapahulu, 808/734-7628, where you will find thousands of the vintage "collectible garments" on display. The best are made from rayon that was manufactured before 1950. Prices can range $100–2,000. Reproductions of these old wearable artworks are also available, as are clothing, jewelry, lamps, figurines, and the like. Nearby at 732 Kapahulu is **Peggy's Picks,** with new and used gifts, treasures, and collectibles from around the world.

Ladies looking for appropriate islandwear that won't break the budget should head for the **Pzazz** "consignment boutique," which sells used designer clothing at 1419 Kalakaua Avenue—beyond the edge of Waikiki.

For **photo finishing and photo supplies** at bargain prices try: **Wolf Camera** in the Waikiki Town Center, Royal Hawaiian Shopping Center, Hilton Hawaiian Village, and at the Sheraton Moana Surfrider; **Island Camera and Gift Shops** at Princess Ka'iulani, Sheraton Waikiki, Royal Hawaiian, and Sheraton Moana Surfrider Hotels; and **Outrigger Photo** at 2335 Kalakaua Ave., 227 Lewers, 2330 Kuhio Ave., and 2169 Kalia Road.

Duty-free goods are always of interest to international visitors. You can find a duty-free store at the Hilton Hawaiian Village. Also, if you want to see a swarm of Japanese jostling for position in a tiny little store trying to feed a buying frenzy, that's the spot. For a larger selection, try **DFS Galleria Waikiki,** 330 Royal Hawaiian Ave., right behind the Bank of Hawaii—how convenient!

Waikiki Shopping Centers

The largest credit card oasis is the **Royal Hawaiian Shopping Center.** This massive complex is three stories of nonstop shopping, running for three blocks in front of the Sheraton and Royal Hawaiian hotels. It's open daily 10 A.M.–11 P.M., 808/922-0588. This complex provides an excellent mixture of small intimate shops, larger national chain stores, and international boutiques, with an overabundance of clothing shops and jewelry stores. If jewelry is an interest of yours, head up to the third floor and have a look at the

O'AHU

Hawaiian Heirloom Jewelry Factory and the intriguing heirloom jewelry museum. Also on the third floor is the Little Hawaiian Craft Shop, which carries an amazing array of high-quality, handmade gift items; most are made by local craftspeople. There's a post office on the third-floor. The second and third floors of this shopping center are pretty quiet. It's off the street so not as many tourists find their way here. It's a good place to do some comparative browsing before making your purchases. If you get hungry while looking from store to store, stop at one of the 11 restaurants or additional snack shops to ease your pangs. While the tastes of Asia predominate, Italian, meat, and seafood are also in the mix. There is an information desk on the first level, about in the middle of the complex. The Waikiki Trolley makes a stop out front, and a parking structure is attached.

Where the Royal Hawaiian Shopping Plaza ends the multilevel **Waikiki Shopping Plaza** begins, but on the other side of the street. The mall's centerpiece is a five-story waterfall, an impressive sculpture of water and Plexiglas, while other fountains grace the lower level. Another feature of this mall is Waikiki Calls, a free hula show. Many inexpensive eateries are on the bottom floor, while fancier Chinese and Japanese restaurants are on the fourth and fifth floors. Clothing and accessory shops seem to predominate. The plaza is open daily 9 A.M.–11 P.M., 808/923-1191. While here, take a ride to the top floor of the Waikiki Business Plaza next door, where you'll get a fine overview of the Honolulu-Waikiki area.

Directly behind the International Market Place at 2301 Kuhio Ave. is the **Waikiki Town Center,** a little older, funkier three-level mall for gifts, fashions, and food. While here, enjoy the free Polynesian Show Monday, Wednesday, Friday, and Saturday 7–7:45 P.M. on the second floor.

The **Hyatt Regency Shopping Center,** also called the **Atrium Shops,** is on the first three floors of the Hyatt Regency Hotel, 2424 Kalakaua Ave., open daily 9 A.M.–11 P.M. The 60 or so shops are mighty classy: if you're after exclusive fashions or a quality memento, this is the place. There's a continental-style sidewalk café, backed by a cascading indoor waterfall. Often free entertainment and fashion shows are put on by the various shops.

King's Village, directly behind the Hyatt Regency, takes its theme from the 1800s, with boardwalks passing 19th-century look-alike shops on two levels, complete with a changing-of-the-guard ceremony nightly at 6:15 P.M., followed by a free hula show on Wednesday, Friday, and Sunday. Apparel and jewelry shops make up the bulk of the stores here, but there are a number of gift shops and restaurants. Around the walkways historical plaques relate, in brief, the reign of the Hawaiian kings and queens. Enter at Ka'iulani and Koa Streets.

The **Waikiki Trade Center** is on the corner of Seaside and Kuhio Avenues with some of Waikiki's most elegant shops, featuring sophisticated fashions, exquisite artwork, and fine dining.

The **Rainbow Bazaar** is a unique mall at the Hilton Hawaiian Village on the far western end of Waikiki. Fun just to walk around, shops feature three main themes: Imperial Japan, Hong Kong Alley, and South Pacific Court. Mostly clothing, gifts, and food.

The newest shopping complex to grace the streets of this already shop-filled town is the **King Kalakaua Plaza.** Nike Town fills a good portion of this building, as does a Banana Republic store.

Outdoor Shops

The **International Market Place** is an open-air shopping bazaar that feels like Asia. Its natural canopy is a huge banyan, and the entire complex is tucked between the Beachcomber and Princess Ka'iulani hotels. This warren of shops opens daily about 9 A.M. and closes when the vendors get tired at night. Among some fine merchandise and a treasure or two is great junk! If you're after souvenirs like bamboo products, shellwork, hats, mats, lotions, alohawear, and carvings, you can't do better than the International Market Place. A food court sits on the Duke's Alley side. The worst thing is that everything starts to look the same; the best is that the vendors will bargain. Make offers and try hard to work your way through the gauntlet of shops without getting scalped.

In **Duke's Alley,** a shortcut between Kuhio and Kalakaua Avenues, you'll find a row of stalls selling basically the same merchandise as in the International Market Place, which is adjacent.

Street Artists and Vendors

You don't have to try to find something to buy in Waikiki—in fact, if you're not careful, the merchandise will come after you! This takes place in the form of street vendors, who have been gaining a lot of attention lately. Some view them as a colorful addition to the beach scene, others as a nuisance. These carnival-type salespeople set up their mobile booths mainly along Kalakaua Avenue, with some on Kuhio Avenue and the side streets in between. In dealing with them you can have a positive experience if you remember two things: they have some pretty nifty junk, and you get what you pay for.

Also, street artists set up their easels along busy thoroughfares, and especially at the entrances to small shopping malls. Most draw caricatures of patrons in a few minutes for a few dollars—fun souvenirs.

Right here under the Waikiki banyan is a gentleman named Coco who makes coconut-frond hats, basically a dying art. Just near the canoe rides, you'll see his hats and baskets. Depending on the hat, you can get one for $15 or so. The baskets, good for holding fruit, incidentals, or whatever, are a real souvenir of Hawaii. With Coco making them right before your very eyes, you can't get more authentic than that. Coco says you can still learn how to weave in the Hawaiian tradition. His dad, Uncle Harry Kuikai, weaves at the Royal Hawaiian Shopping Center every Tuesday and Thursday 9:30–11:30 A.M. He'll teach you the basics of weaving and you can make your own souvenir (free).

Activities and Rentals

Not all activities and sports rentals in Waikiki are done at the umbrella stands set up along Waikiki Beach. For a reputable shop, try **Blue Sky Rentals,** 1920 Ala Moana Blvd., 808/947-0101. Owner Luis Merino can arrange activities and rent equipment for most of your ground, air, and sea needs. Mountain bikes rent for $10 for four hours, $15 for eight hours, or $20 a full day. Mopeds run $18, $23, and $33 for the same time increments. Snorkeling gear or boogie boards are $10 a day. Introductory scuba dives start from about $85 You'll find these and many more options for rental gear and activities at Blue Sky Rentals.

Of the beachside sport rental shops, **Prime Time Sports,** 808/949-8952, is a good bet. At Fort DeRussy Beach in front of the Hale Koa Hotel, it rents all sorts of water equipment and gives scuba, surf, and windsurfing lessons, all at reasonable prices.

As you might expect, **Snorkel Bob's** operates on O'ahu as he does on all the outer islands. Always a good deal, Bob may be a bit higher priced here than on the Neighbor islands, but he still has the same great gear. Depending on the quality, snorkel sets run from $3.50 a day to $29 a week. And if you're traveling to one of the other islands, you can drop your gear off at one of his shops there for free. Find Snorkel Bob's, 808/735-7944, at the corner of Kapahulu and Date Streets, across from the corner of the Ala Wai Golf Course.

O'AHU

M.G.L DOMENY DE REINZI

CENTRAL O'AHU

For most uninformed visitors, central O'ahu is a colorful blur as they speed past in their rental cars en route to the North Shore. Slow down, there are things to see! For island residents, the suburban towns of 'Aiea, Pearl City, Waipahu, Mililani, and Wahiawa are home. The three routes heading north from the coast meet in Wahiawa, the island's most central town. The roads cross just near the entrance to Schofield Barracks, a warm-up target for Japanese Zeros as they flew on their devastating bombing run over Pearl Harbor.

'AIEA, PEARL CITY, AND VICINITY

The twin cities of 'Aiea and Pearl City, except for the World War II military memorials, and perhaps a football game at Aloha Stadium, have little to attract the average tourist. Mainly they are residential areas for greater Honolulu and the large numbers of military families throughout this area. Likewise, Waipahu doesn't hold much attraction to the tourist because of its largely agricultural base, but Hawaii's Plantation Village is an attempt to interpret the importance of plantation culture for visitors.

PEARL HARBOR HISTORICAL SITES

Getting There
There are a few options for how to visit Pearl Harbor and its three historical military sites. If you're driving, the entrance is along Route 99, Kamehameha Highway, about a half mile south of Aloha Stadium; well-marked signs direct you to the ample parking area. If you're on H-1 west, take exit 15A and follow the signs. You can also take TheBus, no. 20 or 47 from Waiki-

To see all three of these memorials—a definite recommendation—plan to be at Pearl Harbor by early midmorning and make a half day of your visit. Start with the USS *Arizona* and then proceed to the other two.

Tour boats operate out of Kewalo Basin doing **Pearl Harbor Cruises.** Costing about $25 for an extensive tour of Pearl Harbor, including a run by the USS *Arizona* Memorial, they are not allowed to drop passengers off at the memorial itself.

USS *Arizona* Memorial

Even as you approach the pier from which you board a launch to take you to the USS *Arizona,* you know that you're at a shrine. Very few spots in America carry such undeniable emotion so easily passed from one generation to another: here, Valley Forge, Gettysburg, not many more. On that beautiful, cloudless morning of December 7, 1941, at one minute before 8 o'clock, the United States not only entered the war, but lost its innocence forevermore.

The first battle of World War II for the United States actually took place about 90 minutes before Pearl Harbor's bombing, when the USS *Ward* sank an unidentified submarine sliding into Honolulu. In Pearl Harbor, dredged about 40 years earlier to allow superships to enter, the heavyweight champions of America's Pacific Fleet were lined up flanking the near side of Ford's Island. The naive deployment of this "Battleship Row" prompted a Japanese admiral to remark that never, even in times of maximum world peace, could he dream that the military might of a nation would have its unprotected chin stuck so far out, just begging for a right cross to the jaw. When it came, it was a roundhouse right, whistling through the air, and what a doozy!

Well before the smoke could clear and the

ki, no. 20, 47, 49, or 52 from Ala Moana Center or downtown, and be dropped off within a minute's walk of the entrance. Depending upon stops and traffic, this trip could take 45 minutes or well over an hour.

Arizona Memorial Shuttle Bus, 808/839-0911, a private operation from Waikiki, takes about 20 minutes and will pick you up at most Waikiki hotels. It charges $6 round-trip; reservations are necessary so call a day in advance. For your return trip, just find the bus in the parking lot and board. Half a dozen buses run to the memorial 6:50 A.M.–1 P.M., and at least as many return 9:50 A.M.–4:45 P.M.

last explosion stopped rumbling through the mountains, 3,566 Americans were dead or wounded, six mighty ships had sunk into the ooze of Pearl, 12 others stumbled around battered and punch-drunk, and 323 warplanes were useless heaps of scrap. The Japanese fighters had hardly broken a sweat, and when their fleet, located 200 miles north of O'ahu, steamed away, the "east wind" had indeed "rained." But it was only the first squall of the American hurricane that would follow.

Visitor Center

The Arizona Memorial Visitor Center, website: www.nps.gov/usar/index.htm, is a joint venture of the U.S. Park Service and the Navy. It's free. The Park Service runs the Visitor Center, and the Navy operates the shuttle boats that take you out to the memorial shrine. The displays, museum, and gift shop at the complex are open daily 7:30 A.M.–5 P.M., with daily programs at the theater and the actual shuttle ride to the memorial itself operating only 8 A.M.–3 P.M. (closed Thanksgiving, Christmas, New Year's Day). If the weather is stormy, or waves rough, they won't sail. For recorded information call 808/422-0561 or 808/422-2771. As many as 5,000 people visit per day, and your best time to avoid delays is before 9:30 A.M. With 1.5 million visitors yearly, this is one of the most heavily visited sites in the state.

As you enter, you're handed a numbered ticket. Until it's called, you can visit the bookstore/gift shop and museum or, if the wait is long, the USS *Bowfin* moored within walking distance (see following). The bookstore specializes in volumes on World War II and Hawaiiana. The museum is primarily a pictorial history, with a strong emphasis on the involvement of Hawaii's Japanese citizens during the war. There are instructions of behavior to "all persons of Japanese ancestry," from when bigotry and fear prevailed early in the war, as well as documentation of the 442nd Battalion, made up of Japanese soldiers, and their heroic exploits in Europe, especially their rescue of Texas's "lost battalion." Preserved newspapers of the day proclaim the "Day of Infamy" in bold headlines.

When your number is called you proceed to the comfortable theater where a 20-minute film includes actual footage of the attack. The film is historically factual, devoid of an overabundance of flag waving and mom's apple pie. After the film you board the launch: no bare feet, no bikinis or bathing suits, but shorts and shirts are fine. Twenty years ago visitors wore suits and dresses as if going to church!

The Memorial

The launch, a large mostly open-air vessel handled and piloted with professional deft by Naval personnel, heads for the 184-foot-long alabaster memorial straddling the remains of the ship that still lies on the bottom. Some view the memorial as a tombstone; others see it as a symbolic ship,

Under attack: The Japanese attack on Pearl Harbor set off a chain of events that would make the U.S. the domineering power of the Pacific.

The USS Arizona Memorial enshrines the names of all those lost during the Pearl Harbor attack.

ROBERT NILSEN

bent by struggle in the middle, but raised at the ends pointing to glory. The USS Arizona became the focus of the memorial because her casualties were so severe. When she exploded, the blast was so violent that it lifted entire ships moored nearby clear out of the water. Less than nine minutes later, with infernos raging and huge hunks of steel whizzing through the air, the Arizona was gone. Her crew went with her; more than 1,100 men were sucked down to the bottom, and only 289 somehow managed to struggle to the surface. To the left and right are a series of black and white moorings bearing the names of the ships that were tied to them on the day of the attack.

The deck of the memorial can hold about 200 people; a small museum holds the ship's bell, and a chapel-like area displays a marble tablet with the names of the dead. Into a hole in the center of the memorial, flowers and wreaths are dropped on special occasions. Part of the superstructure of the ship still rises above the waves, but it is slowly being corroded away by wind and sea water. The flag, waving overhead, is attached to a pole anchored to the deck of the sunken ship. Sometimes, on weekends, survivors from the attack are aboard to give firsthand descriptions of what happened that day. Many visitors are Japanese nationals, who often stop and offer their apologies to these Pearl Harbor survivors, distinguished by special military-style hats. The Navy ordered that

any survivor wishing to be buried with his crew members had that right. Several veterans have been laid to rest with their buddies.

USS Bowfin Submarine Museum and Park
The USS Bowfin, a World War II submarine, is moored within walking distance of the Arizona Memorial Visitor Center. In the museum building, a short pictorial history depicts progress in undersea warfare from Revolutionary times to the present. Battle flags, recruiting posters, photographs, uniforms, military medals, and weapons and hardware are displayed, while a cutaway model of the Bowfin depicts life aboard ship. Unique to the museum, and the only one displayed for public viewing, is a daunting Poseidon C-3 submarine missile. An ongoing film in the mini-theater describes life below the surface for the modern submarine force. For the real aficionado, the museum archives and library of submarine-related literature is open by appointment only. Here and there across the four-acre grounds lie artillery pieces, torpedoes, missiles, and the conning tower and periscope of the **USS Parche.** Next to the museum is a gift shop and snack bar. This park is open daily 8 A.M.–5 P.M., except Thanksgiving, Christmas, and New Year's Day. Guided tours lead into the sub; the last tour starts at 4:30 P.M. Admission to the sub and museum is $8 adults or $4 for the museum only, $3 children ages 4–12 or $2 for the museum only. Children three and under are free for the museum tour

OAHU

but not admitted into the submarine. The rate for *kama'aina,* senior citizens, and active military personnel is $6. (See below for rates combining a visit to both the USS *Bowfin* and USS *Missouri*) The private, nonprofit organization Pacific Fleet Submarine Memorial Association, 808/423-1341, website: www.aloha.net/~bowfin, maintains the park and museum as a memorial and educational exhibit.

Launched one year to the day after the Pearl Harbor attack, the USS *Bowfin* (SS-287) completed nine patrol tours during World War II. Nicknamed the "Pearl Harbor Avenger," she was responsible for sinking an incredible 44 enemy ships before the end of the war. Retired in 1979, restored and opened to the public in 1981, it was put on the National Historical Landmark list in 1986. It's a 312-foot-long sausage of steel with a living area only 16 feet in diameter. As you enter the sub, you're handed a telephone-like receiver; a transmitted message explains about different areas on the sub. The deck is made from teak wood, and the deck guns could be moved fore or aft depending upon the skipper's preference. You'll also notice two anchors. As you descend, you feel as if you are integrated with a machine, a part of its gears and workings. In these cramped quarters of brass and stainless steel lived 90 to 100 men, all volunteers. Fresh water was in short supply, and the only man allowed to shower was the cook. Officers were given a dipper of water to shave with, but all the other men grew beards. With absolutely no place to be alone, the men slept on tiny stacked shelves, and only the officers could control the light switches. The only man to have a minuscule private room was the captain.

Topside, twin 16-cylinder diesels created unbelievable noise and heat. A vent in the passageway to the engine room sucked air with such strength that if you passed under it, you'd be flattened to your knees. When the sub ran on batteries under water, the quiet became maddening. The main bunk room, not much bigger than an average bedroom, slept 36 men. Another 30 or so ran the ship, while another 30 lounged. There was no night or day aboard ship, just shifts. Coffee was constantly available, as well as fresh fruit, and the best mess in all the services. Subs of the day had the best radar and electronics available. Aboard were 24 high-

powered torpedoes, and ammo for the topside gun. Submariners, chosen for their intelligence and psychological ability to take it, knew that a hit from the enemy meant certain death. The USS *Bowfin* is fascinating and definitely worth a visit.

USS *Missouri*

On June 22, 1998, the USS *Missouri* came home. Whereas the destruction of the USS *Arizona* and other ships in the harbor and the incredible loss of life and innocence brought the United States into war with Japan, it was on the deck of the USS *Missouri* that Japan, bruised and bloodied, surrendered to the United States, ending this most costly of world conflicts. Docked on Ford Island just a rifle shot from the USS *Arizona,* it proudly takes its place on "Battleship Row." At 887 feet long and 108 feet wide, this battleship is a behemoth, one of the largest battleships ever built and the last taken off active service. Like a floating city, she had a crew of around 2,500. Commissioned in 1944, this ship

ROBERT NILSEN

USS Missouri

participated in many battles during World War II and later during the Korean War and the Persian Gulf War. Money collected by the private, nonprofit USS Missouri Memorial Association is used to refurbish and maintain the "Mighty Mo." Since January 1999, visitors have been allowed onto the deck, where the signing of the surrender took place, and to view the bridge, climb the stairs from level to level, peer into officers' and enlisted men's quarters, enter the galley and dining rooms, and see the armaments that the ship was well known and feared for. Although later retrofitted with more sophisticated weapons, the original huge 16-inch guns could fire a 2,700-pound shell more than 23 miles, and even the smaller five-inch guns could send their projectiles a respectable nine miles. This was no light-duty ship. For protection, some of its armor plating was 17 inches thick! Several videos and other displays along the way explain the ship's history and function. A plaque on the surrender deck indicates the spot where the table used by representatives of the Japanese, U.S., and Allied governments and militaries signed the surrender document. In future years, other areas of the ship may also be opened to tourists.

Entrance runs $14 adult, $10 kama'aina, $5 military, and $7 children for an unguided tour, or $6 more for guided tours. Shuttle trolleys depart every 10 minutes starting at 9 A.M. from a stand in front of the USS Bowfin Museum and run over the new Ford Bridge to the ship. Tickets are sold at the USS Bowfin ticket office until 4 P.M., and everyone must leave the ship by 5 P.M. For nonmilitary personnel, this is the only way to get to the ship. It's worth a couple of hours and the emotional impact will remain much longer. If you want to combine a tour of the USS Missouri with the USS Bowfin, tickets run $18 self-guided and $24 guided for adults, and $9 unguided and $15 guided for children. For more information contact the USS Missouri Memorial Association, P.O. Box 6339, Honolulu, HI 96818, 808/973-2494, 808/423-2263, or 888/877-6477, website: www.ussmissouri.com.

Visit Ships Program

The Navy used to hold an **open house** on one of its ships berthed at Pearl Harbor on the first Saturday of each month. Unfortunately, it no longer does so, However, on occasion—usually around public holidays—home-port ships are open to the public for tours at Aloha Tower Market Place and at piers on the Neighbor Islands where ships make port calls. For information on when ships will be open for tours, call 808/473-2888.

BEACHES AND SIGHTS

Keaiwa Heiau State Recreation Area

As you travel up 'Aiea Heights Road, you get a world-class view of Pearl Harbor below. It's not glorious because it is industrialized, but you do ride through suburban sprawl Hawaiian style until you come to the end of the road at Keaiwa Heiau State Recreation Area. In the cool heights above 'Aiea, these ancient grounds have a soothing effect the minute you enter. Overnight tent camping is allowed here with a free permit at the exceptionally large sites; for the few other visitors, the gates open at 7 A.M. and close at 7:45 P.M. As you enter the well-maintained park (a caretaker lives on the premises), tall pines to the left give a feeling of alpine coolness. Below, Pearl Harbor lies open, like the shell of a great oyster.

Keaiwa Heiau was a healing temple, surrounded by gardens of medicinal herbs tended by Hawaii's excellent healers, the kahuna lapa'au. From the gardens, roots, twigs, leaves, and barks were ground into potions and mixed liberally with prayers and love. These potions were amazingly successful in healing Hawaiians before the white explorers brought diseases. Walking into the heiau compound, it's somehow warmer and the winds seem quieter. Toward the center are numerous offerings, simple stones wrapped with ti leaves. Some are old, while others are quite fresh. Follow the park road to the **'Aiea Loop Trail,** which heads back 4.8 miles round-trip onto one of the ridges descending from the Ko'olau Mountains. Pass through a forest of tall eucalyptus trees, viewing canyons to the left and right. Notice, too, the softness of the "spongy bark" trees growing where the path begins. Allow three hours for the loop.

Blaisdell County Park

The park's waters, part of Pearl Harbor's East Lock, are too polluted for swimming. It's sad to think that in the late 19th century it was clear

O'AHU

and clean enough to support oysters. Pearl Harbor took its name from Waimomi, "Water of Pearls," which were indeed harvested from the oysters and a certain species of clam growing here. Today, sewage and uncountable oil spills have done their devastation. Recently, oysters from the Mainland's East Coast have been introduced and are being harvested from the mudflats. Supposedly, they're fit to eat. Facilities include a pay phone, tables, and restrooms. From here you can see the back side of Ford Island and a few naval ships parked on its periphery. From this point, the water looks like a lake. Local people gather here on weekends and in the cool of the evening. It's a quiet spot to watch the evening turn to night. Access is off Route 99 near Ka'ahumanu Avenue, about 1.5 miles past Aloha Stadium and just before you enter Pearl City.

Hawaii's Plantation Village

Hawaii's Plantation Village in Waipahu Cultural Park, 94-695 Waipahu St., Waipahu, HI 96797, 808/677-0110, offers a stroll down memory lane into an open-air museum. Below the now-abandoned Waipahu Mill and smokestack, these plantation buildings have been moved from other locations to create this museum-like village. The 30 original structures and the photos, artifacts, and memorabilia they contain testify to the hard work performed by Hawaii's sugar plantation communities and provide insight into the eight ethnic groups represented. From 1852 to 1946, nearly 400,000 immigrants were brought to the islands to work in the field industries. Although the Chinese were first and their numbers amounted to 46,000, the Japanese were the largest group at 180,000. These were followed by Okinawans, Koreans, Portuguese, Puerto Ricans, and a smaller number of northern Europeans. The last major influx was by the Filipinos, whose numbers swelled to about 125,000. Each group contributed greatly to the economic health of the islands and over the following decades became part of the cultural mix that the state is known for today. In the museum building are homey displays illuminating everyday plantation life of the workers and the industry as a whole. The main museum building functions as an education center and is the start of all tours. It houses several displays portraying various aspects of plantation life and is a fine but brief introduction to the reality of the sugar economy in the islands. Out in the yard stands a train engine, once used to pull cane from the fields to the mill. Open for guided tours only Mon.–Fri. 9 A.M.–3 P.M. and Saturday 10 A.M.–3 P.M.; tours run about 90 minutes and start every hour. Admission is $7 for adults, $5 military and kama'aina, $4 for seniors, and $3 for students 5–12. This is a worthy stop.

Hawaiian Railway Line

While no commercial passenger train lines operate in the islands today, two trains do run for tourists: the Sugar Cane Train on Maui and the Hawaiian Railway train on O'ahu. In 'Ewa at 91-1001 Renton Rd., 808/681-5461, the Hawaiian Railway Society gives rides, restores and shows engines and train cars, and maintains an open-air train exhibit and gift shop. This organization does more than give tourist rides; it provides an educational adventure. The 90-minute round-trip, fully narrated rides start at 12:30 P.M. and 2:30 P.M. on Sunday only; $8 adults and $5 for seniors and children under 12. No reservations; first-come, first-served. On the second Sunday of every month, the Dillingham parlor car is added to the train on both runs. Fares for a seat in the parlor car are $15, with no children under age 13 allowed. Group charter rides can be arranged Mon.–Fri. mornings. The train runs about six miles along narrow-gauge track from the 'Ewa station at the end of Renton Road west to the leeward coast, just past the Ko 'Olina Resort. Don't expect a rail burner—this baby moves at a mild 15 miles an hour. All aboard!

At one time, the O'ahu Railway and Land Co. (OR&L) railroad totaled 72 miles of track that ran from Honolulu around Pearl Harbor, up the leeward coast, and across the north coast all the way to Kahuku, with another line up from Honolulu to the inland town of Wahiawa. It was a workhorse of a system, hauling people and goods (mostly sugar and molasses), servicing farms and commercial establishments, and, later, transferring troops and bulk items during World War II. After the war, the railroad couldn't compete with the burgeoning bus and trucking firms and the growing importance of the automobile, so the line was shut down at the end of 1947 after 58 years of service, and most of the track taken up. After much labor was expended restoring a section of the remaining track and some rolling stock, the Hawaiian Railway Society began to offer rides to the public in 1989.

PRACTICALITIES

Accommodations

Except for long-term apartment hotels, accommodations are virtually nonexistent in this area. The **Harbor Arms Apartment Hotel**, 98-130 Lipoa Place, 'Aiea, HI 96701, 808/488-5556, 800/360-5556, fax 808/488-8385, website: www.harborarms.com, email: harborarms@cvc-mail.com, offers fully furnished air-conditioned studios and apartments, all with kitchens and baths, TV, and phone. Rooms start at $67.80 a day with a weekly rate from $417.20; cash only, no credit cards. A laundromat and swimming pool are also available on property, and there's plenty of parking. The Harbor Arms is a three-story cement block affair, not fancy by any means but clean and well-maintained and with all the necessary comforts. Because it's TLA-approved, many military personnel use this facility as temporary housing. Airport transportation provided. Just off Kamehameha Highway and close to H-1, the Harbor Arms is not bothered by traffic noise yet is close to transportation routes and the nearby military bases.

Just down the block at 98-145 Lipoa Pl. is the **Harbor Shores Apartment Hotel**, 808/488-5742, fax 808/486-8537. While a little more contemporary, the Harbor Shores has approximately the same services and amenities, but all units are two-bedroom apartments that run $85 a day, $499 a week, or $1,400 a month. Designed for the family. TLA approved.

Food

Buzz's Steak House, 98-751 Kuahao Pl. (at the corner of Moanalua and Ka'ahumanu), 808/487-6465, is open for lunch 11 A.M.–2 P.M. and again for dinner 5–10 P.M. It's futuristic, like something a kid would build with an erector set. It'd be perfect if it were down by the sea, where you could see something, but from where it's located you can peer at Pearl Harbor in the distance or have a world-class view of the freeway. The steakhouse is owned and operated by an old island family whose business grew into a small chain of restaurants from the original location in Kailua. This is one of the remaining two. Buzz's is an institution where islanders go when they want a sure-fire good meal. There's a salad bar and you prepare your own charbroiled steaks and fish. Generally, you can get lunch sandwiches and entrées for under $12, while the menu has finer meat and fish dishes for up to $28.

In the Waimalu Shopping Plaza, try **Stuart Anderson's Cattle Co. Restaurant**, 808/487-0054, open daily for lunch and dinner. The lounge is open until 2 A.M. weekends, serving huge steaks and all the trimmings. Across the road at 98-1247 Ka'ahumanu is the **Elephant and Castle Restaurant**, 808/487-5591, open daily for lunch and dinner, breakfast on weekends only. This restaurant has done an excellent job of creating an English-style pub atmosphere. The interior is cool and rich with red velvet, heavy chairs, tapestries, and open beams, with a pool table and dartboards in the pub area. Nightly, it's one of the best places in the area for a beer and a chat. The food is good too. Try English fish and chips, a burger platter, hot sandwiches, or soup and sandwich. Specials on weekends are English prime rib dinner, New York steak, and seafood scampi. Enjoy merry old England Hawaiian style. For something more Asian, the Japanese **Kyotaru Restaurant**, 808/487-0091, is almost next door.

Shopping

The main shopping center in 'Aiea is the **Pearlridge Shopping Center**, open Mon.–Sat. 10 A.M.–9 P.M., Sunday until 6 P.M., with prices geared toward island residents, not tourists, so you have a good chance of coming away with a bargain. Some of the larger stores include Liberty House, JCPenney, Sears, Longs, and Waldenbooks. There are also 16 theaters, two food courts with more than 20 restaurants, plus over 150 smaller boutiques and specialty shops. Consisting of two main buildings and several smaller annexes, the entire complex is air-conditioned and serviced by an in-house monorail for your shopping convenience. Plenty of parking.

Across the street to the west is the smaller **Westridge Shopping Center**, and across the highway to the south, the **Pearl Kai Shopping Center**, both clusters of shops and eateries. About one-half mile down Kamehameha Highway to the west is the **Waimalu Shopping Center,** which is little more than a line of ethnic restaurants. Here you can find Japanese, Chinese, Korean, Hawaiian, and Filipino foods, as well as the London Pub sports bar and the Marujyu Market, which is open 24 hours for groceries, pharmacy, and deli.

Farther to the west, along H-1, is the larger **Waikele Shopping Center.** This outlet mall will save you money for fashions, furnishings, and specialty items. You'll only find big name stores here, with no island shops in sight. If you need to travel thousands of miles to spend money at logo wear shops, this is the place. A favorite of locals, it's also well used by visiting Japanese tourists. The Waikele Trolley connects the mall with hotels in Waikiki, leaving various locations in Waikiki twice every morning and returning three times every afternoon and evening; $22 round-trip, $8 for kids. Reservations required. Call 808/591-2561 or have your hotel concierge make the arrangements.

WAHIAWA AND VICINITY

Wahiawa is like a military jeep: basic, ugly, but indispensable. This is a soldiers' town, with servicemen from Schofield Barracks or nearby Wheeler A.F.B. shuffling along the streets. Most are young, short-haired, short-tempered, and dressed in fatigues. Everywhere you look are cheap bars, liquor stores, burger joints, rundown discos perfumed with sweat and spilled beer, pawn shops, tattoo parlors, and used-furniture stores. Route 99 turns into Route 80, which goes through Wahiawa, crossing California Avenue, the main drag, then rejoins Route 99 near the Del Monte Pineapple Variety Garden. Wahiawa has seemingly little to recommend it, and maybe because of its ugliness, when you do find beauty it shines even brighter.

Wahiawa was of extreme cultural and spiritual importance to the early Hawaiians. In town are **healing stones,** whose mystic vibrations were said to cure the maladies of sufferers. In a field not far from town are the **Kukaniloko,** the royal birthing stones, where the ruling *ali'i* labored to give birth to the future nobles of the islands. While in town you can familiarize yourself with O'ahu's flora by visiting the **Wahiawa Botanical Garden,** or take a quick look at a serene Japanese temple.

As you gain the heights of the **Leilehua Plateau,** spread between the Waianae and Ko'olau mountain ranges, a wide expanse of green is planted in pineapple. Just like on supermarket shelves, Del Monte's **Pineapple Variety Garden** competes with Dole's **Pineapple Pavilion,** a minute up the road. As a traveler's way station, central O'ahu blends services and just enough historical sites to warrant stretching your legs, but not enough to bog you down for the day.

SIGHTS

The Healing Stones
Belief in the healing powers of these stones has been attracting visitors since ancient times. When traveling up Kamehameha Highway (Route 80) take a left on California Avenue and follow it to Ka'alalo Place. To glimpse the religion of Hawaii in microcosm, in a few blocks you pass the Ryusenji Soto Buddhist Mission, followed by the healing stones, next door to Olive United Methodist Church. If you've never experienced a Buddhist temple, make sure to visit the grounds of **Ryusenji Soto Mission.** Usually no one is around, and even if the front doors are locked you can peer in at an extremely ornate altar graced by Buddha, highlighted in black lacquer and gold. On the grounds look for a stone *jizo*, patron of travelers and children. In Japan he often wears a red woven hat and bib, but here he has on a straw hat and mu'umu'u.

An HVB Warrior may mark the healing stones, just past the Ka'ala Elementary School, across the street from a beautiful eucalyptus grove. A small, white humble cinder-block building built in 1947 houses the stones right at the edge of the street. When you swing open the iron gate it strikes a deep mournful note, as if it were an instrument designed to announce your presence and departure. Inside the building, three stones sit atop rudimentary pedestals. Little scratches mark the stones, and an offertory box is filled with items like oranges, bread, a gin bottle, coins, and candy kisses. A few votive candles flicker before a statue of the Blessed Virgin.

Kukaniloko Birthing Stones

Follow Route 80 through town for about a mile. At the corner of Whitmore Avenue is a red light: right takes you to Whitmore Village and left puts you on a dirt track that leads to another eucalyptus grove in the midst of pineapple fields marking the birthing stones. About 40 large boulders are in the middle of a field with a mountain backdrop. One stone looks like the next, but on closer inspection you see that each has a personality. It is said they have been used for at least 800 years; the royal wives would come here, assisted by both men and women of the ruling *ali'i*, to give birth to their exalted offspring. The baby's umbilical cord, a sacred talisman, would be hidden in the cracks and crevices of the stones. Near the largest palm tree is a special stone that appears to be fluted all the way around, with a dip in the middle. It, along with other stones nearby, seems perfectly fitted to accept the torso of a woman in a reclining position. Notice that small fires have been lit in the hollows of these stones, and that they are discolored with soot and ashes.

Wahiawa Botanical Garden

In the midst of town is an oasis of beauty, 27 acres of developed woodlands and ravine featuring exotic trees, ferns, and flowers gathered from around the world. At 1396 California Ave., 808/621-7321, just beyond the district park and recreational center, it's open daily except Christmas and New Year's, 9 A.M.–4 P.M., admission free. The parking lot is marked by an HVB Warrior; walk through the main entranceway and take a pamphlet from the box (when available) for a self-guiding tour. When it rains, the cement walkways are treacherously slippery, especially if you're wearing thongs. The nicer paths have been left natural, but they can be muddy. Inside the grounds are trees from the Philippines, Australia, and Africa, and a magnificent multihued Mindanao gum from New Guinea. Fragrant camphor trees from China and Japan and the rich aroma of cinnamon bombard your senses. Everywhere are natural bouquets of flowering trees, entangled by vines and highlighted by rich green ferns. Most specimens have been growing for a minimum of 40 years, so they're well established, and some have been around since the 1920s when this area was an experimental tree farm. This well-kept garden is a delightful little surprise is the midst of this heavily agricultural and military area.

Schofield Barracks

Stay on Route 99 (here called Wilikina Drive), skirt Wahiawa to the west, and go past the entrance to Schofield Barracks. Notice a few shops about 50 yards past the entrance. Stop here and look behind the shops at a wonderful still life created by the Wahiawa Reservoir. Schofield Barracks dates from the early 1900s, named after General John Schofield, an early proponent of the strategic importance of Pearl Harbor. A sign tells you that it is still the "Home of the Infantry, Tropic Lightning." Open to the public, the base remains one of the prettiest military installations in the world, and one of the largest, being home to over 20,000 military personnel and dependents. With permission, you can proceed to the Kolekole Pass, from where you get a sweeping view of inland and coastal O'ahu. You can also visit the small **Tropic Lightning Museum,** 808/655-0438, with its memorabilia going back to the War of 1812. There are tanks from World War II, Chinese rifles from Korea, and deadly *pungi* traps from Vietnam. The museum has lost many of its exhibits in recent years to the U.S. Army Museum at Fort DeRussy in Waikiki, so it remains mostly a portrayal of the history of Schofield Barracks and the 25th Infantry "Tropic Lightning" Division. There is no charge for the museum, which is open Tues.–Sat. 10 A.M.–4 P.M., except federal holidays. Entrance is via the McComb Gate on Wilikina Drive. The museum is straight ahead down the road, but you must follow the signs for parking.

Pineapples

A few minutes past the entrance to Schofield Barracks, Route 803 goes straight ahead to Waialua, while Route 99 bears right and begins passing rows of pineapple. At the intersection of Route 80 is the **Del Monte Variety Garden.** Park along the roadway as there is no parking lot, but please be careful of traffic if you cross the road to the garden. You're free to wander about

PINEAPPLE

Ananas comosus of the family Bromeliaceae is a tropical fruit that originated in southern South America. During the 1500s and 1600s, ships captains took this unusual and intriguingly sweet fruit around the world on their journeys. Pineapples seem to have been brought to Hawaii from somewhere in the Caribbean in the early 1800s, but it wasn't until the mid-1880s that any experimentation was done with them, using the "smooth Cayenne," which is still the dominant commercial fruit variety. The first commercial plots of pineapple production were planted on the Leilehua Plateau at Wahiawa by James Dole just after the turn of the 20th century. For the production of these fruits, he built a cannery there in 1903 and later a second in Iwilei in Honolulu. Expanding his operation, Dole bought the island of Lana'i in 1922 and proceeded to turn the Palawai Basin into one huge pineapple plantation—some 18,000 acres at its greatest extent, producing a million pineapples a day during peak harvest. Relying heavily on canning, Dole made the "king of fruits" a well-known and ordinary food to the American public.

Production of pineapples is a lengthy process. First the ground must be tilled and harrowed to ready the soil for planting. The crowns of the pineapple fruit (which themselves look like miniature pineapple plants) or slips from the stem are planted by hand into long rows—some 30,000 per acre. A drip irrigation system is then installed and the soil covered with ground cloth to help control pests and weeds. Fertilizers and pesticides are then sprayed as needed and the plants grow in the warm tropical sun. After 11–13 months these plants fruit, and some seven months later the first crop is harvested. Generally, each plant yields one fruit, which grows on a center stalk surrounded by sharp and spiky curved leaves. The fruit sprouts again and, about 13 months later, a second crop is taken. Sometimes a third crop is also harvested from these same plants, before the remainders are tilled into the soil to start the process again. Pineapples are picked by hand, a hot, dusty, and prickly job. The fruits are placed on a boom conveyor that dumps them into trucks, which then take them to the cannery. There, all are pressure washed and sorted by size and quality before being canned or fresh-packed into boxes and shipped to market. Generally, about two-thirds are used as fresh fruit; the remainder is canned. All aspects of this production are done on a rotational basis to keep fruits available for market throughout the year.

and read the descriptions of the history of pineapple production in Hawaii and of the genetic progress of the fruit made famous by the islands. Hawaiian pineapple production started in this area at the turn of the 20th century, and it has maintained a strong force in the economy of O'ahu since then. This exhibit is much more educational than the **Dole Pineapple Plantation** just up the road, the one with all the tour buses lined up outside, but it too has a small demonstration garden of pineapple varieties and the giant vegetable garden out in the back. The Dole stop is a monument to retailing with its huge gift shop, open 9 A.M.–6 P.M., where packaged and ready-to-eat pineapples (they sell more than 3,500 a week) and other food items (try the Dole Whip), logo wear, and many other souvenirs made in Hawaii are yours to purchase. While at the Dole Plantation, visit the "World's Largest Maze." Certified by the Guinness Book of World Records, the maze is nearly two acres in area and formed by more than 11,000 native Hawaiian bushes and flowering plants. The maze is open 9 A.M.–5:30 P.M., admission $4.50 adults and $2.50 children. Plan on 20–30 minutes to find your way through—it's a chore and a blast.

PRACTICALITIES

Dot's Restaurant, off California Ave. at 130 Mango St., 808/622-4115, is a homey restaurant specializing in American-Japanese food. It gives a good square meal for your money. The interior is a mixture of Hawaiian/Asian in dark brown tones. Lunch specials include butterfish, teriyaki chicken, pork, or beef plates all for around $6. Miso soup and simple Japanese dishes are also available. The most expensive item on the menu is steak and lobster. Dot's is nothing to write home about, but you definitely won't go hungry. Open 6 A.M.–9 P.M. For something more institutional try **Zippy's** or **L&L Drive-In,** both on the main drag.

The streets of Wahiawa are lined with stores that cater to residents, not tourists. This means that the prices are right, and if you need supplies or necessities, this would be a good place to stock up. Up California Avenue toward the Botanical Garden is **Wahiawa Town Center,** with eateries, Foodland for groceries, Longs Drugs for sundries, a bank, video, and laundry, and the smaller **Wahaiwa Shopping Center** directly adjacent.

DIANA LASICH HARPER

O'AHU

M.G.L DOMENY DE REINZI

THE LEEWARD COAST

The Wai'anae (Mullet Waters) Coast, the lee-ward face of O'ahu, is separated physically from the rest of the island by the Wai'anae Range. Spiritually, culturally, and economically, the sep-aration is even more profound. This area is O'ahu's last stand for ethnic Hawaiians, and for that phenomenal cultural blending of people called *locals*. The idea of "us against them" per-meates the consciousness of the area, but even so, native voices of moderation are raised. Guidebooks, government pamphlets, and word of mouth warn tourists against going to Wai'anae because "the natives are restless." If you follow this poor advice, you miss not only the last of undeveloped coastal O'ahu, but the absolute pleasure of meeting people who will treat you with genuine *aloha*. Along the coast are mag-nificent beaches long known for their surf, new condos and developments nestled in secure val-leys, and prime golfing. Wai'anae is the home of small farms, run-down shacks, and families that hold lu'au on festive occasions, where the food and entertainment are the real article. Anyone lucky enough to be invited into this quickly dis-appearing world will be blessed with one of the last remaining authentic cultural experiences in Hawaii.

The possibility of hassles shouldn't be mini-mized because they do happen, but every ag-gressor needs a victim. The biggest problem is thievery, of the sneak-thief variety. You're marked as a tourist because of your new rental car. If you leave valuables in it, or lying unat-tended on the beach, they have a good chance of disappearing. But who does silly things like this *anywhere* in the United States? You won't be accosted, or held up at gunpoint, but if you both-er a bunch of local guys drinking beer, you're asking for trouble. Moreover, the toughness of Wai'anae is self-perpetuating, and frankly the locals *like* the hard reputation. A few years back a feature writer reported that when he visited Wai'anae some toughs threw rocks at him. No one had ever reported this before, but after a big stink was made about it, more and more people had rocks thrown at them when they vis-ited here. In recent years *pakalolo* has had a tremendous effect on the area. Local guys began

THE
LEEWARD
COAST

growing and smoking it. This brought some money back into the depressed region, and it changed the outlook of some of the residents. They felt a camaraderie with other counterculture people, many of whom happened to be *haole.* They could relax and not feel so threatened with pursuing an often elusive materialistic path. Many became more content with their laid-back lifestyle and genuinely less interested with the materialistic trip all the way around.

In truth, *we* shouldn't be warned about *them,* but vice versa. The people of Wai'anae are the ones being infringed upon, and it is they who, in the final analysis, will be hassled, ripped off, and ultimately dispossessed. A few rocks are poor weapons against developmental progress, which is defined by the big boys with the big dreams and the big bucks to back them up. Some years ago, it was thought that this northeast coast would be the next large region of development, and indeed some was done. However, with the downturn in the Hawaiian economy throughout the 1990s, less was accomplished than some had envisioned. Today, more development is happening in Kapolei and other areas of 'Ewa, closer and more convenient to Honolulu.

'EWA END

Hawaiian Waters Adventure Park
Whether it's barreling down the four-story slide, bodysurfing at the wavepool, leisurely floating down the curvaceous and continuous "river" in an inner tube,

O'AHU

swimming lagoon fronting the Ihilani Hotel at Ko 'Olina Resort

ROBERT NILSEN

or playing with the kids in the *keiki* pool, a day at Hawaiian Waters is good clean fun in a safe environment, with appropriate activities for all ages. Opened in 1999 in Kapolei, this 25-acre water-theme park is the only one of its kind in Hawaii. Other amenities include picnic area, bathrooms and changing rooms, food concessions, gift shops, a musical performance stage, and plenty of free parking. Don't forget your hat and sunscreen. This is the sunniest side of the island! Hawaiian Waters, 808/674-9283, website: www.hawaiianwaters.com, is open daily from 10:30 A.M.; admission runs $29.99 adults and $19.99 for kids ages 4–11.

Ko 'Olina Resort
While still in its early stages of development, the 640-acre Ko 'Olina Resort is set up like other high-class resorts around the islands. Away from the hustle and bustle of the big city, it's a huge manicured property of well-tended and landscaped lawns, tree-lined boulevards, a well-respected golf course, one luxury hotel (for now), the Paradise Cove Lu'au, a marina and public boat launch, four perfectly shaped manmade lagoons for sunbathing and swimming, public access parks, and townhouse properties, with plenty of space for growth. Set between the Barbers Point Harbor and the bottom end of the Wai'anae Mountain Range, this resort has a very good location—it gets the most sun and the least rain. The only drawback, and this should easy to remedy as the resort becomes more built up, is the specter of Campbell Industrial Park down the coast toward Barbers Point.

Barbers Point Beach County Park
This county park is at the end of Olai Road off Kalaeloa Boulevard. The point was named after Captain Henry Barber, who was shipwrecked here in 1795. Few people, even island residents, visit this beach park because the shoreline is rocky, it still hasn't fleshed out to become very pretty, and you have to get to it by driving through the Campbell Industrial Park. One pocket of white-sand beach is open to the public, though it fronts an adjacent residence. The swimming is safe only in summer; snorkeling is better, and you'll find picnic facilities and restrooms.

O'AHU

BEACHES AND SIGHTS UP THE COAST

The Wai'anae Coast is very accessible. One road takes you there. Simply follow the H-1 freeway from Honolulu until it joins the Farrington Highway (Route 93), which runs north, opening up the entire coast. A handful of side roads lead into residential areas, and that's about it! A strange recommendation, but sensible on this heavily trafficked road, is to drive north to the end of the line and then stop at the scenic sights on your way back south. This puts you on the ocean side of the highway, where you won't have to worry about cutting across traffic, which can be a steady stream making it tough to navigate. TheBus no. 51 runs up the Wai'anae Coast to the north end of Makaha and stops at all the beaches on the way.

Note: Four of the beach parks along this coast offer **camping,** but their status periodically changes to no camping without notice. Many of the other campers are local people in semipermanent structures; the status changes quickly to prevent these people from squatting. Also, remember that this is the leeward coast, which gets plenty of sunshine. Many of the beach parks do not have shade trees, so be prepared. June is the prettiest month because all the flowers are in bloom, but it's one of the worst times for sunburn. The entire coast is great for snorkeling, with plenty of reef fish. However, keep your eyes on the swells, and always stay out during rough seas, when waves can batter you against the rocks. The parks listed below run from south to north.

Kahe Point and Tracks
Beach County Parks

These parks are just where the Farrington Highway curves north along the coast. They're the first two *real* Wai'anae beaches, and they're symbolic. You come around the bend to be treated to an absolutely pristine view of the coast with the rolling sea, a white-sand beach, a cove, and the most hideous power plant you've ever seen. Facilities at Kahe Point Beach County Park are restrooms, a phone, a pavilion, and picnic tables. The beach is poor except for a section just north of the improved park, and this

is known as Electric Beach because it sits just opposite the power plant. Swimming is dangerous except on calm summer days. More often, you'll find people surfing and bodysurfing here, and some scuba companies bring guests here to enter the water. Camping is allowed with a county permit, although periodically this camping area closes temporarily.

A short way along is a mostly undeveloped area known as Tracks to island surfers because of the railroad tracks that run along the shore here. The white-sand beach is wide, and the swimming generally safe. The mild waves are perfect for learning how to surf. If you keep your eyes trained out to sea, the area is beautiful. Don't look inland!

Nanakuli Beach County Park

Nanakuli Beach County Park is on the southern outskirts of Nanakuli (Pretend to be Deaf) town, which is the first real town of the Wai'anae Coast. The beach park is community-oriented, with recreational buildings, basketball courts, a baseball diamond, and kiddies' play area. Camping is permitted with a county permit. Lifeguards work on a daily basis, and the swimming is generally safe except during periods of high winter surf. The southern section, called Piliokahe, is fronted by a cliff with a small cove below, and you'll often see fishermen casting off the cliff edge here. This cliff is lithified sandstone overlaying lava. During periods of calm surf, the waters are crystal clear and perfect for snorkeling. The northern end, called Kalaniana'ole, is generally calmer than the southern end. A pathway runs between these sections.

Ulehawa Beach County Park

Ulehawa Beach County Park, just north of Nanakuli and running for a good long way along the coast, offers restrooms, picnic facilities, lifeguards, and sometimes camping. The best swimming is in a sandy pocket near the lifeguard tower at the south end. Surf conditions make for good bodysurfing. Most of the park, along a rocky cliff, is undeveloped. Here you'll find unlimited fishing spots. A shallow lagoon is generally safe for

O'AHU

swimming year-round. As always, it's best to check with the local people on the beach.

Ma'ili Beach County Park

Ma'ili Beach County Park stretches along the length of Ma'ili (Pebbly) town. It lies between two streams coming down from the mountains. Amenities include restrooms, picnic facilities, and lifeguard towers, and much of the park is in a stage of development. The best swimming is in front of the lifeguard towers at the northern end. In wintertime the beach disappears, but it returns wide and sandy for the summer. Plenty of coral pockets offer good snorkeling. Don't just jump in. Ask the locals or swing by the lifeguard tower to make sure that it's safe.

Lualualei Beach County Park

A narrow strip of sand between the road and the water lying directly below Pu'u Ma'ili'ili, a fist of a hill that pushes nearly to the water, Lualualei Beach County Park has restrooms, picnic facilities, and camping during summer months. The entire park is largely undeveloped and lies along low cliffs and raised coral reef. Swimming is almost impossible. It's primarily good for fishing and looking.

Poka'i Beach County Park

Poka'i Beach County Park is one of the nicest along the Wai'anae Coast, just off the main drag in Wai'anae town. It provides restrooms, picnic facilities, lifeguards, and a boat ramp, which brings plenty of small craft into the area. Set on Kane'ilio Point is Kuiluiloa Heiau. Don't be surprised to see a replica of a double-hulled canoe, often used for publicity purposes. It has appeared in a beer commercial. The park is clean, well maintained, reasonably secure, and family-oriented. There's surfing, windsurfing, snorkeling, and safe swimming year-round. If you're heading for one beach along Wai'anae, this is a top choice.

Wai'anae Harbor

To get a look at a small working harbor or to hire a fishing boat, visit Wai'anae Boat Harbor, just across Poka'i Bay from Poka'i Park. Huge installed stones form an impressive manmade harbor, with everything from luxury yachts to aluminum fishing boats. Some cruises and whale-watching tours start from here.

Makaha Beach County Park

Makaha Beach County Park is famous for surfing, and as you approach, you can't help spotting a dominant headland called Lahi Lahi, which was a one-time island. Called "Black Rock" by the local fishermen, and used as a landmark, it still marks Makaha. Surfing competitions have been held here since the Makaha International Surfing Competition began in 1952. In recent years, a local lifeguard named Richard "Buffalo" Keaulana, known to all who've come here, has begun the Annual Buffalo Big Board Riding Championship. Paul Strauch Jr., inventor of the "hang five," comes to Makaha whenever he has a chance, along with Buffalo's sons and other pro surfers, many of whom live in the area. In 1995, Buffalo retired after 36 years as a lifeguard. He has passed the torch on to his son Brian, who now becomes captain of the whole east side. Along with protecting the beach and riding the waves, Brian has a budding acting career as a stunt man for Hollywood.

The swimming can be dangerous during high surf, but excellent on calm days of summer. Winter brings some of the biggest surf in Hawaii. Always pay heed to the warnings of the lifeguards.

Makaha

Although Makaha can translate as "Water Breaking Out to Sea" because of the area's propensity for damming runoff waters from the mountains behind the beach until enough pressure forces it to "break out," there is another meaning for Makaha that doesn't help its image. The second translation, meaning "Fierce," aptly describes a gang of bandits who long ago lived in the surrounding hills and terrorized the region. They would wait for small bands of people walking the road, then swoop down and relieve them of their earthly goods.

If you follow Kili Drive inland, you pass condos and high-rises clinging to the arid walls of this leeward valley. Turning right onto Huipu Drive, or alternately, driving up Makaha Valley Road from the highway, you reach an artificial oasis of green that is the Makaha Golf Club (once a Sheraton Resort) and Makaha Valley Country Club. Continue up Mauanolu Street to visit the **Kane'aki Heiau,** a 17th-century temple restored under the direction of the Bishop Museum in 1970. This temple was dedicated to Lono, the benevolent god of harvest and fertility. The grass and thatched huts used as prayer and meditation chambers, along with a spirit tower, have all been replicated. As the *heiau* is within a private gated community, access is limited to the hours of 10 A.M.–2 P.M. Tues.–Sun. Stop at the guard house and let them know where you're heading.

Once past Makaha, there are plenty of private places to pull off. This crab claw of land, which ends at Ka'ena Point, forms a lightly indented bay. The seascape demands attention, but look into the interior. The mountains seem naturally terraced as they form dry, deep valleys. All are micro-habitats, each different from the other.

Kea'au Beach County Park

Kea'au Beach County Park has restrooms, picnic facilities, and camping. The improved part of the park has a sandy beach, but mostly the park is fronted by coral and lava, and is frequented mostly by fishermen and campers. The unimproved section is not good for swimming, but it does attract a few surfers; it's good for snorkeling and scuba only during calm periods. The improved section is a flat grassy area with picnic tables, shade trees, and pavilions. Farther on is Ohikilili Ranch, a couple of homeless camps along the water, a few private homes, and more strands of solitary beach.

Ka'ena Point State Park

Yokohama Bay is the end of the line; the pavement ends here. If you're headed for Ka'ena Point or beyond to the north coast you'll have to walk through this windswept coastal park. Yokohama Bay is a long stretch of sandy beach that is mostly unimproved. A lava-rock bathhouse is on the right, just after the entrance. The area was named because of the multitude of Japanese fishermen who came to this lonely site to fish. It's still great for fishing! The swimming can be hazardous because of the strong wave action and rough bottom, but the snorkeling is superb. Lifeguards are on duty during the summer months. Mostly the area is used by surfers and local people, including youngsters who dive off the large lava rocks. This is inadvisable for people unfamiliar with the area. Yokohama is a great place to come if you're after a secluded beach. Weekdays, you'll have it to yourself, with a slightly greater number of people on the weekends. Definitely bring cold drinks, and remember that there are no shade trees whatsoever, so a hat or beach umbrella is a necessity. Many camp here unofficially. You can still see cement railroad track abutments, remnants of the sugar cane rail line that once ran around the point to the North Shore. A gigantic golf ball, really a U.S. satellite tracking station, caps the ridge above this park.

Kaneana Cave is a few minutes south of Yokohama Bay on your left as you head back

Long, hot, and dry, the Wai'anae Coast is not frequented by island visitors.

down the coast. You probably didn't notice it on your way north because of the peculiar land formation that conceals the mouth in that direction. Legend has it that this cave was the home of Nanue the shark man. Unfortunately, people have come here with spray cans and beer bottles and trashed the cave. If you can overlook that, it's a phenomenon—a big one. Look for three yellow cement blocks, like road dividers, right in front of the entrance. It's at the foot of a 200-foot outcropping of stone. When you see local people defacing the natural beauty like this, it's hard to believe that the Hawaiians had such a spirit bond with the 'aina.

PRACTICALITIES

ACCOMMODATIONS

Condominiums

Except for camping, the only inexpensive places to stay along the Wai'anae Coast are condos, which rent for about $325 a week and up and usually require a minimum stay of seven days. Some local people let rooms for a good rate, but there is no way to find this out in advance. Your best bet is to check out the bulletin boards at various stores along the coast.

The **Maili Cove,** 87-561 Farrington Hwy., has one-bedroom apartments, a swimming pool, parking, and TV, along with a few hotel units. The **Makaha Beach Cabanas,** 84-965 Farrington Hwy., are in Makaha along the beach just past the high school. All units have a lanai overlooking the water. They're not fancy, but are spotlessly clean and serviceable. All units are fully furnished with complete kitchens.

The **Makaha Shores** are privately owned units that overlook a beautiful white-sand beach and provide great viewing of the surfers challenging the waves below. All units are fully furnished. The least expensive accommodations are at the **Makaha Surfside.** The beach is rocky near the condo, but it makes up for this with two pools and a sauna. All units are individually owned and fully furnished. **Makaha Valley Towers** rise dramatically from Makaha Valley, but they don't fit in. They're either a testament to man's achievement or ignorance, depending on your point of view. The condo provides fully furnished units, a/c, TV, and pool. If you're staying in this ill-fitting high-rise, at least try to get a top floor where you can take advantage of the remarkable view. Just below the Towers is the **Makaha Valley Plantation,** an aesthetic low-rise community that better fits the land, with

upper-end units. Rates vary according to property but generally fall into the $250–450 a week range for studios, $350–550 for one-bedroom units, and up to $750 for two bedrooms per week. Monthly rates are also available, and you get substantial savings for longer rentals.

For rental information on property along this coast, contact Inga's Realty, 808/695-9055, fax 808/695-8060; Sugar Kane Realty, 808/696-5833, fax 808/696-7573; Waianae Coast Realty, 808/696-6366, fax 808/696-6368; or Sun Estates, 808/696-4774, fax 808/696-5817.

Luxury Resort

The courtiers anxiously waited for the grand night when the torches would be lighted and the drums beaten to announce the lovely princess as she was presented to the assembled ali'i. Those closest to the young beauty were confident that their years of training had refined the grace and nobility that matched her dignified heritage. She had proven to be an enthusiastic and willing student, endearing herself to all because of her gaiety, sweetness, and loving heart. But to assume her rightful place with the most powerful in the land, she would have to gain the self-possessed assuredness that only comes from the wisdom of experience. It is much the same with the **J. W. Marriott Ihilani Resort and Spa,** 92-1001 Olani St., Kapolei, HI 96707, 808/679-0079 or 800/626-4446, fax 808/679-0080, website: www.ihilani.com.

The hotel, an alabaster specter floating amidst the emerald-green acres of the Ko 'Olina Resort, rises above a white-sand beach at the southern end of the Wai'anae Coast. It's about a half hour west of the Honolulu airport—simply follow the H-1 expressway to the clearly marked Ko 'Olina exit. You approach the resort by way of a cobblestone drive that winds its way up to a porte cochere where valets and lei-bearing hostesses wait to greet you. The open breezeway leads to a towering glass-domed atrium brightened by cascading trellised flowers and ringed by living green ferns. Below, rivulets trickle through a series of free-form ponds, some like glass-reflecting sculptures, others alive and tinkling a natural refrain. The guest rooms, huge at almost 700 square feet, are pleasantly appointed in pastels and white, and all feature a/c, ceiling fans, louvered doors, remote-control entertainment centers, in-room safes, minibars, and private lanai. Bathrooms, an intricate play of marble and tile, feature double sinks, separate commode and shower stalls, and deep oversize tubs. Evening brings turndown service. Terrace-view rooms run $310, the golf-mountain view rooms $340, while the ocean-view and oceanfront rooms go for $430–495 a night; suites run $800–4,500. Many spa, golf, and tennis packages are also available, and they save a good deal on room rates. Other amenities are 24-hour room service, concierge service, shop boutiques, a *keiki* beachcomber club, tennis courts, and a full-service spa. Free cultural activities are scheduled throughout the week and there's evening entertainment at poolside. For those who desire, a shuttle (fee) runs three times a day from the resort to Waikele Shopping Center, Ala Moana Shopping Center, and points in Waikiki. The terrace is a perfect place to relax after a dip in the freshwater pool, but for a more athletic swim try the gentle lagoon down below. With time and maturity, the Ihilani Resort and Spa, tucked away from the madding crowd, gives every indication of becoming one of O'ahu's premier destinations. In fact, it has received the prestigious AAA five-diamond award for excellence in service and accommodations.

Dining at the Ihilani is a fantastic blending of East and West, relying heavily on locally grown herbs, vegetables, meats, and most importantly, island seafood. It is a blissful marriage built on Mediterranean, Oriental, and Hawaiian cuisine that can easily be influenced by ingredients from around the world. The Ihilani's signature restaurant, a AAA four-diamond award winner, is the dinner-only **Azul,** complemented by a magnificent wine cellar. Here the flavors of fish and seafood are cooked to their finest over the wood-fired oven and grill. Breakfast, lunch, and dinner are served at the open-air **Naupaka Terrace,** with views of the pool and lagoon, and traditional Japanese fare is offered for dinner only at the **Ushio Tei.** And golfers or those into a more casual setting will enjoy clubhouse dining for lunch at the Ko 'Olina Golf Course's **Niblick Restaurant,** which serves a memorable Sunday champagne brunch. For snacks during the day, try the **Poolside Grill** or **Hokule'a Lounge.** In additional to all these options, health-conscious breakfast and lunch spa cuisine is also offered at the Ihilani Spa.

In a separate facility just a short walk across from the main entrance is the **Ihilani Spa,** a magnificently soothing, revitalizing, and uniquely Hawaiian spa experience. This facility is centered around Thalasso water therapy, a computer-controlled water-jet massage utilizing fresh seawater and seaweed. After being immersed in this state-of-the-art tub, you move on to the Vichy Shower, Grand Jet, or Needle Pavilion, where 12 shower heads poke stimulating sprays into every nook and cranny. Next, the superbly trained staff offers hands-on experiences in the form of therapeutic massage including Swedish, *lomi lomi,* or shiatsu. You can also opt for a manicure, pedicure, or skin-rejuvenating facial. To keep trim and supple, head for the fitness facility on the third level where you will find a lap pool, hot tub, aerobics room, and strengthening equipment.

The green velvet of the **Ko 'Olina Championship Golf Course,** designed by Ted Robinson and named as one of the finest courses in America by *Golf Digest,* fronts the hotel. Open since 1990, the course is fully matured and has already hosted prestigious tournaments. If you'd rather play tennis, day or evening, the resort's six artificial grass Kramer surface tennis courts await your pleasure on top of the hotel's parking structure. Court time can be arranged for $24 an hour, and instruction, round robins, and clinics are offered.

SHOPPING, FOOD, AND SERVICES

The new community of Kapolei and the older residential area of Makakilo lie just east of the Ko 'Olina Resort. While there are sparse services in Makakilo, in Kapolei you will find the **Kapolei**

O'AHU

Shopping Center and other nearby shopping areas, perfect for those staying on this coast, comprising a Longs Drug store, a gas station, several fast food joints, a Temps Music, GNC Nutrition Center, Postal Plus for package service, Safeway for food shopping, three banks all with ATM machines, and for food, Loco Moco, Panda Express, and Tasty Korean BBQ for inexpensive dining. A movie theater and post office are a short distance away on Kamokila Boulevard.

Finding a two-scoop plate lunch is no problem. Little drive-in lunch counters are found in almost every Wai'anae town. Each serves hearty island food such as teriyaki chicken, pork, or mahimahi for under $6. A favorite is the **Makaha Drive-In** on Farrington Highway near the Makaha Valley Road intersection.

You also see fruit sellers parked along the road. Their produce couldn't be fresher, and stopping provides you not only with the perfect complement to a picnic lunch but with a good chance to meet some local people.

For your shopping and dining needs in Nanakuli, try the **Pacific Shopping Mall,** where you'll find Sack 'n Save Foods, the largest supermarket in the area for groceries, bakery, and deli. In the complex is **Nanakuli Chop Suey Restaurant,** open 10 A.M.–8:30 P.M., serving standard Chinese fare at local down-home prices. Just behind McDonald's is the **Nanakuli Korean Bar-B-Que,** 808/668-2722, with sit-down and take-out Korean food at moderate prices; open 10 A.M.–9 P.M. daily.

The **Wai'anae Mall** is a complete shopping facility, the largest on the coast. Don't worry about bringing supplies or food if you're on a day excursion. The mall holds all you need, including Waianae Chop Suey, B. K. Ocean Sports, Blockbuster Video, Longs Drugs, and Wai'anae Laundromat. Have no fear if you're addicted to fast food. Some major franchises have decided that your trip to leeward O'ahu wouldn't be complete without something processed in a Styrofoam box. For ethnic flavor try the **Tamura Superette,** which stocks plenty of ingredients used in ethnic foods. An **L&L Drive-In** is here as well for the plate lunch lovers. Perhaps best of all for a quick snack are the hot *malasadas* from Leonard's truck stand at the mall. For banking needs, try the Bank of America branch office. The post office sits across from Tamura's, and you'll spot a number of gas stations in the middle of town, along with a 7-Eleven convenience store.

Arts and Crafts

The **Wai'anae Coast Culture and Arts Society** offers workshops in lei-making, *lau hala* weaving, hula, ceramics, and the Hawaiian language. The center welcomes people either to observe or participate in the programs, residents and visitors alike. The fee to participate is $3 per month plus the cost of supplies. For times and schedules contact the Society at 808/668-1549.

SOUTHEAST O'AHU
MAUNALUA BAY TO MAKAPU'U

It's amazing how quickly you can leave the frenzy of Waikiki behind. Once you round the bend past Diamond Head and continue traveling east toward Koko Head, the pace slackens measurably . . . almost by the yard. A minute ago you were in traffic, now you're cruising. It's not that this area is undeveloped; other parts of the island are much more laid-back, but none so close to the action of the city. In the 12 miles you travel from Honolulu to Waimanalo, you pass the natural phenomenon of Koko Crater, a reliable blowhole, the most aquatically active underwater park in the islands, and a string of beaches, each with a different personality.

Humanity has made its presence felt here, too. The area has some of the most exclusive homes on the island, as well as Hawaii Kai, a less exclusive project developed by the visionary businessman Henry Kaiser, who years ago created this harbinger of things to come. There's Sea Life Park, offering a day's outing of fun for the family, plus shopping centers, the mostly Hawaiian town of Waimanalo, and the inactive Bellows Air Force Base, now one of the finest camping beaches on the island. This lack of development preserves the area as scenic and recreational, prized attributes that should be taken advantage of before this sunny sandbox gets paved over.

SIGHTS, BEACHES, AND PARKS

The drive out this way accounts for half of the 360 degrees of what is called **The Circle Route.** Start by heading over the Pali Highway down to Kailua, hitting the sights on the way, or come this way first along Route 72 as you make the loop back to the city. The only consideration is what part of the day you'd rather stop at the

O'AHU

southeast beaches for a dip. For the most part, the beaches of this area *are* the sights. The road abounds with scenic points and overlooks. This is the part of O'ahu that's absolutely beautiful in its undevelopment. It's hard to find a road on any of the Hawaiian Islands that's going to be more scenic than this. At first the countryside is dry because this is the leeward side. But as you approach Waimanalo it gets much more tropical. The road is a serpentine ribbon with one coastal vista after another, a great choice for a joyride just to soak in the sights. The following listings assume that you follow Route 72 east from Waikiki to Waimanalo.

Maunalua Bay

Maunalua (Two Mountain) Bay is a four-mile stretch of sun and surf between Diamond Head and Koko Head, with a beach park about every half mile. **Wailupe Beach Park** lies on the Waikiki side of the residential Wailupe Peninsula, once a shoreline pond. This pocket-size beach park, clearly marked off the Kalaniana'ole Highway, provides restrooms and picnic facilities. Swimming is officially not recommended. Be careful of the boat channel surrounding the area because the deep drop-off is very abrupt.

After another fancy neighborhood is **Kawaiku'i Beach Park.** No lifeguard, but the conditions are safe year-round, and the bottom is shallow, muddy, and overgrown with seaweed. In times past, islanders came to the confluence of a nearby spring to harvest special *limu* that grow only where fresh water meets the ocean. You'll find unlimited access, parking stalls, picnic facilities, and restrooms. Few people use the park, and it's ideal for sunning, but for frolicking in the water, give it a miss.

In quick succession come **Niu and Paiko Beaches,** lying along residential areas. Although there is public access, few people take advantage of them because the swimming, with a coral and mud bottom, is less than ideal. Some residents have built a pier at Niu Beach past the mudflats,

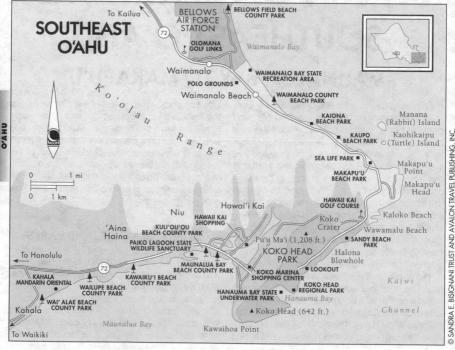

but it's restricted to their private use. Paiko Lagoon is a state bird sanctuary; binoculars will help with sightings of a variety of coastal birds.

On the east side of the Paiko Lagoon is **Kuli'ou'ou Beach Park.** Even with its broad lawns, picnic tables, children's play area, and shallow beach, this "everyman's" park at the end of a string of exclusive neighborhoods is not a very enticing place for swimming.

The residential area in the hills behind **Maunalua Bay Beach Park** is Hawaii Kai, built by Henry Kaiser, the aluminum magnate. The controversial development was often denigrated as "suburban blight." Many felt it was the beginning of O'ahu's ruination. On the oceanside of Kuapa Pond, the park fronts Maunalua Bay. At one time the pond was a huge fishpond, later dredged by Kaiser, who used the dredged material to build the park, which he donated to the city in 1960. The boat launch constitutes the primary attraction of the park, and except for this boat launch (the only one on this side of the island), the area is of little recreational use because of the mud or coral bottom. Outrigger canoe clubs come here to push off for morning canoe practice, and some scuba companies use the boat ramp for their excursions to the outer reef. There are a few tables here for a picnic.

Koke'e and Koko Kai Parks, two undeveloped parks, are along Po'ipu Drive in the Portlock area below Koko Head. The currents and beach conditions make both unsuitable for swimming, but they're popular with surfers. Few others come here, but the views of the bay are lovely.

Hanauma Bay State Underwater Park

One of the premier beach parks in Hawaii is in the sea-eroded crater of an extinct volcano just below Koko Head. People flock here to snorkel, scuba, picnic, and swim. Hanauma Bay, meaning "Curved Bay" and pronounced as three syllables—"ha-nau-ma," gets on average about 3,300 people a day. That's over one million visitors a year! During the day, the parking lot at the top of the hill overlooking the crescent bay below looks like a used car lot, jammed with Japanese imports, vans, and tour buses. Parking is severely restricted, so use TheBus no. 20. If you want to avoid the crowds come in the early morning or after 4 P.M. when the sun dips behind the crater and most tourists leave on cue.

There's still plenty of daylight, so plan your trip accordingly.

The reef protects the bay and sends a maze of coral fingers right up to the shoreline. A large sandy break in the reef, **Keyhole,** is a choice spot for entering the water and for swimming. The entire bay is alive with tropical fish. Many have become so accustomed to snorkelers that they've lost their fear entirely and come nibbling at your fingers for food. The county provides lifeguards from 7 A.M., restrooms, showers, picnic facilities, a pavilion, food concession, and snorkel equipment rental.

Before you enter the water, do yourself a favor and read the large bulletin board near the pavilion that describes conditions. It divides the bay into three areas ranging from beginner to expert, and warns of sections to avoid. Be especially careful of **Witches Brew,** a turbulent area on the right at the mouth of the bay that can wash you into the Moloka'i Express, a notoriously dangerous rip current. Follow a path along the left-hand seacliff to **Toilet Bowl,** a natural pool that rises and falls with the tides. If the conditions are right, you can sit in it to float up and down in a phenomenon very similar to a flushing toilet.

Note: Environmental Alert. Because severe overuse has threatened the fragile ecosystem of the bay, tour companies are now banned from dropping people in the park expressly for snorkeling. Tour buses can now only stop at the top of the hill for a 15-minute overview, and then must leave. People wishing to explore the bay may come by rental car, moped, bicycle, or city bus, which has a stop within the park. However, once the parking lot is filled, it is closed! And, the park is closed to all visitors on Tuesday when sorely needed maintenance is performed. Also, please do not feed the fish. It's illegal to do so and carries a $1,000 fine. Let the fish feed naturally to maintain a better balance and prevent them from becoming food beggars. Most importantly, the very reef is being destroyed by people walking upon it. Please do everything you can to avoid this. Also, leave the sea turtles alone, and all rocks, shells, and coral as you find them. A few tour companies have tried to continue bringing people into the park and have found ways to violate the *spirit,* if not the *letter* of the restrictions. Please do not patronize

O'AHU

them. With care, Hanauma Bay will remain beautiful for all future generations.

One group that you *should* patronize is the volunteer organization **Hanauma Bay Educational Program** (HBEP), a Sea Grant Program out of the University of Hawai'i. The HBEP works toward the conservation and preservation of the bay, and the volunteers run a daily (except Tuesday when the bay is closed) educational tour, starting between 8 and 9 A.M. Come join the tour and learn about this important environmental work.

Koko Head

For a sweeping view, you used to be able to hike to the summit of **Koko Head,** not to be confused with Koko Crater farther east. It's now off limits. The 642-foot summit of Koko (Blood) Head was the last place that young, wandering Madame Pele attempted to dig herself a fiery nest on O'ahu; as usual, she was flooded out by her jealous sister. The bowl of Hanauma Bay lies at the feet of Koko Head; below are two small extinct craters, Nono'ula and 'Ihi'ihilauakea.

Koko Crater

Koko Crater's Hawaiian name is Kohelepelepe (Vagina Labia Minora). Legend says that Pele's sister, Kapo, had a magical vagina that could fly and that she could send anywhere. Kamapua'a, the pig-god, was intent on raping Pele when Kapo came to her aid. She dispatched her vagina to entice Kamapua'a, and he followed it to Koko Crater, where it made the crater and then flew away. Kamapua'a was unsuccessful when taking a flying leap at this elusive vagina.

The rim of Koko Crater rises to 1,208 feet. On the floor is the 60-acre **Koko Crater Botanical Garden,** 808/522-7060, which, due to the unique conditions, specializes in succulents, cacti, and other dry land plants from Hawaii, the Americas, Africa, and Madagascar. Opened in 1958, this garden is little developed and has but one trail and no other amenities. Free admission. Open daily sunrise to sunset, except Christmas and New Year's Day. Expect to spend 90 minutes on the two-mile circle path. To reach the gardens, follow Route 72 east to Wawamalu Beach just past Sandy Beach Park and then take a left on Kealahou Street. Turn left again at a sign that points to a riding stable and botanical garden, and follow the road to its end where a walking path leads into the crater.

Halona Cove

As you round a bend on Route 72 past Hanauma Bay you come to two scenic lookouts and the natural lookout of Halona Cove, which means "The Peering Place," an excellent vantage point from which to see whales in season. Just before Halona stands a monument and stone wall erected by the **Honolulu Japanese Casting Club.** Below on the rocks, men come to cast into the surf. The monument at one time was of

The rocky coastline near the Japanese Casting Club makes a great place to fish.

J.D. BISIGNANI

O'AHU

O Jisan, the Japanese god of protection, but it was destroyed by overzealous patriots during World War II. The current monument was erected after the war, and O Jisan was carved into it. Below is a secluded little beach perfect for sunbathing. The only way to it is to scramble down the cliff. Swim only on calm days, or the waves can pull you out to sea and then suck you into the chamber of the famous **Halona Blowhole** just around the bend. There's a turnout at the blowhole for parking. The blowhole is a lava tube at the perfect height for the waves to be driven into it. The water compresses, and the pressure sends a spume into the air through a hole in its ceiling. Be extremely cautious around the blowhole. Those unfortunate enough to fall in face almost certain death.

Sandy Beach Park

The fine white sand of Sandy Beach forms one of the best bodysurfing beaches on O'ahu, and the most rugged of them all. It's also a great surfing beach—for experts. More necks and backs are broken on this beach than on all the other O'ahu beaches combined. But because of the east-breaking waves, and bottom, the swells are absolutely perfect for bodysurfing. The lifeguards at the two towers use a flag system to inform you about conditions. The **red flag** means "stay out." When checking out Sandy Beach, don't be fooled by bodysurfers who make it appear easy. These are experts, intimately familiar with the area, and even they are injured at times.

Local people refer to the beach as "Scene Beach" because this is where young people come to strut their stuff. This is where the boys are because this is where the girls are. There are restrooms, a large parking area, and two lifeguard towers. Rip-offs have happened, so don't leave valuables in your car. *Kaukau* wagons park in the area, selling refreshments. When wind conditions are right, you may see a whole parade of colorful exotic-shaped kites flying across the sky here. Some even come to practice flying kites to work on skills for kite surfing.

As the road skirts the coastline, it passes a string of beaches that look inviting but are extremely dangerous because there is no protecting reef. The best known is **Wawamalu**, where people come to sunbathe only. Across the road is **Hawaii Kai Golf Course,** an excellent public course.

The lifeguards do a great job at Sandy Beach.

J.D. BISIGNANI

Makapu'u Point

The southeasternmost point of land on O'ahu is Makapu'u (Bulging Eye) Point. This headland overlooks Makapu'u Beach Park and supports an important lighthouse. This lighthouse uses prism glass in its lamp and has been functioning for more than 100 years. Bunkers near the top were constructed during World War II and referred to by James Jones in his novel *From Here to Eternity.* They were manned during the war to protect the deep-water Makapu'u Bay from possible Japanese attack. A moderate one-mile hike over an asphalt road leads to the top. Park along the highway and give yourself at least 90 minutes for the round-trip. It's dry and windy, so bring plenty of water and a hat to shade your eyes. During winter months this is an excellent spot to watch for whales. Some very energetic people bring a picnic lunch and hike down the sheer outer face of this promontory to a rocky tidepool area along the water to sunbathe and fish.

Makapu'u Beach Park

This beach park below Makapu'u Point is a favorite launching pad for hang gliding. Makapu'u is *the* most famous bodysurfing beach in the entire state, and also used for surfing. It can be extremely rugged, however, as more people are

O'AHU

rescued here than at any other beach on O'ahu—except Sandy Beach. In winter the conditions are hazardous, with much of the beach eroded away, leaving exposed rocks. With no interfering reef, the surf can reach 12 feet—perfect for bodysurfing, if you're an expert. In summer, the sandy beach reappears, and the wave action is much gentler, allowing recreational swimming. There are restrooms, lifeguard towers with a flag warning system, and picnic facilities.

Offshore is **Manana (Rabbit) Island.** Curiously, it does resemble a rabbit, but it's so named because rabbits actually live on it. They were released there in the 1880s by a local rancher who wanted to raise them but who was aware that if they ever got loose on O'ahu they could ruin much of the crop lands. During the impotent counterrevolution of 1894, designed to reinstate the Hawaiian monarchy, Manana Island was a cache for arms and ammunition buried on its windward side. Nearby, and closer into shore, is tiny Kaohikaipu Island, which, along with Manana and several other islands along this coast, is reserved as a seabird sanctuary. Efforts are being made by the National Audubon Society to attract albatross to this island from nearby Kaneohe Marine Corps Air Base. Establishing a colony here would keep these ground-nesting animals away from natural predators like mongooses, cats, and dogs.

Sea Life Park Hawaii

Nestled below the lush Ko'olau Mountains inland of Makapu'u Point is Sea Life Park Hawaii, 808/259-2500, website: www.sealifeparkhawaii.com. Within the park, a cluster of tanks hold an amazing display of marine animals that live freely in the ocean just a few hundred yards away. Admission for adults is $25, juniors 4–12 $12.50, under four free. Open daily 9:30 A.M.–5 P.M. A park shuttle bus runs round-trip from major Waikiki hotels for $5 per person, or take TheBus no. 58 from Ala Moana Center or no. 20 from Waikiki past Hanauma Bay. For self-drivers, parking is $3 in the parking lot.

The park hosts a variety of shows throughout the day by trained sea lions, dolphins, and penguins and other activities with turtles and monk seals in the various pools and at the informative Hawaii Ocean Theater. The park's most impressive feature is the **Hawaiian Reef Tank,** a massive 300,000-gallon fish bowl where guests come face to face through walls of glass with more than 2,000 specimens of the island's rich marine life as they descend three fathoms down an exterior ramp. For a more in-depth and intense exposure to the training and care of dolphins, attend **Splash U,** a one-hour interactive dolphin training session where you're behind the scenes and right there with the trainers, or the more intensive **Dolphin Adventure.** Splash U costs $79 adult and $67 for kids up to age 12, the Dolphin Adventure is $130 for adults only. The **Seawalker** program lets guests actually enter the big tank in wet suits and a diver's helmet to meet the fish mask to mouth; $89 for age 12 and up. The newest interactive feature is the **Hawaiian Ray Encounter,** where you enter the stingray tank to float among those graceful creatures; $39 adults or $28 children. All these prices include regular admission to the park. The popular sessions are held several times a day, and reservations must be made well in advance.

A full menu of island food is available at the Sea Lion Cafe for when you've worked up an appetite. Before you leave, pick up a souvenir at one of the gift shops or have a look at the free Pacific Whaling Museum, which houses one of the largest collections of whaling artifacts and memorabilia in the Pacific. Sea Life Park Hawaii is a great learning and entertaining experience for the entire family, or for anyone interested in exploring Hawaii's fascinating marine life.

SERVICES

Except for the excellent camping in Waimanalo, you're limited when it comes to accommodations in this area. Only a few B&Bs and rental homes are available.

One of the first places to pick up supplies as you head east on Route 72 is the Times Super Market in the **Niu Valley Shopping Center,** about halfway between Diamond Head and Koko Head. Aside from foodstuffs, you can also get your prescription filled here, pick out flowers for your sweetie, or grab a sandwich for your trip down the highway. In the shopping center is **The Swiss Inn,** 808/377-5447, an authentic Swiss restaurant where the owner/chef pours love and attention into every dish. The food, like veal medallion Florentino, wienerschnitzel, and baked chicken, is superb, well prepared, and reasonably priced for the quality. Dinner is served from 6 P.M., Sunday brunch 10:30 A.M.–1 P.M. If heavy Germanic food isn't what you're after, perhaps you can try Lung Fung Chinese or Castagnola's Italian. Castagnola's uses only fresh ingredients from the islands and pasta and tomatoes from the Abruzzi region of Italy for natural, flavorful, and wholesome foods cooked to order.

A little less ideal for location and a bit closer to Diamond Head, the **Aina Haina Shopping Center** still has many restaurants, a Foodland Supermarket, two banks, a branch post office, and a gas station. Enter from West Hind Drive.

Hawaii Kai Shopping

On the west side of Kuapa Pond are two shopping malls. Try Marshall's Store, Payless Shoes, General Nutrition Center, Costco, or more than a dozen other shops in the **Hawaii Kai Towne Center.** Safeway, Longs Drugs, Aloha Dive Shop, and numerous other stores and restaurants are in the neighboring **Hawaii Kai Shopping Center** just up the road. The Aloha Dive Shop at the Koko Marina is a full-service dive shop. You can rent or buy snorkeling and scuba gear. So, if you haven't picked up rentals from Waikiki and you're heading out to Hanauma Bay, come here. Dives start at $75 for beginners, featuring all-boat diving at Maunalua Bay, Koko Head, and Diamond Head. Open-water, advanced, and search and rescue certification courses are given for $375. This is the shop of Jackie James, first lady of Hawaiian diving. She's been diving here for more than 25 years.

Note: For Hawaii Kai's outstanding gourmet option, Roy's Restaurant, see the **Waikiki** chapter.

Koko Marina Shopping Center

Along the highway in Hawaii Kai, this center is the largest and easiest-access shopping center that you'll find on the way to Hanauma Bay. There are three banks, several gift shops, Local Motion and other shops for beachwear, and Koko Marina 8 Theaters. Foodland provides most supplies for picnics and camping, and you can dine at Assaggio's Ristorante Italiano, McDonald's, Zippy's, Kokonuts Shave Ice, Bua Khao Thai, Kozo Sushi, or Akasaka for finer Japanese food.

The Japanese own the Koko Marina Center. In the center are water sport and thrill-ride booking agencies that will take non-Japanese tourists, but they are more for the Japanese tourists who come here by the busload and immediately head out on one of these thrill rides. They've already booked from Japan, so it's all set up and off they go.

Hawaii Sport, 808/395-3773, offers more than a dozen water sports to choose from, like a 20-minute banana boat ride for $25, 30-minute jet ski use for $49, parasailing for $49, wakeboarding or water-skiing for $49, and snuba for $79.

Upstairs in the center is **Get Wet Hawaii,** 808/395-7255, which does pretty much the same thing at similar prices, plus offers snorkeling trips to Hanauma Bay, horseback rides, and transportation to and from Waikiki.

Hot Island is a floating complex in Maunalua Bay where you can participate in water activities and splash away to your heart's content. A boat ferries you to the island for a half or full day of adventure. For information, call **Hawaii Ocean Thrills,** 808/539-9400.

On the second floor above McDonald's is **Sea Breeze Water Sports Ltd.,** 808/396-0100. It offers jet skiing at $49 for 30 minutes, speedboat rides for the same price and time, a one-tank scuba dive for $50, and parasailing for $49. Sea Breeze advertises that if you can find a better price anywhere, they will match it.

O'AHU

WAIMANALO

This small rural town was at one time the center of a thriving sugar plantation owned by the *hapa* Hawaiian nobleman, John Cummins, who was responsible for introducing rabbits to Manana Island. It has fallen on hard times ever since the plantation closed in the late 1940s, and now it produces much of Honolulu's bananas, papayas, and anthuriums from small plots and farms, and a great deal of organic greens that end up on the plates of many fine restaurants on the island. The town sits in the center of Waimanalo Bay, which has the longest (three miles) stretch of sand beach on O'ahu, and to many people, especially those from O'ahu, it is also the best. The backdrop for this rather ordinary town is a finely sculpted *pali* that rises precipitously up into a variegated curtain of green—and it's close. Few but adequate travelers' services are in town.

The **Olomana Golf Links,** a relatively easy public course, is close to town. It's also a good place to go for breakfast. You think you're in Waimanalo when you pass the first built-up area, but that isn't it. You keep going about a mile or two and then you'll come to the older section of town, which is Waimanalo proper.

For those who enjoy the sport of kings, polo matches are held at about 2:30 P.M. on Sundays from April (or May) to October at the polo field in Waimanalo across from Waimanalo Bay State Recreation Area. Matches usually last 90 minutes; $3 for adults, kids are free.

Horseback rides are given at **Correa Stables,** just above Kaupo Beach Park on the south end of town.

BEACHES AND PARKS

Kaupo Beach Park
Between Sea Life Park and Waimanalo, this is the first park along the coast that's safe for swimming. The park is undeveloped and has no lifeguards, so you are advised to exercise caution. The shore is lined with a protective reef and rocks, and the swimming is best beyond the reef. Close to shore, the jutting rocks discourage most swimmers. Surfers frequent Kaupo, especially beginners, lured by the ideal yet gentle waves. At the southern end of this park is Makai Research Pier. Part of this pier is open to the public, but the rest is closed for use by government ocean research organizations. Many locals come to fish off the pier or spearfish along the coast. Some companies run scuba tours to the reef offshore.

Waimanalo Beach

ROBERT NILSEN

O'AHU

Kaiona Beach Park

Just before you enter the ethnically Hawaiian town of Waimanalo, you pass Kaiona Beach Park, which you can spot because of the semi-permanent tents pitched there. Local people are very fond of the area and use it extensively. Look inland to view some remarkable cliffs and mountains that tumble to the sea. The area was at one time called Pahonu, "Turtle Enclosure," because a local chief who loved turtle meat erected a large enclosure in the sea into which any turtle that was caught by local fishermen had to be deposited. Parts of the pond perimeter wall can still be seen at low tide. Facilities include restrooms, showers, and a picnic area. Swimming is safe year-round.

Waimanalo Beach County Park

The fine powder sand of Waimanalo beaches stretches virtually uninterupted from Sea Life Park, past the town of Waimanalo, and through Bellows Air Force Base to Wailea Point. At the south end of town, Waimanalo Beach County Park provides camping with a county permit. The beach is well protected and the swimming is safe year-round. Snorkeling is good, and there are picnic tables, restrooms, and recreational facilities, including a ball park, basketball courts, and children's play equipment. The park is right in the built-up beach area, and not secluded from the road. Although the facilities are good, the setting could be better.

Waimanalo Bay State Recreation Area

Just up the road is Waimanalo Bay State Recreation Area, which remains largely undeveloped and is much better situated. This park is good for picnicking and swimming, which can sometimes be rough. The area, surrounded by a dense iron-wood grove, is called "Sherwood Forest" or "Sherwoods," due to many rip-offs by thieves who fancy themselves as Robin Hood, plundering the rich and keeping the loot for themselves. Guess who the rich guys are? Fortunately, this problem of breaking into cars is diminishing, but take necessary precautions. This is the best beach on this section of the island.

Bellows Field Beach County Park

Part of this one-time active Air Force base, now used only as a rest and recreational facility, is now one of O'ahu's finest beach parks, and there's camping too! The water is safe for swimming year-round and lifeguards are on duty on the weekends. Bodysurfing and board surfing are also excellent in the park, but snorkeling is mediocre. After entering the main gates, follow the road for about two miles to the beach area. You'll find picnic tables, restrooms, and cold-water showers. The combination of shade trees and adjacent beach make a perfect camping area and it's often full. The park is marked by two freshwater streams, Waimanalo and Puha, at either end.

FOOD AND SHOPPING

As you enter Waimanalo, look on the right for **Keneke's** plate lunch place, next to the post office. A very local eatery, Keneke's offers plate lunches with a huge list of options for $3.50–6, burgers, sandwiches, shave ice, and smoothies. It's a great place to fill up for an afternoon on the beach, and the crowd at the window tells you what a good reputation it has. Nearby in what looks like an old gas station building is a small "no name" market for sundries and snacks. A short "mile" past Keneke's is **Mel's Market,** where you can pick up almost all supplies and you definitely have a better selection. A gift gallery is next door. Keep going along the Kalaniana'ole Highway for a mile or so to find **Waimanalo Shopping Center** in the middle of town. Here you can do all your business, pick up lunch and supplies, and head on down the road or go to the beach. In the shopping center are **Hawaiian Hidden Treasures** for jewelry, gifts, and souvenirs; **Sumo Connection Hawaii,** where wrestler Akebono's mother presides over sumo memorabilia and aloha shirts; and the well-managed **Waimanalo Laundry.** For food, try **Maria Bonita's Restaurant** for quick Mexican eats at $6.50 or less, **KimoZ Restaurant and Karaoke,** which has some of the best food and drink around in a clean family setting, or **Daves Ice Cream,** open seven days a week 9 A.M.–9:30 P.M. Across the road and down a bit is **Shima's Market,** a small but full-service food and sundries outlet.

M.G.L. DOMENY DE REINZI

WINDWARD O'AHU

O'ahu's windward coast never has to turn a shoulder into a harsh and biting wind. The trades do blow, mightily at times, but always tropical warm, perfumed with flowers, balmy and bright. Honolulu is just 12 miles over the hump of the *pali,* but a world apart. When *kama'aina* families talk of going to "the cottage in the country," they're most likely referring to the windward coast. In the southern parts, the suburban towns of **Kailua** and **Kane'ohe** are modern in every way, with the lion's share of the services on this side. With populations of more than 35,000 each, these two towns together make the second most densely populated area on the island. Kailua has O'ahu's best windsurfing beach and a nearby *heiau,* preserved and unvisited, while Kane'ohe sits on a huge bay dotted with islands and fringed by a reef. The **Kahekili Highway** runs inland to the base of the *pali,* passing the **Valley of the Temples,** resplendent with universal houses of worship. At **Kahalu'u** starts a string of beaches running north, offering the full range of O'ahu's coastal outdoor experience. You can meander side roads into the mountains near the Hawaiian villages of **Waiahole** and

Waikane, where the normal way of life is ramshackle cottages on small subsistence farms.

The coast bulges at **Ka'a'awa,** where the **Crouching Lion,** a natural stone formation, seems ready to pounce on the ever-present tour buses that disturb its repose. North is **Sacred Falls State Park,** a short hike to a peak at O'ahu's beautiful and natural heart (currently closed). Suddenly, you're in manicured **La'ie,** where Hawaii's Mormon community has built a university, a temple perfect in its symmetry, and the **Polynesian Cultural Center,** a sanitized replica of life in the South Seas. The northern tip at **Kahuku** is the site of one of O'ahu's oldest sugar mills. Just outside of town is the **James Campbell National Wildlife Refuge,** and beyond that **Kahuku Point,** where the North Shore begins.

More than a dozen beaches line the 24 miles of the windward coast from Kailua to Kahuku. The majority offer a wide range of water sports and a few have camping. A handful of offshore islands, one or two close enough to wade to, can be visited and explored. Others are refuges for Hawaiian water birds and off limits to visitors.

WINDWARD O'AHU

JAMES CAMPBELL WILDLIFE REFUGE
Ki'i Pond
To Hale'iwa
83
Kahuku
MALAEKAHANA STATE RECREATION AREA
Malaekahana Bay
La'ie Bay
La'ie
LA'IE POINT PARK
POLYNESIAN CULTURAL CENTER
La'ie Beach (Pounder's Beach)
Kokololio Beach
HAU'ULA BEACH PARK
Hau'ula
Punalu'u
Sacred Falls State Park
PUNALU'U BEACH PARK
Mahie Point
MAKAUA BEACH PARK
SWANZY BEACH PARK
Ka'a'awa
KAUHI'IMAKAOKALANI (CROUCHING LION)
KA'A'AWA BEACH PARK
KAHANA VALLEY STATE PARK
Makahonu Point
83
SUGAR MILL RUINS (1864)
KUALOA RANCH
KUALOA COUNTY REGIONAL PARK
Mokoli'i Island (Chinamen's Hat)
Waikane
WAIAHOLE BEACH PARK
Kapapa Island
KANE'OHE MARINE CORPS AIR STATION
SENATOR FONG'S PLANTATION AND GARDEN
Waiahole
Moku Manu
SEABIRD SANCTUARY
Ka'alaea
Wailua Pen.
Mokapu Point
Kahalu'u
Kane'ohe Bay
Pyramid Rock
Mokapu Peninsula
83
HE'EIA STATE PARK
SEE "KANE'OHE" MAP
830
BYODO-IN TEMPLE
Kane'ohe
H3
SEE "KAILUA" MAP
Kailua Bay
Kailua
KAILUA BEACH PARK
H3
Kawainui Marsh
Lanikai
Moku Lua Islands
78
LIKELIKE HWY.
NU'UANU PALI STATE WAYSIDE
H1
70
63
61
PALI HWY.
Mt. Olomana (1,643 ft.)
Waimanalo
BELLOWS FIELD BEACH PARK
Waimanalo Bay
72
HONOLULU
To Honolulu

PACIFIC OCEAN

Ko'olau Range
KAMEHAMEHA HWY

0 2 mi
0 2 km

Moon

O'AHU

© SANDRA E. BISIGNANI TRUST AND AVALON TRAVEL PUBLISHING, INC.

It makes little difference in which direction you travel the windward coast, but the following will be listed from south to north from Kailua to Kahuku. The slight advantage in traveling this direction is that your car is in the right-hand lane, which is better for coastal views. But, as odd as it may seem, this dynamic stretch totally changes its vistas depending upon the direction that you travel. You can come one way and then retrace your steps, easily convincing yourself that you've never seen it before. The road, Kamehameha Highway (Route 83), is clearly marked with mile markers.

KAILUA AND VICINITY

The easiest way into Kailua (Two Seas) is over the Ko'olau Range on Route 61, the Pali Highway. As soon as you pass through a long tunnel just after the Nu'uanu Pali Lookout and your eyes adjust to the shocking brilliance of sunshine, look to your right to see Mt. Olomana. Its 1,643-foot peak is believed to be the volcanic origin of O'ahu, the first land to emerge from the seas. Below lies Kailua and the Kawainui marsh, perhaps the oldest inhabited area on this side of the island. Kamehameha I, after conquering O'ahu in 1795, gave all this land to the chiefs who had fought for him. The area became a favorite of the ruling *ali'i* until the fall of the monarchy at the turn of the 20th century. The Kawainui Canal drains the marsh and runs through Kailua. A good vantage point from which to observe it is along Kalaheo Avenue, the main road running along the coast in Kailua. Kailua is developed with shopping centers, all modern services, and one of the *best* windsurfing beaches in the state. Three golf courses surround the town, and a satellite city hall dispenses camping permits.

SIGHTS

A good touring loop is to continue straight on Route 61 until it comes to the coast. Turn right onto Kalaheo Avenue, which takes you along the coast to Kailua Beach Park. In the waters offshore will be a spectacle of windsurfers, with their sails puffed out like the proud chests of multicolored birds. To the left of the beach is **Mokapu (Sacred District) Peninsula,** home of the Kaneohe Marine Corps Base, closed to civilians except 1–5 P.M. on Sunday when only certain areas are open. Notice that the rock that separates the peninsula creates a large natural archway navigable by sizable boats. Most of the little islands in the bay are bird sanctuaries. The farthest, **Moku Manu,** is home to terns and man-o'-wars, birds famous for leading fishermen to schools of fish.

Follow the road around the shoulder of the headland as it gains the heights from the beach; a pulloff here affords an expansive panorama of the bay below. By daytime it's enjoyable, but in the evening local kids come here to hang out and drink beer. Continuing, the road takes you through an area of beautiful homes until you come to **Lanikai Beach.** At one time trees came down to the shoreline, but it has steadily eroded away. The Navy attempted to start a retaining reef by dumping barge loads of white bath tile just offshore. Their efforts were not successful, but many homes in town now have sparkling new, white-tiled bathrooms! As this road, A'alapapa Drive, loops back toward town, it changes names to Mokulua.

Ulupo Heiau State Monument
Ulupo (Night Inspiration) is dedicated to the Ulu line of *ali'i,* who were responsible for setting up *heiau* involving the sacred births of chiefs. Oftentimes the umbilical cord was cut just as a drum was sounded, then the cord *(piko)* was placed in a shallow rock depression at a *heiau.* This temple, supposedly built by the legendary *menehune,* who usually accomplished their task within the span of one night, shows remarkable stone craftsmanship, measuring 140 feet wide and 30 feet high, although the stepped front wall has partially collapsed by rock fall. Atop the temple is a pathway that you can follow. Notice small stones wrapped in *ti* leaves placed as offerings. The *heiau* overlooks Kawainui marsh, once a huge inland lagoon that provided great quantities of fish for the population. It is estimated that about 6,000 years ago, this marsh was a bay of the ocean. Due to the forces of nature, by 1,000 years ago it had turned into a lagoon. Its

KAILUA

Kailua Bay

KALAMA BEACH PARK

Kailua Beach

KAILUA BEACH CENTER
KALAPAWAI MARKET

Popoʻa Island

KAILUA BEACH PARK

BUZZ'S

KAILUA SHOPPING CENTER

POST OFFICE

WANAʻAO RD.

HAHANI ST.

Kawainui Marsh

HOʻOLAI ST.

HEKILI ST.

HAMAKUA

KAILUA RD. 61

★ ULUPO HEIAU

CASTLE MEDICAL CENTER

KALANIANAʻOLE HWY.

Enchanted Lake

AKUMAU ST.

AKAMAI

KEOLU DR.

KEOLU DR.

AʻULEPE ST.

ENCHANTED LAKE CENTER

HELE ST.

KUPUA ST.

MID-PACIFIC COUNTRY CLUB

Lanikai Beach

Lanikai

AʻALAPAPA DR.

MOKULUA DR.

Kaelepulu Canal

72

0   1 mi
0   1 km

© SANDRA E. BISIGNANI TRUST AND AVALON TRAVEL PUBLISHING, INC.

OʻAHU

size continued to shrink, and by 200 years ago it was a much smaller fishpond, perhaps 400 acres in size. Only in the last century has it become a marsh, due to natural changes and human intervention, and today it's home to many endangered water birds. A second former fishpond to the southeast, similar but smaller, is now known as Enchanted Lake. To get to Ulupo Heiau as you approach Kailua on Route 61, look for a red light and a 7-Eleven store. Turn left onto Uluoa Street, following it one block to Manu Aloha Street, where you turn right. Turn right again onto Manu Oʻo and park in the Windward YMCA parking lot. The *heiau* is directly behind the YMCA building.

Maunawili Demonstration Trail

This is one of Oʻahu's newest trails. The trailhead is just above St. Stephen's Seminary along the Pali Highway, but you can't turn left into the trailhead parking lot when going uphill. Approach it from the Honolulu side or head uphill through the *pali* tunnel and turn off onto Nuʻuanu Pali Drive. Follow this up past the

Nu'uanu Pali Lookout and get back onto the highway going toward Kailua. After passing through the tunnel again, a sign points to a scenic overlook a short ways down. Pull off into the parking area and look for the trail sign and entrance through the highway guardrail a short distance back up the road. This trail can also be accessed by walking down the Old Pali Road from the Nu'uanu Lookout. The beauty of this trail is that it is reasonably flat with little elevation gain or loss as it winds its way along the windward side of the Ko'olau Range. The whine of the Pali Highway abates almost immediately and you are suddenly in a brilliant highland tropical forest. You can continue to the end (upper Waimanalo, about three hours one-way) for a full day's hike, or just find a secluded spot after a mile or so for a picnic. The views are spectacular, and vantage points display the coast all the way from Rabbit Island to Chinaman's Hat. Remember, however, that as with all Hawaiian trails, recent rainfall makes for treacherous footing.

BEACHES

Along the shoreline of an exclusive residential area, just south of Kailua, sits **Lanikai Beach.** Half a dozen clearly marked rights-of-way run off Mokulua Drive, the main thoroughfare, but there is not good parking. No facilities, but good

snorkeling and swimming year-round, with generally mild surf and a long, gently sloping, sandy beach. The beach runs south for almost a mile, broken by seawalls designed to hold back erosion. Many small craft use the sandy-bottomed shore to launch and land. Popular with local people, but not visited much by tourists, this beach is consistently rated as one of the best in the state.

Kailua Beach is the main beach in the area and is often regarded as the best overall beach on the island. It runs for nearly two miles along the front of town, with the Kailua Beach park at its southern end. This beach has become a hot windsurfing spot, and more recently kitesurfers have found it a great place for this new sport. Local people complain that at one time the beach was great for family outings, with safe conditions and fine facilities. Now the wind has attracted a daily flotilla of windsurfers, kayak racers, and jet skiers. The sometimes congested and contested waters can be dangerous for the average swimmer. Many windsurfers are beginners, so if you're a swimmer, be careful of being run over. The conditions are similar to out-of-control skiers found on the slopes of many mountains. The windsurfing area is clearly marked with buoys and the kitesurfing area is farther up the shore.

The park boasts a pavilion, picnic facilities, restrooms, showers, lifeguards, a boat ramp, and sometimes a food concession (they come and go). The surf is gentle year-round, and the

Kailua Beach, the windsurfing capital of O'ahu

J.D. BISIGNANI

swimming safe. Children should be careful of the sudden drop-offs in the channels formed by the Ka'elepulu Canal as it enters the sea in the middle of the beach park. Good surfing and diving are found around Popoi'a Island just off-shore. Follow Route 61 through Kailua to a T-intersection, then turn right onto South Kalaheo Street, following it to the beach park.

Kalama Beach Park is reached by making a left at the T-intersection onto North Kalaheo. Wedged between houses, this beach park has no facilities and is inferior to Kailua Beach Park, but the swimming is good, and sections of the beach have been made off-limits to any surf-riding vehicles.

ACCOMMODATIONS

Most options here are cottages, rental homes, and bed-and-breakfasts.

One of the finest guest homes in Kailua is **Sharon's Serenity,** 808/262-5621 or 800/914-2271. This beautiful property sits on a quiet side street. Sharon goes out of her way to make you feel comfortable and welcome. The coffee is always fresh-perked. Sharon also takes the time to sit with you, giving advice on where to dine, what to see, and a candid description of activities that are worthwhile. The meticulously clean, beautifully appointed home features guest rooms with color TV and refrigerator, Mexican tile throughout, a spacious family room, swimming pool, lanai, and views of the stream, golf course, and mountains beyond. The Blue Room has a queen bed and its own attached private bath. Opening onto the pool, the Poolside Room has both a king bed and a twin. Another bedroom could easily accommodate a small family, with a queen-size bed and a twin bed set up like a daybed. It features in-room sliding doors for privacy and its own bath just across the hall. Rates are $70–75 a night, and the price includes a continental breakfast, which Sharon will have waiting in the morning. Sharon's Serenity is an excellent choice for the windward coast, perfect for getting away from it all.

Kailua Beachside Cottages, 808/262-4128, fax 808/261-0893, has over 30 separate units in Kailua (and two in Waimanalo), ranging in price $65–500 a night. All are fully furnished, and most are within two blocks of the water. The options are broad. These rentals can accommodate those like a young couple out for a week of water activities looking for an inexpensive vacation all the way to a large family needing a five-bedroom luxury beachside home for a family reunion. This company can find the right place to meet your needs. Associated with Kailua Beachside Cottages is **Pat's Kailua Beach Properties,** 808/261-1653, which also has rental properties near the water in Kailua. Both companies use the following email address: pats@aloha.net.

Pacific Hawaii Reservations and **Affordable Paradise Bed and Breakfast,** both reputable agencies with offices in Kailua, list private homes in and around town and throughout the island. Rates and homes differ dramatically, but all are guaranteed to be comfortable and accommodating. Contacts: Ingrid Carvalho, Pacific Hawaii Reservations, 571 Pauku St., Kailua, HI 96734, 808/262-8133, fax 808/262-5030, website: www.oahu-hawaii-vacation.com, email: pir@aloha.net; Barbara Wilson, Affordable Paradise Bed and Breakfast, 332 Ku'ukama St., Kailua, HI 96734, 808/261-1693, fax 808/261-7315, website: www.affordable-paradise.com, email: barbara@affordable-paradise.com.

FOOD

Hahani Street Eateries
Near the post office along Hahani Street is a clutch of small, moderately priced restaurants that include Teddy's Bigger Burger, Maui Taco, Jamba Juice, Saeng's Thai Cuisine, and Mango's Indian Cuisine, so you can choose from food of the world. **Saeng's Thai Cuisine,** 808/263-9727, has been around the longest. Open weekdays for lunch, daily for dinner, it offers spicy Thai food with an emphasis on vegetarian meals. Appetizers and starters are Thai crisp noodles, sautéed shrimp, salads like green papaya salad, *yum koong* shrimp salad, and chicken coconut soup. Specialties include spicy stuffed calamari, Thai red curry, and à la carte beef, pork, and chicken dishes, all under $10. Vegetarians can pick from mixed veggies with yellow bean paste, mixed veggies with oyster

sauce, or zucchini tofu. Saeng's Thai is a good change of pace at a decent price.

Down the street, the **Daiei Food Mart Food Court** holds three quick inexpensive eateries where you order at a counter and eat outside. **Good Friend Chinese Chicken** serves plate lunches along with the usual assortment of Chinese dishes. For something a bit heartier, try **Yummy's Korean Barbecue,** where you can fill yourself with barbecued short ribs, barbecued chicken, noodle soups, or a combination plate. A good place for a breakfast croissant and a coffee pick-me-up is **Baile,** a French sandwich shop.

Hekili Street Eateries

Running into Hahani Street is Hekili Street, along which are several more restaurants. **Princess Chop Suey,** 808/262-7166, is your basic chop suey joint, open Mon.–Sat. 10 A.M.–9 P.M., Sunday 1–9 P.M. Its theme is Naugahyde and Formica, and everything on the menu is under $8.

Next door is **Cisco's Cantina,** 808/262-7337, featuring complete Mexican cuisine, open Sun.–Thurs. 11:30 A.M.–10 P.M., Friday and Saturday 11:30 A.M.–11 P.M. Tostadas, tacos, burritos, enchiladas, and chiles rellenos are all under $15. More expensive dishes are those like fajitas ($19.95, for two $24.95). All come with Mexican corn, sautéed Tex-Mex mushrooms, and salad. Inside, the south-of-the-border atmosphere is created with hanging piñatas, stucco walls, and blue-tile tables.

An easy-going place with linens, **Buona Sera,** 808/263-7696, does reasonably priced Italian food with appetizers in the $6–8 range and main entrées $6–12. Open Sun.–Thurs. 5:30–9 P.M. and Friday and Saturday until 10 P.M.

For more down-home cooking, step next door to **Boots and Kimo's Homestyle Kitchen.**

Uluniu Street Eateries

One block north of the main intersection is Uluniu Street. This street also has several moderate places to eat. First is an authentic but very basic hole-in-the-wall Japanese restaurant, **Kailua Okazuya,** 808/261-1612. It specializes in *donburi,* a bowl of rice smothered with various savories. Try the *o yakodon buri,* chicken and egg with vegetables over rice for under $5. It also serves inexpensive plate lunches and a sushi

special that can't be beat, which includes fresh fish, shrimp, abalone, and octopus. Next door is **Luigi's Place,** 808/263-5678, for Mediterranean cuisine, open Tues.–Sat. 5:30–8:30 P.M., serving pasta for under $11 and other entrées for up to $14. Up the street is the **New Chinese Garden,** 808/262-9090, a basic Chinese restaurant with decent prices that's open daily 10:30 A.M.–9 P.M.

Let the pungent aroma of garlic frying in olive oil lead you to **Assaggio Italian Restaurant,** 354 Uluniu St., 808/261-2772, open for lunch Mon.–Fri. 11:30 A.M.–2:30 P.M., dinner Sun.–Thurs. 5–10 P.M. You are welcomed into a bright and open room done in the striking colors of black, red, teal, and magenta. A wall running down the center of the restaurant separates the bar from the dining room, where tables covered in white linen and black upholstered chairs line the long window area. The typical Italian menu, served with crusty Italian bread, begins with antipasti priced $6–10. Soups like pasta fagioli, minestrone, tortellini imbrodo, or vichyssoise run less. Pasta ranging in price $8–14 includes linguine, fettuccine, and ziti. Dishes are covered in marinara, clam, carbonara, or pesto sauce. Entrées are chicken cacciatore or chicken rolatini, baked ziti with eggplant and mozzarella, or lasagna, and meat dishes such as New York steaks, pork chops, or *osso bucco.* All are priced below $16. From the sea comes fresh fish sautéed in garlic; scallops and shrimp in wine, garlic butter, and snow peas; or calamari alla parmigiana. Desserts are homemade and the full bar serves imported and domestic beers, liquors, coffees, espressos, and plenty of wine varietals.

Around Town

Los Garcia's, at 14 Oneawa St. near the main intersection, 808/261-0306, open daily for lunch and dinner, is a better than average Mexican restaurant. Simple yet tasteful, the south-of-the-border decor is achieved with adobe-like arches, wooden tables, Mexican ceramics placed here and there, and plenty of cacti and hanging plants. The menu features combination dinners of burritos, chiles rellenos, enchiladas, tacos, or tamales all priced under $14. Shrimp and seafood dishes run $14.95 and the special meat plates cost about the same. Less expensive dishes, all around $11, are chimichangas, burritos, tacos rancheros, and pizza Mexicana, while appetizers are half that. There are even a half dozen dishes for the vegetarian. Los Garcia's is definitely worth the money!

Buzz's Original Steakhouse, 413 Kawailoa Rd., 808/261-4661, is really *the* original steakhouse of this small island chain owned by the Schneider family. Buzz's is just across the road from Kailua Beach Park, situated along the canal. This restaurant is an institution with local families. It's the kind of place that "if you can't think of where to go, you head for Buzz's." The food is always good, if not extraordinary. Lunch is served until 3 P.M. and consists of salads and burgers, mostly $6–10. For dinner, some menu items are top sirloin for $16.95, chicken teriyaki at $13.95, rack of lamb for $22.95, and fresh fish that usually runs about $20. Salad bar is included with all entrées, and separately costs $8.95. Everything is charbroiled. Remember, no credit cards.

Family-run **Brent's Restaurant and Delicatessen,** 808/262-8588, in the Kailua Shopping Center, is a slice of New York in paradise. Choose sausage, corned beef, lox, or cheese from the deli case or order a lunch sandwich off the menu. Hearty hot breakfasts are also served as are à la carte dinners. All items on the large menu are reasonably priced. Brent's is open daily except Monday 7 A.M.–8 P.M., Friday and Saturday until 9 P.M.

At the Kailua Beach Center near the beach park is **Kailua Beach Restaurant,** 808/263-2620. Open 9 A.M.–9 P.M., this casual eatery serves egg and griddle items for breakfast and Chinese food the rest of the day. Not gourmet by any means, it gives you plenty food at cheap prices. Nothing on the menu is over $7.50.

For a little pick-me-up, try **Agnes' Portuguese Bake Shop** at Ho'olai and Uluniu Streets for Portuguese-based *malasadas* and *pao dolce,* or soup, salad, cappuccino, or espresso. Open 6 A.M.–6 P.M. except Monday, this is a cool, clean, and inviting place, a popular stop in town. Across the street is **Stircrazy.com Internet Coffee House** for wraps, sandwiches, salads, coffee, and Internet access. Down the street is **Boston North End Pizza.**

Health Foods

A well-established health food store in Kailua is **The Source,** 32 Kainehe St., 808/262-5604. Open weekdays 9 A.M.–9 P.M., Saturday 9 A.M.–6

P.M., and Sunday 10 A.M.–5 P.M., this place has vitamins and minerals, bulk foods, some organic fresh produce, cosmetics and hygiene products, as well as lots of essences, oils, and natural healing products to help with whatever ails you and to keep you on the straight and narrow.

SHOPPING

The two towns of Kailua and Kane'ohe have the lion's share of shopping on the windward coast. You can pick up basics in the small towns as you head up the coast, but for any unique or hard-to-find items, Kailua-Kane'ohe is your only bet. While there are some shops near the main intersection of Kailua Road (Highway 61) and Oneawa, you'll find more in the small shopping centers around town. The **Kailua Shopping Center,** with its new facelift at 540 Kailua Rd., has limited shopping that includes a **Times Supermarket,** open till 10 P.M.; **Under a Hula Moon** for gifts and souvenirs; and the well-stocked **Bookends,** 808/261-1996, open Mon.–Fri. 9:30 A.M.–9 P.M., Saturday 9:30 A.M.–5:30 P.M., Sunday till 5 P.M., for a full range of reading material. Across the street in the **Kailua Center** is a **Liberty House** and **Longs Drugs.** A few steps down Hahani Street is the large **Daiei** store, where you can find just about anything. Also at this shopping center are the Twogood Kayak shop, a crackseed store, Vim 'N Vigor for vitamins and supplements, the Kailua Cinemas, and a Safeway supermarket.

You might pick up an heirloom at **Heritage Antiques,** at the corner of Kailua Rd. and Hamakua St., 808/261-8700, open daily 10 A.M.–5:30 P.M., which is overflowing with Asian, Hawaiian, and Americana antiques. Across the street are **The Hunter,** 808/262-4868, and **Windward Antiques,** 808/262-5526, two other shops for collectibles of all sorts.

Island Treasures, 629 Kailua Rd., 808/261-8131, is an art gallery in Kailua. Owned and operated by Debbie Costello, who comes from a family of artists, the shop is open daily 10 A.M.–6 P.M., Sunday until 4 P.M. Debbie, an artist in her own right, does the beautiful stained glass pieces in the shop. This shop represents Hawaiian artists only and then only if the work has an island flavor.

Kalapawai Market, the closest shop to the beach at the corner of Kailua Rd. and Kalaheo Ave., is open 6 A.M.–9 P.M. daily for basic food and drink supplies, and a deli counter carries items for under $6. Usually parked outside Kalapawai Market are the **Hawaiian Cruisers** quadracycles. These multiperson bicycles rent for $10–40 for one-half hour to four hour periods for a single quadracycle or $20–80 for the double quadracycle. Kitty-corner is the small **Kailua Beach Center.** Aside from the usual places for food, there is a convenience store, a beachwear shop, and Kailua Sailboards for water gear sales and rental and bike rental.

Other smaller malls with additional retail stores are the **Enchanted Lake Shopping Center,** in the Enchanted Lake District around Kaʻelepulu Pond, and **Aikahi Park Shopping Center,** near the Marine Corps base.

SERVICES

Campers can get information and permits at the satellite city hall, 1090 Keolu Dr., near the Enchanted Lake Shopping Center. A post office is at the corner of Kailua and Hahani, just across from the Hawaiian National Bank. Medical aid is available from Castle Medical Center, 808/263-5500, at the intersection of the Pali Highway (Route 61) and Kalanianaʻole Highway (Route 72).

KANEʻOHE AND VICINITY

The bedroom community of Kaneʻohe (Kane's Bamboo) lies along Kaneʻohe Bay, protected by Hawaii's only large barrier reef, easily seen from the Nuʻuanu Pali Lookout high above to the west. Around the edge of the bay lie six of the original 30 fishponds that once graced this fine shore. A lush, fertile land of bountiful farms, historically one of the most productive areas of Oʻahu, Kaneʻohe was the second most populous area on the island. Through the years, the major crops of this coastal town have shifted from taro to rice, sugarcane, pineapples, and bananas, and today a variety is still grown.

Where Route 83 intersects the Likelike Highway on the southern outskirts of Kaneʻohe, it branches north and changes its name from the Kamehameha Highway to the Kahekili Highway until it hits the coast at Kahaluʻu. This four-mile traverse passes two exceptionally beautiful valleys: Haʻiku Valley and the Valley of the Temples. Neither should be missed. Three golf courses grace these green hills, one near the water and two tucked into the folds of the encircling *pali.*

Offshore is Moku O Loʻe, commonly called **Coconut Island.** It became famous as the opening shot in the TV show *Gilligan's Island,* although the series itself was shot in California. Now home to the Hawaii Institute of Marine Biology, in ancient times, it was *kapu* and during World War II served as an R&R camp for B-29 crews. Many of the crews felt the island had bad vibes, and reported having a streak of bad luck. In recent times, Frank Fasi, Honolulu's former mayor, suggested that Hawaii's gate-crashing guests, Ferdinand and Imelda Marcos, should lease Coconut Island. It never happened.

A sandbar, some one mile wide and three miles long, has been building in the center of Kaneʻohe Bay, making a perfect anchorage for yachts and powerboats. These boat people drop anchor, jump off, and wade to the bar through waist-deep, clear waters. It has become an unofficial playground where you can fling a Frisbee, drink beer, fly a kite, or just float around. Part of the sandbar rises above the water and some barbecue chefs even bring their hibachis and have a bite to eat. Surrounding you is Kaneʻohe Bay with Chinaman's Hat floating off to the north and a perfect view of the *pali* straight ahead. The epitome of la dolce vita, Hawaiian style. Fortunately, in recent years, the once crystal-clear bay, which was becoming murky with silt because of development, is clearing again due to conservation efforts.

SIGHTS

Hoʻomaluhia Botanical Garden

At the edge of town and lying below the encircling H-3 freeway is this 400-acre tract, one component of the Honolulu Botanical Gardens system.

Although it includes a 32-acre lake, a dammed reservoir that's part of the flood control for Kane'ohe, no swimming is permitted. The focus of this garden is on trees and plants from various areas of the world, including Hawaii, the Philippines, India, Africa, and tropical America. Day-use and overnight facilities are available, horseback riding is permitted, and walking, jogging, and bicycling are encouraged along its many trails. Free guided nature walks are given 10 A.M. on Saturday, 1 P.M. on Sunday, and Hawaiian plant use walks are run daily 10 A.M.–noon.

The garden, at 45-680 Luluku Rd., Kane'ohe, 808/233-7323, is open daily except Christmas and New Year's Day, 9 A.M.–4 P.M. The entrance is on Luluku Road.

Ha'iku Gardens

Ha'iku (Abrupt Break) Gardens, 46-336 Hai'ku Rd., is a lovely section of a residential area that includes a restaurant and some quiet condominiums. After you pass Kane'ohe District Park and Windward Community College, turn left onto Ha'iku Road and proceed for about one-half mile uphill. The gardens date from the mid-1800s, when Hawaiian *aliʻi* deeded 16 acres to an English engineer named Baskerville. He developed the area, creating spring-fed lily ponds, building estate homes, and planting flowers, fruits, and ornamental trees. Later a restaurant was built, and the grounds became famous for their beauty, often used for outdoor weddings and special gatherings. You're welcome to walk through the gardens, but they are closed at sunset. Proceed from the restaurant down a walkway to the grassy lawn and pond, where perhaps you'll attract an impromptu entourage of ducks, chickens, and guinea fowl that squawk along looking for handouts. Amidst the lush foliage is a gazebo used for weddings. A path leads around the pond, whose benches and small pavilions are perfect for contemplation, and continues under a huge banyan, while a nearby bamboo grove serenades with sonorous music if the wind is blowing.

Valley of the Temples

The concept of this universal faith cemetery is as beautiful as the sculpted *pali* that serves as its backdrop. A rainy day makes it better. The *pali* explodes with rainbowed waterfalls, and the greens turn a richer emerald, sparkling with dewdrops. Don't miss the Valley of the Temples Memorial Park at 47-200 Kahekili Highway. Open daily 8 A.M.–4:30 P.M.; admission is $2 per person, $1 for seniors and children 2–12, or *kamaʻaina* rates of $5 per carload, but you have to prove you're from Hawaii. Admission is charged only until 4:30 P.M. After that, you can walk in to see the grounds, but the buildings will not be open. High on a hill sits a Christian chapel, an A-frame topped by a cross. The views can be lovely from up there, but unfortunately the large windows of the chapel perfectly frame some nondescript tract housing and a shopping center below. Great planning! Different areas are set aside for Catholics, Chinese, and other groups.

The crown jewel of the valley is **Byodo-In Temple** (Temple of Equality), a superbly appointed replica of the 900-year-old Byodo-In of Uji, Japan (depicted on the 10-yen coin). This temple dates from June 7, 1968, 100 years to the day after Japanese immigrants first arrived in Hawaii. It was erected through the combined efforts of an American engineering firm headed by Ronald Kawahara in accordance with a plan designed by Kiichi Sano, a famed Kyoto landscape artist. Remove your shoes before entering the temple. A three-ton brass bell, which you're invited to strike after making an offering, creates the right vibrations for meditation and symbolically spreads the word of Amida Buddha.

The walls hold distinctive emblems of different Buddhist sects. Upstairs wings are roped off, with no entry permitted. Stand on the gravel path opposite the main temple. You'll see a grating with a circle cut in the middle. Stick your face in to see the perfectly framed contemplative

Byodo-In Temple

J.D. BISIGNANI

visage of Buddha. Cross a half-moon bridge to the left of the temple and follow the path to a small gazebo. Here a rock, perfectly and artistically placed, separates a stream in two, sending the water to the left and right. The pagoda at the top of the path is called the Meditation House. Go to this superbly manicured area to get a sweeping view of the grounds. In front of the Meditation House is a curious tree; pick up one of the fallen leaves and feel the natural velvet on the backside.

A small gift shop selling souvenirs, cards, film, and some refreshments is to the right of the temple. If you wish to photograph the complex, it's best to come before noon, when the sun is at your back as you frame the red and white temple against the deep green of the *pali*.

Along the Shore

The shoreline from Mokapu Peninsula past the downtown area is chock-a-block with homes and condos, and a handful of private yacht clubs and marinas. Beyond, it's much more open and rural, more like it was in decades past. Kane'ohe Bay offers the tiny Kane'ohe Beach Park and He'eia State Park, each accessible off Route 830 as it heads northward along the coast. Both are better for the views of Kane'ohe Bay than for any beach activities. They have restrooms and a few picnic tables. The water is safe year-round, but it's murky and lined with mudflats and coral heads. The same conditions hold true for Waiahole Beach Park about four miles north, but that area is much less developed, quieter, and good for beachcombing.

He'eia State Park is designated as an "interpretive park." It sits high on Kealohi Point overlooking He'eia Fishpond below. Kealohi translates as "The Shining," because it was a visible landmark to passing voyagers, but there is a much deeper interpretation. To the Hawaiians this area was a jumping-off point into the spirit world. It was believed that the souls of the recently departed came to this point and leapt into eternity. The right side, He'eia-kei, was the side of light, while the left side, He'eia-uli, was the domain of darkness. The wise *kahuna* taught that you could actually see the face of God in the brilliant sun as it rises over the point. This point is also the site of an ancient *heiau* called Kalae'ulu'ula, but it was removed when sugar

was planted in the 19th century. On the grounds are a main hall, pavilion, restrooms, and various short walks around the entire area with views of Kane'ohe Bay. The park contains numerous indigenous plants and mature trees, the perfect laboratory for the educational goals set by The Friends of He'eia State Park. Because it's an interpretive park, programs are offered for the community and visitors alike.

Below is He'eia Fishpond, the finest remaining example of the many fishponds that once lined this bay. Now privately owned, it is still used to raise mullet (*'ama*), the traditional fish raised by the ancient Hawaiians and *kapu* to all except the *ali'i*.

Just to the north of this park is the state-operated **He'eia Kea harbor.** Generally, small fishing boats and pleasure craft use the boat launch and other facilities, and several water activities companies start their tours here. A gift and snack shop at the end of the pier is a good place to pick up last-minute supplies and to ask about what's operating from the harbor. Club Kona Ocean Sports and the Ocean Queen glass-bottom boat run their operations from here, catering mostly to Japanese visitors. Capt. Bob's caters generally to Western tourists and runs a fun-filled day on the bay for swimming, snorkeling, other water activities, and a barbecue picnic.

For a fun-filled day on the water, far from the crowds of Waikiki, try **North Bay Aquatics,** on the grounds of Schrader's Windward Marine Resort, 47-039 Lihikai Dr., 808/239-5711. A boat runs from the resort property to the sandbar on Tuesday and Saturday, where you can swim, snorkel, kayak, or hydrobike to your heart's content. Departure time is usually around 10:30 A.M. but may depend on the tides, so call a day in advance. Free for those staying at the resort, only $10 for others.

ACCOMMODATIONS

Camp Kokokahi, 47-035 Kane'ohe Bay Dr., 808/247-2124, has private and semiprivate cabins that are only open to visitors when they're not booked for groups. Call for information and reservations no more than 30 days in advance. Cabins are for sleeping only; restrooms, a kitchen, and a laundry facility are separate. Rates are $20 per person in a private cabin, $18 in a shared cabin.

Right over the water opposite the Makani Kai Marina is **Kane'ohe Bay B&B,** 45-302 Pu'uloko Pl., 808/235-4214 or 800/262-9912, fax 808/885-0559, website: www.bestbnb.com, email: bestbnb@aloha.net. The one room with bath not only looks over the bay but also a courtyard swimming pool. Breakfast is served in the lounge. This room runs $125 a night with a two-night minimum. In a quiet residential neighborhood, the room faces east toward the bay and morning sun.

FOOD

Fortunately, or unfortunately, Kane'ohe is a bit of a wasteland as far as tourist services, nightlife, and eating out are concerned. Most people who live here head for the action in Honolulu. The best cheap deal in town is at **Kim Chee One,** 46-010 Kamehameha Hwy., 808/235-5560, which has a few sister restaurants scattered around O'ahu. The setting is plain, but you'll have no trouble finding an excellent Korean mixed barbecue plate for $7.25, or a selection of other Korean and Hawaiianized Korean dishes.

Also offering easy quick food are the Eastern Garden Chinese Restaurant, L&L Drive-In, Tasty Korean BBQ, and the Ko'olau Ranch House restaurant. all at the Kane'ohe Bay Shopping Center, just up the road. The **Ko'olau Ranch House** has hearty favorites like ranch house stew, ranch boy burger, and Ko'olau rib-eye steak, with nothing on the menu over $16.95. A specialty is the Hawaiian buffet served every Friday at 5 P.M. Open for lunch and dinner, but closed 2–5 P.M. The bar serves 4–10 P.M.

Haleiwa Joe's at Ha'iku Gardens, 808/247-6671, true to its name, sits surrounded by a fragrant garden in its lovely, secluded valley. It's considered one of the most beautiful places on O'ahu, and people come here to be married. This restaurant specializes in fresh fish, steak, and prime rib, although the menu is much longer than that, and food is prepared with flavors and spices of the Pacific and Asia. Dinner only is served from 5:30 P.M. Mon.–Sat. and from 5 P.M. on Sunday; the bar opens at 4:30 P.M. and there are bar specials and *pu pu* until 6:30 P.M. It's first-come, first-served; no reservations are accepted.

SHOPPING

The **Windward Mall,** 46-056 Kamehameha Hwy., is open weekdays 9:30 A.M.–9 P.M., Saturday to 5:30 P.M., Sunday 10 A.M.–5 P.M. It's the premier full-service mall on the windward coast. Besides department stores like Liberty House and Sears, shops sell everything from shoes to jewelry.

The **Kane'ohe Bay Shopping Center** across from the Windward Mall is a little more downhome, featuring a Longs Drugs (especially good for photo supplies), a Blockbuster Video, and several restaurants. For those staying in the area, the Safeway and Star Market here are very convenient.

At the corner of Kamehameha Highway and Kane'ohe Bay Drive is the smaller **Windward City Shopping Center.** Here you'll find a Foodland Supermarket, Starbucks Coffee, Longs Drugs, several eateries, and Rainbow Crackseed.

Across from the Valley of the Temples Memorial Park is the **Ko'olau Center,** which provides a gas station, a Times Supermarket, several local eateries, and the Koolau 10 Cinema.

NORTH KANE'OHE BAY

KAHALU'U

This community is at the convergence of Kahekili Highway, Route 83, and Route 830, an extension of the Kamehameha Highway that cuts through Kane'ohe and hugs the coastline heading north from town. This shoreline drive offers some of the most spectacular views of a decidedly spectacular coast, with very few tourists venturing along this side road. Kahalu'u is not much more than a gas station and the Hygienic Store, which sells liquor, groceries, soda, and ice, all you'll need for an afternoon lunch. The store is flanked by stalls selling fruits and shellwork at competitive prices. Although they may not always be around, look for little trucks parked along the road near the Hygienic Store selling hot *ono laulau,* which are snacks that come out of the *imu* oven. Here as well is the large and fancy Noriko's Hawaii, a shop set up to cater to Japanese tour buses making a round-island trip and for those heading to the Polynesian Cultural Center. Contrast this with the Rainbow Plaza up the road, a shop catering to Korean groups, and you'll get the picture of how strong the Japanese influence is and how important their contribution to the local economy, at least in contrast to other groups such as the Koreans.

The Waihe'e Stream, meandering from the *pali,* empties into the bay and deposits fresh water near the ancient **Kahalu'u Fish Pond,** a picture-perfect tropical setting. So picture-perfect is the place that it has provided the background scenery to TV and Hollywood productions such as an episode from *Jake and the Fat Man,* a setting for *Parent Trap II,* and the famous airport and village scene from *The Karate Kid II.* To the west of the fishpond a spit of land holds a wedding chapel, and beyond that, at the mouth of the stream, is Kahalu'u Park, nothing more than a dirt parking lot, a public boat launch well-used by fishers, and a canoe club.

Senator Fong's Plantation and Gardens

Senator Fong's Plantation and Gardens, 47-285 Pulama Rd., just north of Kahalu'u, 808/239-6775, website: www.fonggarden.com, is open daily 10 A.M.–4 P.M., except Christmas and New Year's Day. Admission is $10 adults, $8 seniors, and $6 children 5–12. Guided one-hour tram tours run at 10:30 A.M., 11:30 A.M., 1 P.M., 2 P.M., and 3 P.M., taking visitors through about 200 acres of the garden. The plantation is a labor of love created by former senator Hiram Fong, who served as state senator 1959–77. Upon retirement he returned to his home and ever since has been beautifying the gardens he started in the middle of the 20th century. The result is 725 acres of natural beauty that rise to 2,600 feet at the ridge of the Ko'olau Range above. The valleys and ridges of this garden preserve the native flora and fauna of the land, along with planted flower and fruit gardens, and groves of trees, palms, bushes, and ferns. When you first arrive, a large open-air pavilion houses a snack window serving sandwiches, plate lunches, and saimin. Inside is also a small but well-appointed souvenir shop where you can get everything from aloha shirts to postcards. Notice a table set with baskets of flowers where you can make your own keepsake lei for $6.50.

Accommodations

Schrader's Windward Marine Resort has been operating for years. It overlooks Kahalu'u Fishpond at the end of Wailau Peninsula. At first it may look like a hodgepodge of a place, but it's really a nice little community of about four dozen units in several separate buildings. A number of these units sit along the water while others step up the steep embankment. One-, two-, and three-bedroom units are available, some fully furnished and others with kitchenettes. Surprisingly large, all are neat and clean, with a/c, telephone, television, and daily maid service. A complimentary breakfast is available each morning at the office on the top level of the main building. On property are a swimming pool, laundry, and barbecue pit. Also, a complimentary two-hour pontoon boat cruise into the bay for snorkeling, kayaking, and swimming at the sandbar is open for all guests; $10 for others. The boat leaves every Wednesday and Saturday (days may change) at about 10:30 A.M. Room rates run $60–125 for one-bedroom rooms, $110–190 for two-bedroom units, and $200–320 for three-bedroom suites, but room and car packages are also an option. Ask about off-season and multiple-night discounts. This rural "cottage motel" on the water is a fine alternative for those looking for peace and quiet. For information contact Schrader's Windward Marine Resort, 47-039 Lihikai Dr., Kane'ohe, HI 96744, 808/239-5711 or 800/735-5711, website: www.hawaiiscene.com/schrader.

WAIAHOLE AND WAIKANE

If you want to fall in love with rural, old-time O'ahu, go to the northern reaches of Kane'ohe Bay around Waiahole and Waikane, a Hawaiian grassroots area that has so far eluded development. Alongside the road sit some of the best roadside fruit stands on O'ahu. Do yourself a favor and have one of the coconuts. Sip the juice, and when it's gone, eat the custard-like contents. A real island treat, nutritious and delicious. For a glimpse of what's happening look for the Waiahole Elementary School, and turn left up Waiahole Valley Road. The road twists its way into the valley, becoming narrower. Left and right in homey, ramshackle houses lives down-home Hawaii, complete with taro patches in the back yards and fruit and nut trees to the sides. At the

turn, stop for a bite to eat at the Ono Loa Hawaiian Food restaurant, a very local place. Another road of the same type is about one-half mile up Route 83 just before you enter Waikane. If you're staying in Waikiki, compare this area with Kuhio Avenue only 45 minutes away!

Continuing on, the road passes through what was once sugarcane country. Most of the businesses failed in the 1800s, but you will see the ruins of the Kualoa Sugar Mill a mile or so before reaching Ka'a'awa. The dilapidated mill stands, although it closed more than a century ago; its chimney is the most obvious remnant. Entering is not advised!

Offshore stands a very recognizable island. Mokoli'i (Small Lizard) Island is commonly called **Chinaman's Hat** due to its obvious resemblance to an Asian chapeau. Legend says that Mokoli'i Island is the tail of a lizard that was killed by the goddess Hi'iaka. The body? The flat land near the old overgrown mill ruins.

Kualoa Regional Park

With the *pali* in the background, Chinaman's Hat offshore, and a glistening white strand shaded by swaying palms, Kualoa is one of the finest beach parks on windward O'ahu, and it has one of its longest beaches. Kualoa is one of the most sacred areas on O'ahu, and the *ali'i* brought their children here to be reared and educated. The area is designated in the National Register of Historic Places. It has a full range of facilities

Chinaman's Hat

J.D. BISIGNANI

and services, including lifeguards, restrooms, picnic tables, and an expansive parking area. Because of its exposure to winds, Kualoa is sometimes chilly. The park is popular and often used by athletic groups for games and competitions. The park is open daily 7 A.M.–7 P.M., with overnight camping allowed with a county permit. The swimming is safe year-round along a shoreline dotted with pockets of sand and coral. The snorkeling and fishing are good, but the real treat is walking the 500 yards to Chinaman's Hat at low tide. You need appropriate footgear (old sneakers are fine) because of the sharp coral heads. The island is one of the few around offshore O'ahu that are not official bird sanctuaries, although many shorebirds do use the island and should not be disturbed.

Kualoa Ranch

The 4,000-acre Kualoa Ranch, 49-560 Kamehameha Hwy., 808/237-7321 or 800/231-7321, website: www.kualoa.com, just past Kualoa Regional Park, offers three organized, pre-packaged, outdoor activities tours on its working cattle ranch. Activities run 9 A.M.–3 P.M. Your choice of activities includes horseback riding, jet-ski rides, ATV dune cycle rides, gun range firing, snorkeling, scuba, beach activities, a helicopter ride, a movie set trolley ride, and more. Other games and activities, a petting zoo, and Hawaiian exhibits are also available for free. The Activity Adventure Tour runs $99 for adults and $45 for children 2–11 and includes a full-day pass for up to three activities and discounted rates on others. With the Secret Island and Activity Tour, you get a half day and one activity at the ranch with a movie set tour and a half day of water sports. Rates run $69 for adults and $35 for children 2–11. With both these tours, a helicopter ride may be purchased separately for $39 per person. For $139 adult and $89 for children 2–11, the Deluxe Activity Tour lets you partake in as many activities as you can handle in one day, plus try scuba or take a helicopter ride. For some activities, there are stipulations for the age of participant and adult accompaniment. Individual activities may also be purchased for their set fees. A balanced and filling buffet lunch or sandwich buffet and free transportation from various Waikiki hotels (first pickup is at 7:30 A.M.) are provided with all tours. Ranch activities take place every day. Jet skiing and scuba are offered Mon.–Fri. only; snorkel tours run Mon.–Sat.; mountain biking and fishing are available only Saturday and Sunday; closed on national holidays. The Kualoa Ranch is not a cultural experience. It's an outing for activities, sun, and fun. Call for reservations.

KA'A'AWA TOWN AND VICINITY

SIGHTS AND BEACHES

When you first zip along the highway through town you get the impression that there isn't much here, but there's more than you think. The town stretches back toward the *pali* for a couple of streets. On the ocean side is **Ka'a'awa Beach Park,** a primarily local hangout. Across the road is the post office and the **Ka'a'awa Country Kitchen,** which serves breakfast and plate lunches, where you can easily eat for $5. It has a few tables, but the best bet is to get your plate lunch and take it across the street to the beach park. Behind the post office is **Pyramid Rock,** obviously named because of its shape.

O'ahu's windward *pali* are unsurpassed anywhere in the islands, and they're particularly beautiful here. Take a walk around. Stroll the dirt roads through the residential areas and keep your eyes peeled for a small white cross on the *pali* just near Pyramid Rock. It marks the spot where a serviceman was killed during the Pearl Harbor invasion. His spirit is still honored by the perpetually maintained bright white cross. While walking you'll be treated to Ka'a'awa's natural choir—wild roosters crowing any time they feel like it, and the din of cheeky parrots high in the trees. A pair of parrots escaped from a nearby home some years ago, and their progeny continue to relish life in the balmy tropics.

As you approach the bend of Mahie Point, staring down at you is a very popular stone formation, the **Crouching Lion.** Undoubtedly a tour bus or two will be sitting in the lot of the Crouching Lion Inn. As with all anthropomorphic rock

O'AHU

formations, it helps to have an imagination. Anyway, the inn is much more interesting than the lion. George Larsen built the inn in 1928 from rough-hewn lumber from the Pacific Northwest; the huge stones were excavated from the site itself. The inn went public in 1951 and has been serving tourists ever since.

Four beach parks in as many miles lie between Ka'a'awa Point and Kahana Bay. **Kalae'o'io Beach County Park,** the first, is a very shaded short strip that has roadside parking only. There are a few picnic tables but no restrooms, and while the beach is good the bottom is a bit rocky. The second, a short distance beyond, is **Ka'a'awa Beach County Park,** a popular beach with restrooms, lifeguards, picnic facilities, and limited parking at its northern end. An offshore reef running the entire length of the park makes swimming safe year-round, but perhaps the snorkeling is better. There's a dangerous rip at the south end of the park at the break in the reef. Lots of people come to shore fish this coastal strip.

Swanzy Beach County Park, two minutes north, offers a broad grassy expanse and basketball courts, and has camping with a county permit—weekends only. The sand and rubble beach lies below a long retaining wall, often underwater during high tide. The swimming is safe year-round but is not favorable because of the poor quality of the beach. Swanzy is one of the best squidding and snorkeling beaches on the windward coast. A break in the offshore reef creates a dangerous rip and should be avoided.

Kahana Valley State Park is a full-service park with picnic facilities, restrooms, camping, hiking trails, and a boat launch. Camping is allowed with state permit at the beach; restrooms and information are on the mountain side of the road. It's perfectly situated for a quiet picnic under the coconut trees. Swimming is good year-round, although the waters can be cloudy at times. A gentle shorebreak makes the area ideal for bodysurfing and beginner board riders. This entire beach area is traditionally excellent for *akule* fishing, with large schools visiting the offshore waters at certain times of year. The bay and valley once supported a large Hawaiian fishing village, and many cultural remains dot the area. Remnants of **Huilua Fish Pond** lie just

outside the park boundary a short way back down the road. Running up the valley, past a small in-park residential neighborhood, is the rest of the park. Few visit there. The park encompasses this valley, historically an *ahupua'a,* and runs from water's edge to over 2,600 feet. You can follow two trails, one that goes back about three miles along the stream up the valley and the other a one-mile round-trip along the mountainside past a fish deity shrine to a lookout that was once used to watch for fish in the bay.

PRACTICALITIES

Crouching Lion Inn

There was a time when *everyone* passing through Ka'a'awa stopped at the Crouching Lion Inn. Built in 1928, it was the only place *to* stop for many, many years. The inn has seen its ups and downs, and now, fortunately, is on the upswing again. The inn, along Route 83 in Ka'a'awa, 808/237-8511, is open daily for lunch 11 A.M.–3 P.M., cocktails from 3 P.M. onward, *pu pu* 4–5 P.M., and dinner 5–9 P.M. The inn is beautiful enough to stop at just to have a look, but if you want a reasonably quiet meal, avoid lunchtime and come in the evening when all of the tour buses have long since departed. Sitting high on a verdant green hill, the inn's architectural style is a mixture of English Tudor and country Hawaiian. Inside it is cozy with a few fireplaces as well as open-beamed ceilings, while the view from the veranda is especially grand. Lunch can be a simple order of Portuguese bean soup, or appetizer, salad, and sandwich. Appetizers like royal shrimp cocktail, sautéed mushrooms, or honey garlic shrimp run $7.25–9.50. Salads include Oriental chicken, shrimp parmesan, and fruit of kings salads. Regular lunch entrées are chopped steak, chicken macadamia, or *kalua* pork plate all priced under $11.50. Dinner entrées, accompanied by fresh-baked rolls, soup or salad, vegetables, and choice of rice or potatoes, include Slavonic steak, saut'ed seafood, filet mignon, or rotisserie chicken for $14.95–22.50. Some vegetarian selections complete the menu, which is an expansion of the lunch menu. The inn's famous mile-high coconut pie, macadamia nut cream pie, and double-crusted banana cream pie, for under

$5, are absolutely delicious. The limited-menu early-bird special at $10.95 is a bargain. To complement your menu selection a full bar serves cocktails, beer, wine, and liquors.

On the premises is **Livingston Galleries,** 808/237-7165, open daily 10:30 A.M.–7:30 P.M., which displays original prints, sculptures, some jewelry and gifts, and edition prints of both internationally acclaimed and local island artists; some of the well-known artists shown here are Nisla, Walfrido, David Lee, and Burrows. Predominantly paintings and prints.

PUNALU'U AND HAU'ULA

PUNALU'U

Punalu'u (Coral Diving) is a long and narrow ribbon of land between the sea and the *pali,* a favorite place to come for a drive in the "country." Its built-up area is about a mile or so long but only a hundred yards wide. It has gas, supplies, and camping, along with the several art galleries. In town is **St. Joachim Church.** There's nothing outstanding about it, merely a one-room church meekly sitting on a plot of ground overlooking the sea. But it's real home-grown, where the people of this district come to worship. Just look and you might understand the simple and basic lifestyle that still persists in this area.

On the northern outskirts of town is **Sacred Falls State Park** (closed indefinitely due to a landslide that killed seven hikers in 1999). There is a barricade across the entrance. No admittance. The area's Hawaiian name was Kaliuwa'a (Canoe Leak), and although the original name isn't as romantic as the anglicized version, the entire area was indeed considered sacred. It's a very narrow valley where the gods would show disfavor by dropping rocks onto your head. Hawaiians used to wrap stones with *ti* leaves and leave them along the trail as an appeasement to the gods, so they weren't tempted to brain them. The walls of this deep valley are 1,600 feet high, but the falls drop only 90 feet or so. The pool below was ample for a swim, but the water is chilly and often murky.

HAU'ULA

This speck of a town is just past Punalu'u between mile markers 21 and 22. The old town center is two soda machines, two gas pumps, two limited supply stores, the pink Ching Jong Leong store, and Wu's Sundries. At the estuary of a stream is **'Aukai Beach Park,** a flat little beach right in the middle of town. Rainbow Plaza, a 7-Eleven, and a little church up on the hill with the *pali* as a backdrop add the finishing touches.

Hau'ula Trails
Outdoor enthusiasts will love the little-used Hau'ula Trails. These ridge and valley trails offer just about everything that you can expect from a Hawaiian trail: the mountains, the valleys, and vistas of the sea. Built by the Civilian Conservation Corps during the Depression, these manicured trails are wide, and the footing is great most of the way even in rainy periods. They run up and down two ridges and deep into an interior valley through the extraordinary jungle canopy. The hard-packed ridge trails, covered in a soft carpet of ironwood needles, offer magnificent coastal views once you reach the heights, or you can look inland into verdant gulches and valleys. You'll be passing through miniature ecosystems very reminiscent of the fern forests on the Big Island, but on a much smaller scale. The area flora is made up of ironwoods, passion fruit, thimbleberries, *'ohi'a,* wild orchids, and fiddlehead ferns, among other native and introduced species. All three trails start beyond the end of Makakua Road, which is off Hau'ula Homestead Road. Pass a hunter's check-in station and cross a dry creek bed. On your right is the start of the **Hau'ula Loop Trail.** A short way farther, the **Ma'akua Ridge Trail** heads off to the left, while the **Ma'akua Gulch Trail** goes straight ahead up the valley. Each trail round-trip should take less than two hours.

BEACHES

Right along the highway is **Punalu'u Beach County Park,** with restrooms, picnic tables, lots of shade, decent snorkeling, but no lifeguards. The swimming is safe year-round inside the protected reef. Local fishermen, usually older Filipino men who are surfcasting, use this area frequently. They're friendly and a great source of information for anyone trying to land a fish or two. They know the best baits and spots to dunk a line.

Hau'ula Beach County Park is an improved beach park with picnic facilities, restrooms, pavilion, volleyball court, and camping. There's safe swimming year-round inside the coral reef, with good snorkeling; surfing is usually best in the winter months. Rip currents are present at both ends of the beach at breaks in the reef, and deep holes in the floor of a brackish pond are formed where Ma'akua Stream enters the sea. Across the road are the ruins of the historic **Lanakila Church** (1853), partially dismantled at the turn of the 20th century to build a smaller church near Punalu'u.

Kokololio Beach County Park is next—a fine spot with lots of parking. A little dune protects the beach from road noise. While there is good swimming, many locals come to boogie board, mostly at the northern end where the beach makes a slight curve. With lots of shade trees and picnic tables, it's good for a day trip or to camp with county permit.

PRACTICALITIES

Accommodations

Pat's at Punalu'u is one of the few condos along this coast, and one of the few buildings that approaches the height of coconut trees. Pat's is right on the water, and every unit has a lanai that overlooks the sea. On property are a swimming pool, sauna, patio next to the beach, and parking. Units are fully furnished with kitchens, televisions, and washers and dryers, and run $80–90 for a studio, $100–105 for one bedroom, and $180 for a three-bedroom penthouse, with the addition of a cleaning charge. Weekly and monthly rates can be arranged. A $150 damage deposit is required within 10 days of booking and full payment is to be made one month before arrival. Punalu'u and vicinity is an easy-going area, a throwback to Hawaii as it used to be years ago, yet it's so close to the big city and

all it offers. If you're looking for quiet and relaxation at a decent price, this could be the spot. Room arrangements are made through Paul Comeau Condo Rentals, P.O. Box 589, Ka'a'awa, HI 96730, 808/293-2624 or 800/467-6215, fax 808/293-0618, website: www.tutlebaycondos.com/comeau, email: comeau001@hawaii.rr.com.

Food

Keep a sharp eye out for a truck and a sign featuring shrimp just along the road. Turn in to **Ahi's Restaurant**, operated by Roland Ahi and son, open daily 11 A.M.–9 P.M. At 53-146 Kamehameha Hwy., this is the first place of note after passing the Kahana Valley State Park. The shrimp couldn't be fresher—it comes from local fishermen. In this no-frills but super-friendly restaurant, you can have 30 shrimp cooked to order as scampi, tempura, spicy, or in a cocktail for $10! Shrimp is the pièce de résistance, but basic sandwiches and burgers for under $5.50 are also on the menu, as well as entrées like spaghetti with meat sauce for $6.50, breaded chicken cutlet with gravy at $7.25, and steak and mahimahi combo for $12.95. Complete meals come with green salad, vegetables, bread, rice or potatoes, a soft drink, and sherbet. There are plenty of appetizers and side dishes on the menu and a good selection of beer and wine. On Friday and Saturday nights, various local musicians perform until closing. Ahi's serves all of its great food with authentic *aloha*. Stop in! You'll be glad you did.

Shopping

The **Punalu'u Art Gallery**, in Punalu'u around mile marker 24, 808/237-8221, is the oldest art gallery on windward O'ahu. Open daily 10:30 A.M.–6:30 P.M. Owner and candle artist Scott Bechtol is dedicated to showcasing the works of an assortment of the finest artists that the island has to offer. Scott is well known for his wonderful sculpted candles, all made from the finest beeswax. Some are lanterns shaped like a huge pita bread with the top third cut off. The remainder is sculpted with a scene that glows when the candle is lit. Others are huge tikis, dolphins, or flowers, all inspired by the islands. Some of the larger candles are $70, the man-size tiki is about $800, and Scott's unique "crying tiki" sells for only $25; small tapers go for $5–9. Scott creates all of this beautiful glowing art with just one precision carving tool—a Buck knife! Another artist shown is Bill Cupid, who creates "bananascapes." Bill removes the outer bark from the banana tree, then he tears and cuts it to make a scene of boats or mountains. The result is a three-dimensional piece. Bill's wife is an artist who specializes in seascapes made with seaweed, while Janet Stewart does watercolors and prints. Other beauty is added by Janet Holiday's silk-screen prints and Peter Hayward's landscapes and seascapes in oil. The Punalu'u Art Gallery is a jewel case of manmade beauty surrounded by natural beauty. They harmonize perfectly.

While there, stop next door at **Punalu'u Trading Company** and have a look at its brightly colored sarongs or pick up a cold coconut to drink. A few steps up the way is **Ching Punalu'u Store,** a minimart in an old building for basic food supplies.

Two other galleries here make this a mini-center for viewing art work. At 53-839 Kamehameha Hwy., the **Lance Fairly Gallery** displays colorful landscapes and seascapes by Lance Fairly. His paintings seem to have a luminescence, an inner light, and there's an enhancement of color for a pleasing yet somewhat magical or mystical tone. Lithographs and gicleé available for purchase. website: www.lancefairly.com. Just up the road at 53-866 Kamehameha Hwy. is the **Kim Taylor Reece Gallery,** website: www.alohadirect.com/ktr. Reece is a photographer and most of his large-size prints are of nudes. While the bulk of the work is done in black and white, some prints are hand tinted. This gallery is open noon–5 P.M. Thurs.–Sat. only.

In Hau'ula look for the **Hau'ula Kai Center,** a small shopping center with a post office; Lindy's Foods supermarket for groceries, food, and supplies; and a KFC. Also in Hau'ula is the Rainbow Plaza, an unabashed tourist trap, classic in its obvious tastelessness. Here you'll find beads, baubles, and jewelry. This shop has been taken over by Korean merchants who cater largely to Korean tourist groups.

LA'IE TO KAHUKU

LA'IE

The "Saints" came marching into La'ie (Leaf of the 'Ie Vine) and set about making a perfect Mormon village in paradise. What's more, they succeeded! The town itself is squeaky clean, with well-kept homes and manicured lawns that hint of suburban Midwest America. Dedicated to education, they built a branch of **Brigham Young University** (BYU) that attracts students from all over Polynesia, many of whom work in the nearby Polynesian Cultural Center. The students vow to live a clean life, free of drugs and alcohol, and to not grow beards. In the foyer of the main entrance look for a huge mural depicting La'ie's flag-raising ceremony in 1921, which symbolically established the colony. The road leading to and from the university campus is maze-like but easily negotiable. From the highway, turn onto Hale La'a Boulevard and at the traffic circle follow Kulaniu Street directly to the campus. Alternately, take Naniloa Loop off the highway.

The first view of the **Mormon Temple,** 55-600 Naniloa Loop, La'ie, 808/293-9297, built in 1919, is very impressive. Square, with simple architectural lines, this house of worship sits pure white against the *pali* and is further dramatized by a reflecting pool and fountains spewing fine mists. The visitor's center of this tranquil, shrine-like church is open daily 9 A.M.–8 P.M., when a slide show telling the history of the La'ie colony is presented along with a guided tour of the grounds. The tour guides, while not pushy, definitely want to engage you in a discussion about your beliefs. They are missionaries after all, so it's not surprising, and they'll let you alone if you desire. "Smoking is prohibited, and shirts (no halter tops) must be worn to enter." The temple attracts more visitors than any other Mormon site outside of the main temple in Salt Lake City.

Polynesian Cultural Center

The real showcase is the Polynesian Cultural Center. PCC, as it's called by islanders, began as an experiment in 1963. Smart businessmen said

O'AHU

Mormon Temple

ROBERT NILSEN

it would never thrive way out in La'ie, and tourists didn't come to Hawaii for *culture* anyway. Well, they were wrong, and the PCC now rates as one of O'ahu's top tourist attractions, luring about one million visitors annually. Miracles do happen! PCC is a nonprofit organization, with proceeds going to the La'ie BYU and to maintaining the center itself.

Covering 42 acres, the primary attractions are seven model villages including examples from Hawaii, Samoa, the Marquesas, Fiji, New Zealand, Tonga, and Tahiti. The villages are primarily staffed with people from the representative island homelands. Remember that most are Mormons, whose dogma colors the attitudes and selected presentations of the staffers. Still, all are genuinely interested in dispensing cultural knowledge about their traditional island ways and beliefs, and almost all are characters who engage in lighthearted bantering with their willing audience. Walk through the villages on your own or take a canoe ride over the artesian-fed waterways. Other attractions include a Migrations Museum, art and handicraft shops, and an IMAX theater that presents two shows about Polynesia and the sea. A shuttle tram runs outside the center and will take you on a guided tour to the BYU campus, the temple, and the community. The undeniable family spirit and pride at PCC makes you feel welcome, while providing a clean and wholesome experience, with plenty of atten-

tion to detail. It's this quality approach and good value that has sustained the "miracle."

Throughout the day, there are various cultural presentations at each village. The Pageant of Canoes sails at 2:30 P.M. and is a waterborne show of music and dance. All day, the Keiki Activities program offers children the opportunity to tune into these cultures with kid-oriented experiences. **Horizons,** the center's largest extravaganza, runs 7:30–9 P.M. at the indoor amphitheater. This theater hosts about 3,000 spectators for this show of music, dance, and historical drama, which is put on by nearly 100 performers. The costumes and lighting are dramatic and inspired; it's hard to believe that the performers are not professionals.

Food is available from snack bars, or you can dine at the Ambassador and Gateway restaurants, which serve you dinner as part of packages including the Polynesian extravaganza. Another option is the Ali'i Lu'au, which introduces you to the Hawaiian feast, the ceremony of removing the roasted pig from the *imu* pit, and a reenactment of a royal court procession.

PCC is open daily except Sunday 12:30–6 P.M. for general admission, $27 adult, $16 children, under five free, but dinner is on your own. Packages are also available; they include general admission to the villages and daytime activities, dinner, and preferred seating at the evening show. The Gateway Package, $49 adults and $32 children, includes a buffet dinner; Ali'i Lu'au

Package, $65 adults and $44 children, lets you partake in the lu'au dinner show; and the Ambassador Package, $94 adults and $63 children, serves you a sit-down dinner, gives a guided tour, and offers special souvenirs, gifts, and other perks. For more information contact PCC at 808/293-3333 or 800/367-7060, website: www.polynesia.com. TheBus no. 52 runs to the PCC from Ala Moana Shopping Center but takes about 2.5 hours. PCC runs its own bus transportation to the center from hotels in Waikiki for $15 per person. Most island hotels and tour companies can arrange a package tour to PCC.

La'ie Point

Laniloa Peninsula is a spit of land that pushes out to La'ie Point. It's a residential area that ends in an undeveloped country park, from where you can get scenic views up and down the coast and to the small islands offshore. While the peninsula is a low rocky promontory, beaches line the coast in both directions. Of the offshore islands, there are several legends. One states that Laniloa was a legendary *mo'o* (lizard) that terrorized the inhabitants of this area and anyone who happened to pass this way. The lizard was finally dispatched by the heroic warrior and demi-god named Kana, who had it out for all lizards after one had terrorized his mother. Kana cut this lizard's head into five pieces and threw them into the ocean, and these pieces are now seen as the five small islands off the end of the Laniloa Peninsula.

Malaekahana Bay State Recreation Area

This state recreation area is the premier camping beach and park along the north section of the windward coast. Separated from the highway by a large stand of ironwood shade trees, this 37-acre park offers showers, restrooms, picnic facilities, pavilion, local-style beach houses, and camping. For camping permits, contact Friends of Malaekahana at P.O. Box 305, La'ie, HI 96762, 808/293-1736, fax 808/293-2066; office hours are Mon.–Fri. 10 A.M.–3 P.M.

Malaekahana was Pu'uhonua of La'ie, a place of refuge and, according to legend, the only spot on O'ahu not conquered by King Kamehameha. The recent restructuring of the recreation area was intended to bring back its traditional role as a healing and gathering place. An alternative learning center erected here is connected to Kahuku High School, where students come to reconnect culturally and spiritually.

Offshore is Moku'auia, better known as **Goat Island.** The island is only a stone's throw from shore. Reef walkers or tennis shoes are advised. You can reach this seabird sanctuary by wading across the reef during low tide. You'll find a beautiful crescent white-sand beach and absolute peace and quiet. Relax and look for seabirds, or try to spot hawksbill or green sea turtles. The swimming inside the reef is good, and it's amazing how little used this area is for such a beautiful spot. Farther offshore, about 200–300 yards, are two other small islands, which *you cannot wade to.* It is too far, and the currents are strong. Be aware that there are two entrances to the park. The south entrance, closest to La'ie, puts you in the day-use area of the park, where there are restrooms and showers. The entrance to the camping section is north a minute or two (around mile marker 17) and is marked by a steel gate painted brown and a sign welcoming you to Malaekahana Bay State Recreation Area. Be aware that the gate opens at 7 A.M. and is locked at 7 P.M.

BEACHES

At the southern end of La'ie is **La'ie Beach County Park,** an unimproved beach park with no facilities. The beach here is called **Pounder's Beach,** so named by students of BYU because of the pounding surf. This beach experiences heavy surf and dangerous conditions in the winter months, but its excellent shoreline break is perfect for bodysurfing for those with some skill. The remains of an old pier at which interisland steamers once stopped is still in evidence. The shoreline waters farther into town are safe for swimming inside the reef, but wintertime produces heavy and potentially dangerous surf. Good snorkeling, fishing, and throw-netting.

PRACTICALITIES

Accommodations

The **Best Inn Hukilau Resort,** 55-109 Laniloa St., La'ie, HI 96762, 808/293-9282 or 800/526-4562, fax 808/293-8115, website: www.hawaii-ibestinn.com, email: bestinn@hawaii.rr.com, is just outside the Polynesian Cultural Center on the mountain side of the highway. It's a humble motel-like cinderblock affair—basic, as neat as a pin, and secure. While you won't find luxury, you won't go wrong here. Five two-story buildings with four dozen units surround a quiet and relaxing central courtyard and swimming pool. All rooms have a/c, TV, mini-fridge and microwaves, and island-inspired decorations and amenities; bathrooms have been renovated with new fixtures and accessories. Rooms are $84 queen, $89 double, $94 king, with a $5 reduction during off-season (April, May, September, October); good value. The fee includes continental breakfast, free local telephone calls, and parking. Not only is this inn close to BYU, the PCC, and the Mormon temple, it's near windward and North Shore beaches. Hotel guests have access to a private beach area across the road near a barbecue grill. This is a good choice at reasonable rates.

Lora Dunn's House, 808/293-1000, is at 55-161 Kamehameha Hwy., La'ie, HI 96762, between mile markers 19 and 20, ocean side, just south of Pounder's Beach. Lora admits people on a first-come, first-served basis, but will happily take phone reservations for which she requires a deposit. Chances of turning up and finding a vacancy are poor, so at least call from the airport to check availability. A studio with kitchenette for two people is $50 a day, while the downstairs self-contained, two-bedroom, full-kitchen unit, which is larger and can accommodate up to six people, runs $65 per day for two with $10 for each additional person. There is a two-day minimum. All guests have use of the washer and dryer and there is good off-street parking. Good value in a quiet, if not spectacular, setting. From the house, there's a path to the beach.

A stone's throw from the La'ie Village Shopping Center is the one-unit vacation rental **Ala Mahina,** 808/293-2275. A tropical hideaway set amongst thick vegetation and right on the narrow but sandy beach, it has a good-size sitting room, small but fully furnished kitchen, and one bedroom with air conditioning. All the art hanging on the walls has been done by Michael, the owner. The rate is $150 a night plus a cleaning fee, and weekly rates can be negotiated.

Food and Shopping

When you enter La'ie you will be greeted by the Stars and Stripes flying over the entrance of the Polynesian Cultural Center. Next door is a whopper of a **McDonald's,** and in keeping with the spirit of Polynesian culture, it looks like a Polynesian longhouse. Just up the road at the **La'ie Village Shopping Center** you'll find a large and modern Foodland, along with a Bank of America, a small convenience store, a handful of other shops, La'ie Washerette, L&L Drive-In, La'ie Chop Suey, La'ie Cinemas, and a post office, all that you'll need for a successful vacation.

KAHUKU

This village, and it is a village, is where the *workers* of the North Shore live. Kahuku is "fo' real," and a lingering slice of what *was* not so long ago. Do yourself a favor, and turn off the highway for a two-minute tour of the dirt roads lined by proudly maintained homes that somehow exude the feeling of Asia. The older part of town is to the sea side of the mill; newer homes line well-paved streets up by the school and hospital. When the sugar mill closed, this community like many throughout the state took a nose dive and lost its economic balance. Still looking for equilibrium, some locals have turned to raising freshwater shrimp in several shrimp farms just north of town, and others grow sweet corn. Along the beach is Kahuku Golf Course. Built for plantation workers early in the 1900s, an unusual move by owners for its workers, it is now a public course. On the northern outskirts of town are the two sections of the 164-acre **James Campbell National Wildlife Refuge.** Established in 1976, this refuge consists of marshland and manmade ponds, and harbors many varieties of water birds, including the endemic and endangered Hawaiian stilt, coot, duck, and gallinule. Guided tours are offered periodically for up to 25 people. Call the office at 808/637-6330 to make arrangements.

Practicalities

You can pick up supplies at the **Kahuku Superette,** clearly marked along Route 83, or better yet look for **Giovanni's** white *kaukau* wagon, which sits across the roadway from the school. Daily

10:30 A.M.–6:30 P.M., the wagon sells shrimp scampi, a demonly spicy shrimp, and shrimp in lemon juice that run $11 for a dozen in-the-shell pieces, and this comes with rice and bread. Picnic tables sit under an awning attached to the wagon, and to the side is another *kaukau* wagon selling smoothies. You're guaranteed to get messy eating this meal and you'll use a pile of napkins, but your sticky fingers and sated stomach are your reward. Other similar *kaukau* trucks selling shrimp can also be seen along the highway in the vicinity.

On the north end of town is the **Mill Shopping Center,** which is really the town's old sugar mill recycled. The interior of the old mill, which operated 1893–1971 and is now open daily except Sunday 9 A.M.–5 P.M., is dominated by huge gears and machinery, power panels, crushers, and sign boards that give you a little sugar history lesson. The 10-foot gears and conveyor belts have all been painted with bright colors and seem like a display of modern art pieces. Outside the main mill building under a covered area is a little bazaar of shops, a restaurant, and the Kahuku Theater, but it seems that it's been difficult to keep the shops filled. Also at the shopping center are a gas station, a Leonard J's Hot Malasadas truck, and a post office. Located here is the **Country Kitchen,** 808/293-2110, serving mostly Korean and American standard foods, but, because of the area, it has many shrimp dishes as well. An indoor-outdoor restaurant with a walk-up window, it is open daily 8 A.M.–5 P.M. for breakfast and lunch. Most dishes are in the under-$12 range.

On the second and fourth Saturdays of the month 8 A.M.–noon, the Kahuku Community Hospital sponsors a **farmers' market** for produce, flowers, and crafts, as well as a health screening.

Just a mile past Kahuku, beyond the shrimp farms, is the **Tanaka Plantation Store,** 56-901 Kamehameha Hwy., a refurbished early 1900s company store that now houses a clutch of boutiques and shops. Make sure to visit **The Only Show In Town,** open daily 10:30 A.M.–5:30 P.M., 808/293-1295. Blown to O'ahu's North Shore from Kaua'i by Hurricane 'Iniki, Paul Wroblewski has reopened his antiques and collectibles shop and once again jammed it with Hawaiian artifacts, old bottles, costume jewelry, license plates, Japanese glass fishing floats, netsuke, scrimshaw, a collection of Marilyn Monroe memorabilia, and a full line of antique jewelry. Paul's an amiable fellow and is open to any reasonable offer. Remember, he may price according to your attitude. Also, if you have a collectible that you want to sell or get an estimate of value on, ask Paul to take a look.

Next door is **Imua Shop Polynesia,** open daily 10 A.M.–6 P.M., 808/293-5055, with craft items, carvings, tapa, tiki, aloha shirts, shells, jewelry, Hawaiian quilts, and postcards. If you have any questions on the origin or authenticity of these items, talk to the owner, Doris.

Perhaps the most interesting shop in the complex is the **Amazonian Forest Store,** owned and operated by Brazilian world travelers Cesar Olivera and Katia Ferz. Open daily 11 A.M.–6 P.M., 808/293-5053. It specializes in authentic artifacts gathered from the Amazon and other rainforest regions around the world, including Hawaii and Indonesia. Some of the most amazing artifacts are headdresses and paintings by Brazil's Xindu Indians, along with basketry, parasols, coconut purses, string and cotton hammocks, and semiprecious gemstones gathered from throughout South America. If these aren't enough to make you "bug eyed" perhaps a Brazilian string bikini will. They've added a boutique with ladies' dresses, sundresses, and beach apparel, and men's casual beachwear.

There's usually a truck out front that sells pineapples and other fresh fruit, a good place to buy a fresh snack for the road.

GEOGRAPHICAL NOTE

The following chapter, The North Shore, begins at the west end in Waialua-Hale'iwa and works eastward toward Kahuku. That's because most people visiting the North Shore proceed in this direction, while those heading for windward O'ahu start in Kailua-Kane'ohe and proceed up the coast. So, the end of this chapter follows geographically with the end of The North Shore chapter. Don't let it throw you.

THE NORTH SHORE

This shallow bowl of coastline stretches from Ka'ena Point in the west to Turtle Bay in the east. **Mount Ka'ala,** verdant backdrop to the area, rises 4,020 feet from the Wai'anae Range, making it the highest peak on O'ahu. The entire stretch is a day-tripper's paradise with plenty of sights to keep you entertained. But the North Shore is synonymous with one word: surfing.

Thunderous winter waves, often measuring 25 feet but sometimes up to 40 feet (from the rear!), rumble along the North Shore's world-famous surfing beaches lined up one after the other—**Waimea Bay, Banzai Pipeline, Ehukai, Sunset.** They attract highly accomplished athletes who come to compete in prestigious international surfing competitions. Other beaches, often less well-known, like Mokule'ia Beach, also provide excellent waves without the crowds. Be aware that *all* North Shore beaches experience very heavy surf conditions with dangerous currents from October through April. The waters, at this time of year, are not for the average swimmer. Please heed all warnings. In summertime *moana* loses her ferocity and lies down, becoming gentle and safe for anyone—leap in!.

The main attractions of the North Shore are its beaches, but interspersed among them are a few sights definitely worth your time and effort. The listings below run from west to east. Although the North Shore can easily be approached from Windward O'ahu, the most-traveled route to the North Shore is from Honolulu along the H-2 freeway to Wahiawa, and then directly to the coast from there along Route 99 or Route 803. At Weed Circle or Thompson Corner, where these routes reach the coastal highway, turn left along the Farrington Highway (Route 930), following it to road's end just before Ka'ena Point, or turn right along the Kamehameha Highway (Route 83), which heads around the coast all the way to Kane'ohe.

Hale'iwa is fast becoming the central town along the North Shore. The main street is lined with restaurants, boutiques, art galleries, small shopping malls, and sports equipment stores. **Waialua,** just west, is a former "sugar town" with

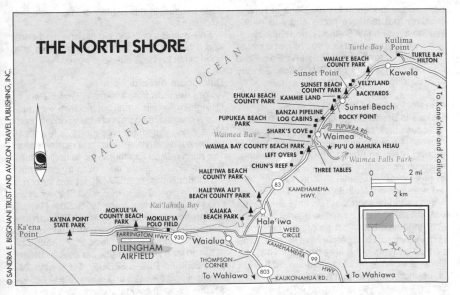

THE NORTH SHORE

an old mill and a few quiet condos for relaxation. Farther west is **Dillingham Airfield,** where you can arrange to fly above it all in a small plane, soar silently in a glider, or give your heart a real jolt by jumping out of a plane for a free-fall parachute ride. The road ends for vehicles not far from there, and then your feet have to take you to Ka'ena Point, where *the* largest waves pound the coast. Heading east, you'll pass a famous *heiau* where human flesh mollified the gods, a monument to a real local hero, and **Waimea Falls Park,** the premier tourist attraction of the North Shore. Then come the great surfing beach-es and their incredible waves. Here and there are tidepools rich with discovery.

Places to stay are quite limited along the North Shore. The best deals are beach homes or rooms rented directly from the owners, but this is a hit-and-miss proposition. You have to check the local papers or the bulletin boards outside stores and shops in Hale'iwa and Waimea. Many better homes are now handled by rental agents. The homes vary greatly in amenities. Some are palaces, others are basic rooms perfect for surfers or those who consid-er lodging secondary.

ALONG THE FARRINGTON HIGHWAY

WAIALUA

The first town is Waialua. In the early 1900s, Waialua, a stop along the sugar-train railway, was a fashionable beach community complete with hotels and vacation homes. Today, it's hard-ly ever visited, and it's not uncommon to see as many horses tied up along the main street as it is to see parked cars in this real one-horse town.

Sundays can also attract a rumble of bikers who kick up the dust on their two-wheeled steeds.

The old sugar mill, an outrageously ugly me-chanical monster, dominates the town. There is no sugar now, but the area does produce some coffee, corn, bananas, and other diversified crops on mostly small plots. Quiet Waialua, with its main street divided by trees running down the middle, *is* rural O'ahu. There's a general store for supplies, a post office, and the **Sugar Bar,** a bar/cocktail lounge in the old Bank of Hawaii building that features pizza and live music Wednesday, Friday, Saturday, and Sunday.

If polo is your game or if you're just curious, head west of town to the Mokule'ia Polo Field and catch a Hawaii Polo Club match, Sunday at 2 P.M. during the season.

Coastal Points of Interest

Mokule'ia Beach County Park is the main public access park along the highway. It provides rudimentary picnic facilities, restrooms, a playground area, and camping. In summertime, swimming is possible along a few sandy stretches protected by a broken offshore reef.

Farther down, **Mokule'ia Army Beach** is a wider strand of sand that has little shade. It's very private, and the only noise interrupting your afternoon slumber might be planes taking off from the airfield. Local people have erected semipermanent tents in this area and guard it as if it were their own. A minute farther toward Ka'ena is an unofficial area with a wide sand beach. During the week you can expect no more than a half dozen people on this 300-yard beach. Remember that this is the North Shore and the water can be treacherous. Careful!

Across from the YMCA camp and up the road a short ways is a trail (30 minutes) that leads uphill to a rock wall that can be seen from the road. Many consider this spot to be the best rock climbing area on the island, and it is indeed unusual in this usually crumbly volcanic landscape.

Five minutes past the airfield, the road ends and a natural area reserve begins. This is a good place to check out giant waves.

Dillingham Airfield

Across the road from Mokule'ia Beach Park is Dillingham Airfield, small but modern, with restrooms near the hangars and a new parking area. Most days, especially weekends, a few local people sell refreshments from their cars or trucks. The main reason for stopping is to take a small biplane flight or glider ride, or to try parachuting. **Glider Rides,** 808/677-3404, takes you on a 20-minute flight. Talk to owner Bill Star, who has been flying from here since 1970. **Soar Hawaii Sailplanes,** 808/637-3147, and **Skysurfing Glider Rides,** 808/637-0590, also do rides of differing lengths. Expect fees in the range of $75–100 for a 20-minute ride per couple. **Stearman Biplane Rides,** 808/637-4461, runs 20-minute flights for $125 and 40-minute flights for $175 in its open-cockpit biplane. Use the west end gate across from the control tower for these attractions.

The first entrance, at the eastern end of the field, will bring you to the three skydive operations: **Pacific International, Drop Zone,** and **Skydive Hawaii.** This is the only place in the state where skydiving is offered commercially. The thrill of a one-minute freefall followed by

skydiving at Dillingham Airfield

five- to 10-minute parachute drop will set you back $150–200. Tandem drops only.

Ka'ena Point State Park

Ka'ena Point lies about 2.5 miles down the dirt track after the pavement gives out. Count on three hours for a return hike and remember to bring water. The point can also be reached from road's end above Makaha on the Waianae (leeward) side of the island. Ka'ena has *the* largest waves in Hawaii on any given day. In wintertime, these giants can reach above 40 feet, and their power, even when viewed safely from the high ground, is truly amazing. Surfers have actually plotted ways of riding these waves, which include being dropped by helicopter with scuba tanks. Reportedly, one surfer named Ace Cool has already done it. For the rest of us mortals . . . "who wants to have that much fun anyway!" Ka'ena Point is the site of numerous *heiau*. Due to its exposed position, it, like similar sites around the islands, was a jumping-off point for the "souls of the dead." The spirits were believed to wander here after death, and once all worldly commitments were fulfilled, they made their "leap" from earth to the land beyond. Hopefully, the daredevil surfers will not revive this tradition! During winter months, chances are good for seeing whales carousing off this point.

Accommodations

Mokuleia Beach Colony, 68-615 Farrington Hwy., is a private gated community of 26 duplexes along a wonderfully uncrowded beach just past the polo grounds. While some owners rent their condos themselves, others are handled by local Realtors. For information and reservations, contact Paradise Realty, 808/637-1997, or Marlanne Abrigo Properties, 808/637-3511.

Just beyond the Colony is **Mokule'ia Sunset Vacation Rentals,** 808/637-2312 or 808/637-4111. Set directly on the beach, this is a quiet place, clean, but a little funky. Other units on the property have long-term residents, but the rentals run: $585 a week for the cottage, $685 weekly for the studio, and $785 a week for the two-bedroom suite that looks right over the water.

Camp Mokule'ia is owned and operated by the Episcopalian Church in Hawaii. This camp runs organized summer programs for kids age 7–17, and offers space for other group meetings and retreats throughout the year. In addition, rooms in their lodge building are open to individuals and families on a space available basis. Reserve no more than 30 days in advance. Plain and simple, rooms and suites run $55–105 per day or $75–120 for a room and light breakfast. Tent camping is also an option at $8 per night for those 18 years old and older and $4 for kids ages 4–17. Meals can be purchased separately. For information and reservations, contact the camp at 68-729 Farrington Hwy., Waialua, HI 96791, 808/637-6241, fax 808/637-5505, website: www.campmokuleia.com.

YMCA Camp H. R. Erdman is next, one of the best-known camps on O'ahu. This YMCA facility is named after a famous Hawaiian polo player killed in the 1930s. The full-service facility is used as a summer camp for children, throughout the year for special functions, and as a general retreat area by various organizations. Access and participation in activities is limited to those staying there. Although cabins are usually rented to groups of eight or more, tenting is available September–May on the weekends and daily through the summer for $7 per person per night, and this includes use of the shower and bathrooms. For information contact YMCA Camp H. R. Erdman, 69-385 Farrington Hwy., Waialua, HI 96791, 808/637-4615, fax 808/637-8874, website: www.camperdman.net.

O'AHU

HALE'IWA AND VICINITY

Hale'iwa (Home of the Frigate Birds) has become the premier town of the region, mainly because it straddles the main North Shore road where the highways over the Leilehua Plateau meet the coast, and it has the majority of shopping, dining, and services along the North Shore. The coastal highway runs through town, but to ease traffic, Hale'iwa now has a bypass, the Joseph P. Leong Highway, around the backside of town. Unless you're really in a rush, follow the brown "Welcome to Historic Hale'iwa Town" sign into town as this is where it's all happening.

Many of the old buildings of town are of the single-story plantation-era variety from the early 1900s. Hale'iwa has managed to keep this old-style look fairly intact, and even the new North Shore Marketplace shopping mall has kept with the style and created single-story false-front stores and covered wooden lanai.

Head eastward and cross the graceful double-arch **Anahulu River Bridge.** Park for a moment and walk back over the bridge. Look upstream to see homes with tropical character perched on the bank with a bevy of boats tied below. The scene is reminiscent of times gone by, and it is said that Queen Liliu'okalani once had a summer house on the banks of this river. Queen

Lili'uokalani has left another mark on the town, this in the guise of the Lili'uokalani Protestant Church on the highway. While the congregation is much older and the original church was from the late 1800s, the present church dates from 1961. If you're heading between Hale'iwa and Waialua take Hale'iwa Road, a back way through residential areas. Look for Pa'ala'a (Sacred Firmness) Road and take it past a Hale'iwa Shingon Mission temple, another old vestige from Hale'iwa's past. This Buddhist mission hosts an Obon festival yearly, traditionally observed in July, which honors the dead—a colorful cultural event. This quiet town with a sugar past and lazy days of surfers and hippies is still strong on cultural activities. If you're in town during the Hale'iwa Arts Festival and the taro festival don't miss them.

PARKS

Hale'iwa Ali'i Beach Park is on the western shores of Waialua Bay, which fronts the town. This beach park is improved with restrooms, lifeguard tower, and a small boat launch. Lifeguards staff the tower throughout the summer, on weekends in winter. The shoreline is rocks and coral

typical rural Buddhist temple, on the outskirts of Hale'iwa

J.D. BISIGNANI

O'AHU

HALE'IWA

PACIFIC OCEAN

Puaena Point

Waialua Bay

To Waimea and Sunset Beach

Ukoa Pond

KAHALEWAI PL.

HALE'IWA BEACH COUNTY PARK

83

KAMEHAMEHA HWY.

JOSEPH P. LEONG HWY.

JAMESON'S BY THE SEA

HALE'IWA GENERAL STORE

SURFHOUSE

SURF AND SEA

HALE'IWA SMALL BOAT HARBOR

Loko Ea Pond

LOKOEA PL.

Anahulu River

HALE'IWA ALI'I BEACH PARK

HALE'IWA JOE'S

ANAHULU RIVER BRIDGE

NAIOIWI LN.

NAIMU RD.

NIUIULA RD.

WAUKANAHELE

MIURA

HALE'IWA BEACH GRILL

MATSUMOTO'S

AOKI

IWA GALLERY

CHURCH

KEWALO

WYLAND GALLERY

AMARA RD.

KAIAKA BEACH COUNTY PARK

KAIAKA

LAWAI LN.

IKEAHIPAKA LN.

FRESH AIR CAMP RD.

Kaiaka Bay

FUJIKA MARKET

HALE'IWA SHOPPING CENTER

WAILUA BAKERY

HALE'IWA ART GALLERY

KILIOE PL.

NORTH SHORE MARKETPLACE

83

KAMEHAMEHA HWY.

HALE'IWA RD.

PA'ALA'A RD.

POST OFFICE

CELESTIAL NATURAL FOODS

CAFE HALE'IWA

JOSEPH P. LEONG HWY.

HALE'IWA SHINGON MISSION TEMPLE

Paurauila Stream

821

82

WAIALUA BEACH RD.

WEED CIRCLE

99

KAMEHAMEHA HWY.

To Wailua

To Wahiawa

MOON

O'AHU

0   0.2 mi

0   0.2 km

© SANDRA E. EISIGN-ANI TRUST AND AVALON TRAVEL PUBLISHING, INC.

with pockets of sand, and although portions can be good for swimming, the park is primarily noted for surfing at a break simply called Hale'iwa. The park is popular with townspeople, and it has become more widely known in the last few years as the popular TV program *Baywatch Hawaii* was based here, and some of the shows were filmed on the beach.

A little farther to the west, on Kaiaka Point, is **Kaiaka Beach County Park.** This is a good swimming and snorkeling beach, and you'll find restrooms and picnic areas here. Camping is allowed with county permit.

Hale'iwa Beach County Park, clearly marked off the highway on the eastern side of Waialua Bay beyond the bridge, is right at the river mouth across from the marina. Here you'll find pavilions, picnic facilities, athletic grounds, lifeguards, restrooms, showers, lots of parking, and food concessions, but no camping. The area is good for fishing, surfing, and, most important, for swimming year-round! It's about the only safe place for the average person to swim along the entire North Shore during winter.

Kawailoa Beach is the general name given to the waterfront stretching all the way from Hale'iwa Beach County Park to Waimea Bay. Cars park where the access is good. None of the shoreline is really suitable for the recreational swimmer. All are surfing areas, with the most popular being Chun's Reef.

ACCOMMODATIONS

On the back side of Lokoea Pond just at the edge of town is **Surfhouse,** 62-202 Lokoea Pl., Haleiwa, HI 96712, 808/637-7146, email: surfhouse@aol.com. A budget accommodation, the Surfhouse offers shared and private rooms in the main house, in a detached bunkhouse, and in a couple of cabins. The bunkhouse has six beds that run $15 a night or $95 a week; private rooms are $45 a night or $280 a week. Campers can find a space on the lawn for $9 a night or $56 a week. Washers and dryers are available and the "Hale'iwa Yacht Club," with its stove, sink, refrigerator, couches, and chairs, serves as the communal eating, sitting, and entertainment area for guests. Bicycles and water equipment can be rented at inexpensive rates.

There's adequate space to park cars. Mostly, young people come to hang out here for a few weeks or stay while looking for a job and more permanent housing, and often a real camaraderie develops among them. Make your arrangements with Sophie or Lee.

For vacation rentals, see the list of agents below under Waimea.

FOOD

Inexpensive Food

Celestial Natural Foods, 808/637-6729, open Mon.–Sat. 9 A.M.–6:30 P.M., Sunday 10 A.M.–6 P.M., is near the western end of town. Up front is a complete natural and health food store. In back, and called **Paradise Found,** is a lunch counter that serves vegetarian meals. Some items are nachos for $4.95, tofu sauté wrap at $4.95, garden burger $5.25, and grilled eggplant and pesto sandwich at $6.50. Smoothies, fresh juice drinks, teas, sodas, and sweets are also available. The food is healthful and nutritious, but portions are definitely not for the hungry.

Cafe Hale'iwa, 808/637-5516, a very casual hole-in-the-wall eatery on your right just as you enter town, serves one of the best breakfasts on O'ahu. Specials of the house are whole-wheat banana pancakes, French toast, spinach and mushroom quiche, huevos rancheros, Breakfast in a Barrel, and steaming-hot Kona coffee. One of the partners is called "the wizard of eggs" and has built up a local following. Lunch options include fish sandwiches and burritos with home fries and potato salad. The café attracts many surfers, so it's a great place to find out about conditions. Hours are Mon.–Fri. 7 A.M.–2 P.M. and Sunday 11 A.M.–2 P.M.

Another tiny place with great treats is **Kua Aina,** for a great assortment of sandwiches and—some claim—the best burgers on the island. There are a few tables out front on the lanai if you're lucky enough to find a spot amongst the hungry mob.

If you're tired or just need a pick-me-up head for the North Shore Marketplace, where you'll find the **Coffee Gallery,** 808/637-5571, open daily 6 A.M.–9 P.M., which has a large selection of fresh roasted gourmet coffee, including Kona coffees and international selections of organi-

O'AHU

cally grown coffee. You can enjoy a steaming cup from its full service espresso bar, along with fresh carrot juice and vegan pastries made without dairy products or eggs. Other more bliss-inducing pastries are blackberry apple crumble pie, super chocolate brownies, fresh fruit bars, and racks of various cookies and muffins. Every day there is a homemade soup, fresh salad, and a fine selection of deli sandwiches that range from a vegetarian garden burger on a whole wheat bun with lettuce and tomatoes, Maui onion, guacamole, and a side of tortilla chips to pita bread filled with eggplant, pesto, and veggies, all priced around $6. It's all vegetarian. Sit outside in the shaded and screened dining area and watch the character-laden "characters" of the North Shore come and go.

For south-of-the-border food, try **Cholo's Homestyle Mexican Restaurant,** 808/637-3059, open 8 A.M.–9 P.M. Plate items, which include rice and beans, run $4–7.50; dinners include rice, beans, salad, chips, salsa, and a choice of meat and go for $6.25–9.50. Many combinations are also available. The walls are festooned with masks, paintings, prints, and other works of art and crafts.

If the smells of fresh-baked bread and pastries don't bring you into the **Wailua Bakery,** nothing will. Aside from the breads, cookies, and muffins, the bakery does filling and delicious sandwiches, smoothies, and juice, right for a "get-me-started" push in the morning or a "keep-me-going" nudge during the day. Although closed on Monday, the bakery is open other days from 8 A.M.

You can tell by the tour buses parked outside that **Matsumoto's** is a very famous store on the North Shore. What are all those people after? Shave ice. This is one of the best places on O'ahu to try this island treat. Not only do the tourists come here, but local families often take a "Sunday drive" just to get Matsumoto's shave ice. Try the Hawaiian Delight, a mound of ice smothered with banana, pineapple, and mango syrup, or any three of nearly two dozen flavors plus ice cream or sweet beans on the bottom. If lines are too long here or if you want to frequent the competition, try **Aoki's** shave ice or **Miura Store,** both only a few steps away. Shave ice cones run about $2.

Its bright colors and modernistic designs might make you think you're in a modern art paint-

ing, but the food at the **Hale'iwa Beach Grill,** 808/637-3394, brings you back to reality. A casual place—plate lunches, sandwiches, burritos, and other simple fare all go for under $6. Order at the counter. The grill is open 11 A.M.–8 P.M.

Rosie's Cantina, 808/637-3538, in the Hale'iwa Shopping Plaza, open daily for breakfast, lunch, and dinner, prepares hearty Mexican dishes for a decent price. The inside is "yuppie Mex" with brass rails, painted overhead steam pipes, and elevated booths. While breakfast is mostly eggs and grill items, most with a south-of-the-border edge, the full lunch and dinner menus are more typically Mexican, from burritos to quesadillas and fajitas. Expect to pay $7–8 for most dishes. Full bar.

Pizza Bob's, 808/637-5095, also in the Hale'iwa Shopping Plaza, has an excellent local reputation, and its little pub serves up not only delicious pizza, but salads, pasta, burgers, and sandwiches. Dinner specials nightly. People are friendly, there's plenty of food, and the price is right. Open most nights until 9 P.M., Fri.–Sat. until 10 P.M., and there is live music on Friday evenings.

Moderate Food

Jameson's by the Sea, 62-540 Kamehameha Hwy., 808/637-4336, open daily for lunch, dinner, and cocktails, is the best that Hale'iwa has to offer. At the north end of town overlooking the sea, its outdoor deck is perfect for a romantic sunset dinner, while inside the romantic mood is continued with track lighting, shoji screens, cane chairs with stuffed pillows, candles with shades, and tables resplendent with fine linen. Appetizers include a salmon pâté for $8.95, stuffed mushrooms with escargot for $7.50, fresh oysters for $8.95, and a bowl of creamy clam chowder for $4.50. Main dishes like mahimahi, stuffed shrimp, shrimp curry with mango chutney, and sesame chicken range $18.50–25. For dessert have the lemon macadamia nut chiffon pie for $4.50. The pub downstairs serves lunch from a slightly different menu that includes sandwiches. It's quiet at night and serves a variety of imported beers. Breakfast is served Sat.–Sun. 9 A.M.–noon. Reservations highly recommended. Request a window seat for the sunset.

Hale'iwa Joe's Seafood Grill, 66-011 Kamehameha Hwy., 808/637-8005, open daily for

O'AHU

lunch from 11:30 A.M. and dinner from 5:30 P.M., is in a green cinder-block building on the left before you cross the Anahulu River bridge. Although purely utilitarian on the outside, the inside is modern and tasteful with a touch of North Shore surfing decor. On the site of the area's first hotel and a precious *heiau*, this fine restaurant looks out over the Hale'iwa boat harbor and some of what's on the menu comes directly from the fishing boats. Dine inside or out. Appetizers like *'ahi* spring roll, Thai fried calamari, and crunchy coconut shrimp run $7–10. Soups and salads are on the menu from a house salad at $3.25 to a grilled salmon spinach salad for $10.75. Main entrées here emphasize fish, but steak and ribs are also available. Fresh mahimahi is always a winner, grilled spicy shrimp starts the taste buds jumping, and the pork ribs marinated in soy-ginger and hoisen sauce tip the hat toward the Orient. Most entrées run $14–20, but the Alaskan king crab legs go for $24.95. Hale'iwa Joe's is good-time place with tasty food in a casual setting.

Casual but one of the best in town is **Portofino,** 808/637-7678, at the North Shore Marketplace. Soups, salads, pasta, pizza, and sandwiches are served for lunch, 11 A.M.–4 P.M. Dinner includes pizza and calzones for $8.95–19.95, but the menu also has full entrées like rosemary chicken for $14.50, barbecue ribs at $16.95, scampi parmesan for $19.75, and various pasta dishes $10–15. An open kitchen emanates aromas. Here they use a wood-fired pizza oven so you know that it's the real McCoy. Eat inside or out, or just stop by for a drink and televised sports in the attached bar.

SHOPPING

In Town

In town you'll find **Miura** general store, in business since the 1918, which has a few basic dry goods but mostly cloth and brightly colored clothing. **Matahari** carries women's fashions.

Along the highway is **Hale'iwa Shopping Center,** which provides all the necessities in one-stop shopping: boutiques, pharmacy, photo store, a Bank of Hawaii, and general food and merchandise. Restaurants include **L&L Drive-In, Pizza Bob's at Hale'iwa,** and **Rosie's Cantina.**

For food and picnic supplies try the **Hale'iwa IGA,** open Mon.–Sat. 8 A.M.–8 P.M., Sunday 8:30 A.M.–5:30 P.M. Almost across the street is the smaller **Fujika** market with a smaller variety but nearly the same hours.

In the same building as Jameson's By the Sea restaurant is **Outrigger Trading Co.,** a shop specializing in gifts and souvenirs. Here you can find high-quality jewelry, prints, T-shirts, candles, books, and many more items. The shop is open daily 10 A.M.–10 P.M.

North Shore Marketplace

The North Shore Marketplace, along the Kamehameha Highway between McDonald's and the Hale'iwa Shopping Center, is a growing complex with some unique shops. Most shops are open 9 A.M.–6 P.M., with restaurants serving until late. One of the most interesting shops is **Jungle Gem's,** with a metaphysical assortment of crystals, crystal balls, African trading beads, and gems. The shop specializes in locally made jewelry that is reasonably priced and of excellent quality. The owners are knowledgeable gemologists and fine jewelers who do much of the work on display. **Silver Moon Emporium** has not only some jewelry but also a fine collection of boutique clothing.

Strong Current Surf Design is a surf shop that also has beachwear, but it's more than that. It's almost like a museum of surfing with all the collectibles on display. Stop in and reminisce about the '50s and '60s classic era of surfing. For water wear and ocean equipment, have a look at **Boardriders Club Northshore** and **Hawaiian Surf** shops. Also in the center is **Patagonia** for high-quality outdoor wear and equipment.

To the left in the rear as you drive into the parking lot is **Barnfield's Raging Isle Surf and Cycle,** 808/637-7707, website: www.raging-isle.com, a full-service mountain bike and surf shop open daily 10 A.M.–6:30 P.M. Aside from selling and repairing bikes, Barnfield's also rents mountain bikes at $40 for 24 hours. The shop also manufactures surfboards here, the only place on the North Shore legally doing so. Board repairs are also made. Casual clothing and surf wear are stocked.

Twelve Tribes International Imports is a multicultural emporium in the back with items from the global village. It's open Mon.–Fri. 10:30 A.M.–5:30 P.M, Sat. 10 A.M.–6 P.M., and Sun. noon–5 P.M. For something more gifty and more island-oriented, have a look at **Polynesian Handicrafts** and **Kama'ainas Hale'iwa.**

Across the way is **North Shore Glass,** where hand-blown art glass is produced in the open-air studio. Most of what the artists make goes to the hotels, but they do have a small rack of retail items that they sell in the studio. Pyrex is used for these delicate figures, many of them dolphins and other sea creatures. Check them out to see how the work is done. Open 10 A.M.–7 P.M. daily.

Next door to North Shore Glass is the **North Shore Surf Museum.** A walk through this compact showplace will teach you a bit about the history of surfing on the North Shore, and you'll have a chance to examine surfboards, clothing, photographs, and other artifacts of surfing life and the culture of the North Shore.

Art Galleries and Shops

Iwa Gallery, open most days 10:30 A.M.–6:30 P.M., is across the street from the Protestant church, which was founded in 1892, and next door to Aoki's Shave Ice. This co-op shows the efforts of local artists who have been juried in order to place their artwork on consignment. Featured are the fine candle sculptures of Scott Bechtol. Other artists displayed at the gallery include: Angela Kanas, a watercolor artist who does fanciful renditions of Hawaiian gods, goddesses, and traditional folk; Janet Stewart, who depicts island themes like Madame Pele lying with the blood of her hot lava flowing from her body or a *keiki* hula dancer with a look of concentration on her face; Bill Cupid uses the bark of banana trees to create entire island scenes like ships departing a sheltered harbor. Serigraphs and cards by Janet Holiday are often depictions of flowers in bold primary colors; Peggy Pai, born and raised in China, creates silk batik with ephemeral, beautiful, cloudy landscapes; James Rack uses his palette and brush to catch scenes of idyllic Hawaii; and Norman Kelly catches children at play or surfers on towering waves in his fluid watercolors.

Wyland Gallery, across the street from the Hale'iwa Shopping Center, 808/637-7498, is open daily 9 A.M.–6 P.M. Wyland is a famous environmental artist known for his huge whale and marine life murals, in addition to watercolors and fine oil paintings. The gallery is large, spacious, and well lit. Everything has a Hawaiian or sea theme, and there's even a huge fish tank filled with tropical fish. There're watercolors of Hawaiian maidens by Janet Stewart, lithographs by Roy Tabora of palm trees and cliffs with Michelangelo skies, waterfall paintings by James Coleman, and bronze sculptures of the sea by Scott Hanson. If the original artwork is too expensive, there are posters, mini-prints, and postcards.

The North Shore Marketplace has two galleries. Hale'iwa Art Gallery lies along the highway, while North Shore Art Gallery sits to the back. **Hale'iwa Art Gallery,** 808/637-3368, shows mostly original works by island artists, many from O'ahu, mostly up-and-comers who have not yet made it big but who show obvious talent. Lots of paintings with a smaller selection of other forms and mediums. The **North Shore Art Gallery,** 808/636-2104, displays paintings of the well-known Walfrido and H. Leung, with some turned wooden bowls and a few petroglyphs. This is quality work and perhaps better because of the warm and "familiar" work of North Shore artist Juno Galang.

Services

The best sources of current general information for the North Shore are the bulletin boards outside many of the shops and restaurants.

As you enter Hale'iwa from the west, you'll pass a Shell gas station and a full-service post office; just east of the bridge is a Chevron station and food mart and the Hale'iwa General Store for basic supplies. A Bank of Hawaii is at the Hale'iwa Shopping Center. **Haliewa Family Health Center,** 808/637-5087, a walk-in clinic at 66-125 Kamehameha Hwy., is open Mon.–Sat. 8 A.M.–5 P.M.

Sporting Rentals and Activities

The following shops are all along the main drag through Hale'iwa.

Barnfield's Raging Isle Surf and Cycle, in the North Shore Marketplace, 808/637-7707, open 10 A.M.–6:30 P.M. daily, is primarily a surf shop and manufacturer of Barnfield's Raging Isle Boards, but it also sells, rents, and repairs bikes.

For surfboards, sailboards, boogie boards, snorkeling equipment, sales and rentals, try **Hawaii Surf and Sail,** 66-214 Kamehameha Hwy., 808/637-5373; **Hawaiian Surf,** 808/637-8316, in the North Shore Marketplace; or **Surf and Sea,** 62-595 Kamehameha Hwy., 808/637-9887, website: www.surfnsea.com. Perhaps the most well-established, Surf and Sea is a mustard yellow and brown building near the bridge that offers great rentals and sales of surfboards, snorkel equipment, scuba gear, and other water toys. Scuba lessons and tours and other lessons are offered daily. Open 9 A.M.–7 P.M. daily.

Another quality company doing scuba lessons is **Deep Ecology,** 808/637-7946, at 66-456 Kamehameha Hwy., website: www.deepecology hawaii.com.

While there is not an overabundance of water activities companies on the North Shore, **North Shore Catamaran Charters,** 808/638-8279, does offer cat rides throughout the year from Hale'iwa harbor on its 40-foot *Ho'o Nanea*. Picnic snorkels run from May to October and whale-watch rides from January to May. Also leaving from Hale'iwa harbor for part- or full-day charter fishing trips along the North Shore is **Chupu Charters,** 808/638-7655.

WAIMEA BAY AND VICINITY

The two-lane highway along the North Shore is pounded by traffic; be especially careful around Waimea Bay. The highway sweeps around till you see the steeple of **St. Peter and Paul Mission** with the bay below. The steeple is actually the remnants of an old rock-crushing plant on the site. **Waimea Bay Beach County Park** has some of the largest rideable waves in the world. This is the heart of surfers' paradise. The park is improved with a lifeguard tower, restrooms, and a picnic area. The steeple overlooks the beach's east end; kids dive off rocks at its western end.

During a big winter swell, the bay is lined with spectators watching the surfers ride the monumental waves. In summertime, the bay is calm as a lake. People inexperienced with the sea should not even walk along the shorebreak in winter. Unexpected waves come up farther than you'd think, and a murderous rip lurks only a few feet from shore. The area is rife with tales of heroic rescue attempts, many ending in fatalities. A plaque commemorates Eddie Aikau, a local lifeguard credited with making thousands of rescues. In 1978, the *Hokule'a,* the Polynesian Sailing Society's double-hulled canoe, capsized in rough seas about 20 miles offshore. Eddie was aboard and launched his surfboard to swim for help. He never made it, but his selfless courage lives on.

Waimea Valley Parks

Look for the well-marked entrance to Waimea Falls Park, mountain side from the bay, and then drive into the lush valley before coming to the actual park entrance. The park is the most culturally significant travel destination on the North Shore, and while providing a wonderful day of excitement, education, and outdoor activity, it has not lost sight of its ancient *aloha* soul. Primarily a botanical garden, with a fascinating display of flowers and plants labeled for your edification, the **Waimea Arboretum** collects, grows and preserves extremely rare specimens of Hawaii's endangered flora. If you choose not to walk, a free open-air tram will take you through, narrating all the way. Within this garden setting is Waimea Falls Park, which presents lessons, demonstrations, and other activities of cultural significance throughout the day at several locations. One thrilling event is the professional diving from the 55-foot rock walls into the pool below Waimea Falls. Culturally enlightening are displays of ancient hula *(kahiko)* performed by very accomplished dancers, a display of Hawaiian games, carving demonstrations, and walks along forest paths that end at fascinating historical sites. All in all, and amidst the beauty of this valley, this is a wonderful learning experience while you have fun at the same time. Free for everyone is a hula show presented every day on the lawn in front of the restaurant near the visitors center. On the property is **Hale o Lono Heiau,** one of the island's largest and most ancient *heiau,* dedicated to the god Lono, and numerous other sites of ancient Hawaiian life and ethnology. As a newer

O'AHU

Waimea Falls Park

accompaniment to this cultural experience, the park offers one-hour-long outdoor tours to those who desire more physical activity as part of the Waimea Adventure Park. Horseback rides, ATV rides, and mountain bike tours are conducted over trails in the adjacent valley, and guided or self-guided kayak tours are operated down the lazy river toward the ocean. Some age and weight restrictions apply.

Waimea Falls Park is open 10 A.M.–5:30 P.M. daily, 808/638-8511. General admission, which allows you access to all shows and cultural tours, is $24 for adults and $12 for juniors ages 4–12. Admission to the adventure park is $59 adults and $47 juniors, and this includes all the cultural shows plus two hour-long outdoor activities or buffet lunch. In addition, single 20-minute outdoor adventures can also be purchased at $20 apiece. The Discover Waimea Package gives you general admission, lunch, and transportation from Waikiki for $39 adults and $29 juniors. At the visitors center, the Pikake Restaurant is open for lunch only 11 A.M.–2 P.M., but plate lunches and other foods can be had throughout the day from the Country Kitchen Snack Shop.

Pupukea Beach Park

A perfect place to experience marine life is the large tidepool next to Pupukea Beach Park, the first one north of Waimea Bay, across the street from the Shell gas station. The beach park has restrooms, picnic facilities, and fair swimming in sandy pockets between coral and rock, but only in summertime. A long retaining wall out to sea forms a large and protected pool at low tide. Wear footgear and check out the pools with a mask. Don't be surprised to find large sea bass. A sign warns against spearing fish, but the local people do it all the time. Be careful not to step on sea urchins, and stay away from the pool during rough winter swells, when it can be treacherous. The western end of this park is called Three Tables. The eastern section of the park is called Shark's Cove, though no more sharks are here than anywhere else. The area is terrific for snorkeling and a major destination for scuba tours in season. The Pupukea Marine Life Conservation District runs from Three Tables Cove past Shark's Cove to Kulalua Point and includes the tidal pools and shoreline. While most water activities are okay, scuba spearfishing is not allowed. If you had to pick a spot from which to view the North Shore sunset, Pupukea Beach Park is hard to beat.

Farther down the road, as you pass mile marker 9 you can't help noticing a mammoth redwood log that has been carved into a giant statue called *Maui Pohaku Loa,* representing an ancient Hawaiian. Peter Wolfe, the sculptor, has done a symbolic sculpture for every state in the union, this being his 50th. This statue is extremely controversial. Some feel that it looks much more like an American Indian than a Hawaiian, and that the log used should have been a native koa instead of an imported redwood from the Pacific Northwest. Others say that its *intention* was to honor the living and the ancient Hawaiians, and that is what's important.

Pu'u O Mahuka Heiau

Do yourself a favor and drive up the mountain road leading to the *heiau* even if you don't want to visit it. The vast and sweeping views of the

O'AHU

offering at Puʻu O
Mahuka Heiau altar

ROBERT NILSEN

coast below to the west are incredible. About one mile past Waimea Bay the highway passes a Foodland on the right. Turn here up Pupukea Road and follow the signs.

Puʻu O Mahuka Heiau, the largest on Oʻahu, covers a little more than five acres. Designated as a national historical landmark, its three sections descend the hillside in huge steps, with one area dropping to another just below. The *heiau* was the site of human sacrifice. People still come to pray, as is evidenced by many stones wrapped in *ti* leaves placed on small stone piles lying about the grounds. In the upper section is a raised mound surrounded by stone in what appears to be a central altar area. The *heiau*'s stonework shows a high degree of craftsmanship throughout, but especially in the pathways. The lower section of the *heiau* appears to be much older and is not as well maintained.

Drive past the access road leading to the *heiau* and in a minute or so make a left onto Alapio Road. This takes you through an expensive residential area called Sunset Hills and past a home locally called **The Mansion**—look for the English-style boxwood hedge surrounding it. The home was purported to be Elvis Presley's island hideaway. This area is a tremendous vantage point from which to view Fourth of July fireworks lighting up Waimea Bay far below. Next to it is a white sculpture called the **World Unity Monument**. The road straight up the hill

leads to the Boy Scout Camp, beyond which a biking/hiking trail leads into the mountains.

The Great Surfing Beaches

Sunset Beach runs for two miles, one of the longest white-sand beaches on Oʻahu. This beach is the site of yearly international surfing competitions. Winter surf erodes the beach, with coral and lava fingers exposed at the shoreline, but in summertime you can expect an uninterrupted beach usually 200–300 feet wide. The entire stretch is technically Sunset Beach, but each world-famous surfing spot warrants its own name though they're not clearly marked and are tough to find . . . exactly. Mainly, look for cars with surfboard racks parked along the road. The beaches are not always well maintained, either. They're often trashed, and the restrooms, even at Waimea Bay, can be atrocious. The reason is politics and money. Efforts all go into Waikiki, where the tourists are. Who cares about a bunch of crazy surfers on the North Shore? They're just a free curiosity for the tourists' enjoyment! Still, some money has been put into this area recently to alleviate this problem, and a few new facilities have been constructed.

The **Banzai Pipeline** is probably the best-known surfing beach in the world. Its notoriety dates from *Surf Safari*, an early surfer film made in the 1950s, when it was dubbed "Banzai" by Bruce Brown, maker of the film. The famous tubelike effect of the breaking waves comes

OʻAHU

from a shallow reef just offshore, which forces the waves to rise dramatically and quickly. This forces the crest forward to create "the Pipeline." A lifeguard tower near the south end of the beach is all that you'll find in the way of improvements. Parking is along the roadway. Look for Sunset Beach Elementary School on the left, and the Pipeline is across the road. You can park in the school's lot on non-school days.

Ehukai Beach County Park is the next area north. It has a lifeguard tower and restroom, and provides one of the best vantage points from which to watch the surfing action on the Pipeline and Pupukea, the area to the right. Convenient for those out for a bit of exercise, a jogging/bicycle path links Ehukai Beach with Sunset Beach up the road.

Don't expect much when you come to **Sunset Beach County Park** itself. Except for a lifeguard tower, there's only a parking lot and bathrooms across the street. Almost as famous as the surfing break is the **Sunset Rip,** a notorious current offshore that grabs people every year. Summertime is generally safe, but never take *moana* for granted.

On the ocean side of the University Livestock Farm is **Waialeʻe Beach County Park.** Its rocky shoreline makes it not so good for swimmers except for a small sandy spot at the southern end, but many fishers come to try their luck. Off the shore here and to the south is Vezlyland, a well-known surfing spot. Across the street may be a stand with fruit and coconuts for sale.

ACCOMMODATIONS

Surfer Rentals

The North Shore of Oʻahu has long been famous for its world-class surfing. The area attracts enthusiasts from around the world who are much more concerned with the daily surfing report than they are with deluxe accommodations. The Kamehameha Highway is dotted with surfer rentals from Haleʻiwa to Turtle Bay. Just outside their doors are famous surfing breaks. Some of these accommodations are terrific, while others are barely livable, and you'll find that most are taken throughout the winter surfing season.

Backpacker's Vacation Inn and Hostel, 59-788 Kamehameha Hwy., 808/638-7838 or 888/628-8882 in Hawaii, fax 808/638-7515 (courtesy phone at airport), website: www.backpackers-hawaii.com, email: backpacker@aloha.net, specializes in budget accommodations for surfers, backpackers, and families. It's in a perfect location, between Waimea Bay and the center of Waimea village, just across from Three Tables Beach. Find it at mile marker 6, the fourth driveway past the church tower coming from Waimea Bay. On the mountain side of the road are two three-story pole-style houses that offer hostel and private room accommodation, while on the ocean side directly across is an additional building with studios. Basic rates in the main house are $15–17 for a bunk in the hostel-style rooms, which includes use of a kitchen, laundry facilities, and TV in the communal room. Each room has four bunks, a shower, and a bath. The feeling is definitely not deluxe, but it is adequate, and there can be a real communal vibe. The back house has several private rooms for two with shared kitchen and bath for $45–54. Studios in the building on the beach rent for $80–114 daily depending upon the season, and each has a complete kitchen or kitchenette, two double beds, a roll-out couch, a ceiling fan, and a world-class view of the beach from the lanai. Weekly rates with discounts are offered and all payments are to be made in advance—no refund policy. This inn and hostel is often full so book ahead. Backpackers is easy but they want you to use common sense, keep the noise down after 11 P.M., and clean up after yourself. It provides free boogie boards and snorkeling gear, Internet access, bike rental for $5–10 a day, and can arrange whale-watching or sunset sails, scuba lessons, kayak rental, and other activities and equipment often at reduced rates. Small valuables can be locked away in an office safe, and larger items can also be stored. Airport transportation for guests is free to and from, and TheBus no. 52 stops directly in front. Friendly and laid-back. A good choice.

About two hundred yards in toward town is the **Plantation Village,** also operated by Backpacker's. The cluster of nine private cottages here, once the homes of real plantation workers, create a small community. These cottages are furnished with cable TV, linens, fans, and a

OʻAHU

full kitchen, and the lanai is a great place to catch the breezes. It's only a three-minute walk to the Foodland store for supplies. Everyone is free to use the washers and dryers and pay phone in the common area. One caveat, however. Some guests have complained that the cottages have, in some cases, been unkempt, in need of supplies, lacking in security, and generally not kept up to the best standards. Use your own judgment. Many of the fruit trees on the grounds provide the guests with complimentary bananas, papayas, and mangos. A bunk in the dorm here goes for $15–18, and a private room for two with shared bath and kitchen is $55–65. The larger, multibedroom cottages that sleep 4–10 people run $110–269. An inexpensive and nutritious evening meal is served each night in the garden area of the village. During surfing season, the Plantation Village is booked up so reserve well in advance. For information and reservations, contact Backpacker's (above).

Shark's Cove Rentals, 808/638-7157 or 808/638-7980, at 59-672 Kamehameha Hwy., website: www.hostel.com/sharkscove, offers share and private rooms in its two houses directly across from Shark's Cove. Clean, safe, and smaller than Backpackers up the road, Shark's Cove contains a common room for everyone to share, a full kitchen, and laundry facilities. A bunk runs $15 a night, $60 for a private room, with a small key and linen deposit; weekly and monthly rates available.

Vacation Rentals

Ke Iki Beach Bungalows is a small beachfront condo complex at 59-579 Ke Iki Rd., Waimea, HI 96712, 808/638-8829. Pass the Foodland supermarket heading east and look for a school sign. Turn left toward the beach. The property has 200 feet of beach with a sandy bottom that goes out about 300 feet (half that in winter). The complex is quiet with a home-away-from-home atmosphere. Rates are $199 for a two-bedroom unit and $150 for a one-bedroom unit on the water, and $130 two-bedroom and $85 one-bedroom on the street side. Three-night minimum required; weekly rates available, with lower rates during low season. A one-time cleaning fee is charged, and this ranges $45–85, depending upon the length of stay. Make inquiries and reservations with the resident manager.

For a room with a view from "up top" in Pupukea, try Lorrie at 808/638-5158. This studio with kitchen and pool runs $75 a night.

Various agencies handle rental homes and condos along the North Shore, mostly between Haleiwa and Turtle Bay. While the range is broad, and prices vary greatly, even season to season, generally you might expect to pay about $100 a night for a studio or condo on the beach, up to $150 for a one-bedroom rental, up to $200 for a two-bedroom unit, and $200–500 for a three or more bedroom home. These homes are fully furnished with all you'll need for a relaxing vacation. Cleaning deposits are usually applied and rental agreements are often for a minimum of one week although sometimes less. By and large, full payment is made in advance. To check on what is available, try the following agencies: **Sterman Realty,** 66-250 Kamehameha Hwy., #D-100, Haleiwa, HI 96712, 808/637-6200, fax 808/637-6100, website: www.sterman.com; **Team Real Estate,** 66-250 Kamehameha Hwy., Suite D103, Haleiwa, HI 96712, 808/637-3507 or 800/982-8602, fax 808/637-8881, website: www.teamrealestate.com; **Juliana Simone, Realtor,** P.O. Box 309, Haleiwa, HI 96712, 808/638-7299, fax 808/638-8018, website: www.sunsethomes.net.

Luxury Resort

The **Hilton Turtle Bay Golf and Tennis Resort** is a first-class resort on Turtle Bay, the northern extremity of the North Shore, 57-091 Kamehameha Hwy., Kahuku, HI 96731, 808/293-8811 or 800/445-8667, fax 808/293-9147, website: www.turtlebayresort.hilton.com. The Hilton was built as a self-contained destination resort and is surrounded by sea and surf on Kuilima Point, which offers protected swimming year-round at Kuilima Cove. The entrance road to the hotel is lined by blooming hibiscus outlining a formal manicured lawn. Both the 27-hole Arnold Palmer–inspired Links at Kuilima and the hotel's tennis facilities have ranked among the best in the country in various surveys. The resort also offers a swimming pool, full water activities including equipment rental and windsurfing and scuba lessons, horseback riding, shopping, and the fanciest dining on the North Shore. Since the hotel is an oasis unto itself, you should always call ahead to book any of these activities, even as a guest staying at the hotel, to avoid disappointment. There's very little shopping in this area, so if you're after film, sundries, or fashions, stop at the hotel's minimall. The resort's seaside Wedding Pavilion is splendid with open-beamed ceiling, stained glass, and eight-foot beveled windows that can be thrown open to allow the ocean breezes to waft through.

All guest rooms in the three-wing main hotel building are ocean view, but not all are oceanfront. Oceanfront is slightly more expensive but is worth the price, especially December–April when humpback whales cavort in the waters off the point. Rooms are furnished with full baths, a mini-fridge, a large vanity, ample closets, a/c, and remote control cable TV. Suites come complete with a library, a large bathroom and changing room, two couches, a sitting area, and a large enclosed lanai. Recently, the hotel has upgraded its carpets, drapes, bedspreads, wallpaper, and upholstered furniture. In addition, about a dozen self-contained cabana cottages line Turtle Bay and Kuilima Cove and offer more seclusion. Rates are $175–285 for a standard ocean-view or oceanfront room, $300 for a cabana, and suites cost $450–1,800; $35 extra person. The Hilton family plan allows children to stay free in a room with their parents. Numerous discount packages are always available. The Hilton is a first-class destination resort, but because of its fabulous yet out-of-the-mainstream location, you get much more than what you pay for. The Hilton Turtle Bay is an excellent choice for a vacation with the feel of being on a Neighbor Island.

Condominiums

Surrounded by golf links on the approach road to the Turtle Bay Hilton resort is **Turtle Bay Condos,** a secure condominium complex of several hundred units that's split into two groups. Within this quiet and landscaped community at Kuilima are private tennis courts, swimming pools, and barbecue facilities, and you're only a short stroll away from the activity, shopping, and dining options at the resort. Vacation rentals in this tropical complex are studios to three-bedroom units, each with a full kitchen, one or more bathrooms, ceiling fans, washer and dryer, entertainment center with TV, telephone, and a lanai

that opens onto the green lawn, palm trees, flowering bushes, and the fairway. Rates for these units run $85–105 studio, $100–145 one-bedroom, $145–165 two-bedroom, and $165–180 three-bedroom. Fees are slightly less during low season, which runs from April through November. There is a two-night minimum stay with a one-week minimum in place over the Christmas holiday. A down payment is required as well as a damage/cleaning deposit. For information and reservations, contact one of the two following companies. **The Estates at Turtle Bay,** 56-565 Kamehameha Hwy., P.O. Box 366, Kahuku, HI 96731, 808/293-0600, fax 808/293-0471, website: www.turtlebay-rentals.com; **Turtle Bay Condos,** 56-565 Kamehameha Hwy., P.O. Box 248, Kahuku, HI 96731, 808/293-2800, fax 808/293-2169, website: www.turtlebaycondos.com.

FOOD

Inexpensive-Moderate

The Sunset Beach store has basic items but is the home of **Ted's Bakery,** where you can get a fine assortment of loaves, pies, and sinfully rich pastries and sweet treats. Ted's also does breakfast omelets and eggs for $3.50–4.50, and burgers, plate lunches, and sandwiches for lunch for $4.50–5.50. No seating; all take-out. Next door to Ted's is **Sunset Beach Store,** which has a few basic necessities and cold drinks, but for a full selection of food supplies, shop **Foodland** along the highway in Waimea. In this town without a restaurant, the deli counter at Foodland could serve as a lunch stop, as there you can get deli salads, cut meat, whole roasted chickens, chicken strips, and sandwiches. Foodland also has a bakery counter. A *kaukau* wagon usually dispenses plate lunches across from Pupukea Beach Park, and **Pupukea Shave Ice** makes island treats.

The **Pikake Restaurant** at Waimea Falls Park is open daily for a lunch buffet 11 A.M. 2 P.M. for $15.95. It's fun to dine here even if you don't enter the park. From the dining room, you can look into some of the nicest gardens while feeding crumbs to the peacocks. A lunch window at the park serves cold sandwiches, burgers, and some hot entrées, mostly for under $6.

Less than half a mile west of Sunset Beach is the **Sunset Diner,** open daily 10:30 A.M.–8 P.M. for plate lunches, burgers, sandwiches, and drinks. It's next to Kammies market, which itself has some basic food supplies, a laundromat, and a gas station.

At the Hilton

The **Sea Tide Room** is synonymous with Sunday brunch. It enjoys a wonderful reputation, and if friends or family come visiting, islanders take them here to impress. Brunch is buffet style 9 A.M.–2 P.M. and features mounds of fresh fruits and pastries, fresh-squeezed fruit juices, imported cheeses, eggs Florentine and Benedict, fresh fish, seafood, sashimi, shrimp, crab claws, and flowing champagne. Reservations are not taken; cost is $26.95 adults and $14.50 for kids 4–11. Expect a wait, which goes quickly as you enjoy the magnificent scenery.

The **Palm Terrace** is the main hotel restaurant for all day dining. Best known for its sumptuous buffets, menu service is also an option. Every evening presents a different theme dinner. The Palm Terrace serves hearty American favorites, supplemented by dishes from around the world. The views overlooking Turtle Bay combined with excellent value for the money make the Palm Terrace the best *ordinary* restaurant on the North Shore.

The **Bay View Lounge** is a casual restaurant/nightclub offering either a taco or pasta buffet. It's open 11:30 A.M.–1 A.M. and serves complimentary *pu pu* around sunset, which is a perfect time to drop in. There is live music nightly. Friday and Saturday the Bay View Lounge is the hotspot disco, ID required after 9 P.M.; dress code is collared shirts and closed-toe shoes. When lounging by the pool, pick up a snack at the **Orchid Snack Bar** or a drink from the **Hang Ten** bar.

GEOGRAPHICAL NOTE

The previous chapter, Windward O'ahu, begins in Kailua-Kane'ohe and works its way up the coast simply because most people visiting that coast approach it from the south. Those heading for the North Shore usually come from Hale'iwa in the west and proceed northeast toward Kahuku. So, the end of this chapter follows geographically with the end of the Windward O'ahu chapter. Don't let it throw you.

O'AHU

KAUA'I

*O, how my spirit languishes
to step ashore in the Sanguishes. . . .*

—Robert Louis Stevenson,
circa 1888

INTRODUCTION

Kaua'i is the oldest of the main Hawaiian Islands, perhaps six million years old, and nature has had ample time to work, sculpting Kaua'i into a beauty among beauties. Flowers and fruits burst from its fertile soil, but the "Garden Island" is much more than greenery and flora—it's the poetry of land itself. Its mountains have become rounded and smooth, and its streams tumbling to the sea have cut deep and wide, giving Kaua'i the only navigable river in Hawaii. The interior is a dramatic series of mountains, valleys, and primordial swamp. The great gouge of Waimea Canyon, called the "Grand Canyon of the Pacific," is an enchanting layer of pastels where uncountable rainbows form prismatic necklaces from which waterfalls hang like silvery pendants. The northwest is the sea cliffs of Na Pali, mightiest in all of Oceania, looming nearly 4,000 feet above the pounding surf.

Only 100 miles by air from Honolulu, everything seems quieter here, rural but upbeat, with the main town being just that, a town. The pursuit of carefree relaxation is unavoidable at five-star hotels, where you're treated like a visiting *ali'i,* or at campsites deep in interior valleys or along secluded beaches where reality *is* the fantasy of paradise.

Kaua'i is where Hollywood comes when the script calls for "paradise." The island has a dozen major films to its credit, everything from idyllic scenes in *South Pacific* to the lurking horror of Asian villages in *Uncommon Valor.* *King Kong* tore up this countryside in search of love, and Tattoo spotted "de plane, boss" in *Fantasy Island.* In *Blue Hawaii,* Elvis's hips mimicked the swaying palms in a famous island grove, while torrid love scenes from *The Thorn Birds* were steamier than the jungle in the background. More recently, parts of *Outbreak* and *Jurassic Park* were filmed here. Perhaps the greatest compliment is that Kaua'i is where other islanders come to look at the scenery.

OVERVIEW

Kaua'i is the most regularly shaped of all the major islands—more or less round, like a partially deflated beach ball. The puckered skin around the coast forms bays, beaches, and inlets, while the center is a no-man's-land of mountains, canyon, valleys, and swamp.

KAUA'I

KAUA'I

KAUA'I

Kaua'i Channel

5 mi

5 km

0

0

MōKōlea Point

Kīlauea Point

'ANINI BEACH
COUNTY PARK

Princeville

Kalihiwai

Kīlauea

Hanalei Bay

Lumahai Beach

Hanalei

HWY

56

Hanalei Valley

Hanalei River

Wai'oli Stream

Lumahai River

Kūhiō

56

Waīniha

Ha'ena

HA'ENA
STATE PARK

Ke'e Beach

KALALAU VALLEY
LOOKOUT

NA PALI COAST
STATE PARK

Na Pali Coast

Na

Pali

Coast

Makaha Point

POLIHALE
STATE PARK

NA PALI
KONA FOREST
RESERVE

PU'U KA PELE
FOREST RESERVE

Makaha Ridge

Kolo Ridge

PACIFIC
MISSILE RANGE
FACILITY

Kaulakahi Channel

KAUMUALI'I

Kekaha

50

550

KŌKE'E RD

WAIMEA CANYON RD

WAIMEA CANYON
STATE PARK

KŌKE'E
STATE PARK

550

Waimea Canyon

Waimea River

Makaweli

Pakala

Waimea

HWY

50

Kaumakani

Olokele

Hanapēpē

Port Allen

SALT POND BEACH
COUNTY PARK

'Ele'ele

540

Numila

Kalaheo

Lāwa'i

Ōma'o

520

530

Koloa

Kukui'ula

PO'IPU BEACH
COUNTY PARK

Po'ipu

50

Kilohana

Last eruption
on Kaua'i

KAUMUALI'I HWY

Puhi

Ha'upu Ridge

Waita Reservoir

Kapaia

583

Kapa'a

581

Wailua

Waīpouli

Kealia

Anahola

HWY

56

Anahola Bay

Anahola Mountains

Moloa'a Bay

KEALIA
FOREST
RESERVE

Mt. Kualapa
(2,129 ft)

KEAHUA
ARBORETUM

580

WAILUA RIVER
STATE PARK

Wailua
Falls

Mt. Wai'ale'ale
(5,148 ft)

WORLD'S
WETTEST SPOT

Mt. Kawaikini
(5,243 ft)

NA PALI-KONA
FOREST RESERVE

Alaka'i Swamp

Waīmea River

Hanapēpē River

Makaweli River

LIHU'E KOLOA
FOREST RESERVE

KAPA'A BEACH
COUNTY PARK

LYDGATE STATE PARK

KUHIO

56

Hanama'ulu

BEACH PARK

LIHU'E AIRPORT

Lihu'e

Nāwiliwili Bay

Kalapaki Beach

Kipu Kai

Alakoko
Fishpond

Kaua'i

Ni'ihau

O'ahu

Moloka'i

Lāna'i

Kaho'olawe

Maui

Hawai'i

KAUA'I

Lihu'e

Almost everyone arrives at the airport in Lihu'e, although some fortunate individuals step ashore at Lihu'e's port, **Nawiliwili Harbor.** Lihu'e is the county seat and major town with government agencies, full amenities, and a wide array of restaurants, shopping, and accommodations; however, most visitors head north to the resort areas of Wailua-Kapa'a or Princeville-Hanalei, or west to the fabulous Po'ipu Beach area. Lihu'e's **Kaua'i Museum** is a must-stop, where you'll learn the geological and social history of the island, immensely enriching your visit.

On the outskirts of town is the remarkably preserved **Grove Farm Homestead,** a classic Hawaiian plantation so intact that all that seems to be missing is the workers. At Nawiliwili Bay you can see firsthand the Menehune's handiwork at the **Alakoko (Menehune) Fishpond,** still in use. A short distance uphill from there on the west edge of town is the bedroom community of **Puhi,** home of **Kaua'i Community College,** the island's only higher educational institution. Just north are the two suburbs of **Kapaia** and **Hanama'ulu.** Here too you'll find shops and restaurants and the junction of Route 583 leading inland through miles of sugarcane fields and terminating at an engaging panorama of **Wailua Falls.**

East Coast

Heading northeast from Lihu'e along Route 56 takes you to **Wailua** and **Kapa'a,** a region known as the Coconut Coast. Wailua is built along the Wailua River, the only navigable stream in Hawaii. At the mouth of the river are two beach parks, a temple of refuge, and petroglyphs, while upstream are more *heiau,* royal birth stones, the heavily touristed yet beautiful **Fern Grotto,** and the **Kamokila Hawaiian Village,** all within the **Wailua River State Park.** Remarkable views overlook the river below and the cascading **'Opaeka'a Waterfalls.** Beyond the falls, the squat compact mountain ridge called the **Sleeping Giant** still presides over town in humble repose. Beyond the giant are upland residential communities and, farther, the **Keahua Arboretum,** the start of several good hiking trails. Heavily damaged by Hurricane 'Iniki, Wailua's Coco Palms Resort was an island institution in the heart of the most outstanding coconut grove on Kaua'i. While it still

lies in devastated disarray, its myth and legend live on.

Along Route 56 toward Kapa'a you pass **The Coconut Marketplace** and half a dozen smaller shopping malls. In the vicinity, affordable condos line the beach. Kapa'a, built on pineapple and sugarcane, is a workers' town with more down-home shopping and good, inexpensive restaurants. Heading north, you pass **Kealia Beach,** an excellent surfing spot; **Anahola Beach,** where the water is fine; and **Moloa'a Bay,** a secluded spot that you can have mostly to yourself. The only town along the way is tiny **Anahola,** where Hawaiians advertise lei strung from flowers grown in their yards.

North Coast

Kilauea, the first town in the Hanalei District and a former sugarcane plantation, begins the north shore. A narrow coastal road leads you through town to **Kilauea Lighthouse,** a beacon of safety for passing ships and for a remarkable array of birds that populate this wildlife sanctuary. In the vicinity numerous sides road lead to "secret beaches," excellent snorkeling spots, and wild surf. **Princeville** is next, one of the largest planned resorts in Hawaii, featuring its own airstrip. Here an entire modern village is built around superb golf courses and an exclusive deluxe resort.

Down the narrowing lane and over a single-lane steel-strut bridge is **Hanalei.** Inland is a terraced valley planted in taro just like in the old days. Oceanside is **Hanalei Bay,** a safe anchorage and haven to seagoing yachts that have made it a port of call ever since Westerners began coming to Hawaii. On the outskirts is **Wai'oli Mission House,** a preserved missionary home dating from 1837. Then comes a string of beaches, uncrowded and well-known for snorkeling. You pass through the tiny village of **Wainiha** and then **Ha'ena,** with the island's "last resort." Just before the end of the road at **Ke'e Beach** are the **wet and dry caves.** Commanding a superb view above the beach are **Kaulu Paoa** and **Kaulu O Laka** *heiau,* dedicated to hula and the veneration of Laka, its bestower, and the location where the beach scenes from *The Thorn Birds* were filmed. From here only your feet and love of adventure take you down the **Kalalau Trail** to back-to-nature camping. You pass along a narrow foot trail down the **Na**

Pali Coast, skirting emerald valleys cut off from the world by impassable 4,000-foot sea cliffs. All along here are *heiau,* ancient village sites, caves, lava tubes, and the romantic yet true **Valley of the Lost Tribe** just beyond trail's end.

South Shore

From Lihu'e west is a different story. Route 50 takes you past the coastal **Ha'upu (Hoary Head) Ridge,** where **Queen Victoria's Profile** squints down at you. **Maluhia Road,** famous for its tunnel-like line of eucalyptus, branches off toward **Koloa,** a sugar town now rejuvenated with shops, boutiques, and restaurants. At the coast is **Po'ipu Beach,** the best on Kaua'i with its bevy of beautiful hotels and resorts. This sunny south coast is where many first-time visitors to Kaua'i head, and it's easy to understand why. At the west end of this strip resort is the **Spouting Horn,** a blowhole in the ceiling of a lava tube that spouts water with each inrushing wave, as regularly as Old Faithful in Yellowstone. In the lower Lawa'i Valley is the **National Tropical Botanical Garden,** managed for the propagation of the earth's tropical plants. Inland, 'Oma'o, Lawa'i, and Kalaheo are strung along the highway running west, each a former sugar town. The largest is **Kalaheo,** where an island philanthropist, Walter McBride, gave the munificent land gift that has become **Kukui O Lono Park.** Here excellent views and a little-played golf course surround a small Japanese garden.

West End

West on Route 50 brings you to **Hanapepe,** a good supply stop famous for its art galleries and inexpensive restaurants. Outside town are **Port Allen Harbor** and **Burns Field** airstrip, both used by numerous activity companies. The best beach between Po'ipu Beach and the far west end is **Salt Pond Beach,** where from ancient times Hawaiians have harvested salt from evaporated sea water. From there, the road skirts the shore, passing **Kaumakani,** a dusty sugar plantation workers' village; **Olokele,** a perfect caricature of a sugar town with its neatly trimmed managers' homes; and **Pakala,** an excellent surfing beach. Quickly comes **Waimea,** where Captain Cook first came ashore, and on the outskirts is the **Russian Fort,** dating from 1817, when all the world powers were present in Hawaii, jockeying to influence this Pacific gem.

In Waimea and farther westward in **Kekaha,** the road branches inland, leading along the rim of **Waimea Canyon.** This is what everyone comes to see, and none are disappointed. The wonderfully winding road serves up lookout after lookout and trail after trail. You end up at **Koke'e State Park** and the **Kalalau Valley Lookout,** where you're king of the mountain, and 4,000 feet below is your vast domain of the Na Pali Coast. West of the sugar town of Kekaha is a flat stretch of littoral farmland vast enough for cane and corn fields, and the military's **Pacific Missile Range Facility** at Barking Sands. The pavement ends and a good tourist-intimidating "cane road" takes over, leading you to the seclusion of **Polihale State Park,** where you can swim, camp, and luxuriate in privacy. If Madame Pele had had her choice, she never would have moved.

THE LAND

Kaua'i, 100 miles northwest of O'ahu, is the northernmost and westernmost of Hawaii's six major islands and the fourth largest. It is approximately 33 miles long and 25 miles wide at its farthest points, with an area of 552 square miles and 90 miles of coastline. The island was built by one huge volcano that became extinct about four million years ago. Speculation holds that Ni'ihau, 20 miles off the west coast, may have been connected to Kaua'i at one time.

A simplified but chronologically accurate account of Kaua'i's emergence is found in a version of the Pele myth retold in *The Kumulipo.* It depicts the fire goddess as a young, beautiful woman who visits Kaua'i during a hula festival and becomes enraptured with Lohiau, a handsome and mighty chief. She wants him as a husband and determines to dig a fire pit home where they can reside in contented bliss. Unfortunately, her unrelenting and unforgiving sea-goddess sister pursues her, forcing Pele to abandon Kaua'i and Lohiau. Thus, she wandered and sparked volcanic eruptions on Oʻahu, Maui, and finally atop Kilauea Crater on Hawaiʻi, where she now resides.

Phenomenal Features of Kauaʻi

Almost smack-dab in the middle of the island are **Mount Kawaikini** (5,243 feet) and adjacent **Mount Waiʻaleʻale** (5,148 feet), the highest points on Kauaʻi. These two high points are thought to be the western rim of the island's collapsed main volcanic crater. Mount Waiʻaleʻale is an unsurpassed "rain magnet," drawing an estimated 450 inches (37.5 feet) of precipitation during the approximately 350 days it rains per year, and earning itself the dubious distinction of being "the wettest spot on earth." Don't be intimidated—this rain is amazingly localized, with only 20 inches per year falling just 20 miles away. Visitors can now enter this mist-shrouded world aboard helicopters that fly through countless rainbows and hover above a thousand waterfalls. The top of the island is buffeted by strong winds, which, along with the cool temperatures, keep the plants that grow here close to the ground.

Draining Waiʻaleʻale is **Alakaʻi Swamp,** a dripping sponge of earth covering about 30 square miles of trackless bog. This patch of mire contains flora and fauna found nowhere else on earth. For example, ʻohiʻa trees, mighty giants of upland forests, grow here as natural bonsai that could pass as potted plants. Bordering the Alakaʻi Swamp on the west is **Waimea Canyon,** where eons of whipping winds, pelting rain, and incessantly grinding streams and rivulets chiseled the red bedrock to depths of 3,000 feet and expanses two miles wide. Up and over the canyon wall from there is the **Na Pali Coast,** an incredibly scalloped, undulating vastness of valleys and *pali* forming a bulwark 4,000 feet high.

Other mountains and outcroppings around the island have formed curious natural formations. The **Haʻupu Ridge,** a diminutive range barely 2,000 feet tall south of Lihuʻe, forms a profile of Queen Victoria. Above Wailua, the **Nounou Ridge** gives the impression of a man in repose and has been dubbed The Sleeping Giant. Another small range in the northeast, the **Anahola Mountains,** had until recently an odd series of boulders that formed "Hole in the Mountain," mythologically created when a giant hurled his spear through sheer rock. Erosion has collapsed the formation, but another hole is forming, as if to continue the legend.

Channels, Lakes, and Rivers

Kauaʻi is separated from Oʻahu by the **Kauaʻi Channel.** Reaching an incredible depth of 10,900 feet and a width of 72 miles, it is by far the state's deepest and widest channel. Inland, man-made **Waita Reservoir** north of Koloa is the largest body of fresh water in Hawaii, covering 424 acres with a three-mile shoreline. The **Waimea River,** running through the floor of the canyon, is the island's longest at just under 20 miles, while the **Hanalei River** moves the greatest amount of water, emptying 140 million gallons per day into Hanalei Bay. But the **Wailua River** has the distinction of being the state's only navigable river, although passage by boat is restricted to a scant three miles upstream. The flatlands around Kekaha were at one time Hawaiʻi's largest body of inland water. These ponds were brackish and were drained in the 19th century to create cane fields.

CLIMATE

Kauaʻi's climate will make you happy. Along the coastline the average temperature is 80° F in spring and summer, and about 75 during the remainder of the year. The warmest areas are along the south coast from Lihuʻe westward, where the mercury can hit the 90s in midsummer. Nighttime temperatures usually drop 10–15°, and may drop into the upper 50s in winter, even along the coast. To escape the heat any time of year, head for Kokeʻe in the mountains, where the weather is always moderate, and may be down-right chilly.

Precipitation

Although Mt. Waiʻaleʻale is "the wettest spot on earth," in the areas most interesting to visitors, rain is not a problem. The driest section of Kauaʻi is the arid Maha Plain near Polihale Beach in the west. From there across the south shore to the Poʻipu Beach resort area, rainfalls run from five inches per year up to a mere 20 inches. Lihuʻe receives about 30 inches. As you head northeast to Kapaʻa and then swing around the coast past Kilauea toward Hanalei, rainfall becomes more frequent but is still a tolerable 45 inches per year. Farther down the coast it may reach 75 inches a year. Cloudbursts in winter are frequent but short-lived.

Hurricanes 'Iwa and 'Iniki

The Garden Island is much more than just another pretty face—the island and its people have integrity. Thanksgiving was not a very nice time on Kaua'i back in November 1982. Along with the stuffing and cranberries came an unwelcome guest who showed no *aloha,* Hurricane 'Iwa. What made this rude 80-mph party-crasher so unforgettable was that she was only the fourth such storm to come ashore on Hawaii since records have been kept and the first since the late 1950s. All told, 'Iwa caused $200 million worth of damage. A few beaches were washed away, perhaps forever, and great destruction was suffered by beach homes and resorts, especially around Po'ipu. Thankfully, no lives were lost. The people of Kaua'i rolled up their sleeves and set about rebuilding. In short order, the island recovered, and most residents thought "that was that."

Unfortunately, on Friday, September 11, 1992, Hurricane 'Iniki, with unimaginable ferocity, ripped ashore with top wind speeds of 175 mph and slapped Kaua'i around like the moll in a Bogart movie. "'Iniki" has two meanings in Hawaiian: "piercing winds" and "pangs of love," both devastatingly painful in their own way. The hurricane virtually flattened or tore to shreds everything in its path. No one was immune from the savage typhoon. Renowned director Steven Spielberg and his cast, including Laura Dern, Jeff Goldblum, Richard Attenborough, and Sam Neill, were on the island filming scenes for the blockbuster *Jurassic Park*. They rode out the storm huddled in the ballroom of the Westin Kauai Lagoons (now the Kaua'i Marriott), along with other guests, bellhops, maids, groundskeepers, and cooks. Afterward, then-mayor JoAnn Yukimura and her staff worked day and night from her roofless office in Lihu'e. Hanalei taro farmers opened their humble doors to homeless neighbors and strangers alike, while a general manager of a luxury resort on the eve of his wedding pleaded with invited guests to give donations to various charitable organizations in lieu of gifts. There was hardly a structure on the entire island that wasn't damaged in one way or another. Proud yachts were thrown like toy boats into a jangled heap; cars were buried whole in the red earth; a full third of Kaua'i's 20,000 homes were broken into splinters; and 4,200 hotel rooms became a tangled heap of steel and jagged glass. By the grace of god, and because of a very competent warning system, only eight lives were lost, and fewer than 100 people had to be admitted to the hospital due to injury. Psychologically, however, many people who lost everything were scared; special counseling services were set up to offer techniques to deal with the stress and sense of loss. Insur-

KAUA'I TEMPERATURE AND RAINFALL

TOWN		JAN.	MARCH	MAY	JUNE	SEPT.	NOV.
Hanapepe	high	79	80	81	84	82	80
	low	60	60	61	65	62	61
	rain	5	2	0	0	2	3
Lihu'e	high	79	79	79	82	82	80
	low	60	60	65	70	68	65
	rain	5	3	2	2	5	5
Kilauea	high	79	79	80	82	82	80
	low	62	64	66	68	69	65
	rain	5	5	3	3	1	5

Note: Temperature is expressed in degrees Fahrenheit; rainfall in inches.

J.D. BISIGNANI

the destruction wrought by Hurricane 'Iniki

ance companies were stressed to the breaking point; some were very slow to pay, and a few literally went broke trying to pay all of the claims brought against them. Undaunted and with pride and will that far surpassed the fury of the storm, Kaua'i's people immediately set about rebuilding homes, while nature took care of the rest. Some philosophical souls believe *Kaua'i* wasn't hurt at all—only a bunch of buildings were destroyed.

They contend that in its millions of years of existence, Kaua'i has been through many storms, and Hurricane 'Iniki was merely a "$1.5 billion pruning . . . for free." Though trees were twisted from the ground and bushes were flattened, Kaua'i is strong and fertile and the damage was temporary. Now, 'Iniki is mostly a memory and Kaua'i has emerged a touch more self-assured and as beautiful as ever.

FLORA AND FAUNA

Kaua'i exceeds its reputation as the Garden Island. It has had a much longer time for soil building and for rooting of a wide variety of plant life, so it's lusher than the other islands. Lying on a main bird migratory route, lands such as the Hanalei National Wildlife Sanctuary have long since been set aside for their benefit. Impenetrable inland regions surrounding Mt. Wai'ale'ale and dominated by the Alaka'i Swamp have provided a natural sanctuary for Kaua'i's own bird and plant life. Because of this, Kaua'i is home to the largest number of indigenous birds extant in Hawaii, though even here they are tragically endangered. As on the other Hawaiian Islands, a large number of birds, plants, and mammals have been introduced in the past 200 years. Most have either aggressively competed for, or simply destroyed, the habitat of indigenous

species. As the newcomers gain dominance, Kaua'i's own flora and fauna slide inevitably toward oblivion.

Indigenous Forest Birds

Kaua'i's upland forests are still home to many Hawaiian birds. You may be lucky enough to spot the **Hawaiian owl** (pueo), one of the friendliest *'aumakua* in ancient Hawaii; the *'elepaio,* an indigenous bird found around Koke'e; and the bright red *'i'iwi.*

'Anianiau is a four-inch yellow-green bird found around Koke'e. Its decline is due to a lack of fear of humans. The *nukupu'u,* extinct on the other islands except for a few on Maui, is found in Kaua'i's upper forests and on the borders of the Alaka'i Swamp. It's a five-inch bird with a drab green back and a bright yellow chest.

KAUA'I

Birds of the Alaka'i Swamp

The following scarce birds are some of the last indigenous Hawaiian birds, saved only by the inhospitableness of the Alaka'i Swamp. All are endangered species and under no circumstances should they be disturbed. The last survivors include: the **'o'u,** a chubby seven-inch bird with a green body, yellow head, and lovely whistle ranging half an octave; the relatively common **Hawaiian creeper,** a hand-size bird with a light green back and white belly, which travels in pairs and searches bark for insects; the *puaiohi,* a dark brown, white-bellied seven-inch bird so rare its nesting habits are unknown.

'O'o'a'a, although its name may resemble the sounds you make getting into a steaming hot tub, is an eight-inch black bird that played a special role in Hawaiian history. Its blazing yellow leg feathers were used to fashion the spectacular capes and helmets of the *ali'i.* Even before white people came, this bird was ruthlessly pursued by specially trained hunters who captured it and plucked its feathers. Finally there is the **'akialoa,** a seven-inch greenish-yellow bird with a long, slender, curved bill.

Marine and Water Birds

Among the millions of birds that visit Kaua'i yearly, some of the most outstanding are its marine and water birds. Many beautiful individuals are seen at Kilauea Point National Wildlife Refuge, where they often nest in the trees on the cliff or on Moku'ae'ae Islet. Among them are the **Laysan albatross** *(moli),* which also nests along Barking Sands; the **wedge-tailed shearwater** *(ua'u kani);* and the **red-footed booby.** Kiting from the same cliffs is the **white-tailed tropic bird,** and one of the most amazing is the **great frigate bird,** which nests at Kilauea Point and is also seen along the Kalalau Trail and even at Po'ipu Beach.

Introduced Common Birds

Kaua'i is rich in all manner of birds, from migratory marine birds to upland forest dwellers. Many live in areas you can visit; others you can see by taking a short stroll and remaining observant. Some, of course, are rare and very difficult to spot. Some of the most easily spotted island birds frequent almost all areas from Kekaha to Kalalau and the upland regions of Koke'e, including the blazing red **northern cardinal;** the comedic, brash **common mynah;** the operatic **western meadowlark,** introduced in 1930 and found in Hawaii only on Kaua'i; the ubiquitous **Japanese white eye;** sudden fluttering flocks of **house finches;** that Arctic traveler the **golden plover,** found along mudflats everywhere; the **cattle egret,** a white, 20-inch-tall heron found anywhere from the backs of cattle to the lids of garbage cans.

ROOSTER ALERT

An ever-present entity on Kaua'i, and to a lesser extent on the other islands, is the feral rooster. Early Polynesians brought chickens with them on their journeys from the South Pacific. Later, Europeans and others brought different varieties of fowl, and the Filipinos brought their fighting cocks. Over the years these animals mingled, mixing breeds. Many were kept in people's backyards for their meat, eggs, or ability to slit the throats of other cocks. As in any rural place, these animals would herald the dawn by crowing. Hurricane 'Iniki changed this bucolic setting in a dramatic way. In its fury, it set many of these previously caged animals free to wander where they might—and they did with abandon. In essence, they've become the island animal kingdom's homeless. Today they seem to be everywhere, and more than that, make a racket at all times of the day. It was impossible to round up all these fugitive birds, so now they roam. To make matters worse, many of the cane fields they used to hunt in search of food are gone, given over to other crops or let grow wild. They look for food where they still can find it, often near residential areas. Many island residents now consider these birds a nuisance, and some hope the state will open a hunting season on them to help control their increasingly more obnoxious population. In the meantime, if you hit one on the road, few will probably care.

KAUA'I BOTANICAL GARDENS

National Tropical Botanical Garden, in Po'ipu, 808/742-2623, is the only research facility for tropical plants in the country and the premier botanical garden on Kaua'i. Tours lasting about 2.5 hours are given daily except Sunday for $25 a person. The visitor center/museum/gift shop is open Mon.–Sun. 8 A.M.–5 P.M. for walk-in visitors. You can take a short self-guided walk around the visitor center garden, but to go into the main gardens you need advance reservations. Pricey but exceptional.

Moir Gardens are at the Kiahuna Plantation Resort in Po'ipu. Over a 27-year period during the mid-1900s, five acres of this former plantation site were cultivated with about 2,500 plants from Africa, the Americas, the Pacific, and India, including cactus and orchid sections. Open daily during daylight hours, free guided tours of the property are given weekdays at 10 A.M.

Smith's Tropical Paradise, 808/821-6892, a finely manicured and well-kept botanical and cultural garden with a bountiful, beautiful collection of ordinary and exotic plants, is on 30 riverfront acres adjacent to the Wailua Marina. Have a look here before heading upcountry. Open 8:30 A.M.–4 P.M.; admission is $5 adults, $2.50 children.

Limahuli Botanical Garden, on Kaua'i's extreme north shore, 808/828-1053, open Tues.–Fri. and again on Sunday 9:30 A.M.–4 P.M., showcases tropical plants both ancient and modern. It's part of the National Tropical Botanical Gardens, and there are both self-guided ($10) and guided ($15) walking tours. As you walk the three-quarter-mile loop trail, you'll pass patches of taro plants introduced to Hawaii by early Polynesians, living specimens of endangered native species, and post-contact tropicals, all while enjoying listening to the legends of the valley.

Introduced Fauna and Game Animals

One terribly destructive predator of native ground-nesting birds is the **mongoose.** Introduced to Hawaii in the 1800s as a cure for a rat infestation, the mongoose has only recently made it to Kaua'i, where a vigorous monitoring and extermination process is underway. Game mammals found in Kaua'i's forests include feral goats and pigs, although they too have caused destruction by uprooting seedlings and by overgrazing shrubs and grasses. Game fowl that have successfully acclimatized include francolins, ring-necked pheasants, and an assortment of quail and dove.

One game animal found in Hawaii only on Kaua'i is the **black-tailed deer.** Kaua'i's thriving herd of 700 started as a few orphaned fawns from Oregon in 1961. These handsome animals, a species of western mule deer, are at home on the hilly slopes west of Waimea Canyon. Although there is little noticeable change in seasons in Hawaii, bucks and does continue to operate on genetically transmitted biological time clocks. The males shed their antlers during late winter months and the females give birth in spring.

HISTORY

Kaua'i is the first of the Hawaiian Islands in many ways. Besides being the oldest main island geologically, it's believed by some that Kaua'i was the first island to be populated by Polynesian explorers. Theoretically, this colony was well established as early as A.D. 200, which predates the populating of the other islands. Even Madame Pele chose Kaua'i as her first home and was content here until her sister drove her away. Her fires went out when she moved on, but she, like all visitors, never forgot Kaua'i.

Written History
The written history of Hawaii began when Captain James Cook sailed into Waimea Bay on Kaua'i's south shore on the afternoon of September 20, 1778, and opened Hawaii to the rest of the world. In the years just preceding Cook's discovery, Hawaii was undergoing a unique change. Kamehameha the Great, a chief of the Big Island, was in the process of conquering the islands and uniting them under his rule. King Kaumuali'i of Kaua'i was able to remain independent from Kamehameha's rule by his use of diplomacy, guile, and the large distances separating his island from the others. Finally, after all the other islands had been subjugated, Kaumuali'i joined Kamehameha through negotiations, not warfare; he retained control of Kaua'i by being made governor of the island by Kamehameha. After Kamehameha died, his successor, Kamehameha II, forced Kaumuali'i to go to O'ahu, where arrangements were made for him to marry the great queen Ka'ahumanu, the favorite wife of Kamehameha, and the greatest surviving *ali'i* of the land. Kaumuali'i never returned to his native island.

Hawaii was in a great state of flux at the beginning of the 1800s. The missionaries were coming, along with adventurers and schemers from throughout Europe. One of the latter was Georg Schaeffer, a Prussian in the service of Czar Nicholas of Russia. He convinced Kaumuali'i to build a Russian fort in Waimea in 1817, which Kaumuali'i saw as a means of discouraging other Europeans from overrunning his lands. A loose alliance was made between Kaumuali'i and Schaeffer. The adventurer eventually lost the czar's support, and Kaumuali'i ran him off the island, but the remains of Fort Elizabeth still stand. Around the same time, George Kaumuali'i, the king's son, who had been sent to Boston to be educated, was ac-

MU AND MENEHUNE

Hawaiian legends give accounts of dwarf-like aborigines on Kaua'i called the Mu and the Menehune. These two hirsute tribes were said to have lived on the island before and after the arrival of the Polynesians. The Mu were fond of jokes and games, while the Menehune were dedicated workers, stonemasons par excellence, who could build monumental structures in just one night. Many stoneworks that can still be seen around the island are attributed to these hardworking nocturnal people.

Anthropological theory supports the legends that say that some non-Polynesian peoples actually did exist on Kaua'i. According to oral history, their chief felt that too much interplay and intermarriage was occurring with the Polynesians. He wished his race to remain pure so he ordered them to leave on a "triple-decker floating island," and they haven't been seen since. If you ask a Kaua'ian whether he or she believes in the Menehune, the answer is likely to be, "Of course not! But, they're there anyway." Speculation holds that they may have been an entirely different race of people, or perhaps the remaining tribes of the first Polynesians. It's possible that they were cut off from the original culture for so long they developed their own separate culture, and the food supply became so diminished their very stature became reduced in comparison to other Polynesians.

companing the first missionary packet to the islands. He came with Reverend Sam Whitney, whom Kaumuali'i invited to stay, and who planted the first sugar on the island and taught the natives to dig wells. Wai'oli Mission House, just north of Hanalei, dates from 1836 and is still standing as a museum. Nearby, Hanalei Bay was a commercial harbor for trading and whaling. From there, produce such as oranges was shipped from Na Pali farms to California. In Koloa, on the opposite side of the island, a stack from the Koloa Sugar plantation, started in 1835, marks the site of the first successful sugar-refining operation in the islands.

Another successful enterprise was Lihu'e Plantation. Founded by a German firm in 1850, it prospered until World War I, when anti-German sentiment forced the owners to sell out. If you go into the Lihu'e Lutheran Church you can view an ornate altar very similar to ones found in old German churches.

During the 1870s and '80s, leprosy raged throughout the kingdom and strong measures were taken. Those believed to be afflicted were wrenched from their families and sent to the hideous colony of Kalaupapa on Moloka'i. One famous Kaua'ian leper, Ko'olau, born in 1862 in Kekaha, refused to be brought in and took his family to live in the mountain fortress of Na Pali. He fought the authorities for years and killed all those sent to take him in. He was made popular by Jack London in his short story, "Ko'olau, the Leper."

When World War II came to Hawaii, Nawiliwili Harbor was shelled on December 31, 1941, but there was little damage. The island remained much the same, quiet and rural until the late 1960s, when development began in earnest. The first resort destination on the island was the Coco Palms Hotel in Wailua, followed by development in Po'ipu and later in Princeville. Meanwhile, Hollywood had discovered Kaua'i and featured its haunting beauty as a "silent star" in dozens of major films. Today, development goes on, but the island remains quiet, serene, and beautiful.

GOVERNMENT

Kaua'i County

Kaua'i County is composed of the inhabited islands of Kaua'i and Ni'ihau and the uninhabited islands of Ka'ula and Lehua. Lihu'e is the county seat. It's represented by two state senators elected from the 6th District—a split district including north Kaua'i and portions of the South, Upcountry, and Hana regions of Maui—and the 7th District, which includes all of southern Kaua'i and Ni'ihau. Kaua'i has three state representatives—from the 12th District, which is again a split district with north Kaua'i and eastern Maui; the 13th District around Lihu'e; and the 14th District, which includes all of southwestern Kaua'i and Ni'ihau. The current mayor of Kaua'i is Maryanne W. Kusaka, a Republican who won a second term of office in 1998.

ECONOMY

The economy of Kaua'i, like that of the entire state, is based on agriculture, the military, and tourism, the fastest-growing sector.

Tourism

Kaua'i is the fourth most visited island after O'ahu, Maui, and the Big Island. Regaining momentum after Hurricane 'Iniki, it is once again attracting just over one million visitors annually. That means that on any given day, on average, there will be just less than 19,000 visitors on the island. Approximately 7,000 accommodation units are available, averaging a 66 percent occupancy rate. At one time, Kaua'i was the most difficult island on which to build a resort because of a strong grassroots antidevelopment faction. This trend has been changing due to the recession that hit everyone after Hurricane 'Iwa and then 'Iniki scared off many tourists. Island residents realized how much their livelihood was tied to tourism, and a recent ad campaign depicting tourists as visitors

KAUA'I

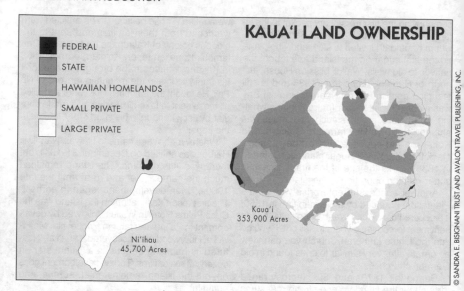

KAUA'I LAND OWNERSHIP

FEDERAL
STATE
HAWAIIAN HOMELANDS
SMALL PRIVATE
LARGE PRIVATE

Kaua'i
353,900 Acres

Ni'ihau
45,700 Acres

(rather than unwelcome invaders) has helped in their acceptance. Also, the resorts being built on Kaua'i are first rate, and the developers are savvy enough to create "destination areas" instead of more high-rise boxes of rooms. That doesn't mean that development on Kaua'i is easy. It's not, as there are many strict regulations to meet, and there is still a vocal opposition to unplanned development.

Agriculture

Agriculture still accounts for a hefty portion of Kaua'i's income. While **sugar,** for decades the backbone of the island's economy, has taken a downward dip, it's still grown commercially on the island although fewer acres are in production and only one mill still processes cane. Kaua'i produces about 12 percent of the state's diversified agricultural crop, with a strong yield in **papayas.** In 1982, California banned the importation of Kaua'i's papayas because they were sprayed with EDB, a fumigant used to control fruit flies. The chemical is no longer used, and the papaya market has rebounded. Hanalei Valley and many other smaller areas produce five million pounds of taro, which is quickly turned into poi, and the county produces two million pounds of guavas, as well as pineapples, beef, and pork

for its own use. A growing aquaculture industry produces prawns, and a tropical flower sector is now emerging. In the mid-1980s, nearly 4,000 acres stretching from 'Ele'ele to Kalaheo were put into coffee, tea, and macadamia nut production. This was, reputedly, the largest economic rediversification project in the state. Since then, coffee on Kaua'i has turned into a thriving industry, and the island now produces more coffee than anywhere in the state, including the famed Kona Coast. On the south shore, some corn is raised and two huge seed production facilities west of Kekaha grow seed corn to be shipped all over the world.

Military

The military influence on Kaua'i is small but vital. With about 125 military personnel and several hundred more civilian contract workers, the only sizable military facility on the island is **Pacific Missile Range Facility** at Barking Sands on the far west end of the island, which supports the testing of missiles, underwater warfare, and communications. In addition, an associated tracking facility sits on Makaha Ridge overlooking the south end of the Na Pali Coast. Operated by the Navy, this facility is available to all branches of the U.S. military, the Department of Defense, NASA, the Department of Energy, and select foreign military units.

Land Ownership

Of Kaua'i's County's total usable land area of approximately 399,000 acres, about 45,700 acres are on the privately owned island of Ni'ihau. The federal government owns just over 3,000 acres; the state has approximately 150,000 acres, of which 20,000 are Hawaiian Home Lands; and the county controls 600 acres, largely in parks. About 196,000 acres are privately owned, or 49 percent of the island. Of this, almost three-quarters is controlled by only half a dozen or so large landholders, mainly Gay & Robinson, Amfac, Alexander & Baldwin, Grove Farm, and Princeville Development Corporation.

PEOPLE

Kaua'i County's 58,300 people, including about 160 on Ni'ihau, account for only 4.8 percent of the state's total population, making it the least populous county. Also, about 325 military personnel and their dependents live on the island. The island density is about 105 people per square mile. The largest town is Kapa'a with 8,200 people, followed by Lihu'e with 5,500. The island's population is distributed as follows: 17,500 along the east coast, 11,200 in Lihu'e and suburban areas, 12,500 in the Po'ipu-Koloa area, 9,200 along the south coast, and 5,400 along the north shore. Ethnically, there is no clear majority on Kaua'i. The people of Kaua'i include: 34 percent Caucasians, 25 percent Filipinos, 20 percent Japanese, 15 percent Hawaiians, and the remaining six percent is made up of Chinese, Koreans, Samoans, and a smattering of African Americans and Native Americans.

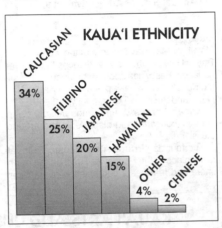

KAUA'I ETHNICITY

CAUCASIAN 34%
FILIPINO 25%
JAPANESE 20%
HAWAIIAN 15%
OTHER 4%
CHINESE 2%

FESTIVALS, HOLIDAYS, AND EVENTS

January

The annual Koke'e Natural History Museum **bird count** is held just at the new year. For avid birders. Call for information, 808/335-9975.

February

The **Hawaii International Scrimshaw Competition,** held throughout the entire month of February and sponsored by Ye Old Ship Store at the Coconut Marketplace, brings the best scrimshanders from around the world to display their phenomenal artwork. Pieces are juried by the public. An excellent opportunity to experience this revived sailors' art.

The two-day **Waimea Town Celebration** is held at Waimea, the spot where Captain Cook first made contact. Food, entertainment, canoe races, rodeo events, a ukulele competition, a softball tournament, and a partial marathon add to the fun. This annual event has been held for more than two decades.

March

Midmonth features feminine beauty and grace at the **Miss Kaua'i Pageant,** at the Kaua'i Community College in Lihu'e.

The **Prince Kuhio Festival,** at Prince Kuhio Park in Po'ipu and in Lihu'e, features festivities from the era of Prince Kuhio along with a canoe regatta, music and dance, a 10K run, and a royal ball in period dress. Held for more than 30 years.

April
Wesak, or **Buddha Day,** is on the closest Sunday to April 8 and celebrates the birthday of the Buddha. Ornate offerings of tropical flowers are placed at temple altars throughout Hawaii. Enjoy the flower festivals, pageants, and dance programs at many island temples.

Enjoy the best that the island has to offer at the **Annual School Art Festival,** at the Kaua'i Museum.

May
May 1, or May Day in some of the world, is **Lei Day** in Hawaii, when everyone dons their flower garlands. Festivities abound throughout Hawaii. On Kaua'i, events take place at the Kaua'i Museum and the Kaua'i Community College.

Armed Forces Week brings military open houses, concerts, and displays in and around the islands.

The four-day **Prince Albert Music Festival** takes place at the Princeville Hotel on the north shore and features a combination of classical music, slack-key guitar, and hula demonstrations, plus fashions, food, and crafts.

June
King Kamehameha Day, June 11, is a state holiday honoring Kamehameha the Great with festivities on all islands. Check local papers for times and particulars. On Kaua'i, enjoy parades, *ho'olaule'a,* and arts and crafts.

Banana Poka Festival at the Koke'e Natural History Museum is an outdoor educational fair that also features foot and bike races.

July
Fourth of July offers parades and other events, including the island's best fireworks show at Vidinha Stadium in Lihu'e. Fireworks are also shot off at the Pacific Missile Range Facility west of Kekaha.

The **Garden Island Championship Canoe Races** takes place at different locations on the island in late July. This and other canoe events are sponsored by Garden Island Canoe Racing Association.

Koloa Plantation Days celebrates Hawaii's plantation life with a parade, crafts fair, entertainment, ethnic foods, rodeo, and sports com-

---

KAUA'I ARTS AND CULTURE INFORMATION

State Foundation on Culture and the Arts, 44 Merchant St., Honolulu, HI 96813, 808/586-0300, website: www.state.hi.us/sfca, was begun by the State Legislature in 1965 to preserve and promote Hawaii's diverse cultural, artistic, and historical heritage. It manages grants and maintains programs in folk arts and art in public places.

Garden Island Art Council, 3116 Elua St., Lihu'e, HI 96766, 808/246-4561, website: www.kauai.net/arts/index.html, email: giac@hawaiian.net, promotes arts and cultural events around the island.

For more than two decades, **Kauai Community Players,** P.O. Box 343, Lihu'e, HI 96766, 808/245-7700, hawaiian.net/~kcp, has been entertaining audiences year-round with adult and children's theater.

The **Kauai Society of Artists,** P.O. Box 3344, Lihu'e, HI 96766, 808/822-7179, email: ksa@hawaiian.net, holds public exhibitions at least three times a year.

Hawaii Children's Theater, 491 Kamalua Rd., Kapa'a, HI 96746, 808/821-7827, presents various live performances during the year.

The **Kauai International Theater,** 808/821-1588, has a 62-seat theater at Kauai Village Shopping Center in Kapa'a for stage presentations. Performances are offered year-round.

College, community, and state events, and concerts, film, theater, and pageants are performed year-round at the **Kaua'i Community College Performing Arts Center** on the campus in Puhi, 808/245-8270, website: www.kauaicc.hawaii.edu/rc/pac/pac.htm.

KAUA'I MUSEUMS AND HISTORICAL SOCIETY

Grove Farm Homestead, P.O. Box 1631, Lihu'e, HI 96766, 808/245-3202, is open by reservation for hour-long tours Monday, Wednesday, and Thursday at 10 A.M. and 1 P.M.; donations requested are adults $5 and children 2–12 $2. This is the homestead of early sugar planter George N. Wilcox. Plantation owner's house, workers' cottages, outbuildings, and garden. Definitely worth a visit.

Kaua'i Historical Society, P.O. Box 1778, Lihu'e, HI 96766, 808/245-3373, was established in 1914. It remains Kaua'i's only general historical archive, preserving printed and audio material, photographs, maps, and other objects. Members work toward the preservation of historical and cultural sites and offer educational programs. The archives are free and open to the public for research weekdays by appointment.

Kaua'i Museum, 4428 Rice St., Lihu'e, HI 96766, 808/245-6931, is open Mon.–Fri. 9 A.M.–4 P.M. and Sat. 10 A.M.–4 P.M.; admission is adults $5, seniors $4, students 13–17 $3, children 6–12 $1. On Monday, Tuesday, and Thursday a free tour at 10 A.M. is included with admission. The history of Kaua'i and Ni'ihau is told through art and ethnic exhibits. Hawaiiana books, maps, and prints are available at the museum shop.

Koke'e Natural History Museum, P.O. Box 100, Kekaha, HI, 96752, 808/335-9975, website: www. aloha.net/~kokee, is open daily 10 A.M.–4 P.M.; free. Exhibits interpret the geology and unique plants and animals of Kaua'i's mountain wilderness. Great to visit while at Waimea Canyon and Koke'e State Park.

Waioli Mission House, 808/245-3202, run by the same group that shows Grove Farm Homestead, is open Tuesday, Thursday, and Saturday 9 A.M.–3 P.M. No reservations are needed. Entrance by donation.

The **Hawaiian Art Museum,** Princeville Center, 808/828-0302, website: www.huna.org, is a small collection of cultural artifacts from Hawaii and the Pacific that belongs to Aloha International, an organization dedicated to the Hawaiian practice of *huna.*

The **Kauai Children's Discovery Museum,** 808/823-8222, under the whale tower at the Kauai Village Shopping Center in Kapa'a, is a hands-on museum dedicated to science, culture, and the arts as it relates to Hawaii, its past, and its environment.

The **Faye Museum** at the Waimea Plantation Cottages, 808/338-1625, is a small museum presenting photographs and artifacts of the sugar plantation years of west Kaua'i. Open daily 9 A.M.–9 P.M. Free.

For a short historical perspective on coffee, a few artifacts, and the story on coffee production and processing on Kaua'i, stop in at the **Kauai Coffee Company Museum** in Numila, 808/335-5497.

petitions. Events take place in and around Koloa.

September
The **Mokihana Festival,** a weeklong event with festivities at some of the big hotels, is a grassroots festival featuring lei-making, hula, and ukulele competitions, along with folk-arts workshops and local entertainment.

October
Aloha Festival is a weeks-long series of events in the fall where everyone celebrates Hawaii's own intangible quality, *aloha.* There are parades, lu'au, historical pageants, balls, and various other entertainments. The spirit of *aloha* is infectious and all are welcome to join in. Check local papers and tourist literature for happenings near you.

The annual one-day **Coconut Festival** held in Kapa'a includes food, games, and crafts.

Eo E Emalani I Alaka'i commemorates Queen Emma's journey to Koke'e and the Alaka'i Swamp. Activities include hula performances, chants, Hawaiian music, and craft demonstrations. Held at the Koke'e Natural History Museum at Koke'e State Park.

November
November 11 is **Veterans Day.** All islands have parades. Get information through the local newspaper or contact the Kaua'i Chamber of Commerce.

KAUA'I

The **Hawaii International Film Festival** brings new and engaging films mainly from Asian and the Pacific to the Performing Arts Center at the Kaua'i Community College in Lihu'e. Call 808/528-3456 or 800/752-8193 for information about what's playing; website: www.hiff.org.

December
The **Christmas Craft Fair** is an annual event known for attracting the island's best in hand-crafted items and home-baked goodies. At the Kaua'i Museum, Lihu'e, 808/245-6931.

SPORTS AND RECREATION

Kaua'i is an exciting island for all types of sports enthusiasts, with golf, tennis, hunting, and water sports, and it's a magnificent island to explore by land, sea, or air. You can rent horses, camp and hike the hidden reaches of the Na Pali Coast, or simply relax on a cruise. The following should start the fun rolling.

BEACHES

Kaua'i has more beach per shoreline mile than any of the other major Hawaiian Islands—about 50 miles of it. With so many beaches to choose from, the problem on Kaua'i is picking which one to visit. If you venture farther than the immediate area of your hotel, the following will help in deciding just where you'd like to romp about. This is a simple listing only. For more details see the specific listings in the appropriate travel chapters.

Lihu'e Area
Kalapaki Beach in Lihu'e is one of the best on the island, convenient to Kaua'i's principal town center. This beach's gentle wave action is just right for learning how to bodysurf or ride the boogie board; snorkeling is fair. Two small crescent beaches lie near Ninini Lighthouse just below the Kauai Lagoons golf course. Water is rougher there, with much exposed rock; snorkeling should be done on calm days only. Also accessible but less frequented is **Hanama'ulu Bay,** just up the coast, with a lagoon, picnic spots, and camping.

East Side
Like its accommodations, the beaches of Wailua are few but very good. **Lydgate Beach** has two lava pools, and the beaches below Wailua Municipal Golf Course offer seclusion in sheltered coves where there's fine snorkeling. **Wailua Beach,** fronting the Coco Palms, is also fine but best during calm weather. **Waipouli Beach** and **Kapa'a Beach** flank the well-developed town of Kapa'a. North of there are **Kealia Beach** and the little-frequented **Donkey Beach,** both known for good surfing. The undertow is quite strong at Donkey Beach, so don't venture out too far if you don't swim well. **Anahola Beach,** at the south end of Anahola Bay, has safe swimming in a protected cove, freshwater swimming in the stream that empties into the bay, picnicking, and camping. Snorkel a short distance up the shore to where the reef comes in close—an area where locals come for shore fishing. Still farther north is **Moloa'a Beach,** a little-visited half-moon swath of sand.

North Kaua'i
Just beyond Kilauea is **Secret Beach,** all that its name implies. At the end of a tiny dirt road, the start of which eludes many people, is a huge stretch of white sand. You're sure to find it nearly empty; no one is around to bother you. A bit farther on is **Kalihiwai Beach,** great for swimming and bodysurfing during the right conditions. A park at **'Anini Beach** is a great place to snorkel because it has the longest exposed reef in Kaua'i, and it's a wonderful place to learn windsurfing because of the shallow water inside the reef.

Hanalei Bay is a prime spot on the north coast. Swim at the mouth of the Hanalei River or at various spots along this long crescent. Experienced surfers ride the waves below the Sheraton; snorkeling is good closer to the cliffs. West of Hanalei is **Lumaha'i Beach,** a beautiful curve of white sand backed by cliffs and thick jungle that was the silent star of the movie *South Pacific*. The inviting water here has a fierce riptide, so enter only when the water is calm. **Ha'ena**

Beach and nearby **Tunnels** are terrific swimming and snorkeling spots. At the end of the road is **Ke'e Beach,** a popular place with some amenities, good swimming in summer, and adequate snorkeling.

Many secluded beaches at the foot of the Na Pali cliffs dot the coast to the west along the Kalalau Trail. **Hanakapi'ai Beach** is reached after one hour on the trail and is fine for sunbathing; the water, especially in winter, can be torturous, so stay out. **Kalalau Beach** is a full day's hike down this spectacular coast. Beyond that, Nu'alolo Kai and Miloli'i beaches can only be reached by boat.

South Kaua'i

The **Po'ipu Beach** area is the most developed on the island—accommodating, tame, and relaxing. You can swim, snorkel, and bodysurf here to your heart's content. The eastern end of this beach is referred to as **Brennecke's Beach.** Fronting the Hyatt Regency is **Shipwreck Beach,** a place where many find the boogie boarding the best. Beyond that is the lonely expanse of **Maha'ulepu Beach** with its windswept dunes.

Down the coast are **Salt Pond Beach,** one of the island's best and good for swimming and windsurfing, and **Pakala Beach,** popular with surfers but also good for swimming and snorkeling. The golden strand of **Kekaha Beach** runs for miles with excellent swimming, snorkeling, and surfing, and stretches into the Pacific Missile Range Facility at Barking Sands, where you can go, with permission, for swimming, surfing, and sunning and good views of Ni'ihau when no military exercises are in progress.

Polihale Beach is the end of the road. Swimming is not the best as the surf is high and the undertow strong, but walk along the shore for a view of the south end of the great Na Pali cliffs. It's a treat.

SCUBA AND SNORKELING

Scuba

With its rich sealife and varied underwater geological formations (ledges, pinnacles, caverns, and coral beds), Kaua'i is an excellent place to scuba dive. Kaua'i's underwater temperature hovers 75–80° year-round, and visibility is often good to 100 feet. Several dozen frequented dive spots surround the island. Most on the south and north shores are good for all levels of divers, and the few off the east and west coasts are generally for experienced divers. The south shore dive sites are mostly between Po'ipu Beach and Spouting Horn, while the north shore dive sites lie between Hanalei and Ke'e Beach. By and large, boat dives go to the south shore in winter and the north shore in summer. There is only one good shore dive spot on Kaua'i and that's at Koloa Landing on the south shore. In addition, some dive tours go to Lehua Island off the north point of Ni'ihau. Not only is Lehua undisturbed, but there is very little runoff from the islands to cloud the water. Lehua reputedly has some of the best diving in the state with exceptionally clear water and deep drop-offs, but it's definitely for experienced and advanced divers only. Companies that offer dive tours vary their sites depending upon weather and water conditions and the skill level of the group.

Scuba Shops and Tour Companies

Fathom Five Divers, 808/742-6991 or 800/972-3078, website: www.fathomfive.com, open daily 9 A.M.–6 P.M. in Koloa, is a retail store and complete diving center offering lessons, certification, rentals, and tours. Maximum of six passengers per boat.

Down the road at Po'ipu Plaza is **Seasport Divers,** 808/742-9303 or 800/685-5889, website: www.kauaiscubadiving.com, a scuba/snorkel shop that does sales, rental, certification, and both diving and snorkeling tours.

Other south shore diving companies are **Ocean Odyssey,** 808/245-8661, and **Mana Divers,** 808/742-9849.

OUTRIGGER CANOE RACING

The **Garden Island Canoe Racing Association** sponsors various racing events around the island from spring through late summer. For information on outrigger canoe competitions, canoe clubs, or public events, contact the association at P.O. Box 43, Lihu'e, HI 96766, 808/822-1944.

KAUA'I

A fine shop with a good reputation in Kapa'a is **Dive Kauai,** 808/822-0452 or 800/828-3483, website: www.divekauai.com, with retail, rental, certification classes, and tours.

Also in Kapa'a are **Bubbles Below,** 808/822-3483, website: www.aloha.net/~kaimanu; **Sunrise Diving Adventures,** 808/822-7333; and **Wet and Wonderful,** 808/822-0211.

On the north shore, try **North Shore Divers,** 808/826-1921.

In addition, many hotels have these or other companies run scuba classes at their hotel pools or organize tours from their beach activities booths.

Snorkeling

The following are some of the best and safest snorkeling sites on Kaua'i. **Ke'e Beach,** at the end of the road at Ha'ena, is tops (definitely stay inside the reef). **Tunnels** has a wonderful view of the mountains (*experienced snorkelers only* at the reef edge; beginners should stay on top of the reef). **'Anini Beach,** almost always gentle and friendly for day outings, is terrific for windsurfing as well. **Lydgate State Park** is the safest for families and children. **Po'ipu Beach,** which is also safe for children, has the best entry to the right of the sand spit. **Koloa Landing,** an entry

point for scuba shore dives, is a frequent haunt of sea turtles and eels. **Prince Kuhio Park** is best known for the turtles. **Lawa'i Beach,** along Lawa'i Rd. leading to the Spouting Horn, has good coral and fish, and sometimes seals.

Before you put your mask on, however, ask at a snorkel shop which locations are best for the season and water conditions. Inquire about types of fish and other sea creatures you might expect to see, water clarity, entry points, surf condition, water currents, and parking.

Snorkel Rentals and Tours

Good old **Snorkel Bob's,** 4-734 Kuhio Hwy. in Waipouli, 808/823-9433, and 3236 Po'ipu Rd. in Koloa, 808/742-2206, website: www.snorkel-bob.com, offers some of the best deals for snorkel rental in Hawaii (free snorkeling maps and advice), and the gear can be taken interisland and turned in at any Snorkel Bob's location.

Kauai Water Ski and Surf Co., 4-356 Kuhio Hwy., Kapa'a, in the Kinipopo Shopping Village, 808/822-3574, open daily 9 A.M.–7 P.M., is a complete water-sports shop that offers snorkel gear by the day or week. Clothing and many other water-sports gear is available.

Across from Po'ipu Beach County Park is **Nukumoi Surf Co.,** 808/742-8019. Open daily

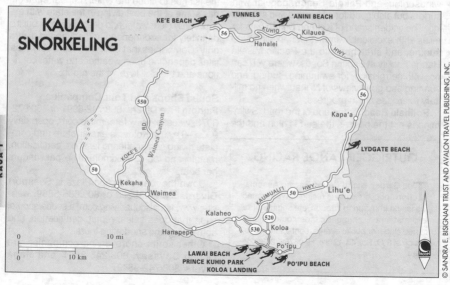

KAUA'I SNORKELING

8:30 A.M.–7 P.M., it rents complete sets of snorkel gear or fins and masks separately. Also available are boogie boards, surf boards, and an assortment of umbrellas, chairs, coolers, and life preservers. It's a retail store, so a full line of water equipment and clothing is for sale.

The **Captain's Cargo Company,** 808/338-0333, in downtown Waimea, also the office of Liko Kaua'i Cruises, rents snorkel gear, arranges boat tours, and sells water clothing.

Other shops to check for snorkel gear are **Seasport Divers,** 808/742-9303 in Po'ipu; **Dive Kauai,** 808/8220452 in Kapa'a; **Pedal and Paddle,** 808/826-9069 in Hanalei, the **Hanalei Surf Co.,** 808/826-9000, also in Hanalei; and **Kayak Kaua'i Outbound,** 808/822-9179 in Kapa'a and 808/826-9844 in Hanalei.

SeaFun Kauai, 808/245-6400, offers half-day shore-based guided snorkeling tours, with equipment and snacks included, for $68.75 adult and $52.50 for children. Location changes depending upon the weather.

Many sailing boats and catamarans incorporate snorkeling into the sailing trip (see below), and some diving and fishing companies also offer snorkeling as an option.

Snuba

Snuba is more than snorkeling, less than scuba. You have a regulator, weight belt, mask, and flippers, and you're tethered to scuba tanks that float above you on a sea-sled. Depth is limited to 20 feet, but the fun isn't. Snuba frees you from being encumbered by tanks and all the scuba apparatus. If you would like to start diving, this is a wonderful and easy way to get a feel for it. **Snuba Tours of Kaua'i,** 808/823-8912, website: www.hshawaii.com/kvp/snuba, offers guided tours off Po'ipu's Lawa'i Beach. The cost is $55 for 90 minutes.

CATCHING WAVES

Surfing

Surfing has long been the premier water sport in Hawaii. Locals and, now, "surfies" from all over the world know where the best waves are and when they come. While Anahola Beach was a traditional surfing spot on Kaua'i for Hawaiians of yesterday, the north shore has the beaches of choice today. The east side of Hanalei Bay provides a good roll in winter for experts, as does Tunnels. Quarry Beach, near Kilauea, and Kealia Beach and Donkey Beach, both north of Kapa'a, are used mostly by locals. On the south coast, the surfers' favorite is the west end of Po'ipu Beach, or west of there, near Pakala. Both Lawa'i Beach and Salt Ponds Beach are used if conditions are right, and waves for all levels can be found along the lengthy Kekaha Beach on the west end. Generally speaking, surf is high on the north shore in winter and flat in summer. On the south shore, it's the reverse, with better surf in summer. As onshore trade winds blow fairly constantly at east shore beaches, the surfing can be decent there any time of year. Listen to local advice as to where and when to ride and why. Check with the shops that sell or rent surfing gear or ask those who give lessons. The sea is unforgiving—and particularly unpredictable in winter.

Boogie boarding is also a fun sport on smaller waves close to shore. Some well-known boogie board beaches are Brennecke Beach and Shipwreck Beach in Po'ipu, Kalihiwai Beach near Kilauea, and Black Pot Beach on Hanalei Bay. Most water sport shops, some activities desks, and hotel beach activities booths rent boogie boards for around $6 a day.

Surfing Lessons and Surf Shops

Surfing lessons are available; they include the free use of a surf board that fits your level, a 60- to 90-minute lesson with free surf time after that, and dry land instruction before entering the water. Most beginning lessons are in small groups of fewer than half a dozen and usually run about $30 an hour, although some companies offer private instruction. Try world champion Margo Oberg and her staff at **Margo Oberg's Surfing School** on Po'ipu Beach. Make reservations through Nukumoi Surf Co., 808/742-8019. In Lihu'e, **Pete's Surf School,** 808/639-4109, and **Aikane Surf School,** 808/639-3559, are two to try. **Hanalei Surf School,** 808/826-9283, and **Learn to Surf,** 808/826-7612, both operate in Hanalei.

Kauai Water Ski and Surf Co., in the Kinipopo Shopping Village, Wailua, 808/822-3574, is a complete water-sports shop that offers

KAUA'I

surfboard and boogie-board rentals by the day or week. Boogie boards run $5–8 a day or $20–30 a week; surf boards $10–15 per day or $40–55 per week, and a car rack with board rental is $5 a day.

Seasport Divers, at the Po'ipu Plaza, 2827 Po'ipu Rd., 808/742-9303 or 800/685-5889, offers rental boards and surfing lessons.

Across from Po'ipu Beach, **Nukumoi Surf Co.,** 808/742-8019, rents hard board surfboards for experienced riders only at $25 a day or $75 a week.

Hanalei Surf Co., 808/826-9000, just a few minutes from a great beginners' surfing area at Hanalei, offers surfing lessons or board rentals without lessons (boogie boards, too). Hanalei Bay goes completely flat in summer, so call ahead for surfing conditions.

Just down the road in Hanalei, **Kai Kane,** 808/826-5594, also sells and rents surfboards and boogie boards.

Windsurfing

Windsurfing has become very popular on Kaua'i in the last few years. Technically called sail-boarding, this sport is commonly known as windsurfing after a major manufacturer of sail-boards. The best spots for beginners are 'Anini Beach on the north coast, Po'ipu Beach on the south, and Kalapaki Beach in Lihu'e. More challenging is Salt Ponds Beach on the west end, and for the advanced only, Ha'ena Beach on the north coast is preferred, or Tunnels just down the way. On the south shore, try Maha'ulepu Beach east of Po'ipu. Ask at water sport shops for other local favorites that would match your ability.

Anini Beach Windsurfing, 808/826-9463, is a one-man operation. Owner Keith Kabe will load his truck with windsurfing gear and come to you. Well known on the north shore, Keith will tailor your windsurfing lesson to fit your ability. Rentals for all levels available.

Windsurf Kauai, 808/828-6838, owned by Celeste Harvel, specializes in beginner lessons. Three-hour group lessons (six people maximum) are $70 with equipment. Those who already know how can rent sailboards here.

Kalapaki Beach Boys, at the Marriott in Lihu'e, 808/246-9661, rents sailboards and offers lessons.

WATER-SKIING

When you think of recreation on Kaua'i, water-skiing doesn't necessarily come to mind. **Kauai Water Ski and Surf Co.,** at Kinipopo Shopping Village in Wailua, is the island's only water-skiing company, and there is only one place where it's permitted to ski. Skimming placid Wailua River, freshwater skiers pass tour boats and kayaks going to and from the Fern Grotto. Water-skiing fees run $55 a half hour and $100 an hour, including boat, driver, gas, skis, and other equipment. Instruction at all levels can be arranged; weekdays only.

OCEAN TOURS

You've only seen half of Kaua'i until you've seen it from the sea. Ocean tours include fishing, sailing, whale-watching, diving, and snorkeling on sailboats, catamarans, and Zodiacs. Most ocean tours run along the Na Pali Coast, but when weather conditions are not good they may travel along the south-central coast. Some run out to Lehua Island, and fishing boats go even farther afield. The majority of tour boats run out of Port Allen Harbor on the south shore near Hanapepe, while others use Nawiliwili Harbor in Lihu'e, Kukui'ula Harbor near Po'ipu, and Kikiaola Harbor west of Waimea.

Zodiacs

The exact opposite experience from the tame Wailua River trip is an adventurous ride down the Na Pali Coast in a very tough, motorized rubber raft. A Zodiac looks like a big horseshoe-shaped inner tube that bends and undulates with the waves like a floating waterbed. These seaworthy craft, powered by twin engines, have separate air chambers for unsinkable safety. Seating 12 or so, they take you for a thrilling ride down the coast, pausing along the way to whisk you into caves and caverns. The wind generally picks up in the afternoon, so for a more comfortable ride, book the morning cruise. Other tours run along the south coast to Kipu Kai, and one company uses larger, rugged hull, soft-sided craft. All are popular so make reservations. Bring a bathing suit, snorkel gear, camera (in a plastic bag for protection), and a windbreaker for the return ride; snacks are provided. Summer weather permits excursions almost every day, but winter's swells are turbulent and these experienced seamen won't go if it's too rough. Take their word for it! Pregnant women and individuals with bad backs are advised not to ride.

Oldest and best known of the Zodiac companies is **Na Pali Zodiac,** 808/826-9371 or 800/422-7824, website: http://planet-hawaii.com/zodiac, owned and operated by "Captain Zodiac," Clancy Greff. This company now operates on Hawai'i and Moloka'i, too. Captain Zodiac runs a winter whale-watching tour to Kipu Kai from Nawiliwili Harbor at Lihu'e for $59 or $49 for kids.

Kauai Z-TourZ, 808/742-6331, website: www.ztourz.com, does summer and winter runs. A five-hour winter whale-watching tour to Kipu Kai and Lawa'i Kai is $90 or $70 for children, and the three-hour tour goes for $60/50. These two go out of Kukui'ula Harbor. The five-hour winter tour up the Na Pali Coast starts at Kikiaola Harbor and costs $120/90.

Another reputable company offering Zodiac tours is **Hanalei Sea Tours,** 808/826-7254 or 800/733-7997, website: www.seatours.net.

The Exploration Company, 808/335-9909 or 800/852-4183, website: www.napali-explorer.com, runs expeditions from Port Allen in two 49-passenger, ridged-bottom inflatable rafts, *Explorer II* and *Explorer III*. These souped-up versions of the typical Zodiacs sport cushioned seats, a shade canopy, a swim step, and a restroom. These craft are not luxury by any means, just larger and more comfortable than the ordinary Zodiac. Five-hour morning and afternoon snorkel rides up the Na Pali Coast run $127 adult and $70 for kids 5–11. If the seas are just too rough to snorkel, they may give you a ride the full length of the coast. A summer snorkel tour around the south side runs $98 adults and $58 for kids. During winter, two-hour whale-watching rides cost $65 adult and $35 for kids. All water equipment is provided, plus snacks on the longer trips. Meet at the Exploration Company office around the side at the 'Ele'ele Shopping Center.

Catamarans and Sailboats

For an adventure with a smooth ride, try a catamaran or a sailboat. Many of the companies that do water adventures on Kaua'i run power cata-marans—only one true sailing ship plies these waters. Catamarans (cats) ride on two widely spaced hulls with a superstructure between; some, called trimarans, have a third hull down the middle. Each comes with some shaded seating area to protect from the sun and on-board toilets and freshwater showers. All provide smooth sailing down the coast and get you back in great comfort. Some of the cats are set up with sails and take advantage of it when the winds are right. These ships primarily run swim/snorkel tours up the Na Pali, but some also have sunset tours along the south coast and, during winter, whale-watching tours. A few offer scuba dives for an extra charge. They offer plenty of fun, give you great views of the coast, and provide complimentary snacks along the way. Those with sails throw in the added experience of slicing through the water without the distraction of motors. Most tour companies run their boats out of Port Allen Harbor, although one goes out of Kikiaola Harbor, and a few use Hanalei as a base. Tours vary, but typically a half-day tour of four hours runs about $110; whale-watching trips cost $60; and, during the summer, sunset tours run close to $80. Due to the weather, more tours are offered during the summer than the winter. Options vary, so when calling, be sure to ask about the particulars of each trip.

Liko Kaua'i Cruises, 808/338-0333, website: www.liko-kauai.com, is owned and operated by a native Hawaiian, Captain Liko Hookano. Unlike the other cruises, Liko Kaua'i takes you on a 49-foot power catamaran down the Na Pali Coast from the west end, departing from Kikiaola Harbor just two miles from Waimea. The four- to five-hour tour meets at 7 A.M. at the offices of Captain's Cargo Company in Waimea. The rates are $115 adults and $75 for children 4–14. During summer months, afternoon snorkel tours and sunset tours for $85 adults and $55 children are also run.

Na Pali Eco Adventures, 808/826-6804, website: www.napali.com, provides environmentally responsible interpretive tours in specially outfitted catamarans (they burn recycled vegetable oil); tours sail from Port Allen Harbor. Aside from the snorkeling, the crew teaches you about marine ecology and the culture of the island. Rates are $115 for a five-hour tour, $100 for a four-hour tour, or $59 for the whale-watching tour, in season.

KAUA'I

Blue Dolphin Charters, 808/742-6731, welcomes you aboard its 63-foot power catamaran, on which you can sail, snorkel, use the water slide, and watch the sun go down. Tours depart from Port Allen Harbor. Tours include a five- to six-hour Na Pali Coast run for $110 and a sunset tour for $75.

Running under sail is possible with Captain Andy of **Capt. Andy's Sailing Adventures,** 808/335-6833, website: www.sailing-hawaii.com. He lets the wind power his 55- and 65-foot catamarans. A real jolly fellow, he will take you for a half day of sailing, snorkeling, and beachcombing for $109, on a four-hour snorkel tour along the south coast for $85, for a two-hour sunset cruise for $59, or on a three-hour sunset cruise for $75, plus whale-watching along the south coast in season. Kids always get discounts.

Holoholo Charters, 808/335-0815, website: www.holoholo-charters.com, also runs out of Port Allen Harbor. Options include a three-hour sunset cruise for $85 and a full-day cruise to Ni'ihau for snorkeling and sightseeing for $160.

Also try **Catamaran Kahanu,** 808/335-3577, at Port Allen, for an intimate experience of the Na Pali Coast for $95 or a whale-watching tour for $55.

One of the few companies to use Hanalei Bay is **Na Pali Catamarans,** 808/826-6853. Here you must canoe from shore to the waiting power catamaran, which is smaller (32 feet) and holds only 15 passengers. From there you cruise the Na Pali Coast from the east. A four-hour snorkel tour runs $125, and a three-hour whale-watching tour is $90.

Hanalei Sea Tours, 808/826-7254, website: www.seatours.net, offers catamaran and Zodiac rides.

Bluewater Sailing, 808/828-1142, runs the 42-foot ketch-rigged yacht *Lady Leanne II* out of Hanalei Bay from May through September and out of Port Allen the rest of the year. This is Kaua'i's only mono-hull charter sailing vessel. Half-day rates are $105 adults or $85 for kids, and sunset sails run $60 adults or $55 for kids. All-day private charters can be arranged.

Kayaking

Kayaking has become very popular in Hawaii, and kayaking in Kaua'i is good. Because Kaua'i is an island state, sea kayaking is predominant,

but at least three rivers can be kayaked as well. Wailua River runs up to Fern Grotto from the town of Wailua, Hule'ia River slides by the Alakoko Fishpond outside Lihu'e, and the Hanalei River skirts the Hanalei Wildlife Reserve on the north shore. Hawaii has no white-water kayaking. The two stretches of ocean most popular with kayakers are the Kipu Kai area just south of Lihu'e on the south shore and the magnificent Na Pali Coast on the north shore. Kipu Kai is a secluded bowl-shaped valley that opens onto a fine beach and is backed by a jagged mountain ridge—only one private road runs to the cattle ranch that occupies this property. It's less than an hour over the water from Lihu'e. Because of water conditions, this stretch is best in the winter. North shore water conditions are better in the summer; water is generally flattest then so you'll be fighting the wind and waves less. Because the north coast sea current runs from east to west, kayak along the Na Pali Coast from Ha'ena to Polihale, not the other way around. Make sure you save enough strength for the return trip.

Check with one of the kayak shops to get the latest information about sea conditions and consider taking an organized tour, offered by many of the kayak shops around the island. At times, permits for tours along both the north and south shores are rescinded, so check to see what's happening when you are there. Whether you paddle on the river or ocean, wear a swimsuit or shorts and T-shirt you don't mind getting wet, and tabi or some type of water shoe or sandal. Be sure to take a brimmed hat and sunglasses, put on sunscreen, take a towel and a dry change of clothes (a dry bag is usually provided on tours), and don't forget drinking water and snacks. A windbreaker is recommended for the open ocean. Most shops want day-rental kayaks back by 5 P.M.

Kayaks (the sit-upon kind) generally rent for about $25 single or $50 tandem. Some shops rent carriers to haul the kayak yourself. A few are near a launch site, but many have shops away from the water, so you have to strap the kayak to a rack and drive to the put-in point.

Outfitters Kaua'i, 808/742-9667 or 888/742-9887, website: www.outfitterskauai.com, offers a seven-hour Kipu Kai Daytrip Tour from September to May for $115 for those in good physical condition, and a full-day Na Pali Daytrip Tour for $135 that runs the whole length of the coast from Ha'ena to Polihale. Also offered are river tours on the Hule'ia and Wailea for $68 and $80, respectively.

Kayak Kaua'i, P.O. Box 508, Hanalei, HI 96714, 808/826-9844 or 800/437-3507, and in Kapa'a at 808/822-9179, website: www.kayak kauai.com, open daily 8 A.M.–5 P.M., has extensive experience—its owners are world-class kayak experts and the staff are sensitive people who provide good service while having a good time. Two-person river kayaks rent for $48 per day, one-person kayaks for $25; sea kayaks are $65 and $35, respectively. Lessons, shuttle service, and storage are also available. From May to September, the company leads ocean kayak tours up the Na Pali Coast for $130. An all-day affair, this tour is for those who are in good shape and do well on the water. A half-day Hanalei River tour is offered year-round for $55. A whirlwind seven-day, six-night Discovery Tour for $1,350 per person includes kayaking, hiking, food, accommodations, and transportation. All of the tours provide good family-style fun. Kayak Kaua'i also rents and sells surfboards, boogie boards, snorkel gear, other beach and water equipment, and camping gear. Staff will rig your car to carry the kayak and provide drop-off and pickup service at Ke'e Beach for $8 or at Polihale State Park for $40—when it's safe to be on the ocean.

Kaua'i Water Ski and Surf, 808/822-3574, in the Kinipopo Shopping Village, Wailua, is a complete water-sports shop that offers daily kayak rentals: $50 a day tandem, $25 a day single seat. Others in the Wailua-Kapa'a area for tours and rentals are: **Paradise Outdoor Adventures,** 808/822-1112, website: www.kayakers.com; **Kayak Ecotours,** 808/822-9078, website: www.kauai-kayaking.com; **Wailua Kayak Adventures,** 808/822-5795; **Kayak Wailua,** 808/822-3388, kayakwailua.com; and **Rainbow Kayak Tours,** 808/822-4000.

For Hule'ia River tours, try **Aloha Canoes and Kayak,** at the Kalapaki Marketplace in Nawiliwili, 808/246-6804. In Hanalei, **Kayak Adventures,** 808/826-9340, website: www.extreme-hawaii.com/kayak, will take care of you.

Whale-watching Cruises

Boats generally run from January through April, but it all depends on how many whales are about and how long they stay. Many of the above Zodiac and catamaran charter companies run whale-watching tours in season.

RIVER CRUISE

Kaua'i has the only navigable river in Hawaii. Covered barges cruise the Wailua River, where *ali'i* once ruled, leaving the Wailua Marina and proceeding a couple of miles upriver to the Fern

ROBERT NILSEN

tourist boat on the Wailua River cruising to the Fern Grotto

KAUA'I

Grotto. This is a tourist activity, pure and simple, but the setting is lovely if you can get beyond the hype and hordes of people. Two companies service this route and run several trips a day for a reasonable fee. See the **Wailua** chapter for details.

FISHING

Deep-sea Fishing Charters

There are excellent fishing grounds off Kaua'i, especially around Ni'ihau, and a few charter boats for hire. Most are berthed at Nawiliwili Harbor, with some on the north coast and at least one in Kekaha.

The following charter boats have good reputations, and all leave from Nawiliwili Small Boat Harbor. **Sea Lure Fishing Charters,** 808/822-5963, offers a modern 28-foot Radon Sportfisher. **Lahela Ocean Adventures,** 808/635-4020, website: www.lahela-adventures.com, runs a 34-foot Radon for the big fish and will do snorkeling and whale-watching tours as well. **Hana Pa'a Charters,** 808/823-6031, has a small Radon for trolling, bottom-fishing, night fishing, or snorkel tours. **True Blue Charters,** 808/246-9662, has the biggest and most luxurious fishing boat on the island, the 55-foot *Konane Star.* Also luxurious are the 38- and 42-foot Bertrams run by **Kai Bear Sportfishing Charters,** 808/826-4556, website: www.kaibearsportfishing.com.

Sport Fishing Kauai, 808/742-7013, website: www.fishing-kauai-hawaii.com, offers 28- and 38-foot Bertrams *(Kauai Kai* and *Vida Del Mar II)* leaving out of Port Allen Harbor and Kukui'ula Harbor, while the 33-foot *Marlin* leaves out of Nawiliwili Small Boat Harbor. Farther to the west, **Kekaha Fishing Company,** 808/337-2700, takes the *Susan Lee* out of the Kikiaola Harbor at Kekaha.

Sea Breeze V from **Anini Fishing Charters,** 808/828-1285, with skipper Bob Kutowski, specializes in sport and bottom fishing. He and Robert McReynolds of **McReynolds Fishing Charters,** 808/828-1379, website: www. aloha.net/~themcrs, both leave from 'Anini Beach and fish the waters of the north coast. Going with either of these guys is perhaps the best introduction to sportfishing in Kaua'i.

Freshwater Fishing

Kaua'i has trout and bass. Rainbow trout were introduced in 1920 and thrive in 13 miles of fishable streams, ditches, and reservoirs in the Koke'e Public Fishing Area. Large and small bass and the basslike *tucunare* are also popular game fish on Kaua'i. Introduced in 1908, they're hooked in reservoirs and in the Wailua River and its feeder streams.

Commercial freshwater fishing operations go for large- and small-mouth bass and peacock bass. For full- and half-day bass fishing excursions, mostly in the reservoirs around Kalaheo and Koloa, contact **Cast & Catch,** 808/332-9707. Its 17-foot bass boat fishes one of Kaua'i's lovely freshwater reservoirs. All tackle, bait, and soft drinks are provided along with airport/hotel pickup and delivery. Also try **J.J.'s Big Bass Tours,** 808/332-9219, with 1993 Big Bass Hawaii State Champion, John Jardin. Tackle, license, refreshments, and hotel pickup are included. **Kauai Freshwater Aquatics,** 808/245-7358, now has an exclusive lease for fishing the Waita Reservoir in Koloa. Half-day trips run $180, full-day trips are $320, which includes all equipment, lunch, the guide and up to two fishermen. No experience necessary. Fishing with these tour operators is all catch and release—your only trophy will be a picture.

CAMPING AND HIKING

Kaua'i is very hospitable to campers and hikers. More than a dozen state and county parks and forest reserves offer camping, and a network of trails leads into the interior. There are different types of camping to suit everyone: you can drive right up to your spot at a convenient beach park, hike for a day through incredible country to camp in total seclusion, or boat to secluded spots along the Na Pali Coast. A profusion of "secret beaches" have unofficial camping; this cannot be recommended, but it's definitely done. Koke'e State Park provides affordable self-contained cabins, and RV camping is permitted at Koke'e and Polihale State Parks and at Ha'ena and Hanama'ulu County Parks.

Hikers can take the Kalalau Trail—perhaps the premier hiking experience in Hawaii—or go topside to Koke'e and follow numerous paths to

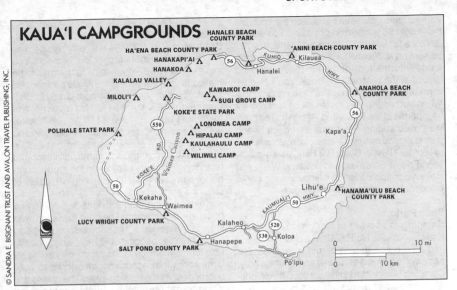

© SANDRA E. BISIGNANI TRUST AND AVALON TRAVEL PUBLISHING, INC.

KAUA'I CAMPGROUNDS

HANALEI BEACH COUNTY PARK
HA'ENA BEACH COUNTY PARK
HANAKAPI'AI
HANAKOA
KALALAU VALLEY
MILOLI'I
'ANINI BEACH COUNTY PARK
KUHIO
Kilauea
56
Hanalei
HWY
KAWAIKOI CAMP
SUGI GROVE CAMP
ANAHOLA BEACH COUNTY PARK
KOKE'E STATE PARK
56
POLIHALE STATE PARK
550
LONOMEA CAMP
HIPALAU CAMP
KAULAHAULU CAMP
WILIWILI CAMP
Kapa'a
KOKE'E RD.
Waimea Canyon
50
Kekaha
Waimea
Lihu'e
HANAMA'ULU BEACH COUNTY PARK
KAUMUALI'I HWY
50
LUCY WRIGHT COUNTY PARK
Kalaheo
520
SALT POND COUNTY PARK
Hanapepe
530
Koloa
Po'ipu
0   10 mi
0   10 km
MOON

breathtaking views over the bared-teeth cliffs of Na Pali. Hunting trails follow many of the streams into the interior; or, if you don't mind mud and rain, you can pick your way across the Alaka'i Swamp. Other fine trails are found in the Wailua area. Wherever you go, enjoy but don't destroy, and leave the land as beautiful as you find it.

General Information

All campgrounds, except for the state parks along the Na Pali Coast and the forest reserve campsites in Waimea Canyon, provide grills, pavilions (some with electricity), picnic tables, cold-water showers, and drinking water. Unfortunately, at some parks, toilets and showers have been vandalized and no longer function, but this may vary according to park maintenance schedules. Camping fuel is not provided, so bring your own wood or charcoal for the grill. No one can camp "under the stars" at official campgrounds; all must have a tent. Campsites are unattended, so be careful with your gear—especially radios, stereos, and cameras—but your tent and sleeping bag are generally okay. Always be prepared for wind and rain, especially along the north shore.

At times, police aggressively issue tickets and hefty fines for illegal camping, especially along north shore beaches. *Sometimes* they merely issue a warning, but definitely do not count on it! Multiple offenders can even be sentenced to jail time.

County Parks

A permit is required for camping at all county-maintained parks with camping facilities, and these are Ha'ena, Hanalei Black Pot, 'Anini, Anahola, Hanama'ulu, Salt Pond at Hanapepe, and Lucy Wright in Waimea; RV camping is permitted at only the Ha'ena and Hanama'ulu parks. Permits are good for up to seven nights per campground. Camping is limited to 60 days total in any one-year period. The permit-issuing office is the Division of Parks and Recreation, 4444 Rice St., Moikeha Bldg., Suite 150, Lihu'e, HI 96766, 808/241-6660, open Mon.–Fri. 8 A.M.–4 P.M. At all other times, including weekends and holidays, you can pick up your permit at the Kaua'i Police Dept., Lihu'e Branch, 3060 'Umi St., 808/241-6711. An application must include the name, address, and telephone number of the principal adult, names and a copy of official identification for all adults in the party, and number of tents that will be used. The cost is $3 per person per day (except Hawaii residents); children under 18 are free if accompanied by parent or guardian.

KAUA'I

Park rangers can issue permits on the spot, but these cost $5 per person per day. If you write in advance for information and reservations, you'll be sent an application. Return it with the appropriate information, and your request will be logged in the reservations book. You'll also receive brochures and maps of the campgrounds. When you arrive, you must pick up and pay for your permit at the Parks and Recreation office or the police station. Be aware that each beach park is closed one day a week for maintenance, except for Hanalei Black Pot Park, which is only open Friday, Saturday, and holidays. When you make your application to camp, ask the parks office for its current closure schedule.

State Parks

Camping is allowed at three state parks on Kaua'i—Koke'e, Na Pali Coast, and Polihale—and a no-cost camping permit is required; RV camping is allowed at Koke'e and Polihale only. Camping is restricted to five consecutive nights within a 30-day period per campground, with one night allowed at Hanakapi'ai when going in along the Kalalau Trail and one night when coming out from the valley, and three-night maximum at Miloli'i farther along the coast. At Polihale, campsites perch on top of the dunes that back the beach, and at Koke'e, the campsite is in the open meadow at the far end from the museum. Permits are issued no more than one year in advance. An application for a permit should be made at the Dept. of Land and Natural Re-

sources (DLNR), Division of State Parks, 3060 'Eiwa St., Rm. 306, Lihu'e, HI 96766, 808/274-3444, Mon.–Fri. 8 A.M.–4 P.M. only. *No* permits will be issued without proper identification. You can also write well in advance for permits to be mailed to you, but you must include photocopies of identification for each camper over 18. Children under 18 will not be issued a permit, and they must be accompanied by an adult. Allow at least one month for the entire process, and no reservations are guaranteed without at least a seven-day notice. Include name, address, and telephone numbers of those in the group, number of campers (with ID photocopies), dates of use, and number of tents.

Koke'e Lodge also provides self-contained housekeeping cabins. They are furnished with stoves, refrigerators, hot showers, cooking and eating utensils, bedding, and linen; wood is available for the fireplaces. The cabins vary from one large room that accommodates three to two-bedroom units that sleep seven. The cabins are tough to get on holidays, during trout-fishing season in August and September, and during the wild plum harvest in June and July. For reservations, write Koke'e Lodge, P.O. Box 819, Waimea, HI 96796, or call 808/335-6061 daily 9 A.M.–3:45 P.M.

Forest Reserves

Camping is allowed in specified sites only within the Na Pali Kona and Pu'u Ka Pele forest reserves. These reserves encompass Waimea

Polihale State Park

J.D. BISIGNANI

and adjacent canyons and the upper Koke'e region. Permits are required and issued free of charge. Applications may be made at the State Division of Forestry and Wildlife, 3060 'Eiwa St., Rm. 306, Lihu'e, 96766, 808/274-3433, Mon.–Fri. 8 A.M.–4 P.M., and must include the names of all campers and the exact dates for which the campsite is requested. Be sure to pick up the very useful *Northwestern Kaua'i Recreational Map* when making your application. Accessible by 4WD vehicles along Camp 10 Road are the Kawaikoi and Sugi Grove campsites. Camping at these camps is limited to three nights total within a 30-day period. The four campsites in Waimea and Koai'e canyons are reachable by foot only, either from Kukui Trail off Koke'e Road or by hiking up the Waimea Canyon from the town of Waimea. Camping is limited to four nights total at these camps. Be sure to sign in and out at the trailheads.

Hiking

More than 90 percent of Kaua'i is inaccessible by road, making it a hikers' paradise. Treks range from overnighters requiring superb fitness and preparedness to 10-minute nature loops just outside your car door. Most trails are well marked and maintained, and all reward you with a swimming hole, waterfall, panoramic overlook, or botanical or historical information.

The premier hike on the Island—considered by some to be the best hike in the state—is the 11-mile long Kalalau Trail. This trail cuts like a ribbon across the cliffs of the north coast from Ke'e Beach at the end of the road to the remote Kalalau Valley. This is a multiple-day hike in and out and requires gear and preparation. The only other well-used trail of note on the north coast is the north half of the Powerline Trail, which goes over the hump of the island from Hanalei to Keahua Arboretum above Wailua. Around the east side are several good day hikes offering plenty of exercise and good vistas. Perhaps the most popular are the three trails on the Sleeping Giant. Farther up onto the mountainside are the Kuilau Trail, Moalepe Trail, and the southern end of the Powerline Trail. By far the greatest concentration of hiking trails on Kaua'i, the trails of Waimea and Koke'e State Parks provide some of the prettiest and most awesome scenery. Here, you have a choice of forest, canyon, or coastal view hikes. It seems that one could walk for a month and not cover all the trails in this area. Further description of each of these trails is found in the appropriate travel chapter below.

Through its various divisions, the Department of Land and Natural Resources, 3060 'Eiwa St., Lihu'e, HI 96766, provides free detailed maps and descriptions of most trails. For state park trails, direct letters to the Department's Division of State Parks; for forest reserve trails, the Division of Forestry.

Tips and Warnings

You *cannot* go from Koke'e down to the valleys of Na Pali. Every now and again someone attempts it and is killed. The cliffs are impossibly steep and brittle, and your handholds and footholds will break from under you. Don't be foolish.

If you're going into the Alaka'i Swamp, remember that all the birds and flora you encounter are unique, and most of them are fighting extinction. Also, your clothes will become permanently stained with swamp mud—a wonderful memento of your trip. Before attempting any of the trails, please sign in at park headquarters.

Rental Equipment and Sales

Kayak Kaua'i Outbound, P.O. Box 508, Hanalei, HI 96714, 808/826-9844 or 800/437-3507, and in Kapa'a at 808/822-9179, open daily 8 A.M.–5 P.M., sells and rents camping equipment. Both locations carry all sorts of camping gear, including metal cups and dishes, packaged foods, insect repellent, backpacks, day packs, ground cloths, camping gas, candles, and tents.

Pedal and Paddle, 808/826-9069, in Hanalei's Ching Young Center, open daily 9 A.M.–5 P.M. in winter, 9 A.M.–6 P.M. in summer, rents and sells backpacking equipment. Rental rates are: two-person dome tent $10 a day, $30 a week; backpack $5 and $20; light sleeping bags $3 and $10; and sleeping pads $3 and $10. A rental day begins at the time you rent and ends at 5 P.M. the following day. Bikes, snorkel gear, surfboards, boogie boards, and kayaks are also available.

Other camping supply outlets are **Dan's Sports Shop,** in the Kukui Grove Center, 808/246-0151, **Kmart,** also in the Kukui Grove Shopping Center, and **Wal-Mart,** near the

KAUA'I

hospital on the north end of Lihu'e. These three shops have basic camping supplies, mostly for the car-camping crowd and not so much for the backpack/hiker variety, but they do carry reasonably inexpensive goods, including dome tents, lanterns, outdoor stoves and fuel, and flannel sleeping bags.

Guided Hikes

Koke'e Natural History Museum offers guided hikes through trails in the state park on weekends during summer. Trails differ each week according to the weather. These hikes leave from the museum at 12:30 P.M.; bring water and all your needed equipment. Call 808/335-9975 to reserve your spot; $3 a head.

Sierra Club announces group hikes in the *Garden Island* newspaper. You can also find the Kaua'i group outing schedule on the Web at www.hi.sierraclub.org.

Guided hikes are offered on the Princeville Ranch, twice daily except Sunday. Hikes run about three hours and the cost is $45–55. Drinking water and all equipment are provided. For information or to reserve, call 808/826-7669.

A child-based program that includes age-appropriate hiking, swimming, snorkeling, and a healthy lunch is offered by **Keiki Adventures Kaua'i,** 808/822-7823.

Whether it's an easy, moderate, or strenuous hike that you're after, **Kaua'i Trail Guides,** 808/821-2345 or 888/677-4453, website: www.hikekauai.com, can find one right for you. With small groups of up to four individuals, this company leads hikes mostly in the high Koke'e State Park and adjoining forest reserve area and along the north shore. All necessary equipment and snacks are provided.

The most education-oriented hikes on the island are done by **Kaua'i Nature Tours,** 808/742-8305 or 888/233-8365, website: www.teok.com. Full-day hikes, all in the easy to moderate level, focus on the natural environment, where you learn about Kaua'i's geology, natural history, and flora and fauna. Various hikes throughout the week go to Waimea Canyon, the Na Pali Coast, Maha'ulepu Beach and dune area, and other beaches around the island. If you want your day to be more than a physical adventure, these hikes may be for you. All hikes run about 9 A.M.–4 P.M. and cost $75.

HORSEBACK RIDING

One of the most exciting and intimate ways to discover Kaua'i is from atop a well-trained horse. All horseback tours are guided. Most of the guides are extremely knowledgeable about the area's unique flora and fauna and are able to talk story about the ancient tales and legends pertaining to the ride site. For your safety and comfort, wear long pants (jeans are best) and closed-toe shoes. Bring a hat and sunblock as well. Most riding stables take riders 10 years old or older, and some have a weight limit—usually around 220 pounds. Snacks and drinks are provided on most rides that go more than a couple of hours. Horseback riding is not allowed on beaches in Hawaii.

Silver Falls Ranch, 808/828-6718, website: www.hawaiian.net/~sfr, on the north shore off Route 56 just west of Kilauea, offers rides daily through private property below Mt. Mamahana, in the shadow of Kalihiwai Ridge. You can choose a 90-minute Greenhorn's Trail Ride for $60; the Hawaiian Discovery Ride, two hours long with refreshment provided for $75; or the Silver Falls Ride, a three-hour ride including a picnic and swim at a private falls for $99. All riders are matched with their horses, and the guides are experienced instructors. More than just a tour operator, the Silver Falls Ranch offers full equestrian services, including lessons, and maintains a stable of only quarter horses.

Princeville Ranch Stables, between Princeville and the Princeville Airport, 808/826-6777, website: www.kauai.net/kwc4, closed Sunday, offers rides through the ranch property and along the bluff that overlooks 'Anini Beach. The deluxe, four-hour ride is $110 and meanders across verdant interior land, ending at an inland waterfall for a swim and picnic. The three-hour ride to 'Anini Bluff runs $100 and includes a snack and swim at the beach. A shorter rides take you to lookouts over Hanalei Valley and into the foothills of the surrounding mountains for $55, while the "cattle drive" at $125 calls for participation.

Esprit De Corps Riding Academy, in the Kapa'a area, 808/822-4688, website: http://kauai-horses.com, will take you on a three-hour ride for

$99, a five-hour ride with snacks for $250, and a deluxe eight-hour ride with lunch and a swim in a mountain stream for $300–350. Reservations are necessary. These rides are geared to riders with some experience and to those who can handle being on a horse for hours. Riders must be age 10 or older. Heading deep into the mountains above Kapa'a, you visit relatively unfrequented spots with good vantage points across the foothills to the coast as well as up toward the island's highest peaks.

You can hire mounts from **CJM Country Stables,** 808/742-6096, website: www.cjmstables.com, about 1.5 miles past the Hyatt in Po'ipu. CJM offers three rides: a secret beach breakfast ride starting at 8:30 A.M. and lasting three hours for $75; a two-hour hidden beach ride twice daily, midmorning and early afternoon, for $65; and a beach, swim, and picnic ride for three hours from noon for $90. No rides are given on Sunday. All rides are taken in the Maha'ulepu Beach and nearby coastal area.

Up the hill from Po'ipu is **Omao Country Stables,** 808/742-8636, which will custom a ride for you and a small party for $125 or take you on a sunset ride at the west end for $140.

BICYCLING

Riding a bike around Kaua'i is fairly easy, thanks to the lack of big hills—except for the road up to Koke'e State Park. Traffic is moderate, especially in the cool of early morning, when it's best for making some distance. Roads are generally good, but shoulders aren't wide and are sometimes nonexistent, particularly on the back roads. Peak season brings a dramatic increase in traffic and road congestion. Take care! Some bike lanes have been constructed, but these are mostly near tourist resorts. Perhaps the best riding is by mountain bike on the cane haul roads that head into the interior. Wherever you ride, watch for rocks, sticks, wet surfaces, crumbled asphalt, and, on gravel back roads, bumps, ruts, and mud puddles.

Mountain biking on most cane roads is not encouraged because you are riding through private property and there is the chance of encountering heavy equipment. Stay off of other private property and do not go beyond locked gates. Some roads leading off the main highways are Route 583 to Wailua Falls (easy); the upland residential roads above Wailua and Kapa'a (easy to moderate); roads uphill between Lawa'i and Kalaheo (slow, steep, and tough); the coastal trail from Kapa'a Beach Park to Anahola (relatively easy), about six miles one-way; and Po'ipu Road past the Hyatt Regency Resort to Maha'ulepu Beach (easy). Others to try are Kealia Road from Kealia up the mountain to the Spauding Monument and from there down to Anahola (moderate uphill and easy down), the back road past Keapana Center to the Spauding Monument (moderate—you must walk the bike a short ways due to the deteriorating condition of the road), and Ko'olau Road near Moloa'a Beach (easy). The 4WD dirt tracks in Koke'e State Park and the adjacent forest reserves are easy to moderate and give you a good workout. Some hiking trails on state forest reserve land are also open to mountain biking, including the 13-mile Powerline Trail over the mountain from Keahua Arboretum to Hanalei (strenuous), the Kuilau and Moalepe Trails, the Kuamo'o Trail on the Sleeping Giant, and the Waimea Canyon Trail on the west end. Remember that there is no biking allowed on any state park trail or forest reserve trail other than those listed above.

Bike Shops
Outfitters Kauai, an ecology-minded sports shop specializing in kayaking and mountain biking, is owned and operated by Rick and Julie Havilend in the Po'ipu Plaza, 2827-A Po'ipu Rd., P.O. Box 1149, Po'ipu Beach, HI 96756, 808/742-9667 or 888/742-9887, website: www.outfitterskauai.com, open daily 9 A.M.–5 P.M. Mountain-bike rentals including helmet, a water bottle, lock, and a map are $20–33 a day, while cruisers run $20 and road bikes are $30 (multiday discounts available). Biking and kayaking incidentals are also available for purchase along with Patagonia clothing. Rick and Julie have lots of information and will do their best to match you and your interest with a great place to ride.

An excellent choice is **Bicycle John's,** along Route 56 in the Kuhio Business Center building as you enter Lihu'e, 808/245-7579, a full-service bicycle shop offering sales, repairs, and rentals. The shop is open Mon.–Fri. 10 A.M.–6

KAUA'I

P.M. and Saturday 10 A.M.–4 P.M. Rental bicycles range from an 18-speed basic cruiser to a custom road bike, and prices range from $25 per day to $65 for four days with a price break for multiday rentals.

You're not required to salute John Sargent, the **Bike Doctor,** who has a shop in Hanalei, 808/826-7799, stocked with everything for both casual and serious cyclists, open Mon.–Sat. 9 A.M.–5 P.M. John sells road bikes, sells and rents Marin mountain bikes, and offers special *wiki*

wiki repair service to visiting cyclists whose equipment has broken down. Rental prices are $25 a day, $100 per seven-day week, including helmet, tool box, and water bottle. The Bike Doctor is intimately familiar with roads and trails all over the island and is happy to give advice on touring. Happy pedaling!

The only bike shop in Kapa'a is the full-service **Kaua'i Cycle and Tour,** 1379 Kuhio Hwy., 808/821-2115, website: www.bikehawaii.com/kauaicycle, open Mon.–Fri. 9 A.M.–6 P.M., Sat-

KAUA'I GOLF COURSES

COURSE	PAR	YARDS	FEES	CART	CLUBS
Grove Farm Golf Course at Puakea 4315 Kalepo Street Lihu'e, HI 96766 808-245-8756	40	3,803	$35 (10 holes) $60 (20 holes)	incl.	$15 (10 holes) $25 (20 holes)
Kaua'i Lagoons Golf Club 3351 Ho'olaule'a Way Lihu'e, HI 96766 808/241-6000 or 808/634-6400	72	6,960 (Mokihana) 7,070 (Kiele)	$100 $150	incl.	$30
Kiahuna Golf Club 2545 Kiahuna Plantation Drive Po'ipu, HI 96756 808/742-9595	70	6,366	$75 morning $55 after 11 a.m. $40 twilight	incl.	$30
Kukuiolono Golf Course 854 Pu'u Road Kalaheo, HI 96741 808/332-9151	36	2,981	$7	$6	$6 $2 handcart
Poipu Bay Golf Course 2250 Ainako St. Koloa, HI 96756 808/742-8711 or 808/858-6300	72	6,959	$145	incl.	$40 $95 after noon $50 twilight
Princeville Makai Golf Course P.O. Box 3040 Princeville, HI 96722 808/826-5070 or 808/826-1105	36 36 36	3,157 (Ocean) 3,149 (Woods) 3,445 (Lake)	$115	incl.	$32
Princeville Prince Course P.O. Box 3040 Princeville, HI 96722 808/826-5070 or 808/826-1105	72	7,309	$155 $100 after noon $50 after 3 p.m.	incl.	$32
Wailua Municipal Golf Course 3-5350 Kuhio Hwy. Lihu'e, HI 96766 808/241-6666	72	6,981	$25 weekdays $35 weekends	$14	$15

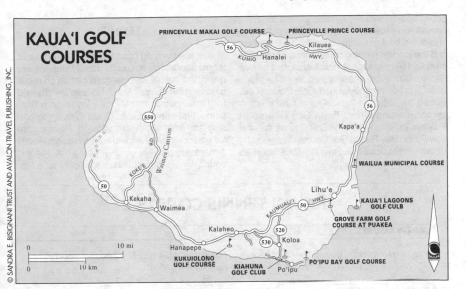

KAUA'I GOLF COURSES

© SANDRA E. BISIGNANI TRUST and AVALON TRAVEL PUBLISHING, INC.

PRINCEVILLE MAKAI GOLF COURSE · PRINCEVILLE PRINCE COURSE
Kilauea
56 · KUHIO · Hanalei · HWY.
550
Waimea Canyon
KOKE'E RD.
56
Kapa'a
50
WAILUA MUNICIPAL COURSE
Kekaha
Waimea
Lihu'e
KAUMUALI'I 50 HWY.
KAUA'I LAGOONS GOLF CULB
GROVE FARM GOLF COURSE AT PUAKEA
Kalaheo
520
Koloa
530
0 ——— 10 mi
0 ——— 10 km
Hanapepe
KUKUIOLONO GOLF COURSE
KIAHUNA GOLF CLUB
Po'ipu
PO'IPU BAY GOLF COURSE

urday 9 A.M.–4 P.M. This shop does sales, repair, and rental, and staff can tell you where it's best to ride on the island. Beach cruisers rent for $15 for 24 hours, front-suspension mountain bikes run $20 a day or $95 per seven-day week, and full-suspension mountain bikes are $35 a day and $150 a week. Each rental includes a helmet, lock, and water bottle. A car rack is available for $5. Unfortunately, this company doesn't run tours anymore.

Pedal and Paddle, in the Ching Young Center in Hanalei, 808/826-9009, rents cruisers at $10 per day or $40 per week, $40 and $80 for a mountain bike; prices include lock, helmet, and car rack if desired.

Kayak Kaua'i Outbound, 808/826-9844 in Hanalei and 808/822-9179 in Kapa'a, website: www.kayakkauai.com, rents mountain bikes and cruisers for $15–20 a day, with multiple-day rates available.

Various activities centers around the island also rent bikes for around $15 per day for a mountain bike and $10 per day for a beach cruiser.

Bicycle Tours

A miniature version of the great Haleakala downhill bike ride is offered on Kaua'i by two tour companies. The 12-mile ride on Kaua'i

starts in the cool mountain air on the rim of Waimea Canyon at about 3,500 feet. From there the group skirts the rim and then heads down the foothills to the coast at Kekaha. All tours are done in groups, and each member is given a helmet, jacket, and gloves to wear. A sag van follows for those who need a rest, and snacks are provided. Closed-toe shoes are a necessity, and long pants may be recommended. Don't forget to bring sunglasses and sunscreen. The cruiser bikes are cushy, with big easy-chair seats, raised handlebars, and extra strong brakes. Sunrise and sunset rides are available and run about $70 per person with reduced rates for kids; count on 4.5–5 hours. If this sounds like a trip for you, contact **Bicycle Downhill,** 808/742-7421, website: www.outfitterskauai.com, or **Kauai Coasters,** 808/639-2412, website: www.aloha.net/~coast.

GOLF

Kaua'i offers varied and exciting golfing around the island at eight golf courses. Kukuiolono Golf Course, a mountaintop course in Kalaheo, is never crowded and is worth visiting just to see the gardens. Wailua Municipal Golf Course is a

KAUA'I

public course with reasonable greens fees; it's considered excellent by visitors and residents—one of the best municipal courses in the country and the longest running on the island. Princeville boasts 45 magnificent holes sculpted above Hanalei Bay. A favorite for years, Kauai Lagoons Golf Club has recently added Kiele Course, designed by Jack Nicklaus. Also in Lihu'e is the up-and-coming Grove Farm Golf Course at Puakea. In Po'ipu, Kiahuna Golf Course and the new Po'ipu Bay Resort Golf Course, designed by Robert Trent Jones Jr., are fabulous courses on the sunny south coast.

TENNIS

The accompanying chart lists private and public tennis courts. Public courts, usually cement, are run by the county and reservations can be made by calling the number listed. No fees are charged for these public courts, but play is on a first-come, first-served basis. Court rules apply and only soft-sole shoes are allowed. Please care for equipment and stick to time limits, especially if there are players waiting. Many hotel tennis courts are open to nonguests, usually for a fee;

KAUA'I TENNIS COURTS

COUNTY COURTS

Under jurisdiction of the County Division of Parks and Recreation, 4444 Rice St., Suite 150, Lieu, HI 96766, 808/241-6277. No fee for use, but reservations are recommended.

TOWN	LOCATION	NO. OF COURTS	LIGHTED
Hanapepe	next to stadium	2	Yes
Kekaha	Faye Park	2	Yes
Kalaheo	Kalawai Park	2	Yes
Kapa'a	New Park	2	Yes
Koloa	Knutsen Park	2	Yes
Wailua	Wailua Homelots Park	4	Yes
Wailua	Wailua Homesteads Park	4	Yes

HOTEL AND PRIVATE COURTS OPEN TO THE PUBLIC

TOWN	LOCATION	TEL. (808)	FEE	NO. OF COURTS	LIGHTED
Princeville	Hanalei Bay Resort	826-6522	$6	8	Yes
Princeville	Princeville Tennis Center	826-3620	$12	6	No
Po'ipu	Poipu Kai Resort	742-2229	$5	8	No
Po'ipu	Hyatt Regency	742-1234	$20	4	Yes
Po'ipu	Kiahuna Tennis Club	742-9533	$10	10	Yes
Lihu'e	Tennis Club at Kaua'i Lagoons	246-2414	$20	8	No
Wailua	Kauai Coconut Beach Hotel	822-3455	$7	3	No

by and large condo tennis courts are reserved for guests only. All private courts are a hard court plexi-pave surface. Although each facility differs, private clubs usually have pro shops, offer equipment rental, and arrange clinics and lessons. Court play is regulated according to accepted rules, and proper attire is required, including proper shoes.

HUNTING

All game animals on Kaua'i have been introduced. Hunters go for feral pigs and goats, and black-tailed deer, which are found only on Kaua'i. Black-tailed deer come from Oregon. Forty were released on Kaua'i in 1961; the herd is now stabilized at around 700 and they're hunted in October by public lottery. Because they thrive on island fruits, their meat is sweeter and less gamy than that of Mainland deer.

A number of game birds are found on Kaua'i. Bag limits and hunting seasons vary, so check with the Department of Land and Natural Resources, Division of Forestry and Wildlife for details at 3060 'Eiwa St., Lihu'e, HI 96766, 808/274-3433. Ring-necked pheasants are one of the best game birds. Also on the list are francolins—gray, black, and Erkel's—chukar, quail, including the Japanese and California varieties, and doves.

Hunting Excursions

Ni'ihau Safaris, Ltd., 808/338-9869, owned and operated by the Robinson family, offers hunting trips to the forbidden island of Ni'ihau. The rate is a very stiff $1,400 and includes round-trip helicopter flight, a personal hunting guide, and a bag limit of one ram and one wild boar. If caught, they are skinned, packed, and readied for mounting. Although the game is plentiful, expect an arduous hunt with the straight-shooting skills left up to you. Also, do not expect to come into contact with any of the island's 230 Hawaiian residents. What you pay for, you get, and that's it!

LAND TOURS

Bus Tours

Most tour companies run vans, but some larger companies also use buses. Though cheaper, tours on full-sized coaches are generally less personalized. Coach tours vary, but typical trips go to the north shore from Lihu'e, to Waimea Canyon and south coast sights, or combine one of these tours with a trip to the Wailua River. Each agency has its own routes and schedules, but all hit the major tourist sites. Rates sometimes include entrance fees and lunch. Half-day fares run $30–60, while full-day fares run $60–80; children's fares are about 25 percent less. Fares may vary according to the area of pickup. Often a tour to the Fern Grotto is considered the highlight—that should say it all! Companies offering these tours include **Polynesian Adventure Tours,** 808/246-0122; **Kaua'i Island Tours,** 808/245-4777; **Roberts Hawaii Tours,** 808/245-9101; and **Kaua'i Paradise Tours,** 808/246-3999, which specializes in German-speaking narration. **North Shore Taxi and Tour,** 808/826-6189, does a version of this combining a van tour of north shore and Coconut Coast sites with a Fern Grotto boat tour and a helicopter ride for $139 per person.

Kaua'i has set the scene for nearly 60 feature films, and now a van tour escorts you to many of the locations, providing details of the film-making, in the comfort of a 15-passenger van that's at least as comfortable as the cushy seats in any silver screen multiplex. **Hawaii Movie Tours,** 808/822-1192 or 800/628-8432, website: www.hawaiimovietour.com, runs a six-hour van tour leaving daily at 9 A.M. from its Kapa'a office. The cost is $85 adult, $68 for kids 11 and under, lunch included. The deluxe version includes a helicopter ride (to see more movie sites) and a lu'au, for $295 per person.

Adventure Van Tours

One unique tour company is **Aloha Kauai Tours,** 1702 Haleukana St., Lihu'e, HI 96766, 808/245-6400 or 800/452-1113, website: www.alohakauaitours.com, email: tours@gte.net. The Mountain Adventure is run by knowledgeable guides who take you up along the Waimea Canyon to Koke'e and into the backcountry over dirt roads by air-conditioned 12-passenger 4WD vans, with an informed narrative on the way. You see a part of Kaua'i not reached by anyone who doesn't walk or bike in. The company's guides, all local people, are excellent and have a tremendous amount of knowledge about

KAUA'I

MOVIES MADE ON KAUA'I

For decades, filmmakers have been drawn to Kaua'i. About five dozen feature films or parts of films have been made on the island. While Kaua'i is varied in its topography and climate, most filmmakers use the lush vegetation, waterfalls, beaches, sheer cliffs, and tropical scenery as backdrops. Everyone seems to know that Kaua'i was used in *South Pacific* with Mitzi Gaynor in 1958 and in *Blue Hawaii* with Elvis in 1961, but others include scenes from *Raiders of the Lost Ark, King Kong, Outbreak, Jurassic Park, Islands in the Stream, Hook, Uncommon Valor,* and *The Man with the Golden Gun.* To fill in the details and the trivia, pick up a copy of *The Kaua'i Movie Book,* by Chris Cook, published in 1996 by Mutual Publishing of Honolulu.

the island's flora, fauna, and history. The daily eight-hour adventure costs $90 plus tax ($62 for children under 12) and includes a deli/picnic lunch (vegetarian too!). Tours start about 8 A.M. with free pickup in the Wailua and Po'ipu areas. This same company also does an excellent Kaua'i Backroads tour by 4WD vans through cane fields up to Kilohana Crater, with commentary about the area on the way. From the crater, the tour then heads to the east Po'ipu seashore near Maha'ulepu through the tunnel in the Ha'upu Ridge, constructed in 1946–47 by Grove Farm to transport cane to the Koloa mill from fields in the Kipu area. Virtually the whole route is on private cane land, behind locked gates, and inaccessible to those without permission. Morning and afternoon tours start at Kilohana. The four-hour tour costs $50 or $43.75 for children; snacks included. Newest of the tours are the weekday-only Blue Hole and Kuilau Trail tours. The half-day Kuilau Trail tour follows the Kuilau Trail on a relatively easy 4.2-mile hike, there and back, opening up sweeping vistas of the island's interior. Fees are $55 adult and $40 children. Full- and half-day Blue Hole tours take you past the Keahou Arboretum into the interior of the island where the waterfalls of Mt. Wai'ale'ale converge. After a rough 4WD ride to the spot where the gate scene of the Jurassic Park movie was filmed, you walk farther

into the wet, dense, and steamy valley. The full-day tour includes a picnic lunch at the arboretum and the Kuilau Trail hike. Half-day fees are $65 adult and $50 children; the full-day fees are $110 adult and $90 children.

ATV Tour

Kaua'i ATV, P.O. Box 800, Kalaheo, HI 96741 (at the corner of Weliwlei and Waikomo Roads in Koloa), 808/742-2734 or 877/707-7088, website: www.kauai.net/kauaiatv, runs four-wheel ATV (all terrain vehicle) tours through former cane land east of Koloa, from the ocean at Maha'ulepu to the Ha'upu Ridge. Three times a day, the 2.5-hour tours run along former cane haul roads, past the Waita Reservoir, and into the half-mile-long tunnel cut through the mountain above the reservoir. Rides are $85 a person; riders 16 years old and older are welcome. Helmets, face shields, gloves, beverages, and instructions are provided; long pants, a long-sleeve shirt, and closed-toe shoes are a must.

AIR TOURS

Helicopter Tours

Flying in a chopper is a thrilling experience, like flying in a light plane—with a twist. It can take you into all kinds of otherwise inaccessible little nooks and crannies. Routes cover the entire island, but the highlights are flying through colorful gorge of the Waimea Canyon, along the giant sea cliffs of the Na Pali Coast, and into the Mt. Wai'ale'ale crater—where it almost never stops raining and where you see dozens of waterfalls and even 360-degree rainbows floating in midair. Earphones cut the noise of the aircraft and play soul-stirring music as a background to the pilot's narration. Each pilot's stories are as different as the pilots themselves, so it's pot luck in that regard, but all are skilled in bringing you up-close to the island. All flights run in a clockwise circle around the island along the same basic route. Longer flights linger at certain scenic spots and dart into more valleys. The basic one-hour around-the-island flight runs about $150 per person; a shorter 45-minute flight is around $100, and longer 75- to 90-minute flights run about $180–210. Some give complimentary videos of your flight or a "standard" flight, while others charge for a video if you want one. Ni'ihau Helicopters also flies periodically to points on Ni'ihau. Its flights are more expensive, but it's the only way to get to see that island up close. Discounts of up to 15 percent from some of the companies are always featured in the ubiquitous free tourist brochures and occasionally available through activities and information centers.

Outdoor purists disparage this mode of transport, saying, "If you can't hike in you shouldn't be there"—but that's tunnel vision and not always appropriate. To go deep into the mist-shrouded interior, especially through the Alaka'i Swamp, the average traveler "can't get there from here"—it's just too rugged and dangerous. The only reasonable way to see it is by helicopter, and, except for the noise, choppers actually have less of an impact on the ecosystem than hikers do! A compromise—limiting numbers and times of flights—seems to be the best answer.

All the helicopter companies are safe and reputable. Remember, however, that the seating arrangement in a helicopter is critical to safety. The pre-flight crew is expertly trained to arrange the chopper so that it is balanced.

Of the dozen helicopter companies on Kaua'i, the majority operate from Lihu'e Airport, with a handful flying from Burns Field in Hanapepe and one flying from the Princeville Airport. For those companies without offices adjacent to the heliports, vans shuttle guests to the tarmac.

The granddaddy of them all is **Jack Harter Helicopters,** 808/245-3774 or 888/245-2001, website: www.helicopters-kauai.com, whose office is along Ahukini Rd., halfway between the airport and downtown Lihu'e. Jack, along with his wife, Beverly, started the helicopter business on Kaua'i, and he has been flying the island for more than 20 years. He and his pilots know countless stories about Kaua'i and just about everywhere to go on the island. Jack Harter runs both six-passenger a/c and four-passenger window-open helicopters. on 60- and 90-minute flights. His old slogan, "Imitated by all, equaled by none"—says it all.

Safari Helicopter, 808/246-0136 or 800/326-3356, website: www.safariair.com, is owned and operated by pilot Preston Myers, who learned to fly in the '60s and has been flying over Kaua'i for more than 12 years. Safari prides itself on offering a luxury tour in its state-of-the-art A-Star

helicopters, complete with two-way sound system, unobstructed view, air-conditioned compartments, and an all-seeing video camera system that records your trip for future enjoyment. A video of your personal tour runs $25. Pre-flight instruction takes place in the Lihu'e office.

Ohana Helicopter Tours, at the Anchor Cove Shopping Center, 808/245-3996 or 800/222-6989, website: www.ohana-helicopters.com, is an owner-operated company that gives personalized service. Ohana offers complimentary shuttle service from its office to the heliport. This company wants you to have the time of your life—not hard to achieve with this experience. The owner, Bogart Kealoha, has years of commercial and military experience and *knows* this island of his birth. His company has a flawless flight record and has grown into one of the largest and best-regarded helicopter companies on the island. From smooth liftoff to gentle landing, you are in good hands with Ohana.

Island Helicopters, 808/245-8588 or 800/829-5999, website: www.islandhelicopters.com, flies about 16 flights a day and has a booth near the Lihu'e commuter terminal. **South Sea Helicopters,** 808/245-2222 or 800/367-2914, website: www.southseahelicopters.com, is owned and operated by Dennis Esaki, a local pilot with plenty of knowledge and experience. South Sea has a counter at the main airport terminal building. **Will Squyres Helicopters,** 808/245-8881 or 888/245-4354, website: www.helicopters-hawaii.com, is a small operation with personalized service from an owner who loves his work. At **Air Kauai,** 808/246-4666 or 800/972-4666, website: www.airkauai.com, owner and pilot Charles DiPiazza takes personal care of you in his air-conditioned AS350B; only seven flights per day are offered.

Several reputable companies fly from Burns Field in Hanapepe. **Bali Hai Helicopters,** 808/335-3166 or 800/325-8687, website: www.balihai-helitour.com, has an office along the highway in town. Almost adjacent is the office of **Hawaii Helicopters,** 808/826-6591 or 800/367-7095, website: www.hawaiiheli.com. Hawaii Helicopters, which flies twin-engine machines, also maintains an office at the airport in Hanalei, the only company to do so, and operates tours on Maui and the Big Island as well. **Inter-Island Helicopters,** 808/335-5009, flies a Hughes 500 four-seater with the doors off to give you a real open-air experience. Besides the basic tour, one includes a waterfall picnic stop on private land. Its office is in the hanger at the west end of town.

Ni'ihau Helicopters, P.O. Box 450, Kaumakani, HI 96747, 808/335-3500 or 877/441-3500, has an office in the old sugar town of Kaumakani but flies out of Burns Field. The primary purpose of Ni'ihau Helicopters is to provide medical and emergency treatment for the residents of Ni'ihau. However, to defray costs, occasional tourist charters are offered on its twin-engine Agusta 109A, when there are enough passengers. The flight runs 3–4 hours, one hour of flight time with about two hours on a beach on Ni'ihau. Rates are $250 per person with six passengers and $338 with four passengers. While it cannot compete for scenery with helicopter companies that regularly fly only over Kaua'i, it does offer you the only way to see Ni'ihau close at hand.

Note: On October 26, 1995, the FAA instituted regulation S472, stipulating that all commercial air-tour operators fly at an elevation of no less than 1,500 feet and maintain a lateral standoff of 1,500 feet from canyon walls. The majority of the helicopter tour operators now have been granted an elevation deviation of 1,000 or 500 feet, but the lateral standoff remains. If you have flown on Kaua'i before and remember descending deep into the canyons and hovering within an arm's length of waterfalls, don't expect a repeat performance. Don't be discouraged, though; despite the new restrictions, the tours are still outstanding and offer the thrill of a lifetime.

Fixed-wing Air Tours

Kumulani Air, 808/246-9123, will take you above Kaua'i's sand and surf in its Piper Chieftan. Tours include a three-island flyover of Ni'ihau, Lehua, and Kaua'i in air-conditioned comfort for $139.

Forty-minute and 60-minute round-island Kaua'i tours go for $49 and $79, respectively. A five-hour "off-island" flight leaves Kaua'i and skirts the north coast of all the islands down to the Big Island, where you will see some volcano activity. After a stop in Hilo for refueling, your return trip is via the south shore of the islands; $240. Also for $240 is a seven-hour flight to Moloka'i, where you get a ground tour and lunch at Kalaupapa National Historical Park, a former lepers' colony. All prices are per person. A two-passenger minimum is needed for the Kaua'i flights, four for the flight of Moloka'i and Kalaupapa, and at least six passengers for the big trip down the state and back. Flights leave from the commuter terminal at the Lihu'e Airport.

Ultralight Power Hang Gliding

Birds in Paradise, 808/822-5309, website: www.birdsinparadise.com, instructs you how to soar above the emerald green and azure blue of Kaua'i in a 70 horsepower ultralight power glider. Instructor Gerry Charlebois has thrilled thousands of brave and slightly wacky souls in the skies above Kaua'i. He describes his apparently skyworthy craft as a "motorcycle with wings" and advertises that it's "the most fun you can have with your clothes on." Safety features include a backup rocket parachute that will bring the entire craft safely to the ground and a surprising structural strength certified twice as strong as a Cessna and capable of withstanding six Gs positive load and three Gs negative. This state-of-the-art tandem glider needs only about 100 feet for takeoff and landing, and Gerry has mounted both a video and a still camera so you can write back home, "Look, Mom. No hands." Prices are $95 for a 30-minute lesson, $165 for one hour. Advanced instructional flights run $240 for 90 minutes and $315 for two hours. All flights leave from Burns Field in Hanapepe.

SHOPPING

Kaua'i has plenty of shops of all varieties. There are several extensive shopping malls, boutiques and specialty stores here and there, food stores in every town, health food stores and farmers' markets, and even a flea market. The following is merely an overview.

SHOPPING CENTERS

In and Around Lihu'e
The **Kukui Grove Shopping Center,** on the west side of Lihu'e along Kaumuali'i Highway (Route 50), is the largest shopping mall on Kaua'i. Anchored by Sears, Liberty House, and Longs Drug Store, its more than 40 shops cluster around an open courtyard and have everything from food to fashions, sports gear to artwork, and general merchandise to gifts. In a new section to the side are Borders Books and Kmart stores; Wal-Mart is across town near the hospital.

Not much is left at the **Lihu'e Shopping Center** near the county building except for a Big Save supermarket, but down Rice Street is the **Rice Shopping Center,** with several local eateries, a laundromat, health food store, and bowling alley. In Nawiliwili is the **Pacific Ocean Plaza,** with several restaurants, and just down the road is the **Anchor Cove Shopping Center,** bright and new with clothing stores, several good restaurants, a convenience store, and various boutiques. Aside from these centers, individual shops are along the main drag, mostly between Hardy Street and Ahukini Road.

On the Coconut Coast
The **Coconut Marketplace,** an extensive shopping mall, is along the Kuhio Highway (Route 56) in Waipouli between Wailua and Kapa'a. While smaller in size, the Coconut Marketplace has more shops than Kukui Grove—nearly 70—in a very attractive open-air setting. Aside from the numerous clothing, jewelry, and gift shops, there are about a dozen restaurant and snack shops, plus a cinema. In its courtyard is a huge banyan tree, a lookout tower, and colorful sculptures made of pipes, fittings, and machinery from old sugar mills.

The **Kauai Village,** built on the theme of a 19th-century Main Street and boasting its own small museum, is modern, large, and diverse. One of Kaua'i's newest shopping centers, Kauai Village offers a Safeway supermarket and Longs Drugs store, a bookshop, two art galleries, clothing and jewelry store, the best health food store on the island, and several restaurants, including the fine-dining A Pacific Cafe.

Along Kuhio Highway in Wailua, Waipouli, and Kapa'a, half a dozen smaller shopping centers line the road. Starting from the Route 580 turnoff at the Wailua River, the first is the Kinipopo Shopping Village. Beyond that, the others include **Waipouli Town Center, Waipouli Plaza,** and **Waipouli Complex,** all on the *mauka* side of the highway in rapid succession. Finally, just before the main part of Kapa'a, is **Kapa'a Shopping Center,** the largest of these complexes, with the greatest variety of stores.

Downtown Kapa'a has many individual shops along its main street, mostly from the Pono Kai condo to the old town park, with a handful of stores beyond that.

Along the North Shore
While Anahola just has a convenience store and an eatery, Kilauea has more shopping. One little cluster is right off the highway as you enter town, but a greater concentration of better shops is a few blocks in at the **Kong Lung Center.** From Kilauea, there is little until you reach Princeville. **The Princeville Center,** the newest and largest on the north shore, provides the main shopping for the residents of this planned community. Here are banks, a supermarket, restaurants, and many clothing, gift, and general merchandise shops. In Hanalei, you'll find a wide selection of stores and eateries at both the **Ching Young Shopping Village** and the **Hanalei Center.**

Koloa and Po'ipu
The raised walkways of Old Koloa Town hold many fine shops, restaurants, and galleries. As a primarily residential area, it holds supermarkets, banks, a medical clinic, and a post office.

Down the road toward Poʻipu is the tiny Poʻipu Plaza, but the main shopping in this resort community is at the **Poʻipu Shopping Center,** an attractive open-air cluster of shops and restaurants geared toward the tourist.

The West End
Kalaheo has a handful of mostly restaurants as you come up the rise into town. Down toward the water is the only mall on this end of the island. It is the proletarian **Eleele Shopping Center** at the turnoff to Port Allen Harbor. Hanapepe, known for its cluster of art galleries along the old main street, also has businesses along the highway. Like Hanapepe, Waimea has a whole gaggle of stores along the highway, some primarily for residents, others geared toward tourists, but no shopping malls. From there on out, there is nothing to the end of the road except a couple of shops in Kekaha and the Kokeʻe Lodge Princeville up the hill in the state park.

SPECIALTY SHOPS, ARTS, AND BOUTIQUES

Fine Art Galleries
The longest-lasting part of a journey is the memory of that journey, which can instantly transport you through space and time to recapture the sublime beauty of the moment. One of the best catalysts for recapturing this memory is an inspirational work of art. **Kahn Galleries** specializes in original artworks and limited-edition prints created by some of the finest artists Hawaii has to offer. Kahn Galleries has several locations: in the old schoolhouse in Hanalei, in Koloa in the main building that faces you as you enter town, at the Kilohana Plantation just west of Lihuʻe, and in the Kauai Village Shopping Center in Kapaʻa. **Island Images,** its discount gallery, is at Coconut Marketplace. The master artists and works displayed by Kahn Galleries include Ray Tabora, who creates dramatic seascapes of wind-whipped palms and crashing surf made magically mysterious by the light of a translucent moon or illuminated by a glorious sunset; H. Leung and his sons, Thomas and Richard, landscape impressionists who blend the techniques of east and west into paintings of provocative, dazzling beauty; world-famous George Sumner,

a much-copied but never equaled environmental impressionist; and the extremely talented Makk family—Meriko, Eva, and A. D.—who work in oil on canvas.

Wyland Galleries, with shops on all the major islands, has galleries at Kauai Village shopping center and the Poʻipu Shopping Village. The artist Wyland is known for his whale murals, of which he has painted dozens around the world. The one you will definitely see here is on a two-story building at the Kauai Village shopping center. Wyland Galleries represents many well-known island artists, including Al Hogue, Jim Warren, John Pitre, and Mike Maiden, mostly painters and sculptors.

Two individual galleries worth noting are the **Ship Store Galleries** at the Coconut Marketplace, which handles predominantly nautical artworks and antiques of all sorts, and the **Kim Taylor Reece Gallery** in downtown Kapaʻa, where photographs are the theme. For a variety of artists' work in one place, visit the shops at **Kilohana,** where numerous well-known and not so well-known artists with works in various mediums are represented in a half dozen galleries. Major hotels also have art galleries in house, but it seems that their artists come from a broader spectrum. Some of the artwork may be by local talent, but much is by Mainland or even foreign artists.

Old Hanapepe Town has a string of more than a dozen fine-art shops and studios along the main drag. The most well known is the James Hoyle Gallery at the west end. James Hoyle uses a mixture of oil, pastel, and polymer, which he applies to canvas in a distinctive style of macro-pointillism with an element of Van Gogh. Each daub, like a melted jelly bean, is a rich color, and the result is an expression of rural culture and naturalism. Other fine artists in town are Dawn Traina, who does multimedia canvas work, watercolorist Arius Hopman, Kim Starr with pastels and serigraphs, and the surrealist Lew Shortbridge.

Specialty Shops
Kauaʻi, like all the islands, has specialty shops worthy of note. The **Kauaʻi Museum Shop** on Rice Street in Lihuʻe has perhaps the island's best selection of Kauaʻian arts and crafts at reasonable prices, as well as books on Hawaii. For

other art and craft items made on Kaua'i, try **Kauai Products Store** in the Kukui Grove Center in Lihu'e. In tiny Kapaia, on the north edge of Lihu'e, is **Kapaia Stitchery**, which has the island's best selection of beautiful handmade quilts. Across the street is **Kapaia Trading Company,** an unusual name for a shop that carries fine handmade furniture from native woods and the island's best selection of cigars and humidors.

The old standby in Kilauea, established over a century ago as an ordinary dry goods store, is **Kong Lung Store,** which now prides itself on being an "exotic gift emporium" and carries craft and gift items, jewelry and fine fashions, and much more. Kilauea is also home to the **Island Soap Co.** Here, and in a second store in Koloa, a husband and wife team hand-pours soap and perfumes the raw bars with heady fragrances like coconut, plumeria, and ginger. They also produce self-pampering products like scented coconut oils, lotions, and bath gels capturing the scents of the islands.

Luxury hotel shops carry high-end fashions and alohawear, art, and sundries.

Flea Markets
Excellent bargains are found at **Spouting Horn Flea Market,** at the end of the road west of Po'ipu Beach, where vendors set up stalls selling cut-rate merchandise.

Bookstores
The most extensive bookstores on Kaua'i are Borders Books and Music and Waldenbooks. **Waldenbooks** has one shop at Kauai Village between Wailua and Kapa'a, 808/822-7749, generally open Mon.–Sat. 9 A.M.–8 P.M. and Sunday 9 A.M.–5 P.M., and featuring racks of books on everything from Hawaiiana to travel, along with maps, postcards, stationery, and some souvenirs. **Borders Books and Music,** 808/246-0862, in the Kukui Grove Shopping Phase II, near Kmart, is an excellent full-service bookstore, music center, and coffee bar. Shelves, attended by a very knowledgeable staff, hold bestsellers, Hawaiiana, children's books, travel guides, and a wide variety of special-interest publications. There is a computer center there and a fine coffee lounge where you can revitalize with a latte and a sweet while perusing your new

PERSONALIZED NOVEL

Perhaps the most one-of-a-kind gift that you can take home from Kaua'i is a book called *Kauai Calling.* This little novel is written with you and your sweetie as the main characters and Kaua'i as the backdrop. Reading and rereading this romantic adventure where you play the main parts should be a kick for you and all your friends and family back home. Written by Ron Christmas and Amy King, your names and some basic information about you are plugged into the text and, like magic (or should I say, like the work of the Menehune), you have your book the next morning, complete, printed, and bound. If it would intrigue you to star in this adventure, contact the authors at Paradise Works, Inc., P.O. Box 1058, Koloa, HI 96756, 808/742-2457, website: www.ParadiseWorks-Inc.com, or stop by the Accents shop at the Hyatt Regency Hotel in Po'ipu to meet one of the authors.

purchase. Open Mon.–Thurs. 8:30 A.M.–10 P.M., Friday and Saturday until 11 P.M., and Sunday until 8 P.M.

Of the independent shops, that with the widest selection of Hawaiiana and Kaua'iana is the gift shop at the **Kaua'i Museum.** Others to check for books on these subjects are the **Koke'e Natural History Museum** in Koke'e State Park, the **National Tropical Botanical Garden Visitor Center** in Po'ipu, the **Lumaha'i Garden Visitor Center** west of Ha'ena, and the **Kilauea Lighthouse Visitor Center** and **Kong Lung Store** in Kilauea. Numerous gift shops throughout the island and hotel sundries shops also carry books on Hawaiian subjects. Books on health, cooking, natural foods, metaphysics, spiritualism, and self-help can be found at **Papaya's Natural Food and Cafe** in Kapa'a and at **Hanalei Natural Foods** in Hanalei.

For books on diving, snorkeling, reef fish, and marine topics, check dive shops and water sport activities shops. Some outdoor adventure shops carry books on camping, hiking, and natural history.

Film and Film Developing
Color slide film and color and black and white print film are available on Kaua'i, but color print

KAUA'I

film is most widely available. Camera shops carry the widest variety but film can also be found at gift shops, sundries stores, most activities outlets, and general merchandise stores throughout the island. For comparison, a roll of ISO 200 or 400, 36-exposure print film generally runs $7–7.50, and color slide film costs $6–8. Standard film developing usually runs about $2.50 for color prints with each print at about 40 cents, or $8 for a roll of 36-exposure slide film.

For film and film developing, **Longs Drugs** in Kapa'a or Lihu'e and **Kmart** and **Wal-Mart** in Lihu'e are as reasonable as anywhere. Independent film developers are found in all major towns on the island. Try: **Westside Fast Photo** in Waimea, **Koloa One Hour Photo** in Koloa, **Photo Spectrum** across from McDonald's along Kuhio Highway in Lihu'e, **Wolf Camera** in the Coconut Marketplace in Wailua, **Cameralab** in Kapa'a, and the **Bali Hai Photo Co.** at the Ching Young Center in Hanalei.

FOOD STORES

Supermarkets

Groceries and picnic supplies can be purchased in almost every town on the island. Many of the markets in the smaller towns also sell a limited selection of dry goods and gifts. The general rule is, the smaller the store the bigger the price. The largest and cheapest stores with the biggest selections are in Lihu'e and Kapa'a.

Kaua'i's own **Big Save** value centers sell groceries, produce, fruit, meats, liquor, health aids, gift items, and magazines in 'Ele'ele, Hanalei, Kapa'a, Koloa, Lihu'e, and Waimea. Most stores are open weekdays 8:30 A.M.–9 P.M., weekends until 6 P.M. Operated by Big Save are the smaller but well-stocked **Menehune Food Marts**, found in Kalaheo, Kekaha, Kilauea, and Lawa'i.

Large **Foodland** supermarkets, open 5 A.M.–midnight, operate at the Waipouli Town Center and the Princeville Center. The Princeville store is the largest and best-stocked market on the north shore.

Star Market has a well-stocked store in the Kukui Grove Shopping Center, open 6 A.M.–11 P.M.

Safeway, in the Kauai Village Shopping Center along the Kuhio Highway in Waipouli between Wailua and Kapa'a, is a large well-stocked supermarket open 24 hours.

Smaller individual markets around the island include **Kojima's** and **Pono Market** in Kapa'a, where you can stock up not only on food items and dry goods, but also on local color. North from Kapa'a are **Whalers General Store** in Anahola and the **Kilauea Farmers' Market** in Kilauea.

Along the south coast, independent groceries include the **Sueoka Store** in Koloa, the **Kukuiula Store** at the turnoff in Po'ipu, and the **Ishihara Market** in Waimea.

Health-food Stores

Papaya's Natural Foods & Cafe, 808/823-0190, open 9 A.M.–8 P.M. daily except Sunday at the Kauai Village Shopping Center in Kapa'a, is the largest and best natural-food store on Kaua'i. Coolers and shelves are stocked with organic fruits and vegetables, beers and wines, wholegrain breads, organic teas and flavored coffees, grains, dried beans, spices, homeopathic medicines, cruelty-free cosmetics, vitamins, minerals, and an assortment of biodegradable cleaning products. The café section has a display case filled with homemade pastries and other goodies, salads and deli entrées, or you can order a freshly made sandwich or full meal to have at the tables outside. If you are into healthy organic food, there is no place better than Papaya's!

If not the best, at least the most down-to-earth health-food store on Kaua'i is **Ambrose's Kapuna Natural Foods,** 808/822-7112, along the Kuhio Highway across from the Foodland Supermarket in Kapa'a. Ambrose is a character worth visiting just for the fun of it. His store is well stocked with juices, nuts, grains, island fruits, vitamins and minerals, and plenty of bananas. Ambrose has one of the largest collections of the big old boards on the island. If he's not in the store just give a holler around the back. He's there!

Vim N' Vigor, 808/245-9053, in the Rice Shopping Center, open Mon.–Sat. 8 A.M.–6 P.M., specializes in vitamins, minerals, and other supplements. The shelves are stocked with a good but limited selection of items from wholewheat flour to spices, organic pastas, and teas. The back deli case holds a small selection of fresh organic vegetables and prepared deli sandwiches.

On the north shore, try **Hanalei Health and Natural Foods,** 808/826-6990, in the Ching Young Village; open daily. Although cramped, this little store has a good vibe and a reasonable selection of bulk foods, fresh produce, hand-squeezed juices, vitamins, and books, as well as a good selection of cosmetics, incense, candles, and massage oils.

General Nutrition Center, 808/245-6657, in the Kukui Grove Center, is a full-service health-food store.

Farmers' Markets

The county-sponsored **Sunshine Farmers' Markets,** featuring mostly organic produce, flowers, and some craft items, are held six days a week at different towns around the island: Monday at noon at the ball park in Koloa; Tuesday at 3:30 P.M. at the Kalaheo Neighborhood Center; Wednesday at 3 P.M. at the New Town Park in Kapa'a; Thursday at 3:30 P.M. at Hanapepe Town Park and also at 4:30 P.M. at the Kilauea Neighborhood Center; Friday at 3 P.M. in Lihu'e at Vidinha Stadium; and Saturday at 9 A.M. at the Kekaha Neighborhood Center. Private farmers' markets are also held on the island: one on Monday at 3 P.M. at the back side of the Kukui Grove Shopping Center, Tuesday 2–4 P.M. in Waipa outside Hanalei, and 9–11 A.M. on Saturday in Kilauea. Farmers bring their produce to town; a large selection of island produce can be had at very good prices. Get there early; the best pickings are gone in the first hour. The stories and local color are even more delicious than the fruit.

Fish Markets

Waters around Kaua'i produce great quantities of excellent fresh fish. Unless you know the captain of a fishing boat, you'll probably have to get your fish from a fish market. Several around the island have good selections and reputations to match. When you're here, have a good look in the deli case for the various fish, seafood, and seaweed preparations, many that you won't find elsewhere.

An excellent fish store is the **Pono Market,** 808/822-0955, in Kapa'a, open Mon.–Sat. 9 A.M.–8:30 P.M. and Sunday till 6 P.M. It has fresh fish daily and often offers specials.

G's Fishco, 4361 Rice St., Lihu'e, 808/246-4440, open weekdays 10 A.M.–8 P.M., Saturday until 7 P.M., and Sunday until 5 P.M., offers cold cases filled with whole fish, *poki,* sashimi, and assorted seafood.

Ara's Sakana-ya, in the Hanama'ulu Plaza in Hanama'ulu, 808/245-1707, open Mon.–Sat. 9 A.M.–7 P.M. and Sunday 9 A.M.–5 P.M., is a takeout deli-restaurant that offers plate lunches, Japanese *bento,* and fresh fish daily.

For fresh fish, fish preparations, and deli foods, try **The Fish Express,** 3343 Kuhio Hwy., Lihu'e, 808/245-9918.

ACCOMMODATIONS

Kaua'i is very lucky when it comes to places to stay. It's been blessed by a combination of happenstance and planning. The island was not a major Hawaiian destination until the early '70s. By that time, all concerned had wised up to the fact that what you *don't do* is build endless miles of high-rise hotels and condos that blot out the sun and ruin the view of the coast. Besides that, a very strong grassroots movement here insisted on tastefully done low-rise structures that blend into and complement the surrounding natural setting. This concept mandates "destination resorts," the kind of hotels and condos that lure visitors because of their superb architecture, artistic appointments, and luxurious grounds. There is room for growth on Kaua'i, but the message is clear: Kaua'i is the most beautiful island of them all, and the preservation of this delicate beauty benefits everyone.

Kaua'i has about 7,000 accommodation units in roughly 175 properties, some 3,000 of which are condominium units. There are three major resort areas on Kaua'i: the Coconut Coast, Po'ipu south shore, and Princeville. The Coconut Coast is the oldest of these areas and has a concentration of condominiums; its occupancy rate and price per room are the lowest of the three main resort areas. Po'ipu, which has the best general-purpose beach and is the most popular destination on Kaua'i, was the first big resort development on the island, and it has a good mix of hotel, condo, B&B, and vacation rental properties. The

KAUA'I

cabin at Kahili Mountain State Park

ROBERT NILSEN

average price per room here and at Princeville is roughly the same. The north shore Princeville development has mostly condos and hotel rooms. In addition to these three areas, Lihu'e, which had the island's first major high-rise hotel, has one excellent destination resort and many modest family-run hotel/motels. On the outskirts of town are two affordable hotel and condo properties. Vacation rentals and B&Bs along the north shore are located primarily in Kilauea, Hanalei, and Ha'ena, and there is one condominium in Ha'ena, literally the last resort. Along the south shore, some rooms are available in Kalaheo, but there is not much from there to the west end, except one relaxing cottage-type property in Waimea. Scattered throughout the rest of the island are mostly vacation rental and B&B accommodations. Long stretches along the coast between the major centers have very little lodging.

Condo Booking and Reservations

The following is a partial list of companies with properties on Kaua'i. Vacation rental agencies listed below can also offer this service for condominiums.

Aston Hotels and Resorts, 2250 Kuhio Ave., Honolulu, HI 96815, 808/931-1400 or 800/922-7886 Mainland, 800/445-6633 Canada, or 800/321-2558 in Hawaii, website: aston-hotels.com

Go Condo Hawaii, 800/452-3463, website: www.gocondohawaii.com

Hawaii Condo Exchange, 800/442-0404, website: http://hawaiicondoexchange.com

Marc Resorts Hawaii, 2155 Kalakaua Ave., Honolulu, HI 96815, 808/926-5900 or 800/535-0085, website: marcresorts.com, email: marc@aloha.net

Outrigger Hotels and Resorts, 2375 Kuhio Ave., Honolulu, HI 96815, 800/688-7444, website: www.outrigger.com

Suite-Paradise, 1941 Po'ipu Rd., Po'ipu-Koloa, HI 96756, 808/742-6464 or 800/367-8020, website: www.suite-paradise.com, email: mail@suite-paradise.com

Vacation Rentals

Emerald Isle Properties, 4244 Kilauea Rd, Kilauea, 808/828-1111 or 800/828-1442, website: www.kauai-vacations-realty.com, handles mostly individual vacation homes in the Kilauea vicinity, with others—including condo units—along the north shore to the end of the road. More than 50 choices.

Garden Island Properties, 4-928 Kuhio Hwy., 808/822-4871 or 800/801-0378, website: www.kauaiproperties.com, email: stricko@kauaiproperties.com, manages more than two dozen vacation rentals and numerous condo units mostly from Kapa'a to Miloli'i on the east side of the island.

Garden Island Rentals, 808/742-9537 or 800/247-5599, fax 808/742-9540, website: www.kauairentals.com, email: gir@kauairentals

.com, rents mostly high-end vacation homes and a few condo units, exclusively in the Po'ipu area. Homes rent by the week for $800–4,500, and condo units cost $100–225 a night with a four-night minimum stay.

Grantham Resorts, 808/742-9469, 800/325-5791 or 800/742-1412, fax 808/742-9093, website: www.grantham-resorts.com, email: info@grantham-resorts.com, is in Koloa and has been managing both condo units and private homes exclusively in Po'ipu since 1984 through its Vacation Homes of Kauai and Po'ipu Vacation Rentals divisions. The condo units range from economy to plush and the private home rentals run from affordable to very expensive.

Hanalei North Shore Properties, Princeville Center, P.O. Box 607, Hanalei, HI 96714, 808/826-9622 or 800/488-3336, website: www.planet-hawaii.com/visit-kauai, email: hnsp@aloha.net, handles more than five dozen vacation rental homes and condos in Princeville and along the north shore from Anahola to Ha'ena.

Kauai Vacation Rentals, 3-3311 Kuhio Hwy., Lihu'e, HI 96766, 808/245-8841 or 800/357-5025, website: www.KauaiVacationaRentals.com, email: aloha@kvrre.com, is the only agency that handles condos and vacation rental homes throughout the island. From Kekaha on the west end to the end of the road on the north shore,

more than 130 units in all price ranges are under its management.

Na Pali Properties, Inc., P.O. Box 475, Hanalei, HI 96714, 808/826-7272 or 800/715-7273, website: www.napaliprop.com, email: nal@aloha.net, at the Ching Young Village, has everything from $500-a-week cottages to $4,500-a-week homes on the beach.

Pacific Paradise Properties, Princeville Center, P.O. Box 3195, Princeville, HI 96722, 808/826-7211 or 800/800-3637, website: www.princeville-vacations.com, email: kaikona@gte.net, also deals almost exclusively with a smaller number of high-end condo and home properties in Princeville.

Real Estate Kauai.Com, at the Princeville Center, P.O. Box 3578, Princeville, HI 96722, 808/826-9675, website: www.real-estate-kauai.com, email: rek@aloha.net, has a limited selection of high-end condo and home rentals almost exclusively in Princeville.

R&R Realty and Rentals, 808/742-7555, 800/367-8022, fax 808/742-1559, website: www.r7r.com, email: randr@r7r.com, arranges low- to midrange condo rentals in Po'ipu.

Hostels

At present, there is only one hostel on Kaua'i—the **Hawaii International Hostel,** 4532 Lehua

---

TIME-SHARES

While time-share accommodations are a factor on all the major islands except Lana'i, Kaua'i has taken to it in a big way. Time-share units, whether condo apartments or hotel suites, are handled in various ways. Generally speaking, specific units are bought for a specified length of time during the year, usually in one-week increments, guaranteeing you vacation accommodations year after year—whether you use them or not. With some organizations, these units can be traded for rooms in other associated time-share complexes around the country (or world). If you do not use your time-share during your time slot, most overseeing companies can rent it for you for that time. With some time-share groups, no specific units are negotiated, but points are bought and these can be used to reserve space wherever the company has properties. The price of purchasing a time-

share unit varies based on its luxury and location, and additional annual fees are charged for maintenance and administration. Units are sold directly through time-share companies, some real estate agents, and time-share resale offices. Time-share companies have requirements for sales that may include, among other things, ownership of a house, specific minimum income level, and U.S. citizenship. One of the favorite means employed by time-share companies to get you to look at their units is to offer greatly reduced activity prices—you'll see these activities booths all over the island—in exchange for your attendance at a seminar and sales session. If you don't mind the sales pitch and accompanying pressure to purchase, try one out. Others wouldn't waste their time with such dealings while on vacation, even if it meant reduced activity rates.

St., Kapa'a HI 96746, 808/823-6142. Rates are $16 for a dorm bunk or $40 for a private room, with reduced rates for those with IYH cards. Dorms are either four- or six-bunk rooms, each with its own bathroom; a female dorm is available. Facilities include a large communal kitchen with good appliances, a lounge with comfortable couches and cable TV, a covered outdoor lanai with a pocket billiard table, a laundry room, and an office safe for valuables. Various daytime tours of the island are also offered for $40.

FOOD

Lu'au

When asked about recommendations for a lu'au on Kaua'i, nearly everyone suggests **Smith's Tropical Paradise Garden Lu'au,** held within the Tropical Paradise Gardens along the banks of the Wailua River. As with most such lu'au, this one starts with an *imu* ceremony, followed by drinks and a full buffet meal. While the food is not necessarily better than anywhere else, the entertainment is different and separate from the meal. Not the typical Polynesian review, here the spectacle includes Hawaiian music, a fiery volcanic eruption, and dances from all the major ethnic groups that have made Hawaii their home. Held Monday, Wednesday, and Friday, the gates open at 5 P.M.; $52 for adults, $27 for children 7–13, and $18 for ages 3–7. Check-in for the pageant only is at 7:30 P.M.; $14 for adults, $7 for kids under age 12. Call 808/821-6895 or 808/821-6896 for reservations—a must—or pick up tickets at the garden entrance or at the Smith's booth across from the entrance to the Coco Palms Hotel on the north side of the river mouth.

The **Kauai Coconut Beach Resort** presents a daily lu'au, 6–8:30 P.M., at its *lu'au halau* under a canopy of stars and palm trees. The *imu* ceremony takes place at 6:15 P.M. so you can see the pig taken from the pit and readied for the meal. Hawaiian- and local-style food is served from 6:30, with cocktails ongoing until the show begins. Afterward, you lean back and watch Hawaiian-only music and dance—no extrava-ganza, just fine sights and sounds. The enthusiastic entertainment is a combination of *kahiko* (ancient hula) and *awana* (modern hula), performed by an accomplished troupe of both men and women. Most numbers are *kahiko*—dignified, refined, and low-keyed portrayals of the tales and myths of ancient Hawaii. Intermixed are *awana* numbers, startling, colorful, and reminiscent of the days when Elvis was still the gyrating king of *Blue Hawaii.* Admission for adults is $55, $50 for seniors, $33 for children age 12–17, and $23 for the little ones 3–11; call 808/822-3455 for reservations.

Reflections of Paradise takes place at the Kilohana Carriage House Monday and Thursday at 6:30 P.M. The evening starts here with a roast pig and other goodies being taken from the *imu.* The full buffet is followed by a show of music and dance from all of Polynesia, both ancient and modern, that you may be invited to participate in. Adults are $49, seniors $45, and children 6–14 $20; call 808/245-9593 for reservations.

Pa'ina 'O Hanalei beachside lu'au is performed at the Princeville Hotel on Monday and Thursday evenings at 6 P.M. near the swimming pool at the hotel. Food is prepared by the hotel kitchen and the performance is a rousing Polynesian review. Many members of the cast also perform at the more casual Tahiti Nui lu'au down in Hanalei. Adults $59.50, children 6–12 $30; seniors get discounts. Call 808/826-2788 for reservations.

Downhome and thoroughly local, **Tahiti Nui** presents a full buffet and Polynesian show every Wednesday 5–8 P.M. in Hanalei. Since 1963, this family-run operation has served real Hawaiian food and offered a show that's not glitzy extravaganza or slick production. This lu'au is very casual Kaua'ian, and everybody has a good time. Adults $52, $30 teens, and $20 for children 3–11; call 808/826-6277 for reservations.

The only lu'au on the south coast is **Drums of Paradise,** held at the Hyatt Regency in Po'ipu every Thursday and Sunday evening 6–8:30 P.M. Presented on the lawn of the lower garden, the full buffet dinner is followed by an elaborate and high-energy Polynesian show. Adult $59.50, children 6–12 years $29.75.

GETTING THERE

Until very recently, there were no nonstop flights to Kaua'i. All passengers had to go through Honolulu to get to Kaua'i. Since 1999, United Airlines has run daily fights from Los Angeles, and weekly summer flights from San Francisco, to Kaua'i, and is currently the only airline with nonstop flights to the island. All other major domestic and foreign carriers fly to Honolulu and have arrangements with either Hawaiian Airlines or Aloha Airlines for getting you to Kaua'i. If you fly from the Mainland with Hawaiian or Aloha, you have the added convenience of dealing with just one airline to get you to Kaua'i. Several charter airlines also fly to Kaua'i nonstop from the Mainland.

Kaua'i's Airport

Lihu'e Airport, less than two miles from downtown Lihu'e, receives all of Kaua'i's commercial flights. On arrival, you're immediately struck by the warm balmy temperature and gentle island breezes. No public transportation to or from the airport is available, so you must either rent a car or hire a taxi. The terminal, long and low, has arrival lounges at both ends and the departure lounge in the middle. In the departure lounge are a restaurant and cocktail lounge, snack shop, flower shop, gift shop, restrooms, public telephones, mailboxes, and change machines. The lobby has a handful of suitcase-size coin lockers; $1 for the first half hour, $1 for each half hour after that, and a 24-hour maximum use for $6. For larger items, overnight storage is available at $3 a bag or $4 for larger bags; contact the porter service 6 A.M.–8:30 P.M. for this service. The gift shop sells pre-inspected island fruit that's boxed and ready to transport. For your entertainment, Hawaiian music is performed in the main lobby 9–11:30 A.M. on Monday, Wednesday, and Friday. Baggage pickup is at either end, Aloha and United to the left as you enter the terminal from the plane, Hawaiian Airlines to the right—follow the signs. Each baggage claim area contains restrooms, public telephones, change machines, and free tourist brochures. Outside the baggage claim areas are tourist information booths (usually staffed) with additional brochures and a courtesy phone for information. Check-in counters are along the outside corridor of the central section—Hawaiian Airlines on the left and Aloha and United on the right as you look at the terminal building. Additional space is used by South Sea Helicopter and the charter airlines, Skyservice USA and Canada 3000. All non-carry-on baggage must go through an agricultural inspection at the terminal entrance; carry-on luggage is run through X-ray machines. All major car rental agencies maintain booths just outside the main entranceway, and each has a base lot beyond the airport ring road that is serviced by van pickup. Public parking is 5:30 A.M.–9:45 P.M. Parking fees run $1 for the first half hour, $1 for each additional hour, with a $7 maximum up to 24 hours. Taxi stands are at both ends of the terminal, and a courtesy taxi phone can be found at each outside tourist information counter.

The old terminal at the Lihu'e Airport, a few hundred yards down Ahukini Road, is now used by flight-see airplane and interisland charter companies. Across the street is the heliport, used actively by eight helicopter companies offering sightseeing tours of the island.

Burns Field (Port Allan Airport) in Hanapepe was the first commercial airstrip on the island, but it hasn't been used as such for years. There are no facilities here whatsoever, and the strip is used only by three helicopter and one ultralight aircraft tour companies.

Princeville Airport, along Route 56 just east of Princeville, served commercial commuter air flights until the mid-1990s, when those routes were discontinued. Today it is used by an occasional private plane that only needs a short runway, but it is frequented much more by the Hawaii Helicopter company and is often referred to by residents of the area as the heliport. The terminal is a cute little building made inconspicuous by the immense beauty surrounding it. Here you'll find a toilet, telephone, an Avis car rental office, and Amelia's Cafe and lounge (upstairs).

Interisland Carriers

The majority of flights from **Hawaiian Airlines,** 800/367-5320 Mainland and Canada, 800/882-8811 statewide, or 808/245-4516 on Kaua'i,

LIHU'E AIRPORT

To Town

AHUKINI RD

570

51

RENTAL CAR OFFICES

KAPULE HWY

RICE ST

51

PARKING

RENTAL CAR BOOTHS

TERMINAL

HELIPORT

OLD TERMINAL

To East Shore

0   0.25 mi

0   0.25 km

© SANDRA E. BISIGNANI TRUST AND AVALON TRAVEL PUBLISHING, INC.

website: www.hawaiianair.com, are to and from Honolulu, with about a dozen and a half per day in each direction. Hawaiian Airlines flights to Lihu'e from Honolulu begin at 5:35 A.M., with flights thereafter about every hour until 8 P.M. Flights from Lihu'e to Honolulu begin at 6:35 A.M. and go all day until 9 P.M. There are nearly as many flights to/from Kahului, Maui, starting around 6:30 A.M. and running until almost 7 P.M. Eleven flights a day go from Lihu'e to Kona on the Big Island, while eight a day go to Hilo, on the opposite side of the island, all spaced throughout the day. Twice a day, Lihu'e is connected with Lana'i and Moloka'i. Hawaiian Airlines partners with American Airlines, Continental Airlines, and Northwest Airlines.

Aloha Airlines, 800/367-5250 Mainland and Canada, 808/245-3691 on Kaua'i, website: www.alohaairlines.com, with its all-jet fleet of 737s, offers more flights to Kaua'i than any other interisland carrier. It flies from Honolulu to Lihu'e about two dozen times per day beginning at 5:30 A.M. with the last flight at 8 P.M.; return flights to Honolulu start at 6:30 A.M., with the last at 9 P.M. Multiple flights throughout the day to/from Maui begin at around 6:30 A.M. and run until after 7 P.M. About a dozen flights a day connect Lihu'e with both Hilo and Kona on the Big Island, spaced throughout the day. Aloha Airlines has no flights from Kaua'i to either Moloka'i or Lana'i. Aloha Airlines partners with United Airlines.

Charter Airlines
I\f you've got the bucks or just need to go when there's no regularly scheduled flight, try **Kumulani Air,** 808/246-9123. Flights leave from the commuter terminal at the Lihu'e Airport.

KAUA'I

GETTING AROUND

The most common way to get around Kaua'i is by rental car. The abundance of agencies keeps prices competitive. As always, reserve during peak season, but in the off-season you may take your chances by shopping around to score a good deal. Kaua'i also has limited shuttle-bus service; expensive taxis; reasonable bicycle, moped, and scooter rentals; and the good old (legal) thumb.

Highway Overview

Kaua'i is nearly round, and one major highway nearly circles the island. Starting in Lihu'e and running north, Highway 56 (Kuhio Highway) goes as far as Ke'e Beach past Hanalei; running west, Highway 50 (Kaumuali'i Highway) runs past Kekaha nearly to Polihale. From the far northern end to the west end, it's about 70 miles and will take about two hours of driving time at a comfortable speed. Only a few major roadways lead off of this coast highway. In and near Lihu'e, they are: Route 570, which runs from the center of town to the airport; Route 51 leading from Hanama'ulu to Nawiliwili Harbor; Route 58 from Kukui Grove Shopping Center also to Nawiliwili Harbor; and Route 583, which goes to Wailua waterfall from Kapaia. North of Lihu'e, Route 580 runs inland from Wailua, and Route 581 circles inland from Kapa'a around the backside of the "Sleeping Giant" to meet Route 580. Along the south shore, Route 520 leaves Route 50 at the Tunnel of Trees and runs down to Koloa and Po'ipu, Route 530 connects Lawa'i and Koloa, and Route 540 sweeps down through the coffee plantation, running from Kalaheo to 'Ele'ele. The longest and most significant highway running off of the coast road is Route 550, connecting Kekaha to Koke'e State Park.

Auto Rental Agencies

The following major firms maintain booths at the Lihu'e Airport. Some companies have cars waiting at the airport, but most shuttle guests to the baseyard just beyond the airport circle road to pick up their vehicle.

Dollar, 808/245-3651 or 800/800-4000 worldwide, website: www.dollarcar.com

Alamo, 808/246-0646 or 800/327-9633, website: www.goalamo.com

National Car Rental, 808/245-5636 or 800/227-7368 nationwide, website: www.nationalcar.com

Avis, 808/245-3512 or 800/321-3712 nationwide, website: www.avis.com.

Budget, 877/283-2468 local or 800/527-0700 worldwide, website: www.drivebudget.com

Hertz, 808/245-3356 or 800/654-3011, website: www.hertz.com

Thrifty, 808/246-6252 or 800/367-2277 worldwide, website: www.thrifty.com

A local company with a reliable reputation is **Westside-U-Drive,** 808/332-8644. Avis is the only company that maintains a small booth at the Princeville Airport, 808/826-9773.

Vanity Cars

Hawaiian Riders, 808/822-5409 or 888/527-9484, website: www.hawaiianriders.com, has two rental offices on Kaua'i, one across from the Waipouli Town Center and the other in Po'ipu. Open 8 A.M.–7 P.M. How about a bright yellow Corvette convertible, or a hot red 1966 Porsche? Maybe a new Plymouth Prowler or the Dodge Viper is more your style. These cars are not cheap; if you want the look, you have to pay. They run from $119 a day for the Porsche to $450 a day for the Viper; part-day rentals can also be made. If you're looking for something more pedestrian, try a Chrysler convertible for $69 a day or $385 a week, or a 4WD Jeep for $79 a day. To rent one of these babies, you must be 21 years old and have a credit card in your name. Hawaiian Riders also rents motorcycles, mopeds, and bikes.

Scooters and Mopeds

These tiny two-wheelers are available from **Hawaiian Riders,** 808/822-5409 or 888/527-9484, with one office in Waipouli and another in Po'ipu. Rental rates range from $20 for two hours to $50 for 24 hours. This company also

KAUA'I

rents full-size motorcycles, exotic cars, and bicycles. To rent a moped or motorcycle, you must be 21 years old; a credit card is required for some, while a cash deposit is all right for others.

ALTERNATIVE TRANSPORTATION

The Kaua'i Bus

One of the benefits to come out of the destruction caused by Hurricane 'Iniki was the establishment of limited public bus transportation. The 'Iniki Express, set up after the hurricane and free at one time, has morphed into **The Kaua'i Bus,** run by the county Department of Transportation, 4396 Rice St., #104, Lihu'e, HI 96766, 808/241-6410. Write or call Mon.–Sat. 7 A.M.–5 P.M. for a current route schedule. Operating times are Mon.–Sat. 5:15 A.M.–6 P.M. (no operation Sunday and holidays). The regular fare is $1 ($25 for a monthly pass) or 50 cents for seniors, students, and people with disabilities if carrying I.D. ($12.50 for a monthly pass). The bus will pick up and drop off only at designated bus stops, and it does not allow large bags or items such as backpacks and boogie boards, but baby strollers are okay.

Each bus displays a route sign at the front and on its curb side. The Kaua'i Bus runs two main routes along the coast highway, north to Hanalei and west to Kekaha, with the addition of one circle route in Lihu'e and one route up to Kapahi above Kapa'a. Although buses have scheduled times, they do not run on regular intervals; there may be as little as one-half hour or as much as 2.5 hours between runs. Please check a current printed bus schedule. Route 100 runs from Kekaha to Lihu'e, and Route 200 makes the reverse run. One bus a day in each direction—early morning and late afternoon—dips down for a circle of Koloa and Po'ipu via Lawa'i before proceeding. Route 400 connects Hanalei to Lihu'e, and Route 500 does the reverse, while Route 600 runs from Lihu'e to Kapahi via Kapa'a and returns. The Lihu'e Extension, Route 700, 8 A.M.–3 P.M. only, starts at the Kukui Grove Shopping Center, runs down to Nawiliwili Harbor, and travels up Rice Street to the County Building. From there it goes along the highway to the Wilcox Hospital before returning to the center of town, Nawiliwili Harbor, and Kukui Grove Shopping Center. Saturday service is reduced by about half, with no service at all on routes 600 and 700. One wonders just how long this bus system will maintain funding—most of the buses seem to run nearly empty. If you do not have a rental car, it is possible to get around by bus, but it will not be convenient nor will it necessarily take you where you want to go.

Shuttle

Run by Trans Hawaiian, the **Coconut Coast Trolley** operates 10 A.M.–10 P.M. daily. The southbound route starts in Kapa'a at the ABC Store and runs via Kauai Village Shopping Center to the Wailua Marina before going on to Lihu'e. Northbound buses run from the Kaua'i Marriott at Nawiliwili Harbor to the Hilo Hattie store, Radisson Kauai Beach Hotel, Holiday Inn Sunspree Resort, and the Coconut Marketplace before continuing on to Kapa'a. A feeder route from the hotels in Po'ipu runs twice a day in each direction. The fare is $2 one-way or $5 for an all-day pass. Call 808/245-5108 for the current schedule.

Taxi

Taxis are all metered and charge a hefty price for their services; all have the same rates. While many are still sedans, minivans are increasing in number. Airport taxis have a monopoly on pickups at the airport, although others can drop off there. Sample fares: $5–8 from Lihu'e to the airport, $30–35 from Po'ipu to Lihu'e, $12–15 from Lihu'e to Wailua, $15–18 from Lihu'e to Kapa'a, $55 from Lihu'e to Waimea, $60 from Lihu'e to Princeville, and $25 from Princeville to Ke'e Beach and the Kalalau trailhead. Reputable taxi companies include **Akiko's,** 808/822-7588, in Kapa'a; **City Cab,** 808/245-3227, in Lihu'e; **Kauai Taxi,** 808/246-9554, also in Lihu'e; and **North Shore Taxi,** 808/826-6189, in Hanalei.

Hitchhiking

Using your thumb to get around is legal on Kaua'i, but you must stay off the paved portion of the road. For short hops in and around the towns—like from Koloa to Po'ipu or from the airport to Lihu'e—thumbing may not be difficult.

But getting out to the Kalalau Trail or to Polihale on the west end when you're toting a backpack and appear to be going a longer distance is tough. As on all the islands, you're most likely to be picked up by a visiting or local *haole.* Sometimes locals in pickup trucks will stop to give you a ride for short distances. Women *should not* hitch alone!

MEDICAL SERVICES

Hospitals

The island's principal medical facility is the full-service **Wilcox Memorial Hospital,** 3420 Kuhio Hwy., Lihu'e, 808/245-1100; dial 808/245-1010 for 24-hour emergencies. Others are **Kaua'i Veterans Memorial Hospital,** in Waimea at 808/338-9431, which is also open for 24-hour medical emergencies; and **Samuel Mahelona Memorial Hospital,** in Kapa'a at 808/822-4961.

Medical Clinics

Medical services are also available from **Kaua'i Medical Group,** 3420 B Kuhio Hwy., Lihu'e, 808/245-1500; after hours call 808/245-1831. The urgent-care clinic runs Mon.–Sat. 9 A.M.–6 P.M. and Sunday 10 A.M.–4 P.M.; the regular clinic runs weekdays 8 A.M.–5 P.M. and weekends 8 A.M.–noon. There are additional offices in 'Ele'ele, Kapa'a, Koloa, Kukui Grove Shopping Center, and Kilauea.

Additional options include the **Hale Lea Family Medicine** clinic, 808/828-2885, in Kilauea; the **Princeville Medical Clinic,** 808/826-7228, at the Princeville Center; and the **Kalaheo Clinic,** 808/332-8523 in Kalaheo. In Kapa'a, the Samuel Mahelona Hospital sponsors a **walk-in clinic,** 808/822-4961.

For the **Natural Health and Pain Relief Clinic,** call 808/245-2277.

Pharmacies

Many pharmacies give senior discounts. Options include **Southshore Pharmacy,** 808/742-7511, in Koloa; **Westside Pharmacy,** 808/335-5342, in Hanapepe; **Shoreview Pharmacy,** 808/822-1447, in Kapa'a; **Longs Drugs,** in the Kukui Grove Shopping Center, 808/245-7771, and in Kapa'a, 808/822-4915. All the hospitals and medical groups also have their own pharmacies.

Alternative Health Care

Many people say they are drawn to the healing powers of Kaua'i. Like all the islands, Kaua'i does seem to have rejuvenescent energy. The ancient Hawaiians knew natural pharmacology and could cure many ailments and diseases, and their healing hands would poke and prod tired muscles with *lomi lomi* massage. Some non-Hawaiians who have come to live on the islands have tapped into this knowledge, and others have brought their own unique experiences that pertain to the healing arts. First, perhaps, were acupuncture and Oriental medicine brought by Asians who came to work the fields. Much later it was chiropractic, western massage, bodywork, naturopathy, reflexology, and a whole host of modern paths. All sorts of alternative medicine—Hawaiian, Asian, and Western—are available on Kaua'i, but aside from those who practice massage (there is a full-page list in the phone book), you'll have to do some research on your own to contact practitioners. To get you started, check out the following to see if they meet your needs: **Kauai Center for Holistic Medicine and Research,** 4504 Kukui St., Kapa'a, 808/823-0994; **Kaua'i's Association of Healing Arts Practitioners,** P.O. Box 160, Kapa'a, HI 96746, 808/923-8088; and **The Health Connection,** 4-1579 Kuhio Hwy. in Kapa'a, 808/822-0200.

KAUA'I

INFORMATION AND SERVICES

For **police, fire,** and **ambulance** anywhere on Kaua'i, dial 911. The **Coast Guard Search and Rescue** can be reached at 800/552-6458. Recorded messages are available 24 hours a day for: **weather,** 808/245-2919, or the National Weather Service, 808/245-6001; **marine and surf report,** 808/245-3564; and **time of day,** 808/245-0212.

Consumer Protection
If you encounter accommodations problems, bad service, or downright rip-offs while on Kaua'i, try the following: Chamber of Commerce, 808/245-7363; Office of Consumer Protection, O'ahu, 808/586-2630; and the Better Business Bureau of Hawaii on O'ahu, 808/536-6956.

Tourist Information
The best information on Kaua'i is dispensed by Kaua'i HVB, 4334 Rice St., Suite 101, Lihu'e, HI 96766, 808/245-3971, website: www.kauai visitorsbureau.org.

For information by radio, convenient while driving, tune to 98.9 FM for a short-range broadcast about area sites.

Post Offices
Normal business hours are Mon.–Fri. 8 A.M.–4:30 P.M., Saturday 9 A.M.–1 P.M. The central post office on Kaua'i is at 4441 Rice St., Lihu'e. Main branches are at Kapa'a and Waimea, with 13 others scattered throughout the island. For information, call 800/275-8777. Most larger hotels offer limited postal services.

Reading Material
The central **library** is at 4344 Hardy St., Lihu'e, 808/241-3222. Branch libraries are in Hanapepe, Kapa'a, Koloa, Princeville, and Waimea. Check with the main library for times and services.

Free **tourist literature** and the narrow-format, magazine-style *This Week Kauai, Spotlight's Kauai Gold,* and *Kauai Beach and Activity Guide* are available at the airport, many hotels, and most restaurants and shopping centers around the island. They come out monthly or quarterly and contain money-saving coupons, information on local events and activities, shopping and restaurants, and island maps. *Kauai Beach Press* has similar content but is in a newspaper format. With a focus on activities and fun things to do, *101 Things to Do on Kauai* is a great resource and also has money-saving coupons. *Menu* is an informative magazine that lists restaurants and details their menus. *Kauai Drive Guide* is available from the car rental agencies and contains tips, coupons, and good maps. The AAA Hawaii *Tourbook* is also very useful. Other publications of interest are *Kauai Magazine* and the in-flight magazines of Aloha and Hawaiian Airlines.

There are two island newspapers: *The Garden Island* is published daily, 50 cents daily and $1 on Sunday, www.kauaiworld.com; and the *Kauai Times* appearsg once a week. Both can be picked up at numerous stands around the island.

Kaua'i Radio Stations
The following stations broadcast on Kaua'i. Occasionally, a high power station from O'ahu can be picked up on Kaua'i as well. KONG 570 AM does news, talk, and sports; KUAI 720 AM plays contemporary music, sports, surf reports, and some Hawaiian oldies; KKCR 91.9 and 90.9 FM are nonprofit community radio stations with various formats; KONG 93.5 FM is the "big boy" on the island, with contemporary music and requests, and Hawaiian music Friday evenings and Sunday mornings; KSRF 95.9 FM offers island sounds; KFMN 96.9 FM plays adult contemporary music; and KSHK 103.3 FM does classic rock and roll.

Island Facts
Kaua'i's nickname is "The Garden Island," and it is the oldest of the main Hawaiian Islands. Its lei is made from the *mokihana,* a small native purple citrus fruit, which is the island's flower.

LIHU'E

The twin stacks of the Lihu'e sugar mill let you know where you are: in a former plantation town on one of the world's most gorgeous islands. Lihu'e (Cold Chill) began growing cane in the 1840s, and its fields were among Hawaii's most productive. Until 1996, when the Lihu'e mill shut down, cane from the surrounding fields was crushed here. Still to be seen around town, cane fields grow cane that's trucked elsewhere for processing. Lihu'e, the county seat, has 5,500 residents, with an additional 4,800 in the nearby bedroom communities of Puhi and Hanama'ulu. With this strong agricultural base and its standing as the county seat, the town has flourished and boasts all the modern conveniences including shopping centers, a library, museum, a hospital, the island's only commercial airport, and its principal harbor. But the feel is still that of a company town that's only slowly expanding its periphery. Only a few short years ago Lihu'e had but two traffic lights; it now has nearly a dozen, with a growing rush-hour traffic problem. It isn't the geographical center of the island, but it is halfway along the coastal road that encircles the island, making it a perfect jumping-off point for exploring the rest of Kaua'i. It has a great concentration of restaurants, a major resort, right-priced accommodations, some entertainment, and the most varied shopping. One of the island's best beaches is within a five-minute drive of downtown, and you can be out of town and exploring long before your shave ice begins to melt.

Lihu'e's two bedroom communities, Puhi to the west and Hanama'ulu to the north, add to the strength and importance of this area. Puhi has the island's only higher educational institution, Kaua'i Community College, and a growing industrial park. Hanama'ulu, an old sugar community, has a stronger past that present but hangs on because of its close proximity to Lihu'e. Its small center has a handful of well-established stores and restaurants, and down at the coast is a fine beach park. Between Lihu'e and Hanama'ulu is the tiny settlement of Kapaia, a wide spot in the road in the Hanama'ulu Stream valley. From here Ma'alo Road (Route 583) runs up through cane fields to Wailua Falls. In town are three shops, the 1884 Immaculate Conception Catholic Church, and Lihu'e Hongwanji Buddhist Temple. The sewing and quilting shop here is perhaps the best on the island, and, oddly enough, the other two shops both sell fine cigars and handmade wood furniture.

SIGHTS

KAUA'I MUSEUM

If you really want to enrich your Kaua'i experience, this is the first place to visit. Spending an hour or two here infuses you with a wealth of information regarding Kaua'i's social and cultural history. The two-building complex is at 4428 Rice St. in downtown Lihu'e, 808/245-6931, open Mon.–Fri. 9 A.M.–4 P.M. and Saturday 10 A.M.–4 P.M.; admission is $5, $4 seniors 65 and older, $3 students 13–17, $1 children 6–12, and free under six. For greater enrichment, museum staff conduct one-hour tours, free with admission, Monday, Tuesday, and Thursday at 10 A.M. Dedicated in 1924 to Albert Spencer Wilcox, son of pioneer missionaries at Hanalei, the main building has a Greco-Roman facade and was the public library until 1970. Its two floors house the main gallery, devoted to ethnic heritage and island art exhibits that are changed on a regular basis. Included here are extensive and fascinating exhibits of calabashes, koa furniture, quilts, and feather lei. One large calabash belonged to Princess Ruth, who gave it to a local child. Its finish, hand-rubbed with the original *kukui* nut oil, still shows a fine luster. The rear of the main floor is dedicated to the Senda Gallery, with its collection of vintage photos shot by W. J. Senda, a Japanese immigrant from Matsue who arrived in 1906. These black and whites are classics, opening a window onto old Kaua'i. Upstairs in the small Oriental Art Gallery are a fine selection of art objects, mostly from China and Japan. Revolving shows, sometimes of contemporary art and craft, are held in a second gallery on this floor.

On the far end of the first floor, the Museum Shop sells books, cards, Hawaiiana prints, and a fine selection of detailed U.S. Geological Survey maps of the entire island. Some inexpensive but tasteful purchases include baskets, wooden bowls, and selections of tapa.

Kaua'i's fascinating natural and cultural history begins to unfold when you walk through the courtyard into the second half of the museum, the William Hyde Rice Building. Notice the large black iron pot used to cook sugarcane. The exhibits are self-explanatory, chronicling Kaua'i's development over the centuries. The windows of the Natural History Tunnel show the zones of cultivation on Kaua'i, along with its beaches and native forests. Farther on is an extensive collection of Kaua'i shells, old photos, and the history and genealogy of Kaua'ian royalty and the ruling class. The central first-floor area has a model of a Hawaiian village, an extensive collection of weapons, some fine examples of adzes used to hollow canoes, and a model of HMS *Resolution* at anchor off Waimea. An excerpt from the ship's log records Captain Cook's thoughts on the day that he discovered Hawaii for the rest of the world.

As you ascend the stairs to the second floor, history continues to unfold. Missionaries stare from old photos, their countenances the epitome of piety and zeal. Just looking at them makes you want to repent! Most old photos record the plantation era. Be sure to see the Spalding Shell Collection, gathered by Colonel Spalding, an Ohio veteran of the Civil War who came to Kaua'i and married the daughter of Captain James Makee, owner of the Makee Sugar Company. Besides shells from around the world are examples of magnificent koa furniture, table settings, children's toys, dolls, and photos of Ni'ihau—about all that the outside world ever sees. Follow the stairs back to the ground floor and notice the resplendent examples of feather capes on the wall. On the main floor, in an alcove by the front door, push the button to begin a short video of Kaua'i. This pictorial is a treat for the eyes; soothing Hawaiian chanting in the background sets the mood.

GROVE FARM HOMESTEAD

Grove Farm is a plantation started in 1864 by George Wilcox, the son of Congregational missionary teachers, who worked for the original owner of the surrounding acreage. The first owner saw no future in the parched land and sold around 500 acres to Wilcox for $12,000,

LIHU'E

ISENBERG PARK

WILCOX HOSPITAL
WAL-MART
HILO HATTIE
WILL SQUYRES HELICOPTERS
SAFARI HELICOPTER
AHUKINI ROAD
TIP TOP MOTEL
LIHUE LUTHERAN CHURCH
LIHU'E SHOPPING CENTER
COUNTY BUILDING
STATE BUILDING
POLICE STATION
ELEMENTARY SCHOOL
SUGAR MILL
POST OFFICE
KAUA'I MUSEUM
HISTORIC COUNTY BUILDING
HVB
LIHUE UNION CHURCH
RICE SHOPPING CENTER
MOTEL LANI
VIDINHA STADIUM
KAUAI GROVE SHOPPING CENTER
HALE LIHUE MOTEL
FIRE STATION
KMART
GROVE FARM GOLF COURSE
GROVE FARM HOMESTEAD

Nawiliwili Stream
Nawiliwili
Nawiliwili Stream

© SANDRA E. BISIGNANI TRUST AND AVALON TRAVEL PUBLISHING, INC.

which he had 10 years of repay in a lease-to-purchase arrangement. Through a system of aqueducts, Wilcox brought water down from the mountains and began one of the most profitable sugar plantations in Hawaii. During the years following, he bought additional surrounding land, and at its height the property encompassed 27,000 acres. Currently it stands at slightly less than 22,000 acres—still sizable, and one of the five largest land holdings on the island.

George Wilcox never married. In 1870, his brother Sam came to live on the homestead, and in 1874, Sam married Emma, the daughter of missionaries from the Big Island. The couple had six children—three boys and three girls. Two of the boys met with tragic early deaths, but Gaylord, the third, not only survived but

managed the farm for years. Of the girls, only Etta, the oldest, married. The two other sisters, Miss Elsie and Miss Mabel, were single all their lives. Elsie became very involved in education and politics, while Mabel went to Johns Hopkins University and earned a degree as a registered nurse. Her parents originally didn't want her to study nursing but acquiesced when she became 25 years old and still desired that calling. She returned in 1911 and eventually opened a public health office on the grounds. The homestead was a working plantation until the mid-1930s, when George died and operations were moved nearby. His nieces, Elsie and Mabel Wilcox, both born here, continued to occupy the dwellings and care for the extensive grounds.

KAUA'I

In 1971, Mabel Wilcox dedicated the family estate to posterity. Well advanced in years but spirited in mind, she created a nonprofit organization to preserve Grove Farm Homestead as a historical living farm. Reap the benefits of her efforts by visiting Monday, Wednesday, or Thursday at 10 A.M. or 1 P.M. A donation of $5, or $2 for children under 12, is requested. Please be prompt! Reservations for tours are preferred, but staff try to accommodate drop-in visitors. Telephone 808/245-3202 at least 24 hours in advance to make arrangements. Mail reservations are accepted up to three months in advance; write to Grove Farm Homestead, P.O. Box 1631, Lihu'e, HI 96766. The homestead is off Nawiliwili Road; precise directions are given when you call. Group size is limited to give full attention to detail and minimize wear and tear on the buildings.

The first thing you might notice when entering Grove Farm are the remains of a narrow-gauge railroad track. The tracks meant sugar, and sugar meant prosperity and change for old Hawaii. A low stone wall partially surrounds the homestead, and beyond the walls are orchards, pasture, and gardens. This is no "glass-case" museum. It's a real place with living history, where people experienced the drama of changing Hawaii. It is part of what was the oldest intact sugar plantation in Hawaii. You meet at the plantation office, where you should notice the old maps on the walls showing the extent of the Wilcox land holdings. Well-informed guides take you on a two-hour tour of the grounds and its various buildings. The grounds are lush and fruitful, with all sorts of trees and plants, many imported, and five kinds of bamboo. At one time the workers were encouraged to have their own gardens. Vegetable and flower gardens, along with fruit and nut orchards, still grace the property. The well-kept homestead buildings include the plantation home and two cottages, the old school that was converted to a public health office for Mabel Wilcox, a fernery, and a simple but homey plantation worker's home. As the tour ends you get a feeling of what Grove Farm is all about—a homestead where people lived, and worked, and dreamed.

George's desk

OTHER SIGHTS

Kilohana
The manor house at Kilohana Plantation was built in 1935 by the wealthy *kama'aina* planter, Gaylord Wilcox, to please his wife, Ethel. She was enamored with Hollywood and its glamorous Tudor-type mansions, which were the rage of the day. Sparing no expense, Gaylord spent $200,000 building an elaborate 16,000-square-foot home; estimates are that it would cost about $3 million in today's dollars. Inside, Gaylord's Restaurant occupies the actual dining room. Original furniture includes a huge table that seats 22 and a stout sideboard fit for a truly regal manor house. On one end is the huge living room, a grand room, almost museum-like, filled with period furniture, rugs, and art pieces on the walls. As you pass from room to room— some of which are occupied by fine boutiques and art galleries—notice the coved ceiling, lustrous wood molding, and grand staircase. A mirror from the '30s (mirrors in Hawaii have a tough

ROBERT NILSEN

The sunny Wilcox living room is filled with embroidery, fine koa furniture, and books.

time holding up because of the moisture) still hangs just inside the tiled main entranceway. From the flagstone rear veranda (also occupied by Gaylord's for alfresco dining), view a living tapestry of mountain and cloud, even more ethereal when mist shrouds magical Mt. Wai'ale'ale in the distance.

At the front, a horse and carriage waits to take visitors on a 20-minute tour of the grounds, 11 A.M.–6 P.M. Mon.–Thurs. at 11 A.M. and 2 P.M., a horse-drawn wagon pulls guests on a one-hour sugar tour through the 35 lush acres that surround the home, which was the center of a working farm—a feeling that lingers. To reach Kilohana, take Route 50 (Kaumuali'i Highway) west from Lihu'e for about two miles toward the tiny village of Puhi, and look on the mountain side for the clearly marked entrance.

Lihu'e's Old Churches

When Route 56 becomes Route 50, just as you pass the Lihu'e Sugar Mill, look for the HVB Warrior pointing you to the **Lihue Lutheran Church.** Just before the bridge, follow Ho'omana Road up the hill through a well-kept residential area. Rebuilt following Hurricane 'Iwa in 1982, the current building is a faithful copy of the original structure built in 1885. It has everything a church should have, including a bell tower and spire, but it's all miniature. The church reflects a strong German influence that dominated Lihu'e and its plantation until World War I. The early

1900s' pastor was Hans Isenberg, brother of the plantation founder and husband to Dora Rice from the old *kama'aina* family. The outside of the church is basic New England, but inside, the ornate altar is reminiscent of baroque Germany. Headstones in the yard to the side indicate just how old this congregation is. In fact, with an active congregation since 1881, it is the oldest Lutheran church in the islands.

Across from the Kukui Grove Shopping Center behind the car dealership along Nawiliwili Avenue is the lava stone **Lihue Union Church,** which was mostly attended by cane workers and their families. Its cemetery is filled with simple tombstones, and plumeria trees eternally produce blossoms for the departed ones. Within the same compound is the **Lihue First Church,** a structure also made of stone, founded in 1840.

Around Town

Many Kaua'i County offices are in the **Lihu'e Civic Center** on the corner of Kuhio Highway and Rice Street, including that of the mayor, property tax, public works, vehicle registration, driver licensing, and county parks. The white and dignified **Historic County Building** faces Rice Street across a wide lawn between 'Ewa and 'Umi Streets. A few county offices still occupy this structure, as does the Kaua'i Historical Society. During the Christmas-New Year's season, this building is decorated inside and out in a

KAUA'I

LIHU'E VICINITY

To Wailua

WAILUA MUNICIPAL GOLF COURSE

ASTON KAUAI BEACH VILLAS AND OUTRIGGER KAUA'I BEACH HOTEL

HANAMA'ULU BEACH COUNTY PARK

AHUKINI RECREATION PIER

Hanama'ulu Bay

Kilohana Crater

Hanama'ulu

Kapaia

SEE "LIHU'E" MAP

Lihu'e

LIHU'E AIRPORT

GROVE FARM GOLF COURSE

KILOHANA PLANTATION

KAUA'I COMMUNITY COLLEGE

Puhi

VIDINHA STADIUM

KAUA'I LAGOONS GOLF COURSE

To Po'ipu and Koloa

ANCHOR COVE

GARDEN ISLAND INN

KAUA'I MARRIOTT

WHALERS BREWPUB

NININI LIGHTHOUSE

KALAPAKI BEACH

Kipu

OVERLOOK

NAWILIWILI HARBOR

SMALL BOAT HARBOR

NIUMALU COUNTY PARK

Alakoko Fishpond

Nawiliwili Bay

Kaua'i Channel

Ha'upu Ridge

Kawai Point

Noku Bay

QUEEN VICTORIA'S PROFILE

© SANDRA E. BISIGNANI TRUST AND AVALON TRAVEL PUBLISHING, INC.

festive holiday spirit and open for everyone's enjoyment. Directly behind is the newer three-story **State Building,** where the Land and Natural Resources office can handle camping and hiking permits on state land, fishing licensing, and hunting permits. Next door is the **State Judiciary** building. Across 'Umi Street are the **police headquarters** and **District Health Office,** while the **fire department** is down Rice Street on the way to Nawiliwili harbor. The main **post office** sits directly across from the Kaua'i Museum, and the **Kaua'i Visitors Bureau** has offices in the Watamull Plaza building, at 4334 Rice Street. Following Hardy Street back around, you'll locate the main **library** across the street from Wilcox Elementary School. Look for the sweep of its roof—like the sail of an outrigger canoe. The library is open Monday and Wednesday 10 A.M.–8 P.M.; Tuesday, Thursday, and Friday 9 A.M.–5 P.M.; and Saturday 9 A.M.–1 P.M. Along the main drag (Kuhio Highway) are three gas stations and farther out is Wilcox Hospital.

Alakoko Fishpond

From Nawiliwili Harbor, follow Wa'apa Road south through the little community of Niumalu, and from there continue onto Hulemalu Road. Along Hulemalu Road, partway around and up the hill, is a lookout, below which is Alakoko (Rippling Blood) Fishpond, commonly known as Menehune Fishpond. Here, you have a sweeping view of Hule'ia Stream and the Ha'upu Ridge on the far side. This fishpond has been used to raise mullet and other commercial fish. Unlike most fishponds, which were built at the edge of the ocean, this pond was constructed along the riverbank by a 900-foot dike, said to be the handiwork of the Menehune. Legend says that these little people built this pond for a royal prince and princess and made only one demand: that no one watch them in their labor. In one night, the indefatigable Menehune passed the stones needed for the project from hand to hand in a double line that stretched for 25 miles. But the royal prince and princess could not contain their curiosity and climbed to a nearby ridge to watch the little people. They were spotted by the Menehune, who stopped building, leaving holes in the wall, and turned the royal pair into the twin pillars of stone still seen on the mountainside overlooking the pond.

About 240 acres of river bottom land surrounding this fishpond, part of the riverbank farther on, and nearby wooded hillsides are now part of **Hule'ia National Wildlife Reserve.** This reserve has been set aside for the protection of the Hawaiian coot, stilt, moorhen, and duck, endangered water birds. No access is allowed.

Wailua Falls

In Kapaia, Route 583 (Ma'alo Road) branches from the highway and heads north into the interior. This paved road lifts up to rolling terrain with a backdrop of lofty mountain peaks. Route 583 runs through cane fields, passes a valley overlook, and ends in a parking area near mile marker 3. Below, Wailua Falls tumbles 80 feet over a ledge into a large round pool, while white-tailed tropicbirds circle above. It's said that the *ali'i* would come here to dive from the cliff into the pool as a show of physical prowess; commoners were not considered to be infused with enough *mana* to perform this feat.

Many of the trees here are involuntary trellises for rampant morning glory. Pest or not, its blossoms are still beautiful as it climbs the limbs. A trail down to the falls is particularly steep and often slippery as the sun doesn't penetrate to dry the ground. Look for it near the end of the guardrail, but be very careful. If you make it down, you may have the falls to yourself, but you'll be like a goldfish in a bowl with the tourists—perhaps jealously—peering down at you. This falls and the river gorge down from here are part of the Wailua River State Park.

BEACHES AND PARKS

Lihu'e has very convenient beaches. You can sun yourself within 10 minutes of anywhere in town, with a choice of beaches on either Nawiliwili or Hanama'ulu Bay. Few tourists head to Hanama'ulu Bay, while Nawiliwili Bay is a classic example of "beauty and the beast." There is hardly a more beautiful harbor than Nawiliwili's, with a stream flowing into it and verdant mountains all around. However, it is a working harbor complete with rusting barges, groaning cranes, and petrochemical tanks. Private yachts and catamarans bob at anchor with their bright colors reflecting off dappled waters, and as your eye sweeps the lovely panorama it runs into the dull gray wall of a warehouse where raw sugar was stored before being shipped to the Mainland to be processed. It's one of those places that separates perspectives: some see the "beauty," while others focus on the "beast."

ROBERT NILSEN

KAUA'I

Wailua Falls

Kalapaki Beach

This most beautiful beach at Nawiliwili fronts the lavish Kaua'i Marriott. Just follow Rice Street until it becomes Route 51; you'll soon see the entrance to the hotel on your left. The hotel serves as a giant folding screen, blocking out most of the industrial area and leaving the lovely views of the bay. Park in the visitors' area at the hotel entrance, or to the rear of the hotel at the north end of Nawiliwili Park, where a footbridge leads across Nawiliwili Stream to the hotel property and the beach. Access to the beach is open to anyone. The wave action at Kalapaki is gentle at most times, with long swells combing the sandy-bottomed beach. Kalapaki is one of the best swimming beaches on the island, fair for snorkeling, and a great place to try bodysurfing, windsurfing, or begin with a board. From here there are great views of the Ha'upu Range and the bay. If you're there on the right day, you can see the SS *Independence* sail in or out of port on its rounds of the islands.

Nawiliwili Park

This park fronts Nawiliwili Bay to the side of Kalapaki Beach. Its lawn provides room for picnic tables, play equipment for kids, and toilets, and although it has shade palm trees for a picnic, it is not nearly as visually pleasing as the landscaped hotel property directly fronting the beach. Local swimmers and surfers come here for beach access, a few come to spearfish, and others come to drink beer and while away the hours under the palms. On occasion, turtles play off the rocks. Follow the road past the enclosed port area to the end of the breakwater for a good view of the inner harbor and Ha'upu Ridge.

Ninini Beach

To the harbor side of Ninini Point and the lighthouse, this small, unfrequented spot, with a narrow sandy beach backed up against the low cliff below Whalers Brewpub, is gentle most of the year, except when the Kona winds blow in from the south. A second smaller beach is closer to the Marriott below the golf course. These se-

cluded beaches are generally frequented by locals. Head past the hotel and turn to the right, going past the few private homes that overlook the bay. Walk along the edge of the golf course until you see the two beaches below, both good for swimming and sunbathing. There is also access from the brewpub parking lot.

To get to **Ninini Point Lighthouse,** take the paved road across from Vidinha Stadium and follow it around between the airport runways and Kaua'i Lagoons Golf Course. This road soon turns to red dirt and is used by joggers. Near the end, one fork leads to the back of the brewpub while the other runs out to the rocky point on which the lighthouse sits. It's about 2.5 miles. The lighthouse, now automated, has operated since 1897; the present yellow structure was built in 1932. There is shoreline access here and a few battered picnic tables.

Niumalu County Park

Just west of the Nawiliwili Small Boat Harbor, this county-maintained park lies along the Hule'ia Stream. It's a very local park, with pavilions, showers, and toilets, but no camping, and home of the Kaiola Canoe Club.

Ahukini State Recreation Pier

As the name implies, Ahukini is simply a pier from which local people fish. And it's some of the best pole fishing around. With the airport to your right, proceed down Ahukini Road until the road ends at a large circular parking lot and breakwater. The airport flight path is directly overhead. The scenery is only fair, and the spot itself is rather unkempt and littered. A skeletal cement framework remains of the old pier, so if you're not into fishing give it a miss. On the way down, sections of train tracks cross the road, a vestige of the sugar era and the means by which cane was transported to waiting ships. Ahukini Pier was used for about 100 years as a major port to ship sugarcane from the island to be processed elsewhere and as such played an important role in the economy of the island.

PRACTICALITIES

ACCOMMODATIONS

If you like simple choices, you'll appreciate Lihu'e; only two fancy resorts and one condo complex are here, the rest are small family-run hotel/motels or apartment hotels. In the smaller places, prices are good because Lihu'e isn't considered a prime resort town. Yet it makes an ideal base, because from Lihu'e you can get *anywhere* on the island in less than an hour. Although it's the county seat, the town is quiet, especially in the evenings, so you won't have to deal with noise or hustle and bustle.

Under $50

The **Tip Top Motel,** 3173 'Akahi St., Lihu'e, HI 96766, 808/245-2333, is a combination motel, restaurant, and bakery popular with local folks. It's a functional, two-story, cinderblock building painted light gray. The check-in lobby/café/bakery is open Tues.–Sun. 6:30 A.M.–3 P.M. and 5:30–9 P.M.; on Monday the hours are 7:30 A.M.–3 P.M. At other hours, check in at Chrissy and Charley's Bar around the side of the building. The rooms are antiseptic in every way—a plus, as your feet stay cool on the bare linoleum floor—and there's virtually no decoration, but

there is a TV in every room and all are air-conditioned. Just to add that mixed-society touch, instead of a Gideon's Bible in the dresser drawer, you get The Teachings of Buddha, placed by the Sudaka Society of Honolulu. Rates are $45 per room, plus a $10 refundable key deposit.

The **Hale Lihue Motel,** 2931 Kalena St., Lihu'e, HI 96766, 808/245-2751, has made an excellent comeback! Don't expect anything fancy from this mocha-colored, 20-room, two-story, cinderblock building, but the manager runs a clean hotel with a screened-in lobby. There are no TVs or phones in the rooms; the television is in the lobby, a pay phone on the front lanai. Perfect for no-frills, budget accommodations. Used mostly by construction workers, backpackers, bicyclists, and budget travelers. Rates are $24.20 single, $27.50 double, or $33 for three people; weekly rates available.

Motel Lani, owned and operated by Janet Naumu, offers clean, inexpensive rooms at 4240 Rice St.; for reservations write Motel Lani, P.O. Box 1836, Lihu'e, HI 96766, 808/245-2965. The lobby is actually an extension of Janet's home, where she and her children often watch TV. There are nine units and, although close to the road, they're surprisingly quiet. Each room has a small desk, dresser, bath, fan, and refrigerator

Kalapaki Beach, one of the best swimming beaches on Kaua'i

ROBERT NILSEN

KAUA'I

and is cross-ventilated. Some have air-conditioning. Janet usually doesn't allow children under three years old, but she's reasonable and will make exceptions. A small courtyard with a barbecue is available to guests. Rates for two nights or more are $32–50 double, $50 and up triple, $14 for an additional person, slightly more for one night. Deposit required.

$50–100

Steve and Susan Layne, owners of the attractive **Garden Island Inn**, 3445 Wilcox Rd., Lihu'e, HI 96766, 808/245-7227, fax 808/245-7603 or 800/648-0154, website: www.gardenisland.com, email: info@gardenisland.com, did a wonderful job of turning the once character-laden but worse-for-wear Ocean View Motel into a bright and cheery inn. Head down Rice Street toward the harbor; the inn is on a cul-de-sac, across from Nawiliwili Beach Park, just a stroll from Kalapaki Beach. Each room has color cable TV, microwave, refrigerator, and coffeemaker with complimentary Kona coffee. The inn also provides boogie boards, snorkeling gear, beach mats, bicycles (if you're nice), and ice chests for a day's outing. The garden view, ground floor rooms, $75 double, are appointed with island prints and flowers from the garden and are cooled by louvered windows and ceiling fans. Second floor rooms, $85 double, are about the same, but each has a/c and its own lanai. The best rooms ($105–125) are on the third floor, from where you look down on a mature banana grove. Is this the tropics or what! More like mini-suites, one- and two-room third-floor units have kitchenettes, a/c, and balconies and give you two full rooms that can easily accommodate four people comfortably. All 21 rooms are nonsmoking. In addition, a two-bedroom condo unit behind the inn with a fully furnished kitchen, cable TV, washer/dryer, and suburb views of the harbor rents for $145–200 per day depending on the number of people (maximum of six) plus a $75 cleaning fee; four-night minimum. From the front of the inn, you can watch the goings on in Nawiliwili Harbor and dock area. For the money, the Garden Island Inn is one of the best deals on Kaua'i.

$200–250

Aston Kauai Beach Villas, 4330 Kauai Beach Dr., Lihu'e, HI 96766, 808/245-7711, 800/922-7866 Mainland and Canada, or 800/321-2558 in Hawaii, is perfectly located midway between the airport and Kapa'a. Along a series of ponds that separate it from the adjacent hotel, it is a fine condominium resort that has consistently earned the AAA three-diamond award. The spacious one- and two-bedroom units differ slightly, but expect a terra-cotta foyer leading to a living room with comfortable bamboo furniture with puffy pillows, a fold-out couch, and remote-control color TV. Fronting each unit is a lanai with outdoor tables, chairs, and lounges that looks out over the richly landscaped garden, ponds, and swimming pool or the ocean. The kitchen, with all necessary appliances and utensils, is accompanied by a dining area, and a washer/dryer combination is tucked into its own utility closet. Master bedrooms have queen-size beds, private baths, and plenty of closet space; the room safe requires a daily fee. Ceiling fans, bedroom air-conditioning, phones, and daily maid service are part of the amenities. Rates are $175–210 for a one-bedroom unit, $240–270 for a two-bedroom with a garden view, and $295–330 for a two-bedroom, ocean-view suite. The four tennis courts, swimming pool, and outdoor cooking grills are for condo residents only, but guests can use the swimming pool at the Radisson Kauai Beach Resort next door and sign for meals at its restaurant.

The **Radisson Kauai Beach Resort** is a low-lying complex on 25 landscaped acres, down the same tree-lined entrance road to and across the ponds from Aston Kauai Beach Villas. Its 345 rooms lie in two- and three-story units that spread from the entrance and lobby like arms around the central garden courtyard with its three swimming pools, hot tub, and grotto waterfall. Free and open to the public, a torch-lighting ceremony is performed in the garden every evening, followed by music in the Mele Lounge. Radisson sank $10 million worth of renovations into the public and private spaces of this hotel when it took over ownership in 2000. Rooms are spacious and tastefully appointed. Each has a full bath, an ocean- or garden-view lanai, an entertainment center, cable TV, small refrigerator, and in-room safe. Dining options include the Terrace Restaurant, which is open for breakfast, lunch, and dinner, and the Cascade Bar and Grill, in the garden, for lunch and light snacks and drinks throughout the day. Activities can be scheduled at the activities desk, while you can find gifts, magazines, and food items at the gift shop or a memento of your trip from the Remember Kauai shop. On the property are tennis courts, two lighted for night play, and a fitness center. Large-group meetings and banquets can also be accommodated in the function rooms. Mountain- and garden-view rooms run $180–199, rooms with a view of the ocean, lagoon, and pool are $200–239, while the oceanfront rooms go for $225–259. Suites are only a bit more at $255–299. For information, contact the Radisson at 4331 Kaua'i Beach Dr., Lihu'e, HI 96766, 808/245-1955 or 888/805-3843, fax 808/246-9085, website: radissonkauai.com.

$250 and up

The **Kaua'i Marriott Resort and Beach Club,** at Kalapaki Beach, Lihu'e, HI 96766, 808/245-5050 or 800/220-2925, fax 808/245-5049, is a testament to humanity's perseverance coupled with the forgiving personality of Mother Nature. Kaua'i's first high-rise hotel was built on Kalapaki beach in the 1960s as the Kauai Surf. It still stands as the Kilohana wing of the Marriott. In 1987, the hotel was completely refurbished and rebuilt, emerging as the Westin—at the time the most luxurious property on Kaua'i. Hurricane 'Iniki then furiously blew ashore, raking the island and mangling the hotel. Afterward, the Marriott chain purchased the property and set about restoring it to its former grandeur. The result is, once again, a fabulous hotel, where about half the rooms are time-share properties. Upon arrival, you enter through a grand foyer. Descending the escalator you emerge on a flagstone path, along the perimeter of Ka Mala O Kalapaki, a formal garden that says "Hawaii" unmistakably, which is surrounded by ballrooms and convention rooms. You'll soon descend a flight of marble stairs on your left into the reception area. Displayed here is a lustrous original koa canoe that belonged to Prince Kuhio. In the care of a local Hawaiian family over the generations, the canoe was leased to Marriott with the understanding that funds be used in a scholarship that directly benefits a child of Hawaiian ancestry. The

central area of the hotel is an extensive pool surrounded by five neoclassical thrust proscenium porticos bubbling with soothing hot tubs and cascades of water; greenery and small private gardens fill other spaces. Overall the hotel is decorated in muted salmon, light green, periwinkle, and island pastel colors, and the halls, walkways, and other public spaces are dotted with an extensive collection of Asian and Hawaiian artworks. Although you're surrounded by luxury at the Marriott, you experience the feeling of a quieter, more casual place. The hotel is very much like the stunning sister who decided to stay close to home instead of heading for the bright lights where her beauty would easily have dazzled everyone.

Rooms are classified as garden view, $259; pool/ocean view, $315; ocean view, $369; and suites, $599–2,400; $25 for an additional adult. Romance, golf, and breakfast packages are also available. Rooms are pure luxury: each has a private lanai, and most overlook the pool or ocean. A comfy bed faces an entertainment center complete with remote-control color TV, while a writing desk, table, chairs, and floor lamps fill out the room. Each room boasts air-conditioning, a mini-fridge, tiled full bath, a steam iron and ironing board, in-room safe, and coffeemaker with complimentary Kona coffee.

The Marriott has four restaurants, one to fit your every need. Amenities include room service, an activities desk, concierge service, a fitness center, children's program, and complimentary airport shuttle. Shops include Lamonts Gifts and Sundries, Collectors Fine Art, Grande's Gems, Tropical Tantrum, Taro Fields, and Shred City. Everything from hair styling to facials and massages is available at Alexander, A Spa Salon. At one end of the quarter-mile-long beach promenade, the beach activity center has gear for all water activities and can arrange activities like scuba, sailing, kayaking, and fishing.

Vacation Rental Agencies

Kauai Vacation Rentals, 3-3311 Kuhio Hwy., Lihu'e, HI 96766, 808/245-8841 or 800/357-5025, website: www.KauaiVacationRentals.com, email: aloha@kvrre.com, handles condos and vacation rental homes throughout the island, with only a handful of condo units overlooking Nawiliwili Bay next to the Marriott.

KAUA'I

FOOD

Dining in Lihu'e is a treat—good to your palate and your budget. The town has many local eateries and a few fast-food chains. Stepping up in class, there are continental, Italian, and Japanese restaurants, while moderately priced establishments serve up hearty dishes of Mexican, Chinese, and good old American fare. Fancier dining is found at the big hotels and a few select restaurants around town.

Inexpensive

If you ask anyone in Lihu'e where you can chow down for cheap, they'll send you to **Ma's Family Inc.,** 4277 Halenani St., 808/245-3142, an institution owned and operated by matriarch Akiyo Honjo, a third-generation Kaua'ian, who is assisted at times by her great-grandchildren. Turn off Rice Street onto Kress and follow it to the corner, where you'll find Ma's. Ma's is open weekdays 5 A.M.–1:30 P.M. and Saturday, Sunday, and holidays 5–11:30 A.M. (or until customers stop coming). The building is old and has seen some wear but is clean. A few tourists find it, but mostly it's local working people who come here for a hearty and filling meal. Lunches are good, but the super deals are breakfast and the Hawaiian specialties. The coffee, free with breakfast and served with condensed milk, arrives in a large pot about as soon as your seat hits the chair. The menu is posted above the kitchen window. You can start the day with The Works, which includes either potatoes or fried noodles, bacon or sausage, and toast for $6. If that's too much, ask for an omelette, French toast, or pancakes. From the Hawaiian menu, try *kalua* pork with two eggs and rice, poi, and *lomi* salmon, or Kaua'i sausage—all for under $6. Ma's also serves hamburgers, an assortment of sandwiches including teriyaki beef, loco moco, and noodles.

Hamura Saimin Stand, 2956 Kress St., 808/245-3271, is just around the corner from Ma's. Open from 10 A.M., people flock to the orange countertops of this restaurant all day long, where they perch on short stools to eat steaming bowls of saimin. Sunday the shop closes at 9:30 P.M., Mon.–Thurs. at 11 P.M., and Fri.–Sat. it stays open until 1 A.M., when all the bars let loose their revelers. There is no decor here (beyond the sign admonishing, Please do not stick gum under counter), just good food. Your first time, try the Saimin Special, which gives you noodles, slivers of meat and fish, vegetables, won ton, and eggs, all floating in a golden broth. Other items on the small menu are variations on the same theme, with nothing more than $6. The bowl size determines your portion: small, medium, large, extra large, special, extra large special. On the counter will be hot sauce, mustard, and *shoyu*—condiments that you mix yourself in the small bowls that accompany your soup. Enjoy not only the saimin, but also the truly authentic Kaua'i experience. Also available as sides are crispy wonton, skewers of beef or chicken, manapua, and lilioko'i pie.

Halo Halo Shave Ice occupies a second counter in the same building 10 A.M.–4:30 P.M.—use the side entrance. Here you can get some of the best throat coolers on the island.

Oki Diner, 3125 Kuhio Hwy., just up from the County government office building, 808/245-5899, has become another favorite for locals in town—and it's open 24 hours a day! This is a spartan place, simple but pleasant. Everything on the menu is available at any time—good quality food at reasonable prices, mostly under $8. At certain times during the day, dim sum is available. A counter at the entrance sells baked goods, so you can leave with sweets for the road or come in to pick up a cake.

Tip Top Cafe/Bakery, 3173 'Akahi St., 808/245-2333, open daily except Monday 6:30 A.M.–2 P.M., doubles as the downstairs lobby of the Tip Top Motel. A local favorite with unpretentious but clean surroundings, the food is wholesome but uninspired—just like the service. Breakfast is the best deal, at around $5, and the macadamia nut pancakes are delish! They are known throughout the island. Plate lunches are under $6, but they say the oxtail soup is the best seller. You can choose anything from pork chops to teriyaki chicken, and you get soup, salad, rice, and coffee. Visit the bakery section and let your eyes tell your stomach what to do. The *malasadas* are fresh daily. Both the bakery and café have been in business since 1916! Sharing this space is the **Sushi Katsu** Japanese restaurant, 808/246-0176, also an inexpensive local eatery. Open daily except Monday 11

A.M.–2 P.M. for sushi only and 5:30–9:30 P.M. for sushi and other Japanese food.

Down the street and almost next to each other across from the Garden Island Newspaper office are **Maria's Mexican Restaurant,** 808/246-9122, with the best Mexican food in Lihu'e, and **Local Boy Restaurant,** 808/246-8898, for friendly service and generous portions of local food.

Dani's, 4201 Rice St., toward Nawiliwili near the fire department, 808/245-4991, is open Mon.–Fri. 5 A.M.–1:30 P.M., Saturday 5 A.M.–1 P.M.. Another favorite with local people, it's been around a while and has a good reputation for giving you a hearty meal for a reasonable price. The food is American-Hawaiian-Japanese. Most full meals range $6–10, and you have selections like *lomi* salmon, tripe stew, teriyaki beef and chicken, and fried fish. Unpretentious, the cafeteria-style interior displays Formica-topped tables and linoleum floors.

Look for an anchor chain marking the two-tone blue **Beach Hut,** open daily 7 A.M.–7 P.M. at the bottom of Rice Street, just before Nawiliwili Harbor. This window-restaurant offers limited seating on the porch or in the upstairs "crow's nest," from where you get a great view of the harbor. With a good reputation among local clientele, it serves breakfast, like omelettes, eggs, and loco moco, Mon.–Sat. 7–10:30 A.M. Lunches of fish and chips, mahimahi, charbroiled chicken, and a variety of sandwiches run $4–9. The specialty is large, juicy buffalo burgers with all the fixings, but turkey burgers and traditional beef burgers are also offered. The Beach Hut is an excellent, laid-back choice for lunch in the Nawiliwili area.

The Fish Express, 3343 Kuhio Hwy., across from Wal-Mart, 808/245-9918, is a retail sales store with a full selection of fresh and frozen fish and seafood that's open daily 10 A.M.–7 P.M., closing Sunday at 5 P.M. If you're looking for something for the road, try the lunch counter Mon.–Fri. 10 A.M.–2 P.M. for plate lunches, sandwiches, and seafood platters, mostly in the $5–8 range. Take-out only.

The Kukui Grove Shopping Center has a number of sit-down and sidewalk restaurants. They include the **Deli and Bread Connection,** a kitchenware store with a deli counter offering sandwiches and an assortment of soups and salads; **Joni-Hana,** a walk-up counter with *bento*

and plate lunches priced reasonably; **Myron's Filipino & Local Food;** and **Ho's Chinese Kitchen** for Cantonese food at very reasonable prices.

Moderate

Restaurant Kiibo, 2991 'Umi St., 808/245-2650, serves authentic Japanese meals without a big price tag. Many Japanese around town come here to eat. The low stools at the counter are reminiscent of a Japanese *akachochin* or *sushiya.* In fact, the sushi bar is a recent addition. The menu listing savory offerings of udon, tempura, teriyaki, and a variety of *teishoku* (specials) includes pictures showing you just what you'll get. The service is quick and friendly; most offerings are under $12. Restaurant Kiibo is *ichiban!* Just off Rice Street, it's open for lunch 11 A.M.–1 P.M. and for dinner 5:30–9 P.M., closed Sunday and holidays.

The **Barbecue Inn,** 2982 Kress St., 808/245-2921, open Mon.–Sat. 7 A.M.–1:30 P.M., then 5–8:30 P.M. Mon.–Thurs. and 4:30–8:45 P.M. Fri.–Sat., has been in business and run by the Sasaki family since 1940, and if you want a testimonial, just observe the steady stream of local people, from car mechanics to doctors, heading for this restaurant. The atmosphere is "leatherette and Formica," but the service is homey, friendly, and prompt. More than 30 entrées—Japanese, American, and local—include tempura, seafood, prime rib, and a dinner plate special. The scampi is perhaps the best for the price on the island. Most meals come complete with soup, salad, a beverage, and dessert, mostly in the $9–17 range. There's always a list of specials, longer than some restaurant's menus. Breakfast and lunch are at bargain prices, the homemade pies are luscious, and cocktails are available.

Tokyo Lobby, 3501 Rice St., in Nawiliwili at the Pacific Ocean Plaza, 808/245-8989, open Mon.–Sat. for lunch 11 A.M.–2 P.M., dinner daily 5–9:30 P.M., prides itself on the freshness of the food, especially the seafood. Appointed with shoji screens, a pagoda-style roof over the sushi bar, paper fans, and paper lanterns, the Tokyo Lobby creates an authentic Japanese atmosphere. Most meals are presented in small wooden boats, the signature of the restaurant. Lunch might be *nigiri* sushi or sashimi, various *don buri,* a bowl of rice with savory bits of meat, egg, and vegetables on top, or *nabeyaki*, assorted seafood with vegetables, and noodles in a broth. The dinner menu includes sashimi and sushi platters, calamari steak, curried chicken, and beef teriyaki, most around $15, or combination dinners like sesame chicken with sashimi for a bit more.

Only a few steps away at the Pacific Ocean Plaza is **Kauai Chop Suey,** 808/245-8790, open daily except Monday for lunch 11 A.M.–2 P.M. and for dinner 4:30–9 P.M. This is a reasonably priced Cantonese restaurant. The restaurant's two dining rooms, separated by a keyhole archway, are alive with plants and brightened by Chinese lanterns hanging from the open-beamed ceiling. Entrées include sizzling shrimp with lobster sauce (Mama Lau, the owner, says this is the best!), boneless chicken with mushrooms, or beef or pork with tomato. House specials are Kauai Chop Suey and a variety of noodle dishes. Kauai Chop Suey also offers plate lunches and dinners to go and has a steady local clientele, a sure sign of good food at reasonable prices.

The **Whalers Brewpub,** 808/245-2000, at the Kaua'i Lagoons Golf Course serves up a full menu, but most come for the location and the beer. Turn at the Marriott entrance and follow the signs for about one mile. One of two brewpubs on the island, the 550–800 barrels of beer brewed here every year is only served on the premises. As you enter, you can see the brewing apparatus through the glass windows to your left. Depending on the season, between five and eight varieties are available. Try the sampler first and then order what suits you the best. Lunches include mostly salads, sandwiches, and burgers in the $8–13 range, while steak, ribs, chicken, and fish are available for dinner for $17–25. Situated about 90 feet above outer Nawiliwili Bay, great sunsets are on the menu nearly every day, as is whale-watching from November to May. Live music, usually by reggae bands, is on tap every Friday until 1 A.M.

The Marriott has three in-house restaurants with better than average fare. **Kukui's Restaurant,** the hotel's open-air main dining room, is open for breakfast, lunch, and dinner and serves Pacific Rim cuisine near the pool. Special are the Friday night prime rib and seafood buffet, Saturday night Pacific Rim sampler buffet, and a Sunday champagne brunch. At the beach end of this dining area next to the bar is **Kukui's Pizza Cafe,** which serves a variety of homemade herbed-crust pizzas. Live Hawaiian music is performed here every evening, with the addition of a torch-lighting ceremony on Monday and Thursday, and a short hula show on Wednesday and Saturday. At the far side of the pool is the **Kalapaki Grill,** which serves up broiled burgers, sandwiches, salads, sides, and drinks during the day. Overlooking the central pool is **Aupaka Terrace.** Cocktails are served on the terrace, as is a continental breakfast, and sushi and Hawaiian *pu pu* in the evening.

Fine Dining

The rear flagstone veranda and original dining room at Kilohana, the restored 1935 plantation estate of Gaylord Wilcox, have been turned into the breezy **Gaylord's,** 808/245-9593, website: www.gaylordskauai.com, open Mon.–Sat. for lunch 11 A.M.–3 P.M. and dinner from 5 P.M., and Sunday for brunch 9:30 A.M.–3 P.M. Reservations are recommended. Lunch might include items like a Kilohana fruit platter, Oriental chicken salad, or Greek roasted vegetable salad, or more substantial dishes like baby-back ribs, fresh fish, or a Reuben sandwich. Dinners begin with a wide selection of appetizers, salads, and soups. Mostly in the $16.95–29.95 range, entrées include herb-crusted whole rack of lamb; chicken breast with papaya, pineapple, and macadamia nut, and cilantro and port wine cream sauce; and Greek-style linguine with grilled chicken, sun-dried tomatoes, olives, and feta cheese. Fish and game lovers will greatly enjoy the seafood rhapsody, fish, prawns, and lobster in a light creamy butter sauce; one of several choices of fresh fish (market price) that can be char-broiled, sautéed, or sesame-crusted; or Gaylord's famous farm-raised venison, which may be offered in a number of daily preparations. Save room for one of Gaylord's memorable desserts and finish your meal with a cappuccino or caffe mocha prepared on a century-old espresso machine, resplendent in its battered yet burnished glory. Gaylord's also prides itself on having one of the largest wine cellars on Kaua'i, featuring more than 100 vintages from around the world representing more than two dozen varietals. The à la carte Sunday brunch features a hearty Plantation Breakfast, strawberry French toast, Gaylord's eggs Benedict, and a vegetarian quiche. Prices for a complete brunch are $8.95–14.95 and include a fresh-baked sweet roll and fruit plate. Gaylord's is a wonderful restaurant to visit just to spend a quiet afternoon or as a special treat for a special occasion. Whether outdoors on the more casual veranda or indoors in the formal dining room, with its starched linens and stemware, the feeling is one of gentility.

J.J.'s Broiler, at the Anchor Cove Shopping Center, 808/246-4422, is open daily 11 A.M.–5 P.M. for lunch, until 10 P.M. for dinner, and from 5 P.M. for cocktails and light meals. Known in Kapa'a for more than 20 years as Kaua'i's original steak house, it was famous for its juicy Slavonic steak—still available. The menu offers grain-fed aged beef from the Midwest and daily choices of fish caught by local captains and delivered fresh. Upon entering, the living landscape of Nawiliwili Bay glistening through the huge windows creates the backdrop for the bi-level interior. The first level is more casual, with a full bar, wooden tables, and bentwood chairs, or you can dine alfresco on the veranda under large umbrellas. The upstairs offers horseshoe booths and intimate tables, along with another full bar and wraparound windows that open to cooling sea breezes. Hanging from the ceiling are replicas of 12-meter racing yachts, exactly like those entered in the America's Cup. Lunch at J.J.'s starts with appetizers like potato skins for $7.75, calamari ringers for $7.25, and mozzarella sticks for $6.95. Soups include the specialties French onion and Hawaiian Ocean Chowder, each for $5.75, and half a dozen salads are available. Sandwiches run $7.65–12.95 and the burgers a little cheaper. Aside from the Slavonic Steak (a thin broiled tenderloin dipped in butter, wine, and garlic sauce) at $17.95 or fresh fish at market price, dinner can be roasted macadamia lamb rack for $23.95, black bean shrimp with Asian polenta for $21.95, or broiled chicken fettuccine for $15.95. Daily specials for both lunch and dinner are offered to help save money, but no matter what you order, large portions will arrive.

The heady aroma of sautéed garlic mixed with the sweet scents of oregano and rosemary floats from the kitchens of **Café Portofino,** on the second level of the Pacific Ocean Plaza,

808/245-2121. This authentic Italian restaurant, owned and operated by Giuseppi Avocadi, is open daily for dinner only 5–10 P.M. Sliding wooden doors open to the distinctive wooden bar—a bold statement of high chic—under the open-beamed wooden ceiling and fancy fans. The main dining room, encased in beveled glass windows, is studded with tables, formally set, and counterpointed by a black-and-white tiled floor. Candlelight and wall sconces set the mood, flowers and ferns add island color, and an outdoor veranda is perfect for a romantic evening. The dinner menu begins with antipasto Portofino for $8, while other appetizer choices run $8–10. Salads include the mixed green house salad for $5; soups, like minestrone or gazpacho, are priced at $4. Tempting Italian entrées include spaghettini alla marinara at $13.50, eggplant parmigiana or pollo porcini (sautéed chicken breast in brandy with a light wild mushroom sauce) for $15, and specialties of the house like osso bucco (veal shank) over fettuccine for $25. Fresh fish (daily quote), broiled, baked, or sautéed, is served with fresh homemade condiments. There is a full wine list, and desserts are complemented by a cup of coffee or cappuccino from the full espresso bar. Every night except Monday, you are serenaded with live contemporary music on saxophone, piano, or harp. Cafe Portofino is an excellent choice for an evening of romance and fine dining. *Buon appetito!*

Duke's Canoe Club, on Kalapaki Bay at the Kaua'i Marriott Resort, 808/246-9599, open daily 5–10 P.M. upstairs for dinner and 11:30 A.M.–11:30 P.M. for drinks, *pu pu,* and light meals at the downstairs Barefoot Bar, with live Hawaiian music Thursday and Friday evenings, is as much a Hawaiian class act as its namesake, the legendary Duke Kahanamoku. Duke's is one of those places, with an exemplary setting just off the beach path and a lustrous wood and thatched interior illuminated by torches and moonlight, that pleasantly overwhelms you with the feeling that you're *really in Hawaii.* At the Barefoot Bar, you feel compelled to quaff a frothy brew and, well . . . kick off your shoes as you listen to the natural melody of wind and waves just a palm tree away. You can order sandwiches, plate lunches, pizza, burgers, and salads, all for well under $10, and you can enjoy a variety of island drinks prepared at the full-service bar (open until midnight). Upstairs, still casual but elegant enough for a romantic evening, the menu offers fresh catch at $19.95, prepared in your choice of five different ways. You can also order shrimp scampi for $17.95, or twist your fork into linguine with basil for a reasonable $9.95, or huli huli chicken at $14.95. The most expensive entrée on the menu is the prime rib of Midwestern aged beef for $23.95. Duke's is Hawaii at its best: relaxed, charming, idyllic, and offering fine cuisine.

Farmers' Market

If you're making your own meals while visiting Kaua'i, remember that locally grown fresh fruit and vegetables are available from vendors at the farmers' market every Friday at 3 P.M. at Vidinha Stadium parking lot in Lihu'e.

A private farmers' market is held every Monday at 3 P.M. at the rear of the Kukui Grove Shopping Center.

ENTERTAINMENT

Lihu'e is not the entertainment capital of the world, but if you have the itch to step out at night, there are a few places where you can scratch it.

The Outrigger Kaua'i Beach Hotel has dancing and entertainment at **Gilligan's,** the island's only active nightclub. It's popular with locals from Lihu'e and Kapa'a who are looking for a night out on the town. The dance floor is seldom empty and the bar is busy. Gilligan's is open Wed.–Sat. with dancing from 9 P.M. until closing. On Wednesday's Western night, line dancing or partner dancing is taught, while Thursday is a mixed bag of music. Friday has music of the '70s and '80s, and Top 40 rules on Saturday. On Thursday and Saturday there is a comedy show at 8 P.M. before the music. There is a dress code. Cover is $2 on Wednesday, $5 other nights, and $12 for the comedy show and dancing.

At the Marriott, stop by Kukui's Bar or Duke's Canoe Club for Hawaiian and contemporary music Thursday and Friday evenings. Kukui's Restaurant also has a sunset hula show on Wednesday and Saturday, and a torch-lighting ceremony on Monday and Thursday. For a more sophisticated evening, try the "A Night of Broadway" dinner show at the Marriott, where three musical acts are performed between courses of your buffet meal. The evening's entertainment runs $68 for adults, with kids age 6–12 about half price. For information and reservations, call 808-246-5166.

The Kukui Grove Shopping Center presents free entertainment, usually of a Hawaiian nature. On Friday at 6 P.M. at the center stage its a **hula show,** but the schedule varies.

Enjoy a night of shared karaoke fun at **Rob's Good Times Grill,** open Mon.–Sat. until 1 A.M. in the Rice Street Shopping Center. A would-be crooner is given the microphone and sings along with the music—the video and words to which are projected on a screen in the corner. A funky, dark little place with booths and Formica tables, it's become a local hangout. Even if your mom used to ask you to stop singing in the shower, here you can join in the fun. Everyone gets applause, and beer and drinks are reasonably priced. Rob's Good Times Grill is one of Lihu'e's only "neighborhood bars," where you can watch sports on a big screen TV, hobnob with the locals, and have a reasonable meal.

The **Hideaway Sports Bar,** 2975 'Ewalu St. (enter around the side), 808/245-3473, open 11 A.M.–2 A.M. is a friendly neighborhood bar where you can have a quiet beer and watch the game

The **Nawiliwili Tavern,** housed in the old Hotel Kuboyama, at the bottom of Rice St. along Paena Loop Rd., 808/245-7267, open 11 A.M.–2 A.M., is a friendly neighborhood bar and restaurant where you can mix with local people and tourists alike who are having fun playing pool, shuffleboard, or darts; music alternates with satellite sports broadcasts. Enjoy a cold beer in the casual and attractive surroundings, or satisfy your appetite by ordering any number of plate lunches or *pu pu.* Happy hour is weekdays 4–6 P.M.

If you're lucky, you can "strike out" at the **Lihue Bowling Center,** in the Rice Shopping Center, 808/245-5263. It's the only bowling alley on the island. The lanes stay open until 11:30 P.M. on Friday and Saturday but usually close about 10:30 P.M. on weekdays depending on how busy things are. Scoring is done with an automatic system.

For movies, try the **Kukui Grove 4 Cinemas,** behind the gas station across Nawiliwili Road from the big Kukui Grove Shopping Center.

For more than two decades, the **Kauai Com-**

munity **Players** have presented the island with its only theatrical performances. Four times a year, this nonprofessional community theater group puts on well-known and experimental plays, usually in the Lihu'e Parish Hall across Nawiliwili Road from the Kukui Grove Shopping Center. For information on what's currently showing, call 808/245-7700.

If you happen to be on Kaua'i on the fourth of July, don't fail to see the fireworks at Vidinha Stadium in Lihu'e. A "do not miss" event, it's reputedly one of the best light shows in the state.

RECREATION

Lihu'e is not the recreational center on the island, but it does offer a variety of options. If you are interested in staying fit or getting fit while vacationing, try the large and well-equipped **Kauai Athletic Club,** across from the Kukui Grove Shopping Center, 808/245-5381. When games are happening, spectator sports can by watched at Vidinha Stadium, which has baseball diamonds and football/soccer fields.

Ho'olaule'a Road runs past the Marriott and leads over two arching bridges to Whalers Brewpub. This road serves as a **jogging path** and, beyond the brewpub, connects with a dirt road that runs in one direction to the Ninini Lighthouse, and in the other direction circles around to Route 51.

Golf and Tennis

Kaua'i Lagoons Golf Club, 808/241-6000 or 800/634-6400, is one of the premier golf courses on the island. Between the Kaua'i Marriott and the airport, the fairways of its two courses are strung along 40 acres of fresh-water meandering ponds. The older Mokihana course is a links course for recreational play, while the Kiele course has been designed as a more challenging championship course. While launches don't cruise these lagoons as they did during the Westin days, the water is still a pleasing backdrop for play. Greens fees run $150 for the Kiele and $100 for the Mokihana. Golf instruction is available, and clinics are held daily. Open 6:30 A.M.–6 P.M., the clubhouse (with restaurant) overlooks one of these lagoons; call ahead for tee times.

Next to the golf clubhouse, the eight plexipave courts of the **Tennis Club at Kaua'i Lagoons,** 808/246-2414, are open to any single or group for an all-day $20 court fee. Ball machines are available for an additional fee, as is private or semi-private instruction. The club's tennis program offers different clinics daily. Call for information, times, and pricing. Except for the 600-seat stadium, these courts are not lighted, so the hours of operation are 7 A.M.–dusk. Operating out of the same office and using the same telephone number, open daily 9 A.M.–7 P.M., is **The Spa,** where you can treat your skin, nails, hands, or whole body to variety of sensual delights and comforts.

A second golf course has opened in Lihu'e, the **Grove Farm Golf Course at Puakea,** 808/245-8756. Currently at 10 holes, it's being expanded to eighteen. Carved from former cane fields, it lies just west of the Kukui Grove Shopping Center on rolling ground and contains a deep ravine, volcanic outcrops, and other natural hazards. Greens fees are $35 or $60 for two times around, $40 twilight. Call the clubhouse/grill for tee times.

Kayaks and Zodiacs

At Nawiliwili small boat harbor, **Island Adventures,** 808/245-9662, website: www.kauaifun.com, rents single- and double-seat kayaks, $10–15 an hour or $30–45 a day, for a trip up Hulei'a Stream. This is the same group—different name—as the Kalapaki Beach Boys, who run the Marriott beach activities center. For a guided tour on the river, try **Aloha Canoes and Kayak,** at the Kalapaki Marketplace in Nawiliwili, 808/246-6804. **Outfitters Kauai,** 808/742-9667 or 888/742-9887, offers a seven-hour Kipu Kai Daytrip Tour from September to May for $115 for those in good physical condition, and a Kipu Falls tour for $68, which requires a two-mile kayak run plus a 1.5-mile hike to the falls, with a shuttle back to the Nawiliwili small boat harbor.

Almost no tour boats operate out of this harbor, but **Na Pali Zodiac,** 808/826-9371 or 800/422-7824, runs a winter whale-watching tour to Kipu Kai for $59 for adultsor $49 for kids.

Fishing

There are a number of charter fishing boats that operate out of Nawiliwili small boat harbor. One

KAUA'I

of these is the 55-foot *Konane Star* run by **True Blue Charters**, 808/245-9662, which is associated with Island Adventures. When not fishing, they will do snorkeling and whale-watching trips. Others are **Kai Bear Sportsfishing Charters**, 808/826-4556; **Sea Lure Fishing Charters**, 808/822-5963; **Lahela Ocean Adventures**, 808/635-4020; and **Hana Pa'a Charters**, 808/823-6031.

SHOPPING

Many good selections and bargains are found in the city. Kaua'ians shop in Lihu'e, and the reasonable prices that local purchasing generates are passed on to you.

Shopping Centers

Not much is left of the **Lihu'e Shopping Center** in downtown Lihu'e except the Big Save Supermarket. Along Route 56 just up from there, you'll see a classic building dating from 1923. Once the home of Garden Island Motors Limited, this and adjacent buildings make up a small strip mall housing Photo Spectrum, offering one-hour film processing, a few apparel shops, and some eateries. The **Rice Shopping Center**, 4303 Rice St., features a laundromat, a bowling alley, inexpensive eateries, a health-food store, and a neighborhood karaoke bar. The real shopping now is done at the newer centers.

The **Kukui Grove Shopping Center**, at the intersection of Kaumuali'i Hwy. and Nawiliwili Rd., just a few minutes west of downtown Lihu'e, is Kaua'i's largest all-purpose shopping mall. The center's main stores include Liberty House and Sears, for general merchandise and apparel; Longs Drugs for sundries, sporting goods, medicines, and photo needs; and Star Market for groceries. Some distinctive boutiques and shops found at the mall include Deja Vu, a surf shop with T-shirts, sun hats, glasses, wraparound dresses, bikinis, boogie boards, surfboards, sandals, and a smattering of dress shirts and shoes; Zales and Prestige Jewelers offer fine jewelry. For anything that beeps or buzzes, head for Radio Shack. Other shops include Dan's Sports Shop, for golf clubs, tennis racquets, baseball caps, mitts, dartboards, and water gear; General Nutrition Center for the health-conscious;

the Deli and Bread Connection for kitchen gadgets and wholesome eats; the Kauai Products Store, which offers quality, mostly island-made goods of all sorts; and half a dozen eateries. A free amateur hula show is performed Friday at 6 P.M. in the central open-air courtyard. General hours are Mon.–Sat. 9:30 A.M.–5:30 P.M., Friday until 9 P.M., and Sunday 10 A.M.–5 P.M. In a separate section to the side are Borders Books and Music and Kmart.

The **Anchor Cove Shopping Center**, at Kalapaki Beach, is a compact shopping and dining mall with a great location. Among the semi-detached kiosks, you will find an ABC Store, open daily 7 A.M.–10:30 P.M., selling sundries, beachwear, groceries, film, drugs, cosmetics, and also liquor; Crazy Shirts, open daily 9 A.M.–9 P.M., with well-made and distinctive T-shirts; and Honolua Surf Co. for casual clothing and resortwear; and Sunglass Hut International, open daily 9 A.M.–9 P.M., which can protect your eyes and enhance your image with sunglasses from famous makers—with 1,700 stores in the chain, it offers excellent prices, and satisfaction is guaranteed even at a store in your home area. Royal Hawaiian Heritage Jewelry sparkles with Hawaiian-inspired jewelry including personalized pendants and bracelets; Sophisticated You, owned and operated by former beauty queen Therese Jasper and open Mon.–Sat. 10 A.M.–5 P.M., Sunday 11 A.M.–3 P.M., features ladies' fine apparel for sale or rent, including wedding gowns and tuxedos, just in case the tropical sun goes to your head and you decide to tie the knot. Other establishments in the center include Ohana Helicopters' office and reservations desk, J.J.'s Broiler, Island Java Roasting Co. for fresh-brewed coffee and more, and Shipwreck Sub and Pizza for a quick meal. Park out front. From another parking lot to the side, a footbridge over the stream connects to Dukes's Canoe Club restaurant and the Marriott property.

The **Pacific Ocean Plaza** is just up from Anchor Cove. Many of its shops are empty, but there are several restaurants here that include Tokyo Lobby, Kauai Chop Suey, and Cafe Portofino. Next to Anchor Cove is the small **Kalapaki Marketplace,** with a handful of shops that include the Aloha Canoe and Kayak office, Lappert's Ice Cream, and a billiards parlor.

Kilohana

On the outskirts of Lihu'e, just past Kukui Grove Shopping Center, Kilohana is a unique collection of shops in a unique setting. Around the time that Gaylord Wilcox moved the business office of Grove Farm from the homestead site, he had the 16,000-square-foot Kilohana plantation house built. After decades of family use, the building was renovated in 1986 and turned into shops that sell arts and crafts. Shops are open 9:30 A.M.–9:30 P.M., closing Sunday at 5 P.M.

The longest-lasting part of a journey is the memory. One of the best catalysts for recapturing your trip is an inspirational work of art. Kahn Galleries at Kilohana specializes in original artworks and limited-edition prints created by some of the finest artists Hawaii has to offer. The Country Store specializes in Hawaiian-inspired souvenirs, wind chimes, wicker picnic baskets, cutlery, pillows, vintage fabric handbags, aloha shirts, hand-blown and hand-etched glass, and lovely silver jewelry. Master crafts from local artists include koa boxes, turned bowls, quilted throws, and cobalt blue hand-blown and -etched glass. Upstairs and down you will also find Sea Reflections, glimmering with glass, jewelry, and marine sculpture; Grande's Gems, for that impulse purchase of a gold bracelet or pearl necklace; the Kilohana Galleries Artisan's Room, offering more artwork, and the Hawaiian Collection Room, which sells Ni'ihau shell lei, coins, and other artifacts. Out front, the Makana Gallery has a unique collection of metal, glass, wood, and pottery gifts. In a separate building out back is Clayworks at Kilohana, which not only sells artists' work but is a place where you can create your own masterpiece.

Artwork isn't the only thing offered here, for Gaylord Restaurant serves some of the most exquisite meals on this side of the island. It also presents the Reflections of Paradise lu'au every Monday and Thursday. Appreciate the house as you wander from shop to shop, but you should also treat yourself to a ride around the plantation grounds in a horse-drawn carriage. For a more extensive look at the grounds, introduction to the history of the plantation, and culture of sugar, try the sugarcane carriage tour; call 808/246-9529 for reservations.

Specialty Shops

Don't pass up **Hilo Hattie's,** 3252 Kuhio Hwy., at the intersection of Ahukini Rd., 808/245-3404, open every day 8:30 A.M.–7 P.M. (Monday from 7:30 A.M.), an institution of alohawear, to at least educate yourself on products and prices. Though the designs may not be one-of-a-kind, nor all made in the state, Hilo Hattie's clothing is very serviceable and well made. Specials are always offered in the free tourist literature and on clearance racks at the store itself. There is a great selection of gifts and souvenirs, food items, and books. Among the abundance of incentives to get you in is the free hotel pickup from Po'ipu to Kapa'a, free refreshments while you look around, and free hemming.

Also at the intersection of Kuhio Highway and Ahukini Road is a **Red Dirt Shirt** outlet. Like its sister stores in Waimea and Kapa'a, this shop carries the famous dirt red T-shirts. Dozens of island designs are available in S-XXXXL. These make good gifts and wearable mementos of your trip to the island.

You knew that it had to happen here as well. Both the big box stores **Kmart** and **Wal-Mart** have stores in Lihu'e. These stores carry everything that the Mainland stores carry with the addition of island-specialty sections. Their introduction has put local stores out of business, but residents can get clothing and household items cheaper here than they were able to previously. Each has a sporting goods section and film developing.

You can find everything you need to try your luck in Kaua'i's waters at **Lihue Fishing Supply,** 2985 Kalena St., 808/245-4930, open Mon.–Sat.

Arts, Crafts, and Souvenirs

Kaua'i Museum Shop, at the Kaua'i Museum has authentic souvenirs and items Hawaiian with competitive prices, which include tapa, wooden bowls, books, cards, prints, and maps.

The **Kauai Products Store,** at the Kukui Grove Shopping Center, 808/246-6753, is a gem. This shop carries art and crafts items, mostly made in Kaua'i, that include paintings, wooden boxes, quilts, metal sculpture, T-shirts, a smattering of jewelry, and food products. It's fine quality at reasonable prices. A good place to stop for a preview of what the island has to offer.

KAUA'I

For antiques and collectibles, try **Time Lapse** behind the Beach Hut burger joint on Nawiliwili Beach.

Remember Kauai, at the Outrigger Kaua'i Beach Hotel, 808/822-0161, specializes in unique Hawaiian jewelry, like necklaces made from shells, beads, wood, and gold. The counters shine with belt buckles, pins, and a large collection of gemstones from around the world. Ni'ihau shellwork is available, and fine specimens run up to $12,000. The scrimshaw, worked by Kaua'i artists on fossilized walrus ivory, adds rich texture to everything from knives to paperweights.

Kapaia Stitchery, 808/245-2281, open 9 A.M.–5 P.M. Mon.–Sat., is where you find handmade quilts and distinctive fashions. This shop is along Route 56 in Kapaia. The owner is Julie Yukimura, who, along with her grandmother and a number of very experienced island seamstresses, creates fashions, quilts, and embroideries that are beautiful, painstakingly made, and priced right. Hung from the ceiling for better display, the quilts are awe-inspiring. If you are considering purchasing a quilt while on the island, this is definitely one of the best places to start your search. For those who sew, the range and quality of material is outstanding, and sewing accessories, patterns, and constructions books are all available. You can't help but be pleased with this fine shop!

The soothing rich aroma of a premium cigar wafts from the **Kapaia Trading Company** into the big dip along Route 56, just at the turnoff to Wailua Falls, across from Kapaia Stitchery, 808/246-6792 or 800/856-6482, website: www.kapaiatrading.com, email: ktct@gte.net, open daily 9 A.M. to sunset. Owned and operated by Bill Carl, this excellent shop is a great place for both men and women to peruse. The swirl of burly koa and other native woods lend natural luster to the handmade humidors and fine furniture that Bill has crafted. If you enjoy a good cigar, write or call Bill in advance to get a list of the many cigar brands he carries. You can pack your purchases in one of many styles of quality humidors, each with a lifetime guarantee (from the builder). From cigar-box-size to a desktop model, these beauties go for from several hundred to several thousand dollars. The hand-built furniture on display includes everything from a dining set to jewelry boxes of solid koa, correspondingly expensive but of rigidly high quality. Everything is available for shipping to the Mainland. The Kapaia Trading Company, more than just a shopping stop, is a real working man's gallery, where years of woodworking experience has been called upon to create exquisite pieces of fine art.

Directly across the street is the smaller **Wailua Falls Gallery** and cigar shop, 808/245-2711. Here too a variety of cigars are displayed in good quality humidors. A limited number of furniture pieces and smaller wood artwork, done by various island artists, are displayed for sale.

Bookshops

Your best bet for all kinds of books in Lihu'e is **Borders Books and Music,** 808/246-0862. Open every day at 8:30 A.M., it closes Mon.–Thurs. at 10 P.M., Fri.–Sat. at 11 P.M., and Sunday at 8 P.M. Borders carries one of the best Hawaiiana sections on the island. After finding your favorite book, browse the CD racks for music or peruse the map section for guidance. Borders also carries select Mainland and international newspapers. Cafe Espresso, within the store, serves up drinks and snacks.

A great place for books relating to Kaua'i and Hawaii is the **Kaua'i Museum Shop**—open museum hours only. Wal-Mart and Kmart both have book sections, but your selection is limited to generic titles.

Photo Needs

For film developing, try **Longs Drugs, Kmart** or **Wal-Mart. Photo Spectrum,** 808/245-7667 offers one-hour film processing and also does studio portraits.

Supermarkets and Health Food Stores

The **Big Save Supermarket,** near the County government building, is open daily 7 A.M.–11 P.M., and a well-stocked **Star Super Market** is at the rear of Kukui Grove Shopping Center. Also at Kukui Grove is **General Nutrition Center** for supplements.

Vim N' Vigor, in the Rice Shopping Center, 808/245-9053, open Mon.–Sat. 8 A.M.–6 P.M., specializes in vitamins, minerals, and other supplements. The shelves are stocked with a good but limited selection of whole-wheat flour to spices, organic pastas, and teas. The back deli case holds a small selection of fresh organic vegetables and prepared deli sandwiches.

Other Needs

As the principal population center of the island, and its county seat, Lihu'e has a five major

banks, four of which are within a few steps of each other along Rice Street. The main post office is across the street from the museum.

The **Lihue Laundromat** is an open-air, 24-hour, self-service laundromat at the Rice Shopping Center.

THE ENVIRONS

PUHI

Sustaining substantial residential growth over the past decade, Puhi has become a bedroom community of Lihu'e. Two road signs tip you off that you're in Puhi—one for **Kaua'i Community College** and the other for the **Queen Victoria's Profile** scenic overlook turnout. It's beneficial to keep abreast of what's happening at the college by reading the local newspaper and free tourist brochures. Often, workshops and seminars concerning Hawaiian culture, folk medicine, and various crafts are offered; most are open to the general public and free of charge. The Hawaii International Film Festival and local theater groups use the college's Performing Arts Center for their performances. About 5,000 students are enrolled at this two-year community college, part of the University of Hawai'i system, most in the fields of business education, health, liberal arts, and vocational technology. Call 808/245-8212 for information about registration and course offerings or visit the college's website: www.kauaicc.hawaii.edu.

Queen Victoria's Profile isn't tremendously remarkable, but a definite resemblance to the double-chinned monarch has been fashioned by nature on the ridge of the Hoary Head Mountains to the south.

Also in Puhi is the head office for Grove Farms Co., a Shell station, and a new warehouse/business park.

Food

Paradise Seafood and Grill, is an easygoing eatery on the highway in Puhi with dining inside or out on the covered veranda at booths or tables. Quick eats include soup, salad, and sandwiches at around $6; burgers for $6–6.50; and fish and chips for $7.50.

Across from the gas station at the intersection is **Puhi Fish And Catering Company,** a small deli with mini-mart attached. Open Mon.–Sat. 6 A.M.–7 P.M., and Sunday 7 A.M.–7 P.M.; the deli is open until 3 P.M. but closed on Sunday. Stop by for an inexpensive plate lunch, deli sandwich, drinks, or a selection of fresh fish. This place does lots of take-out, but you're welcome to eat inside at one of the tables.

HANAMA'ULU

Hanama'ulu is like a "suburb" of Lihu'e and has always been tied to sugar. Here are a post office, an elementary school, a mini-mall, two restaurants, a gas station, and several other shops. From the center of town, follow Hanama'ulu Road, and then Hehi Road down under the highway to Hanama'ulu Beach County Park.

Hanama'ulu Dining

Heading north, in Hanama'ulu and clearly marked along Route 56, is the **Hanamaulu Restaurant Tea House and Sushi Bar,** 808/245-2511, where they must be doing something right—they've lasted in the same location for more than 70 years! Open 10 A.M.–1 P.M. for lunch Tues.–Fri. and 4:30–8:30 P.M. for dinner Tues.–Sun. The menu, which includes sushi, *yakiniku,* and a variety of full-meal Japanese and Chinese dishes, is priced right. An Oriental Buffet is served Sunday evening. Ho Tai, the pudgy happy Buddha, greets you as you enter the room, which has shiny parquet flooring and is partitioned by shoji screens and hanging plants. Next door and part of the same restaurant is the sushi bar with tatami-floored rooms that look over a fishpond and a lovely Japanese garden. In the sushi bar section is an elevated tatami made private by sliding screens. The gardens behind and next door to the restaurant are wonderful and well worth a stroll. This is a local favorite—authentic food at appropriate prices.

JR's Plantation Restaurant, 808/245-1606, also sits along Route 56, a few steps away. Its decoration evokes both the *paniolo* and sugar eras. Drawing from the various ethnic groups on the island, the menu is varied, but the specialty is *kiawe*-broiled prime rib and steak. Most meals run in the $12–18 range, and dinner is served daily 5–9:30 P.M. Open windows let in the breeze as well as the traffic noise along the highway.

In the large green Hanama'ulu Trading Co. building next door (built 1908) are the post office, **Sampaguita's** for take-out, box-lunch Filipino food, and the **Big Wheel Donut Shop,** open early for a quick sugar fix. Across the street are a 7-Eleven and a Shell gas station.

Clearly marked along Route 56, the Hanama'ulu Plaza is right at the intersection of Kuhio Highway and Hanama'ulu Road. It's a small but practical shopping center featuring a laundromat and deli. **Ara's Sakamaya,** 808/245-1707, open Mon.–Sat. 9 A.M.–7 P.M. and Sunday 9 A.M.–5 P.M., is a take-out deli-restaurant that offers plate lunches, Japanese *bento,* and fresh

fish daily. Neat and tidy, **Plaza Laundry** is a full-service laundry with wash, dry, and fold service for those who don't care to do their own. One of the best on the island, it's open Mon.–Sat. 7:30 A.M.–8:30 P.M. and Sunday until 4:30 P.M.

Hanama'ulu Beach County Park
The beach here is fine, and although it's very accessible and good for swimming, few tourists come. To the right of the beach is a lagoon formed by Hanama'ulu Stream. Local families frequent this broad grassy park, and it's particularly loved by children as they can play Tom Sawyer on the banks of the heavily forested stream. If you're lucky, you may see dolphins jumping and spinning at the opening of the bay. There are picnic tables, showers, toilets, a pavilion, and camping (with a county permit) under the ironwood trees that front the beach. At times, homeless people stake out semi-permanent camps here, so it may not be the best for camping or the safest place to leave gear unattended. In Hanama'ulu, turn *makai* (toward the sea) off Route 56 onto Hanama'ulu Road at the 7-Eleven store, take the right fork onto Hehi Road, and follow it under the highway to the park. There is no access directly off the highway.

M.G.L. DOMENY DE REINZI

EAST SHORE

WAILUA

The East Coast of Kaua'i has been called the Coconut Coast, and it's obvious why when you pass through. Even with the extensive development in the area, numerous stands of coconut trees can be seen from the Wailua Golf Course all the way through Kapa'a. The greatest concentration of these stately nut trees, and a fine representation of the area, is at the Coco Palms near the mouth of the Wailua River. It is here that the coconut grove takes on a magical feel and captivates all who see it.

Wailua (Two Waters) is heralded by the swaying fronds of extra-tall royal palms; whenever you see these, like the *kahili* of old, you know you're entering a special place, a place of royalty. The Hawaiian *ali'i* knew a choice piece of real estate when they saw one, and they cultivated this prime area at the mouth of the Wailua River as their own and referred to it as Wailua Nui Ho'ano (Great Sacred Wailua). This was an important gathering place, a spiritual center for the islands,

and through the centuries many *heiau* were built in the area, some where unfortunates were slaughtered to appease the gods, others where the weak and vanquished could find succor and sanctuary. The road leading inland along the Wailua River was called the King's Highway. Commoners were allowed to travel along this road and to approach the royal settlement by invitation only. The most exalted of the island's *ali'i* traced their proud lineage to Puna, a Tahitian priest who, according to the oral tradition, arrived in the earliest migrations and settled here.

Even before the Polynesians came, the area was purportedly settled by the semi-mythical Mu. This lost tribe may have been composed of early Polynesians who were isolated for such a long time that they developed different physical characteristics from their original ancestral stock. Or perhaps they were a unique people altogether, whom history never recorded. But like another Island group, the Menehune, they were

KAUA'I

EAST SHORE

PACIFIC OCEAN

KILAUEA POINT LIGHTHOUSE

Kalihiwai Bay

Kilauea Bay

To Hanalei

Kilauea

56

KUHIO

GUAVA KAI PLANTATION ★

Moloa'a Bay

KOOLAU RD.

MOLOA'A RD.

HWY.

Papa'a Bay

0   2 mi
0   2 km

'ALIOMANU RD. 2nd

Anahola Mountains

'ALIOMANU RD. 1st

Anahola Bay

Anahola

ANAHOLA BEACH COUNTY PARK

Makaleha Mountains

MOON

56

Pohakuloa Point

KEALIA RD.

KUHIO HWY.

KAHUNA RD.

Kumukumu

Kawaihau

KAWAIHAU RD.

Kapahi

KA'APUNI RD.

Kealia

Powerline Trail

Moalepe Trail

HAUIKI RD.

WAIPOULI RD.

'OLOHENA RD.

Kapa'a

Kuilau Trail

'OLOHENA RD.

581

KAPA'A BYPASS RD.

KAPA'A BEACH COUNTY PARK

SEE "KAPA'A" MAP

KEAHUA ARBORETUM

Wailua Reservoir

Sleeping Giant

Waipouli

SEE "WAILUA" MAP

Opaeka'a Falls

Wailua River

580

Wailua

Kaua'i Channel

WAILUA RIVER STATE PARK

Wailua Falls

Wailua Bay

Wailua River

FERN GROTTO ★

56

WAILUA MUNICIPAL GOLF COURSE

583

To Lihu'e ↓   To Lihu'e ↓

KAUA'I

said to be dwarfish creatures who shunned outsiders. Unlike the industrious Menehune, who helped the Polynesians, the Mu were fierce and brutal savages whose misanthropic characteristics confined them to solitary caves in the deep interior along the Wailua River, where they led unsuspecting victims to their deaths.

Inland of Wailua (and also Kapa'a farther up the coast) is an upland district, not terribly high in elevation but located behind Nounou Ridge (Sleeping Giant) and definitely separated from the coast. This is former cane land that has been transformed into hobby farms, pastureland, and small agricultural plots. Numerous roads cut through this pastoral region, creating rural residential areas set amongst the rolling hills, with views of the nearby steep mountain slopes. Here it's easy to spot roosters picking for food along the roadway and cattle egrets standing tall and white in a horse pasture. It is, in a way, a miniature version of Upcountry Maui. For a glimpse of what this area is like, take Kuamo'o Road (Route 580) up from the coast and turn onto Kamalu Road (Route 581), following it around the mountain back to Kapa'a. Alternately, use either end of Opaeka'a Road to get to Pu'u'opae Road and follow this to Olohena Road. There turn uphill and follow it around as it slides down toward the sea via Waipouli Road, or a little farther to the north, Kainahola and Kawaihau Roads.

Wailua today has a population of more than 2,000, but you'd never know that driving past it, as most houses are away from the water, below Nounou Ridge; an additional 4,000 lie scattered on the upland hills of Wailua Homestead. Though it's an older resort area, Wailua is not at all overdeveloped. The natural charm is as vibrant as ever. Depending on conditions, the beaches can be excellent, and hotels, shops, restaurants, and nightlife are close at hand. With development increasing both to the north and south, perhaps now, as in days of old, the beauty of Wailua will beckon once again.

SIGHTS

To the traveling public, Wailua is famous primarily for two attractions: one natural, Fern Grotto, the other manmade, Smith's Tropical Paradise. People flock to these, as they are indeed beautiful spots, but there also exist other spots of historical and cultural significance. Most of these lie within the boundary of **Wailua River State Park,** which runs from the mouth of the Wailua River up the narrow valley, along its south fork to Wailua Falls and its north fork almost to Wailua Reservoir and Keahua Arboretum. Within the arms of this 1,093-acre park are several other waterfalls, including Opaeka'a Falls, half a dozen *heiau,* sacred birthing stones, and vantages for meditative views of the river below. For access to the river park, there is the Wailua Marina on its south bank and the boat/kayak launch on the north bank; the Lydgate Park and Wailua Beach sections front the bay.

Fern Grotto

Nature's attraction is the Wailua River itself, Hawaii's only navigable stream, which meanders inland toward its headwaters at the foot of forbidding Mt. Wai'ale'ale. Along this route is the Fern Grotto, a tourist institution of glitz, hype, and beauty rolled into one. Two local companies run sightseeing trips to the grotto on large motorized barges. As you head the two miles upriver, the crew tells legends of the area and serenades visitors with Hawaiian songs. A hula demonstration is given, and visitors are encouraged to get up and swing along. The grotto itself is a huge rock amphitheater, whose ever-misty walls create the perfect conditions for ferns to grow. And grow they do, wildly and with abandon, filling the cavern with their deep musty smell and penetrating green beauty. Partially denuded of its lush green coat and overhead tree canopy by Hurricane 'Iniki, the grotto is slowly filling in and becoming again the beauty it once was. Although the grotto is smaller than one might imagine, the resonating acoustics are wonderful from inside. Here in the natural cathedral, musicians break into the Hawaiian Wedding Song; over the years a steady stream of brides and grooms have come to exchange vows. The Fern Grotto trip is an amusement ride, and, aside from paddling yourself upriver in a kayak, it's the only way to get there. It's enjoyable and memorable, but you have to stay in the right frame of mind; otherwise, it's too easy to put down. (See Wailua River Cruises below for particulars.)

KAUA'I

Smith's Tropical Paradise

Set along the Wailua River is this 30-acre botanical and cultural garden. A large entranceway welcomes you and proclaims it a "tropical paradise." Inside, most plants are labeled; many are ordinary island foliage, but others are rare and exotic even for the Garden Island. The entire area is sheltered and well watered, and it's easy to imagine how idyllic life was for the original Hawaiians. The array of buildings includes a lu'au house and a lagoon theater used in the evenings for an international musical show and lu'au. Peacocks and chickens pecking beneath the trees are natural groundskeepers, preventing insects and weeds from overpowering the gardens. The "villages"—Japanese-, Philippine-, and Polynesian-inspired settlements—are merely plywood facsimiles. However, the grounds themselves are beautifully kept and very impressive. This garden provides an excellent opportunity to familiarize yourself with Kaua'i's plants, flowers, fruits, and trees. You are welcome to walk where you will, but signs guide you along a recommended route. Scheduled mini-trams carry tourists around the grounds for an additional fee. Entrance fees are $5 adults, $2.50 children 2–11; the tram tour is an additional $3 for adults, $2 for children. Smith's is open 8:30 A.M.–4 P.M., after which the gardens are readied for the evening lu'au and musical entertainment. To get to the gardens, follow the road past the Wailua Marina on the south side of the river; 808/821-6895.

Kamokila Hawaiian Village

Situated at a bend in the Wailua River on the way to the Fern Grotto is Kaua'i's only re-created folk village. Kamokila (Stronghold) has been cut from the jungle on the site of an *ali'i* village, the first of seven ancient villages in this valley; the villages farther up were for common laborers. The prominent ridge across the river indicates the boundary past which the ordinary man could not tread for fear of his losing his life.

The old village sat on terraces on the hillside above the river, and fields were cultivated where the village now lies. Kamokila has been resurrected to give visitors a glimpse of what island

WAILUA

sleeping hale *at Kamokila Hawaiian Village*

ROBERT NILSEN

life was like for the ancient Hawaiians. Opened in 1981, it was destroyed almost immediately by Hurricane 'Iwa in 1982 and badly knocked around again by Hurricane 'Iniki in 1992. It is continually going through renovation to make it more authentic; there are examples of buildings, agricultural plots, fruit trees and medicinal plants, and demonstrations of ancient crafts and activities of everyday life. Taro is grown and poi made, mats and skirts are woven, and traditional medicines prepared. A *hale noa* (chief's sleeping quarters), *hale koa* (warrior's house), *pahoku hanau* (birthing house), *hale ali'i 'akoakoa* (assembly hall), *hale lapa'au* (herbal medicine office), and *lana nu'u mamao* (oracle tower) have been erected. The *imu* pit for cooking is functional, and there is an athletic ground used for games at festival times. There are also tikis (spirit containers) and *'aumakua* (ancestral spirit icons) set up at propitious spots around the village.

A guide escorts you and explains the importance of each site, the methods of creating handicrafts and tools, the use of both the ordinary and medicinal plants, and how the village operated on a daily basis. You may drive down to the village by following a steep one-lane track that skirts the ridge—the turnoff is just above the Opaeka'a Falls overlook on Route 580. The entrance fee is $5 for adults, $2.50 for children under 12; open Mon.–Sat. 9 A.M.–5 P.M. A trip to this inspiring village is well worth the time and effort and will certainly add to your knowledge of the roots of Hawaiian life. For more information, call 808/822-3350. For those who want to combine this tour with a kayak trip up the river, both can be had for $25.

Historical Sites and *Heiau*

The King's Highway (Route 580), running inland from Wailua, and Route 56, the main drag, have a number of roadside attractions and historical sites dating from the precontact period. Most are just a short stroll from your car and well worth the effort. The mountains behind Wailua form a natural sculpture of a giant in repose, aptly called the **Sleeping Giant.** You have to stretch your imagination just a little to see him (his outline is clearer from farther up in Waipouli), and although not entirely a bore, like most giants, he's better left asleep. This giant and his green cover are part of the Nounou Forest Reserve.

Along Route 56, a tall stand of palms on the south side of the Wailua River is part of Lydgate State Park and marks the spot of **Hauola O Honaunau** (Pu'uhonua O Hauola), a temple of refuge that welcomed offending *kapu*-breakers of all social classes. Here miscreants could atone for their transgressions and have their spiritual slates wiped clean by the temple priests, enabling them to return to society without paying with their lives. Both the refuge and **Hiki na a ka la Heiau,** a site of rituals and prayers to the rising sun, are marked by a low encircling wall. The

KAUA'I

area is extremely picturesque here, where the Wailua River meets the sea. Perhaps it's knowledge about the temple of refuge that creates the atmosphere, but here, as at all of these merciful temple sites, the atmosphere is calm and uplifting, as if some spiritual residue has permeated the centuries. It's a good spot to relax in the cool of the grove, and picnic tables are available. At the river mouth and shallowly incised into the river rock are a handful of Kaua'i's few petroglyphs—human and geometric figures. These can usually be seen at low tide and when not covered by sand. Over the road near the entrance to the marina is **Malae Heiau.**

On the low point that forms the northern extent of Wailua Bay, situated on Lae Nani condominium property, is **Kukui Heiau.** As this whole region was once populated by royalty and a point of arrival and departure between the islands, and perhaps also for travelers from islands of the South Pacific, Kukui Heiau was used as a fire beacon site to direct canoes to a proper landing. Perhaps 500 years old and once about 230 feet long by 70 feet wide, only a fragment of its former stone structure is evident today, affirming the skill of its builders and the importance of the site.

As Route 580 starts to meander inland, you pass the state park boat launch area. Almost immediately on your left look for **Holoholoku Heiau,** where the unfortunate ones who didn't make it to the temple of refuge were sacrificed to the never-satisfied gods. This temple is one of Kaua'i's most ancient; the altar itself is the large slab of rock near the front. As if to represent the universality of the life-death cycle, **Pohaku Ho'o Hanau,** the royal birthing stones, are within an infant's cry away. Royal mothers came here to deliver the future kings and queens of the island. The stones somehow look comfortable to lean against, and perhaps their solidity reinforced the courage of the mother. Behind the *heiau,* a silver guardrail leads up the hill to a small, neatly tended Japanese cemetery. The traditional tombstones chronicling the lives and deaths of those buried here have turned green with lichens against the pale blue sky.

Back on Route 580, you start to wend your way uphill. You can see how eroded and lush Kaua'i is from this upland perch. Notice, too, the dark green fresh water as it becomes engulfed by the royal blue of the ocean in the distance. As you climb, look for an HVB Warrior pointing to **'Opaeka'a Falls.** The far side of the road has an overlook; below is the Wailua River and the Kamokila Hawaiian Village. Take a look around to see how undeveloped Kaua'i is. Across the road and down a bit from the 'Opaeka'a turnoff is **Poli'ahu Heiau,** supposedly built by the Menehune and used by King Kaumuali'i, Kaua'i's last king. Nothing is left but a square wall enclosure that has once again been filled with rock to create a level platform. Do not walk on the stones, as it's believed that the spirits of the ancestors are contained in the rocks. Down the ridge, at the end of a gravel track, are the **bell stones;** they were pounded when a royal *wahine* gave birth, and their peals could be heard for miles. From here, there is a great view over the river and down to the coast. It's easy to see why this was a very productive region and one prized by the *ali'i.*

Beaches and Parks

Lydgate Beach is a gem. It's on the south side of the Wailua River, behind the Holiday Inn Sunspree Resort complex. Two large lava pools make for great swimming even in high surf. The smaller pool is completely protected and perfect for tots, while the larger is great for swimming and snorkeling; overseeing the whole beach is a lifeguard. Stay off the slippery volcanic rock barrier. This beach is never overcrowded, and you can find even more seclusion by walking along the coast away from the built-up area. If you head to the river, the brackish water is refreshing, but stay away from the point where it meets the ocean; the collision creates tricky, wicked currents. **Lydgate State Park** also provides sheltered picnic tables under a cool canopy provided by a thick stand of ironwoods, plus grills, restrooms, and showers, but no camping. Here at the park is **Kamalani Playground,** a wonderful kids' play structure created for the community with community input. This is a child's dream come true: slides, swings, steps, tubes, passageways, and different level platforms.

Back down the coast and fronting the golf course is a secluded beach, a continuation of Nukoli'i Beach that's farther down. You can drive to it by following the paved road at the northern end of the course until it becomes dirt and branches toward the sea as a beach access road. The swimming is good in the sheltered coves, and the snorkeling is better than average along the reef. Few people ever come here, and plenty of nooks and crannies are good for one night's bivouac.

Wailua Beach, fronting the Coco Palms, is part of the Kaumuali'i section of Wailua River State Park. It can be treacherous and should only be entered on calm days when lifeguards are in attendance. It's a favorite for people who want to sunbathe, play in the water near shore, or stroll along the water. Surfers come for the breaks on the northern edge of the bay. There is parking under the trees at both ends.

Waipouli Beach County Park fronts the cluster of hotels just north of the Coconut Marketplace. Largely undeveloped, the narrow beach is really not recommended for swimming but is fine for sunbathing.

ACCOMMODATIONS

$100–150

Part of the Hawaiian-owned Sand and Seaside Hotels chain, **Kauai Sands Hotel,** to the side of Coconut Marketplace at 420 Papaloa Rd., Wailua, HI 96746, 808/822-4951 or 800/560-5553, fax 808/822-0978, website: www.sand-seaside.com/kauai.htm, email: info@sand-seaside.com, is a better-than-average moderate hotel with a convenient location, spacious grounds, accommodating staff, a large relaxing lobby, the budget Al & Don's Restaurant, two pools, and beach access. As with all four Sand and Seaside Hotels, this one is reminiscent of earlier days of Hawaiian tourism, a place that would seem familiar to someone who had visited Hawaii in the 1960s or '70s. All rooms have one king-size or two double beds, a refrigerator, air-conditioning, ceiling fans, TVs, telephones, and lanai. What the hotel lacks in luster it makes up for in price. Daily rates, which include breakfast for two, are $98 for a standard room, $125 for the deluxe room, and $135 for a room with kitchenette. Room and car packages are offered for about $30 more. Numerous discounts are offered, including AARP, AAA, military, and Internet booking.

Best Western has taken a former condo complex of 10 two-story buildings and turned the units into the comfortable **Best Western Plantation Hale Suites,** 484 Kuhio Hwy., Kapa'a, HI 96746, 808/822-4941 or 800/775-4253, fax 808/822-5599, website: www.plantation-hale.com, email: ph@aloha.net. Plantation Hale is across the street from Waipouli Beach Park just north of the Coconut Marketplace. This is not an oceanfront property. Accommodations include one-bedroom apartments with full kitchen, bath, dining room, and living area, each with color cable TV and daily maid service. An open-air hallway runs the length of each unit. There are three swimming pools on the property, a spa, putting green, and barbecue areas, and the front has an activities desk. While the road side has a border of trees and bushes, it's a bit close to the highway and some units may get traffic noise. Rates are $135–145 for a suite, $145–155 for garden view, and $155–165 for a scenic view room; $20 for each extra adult. Numerous discounts are offered. It's a decent value all around.

$150–200

A extensive $5 million renovation and property management change has transformed the old Kauai Resort into the 216-room oceanfront **Holiday Inn Sunspree Resort Kaua'i,** 3-5920 Kuhio Hwy., Kapa'a, HI 96746, 808/823-6000 or 888/823-5111, fax 808/823-6666, website: www.holidayinn-kauai.com, email: info@holiday inn-kauai.com. This hotel has a lovely setting at the mouth of the Wailua River just above Lydgate Park. Incorporated into the architecture is a series of cascading pools and a koi pond that boils with frenzied color at feeding time. The main lobby is a huge affair with swooping beams in longhouse style, and the wings of rooms run toward the ocean from there. The feeling you get here is of spaciousness and welcoming. The hotel facilities include two swimming pools, one hot tub, a small fitness room, one tennis court for guests only, volleyball and shuffleboard courts, coin-operated laundry, and a picnic area. For food, there's a restaurant and lounge, a deli-style counter, and poolside snack bar. The hotel rooms are large and many have ocean views; sliding glass doors let in the breeze, but the rooms don't have balconies. The overall color scheme includes muted greens and peach. While the bathrooms are not large, they are tastefully done; one wing has showers and the

COCO PALMS

The Coco Palms was a classic Hawaiian hotel, one of the first tourist destinations built on the island, but it took a terrible beating during Hurricane 'Iniki. The Polynesian-inspired buildings are interspersed through a monumental coconut grove planted by a German immigrant in the early 1800s. His aspiration was to start a copra plantation, and although it failed, his plantings matured into one of the largest stands of coconut trees in the islands. When Hollywood needed "paradise" it came here. The Coco Palms served as movie backdrop for Elvis in *Blue Hawaii* and for Rita Hayworth in the movie *Sadie Thompson,* bringing the hotel (and the island) notoriety. The chapel built for *Sadie Thompson* was left standing, and more than 2,000 marriages were performed there over the years. Some scenes from the movie *South Pacific* were filmed at the Coco Palms, and after Tattoo informed Mr. Roarke of the arrival of "de plane, Boss"

in the popular TV series *Fantasy Island,* it was into the hotel coconut grove that he drove his jeep. Nightly, the hostelry's famous torch-lighting ceremony took place under the palm canopy, which encircles a royal lagoon once used to fatten succulent fish for the exclusive use of the *ali'i.* Everyone, hotel guest or not, was welcome at the ceremony. Some dismissed the ceremony as "fake traditional," but it was the *best* "fake traditional" on the island—both dramatic and fun. This ceremony was started by the now-deceased Grace Guslander—a legend in her own right—a congenial hostess and old-time hotelier famous for her cocktail parties. The Coco Palms was a peaceful garden brought to its knees by the hurricane. It was and still is a landmark. The greenery has rebounded, of course, but one wonders how much of the grounds and the buildings will be saved when the property is finally turned to other uses.

other has bathtubs. Each room contains a small refrigerator, TV, room safe, and iron and ironing board. Room rates run $150–175 and $195–225 for suites. Thirteen two-room cabanas with kitchenettes are separate from the main facility and have unobstructed views of the beach; they run $275 a night. Room and car and romance packages are available. This is a fine, quiet place, where you receive a lot for your money.

Amidst a huge grove of swaying coconut palms, a natural buffer offering peace and tranquillity, with wings encircling a central courtyard, sits the sand-colored **Kauai Coconut Beach Resort,** P.O. Box 830, Kapa'a, HI 96746, 808/822-3455 or 800/222-5642. The palm grove once belonged to the family of the famous swimmer and actor Buster Crabbe, of *Buck Rogers* fame. He and his twin brother, Bud, were born and raised right here, and Buster learned to swim along this very coast. The lobby is alive with trees, flowers, and vines trellised from the balconies; stained glass depicting a sailing canoe departing at sunset and a 40-foot water cascade add comfort and grandeur. A bas-relief encircles the reception area, and as your eyes sweep from panel to panel it tells the story of how the Hawaiians became a "people," migrating

originally from Indonesia until they found their fabled "homeland in the north." All rooms have color TVs, air-conditioning, mini-fridges, safes, coffeemakers with complimentary Kona coffee, and private lanai. Built in 1978 and well used, recent remodeling and upgrades in furniture and amenities keep it fresh and new. Pastels and earth tones predominate, and artwork with Hawaiian themes hangs throughout. Rooms are sizable and the suites that front the ocean are massive. Rates are $150 for a standard room, $160 for a garden room, $210 for an ocean view, and $290 for an oceanfront room. For your convenience, the hotel offers a full-service activities desk, concierge service, a summer children's program, and laundry services. A lobby table is always reserved for local craftspeople, who offer their authentic handmade creations—anything from carvings to quilts. The central courtyard swimming pool and spa are places to relax, but for those looking for more activity, the hotel's three tennis courts, free to guests, offer rentals and lessons and are open to the public for a small fee. An indoor/outdoor restaurant serves breakfast, lunch, and dinner. As the sun sets, find a seat around the courtyard for the free torch-lighting ceremony, then move to the Royal

Coconut Grove Lounge for a drink and nightly entertainment.

Beachside of the Coconut Marketplace is the **Islander on the Beach,** 484 Kuhio Hwy., Kapa'a, HI 96746, 808/822-7417 or 800/847-7417, fax 808/822-1947, website: www.islander-kauai.com, email: islander@aloha.net, a bright white eight-structure complex with a front veranda and decorative balustrades on all levels, giving it something of a Southern plantation look. As a former condo, the studio apartments have been changed into air-conditioned hotel rooms with wet bars, refrigerators, coffeemakers, color TVs, room safes, and lanai, with microwaves in each oceanfront unit and suite. Set right on the beach, the hotel has a pool with jet spa, pool bar, barbecue/picnic area, and sand volleyball net, in addition to an activities desk, gift shop, and guest laundry. The Jolly Roger Restaurant sits adjacent to the parking lot, and only a few steps farther are the myriad shops and eateries of the Coconut Marketplace. Slightly lower during the "value season," room rates run $120 for garden view to $165 for oceanfront, with suites at $210.

Condos

One of the newest condo complexes in the area, and recently renovated, is the luxury **Aston Kaha Lani,** 4460 Nehe Rd., 808/882-9331 or 800/922-7866, fax 808/822-2828. Situated between the Wailua golf course and Lydgate State Park, it's a quiet place with a broad oceanfront lawn, large swimming pool, and tennis courts. These spacious units have living rooms that face the ocean across the lanai, fully equipped kitchens, and separate bedrooms. Each unit is equipped with ceiling fan, color cable TV, and room safe, and a laundry facility is on property. One-bedroom units run $190–215, two-bedroom units $250–265, and three-bedroom units $370–410; $15–50 less during regular season.

A moderately priced condominium on Wailua Bay is the **Kapaa Sands,** 380 Papaloa Rd., Kapa'a, HI 96746, 808/822-4901 or 800/222-4901, fax 808/822-1556, website: www.kapaasands.com, email: ksresort@gte.net, with pool, laundry facilities, and maid service. The oldest condo on the island—open since 1968—the 24-unit Kapaa Sands is kept clean and up to date and has been completely refurbished since Hurricane 'Iniki. It is situated on old Japanese

grounds that once housed a Shinto shrine. The Japanese motif is still reflected in the roofline of the units and the *torii* design above each door number. The well-landscaped grounds are rather compact but manage to include a swimming pool and a grass lawn that fronts a thin sand beach. Each unit has a full kitchen, ceiling fans in all rooms, telephone, TV, VCR, and a lanai. Two-bedroom units occupy two levels, with the bedrooms upstairs. Room rates are $85 and $99 for ocean view and oceanfront studios, and $114 and $129 for two-bedroom ocean view and two-bedroom oceanfront units. Monthly rates are available; the minimum stay is three days except during winter, when it is seven days.

The two classiest places along the north edge of Wailua Bay are Lae Nani and Lanikai. Managed by Outrigger Resorts, **Lae Nani,** 410 Papaloa Rd., Kapa'a, HI 96746, 808/822-4938 or 800/367-7052, Outrigger central reservations 808/688-7777, fax 808/822-1022, offers one- and two-bedroom units on the beach. The rich decor varies by unit, but all have full kitchens, lanai, ceiling fans, TVs, and one and a half baths; most have ocean views. All are immaculately clean. There is a laundry room, daily maid service, one tennis court for guests only, a swimming pool, and poolside barbecue grill. The small Kukui Heiau is on the property beachside, adjacent to a rock-enclosed swimming area that's perfect for kids and others unsure of the waves and tides. One-bedroom units for up to four people are $195–225, and the two-bedroom units are $250–295, maximum six; a two-night minimum stay is enforced. There is public shoreline access at the edge of this property.

Also three stories tall, the **Lanikai** is next door to the Lae Nani at 390 Papaloa Rd., 808/822-7700 or 800/755-2824, fax 808/822-9293. Here there are one- and two-bedroom units with kitchens that rent for $207–303 a day, $25 cheaper during low season. Ask about discounts. For additional information or reservations, contact Castle Resorts, 800/367-5004 Mainland and Canada or 800/272-5275 in Hawaii.

Vacation Rental Agencies

Kauai Vacation Rentals, 3-3311 Kuhio Hwy., Lihu'e, HI 96766, 808/245-8841 or 800/357-5025, website: www.KauaiVacationRentals.com, email: aloha@kvrre.com, handles condos and vacation rental homes throughout the island, but in Wailua it is mostly condo units.

Bed-and-Breakfasts

In the uplands behind the Sleeping Giant is **Lampy's Bed and Breakfast,** 6078 Kolopua St., tel./fax 808/822-0478. This delightful country residence, comfortable and well looked after, holds decorations, crafts, and knickknacks everywhere. Each room has its own bathroom, and the living room has cushy chairs and couches, TV, and audio equipment. The homemade breakfast in served at 8 A.M. either on the patio or in the backyard gazebo. Rooms run $50 single or $55 double, and $65 for the suite. No credit cards or personal checks are accepted. For information or reservations, call Tom or Lampy Lowy.

A short distance away is **Rosewood Bed and Breakfast,** 872 Kamalu Rd., 808/822-5216, fax 808/822-5478, website: www.rosewood-kauai.com, email: rosewood@aloha.net. Creamy yellow with white trim and set behind a neat picket fence, Rosewood is a finely kept plantation-style house with a smaller Victorian house, thatched house, and bunkhouse on the property. Least expensive, at $40–50, are the bunkhouse rooms, which share a bathroom but each has a refrigerator, microwave, and sink. The thatched cottage, one large room with kitchenette and an outdoor shower, and the main house rooms, each with private baths, go for $85. With two floors, two bedrooms, a full kitchen, and porch, the Victorian house runs $115. Breakfast is included for guests of the main house rooms; $10 extra for those in the bunkhouse. Three-night minimum stay.

Managed by Rosewood is **Hale Makani,** a full house with three bedrooms. Although above Sleeping Giant, it has views of the ocean. Bedrooms are upstairs; downstairs is one large room split into living, dining, and kitchen areas. This place is great for a family. The rental rate is $125 a night for up to four people, with a $75 cleaning fee per stay. Contact Rosewood above for information and reservations.

In the same area is **Makana Crest** cottage, P.O. Box 3671, Lihu'e, HI 96766, 808/245-6500, a small single unit with two bedrooms, a bath with shower, and a kitchen.

Across the road from Opaeka'a Falls is **House of Aleva,** 808/822-4606, offering two rooms that

share a bath on the second level. Rates are $40 single or $55 double; no credit cards are accepted. Work out breakfast particulars with owner.

FOOD

Inexpensive

Wah Kung Chop Suey, in the Kinipopo Shopping Village, 808/822-0560, open Tues.–Sat. 11 A.M.–2 P.M. and daily 4–8:30 P.M., is a clean, no-decor restaurant offering Chinese and local food. Lunch specials (all around $5) include items like kung pao with vegetables, rice, or noodles; beef broccoli; fried chicken; lemon chicken; and egg foo young. Soups are $5–6. Standards like chop suey and chow mein are under $7, and the most expensive dishes on the menu are less than $10. Wah Kung has a good reputation with local people.

Stark white with a few ethnic decorations, the **Korean Bar-B-Q Restaurant,** 808/823-6744, is also in the Kinipopo Shopping Village, open daily 10 A.M.–9 P.M., Tuesday from 4:30 P.M. While some items are authentic Korean, there is a mix of Hawaiian and American in the menu. Single plates like kalbi (short ribs) and chapchae (stir-fry clear noodles), mostly run $6–7, while kimchi soup and others are $6.75. The big guys like to come in for the combo plates, $6.25–7.50. Plate dishes come with two-scoop rice and four vegetables, otherwise order à la carte for a few dollars less. Take-out is available.

Directly across the street is **Wailua Family Restaurant,** 808/882-3325, open 6:30 A.M.–9:30 P.M. This place becomes a fairyland of lights in the evening. A full menu is served all day, but many come for the very reasonably priced buffets (under $10) and salad bar.

Surrounded by hotels and condos, the **Coconut Marketplace** has more than a dozen eateries. Among the many, check out **Eggbert's,** a family-style restaurant, open 7 A.M.–9 P.M., that has mostly light fare. **Taco Dude,** which receives high praise from local people, is open for lunch and dinner and serves beef, chicken, or bean tacos, tostadas, burritos, and taco salad. A counter restaurant, it serves fresh food made to order at reasonable prices. **Aloha Kauai Pizza,** 808/822-4511, serves some of the best pizza on the island and is a hit with locals. A short menu of other Italian food is available, many items made from family recipes. Open daily 11 A.M.–9 P.M. **Harley's Ribs and Chicken** says it all with its name. For your sweet tooth, step in to see what mouthwatering delicacies the **Rocky Mountain Chocolate Factory** has to offer or go healthy with **Zack's Frozen Yogurt.**

Moderate

As the main dining room at the Holiday Inn Sunspree, the **Prince Kuhio Court** is open for breakfast, lunch, and dinner. Sit inside or out on the lanai under tiki torches, where you can look out over the garden to the moon reflected off the water and hear soft evening entertainment filter out through the huge open doors. While it serves an à la carte menu at all three meals, it's perhaps best known for its very reasonably priced morning and evening buffets, $9.95 and $19.95, respectively. Evening entrées include baby clams linguini with wine sauce for $12.95, broiled marinated chicken breast with roasted sweet corn cilantro relish for $15.95, and prime beef rib for $21.50. The dining room holds the **Kuhio Lounge** and the **Marketessen,** a deli-style counter for sandwiches, drinks, and food for a picnic. For salads, sides, sandwiches, and burgers at the hotel, try the afternoon-only **Kahanu** cocktail and snack bar at the ocean view pool.

The **Wailua Marina Restaurant,** 808/822-4311, overlooking the Wailua River, offers moderately priced "local-style" food that's filling but not designed for the most refined palate. At this busy marina, the restaurant caters mostly to large tour groups during the day and couples and smaller groups in the evening. If you're going on a Fern Grotto boat trip, consider eating here for lunch 10:30 A.M.–2 P.M. Open 5–8:30 P.M. for dinner, except Monday; entrées run the gamut from chuck ground steak for $9 to fillet of mahimahi at $13.75 to filet mignon at $17.75. Only the lobster and lobster combination plates are more than $20. All entrées include rice or potatoes, a trip to the salad bar, and coffee or tea. Not gourmet, but convenient, and there's never a wait after the last boat uprivor.

Mema, in the Wailua Shopping Plaza, 808/823-0899, is open Mon.–Fri. 11 A.M.–2 P.M. for lunch and nightly 5–9:30 P.M. for dinner. Serving Thai and Chinese cuisine, it's a casual family-operated restaurant with a touch of class. The ornate chairs and tables set the theme, while walls and cabinets are well appointed with decorations. Waiters, dressed in silky Thai clothing, carry their trays past a profusion of potted plants and flowers. The book-like menu starts with crispy noodles, and continues through nearly 50 appetizers, vegetable, chicken, and seafood items, curries, soups, and noodle and rice dishes. Appetizers run $6.95–8.95 and most main entrées and soups range $8.95–17.95. Entrées include satay, spicy lemongrass soup, broccoli with oyster sauce, and seafood red curry cooked in coconut milk with basil and bamboo shoots. Most entrées can be prepared vegetarian, and spiciness can be adjusted. Mema's offers complete wine, beer, cocktail, and dessert menus. If you are looking for a restaurant with excellent exotic food where you can enjoy a romantic evening for a reasonable price, Mema's should be at the top of your list. It's a winner.

Behind the Wailua Shopping Plaza in a converted plantation house, almost hidden under tall trees and behind a prolific bougainvillea, is **Caffé Coco,** 808/822-7990, open daily except Monday 9 A.M.–9 P.M. Using local produce and only fresh fish (no red meat), the tiny kitchen puts nutritious food on your plate, a mix of European, Asian, Mexican, and American cuisine. Some breakfast items are homemade granola, Coco custard French toast, and a house-smoked fish and bagel platter. A midday meal might be a roasted veggie omelette with focaccia bread and roasted potatoes, silver noodle platter with samosa and cup of soup, or an 'ahi nori wrap. For dinner try a fish burrito, cilantro pesto 'ahi, or ono charmoula with curried vegetable samosa, rice, salad, raiita, and chutney. Aside from the daily menu, numerous specials are posted. After dinner, pick one of the many tempting, homemade desserts from the deli case or order coffee from the espresso bar. This is island-casual cuisine at its best—tasty, wholesome, and healthy. Most breakfasts run under $7, lunches about $5–13, and dinners in the $13–16 range. Order at the counter and take a seat out back in the garden under the vine-covered canopy, amongst orchids, bananas, and lime trees. To add to the ambience, live music is performed most evenings of the week. As seating is outside, if

KAUA'I

the mosquitoes get too bothersome, feel free to use the organic "jungle juice" kept at the counter.

At the Coconut Marketplace is **Buzz's Steak and Lobster** restaurant, 808/822-0041, open for lunch 11 A.M.–2:30 P.M. and dinner 4:30–10:30 P.M. *Pu pu* and happy hour are 3–4:30 P.M. and an early-bird special runs 4:30–6:30 P.M. Buzz's started serving steaks and seafood in Waikiki in 1957 and, with its signature restaurant still open on O'ahu, continues to do the same. You enter through large koa doors, where an open kitchen presides over a comfortable dining area, while palm fronds and a hanging canoe add a Polynesian flair. Take time to notice the collection of artifacts, paintings, basketry, lei, and antiques gathered from Tahiti and the islands of the South Pacific. Word on the street says the salad bar here is the best, and it's complimentary with dinner. For lunch, Buzz's offers such items as soup of the day at $2.95, mahimahi and teriyaki chicken sandwiches for $4.50–6.50. Desserts include New York-style cheesecake and homemade ice-cream pie, both priced at $3.95. Appetizers, served at both lunch and dinner, include sautéed mushrooms at $5.50 and teriyaki beef sticks at $4.50. Dinner entrées are mahimahi almondine for $11.95, Pacific shrimp for $16.95, various steaks priced $14.95–17.95, and prime rib (Fri.–Sat. only) at $18.95; lobster and fresh catch at market price.

The **Jolly Roger Restaurant,** 808/822-3451, open 6:30 A.M.–10 P.M., claims to have the longest happy hour on the island—from opening to 8 P.M., when karaoke starts in the lounge. They're not known for exceptional food, but you always get hearty substantial portions no matter what time of day you come to dine, and there are always advertised special deals. Breakfast is served until noon, lunch 11 A.M.–4 P.M., and dinner 3–10 P.M. You can find Jolly Roger between the Coconut Marketplace and the Islander on the Beach.

Expensive

The Japanese legend of Kintaro, a pint-size boy born to an old couple from inside a peach pit, is slightly less miraculous than the excellent and authentic Japanese restaurant named for him, owned and operated by a Korean gentleman,

Don Kim. From the outside, **Restaurant Kintaro,** next to the Kinipopo Shopping Center, 808/822-3341, open daily except Sunday 5:30–9:30 P.M. for dinner only, is nothing special, but inside it transforms into the simple and subtle beauty of Japan. The true spirit of Japanese cooking is presented, with the food as pleasing to the eye as to the palate. The sushi bar alone, taking up an entire wall, is worth stopping in for. The dinners are expertly and authentically prepared, equaling those served in fine restaurants in Japan. If you have never sampled Japanese food before, Restaurant Kintaro is Kaua'i's best place to start. Those who *are* accustomed to the cuisine can choose from favorites like tempura, sukiyaki, a variety of soba, and the old standby teriyaki. Reservations are often necessary.

The **Voyage Room,** at the Kauai Coconut Beach Resort, 808/822-3455, offers a sumptuous breakfast buffet for $11.25, or an à la carte menu for both breakfast and lunch. The special Sunday Brunch, 10 A.M.–1:30 P.M., is a good value at $16.95 adults, $12.95 for children 12–17, and $1 per year for kids 6–11. From 5:30 to 9:30 every evening, the Voyage Room transforms into **The Flying Lobster.** The surf-and-turf-oriented menu begins with appetizers for $4–7.50, soup of the day, and the Never Ending Pasta Bowl for $8.95. Seafood lovers will enjoy entrées like the Ali'i spiny lobster dinner for $29 and shrimp scampi at $17, or a filling combination like fresh catch and top sirloin for $14.50. From the broiler, you can dine on New York strip steak at $17.50 or barbecued baby back ribs for $14. Other selections include the fresh catch of the day at $15.95, which can be broiled or sautéed with lemon butter, and the combination sirloin steak and lobster for $26. Lighter fare, scrumptious desserts, and drinks are also on the menu, and don't forget the early-bird special 5:30–6:30 P.M. Follow the example of the locals who come to the Flying Lobster on Friday and Saturday evenings 5:30–9:30 P.M. for the seafood and prime-rib buffet—lobster, crab, shrimp, oysters, prime rib, and fresh fish cooked to order before your very eyes. Prices are reasonable at $23.95 adults, $14.95 children ages 12–17, and $1 per year for kids 6–11. Sunday evenings bring the prime rib *paniolo* barbecue buffet, a Hawaiian cowboy cookout, also priced at $23.95. Other evening theme buffets are also good values. Reservations are recommended because the buffets are popular with local people, who know quality, quantity, and a good price when they see them.

ENTERTAINMENT

The **Kauai Coconut Beach Resort** offers a little of everything. You can enjoy free *pu pu* and entertainment at Royal Coconut Grove Lounge, just off the gardens and pool deck—happy hour is 4–6 P.M. Follow that with the free torch-lighting ceremony in the central courtyard. Every evening 8–11 P.M., listen to pop, contemporary, and standard hits by local musicians.

Tropical Hawaiian and contemporary music serenades diners nightly at the Prince Kuhio Court dining room at the Holiday Inn Sunspree Resort.

The Coconut Marketplace hosts a free **Polynesian Hula Show** Monday, Wednesday, and Saturday at 5 P.M. The young local dancers and musicians put as much effort into their routines as if this were the big time.

The Coconut Marketplace also has something to offer moviegoers: the **Plantation Cinema 1 and 2.** Call 808/821-2324 for showings and movie times. Adult entrance is $6, seniors, children, and matinee $3.50.

The lounge at the Jolly Roger Restaurant behind the Coconut Marketplace offers karaoke nightly. You can listen, sing, and even dance nightly 8 P.M.–1:30 A.M. The "happy hour" runs all day until karaoke begins, and the drinks are cheaper than at a hotel. The atmosphere is casual and the talk friendly. A good watering hole, where you can find cool drinks, good conversation, and karaoke nightly is **Tradewinds—A South Seas Bar,** at the Coconut Marketplace, 808/822-1621, open 10 P.M.–2 A.M.

Two **lu'au** are performed along this coast. The Kauai Coconut Beach Resort holds its lu'au every evening in the *lu'au halau* amongst the coconut trees starting at 6 P.M. Adult tickets are $55, seniors $50, $33 for children 12–17, and $23 for those 3–11; call 808/822-3455 for reservations. Smith's Tropical Paradise Garden Lu'au hosts a buffet and presents the Golden People of Hawaii musical review on Monday, Wednesday, and Friday starting at 5 P.M. on the banks of the Wailua River. Tickets are $52 for adults, $27 for children 7–13, and $18 for ages 3–7; call 808/821-6895 or 808/821-6896 for reservations.

RECREATION

Golf
Wailua Municipal Golf Course, 808/241-6666, skirts the coast, fronting a secluded beach. Opened in 1920 but rebuilt several times, it is the oldest golf course on the island and supposedly the first built on an outer island. Because of its idyllic setting, it's perhaps the most beautiful public links in Hawaii, and it frequently gets cited as one of the finest municipal courses in the country. On occasion, tournaments are held here. Even if you're not an avid golfer, you can take a lovely stroll over the fairways as they stretch out along the coastline. The greens fees are a reasonable $25 weekdays, $35 weekends ($8 and $12 for residents), carts are $14 and club rental is $15. The driving range is open until 10 P.M. For the convenience of golfers, the clubhouse has a dining room and snack bar open daily.

Wailua River Cruises
You too can be one of the many cruising up the Wailua River on a large, canopied, motorized barge. Most often taken by middle-age and older tourists, anyone can fully enjoy this trip if they let the beauty of the spot surround them. The Fern Grotto, where the boat docks, is a natural amphitheater festooned with hanging ferns—one of the most tourist-visited spots in Hawaii. The oldest company is **Smith's Motor Boat Service,** 808/821-6892 or 808/821-6893, in operation since 1947. The extended Smith family still operates the business, and members serve in every capacity. During the 20-minute ride upriver on their green boats you're entertained with music and a recounting of legends, and at the Fern Grotto a small but well-done medley of island songs is performed. Daily cruises (90 minutes round-trip) depart every half hour from Wailua Marina 9–11:30 P.M., and again 12:30–3 P.M. Monday, Wednesday, and Friday there's an additional 3:30 P.M. cruise. Adults cost $15, children $7.50; discounts for seniors and *kama'aina* are available.

Waialeale Boat Tours, 808/822-4908, with the red barges, is Smith's only competition. Also at the marina, it's a smaller operation with fewer sailings but offers the same type of musical accompaniment and storytelling during the ride. While the daily tour schedule changes periodically depending on the volume of customers, generally boats leave every hour on the half hour between 9:30 A.M. and 1:30 P.M., with additional 9 A.M. and 3 P.M. tours. Tickets are available at the company's marina office and cost $15 adults, $7.50 children; senior and *kama'aina* rates available.

Kayaking

Kayaking in Wailua means kayaking up the gentle and slow-moving Wailua River. The favorite route is to head to Fern Grotto or perhaps a bit beyond to a river's edge swimming hole and rope swing. Do not use the boat dock at Fern Grotto, as they are maintained only for the river barges. Although it has caused some bank degradation, the only way to disembark there is to tie your kayak to a bush on the bank next to the dock and walk along the water to the paved walkway. A second route, now preferred by some, is to head to what is known as "Secret Falls" (or Misty Falls). Going upriver, turn right into the north fork of the river just past Kamokila Hawaiian Village. A short way up—stay to your left—look for the trailhead and tie your kayak up along the bank. From here it's about an hour's walk to the falls. Roughly, follow the south bank until you get to a water gauging station. Just beyond it, cross the stream that comes in from your left. Walk up this stream, cross the right branch, and recross the main stream for a short distance to the falls.

When going either upstream or down on the Wailua River, stay hard to the north bank, as there is frequent barge traffic and periodic motorboats pulling water-skiers.

To rent kayaks for one of these adventures—be sure to ask for a river map—check with one of the following companies. **Wailua Kayak and Canoe,** 808/821-0015, has a booth next to the Smith Motorboat Company booth on Wailua Road, which is the first left turn off Kuamo'o Road (Route 580) after turning inland off of Kuhio Highway (Route 56). As this is the closest place to the river, it's easy to carry the kayak to

the launch site. **Kauai Water Ski and Surf Co.,** 808/822-3575, is in the Kinipopo Shopping Village, while **Kayak Kaua'i Outbound,** 808/822-9179, is at the rear of Coconut Marketplace near the movie theater. Other kayak rental shops can be found farther up the road in Kapa'a. Rates for kayak rentals generally run $25 for a single and $50 for a tandem. If needed, car carriers can also be rented. All places require that you return kayaks by 5 P.M. Kayak launching and retrieval should be done at the state park unit launch site, the third driveway on the left off Route 580 up from Kuhio Highway. Kamokila Hawaiian Village also rents kayaks for $25, which includes a guided tour of the village. If you rent there, you don't have to paddle so far up the river.

Water Skiing

Ever thought of water skiing in paradise? Skimming the smooth waters of Wailua River is the only possibility on Kaua'i, and **Kauai Water Ski and Surf Co.,** in the Kinipopo Shopping Village in Wailua, 808/822-3574, has business to themselves. Open daily 9 A.M.–7 P.M., the shop offers a half hour of skiing for $55 and one hour for $100. Prices include boat, gas, driver, and all equipment. This shop also sells beach clothes and water sports equipment. Rentals include kayaks, surfboards, boogie boards, and snorkeling equipment.

East Kaua'i Hiking Trails

All these trails are in the mountains above Wailua. One trail system crisscrosses Nounou Ridge, otherwise known as the Sleeping Giant, while others start from the Keahua Arboretum at the end of Route 580.

Nounou Mountain Trail, East Side, begins off Haleilio Road just north of Wailua Beach, at the Kinipopo Shopping Village. Follow Haleilio Road for 1.2 miles until it begins to curve to the left. Near pole no. 38, park at the small trailhead parking lot. The trailhead leads to a series of switchbacks that scale the mountain for 1.75 miles. The trail climbs steadily through native and introduced forest and past one large volcanic outcrop. Near the top, it meets the west side trail coming in from the right, and shortly beyond that is a flat, grassy area with a picnic table, shelter, and bench. This is the "chest" of the giant. Stop here a while and take in the views down to Wailua and the coast or up toward the middle of the island. From the picnic area you can proceed along the spine of the mountain, the "throat," to the giant's "face." Although the going gets a little tougher and mountain drops off quickly on both sides, the trail is passable and you may have it to yourself. From the face, you're rewarded with a superb 360-degree view but may not be able to see down the slope due to the thick brush cover.

A parking area and right of way for **Nounou Mountain Trail, West Side** is found at the end of Lokelani Street, off Route 581, north of Route 580. Alternately, a trail right of way leads directly up to this point and the trailhead from Route 581, but there is not much parking along the road. Follow the right of way until it joins the trail at the top end of the pasture. This trail leads you through a forest of introduced trees planted in the 1930s, and includes Norfolk Pine, strawberry guava, and a forest of *hala* trees near the top. About a quarter mile from the start, a fork in the trail locates the junction of the **Kaumo'o Nounou Trail,** which traverses the west side of the mountain, through a bamboo forest and over 'Opaeka'a Stream, from its trailhead on Route 580 across from Melia Street. The West Trail joins the East Trail at the 1.5-mile marker and proceeds to the picnic table and shelter. This trail is slightly shorter, steeper, and more forested than that on the ocean side. Bring water for both, as there is none on the way.

Follow Route 580 until you come to the University of Hawai'i Agriculture Experimental Station. Keep going past the Wailua Reservoir until the pavement ends and then follow the dirt road for almost a mile. A developed picnic and fresh water swimming area is at Keahua Stream, about seven miles in from the highway. This is the **Keahua Arboretum.** Two short trails run on either side of the stream here and another leads into the marshy area beyond the hill. It would have been helpful to have trees in the arboretum named, but it isn't so. The southern end of the **Powerline Trail** starts at the arboretum. Cross the stream and walk up the steep road on the far side. At the top, a hunting trail heads off to the right. This is the start of the Powerline Trail. From here, it's a full day's hike over the mountain

to the trailhead on the Hanalei side, about 13 miles away. This very rugged track is often used by mountain bikers and also by hunters during hunting season.

The **Kuilau Trail** begins about 200 yards before the entrance to the arboretum, on the right. This gradual trail follows a muddy old roadway for a mile or so to a flat spot with a picnic area and shelter. Here are some magnificent views of the mountains. You can look directly out at Mt. Wai'ale'ale and what's known as the Wai'ale'ale crater or farther afield to Kilohana and the Ha'upu Ridge, or follow the powerline as it marches up and over the pass. Like the arboretum below, this is a good area to listen to the birds. Continue on this trail, circling around the hill, and you'll eventually come to a small footbridge. At the bridge, the Kuilau Trail meets the Moalepe Trail, about two miles from the trailhead. After crossing the bridge, the trail climbs through a dense tunnel of trees to a small open flat spot and then turns to the east. The **Moalepe Trail** starts at the end of Olohena Road. From here a dirt track runs for some distance inland to a turnaround, but it may not be passable as it's extremely rutted and often slick in rainy weather. This route, a popular horseback-riding trail, gains the heights and offers some excellent panoramas before joining the Kuilau Trail at the footbridge, almost three miles from Olohena Road. Both these trails bring you to middle elevation mountain slopes.

SHOPPING

Kinipopo Shopping Village

This diminutive seaside mall at 4-356 Kuhio Hwy., just beyond the end of Wailua Beach, offers most of Wailua's one-stop shopping. Aside from Korean and Chinese restaurants, you can find a handful of unique small shops. **Kauai Water Ski and Surf Co.,** 808/822-3574, open daily 9 A.M.–7 P.M., is a complete sales and rental water-sports shop. Bathing suits, bikinis, sun visors, men's shorts, surfboards, boogie boards, wetsuits, fins, masks, snorkels, underwater watches, and even a few backpacks and day packs line the shelves of this small but jam-packed shop. Water-skiing can be arranged and kayaks rented.

KAUA'I

If you are an aficionado of old Hawaii, make sure to drop in to the **Tin Can Mailman,** 808/822-3009, open daily except Sunday 10 A.M.–5:30 P.M. The Tin Can Mailman definitely has a heart for out-of-print books on Hawaii and Polynesia, battered travel guides filled with memories, antique maps, vintage menus, early botanical prints, rare Missionary items, and even new books. The shop is small and bursting with ancient voices still quietly singing their songs. This is the best local bookshop on the island.

Merry-Go-Round Consignment Boutique, open daily, carries an assortment of previously used clothing, including aloha shirts and casual dresses. For something new, try **Kinipopo Fine Art;** for a permanent memento, ask at **Garden Isle Tattoo.** The **Shell Station Mini-Mart,** at the corner, sells sundries, snacks, beer, and packaged foods.

The Coconut Marketplace

Prices at this cluster of more than 70 shops, restaurants, and galleries are kept down because of the natural competition of so many businesses, each of which tries to specialize, which usually means good choices for what strikes your fancy. As you walk around, notice the blown-up photos that give you a glimpse into old Hawaii. Any of the jewelry shops have enough stock on hand to drop even Mr. T to his knees. With so many apparel and footwear shops, the job of finding just the right aloha shirt,

casual dress, or sports clothing shouldn't be a problem.

Ship Store Gallery, 808/822-7758, sets sail for adventure with nautical artwork of tall-masted ships and contemporary Japanese art in a gallery that's filled with cannons, pistols, and swords. This is an amazingly full place that will get the mariner in everyone away from the dock. In addition to the plentiful artwork are fine antiques and collectibles. If the price of original artwork puts too much of a strain on your budget, then **Island Images,** offering fine art prints, posters, and a smattering of original artwork at discounted prices, might have what you need at an affordable price. **Ye Old Ship Store** displays the best collection of scrimshaw on Kaua'i and some sea paintings by local artists.

Make sure to stop into **Kauai Fine Arts,** open daily 9 A.M.–9 P.M., closing Sunday at 6 P.M. Owned by Caribbean islander Mona Nicolaus, who operates the original Kauai Fine Arts in Hanapepe, the boutique specializes in original engravings, antique prints mainly of the Pacific Islands, antique maps, and vintage natural science photos from as far afield as Australia and Egypt. It also houses a collection of antique bottles. Also on display are hand-embroidered pillows and quilts, designed in Hawaii but made on Bali, and tapa imported from Tonga or Fiji. Kauai Fine Arts offers framing and worldwide shipping. If not purchasing, at least stop to browse in the museum-like atmosphere.

courtyard of the Coconut Marketplace

ROBERT NILSEN

KAUA'I

Some other shops include **Liberty House** for men's and women's casual fashion; **Island Surf Shop,** where you can purchase a boogie board, travel bag, a *pareu,* beach hat, and T-shirts; **Russian Treasures,** filled with Russian dolls; and **Products of Kauai,** selling just that. If your heart desires Hawaiian delicacies like Kona coffee, Maui onion mustard, macadamia nuts, island candy, Kauai Kookies, Kukui jams and jellies, or just a souvenir to take home, head for **The Nut Cracker Sweet** and just see if you can pull yourself away. For the ordinary purchase, head for **Whaler's General Store. Wolf Camera** will develop film, and the **Kaua'i Visitors Center** can give you information about things to see, places to go, and adventures to explore.

Specialty Shops and Galleries

Ye Old Ship Store, in the Coconut Marketplace, website: www.scrimshawart.com, distinguished as the center's oldest retail store, is the premier shop on Kaua'i for scrimshaw. The shelves are filled with collectors' pieces and museum-quality artwork scrimmed from fossilized walrus, mammoth, and mastodon ivories that have been worked by extremely talented contemporary artists. Every February, Ye Old Ship Store sponsors the **Hawaii International Scrimshaw Competition,** drawing competitors from throughout the United States and Canada. Pieces created by these master scrimshanders are like any other original works of art, carrying price tags up to $10,000 and beyond. Cases hold other items, not just scrimshaw, in a wide variety of price ranges—Hawaiian fishhooks made from wild pig bone by local hunters; copies of fishhooks from the Philippines; turtles, whale tails, and money clips. Ye Old Ship Store has other interesting items that will delight the entire family. If scrimmed knives, letter openers, and fine jewelry isn't enough, look for the distinctive "Spirit of Aloha Kauai Bottle," made from Kaua'i's land, sea, and air, and each blessed with a Hawaiian prayer, or for an extremely accurate Hawaiian Islands map T-shirt depicting Hawaii during the times of first contact, made more fancy with a border of ancient Hawaiian tattooing. Ye Old Ship Store is a perfect stop to make a purchase that says "Hawaii," or just to have a close-up look at a very intriguing art form.

Set back in the trees behind the Wailua Shopping Plaza, next to Caffé Coco, is **Bambulei,** 808/823-8641, an intriguing little shop that, along with a variety of antiques and collectibles, carries some women's clothing and furniture. Although there is an eclectic mix, much is Asian or Asian-inspired, and there's a heavy predominance of Hawaiiana from the mid-decades of the 1900s. This is worth the stop if a step back in time is of interest to you.

KAPA'A

Kapa'a means "to hold," as in "to hold a canoe on course." In the old days, when the canoes set sail to O'ahu, they'd always stop first at Kapa'a to get their bearings, then make a bee-line directly across the channel to O'ahu. Yachts still do the same today. It was probably a series of fishing villages in days past, but from 1913 to 1960 there was a huge pineapple cannery in Kapa'a, and much of the east shore bristled with these sweet golden fruits. More recently, sugarcane was raised, but that too is all but gone.

The heart of Kapa'a itself is a workers' settlement, a blue collar community with modest homes, utilitarian shops, some downhome eateries, churches, and one hotel. Old Town Kapa'a is where Route 56 and 581 meet. Only in the past few years has there been a move to yuppify shops and restaurants. Yet, the Kapa'a area is one of some contrasts. At the south end along the main drag is **Waipouli** (Dark Water), actually a separate community just north of Coconut Marketplace, though you'd never know it. Clustered here are newish condos, several full-service shopping malls, a multitude of restaurants, and some nightlife—sort of a live-in resort atmosphere. Inland from the center of town are newer, rural bedroom communities that string along the roads that track in toward the mountains. With a population of 8,200, just slightly fewer people live here than in the greater Lihu'e area, but the vibe in Kapa'a is definitely more local. What distinguishes Kapa'a is its unpretentiousness. This is "everyday paradise,"

KAUA'I

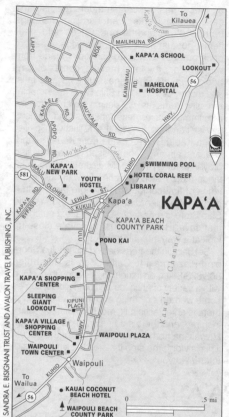

age 11 and under. These informative walks go up as far as the Kapa'a Library before returning via the beach path. Call 808/821-1778 for reservations.

To ease traffic through the heart of this community, the **Kapa'a Bypass Road** skirts around from Wailua to the north edge of Kapa'a. It runs through the agricultural fields behind town and is open 5 A.M.–9 P.M. daily. From where this bypass meets Olohena road near the New Kapa'a Park, jog toward the ocean and turn onto Lehua Street to miss the downtown intersection.

There are few sights per se, although near the middle of this strip, at Kipuni Place, is the **Sleeping Giant Viewpoint** pulloff. From this angle you get a reasonably good look at the mountain, and, using your imagination, you can distinctly see a recumbent figure with head, neck, and chest. Trails up both the front and back of this hill bring you to a picnic spot on the chest, from where a narrow trail leads over the throat to the chin and forehead. While in Kapa'a, spend your time checking out the shops, scanning the color-mottled mountains of the interior, and combing the beaches, especially those to the north. A few minutes up the coast, you're in wide-open spaces. Small oceanside communities pop up, their residents split between beach-house vacationers and settled *kama'aina*. The only town of size is Anahola.

Beach Park

Central Kapa'a's beach begin near Waika'ea Canal, and **Kapa'a Beach County Park** runs north from there for almost a mile until it ends near a community swimming pool and the Kapa'a Library. Small roads lead to the beach through town from the highway. Kapa'a Beach County Park has just over 15 acres, with a pavilion, picnic tables, showers, toilets, and grills. At its south end, a footbridge connects both sides of the canal, where locals often come to fish. A boat ramp backs into the canal here and there is a deep enough channel through the reef for boats to get in and out. This beach is pretty enough to look at, but it is not a typical resort beach. The feeling here is that this area belongs to the locals, although no undue hassles have been reported.

where the visitor is made to feel welcome and stands in line with everyone else at the supermarket. Generally, the weather is cooperative, beaches are fair, and the pace is unhurried. Kapa'a isn't the choicest vacation spot on the island, but you can have a great time here and save money.

To have a free **guided walking tour** of town, complete with snippets of history and culture, contact the Kapa'a History Shop on the main drag. The shop, sponsored by the Kaua'i Historical Society, is open Mon.–Sat. 10 A.M.–4 P.M. The 1.5-hour tours run Tuesday, Thursday, and Saturday and cost $10 adults and $5 children

ACCOMMODATIONS

Under $50

Kauai International Hostel, 4532 Lehua St., Kapa'a, HI 96746, 808/823-6142, welcomes international guests with a friendly multilingual staff. Rates are $16 for a dorm bunk (no reservations, private female dorm available), and $40 for one of the five private rooms with double bed (reservations accepted); $10 key deposit. Reduced rates for those with IYH cards. Although the hostel is open 24 hours, quiet time is at 11 P.M.; checkout is by 10 A.M. Occasionally, staff members or guests organize an impromptu barbecue/lu'au, and the hostel runs van tours for $40—mostly hikes to waterfalls, canyons, and pristine beaches, along with airport pickup on arrival before 10 A.M. and after 6 P.M. Facilities include a large communal kitchen with good appliances, a lounge with comfortable couches and cable TV, a covered outdoor lanai with a pocket billiard table, and a laundry room. Store your valuables in the office safe. Dorm rooms, each with its own sink and private bath, contain either four or six bunks. The private rooms are small but sufficient, and they share a bath. With room for 42, the hostel is clean and well managed. While it has a nominal seven-night maximum stay, there have been some long-term residents. This is a good place to meet young people from all over the world.

Just past the park in Kapa'a, across the street from Kojima's Grocery is **Kapa'a BeachHouse on the Blue Lagoon,** 4-1552 Kuhio Hwy., Kapa'a, HI 96746, 808/822-3424, website: www.kauai-blue-lagoon.com, email: nvb@hawaiian.net. A real beach house converted into a hostel-like accommodation, there are women's and co-ed dorms and a couple of private rooms. Most rooms look out across a grassy lawn to the stillwater "lagoon" inside the reef. The table on the lanai is a gathering place, and a mini-kitchen to the side is for guest use. Also for guests are cable TV, a washing machine (line dry), free weights, and a few exercise machines. The roof can also be used for relaxation. Rooms contain double bed bunks, each with a privacy curtain; rates are $20 single, $35 double, $45 for a private room. The baths are shared. No smoking. The place is amongst a tangle of trees

behind a garage that barely escaped the last hurricane; look for a "Chiropractor" sign and turn in there. Walk up to the second floor to check in. The public bus stops out front. A funky place with easygoing island character, it's not for everyone, but might be right for backpackers, bicycle riders, budget travelers, and anyone who cares more about what they eat than where they sleep.

$50–100

On a back street in downtown Kapa'a, only one block from the water, is **K.K. Bed and Bath,** 4486 Kauwila St., Kapa'a, HI 96746, 808/882-7348 or 800/615-6211 code 32, website: www.aloha.net/~sugi/b&b.html, email: sugi@aloha.net. Owner/manager Richard Sugiyama has turned an old 1930s family warehouse into two clean and bright rental rooms, each with queen bed, refrigerator, color TV, ceiling fan, and bath with shower. Don't expect anything plush, but the place is neat as a pin and Richard is a very accommodating fellow. Daily room rates are $35 single, $50 double, $60 for three adults; no charge for children under 12 when using existing beds. Breakfast is not included. Three-night minimum, no credit cards. Reservations appreciated.

Women looking for an environment that is supportive of women travelers should try **Mahina's Guest House,** 808/823-9364, website: www.mahinas.com, email: mahinas@hawaiian.net, a beach house near the center of Kapa'a. A bed in the shared room is $30 a night, as is the bed on the enclosed lanai. The small private bedroom sleeps one for $40 or two for $47, while the master bedroom with a king bed runs $50–60. The whole house can be rented for $180 a night. Weekly rates are available. For availability, contact Sharon.

Hotel Coral Reef, 1516 Kuhio Hwy., Kapa'a, HI 96746, 808/822-4481 or 800/843-4659, fax 808/822-7705, is relatively inexpensive and definitely has character. Toward the north end of Kapa'a between the main road and the beach, this 25-unit family-style hotel, one of the first built in the area, has a deluxe view of the ocean and a small grove of coconut trees on the lawn. The rates for the recently refurbished rooms are: ocean view $59, oceanfront $89, and two-room suite $79, with a $10 charge for additional guests. The hotel offers room and car packages and *kama'aina* and senior citizen discounts. Rooms feature single and double beds, refrigerators, cable television, and lanai. Rooms downstairs have tile, upstairs, carpet. There is daily maid service, a pay telephone in the lobby, activities bookings, and equipment rental. The Hotel Coral Reef is neat as a pin and very affordable for a family vacation.

Condos

The **Kapa'a Shore** resort condominium is along the main road, across and just up from Kauai Village shopping center, at 4-0900 Kuhio Hwy. It's mostly a time-share property, but one- and two-bedroom, ocean view and oceanfront rental units are available per day or by the week. All units are bright and cheerful, with full kitchens. One-bedroom units run $105–125 per day or $600–700 a week. Two-bedroom units go for $115–135 per day and $700–800 per week. On the property, there is a swimming pool, hot tub, tennis courts, and maid service on request. For reservations, call Garden Island Properties, 808/822-4871 or 800/801-0378.

The **Pono Kai,** 4-1250 Kuhio Hwy., Kapa'a, HI 96746, website: www.ponokai-resort.com, is a 241-unit property on 11 acres, just to the north of the Waika'ea Canal. This is the largest, if not the most luxurious property on the Coconut Coast. While principally a time-share, there are a good number of vacation rental units. Built in 1975 but kept up to date, all units are individually owned and decorated; one-bedroom are $139–179, and two bedrooms $199–229. All have full kitchens, cable TV, and lanai, many have a/c, and each building has laundry facilities. On the property you'll find a swimming pool, jet spa, sauna, shuffleboard lanes, lighted tennis courts for guests only, a small Japanese garden, and numerous barbecue areas. Various craft and cultural activities are offered throughout the week, and the activities desk can arrange excursions for you. For reservations, call RCI Management, 808/822-9831 or 800/438-6493. Marc Resorts manages many units in this complex and maintains front desk staffing 8 A.M.–5 P.M. daily. For information and reservations through Marc Resorts, call 800/535-0085.

Two moderate condos in Waipouli are **Mokihana of Kauai,** 796 Kuhio Hwy., and **Kauai Kailani,** 856 Kuhio Hwy. Both are primarily time-share properties but do vacation rentals when space permits. The Mokihana has all studios with kitchenettes for $65 a day. Kauai Kailani has two-bedroom units with full kitchens for $65–75. For information and reservations, call 800/640-4786.

Bed-and-Breakfasts

For island visitors "who value their personal health, and who seek inner growth and the opening of creative potential," the **Keapana Center,** 5620 Keapana Rd., Kapa'a, HI 96746, 808/822-7968 or 800/822-7968, website: http://planet-hawaii.com/keapana, email: keapana@aloha.net may be the place for you. Gabriela, the multitalented owner, is accommodating and helpful in giving tips on hikes and nature trails. Well-versed in the healing arts, she's in touch with local practitioners and can make arrangements for instruction or sessions of massage and body work, naturopathic medicine, yoga, tai chi, and other healing and wellness programs. Guest rooms in this restful (and nonsmoking) environment are very island, very Hawaiian. The cement floors are covered with sisal matting, and most furniture is rattan or wicker. Floral displays brighten every room, while Balinese masks, Chinese peasant hats, and hula skirts hang from the walls. The common area, open to the elements, is serene with its own indoor/outdoor garden, and, from its rural hilltop setting, offers sweeping vistas over the lush hillside toward the Anahola Mountains. A solar-heated hot tub waits to knead the muscles of intrepid hikers. Rates for the rooms with shared/private baths are $45/$70 single, $55/$75 double; two nights minimum, with weekly discount rates available. Each morning the continental breakfast includes homemade bread, healthy muffins, and island fruits, many of which grow on the property. Bowls of papayas and hands of bananas, all organic and all also from the property, are left in the downstairs area for guests. A kitchenette with refrigerator and microwave is available. Gabriela also offers a freestanding 24-foot yurt with its own kitchen, hot outdoor shower, and compost toilet. The rate is $65–75 for one to three persons, with a five-night minimum, and discounts after two weeks. The yurt can accommodate children, whereas the house is an adults-only atmosphere to ensure the serenity of the environment.

KAUA'I

Inland high above Kapa'a on a working tropical flower farm in an area called Kawaihau is **Kakalina's Bed and Breakfast,** 6781 Kawaihau Rd., Kapa'a, HI 96746, 808/822-2328 or 800/662-4330, fax 808/823-6833, website: www.kakalina.com, email: klina@aloha.net. Kakalina's has three rooms and a separate rental unit. The rooms, a studio with full kitchen, a one-bedroom with kitchenette, and a one-bedroom with full kitchen, run $85–90 a day including a simple fruit, juice, pastry, and coffee breakfast. The one-bedroom house nearby has a complete kitchen and rents for $75 a day, no breakfast included.

Not far away is **Alohilani Bed and Breakfast,** 1470 Wana'ao Rd., Kapa'a, HI 96746, 808/823-0128 or 800/533-9316, website: www.hawaiian.net/~alohila/pg2.html, email: alohila@hawaiian.net. Alohilani has two suites, each for $89 a night, with queen beds, private baths, ceiling fans, refrigerator and microwave. The hot tub is shared, and a continental breakfast is served.

Vacation Rental Agencies
Garden Island Properties, 4-928 Kuhio Hwy., 808/822-4871 or 800/801-0378, website: www.kauaiproperties.com, email: stricko@kauai properties.com, focuses its efforts on the east side of the island. It manages over two dozen vacation rentals and numerous condo units mostly from Kapa'a to Miloli'i but also has several along the north shore as far as Ha'ena, everything from a $65 a night casual oceanside "hut" to a sumptuous three-bedroom house that sleeps 12 for $2,000 a week.

FOOD

From the Waipouli Town Center to the north edge of Kapa'a, there are dozens of places to eat. The vast majority are either inexpensive diners or midpriced restaurants, but there is also one fine dining restaurant, plus the ubiquitous fast-food chains, several bakeries, fruit stands, markets, and grocery stores.

Inexpensive Food in Shopping Malls
The Waipouli Town Center has one of the best moderately priced restaurants on the island, **The King and I,** 808/822-1642, open daily for din-

ner. This Thai restaurant serves wonderful food that will make your taste buds stand up and be counted. Most dinners are $8–12. Serving the same basic type of food at about the same price is **Sukhothai** Thai restaurant, 808/821-1224, in the Kapa'a Shopping Center up the road. Sukhothai is open for lunch and dinner daily.

In the Waipouli Complex, another tiny mall along Kuhio Highway, is the **Aloha Diner,** 808/822-3851. Open daily except Sunday 11:30 A.M.–3 P.M. and 5:30–9 P.M., this diner serves Hawaiian food. It offers ‡ la carte selections like *kalua* pig, chicken lu'au, *lomi* salmon, rice and poi, *haupia,* and *kulolo.* Dinner specials run $6–8, with full dinners around $10. Take-out is available. There is no atmosphere, the service is slow but friendly, and most people eating here are residents who know where to come for filling food.

Papaya's, a natural-food café and market below the Whale Tower at Kauai Village, 808/823-0190, open daily except Sunday 9 A.M.–8 P.M., is not only the largest, but also the best natural-food store and café on Kaua'i. From the café section (the deli counter closes at 7 P.M.) come daily specials like marinated baked tofu over brown rice with green salad for $4.99, a tri-plate with your choice of three salads for $7.50, soup du jour $2.25–3.95 depending upon the size, and two-fisted sandwiches like grilled vegetable at $5.99 and a good old-fashioned tempeh burger for $4.99. Papaya's is famous for its hot entrées, including spinach and herb lasagna and spicy kung pao stir-fry, $5–7.50. Daily specials are always posted. Several American standard breakfasts with a veggie twist and an assortment of homemade pastries are available until 1 P.M. Gourmet coffees, herbed teas, sodas, fresh juices, and smoothies are also specialties. Outdoor tables are available, or sit on the grass in the courtyard. If you are into healthy organic food, there is no place better than Papaya's!

Pony Island Cantina, also at Kauai Village, 808/823-9000, open Mon.–Sat. 11 A.M.–2:30 P.M. and 4:30–9 P.M., Sunday noon–8 P.M., is an eat-in or take-out place that serves fresh Mexican fare with an island twist. Look for the red chili pepper lights strung around the windows. On the menu are the usual salads, tacos, burritos, tostadas, and enchiladas, but the unusual includes such things as seared 'ahi salad for $8.95 and tropical taco with fish for $7.75. Every evening there are specials. With most items you can choose beef, chicken, or vegan mix. Run by a young fellow with just as young a staff, this place offers healthy, wholesome food at decent prices. Give it a try.

Across the shopping center is **Camp House Grill and Bar,** open 6:30 A.M.–9:30 P.M. A clone of the original Camp House Grill in Kalaheo, this family-style place is known for its breakfasts, burgers, Hawaiian *huli* chicken, and barbecue pork ribs. Full bar.

Other Inexpensive Eateries

Kun Ja's II Korean Bar-B-Q, 4-9394A Kuhio Hwy. (next to Taco Bell), 808/821-2088, open Mon.–Sat. 10 A.M.–9 P.M., is a sit-down or take-out restaurant that serves both authentic Korean food and Hawaiianized Korean dishes. Dishes include flame-broiled short ribs and marinated beef strips, mixed rice and vegetables, and various soups and stews, priced $5–7.25. For a really spicy dish try O Jing O Pokum, which is squid and vegetables in a hot sauce, for $6.75. Plate lunches and other local favorites run $5.50–7.50. This restaurant is clean and tidy, with only a few tables.

Marilyn Monroe, skirt tossed by the Kaua'i breeze, and the big bow tie and bigger smile of owner and chief soda jerk Kriss Erickson welcome you to **Breezers,** a vintage '50s soda fountain, at the main intersection in downtown Kapa'a, 808/822-4411, open daily 11 A.M.–10 P.M. Kriss, a bartender for two decades, researched the soda-fountain idea for years before opening Breezers—and actually got his best idea after visiting Disneyland. He scoured Hawaii and then finally the Mainland before finding a real soda fountain. The floor of red, black, and white tiles leads to low stools facing a counter made from glass brick and featuring a light show inside that matches the tunes coming from a real jukebox in the corner. Let your eyes play over the splendid 16-foot mahogany back bar, cabinet, and mirror as you sip your soda, slurp your shake, or savor your sandwich. The ice cream served is Hawaii's own Lappert's—some of the best in the world. Besides standard cones, Breezers serves such scrumptious dishes as an old-fashioned banana split for $6.95 and a Mustang Sally—a rich chocolate brownie with two scoops of creamy vanilla, hot fudge, whipped cream, and nuts—for $6.75. Handmade malts, shakes, and flavored Cokes can be created, or choose a soda, brownie wedge, pie, sandwich, or Sloppy Joe. Breezers is the kind of place where, if you're not smiling going in, you're definitely smiling coming out.

Upstairs of Breezers is **Da Kine Dogs,** 808/821-1668, serving the taste of Chicago in hot dogs, beef and sausage sandwiches, bratwurst, corn dogs, and chili. A few meatless choices are also on the menu, as are fries, baked potatoes, breaded mushrooms, and other sides. No item is over $5.75. Open daily 11 A.M.–9 P.M., except for a noon opening on Sunday and midnight closing on Friday and Saturday. Head up for good quick eats, tropical breezes, and a view over town and the ocean.

Look for yellow and white umbrellas shading a few picnic tables across from the field at the town park that mark **Bubba's,** 808/823-0069, open daily 10:30 A.M.–8 P.M. Here you can have a Bubba burger for $2.50 or a Big Bubba for $4.50. Other menu items include a "Slopper," an open-faced burger smothered in Bubba's famous Budweiser beer chili, for $4.75, and fish and chips, chicken burger, or corn dog, all for under $4.25. Sides include french fries, onion rings, and chili fries. Burgers come on a toasted bun with mustard, ketchup-based relish, and diced onions. Anything else you want on it—cheese, teriyaki, lettuce, or tomatoes—you pay for. Hey, they've been doing things this way since 1936—it's worked. Bubba's is a throwback to the days when a diner owner was also the short-order cook and all the burgers were handmade. Yet, they've also kept up. Try the free Web-TV Internet access or buy a Bubba shirt or hat to take with you. Rock and roll, grease, and Elvis lives, man! Enjoy!

When you don't want to fool around deciding where to get a good meal, head for the north end of Kapa'a and the local favorite, **Kountry Kitchen,** 1485 Kuhio Hwy., 808/822-3511, open daily 6 A.M.–9 P.M. (Tuesday until 2 P.M.). The tables are usually packed with regulars during peak dining hours. Breakfasts are full meals like hefty omelettes, mostly for under $6; lunches of salads, sandwiches, and specialty plates, a few bucks more. Full homestyle dinners of country ribs, sesame shrimp, or baked ham served with soup, bread, potatoes or rice, and veggies are

$8–10. The food is tasty, the service prompt and friendly, and the portions large. True to its advertising, you'll find "no fancy napkins, just good home cooking."

At the north end of Kapa'a, near the neighborhood center and community swimming pool, is the **Killer Juice Bar.** A homespun place, operating out of a roadside stand and parked antique truck, it sells smoothies and fruit drinks, locally grown fruits and vegetables, and homemade treats. A great stop.

Moderate

Just south of the Waipouli Shopping Center, you'll find **Margaritas,** 808/822-1808. Billed as a "Mexican restaurant and watering hole," it's open daily from 4 P.M., dinner is served until 9:30 P.M., and happy hour runs 4–6 P.M. On Friday and Saturday nights 8–11 P.M. it's a happening place with live music. Like any good Mexican restaurant, it has a long menu that includes various burritos, tacos, enchiladas, quesadillas, and fajitas, all priced in the $10.95–16.95 range. Of course, appetizers, salads, sides, and combination plates are also available, as are tropical margaritas and mixed drinks, beers, and wine by the glass. Margaritas is a happy place with a festive atmosphere, and a place to try for lively weekend music.

The **Ono Family Restaurant,** next to the Pono Kai Resort, 808/822-1710, open daily 7 A.M.–2 P.M., is cozy and functional, with nice touches like carpeted floors, ceiling fans, and front lanai seating. An established business, the restaurant gives friendly service, pays attention to detail, and always serves large portions. Creative breakfasts include eggs Canterbury, with turkey, tomatoes, and hollandaise sauce over poached eggs on an English muffin; pancakes; and a variety of omelettes. For lunch, you can't go wrong with a salad or burger, and from the broiler or grill try sirloin steak, barbecued ribs, or teriyaki chicken. The daily fish special is always terrific.

Up the road a few doors is **Tropix Island Style Cafe and Bar,** 808/822-7330. This friendly local place makes you feel at home. Dinner and lunch menus are virtually the same, except you get dessert with dinner. There are several vegetarian dishes, and the vegetables used are organic when possible, but most of the menu is filed with a variety of beef, pork, chicken, and fish dishes, plus sandwiches and burgers. Try the teriyaki beef, chicken katsu, braddah Charley's kalua pork stir-fry, or "supa" sautéed mahimahi. Most lunches run $7–9.50, dinners $9–13. The bar is popular, if you can find a seat, and one of the few bars in town. Live island music plays nightly 8–11 P.M.

If the moon hits your eye like a big pizza pie, go to **Rocco's Italian Restaurant** in downtown Kapa'a across from the ABC store, 808/822-4422, open Mon.–Sat. 11 A.M.–4 P.M. for lunch and daily 5–10 P.M. for dinner. Enter to a valiant attempt at creating a homey Italian atmosphere—red and green curtains, Chianti bottles hanging from an open beamed ceiling, and a recessed bar separated from the downstairs dining area by a glass brick wall. Upstairs, you'll find a more intimate seating area where you can look over a balcony railing festooned with artificial grapes and garlic bunches to the flagstone floor below. Samples from the menu include Caesar salads with shrimp, onion soup, and Sofia's Garden Sub. Pizza by the slice goes for $3 and up, depending on toppings, or choose lasagna, ravioli, eggplant parmigiana, or other standards. Round out your meal with fresh-baked bread, beer and wine by the glass, and a scrumptious dessert. Rocco's food is better than average, and the atmosphere is friendly, with the strong appeal of a cozy neighborhood ristorante.

Norberto's El Cafe, at the intersection of Kukui St. and Route 56 in downtown Kapa'a, 808/822-3362, open Mon.–Sat. 5:50–9 P.M., is a family-run Mexican restaurant. What's it doing in a small town on a Pacific Island, you ask? Gringo, don't look a gift burro in the mouth! Norberto's serves nutritious, delicious, wholesome food and caters to vegetarians—all dishes are prepared without lard or animal fats. The smell of food wafting out of the front door around dinnertime is its best advertisement. This is some of the best Mexican food on the island. Most full-course meals of burritos, enchiladas, and tostadas are under $14; children's plates and à la carte dishes are also available. The best deals are the chef's specials of burrito el café, rellenos tampico, fajitas, and enchiladas grande. Dinners are served with soup, beans, and rice; chips and salsa are complimentary. There's beer on tap, or if you really want to head south of the border (by way of sliding under the table), try a pitcher of margaritas. If you have room after stuffing yourself like a chimichanga, try a delicious chocolate-cream pie or homemade rum cake. The café is extremely popular with local folks and tables don't stay empty.

The Olympic Cafe, a fixture in downtown Kapa'a for more than half a century but torn up by Hurricane 'Iniki, has metamorphosed and is back in business at 1387 Kuhio Hwy., 808/822-2825, open daily 6 A.M.–2 P.M. for breakfast and lunch and 5–9 P.M. for dinner. This casual place has French doors that open onto the sidewalk. The floor is carpeted, the tables are Formica, and contemporary rock plays as background music. At one end, a raised section is filled with reading chairs and shelves of books—browse or buy at 50 percent off cover price. Breakfasts of pancakes, omelettes, or scrambles are mostly under $7, and lunches include sandwiches, burgers, salads, and burritos for $5–8. The dinner menu, priced $8.50–16.95, includes shrimp scampi, coconut curry rice, a variety of pasta dishes, and fresh catch of the day. To accompany any meal are juices, smoothies, Italian sodas, specialty teas, and fine coffees. Order at the counter.

Diners at **Noe's,** in the Kauai Village Shopping Center, 808/821-0110, open daily for lunch 11 A.M.–5 P.M., for dinner 5 P.M.–10:30 P.M., and for happy hour 4–6 P.M., get plenty of hands-on attention from owner Linda Chong. The lunch menu is fairly light with fish and chips and various burgers, mostly under $8. Well-priced dinner specials under $20 include stir-fry local-style beef, chicken, or shrimp, as well as scampi and mahimahi. Every evening there are house specials. Noe's interior is island casual with a touch of Dublin and sports a long bar with stools, and booths or tables with bamboo captain's chairs. A huge hammerhead shark leers beady-eyed from the wall, somewhat like a "hammered" tourist ogling the bikini babes.

Walk the gangplank to enter the **Kapa'a Fish and Chowder House,** in a two-tone blue building on Kapa'a's north end, 808/822-7488, offering a happy hour daily 4–6 P.M. and dinner from 5:30 P.M. Tastefully appointed, this comfortably casual restaurant has a nautical interior featuring a ship's wheel, hanging nets, and ocean-blue carpet. Start with steamed clams, Pacific shrimp cocktail, a pot of clam or fish chowder, or a Cae-

sar salad. Seafood selections include coconut shrimp, Alaskan snow crab clusters, charbroiled lobster tails, or stuffed tiger prawns. Landlubbers can order New York strip steak, ginger chicken, or New York pepper steak, along with multiple combination plates. A selection of pasta dishes includes calamari sauté and shrimp scampi. Appetizers are mostly under $9, entrées run $15–28. The full bar serves wine, beer, and exotic drinks and offers a special every night. The Kapa'a Fish and Chowder House is a decent restaurant, with good value, that has something for everyone.

Fine Dining

Master chef Jean-Marie Josselin knows a good thing when he sees it and, moreover, knows how to prepare it exquisitely. You can enjoy his excellent food at **A Pacific Cafe,** at Kauai Village, 808/822-0013, open 5:30–10 P.M. Although it's in a shopping center, A Pacific Cafe creates a casually elegant atmosphere appointed with a cove and molded ceiling, ferns and flowers placed here and there, bamboo chairs, and an open kitchen so that you can witness the food preparation. Although the menu changes nightly, items below are a sampling of what type of food the kitchen creates. Appetizers range $8.50–10.50 and include such delicacies as deep-fried tigereye 'ahi sushi with wasabi and mustard sauces, or firecracker salmon with Thai chili sauce, cucumber, and ogo sauce. Choose a savory soup and refreshing salad like roasted kabocha pumpkin soup, organic tomato salad, or Indonesian shrimp salad with mango vinaigrette and crispy rice noodles, $6.25–8.95. Order from the wood-burning grill—you can't go wrong! Try grilled 'ahi marinated in miso, with tempura shiitake mushrooms, grilled eggplant, and a sweet soy glaze for $24.50, or the lamb loin with asparagus and garlic mashed potatoes for $25.95. Specialties of A Pacific Cafe include wok-charred mahimahi with garlic sesame crust and lime ginger sauce for $25.95, or lemongrass- and galangal-crusted opah with black rice, shrimp gyoza, and coconut basil sauce for $24.95. If you can't decide, try the prix-fixe menu for $39 and get the works. A Pacific Cafe is an excellent restaurant with the perfect mixture of exceptional food, fine service, superb presentation, and a wonderful wine cellar; by far the best the area has to offer.

ENTERTAINMENT

The night scene in Kapa'a is less than extensive. **Margaritas**, along Kuhio Highway near the Waipouli Shopping Center, jams with live entertainment 8–11 P.M. on Friday and Saturday evenings. Stop in for a Mexican margarita and enjoy the music with other *turistas*. **Tropix Island Style Cafe and Bar** in downtown Kapa'a offers island music nightly 8–11 P.M.; never a cover and always local.

For a cool island drink, canned music, and a local crowd try **Noe's** at the Kauai Village Shopping Center or **Lizard Lounge** at the Waipouli Center.

After years of temporary shelter, the **Kauai International Theater** now has its own home in the Kauai Village shopping center. Stage presentations are performed in the 62-seat theater. For information on what's currently playing and for reservations, call 808/821-1588. Support community arts.

RECREATION

Water Sports

Kayak Kauai, 808/822-9179, open daily 8 A.M.–5 P.M., rents two-person kayaks for $48–60 per day and single kayaks for $25–35 and leads kayak tours. Kayak Kauai has another shop in Hanalei, 808/826-9844, which provides the same services.

Others to see in the Kapa'a-Wailua area for kayaks and kayak tours are the following: **Kauai Water Ski and Surf**, in the Kinipopo Shopping Village, 808/822-3574; **Pardise Outdoor Adventures**, 808/822-1112; **Kayak Ecotours**, 808/822-9078; **Wailua Kayak Adventures**, 808/822-5795; **Kayak Wailua**, 808/822-3388; and **Rainbow Kayak Tours**, 808/822-4000.

Ambrose of **Ambrose's Kapuna Natural Foods**, 808/822-7112, in the funky yellow building across from Foodland in the Waipouli Town Center, is a surfers' advocate, philosopher, and generally good guy. He has one of the largest collections of big boards and old surfboards on the island, and some new ones, too, which he creates out back. If you are a surfer coming on vacation and you let Ambrose know in advance

what you want and are qualified to use, he'll have it waiting when you get here. He doesn't rent boards, but he'll buy back the ones he sells at a very equitable rate. On his neighborhood beaches, Ambrose also offers surfing lessons tailor-made to the individual beginner or advanced board rider. If he's not helping someone in the store, check for him out back.

Snorkel Bob's, just beyond the Coconut Marketplace in Waipouli, 808/823-9433, open 8 A.M.–5 P.M. daily, offers some of the best deals for snorkel rental in Hawaii (and free snorkeling maps and advice). Gear, which includes mask, snorkel tube, and fins, is rented for a 24-hour day or by the week. The basic set is $2.50 a day or $9 per week. Upgrades in quality run $4.50/$19 and $6.50/$29, and for the ultimate optical correction mask the rate is $9 a day or $35 a week. For a "dry" tube add $2 a day. Bob's also rents boogie boards. If you'll be island hopping, Snorkel Bob's allows you to take the gear with you and drop it off at a Snorkel Bob's location on the next island. Bob is now booking various island activities, so you may get free rental on some equipment if you book through him.

Dive Kauai, 976 Kuhio Hwy., 808/822-0452 or 800/828-3483, website: www.divekauai.com, is a full service scuba and snorkel shop. Dive Kauai offers sales and rental of all equipment and carries some water sport clothing and accessories. Scuba gear packages run $40–50, introductory dives are $98 for a one-tank boat or shore dive or $125 for two tanks. For certified divers, most other dives run $80–100. A variety of certification courses are offered, but a basic four- to five-day course runs about $350.

Bicycling

One of the best bike shops on the island for sales and repair is **Kauai Cycle and Tour**, 1379 Kuhio Hwy., 808/821-2115, open Mon.–Fri. 9 A.M.–6 P.M., Saturday 9 A.M.–4 P.M. Stop in and talk to the guys; they can give you great advice on where to ride for your type of bike. Beach cruisers rent for $15 for 24 hours, front-suspension mountain bikes run $20 a day or $95 per seven-day week, and full-suspension mountain bikes are $35 a day and $150 a week. Each rental includes a helmet, lock, and water bottle. A car rack is available for $5. Unfortunately, this place doesn't run tours anymore.

Horseback Riding
Esprit De Corps Riding Academy, 808/822-4688, offers three basic rides, plus specialty rides on request, and riding lessons. These rides, which go into the mountains from upper Kapa'a, tend to be long, so they are better suited to experienced riders. The three-hour Fast ride with trotting and cantering runs $99; the Wow!!! ride runs $250 for five hours, snack included; and the All Day ride is a full-day adventure, with time for a deli lunch and dip in a mountain pool, for $350 each for two to three guests or $300 each for four or more. Riders must be age 10 or older for the trail rides.

Activities Center
Chris The Fun Lady, 4-746 Kuhio Hwy. across from the Waipouli Shopping Center, 808/822-7759, open daily 8 A.M.–6 P.M., offers boogie-board rentals at $5–8 a day; kayaks for $25 single, $50 double with coolers, dry bags, life vests, car racks, and waterproof maps included; top-of-the-line snorkel gear (prescription masks, too), golf clubs, fishing equipment, and surfboards at $10 per day. Chris is an expert at arranging all ocean, air, and lu'au activities, claiming that her years of experience on Kaua'i don't always get you the cheapest but do always gets you the best.

Snorkel Bob's, next door, has also started doing activities. If you rent snorkel equipment from him, he can also hook you up with other island activities for a reasonable price.

Movie Tours
For couch potato movie buffs, **Hawaii Movie Tours** has the van trip for you. This is an escorted tour of the island that stops at many of the sites used by Hollywood to make its feature films. On the way, you'll get regaled by stories of these movies and their actors, see scenes from the movies on the comfy van's TV monitor, and be provided with lunch. The five-hour tour starts at 9 A.M. in Kapa'a at the tour office and costs $85 adult, $68 for kids 11 and under. The deluxe version of this trip includes a helicopter ride (where you see additional film locations) and a lu'au, for $295 per person. Call 808/822-1192 or 800/628-8432 for reservations.

SHOPPING

Kapa'a teems with shopping opportunities. Lining Kuhio Highway are several large and small shopping plazas along with the central downtown shops. All your needs are met by a variety of shops tucked away here and there. Like dealing with the sun in Hawaii, enjoy yourself but don't overdo it.

Kauai Village
Built around a plantation-era main street theme, this modern, large, and very diverse shopping center, one of the newest and best that Kaua'i has to offer, complete with its own museum and visitor center, is at 4-831 Kuhio Highway. It contains a **Safeway** supermarket, open 24 hours; **Longs Drugs,** open Mon.–Sat. 8 A.M.–9 P.M., closing Sunday at 6 P.M., a complete variety store with photo equipment and a pharmacy; an **ABC** store, for everything from suntan lotion to beach mats; and **Waldenbooks,** 808/822-7749, open Mon.–Sat. 9 A.M.–8 P.M. and Sunday 9 A.M.–5 P.M., well stocked with everything from Hawaiiana to travel books. Dining options here include the **A Pacific Cafe,** a fantastic restaurant featuring Pacific Island cuisine prepared by master chef Jean-Marie Josselin; **Papaya's,** the island's best natural health-food store and café; **Camp House Grill,** for food you might have seen on a plantation family's dining table; and **Pony Island Cantina,** for healthy Mexican with a touch of the islands. Other stores are **Sunglass Hut;** the always good **Crazy Shirts; Pai Moana Pearls,** if you're looking for the increasingly popular Tahitian black pearls; and **V.J. Silver and Gold,** which claims to have the island's best selection of silver jewelry. Both **Kahn Galleries** and **Wyland Galleries** are resplendent with some of the finest artworks in Hawaii and offer art lovers a chance to just look or select a favorite to take home as a tangible memory of their island vacation.

Perhaps the best place in the area to look for Hawaiian art and craft items is the **Kaua'i Heritage Center of Hawaiian Culture and the Arts,** 808/821-2070, open Mon.–Fri. 10 A.M.–6 P.M., Saturday until 5 P.M. Aside from the retail business, this organization also runs exhibits, workshops, lectures, and demonstrations on aspects of Hawaiian culture, and displays of high-quality Hawaiian artifacts. Offered here are programs in hula, lei-making, crafts, and legends for adults and children.

Under the Whale Tower toward the back of the center is **Kaua'i Children's Discovery Museum,** 808/823-8222, a hands-on adventure gallery where young kids can learn about science, nature, technology, and culture, particularly as it pertains to Hawaii and Polynesia. Kids can explore an underwater coral reef, learn to navigate an outrigger canoe by the stars, or ride a flight simulator into space. This community-based, volunteer-staffed organization is set up to involve children in their surroundings. On your way out, stop by the gift shop and look over the selection of science toys, educational games, and gifts. The museum is open Mon.–Sat. 2–5 P.M., the gift shop 10 A.M.–5 P.M. Admission is $3.50 for children, $4.50 for adults.

If in need of tourist information or if you want someone to book an activity for you, stop by the **Kaua'i Visitor Center,** 808/882-5113.

Kapa'a Shopping Center

Marked by a Shell station and a Burger King at 4-1105 Kuhio Hwy. is this bite-size, functional shopping center. Here, you'll find a **Big Save,** a well-stocked food store, open daily 7 A.M.–10 P.M.; the full-service Kapa'a post office; an **Ace Hardware** store; an inexpensive restaurant or two; and the Kapa'a clinic of the Kaua'i Medical Group. Here as well is **Kapa'a Laundry Center,** with self-service machines and drop-off service. The laundromat is open 7:30 A.M.–9:30 P.M. and has coin and boxed soap machines. It's the best in the area.

Small Shopping Malls

Across the highway from another Shell station, in the **Waipouli Complex,** are **Aloha Diner** for local Hawaiian food and **Popo's Cookies,** open Thurs.–Sun. Nearby, in the **Waipouli Plaza,** are a variety store with clothing, gifts, and a great fishing/hunting section; a Thai restaurant; and a seashell merchant selling retail and wholesale. Farther down the road, in the **Waipouli Town Center,** you'll find **Foodland,** open 5 A.M.–11 P.M., as well as a Fun Factory arcade for games,

Blockbuster Video for home/condo entertainment, and JM's jewelry store.

Boutiques and Galleries

Next door to Ambrose's Kapuna Natural Foods is **Marta's Boat,** 808/822-3926, open Mon.–Sat. 10:30 A.M.–6 P.M. This is primarily a children's boutique, but the overflowing shelves also hold handmade quilts by local ladies, T-shirts, shorts, casual wear, elegant evening wear, and beautiful lingerie. A rack of games and educational items will help keep the little ones happy on a return plane voyage or during an evening in the condo.

In the old Kawamura Store building, built 1949 and rebuilt 1993, is **Hula Girl,** 808/822-1950, for fine fashions, vintage designwear, Hawaiian craft items, and much more. If you're looking for quality with island flavor, try here. Down the block is **South China Sea Trading Company,** 808/823-8655, with arts and crafts items and tropical furniture from Hawaii and Southeast Asia. Only a few steps away is **Jim Saylor Jewelry,** 808/822-3591, for jewelry and gemstones.

As shiny and glittering as the sunbeams pouring through the windows, **Kela'a Glass Gallery,** in the Hefat Market Place, 4-1354 Kuhio Hwy., Kapa'a, HI 96746, 808/822-4527, owned and operated by Larry Barton, is a showcase for more than 60 contemporary artists working in glass. The gallery features everything from classic vases to free-form sculptures ranging in price from affordable to not affordable. Kela's also sells and ships (disassembled, but with pieces numbered for easy reassembly) wooden flowers that are hand-carved and hand-painted in Indonesia. There are 30 different flowers including hibiscus, irises, calla lilies, various ginger, and heliconia.

Next door is **Kibanu Gallery,** 808/823-6820, a delightful stop to peruse one of the most unusual collections of contemporary art on the island. Here you'll find engaging works of wood, metal, glass, fiber art, and other media.

At the intersection across from the ABC Store, the **Kim Taylor Reece Gallery,** 808/823-8778, displays the evocative and sensual photographs and reproductions of this well-known island artist.

A few shops away, stop in to **East Side Picture and Candle,** 808/654-0503, for original photographs and handmade candles.

Earth Beads, 808/822-0766, owned by Angelika Riskin, open daily except Sunday 10 A.M.–6 P.M., specializes in beads and imported items from India, Africa, and South America. Shimmering in the tiny shop are earrings, belts, incidental bags, and sterling silver jewelry from Thailand, as well as locally made designs. A smattering of primitive basketry, incense, perfumed oils, T-shirts, "jungle" umbrellas and very unusual greeting cards complete the stock of this great little shop.

For a perfectly natural gift, slip down **Orchid Alley** for a beautiful potted plant. Send one home as a reminder of your tropical vacation—they ship. Back down the main drag next to Pono Market is **Flowers and Joys** for some of the best (although not the cheapest) lei on the island.

Walk into the **Island Hemp and Cotton Company,** 808/821-0225, open daily 10 A.M.–6 P.M., and suddenly you're in Asia. Stride across the reed mat floor while the soulful eyes of a Buddha sitting serenely atop a glass counter follow you in. Across from the ABC store in downtown Kapa'a, the shop is owned and operated by Nancee McTernan, a long distance traveler and "old Asia hand" who has personally chosen every item in the store. Some special items include Buddhas from Borneo, baskets from Bali, carved bone necklaces from New Zealand, local puka shell jewelry, and antique wood carvings from all parts of Indonesia. Men's and women's clothing, all made from organic cotton, hemp, and linen, include everything from casual shirts to elegant dresses, and hats to backpacks. If you are after a truly distinctive gift, one-of-a-kind clothing, or an original artifact, visit the shop here or the sister store in Hanalei.

Two Frogs Hugging, 808/823-8777, open Mon.–Sat. 9 A.M.–5 P.M. across from the park in Kapa'a, carries a wonderfully eclectic collection of imported arts, crafts, and furniture from Indonesia and Hawaii, including teak outdoor furniture, mahogany chairs, pottery pots, bamboo window shades, and stone carvings. Look for the two hugging frogs statue out front.

Up near the north end of town, the **Original Red Dirt Shirt** outlet sells many fetching designs made right here on the island using Kaua'i's red earth as a dye. The store carries mostly T-shirts, up to size XXXXL, but also some kids' and toddlers' outfits. Take home the essence of Kaua'i.

Look for **M. Miura Store** at the north end of Kapa'a, mountain side, open Mon.–Sat. 9 A.M.–5 P.M. Local people shop at this dry goods store for alohawear, T-shirts, caps, men's and women's shorts, and a good selection of bikinis.

Photo Needs

Try **Cameralab,** 808/822-7338, near Margaritas Mexican restaurant, or **Longs Drug** at Kauai Village for all your photo finishing needs. In downtown Kapa'a, **Pono Studio** also develops

Don't miss the lively Kapa'a farmers' market.

ROBERT NILSEN

KAUA'I

film, carries photographic equipment, and has a studio for portraits.

Food Shopping

For a full-service supermarket, try **Safeway** at Kauai Village, **Big Save** at the Kapa'a Shopping Center, or **Foodland** at the Waipoili Town Center. Older and more local is **Kojima's** grocery. This well-stocked store is on the mountain side of the road beyond the Aloha Lumber yard at the north end of town, and it carries produce, meat, liquor, beer, and picnic supplies.

Papaya's, at the Kauai Village, 808/823-0190, open daily except Sunday 9 A.M.–8 P.M., is a natural-food market and café. Coolers and shelves hold items like wild tropical guava juice, organic sprouted hot-dog buns, and mainstays like organic fruits and vegetables, yogurt, whole-grain bread, and bulk foods. The owners have added an extensive collection of premium microbrewery beers, along with racks of fine wines. There is also a good selection of organic teas and flavored coffees. Spices, oils, vinegars, organic salad dressings, homeopathic medicines, cruelty-free cosmetics, vitamins, minerals, and an assortment of biodegradable cleaning products are also well represented. A large deli display case holds all kinds of goodies and desserts, and wholesome lunches can be ordered to be eaten outside. If you buy fruit from the produce section, the staff will cut it up for you so you can eat it out front.

There are several other markets and groceries in the Waipouli-Kapa'a area where you can pick up food if you're cooking for yourself. **Ambrose's Kapuna Natural Foods,** in a funky yellow building across from Foodland, 808/822-7112, stocks produce and bulk and health foods. Ambrose and his friends are real storehouses of information about the island; they have the "scoop" on what's happening and where. While visiting Ambrose, take a peek next door at the **Kapa'a Missionary Church,** made from beautifully laid lava rock.

Along the main highway, the local family-run **Pono Market,** open Mon.–Sat. 7 A.M.–8 P.M. (9 P.M. on Friday) and Sunday 8 A.M.–4 P.M., is stuffed to the gills with mini-mart items, along with take-out sushi, *bento,* and deli sandwiches.

As you're coming into Kapa'a heading north look for the **Sunnyside Farmers' Market,** open daily 8 A.M.–8 P.M., where you can get fresh fruits, vegetables, and flowers from around the island, pre-packaged and pre-inspected food items to take home, and a variety of gift, jewelry, clothing, and beach items. The deli in the back serves soups, salads, sandwiches, and other lunch items and drinks.

There's a county-sponsored **farmers' market** every Wednesday at 3 P.M. at the Kapa'a New Town Park, near the armory behind town. This is a lively, local event with great options for vegetables, fruit, and flowers. Stop and pick up food for your evening meal or try coconut milk right out of the shell.

INFORMATION AND SERVICES

Aside from hotel and condo activities desks, the **Kaua'i Visitor Center,** at Kauai Village Shopping Center, 808/822-5113, is a place to get tourist information. They have a complete range of free information on all the island's activities, are able to make reservations, and have an eye for the deals.

Business Support Services, across from the Kapa'a Hongwanji, 808/822-5504, open Mon.–Sat. 8 A.M.–6 P.M., can answer all of your shipping and packing needs. Also available are fax, photocopy, and Internet services, and you can rent time on a typewriter or computer. Off-island faxes run $2.50 for the first page and $1.50 each additional page; Internet use is $5 per half hour, prorated, so you can check your email here.

The two laundromats in the area are **Basuel's** just behind Snorkel Bob's (no soap or change machines) and the larger **Kapa'a Laundry Center** in the Kapa'a Shopping Center, which offers both self-serve and drop-off service. For dry cleaning, head to the **Pono Cleaners** on the main street next to Pono Market.

The Kapa'a **post office** is at the Kapa'a Shopping Center, pretty much in the middle of town. Just north of the Kapa'a Beach County Park is the town **library.**

HEADING NORTH

ANAHOLA AND VICINITY

Route 56 north from Kapa'a is a visual treat. At first, the coastline glides along in an ever-changing panorama. Shortly, the road moves inland through former cane fields, then passes a large dairy farm before moving into orchard and pasture land. Development is sparse until you get to Kilauea in the Hanalei District. To your left are the dominant **Anahola Mountains,** jagged, pointed, and intriguing. Until recently, you could crane your neck and see **Hole-in-the-Mountain,** a natural arrangement of boulders that formed a round *puka* (legend says it was formed by an angry giant who hurled his spear with such force that he made the hole), but time and storms have taken their toll, and the hole has collapsed. More recently, a second hole has begun to open up just below the ridge; this is best seen as you come up 'Aliomanu Road (first section) from the beach.

Kealia

Just north of Kapa'a the road rises slightly around a point. On this point is a **scenic lookout** from where you have decent views both up and down the coast. As soon as you cross Kapa'a Stream you're in the one-store village of Kealia; its school and post office are now closed, but the rodeo corral still gets use. The wide, white strand of **Kealia Beach** curves along the coast for a half mile. It's not a beach park, so there are no facilities, but during calm weather the swimming, bodysurfing, and boogie boarding are good—particularly near the jetty at the north end. Few people are ever here except some local fishermen and surfers, who find the waves most challenging during winter swells.

Donkey Beach

Continue along Route 56 heading north, and just past mile marker 12 you'll find cars parked along the side of the road. Walk to the nearby cane road and continue for 10 minutes until you come to a surfing beach that the locals call Donkey Beach. Look for a tall stand of ironwoods

shadowing the wide sandy beach below. A footpath leads down to it. This area is very secluded and good for unofficial camping; others come here to spend time au naturel. Unfortunately, the undertow is severe, especially during rough weather, and only experienced surfers challenge the waves here. You can sunbathe and take dips, but remain in the shallows close to shore. Bicycle riders who bike the shoreline cane road from Kapa'a to Anahola skirt this beach on their way north.

Anahola

The first village that you come to is Anahola. While the old village is down along the bay, the commercial part of town and newer homes in the Hawaiian Home Lands tract have been built up along the highway. Just before mile marker 14 are the **Whaler's General Store,** open daily 6:30 A.M.–9:30 P.M., selling groceries, souvenirs, vegetables, and liquor, as well as the Anahola post office and a well-known eatery. Anahola Road off Route 56 just before the Whaler's General Store leads to Anahola Beach, a long strand of white sand that forms a series of decent beaches. Just a minute up the road, look to your right for 'Aliomanu Road (first) and follow it for a few minutes to the mouth of the Anahola River as it spills into the bay. Along the curve of the bay north of the river mouth is the narrower and less-frequented section of the beach. Beyond the point is the more secluded 'Aliomanu Beach.

'Aliomanu Road used to run from the highway down to and along the coast before turning inland again to the highway. During one of the last hurricanes, the bridge over a small stream at the north end of 'Aliomanu Beach was washed out and hasn't been replaced. The result is that each section of 'Aliomanu Road is a cul-de-sac. 'Aliomanu Road (second) is the north section of this road.

As you approach Anahola, you'll likely see signs on the highway advertising **lei for sale.** Families here make a few extra dollars by selling these beautiful and fragrant symbols of *aloha*. Although prices vary, expect to pay up to $5 for a *ti-*

Anahola Village church, backdropped by the distinctive Anahola Mountains

loaf lei or $5-10 for a flower lei. Stop and pick one up for your sweetie; many last for several days if refrigerated.

Anahola Beach County Park

Stretching from the river mouth along the south curve of the bay, this park has a developed picnic area, grills, showers, restrooms, and numerous camping spots—county permit required. Tall ironwood trees provide a natural canopy along the narrow strip of sand that slides gently into the water. The swimming is safe in the protected cove and in the fresh water river, good for a refreshing dip. As you walk north the waves and rips get tougher. It's not advisable to enter the deep water, although some experienced board riders do challenge the waves here, as the Hawaiians did long ago, in an area called Kanahawale, which means "easily broken." However, the reef comes close to shore at this end, and wherever you can find a sheltered pocket it's

good for snorkeling. Local anglers love this spot for near-shore fishing. The entire area is popular with local people and at times begins to look like a tent city of semi-permanent campers and squatters. Although the county works to maintain the park, these long-term residents tend to make the area messy at times. This is a place to camp for a few days, or just to stop in for a refreshing plunge on the way to or from the north shore. If you camp, don't leave your stuff unattended for too long.

Moloa'a Beach

The turnoff to Moloa'a (Matted Roots) Bay is between mile markers 16 and 17 near the dairy farm. Turn down the rough Ko'olau Road, follow it to Moloa'a Road, and take this narrow but paved road to the end. Look for the brilliant poinsettias blooming in early winter along Ko'olau Road—they are the island's clue that Christmas and the New Year are near. Moloa'a Bay has a magnificent but rarely visited beach. The road leading down is a luscious little thoroughfare, cutting over domed hillocks in a series of switchbacks. The jungle canopy is thick and then opens into a series of glens and pastures. Off to the sides are vacation homes perched on stilts made from telephone poles. A short drive takes you to road's end and a small cluster of dwellings, where there is limited space to put your vehicle. Park here and follow the right-of-way signs to the beach. Here, a stream comes into the bay providing a great place to wash off the ocean water after a dip. The beach is lovely, bright, and wide, forming a crescent moon. To the north the beach ends in a grassy hillock; south, it's confined by a steep *pali* where the swimming is best. As at all east and north shore beaches, swimming is advised only during calm weather. Snorkeling is good, but you'll have to swim the channel out to the base of the *pali*, which is inadvisable if the waves are rough. Although a few homes are around, Moloa'a is a place of peaceful solitude. Sunsets are light shows of changing color, and you'll probably be a solitary spectator.

Larsen's Beach

From Moloa'a Bay, return to Ko'olau Road (the old coast road) and follow it north as it twists into and then out of the valley. As it comes up on

KAUA'I

the height near an old cemetery, turn seaward and follow a narrow gravel road for half a mile to a small parking lot at the crest of the cliff. From here, a path leads down to Larsen's Beach, named after L. David Larsen, who was a manager of the Kilauea sugar plantation. He built a home for his family nearby. Not particularly good for swimming because of the rocky bottom and close-in reef, this beach is a place where locals come to harvest a type of seaweed or do throw-net fishing. The narrow sand shore may be good for sunbathing, however, and you'll probably have the place to yourself.

Accommodations

Several rental properties line 'Aliomanu Road. **Mahina Kai,** P.O. Box 699, Anahola, HI 96703, 808/822-9451 or 800/337-1134, website: www.vantage21st.com/nahina/mahina.html, email: trudy@aloha.net, is a Japanese-style house with a cobalt blue tile roof that's backed into a hillside and has views of the ocean. An indoor koi pond, open spaces, and paper *shoji* screens help create the atmosphere. The finely landscaped yard is tended with care and there is even a small *heiau* on the property. Down below the house, set in a walled garden amidst thick vegetation, is the very private free form swimming pool. Above the main house, the "tea house" has enough room for workshop activities and small group meetings. Each with its own bathroom and refrigerator, the three rooms run $125 a night. These rooms share a kitchenette. With its own entrance, the downstairs apartment has its own small kitchen and goes for $150. There is a three-night minimum, and it's gay friendly here.

Paradise Vacation Rentals, 4760 'Aliomanu Rd., 808/822-5754, is on the beach side of the road in a quiet, relaxed compound. Here you have a choice of a cabin at $50, studio at $75, or the house at $100. The cabin and studio have queen beds, TV, and small kitchenette, while the house has king beds and a full kitchen. For information, write P.O. Box 108, Anahola, HI 96703.

Moloa'a Kai on Moloa'a Bay gives you all the amenities of a two-bedroom, two-bath house right on the beach. This house can sleep up to seven and rents for a week at $785–995. Daily rental—three-night minimum—is also an option. Contact Hawaii Beachfront Vacation Homes, 46-535 Haiku Plantation Place, Kane'ohe, HI 96744, 808/247-3637, fax 808/235-2644, website: www.hotspots.hawaii.com/beachrent1.html, email: hibeach@lava.net.

Other vacation rentals can be arranged through **Garden Island Properties,** 808/822-4871 or 800/801-0378 in Kapa'a, or **Emerald Isle Properties,** 808/828-1111 or 800/828-1442 in Kilauea.

Food

Duane's Ono Char Burger, open Mon.–Sat. 10 A.M.–6 P.M. and Sunday 11 A.M.–6 P.M., is known far and wide. It's a clean, friendly roadside stand where you can get burgers, fish and chips, sides, and drinks. Some of the double-fisted burgers include the Ono; an Old Fashioned, with cheddar, onions, and sprouts on a Kaiser roll; the Local Boy, made with teriyaki, cheddar cheese, and pineapple; a Local Girl, made with teriyaki and Swiss cheese; and even a meatless Boca Burger. The burgers are oversize and heavy with cheese and trimmings, and everything is under $6. For an extra treat, try a delicious marionberry shake. Umbrella tables are to the side, but hold your appetite for a few minutes and make it a picnic at the nearby beach.

Across the road from Duane's and up a bit, look for the Anahola Baptist Church and a small lane leading to the **Polynesian Hide-a-way,** a local Hawaiian restaurant, open Tues.–Sat. 10 A.M.–5 P.M., Sun.–Mon. 11 A.M.–6 P.M. The Hide-a-way is a hut in a grove of trees for eat-in or take-out that offers plate lunches such as a *huli huli* chicken, *laulau, kalua* pig, and fish and chips. Polynesian Hide-a-way is downhome, clean, friendly, inexpensive, delicious, and filled with the *aloha* spirit. You can't go wrong.

KAUA'I

NORTH SHORE

The north shore is a soulful song of wonder, a contented chant of dream-reality, where all the notes of the Garden Island harmonize gloriously. The refrain is a tinkling melody, rising, falling, and finally reaching a booming crescendo deep in the emerald green of Na Pali. In so many ways this region is a haven: tiny towns and villages that refused to crumble when sugar pulled out; a patchwork quilt of diminutive *kuleana* of native Hawaiians running deep into luxuriant valleys, where ageless stone walls encircle fields of taro; a winter sanctuary for migrating birds and gritty native species desperately holding on to life; a refuge for myriad visitors—the adventuring, vacationing, life-tossed, or work-weary who come to its shores seeking a setting to find peace of body and soul.

The north shore is only 30 miles long, but, oh, what miles! Along its undulating mountains, one-lane roads, and luminescent bays are landlocked caves still umbilically tied to the sea; historical sites, the remnants of peace or domination once so important and now reduced by time; and living movie sets, some occupied by villas of stars or dignitaries. Enduring, too, is the history of old Hawaii in this fabled homeland of the Menehune, overrun by the Polynesians who set up their elaborate kingdoms built on strict so-cial order. The usurpers' *heiau* remain, and from one came the hula, swaying, stirring, and spreading throughout the island kingdoms.

Starting in **Kilauea,** an old plantation town, you can marvel at the coastline from bold promontories pummeled by the sea and observe seabirds at the wildlife sanctuary. Then there are the north shore beaches—fans of white sand, some easily visited as official parks, others hidden, the domains of simplicity and free spirits. **Princeville** follows, a convenient but incongruous planned community, vibrant with its own shopping mall and flexing condo muscles. Over the rise is **Hanalei,** even more poetic than its lovely name, a tiny town, a yachties' anchorage with good food, spirited, slow, a bay of beauty and enchantment. Movie cameras once rolled at neighboring **Lumaha'i Beach,** and an entire generation shared the dream of paradise when they saw this spot in *South Pacific.* Next in rapid succession are **Wainiha** and **Ha'ena,** with its few amenities, a little of the world's most relaxed lifestyle. The road ends at **Ke'e Beach,** where adventure begins with the start of the **Na Pali Coast Trail.** The north shore remains for most visitors the perfect setting for seeking and maybe actually finding peace, solitude, the dream, yourself.

KAUA'I

KILAUEA

There's no saying *exactly* where it begins, but Kilauea is generally considered the gateway to the north shore. The village proper was built on sugar, but that foundation melted away almost 40 years ago. Now the town holds on as a way station to some of the most intriguing scenery along this fabulous coast. Notice the bright, cheery, well-kept homes as you pass through this community. The homeowners may be short on cash but are nonetheless long on pride and surround their dwellings with lovingly tended flower gardens. The bungalows—pictures of homey contentment—are ablaze with color.

To get into town, look for mile marker 23 and a Shell gas station on your right, along with the Menehune Food Mart, a small store selling sundries and general groceries. This is where you turn onto Kolo Road, following the signs to Kilauea Lighthouse and the National Wildlife Refuge. The promontory that the lighthouse occupies, Kilauea Point, is the northernmost point of the main Hawaiian Islands. A second way into Kilauea is by turning off the highway just before mile marker 23 at Hookui Road. Go one block and turn left onto Kolo Street. Pass St. Sylvester's Church and proceed over a bridge, past the Kilauea School, and on into town. Kilauea's first commercial area is at the corner of Kolo Street and Kilauea Road near the gas station. Down Kilauea Road at Keneke Street are the Kong Lung Center and other concerns, the real business hub of town. Behind this group of businesses is a small community park. One block away on Oka Street are two medical clinics and bakery/café.

SIGHTS

Just before you arrive at the turnoff to Kilauea, turn inland on Kuawa Road and follow the signs to the 480-acre **Guava Kai Plantation,** the largest guava producing and processing venture in the nation. Proceed along the access road lined with ferns, banana trees, ironwoods, and flowering bushes, and stop in at the visitor center/snack shop, 808/828-6121, open daily 9 A.M.–5 P.M., where you can learn about guava processing; taste guava juice, jams, and jellies; or purchase a guava product, T-shirt, or sundry item. The free self-guided tour is actually just a view of the beginning stages of fruit processing, as you are not allowed into the factory itself. Come early, as much of the work in this outdoor receiving area starts before 6 A.M. You're invited to pick a handful of guava fruit from the orchard at no charge as a take-away treat—staff members will point you to an area where the fruit is ripe. Don't hurry away, however, treat yourself to a stroll through the botanical garden. Follow a well-trodden path through a covered archway where tropical plants grow, and cross a tiny stream to find many of Hawaii's flowers and plants labeled by name. The path winds along for just 10 minutes and leads to a pond surrounded by taro, bird of paradise, hibiscus, torch ginger, ferns, and various palms. Near the pond, you'll find a round, thatched gazebo, and a picnic table for your enjoyment. Finally, cross the stream on two wooden half-moon bridges while listening to the babbling water and whispering wind, just as the ancient Hawaiians did while tending their water-terraced fields. Before leaving, stop at the snack shop for guava juice, a juice float or slush, ice cream cone, or bowl of saimin.

Where Kolo Road intersects Kilauea Road sits **Christ Memorial Episcopal Church** on the right. Hawaii seems to sprout with as many churches as bamboo shoots, but this one is special. The shrubbery and flowers immediately catch your eye, their vibrant colors matched by the stained-glass windows, imported from England. The present church was built in 1941 from cut lava stone. Inside is a hand-hewn altar, and surrounding the church is a cemetery with several tombstones of long-departed parishioners. Go in, have a look, and perhaps meditate for a moment. Before turning on Kilauea Road have a look at **St. Sylvester's Catholic Church.** This house of worship is octagonal, with a roof resembling a Chinese hat. Inside are murals painted by Jean Charlot, a famous island artist. The church, built by Friar John Macdonald, was an attempt to reintroduce art as one of the bulwarks of Catholicism.

NORTH SHORE

OCEAN

PACIFIC

KILAUEA LIGHTHOUSE

Moku'ae'ae Island · Kilauea Point

Kauapea Beach · Kilahiwai Bay · Mokolea Bay

Mokolea Point

PRINCEVILLE MAKAI GOLF COURSE

'ANINI BEACH COUNTY PARK

'Anini Beach · Kalihiwai Bay

HANALEI BEACH COUNTY PARK

Princeville · PRINCEVILLE PRINCE COURSE · Kalihiwai · Kalihiwai Falls · Kilauea

Pu'u Po'a Point

To Kapa'a

HA'ENA BEACH COUNTY PARK

HA'ENA STATE PARK

Ke'e Beach

Ha'ena Point · Lumahai Beach · Wainiha Bay

Ha'ena · Wainiha

Hanalei Bay · Hanalei

PRINCEVILLE AIRPORT

GUAVA KAI PLANTATION

Hanakapi'ai Beach

Kalalau Trail

Hanakapi'ai Stream

NA PALI COAST STATE PARK

To Kalalau Valley

Wainiha River · Lumahai River · Wai'oli Stream · Hanalei River · Kalihiwai River · Kalihiwai Stream · Halaulani Stream

SEE "NA PALI COAST" MAP

SEE "ROAD'S END" MAP

SEE "HANALEI" MAP

SEE "PRINCEVILLE" MAP

0   2 mi
0   2 km

Kilauea Point National Wildlife Refuge

Head down Kilauea Road (sometimes referred to as Lighthouse Road) past the Kong Lung Center, following it as is makes a hard swing to the left, then winds around, ending at Kilauea Point National Wildlife Refuge and **Kilauea Lighthouse,** a designated national historical landmark. This facility, built in 1913, was at one time manned by the Coast Guard but is now under the jurisdiction of the Department of the Interior's Fish and Wildlife Service. Stately and solid, it stands about 50 feet tall, the base more than 200 feet above the sea. Boasting the largest "clamshell lens" in the world, it was capable of sending a beam 20 miles out to sea. The clamshell lens was discontinued in 1976, when a small, high-intensity beacon was activated as the reference point for mariners.

The refuge, which encompasses the high cliffs from Kilauea Point past Crater Hill to Mokolea Point (one half of an ancient and eroded crater rim), is alive with permanent and migrating seabirds. Keep your eyes peeled for the great frigate bird kiting on its eight-foot wingspan, and the red footed booby, a white bird with black wingtips darting here and there, always wearing red dancing shoes. The *nene,* wedgetail shearwaters, and red- and white-tailed trop-

icbirds are also common here. The wildlife refuge is attempting to relocate albatross from the Midway Islands, where they have virtually taken over the island. More than 40 have been successfully relocated, and you can watch them floundering around on nearby Albatross Hill. At certain times of the year, Hawaiian monk seals and green sea turtles can be seen along the shore and around Moku'ae'ae Island just off Kilauea Point. Dolphins are also spotted offshore during spring and summer, and whales play in these waters, part of the Hawaiian Islands Humpback Whale National Marine Sanctuary, during winter and spring.

A leisurely walk takes you out onto this amazingly narrow peninsula to the lighthouse and visitor center. Don't keep your eyes only in the air, however. Look for the coastal *naupaka* plants, which surround the parking lot and line the walk to the lighthouse. Common along the seashore and able to grow even in arid regions, these plants have bunches of bright green, moisture-retaining, leathery leaves; at their centers are white half-flowers the size of a fingernail and small white seeds. Information at the visitors center gives you a fast lesson in bird life, plant life, and a pictorial history of the lighthouse—worth reading. Also available are a good selection of books

KAUA'I

Kilauea Lighthouse

ROBERT NILSEN

KAUA'I

on Hawaiian flora, fauna, history, and hiking, as well as maps of the islands. There are usually informative docents in the yard, and the center often sets up binoculars on tripods trained on particular birds or nesting sites on the nearby cliffs.

The refuge has established a one-mile-long walking trail from Kilauea Point east to Crater Hill that is used strictly for tours led by refuge personnel. The hiking tour leaves at 10:15 A.M. from the visitor center; make your reservation by calling 808/828-0168. From Crater Hill, 568 feet straight up from the water, the wide Pacific stretches virtually unobstructed until it hits the Aleutian Islands of Alaska. This sea cliff is like a giant stack of pancakes, layered and jagged, with the edges eaten by age, and covered with a green syrup of lichen and mosses. The cliff is undercut and gives the sensation of floating in midair. There is a profusion of purple and yellow flowers all along the edge. Like Kilauea Point to the west and Mokolea Point to the east, these

cliffs serve as a giant rookery for seabirds. The military found it a perfect spot, too, and erected a radar station here during World War II.

This lighthouse and sanctuary are open daily 10 A.M.–4 P.M., except federal holidays. The entrance fee is $2 adults, free for children under 16; the cost of an annual refuge permit is $10. Golden Eagle, Golden Access, and Golden Age Passes, and a Federal Duck Stamp are honored for free entrance.

Beaches

The Kilauea area has some fantastic beaches.

Kilauea Bay offers great fishing, unofficial camping, and beautiful scenery. Proceed through Kilauea past Kong Lung Store. Take the second dirt road to the right (if it's open), or walk; it angles through what used to be cane fields. Follow this rutted road a mile and a half down to what the local people call **Quarry Beach,** also known as Kahili Beach. At the end of the road is the now-abandoned Kahili Quarry. Characteristic of Kaua'i, Kilauea Stream runs into the bay. You must wade across the stream to the seldom-visited sandy beach. The swimming is good in the stream and along the beach, but only during calm periods. Some local residents come here to surf or use boogie boards. Plenty of places along the streambank or on the beach are good for picnicking and camping. Many local fishermen come here to catch a transparent fish called 'o'io, which they often use for bait. It's too bony to fry, but they have figured out an ingenious way to get the meat. They cut off the tail and roll a soda pop bottle over it, squeezing the meat out through the cut. They then mix it with water, hot pepper, and bread crumbs to make delicious fish balls.

Kauapea Beach, more commonly called **Secret Beach,** deserves its name. After passing through Kilauea, look for Banana Joe's tropical fruit stand on the left; just past it is Kalihiwai Road. Make a right here and then take the very first dirt road on the right, through the cut in the roadbank, and down to a parking area. Follow the trail along the horse pasture barbed-wire fence and then steeply down the slippery ravine before emerging at the beach in less than 15 minutes. Even some local residents ruefully admit that the secret is out. However, if you venture to this beach, be conscious that there are private homes nearby and that it's a place locals come to enjoy themselves away from the crowds of tourists. If you expect Secret Beach to be small, you're in for a shock. This white-sand strand is huge and backed by steep cliff walls. Reasonably calm during summer months, waves thunder in and crash on the beach during winter. Dolphins seem to like this area as well—please give these intelligent animals plenty of space—and whales can be seen offshore during the winter months. Secret Beach is a de facto nude beach and is accepted as such by most local residents. Beyond the far end of the beach you can see Kilauea Lighthouse, proud and dominant and dazzling white in the sun. Along the beach is a fine stand of trees providing shade and perfect for pitching a tent, but be aware that police sometimes patrol here and issue tickets for camping without a permit! Nonetheless, some people make this beach home for a few weeks or months at a time—unofficially, of course. For drinking water, head along the beach and keep your eyes peeled for a fresh water spring coming out of the mountain. What more can you ask for?

Kalihiwai Beach is at the end of Kalihiwai Road. If you go over the Kalihiwai River, you've gone too far—even though another section of the Kalihiwai Road also leads from there down to the coast. This road was once part of the coastal road, but the devastating tsunami of 1946 took out the lower bridge, and the road is now divided by the river. As on many such rivers in Kaua'i, a ferry was used here to ease early transportation difficulties. In less than half a mile down the first Kalihiwai Road you come to an off-the-track, white sand beach lined with ironwoods. The swimming, bodysurfing, and boogie boarding are outstanding here, given the right conditions. The river behind the ironwoods forms a fresh water pool for rinsing off, but there are no amenities whatsoever. People sometimes camp among the ironwoods. The second Kalihiwai Road—take the right fork in the road—leads you to the west side of the river, where some people come to fish.

On the way to the second Kalihiwai Road you cross Kalihiwai Stream. Just before the bridge is a scenic overlook where you can take in this lush valley and its waterfall. Before you get back into your car to head on, go back up the road a hundred yards or so where a tall thin falls slices through a tight ravine right at the road's edge, almost out of view of traffic. As this spot is directly on the busy highway, pull your car all the way off the roadway and be extra cautious as you walk along.

Go over the bridge and turn right on the second Kalihiwai Road. Follow this to a Y, take the left fork—'Anini Road—and follow it to its end at the remarkable **'Anini Beach County Park.** This area was known as one of the best fishing grounds and was reserved for the exclusive use of the *ali'i.* 'Anini was traditionally called *W'anini.* But time and sea air weathered a latter-day sign until the "W" rusted off completely. Newcomers to the area mistakenly called it 'Anini, and the name stuck. The reef here, at two miles, is the longest exposed reef off Kaua'i; consequently, the snorkeling is first-rate. It's amazing to snorkel out to the reef in no more than four feet of water and then to peer over the edge into waters that seem bottomless. Windsurfers also love this area, and their bright sails can be seen year-round. Those in the know say this is the best spot on Kaua'i for beginning windsurfers, as the trade winds generally blow gently and steadily toward the shore, the water is shallow, and the beach protected. Beginning lessons are often given here. Longer than the reef, the beach is fine sand, and swimming is excellent. Follow the road to the end, where a shallow, brackish lagoon and a large sandbar make the area good for wading. This park has full amenities—toilets, picnic tables, grills, and a pavilion. Camping by county permit is allowed in designated areas; the day use picnic spot is at the other end of the park. There are private homes and vacation rentals at both ends of this beach, so be considerate when coming and going.

A polo ground is across the road from the open camping area. On Sundays from April to August, matches are held here beginning at 3 P.M. and lasting until about

great frigate bird

KAUA'I

LOUISE FOOTE

5 P.M. Admission is $3 per person or $6 per car. The exciting matches are both fun and stylish. The local horsemen are excellent players who combine with their trusty mounts to perform amazing athletic maneuvers. Call the Kauai Polo Club, 808/828-0273, for information.

PRACTICALITIES

Accommodations

For a quiet restful stay on an orchid farm, try the vacation rental at **Makai Farms**, P.O. Box 93, Kilauea, HI 96754, 808/828-1874, fax 808/828-0148, website: www.makaifarms.com, email: makai@aloha.net. The cottage here sleeps up to four. Upstairs is the bedroom, downstairs the kitchen and bathroom. Sit outside in the trade winds and savor fruit picked off the trees on the property. The rate is $80 for a couple, $10 for each additional adult; two nights' minimum preferred.

For a self-contained studio that looks out over the river and ocean, with private bath and kitchenette, contact Margaret Neumann at 808/828-1300. It rents for $85 a night. Breakfast is not included.

Hale Ho'o Maha, 808/828-1341 or 800/851-0291, website: www.aloha.net/~hoomaha, email: hoomaha@aloha.net, is in Kalihiwai on five acres, a few minutes' walk from the bay and Secret Beach. This bed-and-breakfast has four rooms at $55–80 a night, with breakfast included. Two rooms share a bath, and two rooms have a three-night minimum. Contemporary island style.

Along 'Anini Beach Road are numerous vacation rentals. **'Anini Beach Hale** is a two-bedroom, two-bath house, with full kitchen, laundry facilities, and entertainment center. It sleeps four adults and two children. Rates are $175 a night or $1,100 a week, plus a $75 cleaning fee. For information and reservations, contact P.O. Box 419, Kilauea, HI 96754, 808/828-6808 or 877/262-6688, website: www.yourbeach.com, email: bebe@aloha.net.

For the large family, the 2,000-square-foot **'Anini Hale** will fit the bill with its three bedrooms, two baths, complete kitchen, laundry room, large living and dining rooms, and wraparound lanai. The house goes for $170 a day for two, $15 for each extra person, or $1,300 a

week and $100 for each additional person. A smaller cottage in the back, also with full amenities, rents for $100 a night or $650 a week. For reservation information write P.O. Box 989, Hanalei, HI 97814; call 808/826-6167, fax 808/826-6067, check out the website at www.'aninihale.com, or email rappbob@gte.net.

Vacation Rental Agencies

Emerald Isle Properties, 4244 Kilauea Rd., 808/828-1111 or 800/828-1442, website: www.kauai-vacations-realty.com, can match you with a rental home in Kilauea or anywhere along the north coast. This agency generally does bookings into individual homes, but they handle a few condo units as well.

Also handling many vacation rentals from Anahola to Ha'ena is **Hanalei North Shore Properties,** 808/826-9622 or 800/488-3336, website: www.planet-hawaii.com/visit-kauai, email: hnsp@aloha.net.

Covering pretty much the same ground and offering upscale vacation rentals is **Harrington's Paradise Properties,** 808/826-9655 or 888/826-9655, email: chisholm@gte.net.

Kauai Vacation Rentals, 3-3311 Kuhio Hwy., Lihu'e, HI 96766, 808/245-8841 or 800/357-5025, website: www.KauaiVacationRentals.com, email: aloha@kvrre.com, handles many midrange homes in the Anahola to 'Anini Beach area.

Food

The **Roadrunner Bakery and Cafe,** 2430 Oka St. (turn one block before Kong Lung Center), 808/828-8226, open daily for breakfast, lunch, and dinner (except Sunday), would make even Wile E. Coyote give up Acme Exploding Enchiladas with its excellent and very affordable Mexican food. The brightly painted wall murals of rural Mexican scenes put you in a south-of-the-border mood. Chew your enchiladas while Aztec Indians tend their crops, horses gallop past, buses laden with chickens and baggage cruise along through cactus fields, and *charros* roast a side of beef over a campfire. Breakfast gets you rolling with huevos rancheros, Mexicana or Americano. Lunch brings appetizers like chips and salsa and entrées like chicken flautas. The dinner menu has a range of appetizers and salads priced $4.75–8.95. Regular Mexican fare includes tostadas smothered with roasted chicken, pork, steak, or fresh catch, all under $10.95; and cheese, chicken, or eggplant enchiladas for $9.95. Roadrunner also offers tacos, chilis rellenos, burras, and burgers, all handmade fresh on the premises, and there are many fish and vegetarian options. Nothing on the menu costs more than the chili relleno combination with fresh island fish, enchiladas, or sope for $13.95. From the bakery you can order Hanalei taro rolls, bagels, or sourdough, cracked pepper, honey wheat, and Rhine molasses breads, along with all sorts of goodies. The bakery entrance is through a separate corner door. Roadrunner is a hands-on business run with pride, friendliness, and a commitment to fresh and excellent food at reasonable prices.

Just behind Kong Lung Co. is the **Kilauea Bakery and Pau Hana Pizza**, 808/828-2020, open daily except Sunday 6:30 A.M.–9 P.M. (pizza from 11 A.M.). Using all natural ingredients, Kilauea Bakery supplies some of the best restaurants along the north shore. The extensive selection of baked goods is tempting, the bread sticks famous, and occasionally something a bit offbeat like pumpkin coconut muffins is for sale. As with the other shops in this little complex, Kilauea Bakery succeeds in offering something special. The pizzas are made with garlic-infused olive oil, whole-milk mozzarella, and homemade sauce on a whole-wheat or sourdough crust. All are gourmet, topped with sautéed mushrooms, feta cheese, grated Parmesan, homemade pesto, sun-dried tomatoes, locally grown peppers, or the like, priced from $7.25 for a small to $27.85 for a 16-inch large with six toppings, or $2.75 by the slice. Specialty pizzas are also available. Enjoy your treat inside, or sit on the tiny veranda under a shade umbrella. Coffee, made by the cup, is also served at the espresso bar.

Next door to Kong Lung Center is **Lighthouse Bistro**, 808/828-0480, open since late 1999. Guests will be comfortable in this plantation-style building with windows that open wide to catch the breezes and the cushy rattan furniture. Appetizers and antipasti run $8–15. Entrées, $17–25, include stuffed shrimp in phyllo, mango cherry chicken, seafood linguini, and Cajun barbecue shrimp. This is the town's fine dining restaurant and you can enjoy dinner accompanied with light piano music on Friday and Saturday evenings.

A few steps away is the Kilauea Theater, and beyond that, **Kilauea Farmers' Market**, 808/828-1512, a deli/grocery store/lunch counter, open daily 8:30 A.M.–8:30 P.M., until 7:30 P.M. on Sunday. The deli carries food items and beverages and makes filling homemade soups, garden salads, and sandwiches for those who want to eat something substantial but don't want a full sit-down meal. Much of the limited selection of produce is organic, and the market has packaged natural foods and a gourmet section with imported cheeses, fine food items, wines, and microbrews.

Look for the kiosk in a banana grove marking **Mango Mama's Cafe** at the Hookui Road turnoff along Route 56. Mango Mama's is ripe with papayas, bananas, macadamia nuts, fresh juices, smoothies, sugarcane, honey, and healthful sandwiches; open daily 7:30 A.M.–6 P.M. Mango Mama has information on north shore activities as well.

After visiting all these places, you need a rest. The perfect stop is just west of town at **Banana Joe's** fruit stand, *mauka* of the highway (toward the mountains), 808/828-1092, open 9 A.M.–6 P.M. daily. Run by Joe Halasey, his wife, and friends, this little yellow stand offers fresh fruit, smoothies and other drinks, packaged fruit baskets, baked goods with fruit, and locally produced honey. They have more kinds of fruit than you've ever heard of—try something new. If you're interested and they have the time, you may be able to visit the farm behind the stand and talk to Banana Joe himself, but you'll have to ask first. After Banana Joe's and Mango Mama's, what's next in the related-to-a-tropical-fruit department? Sister Soursop and Brother Breadfruit?

Two **farmers' markets** are held each week in Kilauea. The county-sponsored market is Thursday at 4:30 P.M. at the Kilauea Neighborhood Center in the middle of town, and the private Saturday market is held at Christ Memorial Church 9 A.M.–noon. Each has the usual collection of organic food and flower stands, but some say the Saturday market is bigger and better.

Shopping and Services

In Kilauea across from the Shell station look for **Shared Blessing Thrift Shop**, open Tuesday and Thursday 2–5 P.M. and Wednesday and Saturday 9:30 A.M.–2:30 in a vintage plantation

KAUA'I

building, a good place to pick up secondhand treasures or curios from Kaua'i, among everything from binoculars to boogie boards. For modern fashions, try **Jungle Girl** near the intersection of Kilauea Road.

An institution in this area is **Kong Lung Co.,** along Kilauea Road at the intersection of Keneke Street, 808/828-1822, open Mon.–Sat. 9 A.M.–6 P.M., Sunday 10 A.M.–5 P.M., which has been serving the needs of the north shore plantation towns for more than a century. But don't expect bulk rice and pipe fittings. Rather, this is a collection of fine fashions and jewelry, bath products, antiques, art and crafts, and home accessories, much of which has a distinctive Asian flavor. It bills itself as an "exotic gift emporium," and you'll agree. The upstairs section of the store is called **Reinventions** and sells consignment clothing for both men and women, as well as Hawaiian quilts and other quilted pieces.

Kilauea is also home to the **Island Soap and Candle Works,** directly behind the Kong Lung Co. store, 808/828-1955, website: www.handmade-soap.com, open Mon.–Sat. 9 A.M.–8 P.M., Sunday 11 A.M.–6 P.M. The owners, a husband and wife team, hand-pour the soap, perfuming the raw bars with coconut, plumeria, and ginger. They also produce scented coconut oils, lotions, and bath gels capturing the scents of the islands, and a wide variety of scented candles. Business has been good, and they've opened a second shop in Koloa on the south shore. Island Soap products are available at boutiques throughout Hawaii and can also be purchased by mail: call 888/528-7627 or write P.O. Box 548, Koloa, HI 96756.

To experience the living beauty of your trip to Kaua'i, try a bouquet of lovely orchids from **Makai Farms,** 808/828-1874, by appointment only. Look for the sign to the entrance along a white fence, *makai* past mile marker 21. Up Waiakalua Street (follow the signs) is **Kauai Orchids,** 808/828-0904, open Wed.–Sun. 10 A.M.–4 P.M. or by appointment. Also open nearby for the tropical flowers and palms the islands are so well known for is **Emmalani's Nursery and Garden,** 808/828-1800. All have plants certified to ship or carry to the Mainland.

The **Kilauea Theater** shows films, including the annual International Film Festival films, and hosts many community events.

For medical emergencies while on the north shore, stop in at **Hale Le'a Family Medicine Clinic,** on Oka Street, 808/828-2885. Next door is the **North Shore Pharmacy,** and a few steps away the **North Shore Clinic,** 808/828-1418.

Recreation

On a 400-acre property, two miles into the mountains above the highway, is **Silver Falls Ranch,** 808/828-6718, a professional equine organization that treats its horses well, like it does its guests. Three horseback rides are offered, a 90-minute Greenhorn Ride for beginners at $60, a two-hour Hawaiian Discovery Ride at $75 that takes you farther into the hills below Mt. Namahana, and a three-hour Silver Falls Ride for $99 that includes a stop for lunch and a swim at the pool below a cascade falls. This is fun for every level of rider, and the rides surround you with wonderful scenery between Kalihiwai and Kamo'okoa Ridges.

PRINCEVILLE

Princeville is 9,000 acres of planned luxury overlooking Hanalei Bay. This bluff top plateau was considered by the ancient Hawaiians as a place of *mana* and appropriately was the site of various *heiau*. When Europeans first surveyed the island, they knew that this point could have strategic importance. In the early 1800s, the Russian Fur Trading Company built Fort Alexander on this headland, one of three forts it constructed on Kaua'i in order to establish and maintain influence over the independent Kaua'ian King Kau-

muali'i. This fort served the company only for a few short months before the newcomers were forced to leave the island. It, and a fort erected in Hanalei below, fell into disrepair, and the stones were carted away for other purposes. Only the remains of stone walls at Fort Elizabeth in Waimea on the south coast of the island remain to hint at the scope of these Russian fortifications.

In the 1800s, the surrounding countryside was a huge sugar and coffee plantation—Kaua'i's oldest, established in 1853 by the Scots-

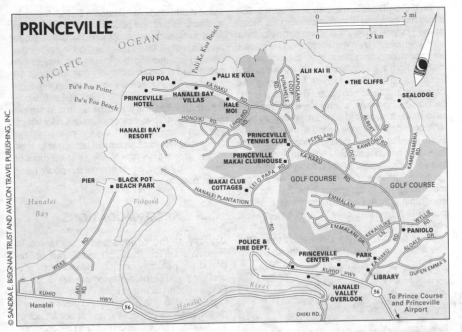

man R. C. Wyllie. After an official royal vacation to the ranch by Kamehameha IV and Queen Emma in 1860, the name was changed to Princeville in honor of the royal son, Prince Albert. The young heir unfortunately died within two years, and his heartbroken father soon followed. In 1865, Wyllie also died, and the plantation was sold. While coffee never really did well here, sugar continued to be raised and milled in Hanalei. The operation turned to cattle ranching around 1900, and this lasted until 1969 when the land changed hands again.

That year, Consolidated Gas and Oil of Honolulu took these acres and began developing them into a prime vacation community designed to keep the humdrum world far away. Bought by the Princeville Development Corporation, a subsidiary of Quitex Australia, the hotel went through a major renovation and other development was started. Then in 1990, the Princeville resort was taken over by the Japanese consortium of Suntory, Mitsui, and Nippon Shinpan. Unfortunately, Hurricane 'Iniki struck in 1992, necessitating major repairs to the hotel, condos,

homes, and other facilities. The Princeville community now provides everything: accommodations, shopping, dining, a community park, the island's newest public library, golf and tennis facilities, a gas station, banks, and even a fire and police force. First-rate condos are scattered around the property, private luxury homes cluster around the golf links, and the refurbished multi-tiered Princeville Hotel perches over the bay. The guests expect to stay put, except for an occasional day-trip. Management and clientele are in league to provide and receive satisfaction. And without even trying, it's just about guaranteed. The community maintains a website at www.princeville.com.

BEACHES

Set on a high headland, Princeville is not known for its beaches. Yet, there are a few fairly isolated sandy spots tucked into the cliff face that are used for sunning and more often as entry points for surfers. The largest and most easily accessed is **Puʻu Poa Beach,** the beach directly below the Princeville Hotel. Stretching toward the mouth of the Hanalei River, the white sandy bottom here is enclosed by a narrow reef and is decent for swimming when the surf is not high. If not coming from the hotel pool area, try the beach access steps that lead down from the guard house at the hotel entrance. There is a small public parking lot here. **Pali Ke Kua Beach** is reached by a steep and sometimes slippery public access path that runs between the Princeville Hotel parking lot and the Puu Poa condo complex. This beach is actually split into two pocket-like sections, separated by a rocky outcrop. To get to the other end of this beach, use the cement path that leads down from Pali Ke Kua condominium. A sign here may say that the beach is for guests only, but all beaches in Hawaii are open to everyone.

Other paths down the cliff lead to the rocky shoreline and not to sandy beaches. One of these paths leads to **"Queen's Bath,"** basically a large crescent tide pool gouged out of the lava shelf at water's edge. Where Punahele Road and Kapiʻolani Loop meet, a sign indicates the parking lot and another points the way to the trail. Head down the slippery trail for about 10 minutes, which follows a small stream that tumbles into a crevasse in the lava shelf at the bottom, then follow the shoreline around to the left another 10–15 minutes or so, to this pool where you can swim right at the edge of the ocean. On calm days you can almost lie with your toes in the pool and hands in the sea; on days of heavy surf, waves crash against the pool's outer edge in white thunder.

ACCOMMODATIONS

Virtually all the condos and hotel rooms in Princeville fall into the $250 and up range. The best deals naturally occur off-season (fall), especially if you plan on staying a week or more. Oddly enough, a project like Princeville should make booking one of its many condos an easy matter, but it's sadly lacking on this point. Lack of a centralized organization handling reservations causes the confusion. Each condo building can have half a dozen booking agents, all with different phone numbers and widely differing rates. The units are privately owned, and the owners simply choose one agency or another. If you're going through a travel agent at home, be aware of these discrepancies and insist on the least-expensive rates. A situation that reduces the number of units available is that many of the condos are moving to exclusively time-share programs, while others still offer rental units along with the time-share units, so check out the possibilities.

Princeville Hotel

The Princeville Hotel, 5520 Ka Haku Rd., Princeville, HI 96722, 808/826-9644 or 800/325-3589, fax 808/826-1166, is a dramatic architectural opus, built in four cascading tiers on an extreme point of rugged peninsula. From its perch, all but 16 of the 252 rooms offer breathtaking views of the frothing azure of Hanalei Bay as it stretches toward the emerald green of Mt. Makana (Bali Hai) down the coast. The other

ROBERT NILSEN

At Queen's Bath, a large, crescent-shaped tide pool, you can swim at the edge of the ocean.

KAUAʻI

rooms offer panoramic views of Puu Poa Marsh, a wildlife wetlands that offers sanctuary to exotic bird life. This is Kaua'i's most opulent hotel. The main lobby offers elegance on a grand scale, with gold-capped Corinthian columns, teardrop chandeliers, and a central reflecting pool set in a floor of swirled black and white marble that's studded with Louis XIV chairs and plush couches. Here you'll find the concierge and activities desks. Opposite the front desk is the Living Room, a dignified area serving as library, cocktail lounge, and music room. Choose a plush chair just before sunset and sip a cocktail as the sun streaks the sky with lasers of light dancing across the endless blue of the wide Pacific. There is entertainment here every night: Hawaiian and contemporary music, and twice-weekly sonorous Hawaiian chanting and hula. In addition, an artisans program with demonstrations of Hawaiian arts and crafts is held here daily. This lobby level has a small mini-mall with a cluster of shops, below which is a small cinema, and the grand staircase at the far end leads to the hotel's two fine dining restaurants. The hotel entrance is on level nine. Taking elevators and walkways to level one deposits you at the swimming pool and poolside Beach Restaurant and Bar, next to which the twice-weekly lu'au is performed. A few steps away are the beach and beach activities center. The white sand beach fronting the hotel is perfect for swimming, and the reef below, alive with tropical fish, is excellent for snorkeling. At dusk, descend to the pool area and immerse yourself in one of the hot tubs to watch the sun melt into the Pacific as you melt into the foaming bubbles. For parents who wish for some time alone, let the Keiki Aloha children's program look after your kids with entertaining excursions and arts and crafts. A free drop-off and pickup shuttle service is offered anywhere in the Princeville resort area, including the Prince Golf Course clubhouse and the heliport. Request a shuttle ride from the bell desk—be sure to ask for the telephone number to call for a return ride. No matter how formal the surroundings may seem, the staff infuse this property with the casual and genuine spirit of Hawaiian *aloha.*

All rooms feature bathrooms with double vanities, separate toilets, terry robes, slippers, and deep immersion tubs, some of which are mini-spas. Bathroom windows are of liquid crystal that can be controlled to change from opaque for privacy to clear so that you can enjoy the view while you soak. These finely decorated rooms in beige or green also feature king beds, refrigerators, remote-control color TVs, safes, ironing boards, and 24-hour room service; suites have an extra large and plush sitting area with dining table. A mountain/garden view room runs $360, partial ocean view and ocean view rooms $410–510, and junior suites are $595; other suites run $1,000–3,500. There is a $50 extra person charge, with a maximum of four to a room. Children under 18 room for free in existing beds.

Hanalei Bay Resort

The Hanalei Bay Resort and Suites, 5380 Honoiki Rd., Princeville, HI 96722, 808/826-6522 or 800/827-4427, fax 808/826-6680, is a condo resort with some private units. You enter through a spacious open foyer paved with flagstone and face the Happy Talk lounge, done in longhouse style with a palm-frond roof, magnificent koa long bar, and matching koa canoe. From the bar, you have a spectacular panorama of distant Bali Hai dappled by passing clouds and Hanalei Bay, a sheet of foam-fringed azure. Evening brings live music, with everything from jazz to a local slack-key combo. Just as good for views of the bay and the waterfalls on the mountains is the Bali Hai Restaurant. Stepping down the hillside from the bar is the resort's free-form pool, complete with one sand edge, a 15-foot waterfall, and whirlpool grotto—all surrounded by landscaping inspired by the area's natural beauty. The cobalt blue tile of the second pool matches the color of the bay beyond. For a swim in the bay, take the beach path down the hill to the water. The resort's 16 buildings are situated along walking paths, and all units have a stupendous view. There is no driving on the property, so you must leave your car in the parking lot at the front and you and your luggage will be shuttled to your unit by small van. Renovated extensively in 1995, the resort has amenities including TV, phone, and air-conditioning, full kitchens in the suites (no kitchens in the single hotel rooms), and laundry facilities. For those who care to do more than sit by the pool, daily cultural activities are scheduled. Sign up for these at the concierge desk, where other island activities can also be booked. The eight tennis here courts are open to guests and nonguests, and the pro shop arranges clinics and round robins. Single hotel rooms and one-, two-, and three-bedroom suites in mountain and ocean view categories are available; rates start at $170 for a room and run $320–725 per night for the suites. A made-to-order breakfast and two afternoon cocktails daily are complimentary with each suite.

Condos

There are more than 15 condominium properties in Princeville. Most of the high-end condos are located far into the development near the Princeville Hotel or strung along the cliff edge overlooking the pounding surf. They are out to please and don't skimp on the luxuries. About a third are managed strictly as time-share properties, and several others have blocks of units that are also managed that way. Even in this luxury development there are a few small median-range complexes. Although low-end properties and subsidized housing were supposed to be incorporated into this development, it seems all of those have been shifted down the road to Kilauea. What follows is a sampling of what's available.

Marc Resorts Hawaii manages units in the four properties closest to the Princeville Hotel. Sleek and modernistic, with its curved exterior and step-terrace construction, **Puu Poa** is perhaps the most luxurious. It has spacious two-bedroom, two-bath units with complete kitchens that run $249–299 for up to six people, and guest-use tennis courts and a swimming pool. Next along the cliff is **Pali Ke Kua,** which boasts one of the best restaurants on the north coast. This property is a mix of one- and two-bedroom, garden, ocean view, and oceanfront units, priced $179–299. Comfortable and well furnished, each unit has cable TV, washers and dryers, and a full kitchen—just right for families. Swim in the pool topside or walk the path down to the gazebo and secluded beach to sunbathe. Across the road, overlooking the golf course, are Hale Moi cottages and Hanalei Bay Villas. Most economical are the **Hale Moi** cottages—four-plexes with pleasing mountain views. Available here are hotel room-like master bedroom units, suites, and one-bedroom units for $119–179. All except the master bedroom units have kitchens.

The more luxurious **Hanalei Bay Villa** is one of the area's newest vacation rental properties, and each of these buildings perches on stilts like a bird cage overlooking the glen and fairway. Running $249–289, all units have two bedrooms, full kitchens, and mountain or bay views. There is a two-night minimum at these Marc Resorts Hawaii properties. For information and reservations, call 800/535-0085.

Set high on the bluff overlooking the Pacific Ocean is **The Cliffs at Princeville,** 808/826-6219, 808/622-6219, or 800/367-7052, website: www.cliffs-princeville.com. These one-bedroom condo units have two full-size baths, a fully equipped kitchen, and a large living room. Two large lanai, one at each end of the unit, offer both ocean and mountain views. Although all units are individually owned, furnishings are basically of a contemporary style. The bedrooms have king-size beds and the cushy living-room couches pull out to sleep two more. Units have color TVs, video and stereo systems, compact washers and dryers, irons and ironing boards, small safes for valuables, and daily maid service. Some third-floor units have a loft, and the living-room ceiling slants up to the second floor. One-bedroom units are $155–175, with lofts $205–225; there's a two-night minimum. The property also has a pool with spa, putting green, volleyball court, four tennis courts free to guests, a breezy rec room with TV and reading material, and a laundry room. The activities desk will gladly arrange tours for you, offer suggestions for day-trips, or rent you a bicycle.

The weathered gray Cape Cod-ish **Sealodge** condos have one of the best locations for views along this coast. All individually owned, these units all have full amenities and most have washers and dryers. Although rates vary a little, expect to pay $95 for a one-bedroom or $125 for a two-bedroom unit with a $45–55 cleaning charge; weekly rates are available. Most of the units here are managed by Jack Waring, 800/446-4384; Herb Hubbard, 800/585-6101; and Carol Goodwin, 650/573-0636.

Other good locations include the **Alii Kai II,** contact Oceanfront Realty, 800/222-5541, and **Makai Club Cottages** 800/367-7090, which is a time-share complex that rents its one- and two-bedroom units for $600–1,200 a week when available.

The **Paniolo,** 808/826-5525, and **Puamana,** 808/826-9768, are lower-end complexes for this development, where you would expect a better deal.

Vacation Rentals

Handling vacation rentals in Princeville only is **Real Estate Kauai.Com,** at the Princeville Center, 808/826-9675, website: www.real-estate-kauai.com, email: rek@aloha.net. Most of these properties are high-end condos and homes that rent for $800–2,400 a week.

Also dealing almost exclusively with high-end condo and home properties in Princeville is **Pacific Paradise Properties,** 808/826-7211 or 800/800-3637, website: www.princeville-vacations.com, email: kaikona@gte.net.

Hanalei North Shore Properties, 808/826-9622 or 800/488-3336, website: www.planet-hawaii.com/visit-kauai, email: hnsp@aloha.net, handles about 150 economy to high-end vacation rental homes and condos in Princeville and along the north shore from its office at the Princeville Center. They can find the right place for you.

Also try **Hanalei Vacations,** 808/826-7288 or 800/487-9833, website: www.hanalei-vacations.com, email: rentals@aloha.net, which manages a full range of condos in Princeville and homes and cottages in Ha'ena.

FOOD

Fine Dining

Fine dining in Princeville means eating at the hotel restaurants. The **Bali Hai Restaurant,** at the Hanalei Bay Resort, 808/826-6522, enjoys an excellent reputation not only for its food but also for its superb atmosphere and prize-winning view of the sunset through the wraparound windows of this bi-level and informal yet elegant restaurant. Reminiscent of a Polynesian longhouse, with a vaulted thatched roof, it's open daily for breakfast 7–11 A.M., lunch 11:30 A.M.–2 P.M., and dinner 5:30–10 P.M. Appropriately named, you look out between tall coconut trees, across the spectacular view of Hanalei Bay, and down the coast toward Bali Hai (Mt. Makana), the sentinel of the north coast. The Bali Hai chefs grow their own herbs on the premises and insist on fresh local vegetables, meat, and fish

prepared in a mixture of continental and Pacific Rim cuisine. Start your day with chilled fresh fruit or a continental breakfast that includes fresh fruit juices, bakery items, and Kona coffee, or go local with a taro patch breakfast of two fried eggs, Portuguese sausage, poi pancakes, and taro hash browns. Lunchtime brings soups and salads, sandwiches, and an assortment of burgers. For dinner, you can start with appetizers like blackened 'ahi or Bali Hai crabcakes for $12.75, or a Caesar salad for $7.75. Entrée specialties are fresh island fish prepared with a variety of tempting sauces including shiitake mushroom, chili and peanut satay, and pineapple fruit salsa. Standard but wonderful offerings are linguini with sautéed breast of chicken at $18.50, pan-seared shrimp and scallops for $22.75, and broiled tenderloin with Boursin cheese and Burgundy sauce for $32.

The Princeville Hotel is home to three restaurants. The **Cafe Hanalei,** open for breakfast 6:30–11 A.M., lunch 11 A.M.–2:30 P.M., dinner 5:30–9:30 P.M., offers indoor or outdoor seating in a casual setting. It's continental with a heavy dose of Oriental. Breakfast at Cafe Hanalei is either continental for $16 or full buffet for $20.95; à la carte and Japanese breakfasts are also available. The continental breakfast is much more than you might expect, and the full breakfast buffet is complete with an omelette station and an array of savory breakfast meats. On Sunday, breakfast stops early and gives way to Sunday brunch 10 A.M.–2 P.M. for $33.95 or $38.50 with champagne. Lunch may be a reasonably priced Japanese noodle salad with fish cake, Thai coconut curry with chicken and vegetables, a Caesar salad, or any of a number of gourmet sandwiches, wraps, or seafood dishes. Dinner entrées are barbecued lamb chop, Hawaiian bouillabaisse, grilled 'ahi, or breast of chicken, mostly in the $27–34 range. Finish with desserts like liliko'i cheesecake, crème brûlée, or chocolate torte with minted truffle cream, all delicious and prepared daily. If this is not enough to tempt your taste buds, a sushi bar menu is added Tuesday, Wednesday, Saturday, and Sunday 5–9:30 P.M., which can also be served in the Living Room one level up.

Down a flight of steps from the main lobby, **La Cascata,** open nightly for dinner 6–10 P.M.,

KAUA'I

offers tremendous views of the island's inland waterfalls as you dine in this elegant ristorante. Designed after a famous restaurant in Positano, Italy, it features elegant decor including hand-painted terra cotta floors, inspiring murals, and formally set tables. After antipasti and insalata, the Italian menu features such items as sautéed lobster, shrimp, scallops, and clams over linguini pasta, pork tenderloin with candied red cabbage, fontina-stuffed breast of chicken, pesto roasted pink snapper, and veal piccata with lemon and capers. Meals are perfectly finished with desserts like classic tiramisu, mango cheesecake, macadamia nut pie, or with a cup of espresso or cappuccino, or a glass of fine port.

For light meals 11 A.M.–5:30 P.M., try the hotel's casual, pavilion-type **The Beach Restaurant and Bar,** where you can order snacks, salads, or sandwiches. Try the crispy taco salad with black beans and vegetables, spicy buffalo wings, Black Angus burger, or fresh island fish sandwich, all priced $7.95–14.95. A children's menu helps keep prices down for the little ones. On Monday and Thursday from 6 P.M., the courtyard and accompanying stage area are transformed into the Pa'ina 'O Hanalei lu'au and Polynesian show. For afternoon tea, a sunset cocktail, or early evening *pu pu,* try the **Living Room,** just off the main lobby, or swim up to the pool's water bar until sunset for a mid-lap mai tai.

The **Beamreach Restaurant,** 808/826-6143, in a freestanding building on the grounds of the Pali Ke Kua condo complex, is a casual fine dining restaurant where the chef offers a mix of island-style and classic American dishes. Open nightly for dinner 5:30–9:30 P.M. (reservations suggested); reduced-price Sunset Specials run 5:30–6:30 nightly. The bi-level dining room, subdued in shades of tan and brown, is lightly appointed with hanging baskets, throw nets, frescoes depicting Hawaiian mythology, and a display case holding ancient artifacts. A very good sign is that all soups, salad dressings, and rolls are made on the premises, and fresh organic greens and vegetables are used as much as possible. Stimulate your palate with appetizers like *poki,* offered raw or seared; teriyaki meat sticks; or a pot of fresh steamed clams. Move on to entrées, priced $14–25, like ground sirloin, filet mignon, macadamia nut chicken with tropi-

cal sauce, or fresh fish sautéed, broiled, or blackened. Your sweet tooth will be happy with desserts such as Tahitian Lime Pie, tropical fruit sherbet, or a rum, caramel, or chocolate sundae. The Beamreach also has a full-service bar stocked with fine wine, a good selection of beer, and house specialty tropical drinks.

Princeville Center and Beyond

At the Princeville Center you'll find **Chuck's Steak House,** 808/826-9700, open for lunch Mon.–Fri. 11:30 A.M.–2:30 P.M., nightly for dinner 6–10 P.M. Chuck has a very loyal clientele that comes not only for the juicy steaks but for the fresh fish as well. Chuck's is "casual country," with an open-beamed ceiling, a choice of booth or table inside or on the lanai, and a few saddles and barrels placed here and there for effect. The lunch menu has salads and *pu pu* such as "loaded fries," which are covered with bacon, cheese, and sour cream, and Caesar salad. Burgers and sandwiches go from a simple burger to a barbecue prime rib sandwich for under $12. Dinner is delicious, with the fresh catch charbroiled or sautéed for $19.95, shrimp Hanalei for $22.95, juicy prime rib for $17.95–25.95 depending on the cut, barbecued baby-back pork ribs for $18.95, teriyaki chicken breast at $16.95, and an assortment of combination dinners priced $20.95–27.95. A senior and children's menu relieves the bottom-line total. Chuck's has a full-service bar separate from the dining area, 11:30 A.M.–10:30 P.M., with Hawaiian music Thursday through Saturday. Chuck's is a good choice for a family-style restaurant offering hearty portions.

Follow the rich aroma of brewing coffee to **Hale O Java,** an upscale, friendly, indoor/outdoor, casual restaurant behind Chuck's Steak House, 808/826-7255, open daily for breakfast, lunch, and dinner; they'll even deliver from 5 P.M. until closing. The breakfast menu offers Belgian waffles, tropical granola, and an early-bird special of two eggs, bacon, toast, and Americano coffee. A steaming coffee, latte, cappuccino, or mocha in a large Italian-style cup costs around $2; or try a fruit slush or smoothie just to cool off. A glass case is filled with pastries—from sticky buns to bagels—made fresh on the premises. The lunch menu is basically *panini,* Italian sandwiches made with an assortment of lunch meats and smothered with mozzarella, sliced tomatoes, and fresh pesto, served on focaccia bread for about $8. Pizza, a specialty of Hale O Java, is priced $9.50–19.50—extra with more toppings. Dinner brings a variety of pasta dishes plus such items as firecracker salmon and blackened shrimp, most in the under-$15 range. This place is a step or two off the normal tourist track, but it's quiet and offers well-prepared food and decent prices with a friendly staff to make you feel welcome.

Also at the Princeville Center, you can get a brew and a burger at the **Paradise Bar and Grill,** and **Lappert's Ice Cream** will fill a cone for you.

The **Princeville Restaurant and Bar,** at the Prince Golf Course clubhouse, 808/826-5050, serves breakfast 8–11 A.M., lunch 11 A.M.–3 P.M., and cocktails 11 P.M.–6 P.M., as well a Sunday brunch and a Monday night sushi bar. The breakfast menu includes the usuals, like eggs, waffles, omelettes, and fruit plates ranging $5.25–8. Salads, sandwiches (with names like Birdie, Double Eagle, and Bogey), and sides are served for lunch, and run under $9.50. This is a perfect spot in well-appointed surroundings for a day on the links.

ENTERTAINMENT

There is little in the way of evening entertainment in Princeville, however, the following are definitely worth checking out.

The **Happy Talk Lounge,** with an outrigger canoe suspended from its ceiling, mixes its fantastic views of Hanalei Bay with exotic drinks, wine by the glass, and frothy beers for a night of relaxation and entertainment. A limited menu is served in the evening after the 4–6:30 P.M. happy hour with free *pu pu.* The bar swings with live entertainment Mon.–Sat. 6:30–9:30 P.M.—everything from contemporary music to Hawaiian ballads performed by slack-key artists. A very special performance that shouldn't be missed is the free jazz jam every Sunday 3–7 P.M. Local musical talent is fantastic, but to make things even better, top-name musicians who happen to be on the island are frequently invited to join in. If you love jazz, you can't find a more stunning venue than the Happy Talk.

The **Living Room,** in the main lobby of the Princeville Hotel, is a dignified venue of couches and stuffed chairs for a variety of island-themed entertainment including Hawaiian music, chanting, and hula that's open to everyone 7–11 P.M. nightly. In keeping with the grand setting, an afternoon tea is served 3–5 P.M., *pu pu* are available 5–9:30 P.M., desserts until 10 P.M., and cocktails can be ordered 3 P.M. to midnight.

Don't forget **Amelia's,** open daily at noon, upstairs at the old Princeville Airport. This friendly neighborhood-style pub serves sandwiches, hot dogs, chili, and nachos and has four TVs for live satellite sports. The bar closes at 7–8 P.M. on weekdays but stays open until the band stops playing on Friday, Saturday, and Sunday. On occasion there is a cover. Friday and Saturday are for rock and roll; Sunday it's the blues.

Pa'ina 'O Hanalei beachside lu'au, performed Monday and Thursday at 6 P.M. near the swimming pool at the Princeville Hotel, is the only lu'au in this resort community. While not given the highest marks, the food is good and the island music and dance performance are rousing. Many show members also perform on Wednesday for the more casual Tahiti Nui lu'au down in Hanalei. Adult tickets are $59.50, children 6–12 $30; senior tickets are discounted. Call 808/826-2788 for reservations.

The **Hawaiian Art Museum,** at the Princeville Center on the second floor next to Foodland, is the home of **Aloha International,** 808/828-0302, website: www.huna.org, open Mon.–Fri. 2–5 P.M., founded by Serge King and dedicated to the practice and philosophy of *huna.* The shelves and counters of this small collection hold artifacts like poi pounders and bowls, a remarkable carved statue of a god doing a handstand, a model village alive with dancers and warriors, descriptions of different canoes, *makini* masks with distinctive owl-like eyes, ferocious-looking *palau* war clubs, and Hawaiian musical instruments. On Sunday morning 10 A.M.–noon there is a session on Hawaiian philosophy and culture by Serge King, an internationally known author and lecturer proficient in his knowledge of *huna* and ancient Hawaiian arts and crafts. Throughout the week are groups on hula, meditation, and healing.

SHOPPING

Aside from the shops at the hotels, the shopping in Princeville is clustered in the **Princeville Center,** with most shops open daily 8 A.M.–8 P.M. Since Princeville is a self-contained community, many of these are practical shops: bank, hardware store, gas station, real-estate offices, post office, restaurants, and a medical clinic. **Foodland,** open daily 6 A.M.–11 P.M., is important because it offers the cheapest food on the north shore. Before it was built, the local people would drive to Kapa'a to shop; now they come here.

Some of the shops here include **Lappert's Ice Cream,** for a quick pick-me-up; **J Ms Jewels** for a quick pick-*her*-up; the **Kauai Kite and Hobby Company,** a bursting crayon box filled with stuffed animals, toys, and, of course, kites; **Hanalei Photo Company,** a full-service photography store offering developing, cameras, photo supplies, and gadgets; and **Sandudes,** a clothing boutique for men and women with sandals, sun hats, waterproof watches, perfume, ladies' dresses, jewelry, T-shirts, and beach bags. **Pretty Woman** sells name-brand ladies' fashions, jewelry, evening dresses, hats, and accessories. Not-so-pretty men are also welcome—especially if they have rolls of wrinkled-up bills bearing pictures of dead presidents, who were not so pretty either.

RECREATION

Those addicted to striking hard, dimpled white balls or fuzzy soft ones have come to the right spot. In Princeville, golf and tennis are the royal couple. However, they are not the only sporting options available. Horseback riding and hiking are becoming popular, and for those less inclined to the physical, a wagon ride or helicopter ride are better suited. To help keep yourself in condition or to ease your tired muscles after a hard day of exercise, pay a visit to the health spa.

Golf
The **Princeville Makai Golf Course,** 808/826-5070, offers 27 holes of magnificent golf designed by Robert Trent Jones Jr. in 1971. This course, rated the #6 golf course in Hawaii by

Golf Digest in 1998, has hosted the 26th annual World Cup in 1978, the LPGA Women's Kemper Open 1986–1989, and the 1990 first Itoman LPGA World Match Play Championship. Radiating from the central clubhouse are three nine-hole, par-36 courses you can use in any combination. They include the Woods, Lake, and Ocean courses—the names highlighting the special focus of each. The cliff-top Ocean 7 is a challenging hole as you must shoot over a deep ravine, and the Lake 9 sets two lakes in your way, but the most difficult hole is Woods 6, which features a long dogleg into the trade winds. The pro shop will set you up with a tee time, and the snack shop offers reasonably priced sandwiches, burgers, and drinks. Greens fees are $115, with many discounts and packages available.

Opened in 1987, the 18-hole **Prince Course,** 808/826-5070, set on the bluff above 'Anini Beach, also welcomes the public. It's off Highway 56 about one mile east of the Princeville Resort entrance and has its own clubhouse. For this course, accuracy and control are much more important than power and distance. Many expert golfers judge the Prince extremely difficult. With a course rating of 75.3 and slope of 145, it's one of the most challenging in Hawaii and is continually rated one of the top courses in the state and one of the top 50 in the country. Greens fees are $155. Fitting into its natural environment, thick tropical woods, deep ravines, and streams are among the obstacles. The driving range is open during daylight hours. The clubhouse has an extensive pro shop and houses the Princeville Health Club and Spa, and on the lower level, the Princeville Restaurant and Bar.

The **Princeville Health Club and Spa,** at the Prince Course clubhouse, 808/826-5030, keeps you healthy with aerobic classes, free weights, a complete set of conditioning machines, a lap pool, hot tub, steam room, sauna, massage by appointment, and skin and body treatments. Nutrition programs can be set up with the staff, who also have information about running courses. One such **jogging path** runs between this clubhouse and the Princeville main entrance gate—about one mile. To enhance these offerings are spectacular views out the plate glass windows toward waterfall-draped mountains and over the rolling fairways to the Pacific Ocean. There's nothing like fabulous surroundings to help increase your aerobic exercise. The daily admission fee is $12, weekly and monthly rates are also available. Hours: Mon.–Fri. 6:30 A.M.–8 P.M., Saturday 8 A.M.–8 P.M., and Sunday 8 A.M.–6 P.M.

Tennis

You can charge the net on six professional plexipave tennis courts at the **Princeville Tennis Club**, 808/826-3620. Open daily 8 A.M.–6 P.M. just down the rise from the Makai Golf Course clubhouse, there is a pro shop, private lessons by appointment, and racquet and ball machine rental. Court fees for a 90-minute reserved time are $12 ($10 for Princeville guests); weekly, monthly, quarterly, and annual memberships also available.

The **Hanalei Bay Resort Tennis Club**, 808/826-6522, has eight courts open to the public; court fee is $6 per person. Men's and women's clinics and round robins are scheduled, and equipment is rented. Call to reserve a court. Several condos in Princeville also have tennis courts for guests only.

Princeville Ranch

Princeville Ranch Stables, 808/826-6777, a half mile east of Princeville Center, is open Mon.–Sat. You can rent a mount here for group rides that take you throughout the area's fascinating countryside. Prices are $55, $100, $110, and $125 for the Hanalei Valley, 'Anini Bluff, waterfall picnic ride, and participatory "cattle ride." The Hanalei Stampede, Kaua'i's largest rodeo, is held at the stables in early August.

The ranch also offers an easygoing wagon ride and day hikes on its property. The office for the wagon ride and day hikes is across the highway from the stable office. Four **wagon rides** are offered: a 45-minute quickie tour for $25 a head; a two-hour lunch tour for $45; a three-hour sunset ride, $85 adults and $45 children 5–10 years old; and a three-hour waterfall swim and lunch ride for $65 a person. On the lunch (except Sunday) and sunset tours, a barbecue meal is cooked by the trail hands. For reservations, call 808/826-1677.

Two different **guided hikes** are also offered on ranch property, twice daily except Sunday. The Hidden Hanalei hike costs $45, and the Waterfall Excursion is $55. All hikes run about three hours. Drinking water and all equipment are provided. Call 808/826-7669 to reserve a spot.

Helicopter Tour

The only helicopter company currently operating at the Princeville Airport in **Hawaii Helicopters**, 808/826-6591 or 800/367-7095. Hawaii Helicopters also flies out of Burns Field in Hanapepe and operates tours on Maui and the Big Island as well. Flying twin-engine machines, the company offers 45- and 60-minute circle-island flights, plus one that includes a stop at Hanapepe for a tour of the town and a swim at Salt Ponds Beach County Park, for $135–179.

SERVICES

Princeville Service Center, 808/826-7331, has postal, shipping, and packaging supplies and services, email access, and copy machines.

The new **Princeville Library** is at the Princeville entrance. Open Tuesday, Thursday, Friday, and Saturday 9 A.M.–5 P.M., Wednesday noon–8 P.M. Its elegant design with arched ceiling and chandelier fits well in this resort community.

Need to check your email? Akamai Computer's **Internet café**, 808/826-1042, on the second floor at the front of the center is open Mon.–Fri. 9 A.M.–5 P.M.

The shopping center has a **Bank of Hawaii** branch office with ATM machine.

The **Princeville Medical Clinic**, 808/826-7228, specializing in preventive medicine, is open Mon.–Fri. 9 A.M.–1 P.M. and 2:30–5 P.M. and Saturday 10 A.M.–1 P.M. Mornings are best for walk-in patients.

The last **gas station** on the north shore is Princeville Chevron, open daily 8 A.M.–5 P.M. If your gauge is low, make sure to tank up if you're driving back down the coast.

Avis, 808/826-9773, maintains a small rental car booth at the Princeville Airport.

KAUA'I

HANALEI

If Puff the Magic Dragon had resided in the sunshine of Hanalei instead of the mists of Hanalee, Little Jackie Paper would still be hangin' around. You know you're entering a magic land the minute you drop down from the heights and cross the Hanalei River. The narrow, one-lane bridge is like a gateway to the enchanted coast, forcing you to slow down and take stock of where you are.

Hanalei (Crescent Bay) compacts a lot into a little space. You're in and out of the town in two blinks, but you'll find two small shopping centers, some terrific restaurants, the beach, ocean activities, and historical sites. You also get two superlatives for the price of one: the epitome of a laid-back north shore village, and a truly magnificent bay. In fact, if one were forced to choose the most beautiful bay in all of Hawaii, Hanalei would definitely be among the finalists.

Mile markers on Highway 56 going west are renumbered from one at Princeville. It is 10 miles from there to the end of the road at Ke'e Beach. On occasion, during periods of heavy rain when water threatens to swallow the bridge, it will be closed to traffic and the road blocked by gates. That means no cars in or out until the water recedes!

SIGHTS

The sights around Hanalei are exactly that—beautiful sweeping vistas of Hanalei Valley and the sea, especially at sunset. People come just for the light show and are never disappointed. When you proceed past the Princeville turnoff, keep your eyes peeled for the Hanalei Valley **scenic overlook.** Don't miss it! Drifting into the distance is the pastel living impressionism of Hanalei Valley, most dramatic in late afternoon, when soft shadows from deeply slanting sun rays create depth in this quilt of fields. Down the center, the liquid silver Hanalei River flows until it meets the sea, where the valley broadens into a wide flat fan. Along its banks, impossible shades of green vibrate as the valley steps back for almost nine miles, all cradled in the protective arms of 3,500-foot *pali*. Controlled by rains, waterfalls either tumble over the *pali* like lace curtains billowing in a gentle wind or with the blasting power of a fire hose. Local wisdom says, "When you can count 17 waterfalls, it's time to get out of Hanalei." The valley has always been one of the most accommodating places to live in all of Hawaii, and its abundance was ever-blessed by the old gods. Madame Pele even sent a thunderbolt to split a boulder so that the Hawaiians could run an irrigation ditch through its center to their fields.

Unlike the Princeville bluff, Hanalei was an area for the common man. In the old days, Hanalei produced taro, and deep in the valley the outlines of the ancient fields can still be discerned. The bay produced great quantities of fish, and others were raised in ponds, one of which still remains between the town and a twist in the river. Then the white man came and planted coffee that failed and sugarcane that petered out, and finally raised cattle that over-grazed the land. During these times, Hanalei had to *import* poi from the Kalalau Valley to the west. Later, when Chinese plantation laborers moved in, the valley was terraced again, but this time the wet fields were given to rice. This crop proved profitable for many years and was still grown as late as the 1930s. Then, amazingly, the valley began to slowly revert back to taro patches.

In 1972, 917 acres of the Hanalei Valley were designated **Hanalei National Wildlife Refuge;** the endangered native water birds Hawaiian coot, black-necked stilt, *koloa* duck, and gallinule, as well as several migrant species, loved it and reclaimed their ancient nesting grounds. Today, the large, green, heart-shaped leaves of taro carpet the valley, and the abundant crop supplies about half of Hawaii's poi. You can go into Hanalei Valley; however, you're not permitted in the designated wildlife areas except to fish or hike along the river. Never disturb any nesting birds. Look below to where the one-lane bridge crosses the river. Just there, 'Ohiki Road branches inland. Drive along it slowly to view the simple and quiet homesteads, the historic Haraguchi Rice Mill, nesting birds, wildflowers, and terraced fields of this enchanted land.

In addition, and more recently, the **Hanalei River** itself has been designated an American Heritage River, one of only 14 in the nation to be so noted and the only one whose total length is so designated. Federal moneys will be used to help protect its unique character and enhance its preservation.

Wai'oli Mission House Museum

As you leave town, look to your left to see the deep green clapboard and shingle **Wai'oli Hui'ia Church.** If you're in Hanalei on Sunday, do yourself a favor and go to the 10 A.M. service; you will be uplifted by a choir of rich voices singing enchanting hymns in Hawaiian. Justice is done to the word *wai'oli,* which means "joyful water." Although the congregation was established in 1834, the church was built in 1912 on land given to the congregation by the then governor of Kaua'i. American Gothic in style, it looks as if it could have been plunked down here from some sleepy New England community—except, perhaps, for the steeple's typically Hawaiian double pitch hip roof. Inside, pay attention to the stained

glass windows that mimic the rich colors of the surrounding sea, land, and sky, and appreciate the delicate but sturdy open-beam supports upholding the roof. This church was part of a mission station that also included a home for the preacher, a school for Hawaiian boys, and accommodations for the teacher.

Set to the side of the church, the **Wai'oli Mission House,** 808/245-3202, was the teacher's house. You know you're in for a treat as soon as you pull into the parking lot, which is completely surrounded by trees, creeping vines, ferns, and even papaya. Walk over stepping-stones through a garden with the jagged mountains framing a classical American homestead; the acreage was also a self-sufficient farm where the resident teacher and family raised chickens and cattle. Most mission homes are New England-style, and this one is, too, inside. But outside, it seems somehow different. It was built by Reverend William P. Alexander, who arrived with his wife, Mary Ann, in 1834 by double-hulled canoe from Waimea. The home's second occupants moved in 1837, and in 1846, Abner and Lucy Wilcox

KAUA'I

The spacious guest bedroom at the Wai'oli Mission House Museum is filled with period furniture.

ROBERT NILSEN

arrived and took up residence. They lived here until 1865, the year they both passed away on a trip to New England. This home became synonymous with the Wilcox family. Indeed, it was owned and occupied by the family until very recently. It was George, the son of Abner and Lucy, who founded Grove Farm on the south side in Lihu'e. His niece, Miss Mabel, created the nonprofit organization that operates both the Wai'oli Mission House and the Grove Farm Homestead.

You enter the parlor, where Lucy Wilcox taught native girls who'd never seen a needle and thread to sew. In the background, an old clock ticks. Paintings of the Wilcoxes line the walls, and Abner's books line the shelves. Mr. Wilcox, in addition to being a missionary, was a doctor, teacher, public official, and veterinarian. His preserved letters show that he was a very serious man, not given to humor. He and Lucy didn't want to come to Wai'oli at first, but they learned to love the place. He worried about his sons and about being poor. He even wrote letters to the king urging that Hawaiian be retained as the first language, with English as the second.

During the time that this was a mission household, eight boys were raised here—four born in the main bedroom. Behind it is a nursery, the only room that has had a major change; a closet was built and an indoor bathroom installed there in 1921. Upstairs is a guest bedroom that the Wilcoxes dubbed the "room of the traveling prophet" because it was invariably occupied by visiting missionaries. It was also used by Abner Wilcox as a study, and the books in the room are the original primers printed on O'ahu.

The house has been added to several times and is surprisingly spacious. Around the home are artifacts, dishes, knickknacks, and a butter churn from the 1800s. Lucy Wilcox churned butter, which she shipped to Honolulu in buckets and which brought in some good money. Most of the furniture is donated period pieces; only a few were actually used by the Wilcoxes. From an upstairs window, you can still see the view that has remained unchanged from the 19th century: Hanalei Bay, beautifully serene and timeless. The Wai'oli Mission House is open Tuesday, Thursday, and Saturday 9 A.M.–3 P.M., and is free! At the end of the tour, there is a leather chest for donations; please be generous.

BEACHES

Since the days of the migrating Polynesians, Hanalei Bay has been known as one of the Pacific's most perfect anchorages. Used as one of Kaua'i's three main ports until very recently, it's still a favorite port of call for world-class yachts. They start arriving in mid-May, making the most of the easy entrance and sandy bottom, and stay throughout the summer. They leave by October, when even this inviting bay becomes rough, with occasional 30-foot waves. The

KAUA'I

Hanalei Pier was constructed in 1912 to transport rice from this fertile valley but was discontinued as a commercial port of call with the decline of that commodity. It has, however, continued to serve boaters and is still a favorite of fishermen. When you drive to the bay, the section under the trees between the pier and the river is called **Black Pot**. It received this name from an earlier time, when the people of Hanalei would greet the yachties with island *aloha,* which, of course, included food. A fire was always going with a large black pot hanging over it, into which everyone contributed and then shared in the meal. Across the road and upriver a few hundred yards is **Hanalei Canoe Club**. This small local club has produced a number of winning canoe teams in statewide competitions, oftentimes appearing against much larger clubs.

The sweeping crescent bay is gorgeous—nearly two miles of narrow beach that sweeps out gently to a sandy bottom. The Hanalei River and three smaller streams empty into it, and all around it's protected by embracing mountains. A long pier slices into it, and two reefs front the bay: Queen to the left and King to the right. The bay provides excellent sailing, surfing, and swimming—mostly in the summer when the water can be as smooth as a lake. The swimming is good near the river and at the west end, but rip currents can appear anywhere, even around the pier area, so be careful. The best surf rolls in at the outside reef below Pu'u Poa Point on the east side of the bay, but it's definitely recommended only for expert surfers who often come to catch the bigger waves of winter. Beginners should try the middle of the bay during summer, when the surf is smaller and gentler. The county maintains two parks on the bay: **Black Pot**, at the Hanalei River mouth, and **Hanalei Pavilion** in the middle of the bay near a section known as Pine Trees. Black Pot and Hanalei Pavilion have picnic areas, grills, restrooms, and showers, although these amenities are sometimes vandalized and unusable. You'll find additional beach access and parking at the end of He'e, Ama'ama, and Ana'e Roads and down the way at Waipa. Camping is permitted at Black Pot only on Friday, Saturday, and holidays. A small *kaukau* wagon selling plate lunches is often near the river here; local fishermen launch their boats in the bay and are often amenable to selling their catch.

ACCOMMODATIONS

There are no hotels in Hanalei, only a handful of bed-and-breakfasts, one small motel-like inn, and plenty of vacation rental homes. Many of the rental homes, which range from economy to sumptuous, are right on the beach (or nearly), while more are farther along the coast toward the end of the road. Wherever you stay, however, you're never far from the beach and always surrounded by exquisite scenery.

You can almost still smell the sweet incense that permeates the **Historic Bed and Breakfast,** 5-5067 Kuhio Hwy., P.O. Box 1662, Hanalei, HI 96714, 808/826-4622, website: www.bubbaburger.com/bnb/for.html, email: jb-shepd@aloha.net. Housed in Kaua'i's oldest Buddhist Temple, the simple but elegant structure built in 1901 served the Japanese community until 1985, when it began to fall into disrepair. Neglected and deteriorating, the temple was saved by a consortium of local business people who moved it from its original location. It now has the distinction of being listed on both the National and State Historic registers. This painstaking and extensive effort refurbished much of the original structure including the lustrous hardwood floor, polished over the decades by the stockinged tread of devout parishioners. This B&B is now owned and operated by Jeff and Belle Shepherd, who welcome you to four bright and airy rooms cooled by ceiling fans. Decorated with original art and exuding more character, the three downstairs rooms, priced $59 single or $68 double, are separated by shoji screens and feature beds covered with antique quilts. You are free to relax in the comfortable common area—part of which serves as a dining room for breakfast—or to stroll outdoors to a small garden, perfect for an evening cup of tea. The shared bathrooms have deep Japanese-style *ofuro* tubs where you can soak away to your heart's content. In a more modern style, the upstairs suite has its own bathroom and runs $85. Two nights minimum, no small children or pets. Historic Bed and Breakfast is centrally located, only a five-minute walk to the downtown area or the beach.

Bed, Breakfast, and Beach, P.O. Box 748, Hanalei, HI 96714, 808/826-6111, owned by

Carolyn Barnes, is a neo-classic tri-level plan-tation-style home in a quiet residential area only a minute's walk from the beach. It gives you a strong feeling that you are part of the communi-ty. Upstairs offers a wide, covered lanai, perfect for catching the breeze or listening to the soft patter of a morning shower while eating break-fast. On the upper levels you'll find plenty of win-dows from which to enjoy a postcard view of the surrounding mountains. The common area, a casual lounging parlor, is cool and inviting with smooth parquet floors, an open-beamed ceil-ing, and knotty-pine paneling. The decor through-out is a mixture of classic Hawaiian and tasteful New England antique. Nooks and crannies are filled with objets d'art and plenty of reading ma-terial. From the common area, a staircase as-cends to the Bali Hai Suite, a 700-square-foot unit that occupies the entire top floor. Off the central area is the Pualani Suite—smaller, but alive, like a living floral arrangement with pastel blooms from ceiling to bedspread. At ground level, two units, called the Garden Lanai and Maki, offer kitchenettes and outdoor showers (Garden Lanai has an indoor shower as well). Bed, Breakfast, and Beach is an excellent choice of accommodation for relaxation, a feeling of homeyness, and extremely good value. Rates are $65–110; children are welcome except in the Bali Hai Suite.

The **Hanalei Plantation House** looks out across the coast road to the beach in Waipa, just past mile marker 4. A new two-level building, it has four one-bedroom units, each styled in an eminently comfortable, island contemporary man-ner. Enter to a large bedroom, with queen bed, writing desk, and entertainment center. Large windows let in plenty of light. Just beyond is a kitchenette and spacious bathroom. A simple continental breakfast is served on the second floor lanai. Light and cheery, and neat as a pin, this is a good spot for adventures either way along the road. Extra towels and beach gear can be borrowed for a day out, and an outdoor show-er should be used to wash off beach sand. All four rooms here run $125 a night. Make arrange-ments through Bed, Breakfast, and Beach, P.O. Box 748, Hanalei, HI 96714, 808/826-6111.

The moderately priced **Hanalei Inn,** P.O. Box 1373, Hanalei, HI 96714, 808/826-9333, is on the west side of town across from the school. It's

tucked in among flowering bushes and trees; with only five studio apartments, it's a quiet place. Each unit has a living/bedroom area with queen-size bed, an efficiency kitchen sufficient to make light meals (one unit has no kitchen), a full bath, and a coin-operated washer and dryer to the rear of the overgrown pavilion. Rates from $65 ($55 for the unit with no kitchen); no credit cards or personal checks. In addition, the inn rents a small one-bedroom house nearby for $85. Not exceptional in any way, nor with any particular character, it still offers some of the least expen-sive beds in town.

Vacation Rental Agencies

With its office along the highway toward the west end of Hanalei, **Harrington's Paradise Prop-erties,** 808/826-9655 or 888/826-9655, email: chisholm@gte.net, offers many upscale vaca-tion rentals in town and along the north shore.

Na Pali Properties, Inc., at the Ching Young Village, 808/826-7272 or 800/715-7273, web-site: www.napaliprop.com, email: nal@aloha.net, has everything from $500 a week cottages to $4,500 a week homes on the beach.

Hanalei North Shore Properties, in the Princeville Shopping Center, 808/826-9622 or 800/488-3336, website: www.planet-hawaii .com/visit-kauai, email: hnsp@aloha.net, handles many vacation rentals in Hanalei as well as along the entire north shore from Anahola to Ha'ena.

Emerald Isle Properties, Kilauea, 808/828-1111 or 800/828-1442, website: www.kauai-va-cations-realty.com, can match you with a rental home anywhere along the north coast.

Kauai Vacation Rentals, 3-3311 Kuhio Hwy., Lihu'e, HI 96766, 808/245-8841 or 800/357-5025, website: www.KauaiVacationRentals.com, email: aloha@kvrre.com, also has numerous rentals mostly in the medium to expensive range all the way to the end of the road.

FOOD

Hanalei has a number of eating institutions, rang-ing from excellent restaurants to *kaukau* wagons. The food is great at any time of day, but those in the know time their meals to coincide with sunset. They watch the free show and then go for a great dinner.

KAUA'I

Inexpensive

One of the few early morning places in town is **Hanalei Wake-Up Cafe,** 808/826-5551, open daily 5:30 A.M.–2 P.M. Cubbyhole small, it also has a few tables out on the veranda. The cheery help, the smell of freshly brewed coffee, and the good home cookin' should help start your day off on the right foot. With plastic chairs and pictures on the walls, there is nothing high-class here, just good food.

In a freestanding building in the Hanalei Center follow the aroma of fresh brewed coffee to the **Old Hanalei Coffee Company,** 808/826-6717, open daily 8 A.M.–5 P.M., where you can revitalize with a cup of espresso, cappuccino, latte, café au lait, or an old-fashioned hot chocolate made with Hershey's syrup and milk. If you're in the mood for something else, try a frosted mocha or a flavored Italian soda. The Old Hanalei Coffee Company serves a limited breakfast and lunch menu until 2 P.M.; you can eat inside or out on the lanai. Smaller items—all made on the premises—include muffins and cheesecake, or you might like to bring home a pound of bulk coffee. Just outside is **Shave Ice Paradise.** Here you can choose from 17 flavors of traditional shave ice including coconut and papaya, with fruit cocktail and adzuki beans thrown in for good measure. There's ice cream and a signature drink called a Summer Breeze, somewhat like an Orange Julius with a special twist. Staff members scoop the ice cream and make the shave ice as if they were doing it for family and friends. Your only problem is to lick faster than these hefty babies can melt.

Hanalei Mixed Plate, 808/826-7888, in a freestanding building in the Ching Young Village, serves up plate lunches of rice with one, two, or three entrées ($4.95–7.95) that might include shoyu ginger chicken, kalua pork and cabbage, and vegetable stir-fry. Hearty sandwiches ($6.95–10.95) of sautéed mahimahi, marinated and grilled teriyaki chicken, and the like are also on the menu, as are salads, flame-broiled (beef, buffalo, garden, or tempeh) burgers and fries, and hot dogs. Hanalei Mixed Plate is basically a walk-up counter with outdoor bar stool seating where prices are reasonable, servings generous, and the music is reggae. Next door is **Zababaz,** where you can refresh yourself with a shave ice or a Lappert's ice cream cone.

Bubba Burger, 808/826-7839, open daily 10 A.M.–6 P.M., is still doing what it's always done: serving up double-fisted burgers, individually made, at great prices. It's mostly a window restaurant, but there is seating on the lanai, with a few tables inside. Bubba's burgers range in price $2.50–5.75, with other offerings on the menu like Italian sausage or a fish burger, and a Hubba Bubba—rice, a burger patty, and hot dog, all smothered with chili. Try side orders like chili fries or Caesar salad, all light on the wallet but not so light on the waistline.

taro fields in the Hanalei Valley, from which the majority of Hawaii's poi is made

ROBERT NILSEN

KAUA'I

In the Ching Young Village, **Pizza Hanalei,** 808/826-9494, is open daily 11 A.M.–9 P.M. Made with thin, white, or whole-wheat crust, these pizzas run $9.40 for plain cheese to $34.45 for the Lizzy Special. There is pizza by the slice ($2.50–2.85) 11 A.M.–4 P.M. Green salads, garlic bread, spinach lasagna, and pizzaritos (pizza filling rolled up in a pizza shell like a burrito) are also on the menu.

At Tahiti Nui is the **Bamboo Room,** 808/826-1078, a reasonably priced, mostly Thai restaurant that also has some Chinese items on the menu. Open daily from 11:30 A.M.

Moderate

The **Hanalei Gourmet,** in the old schoolhouse at the Hanalei Center, 808/826-2524, open daily 10:30 A.M.–10:30 P.M. for lunch and dinner, is a born-again-hippie, semi-yuppie, one-stop nouveau cuisine deli, gourmet food shop, and good-time bar. To top it off, it's friendly, the food is exceptionally good, the prices are right, and there's even live nightly entertainment. It is broken into two sections: to the right is the deli, with cases filled with lunch meats, cheeses, salads, and smoked fish; while to the left is the bar/dining area. Here, ceiling fans keep you cool, while blackboards, once used to announce hideous homework assignments, now herald the daily specials. Behind the bar, windows through which kids once stared amid daydreams of summer now open to frame green-silhouetted mountains. Original hardwood floors, white walls bearing local artworks and hanging plants, two big-screen TVs for sports enthusiasts, and a wide veranda with a few tables for dining alfresco complete the restaurant. Lunch sandwiches, all around $8, are huge wedges. Dinners are served 5:30–9:30 P.M. and feature specialty pasta, fresh fish, ginger chicken, and various grill items. Most salad and grill items are under $9 and dinner entrées under $19. You can also order a picnic lunch to go, side salads, plenty of baked goods, and even a fine bottle of wine. The Hanalei Gourmet definitely lives up to its name and is the perfect spot for a meal or a social beer.

At the first building on the right as you enter town, look for a hanging golden dolphin marking the **Hanalei Dolphin Restaurant,** 808/826-6113, open daily 11 A.M.–10 P.M., almost hidden in the dense tropical foliage on the banks of the Hanalei River. The interior is casual, with an open-beamed ceiling, corrugated roof, shutters that hinge open to the garden, trophy fish, hanging glass floats, and ship's lanterns. Lunch is mostly salads, sandwiches, and sides. Appetizers include ceviche at $5 and stuffed mushrooms for $7. Seafood, mainly from the owners' fish market around back, includes fresh catch at market price, teriyaki shrimp for $22, and calamari for $18. Fish is the specialty here, charbroiled or blackened, but Hawaiian chicken for $16.50, New York steak at $23, and other items are also on the menu. All entrées are served with family-style salads, pasta, steak fries or rice, and hot homemade bread. There's a full bar for tropical cocktails. Open for years, the Dolphin serves consistently good but not memorable food.

Zelo's, 808/826-9700, established in Princeville for seven years, moved to Hanalei in late 1995 after the hurricane. It's open daily 11 A.M.–9:30 P.M. with happy hour 3:30–5:30 P.M. and sometimes music on weekends. The interior of this indoor/outdoor restaurant is distinctive, with a bamboo bar covered with a corrugated roof supported by old beams and tree trunks, and *lau hala* matting on the walls. The lunch menu offers salads ranging from a petite for $4 to a Chinese chicken salad for $10. Sandwiches include a Philadelphia steak sandwich for $8.95 and turkey and cheese at $6.25. There is a full range of burgers with all the fixings—including teriyaki, pesto, and a Cajun fish burger—priced $5.25–8.95. Other items are nachos, gourmet onion rings, all-you-can-eat spaghetti at $9.95, and a variety of other pasta, steak, and fish dishes for $12.95–22.95. The atmosphere is pleasant, the staff friendly, and the prices reasonable.

Upstairs in the Ching Young Village, serving sushi, sashimi, rice rolls, and other Asian-inspired dishes is **Sushi Blues and Grill,** 808/826-9701, open Tues.–Sun. from 5:30 P.M. Special rolls run $3.95–11.95 and entrées mostly in the $13–19 range. In addition to these tasty treats are a full selection of beers, sake, wine, and tropical drinks, and there is music every Wednesday and Sunday evenings.

Fine Dining

A great place to write home is the covered veranda of the 100-year-old plantation home that was once the Hanalei Museum. The owners of **Postcards,** 808/826-1191, a gourmet natural food restaurant, have refurbished the building to a condition as close to the original as possible, and today it is listed on the National Register. Enjoy breakfast here 8–11 A.M. (until noon on Sunday) with a steaming cup of cappuccino and a homemade muffin and watch north shore life go by. Dinners are served daily 6–9 P.M., inside or out on the front and side porches. Tables are covered with old postcards under glass, and the restaurant is always full. Postcards is an upbeat, health-conscious vegetarian restaurant that prides itself on using organic ingredients and making every dish and sauce from scratch. While the menu changes periodically, vegetables, pasta, and seafood are the mainstays—no red meat or poultry is served. Dishes are simple but hearty, and while not inexpensive, the quality is excellent. Save room for dessert; they're all made here in the kitchen. Postcards is wheelchair friendly, while smokers are completely prohibited from lighting up even outside. Reservations recommended. Postcards is an excellent choice.

Other Food Options

The **Hanalei Dolphin Fish Market,** around back behind the restaurant is open daily 11 A.M.–8 P.M., selling fresh, locally caught fish, some ready-to-cook prepared items, sauces and dressings. It can—with a day's notice—create a luscious sashimi and sushi platter.

Hanalei Health and Natural Foods, 808/826-6990, is open daily at the Ching Young Center. Inside are bulk foods, fresh fruits and vegetables, a variety of baked breads, freshly squeezed juices, deli foods, and sandwiches, as well as books and vitamins. The deli counter in the back is open 11 A.M.–2 P.M. for soups and sandwiches. There is also a good selection of cosmetics, incense, candles, and massage oils. If you're into natural foods and healthful living, stop in, look around, and chat.

Every Tuesday 2–4 P.M., pick up some farm-fresh fruit and vegetables from the Hawaiian Farmers of Hanalei **farmers' market,** a half mile west of town, in Waipa, on the road to Ha'ena. Look for the sign along the road on the left.

ENTERTAINMENT

Hanalei is a quiet town but there are a few options for at least some entertainment.

The **Hanalei Gourmet** offers light-hearted live music every night; Wednesday and Sunday evenings bring music to **Sushi Blues and Grill,** upstairs in the Ching Young Village; and **Tahiti Nui** often has someone playing on Friday and Saturday evenings from about 8 P.M. You've got to stop at the Tahiti Nui, 808/826-6277, if just to look around and have a cool drink. The owner, Louise Marston, a real Tahitian although her name doesn't sound like it, is dedicated to creating a friendly family atmosphere, and she succeeds admirably. Inside, it's pure Pacific Island. The decorations are modern Polynesian longhouse, with blowfish lanterns and stools carved from palm tree trunks. The bar, open from noon to midnight, is the center of action; happy hour is 4–6 P.M. daily. Old-timers drop in to "talk story," and someone is always willing to sing and play a Hawaiian tune. The mai tai are fabulous. Just sit out on the porch, kick back, and sip away.

Perhaps the most downhome and local lu'au in the state is put on right here in Hanalei. **Tahiti Nui** presents a full buffet and Polynesian show every Wednesday 5–8 P.M.—unless there are not enough customers to make it a go. This is a family-run operation that's been going since 1963. The food is real Hawaiian and the show is no glitzy extravaganza or slick production. There's singing, dancing, and good cheer all around—a perfect time to mingle with the local people. This lu'au is very casual Kaua'ian, and everybody has a good time; adults $52, $30 teens, and $20 for children 3–11. Call 808/826-6277 for reservations.

SHOPPING

The Hanalei Trader is the first building as you enter town. Here you'll find **Ola's,** 808/826-6937, open daily late morning to late evening., an "American" craft store with eclectic assortment of items from all 50 states, like glass work from Oregon, ceramics from California, wood products from Hawaii, and jewelry from New York. Other unique items are wildflower honey bath salts, greeting cards, hairbrushes, wooden boxes, leather purses, and pottery.

Kai Kane, 808/826-5594, a.k.a. The Water Man, also in the Hanalei Trader, not only catches your eye but also helps keep the sun out of it with a display of hats for both men and women. It also sells a large selection of alohawear and casual beachwear. Glass cases hold watches and sunglasses, while a canoe fashioned from breadfruit hangs overhead and surfboards line the walls. Although Kai Kane doubles as a clothing shop, its primary function is as a surf shop. Upstairs is filled with surfboards, along with a wide selection of wetsuits, leashes, and shorts.

Two shops just near Tahiti Nui are the **Hanalei Photo Company,** with one-hour developing, cameras, and a fax service, and **Kiki's Bikini's,** where ladies might find that just-right swimsuit

Around the side is **Island Hemp and Cotton Company,** 808/826-7565, sister store to the shop in Kapa'a, open daily 10 A.M.–6 P.M. Owned by an "old Asia hand," this shop carries cotton and natural fiber clothing for women, accessories, craft items from South East Asia, and jewelry.

The **Ching Young Village Shopping Center** in the center of town includes a small shopping center plus nearby freestanding buildings. Among its attractions are a Big Save Supermarket, open daily 7 A.M.–9 P.M., the only food retailer from here to the end of the road; Hanalei Video and Music; Peddle and Paddle, for sports equipment rental and clothing; a few other casual clothing stores; and public restrooms. The Artists Gallery of Kaua'i sells art and crafts items done mostly on the island, and On The Road To Hanalei carries gifts and jewelry. Restaurants here include Hanalei Mixed Plate, Zelo's, Sushi Blues, and Pizza Hanalei. Although small and somewhat crowded, Hanalei Natural Foods carries bulk and packaged foods, and supplements.

The **Hanalei Center,** the newest in town, has an excellent assortment of shops and boutiques. Some impressive ones are Rainbow Ducks, specializing in children's wear; Sand People, which offers casual island clothing for men and women, gifts, and jewelry; and Yellowfish Trading Company, which is stuffed from floor to ceiling with Hawaiiana, antiques, collectibles, hula-doll lamps, classic Hawaiian aloha shirts, kuchi-kuchi dolls, costume and silver jewelry, floral day bags,

candles, swords, antique hats, Matson Steamship Line posters, and koa carvings and incidentals. Here, too, is Whalers General Store, open daily 8 A.M.–8 P.M., selling groceries, liquor, sundries, and souvenirs. In the old Hanalei School section of the center are several additional shops including the Hanalei Surf Company, with boards, water gear, and clothing; and Tropical Tantrum, a small Hawaii chain that designs its own fabrics, which are then turned into original clothing in Indonesia. At Tropical Tantrum, women can rage in the most vibrant colors of purple, blue, red, green, and yellow, transforming themselves into walking rainforests. The most distinctive shop, Kahn Galleries, 808/826-6677, specializes in original artworks and limited edition prints created by some of the finest artists Hawaii has to offer.

The Hanalei Valley not only grows taro, but some tropical flowers are raised here as well. **Kauai Exotix** will send mixed bouquets of flowers grown on its farm to anywhere in the United States or Canada. To find out what's available, contact: P.O. Box 371, Hanalei, HI 96714, 808/826-7133 or 800/718-1018, fax 808/826-7912, website: www.besttropicals.com, email: aloha@kexotix.com.

RECREATION

Hanalei is alive with outdoor activities. The following is merely a quick list of what's available.

Until August 1998 motorized boats could use Hanalei Bay for commercial purposes, many starting right from the river mouth. After that date, by governor's decree, only nonmotorized uses of the bay were allowed, to the consternation of many in the business sector. However, the reduced activity in the bay has made it a much quieter place, less busy, and more enjoyable for the nonmotorized recreational users.

The company to see for a kayaking adventure up the Hanalei River or, during summer, along the Na Pali Coast, is **Kayak Kaua'i Outbound,** 808/826-9844 or 800/826-9844. Rental rates per day are $25 for a single river kayak and $48 for a double, $35 and $60, respectively, for the sea kayaks; multi-day and weekly rates are also available. Lessons, guide service, shuttle support, and storage can be arranged. Other water equipment—snorkel gear, surfboards, boogie boards—are also rented, as are camping gear and bikes. Mountain bikes run $20 a day while beach cruisers are $15; backpacks go for $8 a day, two-person tents $8, sleeping bags $6, and pads $3. All rentals can be returned in Hanalei or at the Kapa'a store. If you want to buy, Kayak Kaua'i is one of the few places on the island that sells good quality camping and backpacking equipment.

For catamaran adventures along the Na Pali Coast, try **Na Pali Catamarans,** 808/826-6853, or **Hanalei Sea Tours,** 808/826-7254, website: www.seatours.net.

The **Hanalei Surf Co.,** in the Hanalei Center, 808/826-9000, is a water sports shop that rents and sells snorkeling equipment, boogie boards, surfboards, and other water equipment. Rental rates for surfboards run $12–15 per day or $50–65 a week, boogie boards are $5 or $7 with fins, and snorkel equipment is $3–5 or $15–29 a week; three- and five-day rates are also available on all rentals. Hanalei Surf Co. has a "rent to buy" option on its snorkel equipment—ask. The store is also stocked with a good selection of shirts, shorts, thongs, bathing suits, incidental bags, sunglasses, sunblock, and dresses.

Pedal and Paddle, in the Ching Young Village, 808/826-9069, open daily 9 A.M.–5 P.M. in winter, 9 A.M.–6 P.M. in summer, rents snorkel gear, boogie boards, kayaks, mountain bikes, and some camping gear. Prices are: snorkel gear $5 a day, $20 per week; boogie boards $5 and $20; cruiser bikes $10 and $40; ordinary mountain bikes $20 and $80, two-person dome tents $10 and $30; backpacks $5 and $20; light sleeping bags $3 and $10; and sleeping pads $3 and $10. A rental day begins the hour you rent and ends at 5 P.M. the following day. Pedal and Paddle does not sell bikes or kayaks but has snorkel and camping gear, hats, and sandals for sale.

John Sargent's **Bike Doctor,** in Hanalei, 808/826-7799, open Mon.–Sat. 9 A.M.–5 P.M., does bike repair and is stocked with everything for the casual and serious cyclist. John is also intimately familiar with roads and trails all over the island and is happy to give advice on touring. The Bike Doctor is the only shop in town that rents high-quality mountain bikes for the serious off-road rider.

North Coast Trail
The only hiking trail of length in the Hanalei area is the **Powerline Trail,** which runs across the island to the Keahua Arboretum above Wailua. Along this route you get masterful views of the Hanalei region and the core of the island's central mass, plus a view of both the north and south shores. Unless you have cars at both ends of this trail, just hike up as far as you like—or the weather permits—and return. To reach the trailhead, turn at the Princeville Stables. Continue uphill on this paved road about two miles until the pavement gives out. Proceed a bit farther until you reach an area to park near a water tank where the road starts to get worse. This trail is often used by mountain bikers.

SERVICES AND INFORMATION

The **post office** in Hanalei is next to Ching Young Village.

North Shore Cab, 808/826-6189, not only runs a pickup and delivery service, but also does tours. The ordinary fare from Hanalei to Princeville is $15, to the end of the road at Ke'e Beach is about $25, and to the Lihu'e Airport about $60. North Shore Cab also offers luxury service with one of its stretch limos for considerably more. You must pre-arrange the luxury service, and the driver will be waiting, resplendent in his casual chauffeur's uniform. Group tours can also be arranged, and these fares can be negotiated.

Paradise Adventures, along the highway in Hanalei next to the post office, P.O. Box 1379, Hanalei, HI 96714, 808/826-9999 or 888/886-4969, fax 808/826-9998, email: byron@aloha.net, is the best place in town to stop for activities information and bookings for anywhere on the island. Having operated a company that ran boat tours along the Na Pali Coast, the owners, Byron and Dot, keep in touch with what's happening on the island and know the ins and outs of the tourist industry. This is a full-service company that can put you not only on the water in a boat or kayak, but also on a land tour, on the back of a horse, or up in a helicopter. The owners will also help you book a room or arrange a meal or lu'au.

KAUA'I

Paradise Adventures works only with those companies that offer the highest quality service so that your experience is a rewarding one.

Across from Zelo's is **Hanalei Town Activi-** **ties and Information Center,** 808/826-1913, where you can collect information about the area, book an activity, or rent snorkel equipment or a boogie board.

ROAD'S END

Past Hanalei you have six miles of pure magic until the road ends at Ke'e Beach. To thrill you further and make your ride even more enjoyable, you'll find historical sites; natural wonders; an oceanside resort; the *heiau* where hula was born, overlooking a lovely beach; and the trailhead to Kaua'i's premier hike, the Kalalau Trail. The Hanalei Valley is the largest along this coast; nearly as large but more serpentine is the Wainiha Valley. Between these lie the deep and green Wai'oli, Waipa, and Lumaha'i Valleys. At mile marker 7 is the tiny village of Wainiha, and beyond that the small community of Ha'ena, not a town per se, more a state of mind. The Wainiha Valley is said to have been inhabited long ago by the race of dwarfish Mu people. While many legends revolve around these mythical pre-Hawaiians, an official census from the late 1700s mentions 65 Mu living in Wainiha Valley. As you drive along, you cross one-lane bridges, travel through tunnels of trees, and pass little beaches and bays, one after another, invariably with small streams flowing into them. Try not to get jaded peering at "just another gorgeous north shore beach."

SIGHTS

Lumaha'i Beach is a femme fatale, lovely to look at but treacherous. This hauntingly beautiful beach (whose name translates as "Twist of Fingers") is what dreams are made of: white sand curving perfectly at the bottom of a dark lava cliff with tropical jungle in the background. The riptides here are fierce even with the reef, and the water should never be entered except in very calm conditions during the summer. Look for a vista point after mile marker 5, just beyond the west end of Hanalei Bay. Cars invariably park here. It's a sharp curve, so make sure to pull completely off the road or the police may ticket you. An extensive grove of hala trees appears just as you set off down a steep and often muddy footpath leading down to the east end of the beach. The best, easiest, and safest place to park is among the ironwood trees at the west end of the beach near the bridge that crosses the Lumaha'i River; an emergency phone is across the road from this parking area. From here you can walk to the south end if you want seclusion.

About six-tenths of a mile past YMCA, a

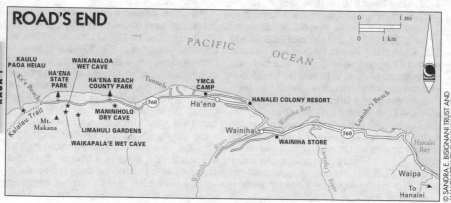

ROAD'S END

ROAD ETIQUETTE

The narrow north shore road, with its many one-lane bridges, requires that you drive with a certain degree of caution and road etiquette. First of all, slow down and enjoy the scenery. This road is full of curves, so drive defensively. If you need to stop, pull all the way off the roadway so other cars can get by safely. White lines on the road and yield signs alert you to where you must stop at one-lane bridges to let traffic from the other direction pass. There is not always a good line of sight at these bridges, so be cautious. If two cars approach a bridge at the same time, let the other car go first. If you are in a line of cars that is crossing the bridge when others are waiting to cross from the other direction, and if you are in the first half dozen of this line of cars, cross. Otherwise, stop and let the oncoming traffic cross before you proceed. Above all, always be polite, smile, and give the other cars that wait the *shaka* sign.

short dead-end road turns off the highway and a trail through the trees leads to Makua Beach, commonly known as **Tunnels.** It's superb for snorkeling and scuba diving, perhaps the best on the island, with a host of underwater caves off to the left as you face the sea. Look for the small fish inside the reef, for the bigger fish (experienced snorkelers and divers only) you must go into the sea caves or over the edge of the awesome drop off. Both surfing and windsurfing are great, and so is the swimming if the sea is calm. Watch out for boats that come inside the reef. Off to the right and down a bit is a nude beach. There are no facilities here and parking is limited along the roadway, but it's less than half a mile east down the beach from Ha'ena Beach Park.

Ha'ena Beach County Park, just a mile before road's end, is a large, flat, field-like area, where you stake out your own camping site. For your convenience, the county provides tables, a pavilion, grills, showers, and camping (permit required). The sand on this long crescent beach is rather coarse, and the swimming is good only when the sea is gentle, but in summertime a reef offshore is great for snorkeling. The cold stream running through the park is always good for a dip.

Across the road is **Maniniholo dry cave.** Notice the gorgeous grotto of trees, and the jungle wild with vines. You walk in and it feels airy, like it would be nice living quarters, but it has never been suggested that the cave was used for permanent habitation. Luckily, even with all the visitors going in and out, it hasn't been trashed.

Limahuli Botanical Garden, in the last valley before the beginning of the Kalalau Trail, a half mile past mile marker 9, 808/826-1053, open Tues.–Fri. and Sunday 9:30 A.M.–4 P.M., showcases tropical plants both ancient and modern. This garden is part of the National Tropical Botanical Gardens; the 14 original acres were donated by Juliet Rice Wichman in 1976, later expanded to 17 acres, and an additional 985-acre preserve in the valley above was donated by her grandson, Chipper Wichman, the garden's director, in 1994. There are both self-guided ($10) and guided ($15) walking tours of the gardens; guided tours are 10 A.M. and 2 P.M. only—by reservation. Wear good shoes; umbrellas are provided. Tours start at the visitors center, which has a fine collection of books on Hawaiian flora and other subjects. As you walk through this enchanted area you'll pass taro patches growing behind stone terraces believed to be at least 900 years old, plants introduced to Hawaii by the early Polynesians, living specimens of endangered native Hawaiian species, and post-contact tropicals; your guide treats you to legends of the valley (or you can read them in your brochure) as you follow the three-quarter-mile loop trail. Only this garden with its trail is open to the public; the vast interior of the preserve is only accessible to biologists and botanists doing research. For those who love the living beauty of plants and flowers, a trip to Limahuli Botanical Garden is well worth the effort.

Up the road, just after entering **Ha'ena State Park,** an HVB Warrior points the way to the **wet caves;** right along the road is **Waikanaloa,** and 150 yards up the side of a hill is **Waikapala'e.** Their wide openings are almost like gaping frogs' mouths, and the water is liquid crystal. Amazingly, the dry cave is down by the road, while Waikapala'e, subject to the tides, is inland and up-hill. Look around for *ti* leaves and a few scraggly guavas. Straight up, different lava that has flowed over the eons has created a stacked pancake

KAUA'I

FIRE SHOWER

After Hanalei Bay, the most notable feature along the north coast is the towering spire of Mt. Makana. Rising directly above Ke'e Beach at the end of the road, **Mt. Makana** is popularly known as Bali Hai—made famous in the movie *South Pacific*. This peak was one of the two spots on the island—the other being the ridge end above Nu'alolo Beach just down the coast to the west—where, for special occasions, fire throwers would toss burning branches of *papala* or *hau* trees off the cliff at night in a Fourth of July–style spectacular similar to the old firefalls at Yosemite National Park. Updrafts of wind would carry these burning pieces of wood out to sea in a shower of red sparks. Crowds would gather along the shore and in canoes on the water to watch, and those whose firebrands went the farthest would be accorded great acclaim.

effect. The best time to come is in the hour before and the hour after noon, when the sun shoots rays into the water. If azure could bleed, it would be this color. The 66-acre Ha'ena State Park not only encompasses these caves but also Ke'e Beach and the trailhead for the Kalalau Trail.

The road ends at **Ke'e Beach,** a popular spot with restrooms and showers. Here is the beginning of the Kalalau Trail. Although there are many parking spaces, the lot begins to fill early, particularly on warm, dry days. As always, the swimming is good only in the summertime, but snorkeling inside the wide reef is great most of the year. Around the point to the right you might find the beach less crowded, and it was up in the trees here that Taylor Camp, the most well known of the north coast hippie communities of the '60s, was located. If conditions are right and the tide is out, you can walk left along the shore to get a dazzling view of the Na Pali cliffs. Don't attempt this when the sea is rough! This path takes you past some hidden beach homes. One was used as the setting for the famous love rendezvous in the miniseries *The Thorn Birds*. Past the homes, another path takes you up the hill to the ancient sites of **Kaulu Paoa Heiau** and **Kaulu O Laka Heiau,** birthplace of the hula, where the goddess Laka bestowed to the Hawai-

ians this wonderful expression of dance and story. The views from up here are remarkable and worth the short climb, especially during winter, when the sun drops close to the cliffs and backlights Lehua Island, then sinks into its molten reflection. In the past, after novitiates had graduated from the hula *heiau,* they had to jump into the sea below, swimming around to Ke'e Beach as a sign of dedication. Tourists aren't required to perform this act.

ACCOMMODATIONS

If you're looking for a real quiet and secluded place to stay, you'll find it at the **Jungle Bungalow** on the island in the Wainiha River, P.O. Box 1379, Hanalei, HI 96714, 808/826-9999 or 888/886-4969, website: www.paradise-adventures.com/bungalow, email: byron@aloha.net. Surrounded by thick tropical greenery and the sound of the rushing river, this two-story cottage offers a real tropical hideaway. Downstairs is a complete kitchen and living room, upstairs in the master bedroom and toilet. Outside, the lanai fronts a large private lawn, and around the side, surrounded by greenery for your privacy, is a clawfoot tub and shower. The bungalow goes for $115 for a couple and $10 each additional person up to five; four nights minimum. A few yards up the driveway is the Jungle Cabana, a smaller single-level unit that sleeps two with a similar bathing setup outside. Inside are a living/sleeping area, kitchen, and toilet; the Cabana goes for $95 a night. Both units are basic, simple, and comfortable, and envelop you with the sounds of the forest.

Next up, look for signs to the five-acre, 48-unit **Hanalei Colony Resort,** P.O. Box 206, Hanalei, HI 96714, 808/826-6235 or 800/628-3004, fax 808/826-9893. website: www.hcr.com, email: hcr@aloha.net—literally the last resort and the only resort on the beach along the north coast. You can rent very comfortable, spacious, two-bedroom condos here, each with a full kitchen, shower/tub, and lanai. The brown board-and-batten buildings blend into the surroundings. Now past 30 years old, this property is still well looked after but not luxurious, and the oceanfront units have some of the most spectacular views anywhere along this coast.

The resort has a hot tub and swimming pool, barbecue grills, coin-operated washers and dryers, Hawaiiana classes, and twice-weekly maid service, but no television or phones. The beach in front of the resort is great for a stroll at sunset, but be very careful swimming during winter months or periods of high surf. Based on single or double occupancy, units cost from $170 for a garden view to $265 for a premium oceanfront, $25 less during low season, with the seventh night free for a weeklong stay. Car-rental packages are available if arranged before arriving on Kaua'i.

Just past Hanalei Resort, between mile markers 7 and 8 on the highway, look for the entrance to **YMCA Camp Naue.** The turnoff is at the road entrance by the phone booth. Here, several buildings are filled with bunks with a separate toilet area and cooking facilities. The camp caters to large groups but is open to single travelers on a first come, first served basis for the staggering sum of $12 per night. The cost for tent camping is $10, with each additional person in the tent at $7. The bunkhouses lie under beachside trees, and campers stay in the yard. All guests must provide their own sleeping bag or bedding. Hot showers are available to all, but the cooking facilities are only for groups. On the property is a pavilion with grills, but you must provide your own wood or bring a camp stove. As with most YMCAs, there are many rules to be followed. You can get full information from YMCA headquarters in Lihu'e or by writing YMCA of Kauai, P.O. Box 1786, Lihu'e, HI 96766, 808/246-9090, or 808/826-6419 in Ha'ena.

FOOD

Over a small white bridge in the village of **Wainiha** (Angry Water) is the tiny **Wainiha Store,** 808/826-6251, open daily 9:30 A.M.–7 P.M. Here, you can pick up a few supplies and sundries. People from around the area come to the store to post fliers if they have rooms to rent. This way, you can still get a shack on the beach or in among the banana trees. Attached to the store are a sandwich window and a gift shop.

On the premises of the Hanalei Colony Resort, taking over where "hoochy-koochy" Charo had reigned for years, is **Sert's on the Beach,** 808/826-0060. This restaurant, like its sister restaurant at Volcano on the Big Island, offers an imaginative Asian-French fusion menu with lunch noon–4 P.M. and dinner 4–9 P.M. While items on the menu change periodically, expect appetizers like shrimp and shiitake mushroom gyoza or crispy Parmesan calamari for $4.95–10.95, and house or Caesar salad. Entrées might include charbroiled striploin and scalloped potatoes with a caramelized Maui onion peppercorn brandy sauce, or fresh fish sautéed with cilantro and a sweet chili nori butter, most under $24. Sert's is a fine restaurant deserving of your patronage—and the only place for meals between Hanalei and the end of the road. In a separate shop near the restaurant entrance is the **Steam Vent Cafe,** open for coffee, tea, juice, and pastries in the morning and pre-made salads and sandwiches during the day. The Steam Vent is set up with help-yourself counter service only, but there are a few tables outside.

KAUA'I

NA PALI COAST

The Na Pali Coast, from Ke'e Beach on the north shore to Polihale Beach on the west end, is less than 15 miles long—but, oh, what miles! You must speak in superlatives to describe it. Here the sea cliffs rise sharply out of the water to nearly 4,000 feet in height. Along its length are numerous valleys, the largest and most majestic is Kalalau Valley, the site of ancient habitation, numerous archaeological remains, and many myths and legends. Deep cuts in this rock face have created numerous narrower chasms, including several hanging valleys, and these hold evidence of other inhabited sites. Rain is abundant along this coast, and streams course through each lush valley, creating many refreshing waterfalls; a few that fall directly into the sea were used by Hawaiians like a faucet, to fill fresh water containers. While all sorts of huge trees, native and introduced, bushes, flowers, and vines fill the large Kalalau Valley and other valley floors, much of the steep valley walls are covered in a variety of ferns. A handful of sea caves, one with a collapsed ceiling, puncture this rampart at water level, and several beaches dot the coast. Fishing is good, particularly inside the fringe reefs at Ke'e, Nu'alolo Kai, and Miloli'i. The Na Pali Coast is home to a large community of spinner dolphins that often play in the wake of passing boats, and gracefully slow green sea turtles are spotted periodically. During winter months, whales migrate from the cold waters of the north Pacific to bask in the warmer Hawaiian waters to birth, nurse, and raise their young.

Accessibility

No roads enter the Na Pali Coast area, so your options are limited in that way. However, it is not inaccessible. It can be approached by land, air, and water. Sea kayaks can be rented for a trip down the coast—during calm summer weather only. Non-motorized and quiet, this is undoubtedly as close an experience to early Hawaiian outrigger canoe travel along the Coast that most can get these days. Boat tours from the west end and south shore regularly make trips to this section of the island for a close-up look at the

cliffs and valleys from the water—a truly awe-inspiring sight. Helicopters fly overhead, offering riders an unparalleled view of the entire coastline and dipping into valleys along the way, bringing you up nose to nose with these green chasms. Even though there are flight restrictions, helicopter tours along this coast, as in other areas of the island, are not without critics, as they intrude on the serenity of an otherwise solitary and tranquil place. The Na Pali can also be seen by looking down from the Kalalau Valley overlooks and from several trails that traverse the razor ridges above the coast's deep valleys. Perhaps the best way to get up-close and personal with the Na Pali Coast is to hike in on the Kalalau Trail, which starts at road's end at Ke'e Beach.

Na Pali Coast State Park

The Kalalau Valley and the trail leading to it, plus strips at Nu'alolo Kai and Miloli'i are all part of the sprawling 6,175-acre Na Pali Coast State Park. The remainder of the coastline, cliffs, and valleys are either state forests or natural area reserves. A ranger at Kalalau Valley oversees the park. For those hiking in, the trailhead has a box where you sign in. Day-use permits are required beyond Hanakapi'ai (two miles in); camping permits are required to stay overnight at Hanakapi'ai, Hanakoa, or Kalalau. You can camp for up to five nights, but no two consecutive nights are allowed at either Hanakapi'ai or Hanakoa. You need a good waterproof tent, sleeping bag, mosquito repellent, first-aid kit, biodegradable soap, food, and toiletries. There are many streams along the trail, but the water can be biologically contaminated and cause horrible stomach distress. Boil it or use purification tablets. Little firewood is available, and you can't cut trees, so take a stove. Don't litter; carry out what you carried in.

Because of heavy use and environmental concerns, the Kalalau Trail and/or Hanakoa campsite have been closed from time to time during the past decade for repair and rejuvenation. Make sure to check with the DLNR State Parks office at 808/274-3444 for the current status on use and accessibility.

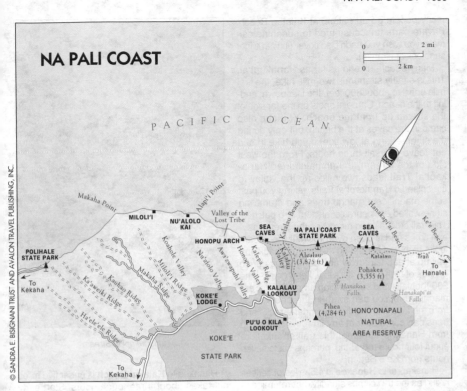

The Nu'alolo Kai and Miloli'i sections can only be reached by boat or kayak. While Nu'alolo Kai is reserved for day use only (commercial boat tours stop here during the summer months), primitive campsites are available at Miloli'i for a maximum of three nights for those who desire real isolation.

The Kalalau Trail

Originally carved out by Hawaiians who needed an overland route between the Kalalau Valley and Ha'ena, the Kalalau Trail not only leads you physically along the Na Pali Coast, but back in time to classic romantic Hawaii. You leave the 20th century farther and farther behind with every step and reenter a time and place where you can come face to face with your *nature self.*

Getting to the trailhead is simple: follow Route 56 until it ends and then hike. This hike is *the* premier hike on Kaua'i and perhaps in the entire state. The Kalalau is a destination in and of itself, and those who have walked these phenomenal 11 miles never forget it. The trail leads down the Na Pali Coast—as close as you can get to the Hawaiian paradise of old. The trail is well marked by countless centuries of use, so you won't get lost, but it's rutted, root strewn, and muddy. Remnants of mileage posts are all along the way. Streams become torrents during rains but recede quickly—just wait it out. Mountain climbing is dangerous because of the crumbly soil, and the swimming along the coast is unpredictable, with many riptides. Summers, when the wave action returns sand to the beach, are usually fine, but stay out of the water September–April. At Hanakapi'ai, a grim reminder reads, "This life-saving equipment was donated by the family and friends of Dr. Rulf Fahleson, a strong swimmer, who drowned at Hanakapi'ai in March 1979." Pay heed! Also, in keeping with the tradition of "Garden of Eden,"

KAUA'I

many people go au naturel at Kalalau Beach. Private parts unaccustomed to sunshine can make you wish you hadn't, so cover up with either sunblock or clothing.

Many people hike in as far as **Hanakapi'ai.** This is a fairly strenuous two-mile hike, the first mile uphill to about 800 feet, the last down, ending at the beach. Camp at spots on the far side of the stream up from the beach. You can also camp in the caves at the beach, but only during the summer and at low tide. If you hike in and out, leave yourself three hours. From the west side of the stream, the unmaintained **Hanakapi'ai Trail** leads two miles up the valley to the splendid **Hanakapi'ai Falls,** taking you past some magnificent mango trees and crumbling stone-walled enclosures of ancient taro patches. This trail crosses and recrosses the stream several times and is often overgrown. If the stream looks high and is running swiftly, turn back; the trail up ahead is narrow and dangerous during periods of high water. If it's low, keep going—the 300-foot falls and surrounding amphitheater are magnificent. You can swim in the pools away from the falls, but not directly under—rocks and trees can come over at any time. As a side trip from Hanakapi'ai camp, this trail should take about four hours round-trip, perhaps six to seven hours from Ke'e Beach.

Hanakapi'ai to **Hanakoa** is 4.5 miles of serious hiking as the trail climbs steadily, not returning to sea level until reaching Kalalau Beach nine miles away. Switchbacks take you 600 feet out of Hanakapi'ai Valley. Although heavily traversed, the trail can be very bad in spots. Before arriving at Hanakoa, you must go through **Ho'olulu** and **Waiahuakua** hanging valleys. Both are lush with native flora and are parts of Honoonapali Nature Area Preserve. Shortly, Hanakoa comes into view. Its many wide terraces are still intact from when it was a major food-growing area. Coffee plants gone wild can still be seen. Hanakoa is rainy, but the rain is intermittent, and the sun always follows. The swimming is fine in the many stream pools. A one-third-mile hike up the east fork of the stream, just after the six-mile marker, takes you past more terraces good for camping before coming to **Hanakoa Falls.** The terraces are wonderful, but the trail is subject to erosion and is treacherous with many steep sections.

Hanakapi'ai Stream

ROBERT NILSEN

Hanakoa to **Kalalau Beach** is under five miles but takes about three tough hours. Start early in the morning; it's hot, and although you're only traveling five miles, it gets noticeably drier and more open as you approach Kalalau. The views along the way are ample reward. The power and spirit of the incomparable *'aina* become predominant. Around the seven-mile marker you enter land that until the late 1970s was part of the Makaweli cattle ranch. The vegetation turns from lush foliage to lantana and sisal, a sign of the aridness of the land. After crossing Pohakuao Valley, you climb the *pali;* on the other side is Kalalau. The lovely valley, two miles wide and three deep, beckons with its glimmering fresh water pools. It's a beauty among beauties and was cultivated until the 1920s. Many terraces and house sites remain. Plenty of guava, mango, and Java plum trees can be found. You can camp only in the trees fronting the beach or in the caves west of the waterfall. You are not allowed to camp along the stream, at its mouth, or in the valley. The waterfall has a fresh water pool, where feral goats come in the morning and evening to water.

A *heiau* is atop the little hillock on the west side of the stream. Follow the trail here up-valley for two miles to **Big Pool**, making one stream crossing on the way. Big Pool is really two pools connected by a natural water slide. Riding it is great for the spirit but tough on your butt. Enjoy! Along the way you pass Smoke Rock, where *pakalolo* growers at one time came to smoke and talk story.

Honopu, Nuʻalolo Kai, Miloliʻi

Less than a half mile to the west of Kalalau Valley is **Honopu Valley.** This valley is known as the "Valley of the Lost Tribe," as legend tells of a race of small people inhabiting it in great isolation. These Mu were also said to have lived in the Wainiha Valley to the east. The two-part beach at Honopu is unique in that it's split by a huge rock arch; it has been the setting of at least two movie sequences.

Beyond Awaʻawapuhi Valley is **Nuʻalolo Kai,** an area of beach and dunes backed up tight against the cliff. Nuʻalolo Kai was inhabited by a small community of Hawaiians until 1919, and remains of their habitation still exist in stone enclosures, walls, and *heiau* platforms. Fishing was good within the protected reef, and taro was raised in the adjoining Nuʻalolo Aina Valley. Between these two areas, however, is a sheer cliff, so a rope ladder was hung from a ledge above, from where a trail led around the point to the fields. Because of the reef, there was good anchorage here at Nuʻalolo Kai, and it was often used as a rest stop by canoes going between Hanalei and Waimea.

About a mile to the west is **Miloliʻi,** also an ancient inhabited site. Here the valley is more easily accessible, and small amounts of taro were cultivated to sustain a small population. There is anchorage on the beach for boats, a primitive camping area with restrooms and a shelter, and down the beach a *heiau* site. You will notice that Miloliʻi is much drier than the rest of the Na Pali Coast—the heavy rains that pelt Kalalau Valley peter out before they make it this far, and Miloliʻi gets only about 20 inches a year.

KAUAʻI

M.G.L. DOMENY DE REINZI

SOUTH SHORE

The Kaumuali'i (Royal Oven) Highway (Route 50) steps west from Lihu'e, with the Ha'upu Ridge (Hoary Head Mountains) adding a dash of beauty to the south and Queen Victoria's Profile winking down from the heights. Inland is Kilohana Crater, and between it and the Ha'upu Ridge are still productive cane fields. The road rises gently over the Knudsen Gap and you enter the Koloa District, which stretches to the east bank of the Hanapepe River. Soon, Maluhia (Peaceful) Road (Route 520) branches to the south through an open lei of fragrant eucalyptus trees lining the route to the old sugar town of Koloa and on to the much newer resort community of Po'ipu. Continuing west on the highway, coming in quick succession, are the small inland towns of 'Oma'o, Lawa'i, and Kalaheo, way stations on the road. Hereabouts are the remains of the area's once vibrant sugar industry, wide acres of the area's new crop, coffee, an exquisite tropical botanical garden, beautiful white sand beaches, and a few of the island's newest and most luxurious resorts.

KOLOA

As you head down Maluhia Road, you pass through the **Tunnel of Trees,** a stand of rough-bark *Eucalyptus robustus,* sometimes referred to as "swamp mahogany." Brought from Australia and planted by the Knudsen family, the largest landowner in this area, to help stabilize the then soggy road over the Knudsen Pass, they're now well established, adding beauty, a heady fra-grance, and shade to more than a mile of this country lane.

The town of Koloa attracts a large number of tourists and packs them into a small area. On the site of what was the island's oldest sugar mill, Koloa has been transformed from a tumble-down sugar town to a thriving tourist community where shops, restaurants, and boutiques line its wooden sidewalks. Nearly all the old shops are re-modeled plantation buildings. Dressed in red paint and trimmed with white, they are festooned with strings of lights as if decorated for a per-petual Christmas festivity. Most businesses line the town's main street, but others are found along Po'ipu Road as it heads down toward the coast. Traffic can be hectic with morning and evening mini-rush hours, and parking is always a problem. There are a few small parking lots, but you usually have to find a spot along the main drag or on one of the side streets—respect all signage.

In accord with its strong economic position, Koloa was the major population center on Kaua'i from 1835 to 1880. During this time, Koloa Land-ing in Po'ipu was reputedly one of the three most active whaling ports in Hawaii. Sugar was shipped from the Koloa Landing, which was then one of the main ports of entry for the island. Sugar remained strong here throughout most of the 20th century, but the newest mill shut down in 1996, a victim of the statewide declining sugar industry, and its lifeless edifice can still be seen east of town at the end of Maha'ulepu Road. Active cane fields in this area are now gone, replaced by limited cattle ranching, cof-fee, and corn production.

One meaning for *Koloa* is "duck"; the area was probably so named because of the pre-ponderance of ponds throughout the district that attract these water-loving fowl. In fact, before the development of the sugar industry, the Koloa District was known for its taro production, which employs flooded fields and necessitates much water. Today, numerous reservoirs dot the hill-sides, including **Waita Reservoir** at the east-ern edge of town, the largest man-made water catchment on the island and in the state.

SIGHTS

Just as you enter town, look to your right to see a weathered stone chimney standing alone in a little overgrown field. This unmarked edifice is what's left of the **Koloa Sugar Plantation,** established in 1835, site of the first successful at-tempt at refining sugar in the Hawaiian Islands. Although of major historical significance, the chimney is in a terrible state of disrepair. Shrubs are growing off the top and a nearby banyan

On the left side of the image:

© SANDRA E. BISIGNANI TRUST AND AVALON TRAVEL PUBLISHING, INC.

KOLOA

To Lihu'e

KNUDSEN PARK

MALUHIA

520

WAILA'AU RD.

POST OFFICE   BANK

KOLOA SUGAR   KAHN GALLERIES   KOLOA RD.
PLANTATION   BIG SAVE

MEDICAL   ISLAND SOAP AND
CLINIC   CANDLE WORKS

                WELIWELI RD.

GAS   KAUAI
         SUEOKA'S STORE   ATV
To   KOLOA HISTORY CENTER
Kalaheo   To
         SNORKEL BOB'S   Koloa-Po'ipu
FATHOM   Bypass
FIVE
DIVERS   PO'IPU

                OLD KOLOA HOUSE

         KOLOA
         UNION CHURCH
                        RD.
         KOLOA CHURCH
                WAIKOMO

To
Po'ipu   SCALE NOT AVAILABLE

KAUA'I

has thrown off an aerial root and is engulfing the structure. Unless action is taken soon, this historical site will be lost forever.

On this overgrown corner lot is a circle of more than a dozen varieties of sugarcane, each with a short explanation of its characteristics and where it was grown. A plaque and sculpture have recently been added to this site. Reading the plaque will give you an explanation of and appreciation for the sugar industry on Hawaii, the significance of the Koloa Sugar Plantation, and the people who worked the fields. The bronze sculpture portrays individuals of the seven ethnic groups that provided the greatest manpower for the sugar plantations of Hawaii: Hawaiians, Chinese, Japanese, Portuguese, Puerto Ricans, Koreans, and Filipinos. (From the 1830s to about 1910, smaller numbers of Englishmen, Scots, Germans, Scandinavians, Poles, Spaniards, American blacks, and Russians also arrived to work. All in all, about 35,000 immigrants came to Hawaii to make the sugar industry the success it has been.) Koloa is the birthplace of the Hawaiian sugar industry, the strongest economic force in the state for more

than a century. More than anything else, it helped to shape the multiethnic mixture of Hawaii's population. To help celebrate Hawaii's plantation life, the annual **Koloa Plantation Days Festival** takes place in late July in Koloa and the surrounding area.

While its name makes it sound more prestigious that it actually is, the **Koloa History Center** does have a few small displays and pictorials. In a courtyard near the stream, it's a good place for an introduction to the historical significance of Koloa and the surrounding area. With picnic tables and a small garden, this courtyard is good for a midday rest. The courtyard, Waikomo Stream, the roadway, and nearby buildings are all shaded by the branches of a huge monkeypod tree.

The tall steeple on the way to Po'ipu belongs to **Koloa Church,** locally known as the White Church. Established as a congregation in 1835, this structure was built in 1859. It was remodeled in 1929. For many years the steeple was an official landmark used in many land surveys and was often used by sailors to direct their boats to shore. Next to it stands the **Koloa Union Church,** equally old. If you take Weliweli Road out of town, and then follow Hapa Road to its end, you come to **St. Raphael's Catholic Church,** marking the spot where a Roman Catholic mission was first permitted in the islands, in 1841. The stone church itself dates from 1856, when it was built by Friar Robert Walsh. This is a quiet spot, and the church has obviously done well. The roof of the church can be seen sticking above the trees from Kiahuna Golf Club in Po'ipu, a short distance away.

Past Hapa Road, a continuation of Weliweli Road had been cut through the fields to become the **Koloa-Po'ipu Bypass,** a shortcut from Koloa town to the eastern end of the Po'ipu strip, emerging just near the Hyatt Regency Resort.

ACCOMMODATIONS

A plantation manager's house from the early 20th century, originally located at Kukui'ula Harbor, **Old Koloa House** now sits on a quiet street in Koloa along a small stream. It offers one large suite that opens through a double French door to the back lawn and garden. The owners collect antiques, so there are a few older pieces of furniture and decorative items around the suite that elicit a sense of an older, slower time. It's a charming place. A queen-size bed with mosquito netting, ceiling fan, TV, CD player, and books add to the homey, comfortable feel. Other amenities include a telephone, mini-fridge, microwave, coffeemaker, hair dryer, iron, and ironing board. The private bath has a clawfoot tub with shower. For the first morning, a simple continental breakfast is left in the refrigerator; after that you're on your own. The owners are helpful and engaging and can offer suggestions for activities and food. Old Koloa House seems a perfect place for newlyweds or other couples who desire a romantic escape. The room rate is $78 a night, two nights minimum. For information and reservations, call 808/742-2099, write 3327 Waikomo Road, Koloa, HI 96756, visit www.aloha.net/~keane, or email oldkoloahouse@webtv.net.

Lying below the imposing Kahili peak, **Kahili Mountain Park** is a gem, *if* you enjoy what it has to offer: It's like a camp for big people. To get there, follow Route 50 west about a half mile past the turnoff to Koloa, and look for the sign pointing mountainside up a well-graded dirt road. Follow it for about one mile to the entranceway. The surroundings are absolutely beautiful, and the only noises, except for singing birds, are from an occasional helicopter flying into Waimea Canyon and the children attending the school on the premises. The broad meadow is surrounded by mountains, with the coast visible and Po'ipu Beach about 15 minutes away. In the middle of the meadow is a cluster of rocks, a mini replica of the mountains in the background. One strenuous trail from the property runs up to Kahili peak above; a shorter and much easier stroll brings you to a grove of Norfolk pines. A spring-fed pond is chilly for swimming, but great for catching bass that make a tasty dinner. There are three types of accommodations: cabinettes, cabins, and new cabins. A cabinette is a one-room unit with five twin beds and kitchenette. A few of the original rustic cabinettes still remain, with bare wood walls, open ceilings, and cement floors, but the majority didn't survive Hurricane 'Iniki. The cabinettes are in a cluster facing a meadow, and each is surrounded by flower beds and trees. Bathrooms and showers are in a central building, with separate laundry facilities available. A relaxing Japanese *ofuro* (hot tub) is also open to guests. The cabins are raised, wooden-floored houses with full kitchens, inside toilets, outdoor showers, and bedrooms with chairs, tables, and dressers. Each has two twin beds and one double bed. New cabins, built after the hurricane, are a bit larger and upgraded with one queen-size and two twin beds, indoor bathroom with showers, complete kitchens with large refrigerators, and a screened porch. Rates are based on double occupancy, with $10 extra for persons over eight years of age: cabinette, $40; cabin, $50; new cabin, $60. Two additional

honoring contributors to Hawaii's sugar industry at the Koloa Sugar Plantation

ROBERT NILSEN

KAUA'I

cabins, a bit more luxurious, run $78 and $88. All linens, towels, toilet paper, and kitchen utensils are provided, but you must do all your own housekeeping. Kahili Mountain Park is owned and operated by the Seventh-Day Adventist Church, which also runs the school on the property. For information and reservations, call 808/742-9921 or write P.O. Box 298, Koloa, HI 96756.

FOOD

While there are not many restaurants in town, **Pizzetta**, 808/742-8881, is perhaps the best of the bunch and is establishing a fine reputation among locals. Right in the center of town, its front tiled section with a counter window gives way to a wood-floor raised back portion and lanai. Pictures of Italian scenes line the walls, soft jazz fills the air, and a full-service bar mixes drinks. Appetizers such as pepperoni sticks and stuffed mushrooms are $4.95–5.95, soups and salads are under $7.95. A variety of pasta dishes, calzones, and other entrées are tempting and reasonably priced at $6.95–13.95. But Pizzetta is best known for its pizza—handmade crust, homemade sauce—which can be ordered as a whole pie or by the slice, eaten in or taken out; free delivery is available. Standard or make-your-own pizzas run $10.95–23.95 or more depending on the number of toppings.

An easygoing casual place that's a hit with the tourist crowd is **Tomkat's Grill**, 808/724-8887. Enter via a hallway and proceed to the back, where seating is in two sections next to a small courtyard koi pond. The menu is heavy on sandwiches and burgers, most under $7, and deep fried *pu pu*. Other lunch items are a chef salad, one-half rotisserie chicken, and teriyaki steak plate. The limited number of dinner specials, served after 5 P.M., include barbecued pork ribs, garlic seafood pasta, and fresh fish, all for under $16.95. A short children's menu helps keep prices down. Order drinks from the bar or pick out a fresh pastry from the case. Take-out is available on all items.

Da'li Deli and Cafe, 808/742-8824, across from the post office, is open for breakfast and lunch; eat in or take out. Breakfast specials are mostly under $6, while lunch sandwiches are

no more than $7. While many come to start their day here, others come for the bagels, pastries, bread, and deli items, or the many gourmet food items that line the side shelf. This is an up and coming place offering healthy, gourmet food in an easy atmosphere.

Next door to Da'li Deli is **Koloa Fish Market**, open every day except Sunday, for the freshest whole fish and seafood in town, plate lunches, *pu pu,* and beer.

For local atmosphere and inexpensive food to match, try **Kauai Kitchens,** 808/742-1712, next to the supermarket. Open for breakfast and lunch.

Adjacent to Sueoka's Store in downtown Koloa is a **plate-lunch window** that dishes out hearty, wholesome food until early afternoon. It's difficult to spend more than $6.

Lappert's Aloha Ice Cream, downtown Koloa, 808/742-1272, dishes up creamy scoops of delicious Kaua'i-made ice cream. Connoisseurs of the dripping delight consider it among the best in the world. The ice-cream parlor doubles as an espresso bar, with pastries thrown in for good measure.

In Koloa, a **Big Save Supermarket** is at the junction of Koloa and Waikomo Roads. A full-service grocery store, it's open 7 A.M.–11 P.M. daily. **Sueoka's Store,** in downtown Koloa, is a family-owned, local grocery and produce market, open 8 A.M.–8:30 P.M. Both carry virtually everything that you'll need for condo cooking.

Pick up fresh fruits and vegetables at the **farmers' market** held every Monday at noon at Koloa (Knudsen) Park. Depending on what's happening on the farms, you can get everything from coconuts to fresh-cut flowers while enjoying a truly local island experience.

SHOPPING

In Koloa, shops and boutiques are strung along the road like flowers on a lei. You can buy everything from original art to beach towels. There are shops selling jewelry, swimwear, casual clothing, gifts, and candles, and even a specialty shop for sunglasses; Old Koloa Town packs a lot of shopping into a little area. Besides, it's fun just walking the raised sidewalks of what looks very much like an old Western town.

KAUA'I

Look for **Jungle Girl,** next to Lappert's Aloha Ice Cream, offering alohawear and casual clothing; **Crazy Shirts,** a Hawaiian firm selling some of the best T-shirts and islandwear available; **Progressive Expressions,** for surfboards, surf gear, and islandwear; and **Emperors Emporium,** for the usual postcards, cheap jewelry, outlet alohawear, and souvenirs. Casual resortwear is available from **Paradise Clothing,** with a good assortment of bathing suits, beach dresses, men's and women's hats and shorts, and a sampling of clothing for children. Much more unique is **The Blue Orchid** at the upper end of town, a ladies' boutique selling dresses, alohawear, earrings, jewelry, and fresh-cut flowers. The owner hand-paints the dresses and T-shirts, all of which are made from cotton, rayon, or silk.

Also along the strip you'll find **Atlantis Gallery and Frames,** featuring prints, posters, and framing; **Kahn Galleries,** with its exceptional collection of paintings featuring some of the most prominent island artists; and **Kahana Ki'i Art Gallery** if you're looking for quality island art.

Just before the elevated walkway begins, you'll find **Hula Moon Gifts.** The shelves at Hula Moon bear mostly arts and crafts made in Hawaii, with some of the gift items fashioned in Indonesia. Featured items include vests imprinted with a tapa design and antique print; lifelike Hawaiian dolls made from resin; tiles, platters, and red-dirt pottery; handmade (and numbered) ukulele; koa bowls; and less-expensive items like shark-teeth necklaces, barrettes, bracelets, mirror and comb sets, and koa bookmarks.

At the upper end of the raised walkway is **Island Soap and Candle Works,** 808/742-1945, website: www.handmade-soap.com, open daily 9 A.M.–9 P.M. You can't miss this shop as the lovely aromas waft out the store onto the sidewalk. It's a heady smell, and this is definitely not the place for those sensitive to fragrance. For others, head on in to an eye-popping variety of soaps, beeswax candles, lotions, gels, and oils. All handmade, these products are available at boutiques throughout Hawaii and can also be ordered by mail or phone: call 888/528 7627 or write P.O. Box 548, Koloa, HI 96756. A second store is at Kong Lung Center in Kilauea on the north shore.

Koloa One Hour Photo, along Po'ipu Road in Koloa, 808/742-1719, offers camera needs, film, and processing.

RECREATION

Fathom Five Divers, about 100 yards down from the Chevron station in Koloa, 808/742-6991 or 800/972-3078, open daily 9 A.M.–6 P.M., owned and operated by Karen Long-Olsen, is a complete diving center offering lessons, certification, and rentals. Two-tank boat dives for certified divers, including gear, are $90. Introductory dives, including lesson and gear, are $135; a one-tank shore dive is $95. Certification courses take five days and runs $369 with a small group. Tank refills are also available. Fathom Five also does half-day snorkeling cruises that include lessons and gear for $65. Snorkel rental is $5 per day, $15 per week. Boat dives go out of Kukui'ula Harbor near the Spouting Horn and shore dive at Koloa Landing.

Snorkel Bob's, just past Koloa Chevron along Po'ipu Road, 808/742-2206, rents inexpensive snorkel gear that can be taken interisland. Snorkel Bob's has some of the best prices, equipment, and services on the island. Gear, which includes mask, snorkel tube, and fins, is rented for a 24-hour day or by the week. The snorkel set runs from $2.50 per day or $9 a week to $9 a day or $35 a week, depending on the quality. Rental boogie boards are also available. Bob is now booking various island activities, so you may get free or discounted equipment rental if you book through him.

Kauai ATV, on the corner of Weliwlei and Waikomo Roads, 808/742-2734, website: www.kauai.net/kauaiatv, runs four-wheel ATV (all terrain vehicle) tours through former cane land east of Koloa, three times a day for 2.5 hours; $85 a person. Riders must be 16 years old or older. Helmets, face shields, gloves, beverages, and instructions are provided; long pants, a long-sleeve shirt, and closed-toe shoes are a must.

Aside from its ball fields, Koloa Park has tennis courts that are open to the public, free, and lighted at night; they operate on a first-come, first-served basis.

KAUA'I

SERVICES

The Koloa **post office** is along Koloa Road, 808/742-6565. At the end of Koloa Road just beyond the post office is a branch of First Hawaiian Bank, the only bank in the Koloa-Po'ipu area. At the intersection of Koloa and Po'ipu Roads is the only **gas station** in town.

The Kaua'i Medical Group's **Koloa Clinic,** 808/742-1621 (808/245-1831 after hours), offers medical services Mon.–Fri. 8:30 A.M.–12 P.M. and 1:30–5 P.M. This clinic is by the stream next to the Koloa Sugar Mill chimney. The **South Shore Pharmacy** in downtown Koloa, 808/742-7511, open Mon.–Fri. 9 A.M.–5 P.M., not only has a prescription service but also first-aid supplies and skin- and health-care products. The **Koloa Chiropractic Clinic,** 3176 Po'ipu Rd., 808/742-9555, can also help with medical problems. (If they can't help, the Kauai Mortuary is right down the street.)

PO'IPU

Po'ipu Road continues south from Koloa for two miles until it reaches the coast. En route it passes a private cane road, which runs west to Numila, and a bit farther branches at a Y. Here, Lawa'i (Beach) Road turns right and hugs the coast past condos, private homes, and a string of vacation rentals, terminating at the Spouting Horn and the entrance to the National Tropical Botanical Gardens. Po'ipu Road itself bends left past a string of condos and hotels, into what might be considered the town, except that nothing in particular makes it so. From Po'ipu Road, Kapili, Ho'owili, and Pe'e Roads lead to the beach. Ho'onani Road also runs along the water here, splitting from Lawa'i Road and crossing the Waikomo Stream just above Whaler's Cove. At the mouth of the stream you pass **Koloa Landing,** once the island's most important port. When whaling was king, dozens of ships anchored here to trade with the natives for provisions. Today nothing remains, but it is a favorite entry point for shore dives and a good place to watch for turtles in the morning and evening. Snorkeling and scuba diving are best to the sides of the bay, away from the sandy middle.

Po'ipu is the most well-established and developed tourist area on Kaua'i, but it's now fielding competition from developments in Kapa'a and Princeville. On the oceanfront in Po'ipu, luxury accommodations and fine restaurants front the wide beaches, the water beckons, and the surf is gentle. Behind this resort community on the east end is **Pu'u Hi** cone, where the last volcanic eruption occurred on the island about 1.5 million years ago; to the west, beyond Prince Kuhio's birthplace, is the Spouting Horn, a plume of water that jets up through an opening in the volcanic rock shore with every incoming wave. Whether you're exploring the sights, cultivating a tan on the beach, combing the shops for your gift list, or sampling island treats, Po'ipu will not fail to provide.

Hurricane 'Iniki pummeled Po'ipu like a boxer hitting a punching bag. In the aftermath, it took years for the devastated Po'ipu area to recover and rebuild. By the end of 1999, all hotel and condo properties were again up and running, except for the former Waiohai Hotel. Only slowly have other properties been developed. Although it continues to face some strident opposition by local activists and must meet strict county requirements, the largest new development planned in Po'ipu is for the Kukui'ula Bay area near Spouting Horn. Alexander and Baldwin plan a 200-room hotel fronting the lagoon basin, expansion of Kukui'ula Harbor facilities, greenways and bike paths, an 18-hole golf course, a shopping center, and over 3,000 condo units and residential lots that would stretch back to Po'ipu Road. In order to service this huge integrated development, a new road would have to be cut through former cane land to ease traffic on Lawa'i Road. While not fronting the water, this development will undoubtedly and dramatically change the face of Po'ipu.

SIGHTS

The Great Po'ipu Beaches

Although given a lacing by Hurricane 'Iniki, **Po'ipu Beach County Park** is on the mend and is Po'ipu's best-developed beach park. At the eastern end of Po'ipu, it provides a pavilion, tables, showers, toilets, a playground, walkways, and lifeguards on duty daily. There's plenty of parking along Ho'one Road or across the street. The swimming, snorkeling, and bodysurfing are great. Po'ipu Beach has something for just about everyone. A sheltered pool rimmed by lava boulders is gentle enough for any swimmer, and going just beyond it provides the more exciting wave action often used by local surfers. Follow the rocks out to Nukumoi Point, where there are a number of tide pools; snorkeling is best on the right side. Waves come in all sizes, and instructors use Po'ipu Beach for beginning surf lessons. The far eastern end of Po'ipu Beach is called **Brennecke's Beach.** Popular with locals, it's one of the best spots on the island for boogie boarding and bodysurfing. Following the shoreline around to the west are two additional crescent beaches, one in front of the Kiahuna Plantation Resort and the other fronting the Sheraton Kauai Resort. Both slope gently into the water and often are the haunt of seals and turtles.

At the eastern end of the Hyatt is an access road leading to **Shipwreck Beach,** now improved with a pavilion containing restrooms and showers. Shipwreck Beach is a half-mile strand of white sand. One of the only beneficiaries of Hurricanes 'Iwa and 'Iniki, the beach was broadened and widened with huge deposits of sand, making it bigger and better than ever. The swimming is good, but, as always, use caution. The beach is perhaps best known for boogie boarding and bodysurfing, and these usually take place at the far eastern end near the sandstone bluff. It is below this bluff that a boat wreck lay for many years. Now only the heavy motor still lies here, exposed at times of heavy surf, the rest having been torn away by the last hurricane. Also near here, etched into the hardened sandstone and buried under beach sand most of the year, is one of the few petroglyphs on the island. In order to see it, you have to be lucky enough to be there when the water pulls the sand away to expose these rock carvings. The Hyatt Hotel has developed a walkway running east along the golf course, affording fantastic seascapes as you amble above the bluff.

Continue along Po'ipu Road—no longer paved—past the golf course and turnoff to CJM Stables. Take the first right turn onto another dirt road that runs down toward the water. Access to **Maha'ulepu Beach** is across private land, and the landowner sometimes posts a security guard who asks to see your driver's license and may have you sign a liability release. Be sure to note the time because this gate is locked 6 P.M.–7:30 A.M. The dirt access road leads down to a parking lot just behind the sand dunes; a track to the left behind the dunes leads to a smaller parking spot. Maha'ulepu Beach is long. Its western extent is rather straight and exposed but at the eastern end it slips around into a nice protected cove good for swimming. Sand dunes back the beach through most of its length, and more are found beyond the beach before the mountains begin. Not many people frequent this beach—although George C. Scott came here to play Ernest Hemingway for the movie *Islands in the Stream*—but fishermen come, as do au naturel sunbathers, and, when the waves are right, surfers. When the waves are not too strong, swimming is good within the reef, which is also used by windsurfers. There is no official camping here, but local people sometimes bivouac in the ironwoods at the east end. There are no facilities. A trail along the lithified sandstone bluff runs by the golf course from Shipwreck Beach to near the CJM Stables, a distance of a mile or so, from where it's a short walk beyond to Maha'ulepu Beach.

Just west of Kuhio Park, fronting Lawa'i Beach Resort, is the narrow, roadside **Lawa'i Beach,** also called Beach House Beach. Not particularly good for swimming because of its rocky bottom and shoreline, these characteristics make it one of the best, and most family-safe, snorkeling spots in the area. Enter at the sandy end near the Beach House Restaurant. Surfers and body boarders also come here for the breaks created by the reef. Back down the coast a few hundred yards, on the east side of Kuhio Park, is **Keiki Beach** (Baby Beach). Somewhat protected by the reef, with a narrow sand strip, this beach is secluded and used mostly for sunbathing.

East End

Along Po'ipu Road, look for the driveway into the Kiahuna Plantation Resort on the right across from the Po'ipu Shopping Village. This is the site of the **Moir Gardens.** These grounds, originally

KAUA'I

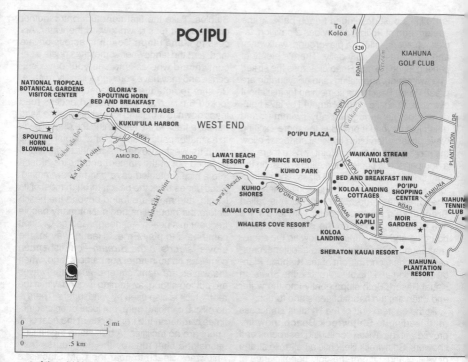

PO'IPU

To Koloa

520

KIAHUNA GOLF CLUB

NATIONAL TROPICAL BOTANICAL GARDENS VISITOR CENTER

GLORIA'S SPOUTING HORN BED AND BREAKFAST

COASTLINE COTTAGES

KUKUI'ULA HARBOR

WEST END

SPOUTING HORN BLOWHOLE

PO'IPU PLAZA

LAWA'I

AMIO RD.

ROAD

LAWA'I BEACH RESORT

PRINCE KUHIO

KUHIO PARK

WAIKAMOI STREAM VILLAS

PO'IPU BED AND BREAKFAST INN

KUHIO SHORES

HO'ONA RD.

KOLOA LANDING COTTAGES

PO'IPU SHOPPING CENTER

KAUAI COVE COTTAGES

WHALERS COVE RESORT

KOLOA LANDING

PO'IPU KAPILI

MOIR GARDENS

KIAHUNA TENNIS CLUB

SHERATON KAUAI RESORT

KIAHUNA PLANTATION RESORT

PLANTATION DR.

0   .5 mi
0   .5 km

part of the old Koloa Sugar Company manager's estate, were a "cactus patch" started by Sandie Moir, wife of the manager, Hector Moir, back in 1938. Over the years, the gardens grew more and more lavish, with the inclusion of succulents, orchids, bromeliads, dry land trees, and several ponds, until they became a standard Po'ipu sight. Mrs. Moir was a horticulturist enamored of cacti. Whenever she went to the Mainland she collected these amazing plants, mainly from Texas and the Southwest, and transported them back to Hawaii to be planted in her cactus garden. However, before planting them she would invite a *kahuna* to bless the land and to pray for their acceptance. The Kiahuna Plantation Resort has greatly expanded the original gardens; the property's 35 lovely acres are adorned with more than 3,000 varieties of tropical flowers, trees, and plants, and a lovely lagoon. Many plants are identified. The cactus garden has flourished and by magic or mystery was the only thing in the entire area left untouched when Hurricane 'Iniki swept

away everything else in sight like a huge broom. The rest of the property was heavily battered by the hurricane, but the two dozen full-time gardeners have restored everything to its former beauty. The gardens are open free of charge to the public during daylight hours.

West End

Turn onto Lawa'i Road to pass **Prince Kuhio Park,** locally known as "PK," the birthplace of Prince Kuhio, Jonah Kalaniana'ole. Loved and respected, Prince Cupid—a nickname by which he was known—was Hawaii's delegate to Congress from the turn of the century until his death in 1922. In this capacity, he advocated for the rights of Hawaiians and fought for their respect. This "People's Prince" often returned to the shores of his birth whenever his duties permitted. Containing a statue and monument, terraced lava walls, a *heiau,* palm trees, and the remains of a fishpond, this well-manicured acre faces the sea. Turtles often congregate off the rocks across the road.

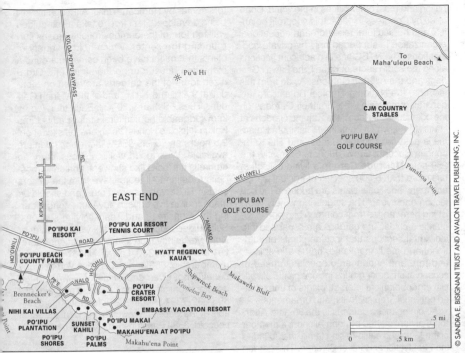

To
Maha'ulepu Beach

Pu'u Hi

CJM COUNTRY
STABLES

KOLOA-PO'IPU BAY PASS RD

PO'IPU BAY
GOLF COURSE

WELIWELI RD

Punahoa Point

EAST END

PO'IPU BAY
GOLF COURSE

'AINAKO

KIPUKA ST

PO'IPU KAI
RESORT

PO'IPU KAI RESORT
TENNIS COURT

PO'IPU RD

KOHU

PO'IPU BEACH
COUNTY PARK

HYATT REGENCY
KAUA'I

Shipwreck Beach

Makawehi Bluff

Keoneloa Bay

PE'E

Brennecker's
Beach

NALO

RD

PO'IPU
CRATER
RESORT

NIHI KAI VILLAS

EMBASSY VACATION RESORT

PO'IPU
PLANTATION

SUNSET
KAHILI

PO'IPU MAKAI

PO'IPU
SHORES

PO'IPU
PALMS

MAKAHU'ENA AT PO'IPU

Makahu'ena Point

HO'OHU RD

0   .5 mi

0   .5 km

© SANDRA E. BISIGNANI TRUST AND AVALON TRAVEL PUBLISHING, INC.

Farther along is **Kukui'ula Bay.** Before Hurricane 'Iwa and later 'Iniki pummeled this shoreline, the bay was an attractive beach park where many small boats anchored. Today, it's coming back, and you can still launch a boat or kayak here. A handful of sailing, diving, and fishing companies leave from the Kukui'ula Harbor, shore fishermen come to try their luck, and scuba divers explore the coral reef offshore. At the end of Amio Road, the park offers new and clean picnic tables, grills, and restrooms.

In a moment, you arrive at the **Spouting Horn.** A large parking area has many stalls marked for tour buses; at the flea market here, you can pick up trinkets, jewelry, and souvenirs. Don't make the mistake of looking just at the Spouting Horn. Have "big eyes" and look around at the full sweep of this remarkable coastline. The Spouting Horn is a lava tube that extends into the sea, with its open mouth on the rocky shore. The inrushing wave action causes the spouting phenomenon through a hole in the cave

roof, which can blow spumes quite high, depending on surf conditions. They say it shot higher in the old days, but when the salt spray damaged the nearby cane fields, plantation owners supposedly had the opening made larger so the spray wouldn't carry as far. Photographers wishing to catch the Spouting Horn in action have an ally. Just before it shoots, a hole behind the spout makes a large belch—a second later, the spume flies. Be ready to click. For your safety, stay behind the guard rail.

National Tropical Botanical Garden

The National Tropical Botanical Gardens (NTBG) constitute the only tropical plant research facility in the country. Its primary aims are to preserve, propagate, and dispense knowledge about tropical plants. This is becoming increasingly important as large areas of the world's tropical forests are being destroyed, and Hawaiian native plants are now threatened or endangered at a rate far greater than anywhere else in the nation and most other places in the world. Chartered by Congress in 1964, this nonprofit botanical and horticultural research and educational organization is supported only by private contributions. The NTBG has two adjacent sections along the south shore of Kaua'i: the Lawa'i Gardens and the Allerton Gardens. Aside from this location, the National Tropical Botanical Gardens also maintains the Limahuli Gardens on the north coast of Kaua'i; the Kahanu Gardens at Hana, Maui, which contains Pi'ilanihale Heiau, the largest *heiau* in the islands; and The Kampong in Coconut Grove, Florida. Currently, the 259-acre **McBryde Garden's** living collection has more than 6,000 species of tropical plants, and many additional plants are added to the collection each year. The staggering variety flourishing here ranges from common bamboo to romantic orchids. The gardens are separated into individual sections that include plants of nutritional and medicinal value, herbs and spices, and rare and endangered species in need of conservation; other groups include plants of special ethnobotanical interest, plants of unexploited potential, tropical fruits, and ornamentals.

Adjoining these gardens is the 80-acre **Allerton Garden,** started by John Allerton, a member of the Mainland cattle-raising family that founded the First National Bank of Chicago. This garden dates from the 1870s, when Queen Emma made the first plantings here at one of her summer vacation homes. In 1938, Robert Allerton bought this property, and for 20 years, he and adopted son John, helped by a host of gardeners, cleared the jungle and planted. John scoured the islands of the South Pacific to bring back their living treasures, and oftentimes, old *kama'aina* families would send cuttings of their rarest plants to be included in the collection. The Lawa'i River runs through the property, and pools, statuary, and garden "rooms" help set the mood.

These gardens are so enchanting that many visitors regard them as one of the real treats of their trip. The visitors center, 808/742-2623, open Mon.–Sat. 8 A.M.–5 P.M., with its interpretive displays and small gift shop, is a restored plantation manager's house across from the Spouting Horn. Particularly nice are its selection of Ni'ihau shell leis, fine quilts, and books on Hawaii. This center was opened in 1997, following the total destruction of the former visitors center by Hurricane 'Iniki. Although it's still being developed, feel free to take a self-guided walking tour of the demonstration gardens surrounding the center, which hold a variety of plants that might have been common around a plantation house during the sugar era. Organized tours of the gardens are given on Monday at 9 A.M. and 1 P.M., and of the Allerton Gardens Tues.–Sat. at 9:30 A.M. Each tour, led by knowledgeable horticultural staff or a Na Lima Kokua (Helping Hands) volunteer, lasts for about 2.5 hours and costs $30—*kama'aina* rates are available. Wear good walking shoes, carry an umbrella if it looks like showers, and bring mosquito repellent! All tours leave from the visitors center. Reservations are a must and should be made four to five days in advance—longer during the Christmas and Thanksgiving seasons. Self-guided tours $15. Call the visitors center or write well in advance to the reservations secretary at P.O. Box 340, Lawa'i, HI 96765. Annual membership, $50 and up, entitles you to many benefits not given casual visitors—write to the development office at the address above or call 808/332-7324. Additional information is available at the website www.ntbg.org. Contact: Janet Leopold, 3530 Papaluna Rd., Kaleheo, HI 96741.

ACCOMMODATIONS

Most of Po'ipu's available rooms are found in medium- to high-priced condos; however, there are a handful of cottages, several bed-and-breakfasts, and two first-class hotels.

$250 and up

A parade of royal palms lines the grand boulevard that ends at the elegant porte cochere where towering panes of glass open to a roiling sea frothing against periwinkle sky at the **Hyatt Regency Kauai Resort and Spa,** 1571 Po'ipu Rd., Koloa, HI 96756, 808/742-1234 or 800/633-7313, website: www.kauai-hyatt.com. The Hyatt is a grand hotel in grand dimension that bespeaks the luxury of 1920s and 1930s Hawaii. This magnificent, 600-room hotel, deceptive in size, is architecturally designed so that its five floors rise no taller than the surrounding palms. Through the entry are the main reception and concierge desks, and to the sides in both directions are the

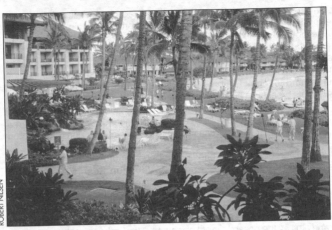

ROBERT NILSEN

the luxurious and tasteful Sheraton Kauai Resort

numerous resort shops. To one side of the inner courtyard is Stevenson Library, one of the Hyatt's bars, with over-stuffed chairs, pool and billiard tables, a grand piano, and ornate chess sets waiting for the first move. Live jazz is performed here nightly. The main courtyard opens onto a terrace that overlooks the oceanside grounds of the hotel. Walking paths scented by tropical blooms lead through acres of pools, both fresh and saltwater, featuring slides, a rivulet flowing through a "gorge," and the watery massaging fingers of cascading waterfalls and bubbling whirlpools. Through the heart of the hotel, greenery and flowers, both wild and tamed, compose a living lei of floral beauty. Lustrous koa tables bear flowers ablaze with color. Artworks, tapa wall hangings, and birdcages filled with flitting plumage and trilling songs line the hallways, while the interplay of marble floors and rich carpets is counterpointed by weathered bronze.

Heavy mahogany doors open into large guest rooms, all done in soothing pastels with white on tan textured wallpaper. Each room features a full entertainment center, private lanai with outdoor furniture, a mini-bar, double closets, and spacious bathrooms. Mahogany furniture, overstuffed chairs and footstools, and Chinese-style lamps ensure tasteful relaxation, and Hawaiian quilts cover the beds. Rates range from $335 for a garden view to $495 for a deluxe oceanfront room; $565 for Regency Club; and $825 to $3,100 for suites.

The five restaurants at the Hyatt range from casual to elegant, and five lounges offer libations in poolside to formal settings; additionally, there is the Po'ipu Bay Grill and Bar next door at the golf course clubhouse. A myriad of cultural activities are scheduled throughout the week, and of great interest is the nightly Hawaiian music program accompanied by a torch-lighting ceremony and/or a *keiki* hula show. Drums of Paradise lu'au is held every Thursday and Sunday in the lower courtyard, and the on-property Anara Spa is perfect for those seeking a rejuvenative health retreat. Camp Hyatt keeps the kids busy while parents are off doing other things, and of course, the hotel's tennis courts and adjacent golf links are for those who desire physical activity.

Following a $45 million remodel, the **Sheraton Kauai Resort,** 2440 Ho'onani Rd., Po'ipu Beach, Koloa, HI 96756, 808/742-1661 or 800/782-9488, website: www.sheraton-kauai.com, reopened in 1997, the last of the major hotels on Kaua'i to do so after the devastating effects of Hurricane 'Iniki. Sheraton's two former properties have been combined into a 413-room resort with ocean, beach, and garden wings, on 20 lovely acres. Casually elegant and elegantly modern, the Sheraton Kauai Resort is a tasteful, eminently comfortable accommodation, no taller than the coconut trees on property, where the tropics surround you and pretense is left at the door.

The porte cochere opens onto the open-air reception area. Check in and inquire about

KAUA'I

events or book activities at the concierge and activities desks. Notice the lovely mural of a Hawaiian family gracing the lobby. Surrounding the courtyard beyond are the library; retail shops for resortwear, sundries, and jewelry; a fitness center; beauty salon and massage center; and the hotel's main restaurant and lounge. The Shells restaurant is known for its breakfasts and seafood dinners, and for the perfect sunset spot, find a seat at The Point lounge. Across the road in the garden section are a cultural center where daily programs are offered and craft items displayed and sold, and, in a quiet corner off a koi pond, the Naniwa restaurant offers a taste of Japan. On the property are two swimming pools, one in the garden, surrounded by waterfalls, and the other, just off the beach, boasting a hot tub and water slide. Lighter fare is served throughout the day at the Oasis Bar and Grill by the oceanside pool. The beach activities center offers rental of water equipment, and the tennis courts are open to guests only 7 A.M.–10 P.M. Kids ages 5–12 years old can have great fun in supervised play through the Keiki Aloha Club. A complimentary resort shuttle operates hourly 7 A.M.–10 P.M. to the Po'ipu Shopping Village, Po'ipu golf courses, or up the road to Koloa.

Each spacious room is appointed with amenities for your comfort, including a/c, entertainment center, refrigerator, personal safe, and private lanai. Rates range from $285 for a garden view room to $750 for an oceanfront suite. In addition, there is a $10 per room resort activities fee. Guests at this resort can also use the facilities at the Princeville Hotel on the north shore and charge all expenses to their rooms.

Condos

Although the prices in Po'ipu can be a bit higher than elsewhere on Kaua'i, you get a lot for your money. More than a dozen well-appointed modern condos are lined up along the beach and just off it, with thousands of units available. Most are a variation on the same theme: comfortably furnished, fully equipped, with a tennis court here and there, always a swimming pool, and maid service available. Most require a minimum stay of at least two nights, with discounts for longer visits. The following condos have been chosen to give you a general idea of what to expect. You can get excellent brochures listing most Po'ipu-area accommodations by writing to Po'ipu Beach Resort Association, P.O. Box 730, Koloa, HI 96756, 808/742-7444. The Po'ipu Beach Resort Association also offers a "one stop shop" online information and reservation system for participating association properties, where you can find availability, pricing, and amenities, and book online all from one site. This service, which handles not just condos, but all types of accommodations in the Po'ipu area, can save you the time of checking different properties independently. For this free service, access http://poipu-beach.org/reservations.

Embassy Vacation Resort Po'ipu Point, managed by Marc Resorts Hawaii, at 1613 Pe'e Rd., Po'ipu, HI 96756, 808/742-1888 or 800/535-0085, is a marriage of luxury condo and time-share units that sits on 23 manicured, oceanfront cliff acres. The Embassy is grand in scope but not pretentious. Upon arrival, you enter through a white porte cochere to the main lobby with its guest reception and concierge desk, which opens to the gardens below. The 10 neo-classic plantation-style buildings surround a central courtyard where you will discover, fronting a sandy beach, a large pool with one side tiled and the other sand-bottomed. At poolside you will find a hot tub and, nearby, a complete fitness center. Mornings bring a complimentary healthy breakfast in an outdoor dining area near the pool. Here and there throughout the property you'll find little picnic nooks complete with tables and barbecue grills for your enjoyment. Notice a thick grove of ironwoods completely surrounded by a hedge; these protect the site of an ancient *heiau* that the resort is dedicated to preserving. Just below the pool area lies a stretch of dramatic coastline pounded by heavy wave action, frothing misty azure against the coal-black lava. These waters are too treacherous for recreational swimming, but a two-minute walk takes you to Shipwreck Beach. The one- and two-bedroom units, air conditioned with ceiling fans throughout, feature full kitchens with marble-topped counters and all amenities and a dining/living room that open to a wraparound lanai. Each unit has its own washer and dryer, along with steam iron and ironing board. Room charges (no extra charge for additional guests) range $299–450 for one-bedroom units and $350–565 for two-bedroom suites; package rates available.

The **Po'ipu Shores** condo is at the east end of the beach, surrounded by other small condos. They're slightly less expensive than the rest, allowing up to six people at no extra charge in certain two- and three-bedroom units. The one-bedroom units run $110; a standard two-bedroom is $150, a deluxe two-bedroom is $160, and a three-bedroom unit runs $165. Rates are $10–20 cheaper off-season. There is a three-night minimum stay. Maid service is provided free every other day. All units are clean, spacious, and airy, and the area's best beaches are a short stroll away. Write Po'ipu Shores, 1775 Pe'e Rd., Koloa, HI 96756, 808/742-7700, 800/367-5004 Mainland and Canada, or 800/272-5275.

With 110 acres, **Po'ipu Kai Resort** has the largest grounds in the area—one corner of which runs down to the ocean. Through this finely landscaped property, a walking path connects Brennecke's Beach with Shipwreck Beach. Set among broad gardens, most units look out onto a swimming pool or the tennis courts. There are one-, two-, three-, and four-bedroom units, in numerous floor plans. Some are Hawaiian in theme; others are Spanish, with stucco and arched entryways; modern units show more glass and chrome; and a few may resemble your own Mainland abode. A handful of multi-bedroom homes are also available in the adjacent housing estate. Facilities on the grounds include nine tennis courts (free for guests), a pro shop with a resident tennis pro, six swimming pools, two outdoor hot tubs, numerous barbecue grills, and an activities center. Next to the resort office is the House of Seafood, the area's premier seafood restaurant, open only for dinner. A complex structure of room rates exists, depending upon the season and length of stay, but generally the one-bedrooms run $147–270 during regular season, two-bedroom units $170–307, three-bedroom units $229–274, and four-bedrooms units $352. For reservations, write to Po'ipu Kai Resort, 1941 Po'ipu Rd., Po'ipu-Koloa, HI 96756, or call 808/742-6464 or 800/367-8020, visit www.suite-paradise.com, or email mail@suite-paradise.com. Aston Hotels and Resorts also manages numerous units at Po'ipu Kai. For information on its units and rates, contact Aston at 1775 Po'ipu Road, Koloa, HI 96756, 808/742-7424 or 800/922-7866.

The **Kiahuna Plantation Resort,** 2253 Po'ipu Road, Koloa, HI 96756, 808/742-6411 or 800/688-7444, is operated by Hawaii's own Outrigger Resorts; some units are managed by Castle Resorts and Hotels, 800/367-5004. It first opened its doors and grounds to the public in 1972. Previously, it was the estate of Mr. and Mrs. Hector Moir, a manager of the Koloa Sugar Company. Their private home, now serving as the reception center, is a breezy but stout lava-rock structure in the classic plantation style. Their living room and adjoining rooms, appointed in lustrous koa, now serve as the dining room of the Italian restaurant **Piatti.** Fronting the house is Moir Gardens, a unique mix of cacti and tropical flowers and trees. The property, comprising 35 lush acres fronting Po'ipu Beach, houses just over 300 units, divided into separate buildings. Contemporary in design, they are white inside and out with dark trim. Interior styling differs from one unit to another since each is individually owned, yet all are well appointed, as they must meet high standards. You enter the large one-bedroom units through louvered doors. Sliding doors at the far end allow breezes to filter through, assisted by ceiling fans in every room. The bedroom features a king- or queen-size bed, and across the hall, the bathroom has a shower and tub, dressing area, and handy hallway closets with complimentary safes. The comfy living room, separate dining area, and full modern kitchen are on the ocean side. Here you'll find all the amenities and comforts of home and, what's more, you have daily housekeeping service. Each unit has a covered lanai with table, chairs, and lounges overlooking the grounds. With the sea in the distance you'll feel like a transplanted flower in this magnificent garden, set amongst red ginger, yellow plumeria, and a painter's palate of greens. The two-bedroom units are bi-level and the size of most homes. All units are only a minute's walk from the beach, home to the Hawaiian monk seal March–July. Full beach service is provided, and the concierge desk can make arrangements for any activity on the island. The resort tennis courts are across the road. Laundry facilities are on the premises. One-bedroom suites (maximum four guests) run $190–420, two-bedroom suites (for up to six) are $330–470. Prices depend on the view; numerous packages are available.

The Kiahuna Plantation Resort is a first-rate condominium, expertly managed, with a superb location.

Poʻipu Kapili, 2221 Kapili Rd., Koloa, HI 96756, 808/742-6449 or 800/443-7714, fax 808/742-9162, website: www.poipukapili.com, email: aloha@poipukapili.com, is a three-story, upscale condo complex with only 60 units on five acres that has a touch of the Hawaiian plantation style, across the road from a rocky shoreline. All units have ocean views. The pool is in the center of the property, surrounded by gardens and lawn. Also on the premises are free, lighted tennis courts, and racquets and balls are provided. Each unit is huge. Bedrooms have ceiling fans and wicker furniture, kitchens are spacious and furnished with modern appliances, and the large living area opens onto a private lanai that overlooks the pool and garden. Rates range $195–210 for a one-bedroom unit to $260–285 for a two-bedroom, regular season; monthly and weekly discounts are available, as are several packages. The condo also offers a convenient activities desk that will book you into any activity that strikes your fancy.

On the far side of Koloa Landing is **Whaler's Cove,** 2640 Puuholo Rd., Koloa, HI 96756, 808/742-7571 or 800/225-2683, fax 808/742-1185, website: www.whalers-cove.com, email: whalers@hawaiian.net, a deluxe accommodation with only 38 units offering you an excellent sense of privacy and manageability. Set right on the point, Whaler's Cove opens to and embraces the sea. All individually owned, most units are tastefully decorated in a contemporary island style. Here you'll find full kitchens and baths with all the amenities, daily housekeeping, laundry facilities, and a private swimming pool set above the rocky water's edge. One-bedroom units here run $295–400 and two-bedroom units are $360–470; units are $25–40 extra during holiday season.

Other condos also stretch along this wonderful shore. The smaller ones generally cluster at the east end of the beach; others are near Koloa Landing and Kuhio Park. **Makahuʻena at Poʻipu** sits on Makahuʻena Point, with the crashing waves below. Managed by Castle Resorts, here you'll find one-, two-, and three-bedroom units with full kitchens, and swimming pool and tennis courts on the property for guests to use. Rates

run $146–324 during regular season, $25 more during high season. Call 808/742-2482 or 800/367-5004 for information. **Poʻipu Crater Resort** snuggles inside a small seaside caldera. The Polynesian-inspired buildings are surrounded by greenery and on the property are a swimming pool and tennis courts. It's managed by Suite Paradise, 808/742-7400 or 800/367-8020. **Poʻipu Makai,** 808/245-8841 or 800/367-5025; **Poʻipu Palms,** 800/367-8022; and **Sunset Kahili,** 808/742-7434 or 800/827-6478, website: www.sunsetkahili.com, all run in quick succession across the cliff at the east end of Poʻipu Beach. The small and newer family-run **Poʻipu Plantation,** 808/742-6757 or 800/634-0263, website: www.poipubeach.com, has only nine units that range $95–130 and is tucked behind a plantation-era bungalow. Just a few steps from Brennecke's Beach is the posher **Nihi Kai Villas,** 808/742-7220 or 800/325-5701. On the west end, **Waikomo Stream Villas,** 808/742-7220 or 800/325-5701, is just inland and backs up against the stream above Koloa Landing. At Lawaʻi Beach are **Lawaʻi Beach Resort,** 808/742-5152, a time-share property that rents out condo units for $145 a day when they are available; **Kuhio Shores,** 808/742-1391; and **Prince Kuhio,** 808/742-1409.

East End B&Bs and Vacation Rentals

Pua Hale (Flower House), at 2381 Kipuka St., Koloa, HI 96756, 808/742-1700 or 800/745-7414, website: www.portraitsofhawaii.com, email: poh@aloha.net, is a lovely, deluxe 750-square-foot house where your privacy and serenity are assured. With a touch of Japan, Pua Hale features shoji screens, cool wooden floors, a relaxing *ofuro,* custom furniture and decorating, and a complete kitchen and laundry. This self-contained unit, only minutes from Poʻipu, is surrounded by a privacy fence and a manicured garden, so you can choose whether you want to socialize or simply enjoy the glorious quietude on your own. Rates are a reasonable $120 per night, or $750 per week. You can't find better.

Built in 1998, one new and upscale rental home at the eastern end of Poʻipu is **Maluhia ma ka Honua.** With three bedrooms, four bathrooms, full kitchen, huge living/dining room, and wraparound lanai, this house is suited for families. It has all electric appliances in the kitchen and the amenities are modern throughout. Maluhia ma ka Honua makes you feel at home, and you can't help but relax and have a restful time. The rent rate is $1,575 per week, with a $150 cleaning fee. Contact Garden Island Rentals for reservations, 808/742-9537 or 800/247-5599.

Situated right on the water just east of Brennecke's Beach is the upscale **Honu Kai Villas,** 1871 Pe'e Road, Koloa, HI 96756, 808/742-9155 or 800/854-8363, fax 808/742-7940, website: www.honukai.com, email: rjr@honukai.com. The location couldn't be better. Within this tight compound are six spacious units and a swimming pool. Modern in design, each unit shows fine craftsmanship and has full kitchen and laundry facilities. The one-bedroom units run $200 a day or $1,400 a week, and the two-bedroom units $233–250 a day or $1,500–1,600 a week; five-night minimum. Three-bedroom, three-bath units are $2,800–3,000 a week. A $85–125 cleaning fee is levied on all units. No breakfast is served.

Directly up from Brennecke's Beach is **Plantation Cottage** vacation rental, 2254 Pane Rd., 808/742-6688. Built in 1924 and restored in 1996, this building evokes the sugar era with its spaciousness and front veranda. A two-bedroom, one-bath home that sleeps five, it rents for $155 a night or $775 a week; the rate changes depending on the season.

Po'ipu Plantation, 1792 Pe'e Road, Koloa, HI 96756, 808/742-6757 or 800/634-0263, website: www.poipubeach.com, email: plantation@poipubeach.com, is a three-bedroom plantation-era home that's just up the street from Brennecke's Beach. The front lanai serves as a common room, and all three rooms go for $85 a night.

Adjacent to the Po'ipu Bay Golf Course and within easy walking distance of both Shipwreck and Brennecke's Beaches is **Hale Hyette B&B,** which offers one room with private entrance, bath, and a lanai with views, and a simple continental breakfast each morning. The room rate is $100 a night, two nights minimum; no credit cards. For reservations and information call 808/742-2877.

West End B&Bs and Vacation Rentals
Po'ipu Bed and Breakfast Inn, 2720 Ho'onani Rd., Koloa, HI 96756, 808/742-1146 or 877/552-0095, fax 808/742-6843, website: www.poipu.net, email: poipu@aloha.net, is a large and spacious renovated plantation house from the 1930s. Stained in tropical colors, this wooden house has all the comforts of home, plus antiques, art, and crafts from the island. If you have a childlike affection for carousel rides, you'll love this place because there are several carousel horses in the house. The bedrooms are on either side of the large, central sitting room. Each has a color TV, ceiling fan, and private bath. The sitting room has a TV, videotapes, books, and games. Smoking is not allowed inside the house; sit out on the large, comfortable lanai or walk in the garden. Children are welcome. Daily room rates, including a continental breakfast, are $120–150. Rooms can be combined into two-bedroom, two-bath suites, and the entire house can be rented. An extra $15 is charged for an additional person, and there's a discount for single occupancy. Discounts are also given on prepaid weeklong or longer stays, and Christmas holiday rates are about $40 extra. The owners also rent a unit in the nearby Whaler's Cove condominium for $325–450 depending on the season and number of guests; two nights minimum.

Next door is **Koloa Landing Cottages,** 2704-B Ho'onani Road, Koloa, HI 96756, 808/742-1470 or 800/779-8773, fax 808/332-9584, planet-hawaii.com/koloa, email: dolphin@aloha.net. These basic units are some of Po'ipu's least-expensive accommodations. Two-bedroom, two-bath units, the main house, and five cottages each sleep up to six people and have a full kitchen and color television. Rates are $125 for the house and $110 for the cottages for up to four, and $10 for each additional person. For one bedroom it's $80, and studios, also equipped with kitchen and color TVs, run $70. A cleaning fee of $20–60 is added to the price of the room. Four nights minimum. Laundry facilities are on the premises. Reservations are suggested; a $125 deposit is required, and 25 percent discount is offered for stays longer than 14 days. Contact Sylvia or Hans to reserve.

Garden Isle Cottages, 2660 Puuholo Rd., Koloa, HI 96756, 808/742-6717 or 800/742-6711, fax 808/742-1933, website: www.oceancottages.com, email: vacation@oceancottages.com, are perched on the craggy rocks above Koloa Landing surrounded by lush foliage, offering privacy. The cottages are operated by artists Robert and Sharon Flynn, whose original works highlight each of the units, and each of the four cottages are decorated in an Oriental, Indonesian, Heritage, or Polynesian theme. The cottages are two duplexes, each with upper and lower units. All the units have one bedroom and one bath and are self-contained and fully equipped; downstairs units have kitchens, upstairs units have kitchenettes. The price is $140 high season and $125 low season, plus $10 for each person beyond two. Four nights' deposit is required; weekly and monthly rates can be arranged.

Of contemporary design, **Turtle Cove Suites** overlook Whalers Cove. The four units offer full amenities, two with full kitchens and two with kitchenettes, and a small private swimming pool. Rates run $100–175, three nights minimum; $300 holds the reservation, and no credit cards are accepted. For information: P.O. Box 1899. Koloa, HI 96756, 808/742-8978, fax 808/742-7071, planet-hawaii.com/poipubeach, email: turtles@aloha.net.

Nearby along the same quiet residential road are **Kauai Cove Cottages,** 2672 Puuholo Rd., #A, Po'ipu, HI 96756. 808/742-2562 or 800/642-9945, website: www.kauaicove.com, email: info@kauaicove.com. Set close to the road and lined up like a row house, they are not much to look at from the outside, but they are a surprise on the inside. Not overly large, but modern in style and well designed in light colored hardwood and bamboo, each of the three studios is adorned in island tropical decor with island-inspired artwork on the walls. Tall cathedral ceilings make the rooms appear more spacious, and a kitchen is set up for full meal preparations. Each room comes with color TV and a CD player with a selection of contemporary Hawaiian music, and the queen bed is replete with old-style hanging mosquito netting. These are comfortable units that remind you in every way that you are on vacation in the tropics. Rates are $85 a night with a $25 cleaning fee for stays of three days or less.

Hale Pilialoha is a pleasant house in a quiet neighborhood. Airy and spacious, the home's nine French doors open onto gardens and lanai. The main room and full kitchen complement the two bedrooms to accommodate a family. Rent is $200 a night for two people, $25 a person additional, plus $75 cleaning fee. Contact Rosewood, 872 Kamalu Rd., Kapa'a, HI 96746 for information and reservations, call 808/822-5216, fax 808/822-5478, visit rosewoodkauai.com, or email rosewood@aloha.net.

Along Lawa'i Road near Kukui'ula Harbor, three plantation-era buildings, aquamarine with yellow highlights, sun themselves contentedly on the well-landscaped lawn below tall palms and just back from the water, a perfect picture of old-style Hawaii from decades past. These renovated buildings are **Coastline Cottages,** and all have been brought up to date with modern comforts. The four units, a studio, a one-bedroom/two-bath, a two-bedroom/two-bath, and a three-bedroom/four-bath, run $185–650 a night with a three-night minimum. Barbecue grill and laundry facilities are on the premises. Contact P.O. Box 287, Kalaheo, HI 96741, 808/332-9688, fax 808/332-7620, email: jds@aloha.net.

You will find no bedroom closer to the gentle surf than at **Gloria's Spouting Horn Bed and Breakfast,** 4464 Lawa'i Beach Rd., Koloa, HI 96756, tel./fax 808/742-6995, website: www.best.com/~travel/gloria, email: glorbb@hotmail.com. Leveled by Hurricane 'Iniki, the one-time humble plantation house has come back as a perfectly designed and highly attractive B&B, with your comfort and privacy assured. Created by Bob and Gloria with the help of a California architect, the stout, hurricane-resistant, natural-wood post-and-beam structure supports a Polynesian longhouse-style roof. None of the three guest rooms share a common wall, and the entire home is designed for maximum exposure to the outdoors. Wide bay windows with louvers underneath bring you as close as possible to the outdoors when opened simultaneously. A nubbed burgundy carpet (no shoes inside, please) massages your feet as you pad the hall to your cross-ventilated suite, which is further cooled by ceiling fans in the main bedroom and in your private bath. Skylights let in the sun or stars, and floral wallpaper and antique tables suggest a Victorian theme. Every suite opens to a private lanai where the rolling surf and dependable whoosh of the Spouting Horn serenade you throughout the evening. All baths are private, spacious, and offer a shower, commode, and Japanese *ofuro*. Descend a central stairway to a small bar that holds port, brandy, and different liqueurs for your evening enjoyment. Breakfast is a combination of fresh fruits, fresh juices, piping hot coffee and tea, and perhaps a pizza pancake crunchy with macadamia nuts and smothered with home-made banana topping. Room rates are $225 per night, three nights minimum; no credit cards. Only a few steps from the Spouting Horn, traffic disappears at night and the quiet settles in at this absolutely excellent accommodation.

Vacation Rental Agencies

R&R Realty and Rentals, 808/742-7555 or 800/367-8022, fax 808/742-1559, website: www.r7r.com, email: randr@r7r.com, arranges only condo rentals in Po'ipu. R&R has over four dozen units in six properties, mostly in the low to midrange complexes. Studios start about $75 a night, one-, two-, and three-bedroom units run $125–175, but rates are cheaper at four nights or longer.

Po'ipu Connection Realty, 808/742-2233 or 800/742-2260, fax 808/742-7382, website: www.poipuconnection.com, email: poipu@hawaiian.net, handles private vacation condo rentals exclusively along the Po'ipu Coast. From the large complexes to a small six-plex, these units range from $75 a night for a studio to $300 a night for a deluxe oceanfront unit.

Garden Island Rentals, 808/742-9537 or 800/247-5599, fax 808/742-9540, website: www.kauairentals.com, email: gir@kauairentals.com, rents mostly high-end vacation homes and a few condo units, exclusively in the Po'ipu area. Nearly all are on or very close to the water. The condo units run $100–225 a night with a four-night minimum stay, and the homes range $800–4,500 a week with a seven-night minimum.

Grantham Resorts, 808/742-9469, 800/325-5791, or 800/742-1412, fax 808/742-9093, website: www.grantham-resorts.com, email: info@grantham-resorts.com, is in Koloa and manages both condo units and private homes, exclusively in Po'ipu. Most of its condo units are in the Waikomo Stream Villas and Nihi Kai Resort, but there are units in eight other complexes. Private home rentals run from a two-bedroom, two-bath bungalow near Koloa Landing for $160 a day to a four-bedroom, four-bath house that sleeps 10 on Po'ipu Beach for $1,375 a day. Well established, Grantham has been matching people with places since 1984.

Kauai Vacation Rentals, 3-3311 Kuhio Hwy., Lihu'e, HI 96766, 808/245-8841 or 800/357-5025, website: www.KauaiVacationRentals.com, email: aloha@kvrre.com, handles condo and vacation rental homes in Po'ipu, mostly low to midrange.

FOOD

Inexpensive

A casual place for Mexican fare is **Amigo's** at the Po'ipu Shopping Village, 808/742-2449. Order at the counter and eat in the breezeway. Everything on the menu is under $10, and choices include all the usual Mexican offerings like burritos, tacos, chimichangas, enchiladas, and the like. Vegetarian dishes are available, and vegetable oil is used instead of lard or animal fat. Take-out available. Open for lunch and dinner, 11 A.M.–9 P.M.

Brennecke's Beach Deli is just off Po'ipu Beach, below Brennecke's restaurant. The best deals are take-out hot dogs, burgers, and filling plate lunches, but it also has pastries, ice cream, and beer. For a bit more sophistication, try one of the hotel's poolside grills and cafés for a light lunch.

Joe Batteiger is a football fanatic from Cleveland, Ohio, who spent many a fall afternoon in that city's "Dog Pound." After the game, Joe and his buddies wanted to wrap their meaty fists around man-size sandwiches and wash them down with cold ones. No froufrou food for these bruisers. So Joe moved to Kaua'i and opened **Joe's Courtside Cafe,** adjacent to the Kiahuna Tennis Club (look for a sign *mauka* just past the Po'ipu Shopping Plaza), 808/742-6363, open for breakfast 7–11 A.M., lunch 11 A.M.–2 P.M., and cocktails daily. Joe serves up his fare on an elevated portico with a brick and tile floor. Start the day with eggs Benedict for $8.75, biscuits and gravy for $6.95, or you can also create your own omelettes for $7.50. Lunch selections are heartier sandwiches and grilled items. Joe has apparently done so well that he has open a second joint, **Joe's on the Green,** at the Kiahuna Golf Club clubhouse, 808/742-9696. Breakfast is pretty much the same here, with an early-bird breakfast special Mon.–Sat. 7–9 A.M. Lunch brings a personalized house salad that you build yourself for $5.75, grilled chicken breast at $8.25, and a variety of sandwiches priced $6.50–7.95. The grill serves up such treats as a Joe Mama burger for $6.75, a grilled chicken breast sandwich for $7, and A Dog Named Joe for $5.25, served with a wedge of kosher pickle and authentic stadium mustard imported from Cleveland. Happy hour runs 3–5:30 P.M., and dinners are now served Thursday and Friday 5:30–9 P.M. Both Joe's places are sleepers, known mostly to local people who come time and again to get a fine breakfast or lunch at a reasonable price. Some swear it's the best breakfast in town.

Moderate
La Griglia, at the Po'ipu Shopping Village, 808/742-2147, open 7 A.M.–10 P.M., offers American standards and Italian dishes directly from Calabria created by owner Cathy Gargalonne. Breakfast brings omelettes and eggs for around $7, and the homemade cinnamon rolls and various muffins sell out quickly. Lunch, served 11 A.M.–5 P.M., and dinner, 5–10 P.M., bring out the real Italian with various antipasto, pasta, salads, and casseroles. The lunch and dinner menus are similar but prices are a few bucks less at lunch, when you'll also find layered sandwiches on the menu. Dinner entrées mostly run $9.95–14.95 and include meat or veggie lasagna, chicken or eggplant parmigiana, lemon chicken angel hair pasta, spaghetti with meatballs, and fettuccine quattro fromaggio. Pizzas for $14.95–21.95 are served all day. Beside the espresso bar, beverages include wines by the bottle or glass and beer; happy hour is 3–6 P.M. daily.

Representing foods from the many ethnic groups of the islands is **The Plantation House,** 808/742-7373, a casual open-air restaurant at the Po'ipu Shopping Village. Served 7–10 A.M., breakfast might be buttermilk pancakes or *loco moco,* all for under $7.25. Lunch, 11 A.M.–3 P.M. includes Portuguese bean soup, Chinese chicken salad, and tempura mahimahi sandwich. Stop in 5–9 P.M. for dinner, when most entrées are in the $15–19 range, like Hawaiian-style barbecued chicken, hot and spicy chili shrimp, and New York steak. Pizza can be ordered, and kids have a special menu; cocktails are available.

An indoor/outdoor café, **Pattaya Asian Cafe,** at the Po'ipu Shopping Village, 808/742-8818, is open 11:30 A.M.–2:30 P.M. for lunch and 5:30–9:30 P.M. for dinner. This is a very tasteful, moderately priced restaurant appointed with a flagstone floor and Thai mahogany tables and chairs. The ornate mahogany bar, covered by a pagoda roof, flashes with mirrors embedded in two gold and blue swans. The exotic menu starts with *mee grop,* a dish of crispy noodles, chicken, bean sprouts, and green onions; Bangkok wings, a concoction of long rice, onion, black mushrooms, carrots, and ground pork served with the house peanut sauce; and delicious fish cakes or sautéed calamari, ranging in price $7.95–9.25. Soups and salads are spicy lemongrass soup for $10.95, a Thai ginger coconut soup with chicken or seafood at $7.25–10.95, and fresh island papaya salad for $5.95. More substantial meals include *pad Thai,* a traditional noodle dish for $9.25; spicy fried rice ranging $6.95–9.25 depending upon ingredients; red, green, and yellow curry made with chicken, pork, beef, or shrimp $7.95–14.95; and plenty of vegetarian selections. All dishes can be ordered to the spice level you desire. Pattaya Asian Cafe is a terrific and authentic restaurant with friendly service and good prices, and you know the food will be good because the owner uses herbs from his own garden.

You can find other midpriced restaurants at the hotels and clubhouses in Po'ipu. Try the **Po'ipu Bay Bar and Grill** at the Po'ipu Bay Golf Course clubhouse, 808/742-1515. Open 6:30 A.M.–3 P.M. for breakfast and lunch, with *pu pu* and happy hour until 7 P.M., this moderately priced restaurant serves mostly American standards, with the addition of a Japanese breakfast and various plate lunches. On Thurs.–Sat. evenings, the grill and bar stay open until 10 P.M. or 11 P.M., with the accompaniment of live entertainment. Seated inside or out, you'll have fantastic views over the fairways of the Ha'upu Ridge and coastline.

Two restaurants in the Po'ipu area that are more expensive than moderate places, but not quite in the fine dining category are Brennecke's Beach Broiler and Keoki's Paradise. **Brennecke's Beach Broiler,** an open-air, second-story deck directly across from Po'ipu Beach County Park, 808/742-7588, offers a superb view. Seafood is the dinner specialty, but pasta and *kiawe*-broiled meat and chicken are also served. Dinner prices range $16.50–22.95. Salads and sandwiches are served for lunch, and *pu pu* until closing. There is a children's menu for both lunch and dinner. Lunch is 11 A.M.–4 P.M., happy hour 2–5 P.M., dinner 4–10 P.M., and early dinner special 4–6 P.M. Brennecke's is a fun, casual place with tasty food, a good choice for a family on vacation. As it's popular and not a big place, call for a reservation.

Keoki's Paradise, at the Po'ipu Shopping Village, 808/742-7534, is an excellent choice for dinner or a night's entertainment. Enter past a small fountain into the longhouse-style interior with stone floor and thatched roof. Choose a seat at the long bar for a casual evening or at one of the tables overlooking the garden surrounding the restaurant. The varied menu lists savory items including Thai shrimp sticks for $8.95; fresh catch for $19.95 prepared a variety of ways including baked, herb-sautéed, teriyaki-grilled, or in an orange ginger sauce; pesto macadamia shrimp for $16.95; or beef dishes like top sirloin at $16.95 and prime rib for $23.95. Keoki's renowned dessert is its Hula Pie, a mound of ice cream filling an Oreo cookie crust, that's big enough for at least two. Simpler and cheaper, the Cafe Menu (available 11 A.M.–11:30 P.M. at the bar), includes *pu pu,* burgers, salads, sandwiches, and plate lunches. "Aloha Fridays" brings food and drink specials 4:30–7 P.M. A great selection of beer and mixed drinks adds to an enjoyable evening. Have an island drink before going in to dinner, served 5:30–10 P.M. Live entertainment is offered Thurs.–Sat. by local bands specializing in contemporary Hawaiian music, and again Sunday 3–6 P.M. Keoki's is a feel-good place that fills you up with large portions of tasty food.

In 2000, **Casa di Amici** moved from its north shore location to the south shore, for a good view overlooking the Po'ipu coastline. Upscale down-home, Casa di Amici serves Italian cuisine with a touch of Asia and France mixed in. It's about one block from the beach at 2301 Nalo Rd; call 808/742-1555 for reservations.

Fine Dining

Exquisite dining can be enjoyed at various restaurants, some overlooking Po'ipu's beaches—perfect for catching the setting sun—and others in elegant gardens bathed by tropical breezes. Prices are high, but you definitely get a full measure of what you pay for. Reservations are recommended at all these fine-dining establishments.

At the Kiahuna Plantation Resort in what once was the plantation manager's home, under towering trees and surrounded by lush greenery, **Piatti** restaurant, 808/742-2216, open nightly 5:30–10:30 P.M., serves northern Italian food with a strong influence of Pacific Rim style. Start with a cold poached shrimp or Thai beef salad appetizer, $7.95–10.95. Salads or gourmet pizzas could follow, or try an entrée such as rotisserie chicken, sugarcane pork tenderloin, miso shiitake risotto with sesame fish, or lobster and taro linguine, $15.95–27.95. The combinations of tastes are tantalizing and the creations unique. Full bar.

At the Po'ipu Shopping Village, culinary magic is created at **Roy's Po'ipu Bar and Grill,** 808/742-5000, open nightly for dinner 5:30–9:30 P.M. Here, in an open kitchen—one of Roy's trademarks—the chef de cuisine and a superbly trained staff create an array of marvelous dishes from the island's freshest meats, fish, poultry, fruits, and vegetables. The chef's "specials sheet" changes nightly, but a sampling of the delectable dishes that you may enjoy includes dim sum appetizers like crispy smoked duck gyoza, crispy Asian spring rolls, sweet basil-crusted beef sauté, and ravioli with shiitake and spinach. Healthy green salads and *imu*-baked pizzas are also available. A few entrées usually on the menu are lemongrass-crusted chicken, grilled shrimp, and pot roast trimmed with mashed potatoes and old-fashioned apple ginger pineapple sauce. The specials sheet always has fresh fish and seafood, like basil-seared *ono* with Thai red curry and lobster sauce, macadamia-nut-crusted *hevi* with a mango and coconut sauce, and sesame-seared *uku* with a shiitake cream sauce, all at market price. Most entrées are in the $15–25 range. Roy's offers a memorable dining experience.

Another superb eatery is the **Beach House Restaurant,** 808/742-1424, open daily for dinner 5:30–10 P.M. The menu varies nightly, but expect a blending of East and West with a Mediterranean flair. Sunset at the Beach House couldn't

KAUA'I

be better. This restaurant had new owners beginning in January 2000, so only time will tell if they keep the standard set by former restaurateur and chef Jean-Marie Josselin.

The **House of Seafood** at Po'ipu Kai Resort, 808/742-6433, has windows framing living still-lifes of palm fronds and flower gardens against a background of the distant ocean. It consistently has the largest selection of fresh fish in the area, often with at least 10 varieties, and its dishes are very creative—baked in puff pastry, sautéed with macadamia nut sauce, or steamed in a ginger sauce, to name a few. Ask the waiter for the best choice of the day. Although fish and seafood are its specialty, steak and chicken are also on the menu. Start your meal off with an appetizer, soup, or salad, and finish with a creamy island-fruit dessert or drink. Entrées run $20–39, a children's menu $7–13. The House of Seafood is a restaurant for a special occasion; locals speak highly of the quality of its food. Open nightly for dinner only, with happy hour and *pu pu* 3–5 P.M.

The main dining room at the Hyatt is the **Ilima Terrace,** 808/742-1234, open daily for breakfast, lunch, and dinner, with both buffet and à la carte menus. Descend a formal staircase and step onto a slate floor covered with an emerald green carpet. Floor-to-ceiling beveled glass doors look out onto the lovely grounds, and seating is pleasant inside or out. Start your day with a choice of fresh chilled juices, hearty omelettes, or griddle items, where most selections are under $10. If it's hard to choose, try the Ilima Breakfast Buffet at $17.50 daily, $19.75 on Sunday, or sleep in Sunday for the hearty champagne brunch for $28.95. Lunch is à la carte and brings starters like smoked chicken quesadillas, deli board items of soup, salad, and sandwiches. Move on to seared 'ahi, prawn noodles, or your choice of pizza, with nothing over $16. The à la carte dinner menu is an expanded version of lunch offerings, but you may also choose the buffet for $28.95, that rotates daily to Italian, Hawaiian seafood, or prime rib. Desserts include triple chocolate torte, coconut cream pie, and chocolate crème brûlée. Children can get reduced portions for half price. There is a full-service bar, with wine, beer, and cappuccino.

Dondero's, featuring classic Italian cuisine, is the Hyatt's signature restaurant, 808/742-1234, open for dinner only 6–10 P.M. The continental room is formal, and the view through floor-to-ceiling windows is of the manicured gardens. Dinner begins with antipasti, such as calamari fritti and carpaccio, for $8.50–12.50, and moves on to soups and salads, mostly under $10. Rigatoni alla Bolognese and other traditional pastas, osso bucco, cioppino, and many other fish and meat selections fill the menu and cost $16.50–28.25. Round out your meal with tiramisu or another dessert, and coffee or cordials. In addition to dessert wines, Dondero's has table wine to complement any entrée. Resort attire is a must.

Slightly more casual is the Hyatt's **Tidepool Restaurant,** 808/742-1234, open for dinner only 6–10 P.M., a mushroom cluster of thatched South Sea "huts" supported by huge beams forming an indoor/outdoor restaurant overlooking the tide pools. Low-light and romantic, the Tidepool boasts fresh fish, sautéed, seared, grilled, or steamed, with a medley of sauces and toppings to choose from. This contemporary Hawaiian cuisine also includes grilled steak and ribs. Entrées run $23–36.

The Sheraton also offers sumptuous food in fine settings. **Shells,** 808/742-1661, the Sheraton's signature restaurant, is set on a rocky point almost at water's edge. Facing east and commanding a superb view of the white sand and rich blue water of the bay, it's a perfect place to start the day. Served 6:30–11 A.M., Shells' breakfast has a well-deserved reputation. It includes traditional American and some international selections, off the menu or as a buffet. For an evening meal, order either as complete dinner or à la carte. Items include any number of fresh fish, broiled, baked, steamed, or sautéed and covered in saffron cream, citrus glaze, teriyaki, beurre blanc, or tartar sauces. Other choices are roast prime rib, pork loin, macadamia- and panko-crusted chicken breast, and a variety of pasta dishes. The salad bar always includes locally grown greens. Entrées run $23.95–35.95, or $9 less à la carte. In addition to the usual menu, the Friday Night Seafood Buffet is making a reputation for itself; it runs $34.95. Dinner is served 5:30–9:30 P.M. daily.

The traditional-style Japanese restaurant **Naniwa** overlooks a koi pond in the Sheraton's garden wing, 808/742-1661. Sushi is a favorite here, as are the fish preparations. Naniwa is perhaps best known for its Saturday Evening Buffet at $31.95 a person. Open daily except Monday and Friday 5:30–9:30 P.M..

ENTERTAINMENT

If, after a sunset dinner and a lovely stroll along the beach, you find yourself with dancing feet or a desire to hear the strains of your favorite tunes, Po'ipu won't let you down. Several hotel restaurants and lounges in the area feature piano music or small combos, often with a Hawaiian flair.

The Point lounge at the Sheraton gives you a ringside seat for sunset and perhaps the best coastal view in Po'ipu, open for drinks and cocktails 11 A.M.–1 A.M. Light meals of soups, salads, and sandwiches are served 11 A.M.–3 P.M., and *pu pu* 5–10 P.M. **The Point** follows sunset with the soft sounds of light jazz and contemporary music Wed.–Fri. 8:30–11:30 P.M., and Saturday 10 P.M.–1 A.M. For live jazz nightly try **Stevenson's Library** at the Hyatt. This is the poshest lounge on the island—resortwear requested.

Free Hawaiian music is presented nightly starting around sundown at the Hyatt's **Seaview Terrace,** and this show is accompanied by a torch-lighting ceremony every evening except Tuesday and Sunday, which bring a *keiki* hula show. Come for *pu pu* and cocktails and enjoy the captivating entertainment.

Keoki's, in the Po'ipu Shopping Village, gently sways with contemporary Hawaiian music Thurs.–Sat. evenings, and again on Sunday 3–6 P.M. Come for dinner or a quiet beer and *pu pu,* and let your cares drift away. The small dance floor is popular with those from the area.

A perk for those perusing the shops at the Po'ipu Shopping Village are the **free dance shows** performed every Monday and Thursday at 5:30 P.M. in the center's outdoor courtyard.

Every Thursday and Sunday evening 6–8:30 P.M., the **Drums of Paradise** lu'au is presented at the Ilima Garden at the Hyatt Regency. A full buffet dinner includes the usual complement of Hawaiian and Pacific foods, and the meal is followed by an enthusiastic and high-energy Polynesian show. Adult tickets are $59.50 while children 6–12 years old get in for half price. This is the only lu'au performed along the entire south coast.

SHOPPING

Shopping in Po'ipu is varied and reasonably extensive for such a small area. The Po'ipu Shopping Village has the largest concentration of shops, but don't forget Po'ipu Plaza, the hotel arcades, and the Spouting Horn flea market.

Po'ipu Shopping Village

The Po'ipu Shopping Village offers unique one-stop shopping. The **Ship Store Gallery,** open daily 9 A.M.–9 P.M., provides all things nautical including sea-inspired art, especially of the great sailing days of discovery. Next door is **Wyland Galleries,** featuring some of the island's best painters and sculptors. **Hale Mana** carries fine arts and Asian antiques. **The Black Pearl Collection** sells pearls and jewelry; **Xan** does designer jewelry. **Sand Kids** features distinctive children's wear, while half a dozen shops cater to adults. Next door to each other you'll find **Overboard For Men** and **Overboard For Women,** both featuring casual to elegant alohawear. **Bamboo Lace** offers dresses, blouses, hats, jewelry, and a smattering of alohawear. It's owned and operated by Nadine, who handpicks fashionable clothing from the continent. Shelves also hold bath and skin-care products, gift items, lingerie, fancy shoes, and straw hats. For general merchandise items, stop at the **Whalers General Store.**

Food Stores

Po'ipu is home to the generally well-stocked **Kukui'ula Store,** at Po'ipu Plaza, open Mon.–Fri. 8 A.M.–8:30 P.M. and Sat.–Sun. until 6:30 P.M., where you'll find groceries, produce, bakery goods, sundries, and liquor. **Whaler's General Store,** at Po'ipu Shopping Village, open daily 7:30 A.M.–10 P.M., is a well-stocked convenience store with a good selection of wines and liquors, souvenirs, and gifts; **Brennecke's Beach Deli,** across from Po'ipu Beach County Park has a small selection of canned and packaged goods and food to go.

If you're staying in a Po'ipu condo and are buying large quantities of food, you may save money by making the trip to one of the larger markets in Koloa.

For fresh fruit and vegetables and a number of ready-made gift baskets, try the open-air **Po'ipu**

KAUA'I

South Shore Market, at the corner of Po'ipu Road and the Koloa-Po'ipu Bypass. Local farmers also have a stand set up along Po'ipu Beach Road near the cane haul road between Koloa and the coast.

Photo Needs

Po'ipu One Hour Photo, at the Po'ipu Plaza, 808/742-9303, does film developing.

RECREATION

Golf

Designed by Robert Trent Jones Jr., the **Kiahuna Golf Club,** 808/742-9595, is an 18-hole, par 70 course just up the road from Po'ipu Shopping Village. Undulating over land up from the coast, this course preserves several archaeological sites. The course is open for play 7 A.M. until sunset, the pro shop hours are 6:30 A.M.–6:30 P.M., and a restaurant is available throughout the day. Greens fees run $38 for 9 holes and $75 for a full 18 holes; midday, twilight, hotel guest, resident, junior, and package rates are also available. Lessons can be arranged.

The Po'ipu Bay Golf Course, 808/742-8711 or 800/858-6300, the site of the PGA Grand Slam of Golf since 1994, is a par-72 Scottish links-style course also designed by Robert Trent Jones Jr. and opened in 1991. With 6,959 magnificent yards (gold tees) rolling along the oceanside cliffs with the mountains as backdrop, it's noted for stunning views and is described as the Pebble Beach of the Pacific. Seven of the 18 holes have water hazards, making for challenging play. For practice, try the driving range, putting greens, and practice bunker. The excellent pro shop is open 6:30 A.M.–6 P.M.; call for tee times or for use of the driving range. At the clubhouse, the Po'ipu Bay Grill and Bar serves light meals until 3 P.M. and drinks until 7 P.M., later on the weekends. Fees run $145, $95 after noon, and $60 for twilight. Lessons, club rental, and the practice range are extra.

Tennis

Several hotels and condominiums in the Po'ipu area have tennis courts for their guests, but three are open to anyone. The largest is the **Kiahuna Tennis Club,** just east of the Po'ipu Shopping Village and across the street from the Kiahuna Plantation Resort, 808/742-9533. Kiahuna has 10 plexipave courts, a pro shop, and rental equipment. Court fees are complimentary for Kiahuna Plantation Resort guests but $10 per court time for others. Ball machines are $20 an hour, basket of balls $10, racquet and shoes $5 apiece. Clinics are available for $10–12, and it's $45 for a one-hour private lesson. Call for court times and inquiries about clinics and lessons. The Kiahuna Plantation Resort swimming pool is at the tennis club; both pool and club are open 7:30 A.M.–6 P.M. Adjacent to the pro shop and open for breakfast and lunch is Joe's Courtside Cafe.

The second well-equipped tennis facility is the **Po'ipu Kai Resort Tennis Center,** 808/742-2229, open 7 A.M.–6 P.M. with eight plexipave courts. Free to resort guests, there is a $5 an hour charge for others. Although it's more relaxed here than at the Kiahuna Tennis Club, proper attire is required and you should leave the court ready for those who follow you. Round robins and clinics are held throughout the week for $6–10, and private lessons run $30 an hour. Racquets and ball machines can be rented.

The Hyatt Regency **Tennis Garden,** 808/742-1234, has four hard courts and is open 7 A.M.–6 P.M. Court fees are $20 an hour, racquets can be rented for $5, and a ball machine costs $10 an hour. Morning clinics are scheduled and private lessons can be arranged for $50 an hour.

Bicycling and Kayaking

Outfitters Kauai, in the Po'ipu Plaza, 808/742-9667 or 888/742-9887, website: www.outfitterskauai.com, open daily 9 A.M.–5 P.M. is a kayak and biking shop. Daily rental rates for bicycles are $20 for a cruiser, $30 for a road bike, and $20–33 for a mountain bike. All come with a helmet, lock, and water bottle. Outfitters Kauai also organizes a Bicycle Downhill bike ride that brings you up the Waimea Canyon so you can glide down to the coast. Rental kayaks and various guided kayak tours are also available. Outfitters Kauai retails biking and kayaking incidentals in its shop along with Patagonia clothing—shorts, sweatshirts, shirts, and even hats.

Water Sports

Seasport Divers, at Po'ipu Plaza, 2827 Po'ipu Rd., 808/742-9303 or 800/685-5889, website:

www.kauaiscubadiving.com, is a full-service snorkel/scuba/surf shop. Rentals include snorkel masks, fins, and snorkels at $5 per hour, $15 per day, and surfboard rentals differ depending on quality. Two-tank introductory boat or shore dives run $110, and a one-tank shore dive is $85. A full-day three-tank boat dive to Ni'ihau runs $230–270. A three-day certification courses for small groups goes for $350 or $495 for private lessons. Seasport Divers is also a sports boutique with boogie boards, surfboards, and all sorts of water equipment, and within the shop is a clothing section and a one-hour photo finisher.

World surfing champion Margo Oberg or one of her staff members will teach you how to mount a board and ride gracefully over the shimmering sea. Beginning classes of one hour of instruction and a half hour of practice at Po'ipu Beach run $45 per person. Make reservations through Nukumoi Surf Co., 808/742-8019.

Across from Brennecke's Beach is **Nukumoi Surf Co.**, 808/742-8019, open 8:30 A.M.–7 P.M. daily. Not only does this shop arrange surf lessons with Margo Oberg, they rent surf boards and other water equipment. Boogie boards or snorkel gear go for $5 a day or $15 a week. Nukumoi is very convenient to the beach. This is also a retail shop, so a full line of water equipment and clothing is for sale.

Kauai Z-TourZ, 808/742-6331, website: www.ztourz.com, does Zodiac tours from Kukui'ula Harbor to Kipu Kai and Lawa'i Kai. The cost is $90 adult and $70 for children for a five-hour tour, and the three-hour tour goes for $60 for adults and $50 for kids. A five-hour winter tour up the Na Pali Coast starts at Kikiaola Harbor near Waimea and costs $120 for adults and $90 for kids.

Horseback Riding

If you're into horseback riding, try **CJM Country Stables**, 808/742-6096, for any of its three scheduled rides. The two-hour, easy beach ride leaves at 9:30 A.M. and 2 P.M. and costs $65. Departing at 8:30 A.M., the beach breakfast ride takes you to a secluded beach girdled by high mountains where you relax while breakfast is prepared for you; it costs $75 and runs three hours. The longer beach, swim, and picnic ride leaves at noon and costs $90. Not all rides are offered every day. CJM is about 1.5 miles past the Hyatt Regency on Po'ipu Road.

Hike

Every other Monday at 9 A.M., the Hyatt Regency, 808/742-1234, offers a free two-hour guided hike along the coastal bluffs and dunes toward Maha'ulepu Beach. The Anara Spa, also at the Hyatt, sponsors morning walks along the beach and golf course.

An exclusive jogging/biking path has opened in Po'ipu for those who don't want to worry about vehicular traffic. The gated pathway starts next to the Kiahuna Tennis Courts and runs for 1.2 mile up toward Koloa.

Spa

In its own facility at the Hyatt Regency is the distinctive green tile roof of the horseshoe-shaped **Anara Spa**, 808/742-1234. This spa offers total immersion into health and fitness, and general pampering of aching muscles and jangled nerves 6 A.M.–8 P.M. daily. The treatment rooms offer ancient Hawaiian and modern remedies for energy and rejuvenation. All rooms are indoor/outdoor, with mini-gardens and the serenade of falling waters to help relax and soothe. Various massages, facials, body treatments, and aromatherapies can be booked individually or as packages, and the salon offers hair, makeup, nail, and waxing services. The Anara Spa also offers a lap pool, aerobics room, complete training equipment, fitness assessment, personal training, and a morning walk along the beach or sand bluffs near the golf course. After a serious workout, relax at the spa's poolside Kupono Cafe for a health-conscious, low-calorie meal.

Other

The Hyatt Regency hotel offers an **astronomy show** at 8 and 9:30 P.M. nightly, weather permitting, except for the period of about 10 nights around the full moon, when it's just too bright. Led by a local astronomer, you will peruse the sky by naked eye and telescope. The cost is $25, limit eight people. Sign up at the hotel concierge desk or call 808/742-1234.

INFORMATION

General Information

The **Po'ipu Beach Resort Association**, P.O. Box 730, Koloa, HI 96756, 808/742-7444 or

800/262-1400, website: http://poipu-beach.org, email: info@poipu-beach.org, is an excellent nonprofit organization that can help you plan your trip in the Po'ipu area. It can provide brochures and tips on everything from dining to accommodations, and provides an online reservation system; ask for its 36-page planning brochure, also available on the Web.

Brennecke's Beach Center, 808/742-7505, offers information and can set you up with any kind of activity on the island. Rental beach gear is offered at affordable rates.

There are no banks in Po'ipu, but the two hotels will cash traveler's checks for their guests. The closest bank is in Koloa, as is the nearest post office and medical clinic.

INLAND TOWNS

LAWA'I

In times past, *ali'i* from throughout the kingdom came to Lawa'i to visit an ancient fishpond in the caldera of an extinct volcano. Legend says that this was the first attempt by Madame Pele to dig herself a fiery home. From more recent times, look into the valley below town to see an abandoned pineapple factory.

Accommodations

Perched on a steep hillside above a green pasture and facing the high mountains at the center of the island, **Marjorie's Kauai Inn,** P.O. Box 866, Lawa'i, HI 96765, 808/332-8838 or 800/717-8838, website: www.planet-hawaii.com/marjorie, email: ketcher@aloha.net, has an unbeatable location. You have your choice of three private rooms, two with showers and one with a bath, each with private mini-kitchen, cable TV, radio, phone, and its own entrance. Also included are access to a hot tub, a barbecue grill, and laundry facilities. Light, bright, and cheery, all rooms open onto a lanai that overlooks the valley. Very accommodating, Marjorie can arrange activities for you and will encourage you to have wonderful adventures during your stay. This place is a find, quiet and rural. Room rates are $78 and $88, and $15 for each additional person over two.

Set amongst thick vegetation on a quiet cul-de-sac, with a fine view of the distant ocean, is **Victoria Place B&B,** P.O. Box 930, Lawa'i, HI 96765, 808/332-9300, fax 808/332-9465, website: www.hshawaii.com/kvp/victoria, email: edeev@aloha.net. Presided over by the gracious and warmhearted Edee Seymour, a transplant from the Mainland, Victoria Place is more like a home than a guest house. Edee fills you with a hearty breakfast and pastries, can clue you in on what to see and where to go, and always respects your privacy. The three rooms, one handicapped-accessible and another set up for a single traveler only, all have private bathrooms and run $60–80. These open onto the swimming pool at the front of the house. Down below, Victoria's Other Secret is a studio apartment with its own entrance, bath, and kitchen that goes for $100 a night. For any of the rooms, add $10 per room for one-night stays. No credit cards accepted. Everyone shares the back lanai and can borrow books from Edee's huge collection.

Food

In town next to the post office, at mile marker 10, is the **Lawa'i Restaurant,** 808/332-9550, open Mon.–Thurs. 10 A.M.–8 P.M. and Fri.–Sat. 9 A.M.–9 P.M., closed Sunday. This very local restaurant serves American standards and Asian food at very reasonable prices. You know this has to be a decent place as the police regularly make it their lunch stop. Next door is **Menehune Food Mart,** a reasonably well-stocked way station open daily.

Mustard's Last Stand at the Hawaiian Trading Post features more than a dozen varieties of hot dogs and sausages, burgers, sandwiches, fish and chips, and delicious scoops of island-flavored Lappert's ice cream. The place lives up to its name—the self-serve condiment/mustard table has a dozen and a half trimmings to flavor your dog. Picnic tables in a pleasant grove of coconut, breadfruit, orange African tulip, and purple Hong Kong orchid trees sit across the parking lot. Everything at Mustard's (except the food) is made out of old surfboards. Notice the bottles that have been embedded in the cement floor, and the wave to the rear, fashioned from

Mustard's Last Stand, featuring all the trimmings for your dog

J.D. BISIGNANI

plaster, where you can stand on a surfboard and have your picture taken. Mustard's is excellent for what it has to offer, and the service is friendly. It's a big hit with the kids and reminds parents of roadside joints of times past. Most everything on the menu is less than $4.

Shopping

At the intersection of Koloa Road and Kaumuali'i Highway (Rts. 50 and 530), is the **Hawaiian Trading Post** gift shop. Referred to by locals as "the tourist trap," the Hawaiian Trading Post sells a mind-boggling variety of hand-crafted items as well as a large selection of souvenirs, treasures, and tourist junk. Other selections include T-shirts, jewelry, black pearls, post cards, and carvings, and an excellent display of Ni'ihau shell lei that should be featured but are stuck away in the back. These Ni'ihau shell lei, some for display only and some for sale, are perhaps the best collection of shell lei on the island—worth the stop by themselves. Occupying a portion of the same building is **Lee Sands,** featuring goods made from eel skin and other exotic leathers.

A short way down Koloa Road is **Lawa'i General Store,** for sundries and a few groceries.

KALAHEO

The area around Kalaheo is springing up with many new housing subdivisions, and large tracts of coffee, tea, and macadamia nut trees are tinting the hillsides in new shades of green. Throughout the state there are pockets of population groups with heavier concentrations than elsewhere; for Kalaheo, it's the Portuguese. In town are three gas stations, a liquor store, post office, a medical clinic and pharmacy, restaurants, a mini-mart, and a new office/shopping plaza, all along Route 50, making Kalaheo the first sizable town between Lihu'e and Hanapepe where you can pick up anything you may need before continuing west.

For a great view over the lowlands from the heights, take a drive up Puulima Road, Kikala Road, or Wawae Road above town. Drive slowly and cautiously—the roads are very steep—and it is a residential area.

Kukui O Lono Park

Kukui O Lono Park is a personal gift from Walter D. McBryde, the well-known plantation owner who donated the land to the people of Kaua'i in 1919. Accept it! It's off the beaten track but worth the trip. Turn left in Kalaheo at the Menehune Food Mart and go along Papalina Road for one mile until you come to the second Pu'u Road—the first turnoff to Pu'u Road skirts the hill below the park and circles back to the second Pu'u Rd. turnoff. A sharp right turn brings you through the large stone-and-metal gate (open 6:30 A.M.–6:30 P.M.) Inside the park is a public golf course and Japanese-style garden. The entrance road leads through a tunnel of eucalyptus trees to a commemorative plaque to McBryde. A

KAUA'I

flock of green parrots that nest in the tall euca-lyptus trees on the grounds can be heard in a symphony of sound in the early evening.

For the gardens and McBryde's memorial, go straight ahead to the parking lot; to get to the clubhouse, follow the road to your right for about a half mile. As the park is set on top of a hill, the sweeping views in all directions are striking. During the winter months, you may be able to spot whales spouting along the coast below. Unfortunately, perfectly placed in the center of one of the nicest views is a microwave antenna and dish. Set amidst a grove of towering trees, the Japanese garden offers peace and tranquil-lity. Occasionally, weddings are held here. The whole scene is conducive to Zen-like medita-tion. Enjoy it.

At the **Kukuiolono Golf Course** clubhouse, 808/332-9151, are a pro shop and snack bar. A round of golf on the par-36 course is $7; carts and clubs are rented at a similarly reasonable rate. Lessons are $15 a half-hour and must be arranged with the pro. Having opened in 1929 for the workers of the McBryde sugar plantation, this is the second oldest golf course on the island.

Accommodations

Classic Vacation Cottages, 2687 Onu Pl., P.O. Box 901, Kalaheo, HI 96741, 808/332-9201, fax 808/7645, website: www.classiccottages.com, email: clascot@hawaiian.net, has five homey units where you can expect low daily rates while enjoying excellent access to nearby attractions. Rates are $45 and $60 for the two studios, $70–75 for the two cottages, and $85 for the house that sleeps up to six; for more than two people, add $10 a person. No credit cards ac-cepted. Each unit has at least one stained-glass window, and all have kitchen facilities, cable TV, and ceiling fans. No breakfasts are served, but guests have free use of snorkel gear, tennis rac-quets, and golf clubs. Good value and seclusion.

The restored plantation home of District Judge Jardine, constructed in 1926, is now the **Kalaheo Plantation Estate** vacation home, 4579 Pu'uwai Rd., P.O. Box 872, Kalaheo, HI 96741, 808/332-7812 or 888/332-7812, website: www.kala-heo-plantation.com, email: kalaheo1@gte.net. Although some attempt has been made to keep with the old style, much of the renovation is mod-ern in tone and still needs a loving hand in places. The Magnolia, Orchid, and Hibiscus suites include private baths, kitchens, seating areas, and lanai, while the Blue Ginger Room has a kitchenette and bath with shower. Each has a private entrance, and all guests can use the screened front lanai. No breakfast is served. Rates run $55–75 a night; weekly and monthly rates are available, or the whole house can be yours for $200 for eight people or $300 for up to 14. No credit cards.

Behind the Kalaheo Steak House is the **Kala-heo Inn,** P.O. Box 584, Kalaheo, HI 96741, 808/332-6023, or 888/332-6023, fax 808/742-6432, website: www.kalaheoinn.com, email: chet@aloha.net. Once a ratbag dive for overnight and long-term stays, this inn has been totally re-modeled into a bright and cheery place with lots of local character. These are basic apartment-like units, reasonably priced, and great for those who care more about what they eat and see than where they sleep. Each unit has separate living room, bedroom, and kitchen or kitchenette areas, queen or twin beds, ceiling fans, TV, and a bath with shower. New tile and vinyl flooring take the place of carpet. There are washers and dryers on the premises. Rooms run $65–75.

Food

Local people out for an evening meal at rea-sonable prices give the nod to **Kalaheo Steak House,** 4444 Papalina Rd., 808/332-9780, open daily 5:30–9:30 P.M., where you can get a well-prepared and hearty portion of steak, seafood, pork, or poultry, and, reputedly, one of the best dinner salads on the island. While you wait for your main dish, try the steamer clams, brought to your table in a bucket, or the wonderful Por-tuguese bean soup. Most menu items are in the $14–20 range. Make a left at the signal along Route 50 in Kalaheo and look for a green build-ing on the left with an awning. The interior, very much in steakhouse motif, is completely knotty pine—simple, but tasteful, offering seating at a combination of black leatherette booths and ta-bles with captain's chairs. A mural of tropical fish completes the decor. Local lore has it that when you leave Kalaheo Steak house, the *dog-gie bag* contains more food than you're usually served at most restaurants.

If you're interested in a pizza, stop in at **Brick Oven Pizza,** 808/332-8561, open Tues.–Sun.

11 A.M.–10 P.M., on the mountain side just as you enter Kalaheo. Pizzas range in price from $8.75 for a 10-inch cheese pizza to $26.35 for a large 15-inch deluxe with all the toppings, on whole wheat or white crust with garlic butter glazing. Brick Oven also prepares oven-baked sandwiches for around $6.50, pizza bread for $2.75, and a variety of salads. Wine, beer, and soft drinks are available. If you're heading to Waimea or Polihale, call ahead to have a pizza ready for you. While a bit on the pricey side, Brick Oven has a well-deserved excellent local reputation.

Chefs Tony and Rosario serve a mix of traditional northern and southern Italian cuisine at **Pomodoro Ristorante Italiano,** in the Rainbow Plaza on the left as you enter Kalaheo, 808/332-5945, open nightly 5:30–10 P.M. The menu opens with classics like mozzarella, prosciutto, or calamari antipasti, ranging in price $6.50–9.50, a mixed green salad at $4.95, and a Caesar for $5.95. Pasta is spaghetti with meatballs or Italian sausage for $11.95, linguine shrimp marinara at $16.95, fettuccine Alfredo for $11.50, and an assortment of ravioli, cannelloni, manicotti, and lasagna in different sauces priced at $13.95–14.95. Specialties are veal parmigiana or piccata at $18.95, eggplant parmigiana at $16.95, and chicken saltimbocca for $17.95. The wine list, by the bottle or glass, includes wines from California and Italy. Top off your meal with an espresso and an Italian dessert made fresh daily. The dining room is small, intimate, and island-flavored, and the waitstaff are professional. You'll be happy you came, and you'll leave a well-fed individual.

Another option for food is the blue-and-white **Camp House Grill,** across from the Menehune Food Mart at the stop light, 808/332-9755. Specializing in burgers and Hawaiian-style barbecued chicken, the Camp House Grill is open for breakfast daily 6:30–10:30 A.M. and for lunch and dinner 11 A.M.–9 P.M. Menu items are basic American standards with a Hawaiian twist and include the famous Camp House breakfasts, like a flour tortilla stuffed with scrambled eggs, sausage, and cheeses, topped with sauce and served with rice or Camp House hash browns at $4.95, a variety of omelettes for around $6.95, and early-bird specials for as little as $2.55. Lunches and dinners start with salad, soup, and chili, but it's most famous for its burgers and fries, ranging $3.95–4.95, some with unusual toppings like grilled pineapple and teriyaki sauce. Evening specialties are barbecued pork ribs at $14.95 and huli chicken at $7.95. All the luscious home-made pies, like macadamia nut pie, pineapple cream cheese pie, and sour cream apple pie, are baked here in the kitchen. A nice homey touch is an ongoing children's placemat-coloring contest. When completed, the entries are pinned to the wall as permanent mementos, and prizes include free meals and coloring sets. Although not gourmet, the Camp House Grill offers honest, filling, and moderately priced food.

For coffee in all its permutations, try the **Kalaheo Coffee Co. and Cafe,** 808/332-5858, near the main intersection in town. Aside from getting coffee by the cup, you can buy pound and half-pound packages of (mostly) Hawaiian coffee, whole bean or ground, blended or unblended, and even have it shipped. Breakfast items like omelettes, eggs, and pancakes are served 6–11 A.M. and lunch runs 10:30 A.M.–4 P.M. (grill closes at 3:30 P.M.) for salads, sandwiches, and grill items you order at the counter. Wholesome, healthy, and filling, nearly everything on the menu is under $7.

At the signal along Route 50 in Kalaheo, you'll find the **Menehune Food Mart** with **Steve's Mini Mart** across the street. Both can supply you with any sundries or light groceries that you may need.

Every Tuesday at 3:30 P.M., a **farmers' market** is held at the Kalaheo Neighborhood Center along the highway for locally grown produce, fruits, and flowers. Check it out for good fresh food and a local experience.

Between Lawa'i and Kalaheo, stop at the **Kukui Tropics** for pre-packaged, gift fruit items, like jams, jellies, preserves, mustard, sauces, macadamia nuts, and coffee.

Services

Next to the post office near the traffic light, the **Kalaheo Clinic,** 808/332-8523, is open for checkups and minor emergencies Mon.–Fri. 8 A.M.–8 P.M., Saturday 8 A.M.–noon, and Sunday 1–4 P.M.

M.G.L. DOMENY DE REINZI

WEST END

After Kalaheo, the highway dips south again and passes 'Ele'ele, the still-active Port Allen Harbor, and Hanapepe at the mouth of the Hanapepe River, whose basin has long been known as one of the best taro lands in the islands. You pass tiny "sugar towns" and hidden beaches until you enter Waimea, whose east flank was once dominated by a Russian fort, the last vestige of a dream of island dominance gone sour. Captain Cook landed at Waimea in the midafternoon of January 20, 1778; a small monument in the town center commemorates the great event. A secondary road leading north from Waimea and another from Kekaha farther west converge inland, then meander along Waimea Canyon, the Pacific's most superlative gorge. Kekaha, with its now-silenced sugar stacks, marks the end of civilization, and the hard road gives out just past the Pacific Missile

Range Facility. A cane road picks up and carries you to the wide, sun-drenched beach of Polihale, the end of the line, and the southernmost extremity of the Na Pali Coast.

This is the **Waimea District,** the broad and diverse west end of the island. Waimea means "red water," and the area was so named for the distinctive color of the Waimea River, which bleeds from Mt. Wai'ale'ale. It cuts through Waimea Canyon, depositing the rich red soil at its mouth.

The sometimes turbulent but forever enduring love affair between non-Polynesian travelers and the Hawaiian Islands began in west Kaua'i, when Captain Cook arrived off Waimea Bay and a longboat full of wide-eyed sailors made the beach. Immediately, journals were filled with glowing descriptions of the loveliness of the newly found island and its people, and the liaison has continued unabated ever since.

WEST END

HANAPEPE VICINITY

'ELE'ELE AND PORT ALLEN

As you roll along from Kalaheo to Hanapepe, you're surrounded by former sugarcane fields, now acres of coffee trees. About halfway there, along the inland side of the highway, an HVB Warrior points to an overlook. Stop. **Hanapepe Valley Overlook** is no farther away than your car door, served up as easily as a fast-food snack at a drive-through window. For no effort, you get a remarkable panorama of a classic Hawaiian valley, with some taro still planted at its lower end.

In a moment, you come to **'Ele'ele** and **Port Allen,** separate communities on the east side of the Hanapepe River. Predominantly residential, 'Ele'ele sits mostly on the bluff along the highway, but the 'Ele'ele Shopping Center lies at the curve where the highway turns down to Hanapepe. Turn off the highway and follow the road (Route 541) from the shopping center down to Port Allen, past several small businesses to the commercial and small boat harbors. Numerous tour boat companies and fishing charters run out of Port Allen, and the Coast Guard keeps a few boats here as well. Kauai Electric has a power plant off to the side that generates about 85 percent of the island's electricity. The remainder is produced by four small hydroelectric plants at other locations on the island. After Hurricane 'Iniki, the powerline that cuts across the island from west to east and then over the mountain to Hanalei was erected, replacing the electrical lines that ran around the island along the highway. Although a shorter route to get electricity to its end users, the powerline is a transgression on the otherwise pristine landscape of Kaua'i. Just beyond the power plant is a small beach known as Glass Beach. It's more or less picked over now and pretty junky, but people came for years to collect colored glass from the dark sand to fashion into art objects. This beach is sometimes used by shore fishermen now.

There is a second route from Kalaheo to Hanapepe. Just outside Kalaheo the road splits, and Highway 540 (Halewili Road) slopes down toward the ocean to the tiny town of Numila, where it turns and shoots across to meet the main highway at 'Ele'ele. **Numila** is a dusty former sugar town, rather disheveled and unkempt. Once a thriving, well-kept community, it now looks as if it's taking on the color of the ground on which it lies. Yet, it's still possible to see fine examples of plantation-era vernacular housing here and imagine what it was like during the good years. The McBryde sugar mill once kept this town vibrant, but now its offices house the Kauai Coffee Company.

If you use Route 540, and particularly if you're a coffee connoisseur, stop at the **Kauai Coffee Company Visitor Center and Museum,** just beyond Numila, 808/335-5497 or 800/545-8605, website: www.kauaicoffee.com. Over 150 years ago, coffee was planted in this region of Kaua'i as the first coffee plantation in the Hawaiian Islands. After some years and little success, coffee production was discontinued here but took hold on the Big Island, at Kona. Today, coffee is grown not only on the Big Island, but also on Maui, Moloka'i, O'ahu, and once again on Kaua'i, where it's relatively big business. The Kauai Cof-

---

KAUA'I RED DIRT

While it is true of several of the Hawaiian Islands, Kaua'i in particular has especially red dirt, due to the high mineral bauxite content. As the oldest of the major islands, Kaua'i has been exposed to the elements for the longest time, allowing the hard volcanic rock to break down into fine red particles. Seeing opportunity where others saw trouble, at least one entrepreneur decided to make use of this ubiquitous island commodity and dye clothing with it. These are the increasingly popular Red Dirt Shirts of Kaua'i. But what dyes also stains, and you might not want it to stain your clothes. If you venture out of the beaches and away from paved roads and walkways, you will undoubtedly encounter red dirt during your stay. Be aware, treat it with respect, and know that at least your shoes will take on a slightly reddish tinge.

COFFEE PROCESSING

Coffee grows on short trees or bushes, and the first harvest usually occurs about five years after planting. The fruits, which grow close to the tree's branches, are green when immature but turn bright red and are called "cherries" when they ripen in mid- to late fall. While much coffee is hand-picked—a labor-intensive process—the Kauai Coffee Company uses machines to pick the cherries; the machines straddle the trees and shake the cherries loose from the branches. Once collected, the cherries are trucked to the mill for wet processing. The ripe cherries are separated from the overripe and immature, and the skin and pulp are removed to reveal the beans (usually two per cherry) inside. These beans are then washed and dried mechanically to a set moisture content, after which the parchment covering and silver-like skin are removed. Sorting is done by size, color, and density, and finally by hand if necessary to remove any stray unacceptable beans. After grading, samples from each batch are roasted and tasted as a final test, then bagged, inspected, and shipped.

fee Company has a 3,400-acre plantation of drip-irrigated Hawaiian *arabica* coffee bean plants and in 1999 produced nearly five million pounds of coffee. This is the largest single coffee estate in Hawaii and captures about 65 percent of the Hawaiian coffee market. Refurbished plantation buildings now hold the gift shop and museum, open daily 9 A.M.–5 P.M. Stop in to peruse the historical artifacts and learn how coffee is handled at each stage from tree to cup. Sample tastes are always available for you to try. Aside from the usual gift items, you can purchase a bag or case of estate-grown ground or whole bean coffee in any of the numerous roasts.

Food

Toi's Thai Kitchen, 808/335-3111, family operated and one of the best Thai restaurants on Kaua'i, is in the back corner of the 'Ele'ele Shopping Center and open weekdays 10:30 A.M.–2:30 P.M. and Saturday 11:30 A.M.–2:30 P.M. for lunch, and daily 5:30–9:30 P.M. for dinner. Prepared by Mom and served by her lovely daughters,

the menu starts with items like spicy sour soup with lemongrass and ginger, priced $7.95–10.95 depending upon whether you add pork, beef, or seafood, and spring rolls or deep fried tofu for $6.95. Entrées include stir-fried eggplant and tofu in a spicy sauce with your choice of meat, $7.95–10.95; savory satay priced $7.95–10.95; and yellow curry with your choice of meat for $7.95–9.95. For most items, you have your choice of meat, poultry, fish, seafood, eggplant, or vegetarian. One of the sweet Thai desserts comes with some meals, but if not, order one—it's a treat. Beer and wine are served. Although some Thai decorations adorn the walls, it's not for the decor that you come, but for the tasty and reasonably priced food.

In a separate building at the shopping center is **Grinds Espresso,** 808/335-6027, open daily 5:30 A.M.–9 P.M., a local place serving mostly local foods at reasonable prices. Egg and grill items are served up for breakfast; for the rest of the day, sandwiches and plate lunches are the norm. Any time of the day is coffee time here. Except for pizza, nothing on the menu is more than $7.50. Eat in or pick up orders to go.

Practicalities

At mile marker 16, in the shadow of McDonald's golden arches, is the **'Ele'ele Shopping Center.** Here, along with various eateries are a post office and First Hawaiian Bank branch, a laundromat, Big Save Supermarket (open Mon.–Sat. 7 A.M.–10 P.M.), Ace Hardware store, and the 'Ele'ele Clinic, 808/335-0499. The laundromat is open 24 hours a day but has no change machine or soap dispenser. Check with one of the three tour boat companies that have offices here, Holo Holo Charters, The Exploration Company, and Captain Andy's Sailing Adventures, for a day of fun on the water.

What began as a slap from Mother Nature turned **Paradise Sportswear,** 808/335-5670, in a large industrial building just before Port Allen Small Boat Harbor, from an obscure tiny company into one of the most famous in the state. After Hurricane 'Iniki ravaged Kaua'i in 1992, the staff returned to find the roof of the building completely torn off and the warehouse, containing shirts jobbed from other companies, inundated with red dirt and the shirts rendered unsellable—or maybe not! Amidst the devastation, the future seemed bleak, but as legend would have it, one person said, in effect, "Ah, these shirts actually look pretty cool." Perhaps spurred by desperation, the forlorn faces, after rolling their eyes heavenward, slowly reconsidered and began to smile. Voilà, the **Red Dirt Shirt** was born. Dedicated to the community, Paradise Sportswear is a true cottage industry, employing local families who pick up ordinary white shirts, take them home, and repeatedly dip them in vats of Kaua'i's famous red dirt. After bringing them back, other local people working on the premises apply original silk-screen designs. Since absolutely no chemicals or dyes are used, no two shirts—which range in color from deep copper to burnt orange—are the same. Tour the factory Mon.–Thurs. to watch the silk-screening process, and make sure to stop in at the retail shop, where you can choose from countless designs and styles, ranging from tiny tank tops for tots to XXXXXLs for walking Sherman tanks, and take advantage of discounts on factory seconds. The largest Red Dirt T-shirt made, a special order 8XL, was for a Hawaiian sumo wrestler! Retail outlets featuring Red Dirt Ts are found on every island, with innumerable boutiques and shops carrying these very distinctive souvenirs. On Kaua'i, visit the outlet shops in Waimea, Lihu'e, and Kapa'a. Mainlanders can even find them at outlets in St. George and Moab, Utah—where, incidentally, you also find red dirt. For mail orders, call 800/717-3478 or go to www.dirtshirt.com.

Recreation

The Exploration Company, 808/335-9909 or 800/852-4183, website: www.napali-explorer.com, runs 49-passenger, rigid-bottom inflatable rafts up the Na Pali Coast during winter and along the south coast in summer. Meet at the Exploration Company office around the side at the 'Ele'ele Shopping Center.

For other boating adventures, all of the following use Port Allen Harbor. For catamaran tours, try **Na Pali Eco Adventures,** 808/826-6804; **Blue Dolphin Charters,** 808/742-6731; **Capt. Andy's Sailing Adventures,** 808/335-6833; **Holoholo Charters,** 808/335-0815; and **Catamaran Kahanu,** 808/335-3577. The only true commercial sailing ship in Kaua'i, *Lady Leanne II,* run by **Bluewater Sailing,** 808/828-1142, uses Port Allen October through April.

HANAPEPE

Hanapepe (Crushed Bay), billing itself as "Kaua'i's Biggest Little Town," has had a more glorious past than its present, although it is reemerging as a center of the arts and has the greatest concentration of artists' studios on the island. Hawaiians cultivated taro in Hanapepe Valley, making this a great settlement. Later, the Chinese and others came to grow rice. From the early 1900s until just after World War II, Hanapepe was a bustling town. With a growing population, Hanapepe became an economic center with its main street chockablock with shops and businesses, two movie theaters, and three skating rinks. During the 1940s, thousands of GIs were trained and billeted here before being shipped to the Pacific for overseas duty. Burns Field became the first commercial airstrip on the island, now used only by air tour companies, and its harbor (Port Allen) remains the island's second largest commercial port and one of the principal harbors for boat tours.

Hanapepe is divided into two sections. As you approach town from the east, look up to your right; if it's early winter, you'll see an entire hillside of bougainvilleas ablaze with a multicolored patchwork of blossoms. The newer section to town lies along Route 50, the other is Old Hanapepe, a "must-see" along Hanapepe Road; the Y-intersections at both ends of town direct you by sign to the historic main street that parallels the highway. Along Route 50 are the police and fire departments, a library, the Westside Pharmacy, the Hanapepe Hongwanji, a restaurant, and a gas station in rapid succession before the bridge. Beyond the bridge are more shops and restaurants, the Hawaii Helicopter and Bali Hai Helicopter offices, and the Hanapepe Park and stadium, often lit at night for ball games. Keep a lookout for the **Soto Zen Temple Zenshuji** on your left. It's quite large and interesting to people who haven't visited a temple before. At the western end of town is the famous **Kauai Kookie Kompany,** whose macadamia shortbread, Kona coffee, guava macadamia, and coconut krispies cookies, among others, are now available statewide. Just beyond that, at the Y-intersection, is a small gift shop called Giorgio's where you'll find unique

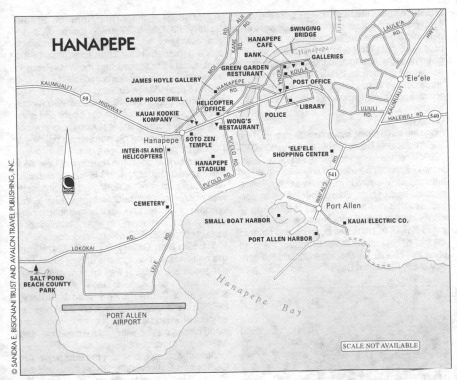

HANAPEPE

© SANDRA E. BISIGNANI TRUST AND AVALON TRAVEL PUBLISHING, INC.

SCALE NOT AVAILABLE

coconut postcards and painted surfboard art. Just before the turnoff for Salt Pond Beach County Park you'll find the **Inter-Island Helicopter** office way in the back in the hangar.

Old Hanapepe is a time-frozen still life of vintage false front buildings housing a palette of art studios, local dry-goods stores, two banks, an excellent restaurant, and a swinging foot bridge. Like the newer section of town, it lies on both sides of "the bridge." On the west side of this one-lane bridge (built 1911) are the art gallery of the best-known artist in Hanapepe and an orchid nursery. In 1943, when the entire world was ugly with war, Matsuuki Shimonishi looked for simple beauty, which he found in the delicate blooms of orchids. Until his death in 1989, he worked daily with the flowers, hybridizing many, one of which he named *dandrobum tokiwa shimonishi* for his wife, Tokiwa. **Shimonishi Orchid Nursery,** open daily except Sunday and

Wednesday 9 A.M.–noon and again 1–4 P.M., 808/335-5562 or 800/510-8684, is now in the care of his daughter. Born and raised on Kaua'i, Elsie and her husband returned to the island in 1984 to help restore the nursery after it was ravaged by Hurricane 'Iwa and have run the nursery full time since then. You are welcome to tour the nursery to find that perfect flower to take with you or have shipped back to the mainland.

Friday Art Night

Following in the footsteps of Lahaina, Maui, Hanapepe has established "Friday Art Night," to celebrate its strong and growing connection with the Hawaiian art community. Of the 11 galleries in town, most are one-artist shops. Every Friday evening 6–9 P.M., eight galleries along the old main drag keep their doors open, catering to art lovers and others looking to peruse or buy. Most artists are available at their galleries and proudly display their latest works. Some may even pull their easels out on the sidewalk and demonstrate there. Refreshments are often available, and musical performances are usually given near the entrance to the swinging bridge. As casual a place as this is, the scene sometimes carries a main street block party atmosphere. For more information, call 808/335-0343.

Galleries

Along the main street, make sure to stop in at the fine art studio of **Dawn Traina Gallery,** 808/335-3993, who, knowing she wanted to be an artist since childhood, pursued an education in art on both coasts. Working in multimedia with acrylics, pastels, and pencils, Dawn specializes in portraiture. She not only captures the feeling of what's current today, but somehow, since moving to Hawaii in 1979, has been able to tap into the lore of Hawaii and to visibly render the spirit of ancient chants, dances, legends, and the gentility of the Plantation Days.

ROBERT NILSEN

KAUA'I

Hanapepe's swinging footbridge, built in 1911

Next door is the **Arius Hopman Studio Gallery,** 808/335-0227, featuring mostly landscape watercolors. Painted on location, each piece demonstrates a connectedness to the spot. Colors are vibrant and there is feeling in every stroke. Commissions accepted.

The **Kauai Village Gallery,** on the left as you enter town, 808/335-0343, website: www.hawaii-iart.com, offers a collection of pottery and photographs by local artists, featuring gallery owner Lew Shortbridge and his surrealistic paintings. Prices are reasonable. Open daily.

A little farther down the road is the **Lele Aka Studio and Gallery,** 808/345-5267, website: www.hawaiiart.com, featuring art ranging from wild mythological creatures to portraits of the children of Kaua'i. The work is mystical, otherwordly, with overlapping images. Although the tone is otherwise, dark colors predominate.

The **Kim Starr Gallery,** 808/335-0381, shows the paintings and serigraphs of Kim Starr. Her cat series is becoming well known, as are her human figures. A few steps away is the **Kama'aina Cabinets/Koa Wood Gallery,** 808/335-5483, closed Sunday, showing fine examples of wood carvings, furniture, and other wood pieces crafted with skill, experience, and a feeling of movement.

Almost across the street is **Hanapepe Art Center and Gallery,** 808/335-3442, which displays a wide eclectic collection of multi-media artworks, many by owners Rick and Anna Ramondi, but other artists are featured as well. Although not on the main drag, **8-Bells Gallery,** 808/335-0550, website: www.hawaiiart.com, features paintings and prints and some sculpture by local artists. This gallery can frame artwork if you find something special here that you want to take with you.

On the far side of the bridge is the **James Hoyle Gallery,** 808/335-3582, open daily 9 A.M.–6 P.M. and by appointment. James Hoyle has been able to capture the spirit of Hawaii through fantastic color and movement. The sense that permeates all of Hoyle's work is that in Hawaii, humanity cannot conquer nature but must learn to live in harmony with the 'aina. These fine works range in price $800–40,000. If you can't afford an original, serigraphs finished and embellished in vivid color by the artist go for around $700. Hoyle uses bright colors, strong brush strokes, and heavy gobs of pastels in a manner similar to the impressionists like Van Gogh and Paul Gauguin.

As you enter town on the right, **Kauai Fine Arts,** 808/335-3778, website: www.brunias.com, open 9 A.M.–5 P.M. daily, stocks prints, antique maps, and some tribal art from around the world. A great place to get lost in the age of exploration or early 20th-century Hawaii. A sister store at Coconut Marketplace has a larger and more varied collection.

Beach

On the western outskirts of town, a sign points *makai* (toward the sea) down Route 543. Follow the sign past a small veterans' cemetery, where an HVB Warrior points down Lele Road to **Salt Pond Beach County Park,** the best beach and windsurfing spot on this end of the island. This beach is at the west end of the Port Allen Airport (Burns Field) runway, once the major airport for the island but now only an airstrip with no facilities that three helicopter companies and one ultralight aircraft company use.

Local people from around Hanapepe enjoy this popular beach park. The swimming is excellent—a natural breakwater in front of the lifeguard stand makes a pool safe for tots—and snorkeling is fair out on the periphery of the bay. Surfers enjoy the breaks here, and a constant gentle breeze makes the area popular with windsurfers. Bring a picnic lunch and make a day of it; on the weekends you might find a *kaukau* wagon parked here for light snacks. Amenities include several pavilions and picnic tables, toilets, and showers, and camping is allowed with a county permit.

Along the road to Salt Pond Beach, you pass the actual salt ponds, evaporative basins cut into the red earth that have been used for hundreds of years. The sea salt here is still harvested but isn't considered pure enough for commercial use. The local people know better; they harvest the salt in the spring and summer, and because of its so-called impurities (which actually add a special flavor), it is a sought-after commodity and an appreciated gift for family and friends. If you see salt in the basins, it belongs to someone, but there won't be any hassles if you take a *small* pinch to taste. Don't scrape it up with your fingers because the sharp crystals can cut you—and you'll rub salt into your wounds in the process.

Food

The **Green Garden Restaurant,** 808/335-5422, an old standby along the highway, is marked by a tangle of vegetation that almost makes the building look overgrown. It's open daily 7 A.M.–2 P.M. for breakfast and lunch and daily except Tuesday 5–9 P.M. for dinner. Since 1948, this family-owned restaurant offers tourist-quality food in large portions, with *aloha* service. The new section of the restaurant is set up to hold busloads of tourists who arrive for lunch; go a little before or a little after noon. The old room has a few plants, but the name is really held up by the decor—green walls, chairs, tables, place mats, bathrooms. If you see anything on the menu that you might want to mix and match, just ask. Substitutions are made cheerfully. Lunches run mostly under $10, with full-meal dinner selections including beverage $12–19. The homemade pies are famous and always delicious.

Over the bridge and on your left is another island institution, **Wong's Restaurant,** 808/335-5066, open daily except Monday for breakfast, lunch, and dinner. Wong's is one giant dining room reminiscent of a small-town banquet hall that caters to local bowling leagues and wedding receptions. It's a favorite of the tour buses and can be crowded. The service is friendly, the portions large, and the food, while not memorable, is very reasonably priced; you won't complain, but you won't be impressed, either. Wong's specialties are Chinese and Japanese dishes, all under $10, with many around $7–8. If that isn't enough, **Omoide's Deli and Bakery** occupies a second section of the same building where you can pick up a sandwich or pizza, birthday cake, or slice of its island-famous homemade liliko'i chiffon pie.

Even if you tried, you couldn't miss **Camp House Grill and Cantina,** 808/335-5656, open daily for lunch and dinner. It's a huge piñata of a bright turquoise metal building trimmed in yellow and green, and the inside is more colorful than a Kaua'i sunset. Dishes include spicy Mexican fare like burritos, chile verde, carne asada, and pollo poblano, which run $8–14 for lunch, a few dollars more for dinner. The bar serves imported beers and mixed drinks with happy-hour prices 4–6 P.M. daily.

KAUA'I

As you come into the old town from the east, the first store on your left—in an old house—is **Taro Ko,** a tiny mom-and-pop, house-front shop selling taro chips. It is nothing to look at from the outside, but it's the flavors of the chips that draw people here. While mama is inside looking after the deep-fryers, papa might be out lounging under the tree.

Hanapepe Cafe and Espresso Bar, 808/335-5011, open daily 8–11 A.M. for breakfast, 11 A.M.–2 P.M. for lunch, and Thurs.–Sun. 6–9 P.M. for dinner with live music, is a fantastic eclectic restaurant for mind and body. Housed in the old town drugstore (circa 1939), the espresso bar/restaurant section is fashioned from the original soda fountain counter, tastefully modernized with a black-and-white checkerboard motif. All the food served is health-conscious vegetarian with an attempt at organic and locally grown whenever possible, but always fresh and definitely savory and satisfying. Breakfast is terrific, with homemade pastries and pies washed down with steaming cups of espresso, hot chocolate, cappuccino, caffe latte, and an assortment of herbal teas all reasonably priced. Lunch brings a garden burger, Caesar salad, and homemade minestrone soup, all served with fresh bread. Dinner is always vegetarian Italian à la Hawaii and could be baked lasagna al forno, linguine with pesto, or artichokes with cannelloni, all served with soup, salad, and bread for around $20. Dinner music is usually provided by a solo local performer playing anything from slack-key to classical flute music. If you are craving a snack, quiet cup of coffee, or a full meal, you can't beat the Hanapepe Cafe and Espresso Bar. Reservations recommended for dinner. Bring your own bubbly. The entry to the café takes you through **Uncle Eddie's Aloha Angels.** The focus of Uncle Eddie's is angels in all their manifestations. If you're unsure of what to expect after your visit from the Grim Reaper, try this tiny shop for a sneak preview of kingdom come.

For local food at moderate prices, try **Linda's Restaurant,** offering breakfast specials and inexpensive dinners; or the **Da Imu Hut Cafe,** offering a full assortment of local grinds and refreshing drinks.

On Thursday 3:30–5:30 P.M. a **farmers' market** is held at Hanapepe Town Park behind the

fire station. Stop by for the freshest in local organic produce.

Recreation

Bali Hai and Hawaii Helicopter companies both have offices along the highway in Hanapepe on the west side of the bridge. **Bali Hai Helicopters,** 808/335-3166 or 800/325-8687, flies 45- and 60-minute circle island flights daily, $120 and $159, in its four-passenger Bell Ranger that's painted in bright rainbow colors. **Hawaii Helicopters,** 808/826-6591 or 800/367-7095, flies twin-engine machines and does basically the same routes for similar rates. Using Hughes 500 four-seater machines with their doors off for an open-air experience, **Inter-Island Helicopters,** 808/335-5009, also flies the circle-island route but adds one tour with a waterfall picnic stop. Its office is in the hangar at the west end of town. Although based in Kaumakani, a few miles farther to the west, **Ni'ihau Helicopters,** 808/335-3500, office open Mon.–Sat. 8 A.M.–2 P.M., also uses Burns Field. Set up to provide medical services for the residents of Ni'ihau, the helicopter is employed for occasional tours in its twin-engine Agusta 109A—when there are enough passengers. Ni'ihau Helicopter runs completely different tours than all other helicopter companies on Kaua'i. Its flight runs three to four hours, takes you to Ni'ihau and back, and gives you plenty of time on a Ni'ihau beach. Rates are $250 per person with six passengers and $338 with four passengers. This is virtually the only way to get to Ni'ihau unless you are an invited guest. The company also offers hunting safaris.

Also flying out of Burns Field in a 70-horsepower ultralight power glider is **Birds in Paradise,** 808/822-5309. With the instructor, you can have a truly unique experience soaring above terra firma in this "motorcycle with wings." Prices are $95 for a 30-minute lesson, $165 for one hour. Advanced instructional flights run $240 for 90 minutes and $315 for two hours.

SUGAR TOWNS

The road hugs the coast after Hanapepe, bypassing a series of still-working sugar towns until you arrive in Waimea. **Kaumakani,** a small cluster of vernacular homes with a few dirt lanes

KAUA'I

where sugar plantation workers live, has a post office, mini-mart and bakery, and the Ni'ihau Helicopter office. Here, everything seems to be tinged with red. *Mauka* of the highway, surrounded by cane fields, is the refurbished, plantation-style United Methodist Church, established 1901, the oldest Methodist church on the island.

Less than a half mile west is **Olokele.** As counterpoint to the disheveled and dusty look of Kaumakani, Olokele is a one-street community of larger and better-kept houses, wide green lawns, and towering canopy-like Monkeypod trees. Manifesting an air of an easier life from earlier decades, quaint lampposts line this road as it dips down to the still-active sugar mill, and at night displays a genteel quality. This is where the plantation managers and mill higher-ups live. Take a drive through, drawing your own conclusions on the quality of life. Gay and Robinson, owners of the mill, offer two-hour bus and walking tours of the mill and surrounding fields as an overview of the sugar production process and everyday mill operation. Pants (or shorts) and closed-toe shoes must be worn, and it's a good idea to wear clothing that you wouldn't mind getting stained by the rich red dirt in the fields. Hard hats and goggles are provided for the part of the tour that goes through the mill. Per-

haps the best time to visit is April–October, when the mill is most active. These **sugar plantation tours** start at the visitors center (open 8 A.M.–4 P.M. Mon.–Fri.), near the mill office, where there are displays of artifacts relating to the sugar industry. Tours are offered at 8:45 A.M. and 12:45 P.M. Mon.–Fri., except holidays, and run $31.25 per person for adults with a 30 percent discount for children 8–15; call 808/335-2824 to make a reservation or visit www.gandrtours-kauai.com on the Web.

Next is **Pakala,** noted more for its surfing beach than for the town itself. At mile marker 21, a bunch of cars pulled off the road means the surf's up. Follow the pathway to try the waves yourself or just to watch the show. This beach is not an official park. Walk down past the bridge to a well-worn pathway leading through a field. In a few minutes is the beach, a 500-yard-long horseshoe of white sand. Off to the left is a rocky promontory popular with local fishermen. The swimming is fair, and the reef provides good snorkeling, but the real go is the surf—the beach is nicknamed "Infinity" because the waves last so long; they come rolling in in graceful arcs to spill upon the beach, then recede in a regular, hypnotic pattern, causing the next wave to break and roll perfectly. Sunset is a wonderful time to come here for a romantic evening picnic.

WAIMEA

Like the Hanapepe Valley back down the coast, the area near the mouth of the Waimea River was historically a large settlement area and the river valley used for taro production, some of which carries on today. Kaumuali'i, the last great king of Kaua'i, maintained a household here, so Waimea for a time was a seat of power.

The town of Waimea has only a few sights of interest. You can walk to see its old buildings, churches, the Captain Cook landing site, the sugar mill ruins, and a royal coconut grove; a Russian fort lies across the river on the far bank. Waimea does have one fine accommodation, a brewpub, some reasonably good restaurants, and limited shopping. In addition, you'll find two supermarkets, three gas stations, a boat tour company, a laundromat, a photography supply store, a library, two banks, a sporting goods

store, and a pharmacy. Near the western edge of the downtown area is a Red Dirt T-Shirt outlet, so if you haven't picked up one before now, you can get it here before heading out to the beach. A couple of blocks up Waimea Canyon Road is Kaua'i Veterans Memorial Hospital. As the gateway to the Waimea Canyon and Koke'e state parks, one of the two roads up the mountain starts here in town.

SIGHTS

The remains of a Russian fort still guard the eastern entrance to Waimea town. Turn left at the sign for **Russian Fort Elizabeth State Historic Park;** the remains are right there. The fort, roughly shaped like an eight-pointed star, dates from 1817 when a German doctor, Georg Anton Schaeffer, built it in the name of Czar Nicholas of Russia, naming it after the potentate's daughter. Schaeffer, a self-styled adventurer and agent for the Russian-American Company, saw great potential in the domination of Hawaii and built two other forts on Kaua'i, one on the bluff at Princeville, which overlooks Hanalei Bay, and the other down along Hanalei Bay. Due to political maneuverings with other European nations, Czar Nicholas never warmed to Schaeffer's enterprises and withdrew official support. For a time, Kaua'i's King Kaumuali'i flew the Russian flag, perhaps in a subtle attempt to play one foreign power against another. Soon, Schaeffer was unceremoniously kicked off Kaua'i, sent to Honolulu, and then forced to leave the islands al-

together. The fort fell into disrepair and was virtually dismantled in 1864, when 38 guns of various sizes were removed. The stout walls, once 30 feet thick, are now mere rubble, humbled by encircling, nondescript underbrush. However, if you climb onto the ramparts you'll still get a commanding view of Waimea Bay. Pick up a brochure at the entrance and walk the path inside and around the fortification.

Just after you cross the Waimea River, signs point to **Lucy Wright Beach County Park,** a five-acre park popular with the local folk. There's a picnic area, restrooms, showers, a playground, and tent camping with a county permit. The park is situated along the mouth of the river, which makes the water a bit murky. The swimming is fair if the water is clear, and the surfing is de-

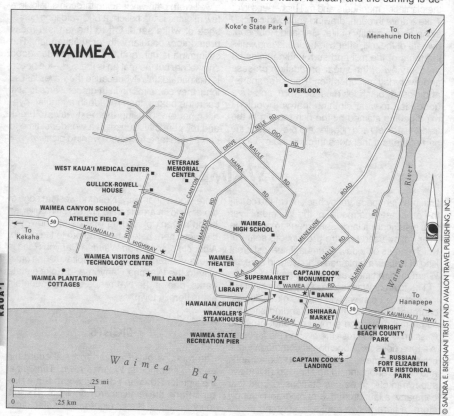

© SANDRA E. BISIGNANI TRUST AND AVALON TRAVEL PUBLISHING, INC.

cent around the river mouth. The Kilohana canoe club launches here to practice on the bay. A few hundred feet to the west of this park is the **Waimea State Recreation Pier,** open for picnicking and good for open-ocean pole fishing and crabbing. Reach it by walking along the beach or down a backstreet behind the Waimea Library. The beach at both of these parks is not really recommended for swimming and is often full of driftwood.

Captain Cook's achievements were surely deserving of more than the uninspiring commemorative markers around Waimea. Whether you revere him as a great explorer or denigrate him as an opportunistic despoiler, his accomplishments in mapping the great Pacific were unparalleled and changed the course of history. In his memory are **Captain Cook's Landing,** a modest marker attached to a boulder at Lucy Wright Beach Park, commemorating his "discovery" of the Sandwich Islands at 3:30 P.M. on September 20, 1778, and **Captain Cook's Monument,** on the median strip Hofgaard Park in downtown Waimea.

If you're fascinated by Kaua'i's half-legendary little people, you might want to take a look at the **Menehune Ditch** *(Kiki a Ola),* a stone wall encasing an aqueduct curiously built in a fashion unused by and apparently unknown to the Polynesian settlers of Hawaii, in which mating stones are cut to match. The road now covers much of the ditch, which was cut into the riverside cliff face. The oral tradition states that the ditch was built by order of Ola, high chief of Waimea, and that he paid his little workers in *'opae,* a tiny shrimp that was their staple. On payday, they supposedly sent up such a great cheer that they were heard on O'ahu. Said to have once stretched 25 miles up the valley, today the site is greatly reduced as many of the distinctively hand-hewn boulders have been removed for use in buildings around the island, especially in the Protestant church in Waimea. Some steadfastly maintain that the Menehune never existed, but legends abound and works attributed to them are seen here and there around the island. Similar to that in Hanapepe, a pedestrian footbridge crosses the river here, used mostly in times of high water when it's impossible to drive a vehicle through the ford. It perhaps is a remnant of a time when Waimea was a much more thriving community.

As a testament to its former importance, Waimea has numerous, well-maintained **old structures.** Standing across from the Captain Cook Monument in Hofgaard Park in the middle of town is the 1929 First Hawaiian Bank Building. Around the corner is the older Electric Light Co. building (1907). Across from the fire station is the Hawaiian Church (there's been a congregation since 1820), built in 1865 and renovated in 1995. Across the street, now a store for antiques and collectibles is the Fah Inn (1890), and one block up on either side of the intersection are the Yamase and Masuda buildings, both from 1919. The 1938 Waimea Theater, renovated in 1999, is a few steps up the road and once again open for movies and theatrical plays. Established in 1859, the United Church of Christ building is the oldest church extant in town. Perhaps the oldest building is the Gullick-Rowell House (1829), at the entrance to the hospital and still occupied by descendants of the missionary family.

From 1884 to 1946, Waimea was the home of a thriving yet small sugar mill and center for a plantation community. While the mill structure is in a state of disrepair, a number of the worker's houses survive, and the back lanes of this "camp" give evidence of what life in the former plantation was like. A guided **mill camp walking tour** starts at the small museum in the administration building of Waimea Plantation Cottages, in the coconut grove at the west end of town. Led by volunteers, this tour focuses on the laborers' homes and gardens and the social role of such camp communities in past plantation life on the island. Tours are offered at 9 A.M. on Tuesday, Thursday, and Saturday and last about 90 minutes. The cost is $10 adult, $8 for seniors, and $5 for children 6–12. All proceeds go to help preserve the historic structures and support community events. Reservations are a must, as groups are kept to 12 or less; call 808/338-0006.

For a quick look at the history of Waimea and the surrounding region, stop for a look at the new **Waimea Visitor and Technology Center** on the west end of town where Waimea Canyon Road meets the highway. Here audiovisual displays and a few historical artifacts help illustrate the area's sugar past and technological present.

KAUA'I

ACCOMMODATIONS

Aside from a few private rental homes, **Waimea Plantation Cottages,** 9600 Kaumuali'i Hwy., #367, Waimea, HI 96796, 808/338-1625 or 800/992-4632, fax 808/338-2338, website: www.waimea-plantation.com, email: waiple@ aloha.net, is virtually the only place to stay along the south shore west of Kalaheo—and what a place it is. Owned by the Kikiaola Land Company, Ltd., and operated by Aston Hotels and Resorts, 800/922-7866 or 800/321-2558 in Hawaii, this oceanfront property is set in a grove of more than 750 coconut palms and a few huge banyan trees at the west end of Waimea. Not victimized by big bucks or modern resort development, workers' and supervisors' cottages and the manager's house from the former Waimea sugar plantation have been renovated and preserved, and the grounds maintained in an old-style way. Here you are treated to a touch from the past. While some modern amenities such as full kitchens, bathrooms, and color cable TVs have been added for comfort and convenience, an effort has been made to keep each unit as much in its original state (1920–30s era) as possible; period furniture and other furnishings add to the feel of that bygone era. Most buildings have bare wood floors and painted wood walls. Nearly all have ceiling fans and lanai. Weekly housekeeping and linen service are included. Complimentary washers and dryers are available on the premises. A swimming pool in the 1930s style has been constructed on the lawn, and there's croquet, horseshoes, and volleyball, along with a restaurant and brewpub. In accordance with this philosophy of preservation, some longtime employees of the plantation (no longer a functioning entity) are still offered low- or no-rent cottages in the mill camp rather than being turned out to make way for development of the land. On check-in at the administration building, have a look at the small **Faye Museum,** which presents artifacts and photographs of the early days of sugar in West Kaua'i.

Presently, there are about 50 units, including 11 cottages moved from the Kekaha Plantation and others from the former town of Mana. Rates for the cottages range from a one-bedroom for $195 to a three-bedroom unit for $330; weekly discounts, specials, and *kama'aina* rates are available, and a $20 price cut applies during low season. The two-story, five-bedroom, two-bath Manager's House is available for $515 a night. The average length of stay is a 7–10 days, with a 35 percent return rate; make your reservations several months in advance. (The six-bedroom Faye estate and adjoining one-bedroom cottage directly on the beach in Hanalei are also operated by Waimea Plantation Cottages.) Low-key and unpretentious, this institution aims to please and offers an opportunity for seclusion and serenity. What could be better than to relax and read a favorite book on your breezy lanai, watch the sunset through the coconut grove, or take a moonlight stroll along the gently lapping shore? Make reservations with Waimea Plantation directly or through Aston Hotels.

FOOD

It's easy to imagine a grizzled *paniolo* contentedly dangling his spurs over the banister of the distinctive veranda at the **Wrangler's Steakhouse,** in downtown Waimea at 9852 Kaumuali'i, 808/338-1218, open Mon.–Sat. for lunch 11 A.M.–5 P.M. and for dinner 5–9 P.M. The interior is a large open-beamed room with hardwood floors, cooled by ceiling fans. You can choose to dine inside at a private booth or table, or alfresco on the big veranda out front or in the red blaze—a ginger garden out back. To enhance the atmosphere, soft dinner music is played nightly. A full-service bar is stocked with a complete assortment of liquors, wines, and beers to complement all meals. The lunch menu has burgers, sandwiches, and Mexican plates, mostly under $8.50. As you might expect, the Wrangler dinner menu is heavy on the steaks and red meats, with some poultry, seafood, combination, and a few Mexican selections. The house specialty is a sizzling 16-ounce New York steak served with sautéed mushrooms and baked potato. Entrées, $10.75–19.95, come with homemade chips and salsa and soup. The Wrangler Steak House is excellent, friendly, and priced right. While you're here, take a few minutes and have a look at the gift shop and small *paniolo* museum.

For a simpler, quicker meal, try **Pacific Pizza and Deli,** 808/338-1020, for pizza, calzones, deli sandwiches, drinks, and ice cream. Along with the ordinary pizzas, you have your choice of Thai, Japanese, Mexican, and other unusual pizza offerings. Refreshing drinks include Tropical Smoothies with pineapple, mango, or papaya, home-brewed ice tea, and coffee drinks from espresso to latte. Pacific Pizza shares the Wrangler Restaurant building and is connected to the restaurant.

Establishing itself as a fine place for coffee, pastries, ice cream, and light meals is **John's Place,** 808/338-0330, across from the Captain Cook Monument. Breakfast, served until 11 A.M., is mostly eggs, pancakes, hot muffins, bagels, and croissants. Served until closing at 6 P.M. are fish and chips, burritos, wraps, and any number of sandwiches, all under $7.95. Many come for the espresso, but you can also get fountain drinks, juices, and smoothies. Good eats and good prices.

Paulani's Farmers' Market at the west end of town not only has local fruit and vegetables but also sandwiches, frosties, and smoothies. Directly across the street is **Betty's** for inexpensive local grinds and fast food. **Subway, TCBY,** and a shave ice place are also doing business here.

The **Waimea Brewing Company,** 808/338-9733, is open daily for lunch and dinner on the property of Waimea Plantation Cottages, next to the registration office. The breezy plantation-style building has large open windows, high ceilings, and ceiling fans. The hand-crafted beers, usually a half dozen or more ranging from light lagers to thick stouts, are brewed in a room seen through the glass window behind the bar. These beers can only be sold here. Stop for a repast and cool yourself down with one of these sudsy drinks. If you have trouble deciding which beer will fit your palate best, try the sampler for $5. Some of what appears on the menu are appetizers like smokin' wings, taro leaf goat cheese dip, and gado gado skewers for $3.75–6.75. Salads and sandwiches are favorites and run $3.95–8.95. Dinner entrées include fresh catch at $15.95, kalbi beef ribs for $13.95, and a saimin bowl for $5.95, and every evening there are specials. Sit inside so you can see the bar or outside on the veranda under the stars—either way it's a very pleasant, relaxing experience. Hours are 11 A.M.–11 P.M. daily, with food served until 9 P.M. Reservations are not always necessary but may be a good idea on the weekend. Picnic basket lunches can be ordered, very convenient if you're going out to Polihale or up to Koke'e, but anything on the menu can be ordered to go.

Along the main road, facing Captain Cook's statue, is **Ishihara Market,** open 6 A.M.–8 P.M. daily, where you'll find all the necessities; it now sells some prepared hot meals. Kitty-corner across the intersection is the police station; the street running inland from there goes to the Menehune Ditch. Across the street is a well-stocked **Big Save Supermarket.** Its lunch counter, believe it or not, features terrific local dishes at very reasonable prices. For liquor of all sorts, try **Da Booze Shop.**

RECREATION

The **Captain's Cargo Company,** and office of **Liko Kaua'I Cruises,** 808/338-0333 or 888/732-5456, website: www.liko-kauai.com, email: liko@aloha.net, is operated by Debra Hookano, wife of Captain Liko. Across from the Captain Cook Monument in the center of town, the small but tasteful Captain's Cargo Company boutique, open daily 8 A.M.–5 P.M., offers jewelry, fashionable dresses, shorts, T-shirts, and even brocaded vests. The boutique also rents and sells surfboards, boogie boards, and snorkel equipment. Captain Liko runs his 49-foot power catamaran out of the tiny Kikiaola Harbor just up the road. This is the closest departure point for trips to the Na Pali Coast, so it gives you the shortest "commute." Born and raised on Kaua'i, Captain Liko worked for 10 years as a supervising lifeguard on the west end, and no one knows these waters better than he. After you board, Captain Liko begins telling Hawaiian tales, especially about Ni'ihau, the island of his ancestors. Captain Liko not only offers spectacular sights but also a chance to snorkel and swim if the weather is cooperating; he brings along snacks and drinks for the ride. If you are lucky, dolphins will play alongside the boat as you cruise, or you may see whales frolicking during the winter months. On the way back, since the boat is completely outfitted for fishing charters, some lucky person gets to reel in whatever bites. Morning cruises with check-in at 7 A.M. run about four hours long, $115 for adults and $75 for children 4–14 years. During the summer months, an afternoon cruise is added. Weather permitting, sunset cruises run 3–6 P.M. and are $85 adult and $55 children.

TO THE END OF THE ROAD

KEKAHA

Back on Highway 50 going west, you enter Kekaha, passing the former plantation workers' homes trimmed in neat green lawns and shaded from the baking sun by palm and mango trees. Japanese gardens peek from behind fences. Kekaha was a planned plantation town, a model community by some regards, that was built and maintained by sugar and thrived for a century. The highway skirts town, running right along the water, while the main street, Kekaha Road, Ys off near Kikiaola Harbor and runs into town past the old sugar mill to the shopping plaza at Alae Road. Along the main street are one gas station—your last chance if heading west or up Waimea Canyon—**Thrifty Mini Mart,** and a post office. Until 1996, cane trucks, like worker bees returning to the hive, carried their burdens into the ever-hungry jaws of the **Kekaha Sugar Company,** whose smokestack owns the skyline but belches black soot no more. Still, a sweet molasses smell lingers in the air. Even with the closing of the mill, the town remains well-trimmed and ostensibly prosperous, perhaps because of the work available at both the seed corn companies up the road and at Barking Sands, the Pacific Missile Range Facility farther on.

Route 550, the western road leading to Waimea Canyon and Koke'e state parks, branches off in the center of town. At this intersection you'll find the Waimea Canyon Plaza, a small mall with shops like the **Menehune Food Market,** your last chance for snacks and sundries; **Waimea Canyon Snack Shop** for burgers, *bento,* and plate lunches; **Lappert's Ice Cream;** and **Emperors Emporium** and **Waimea Canyon General Store,** side-by-side shops for postcards, cheap jewelry, outlet alohawear, and souvenirs. At the first major cane road intersection on the road out of town toward the mountain, a traffic light was hung in 1957—the island's first.

Route 50, Kaumuali'i Highway, proceeds west along the coast. When still in town, you pass **H.P. Faye Park.** The Kekaha Neighborhood Center is nearby and is the site of the Saturday 9 A.M. **farmers' market.** Across the road is **Kekaha Beach County Park** with pavilion, tables, toilets, and grills. Then the golden sands of the beach park stretch for miles, widening as you head west, with pulloffs and shade-tree clusters now and again. The sun always shines, so pick your spot anywhere along the beach. The area is good for swimming and snorkeling during calm weather, and fair for surfing, although the reef can be quite shallow in spots. The beach across the road from the Catholic church is perhaps the best for little kids. Since there's no tourist development in the area, it's generally quite empty.

At the east end of Kekaha, **Kikiaola Harbor** serves the needs of area residents with a boat launch and is where Liko Kaua'i starts its tours. There are a few picnic tables and restrooms here, but no camping is allowed.

There are no hotels or condominiums in Kekaha, only a couple of vacation rentals and B&Bs. **Kekaha Vacation Rentals,** 808/337-9565 or 800/677-5959, website: http://wwte.com/hawaii/kauai/kekaha1.htm, offers six rental units ranging from a one-bedroom suite to a three-bedroom house; all are directly across the highway from the ocean. All units are comfortably furnished, supply all linens and towels, and have complete kitchens, TV, and washing machines. Bicycles and boogie boards are available for guests to use. These units range $500–1,000 a week, with an additional $50 cleaning fee; four nights minimum. For B&Bs, try one of the B&B agencies listed in the Introduction of this book.

PACIFIC MISSILE RANGE FACILITY

The sea sparkles, and the land flattens wide and long, with green cane billowing all around. Dry gulches and red buttes form an impromptu

MANA PLAIN

Unlike the rest of the island, which is volcanic in nature, the Mana Plain is sedimentary, perhaps a combination of dirt swept down from the hills and sand pushed up from the sea. It stretches from the Waimea River to the Na Pali cliffs at Polihale, about 16 miles along its coastal periphery. Prior to the 1900s, the Mana Plain was marshy with numerous ponds and inland waterways—a great wildlife area for birds—and it was possible to boat from the former town of Mana on its west end to Waimea. The old town of Mana, which no longer exists, was a thriving sugar community in the mid-1800s but shrank to nothing with the decline of the sugar industry. The early Hawaiians lived along the coast and near the cliff, and when immigrants moved into the area, rice was cultivated. In the early 20th century, the wetlands were drained to create productive sugarcane land, and much is still used as such today. Recently, some of this land has been turned over to other uses. One huge strip along the coast, the Pacific Missile Range Facility at Barking Sands, has been in military hands since World War II, and large acreage is planted in seed corn by two mainland companies. The Barking Sands airfield was originally built in 1928 by the Kekaha sugar plantation and later used by both Hawaiian Airlines interisland flights and Pan Am transpacific flights between the U.S. West Coast and Asia.

inland wall. In six miles are the gates of the Pacific Missile Range Facility (PMRF), also known as **Barking Sands.** Here howl the dogs of war, leashed but on guard. Run by the Navy but used by all sectors of the U.S. military, allied foreign military units, and select civilian and educational agencies, PMRF is a training ground for air, surface, underwater, and coastal maneuvers, target practice, electronic warfare and communication, and tracking. In essence, it's a training facility for sea warfare. As one of its brochures states, "PMRF is the world's largest instrumented, multi-dimensional testing and training range." Its range covers 42,000 square miles to the west and south with the addition of 1,000 square miles underwater. Along with the main 2,000-acre facility along the coast, which boasts a 6,000-foot runway, an associated base, where training exercises are held, lies a short way up the Na Pali Coast on the end of Makaha Ridge. Built originally by NASA in 1960 to track the Mercury space craft, it's a state-of-the-art facility that is integral to maintaining the U.S. military's combat readiness.

In late 1996, NASA announced that one of the most advanced studies of the earth's atmosphere was to be conducted at the Pacific Missile Range Facility. That research featured "Pathfinder," an experimental remote-controlled light aircraft that was fueled entirely by solar power. This slow-speed "flying wing" was powered by six electric motors and reached a height of over 80,000 feet. It was followed by other high-altitude versions including the Centurion and Helios. NASA officials chose Kaua'i because its weather provides 360 clear days, offering perfect flying in virtually unobstructed air space. The program brought a substantial amount of money into the local economy and provided hands-on experience for some lucky students at Kaua'i's community college.

PMRF is home to over 100 military personnel and their families, and many times that number of civilian workers are employed on the base. Most of its facilities are open only to these personnel, but some of the base is open to the public for swimming, camping, and fishing. The base maintains two recreational areas and the **Major's Bay Beach** for public use. Rec. I (Barking Sands, Nohili dune area) and Rec. II (Kini Kini area) are open from 4 P.M. (6 P.M. for Rec. II) to 6 A.M. during the week and all day on weekends and holidays but may be closed at any time due to exercises and training maneuvers. Call 808/335-4229 for current information on closures. Major's Bay Beach, one of the broadest beaches on the island, is open 24 hours a day for swimming, surfing, and sunbathing—it's hot and shadeless. There is a new pavilion and toilet/shower facility up in the trees. You can camp here as well, but all camping must be done on the sand below the vegetation level. No camping permit is required, but you must get a recreation pass from the security guard at the

KAUA'I

front gate. Major's Bay Beach affords the best view of Ni'ihau, a purple Rorschach blot on the horizon—this is the closest you're likely to get to the "Forbidden Island." The Barking Sands has the largest sand dunes on Kaua'i, due to the ocean's shallowness between the two islands. Supposedly, if you slide down the dunes, made from a mixture of sand and ground coral, the friction will cause a sound like a barking dog, an effect that's most evident during the heat of the day when the sand is totally dry. Some locals come to the beaches at PMRF (and to Polihale Beach) to drive on the sand. If you choose to do so, be very cautious as vehicles can and do get stuck very easily. There is no tow service on the base—you would have to get assistance from town—and no gas service is available to guests, but if you've let air out of your tires to drive on the sand, you can refill your tires with air at the base service station. For any use of the base, you must register for a pass at the front gate security office, 808/335-4221. For nonresidents, your driver's license and rental car agreement will be sufficient. The main gate is open 6 A.M.–6 P.M. Mon.–Fri.; for all other times go to the secondary gate about one mile back down the highway toward Kekaha.

On occasion, missile launches can be seen at the base. During these training operations, access to the base is restricted and the Navy blocks boat traffic past the facility. However, these launches can be seen from Polihale State Park and from the highway.

Aside from its beaches, most use of the base is for movies and stargazing, and for the annual Fourth of July fireworks show. The base movie theater, an outdoor affair with medium-size screen and stadium seats (you could bring your own lawn chair and sit on the grass), shows free first-run movies Wed.–Sun.; all you need is a base pass. Showtime varies by season but is usually 7:30 P.M. in winter and 8 P.M. during the summer. Call 808/335-4210 for the current movie schedule and showtime.

The Kauai Educational Association for Science and Astronomy, a.k.a. **KEASA**, welcomes islanders and visitors of all ages to peer through its 14-inch computerized telescope every month on the Saturday nearest the new moon at its observatory on PMRF, beginning at sunset. (Additional stargazing opportunities are held the fol-

lowing weekend at the Hyatt Hotel in Po'ipu and the Princeville Hotel in Princeville.) For further information and current meeting dates and times, call 808/245-8250. To get to either the movie theater or the observatory, use the base gate closest to Kekaha and inform the guard of your destination.

POLIHALE STATE PARK

Route 50 curves to the right after you pass the missile range. After the asphalt peters out, an HVB Warrior points left to Polihale State Park at a stop sign at a crossroads. You go in by five miles of dirt cane road that doesn't seem to get much attention. The earth is a definite buff color here, unlike the deep red that predominates throughout the rest of the island. You can day-trip to soak up the sights, and you'll find pavilions, showers, toilets, and grills. This area is hot and dry, so bring plenty to drink. Both RV and tent camping are allowed with a state park permit. The camping area is on the top of the dune on the left before you get to the day-use pavilions at the far end. There are generally no hassles, but the rangers do come around, and you should have a permit with you—it's a long way back to Lihu'e to get one.

From the parking area, walk over the dune and down to the beach. The broad powdery white sand beach stretches for nearly three miles, pushing up against the Na Pali cliffs to the north and skirting a hill on the military base to the south. However, this beach actually continues around the bend, running uninterrupted (although it narrows substantially in spots) all the way to Kekaha, a distance of about 15 miles, basically edging the Mana Plain. It is the longest beach by far in the state. The swimming can be dangerous, as currents are strong, but the hiking is grand. With a small reef offshore, the most protected spot is known as Queen's Pond; it's at the far southern end of the beach. You'll have your best chance to swim in summer. When the sea is not too rough, experienced surfers come to ride the waves.

Literally at the end of the road, this beach takes you away from the crowds, but you'll hardly ever be all by yourself. Here the cliffs come down to the sea, brawny and rugged with the Na Pali Coast beginning around the far bend. Where the cliffs meet the sea is the ruin of **Polihale Heiau**. This is a powerful spot, where the souls of the dead made their leap from land into infinity. Their goal was the land of the dead, a mythical submerged mountain a few miles off the coast. The priests of this temple chanted special prayers to speed them on their way, as the waters of life flowed from a sa-

cred spring in the mountainside. Even if you are not pulled here because of the mystical, this is a marvelous place for a picnic and beach walk. As it rains so little here and distant clouds often do not hamper the view, sunsets are super, and seeing the green flash is a definite possibility. With no lights or air pollution to speak of, stargazing at Polihale can be exceptional.

MOUNTAIN PARKS

WAIMEA CANYON STATE PARK

The "Grand Canyon of the Pacific" is an unforgettable part of any trip to Kaua'i, and you shouldn't miss it for any reason. Waimea Canyon Drive begins in Waimea, heading inland past sugarcane fields for seven miles, where it joins Koke'e Road (Route 550) coming up from Kekaha. This serpentine route runs along a good but narrow road into Kaua'i's cool interior, with plenty of fascinating vistas and turnouts along the way. Going up, the passenger gets the better view. Behind you, the coastal towns fade into the pale blue sea, while the cultivated fields are a study of green on green. Waimea Canyon Drive is narrower, windier, and steeper in parts than the more gradually graded and better paved Route 550, a gentle roller-coaster of a road. Ei-

ther route is worthwhile, and you can catch both by going in on one leg and coming out on the other. Less than a mile before these two roads meet, you enter Waimea Canyon State Park, a ridgetop park of more than 1,800 acres that flanks the road to Koke'e and overlooks the canyon and ridges beyond, most of which lie within the boundaries of Pu'u Ka Pele and Na Pali Kona Forest Reserves.

Ever climbing, you feel as though you're entering a mountain fortress. The canyon yawns, devouring clouds washed down by draughts of sunlight. The colors are diffuse, blended strata of gray, royal purple, vibrant red, russet, jet black, and bubble-gum pink. You reach the thrilling spine, where the trees on the red bare earth are gnarled and twisted. The road becomes a roller coaster whipping you past raw beauty, immense and powerful. Drink deeply, contemplate, and

A visit to Kaua'i is not complete without a stop at Waimea Canyon—the "Grand Canyon of the Pacific."

ROBERT NILSEN

KAUA'I

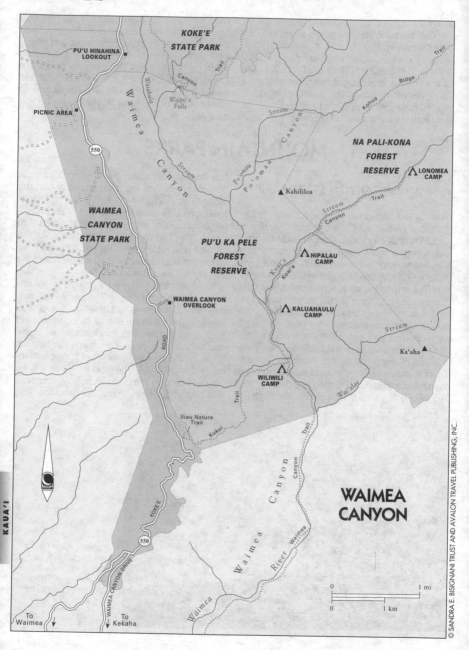

KOKE'E STATE PARK

PU'U HINAHINA LOOKOUT

PICNIC AREA

Waialae

Canyon

Trail

Waipo'o Falls

Stream

Kohua Ridge

Trail

NA PALI-KONA FOREST RESERVE

LONOMEA CAMP

Waimea Canyon

Po'omau

Po'omau Canyon

Stream

Kahililoa

WAIMEA CANYON STATE PARK

PU'U KA PELE FOREST RESERVE

WAIMEA CANYON OVERLOOK

Koai'e

Koai'e

Stream

Canyon

Trail

HIPALAU CAMP

KALUAHAULU CAMP

Stream

Ka'aha

ROAD

WILIWILI CAMP

Wai'alae

Trail

Iliau Nature Trail

Kukui

Canyon Trail

Waimea Canyon

KOKE'E

550

WAIMEA CANYON

Waimea River

Waimea

To Waimea

WAIMEA CANYON DRIVE

To Kekaha

0   1 mi

0   1 km

KAUA'I

© SANDRA E. BISIGNANI TRUST AND AVALON TRAVEL PUBLISHING, INC.

move on into the clouds at the 2,000-foot level, where the trees get larger again. This mountain fastness took the full brunt of Hurricane 'Iniki. Along the highway—and farther into this arboreal wilderness—you will see evidence of 'Iniki's fury in the form of skeletal dead trees. Luckily, Mother Nature is able to regenerate herself quickly, so much of the destruction has disappeared behind new growth.

As you climb, every lookout demands a photo. At **Waimea Canyon Overlook** (3,400 feet) you have the most expansive view of the canyon and across to valleys that slice down from the lofty peak. From here it's obvious why this canyon was given its nickname. Keep a watch out for soaring birds, mountain goats, and low-flying helicopters. The colors are quite amazing here, and the best time for photos is either early morning or late afternoon when shadows play across these mottled and deeply etched walls.

From **Pu'u Ka Pele Overlook,** Waipo'o Waterfall is seen tumbling forcefully off the hanging valley up the canyon. This overlook may be inaccessible and unsigned as it has recently undergone revegetation work to help stem erosion. A small rest area with a few picnic tables lies across the road. **Pu'u Hinahina Overlook** (3,500 feet) provides the best views down the canyon toward the ocean. Walk up a short trail behind the restrooms and you may have a good view of Ni'ihau adrift in the ocean to the west, if not obscured by clouds. A little farther along is a NASA space flight tracking station, and at the same turnoff is a track that leads into the Halemanu Valley. Beyond this point is Koke'e State Park, and from here on you start to see more forest birds.

Trails

One of the best trails off Koke'e Road is the Kukui Trail. The well-marked trailhead is between mile markers 8 and 9. As there is not much parking here, pull all the way off the roadway. The trail starts with the **Iliau Nature Loop,** an easy, 15-minute, self-guided trail at about 3,000 feet in elevation. Notice the pygmy palm-like lobelia among the many varieties of plants and flowers. Some signage here helps to explain the various plants. The *iliau,* after which the trail is named, is a relative of the silversword

that grows high on Haleakala on Maui and the greensword that grows on the Big Island. This rare plant grows only on the dry western mountain slopes of Kaua'i, and it seems that the greatest concentration is here. After years of growth, a tall spire shoots up in late spring bedecked with a profusion of small blossoms, only to die. Don't keep your nose to the ground here, however, because you can sometimes see white-tailed tropicbirds flying gracefully over the canyon or the brown-and-white *pueo* (Hawaiian owl) searching for its next meal.

The sign-in hut for the **Kukui Trail** is at the end of the Nature Loop; a pavilion stands nearby. Read some of the comments before heading down. The trail descends 2,000 feet through a series of switchbacks in 2.5 miles. At the one-half-mile and one-mile points along the trail are benches that offer grand views of the canyon vistas. Turn around here if you think that the hike so far has been enough for you. Continuing down, the trail ends on the floor of the canyon at Wiliwili Campsite. From here the hale and hardy can head up the Waimea River for a half mile, either to the dam or on the opposite side of the river to Kaluahaulu Camp and the beginning of the **Koai'e Canyon Trail.** This three-mile trail takes you up the south side of Koai'e Canyon, along which are plenty of pools and two additional campsites. This trail *should not* be attempted during rainy weather because of flash flooding. You can also branch south from the Kukui Trail and link up with the **Waimea Canyon Trail,** which takes you eight miles, mostly via a 4WD track, to the town of Waimea. Because it crosses a game management area, you must have a special permit (available at the trailhead). There is no camping south of Wai'alae Stream, the southern boundary of the forest reserve. The Waimea Canyon Trail is sometimes used by mountain bikers.

KOKE'E STATE PARK

After passing Pu'u Hinahina Overlook, you enter Koke'e State Park and soon reach park headquarters, the lodge, and museum. At the museum, helpful staff can provide you with a map of walking trails in the park and some information about the region's flora and fauna. Koke'e ranges

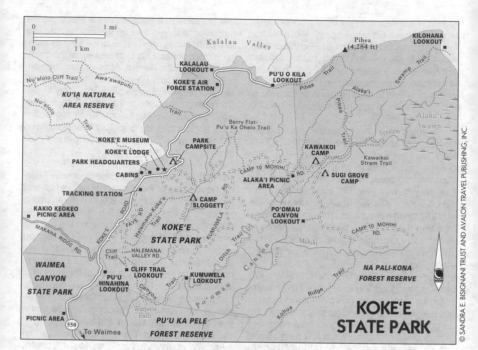

KOKE'E
STATE PARK

© SANDRA E. BISIGNANI TRUST AND AVALON TRAVEL PUBLISHING, INC.

3,200–4,200 feet in elevation and is a huge 4,345 acres in breadth. Although its forest is mixed, koa and 'ohi'a predominate. Temperatures here are several degrees cooler than along the coast and can be positively chilly at night, so bring a sweater or jacket. In January, the average daytime temperature is 45° and in July it's 68°. The average monthly rainfall is 70 inches a year, with most of that coming from October to May. Wild boar hunting and trout fishing are permitted within the park in prescribed areas at certain times of the year, but check with the Department of Land and Natural Resources on the third floor of the state office building in Lihu'e about licenses, limits, season, etc., *before* coming up the mountain. Trout fishing permits are also issued at the park headquarters during fishing season only. To see wildlife anywhere in the park, it's best to look early in the morning or late in the afternoon when animals come out to feed. Aside from the views, the native forest birds attract many visitors to the park, and you don't always have to hike off the main roads to see

them. What you might see are the reddish *'apapane* and *'i'iwi,* the green-yellow *'amakihi* and *'anianiau,* and the brownish *'elepaio.* Of the non-native birds, you probably will catch sight of the red-crested cardinal, the shama—a black bird with chestnut colored breast and white on the tail—and, of course, the feral roosters.

Two spectacular lookouts await you farther up the road. At **Kalalau Lookout** (4,120 feet), mile marker 18, walk a minute and pray that the clouds are cooperative, allowing lasers of sunlight to illuminate the humpbacked, green-cloaked mountains, silent and tortured, plummeting straight down to the roiling sea far, far below. There is a picnic area here with toilets. **Pu'u O Kila Lookout** (4,176 feet), another mile farther, is the end of the road. From here you not only get a wonderful view into the Kalalau Valley—the widest and largest valley along the Na Pali Coast—but also up across the Alaka'i Swamp to Mt. Wai'ale'ale if the clouds permit. One trail starts here and runs along an abandoned road construction project to Pihea, where it turns south into the Alaka'i Swamp.

There is another fine viewpoint in this high mountain region that is not along Route 550, but a wonderful spot nonetheless. A short distance up from Pu'u Hinahina Lookout, take the only paved road leading off to the left as you go up the mountain. There is no sign at the intersection, but this is Makaha Ridge Road. This narrow road—drive defensively and watch for oncoming traffic—leads steeply down the ridge, passing **Kakio Keokeo Picnic Area,** and continuing about four miles to PMRF tracking station—no entry. Cut through dense forest, the road affords no sweeping views. Almost to the end of the road, a secondary dirt road—for 4WD only—turns off to the left and runs for a little over one mile to the **Pine Forest Drive Picnic Area,** a great spot for a picnic and romantic sunsets.

Koke'e Natural History Museum

Open 10 A.M.–4 P.M. daily, the Koke'e Natural History Museum, 808/335-9975, website: www.aloha.net/~kokee, email: kokee@aloha.net, is to the side of a meadow just beyond the 15 mile marker. Be sure to stop; it's free. It's a good place to get detailed hiking maps of the park and the surrounding national forest lands and additional information about the mountain environment of Kaua'i. Inside are displays of native birds, descriptions of plants and animals found in the park, Hawaiian culture, an exhibit on weather with a focus on Hurricane 'Iniki and its aftermath, books on Kaua'i and Hawaii, local Kaua'i crafts, and a relief map of the island. The nonprofit museum sponsors periodic work crews to help remove alien plants and maintain native species, conducts an annual environmental fair, and holds the annual Emmalani Festival. By reservation, the museum offers easy to moderate free guided walks appropriate for kids and adults on Sundays during summer months.

Accommodations and Food

Koke'e Lodge, P.O. Box 819, Waimea, HI 96796, 808/335-6061, provides a dozen self-contained cabins, furnished with stoves, refrigerators, hot showers, cooking and eating utensils, and bedding; wood is available for woodstoves. The cabins cost $35 or $45 per night (five-night maximum; two-night minimum if one of the nights is Friday or Saturday) and vary from one large room for up to three people to two-bedroom units that sleep seven. The cabins are tough to get on weekends and holidays, in the August–September trout-fishing season, and during the wild plum harvest in June and July. For reservations, write well in advance (six months perhaps) and include a SASE, number of people, and dates requested. Full payment is required within two weeks of making reservations, with a refund possible (less a $15 service fee) if reservations are canceled at least one week before arrival. Check-in is 2 P.M., checkout is 11 A.M.

The Koke'e Lodge **restaurant, lounge, and gift shop** are open 9 A.M.–4 P.M. daily. The restaurant serves a full breakfast 9–11 A.M. and lunch 11 A.M.–3:30 P.M. The cool weather calls especially for a slice of homemade pie, a steaming pot of coffee, or a cup of hot chocolate with a mountain of whipped cream. Cocktails can be bought at the lounge. Prices for food and drink are on the high side, but, after all, everything has to be trucked up the mountain. The next nearest restaurant or bar is 15 miles down the road at either Waimea or Kekeha. Also in the lodge is a shop that sells postcards, T-shirts, snacks, sundries, and souvenirs; outside are a few picnic tables and a public telephone.

Tent camping is allowed at Koke'e State Park at a developed campground a few hundred yards across the meadow from the museum, with a permit. Camping permits are issued free at the state parks office in Lihu'e. Picnic tables and toilets are provided. In addition, two forest reserve campgrounds along Camp 10 Road and four primitive campgrounds in Waimea and Koai'e Canyons are open to campers with permit from the State Division of Forestry and Wildlife, which occupies the same office in Lihu'e as the state parks office.

The YWCA maintains **Camp Sloggett** within Koke'e State Park for group and individual hosteling and tent camping. Tent campers use raised platforms. Hostel guests use the bunkhouse on a first-come, first-served basis, unless a group of 25 or more has arranged to use the entire camp. The bunkhouse has single or bunk-style beds, and everyone has access to hot showers and a kitchen. Hostel guests must provide their own bedding and towels. Space can be arranged through the resident caretaker, who also has information about hiking. Rates are $10 for tent camping, $20 for hostel campers. Call 808/335-6060 for space availability, and 808/245-5959 for group reservations. To reach the camp, take the first right turn after passing the Koke'e Lodge, and follow the dirt road to a clearing and camp entrance. While this road may be somewhat rugged, it is open year-round and can be traversed by two-wheel-drive rental cars.

Koke'e State Park Trails

Maps of Koke'e's trails are available at the Koke'e Natural History Museum. Two of the best are Hawaii Nature Guide's *Kokee's Trails* map and the more detailed and broader scope *Northwestern Kaua'i Recreational Map* by Earthwalk Press. The list of trails below is not meant to be comprehensive; these are only several of the many trails in the area. The trail entries are not detailed accounts but general descriptions to characterize the trails. Please check at the Koke'e museum for up-to-the-minute trail information and use one of the popular trail books listed in the "Hiking" section in the main introductory material for more in-depth details of each trail.

Koke'e has about 45 miles of trails. A number of trails start along Koke'e Drive or the dirt roads that lead off from it; most are marked and well maintained. Generally speaking, these trails are of four kinds: Na Pali Coast overlook trails; Alaka'i Swamp trails; forest trails; and canyon overlook trails. These trails are for hiking only. Bikes, horses, and motorcycles should be used on the park and forest reserve dirt roads only. There is *no* trail to the top of Mt. Wai'ale'ale. Although the ancient Hawaiians did maintain a path to the summit to perform ceremonies at a *heiau* that was there, due to its extreme environmental sensitivity the summit area is now restricted and closed to all casual entry. Fines will be levied against all those who try to reach the top without duly authorized permission for scientific research.

The first trails you encounter heading up from the coast are off Halemanu Road. **Cliff Trail** is only a few hundred yards long and leads to a spectacular overview of the canyon. Look for feral goats on the canyon ledges. **Canyon Trail** continues off Cliff Trail for 1.5 miles. It's a strenuous trail that dips down to Waipo'o Waterfall before climbing out of the canyon to the end of Kumuwela Road at Kumuwela Lookout, and it

should take no more than three hours round-trip. Waipo'o Waterfalls, in two sections and cascades, is the highest on the island at about 800 vertical feet. To make an easy circle, take Halemanu Road to its end. There, cross the wooded valley by the short **Unnamed Trail** to reach an undrivable section of Faye Road, which leads back up to the highway not too far from the Halemanu Road turnoff. **Halemanu-Koke'e Trail** leaves Halemanu Road and runs through the forest to a secondary road off Camp 10 Road. It travels just more than a mile and is a self-guiding nature trail. With plenty of native plants and trees, it's a favorite area for indigenous birds. Perhaps the easiest nature trail to access is the **Nature Trail** that starts near the Koke'e museum and requires less than half an hour to the end and back. This is a favorite and good for small children.

At pole no. 320 near park headquarters, you find the beginning of **Camp 10-Mohihi Road.** For this road, 4WDs are recommended, but it might be crossed with a two-wheel-drive car *only* in dry weather. It leads to a number of trails, mostly heading into the forest; others run out along ridges for canyon views; still others head into the Alaka'i Swamp. **Berry Flat-Pu'u Ka Ohelo Trail,** an easy one-mile loop, gives you an up-close look at a vibrant upland forest. Under the green canopy are specimens such as *sugi* pine, California redwoods, Australian eucalyptus, and native koa. Locals come here to harvest the methley plums, for which the area is famous. There is a midsummer season and limits for picking these plums, so check with the park headquarters first. Less than half a mile up ahead is the trailhead to the newly reopened **Ditch Trail,** which gives views into Po'omau Canyon. Set aside at least a half day for this trail. A short way farther is **Sugi Grove,** where camping is limited to three days. This is the trailhead to the **Kawaikoi Stream Trail,** a 3.5-mile round-trip, moderate forest trail known for its scenic beauty. It follows the south side of the stream, crosses over, and loops back on the north side. Avoid it if the stream is high. About halfway up this trail, you can cross the stream to connect with the Pihea Trail.

The **Alaka'i Swamp Trail** is otherworldly and magical, crossing one of the most unusual pieces of real estate in the world. It begins off Camp 10 Road near the state park-forest reserve boundary. The nearby **Alaka'i Picnic Area** offers views into the Waimea Canyon. The trail heads into the swamp for 3.5 miles. Once you had to slog through the bogs, now much of the way is over a raised walkway—easier for you and more protection for the fragile environment. Still, it's a rainy area, so be prepared to get wet and muddy. If you smell anise along the way, that's the *mokihana* berry, used with *maile* for fashioning wedding lei. This trail, great for the unique vegetation, is also very good for birding. The trail ends at the Kilohana Lookout, where there's an expansive vista of Wainiha and Hanalei Valleys on a very rare clear day; otherwise you might only see a few dozen yards ahead of you. This trail is a real gamble for views. An alternate route to the Alaka'i Swamp, providing easier access, starts by taking **Pihea Trail** from the end of the paved road near the Pu'u O Kila Overlook. This is a good general-interest trail because it gives you wonderful views into Kalalau Valley virtually all along its length. Don't forget to turn around, however, for the views over the inner valleys and up to Mt. Wai'ale'ale are superb. About one mile along, the trail turns south and descends into the forest where the Alaka'i Swamp Trail, which comes in from the right, bisects it. This trail is also good for birding, and aside from the native birds, you might run into *moa,* wild jungle fowl. Continuing straight through this trail intersection, the Pihea Trail eventually dips down to Kawaikoi Stream and ends at Kawaikoi Campsite, from where you can return via Camp 10

Road for an amazing loop of the area. Count on a long day to do the loop, or be dropped off at Pu'u O Kila Overlook and picked up at Kawaikoi campsite, a distance of about four miles.

One of the most rewarding trails for the time and effort is **Awa'awapuhi Trail.** The trailhead is after park headquarters, just past pole no. 152 at the crest of the hill. It's three miles long and takes you out onto a thin finger of *pali,* with the sea and an emerald valley 2,500 feet below. The sun dapples the upland forest that still bears the scars of Hurricane 'Iniki. Everywhere flowers and fiddlehead ferns delight the eyes, while wild thimbleberries and passion fruit delight the taste buds. The trail is well marked and slightly strenuous. Connecting with the Awa'awapuhi at the three-mile marker is the **Nu'alolo Cliff Trail,** which connects with the **Nu'alolo Trail.** The Nu'alolo Trail starts near park headquarters and is the easiest trail to the *pali* with an overview of Nu'alolo Valley. It's 3.4 miles to the Nu'alolo Cliff Trail junction and 3.8 miles to the vista point at the Nu'alolo Trail terminus. Either the Awa'awapuhi or Nu'alolo ridge trails can be done separately, without using the Nu'alolo Cliff Trail, but all three together make a nice loop. Remember that the trail going in is downhill and coming out is uphill—over 1,500 feet elevation gain. Pace yourself. It's recommended that this loop be done counterclockwise, going in on the Awa'awapuhi Trail and coming out on the Nu'alolo Trail. As it's over 10 miles, give it a full day, although it can be done in a strong half day.

NI'IHAU AND THE NORTHWESTERN ISLANDS
NI'IHAU: THE FORBIDDEN ISLAND

The only thing forbidding about Ni'ihau is its nickname, "The Forbidden Island." Ironically, it's one of the last real havens of peace, tranquillity, and tradition left on the face of the earth. This privately owned island, operating as one large cattle and sheep ranch, is staffed by the last remaining pure Hawaiians in the state. To go there, you must have a personal invitation by the owners or one of the residents. Some people find this situation strange, but it would be no stranger than walking up to an Iowa farmhouse unannounced and expecting to be invited in to dinner. The islanders are free to come and go as they wish and are given the security of knowing that the last real Hawaiian place is not going to be engulfed by the modern world. Ni'ihau is a reservation, but a *free-will* reserva-

tion—something you'll admire if you've ever felt that the world was too much with you.

The Land and Climate
The 17-mile **Kaulakahi Channel** separates Ni'ihau from the western tip of Kaua'i. The island's maximum dimensions are 18 miles long by six miles wide, with a total area of 70 square miles. The highest point on the island, Pani'au (1,281 feet), lies on the east-central coast. There are no port facilities on the island, but the occasional boats put in at Ki'i and Lehua Landings, both on the northern tip. Since Ni'ihau is so low and lies in the rainshadow of Kaua'i, it receives only 30 inches of precipitation per year, making it rather arid. Oddly enough, low-lying basins, eroded from the single shield volcano

that made the island, act as a catchment system. In them are the state's largest naturally occurring lakes, 182-acre Lake Halulu and the larger Halali'i. Two uninhabited islets join Ni'ihau as part of Kaua'i County: Lehua, just off the northern tip and exceptional for scuba diving, and Ka'ula, a few miles off the southern tip; each barely covers one-half square mile.

HISTORY

After the goddess Papa returned from Tahiti and discovered that her husband, Wakea, was playing around, she left him. The great Wakea did some squirming, and after these island-parents reconciled, Papa became pregnant and gave birth to Kaua'i. According to the creation chants found in the *Kumulipo,* Ni'ihau popped out as the afterbirth, along with Lehua and Ka'ula, the last of the low reef islands.

Ni'ihau was never a very populous island because of the relatively poor soil, so the islanders had to rely on trade with nearby Kaua'i for many necessities, including poi. Luckily, the fishing grounds off the island's coastal waters are the richest in the area, and Ni'ihauans could always trade fish. The islanders became famous for Ni'ihau mats, a good trade item, made from *makaloa,* a sedge plant that's plentiful on the island. Craftsmen also fashioned *ipu pawehe,* a geometrically designed gourd highly prized in the old days. When Captain Cook arrived and wished to provision his ships, he remarked that the Ni'ihau natives were much more eager to trade than those on Kaua'i, and he secured potatoes and yams that seemed to be in abundant supply. Today, aside from raising livestock, Ni'ihau residents make charcoal, gather honey and produce excellent-quality (and very expensive) shell lei.

Kamehameha IV Sells

Along with Kaua'i, Ni'ihau became part of the kingdom under Kamehameha. It passed down to his successors, and in 1864, Kamehameha IV sold it to the Sinclair family for $10,000. Originally the king didn't want to sell this island and offered them another property, a swampy beach area, but much closer to the center of island power. That property was Waikiki. The Sinclairs

NI'IHAU

© SANDRA E. EISIGNANI TRUST AND AVALON TRAVEL PUBLISHING, INC.

turned the king down. Apparently, Ni'ihau was in great form after a fine spring and looked like a much better deal. This Scottish family, which came to Hawaii via New Zealand, has been the sole proprietor of the island ever since, although they now live on Kaua'i. They began a sheep and cattle ranch, hiring the island's natives as workers. No one can say exactly why, but it's evident that this family felt a great sense of responsibility and purpose. Tradition passed down over the years dictated that islanders could live on Ni'ihau as long as they pleased, but that visitors were not welcome without a personal invitation. With the native Hawaiian population so devastated, the Robinsons (descendants of the Sinclairs) felt that these proud people should have at least one place to call theirs and theirs alone. To keep the race pure, male visitors to the island were generally asked to leave by sundown.

Ni'ihau Invaded

During World War II, Ni'ihau was the only island of Hawaii to be occupied by the Japanese. A Zero pilot developed engine trouble after striking Pearl Harbor and had to ditch on Ni'ihau. At first the islanders took him prisoner, but he some-

NI'IHAU SHELLWORK

The finest shellwork made in Hawaii comes from Ni'ihau, in a tradition passed down over the generations. The shells themselves—tiny and very rare *kahelelani* and *kamoa*—are abundant only in the deep waters off the windward coast. Sometimes, the tides and winds are just right and they are deposited on Ni'ihau's beaches, but rarely more than three times per year. When that does happen, islanders stop everything and head for the shore to painstakingly collect them. The shells are sorted according to size and color, and only the finest are kept: 80 percent are discarded. The most prized are so tiny that a dozen fit on a thumbnail. Colors are white, yellow, blue, red, and the very rare gold. The best shells are free from chips or cracks. After being sorted, the shells are drilled. Various pieces of jewelry are fashioned, but the traditional pieces are necklaces and lei. The lei are often done in a pattern imitating flower lei of the other islands, as few natural flowers grow on Ni'ihau. These works can be short, single-strand chokers or heavy multi-strand pieces. The rice motif is always popular; these are usually multi-stranded with the main shells clipped on the ends with various colored shells strung in as highlights.

A necklace takes long hours to create, with every shell connected by intricate and minute knots. Usually the women of Ni'ihau do this work. Clasps are made from a type of cowry shell found only on Ni'ihau. No two necklaces are exactly alike. They sell by the inch, and the pure white and golden ones are very expensive—most are handed down as priceless heirlooms. Although Ni'ihau shellwork is available in fine stores all over the state, Kaua'i, perhaps because it's closest, seems to get the largest selection. For an introduction, have a look at the collection at the Hawaiian Trading Company in Lawa'i. If you're after a once-in-a-lifetime purchase, consider Ni'ihau shellwork.

The most comprehensive book covering this artistic subject is *Ni'ihau Shell Leis,* by Linda Paik Moriarty, published by the University of Hawai'i Press.

LOUISE FOOTE

---

how managed to escape and commandeer the machine guns from his plane. He terrorized the island, and the residents headed for the hills. One old woman who refused to leave was like a Hawaiian Barbara Fritchie. She told the Japanese prisoner to shoot her if he wished, but to please stop making a nuisance of himself—it wasn't nice! He would have saved himself a lot of trouble if he had only listened. Fed up with hiding, one huge *kanaka,* Benehakaka Kanahele, decided to approach the pilot with *aloha.* He was convinced the intruder would see the error of his ways. This latter-day samurai shot Mr. Kanahele for his trouble. Ben persisted and was shot again. An expression of pain, disgust, and disbelief at the stranger's poor manners spread across Ben's face, but still he tried pleading with the prisoner, who shot him for the third time. Ben had had enough, and grabbed the astonished pilot and flung him headlong against a wall, cracking his skull and killing him instantly.

This incident gave rise to a wartime maxim—"Don't shoot a Hawaiian three times or you'll make him mad"—and a song titled, "You Can't Conquer Niihau, Nohow." Mr. Kanahele lived out his life on Ni'ihau and died in the 1960s.

LIFE TODAY

The only reliable connection that the islanders have with the outside world is a World War II-vintage landing craft, which they use to bring in supplies from Kaua'i, and a new Agusta helicopter used for medical emergencies, supplies, and aerial tours. For years, homing pigeons were used to send messages, but they have been replaced by two-way radios. There's no communal electricity on the island, but people do have generators to power refrigerators and TVs. Battery radios are very popular, and most people get around either on horseback or in pickup trucks.

The population numbers around 230 people, 95 percent of whom are Hawaiian, the other 5 percent Japanese, and the main community is Pu'uwai, about midway down the west coast. There is one elementary school, in which English is used, but most people speak Hawaiian at home. The children go off to Kaua'i for high school, but after they get a taste of what the world at large has to offer, a surprisingly large number return to Ni'ihau.

After Hurricane 'Iwa battered the island and Hurricane 'Iniki followed suit in 1992, the state was very eager to offer aid. The people of Ni'ihau thanked them for their concern but told them not to bother—that they would take care of things themselves. Ni'ihau was the only island to reject statehood in the plebiscite of 1959. In November 1988, when a group of environmentally conscious Kaua'ians took a boat to Ni'ihau to try to clear some of the beaches of the floating sea junk that had washed up on shore, the Ni'ihauans felt that the island was being trespassed—they didn't want such help in any case—and a few shots were fired, a warning to back off. Still unsettled, the controversy focuses on the question of who owns the beach—all beaches in Hawaii are open to free access, yet the whole island of Ni'ihau is privately owned. Occasionally, boaters still try to land on the island and some have their craft confiscated.

Today, some people accuse the Robinson family of being greedy barons of a medieval fiefdom, holding the Ni'ihauans as virtual slaves. This idea is utter nonsense. Besides the fact that the islanders have an open door, the Robinsons would make immeasurably more money selling the island off to resort developers than running it as a livestock ranch. As if the spirit of old Hawaii was trying to send a sign, it's interesting that Ni'ihau's official lei is fashioned from the *pupu,* a rare shell found only on the island's beaches, and the island's official color is white, the universal symbol of purity.

Tours
Ni'ihau Safaris offers two different types of tours to the island, one a helicopter tour and the other a hunting tour. Aside from being invited to the island, these are the only ways to get a close-up look at Ni'ihau. Although it has no fixed schedule, **Ni'ihau Helicopters** flies charter tours on its twin-engine Agusta 109A when there are enough people to make a go of it. This three- to four-hour flight is not a sightseeing flight per se, but takes you to the island and lets you enjoy the beach for a couple of hours to play in the water and walk on the sand. Don't expect to meet any island residents, however, as they usually set you down away from where the people live. Rates are $250 per person with six passengers and $338 with four passengers. Alternately, a **hunting expedition** can be arranged for wild pig and feral sheep. The hunting rules for the island are strict but fair for a free chase hunt. Rates are up to $1,500 a day per hunter, with a maximum of four hunters, and this fee includes transportation, guide, lunch, up to one animal each, and care and packing of all shot animals. For more information on either of these tours, call 808/335-3500 or 877/441-3500, or write P.O. Box 450, Kaumakani, HI 96747.

THE NORTHWESTERN ISLANDS

Like tiny gems of a broken necklace, the Northwestern Hawaiian Islands spill across the vast Pacific. Popularly called the **Leewards,** most were discovered in the 19th century, oftentimes by hapless ships that ground to a sickening halt on their treacherous, half-submerged reefs. Even today, craft equipped with the most modern navigational devices must be wary in these waters. They remain among the loneliest outposts on the face of the earth.

Land and Climate
The Leewards are the oldest islands of the Hawaiian chain, believed to have emerged from the sea 25–30 million years! Slowly they floated northward past the suboceanic hot spot as the other islands were built. Measured from **Nihoa Island,** about 100 miles off the northwestern tip of Kaua'i, they stretch for just under 1,100 miles to **Kure Atoll.** There are a dozens of islets, shoals, and half-submerged reefs in this chain.

NI'IHAU

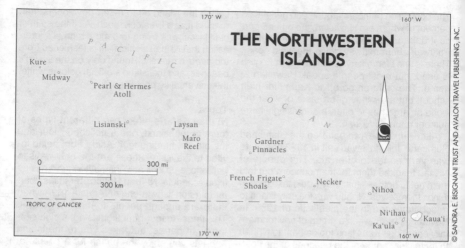

Most have been eroded flat by the sea and wind, but a few tough volcanic cores endure. Together they make up a landmass of approximately 3,500 acres, the largest being the three Midway islands—taken together—at 1,580 acres, and the smallest the **Gardner Pinnacles** at six acres. The climate is similar to that of the main islands with a slightly larger variance. Temperatures, usually 70–85 degrees, sometimes dip as low as 50 degrees and climb as high as 90 degrees. Rainfall can come any month of the year, but is more frequent in the winter. The average annual total is about 40 inches.

Administration and History

Politically, the Leewards are administered by the City and County of Honolulu, except for the Midway Islands, which are under federal jurisdiction. None, except Midway, are permanently inhabited, but there are some lonely wildlife field stations on Kure and the French Frigate Shoals. All, except for Midway Atoll, are part of the **Hawaiian Islands National Wildlife Refuge,** established at the turn of the 20th century by Theodore Roosevelt. In 1996, following the closure of the Naval Air Base on Midway Island, Midway Atoll was turned over to the Department of the Interior and is now administered as the **Midway Atoll National Wildlife Refuge.**

In precontact times, some of the islands supported a culture markedly different from the one that emerged on the main Hawaiian Islands. Necker Island, for example, was the only island in the entire Hawaiian archipelago on which the inhabitants carved stone figures with a complete head and torso. On others, remains of *heiau* and agricultural terracing allude to their colonization by precontact Hawaiians. Over the years, natives as well as Westerners have exploited the islands for feathers, fertilizer, seals, and fish.

The islands are now closely monitored by the U.S. Fish and Wildlife Agency. Permission to land on them is granted only under special circumstances. Studies are underway to determine if the waters around the islands can support commercial fishing, while leaving a plentiful supply of food for the unique wildlife of these lonely islands.

Wildlife

Millions of seabirds of various species have found permanent sanctuary on the Leewards, using them as giant floating nests and rookeries. Today the populations are stable and growing, but it hasn't always been so. On Laysan, in the early 1900s, egg hunters came to gather countless albatross eggs, selling the albumen to companies making photographic paper. They brought their families along, and their children's pets, which included rabbits. The rabbits escaped and multiplied wildly. In no time they invaded the territories of the **Laysan honeycreeper, rail,** and **millerbird,** rendering them extinct. Laysan has recovered and is refuge to more than six million birds, including the rare and indigenous **Laysan teal** and **finch.**

An amazing bird using the rookeries is the **frigate bird.** During mating rituals, the male can inflate its chest like a giant red heart-shaped balloon. Also known as man-o'-war birds, they oftentimes pirate the catches of other birds, devour chicks, and even cannibalize their own offspring.

Some of the most prolific birds of the Leewards are terns, both the delicate all-white **fairy tern** and its darker relative the **sooty tern.** Other distinctive species include a variety of boobies, and the **Laysan albatross,** which has a wingspan of 10–12 feet, the world's largest.

Besides birds, the islands are home to the **Hawaiian monk seal,** one of only two species of indigenous Hawaiian mammals. These beautiful and sleek animals were hunted to near extinction for their skins. Humans encroached on their territory more and more, but now they are protected as an endangered species. About 1,000 individuals still cling to existence on various islands.

The **green sea turtle** is another species that has found a haven here. They were hunted to near extinction for their meat and leather, and of the few colonies around the world, the largest in the United States is on the French Frigate Shoals.

MIDWAY ISLANDS

Midway Atoll is about 1,200 miles northwest of and an hour behind Honolulu. It is only 150 miles or so east of the international date line. The atoll is comprised of three separate islands, Sand, Eastern, and Spit, within a 25 square mile lagoon. Together, at about three square miles, the islands comprise about one half of the total land area of all the Northwestern Islands. These three islands and surrounding reef are coral growths that rise some 500 feet above the underlying volcanic peak.

First discovered in 1859 and named Brooks Islands, they were renamed Midway when annexed by the United States in 1867. In 1903,

Pres. Theodore Roosevelt put the islands under the control of the U.S. Navy to help stem the loss of bird life by Japanese sailors, who gathered bird eggs and feathers there. In the first decade on the 1900s, employees of a cable company were the first permanent resident on the islands. This communications station was a strategic link between the United States and Asia. From 1935 until the early '60s, Midway was a refueling station for most transpacific air routes to the Orient, first used by clipper seaplanes and later by prop and jet planes. With the growing concern about Japanese aggression in Asia, a naval base was begun on Midway in 1940. This installation was bombed on December 7, 1941, after the attack on Pearl Harbor earlier in the day. In June of the following year, the Battle of Midway took place in the ocean off the atoll, and was a turning point in the war of the Pacific. Until 1993, Midway continued to be used as a military base, housing up to 4,000 personnel during the 1960s. With the closure of the naval facility, Midway Atoll has become the **Midway Atoll National Wildlife Refuge,** administered from 1996 by the U.S. Fish and Wildlife Service for the Department of the Interior. Today, Midway has 150–200 permanent residents that run its facilities, maintain the refuge, and conduct scientific study. Tourists are allowed to visit the island, but only in strictly limited numbers—up to 100 persons a week. For all visitors, there is a $5 per person per day users fee which goes toward the administration of the refuge. Midway's weather and climate is similar to that of the main Hawaiian Islands. The average daytime summer temperature is 78° F, dropping to 55–65 from January to March, with about 40 inches of rain a year.

Hawaiian monk seals, green sea turtles, spinner dolphins, and close to 200 varieties of colorful **reef fish** inhabit the lagoon, while more than a dozen species of seabirds live and nest around the atoll. The world's large colony of **Laysan albatross,** about 2 million birds, inhabit the island, as do **great frigate birds, red-tailed tropic birds, terns, boobies, petrels,** and **wedge-tailed shearwaters.**

You can visit Midway to bird-watch, snorkel, dive, or fish. Bird-watching and snorkeling are free, but other activities are run by concessionaires. Fishing and diving operations are conducted by Destination Pacific. Contact them at

NI'IHAU

888/244-8582, or website: www.fishdive.com/midwayatoll.html. The Oceanic Society is a non-profit organization that also runs ecotours to Midway. Find information about their tours online at www.oceanic-society.com.

Transportation to the atoll is provided only by Aloha Airlines, 800/367-5250, which runs a once-weekly 2.5-hour charter from Honolulu on Saturday afternoon, returning Saturday evening, for $535 round-trip. Occasional Wednesday flights are also run, but these are generally not scheduled more than a month or so in advance. Flights are scheduled late in the day and early evening to avoid problems with birds and bird flight. Midway is considered outside the United States for customs and immigration purposes, so proper identification, and a visa if necessary, are required for your return trip. Accommodations for visitors to the island are in two remodeled officers' quarters that have queen or double beds, a/c, television, and telephones. A room with shared bath runs $125 a night, a room with private bath is $165, two-room suites go for $215, and the three-room suite is $300. The refuge cafeteria serves breakfast, lunch, and dinner, and The Clipper House restaurant offers fine French cuisine for breakfast and dinner. For sundries and supplies, T-shirts, gifts, and basic necessities, visit the Ship Store. Bike rental is $5 a day.

For more information on Midway Atoll and visiting this far outpost, contact: Midway Phoenix Corp., P.O. Box 29460, Honolulu, HI 96820, 808/599-5400 or 800/643-9291, website: www.midwayisland.com; or the Midway Atoll National Wildlife Refuge, 808/599-3914, website: www.r1.fws.gov/midway.

BOOKLIST

Many publishers print books of Hawaii. The following focus on Hawaiian topics. **University of Hawai'i Press,** website: www.uhpress.hawaii.edu, had the best overall general list of titles on Hawaii. The **Bishop Museum Press,** www.bishopmuseum.org/bishop/press, puts out many scholarly works on Hawaiiana, as does **Kamehameha Schools Press,** www.ksbe.edu/pubs. Also good are **Bess Press,** www.besspress.com; **Mutual Publishing,** www.mutualpublishing.com; and **Petroglyph Press,** www.basicallybooks.com. Two websites specifically oriented to books on Hawaii, Hawaiian music, and other things Hawaiian are Island Bookshelf at www.islandbookshelf.com and Hawaii Books at hawaiibooks.com.

ASTRONOMY

Bryan, E. H. *Stars over Hawaii.* Hilo, HI: Petroglyph Press, 1977. An introduction to astronomy, with information about the constellations and charts featuring the stars filling the night sky in Hawaii, by month. An excellent primer.

Rhoads, Samuel. *The Sky Tonight—A Guided Tour of the Stars over Hawaii.* Honolulu: Bishop Museum, 1993. Four pages per month of star charts—one each for the horizon in every cardinal direction. Exceptional!

COOKING

Alexander, Agnes. *How to Use Hawaiian Fruit.* Hilo, HI: Petroglyph Press, 1984. A slim volume of recipes using delicious and different Hawaiian fruits.

Beeman, Judy, and Martin Beeman. *Joys of Hawaiian Cooking.* Hilo, HI: Petroglyph Press, 1977. A collection of favorite recipes from Big Island chefs.

Choy, Sam. *Cooking From the Heart with Sam Choy.* Honolulu: Mutual Publishing, 1995. This beautiful, hand-bound cookbook contains many color photos by Douglas Peebles.

Fukuda, Sachi. *Pupus, An Island Tradition.* Honolulu: Bess Press, 1995.

Margah, Irish, and Elvira Monroe. *Hawaii, Cooking with Aloha.* San Carlos, CA: Wide World, 1984. Island recipes, as well as hints on decor.

Rizzuto, Shirley. *Fish Dishes of the Pacific—from the Fishwife.* Honolulu: Hawaii Fishing News, 1986. Features recipes using all the fish commonly caught in Hawaiian waters (husband Jim Rizzuto is the author of *Fishing, Hawaiian Style*).

CULTURE

Dudley, Michael Kioni. *Man, Gods, and Nature.* Honolulu: Na Kane O Ka Malo Press, 1990. An examination of the philosophical underpinnings of Hawaiian beliefs and their interconnected reality.

Hartwell, Jay. *Na Mamo: Hawaiian People Today.* Honolulu: 'Ai Pohaku Press, 1996. Profiles 12 people practicing Hawaiian traditions in the modern world.

Heyerdahl, Thor. *American Indians in the Pacific.* London: Allen and Unwin Ltd., 1952. Theoretical and anthropological accounts of the influence on Polynesia of the Indians along the Pacific coast of North and South America. Though no longer in print, this book is fascinating reading, presenting unsubstantiated yet intriguing theories.

Kirch, Patrick V. *Feathered Gods and Fishhooks: An Introduction to Hawaiian Archaeology and Prehistory.* Honolulu: University of Hawai'i Press, 1997. This scholarly, lavishly illustrated, yet very readable book gives new insight into the development of pre-contact Hawaiian civilization. It focuses on the sites and major settlements of old Hawaii and chronicles the main cultural developments while weaving in the social climate that contributed to change. A very worthwhile read.

FAUNA

Boom, Robert. *Hawaiian Seashells.* Honolulu: Waikiki Aquarium, 1972. Photos by Jerry Kringle. A collection of 137 seashells found in Hawaiian waters, featuring many found nowhere else on earth. Broken into categories with accompanying text including common and scientific names, physical descriptions, and likely habitats. A must for shell collectors.

Carpenter, Russell, and Blyth Carpenter. *Fish Watching in Hawaii.* San Mateo, CA: Natural World Press, 1981. A color guide to many of the reef fish found in Hawaii and often spotted by snorkelers. If you're interested in the fish that you'll be looking at, this guide will be very helpful.

Fielding, Ann, and Ed Robinson. *An Underwater Guide to Hawai'i.* Honolulu: University of Hawai'i Press, 1987. If you've desired to snorkel/scuba the living reef waters of Hawaii and be familiar with what you're seeing, get this small but fact-packed book. The amazing array of marine life found throughout the archipelago is captured in glossy photos with accompanying informative text. Both the scientific and common names of specimens are given. This book will enrich your underwater experience and serve as an easily understood reference guide for many years.

Goodson, Gar. *The Many-Splendored Fishes of Hawaii.* Stanford, CA: Stanford University Press, 1985. This small but thorough "fishwatchers" book includes entries on some deep-sea fish.

Hawaii Audubon Society. *Hawaii's Birds.* Honolulu: Hawaii Audubon Society, 1981. Excellent bird book, giving description. range, voice,

and habits of the over 100 species. Slim volume; good for carrying while hiking.

Hobson, Edmund, and E. H. Chave. *Hawaiian Reef Animals.* Honolulu: University of Hawai'i Press, 1987. Colorful photos and descriptions of the fish, invertebrates, turtles, and seals that call Hawaiian reefs their home.

Kay, Alison, and Olive Schoenberg-Dole. *Shells of Hawai'i.* Honolulu: University of Hawai'i Press, 1991. Color photos and tips on where to look.

Mahaney, Casey. *Hawaiian Reef Fish, The Identification Book.* Planet Ocean Publishing, 1999. A spiral-bound reference work featuring many color photos and descriptions of common reef fish found in Hawaiian waters.

Nickerson, Roy. *Brother Whale, A Pacific Whalewatcher's Log.* San Francisco: Chronicle Books, 1977. Introduces the average person to the life of earth's greatest mammals. Provides historical accounts, photos, and tips on whale-watching. Well-written, descriptive, and the best "first time" book on whales.

Pratt, H. D., P. L. Bruner, and D. G. Berrett. *The Birds of Hawaii and the Tropical Pacific.* Princeton, NJ: Princeton University Press, 1987. Useful field guide for novice and expert bird-watchers, covering Hawaii as well as other Pacific Island groups.

Tomich, P. Quentin. *Mammals in Hawai'i.* Honolulu: Bishop Museum Press, 1986. Quintessential scholarly text on all mammal species in Hawaii, with description of distribution and historical references. Lengthy bibliography.

van Riper, Charles, and Sandra van Riper. *Field Guide to Mammals in Hawaii.* Honolulu: Oriental Publishing, 1995. A guide to the surprising number of mammals introduced into Hawaii. Full-color pages document description, uses, tendencies, and habitat. Small and thin, this book makes a worthwhile addition to any serious hiker's backpack.

FLORA

Kepler, Angela. *Exotic Tropicals of Hawaii: Heliconias, Gingers, Anthuriums, and Decorative Foliage.* Honolulu: Mutual Publishing, 1999. This book features the photography of Jacob Mau.

Kepler, Angela. *Hawaiian Heritage Plants.* Honolulu: University of Hawai'i Press, 1998. A treatise on utilitarian plants used by the early Hawaiians.

Kepler, Angela. *Hawai'i's Floral Splendor.* Honolulu: Mutual Publishing, 1997. A general reference to flowers of Hawaii.

Kuck, Lorraine, and Richard Togg. *Hawaiian Flowers and Flowering Trees.* Rutland, VT: Tuttle, 1960. A classic, though no longer in print, field guide to tropical and subtropical flora illustrated in watercolor. A "to the point" description of Hawaiian plants and flowers with a brief history of their places of origin and their introduction to Hawaii.

Merrill, Elmer. *Plant Life of the Pacific World.* Rutland, VT: Tuttle, 1983. The definitive book for anyone planning a botanical tour to the entire Pacific Basin. Originally published in the 1930s, it remains a tremendous work, worth tracking down through the out-of-print book services.

Miyano, Leland. *Hawai'i, A Floral Paradise.* Honolulu: Mutual Publishing, 1995. Photographed by Douglas Peebles, this large-format book is filled with informative text and beautiful color shots of tropical flowers commonly seen in Hawaii.

Sohmer, S. H., and R. Gustafson. *Plants and Flowers of Hawai'i.* Honolulu: University of Hawai'i Press, 1987. Sohmer and Gustafson cover the vegetation zones of Hawaii, from mountains to coast, introducing you to the wide and varied floral biology of the islands. They give a good introduction to the history and unique evolution of Hawaiian plantlife. Beautiful color plates are accompanied by clear and concise plant descriptions, with the scientific and common Hawaiian names listed.

Teho, Fortunato. *Plants of Hawaii—How to Grow Them.* Hilo, HI: Petroglyph Press, 1992. A small but useful book for those who want their backyards to bloom into tropical paradises.

Wagner, Warren L., Derral R. Herbst, and H. S. Sohner. *Manual of the Flowering Plants of Hawai'i.* Rev. ed. 2 vols. Honolulu: University of Hawai'i Press in association with Bishop Museum Press, 1999. Considered the Bible for Hawaii's botanical world. Scholarly.

HEALTH

Gutmanis, June. *Kahuna La'au Lapa'au.* Honolulu: Island Heritage, 1987. Text on Hawaiian herbal medicines: diseases, treatments, and medicinal plants, with illustrations.

McBride, L. R. *Practical Folk Medicine of Hawaii.* Hilo, HI: Petroglyph Press, 1975. An illustrated guide to Hawaii's medicinal plants as used by the *kahuna lapa'au* (medical healers). Includes a thorough section on ailments, diagnosis, and the proper folk remedy. Illustrated by the author, a renowned botanical researcher and former ranger at Volcanoes National Park.

Wilkerson, James A., ed. *Medicine for Mountaineering and Other Wilderness.* 4th ed. Seattle: The Mountaineers, 1992. Don't let the title fool you. Although the book focuses on specific health problems that may be encountered while mountaineering, it is the best first-aid and general health guide available today. Written by doctors for the layperson to use until help arrives, it is jam-packed with easily understandable techniques and procedures. For those intending extended hikes, it is a must.

HISTORY

Apple, Russell A. *Trails: From Steppingstones to Kerbstones.* Honolulu: Bishop Museum Press, 1965. This "Special Publication #53" is a special-interest archaeological survey focusing on trails, roadways, footpaths, and highways and how they were designed and maintained throughout the years. Many "royal highways" from pre-contact Hawaii are cited.

Ashdown, Inez MacPhee. *Kahoʻolawe.* Honolulu: Topgallant Publishing, 1979. The tortured story of the lonely island of Kahoʻolawe by one of the family who owned the island until it was turned into a military bombing target during World War II. A first-person account of life on the island.

Ashdown, Inez MacPhee. *Ke Alaloa o Maui.* Wailuku, HI: Kamaʻaina Historians Inc., 1971. A compilation of the history and legends connected to sites on the island of Maui. Ashdown was at one time a "lady in waiting" for Queen Liliʻuokalani and was later proclaimed Maui's "Historian Emeritus."

Barnes, Phil. *A Concise History of the Hawaiian Islands.* Hilo, HI: Petroglyph Press, 1999. An examination of the main currents of Hawaiian history and its major players, focusing on the important factors in shaping the social, economic, and political trends of the islands. An easy read.

Cameron, Roderick. *The Golden Haze.* New York: World Publishing, 1964. An account of Captain James Cook's voyages of discovery throughout the South Seas. Uses original diaries and journals for an "on the spot" reconstruction of this great seafaring adventure.

Cox, J. Halley, and Edward Stasack. *Hawaiian Petroglyphs.* Honolulu: Bishop Museum Press, 1970. The most thorough examination of petroglyph sites throughout the islands.

Daws, Gavan. *Shoal of Time, A History of the Hawaiian Islands.* Honolulu: University of Hawaiʻi Press, 1974. A highly readable history of Hawaii dating from its "discovery" by the Western world down to its acceptance as the 50th state. Good insight into the psychological makeup of influential characters who helped form Hawaii's past.

Finney, Ben, and James D. Houston. *Surfing, A History of the Ancient Hawaiian Sport.* Los Angeles: Pomegranate, 1996. Features many early etchings and old photos of Hawaiian surfers practicing their native sport.

Fornander, Abraham. *An Account of the Polynesian Race; Its Origins and Migrations, and the Ancient History of the Hawaiian People to the Times of Kamehameha I.* Rutland, VT: C. E. Tuttle Co., 1969. This is a reprint of a three-volume opus originally published 1878–85. It is still one of the best sources of information on Hawaiian myth and legend.

Free, David. *Vignettes of Old Hawaii.* Honolulu: Crossroads Press, 1994. A collection of short essays on a variety of subjects.

Fuchs, Lawrence. *Hawaii Pono.* Honolulu: Bess Press, 1961. A detailed, scholarly work presenting an overview of Hawaii's history, based upon ethnic and sociological interpretations. Encompasses most socio-ethnological groups from native Hawaiians to modern entrepreneurs. A must for social historical background.

Handy, E. S., and Elizabeth Handy. *Native Planters in Old Hawaii.* Honolulu: Bishop Museum Press, 1972. A superbly written, easily understood scholarly work on the intimate relationship of pre-contact Hawaiians and the *'aina* (land). Much more than its title implies, this book should be read by anyone seriously interested in Polynesian Hawaii.

Ii, John Papa. *Fragments of Hawaiian History.* Honolulu: Bishop Museum, 1959. Hawaii's history under Kamehameha I as told by a Hawaiian who actually experienced it.

Joesting, Edward. *Hawaii: An Uncommon History.* New York: W. W. Norton Co., 1978. A truly uncommon history told in a series of vignettes relating to the lives and personalities of the first Caucasians in Hawaii, Hawaiian nobility, sea captains, writers, and adventurers. Brings history to life. Absolutely excellent!

Joesting, Edward. *Kauai: The Separate Kingdom.* Honolulu, University of Hawai'i Press, 1984. The history of Kaua'i through the end of the Hawaiian monarchy. Joesting brings the story of the island to life through the people who shaped it.

Kamakau, S. M. *Ruling Chiefs of Hawaii.* Rev. ed. Honolulu: Kamehameha Schools Press, 1992.

Krauss, Robert. *Grove Farm Plantation: The Biography of a Hawaiian Sugar Plantation.* Palo Alto, CA: Pacific Books, 1984. A history of the Grove Farm, the Wilcox family, and the economy of sugar on Kaua'i.

Kurisu, Yasushi. *Sugar Town, Hawaiian Plantation Days Remembered.* Honolulu: Watermark Publishing, 1995. Reminiscences of life growing up on sugar plantations on the Hamakua Coast of the Big Island. Features many old photos.

Lili'uokalani. *Hawaii's Story by Hawaii's Queen.* 1898. Reprint, Honolulu, Mutual Publishing, 1990. A moving personal account of Hawaii's inevitable move from monarchy to U.S. Territory by its last queen, Lili'uokalani. The facts can be found in other histories, but none provides the emotion or point of view expressed by Hawaii's deposed monarch. A "must-read" to get the whole picture.

McBride, Likeke. *Petroglyphs of Hawaii.* Hilo, HI: Petroglyph Press, 1997. A revised and updated guide to petroglyphs found in the Hawaiian Islands. A basic introduction to these old Hawaiian picture stories.

Nickerson, Roy. *Lahaina, Royal Capital of Hawaii.* Honolulu: Hawaiian Service, 1978. The story of Lahaina from whaling days to present, spiced with ample photographs.

Tabrah, Ruth M. *Ni'ihau: The Last Hawaiian Island.* Kailua, Hawaii: Press Pacifica, 1987. Sympathetic history of the privately owned island of Ni'ihau.

INTRODUCTORY

Carroll, Rick, and Marcie Carroll, eds. *Hawai'i: True Stories of the Island Spirit.* San Francisco: Travelers' Tales Guides, 1999. A collection of stories by authors who were chosen to elicit the essence of Hawaii and Hawaiian experiences. A great read.

Cohen, David, and Rick Smolan. *A Day in the Life of Hawaii.* New York: Workman, 1984. On December 2, 1983, 50 of the world's top photojournalists were invited to Hawaii to photograph the variety of daily life on the islands. The photos are excellently reproduced, accompanied by a minimum of text.

Day, A. G., and C. Stroven. *A Hawaiian Reader.* 1959. Reprint, Honolulu: Mutual Publishing, 1984. A poignant compilation of essays, diary entries, and fictitious writings that takes you from the death of Captain Cook through the "statehood services."

Department of Geography, University of Hawai'i, Hilo. *Atlas of Hawai'i.* 3rd ed. Honolulu: University of Hawai'i Press, 1998. Much more than an atlas filled with reference maps, this also contains commentary on the natural environment, culture, and sociology; a gazetteer; and statistical tables. Actually a mini-encyclopedia.

Michener, James A. *Hawaii.* New York: Random House, 1959. Michener's fictionalized historical novel has done more to inform *and* misinform readers about Hawaii than any other book ever written. A great tale with plenty of local color and information, but read it for pleasure, not facts.

Piercy, LaRue. *Hawaii This and That.* Honolulu: Mutual Publishing, 1994. Illustrated by Scot Ebanez. A 60-page book filled with one-sentence facts and oddities about all manner of things Hawaiian. Informative, amazing, and fun to read.

Steele, H. Thomas: *The Hawaiian Shirt: Its Art and History.* New York: Abbeville Press, Inc., 1984.

LANGUAGE

Elbert, Samuel. *Spoken Hawaiian.* Honolulu: University of Hawai'i Press, 1970. Progressive conversational lessons.

Elbert, Samuel, and Mary Pukui. *Hawaiian Dictionary.* Honolulu: University of Hawai'i, 1986. The best dictionary available on the Hawaiian language. The *Pocket Hawaiian Dictionary* is a less expensive, condensed version of this dictionary, adequate for most travelers with a general interest in the language.

Pukui, Mary Kawena, Samuel Elbert, and Esther T. Mookini. *Place Names of Hawaii.* Honolulu: University of Hawai'i Press, 1974. The most current and comprehensive listing of Hawaiian and foreign place-names in the state, giving pronunciation, spelling, meaning, and location.

Schutz, Albert J. *All About Hawaiian.* Honolulu: University of Hawai'i Press, 1995. A brief primer on Hawaiian pronunciation, grammar, and vocabulary. A solid introduction.

MYTHOLOGY AND LEGENDS

Beckwith, Martha. *Hawaiian Mythology.* 1970. Reprint, Honolulu: University of Hawai'i Press, 1976. Since its original printing in 1940, this work has remained the definitive text on Hawaiian mythology. Beckwith compiled this book from many sources, giving exhaustive cross-references to genealogies and legends expressed in the oral tradition. If you are going to read one book on Hawaii's folklore, this should be it.

Beckwith, Martha. *The Kumulipo.* 1951. Reprint, Honolulu: University of Hawai'i Press, 1972. Translation of the Hawaiian creation chant.

Colum, Padraic. *Legends of Hawaii.* New Haven: Yale University Press, 1937. Selected legends of old Hawaii, reinterpreted but closely based upon the originals.

Elbert, S., ed. *Hawaiian Antiquities and Folklore.* Honolulu: University of Hawai'i Press, 1959. Illustrated by Jean Charlot. A selection of the main legends from Abraham Fornander's great work, *An Account of the Polynesian Race.*

Kalakaua, David. *The Legends and Myths of Hawaii.* Edited by R. M. Daggett, with a foreword by Glen Grant. Honolulu: Mutual Publishing, 1990. Originally published in 1888, this book by Hawaii's own King Kalakaua draws upon his scholarly and formidable knowledge of the classic oral tradition to bring alive ancient tales from pre-contact Hawaii. A powerful yet somewhat Victorian voice from Hawaii's past speaks clearly and boldly, especially about the intimate role of pre-Christian religion in the lives of the Hawaiian people.

Melville, Leinanai. *Children of the Rainbow.* Wheaton, IL: Theosophical Publishing, 1969. A book on higher spiritual consciousness attuned to nature, which was the basic belief of pre-Christian Hawaii. The appendix contains illustrations of mystical symbols used by the *kahuna.* An enlightening book in many ways.

Pukui, Mary Kawena, and Caroline Curtis. *Hawaii Island Legends.* Honolulu: The Kamehameha Schools Press, 1996. Hawaiian tales and legends for the pre-teen.

Pukui, Mary Kawena, and Caroline Curtis. *Tales of the Menehune.* Honolulu: The Kamehameha Schools Press, 1960. Compilation of legends relating to Hawaii's "little people."

Pukui, Mary Kawena, and Caroline Curtis. *The Waters of Kane and other Hawaiian Legends* Honolulu: The Kamehameha Schools Press, 1994. Tales and legends for the pre-teen.

Thrum, Thomas. *Hawaiian Folk Tales.* 1907. Reprint, Chicago: McClurg and Co., 1950. A collection of Hawaiian tales from the oral tradition as told to the author from various sources.

Westervelt, W. D. *Hawaiian Legends of Volcanoes.* 1916. Reprint, Boston: Ellis Press, 1991. A small book concerning the volcanic legends of Hawaii and how they related to the fledgling field of volcanism in the early 20th century. The vintage photos alone are worth a look.

Wichman, Frederick B. *Kaua'i: Ancient Place Names and Their Stories.* Honolulu: University of Hawai'i Press, 1998. A very readable explanation of stories and legends relating to places on Kaua'i and the meanings of place-names.

NATURAL SCIENCES

Carlquist, Sherwin. *Hawaii, a Natural History: Geology, Climate, Native Flora and Fauna above the Shoreline.* Lawai, HI: Pacific Tropical Botanical Garden, 1984. Definitive account of Hawaii's natural history.

Hazlett, Richard, and Donald Hyndman. *Roadside Geology of Hawai'i.* Missoula, MT: Mountain Press Publishing, 1996. Begins with a general discussion of the geology of the Hawaiian Islands, followed by a road guide to the individual islands offering descriptions of easily seen features. A great book to have in the car as you tour the islands.

Hubbard, Douglass, and Gordon Macdonald. *Volcanoes of the National Parks of Hawaii.* 1982. Reprint, Volcanoes, HI: Hawaii Natural History Association, 1989. The volcanology of Hawaii, documenting the major lava flows and their geological effect on the state.

Kay, E. Alison, comp. *A Natural History of the Hawaiian Islands.* Honolulu: University of Hawai'i Press, 1994. A selection of concise articles by experts in the fields of volcanism, oceanography, meteorology, and biology. An excellent reference source.

Macdonald, Gorden, Agatin Abbott, and Frank Peterson. *Volcanoes in the Sea.* Honolulu: University of Hawai'i Press, 1983. The best reference to Hawaiian geology. Well-explained for easy understanding. Illustrated.

PERIODICALS

Hawaii Magazine. 3 Burroughs, Irvine, CA 92618. This magazine covers the Hawaiian Islands like a tropical breeze, featuring articles on all aspects of life in the islands, with special departments on travel, events, exhibits, and restaurant reviews. Up-to-the-minute information—a fine read.

Naturist Society Magazine. P.O. Box 132, Oshkosh, WI 54920. This excellent magazine not only uncovers bathing-suit-optional beaches throughout the islands, giving tips for naturalists visiting Hawaii, but also reports on local politics, environment, and conservation measures from the health-conscious nudist point of view. A fine publication.

PICTORIALS

La Brucherie, Roger. *Hawaiian World, Hawaiian Heart.* Pine Valley, CA: Imagenes Press, 1989.

POLITICAL SCIENCE

Albertini, Jim, et al. *The Dark Side of Paradise, Hawaii in a Nuclear War.* Honolulu: cAtholic Action of Hawaii. Well-documented research outlining Hawaii's role and vulnerability in a nuclear world. This book presents the antinuclear and antimilitary side of the political issue in Hawaii.

Bell, Roger. *Last Among Equals: Hawaiian Statehood and American Politics.* Honolulu: University of Hawai'i Press, 1984. Documents Hawaii's long and rocky road to statehood, tracing political partisanship, racism, and social change.

SPORTS AND RECREATION

Alford, John D. *Mountain Biking the Hawaiian Islands: Mauka to Makai*. Honolulu: 'Ohana Publishing, 2000. Good off-road biking guide to the main Hawaiian Islands.

Ambrose, Greg. *Surfer's Guide to Hawai'i*. Honolulu: Bess Press, 1991. Island-by-island guide to surfing spots.

Ball, Stuart. *The Hikers Guide to the Hawaiian Islands*. Honolulu: University of Hawai'i Press, 2000. Very excellent. Forty-four hikes on each of the four main islands. Ball also has *The Hikers Guide to O'ahu.*

Cagala, George. *Hawaii: A Camping Guide*. South Boston: Hunter Publishing, 1994. Useful.

Chisholm, Craig. *Hawaiian Hiking Trails: The Guide for All Islands*. Lake Oswego, OR: Fernglen Press, 1999. Also *Oahu Hiking Trails.*

Cisco, Dan. *Hawai'i Sports*. Honolulu: University of Hawai'i Press, 1999. A compendium of popular and little-known sporting events and figures, with facts, tidbits, and statistical information. Go here first for a general overview.

Lueras, Leonard. *Surfing, the Ultimate Pleasure*. Honolulu: Emphasis International, 1984. One of the most brilliant books ever written on surfing.

McMahon, Richard. *Camping Hawai'i: A Complete Guide*. Honolulu: University of Hawai'i Press, 1997. This book has all you need to know about camping in Hawaii, with descriptions of different campsites.

Morey, Kathy. *Oahu Trails*. Berkeley, CA: Wilderness Press, 1997. Morey's books are specialized, detailed hiker's guides to Hawaii's outdoors. Complete with useful maps, historical references, official procedures, and plants and animals encountered along the way. If you're focused on hiking, these are the best to take along. *Maui Trails, Kauai Trails,* and *Hawaii Trails* are also available.

Rosenberg, Steve. *Diving Hawaii*. Locust Valley, NY: Aqua Quest, 1990. Describes diving locations on the major islands as well as the marine life divers are likely to see. Includes many color photos.

Smith, Robert. *Hawaii's Best Hiking Trails*. Kula, Hawaii: Hawaiian Outdoor Adventures, 1991. Other guides by this author include *Hiking Oahu, Hiking Maui, Hiking Hawaii,* and *Hiking Kauai.*

Sutherland, Audrey. *Paddling Hawai'i*. Rev. ed. Honolulu: University of Hawai'i Press, 1998. All you need to know about sea kayaking in Hawaiian waters.

Thorne, Chuck. *The Diver's Guide to Maui*. Hana, HI: Maui Dive Guide, 1994. A no-nonsense snorkeler's and diver's guide to Maui waters. Extensive maps, descriptions, and "straight from the shoulder" advice by one of Maui's best and most experienced divers. A must for all levels of divers and snorkelers.

Valier, Kathy. *On the Na Pali Coast; A Guide to Hikers and Boaters*. Honolulu: University of Hawai'i Press, 1988. An invaluable guide to what you encounter along Kaua'i's spectacular North Coast. Natural, historical, and cultural references.

Wallin, Doug. *Diving and Snorkeling Guide to the Hawaiian Islands*. 2nd ed. Houston: Pisces Books, 1991. A guide offering brief descriptions of diving locations on the four major islands.

TRAVEL

Clark, John. *Beaches of O'ahu*. Honolulu: University of Hawai'i Press, 1997. Definitive guide to beaches, including many off the beaten path. Features maps and black-and-white photos. Also *Beaches of the Big Island, Beaches of Kaua'i and Ni'ihau,* and *Beaches of Maui County.*

Stanley, David. *Moon Handbooks: South Pacific.* 7th ed. Emeryville, CA: Avalon Travel Publishing, 1999. The model upon which all travel guides should be based. Simply the best book in the world for travel throughout the South Pacific.

ACCOMMODATIONS INDEX

BIG ISLAND

aaah, The Views: 295
Affordable Hawaii at Pomaika'i "Lucky" Farm B&B: 264
Akaka Inn: 350–351
Akiko's Buddhist Bed and Breakfast: 353
Arnott's Lodge: 209, 333–334
Aston Keauhou Beach Resort: 233
Aston Royal Sea Cliff Resort: 234
Bay Club: 278
The Bay House B&B: 334
Beck's Paradise Bed & Breakfast: 413
Bed and Breakfast Mountain View: 380
Bougainvillea Bed and Breakfast: 417
Carson's Volcano Cottages: 386
Chalet Kilauea: 387
Cliff House: 360, 373
Cook's Cottage: 305
Country Goose Bed and Breakfast: 383
Dolphin Bay Hotel: 333
Dragonfly Ranch: 265
Friends of Friends: 335
The Guesthouse at Volcano: 383–384
Hale Kai: 334
Hale Kilauea: 386
Hale Kipa O Kiana: 378
Hale Kona Kai: 234
Hale Maluhia Country Inn Bed and Breakfast: 254
Hale Ohia: 385–386
Hale Puu Mamo: 305
Hapuna Beach Prince Hotel: 282–283
Hawaiian Naniloa Resort: 332
Hawaii's Best Bed and Breakfast: 295
Hilo Hawaiian Hotel: 332
Hilo Seaside Hotel: 331
Hilton Waikoloa Village: 278–279
Holmes' Sweet Home B&B: 335
Holo Holo In: 209, 383
Holualoa Inn Bed and Breakfast: 253
Hotel Honoka'a Club: 209, 356
Ironwood House B&B: 335
Jacaranda Inn: 295
Ka Hale Iki Kilauea: 386
Kailua Plantation House B&B Inn: 233

Kaimana Guest House and Hostel: 209, 267
Kalani Oceanside Resort: 378
Kamuela Inn: 294
Kanola at Kona: 234
Keauhou Resort: 234
Kilauea Lodge: 384
Kilauea Military Camp: 406
King Kamehameha's Kona Beach Hotel: 232
Kohala Country Adventures Guest House: 309
Kohala's Guest House: 309
Kohala Village Inn: 305
Kona Bali Kai: 234
Kona Bay Hotel: 232
Kona Billfisher: 234
Kona by the Sea: 235
Kona Hotel: 253
Kona Islander Inn: 234
Kona Magic Sands Resort: 233–234
Kona Reef: 234
Kona Seaside Hotel: 232
Kona Tiki Hotel: 232
Kona Village and Four Season Resorts: 275, 276–277
Kulaniapia: 335
Lihi Kai B&B: 334
Lion's Gate: 265
Log Cabin: 357
Macadamia Meadows B&B: 414
Maid's Quarters, The: 384
Manago Hotel: 264
Margo's Corner: 414
Mauka Bed and Breakfast: 357
Mauna Kea Beach Hotel: 281–282
Mauna Kea Resort: 275
Mauna Lani Bay Hotel and Bungalows: 280
Mauna Lani Resort: 275
Mauni Lani Condominiums: 281
Maureen's Bed and Breakfast: 335
Merryman's Bed and Breakfast: 264
Moo's Log Cabin: 361
Mountain Meadow Ranch B&B: 356–357
My Island Bed and Breakfast: 383
Off the Wall Mini Hotel: 333
Oma's Hapu'u Hideaway: 384
The Orchid (Mauna Lani): 279
Our Place Papaikou's B&B: 334

Outrigger Waikoloa Beach Hotel: 277
Paauhau Plantation: 357
Patey's Place: 209, 231
Pearl's Shell B&B: 373
Pineapple Park B&B Hostel: 209
Rainbow Plantation B&B: 265
Rosey's Rest: 254
Royal Kona Resort: 233
Sea Mountain Resort: 411
Shipman House B&B Inn: 336
Shirakawana Motel: 414
Sunny Branch Acres: 373
Teshima's Inn: 255
Tutu's Place: 386
Uncle Bill's Hilo Bay Hotel: 331–332
vacation rental agencies: 208, 235; Kona 235;
    South Kohala 283–284
Volcano Country Cottages: 385
Volcano House: 406
Volcano Inn: 383
Waiakea Villas Hotel: 332
Waikoloa Resort: 275
Waikoloa Villas: 283
Waimea Country Lodge: 295
Waipio Wayside: 360
Whimsies: 373
Wild Ginger Inn: 333

KAUA'I

Alii Kai II: 1078
Alohilani Bed and Breakfast: 1055
'Anini Beach Hale: 1072
'Anini Hale: 1072
Aston Kaha Lani: 1043
Aston Kauai Beach Villas: 1022
Bed, Breakfast and Beach: 1087–1088
Best Western Plantation Hale Suites: 1041
Classic Vacation Cottages: 1128
Cliffs of Princeville: 1078
Coastline Cottages: 1118
Embassy Vacation Resort Po'ipu Point: 1114
Garden Island Inn: 1022
Garden Isle Cottages: 1117–1118
Gloria's Spouting Horn Bed and Breakfast:
    1118–1119
Hale Ho'o Maha: 1072
Hale Hyette B&B: 1116
Hale Lihue Motel: 1021
Hale Makani: 1044

Hale Moi: 1078
Hale Pilialoha: 1118
Hanalei Bay Resort: 1077–1078
Hanalei Bay Villa: 1078
Hanalei Colony Resort: 1096–1097
Hanalei Inn: 1088
Hanalei Plantation House: 1088
Hawaii International Hostel: 1005–1006
Historic Bed and Breakfast: 1087
Holiday Inn Sunspree Resort Kau'i: 1041–1042
Honu Kai Villas: 1117
House of Aleva: 1044
Hyatt Regency Kauai Resort and Spa:
    1112–1113
Islander on the Beach: 1043
Jungle Bungalow: 1096
Kahili Mountain Park: 1105–1106
Kakalina's Bed and Breakfast: 1055
Kalaheo Inn: 1128
Kalaheo Plantation Estate: 1128
Kapa'a Shore: 1054
Kapa'a Sands: 1043
Kauai Coconut Beach Resort: 1042
Kauai Cove Cottages: 1118
Kauai Kailani: 1054
Kauai Marriott Resort and Beach Club: 1023
Kauai Sands Hotel: 1041
Keapana Center: 1055
Kiahuna Plantation Resort: 1115–1116
Koke'e Lodge: 1151
Kola Landing Cottages: 1117
Kuhio Shores: 1116
Lae Nai: 1043
Lampy's Bed and Breakfast: 1044
Lanikai: 1043
Lawa'i Beach Resort: 1116
Mahina Kai: 1066
Makahu'ena at Po'ipu: 1116
Makai Club Cottages: 1078
Makai Farms: 1072
Makana Crest: 1044
Maluhia ma ka Honua: 1116–1117
Marjorie's Kauai Inn: 1126
Mokihana of Kauai: 1054
Molo'a Kai: 1066
Motel Lani: 1021–1022
Nihi Kai Villas: 1116
Old Koloa House: 1105
Pali Ke Kua: 1078
Paniolo: 1079
Paradise Vacation Rentals: 1066

Plantation Cottage: 1117
Po'ipu Bed and Breakfast Inn: 1117
Po'ipu Crater Resort: 1116
Po'ipu Kai Resort: 1115
Po'ipu Kapili: 1116
Po'ipu Makai: 1116
Po'ipu Palms: 1116
Po'ipu Plantation: 1116, 1117
Po'ipu Shores: 1115
Pono Kai: 1054
Prince Kuhio: 1116
Princeville Hotel: 1076–1077
Pua Hale: 1116
Puamana: 1079
Puu Poa: 1078
Radisson Kauai Beach Resort: 1022
Rosewood Bed and Breakfast: 1044
Sealodge: 1078
Sheraton Kauai Resort: 1113–1114
Sunset Kahili: 1116
Tip Top Hotel: 1021
Turtle Cove Suites: 1118
vacation rentals agencies: 1004–1006, 1023,
    1043–1044, 1055, 1072, 1079, 1088, 1119
Victoria Place B&B: 1126
Waikomo Stream Villas: 1116
Waimea Plantation Cottages: 1142
Whaler's Cove: 1116
YMCA Camp Naue: 1097

MAUI, LANA'I, MOLOKA'I

Ali'i Hono Hu'ako Tropical Gardens: 638
Aloha Cottages: 646
Aloha Lani Inn: 515
Aston Kaanapali Shores: 549
Aston Maui Kaanapali Villas: 540
Babson's Bed and Breakfast: 575
Bambula Inn Bed and Breakfast: 515
Banana Bungalow: 468, 493
Blue Horizons B&B: 552
By the Sea B&B: 574–575
Camp Grande: 588
Diamond Resort: 590
Dreams Come True: 685
Ekahi Village: 590
Ekena: 648
Ekolu Village: 590
Elua Village: 590
Embassy Vacation Resort: 552

Eva Villa: 575
Four Seasons Resort Wailea: 588–589
Garden Gate Bed and Breakfast: 516
Grand Champions: 590
Grand Wailea Resort and Spa: 587–588
Hale Ho'okipa Inn: 605
Hale Kai O Kihei: 573–574
Hale Maui: 548
Hale Moe: 685
Hale O Lana'i: 685
Hale Ono Loa: 548
Halfway to Hana House: 637–638
Hana Accommodations: 647
Hana Ali'i Holidays: 647–648
Hana Hale Malamalama: 648
Hana Kai Maui Resort: 648
Hana Maui Vacation Rental: 646
Heavenly Hana Inn: 649
Homoa Bay House and Bungalow: 648
Honokowai Palms: 547
Hotel Hana-Maui: 649–650
Hotel Lana'i: 682–683
Hotel Moloka'i: 722
House of Fountains: 516
Huelo Point Lookout: 639
Hyatt Regency Maui: 536
Joe's Place: 646
Josie's Hana Hideaway: 647
Kaanapali Alii: 539
Kaanapali Alii Royal: 539
Ka'anapali Beach Hotel: 538
Ka Hale Mala: 730
Kahana Sunset: 550
Kahana Village: 551
Kahana Villa Maui: 548
Kailua Maui Gardens: 638
Kaluakoi Condos: 742
Kaluakoi Hotel: 742
Kamalo Plantation: 731
Kamole Sands: 574
Kapalua Bay Hotel: 560
Kauhale Makai: 573
Kea Lani Hotel: 589–590
Kuau Cottages: 627
Kuau Plaza Condo: 627
Kula Lodge: 613
Kula View Bed and Breakfast: 614
Kulani's Hideaway: 646
Kumu'eli Farms B&B: 731
Lahaina Inn: 513
Lahaina Roads: 514

Lahaina Shores: 514
Lana'i Conference Center: 685
Leinaala: 573
Lihi Kai Cottages: 574
Lodge at Ko'ele: 683–684
Maalaea Surf Resort: 572–573
Mahana at Kaanapali: 551
Makai Inn: 512–513
Makena Surf: 590
Maluhia Hale B&B: 638
Mama's Beachfront Cottages: 627
Manele Bay Hotel: 684–685
Man Kai Maui: 574
Maui Beach Hotel: 482
Maui Coast Hotel: 572
Maui Eldorado Resort: 539
Maui Hill: 575
Maui Islander: 514
Maui Kai: 549
Maui Lu Resort: 572
Maui Marriott: 538
Maui Oceanfront Inn: 572
Maui Park: 548
Maui Prince Hotel: 597–598
Maui Seaside Hotel: 483
Maui Vista: 574
Menehune Shores: 573
Moanui Beach House: 731
Mokapu Beach Club: 586
Molina's: 493–494
Moloka'i Ranch: 744
Molokai Shores: 722
Nalu Kai Lodge: 627
Nani Kai Hale: 572
Napili Kai Beach Resort: 550
Napili Point Resort: 551
Napili Sunset: 549
Napili Surf Beach Resort: 548
Noelani: 548
Nona Lani Cottages: 573
Northshore Inn: 468, 493
Old Lahaina House: 515
Old Wailuku Inn at Ulupono: 494
Outrigger Wailea Beach Resort: 586
Paki Maui Resort: 549
Patey's Place Maui Hostel: 468, 512
Peace of Mind: 606
Pineapple Park B&B Hostel: 468
Pioneer Inn: 513
Plantation Inn, The: 514
Polo Beach Club: 589

Puamana: 515
Pu'u O Hoku Country Cottage: 731–732
Renaissance Wailea Beach Resort: 585–586
Ritz-Carlton Kapula: 559
Royal Kahana Resort: 550
Royal Lahaina Resort: 538
Sands of Kahana: 549
Sheraton Maui: 537
Silvercloud Upcountry Guest Ranch: 615
Sugar Beach Resort: 572
Tea House Cottage: 638
Tradewinds Cottages: 648
vacation rental agencies: 467, 476, 552, 560,
   575
Waialua Beach House: 731
Wailana Inn: 573
Wai Ola Vacation Paradise: 516
Wavecrest Resort: 730
Westin Maui: 537
Whaler on Kaanapali Beach, The: 539

O'AHU

Adam and Eve B&B: 826
Affordable Paradise Bed and Breakfast: 925
Airport Mini-Hotel: 825
Ala Mahina: 942
Ala Moana Hotel: 824
Aston Aloha Surf Hotel: 862
Aston at the Executive Center: 824
Aston Coconut Plaza Hotel: 860
Aston Honolulu Prince: 872
Aston Pacific Monarch: 873
Aston Waikiki Beachside Hotel: 865
Aston Waikiki Beach Tower Hotel: 873
Aston Waikiki Circle Hotel: 863
Aston Waikiki Joy Hotel: 863
Aston Waikiki Shores Condominium: 873
Aston Waikiki Sunset Hotel: 865
Backpacker's Vacation Inn and Hostel: 787
Banana Bungalow Waikiki Beach: 787, 859
Best Inn Hukilau Resort: 941–942
Big Surf Hotel: 860
Breakers: 861
Camp Kokokahi: 931–932
Camp Mokule'ia: 947
Crouching Lion Inn: 936–937
Diamond Head Beach Hotel: 864
Doubletreee Alana Waikiki Hotel: 865–866
Hale Aloha Youth Hostel: 787, 859
Hale Koa: 858

Halekulani: 870
Harbor Arms Apartment Hotel: 897
Harbor Shores Apartment Hotel: 897
Hawaiiana Hotel: 861
Hawaii Prince Hotel: 868
Hilton Hawaiian Village: 866–867
Hilton Turtle Bay Golf and Tennis Resort: 958–959
Holiday Inn Waikiki: 861–862
Honolulu International Youth Hostel: 787, 824
hotel/condo booking agencies: 786
Hyatt Regency Waikiki: 867–868
'Ilima Hotel: 863–864
Inn on the Park: 861
InterClub Waikiki: 787, 859–860
Island Hostel: 787, 860
J.W. Marriott Ihilani Resort and Spa: 909–910
Kahala Mandarin Oriental: 871–872
Kailua Beachside Cottages: 925
Kane'ohe Bay B&B: 932
Ke Iki Beach Bungalows: 958
Lora Dunn's House: 942
Manoa Valley Inn: 825–826
Marc Resorts: 872
Miramar: 862
Mokuleia Beach Colony: 947
Mokule'ia Sunset Vacation Rentals: 947
New Otani Kaimana Beach Hotel: 864
Ohana Hotels: 861
Outrigger East: 863
Outrigger Islander Waikiki: 863
Outrigger Reef: 863
Outrigger Waikiki: 863
Pacific Beach Hotel: 865

Pacific Hawaii Reservation: 925
Pagoda Hotel: 823
Pat's at Punalu'u: 938
Pat's Kailua Beach Properties: 925
Plaza Hotel: 825
Polynesian Hostel Beach Club: 787, 859
Queen Kapiolani Hotel: 862
Ramada Vacation Suites: 862
Royal Grove Hotel: 860
Royal Hawaiian Motel: 869–870
Schrader's Windward Marine Resort: 933–934
Sharon's Serenity: 925
Sheraton Moana Surfrider: 868
Sheraton Princess Ka'iulani Hotel: 886
Sheraton Waikiki: 868
Shower Tree: 825
Surfhouse: 787, 950
Town Inn: 823
Turtle Bay Condos: 959
W Hotel Honolulu: 872
Waikiki Beachcomber Hotel: 865
Waikiki Beach Marriott Resort: 866
Waikiki Beachside Hotel and Hostel: 859
Waikiki Gateway Hotel: 862
Waikiki Hana Hotel: 860
Waikiki Parc Hotel: 864–865
Waikiki Prince Hotel: 860
Waikiki Sand Villa: 862
Waikiki Shores: 863, 864
YMCA Atherton Branch: 824
YMCA Camp H.R. Erdman: 947
YMCA Central Branch: 823s
YMCA Fernhurst: 823
YMCA Nu'uanu: 823

RESTAURANT INDEX

BIG ISLAND

Aioli's Restaurant: 297
Aki's Cafe: 236
Aloha Akaka Plate Lunch: 351
Aloha Theatre Cafe: 255 245
Bad Ass Coffee Company: 257
Bangkok House: 240
Basil's Pizzaria and Restaurant: 237
Bay Terrace: 280
Beach Grill: 284
Beach Tree Bar and Grill: 277
Bear's Coffee Shop: 338
Big Island Candies: 339
Big Island Steakhouse: 284
Billy Bob's Pork 'n Park: 265
Blue Dolphin Restaurant: 284
Bree Garden Restaurant: 297
Brown's Beach House: 280
Bubba Gump's: 240
C.C. Jon's: 358
Café Pesto: 285, 341
Cafe 100: 337
Cafe Il Mondo: 357–358
Cafe Sibu: 239
Canoe House: 280
Canoes Cafe: 339
Captain Bean's Dinner Cruise: 245
Caqnaan Deli: 259
Cassandra's Greek Taverna: 239
Charlie's Bar and Grill: 379
Chart House: 242
Chili by Max: 237
Chris's Bakery: 259
Clipper Lounge: 278
Daizen Okazuya: 295
Don's Family Deli: 309
Don's Pake Kitchen: 296
Donatoni's: 279
Dotty's Family Restaurant: 338
Drysdale's Too: 241
Edelweiss: 297
Evie's Natural Foods: 257
Fiasco's: 340
Flashback's Bar and Grill: 240
Freddie's: 338

French Bakery: 236
Gallery Restaurant: 280
Grand Palace Chinese Restaurant: 284
Hama Yu Japanese Resaurant: 284
Hang Ten: 279
Happy Valley Seafood Restaurant: 339
Harbor House: 236
Hard Rock Cafe: 240
Harrington's: 341

LU'AU

Big Island
Hale Ho'okipa-Friday Night Lu'au: 209
Island Breeze Lu'au: 209, 243
Kona Village Resort: 286
Legends of the Pacific: 209, 279, 286
Old Hawaii Aha'aina Lu'au: 209, 286
Paniolo Night: 209, 286
Royal Lu'au: 209, 278, 286
Tihati's Drums of Polynesia lu'au: 209, 243

Kaua'i
Drums of Paradise: 1006
Kaual Coconut Beach Resort: 1006
Pa'ina 'O Hanalei: 1006
Reflections of Paradise: 1006
Tahiti Nui: 1006

Maui
Drums of the Pacific: 468, 543
The Feast of Lele: 468, 523
Maui Marriott: 468, 543
Old Lahaina Lu'au: 468, 523
Renaissance Wailea Beach Resort: 468
Royal Lahaina Lu'au: 468, 543
Wailea Sunset Lu'au: 593
Wailea's Finest Lu'au: 468, 593

O'ahu
Ali'i Lu'au: 787
Germaine's Lu'au: 787
Paradise Cove Lu'au: 787
Royal Hawaiian Lu'au: 787

PACIFIC RIM/HAWAIIAN REGIONAL CUISINE

Big Island
Bamboo Restaurant: 306
Cafe Sibu: 238
Hawaiian Style Cafe: 296
Kalaiki Plate Lunch: 413
Kawaihae Harbor Grill: 285
Maha's Cafe: 296
Merriman's: 297–298
Orchid Court: 280
Restaurant Yokohama: 238–239
Sam Choy's Kaloko Restaurant: 240
Super Js: 265
Teshima's Restaurant: 255

Kaua'i
Bali Hai Restaurant: 1079
Camp House Grill and Cantina: 1137
Da Imu Hut Cafe: 1138
Green Garden Restaurant: 1137
Hanapepe Cafe and Espresso Bar: 1138
Linda's Restaurant: 1138
Omoide's Deli and Bakery: 1137
Pacific Cafe: 1058
Polynesian Hide-a-way: 1066
Tidepool Restaurant: 1122
Wong's Restaurant: 1137

Maui
Aloha Mixed Plate: 517
Anuenue Room: 561

Bamboo Bistro: 568
Banyan Tree: 561
Bay Club: 561
Haliimaile General Store: 607
Hula Moons Restaurant: 591
Humuhumunukunukuapua'a: 591
Local Food: 517
Mama's Fish House: 629
Nick's Fishmarket: 592
A Pacific Cafe, Honokowai: 554
Pacific Cafe Maui: 578
Rabang's: 723
Saeng's: 494
SeaWatch: 593

O'ahu
3660 On the Rise: 833
Alan Wong's: 833
Chai's Island Bistro: 830
Chef Mavro Restaurant: 833–834
Haleiwa Joe's at Ha'iku Gardens: 932
Hawaii Theatre: 840
Helena's Hawaiian Food: 830
Indigo: 833
On Jin's Cafe: 833
Ono Hawaiian Foods: 882
Peacock Dining Room: 876
Sam Choy's Breakfast, Lunch, and Crab: 832–833

Hawaii Calls Restaurant: 278
Hawaiian Chili by Max: 284
Herb's Place: 358
Hilo Homemade Ice Cream: 339
Holualoa Cafe: 255
Honu's Nest: 340
Hualalai Club Grille and Bar: 277
Huggo's Restaurant: 241
Hula La's Burrito Bar: 306
Huna Ohana: 373
Island Grinds: 339
Jameson's-by-the-Sea: 241
Java on the Rock: 238
Kalaiki Plate Lunch: 413
Kamuela Deli: 296
Kamuela Provision Co.: 279

Kawaihae Harbor Grill: 285
Ke'ei Cafe: 265
Kea'au Cafe: 379
Kea'au Chop Suey House: 378
Ken's House of Pancakes: 339
Keoki's Coffee Company: 358
Keoki's Place: 355
Kilauea Lodge Restaurant: 387
Kimo's Family Buffet: 237
King Yee Lau: 237
Kirin: 279
Koa House: 297
Kohala Coffee Mill: 306
Kona Beach Restaurant: 242
Kona Brewing Company: 242
Kona Galley: 239

Kona Grill: 237
Kona Inn Restaurant: 241–242
Kona Ranch House: 239
Kona Theater Cafe: 265
Korner Pocket Bar and Grill: 258–259
La Bourgogne: 241
Lanky's Pastries and Deli: 339
Lava Java: 237
Lava Rock Restaurant: 388
Low International Food: 337
Luquin's Place: 373
Mady's Cafe Makana: 373
Mamane Street Bakery & Café: 357
Manago Hotel Restaurant: 265
Mark Twain's Square Café and Gift Shop: 414
Matthew's Place: 309
Michaelangelo's: 242
Miyo's: 339
Morelli's Pizza: 297
Mun Cheong Lau: 338
Na'alehu Coffee Shop: 413
Nalu Bar and Grill: 278
Nihon Restaurant: 3440
Nori's Saimin and Snacks: 338
Nuang Mai: 340
Ocean Grill: 280
Ocean Sushi: 339
Ocean View Inn: 236
Oodles of Noodles: 240
Orchid Cafe: 279
Orchid Court: 280
Palm Terrace: 279
Pancho and Lefty's: 239
Paniolo Country Inn: 296
Paniolo Plantation Inn: 358
Parker Ranch Grill: 297
Pescsatore: 341
A Piece of the Apple: 238
Pot Belli Deli: 238
Puhu I'a Restaurant: 277
Punalu'u Bake Shop and Visitor's Center: 412
Queen's Court Restaurant: 340
Quinn's: 239
Rainbow Moon Pizza: 388
Restaurant Miwa: 339
Reuben's Mexican Food: 340
Rocky's Pizza: 237
Roussols Waikoloa Villlage: 206
Roy's Waikoloa Bar and Grill: 284
Royal Jade Garden: 236
Royal Siam Thai Restaurant: 339

Sam Choy's Kaloko Restaurant: 240
Sandalwood Room: 341
Satsuki's: 338
Sawasdee Thai Cuisine: 373
Seaside Restaurant: 341
Sert's at Volcano Village: 387
Shaka Restaurant: 413
Simply Natural Ice Cream Parlor and Deli: 358
Stan's Restaurant: 236
Steam Vent Cafe: 388
Su's Thai Kitchen (Kona): 236
Su's Thai Kitchen (Waimea): 297
Teshima's Restaurant: 255
Tex Drive In and Restaurant: 358
Thai Thai Restaurant: 388
The Grill: 280
Tres Hombres: 240
Tres Hombres Beach Grill: 285
Tropical Dreams: 238
Tropical Dreams Ice Cream: 339
Tsunami Grill: 338
Verna's: 339
Verna's Drive-In: 237
Verna's V Drive in: 378
Volcano Golf and Country Club: 381, 388
Volcano House Restaurant: 407
Waimea Coffee Company: 296
Young's Kalbi: 295

KAUA'I

Aloha Diner: 1055
Aloha Kauai Pizza: 1044
Amigo's: 1119
Ara's Sakamaya: 1034
Aupaka Terrace: 1026
Bamboo Room: 1080
Barbecue Inn: 1025
Beach House Restaurant: 1121–1122
Beach Hut: 1025
Beach Restaurant and Bar: 1080
Beamreach Restaurant: 1080
Big Wheel Donut Shop: 1034
Breezer's: 1056
Brennecke Beach Deli: 1119
Brennecke's Beach Broiler: 1120–1121
Brick Oven Pizza: 1128–1129
Bubba Burger: 1089
Bubba's: 1056
Buzz's Steak and Lobster: 1046
Cafe Hanalei: 1079

Cafe Portofino: 1027
Caffé Coco: 1045–1046
Camp House Grill: 1129
Camp House Grill and Bar: 1056
Casa Di Amici: 1121
Chuck's Steak House: 1080
Da Kine Dogs: 1056
Da'li Deli and Cafe: 1106
Deli and Bread Connection: 1025
Dondero's 1122
Duane's Ono Char Burger: 1066
Duke's Canoe Club: 1027–1028
Eggbert's: 1044
Fish Express: 1025
Flying Lobster: 1046
Gaylord's: 1026–1027
Grinds Espresso: 1133
Hale O Java: 1080
Halo Halo Shave Ice: 1024
Hamura Saimin Stand: 1024
Hanalei Dolphin Restaurant: 1090
Hanalei Gourmet: 1090
Hanalei Mixed Plate: 1089
Hanalei Wake-Up Cafe: 1089
Hanama'ulu Restaurant Tea House and Sushi
   Bar: 1033–1034
Harley's Ribs and Chicken: 1045
Hawaiian Art Museum: 1081
Ho's Chinese Kitchen: 1025
House of Seafood: 1122
J.J.'s Broiler: 1027
Joe's Courtside Cafe: 1119
Joe's on the Green: 1119–1120
John's Place: 1143
Jolly Roger Restaurant: 1046
Joni-Hana: 1025
JR's Plantation Restaurant: 1034
Kalaheo Coffee Co. and Cafe: 1129
Kalaheo Steak House: 1128
Kalapaki Grill: 1026
Kapa'a Fish and Chowder House: 1058
Kauai Chop Suey: 1026
Kauai Kitchens: 1106
Keoki's Paradise: 1121
Kilauea Bakery and Pau Hana Pizza: 1073
King and I: 1055
Koloa Fish Mardet: 1106
Korean Bar-B-Q Restaurant: 1044
Kountry Kitchen: 1056–1057
Kukui's Pizza Cafe: 1026
Kukui's Restaurant: 1026

Kun Ja's II Korean Bar-B-Q: 1056
La Cascata: 1079–1080
La Griglia: 1120
Lawa'i Restaurant: 1126
Lighthouse Bistro: 1073
Llima Terrace: 1122
Local Boy Restaurant: 1025
Ma's Family Inc.: 1024
Mango Mama's Cafe: 1073
Margaritas: 1057
Maria's Mexican Restaurant: 1025
Mema: 1045
Mustard's Last Stand: 1126–1127
Myron's Filipino & Local Food: 1025
Noe's: 1058
Norberto's El Cafe: 1057–1058
Oki Diner: 1024
Old Hanalei Coffe Company: 1089
Olympic Cafe: 1058
Ono Family Restaurant: 1057
Pacific Pizza and Deli: 1143
Papaya's: 1055
Paradise Bar and Grill: 1081
Paradise Seafood and Grill: 1033
Pattaya Asian Cafe: 1120
Piatti: 1121
Pizza Hanalei: 1080
Pizzetta: 1106
Plantation House: 1120
Po'ipu Bay Bar and Grill: 1120
Pomodoro Ristorante Italiano: 1129
Pony Island Cantina: 1055–1056
Postcards: 1091
Prince Kuhio Court: 1045
Princeville Restaurant and Bar: 1081
Puhi Fish and Catering Company: 1033
Restaurant Kiibo: 1025
Restaurant Kintaro: 1046
Roadrunner Bakery and Cafe: 1072–1073
Rocco's Italian Restaurant: 1057
Rocky Mountain Chocolate Factory: 1045
Roy's Po'ipu Bar and Grill: 1121
Sampaguita's: 1034
Sert's on the Beach: 1097
Shave Ice Paradise: 1089
Shells: 1122
Steam Vent Cafe: 1097
Sukhothai: 1055
Sushi Bar and Grill: 1090
Sushi Katsu: 1024–1025
Taco Dude: 1044

Tip Top Cafe/Bakery: 1024
Toi's Thai Kitchen: 1133
Tokyo Lobby: 1025–1026
Tomkat's Grill: 1106
Tropix Island Style Cafe and Bar: 1057
Voyage Room: 1046
Wah Kung Chop Suey: 1044
Wailua Family Restaurant: 1044
Wailua Marina Restaurant: 1045
Waimea Brewing Company: 1143
Whaler's Brewpub: 1026
Wrangler Steakhouse: 1142
Zababaz: 1089
Zelo's: 1090

MAUI

Alexander's: 576
Aloha Pavillion: 542
Anthony's Coffee: 629
Asian Cuisine Yakiniku and Sports Bar: 483
Azeka's Ribs and Snack Shop: 576
B.J.'s Chicago Pizzeria: 520
Bamboo Cafe: 517
Bangkok: 628
Basil Tomatoes: 541
Beach Club: 553
Beachcombers: 541
Beachwalk Market and Pantry: 542
Bella Luna: 592
Bistro Molokini: 591
Biwon Restaurant: 496
Blue Ginger Cafe: 686
Buzz's Wharf: 568
Café O Lei: 607
Cafe Ciao: 592
Cafe Kiowa: 598
Cafe Kula: 591
Cafe Navaca: 578
Canton Chef: 578
Carrelli's On the Beach: 579
Casanova Italian Restaurant and Deli: 606
Cascades Grille and Sushi Bar: 542
Castaway Cafe: 541
Charley's: 628
Cheeseburger in Paradise: 518
Chez Paul: 521–522
China Boat: 553
Chuck's Steak House: 577
Clubhouse at the Experience at Ko'ele: 686
Clubhouse Restaurant: 687–688

Coffee Shop, The: 552
Coffee Store, The: 483
Coffee Works: 686
Compadres Mexican Bar and Grill: 520
Coral Reef, The: 543
Courtyard Cafe: 607
Cucina di Malia Trattoria: 569
David Paul's Lahaina Grill: 521
Dollie's: 553
Erik's Seafood Grotto: 554
Ferraro's at Seaside: 592
Fish and Game Brewing Company and
    Rotisserie: 555
Five Palms: 578
Fleming's Restaurant: 562
Fujiya: 494
Gardenia Court: 561
Gazebo: 553
Gerard's: 521
Grand Dining Room Maui: 591
Grateful Bread: 610
Greek Bistro: 578
Hakone: 598
Hana Gion: 591
Hana Ranch Restaurant: 650
Happy Valley Cafe: 495
Hard Rock Cafe: 518
Harry's Sushi Bar: 593
Hawaiian Moon's Deli and Natural Foods: 577
Heckock's: 519
Henry Clay's Rotisserie: 686
Hideaway: 484
Honokowai Okozuya Deli: 552
Hotel Hana-Maui: 650
Hotel Moloka'i Restaurant: 724
Hula Grill and Barefoot Bar: 540–541
Hulopo'e Court: 687
I'o: 520–521
Ichiban Okazuya: 495
Ichiban Restaurant: 483
Ihilani Dining room: 687
International House of Pancakes: 576
Jacques Bistro: 628
Jacques on the Beach: 577
Jameson's Grill and Bar: 562, 578
Joe's Bar and Grill: 593
Johnny's Burger Joint: 540
Ka'anapali Mixed Plate: 542
Kabi House: 576
Kahana Terrace Restaurant: 553
Kanemitsu Bakery: 723

Kay's Cafe and Deli: 577
Kea Lani: 592
Keka'a Terrace: 543
Kihei Caffe: 576
Kihei Prime Rib and Seafood House: 578
Kimo's: 519
Kincha: 591
Kitada's Kau Kau: 607
KKO Kai Ku Ono: 578
Kobe Japanese Steak House: 518
Ko'Ala: 542
Koho Grill and Bar: 484
Koho's Grill and Bar: 553
Komoda's: 607
Kula Lodge Restaurant: 613
Kuma Bar and Grill: 591
Lahaina Coolers: 519
Lahaina Fish Company: 519
Le Gunji: 592
Leilani's on the Beach: 540
Lobster Cove Restaurant: 593
Lodge at Ko'ele Formal Dining Room: 686
Local Boys: 483
Longi's: 520
Lourdes Kitchenette: 552
Luigi's: 540
Made in the Shade: 541
Makawap Steak House: 606–607
Makena Club House: 598
Mama's Ribs 'N Rotosserie: 552
Marco's Grill and Bar: 484
Margarita's Beach Cantina: 577
Matsu Restaurant: 483
Maui Bake Shop and Deli: 495
Maui Bakery, Bagelry and Deli: 482
Maui Coffee Roasters: 483
Maui Mixed Plate: 483
Maui Onion: 591
Maui Taco: 517, 552
Maunaloa Dining Room: 745
Milagros Bar and Restaurant: 628
Moana Bakery and Cafe: 628
Moloka'i Drive-in: 723–724
Moloka'i Pizza Cafe: 724
Moondoggy's: 484
Moose McGillycuddy's: 518
Nalu Sunset Bar: 542
Nazo's Restaurant: 496
Norm's Cafe: 496
Ohia Lodge: 743
'Ono Surf Bar and Grille: 542

Orient Express: 554
Outback Steakhouse: 553
Oviedo's Lunch Counter: 723
Pacific Grill: 592
Pacific'O Cafe: 520
Paia Coffee Compant: 629
Paia Fish Market Restaurant: 628
Palm Court: 590
Peggy Sue: 576
Pele's Other Garden: 686
Picnic's: 627–628
Pioneer Inn Bar and Grill: 518
Pizza Hut: 552
Plantation House: 562
Polli's Mexican Restaurant: 606
Polo Beach Grill and Bar: 592
Pool Grille: 687
Prince Court: 598
Pukalani Country Club: 610
Rainbow Dining Room: 483
Ramon's: 494
Red Dragon Restaurant: 483
Red Lantern: 518
Reilley's Steak and Seafood House: 540
Restaurant Isana: 577
Restaurant Mushroom: 495
Ritz-Carlton Restaurants: 561
Roy's Kahana Bar and Grill: 554
Roy's Nicolina Restaurant: 554–555
Royal Ocean Terrace: 541
Royal Scope Ice Cream Parlor: 541
Rusty Harpoon: 541
Ruth's Chris Steak House: 520
Sam Choy's Kahului: 484
Sam Choy's Lahaina: 520
Sam Sato's: 495–496
Sansei: 561–562
Sea House Restaurant: 555
Seasons: 591–592
Sen Ju Sushi: 542
Shishodo Manju Shop: 496
Siam Thai: 494
Silk Road: 495
Simple Pleasures Cafe: 495
Siu's Chinese Kitchen: 483
Smokehouse BBQ: 517
Spats Trattoria: 542
Sport's Page Bar and Grill: 577
Stella Blue's Cafe: 575–576
Stillwells Bakery and Cafe: 495
Stopwatch Bar and Grill: 607

Sundown Deli: 723
Sunrise Cafe: 517
Sunset Terrace: 590
Swan Court: 542
Swiss Cafe: 517
Taiko: 592
Tanigawa's: 686
Tasty Crust Restaurant: 495
Teppan Yaki Dan: 542
Terrace Restaurant: 561
Terrace: 687
Thai Chef: 517
Thai Chef Restaurant: 577–578
Tiki Bar and Grill: 542
Tiki Terrace: 541
Tokoyo Tei: 496
Tony Roma's: 577
Trattoria Haiku: 630
Tu-Tu's: 650
Upcountry Cafe: 610
Va Bene: 542
Vegan Restaurant: 628
Vi's Restaurant: 483
Village Grill: 745
Wailea Steak and Seafood: 592–593
Waterfront Restaurant: 568
Woody's Ocean Front Grill: 519
Yakiniku Lahaina: 518
Zoolu Bar and Grill: 519
Zushi's: 517

O'AHU

Ahi's Restaurant: 938
Ala Moana Poi Bowl: 826
Aoki's: 95
Assaggio: 827
Assaggio Italian Restaurant: 926
Auntie Pasto's: 832
Bali by the Sea: 880
Bay View Lounge: 960
Benihana: 878
Benkei: 827
Big City Diner: 831
Boci: 830
Boots: 926
Brent's Restaurant and Delicatessen: 927
Brew Moon Restaurant and Micro Brewery: 828
Buddhist Vegetarian Restaurant: 843
Buona Sera: 926
Buzz's Original Steakhouse: 927
Buzz's Steak House: 897
Cafe Hale'iwa: 950
Caffelatte: 875–876
Chart House: 833
Cheeseburger in Paradise: 875
China House: 827
Cholo's Homestyle Mexican Restaurant: 951
Chowder House: 827
Chuck's Steakhouse: 876
Ciao!: 877–878
Cisco's Cantina: 926
Coffee Gallery: 950–951
Compadres Mexican Bar and Grill: 828
Contemporary Cafe: 831
Da Smokehouse: 874–875
Diamond Head Grill: 879
Don Ho's Island Grill: 829
Doong Kong Seafood Restaurant: 843–844
Dot's Restaurant: 901
Duke's Canoe Club, Waikiki: 877
Dynasty Restaurant: 874
Eggs and Things: 874
Elephant and Castle Restaurant: 897
Ezogiku: 875
Fisherman's Wharf: 831–832
Forum Restaurant: 832
Furusato Sushi: 880
Garden Cafe: 831
Golden Dragon: 879
Good Friend Chinese Chicken: 926
Gordon-Biersch Brewery & Restaurant: 829
Ha Bien: 844
Hakone: 879
Hale Vietnam: 831
Hale'iwa Beach Grill: 951
Hale'iwa Joe's Seafood Grill: 951–952
Hank's Cafe Honolulu: 843
Hanohano Room: 880–881
Hard Rock Cafe: 877
Hideaway Restaurant: 832
House of Hong: 876
House Without a Key: 878
Hungry Lion: 830
Hy's Steakhouse: 880
India House: 832
Irifune Japanese Restaurant: 882
Island Burger: 826
Jameson's by the Sea: 951
Josie's: 830
K C Drive-in: 882
Ka'a'awa Country Kitchen: 935

Kailua Beach Restaurant: 927
Kailua Okazuya: 926
Keo's in Waikiki: 877
Keo's Thai Cuisine: 827
Kim Chee One: 932
Kimo's Homestyle Kitchen: 926
Kincaid's Fish Chop & Steak House: 827
Ko'oloau Ranch House: 932
Korean Barbecue Express: 827
Kua Aina: 950
Kyo-ya: 880
L&L Drive-in: 827
La Mer: 880
Lahaina Chicken: 826
Legend Seafood Restaurant: 832
Leonard's Bakery: 882
A Little Bit of Saigon: 844
Lou Garcia's: 926–927
Luigi's Place: 926
Makai Food Court: 827
Mama's Spaghetti: 826
Man Lee's Chinese Restaurant: 875
Matsumoto's: 951
Matteo's: 879
Maxime Vietnamese Restaurant: 844
Mekong I and II: 828
Michel's: 879
Mini Garden Noodle House: 843
Miura: 951
Miyako Kacho: 880
Mocha Java Cafe: 827
New Chinese Garden: 926
Nick's Fishmarket: 881
Oceanarium: 876–877
Old Spaghetti Factory: 827
Orchids Dining Room: 878–879
Padovani's Bistro: 878
Palm Terrace: 960
Paradise Found: 950
Payao Thai Restaurant: 830
Penny's Lunch Wagon: 831
People's Cafe: 830
Pepper's: 876
Perry's Smorgy: 875
Pier Seven Restaurant: 830

Pikake Restaurant: 959
Pizza Bob's: 951
Planet Hollywood Honolulu: 877
Portofino: 952
Princess Chop Suey: 926
Pyramids: 882
Rainbow Drive-in: 881–882
Restaurant Suntory: 880
Rosarina Pizza: j843
Rosie's Cantina: 951
Roy's Restaurant: 878
Royal Kitchen: 844
Ruffage Natural Foods: 875
Ruth's Chris Steakhouse: 830
Ryan's Grill: 828
Saeng's Thai Cuisine: 925–926
Saigon Cafe: 874
Sam Choy's Diamond Head Restaurant: 881
Sansei Seafood Restaurant and Sushi Bar: 829
Scoozees a GoGo Bakery and Deli: 828
Sea Tide Room: 960
Sekiya's Restaurant and Deli: 830
Shogun Restaurant: 877
Shore Bird Beach Broiler: 876
Shung Chong Yuein: 843
Stuart Anderson's Cattle Co. Restaurant: 897
Suehiro's: 830
Sunset Diner: 960
Sunset Grill: 830
Super Chef Gourmet Restaurant: 876
Sushi Mesa: 828
Ted's Bakery: 959
Ting Yin Chop Suey: 843
To Chau Vietnamese Restaurant: 844
Top of Waikiki: 880
Trattoria: 877
Tsuruya Noodle Shop: 826
Wailua Bakery: 951
Won Kee Seafood Restaurant: 832
Yat Tug Chow: 843
Yum Yum Tree: 828
Yummy Korean BBQ: 826
Yummy's Korean Barbecue: 926
Zaffron: 843

INDEX

A

a'a: 5–6
Academy Art Center at Linekona: 818–819
accommodations: 113–117; *see also specific place*; Accommodations Index
agricultural inspection: 131
'Ahihi-Kina'u Natural Reserve: 597
Ahu'ena Heiau: 222
Ahukini State Recreation Pier: 1020
'Aiea: 891–898
'Aina Moana (Land form the Sea) Recreation Area: 821–822
airfares: 129–190
airports: Dillingham Airfield 946–947; Hana 644; Hilo International Airport 211; Honolulu International Airport 788; Kahului Airport 469; Kapula-West Airport 469; Kaua'i Airport 1007; Kona International Airport 211–212; Maui 469–471; Moloka'i Airport 718; Princeville Airport 1007; Waimea-Kohala Airport 212; Upolu Airport 212
air tours: Kaua'i 996–998; Maui 460–461; O'ahu 781
'Akaka Falls State Park: 352
'akepa: 170
'akiapola'au: 169
Alakoko Fishpond: 1019
Ala Moana Beach Park: 821
Alexander and Baldwin Sugar Mill Museum: 434, 480–481
Ali'i Drive: 226–228
Allerton Garden: 1112
Aloha International: 1081
Aloha Tower: 808–809
'amakihi: 15
Amy B.H. Greenwell Ethnobotanical Garden: 168, 258
'Anaeho'omalu Bay: 273
Anahola: 1064–1066
Anahola Beach County Park: 1065
Anahola Mountains: 1064
Anahulu River Bridge: 948
Anara Spa: 1125
'Anini Beach County Park: 1071–1072
archery: 677
art: 83–91; *see also specific place*

Atlantis Submarine: 244
ATV tours (Big Island): 201
auto rentals: *see* transportation *under specific place*
axis deer: 668

B

Bailey House Museum: 434, 489–490
Baldwin Home: 434, 507
Banyan Tree, The: 505
Banzai Pipeline: 956
Barbers Point Beach County Park: 904
Barking Sands: 1145
Battle of Moku'ohai: 261
bed-and-breakfasts: 116–117 *see also specific place;* Accommodations Index
Bellows Field Beach County Park: 919
bicycling: 108; Big Island 194–195; Hamakua Coast 365; Hilo 343; Kaua'i 991–993; Kona 244; Maui 453; Moloka'i 714–715; O'ahu 774; Po'ipu 1124; Waipi'o 366
Big Five Corporations: 53
Big Island: 168–420; accommodations 207–209; economy 174; festivals, holidays, and events 176–179; flora and fauna 167–171; food 209; government 173; history 172; information and services 217; land 164–166; people 176; shopping 204–206; sports and recreation 180–203; travel 210–216
Big Island Botanical Garden: 168
billfish: 171
birds/bird-watching: 14–20, 169, 191, 667–668, 755–756, 969–970, 1159
Bishop Museum: 762, 815–818
black marlin: 171
Black Pot: 1087
Blaisdell County Park: 895–896
bodysurfing: Homoa Beach 645–646; Kama'ole I, II, III 571; Makapu'u Beach Park 915–916; Pounder's Beach 941; Sandy Beach Park 915; Wailea Beach 585; *see also beaches*
Boiling Pots: 327
Bond Estate: 308
boogie boards: 101
Brennecke's Beach: 1109

BEACHES

'Ahihi-Kina'u Natural Reserve: 597
Ala Moana Beach Park: 821
'Anaeho'omalu Bay: 273
Anahola Beach County Park: 1065
'Anini Beach County Park: 1071–1072
Banzai Pipeline: 956
Barbers Point Beach County Park: 904
Bellows Field Beach County Park: 919
Big Island: 180
Brennecke's Beach: 1109
Cape Kina'a: 597
Carlsmith Beach County Park: 330
Donkey Beach: 1064
D.T. Fleming Beach: 437
D.T. Fleming Beach Park: 558
Ehukai Beach County Park: 957
Fort DeRussy Beach: 855
Gray's Beach: 855
Green Sands Beach: 180, 415–416
Ha'ena Beach County Park: 1095
Halawa Bay: 710, 729–730
Hale'iwa Ali'i Beach Park: 948–950
Hale'iwa Beach County Park: 950
Hana Beach County Park: 641
Hanaka'o'o Beach Park: 535
Hanalei Bay: 1086–1087
Hanama'ulu Beach County Park: 1034
Hapuna Beach State Recreation Area: 181, 274
Hau'ula Beach County Park: 938
He'eia Kea Harbor: 931
Hilo Bayfront Park: 330
Holoholokai Beach Park: 274
Homoa Beach: 645–646
Honokohau Beach: 230
Honokowai Beach Park: 546
Ho'okena Beach County Park: 266
Ho'okipa Beach Park: 626
H.P. Baldwin Beach: 437
H.P. Baldwin County Park: 626
Isaac Hale Beach County Park: 375
Ka'a'awa Beach County Park: 935, 936
Ka'alawai Beach: 858
Ka'anapali Beach: 535
Ka'ena Point State Park: 907, 947
Kahaku'u Beach Park: 180, 229–230
Kahala Beach: 858
Kahana Beach: 437, 546
Kahanamoku Beach: 855
Kahe Point Beach County Park: 905

Kaiaka Beach County Park: 950
Kailua Beach: 924
Kaimu Beach Park (Black Sand Beach): 376
Kaiona Beach Park: 919
Kalae'o'io Beach County Park: 936
Kalalau Beach: 1101
Kalama Beach Park: 925
Kalama Park: 571
Kalepolepo Beach Park: 570
Kalihiwai Beach: 1071
Kaluahole Beach: 857
Kamakahonu Beach: 229
Kama'ole I, II, III: 571
Kama'ole Beach: 437
Kanaha Beach County Park: 479
Kaneana Cave: 907–908
Kapa'a Beach County Park: 303, 1052
Kapalua Bay Beach: 437
Kapalua Beach: 448
Kauna'oa Beach (Mauna Kea Beach): 181, 274
Kaupo Beach Park: 919
Kawaiku'i Beach Park: 912
Kawailoa Beach: 950
Kawakiu Beach: 710, 741
Kea'au Beach County Park: 907
Kealia Beach: 1064
Keawakapu Beach: 437, 585
Ke'e Beach: 1096
Kehena Beach: 376
Keiki Beach: 1109
Kekaha Beach County Park: 1144
Keokea Beach: 308–309
Koke'e Park: 913
Kokololio Beach County Park: 938
Koko Pai: 913
Kona Coast State Park: 231
Kua Bay: 231
Kualoa Regional Park: 934–935
Kuapoa Beach: 744
Kuilei Cliffs Beach Park: 857–858
Kukui'ula Bay: 1111
Kuli'ou'ou Beach Park: 913
La'ia Beach County Park: 941
Lahaina Beach: 437, 511–512
Lanikai Beach: 924
La Pérouse Bay: 597
Larsen's Beach: 1065–1066
Launiupoko Beach: 437
Lawa'i Beach: 1109

Lehia Park: 331
Leleiwi Beach County Park: 331
Little Maken: 597
Lualualei Beach County Park: 906
Lucy Wright Beach County Park: 1140
Lumaha'i Beach: 1094
Lydgate Beach: 1040
Ma'alaea Beach: 567
Maha'elpu: 1109
Mahaiula Beach: 231
Mahukona Beach County Park: 303
Ma'ili Beach County Park: 906
Mai Poina 'Oela'u Beach Park: 570
Major's Bay Beach: 1145–1146
Makaha Beach County Park: 906–907
Makalawena Beach: 231
Makalei Beach County Park: 857
Makapu'u Beach Park: 915
Makena Beach: 437, 597
Makena State Park: 597
Malu'aka Beach: 596–597
Manini Beach: 261
Mauna Kea: 181, 274
Maunalua Bay: 911–917
Maunalua Bay Beach Park: 913
Mile Marker 20 Beach: 729
Miloli'i Beach: 267
Miloli'i Beach County Park: 267
Mokapu Beach: 585
Mokule'ia Army Beach: 946
Mokule'ia Beach County Park: 946
Moloa'a Beach: 1065
Mo'omomi Beach: 710, 740
Nahuna (Five Graves) Point: 596
Napili Bay: 547
Napo'opo'o Beach County Park: 261
Ninini Beach: 1020
Niu Beach: 912
North Ka'anapali Beach: 536
North Kona Beaches: 230–231
Old Kona Airport State Recreation Area: 230
Olowalu Beach: 437
Omeola Beach: 597
One Ali'i Beach Park: 710, 726–727
Onekahakaha Beach County Park: 330
Paiko Beach: 912–913
Palauea Beach: 596
Pali Ke Kua Beach: 1076
Papohaku Beach: 710, 741
Pine Trees Surfing Beach: 230–231

Pohoiki Bay: 375
Poka'i Beach County Park: 906
Polihua Beach: 698
Polo Beach: 585
Po'olenalena: 596
Pounder's Beach: 941
Prince Kuhio Beach and Beach Park: 856
Puamana Beach: 437
Puamana Beach County Park: 512
Punalu'u Beach County Park: 414, 937–938
Pupukea Beach Park: 955
Pu'u Poa Beach: 1076
Quarry Beach: 1070
Queens Beach: 857
Red Sand Beach: 437, 645
Reeds Bay Beach Park: 330
Richardson's Beach Park: 331
Royal Moana Beach: 855
Salt Pond Beach County Park: 1137
Sandy Beach Park: 915
Sans Souci Beach: 857
Secret Beach: 1070–1071
Shipwreck Beach: 665, 695–696, 1109
Spencer Beach: 274
Spencer Beach County Park: 274–275
Sunset Beach: 956
Sunset Beach County Park: 957
Sunset Rip: 957
Tracks Beach County Park: 905
Ulehawa Beach County Park: 905–906
Ulua Beach: 585
Waialae Beach County Park: 858
Waiale'e Beach County Park: 957
Waialua Beach: 729
Wai'anae Harbor: 906
Wai'anapanapana Beach: 437
Waiehu Beach County Park: 498
Waihe'e Beach County Park: 499
Waikiki Marine Conservation District: 857
Wailea Beach: 585
Wailua Beach: 1041
Wailupe Beach Park: 912
Waimanalo Beach County Park: 919
Waimea Bay Beach County Park: 954
Waipi'o Beach: 365
Waipouli Beach County Park: 1041
Waipu'ilani Park: 571
Wawaloli Beach: 231
White Sands Beach County Park: 180, 229
Whittington Beach County Park: 412

BOTANICAL GARDENS

Allerton Garden: 1112
Amy B.H. Greenwell Ethnobotanical Garden: 168, 258
Big Island Botanical Garden: 168
Enchanting Floral Gardens: 611
Foster Botanical Gardens: 756, 819
Garden of Eden Botanical Gardens: 635
Ha'iku Gardens: 756, 929–930
Hawaii Tropical Botanical Garden: 168, 329
Hilo Forestry Arboretum: 168, 328
Ho'omaluhia Botanical Garden: 756, 929
Kahanu Gardens: 643
Ke'anae Arboretum: 635–636
Koko Crater Botanical Garden: 914
Kula Botanical Gardens: 611
Lawa'i Garden: 1112
Lili'uokalani Botanical Garden (O'ahu): 756
Lili'uokalani Gardens (Big Island): 325
Limahuli Botanical Garden: 971, 1095
Lyon Arboretum: 756, 815
Mauna Loa Macadamia Nut Factory: 328
Moanalua Gardens: 756, 819–820
Moir Gardens: 971, 1109–1110
Nani Mau Gardens: 168, 329
National Tropical Botanical Garden: 971, 1111–1112
Purdy's Macadamia Nut Farm: 734
Senator Fong's Plantation and Gardens: 933
Smith's Tropical Paradise: 971, 1038
Wahiawa Botanical Garden: 756, 899
Waimea Arboretum and Botanical Garden: 756, 954
World Tropical Botanical Gardens: 168, 354

Brigham Young University: 939
Burn's Field: 1007
bus tours see transportation under specific place

C

camping: 103–108; Big Island 188–190; Haleakala 621–622; Kaua'i 986–989; Kipahulu 655; Lana'i 673; Malaekahana Bay State Park 941; Maui 450
Canada-France-Hawaii Telescope: 315
Cape Kina'a: 597
Cape Kumukahi: 374
Captain Cook: see Cook, Captain James

Captain Cook (town of): 260–267
Captain Cook's Landing: 1141
Captain Cook's Monument: 1141
Carlsmith Beach County Park: 330
carnations: 427
car rentals see transportation under specific place
Carthaginian II: 434, 506
cattle: 174
central O'ahu: 752
Chain of Craters Road: 392, 401–402
China Art Collection: 323
Chinaman's Hat: 934
Chinatown: 840–844
Chinese Chamber of Commerce: 840
Chinese medicine: 843
Christ Church Episcopal: 257
Christ Memorial Episcopal Church: 1068
climate: 7–10; Big Island 166–167; Kaua'i 967–968; Maui 425–426; O'ahu 754–755
Coconut Island: 325, 928
coffee: 125, 174
Coffees of Hawaii: 733
Contemporary Museum: 762, 819
cook pines: 667
Cook, Captain James: 27–31, 58, 85, 173, 262, 972
Cooking School at Akaka Falls Inn: 350
Crater Rim Drive: 396, 398
crested honeycreeper: 15
Crouching Lion: 935–936
cruises: see river cruise, sunset dinner cruise, and underwater cruises

D

Dai Fukuji Buddhist Temple: 255
Damien Museum: 762, 854
Daughters of Hawaii: 226
David Douglas Historical Monument: 354
Department of Land and Natural Resources: 105
Devastation Trail: 399
Diamond Head: 850–851
Dillingham Airfield: 946–947
dinner sails (Maui): 444–445
diving: see scuba/snorkeling
Donkey Beach: 1064
drinking laws: 125
drugs: see illegal drugs
D.T. Fleming Beach: 437
D.T. Fleming Beach Park: 558

E

Earth Heritage Gallery: 323
earthquakes: 7
East-West Center: 814
economy: 47–54; *see also specific place*
ecotourism: 49; *see also specific place*
Ehukai Beach County Park: 957
electric car rental (Kona): 244
'Ele'ele: 1132–1134
'elepaio: 16
Enchanting Floral Gardens: 611
Episcopal Cemetery: 509

F

Fagan Memorial: 641–642
Falls of Clyde: 807
Father Damien: 736–737
fauna: 14–24; *see also specific place*
Faye Museum: 977, 1142
Fern Grotto: 1037
ferns: 167–168
festivals, holidays and events: 94; *see also specific place*

FISHING

introduction: 101–103, 122–123
Ala Wai Canal: 854
Big Island: 187
Hale'iwa Beach County Park: 950
Hanalei Bay: 1086–1087
Hilo Bayfront Park: 330
Hulopo'e Bay: 691
Kapa'a Beach County Park: 1052
Kaumalapa'u Harbor: 691–692
Kaua'i: 986
Kualoa Regional Park: 934–935
Lana'i: 673
Larsen's Beach: 1065–1066
Maui: 447
Midway Islands: 1159–1160
Moloka'i: 711–712
Nawiliwili Small Boat Harbor: 1029
O'ahu: 770
Polo Beach: 585
Punalu'u Beach County Park: 937–938
Reeds Bay Beach Park: 330
Spencer Beach County Park: 274–275
Waialae Beach County Park: 858
Waiale'e Beach County Park: 957

fixed-wing air tours (Big Island): 203
flora: 10–14; *see also specific place*
food and drink: 117–125; *see also specific place;* Restaurant Index
forest birds: 170
Fort DeRussy Beach: 855
Foster Botanical Gardens: 756, 819
Fuku-Bonsai Cultural Center: 379

G

Gardner Pinnacles: 1158
Garden of Eden Botanical Gardens: 635
Garden of the Gods: 697–698
glass-bottom boats: 186–187
Goat Island: 941
golf: 109; Big Island 197–198; Hilo 343; Kapalua 563; Kaua'i 993–994; Lahaina 544; Lana'i 675; Maui 455–458; Moloka'i 715; O'ahu 775–778; Po'ipu 1124; South Kohala 286; Wailua 1047
government: 44–47; *see also specific place*
Gray's Beach: 855
Green Sands Beach: 180, 415–416
green sea turtle: 273, 1159
Grove Farm Homestead: 977, 1014–1016
Guava Kai Plantation: 1068

H

Ha'ena Beach County Park: 1095
Ha'ena State Park: 1095
Ha'iku: 630–631
Ha'iku Gardens: 756, 929–930
Hakalau Forest National Wildlife Refuge: 171–172
Halawa Bay: 710, 729–730
Halawa Valley: 727–732
Hale Halawi O Holualoa Congregational Church: 227
Hale'iwa: 948–954
Hale'iwa Ali'i Beach Park: 948–950
Hale'iwa Beach County Park: 950
Hale Oloha: 509
Hale O Lono Heiau: 954–955
Hale Pa'i: 434
Hale Pohaku: 313
Haleakala National Park: 447–449, 616–622
Halema'uma'u Crater: 399
Halema'uma'u Overlook: 399
Hali'imaile: 605
Halona Cove: 914
Hamakua: 164

Hamakua Coast: 349–368
Hamakua Music Festival: 356
Hamoa Beach: 437
Hana: 639–652; accommodations 646–650; beaches 645–646; history 639–641; practicalities 650–652; sights 641–645
Hana Airport: 469
Hana Bay: 437, 641
Hana Beach County Park: 641
Hana Cultural Center: 434, 642–643
Hanaka'o'o Beach Park: 535
Hanakapi'ai Trail: 1100
Hanakoa Falls: 1100
Hanalei: 1084–1094
Hanalei Bay: 1086–1087
Hanalei Canoe Club: 1087
Hanalei National Wildlife Refuge: 1084
Hanalei Pavilion: 1087
Hanalei River: 1085
Hanalei Scenic Overlook: 1084
Hanalilolilo Trail: 733
Hanama'ulu: 1033–1034
Hanama'ulu Beach County Park: 1034
Hanapepe: 1134–1139
Hanapepe Valley Overlook: 1132
Hanauma Bay State Underwater Park: 913
Hansen's disease (leprosy): 735–738
Hapai Ali'i Heiau: 227
Hapuna Beach State Recreation Area: 181, 274
Hauola O Honaunau: 1039
Hau'ula: 937
Hau'ula Beach County Park: 938
Hawaiian Art Museum: 977, 1081
Hawaiian beliefs: 73–81
Hawaiian coot: 15
Hawaiian crow: 169
Hawaiian folk medicine: 147–148
Hawaiian hawk: 169
Hawaiian Home Lands Agency: 415
Hawaiian Islands Humpback Whale National Marine Sanctuary: 21
Hawaiian Islands National Wildlife Refuge: 1158
Hawaiian language: 68–72
Hawaiian Railway Line: 897
Hawaiian stilt: 15
Hawaiian thrush: 170
Hawaiian Trail and Mountain Club: 105
Hawaiian Volcano Observatory: 398
Hawaiian Waters Adventure Park: 903–904
Hawaii Audubon Society: 106
Hawaii Chinese Historical Center: 841

Hawaii Convention Center: 854
Hawaii Heritage Center: 840–841
Hawaii Maritime Center: 762, 806–807
Hawaii Nature Center: 106; 'Iao Valley 491
Hawaii's Plantation Village: 762, 896
Hawaii State Capitol: 802
Hawaii State Library: 802
Hawaii Theatre: 840
Hawaii Tropical Botanical Garden: 168, 329
Hawaii Volcanoes National Park: 189–190, 390–407
Hawi: 301, 305–307
hawksbill turtle: 171
healing stones: 898–899
health and safety: 144–152; *see also specific place*
He'eia Kea Harbor: 931
He'eia State Park: 931
heiau: 74; *see also specific place*; specific *heiau*
Hele-On Bus: 214
helicopter tours: Big Island 202; Maui 460
Hi'ilawe Waterfall: 361
Hikaiu Heiau: 261–262
Hiki na a ka la Heiau: 1039–1040
hiking: 103–108; Big Island 188–192; East Kaua'i 1048–1049; Haleakala 620–621; Kaua'i 989–990; Kilauea Caldera 399–400; Kula 612–613; Lahaina 525; Maha'ulepu Beach 1125; Maui 450; Mauna Kea 314; Mauna Loa 395; Moloka'i 713; Wailua 1048
Hilian Pali Lookout: 403
Hilo: 163, 319–348; accommodations 331–336; food 337–341; practicalities 342; sights 321–330
Hilo Arboretum: 168
Hilo Bayfront Park: 330
Hilo Forestry Arboretum: 168, 328
Hilo International Airport: 211
Historic County Building: 1017–1018
history: 24–43 *see also specific place*
hitchhiking: 143–144, 215–216
Hokuji Mission Shingon Buddhist Temple: 509
Hokul'ea: 807–808
Hokuloa Church: 272, 411
Hole in the Mountain: 1064
Holoholokai Beach Park: 274
Holoholoku Heiau: 1040
Holualoa: 250–255; accommodations: 253–254; coffee plantations 253; food 255; shops and galleries 251–253
Holy Ghost Catholic Church: 613

Holy Innocents Episcopal Church: 509
Holy Rosary Church: 626
Homoa Beach: 645–646
Honaka'a: 355–361
Honalo: 255–257
honeycreeper: 15, 169
Hongwanjii Temple: 509
Honoapi'ilani Highway: 533
Honoka'a: 355
Honokahau Harbor: 228
Honokohau Bay: 558–559
Honokohau Beach: 230
Honokowai: 546–556
Honokowai Beach Park: 546
Honolua Bay: 558
Honolulu: 752, 797–844; accommodations 823–826; entertainment 834–836; food 826–834; shopping 836–839; sights 799–822
Honolulu Academy of Arts: 762, 818
Honolulu Beaches and Parks: 820–822
Honolulu International Airport: 788
Honolulu Zoo: 851
Honomanu County Park: 635
Honomu: 349–355
Honopu: 1101
Honopu Valley: 1101
Ho'okena: 266
Ho'okena Beach County Park: 266
Ho'okipa: 437
Ho'okipa Beach Park: 626
Ho'olulu County Park: 325
Ho'omaluhia Botanical Garden: 756, 929
horseback riding: 108; Big Island 192–193; Kaua'i 991; Kona 259–260; Lana'i 674; Maui 450–451; Moloka'i 713–714; O'ahu 773–774; Po'ipu 1125; Waipi'o 364
H.P. Baldwin Beach: 437
H.P. Baldwin County Park: 626
Hualalai Road: 250
Huelo: 633
Hui Aloha Church: 656
Hui No'eau Visual Arts Center: 605
hula: 90–91
Hulihe'e Palace: 179, 225–226
Hulopo'e Bay: 691
humpback whales: 171
hunting: 110–111; Big Island 199; Kaua'i 995; Lan'i 676; Moloka'i 716; O'ahu 775
hurricanes: 10; Hurricane 'Iniki 968–969; Hurricane 'Iwa: 968–969

I
'Iao State Park: 491–492
'Ili'ili'opae Heiau: 728
illegal drugs: 150–151
'Imiola Church: 293
information and services: 154–158; *see also specific place*
interisland travel: 136–139; Big Island 212; Kaua'i 1007–1008; Maui 471
'Iolani Palace: 762, 801–802
Isaac Hale Beach County Park: 375
Island Heritage Gallery: 323
Island Marine Institute: 24
'i'iwi: 15

J
James Cambell National Wildlife Refuge: 942
James Clerk Maxwell Telescope: 315
jet skiing (O'ahu): 768
John Palmer Parker: 289–292
John Young's Homestead: 272
Judd Trail: 822
J.W. Marriott Ihilani Resort and Spa: 909–910

K
Ka'a'awa: 935–937
Ka'a'awa Beach County Park: 935, 936
Ka'aha Trail: 404
Ka'ahumanu: 35
Ka'ahumanu Church: 489
Ka'alawai Beach: 858
Ka'anapali: 533–545
Ka'anapali Beach: 437, 535
Ka'eleku Caverns: 643
Ka'ena Point State Park: 907, 947
Kahakuloa: 498–500
Kahaku'u Beach Park: 180, 229–230
Kahala Beach: 858
Kahalu'u: 933
Kahalu'u Fish Pond: 933
Kahana: 546
Kahana Beach: 437, 546
Kahanamoku Beach: 855
Kahana Valley State Park: 936
Kahanu Gardens: 643
Kahauku: 942–943
Kahekili's Leap: 693
Kahe Point Beach County Park: 905
Kahikolu Congregational Church: 261
Kaho'olawe: 658–662; history 660–662; land 658–659

Kahului: 477–500; accommodations/food 482–484; shopping/services 485–487; sights 477–482
Kahului Airport: 469
Kahului Harbor: 479
kahuna: 76
Kahuwai Bay: 273
Kaiaka Beach County Park: 950
Kailua: 633, 923–928
Kailua Beach: 924
Kaimu: 377–378
Kaimu Beach Park (Black Sand Beach): 376
Kainaliu: 255–257
Kaiona Beach Park: 919
Kaka'ako (Point Picnic) Waterfront Park: 821
Kakio Keokeo Picnic Area: 1151
Kala'e Cocks: 735
Kalae'o'io Beach County Park: 936
Kalaheo: 1127–1129
Kalahikiola Church: 301, 308
Kalakaua Park: 324
Kalalau Beach: 1101
Kalalau Lookout: 1151
Kalalau Trail: 1099–1100
Kalama Beach Park: 925
Kalama Park: 571
Kalapaki Beach: 1020
Kalaupapa: 735–739
Kalaupapa Overlook: 735
Kalepolepo Beach Park: 570
Kalihiwai Beach: 1071
Kalopa State Recreation Area: 355
Kalua'aha Church: 728
Kaluahole Beach: 857
Kamakahonu Beach: 229
Kamakou Preserve: 733
Kamalani Playground: 1040–1041
Kamalo Wharf: 727
Kama'ole Beach: 437
Kama'ole I, II, III: 571
Kamehameha: 31–35, 172–173, 641
Kamehameha III: 37
Kamehameha IV: 1155
Kamehameha 'Akahi 'Aina Hanau: 305
Kamehameha County Park: 308
Kamehameha Iki Park: 508
Kamehameha's Birthplace: 303
Kamokila Hawaiian Village: 1038–1039
Kamuela Museum: 179, 293–294
Kanaha Beach County Park: 479
Kanaha Pond State Wildlife Sanctuary: 477–479

Kanaloa: 75–76
Kane: 75–76
Kaneana Cave: 907–908
Kane'ohe: 929–939
Kanepu'u Preserve: 697
Kapa'a: 1051–1063; accommodations 1053–1055; entertainment 1059; food 1055–1058; information and services 1063; recreation 1059–1060; shopping 1060–1063
Kapa'a Beach County Park: 303, 1052
Kapa'a Bypass Road: 1052
Kapa'au: 307–310
Kapalua Bay Beach: 437
Kapalua Beach: 448
Kapapala Ranch: 410
Kapi'olani Park Kiosk: 849
Kapi'olani Regional Park: 856–857
Kapoho: 375
Kapuaiwa Coconut Grove: 720
Kapula: 557–569
Kapula-West Airport: 469
Kapunanoni Heiau: 227
kapu system: 78–81
Ka'u: 408–417
Kaua'i: 963–1012; accommodations 1003–1007; economy 973–975; festivals, holidays, and events 975–978; flora and fauna 969–971; government 973; history 972–973; information and services 1011–1012; land 966–969; people 975; shopping 999–1003; sports and recreation 978–998; transportation 1007–1010
Kaua'i Airport: 1007
Kaua'i Children's Discovery Museum: 977
Kaua'i Coffee Company Museum: 977, 1132–1133
Kaua'i Community College: 1033
Kaua'i County: 973
Kauai Educational Association for Science and Astronomy (KEASA): 1146
Kaua'i Historical Society: 977
Kauai Kookie Kompany: 1135–1146
Kaua'i Museum: 977, 1014
Ka'u Desert: 392, 403
Ka'u Desert Trail: 403
Ka'uiki Hill: 641
Kauladahi Channel: 1155
Kaulanapueo Church: 633
Kaumakani: 1138–1139
Kaumalapa'u Harbor: 691–692
Kaumana Caves: 327
Kaunakakai: 720–726

Kaunakakai Wharf: 720
Kauna'oa Beach (Mauna Kea Beach): 181, 274
Kaunolu: 692–694
Kaunolu Bay: 665
Kaupo Beach Park: 919
Ka'upulehu Petroglyphs: 271
Kawaihae Town: 273
Kawaiku'i Beach Park: 912
Kawailoa Beach: 950
Kawakiu Beach: 710, 741
Kawela: 727
kayaking: 186, 306; Kaua'i 984–985; Maui
  446–447; Moloka'i 711; O'ahu 770; Po'ipu
  1124; Wailua 1048
Kea'au Beach County Park: 907
Keaiwa Heiau State Recreation Area: 89
Kealakekua: 255, 257–260
Kealakekua Bay: 261–262
Kealia: 255, 1064
Kealia Beach: 437, 1064
Kealia Pond National Wildlife Refuge: 567–568
Ke'anae: 635
Ke'anae Arboretum: 635–636
Ke'anae Peninsula: 636
Keauhou Bay: 227
Keawakapu Beach: 437, 585
Keawala'i Church: 596
Keawanui Fishpond: 728
Ke'e Beach: 1096
Ke'ehi Lagoon Beach Park: 820
Ke'ei: 261
Ke'eku Heiau: 227
Kehena Beach: 376
Keiki Beach: 1109
Kekaha: 1144
Kekaha Beach County Park: 1144
Keokea: 255
Keokea Beach: 308–309
Keomuko: 694
Keopuolani Park: 480
Kepaniwai Park: 490–491
Kewalo Basin Park: 821
Keyhole: 913
Kihei: 437, 569–583; accommodations 571–575;
  beaches 570–571; food 575–579; practicalities
  579–583
Kihei Boat Ramp: 571
Kiholo Bay: 273
Kikiaola Harbor: 1144
Kilauea: 1068–1074
Kilauea Caldera: 397–400

Kilauea Iki: 399
Kilauea Lighthouse: 1069–1070
Kilauea Military Camp: 398
Kilauea Overlook: 398
Kilauea Point National Wildlife Refuge:
  1069–1070
Kilohana Plantation: 1016–1017
King Kalakaua: 24
Kipahulu: 653–655
Kipuka Puaulu: 404
Kipuka Pu'u Huluhulu: 318
kitesurfing: 101; Kanaha Beach County Park
  479; see also surfing
koa: 12–13
Koai'e Canyon Trail: 1149
Kohala: 163
Kohala Ditch: 310
Kohala Historical Sites Monument: 305
Koke'e Natural History Museum: 977, 1151
Koke'e Park: 913
Koke'e State Park: 1149–1153
Koke'e State Park Trails: 1152
Koki Beach: 645
Koko Crater: 914
Koko Crater Botanical Garden: 914
Koko Head: 914
Kokololio Beach County Park: 938
Koko Pai: 913
Kolekole: 353
Koloa: 1103
Koloa Sugar Plantation: 1103–1104
Komoa Wind Farm: 415
Kona: 162–163, 219–267; accommodations
  231–235; beaches and parks 229–231; en-
  tertainment 242–243; food 236–242; recre-
  ation 243–245; services and information
  249–250; shopping 245–249; sights 222–229;
  transportation 250
Kona Coast State Park: 231
Kona Historical Society Museum: 179, 258
Kona International Airport: 211–212
kona winds: 10
konane: 263
Ko 'Olina Resort: 904
Ku: 75
Kua Bay: 231
Kualapu'u: 733–734
Kualoa Ranch: 935
Kualoa Regional Park: 934–935
Kuan Yin Temple: 841
Kuapo: 656–657

Kuapoa Beach: 744
Ku'emanu Heiau Temple: 227
Kuilei Cliffs Beach Park: 857–858
Kukaniloko Birthing Stones: 899
kukui: 13, 704
Kukuihaele: 360–361
Kukui Heiau: 1040
Kukui O Lono Park: 1127–1128
Kukui Trail: 1149
Kukui'ula Bay: 1111
Kula: 610–615
Kula Botanical Gardens: 611
Kula Kai Caverns: 417
Kuli'ou'ou Beach Park: 913
Kumulipo, The: 25, 421
Kure Atoll: 1157–1158

L
La'ia Beach County Park: 941
La'ie: 939–942
La'ie Point: 941
Lahaina: 501–532; accommodations 512–516; entertainment/shopping 522–532; food 516–522; services 532; sights 505–512;
Lahaina Beach: 437, 511–512
Lahaina Jodo Mission: 509–510
Lahainaluna: 510–511
Lahaina Pali Trail: 525
Lahaina Restoration Foundation: 434, 502
Lake Waiau: 314
La Mariana Yacht Sailing Club: 820–821
Lana'i: 663–680; flora and fauna 667–671; land 666–667; people 671–672; services and information 679–680; sports and recreation 672–677; travel 677–679
Lana'i Airport: 677
Lana'i City: 680–689
land: 4–10; *see also specific place*
land ownership: 175
land tours: Kaua'i 995–996; O'ahu 775–781
language: 66–73
Lanikai Beach: 924
Lapakahi State Historical Park: 301, 303
La Pérouse Bay: 597
Larsen's Beach: 1065–1066
Launiupoko Beach: 437
Laupahoehoe: 354–355
Laupahoehoe Point County Park: 354
Laupahoehoe Train Museum: 179, 354
lava: 5–6
Lava Tree State Monument: 372

lava tube: 6
Lawa'i: 1126–1127
Lawa'i Beach: 1109
Lawa'i Garden: 1112
Leewards: 1157
Lehia Park: 331
lei: 88–90
Leke Lake Burial Grounds: 228
Leleiwi Beach County Park: 331
leprosy: *see* Hansen's disease
Lihu'e: 1013–1034; environs 1033–1034; practicalities 1021–1033; sights 1014–1020
Lihue First Church: 1017
Lihue Lutheran Church: 1017
Lihue Union Church: 1017
Lili'uokalani: 41–42
Lili'uokalani Botanical Garden (O'ahu): 756
Lili'uokalani Gardens (Big Island): 325
Limahuli Botanical Garden: 971, 1095
Little Blue Church: 227
Little Maken: 597
Lo'ihi Seamount: 411
Lono: 77
lu'au: 117; 119–120; *see also* Restaurant Index
Luahiwa Petroglyphs: 690–691
Lualualei Beach County Park: 906
Lucy Wright Beach County Park: 1140
Lumaha'i Beach: 1094
Lydgate Beach: 1040
Lydgate State Park: 1040
Lyman Mission House and Museum: 179, 321
Lyon Arboretum: 756, 815

M
Ma'alaea: 565
Ma'alaea Beach: 567
MacKenzie State Recreation Area: 376
Madame Pele: *see* Pele
Maha'elpu: 1109
Mahaiula Beach: 231
Mahukona Beach County Park: 303
Mailelomo Heiau: 272
Ma'ili Beach County Park: 906
Maili Cove: 908
Main Forest Road: 732
Mai Poina 'oela'u Beach Park: 570
Major's Bay Beach: 1145–1146
Makaha: 906–907
Makaha Beach Cabanas: 908
Makaha Beach County Park: 906–907
Makaha Shores: 908

MUSEUMS

Alexander and Baldwin Sugar Mill Museum: 434, 480–481
Bailey House Museum: 434, 489–490
Baldwin Home: 434, 507
Bishop Museum: 762
Carthaginian II: 434, 506
China Art Collection: 323
Contemporary Museum: 762, 819
Damien Museum: 762, 854
Earth Heritage Gallery: 323
Faye Museum: 977, 1142
Grove Farm Homestead: 977, 1014–1016
Hale Pa'i: 434
Hana Cultural Center: 434
Hawaiian Art Museum: 977, 1081
Hawaii Maritime Center: 762, 806–807
Hawaii's Plantation Village: 762, 896
Honolulu Academy of Arts: 762, 818
Hui No'eau Visual Arts Center: 605
Hulihe'e Palace: 179, 225–226
'Iolani Palace: 762, 801–802
Island Heritage Gallery: 323
Kamuela Museum: 179, 293–294
Kaua'i Children's Discovery Museum: 977
Kaua'i Coffee Company Museum: 977, 1132–1133
Kaua'i Historical Society: 977
Kaua'i Museum: 977, 1014
Kohala Historical Sites Monument: 305
Koke'e Natural History Museum: 977, 1151

Kona Historical Society Museum: 179, 258
Lahaina Restoration Foundation: 434
Laupahoehoe Train Museum: 179, 354
Lyman Mission House and Museum: 179, 321
Maui Arts and Cultural Center: 479–480
Maui Historical Society: 434
Mission House Museum: 762, 803–805
Moloka'i Museum and Cultural Center: 734
Onizuka Space Center: 179
Pacific Aerospace Museum: 762
Pacific Tsunami Museum: 179, 324
Paper Airplane Museum: 434, 480
Parker Ranch Museum: 179
Parker Ranch Visitor Center and Museum: 293
Polynesian Cultural Center: 939–941
Queen Emma Summer Palace: 763, 809–810
Queen's Medical Center Historical Room: 763
Royal Kona Coffee Mill and Museum: 260
Teshima's Restaurant: 255
Thomas A. Jaggar Museum: 398
Tropic Lightning Museum: 763
U.S. Army Museum of Hawaii: 763, 852–853
USS *Arizona* Memorial: 763, 891–893
USS *Bowfin* Submarine Museum: 763, 893–894
USS *Missouri:* 763, 894–895
Volcano Art Center: 397
Waioli Mission House: 977
Whaler's Village Museum: 434, 534

Makaha Valley Plantation: 908
Makaha Valley Towers: 908
Makahiki: 77
Makalawena Beach: 231
Makalei Beach County Park: 857
Makapu'u Beach Park: 915
Makapu'u Point: 915
Makawao: 601–609
Makawao Rodeo: 603
Makawao Union Church: 627
Makena: 595–599
Makena Beach: 437, 597
Makena State Park: 597
Makiki Valley Trail: 822
Malae Heiau: 1040
Malaekahana Bay State Recreation Area: 941

Mala Wharf: 510
Malu'aka Beach: 596–597
Malu'ulu O Lele Park
mammals: 170
Mana'e Canoe Club: 728
Mana Hale: 292
Manana (Rabbit) Island: 916
Manele Bay: 665, 691
Maninholo dry cave: 1095
Manini Beach: 261
Manoa Valley: 814–815
Manuka State Wayside: 417
maps: 106, 192
Mapulehu Mango Grove: 728
Maria Lanakila Church: 266
marijuana: *see* illegal drugs

Mark Twain Monkeypod Tree: 414
Masters and Servants Act: 52
Maui: 421–476; accommodations 466–468; festivals, holidays, and events 433–436; flora and fauna 426–428; food 468; government/economy 428–433; history 428–430; information and services 475; land 424–426; people 433; shopping 463–466; sports and recreation 436–463; transportation 469–475
Maui Arts and Cultural Center: 479–480
Maui Community College: 479
Maui Historical Society: 434
Maui Ocean Center: 567
Maui parrotbill: 15
Maui Tropical Plantation: 492–493
Mauna Iki Trail: 404
Mauna Kea: 181, 274, 313–314
Mauna Kea Ice Age Natural Area Reserve: 314
Mauna Kea Observatory Complex: 314–317
Mauna Loa: 318, 395
Mauna Loa Macadamia Nut Factory: 328
Mauna Loa NOAA Observatory: 318
Maunalua Bay: 911–917
Maunalua Bay Beach Park: 913
Maunawili Demonstration Trail: 923–924
Menehune: 57
Menehune Ditch: 1141
Midway Atoll National Wildlife Refuge: 1158, 1159
Midway Islands: 1159–1160
Mile Marker 20 Beach: 729
military: 174; Kaua'i 974–975
Miloli'i: 266, 1101
Miloli'i Beach: 267
Miloli'i Beach County Park: 267
missionaries: 36–38, 81–83
Mission House Museum: 762, 803–805
Moanalua Gardens: 756, 819–820
Moa'ula Falls: 730
Moir Gardens: 971, 1109–1110
Mokapu Beach: 585
Moku'aikaua Church: 224–225
Mokule'ia Army Beach: 946
Mokule'ia Bay: 558
Mokule'ia Beach County Park: 946
Moloa'a Beach: 1065
Moloka'i: 699–746; accommodations and food 717–718; economy 707–708; flora and fauna 703–704; history 704–706; information and services 719–720; land 702–703; overview 699–702; people 708–709; sports and recreation 709–717; transportation 718–719
Moloka'i Airport: 718
Moloka'i Brewing Company: 724
Moloka'i Museum and Cultural Center: 734
Molokai Ranch: 705
money: 156
mongoose: 971
Mo'omomi Beach: 710, 740
mopeds: 143, 214
Mormon Temple: 939
motorcycles: 143, 214
motor homes: 214
mouflon sheep; 668
Mu: 57
mule rides: 193–194, 714
Muliwai Trail: 368
Munro Trail: 664, 689–690
music: 91–94; *see also specific place*

N
Na'alehu: 412
Naha: 694
Nahiku: 637
Nahuna (Five Graves) Point: 596
Nani Mau Gardens: 168, 329
Naniwa: 1122–1123
Na Pali Coast State Park: 1098–1099
Napili: 546–556
Napili Bay: 547
Napo'opo'o: 261
Napo'opo'o Beach County Park: 261
National Energy Laboratory of Hawaii Authority (NELHA): 228
national parks: 106; *see also specific place*
National Tropical Botanical Garden: 971, 1111–1112
Nawiliwili Park: 1020
nene: 16, 169, 395
Nihoa Island: 1157
Ni'ihau: 1154–1160
Ninini Beach: 1020
Ninini Point Lighthouse: 1020
Ninole: 411–412
Ninole Cove Park: 411
Niu Beach: 912
Niumalu County Park: 1020
North Bay Aquatics: 931
North Coast Trail: 1093
North Ka'anapali Beach: 536
North Kohala: 301–313
North Kona Beaches: 230–231

North Shore O'ahu: 753
Northwestern Islands: 1157–1160
Nua'auilua Bay: 635
Nu'alolo Kai: 1101
Nu'uanu Pali Lookout: 811

O
O'ahu: 749–779; accommodations and food 785–787; economy 757–759; festivals, holidays, and events 760–765; flora and fauna 755–756; government 757; information and services 795–796; land 754–755; overview 749–754; people 759–760; shopping 783–785; sports and recreation 765–782; transportation 788–795
'O'ahupaeka'a Falls: 1040
ocean tours: Big Island 184; Kaua'i 982–984; Maui 444–445; O'ahu 768–769
Ocean View: 416
Odaishan: 350
Office of Hawaiian Affairs (OHA): 46
'Ohe'o Gulch: 655
'ohi'a: 12–13
'Ola'a Track: 405
Old Kona Airport State Recreation Area: 230
Olokele: 1139
Olowalu Beach: 437
Olowalu Massacre: 33
Omeola Beach: 597
One Ali'i Beach Park: 710, 726–727
Onekahakaha Beach County Park: 330
Oneloa Beach: 558
Onizuka Center for International Astronomy: 316
Onizuka Space Center: 179, 229
Onomea Scenic Drive: 349
Our Lady of Sorrows Church: 728

P
Pacific Aerospace Museum: 762, 789
Pacific Missile Range Facility: 1145–1146
Pacific Rim/Hawaiian Cuisine: 119; see also Restaurant Index
Pacific Tsunami Museum: 179, 324
Pacific Whale Foundation: 24
packing: 152–153
Pahala: 409
Pahoa: 371–372
pahoehoe: 5–6
Pa'ia: 624–630
Paiko Beach: 912–913
Painted Church: 377

Pakala: 1139
pakalolo: 150–151
Pala'au State Park: 735
Palauea Beach: 596
Pali Highway: 809–810
Palikea Stream: 424
Pali Ke Kua Beach: 1076
Pana'ewa Equestrian Center: 328
Pana'ewa Rainforest Zoo: 328
Papalaua Wayside: 437
papayas: 974
Paper Airplane Museum: 434, 480
Papohaku Beach: 710, 741
Paradise Park: 815
paragliding: Maui 443, 461, O'ahu 768
parasailing: 185
Parker Ranch: 289, 292
Parker Ranch Museum: 179
Parker Ranch Visitor Center and Museum: 293
Pearl City: 890–898
Pearl Harbor: 43; historical sites 890–895
pedicabs (Waikiki): 849
Pe'epe'e Falls: 327
Pele: 4, 76, 392–393
people: 54–65: see also specific place
Pepe'opae Trail: 733
petroglyphs: 271, 402, 690–691, 693, 696; see also specific place
pets and quarantine: 131
Phallic Rock: 735
pidgin: 66–68
Pihana Heiau State Monument: 498
Pi'ilanihale: 643–644
pineapples: 52, 669–670, 899–900
Pine Trees Surfing Beach: 230–231
Pioneer Inn: 507
Pohaku Ho'o Hanau: 1040
Pohakuloa: 317–318
Pohakuloa Military Camp: 318
Pohoiki Bay: 375
Po'ipu: 1109–1126; accommodations 1112–1119; entertainment 1123; food 1119–1123; information 1125–1126; recreation 1124–1125; shopping 1123–1124; sights 1109–1112
Po'ipu Beach County Park: 1108–1109
Poka'i Beach County Park: 906
Poli'ahu Heiau: 1040
Polihale State Park: 1146–1147
Polihua Beach: 698
Polo: 604
Polo Beach: 585

Pololu Valley: 310–311
Pololu Vally Lookout: 301
Polopoli Spring State Recreation Area: 612
Polynesian Cultural Center: 939–941
Po'olenalena: 596
po'ouli: 15
Port Allen: 1132–1134
Pounder's Beach: 941
prickly pear cactus: 427–428
Prince Kuhio Beach and Beach Park: 856
Prince Kuhio Park: 1110
Princeville: 1075–1083
Princeville Airport: 1007
Princeville Makai Golf Course: 1082
prostitution: 149–150
protea: 426–427
Puako: 271–272
Puako Petroglyphs: 271
Puala'a Park: 375
Puamana Beach: 437
Puamana Beach County Park: 512
public transportation: 143; see also specific
    place
pueo: 16
Puhi: 1033
Pukalani: 609–610
Puna: 164, 369–389
Puna Coast Trail: 404
Punalu'u: 411–412, 937
Punalu'u Beach County Park: 414, 937–938
Punchbowl (National Cemetery of the Pacific):
    811–813
Punualu'u Beach County Park: 411, 937–938
Puohokamoa Falls: 635
Pu'opelu: 292
pu-pu: 123; see also specific place
Pupukea Beach Park: 955
Purdy's Macadamia Nut Farm: 734
Pu'u Hinahina Overlook: 1149
Pu'uhonua O Honaunau National Historical Park:
    262–264
Pu'u Ka Pele Overook: 1149
Pu'u Keka'a: 534
Pu'ukohola Heiau: 270, 272
Pu'u Kukui: 423, 424
Pu'u Kukui Preserve: 557
Pu'u Loa Petroglyphs: 402
Pu'u O Kila Lookout: 1150–1151
Pu'u O Mahuka Heiau: 955–956
Pu'u O'o Trail: 318
Pu'u Poa Beach: 1076

QR
Quarry Beach: 1070
Queen Emma Summer Palace: 763, 809–810
Queens Beach: 857
Queen's Medical Center Historical Room: 763
Queen Victoria's Profile: 1033
rafting (Maui): 446
rainforests: 14
Recollections of Kaho'olawe: 662
Red Sand Beach: 437, 645
Reeds Bay Beach Park: 330
religon: 73–83
rental cars: 139–143 see also transportation
    under specific place
Richardson's Beach Park: 331
Rinzai Zen Mission: 626
river cruise (Kaua'i): 985–986, 1047–1048
Route 250: 302
Royal Hawaiian Hotel: 853
Royal Kona Coffee Mill and Museum: 260
Royal Moana Beach: 855
Russian Fort Elizabeth State Historic Park:
    1139–1140

S
Saddle Road: 163, 312–318
sailboarding: 100; see also specific place
sailing: 185–186; see also specific place
saimin: 121; see also Restaurant Index
Saint Joseph Church: 727–728
Salt Pond Beach County Park: 1137
Sandalwood Measuring Pit: 732
Sand Island State Recreation Area: 820
Sandy Beach Park: 915
Sans Souci Beach: 857
Schofield Barracks: 899
scrimshaw: 87–88
Sea Life Park Hawaii: 916
Sea Mountain Resort and Golf Course: 411
Seamen's Cemetery: 509
seasickness: 102
Secret Beach: 1070–1071
Senator Fong's Plantation and Gardens: 933
Sheraton Moana Surfrider: 853
shield volcanoes: 5
Shipwreck Beach: 665, 695–696, 1109
shopping: see specific place
shuttle services: 215
Sierra Club, Hawaii chapter: 105
silversword: 426
skiing (Big Island): 195–196

SCUBA/SNORKELING

introduction: 95–100
'Anini Beach County Park: 1071–1072
Annahola Beach County Park: 1065
Barbers Point Beach County Park: 904
Big Island: 181–184
Brennecke's Beach: 1109
Ha'ena Beach County Park: 1095
Hanauma Bay State Underwater Park: 913
Hapuna Beach State Recreation Area: 181, 274
Hau'ula Beach County Park: 938
He'eia Kea Harbor: 931
Hilo: 343
Homoa Beach: 646
Honokowai Beach Park: 546
Ka'a'awa Beach County Park: 936
Ka'anapali Beach: 535
Kalapaki Beach: 1020
Kaloko Beach: 230
Kapalua Bay Beach: 437, 558
Kapoho: 375
Kaua'i: 979–980
Kekaha Beach County Park: 1144
Keyhole: 913
Kona: 243
Kualoa Ranch: 935

Kualoa Regional Park: 934–935
Kuilei Cliffs Beach Park: 857–858
Kukui'ula Bay: 1111
Lana'i: 672
Lanikai Beach: 924
Lydgate Beach: 1040
Ma'ili Beach County Park: 906
Maui: 437–438, 440–441
Midway Islands: 1159–1160
Moloa'a Beach: 1065
Moloka'i: 711
Napili Bay: 546, 547
North Ka'anapali Beach: 535
O'ahu: 765–767
Old Kona Airport State Recreation Area: 230
Olowalu Beach: 437
Pohoiki Bay: 375
Poka'i Beach County Park: 906
Polo Beach: 585
Richardson's Beach Park: 331
Salt Pond Beach County Park 1137
snorkel boats: 183–184
Spencer Beach County Park: 274–275
Tunnels: 1095
White Sands Beach County Park: 180, 229

Sleeping Giant: 1039
Sleeping Giant Viewpoint: 1052
Smith and Bronte Landing Site: 728
Smith's Tropical Paradise: 971, 1038
snorkel boats: 183–184
snuba: 100, 184; Kaua'i 981; Maui 441; O'ahu 767
Soto Zen Temple Zenshuji: 1134
South Kohala: 268–288; accommodations 275–284; food 284–286; recreation 287–288; sights 271–275
South Kona: 255–267
South Point: 414–416
Southwest Rift: 399
Spencer Beach: 274
Spencer Beach County Park: 274–275
sporting clays: 458, 676
sports and recreation: 95–11; *see also specific place*
Spouting Horn: 1111
St. Andrew's Cathedral: 803

State Archives: 802
statehood: 43
state parks: 106 *see also specific place*
Statue of King Kamehameha: 799
St. Augustine Catholic Church: 854
St. Benedict's Painted Church: 260–261
steam vents: 398
St. Joseph's Church: 656
St. Paul's Catholic Church: 255
St. Peter's Catholic Church: 226
Strifes of Maui: 76
submarines: 187, 244, 763, 893–894
sugar: 39–40, 51–52, 174, 432, 974
Sulfer Banks: 398
Sunset Beach: 956
Sunset Beach County Park: 957
sunset dinner cruise (Kona): 245
Sunset Rip: 957
swimming: *see specific place*/beach
Sylvester's Catholic Church: 1068–1069

SURFING

introduction: 80, 100
Banzai Pipeline: 956
Big Island: 184
Donkey Beach: 1064
D.T. Fleming Beach Park: 558
Gray's Beach: 855
Hale'iwa Beach County Park: 950
Hamoa Beach: 645
Honoli'i Beach County Park: 331
Honolua Bay: 558
Ka'alawai Beach: 858
Ka'anapali Beach: 535
Kaluahole Beach: 857
Kaua'i: 981–982
Kauna'oa Beach (Mauna Kea Beach): 181, 274
Koki Beach: 645
Lucy Wright Beach County Park: 1140
Major's Bay Beach: 1145–1146
Maui: 441–443
Moloka'i: 711
Napili Bay: 547
O'ahu: 767–768
Pine Trees Surfing Beach: 230–231
Pohokoi Bay: 375
Prince Kuhio Beach and Beach Park: 856
Royal Moana Beach: 855
Salt Pond Beach County Park: 1137
Sunset Beach: 956
Wailua Beach: 1041
Waimea Bay Beach County Park: 954
White Sands Beach County Park: 229

T
Tantalus Valley Trail: 822
taxis: 215
Tedeschi Winery: 614–615
tennis: 109–110; Big Island 199; Kapula 563–564; Kaua'i 994–995; Kona 243; Lahaina 544; Lan'i 675; Maui 455, 458; Moloka'i 715; O'ahu 775, 779; Po'ipu 1124; Princeville 1083; South Kohala 286–287
Teshima's Restaurant: 255
theft: 151–152
Thomas A. Jaggar Museum: 398
Thurston Lava Tube: 392, 399
tidal wave: *see* tsunami

time zones: 155
tourism: 175
tours: 111; *see also specific place*
Tracks Beach County Park: 905
trade winds: 9–10
transportation: 127–144; *see also specific place*
travelers with disabilities: 142–143; 148–149
tree molds: 404
Tropic Lightning Museum: 763
tsunami: 6–7, 166
Tunnel of Trees: 1102
Tunnels: 1095
Twin Falls: 633

U
Ulehawa Beach County Park: 905–906
Ulua Beach: 585
Ulupo Heiau State Monument: 922–923
underwater cruises (O'ahu): 770
University of Hawai'i: 813–814
University of Hawai'i Agricultural Experimental Station: 611–612
Upolu Airport: 212
Urusenke Teahouse: 854
U.S. Army Museum of Hawai'i: 763, 852–853
USS *Arizona* Memorial: 763, 891–893
USS *Bowfin* Submarine Museum: 763, 893–894
U.S. Seamen's Hospital: 510
USS *Missouri:* 763, 894–895

V
Valley of the Temples: 930–931
visas: 131
Volcano Art Center: 397
volcanoes: 4
Volcano Golf and Country Club: 361
Volcano Village: 381–389
Volcano Winery: 381–382
Von Holt Memorial Park: 303

WXYZ
Wa: 57
wagon ride: 714
wagon tour (Waip'o): 365–366
Waha'ula Heaiau: 403
Wahiawa: 898–901
Wahiawa Botanical Garden: 756, 899
Waiahole: 934
Waialae Beach County Park: 858
Waialea Bay Marine Life Conservation District: 272

Waiale'e Beach County Park: 957
Waialua: 945–947
Waialua Beach: 729
Wai'anae Harbor: 906
Wai'anapanapa Caves: 644
Wai'anapanapa Beach: 437
Wai'anapanapa State Park: 644
Wai'ohinu: 413–414
Wai'oli Hul'ia Church: 1085
Wai'oli Mission House: 1085–1086
Waiehu Beach County Park: 498
Waihe'e Beach County Park: 499
Waihou Spring Trail: 605
Waikamoi Ridge: 633
Waikane: 934
Waikiki: 752, 845–889; accommodations
    858–873; beaches and parks 854–858; en-
    tertainment 882–886; food 874–882; history
    845–848; shopping 886–889; sights 850–854
Waikiki Aquarium: 851–852
Walkiki Marine Conservation District: 857
Waikoloa Petroglyphs: 271
Waikoloa Village: 273
Waikolu (Three Waters) Overlook: 733
Wailea: 353, 437, 584–594
Wailea Beach: 585
Wailoa River State Park Recreation Area: 326
Wailua (Kaua'i): 1035–1051; accommodations
    1041–1044; entertainment 1047; food
    1044–1047; recreation 1047–1049; shopping
    1049–1051; sights 1037–1041
Wailua (Maui): 636–637
Wailua Beach: 1041
Wailua Falls: Kaua'i 1019, Maui 653
Wailua Wayside Park: 637
Wailuku: 487–497; accommodations 493–494;
    entertainment/services 496–497; food
    494–496; sights 489–493
Wailupe Beach Park: 912
Waimanalo: 918–919
Waimanalo Bay State Recreation Area: 919
Waimanalo Beach County Park: 919
Waimea (Big Island): 289–300; accommoda-
    tions 294–295; food 295–298; history
    291–292; recreation 298; services and infor-
    mation 300; sights 292–294
Waimea (Kaua'i): 1139–1144
Waimea Aboretum and Botanical Garden: 756,
    954
Waimea Bay: 954–960
Waimea Bay Beach County Park: 954
Waimea Canyon Overlook: 1149
Waimea Canyon State Park: 1147–1149
Waimea Canyon Trail: 1149
Waimea District: 1130
Waimea Falls Park: 955
Waimea-Kohala Airport: 291
Waimea State Recreation Pier: 1141
Waimea Valley Parks: 954–955
Waimea Visitor and Technology Center:
    1141–1142
Waimoku Falls: 654–655
Waine'e Church: 508
Waioka Pool: 652
Waioli Mission House: 977
Waipi'i Treehouse: 367–368
Waipi'o Beach: 180, 364, 365
Waipi'o Valley: 361–368
Waipi'o Valley Overlook: 360
Waipouli: 1051–1052
Waipouli Beach County Park: 1041
Waipu'ilani Park: 571
Waita Reservoir: 1103
Wananulua Church: 642
War Memorial: 803
War Memorial Park and Center: 480
Washington Place: 802
water skiing: Kaua'i 982; Wailua 1048
Wawaloli Beach: 231
weather (Haleakala): 617
West Maui Mountains: 424
Whaler's Village: 434
Whaler's Village Museum: 434, 534
whales/whale-watching: 20–24, 186; see also
    specific place
White Sands Beach County Park: 180, 229
Whittington Beach County Park: 412
wildlife refuges: 18–19 see also specific place
windsurfing: Big Island 184; Kanaha Beach
    County Park 479; Kaua'i 982; Ma'alaea Beach
    567; Mai Poina 'oela'u Beach Park 570; O'ahu
    768; see also surfing
W.M. Keck Observatory: 315
Wo Hing Temple: 509
Wood Valley Temple: 409
World Tropical Botanical Gardens: 168, 354

ABOUT THE AUTHOR

Robert Nilsen was born and raised in Minnesota. His first major excursion from the Midwest was a two-year stint in South Korea with the Peace Corps. Following that eye-opening service, he stayed on in Korea independently, teaching and traveling. Setting his sights on other lands and cultures, he made a two-year trek through Asia before returning home to the United States, and since then has had the good fortune to return to Asia and the Pacific on numerous occasions. Robert has written *Moon Handbooks: South Korea* for Avalon Travel Publishing and has contributed to *Moon Handbooks: Indonesia*. Since the passing of his good friend J. D. Bisignani, he has shouldered full responsibility for the revision of the Hawaii series of Moon Handbooks, which includes *Moon Handbooks: Hawaii, Moon Handbooks: Maui, Moon Handbooks: Kaua'i, Moon Handbooks: Big Island of Hawai'i,* and *Moon Handbooks: O'ahu.*

U.S.~METRIC CONVERSION

1 inch = 2.54 centimeters (cm)
1 foot = .304 meters (m)
1 yard = 0.914 meters
1 mile = 1.6093 kilometers (km)
1 km = .6214 miles
1 fathom = 1.8288 m
1 chain = 20.1168 m
1 furlong = 201.168 m
1 acre = .4047 hectares
1 sq km = 100 hectares
1 sq mile = 2.59 square km
1 ounce = 28.35 grams
1 pound = .4536 kilograms
1 short ton = .90718 metric ton
1 short ton = 2000 pounds
1 long ton = 1.016 metric tons
1 long ton = 2240 pounds
1 metric ton = 1000 kilograms
1 quart = .94635 liters
1 US gallon = 3.7854 liters
1 Imperial gallon = 4.5459 liters
1 nautical mile = 1.852 km

To compute celsius temperatures, subtract 32 from Fahrenheit and divide by 1.8. To go the other way, multiply celsius by 1.8 and add 32.

Planning Your Vacation Just Got Easier

AVALON
TRAVEL
publishing

How far will our travel guides take you? As far as you want.

Discover a rhumba-fueled nightspot in Old Havana, explore prehistoric tombs in Ireland, hike beneath California's centuries-old redwoods, or embark on a classic road trip along Route 66. Our guidebooks deliver solidly researched, trip-tested information—minus any generic froth—to help globetrotters or weekend warriors create an adventure uniquely their own.

And we're not just about the printed page. Public television viewers are tuning in to Rick Steves' new travel series, *Rick Steves' Europe*. On the Web, readers can cruise the virtual black top with *Road Trip USA* author Jamie Jensen and learn travel industry secrets from Edward Hasbrouck of *The Practical Nomad*.

In print. On TV. On the Internet.

We supply the information. The rest is up to you.

Avalon Travel Publishing

Something for everyone

www.travelmatters.com

Avalon Travel Publishing guides are available at your favorite book or travel store.

MOON HANDBOOKS

provide comprehensive coverage of a region's arts, history, land, people, and social issues in addition to detailed practical listings for accommodations, food, outdoor recreation, and entertainment. Moon Handbooks allow complete immersion in a region's culture—ideal for travelers who want to combine sightseeing with insight for an extraordinary travel experience in destinations throughout North America, Hawaii, Latin America, the Caribbean, Asia, and the Pacific.

WWW.MOON.COM

Rick Steves shows you where to travel and how to travel—all while getting the most value for your dollar. His Back Door travel philosophy is about making friends, having fun, and avoiding tourist rip-offs.

Rick has been traveling to Europe for more than 25 years and is the author of 22 guidebooks, which have sold more than a million copies. He also hosts the award-winning public television series *Rick Steves' Europe*.

WWW.RICKSTEVES.COM

ROAD TRIP USA

Getting there is half the fun, and Road Trip USA guides are your ticket to driving adventure. Taking you off the interstates and onto less-traveled, two-lane highways, each guide is filled with fascinating trivia, historical information, photographs, facts about regional writers, and details on where to sleep and eat—all contributing to your exploration of the American road.

"[Books] so full of the pleasures of the American road, you can smell the upholstery."
~BBC radio

WWW.ROADTRIPUSA.COM